THE OXFORD
TURKISH–ENGLISH
DICTIONARY

TÜRKÇE-İNGİLİZCE SÖZLÜK

H. C. HONY ve FAHİR İZ

ÜÇÜNCÜ BASKI

A. D. ALDERSON ve FAHİR İZ

OXFORD
AT THE CLARENDON PRESS
1984

THE OXFORD
TURKISH–ENGLISH
DICTIONARY

H. C. HONY and FAHİR İZ

THIRD EDITION

A. D. ALDERSON and FAHİR İZ

OXFORD
AT THE CLARENDON PRESS
1984

Oxford University Press, Walton Street, Oxford OX2 6DP

London New York Toronto
Delhi Bombay Calcutta Madras Karachi
Kuala Lumpur Singapore Hong Kong Tokyo
Nairobi Dar es Salaam Cape Town
Melbourne Auckland

and associated companies in
Beirut Berlin Ibadan Mexico City Nicosia

Oxford is a trade mark of Oxford University Press

Published in the United States
by Oxford University Press, New York

© *Oxford University Press 1984*

First Edition 1947
Second Edition 1957
Third Edition 1984

British Library Cataloguing in Publication Data
Hony, H. C.
The Oxford Turkish–English dictionary.—3rd ed.
1. Turkish language—Dictionaries—English
2. English language—Dictionaries—Turkish
I. Title II. İz, Fahir III. Alderson, A. D.
494'.35321 PL191
ISBN 0-19-864124-9

Typeset at the University Press, Oxford
Printed in Great Britain
by Thomson Litho Ltd., East Kilbride

PREFACE

The Turkish language experienced one, instant reform in 1928 when Kemal Atatürk decreed the change from the Arabic to the Roman alphabet. In the years since then a more gradual and subtle—but equally effective—reform has taken place in the field of vocabulary. Originally sponsored by the government and supported all the way by the majority of writers, it has resulted in the creation of a new written and spoken language. Apart from changes in the conversational, literary, and commercial vocabulary, with some four to five thousand neologisms of everyday use replacing loan-words from Arabic and Persian, the whole scientific terminology (based originally on Arabic) has been replaced by one based largely on western European languages.

It is not the purpose of this dictionary to make any value judgement on these changes but to record them as faithfully as possible and as fully as space allows. To keep the text within reasonable limits a great deal of the obsolete Arabic–Persian heritage has been omitted; this has been balanced by the incorporation of a large proportion of the Turkish neologisms and of the European loan-words. While some Turks of the older generation consider these changes a mixed blessing, it is felt that the majority of them are permanent; even if some neologisms do not survive, they may serve as a guide in the interpretation of others.

The other major change in this new edition of the dictionary has been the complete rearrangement of idiomatic material; in the earlier editions phrases were entered under the 'less common/more difficult' word, as being the one the user would most probably turn to first. Here, however, the method followed in all modern Turkish dictionaries has been adopted and all idioms are to be found under the first word of the phrase, with only a non-essential *bu*, *şu*, *bir* being relegated to the end of the phrase.

A dictionary of this scope depends greatly on the work and help of others. It is an extension of the two previous editions by H. C. Hony and F. İz and, as in the case of the companion English–Turkish volume, Professor F. İz, now of the Boğaziçi University, indicated the changes he would like to see in the Turkish vocabulary, made many suggestions as to the general treatment, and read the final text. The Türk Dil Kurumu is *the* authority on the Turkish language and it is only fitting to record here the debt owed to so many of its publications and in particular to the *Türkçe Sözlük* (1974) and the *Yeni Yazım Kılavuzu* (1977).

Once more my thanks go to Professor E. Toğrol, Rector of the Boğaziçi University, and to Dr. G. L. Lewis of Oxford University, both of whom read the text and made many useful suggestions. I am equally grateful to the staff of the Oxford University Press and in particular to Dr. R. W. Burchfield, CBE, Mr. B. L. Phillips, and Mr. B. Townsend, for their continued guidance. My secretary, Mrs. C. Crane, typed the whole manuscript with the skill and accuracy she has always applied to so many different linguistic texts. Finally—and the repetition is a measure of my gratitude—I wish once again to express my deep appreciation of my wife's understanding and encouragement in a task which has occupied so much of our time.

April 1984 A.D.A.

ÖNSÖZ

Türk dili, Kemal Atatürk'ün Arap harflerinden Roma alfabesine geçilmesi kararı ile 1928'de ani bir değişim geçirdi. Dilin o yıllardanberi geçirdiği yavaş ancak etkili değişim ise daha çok, kullanılan sözcükleri etkiledi. Devlet tarafından başlatılan ve yazarların çoğunca desteklenen bu tutum, yeni bir yazı ve konuşma dilinin yaratılması ile sonuçlandı. Konuşma, edebiyat ve ticaret diline Arapça ve Farsçadan geçmis olan 4000–5000 sözcüğün yerini gündelik dilde kullanılanların almasının dışında, kökeni Arapçaya dayalı bilimsel terimlerin hepsi Batı Avrupa dillerinden alınan karşılıklarıyla değiştirildi.

Bu sözlüğün amacı yapılan değişiklikler üzerine değer yargıları belirtmek değil, onlara olabildiğince sadakatle, eserin kapsamı elverdiği ölçüde yer vermek. Eseri kabul edilir uzunlukta tutabilmek için artık yaygın olarak kullanılmayan Arapça–Farsça dil mirasının büyük bir kısmı çıkarılmıştır. Bu boşluğu dengelemek için ise sözlüğe çok sayıda Türkçe sözcük ile Avrupa dillerinden ödünç alınanlar katılmıştır. Her ne kadar eski kuşak Türkler bu değişiklikler konusunda kararsızlarsa da bunların pek çoğunun kalıcı olacağını kestirmek güç değil. Üstelik, bu sözcüklerin bir kısmı, yaşamasalar bile başka sözcüklerin yorumlanmasında yol gösterici olabilirler.

Sözlüğün bu baskısındaki en önemli diğer değişiklik deyimlerin tamamen farklı bir düzende sunulmasıdır. Daha önceki baskılarda deyimler, 'daha az yaygın/daha zor' sözcüğün altında verilmişti. Bu kez, diğer bütün Türkçe sözlüklerde izlenen yöntem benimsenerek tüm deyimler ilk kelimenin altında gruplanmış, yalnızca *bu*, *şu*, *bir* gibi gerekli olmayan sözcükler sona aktarılmıştır.

Böylesine kapsamlı bir sözlük, büyük ölçüde başkalarının çalışma ve yardımına dayanır. Bu eser, H. C. Hony ve Fahir İz'in hazırladığı daha önceki iki basımın genişletilmesiyle ortaya çıkmıştır. Boğaziçi Üniversitesinden Prof. Fahir İz Türkçe sözcüklerde görmeyi beklediği değişiklikleri belirtmiş, genel elealınışa ilişkin pek çok öneri ileri sürmüş, metnin son düzeltmelerini yapmıştır. Bu eser, Türk dili konusundaki tek otorite olan Türk Dil Kurumuna, kurumun yayınlarına ve özellikle *Türkçe Sözlük* (1974) ve *Yeni Yazım Kılavuzu*'na çok şey borçludur.

Metni okuyarak pek çok yararlı öneride bulunan Boğaziçi Üniversitesi Rektörü Prof. E. Toğrol'a ve Oxford Üniversitesinden Dr. G. L. Lewis'e tekrar teşekkürlerimi sunarım. Sürekli yol gösterilerinden ötürü Oxford Press mensuplarına ve özellikle Dr. R. W. Burchfield, CBE, Bay B. L. Phillips ile Bay B. Townsend'e minnettarım. Bütün el yazmasını, başka dillerde pek çok metne daima gösterdiği dikkat ve beceri ile sekreterim Mrs. C. Crane daktilo etti. Son olarak, bu eserin ortaya çıkması sırasında geçirdiğimiz uzun zaman boyunca eşimin gösterdiği anlayış ve teşvikten ötürü duyduğum takdir duygusunu bir kez daha dile getirmek isterim.

Nisan 1984   A.D.A.

INTRODUCTION

1. *Economy of space*

To make the most effective use of the space available various means have been adopted.

1. Where an adjective or noun has been explained with a long series of meanings, only one or two of these, followed by 'etc.', may be given for related nouns or verbs; in these cases look back to the root-word: compare **sert** and **sertlenmek**.

2. The oblique stroke (/) is frequently used to indicate synonyms and at the same time avoid repetition. Thus:

> **eder,** . . . ~ **çizelgesi/** ~ **lik** = **eder çizelgesi** *veya* **ederlik**.
> **halt** stupid/improper speech/deed = stupid *or* improper speech *or* stupid *or* improper deed.

Note that in phrases with these alternatives only the last is inflected:

> **dümeni sağ/sola kırmak** = **dümeni sağa** *veya* **sola kırmak**.

3. The double oblique stroke (//) is used to show that the phrase is applicable to two quite distinct concepts:

> **aboneyi kesmek//yenilemek** = cancel//renew a subscription.
> **santimetre kare//küp** = square//cubic centimetre.
> **eksik çıkmak** = be defective//short/under weight.

4. Parentheses ( ) are used in two ways.

(*a*) They may suggest typical ideas which could be replaced by other similar ones:

> **insan (su)suz nasıl edebilir?** = how can a man live without (water)?
> **(et)siz** (meat)?
> **(hava)sız** (air)?

> **kökten sürme (ressam)dır** = he's a born (artist)
> **(heykeltraş)** (sculptor)
> **(yazar)** (writer).

(*b*) They are also used to give extensions of the concept:

> **Dış İşleri Bakan(lığ)ı**, the Foreign Minis·ter/(-try) = **Dış İşleri Bakanı** *veya* **Bakanlığı**, the Foreign Minister *or* Ministry.
> **ödeme güç(süzlüğ)ü**, (in)solvency = **ödeme gücü** *veya* **güçsüzlüğü**, solvency *or* insolvency.

5. Wherever convenient the compounds of Turkish words are grouped together. The shoulder-heads take this into account.

> **albay(lık)** (duties, rank of) colonel
> **bağırt·ı** . . . ~ **kan** . . . ~ **lak** . . . ~ **mak**.

6. In the English text, the articles, *a, the*, are omitted before nouns unless essential to the meaning of the phrase, and *to* as the sign of the infinitive is similarly omitted before verbs.

7. In the case of European loan-words, those beginning with the same prefix have sometimes been grouped together even though not related in etymology or meaning; see **desi-, egz-, eks-, mülti-,** etc. This also applies to a few Arabic and Persian loan-words.

2. *Vocabulary*

The general aim has been to give a picture of the Turkish vocabulary as it existed *c*.1980—it must be remembered that there is always a time-lapse in the publication of a dictionary. There are many changes as compared with what was included in or excluded from the previous edition nearly thirty years ago.

1. *Arabic and Persian words.* With a few exceptions only those words given in the *Türkçe Sözlük* (1974) have been included in this edition.

2. *Neologisms.* Here again the *Türkçe Sözlük* (1974) has been taken as a guide, and all the neologisms it lists have been included. To these have been added those words listed in the *Özleştirme Kılavuzu* (1978) and many of the technical words given in the numerous glossaries also published by the Türk Dil Kurumu. Reference has also been made to A. Püsküllüoğlu, *Öztürkçe Sözlük* (1979) and to *Zemin Mekaniği ve Temel Mühendisliği Terimleri Sözlüğü* (1980) and obviously much more has been culled from the reading of contemporary books and periodicals.

3. *English and French words.* Apart from numerous words of everyday conversation, these form the basis—as in most modern languages—of the scientific terminology in use; they have been given a larger place than some of my colleagues considered appropriate.

The transliteration of English and French words into Turkish often renders them unrecognizable to the English user, who in any case may not be fluent in French:

> **fayrap,** (*naut.*) fire up!—**nakavt,** (*sp.*) knock-out—**aperkat,** (*sp.*) upper-cut—**blakavt,** black-out—**bleyt,** (*eng.*) blade—**şanjman,** (*mot.*) *changement,* gear-box—**jaketatay,** (*mod.*) *jaquette à taille,* morning-coat—**jön-prömiye,** (*th.*) *jeune premier,* juvenile lead—**rekortmen,** (*sp.*) *recordman,* record-holder—**sanzatu,** (*gamb.*) *sans-atout,* no trumps—**tuvenan,** (*min.*) *tout-venant,* aggregate—etc., etc.

Further, the Turkish user will want confirmation that the word he uses in its Turkish form has the same or a similar form, and the same meaning, in English; there are too many 'false friends' in the translator's world.

3. *Arrangement*

1. *Word order.* All the entries (words, compound words, affixes, and abbreviations) have been arranged in a single alphabetical order. The two exceptions are where:

(*a*) a very brief compound-word entry is moved up or down not more than a couple of lines to/within the main entry, in order to save space: **metal·bilim/ ∼ ürji;**
(*b*) the compound-word entries of two homonyms are kept respectively together; compare the entries under **esrar**[1] and [2] and **yüzlü**[1] and [2].

2. *Headwords.* In each entry the definition of the headword is given first, synonyms being separated by commas and more distinct meanings by semicolons. This is followed by phrases in which the headword occurs, first in the uninflected form and then in the various inflected forms:

ocak . . . ~ (ayı): ~ başı: ~ külahı: ~ı daim yanan: ~ına düşmek: ~ını söndürmek.

Such phrases are always given in the third-person singular form, unless the idiom is specific to the first or second person or to the third person plural.

3. *Inflected forms.* These are always given in alphabetical order, which means that—in accordance with the rules of vowel harmony—the cases do not always occur in the same order:

ev, evde(n), eve, evin.
okul, okula, okulda(n), okulun.
mekte'pᵇⁱ, mektebe, mektebin, mektepte(n).

Where inflections may, or in some Arabic words may not, involve a modification of the final syllable of the basic word this has been indicated by showing the accusative case as follows:

fak'irʳⁱ = fakir, fakri.	böre'kᵍ¹ = börek, böreği.
kut'upᵇᵘ = kutup, kutbu.	çeki'çᶜⁱ = çekiç, çekici.
kabahatⁱ = kabahat, kabahati.	re'tᵈᵈⁱ = ret, reddi.
mevlu'tᵈᵘ = mevlut, mevludu.	rahi'pᵇⁱ = rahip, rahibi.

If the modified forms occur at some distance alphabetically from the headwords, then a cross-reference is given:

redd- = RET.   rahib- = RAHİP.

In the case of words such as **Allah, baş, kafa, yan, yüz**, etc., which have very rich idiomatic phraseology, the phrases for each inflected form are grouped together in separate sub-paragraphs.

4. *Compound words.* Usage with regard to compound concepts varies in Turkish, as it does in English; sometimes they occur as two separate words, sometimes as one single word (but very seldom as hyphenated words). Here the rules of spelling set out in *Yeni Yazım Kılavuzu* (1977) have been followed. As two words the concept appears in correct alphabetical position under the simple headword; if it also occurs as one word, then a cross-reference is given in small capitals. If it only occurs as a single word, then the cross-reference alone is given. Where considered necessary, a similar cross-reference is given back from the single word to the two-word form:

kara: ~ELMAS refers on to **karaelmas**;
karasu: = KARA¹ refers back to **kara suları**.

In general it will be advisable to start the search by looking up the compound word under its first element.

5. *Verb forms.* Unusual aorist forms are indicated thus:

gi'tmekᵈᵉʳ = gider.   e'tmekᵈᵉʳ = eder.   zikr'etmekᵉᵈᵉʳ = zikreder.

In the case of a verb like **yemek**, with several irregular forms, these are given separately with a cross-reference back to the infinitive, where they are shown in parentheses after the headword:

yemek² (yer, yiyecek, yiyen, yiyor).

The passive, causative, reciprocal, and other forms of the verb have generally been included as infinitives, with a cross-reference to the simple active verb, if that entry is at some distance alphabetically:

verdirmek *vc.* = VERMEK.

An indication of the meaning of these various forms is only given if it is not immediately obvious, or it is definitely idiomatic. Idiomatic verbal phrases are given in full immediately after the infinitive, cf. **durmak, gülmek.**

6. *Complements.* Suffixes in brackets after verbs and postpositions indicate the appropriate inflections of the complements governed by them:

ödetmek (-i, -e), let/make (s.o.) pay (stg.) to (s.o.)
ölçüşmek (-le), compete with one another.
önce (-den), prior to (stg.), in front of (s.o.)

7. *Numerals.* Turkish is very rich in idioms and phrases connected with numbers. Where they are explicit to a particular number they are naturally shown under that headword:

dört nala gitmek; bin dereden su getirmek; yedi canlı; yetmiş yedi göbeğinden beri.

Where it is possible to substitute any other number, the phrases have been collected under **beş** for numbers 1 to 9, and under **kırk** for higher numbers.

4. *Spelling*

After a long period of uncertainty, the Türk Dil Kurumu has now established a clear and precise system of orthography, and the recommendations given in its *Yeni Yazım Kılavuzu* (1977) have been followed throughout this dictionary. If a word cannot be traced under one form of spelling, it may be found under one of the likely variations, as follows: **a/e; ı/i; ö/ü; u/ü;—c/ç; d/t; ğ/v; p/b.** Genuine alternative spellings are cross-referenced.

It should be noted that the use of the circumflex (^) has been practically phased out, except to distinguish between homonyms: **adet/âdet; alem/âlem;** and in certain Arabic words (see Pronunciation).

All English words are spelt according to English and not American usage.

5. *Pronunciation*

The modern Turkish alphabet is completely phonetic, easy to learn, and without any great difficulties as to pronunciation.

(*a*) *Vowels*

a as *u* in *sun*
e as *e* in *bed*
ı as *i* in *cousin*
i as *i* in *sit*
â as *a* in *far* (after **g/k** it becomes *ya*)
û as *u* in *rule* (after **g/k** it becomes *yu*)

o as *o* in *got*
ö as *eu* in French *peu*
u as *u* in *bull*
ü as *u* in French *tu*

(*b*) *Consonants.* These are pronounced as in English with the exception of the following six:

c as *j* in *jar*
ç as *ch* in *church*

j as *s* in *measure*
ş as *sh* in *shut*

ğ with hard vowels a guttural and barely perceptible **g** (**dağ**); with soft vowels as
y (**eğer** = *eyer*).

v between the English *v* and *w*; it is sometimes interchangeable with **ğ**: **dövmek**
or **döğmek**.

(*c*) *Stress.* In Turkish words the stress is more evenly divided than in English, but
normally falls on the last syllable except in place-names and adverbs:

kitáp; konuşmák; bizimkilér; elindekilerindén; Ánkara; yálnız (only) but **yalníz**
(alone).

The main exceptions to this are:

(i) there is a strong stress on the syllable preceding the negative **-me** and an even
stronger stress before the interrogative **mi**: **yápmadı; yaptí mı; yapmadí mı**.
(ii) in compound words the stress falls on the last syllable of the first element:
báşmüdür; itimátname; kanátayaklıgiller.
(iii) in foreign loan-words the original accent is generally retained: **élbet; záten;
jiroskóp; lokánta; yóga; nákavt; zirkónyum**. However, Arabic and Persian
words are tending towards the Turkish usage.

6. *Idiomatic phrases*

Idiomatic phrases are not translated literally but are expressed/explained with
the nearest English equivalent.

7. *Points of grammar*

It is assumed that users of the dictionary recognize the various parts of
speech; they have therefore only been indicated:

(*a*) in the case of homonyms:

yemek[1] *n*(*oun*)—**yemek**[2] *v*(*erb*);

(*b*) to distinguish the various verbal forms, transitive, intransitive, passive, causative,
etc. (see Arrangement, Verb forms);
(*c*) to differentiate between a word being used as a noun and as an adjective, etc.:

serin *a*(*djective*) Cool. *n*(*oun*) Cool air/weather.

Most of the grammatical suffixes are given separately, with brief explanations. However, to assist those who wish to study points of Turkish grammar
in greater detail, a full system of cross-references to G. L. Lewis, *Turkish
Grammar* (Oxford, 1967), has been included; these are indicated by page
numbers in square brackets, [82], normally placed immediately after the
headword.

8. *Categories*

Where a word is used in many different contexts with different meanings, these
have been indicated by abbreviated guide-words: *mil*(*itary*); *eng*(*ineering*). A
full list of these is given in the Table of Abbreviations. To avoid a profusion of
such guide-words, the categories have been selected as having as wide a scope
as possible; nor are they unnecessarily repeated.

9. *Abbreviations*

Within the general alphabetical order have been included the most commonly used and generally accepted abbreviations to be found in Turkish; again, bear in mind that these relate to about 1980. If they represent Turkish words, these are given in full without any translation; if foreign words, then their full meaning is given in the appropriate language:

DTCF = Dİl ve Tarİh-Coğrafya Fakültesİ.
FAO = (*Food and Agriculture Organization*).

ABBREVIATIONS
KISALTMALAR

a.	adjective	sıfat
adm.	administration	idarecilik
adv.	adverb	belirteç
aer.	aeronautics, astronautics	havacılık, astronotik
agr.	agriculture, farming	tarım, çiftçilik
Amer.	America(n)	Amerika(n)
arch.	architecture, building	mimarlık, yapıcılık
archaeol.	archaeology	arkeoloji
art	art	sanat
ast.	astronomy	gökbilim
aux. v.	auxiliary verb	yardımcı eylem
bio.	biology, anatomy	yaşambilim, anatomi
bot.	botany	bitkibilim
carp.	carpentry, furniture	dülgerlik, mobilya
chem.	chemistry, pharmacy	kimya, eczacılık
child.	children's language/games	çocuk dil/oyunları
ch.s.	chemical symbol	kimya simgesi
cin.	cinema, photography	sinema, fotoğrafçılık
col.	colloquial	konuşma dili
conj.	conjunction	bağlaç
cul.	culinary, food, drink	aşçılık, yiyecek, içecek
(-de)	verb taking a locative complement	-de'li tümleç alan eylem
(-den)	verb taking an ablative complement	-den'li tümleç alan eylem
dial.	dialect	lehçe
dom.	domestic	eve ait
E.	East(ern)	Doğu(+)
(-e)	verb taking a dative complement	-e'li tümleç alan eylem
ech.	echoic	yansıma
ed.	education	eğitim
e.g.	for example	örneğin
el.	electricity, electronics	elektrik, elektronik
eng.	engineering, mechanics	mühendislik, mekanik
ent.	entomology	böcekbilim
esp.	especially	özellikle
etc.	et cetera	ve benzerleri
ethn.	ethnology	budunbilim

etm.	to do	etmek
Eur.	European	Avrupalı
fem.	feminine	dişil
fig.	figuratively	mecazi olarak
fin.	finance, economics, commerce	maliye, ekonomi, tecim
for.	forestry	ormancılık
fut.	future	gelecek zaman
gamb.	gambling, card-playing	kumar, kâğıt oyunları
gen.	generally	genellikle
geo.	geography	coğrafya
geol.	geology	yerbilim
his.	history	tarih
(-i)	verb taking an accusative complement	-i'li tümleç alan eylem
ich.	ichthyology	balık bilimi
imp. v.	impersonal verb	özne almayan eylem
(-in)	possessive case	-in hali; iyelik eki
ind.	industry	endüstri, sanayi
int.	interjection	ünlem
iron.	ironically	istihzalı olarak
jok.	jokingly	alay yollu söylenir
(-le)	verb taking a 'with' complement	-le'li tümleç alan eylem
leg.	legal	hukuksal
ling.	linguistics, grammar, phonetics	dilbilim, dilbilgisi, sesbilim
lit.	literature	yazın, edebiyat
live.	livestock farming	hayvancılık
masc.	masculine	eril
math.	mathematics	matematik
med.	medicine, dentistry	tıp, dişhekimliği
met.	meteorology	meteoroloji
mil.	military	askerlikle ilgili
min.	mining, metallurgy	madencilik, metalbilim
mod.	fashion, clothing, cosmetics	moda, giyim, kozmetik
mot.	motor vehicles, roads	motorlu taşıtlar, yollar
mus.	music	müzik
myc.	mycology	mantarbilim
myth.	mythology	mitoloji
N.	North(ern)	Kuzey(+)
n.	noun	ad, isim
naut.	seamanship and ships	denizcilik, gemiler
neg.	negative	olumsuz
now	now, the present	şimdi
obs.	obsolete	bugün kullanılmayan
olm.	to be	olmak

Or.	Oriental	Doğu+
orn.	ornithology	ornitoloji
o.s.	oneself	kendisi
part.	participle	ortaç
pej.	pejorative	yermeli
phil.	philosophy, logic, ethics	felsefe, mantık, törebilim
phys.	physics	fizik
pl.	plural	çoğul
poet.	poetic	şiirde kullanılır
pol.	politics	politika
post.	postposition	ilgeç, edat
pref.	prefix	önek
pr.n.	proper noun	özel ad
pron.	pronoun	adıl
psy.	psychology	ruhbilim, psikoloji
pub.	publishing, printing	basın, basmacılık
rad.	radio, TV, radar	radyo, TV, radar
rel.	religion	din
rly.	railways	demiryolları
S.	South(ern)	Güney(+)
s.	singular	tekil
sl.	slang	argo
s.o.	someone	bir kimse
soc.	sociology	toplumbilim
sp.	sport, gymnastics	spor, jimnastik
stg.	something	bir şey
suf.	suffix	sonek
tex.	textiles, weaving	mensucat, dokumacılık
th.	theatre	tiyatro
Tk.	Turkish	Türk+
v.	verb	eylem
vc.	verb causative	ettirgen eylem
vi.	verb intransitive	geçişsiz eylem
vn.	verbal noun	eylem adı, ad-fiil
vp.	verb passive	edilgen eylem
vt.	verb transitive	geçişli eylem
vulg.	vulgar(ly)	kaba(ca)
W.	West(ern)	Batı(+)
zoo.	zoology	hayvanbilim, zooloji

SIGNS

İŞARETLER

=	equals; see word(s) in small capitals separately	demek; küçük punto büyük harfle yazılan sözcük(ler)e ayrıca bakınız
~	in place of repeating a word or root	bir sözcük veya kökü tekrarlamamak için
= ~...	see the compound form	bileşik şekline bakınız
.../...	separates alternatives	'ya da' anlamındadır; ayrı kullanılışı gösterir
...//...	separates two different expressions	iki ayrı deyim gösterir
·	indicates end of word-root [ol·mak]	sözcük kökünden sonra konur
ı	indicates where the spelling changes for the inflected forms [kita'pᵇı]	ad durumuna göre yazımın değiştiğini gösterir
+	indicates use of the noun in the possessive ('izafet') construction [Türk+]	adın bir ad tamlamasında kullanılmasını gösterir
[82]	see G. L. Lewis, *Turkish Grammar*, p. 82	bk. G. L. Lewis, *Turkish Grammar*, s. 82

A

A, a[1] [a] First Tk. letter, A; first (in a class/series); (*bio.*) blood-group A; (*chem.*) vitamin A; (*mus.*) la. ~'**dan Z'ye kadar**, from A to Z, from top to bottom, entirely.

a[2] *int.* Ah!, eh?, oh!; then!, so!

A, a. = (*ling.*) AD; AKŞAM; (*mil.*) ALAY; ALMANCA/ (-DAN); (*el.*) AMPER; ANGSTROM; ANKARA; AR; (*el.*) ANOT; (*ch.s.*) ARGON; AT (chess); (*in compound titles*) ATATÜRK.

-a[1] *fem. n. suf.* [25] = -E[1] [REFİKA].

-a[2] *dative n. suf.* [28] = -E[2] [AKŞAMA].

-a[3] *v. suf.* [174] = -E[3] [OLA, KALA].

-a[4] *adv. suf.* [196] [FARAZA].

-a-[5] *v. suf.* [227] = -E-[4] [HARCAMAK].

A.a. = ATOM AĞIRLIĞI.

AA = ANADOLU AJANSI.

ab (*obs.*) Water; river; fountain; juice; wine; tears.

a.b. = (*bio.*) ALT-BÖLÜM.

AB = (*bio.*) Blood-group AB.

aba (*tex.*) Coarse woollen cloth; (*mod.*) aba, cloak. ~ **altından değnek göstermek**, threaten with soft words, use an iron hand in a velvet glove: ~ **gibi**, (*tex.*) thick, coarse: ~**yı yakmak (-e)**, fall in love with s.o.

aba·cı Aba maker/seller: ~ **kebeci sen neci?**, what is it to you? ~**cılık**, aba making.

abad·(an) Prosperous, flourishing. ~**anlık**, prosperity.

abadi A glazed yellow writing-paper.

abajur Lampshade; roller-blind.

abak[1] (*eng.*) Chart, diagram; (*aer.*) spinner. ~(**üs**), abacus.

abalı Wearing an aba; poor, wretched; = VURMAK. ~**memeliler**, (*zoo.*) dermoptera, flying lemurs.

abandırmak (-i, -e) Make lean over/kneel down.

abandone ~ **etm.**, (*sp.*) abandon (match).

abani Silk-cloth (with yellow design).

abanmak (-e) Lean over/against; push against; reject; (*sl.*) live off s.o., batten on s.o.

abanoz (*carp.*) Ebony. ~ **ağacı**, (*bot.*) ebony tree: ~ **gibi**, jet black: ~ **kesilmek**, become as black/ hard as ebony: ~ **yürekli**, hard-hearted. ~**giller**, (*bot.*) Ebenaceae.

abart·ı/-ma Exaggeration. ~**ıcı**/~**macı**, exaggerator. ~**ılı**/~**malı**, exaggerated. ~**ılmak**, *vp.* be exaggerated. ~**mak (-e)**, exaggerate.

abaşo *a.* (*naut.*) Lower; bottom.

Abbas *pr.n.* ~ **yolcu (duramaz)**, Abbas is about to go (said of s.o. about to die/travel/be dismissed).

AB·C = ABECE; ATOM BİYOLOJİ KİMYA. ~**D** = AMERİKA BİRLEŞİK DEVLETLERİ.

abdal[1] *n.* Wandering dervish. ~**a malum olur**, (*jok.*) prophet(ic).

Abdal[2] *pr.n.* (Member of) Turkish tribe in Afghanistan/nomadic tribe in Anatolia.

ab·dal[3] *a.* = APTAL. ~**dest** = APTES.

abdük·siyon (*bio.*) Abduction. ~**tör**, abductor.

abdülleziz (*bot.*) Earth-almond.

abece Alphabet. ~**li**, alphabetic(al): ~ **sayılı**, alphanumerical. ~**sel**, alphabetic(al).

aber·an (*ast., psy.*) Aberrant. ~**asyon**, aberration.

abes *a.* Useless; stupid; low-down. *n.* Useless thing; absurdity, nonsense. ~ **kaçmak**, be spoken out of turn: ~ **yere**, in vain, to no purpose; an exercise in futility: ~**le uğraşmak**, pass the time with trifles.

abı·hayat[1] The water of life; excellent water; (*jok.*) raki: ~ **içmiş**, one who never grows old. ~**ru**, honour, self-respect: ~ **dökmek**, beg humbly, humiliate o.s.

abi (*col.*) = AĞABEY.

abide Monument. ~**leşmek**, *vp.* be remembered. ~**leştirmek (-i)**, commemorate. ~**vi**, monumental.

-abil- *v. suf.* [151] = -EBİL- [YAPABİLMEK].

abis (*geo.*) Abyss. ~**el**, abyssal, bottomless.

abiyogenez (*bio.*) Abiogenesis, spontaneous generation.

abla Elder sister; elderly female domestic.

ablak Chubby, round. ~ **yüzlü**, round-faced.

ablalı·k[g1] Being an elder sister. ~ **etm.**, behave protectively (like an elder sister).

abla·syon (*geo., phys.*) Ablation. ~**tif**, (*ling.*) ablative.

ablatya Large fishing-net.

abli (*naut.*) Sheet. ~**yi bırakmak/kaçırmak**, (*sl.*) lose control of o.s.

abluka Blockade. ~ **altına almak**/~ **etm.**, blockade: ~ **kaçağı**, blockade runner: ~**yı bozmak**/ **yarmak**, run the blockade: ~**yı kaldırmak**, raise the blockade.

abone Subscriber; reader; subscription. ~ (**bilet**/ **kartı**), season-ticket: ~ **olm.**/**yazmak (-e)**, subscribe to: ~ **ücreti**, subscription-fee: ~**yi kesmek**// **yenilemek**, cancel//renew a subscription.

abon·eli *a.* Subscription. ~**elik**, *n.* subscriber; subscription. ~**man** = ABONE; agreement for supply of gas/water, etc.: ~ **sigortası**, (*fin.*) floating insurance.

aborda (*naut.*) Boarding. ~ **etm. (-e)**, go alongside; (*sl.*) accost.

abortif Abortive.

abosa (*naut.*) Avast! ~ **etm.**, moor; (*sl.*) stop, pack up.

abra Make-weight, tare. ~**ma**, (*naut.*) handling. ~**mak (-i)**, handle/steer/con (ship).

abra·sif Abrasive. ~**zyon**, abrasion.

abraş Speckled; piebald; (*bot.*) chlorotic; (*med.*) leprous. ~**lık**, (*bot.*) chlorosis; (*med.*) leprosy.

abs- *Also* = APS-. ∼ **olü(tizm)**, absolu·te/(-tism).

ab·sorbe Absorbed: ∼ **etm.**, absorb. ∼ **sorpsiyon**, absorption.

ab·straksiyon(izm) (*art.*) Abstraction(ism). ∼ **stre**, abstract.

abu *int.* (*of fear/surprise*) Ah!, oh!

abuhava Climate.

abuk sabuk Incoherent, nonsensical. ∼ **söylemek**, talk nonsense: ∼ **söz**, nonsense.

abuli (*psy.*) Ab(o)ulia, loss of will-power.

abullabut Stupid; loutish, boorish.

abur cubur Incongruous mixtures (of food etc.); unwholesome; trash. ∼ **kimseler**, riff-raff.

abus Sour-faced, grim, morose; frowning.

abuzambak = ABUK SABUK.

Ac. = (*ch.s.*) AKTİNYUM.

acaba I wonder if . . .!; is it so?

-acağı- *v. suf.* [163, 186] = -ECEĞİ- [ALACAĞINDAN].

acaibisebaiâlem The seven wonders of the world.

acaip = ACAYİP.

-acak *v. suf.* [112, 158] = -ECEK [ALACAK]. ∼ **bir sebep yok**, there's no reason to . . ..

acar Bright; self-reliant; enterprising; plucky; new. ∼ **lık**, enterprise.

acayi¹pᵇⁱ *a.* Wonderful; bizarre, eccentric, strange. *int.* How strange!; you don't say! ∼ **karşılamak**, find/consider strange: ∼ **olm.**/∼ **leşmek**, *vi.* become strange/different: ∼ **ine gitmek**, seem strange. ∼ **çe**, strangely. ∼ **lik**, strangeness; oddity.

acelacayip Very strange; queer.

acele *n.* Haste, hurry; dispatch. *a.* Hasty, hurried, cursory; emergency, express, urgent. *adv.* Hastily, hurriedly, urgently. ∼ ∼, very hurriedly, in a rush: ∼ **etm.**, hasten; be in a hurry: ∼ **ile**, hastily: ∼ **işe şeytan karışır**, more haste less speed: ∼ **mektup// teslim**, express letter//delivery: ∼ **si olm.**, have to hurry: ∼ **si var**, it's urgent: ∼ **(si) yok**, there's no hurry (for it): ∼ **ye gelmek**, be done in a hurry/ carelessly: ∼ **ye getirmek**, profit by s.o.'s haste (to cheat him); do stg. in a hurry.

acele·ci In a hurry; hasty/impatient/restless (person). ∼ **cilik**, hastiness. ∼ **leştirmek (-i)**, hasten.

Acem *pr.n.* (*ethn.*) Persian, Iranian. ∼ +, *a.* Persian, Iranian: ∼ **halı//seccadesi**, Persian carpet//rug: ∼ **kama//kılıcı**, two-edged dagger//sword: ∼ **kılıcı gibi**, double-faced/-dealing: ∼ **mübalağası**, over-exaggeration: ∼ **pilavı**, (*cul.*) rice stewed with meat.

acem(aşiran/ ∼ **buselik/** ∼ **kürdü)** (*Or. mus.*) Tk. melodies.

Acemce (*ling.*) Persian, Farsi.

acemi *n.* Beginner, novice; stranger; raw recruit; cub. *a.* Awkward, clumsy, inexperienced, unskilled; callow, raw. ∼ **beygir**, (*live.*) unbroken horse: ∼ **çaylak (bu kadar uçar)**, (that's all you can expect from) a clumsy fellow: ∼ **deposu**, (*mil.*) recruiting centre: ∼ **er/nefer**, (*mil.*) recruit: ∼ **öğretmeye vaktim yok**, I've no patience for/with him: ∼ **talebe**, apprentice.

acemi·ce Clumsily. ∼ **lik**, inexperience; awkwardness: ∼ **çekmek**, suffer from inexperience. ∼ **oğlan**, (*his.*) Janissary recruit.

Acem·istan (*geo.*) Iran, Persia. ∼ **lalesi**ⁿⁱ, (*bot.*) a saxifrage.

acent·a/-e (*fin.*) Agent, broker, factor, representative; agency, branch. ∼ **elik**, agency.

acep = ACABA.

aceze *pl.* The destitute; waifs and strays.

acı¹ *a.* Bitter, acerbic; caustic, sharp, pungent, acrid; rancid (oil); glaring (colour); dismal, pitiable; harsh, brutal. ∼ ∼, bitterly: ∼ ∼ **feryat etm.**, scream blue murder: ∼ AĞAÇ: ∼ BADEM: ∼ BAKLA: ∼ **bir hayal kırıklığı**, a rude awakening: ∼ **çeken**, worried; suffering: ∼ ÇİĞDEM: ∼ **dil**, harsh words: ∼ **göl**, (*geo.*) salt lake: ∼ **gülme**, bitter sardonic laugh: ∼ HIYAR: ∼ **kahve**, (*cul.*) Tk. coffee with little sugar: ∼ **kuvvet**, brute force: ∼ MARUL: ∼ **patlıcanı kırağı çalmaz**, you can't spoil what is already spoiled: ∼ **soğan kuru ekmek**, in reduced circumstances: ∼ **soğuk**, (*met.*) bitter cold: ∼ **söylemek**, speak the unvarnished truth: ∼ **söz**, harsh words, reproaches: ∼ **su**, hard/salty/ brackish water: ∼ YONCA.

acı² *n.* Pain, ache; suffering; distress; grief, sorrow. ∼ **çekmek/duymak** = ∼ MAK: ∼ **gelmek**, be hurtful: ∼ **görmüş**, who has suffered: ∼ **yit(ir)imi**, (*med.*) analgesia: ∼ **sı içine çökmek/yüreğine işlemek**, feel stg. bitterly; worry about stg.: ∼ **sı sonra çıkar**, there'll be the devil to pay: ∼ **sı tepesinden çıkmak**, feel very sore about stg.; suffer great pain: ∼ **sına katlanmak**, bear the brunt of: ∼ **sını çekmek**, pay the penalty for stg.: ∼ **sını çıkarmak**, take revenge for stg.; get one's own back: ∼ **yı tatmıyan tatlıyı anlıyamaz**, one only appreciates happiness through sadness.

acı·aga¹çᶜ¹ (*bot.*) Bitter-wood, quassia. ∼ **badem**, (*bot.*) bitter almond; (*fig.*) shrewd, hard-boiled: ∼ **kurabiyesi**, (*cul.*) macaroon. ∼ **bakla**, (*bot.*) horse bean; lupin. ∼ **balık**, (*ich.*) bitterling. ∼ **ca**, bitterish. ∼ **çiğdem**, (*bot.*) meadow saffron: ∼ **giller**, Colchicaceae. ∼ **daş**, fellow-sufferer. ∼ **elma/** ∼ **hıyar**, (*bot.*) colocynth. ∼ **kabuk/** ∼ **kök**, (*bot.*) quassia.

acı¹kᵍ¹ ¹ Grief, sorrow; tragedy; anger. ∼ **ı tutmak**, (*obs.*) get angry. ∼ **ılmak**, *imp. v.* one be hungry. ∼ **lanmak**, *vi.* grow sad/mournful. ∼ **lı**, painful; pathetic, tragic, tearful: ∼ **komedi**, (*th.*) tragicomedy: ∼ **olay**, tragedy. ∼ **ma**, *vn.* hunger. ∼ **mak**, *vi.* be/feel hungry. ∼ **tırmak (-i)**, make hungry, give a keen appetite.

acık² (*col.*) = AZICIK.

acı·lanmak/ ∼ **laşmak** *vi.* Become bitter/harsh/ pungent/rancid, etc.; get cross; be worried. ∼ **lı**, grieved, sad; dramatic; bitter; spicy. ∼ **lık**, grief; bitterness; acerbity.

acı·ma *vn.* Compassion, pity; aching; (*cul.*) rancidity. ∼ **mak**, *vi.* feel pain, ache, hurt; feel pity, be sorry; (*cul.*) become rancid/sour: (-e), pity/feel pity for/commiserate with s.o.; grudge stg.; deplore stg.; regret the loss/waste of stg.: = ACILAŞMAK: **acıyarak**, compassionately. ∼ **malı**, merciful, compassionate. ∼ **marul**, (*bot.*) endive; chicory. ∼ **masız**, hard-hearted, pitiless, cruel. ∼ **masızlık**, pitilessness, cruelty. ∼ **mık**, (*bot.*) common darnel; corn-cockle. ∼ **mış**, (*cul.*) rancid. ∼ **msı/** ∼ **mtırak**, bitterish.

acın·acak Pitiable; deplorable, regrettable. ∼ **aklı**,

pitiable. ~**ası**, strange (person). ~**dırmak (-i, -e)**, arouse pity for s.o./o.s.; ask for sympathy. ~**ma**, *vn.*; regret. ~**mak (-e)**, be pitied/regretted; grieve for s.o./stg. ~**sı**, perplexed, wretched.
acı·pelin (*bot.*) Wormwood. ~**rak**, slightly bitter. ~**rga**, (*bot.*) horse-radish. ~**sız**, without pain/ bitterness; painless: ~ **ölüm**, euthanasia. ~**tmak (-i)**, cause pain/suffering; hurt; (*cul.*) make bitter, turn. ~**yıcı**, sad, bitter. ~**yonca**, (*bot.*) bogbean.
acibe Strange/wonderful thing. ~**i hilkat**, monster.
acil Hurried; hasty; fleeting; urgent; prompt; pressing. ~**en**, promptly; hastily; urgently.
acip Wonderful; strange.
aci·tato (*mus.*) Agitato. ~**yo** = ACYO.
ac'iz^zi Incapacity, inability; impotence; poverty. ~ **hali**, (*fin.*) insolvency: ~ **halinde**, insolvent: ~**e düşmek**, fail, become insolvent.
âciz Incapable; weak; impotent; poor, humble. ~ **bırakmak**, baffle: ~ **kalmak (-den)**, be incapable of.
âciz·ane (*obs.*) Humbly, modestly. ~**leri**, (*obs.*) your humble servant. ~**lik**, inability; humbleness.
acul^ü Impatient; precipitate, impetuous.
acun (*ast.*) Cosmos, universe. ~ +, *a.* Cosmic; cosmo-. ~**bilim**, cosmology. ~**doğum**, cosmogony. ~**sal**, cosmic.
acur^1 (*bot.*) Hairy cucumber. ~ ^2(**lu**) = AJUR(LU).
acuze Old woman; shrew, hag. ~**lik**, malicious act.
acyo (*fin.*) Agio; premium. ~**cu**, speculator. ~**culuk**, agiotage.
acz- = ACİZ.
aç^1 Hungry; empty; destitute; covetous; insatiable. ~ **açık**, hungry and homeless: ~ ~**ına**, without food; with an empty stomach: ~ **aman bilmez**, the starving show no mercy: ~ **ayı oynamaz**, don't grudge the worker his food/wages; feed him first then expect service: ~ **bırakmak/koymak (-i)**, starve s.o.: ~ **biilaç**, starving, utterly destitute: ~ **çıplak**, without food or clothing: ~ **doyurmak**, feed the destitute: ~ **durmak/kalmak**, *vi.* go without food; starve; fast: ~ **gezmektense tok ölmek yeğdir**, death is preferable to starvation: ~GÖZLÜ: ~ **karnına (alınacak ilaç)**, (medicine to be taken) on an empty stomach: ~ **kurt gibi**, like a ravenous wolf: ~ **suzuz kalmak**, be destitute: ~ **taksir**, fasting; starving: ~ **tavuk kendini arpa ambarında sanır**, the destitute live on illusions: ~ **yanından kaç!**, beware of the hungry!: ~**ın karnı doyar gözü doymaz**, the starving are never satisfied: ~**ın koynunda ekmek durmaz**, those who are starving can't save money: ~**ından ölmek**, die of hunger; starve.
-aç *n. suf.* [225] = -GEÇ [KALDIRAÇ].
açaca'k^ğı Tool for opening, (tin-)opener; key; pencil-sharpener.
açalya (*bot.*) Azalea.
aç·an Opener; (*bio.*) (ex)tensor. ~**ar**, opener, key; (*eng.*) valve; (*cul.*) apéritif, appetizer.
aççelerando (*mus.*) Accelerando.
açevele (*naut.*) Span, sprit; hammock stretcher.
açgözlü Covetous, avaricious; avid, greedy, insatiable. ~**lük**, avarice, cupidity; greed, etc.: ~ **etm.**, covet, desire: ~ **her şeyi kaybettirir**, covet all lose all.

açı (*math.*) Angle; (*eng.*) elbow; (*fig.*) view(point), direction. ~ +, *a.* Angular: ~ **çekimi**, (*cin.*) angle shot: ~ **uzaklığı**, angular distance: ~**dan (bu)**, from (this) point of view: ~**nın kenarlar**//**tamam**// **tepesi**, (*math.*) arms//complement//point of the angle.
açı·cı *a.* Opening. *n.* Opener; (customs) examiner; expander; (*bio.*) extensor. ~**d-** = AÇIT.
açık^1 *a.* Open; uncovered; unobstructed; exposed (to); clear, cloudless, bright; naked, bare; (*fin.*) unpaid, deficient, missing; lacking; vacant, unoccupied, empty; audible, distinct; light/pale (colour); plain (language), not in cipher; blunt, bluff, free in manner, impudent; saucy, obscene (book); (*fin.*) blank (bill/cheque, etc.) *adv.* Openly; freely; frankly; clearly. ~ ~, openly, nothing concealed: ~ **adım**, stride: ~AĞIZ: ~ **ağızlı**, babbling; stupid: ~ **alınla**, successfully and honourably: ~ **anlaşma**, (*fin.*) open-ended contract: ~ **artırma**, public auction: ~ **ateş**, (*mil.*) direct fire: ~ **baş**, bareheaded; bald: ~ **bildirme**, public announcement: ~ **bir hava**, cloudless sky/weather: ~ **bono vermek (-e)**, give s.o. (*fin.*) a blank cheque// (*fig.*) carte blanche/complete authority: ~ **boyalı**, (*med.*) hypochromic: ~ **bölge**, (*fin.*) free zone: ~ **bulunmak**, be vacant: ~ **ciro**, (*fin.*) blank endorsement: ~ **çek**, (*fin.*) blank cheque: ~ **deniz**, *n.* (*naut.*) the open sea, the deep; the high seas; *a.* offshore: ~ **devre**, (*el.*) open/isolated circuit: ~ **doru**, light bay (horse): ~ **durmak**, stand aside, not interfere: ~ **duruşma**, (*leg.*) public hearing: ~ **eksiltme**, (*fin.*) Dutch auction; open tender: ~ **ela**, greenish grey: ~ **elli**, generous, open-handed: ~ **fikirli**, broad-minded, enlightened: ~GÖZ: ~ **hava**, cloudless sky; open-air (cinema etc.): ~ **hava ocağı**, (*min.*) opencast mine: ~ **hava resmi**, (*art.*) landscape: ~ **hava toplantısı**, (*pol.*) meeting: ~HAVA: ~ **hece**, (*ling.*) open syllable: ~ **imza**, signature on a blank cheque, etc.: ~ **işletme**, (*min.*) opencast mining: ~ **itibar**, (*fin.*) overdraft: ~ **kafalı**, clearheaded: ~ **kalp ameliyatı**, (*med.*) open-heart surgery: ~ **kalpli**, open-hearted, loyal; good-natured, kindly: ~ **kapı**, (*adm.*) open-door (policy); (*fig.*) hospitable person; hospitality: ~ **kapı bırakmak**, keep the negotiations open: ~ **konuşmak**, speak openly/frankly: ~ **kredi**, (*fin.*) overdraft: ~ **liman**, (*mil.*) open//(*fin.*) free port: ~ **mektup**, unsealed letter; (*pub.*) open letter: ~ **meşrep**, immoral, libertine: ~ **ocak (işletme)**, (*min.*) opencast (mining): ~ **olm.**, be open/clear/frank, etc.; (-e), be welcoming: ~ **ordugâh**, (*mil.*) bivouac, camp: ~ **oturum**, (*adm.*) public meeting, open session: ~ **oyuncu**, (*sp.*) winger: ~ **öz tok söz**, sincerely and frankly: ~ **rastık**, (*myc.*) loose smut: ~ **renk**, light/ pale colour: ~ **saçık**, immodestly dressed; indecent (words, etc.), dirty, bawdy; disorderly, untidy: ~ **saçık yayın**, (*pub.*) pornography: ~ **satış** = ~ ARTIRMA: ~ **seçik**, very clear(ly): ~ **söylemek**, speak clearly/frankly/openly: ~SÖZLÜ: ~ **şehir**, (*mil.*) open city: ~ **taşıt**, open/uncovered vehicles: ~ **yer**, open space; (*adm.*) vacant post: ~ **yer korkusu**, (*psy.*) agoraphobia: ~ **yol**, (*mot.*) throughway: ~ **yürekle**, openly; sincerely: ~

yürekli(lik), open-hearted(ness), honest(y), loyal(ty).

açı'kᵍ¹ ² *n.* Open air; open country; (*naut.*) open sea; offing; high seas; gap, vacant space; (*adm.*) vacant position; (*fin.*) deficit; (*sp.*) outside. ~ **maaşı**, (*fin.*) half-/redundancy pay: ~ **vermek**, (*fin.*) produce a deficit; (*fig.*) reveal one's soft spot: ~ **a çıkarma**, (*adm.*) dismissal; display: ~ **a çıkarmak (-i)**, dismiss s.o.; display, reveal, make known: ~ **a çıkmak**, be dismissed/without work; become clear, be understood; (*chem.*) result from a reaction: ~ **a varmak**, reach the open sea: ~ **a vermek (-i)**, make clear: ~ **a vurma**, disclosure: ~ **a vurmak**, *vi.* become clear: **(-i)**, *vt.* lay bare, expose, proclaim to the world, declare openly; divulge (a secret, etc.): ~ **ı çıkmak**, show a deficit, be short in one's accounts: ~ **ı kapatmak**, meet a deficit; close the gap: ~ **lar livası**, (*iron.*) the unemployed: ~ **ta**, in the open air, outdoors; (*ind.*) unemployed; (*naut.*) offshore: ~ **ta bırakmak (-i)**, leave outside/ homeless/uncared for/without work: ~ **ta kalmak/ olm.**, be out in the cold/homeless/uncared for/ without work: ~ **ta yatmak**, bivouac: ~ TAN.

açık·ağ'ızᶻ¹ Babbler; imbecile; astonishment; (*bot.*) rocket. ~ **ça**, openly; clearly, distinctly; bluntly; above-board: ~ **söylemek**, declare, confess. ~ **çası**, in plain words. ~ **çı**, (*fin.*) bear. ~ **-gagalı leylek**, (*orn.*) African open-bill stork. ~ **göz**, wide awake, sharp, cunning (fellow), cagey: ~ **dür!**, he's all there! ~ **göz(lü)lük**, alertness, sharpness, cunning; being wide awake: ~ **etm.**, be wide awake/practical; have an eye on the main chance. ~ **hava**, (*phys., met.*) atmosphere. ~ **lama**, clarification, description, comment(ary); statement: ~ **isteme**, asking for an explanation: ~ **noktası**, (*ling.*) colon: ~ **yapmak/~ da bulunmak**, make a statement. ~ **lamak (-i)**, make public, divulge; explain, clarify, comment on. ~ **lanış**, publicity. ~ **lanmak**, *imp. v.* be explained/made clear, etc.; become common knowledge/public; throw off disguise/concealment. ~ **layıcı**, explanatory; (*ling.*) in apposition: ~ **ad**, (*pub.*) sub-title. ~ **lı**, ~ **koyulu**, (*art.*) with light and dark colours, chiaroscuro; variegated; dappled. ~ **lık**, open space; break, interval; opening, door, etc., gap; (*eng.*) clearance; (*cin.*) aperture; (*fig.*) freedom of manner, bluffness; indecency; clearness (weather/expression); lightness/paleness (colour); openness; spaciousness. ~ **lıkla**, openly, clearly. ~ **lıkölçer**, (*phys.*) aperture-meter. ~ **sözlü(lük)**, outspoken/ (-ness). ~ **tan**, *adv.* without effort; from a distance/ the open sea: ~ **açığa**, openly, frankly: ~ **para kazanmak**, receive unexpected money, have a windfall: ~ **satış**, (*fin.*) bear/short sale. ~ **tohumlular**, (*bot.*) gymnosperms.

açı·lama Reconnaissance, survey; explanation, commentary; (*cin.*) shooting from different angles. ~ **lamak (-i)**, reconnoitre, survey. ~ **lı**, angular, angled: ~ **olma/~ lık**, angularity.

açıl·ım Opening; (*ast.*) declination; (*math.*) development, expansion. ~ **ır**, *v.* = AÇILMAK: *a.* opening, sliding open: ~ **kapanır**, folding, collapsible (chair, etc.); extending/drop-leaf (table): ~ **yemiş**, (*bot.*)

dehiscent fruit. ~ **ış**, opening; inauguration; (*eng.*) clearance; (*naut.*) clearing: ~ **gece//günü**, opening night//day: ~ **nutuk//töreni**, inaugural speech// ceremony. ~ **ma**, opening; development; (*cin.*) fade-in; (*bot.*) dehiscence; (*phys.*) dilation; (*mil.*) deployment, open order: ~ **saati**, opening-time.

açılmak *vi.* Be opened; be discovered; be widened; develop; dilate; become more spacious; be amused; be refreshed; escape from boredom; recover (from faintness etc.); (*met.*) (weather) clear; (*adm.*) (post) become vacant; be cleaned; develop; open out; blossom out; throw off restraint, become more easy in manner; be morally corrupted; recede, draw away from, shun; (*naut.*) put to sea; (swimmer) go far out: **(-e)**, open one's heart to s.o.; (door, etc.) open/give on to. **açıl Susam açıl!**, open Sesame!: **açılıp saçılmak**, be scattered; dissipate one's forces; be immodestly dressed; spend extravagantly: AÇILIR: **açılmadık kutu**, a secretive/uncommunicative person: **açılmaz yemiş**, (*bot.*) indehiscent fruit.

açım Invention; opening. ~ **cı**, inventor. ~ **(lama)**, annotation: ~ **yazmak/~ lamak (-i)**, annotate. ~ **lı**, ~ **doğurtma**, (*med.*) caesarian birth.

açın Development; discovery. ~ **dırma**, (*math.*) development; expansion. ~ **dırmak (-i)**, develop; expand. ~ **ım**, (*math.*) development. ~ **lama**, (divine) inspiration, revelation. ~ **lamak (-i)**, discover. ~ **mak**, *vi.* (*bio.*) develop, expand. ~ **sama**, exploration. ~ **samak (-i)**, explore.

açı·ortay (*math.*) Angle bisector: ~ **düzlemi**, bisecting plane. ~ **ölçer**, protractor. ~ **sal**, angular: ~ **hız**, angular velocity.

açış Opening, inauguration. ~ **+**, *a.* Opening; inaugural.

açı'tᵈ¹ (*arch.*) Opening, door, window, etc.

açkı (Wax-)polish, gloss; (*eng.*) reamer; opener; key. ~ **cı**, polisher. ~ **lamak (-i)**, polish, burnish; buff. ~ **lı**, polished.

açlı·kᵍ¹ Hunger; starvation, famine; greed; emptiness. ~ **çekmek**, go hungry; endure poverty: ~ **grevi**, hunger-strike: ~ **ta darı ekmeği helvadan tatlıdır**, hunger is the best cook: ~ **tan gözü kararmak**, be very hungry: ~ **tan kırılmak**, be starved: ~ **tan nefesi kokmak**, be destitute: ~ **tan ölmek**, die of hunger, starve to death: ~ **tan ölmeyecek kadar**, very little (food); without appetite.

açma *vn.* (Act of) opening; inauguration; clearing, solving; (*agr.*) deforestation; field cleared of bushes etc. (ready for cultivation); (*eng.*) decoupling, disconnecting; hole, orifice. ~ **beyazı**, (*pub.*) transparent white: ~ **ipi**, (*aer.*) ripcord. ~ **cılık**, (*agr.*) clearing, deforestation.

açmak (-i, -e) *vt.* Open; begin (discussion, war, etc.); declare open (meeting, etc.); reveal (secret); solve (difficulty); lay bare; undo, unravel; whet (appetite); dilate; unfold; cheer up; (*naut.*) set (sails); clear away (obstruction); lighten (colour); (*el.*) break (circuit); switch/turn on (light, radio, etc.); dial (a telephone number); sink (well); (*cul.*) roll out (pastry); rub up, polish; uncover; (*math.*) develop; (*fin.*) establish (a business); (*agr.*) bring into cultivation; explain (a subject) more fully; bring out, show at its best; suit, please, become. *vi.* (Flower) bloom; (sky/weather) clear. **aç başı!**, (*sl.*) buzz off!, scram!: **aç gözünü açarlar gözünü**, keep your eyes open or you will have them opened for you: **açarak alıştırma**, (*eng.*) expansion fit: **açıp genişletmek**, open out: **açıp kapama**, (*el.*) on-off: **açtı ağzını yumdu gözünü**, he cursed him up hill and down dale.

açmalı¹k^g¹ Soap; detergent.

açmaz *a.* Reserved, discreet, secretive. *n.* Difficult position; check (in chess, etc.); dilemma, impasse; deceit, trick. ~ **oynamak**, trick, lay a trap: ~**a düşmek/gelmek**, fall into a trap: ~**a getirmek**, play a trick on, lay a trap for. ~**lık**, reserve, discretion; secretiveness.

açtırmak (-i, -e) *vc.* = AÇMAK. Cause to open, etc.; uncover; (*agr.*) clear/reclaim (land). **açtırma çuvalın ağzını/kutuyu söyletme kötüyü**, don't broach the subject for you'll only hear evil.

ad^di ¹ Counting, enumeration.

ad¹ ² Name; reputation; (*ling.*) noun, substantive; (*pub.*) title. ~ +, *a.* (*ling.*) Nominal: ~ **almak**, gain a reputation: ~ **çekimi**, (*ling.*) personal suffixes; declension, inflexion: ~ **damgası**, seal: ~ **durumu**, (*ling.*) case: ~ **gövdesi**, (*ling.*) noun stem: ~ **kazanmak**, make a name for o.s.: ~ **koymak/ vermek (-e)**, give a name to; designate; name, christen: ~ **kökü**, (*ling.*) noun root: ~ **soylu**, (*ling.*) nominal: ~ **tamlaması** (*ling.*) possessive construction: ~ **takmak (-e)**, give a bad name/ nickname to.

ad-: ~**a yazılı**, (*fin.*) to order: ~**dan türeme**, (*ling.*) denominative formation.

adı: ~ **anılan**, the afore-mentioned: ~ **batası(ca)**, *a.* accursed, confounded; abhorred: *n.* that dreadful illness; that damned fellow!: ~ **batmak**, pass into oblivion: ~ **belirsiz**, unknown, of obscure origin: ~ **bile okunmamak (-in)**, be of no importance: ~ **bozulmak**, lose one's good name/reputation: ~ **çıkmak**, become known; get a bad name: ~ **çıkmak (-e)**, be known as . . .; get the reputation of . . .: ~ **çıkacağına canı çıksın/çıkmış dokuza inmez sekize**, give a dog a bad name: ~ **deliye çıkmak**, be reputed mad: ~ **duyulmak**, be(come) known: ~ **fenaya çıkmak**, get a bad name: ~ **geçen**, the above-mentioned: ~ **geçmek**, be remembered; be mentioned: ~ **kalmak (-in)**, be remembered only by name: ~ **karışmak (-e)**, s.o.'s name be connected with stg.: ~ **kazanmak**, gain a reputation: ~ **kötüye çıkmak**, get a bad name: ~ **nedir?**, what is his name?: ~ **olm.**, have an unfounded reputation: ~ **sanı**, one's name and reputation: ~ **sanı yok**, of no account/repute: ~ **üstünde**, as the name implies; as befits the name: ~ **var**, famous; it exists only in name (not in reality): ~ **verilmek**, be named/given a name: ~ **mız sanımız**, our good name.

adına: in the name of/on behalf of/for s.o./stg.: ~ **davranan/davrancı**, agent, representative: ~ **hareket etm.**, act for s.o.: ~ **sunmak**, dedicate stg. to s.o.

adını: ~ **almak**, be named: ~ **ağza almamak**, refuse to mention s.o.'s name; have nothing more to do

with s.o.: ~ **anmamak**, not mention s.o. at all: ~ **bağışlamak**, give one's name (when asked): ~ **koymak**, give (a child) a name; (*fig.*) come to a decision; define precisely, make clear; (*fin.*) decide on a price for stg.: ~ **vermek**, mention s.o.'s name; denominate.

adıyla sanıyla, by his/its well-known name.

ad. = (*geo.*) ADASI; (*ling.*) ADIL.

a.d. = (*bio.*) ALTDAL.

AD = ANADİLDEN DERLEMELER; ANKARA DEVLET . . . .

ada Island; (*adm.*) ward; (*arch.*) block of buildings/ land. ~ **çiçeği**, (*bot.*) meadow buttercup: ~ **gibi**, very big (ship): ~ **yavrusu**, fisherman's rowing-boat. ~**balığı^nı**, sperm whale. ~**LAR**.

adab- = ADAP. ~**ımuaşeret^i**, rules of social behaviour/conduct; etiquette.

adacı¹k^g¹ Small island, islet; traffic island.

adacyo (*mus.*) Adagio.

adaçayı^nı (*bot.*) Garden sage.

ada¹k^g¹ Vow; votive offering; threat. ~ **adamak/ etm.**, pledge, vow; promise, threaten. ~**lı**, promised; fiancé(e); s.o. who has made a vow. ~**lık**, *a.* votive (animal): *n.* votive place.

Adalar (*geo.*) Princes' Islands (Marmora); Aegean Islands. ~ **denizi**, Aegean Sea.

adale (*bio.*) Muscle. ~ +, Muscular: ~ **büzülmesi**, cramp: ~**ler dermansızlığı**, (*med.*) muscular dystrophy. ~**li**, muscular; brawny.

adalet^i (*leg.*) Justice; courts; equity. ~ **Bakan(lığ)ı**, (*adm.*) Minis·ter/(-try) of Justice: ~ **Divanı**, International Court of Justice (The Hague): ~ **Partisi**, (*pol.*) Justice Party: ~ **sarayı**, law-courts.

adalet·çi Just man. ~**le**, justly. ~**li**, just, equitable. ~**siz**, unjust, inequitable. ~**sizlik**, injustice, inequity.

adalı *n.* Islander, *esp.* Aegean islander. *a.* Island.

adali Muscular.

adam *n.* Man; human being; person; good/fine man; servant; agent; partisan. *imp. pron.* One. *suf.* -er, -ist, -man. ~ ~**a**, man to man: ~ **ahbabından belli**, a man is known by the company he keeps: ~AKILLI: ~ **almak**, recruit: ~ **almamak**, (streets, etc.) be overcrowded: ~ **azmanı**, well-built man: ~ **başına**, apiece, each, per head/person: ~ **beğenmemek**, be over-critical: ~ **beni hiç sarmadı**, I didn't take to the man at all: ~ **bir ibret!**, what an impossible man!: ~ **boyu**, as tall as a man: ~ **bu!**, there's a man for you!: ~ **çekiştirmek**, slander: ~ **değil cudam**, 'don't call him a man': ~ **değiştirme**, (*sp.*) substitution: ~ **etm. (-e)**, make a man of, bring up well: ~ **evlat/oğlu**, well-bred man: ~ **gibi**, manly, like a gentleman: ~ **içine çıkmak**, mix with people: ~ **içine karışmak**, become important: ~ **kaldırmak**, kidnap, abduct: ~ **kıtlığı**, (*ind.*) manpower shortage: ~ **kullanmak**, employ, manage: ~ **müsvedde/ taslağı**, apology for a man, lout: ~ **oğlu** = ~ EVLADI: ~ **olacak çocuk bakış/bokundan bellidir**, (*vulg.*) from his looks you can tell which child will make a fine man: ~ **oldum sanıyor!**, he thinks he's a man now!: ~ **olm.**, grow up; have a good career: ~ **olmaz**, hopeless, incorrigible: ~OTU: ~ **öldürme**, homicide, manslaughter: ~ **sarrafı**, good judge of character/people: ~ **satma**, betrayal, infidelity: ~ **(sen de)!**, come along!, you can do it!, don't worry!: ~ **senin dengin değil**, this man is not your equal (in position/capacity): ~ **sırasına geçmek/girmek**, (*iron.*) become important: ~ **takmak**, appoint one man to accompany another: ~ **taslağı** = ~ MÜS-VEDDESİ: ~ **tutmak**, (*sp.*) mark a man: ~ **vurmak**, murder s.o.: ~ **yerine koymak/~dan saymak (-i)**, hold in esteem, consider important: ~ **yokluğunda (ben geldim)**, for want of s.o. better (I've come).

adama: ~ **bağlı**, it depends on the man in question: ~ **dönmek**, become presentable; improve: ~ **laf anlatmak deveye hendek anlatmaktan zor**, it's impossible to make the man see the point: ~ **o kadar kızdım ki . . .**, I was so angry with the man that . . .: ~ **vurmak**, strike a man: ~ **yazık oldu**, it all happened pointlessly to the man: ~ **zırnık vermez**, he's terribly mean.

adamın: ~ **başında ateş yanıyor**, the man is haunted by disaster: ~ **hallerini beğenmiyorum**, I don't like the way the man carries on: ~ **işi gücü**, a man's job, his daily work: ~ **kuyruğudur**, he follows the man about like his shadow: ~ **a çatmak**, (a quarrelsome man) meet his match: ~ **a düşmek**, find the right man for the job: (*fig.*, *iron.*) come across s.o. unreliable: ~ **a göre**, according to/considering the individual.

adamla işim var, I've a job looking after the man; he's a damned nuisance.
adamak (-i, -e) Vow; offer stg. (to fulfil a vow). ~ **la mal tükenmez**, promises cost nothing.
adam·akıllı Proper, reasonable; thoroughly, fully: ~ **ıslatmak**, give s.o. a sound thrashing: ~ **yorulmuş**, worn-out. ~ **ca(sına)**, in a human manner; in the proper way; as a man should. ~ **cağız**, good fellow; poor chap. ~ **cık**ᵏᵍ¹, little man; wretch. ~ **cıl**, tame; domestic; shy; misanthrope; vicious (horse). ~ **cılayın**, properly, decently. ~ **kökü/ ~otu**ⁿᵘ, (*bot.*) mandrake. ~ **lık**, decent/honest behaviour; best clothes. ~ **sendeci**, s.o. always saying ADAM SEN DE! and avoiding the work. ~ **sendecilik**, so saying and doing; indifference, lack of interest. ~ **sız (kalmak)**, (be) without servants/help; unmanned. ~ **sızlık**, lack of employees/servants//protection.
adan(ıl)mak (-e) Be promised/vowed.
adaⁱ**p**ᵇ¹ *pl.* = EDEP. Customs; proprieties. ~ **ve erkân**, customary practices.
adap·tasyon (*lit.*, *zoo.*) Adaptation. ~ **te**, adapted: ~ **etm.**, adapt: ~ **olm.**, be adapted/suitable. ~ **tör**, (*el.*, *eng.*) adaptor.
ada·soğanıⁿ¹ (*bot.*) Squill. ~ **tavşanı**ⁿ¹, (*zoo.*) rabbit.
adaş Having the same name; namesake.
ada·şmak *vi.* Vow mutually. ~ **tmak (-i, -e)**, *vc.* = ADAMAK.
adavetⁱ Hostility, enmity; hate.
aday Candidate; applicant; (*dial.*) betrothed. ~ **lık**, candida·cy/-ture: ~ **ını koymak**, be a candidate/ apply for; contest an election.
ad·bilim (*ling.*) Study of names/nouns. ~ **cı(lık)**,

(*phil.*) nominal·ist/(-ism). ~ **çekme/ ~çekimi**, ballot, draw. ~ **çekmek**, *vi.* ballot/draw lots (for).
addaks (*zoo.*) Addax (antelope).
add·edilmek/~olunmak *vp.* Be counted/considered. ~ ⁱ**etmek**ᵉᵈᵉʳ **(-i)**, count; enumerate; assume, consider; esteem.
addeğişimiⁿⁱ (*lit.*) Metonymy.
ade·d- = ADET. ~ **di**, numerical, arithmetical.
adele = ADALE.
adem Non-existence; lack of; absence. ~ **i** (+ *noun*) absence of: ~ **emniyet**, insecurity: ~ **icabet**, (*fin.*) non-acceptance: ~ **icra**, (*adm.*) non-execution/ -performance: ~ **itimat**, (*pol.*) no confidence: ~ **kabiliyet**, incapacity: ~ **kabul**, (*fin.*) non-acceptance: ~ **merkeziyet**, (*adm.*) decentralization: ~ **merkezileştirmek**, decentralize: ~ **muvaffakiyet**, failure: ~ **tecavüz**, (*adm.*) non-aggression: ~ **tediye**, non-payment: ~ **teslim**, non-delivery.
Âdem *pr.n.* Adam. ~ **elması**ⁿ¹, (*bio.*) adam's apple. ~ **i**, *a.* human. ~ **iyet**ⁱ, humanity; humaneness. ~ **oğlu**ⁿᵘ/ ~ **zade**, mankind, people. ~ **otu** = ADAMOTU.
Aden (*geo.*) Aden; (*rel.*) the Garden of Eden.
aden·itⁱ (*med.*) Adenitis. ~ **oit**ⁱ, (*bio.*) adenoids.
adese (*phys.*, *bio.*) Lens; (*bot.*) lenticel; (*med.*) black measles. ~ **kıl çaprazı**, reticule: ~ **perdesi**, (*cin.*) shutter, diaphragm. ~ **li**, optical.
adeⁱ**t**ᵈⁱ Number; numeral; total, quantity; unit; piece: (*live.*) head. ~ + , *a.* Arithmetical.
âdetⁱ Custom, convention, habit; (*bio.*) menstruation, periods; (*his.*) tax. ~ **bezi**, (*med.*) sanitary towel: ~ **dışı**, *ad hoc*: ~ **edinmek/etm.**, acquire/ contract/get into a habit: ~ **görmek**, (*bio.*) menstruate, have one's periods: ~ **ikinci tabiattır**, habit is second nature: ~ **kalkmak**, a custom fall into disuse: ~ **olm.**, become a custom/habit: ~ **olmuştur**, it is customary/established practice: ~ **romanı**, (*lit.*) novel of manners: ~ **üzere**, as usual: ~ **yerini bulsun diye**, as a mere formality: ~ **e düşkün**, conventional (person): ~ **e uygun**, conventional: ~ **ten hariç**, out of the ordinary, unusual: ~ **ten kesilme**, (*bio.*) menopause: ~ **ten vazgeçmek**, break/drop a habit: ~ **ten vazgeçirmek (-i)**, break s.o. of a habit.
âdet·a *adv.* [198] As usual; merely, simply; as it were, sort of; nearly, virtually, as good as; (*mil.*) walking (a horse)! ~ **çe**, as usual.
adetçe Numerically.
adez·iv Adhesive. ~ **yon**, adhesion.
adıl (*ling.*) Pronoun.
adım Step; pace; (*eng.*) pitch (of a screw). ~ **açmak**, stride out; go faster: ~ ~, step by step, gradually: ~ ~ **gezmek (-i)**, visit every corner of: ~ **atla(ma)**, (*sp.*) hop step and jump: ~ **atmak**, walk; (take the first) step, begin; advance: ~ **atmamak (-e)**, not visit: ~ **başında**, at every step; frequently; close by: ~ **ölçeği**, pedometer: ~ **uydurmak**, fall in step; (*fig.*) fall into line: ~ **uzunluğu**, (*sp.*) length of stride: ~ **ını alamamak**, be unable to refrain (from doing stg.): ~ **ını attırmamak**, prevent s.o. going out: ~ **ını denk/tek almak**, proceed cautiously: ~ **ını geri almak**, retreat: ~ **ını tetik almak**, proceed with caution: ~ **la ölçmek**, pace out: ~ **larını**

açmak/sıklaştırmak, walk faster; hasten: ~ **larını seyrekleştirmek**, walk more slowly.

adım·lamak (-i) Pace; measure by paces. ~ **lık**, distance (measured in steps). ~ **sayar**, pedometer.

adi Customary, usual, ordinary; simple, elementary; banal, common(-place); base, coarse, vulgar, cheap, mean; (*orn.*) common; (*fin.*) inferior (quality). ~ **balıkçıl**, (*orn.*) grey heron: ~ **bilet**, (*rly., etc.*) single ticket: ~ **buhar**, (*phys.*) saturated steam: ~ **çek**, normal crossed cheque: ~ **gün**, week-day, working day: ~ **hisse (senedi)**, (*fin.*) ordinary share: ~ **içtima**, (*adm.*) ordinary meeting: ~ **ispinoz**, (*orn.*) chaffinch: ~ **katar**, (*rly.*) slow/stopping train: ~ **kesir**, (*math.*) vulgar fraction: ~ **küçük kabak**, (*bot.*) ornamental gourd: ~ **mallar**, inferior goods: ~ **martı**, (*orn.*) herring-gull: ~ **pullu**, (*ich.*) carp: ~ **yazı**, longhand: ~ **ye düşme**, anticlimax.

adil Just; lawful; equitable, fair, impartial; legally competent (witness). ~ **ane**, justly; equitably, fairly.

adi·leşmek *vi.* Become common/vulgar/inferior. ~ **leştirmek (-i)**, banalize. ~ **lik**, commonness, vulgarity; baseness.

adi·syon (*fin.*) Bill. ~ **tif**, (*chem.*) additive.

adiyabatik (*met.*) Adiabatic.

adl. = (*geo.*) ADALARI.

ad·landırma (*med.*) Nomenclature, terminology. ~ **landırmak (-i)**, give a name to; refer to. ~ **lanmak**, *vi.* be named; earn a bad name. ~ **laşmak**, *vi.* (*ling.*) become a noun. ~ **lı**, named; famous: ~ **adı ile**, with a well-known name: ~ **sanlı**, famous, celebrated. ~ **lık**, name-plate; (*sp.*) shield.

adli Pertaining to law/justice; judicial. ~ **hata**, judicial error: ~ **sicil**, criminal record: ~ **subay**, (*mil.*) provost-marshal: ~ **tasfiye**, (*fin.*) liquidation: ~ **tıp**, forensic medicine: ~ **yıl**, legal year.

adliye Justice; judicial procedure; law-court. ~ **encümeni**, judicial commission: ~ **işleri**, jurisprudence: ~ **Nazır/Vekili**, (*obs.*) Minister of Justice: ~ **Nezaret/Vekâleti**, (*obs.*) Ministry of Justice: ~ **sarayı**, law court(s). ~ **ci**, jurist, legal authority; Ministry of Justice official.

AD·MMA = ANKARA DEVLET MİMARLIK VE MÜHENDİSLİK AKADEMİSİ. ~ **N** = (*Allgemeine Deutsche Nachrichten*), East-German Press Agency. ~ **OB** = ANKARA DEVLET OPERA VE BALESİ.

adr. = ADRES.

adrenalin (*bio.*) Adrenalin(e).

adres Address. ~ **(baskı) makinesi**, addressograph: ~ **bırakmak/göstermek/vermek**, leave/give one's address: ~ **defter/rehberi**, address-book, directory: ~ **sahibi**, addressee, consignee: ~ **yazmak**, address. ~ **li**, addressed; consigned (to).

Adriya ~ **denizi/** ~ **tik** (*geo.*) Adriatic (Sea).

adsız Nameless; anonymous; unknown; without reputation. ~ **parmak**, ring-finger.

ADSO = ANKARA DEVLET SENFONİ ORKESTRASI.

adsor·be Adsorbed. ~ **plama/** ~ **psiyon**, adsorption. ~ **plamak (-i)**, adsorb.

-adurmak *v. suf.* [191] = -EDURMAK [KONUŞ-ADURMAK].

adveksiyon (*met.*) Advection.

AEO = AVRUPA EKONOMİK ORTAKLAŞMASI.

aer. = AERODİNAMİK.

aero- *pref.* Aero-. ~ **dinami¹kᵍⁱ**, *a.* aerodynamic; streamline(d): *n.* aerodynamics. ~ **faji**, (*med.*) aerophagia. ~ **fobi**, (*psy.*) aerophobia. ~ **fotogrametri**, aerial survey(ing). ~ **litⁱ**, (*ast.*) aerolite. ~ **mekani¹kᵍⁱ**, aeromechanic(s). ~ **¹pᵇᵘ**, (*zoo.*) aerobe. ~ **sol**, aerosol. ~ **statik**, aerostatics. ~ **terapi**, (*med.*) aerotherapy.

AET = AVRUPA EKONOMİK TOPLULUĞU.

afᶠ¹ Pardon, amnesty; forgiveness; exemption; excusing; dismissal. ~ **buyurunuz!**, I beg your pardon!: ~ **dilemek**, beg pardon: ~ **kanunu**, amnesty law: ~ **a uğramak**, be pardoned.

a.f. = (*bio.*) ALTFAMİLYA.

afacan Unruly, undisciplined, mischievous, naughty (child); rascal; urchin. ~ **laşmak**, become/grow unruly, etc. ~ **lık**, unruliness, indiscipline, naughtiness: ~ **etm.**, be unruly, etc.

afakan Palpitation; discomfort, worry. ~ **lar basmak/boğmak**, be worried.

afaki¹ (*med.*) Aphakia.

afaki² Here and there; superficial; futile (language): (*leg.*) objective, impartial. ~ **olarak**, objectively: ~ **sözler**, generalities; small-talk. ~ **lik**, objectivity; superficiality.

afal ~ ~, with staring eyes; astonished. ~ **ina**, (*zoo.*) bottle-nosed dolphin. ~ **la(ş)mak**, *vi.* be astonished/taken aback/stupefied. ~ **laştırmak/** ~ **latmak (-i)**, astonish, amaze, stupefy.

afat¹ *pl.* = AFET. Calamities, disasters, tragedies.

afazi (*med.*) Aphasia.

aferin Bravo!, capital!, well done!; (*iron.*) oh dear!; (*ed.*) good mark. ~ **almak**, (*ed.*) receive a good mark/report.

aferist¹ Speculator, profiteer.

afet¹ Disaster, calamity, cataclysm, tragedy; bane, blight; a bewitching beauty. ~ **zede**, disaster-stricken.

aff- = AF. ~ **edilmek/** ~ **olunmak**, *vp.* be pardoned. ~ **¹etmek**ᵉᵈᵉʳ**/** ~ **eylemek (-i)**, pardon, forgive; (*pol.*) amnesty; excuse, condone; give leave to go; dismiss: **affedersiniz!**, excuse me!, I beg your pardon! ~ **ıumumi**, (*leg.*) general amnesty.

affettuoso (*mus.*) Affettuoso.

Afgan *a.* Afghan. ~ **ca**, (*ling.*) Pushtu. ~ **istan**, (*geo.*) Afghanistan. ~ **lı**, *n.* (*ethn.*) Afghan.

afi (*sl.*) Showing off, swagger. ~ **kesmek/satmak/ yapmak**, cut a dash, swagger. ~ **li**, swaggering.

afif Chaste; virtuous; innocent.

a. fil. = (*bio.*) ALTFİLUM.

afiş (*pub.*) Advertisement, bill, placard, poster. ~ **harfleri**, (*pub.*) display type: ~ **yutmak**, (*sl.*) tell a lie; boast: ~ **te kalmak**, (*th.*) be rehearsed a long time.

afiş·çi Bill-poster. ~ **e**, displayed: ~ **etm.**, declare, fix; risk a bad reputation: ~ **fiyat**, (*fin.*) published/ fixed price.

afita¹pᵇ¹ Sun; (*fig.*) beautiful face. ~ **perest**, (*rel.*) sun-worshipper.

afiyet[i] Health; well-being. ~ **bulmak**, regain one's health: ~ **ola!/olsun!**, '*bon appétit!*'; may it do you good (to one about to eat/drink): ~**le (yemek)**, (eat) with a good appetite.

afoni (*ling.*) Aphonia.

aforizma Aphorism.

aforoz (*rel.*) Excommunication; (*adm.*) banishment. ~ **etm.**/~**lamak (-i)**, excommunicate; anathematize; banish; send to Coventry; (*sl.*) sack, fire. ~**lu**, excommunicated; banished; sent to Coventry.

afortiori *A fortiori*.

AFP = (*Agence France Presse*), French Press Agency.

Afr. = AFRİKA(LI).

afra tafra Pompously; arrogantly, swaggering.

Afrika (*geo.*) Africa. ~ +, *a.* African; Afro-. ~ **çam ağacı**, (*bot.*) Atlas cedar: ~ **karsağı**, (*zoo.*) fennec. ~**domuzu**[nu], (*zoo.*) warthog. ~**lı**, *n.* (*ethn.*) African.

afro·dit[i] (*myth.*) Aphrodite. ~**dizyak**[1], (*med.*) aphrodisiac.

afsun Spell, charm, incantation; crafty tale. ~**cu**/~**ger**, sorcerer, witch. ~**culuk**, witchcraft. ~**lamak (-i)**, bewitch. ~**lu**, bewitched; magical.

Afşar Turkoman tribe (in N. Iran/S. Anatolia).

aft(a) (*med.*) Aphtha. ~ +, *a.* Aphthous.

aftos (*sl.*) Mistress. ~**piyos**, useless, worthless: ~ **iki tavuk bir horoz**, hocus-pocus.

afur tafur With a superior air. = AFRA.

afyon Opium. ~ **çiçeği**, (*bot.*) (opium) poppy: ~ **ruhu**, (*med.*) laudanum: ~ **tekeli**, (*adm.*) opium monopoly: ~ **tiryakisi**, opium addict: ~**u başına vurmak**, go berserk: ~**unu patlatmak**, (*sl.*) disturb and anger s.o.

afyon·cu(luk) (Work of) opium-grower//-dealer. ~**keş(lik)**, opium addict(ion). ~**lamak (-i)**, put to sleep, drug; (*fig.*) lead into evil ways. ~**lanmak**, *vp.* ~**lu**, containing opium; drugged, intoxicated.

Ag. = (*ch.s.*) GÜMÜŞ.

agâh Aware, informed, knowing; wary, vigilant. ~ **etm.**, inform: ~ **olm.**, know, be aware of.

agamagiller (*zoo.*) Agamidae.

aganta (*naut.*) ~ **etm.**, hold fast, haul taut, belay.

agaragar (*bot.*) (Gelatine from) agaragar seaweed.

ag·at (*min.*) Agate. ~**av**, (*bot.*) agave.

agel (*mod.*) Agal (part of Arab headdress).

-agelmek *v. suf.* [191] = -EGELMEK [KORKUTAGEL-MEK].

-agitmek *v. suf.* [192] = -EGİTMEK [DAYANAGİT-MEK].

ag·lomera (*min.*) Agglomerate. ~**lütinasyon**, (*med.*) agglutination. ~**lütinin**, agglutinin. ~**lüti-nojen**, agglutinogen.

agnos·i (*med.*) Agnosia. ~**tik**, (*phil.*) agnostic. ~**tisizm**, agnosticism.

Agop Jacob. ~**'un kazı gibi bakmak**, gape stupidly.

agora Agora. ~**fobi**, (*psy.*) agoraphobia.

-agörmek *v. suf.* [191] = -EGÖRMEK [ÇALIŞAGÖR-MEK].

agraf Clasp; staple. ~ **iğne**, safety-pin.

agrafi (*psy.*) Agraphia.

agrandis·e ~ **etm.**, enlarge, exaggerate. ~**man**, (*cin.*) enlargement: ~ **etm.**, enlarge. ~**ör**, enlarger.

agre·ga (*min.*) Aggregates. ~**je**, (*ed.*) s.o. passing an exam to be a professor. ~**man**, (*adm.*) credentials.

agu (*ech.*) Baby's gurgle of pleasure. ~**cuk**, (*iron.*) baby; overgrown boy: ~ **bebecik!**, naughty boy!; immature person. ~**lamak**, *vi.* gurgle. ~**ş**, (*fig.*) bosom.

ağ Net; network, netting; screen; grid; (spider's) web; snare; (*mod.*) (trousers) crotch. ~ **atmak/ bırakmak**, cast a net: ~ **gemisi**, (*naut.*) minesweeper: ~ **gibi**, reticulated: ~ **gözü**, mesh: ~ **kat/ tabaka**, (*bio.*) retina: ~ **örmek**, weave a net: ~ **şeklinde**, as a net; reticular: ~ **torba**, string-bag: ~ **yatak**, hammock: ~**a tutulmak/**~**da yakalan-mak**, be caught/ensnared: ~**ı çekmek**, cast a net: ~**ına düşürmek (-e)**, ensnare: ~**la tutmak**, enmesh.

ağa Agha; landlord; lord, master, gentleman; (*his.*) title of many officials; (*obs.*) title given to an illiterate man. ~ **baba**, grandfather, old man: ~ **divan//kapısı**, (*his.*) court//residence of YENİÇERİ AĞASI. ~**baba**, grandfather; senior; old-fashioned man. ~**bey(lik)**, (being/behaving like an) elder brother//senior colleague, etc.

ağa[1]**ç**[c1] (*bot.*) Tree; (*for.*) wood, timber; mast, pole. *a.* Wooden; timbered. ~ +, Wood-, tree-, dendro-; arboreal: ~ **bacak**, peg-leg: ~ **balı**, resin: ~ **bilgi/ bilimi**, dendrology: ~ **biti**, (*ent.*) psylla, plant-louse: ~ **budamak**, prune trees: ~ **burgusu**, (*carp.*) auger, gimlet: ~ **çatı/çerçeve**, timber frame: ~ **çiçeği (açmak)**, *n.* (*v.*), blossom: ~ **çivi**, (*carp.*) wooden peg; dowel; tree nail: ~ **damarı**, wood grain: ~ **delgisi**, (*carp.*) auger, gimlet: ~ **devirmek**, fell a tree: ~ **dikmek**, plant trees: ~ **ebegümeci**, (*bot.*) tree-mallow: ~ **fulü**, (*bot.*) mock-orange: ~ **gövdesi**, trunk: ~ **hamuru**, wood-pulp: ~ **incir kuşu**, (*orn.*) tree-pipit: ~ **işleme**, wood-working: ~ **işleri**, woodwork: ~ **kabuğu**, bark: ~ **kalemi**, (*carp.*) chisel: ~ **kanseri**, (*ent.*) canker: ~ **kaplama**, (*carp.*) veneer: ~ **kesmek**, fell trees; cut timber: ~ **kiriş**, (*carp.*) baulk; beam: ~ **kömürü**, charcoal: ~ **kökü**, stump: ~ **kundura**, (*mod.*) clog, sabot: ~ **kurbağası**, (*zoo.*) tree-frog: ~ **kurdu**, (*ent.*) wood-worm: ~ **kütüğü**, log: ~ **lalesi**, (*bot.*) tulip-tree: ~ **oyma**, (*pub.*) wood-engraving: ~ **sansarı**, (*zoo.*) pine marten: ~ **sınırı**, (*geo.*) tree-/timber-line: ~ **sütleğeni**, (*bot.*) tree spurge: ~ **tahniti**, wood-preservation: ~ **tahtakurusu**, (*ent.*) shield/plant bug; forest bug: ~ **tarlakuşu**, (*orn.*) wood lark: ~ **tavuğu**, (*orn.*) curassow: ~ **taze/yaş iken eğilir**, (*fig.*) train the mind while it is young: ~ **tokmak**, (*carp.*) mallet: ~ **torna tezgâhı**, (*carp.*) wood-lathe: ~ **yaprağı**, leaf; foliage: ~**a çıksa pabucu yerde kalmaz**, he is very smart; he knows his business: ~**lara su yürümek**, the sap begin to rise in the trees, trees begin to shoot: ~**tan**, (made) of wood.

ağaç·çı[1]**k**[g1] (*bot.*) Small tree; bush, shrub. ~**çıl**, (*zoo.*) tree-loving/-frequenting: ~ **tarlakuşu**, (*orn.*) wood lark. ~**çılık**, (*for.*) arboriculture. ~**çileği**[ni], (*bot.*) raspberry. ~**kakan**, (*orn.*) woodpecker. ~**kavunu**[nu], (*bot.*) citron. ~**kesen**, (*ent.*) sawfly. ~**la(ndır)mak (-i)**, (*for.*) plant with trees, afforest.

~ **lanmak**, *vp.* be covered with trees. ~ **lı**, wooded; lined/covered with trees. ~ **lık**, *a.* full of trees; timbered, well wooded: *n.* copse, grove, wood, bush. ~ **lıklı**, tree-lined (avenue). ~ **sakızı**, (*bot.*) resin. ~ **sı**, (*geol.*) dendrite. ~ **sı(l)**, (*bot.*) arboreal; ligneous, woody; wooden. ~ **sız**, treeless. ~ **sızlan-(dır)ma**, deforestation.

ağa·lanmak *vi.* Become proud (like an Agha); give o.s. airs. ~ **lık**, state/title of an Agha; pride; generosity, magnanimity.

ağan (*ast.*) Meteor, shooting-star. ~ **lar**, (*soc.*) ascendants.

ağar·ma *vn.* Growing white; dawning, daybreak. ~ **mak**, *vi.* grow white/pale; blanch; become light (dawn). ~ **tı**, a growing grey/light; whiteness; (*cul.*) curd; dairy products. ~ **tıcı**, (*chem.*) whitening (material), bleach. ~ **tma**, making white; silver-cleaning: ~ **tozu**, bleaching powder. ~ **tmak (-i)**, whiten, bleach; clean; clear (s.o.'s honour).

ağ·bene'k^{gi} (*myc.*) Net blotch (on barley). ~ **cık**, (*bio.*) reticulum.

ağda (*cul.*) Semi-solid sweet (of sugar, etc.); molasses, thick syrup. ~ **kullanmak/yapıştırmak/yapmak**, apply AĞDA as a depilatory. ~ **lanmak/**~**laşmak**, *vi.* become viscous; thicken. ~ **lı**, viscous; (*lit.*) heavy/involved (style). ~ **(lı)lık**, viscosity.

ağdır·ma *vn.* (*phys.*) Gravity, gravitation. ~ **mak (-i)**, make semi-solid (by boiling); cause to rise: *vi.* become heavier on one side. ~ **malı**, *a.* gravity.

ağı (*chem.*) Poison. ~ **gibi**, very bitter//hard. ~ **ağacı**, (*bot.*) oleander. ~ **keser**, (*med.*) antivenin.

ağıd- = AĞIT.

ağıl (*live.*) Sheep-pen/-fold; (*ast.*, *cin.*) halo, halation. ~ **kenesi**, (*ent.*) soft tick: ~ **a kapamak**, fold.

ağı·lamak (-i) Poison; (-e), add poison to. ~ **lanım**, intoxication. ~ **lanmak**, *vi.* poison o.s.: *vp.* be poisoned. ~ **latmak (-i, -e)**, *vc.* ~ **lı**, poisoned; toxic, poisonous: ~ **baldıran**, (*bot.*) hemlock. ~ **lıböcek**, (*ent.*) ground beetle. ~ **lılık**, toxicity.

ağıl·lanmak *vi.* (Sheep) be folded/penned; (*ast.*) have a halo. ~ **önler**, (*cin.*) antihalo.

ağım (*bio.*) Instep. ~ **lı**, with a high instep.

ağınma (*chem.*) Sublimation.

ağınmak *vi.* (Animal) roll in the grass/dust.

ağıotu (*bot.*) Hemlock.

ağır *a.* Heavy; weighty; serious, dignified; dull; slow (action/time); lazy; (*cul.*) unwholesome; (*met.*) close, unhealthy; critical, severe (illness/loss/ punishment); dangerous, harmful; repressive (tax); valuable, expensive (clothes/goods); dense (liquid); cumbersome; fatiguing; (*bio.*) pregnant; (*phys.*) bary-. *adv.* Slowly; unhurriedly; heavily; sedately; seriously. ~ **adam**, slow-moving/serious-minded man; dull person, bore: ~ ~, slowly, gradually: ~ ~ **pişirmek**, (*cul.*) stew: ~ **aksak**, very slowly: ~ **almak (-i)**, do stg. unhurriedly: ~ **basmak**, press/weigh heavily; be influential, carry weight; overpower, impose one's will; (-i), have nightmares: ~ **boy**, excellent, outstanding: ~ **canlı**, lazy; indifferent; tedious: ~ **ceza**, (*leg.*) severe punishment, penal servitude, hard labour: ~ **ceza mahkemesi**, criminal court: ~ **davranışlı**, discreet: ~ **davranma**, reluctance: ~ **dilli**, foul-mouthed:

~ **duymak**, be hard of hearing/deaf: ~ **elli**, heavy-handed: ~ **ezgi, fıstıki makam**, (*jok.*) slow and unperturbed: ~ **gelmek (-e)**, come hard to s.o.; find stg. difficult: ~ **gövde, fat**: ~ **hapis cezası**, (*leg.*) solitary confinement; life imprisonment; imprisonment with hard labour: ~ **hareket(li)**, slow-motion, delayed action: ~ **hastalık**, (*med.*) fatal/ serious illness: ~ **hava**, close/unhealthy weather; fug; (*mus.*) mournful tune: ~ **hidrojen**, (*chem.*) deuterium: ~ **hizmet**, (*ind.*) heavy-duty: ~ **ihmal**, (*leg.*) gross negligence: ~ **iş**, hard work; heavy duty: ~ **işçi**, (*sl.*) prostitute: ~ **işitmek** = ~ DUYMAK: ~ **kaçmak**, be offensive: ~ **kanlı**, lazy, sluggish, torpid: ~ **kayıp**, great losses (in mil./natural disaster): ~ **kazan geç kaynar**, great things take time: ~ **kira**, (*fin.*) high rent: ~ **kruvazör**, (*naut.*) battle-cruiser: ~ **kusur**, (*leg.*) gross negligence: ~ **mal**, expensive goods: ~ **ol!**, be serious/patient!; go slowly!: ~ **oturmak**, prove/work out expensive: ~ **para cezası**, (*leg.*) (heavy) fine: ~ **sanayi**, heavy industry: ~ SIKLET: ~ **söylemek**, speak bitterly/ harshly: ~ **sözler**, harsh words: ~ SU: ~ **suç**, (*leg.*) serious crime: ~ **surette**, heavily; slowly: ~ **toplar**, (*mil.*) heavy artillery: ~ **tortu**, (*geol.*) placer: ~ **yanan**, slow burning: ~ **yaralı**, severely wounded: ~ **yol!**, (*naut.*) reduce speed!: ~ **yongayı yel kaldırmaz**, (*fig.*) he has influential friends and can't easily be removed: ~ **yük arabası**, dray: ~ **yüklü**, heavy-laden: ~ **yürekli**, heavy-hearted: ~ **dan almak**, take things easily; slack; show indifference/ reluctance; (*ind.*) work to rule: ~ **ına gitmek**, give offence, hurt s.o.'s feelings: ~ **ını takınmak**, behave with great decorum.

ağır·ayak (*bio.*) Heavy with child, pregnant. ~ **başlı**, grave, serious, dignified (man). ~ **başlılık**, gravity, dignity, equanimity. ~ **ca**, rather heavy; heavily. ~ **cık**, (*phys.*) baryon. ~ **küre**, (*geol.*) bary-sphere. ~ **lama**, entertainment; respect; reluctance: ~ **günü**, (*art.*) private-view day. ~ **lamak (-i)**, *vt.* treat with respect, honour; entertain, show hospi-tality to: *vi.* slow down, lag. ~ **lanmak**, *vi.* be treated with respect; become heavy. ~ **laşmak**, *vi.* become heavier/more difficult/slower/more serious; (*cul.*) go bad; (*met.*) become overcast. ~ **laştırmak (-i)**, burden; aggravate. ~ **latmak (-i)**, make heavy/ slow; aggravate. ~ **latıcı**, (*leg.*) aggravating (cir-cumstances). ~ **layıcı**, hospitable; kind.

ağırlı'k^{g1} Weight, heaviness; (*phys.*) (force of) gravity, gravitation; burden; responsibility; slow-ness; stupidity; seriousness; hardness of hearing; nightmare; oppressiveness (heat/boredom); un-healthiness; (money for) trousseau; jewellery; bag-gage; (*mil.*) heavy transport. ~ +, *a.* (*phys.*) Gravity; baro-, bary-: ~ **basmak**, (sleep) come upon s.o.; (nightmare) oppress s.o.: ~ **fazlası**, excess weight: ~ **incelemesi**, (*med.*) gravimetric analysis: ~ **kazanmak**, (*fig.*) gain weight/importance: ~ **libresi**, pound avoirdupois: ~ **merkezi**, (*phys.*) centre of gravity; (*fig.*) important part: ~ **olm. (-e)**, be a burden to: ~ **oturmak**, be costly: ~ **vermek (-e)**, attach importance to. ~ **lı**, weighted, loaded; (*fig.*) esteemed, respected.

ağır·samak (-i) Find burdensome; treat coldly.

~ **sıklet**[i], (*sp.*) heavyweight (79 kg. +). ~ **su**, (*nuc.*) heavy water. ~ **şa¹k**[ġ1], disc; spindle whorl; (*bio.*) pimple; (*phys.*) counter-weight. ~ **şaklanmak**, *vi.* (pimple) be formed. ~ **yağ**/~ **yakıt**, heavy fuel (-oil). ~ **yuvar** = ~ KÜRE.

ağış Rising (of vapour, mist, etc.).

ağı¹t[d1] *n.* Dirge, lament, keening; mourning. ~ **koparmak**/**yakmak**, wail, lament, keen. ~ **çı**, professional mourner. ~ **lama**, lament; funeral oration. ~ **sal**, *a.* mourning.

ağıtutar (*med.*) Antitoxin.

ağız[¹ ¹] (*live.*) First milk, beestings.

ağ¹ız[z1 2] Mouth; (*orn.*) bill; (*ling.*) speech, manner of speaking/singing, accent, dialect; talk; persuasive words; entrance, opening; junction, crossroads; (*geo.*) inlet, estuary, river-mouth; edge/ brink (of danger); brim (cup); muzzle (gun); edge/ blade (knife, etc.); each successive baking in the oven, *hence* ILK ~; one time. ~ +, *a.* Mouth-; oral: ~ **açısı**, (*eng.*) clearance angle: ~ **açmak**, speak; talk: ~ **açmamak**, not utter a word: ~ **açtırmamak**, not let s.o. speak: ~ ~**a** (**dolu**), brimful; completely, utterly: ~ ~**a vermek**, whisper to each other: ~ **alışkanlığı**, manner of speech: ~ **aramak**, sound out s.o.: ~ **armonikası**, (*mus.*) mouth organ: ~ **atmak**, brag: ~ **bağı**, (*naut.*) mousing: ~ **bir etm.**, agree to tell the same story: ~ **birliği**, unanimity of expression: ~ BİRLİĞİ: ~ **boşluğu**, mouth cavity: ~ **bozmak**, abuse, vituperate: ~ **bozukluğu**, cursing and swearing: ~ **burun birbirine karışmak**, (face) be worn and lined: ~ **çevresi**, (*dom.*) embroidered guest napkin: ~ **dalaşı**, bickering, battle of words: ~ **değişikliği**, (*cul.*) a variety of food; a change: ~ **değiştirmek**, change one's tune: ~ **dil vermemek**, be too ill to speak: ~ **dolusu (küfür)**, without restraint, unreservedly; at the top of one's voice; (continuous swearing): ~ **etm.** (**-e**), try to persuade s.o.: *vi.* speak one's mind; boast, speak theatrically: ~ **kalabalığı(na getirmek)**, (disconcert by) a spate of words: ~ **kavafı**, s.o. who tries to deceive with too many words: ~ **kavgası (etm.)**, *n.* altercation; (*v.* quarrel): ~ **kokusu**, foul breath; (*fig.*) moodiness, caprice: ~ **kullanmak**, speak carefully, manage one's words: ~ **mızıkası**, (*mus.*) mouth-organ: ~OTU: ~ **patlangacı**, (*cul.*) bubble-gum: ~ **persenk**/**sakızı**, constant refrain/ harping on stg.: ~ **satmak**, boast; blow one's own trumpet: ~ **suyu**, saliva, spittle: ~ **sütü**, (*bio.*) colostrum: ~ **şakası**, joke, jesting: ~ **tadı**, enjoyment (meal); peace, harmony (in a group): ~ **tadıyla**, with pleasure/zest: ~ **tamburası** (**çalmak**), *n.* Jew's harp; (*v.* speak disconcertingly; try to fool s.o.; one's teeth chatter from cold): ~ **tavanı**, (*bio.*) palate: ~ **torbası**, (*live.*) muzzle: ~ **tüfeği**, (*mil.*) muzzle-loader: ~ **tütünü**, chewing tobacco: ~ **yapmak**, try to make stg. appear different: ~ **yaymak**, avoid the truth: ~ **yilimi**, (*bio.*) phlegm, mucus: ~ **yormak**, talk/plead in vain.

ağızdan, verbally, by word of mouth; rumoured, unauthentic; (*med.*) orally: ~ **ağza dolaşmak**, be rumoured: ~ **dolma**, (*mil.*) muzzle-loading: ~ **işitme**, hearsay: ~ **kapmak**, learn by listening to others.

ağza: ~ **alınmaz**, inedible; unmentionable, obscene: ~ **almak**, mention; refer to: ~ **düşmek**, be gossipped about; get a bad reputation: ~ **koyacak bir şey**, stg. to eat: ~ **tat boğaza feryat**, a morsel of delicious food.

ağzı: ~ **açık (kalmak)**, *a.* open, uncovered; astonished, gaping; (*v.* gape with astonishment): ~ **aya**, gözü **çaya bakmak**, do things haphazardly: ~ **bir**, in agreement: ~ **boş**, indiscreet, telling secrets: ~ **bozuk**, abusive, foul-mouthed: ~ **burnu yerinde**, beautiful, attractive: ~ **büyük**, loud-mouthed, pretentious: ~ **çelikli**, endless talker: ~ **değişmek**, change one's tune: ~ **dört köşe olm.**, (*sl.*) be in a good humour: ~ **gevşek**, who can't hold his tongue; indiscreet; garrulous: ~ **havada**, crazy, stupid: ~ **kalabalık**, noisy, garrulous: ~ **kapanmak**, be reduced to silence: ~ **kara**, delighting in giving bad news; making the worst of what he hears: ~ **kilitli**, discreet, secretive: ~ **kokmak**, have bad breath; (*fig.*) be foul-mouthed: ~ **kulaklarına varmak**, grin from ear to ear; be very pleased: ~ **kuruyası!**, may his tongue be withered! ~ **laf**/**lakırdı yapmak**, sound important: ~ **mühürlü**, s.o. whose lips are sealed: ~ **oynamak**, eat; talk: ~ **pek**/**sıkı**, discreet, reliable; secretive, tight-lipped, reticent; taciturn: ~ **pis**, s.o. always swearing: ~ **sulanmak**, (mouth) water; be envious: ~ **süt kokmak**, be young/inexperienced; be tied to s.o.'s apron-strings: ~ **teneke kaplı**, (*jok.*) able to eat/drink very hot things: ~ **torba değil ki büzesin**, you can't stop people talking: ~ **var dili yok**, very silent; submissive: ~ **varmamak**, be reluctant/not bring o.s. to say stg.: ~ **vidalı**, screw-top (bottle): ~ **yanmak** (**-den**), 'burn one's fingers'/have a bitter experience with: ~ **yayvan**, garrulous: ~ **yok**, quiet, mild-spoken; defenceless; helpless.

ağzım: ~**a çöp koymadım**, I haven't eaten a single morsel: ~**ın tadını bozma!**, don't spoil my enjoyment/pleasure.

ağzına: ~ **almamak** (**-i**), not mention: ~ **aptesle almak**, speak of s.o. very respectfully: ~ **atmak** (**-i**), put in one's mouth: ~ **bakakalmak**, be astonished at s.o.'s words: ~ **bakmak**, follow/obey s.o. blindly; do as s.o. says: ~ **baktırmak**, speak very persuasively: ~ **bir parmak bal çalmak**, try to buy off/ silence s.o. with a trifle; soothe s.o. (with honeyed words): ~ **bir çöp**/**şey koymamak**, not eat at all: ~ **bir zeytin verir altına tulum tutar**, expect much in return for little: ~ **burnuna bulaştırmak**, make a mess of stg.: ~ **değin**, brimful: ~ **geldiği gibi**, without thought/reflection: ~ **geleni söylemek**, say disagreeable things; speak without due thought: ~ **gem vurmak**, (*fig.*) muzzle s.o.: ~ **kadar**, brimfull; full up: ~ **koymamak**, not eat: ~ **layık**, that was a really good meal!: ~ **sürmemek** (**-i**), eat nothing of it at all: ~ **taş almış**, not talkative, silent: ~ **verilmesini beklemek**/**istemek**, expect to be waited on hand and foot: ~ **vur lokmasını al**, he can't say boo to a goose: ~ **yakışmamak**, speak rudely/unsuitably.

ağzında: ~ **bakla ıslanmaz**, s.o. unable to keep a secret; chatterbox: ~ **büyümek**, be unable to swallow: ~ **gevelemek**, mumble: ~ **torba mı var?**, have you lost your tongue?: ~ **tükürüğü kurudu**, he talked himself hoarse.

ağzından: ~ **baklayı çıkarmak**, lose patience and speak out: ~ **bal akmak**, be quick-witted and intelligent; speak pleasantly: ~ **çıkanı kulağı işitmemek**, not realize what one says; be carried away: ~ **çıkmak/kaçırmak**, let slip unintentionally, blurt out: ~ **dökülmek**, be clear from one's speech that . . .: ~ **düşürmemek**, never stop talking about stg.: ~ **girip burnundan çıkmak**, try to cajole s.o.: ~ **işitme**, rumour, hearsay: ~ **kaçmak**, (a word) slip out inadvertently: ~ **kapmak**, worm a secret out of s.o.: ~ **laf alamazsın**, he won't be drawn: ~ **laf/söz almak**, (by dint of talking) get s.o. to say what one wants: ~ **lokmasını almak**, take from s.o. what is rightfully his: ~ **söz dirhemle çıkıyor**, it's hard to get a word out of him: ~ **tekrarlamak**, quote/repeat s.o.'s words.

ağzını: ~ **açacağına gözünü aç!**, don't just gape, open your eyes!: ~ **açmak**, give vent to one's feelings: ~ **açıp gözünü yummak**, lose one's temper and say bitter things without reflection; let o.s. go: ~ **açmamak**, say nothing; be silent: ~ **aramak**, try to draw/sound out s.o.: ~ **bıçak açmamak**, be too upset to speak; be very depressed: ~ **bozmak**, vituperate; curse; swear: ~ **çalkamak**, (*med.*) gargle: ~ **çarşamba pazarına çeviririm**, (*sl.*) I'll smash your face in: ~ **faraş gibi açmak**, speak impertinently: ~ **hava/poyraza açmak**, be disappointed; get nothing: ~ **kapamak**, close one's mouth, be silent: ~ **kapatmak**, silence s.o.: ~ **kiraya vermek**, keep silent (about stg. that concerns one): ~ **öpeyim!**, I could kiss you for such good news/words!: ~ **pek/sıkı tutmak**, keep secret: ~ **sulandırmak**, (*cul.*) make one's mouth water: ~ **tıkamak**, silence s.o.: ~ **topla!**, mind your language!, don't be impudent!: ~ **tutmak**, hold one's tongue; keep silent: ~ **yoklamak**, sound s.o.; try to discover s.o.'s opinions/intentions: ~ **yormak**, talk to no purpose.

ağzının: ~ **aşı olmamak**, be beyond one's ability: ~ **içine bakmak**, hang on s.o.'s lips: ~ **kaşığı olmamak (-in)**, be too deep to be understood by s.o.; be above one's head/capacity: ~ **kokusunu çekmek (-in)**, put up with s.o.'s ill-natured gossip/continuous talk: ~ **mührü ile**, fasting: ~ **ölçüsünü vermek (-e)**, give s.o. a piece of one's mind; put s.o. in his place: ~ **payını almak**, be snubbed: ~ **payını vermek**, snub s.o.: ~ **suyu akmak**, desire stg. strongly: ~ **tadını almak (-den)**, suffer bitter experience (with stg.): ~ **tadını bilmek**, be a gourmet: ~ **tadını kaçırmak**, upset s.o.; spoil s.o.'s pleasure.

ağzıyla: ~ **aslan tuttuğunu söylemek**, boast of incredible deeds: ~ **kuş tutsa faydası yok**, whatever he does it won't help now.

ağız·birliği ~ **etm.**, agree to tell the same story. ~**lamak (-i)**, (*eng.*) fit a part (in its housing); (*naut.*) reach the entrance (bay, harbour). ~**laşma**, *vn.* (*bio.*) anastomosis. ~**laşmak (-le)**, *vi.* (*bio.*) (artery, etc.) intercommunicate, anastomose. ~**latmak (-i)**, *vc.* ~**lı**, having a mouth; -mouthed;

(gun) -barrelled; (knife) -bladed. ~**lık**, mouthpiece (pipe, telephone, etc.); cigarette-holder; muzzle (dog); stone surround (well); leaf-cover (basket of fruit); funnel: ~ **kayışı**, (*live.*) curb-rein. ~**lıkçı**, cigarette-holder maker/seller. ~**lıklı**, ~ **sazlar**, (*mus.*) brass wind-instruments. ~**otu**, priming (gun). ~**sal**, (*med.*) oral. ~**sıl**, related to the mouth; (*ling.*) oral. ~**sız**, soft-spoken; submissive.

ağ·katman (*bio.*) Retina. ~**kepçe**, (*sp.*) angler's long-handled net. ~**kurdu**, (*zoo.*) webworm.

ağla·ma Weeping; lamentation: ~**dan**, dry-eyed. ~**mak**, *vi.*/(**-e**), cry/grieve (for), bewail; (*bot.*) (sap) flow: ~ **sıklamak**, weep and lament: **ağlama ölü için ağla diri için**, weep for the living not the dead: **ağlamayan çocuğa meme vermezler**, you get nothing without fighting for it: **ağlarsa anam ağlar, gerisi/kalanı yalan ağlar**, don't expect others to worry about you: **ağlayası gelmek**, feel like crying. ~**ma(k)lı**, on the brink of tears, tearful. ~**mış/** ~**msık**, tearful; snivelling, whining; plaintive. ~**msamak**, *vi.* whine, whimper. ~**nmak**, *vp.* be mourned/missed. ~**şmak (-le)**, *vi.* weep together; complain bitterly. ~**tı**, tragedy. ~**tıcı/** ~**tısal**, tragic. ~**tmak (-i)**, cause to weep. ~**ya/** ~**ya**, *adv.* weeping. ~**yış**, *n.* weeping; complaint.

ağ·ma *vn.* (*ast.*) (Shooting) star. ~**mak**, *vi.* rise; evaporate; hang down.

ağmantarlar (*myc.*) Web fungi, hyphomycetes.

ağnam *pl.* (*live.*) Sheep; goats; flocks. ~ **vergisi**, (*fin.*) tax on livestock (sheep, camels, etc.). ~**cı**, livestock-tax collector.

ağnamak = AĞINMAK.

Ağrı[1] (*geo.*) Ararat. ~ **dağı**, Mount Ararat. ~**boz**, Euboea.

ağrı[2] (*med.*) Pain; ache. ~ **kesimi**, (*med.*) analgesia; anodyne, pain-killer: ~ **verici**, painful: ~**lar**, labour pains: ~**sı tutmak**, (labour pains) come on: ~**sına gitmek**, hurt s.o.'s feelings: ~**yı kesmek**, stop the pain.

ağrı·kesen (*med.*) Analgesic. ~**(k)lı**, diseased, unhealthy; aching, painful. ~**ma**, *vn.*; (*live.*) sheep disease (causing loss of wool), Texas fever. ~**mak**, *vi.* ache, hurt: (**başım**) **ağrıyor**, (my head) aches. ~**sız**, without pain; (*fig.*) without cares: ~ **baş mezarda gerek**, only death ends all troubles: ~ **baş yastık istemez**, don't fuss about s.o. healthy. ~**tmak (-i)**, cause pain to, hurt.

ağs- = AKS-.

ağ·sı (*bio.*) Reticular. ~**tabaka**, retina. ~**tonoz**, (*arch.*) fan-tracery/-vaulting.

ağu = AĞI.

ağustos August. ~ **gülü**, (*bot.*) dog-rose: ~ **ördeği**, (*orn.*) garganey: ~**ta bokun mu dondu?**, how can you feel cold on such a hot day?: ~**ta suya girse balta kesmez buz olur**, he never has any luck. ~**böceği**[ni], (*ent.*) cicada; (*fig.*) chatterbox.

ağyar *pl.* = GAYR. Others; foreigners; foe.

ağz- = AĞIZ.

ah[1] *int.* Ah!; oh!; alas. ~ **deyip** ~ **işitmek**, be alone and helpless: ~ **ü figan etm.**, bemoan: ~ **(ü) vah**, sighs and laments.

ah[2] *n.* Sigh; curse. ~**(ını) almak**, be cursed for one's deeds: ~ **çekmek/etm.**, *vi.* sigh; groan; curse: ~

salmak, heave a sigh: ~**a gelmek**/ ~**ına uğramak**, get one's deserts: ~**ı tutmak**, (one's curse) take effect: ~**ı yerde kalmamak**, (s.o.'s curse) take effect sooner or later: ~**ım şahım bir şey değil**, it's not worth sighing over; it's over-rated in value, nothing to write home about.

A/h = (fin.) AÇIK HESAP; (el.) AMPER-SAAT.

AH = AMME HUKUKU.

aha int. Aha!; there it is!

ahali pl. = EHİL. Inhabitants; people; the public. ~ **mübadelesi**, exchange of (pol.) populations/ (his.) Greek and Tk. minorities (1923): ~ **sokağa uğramış**, everybody is out in the streets.

ahar n. (pub.) Size; (tex.) dressing. ~**lamak (-i)**, calender, size, dress. ~**lı**, sized, dressed, glossy. ~**lılık**, gloss.

âhar a. Other; different. ~ **bir kimse**, another person.

ahbaᵇpᵇⁱ Friend; acquaintance, companion. ~ **çavuşlar**, chums, cronies, pals: ~ **olm.**, be(come) friends.

ahbap·ça Amicably, like friends. ~**laşmak**, vi. become friends. ~**lık**, acquaintanceship, friendship: ~ **etm.**, behave like/be friends: ~**a dökmek**, show excessive concern/sympathy.

ahçı, etc. = AŞÇI.

ahd- = AHİT. ~**en**, by treaty; as a pact. ~ᵗ**etmek**ᵉᵈᵉʳ, vi. take an oath; solemnly promise; make an agreement: vt. contract/covenant/undertake to do stg.; enjoin. ~**i**, contractual: ~ **tarife**, international customs tariffs.

Ahdi-atikⁱ (rel.) Old Testament. ~**cediᵗtᵈⁱ**, New Testament.

ahenᵏkᵍⁱ Purpose, intention; accord, consonance, harmony; music, air. ~ **bilgisi**, (phys.) harmonics: ~ **kaidesi**, (ling.) vowel harmony: ~ **kapak/tahtası**, (mus.) sounding-board: ~ **kurmak**, harmonize, ensure agreement: ~ **sağlamak**, create unity: ~**i bozmak**, create disorder, disarrange; disunite.

ahenk·leşmek vi. Harmonize; be harmonious. ~**leştirmek (-i)**, harmonize; coordinate. ~**li**/~**tar**, (phys.) harmonic; (fig.) harmonious, in accord; euphorious; in time; in order; symmetrical. ~**lilik**, harmony, accord. ~**siz**, disunited; discordant; (phys.) anharmonic; (mus.) atonal, cacophonous, dissonant. ~**sizlik**, disunity; discord(ance); cacophony, dissonance.

aheste Slow; gentle; calm; (mus.) soft. ~ **beste**, slowly; gently; calmly, nonchalantly.

AHF = (ed.) ANKARA HUKUK FAKÜLTESİ.

ahfaᵇtᵈⁱ pl. = HAFİT. Grandchildren, descendants.

ahı Generous; = AHİ.

ahır Stable, cowshed. ~ **bölmesi**, box, stall: ~ **gibi**, very untidy: ~**a çekmek/koymak**, stable: ~**a çevirmek**, make filthy/untidy. ~**lamak**, vi. (live.) become soft from staying in the stable.

âhır a. Last; latter. adv. After; in the end; lastly. ~ **nefes**, one's last breath: ~ **vakit**, one's last years: ~ **zaman**, the end (of the world): ~ **zaman Peygamberi**, the last Prophet, Muhammad.

Ahi (his.) Member of a semi-religious fraternity/ trade guild; s.o. generous. ~**lik**, system of fraternities/trade guilds; brotherhood; chivalry, generosity: ~ **ocağı**, trade guild.

ahir Last, latter. ~**en**, lastly, finally; recently.

ahᵇitᵈⁱ Oath; promise; pact, treaty; undertaking; injunction; (obs.) epoch, period. ~**leşmek**, vi. swear together; make a solemn agreement. ~**li**, bound by oath, etc. ~**name**, covenant, pact, agreement.

ahᵇizᶻⁱ Taking, receiving. ~**e**, (el., rad.) receiver.

ahkâm pl. = HÜKÜM. Judgements; laws; rules; provisions; opinions; inferences (from observations); absurd opinions, etc. ~ **çıkarmak**, draw arbitrary conclusions; make absurd suggestions: ~ **kesmek**, decide arbitrarily: ~ **kurmak**, lay down the law pompously: ~**ından geçilmemek**, be unbearably conceited.

ahl(b). = AHLAK(BİLİM).

ahlaf pl. = HALEF. Successors; descendants; posterity.

ahlak¹ Moral qualities; morals; character. ~ **bozukluğu**, depravity: ~ **duygusu**, moral sense: ~ **düşkünlüğü**, decline in morals: ~ **hocalığı etm.**, set o.s. up as a guardian of public morals: ~**a aykırı**, immoral: ~**ı bozuk**, debauched, depraved: ~**ını bozmak**, demoralize, deprave: ~**ını değiştirmek**, change one's character.

ahlak·bilim (phil.) Moral philosophy, ethics. ~**çı**/ (-lık), moral·ist/(-ism). ~**dışı**, amoral. ~**dışıcı(lık)**, amoral·ist/(-ism). ~**dışılık**, amorality. ~**ıyatı**, ethics. ~**i**, concerning morals; moral. ~**lı**, moral; decent, well-behaved. ~**lılık**, good conduct, morality, decency. ~**sal**, moral. ~**sız**, immoral, dissolute. ~**sızca**, immorally, indecently. ~**sızlık**, immorality, vice; depravity, debauchery.

ahlamak vi. Sigh. **ahlayıp vahlamak**, sigh and moan.

ahlat¹ ¹ (bot.) Wild pear; (fig.) boor. ~**ın iyisini (dağda) ayılar yer**, the best things go to the undeserving.

ahlat¹ ² ~**ı erbaa**, (phil.) the body's four humours.

ahmaᵏkᵍ¹ a. Stupid, foolish. n. Fool, idiot; dullard. ~ **ıslatan**, fine drizzle. ~**ça**, a. rather foolish: adv. foolishly. ~**laşmak**, vi. become stupid/confused. ~**lık**, stupidity, foolishness; dullness.

ahret¹ Next world, future life. ~ **adamı**, otherworldly man: ~ **babası**, etc., father, etc. by adoption: ~ **evi**, the next world: ~ **suali (sormak)**, n. endless questions, cross-examination; (v. cross-examine): ~ **yolculuğu**, death: ~**e varmak**/~**i boylamak**, die: ~**ini yapmak/zenginleştirmek**, acquire merit (in Heaven): ~**te on parmağı yakasında olm.**, make s.o. pay for it in the next world. ~**lik**, stg. connected with the next world; a devout man; an orphan/needy girl brought up as a servant.

ahşa pl. (bio.) Guts, intestines; viscera.

ahşaᵇpᵇⁱ Wooden, (made of) timber.

ahtapotᵘ (zoo.) Octopus: polyp(us); (med.) cancerous ulcer, polyp; (fig.) hanger-on, sponger. ~ **gibi**, importunate.

ahu (zoo.) Gazelle. ~ **gibi**, very beautiful (girl): ~ **gözlü**, with beautiful eyes. ~**baba**, friendly old man. ~**duduⁿᵘ**, (bot.) raspberry.

ahvalⁱ pl. = HAL. Conditions; circumstances. ~ **böyle iken**, at this juncture: ~**i sıhhiye**, state of s.o.'s health: ~**i şahsiye**, civil status: ~**i umumiye**, general situation.

ahz- = AHİZ. ~ **¹etmek**ᵉᵈᵉʳ, take; receive. ~ **üita**, trade, commerce: ~ **etm.**, trade, deal.

AID = (*Agency for International Development*).

aidat¹ *pl.* Revenues; income; contribution, dues; subscription; allowance; remuneration.

aidiyet¹ A belonging to; a concerning; (*leg.*) competence.

aile Family; relations; social group; wife; (*ling.*, *bio.*) family. ~ **ad/ismi**, family name, surname: ~ **bahçe/gazinosu**, (*soc.*) place for family entertainment (no alcohol!): ~ **cüzdanı**, (*fin.*) savings account: ~ **kızı**, girl of good family: ~ **ocak/ yurt/yuvası**, home: ~ **ödencesi**, family allowance: ~ **pansiyonu**, family hotel: ~ **planlaması**, family planning: ~ **reisi**, householder, head of the family: ~ **vakfı**, (*leg.*) family trust: ~ **yardım/zammı**, (*fin.*) family allowance: ~**yi geçindirmek**, keep the pot boiling. ~**ce(k)**, as a family. ~**sel/**~**vi**, *a.* family, domestic, private.

ait [89] Relative to; concerning; belonging; (*leg.*) competent. ~ **olm.** (**-e**), belong to; concern.

ajan Agent; spy. ~**da**, diary; memorandum. ~**lık**, agency. ~**s**, news-agency; branch of a company: ~ **bülteni**, news-agency bulletin.

ajur (*tex.*) Open-work embroidery; hemstitch. ~**lu**, open-worked: ~ **dikiş**, hemstitch.

ak¹ *a.* White; clean; honest. *n.* White colour; white (of an egg/eye). ~AĞA: ~AĞAÇ: ~AMBER: ~ **akçe**, silver money: ~ **akçe kara gün içindir**, money saved is for a rainy day: ~ **alaca**, white-spotted: ~ **altın**, white gold, platinum: ~ **Arap**, (*ethn.*) real Arab (not a Negro): ~ASMA: ~BABA: ~BALIK(ÇIL): ~BASMA: ~BAŞ: ~ **baykuş**, (*orn.*) short-eared owl: ~BENEK: ~ **çam**, (*bot.*) silver fir: ~CİĞER: ~DİKEN: ~ **don**, (*met.*) hoar-frost: ~ **düşmek**, (hair, etc.) begin to turn white: ~ **göt** = ~ KÖPEK: ~ **göz**, coward: ~ **gözlü**, light-coloured eyes; (*fig.*) hardhearted: ~ **gül**, (*bot.*) sweet briar: ~ **kirpani**, white but dirty: ~ **koç kara koç o dövüşte olacak**, that fight will show who is the better man: ~ **koyunun kara kuzusu da olur**, there can be black sheep in the best of families: ~ **köpek kara köpek**, ill-assorted group of people: ~ **köpek kara köpek geçitte belli olur**, one's character becomes clear in times of trouble: ~KUYRUK: ~MADDE: ~MANTAR: ~ **mermer**, (*geol.*) alabaster: ~ **mı kara mı, önüne düşünce görürsün**, things will become clear with time: ~ **mukallit**, (*orn.*) olivaceous warbler: ~ **oda**, bridal chamber: ~ **pak**, bright and clean; whitehaired: ~PAS: ~ **saçlı**, white-haired: ~SAKAL: ~ **sakal kara sakal**, high and low, rich and poor; everyone: ~ **sakaldan yok sakala gelmek**, lose all one's strength with age: ~ **sakaldan yok sakala kadar**, everybody, old and young alike: ~ **sakallı**, white-bearded: ~SU: ~SÜLÜMEN: ~ **şeytan kara şeytan**, with great difficulty: ~TAVŞAN: ~ **tilki**, (*zoo.*) Arctic fox: ~ **toz ağacı**, (*bot.*) aspen: ~YUVAR: ~ **zaç**, (*chem.*) sulphate of zinc: ~**ı** ~ **karası kara**, with white complexion but black eyes and hair: ~**ın adı karanın tadı**, darkly handsome: ~**la karayı seçmek**, have the greatest difficulty in doing stg., be in a predicament.

-ak *a./n. suf.* [223] = -EK [DURAK].

akabe Steep road; pass; danger. *pr.n.*, Aqabah.

akabinde Immediately afterwards; subsequently.

aka¹çᶜ¹ Drain-pipe. ~**lama**, (*agr.*) drainage: ~ **havzası**, catchment basin. ~**lamak** (**-i**), (*agr.*, *med.*) drain.

akademi Academy; institution of higher education. ~ **armağanı**, (*cin.*) Academy award: ~ **üyesi/**~**ci**, academician, fellow. ~**k/**~**sel**, *a.* academic, university. ~**syen**, academician.

ak·ağa (*his.*) White eunuch. ~**ağa¹ç**ᶜ¹, (*bot.*) silverbirch.

akai¹tᵈ¹ *pl.* = AKİDE². (*rel.*) Articles of faith, catechism.

akaju (*bot.*) Mahogany.

aka¹kᵍ¹ (*geo.*) River-bed; valley; (*eng.*) conduit, duct; running water.

akala (*bot.*) Type of cotton plant.

akalınlı White-browed. ~ **deniz kırlangıcı**, (*orn.*) least tern.

akalliyet¹ (*soc.*) Minority (community in Turkey). ~**in hakları**, (*leg.*) minority rights.

-akalmak *v.suf.* [191] = -EKALMAK [BAKAKALMAK].

akamber (*zoo.*) Ambergris; (*bot.*) hymena resin.

akamet¹ Sterility; (*fig.*) lack of success, failure. ~**e uğramak**, fail: ~**e uğratmak**, spoil, upset.

akan *v.* = AKMAK. *a.* Flowing. ~ **sular durur**, that settles the matter; I am/he is non-plussed. ~ **yıldız**, (*ast.*) shooting-star.

akar¹/~**et¹** Landed property; house, etc. for letting.

akar² (*ent.*) Mite. ~**lar**, mites and ticks.

akar³ *a./n.* Flowing; liquid; hydraulic; hydro-; running (water); leaky. ~ **bilgisi**, (*phys.*) hydraulics: ~ **hali**, fluid state: ~ **mallar**, wet goods: ~**ı kokarı yok**, in perfect order.

akar·amber (*bot.*) Liquidambar. ~**ca**, (*med.*) flux; fistule; (*geo.*) brook. ~**kum**, (*geol.*) quicksand. ~**su**, running water, river; single necklace (diamonds/pearls): ~ **bilimi**, potamology: ~ **oyuğu**, gully. ~**yakı¹t**ᵈ¹, liquid fuel: ~ **depo alanı**, tank farm.

akasma (*bot.*) White bryony; white clematis.

akasya (*bot.*) Acacia; mimosa. ~ **sakızı**, gum arabic.

Aka¹tᵈ¹ (*his.*) Akkad.

ak·baba (*orn.*) Vulture; (*fig.*) white-haired: ~ **kralı**, king vulture: ~**ya dönmek**, become whitehaired. ~**balı¹k**ᵍ¹, (*ich.*) dace; bleak. ~**balıkçıl**, (*orn.*) great white heron. ~**balina**, (*zoo.*) white whale, beluga. ~**ballıbaba**, (*bot.*) white deadnettle. ~**basma**, (*med.*) cataract. ~ **baş**, (*orn.*) brent-goose. ~**başlı**, yelve, (*orn.*) pine bunting. ~**bene¹k**ᵍ¹, (*med.*) leucoma. ~**bıyıklı**, ~ **deniz kırlangıcı**, (*orn.*) whiskered tern. ~**borsa**, (*fin.*, *col.*) official stock-exchange. ~**burça¹k**ᵍ¹, (*bot.*) vetchling.

akciğer (*bio.*) Lungs. ~ +, *a.* Bronchial, broncho-; pulmonary. ~ **atardamarı**, pulmonary artery: ~ **borucukları**, bronchioles: ~ **borusu**, bronchus: ~ **gözcük/petekleri**, pulmonary alveoli: ~ **iltihap/ yangısı**, (*med.*) pneumonia: ~ **kasabaları**, bronchi: ~ **kılkurdu**, (*zoo.*) lungworm: ~ **kovuğu**, (*bio.*) pleural cavity: ~ **sönüğü**, (*med.*) atelectasis: ~

tozancası, pneumoconiosis: ~ **yelpiği**, bronchial asthma: ~ **zarı**, (*bio.*) pleura. ~**li**, (*zoo.*) pulmonate: ~ **barramunda**, (*ich.*) Australian lungfish. ~**siz**, lungless.

akça[1] *a.* Whitish, pale, faded. ~ **pakça**, rather pretty. ~**ağaç**, (*bot.*) maple: ~ **şekeri**, (*cul.*) maple syrup. ~**ağaçgiller**, (*bot.*) acers. ~**kavak**, (*bot.*) white poplar. ~**pa¹k^{ğı}**, (*ich.*) silver bream. ~**yel**, (*met.*) SE wind.

akça²/akçe *n.* Coin; asper; (sum of) money; (*his.*) 1/3rd PARA. ~ **adama akıl öğretir**, money makes one wise: ~ **düşkünü**, money-grubber: ~ **etmez**, valueless: ~ **farkı**, (*fin.*) rate of exchange: ~ **kesmek**, mint money; (*fig.*) have a mint of money: ~**nın yüzü sıcaktır**, the sight of money opens doors. ~**lama**, *vn.* financing. ~**lamak (-i)**, finance. ~**lı**, financial, monetary: ~ **adamdan dağlar korkar**, money is power. ~**sız(lık)**, penniless(ness).

akçıl Whitish; faded. ~**laşmak**, *vi.* fade. ~**lık**, fading.

ak·çöpleme (*bot.*) White hellebore. ~**darı**, (*bot.*) millet. ~**demir**, (*min.*) wrought iron. ~**deniz**, *pr.n.* (*geo.*) the Mediterranean: ~ **adaları**, the Archipelago: ~ **boğazı**, the Dardanelles.

akd- = AKİT. ~**¹etmek**^{eder} **(-i)**, bind, tie; conclude (bargain), sign (treaty); contract (marriage); set up, establish (council); organize (meeting).

ak·diken (*bot.*) Buck-/haw-thorn. ~**doğan**, (*orn.*) gerfalcon. ~**gö¹t**^{dü}, (*orn.*) stonechat. ~**günlü**, lucky. ~**günlük**, (*bot.*) frankincense. ~**gürgen**, (*bot.*) beech. ~**hardal**, (*bot.*) white mustard.

akı¹ *a.* Generous.

akı² *n.* (*phys.*) Flux, flow.

akıbet[i] *n.* End; consequence, result; near future, destiny. *adv.* Finally. ~**ine uğramak**, meet one's fate.

akıcı *n.* Fluid. *a.* Flowing; easy; (*lit.*) fluent; (*ling.*) liquid, trilled. ~ **kum**, (*geol.*) quicksand. ~**lık**, fluidity; fluency; (*cin.*) continuity.

ak¹ıl^{lı} Intelligence, reason, sense, wisdom; comprehension; prudence; memory; opinion. ~ ~**dan üstündür**, it pays to ask advice: ~ **almak/danışmak**, consult: ~ **almamak**, not comprehend: ~ **almaz**, unimaginable; incomprehensible; incredible: ~ **bırakmamak**, upset s.o.'s train of thought: ~ **defteri**, notebook: ~ **dengesi**, sanity: ~ **erdirmek**, conceive (idea); **(-e)**, come to understand stg.: ~ **ermek**, understand: ~ **etm. (-i)**, think of (plan, etc.): ~ **hasta·lığı//-nesi//-sı**, mental illness// hospital//patient: ~ **hoca/kethüdası**, mentor, (interfering) adviser: ~ **hocalığı yapmak**, give good advice (pretentiously): ~ **için yol birdir**, the wise all reach the same solution: ~ **iş/kârı değil**, unreasonable; not sensible: ~ **kutusu**, (*jok.*) inventive; trouble-shooter: ~ **öğretmek/vermek**, advise: ~ **sağlığı**, (*med.*) mental health: ~ **sır erecek gibi değil**, unintelligible, inexplicable, mysterious: ~ **terelelli (-de)**, frivolous: ~ **var izan/yakın var**, it's obvious!, it's only common sense, what's the problem?: ~ **verme (kutusu)**, suggestion(-box): ~ **yaşta değil baştadır**, age is no guarantee of wisdom: ~ **zayıflığı**, mental deficiency, feeblemindedness: ~ **züğürdü**, of poor intelligence.

akıl-: ~**da kalmak**, be borne in mind/remembered: ~**da tutmak**, bear in mind, remember: ~**dan**, from memory: ~**dan çıkarmak**, forget about: ~**dan çıkmamak**, be unable to forget: ~**dan hesap**, mental arithmetic: ~**la gelmedik**, unimaginable: ~**la sığar**, it's reasonable: ~**lar durdurmak**, dumbfound s.o.: ~**lara durgunluk verecek derecede**, to an astounding degree: ~**lara durgunluk vermek**, be incredible/astonishing: ~**ları pazara çıkarmışlar herkes yine kendi aklını almış**, we each prefer our own opinions.

akla: ~ **durgunluk vermek**, astound: ~ **gelmedik**, unthinkable: ~ **gelmek**, occur to the mind; think about; remember: ~ **gelmeyen başa gelir**, the unexpected always happens: ~ **gelmez**, unthinkable: ~ **getirmek**, remind: ~ **hayale gelmez**, incredible: ~ **sığar**, plausible; admissible: ~ **sığmamak**, be unthinkable: ~ **uygun/yatar**, reasonable: ~ **yakın**, reasonable, clear; plausible: ~ **zarar**, very surprising.

aklı: ~ **almamak**, not understand; not believe possible: ~ **başına gelmek**, come to one's senses; see reason: ~ **başında**, he knows his business, he's 'all there': ~ **başında olmamak**, be unable to think clearly: ~ **başından bir karış yukarı**, thoughtless; absent-minded: ~ **başından gitmek**, lose one's head: ~ **bokuna karışmak**, (*vulg.*) be confused from fear: ~ **bozulmuş**, deranged: ~ **çalık**, crazy: ~ **çıkmak**, worry, be anxious, fear: ~ **durmak (-e)**, be dumbfounded/unable to think: ~ **ermek**, understand; grasp (idea): ~ **evvel**, very clever: ~ **fikri**, lost in thought: ~ **fikri birbirine karışmak**, be bewildered: ~ **gitmek**, be astonished: ~ **karışmak**, be confused: ~ **kasıranemce**, in my humble opinion: ~ **kesmek**, decide, judge; realize; believe possible: ~ **kısa**, of limited intelligence: ~ **oynamak**, go off one's head: ~ **sana kim öğretti (bu)?**, who put the idea into your head?: ~ **sıra**, (*iron.*) according to him: ~ **sonradan gelmek**, think of stg. too late, be wise after the event: ~ **takılmak (-e)**, apply one's mind to: ~ **tepesinden yukarı**, thoughtless(ly), absent-minded(ly): ~ **yatmak (-e)**, be convinced/ satisfied about.

aklı-: ~**m ermez (-e)**, it's beyond me!: ~**ma gelen başıma geldi**, what I feared happened: ~**mda!**, I haven't forgotten!: ~**n dikliğine gitmek**, be obstinately perverse.

aklına: ~ **dokunmak**, derange s.o.: ~ **düşmek**, remember; have an idea: ~ **esmek**, feel like doing stg.; take it into one's head to do stg.: ~ **esen/ geleni söylemek**, talk at random/without thought: ~ **gelmek**, come to mind; imagine: ~ **getirmek**, remind s.o.; recollect stg.: ~ **hiffet getirmek**, go off one's head: ~ **koymak**, decide definitely; suggest stg. to s.o.: ~ **sığdırmak**, accept, understand: ~ **şaşayım**, I'm surprised at you; what an idea!: ~ **takmak**, think hard and long about stg.: ~ **turp sıkayım!**, (*sl.*) you're crazy!; what rot!, keep your advice to yourself!: ~ **uymak**, follow one's own whims; yield to some temptation: ~ **yelken etm.**, behave thoughtlessly.

aklın-: ~**da kalmak/olmak/tutmak,** not forget; remember: ~**da zoru var,** he's off his head: ~**dan çıkmak,** forget: ~**dan çıkaramamak,** have stg. on the brain: ~**dan geçirmek,** happen to think of stg.: ~**dan geçmek,** occur to s.o.: ~**dan zoru olm.,** be disturbed in mind.

aklını: ~ **başına almak/toplamak,** pull o.s. together, collect one's wits: ~ **başından almak,** make s.o. unable to think: ~ **bozmak/kaçırmak,** lose one's reason; go mad: ~ **çelmek,** captivate the mind; bias; persuade, dissuade: ~ **oynatmak,** go mad: ~ **peynir ekmekle mi yedin?,** have you gone out of your senses?: ~ **şaşırmak,** go crazy.

aklı-: ~ **nın terazisi bozulmak,** the balance of one's mind be disturbed. ~**nla bin yaşa!,** (*iron.*) what a bright idea!

akıl·cı (*phil.*) Rationalist. ~**cılık,** rationalism. ~**dışı,** irrational. ~**dişi**ni, (*bio.*) wisdom-tooth.

akılgın (*bot.*) White tamarisk.

akılık Generosity.

akıl·lanmak *vi.* Become wiser (by experience). ~**lı,** clever, intelligent; reasonable; prudent; discerning; well-advised: ~ **adamın harcı,** the way a wise man would act: ~ **düşman akılsız/cahil dosttan yeğdir,** an intelligent enemy is preferable to a stupid friend: ~ **geçinmek,** pass for a wise man: ~ **ol da deli sansınlar,** act wisely and let them think you a fool: ~ **uslu,** reasonable; wise. ~**lıca,** reasonably. ~**lılık,** wisdom, intelligence. ~**sız,** stupid, empty-headed; imprudent; ill-advised: ~ **başın ceza/ zahmetini ayak çeker,** thoughtlessness makes hard work for the feet. ~**sızlık,** stupidity; imprudence: ~ **etm.,** behave stupidly/thoughtlessly.

akım (*phys., el.*) Current, flow; (*pol.*) current, movement, trend; (*art.*) style, trend. ~ **çevirgeci,** (*el.*) change-over switch: ~ **devresi,** (*el.*) current circuit: ~ **kesici,** (*el.*) cut-out, circuit-breaker: ~**ı kesmek,** de-energize.

akım·la Electro-. ~**lı,** live (wire). ~**lık,** (*eng.*) conduit. ~**sız,** (*el.*) dead (line). ~**toplar,** (*el.*) accumulator.

akın (*mil.*) (Commando-)raid; foray; rush; stream (people, etc.); (*ich.*) shoal (fish). ~ ~, rushing/ surging in crowds: ~ **etm./saldırmak,** raid; foray; rush (in crowds): ~ **kayası,** (*ich.*) goby.

akın·cı *a.* (*mil.*) Raiding, pioneering: *n.* raider; commando; (*his.*) member of a light cavalry corps; (*sp.*) forward, striker: ~ **katı,** (*sp.*) forward line: ~ **kuvvetler,** (*mil.*) expeditionary force. ~**cıl,** attacking, offensive.

akındırı·kğı (*bot.*) Resin.

akıntı Current, stream; flow, leak; (*med.*) streaming cold, etc.; incline. ~ **açısı,** (*naut.*) drift angle, leeway: ~ **ağı,** drift net: ~ **aşağı,** downstream: ~ **çağanozu,** (*zoo.*) crab caught in the current; (*jok.*) very distorted body: ~ **demiri,** (*naut.*) drift anchor: ~ **ortası,** midstream: ~ **yukarı,** upstream: ~**ya kapılmak,** be caught in/go with the current; (*fig.*) be swayed by the crowd: ~**ya karşı,** upstream: ~**ya kürek çekmek,** row against the current; struggle in vain. ~**lı,** flowing; sloping. ~**sız,** currentless, still.

akıölçer (*el.*) Induction meter.

akış Course; flow; passing; incline; trip, run. ~ **ağ/ çizelgesi,** flow diagram: ~ **aşağı,** downstream: ~ **çizgisi,** stream-line: ~ **oranı,** flow rate; discharge: ~ **ölçeği,** flowmeter: ~ **yukarı,** upstream.

akışkan *a., n.* (*phys.*) Fluid. ~**laştırıcı,** fluidizing agent. ~**laştırmak (-i),** fluidize. ~**lık,** fluidity. ~**sı(lık),** vis·cous/(-cosity).

akış·lı Flowing. ~**mak,** *vi.* flow together. ~**maz/ (-lık),** vis·cous/(-cosity).

akıt·a¹**ç**cı (*med.*) Drain. ~**ılır,** (*min.*) ductile. ~**ım,** drainage. ~**ma,** *vn.* discharging; drainage; pouring; making flow; (*min.*) cast (iron); blaze (on horse); (*cul.*) pancake. ~**mak (-i, e),** *vc.* = AKMAK; make/let flow; drain; shed (tears).

akız Fluidity; flow(ing).

akide¹ (*cul.*) ~ **(şekeri),** sugar candy.

akide² (*rel.*) Faith, creed, doctrine, dogma. ~**si bozuk,** unsound in faith: ~**yi bozmak,** go against one's beliefs.

akifer (*geol.*) Aquifer(ous), water-bearing.

akiki (*geol.*) Agate, cornelian.

akil Reasonable. ~ **baliğ,** adolescent. ~**ane,** reasonably.

akim Sterile, barren; without result. ~ **kalmak,** *vi.* fail; (*mil.*) abort: ~ **kalmış,** abortive.

ak·issi *n.* (*phys.*) Reflection; reverse side; converse; echo; reaction; reverberation. ~ **sondası,** echo-sounder: ~ **uyandırmak,** produce a reaction: ~**ini anlamak,** understand exactly the opposite of stg.: ~**ini ispat etm.,** disprove stg.: ~**ini söylemek,** contradict.

akis·e (*phys.*) Reflector. ~**li,** reflecting. ~**siz,** (*rad.*) anechoic.

ak·itti/di Compact, treaty; bargain; marriage; conclusion (of a treaty, etc.). ~**in bozulması,** cancellation/violation of the contract: ~**ten doğan,** contractual.

âkiti Contracting party; signatory.

Akka (*geo.*) Acre.

ak·kan (*bio.*) Lymph: ~ **düğümu,** lymph node: ~ **göze,** lymphocyte. ~ **kanatlı,** (*orn.*) white-winged. ~**karınca,** (*ent.*) white ant: ~**lar,** termites: ~**karınlı,** white-bellied: ~ **sağan,** (*orn.*) Alpine swift. ~**kava**¹**k**ğı, (*bot.*) white poplar. ~**kefal,** (*ich.*) bleak. ~**kelebe**¹**k**ği, (*ent.*) black-veined white butterfly. ~**kor(lu),** (*phys.*) incandescent; white-hot, glowing. ~**korısı/~korluk,** incandescence. ~**kömür,** (*phys.*) white coal, electricity. ~**kulaklı,** white-eared. ~**kuyru**¹**k**ğu, (*bot.*) green tea. ~**kuyruklu,** white-tailed. ~**kü** = AKÜ.

akl- = AKIL.

akla·ma *vn.* (*leg.*) Acquittal. ~**mak (-i),** whiten, brighten; (*leg.*) acquit; clear s.o.'s honour.

aklan (*geo.*) Mountain-slope; catchment area; stream.

aklan·ma *vn.* (*leg.*) Acquittal; discharge. ~**mak,** *vi.* become white/bright; (*leg.*) be acquitted.

akl·en By reason/intuition. ~¹**etmek**eder = AKIL ETM.

ak·leyle¹**k**ği (*orn.*) White stork. ~**lı,** *a.* with white (spots): ~ **karalı,** black and white; piebald. ~**lık,** whiteness; white face-paint; innocence; (*ast.*) albedo.

aklı·nca According to his idea. ~**selim**, commonsense: ~ **sahibi**, a man of common-sense.
akli *a.* Mental; reasonable. ~**yat**[1], knowledge got by reasoning. ~**ye**, (*psy.*) mental diseases//clinic; (*phil.*) rationalism. ~**yeci**, mental specialist, alienist, psychiatrist.
aklimlemek (-i) Air-condition.
AKM = ATATÜRK KÜLTÜR MERKEZİ.
akma *vn.* Flowing, running; flow; current; (*phys.*) yield; (*fin., geol.*) liquidity; effluence; effusion; (*bot.*) resin; (*ast.*) shooting-star. ~ **biçim(l)i**, streamline(d): ~ **sınırı**, (*phys.*) yield point.
akmadde (*bio.*) White matter.
ak·mak *vi.* Flow, discharge; drain away; leak; drip; (*phys.*) yield; (*tex.*) become frayed/ravelled; (stocking) ladder; (*sl.*) run away, do a bunk: **akacak kan damarda durmaz**, fate is unavoidable: **akmasa da damlar**, a little is better than nothing: **akmış çorap//kumaş**, (*tex.*) laddered stocking//frayed cloth. ~**maz**, *a.* stagnant, still; non-liquid.
ak·mantar (*myc.*) Field mushroom. ~**meşe**, (*bot.*) white oak.
akne (*med.*) Acne.
akompan·yatör/ ~ yatris (*mus.*) Male/female accompanist. ~**ye**, ~ **etm. (-e)**, be with; (*mus.*) accompany. ~**yeci**, accompanist.
akonitin (*med.*) Aconitine.
akont[u] (*fin.*) Instalment, part-payment.
akord- = AKORT. ~**eon**, (*mus.*) accordeon; (*tex.*) pleats.
akor[t][du] Harmony; agreement; (*mus.*) being in tune; chord. ~ +, *a.* (*el., mus.*) Tuning-: ~ **anahtar//çatalı**, tuning-key//-fork: ~ **etm.**/ ~**lamak**, tune (an instrument): ~**u bozuk orkestra gibi**, all out of tune/in disagreement.
akort·çu Tuner. ~**lu**, tuned; in tune. ~**suz**, out of tune. ~**suzluk**, discord, disharmony.
akoz (*sl.*) ~ **etm.**, shut up. ~**lamak (-i)**, whisper.
akpas (*myc.*) White blister/rust (on crucifers).
akraba *pl.*; *used as s.* Relative(s). ~ **arasında teklif tekellüf olmaz**, there must be no standing on ceremony among relatives: ~ **kayırıcılığı**, nepotism: ~ **namına kimsesi yok**, he has no relations. ~**lık**, relationship.
akran Equal (in age/size, etc.); contemporary.
akreditif ~ **(mektubu)** (*fin.*) letter of credit.
akre[l][b][i] (*zoo.*) Scorpion; hour-hand (watch); (*sl.*) policeman. ~ **Burcu**, *pr.n.* (*ast.*) Scorpio: ~ **gibi**, always speaking to harm others: ~ **otu**, (*bot.*) heliotrope: ~ **Yüreği**, (*ast.*) Antares.
akrilik (*chem.*) Acrylic.
akro·basi/-batlık Acrobacy; acrobatics. ~**bat**[l], acrobat. ~**matik**, (*phys.*) achromatic. ~**matin**, (*bio.*) achromatine. ~**matopsi**, colour-blindness. ~**megali**, (*bio.*) acromegaly. ~**pol**[ü], acropolis; (*arch.*) the Acropolis in Athens. ~**stiş**, (*lit.*) acrostic. ~**şaj**, (*rad.*) oscillation.
aks Axis; (*eng.*) axle, journal.
aks- = AKİS.
aksa Hitch, snag.
aksak Lame; limping; lop-sided; interrupted, delayed.
aksakal Village elder. = AK SAKAL.

aksak·lık Lameness; limping behind others; interruption; hitch, defeat. ~**sız**, without limping//hitch.
aksam *pl.* = KISIM. Parts; (*eng.*) spare parts.
aksa·ma *vn.* Limping; hitch; emergency (light, etc.). ~**madan**, regularly. ~**mak**, *vi.* limp; falter; have a hitch.
aksan (*ling.*) Accent; stress. ~ **koymak**, accentuate. ~**lı**, with an . . . accent.
aksata Trade, commerce. ~ **etm.**, do business.
aksatmak (-i) *vc.* = AKSAMAK. Make limp; hinder/ delay.
akse (*med.*) Fit; attack; paroxysm; reflex.
aksedir (*bot.*) American arbor-vitae.
aksele·rasyon (*mot.*) Acceleration. ~**ratör**, accelerator. ~**re**, ~ **etm.**, accelerate. ~**rometre**, accelerometer.
aksep·tans (*ed., fin.*) Acceptance. ~**tör**, acceptor.
aksesuar Accessory; spare part; (*cin., th.*) props; (*mod.*) accessories. ~**cı**, (*cin., th.*) property-man.
aks[l]**et·mek**[eder] *vi., vt.* Reflect; be reflected; project; reverberate, re-echo; become known. ~**tirici**, reflecting. ~**tirmek (-i, -e)**, reflect; echo; cause to be known.
aksır·ı[l]**k**[ğı] Sneeze. ~**ıklı**, ~ **tıksırıklı**, coughing and sneezing; old and in bad health. ~**ma**, *vn.*: ~ **otu**, (*bot.*) sneezewort. ~**mak**, *vi.* sneeze. ~**tıcı**, sneeze-provoking. ~**tmak (-i)**, *vc.*
aksi *a.* Contrary; awkward, disagreeable, perverse, contrary; unlucky, adverse; counter-, contra-; reciprocal. ~ **akım/cereyan**, counter-current: ~ **çıkmak**, happen contrary to expectation: ~ **gibi**, unfortunately, just to be awkward [**o gün ~ gibi yağmur yağdı**, of course it *would* rain that day]: ~ **gitmek**, (things) go wrong: ~ **hal/takdirde**, otherwise, if not: ~ **istikamet/yön**, opposite direction: ~ **olarak**, on the contrary: ~ **şeytan!**, as bad luck would have it!; what a nuisance!: ~ **tesadüf**, unfortunate coincidence: ~ TESİR.
aksi·lenmek/ ~ leşmek *vi.* Show resentment; be awkward/difficult/obstinate. ~**lik**, perversity, contrariness; obstinacy; difficulty, hitch; misfortune, mishap: ~ **çıkmak**, an obstacle arise: ~ **etm.**, make difficulties. ~**ne**, on the contrary; in a contrary manner. ~**seda**, echo. ~**tesir**, reaction, counterstroke.
aksi·yal (*eng.*) Axial. ~**yom**, (*phil.*) axiom. ~**yon**[1], action, event, development. ~**yon**[2]**(er)**, (*fin.*) share(holder). ~**yonoterapi**, (*med.*) activity therapy.
aksolotl (*zoo.*) Axolotl.
akson (*bio.*) Axon.
ak·soy(lu) Noble, well-born. ~**söğül't**[dü], (*bot.*) white willow. ~**su**, (*med.*) cataract, amaurosis. ~**sungur**, (*orn.*) gyrfalcon.
aksü-lamel Reaction, catalysis: ~ **yapmak**, (*chem.*) react. ~**lümen**, (*chem.*) corrosive sublimate, mercuric chloride.
akşam *n.* Evening; the sunset hour. *adv.* In the evening; this/last evening. ~ **ahıra sabah çayıra**, 'life is just eating and sleeping': ~ **(alaca)karanlığı**, dusk: ~ **ezanı**, (*rel.*) sunset call to prayer: ~ **ezanında**, at sunset: ~ **elbise/kıyafet/tuvaleti**, evening dress/clothes: ~ **namazı**, (*rel.*) evening

prayers: ~ **okulu**, (ed.) night school, evening classes: ~ **olm.**, get dark: ~ **sabah**, constantly, all the time: ~ **sabah demez gelir**, he comes at all sorts of (inconvenient) times: ~ **sularında**, around evening-time: ~ **tavus kelebeği**, (ent.) eyed hawkmoth: ~ **vakti**, in the evening: ~ **yediğini sabaha unutmak**, be very absentminded: ~ **yemeği**, dinner, supper: ~ **ziyafeti**, dinner-party.

akşam-: ~**a doğru/**~**dan**, towards evening: ~**a sabaha**, very soon, shortly: ~**dan** ~**a**, every evening: ~**dan kal·ma/-mış**, having a hangover: ~**dan kavur sabaha savur**: he's a spendthrift: ~**dan sonra merhaba!**, it's a bit late for that!: ~**ı bulmak/etm.**, last/stay till evening: ~**lar**, in the evenings: ~**lar/** ~ **şerifler hayrolsun!**, good evening!: ~**ları**, in the evenings.

akşam·cı Night-shift worker; (ed.) evening-class student; (sl.) habitual (evening) drinker. ~**cılık**, regular drinking. ~**güneşi**ⁿⁱ, a. yellowish pink: n. afternoon sun; (fig.) extreme old age: ~ **gibi**, fleeting, transitory. ~**ki**, a. evening. ~**lamak**, vi. spend the whole day doing stg.; stay the night; (moon) rise late. ~**latmak (-i)**, put s.o./stg. off till evening; keep s.o. busy all day; entertain s.o. for the night. ~**leyin**, in the evening. ~**lı**, ~ **sabahlı**, morning and evening, every day. ~**lık**, evening clothes, etc.: ~ **sabahlık**, unavoidably soon. ~**üstü/** ~**üzeri**, [201] at sunset/dusk; towards evening. ~**yıldızı**, (ast.) Venus.

ak·şar/~**şın** (bio.) a. Albino. ~**şınlık**, albinism.

aktar Druggist('s), herbalist('s); haberdasher('s); 'corner'-shop(keeper). ~ **lık**, herbalist's//haberdasher's trade/goods.

aktar·ıcı (arch.) Tiler; (sp.) passer; (rad.) transmitter; (lit.) translator, adaptor. ~ **ılır**, (fin.) negotiable. ~**ılmak**, vp. be changed/transferred, etc. ~**ım**, change; (mus.) transposition; (sp.) transfer; (fin.) endorsement. ~**ımcı**, (mus.) transposer. ~**ma**, (rly.) change, connection; transfer, transshipment; (lit.) excerpt, adaptation, quotation; (sp.) pass; relay changeover; (fin.) virement, clearing; (leg.) cession, assignment; (rad.) transmission; (agr.) first and second ploughing of a field: ~ **bileti**, (rly.) transfer ticket: ~ **eşyası**, (fin.) goods in transit: ~ **etm.**, transfer, trans-ship: ~ **treni**, connecting train, etc.: ~ **tümce**, (ling.) indirect speech: ~ **yapmak**, change (trains, etc.). ~**macı**, (lit.) adaptor, quoter. ~**macılık**, adaptation, quoting; translating; (phil.) system of thought. ~**mak (-i, -den, -e)**, transfer (to another receptacle); trans-ship; (rly.) change (trains); empty contents; (rad.) transmit; (lit.) adapt; quote; translate; (mus.) transpose; (sp.) pass; transfer; (fin.) endorse; (leg.) assign, cede; (arch.) re-tile, etc. (as necessary); (agr.) plough for the first and second time. ~**malı**, connecting (train, etc.); indirect. ~**masız**, without change/transfer; direct, through.

aktavşan¹ (zoo.) Jerboa, desert rat.

akt- = AKİT. ~**en**, contractually. ~**etmek** = AKDETMEK.

aktif a. Active; lively; hard-working; effective; (ling.) active/transitive (verb). n. (fin.) Asset(s). ~

metot, (ed.) active method (of learning). ~ **leştirmek (-i)**, activate.

aktin·ik (phys.) Actinic. ~**i**ⁱ**t**ᵈⁱ, (chem.) actinide. ~**o-**, actino-. ~**yum**, (chem.) actinium.

akti·vasyon (chem.) Activation. ~**ve**, activated. ~**vist**, (pol.) activist. ~**vite**, activity. ~**vizm**, activism.

ak·tör (cin., th.) Actor. ~**tris**, actress.

aktöre (phil.) Good conduct; morals. ~**cilik**, moralism. ~**li/**~**sel**, well-behaved; moral.

aktutma (med.) Albuminuria.

aktü·alite Actuality; news: ~ **(filmi)**, (cin.) newsreel. ~**alizm**, (phil.) actualism. ~**atör**, (eng.) actuator. ~**el**, contemporary; up-to-date. ~**elleştirmek (-i)**, bring up to date. ~**er**, (fin.) actuary.

aku. = AKUSTİK.

aku·ple ~ **etm.**, (el.) connect. ~**plıman**, (eng.) coupling. ~**punktur**, (med.) acupuncture. ~**stik**, (phys.) a. acoustic: n. acoustics. ~**söz**, (med.) midwife. ~**t**, (med.) acute (illness). ~**zatif**, (ling.) accusative case.

akü(mülatör) (el.) Accumulator; (storage) battery. ~ **doldurucusu**, battery charger. ~**lü**, battery-powered/-operated.

akvam pl. = KAVİM. Peoples, nations. = CEMİYETİ.

akvar·el (art.) Water-colour. ~**yum**, (zoo.) aquarium.

akya(balığıⁿⁱ**)** (zoo.) Leer-fish.

ak·yazı(lı) Luck(y). ~**yel**, (met.) dry south wind. ~**yem**, (ich.) fish used as bait. ~**yıldız**, (ast.) the Dog-star; (fig.) luck. ~**yuvar**, (bio.) leucocyte; white corpuscle. ~**zamba**ⁱ**k**ᵏⁱ, (bot.) the Madonna lily. ~**zar**, (bio.) fascia.

al¹ n. Trick, fraud. ~ **etm.**, deceive, trick.

al² a. Red, vermilion, crimson; chestnut (horse). n. Red colour; rouge; (med.) erysipelas; puerperal fever. ~ **basmak**, blush; (med.) catch puerperal fever: ~BASTI: ~ **bayrak**, the Turkish flag: ~ **elmaya taş atan çok olur**, there are always many to be jealous of and harm the successful: ~ **giymedim ki alınayım**, it doesn't concern me so why should I take offence?: ~ **gömlek gizlenemez**, the truth can't be hidden: ~ **kanlara boyanmak**, be wounded/killed, die a martyr: ~ **kiraz üstüne kar yağmış**, the unexpected can always happen: ~ **sancak** = ~ BAYRAK: ~**ı moru mor**, flushed and out of breath (from confusion/exertion). [Also = KIRMIZI; KIZIL.]

al³ = ALAŞAĞI: ALMAK.

alⁱ⁴ n. (obs.) Dynasty; important man's family. ~**i Osman**, the Ottoman dynasty: ~**i Resul**, the Prophet Muhammad's family.

Al. = ALMAN(YA); ALMANCA(DAN); (ch.s.) ALÜMİNYUM.

-al¹ a. suf. [65] = -EL¹ [ATOMAL].

-al-² v. suf. [229] = -EL-² [BOŞALMAK].

ala a. Variegated; speckled; pied; light-brown. ~ ÇAM: ~ DOĞAN: ~ GEYİK: ~ GÜN: ~ KARGA: ~ kır, dappled grey.

âlâ a. comp. = ÂLİ. Higher; highest; good, excellent. ... ~, **sözüm yok**, well and good, I should have nothing to say against it.

ala ala *int.* Hey! ~ ~**ya kalkmak**, (*pol.*) demonstrate noisily.

ala- *pref.* [95] In the style of, *à la* [ALATURKA].

ala·baca'kᵍ¹ White sock (of a horse). ~**balı'k**ᵍ¹, (*ich.*) brown/sea trout. ~**balıkgiller**, (*ich.*) salmons.

alabanda (*naut.*) Inner side of a ship; 'about ship!' order; (*fig.*) violent abuse; severe scolding. ~ (**ateş**), broadside: ~ **etm.**, put the helm hard over: ~ **iskele//sancak**, hard to port//starboard: ~ **kaplaması**, side battens: ~ **olm.**, (*sl.*) be attacked: ~**dan** ~**ya**, athwartships: ~**yı yemek**, (*sl.*) be severely scolded.

ala·baş (*bot.*) Cabbage. ~**bık**, two-faced, hypocritical.

alabil·diğine *adv.* To the utmost; at full speed; continually; incredibly. ~**irlik**/~**me**, ~ **gücü**, capacity.

ala·bora/~**bura** (*naut.*) ~ **etm.**, hoist a flag; salute by raising oars on end; furl sails: ~ **olm.**, capsize. ~**borina**, before the wind, on a bowline.

alabros (*mod.*) Crew-cut (men's hair).

alaca¹ ~ **verece**, the completion of a purchase.

alaca² *a.* Variegated; motley; piebald. *n.* Striped material; fruit first to ripen. ~ **ağaçkakan**, (*orn.*) great spotted woodpecker: ~ **akik**, (*geol.*) onyx, chalcedony: ~ **baykuş**, (*orn.*) tawny owl: ~ **bulaca**, daubed with incongruous colours: ~ **dostluk**, fickle friendship: ~ **düşmek**, (fruit) become ripe: ~ **karga**, (*orn.*) rook: ~ **kargaya borçlu**, hopelessly in debt: ~ **kelebekler**, (*ent.*) fritillaries and vanessids: ~MENEKŞE: ~ **mersin**, (*ich.*) sturgeon: ~ **sülün**, green pheasant: ~**sı içinde**, sly, shifty.

alaca·balıkçıl (*orn.*) Squacco heron. ~**doğan**, (*orn.*) peregrine falcon; (?) common kestrel; (?) goshawk. ~**karanlık**, twilight, dusk.

alaca'kᵍ¹ *n.* (*fin.*) Money owed to s.o.; credit; asset. ~ **ve borçlar**, assets and liabilities: ~ **verecek** = ALIŞVERİŞ: ~**ı olsun!**, I'll make him pay for it: ~**ım var (-den)**, (he) owes me money: ~**ına şahin vereceğine karga**, eager to borrow but slow to pay up: ~**la verecek ödenmez**, a debt owed to you won't pay your debts. ~**lı**, (*fin.*) creditor: ~ **bakiye**, credit balance: ~ **ile anlaşmak**, compound a debt: ~ **taraf**, credit side.

alaca·lanmak *vi.* Become speckled/variegated. ~**lı**, mottled, multicoloured. ~**menekşe**, (*bot.*) pansy.

alacı'kᵍ¹ (Nomad's) felt tent/wattle hut.

ala·çam (*bot.*) Cluster pine. ~**doğan** = ALACA-/KIZILDOĞAN.

alafranga *a.* European; Occidental; in the European fashion. ~ **hela taşı**, (*dom.*) WC (bowl and seat): ~ **müzik**, Occidental music: ~ **saat**, European time (= ALATURKA): ~ **takvim**, (*ast.*) Gregorian calendar: ~ **yemekler**, (*cul.*) European cuisine: ~**nın bebesi**, (*sl.*) ignorant, inexperienced. ~**cı(lık)**, imita·tor/(-tion) of European ways; (*fig.*) snobbery. ~**laşmak**, imitate European ways.

alagarson (*mod.*) Eton-crop (women's hair).

ala·geyi'kᵍ¹ (*zoo.*) Fallow-deer. ~**gün**, (clouds causing) shadowy light. ~**imisema**, (*met.*) rainbow.

alaka Connection; relationship; affinity; attachment; love; interest; concern. ~ **duymak (-e, karşı)**,

be interested in; have relations with: ~ **göstermek (-e)**, show/take interest in: ~ **uyandırmak**, arouse interest: ~ **verici**, interesting: ~**sı olm. (-le)**, be interested in: ~**sını**/~**yı kesmek (-le)**, break off/sever relations with; dissociate o.s. from.

alaka·bahş Interesting. ~**dar**, connected, concerned, interested: ~ **etm. (-i)**, interest; concern: ~ **olm. (-le)**, be interested in/concerned with. ~**landırmak (-i)**, interest; affect. ~**lanmak (-le)**, be interested in; be concerned/involved with stg. ~**lı**, associated, connected; interested; involved: ~ **kimse**, interested party: ~ **makam**, (*adm.*) the competent authority.

alakarga (*orn.*) Jay.

alakart (*cul.*) (Food, meal) *à la carte.*

alakasız Uninterested, indifferent; unconnected. ~**lık**, lack of interest, indifference; apathy.

alakok (*cul.*) Boiled (egg).

alako(y)mak (-i, -e) = ALIKOYMAK.

alala·ma *vn.* (*mil.*) Camouflage. ~**mak (-i)**, camouflage.

alamana (*naut.*) Large fishing/timber-carrying boat. ~ **ağı**, large trawl-net.

Alaman(ya) *pr.n.* = ALMAN(YA).

alametⁱ Sign; mark; badge; symbol; ensign; augury; character, *cachet*; symptom; trace; (*stg.*) enormous; monstrous. ~ **olm.**, augur: ~**i farika**, distinguishing mark; (*fin.*) trademark.

ala·minütⁱⁱ *a., adv.* Very quick(ly); immediate(ly); (*cul.*) 'while you wait!' ~**mo'lt**ᵈⁱ, in the fashion.

alan¹ *n.* (*fin.*) Taker, receiver; buyer, purchaser. ~ **razı satan razı**, since those concerned are satisfied others shouldn't interfere.

alan² *n.* (Forest) clearing; open space; (town) square; zone; (*fig.*) domain; field/sphere (of work); position, site; (*aer.*) air-field: (*math.*) area; (*cin.*/*phys.*) field; (*sp.*) field, arena, court. ~ **araştırması**, (*soc.*) field work/research: ~ **genişletici**, (*cin.*) wide-angle lens: ~ **hızı**, (*rad.*) sweep speed: ~ **korku/ürküsü**, (*psy.*) agoraphobia: ~ **topu**, (*sp.*) tennis-ball. ~**ölçer**, planimeter. ~**topu**ⁿⁱ, (*sp.*) (game of) tennis.

alan talan/taran In utter confusion. ~ **etm.**, upset completely; vandalize.

alanglez (*mod.*, *etc.*) In the English style/way.

alarga (*naut.*) *int.* Cast off!; stand away/clear! *n.* Open sea. *a.* Distant, apart. ~ **durmak**, (*naut.*) give a wide berth to; (*sl.*) remain aloof: ~ **etm.**/~**ya çekmek**, put out to sea; (*sl.*) withdraw: ~**da**, in the offing; clear of: ~**da durmak**, remain at a distance: ~**da yatmak**, (*naut.*) anchor in the roadsteads: ~**dan**, from far: ~**dan gelmek**, not care two hoots about: ~**dan seyretmek**, watch from a distance.

alarm Alarm (signal). ~ **düdüğü**, siren: ~ **işaretini çalmak**, (*mil.*) sound the alert: ~ **kalkışı**, (*aer.*) scramble.

alasulu Half-ripe (fruit, etc.).

alaşağı ~ **etm.**, beat/knock down; depose, dethrone.

Alaşehir (*his.*) Philadelphia (in Asia Minor).

alaşım (*min.*) Alloy. ~**lamak (-i)**, alloy. ~**lı**, alloyed: (**bakır**) ~ **çelik**, (copper-)steel alloy.

alatav (*agr.*) Moist (earth).

alaturka In the Ottoman/Turkish style. ~ **hela taşı**, (*dom.*) Tk. style WC.: ~ **müzik**, Tk. music: ~ **saat**, (*rel.*) prayer-time (reckoned from sunset): ~ **yemekler**, (*cul.*) Tk. cuisine. ~**cı**, lover/player/ singer of Tk. music. ~**cılık**, love/promotion of Tk. music. ~**lık**, the Tk. style.

alavere Passing/throwing stg. from hand to hand; (*naut.*) gangway for (un)loading goods; (*fig.*) utter confusion; (*fin.*) speculation. ~ **dalavere çevirmek/ yapmak**, cheat, play a trick: ~ **tulumbası**, force-pump. ~**cı**, (*fin.*) jobber, speculator.

alay[1] (*mil.*) Regiment; parade, procession; ceremony; crowd, troop; everyone. ~ +, *a.* Regimental; ceremonial: ~ ~, in great numbers; in crowds: ~ **arabası**, state coach: ~ **bağlamak**, draw up troops in line of battle: ~ **beyi**, (*his.*) gendarmerie commandant: ~BOZAN: ~ **elbisesi**, parade uniform: ~ **geçirmek**, review the troops: ~ **kelebekleri**, (*ent.*) processionary caterpillar moths: ~ **komutanı**, (*mil.*) regimental commander: ~ **malay**, all together; in a crowd: ~ **meydanı**, parade ground: ~ **sancakları**, flags for dressing ship, etc.: ~ **topu**, saluting gun: ~**a çıkarmak** (-i), transfer (officer) from academy to regiment.

alay[2] Joke; banter, derision, mockery, ridicule. ~ **etm.** (-le), deride: ~ **etme!**, joking apart!, tell me seriously!: ~ **geçmek/kesmek**, (*sl.*) make fun of, mock: ~ **gibi gelmek** (-e), seem unbelievable: ~ **için**, for fun: ~ **yollu söylenir**, jokingly: ~**a almak**, make fun of; caricature: ~**ın sırası değil!**, the joke is out of place!: ~**ında olm.**, not take stg. seriously.

alay·bozan Matchlock gun; (*fig.*) spoilsport. ~**cı**, *n.* joker, mocker: *a.* cynical; mocking, derisive: ~ **kuş**, (*orn.*) mocking-bird. ~**cılık**, joking; mockery.

alayı·k[ğı] (*med.*) Horse syphilis.

alay·iş Pomp, display; showiness. ~**lı**[1], ceremonious, pompous; (*mil.*) officer risen from the ranks. ~**lı**[2], joking, mocking: ~ **gülümseme**, wry smile. ~**sı**, half-joking half-serious. ~**sılama**, irony.

alaz Flame. ~**lama**, *vn.*; (*med.*) erythema. ~**lamak** (-i), scorch, singe; brand. ~**lanmak/~laşmak**, *vi.* be singed/branded; (*med.*) (skin) be inflamed/come out in spots.

Alb. = ALBAY.

albastı (*med.*) Puerperal fever.

albatr (*min.*) Alabaster. ~**os**, (*zoo.*) albatross.

albay (*mil.*) Colonel; (*naut.*) captain; (*aer.*) group-captain. ~**lık**, colonelcy; (group-)captaincy; rank of colonel, etc.

albeni Attractiveness, charm; sex-appeal. ~**li**, attractive, charming. ~**siz**, unattractive.

albi·nizm (*bio.*) Albinism. ~**no(s)**, albino.

albüm (Photograph, etc.) album; scrap-book.

albümin (*chem.*) Albumin. ~ **hali**, (*med.*) albuminuria: ~ **özü**, protein. ~**li**, albuminous.

alçacık Rather/very low; humble.

alçak Low; short; vile, base, abject, despicable; cowardly. ~ **arazi**, lowland: ~ **basınç**, (*phys.*) low pressure; vacuum; (*met.*) depression: ~ **boylu**, short (in stature): ~ **eşeğe kim olsa biner**, the willing horse gets exploited: ~ **eşek**, fool; booby: ~

frekans, (*rad.*) low frequency: ~ **gönüllü**, humble, meek, modest; affable: ~ **gönüllülük**, humility, modesty: ~ **herif**, scoundrel: ~ **kabartma**, (*art.*) low relief, bas-relief: ~ **kavuşum**, (*ast.*) inferior conjunction: ~ **ruh/tabiatli**, of base nature: ~ **ses**, soft noise; (*mus.*) deep voice: ~ **takım**, the scum of the people: ~ **tazyik** = ~ BASINÇ: ~**tan almak**, adopt a friendly/modest/conciliatory attitude; change one's tune: ~**tan görüşmek**, speak in a quiet/modest manner: ~**tan uçuş**, (*aer.*) low-level flying.

alçak·ça Rather low; abjectly, in a cowardly manner. ~**lık**, lowness; depression; shortness; baseness, meanness; cowardice; enormity.

alçal·ma *vn.* Stooping; descent; degradation; humiliation; reduction; (*geol.*) settling; subsidence; ebb-tide. ~**mak**, *vi.* bend down, stoop: descend; lose value; abase o.s.; condescend. ~**tıcı**, degrading, humiliating; belittling. ~**tmak** (-i), drop, lower; lessen; debase; degrade; belittle, humiliate; depress.

alçarak Lowish.

alçı (*chem.*) Plaster of Paris, gypsum. ~ **kalıp**, plaster mould: ~**da**, in plaster: ~**ya almak/ koymak**, (*med.*) put in plaster.

alçı·cı Plasterer. ~**lamak** (-i), coat with plaster of Paris. ~**lı**, plastered. ~**taşı**[nı], (*geol.*) gypsum.

alda·¹ç[cı] Trick, plot. ~**nç/~ngaç**, easily cheated/ deceived. ~**ngı¹ç**[cı], trick. ~**nmak**, *vi.* be deceived; be enticed; be taken in; be mistaken; (*bot.*) bloom early. ~**tan**, deceiver; imposter; (*fin.*) shark. ~**tı**, trick, deception. ~**tıcı**, deceptive; deceitful; deceiving; cheating. ~**tılmak**, *vp.* be deceived; rise to the bait. ~**tma**, *vn.* deception. ~**tmaca**, trick, catch; plot. ~**tmak** (-i), deceive, defraud, dupe, cheat; (*sp.*) fake, feint; be unfaithful (to wife/husband): **aldatayım diye aldanır**, hoist with his own petard.

aldehi·t[di] (*chem.*) Aldehyde.

aldı (*med.*) Intake.

aldır·ış Attention, regard; care: ~ **etm.**, (*usually neg.*) pay (no) attention; take (no) action: ~ **etmez**, easy-going. ~**ışsız**, careless; indifferent. ~**mak** (-i, -e), *vc.* = ALMAK; fetch, take away, collect: *vi.* (*usually neg.*) take (no) notice of, pay (no) attention to; disregard; (not) bother about. ~**mayış**, disregard. ~**maz**, careless; indifferent; thick-skinned. ~**mazlık**, carelessness; indifference: ~**tan gelmek**, pretend to be indifferent, not care. ~**tmak** (-i), *vc.* = ALDIRMAK.

alegori (*lit.*) Allegory. ~**k**, allegorical.

aleksi (*ed.*) Alexia; dyslexia, word-blindness.

alel·acayip Very strange, surprising. ~**acele**, very quickly, hastily. ~**ade**, ordinary, common(place), normal, usual: ~ **topluluk**, multitude; the common herd. ~**adeleşmek**, *vi.* become normal, etc. ~**adelik**, ordinariness, normality. ~**fevr**, in a hasty manner, on the spur of the moment. ~**hesa¹p**[bı], (*fin.*) on account/advance (payment). ~**husus**, especially. ~**ıtlak**, absolutely; unreservedly; universally. ~**umum**, generally, in general. ~**usul**, in customary manner; as a mere formality.

alem Sign; mark; flag; proper name; high mountain; peak of a minaret; crescent(-and-star) on the top of a mosque. ~ **olm.**, become a distinctive name/ epithet for . . .; be known as . . . . ~**ci**, (*arch.*) worker on a mosque/minaret. ~**dar**, (*mil.*) standard-bearer; leader.

âlem World; universe; all the world, everyone; (*zoo.*) kingdom, class of beings; state of health; amusement, entertainment, party; surprising state of affairs. ~ **+**, *a.* Cosmic: ~ **yapmak**, have a party/entertainment: ~**de . . .**, would that . . ., how I wish that . . .; . . . for the world: ~**e ne?**, what is it to other people?: ~**e sakal dağıtmak**, (*fig.*) wish to teach people a lesson: ~**i mana(da görmek)**, (see in a) dream: ~**i mi (-in)?**, what sense is there (in . . .)?: ~**i var mı (. . . etmenin)**:, does one do that sort of thing?: ~**i yok (. . . etmenin)!**, that sort of thing's not done!: ~**in ağzı torba değil ki büzesin!**: you can't stop tongues wagging!: ~**in ağzında sakız olm.**, be a matter of common talk: ~**in götünde parmak çalmak/götünü yalamak**, (*vulg.*) toady to everyone: ~**lere düşkün**, convivial. ~**penah**, (*his.*) the Refuge of the World, the Sultan. ~**şümul**ü, world-embracing; universal; cosmopolitan.

alen·en Publicly, openly. ~**girli**, (*sl.*) handsome; showy. ~**i**, *a.* public; openly said/done: ~ **celse**, (*leg.*) public hearing/session. ~**iyet**i, publicity; openness: ~**e vurmak**, do openly/publicly; make known, reveal.

aler·jen (*med.*) Allergen. ~**ji**, allergy: ~**si olm. (-e)**, be allergic to. ~**jik**, allergic.

ales·sabah Early in the morning. ~**seher**, at dawn.

alesta (*naut.*) Ready, prepared; now, instantly. ~**!**, *int.* stand by!, (make) ready! ~ **beklemek**, be ready.

aleti Tool; instrument; utensil; apparatus, appliance; device; (*bio.*) member/organ (of the body). ~ **çantası**, tool-bag: ~ **edevat**, tools: ~ **etm. (-i)**, employ s.o. unsuitably: ~ **gibi kullanmak (-i)**, employ/use s.o. as a means to . . .: ~ **kutusu**, tool-box/-chest/-kit: ~ **olm.**, be a means to . . ., be instrumental in . . ., serve as . . .; (*pej.*) be a tool: ~ **sapı**, tang: ~ **tablosu**, (*mot.*) dashboard, instrument panel: ~ **ustası**, tool-maker. ~**çi(lik)**, (*phil.*) instrumental·ist/(ism). ~**sel**, instrumental.

alev Flame; blaze; (*mil.*) pennant. ~ ~/~ **içinde**, aflame, blazing: ~ **alır**, inflammable: ~ **almak**, catch fire: ~ **almaz**, flameproof: ~ **cıhaz/makinesi**, (*mil.*) flame-thrower: ~ **kesilmek**, (*fig.*) flare up: ~ **lambası**, blow-lamp: ~ **parıltısı**, blaze: ~ **saçağı sarmak**, be in a very dangerous position; be out of control: ~**in tepmesi**, (*ind.*) flashback.

Alevi (*rel.*) Partisan of Ali; Alaouite, Shiite. ~**lik**, Shiism.

alev·lendirmek (-i) *vc.* Cause to blaze; set fire to; blast off (a rocket); (*fig.*) make angry/excited. ~**lenir**, inflammable. ~**lenme**, *vn.* blaze; inflammation; excitement: ~ **noktası**, (*phys.*) flash-point. ~**lenmek**, *vi.* blaze, burst into flame; (rocket) blast off; (*fig.*) become angry/excited. ~**lenmez**, non-inflammable. ~**li**, blazing, flaming; in a passion. ~**siz**, flameless.

aleyh *post.* [94] Against; anti; contra-. ~**e dönmek**, turn against: ~**inde bulunmak/söylemek (-in)**, criticise/reproach s.o.: ~**inde olm. (-in) (tamamen)**, be (dead) against s.o.; oppose s.o.; be unfavourable to

s.o.: ~**ine çevirmek**, antagonize: ~**ine olm. (-in)**, be disadvantageous/unfavourable to s.o.: ~**te olm.**, be opposed to: ~**te rey**, (*adm.*) negative vote, 'no'; defeat. ~**tar**, *a.* against, hostile to, opposed to: *n.* opponent. ~**tarlık**, opposition.

aleykümselam Peace be to you! (*the reply to the Muslim greeting:* SELAMÜNALEYKÜM).

alfa (*ling.*) Alpha (α). ~ **ışınları**, (*phys.*) alpha-rays: ~ **taneciği**, alpha particle. ~**-sayısal**, alpha-numeric.

alfabe (*ling.*) Alphabet, ABC; (*ed.*) primer; (*fig.*) beginning. ~ **dışı**, letter not in an(other) alphabet; (*ed.*) analphabetic: ~ **düzen/sırasıyla**, in alphabetic order. ~**tik**, alphabetic(al); in alphabetic order.

alfeni·lᵗᵈⁱ (*min.*) Silver alloy (for cutlery), alfenide.

algarina (*naut.*) Floating crane; sheer-hulk.

algı¹ (*agr.*) Spoon to collect raw opium; (*fin.*) purchase.

algı² (*phil., psy.*) Apprehension; perception; understanding; feeling. ~**cı(lık)**, perception·ist/(-ism). ~**lama**, *vn.*; perception. ~**lamak (-i)**, apprehend, perceive. ~**lanabilirlik**, perceptibility. ~**lanır**, perceptible. ~**lanmak**, be perceived. ~**layıcı**, (*el.*) detector. ~**sal**, perceived.

algın Pale, sickly; (*fig.*) lovesick. ~**lık**, weakness.

algler (*bot.*) Seaweeds.

algoncar (*bot.*) Sloe; bullace.

algoritma (*math.*) Algorithm.

-alı *v. suf.* [181] = -ELİ (BAKALI).

alıcı *n.* (*fin.*) Buyer, customer; acceptor; addressee; (*el.*) (telephone) receiver; (*rad.*) receiver, set; (*eng.*) intake; (*cin.*) motion-picture/ciné camera. *a.* Taking, receiving; dazzling; attractive. ~ **fiyatı**, bid price: ~ **gözüyle bakmak**, look at stg. with a buyer's eye; regard earnestly/with serious intention: ~ **kuş**, (*orn.*) bird of prey: ~ **melek**, (*rel.*) the Angel of Death: ~ **radyo**, radio receiver: ~ **verici**, s.o. who takes back a gift he has given: ~ **verici radyo**, transceiver: ~ **yönetmeni**, (*cin.*) cameraman.

alıçᶜⁱ (*bot.*) Azarole thorn; (?) mountain ash.

alıkᵍⁱⁱ *n.* Saddle cloth; old clothes, rags.

alık² *a.* Stupid; imbecile. ~ ~, stupidly. ~**lanmak**/ ~**laşmak**, *vi.* become imbecile. ~**lık**, stupidity; imbecility; stupid act.

alıko·n(ul)mak *vp.* Be kept/retained/arrested/ detained. ~**(y)ma**, *vn.* arrest, detention; retention. ~**(y)mak (-i, -e, -den)**, keep (back); arrest, detain; hinder, stop; retain, withhold; put aside (for s.o.). ~**yucu**, (*el.*) capacitor.

alım (*fin.*) Taking; buying; acquisition, purchase; (*fig.*) attraction, charm; range. ~ **fiyatı**, purchase price: ~ **öndeliği**, (*fin.*) earnest money: ~ **satım**, business, trade.

alım·cı Creditor; tax-collector. ~**lı**, attractive, charming: ~ **çalımlı**, striking, beautiful. ~**lılık**, beauty, charm, attraction. ~**sız**, unattractive, ugly. ~**sızlık**, unattractiveness.

al·ınⁿⁱ Forehead; brow; face; front; boldness, shamelessness; (*geol.*) breast, face; (*met.*) front; (*min.*) butt. ~ **damarı çatlamak**, lose all sense of shame: ~ **dikişi**, (*min.*) butt-weld: ~ **dişlisi**, (*eng.*) spur gear/wheel: ~ **düzlemi**, (*math.*) front(al) plane: ~ **kas**//**kemiği**, (*bio.*) frontal muscle//bone: ~ **teri**, sweat of the brow, hard work: ~ **teri dökmek**, work hard, make great efforts: ~ **teriyle geçinmek/kazanmak**, live by the sweat of one's brow: ~ YAZISI.

alnı: ~ **açık (yüzü ak)**, innocent, blameless: ~ **davul derisi**, brazen-faced: ~ **na öyle yazılmıştır**, it was predestined for him: ~ **nda yazılmış olm.**, one's destiny/fate to be fixed: ~ **nı çatmak**, frown: ~ **nı karışlamak**, challenge, defy: ~ **nın akı ile**, without a stain on his character.

alındı (*fin.*) Receipt. ~ **lı**, registered (letter).

alın·gaç/ ~ **gan** Touchy. ~ **ganlık**, touchiness.

alın·lı With a broad forehead; shameless. ~ **lık**, (*mod.*) ornament on the forehead; frontlet; (*arch.*) inscription/sign on a house front; pediment.

alın·mak *vp.* = ALMAK. Be taken, etc.: (**-e, -den**), be hurt; take offence. ~ **mış**, assumed.

alın·teri = ALIN. ~ **yazısı**, fate, destiny.

alıntı·(lama) (*lit.*) Adaptation; borrowing, citation, quotation. ~ **lamak (-i)**, adapt; borrow, cite, quote.

alıp ~ **götürmek/vermek**, *etc.* = ALMAK.

alırlı·lıkᵍ¹ (*psy.*) Understanding, perception, receptivity.

alış *vn.* = ALMAK. Action of taking/receiving/buying, etc.; purchase; (*eng.*) intake, admission. ~ **doğruluğu**, (*rad.*) fidelity (of reception): ~ **gücü**, purchasing power: ~ **kabiliyeti**, capacity.

alış·agelmek (-e) Be accustomed to . . . for a long time. ~ **ık**, accumstomed/used to; tame; familiar; regular (client, etc.); (machine) working smoothly. ~ **ıklık**, being accustomed; tameness; familiarity. ~ **ılagelen**, customary, as usual. ~ **ılmak**, *vp.* ~ **ılmış**, customary, habitual. ~ **kan**, accustomed; familiar. ~ **kanlık**, custom; habit; being accustomed; familiarity. ~ **kı**, custom, habit. ~ **kın**, being used to doing stg.; (*med.*) habitual: ~ **göz**, practised eye. ~ **kınlık** = ~ KANLIK. ~ **mak (-e)**, be accustomed (to); become familiar (with); become addicted to; become tame; work smoothly; adjust o.s. to; be acclimatized to: **alışmış kudurmuştan beterdir**, it is difficult to change one's habits. ~ **tıra** ~ **tıra**, gently. ~ **tırı**, (*med.*) exercise. ~ **tırıcı**, (*med.*) addictive. ~ **tırma**, *vn.*; (*sp.*) exercise; training; (*eng.*) fit: ~ **defteri**, (*ed.*) exercise book: ~ **yapmak**, (*sp.*) train. ~ **tırmak (-i, -e)**, accustom, familiarize; (*med.*) addict; adjust; condition; acclimatize; break in/tame (an animal); instruct; (*sp.*) train; (*eng.*) get into running order: **alıştırarak haber vermek (-i)**, break the news gently to s.o.

alışveriş Buying and selling; commerce, trade; (*fig.*) connection; relation. ~ **etm. (-le)**, do business/have dealings with: ~ **miskalle**, business is business: ~ **tıkırında**, business is good.

Ali *pr.n.* Ali. ~ **aşağı** ~ **yukarı**, it's nothing but 'Ali' all the time: ~ **kız**, (*col.*) tomboy: ~ **Paşa vergisi**, gift that is taken back: ~ **Veli**, Tom, Dick and Harry: ~ **nin külahını Veliye, Velinin külahını** ~ **ye giydirmek**, earn one's living by little tricks, rob Peter to pay Paul.

âli High, exalted. ~ **cena'p**ᵇ¹, majestic; eminent;

chivalrous, magnanimous, generous. ~ **cenaplık**, magnanimity, generosity.

alicengiz ~ **oyunu**, a dirty trick.

alifatik (*chem.*) Aliphatic.

alikıran ~ **baş kesen/koparan**, bully, despot.

alil Ill; invalid; blind.

alim *a.* Knowing; who knows. ~ **allah!**, *int.* by God!; as God is my witness!; I warn you!

âlim *a.* Learned (person). *n.* Scholar. ~ **ane**, learned (book). ~ **lik**, learning, scholarship.

ali·terasyon (*lit.*) Alliteration. ~ **vre**, (*fin.*) for future delivery: ~ **satış**, time bargain. ~ **vyon** = ALÜVYON. ~ **zarin**, (*chem.*) alizarin, madder. ~ **ze**, (*met.*) trade-wind.

al·jesi/ ~ **jezi**, (*med.*) Algesia. -~ **ji**, *suf.* -algia. ~ **jinik**, ~ **asit**, (*chem.*) alginic acid.

alkal·i (*chem.*) Alkali. ~ **ik/** ~ **ili**, alkaline. ~ **ilik**, alkalinity. ~ **imetre/** ~ **ölçer**, alkali-meter. ~ **oi'**ᵗᵈⁱ, alkaloid.

alkarna Net for dredging shell-fish.

alkım (*met.*) Rainbow.

alkış Applause; acclamation. ~ **toplamak**, be much applauded: ~ **tufanı (toplamak)**, (receive) loud applause/a standing ovation; (*th.*) (bring down the house): ~ **tutmak**, clap, cheer, applaud.

alkış·çı Cheer-leader; (*th.*) 'claque'; (*pej.*) toady. ~ **çılık/** ~ **lama**, cheering, applause. ~ **lamak (-i)**, clap, cheer, applaud, acclaim. ~ **lanmak**, *vp.*

alki·l (*chem.*) Alkyl. ~ **l'**ᵗᵈⁱ, alkyd.

alkolü Alcohol. ~ **arama**, (*leg.*) blood-test for alcohol: ~ **lambası**, (*dom.*) spirit-lamp. ~ **ik**, *a.*, *n.* alcoholic (person); drunkard. ~ **izm**, alcoholism: ~ **meselesi**, the drink problem. ~ **lü**, *a.*, alcoholic, intoxicating: *n.*, drinker. ~ **ölçer**, (*chem.*) alcoholo-meter. ~ **süz**, (*cul.*) non-alcoholic.

alkuşaklı (*orn.*) ~ **ördek**, common shelduck.

Allah *n.* Allah, God. *int.* How wonderful!, really! ~ **acısın (-e)**, may God have mercy on him!: ~ **adamı**, man of God: ~ **akıl(lar)/akıl fikir versin (-e)**, I am surprised (at s.o.); how foolish (of him)!: ~ ~ **!**, by God!, good Lord!: ~ **aratmasın**, it may not be perfect but it might be worse: ~ **artırsın**, may God increase your prosperity: ~ **aşkına**, for Heaven's sake!: ~ **bağışlasın (-i)**, may God bless s.o.: ~ **belasını versin**, curse him!: ~ **beterinden esirgesin/saklasın (-i)**, may God protect s.o. from stg. worse!: ~ **bilir**, only God knows; who can tell?: ~ **bir**, I swear it: ~ **bir kapı kaparsa bin kapıyı açar**, if you fail in one thing there are many more to try: ~ **bir yastıkta kocatsın**, (married couple) may they grow old together: ~ **büyüktür**, God is great; God will put things right: ~ **canını alsın/cezasını versin**, curse him: ~ **dağına göre kar verir**, we are given strength according to our needs: ~ **derim**, words fail me!; it's hopeless: ~ **dirlik düzen versin!**, God grant you happiness! (to newly married couple): ~ **dokuzda verdiğini sekizde almaz**, you can't change your destiny: ~ **dört gözden ayırmasın**, may God protect the child from being orphaned: ~ **düşmanıma vermesin**, I wouldn't wish it on my worst enemy: ~ **ecir sabır versin**, may God give you patience and help you bear your loss: ~ **eksik etmesin**, may you not want for anything:

~ **eksikliğini göstermesin**, I don't complain but
. . .: ~ **emeklerini eline vermesin**, may you not toil
in vain: ~ **esirgesin/etmesin/göstermesin/korusun/
saklasın/vermesin!**, God preserve us!, God forbid!:
~ **evi**, the house of God, the mosque: ~ **feyzini
artırsın!**, I wish you all success: ~ **gani gani rahmet
eylesin!**, may God rest his soul! (only said when
mentioning the deceased's good deeds): ~ **gecin-
den versin!**, I hope it won't be for many years
(speaking to s.o. of his own death): ~ **hakkı için**,
in God's name!: ~ **hayırlı etsin**, may God make it
fruitful/profitable (new work, etc.): ~ **herkesin
gönlüne göre verir**, God gives to each according to
his heart's desire: ~ **için**, for God's sake; really,
truly; to be fair: ~ **iflah etsin!**, may God reform
him!: ~ **(seni) inandırsın**, may God make you
believe me; as God is my witness: ~ **isterse**, God
willing: ~ **işinizi rast getirsin!**, may God grant you
success!: ~ **kerim**, God is gracious, trust in Him:
~ **kimseye gördüğünden yad etmesin**, Heaven save
one from coming down in the world: ~ **kimseyi
diline düşürmesin!**, may God preserve anyone from
his tongue!: ~ **korusun** = ~ ESİRGESİN: ~ **layık/
müstahakını versin!**, may God give him his deserts!;
curse him!; confound it!: ~ **muinin olsun**, God help
you!: ~ **ömürler versin!**, God grant you long life!:
~ **övmüş de yaratmış**, how beautiful!: ~ **rahatlık
versin!**, sleep well!, good-night!: ~ **rahmet eylesin**,
may he rest in peace: ~ **razı olsun**, may God reward
(you): ~ **rızası için**, for God's sake (!): ~ **saklasın!**
= ~ ESİRGESİN!: ~ **selamet versin!**, may God protect him!: ~ **senden razı olsun**, may God be pleased
with you: ~ **son gürlüğü versin**, may God give him
happiness and prosperity in old age: ~ **sonunu
hayır etsin**, let's hope things turn out well: ~
taksimi, unequal division/share: ~ **taksiratını
affetsin**, may God pardon (a dead person): ~(ı)
var, as God is my witness; we must be fair: ~
vere de . . ., God grant that . . .: ~ **vergisi**,
talent: ~ **versin**, (to a beggar) may God help you;
(*iron.*) congratulations!: ~ **yapısı**, a work of God:
~ **yarattı dememek**, show no mercy/pity: ~ **yazdı
ise bozsun**, God forbid!, may it never happen: ~
yürü ya kulum demiş, (*said of*) the *nouveaux riches*.

Allaha: ~ **emanet**, may God protect s.o.; farewell!,
good-bye!: ~ISMARLADIK: ~ **sığındık**, I trust in
God: ~ **şükür!**, thank God!: ~ **vergi**, only God
can do that.

Allahı: ~ **çok insanı az bir yer**, very remote/
deserted place: ~ **seversen**, for God's sake: ~**m!**,
my God!

Allahın: ~ **belası**, pest; blighter; confounded
nuisance: ~ **cezası**, s.o. very naughty: ~ **evi**, the
human heart: ~ **gazabı**, stg. very troublesome: ~
günu, every blessed day: ~ **hikmeti**, divine dis-
pensation; stg. incredible; 'Heaven knows why!',
'strangely enough!', 'for some mysterious reason!':
~ **kulu**, person, human-being: ~**a kavuşmak**, go
to join one's Maker.

Allahtan: natural, inborn; thank goodness that . . .;
it's a good thing that . . .; fortunately!: ~ **bulsun!**,
may God punish him!: ~ **ki**, naturally: ~ **kork!**,

shame!, don't do it!: ~ **korkmaz**, impious; cruel;
pitiless.

Allahü: ~ **âlem**, probably; God knows: ~ **ekber**,
Allah is the greatest.

Allah-aısmarladık May God be with you!, goodbye! ~**lık**, *n.* deity; godliness: *a.* beyond man's
cômprehension/ability; useless but harmless
(man); imbecile. ~**sız**, atheist, unbeliever; merciless ~**sızlık**, atheism.

allak[1] Tricky, deceitful; fickle. ~**lık**, deceit.

allak[2] **bullak** Pell-mell; in utter confusion; topsy-
turvy. ~ **etm.**, throw into confusion; confuse s.o.:
~ **olm.**, be chaotic; be confused.

allamak allayıp pullamak (-i), deck out, decorate.

allame Very learned/knowledgeable.

allasen (*col.*) = ALLAHI SEVERSEN.

allegr(ett)o (*mus.*) Allegr(ett)o.

allem ~ **etm. kallem etm.**, use every trick to attain
one's purpose: ~ **kallem**, vague words; tricks,
dodges: ~ **kallem etm.**, put s.o. off with words;
trifle with s.o.

al-lı With red colouring: ~ **güllü/pullu**, brightly
coloured/decorated. ~**lık**, redness; red colour;
rouge.

Alm. = ALMAN; ALMANCA(DAN); ALMANYA.

al-ma *vn.* Taking; reception; purchasing; admission;
(*eng.*) intake. ~**ma'ç**cı, (*el.*) receiver; motor; (*bio.*)
receptor.

almak (-i) Take; get, obtain; buy; receive; accept;
hold, take in, contain; marry; carry away/off; catch
(illness; fire); put on (clothes); move stg.; comprehend; assume, take on; conquer, capture; (*naut.*)
row, pull; eat/drink/smoke stg.; steal. *vi.* Catch fire;
(contagion) take hold, affect. **al(ın)!**, there!: **al aşağı
vur yukarı**, bargaining: **al benden de o kadar**, it's
the same with me: **al birini çarp/vur ötekine**, there's
nothing to choose between them: **al gülüm ver
gülüm**, know how to give as well as take: **al sana bir
. . . daha**, here's another one for you: **al takke ver
külah**, squabbling with each other; becoming very
intimate: **alıp götürmek**, carry away/off: **alıp vere-
ceği olmamak**, have no dealings/relations with s.o.:
alıp verememek (-le), have a disagreement with s.o.:
alıp vermek, get excited: **alıp yürümek**, make swift
progress; become the fashion, 'catch on'.

almamazlık Refusal.

Alman *n.* (*ethn.*) German. ~ +, *a.* German: ~
rakısı, (*jok.*) brandy mixed with purgatives: ~
usulü(yle ödemek), *n.* Dutch treat (*v.* go Dutch).

almana'kğı Almanac.

Alman-ca (*ling.*) German. ~**gümüşü**nü (*min.*)
nickel silver. ~**ya**, (*geo.*) Germany: ~ **işçisi**, guest-
worker: ~ **sancısı**, problems of a guest-worker.
~**yalı**, (*ethn.*) German.

almaş *n.* Alternative; permutation; exchange. ~**ık**,
a. alternative; (*bot.*) alternate (leaves). ~**ır**, (*el.*)
alternator.

aln- = ALIN. ~**a'ç**cı, front; (*arch.*) elevation.

alo *int.* Hallo! (on telephone).

alo-pati (*med.*) Allopathy. ~**pesi**, alopecia. ~**trop**,
(*chem.*) allotrope. ~**tropi(k)**, allotro·py/(-pic).

alp[1] Hero; brave man. ~**lık**, heroism.

Alp 23 altınbaş

Alp[i2] (*geo.*) Alp. ~ +, *a.* Alpine. ~ **inist**[i], alpinist, mountain climber. ~ **ler**, the Alps. ~ **yıldızı**[nı], (*bot.*) edelweiss.

alpaka (*zoo.*) Alpaca, llama; (*tex.*) alpaca.

Alsas (*geo.*) Alsace. ~ **çoban köpeği**, (*zoo.*) alsatian: ~ **Loren**, (*geo.*) Alsace Lorraine.

alşimi Alchemy. ~ **st**[i], alchemist.

alt[1] *n.* [90] Lower/under part of stg.; underneath; underside; bottom; base; infra-; hypo-; sub-; continuation. *a.* Lower, inferior, under; basic; (*bio.*) sub-. ~ **akıntı**, undercurrent: ~ ~ **a üst üste** (**boğuşma**), one on top of the other; (a tough struggle): ~ **bacak**, (*bio.*) calf: ~ **baş**, the lower end of stg.: ~ **başında**, immediately below; near, next: ~ **başından**, from the very bottom: ~ **başlık**, (*pub.*) sub-heading: ~ **baştan başlamak**, begin at the end: ~ **bodrum**, sub-basement: ~ **çeneden girip üst çeneden çıkmak**, talk s.o. over: ~CİNS: ~ **değirmentaşı**, nether millstone: ~ **derece**, infra-: ~DERİ: ~ **düzen**, under-carriage, bogie, chassis: ~ **etm.**, conquer, overthrow: ~FAMİLYA: ~GEÇİT: ~ **güverte**, (*naut.*) orlop, lowest deck: ~ **havayuvarı**, (*geo.*) lower atmosphere: ~KARŞIT: ~ **kat**, lower storey; first coat/layer (paint, etc.): ~KIRMIZI: ~ **olm.**, be defeated: ~SINIF: ~ **tabaka**, bottom layer; (*geol.*) substratum: ~TAKIM: ~ **tarafı**, underside; sequel; (cost) at most . . .: ~ **tarafı çapanoğlu çıkar**, there's a 'fly in the ointment'/'snag somewhere': ~ **tetik**, half-cock: ~TOPRAK: ~ÜST: ~ **yanı çıkmaz sokak**, this leads nowhere: ~ **yanını sormak (-in)**, inquire further into stg., get to the bottom of the matter: ~YAPI: ~ **yazı**, (*pub.*) footnote; (*cin.*) subtitle.

alt-: ~ı **alay üstü kalay**, (*mod.*) smart exterior but shabby underneath: ~ı **çizilmiş kelime**, the underlined word: ~ı **kaval üstü şişane**, a paradoxical absurdity; wearing clothes that do not match: ~ına **almak/alıp dövmek**, give s.o. a good thrashing: ~ına **etm./kaçırmak/koyuvermek**, foul one's bed/clothing: ~ına **imza atmak**, undersign: ~ında, under(neath): ~ında **kalmak**, have no answer (to stg.): ~ında **kalmamak**, not be out-done; not be under an obligation: ~ından, from under(neath): ~ından **girip üstünden çıkmak**, squander (a fortune): ~ından **kalk(ma)mak**, be (un)successful: ~ından **kesmek**, (*min.*) undercut: ~ından **ne çıkacak bilinmez**, the outcome is uncertain: ~ını **çaldırmak**, give o.s. away: ~ını **çizmek**, underline; (*fig.*) emphasize: ~ını **ıslatmak**, wet o.s., be incontinent: ~ını **kazmak**, undermine: ~ını **üstüne çevirmek/getirmek**, turn upside down/topsy-turvy: ~ta **kalmak**, be defeated; come off badly: ~ta **kalanın canı çıksın!**, woe to the conquered!: ~tan, from below; bottom: ~tan **almak**, behave weakly: ~tan ~a, by implication; between the lines; in an underhand way: ~tan ~a **anlatmak**, hint at, imply: ~tan **bindirme**, (*geol.*) underthrust: ~tan **görünüş**, worm's-eye view: ~tan **oymak/yemek**, undermine: ~tan **vuruş**, (*sp.*) uppercut.

-alt- *v. suf.* [229] = -ELT- [AZALTMAK].

alt·bilin[i]**ç**[ci] *n.* (*psy.*) Subconscious. ~**bilinçsel**, *a.* subconscious. ~**bölüm**, (*lit.*) sub-section; (*bio.*) subdivision. ~**cins**, (*bio.*) sub-genus. ~**çene**, (*bio.*)

mandible, lower jaw. ~**dal**, (*bio.*) sub-cladus. ~**dama**[ı]**k**[ğı], (*bio.*) lower palate. ~**deri**, (*bio.*) derma, corium. ~**deyim**, (*phil.*) sub-expression. ~**duda**[ı]**k**[ğı], (*bio.*) lower lip.

alter·asyon Alteration. ~**e**, altered: ~ **etm.**, alter, modify. ~**natif**, *a.* (*bot.*) alternate; (*el.*) alternating: *n.* alternative: ~ **akım**, (*el.*) alternating current. ~**natör**, (*el.*) alternator.

altes His/Her Highness (prince(ss)'s title).

alt·ev (*arch.*) Ground-floor (room). ~**familya**, (*bio.*) sub-family. ~**filum**, (*bio.*) sub-phylum. ~**geçi**[ı]**t**[di], (*eng.*) underpass, subway. ~**geçici**, (*el.*) subtransient. ~**gergi**, (*arch.*) tie-beam.

altı Six; hexa-. ~ **aylık**, (*pub.*) biannual: ~ **bazlı**, (*chem.*) hexabasic: ~ **değerli**, hexavalent: ~ **kapıya almak**, (*sl.*) have complete control over s.o.: ~ **karış beberuhi**, (*jok.*) dwarf: ~ **kat**, sixfold: ~ **okka etm. (-i)**, frogmarch s.o.: ~ **oklu bayrak**, (*pol.*) six-arrow flag (of HALK PARTİSİ): ~ **tekerlekli**, (*mot.*) six-wheel(er): ~**da bir**, one sixth: ~**dan yemek**, (s.o. ill) eat normally. ~**atar**, (*mil.*) six-shooter. ~**gen**/~**köşe(li)**, (*math.*) hexagon(al). [*Further phrases* = BEŞ].

altı[ı]**k**[ğı] (*phil.*) Subaltern. ~**lık**, specificity; sub-alternation.

Altı·kardeş (*ast.*) Cassiopeia constellation. ~**lı**, *n.* (*gamb.*) six: *a.* six-(sided, etc.); (*chem.*) hexavalent. ~**lık**, containing six (parts); worth six (units); (*ast.*) sextant.

altın *n.* Gold; (*chem.*) aurum; gold coin; wealth. *a.* Golden; gold-coloured. ~ +, *a.* Aur-; chrys-: ~ **adı pul olm.**, be discredited: ~ **adını bakır etm.**, bring dishonour upon an honoured name: ~ **anahtar her kapıyı açar**, money talks/opens all doors: ~ **arayıcı**, gold-digger/-prospector: ~ **ayarı**, assay: ~ **babası**, s.o. immensely wealthy; a Croesus: ~BAŞ: ~ **başak**, (*bot.*) golden rod: ~ **bilezik**, gold bracelet; (*fig.*) skill that will earn one's living: ~**böcek**: ~ **çağ/devri**, golden age: ~ **çiçeği**, (*bot.*) buttercup: ~ **dolgulu**, gold-filled (tooth): ~ **dövücü**, goldbeater: ~ **eli bıçak kesmez**, the rich can't be hurt: ~ **esas/kural/miyarı**, (*fin.*) gold standard: ~ **kakma**, gold inlay: ~ **kaplama(lı)**, gold-plate(d): ~ **kartal**, (*orn.*) golden eagle: ~ **keseği**, (*min.*) gold nugget: ~ **kesmek**, be very rich: ~ **Kıyısı**, *pr.n.* (*geo.*) Gold Coast: ~KÖKÜ: ~ **kuyumcusu**, goldsmith: ~ **külçesi**, gold bullion: ~ **küpü**, a Croesus: ~ **leğene kan kusmak**, live in misery; suffer in spite of one's wealth: ~ **Ordu**, (*his.*) Golden Horde: ~ **pas tutmaz**, slander can't hurt a good person: ~ **rengi**, golden, aureate: ~ **sarısı**, golden blonde: ~SUYU: ~ **şartı**, (*fin.*) gold clause: ~ **tasa kan kusmak**, rich man have troubles: ~TOP: ~ **topu (gibi)**, chubby baby: ~ **tutsa toprak olur**/~**a yapışsa elinde bakır kesilir**, he's always unlucky: ~ **varak**, gold leaf: ~ **yağmurcun**, (*orn.*) Eurasian golden plover: ~ **yaldız**, gilt: ~ **yaldız(lama)**, gilding: ~ **yedeği**, (*fin.*) gold reserve: ~ **yıldönümü**, golden-wedding anniversary: ~ **yumurtlayan tavuk**, s.o. well off; (*fig.*) the goose that lays the golden eggs; foreign tourist: ~**dan**, gold(en).

altın·baş Golden head; (*bot.*) kind of melon; (*cul.*)

kind of raki: ~ **kefal**, (*ich.*) golden mullet.
~**böce¹kᵍⁱ**, (*ent.*) rose chafer. ~**cı¹**, *n.* goldsmith.
altıncı² (6.) *a.* (*math.*) Sixth.
altın·cı¹kᵍ¹ (*bot.*) Pot-marigold. ~**ımsı**, like gold,
golden. ~**kamışı**ⁿⁱ, (*bot.*) yellow loosestrife.
~**kökü**ⁿü, (*bot.*) ipecacuanha root. ~**lamak (-i)**,
gild. ~**lı**, (*geol.*) auriferous; (*mod.*) ornamented
with gold; (*fig.*) rich. ~**olu¹kᵍu**, (*tex.*) gold-
embroidered striped fabric. ~**otu**ⁿu, (*bot.*) hart's
tongue fern. ~**suyu**ⁿu, (*chem.*) *aqua regia.* ~**tavuk**,
(*orn.*) Himalayan monal pheasant. ~**top**u, (*bot.*)
grapefruit; daffodil: = ~ TOPU.
altı·parma¹kᵍ¹ Six-fingered/-toed (person); (*ich.*)
large PALAMUT; (*tex.*) cloth striped in six colours.
~**patlar**, six-shooter, revolver. ~**şar**, six each; in
sixes, six at a time. ~**z**, sextuplet.
altimetre (*aer.*) Altimeter.
alt·karşıt¹ (*phil.*) Subcontrary. ~**kırmızı**, (*phys.*)
infra-red. ~**kuram**, sub-theory. ~**kurul**, (*adm.*)
sub-committee. ~**lamak (-i)**, (*phil.*) subsume. ~**lı**,
~ **üstlü**, (*arch.*) on two floors; (*mod.*) in two parts,
costume, twin-set. ~**lık**, under-layer; pedestal;
mount, support; pad; (*dom.*) table-mat, coaster.
altmış Sixty. ~**altı**, (*gamb.*) a card game: ~**ya**
bağlamak, (*sl.*) put s.o. off with vague promises.
~**ar**, sixty each; sixty at a time. ~**dörtlük**, (*mus.*)
1/64th of a semibreve. ~**ıncı (60.)**, sixtieth. ~**lık**,
sixty years old; containing sixty (parts); worth sixty
(units). [*Further phrases* = KIRK].
alto (*mus.*) Alto.
altrü·ist Altruist. ~**izm**, altruism.
alt·sınıf (*bio.*) Sub-class. ~**şube**, (*fin.*) sub-branch.
~**takım**, (*bio.*) sub-order. ~**toplum**, (*soc.*) lower
classes. ~**toprak**, (*geol.*) subsoil. ~**tür**, (*bio.*) sub-
species. ~**ulaşım**, (*rly.*) underground, metro.
altuni Golden-coloured.
altüst Upside-down; topsy-turvy. ~ **böreği**, (*cul.*)
pasty baked on both sides: ~ **etm.**, disorganize,
dislocate: ~ **olm.**, be in disorder; be upset/dis-
turbed.
alt·yapı (*arch.*) Underground services, substruc-
ture; foundation; (*eng.*) chassis; (*phil.*) infrastructure, basic concept. ~**yapısal**, basic. ~**yazı**, (*pub.*)
footnote; (*cin.*) subtitles.
alüfte Tart, cocotte, prostitute.
alümin (*min.*) Alumina. ~**at**, aluminate. ~**yum**,
(*chem.*) aluminium: ~**la kaplamak**, aluminize.
~**yumlu**, aluminous. ~**yumtaşı**, (*geol.*) bauxite.
alüv·yon (*geol.*) Alluvium, alluvion. ~**yon+/**
~**yonel**/~**yonlu**, alluvial. ~**yum**, alluvium.
al·yaj (*min.*) Alloy. ~**yans**, wedding-ring.
al·yanaklı Red-cheeked. ~ **maymun**, (*zoo.*) rhesus
monkey. ~**yuvar**, (*bio.*) red blood-corpuscle, erythrocyte.
am (*bio.*; *vulg.*) Vulva. ~ **biti**, (*ent.*) crab-louse.
Am. = AMERİKA(N); (*ch.s.*) AMERİKYUM.
ama = AMMA. *conj.* [120] But, yet, still; be sure to
. . .!; mind you . . .!; though! ~**sı (maması) yok**,
there's no 'but' about it; 'but me no buts!': ~**sı**
var, it has hidden defects, *caveat emptor.*
âmâ Blind. ~**lık**, blindness.
-ama- *v. suf.* [151] = -EME- [ANLIYAMAM].
amabile (*mus.*) Amabile; pleasantly.

ama¹çᶜ¹ Target; aim, purpose, intention, design,
object. ~ **edinmek**, have a goal/aim: ~ **gütmek**,
strive for stg.: ~**ına ulaşmak**, achieve one's aim:
~**ıyla**, with an eye to . . . .
amaç·lama *vn.* Intention, aim. ~**lamak (-i)**, aim at/
intend stg. ~**layarak**, intentionally. ~**lı**, having/
with a purpose; motivated; purposeful: ~ **dokunca**,
(*leg.*) barratry. ~**lılık**, purposefulness. ~**sız(lık)**,
aimless(ness).
amade Ready, prepared.
amalⁱ¹ *pl.* = AMEL. Actions, deeds.
amalⁱ² *pl.* = EMEL. Desires, hopes, ambitions.
amalgam (*chem.*) Amalgam. ~**asyon**, (*fin.*) amalgamation. ~**e**, amalgamated: ~ **etm.**, amalgamate.
aman *n.* Pardon, mercy. *int.* [137] Help!; mercy!;
alas!; for goodness sake! ~ ~!, oh my!, good
heavens!: ~ ~ **değil**, it's nothing special: ~ **bu**
yumurcak!, drat the child!: ~ **bulmak**, be saved:
~ **dedirtmek (-i)**, make s.o. cry for mercy/yield:
~ **demeye kalmaz**, before one could say a word:
~ **derim!**, don't do such a thing!: ~ **dilemek/**
istemek (-den), ask for mercy/quarter: ~ **efendim!**,
please don't!: ~ **faş olmasın!**, I hope to goodness
people don't hear of it: ~ **ne çiçek!**, (a girl who
suddenly becomes) forward/flighty!: ~ **üstümde**
kalmasın, before I forget (s.o.'s greetings): ~ **ver-**
(me)mek, show (no) mercy: ~ **yarabbi!**, dear dear!,
dear me!: ~ **zaman!**, mercy!, mercy!: ~ **zaman din-**
lemez, merciless: ~**a düşürmek/getirmek (-i)**
= ~ DEDİRTMEK: ~**a gelmek**, come to terms, yield:
~**ı kesilmek**, have no strength/recourse left: ~**ı**
zamanı yok, there's no getting out of it; you must!:
~**ın!**, help!; mercy! ~**sız**, pitiless, without mercy;
deadly.
Amasya (*geo.*) Amasia. ~**nın bardağı biri olmazsa**
bir(i) daha, there are as good fish in the sea as ever
came out of it; nothing is indispensible.
AMAT = (*American Mission for Aid to Turkey*).
amatol (*chem.*) Amatol.
amatör (*art.*, *sp.*) Amateur; dilettante. ~ **işi**/~**ce**,
amateurish. ~**lük**, amateurism.
Amazon (*geo.*) Amazon; (*myth.*) Amazon; (*sp.*)
woman horserider. ~ **taşı**/~**it**ⁱ, (*geol.*) amazonite.
amba·laj Packing; package, container; wrapping;
~ **kâğıdı**, wrapping paper: ~ **sandığı**, crate: ~
yapmak/~**lamak (-i)**, pack; wrap up. ~**lajcı**,
packer, crater. ~**le**, confused: ~ **olm.**, become
confused/bewildered.
ambar Barn, granary; store(house), warehouse;
depository; (*mil.*) magazine; (*naut.*) hold; bin (for
measuring bulk). ~ **ağzı**, (*naut.*) hatchway: ~ **ağzı**
mezarnası, hatch-coaming: ~ **faresi**, s.o. very fat:
~ **kapağı**, (*naut.*) hatch: ~**dan çıkarmak**, (*ind.*)
break bulk. ~**cı**, storekeeper; warehouseman.
~**lamak (-i)**, store.
ambargo (*adm.*) Embargo. ~ **koymak (-e)**, (impose
an) embargo: ~**yu kaldırmak (-den)**, lift the embargo.
amber Ambergris; perfume, fragrance. ~**ağacı**ⁿⁱ,
(*bot.*) type of mimosa, (?) styrax. ~**balığı**ⁿ, (*zoo.*)
sperm whale. ~**baris**, (*bot.*) marberry, berberis.
~**bu**, (*cul.*) large-grained rice. ~**çiçeği**ⁿⁱ, (*bot.*)
musk-mallow; musk-seed. ~**li**, with ambergris.

amblem Emblem, sign, symbol.
amboli (*med.*) Embolism.
ambreye Coupled, connected.
ambrosya (*myth.*) Ambrosia.
ambulans Ambulance.
ambuvatman (*carp.*) Encasing; (*eng.*) housing.
amca Paternal uncle; *familiar address to an older man*. ~ **gibi**, avuncular: ~ **kız/oğlu**, (paternal) cousin: ~ **torunu**, first cousin once removed: ~ **mla dayım hepsinden aldım payım**, I've had enough of my relations. ~ **lık**, unclehood; step-uncle: ~ **etm.**, behave like an uncle. ~ **zade**, (paternal) cousin.
amden (*leg.*) Intentionally; deliberately.
amel Action, deed; labour, job, work; execution; catharsis; (*med.*) movement of the bowels, diarrhoea; practice; performance. ~ **etm.**, act, proceed: ~ **ilacı**, (*med.*) purgative: ~ **olm.**, (*med.*) have diarrhoea: ~ **olunmak**, (*adm.*) be proceeded with: ~ **vermek**, (*med.*) purge: ~ **e gelmek**, (*adm.*) take effect: ~ **e getirmek**, apply, enforce.
amele *pl.* = AMIL[1]. Workers. *s.* Workman, labourer. ~ **birliği**, trade union: ~ **hukuku**, labour law/legislation.
ameli Practical (not theoretical); (*math.*) applied. ~ **manda**, unable to work; past work; invalided. ~ **yat**[1] *pl.* = ~ YE; practical deeds; (*mil.*) operations; *s.* (*ind.*) process; (*med.*) operation; -ectomy: ~ **etm.**, operate: ~ **masası**, operating table: ~ **olm.**, undergo an operation. ~ **yathane**, (*med.*) theatre. ~ **ye**, (surgical) operation; work; (*chem.*) process.
amenajman (*for.*, *min.*) Management.
amen·na *int.* Admitted!, agreed! ~ **tü**, (*rel.*) creed.
amer (*cul.*) Bitters (drink).
Amerika (*geo.*) America. ~ +, *a.* American; (*sl.*) very rich: ~ **ateş çiçeği**, (*bot.*) poinsettia: ~ **bıldırcını**, (*orn.*) bobwhite: ~ **Birleşik Devletleri**, the United States of America; USA: ~ **bizonu**, (*zoo.*) bison: ~ **devekuşu**, (*orn.*) greater rhea: ~ **karaağacı**, (*bot.*) white elm; hop-tree: ~ **timsahı**, (*zoo.*) alligator: ~ **yerlisi**, (*ethn.*) Red Indian.
Amerika·armudu[nu] (*bot.*) Avocado pear. ~ **bademi**[ni], (*bot.*) styrax (tree producing benzoin). ~ **elması**[nı], (*bot.*) cashew-nut/-tree. ~ **lı**, *a.*, *n.* [44] (*ethn.*) American. ~ **lılaşmak**, *vi.* become an American/americanized. ~ **lılaştırmak (-i)**, americanize. ~ **n**, *a.*, *n.* [44] American: ~ **aynası**, (*eng.*) universal chuck: ~ **bar**, drinks bar: ~ (**bezi**), (*tex.*) unbleached calico: ~ **cevizi**, (*bot.*) hickory nut: ~ **fıstığı**, (*bot.*) peanut: ~ **makabı**, (*eng.*) twist-drill: ~ **pazarı**, shop selling American goods: ~ **sığırı**, (*zoo.*) moose. ~ **piresi**[ni], (*zoo.*) sand-flea, jigger. ~ **tavşanı**[nı], (*zoo.*) chinchilla. ~ **üzümü**[nü], (*bot.*) common pokeweed.
amerikyum (*chem.*) Americium.
ametal (*chem.*) Non-metallic (element).
ametist[i] (*geol.*) Amethyst.
amfetemin (*chem.*) Amphetamine.
amfi (*col.*) Amphitheatre; lecture-room. ~ -, *pref.* amphi-. ~ **bi**, *a.* amphibian, amphibious: ~ **harekât**, (*mil.*) amphibious operation. ~ **bol**[ü], (*min.*) amphibole. ~ **byum**, *n.* amphibian. ~ **teatr**, (*th.*) amphitheatre; circus; (*ed.*) lecture-room.

Amharca (*ling.*) Amharic.
amib- = AMİP. ~ **oyid**, amoeboid.
amigdalit[i] (*med.*) Tonsilitis.
amigo (*sp.*) Cheer-leader.
amil[1] *a.* Doing; working; active. *n.* Workman; factor; manufacturer; author, agent.
ami·l[2] (*chem.*) Amyl. ~ **n**, amine: ~ +, amino-.
âmin *int.* Amen!, so be it! ~ **demek**, agree. ~ **ci**, yes-man.
ami[l]**p**[bi] (*zoo.*) Amoeba. ~ + / ~ **li**, amoebic.
amir *a.* Commanding. *n.* Commander; superior; chief; boss; foreman. ~ **hükümler**, (*leg.*) mandatory provisions/rules: ~ **i ita**, (*adm.*) official authorizing payments.
amiral[i] (*naut.*) Admiral; flag-officer. ~ **gemisi**, flagship: ~ **yaveri**, flag-lieutenant. ~ **lik**, admiral's rank/office; admiralty.
amir·ane *adv.* In an imperious/commanding manner. ~ **lik**, commander's rank/office/manner.
ami[l]**t**[di] (*chem.*) Amide. ~ **oz**, (*bio.*) amitosis.
amiyane Vulgar, common. ~ **tabiriyle**, in common parlance/popular speech.
amiz Mixture, combination; association. - ~ , *suf.* mingled with . . .; provoking . . . [HİKMETAMİZ]. ~ **iş**, association; intercourse; mixture.
amma = AMA. *conj.* [210] But. *adv.* How . . .!, what a . . .! ~ (**da**) **yaptın ha!**, get along with you!; now you've done it!
amme *n.* The public; everyone. *a.* General; public. ~ **alacağı**, (*fin.*) public revenue: ~ **arazisi**, state land: ~ **davası**, (*leg.*) public prosecution: ~ **efkârı**, public opinion: ~ **hizmeti**, (*adm.*) public/civil service: ~ **hukuku**, public law: ~ **idaresi**, public administration: ~ **işletmeleri**, public utilities/works: ~ **malları**, public/state property: ~ **menfaatı**, national/public interest: ~ **müesseseleri**, public institutions.
amnezi (*med.*) Amnesia.
amnios (*bio.*) Amnion. ~ **mayii**, amniotic fluid.
amoni[l]**t**[di] (*zoo.*) Ammonite.
amon·ya[l]**k**[ğı] (*chem.*) *n.* Ammonia: *a.* ammoniac. ~ **yaklı**, ammoniated. ~ **yum**, ammonium.
amoral (*phil.*) Amoral. ~ **ist**, amoralist. ~ **izm**, amorality, amoralism.
amorf (*geol.*) Amorphous. ~ **olm.**, (*sl.*) be ashamed; get a beating.
amoroz (*med.*) Amaurosis.
amorsaj (*eng.*) Starting up.
amorti (*fin.*) Paid off/up; 'money back' (in a lottery). ~ **edilmek**, depreciate: ~ **etm.**, redeem, amortize; pay off: ~ **karşılığı**, sinking fund. ~ **sman**, amortization, depreciation, redemption: ~ **fonu**, sinking fund: ~ **karşılığı**, depreciation reserve. ~ **sör**, (*eng.*) shock-absorber; damper, dash-pot: ~ **lü uçak dikmesi**, (*aer.*) oleo-leg.
amper (*el.*) Ampere. ~ **aj**, amperage. ~ **metre**/ ~ **olçer**, ammeter. ~ **saat**[i], ampere-hour.
ampir (*mod.*) Empire-style. ~ **ik**, (*phil.*) empiric(al). ~ **ist**[i], empericist. ~ **izm**, empiricism.
ampli·fikasyon (*rad.*) Amplification. ~ **fikatör**, amplifier. ~ **fiye**, amplified: ~ **etm.**, amplify. ~ **tü**[l]**t**[dü], (*phys.*) amplitude.

ampulü (*el.*) Bulb, lamp; (*med.*) ampoule. ~ **duyu**, lamp-holder/-socket.
ampütasyon (*med.*) Amputation.
Amu ~ **Derya**, (*geo.*) River Oxus.
amu·di *a.* Perpendicular, normal, vertical. ~ **dufıkari**, (*bio.*) spine, backbone. ~ ¹t^{du}, *n.* vertical; perpendicular: ~ **a kalkmak**, (*sp.*) do a handstand.
amyant¹ (*geol.*) Asbestos. ~ **lı çimento**, asbestos cement.
an¹ (*psy.*) Mind, intelligence; perception; memory.
an² Moment, instant; (*phys.*) moment, torque.
an³ (*agr.*) Boundary between fields; ba(u)lk.
-an¹ *adv. suf.* [196] = -EN¹ [ŞER'AN].
-an² *v. suf.* [158, 180] = -EN² [BAKANLAR].
ana = ANNE. *n.* Mother; (*zoo.*) dam; principal part/ main body (of stg.); origin, basis; (*fin.*) capital, stock, principal. *a.* Main, principal; key, basic; master, major, fundamental, prime; (*el.*) primary; (*fin.*) parent, controlling. ~ **akçe**, (*fin.*) capital; principal: ~ ARI: ~ **aşaması**, (*eng.*) main stage: ~ **atardamar**, (*bio.*) aorta: ~ **baba**, parents: ~ **baba bir**, children of the same parents: ~ **baba günü**, doomsday; great confusion: ~ **baba yavrusu**, darling child: ~ **bir baba ayrı**, children of the same mother (but different fathers): ~ **boru**, (*eng.*) (main) drain: ~ **cadde**, main/high street: ~ **çark**, (*eng.*) driving wheel: ~ **çizgi/doğru**, base line, (*math.*) generator; (*th.*) main plot: ~ **defter**, (*fin.*) ledger, analysis book: ~ **demiryolu**, (*rly.*) main line: ~ DİL: ~ **direk**, (*naut.*) main/lower mast: ~ **dizi**, (*phys.*) standard rating: ~ **duvar**, (*arch.*) bearing wall: ~ **gemi**, (*naut.*) mother-/store-ship: ~ **gibi**, motherly: ~ **güverte**, (*naut.*) main deck: ~ **hakkı**, the duty owed to one's mother: ~ **hat**, (*rly.*) main/trunk line; (*el.*) feeder: ~ **hatlar**, outline(s): ~ **kapı**, (*arch.*) main/front door; gateway: ~ KARA: ~ **kız**, mother and daughter: ~ **kızına taht kurmuş baht kuramamış**, a girl's happiness comes from the husband not the mother: ~ **kök**, (*bot.*) tap-root: ~ **kucağı**, mother's bosom: ~ **kuzusu**, babe-in-arms; spoilt child: ~ **lağım**, (*eng.*) main sewer: ~ **makinesi**, (*live.*) incubator: ~ MAL: ~ **mastar**, (*eng.*) master gauge: ~ **mektebi** = ~ OKULU: ~ **mili**, (*eng.*) lead screws (of a lathe): ~ **oğul**, mother and son: ~ **ortaklık**, (*fin.*) holding/ parent company: ~ PARA: ~ SANLI: ~ **sütü**, (*bio.*) breast-milk: ~ **şalter**, (*el.*) master-switch: ~ **şose**, arterial highway: ~ TERİM: ~ **toplardamar**, (*bio.*) vena vaca: ~ **tüyü**, (*zoo.*) down: ~ TÜZÜK: ~ VATAN: ~ **yapı**, (*arch.*) main building/structure: ~ **yarısı**, like/replacing one's mother; (*fig.*) aunt: ~ YASA: ~ YOL: ~ YÖN: ~ YURT: ~ **yüreği**, mother-love.
ana-: ~ **dan doğma**, from birth, born, congenital; stark naked: ~ **dan doğmuşa dönmek**, achieve a peaceful existence: ~ **lar kusuru**, poor sort of mother: ~ **m!**, *int.* (*of strong feeling*) mother!; my dear!: ~ **m avradım olsun!**, (*vulg.*) I swear!: ~ **m babam!** (*sl.*) my dear fellow!: ~ **mın sütü gibi helal olsun**, you are quite entitled to it; have no qualms in accepting it: ~ **n yahşi baban yahşi**, I pleaded with him: ~ **nın örekesi!**, (*vulg.*) stuff and nonsense!

anası: ~ **ağlamak**, suffer great pain/misfortune: ~ **danası**, (*col.*) mother and daughter/son: ~ **kadir gecesi doğurmuş**, very lucky!: ~ **na bak kızını al, kenarına bak bezini al**, judge the daughter by her mother, the cloth by its selvage: ~ **ndan doğduğuna pişman**, regret being born, wretched: ~ **ndan emdiği süt burnundan gelmek**, suffer extreme hardship: ~ **nı ağlatmak/bellemek**, (*vulg.*) give s.o. a good hiding; ill-treat s.o.: ~ **nı eşek kovalasın!**, (*vulg.*) I'm fed up!: ~ **nı satayım!**, (*sl.*) I don't care two hoots!: ~ **nın gözü**, (*sl.*) very cunning: ~ **nın ipini satmış/pazara çıkarmış**, a real scoundrel: ~ **nın kızı**, her mother's daughter: ~ **nın körpe kuzusu**, mother's little darling: ~ **nın nikâhını istemek**, ask too much money for stg.: ~ **yla dana** = ~ DANASI.
ana·arı (*ent.*) Queen-bee. ~ **babula**, chaos.
anabatik (*met.*) Anabatic (winds).
ana·cıl Very fond of one's mother. ~ **cı¹k**^{ğı}, little mother.
ana¹ç^{cı} (Animal/child) able to look after itself; (animal/tree) mature; grown up, big; (*fig.*) brought up to a business; experienced, shrewd. ~ **laşmak**, *vi.* reach maturity. ~ **lık**, maturity.
ana·dil (*ling.*) Parent language. ~ **dili**, mother-tongue.
Anadol·u (*geo.*) Anatolia; Asia-Minor: ~ +, *a.* Anatolian: ~ **Ajansı**, Tk. Press Agency: ~ **palamut ağacı**, (*bot.*) Turkey oak: ~ **yakası**, (*geo.*) Asiatic coast (of Bosphorus). ~ **(u)lu**, *n.* Anatolian.
ana·du¹t^{du} (*agr.*) Hayfork, pitchfork. ~ **erki**, (*soc.*) matriarchy. ~ **erkil**, matriarchal. ~ **fikir**, (*lit.*) main theme.
anafor Eddy; counter-flow; (*sl.*) stg. got for nothing; illicit gain; bribe. ~ **etm.** = LAMAK: ~ **a konmak**, get stg. for nothing: ~ **dan**, (*sl.*) illicitly.
anafor·cu One who lives at another's expense, parasite; profiteer; one who makes illicit gains. ~ **culuk**, parasitism; profiteering. ~ **lamak (-i)**, (*sl.*) make illicit gains, profiteer. ~ **lu**, with an eddy/ current.
ana·glif (*cin.*) Anaglyph. ~ **gram**, (*lit.*) anagram.
anahtar Key; clue; code; (*eng.*) spanner, wrench; (*el.*) switch; (*mus.*) key, clef. ~ **ağzı**, (*eng.*) wrench jaws: ~ **deliği**, keyhole: ~ **kolu**, (*eng.*) spanner arm: ~ **sözcüğü**, keyword, catchword: ~ **taşı**, (*arch.*) keystone: ~ **teslimi (tesis)**, (*fin.*) turnkey (job): ~ **uydurmak**, use a false key; (*fig.*) intrigue: ~ **vermek (-e)**, (*th.*) give s.o. his cue.
anahtar·cı Locksmith; keeper of the keys, warden; (*sl.*) burglar. ~ **cılık**, locksmith's work. ~ **lı**, key-operated. ~ **lık**, key-ring/-case.
ana·kara (*geo.*) Continent, mainland. ~ **kaya**, bed-rock.
anakonda (*zoo.*) Anaconda.
anakronik Anachronistic.
analfabet (*ed.*) Illiterate. ~ **izm**, illiteracy.
ana·lı Having a mother: ~ **kuzu kınalı kuzu**, the joy of children who have parents. ~ **lık**, motherhood, maternity; motherly woman; adoptive mother: ~ **etm. (-e)**, look after s.o. like a mother: ~ **ocak**, maternal family: ~ **sigortası**, maternity insurance: ~ **ta**, in pregnancy.
anali·tik (*math.*, *chem.*) Analytic(al). ~ **z**, (*chem.*)

analysis; (*fin.*) breakdown: ~ **etm.**/~**lemek**, analyse. ~**zör**, analyser.
analjezi (*med.*) Analgesia. ~ + /~**k**, analgesic.
ana·log Analogous. ~**loji**, (*lit.*) analogy; (*bio.*) resemblance.
ana·mal (*fin.*) Capital: ~ **kaçırımı**, hot money. ~**malcı(lık)**, capital·ist/(-ism). ~**mallı**, *a.* capitalist. ~**maya**, (*bio.*) enzyme. ~**metal**, base metal.
ananas (*bot.*) Pineapple. ~**giller**, Bromeliaceae.
anane Tradition. ~**siyle (anlatmak)**, (explain) in/ with all its details. ~**ci(lik)**, traditional·ist/(-ism). ~**peresti**, traditionalist; (*pej.*) ultra-conservative. ~**vi**, traditional.
ananeti (Male) impotence.
ana·okulunu (*ed.*) Kindergarten; nursery-/play-school. ~**para**, (*fin.*) capital.
anar·şi Anarchy. ~**şik**, anarchic. ~**şisti**, anarchist. ~**şizm**, anarchism. ~**tri**, (*med.*) anarthria, inability to speak.
ana·saat (*ast.*) Master-clock. ~**sanlı**, matronymic. ~**sıl**, by origin, originally. ~**sınıfı**, (*ed.*) master class.
anasır *pl.* = UNSUR. Elements.
anason (*bot.*) Anise; (*cul.*) aniseed.
anasoy (*ethn.*) Race. ~**cu**, *n.* rac(ial)ist. ~**cul**, *a.* racist. ~**culuk**, rac(ial)ism.
anastigmatik (*phys.*) Anastigmatic.
anat¹ *pl.* Shades of meaning, nuances; moments.
anat. = ANATOMİ.
ana·temel Foundation; source. ~**terim**, principal term, main heading.
anatomi (*med.*) Anatomy. ~**ci**, anatomist. ~**k**, anatomical.
anatüzük (*leg.*) Articles of association; statute.
anavasya Fish-migration (Mediterranean to Black Sea).
anavata (*tex.*) Satin-stitch embroidery.
ana·vatan Mother-country; original home(land). ~**yasa**, (*leg.*, *pol.*) constitution: ~ +, *a.* constitutional: ~ **dışı**, unconstitutional: ~ **yanlısı**/~**cı**, constitutionalist. ~**yasal**, *a.* constitutional. ~**yol**, arterial road, (main) highway. ~**yön**, (*geo.*) cardinal point (N, E, S, W). ~**yurltdu** = ~VATAN.
anbean *adv.* [196] From moment to moment; from time to time; gradually; one after the other.
anca Hardly, barely; just. ~ **beraber kanca beraber**, inseparable (friends, etc.); 'we must stick together'.
ancak *adv.* [211] Hardly, barely, only, just; at the earliest. *conj.* But; on the other hand, however. ~ **teneşir paklar**, he's a great scoundrel: ~ **ve** ~, simply and solely.
ançüez (*ich.*) Anchovy. ~ **ezmesi**, (*cul.*) anchovy paste.
And ~ **dağları**, (*geo.*) Andes.
and- = ANT.
andalçc¹ Gift, souvenir; *pl.* memoirs.
andant·e (*mus.*) Andante. ~**ino**, andantino.
andavallı (*sl.*) Simpleton, imbecile.
andez·in (*geol.*) Feldspars. ~**iti**, andesite.
andılç¹ Memorandum, note; diary.
andılkğ¹ (*zoo.*) Species of hyena.
andır·an *a.* Analogous; reminiscent of: *n.* (*phil.*) analogue. ~**ı**, note, reminder. ~**ış**, analogy, simi-

larity. ~**ışma**, remembrance; ambiguity. ~**ışmalı**, ambiguous. ~**ma**, *vn.*; resemblance. ~**mak (-i, -e)**, bring to mind; bear a striking resemblance to, remind one of.
andız(otunu) (*bot.*) Elecampane, inula.
an·do- (*bio.*) = ENDO-. ~**dro-**, (*bio.*) andro-: ~**gen**, androgen.
ane (*bio.*) Pubes; private parts.
-ane¹ *n. suf.* [6, 66] = -HANE [POSTANE].
-ane² *suf.* [66] (i) *adj. to adv.* [mest, drunk: ~ **ane**, drunkenly]. (ii) *adj. describing person to adj. describing act/thing* [âlim, learned (man): ~ **ane**, learned (book)]. (iii) *n. to adj./adv.* [peder, father: ~ **ane**, paternal(ly)].
anekdotu (*lit.*) Anecdote.
anele (*naut.*) Iron ring (of an anchor).
anemi (*med.*) Anaemia. ~**k**, anaemic.
ane·mometre (*met.*) Anemometer. ~**mon**, (*bot.*) wood-anemone.
ane·roiltdi (*phys.*) Aneroid (barometer). ~**stetik**, *n.* (*med.*) anaesthetic. ~**stezi**, (*med.*) anaesthesia: ~ **veren**, anaesthetist: ~ **yapmak**, anaesthetize: ~ + /~**k**, *a.* anaesthetic. ~**vrizma**, (*med.*) aneurism.
angaj·e (*lit.*) Committed; occupied: ~ **etm.**, book, reserve: ~ **olm.**, be booked/reserved. ~**man**, (*fin.*) undertaking; engagement: ~ **a girmek**, undertake.
angarya *n.* Forced labour; unpaid job; hard task; (*mil.*) fatigue; burden; infliction. *adv.* Carelessly, perfunctorily; unwillingly. ~**cı**, *s.o.* inflicting forced labour, etc.
angı Memory; souvenir; reputation; fame. ~ **çağrısı**, recollection, remembrance: ~**ların saptanımı**, (*psy.*) fixation of memories.
angılç¹ (*agr.*) (Horse-cart with) wood-slat panels.
an·gın Famous. ~**gıt** = ANGUT.
Angli·kan(izm) (*rel.*) Anglican(ism). ~**sizm**, (*ling.*) anglicism.
Anglo·fil Anglophile. ~**fobu**, Anglophobe. ~**sakson**, (*his.*) Anglo-Saxon (tribes); (*ling.*) English-speaking (nations).
Angstrom (*phys.*) ~ **birimi**, Ångström unit.
angu·di Ruddy. ~**ltdu**, (*orn.*) ruddy shelduck; (*sl.*) fool.
anı (*psy.*) Memory; remembrance. ~**lar**, memories; (*lit.*) memoirs: ~**sını yaşatmak**, commemorate. ~**cı**, memoir-writer. ~**lık**, diary.
anık Ready; present; apt; talented. ~ **bulun(ma)-mak**, be present//(absent). ~**lamak (-i)**, prepare; (*psy.*) reproduce (memories). ~**lık**, readiness; aptitude; talent. ~**sız**, untalented.
anıl·mak *vp.* = ANMAK. Be remembered/commemorated; be mentioned/called. ~**ır**, commemorable.
anımsa·ma Reminiscence. ~**(t)mak** = ANSI(T)MAK.
anırmak *vi.* (Donkey) bray; (*fig.*) boast.
anıştır·ma (*lit.*) Allusion. ~**mak (-i)**, allude to.
anıt¹ Monument; memorial; (*mil.*) cenotaph. ~ **Tepe**, (*geo.*) site of ~KABİR. ~**kabirri**, mausoleum; *pr.n.* Atatürk's tomb. ~**laşmak**, *vp.* be remembered/commemorated. ~**laştırmak (-i)**, commemorate. ~**mezar**, mausoleum. ~**sal**, monumental.

anız (*agr.*) Stubble. ~**bozma**, breaking up the stubble. ~**lık**, field of unbroken stubble.
ani Instantaneous; momentary; abrupt, sudden, unexpected. ~ **artış**, surge: ~ **gereklik**, emergency: ~ **hareket/tesir**, impulse: ~ **söz**, exclamation: ~ **suç**, (*leg.*) unpremeditated crime: ~ **tehlike**, emergency: ~ **yanma**, instantaneous combustion. ~**de**, on the instant, instantly. ~**den**, suddenly.
ani·dri¹tᵈⁱ (*chem.*) Anhydrite. ~**lin**, aniline.
anilmerkez (*phys.*) Centrifugal.
ani·masyon (*cin.*) Animation: ~ **filmi**, animated cartoon. ~**mato**, (*mus.*) animato. ~**mizm**, (*rel.*) animism.
an·iyon (*phys.*) Anion. ~**iso-**/~**izo**, (*bio.*, *etc.*), aniso-. ~**izotropi(k)**, anisotrop·y/(-ic).
anjin (*med.*) Angina.
Ank. = ANKARA.
anka (*myth.*) Legendary bird; phoenix; (*fig.*) imaginary thing; s.o. immensely rich. ~ **gibi**, nonexistent.
Ankara (*geo.*) Ankara; (*his.*) Ankyra, Angora. ~ **keçi//kedisi**, (*zoo.*) Angora goat//cat: ~ **sofu**, (*tex.*) mohair: ~ **taşı**, (*geol.*) andesite: ~ **yünü**, (*tex.*) Angora wool. ~**lı**, inhabitant of Ankara.
an·karip Shortly, soon. ~**kasdin**, intentionally.
an·kastre Built-in. ~**kesman**, (*fin.*) collection; paying-in. ~**ket**ⁱ, (*lit.*) investigation, inquiry: ~ **yapmak**, investigate. ~**ketçi**, investigator, reporter. ~**kiloz**, (*med.*) ankylosis. ~**klav**, (*adm.*) enclave. ~**kole**, (*tex.*) starched, sized. ~**konsinyasyon**, (*fin.*) on consignment. ~**kraj**, (*eng.*) anchor(age). ~**kre**, ~ **etm.**, anchor.
anl. = ANLAMDAŞ.
anla¹kᵍ¹ (*psy.*) Intelligence, brains. ~ **geriliği**, mental deficiency, backwardness. ~**alır**, intelligible. ~**almaz**, unintelligible. ~**lı**, intelligent, clever. ~**sal**, intellectual.
anlam (*ling.*) [225] Meaning; sense, signification; construction. ~ +, *a.* Semantic: ~ **aykırılığı**, contradiction in terms: ~ **bayağılaşması**, pejorative semantic change: ~ **çokluğu**, polysemy: ~ **daralma//değişme//genişleme//kayması**, semantic restriction//change//evolution//displacement: ~**ı taşımak**, mean, have the meaning: ~**ına gelmek**, (come to) mean.
anla·ma *vn.* Knowledge; understanding; (*psy.*) comprehension; apprehension: ~**ya çalışmak**, seek to understand. ~**mak (-i)**, understand; comprehend; apprehend; ascertain; appreciate: **(-den)**, understand, know about; make use of; be appreciative of; find pleasure in: **anladığım kadar**, as far as I (can) understand: **anladımsa Arap olayım**, I've understood nothing at all; it's all Greek to me: **anlamaz görünmek**, feign ignorance: **anlayana sivrisinek saz anlamayana davul zurna az**, a whisper is enough for a wise man, a shout won't make a fool understand: **anlıyamadım gitti**, I just couldn't understand. ~**(ma)mazlık**, lack of understanding: ~**tan gelmek**, feign ignorance.
anlam·bilim (*ling.*) Semantics. ~**ca**, regarding the meaning. ~**daş**, synonymous. ~**daşlık**, synonymity; ambiguity. ~**landırma**, *vn.* explanation; interpretation. ~**landırmak (-i)**, give/explain the

meaning. ~**lı(lık)**, meaningful(ness). ~**sal**, semantic. ~**sız(lık)**, meaningless(ness).
anlaş·amamazlık Misunderstanding. ~**ık**, (*leg.*) party (to an agreement): ~ **Devletler, (**his.) Entente Powers. ~**ılan**, *adv.* so it seems; probably; apparently. ~**ılır**, *a.* intelligible, clear; explicit: ~ **anlaşılmaz**, imperceptible. ~**ılmak**, *vp.* [150] = ANLAMAK; be understood; be evident. ~**ılmaz**, incomprehensible; unintelligible; illegible: ~ **insansın vesselâm!**, you're a strange creature and that's all about it!: ~ **iş**, enigma. ~**ılmazlık**, acatalepsy, incomprehensibility. ~**ım** = ANLAŞMA; consensus. ~**ıt**, compromise.
anlaş·ma *vn.* Agreement, accord, contract, covenant; understanding; (*fin.*) composition; (*rel.*) concordat: ~ **akdetmek/yapmak**, sign/make an agreement: ~**ya varmak (-le)**, reach an agreement with s.o. ~**mak (-le)**, understand one another; come to an agreement; settle one's differences. ~**malı**, contracting, contractual: ~ **memleketler**, (*fin.*) countries with mutual clearing agreements: ~ **tarife**, (*fin.*) international customs tariff. ~**(ma)mazlık**, disagreement; discord; misunderstanding; difference of opinion.
anlat·ı Story-telling; narrative. ~**ıbilim**, the art of story-telling; the science of explanation. ~**ıcı**, *a.* descriptive: *n.* story-teller. ~**ılmak**, *vp.* be recounted; be explained. ~**ım**, explanation; description: ~ **titremi**, intonation, expression. ~**ımcı(lık)**, (*phil.*) expression·ist/(-ism). ~**ımlamak (-i)**, explain. ~**ımlı/**~**ımsal**, explanatory; descriptive. ~**ış**, mode of explaining; explanation; description: ~ **vurgusu**, (*ling.*) logical accent: ~**tan** ~**a fark var**, how the case is presented makes a difference. ~**ma**, *vn.*, explanation, description. ~**mak (-i, -e)**, explain, expound; describe; narrate; make known.
anlayış Understanding; comprehension; discernment; intelligence; sagacity. ~ **göstermek**, show understanding, be receptive. ~**lı**, intelligible; intelligent, sensible, discerning. ~**lılık**, intelligence, discernment. ~**sız**, unintelligent; thick-headed, stupid. ~**sızlık**, lack of intelligence; stupidity.
anlı ~ **sanlı/şanlı**, glorious; famous.
anlı¹kᵍ¹ (*phil.*) Intellect, understanding. ~**çı(lık)**, *n.* intellectual(ism). ~**sal**, *a.* intellectual. ~**yoğrum**, (*psy.*) intelligence.
an·ma *vn.* Remembrance; commemoration; mention; (*mil.*) citation: ~ **gün//töreni**, (*mil.*) remembrance day//ceremony: ~ **imleri**, (*ling.*) quotation marks. ~**mak (-i)**, call to mind; mention; name; commemorate. ~**malık**, souvenir.
anne = ANA. Mother. ~ **olm.**, become a mother, have a child: ~**min ölüsünü öpeyim ki**, (an oath) may my mother die if . . .! ~**anne**, maternal grandmother. ~**ciğim**, dearest mother; mummy!
ano·din (*med.*) Anodyne. ~**fel**, (*ent.*) anopheles mosquito. ~**mal(i)**, anomal·ous/(-y). ~**nim**, anonymous: ~ **ortaklık/şirket**, (*fin.*) joint-stock/limited company. ~**nimlık**, anonymity.
anon·s Announcement. ~**se**, ~ **etm./vermek**, announce.
anorak (*mod.*) Anorak.
anor·eksi (*med.*) Anorexia. ~**ganik**, (*chem.*)

inorganic. ~**mal**[i], abnormal. ~**malleşmek**, *vi.* become abnormal. ~**mallik**, abnormality; perversion.

ano[l]**t**[du] (*el.*) Anode. ~ +, *a.* Anodic. ~**laştırmak** (-i), anodize. ~**sal**, anodic.

anölçer Chronometer, stop-watch.

ansal *a.* (*psy.*) Intellectual, mental.

ansambl The whole; (*mod.*) suit; (*mus.*) group, ensemble.

ansefal·it[i] (*med.*) Encephalitis. ~**ografi**, encephalograph.

ansı·ma Remembering. ~**mak** (-i), remember, recall. ~**nmak**, *vp.* be remembered. ~**tmak** (-i, -e), remind.

ansız[1] *n.* Bastard.

ansız[2] / ~ **ın** *adv.* Suddenly; abruptly; without warning.

ansiklopedi Encylopaedia. ~**k**, encyclopaedic; ~ **sözlük**, encyclopaedic dictionary.

ansuit (*arch.*) En suite.

an[l]**t**[dı] Oath; vow. ~ **etm./içmek**, take an oath; swear stg.: ~ **içirmek/verdirmek** (-e), let/make s.o. swear stg.: ~ **kardeşi**, blood brother: ~ **vermek**, conjure; adjure: ~**ı olm.**, be agreed and sworn: ~**ını bozmak**, violate one's oath.

An·takya (*geo.*) Antioch. ~**talya**, (*geo.*) Adalia; (*his.*) Attaleia.

antant[1] (*adm.*) Treaty, agreement, *entente.* ~ **kalmak** (-le), reach an agreement with s.o.

Antarktik (*geo.*) *a.* Antarctic. ~ **kara**/~**a**, *n.* the Antarctic, S. Polar region.

anten (*rad.*) Antenna, aerial; (*ent.*) antenna, feeler; (*naut.*) spar. ~ **dizisi**, (*rad.*) antenna array: ~ **kubbesi**, (*aer.*) radome.

antepfıstığı[n] (*bot.*) Pistachio (nut/tree).

anterit[i] (*med.*) Enteritis.

anterlin (*pub.*) Inter-line.

antet[i] Headline, letter-head.

anti- *pref.* Anti-. ~ **alkolizm**, (*med.*) anti-alcoholism. ~**beybi**, (*med.*) contraceptive. ~**biyotik**, *a.*, *n.* antibiotic. ~**demokratik**, (*pol.*) antidemocratic. ~**faşist**, (*pol.*) anti-fascist. ~**friz**, (*chem.*) antifreeze. ~**jen**, (*bio.*) antigen.

antik *a.* Antique; ancient. ~ **a**, *n.* antique; (*sl.*) figure of fun, curiosity; (*mod.*) hemstitch: *a.* antique, rare; comic; eccentric: ~ **meraklısı**, antiquarian: ~**nın biridir**, he's a queer card. ~**acı**, antique-dealer. ~**acılık**, dealing in antiques. ~**alık**, antiqueness; eccentricity. ~**çağ**/~**ite**, antiquity.

anti·kiklon (*met.*) Anticyclone. ~**klinal**, (*geol.*) anticline. ~**komünist**, (*pol.*) anti-communist. ~**kor**, (*med.*) antibody. ~**logaritma**, (*math.*) antilog(arithm).

Antil ~ **adaları**, (*geo.*) Antilles, West Indies: ~ **denizi**, Caribbean Sea.

antilo[l]**p**[bu] (*zoo.*) Antelope.

anti·manyetik (*el.*) Antimagnetic. ~**militarist**, (*soc.*) anti-militarist. ~**mon(lu)**, (*chem.*) antimo·ny/(-nial). ~**nomi**, (*phil.*) antinomy. ~**pati**, antipathy. ~**patik**, antipathetic, cold, distasteful; unattractive: ~ **bulmak** (-i), find s.o. unattractive: not warm to s.o. ~**semitizm**, (*ethn.*) anti-Semitism. ~**sepsi**, (*med.*/) antisepsis. ~**septik**, antiseptic; disinfectant.

~**siklon**, (*met.*) anticyclone. ~**simetrik**, (*chem.*) antisymmetric(al). ~**tank**, (*mil.*) anti-tank. ~**te**, (*phil.*) entity. ~**tetanik**, (*med.*) anti-tetanus. ~**tez**, (*lit.*) antithesis. ~**toksik**, (*chem.*) antitoxic. ~**toksin**, antitoxin. ~**toros**, *pr.n.* (*geo.*) Anti-taurus.

ant·laşma (*adm.*) Treaty, covenant, *entente*; (*leg.*) agreement. ~**laşmak**, *vi.* take an oath together; (-le), agree with s.o. ~ **lı**, bound by an oath; sworn: ~ **bildiri**, (*leg.*) affidavit.

antoloji (*lit.*) Anthology. ~**yi tertip eden**, anthologist.

antomo·log (*bio.*) Entomologist. ~**loji**, (*bio.*) entomology.

antraks (*med.*) Anthrax.

antrakt[1] (*th.*) Entr'acte.

antrasit[i] (*min.*) Anthracite.

antrdö (*mod.*) Insert.

antre (*arch.*) Entry, entrance; entrance-fee; (*soc.*) *entrée.*

antren·man (*sp.*) Training: ~ **fanilası**, sweat-shirt: ~ **yapmak**, *vi.* train: ~ **yaptırmak**, *vt.* train/coach s.o. ~**ör**, trainer, coach. ~**örlük**, coaching.

antr·epo (*fin.*) Bonded warehouse; *entrepôt*: ~**da bulunmak**, be in bond: ~**ya konulmuş**, bonded. ~**kot**[u], (*cul.*) (beef) rib steak. ~**ok**[u], (*geol.*) entrochite. ~**opi**, (*phys.*) entropy. ~**parantez**, besides.

antropo- *pref.* Anthropo-. ~**faj**, cannibal. ~**log**, anthropologist. ~**loji(k)**, anthropolo·gy/(-gical). ~**metri**, anthropometry. ~**morf(izm)**, anthropomorph·ous/(-ism). ~**santrizm**, (*phil.*) anthropocentrism. ~**yidler**, (*zoo.*) anthropoids. ~**zoik**, (*geol.*) anthropozoic.

anut[u] Obstinate, stubborn.

anüs (*bio.*) Anus. ~ +, *a.* Anal: ~ **yüzgeci**, anal fin.

anyon (*chem.*) Anion. ~**ik**/~**lu**, anionic.

Anzac = (*Australian and New Zealand Army Corps*).

anzarot Sarcocolla resin; (*sl.*) raki, arrack. ~ **ağacı**, sarcocolla tree.

AO = Anonİm Ortaklık. ~**Ç** = Atatürk Orman Çİftlİğİ.

aort[u] (*bio.*) Aorta.

ap- *pref.* Very, completely [apaci; apaçık, etc.].

AP = Adalet Partİsİ; (*Associated Press*). ~**A** = Avrupa Para Anlaşması.

ap·acı Very bitter. ~**açık**, wide open; very clear/evident. ~**açıklık**, wide-openness; clearness; evidence. ~**ağır**, very heavy. ~**ak**, very white; pure white. ~**alaca**, very variegated. ~**alak**, big and chubby (baby).

apandis (*bio.*) Appendix. ~**it**[i], (*med.*) appendicitis: ~ **ameliyatı**, appendectomy.

apansız(ın) All of a sudden; quite unexpectedly.

apar *n.* (*th.*) Aside. ~ **topar**, *adv.* with surprising suddenness; headlong, helter-skelter.

aparat Apparatus.

aparmak (-i) Carry off; make off with, steal.

apart(ı)man (*arch.*) Block of flats; flat. ~ **dairesi**, flat; suite of rooms. ~**laşma**, development/building of flats.

apaş Apache; gangster, tough guy.

ap·aşikâr Very evident. ~**aydın**, very bright.

~ **aydınlık**, great brightness. ~ **ayrı**, quite different/ distinct.

apati (*psy.*) Apathy.

apaz (*bio.*) Palm of hand; handful. ~ **lama**, (*met.*) beam wind. ~ **lamak (-i)**, grasp with the hand: *vi.* (*naut.*) sail with a beam wind.

apeks (*math.*) Apex.

apel (*th.*) Call.

aperitif (*cul.*) Apéritif; appetizer.

aperiyodik (*ast.*) Aperiodic.

aperkat[1] *sp.* Upper-cut.

apertometre (*cin.*) Aperture-metre.

apış (*bio.*) Fork (of the body), crotch. ~ **açmak**, stand with legs apart: ~ **arası**, (*polite for*) 'private parts'.

apış·ak With legs astride; too tired to walk. ~ **ık**, (animal) with its tail between its legs; weary; dejected; dazed. ~ **lık**, (*mod.*) crotch gusset. ~ **mak**, *vi.* (animal) collapse from weariness; be weary and helpless: **apışıp kalmak**, be baffled/completely nonplussed: **apışmış olarak**, astraddle. ~ **tırmak (-i)**, tire out (an animal) completely; make s.o. weary and helpless; (*naut.*) moor fore and aft.

apiko (*naut.*) Anchors aweigh!; (*fig.*) ready; agile; on the *qui vive*, alert; smart. ~ **luk**, agility; elegance.

aplanatik (*phys.*) Aplanatic.

apli'k[ği] (*dom.*) Wall-light. ~ **asyon**, (*tex.*) appliqué; (*arch.*) staking out a plot of land. ~ **e**, (*tex.*) appliqué.

apolet[i] (*mod.*) Epaulette.

apopleksi (*med.*) Apoplexy.

aport *int.* (*sp.*) Bring!, fetch! (order to a dog).

aposteriori *A posteriori*.

apostrof (*ling.*) Apostrophe.

apoşi Bag-shaped large-meshed fishing-net.

apote'k[ği] (*bot.*) Apothecium.

appassionato (*mus.*) Appassionato.

apraksi (*med.*) Apraxia.

apre (*tex.*) Finishing; (*arch.*) primer.

apriori *A priori*.

apron (*aer.*) Apron.

Aprt. = APARTMAN.

apse (*med.*) Abscess. ~ **yapmak**, form an abscess.

apsent[i] (*bot.*) Absinth(e). ~ **izm**, (*med.*) absinthe poisoning.

apsis (*math.*) Abscissa; coordinate; (*arch.*) apse. ~ **ekseni**, axis of *x*.

apsür't[dü] (*th.*) Absurd.

Apt. = APARTMAN.

aptal *n.* Silly fool, simpleton; imbecile. *a.* Stupid; dense, dumb; imbecile; feckless. ~ **değilim**, I wasn't born yesterday: ~ **olm.**, be stupid, etc.

aptal·ca Stupid(ly): ~ **(balık)**, (*ich.*) white bream. ~ **laşmak**, *vi.* become stupid. ~ **lık**, stupidity: ~ **etm.**, make a fool of o.s.; play the fool; act stupidly. ~ **sı**, naïve.

apteriks (*zoo.*) Kiwi, apteryx.

aptes (*rel.*) Ritual ablutions; (*bio.*) bowel movement. ~ **aldırmak (-e)**, (*sl.*) wash stg.: ~ **almak**, perform such ablutions: ~ **bozmak**, relieve nature; have a bowel movement: ~ **tazelemek**, repeat ablutions: ~ **i bozulmak**, need to repeat ablutions: ~ **i gelmek**, need to relieve nature: ~ **i kaçmak**,

need but be unable to relieve nature: ~ **inden şüphesi olmamak**, be certain one is not at fault: ~ **ini vermek (-e)**, scold s.o.

aptes·bozan (*bio.*) Beef tapeworm. ~ **bozanotu**[nu], (*bot.*) great burnet. ~ **(h)ane**, latrine, water-closet. ~ **li**, ritually clean. ~ **lik**, *n.* washroom: *a.* used in ablutions. ~ **siz**, (*rel.*) not having performed one's ablutions; impure: ~ **yere basmamak**, be exceedingly religious.

apukurya Carnival; shrove-tide.

apul apul *adv.* Swaying; waddling.

ar[1] (*math.*) Are (100 m² = 120 sq. yds.).

ar[2] Shameful deed; shame, bashfulness, modesty. ~ **belası**, need to consider one's reputation: ~ **çekmekten bar çekmek evladır**, better to bear a burden than shame: ~ **damarı çatlamak**, feel no sense of shame: ~ **etm.**, be ashamed: ~ **namus tertemiz**, shameless: ~ **yılı değil, kâr yılı**, of course one wants to make a profit; (*iron.*) he won't miss a chance to make money.

Ar. = ARAP; ARAPÇA(DAN); (*ch.s.*) ARGON.

-ar[1] *v. suf.* [116] = -R [YAPAR].

-ar-[2] *v. suf.* [145] = -DİR-; -ER-[2, 3] [ONARMAK].

-ar[3] *a. suf.* [83] = -ER[4] [ALTIŞAR].

-ar -maz *v. suf.* [182] = -İR -MEZ [ÇALAR ÇALMAZ].

ara *n.* [92] Interval/space (in place/time); gap; break; pause; (*sp.*) half-time, time-out; relationship/understanding (between two persons); intermediary. *a.* Middle, interim; intermediate; communicating, linking. *In phrases*, among(st); between. ~ **alkışı**, spontaneous applause: ~ **astar**, (*mod.*) interlining: ~ **bağı**, (*bio.*) septum: ~ **bilançosu**, (*fin.*) interim balance-sheet: ~ **boşluğu**, (*eng.*) clearance space: ~ **boşu**, (*pub.*) space: ~ BOZANLIK: ~ **bölge**, (*adm.*) buffer zone: ~ **bulmak**, find a way/ opportunity; mediate, reconcile: ~ BULUCU: ~ CÜMLE: ~ **değer bulma**, (*math.*) interpolation: ~ **devlet**, (*pol.*) buffer state: ~ **duvar**, (*arch.*) partition; party-wall: ~ **kapı**, (*arch.*) access/communicating door: ~ **kararı**, (*leg.*) provisional judgement: ~ **kat**, (*arch.*) mezzanine floor: ~ **limanı**, (*naut.*) port of call: ~ **mal**, (*ind.*) semi-processed goods: ~ **nağmesi**, (*mus.*) intermezzo, interlude: ~ **oyunu**, (*th.*) interlude: ~ **parçası**, (*eng.*) adaptor: ~ **seçimi**, (*adm.*) by-election: ~ **sıra**, *adv.* at intervals, now and again, occasionally: ~ SÖZ: ~ **tabaka**, priming coat (of paint): ~ **tesir**, interference: ~ **verme**, holiday: ~ **vermek**, pause; make a break, interrupt; suspend: ~ **vermeksizin**, without interruption.

arada, sometimes: ~ **bir**, here and there: ~ **çıkarmak**, find an opportunity (to do stg. while busy): ~ **gitmek**, pass unnoticed (in a crowd): ~ **kalmak**, be mixed up in an affair: ~ **kaynamak**, be lost in the midst of confusion: ~ **sırada**, here and there; now and again: ~ **söylemek**, speak of stg. connected.

aradan, from then till now; in the meantime: ~ **çıkarmak**, remove stg., get (one job) out of the way in order to do others: ~ **çıkmak**, leave others; cut relations with others; not interfere; take no further part in stg.

araları: ~ açık, their relations are strained, they are not on good terms: ~ açılmak, quarrel: ~ soğumak, their relations become strained: ~ şekerrenk, relations are cool: ~ yağ bal, all is well between them; they get on well together: ~na girmek, come between: ~na kara kedi sokmak, set people by the ears, put the cat among the pigeons: ~nda dağlar kadar fark olm., be poles apart; be as different as chalk and cheese: ~nda husumet var, there is bad blood between them: ~ nda karlı dağlar olm., be very far apart/widely separated: ~ndan kara kedi geçmek, quarrel: ~ndan su sızmaz, they are very close friends; they are as thick as thieves: ~nı açmak/bozmak, spoil a friendship, cause bad blood: ~nı bulmak, reconcile.

ara-: ~mızda hukukumuz var, we are old friends: ~nızda kara kedi mi geçti?, have you quarrelled?

arası: ~ açık (-le), at enmity with: ~ geçmeden, immediately, straight away: ~ hoş/iyi değil, they are not on good terms: ~ soğumak, (with time) stg. become less important; be forgotten/neglected: ~na, [90] amongst, between: ~nda, amongst, between: ~ndan, from among/between; between, through.

araya: ~ almak, surround, hem in: ~ gelmek (bir), come together, meet: ~ girmek, mediate between; interfere with; prevent by interfering: ~ gitmek, be lost/sacrificed: ~ koymak (-i), put s.o. in as intermediary: ~ lakırdı karıştı, another subject cropped up (to change the conversation): ~ soğukluk girmek, the friendship be upset: ~ vermek, waste one's money.

arayı: ~ soğutmak, strain relations.
Arab- = ARAP.
araba Carriage; cart; wagon; barrow; (eng.) sliderest; cartload. ~ atı, carriage-horse: ~ devrilince/kırılınca yol gösteren çok olur, there are plenty of helpers when it's too late: ~ dingili, axle-tree: ~ dolu/yükü, cartload: ~ durağı, cab-rank/-stand: ~ izi, cart-track, rut: ~ koşmak, harness horses to the cart: ~ marangozu, cartwright, coach-builder: ~ parkı, (mil.) transport fleet: ~ ücreti yanına kalmak için, to save the carriage/coach fare: ~ vapuru, car-ferry: ~ yayları, coach springs: ~sını düze çıkarmak, put matters straight, overcome difficulties: ~yı çekmek, (sl.) be off!, clear out!
araba·cı Driver, cabman, coachman; cartwright. ~cılık, driving. ~lık, coach-house; garage; cartful, cartload.
arab·esk (art.) Arabesque. ~i, a. Arab(ian): n. (ling.) Arabic. ~istan, (geo.) Arabia. ~istandefnesi[ni], (bot.) flax-leaf daphne. ~iyat, Arab literature/science.
ara·bozan/~bozucu Mischief-/trouble-maker. ~bozanlık/~bozuculuk, trouble-making. ~bozukluğu, discord, strife. ~bulma, reconciliation, mediation. ~bulucu, go-between; conciliator, mediator, peacemaker. ~buluculuk, peacemaking, conciliation, mediation. ~cı, mediator; (fin.) intermediary, agent, broker, middle-man: ~manav, wholesale fruiterer. ~cılı, indirect. ~cılık,

[147] mediation; intervention: ~ akçe/parası, commission: ~ etm., act as a go-between; mediate: ~ıyla, through the agency of. ~cısız, direct. ~cümle, (ling.) parenthetic clause.
ara[i]ç[c1] Means; medium; tool; apparatus, device, implement; vehicle. ~çılık, (phil.) instrumentalism. ~lı, indirect. ~lık, means, assistance. ~sız, direct.
ara·da/~dan = ARA.
Aradeniz (geo.) The Mediterranean Sea.
araek (ling.) Infix.
Araf (rel.) Purgatory.
ara·faz (el.) Intermediate phase. ~gelir, (fin.) interim dividend.
aragonit[i] (geol.) Aragonite.
arak[1] (cul.) Raki, arrack; (obs.) sweat; (sl.) theft.
-arak v. suf. [176] = -EREK [ÇALIŞARAK].
araka (bot.) Large-sized pea, green pea.
arakapa[i]k[ğ1] (pub.) Fly-leaf.
arakçı (sl.) Thief. ~lık, thieving.
arakesit[i] (math.) Intersection.
arakıye Soft felt cap (under turban); (mus.) fife.
araklamak (-i) (sl.) Remove/steal adroitly; pilfer.
arakonakçı (bio.) Intermediate host (for a parasite).
arakorunca[i]k[ğ1] (fin.) Entrepôt, bonded warehouse.
aral (geo.) Archipelago. ~ Gölü, Aral Sea.
arala·mak (-i) Make a space between (things); half-open (a door); leave ajar. ~nmak (-den), vi. (sl.) go away, leave s.o. ~şmak (-le), become separated. ~tmak (-i, -e), vc. ~yıcı, (eng.) spacer.
ara·lı Intermittent; periodic; indirect. ~lık, n. space; interval (place/time); chink, crevice, crack; alley; aperture, opening; (phys.) range; (eng.) backlash, clearance; passage; interruption, break: a. scattered; at intervals; half-open, ajar: ~ arazi, (mil.) no-man's-land: ~ (ayı), (obs.) month of ZİLKADE, (now) December: ~ bırakmak, leave open a space: ~ etm., leave ajar/half-open: ~ oyunu, (th.) interlude: ~ vermek, put off stg. for a time: ~ vermeden (konuşmak), (talk) continuously: ~a gitmek, fall between the cracks, i.e. be lost/forgotten: ~ta, in the meantime. ~lıklı, a. spaced out; intermittent; (sp.) staggered: adv. disjointedly; brokenly. ~lıksız, uninterrupted(ly).
araltı (live.) Pole separating stalls in a stable.
ara·ma vn. Search(ing); exploration; investigation: ~ aleti, detector: ~ belge/buyruğu, (leg.) search-warrant: ~ hakkı, right of search: ~ kılavuzu, (pub.) directory: ~ tarama, (police) searching/frisking s.o.; (naut.) mine-sweeping: ~ tarama gemisi, mine-sweeper: ~ ve kurtarma, (aer.) search and rescue: ~ yapmak, carry out a search. ~ma[i]ç[c1], (archaeol.) excavation, dig. ~mak (-i), seek, look for; look s.o. up; search (for); examine, investigate; hope/long for; feel the absence of, miss: vi. (col.) look for trouble: ~ taramak, search carefully: ~la bulunmaz, stg. very rare: arıyorsun, şimdi dayağı yersin, you've asked for trouble, now you'll get it: aradığını buldu, he got his deserts!: arayıp da bulamamak, have a pleasant surprise: arayıp sormak (-i), make inquiries about s.o.'s

health/circumstances: **arayıp soranı bulunmaz/yok!**, he's all alone!

Arami (*ling.*) Aramaic.

aranağme (*Or. mus.*) Instrumental passage; (*fig.*) refrain.

aran'ç[c1] (*leg.*) Lawsuit; claim; petition. ~ **konusu**, suit, claim: ~ **yöneltmek**, bring a suit: ~**a katılmak**, intervene. ~ **çı**, claimant, plaintiff. ~ **lı**, defendant.

aranedencilik (*phil.*) Occasionalism.

aran(ıl)mak *vp.* = ARAMAK. Be sought; be searched; search o.s./one's pockets, etc.; search one's mind; be sought after; be desired/appreciated too late; be missed.

aranj·e (*mus.*) ~ **etm.**, arrange. ~**man**, arrangement.

Ara'p[b1] *n.* Arab; Ethiopian; (*pej.*) = ZENCİ, Negro. *a.* Very dark, black. ~ +, *a.* Arab(ian); Negro: ~ **aklı**, stupidity: ~ **ardında**, the bogeyman's behind you: ~ **aşiretleri**, Bedouin tribes: ~ **atı**, Arab horse: ~ **bacı**, Negro nurse: ~ **Birliği**, (*pol.*) Arab League: ~ **böcek**, (*ent.*) negro bug: ~ **çorap**, (*col.*) Negroes: ~ **darısı**, (*bot.*) buck-wheat: ~ **dilini çıkarmış gibi**, not matching: ~ **doyuncaya yer**, Acem **çatlayıncaya**, an Arab eats till he is full, a Persian till he bursts: ~ **gibi olm.**, be pitch black: ~ **inciri**, (*bot.*) prickly pear: ~ **olayım** (. . . sa), I'm hanged if . . .: ~ **oynamak (-in)**, be lucky: ~ **rakamları**, (*math.*) Arabic numerals: ~ **tavşanı**, (*zoo.*) jerboa, desert rat: ~ **tavuğu**, (*orn.*) pin-tailed sandgrouse: ~ **uyandı/**~**ın gözü açıldı**, he's learnt a lesson: ~ **yazısı**, Arabic writing: ~**ın yalellisi gibi**, unending, monotonous.

Arap·ça (*ling.*) Arabic; in the Arabian manner; (*pej.*) unintelligible: ~**dır benim için!**, it's all Greek to me!: ~ **değil mi? Uydur uydur söyle!**, you can say what you like, it's all Greek to us! ~ **çalaştırmak**, arabicize. ~**çı**, fanatical Arabophile. ~**sabunu**[nu], soft soap. ~**saçı**[nı], fuzzy/woolly hair; (*fig.*) a tangled affair; a mess; (*bot.*) yarrow, milfoil: ~ **gibi**, tangled, confused, intricate: ~**na dönmek**, be difficult to sort out; (traffic) get snarled up. ~**zamkı**[nı], gum arabic.

ararot[u] (*bot.*) Arrowroot. ~ **kamışı**, arrowroot plant.

Arasat (*rel.*) Place where Muslims will gather on the Day of Judgement.

ara·sı = ARA. -~**sı**, *a. suf.* inter- [ULUSLARARASI]. ~**sıra** = ARA SIRA. ~**sız**, without interruption, continuously. ~**söz**, (*th.*) aside: ~ **olarak**, by the bye.

arasta Street in the bazaar for one trade; fair; (*mil.*) sutler's camp.

araşit[i] (*bot.*) Peanut, earth-nut, ground-nut.

araştır·ıcı Investigator; (*ed.*) researcher; (*geo.*) explorer; (*geol.*) prospector; (*fig.*) curious person. ~**ıcılık**, investigation. ~**ma**, *vn.* research, investigation; survey; (*geol.*) prospecting: ~ **enstitüsü**, (*ed.*) research institute: ~ **filmi**, research film, documentary: ~**-geliştirme**, research and development. ~**macı**, investigator. ~**mak (-i)**, search; investigate; do research into.

arat·mak (-i, -e) *vc.* = ARAMAK. Make s.o. regret/long for stg. ~**mamak (-i)**, make stg. not be missed; be a complete substitute for stg.

ara·tümce (*ling.*) Parenthesis, aside. ~**ya**//~**yı** = ARA.

ara·yıcı *n.* Seeker; customs inspector; beachcomber; (*ast.*) finder (telescope): *a.* wandering about as if in search of stg.: ~ **fişeği**, jumping cracker. ~**yış**, searching.

ara·yığımlık (*fin.*) Entrepôt. ~**yüzey**, (*phys.*) interface.

araz *pl.* Attributes; symptoms; accidents.

arazbar (buselik) (*Or. mus.*) Compound melodies.

arazi Land, country; ground; domain, estate, real property; site, field (of work). ~ +, *a.* Land; territorial: ~ **açma**, land clearance: ~ **arabası**, (*mot.*) estate-car, land-rover: ~ **bilgisi**, topography: ~ **çöküntüsü**, (*geol.*) ground subsidence: ~ **kazanma**, (*agr.*) land reclamation: ~ **ölçme**, surveying: ~ **ölçme bilgisi**, geodesy: ~ **noktası**, landmark: ~ **sahibi**, landowner: ~ **terki**, (*pol.*) cession of territory: ~ **vasıtası**, estate vehicle: ~ **vergisi**, (*fin.*) land tax: ~ **yarışı**, (*sp.*) steeplechase: ~**den istifade**, land utilization: ~**ye uymak**, (*sl.*) hide.

arbede Quarrel, affray; free fight; row; noise.

arbitraj (*fin.*) Arbitrage, jobbing.

ard- = ART.

arda (*carp.*) Turner's chisel; marking-peg.

arda'k[ğ1] (*myc.*) Fungal rot on trees, (?) honey fungus.

ardala Bell (on the last camel of a caravan); cushion (for an animal's back); pillion.

ardaşık = ARDIŞIK.

ardı'ç[c1] (*bot.*) Juniper. ~ **bülbülü**, (*orn.*) thrush nightingale: ~ **katranı**, (*chem.*) oil of savin: ~ **rakı/suyu**, gin. ~**kuşu**[nu], (*orn.*) fieldfare. ~**kuşugiller**, thrushes.

ardıl *a.* Consecutive; consequent. *n.* (*leg.*) Successor. ~**lık**, succession. ~**mak (-e)**, cling to s.o.'s back; (*fig.*) pester s.o.

ard·ın ~ ~, backwards. ~**ınca**, immediately behind. ~**ısıra** = ART. ~**ışık**, successive; progressive; (*math.*) consecutive; alternate, alternating. ~**ışıklık**, succession. ~**ışma**, *vn.* following on. ~**ışmak**, *vi.* follow on.

ardiye Warehouse, depository; entrepôt; storage fee; demurrage.

ard·lama (*geol.*) Succession. ~**uvaz**, (*geol.*) slate.

arena (*sp.*) Arena.

areometre (*phys.*) Hydrometer, areometer.

arg. = ARGO.

arga'ç[c1] (*tex.*) Weft. ~**lamak (-i)**, weave in its weft.

argalı (*zoo.*) Wild sheep, argali.

argı·mak *vi.* Grow thin. ~**n**, thin, exhausted. ~**nlık**, emaciation, exhaustion. ~**tmak (-i)**, *vc.*

argı't[d1] (*geo.*) Mountain pass; watershed.

argo (*ling.*) Argot, cant, slang. ~**msu**, slangy.

argon (*chem.*) Argon.

argonot[u] (*zoo.*) Paper nautilus.

argüman (*phil.*) Argument, opinion.

arı[1] *a.* Clean; unadulterated; pure; innocent; net (weight); (*ling.*) pure (of foreign words). ~ **ispirto**, (*chem.*) absolute alcohol: ~ **kan**, (*live.*) pure-blooded; thoroughbred: ~ **sili**, very clean: ~ **su**, distilled water.

arı[2] *n.* (*ent.*) Bee. ~ **bal alacak çiçeği bilir**, clever men know where their profit lies: ~ **diken/iğnesi**, bee's sting: ~ **gibi**, hard working: ~ **gibi sokmak**, sting; speak bitter words: ~ **kovanı**, bee-hive: ~ **kovanı gibi işlemek**, swarm with activity: ~ KUŞU: ~ **sürüsü**, swarm of bees: ~ SÜTÜ: ~ ŞAHİNİ: ~ **yiyen çaylak**, (*orn.*) honey-buzzard: ~ **yuvası**, hornet's nest: ~ **dan korkan bal yemez**, nothing venture nothing win: ~ **lar**, bees, Apidae: ~ **nın yuvasına kazık dürtmek/sokmak**, stir up a hornet's nest.

arı·beyi[ni] Queen-bee. ~ **cı**, apiarist, beekeeper. ~ **cılık**, apiculture, beekeeping. ~ **çıl**, (*zoo.*) apivorous.

arık Lean, emaciated; clean, pure, honourable. ~ **lamak**, *vi.* become lean, etc. ~ **laşmak**, *vi.* be lean, etc. ~ **latmak (-i)**, make lean, etc. ~ **lık**, leanness, emaciation; cleanness, purity.

arıkil (*geol.*) Kaolin, china clay.

arı·kuşu[nu] (*orn.*) Bee-eater. ~ **lık**[1], bee-hive platform, apiary.

arı·lamak (-i) Cleanse. ~ **laşmak**, *vi.* grow/become pure; be unadulterated. ~ **laştırmak (-i)**, make pure, refine; filter. ~ **lık**[2], cleanliness; purity; innocence; (*ling.*) purity; clarity, simplicity.

arın·dırmak (-i) Cleanse. ~ **ık**, (*med.*) abacterial. ~ **ma**, cleansing; catharsis; purification. ~ **mak**, *vi.* become clean; be purified; be rid of stg.: **arınıp tarınmak**, be thoroughly cleaned.

arı·özü/~ sütü[nü] Food for bee larvae. ~ **şahini**[ni], (*orn.*) honey-buzzard.

arış Forearm, cubit; (ox-cart) pole; (*tex.*) warp.

arıt·ıcı ~ (**madde**), detergent. ~ **ık**, refined. ~ **ılma/~ ım**, purification; refining; antisepsy; cleansing. ~ **ımevi/~ ımyeri**[ni], refinery. ~ **kan**, antiseptic.

arıtla·ma Recommendation, testimonial. ~ **mak (-i)**, recommend, give a testimonial.

arıt·ma Cleansing; refining; (*fin.*) liquidation. ~ **macı(lık)**, (*art.*) pur·ist/(-ism). ~ **mak (-i)**, cleanse, purify; clarify, refine.

arız That which occurs/happens; accidental; intercepting, impeding, obstructing. ~ **olm.**, happen, occur, befall.

arıza Accident; incident; defect, fault; obstruction. ~ **bulucu**, fault-finder, (*ind.*) trouble-shooter: ~ **yapmak**, be spoilt; break down: ~ **ya uğramak**, meet with an accident.

arız·alanmak *vi.* Be defective/uneven. ~ **alı**, uneven, broken (country); full of difficulties and obstacles; defective, faulty. ~ **asız**, unobstructed; level; free from difficulties; without hitch; without defects, undamaged. ~ **i**, accidental; adventitious; casual; temporary.

Ari *n.*, *a.* (*ling.*, *ethn.*) Aryan.

arif Wise; intelligent; skilled, expert. ~ **olan anlar/~ e tarif ne hacet?**, a wise man needs no explanation, verb. sap. ~ **ane**[1], *adv.* skilfully, cleverly.

arifane[2] *n.* Picnic/feast to which all contribute; Dutch treat. ~ **ile**, sharing, contributing.

arife Eve (festival); verge, threshold (event). ~ **günü**, the eve of a Bairam.

arina (*dom.*) Sand for scouring; bath-brick.

Aristo Aristotle. ~ **cu(luk)**, (*phil.*) Aristotelian(ism).

aristokra·si (*soc.*) Aristocracy. ~ **t**[1], *n.*/(*a.*) aristocrat(ic). ~ **tlık**, aristocracy.

aritmeti[k][ği] *n.*, (*a.*) Arithmetic(al). ~ **dizi**, arithmetical series/progression: ~ **işlem**, arithmetical operation. ~ **çi**, arithmetician.

aritmik (*mus.*) Arhythmic.

ariya (*naut.*) Dipping, lowering. ~ **etm.**, dip the flag.

ariyet[i] Stg. borrowed/lent; loan. ~ **almak**, borrow: ~ **vermek**, lend: ~ **(en) kullanmak**, make temporary use of stg.

ariza Petition; letter to a superior.

arizamik *adv.* Fully, in great detail.

Arjantin (*geo.*) Argentina. ~ +, *a.* Argentinian. ~ **li**, *n.* (*ethn.*) Argentinian.

ark[1][1] (*agr.*) Dike, ditch; conduit; irrigation canal.

ark[1][2] (*el.*) Arc. ~ **kaynağı**, arc-weld: ~ **lambası**, arc-lamp: ~ **yapmak**, arc.

ark. = ARKEOLOJİ.

arka *n.* [90] Back; back part; far/other/reverse side; posterior; (*lit.*) continuation, sequel, end; protection, support; supporter, backer, patron. *a.* Back; rear; tail; (*naut.*) aft(er); other. ~ **arabası**, trailer: ~ ~ **ya**, one after the other; tandem; back to back: ~ ~ **ya beş gün**, for five whole days: ~ ~ **ya gelmek**, succeed each other steadily: ~ ~ **ya vermek**, stand back to back/join together (for mutual protection): ~ **avlu**, backyard: ~ **ayak**, (*zoo.*) rear leg: ~ **bulmak**, find protector/patron: ~ **cam**, (*mot.*) rear window: ~ **çantası**, haversack, rucksack: ~ **çevirmek (-e)**, (*fig.*) turn one's back on/shun s.o.: ~ **çıkmak**, befriend, protect: ~ **çizgi**, (*sp.*) base line: ~ **damak** = ART: ~ **dayağı**, backrest: ~ **feneri**, (*mot.*) tail-/rear-lamp: ~ **güverte**, (*naut.*) afterdeck: ~ **kapak**, (*mot.*) tailgate: ~ **kapıdan çıkmak**, leave school a failure: ~ **müziği**, (*th.*, *cin.*) background music: ~ **olm. (-e)**, back/support s.o.: ~ **plan**, background: ~ **sokak**, back street: ~ **tarafı**, continuation, sequel; (*aer.*) afterbody: ~ **üstü düşmek//yatmak**, fall//lie on one's back: ~ **vermek**, support: ~ **yüz**, reverse, verso.

arkada, (*naut.*) astern: ~ **bırakmak (-i)**, go ahead of; leave behind/astern: ~ **kalanlar/~ kiler**, those left behind: ~ **kalma**, time-lag: ~ **kalmak**, stay/be left behind; keep in the background: ~ **koymak**, leave behind: ~ **oturmak**, take a back seat.

arkadan, from the rear; subsequently: ~ **almak**, back off: ~ **arkaya**, secretly; behind s.o.'s back: ~ **desteklemek**, support: ~ **gelmek**, loiter; follow: ~ **görüş**, rear-view: ~ **söylemek**, criticise/gossip behind s.o.'s back; backbite: ~ **vurmak**, (*fig.*) stab s.o. in the back: ~ **yetişmek**, overtake.

arkası: ~ **alınmak**, be brought to an end; be halted: ~ **gel(me)mek**, (*pub.*, *ind.*) be (dis)continued: ~ **kesilmek**, be cut off/terminated; come to an end; become extinct: ~ **ol(ma)mak**, (not) have a 'backer'/support/'influence' (in one's career): ~ **pek**, who is strongly supported; (*mod.*) warmly dressed: ~ **sıra**, following, just behind: ~ **var**, (*pub.*) to be continued/concluded; (*fig.*) having support: ~ **yere gelmemek**, be firmly established; have powerful backers: ~ **yufka**, there's nothing more to eat; you've had the best (of the meal).

arkasına: ~ **adam takmak**, collect followers; have s.o. pursued: ~ **bakmadan**, without thinking of those left behind: ~ **düşmek/takılmak**, work very hard to complete stg.; pursue s.o. very closely.

arkasında: ~ **dolaşmak/gezmek**, try to complete stg.: ~ **koşmak**, chase; follow up: ~ **yumurta küfesi yok ya!**, there's nothing to stop him changing his mind!

arkasından, from behind; after; behind his back, in his absence: ~ **atlı kovalar gibi**, in great haste: ~ **çekiştirmek**, backbite: ~ **koşmak**, chase s.o. to complete stg.: ~ **sürüklemek**, trail behind s.o.: ~ **teneke çalmak**, boo s.o. in public.

arkasını: ~ **almak**, complete stg.: ~ **bırakmak**, not follow up/stick to s.o.: ~ **çevirmek (-e)**, pay no attention to: ~ **dayamak (-e)**, support s.o.: ~ **getirememek**, be unable to complete stg.: ~ **vermek**, support/protect s.o.

arkaya: ~ **atmak/bırakmak/koymak**, put off/delay stg.: ~ **kalmak**, stay behind: ~ **yatmak**, lean back, recline: ~ **yayık**, (*aer.*) swept-back: ~ **yıkılmak**, fall backwards.

arka·bölge (*geo.*) Hinterland. ~**cı**, (*mil.*) rearguard.

arka¹çᶜ¹ Mountain pasture, plateau.

arkadaş Companion, friend; colleague; confederate; associate. ~ **canlısı**, s.o. very friendly: ~ **değil arka taşı**, a false 'friend': ~ **olm.**, be(come) friends.

arkadaş·ça Like friends; in a friendly manner. ~**lık**, companionship, friendship: ~ **etm.**, be together; be friends: ~ **icabı**, as friendship requires.

arka·ik Archaic; (*art.*) primitive. ~**izm**, archaism.

arka·lamak (-e) Support, back; protect. ~**lanmak**, *vp.* be supported; **(-e)**, rely on s.o. ~**lı**, s.o. with supporters/'friends at court'. ~**lık**, porter's saddle; sleeveless jacket; (chair, etc.) back; (bicycle) carrier. ~**lıksız**, (chair, etc.) backless. ~**sız**, without backers, lacking support: ~ **iskemle**, (*dom.*) stool. ~**üstü (yatar)**, (lying) on one's back. ~**yüz**, (*pub.*) verso.

arkdüzen (*agr.*, *arch.*) Drainage.

arkebüz (*mil.*) Arquebus.

arkeen (*geol.*) Archaean.

arkegon (*bot.*) Archegonium.

arkeo·log Archaeologist. ~**loji(k)**, archaeolo·gy/ (-gical). ~**pteriks**, (*zoo.*) (fossil) archaeopteryx.

arkoz (*geol.*) Millstone-grit, arkose.

Arktik *a.* (*geo.*) Arctic. ~ **kuşak**, Arctic zone.

arlan·mak *vp.* Be ashamed. ~**maz**, shameless, brazen-faced.

arma (*his.*) Armorial bearings, coat of arms; (*naut.*) ship's rigging; (*sl.*) jewellery. ~ **başlığı**, crest: ~ **budatmak/uçurmak**, (*naut.*) (storm) carry away the rigging: ~ **donatmak/etm. (-i)**, (*naut.*) rig: ~ **soymak**, (*naut.*) dismantle the rigging.

arma·cılık Heraldry. ~**da**, (*naut.*) armada, fleet. ~**dor**, (*naut.*) rigger: ~ **çeliği**, belaying-pin. ~**dura**, belaying-pin rack.

armağan Present, (free) gift; (*lit.*) Festschrift. ~ **etm.**, give, make a gift of stg. ~**lamak (-i)**, make gifts to s.o.

armatör (*naut.*) Ship-owner. ~**lük**, ship-owning.

armatur (*el.*) Armature; condenser plate.

armon·i (*mus.*) Harmony. ~**ik(a)**, harmonica; accordeon. ~**ikler**, (*phys.*) harmonics. ~**yum**, harmonium.

armudi(ye) Pear-shaped (gold coin/ornament).

armu¹tᵈᵘ (*bot.*) Pear; (*sl.*) stupid; (*el.*) pear-shaped switch. ~ **ağacı**, pear-tree: ~ **ağacı elma vermez**, one can only do one's best: ~ **gibi**, very stupid: ~ **kurusu**, (*cul.*) dried pears: ~ **piş ağzıma düş!**, s.o. who expects everything to fall into his lap without effort: ~**un iyisini ayı yer!** = AHLAT: ~**un sapı var, üzümün çöpü var demek**, always find fault, be very hard to please.

armut·kabağıⁿ¹ (*bot.*) Ornamental gourd. ~**kaplanı**, (*ent.*) lace-bug. ~**top**ᵘ, (*sp.*) punch-ball.

armuz (*naut.*) Plank-seam. ~**lu**, carvel-built (boat).

Arn. = ARNAVUTÇA(DAN); ARNAVUTLUK.

Arnavu¹tᵈᵘ *n.* (*ethn.*) Albanian. ~ **+**, *a.* Albanian: ~ **bacası**, (*arch.*) dormer window: ~ **besası**, (*pej.*) agreement soon to be broken; treachery: ~ **biberi**, (*bot.*) red pepper: ~ **darısı**, (*bot.*) millet.

Arnavut·ciğeriⁿⁱ (*cul.*) Fried liver. ~**ça**, (*ling.*) Albanian. ~**kaldırımı**ⁿ¹, cobblestone pavement. ~**luk**, (*geo.*) Albania; Albanian character: ~ **damarı/~u tutmak**, act/speak violently; be very obstinate.

arnika (*bot.*) Mountain arnica.

arnuvo Art nouveau.

aromatik (*chem.*) Aromatic.

arozöz (*agr.*) Sprinkler; water-cart.

arpa (*bot.*) Barley. ~ **boyu kadar**, a very short distance: ~ **ektim darı çıktı**, it was a bitter disappointment; I was disillusioned: ~ **mı buğday mı?**, is it a boy or a girl?: ~ **öz(üt)ü**, malt extract: ~SUYU: ~ **şehriye**, (*cul.*) grain-shaped macaroni: ~ **şırası**, barley-water: ~ **tanesi**, barleycorn.

arpa·cı Barley-seller; (*sl.*) thief: ~ **kumrusu gibi düşünmek**, be very pensive. ~**cık**, (*med.*) stye; (*mil.*) (gun) foresight; bead: ~ **soğanı**, (*agr.*) onion-set; (*bot.*) shallot. ~**cılık**, dealing in barley. ~**lama**, *vn.* (*live.*) founder (horse's hoof disease). ~**lamak**, *vi.* (horse) be overfed with barley. ~**lık**, barley-field; barley-bin; mark on a horse's teeth (indicating age); (*his.*) fief; = BAŞMAKLIK. ~**suyu**ⁿᵘ, (*jok.*) beer.

arpağ Magic spell, incantation. ~**cı**, wizard, sorcerer.

arpej (*mus.*) Arpeggio.

arsa Building plot. ~ **parçası**, block: ~ **tellalı**, land-agent.

arseni¹kᵍⁱ Arsenic. ~**li**, arsenical.

arsız Shameless, barefaced; cheeky; impudent; importunate; (*fig.*) (plant) that grows everywhere.

arsız·ca Unashamedly; cheekily, impudently. ~**lanmak**, *vi.* act shamelessly; be impudent. ~**laşmak**, *vi.* become shameless/impudent. ~**lık**, shamelessness; impudence: ~ **istemez!**, none of your cheek!

arslan = ASLAN. Lion.

arş[1] = ARIŞ.
arş[2] (*mil.*) March!
arş[3] (*rel.*) Throne of God; (*arch.*) pavilion, booth; roof, ceiling.
arş[4] (*el.*) Current-collector (tram-car/trolley-bus).
arşe (*mus.*) Violin bow.
arşın (*math.*) Tk. yard (approx. 68 cm.); yardstick. ∼**la satmak**, sell by the yard: ∼**ları açmak**, stride out. ∼**lamak (-i)**, pace out, measure in yards; *vi.* step out, walk quickly. ∼**lık**, stg. sold by the yard; stg. a yard in length.
arşi- *pref.* Arch(i)-. ∼**dük**[ü], archduke. ∼**mandrit**[i], (*rel.*) archimandrite. ∼**tekt**, architect. ∼**v**, (*adm.*) archives. ∼**vci**, archivist.
arı**t**[d1] *n.*, *a.* [90] Back; behind; rear, hinder part; sequel, end. ∼ ∼**a**, one after the other; consecutive: ∼ AVURT: ∼ **boyunlu**, (*leg.*) secondary surety: ∼ BÖLGE: ∼ DAMAK: ∼ **düşünce//niyet**, real/concealed thought//intention: ∼ **elden**, secretly, furtively: ∼ **eteğinde namaz kılınır**, s.o. very virtuous: ∼ **ısıtıcı**, (*eng.*) reheater: ∼ **kenar**, (*aer.*) trailing edge: ∼ ODA: ∼ **oyun**, (*th.*) epilogue, tail-piece: ∼ **teker**, (*mot.*) rear/drive wheel: ∼ **ünlü**, (*ling.*) back vowel: ∼ **yakıcı**, (*eng.*) after-burner.

ard-: ∼**a düşmek**, lag behind: ∼**ı arası kesilmeden/** ∼**ına**, continuously, uninterruptedly: ∼**ı arkası gelmeyen**, endless: ∼**ı kesilmek**, cease, come to an end: ∼**ı sıra**, one behind the other, in series; immediately following: ∼**ı sıra gitmek**, follow after s.o.: ∼**ılı**, with a following: ∼**ıma/**∼**ımca/**∼**ımda**, behind me, after me: ∼**ına adam takmak**, collect followers: ∼**ına düşmek**, pursue, follow: ∼**ına kadar açık**, wide-open (door, etc.): ∼**ınca**, from behind: ∼**ında gezmek**, run after s.o.; try to get stg.: ∼**ında yüz köpek havlamıyan kurt kurt sayılmaz**, all great men have their critics: ∼**ından**, subsequently: ∼**ından atlı/cellat kovalamak**, be in a great (unnecessary) hurry: ∼**ından koşmak**, run after s.o.: ∼**ından sapan taşı yetişmez**, stg. moving very fast: ∼**ını bırakmamak**, have s.o. pursued: ∼**ını kesmek**, hinder, stop, prevent: **artta kalmak**, remain behind; survive, outlive.
artağan Fruitful. ∼**lık**, fruitfulness, plenty.
arta·kalan Remaining behind; surviving. ∼**(kal)-mak**, *vi.* remain over; survive. ∼**n**, increasing; exceeding.
artam Excellence, merit. ∼**lı**, excellent, meritorious.
art·avurı**t**[du] (*bio.*) Rear of the cheek: ∼ **ünsüzü**, (*ling.*) velar lateral consonant. ∼**bileşen**, (*phil.*) consequent. ∼**bölge**, (*geo.*) hinterland. ∼**çevirme**, (*phil.*) obversion. ∼**çı**, *n.* (*mil.*) rearguard: *a.* (*art.*) traditionalist. ∼**çılık**, (*mil.*) duties of the rearguard. ∼**dama**ı**k**[g1], (*bio.*) rear of the palate: ∼ **ünsüzü**, (*ling.*) postpalatal/velar consonant. ∼**ek**[i], suffix.
arte·fakt (*archaeol.*) Artefact. ∼**r(i)**, (*bio.*) artery. ∼**rit**[i], (*med.*) arteritis. ∼**riyoskleroz**, (*med.*) arteriosclerosis. ∼**zyen (kuyusu)**, artesian well.
artı *n.* Plus sign (+). *a.* Positive. ∼ **eksi**, plus or minus (sign) (±): ∼ **kutup//uç**, (*el.*) positive pole//terminal: ∼ **sayı**, (*math.*) positive number.
artı·cı (*eng.*) Booster. ∼**cık**, (*phys.*) positron.

artıı**k**[g1] *a.* Left, remaining; additional, extra; superfluous; more; (*phys.*) residual. *n.* What is left; residue; remnant; (*ind.*) waste; (*fin.*) balance; end, stub. *adv.* [203] At last!; well now! henceforth! ∼ **bizden geçti**, I'm past/too old for that sort of thing: ∼ **bu kadarı da fazla**, that's more than enough: ∼ **canıma yetti**, I've had enough of it!: ∼ **çok oldu!**, well, I'm damned!: ∼ **eksik**, deficiencies; more or less: ∼ **ısı**, (*phys.*) residual heat: ∼ **insafına kalmış**, it all depends on his sense of fair play now: ∼ **iş bir eve kaldı!**, now all that we need is a house!: ∼ **mal göz çıkarmaz**, one can never own too much: ∼ **senden bıktım!**, (*vulg.*) I've had enough of you!: ∼ **su**, waste water, effluent: ∼ **yeter!** enough!
artık·değer (*fin.*) Capital gain. ∼**gün**, (*ast.*) leap-year day (29 February). ∼**lama**, (*lit.*) parenthesis; digression; padding. ∼**lık**, superfluity; redundancy. ∼**yıl**, (*ast.*) leap-year, bissextile.
art·ım Increase; (*math.*) increment. ∼**ımlama**, (*lit.*) pleonasm, padding. ∼**ımlı**, swollen, increased in size (as cooked rice). ∼**ın**, (*phys.*) cation. ∼**ırgan**, (*med.*) adjuvant. ∼**ırıcı**, booster; multiplier. ∼**ırılmak**, *vp.* be increased/augmented. ∼**ırım**, economy, saving. ∼**ırma**, *vn.* act of increasing; economizing; overbidding; auction. ∼**ırmak (-i)**, increase, augment; economize, save, put by; raise a bid (at auction); collect; go too far, exceed the bounds. ∼**ırmalı satış**, auction. ∼**ış**, increase. ∼**ıu**ı**ç**[cu], (*phys.*) anode.
artifisyel Artificial, false.
artist[i] Artist; (*th.*) actor, actress, performer. ∼ **gibi**, showily attractive. ∼**ik**, artistic. ∼**lik**, work/position of an artist.
artkafa (*bio.*) Occiput. ∼ **kemiği**, occipital bone.
art·ma Stg. left over; residue. ∼**mak**, *vi.* increase, multiply; remain over; rise (prices, tide, etc.).
artoda (*bio.*) Posterior chamber (of the eye).
artr·it[i] (*med.*) Arthritis. ∼**itik**, arthritic. ∼**itizm**, arthritism: ∼**oz**, arthrosis.
art·sız ∼ **arasız**, uninterruptedly. ∼**ülke**, (*geo.*) hinterland. ∼**zamanlı(lık)**, (*ling.*) diachron·ic/ (-ism).
aruseı**k**[gi] Irridescent green/pink mother-of-pearl.
aruz (*lit.*) Prosody.
arya[1] (*naut.*) ∼ **etm.**, lower (flag, etc.). ∼**direk**, jury-mast.
ary·a[2] (*mus.*) Aria. ∼**etta**, arietta. ∼**oso**, arioso.
Aryanizm (*rel.*) Arianism.
arz[1] Representation; petition; expression of opinion; submission of stg. (for consideration). ∼ **etm.**, present (a petition); submit (a proposal); offer (an opinion); express (a sentiment); present (one's respects): ∼ **odası**, audience chamber: ∼ **üzerine**, on request: ∼ **ü/ve talep**, (*fin.*) supply and demand: ∼**ı didar etm.**, appear: ∼**ı endam etm.**, make an appearance, present o.s.: ∼**ı hürmet ederim**, I present my respects.
arz[2] Width, breadth; (*geo.*) latitude. ∼ **dairesi**, a parallel of latitude. ∼ **ani**, transverse, lateral, cross. ∼**i**, latitudinal.
arz[3] The earth; land; country. ∼**iyat**[i], geology.
arzu Wish, desire. ∼ **etm.**, wish, desire: ∼**sunda bulunmak/olm.**, have a wish to . . .: ∼ **talep** = ARZ[1].

arzu·hal[i] Written petition. ~**halci(lik)**, (work of) petition-writer/street letter-writer. ~**keş**/~**lu**, wishful, desirous. ~**lamak (-i)**, desire, long for. ~**suz(luk)**, unwilling(ness).

as[1] (*zoo.*) Ermine.

as[2] Ace (cards); (*fig.*) ace, star performer.

as- *pref.* = AST. Second-; vice-; deputy-; sub-.

As. = (*ch.s.*) ARSENİK; (*ed.*) ASİSTAN; ASKER(İ); ASKERLİK.

A-s. = (*el.*) AMPER-SAAT.

a.s. = (*bio.*) ALT-SINIF; (*chem.*) ATOMSAL SAYI.

asa Stick; baton; sceptre.

ASA =(*American Standards Association*).

asab- = ASAP. ~**i**, nervous; neurotic; irritated; on edge. ~**ileşmek**, *vi.* have one's nerves on edge; become irritated. ~**ilik**, nervousness; irritability. ~**iye**, (*med.*) nervous diseases. ~**iyeci**, neurologist. ~**iyet**[i], nervousness; nervous irritation; (*obs.*) fanaticism; sensitiveness.

asal Basic; fundamental; principal; (*math.*) prime (factor/number). ~ **gazlar**, (*chem.*) noble gases: ~ **gerilme**, (*eng.*) principal stress: ~ **odak noktası**, (*phys.*) principal focal point: ~ **olmıyan**, (*math.*) compound: ~ **sayı**, (*math.*) prime number.

asala[k]ᵍ¹ (*bio.*) Parasite; (*fig.*) parasite, sponger. ~**bilim**, parasitology. ~**kıran**, parasiticide. ~**lık**, parasitism. ~**sal**, parasitic.

asalet[i] Nobility of birth; performing a duty in person; (*leg.*) personal appearance; (*lit.*) nobility of style. ~ **bellidir**, blood will tell. ~**en**, in person; (*leg.*) acting as principal (not agent).

asansör Lift, elevator. ~ **kafes/odası**, lift cage. ~**cü**, lift-operator. ~**lü**, (*arch.*) with lift.

asa[p]ᵇ¹ *pl.* Nerves. ~ **bozukluğu**, nervous disorder; shock: ~**ı bozulmak**, get nervous/upset.

asar *pl.* = ESER. Works; monuments; signs, traces, remains; legends. ~**ı metruke**, (*lit.*) posthumous works. ~**ıatika**, ancient monuments, antiquities.

asayiş Quiet; repose; security. ~ **berkemal**, perfectly quiet//secure: ~ **sorunu**, security problem/question: ~ **toplantısı**, (*adm.*) security council/meeting: ~**i iade etm.**, restore order. ~**sizlik**, disorder; insecurity.

asbaşkan(lık) (*adm.*) Deputy-chairman(ship); vice-presiden·t/(-cy).

asbest[i] (*geol.*) Asbestos.

As. CK = ASKERİ CEZA KANUNU.

aselben[t]ᵈⁱ (*bot.*) *Styrax officinalis*; (*chem.*) benzoin; storax. ~ **eriyiği**, friar's balsam.

asenkron (*phys.*) Asynchronous.

asep·si (*med.*) Asepsia. ~**tik**, aseptic.

ases (*his.*) Night-watchman; night patrol. ~**başı**, (*his.*) Chief of Police.

aset·al (*chem.*) Acetal. ~**at**, acetate. ~**ik (asit)**, acetic (acid). ~**ilen**, acetylene. ~**on**, acetone.

asfalt[1] *n.* Asphalt; motorway. *a.* Asphalt(ed). ~ **yol**, asphalted/made-up road: ~**la döşemek/ kaplamak**/~**lamak (-i)**, asphalt. ~**lanmak**, *vp.* be asphalted. ~**laş(tır)mak**, *vi.* (*vt.*) bituminize. ~**lı**, asphalt(ic).

asgari Smallest, least, lowest; (*math.,fin.*) minimum.

asha[p]ᵇ¹ *pl.* = SAHİP. Masters; (*rel.*) companions/ disciples of the Prophet Muhammad.

ası[1] Suspension; garland. ~**da kalmak/olm.**, be in suspense/uncompleted. ~**cı**, (*bot.*) suspensor.

ası[2] Profit, benefit; (*pub.*) placard, poster. ~**cıl**, self-seeking.

-ası *v. suf.* [115, 161] = -ESİ [OLASI].

asık Cross; hanged; hanging. ~ **yüzlü**, sulky, surly.

as[ı]l¹¹ *n.* Foundation; base; reality; origin, source; root; race, stock; essential part/substance. *a.* Real; true; genuine; essential; main, principal; primary; fundamental; inherent; original. ~ **mahsul**, original product: ~ **nüsha**, original/master copy: ~ **sayılar**, (*math.*) cardinal numbers: ~ **üye**, (*adm.*) foundation/full member: ~ **vurgu**, (*ling.*) main/ primary stress: ~**ı astarı (-in)**, its real form/reality; the real truth of a matter: ~**ı astarı/faslı olmamak**, be entirely unfounded/devoid of truth: ~**ı çıkmak**, the truth become known: ~**ı nesli**, his origin and family: ~**ı yok**, unfounded, untrue: ~**ına bakarsan**, the truth of the matter is: ~**ında**, originally: ~**ını ararsan**, in point of fact: ~**ıyla mukabele etm.**, compare stg. with its original.

asıl·aca[k]ᵏᵍ¹ *a.* About to be hanged. *n.* Gallows-bird; criminal: ~ **suya boğulmaz**, the gallows-bird won't get drowned. ~**ı¹**, hanging; suspended; overhead; (*arın*) in a sling; hanged (executed): ~ **kalmak**, be suspended: ~ **olm.**, be dependent.

ası·lanmak (-den) Profit from stg. ~**lı²**, profitable, advantageous.

asıl·mak *vi.* Hang; be hanged//hung/suspended; lean out of/over; insist; be obstinate: (-e), cling to; pull: **asılırsan, İngiliz sicimiyle asıl**, always buy/use the best quality: **asılıp kuru(t)mak**, (*tex.*) drip-dry: **asılıp sallan(dır)mak**, dangle. ~ **mışadam**, (*bot.*) man-orchid.

asıl·sız Without foundation/truth; baseless. ~**tı**, (*chem.*) suspension. ~**zade(lik)** = ASİLZADE.

asım *n.* Hanging. ~ **takım**, jewellery, ornaments.

asıntı *n.* Putting off, delaying; pestering; (*col.*) unpaid debt. ~**da kalmak**, leave in the air/ unfinished: ~**ya bırakmak**, put off, delay.

as[ı]rʳ¹ Age; time; epoch; century. ~**ı Saadet**, the lifetime of the Prophet Muhammad: ~**larca**, for centuries. ~**dide**, age-old, immemorial. ~**lık**, *a.* (so many) centuries old: *n.* centenarian: ~ **düşman**, sworn enemy.

-asıya *v. suf.* [180] = -ESİYE [ÇILDIRASIYA].

asi *n.* Rebel, insurgent; brigand; sinner. *a.* Rebellious; refractory.

asid- = ASİT.

aside (*cul.*) Rice//barley meal, meat and okra.

asid·ik (*chem.*) Acidic. -**imetre**/~**ölçer**, acidimeter. ~**oz**, (*med.*) acidosis.

asiklik (*el.*) Acyclic.

asil *a.* Of noble birth; noble; chivalrous. *n.* (*fin.*) Principal (not agent); (*adm.*) permanent (not acting/temporary). ~ **kanlı**, blue-blooded.

asi·leşmek *vi.* Rebel. ~**lik**, rebellion: ~ **etm.**, rebel.

asil·leştirmek (-i) Ennoble. ~**lik**, nobility. ~**zade**, nobleman, peer; aristocrat; (*sl.*) pimp. ~**zadelik**, nobility.

asimetri(k) Asymme·try/(-trical).

asimi·lasyon (*bio., ed.*) Assimilation. ~**le**, ~ **etm.**, assimilate.

asi·m(p)tot[u] (*math.*) Asymptote. ~ **nkron**, asynchronous. ~ **smik**, (*geol.*) aseismic.
asistan (*ed.*) Assistant to a professor; (*med.*) assistant doctor, intern. ~ **lık**, assistantship, internship.
asi¹t[di] (*chem.*) *n.* Acid. ~ + , *a.* Acid(ic): ~ **aljinik//asetik // askorbik // borik // hidroklorik // karbolik// karbonik// nitrik// oksalık// pikrik// sitrik// sülfürik// ürik**, alginic// ascetic// ascorbic// bor(ac)ic// hydrochloric// carbolic// carbonic// nitric// oxalic// picric// citric// sulphuric// uric acid: ~ **denemesi**, acid test: ~ **derecesi**, acidity: ~ **kökü**, acid radical: ~ **e dirençli**, acid-proof/-resistant. ~ **li**, acid(ic). ~ **leş(tir)mek**, *vi.*/(*vt.*) acidify. ~ **lik**, acidity. ~ **ölçer**, acidimeter.
As. İz. = ASKERİ İNZİBAT.
ask. = ASKER(İ); ASKERLİK.
askat¹ (*math.*) Sub-multiple; (*geol.*) substage.
asker *n.* Soldier; military service; troops; (*sl.*) money. *a.* Soldierly; military. ~ **çıkarmak**, (*naut.*) land troops: ~ **kaçağı**, absent-without-leave, deserter: ~ **nakliye gemi// uçağı**, troop-ship// -plane: ~ **ocağı**, place for military service (barracks, camp, ship, etc.): ~ **olm./** ~ **e gitmek**, enlist; join the army; be called up: ~ **tayını**, soldier's rations: ~ **terhisi**, demobilization: ~ **toplamak**, recruit: ~ **yazılmak**, enlist, join up: ~ **den kaçmak**, desert: ~ **e alınmak**, be conscripted/sent to training camp: ~ **e almak**, conscript, enlist: ~ **e çağrılmak**, be called up: ~ **e gönüllü yazılmak**, enrol/join up as a regular soldier.
asker·i *a.* Military; martial; ~ **ataşe**, (*adm.*) military attaché: ~ **bando**, (*mus.*) military band: ~ **bölge/mıntıka**, military zone: ~ **ceza kanunu**, military penal code: ~ **fesat**, (*his.*) mutiny: ~ **heyet**, military mission: ~ **hizmet**, military service: ~ **İnzibat/Karakol**, Military Police: ~ **isyan**, mutiny: ~ **izin**, leave of absence: ~ **konak**, billet, camp: ~ **mahkeme**, military tribunal: ~ **mühendis**, ordnance engineer: ~ **talebe**, cadet: ~ **yardım**, (*pol.*) military aid/assistance. ~ **ileşmek**, *vp.* be militarized. ~ **ileştirmek (-i)**, militarize. ~ **lik**, military/national service; enlistment, recruitment: ~ **ataşesi**, military attaché: ~ **çağı**, period of liability to military service: ~ **dairesi**, regional call-up/recruiting office: ~ **(dersi)**, (*ed.*) military education in school: ~ **etm./yapmak**, do military service; bear arms: ~ **görev/hizmeti**, military/conscript service: ~ **kurulu**, military selection board: ~ **öğrenimi**, drill: ~ **yoklaması**, roll-call: ~ **e elverişli**, fit for military service.
askı Stg. hanging (esp. a bowl for flowers); pendant; rack; fruit (hung up to ripen); (*mod.*) braces; suspenders; clothes-hanger; (*dom.*) coffee-cup tray; (*bot.*) bush for silkworm cocoons; (*med.*) sling; (*aer.*) suspension; (*arch.*) king-post; (*fig.*) delay, postponement; suspense, doubt; (*adm.*) display of official notices/banns. ~ **da**, suspended; floating, deferred: ~ **da bırakmak**, leave in doubt/suspense: ~ **da kalmak**, remain in suspense, await the conclusion; (banns) be published: ~ **ya almak**, prop up, support; (*naut.*) raise a sunken ship: ~ **ya çıkmak**, (*ent.*) (silkworm) start spinning cocoons: ~ **ya çıkarmak**, publish the banns.
askı·cı (*sl.*) Who does not pay his debts. ~ **lı**,

suspended: ~ **yatak**, hammock. ~ **lık**, coat-hanger. ~ **yeri**, coatstand.
ask·lı (*myc.*) Sac fungus, ascomycete. ~ **orbik**, (*chem.*) ascorbic. ~ **ospor**, ascospore.
asl- = ASIL.
asla *adv.* Never; in no way. *int.* Never!, decidedly not!
aslan¹ = ASLEN.
aslan² (*zoo.*) Lion; (*fig.*) hero. ~ **ağzında olm.**, be in a difficult situation: ~ **(burcu)**, (*ast.*) Leo: ~ **gibi**, like a lion, well-built: ~ **kesilmek**, be strong and brave as a lion: ~ **maymunu**, (*zoo.*) golden lion tamarin: ~ **payı**, the lion's share: ~ **sütü**, (*jok.*) rakı: ~ **yatağından belli olur**, a man is judged by his surroundings: ~ **yavrusu**, lion's whelp, lion-cub: ~ **yürekli**, lion-hearted: ~ **ım!**, my young lion!
aslan·ağzı[nı] (*bot.*) Antirrhinum; snapdragon; (*arch.*) lion's-head stone gargoyle. ~ **ca**, like a lion. ~ **cı**, lion-keeper/-trainer. ~ **gil**, feline. ~ **giller**, (*zoo.*) cat family, Felidae. ~ **kuyruğu**[nu], (*bot.*) common motherwort. ~ **lık**, great bravery. ~ **pençesi**[ni], (*bot.*) lady's mantle; (*med.*) large carbuncle.
aslen Originally; fundamentally; essentially.
aslık (*med.*) (Woman) with defective genitalia.
asli Fundamental; radical; essential; (*soc.*) aboriginal, autochthonous. ~ **adet/sayı**, (*math.*) prime number: ~ **maaş**, (*adm.*) basic salary: ~ **metal**, noble metal: ~ **nüsha**, (*pub.*) original text. ~ **ye (mahkemesi)**, (*leg.*) court of first instance.
asma¹ *vn. a.* Suspended; hanging; pendant. ~ **kat**, (*arch.*) mezzanine floor: ~ **kilit**, padlock: ~ **köprü**, suspension-bridge: ~ **merdiven**, (*naut.*) gangway: ~ **pusula**, (*naut.*) telltale compass: ~ **saat**, wall-clock: ~ **yatak**, hammock, cot.
asma² *n.* (*bot.*) Vine (especially on a trellis); grape-vine. ~ **bıyığı**, tendril: ~ KABAĞI: ~ **kütüğü**, vinestock: ~ YAPRAĞI.
asma·bahçe Hanging garden. ~ **biti**[ni], (*ent.*) grape phylloxera. ~ **giller**, vines, Vitaceae.
asmak (-i, -e) Hang; suspend; put off paying (a debt); cease (work); play truant (from school), 'cut' (a lecture, etc.). **asıp kesmek**, behave in an arbitrary/ despotic manner: **astığı astık kestiği kestik olm.**, wreak one's will, be answerable to no one for one's actions.
asma·kabağı[nı] (*bot.*) Long edible gourd (grown on a trellis). ~ **kurdu**, (*ent.*) pyralis, meal moth. ~ **lı**, having a vine. ~ **lık**, place planted with vines; (*arch.*) picture-rail. ~ **yaprağı**[nı], (*cul.*) vine leaves (for making DOLMA).
aso Ace; star performer; = AS². ~ **r Adaları**, *pr.n.* (*geo.*) the Azores. ~ **rti**, (*mod.*) matching. ~ **syasyon**, (*psy.*) association.
aspi·distra (*bot.*) Aspidistra. ~ **ratör**, aspirator, suction mechanism; vacuum-cleaner; ventilator. ~ **rin**, (*med.*) aspirin.
aspur (*bot.*) Safflower; (*tex.*) red dye (from it).
asr- = ASIR. ~ **i**, modern; up-to-date; contemporary; fashionable. ~ **ileşme**, *vn.* modernization. ~ **ileşmek**, *vi.* become modern. ~ **ileştirmek (-i)**, modernize. ~ **ilik**, modernization; modernity; up-to-dateness.

assai (*mus.*) Very.
Asst. = ASİSTAN.
assubay Non-commissioned/junior officer; (*mil.*) warrant-officer; (*naut.*) petty-officer: (1. ~ **çavuş**, sergeant; 2. ~ **üsçavuş**, company quarter-master sergeant; 3. ~ **başçavuş**, company sergeant-major; 4. ~ **kıdemli başçavuş**, regimental sergeant-major). ~**lık**, rank/duty of a junior officer.
ast[1] *a.* Under; below; (*mil.*) junior. *n.* Subordinate.
ast. = ASTRONOMİ.
AST = ANKARA SANAT TİYATROSU.
astar (*tex.*) Lining; (paint) priming, undercoat; (*eng.*) casing; (*naut.*) protective patch on sails. ~ **boyası**, (*art.*) priming coat: ~ **kaplama**, (*carp.*) reinforcing sheets in plywood: ~**ı yüzünden pahalı**, accessories costing more than the main part; (*fig.*) unprofitable enterprise; game not worth the candle.
astar·lamak (-i) (*tex.*) Line; apply priming. ~**lı**, lined; (*fig.*) backed, supported. ~**lık**, material (suitable) for lining. ~**sız**, unlined; uncoated.
astasım (*phil.*) Episyllogism.
asta·tik (*phys.*) Astatic. ~**tin**, (*chem.*) astatine.
asteğmen(lik) (*mil.*) Second-lieutenant(cy); (*naut.*) midshipman(ship); (*aer.*) pilot officer('s rank).
asteni (*med.*) Asthenia. ~**k**, asthenic.
asterisk (*pub.*) Asterisk.
astım/astma (*med.*) Asthma. ~**lı**, asthmatic.
astırmak (-i, -e) *vc.* = ASMAK.
astigmat (*med.*) Astigmatic. ~**izm**, astigmatism.
astr. = ASTRONOMİ.
astragal (*bio.*) Astragalus.
astra·gan (*mod.*) Astrakhan fur. ~**kan**, (*geo.*) Astrakhan.
astro- *pref.* ~**fizi**ˡkᵍⁱ, astro-physics. ~**log**ᵘ, astrologer. ~**loji**, astrology. ~**nom**, astronomer. ~**nomi**, astronomy. ~**nomik**, astronomic(al); celestial; (*fig.*) astronomical (price, etc.). ~**not**ᵘ**(luk)**, astronaut(ics).
astropika(l) (*geo.*) Sub-tropic(al).
asude Tranquil; at rest. ~**lik**, tranquility, peace.
asuman (*lit.*) The heavens, sky. ~**i**, celestial; azure.
Asur (*his.*) Assyria. ~ +, *a.* Assyrian. ~**ca**, (*ling.*) Assyrian. ~**lu**, *n.* (*ethn.*) Assyrian.
asürans (*fin.*) Insurance.
Asya (*geo.*) Asia. ~ +, *a.* Asian; Asiatic. ~**lı**, *n.* (*ethn.*) Asian, Asiatic.
asyön (*geo.*) Intermediate compass point (NE, SE, SW, NW).
aş (*cul.*) Cooked food. ~ **damı**, kitchen: ~ **deliye kalıyor**, when wise men fall out fools profit: ~ **kabı**, (*mil.*) mess-tin: ~ **ocağı**, soup-kitchen, canteen: ~ **otu**, (*cul.*) herbs: ~ **pişti bayram geçti!**, back to business!: ~ **pişti kaşık üstüne dikildi!**, all is ready!: ~ **taşınca kepçeye paha olmaz**, in difficult times trifles assume importance: ~**ta tuzu bulunmak**, contribute however little to stg., 'the widow's mite'.
-aş *n. suf.* [64] = -DEŞ [OYNAŞ].
AŞ, Aş = ANONİM ŞİRKET.
aşağı *adv.* [198] Down; below. *a.* Lower; low, common, inferior (object). *n.* Lower part. ~ **almak**, overturn: ~ **atmak**, ignore, disregard: ~ **bitkiler**, (*bot.*) lower orders of plants: ~ **çeken kas**,

(*bio.*) depressor: ~ **çekişli**, (*eng.*) down-draught: ~ **düşmek**, (level/quality) become lower: ~ **görmek/ tutmak**, under-estimate; despise: ~ **görülen**, despicable: ~ **inhiraf**, (*aer.*) downwash: ~ **kalır yan/ yeri yok (-den)**, quite the equal of: ~ **kal(ma)mak (-den)**, (not) fall short of: ~ **kurtarmaz (-den)**, nothing less will do/pass: ~ **tazyik**, (*phys.*) low pressure: ~ **tutmak**, despise: ~ **tükürsem sakalım**, **yukarı tükürsem bıyığım**, between the Devil and the deep blue sea; on the horns of a dilemma: ~ **vurmak**, (*fin.*) reduce, knock down: ~ **yukarı**, roughly speaking, more or less, about, approximately: ~**da**, below; down(stairs): ~**daki**, the following, the undermentioned: ~**dan**, from below: ~**dan almak**, begin to sing small; return a soft answer: ~**sı**, the lower/following part; sequel: ~**ya**, down(wards).
aşağı·lama *vn.* Contempt. ~**lamak**, *vi.* come down; come lower; fall in esteem, be discredited; become cheap/common. ~**laşmak**, *vi.* become lower, etc. ~**latmak (-i)**, lower, degrade; treat as inferior; reduce. ~**lı**, ~ **yukarılı**, both upstairs and downstairs. ~**lık**, *a.* base; common; inferior; coarse; despicable, contemptible: *n.* baseness; lowness: ~ **adam**, coarse/primitive man: ~ **duygu/karmaşa/ kompleksi**, (*psy.*) inferiority complex. ~**sama**, contempt, derision. ~**samak (-i)**, treat lightly; deride; hold in contempt.
aşama (*mil.*) Rank; grade; phase, stage; gradation; (*fin.*) rate, limit. ~ ~, gradually: ~ **düşürümü**, (*adm.*) demotion: ~ **düzen/sırası**, (*adm.*) hierarchy: ~ **nizamı**, echelon: ~**sını düşürmek**, break an officer; demote; (*naut.*) disrate. ~**lı**, in echelon; by stages, gradually; (*sp.*) staggered (start).
aşar *pl.* (*math.*) Tenths; (*fin.*) tithes. ~**i**, *a.* (*obs.*) decimal.
aşçı (*cul.*) Cook. ~ **baltası**, chopper: ~ **çok olursa çorba bozulur/yanar**, too many cooks spoil the broth: ~ **dükkânı**, eating-house: ~ **kadın**, woman cook: ~ **yamağı**, under-cook; kitchen-maid. ~**başı**, head-cook, chef. ~**lık**, *n.* cooking, cookery, cuisine: *a.* culinary, cookery: ~ **etm.**, be/work as a cook.
aşerat[1] *pl.* (*obs.*) The tens (column).
aş·ermek (-i, -e) (*cul.*) (Pregnant woman) long for unusual foods. ~**evi**ⁿⁱ/ ~**hane**, cook-house; kitchen; restaurant; eating-house, soup-kitchen.
aşı (*agr.*) Graft; (*med.*) vaccination; inoculation. ~ **çeliği**, grafting shoot: ~ **iğnesi**, hypodermic needle: ~ **kâğıdı**, vaccination certificate: ~ **kalemi**, (*agr.*) cutting for grafting, scion: ~ **tutmak**, graft// inoculation take: ~ **vurmak**, graft, bud; inoculate.
aşı·boyalı Painted red. ~**boyası**ⁿⁱ, *n.* red ochre paint: *a.* brick-red. ~**cı**, (*agr.*) grafter; (*med.*) inoculator, vaccinator.
aşıˡkᵍⁱ (*bio.*) Knuckle-bone; (*arch.*) purlin. ~ **atılamaz kimse**, s.o. to be wary of: ~ **atmak/ oynamak**, *vi.* play knuckle-bones: (-le), compete/vie with: ~**ı cuk oturmak**, be lucky/successful. ~**kemiği**, (*bio.*) ankle-bone, astragalus.
âşıkˡkᵍⁱ *n.* Lover, admirer; wandering minstrel; dervish in ecstasy; (*col.*) dear! *a.* In love; enraptured, in ecstasy. ~ **gözü kör derler**, they say love is

blind: ~ **olm.** (-e), fall in love with: ~**a Bağdat sorulmaz**, nothing is too much for s.o. in love: ~**la aşık atılmaz**, don't argue with s.o. in love.

âşık·ane/~**ça** Amatory, amorous, loving. ~**lı**, in love; lover: ~**sı** (-**in**), amateur/fan/lover of stg. ~**lık**, being in love. ~**taş**, each of a pair of lovers; flirt, sweetheart. ~**taşlık**, love-affair, flirtation: ~ **etm.**, flirt, have a love-affair. ~**yolu**, (*carp.*) fretwork, meander.

aşı·lama *vn.* (*agr.*) Grafting; (*med.*) vaccination; inoculation; addition of cooling/warming water: *a.* grafted; cooled/warmed. ~**lamak** (-**i**, -**e**), (*agr.*) graft, bud; (*med.*) vaccinate, inoculate; pass on an illness; add cooling/warming water; (*fig.*) suggest, inspire. ~**lanmak**, *vp.* ~**latmak** (-**i**, -**e**), *vc.* ~**layım** = ~**LAMA**. ~**lı**, (*agr.*) grafted; (*med.*) vaccinated, inoculated.

aşım (*bio.*) Mating a male animal with the female; (*mus.*) disharmony (between two melodies).

aşın·dırgan/~**dırıcı** (*min.*) Abrasive; corrosive; (*geol.*) erosive. ~**dırma**, *vn.* abrasion; corrosion; erosion; (*fig.*) attrition: ~ **savaşı**, (*mil.*) war of attrition. ~**dırmak** (-**i**), abrade, wear out (by friction); corrode, eat away; erode. ~**ım**, (*geol.*) erosion. ~**ma**, *vn.* abrasion; corrosion; erosion; (*fin.*) depreciation, amortization: ~ **ve yıpranma**, wear and tear. ~**mak**, *vi.* be abraded/eroded; wear thin; be effaced; depreciate. ~**maz**, non-corrosive. ~**tı**, eroded place.

aşı'ır^{rı} (*rel.*) Reading of verses from the Koran.

aşıramento (*sl.*) Stealing. ~ **etm.**, steal. ~**cu**, thief.

aşırı *n.* Space beyond stg.; other side; interval; overseas. *a.* [199] Excessive, exaggerated; extreme, beyond bounds; extra-, hyper-; over-, super-. *adv.* Excessively, extremely; beyond, over-. ~ **akım**, (*el.*) overcurrent; (*pol.*) extremist trend: ~ **derecede**, excessively, 'to a fault': ~ **doygun**, (*phys.*) super-saturated: ~ **gitmek**, go beyond the bounds, exceed the limit: ~ **ısıtma**, superheating: ~ **ışıklı**, (*cin.*) overexposed: ~ **istek**, passion, greed: ~ **şişmanlık**, obesity: ~ **uç**, (*pol.*) extreme left/right wing: ~ **yeni**, ultra-modern.

aşırı·bellem (*psy.*) Very retentive memory; hypermnesia. ~**besi**, over-eating/-feeding; (*med.*) hypertrophy. ~**cılık**, extremism, excess. ~**doyma**, (*phys.*) super-saturation. ~**duyu**, excessive sensitivity; hyperesthesia. ~**ergime**, (*phys.*) superfusion; super-cooling. ~**lık**, excess; exaggeration; extremism; over-abundance.

aşır·ılmak *vp.* Be passed over; be stolen. ~**ma**, *vn.* passing over/beyond; theft; (*lit.*) plagiarism; (*arch.*) purlin; small bucket; (*sp.*) lob: *a.* conveyed over; smuggled; stolen: ~ **kayış**, (*eng.*) drivebelt. ~**macılık**, stealing; (*lit.*) piracy, plagiarism. ~**mak** (-**i**, -**den**), convey over a height; pass over; escape (danger); go beyond (the limit); smuggle; steal, pilfer; (*lit.*) plagiarize; abstract; get rid of s.o. ~**tı**, (*fin.*) defalcation, embezzlement. ~**tıcı**, embezzler. ~**tma**, *a.* passed over; indirect; stolen: *n.* saddlegirth; (*sp.*) lob: ~ (**topçu**) **ateşi**, (*mil.*) indirect fire. ~**tmak** (-**i**), *vc.*

aşı·sız Not (*agr.*) grafted//(*med.*) vaccinated/inoculated. ~**'t^{dı 1}**, point of (*agr.*) grafting//(*med.*)

vaccination; (*geo.*) mountain pass. ~**taşı^{nı}**, crude ochre.

aşıt^{ı 2} Footbridge; viaduct.

aşikâr Clear, evident; apparent; distinct, conspicuous. ~**e**, clearly; openly, publicly. ~**lık**, openness.

Aşil (*myth.*) Achilles. ~ **kirişi**, (*bio.*) Achilles tendon.

aşina *n.* Acquaintance. -~, *n. suf.*, expert in . . ., understanding . . .; [LİSANAŞİNA]. ~**lık**, acquaintance; intimacy; expert knowledge: ~ **göstermek**, be interested in s.o.: ~**ı olm.** (-**le**), know s.o. to speak to.

aşiretⁱ (*soc.*) Tribe (*esp.* a nomadic tribe).

aşk^ı Love; passion. ~ **etm.** (-**e**), strike s.o. sharply: ~ **macerası**, love affair: ~ **olmayınca meşk olmaz**, nothing is achieved without passion/enthusiasm: ~**OLSUN**: ~**a gelmek**, get excited/ecstatic.

aşkın Past; exceeding, over, beyond; excessive; furious, impetuous; (*phil.*) transcendent(al). ~**lık**, transcenden·ce/-talism.

aşkolsun *int.* Bravo!, well done!; (*of disappointment*) that's too bad of you!

aşlama(k) = AŞILAMA(K).

aşlık (*agr., cul.*) Provisions, foodstuffs; cereals; store of provisions. ~ **ambarı**, barn. ~**çı**, provision-merchant; storeman.

aş·ma (*carp.*) Overlap; (*geo.*) drift. ~**mak** (-**i**), pass over/beyond; (*live.*) (stallion) cover a mare; exceed (time): *vi.* pass the limit; exceed; override; be extravagant; overflow; overlap; outgrow; (*sl.*) run away.

aşna ~ **fişne**, (*sl.*) coquetry, flirting; secret friend(ship). ~**lık**, ~ **etm.**, greet, salute.

aşnı Ancient; archaic. ~**lama**, (*chem.*) ageing; (*cin., th.*) creating the appearance of age/neglect. ~**lık**, (*ling.*) archaism.

aşoz (*carp.*) Rabbet, rebate. ~**lu**, rabbeted.

aştırmak (-**i**, -**e**) *vc.* = AŞMAK; (*live.*) mate animals.

aşure Tenth day of Muharrem; (*cul.*) sweet dish (prepared for that day), Noah's pudding. ~ **ayı**, Muharrem. ~**lik**, *a.* used in making AŞURE.

aşüfte Coquette; prostitute. ~**lik**, coquetry.

aşyermek = AŞERMEK.

at^ı Horse; knight (chess). ~ +, *a.* Horse; equine: ~ **ahırı**, stable: ~ **anası** = ATLAR: ~ **BALIĞI**: ~ **başı beraber/bir**, on a level with, neck and neck with: ~ **başlığı**, bridle: ~ **binicisine göre eşinir**, people do what their leader says: ~ **binicisini bilir**, the horse knows his rider: ~ **bulunur eyer/meydan bulunmaz eyer/meydan bulunur** ~ **bulunmaz**, stg. you need is always sure to be lacking: ~ **cambazı**, circus-rider; rough-rider; horse-coper/-dealer: ~ **cambazhanesi**, circus: ~ **cambazlığı**, circus-riding; horse-dealing; horse-breaking: ~ **çalındıktan sonra ahırın kapısını kapamak**, close the stable door after the horse has bolted: ~ **çatlatmak**, ride a horse to death: ~ **çulu**, horse-cloth: ~ **derisi**, horse hide: ~ **dili**, (*bot.*) large butcher's broom: ~ **frengisi**, (*med.*) horse syphilis: ~ **gibi**, horse-like, horsey, big (woman): ~ **görünce aksar su görünce susar**, s.o. who wants whatever he sees: ~ **hırsızı gibi**, his appearance is against him: ~ **ile avratta uğur vardır**, a horse and a wife bring luck: ~ **izi it izine karışmak**, good and bad things get hopelessly mixed up: ~**KAFALI**: ~ **kasnısı**, (*bot*.) giant fennel: ~**KESTANESİ**: ~ **kılı**, horse-hair: ~ **koşmak**, harness (to a carriage): ~ **koşusu**, horse-race: ~ **kuyruğu**, horse's tail: ~**KUYRUĞU**: ~ **meydanı**, hippodrome: ~ **nalı**, horseshoe: ~ **nalı kadar**, (*iron*.) s.o. plastered with medals/jewels, etc.: ~ **nalı yengeç**, (*zoo*.) horseshoe crab: ~ **olur . . .**, = ~ BULUNUR: ~ **oynatmak**, ride skilfully; race horses; (*adm*.) have authority in a place; (*fig*.) have complete mastery of a subject: ~ **panayır//pazarı**, horse-fair//-market: ~ **sağrısı**, (*med*.) croup: ~ **sahibine göre eşer** = ~ BİNİCİSİNE: ~SİNEĞİ: ~SÜLÜĞÜ: ~ **sürmek**, drive/push a horse on: ~ **takımı**, harness, tack: ~ **tellalı**, horse-coper: ~ **tepmek**, (horse) kick; spur on a horse: ~ **topuğu**, (*bio*.) fetlock: ~ **uşağı**, groom: ~ **yarışı**, horse race: ~ **yemliği**, manger.

ata: ~ **arpa yiğide pilav**, to each his own: ~ **biner gibi**, astraddle, astride: ~ **binmeden ayaklarını sallamak**, count one's chickens before they are hatched: ~ **binmek**, mount/ride a horse: ~ **deveye değil ya!**, not so very expensive after all!: ~ **dona bakma binmiş cana bak!**: never mind his horse or his clothes just look at the rider: ~ **et ite ot vermek**, give the wrong thing to the wrong man: ~ **gem vurmak**, curb, rein in.

atı: ~ **alan Üsküdar'ı geçti**, the opportunity has been missed; it's too late already: ~ **dört nala kaldırmak**, put one's horse into a gallop.

atın: ~ **başı zapt olunmamak**, (horse) bolt with his rider: ~ **ölümü arpadan olsun**, don't deprive yourself for fear of the consequences; I shall go on with it whatever happens: ~**ı salmak**, let one's horse go at full speed.

at-: ~**la arpayı dövüştürmek**, try to set friends at loggerheads: ~**lar anası**, big masculine woman: ~**lar nallanırken kurbağalar ayak uzatmaz**, each man must know his place: ~**lar tepişir, arada eşekler ezilir**, the weak suffer when the mighty fall out: ~**tan inip eşeğe binmek**, come down in the world; lose 'face'/position.

At. = (*ch.s.*) ASTATİN.

-at *n. pl. suf.* [27] [HAŞARAT, GİDİŞAT].

a.t. = (*bio*.) ALTTAKIM.

ata Father; ancestor; elder; *pr.n.* Atatürk. ~**dan kalma**, traditional.

ata. = ATASÖZÜ.

ata·bey/~**bek** (*his*.) Prince's tutor. ~**cılık**, atavism. ~**lıç**[c1], atavistic, traditional. ~**erki(l)**, patriarch·y/ (-al).

ata[c1 2] (*gamb*.) Counter, chip.

atak[1] *a*. [223] Testy; irritable; reckless; bold, daring. ~**lık**, boldness, recklessness; impulse.

atak[1 2] *n*. (*sp., mil*.) Attack; (*mus*.) entry. ~**e**, ~ **etm.**, attack. ~**si**, (*med*.) ataxia.

atalet[i] Idleness; unemployment; (*phys*.) inertia. ~**e sürüklemek**, bring to a standstill; render useless.

atalık Fatherly behaviour; guardian, tutor.

ata·ma *vn*. (*adm*.) Appointment. ~**mak** (-i, -e), appoint. ~**nma**, *vn*. being appointed. ~**nmak** (-e), *vp*. be appointed.

ataman Cossack elected-chief, hetman.

atan (*sp*.) Server. ~ **ilerde**, advantage in/server.

ataraksiya (*phil*.) Ataraxy.

atar·ca (*ast*.) Pulsating. ~**damar**, (*bio*.) artery: ~ **yangısı**, (*med*.) arteritis. ~**kanal**. spermiduct. ~**-toplardamar** +, arterio-veinous.

atasözü[nü] (*lit*.) Proverb, adage, saying.

ataş (*eng., tex*.) Fastener. ~**e**, (*adm*.) attaché.

Atatürkçü *a., n*. Ataturkist, Kemalist. ~**lük**, Ataturkism, Kemalism.

ata·vik Atavistic. ~**vizm**, atavism.

at·baklası[n1] (*bot*.) Small kind of bean. ~**balığı**[n1], (*ich*.) European catfish, sheatfish, wels. ~**çağız**, little horse. ~**çı**, horse-breeder. ~**çılık**, horse-breeding/-racing/-showing.

ateh (*psy*.) Senility, dotage. ~ **getirmek**, become senile, reach one's second childhood.

ate·ist (*phil*.) Atheist. ~**izm**, atheism.

atelye Workshop; = ATÖLYE. ~ **resmi**, (*eng*.) detail drawing.

aterina (*ich*.) Sand-smelt.

ateş Fire; conflagration; heat; hearth; ardour, vehemence; (*med*.) fever, temperature; danger, disaster. ~**!**, (*mil*.) fire!: ~ **açmak**, open fire: ~ **almak**, catch fire; become anxious; (gun) fire: ~ **almamak**, misfire; fail: ~ **almaya mı geldin?**, you've only stayed a minute!: ~ **altında**, in danger, vulnerable; (*mil*.) under fire: ~ **baca/saçağı sarmak**, (fire) get out of control: ~BALIĞI: ~ **barajı**, (*mil*.) curtain fire: ~ **basmak**, feel hot (from shame/anger): ~ **bastırmak**, (fever) set in: ~ **başı**, fireside: ~ **boy/hattı**, (*mil*.) firing-line: ~BÖCEĞİ: ~ **çakmak**, strike fire: ~ **çıkmak**, (fire) break out: ~ **dikeni**, (*bot*.) firethorn, pyracanthus: ~ **düştüğü yeri yakar**, calamity only hurts those it actually strikes: ~ **düşürücü**, (*med*.) antipyretic: ~ **etm.**, discharge (a gun); shoot: ~ **gecesi**, bonfire celebration (eve of John the Baptist's feast, 24 June): ~ **geç(ir)mez**, fireproof: ~ **gemisi**, fireship: ~ **gibi**, very hot; skilful and hard-working: ~ **gibi yanmak**, have a very high temperature: ~ **gömleği**, (*med*.) erysipelas: ~ **idaresi**, (*mil*.) fire-control: ~ **kes!**, cease fire!: ~KES: ~ **kesmek**, cease fire/firing: ~ **kıtası**, (*mil*.) firing squad: ~ **kili**, (*ind*.) refractory clay: ~ **koymak**, set on fire: ~ **olmayan yerden duman çıkmaz**, there's no smoke without fire: ~ **olsa cirmi kadar yer yakar**, there's nothing to be feared from him: ~ **pahasına**, at an exorbitant price: ~ **parçası**, very lively, hardworking, skilful, naughty (child): ~ **porseleni**, (*dom*.) flame-proof pottery: ~ **püskürmek/saçmak**, spit fire; be furiously angry: ~ **saçağı sardı**, things are pretty desperate: ~ **sahası**, (*mil*.) field of fire: ~ **sayımı**, (*mil*.) count-down: ~ **tanzim kapağı**, (*eng*.) damper: ~ **toprağı**, fire-clay: ~ **tuğlası**, fire-brick: ~ **tutuşturmak/yakmak**, light a fire: ~ **vermek**, set on fire, burn: ~ **yutan**, (*th*.) fire-eater.

ateşe: ~ **atmak (kendini)**, sacrifice o.s.; knowingly take a great risk: ~ **dayanıklı**, fire-resistant: ~ **dayanıklı/dayanır**, fireproof: ~ **göstermek**, air/dry (clothes): ~ **tapan**, (*rel*.) fireworshipper: ~ **tutmak**, warm stg.; fire at: ~ **vermek**, set on fire; cause a panic; start a cold war: ~ **vurmak**, put on the fire to cook: ~ **vursan duman vermez**: s.o. very mean: ~ **yanmak**, suffer loss/misfortune.

ateşi: ~ **başına vurmak**, become very angry/nervous/excited: ~ **çıkmak/yükselmek**, (*med.*) (temperature) rise; become feverish: ~ **düşmek**, (temperature) drop: ~ **uyandırmak**, stir up a dying fire: ~ **ne yanmak**, suffer (through s.o. else).

ateş-: ~ **le barut bir arada olmaz**, two young lovers should not be left alone together: ~ **le oynamak**, play with fire, take risks: ~ **ler içinde**, (*med.*) with a very high temperature: ~ **ten gömlek**, a pitiable situation; a great ordeal.

ateş·balığı^{nı} (*zoo.*) Sardine. ~ **baz**, (*th.*) firework specialist; fire-swallower. ~ **böceği**^{ni}, (*ent.*) fire-fly; glow-worm: ~ **ni görse yangın sanır**, he always exaggerates (the worst). ~ **böcekleri**, (*ent.*) Lampyridae. ~ **çi**, (*eng.*) stoker, fireman. ~ **çiçeği**^{ni}, (*bot.*) scarlet sage, salvia. ~ **i**, fiery; fiery red. ~ **in**, hot; fiery. ~ **kayığı**^{nı}, boat for sardine-fishing. ~ **kes**, (*mil.*) cease-fire; armistice. ~ **leme**, *vn.* firing; (*eng.*) spark, ignition. ~ **lemek (-i)**, set fire (to), ignite; fire; stir up (trouble). ~ **lendirmek (-i)**, stir up, excite s.o. ~ **lenmek**, *vi.* catch fire; fly into a rage. ~ **letmek (-i, -e)**, *vc.* order to be burnt. ~ **leyici**, (*eng.*) igniter. ~ **li**, burning, fiery; ardent, passionate; temperamental; (*med.*) having a temperature: ~ **silahlar**, (*mil.*) fire-arms. ~ **lik**, *n.* hearth, fireplace: *a.* for burning. ~ **lilik**, passionateness, impulsiveness.· ~ **pare**, spark; (*fig.*) s.o. full of fire, a bright spark. ~ **perest**^{i}, (*rel.*) fire-worshipper, Zoroastrian. ~ **perestlik**, fire-worship. ~ **siz**, (*med.*) afebrile. ~ **yuvar**, (*geol.*) pyrosphere.

atf- = ATIF. ~ **en**, with reference to; considering; attributed to. ~ ^{l}**etmek**^{eder} **(-e)**, direct, incline; ascribe, attribute; impute. ~ **olunur**, attributable.

atgiller (*zoo.*) Horses; Equidae.

Atğm. = ASTEĞMEN.

atıcı Marksman, good shot; launcher; ejector; (*fig.*) braggart, boaster. ~ **lık**, marksmanship; (*fig.*) boasting, lying: ~ **bilgisi**, ballistics.

at^l**ıf**^{fı} Inclination; turning towards; favour; attributing, ascribing; joining two words/sentences together. ~ **edatı**, (*ling.*) coordinating conjunction.

atıfet^i Affection; sympathy, pity; benevolence.

atı^l**k**^{ğı} Small churn.

atıl Idle, lazy; inactive; (*chem.*) inert. ~ **kalmak**, be inactive; be abandoned/out of use. ~ **lık**, inaction; inertia.

atılgan Dashing, reckless, bold; enterprising, pushing. ~ **lık**, dash, pluck; enterprise.

atıl·ım/ ~ **ış** Rush forward, advance; development; attack; thrust; (*psy.*) dash. ~ **ımcı**, (*art.*) avant-gardist. ~ **mak (-e, -den)**, *vp.* = ATMAK; be thrown; be discharged/abandoned/thrown away; be discredited; (*adm.*) be dismissed/expelled; burst into (conversation); rush; hurt o.s. on stg.

atım (*mil.*) Discharge (gun); range (gun); charge (powder, shot); round; (*med.*) beat, pulsation; ejaculation. ~ **cı**, (*tex.*) cotton/wool carder/fluffer. ~ **lık**, charge. ~ **yolu**, (*bio.*) spermiduct.

atış (*mil.*) Act of firing (a gun); (*sp.*) service. ~ **+**, *a.* Ballistic: ~ **alan/meydan/yeri**, rifle/artillery range,

butts: ~ **hareketi**, (*phys.*) projectile motion: ~ **ilmi**, ballistics. ~ **ma**, *vn.* quarrel. ~ **mak (-le)**, *vi.* quarrel; bicker, have a tiff. ~ **tırmak (-i)**, bolt (food), gobble up; *vi.* begin to snow/rain.

ati *a.* Future; subsequent. *n.* Future; tomorrow. ~ **de**, in the future; (*pub.*) below, what follows.

atik$^{i\,1}$ Ancient, antique; (*arch.*) Attic.

ati^l**k**$^{ği\,2}$ Quick, alert, agile. ~ **tetik**, very agile. ~ **lik**, alertness; agility.

Atina (*geo.*) Athens. ~ **+**, *a.* Athenian. ~ **lı**, *n.* (*ethn.*) Athenian.

at·kafalı Stupid. ~ **kestanesi**^{ni}, (*bot.*) horse-chestnut. ~ **kestanesigiller**, Hippocastanaceae.

atkı (*tex.*) Weft; (*agr.*) hay-fork; (*mod.*) scarf, shawl; shoe-buckle; (*arch.*) lintel. ~ **ile sarılı**, wrapped in a shawl. ~ **lamak**, *vi.* weave.

atkuyruğu^{nu} (*bot.*) Marestail; (*mod.*) (hair) ponytail. ~ **giller**, (*bot.*) marestails.

atla·ma *vn.* Bound, jump, leap, spring; (*el.*) arcing; (*sp.*) diving; jumping; (*lit.*) skipping/omission (of a passage); (*ling.*) dropping (a letter/word): ~ **beygir/sehpası**, (*sp.*) vaulting horse: ~ **çizgisi**, (*sp.*) take-off line: ~ **havuzu**, jumping pit: ~ **ipi**, skipping-rope: ~ **kasa/tahtası**, (*sp.*) springboard: ~ **taşı**, stepping-stone: ~ **taşı yapmak**, make use of (s.o./stg. to progress). ~ **mak (-den)**, jump from, leap over/through: **(-e)**, jump on/into: **(-i)**, jump over; skip/omit stg.: (*pub.*) miss (an item of news); (*fig.*) narrowly escape (danger, etc.): **(-de)**, be deceived: *vi.* jump, leap, spring: **atladı gitti genç Osman!**, that job's finished!; the danger is over! ~ **mba**^{l}**ç**^{cı}, children's jumping game.

atlan·dırmak (-i) Mount s.o. on a horse; give s.o. a riding-horse. ~ **gı**^{l}**ç**^{cı}, stepping-stone. ~ **ılmak (-den)**, *imp. v.* one jump from. ~ **mak**^{1}, *vp.* be jumped; be omitted. ~ **mak**^{2}, *vi.* mount/obtain a horse.

Atlanti^l**k**^{ği} ~ /**Atlas**^{1} **Okyanusu** (*geo.*) Atlantic Ocean. ~ **demeci**, (*pol.*) Atlantic Charter: ~ **gemisi**, (*naut.*) trans-Atlantic liner: ~ **mersin balığı**, (*ich.*) common sturgeon.

atlas^2 (*geo.*) Atlas; (*pub.*) illustrated section (of book).

atlas^3 ~ **kemiği**, (*bio.*) atlas(-bone).

atlas^4 (*tex.*) Satin. ~ **dikişi**, satin stitch: ~ **perdahı**, (*min.*) satin finish. ~ **ağacı**^{nı}, (*bot.*) satinwood. ~ **çiçeği**^{ni}, (*bot.*) cactus. ~ **çiçeğigiller**, cacti. ~ **sediri**^{ni}, (*bot.*) Atlas cedar.

atlat·ılmak *vp.* Be overcome; be passed over. ~ **ma**, *vn.*: ~ **haber**, (*pub.*) scoop, exclusive. ~ **mak (-i, -e, -den)**, *vc.* = ATLAMAK; cause to jump; pass over; overcome (danger/illness); put off stg.; deceive/baffle s.o.; put off/get rid of s.o. (by empty promises).

atla·yıcı (*sp.*) Jumper. ~ **yış**, jump(ing).

atlet^i *n.* (*sp.*) Athlete, sportsman. *a.* Athletic; well-built. ~ **ayakkabısı**, track-shoe: ~ **fanilası**, sports-vest. ~ **ik**, athletic. ~ **izm**, athleticism; athletics.

atlı *n.* Horseman, rider, cavalier. *a.* Mounted on horseback; horse-drawn; having (so many) horses; equestrian. ~ **asker**, cavalryman: ~ **kovalamak**, hurry unnecessarily: ~ **polis**, mounted police.

~**karınca**, roundabout, merry-go-round, carouselle.

atm. = ATMOSFER.

atma[1] *vn.* = ATMAK. Throwing, etc. *a.* Ballistic. ~ **füzesi**, ballistic missile: ~**lar**, (*sp.*) throwing events. ~**lık**, (*fin.*) token; (*gamb.*) counter, chip.

atma[2] (*arch.*) Crosspiece; (*mod.*) shoe-strap.

atmaca (*orn.*) Sparrow-hawk; (boy's) catapult. ~ **kartalı**, (*orn.*) Bonelli's eagle: ~ **kuşu**, accipiter.

at¹mak[ar] (**-i, -e**) Throw; throw away; dump; eject; drop; put into; postpone; fire (a gun): shoot (an arrow, etc.); blow up (a bridge, etc.); aim at; give (a kick); step (a pace); cast (an imputation); tell (lies); drink off (a glass of beer, etc.); (*sp.*) serve. *vi.* Splinter, crack, split; (gun) go off; (magazine) blow up; (heart) beat; boast; invent stories; tell lies; (dawn) break; (colour) fade. **atıp savurmak**, bluster: **atıp tutmak**, rant, declaim; inveigh against; blame, criticise: **atma Recep, din kardeşiyiz!**, don't tell me such stories!: **atmaz boya**, (*tex.*) fast dye: **atmış**, (*sl.*) = ALTMIŞ: **atsan atılmaz, satsan satılmaz**, I don't know what to do about it; I'm completely puzzled/baffled: **attığı tırnağa benzemez** (**-in**), worthless (as compared with s.o.): **attığını vuruyor**, he's a dead shot, he never misses the mark; he always achieves his aim.

atmalık (*gamb.*) Chip, counter.

atmasyon (*sl.*) [172] Bragging, boast; bluff; lie. ~**cu**, braggart; boaster; liar. ~**culuk**, boasting; lying.

atmı¹k[ğı] (*bio.*) Sperm. ~ **kanalı**, spermiduct.

atmosfer (*phys.*) Atmosphere. ~+/~**ik**, atmospheric. ~ **basıncı**, atmospheric pressure. ~**lik**, atmosphere (unit).

atol[ü] (*geo.*) Atoll.

atom (*phys.*) *n.* Atom. ~+, *a.* Atom(ic); nuclear: ~ **ağırlığı**, atomic weight: ~ **ayırıcı**, atomic reactor: ~ **bilgisi**, nucleonics: ~ **bombası**, atom bomb: ~ **bölünme/parçalanması**, atom fission/splitting: ~ **çağı**, atomic age: ~ **çekirdeği**, atomic nucleus: ~ **enerji/gücü**, atomic energy: ~ **numara/sayısı**, atomic number: ~ **reaktörü**, nuclear/chain reactor: ~ **savaşı başlığı**, (*mil.*) atomic warhead: ~ **savaş(mas)ı**, nuclear warfare: ~ **silahları**, atomic weapons: ~**lara ayırmak**, (*phys.*) atomize.

atom-al/~ik *a.* Atomic: ~ **ağırlık**, atomic weight. ~**culuk**, (*phil.*) atomism. ~**izasyon**, (*chem.*) atomization. ~**lamak**, *vi.*, (*ed. sl.*) repeat a class. ~**lu**. atomic, nuclear. ~**luk**, atomicity. ~**sal**, atomic.

aton (*med.*) Atony. ~**al**, (*mus.*) atonal.

Atos ~ **dağı** (*geo.*) Mount Athos.

atölye (*art.*) Atelier, studio; (*ind.*) factory, workshop. ~ **resmi**, (*eng.*) working drawing.

atraksiyon (*th.*) Cabaret/entertainment number.

atriyum (*arch., bio.*) Atrium.

atrofi (*bio.*) Atrophy.

atropin (*chem.*) Atropine.

atsız[1] = ADSIZ.

at-sız[2] Horseless; on foot. ~**sineği**[ni], (*ent.*) forest-fly. ~**sülüğü**[nü], (*ent.*) horseleech.

attar = AKTAR.

attırmak (**-i, -e, -den**) *vc.* = ATMAK.

Au. = (*ch.s.*) ALTIN.

aut (*sp.*) Out (of play). ~ **olm.**, be out. ~**bord**, ~ **motor**, (*naut.*) outboard engine.

AÜ = ANKARA ÜNİVERSİTESİ; ATATÜRK ÜNİVERSİTESİ (Erzerum).

av The chase; hunting, shooting, fishing; game; prey; booty. ~ **aramak**, hunt for game; search for stg. (to lay hands upon): ~ **avlamak**, hunt: ~ **avlanmış tav tavlanmış**, it's all over and done with: ~ **bıçağı**, bowie(-knife): ~ **çantası**, game-bag: ~ **çiftesi**, double-barrelled shot-gun: ~ **et//hayvanı**, (*cul.//sp.*) game: ~ **havası**, (*met.*) good hunting weather; (*fig.*) thieves' opportunity: ~ **hukuku**, hunting/game laws: ~ **korucusu**, game-keeper: ~ **köpeği**, hunting-/sporting-dog, hound: ~ **kurşunu**, buckshot: ~ **kuşu**, game bird; wild fowl: ~ **takımı**, shooting/fishing tackle: ~ **tezkeresi**, hunting/gun licence: ~ **tüfeği**, shot-gun: ~ **uçaği**, (*aer.*) fighter plane: ~ **yasağı**, out-of-season: ~ **yatağı**, place frequented by game: ~**a çıkmak**, go out hunting; set up a line of beaters/skirmishers.

Av. = (*leg.*) AVUKAT.

-av *n. suf.* [236] = -EV [SINAV].

avadan-cı (*his.*) Class of Palace servants. ~**lık**, materials, supplies; (workman's) set of tools; gear, kit; (*sl.*) penis.

aval[i 1] *n.* (*fin.*) Endorsement, guarantee; guarantor. ~ **etm./vermek**, back a bill.

aval[2] *a.* (*sl.*) Half-witted, stupid. ~ ~, stupidly.

avam *pl.* = AMME. The public, the common people. ~ **dili**, (*ling.*) demotic, vernacular: ~ **kamarası**, (*adm.*) the House of Commons: ~ **tabaka/takımı**, (*soc.*) the lower classes. ~**ca**, vulgar. ~**firip**, (*pol.*) demagogue.

avana¹k[ğı] (*sl.*) Gullible; simpleton. ~**lık**, gullibility: ~ **etm.**, behave stupidly.

avan-gard[1] (*art., lit.*) Avant-garde. ~**proje**, (*arch.*) draft plan.

avans (*fin.*) Advance; credit. ~ **vermek**, make an advance; (*sl.*) make advances to s.o.

avanta (*sl.*) Advantage; (illicit) profit; fringe benefit. ~ **almak/etm.**, get stg. for nothing: ~**dan**, gratis, for nothing. ~**cı**, s.o. making illicit gains/wanting stg. for nothing; sponger. ~**cılık**, wanting stg. for nothing, sponging.

avan-taj (*fin.*) Benefit, profit; (*sp.*) advantage; handicap. ~**tür(iye)**, adventure(r).

avara *int.* (*naut.*) Cast off!; (*sl.*) shove off!; clear out! *a.* (*eng.*) Idle, not in gear. *n.* (*naut.*) Standing off, making for the open sea. ~ **çalışma**, (*eng.*) idling: ~ **gönderi**, (*naut.*) barge-pole: ~ **kasnak**, (*eng.*) idle pulley: ~ **kasnak işlemek**, idle: ~ **kolu**, disengaging lever: ~**lı kavrama**, loose coupling: ~**ya almak**, disengage, throw out of gear.

avare Vagabond; good-for-nothing; beatnik; drifter; out-of-work; gadabout; wild (child); (*geol.*) erratic. ~ **dolaşmak**, drift about: ~ **etm.**, interfere with s.o.'s work (by talking, etc.).

avare-leşmek *vi.* Drift idly about. ~**lik**, idleness, vagrancy.

avarız *pl.* = ARIZA. Obstacles, etc.; (*his.*) levy, extraordinary taxes.

avarya (*naut.*) Damage to goods in transit; average. ~ **muhammini**, average adjuster. ~**lı**, damaged.

avaz Loud voice. ~ ~/~ı çıktığı kadar bağırmak, shout at the top of one's voice.

avcı Hunter; (*mil.*) skirmisher. ~ **avında yolcu yolunda gerek**, each man to his business: ~ **kedi**, (*zoo.*) good mouser: ~ **köpeği**, hunting-dog, hound: ~ **kuş**, (*orn.*) bird of prey: ~ **kulübesi**, hunting-lodge: ~ **mangası**, (*mil.*) skirmishers: ~ **sinek**, (*ent.*) robber fly: ~ **tahtakurusu**, (*ent.*) assassin bug: ~ **uçağı**, (*aer.*) fighter plane.

avcı-lık Hunting; shooting; (*fig.*) courting (a woman): ~ **etm.**, hunt. ~**otu**^{nu}, (*bot.*) pheasant's eye.

avdet^i Return. ~ **etm.**, return, turn back. ~**çi**, homecomer; returned emigrant. ~**i** = DÖNME. ~**name**, (*adm.*) letters of recall.

avene *pl.* Helpers; accomplices.

-aver *a. suf.* Bringing/causing/possessing . . . [CENGAVER].

avgın (*arch.*) Drainage-hole; covered conduit; water-course; (*naut.*) scupper.

avi (*fin.*) Advice-note. ~**sto**, (*fin.*) on sight.

avize Chandelier; hanging-lamp. ~**ağacı**^{nı}, (*bot.*) yucca.

avizo (*naut.*) Dispatch-boat.

av·lak Good hunting-ground. ~**lama**, *vn.* hunting; the chase; (*sp.*) placing (volleyball). ~**lamak (-i)**, hunt; shoot; fish for; entice, allure: *vi.* go out hunting, etc. ~**lanmak**, *vp.* be hunted: be caught: *vi.* go out hunting. ~**lı**, with much game.

avlu (*arch.*) Courtyard; area.

avniye (*obs.*) Hooded raincoat.

avo·kat = AVUKAT. ~**set**^{i}, (*orn.*) avocet.

Avrasya (*geo.*) Eurasia. ~ +, *a.* Eurasian. ~**lı**, *n.* (*ethn.*) Eurasian.

avra^{ltdı} (*dial.*) Woman; wife. ~ **almak**, take a wife: ~ **boşamak**, divorce/repudiate a wife: ~ **pazarı**, (*his.*) female slave market; (*now*) market where women sell odds and ends.

avret^i (*bio.*) ~ **(yerleri)**, privy parts. ~**çe**, womanly.

Avrupa (*geo.*) Europe. ~ +, *a.* European: ~ **alabalığı**, (*ich.*) brown trout: ~ **bizonu**, (*zoo.*) 'aurochs'; European bison: ~ **Ekonomik Ortaklaşma/Topluluğu**, (*fin.*) European Economic Community: ~ **engereği**, (*zoo.*) asp viper: ~ **görmüş**, having acquired some culture/*savoir-vivre*: ~ **İktisadi İşbirliği Teşkilatı**, (*pol.*) Organization for European Economic Cooperation: ~ **İnsan Hakları Divan/Komisyonu**, (*leg.*) European Court/Commission for Human Rights: ~ **kekliği**, (*orn.*) grey partridge: ~ **kızılcığı**, (*bot.*) dogwood: ~ **Konsey/Meclisi**, (*pol.*) Council of Europe: ~ **Kömür ve Çelik Topluluğu**, (*ind.*) European Coal and Steel Community: ~ **Para Antlaşması**, (*fin.*) European Monetary Association: ~ **Tediyeler Birliği**, (*fin.*) European Payments Union: ~ **Toplulukları**, (*pol.*) European Communities: ~ **Türkiyesi**, (*geo.*) Turkey in Europe, Tk. Thrace: ~ **yabanatı**, (*zoo.*) tarpan: ~**dan gelme**, imported from Europe.

Avrupa·i In the European manner/style. ~**lı**, *n.* (Western) European. ~**lılaşmak**, *vi.* become Europeanized. ~**lılaştırmak (-i)**, Europeanize.

Avşar = AFŞAR.

avu^{l}ç^{cu} Palm of the hand; handful. ~ **açmak**, beg: ~ ~, by the handful, a handful each; (money) freely, lavishly, in large quantities: ~ **dolusu**, handfuls/heaps (of money): ~ **içi**, hollow of the hand; palm: ~ **içi kadar**, very tiny (place): ~**u kaşınıyor**, he has an itching palm, he will accept money: ~**una saymak**, pay in advance: ~**unu yalamak**, (*jok.*) go away empty-handed: ~**unu yala!**, you'll get nothing here!: ~**unun içi gibi bilmek**, know (a place) like the palm of one's hand: ~**unun içinde tutmak (-i)**, hold s.o. in the palm of one's hand/completely in one's power: ~**unun içine almak (-i)**, get complete control over s.o. ~**lamak (-i)**, grasp in the hand; take a handful of. ~**lanmak**, *vp.*

avukat^ı Advocate; lawyer, barrister, counsel, attorney; (*fig.*) fluent talker, s.o. loquacious. ~**lık**, advocacy; profession/work of a barrister, etc.; loquacity: ~ **ücret (tarifesi)**, (scale of) legal fees.

avun·^{l}ç^{cu} Consolation. ~**durmak (-i)**, console. ~**ma**, *vn.* being distracted/consoled. ~**mak**, *vi.* be distracted/consoled; distract o.s.; have one's mind taken off stg.; (animal) be in calf, etc. ~**tu**, distraction; consolation.

avur^{l}t^{du} Hollow inside the cheeks; (*fig.*) boasting. ~ **kesmek**, play the hero: ~ **satmak/** ~ **zavurt etm.**, give o.s. airs, assert o.s., bluster about: ~ **şişirmek**, puff out one's cheeks with conceit: ~ **ünsüzü**, (*ling.*) lateral consonant: ~ **zavurt**, bluster, self-assertion: ~**ları çökmek**, look very weak: ~**u una çökmüş/geçmiş**, with sunken cheeks. ~**lamak (-e)**, *vi.* boast, bluster. ~**lu**, puffed up; conceited; swaggering.

Avus. = AVUSTRALYA(LI); AVUSTURYA(LI).

Avustralya (*geo.*) Australia. ~ +, *a.* Australian: ~ **kara kuğu kuşu**, (*orn.*) black swan: ~ **yünü**, botany wool. ~**karatavuğu**^{nu}, (*orn.*) lyre bird. ~**lı**, *n.* (*ethn.*) Australian.

Avusturya (*geo.*) Austria. ~ +, *a.* Austrian. ~**lı**, *n.* (*ethn.*) Austrian.

av(u)t (*sp.*) = AUT.

avut·mak (-i) Console; delude; delay/distract s.o. with stg.; keep (a child) amused/occupied. ~**turmak (-i, -e)**, *vc.* ~**ulmak**, *vp.*

ay^1 *int.* (*of sudden pain/emotion*). Ah!; Oh!

ay^2 *n.* (*ast.*) Moon; (lunar) month; crescent; beautiful face. ~ +, *a.* Lunar; luni-; crescent-shaped: ~ **ağılı**, lunar halo: ~**BALIĞI**: ~ **balta**, (*mil.*) crescent-shaped battle-axe: ~ **başı**, first days of a month; = ~**BAŞI**: ~ **bilgisi**, selenology: ~**ÇİÇEĞİ**: ~ **dede**, (*child.*) man in the moon: ~ **dedeye misafir olm.**, sleep in the open: ~**DEMİR**: ~ **doğdu**, the new moon: ~ **doğuşu**, moonrise: ~ **francalası**, moon crescent; (*cul.*) *croissant*: ~ **gibi**, beautiful: ~ **gün takvim//yılı**, (*ast.*) luni-solar calendar//year: ~ **harmanlanmak**, the moon be surrounded by its halo: ~ **ışığı**, moonlight; brightness of the full moon: ~ **ışını**, moonbeam: ~ **karanlığı**, light from a cloud-covered moon: ~ **modülü**, (*aer.*) lunar module: ~ **ötesi**, translunar: ~ **parçası**, a beauty (girl/woman): ~ **takvimi**, (*ast.*) lunar calendar: ~ **tedirginliği**, (*ast.*) evection: ~ **tutulması**, (*ast.*)

lunar eclipse: ~ **yıldız**, star and crescent (on the Turkish flag): ~ **yılı**, (*ast.*) lunar year.

ay-: ~**da (beş)**, (five) a/per month: ~**da âlem/yılda bir**, very rarely, once in a blue moon: ~**ı gördüm yıldıza itibarım yok**, only the best is good enough for me: ~**ın dört çarşambası bir araya gelmiş**, all my troubles have come together with a rush: ~**ın evreleri**, (*ast.*) phases of the moon: ~**ın halkası**, (*ast.*) halo round the moon: ~**ın kaçı?**, what day of the month is it?: ~**ın kaçında...?**, on which day of the month...?: ~**ın on dördü**, the full moon: ~**ın on dördü gibi**, very beautiful (girl).
ay. = AYRICA. ~ **bk.** = AYRICA BAKINIZ.
-ay *n.*, *a. suf.* [226] = -EY [OLAY; YATAY].
aya[1] (*bio.*) Palm (of the hand); sole (of the foot).
aya[2] (*rel.*) Holy. ~ **İrini//Sofya**, St. Irene//Sophia.
aya[1]**k**[ğ1] *n.* (*bio.*) Foot; leg; step; (*math.*) foot (30 cms.); gait, pace, walking speed; stair; rung (of a ladder); pedal (of a machine); (*geo.*) outlet (of a lake); tributary (of a river); (*arch.*) pedestal, plinth; pier, column, pillar; abutment; base, support; (*lit.*, *col.*) rhyme. *a.* Standing; on foot. ~ **altı**, just under one's feet; in one's way: ~ALTI: ~ **altında kalmak**, be trodden underfoot: ~ **atmak (-e)**, visit for the first time; take a step: ~ **atmamak (-e)**, never visit a place: ~ ~ **üstüne atmak**, cross one's legs: ~ **bağı**, fetter; hobble; tether; (*fig.*) impediment, hindrance; tie, burden: ~ **bağını çözmek**, be divorced: ~ **bakımı**, (*med.*) pedicure: ~ **baskısı**, (*mot.*) pedal: ~ **basmak (-e)**, enter/set foot (in a place); put one's foot down, insist: ~ **basmamak**, never visit: ~BASTI: ~ **bileği**, (*bio.*) ankle(-bone), tarsus: ~ **bileziği**, (*mod.*) anklet: ~ **değiştirmek**, (*mil.*) get into step: ~ **değmemiş**, untrodden: ~ **diremek**, put one's foot down, insist: ~ **divanı**, (*adm.*) ad hoc/on-the-spot council meeting: ~ **freni**, (*mot.*) foot-brake: ~ **işi**, light work; errand: ~ **izi**, footprint: ~KABI: ~ **kavafı**, s.o. always seen about town: ~ **kemeri**, (*bio.*) arch of the foot: ~ **kirası**, fee/tip (for a messenger): ~ **kolu**, (*eng.*) foot-lever: ~ **makarası**, castor(-wheel): ~ **makinesi**, foot-operated machine: ~ **parmağı**, (*bio.*) toe: ~ **patırdısı**, the noise of footsteps; a mere threat; a false alarm: ~ **satıcısı**, hawker, peddlar, street-salesman: ~ **sesi**, footstep: ~ **sürmek**, do stg. slowly and unwillingly: ~ **sürtmek**, walk about: ~ **sürümek**, shuffle along; try to avoid doing stg.: ~ **tabanı**, (*bio.*) sole of the foot: ~ **tarağı**, (*bio.*) metatarsus: ~ **tedavisi**, (*med.*) out-patient treatment: ~ **teri**, (*med.*) athlete's foot; = ~TERİ: ~UCU: ~ **uydurmak (-e)**, fall into step with s.o.; fit in with stg.: ~ **uzatmak**, stride out: ~ÜSTÜ: ~ÜZERİ: ~ **yapmak (-e)**, (*sl.*) cheat, fool: ~ **yerden kesilmek**, find some means of transport (other than walking): ~ **zarı**, (*zoo.*) web(bing).

ayağa: ~ **düşmek**, (*fig.*) be cheapened: ~ **fırlamak**, stand up hurriedly: ~ **kaldırmak**, instigate, stir up, alarm (people); cause to rebel: ~ **kalkmak**, rise to one's feet, stand up; get excited/alarmed; rebel; (*med.*) (patient) get better, recover; stand (out of respect for s.o.): ~ **sarılmak**, clasp s.o.'s legs in entreaty.

ayağı: ~ **alışmak (-e)**, frequent (a place): ~ **birbirini dolaşmak**, be thrown into confusion: ~ **çelmek**, trip up: ~ **dolaşmak**, trip up; make a mistake: ~ **düşmek (-e)**, pass through (a place): ~ **düze basmak**, step on to level ground; reach safety; get out of difficulties: ~ **ile gelmek (kendi)**, come of one's own accord; be obtained without effort: ~ **kaymak**, slip: ~ **kesilmek**, be prevented from going: ~ **suya ermek/girmek**, understand the position/realize the truth too late; be disappointed: ~ **uğurlu**, s.o. who brings good luck: ~ **uğur·lu//-suz gelmek**, bring good//bad luck: ~ **uyuşmak**, one's foot go to sleep: ~ **üzengide**, about to set forth: ~ **vuruşu**, stamping: ~ **yerden kesilmek**, lose contact with the ground; ride (instead of walking); get out of one's depth: ~ **yere basmamak**, jump for joy, walk on air.

ayağına: ~ **bağ vurmak**, hinder s.o.: ~ **çabuk**, light-footed, agile: ~ **çağırmak**, call to one's side: ~ **çelme takmak**, trip s.o. up; hinder s.o.'s progress: ~ **dolanmak/dolaşmak**, be in the way; obstruct s.o., be hoist with one's own petard: ~ **düşmek/kapanmak/sarılmak**, implore s.o. for mercy: ~ **geçirmek**, put on stg. hurriedly: ~ **(kadar) gelmek**, be good enough/condescend to visit s.o.; (luck, success, etc.) come to s.o. (without his making any effort): ~ **gitmek**, visit s.o. personally: ~ **ip takmak**, try to discredit s.o.: ~ **kara su inmek**, get tired from standing too long: ~ **kira mı istiyorsun?**, why can't you take the trouble to come/go?: ~ **pabuç olamamak**, be unworthy of/beneath s.o.: ~ **sıcak su mu dökelim, soğuk su mu?**, an expression of joy (on seeing a rare visitor): ~ **sıkı**, a good walker ~ **yüz sürülecek bir adam**, a man worthy of the highest respect.

ayağında: ~ **donu yok, başına fesleğen ister/takar**, he spends on luxuries when he can't afford the necessities of life.

ayağını: ~ **alamamak**, be unable to move one's foot; **(-den)**, be unable to give up/refrain from stg. ~ **almak**, slander s.o.: ~ **altına almak**, draw up and sit on one leg: ~ **bağlamak (-in)**, hinder s.o.: ~ **çabuk tutmak**, hurry: ~ **çekmek (-den)**, stop visiting (a place): ~ **çıkarmak**, take off one's shoes: ~ **denk/tetik almak**, be alert/on one's guard; watch one's step: ~ **denk basmak**, act carefully; step warily: ~ **giymek**, put on one's shoes: ~ **kaydırmak**, make s.o. lose his job: ~ **kesmek (-den)**, cease to visit; **(-in)**, prevent s.o. from going: ~/~**n altın öpeyim**, I implore you: ~ **sürümek**, drag one's feet: ~ **tek atmak**, tread warily, be about to leave/die: ~ **yorganına göre uzatmak**, cut one's coat according to one's cloth; accommodate to circumstances.

ayağının: ~ **altına almak (-i)**, thrash s.o.; destroy stg.: ~ **altına karpuz kabuğu koymak**, intrigue against s.o., cause s.o.'s downfall: ~ **altında olm.** (a place) be at one's feet: ~ **bağını çözmek**, divorce (one's wife): ~ **bastığı yerde ot bitmez**, who ruins, destroys a place, who carries out a 'scorched earth' policy: ~ **pabucunu başına giymek**, get the better o s.o.: ~ **tozu ile**, as soon as s.o. comes; without delay: ~ **türabı olm.**, humiliate o.s. before s.o. **ayakla**, on foot, by walking: ~ **basmak**, tread; stamp.

ayaklar: ~ **altına almak**, disregard, trample upon: ~ **baş, başlar ayak oldu**, the social order has been turned upside down: ~ı **dolaşmak**, trip over: ~ı **geri geri gitmek (-e)**, go unwillingly, drag one's feet; draw back (in fear, etc.): ~ı **yere değmemek**, be very pleased: ~ım **buz kesildi**, my feet are like ice: ~ın **ucuna basarak**, on tiptoe: ~ına **dolaşmak (-in)**, be a handicap/hindrance to s.o.: ~ını **yerden kesmek**, avoid walking; (sp.) lift s.o. off the ground.

ayakta, on foot, standing; excited, worried: ~ **durmak**, remain standing: ~ **duramamak**, be ready to drop (from fatigue): ~ **kalmak**, find nowhere to sit down; remain standing, not collapse: ~ **tutmak (-i)**, keep s.o. standing; prevent s.o. falling (into a trap); ensure stg. continues; maintain: ~ **uyumak**, be excessively tired.

ayaktan, (live.) alive, on the hoof; (med.) ambulatory.

ayakaltı[n1] (bio.) Sole (of the foot); ground underfoot; much-frequented place. ~**nda**, on this very spot: ~**nda bırakmak**, allow s.o. to be crushed/destroyed: ~**nda dolaşmak**, get under people's feet, be in the way: ~**nda kalmak**, be crushed.

ayak·bastı[y1] ~ **parası**, toll/tribute levied on travellers/goods. ~**ça**[l**k**ğ1], steps, stairs; = ~ LIK. ~**çı**, servant for light outdoor jobs; errand-boy; s.o. employed for a particular job. ~**çın**, (tex.) loom treadle.

ayakkabı[y1] Footwear, boots, shoes, etc. ~ **bağı**, boot-/shoe-lace: ~ **boyacısı**, boot-black: ~ **boyası**, shoe-polish: ~ **çekeceği**, shoehorn: ~ **kalıbı**, shoe-tree: ~ **pençesi**, sole: ~ **tamircisi**, cobbler: ~ **vurmak**, (shoe) hurt the foot: ~**larını çevirmek**, hint to s.o. that it is time to leave.

ayakkabı·cı Shoemaker; shoe-seller; cobbler. ~**cılık**, shoemaking; shoe trade. ~**lık**, n. shoe-cupboard: a. suitable for shoe-making. ~**sız**, shoeless; barefoot.

ayak·lamak (-i) Trample on; measure out by pacing. ~**lanış/**~**lanma**, vn. (leg.) breach of the peace; (pol.) uprising, rebellion. ~**lanmak**, vi. (patient) be able to walk; (child) begin to walk; rise to one's feet (-e karşı), rise in rebellion/protest against stg. ~**lı**, having feet; on foot; longlegged (animal); movable, ambulatory: ~ **bardak**, (dom.) wineglass: ~ **canavar**, a perfect brute; (child.) bogy-man: ~ **kütüphane**, (fig.) a walking encyclopedia: ~ **lamba**, (el.) standard lamp. ~**lık**, stg. serving as a foot; stg. one foot in length; pedal; stilts. ~**sız**, footless, legless. ~**sızlar**, (zoo.) Apoda. ~**takımı**[n1], (soc.) the lower classes; the common people; the rabble: ~ **ağzı**, (ling.) slang. ~**taş**, companion, comrade; accomplice. ~**teri**[ni], doctor's fee (for a house-call); fee paid to s.o. (for working away from home); = ~ TERİ. ~**topu**[nu], football. ~**ucu**[nu], foot (of a bed, etc.); (ast.) nadir; (sp.) tiptoe: ~**nda/**~ **uçlarında**, (sp.) on the toes. ~**üstü/**

~**üzeri**, standing about, on foot; in haste; frequented (place): ~ **anlatılmaz**, it's a long story. ~**yolu**[nu], latrine, lavatory, water-closet: ~**na çıkmak/gitmek**, use the lavatory/toilet.

ayal[i] pl. = AİLE. Families; dependants. s. (col.) Wife, family.

ayalamak (-i) Gather/collect in the palm/hand.

ayan[1] a. Manifest, clear, evident. ~ **beyan**, very evident, clearly; in every detail: ~ **olm.**, be clear, be known.

ayan[2] n. pl. (soc.) Notables; chiefs; senators. s. (obs.) Village headman. ~ **azası**, senator: ~ **meclisi**, (adm.) Senate.

ayandon (met.) Storm (beginning on 28 January).

ayar Standard of fineness (gold/silver); carat; gauge; accuracy (scales, watch, etc.); alignment; setting; (aer.) trim; degree; grade; disposition, temper. ~ +, a. Regulating, adjusting; (aer.) trimming: ~ **bobini**, (rad.) tuning coil: ~ **bozukluğu**, out of true: ~ **bulmak**, assay; adjust: ~ **damgası**, (min.) hallmark; assay mark: ~ **etm.**, regulate; calibrate; adjust; compensate: ~ **kademesi**, (el.) tapping: ~ **valfı**, regulating valve: ~ **vidası**, set-screw: ~ı **bozuk**, out of order; not regulated: ~**ını bozmak**, debase stg.: ~**ını tayin etm.**, assay.

ayar·cı (obs.) Inspector of weights and measures. ~**lama**, vn. testing; adjustment; calibration. ~**lamak (-i)**, assay; test; adjust; regulate; calibrate; (aer.) trim; (ast.) collimate; (cin.) focus; (fin.) verify weights and stamp them. ~**lanır**, adjustable. ~**lanmak**, vp. ~**latmak (-i)**, vc. ~**layıcı**, regulator. ~**lı**, of standard fineness; regulated; adjusted; adjustable: ~ **bomba**, time-bomb: ~ **kanatlı**, adjustable-pitch (blade, etc.). ~**sız**, below standard; not adjusted; out of order; uncontrolled.

ayart·ı Corruption, perversion; enticement, seduction. ~**ıcı**, corrupting, perverting; enticing. ~**ıcılık**, action of corrupting, etc. ~**ılmak**, vp. be led astray/perverted, etc. ~**ma**, vn. deception; seduction. ~**mak (-i)**, lead astray, corrupt, pervert; entice; seduce.

Aya·sofya (arch.) St. Sophia. ~**stefanos**, (his.) San Stefano; (now) Yeşilköy.

ayaz n. Frost (at night); dry cold (daytime). a. (sl.) Dangerous, harmful; difficult. ~ **almak**, get nothing: ~ **kesmek**, suffer long exposure to the cold: ~ **Paşa kol geziyor**, (jok.) it's frightfully cold outside: ~ **vurmuş**, (bot.) frost-bitten: ~**a çekmek**, (weather) turn frosty: ~**a kalmak**, be too late for stg.: ~**da kalmak** = ~ LAMAK.

ayaz·ağa (sl.) Harsh/severe schoolmaster. ~**lamak**, vi. pass a frosty night in the open; be cold; (sl.) wait in vain. ~**lanmak**, vi. (night) become clear and cold; be exposed to the frost; catch a chill. ~**latmak (-i)**, expose to the frost/cold. ~**lık**, (arch.) balcony; terrace, verandah.

ayazma (rel.) Sacred spring (of Greeks).

-ayazmak aux. v. suf. [191] = YAZMAK.

ay·balığı[n1] (zoo.) Common ocean sun-fish. ~**başı**[n1], (bio.) menstruation: ~ +, a. menstrual: ~ **görmek**, menstruate: ~ **kesimi**, menopause: also = AY BAŞI. ~**ça**, (ast.) crescent moon. ~**çiçeği**[ni], (bot.) common sunflower. ~**demir**, cooper's adze.

aydın *a.* Bright; luminous; clear; educated, brilliant, enlightened. *n.* Light; intellectual.
aydın·cılık Intellectualism. ~**ger**, (*art.*) tracing paper. ~**lanma**, *vn.* illumination; clarification; enlightenment. ~**lanmak**, *vi.* become bright/luminous; become clear. ~**latıcı**, *a.* light-giving; clarifying, explanatory: ~ **ek**, (*phil.*) epexegesis. ~**latılmış**, enlightened, intellectual. ~**latma**, *vn.* illumination; (*th.*) lighting system; (*fig.*) clarification, enlightenment: ~ **ampulü**, (*el.*) floodlight: ~ **bombası**, (*mil.*) flare. ~**latmak** (**-i**), illuminate, light up; clarify, elucidate, enlighten. ~**lık**, *n.* illumination, light; daylight; clearness; (*arch.*) light-shaft, well; skylight: *a.* bright; clear. ~**lıkölçer**, (*cin.*) photometer, lightmeter.
aydırmak (**-i**) Restore to consciousness, bring to.
ayet[i] (*rel.*) Verse of the Koran; sign; miracle. ~**üllah**, a leader of the Shiite Muslims.
ayevi[ni] (*ast.*) Moon's halo.
aygın ~ **baygın**, languid; half-asleep.
aygır (*zoo.*) Stallion. ~ **deposu**, large stable; stud: ~ **gibi**, violent, unruly (man).
aygıt[1] Apparatus; equipment; instrument; contrivance, device; (*bio.*) system. ~**çı(lık)**, (*phil.*) instrumental·ist/(-ism).
ayı (*zoo.*) Bear; (*fig.*) boor; clumsy lout. ~ **dutu**, (*bot.*) blackberry: ~ **gibi**, huge: ~ **gülü**, (*bot.*) peony: ~KULAĞI: ~ **oynatıcısı** = ~CI: ~ **pavuryası**, (*zoo.*) spider crab: ~ PENÇESİ: ~ **postu**, bearskin: ~ **sarmısağı**, (*bot.*) ramsons: ~ **şakası**, rough practical joke: ~ **tabanı**, clumsy man: ~ÜZÜMÜ: ~ **yavrusu**, bear-cub: ~YONCASI: ~ **yürüyüşü**, walking on all fours: ~**nın kırk türküsü var, kırkı da ahlat üstüne**, (*pej.*) he's always harping on the same subject: ~**ya kaval çalmak**, try to make a stupid person understand: ~**yı vurmadan postunu satmak**, count one's chickens before they are hatched.
ayıb- = AYIP.
ayı·bacağı[nı] (*naut.*) Spinnaker. ~**balığı**[nı], (*zoo.*) seal. ~**boğan**, big uncouth man. ~**cı**, bear-leader; (*fig.*) coarse rough man. ~**giller**, (*zoo.*) bears, Ursidae. ~**gülü**[nü], (*bot.*) garden peony.
ayık In full possession of one's senses; wide awake; sober (after being drunk).
ayık·lama *vn.* Cleaning; selecting. ~**lamak** (**-i**), clear of refuse; (*cul.*) shell (peas, etc.); clean; clean off; pick and choose, sort out, select; (*lit.*) expurgate: **ayıkla şimdi pirincin taşını!**, here's a pretty mess! ~**lanma**, *vn.*; (*bio.*) natural selection. ~**lanmak**, *vp.* ~**latmak** (**-i, -e**), *vc.*
ayık·lık Soberness; recovery (from fainting, etc.); consciousness. ~**mak**, *vi.* recover consciousness; wake up; come to one's senses.
ayıkulağı[nı] (*bot.*) Primula auricula, bear's ear.
ayıl·mak *vi.* Recover (from drunkenness, etc.); come round (after fainting); realize the facts of stg.: ~ **bayılmak**, have hysterical fits of weeping: **ayılıp bayılmak** (**-e**), love s.o. excessively. ~**mış**, conscious. ~**tı**, sobering up. ~**tmak** (**-i**), *vc.* bring round.
ayın·ga/~**ka** (*sl.*) Chopped-up tobacco. ~**gacı**, tobacco smuggler.

ayı·p[bı] *n.* Shame; disgrace; something 'not done'; fault, defect. *a.* Shameful, disgraceful, unmannerly. ~ (**tır**)!, for shame!; you ought to be ashamed of yourself!: ~ **aramak**, seek an excuse to blame s.o.: ~ **davası**, (*leg.*) suit for material damages: ~ **değil**, there's no harm in it; it's quite permissible: ~ **etm./sallamak/yapmak**, behave disgracefully/ shamefully: ~ **olmasın (sormak)**, I hope you don't mind my (asking): ~ **yerler**, (*bio.*) privy parts: ~**ı var**, he has stg. to be ashamed of: ~**tır söylemesi**, it is shameful to tell; excuse the expression but . . . .
ayıpençesi[ni] (*bot.*) Acanthus, bear's breech.
ayıp·lama *vn.* Blame. ~**lamak** (**-i**), find fault with, censure, condemn. ~**lanacak**, *a.* discreditable. ~**lanmak**, *vp.* be censured/blamed. ~**lanmaz**, it's only human; it's excusable. ~**lı**, shameful; defective. ~**sız**, without defect; irreproachable; innocent.
ayır·a·lç[c1] (*chem.*) Reagent; (*lit.*) criterion. ~**an**, (*phys.*) dispersive; (*math.*) discriminating. ~**ga**, discord, strife. ~**ıcı**, *a.* separating; distinctive: *n.* separator; grader; insulator. ~**ım**, (act of) separation; insulation; grading; selection; allocation; discrimination: ~ **yapmak**, separate, distinguish. ~**ımcı**, (*fin.*) discriminatory. ~**ma**, *vn.* separation; distinction; division; selection; (*chem.*) cracking; (*eng.*) spreader, spacer: ~ **yetisi**, (*psy.*) discrimination. ~**ma·lç**[c1], characteristic; distinguishing mark; trade-mark. ~**mak** (**-i, -e, -den**), separate; divorce; sever; (*chem.*) crack; decompose; divide; insulate; disconnect, detach, disengage; (**. . . için**), allocate, assign, set apart, reserve, earmark/destine (for); choose; distinguish; discriminate; dissociate; disunite; draw apart: **ayırıp öldürmek**, (*live.*) cull (weak animals).
ayır·t[d1] Difference; distinction; characteristic. ~ **edici**, distinctive; characteristic: ~ **edilmek** (**-den**), be distinguished/separated: ~ **edilmez**, indistinguishable: ~ **etm.** (**-i, -den**), distinguish; differentiate/discriminate between.
ayırt·a·lç[c1] (*fin.*) Trade-mark. ~**edim**, (*med.*) identification. ~**ı**, slight difference, distinction; grade, nuance; (*th.*) shade of meaning. ~**ım**, separation; reservation: ~ **gücü**, (*psy.*) discrimination. ~**kan(lık)**, *a.*, (*n.*) characteristic: ~ **vermek**, characterize. ~**lamak** (**-i**), separate; distinguish; select. ~**mak** (**-e, -i, -den**), *vc.* = AYIRMAK. ~**man**, (*ed.*) invigilator.
ayı·üzümü[nü] (*bot.*) Bearberry; bilberry. ~**yoncası**[nı], (*bot.*) acanthus, bear's breech.
ayin (*rel.*) Rite; ceremony; service; music played during Mevlevi worship. ~**i Cem**, (*rel.*) a Bektashi ceremony; (*fig.*) a Bacchic feast, drinking bout: ~**i ruhani**, requiem, memorial service.
ayine (*obs.*) Mirror = AYNA. ~**si iştir kişinin lafına bakılmaz**, it's deeds that count not words.
aykırı *a.* [89] Crosswise, transverse, athwart; anomalous, discordant; incongruous; perverse, illnatured, eccentric; inclined, sloping; (**-e**) contrary (to), against, not in accordance with. ~ **düşmek**, not be suitable; be in the wrong direction: ~ **geçmek**, traverse: ~ **gitmek**, swerve from the straight path; go on in an extravagant manner: ~

katmanlaşma, (geol.) discordant stratification: ~ **olm.**, be the opposite: ~ **sofu(luk)**, fanatic(ism). **aykırı·kanı** (phil.) Paradox. ~**lamak**, vi. become oblique. ~**laşmak**, vi. become the opposite, etc. ~**lık**, anomaly; antithesis; irregularity; infringement; offence; eccentricity.

ayla (ast.) Halo.

ayla¹kᵍ¹ a. Unemployed; involuntarily idle; dilatory. n. Loafer, tramp. ~ **olm.**, have nothing to do. **aylak·ça** Dilatorily. ~**çı**, casual labourer: parttimer. ~**çılık**, casual labour. ~**lık**, idleness; unemployment: ~ **etm.**, remain idle, not work: ~ **yardımı**, (soc.) unemployment benefit.

aylandız (bot.) Tree of heaven, ailanthus.

aylanmak (vi.) Revolve; rotate; circulate; eddy.

aylı With a (crescent) moon shape (on it); moonlit.

aylı¹kᵍ¹ a. Monthly; a month old; lasting a month. n. (fin.) Monthly salary/instalment; (pub.) monthly magazine. ~ **bağlama**, monthly allowance: ~ **maaş**, salary: ~ **sayışımı**, payroll: ~**a geçmek**, start to have a salary; join the staff. **aylık·çı** (adm.) S.o. who receives a salary/lives only on his salary. ~**lı**, salaried; paid monthly: ~ **memur**, (adm.) established official.

ay·mak vi. Come to, recover consciousness; awaken, wake up. ~**maz**, careless, unwary. ~**mazlık**, carelessness, unwariness.

ayna n. Mirror, looking-glass; (naut.) telescope; oar-blade; smooth surface of an eddy, etc.; (carp.) panel; (th.) curtain (for shadow-plays); (eng.) chuck; (geol.) face; (bio.) knee-cap (of a horse). a. (sl.) Perfect, doing well. ~ **aksi**, mirror image: ~ **cam/kristalı**, mirror/plate glass: ~ **gibi**, sparkling: ~ **telgrafı**, heliograph: ~ **testere**, (carp.) circular saw: ~ **tırnağı**, wall-support (for a mirror); (eng.) chuck-jaw: ~**ya bakmak**, look at o.s. in the mirror.

ayna·cı Maker/seller of mirrors; (fig.) trickster, cheat. ~**lı**, having a mirror; metallized; reflecting; (phys.) catoptric; (sl.) fine, excellent: ~ **dolap**, (dom.) wardrobe with mirror. ~**lık**, (naut.) transom: ~ **tahtası**, back of the stern thwart. ~**sız**, a. without mirror; unpleasant, awkward: n. (sl.) policeman; (gamb.) backgammon piece. ~**taşı**ⁿ¹, (arch.) ornamental stone.

aynaz (th.) Director of folk games/plays.

aynen In exactly the same way; without change; textually; integrally; (payment) in kind.

aynı [76] a. Identical; the same; veritable; iso-. n. Copy, duplicate, facsimile. ~ **ağzı kullanmak**, say the same thing: ~ **bir kapıya çıkar**, it all leads to the same thing: ~ **cinsten**, homogeneous; (bio.) congener: ~ **çatı içinde**, under the same roof; intimate with one another; 'in the same boat': ~ **derecede/ile**, equally: ~ **fikirde olm. (-le)**, see eye to eye with: ~ **kökten**, (ling.) conjugate: ~ **ölçülü**, isometric: ~ **sınıftan**, (bio.) congener: ~ **soydan**, cognate: ~ **şekilde**, in the same way: ~ **şey**, it makes no difference: ~ **yer**, (pub.) ibid(em): ~ **yola çıkmak**, reach the same conclusion: ~ **zamanda**, at the same time, simultaneously; meanwhile.

aynı·lık Sameness; identity. ~**sefa**, (bot.) field marigold. ~**yla**, exactly the same.

ayni¹ a. Ocular.

ayni² a. In error = AYAN¹.

ayni³ a. Essential; (leg.) real (not personal); (fin.) in kind. ~**yat**¹, (fin.) goods in hand; inventory; (adm.) priced requisition form.

ayniyetⁱ Being identical; identity.

Aynoroz (geo.) Mount Athos.

aynştaynyum (chem.) Einsteinium.

ayol int. (Mostly women) You there!, say!, well!

ayra¹çᶜ¹ (Round) bracket ( ), parentheses. ~ **açmak**, interject, interpose: ~ **içinde**, in brackets. **ayral** Exceptional. ~**lık**, exception. ~**sız**, without exception.

ayran (cul.) Drink made with YOĞURT and water; buttermilk. ~ **ağızlı/delisi**, (sl.) simpleton: ~**ı kabarmak**, lose control of o.s. (from temper/drink); be infuriated: ~**ı yok içmeye, at/tahtırevanla gider sıçmaya**, (vulg.) s.o. penniless who wants to show off. ~**cı**, AYRAN-maker/seller. ~**lı**, quick-tempered, fiery.

ayrı Apart; separate(d); alone; isolated; other; distinct; exceptional; (math.) discrete. ~ ~, separately; one by one; by oneself: ~ **baş çekmek**, go one's own way; be a law to o.s.: ~ **çanakyapraklılar**, (bot.) dialysepalous plants: ~ **eksenli**, (eng.) eccentric: ~ **gayrı bilmemek/**~**sı gayrısı olmamak**, no need for ceremony; indiscriminately, without any exception, all alike: ~ **koymak**, put aside: ~**mız gayrımız yok**, we have everything in common; there is no difference between us; we don't stand upon ceremony: ~ **olarak**, under separate cover: ~ **seçi**, difference, disparity: ~ **seçi olm.**, separate one's possessions: ~ **seçi yapmak**, differentiate in the treatment of people, discriminate: ~ **seçi yok!**, without distinction!: ~ **taçyapraklılar**, (bot.) dialypetalous plants: ~ **tutmak**, behave differently.

ayrı·basım (pub.) Reprint/offprint (of an article). ~**ca**, separately; apart; in brackets; otherwise; in addition; concessionary. ~**calı**, exceptional. ~**calık**, (leg.) concession, privilege; (ed.) speciality. ~**calıklı**, (fin.) preferential; (leg.) privileged; licensee. ~**cinsten**, heterogeneous.

ayrı¹çᶜ¹ Bifurcation, parting, separation.

ayrık Separated; divorced; exceptional; disjunctive; (eyes) wide apart; (hair) parted; (geol.) clastic; split.

ayrık·laşma (geol.) Disintegration; (leg.) sequestration. ~**lı**, exceptional. ~**lık**, exception; (phil.) disjunction; (ast.) anomaly: ~ **daneli**, (geol.) granular. ~**otu**ⁿᵘ, (bot.) couch grass. ~**sı**, different; abnormal, eccentric; (ast.) anomalistic. ~**sılık**, abnormality; anomaly; eccentricity. ~**sın**, eccentric. ~**sız**, without exception; indiscriminate(ly); bar none.

ayrı·lanma vn. Separation, being apart. ~**lanmak**, vp. be separated. ~**laşma**, vn. differentiation. ~**laşmak**, vi. become different/separate. ~**lı**, separated. ~**lık**, separation; deviation; isolation; difference; exception; absence; (leg.) separation: ~ **acısı**, (psy.) mental pain, bitterness of heart:

~ **çeşmesi**, a well outside the village where good-byes are said: ~ **davası**, legal separation suit. ~ **lım**, (*med.*) detachment. ~ **lır**, separable, divisible. ~ **lış**/~ **lma**, *vn.*; separation, leaving, departure; (*med.*) ablation; (*phys.*) deviation, divergence; diffusion, dispersion; fission. ~ **lmak (-e)**, *vp.* = AYIRMAK; be allocated to; **(-den)**, be separated/parted; differ; be distinguished; divide; diverge; deviate; disagree, dissent; decompose; come apart/asunder; depart, leave, go away, drive off; (*pol.*) defect; (*chem.*) crack; split open; (*sp.*) break away; *vi.* be divorced. ~ **lmaz**, inseparable: ~ **parça**, integral part. ~ **lmazlık**, inherence. ~ **lmış**, set aside/apart; reserved (book, etc.); (*el.*) isolated; (*fin.*) allocated. ~ **ltı**, (*leg.*) article.

ayrım Distinction; difference; disparity; (*soc.*) apartheid; (*fin.*) allocation; (*pub.*) part, fascicule; (*cin.*) sequence.

ayrım·cı (*fin.*) Discriminatory, differential. ~ **lama**, (*cin.*) continuity. ~ **laşım**/~ **laşma**, *vn.* differentiation. ~ **laşmak**, *vi.* (*bio.*) become differentiated. ~ **lı**, different; separate; (*chem.*) differential. ~ **lılık**, difference. ~ **sal**, (*math.*) differential; analytical: ~ **damıtma**, (*chem.*) fractional distillation. ~ **samak**, *vi.* perceive, realize. ~ **sız**, similar, without distinction. ~ **sızlık**, similarity.

ayrıntı Detail, accessory; circumstance. ~ **çekimi**, (*cin.*) close-up: ~ **soyundan**, secondary: ~ **lar**, details, data. ~ **lı**, detailed; diffusive; circumstantial: ~ **çizim**, (*eng.*) working drawing.

ayrış·çılık Opposition. ~ **ık**, (*chem.*) decomposed; separated; different, various; variable; (*phys.*) differential; heterogeneous. ~ **ıklık**, being decomposed/differentiated. ~ **ım**/~ **ma**, *vn.* (*chem.*) decay; decomposition; (*geol.*) weathering; (*phys.*) dissociation. ~ **mak**, *vi.* (*chem.*) decompose. ~ **mış**, (*chem.*) decomposed; (*geol.*) weathered. ~ **tırma**, *vn.* decomposition. ~ **tırmak (-i)**, (*chem.*) decompose.

ayrıt[1] (*math.*) Edge, line of intersection.

ay·sar (*psy.*) S.o. whose disposition changes with the moon's phases; moonstruck. ~ **sız**, moonless.

ays·berk[i] (*geo.*) Iceberg. ~ **filt**[i], icefield.

ayşekadın (*bot.*, *cul.*) ~ **(fasulyesi)**, French green beans.

ay·ta (*th.*) Declamation; oratory: ~ **+**, oratorical. ~ **tışma**, learned discussion. ~ **tışmak (-i)**, discuss.

ayva (*bot.*) Quince. ~ **ağacı**, quince-tree: ~ **gibi**, very pale: ~ **göbekli**, with a sunken stomach: ~ **tatlısı**, (*cul.*) quince cheese: ~ **tüyü**, down (on fruit/cheeks): ~ **yı tutmak**, (*sl.*) get tipsy: ~ **yı yemek**, (*sl.*) get into difficulties. ~ **lık**, quince orchard.

ayvan Room with one side open; balcony, veranda.

ayvaz (*obs.*) Steward, major-domo; (*naut.*) sickbay attendant. ~ **kasap hep bir hesap**, it all comes to the same thing.

ayyar *n.* Cheat, rogue. *a.* Crafty, deceitful.

ayyaş Alcoholic; drunkard, toper. ~ **lık**, alcoholism; drunkenness.

Ayyuk[u] (*ast.*) Capella; (*fig.*) the highest point of the heavens. ~ **a çıkmak**, rise to the skies, boast; cry out.

az *a.* [75] Little; few; insignificant; low. *adv.* Little; seldom. ~ **(-den)**, [54] less . . . than: ~ ~, gradually, slowly: ~ **bir şey**, just a little: ~ **buçuk**, (*col.*) [81] somewhat; slight; just a little, a handful of: ~ **bulmak**, consider insufficient: ~ **bulunur**, rare: ~ **buz şey değil**, it's no small matter: ~ **çok**, in some degree, more or less; a certain number: ~ **daha**, all but, almost, well nigh: ~ **daha yüreğime iniyordu**, I nearly died of shame: ~ **değer biçmek**, undervalue, undercharge: ~ **değil**, appearances are deceptive: ~ **devirli**, (*eng.*) low-speed: ~ **dumanlı**, (*chem.*) almost smokeless: ~ **farkla**, close: ~ **GELİŞMİŞ**: ~ **gelmek**, be insufficient: ~ **görmek**, deem/find stg. too little: ~ **görülen**, unusual, rarely seen: ~ **günün adamı olmamak**, be a man of experience, not be born yesterday: ~ **işlek**, unproductive: ~ **kaldı/kalsın** . . ., almost: ~ **konuştu fakat öz konuştu**, he spoke little but to the point: ~ **olsun öz olsun**, it's quality not quantity that counts: ~ **sonra**, soon after: ~ **sözlü**, reticent: ~ **şekerli**, (*cul.*) coffee with little sugar: ~ **tamah çok ziyan getirir**, a little greed can bring great harm; don't spoil the ship for a ha'p'orth of tar: ~ **veren** . . . = ÇOK VEREN . . .: ~ **yapım**, (*ind.*) under-production: ~ **a çoğa bakmamak**, make do, make the best of it: ~ **a sormuşlar nereye çoğun yanına demiş**, to those that have shall be given: ~ **dan** ~, very few/little: ~ **ı çoğa saymak/tutmak**, take the will for the deed.

Az. (*obs.*) = (*ch.s.*) AZOT.

aza *pl.* = UZUV. (*bio.*) Limbs. *s.* (*adm.*) Member. ~ **kaydolunmak (-e)**, *vp.* be enrolled a member of.

azab- = AZAP[1, 2].

az·acık = AZICIK. ~ **ad-** = AZAT.

azade Free, not confined: **(-den)**, freed from; absolved.

Aza¹k[g1] (*geo.*) ~ **Denizi**, the Sea of Azov. ~ **eyiri**, (*bot.*) sweet flag.

azalık Membership. ~ **aidat/ücreti**, membership fees/dues.

azal·ma *vn.* Reduction; abatement. ~ **mak**, *vi.* diminish; decrease; be reduced; (*ast.*) decay; ebb; be lowered; drop away: **azalıp çoğalmak**, fluctuate, ebb and flow. ~ **tıcı**, *a.* extenuating: *n.* reducer; (*el.*, *th.*) dimmer(-switch). ~ **tma**, *vn.* cut-back, decrease, reduction; detraction; alleviation. ~ **tmak (-i)**, decrease, deplete, diminish, lessen, reduce; lower; attenuate; detract from; allay, alleviate, assuage (pain, etc.): **azaltan nedenler**, (*leg.*) extenuating circumstances.

azamet[i] Greatness; grandeur; pride, conceit; ostentation. ~ **satmak/taslamak**, give o.s. airs, be conceited: ~ **inden yanına varılmıyor**, he exudes conceit: ~ **ini görme!**, you never saw such conceit!. ~ **li**, magnificent, imposing, proud; ostentatious.

azami Greatest; ultimate; (*math.*) maximum; in the highest degree. ~ **fiyat**, (*fin.*) maximum price; ceiling: ~ **hızla**, with all speed: ~ **irtifa**, (*aer.*) ceiling: ~ **olarak**, at most; to the utmost: ~ **uçuş ağırlığı**, (*aer.*) maximum all-up weight: ~ **yüklü ağırlığı**, (*mot.*) maximum loaded weight.

aza¹p[b1 1] *n.* Farm-labourer; bachelor; (*his.*) marine.

aza'p[b1 2] *n.* Pain; torment, torture; great trouble, distress. ~ **çekmek,** suffer, be in difficulties; suffer torment (in hell): ~ **vermek,** cause pain/suffering/annoyance.

azar[1] ~ ~, [194] little by little, gradually: ~ ~ **dağıtmak,** dole out.

azar[2] Reprimand; reproach; scolding. ~ **işitmek,** be scolded. ~ **lama,** *vn.* reprimand; scolding. ~ **lamak (-i),** reprimand; reproach; admonish, chide, scold. ~ **lanmak,** *vp.* be scolded, etc.; be on the carpet/mat. ~ **latmak (-i, -e),** *vc.*

aza'lt[d1] *a.* Free; freeborn. *n.* Liberation; (*ed.*) dismissal from school; the giving of a holiday; (*leg.*) manumission. ~ **buzat cennette bizi gözet,** we set you free so look after us in Paradise (*said when freeing a captured bird*): ~ **etm.** = ~ LAMAK.

azat·lamak (-i) Set free, emancipate; let (children) out of school; (*leg.*) manumit. ~ **lı,** set at liberty; (*leg.*) manumitted, freed man. ~ **lık,** *n.* emancipation, freedom, liberty; *a.* (slave) about to be freed. ~ **sız,** that cannot be freed.

az·ca Rather few/little. ~ **cık** = AZICIK.

azdır·ılmak *vp.* Be led astray; be spoilt. ~ **mak (i),** lead astray; spoil (a child); rouse, excite; allow a small evil to become great.

az·dik[i] (*naut.*) Asdic. ~ **elya,** (*bot.*) azalea. ~ **eotrop,** (*chem.*) azeotrope.

Azer·baycan (*geo.*) Azerbaijan. ~ **baycanlı,** *n.* (*ethn.*) Azerbaijani. ~ **i,** *n.* (*ethn.*) Azerbaijani: ~ +, *a.* belonging to Azerbaijan. ~ **ice,** (*ling.*) Azerbaijani, Azeri.

azgelişmiş (*soc.*) Backward; (*adm., fin.*) underdeveloped. ~ **lik,** backwardness; underdevelopment.

azgın Furious; mad; unbridled; desperate; extreme, excessive; rebellious; astray; (river) in flood.

azgın·laşmak *vi.* Become furious, etc.; have excessive sexual desires; (animal) be on heat, rut. ~ **lık,** excessiveness; wildness; depravity.

azı/ ~ **dişi**[ni] (*bio.*) Molar tooth; tusk.

azıcık Very little/few; a little/few. ~ **aşım kavgasız başım,** not rich but carefree.

azı'k[ğ1] Food; provisions; fodder. ~ **çı,** forager; (*obs.*) sutler. ~ **lanmak,** *vi.* obtain provisions; eat. ~ **lı,** having food; well off; charitable. ~ **lık,** provisions; food receptacle.

azılı Having molar teeth/tusks; ferocious, savage; dangerous, violent, unbridled; (*med.*) pernicious. ~ **hırsız,** notorious thief: ~ **köpek,** wild dog: ~ **müfrit,** (*pol.*) ultraradical.

azımsamak (-i) Think stg. inadequate; disdain stg.

azın (*bio.*) Minimum. ~ **lık,** (*adm.*) minority: ~ **oy,** minority vote: ~ **lar,** (*soc.*) the non-Muslim minorities in Turkey: ~ **ta kalmak,** (*adm., soc.*) be in the minority.

azış Violence. ~ **ık,** violent, oppressive. ~ **mak,** *vi.* become aggravated. ~ **tırmak (-i),** aggravate.

azıt·mak *vi.* Grow excessively; overflow; rebel; go astray; go too far; become unreasonable; become insolvent: (-i), *vt.* let get out of hand; aggravate. ~ **tırmak (-i),** *vc.* = AZMAK[2].

az'il[li] (*adm.*) Dismissal; removal (from office).

az'im[mi] Resolution, determination; firm intention. ~ **li,** resolute, determined, dogged: ~ **tavır,** an air of determination.

azimet[i] Departure; setting out on a journey. ~ **etm.,** depart.

azimut (*ast.*) Azimuth.

aziz *a.* Dear; precious; rare; highly prized; mighty; glorious; saintly. *n.* Saint. ~ **tutmak,** cherish: ~ **im!,** my dear fellow! ~ **lik,** preciousness, etc.; saintliness; practical joke, mischief-making: ~ **etm.,** play practical jokes; make mischief.

azl- = AZİL. ~ **edilmek/** ~ **olunmak,** *vp.* be dismissed; be retired. ~ **'etmek**[eder] (-i), (*adm.*) dismiss (from office); depose.

azlık Scarcity; paucity; (*adm.*) minority; (*med.*) deficiency. ~ **çokluk,** (*ling.*) quantity.

azma *n.* Hybrid; monstrosity: *vn.* = AZMAK[2]; exacerbation.

azma'k[ğ1 1] *n.* River in spate; overflow (from a dam); marshy hollow; drainage canal.

azmak[2] *vi.* Go astray; become furious/mad/unmanageable; become depraved; (animal) be on heat, rut; (river) be in flood; (*bio.*) be a hybrid. **azmış,** enraged; excited; furious; (animal) on heat.

azman *a.* Monstrous, enormous; hybrid. *n.* (*arch.*) Beam, baulk of timber.

azm- = AZİM. ~ **'etmek**[eder] (-e), resolve upon, decide, determine; intend; be bent on. ~ **ettirmek (-i, -e),** *vc.*

aznavur Wild brigand. ~ **gibi,** awe-inspiring, frightening.

aznif A kind of dominoes (game).

azoi'k[ği] (*geol.*) Without fossils; azoic.

azot[u] (*chem.*) Azote, nitrogen. ~ **un saptanması,** nitrogen fixation. ~ **lama,** *vn.* nitrogenization. ~ **lamak (-i),** nitrogenize. ~ **lu,** nitrogenous, nitrous. ~ **ometre,** nitrometer.

Azrail (*rel.*) The archangel Azrael; the Angel of Death. ~ **in elinden kurtulmak,** be saved from death.

azrak Rare, unusual. ~ **eleman,** (*chem.*) trace element: ~ **toprak,** (*chem.*) rare earth.

B

B, b [be] Second Tk. letter, B; second (in a class/ category); (*mus.*) B, te. ~ **vitamini,** (*bio.*) vitamin B.
B, b. = (*ling.*) BAĞLAÇ; BAKINIZ; (*pub.*) BASKI; (*mus.*) BASSO; BATI; BAY; (*ling.*) BİLEŞİK; (*mil.*) BİRLİK; (*ch.s.*) BOR; (*bio.*) BÖLÜM; (*British*); BÜYÜK.
-b- *Replaces* **p** *before a vowel suffix* [BAP + I = BABI].
Ba. = (*ch.s.*) BARYUM; BATI.
bab- = BAP.
baba Father; forefather; venerable man; head of a religious order; (*arch.*) knob; newel-post; king-post; (*naut.*) bollard, bitts. ~ +, *a.* Paternal; fatherly: ~ **adam,** elderly/honest/mature man: ~ **bucağı,** inherited property: ~ **değil trabzan** ~ **sı,** a father without authority: ~ **dostu,** an old friend of the family: ~ **ev/ocak/yurdu,** the family house; home: ~ **hakkı,** a father's due: ~ **hindi,** (*orn.*) turkey-cock: ~ **malı,** patrimony, inheritance: ~ **olm.,** be(come) a father; beget: ~ **yurdu,** paternal home: ~ **dan** ~ **ya,** antecedents, ancestors: ~ **dan kalma,** *n.* inheritance; *a.* inherited: ~ **dan kalmak,** be inherited: ~ **dan oğula,** from father to son: ~ **ları tutmak/üstünde olm.,** (*psy.*) become angry; (Negroes) have a fit, run amok: ~ **larımı ayağa kaldırma!,** don't infuriate me!: ~ **larımız,** our forefathers/predecessors: ~ **m,** *informal address* (*for a man*): ~ **m da bilir/olur/yapar,** that's easy; anyone knows/can do that: ~ **na rahmet!,** many thanks!: ~ **na yuttur,** (*mod. sl.*) falsies: ~ **nın canına değsin,** (*expresses thanks for an action*): ~ **sına çekiyor,** he takes after his father: ~ **sına rahmet okumak,** think well of s.o.: ~ **sının hayrına (değil ya),** (not) 'just for love', (not) in a disinterested manner: ~ **sının oğlu,** the spit and image of his father: ~ **sının yüzü suyu hürmetine,** out of respect for/thanks to his father.
baba·anne Paternal grandmother. ~ **ca,** fatherly; in a fatherly manner: ~ **konuşmak,** talk like a Dutch uncle. ~ **can,** kindly, good-natured, easy-going. ~ **canlaşmak,** *vi.* behave kindly. ~ **canlı,** kindness, good nature, pleasantness. ~ **cığım,** daddy. ~ **cığımcılık,** (*sl.*) mugging. ~ **ᶦçᶜ¹,** *n.* (*orn.*) big (turkey) cock: *a.* swaggering. ~ **çko,** (*sl.*) stout; swaggering. ~ **fingo,** (*naut.*) top-gallant (sail/yard). ~ **köş,** (*zoo.*) slow-worm. ~ **lanmak,** *vi.* become angry. ~ **lı,** having a father; (*psy.*) running amok, having nervous fits; bad-tempered. ~ **lık,** *n.* paternity; fatherly affection; adoptive father; guardian; simple old man: *a.* good and sincere; simple, ingenuous: ~ **davası,** (*leg.*) affiliation suit: ~ **fırın has işler!,** he lives well off his father: ~ **ını ispat,** affiliation. ~ **sız,** orphaned. ~ **tatlısıⁿ¹,** (*cul.*) Tk. savarin; a leavened pastry. ~ **torik,** (*vulg.*) penis. ~ **yani,** fatherly; unpretentious, easy-going; shabby. ~ **yiğiᶦtᵈ¹,** *n.* full-grown strong young man;

'stout fellow': *a.* brave, virile. ~ **yiğitlik,** bravery, virility.
Babıâli (*his.*) The Sublime Porte; the Ottoman Government; (*now*) 'Fleet Street'. ~ **efendisi gibi konuşmak,** speak very loftily.
Babil (*geo.*) Babylon; Babel. ~ +, *a.* Babylonian. ~ **li,** *n.* Babylonian. ~ **istan/** ~ **onya,** Babylonia.
babu(i)n (*zoo.*) Baboon.
BAC = BİRLEŞİK ARAP CUMHURİYETİ.
baca Chimney, flue; (*naut.*) funnel; skylight; shaft; (sewer) manhole. ~ **başı,** stone mantelpiece: ~ **başlık/fırıldağı,** (chimney) cowl: ~ **deliği,** flue: ~ **kara sağanı,** (*orn.*) chimney swift: ~ **kırlangıcı,** (*orn.*) swallow: ~ **kulağı,** shelf at the side of the fireplace: ~ **külahı,** chimney-pot: ~ **tomruğu,** chimney-stack: ~ **sı eğri olmuş . . .,** no matter as long as . . .: ~ **sı tütmek,** (family) live well: ~ **sı tütmez,** (family) in poor circumstances, destitute, scattered.
bacaᶦkᵍ¹ Leg; thigh; (*gamb.*) knave. ~ ~ **üstüne atarak (oturmak),** (sit) cross-legged: ~ **gösterisi,** (*th.*) leg-show: ~ **kadar,** knee high, small: ~ **kalemi,** (*bio.*) fibula.
bacak·lı With legs; having . . . legs; tall, long-legged: ~ **yazı,** bold/legible writing. ~ **sız,** legless; short-legged, squat; precocious (child).
bacanaᶦkᵍ¹ Wife's sister's husband, brother-in-law.
bacı Elder sister; wife; elderly (Negro) female servant; (*obs.*) wife of the head of a religious order.
baç¹ (*his.*) Toll; tribute; tax; customs-duty.
badana Whitewash; distemper. ~ **etm./** ~ **vurmak** = ~ LAMAK. ~ **cı,** whitewasher. ~ **lamak (-i),** whitewash; distemper. ~ **lanmak,** *vp.* ~ **lı,** white-washed; distempered; (*fig.*) too much made-up (woman).
badas Grain mixed with earth (from the threshing floor).
badaş = BAĞDAŞ.
badaᶦtᵈ¹ (*bot.*) Jerusalem artichoke; (?) white truffle.
bade¹ *n.* Wine; alcoholic drink; wine-glass.
bade² *prep.* After . . . .. ~ **harabül Basra,** after that it's too late; the damage is already done. ~ **hu,** after that, then.
badem (*bot.*) Almond. *a.* Almond-shaped. ~ **ağacı,** almond tree: ~ **ezmesi,** (*cul.*) almond-paste, marzipan: ~ **gibi,** fresh and crisp (for a salad): ~ **gözlü,** almond-eyed: ~ **helvası,** (*cul.*) almond HELVA: ~ **içi,** (*bot.*) almond kernel: ~ **kurabiyesi,** (*cul.*) macaroon: ~ **kürk,** (*mod.*) fur (made from legs of fox-skin): ~ **parmak,** thumb: ~ **şekeri,** (*cul.*) sugar-almond; (*sl.*) bullet: ~ **tırnak,** long almond-shaped finger-nail.
badema (*obs.*) From now on; in this way.

badem·ci'k^{ği} (*bio.*) Tonsil: ~ **iltihabı**, (*med.*) tonsilitis: ~ **leri almak/çıkarmak**, remove s.o.'s tonsils. ~ **li**, (*cul.*) with/containing almonds. ~ **lik**, (*agr.*) almond orchard. ~ **si**, almond-shaped, amygdaloid. ~ **yağı**^{nı}, (*cul.*) almond oil.

baderna (*naut.*) Serving, parcelling (of a rope).

badı'ç^{cı} (*bot.*) Pod (of beans, peas, etc.).

badi (*orn.*) Duck. ~ ~ **yürümek/ ~ klemek**, waddle. ~ **k**, *n.* duck(ling): *a.* (*fig.*) short-legged; small.

badire Unexpected calamity; difficult situation.

badiye Desert; wilderness.

badya Broad and shallow wooden/earthen bowl; tub.

BA·E Bİrleşİk Arap Emİrlİklerİ. ~ **F** = Batı Almanya Federasyonu.

Baf *pr. n.* (*geo.*) Paphos (Cyprus).

bagaj Baggage, luggage. ~ **vagonu**, (*rly.*) luggage-van: ~ **(yeri)**, (*mot.*) boot; (*rly.*) luggage-rack.

bağ¹ *n.* Bond, brace; cord, tie; fastener; bandage; bunch; bundle; (*fig.*) impediment, restraint; relationship; link, connection; (*bio.*) tendon; ligament; (*bio.*) desmo-; (*chem.*) bond; (*ling.*) copula; (*naut.*) knot. ~ **dokusu**, (*bio.*) connective tissue.

bağ² *n.* Vineyard; orchard; garden. ~ **bahçe sahibi**, a man of property: ~ **bozmak**, harvest the last grapes: ~ **budamak**, prune a vineyard: ~ **dua değil çapa ister!**, hard work is needed—not prayers!: ~ **kuduzu**, (*ent.*) grape phylloxera: ~ **kütüğü**, (*bot.*) vine-stock: ~ **mildiyusu**, (*myc.*) vine downy mildew: ~ **salyangozu**, (*zoo.*) Roman snail: ~ **yaprağı**, (*bot.*) large plantain.

bağ. = (*ling.*) BAĞLAÇ.

bağa (*zoo.*) Turtle-shell; tortoise-shell; (*med.*) tumour. ~ **gözlük**, horn-rimmed spectacles.

bağan Still-born child/animal; skin of a still-born lamb.

bağ·boğan (*bot.*) Common dodder. ~ **bozumu**^{nu}, (*agr.*) harvesting of the grapes; the vintage; autumn: ~ **fırtınası**, (*met.*) autumnal storm. ~ **cı**, vine-grower: ~ **bıçağı**, pruning-knife. ~ **cılık**, vini-/viti·culture.

bağcı'k^{ğı} Strap, tape.

bağdadi¹ *n.* (*arch.*) Lath and plaster work; half-timbered.

Bağdadi² *n.* Native of Baghdad.

bağda·lamak (-i) Trip s.o. ~ **mak (-i)**, intertwine, tie together; put s.o. in an impasse.

bağdaş Sitting cross-legged (in the Or. fashion). ~ **kurmak**, sit cross-legged.

bağdaş·ık In harmony, coherent; homogeneous. ~ **ıklık/ ~ ım**, harmony, coherence; homogeneity. ~ **ma**, blending together; correlation; getting on well together. ~ **mak (-le)**, blend/fit together; harmonize; reach an agreement; be reconciled; get on well together; choose a partner (children's games). ~ **maz**, incoherent. ~ **mazlık**, disharmony, incompatibility, discord; incoherency; misunderstanding. ~ **tırıcı**, bringing harmony. ~ **tırmak (-i)**, ensure/produce harmony; correlate; reconcile.

Bağda'^{dı}(*geo.*)Baghdad. ~ **çıbanı**,(*med.*)Baghdad boil, Aleppo button: ~ **harap oldu**, I'm starving: ~ **ı tamir etm.**, (*jok.*) fill one's stomach, eat well.

bağ·değer (*chem.*) Valency. ~ **dokusu**^{nu} (*bio.*) connective tissue, conjunctiva: ~ **iltihabı**, (*med.*) conjunctivitis. ~ **fiil**, (*ling.*) gerund.

bağı Magic; spell, incantation. ~ **cı**¹, *n.* sorcerer.

bağıcı² *a.* Binding, tying together; corrupting.

bağıd· = BAĞIT.

bağıl (*phys.*) Dependent; relative. ~ **hata/yanılgı**, (*math.*) relative error: ~ NEM.

bağılda'k/bağırda'k^{ğı} Strap holding a baby in its cot.

bağıl·değer (*math.*) Relative value. ~ **lık**, relativity. ~ **nem**, (*met.*) relative humidity. ~ **yoğunluk**, (*phys.*) relative density.

bağım Dependence, subjection. ~ **lanmak**, *vi.* become dependent. ~ **laşma**, inter-dependence. ~ **lı**, dependent; subsidiary: ~ **olm. (-e)**, be connected to/with: ~ **sıralı tümce**, (*ling.*) sentence with dependent clauses. ~ **lılık**, dependence, subjection. ~ **sız**, detached, independent; competitive; (*rel.*) autocephalous: ~ **barınak**, (*naut.*) free port: ~ **sıralı tümce**, (*ling.*) sentence with independent clauses. ~ **sızca**, independently. ~ **sızlaşmak**, *vi.* become/grow independent. ~ **sızlık**, independence. ~ **sızlıkçı(lık)**, defen·dant/(-ce) of independence.

bağıntı Relation; connection; (*math.*) ratio, equation. ~ **cı(lık)**, (*phil.*) relativ·ist/(-ism). ~ **lı**, relative. ~ **(lı)lık**, relativeness, relativity.

bağ'ır^{rı} (*bio.*) The middle part of the body; bosom; breast; internal organs; middle/front (of anything). ~ **yeleği**, (*mil.*) leather jerkin (worn under armour): ~ **ı yanık**, afflicted, distressed: ~ **ı yanmak**, suffer; be in great pain; be very thirsty: ~ **ına basmak**, cherish, embrace; take great interest in: ~ **ına taş basmak**, resign o.s., suffer without complaint; restrain/hide one's grief: ~ **ını delmek**, wound deeply. ~ **dak** = BAĞILDAK.

bağır·ış Shouting, yelling: ~ **çağırış**, clamour, clangour, blaring noise. ~ **mak**, *vi.* shout; clamour, bawl, yell, raise an outcry; (crow) caw: **(-e)**, shout at, rebuke loudly.

bağırsa'k^{ğı} (*bio.*) Intestine; bowel; gut; (*cul.*) (sausage) casing. ~ **+**, *a.* Intestinal; gastral; entero-: ~ **askısı**, mesentery: ~ **çıkıntısı**, (*sl.*) boy's penis: ~ **ingin/yangısı**, (*med.*) enteritis: ~ **kazıntısı**, discharge from the large intestine; (*col.*) runt of the litter: ~ **oluşumu**, (*bio.*) gastrulation: ~ **solucanı**, (*zoo.*) large roundworm: ~ **teli**, catgut: ~ **tümörü**, (*bio.*) intestinal villi: ~ **ını deşmek**, (threaten to) kill s.o.: ~ **lar**, entrails: ~ **larını çıkarmak**, disembowel, eviscerate.

bağırt·ı Shouting; outcry, yell. ~ **kan**, noisy, always shouting. ~ **lak**, (*orn.*) garganey: ~ **kuşu**, (?) Pallas's/black-bellied sandgrouse: ~ **mak (-i)**, *vc.* BAĞIRMAK.

bağış Gift, donation; act of giving; (*fig.*) tip. ~ **ve kredi**, (*fin.*) lease-lend: ~ **ta bulunmak**, make a donation.

bağışık (-den) Excused, exempt; duty-free; (*med., pol.*) immune. ~ **lama**, *vn.* exemption; (*med.*) immunization. ~ **lamak (-i)**, exempt; (*med.*) immunize. ~ **lık**, exemption; immunity. ~ **lıkbilim**, (*med.*) immunology.

bağışla·ma Giving, donation; grant; pardon. ~ **mak** (-i, -e), give gratis; grant; give to charity, donate; make allowances for; pardon; spare s.o.'s life: **bağışlayın(ız)!**, pardon!, excuse me! ~ **nmak**, *vp.* ~ **tıcı**, ~ **neden**, excuse. ~ **tmak** (-i), *vc.* ~ **yıcı**, forgiving.

bağı·ı̇t[d1] (*leg.*) Compact, agreement, contract. ~ **tan doğan**, contractual. ~ **çı**, contracting party. ~ **laşmak** (-le), reach an agreement with. ~ **lı**, contracted; contractual; registered (letter, etc.). ~ **sız**, uncommitted.

bağkesen (*ent.*) Grape-cutter beetle.

bağla (*eng.*) Dam, barrage.

bağla·ç[c1] Paper-clip; (*ling.*) conjunction. ~ **grubu**, (*ling.*) coordinated group of words. ~ **lı**, (*ling.*) having a conjunction: ~ **tamlama**, coordinated word relationship: ~ **yancümle**, relative clause introduced by kİ. ~ **sız(lık)**, without a conjunction/ (asyndeton).

bağlak (*th.*) Epilogue.

bağla·m Bunch/bundle (of similar things); (*phys.*) binding; (*rad.*) beam; (*phil.*) context; consistency; coherence (of ideas). ~ **ma**, *vn.*; (*soc., pol.*) participation; (*fin.*) allowance; (*naut.*) mooring; (*mus.*) lute with three double-strings; (*arch.*) crossbar, tie-bar, beam: *a.* tied, bound: ~ +, *a.* connecting, coupling, engaging: ~ **çizgisi**, (*ling.*) hyphen: ~ **demiri**, (*rly.*) fish-plate: ~ **barınak/limanı**, (*naut.*) port of registration: ~ **ulacı**, (*ling.*) co-ordinating gerund. ~ **macı**, lute-maker/-seller/-player. ~ **mak** (-i, -e), tie, bind, clamp, fasten, attach; bandage; (*el.*) connect; (*naut.*) bend, tie up, moor; produce/form (skin, ice, seed, etc.); make (a bundle); tie/wrap up (a parcel); dedicate to; (*fin.*) allocate, assign; make a contract about stg.; dam (a stream); occupy (s.o.'s time); win (s.o.'s support/ affection); interrupt (movement); bring to an end; end up by doing stg. ~ **msal**, (*phil.*) contextual.

bağlan = BAKLAN.

bağla·nım Tying, binding, fastening, etc.; (*adm.*) taking sides. ~ **nma**, affiliation; (*phys.*) bonding. ~ **nmak**, *vp.* = ~ MAK; be tied, etc.; be obliged; be occupied (with stg.); be engaged (to do stg.); (-e) love/be fond of s.o. ~ **ntı**, connection, link, tie; (*ling.*) liaison; (*eng.*) coupling; (*phil.*) relation; coordination: ~ **bileziği**, (*eng.*) sleeve: ~ **borusu**, (*arch.*) branch soil-pipe: ~ **kesmek**, disconnect, disengage: ~ **kurmak** (-le), establish a connection with: ~ **kutusu**, (*el.*) junction-box: ~ **parçaları**, (*eng.*) fittings: ~ **ünlüsü**, (*ling.*) connecting vowel: ~ **yıldız**, (*ast.*) reference star. ~ **ntılı**, (inter-)connected; coordinate; dependent. ~ **ntısız**, independent: ~ **ülkeler**, (*pol.*) non-aligned nations. ~ **şık**, linked, coupled, connected, allied. ~ **şma**, *vn.* union. ~ **şmak** (-le), be united, join together; reach an agreement. ~ **tmak** (-i), *vc.* = ~ MAK. ~ **yıcı**, binding, linking, connecting; bridging; (*chem.*) fixing, stabilizing; (*leg.*) mandatory: ~ **(madde)**, (*chem.*) binder.

bağ·lı[1] *a.* Having vineyards: ~ **bahçeli**, rich, well-to-do, a man of property. ~ **lık**, *a./n.*, (place) full of vines: ~ **bahçelik**, (place) with vineyards and gardens.

bağlı[2] *a.* Bound; tied; (*aer.*) captive; conditional; (*chem.*) bonded; impotent; (*leg.*) (agreement) settled, concluded; (*fin.*) (income, etc.) assigned, allocated; (-e), ancillary to, dependent on, connected to/with. ~ **balon**, (*aer.*) captive/tethered balloon: ~ **muamele**, subordinate transaction. ~ **bağış**, pious foundation: ~ **belgiti**, deed of trust. ~ **laşık**, (*phil.*) correlative. ~ **laşım**, (*phil.*) correlation. ~ **laşma**, (*phil.*) mutual relationship, correlation. ~ **lık**, attachment; correlation; allegiance; loyalty; dependence; devotion: ~ **inancası**, (*fin.*) fidelity bond.

bağmak (-i) Bewitch, put a spell on s.o.

bağnaz Fanatic(al). ~ **lık**, fanaticism.

bağr- = BAĞIR, ~ **ıkara**, (*orn.*) a kind of titmouse.

bağrış·ma Shouting together. ~ **mak** (-le), shout together/at each other: **bağrışa çağrışa**, making a great noise.

bağsız(lık) (*phil.*) Free(dom); indepen·dent/ (-dence).

baha = PAHA.

bahadır *a.* Brave, gallant. *n.* Hero, champion.

Bahai(lik) (*rel.*) Bahai(ism).

bahane Pretext; cover; excuse. ~ **aramak**, look for an excuse: ~ **etm.**, make an idle excuse; allege: ~ **siyle**, on the pretext that; under cover of.

bahar[1] *n.* Spring (season); spring flowers/blossom; (*fig.*) youth. ~ **Bayramı**, Spring festival/holiday (1 May): ~ **noktası**, (*ast.*) spring equinox: ~ **yıldızı**, (*bot.*) creeping gypsophila. ~ **iye**, (*lit.*) ode in praise of spring.

bahar[2] *n.* (*cul.*) Spice. ~ **at**[1], spices: ~ **adaları**, (*geo.*) Spice Islands, Moluccas: ~ **katılması**, (*cul.*) seasoning. ~ **atçı**, herbalist, spice-merchant. ~ **atçılık**, spice-selling. ~ **lı**, spiced: ~ **koku (saçan)**, aroma/ (-tic).

bahçe Garden. ~ **bülbülü**, (*orn.*) garden warbler: ~ **kekiği**, (*bot.*) garden thyme: ~ **kızılkuyruğu**, (*orn.*) redstart: ~ **mimarisi**, landscape gardening: ~ **musluğu**, lawn sprinkler: ~ **ötleğeni**, (*orn.*) garden warbler: (?) blackcap: ~ **şemsiyesi**, garden umbrella, sunshade: ~ **teresi**, (*bot.*) (garden) cress: ~ **tırmaşık kuşu**, (*orn.*) short-toed tree-creeper: ~ **yelvesi**, (*orn.*) ortolan bunting.

bahçe·ci(lik) Garden·er/(-ing). ~ **li**, with a garden; garden-: ~ **ev**, villa: ~ **lokanta**, garden-restaurant. ~ **lik**, place full of/suitable for gardens; garden-plot. ~ **-sokak**, boulevard.

bahçıvan Gardener. ~ **lık**, gardening, horticulture.

bahi (*obs.*) Erotic.

bah·ir[ri] (*obs.*) Sea; (*lit.*) a poetic metre.

bah·is[si] Discussion; inquiry; subject/topic of discussion/inquiry; (*gamb.*) bet, wager. ~ **açmak**, open the discussion: ~ **konu/mevzuu**, subject under discussion: ~ **konu/mevzuu olm.**, be discussed/ treated: ~ **koymak**, lay a bet: ~ **tazelemek**, return to a subject: ~ **tut(uş)mak**/~ **e girişmek**, bet, wager with s.o.: ~ **e girmek**, wager (backing one's own opinion): ~ **i geçen**, the above-mentioned: ~ **i kabul etm.**, take/accept a bet: ~ **i kaybetmek**, lose the bet: ~ **i müşterek**, (*gamb.*) totalizator, tote.

bahname (*lit.*) Pornographic/obscene writing.

Bahreyn (*geo.*) Bahrein.

bahri[1] *n.* (*orn.*) Great crested grebe.
bahri[2] *n.* = BAHİR. *a.* Maritime; naval; nautical. ~ **ahmer**, (*obs.*) the Red Sea. ~ **lut**, (*obs.*) the Dead Sea. ~ **muhit**, (*obs.*) ocean: ~ **i Atlasi**, the Atlantic (Ocean): ~ **i Kebir**, the Pacific (Ocean). ~ **sefid**, (*obs.*) the Mediterranean. ~ **siyah**, (*obs.*) the Black Sea. ~ **ye**, navy: ~ **Bakan(lığ)ı**, the Minis·ter(-try) for the Navy: ~ **Nezaret/Vekâleti**, (*obs.*) the Ministry of Marine: ~ **zabiti**, naval officer. ~ **yeli**, seaman; naval cadet.
bahs- = BAHİS. ~ **¹etmek**ᵉᵈᵉʳ **(-den)**, discuss; mention; talk about; treat of; (*gamb.*) bet, wager.
bahş Gift; giving; forgiving. ~ **¹etmek**ᵉᵈᵉʳ **(-i, -e)**, give, grant; forgive, pardon. ~ **iş**, tip, baksheesh; gratuity, gift; bribe: ~ **atın dişine bakılmaz**, don't look a gift horse in the mouth.
baht[1] Chance, luck, fortune; good luck; destiny. ~ **işi**, a matter of chance; fluke: ~ **a bağlı**, (*leg.*) aleatory: ~ **ı açık**, lucky: ~ **ı açık olm.** (-den), be lucky in stg.: ~ **ı kara**, unlucky: ~ **ın gür olsun!**, good luck!: ~ **ına küsmek**, curse one's fate.
baht·iyar Lucky; blissful, happy. ~ **iyarlık**, good fortune; bliss, happiness. ~ **sız**, unfortunate, unlucky, ill-starred. ~ **sızlık**, ill-fortune.
bahusus Especially; particularly; above all.
Bak. = BAKAN(LIK); BAKTERİYOLOJİ.
baka·lçc[1] (*cin.*) Variable-focus viewfinder.
baka·durmak/~ **kalmak** *vi.* Stand in astonishment/bewilderment; (-e), stare at.
bakalit[1] (*chem.*) Bakelite.
bakalorya (*ed.*, *obs.*) School-leaving certificate; baccalaureate.
bakalyaro (*ich.*) (Salted) cod.
bakam (*bot.*) Logwood, campeachy tree. = BAKKAM.
bakan *n.* S.o. who looks; (*adm.*) minister, secretary of state. ~ **(-e)**, *a.* with a view of: ~ **lar Kurulu**, *pr.n.* (*adm.*) Council of Ministers, Cabinet. ~ **lık**, (*adm.*) ministry, department.
bakana·lkᵍ¹ (*zoo.*) Cloven hoof.
bakar (*zoo.*) Ox. ~ **i**, bovine.
bakara (*gamb.*) Baccarat.
bakarkör A blind man whose eyes seem normal; (*fig.*) s.o. very unobservant.
bakaya *pl.* = BAKİYE. Residues; arrears; back-pay; remains; (*mil.*) deserter.
bakı (*geo.*) Aspect; (sur)face; omen, augury; (*med.*) examination, inspection. ~ **cı**, attendant, nurse; soothsayer, fortune-teller. ~ **cılık**, nursing; fortune-telling.
bakılmak (-e) *imp. v.* Be attended to; be looked after; be considered; be followed as a rule; (*leg.*) be heard.
bakım Look, glance; aspect, viewpoint, point of view; (*med.*) care, attention; (*eng.*) maintenance, overhaul, upkeep. ~ **odası**, sick-bay: ~ **yurdu**, old people's home: ~ **ından**, *post.* [93] on account of, from the point of view of, with regard to.
bakım·cı Attendant; (*sp.*) trainer, manager. ~ **evi**ⁿⁱ, crèche, children's hospital; dispensary, outpatients' hospital/ward. ~ **lı**, well-cared for, well-kept. ~ **lık**, (*cin.*) small film projector, hand-viewer. ~ **sız**, neglected, uncared for. ~ **sızlık**, neglect, lack of care.

bakın·a·lkᵍ¹ (*med.*) Polyclinic. ~ **ca**, considering. ~ **cak**, adjustable backsight (of a gun). ~ **dı**, *int.* [138] just look! ~ **mak (-e)**, *vi.* look about/around; be bewildered: *vp.* (*med.*) be examined (by).
bakır (*chem.*) Copper; copper utensil. ~ **+**, *a.* (Made of) copper; (*geol.*) chalco-; (*chem.*) cupro-: ~ **basması**, (*pub.*) copperplate printing: ~ **çağı**, (*his.*) Chalcolithic Age: ~ **çalmak/çalığı olm.**, (*cul.*) be tainted with copper (from an untinned copper vessel): ~ **denizi**, (*naut.*) a head sea: ~ **hâsıl eden**, (*geol.*) cupriferous: ~ **kafalı engerek**, (*zoo.*) copper-head: ~ **kaplama**, copper-plated: ~ **kaplamak**, copper(-plate): ~ **kaplanmış**, copper-bottomed: ~ **kaplı**, copper-sheathed: ~ **kargası**, (*orn.*) blue roller: ~ **levha**, copper plate/sheet: ~ **para**, copper money; coppery: ~ **varak**, copper foil.
bakır·cı(lık) (Work/business of) coppersmith. ~ **hane**, coppersmithy. ~ **lamak (-i)**, copper. ~ **laşmak**, *vi.* become copper-coloured. ~ **lı**, coppery; (*chem.*) cupreous. ~ **sı**, coppery. ~ **taşı**ⁿ¹, (*geol.*) malachite.
bakış Look; care. ~ **+**, *a.* Visual. ~ **ık**, (*math.*) symmetrical. ~ **ım**, symmetry. ~ **ımlı**, symmetrical. ~ **ımsız**, asymmetrical. ~ **ımsızlık**, asymmetry. ~ **lı**, having a . . . way of looking. ~ **mak (-le)**, look at each other.
bakıt·ım (*leg.*) Examination. ~ **mak (-i)**, examine.
baki *a.* Permanent; enduring, lasting; remaining. *n.* Remainder. *adv.* Finally; as to the rest. ~ **kalmak**, remain over; survive: ~ **kalan bu kubbede bir hoş sada imiş**, only a happy memory remains; try to leave stg. to be remembered by.
bakir *a.* Virgin; untouched. ~ **orman**, (*for.*) virgin forest. ~ **e**, *n.* (*bio.*) virgin, maiden.
bakiye Remainder; residue; (*fin.*) arrears; balance; (*lit.*) sequel. ~ **yekûn**, total balance.
bakkal Grocer('s shop). ~ **çakkal**, grocers and the like: ~ **defteri değil!**, write neatly!: ~ **dükkânı**, grocer's shop: ~ **kâğıdı**, coarse wrapping paper: ~ **terazisi**, counter scales: ~ **a bırakma!**, (*jok.*) get on with the job! ~ **iye**, groceries; big grocer's shop. ~ **lık**, grocer's business.
bakkam (*chem.*) A non-fast die, haematoxylin. = BAKAM.
bakla (*bot.*) Bean; (*cul.*) (small) broad-bean; (*eng.*) link (of a chain). ~ **atmak/dökmek**, tell fortunes with beans: ~ **kadar**, very big (of a tiny insect): ~ **oda . . .** = NOHUT: ~ **yı ağzından çıkarmak**, spill the beans, let the cat out of the bag.
bakla·çiçeğiⁿⁱ A dirty yellowish-white colour. ~ **giller**, (*bot.*) Leguminosae. ~ **kırı**ⁿ¹, dapple-grey (horse). ~ **msı**, bean-shaped: ~ **meyve**, bean-pod.
baklan (*orn.*) Ruddy shelduck.
baklava (*cul.*) A sweet pastry-cake (with nuts and honey, cut in lozenges). ~ **biçim/dilimi**, diamond-shaped, rhomboid: ~ **börek (yanında)**, very easy (compared with), a piece of cake: ~ **börek olsa yemem**, I couldn't eat another mouthful.
baklava·cı(lık) (Work of) BAKLAVA maker/seller. ~ **lık**, used/useful in making BAKLAVA.
bakliy·at[1] (*cul.*) Legumes, pulses; dried beans. ~ **e**, (*bot.*) Leguminosae.

bakmak *vi.* (-e) Look; look at; eye; examine; care for, look after, tend; attend to, see to; consult (a book, etc.); look at (s.o. for guidance); (-e), face towards, look out on. ~ şartıyla, (*leg.*) on condition to look after s.o.: **bak!**, look!; attention!; just look!, good heavens!: **bak kerataya!**, look at the little fellow: **bak yediği naneye!** = YEDİĞİ: **bakalım!**, *int.* (*of doubt/threat/encouragement*) well!; we'll see!: **bakan göze yasak olmaz**, you can't stop people looking; a cat may look at the queen: **bakarak (-e)**, compared with: **bakarmısın(ız)?**, will you please look?; could you please help?: **bakarsan bağ olur bakmazsan dağ olur**, success requires effort: **bakmaya kıyılmaz bir manzara**, a view one never tires of looking at: **baksan(ız)a!**, look here!; be careful!; listen to me!: **baktıkça alır**, not immediately attractive/striking: **baktıkça bakacağı gelmek**, be unable to stop looking; want to look.

bakra'ç[c1] Copper bucket.

bakteri (*bio.*) Bacterium, microbe. ~ +, Bacterio-: ~ **yok eden madde**, bactericide. ~**di**, anthrax bacillus. ~**giller**, (*bot.*) Bacteriaceae. ~**sit**, bactericidal. ~**yolog**, bacteriologist. ~**yoloji**, bacteriology.

baktırmak (-i, -e) *vc.* = BAKMAK.

Baküs (*myth.*) Bacchus. ~ +, Bacchic.

bal Honey, syrup; oozing sap. ~ **alacak çiçeği bilmek/bulmak**, know/find s.o./stg. that will be profitable/useful: ~ARISI: ~ **ayısı**, (*zoo.*) honey-bear: ~ (~) **demekle ağız tatlılanmaz**, talking is not enough: ~ **başı**, the purest honey; ~ **dök de yala**, very clean (*cp.* the floor is clean enough to eat your food off): ~ **gibi**, pure as honey, unadulterated; easily, properly, certainly: ~ **gibi yalan**, a lie pure and simple: ~ **gugukları**, (*orn.*) honeyguides: ~GÜMECİ: ~KABAĞI: ~ **kelebeği**, (*ent.*) honeycomb moth: ~ **otu**, (*bot.*) nodding melic: ~ **peteği**, honeycomb: ~ **sağmak**, take the honey from the hive: ~ **tutan parmağını/ parmak yalar**, he will get some profit from it: ~**la sarmısak yemesini icat etm.**, invent stg. useless.

bal. = BALE[2].

bala Child, baby.

balaban (*zoo.*) Tame bear; (*fig.*) enormous man/ animal; large drum. ~**kuşu**[nu], (*orn.*) Eurasian bittern. ~**laşmak**, grow very large/fat.

balad (*lit.*) Ballad(e). ~**ör**, (*eng.*) sliding-gear; selector.

bala'k[g1] (*zoo.*) Any young animal, cub; buffalo calf.

balalayka (*mus.*) Balalaika.

balama (*th.*) Typical Greek/European character.

balan·çina/ ~**sine** (*naut.*) Main boom topping-lift.

balans Balance. ~ **ayarı**, balancing (of car wheels).

balar (*carp.*) Thin board; rafter.

balarısı[nı] (*ent.*) Honey-bee.

balast[1] (*rly.*) Ballast.

balata (*eng.*) Brake-disc/-lining.

bal·ayı[nı] Honeymoon. ~**bal**, (*bot.*) stele; saltwort. ~**cı**, apiarist, bee-keeper, dealer in honey; (*orn.*) honey-eater. ~**cılık**, bee-keeping, honey-selling.

balça'k[g1] Guard of sword hilt.

balçı'k[g1] Wet clay; potter's clay; sticky mud.

~ **balığı**, (*ich.*) lungfish: ~ **hurma//inciri**, crushed dried dates//figs. ~**lamak (-i)**, coat/dirty with clay. ~**lı**, clayey. ~**yiyen**, (*ich.*) weather-fish.

baldır (*bio.*) Calf (of the leg). ~ **kemiği**, shin-bone, tibia: ~**ı çıplak**, bare-legged; (*fig.*) a rough/rowdy person. ~**ak**, (*mod.*) lower part of the leg; leggings; (*mil.*) loop of sword-belt.

baldır·an (*bot.*) Hemlock: ~ **şerbeti**, (*fig.*) the benefit (after much toil and sweat). ~**anlık**, where hemlock grows freely. ~**gan**, (*bot.*) ferula asafoetida. ~**ıkara**, (*bot.*) maidenhair fern. ~**sokan**, (*ent.*) stable-fly, biting horse-fly.

baldız Sister-in-law (wife's sister).

baldudak Sweet-spoken.

bale[1] *n.* (*el.*) Brush, contact.

bale[2] *n.* (*mus.*) Ballet. ~**ci**, ballet-dancer. ~**rin**, ballerina. ~**toman**, balletomane.

balgam (*bio.*) Mucus, phlegm. ~ **atmak**, (*vulg.*) drop malicious hints: ~ **çıkarmak**, expectorate; spit: ~ **söktürücü**, (*med.*) expectorant.

balgam·lamak (-i) Smear with mucus. ~**lı**, covered with mucus, mucous. ~**taşı**[nı], (*geol.*) jasper, onyx.

balgümeci[ni] Honeycomb; (*tex.*) honeycomb pattern.

balı'k[g1] (*ich.*) Fish; (*ast.*) Pisces. ~ **avcısı**, angler: ~ **avı**, fishing, angling: ~ **baştan kokar**, corruption starts at the top: ~ **bilimi**, ichthyology: ~ **ezmesi**, fish-paste: ~ **gübresi**, (*agr.*) guano: ~ **istifi**, packed like sardines: ~ **kanadı**, (*ich.*) fin: ~ **kartalı**, (*orn.*) osprey: ~ **kavağa çıkınca**, (*jok.*) never: ~ **kılçığı**, (*ich.*) fish-bone; herring-bone (pattern): ~ **köftesi**, (*cul.*) fish ball/cake/finger: ~ **pastırması**, (*cul.*) dried/smoked fish: ~ **pilakisi**, (*cul.*) spiced cold fish: ~ **tavası**, (*cul.*) fried fish: ~ **tutkalı**, fish-glue, isinglass: ~ **tutmak**, catch fish; (*sl.*) be lucky: ~ **yavrusu**, fry: ~**a çıkmak**, go out fishing: ~**ın belkemiğini bulmak**, solve the problem.

balık·adam Skin-diver. ~**ağı**[nı], fishing-net. ~**çı**, fisherman; fishmonger. ~**çıl**[1], *a.* piscivorous, fish-eating. ~**çıl**[2], *n.* (*orn.*) heron. ~**çılık**, fishing; dealing in fish. ~**çıllar**, (*orn.*) herons. ~**çın**, (*orn.*) common tern. ~**eti(nde)**, well-fleshed, neither fat nor thin. ~**gözü**[nü], (*mod.*) eyelet (for belt/strap). ~**hane**, custom-house for dues on fish; wholesale fish-market. ~**kaçtı**, (*obs.*) game played by women. ~**lama**, (*sp.*) head-first dive: ~ **dalmak**, dive headfirst. ~**lava**, good fishing-ground. ~**lı**, containing fish. ~**nefsi**[ni], (*zoo.*) spermaceti. ~**otu**[nu], (*bot.*) Indian-/fish-berry plant. ~**pulu**[nu], (*ich.*) fish scale. ~**sırtı**[nı], cambered, hog-backed (road); (*mod.*) herring-bone pattern. ~ **yağı**[nı], (*chem.*) fish oil; codliver oil. ~**yiyen**, (*zoo.*) fish-eating. ~ **yumurtası**[nı], (*ich.*) fish-roe; (*cul.*) caviar.

baliğ *a.* Reaching, attaining; amounting (to); adult, mature; perfect. *n.* Amount, sum. ~ **olm.**, reach the age of discretion/puberty; (-e), amount/come to.

balina (*zoo.*) Whale; (*mod.*) whalebone. ~ **avcı(lığ)ı**, whal·er/(-ing): ~ **çubuk/dişi**, (*zoo.*) whalebone: ~ **yağı**, blubber. ~**giller**, whales, dolphins, Cetacea. ~**lı**, (*mod.*) with whalebone.

bali·sti'k[g1] (*mil.*) Ballistics. ~**z**, (*rad.*) beacon.

balkabağı[nı] (*bot.*) Pumpkin; squash; (*fig.*) idiot.

balkan (*geo.*) Wooded mountain range. ~ +, *a*. Balkan: ~ **yarımadası,** the Balkan Peninsula: ~**lar,** the Balkans. ~**laştırmak (-i),** Balkanize. ~**lı,** a native of the Balkans. ~**lık,** *a*. wooded, mountainous.

Balkar Branch of Kipchak Turks (in the Caucasus). ~**ca,** (*ling.*) Balkar dialect of Kipchak.

balkelebeğini (*ent.*) Wax-moth.

balkı·mak *vi.* Shimmer, glimmer; (wound) throb. ~**r,** glitter, gleam; lightning.

balkon (*arch., th.*) Balcony; (*sl.*) bosom. ~**lu,** with a balcony; (*sl.*) with a large bosom.

ballan·dırmak (-i) Smear with honey; extol extravagantly; (*sl.*) hand over, cough up: ~**dıra** ~**dıra anlatmak,** relate in terms of extravagant praise. ~**mak,** *vi.* become viscous like honey; be spread with honey; (*fig.*) become sweet and attractive.

bal·lı Honeyed: ~ **börek,** (*cul.*) honey pasty; (*fig.*) heart's desire. ~**lıbaba(giller),** (*bot.*) dead-nettle, (Lamiaceae). ~**lıbasra,** (*ent.*) fig wax-scale. ~**lık,** (*bot.*) nectary; (*myc.*) vine mildew. ~**mumcu,** beeswax seller. ~**mumu**nu, (bees)wax; sealing-wax; cero-: ~ **çiçeği,** (*bot.*) wax flower, hoya: ~ **gibi erimek,** (*fig.*) become very thin: ~ **macunu,** wax (for repairing furniture): ~ **müzesi,** waxworks: ~ **yapıştırmak,** stick wax on stg.; (-e), (*fig.*) note down (to remember stg.); mark s.o. down (for revenge, etc.).

balo Ball, dance. ~ **tertip etm./vermek,** give a ball.

balon Balloon; (*naut.*) ship's fender; balloon flask; (*pub.*) fake. ~ **balığı,** (*ich.*) pufferfish: ~ **barajı,** (*aer.*) balloon barrage: ~ **floku,** (*naut.*) spinnaker: ~ **lastik,** (*mot.*) balloon tyre: ~ **sepeti,** (*aer.*) gondola: ~ **uçurmak,** (*fig.*) fly a kite. ~**cu,** balloonist. ~**lu,** ~ **ayıbalığı,** (*zoo.*) hooded seal.

balotaj (*adm.*) Failure to gain an absolute majority.

baloz Low class *café chantant*.

bal·özünü (*bot.*) Nectar. ~**özülük,** nectary. ~ **peteği**ni, honeycomb. ~**rengi**ni, honey colour.

balsam (*bot.*) Balsam (resin).

balsıra (*myc.*) Manna; honeydew, mildew.

balta Axe. ~ **burun,** hook-nosed: ~ **değmemiş/ girmemiş/görmemiş orman,** virgin forest; the backwoods: ~ **olm./~yı kapıya asmak,** (*fig.*) be tiresome; bore, pester: ~**sı kütükten çıkmak,** overcome an obstacle, solve a problem: ~**yı taşa basmak/ vurmak,** do/say stg. unseemly; make a *faux pas*. (a girl) she has a young man: ~**yı taşa basmak/ vurmak,** do/say stg. unseemly; make a *faux pas*.

balta·baş/~burun (*naut.*) Straight-stemmed (ship). ~**cı,** maker/seller of axes; woodcutter; (*mil.*) sapper, pioneer: (*his.*) halberdier; fireman using an axe. ~**cı**lkgı, hatchet, adze. ~**lama,** *vn.* demolition; (*pol.*) sabotage. ~**lamak (-i),** cut down with an axe; demolish; extirpate; destroy (hope, etc.); (*pol.*) sabotage. ~**layıcı,** saboteur. ~**lık,** forest area where villagers have wood-cutting rights; copse: ~ **hakkı,** wood-cutting rights.

Baltılkgı (*geo.*) ~ **(denizi),** the Baltic (Sea).

baltrap Clay-pigeon trap.

balüzümünü (*bot.*) A scented white grape.

balya Bale. ~**lamak (-i),** bale. ~**lı,** baled.

balyemez (*his.*) Long-range siege gun.

balyos (*his.*) Title of European (*esp.* Venetian) ambassadors, bailo; ruler of a Venetian colony.

balyoz Sledge-hammer. ~ **gibi,** very big/heavy. ~**lamak (-le),** beat/strike with a sledge-hammer.

balza ~ **(ağacı)** (*bot.*) Balsa (wood).

bambaşka Utterly different.

bambu (*bot.*) Bamboo. ~ **perdeli sınır,** (*adm.*) bamboo curtain.

bambul (*ent.*) (?) Corn-chafer.

bamtelini (*mus.*) String giving the lowest note; (*mod.*) imperial (beard); (*fig.*) vital point, sore spot. ~**ne basmak/dokunmak,** tread on s.o.'s corns, touch his sore spot.

bamya (*bot.*) Okra, lady's fingers. ~ **tarlası,** (*sl.*) cemetery.

ban (*adm., his.*) Ban (of Croatia/Hungary).

bana *dative* = BEN². To me. ~ **bak!,** look here!, hi!: ~ **bakma!,** never mind what I do!; don't count on me!: ~ **da . . . demesinler,** I'll do it, never fear; of course I can do/say it: ~ **düşmez,** it's not up to me . . .: ~ **gelince,** as for me; as far as I am concerned: ~ **göre hava hoş,** it suits me; it's all the same to me: ~ **kör diyen kendisi badem gözlü olsa!,** people who live in glass houses shouldn't throw stones: ~ **kalırsa,** if it's left to me . . .: ~ **mısın dememek,** be very thick-skinned; have no effect: ~ **ne?,** what's that to me?; I don't care!: ~ **öyle geliyor ki,** it seems to me that . . .: ~ **sorarsan!,** for all I care!; if you ask me!: ~ **söylemez,** it means nothing to me: ~ **şaka gibi geliyor,** it's incredible: ~ **vız gelir tırıs gider,** I don't care two hoots/a brass farthing.

banağacını (*bot.*) Horseradish tree.

banco(cu) (*mus.*) Banjo(-player).

band- = BANT.

bandaj (*med.*) Bandage; (*eng.*) belt; (*rly.*) tyre.

bandıra (Foreign) flag; national colours. ~**lı,** sailing under . . . colours.

bandırma (*cul.*) Sweetmeat (walnuts, etc.), strung on a thread and soaked in grape-juice).

bandırmak (-i, -e) Dip stg. (into stg.).

band(ı)rol Monopoly tax label.

bandikut (*zoo.*) Bandicoot.

bando (*mus.*) Military/brass band. ~ **şefi,** bandmaster, drum-major.

bangır ~ ~, yelling, screaming. ~**damak,** *vi.* yell, scream.

bani Builder, constructor; founder.

bank[1] (*fin.*) Bank (*as part of pr.n.* = ETİBANK). (*dom.*) garden-seat; (*naut.*) (sand-)bank.

banka (*fin.*) Bank; (*sl.*) brothel. ~ +, *a*. Bank(ing): ~ **cüzdanı,** bank-book: ~ **havalesi,** bank giro/ transfer: ~ **hesap/sayışımı,** bank-account: ~ **indirim sınırı/iskonto haddi,** bank-rate: ~ **işlemleri,** banking (operations): ~ **ödeği,** bank bill: ~ **ödeme emri,** banker's order: ~ **yedekleri,** bank reserves: ~**ya koymak/yatırmak (-i),** bank, deposit.

bank·acı(lık) Bank·er/(-ing), ~**er,** banker; money-changer; (*fig.*) s.o. very rich. ~**et**i, soft verge (of metalled road); shoulder. ~**iz,** (*geo.*) ice-floe, ice-pack. ~**not**u, (*fin.*) bank-note. ~**o,** *n.* garden-seat; (*fin.*) counter: *int.* (*gamb.*) "bank!": ~ **tutan,** (*gamb.*) banker.

banliyö Suburb. ~ +, *a*. Suburban. ~ **bölgesi,**

commuter-belt: ~ **treni**, commuter/suburban train: ~ **yolcusu**, commuter.
banmak (**-i, -e**) Dip/soak stg. (in stg.).
banotuⁿᵘ (*bot.*) Henbane.
ban¹tᵈ¹ (*el., med.*) Band, tape; ribbon, strip; (*el.*) magnetic tape; (*eng.*) belt. ~ **geçirici**, (*el.*) band-pass: ~ **izole**, insulating tape: ~**a almak**, (record on) tape.
ban·yağı (*chem.*) Ben-oil. ~ **yan**, (*bot.*) banian-tree.
banyo Bath; bathe; bathtub; bathroom; (*cin.*) developing dish; development. ~ **etm./yapmak**, bath; bathe: ~ **süngeri**, (*zoo.*) (bath/toilet) sponge.
baoba¹pᵇ¹ (*bot.*) Baobab tree.
ba¹pᵇ¹ (*arch.*) Door; gate; (*pub.*) chapter; subdivision; class, category; connection; subject.
bar¹ *n.* (*mus.*) E. Anatolian folk-dance.
bar² *n.* Coating, tarnish (on glass); (*med.*) fur (on the tongue).
bar³ *n.* Night-club; drinking bar/saloon.
bar⁴ *n.* (*phys.*) Bar.
bar⁵ *adv.* ~ ~ **bağırmak**, shout loudly and continuously.
bâr Load, burden; time, turn; fruit. ~ **olm.** (**-e**), be a burden to s.o.
-bar *suf.* Pouring . . .; spreading . . . [EŞKBAR].
baraj Dam, barrage. ~ **ateşi**, (*mil.*) barrage (of gunfire): ~ **balonu**, barrage-balloon.
bara¹kᵍ¹ *a.* (*zoo.*) Long-haired; (*tex.*) thick-piled. *n.* (*tex.*) Plush; (*bot.*) a climbing vine.
baraka Hut, booth, shed; (*fig.*) barracks.
baran¹ *n.* (*met. obs.*) Rain.
baran² *n.* (*agr.*) Row of vines; furrow.
barata (*his.*) Cloth cap; (*bot.*) Turk's cap lily.
baratarya (*naut.*) Barratry.
barba (*col.*) Uncle! (to a Greek publican, etc.).
barbakan (*mil.*) Barbican, loophole; (*eng.*) seep-hole.
barbar Barbarian; barbarous, barbaric. ~**ca**, barbarous(ly), brutal(ly). ~**izm**, (*ling.*) barbarism. ~**laşmak**, *vi.* behave barbarously. ~**lık**, barbarity.
barbata (*mil.*) Parapet, machicolation, castellation.
barbekü (*cul.*) Barbecue.
barbiturat¹ (*chem.*) Barbiturate.
barbunya (*ich.*) Red/striped/sur-mullet; (*sl.*) ten-lira note; (*ed. sl.*) full marks. ~ (**fasulyesi**), (*bot.*) small reddish bean. ~**giller**, (*ich.*) Mullidae.
barbutᵘ (*gamb.*) A game with dice.
barça (*his.*) Galley; ancient warship.
barça¹kᵍ¹ = BALÇAK.
barda Cooper's adze.
bardacı¹kᵍ¹ Small cup; (*bot.*) type of fresh fig.
barda¹kᵍ¹ Drinking-mug; glass for water, wine, etc.; pitcher, ewer. ~ **likeni**, (*myc.*) cup lichen: ~ı **taşıran damla**, the last straw: ~**taki fırtına**, storm in a teacup: ~**tan boşanırcasına yağmur yağıyor**, it's raining in torrents. ~**altı**, (*dom.*) coaster, mat. ~**eriği**ⁿⁱ, (*bot.*) egg-plum.
barem Ready-reckoner; (*adm.*) scale of official salaries. ~ **kanunu**, law regulating official salaries: ~**e girmek**, (civil servant) become established.
barfiks (*sp.*) Horizontal bar.
bargam (*ich.*) A type of bass.
barhana = BERHANE.

barı Fence. ~**lanmak**, *vi.* retire, shut o.s. up. ~**mak** (**-i**), shelter, shield; assist.
barın (*phys.*) Barn.
barın·a¹kᵍ¹ Shelter; hiding place; port; (*pol.*) asylum; boarding-house: ~ **böcekleri**, (*ent.*) household pests. ~**akçı(lık)**, (work of) boarding-house keeper. ~**dırmak** (**-i, -e**), give shelter to; lodge, house. ~**ıcı**, boarder. ~**ma**, *vn.*: ~ **limanı**, (*naut.*) port of refuge. ~**mak** (**-de**), take refuge/shelter in; lodge. ~**malı¹k**ᵍ¹, barricade.
barış Reconciliation; peace, concord. ~ **etm.**, make peace: ~ **görüş olm.**, be reconciled: ~ **harekâtı**, (*pol.*) peace-movement: ~ **ordusu**, (*mil.*) standing army: ~ **yargıcı**, (*leg.*) justice of the peace: ~**a karşı suç**, (*leg.*) breach of the peace: ~ı **tehdit**, threat to peace: ~**ta**, peaceable.
barış·çı(l) Peace-loving; 'dove'; pacifist: ~ **çözüm**, peaceful solution. ~**çılık**, pacifism. ~**ık**, at peace; reconciled; in agreement. ~**ıklık**, mutual peace, harmony, reconciliation. ~**landırma**, pacification. ~**ma**, reconciliation. ~**mak** (**-le**), be reconciled, make peace. ~**sever**, peace-loving; pacifist. ~**severlik**, pacificism. ~**tırıcı**, *n.* conciliator, peace-maker: *a.* conciliatory. ~**tırmak** (**-i, -le**), reconcile, conciliate, make peace (among).
bari For once; at least; if only. ~ **haberini alsam**, if only I could get news of him.
bari·kat¹ Barricade: ~ **kurmak**, (set up a) barricade. ~**yer**, barrier.
bari·sfer (*geol.*) Barysphere. ~**ton**, (*mus.*) baritone.
barit(in) (*geol.*) Barite.
bariz Manifest; open; conspicuous, prominent. ~**lik**, being manifest; conspicuousness, prominence.
bark¹ = EV BARK. ~**lanmak**, *vi.* set up house; start family life.
bark·a (*naut.*) Large rowing boat. ~ **arol**ᵘ, (*mus.*) barcarole. ~**o**, (*naut.*) barque.
barlam (*ich.*) Hake.
bar·men Barman, bar-tender. ~**n**, (*phys.*) = BARIN.
barname (*fin.*) Manifest, bill of lading.
baro (*leg.*) Bar. ~**graf**, (*phys.*) barograph.
barokᵘ (*art.*) Baroque.
baro·metre (*phys.*) Barometer. ~**metrik**, barometric. ~**skop**ᵘ, baroscope.
baron·(es) (*soc.*) Baron(ess). ~**luk**, barony.
barsak = BAĞIRSAK.
barsam (*ich.*) (Lesser) weaver, sting-fish.
barsama (*bot., cul.*) Cooking herbs (mint, thyme, etc.).
barudi Slate-coloured, dark grey.
barutᵘ Gunpowder; very pungent drink; (*fig.*) hot-tempered man. ~ **ambarı**, powder magazine: ~ **fıçısı**, powder-barrel/-keg: ~ **fıçısı gibi**, (*fig.*) dangerous place, trouble-making spot: ~ **gibi**, hard/irascible (person); sharp/bitter (taste): ~ **hakkı**, charge of powder: ~ **kesilmek/olm.**, fly into a rage: ~ **kokusu gelmek**, sense the danger of war: ~ **yoktu kaptanım**, (*fig.*) no further explanation is needed: ~**la oynamak**, (*fig.*) play with fire.
barut·çu Powder-maker. ~**hane**, powder-mill; powder magazine. ~**luk**, powder flask.
baryum (*chem.*) Barium.

bas[1] *n.* Operating lever/button (of WC).
bas[2] *n.* (*mus.*) Bass (voice/instrument). ~ **bariton,** bass-baritone: ~ **tutmak,** (bass instruments) accompany.
bas. = BASIN; BASMACILIK; BASSO.
basa¹çᶜ¹ (*eng.*) Compressor; pump.
basamak *n.* Step, stair; tread/round/rung (of a ladder); foot-rest; (*math.*) order; column (of figures); degree, stage; (*carp.*) workbench. ~ ~, (rise) gradually: ~ **yapmak,** make use of s.o./stg. to rise. ~ **lı,** having steps, etc.; stepped; (*math.*) scalar: ~ **tiyatro,** classical (amphi)theatre. ~ **sı,** (*bot.*) scalariform.
basan *a.* Pressing; treading. *n.* (*pub.*) Printer; = KARA ~.
basar Sight, vision; mental perception. ~ **i,** optical.
basar·ı¹kᵍ¹ (*eng.*) Treadle. ~ **ma,** (*naut.*) lifting (one side of stg.). ~ **na,** (*eng.*) lever, jack.
basbayağı *a.* Very common/ordinary. *adv.* Altogether; entirely.
basen (*bio.*) Pelvic zone; hip measurement.
bas·ga¹çᶜ¹ (*min.*) Press. ~ **ı,** (*pub.*) printing; impression. ~ **ıcı,** printer. ~ **ık,** compressed; flattened; low; dwarf; mumbling. ~ **ıklık,** flatness; lowness; (*math.*) oblateness.
basıl·a! (*pub.*) (Order to) print! ~ **ı,** flattened; (*pub.*) printed: ~ **kâğıt,** printed matter. ~ **mak,** *vp.* = BASMAK; be pressed; be printed, etc.; be overcome; be extinguished: **basılmış eser/yapıtlar,** printed matter.
basım (*pub.*) Printing, typography. ~ **cı,** printer; editor. ~ **cılık,** work of printing. ~ **evi**ⁿ¹, printing-house, press.
basın (*pub.*) The press, newspapers. ~ **ajansı,** press agency: ~ **ataşesi,** (*adm.*) press attaché: ~ **hürriyet/ özgürlüğü,** freedom of the press: ~ **kartı,** press card: ~ **sözcüsü,** press officer: ~ **toplantısı,** press conference.
basın·ç¹çᶜ¹ (*phys.*) Pressure; (*geol.*) compression: ~ **birimi,** bar: ~ **düşüklüğü** (*met.*) depression: ~ **ölçme aleti,** pressure gauge: ~ **yapmak,** compress. ~ **nçlı,** compressed; pressurized. ~ **nçölçer,** (*phys.*) barometer, pressure-gauge. ~ **ölçer,** (*phys.*) manometer, pressure-gauge.
basır (*obs.*) Sharp-sighted; quick-witted. ~ **a,** the visual faculty, sight. ~ **ganmak,** *vi.* have nightmares.
basış *vn.* = BASMAK.
basil (*bio.*) Bacillus. ~ **li,** bacillary.
basir Intelligent, discerning. ~ **et**ⁱ, perception, insight; circumspection; foresight: ~ **i bağlanmak,** lose one's common-sense; be blind to one's own interests. ~ **etli,** clear-sighted; far-seeing; cautious, circumspect. ~ **etsiz,** lacking foresight. ~ **etsizlik,** lack of foresight.
basitⁱ Simple; plain; ordinary; easy; basic, elementary. ~ **kesir,** (*math.*) simple fraction: ~ **sözcük,** (*ling.*) simple/non-compound word: ~ **tümce,** (*ling.*) simple sentence.
basita Sundial. ~ **mili,** gnomon.
basit·leşmek *vi.* Become common/simple, etc. ~ **leştirmek (-i),** simplify; popularize. ~ **lik,** simplicity.
Bask (*ethn.*) Basque. ~ **ça,** (*ling.*) Basque.

basket·bolü (*sp.*) Basketball. ~ **çi,** basketball player.
baskı (*pub.*) Press; stamp; (state of a) printed copy; circulation; edition; (*phys.*) pressure, compression; (*mod.*) hem; (*fig.*) oppression, restraint; discipline; (*sp.*) marking (an opponent). ~ **altına almak,** oppress, tyrranize: ~ **altında,** under discipline/ pressure: ~ **altında tutmak,** restrain, restrict s.o.: ~ **kalıbı,** printing stamp: ~ **kolu,** pump-handle; (*eng.*) cantilever: ~ **makinesi,** printing-press: ~ **sayısı,** (*pub.*) number printed, circulation: ~ **yapmak,** pressurize; constrain, use force, force s.o. to do stg.: ~ **da,** in the press: ~ **sını gidermek,** (*phys.*) depressurize: ~ **ya girmek,** (*pub.*) go to press: ~ **yı azaltma (hücresi),** (*phys.*) decompression (chamber).
baskı·cı (*pub.*) Press operator; (*tex.*) stamper. ~ **cılık,** stamping. ~ **lık,** paperweight. ~ **sal,** *a.* pressure. ~ **sız,** undisciplined. ~ **sızlık,** indiscipline.
baskın *a.* Heavy; overpowering; **(-den),** superior; surpassing; (*bio.*) dominant. *n.* Sudden attack; night attack; (police-)raid: ~ **basanındır,** the attacker wins: ~ **çıkmak,** come off best; **(-den),** get the better of; be superior to: ~ **etm./** ~ **yapmak/** ~ **a uğratmak,** raid, attack by surprise: ~ **gelmek,** seem heavy/irresistible: ~ **grev,** (*ind.*) lightning strike: ~ **vermek/** ~ **a uğramak,** be raided/attacked by surprise; suffer stg. ~ **cı,** raider, attacker.
basklarnetⁱ (*mus.*) Bass-clarinet.
baskül Weighing machine; weighbridge. ~ **lü,** ~ **sandalye,** rocking-chair.
basma *vn.* = BASMAK. Print; (*tex.*) printed (*esp.* cotton) goods; (*pub.*) printed matter; (*geol.*) dominance; (*gamb.*) a card game. *a.* Pressed; forced; printed. ~ **devre,** (*el.*) printed circuit: ~ **kalıbı,** (*eng.*) pressure mould; = ~ KALIP. ~ **cı(lık),** (work of) s.o. who makes/sells printed goods. ~ **hane,** (*tex.*) print-works.
basmak (-i) *vt.* Stamp; print; attack suddenly, surprise; raid; overpower; give (a blow); utter (a cry): **(-e),** press; tread on; oppress; flavour (food) too much; reach an age. *vi.* Tread; be oppressive; settle, sag; (cold/darkness) set in; (water) flood, overflow; (several people) arrive suddenly, crowd in. **bas!,** (*sl.*) get out!, go to hell!: **basıp geçmek,** (*sp.*) overtake the leader (in a race): **basıp gitmek,** go off (without caring a straw): **bastığı yeri bilmemek,** not choose one's steps carefully; (*fig.*) walk on air.
basmakalı¹pᵇ¹ Stereotyped, banal (remark, etc.); cliché. ~ **söz,** banality, cliché.
Basra (*geo.*) Basra. ~ **harap olduktan sonra,** too late!: ~ **körfezi,** the Persian Gulf.
bas(s)o (*mus.*) Bass. ~ **n,** bassoon.
bastarda (*his.*) War galley; flagship.
bastı (*cul.*) Vegetable stew; (*mod.*) ribbon.
bastıbaca¹kᵍ¹ *a.* Short-/bandy-legged. *n.* Urchin; precocious child.
bastı¹kᵍ¹ = PESTİL.
bastır·ılmak *vp.* ~ **mak (-i, -e),** *vc.* = BASMAK: depress, push down, press, compress; overwhelm; damp, extinguish; suppress; repress; hide, hush up (a scandal, etc.); catch unawares; (*tex.*) tack; relieve (the stomach); cry out; speak derisively; (cold, darkness, etc.) set in.

bastika (*naut.*) Snatchblock.
baston (Walking-)stick, cane; (*naut.*) jib-boom.
~ **francala**, (*cul.*) (stick-shaped) loaf of bread: ~
(**yutmuş**) **gibi**, as stiff as a poker, like a ramrod: ~
yüksüğü, ferrule.
basur (*med.*) Piles, haemorrhoids. ~ **memesi**, a
haemorrhoid. ~**otu**[nu], (*bot.*) lesser celandine, pile-
wort.
basübadelmevt[i] (*rel.*) The resurrection of the dead.
basya (*bot.*) A gum-tree, (?) bassia.
baş *n.* Head; top; crown; (*geo.*) peak; knob; (*eng.*)
ram; (*naut.*) bow, prow; (*naut.*) course, heading;
beginning, source; foundation; (*live.*) [80] head (of
cattle, etc.); captain, leader, chief(tain); intelligence, understanding; (*fin.*) moneychanger's commission; (one)self. *a.* Head, chief; arch-; capital;
primary; cardinal; (*naut.*) fore-; (*bio., med.*)
cephalo-; [*usually written as a compound*: BAŞ-
BAKAN, etc.]. *post.* [90] Immediate vicinity [= OCAK
BAŞI]. ~ **açmak**, uncover the head: ~ **ağrısı**, (*med.*)
headache: ~ **ağrısı olm.**, be a nuisance: ~ **ağrıtmak**,
disturb/tire s.o. with talking: ~ **alamamak (-den)**,
be too busy with stg. (to do other things), miss the
opportunity: ~ **aşağı**, head first, headlong; inverted, upside-down: ~ **aşağı gitmek**, go steadily
downhill, become a failure: ~ **bağlamak**, (*bot.*)
(corn) produce ears; cover the head; be(come)
connected with: ~ ~**a**, [195] together, tête-à-tête,
face to face; confidentially: ~ ~**a kalmak**, be left
alone with: ~ ~**a varış**, (*sp.*) dead-heat: ~ ~**a**
vermek, have a tête-à-tête, collaborate, put heads
together: ~ **belası**, source of trouble/annoyance:
~ **biti**, (*ent.*) human louse: ~ **bulmak**, (*fin.*) leave a
profit: ~ **çanağı**, (*bio.*) skull: ~ÇAVUŞ = ASSUBAY:
~ **çekimi**, (*cin.*) close-up: ~ **çekmek**, take the lead,
guide: ~ **çevirmek (-den)**, withdraw one's favour
from; abandon (idea, project): ~ **dalgası**, (*naut.*)
bow wave: ~ **döndürücü**, vertiginous, making
dizzy: ~ **dönmesi**, dizziness: ~ **edebilmek (-le)**, (be
able to) cope with: ~ **edememek (-le)**, be unable to
cope with: ~ **eğmek**, bow; (*fig.*) bow one's head,
submit; (*fig.*) take a back seat: ~ **elde iken**, while
still living, in his lifetime: ~ **etm.**, succeed, overcome: ~ **film**, (*cin.*) feature film: ~ **gelmek**, come
into power; conquer, defeat: ~ **göstermek**, show
o.s., appear, become visible; (revolt) break out: ~
göz etm., marry off: ~ **göz sadakası**, a sacrifice (to
avert a mishap): ~ **göz yarmak**, bungle things; do
stg. unseemly: ~ **kaldırmak**, raise the head;
= ~KALDIRMAK: ~ **kaldırmamak**, work unceasingly: ~ **kasarası**, (*naut.*) fo'c'sle: ~ **kesmek**,
bow in greeting: ~ **kıç vurmak**, (*naut.*) pitch and
toss: ~ **kıç yok**, there's neither leader nor led: ~
kırılır fes içinde kol kırılır yen içinde, wash your
dirty linen at home, not in public: ~ **ko(y)mak (-e)**,
stake one's life on stg.: ~ **koşmak**, be obstinate/
insistent: ~ **köşe**, seat of honour: ~MAKALE:
~ **nereye giderse ayak da oraya gider**, children must
follow the grown-ups' example: ~ **ol da, istersen**
soğan ~**ı ol**, always try to be at the head/in the
lead: ~ **omuzluğu**, (*naut.*) bow: ~ **örtüsü**, (*mod.*)
headscarf: ~ **paçası**, (*cul.*) sheep's-head jelly: ~ **rol**,
(*th.*) lead(ing part): ~ **sağlığı dilemek**, express one's

condolences (on a relative's death): ~ **sallamak**
(-e), nod in agreement with; listen without paying
attention: ~ **sedire geçmek**, take the first/top seat;
be very important: ~ **tacı**, crown; (*fig.*) much
loved/respected person: ~ **tutmak (-e)**, (*naut.*) head
for: ~ **tutmamak**, (*naut.*) not answer the helm: ~
ucuna dikilmek, pester s.o.: ~ **üstünde tutmak**,
honour highly: ~ **üstünde yeri olm.**, be highly
venerated/loved: ~ **üstüne!**, *int.* at your service!;
it shall be done!; with pleasure!, you are welcome!, very good!: ~ **vermek**, give one's life
(for stg.); show its head, begin to appear: ~
vurmak, (*naut.*) pitch; **(-e)** = ~VURMAK: ~ **yapıt**,
masterpiece: ~ **yastığı**, pillow: ~YAZI: ~ **yemek**,
n. the best dish (of the meal); *vt.* cause s.o.'s death/
dismissal.

başa: ~ **baş**, [195] on equal terms: ~ **baş gelmek/**
kalmak, (*sp.*) be equal, draw: ~ **bela**, source of
trouble: ~ **çıkartmak (-i)**, fuss over s.o.: ~ **çıkmak**,
succeed, accomplish; **(-le)**, cope with, master,
succeed with: ~ **çıkmamak**, have insufficient time,
etc. (for a job): ~ **geçmek**, take the lead: ~ **gelen**
çekilir, what can't be cured must be endured: ~
gelmek, befall, happen, occur: ~ **güreşmek**, (*sp.*)
contest in the first class; (*fig.*) tackle the hardest
side of stg.: ~ **kakmak (-i)**, remind of a former
kindness, taunt, rub in (one's favours).

başı: ~ **açık**, bare-headed; clear, obvious: ~
açılmak, begin to go bald: ~ **ağrımak**, be troubled: ~
~ **bağlı**, attached, not free; engaged, married: ~
bela/dertte, in an awkward situation: ~ **bela/derde**
girmek, get into difficulties: ~ **bütün**, with
husband/wife living: ~ **çatlamak**, have a splitting
headache: ~ **daralmak**, fall into financial difficulties: ~ **darda kalmak**, be in straitened circumstances: ~ **derde düşmek**, get into trouble: ~
derdine düşmek, be preoccupied with one's own
troubles: ~ **devletli**, lucky, fortunate: ~ **dinç**, free of all
anxiety/sorrow: ~ **dönmek**, feel dizzy/giddy; (*fig.*)
be out of one's depth: ~ **dönük**, giddy; bewildered:
~ **dumanlı**, (mountain) wreathed in mist; (*fig.*)
dazed, drunk, lovesick: ~ **göğe ermek**, (*jok.*) meet
with unexpected happiness, rejoice: ~ **göğe erdi**
sanıyor, he thinks he did stg. wonderful: ~ **havada**,
conceited: ~ **hoş olmamak (-le)**, be displeased with
stg.: ~ **için (-in)**, for the sake of . . .: ~ **kalabalık**,
surrounded/having to deal with many people: ~
kazan gibi olm., one's head be throbbing (with all the
noise): ~ **nara yanmak**, suffer because of s.o. else:
~ **önünde**, quiet, unassuming, satisfied; harmless,
submissive: ~ **sıkılmak**, be in difficulties: ~ **sıkıya**
gelmek, be worn out with trouble: ~ **şişmek**, get
swollen-headed: ~ **tas**, bald-headed: ~ **taşa değdi**
geldi, he has had a bitter experience: ~ **tutmak**,
have a headache: ~ **üstünde yeri olm.**, be highly
respected: ~ **yastık (yüzü) görmemek**, not to sleep a
wink: ~ **yerine gelmek**, collect o.s.; recover one's
wits: ~ **yukarıda**, self-satisfied, conceited; proud;
ambitious: ~ **yumuşak**, quiet-spoken, reasonable.

baş-: ~**ıma gelenler!**, the things that I suffer/
happen to me!: ~ **ımda bu iş var**, I've got this job to

do: ~ **ımla beraber**, with the greatest pleasure!: ~ **ın sağ olsuna gitmek**, go to offer one's condolences.
başına, each, per head, per person: ~ **bela açmak/getirmek/olm.**, cause s.o. trouble, vex: ~ **belayı satın aldı**, he got more than he bargained for: ~ **bir hal gelirse**, if he should die: ~ **bitmek**, pester: ~ **buyruk**, a law unto himself: ~ **çalmak (-ın)**, give back a gift angrily/with disgust: ~ **çalsın**, now he can whistle for it!: ~ **çıkarmak**, fuss over/spoil s.o.: ~ **çıkmak (-ın)**, presume on s.o.'s kindness: ~ **çorap örmek**, plot against s.o.; ~ **dert açmak**, bring trouble on o.s.: ~ **dert etm.**, worry about stg.: ~ **devlet kuşu konmak**, have a great stroke of luck: ~ **dikilmek**, stay close to s.o., keep control over s.o.; watch over and make s.o. work: ~ **dikmek**, appoint s.o. to protect s.o./stg.; drink stg. to the last drop: ~ **dolamak**, burden s.o.: ~ **ekşimek (-ın)**, be a heavy burden to; dominate: ~ **geçirmek**, (*mod.*) put stg. on one's head; (*fig.*) beat s.o. about the head with stg.: ~ **geçmek**, set s.o. to work; take over the management (of work); become the leader: ~ **gelmek**, befall, happen (to): ~ **güneş geçmiş**, he's feeling the effects of the sun: ~ **hal gelmek**, be hard put to it: ~ **iş açmak/çıkarmak**, cause trouble to s.o.: ~ **iş çıkmak**, have an unpleasant surprise: ~ **kalmak**, be forced to do stg.: ~ **karalar bağlamak**, be very sorrowful: ~ **oyun açmak** = ~ **iş**: ~ **sarmak**, wind stg. round one's head; (wine) go to one's head; pester s.o. (with stg.): ~ **taç etm.**, respect/revere s.o.: ~ **teller taksın!**, that's one up to him!: ~ **vur ağzından lokmasını al!** = AĞZINDAN: ~ **vurmak**, (drink/ wealth, etc.) go to one's head; bring on a headache.

başında: ~ **beklemek/durmak**, watch over s.o.: ~ **değirmen çevirmek/döndürmek**, disturb s.o. with noise: ~ **kavak yelleri esmek**, have fantastic ideas/ projects; not know what one is doing: ~ **olm.**, be in the same awkward situation; be the leader: ~ **torba/yuları eksik**, (*vulg.*) he's a beast/donkey.

başından, basically, essentially: ~ **aşağı kaynar sular dökülmek**, have a terrible shock: ~ **atmak**, put off/get rid of s.o.: ~ **beri**, all along/the time: ~ **büyük işlere girişmek**, bite off more than one can chew: ~ **geçmek**, have happened to s.o. before: ~ **kesmek**, remove completely: ~ **korkmak**, fear to be involved (because of the consequences): ~ **savmak**, get rid/dispose of s.o.

başını: ~ **ağrıt(ma)mak**, (not) worry s.o. (with endless details): ~ **alamamak (-den)**, be too busy with stg. (to do anything else): ~ **alıp gitmek**, go off without leave/notice: ~ **ateşler/nara yakmak**, create trouble for s.o.: ~ **bağlamak**, betroth/marry off s.o.: ~ **beklemek**, observe stg.: ~ **belaya sokmak**, burn one's fingers: ~ **bir yere bağlamak**, find work for s.o.; save s.o. from destitution: ~ **boş bırakmak**, leave s.o. free/unfettered: ~ **çatmak**, tie a scarf round one's head (to prevent it aching): ~ **derde sokmak**, get into trouble, bring trouble upon o.s.: ~ **dinlemek**, rest: ~ **dinlendirmek**, blow away the cobwebs: ~ **ezmek**, crush, put out of action: ~ **gözünü yarmak**, do stg. badly/not as one wanted: ~ **istemek**, want s.o. dead: ~ **kaldır(a)-**

mamak, make a job last; (*med.*) not get better: ~ **kaşımaya vakti olmamak**, not have a moment to spare (for stg.): ~ **kes!**, duck your head!: ~ **koltuğunun altına almak/ortaya koymak**, take one's life in one's hands: ~ **kurtarmak**, save one's life; manage to survive: ~ **okutmak**, (*rel.*) have prayers recited (over the sick): ~ **rüzgâra çevirmek**, (*naut.*) bring to: ~ **sokacak bir yer**, a place to rest/a roof over one's head (however modest): ~ **sokmak (-e)**, find some sort of protection (in): ~ **(taştan) taşa vurmak**, sincerely repent: ~ **toplamak/yapmak**, (woman) arrange her hair: ~ **vermek**, sacrifice o.s.: ~ **yakmak**, get into difficulties: ~ **yemek**, ruin/kill s.o.

başının: ~ **altında**, under one's pillow: ~ **altından çıkmak**, (plan, etc.) be hatched out in s.o.'s head: ~ **belasını aramak**, ride for a fall: ~ **çaresine bakmak**, look after one's own affairs; fend for o.s.: ~ **derdine düşmek**, be preoccupied with one's own troubles: ~ **dikine gitmek**, believe in o.s., not listen to others' advice: ~ **etini yemek**, worry the life out of s.o., badger/nag s.o.: ~ **gözünün sadakası**, an involuntary sacrifice (to avert a mishap); a thank-offering (given grudgingly).

başınız sağ olsun!, my condolences to you!

başta, at the top; at the head; first; before everything; (*naut.*) (a)fore: ~ **bulunmak**, be in charge of stg.: ~ **gelmek**, come first, be dominant: ~ **gitmek**, be in the lead: ~ **taşımak**, show great respect.

baştan, again; from the beginning; overhead: ~ **aşağı/ayağa/başa** = BAŞTANBAŞA: ~ **aşmak**, be too much: ~ **çıkarmak**, seduce, debauch, pervert: ~ **çıkmak**, throw off restraint; get out of control; be led astray: ~ **kalma/kalmış**, second-hand: ~ **kara etm.**, (*naut.*) run ashore, go aground; (*fig.*) make a last desperate effort: ~ **kara gitmek**, head for disaster: ~ **kıça kadar**, (*naut.*) fore and aft: ~ **savma**, careless, perfunctory, superficial, negligent: ~ **savma cevap**, evasive answer: ~ **savmak**, do stg. carelessly/superficially: ~ **sona dek**, from start to finish.

baş·abaş Entirely, completely; (*fin.*) at par: ~**tan aşağı//yukarı**, below//above par. ~**ağa¹çı**, (*carp.*) cross-cut/end-grained timber. ~**ağırlık**, (*sp.*) heavyweight. ~**ağrısı**ⁿ¹, (*med.*) headache; (*fig.*) nuisance, pest, worry.

başa¹kᵍ¹ (*bot.*) Ear of corn. ~ **bağlamak/tutmak** = LANMAK: ~ **bıyığı**, awn: ~ **burcu**, (*ast.*) Virgo: ~ **dikeni**, (*bot.*) beard: ~ **etm./toplamak**, glean: ~ **samanı**, chaff.

başak·çı (*agr.*) Gleaner. ~**çık**, (*bot.*) spicule. ~**çılık**, gleaning. ~**lanmak**, *vi.* (*bot.*) come into ear. ~**lı**, in ear, bearing spikes. ~**sız**, earless.

baş·aktör//~aktris (*th.*) Leading actor//actress. ~**altı**ⁿ¹, (*sp.*) second class (in wrestling); (*naut.*) forward crew-quarters. ~**amiral**ⁱ, (*naut.*) admiral-in-chief.

başarı Success; achievement; accomplishment: ~ **göstermek**, be successful: ~**ya ulaşmak**, achieve success.

başar·ıcı/~ılı Successful. ~**ıcılık**, ability. ~**ılılık**, success. ~**ılmak**, *vp.* be successfully completed.

~ **ım,** performance. ~ **ısız,** unsuccessful. ~ **ısızlık,** lack of success, failure. ~ **mak (-i),** bring to a successful conclusion; carry the day; succeed in, accomplish, achieve. ~ **mamak,** *vi.* fail.

başasistan(lık) (*ed., med.*) (Rank/work of) chief assistant/intern.

başat (*bio.*) Dominant. ~ **lık,** dominance: ~ **yasası,** law of dominance.

baş·bakan(lık) (*adm.*) (Rank/duty/office of) prime minister. ~ **bakman** = ~ MÜFETTİŞ. ~ **başa,** (*eng.*) butt. ~ **buğ,** (*mil.*) commander-in-chief; head of irregular troops; leader. ~ **çavuş(luk),** (rank of) (*naut.*) petty-officer//(*mil.*) sergeant-major. ~ **çı,** foreman; boss; seller of sheep's-heads, etc. ~ **çık,** (*bot.*) anther; (*pub.*) article. ~ **diz(g)ici,** (*pub.*) chief compositor/typesetter. ~ **düşman,** arch-enemy. ~ **eski,** senior (servant, etc.). ~ **garson,** head-waiter, *maître d'hôtel.* ~ **gedikli,** (*mil.*) sergeant-major. ~ **hakem,** (*sp.*) referee. ~ **hekim(lik),** (*med.*) (post/work of) head doctor in a hospital/medical director. ~ **hemşire(lik),** (*med.*) (post/work of) matron//senior sister. ~ **heykeli,** (*art.*) bust. ~ **ıboş,** vagabond; (animal) not tethered/tied up; free, unfettered: ~ **bırakmak,** leave untethered/uncontrolled; leave to o.s.: ~ **kalmak,** be left free, be independent: ~ **koşmak,** career about wildly. ~ **ıboşluk,** freedom, independence. ~ **ıbozuk,** *n.* (*mil.*) irregular soldier, bashibazouk; civilian: *a.* in disorder, undisciplined. ~ **ıbozukluk,** (*mil.*) being an irregular; disorder, indiscipline. ~ **ıkabak,** *a.* all the hair fallen out/cut very short: *adv.* bareheaded. ~ **imam,** (*rel.*) chief imam.

başka *pron.* [76] Other; another; in addition; different; apart. *post.* **(-den)** [89] Other than; else than; apart from; besides. ~ ~ , separately, one by one: ~ **bir deyişle,** in other words: ~ **biri,** another; s.o./ stg. else: ~ **çare yok,** there's no alternative: ~ **işi yok mu?,** why is he interfering?: ~ **kapıya müracaat!,** you'd better try somewhere else: ~ **ları,** others; other people: ~ **larına bakınca/göre,** in comparison, relatively: ~ **sı**[nı], *pron.* [76] another; s.o. else; (*leg.*) third party: ~ **sı adına,** (*fin.*) nominee: ~ **sı değil yine o!,** it's just him again: ~ **sının derdine yanmak,** suffer because of/for s.o. else: ~ **sının yalancısıyım,** that's what I was told (but it may be a lie).

başka·ca Separately, independently; rather different; otherwise; further. ~ **lamak (-i),** change. ~ **laşım/** ~ **laşma,** (*bio., geol.*) metamorphosis. ~ **laşmak,** *vi.* alter, grow different; (*bio., geol.*) metamorphose. ~ **laşmış,** (*geol.*) metamorphic. ~ **laştırmak (-i),** alter. ~ **lık,** diversity; alteration; change in appearance.

başkaldır·an/ ~ **ıcı** Rebel; opponent. ~ **ı/** ~ **ma,** revolt; uprising; opposition. ~ **mak (-e),** revolt/rise against; oppose.

baş·kan (*adm.*) President; manager; chairman; chieftain: ~ **ın oyu,** casting-vote. ~ **kanlık,** presidency; chairmanship; chieftaincy: ~ **etm.,** preside over, take the chair at (a meeting). ~ **kâti'p**[bi], first secretary; chief clerk. ~ **kâtiplik,** post of first secretary; chief clerkship. ~ **kent**[i], (*adm.*) capital. ~ **kesi't**[di], (*carp.*) cross-cut, end-grain. ~ **kiriş,** (*arch.*) architrave. ~ **kişi,** hero. ~ **komutan/**

kumandan(lık), (*mil.*) (rank/office/duties of) commander-in-chief. ~ **konakçı,** (*bio.*) primary host. ~ **konsolos,** (*adm.*) consul-general. ~ **konsoloshane,** (*arch.*) consulate-general. ~ **konsolosluk,** (*adm.*) consulate-general; consul-generalship. ~ **koşul,** precept, obligation. ~ **kurt,** *pr.n.* branch of the Kipchak Turks (in the Urals). ~ **lahana,** (*bot.*) cabbage. ~ **lam,** (*pub.*) article.

başla·ma *vn.* Beginning, start; introduction; (*sp.*) kick-off: ~ **atışı,** (*sp.*) service: ~ **değişimi,** change of service: ~ **dan menetmek,** nip in the bud. ~ **mak,** *vi.*; **(-i),** *vt.* begin, commence, start; develop; appear: **başla!,** (*cin.*) action! ~ **ngı'ç**[cı], beginning, commencement, start; (*math.*) origin; (*aer.*) threshold; (*lit.*) preface: ~ +, *a.* initial; incipient: ~ **noktası,** starting-point; (*math.*) point of origin. ~ **n(ıl)mak,** *vi.* be begun; (*bot.*) form a bulb/head, etc. ~ **ntı,** (*mus.*) overture. ~ **tıcı,** (*sp.*) starter. ~ **tım,** (*med.*) induction. ~ **tmak (-i, -e),** *vc.* make/let begin; (*ed.*) put (a child) to school. ~ **yıcı,** *n.* beginner: *a.* beginning. ~ **yış,** *n.* beginning; (chess) opening.

başlı Having a head; principal, important; rounded; with a knob; (*naut.*) down by the head; (*bio.*) cephalo-; (*orn.*) -headed, -capped.

-başlı *suf.* (*bio.*) -cephalic, -cephalous.

baş·lıbaşına Independently, on one's own. ~ **lıca,** *a.* principal, chief: *adv.* principally, above all. ~ **lık,** (*adm.*) headship, presidency; (*dom.*) headrest; (*mod.*) headgear; helmet; (*arch.*) cowl; (*live.*) bridle; (*arch.*) capital; (*el.*) terminal; (*eng.*) cap(ping); (*pub.*) caption, title, heading, headline; (*naut.*) masthead; (*soc.*) sum paid by the bridegroom to the bride's family: ~ **atmak/koymak,** (*pub.*) give a title to stg. ~ **lıklı,** having/with a BAŞLIK; headed (note-paper); (*bio.*) cucullated: ~ **maymun,** (*zoo.*) capuchin monkey. ~ **lıksız,** without a BAŞLIK.

başmak *n.* (*obs.*) Slipper, shoe. ~ **çı,** shoe-maker/ -seller; (in mosques) man in charge of shoes taken off. ~ **lık,** material for making shoes; (*his.*) pin-money for the Sultan's mother/daughters; (in mosques) shoe-rack.

baş·makale = ~ YAZI. ~ **mal,** (*fin.*) capital. ~ **man,** primate, leader. ~ **muallim** = ~ ÖGRETMEN. ~ **muharrir** = ~ YAZAR. ~ **murakı'p**[bı], (*fin.*) controller-in-chief. ~ **müdür(lük),** (*adm.*) (office/duties of) chief manager, director. ~ **müfettiş,** (*adm.*) chief inspector. ~ **mühendis,** chief engineer. ~ **müretti'p**[bi] = ~ DİZİCİ. ~ **müşavir,** (*adm.*) chief consultant. ~ **oyuncu,** (*cin., th.*) feature-/leading player. ~ **öğretmen,** (*ed.*) head-teacher. ~ **örtü(sü)**[nü], (*mod.*) (woman's) headgear; veil. ~ **örtülü,** (woman) veiled/with head covered. ~ **parmak,** (*bio.*) thumb; big toe. ~ **pehlivan,** (*sp.*) champion wrestler. ~ **piskopos(luk),** (*rel.*) archbishop(ric). ~ **resmi,** (*art.*) portrait. ~ **rol,** (*cin., th.*) leading part/role. ~ **sağ(lığı)**[nı], (offering of) condolences: ~ **dilemek,** offer one's condolences: ~ **satıcı,** main supplier. ~ **savcı(lık),** (*leg.*) (office/duties of) attorney-general, public prosecutor. ~ **sız,** headless; without a leader/manager; (*bio.*) acephalous. ~ **sızcılık,** anarchism. ~ **sızlık,** being headless/ without a leader: (*soc.*) anarchy. ~ **şehir** = ~ KENT. ~ **tabi'p**[bi] = ~ HEKİM.

baş·tanbaşa (*adv.*) [195] From end to end; completely, entirely, fully, thoroughly; (*lit.*) in depth: ~ **okumak**, read from cover to cover: ~ **resimli**, (*pub.*) fully illustrated. ~ **tanımaz(lık)**, (*pol.*) anarch·ist/(-ism). ~ **tankara,** (*orn.*) (great) tit. ~ **ucu**[nu], head(-end); bedside; (*ast.*) zenith: ~ **uzaklığı**, (*ast.*) zenith distance: ~ **nda**, at his (bed)side. ~ **uzman(lık)**, (post of) chief expert/specialist. ~ **ülke**, (*pol.*) home-land/mother-country (of an empire). ~ **vekâlet** = ~ BAKANLIK. ~ **vekil** = ~ BAKAN. ~ **vura(ca)ğı**[nı], (*leg.*) competent authority. ~ **vurma**, having recourse to, applying for; application. ~ **vurmak (-e)**, have recourse to; apply for; (*leg.*) appeal; (fish) bite, take the bait. ~ **vuru**, application; (*eng.*) datum: ~ **kitap**, reference book. ~ **vurucu**, applicant. ~ **yapıt**[1], (*art.*, *lit.*) masterpiece, classic. ~ **yardımcı**, (*adm.*) chief-assistant. ~ **yargıcı**[y1], (*sp.*) referee, umpire. ~ **yarış**, championship. ~ **yasa**, principle. ~ **yaver**, (*mil.*) chief aide-de-camp. ~ **yazar(lık)**, (*pub.*) (office/duties of) editor-in-chief/principal leader-writer. ~ **yazı**, (*pub.*) editorial, leader. ~ **yazman**, (*adm.*) first secretary; chief clerk. ~ **yıldız**, (*ast.*) primary (of a double-star). ~ **yönetmen**, (*adm.*) director.

bat (*eng.*) Swage (for lead pipes).

bata·k[ğı] *n.* Quagmire; bog, marsh. *a.* Boggy; (*fin.*) fraudulent; about to sink/perish; desperate (condition/affair). ~ **para**, bad debt.

batak·çı Fraudulent borrower; swindler, cheat: ~ **ya mal kaptırmış gibi**, s.o. eager to get back a loan. ~ **çıl**, (*bot.*) marsh-loving (plants). ~ **çılık**, fraudulence; swindling. ~ **çulluğu**[nu] = ~ LIK ÇULLUĞU. ~ **hane**, gambling den; den of thieves; dangerous spot. ~ **lı**, marshy. ~ **lık**, marshy place, bog, fen; quicksand: ~ **ardıcı**, (*orn.*) marsh warbler: ~ **baştankarası**, (*orn.*) marsh tit: ~ **baykuşu**, (*orn.*) short-eared owl: ~ **çulluğu**, (*orn.*) common snipe: ~ **humması**, (*med.*) ague: ~ **kaplumbağası**, (*zoo.*) Eur. pond tortoise: ~ **kırlangıcı**, (*orn.*) collared pratincole: ~ **kiraz kuşu**, (*orn.*) reed bunting: ~ **kunduzu**, (*zoo.*) coypu: ~ **marnı**, (*geol.*) boglime: ~ **ötleğen/saz bülbülü**, (*orn.*) marsh warbler: ~ **samuru**, (*zoo.*) Eur. mink: ~ **serçesi**, (*orn.*) Spanish sparrow: ~ **süseni**, (*bot.*) iris: ~ **tavuğu**, (*orn.*) spotted crake. ~ **lıkketeni**[ni], (*bot.*) cottongrass. ~ **lıkkömürü**[nü], peat. ~ **lıkkuşları**, (*orn.*) marshbirds. ~ **sal**, *a.* marsh-; marshy.

batar (*med.*) Pneumonia.

bat·ardo (*eng.*) Caisson, cofferdam; (*arch.*) bulkhead. ~ **arya**, (*mil.*) battery (of artillery); (*naut.*) port/starboard guns of one deck; (*el.*) battery; (*eng.*) set, group. ~ **eri**, (*mus.*) group of percussion instruments. ~ **erist**[i], percussion instrumentalist.

batı *n.* (*geo.*) The West; Western countries; the Occident; Europe; (*met.*) the west wind. *a.* West/(-ern); Occidental. ˙~ **karayel**, (*naut.*) west-north-west: ~ **kerte karayel//lodos**, west by north//south: ~ **lodos**, west-south-west: ~ **özentili**, (*soc.*) aping Western ways. ~ **cı(lık)**, (*soc.*) westerniz·er/(-ation).

batık Submerged; sunken. ~ **gözlü**, hollow-eyed. ~ **meşe**, (*bot.*) bog-oak.

batıl False; erroneous; (*leg.*) invalid; vain; useless. ~ **itikat**, superstition.

batılı *a.* (*soc.*) Western, occidental. *n.* Western(er), Occidental. ~ **ca(lık)**, (being) in European style. ~ **laşma**, westernization. ~ **laşmak**, *vi.* become westernized. ~ **laşmışlık**, state of being westernized. ~ **laştırmak (-i)**, westernize.

batın[nı] (*bio.*) Abdomen, stomach; (*soc.*) family; clan; generation. **bir ~ da üç çocuk**, three children at one birth.

batıni *a.* (*phil.*) Hidden; mysterious; inner; spiritual; esoteric. *pr.n.* (*rel.*) Member of the ~ YE sect. ~ **ye**, (*rel.*) sect believing in the hidden meaning of the Koran.

bat·ırılmak *vp.* Be submerged/sunk/dipped. ~ **ırmak (-i, -e)**, submerge; sink; dip; thrust into; (*fin.*) ruin, reduce to bankruptcy; decry, speak ill of. ~ **ış**, submerging, sinking; decline, ruin; setting (of the sun): ~ **noktası**, west point.

bati Slow, tardy; dilatory, slothful.

bati·k (*tex.*) Batik. ~ **skaf**, (*naut.*) bathyscaph. ~ **sta**, (*tex.*) batiste.

batkı *n.* (*fin.*) Bankruptcy, failure. ~ **sözleşmesi**, composition (with creditors): ~ **ya düşmek**, fail. ~ **n**, *a.* bankrupt; deep, hollow. ~ **nlık**, bankruptcy; depth, hollowness.

Batlamyos (*his.*) Ptolemy. ~ +, Ptolemaic.

bat·ma *vn.* Sinking; setting; (*soc.*) collapse, failure. ~ **mak**, *vi.* sink; submerge; go to the bottom; (*ast.*) set; (money) be lost; (*soc.*) be destroyed, pass out of existence; (*fin.*) be ruined, go bankrupt: (-e), *vt.* penetrate; enter deeply; prick, sting; get on s.o.'s nerves, irk: **bata çıka**, with the greatest difficulty: **battı balık yan gider**, sink or swim, come what may. ~ **mayan**, (*ast.*) circumpolar.

batman[1] *n.* (*obs.*) Weight (*variable* = 2-8 OKKA; 2-10 kg.).

batman[2] (*phys.*) Thrust.

batn- = BATIN.

baton (*mus.*) Baton. ~ **sale**, (*cul.*) salty stick-biscuit.

battal *a.* Useless, worthless; unemployed, idle; large and clumsy; obsolete; (*leg.*) abrogated, cancelled, void. *n.* Large-sized paper; documents no longer valid. ~ **boy**, (*pub.*) folio: ~ **etm.**, render null and void; cancel.

battaniye (*dom.*) Blanket.

batur Brave, heroic.

batyal (*naut.*) Deep (sea), 200-1,000 m.

bav Training (dogs, hawks, etc.) to hunt. ~ **cı**, trainer. ~ **lı**, *a.* trained: *n.* lure, etc. (for training). ~ **lımak (-i)**, train to hunt.

bavul Traveller's trunk, suitcase.

Bavyera (*geo.*) Bavaria. ~ **lı**, *a.*, *n.* Bavarian.

bay (*obs.*) Man of property, rich man; (*now*) gentleman; Mr. ~ **lara**, (toilet, etc.) for men, 'gentlemen', 'the gents'.

bayağı *a.* Common, banal, normal, ordinary; drab; rough, coarse, vulgar. *adv.* Simply, merely, just; thoroughly, pretty well. ~ **dil**, (*ling.*) vulgarism: ~ **engerek**, (*zoo.*) viper, adder: ~ **gün**, ordinary/working day: ~ **kaçmak**, be inappropriate/out of place.

bayağı·kesir (*math.*) Vulgar fraction. ~ **laşmak**, *vi.* become common/coarse, etc. ~ **laştırmak (-i)**, make common/coarse, etc. ~**lık**, commonness; coarseness; vulgarity.

bayan Lady; Mrs., Miss, Ms. ~ **elçi**, (*adm.*) lady ambassador, ambassadress: ~**lar, baylar!**, ladies and gentlemen!: ~**lara**, (toilet, etc.) for women, 'ladies', powder-room.

bayat[1] (*cul.*) Stale; not fresh; (*fig.*) insipid; out-of-date; (*sl.*) backward. ~**lamak**, *vi.* become stale, lose its freshness. ~**latmak (-i)**, wait for stg. to become stale (before using it). ~**lık**, staleness.

bayati (*Or. mus.*) An old melody.

bay·gı(lı) (*med.*) Coma(tose). ~**gın**, fainting; unconscious; dazed; languid; faint; drooping (flowers); heavy (smell): ~ ~, languidly; amorously: ~ **düşmek**, be(come) very tired. ~**gınlaşmak**, *vi.* begin to look languid; become sleepy. ~**gınlık**, swoon, fainting condition; languor; drooping (of a flower). ~**gıntı**, (*zoo.*) silkworm's inability to make a cocoon.

bayıl·dı = İMAMBAYILDI. ~**mak**, *vi.* faint, swoon; have a black-out; (*bot.*) droop; (*naut.*) list: **(-den)**, be sick from/exhausted with: **(-e)**, be passionately fond of/addicted to: **(-i)**, (*sl.*) give, pay, spend: ~**a** ~ **a**, willingly, eagerly. ~**tıcı**, sickly/nauseating (smell, taste); causing to faint; (*med.*) anaesthetic. ~**tmak (-e)**, cause to faint; cause slight nausea; (*med.*) anaesthetize.

bayındır Prosperous; developed. ~**laşmak**, *vi.* become prosperous; be developed. ~**laştırma**, development. ~**laştırmak (-i)**, make prosperous; develop. ~**lık**, prosperity; development: ~ **Bakan(lığ)ı**, (*adm.*) Minis·ter(-try) of Public Works: ~ **işleri**, public works: ~ **mühendis(liğ)i**, civil engineer(ing). ~**ma**, development. ~**mak (-i)**, develop, improve. ~**sız**, undeveloped; uncultivated.

bayır Slope; ascent, slight rise; hill. ~ **asağı**// **yukarı**, down-//up·hill. ~**kuşu**[nu], (*orn.*) woodlark. ~**laşmak**, *vi.* become steep, rise. ~**turpu**[nu], (*bot.*) horse-radish.

bayi[i] Seller, vendor; salesman; retailer (of monopoly goods), tobacconist; wholesale distributor.

Baykal ~ **deniz/gölü**, Lake Baikal.

baykuş (*orn.*) Owl. ~ **gibi**, owlish; (*fig.*) ill-omened: ~ **papağanı**, kakapo. ~**giller**, Strigidae.

baylan *n.* (*art.*) Artificiality. *a.* Spoilt (child); coy.

baypas (*eng.*) Bypass. ~ **yol**, bypass, relief road.

bayra[1]**k**[gı] Flag, ensign, standard; (*mil.*) colours. ~ **açmak**, unfurl a flag; collect volunteers; defy; revolt: ~ **altı**, military service: ~ **çekmek**, hoist the flag: ~ **direği**, flag-pole/-staff: ~ **esası**, (*leg.*) law of the flag: ~ **koşu/yarışı**, (*sp.*) relay-race: ~ **kumaşı**, (*tex.*) bunting: ~ **sopası**, (*sp.*) baton: ~**ı (yarıya) indirmek**, lower the flag (to half-mast): ~**ları açmak**, become insolent/abusive: ~**larla donatmak**, (*naut.*) dress ship.

bayrak·lı Beflagged: ~ **cennetkuşu**, (*orn.*) King of Saxony bird of paradise. ~**lık**, (*tex.*) bunting. ~**tar**, (*mil.*) flag-/standard-bearer; colour-sergeant. ~**tarlık**, standard-bearer's duties: ~ **etm.**, take the lead; show the way: ~**ını yapmak**, be in the vanguard.

bayram Religious feast day (esp. following the fast of Ramadan), Bairam; national holiday; festival; festivity. ~ **arifesi**, the eve of Bairam: ~ **ayı**, lunar month of ŞEVVAL: ~ **etm./yapmak**, celebrate, rejoice: ~ **haftasını mangal tahtası anlamak**, (*jok.*) completely misunderstand stg.: ~ **havası**, pleasant/ joyful atmosphere: ~ **koçu gibi**, showily and tastelessly decorated: ~ **şekeri**, (*cul.*) sweetmeat offered at Bairam: ~ **tebriki**, Bairam con-gratulations//greeting-card: ~ **üstü**, just before Bairam: ~**da seyranda**/~**dan** ~**a**, seldom, rarely, once in a blue moon: ~**dan sonra şekeri nidem**, it's no use to me now, it's too late.

bayram·laşmak (-le) Exchange festival greetings; rejoice (with s.o.). ~**lık**, *a.* festive; fit for the Bairam: *n.* Bairam present; one's best clothes: ~ **ad**, taking an insult as a compliment. ~**yeri**[ni], fairground.

bayrı Antique; very old. ~**lık**, antiquity; oldness, seniority.

baysal(lık) Tranquil(lity); peaceful(ness).

baysungur (*orn.*) A bird of prey; lammergeyer.

baytar Veterinary surgeon. ~**lık**, veterinary surgery.

baz (*chem.*) Base. ~**al**[i], basal, essential.

-baz *n. suf.* Playing with [CAMBAZ; DÜZENBAZ]

bazalt[1] (*geol.*) Basalt.

baz·an/~**en** Sometimes; now and then.

bazı *a.* [74] Some; a few; certain. *adv.* Sometimes. ~ **adam(lar)**, some people; certain people: ~ ~, at times, now and then: ~ **kere**, sometimes: ~**ları**/ ~**sı**, some of them: ~**ları nebi** ~**ları veli dediler**, it's not quite certain what is meant: ~**mız**, some of us: ~**nız**, some of you.

baziçe (*obs.*) Toy, plaything; laughing-stock.

bazi·diyospor (*myc.*) Basidiospore. ~**k**, (*chem.*) basic. ~**t**[i], (*myc.*) basidium.

bazilika (*arch., rel.*) Basilica; (*his.*) palace, law-court.

bazlama(¹**ç**ᶜ¹) (*cul.*) Pastry cooked on a griddle.

bazu = PAZI.

bazuka (*mil.*) Bazooka.

B·B = BAYINDIRLIK BAKANLIĞI. ~**BC** = (*British Broadcasting Corporation*). ~**CG** = (*med.*) (*BCG vaccine*). ~**çvş** = (*mil.*) BAŞÇAVUŞ.

be[1] *n.* (*ling.*) The Tk. letter B, b.

be[2] *int.* (*col.*) Hi!, heh you!, I say!

Be., be. = (*ling.*) BELİRTEÇ; (*ch.s.*) BERİLYUM.

bebe (*col.*) Baby. ~**cik**, little baby; (*iron.*) flippant old person.

bebe[1]**k**[gi] Baby; doll. ~ **gibi**, babyish; (*fig.*) very pretty (woman): ~ **beklemek**, be pregnant/about to give birth.

bebek·çe Babyish. ~**çik**, little baby. ~**leşmek**, *vi.* behave childishly. ~**lik**, babyhood; childishness: ~ **etm.**, behave childishly.

beberuhi Pygmy; dwarf; (*th.*) character in KARAGÖZ.

bebit[i] ~ **metal**, Babbitt metal.

becayiş (*adm.*) Exchange of posts (by two officials). ~ **etm.**, exchange posts.

becelleşmek *vi.* Struggle/fight with one another.

beceri(¹**k**ᵍⁱ) Resourcefulness; tact; ability; skill; (*sp.*) agility. ~**li**, resourceful; capable, efficient; clever; adroit, deft, skilful. ~**lilik**, resourcefulness;

dexterity, skill. ~siz, a. clumsy, incapable, maladroit: n. bungler; duffer. ~sizce, clumsily. ~sizlik, clumsiness; incapacity.

becer·mek (-i) Carry out stg. skilfully; contrive; do stg. successfully; (iron.) spoil, ruin; (fig.) injure/violate/kill s.o. ~tmek (-i, -e), vc.

becet[i] (orn.) A sparrow-like bird.

becit Important, necessary, essential.

be[l]ç[ci] [1] n. (mod.) Badge.

Be[l]ç[ci] [2] n. (his.) Vienna. ~li, Viennese. ~tavuğu[nu], (orn.) helmet guinea-fowl.

bed- = BET[3].

bedahet[i] Obviousness; improvisation, extempore speech.

bedava Gratis, free, for nothing; very cheap, for next to nothing. ~ sirke baldan tatlıdır, free vinegar is sweeter than honey. ~cı, s.o. always expecting stg. for nothing; sponger. ~cılık, always expecting things for nothing; sponging.

bed·baht[i] Unfortunate, unlucky; unhappy. ~bahtlık, misfortune; unhappiness. ~bin, despondent, pessimistic; cynical. ~binleşmek, vi. become pessimistic/cynical. ~binlik, despondency; pessimism; cynicism. ~dua, curse, malediction: ~ etm. (-e), curse s.o.: ~sı sinmek (-e), things go wrong for s.o. (because of a curse): ~sını almak, be cursed.

bedel n. Substitute; equivalent; allowance; compensation; price; (obs.) sum paid for exemption from military service; s.o. performing military service/making a pilgrimage for s.o. else. ~ (-e), in place of...; in exchange for...; as a substitute for...: ~ ve navlun, cost and freight (C & F). ~ci/~li, s.o. who has paid military exemption tax. ~siz, without cost/price.

beden (bio.) Trunk; body; (arch.) castle wall; tower; (naut.) bight (of rope). ~ +, a. Physical; corporal: ~ bağı, (naut.) rolling hitch: ~ cezası, (leg.) corporal punishment: ~ eğitim/terbiyesi, (sp.) physical culture/education/training; gymnastics, athletics: ~ini işletmek, exercise o.s.

beden·ce Physically. ~en, in person; personally; physically. ~i/~sel, physical; corporal; bodily.

bedesten Covered market (for valuable goods).

bedevi Nomad; Bedouin. ~lik, Bedouinism.

bedhah Malevolent; evil-natured; vicious.

bedihi Axiomatic, obvious; self-evident. ~dir, it goes without saying.

bedii Aesthetic. ~yat, aesthetics.

bed[l]ir[ri] Full moon.

bed·lik Ugliness; wickedness. ~nam, of ill repute.

begonya (bot.) Begonia. ~giller, Begoniaceae.

begüm (soc.) Begum.

beğen·ce (pub.) Favourable review; appreciation/preface (by an important writer). ~di = HÜN-KÂRBEĞENDİ. ~dirmek (-i, -e), cause s.o. to like/approve stg. ~i, (art.) aesthetic feeling; (good) taste. ~ili(lik), tasteful(ness). ~ilmek, vp. be desired/liked/admired/approved. ~isiz, lacking taste. ~isizlik, (art.) lack of taste; bad taste. ~mek (-i), like; fancy; approve; admire; select: beğen beğendiğini seç!, choose whichever you like!, take your choice!: beğenirsiniz!, you'll never guess!:

beğenmeye bağlı, on approval. ~memek (-i), not like; dislike; deprecate, disapprove of; be doubtful about; be particular about stg.; belittle stg.: beğenmiyen beğenmesin/kızını vermesin, if you don't like it you can lump it! ~mezlik, not liking; dislike.

behavyor·ist (psy.) Behaviourist. ~ism, behaviourism.

behemehal In any case; whatever happens.

beher To each; for each. ~ gün, daily: ~ nüfusa, for each one: ~i, each one: ~ine, apiece, per head.

behey int. (of irritation). Hi!; you there!

behimi a. Animal, brutish (feelings). ~yet[i], bestiality (esp. sexual).

behre Share, lot, portion; advantage; knowledge; capacity. ~dar/~li, having a share (of goods/knowledge). ~siz, without a share; unfortunate; poor; incapable.

be[l]is['si] Harm; obstacle; unsuitability. ~ görmemek, see no objection: ~ yok!, no matter!, never mind!

bej Beige.

bek[i] [1] n. (sp.) Full-back.

bek[i] [2] n. (dom.) Gas-burner/nozzle.

bek[i] [3] n. (prov.) Lookout. ~ kulesi, watch-tower; (sp.) hide.

beka Permanence; stability; what remains; sequel.

bekar (mus.) 'Natural' sign.

bekâr a. Celibate. n. Bachelor; a provincial alone in the city. ~ odası, hostel for such provincials. ~et[i], virginity. ~lık, celibacy; being unmarried; bachelorhood: ~ sultanlıktır, a bachelor's life is a king's life.

bekas (orn.) Eurasian woodcock. ~in, (orn.) common snipe.

bekaya = BAKAYA.

bekçi(lik) (Duties of) watchman, esp. night-watchman; sentry; forest-guard. ~ parolası, watchword.

bekin·me vn. Insistence. ~mek, vi. insist.

bekle·me Waiting; expectance: ~ hakkı, (fin.) option: ~ kulübesi, (mil.) sentry-box: ~ oda/salonu, waiting-room: ~ süresi, waiting period; (fin.) lay days, demurrage. ~mek, vi. wait; remain in expectation: (-i, -den), vt. await; watch; guard; lie in wait for; anticipate; expect, hope for: bekle bre bekle, he/we waited and waited: bekle yârın köşesini!, keep on hoping!: beklemiş et, (cul.) meat that has been kept/hung: bekleyen derviş muradına ermiş, everything comes to him who waits. ~mesiz, (rly.) express. ~ndik/~nen, expected, due, anticipated. ~n(il)mek, vp. be awaited; be expected/hoped for. ~nmedik, unexpected: ~ hal, contingency: ~ olay, accident. ~nmezlik, being unexpected: ~ eylemi, (ling.) verb expressing sudden/unexpected action. ~nti, expectation. ~r, a. stand-by, reserve: ~ ulak/yazılım, poste-restante. ~şmek, vi. wait together. ~tim, (fin.) blocking, freezing. ~e almak, block, freeze. ~tme, vn. holding; storage. ~tmek (-i, -e), cause to wait; keep waiting; have stg. watched/guarded; (adm., sp.) block (s.o./an action); (aer.) hold.

bekri Habitual drunkard; toper. ~lik, drunkenness.

Bektaşi (rel.) Dervish of the Bektashi sect; (fig.)

freethinker; dissolute. ~ **sırrı**, a great mystery/ secret. ~**kavuğu**nu, (*bot.*) echinocactus. ~**lik**, the Bektashi sect; being a Bektashi dervish. ~**üzümü**nü, (*bot.*) gooseberry.

bel[1] *n.* Sign; (*el.*) bel.

bel[2] *n.* (*agr.*) Spade, gardener's fork. ~ **bellemek**, dig.

bel[3] *adv.* ~ ~ **bakmak**, stare vacantly, gape.

bel[4] *n.* (*bio.*) Waist; loins; middle of the back; (*naut.*) midship(s); (*geo.*) col, mountain pass. ~ **ağrısı**, (*med.*) backache, lumbago: ~ **bağlamak (-e)**, rely upon, trust to: ~ **bölgesi**, (*bio.*) lumbar region: ~ **bükmek**, bow down: ~ **eğmek**, bow down: ~ **geçidi**, (*geo.*) mountain pass: ~ **gevşekliği**, (*med.*) impotence: ~KEMİĞİ: ~ **kıra kıra**, swaying from side to side: ~ **kırmak**, bend to left and right: ~ **kündesi**, (*sp.*) a wrestling hold: ~SUYU: ~ **vermek**, (*min.*) buckle; (*arch.*) bulge, sag; yield; collapse: ~**i açılmak**, need to urinate: ~**i anahtarlık kadın**, careful and efficient housewife: ~**i boğuk bardak**, narrow-waisted glass: ~**i bükülmek**, be bent double, with age; be handicapped; feel weak; be unable to do stg.: ~**i çökmek**, become hunchbacked: ~**i gelmek**, (*bio.*) eject semen: ~**i kırılmak**, be exhausted; (*fig.*) be discouraged: ~**inden gelmek (-in)**, be the child of: ~**ini bükmek (-in)**, break the back of, defeat; (illness) cripple; (*sl.*) make short work of stg.: ~**ini doğrultmak**, recover: ~**ini kırmak**, (*fig.*) ruin, cripple; break s.o.'s back.

bel. = (*ling.*) BELİRTEÇ.

bela Trouble; misfortune; calamity, disaster; grief; difficulty; punishment; curse. ~ **çıkarmak**, start a quarrel: ~ **dur vardım/geliyorum demez**, misfortunes come without warning: ~**lar mübareği**, the last straw!: ~**sı (-in)**, for the sake of ... [= NAMUS]: ~**sını aramak**, court disaster: ~**sını bulmak**, get the punishment one deserves: ~**ya çatmak/girmek/ uğramak**, get into trouble, meet with misfortune: ~**yı aramak**, ask/look for trouble: ~**yı berzah**, deep trouble: ~**yı satın almak**, get into difficulties with one's eyes open.

belagat[i] Eloquence; rhetoric; hidden meaning.

belahat[i] Stupidity; idiocy.

belalı *a.* Troublesome; difficult; calamitous; quarrelsome. *n.* Pimp; bully. ~ **alacaklı**, dun.

belce (*bio.*) Space between the eyebrows.

belci Spade-maker/-seller; (*agr.*) labourer.

B. Elçi = (*adm.*) BÜYÜKELÇİ.

Belçika (*geo.*) Belgium. ~ +, *a.* Belgian. ~**lı**, *n.* Belgian.

belde Town. ~**i tayyibe**, (*geo.*) Medina.

beledi *a.* Relating to a town; local; municipal, civic. *n.* (*tex.*) Thick cotton material; (*ich.*) chub. ~**ye**, municipality: ~ **başkan/reisi**, mayor: ~ **makamları**, civic authorities: ~ **meclisi**, borough/ municipal/town council: ~ **rüsumu**, municipal taxes: ~ **suçları**, breaches of municipal bye-laws. ~**yeci**, municipal employee. ~**yecilik**, municipal work.

bele·mek (-i, -e) Swaddle (a child); strap into the cradle; smear with stg. ~**nmek (-e)**, *vp.*

belemir (*bot.*) Cornflower.

belen (*geo.*) Mountain pass.

beler·mek *vi.* (Eyes) be wide open; stare. ~**tmek (-i)**, open the eyes wide and stare (in fear/anger).

beleş (*sl.*) Gratis, free of charge. ~ **atın dişine bakılmaz** = BAHŞİŞ: ~**e konmak**, get stg. for nothing. ~**çi**, sponger, scrounger, parasite.

belge Document; certificate; report; voucher; (*th.*) argument; *pl.* documentation. ~ **almak**, (*ed.*) be expelled from school (after failing the same class/ examination two years running): ~**ye bağlamak**, prove.

belge·ci (*cin.*) Documentary-film maker. ~**bilim**, documentation. ~**cik**, coupon. ~**-film**, (*cin.*) documentary film. ~**leme**, *vn.* confirming, documenting, proving. ~**lemek (-i)**, confirm, prove. ~**lendirmek (-i)**, prove by documentary evidence; patent. ~**lenmek**, *vp.* be confirmed/proved. ~**li**, (*adm.*) certified, documented; (*ed.*) expelled pupil. ~**lik**, (*adm.*) archives. ~**sel**, documentary. ~**siz**, unpatented.

belgi (*dial.*) Sign; distinguishing mark. ~**li**, definite; distinct.

belgin (*phil.*) Precise, clear, definite. ~**leştirme**, *vn.* ~**leştirmek (-i)**, make clear/explicit. ~**lik**, precision, clarity.

belgisiz Indefinite. ~ **adıl//sıfat**, (*ling.*) indefinite pronoun//adjective. ~**lik**, imprecision, indefiniteness.

belgi[i]t[di] (*phil.*) Proof, evidence; receipt; (*leg.*) deed. ~**leme**, providing proof. ~**lik**, wallet, portfolio.

Belgrad (*geo.*) Belgrade.

beli (*dial.*) Yes.

beliğ Eloquent.

beli[i]k[gi] (*mod.*) Plait of hair.

belinlemek *vi.* Wake up with sudden fear; be startled.

belir·ge (*leg.*) Presumption. ~**gi**, (*med.*) syndrome. ~**gin**, clear, manifest. ~**ginleşmek**, *vi.* become clear. ~**ginlik**, clarity.

belir·imsizlik (*phil.*) Indefiniteness. ~**leme**/ ~**lenim**/ ~**leyim**, determination, definition. ~**lemek (-i)**, determine, define; limit, restrict. ~**lenimci(lik)**, (*phil.*) determin·ist/(-ism). ~**lenmek**, *vi.* be determined, become definite. ~**lenmezlik**, indeterminacy. ~**leyici**, characteristic.

belirli Determined; given, fixed, specified; specific; clear. ~ **belirsiz**, not clear/distinct; hardly perceptible: ~ **geçmiş zaman**, (*ling.*) past definite/perfect tense: ~ **süreli**, (*naut.*) fixed time (charter). ~**lik**, being determined/fixed; definiteness.

belir·me *vn.* Appearance; embodiment. ~**mek**, *vi.* appear, become visible; become clear; become conspicuous. ~**siz**, indistinct, dim, not clear; uncertain, equivocal, ambiguous, doubtful; indefinite; unknown: ~ **geçmiş zaman**, (*ling.*) past indefinite tense. ~**sizleşmek**, *vi.* become dim/faded, etc. ~**sizlik**, indistinctness, ambiguity; uncertainty; indefiniteness.

belir·te[i]ç[ci] (*ling.*) Adverb; (*chem.*) reagent; indicator. ~**ten**, (*ling.*) determinative. ~**ti**, indication, mark, sign, symbol; (*math.*) characteristic; (*med.*) symptom; (*leg.*) proof, circumstantial evidence. ~**tici**, descriptive. ~**tik**, explicit, clear. ~**tilen**, word qualified (by an adjective). ~**tili**, marked, with a sign; determined, qualified; determinative: ~ **nesne**, (*ling.*) definite direct object: ~ **tamlama**, (*ling.*) genitival/possessive construction. ~**tilmek**, *vp.* be made clear/definite; be determined. ~**tilmezlik**, uncertainty. ~**tisiz**, without mark/sign; indeterminate, indefinite: ~ **tamlama**, (*ling.*) 'shortened'/indeterminate genitival construction. ~**tisizlik**, indeterminacy. ~**tke**, emblem, sign. ~**tken**, determinant. ~**tme**, determination, definition; clarification: ~ **durumu**, (*ling.*) accusative case: ~ **grubu**, (*ling.*) qualified noun phrase: ~ **sıfatı**, (*ling.*) demonstrative/determinative adjective. ~**tmek** (-i), make conspicuous/clear; accentuate; make known; reveal; determine, define; expound; point out; specify.

beli¹t^{di} (*phil.*, *math.*) Axiom. ~**ke**, axiomatics. ~**sel**, axiomatic.

bel·kemiği^{ni} (*bio.*) Backbone, spine; spinal column; (*fig.*) basis, foundation, backbone. ~**kemikli**, vertebrate.

belki Perhaps, maybe; even, but. ~ **de**, as likely as not ~**li**, (*phil.*) probable, possible.

Bel·kis (*his.*) Queen of Sheba. ~**kiz**, (*his.*) Aspendos.

belladon (*bot.*) Deadly nightshade.

bel·lek Memory: ~ **karışıklığı**, (*psy.*) confused memory: ~ **yitimi**, (*psy.*) loss of memory, amnesia. ~**lem**, ability to remember, memory. ~**lemsel**, related to memory.

belleme¹ *n.* (*tex.*) Numnah, horse-blanket.

belle·me² *vn.* (*agr.*) Digging. ~**mek**¹ (-i), dig. ~**nmiş**¹, dug with a spade.

belle·me³ *vn.* Remembering, memorizing. ~**mek**² (-i), commit to memory, memorize, learn by heart. ~**nmek**, *vp.* be remembered. ~**nmiş**², committed to memory; well-known. ~**te¹çci**, mnemonics. ~**ten**, (*pub.*) learned journal. ~**tici**, (*ed.*) tutor, crammer; teaching. ~**tmek** (-i, -e), cause to remember, remind.

belli Known; evident; clear. ~ **başlı**, eminent, notable, well-known; chief, main, principal; definite: ~ **belirsiz**, imperceptible, hardly visible: ~ **beyan**, very evident: ~ **etm.**, make clear/evident/understood; make known: ~ **olm.**, be understood; be clear: ~ **olmaz**, it all depends. ~**lik**, clarity; obviousness. ~**siz**, unknown; imperceptible.

bellik Distinctive sign/mark.

bel·soğukluğu^{nu} (*med.*) Blennorrhea; gonorrhea: ~**na uğratmak**, (*vulg.*) interrupt by interfering. ~**suyu**^{nu}, (*bio.*) sperm.

bembeyaz Extremely white; 'whiter than white'. ~ **kesilmek/olm.**, turn white with fear.

bemol^{ü} (*mus.*) Flat.

ben¹ *n.* (*bio.*) Mole; beauty-spot.

ben² (*sp.*) Bait (for fishing).

ben³ *pron.* [67] I; myself. = BANA; BENIM. ~ **ağa**... = SEN AĞA: ~ **artık kaçayım**, I must be going: ~ **böyleyim**, I am what I am: ~ **bu fikirde değilim**, I beg to differ, I don't agree: ~ **(bu işte) yokum**, I'm not interfering; it's nothing to do with me: ~ **de**, in return: ~ **faka basmam yağma yok!**, you don't catch me!: ~ **hancı sen yolcu iken (elbette bir gün gene görüşürüz)**, we may be glad of each other's

help one day: ~ **karışmam!**, I'm not interfering!; (after giving advice) don't blame me if things go wrong!: ~ **oldum bittim**, ever since I can remember: ~ **şahımı bu kadar severim**, I can't do more than that; don't expect a greater sacrifice from me: ~ **yaşta**, of my age: ~ **yazdım sen değil**, it is *I* who wrote not you: ~**de**, on/with me; = BENDE: ~**de buna takat yok**, I can't afford so much; I can't bear it: ~**de**...**var**, I have/possess...: ~**de**...**yok**, I don't have/possess...: ~**den**, from/by/through me: ~**den paso!**, I've had enough of it!; don't count on me any more: ~**den söylemesi!**, well, I've warned you/said enough!: ~**den yana umudunu kes!**, you won't get much change out of me!: ~**i**, me: ~**i buralarda yüzüstü bırakma**, don't leave me here to my fate: ~**i günaha sokma!**, don't provoke me!; don't insist too much!: ~**i hiç ilgilendirmez**, that leaves me cold: ~**i rahat bırak!**, don't bother me!; leave me alone!: ~**i sarmıyor**, it doesn't appeal to me: ~**i sokmayan yılan bin yaşasın**, I don't mind as long as he doesn't hurt me: ~**i tilki yiyeceğine aslan yesin**, it's best to suffer at the hands of s.o. noble: ~**im** = BENIM.

ben·benci Self-satisfied; conceited. ~**ce**, according to me, in my opinion; for my part, as for me: ~ **hepsi bir**, it's all the same to me. ~**ci**, s.o. always talking about himself, conceited. ~**cil**, egotistic, selfish; conceited; egoistic. ~**cileyin**, *adv.* [205] like me. ~**cilik**, conceit; egotism, selfishness; (*phil.*) egoism. ~**cilleşmek**, *vi.* behave selfishly, etc. ~**cillik**, egotism, selfishness.

bend- = BENT.

bende Slave; servant. ~**niz**, [68] 'your humble servant', (*polite for*) 'I': ~**niz cennet kuşu . . .**, (*jok.*) (*on introducing o.s.*) 'your most humble servant . . .'. ~**gân**, slaves.

bende(n) = BEN³.

bendeğil (*phil.*) Non-ego.

bender Commercial port; fortress controlling the sea.

bend¹etmek^{eder} (-i) Bind, tie, fasten; captivate; attach to o.s.; enslave.

bene¹k^{ği} Small spot (on skin/coat); smudge; (*ast.*) facula. ~**lemek** (-i), dapple. ~**li**, dappled, spotted: ~ **alaca**, (*ich.*) platy: ~ **çulluk//kızılbacak**, (*orn.*) spotted sandpiper//redshank: ~ **kırlangıçbalığı**, (*ich.*) grey gurnard: ~ **köpekbalığı**, (*ich.*) lesser spotted dogfish: ~ **levrek**, (*ich.*) black bass: ~ **su yelvesi**, (*orn.*) spotted crake: ~ **yılanyastığı**, (*bot.*) cuckoo-pint.

bengi Immortal, everlasting; endless. ~**lemek** (-i), immortalize. ~**leşmek**, *vi.* become immortal. ~**lik**, endlessness; immortality; infinite time. ~**su**, the water of life; elixir.

beni·âdem Sons of Adam, mankind. ~**beşer**, human beings. ~**İsrail**, the Israelites.

beniçinci (*phil.*) Egocentric. ~**lik**, egocentricity.

benim¹ *v.* I am.

benim² = BEN³. *pron.* Mine. *a.* My. ~ **Arap oynadı**, (*sl.*) I'm having a spell of good luck: ~ **diyen**, s.o. who thinks he can do everything: ~ **gibiler**, people like me: ~ **harcım değil**, that's not for me, I can't

afford it: ~ **katımda**, as for me; in my opinion: ~**le refikam**, I and my wife.
benim·ki The one belonging to me, mine. ~**leme**/~**seme**, appropriation. ~**lemek**/~**semek (-i)**, appropriate/lay claim to stg. (not one's own); adopt as one's own; assimilate; assume as a personal obligation/interest. ~**senmek**, *vp.* ~**setmek (-i, -e)**, *vc.*
ben¹izᶻⁱ Colour of the face; complexion. ~**i atmak/ uçmak**, bleach, turn pale: ~**i kül gibi olm.**, turn very pale, the blood drain from the face: ~**inde kan kalmamak**, be very pale: ~**ine kan gelmek**, the colour return to one's cheeks/face.
ben¹kᵍⁱ Narcotic drug from hemp, bhang.
benli¹ *a.* (*bio.*) Having moles on the skin.
benli² *adv.* = SENLİBENLİ.
benli¹kᵍⁱ Personality; individuality; self-respect; pride, egoism. ~ **davası**, self-conceit; feeling of personal superiority: ~ **ikileşmesi**, split personality: ~ **yitimi**, loss of personality: ~**inden çıkmak**, behave unnaturally, act out of/change character: ~**ine düşkün**, proud, arrogant.
benlikçi S.o. with great self-conceit. ~**lik**, feeling of great self-conceit; excessive individualism.
benmari (*cul.*) Double-saucepan.
ben·olmayan = BENDEĞİL. ~**özekçi(lik)**, egocentric(ity). ~**siz¹**, *adv.* without me/my assistance.
bensiz² *a.* Without a mole/blemish.
ben¹tᵈⁱ Bond, tie, fastening; (*eng.*) dyke, embankment, barrage, dam, reservoir; (*leg.*) clause, paragraph, article; (*lit.*) stanza.
bentoni¹tᵈⁱ (*geol.*) Bentonite.
benz- = BENİZ.
benze·k (*lit.*) Pastiche; (*art.*) imitation; (*pub.*) reproduction. ~**mek (-e)**, *vi.* be like, resemble; look as if . . . . ~**memek**, *vi.* differ; be different. ~**meyiş**, dissimilarity. ~**miyen**, different; disparate.
benzer *a.* Like, resembling, similar; analogous; (*ling.*) cognate; (*math.*) congruent. *n.* (*cin.*) Double, stand-in. ~**i**, replica, copy; (*cin.*) double, stand-in: ~ **yok**, unique. ~**lik**, likeness, resemblance, similarity; analogy; (*bio.*) mimicry; (*math.*) congruence. ~**siz(lik)**, unique(ness).
benzeş Similar; comparable. ~**en**, analogous; (*ling.*) assimilated (letters). ~**ik**, homogeneous. ~**im**, analogy; resemblance, similarity. ~**(im)lik**, similarity. ~**me**, *vn.* affinity; (*ling.*) assimilation. ~**mek**, *vi.* resemble one another. ~**mezlik**, differentiation, dissimilation. ~**tirmek (-i)**, assimilate.
benze·tⁱ Imitation. ~**tçi**, imitator. ~**ti**, (*art.*) copy, duplicate; replica; (*lit.*) comparison: ~ **ressam**, copyist; imitator. ~**tici**, *a.* (*art.*) copying; forging: ~ **ressam**, copyist; forger. ~**tili**, similar; imitating. ~**tilmek**, *vp.* ~**tim**/~**tme**, (*lit.*) simile, comparison. ~**tiş**, copying. ~**tlemek (-i)**, copy, forge. ~**tlemeli**, forged. ~**tmek (-i, -e)**, liken, compare; assimilate; make an imitation/copy of stg.; mistake (A for B); see a resemblance (in A to B); (*fig.*) spoil, destroy; (*fig.*) give s.o. a good hiding: ~ **gibi olmasın**, comparisons are odious. ~**yiş**, resemblance, similarity; assimilation.
benz·in (*chem.*) Petrol; benzine: ~ **deposu**, petrol

tank: ~ **istasyonu**, filling station. ~**oik**, benzoic. ~**ol**ᵘ, benzol(e).
beraat¹ Innocence; acquittal. ~ **etm.**, be acquitted: ~ **ettirmek**, acquit: ~**ı zimmet**, freedom from debt/obligation: ~**ı zimmet asıldır**, one is presumed innocent until proved guilty.
beraber Together; in company with; abreast, equal; in the same direction; on the same level. ~ **(-le)**, together with: ~ **bulunmak (-le)**, accompany s.o. ~**e**, (*sp.*) drawn game; deuce: ~ **bitmek**, (*sp.*) finish in a dead heat: ~ **kalmak**, (*sp.*) be equal, finish level; draw, tie. ~**lik**, being equal/abreast; being together; solidarity, cooperation: ~ **müziği**, orchestral/choral music: ~ **sağlamak**, (*sp.*) equalize.
berat¹ Patent; warrant; order conferring a dignity/ decoration; (*fin.*) charter. ~ **gecesi**, (*rel.*) feast celebrating the revelation of his mission to the Prophet Muhammad (15 ŞABAN]. ~**lı**, holder of a patent, etc.; privileged.
berbat¹ Destroyed; scattered; ruined, spoilt; filthy; soiled; abominable, detestable. ~ **etm.**, bungle, spoil, ruin. ~**lık**, hopeless situation.
berber¹ *n.* Barber; hairdresser. ~ **aynası**, hand-mirror. ~**balığı**ⁿⁱ, (*ich.*) (?) threadfin. ~**lik**, barber's trade; hairdressing; (*fig.*) excessive flattery.
Berber² *pr. n.* (*ethn.*) Berber. ~ **maymunu**, (*zoo.*) Barbary ape. ~**i**, *n./a.* Berber. ~**ice**, (*ling.*) Berber language. ~**istan**, (*geo.*) Barbary (Coast).
berdevam *a.* Lasting; continuous. *adv.* Continuously; uninterruptedly. ~**dır (-de)**, he continues to . . .: ~ **olm.**, continue to exist.
berduş Vagabond, tramp.
bere¹ *n.* (*med.*) Bruise; contusion; ecchymosis.
bere² *n.* (*mod.*) Beret.
bereketⁱ Abundance; increase; blessing; fecundity. ~ **boynuzu**, (*art.*) horn of plenty: ~ **versin**, may God bless you!; thank you!: ~ **(versin) ki**, fortunately, as good luck would have it.
bereket·lenmek *vi.* Increase; be abundant. ~**li**, fruitful, fertile; abundant: ~ **olsun!**, may it be plentiful! ~**lilik**, fruitfulness, fertility; abundance. ~**siz**, unfruitful; infertile. ~**sizlik**, unfruitfulness.
bere·lemek (-i) (*med.*) Bruise; contuse, dent. ~**lenmek**, *vi.* be(come) bruised/dented. ~**li**, bruised; dented.
Bergama (*his.*) Pergamum; (*geo.*) Bergama.
bergamotᵘ (*bot.*) Bergamot orange, citrus tree.
ber·güzar Memento; souvenir. ~**hane**, large rambling house (in ruins); trading caravan: ~ **gibi**, (house) too big, barn-like. ~**hava**, carried into the air; destroyed; annihilated: ~ **etm.**, blow stg. up: ~ **olm.**, be blown up; be annihilated. ~**hudar**, successful, prosperous: ~ **ol!**, I wish you prosperity, (I thank you).
beri *n.* The near side; this side. *adv.* Here, hither; the time since; until now. **(-den)**, *post.* [89] Since; this side of. ~ **taraf**, this side. ~**deki**, *pron.* that which is on this side.
beriberi (*med.*) Beriberi disease.
berikiⁿⁱ *pron.* [72] The one on this side; the nearest; the last mentioned.

beril (*geol.*) Beryl. ~**yum**, (*chem.*) beryllium.

berjer (*dom.*) Bergère, large cushioned chair.

berk[i] Hard; firm, solid; rugged, strong.

Berka (*geo.*) Cyrenaica.

berkelyum (*chem.*) Berkelium.

berk·inmek *vi.* Become firm/strong. ~**itmek** (-i), render solid/firm; reinforce; consolidate; strengthen; back, support; affirm, confirm: **berkitilmiş borçlar**, (*fin.*) consolidated debts. ~**lik**, strength; firmness, hardness.

Berlin (*geo.*) Berlin. ~**li**, Berliner.

ber·mucibi In conformity with; as required. ~**murat**, satisfied, happy: ~ **olm.**, have one's wish. ~**mutat**, as usual.

bermuda (*mod.*) Bermuda shorts.

Bern (*geo.*) Berne.

berrak Clear; cloudless; limpid; brilliant, sparkling. ~**laşmak**, *vi.* become clear, etc. ~**laştırmak** (-i), clarify. ~**lık**, clarity; brilliance.

berri *a.* Terrestrial, land-, continental. ~**ye**, (*mil.*) land forces; (*geo.*) desert.

bertaraf Aside; out of the way; putting aside; apart from. ~ **etm.**, avert; put aside; dispose of; eliminate; discard, get rid of: ~ **olm.**, be put aside; disappear.

bertik Sprained, slightly injured. ~**ilmek**, *vp.* be sprained/injured. ~**mek** (-i), sprain, injure slightly.

berzah (*geo.*) Isthmus.

be's- = BEİS.

besa Truce (*esp.* in a blood-feud); compact.

Besarabya (*geo.*) Bessarabia.

bes·bedava Absolutely gratis. ~**belli**, perfectly clear/obvious. ~**beter**, very much worse.

bese·lemek = ESELEMEK. ~**rmek** = ESERMEK.

besi (*live.*) Place where animals are fattened; battery-farm; fattening of animals; (*fig.*) support, prop. ~**ye çekmek**, fatten, feed up; ~**ye komak**, put (out) to fatten up.

besi·bilim(ci) (*med.*) Diete·tics/(-tician). ~**bilimsel**, dietetic. ~**ci(lik)**, (*live.*) stock-breed·er/(-ing). ~**doku**, (*bot.*) endosperm, albumen. ~**düzen(sel)**, diet(ary). ~**li**, fattened. ~**n**, (*bio.*) food(stuff); diet: ~ **ve Tarım Örgütü**, Food and Agriculture Organization. ~**nsizlik**, lack of food; starvation. ~**örü**, (*bot.*) albumen, endosperm. ~**suyu**[nu] (*bot.*) sap. ~**yeri**, (*bio.*) culture medium.

bes·lek Servant-girl. ~**leme**, *vn.* act of feeding/fattening; servant-girl: ~ **gibi**, poorly/unsuitably dressed (girl): ~ **kılıklı**, slatternly. ~**lemek** (-i), feed, nourish; (*live.*) fatten, breed, rear; (*fig.*) support, prop; take into one's service: **besle kargayı oysun gözünü**, nourish a viper in one's bosom. ~**lemelik**, servant-girl. ~**lenen**, (*phys.*) sustained, undamped. ~**lenilmek**, *vp.* be fed, etc. ~**lenim**/ ~**lenme**, *vn.*; nutrition, alimentation: ~ **bölgesi**, (*geo.*) catchment area: ~ **çantası**, school-meal bag: ~ **eğitimi**, (*med.*) dietetics. ~**lenmek**, *vi.* feed o.s.: *vp.* be fed, etc. ~**letmek** (-i, -e), *vc.* ~**leyici**, *n.* feeder, fattener; *a.* nutritious, wholesome, alimentary. ~**leyiş**, nutrition. ~**li** = BESİLİ.

besmele The formula BİSMİLLAH(İRRAHMANİR-RAHİM). ~ **çekmek/okumak**, pronounce this formula. ~**siz**, of evil omen; rogue; bastard (child).

Bessemer ~ **çelik**//**usulü** (*min.*) Bessemer steel//process.

beste (*mus.*) Tune, composition. ~**ci**/~**kâr(lık)**, compos·er/(-ing). ~**lemek** (-i), compose, set to music. ~**lenmek**, *vp.* ~**li**//~**siz**, with//without music.

beş Five; penta-. ~ **aşağı** ~ **yukarı**, close bargaining: ~ **aşağı** ~ **yukarı uyuşmak**, reach an understanding, compromise: ~ **aya kalmaz**, in less than five months: ~ ~ **daha on eder**, five and five makes ten: ~ ~ **sayıyor**, he thinks his gift is wonderful: ~ **bin lira içeri girdim**, (*sl.*) I lost five thousand liras: ~ **birim**, five units; five off: ~ **dakikada şıpınişi bitirim**, I'll finish it off in five minutes: ~ **duyu**, (*bio.*) the five senses: ~ **gözlü**, (*arch.*) five-arched (bridge): ~ **gün içinde**, within five days: ~ **gün kala** (-e), five days until . . .: ~ **günlük çocuk**, a five-day-old baby: ~ **günlük yol**, a five-day journey: ~ **günlük zahire**, provisions for five days: ~ **haneli rakam**, (*math.*) five-figure number: ~ **kadar**, about five: ~ **kala** (-e), five minutes to . . .: ~ **kalem eşya**, five items: ~ **kap yemek**, five portions of food: ~ **kapı aşırı**, at the sixth door along: ~ **kardeş**, (*jok.*) slap, box on the ears: ~ **kardeşin tadını tatmamış**, he needs a good smacking: ~ **kere dört**, five times four: ~ **kıta**, five off, five units of . . .: ~ **kişilik**, (*stg.*) for five people: ~ **köşe(li)**, (*math.*) pentagon(al): ~ **kuruş eksik**, five KURUŞ short: ~ **kuşaklık**, for five generations: ~ **küsur yıldır**, it's just over five years since: ~ **lira hakkım var**, I am owed five liras: ~ **lira verdim** (-e), **vermedi**, I offered him five liras for . . ., but he wouldn't sell it: ~ **misli**, fivefold: ~ **on**, a little: ~ **on kuruş çıkarmak**, earn a little: ~ **para almamak**, earn nothing: ~ **para etmez**, worthless: ~ **para ver söylet on para ver sustur**, she would talk the hind leg off a donkey: ~ **paralık etm.**, scold, criticize: ~ **parmak bir olmaz**, all men are not alike: ~PARMAK: ~ **saat çekmek**, last/take five hours: ~ **saat kadar**, for about five hours: ~ **saat yüründü**, it was a five-hour walk: ~ **saate kadar**, in about five hours: ~ **saatle gidilir gelinir**, you can go there and back in five hours: ~ **saatte bir**, every five hours, once in five hours: ~ **sabıkası bulunan bir yankesici**, (*leg.*) a pick-pocket with five previous convictions: ~ **sene gider**, (clothes) it will last five years: ~ **sene küreğe mahkûm oldu**, (*leg.*) he was sentenced to five years hard labour: ~ **şeritli**, (*mot.*) five-lane (road): ~ **tane**, five (units): ~ **vakit namaz**, (*rel.*) the five daily prayers: ~ **yıl önce**, five years ago: ~ **yıldız**, (*sl.*) catamite: ~ **yıllık plan**, (*adm.*) five-year plan: ~ **yüz liraya patladı**, I blew 500 liras on it: ~ **yüz metre kala** (-e), 500 metres short of . . .: ~**e kadar**, up to five: ~**te bir**, one fifth; one in five: ~**ten ona kadar**, from five to ten.

beşaret[i] Good news; innovation.

beş·bıyı'k[ğı] (*bot.*) Medlar. ~**er**[1], *a.* five of each, five at a time: ~ **yüz**, five hundred each.

beşer[2] *n.* Mankind. ~ **hakları**, human rights: ~ **şaşar**, to err is human. ~**i**, human; anthropo-. ~**iyet**[i], humanity; human nature.

beşere (*bio.*) Epidermis, cuticle.

beşgen (*math.*) Pentagon. ~**(li)**, *a.* pentagonal.

beşibir·arada/ ~ **lik/** ~ **yerde** Tk. 5-lira gold coin (worn as an ornament).

beşi[l]k[ği] Cradle; (*fig.*) cradle; (*aer.*) nacelle; (*mil.*) gun-carriage. ~ **kertiği/kertme nişanlı**, betrothed while still in the cradle: ~ **salıncak**, swing-boat: ~ **sandalye**, rocking-chair.

beşik·çatı (*arch.*) Saddle-roof. ~ **çi**, maker/seller of cradles. ~ **kemer**, (*arch.*) arched frame. ~ **örtüsü**[nü], (*arch.*) saddle-back. ~ **taş**, sarcophagus. ~ **tonoz**, (*arch.*) barrel-vault.

beş·inci (5.) Fifth: ~ **delmek**, (*sp.*, *etc.*) finish fifth: ~ **kol**, (*pol.*) fifth column. ~ **iz**, quintuplet. ~ **izli**, fivefold; having five . . .. ~ **leme**, *vn.* dividing into five (parts). ~ **lemek**, *vi.* divide into five (parts); make up to five; do stg. five times. ~ **li**, pentad; worth five (units); having five (parts); (*mus.*) quintette; (*gamb.*) the five; fivefold: ~ **yarış**, (*sp.*) pentathlon. ~ **lik**, five (unit) coin; stg. having/ worth five (units). ~ **me**, (*tex.*) cloth striped in five colours; (*carp.*) post of a lathe. ~ **parma[l]k**[ğı], (*zoo.*) starfish; (*tex.*) = ~ **ME**. ~ **parmaklı**, (*zoo.*) five-fingered/-toed; pentadactyl. ~ **parmakotu**[nu], (*bot.*) creeping cinquefoil. ~ **pençe**, (*zoo.*) starfish. ~ **taş**, (*child.*) jackstone. ~ **yüzlük**, (*fin.*) note for £T.500; having/containing five hundred (units).

beşuş Smiling, happy.

bet[i 1] *n.* Face. ~ **beniz kalmamak**, have no colour left: ~ **i benzi kireç kesilmek**, turn as white as chalk.

bet[i 2] *n.* ~ **bereket**, abundance, prosperity: ~ **i bereketi kalmamak**, become scarce, come to an end.

be[l]t[di 3] *a.* Bad; ugly; unseemly. ~ ~ **bakmak**, look with evil intentions: ~ **suratlı**, having an evil look: ~ **ine gitmek**, vex/annoy s.o.

beta (*ling.*) Beta (β). ~ **ışınları**, (*phys.*) beta rays. ~ **tron**, betatron.

betelemek (-i) Quarrel with s.o.

beter (*comp.* = BET[3]) Worse. ~ **in** ~ **i var**, there is always stg. worse.

beti (*art.*) Figure; form, shape. ~ **li**, having figures; figurative, concrete. ~ **siz**, without figures, abstract.

beti[l]k[ği] (*pub.*) Small book; short letter, document.

betim (*lit.*) Image; picture; description. ~ **leme**, *vn.* description. ~ **lemek (-i)**, describe. ~ **lemeli**, with (full) description. ~ **leyici**, (*phil.*) descriptor. ~ **sel**, descriptive: ~ **gövdebilim**, (*med.*) descriptive anatomy.

beton (*arch.*) Concrete. ~ **gibi**, very strong; resistant. ~ **arme**, reinforced concrete, ferrocrete. ~ **cu**, concrete worker. ~ **karar/** ~ **yer**, concrete-mixer. ~ **lamak (-i)**, concrete stg.

bev·[l]il[li] (*med.*) Urine. ~ **l[l]etmek**[eder], urinate. ~ **li**, (*chem.*) uric; (*med.*) urinary. ~ **liye**, (*med.*) urology. ~ **liyeci**, urologist.

bey Gentleman; (*adm.*) prince, chief; (*gamb.*) ace; (*his.*) bey, commander; lord; rich/important man. ~ **BABA/** ~ **EFENDI**. ~ **gibi yaşamak**, live like a lord.

beyaban Desert; the wilds.

beyan Declaration; explanation; expression; style. ~ **etm.**, announce, attest; declare, explain: ~ **eden/ sahibi**, declarer.

beyan·at[1] *pl.* Declarations; *sing.* discourse, speech:

~ **ta bulunmak**, hold forth, make a speech; give an explanation; make an announcement. ~ **name**, (*adm.*) manifesto, declaration; (*leg.*) affidavit.

beyarı (*ent.*) Queen bee.

beyaz White (colour); white (of an egg/eye); (*fin.*) blank; (*pub.*) fair copy; (*sl.*) heroin. ~ **alınlı//bıyıklı deniz kırlangıcı**, (*orn.*) least//whiskered tern: ~ **ayı**, (*zoo.*) polar bear: ~ **balıkçıl**, (*orn.*) great white heron: ~ **baykuş**, (?) snowy owl: ~ **bayrak**, (*mil.*) white flag: ~ **çakıl kuşu**, (*orn.*) sanderling: ~ **etm.**, make a fair copy: ~ **gözlügiller**, (*orn.*) white-eyes: ~ **kanatlı deniz kırlangıcı**, (*orn.*) white-winged black tern: ~ **karınca**, (*ent.*) termite: ~ **karınlı sağan//yeşilbacak**, (*orn.*) Alpine swift//common sandpiper: ~ **kitap**, (*adm.*) white paper: ~ **kuyruklu kartal**, (*orn.*) white-tailed eagle: ~ **kuyruklu yeşilbacak**, (*orn.*) green sandpiper: ~ **mukallit**, (*orn.*) olivaceous warbler: ~ **oy**, vote of approval: ~ **Rus**, (*ethn.*) White Russian: ~ **sabun**, curd soap: ~ **Saray**, (*adm.*) the White House: ~ **sırtlı**, white-backed: ~ **tarak dişli ördek**, (*orn.*) smew: ~ **zehir**, (*col.*) morphine, cocaine, etc.: ~ **a çekmek**, make a fair copy: ~ **a çıkarmak (-i)**, stand up for s.o., clear his character. [*Also* = AK.]

beyaz·gerdan: ~ **ötleğen kuşu**, (*orn.*) whitethroat. ~ **ımsı/** ~ **ımtırak**, whitish; quite white. ~ **ırk**, (*ethn.*) Caucasian/white race. ~ **kömür**, (*el.*) hydro-electricity. ~ **lanmak/** ~ **laşmak**, *vi.* become white. ~ **laştırmak (-i)**, whiten, bleach. ~ **latılmak**, *vp.* be made white. ~ **latmak (-i)**, make white, whiten; (*cul.*) blanch; (*tex.*) bleach. ~ **lı**, white; with white in it; wearing white. ~ **lık**, whiteness; growing light. ~ **perde**, (*cin.*) the silver screen. ~ **peynir**, (*cul.*) (goat/sheep's) white curd cheese. ~ **sine[l]k**[ği], (*ent.*) (?) white fly.

bey·baba Father, old gentleman. ~ **efendi**, (*respectful address*) Sir! ~ **erki**, aristocracy.

beygir (*live.*) Horse; cart-horse; pack-horse; (*sp.*) (wooden) horse. ~ **bakımı**, horse-breeding: ~ **değirmeni**, horse-powered mill: ~ **gibi**, clumsy, stupid: ~ **otu**, (*bot.*) field horsetail. ~ **ci**, hacking stableman. ~ **(gücü**[nü]), (*phys.*) horse-power.

beyhude *a.* Vain, useless. *adv.* In vain. ~ **yere**, in vain, unnecessarily.

bey·[l]in[ni] *n.* (*bio.*) Brain; cerebrum; brains; intelligence, mind. ~ +, *a.* Brain-; cerebral; cerebro-; encephalo-: ~ **iltihap/yangısı**, (*med.*) encephalitis: ~ **kabuğu**, (*bio.*) cerebral cortex: ~ **kanaması**, (*med.*) cerebral haemorrhage: ~ **kızartma/tavası**, (*cul.*) brain fritters: ~ **sapı**, (*bio.*) brain stem: ~ **sarsılması**, (*med.*) concussion: ~ **takımı**, (*cul.*, *fig.*) set of brains: ~ **yıkamak**, brain-wash s.o.: ~ **zarı veremi**, (*med.*) cerebral meningitis: ~ **i atmak**, fly into a rage: ~ **i bulanmak**, be dazed; suspect stg., smell a rat: ~ **i dağınık**, scatter-brained: ~ **i karıncalanmak**, be too exhausted to think: ~ **i sulanmak**, be(come) senile; (*med.*) have water on the brain: ~ **i yıkanmış**, brain-washed. ~ **inde şimsek çakmak**, have a sudden inspiration: ~ **inden vurulmuşa dönmek**, be thunderstruck: ~ **ine vurmak**, be befuddled (with drink): ~ **ini patlatmak**, beat s.o.'s brains out.

beyin·ci[l]k[ği] (*bio.*) Cerebellum. ~ **li**, having a brain;

(*suf.*) -brained. ~-**omurilik**, (*bio.*) cerebro-spinal. ~**orağı**ⁿⁱ, (*bio.*) falx cerebelli. ~**sel**, (*bio.*) cerebral. ~**si**, (*bio.*) cerebroid. ~**siz(lik)**, brainless(ness), stupid(ity). ~**üçgeni**ⁿⁱ, (*bio.*) fornix cerebri. ~**zarları**, (*bio.*) meninges.

bey¹itᵗⁱ (*lit.*) Verse, couplet, distich.

beyiye (*fin.*) Commission/percentage (on a sale).

beykoz (*gamb.*) Ace.

beyler (*naut.*) Bailer.

beylerbeyiⁿⁱ (*his.*) Governor of a province.

beyli'kᵍⁱ *a.* Belonging to the State; governmental; public; conventional, stereotyped. *n.* (*adm.*) Title/ status of//district governed by a BEY; gentle birth; the Government/Establishment; (*mil.*) small blanket. ~ **cevap**, stereotyped reply: ~ **çeşmeden su içme!**, beware of being a government employee: ~ **fırın has çıkarır**, (*jok.*) government employment is profitable: ~ **gemi**, (*naut.*) battleship: ~ **kapısı**, (*adm.*) ministry: ~ **satmak**, behave like a little lord, give o.s. airs. ~ **çi**, (*his.*) head of Chancery.

beyn- = BEYİN.

beynamaz (*rel.*) S.o. precluded from prayer (by ritual uncleanness); unbeliever. ~ **özrü**, a lame excuse.

beyn·elmilel International. ~**imizde**// ~**inizde**// ~**inde**, among/between us//you//them.

Bey·oğluⁿᵘ (*geo.*) Pera. ~**rut**, (*geo.*) Beirut.

beysbol(cu) (*sp.*) Baseball(-player).

beysoylu (*soc.*) Aristocrat.

beyt- = BEYİT.

beytⁱ House. ~**ullah**, (*rel.*) the Kaaba (at Mecca); the house of God. ~**ülmal**, (*his.*) the Treasury.

beyyine (*leg.*) Proof; evidence.

beyz·a (*obs.*) Egg. ~**i**, oval.

beyzade Son of a BEY; noble.

bez¹ *n.* (*tex.*) Linen/cotton material; fabric, cloth; rag; (*dom.*) duster; (*art.*) canvas. ~ **ciltli**, (*pub.*) cloth-backed/-bound: ~**i herkesin arşınına göre vermezler**, no man is above the law. ~**ci**, cloth-seller, draper.

bez²/beze¹ *n.* (*bio.*) Gland. ~ +, *a.* Glandular.

bezdir·ilmek *vp.* ~**mek** (-i, -den), annoy, plague s.o.

beze² *n.* (*cul.*) Lump of dough; meringue.

beze'kᵍⁱ Ornament; decoration; (*pub.*) vignette. ~ **çi**, interior decorator; (*obs.*) woman who dressed brides. ~**çil**, ornamental. ~**leme**, ornamentation, adornment. ~**sel**, decorative.

bezel (*bio.*) Glandular; adenoid.

bezele·mek (-e) (*cul.*) Make lumps of dough. ~**nmek**, *vp.*

bezelye (*bot.*) Green pea(s). ~ **taşı**, (*geol.*) pisolite.

beze·m (*th.*) Décor. ~**mci**, decorator, designer. ~**me**, *vn.* adornment, decoration. ~**mek** (-i), adorn, bedeck, decorate. ~**meli(k)**, ornamented, decorated; decorative. ~**mlemek** (-i), decorate. ~**msel**, decorative. ~**n**, decoration, ornament. ~**nmek**, *vi.* be decorated, etc.; embellish o.s. ~**yici**, (*art.*) decorator.

bezesten = BEDESTEN.

bezgin (*psy.*) Tired of life; disgusted; discouraged. ~**lik**, weariness, lethargy; depression.

bezikⁱ (*gamb.*) Bezique.

bez'irʳⁱ (*bot.*) Flaxseed, linseed (oil).

bezirgân Merchant, pedlar; (*pej.*) exploiter. ~**lık**, cunning dealing.

bezir·lemek (-i) (*carp.*) Coat wood with linseed oil. ~ **yağı**ⁿⁱ, linseed oil.

bez·mek (-den) Be tired of life/depressed; become sick of/disgusted with. ~ **miş**, wearied; depressed.

beztüyler (*bot.*) Glandular down/hairs.

bezzaz (*obs.*) Linen-draper. ~ **lık**, drapery; draper's trade.

bıcıl (*gamb.*) Knucklebone (used as dice).

bıcılgan Infected (wound); cracked heel (of horse).

bıcırgan (*eng.*) Reamer; burnisher.

bıça'kᵍⁱ Knife; (*eng.*) cutter. ~ **ağzı**, cutting edge: ~ **altına yatmak**, have an operation: ~ **atmak**, throw knives; wound; operate: ~ ~**a gelmek**, be at daggers drawn; come to blows: ~ **çekmek**, be ready to attack s.o.: ~ **gibi kesmek**, cease immediately; remove completely: ~ **kemiğe dayanmak**, become unbearable: ~ **kınını kesmez**, don't harm your protectors: ~ **sırtı**, blunt edge: **sırtı kadar (fark)**, a very small (difference): ~ **sırtı kalmak** (-e), all but/almost do stg.: ~ **silmek**, finish off a job: ~ **yarası onulur dil yarası onulmaz**, a knife wound heals but cruel words are never forgotten: ~ **yemek**, be stabbed.

bıçak·çı Cutler; (*fig.*) s.o. too ready with his knife, quarrelsome. ~ **çılık**, cutler's work/trade. ~**lamak** (-i), stab/knife s.o. ~**lanmak**, *vp.* ~**laşmak**, *vi.* fight with knives. ~**lı**, armed with a knife. ~**lık**, *n.* knife-case, sheath: *a.* suitable for cutlery. ~**yeri**ⁿⁱ, knife-wound scar.

bıçkı (*carp.*) Cross-cut saw; saddler's saw. ~ **talaş/ tozu**, sawdust: ~ **tezgâhı**, sawmill. ~**cı**, sawyer.

bıçkın A quarrelsome tough; vagabond. ~**laşmak**, *vi.* behave like a tough.

bıdık Short and tubby.

bık·ılmak (-den) *vp.* Be tired of. ~**kın**, disgusted; satiated; bored. ~**kınlık**, disgust; boredom. ~**mak**, *vi.* be disgusted/satiated: (-den), be sick of stg.: **bıkıp usanmak**, be very discouraged: **bıktım artık!**, I'm sick of it!; I've had enough of it! ~**tırıcı**, sickening, disgusting. ~**tırmak** (-i, -den), sicken, disgust; discourage.

bıldır *adv.* [204] (*col.*) Last year; a year ago.

bıldırcın (*orn.*) Common quail; (*fig.*) plump and attractive little woman. ~ **kılavuzu**, (*orn.*) corn-crake: ~ **otu**, (*bot.*) common monkshood: ~ **ördeği**, (*orn.*) garganey.

bıllık ~ ~, plump.

bıngıl ~ ~, quivering like a jelly; well-nourished, fat. ~**dak**, (*bio.*) fontanelle. ~**damak**, *vi.* quiver (like jelly).

bırak·ı (*fin.*) Laissez-faire; assignment. ~**ılmak**, *vp.* ~**ılmış**, abandoned; deserted. ~**ım**, (*chem.*) deposition; (*ind.*) strike. ~**ımcı**, (*ind.*) striker. ~**ımızcılık**, (*adm.*) liberalism, private enterprise, *laissez-faire*. ~**ıntı**, (*chem.*) deposit. ~**ışma**, (*mil.*) cessation of hostilities, armistice. ~**ışmak** (-i), cease hostilities. ~**ıt**¹, (*leg.*) dead man's estate, inheritance. ~**ma**, *vn.* leaving, abandonment, etc. ~**mak** (-i, -e), leave; leave/let go; release; abandon, quit; put off; put down; deposit; leave off, desist, cease from; give up (a habit); entrust stg. to s.o.; allow; grow (beard, etc.); divorce; cede; bequeath; (*ed.*) keep a pupil down, not promote him: *vi.* come away/unstuck: **bırak ki!**, let alone . . .!: **bırakıp kaçmak**, (*mil.*) desert: **bıraktığı yerde otluyor**, he's never made any progress. ~**maz**, clinging. ~**tırmak (-ı, -e)**, *vc.*

bıyıꞁkᵍˡ Moustache; (*zoo.*) whisker; (*bot.*) tendril. ~ **altından gülmek**, laugh up one's sleeve: ~ **bırakmak**, grow a moustache: ~ **burmak**, curl one's moustache; (young man) swagger slightly, show o.s. off to the girls: ~**ı terlemek**, one's moustache grow: ~**ına gülmek**, mock s.o. to his face: ~**ını balta kesmez olm.**, be a tough fellow, fear no one: ~**ını silmek**, consider the job finished: ~**ları ele almak**, become a man.

bıyık·lanmak *vi.* Grow a moustache. ~**lı**, having a moustache; whiskered: ~ **baştankara**, (*orn.*) bearded reedling: ~ **doğan** (*orn.*) lanner falcon. ~**lıbalık**, (*ich.*) barbel. ~**sız**, cleanshaven.

bızbız (*mus.*) Left-hand drum-stick.

bızdıꞁkᵍˡ (*jok.*) Little child.

bızır (*bio.*) Clitoris.

bi-ˡ *pref.* Without, -less, un- [BİÇARE].

bi-² *pref.* Bi- [BİKROMAT].

Bi. = (*ch.s.*) BİZMUT.

biatⁱ (*his.*) (Oath of) allegiance; homage (to the Sultan-Caliph); fealty. ~ **etm. (-e)**, do homage.

bi·baht Unfortunate. ~**behre**, without a share (of knowledge/capacity); unfortunate; incapable.

biber (*bot.*, *cul.*) Pepper (black, red). ~ **dolması**, (*cul.*) stuffed peppers: ~ **ekmek (-e)**, put pepper on: ~ **gibi**, sharp, pungent: ~ **gibi yanmak**, (eyes, etc.) be very painful: ~ **tanesi**, peppercorn.

biber·iye (*bot.*, *cul.*) Rosemary. ~**lemek (-i)**, add/sprinkle with pepper. ~**li**, (*cul.*) peppered, peppery; pungent. ~**lik**, pepper-pot.

biberon Baby's bottle.

bibi (*col.*) Paternal aunt.

bibliyo·fil (*lit.*) Bibliophile. ~**graf**, bibliographer. ~**grafi**/~**grafya**, bibliography. ~**grafik**, bibliographical. ~**man**, bibliomaniac, book-collector. ~**mani**, bibliomania, book-collecting.

biblo Trinket; curio; knick-knack; ornament. ~ **gibi**, small and attractive (girl/house): ~**lar**, bric-a-brac.

biçare(lik) Helpless(ness); hopeless(ness); wretched(ness).

biçem (*art.*, *lit.*) Style. ~**bilim**, stylistics. ~**leme**, *vn.* stylization. ~**lemek (-i)**, stylize. ~**sel**, stylistic.

biçer·bağlar (*agr.*) Reaper-binder, harvester. ~**döver**, reaping-threshing machine, combine-harvester.

biçil·mek *vp.* = BIÇMEK; be cut, etc. ~**miş**, ~ **kaftandır (için)**, appropriate, well-adapted; 'cut out' for the job; 'just made' for s.o.

biçim (*mod.*) Cut (of a coat, etc.); (*art.*) form, shape; build; manner; sort; (*agr.*) reaping. ~ **almak**, take shape: ~ **bilgisi**, (*ling.*) accidence: ~ **bozma**/**değiştirme**, deformation, distortion: ~ **bozukluğu**, deformity: ~ **vermek**/~ **e sokmak**, put in order: ~**i bozmak**, disfigure, distort, deform: ~**ine getirmek**, find a suitable opportunity for.

biçim·bilgisiⁿⁱ (*ling.*)// ~**bilim** (*bio.*) Morphology. ~**birim**, (*ling.*) morpheme. ~**bozumu**, distortion.

~**ce**, in form. ~**ci(lik)** (*art.*, *phil.*) formal·ist/(-ism). ~**deş(lik)**, (*bio.*) homomorph·ic/(-ism); (*phil.*) isomorph·ic/(-ism). ~**leme**, *vn.* design(ing); shaping. ~**lemek (-i)**, design; (*sl.*) shame. ~**lendirmek (-i)**, form/shape stg.; give shape to. ~**lenim**, (*min.*) morphology. ~**lenme**, formation; taking shape. ~**lenmek**, *vi.* be formed/shaped; take shape. ~**li**, well-cut/-shaped; shapely; clean-cut. ~**lik**, (*eng.*) template. ~**sel**, connected with shape; formal. ~**sellik**, conformity. ~**siz**, amorphous; ill-shaped, unsymmetrical; (*fig.*) ugly, unpleasant; clumsy; bizarre; out-of-place; unsuitable. ~**sizleşmek**, *vi.* become ill-shaped/ugly, etc. ~**sizlik**, ugliness; unsuitability.

biç·intilik/ ~**iꞁt**ᵈⁱ (*mod.*) Pattern. ~**ki**, cutting-out: ~ **ev**//**yurdu**, tailoring workshop//school. ~**me**, *vn.* cutting; (*math.*) prism; (*arch.*) dressed stone. ~**mek (-i)**, cut out; cut up; cut through; divide; (*agr.*) reap, mow; (*fin.*) estimate/fix a price. ~**tirmek (-i, -e)**, *vc.*

bid'atⁱ (*rel.*) Innovation (which is evil), heresy.

bidayetⁱ Beginning, commencement. ~ **mahkemesi**, (*leg.*) court of first instance, lower court.

bid·e (*dom.*) Bidet. ~**on**, can, drum, metal container.

bi·düziye Uninterruptedly. ~**edep**, unmannerly, ill-bred. ~**esas**, without foundation.

biftekⁱ (*cul.*) Beefsteak.

bi·gâne Foreign; strange, aloof; disinterested, indifferent. ~ **gayrı**, ~ **hakkın**, unjustly.

bigudi (*mod.*) Hair-curler/-roller.

bi·günah Innocent, blameless. ~**haber**, unaware, ignorant./ ~**had**, without limit, indefinite. ~**hakkın**, rightly, deservedly; as it should be; perfectly. ~**hesap**, countless. ~**huş**, unconscious; bewildered. ~**huzur**, uneasy, uncomfortable. ~**kes**, friendless; destitute; orphan.

bikarbonatⁱ (*chem.*) Bicarbonate.

bikini (*mod.*) Bikini (swimsuit).

bik·irʳⁱ Virginity; virgin. ~**ini izale etm.**, deflower.

bi·kloridⁱ (*chem.*) Bichloride. ~**kromat**ˡ, (*chem.*) bichromate.

bil. = BİLHASSA.

bila- *pref.* Without, -less, un-. ~ **bedel**, free of charge.

bilad *pl.* = BELED, BELDE. Regions; cities.

biladerağacıⁿⁱ (*bot.*) Cashew-nut tree.

bila·fasıla Uninterruptedly. ~**hara**, later on. ~**ihtiyar**, without option: ~ **bunu söylemiş**, he couldn't help saying this. ~**istisna**, without exception. ~**ivaz**, without stg. in exchange; disinterestedly. ~**kis**, on the contrary; far from it.

bilanço (*fin.*, *fig.*) Balance-sheet. ~ **çıkarmak**, strike a balance: ~ **düzenlemek**, draw up a balance-sheet.

bilar (*naut.*) Caulking mixture.

bilardo (*sp.*) Billiards. ~**bilye**//**çuha**//**istekası**, billiard ball//cloth//cue.

bila·sebep Without cause/reason. ~**tereddüt**, without hesitation.

bilateral (*adm.*) Bilateral.

bila·ücret Without payment/reward. ~**vasıta**, directly, without intermediary. ~**veled**, without issue.

bilcümle *a.* All. *adv.* In all, totally.
bildiⁱkᵍⁱ *a.* Known; not a stranger. *n.* Acquaintance. ~ **çıkmak**, prove to be an old acquaintance: = BİLMEK.
bildir·ge *(adm.)* Declaration; advice; *(fin.)* entry. ~ **i**, *(adm.)* communiqué, bulletin; proclamation; *(ed.)* communication, paper; *(lit.)* message: ~ + , *a.* didactic: ~ **tahtası**, notice-board; *(sp.)* results board: ~ **yi almak**, be informed. ~ **ilme**, *vn.*: ~ **den**, without notice; on call. ~ **ilmek**, *vp.* be made known. ~ **im**, communication; notification: ~ **de bulunmak**, declare. ~ **imci**, correspondent; declarer. ~ **imlik**, declaration. ~ **imsiz**, without notice. ~ **işim**/~ **işme**, intercommunication, correspondence. ~ **işmek (-le)**, intercommunicate; reach an understanding by signs and sounds. ~ **me**, statement, declaration; advice: ~ **kipleri**, *(ling.)* indicative mood (tenses): ~ **tümcesi**, *(ling.)* indicative sentence: ~ **yazılımı**, *(fin.)* advice note. ~ **mek (-i, -e)**, make known; communicate; notify. ~ **melik**, *(fin.)* tariff: ~ **savaşı**, tariff war. ~ **men**, *(pub.)* correspondent, reporter. ~ **sel**, declaratory.
bile¹ *adv.* [197] Even; already; even if.
bile² *adv.* ~ ~ , deliberately; knowingly; with one's eyes open; in cold blood: ~ ~ **lades**, knowingly let s.o. be tricked: ~ **isteye**, intentionally. ~ **cen(lik)**, conceited(ness); pretentious(ness).
bileği *(eng.)* Sharpening instrument. ~ **çarkı**, grindstone: ~ **kayışı**, (razor-)strop. ~ **taşı**ⁿ¹, whetstone.
bileⁱkᵍⁱ *(bio.)* Wrist(-bones); carpus; *(zoo.)* pastern. ~ **damarı**, ulnar artery: ~ **gibi (akmak)**, (flow) abundantly: ~ **kuvveti**, *(fig.)* elbow-grease: ~ **saati**, wristwatch: ~ **inde altın bileziği olm.**, have a profitable occupation: ~ **ine güvenmek**, rely on s.o.'s skill/strength. ~ **li**, strong-wristed. ~ **lik**, *(sp.)* wrist-strap.
bile·me *vn.* Sharpening: ~ **taşı**, whetstone. ~ **mek (-i)**, sharpen, whet, grind. ~ **nmek**, *vp.* be sharpened, etc.
bil·en Knowing, understanding. ~ **erek**, knowingly; intentionally. = ~ MEK.
bileş·en *a., n. (math., phys.)* Component, constituent. ~ **ik**, *a., n.* combined, joint; bulk; compound, composite, synthesis: ~ **faiz**, *(fin.)* compound interest: ~ **göz**, *(bio.)* composite eye: ~ **iyelik**, joint ownership: ~ **kesir**, *(math.)* compound fraction. ~ **ikgiller**, *(bot.)* composite flowers. ~ **ikleşme**, composition, combination. ~ **ikleşmek**, *vi.* compose, combine, form a compound. ~ **ikleştirme(k)** = BİLEŞTIRME(K). ~ **iklik**, compound state; composition. ~ **im**, *n. (chem.)* compound; composition. ~ **ke**, *(phys.)* resultant. ~ **ken**, component. ~ **me**, *vn. (phys., chem., ling.)* formation of a compound. ~ **mek (-le)**, combine with, form a compound (with). ~ **tirici**, composing, compounding; mixing. ~ **tirme**, *vn.* forming a compound, combining. ~ **tirmek (-i, -le)**, compose, form a compound; constitute.
bileti Ticket. ~ **almak**, buy a ticket, book a seat: ~ **farkı**, excess fare: ~ **kesmek**, issue a ticket: ~ **(satış) gişesi**, *(rly.)* ticket-office: *(th.)* box-office.
bilet·çi(lik) (Work of) ticket-collector/-seller//bus-/

tram-conductor. ~ **siz**, without a ticket: ~ **kalmıyalım!**, any more fares, please?
bile·tmek (-i, -e) *vc.* Get stg. sharpened. ~ **yici(lik)**, knife-grind·er/(-ing). ~ **ylemek (-i)**, *(prov.)* = BİLEMEK. ~ **ytaşı**, *(carp.)* whetstone.
bileziⁱkᵍⁱ *(mod.)* Bracelet, bangle; *(eng.)* collet; well-head; *(eng.)* metal ring; *(pub.)* brace; *(sl.)* handcuffs.
bil·farz Supposing that. ~ **fiil**, in fact; actually; *de facto*.
bilge *a.* Learned, wise. *n.* Wise man, scholar. ~ **lik**, learning; wisdom.
bilgi Knowledge, learning, science; cognizance. ~ + , *a.* Informatory: *n.* ~ **(ler)**, data; information: ~ **bankası**, data bank: ~ **belgesi**, form: ~ **dalı**, *(ed.)* branch, field, discipline: ~ **edinmek**, be informed; obtain information: ~ **işlemi**, data processing: ~ **kaydedici**, data recording: ~ **sahibi olm. (hakkında)**, be cognizant of stg.: ~ **satmak**, air/ parade one's knowledge: ~ **toplam**//**ulaşımı**, data collection//retrieval: ~ **vermek**, acquaint; *(mil.)* brief.
bilgi·ci(lik) Sophist(ry). ~ **lç**ᶜⁱ, wise man; *(pej.)* pedant; know-all. ~ **çane**, pedantically. ~ **çlik**, (pretentious) learning; *(pej.)* pedantry: ~ **taslamak**, make a pretence of knowledge. ~ **kuram(sal)**, *(phil.)* epistemolo·gy/(-gical). ~ **li**, learned; well-informed. ~ **lik**, encyclopaedia. ~ **lilik**, learning; knowledge. ~ **n**, learned man; bookman; scholar; scientist; expert, authority: ~ **olm. (-de)**, be an authority on. ~ **nce**, academic. ~ **nlik**, learning, scholarship; bookishness. ~ **sayar**, computer, electronic calculator: ~ **sayım**, informatics. ~ **sel**, *(phil.)* epistemic. ~ **siz**, unaware, ignorant, lacking information. ~ **sizlik**, unawareness; ignorance.
bilhassa Especially, in particular. ~ **ve** ~ , above all.
bili *(phil.)* Knowledge, information. ~ **ci**, knowing.
bilibili *int. (ech.)* Chuck-chuck!
bililtizam On purpose, intentionally.
bilim Science, branch of knowledge. ~ + , *a.* Scientific: ~ **adamı**, a man of learning/science; scholar: ~ **dalı**, *(ed.)* discipline, field, branch: ~ **dergisi**, *(pub.)* learned journal: ~ **dışı**, unscientific.
bilim·ci/~ **eri** Scientist, scholar. ~ **cilik**, *(phil.)* scientism. ~ **kurgu**, *(lit.)* science-fiction. ~ **leştirme**, making known, publishing. ~ **leştirmek (-i)**, make known, publish. ~ **sel**, scientific. ~ **sellik**, relating to science/knowledge. ~ **siz**, unscientific.
bilinⁱçᶜⁱ *(psy.)* Consciousness; the conscious (mind.) ~ **altı**ⁿ¹, the subconscious (mind). ~ **dışı**ⁿ¹, the unconscious (mind). ~ **lendirmek (-i)**, make conscious/aware (of stg.); *(sl.)* indoctrinate. ~ **lenmek**, *vi.* become conscious/aware (of stg.) ~ **li(lik)**, conscious(ness), aware(ness). ~ **siz(lik)**, unconscious(ness), unaware(ness).
bilin·diⁱkᵍⁱ *(math.)* Known quantity. ~ **emez**, *(phil.)* that can not be known. ~ **emezci(lik)**, uncertain(ty); agnostic(ism). ~ **en**, *(math.)* known quantity. ~ **mediⁱk**ᵍⁱ, unknown quantity. ~ **mek**, *vp.* = BİLMEK; be known, etc.; be acceptable/gratefully received. ~ **meyen**, *(math.)* unknown (quantity).

~**mez**, unknown; incomprehensible; uncertain. ~**mezlik**, incomprehensibility; uncertainty.

bilir *a.* Knowing, aware of. ~ **bilmez**, [182] half-knowing, with a little knowledge. ~**kişi**, expert. ~**kişilik**, expert's survey/report; expertise.

bilisiz Unaware, ignorant, lacking information. ~**lik**, unawareness; ignorance; (*phil.*) agnosia.

bilistifade Profiting by, taking advantage of.

biliş A knowing; knowledge; acquaintance. ~ **tanış**, friends and acquaintances. ~**i**, information. ~**im**, data processing. ~**mek (-le)**, know one another, be acquainted; strike up an acquaintance.

bil·iştirak Jointly. ~**ittifak**, by common agreement; unanimously. ~**kuvve**, inherent; virtual(ly); potentially. ~**lahi!**, (*int.*) I swear by God!; believe me!

billur Crystal; (*geol.*) rock-crystal; cut-glass. ~ +, *a.* Crystal(line): ~ **gibi**, crystalline; crystal-clear; very white and spotless (skin): ~ **a bakarak falcılık**, crystal-gazing.

billur·bilimi Crystallography. ~**cisim**, (*bio.*) crystalline lens. ~**iye**, cut-glass ware. ~**laş(tır)-ma**, *vn.* crystallization. ~**laş(tır)mak**, *vi./(vt.)* crystallize. ~**lu**, crystalline. ~**sal**/~**su**, crystalloid; crystalline.

bilme *vn.* = BİLMEK. Knowing, etc. ~ **yeteneği**, (*phil.*) cognition. ~**ce**, riddle, enigma: ~ **bulmaca**, puzzle. ~**den**, without knowing/counting the cost. ~**dik**, who does not know; unknown: ~ **kimse kalmadı**, everyone knows it.

bil·mekir **(-i)** Know; learn; recognize; guess; consider; believe; hold (s.o.) responsible. *aux. v.* (*with the gerund in* -e) Be able to [**gidebilmek**, be able to go: **yapabilmek**, be able to do]. **bildiğinden kalmamak/şaşmamak**, go one's own way, not heed/be deterred by others: **bildiği okumak**, stick to one's guns, insist on one's own way: **bildiğini söylemek**, testify: **bildiğini yapmak**, follow one's own judgement, only pretend to heed advice: **bildiği yedi mahalle bilmez**, s.o. very cunning: BİLDİK: **bildim bileli**, from of old: BİLE[2]: **bilemedin(iz)**, at most: BİLEREK: BİLİR: BİLMEDEN: **bilmem hangi/kim . . .**, I don't know which/who . . .: **bilmem ki . . .**, I wonder what . . .: **bilmem neden buldu buldu da beni buldu**, I don't know why he picked on me (of all people): **bil(me)mezlikten gelmek**, pretend not to know; affect/feign ignorance: **bilmeyerek**, accidentally.

bilmesinlercilik (*col.*) Obscurantism.

bilmez Who does not know; ignorant; ungrateful. ~ **gibi soruyor**, he asks as though he does not know/pretending not to know. ~**lemek (-i)**, prove/show up s.o.'s ignorance. ~**lenmek**, *vi.* appear ignorant; feign ignorance. ~**lik**, (feigned) ignorance: ~**e vurmak**/~**ten gelmek**, feign ignorance.

bil·misil In a similar way. ~**mukabele**, in return/retaliation. ~**umum**, in general, on the whole; all. ~**vasıta**, indirectly. ~**vesile**, on the pretext of.

bilseme Curiosity, the desire to know.

bil·ya/~**ye** (*child.*) Marble; bead; (*sp.*) billiard ball; (*eng.*) ball(-bearing). ~**yeli**, (*eng.*) with a ball: ~ **kalem**, ball-point pen: ~ **mafsal**, ball-joint: ~ **valf**, ball valve: ~ **yatak/yuva**, ball-bearing.

bilyon (*math.*) Billion (10^9).

bim (*arch.*, *rad.*) Beam.

bimar Ill. ~**hane**, mental hospital.

bimetalik (*min.*) Bimetallic.

bin[1] *a.* (*math.*) Thousand; a great many. ~ **beladan artakalmak**, have suffered much: ~ **bela ile**, only with the greatest difficulty: ~ **bir**, a thousand and one; very many, countless; ~ BIR: ~ **bir ayak bir ayak üstüne**, very crowded, all treading on each other's toes: ~ **bir kapının ipini çekmek**, lead a wandering life: ~ **bir yaprak tatlısı**, (*cul.*) mille-feuille: ~ **can ile**, with the greatest eagerness: ~ **dereden su getirmek**, make all sorts of excuses; raise countless difficulties: ~ **işçi bir başçı**, there must be many followers but only one leader: ~ **işit bir söyle**, silence is golden: ~ **kalıba girmek**, be always changing shape/clothes: ~ **kat**, a thousandfold: ~ **küsur**, a thousand off: ~ **lira içeri girdim**, I lost £T1,000: ~ **nasihatten bir musibet yeğdir**, experience is the best teacher: ~ **ölçüp bir biçmeli**, look before you leap: ~ **parça olm.**, break into a thousand pieces: ~ **pişman olm.**, be very sorry/repentant: ~ **renge girmek**, keep changing colour; (*fig.*) be inconsistent; use every kind of subterfuge: ~ **tarakta bezi var**, he has many irons in the fire: ~ **yaşa(sın)!**, long live . . .!: ~ **yılın bir başı**/~**de bir**, very rarely: ~**de bir**, (*math.*) one thousandth: ~**i bir paraya**, abundant; very cheap, ten a penny: ~**in yarısı beş yüz**, a penny for your thoughts!; what have you got to worry about?: ~**lerce**, thousands of.

bin[2] (*obs.*) Son of [**Ali** ~ **Hasan**, Ali son of Hassan]. **-bin** *suf.* -seeing [BEDBİN].

bina Building, fabric, edifice; act of building, construction; a basing (a claim, etc.); (*obs.*) an Arabic grammar book; (*ling.*) voice. ~ **etm.**, build, construct.

binaen On account of; in consequence of; based on. ~**aleyh**, consequently, therefore.

binam Nameless. ~ **ve nişan**, without name or trace.

bin·başıy[1]**(lık)** (Rank/duties of) (*mil.*) major// (*naut.*) commander//(*aer.*) squadron-leader; (*his.*) bimbashi. ~**birgece Masalları**, (*lit.*) A Thousand and One/The Arabian Nights. ~**dallı**, (*tex.*) (purple) velvet embroidered with leaves and flowers.

bindi Bearer, support.

bindir·gi (*art.*) Easel. ~**ilmek**, *vp.*: **bindirilmiş kuvvet**, (*mil.*) motorized force. ~**im**, (*fin.*) increase in price. ~**imli**, increased in price. ~**me**, *vn.*; (*carp.*) joint, overlap; (*geol.*) overthrust: *a.* mounted on, resting on: ~ **kaplamalı**, (*naut.*) clinker-built: ~ **kaynak**, (*min.*) overlap weld: ~ **limanı**, (*naut.*) port of embarcation. ~**mek (-i, -e)**, *vc.* = BİNMEK; cause to mount; cause to rest on/overlap: **(-e)**, (*naut.*) collide with, ram; add to.

bine·lkgi *a.* Connected with riding. *n.* Mount (horse, etc.). ~ **arabası**, carriage: ~ **otomobili**, passenger-car: ~ **tavlası**, riding-stable. ~**atı**n[1], saddle-/riding-horse. ~**taşı**n[1], mounting-block.

biner One thousand each.

bingi (*arch.*) Pendentive, sconce.

bingözotunu (*bot.*) Scammony.

bini Mounting, riding; (*carp.*) overlapping edge. **~ci**, *a.* riding; equestrian: *n.* rider, good horseman; jockey. **~cilik**, horsemanship; equitation. **~lmek** (-e), be mounted.

bininci (1000.) Thousandth.

bin·iş *vn.* = BİNMEK; act/method of riding; (*his.*) riding procession, cavalcade; (*mod.*) riding cloak: **~ kartı**, (*aer.*) boarding-card. **~işmek**, *vi.* ride together; (*bio.*) overlap. **~iti**, mount; (*cul.*) caketray.

bin·lerce In thousands; thousands of. **~lik**, 1,000 lira note; 3-litre bottle: **~ basamağı**, (*math.*) thousands column.

binmek (-e) Mount; ride; get into, climb onto; board (plane, ship, train, etc.); overlap; assume an attitude/condition. **bindiği dalı kesmek**, cut the ground from under one's own feet.

binom (*math.*) Binomial. **~inal**, binominal.

bint[i] (*obs.*) Daughter; girl.

bin·yapra'k[ğı] (*bot.*) Yarrow. **~yapraklı**, water milfoil. **~yıl**, (*his.*) millennium.

bi·payan Endless; infinite; everlasting. **~perva**, fearless; unscrupulous.

bir *a.* [53, 79] One; a; the same; equal. *adv.* [197] In such a way; once; alone, only; just [**~ gidip bakalım!**, let's just have a look!]; (*emphasis*) [**~ yağmur ~ yağmur!**, you never saw such rain!]. **~ abam var atarım, nerde olsa yatarım**, by yourself you can choose where to stay: **~ adet**, one (off), one piece: **~ adımlık yer**, only a step away, close by: **~ ağızdan**, with one voice, in unison: **~ ağızdan çıkan bin dile yayılır**, rumours soon spread: **~ akçe ile dokuz kubbeli hamam yapmak**, build castles in Spain: **~ alay**, much, many: **~ âlem**, a wonder!: **~ an evvel/önce**, [195] as soon as possible: **~ an için**, just for a moment: **~ ara(lık)**, whenever; for a moment; some time or other: **~ araba**, a wagonload; (*fig.*) a load/lot of ..., many: **~ arada**, all together; at one go; at the same time, simultaneously; in the same place together: **~ arada bulundurmak**, combine; bring together: **~ araya gelmek**, come together; meet at the same place; coincide: **~ araya getirmek**, collect: **~ aşağı ~/beş yukarı**, up and down, backwards and forwards: **~ atımlık barutu kalmak/olm.**, be down to one's last shot, have nothing in reserve: **~ avuç**, little/a few (stg. big); much/many (stg. small): **~ ayağı çukurda olm.**, have one foot in the grave: **~ ayak evvel**, as soon as possible: **~ ayak üzerinde**, quickly: **~ bakıma**, in one respect; from one point of view: **~ baltaya sap olm.**, find a career; amount to stg. in life: **~ bap ev**, one house: **~ bardak suda fırtına koparmak**, raise a storm in a teacup: **~ başına**, alone, by oneself: **~ ben ~ de Allah bilir**, only God and I know the truth of it: **~ ~**, [194] one by one: **~BİRİ: ~ boy**, once: **~ boyda**, equal in height: **~ böylesi gözümde tütüyor**, I long for one like that: **~ bu eksikti**, that's the last straw!: **~ buçuk**, one and a half: **~ cihetli ~ bitaraflık**, a one-sided neutrality: **~ çatı altında**, under the same roof; intimate with one another; 'in the same boat': **~ çırpıda**, easily and quickly: **~ çiçekle bahar/yaz olmaz**, one swallow doesn't make a summer: **~**

çift, a pair; one or two (words): **~ çöplükte iki horoz ötmez**, there can only be one boss at a time: **~ çuval inciri berbat etm.**, ruin everything; upset the apple-cart: **~ daha**, once more; (+ *neg.*) [204] never!; no more; not again: **~ daha yüzüne bakmamak**, sever relations with s.o.: **~ dalda durmamak**, be fickle/capricious: **~ damla**, very little: **~ de**, *adv.* [197] and another thing, in addition, besides, moreover, furthermore; and all of a sudden: **~ de ne göreyim**, and all of a sudden: **~ dediği ~ dediğini tutmamak**, not make sense: **~ dediği iki olmaz**, highly esteemed, revered: **~ dediğini iki etmemek (-in)**, be able to refuse nothing to s.o.: **~ defa**, once; to begin with; first of all: **~ derece(ye kadar)**, somewhat, to some extent: **~ deri ~ kemik**, nothing but skin and bones; emaciated: **~ dikişte içmek**, drink off/up at one go: **~ dirhem**, (+ *neg.*) not an ounce of: **~ dirhem et bin ayıp örter**, a little plumpness hides all the defects: **~ dokun bin ah dinle kâsei fağfurdan**, everyone has his own troubles: **~ dostluk kaldı!**, (almost) everything has been sold!: **~ dövdü ki**, he gave him such a beating: **~ düzüye**, uninterruptedly, continuously [= BİDÜZİYE]: **~ el**, one shot: **~ el ~ eli yıkar, iki el ~ yüzü yıkar**, one needs help sometimes: **~ elden**, from the same person/place: **~ elden satılmak**, be sold *en bloc*/at one go: **~ elini bırakıp ötekini öpmek**, be over-respectful: **~ eli yağda ~ eli balda**, very comfortably off, well-to-do: **~ elinin verdiği öbür elin duymasın**, 'let not your right hand know what your left hand doeth': **~ elle verdiğini öbür elle almak**, give with one hand and take with the other: **~ elmanın ~yarısı ~i, ~ yarısı ~i**, as like as two peas in a pod: **~ etm.**, bring together, unite: **~ eyyam**, at one time, formerly: **~ fincan kahvenin kırk yıl hatırı var**, a kindness is never forgotten: **~ fit bin büyü yerine geçer**, one malicious hint can do a power of evil: **~ gelmek**, be equal: **~ gömlek aşağı//üstün olm.**, be a shade inferior//superior: **~ gömlek farklı olm.**, be little (if any) superior: **~ gömlek fazla eskitmiş olm.**, be older and wiser than s.o.: **~ görmek = ~ TUTMAK: ~ göz(ü) gülmek**, be laughing and crying at the same time; have mixed feelings: **~ gün**, one day, sometime: **~ gün bile sek(tir)mez**, he never misses a single day: **~ gün evvel**, as soon as possible: **~ gün olur ki**, the day will come that . . .: **~ günlük beylik beyliktir**, enjoy yourself while you can: **~ güzel**, thoroughly: **~ hal olm.**, meet with trouble, die; be bored stiff; be in a state, get into a temper: **~ hamlede**, at a single bound: **~ hayli**, quite a lot: **~ hoş olm.**, feel uncomfortable; be disconcerted/offended: **~ hoşluğu olm.**, feel 'queer'/unwell: **~ içim su**, delicious; delightful (woman): **~ iki**, one or two; a few: **~ iki demeden/derken**, all of a sudden; without hesitation: **~ iki derken işler fenaya varır**, small faults unnoticed soon become bad habits: **~ iki tek atalım**, let's have a couple of drinks: **~ işe balta ile girişmek**, set about stg. in a clumsy/tactless manner: **~ işi sağlam tutmak**, start stg. on a sound basis: **~ işte eli olm.**, have a finger in the pie: **~ kaç = BİRKAÇ: ~ kafada**, of one mind: **~ kalemde**, at one go; instantly: **~ kapıya çıkmak**, reach the same conclusion: ~ **kararda/karar üzere**, in an unvarying degree, in a uniform manner: ~ **kararda** ~ **Allah**, man proposes God disposes: ~ **karış**, very short/little: ~ **karış beberuhi**, (*jok.*) a very short person: ~ **kaşık suda boğmak** = ELİNDEN: ~ **kat çamaşır**, a change of underwear: ~ **kat daha**, one more of the same; twice as much: ~ **kat elbise**, a suit of clothes: ~ **kazanda kaynamak**, be in complete agreement; get on very well together: ~ **kenara**, aside: ~ **kere**, once; just; let it be said that . . .; for one thing . . .; to begin with: ~ **kere daha**, once again, once more: ~ **kere denemek**, take a chance: ~ **kerecik**, once: ~ **kıyamettir gitmek/kopmak**, an uproar break out; all hell break loose: ~ **kızarsa pir kızar**, he seldom loses his temper but when he does . . .: ~ **kol çengi**, s.o. who talks loudly and heartily; be the life and soul of the party: ~ **koltuğa iki karpuz sığmaz**, one can't do two things at once: ~ **koşu**, quickly, with a dash: ~ **koyundan iki post çıkmaz**, you can't do the impossible: ~ **köroğlu** ~ **ayvaz**, just a husband and wife without any children: ~ **köşede**, by oneself: ~ **köşeye atmak (-i)**, put stg. aside till needed: ~ **köşeye çekilmek**, go into seclusion, withdraw from public life: ~ **kulağı sağır olm.**, condone stg.: ~ **kulağından girip öbür kulağından çıkmak**, go in at one ear and out at the other: ~ **lafa omuz vermemek**, ignore what s.o. says: ~ **lokma** ~ **hırka**, just enough to keep body and soul together: ~ **metelik etmez**, it's not worth a brass farthing: ~ **mevsim süren**, (*bot.*) annual: ~ **miktar**, a small amount: ~ **misli artmak**, double: ~ **musibet bin nasihatten evla/yeğdir**, experience is the best teacher: ~ **müddet**, for a while: ~ **nefeste**, uninterrupted (talking/drinking): ~ **nice**, quite a lot, a good many: ~ **numaralı**, number one, the first; the best: ~ **o kadar**, as much again: ~ **o yana** ~ **bu yana**, to many places: ~ **olm.**, be quick; be at one, agree; be wearied: ~ **oldu ama pir oldu**, it was a great success: ~ **olur iki olur!**, once or twice (but not always): ~ **ölçüde**, relatively: ~ **önceki**, a previous one: ~ÖRNEKLİK: ~ **paralık etm.**, vilify, ruin s.o.'s reputation: ~ **parça**, a bit, a little, a moment: ~ **parmak bal olm.**, be the subject of gossip: ~ **pereseye geldi ki**, it came to such a point that . . .: ~ **pul etmemek**, be worthless: ~ **püf noktası var**, there's a catch in it: ~ **saat evvel**, as soon as possible: ~ **saliste**, in a flash: ~ **sıçrarsın çekirge, iki sıçrarsın çekirge, üçüncüsünde avucuma düşersin çekirge!**, 'softly softly catchee monkey!': ~ **sıkımlık canı var**, you could knock him down with a feather (he's so weak): ~ **sıra kazalar**, a chapter of accidents: ~ **sıraya**, one after the other: ~ **solukta**, in a flash: ~ **söyledi pir söyledi**, he spoke briefly but to the point: ~ **sözünü iki etmemek** = BİR DEDİĞİNİ . . .: ~ **suretle**, in some way or other; to such a degree that . . .: ~ **sürü**, very many: ~ **şey**, a thing; something: ~ **şey çıkmaz**, it doesn't matter: ~ **şey değil**, it's nothing; it doesn't matter; (*in reply to thanks, etc.*) not at all!: ~ **şey(ler) olm.**, change (in manner); feel strange/unwell: ~ **şey sanmak**, over-rate s.o.: ~ **şeyde karar kılmak**, abide by a decision: ~ **şeydir oldu**, I'm sorry but it can't be helped now: ~ **şeye**

benzememek, it's like nothing on earth, it's useless: ~ **şeyin dahilinde**, inside a thing: ~ **şeyle bozmak**, have a bee in one's bonnet about stg., be obsessed by stg.: ~ **şeyler**, something or other: ~ **şeyler dönüyor**, there's stg. brewing: ~ **tahtada**, at once, at one go: ~ **tahtası eksik**, 'having a screw loose'; half-witted: ~ **takım . . .**, [75] a set of . . .; = ~ TAKIM: ~ **takriple**, by some means: ~ **tane**, just one: ~ **tarafa bırakmak/koymak**, put on one side: ~ **tarafa çekmek**, draw aside: ~ **taşla iki kuş vurmak**, kill two birds with one stone: ~ **tek**, one and only: ~ **tek atmak**, (*sl.*) have a drink: ~ **teviye** = BİTEVİYE: ~ **tuhaflığım var**, I feel queer/unwell: ~ **tutmak**, consider equal: ~ **türlü**, some kind of . . .; in some way, somehow; (+ *neg.*) *adv.* [197] not at all, on no account: ~ **uçtan** ~ **uca**, from end to end: ~ **vakit(ler)**, once (upon a time): ~ **varmış** ~ **yokmuş**, (*lit.*) once upon a time there was . . .: ~ **vuruşla ağaç devrilmez**, you need patience/tenacity: ~ **yana**, apart from, leave alone . . .: ~ **yana bırakmak**, put on one side; disregard: ~ **yandan**, at the same time: ~ **yandan** ~ **yana**, from one side to the other: ~ **yastığa baş koymak**, get married: ~ **yastıkta kocamak**, have a long married life: ~ **yaşına daha girmek**, be astonished; be older and wiser: ~ **yere getirmek**, bring/collect together: ~ **yere kadın getirmek**, bring a woman to a place for immoral purposes: ~ **yığın**, many: ~ **yiyip bin şükretmek**, be thankful for small mercies; be very pleased with life: ~ **yol**, once: ~ **yolunu bulmak**, find a way of doing stg.: ~ **zaman(lar)**, at one time; formerly; once: ~**den** ~**e** = ~DENBİRE: ~**e bin katmak**, greatly exaggerate: ~**e** ~ = ~EBİR: ~**e . . . vermek**, (*agr.*) yield onefold: ~**i (-den)**, one of them: ~**i** ~**i** = ~BİRİ. [*For further phrases* = BEŞ.]

Bir., bir. = BİRLEŞMİŞ; BİRLİK.

bira Beer. ~ **fabrikası**, brewery: ~ **mayası**, (*cul.*) barm, yeast. ~**cı**, brewer; beer-drinker. ~**cılık**, brewing. ~**hane**, beerhouse; public-house; brewery.

birader Brother; fellow-mason; (*int.*) friend!

biraz [75] A little, rather. ~ **insafı ele al!**, be fair/a bit reasonable!: ~ **rahat yüzü görmek**, find a little peace. ~**cık**, the smallest. ~**dan**, in a moment, soon; shortly afterwards.

birbiçimli(lik) Uniform(ity).

birbiri[ni] *pron.* [76] One another. ~ **ardından**, one after the other: ~**nden ayırmak**, disconnect: ~**nden iyi**, one better than the other: ~**nden uzaklaşmak**, diverge: ~**ne aykırı**, contrasting: ~**ne bağlı**, interdependent; interlocking: ~**ne danışmak**, consult each other: ~**ne düşürmek**, set two people at loggerheads: ~**ne geçmek**, fit into one another; interlock; intertwine; fall into confusion; quarrel with one another: ~**ne girmek**, quarrel; be seized with panic: ~**ne katmak**, incite one against the other: ~**ne uyma**, consistency: ~**ne uymaz**, inconsistent, incompatible: ~**ne yakın**, close-set: ~**ni didiklemek**, tear one another to pieces: ~**ni tutmamak**, conflict with each other: ~**ni tutmaz**, incompatible, inconsistent; not tallying: ~**ni yemek**, turn against each other: ~**nin adamı olm.**, join s.o., be s.o.'s supporter: ~ **nin ağzına tükürmek**, tell exactly the same story: ~ **nin can düşmanı olm.**, be at daggers drawn: ~ **nin gözünü boyamak**, pretend to believe stg. (when each knows the other doesn't believe it): ~ **nin gözünü çıkarmak**, beat each other mercilessly: ~ **nin gözünü oymak**, be at daggers drawn: ~ **yle birleştirmek**, amalgamate.

bir·ci(lik) (*phil.*) Mon·ist/(-ism). ~ **cinsten**, (*phys.*) homogeneous. ~ **çenekliler**, (*bot.*) monocotyledons. ~ **çenetli**, (*bot., zoo.*) single-shelled/ univalve. ~ **çoğu**nu, *pron.* [75] a good deal of it. ~ **çok**, a good few; a lot. ~ **çokları**, a good many of them. ~ **delikliler**, (*zoo.*) monotremes.

bir·den Together; at the same time; instantaneous; suddenly. ~ **denbire**, [195] abruptly, all at once; all of a sudden; out of a clear sky: ~ **bulmak**, alight upon: ~ **çıkmak**, burst forth: ~ **düşmek**, (*fin.*) slump: ~ **kır(ıl)mak**, snap: ~ **ölmek**, die suddenly: ~ **parlamak**, blaze up: ~ **saldırmak**, assault. ~ **dirbir**, (*sp.*) leap-frog.

birebir Most efficacious (remedy); equal to the occasion; 'just the thing'; (*phil.*) one-to-one. ~ **gelmek**, be the one and only cure.

birer *a.* [83] One apiece, one each. ~ ~, *adv.* [194] one by one: ~ ~ **saymak**, enumerate; count out: ~ **ikişer**, one or two each: ~ **liraya**, at one lira each: ~ **tane çakalım**, (*sl.*) let's have a drink.

bir·eşeyli (*bio.*) Unisexual. ~ **evcikli**, (*bot.*) monoecious.

bireşim (*chem., phil.*) Synthesis; = BİLEŞİM. ~ **li**/ ~ **sel**, synthetic.

birey *n.* Individual. ~ **ci**, *a.* individualist. ~ **cilik**, (*soc.*) individualism. ~ **leşmek**, *vi.* become an individual. ~ **leştirmek (-i)**, individualize; consider as an individual. ~ **lik**, individuality. ~ **oluş**, (*bio.*) ontogenesis. ~ **sel**, *a.* individual. ~ **selleştirmek (-i)**, individualize. ~ **sellik**, state of individuality. ~ **üstü(lük)**, supra-individual(ity).

bir·gözeli/ ~ **hücreli** (*bio.*) Unicellular: ~ **hayvanlar (bilimi)**, proto·zoa/(-zoology). ~ **gözlü**, (*bio.*) monocular.

biri(si)ni *pron.* [74] One of them; an individual; someone. ~ ~, one another: ~ **gelir** ~ **gider**, one goes another comes: ~ **miz**, one of us: ~ **nden** ~, one of them: ~ **nden geçinmek**, live/sponge on s.o.: ~ **ni bir şeyden etm.**, cause s.o. to lose stg., deprive s.o. of stg.: ~ **nin**, someone's: ~ **nin hesabına**, at s.o.'s cost: ~ **nin lehinde**, on s.o.'s behalf: ~ **niz**, one of you. ~ **bir** = BİRBİRİ. ~ **cik**, *a.* unique; one only; a small one.

birik·i (*min.*) Reserve. ~ **ici**, cumulative. ~ **im**, accumulation; (*fin.*) stock; (*geol.*) deposit. ~ **imlik**, container, tank. ~ **inti**, accumulation; heap; garbage; (*bio.*) detritus; (*geol.*) deposit, till: ~ **konisi**, (*geol.*) alluvial cone/fan. ~ **işme**, (*zoo.*) agglutination (of cells). ~ **me**, *vn.* accumulation: ~ **havzası**, (*geo.*) catchment area/basin. ~ **mek**, *vi.* come together, assemble; accumulate; agglutinate, coalesce. ~ **miş**, accumulated; (*fin.*) cumulative; backlog (of work, orders, etc.). ~ **tiren**, accumulator. ~ **tirici**, *a.* accumulative: *n.* reservoir. ~ **tirim**, accumulation, agglutination. ~ **tirme**, *vn.*

(ac)cumulating, etc. ~ **tirmek (-i, -e)**, let stg. accumulate; collect; agglutinate; assemble; amass; save up (money).

birileri *pron.* Some (people).

birim (*math. etc.*) Unit; unity. ~ +, *a.* Unit, unitary; specific: ~ **bedel/fiyatı**, unit price: ~ **hacim ağırlığı**, bulk weight, unit weight, specific gravity: ~ **maliyet/tümdeğeri**, unit cost: ~ **ler bölüğü**, the class of simple numbers (1–999). ~ **li**/ ~ **sel**, unitary.

birincas(ı)f (*bot.*) Mugwort.

birinci (1.) *a.* First; primary; chief. *n.* (*sp.*) Champion. ~ **balkon**, (*th.*) dress circle: ~ **çıkmak**/ **gelmek**, (*sp., etc.*) come first: ~ **elden**, first-hand: ~ **ifrattı ikincisi tefrit oldu**, the first was excessive the second insufficient: ~ **kânun**, (*obs.*) December: ~ **kaptan**, (*naut.*) captain: ~ **kişi**, (*ling.*) first person: ~ **mevki**, (*rly., etc.*) first-class: ~ **olm.**, be first: ~ **sınıf**, (*rly., etc.*) first-class; (*fig.*) high-class; first-rate: ~ **temsil**, first (*pub.*) edition//(*th.*) performance: ~ **teşrin**, (*obs.*) October: ~ **zaman**, (*geol.*) palaeozoic era.

birinci·l Primary; proto-; primitive: ~ **sünger**, (*bio.*) primary meristem. ~ **lik**, first prize; first place: ~ **ler**, (*sp.*) championship competition. ~ **zar**, (*bot.*) primine.

bir·isini = BİRİ. ~ **kaç**ı, *a.* [76] a few; some; several: ~ **adım ötesi**, a few paces away: ~ **defa**, several times: ~ **ı**nı, *pron.* some; several.

birle·me *vn.* Uniting; making one. ~ **mek (-i)**, unite; make one.

birleş·en (*math.*) Concurrent; intersecting. ~ **e**lk^{ği}, (*bio.*) commissure. ~ **ik**, united; joint; connected; conjoint; (*bio.*) compound, composite, conjugate; (*ling.*) compound (noun/verb/tense, etc.): ~ **Amerika Devletleri**, (*pol.*) United States of America: ~ **Arap Cumhuriyet//Emirlikleri**, (*pol.*) United Arab Republic//Emirates: ~ **harf**, (*ling.*) digraph, trigraph: ~ **Milletler**, (*pol.*) United Nations: ~ **oturum**, (*adm.*) joint session. ~ **ilmek**, *vp.* be joined/ united. ~ **im**, union, joining; combination; (*adm.*) meeting, sitting, session; (*bio.*) coupling, copulation, mating. ~ **ke**, (*fin.*) cooperative. ~ **keci(lik)**, cooperativ·ist/(-ism). ~ **me**, *vn.* union, joining; coalition; cohesion; combination; confluence; conjugation; (*fin.*) fusion, merger; (*chem.*) valence; (*bio.*) conjugation: ~ **borusu**, (*eng.*) collector, manifold: ~ **değeri**, (*chem.*) valency: ~ **eğilimi**, affinity. ~ **mek (-le)**, unite; re-unite; assemble; agree; ally with; be reconciled; combine with; coalesce. ~ **miş**, united; (*bot.*) fasciated: ~ **Milletler (Teşkilatı)**, (*pol.*) the United Nations (Organization). ~ **tiren**, (*ling.*) copulative; conjunctive. ~ **tirici**, *a.*/ ~ **tirme**, *vn.* assembling; combining; joining: ~ **boru/cihazı**, (*eng.*) coupling; joint. ~ **tirmek (-i, -le)**, unite; join; cement; combine; assemble; couple; connect; agglutinate; consolidate; ally.

birli (*gamb.*) Ace (cards); one (dominoes, etc.).

birli·k^{ği} Unity; union; combination; agreement; consolidation; association, trade-union; alliance; (con)federation; (*fin.*) cooperative; (*mil.*) unit; equality; similarity; identity; (*bio.*) synapsis; (*mus.*)

whole note. ~ **kurmak**, unite, combine: ~ **kurulu**, (*fin.*) consortium: ~ **olm.**, agree. ~**siz**, disunited.
birlik·te *adv.* [261] Together; as a whole; in company; jointly: *a.* joint; collective; co-: ~ **akma**, confluence: ~ **çalışmak**, cooperate: ~ **doğmuş**, (*zoo.*) connate: ~ **ögretim**, coeducation. ~**teş**, (*pol.*) federate.
Birmanya (*geo.*) Burma. ~+, *a.* Burmese. ~**ca**, (*ling.*) Burmese. ~**lı**, *n.* (*ethn.*) Burmese.
birörnek *a.* Uniform; of the same pattern. ~**lik**, uniformity, homogeneity.
birsam Hallucination.
bir·seslilik (*mus.*) Unison. ~**takım**, *a.* [75] a quantity; some; several: ~**(lar)ı**, *pron.* some. ~**terimli**, (*math.*) monomial. ~**türlü**, (+ *neg.*) by no means; in no way. ~**yapımlama**, (*chem.*) homogenization. ~**yapımlı(lık)**, homogene·ous/(-ity).
bisikleti Cycle; bicycle. ~ **yolu**, cycle track: ~**e binmek**/~**le gitmek**, cycle. ~**çi(lik)**, cycl·ist/(-ing).
Biskay ~ **körfezi**, (*geo.*) Bay of Biscay.
bisküviyi (*cul.*) Biscuit, cracker.
bismillah (*int.*) In the name of God! (*said before starting an undertaking*). ~ **demek/ile başlamak**, start on some work. ~**irrahmanirrahim!**, (*rel.*) in the name of God the Compassionate the Merciful!
bisturi (*med.*) Bistoury; surgeon's knife.
bişey (*col.*) = BİR ŞEY.
biti (*ent.*) Louse. ~**i canlanmak/kanlanmak**, recover one's spirits/money, etc.; get uppish: ~**ler**, lice.
bita = BİTE.
bitaıpbı Exhausted; without strength. ~ **düşmek**, get exhausted; become feeble.
bitaraf·(lık) Impartial(ity); neutral(ity). ~**laşmak**, *vi.* be(come) neutral. ~**laştırmak (-i)**, *vc.*
bite (*naut.*) Bitts, cleat, bollard.
bitek1 (*col.*) = BİR TEK.
bite·k2 *a.* (*agr.*) Fertile. ~**ksiz**, infertile. ~**lge**, fertility.
biter *n.* = BİTTER. *v.* = BİTMEK.
bitevi(ye) *a.* All of a piece; complete. *adv.* Uninterruptedly, continuously. ~**lik**, continuousness.
bitey (*bot.*) Flora.
bitik Worn out; bad; in love. ~**lik**, exhaustion.
bitim End, ending, finish; conclusion; completion; limit. ~**li**, finite; limited. ~**siz**, infinite; boundless, limitless.
bitir·ilmek *vi.* Be finished/concluded. ~**im** = BITIM, (*sl.*) smashing!: ~ **yeri**, (*sl.*) gambling den. ~**imci**, (*sl.*) gambling-den operator. ~**me**, *vn.* ending; conclusion; completion: ~ **araştırması**, (*ed.*) thesis: ~ **belgesi**, (*ed.*) certificate: ~ **eylemi**, (*ling.*) compound verb: ~ **pazarı**, (*fin.*) final offer. ~**mek (-i)**, *vc.* = BİTMEK; finish; complete; terminate, bring to an end; close down; conclude; destroy; exhaust; (*bot.*) cause to grow/sprout. ~**melik**, (*ed.*) certificate. ~**miş**, experienced; cunning; (*ed.*) graduate.
bitiş *vn.* = BİTMEK. Ending, finish; conclusion; (*th.*) finale. ~ **sözleri**, (*th.*) epilogue.
bitişiılkği *a.* Touching; adjacent; contiguous, neighbouring; integral with. *n.* Next-door house; neighbour: ~ **çanakyapraklı**, (*bot.*) gamopetalous: ~ **ikizler**, (*bio.*) Siamese twins: ~ **olm.**, be touching; abut on: ~ **taçyapraklı**, (*bot.*) gamosepalous.

bitiş·iklik Contiguity. ~**im(li)**, (*ling.*) aggluti na·tion/(-tive). ~**ken(lik)**, (*ling.*) agglutina·tive (-tion). ~**mek**, *vi.* be contiguous; join; adhere abut on. ~**tirici**, (*phil.*) conjunctive. ~**tirim**, juxta position. ~**tirmek (-i)**, cause to touch/adhere, etc
bitki (*bot.*) Plant. ~ +, *a.* Vegetal, vegetative phyto-; plant-: ~ **bilgini**, botanist: ~ **bitleri**, (*ent.* aphids, plant-lice: ~ **evreni**, vegetable/plant king dom: ~ **gübresi**, (*agr.*) compost: ~ **kesen kuşları** (*orn.*) leafcutters: ~ **kömürü**, charcoal: ~ **örtüsü** (*geo.*) vegetation: ~ **sapı**, (*bot.*) culm: ~ **uyuzu** (*myc.*) gall: ~**ler bilgisi**, botany.
bitki·bilim(ci) Botan·y/(-ist). ~**cil**, (*zoo.*) phyto phagous, herbivorous. ~**lenme**, (*geo.*) vegetation ~**msi**, plant-like: ~ **hayvanlar**, (*zoo.*) phytozoa.
bitkin Exhausted; decrepit; worn-out; 'all in'. ~ **bi halde**, dead-beat: ~ **düşmek**, become exhausted etc. ~**lik**, exhaustion; weariness.
bitkisel *a.* Vegetable, vegetal; phyto-. ~ **örtü**, (*geo. vegetation: ~ **tel**, (*bot.*) fibre: ~ **toprak**, (*agr. topsoil: ~ **yaşam**, (*med.*) cabbage/vegetabl existence.
bit·lemek (-i) Delouse s.o.; (*sl.*) pick a quarre ~**lenmek**, *vi.* be infested with lice; be deloused delouse o.s.; (*sl.*) be lousy with money. ~**li**, lousy (*sl.*) fairly rich: ~ **baklanın kör alıcısı olur**, a buye can always be found for the shoddiest of articles: ~ **kokuş**, (*pej.*) slut.
bitmek1 *vi.* (Hair, plants, etc.) grow/sprout.
bitmek2 *vi.* Come to an end, cease, finish; b completed; be exhausted; be ruined/destroyed: **(-e)** be very fond of s.o. ~ **tükenmek bilmemek**, neve come to an end: **bitinceye kadar**, for the duratio of . . .: **bitmedi**, (*pub.*) to be continued: **bitme tükenmez**, interminable, endless, inexhaustibl **bitmiş**, (*bio.*) extinct.
bitniılkği (*soc.*) Beatnik.
bit·otunu (*bot.*) Lousewort; an insecticide ~**pazarı**mı, flea-market, old-clothes marke ~**sirkesi**ni, (*ent.*) nit. ~**yeniği**ni, louse-bite; (*fig. doubtful/tender spot; secret anxiety.
bittabi Naturally, of course.
bitter (*cul.*) Bitter (ale/chocolate); type of gin.
bitüm (*min.*) Bitumen; asphalt. ~**lemek (-i)** asphalt. ~**leş(tir)mek**, *vi./(vt.*) bituminize. ~**lü** bituminous.
bivefa Faithless; inconstant.
biy. = BİYOLOJİ.
biye (*mod.*) False tuck. ~**l**, (*eng.*) ~ **başı**, big end: ~ **(kolu)**, con(necting)-rod.
biyo- *pref.* Bio-. ~**coğrafya**/~**jeografi**, biogeo graphy. ~**elektronik**, bionic: ~ **bilgisi**, bionics ~**fizik**, biophysical: ~ **bilgisi**, biophysics ~**fizikçi**, biophysicist. ~**grafi**/~**grafya**, bio graphy. ~**grafik**, biographical. ~**kimya**/~**şimi** biochemistry. ~**kimyacı**/~**şimist**i, biochemis ~**log**, biologist. ~**loji(k)**, biolo·gy/(-gical) ~**meteoroloji**, biometeorology. ~**nik**, bionic(s) ~**psi**, (*med.*) biopsy: ~ **yapmak**, carry out biopsy. ~**sfer**, biosphere. ~**tit**i, (*min.*) biotite.
biz1 *pron.* [67] We; (*col.*) I. ~ **artık geçtik**, I'm to old for/past that: ~ ~**e**, on our own: ~ ~**e kalma (-le)**, have a tête-à-tête with s.o.: ~ **yaştakile**

people of our age: ~ce, according to us; in our opinion: ~celeyin, like us: ~de, with us; at home: ~de para pul arama!, don't think we've got any money!: ~den, from us; one of us; (*sl.*) cunning: ~e, to us: ~e yol göründü, we must be going: ~i, us: ~i çiğneyip geçtiniz, (*jok.*) you passed without even deigning to notice us. ~im, our: ~ için, for us. ~imki, ours; (*col.*) my wife/husband: ~leri yadırgıyorum, our own people are strangers to me. ~ler, (*col.*) we.

biz² *n.* (*carp.*) Awl, bradawl.

Bizans (*hist.*) Byzantium. ~+, *a.* Byzantine. ~lı, *n.* (*ethn.*) Byzantine.

bizar Tired; sick of stg. ~ etm., distress; annoy.

bizatihi In itself; intrinsically.

biz·ce/~de/~den/~e/~im = BİZ¹. ~egöre(lik), relativ·e/(-ity).

bizlemek (-i) Pierce with an awl.

bizmut^u (*chem.*) Bismuth.

bizon (*zoo.*) Bison.

bizzat In person, personally. ~ ihkakı hak etm., take the law into one's own hands.

bk(z). = BAK(INIZ).

Bk. = (*ch.s.*) BERKELYUM.

BK = (*leg.*) BORÇLAR KANUNU.

Bl. = (*mil.*) BÖLÜK. ~K., BÖLÜK KOMUTANLIĞI.

blakavt (*mil.*) Black-out.

blanketⁱ (*pub.*) Blanket.

bla·sto- *pref.* (*bio.*) Blasto-. ~stula, (*bio.*) blastula.

blazer (*mod.*) Blazer.

blefaro- *pref.* (*bio.*) Blepharo-.

blendaj (*el.*) Screening.

bleytⁱ (*eng.*) Blade.

blok Block; (*geol.*) boulder; (*adm., arch.*) block, unit. ~ inşaat, block of buildings. ~aj, (*fin.*) blocking; (*arch.*) ballast foundation for concrete-work: ~ taşı, cobble-stone. ~e, (*fin.*) blocked: ~ etm., block; stop. ~havz, (*mil.*) blockhouse. ~laşmak, *vi.* (*arch.*) lay down a block foundation; (*pol.*) form a block. ~lu, in/with blocks: ~ kil, (*geol.*) boulder clay. ~not^u, block-notebook, writing-pad. ~suz, (*pol.*) non-aligned.

blöf Bluff. ~ yapmak, bluff: ~e aldırmamak, call s.o.'s bluff. ~çü, s.o. who bluffs.

blu·cin (*mod.*) Blue-jeans. ~m, a gambling game.

bluz (*mod.*) Blouse; (*mus.*) blues. ~on, (*mod.*) jacket.

blüm (*min.*) Bloom.

BM = BİRLEŞMİŞ MİLLETLER. ~M = BÜYÜK MİLLET MECLİSİ. ~T = BİRLEŞMİŞ MİLLETLER TEŞKİLATI.

Bn. = BAYAN. ~b. = BİNBAŞI.

bo- *Also* = PO-.

boa (*zoo.*) Boa; (*mod.*) fur scarf. ~ yılanı, (*zoo.*) boa constrictor. ~giller, boas.

bobin (*tex.*) Bobbin; (*cin.*) spool; (*el.*) coil, armature. ~ kâğıdı, (*pub.*) newsprint.

bobstil = BOPSTİL.

boca (*naut.*) Leeward (side of ship); cant; (*fig.*) act of pouring/decanting. ~ alabanda!, veer ship!: ~ etm., veer to leeward; (*fig.*) tilt; turn over; transport; pour out, empty.

bocala·ma *vn.* ~mak, *vi.* (*naut.*) veer/bear away;

run before the wind; (*fig.*) turn from side to side; stumble, falter; fail; (*lit.*) get confused; (*phys.*) fluctuate.

boci Heavy two-wheeled hand-cart.

bocu^lk^{ğu 1} *n.* (*rel.*) Christmas. ~ domuzuna dönmek, become very fat.

bocu^lk^{ğu 2} *n.* (*dial.*) Pig, hog.

bocur·gat¹ (*naut.*) Capstan; winch: ~sız iş görmez, s.o. who will only work under pressure. ~um, mizzen-sail (of a yawl).

bodoslama (*naut.*) Stem-/stern-post.

bodrum Subterranean vault; dungeon; basement; *pr.n.* (*his.*) Halicarnassus. ~ gibi, dark and airless: ~ katı, basement: ~ mantarı, (*myc.*) cellar fungus. ~lu, with a basement/cellar.

bodu^lç^{cu} (*dial.*) Wooden jug; earthenware bowl.

bodur Short; dwarf; squat. ~ çapak, (*ich.*) white/silver dream: ~ meşe, (*bot.*) common/pedunculate oak: ~ söğüt, (*bot.*) dwarf willow: ~ tavuk her dem/gün piliç/taze görünür, small women always look young.

bodur·laşmak *vi.* Become short/dwarfed/squat. ~luk, shortness, etc. ~pas, (*myc.*) barley/brown/leaf rust.

bofa = BUFA.

Bofor *pr.n.* ~ rüzgâr cetveli, (*met.*) Beaufort scale.

bogi (*sp.*) Bogey (at golf); (*eng.*) bogie.

boğa (*zoo.*) Bull. ~ antilopu, eland: ~ burcu, (*ast.*) Taurus: ~ dövüş/güreşi, bull-fight(ing): ~ güreş-çisi, matador, toreador.

boğaça (*cul.*) = POĞAÇA.

boğada (*dom.*) Preparing the laundry with lye.

boğa^lk^{ğı} (*med.*) Quinsy; angina; croup.

boğalı^lk^{ğı} (*live.*) Young bull (for breeding).

boğana^lk^{ğı} (*met.*) Sudden squall.

boğanotu^{nu} (*bot.*) Aconitum.

boğa·sak (*live.*) Cow on heat. ~samak, *vi.* be on heat.

boğası (*tex.*) Thin twill (for linings).

boğata (*naut.*) Dead-eye.

boğaz (*bio.*) Throat; neck (of a bottle, etc.); (*med.*) fauces; (*geo.*) mountain-pass, defile; channel, strait(s); mouth (of a river); (*fig.*) mouth to be fed; food and drink; board (of a servant). ~ açılmak, get hungry, have an appetite: ~ açmak, (*agr.*) break-up ground round trees: ~ ağrısı, (*med.*) sore throat, angina: ~a gelmek, fly at each other's throats; quarrel violently: ~ dert/kavgası, the struggle for existence: ~ derdine düşmek, be mainly concerned with the problem of food: ~ dokuz boğumdur!, watch your tongue!: ~ doldurma, (*agr.*) earthing up: ~ ola!, (*int.*) may it (the food) do you good!: ~ olm., (*med.*) have swollen glands/sore throat: ~ tokluğuna çalışmak/hizmet etm., work for one's board: ~ uru, (*med.*) goitre, Derbyshire neck.

boğaz-: ~dan bahsetmek, talk about food: ~dan yatmak, be in bed with a sore throat: ~ı açılmak, get an appetite: ~ı düğümlenmek, choke with worry: ~ı inmek, (*med.*) the tonsils be swollen/inflamed: ~ı kurumak, be parched/thirsty: ~ı tok, satiated: ~ına dizilmek, have no appetite (from worry): ~ına düğümlenmek, be unable to speak (from excitement, etc.): ~ **ına düşkün**, gourmet, fond of food: ~ **ına iyi bakar**, he does himself proud: ~ **ına kadar borca batmak/girmek**, be up to one's ears in debt: ~ **ına sarılmak**, throttle s.o.; put pressure on, insist: ~ **ına tıkamak**, not let s.o. speak: ~ **ında kalmak**, stick in one's throat: ~ **ından artırmak/kesmek**, economize on food: ~ **ından geçmemek**, be unable to enjoy a meal (because of s.o.'s absence): ~ **ını çıkarmak**, earn just enough to eat: ~ **ını doyurmak**, satisfy one's hunger: ~ **ını sevmek**, be very fond of food: ~ **ını sıkmak**, strangle/throttle s.o.: ~ **ını yırtmak**, shout o.s. hoarse: ~ **lar**, *pr.n.* (*geo.*) the Straits (Bosphorus + Dardanelles): ~ **lar meselesi**, (*pol.*) the Straits question.

Boğaz·içi[ni] (*geo.*) The Bosphorus. ~ **kesen**, (*mil.*) fortress commanding a strait/surrounded by water; narrow street; mountain gorge. ~ **köy**, (*his.*) Hattusa. ~ **la**[lk][g1], (*med.*) goitre, Derbyshire neck. ~ **lamak (-i)**, cut the throat of; strangle. ~ **lanmak**, *vp.; (fig.)* acquire a good appetite; (*sl.*) be cheated. ~ **laşmak (-le)**, strangle each other; struggle. ~ **latmak (-i)**, *vc.* ~ **layan**, (*sl.*) clip joint, den of thieves. ~ **lı**, gluttonous, greedy, gourmand. ~ **lık**, wrapper for the throat; fur collar; food. ~ **sız**, who eats little; without appetite. ~ **yangısı**[nı], (*med.*) angina.

Boğdan = BUĞDAN.

boğ·durmak (-i, -e) Cause/order s.o. to be drowned/strangled. ~ **maca**, ~ **(öksürüğü)**, (*med.*) whooping-cough. ~ **mak**[1] **(-i)**, *vt.* constrict; choke, strangle; asphyxiate; suffocate; drown; (colours) be unsuitable for s.o.: **(-e)**, overwhelm.

boğma[lk][g1 2] *n.* (*bio.*) Node; joint; articulation. ~ **kemikleri**, (*bio.*) phalanges. ~ **lı**, articulated. ~ **lıkuş**, (*orn.*) calandra lark.

boğ·ucu Choking, suffocating; stuffy; stifling; (*sl.*) cheating: ~ **gaz**, (*min.*) choke-damp. ~ **uk**, suffocated: ~ ~, hoarse (voice). ~ **uklaşmak**, *vi.* become hoarse. ~ **ulma**, *vn.* asphyxia. ~ **ulmak**, *vp.* = BOĞMAK[1]; be choked/drowned, etc.; gasp for breath; choke (with anger/laughter); (*sl.*) be fleeced. ~ **ulum**, (*med.*) asphyxia.

boğum (*bio.*) Node; articulation, joint; choke (of a gun). ~ **la(n)ma**, *vn.*; (*ling.*) articulation: ~ **bölge//noktası**, zone//point of articulation. ~ **lanmak**, *vi.* (*bio.*) form a joint/node; (*ling.*) articulate. ~ **lu**, articulated; knotty; wrinkled: ~ **tüfek**, choke bore.

boğun = BOĞUM; (*arch.*) hole in the roof (for ventilation). ~ **tu**, suffocation; oppression; swindling; cheating; profiteering: ~ **yeri**, (*sl.*) gambling den: ~ **ya getirmek**, gull s.o. ~ **uk**, hoarse-sounding.

boğuş·mak (-le) Fly at one another's throats; quarrel; fight. ~ **turmak (-i)**, *vc.*

bohça Square of cloth for wrapping; bundle; pack; parcel; square shawl; selected and finely cut tobacco; (*sl.*) buttocks. ~ **etm.**, wrap up in a bundle: ~ **sını bağlamak**, pack up one's traps: ~ **sını koltuk/eline vermek**, give s.o. the sack.

bohça·böreği[ni] (*cul.*) Bundle-shaped pastry. ~ **cı**, (*obs.*) woman pedlar of small draperies. ~ **lamak (-i)**, wrap up, make a parcel of. ~ **lanmak**, *vp.*

bohem *a., n.* (S.o.) living a bohemian life. ~ **yaşamı**,

bohemian existence. ~ **ya**, *pr.n.* (*geo.*) Bohemia. ~ **yalı**, *n.* (*ethn.*) Bohemian.

boji (*rly.*) Bogie.

bok[u] (*vulg.*) *n.* Excrement, dung, shit; ordure; copro-; (*fig.*) difficult situation. *a.* Worthless. ~ **atmak/bulaştırmak**, throw/smear dirt (on); slander: ~ **canına olsun!**, curse you!: ~ **etm.**, spoil; ruin: ~ **karıştırmak**, make a mess of things: ~ **püsür**, rubbish: ~ **üstünde** ~, terrible: ~ **yedi başı**, always interfering, a meddler: ~ **yemek**, commit an indiscretion, make a blunder: ~ **yemenin Arapça/gülpembesi**, an awful blunder: ~ **yoluna gitmek**, lose one's life unnecessarily/in a worthless cause: ~ **a basmak**, get into a mess: ~ **a nispetle tezek amberdir**, the lesser of two evils: ~ **tan (künet/terazi)**, made of rubbish; useless; worthless: ~ **u una**, in vain, senselessly: ~ **u çıkmak**, the ugly side of s.o./stg. be revealed: ~ **u ile kavga etm.**, be angry with everything: ~ **un soyu**, (*int.*) cursed!: ~ **unda boncuk bulmak/inci aramak**, over-estimate s.o.: ~ **unu çekmek**, suffer the evil consequences of s.o. else's actions: ~ **unu çıkarmak** = ~ ETM.

bok·böcegi[ni] (*ent.*) Dor-/dung-beetle; sacred beetle/scarab. ~ **çu**, dung seller; cesspool cleaner. ~ **çul**, coprophagous. ~ **lamak (-i)**, (*vulg.*) soil, befoul; besmirch, bring into disrepute; mismanage. ~ **laşmak**, *vi.* (*vulg.*) become bad/difficult; be annoyed/bored; meddle. ~ **lu**, fouled with dung; filthy. ~ **luca**, thicket: ~ **bülbülü** (*orn.*) wren; (*fig.*) pert and talkative person. ~ **luk**, dung heap; filthy place; state of disorder/misery. ~ **sineği**[ni], (*ent.*) drone-fly.

boks (*sp.*) Boxing. ~ **yapmak**, box. ~ **ör**, boxer.

boksit[i] (*geol.*) Bauxite.

bol[ü 1] *n.* (*cul.*) (The drink) punch; (*dom.*) (finger-) bowl.

bol[ü 2] (*sp.*) Bowls; -ball.

bol[ü 3] (*med.*) Large soft pill, bolus.

bol[4] *a.* Wide; loose/baggy (clothes); ample; copious; abundant, plentiful. ~ **ahenk**, fond of gaiety: ~ / ~ **bulamaç**, abundantly, amply; in armfuls; generously: ~ **bulamak**, lay on thickly; give abundantly: ~ **doğramak**, spend freely: ~ **keseden**, generously: ~ **keseden atmak/bağışlamak/vaat etm.**, make extravagant promises; talk wildly about spending money: ~ **paça**, (*mod.*) wide trouser-legs. ~ **armak** *vi.* = ~ LAŞMAK. ~ **ca**, loosely; abundantly, amply: ~ **bulunmak**, abound.

bolero (*mod., mus.*) Bolero.

boliçe Jewish woman.

Bolivya (*geo.*) Bolivia. ~ +, *a.* Bolivian. ~ **lı**, *n.* (*ethn.*) Bolivian.

bol·lanmak/ ~ laşmak *vi.* Become wide/loose; become copious/abundant. ~ **laştırmak/ ~ latmak (-i, -e)**, *vc.* make wide, etc. ~ **luk**, wideness; looseness (of fit); abundance, plenty: ~ **bir memleket**, a land of plenty.

Bolşevi[lk][gi] Bolshevik, Bolshevist. ~ **lik**, Bolshevism.

bom (*sl.*) Lie. ~ **atmak**, tell a lie.

bomba[1] *n.* (*naut.*) Boom.

bomba[2] *n.* (*mil.*) Bomb; grenade; big barrel; (gas-) cylinder. ~ **deliği**, (*aer.*) bomb-door: ~ **gibi**, strong, healthy; (*ed.*) well-prepared (pupil): ~ **gibi patlamak**, burst out angrily; (news) astonish everyone: ~ **körletme/yoketmesi**, (*mil.*) bomb disposal: ~ **uçağı**, (*aer.*) bomber-plane: ~ **yuvası**, (*aer.*) bomb-bay.

bomba·cı (*mil.*) Bombardier; bomber; bomb-maker. ~**lama**, *vn.* aerial bombing; bombardment: ~ **vizörü**, (*aer.*) bomb-sight. ~**lamak (-i)**, bomb (from the air). ~**lanmak**, *vp.* be bombed. ~**lanmış yer**, bomb-site. ~**rdıman**, bombardment; bombing: ~ **etm.**, bombard; bomb: ~ **uçağı**, (*aer.*) bomberplane. ~**rdon**, (*mus.*) bombardon.

bombe(li) Convex, dished; (*eng.*) camber(ed).

bom·bok (*vulg.*) Utterly spoilt; quite useless. ~ **boş**, quite empty; utterly nonsensical. ~**cu**, (*sl.*) liar.

bonbon (*cul.*) Bonbon, sweet.

boncuˡkᵍu Bead (*esp.* a blue bead against the evil eye). ~ **gibi**, beadlike; beady (eyes); very distinct: ~ **illeti**, (*med.*) infantile convulsions: ~ **mavisi**, turquoise blue: ~ **tutkalı**, beadlike glue.

boncuk·lanmak *vi.* (Tears, etc.) become like beads. ~**lu**, beaded: ~ **kertenkele**, (*zoo.*) gila monster, beaded lizard.

bonderlemek (-i) (*tex.*) Bonderize.

bone (*mod.*) Bonnet.

bon·file (*cul.*) Best undercut of beef. ~**jur**, (*mod.*) cut-away/morning coat; (*int.*) good-morning! ~**kör(lük)**, gener·ous/(-osity). ~**nüvi**, good-night! ~**o**, (*fin.*) bond; bill: ~ **kırdırmak**, cash in a bill. ~**sans**, commonsense. ~**servis**, testimonial, certificate of good character. ~**suvar**, good evening! ~**şans**, good luck. ~**voyaj**, good journey!

bopstil (*mod.*) Bob-style, exaggerated style; dandy.

borˡ¹ *n.* (*agr.*) Waste/fallow/unploughed land; dregs.

bor² *n.* (*chem.*) Boron. ~ +, *a.* Boro-.

bor- *pref. See also* BUR-.

bora (*met.*) Squall, tempest, blast; (*fig.*) violent abuse/reproach. ~ **koptu**, the storm burst: ~ **patlatmak**, (*sl.*) get very angry: ~ **yemek**, be exposed to a storm of wind/words. ~**ğan** = BURAĞAN.

borak (*agr.*) Infertile.

boraks (*chem.*) Borax. ~**lı**, boracic.

boran (*met.*) (Summer) thunderstorm. ~**bulut**, cumulonimbus.

borani (*cul.*) Dish of vegetables, rice and yoghurt.

bor·asik (*chem.*) Boracic. ~**asik**ⁱ, (*geol.*) boracite. ~**at**ⁱ, (*min.*) borate.

borazan (*mus.*) Trumpet; (*obs.*) trumpeter. ~ **kuşu**, (*orn.*) agami, trumpeter. ~**cı**, (*mil.*) trumpeter; bugler. ~**cıbaşı**ⁿⁱ, trumpeter; trumpet-major. ~**lı**, ~ **kuğu kuşu**, (*orn.*) trumpeter swan.

borˡçᶜu Duty, obligation; (*fin.*) debt; loan, advance. ~ **almak**, borrow: ~ **belgiti (iyesi)**, (*fin.*) debenture (holder): ~ **bini aşmak**, have a pile of debts: ~ **etm./yapmak**, incur a debt: ~ **gırtlağa çıkmak**, be up to one's ears/eyes in debt: ~ **harç**, getting money by hook or by crook: ~ **kapamak**, extinguish a debt: ~ **ödenir kira ödenmez**, it is better to borrow to buy a house than rent one: ~ **para**, a loan: ~ **senedi**, (*fin.*) bill, bond: ~ **vermek**, lend; give credit/a loan: ~ **vermekle yol yürümekle tükenir**, debts can be paid even if slowly: ~ **yemek**,

live by borrowing: ~**a**, as a loan: ~**a almak/ alışveriş etm.**, buy on credit: ~**a girmek**, get/run into debt: ~**tan kurtarma**, discharge (of a debtor): ~**una saymak/tutmak (-i)**, consider stg. as part payment of a debt: ~**unu kapatmak/ödemek/ vermek**, pay off/repay a debt/loan.

borç·lancı Guarantor. ~**lancılık**, guarantee, security, caution-money. ~**landırılmak**, *vp.* be forced into debt. ~**landırmak (-i)**, force s.o. into debt; debit, charge. ~**lanılmak**, *imp. v.* debt be incurred. ~**lanım**, bond; guarantee. ~**lanma**, *vn.* borrowing. ~**lanmak (-e)**, borrow; take a loan; owe, be in debt. ~**lu**, *a.* indebted; beholden: *n.* debtor: ~ **çıkmak**, be in debt/'in the red'. ~**luluk**, indebtedness. ~**suz**, without any debts: ~ **harçsız**, without borrowing. ~**suzluk**, being without any debts.

borda (*naut.*) Ship's side; broadside. ~ **ateşi**, broadside (of guns): ~, side by side: ~ ~**ya**, alongside: ~ ~**ya getirmek**, lay alongside: ~ **etm.**, board (an enemy ship): ~ **fenerleri**, port and starboard lights: ~ **hattı**, line abreast: ~ **iskelesi**, accommodation ladder: ~**da**, abeam, abreast. ~**lamak (-i)**, board (a ship).

bor·do *a.* Claret red. *n.* Bordeaux wine, claret. ~**dro**, (*fin.*) memorandum; detailed account; docket. ~**dür**, edge; kerb. ~**ik**, (*chem.*) boric, boracic: ~ **asit**, boric acid. ~**ina**, (*naut.*) bow-line.

bornoz/bornus (*mod.*) Bath-robe; burnous, Arab cloak; barber's jacket.

borsa (*fin.*) Bourse; stock-exchange. ~ **acente/ temsilcisi**, stock-broker: ~ **çizelge/işlemleri**, exchange quotation//transactions: ~ **oyunculuğu**, stock-jobbing: ~ **oyuncusu**, stock-jobber: ~ **oyunu**, speculation. ~**cı**, jobber; speculator.

boru (*eng.*) Tube, pipe; (*mus.*) trumpet; (*fig.*) idle talk, nonsense. ~ **ağı**, (*eng.*) pipe network: ~ **anahtarı**, pipe wrench: ~ **askısı**, pipe bracket: ~ **bileziği**, ornamental ring (on a stove-pipe): ~ **bükmesi**, pipe-bending: ~ **çalmak**, (*mus.*) blow/ signal with the trumpet: ~ **çekmesi**, (*eng.*) pipedrawing: ~ **değil/mu bu?**, it's no small matter!: ~ **hattı**, (*eng.*) pipeline: ~ **işareti**, (*mil.*) bugle-call: ~ **kangalı**, (*eng.*) coil: ~ **kelepçe/mengenesi**, pipeclamp//-vice: ~ **su ötmek**, (*fig.*) be the 'big noise'/ influential: ~**sunu çalmak**, blow s.o. else's trumpet.

boru·cu Maker/seller of pipes/tubes/trumpets; (*mus.*) trumpeter; (*eng.*) pipe-fitter. ~**cuk**, (*bio.*) tubule. ~**çiçeği**ⁿⁱ, (*bot.*) datura, trumpet-flower. ~**çiçeğigiller**, Campanulaceae. ~**kabağı**ⁿⁱ, (*bot.*) a cylindrical squash. ~**msu**, pipe-shaped; (*bio.*) tubiform. ~**yolu**ⁿᵘ, (*min.*) pipe-line.

bos(lu) = BOY(LU).

Bosna (*geo.*) Bosnia. ~ +, *a.* Bosnian. ~**lı**, *n.* (*ethn.*) Bosnian. ~**sarayı**, (*geo.*) Sarajevo.

bostan (*agr.*) Vegetable (*esp.* melon) garden; (*bot.*) melon. ~ **beygiri**, horse turning the water-wheel: ~ **beygiri gibi dolaşmak/dönmek**, walk aimlessly round and round; stick to routine; make no progress: ~ **çukuru**, manure pit: ~ **dolabı**, irrigation water-wheel: ~ **korkuluğu**, scarecrow; (*fig.*) lazy/incapable person: ~ **sineği**, (*ent.*) crane-fly: ~ **tahtası**, garden-bed.

bostan·cı Gardener; (*his.*) a bodyguard of the Sultan: ~ **başı**, (*his.*) commander of the Sultan's bodyguards. ~**cılık**, gardening; guard's duties. ~**patlıcanı**[n1], (*bot.*) a large egg-plant.

boş Empty; blank; bare; clear; empty-handed; vain, useless; (*eng.*) idle, disengaged; unoccupied; unemployed; divorced; loose, slack; untethered; (*bio.*) coelo-. ~ **(unu) almak**, take up the slack; (*fig.*) trim an unlikely story to make it plausible: ~ **atıp dolu tutmak**, 'draw a bow at a venture'; make a lucky shot; learn stg. by subtle questioning: ~ **bağırsak**, (*bio.*) jejunum: ~ **bırakmamak (-i)**, help s.o.: ~ **böğür**, (*bio.*) small of the back: ~ **bulunmak**, be taken unawares; be surprised: ~ **çekmek**, draw a blank (in a lottery): ~ **çıkmak**, hopes come to nothing: ~ **çıkmamak (-den)**, make some small profit from: ~ **çuval ayakta durmaz**, some talent is needed to succeed: ~ **durmak**, remain idle: ~ **durmamak**, never be idle; respond to s.o.'s action: ~ **düşmek**, (*obs.*) (woman) be divorced: ~ **film**, (*cin.*) unexposed film: ~ **gezenin** ~ **kalfası**, ne'er-do-weel, vagabond: ~ **gezmek**, idle about; be without work: ~**İNANÇ**: ~ **kafalı**, empty-headed: ~ **kâğıdı**, (*obs.*) man's written declaration of divorce: ~ **kile . . .** = DİPSİZ KİLE: ~ **ko(y)mak**, leave s.o. to his own resources: ~ **makara**, (*eng.*) idling pulley: ~ **ol(sun)!**, (*obs.*) (man's verbal declaration) be divorced!: ~ **olm.**, be empty/useless/unoccupied: ~ **olmamak**, be not without reason: ~ **vermek**, (*sl.*) pay no attention: ~ **yere**, in vain: ~ **yere tüketmek**, waste: ~**a almak**, slacken; (*mot.*) disengage the clutch: ~**a çıkmak**, (hope, etc.) be blighted, come to nothing, fail: ~**a gitmek**, be in vain; be wasted: ~**a koysan dolmaz doluya koysan almaz**, it doesn't work whichever way you do it: ~**ta** = BOŞTA: ~**u** ~**una**, completely in vain: ~**una** = BOŞUNA.

boş·alım Discharge. ~**alma**, *vn.* discharge, emptying; pouring out one's worries to s.o. ~**almak**, *vi.* be discharged/emptied; run out; get stg. off one's chest; (animal) get loose; defecate. ~**alta**[l]**çı**[cı], (*phys.*) vacuum pump. ~**altılmak**, *vp.* be emptied, etc. ~**altı(m)**, cleaning out; (*bio.*) excretion: ~ **aygıtı**, (*bio.*) excretory organs. ~**altma**, *vn.* emptying, draining; unloading; discharge: ~ **borusu**, drainage pipe: ~ **havzası**, (*geo.*) drainage basin: ~ **kuyusu**, (*eng.*) bleeder well: ~ **limanı**, (*naut.*) port of discharge: ~ **tığı**, broach: ~ **tulumbası**, (*phys.*) vacuum pump. ~**altmak (-i, -e)**, empty; (*phys.*) evacuate; pour out; spill; discharge (firearms); (*eng.*) bleed (air, etc.); clean/clear out; excrete. ~**ama**, *vn.* (*obs.*) divorce. ~**amak (-i)**, (*obs.*) divorce one's wife. ~**andırmak (-i)**, *vc.* = BOŞANMAK; (*leg.*) divorce (a couple). ~**anma**, *vn.* divorce: ~ **davası**, divorce suit. ~**anmak (-den)**, (*leg.*) be divorced; be unharnessed; be loosed, break loose, escape; be poured; flow freely; pour with rain; be emptied/unloaded; (firearms) be discharged; burst into tears; pour out one's heart. ~**atılmak**, *vp.* ~**atmak (-i, -den)**, *vc.* = BOŞA(N)MAK. ~**ay(lı)**, *n.*/(*a.*) vacuum. ~**boğaz**, garrulous, indiscreet. ~**boğazlık**, idle talk, indiscreet babbling: ~ **etm.**, babble stg. out. ~**inan(**[l]**çı**[cı]**)**,

(*rel.*) superstition; false conviction; credulity. ~**lamak (-i)**, loose, let go; abandon, neglect; ignore. ~**luk**, emptiness; vacant space; cavity; gap; (*eng.*) clearance; (*eng.*) backlash; (*fin.*) ullage; (*phys.*) vacuum; (*met.*) pocket; (*fig.*) vanity; uselessness; leisure: ~ **tulumbası**, (*phys.*) vacuum pump. ~**luklu**, (*geol.*) cavernous.

Boşnak (*ethn.*) Bosnian. ~ **güzeli**, a beautiful blonde. ~**ça**, (*ling.*) Bosnian.

boş·ta Out of work; idly; in the open: ~ **gezmek**, wander idly about: ~ **kalmak**, be unemployed. ~**u** ~**una** = BOŞ. ~**una**, in vain, to no end/purpose: ~ **harcama**, extravagance.

bot[u 1] (*naut.*) Small ship; patrol-boat; dinghy.

bot[u 2] *n.* (*mod.*) Boots.

bot. = BOTANİK.

botani[l]**k**[gi] *n.* Botany. *a.* Botanic(al). ~ **ağaç bahçesi**, arboretum: ~ **âlim/bilgini**/~**çi**, botanist.

botulizm (*med.*) Botulism.

boy[1] *n.* (*soc.*) Branch of a race; clan, tribe. ~ **beyi**, chieftain.

boy[2] *n.* Length; height; depth; stature; size; (*pub.*) format; (*geo.*) bank, shore. ~ **almak/atmak/çekmek/sürmek**, increase in height/length: ~ **aptesi**, (*rel.*) ablution of the whole body: ~ **aynası**, full-length mirror: ~[u] **bos**[u], figure, stature: ~ ~, of different sizes/qualities: ~ **göstermek**, put in an appearance (but do nothing): ~ **menteşesi**, (*carp.*) piano hinge: ~ **ölçmek (-le)**, try conclusions with s.o.: ~ **ölçüşmek**, challenge/compete with s.o.: ~ **paltosu**, (*mod.*) full-length overcoat: ~ **salmak**, (young trees, etc.) grow: ~ **sürmek**, grow tall shoot up: ~ **vermek**, (water) be too deep for s.o. measure the water's depth against one's body: grow: ~ **vermemek**, (water) be shallow; not be too deep for s.o.: ~**a çekmek**, (child) grow taller (but not broader in proportion): ~**dan** ~**a**, from end to end; completely: ~**u bosu yerinde**, tall and well built: ~**u devrilsin!**, curse him!; may he die! ~**una** = BOYUNA. ~**unca**, *adv.* lengthwise; according to its length: *post.* [94] along; during; throughout: ~**un(c)a beraber**, of the same height: ~**un(c)a çocuğu olm.**, have a mature child: ~**unca kalıbın basmak**, put great trust in: ~**undan utan!**, you should be ashamed to do this at your age!: ~**unun ölçüsünü almak**, get one's deserts, learn one's lesson by painful experience.

boya Dye; paint; colour; ink; (*fig.*) deceptive appearance. ~ **çekmek/vurmak**, paint, dye: ~ **çıkarıcı**, paint-stripper: ~ **eczası**, dye-stuff: ~ **(püskürtme) tabancası**, paint-gun/-sprayer: ~ **sürmek**, lay on paint: ~ **tabakası**, a coat of paint ~ **tutmak**, (cloth) take a dye; (dye) become fast. ~**sı atmak**, fade.

boya·alır (*bio.*) Chromophile. ~**almaz**, chromophobe. ~**cı**, dyer; colourman; shoe-black; (*fig.* deceptive in appearance: ~ **kedi/köpeği gibi**, multi coloured, crudely dyed: ~ **küpü**, dyer's vat: ~ **küpü mü bu?/değil ya?**, it's not so easy as all that!: ~ **sandığı**, the shoe-black's box-cum-stand. ~**cılık** making/selling of dyes, paints, etc.; shoe-black' trade. ~**gözesi**, (*bio.*) chromatophore. ~**hane**, dye house; paint-works; colourman's shop. ~[l]**k**[g1], pig ment. ~**lamak (-i)**, paint haphazardly; smear with paint. ~**lanmak**, *vp.* be smeared with paint. ~**lı**, painted; dyed; coloured; (woman) made-up. ~**m**, (*art.*) painting. ~**ma**, *vn.* action of painting, etc.: *a.* coloured, painted, dyed; false, imitation: ~ **maddesi**, pigment. ~**mak (-i, -e)**, paint, dye; decorate. ~**nmak**, *vp.* be painted/dyed; (woman) make o.s. up.

boyan = MEYAN.

boyana (*naut.*) Working a boat with a single stern oar. ~ **etm.**, steer/scull (a boat): ~ **küreği**, single stern oar, scull.

boyar (*his.*) Boyar, Slav nobleman/landowner.

boyarmadde (*chem.*) Colouring matter, pigment; (*bot.*) pigment.

boya·sız Unpainted, undyed; colourless; (woman) without make-up. ~**tmak (-i, -e)**, *vc.* = ~MAK.

boy·bos = BOY². ~**ca**, as regards height/length; lengthwise: ~ **evlat**, practically grown-up child: ~ **günaha girmek**, commit a great sin. ~**çekme**, (*carp.*) lengthwise shrinkage (of timber). ~**daş**, *a.* equal in height: *n.* equal, peer. ~ **daşlık**, equality (in height). ~**kesit**, (*math.*) longitudinal profile.

boykot[u] Boycott; sending to Coventry. ~ **etm.**, boycott; send to Coventry. ~**aj**, boycotting. ~**çu**, boycotter.

boylam (*ast., geo.*) Longitude, meridian. ~ +, *a.* Longitudinal.

boy·lamak (-i) Measure the height/length of; traverse the length of; (*sl.*) run off to. ~**lanmak**, *vi.* grow/become long/tall; go further. ~**latmak (-i, -e)**, *vc.* make grow in height/length; make s.o. go to a far place.

boyler (*eng.*) Boiler, water container.

boylu Having height/length; tall. ~ **boslu**, tall, well-built, well-developed: ~ **boyuna**, at full length: ~ **boyunca**, in its entire length.

boyn- = BOYUN².

boyna = BOYANA.

boynuz *n.* (*zoo.*) Horn; antler; (*ent.*) antenna; (*med.*) cupping-glass; (*mus.*) horn. *a.* Made of horn. ~ +, *a.* Horn; cerato-: ~ **çekmek**, (*med.*) cup: ~ **dikmek/takmak/yaldızlamak**, be cuckolded: ~ **diktirmek/taktırmak (-e)**, make a cuckold of s.o.: ~ **kulağı geçmek**, surpass (s.o. bigger): ~ **maddesi**, (*zoo.*) keratin: ~ **sineği**, (*ent.*) horn fly: ~ **vurmak** = ~LAMAK.

boynuz·lamak (-i) Gore s.o. ~**lanmak**, *vi.* grow horns: *vp.* be cuckolded; be gored. ~**latmak (-i)**, cuckold s.o. ~**lu**, horned; (*fig.*) cuckold; pimp: ~ **anhima** = ~LUKUŞ. ~**lugalı**, (*orn.*) hornbill. ~**lugiller**, (*zoo.*) cattle. ~**lukuş**, (*orn.*) horned screamer. ~**luteke**, (*ent.*) long-horned beetle. ~**otu**[nu], (*bot.*) hellebore.

boy·otu[nu] (*bot.*) Fenugreek. ~**suz**, short of stature.

boyun[1] = BOY[1,2].

boy·un[nu 2] *n.* (*bio.*) Neck; cervix; (*geo.*) col, pass; (*eng.*) shank; (*fig.*) responsibility. ~ALTI: ~ATKISI: ~ **borcu**, binding duty, obligation: ~ **bükmek**, bow: ~ **çeviren**, (*orn.*) wryneck: ~ **eğdirmek**, force to submit: ~ **eğer**, compliant, submissive: ~ **eğme**, *vn.* base compliance: ~ **eğmek**, bow the neck, submit; humiliate o.s.: ~ **eğmez**, challenging,

independent: ~ **kesmek/kırmak**, bow the head (in respect/humility): ~ **noktası**, (*geo.*) lowest point between two hills: ~ **olm.**, stand guarantor: ~ **omuru**, (*bio.*) cervical vertebra: ~ **toplardamarı**, (*bio.*) jugular vein: ~ **tutmak**, protest: ~ **vermek**, obey.

boynu: ~ **altında kalsın!**, may he perish!: ~ **bükük**, wretched: ~ **eğik/eğri**, hanging one's head in shame, humiliated: ~ **tutulmak**, have a stiff neck: ~**m(uz) kıldan ince!**, I am at your mercy!; upon my head be it!: ~**na almak**, take upon o.s.: ~**na atmak**, impute to s.o.: ~**na binmek**, dun/persecute s.o.: ~**na borç**, a duty: ~**na geçirmek**, take possession of stg.: ~**na sarılmak**, throw one's arms round s.o.'s neck: ~**nda kalmak**, (obligation) remain unfulfilled: ~**nu bükmek**, be in a pitiful state; accept one's fate: ~**nu kırmak**, take o.s. off: ~**nu tutulmak**, have a stiff neck: ~**nu uzatmak**, crane one's neck; submit o.s.: ~**nu vurmak**, decapitate.

boyuna Lengthwise; according to its length; (*geo., phys.*) longitudinal; continually. ~ **eğim**, (*eng.*) grade, gradient: ~ **kesit**, (*math.*) longitudinal section: ~ **rıhtım**, wharf, quay.

boyun·altı ~ **bezi**, (*bio.*) thymus. ~**atkısı**[nı], scarf; comforter. ~**bağı**[nı], necktie, cravat; scarf; dog-collar. ~ **buran** = DÖNERBOYUN. ~**ca** = BOY². ~**ca**[ğı], necklace. ~**cu**[k ğu], (*bot.*) style. ~**duru**[k ğu], (*agr.*) yoke; (*arch.*) lintel; (*sp.*) head-lock; (*naut.*) crowfoot; (*fig.*) oppression: ~ **altına almak/** ~**a vurmak**, put under the yoke; reduce to submission/servitude: ~ **parası**, (*soc.*) money given to bride's friends by her father-in-law. ~**lu**, having a neck; -necked; (*leg.*) responsible; guarantor. ~**luk**, scarf; collar. ~**luluk**, guarantee, surety.

boyut[u] (*math.*) Dimension; size; exponent. ~ +/ ~**lu**/~**sal**, dimensional. ~**tutar**, fixture.

boz Grey; dun; uncultivated (land). ~ **kaz**, (*orn.*) greylag goose: ~ **ördek**, (*orn.*) gadwall: ~ **sırtlan**, (*zoo.*) brown hyena.

boza (*cul.*) Boza (drink from fermented millet). ~ **gibi**, dense, cloudy (liquid): ~ **olm.**, (*fig.*) be ashamed. ~**cı(lık)**, (work of) maker/seller of boza.

-bozan *suf.* Spoiling [OYUNBOZAN].

boz·armak *vi.* Become/turn grey. ~**ayı**, (*zoo.*) brown bear. ~**bakkal**, (*orn.*) field-fare. ~**ca**, *a.* greyish; *n.* uncultivated land. ~**caada**, *pr.n.* (*geo.*) Tenedos. ~**doğan**, (*orn.*) grey falcon; (*bot.*) a type of pear; (*his.*) a mace.

bozdur·(t)mak (-i, -e) *vc.* ~**ulmak**, *vp.* = BOZMAK.

bozgun *a.* Routed, defeated. *n.* Rout, débâcle, defeat; discomfiture. ~ **vermek/** ~**a uğramak**, be routed. ~**cu**, defeatist; trouble-maker. ~**culuk**, defeatism. ~**luk**, defeat; discomfiture.

boz·kır *a.* Pale grey (horse): *n.* steppe(-land): ~ **antilopu**, (*zoo.*) saiga: ~ **doğanı**, (*orn.*) prairie falcon: ~ **tavşanı**, (*zoo.*) jack-rabbit. ~**kurt**, (*zoo.*) grey wolf; (*myth.*) a wolf that led the Turks across mountains to the open world. ~**lak**, (*mus.*) a folk melody.

bozla·mak *vi.* (Camel) bellow. ~**tmak (-i)**, *vc.*

bozma *vn.* = BOZMAK. Act of spoiling, etc. *a.* Spoilt; demolished; (*eng.*) made out of cannibalized materials. ~sı (-in), an apology for . . .. ~cı, s.o. who buys old things to cannibalize them.

bozmadde (*bio.*) Grey matter.

bozmak (-i) Derange; disrupt; damage, cripple; spoil; adulterate; bungle, ruin, destroy; deprave, corrupt; deflower; abash, disconcert, discomfit, confuse; (*leg.*) annul, cancel; invalidate; break, contravene (oath/treaty); (*fin.*) change (money); (*sp.*) violate; (*mil.*) defeat, rout; (*agr.*) gather the final crop (of grapes, vegetables, etc.); (*eng.*) cannibalize: *vi.* go mad; (weather) deteriorate: (-le), be crazy about stg.

bozrak Light greyish in colour.

bozucu *a.* Disconcerting; confusing; corrupting, etc. *n.* Demolisher; (*eng.*) spoiler; ship-breaker.

bozu¹kᵍᵘ¹ *n.* (*mus.*) Type of lute; (?) bouzouki.

bozuk² *a.* Destroyed; spoilt; unserviceable, out of order, not working; ruined; broken; deranged; depraved, corrupt. ~ oluşum, (*med.*) malformation: ~ para, (*fin.*) small change: ~ para gibi harcamak, try to profit from/exploit s.o.: ~ ses, (*mus.*) cacophony.

bozuk·düzen Disordered; irregular. ~luk, ruin; being out of order/broken down; disturbance; defeat; (*fin.*) small change; (*psy.*) corruption.

bozul·gu Damage, loss. ~ma, *vn.* depravation; discomposure; (*chem.*) breakdown, decay, decomposition; (*nuc.*) breakdown; (*rad.*) distortion. ~mak, *vp.* = BOZMAK; be spoilt, etc.; get out of order; break down; deteriorate; (*cul.*) go bad; be taken aback/disconcerted; look vexed; grow thin; become pale/ill: **bozulmamış**, virgin, untouched: **bozulup büzülmek**, retire into one's shell.

bozum *vn.* = BOZMAK. ~ etm., (*sl.*) put to shame: ~ havası, the embarrassment caused by s.o. else's discomfiture: ~ olm., be disconcerted. ~ca, (*zoo.*) a grey lizard.

bozun·ma (*phys.*) Decomposition. ~tu, discomfiture, embarrassment; old materials, scrap; = BOZMA: ~su (-in), a mere parody of a . . .: ~ya uğramak, be embarrassed/discomfited: ~ya vermemek, not let o.s. be disconcerted. ~um, (*eng.*) deformation.

bozuş·ma *vn.* Discord; dissension; quarrelling. ~mak (-le), quarrel with each other; disagree; dissent from; become estranged; break with s.o. ~uk, who has quarrelled; on bad terms.

bozu¹tᵈᵘ Intrigue; malice; disorder. ~çu, mischief-/trouble-maker.

boz·yel (*met.*) South-west wind. ~yürük, (*zoo.*) sand boa.

böbre¹kᵍⁱ (*bio.*) Kidney. ~+, *a.* Renal: ~ havuzcuğu, (*bio.*) renal pelvis: ~ yağı, (*cul.*) suet: ~ yangısı, (*med.*) nephritis. ~sel, renal. ~üstü, suprarenal, adrenal: ~ bezi, adrenal gland.

böbür (*zoo.*) Syrian rock hyrax/dassie cony. ~lenmek, *vi.* assume an arrogant air, boast. ~tü, boasting, arrogance.

böce¹kᵍⁱ (*ent.*) Insect; bug; (*zoo.*) crawfish, spiny lobster. ~ çıkarmak, breed silkworms: ~ gibi, small and dark (child): ~ tozlanması, (*bot.*) entomophily: ~ler, (*ent.*) order of insects: ~leri yokedici ilaç, insecticide.

böcek·başıⁿⁱ (*his.*) Chief of the Palace detectives. ~bilim, (*zoo.*) entomology: ~ uzmanı, entomologist. ~çil, (*bot.*, *zoo.*) insectivorous. ~hane = ~LİK. ~kabuğu**ⁿᵘ, bright greenish-blue colour; shot, irridescent. ~kapan, (*bot.*) insect-eating plant. ~lenmek, be infested with insects. ~li, containing/infested with insects. ~lik, silkworm breeding shed. ~siz, without/free of insects.

böcü (*ent.*) Larva; mite: insect.

böcül ~ ~, squinting to both sides.

böğ(ü) (*ent.*) Common barrel-spider.

böğ¹ürʳü (*bio.*) Side; flank; small of the back.

böğürtlen (*bot.*) Blackberry; (*sl.*) vomit. ~ çalısı, bramble. ~lik, thicket of brambles.

böke (*sp.*) First, champion.

böl·dürmek (-i) *vc.* = BÖLMEK. ~e, (*soc.*) cousin; (*pub.*) fascicle. ~eci¹k**ᵍⁱ, part, piece. ~e¹ç**ᶜⁱ, (*bio.*, *phys.*) diaphragm. ~e¹k**ᵍⁱ, (*fin.*) rate, instalment; (*soc.*) clique. ~ekleşmek, *vi.* form a clique. ~en, (*math.*) divisor, denominator.

bölge District; division; area; region; zone. ~ ve şehir planlaması, town and country planning. ~ci(lik), (*adm.*) devolution·ist/(-ism); regional·ist/ (-ism). ~lerarası, inter-regional. ~lik, localized. ~sel, local; regional; divisional; district. ~sellik, regionalism.

böl·me *vn.* Division; (*arch.*) partition; dividing wall; (*bio.*) septum; (*naut.*) bulkhead; compartment; chamber; (*aer.*) bay, pod: ~ kapısı, watertight door: ~ (levhası), (*eng.*) baffle: ~ perdesi, (*eng.*) diaphragm. ~mek (-i), separate; divide; split; cut up; compartmentalize. ~meleme, (*phys.*) partitioning. ~ü, (*math.*) division sign (÷); divided by, over. ~ücü, (*math.*) dividing; (*soc.*) separatist. ~ücülük, division; separatism; class warfare. ~ü¹k**ᵍü, part; (sub)division; compartment; (*math.*) class; (*mil.*) company, squad(ron): ~ ~/~ pörçük, bit by bit, in bits: ~ emini, (*mil.*) pay-/quartermaster. ~üklü, (*cin.*, *lit.*) serial.

bölüm Act of dividing; portion; slice; batch; (*pub.*) chapter, article; section, class; (*adm.*) department; (*bio.*) division; (*math.*) fraction, quotient; (*geol.*) epoch; (*fin.*) instalment; (*th.*) act. ~ ~, in succession: ~ duvarı, (*arch.*) partition wall: ~lere ayırmak, departmentalize.

bölüm·ce (*pub.*) Paragraph. ~cü¹k**ᵍü, (*bio.*) lobule. ~leme, *vn.* classification. ~lemek (-i), classify; compartmentalize. ~lenmek, *vp.* ~sel, partial.

bölün·ce (*pub.*) Paragraph. ~¹ç**ᶜü, (*fin.*) instalment. ~ebilirlik/ ~ebilme, (*math.*) divisibility. ~en, (*math.*) dividend; numerator. ~me, *vn.*; division; separation; distribution; (*zoo.*) segmentation; (*bot.*) division; (*sp.*) break-up of the pack. ~mek, *vp.* be divided/separated. etc. ~mez, indivisible: ~ sayı, (*math.*) prime number. ~müş, divided: ~ yol, dual carriageway. ~tü, part, fraction (of stg.); (*pub.*) fascicle. ~tüler, divisions, sections.

böl·üşmek (-i, -le) Divide up; share out. ~üştürmek (-i, -e), *vc.* ~üşüm, dividing up, sharing out; allocating. ~üt**ü, lot, batch; (*bio.*) segment, metamere. ~ütlenme, (*bio.*) metamerization.

bön Silly; naive; vacant; imbecile. ~leşmek, *vi.*

become silly, etc. ~**lük**, silliness; naivety; imbecility. ~**sümek**, *vi.* behave like an imbecile.
böre¹kᵍⁱ (*cul.*) (Various kinds of) flaky pastry, pasty, pie. ~**çı(lik)**, (work of) maker/seller of BÖREK. ~**lik**, suitable for/used in making BÖREK.
börkü (*mod., obs.*) Felt cap.
börkene¹kᵍⁱ (*zoo.*) Second stomach (of ruminants); crop (of birds).
bört·mek *vi.* (*cul.*) Cook slightly. ~**türmek (-i)**, *vt.* cook slightly. ~**ük**, stg. slightly cooked. ~**ülmek**, *vp.* be slightly cooked.
börtü ~ **böcek**, all sort of insects.
börülce (*bot., cul.*) Cherry-bean, cow-pea.
bösmek *vi.* Vaporize and explode.
böyle *a.* [72] Such; this kind of; similar to this. *adv.* [195] So; thus; in this way. ~ **değilse kellemi keserim**, if it's not so I'll eat my hat: ~ **gelmiş** ~ **gider**, it'll always be like that; don't expect any improvement: ~ **iken**, while it is/was thus; notwithstanding: ~ **ise**, if so, in that case: ~ **işler varlıkla olur**, you must be well-off to do such things: ~ **olunca**, in that case: ~ **söyledi ha!**, so he said that did he!: ~ **yalanlara karnım tok**, I won't be taken in by such lies: ~ **yapanlar yok değildir**, there are many who behave like this: ~ **yapmıyalım, laf olur**, don't let's do this or people will talk.
böyle·ce *adv.* [195] Thus, in this way. ~**likle**, in this manner; in the end. ~**mesine**, in this fashion/way. ~**si**, this kind of person. ~**sine**, so excessively; to such a one as this.
BP = BİRLİK PARTİSİ.
Br. = (*ch.s.*) BROM; (*geo.*) BURUN.
bradi- *pref.* (*zoo.*) Brady-.
Brahman·(lık)/ ~ **cı(lık)** (*rel.*) Brahmin(ism).
braki- *pref.* (*zoo.*) Brachy-. ~**sefal**, brachycephalous.
branda (*naut.*) Hammock; (*mot.*) hood. ~ **bezi**, sailcloth.
branş (*fin.*) Branch; sector; (*ed.*) subject.
bravo *int.* Bravo!, well done!
bre *int.* (*col.*) Now then!, hi, you!; wonderful!
Brehmen = BRAHMAN.
brendi (*cul.*) Brandy.
breş (*geol.*) Breccia.
Bretanya (*geo.*) Brittany. ~**lı**, (*ethn.*) Breton.
Brezilya (*geo.*) Brazil; (*bot.*) brazilwood. ~ +, *a.* Brazilian: ~ **kestanesi**, (*bot.*) brazil-nut. ~**lı**, *n.* (*ethn.*) Brazilian.
briçⁱ (*gamb.*) Bridge.
briçka One-horse open carriage.
brifing (*mil.*) Briefing.
brikⁱ (*naut.*) Brig; (*mot.*) break, light carriage.
briketⁱ (*min., arch.*) (Coal) briquette. ~**çi**, briquette maker/seller. ~**lemek (-i)**, make briquettes.
Brit. = (BÜYÜK) BRİTANYA; İNGİLTERE.
Britanya (*geo.*) (Great) Britain. ~ +, *a.* Britannic, British. ~**lı**, *n.* (*ethn.*) Briton, Englishman.
briyantin Brilliantine.
briz (*met.*) Breeze. ~**briz**, (*dom.*) short window curtain.
bro·de (*tex.*) Embroidery. ~**kar**, (*tex.*) brocade.
brom·(in) (*chem.*) Bromine: ~ +, bromo-: ~ **asidi**,

bromic acid. ~**at**¹, bromate. ~**lu**, bromic. ~**ür**, bromide.
bronş (*bio.*) Bronchus, windpipe. ~**lar**, bronchi(a). ~**çu¹k**ᵍᵘ, bronchiole. ~**it**ⁱ, (*med.*) bronchitis.
bronz (*min.*) Bronze. ~**it**ⁱ, bronzite. ~**laşmak**, *vi.* become bronze in colour.
broş Brooch. ~**ür**, (*pub.*) brochure, fascicule.
brovnik (*mil.*) Browning automatic pistol.
bröve (*ed.*) Certificate (of capabilities).
Brüksel (*geo.*) Brussels. ~ **lahanası** = BÜRÜK-SELLAHANASI.
brülör Burner (gas-, bunsen-, etc.).
brüt (*fin.*) Gross (weight, etc.); without deduction.
bşk. = BAŞKA.
Bş·k = BAŞKAN(LIK). ~**tbp** = BAŞTABİP.
BŞK = BAŞKOMUTAN.
buⁿᵘ *a. This. pr.* [71] This (one); (*pl.* **bunlar** these); the above-mentioned, the aforesaid. ~ **ahvalde**, under the circumstances: ~ **aptesle daha çok namaz kılınır**, it will serve many more useful purposes: ~ **arada**, during this period; at the same time; including/amongst these: ~ **aralık**, at this time; then; meanwhile: ~ **bakımdan**, from this viewpoint: ~ **bapta**, on this subject; in this connection: ~ **böyle sökmez**, you won't get any further like this; this won't do: ~ **cümle ile**, nevertheless: ~ **cümleden**, as an instance of this: ~ **da caba**, and what's more, and into the bargain: ~ **da geçer**, this too will pass!, never mind!: ~ **defa**, this time, now: ~ **gibi**, such, like this: ~ **gibiler**, the likes of these; people like this: ~ **giz**, this time; for this once: ~ **gözle**, with this understanding: ~ **günahına (bile) değmez**, the game is not worth the candle: ~ **günlerde/yakınlarda**, quite soon: ~ **haysiyetle** = ~ BAKIMDAN: ~ **hepsinden beter/hepsine tüy dikti**, that beats everything!: ~ **hususta/münasebetle**, in this respect/connection: ~ **imalı sözler**, words alluding to this; these allusions: ~ **iş sökmez/yürümez**, this sort of thing can't go on!: ~ **itibarla**, and therefore; and so: ~ **kabilden**, of this kind/sort: ~ **kadar**, this much, so many; to this extent; . . . odd [**kırk bu kadar yıl**, forty odd years]: ~ **kadar olur/kadarı da fazla**, this is a bit too much of a good thing!: ~ **kadar kusur kadı kızında da bulunur**, that's a very trifling fault: ~ **kadarcık**, just this much: ~ **kadarla kalsa iyi**, it wouldn't have mattered if that had been all: ~ **kadarcık şeyi bilmeliydiniz**, you ought to have known better: ~ **kafada adamlar**, these kind of people: ~ **kafayı bırak!**, you must give up these sort of ideas: ~ **kere**, this time; now, recently: ~ **kez**, this time: ~ **ne demek?**, what does that mean?: ~ **ne naz?**, why so coy/reluctant?: ~ **ne perhiz** ~ **ne lahana turşusu!**, what a contrast!; it's not consistent/in keeping!: ~ **neden/sebeple**, for this reason; therefore: ~ **olmaz!**, this won't do!: ~ **olmazsa Arap olayım**, if it's not so I'm a Dutchman: ~ **sevdadan vazgeç!**, give up this idea!: ~ **sıcağa kar mı dayanır**, the force of circumstances brings sudden changes: ~ **surette**, in this way: ~ **takdirde**, in this case: ~ **yakınlarda** = ~ GÜNLERDE: ~ **yana (-den)**, [89] since; until now.
buna, to this: ~ **da eyvallah!**, God's will be done!; I'm thankful for small mercies: ~ **gülünmez!**, it's no

laughing matter!: ~ **mukabil**, on the other hand: ~ **ne denir?**, what is this called?: ~ **ne dersiniz (-de)?**, how/what do you do call this in (English)?; (*fig.*) what about this?: ~ **pes!**, it's beyond me!, it's the limit!: ~ **rağmen**, even then.

bunda: ~ **bir iş var!**, there's stg. funny/strange about this.

bundan, from/through/by this: ~ **başka çare yok**, there's no other way out; this is the only solution: ~ **böyle**, [203] henceforth, from now on: ~ **böyle**... **denecek,** hereinafter referred to as . . .: ~ **dolayı**, on account of this: ~ **evvel/önce**, before this, previously: ~ **iyisi can sağlığı**, the best one can have: ~ **maada**, furthermore; besides this: ~ **ötesine karışmam**, beyond that I'm not concerned: ~ **sonra**, after this: ~ **sonrası**, what happens next: ~ **şu kadar sene evvel**, many years ago.

bunu, this: ~ **al da başına çal!**, (angrily) 'here, take it back, I don't want it!': ~ **benden esirgeme**, don't grudge me this: ~ **saymayız, sizi yine bekleriz!**, I don't call this a visit—you must come again!: ~ **yanına koymam!**, I shan't forget that (you'll pay for it!): ~ **yapmam dedi dayattı**, he insisted he would not do it: ~ **yapman için kırk fırın ekmek yemen lazım**, it will be a long time before you are capable of doing this: ~ **yapmasa nesi eksilir?**, if he doesn't do this what will he miss?

bunun, of this: ~ **burası**, this place here: ~ **daniskasını bilir**, he knows it from A to Z: ~ **fevkinde**, above this: ~ **gibisi**, one like this: ~ **hakkında**, about this: ~ **için**, for this reason/purpose: ~ **kadar büyük**, as big as this: ~ **sonu yoktur**, no good will come of this: ~ **üstüne soğuk/bir bardak su iç!**, you can write that off!, you'll never see that again: ~ **üzerine**, then, thereupon: ~ **la beraber/birlikte**, [211] at the same time; nevertheless; however, in spite of this.

buat¹ (*el.*) Junction-box; (*th.*) night-club.
buca¹kᵍⁱ Corner; angle; (*adm.*) quarter, district, commune. ~ ~ **aramak**, search in every nook and cranny: ~ ~ **kaçmak**, run away to avoid s.o./stg.: ~ **müdürü**, (*adm.*) district commissioner.
buçu¹kᵍᵘ [81] Half (after numerals) [iki ~, two and a half]. ~ **lu**, having halves/fractions.
bud- = BUT.
Buda (*rel.*) Buddha. ~ **dini**, Buddhism.
buda¹k/budacı¹kᵍⁱ (*for.*) Twig; shoot; knot (in timber). ~ **lamak (-i)**, (*for.*) bud-graft. ~ **lanmak**, *vi.* send forth shoots; become knotty; (*fig.*) become complicated/difficult. ~ **lı**, knotty (wood).
budala Silly fool; ass; imbecile; greedy. . . . ~ **sı**, mad on . . .. ~ **laşmak**, *vi.* behave foolishly. ~ **lık**, foolishness: ~ **etm.**, behave foolishly; make an ass of o.s. ~ **msı**, foolish.
buda·ma *vn.* (*agr.*, *th.*) Cutting. ~ **mak (-i)**, prune; lop, trim; (*fig.*) reduce, deduct. ~ **nmak**, *vp.* be pruned/trimmed: *vi.* apply o.s. assiduously to stg. ~ **tı**, loppings, prunings. ~ **tmak (-i, -e)**, *vc.*
Bud·apeşte (*geo.*) Budapest. ~ **in**, Buda.
Bud·ist¹ Buddhist. ~ **izm**, Buddhism.
budun (*soc.*) Tribe, people, nation. ~ **betim(ci)**, ethnograph·y/(-er). ~ **betimsel**, ethnographical.

~ **bilim(ci)**, ethnolo·gy/(-gist). ~ **bilimsel(lik)**, ethnological (quality/nature). ~ **sal**, tribal, ethnic. ~ **su**, primitive tribe.
buduvar (*dom.*) Boudoir.
bufa ~ (**balığı**), (*ich.*) lamprey.
bugün (*adv.*) [201] Today. ~ **bana ise yarın da sana!**, it will be your turn tomorrow!: ~ **olmazsa yarın var**, there's always tomorrow: ~ **yarın**, soon: ~ **den tezi yok**, straight away: ~ **den yarına**, shortly: ~ **e** ~, don't forget that . . .: ~ **e değin/~edek**, today: ~ **lerde**, in these days, nowadays: ~ **ü yarınına uymamak**, for one's circumstances/moods be liable to change.
bugün·kü Of today, today's; current, modern, up-to-date: ~ **günde**, now at this time: ~ **tavuk yarınki kazdan iyidir**, a bird in the hand is worth two in the bush: ~ **ler**, modern (people, etc.). ~ **lük**, *adv.* just for today: ~ **yarınlık**, that may happen any moment.
Buğdan (*his.*) Moldavia. ~ **lı**, (*ethn.*) Moldavian.
buğday Wheat; corn. ~ **açık rastığı**, (*myc.*) loose wheat smut: ~ **başak verince orak pahaya çıkar**, when they are needed things become expensive: ~ **benizli**, light-brown complexioned: ~ **böcek/kenesi** = ~ **BİTİ**: ~ **karıncası**, (*ent.*) harvester ant: ~ **kurdu**, (*ent.*) grain larva: ~ **küllemesi**, (*myc.*) grain mildew: ~ **rastığı**, (*myc.*) smut ball.
buğday·bitiⁿⁱ (*ent.*) Grain weevil. ~ **cıl (bülbül)**, (*orn.*) bluethroat. ~ **giller**, (*bot.*) grain, cereals. ~ **güvesi**ⁿⁱ, (*ent.*) grain moth. ~ **pası**ⁿⁱ, (*myc.*) black/stem rust. ~ **sı**, (*bot.*) grain-like: ~ **tohum**, tightly coalesced seed: ~ **yemiş**, caryopsis. ~ **sılar**, (*bot.*) Gramineaceae. ~ **sürmesi**, (*myc.*) wheat bunt.
buğu Steam; condensation, vapour; mist; damp, moisture. ~ **evi**ⁿⁱ, vapour-bath; sterilizer. ~ **lama**, *vn.* steaming; misting over; (*cul.*) steamed food: *a.* (*cul.*) steamed. ~ **lamak (-i)**, steam; cover with steam/mist. ~ **landırmak (-i)**, cause to be steamed/misted over. ~ **lanmak**, *vi.* be enveloped in vapour/steam; be misted over. ~ **laşmak**, *vi.* become steam, vaporize. ~ **laştırıcı**, *a.* vaporizing: *n.* vaporizer. ~ **laştırmak (-i)**, evaporate. ~ **lu**, steamed/misted over.
buğur (*zoo.*) Adult male camel.
buhar Steam; vapour; exhalation. ~ **düdüğü**, steam whistle, buzzer: ~ **kazanı**, steam boiler: ~ **kurutucusu**, steam dryer: ~ **makinesi**, steam-engine.
Buhara (*geo.*) Bokhara. ~ **halısı**, (*tex.*) Bokhara rug.
buhar·lama *vn.* (*for.*) Steaming (of timber). ~ **lanmak**, *vi.* vaporize; be exposed to steam; give off steam. ~ **laşma**, evaporation. ~ **laşmak**, *vi.* become steam; vaporize. ~ **laştırmak (-i)**, evaporate. ~ **lı**, steamy; with steam power: ~ **ısıtma**, steam heating.
buhran Crisis; emergency; (*fin.*) depression.
buhur Incense; fumigation. ~ **dan(lık)/~luk**, censer, incense-burner. ~ **umeryem**, (*bot.*) cyclamen.
buji (*el.*) Spark-plug.
bukağı Fetter (for people); (*mod.*) anklet; (*live.*) hobble. ~ **lamak (-i, -e)**, fetter s.o. ~ **lamak (-i)**, hobble.

~**lı**, fettered; hobbled; (horse) with white socks. ~**lık**, (*zoo*.) pastern.

bukalemun (*zoo*.) Chameleon; (*fig*.) fickle/changeable person; (*tex*.) shot silk.

buk·et[i] Bouquet (of flowers). ~**le**, lock of hair; curl: ~ **yapmak**, *vt*., curl, make curls. ~**let**[i], (*tex*.) knop wool.

bukran Wool clippings (used by saddlers).

buku[l]**k**[ğu] (*med*.) Goitre, Derbyshire neck.

bul (*carp*.) Plank sawn on two sides only.

Bul. = BULVAR(I).

bulaca = ALACA.

bul·aç (*pub*.) Bookmark.

bulada (*live*.) Chicken.

bula[l]**k**[ğı] (*geo*.) Spring, source.

bula·ma (*cul*.) Grape-juice (reduced till like honey); molasses. ~**maç**, (*cul*.) watery paste; thick soup; (*ind*.) slurry. ~**mak** (-i), smear; bedaub; dirty, soil; mix; (-e), (*cul*.) coat/cover with.

bulan·dırılmak *vp*. ~**dırmak** (-i, -e), *vc*. make turbid/muddy; dim; cloud (the eye/mind); turn (the stomach), nauseate. ~**ık**, turbid; blurred, dim, clouded; (*met*.) cloudy, overcast: ~ **suda balık avlamak**, fish in muddy waters. ~**ıklık**, turbidity; cloudiness. ~**mak**, *vi*. become cloudy/turbid; become nauseated, feel sick; (eye) become bloodshot/opaque; (eye/mind) be clouded/dimmed. ~**tı**, nausea.

bulaş·ıcı (*med*.) Contagious, infectious: ~ **hastalık**, contagious/infectious disease. ~**ık**, *a*. smeared over; soiled, dirty; contaminated; (*med*.) infected; catching, contagious; suspect (of contact with infection); compromised; (*naut*.) not having a clean bill of health; (*pej*.) importunate, too familiar: *n*. dirt; contagion; dirty kitchen utensils: ~ **bezi**, (*dom*.) dishcloth: ~ **deniz**, (*naut*.) mined area of sea: ~ **gemi**, ship with foul bill of health: ~ **hastalık**, (*med*.) contagious disease; contagion: ~ **iş**, a dirty job: ~ **makinesi**, (*dom*.) dish-washer: ~ **suyu**, dish-water: ~ **suyu gibi**, (*cul*.) tasting like dish-water, tasteless. ~**ıkçı(lık)**, dishwasher/(washing up). ~**ılmak** (-e), be involved; be contaminated. ~**ım**/~**ma**, *vn*. (*med*.) contamination, infection. ~**kan**, *a*. sticky, adhesive, contaminating; always quarrelling. ~**kanlık**, stickiness; quarrelsomeness. ~**kıran**, *a*. disinfectant. ~**kırım**, (*med*.) asepsis. ~**mak**, *vi*. be smeared/stuck; become dirty; be defiled: (-e), be contaminated by, come into contact with (contagion); be involved in (an affair); take in hand; have to do with. ~**sızlaştırmak** (-i), disinfect. ~**tırıcı**. contaminating; soiling, dirtying. ~**tırmak** (-i, -e), daub, smear; stick on; dirty; infect, contaminate; involve in (stg. unpleasant).

bul·do[l]**k**[ğu] (*zoo*.) Bulldog. ~ **yarasası**, hare-lipped/bulldog bat. ~**dozer**, (*eng*.) bulldozer.

bul·dumcuk ~ **olm**., be overjoyed at finding stg. greatly desired. ~**dura**[l]**çı** = BUL-AÇ. ~**durmak** (-i, -e), *vc*. = BULMAK.

bulgar *n*. (*ethn*.) Bulgarian. ~ +, *a*. Bulgarian. ~**ca**, (*ling*.) Bulgarian. ~**i**, (*mus*.) type of four-stringed guitar. ~**istan**, (*geo*.) Bulgaria. ~**istanlı**, *n*. (*ethn*.) Bulgarian.

bulgu A finding; discovery; invention. ~ **belgesi**, patent. ~**cu**, discoverer; inventor. ~**lama**, *vn*. discovering, inventing; (*phil*.) heuristics. ~**lamak** (-i), discover; invent. ~**sal**, inventive; (*phil*.) heuristic.

bulgur (*cul*.) Boiled and pounded wheat; (*met*.) fine hail. ~ ~, like hail. ~**cu**, maker/seller of BULGUR. ~**cuk**, (*ast*.) granular element; (*geol*.) grain. ~**lanma**, (*ast*., *geol*.) granulation. ~**luk**, *a*. used in making BULGUR.

Bulgurlu (*geo*.) Village near Üsküdar. ~ **ya gelin mi gideceksin?**, why all this unnecessary fuss/hurry?

bullak = ALLAK.

bul·ma *vn*. Finding, discovery. ~**maca**, (*pub*.) (crossword) puzzle. ~[l]**mak**[ur] (-i), find; detect; discover; invent; obtain; contrive; reach; remember, call to mind; have an opinion about; choose; be punished: (-e), impute (blame): **buldukça bunamak**, never be content; always be grumbling; always asking for more: **bulup buluşturmak**, find at any cost: **bulup çıkarmak**, invent, find out, discover.

bul·on (*eng*.) Bolt. ~**teryer**, (*zoo*.) bull-terrier.

bulucu Inventor; discoverer; (*phys*.) detector. ~**k**, (*lit*.) witty remark. ~**kçu**, witty. ~**luk**, inventiveness.

buluğ Maturity; adulthood. ~**a ermek**, reach maturity: ~**a varmamış**, adolescent: ~**a varmış**, adult.

bulun·a[l]**k**[ğı] Address. ~**an**, existing, present.

bulun[l]**ç**[cu] Conscience.

bulun·durmak (-i) Make/let be present; have ready; keep, have in stock. ~**durulmak**, *vp*. be made to be present, etc. ~**mak**, *vp*. = BULMAK: *vi*. be present; find o.s., be, exist, stay: **bulunduğum vaziyeti yadırgadım**, I found my position strange: **bulunmuş eşya**, treasure-trove: **bulunsun diye!**, in case of need. ~**mayış**, absence. ~**maz**, not to be found; rare, choice: ~ **hint kumaşı değil**, he/it is no great catch. ~**tu**, (*archaeol*.) a find, antique; (*soc*.) foundling.

buluş Act of finding; invention, discovery; creation, contrivance. ~ **belgesi** (*leg*.) patent. ~**ma**, *vn*. appointment, rendezvous, meeting: ~ **yeri**, meeting-place, rendezvous. ~**mak (-le)**, be together with others, meet. ~**turmak (-i, -le)**, bring together; arrange a meeting of/with. ~**turucu(luk)**, (work of) keeper of illicit-meetings house. ~**ulmak**, *vp*. be brought together. ~**um**, meeting, rendezvous. ~**umevi**, brothel; house for illicit meetings.

bulut[u] (*met*.) Cloud. ~ **gibi (sarhoş)**, dead drunk: ~**a uçma**, (*aer*.) cloud-hopping: ~**tan nem kapmak**, be very touchy/suspicious.

bulut·lanmak *vi*. Become cloudy, cloud over; become opaque. ~**lu**, cloudy; overcast; dim, hazy; opaque. ~**luluk**, nebulosity. ~**su**, (*ast*.) *n*. nebula; *a*. nebular, nebulous. ~**suz**, cloudless; azure, clear.

bulvar Boulevard. ~ **tiyatrosu**, (*th*.) theatre showing light/entertaining plays.

bum (*ech*.) Boom, bang. ~**ba**, (*naut*.) boom.

bumbar (*bio*.) Large intestine; colon; (*cul*.) sausage, etc.; (*dom*.) draught excluder.

bun Anxiety, distress; crisis.

buna = BU.

bun·ak *a.* Imbecile; in one's second childhood, senile, doting. ~**aklık**, imbecility; senility, dotage. ~**algı**, (*phys.*) critical. ~**alım**, crisis; (*fin.*, *med.*) depression, collapse. ~**almak**, *vi.* be stupefied; be suffocated (smoke, etc.); be utterly bored/wearied. ~**almış**, doddery. ~**altı**, anxiety, worry. ~**altıcı**, stupefying; worrying. ~**altmak** (**-i**), stupefy; weary, etc. ~**ama**, *vn.* senility, dotage. ~**amak**, *vi.* become senile; reach one's dotage.

bun·ca In this fashion; this much: ~ **kere**, so many times: ~ **yıllık dost**, a very old friend: ~ **zaman**, so long a time. ~**cağız**, this poor little thing. ~**cılayın**, so much/many; in this way.

bu·nda(n)/~**nlar**/~**nu(n)** = BU.

bungalow (*arch.*) Bungalow.

bun·gun Worried. ~**lu**, anxious, distressed, depressed. ~**luk**, uneasiness, depression; crisis. ~**mak** (**-i**), dislike; find unsatisfactory.

bunsen ~ **bek/lambası**, (*chem.*) Bunsen burner.

bur. = (*geo.*) BURUN.

bura [199] This place; this condition; this point. ~ **ahalisi**, the people of this place: ~ ~ = BURMAK: ~**da**, here, in this place: ~**da kalınır mı?**, can one stay here?: ~**da uyunur mu?**, can one get any sleep here?: ~**da zorbalık sökmez**, force won't get you anywhere here: ~**dan**, from here; hence: ~**dan geçilir/inilir**, *etc.*, one goes through/down, etc. here: ~**dayım diye bağırmak**, stare one in the face: ~**larda**, hereabouts, in these parts: ~**lı**, of/belonging to this place, native: ~**lıyım**, I belong here: ~**m**[1], this part of me: ~**sı**[n1], [199] this place, here. ~**sı kavak gölgesi değil!**, if you sit in my café you must order stg.: ~**sı neresi?**, what place is this?: ~**sı yol geçen hanı değil!**, where do you think you are!; you must behave yourself here!: ~**ya**, to this spot; here, hither: ~**ya geleli tam bir saat oldu**, I've been here an hour already.

burağan (*met.*) Whirlwind; tempest.

buram[2] ~ ~, whirling; eddying; like a whirlpool; excessively: ~ ~ **terlemek**, sweat profusely.

buran = BORAN. ~**da** = BRANDA.

burcu Pleasant smell, odour. ~ ~, sweet-smelling. ~**mak**, *vi.* smell pleasantly, perfume.

bur·ç[cu 1] *n.* (*arch.*) Tower; (*ast.*) constellation/sign of the Zodiac. ~ +, *a.* zodiacal: ~**lar kuşağı**, Zodiac.

bur·ç[cu 2] *n.* (*bot.*) Mistletoe. ~**a**[lk g1], *n.* (*bot.*) vetch: *a.* screwed, wound round itself. ~**un**, (*zoo.*) female roedeer.

bur·ç[cu 3] = MURÇ.

burda(n) = BURADA(N).

bur·gacı[lk g1] = KARGACIK. ~**ga**[lç c1], twist, bend; (*phys.*) vortex; (*geo.*) eddy, whirlpool. ~**gaçlı**, serpentine. ~**gan**, (*carp.*) vice screw. ~**gata**, (*naut.*) unit of thickness for rope (= 2·5 cm.). ~**gu**, (*carp.*) auger; bit; gimlet; (*dom.*) corkscrew; (*min.*) drill, auger, borer: ~ **kuyusu**, artesian well: ~ **salma**, boring. ~**gulamak** (**-i**), bore; drill. ~**gulanmak**, *vp.*

burhan (*leg.*) Proof, evidence.

burjuva (*soc.*) Bourgeois; burgher; (*phil.*) materialist. ~**lık**, materialism. ~**zi**, bourgeoisie.

burk·mak (**-i**) Twist, turn. ~**uk**, twist. ~**ulma**, *vn.*

distortion; (*eng.*) buckling; (*med.*) twist, sprain, crick. ~**ulmak**, *vp.* ~**utmak** (**-i**), sprain.

burlesk[i] (*th.*) Burlesque.

bur·ma *vn.* Twisting; screw; convolution; (*med.*) castration; griping of the stomach; (*cul.*) a sweet = SARIĞIBURMA: *a.* screwed; contorted, twisted; spiral; castrated. ~**ma**[lç c1], (*dom.*) corkscrew. ~**mak** (**-i**), twist; wring; contort; castrate; dislocate; (the bowels) gripe; bore (a hole): **bura bura oynamak**, dance with wild contortions.

burn- = BURUN. ~**az**, (*obs.*) big-nosed.

burnuz = BORNOZ.

burs (*ed.*) Scholarship, bursary. ~**iye**/~**lu**, having a scholarship.

Bursa (*geo.*) Bursa; (*his.*) Brusa, Prusa.

burtla[lk g1] (*live.*) Piglet, sucking-pig.

bur·u (*med.*) Griping (of the bowels); labour pains. ~**uk**, twisted; sprained; acerbic; acrid, sour; (*carp.*) warped. ~**ukluk**, sharpness, sourness; acerbity. ~**ulma**, *vn.* twisting; writhing; (*phys.*) torque. ~**ulmak**, *vp.* = BURMAK; be twisted; be contorted; writhe (with pain); be offended. ~**ulmalı**, (*eng.*) torsional. ~**ulmuş**/~**ulu**, twisted, screwed; strangled; castrated. ~**ultu**, (*min.*) twist. ~**um**, torsion; contortion: ~ ~, contorted; griped.

bur·un[nu] Nose; point, tip; (*orn.*) beak; (*geo.*) cape, headland, promontory; (*fig.*) pride, arrogance. ~ +, *a.* Nasal: ~ **boşluğu**, (*bio.*) nasal cavity: ~ ~ (**gelmek**), (come) very close and face to face: ~ **deliği**, (*bio.*) nostril: ~ **kanadı**, (*bio.*) ala nasi: ~ **kanatmamak**, act gently/without bloodshed: ~ **kanı**, blood-red: ~ **kemiği**, (*bio.*) ethmoid bone: ~ **kırmak**, screw up the nose (in dislike/ contempt): ~ **kıvırmak**, consider unimportant, dislike: ~ **perdesi**, (*bio.*) nasal septum: ~ **sişirmek**, become conceited: ~ **yapmak**, look superior.

burnu: ~ **bir karış havada**, very conceited: ~ **büyük**, conceited, proud: ~ **büyümek**, become conceited: ~ **havada**, very pleased with o.s.: ~ **Kaf dağında**, very conceited: ~ **kanamamak**, escape without a scratch: ~ **sürtülmek**, eat humble pie; learn one's lesson: ~**na çıkmak**, become intolerable: ~**na girmek**, come too close to s.o.: ~**nda tütmek**, crave/long for.

burnundan: ~ **düşen bin parça olm.**, be in the worst of tempers: ~ **düşmüş** = HIK DEMİŞ . . .: ~ (**fitil fitil**) **gelmek**, s.o.'s pleasure be completely spoilt: ~ **getirmek**, make s.o. sorry for stg.: ~ **kıl aldırmamak** be very stand-offish and superior; not yield an inch: ~ **solumak**, pant heavily; snort with anger: ~ **yakalamak** (**-i**), catch s.o. well and truly.

burnunu: ~ **çekmek**, sniff; go away emptyhanded: ~ **kırmak**, take the conceit out of s.o.: ~ **sıksan canı çıkacak**, weak and impotent: ~ **silmek**, blow/wipe one's nose: ~ **sokmak** (**-e**), stick one's nose in, interfere, butt in: ~ **tıkamak**, hold one's nose: ~ (**yere**) **sürtmek** = BURNU SÜRTÜLMEK.

burnunun: ~ **dip/ucunda**, right under one's nose: ~ **dik/doğrusuna gitmek**//~ **doğrusundan ayrılmamak**, be above taking any advice, be too conceited to listen to others: ~ **direği kırılmak**, be quite overcome by a smell: ~ **direk/kemiği sızlamak**, feel very sad: ∼ **ucunu görmemek**, be blind with pride; be very drunk: ∼ **yeli harman savuruyor**, s.o. very conceited.

burun·duru¹k^{ğu} Twitch (for holding an unruly horse). ∼**lu**, having a nose; pointed; proud, conceited. ∼**luk**, (animal's) nose-ring; iron toe-cap (of a boot). ∼**otu**^{nu}, snuff. ∼**sa¹k**^{ğı}, device to prevent a calf suckling. ∼**sal**, (*ling.*) nasal(ized). ∼**salı¹k**^{ğı}, muzzle. ∼**suz**, noseless; with a very small nose; (*mot.*) cab over the engine.

buruntu (*med.*) Colic.

buruş Wrinkle; (*tex.*) crease; (*min.*) buckle, corrugation. ∼ ∼, very wrinkled/crumpled. ∼**ma**, *vn.* creasing; buckling. ∼**mak**, *vi.* be creased/crumpled/wrinkled/puckered; (*min.*) buckle; (*fig.*) have one's teeth set on edge. ∼**mamazlık**, crease-resistance. ∼**turmak (-i)**, *vt.* crease, crumple, crush, wrinkle; frown; corrugate; (*min.*) buckle; (*fig.*) set the teeth on edge. ∼**uk**, puckered; (badly) creased, crumpled, wrinkled; ruffled; buckled. ∼**ukluk**, creasing, wrinkling, etc.

buse Kiss. ∼ **almak**, kiss.

buselik (*mus.*) An Or. melody.

bust(er) (*eng.*) Boost(er).

buşon (*el.*) Wall plug; (*mil.*) fuse-plug.

bu¹t^{du} (*bio.*) Thigh; buttock; (*cul.*) leg of meat. ∼**lu**, (*orn.*) rumped, vented.

butik^{i} Boutique.

butlan *n.* (*leg.*) Error; nullity, invalidity; being void.

bu¹ut'^{du} (*math.*) Distance; dimension. ∼**lu**, -dimensional.

buy·durma *vn.* (*phys.*) Cooling, chilling, freezing: ∼ +, *a.* cryo-: ∼ **bilgisi**, cryogenics: ∼ **biyolojisi**, cryobiology: ∼ **odası**, chilling room. ∼**durmak (-i)**, chill, cool, freeze. ∼**durucu**, chiller. ∼**mak**, *vi.* be very cold; freeze; freeze to death.

buyot^{u} Hot-water bottle.

buy·ru¹k^{ğu} Order, command, behest: ∼**lusuna**, (*fin.*) to order: ∼**u altına girmek**, be forced to obey s.o. ∼**rulmak**, *vp.* be ordered. ∼**rultu**, (*adm.*) order; (*his.*) decree; mandate. ∼**rultucu**, (*col.*) bossy person. ∼**rum**, (*psy.*) will-power. ∼**rumlu**, strong-willed. ∼**rut**, (?) gene ∼**urgan(lık)**, despot(ism); dictator(ship); tyran·t/(-ny). ∼**urma**, *vn.* ordering, commanding. ∼**urmak (-i, -e)** [155], order, command; speak; come, go, pass, enter; take; deign/condescend to do (*used out of deference/politeness instead of* ETMEK): **buyur?**, I beg your pardon, what did you say?: **buyurun(uz)!**, please (sit down/come in, etc.): **buyurun cenaze namazına!**, (*jok.*) we're done for!: **buyurun da bir acı kahve içelim!**, come and have a little drink in my house! ∼**uru**, order, command. ∼**urucu**, chief commander.

buz *n.* Ice. *a.* Very cold; frozen; (*fig.*) cold. ∼ +, *a.* cryo-; ice-: ∼ **bacası**, serac: ∼ **bağlamak**, form ice, freeze over: ∼ **başlık**, (*geo.*) ice-cap: ∼ **çağı** = BUZUL: ∼ **çözmek/eritmek**, defrost, de-ice: ∼ **dalgıcı**, (*orn.*) common loon: ∼ **gibi**, very cold, as cold as ice; new and clean; fresh and tender (meat); (*fig.*) (as a matter) of course: ∼ **gibi soğumak (-den)**, be disgusted with, loathe s.o.: ∼ **hokeyi**, (*sp.*) ice-hockey: ∼ **kesesi**, (*med.*) ice-pack: ∼ **kesilmek**, be frozen; be petrified (with fear, etc.): ∼

kesmek, feel very cold, be frozen stiff: ∼ **mahmuzu**, (*sp.*) crampon: ∼ **tutmak**, be frozen over: ∼ **üstüne yazı yazmak**, do stg. that will not last, build on sand: ∼ **yalağı**, (*geo.*) cirque: ∼ **yarığı**, (*geo.*) crevasse: ∼ **yığını**, (*geo.*) pack-ice: ∼**lar çözülmek**, (ice) begin to melt/thaw; (*fig.*) (atmosphere) begin to thaw, become genial.

buzağı (*live.*) Sucking calf. ∼**lamak**, calve.

buz·çözer (*chem.*) Defroster. ∼**dağı**^{nı} (*geo.*) iceberg. ∼**dolabı**^{nı}, (*dom.*) refrigerator; ice-box. ∼**hane**, (*ind.*) ice-house; ice factory; cold-storage plant. ∼**kıran**, (*naut.*) ice-breaker. ∼**la**, (*geo.*) pack-ice: ∼**lanma**, *vn.* (*aer.*) icing. ∼**lanmak**, *vi.* become ice; be covered with ice; ice up; lose polish, become dull. ∼**lu**, icy; iced; dulled; frosted (glass). ∼**lucam**, ground/frosted glass. ∼**luğan**, (*geo.*) perpetually snow-covered peak. ∼**luk**, (*dom.*) ice-box; freezer; (*ind.*) ice-factory; ice-house.

buzul (*geo(l).*) Glacier. ∼ +, *a.* Glacial; ice-: ∼ **ara dönemi**, interglacial period: ∼ **balinası**, (*zoo.*) Biscayan whale: ∼ **çağ/devri**, (*geol.*) ice age: ∼ **kaynak//seli**, glacial spring//flood.

buzul·altı Sub-glacial. ∼**kar**, névé. ∼**laşma**, *vn.* glaciation. ∼**masası**^{nı}, ice-table. ∼**taş**, moraine.

bü. = BÜYÜK.

BÜ = BOĞAZİÇİ ÜNİVERSİTESİ.

bücür Short, squat, dwarf; 'cute' (child). ∼**leşmek**, *vi.* become short, etc. ∼**lük**, shortness, etc.

Büdü = EDİ.

büfe (*dom.*) Sideboard, dresser; dining-table; buffet. ∼ **vagonu**, (*rly.*) buffet-car. ∼**ci(lik)**, (work of) buffet-manager.

büğe(lek) = BÜVE.

büğe·mek (-i) (*eng.*) Dam (a stream). ∼**t**^{i}, dam, weir; reservoir.

büğlü (*mus.*) Bugle.

büğrü = EĞRİ.

bühtan False accusation; calumny. ∼**cı**, calumniator.

bük^{ü} (*for.*) Waterside thicket.

büken (*bio.*) Flexor.

bükey (*math.*) Curve.

bük·lüm Twist; convolution; manifold; (hairpin) bend; fold; curl: ∼ ∼, very twisted; in curls: ∼ **halinde**, convolute. ∼**lümboru**, (*eng.*) coil. ∼**me**, *vn.* twisting; curling; contortion; (*sp.*) bending; (*tex.*) twisted thread, twine: *a.* twisted, bent, folded, curled. ∼**mek (-i)**, twist (together); spin; curl; contort; distort; buckle; bend; fold (over): **büke büke**, *adv.* twisting and turning.

Bükreş (*geo.*) Bucharest.

bük·ük Curved; twisted; bent; contorted; distorted; crooked. ∼**ülgen**, flexible; = ∼ÜNLÜ. ∼**ülgenlik**, flexibility. ∼**ülme**, *vn.* (*phys.*) distortion. ∼**ülmek**, *vp.* = BÜKMEK. ∼**ülmez(lik)**, stiff(ness), rigid(ity). ∼**ülü**, bent, twisted, etc. ∼**üm**, *n.* bending, twisting, etc.; torsion; bend, twist; (*tex.*) skein, yarn. ∼**ün**, (*ling.*) (in)flexion. ∼**üngen**, (*ling.*) declinable, inflexional. ∼**ünlü**, (*ling.*) flexional, inflected: ∼**dil**, inflexional language. ∼**ünmek**, *vi.* double up (with pain). ∼**üntü**, fold; twist; knot; (*tex.*) hem(-stitch); (*mot.*) road-bend; (*med.*) intestinal pain.

bülbül (*orn.*) Nightingale. ∼ **çanağı gibi**, tiny

(bowl): ~ **gibi konuşmak/okumak**, speak/read fluently: ~ **gibi söylemek**, tell the whole story: ~ **gibi şakımak**, speak pleasantly: ~ **kesilmek**, speak under compulsion: ~**ler**, (*orn.*) robins: ~**ün çektiği dili belasıdır**, one's tongue is apt to get one into trouble. ~**yuvası**[n1], (*cul.*) a pastry made with pistachio nuts.

bülen¹t[di] High, tall; exalted. ~ **avaz**, loud-voiced: ~ **pervaz**, ambitious; presumptuous.

bülten (*pub.*) Bulletin; journal; magazine.

bülüğ = BULUĞ.

bünye (*arch.*) Edifice; (*bio.*) structure; constitution. ~ **sertleştir(il)mesi**, (*min.*) case-hardening: ~**si demir gibidir**, he has an iron constitution. ~**vi**, structural.

bürçü¹k[ğü] (*bot.*) Corymb; (*ast.*) coma.

büret[i] (*chem.*) Burette.

bürgü (*mod.*) Covering; cloak; veil; (*bot.*) perianth. ~**msü**, (*bot.*) bracteal.

bürhan (*leg.*) Proof, evidence.

büro (*adm.*) Bureau, office. ~**krasi**, bureaucracy; red tape. ~**krat**, bureaucrat: ~ **gibi/**~**ik**, bureaucratic.

bürudet[i] Cold; coldness; (*fig.*) coolness.

bürüksellahanası[n1] (*bot.*) Brussels sprouts.

bürü·lü Wrapped up; enfolded. ~**m**, a wrapping up, folding; fold. ~**mce¹k**[ği], stg. wrapped up like a cocoon. ~**mcü¹k**[ğü], (*tex.*) raw silk; crêpe; gauze. ~**me**, *vn.* invasion. ~**mek (-i)**, wrap (up); enfold; cover up; invade; infest. ~**nmek (-e)**, wrap o.s. up in.

büsbütün Altogether; entirely; quite. ~ **elden çıkmak**, go by the board: ~ **içleniyorum**, I am quite overcome by my feelings.

büst[ü] (*bio., art.*) Bust.

büta·diyen (*chem.*) Butadiene. ~**n**, butane.

bütçe (*fin.*) Budget; income. ~ **+**, *a.* Budgetary: ~ **yılı**, financial year: ~**nin dengeliği**, (*fin.*) balancing of the budget. ~**leme**, *vn.* budgeting. ~**lemek**, *vi.* budget.

bütil (*chem.*) Butyl. ~**en**, butylene.

bütün *a.* [76] (+ *sing.*) Whole, entire, complete; total: (+ *pl.*) all. *n.* A/the whole; (*math.*) the total. *adv.* Wholly, completely. ~ **bunlar kuru laf!**, that's all my eye!: ~ ~, altogether: ~~**e**, completely, entirely: ~ **cesaretini toplamak**, take one's courage in both hands: ~ **enli**, full width: ~ **gün**, the whole day: ~ **ömrümde**, in all my born days: ~ **varlığımızla dileriz**, we wish with all our hearts that . . ..

bütün·cül(lük) (*pol.*) Totalitarian(ism). ~**leme**, *vn.* completion: ~ **sınavı**, (*ed.*) second examination (for those who failed first time): ~**ye kalmak**, (*ed.*) have to take an examination the second time. ~**lemeci**, interior designer. ~**lemek (-i)**, complete; repair. ~**lemeli**, (*ed.*) pupil having to repeat an examination. ~**lenmek**, *vp.* ~**ler**, *a.* complementary, supplementary; additional: ~ **açı**, (*math.*) supplementary angle. ~**leşme**, *vn.* (*soc.*) integration. ~**leşmek**, *vi.* become complete. ~**leyin**, completely. ~**lük**, totality, entirety. ~**sel(lik)**, total(ity).

büve(lek) (*ent.*) Warble-fly.

büvet[i] Refreshment bar (for drinks).

büyü Spell, charm, incantation; sorcery. ~ **otu**, (*bot.*) thorn-apple: ~ **yapmak**, practise sorcery; cast a spell; conjure: ~ **yaptırmak**, try to get control of s.o.: ~**yü bozmak**, break a spell. ~**cü**, sorcerer, magician. ~**cülük**, sorcery, magic, the black art.

büyücek Quite/fairly large.

büyü¹k[ğü] Great, large; high; capacious; considerable; important, chief; adult, elderly; (*phil.*) major; (*zoo.*) great(er), large(r), macro-. ~ **acı**, distress: ~ **aptes**, (*rel.*) full ablution; (*bio.*) bowel movement: ~ **aptesi gelmek**, feel the need to relieve the bowels: ~ **atardamar**, (*bio.*) aorta: ~ **avarya**, (*fin., naut.*) general average: ~ **avlu**, (*arch.*) compound: ~ **ayraç**, (*pub.*) large brackets { }: ~ **bağırgan kartal**, (*orn.*) spotted eagle: ~ **balık küçük balığı yutar**, the great and powerful crush the weak: ~ **başın derdi** ~ **olur**, heavy the head that wears the crown: ~ **baştankara**, (*orn.*) great tit: ~ **beyaz balıkçıl**, (*orn.*) great egret: ~ **bilmek/görmek/tutmak**, consider/ esteem highly: ~ **boy**, large-size: ~ **Britanya**, *pr. n.* (*geo.*) Great Britain: ~ **cennet kuşu**, (*orn.*) greater bird of paradise: ~ **çağlayan**, (*geo.*) cataract: ~ **çaplı**, (*eng.*) large-bored, big calibre: ~ **çekirdek**, (*bio.*) macronucleus: ~ **çiçekli**, (*bot.*) large-flowered, grandiflora: ~ **daire**, (*geo.*) great circle: ~ **değer**, (*math.*) maximum (value): ~ **devedikeni**, (*bot.*) cardoon: ~ **dolaşım**, (*bio.*) systematic circulation: ~ **donanma**, (*naut.*) armada: ~ **gelim//gidim**, (*geo.*) high-//low-water: ~ **gösteri**, spectacle: ~ **hap**, (*med.*) bolus: ~ **harf (kasası)**, (*pub.*) capital letter/(upper case): ~ **Hindistan cevizi**, (*bot.*) coconut: ~ **ikramiye**, first prize (in lottery, etc.): ~ **kafalı**, highly intelligent: ~ **kalori**, (*phys.*) kilocalorie: ~ **kar kazı**, (*orn.*) greater snow goose: ~ **karga**, (*orn.*) raven: ~ **karıncayiyen**, (*zoo.*) giant ant-eater: ~ **karides**, (*zoo.*) prawn: ~ **kervan çulluğu**, (*orn.*) Eurasian curlew: ~ **laf etm./söz söylemek**, dogmatize; boast; talk big; be too cocksure: ~ **lokma ye** ~ **söz söyleme!**, don't boast about the future!: ~ **mağaza**, (*fin.*) supermarket; department store: ~ **mavi balıkçıl**, (*orn.*) great blue heron: ~ **mevlit ayı**, (*rel.*) lunar month of REBİ-YÜLEVVEL: ~ **Millet Meclisi**, (*adm.*) (Tk.) Grand National Assembly: ~ **mirahor**, (*his.*) grand master of the horse: ~ **Okyanus**, *pr. n.* (*geo.*) the Pacific Ocean: ~ **orman bahçıvanı**, (*ent.*) pine-bark beetle: ~ **oynamak**, (*gamb.*) play for high stakes: ~ **örümcek kuşu**, (*orn.*) northern shrike: ~ **para**, much money: ~ **rağbet**, (*soc.*) cult; (*fin.*) boom: ~ **(söz) söylemek**, boast; talk big: ~ **sözüme tövbe!**, don't wish to boast but . . .!: ~ **su dökmek**, (*bio.*) make/pass water: ~ **tavus kelebeği**, (*ent.*) peacock moth: ~ **tazı**, (*live.*) deerhound: ~ **testere gagalı ördek**, (*orn.*) common merganser, goosander: ~ **toy kuşu**, (*orn.*) great bustard: ~ **tövbe ayı**, (*rel.*) lunar month of CEMAZİYÜLEVVEL: ~ **ünlü uyumu**, (*ling.*) palatal/major vowel harmony: ~**le** ~ **küçükle** küçük olm., mix easily with all kinds of people: ~**ler**, elders; adults: ~**ten** ~**e**, (*leg.*) from the eldest to the next eldest (heir).

Büyük·ada (*geo.*) Prinkipo Island. ~**amiral**[i], (*naut.*) admiral of the fleet, high admiral. ~**ana/**~**anne**, grandmother. ~ **ayı**, (*ast.*) the Great Bear. ~ **baba**, grandfather. ~ **baldıran**, (*bot.*) common hemlock. ~ **baş(lar)**, (*live.*) cattle. ~ **çe**, quite/rather big. ~ **elçi**, (*adm.*) ambassador. ~ **elçilik**, embassy. ~ **hanım**, eldest lady of the house. ~ **lenme**, *vn.* pride, conceit. ~ **lenmek**, *vi.* become proud. ~ **lenmiş**, conceited. ~ **lü**, ~ **küçüklü**, young and old together. ~ **lük**, size; greatness; generosity; (*math.*) magnitude: ~ **deliliği**, (*psy.*) megalomania: ~ **delisi**, megalomaniac: ~ **göstermek**, be generous/ magnanimous: ~ **taslamak**, be full of self-importance. ~ **semek**, *vi.* exaggerate one's own importance. ~ **sü**, big; well-off.

büyü·leme *vn.* Casting a spell; captivation, charm. ~ **lemek** (**-i**), cast a spell over; enchant; captivate, charm. ~ **lenmek**, *vp.* be under a spell; be captivated/charmed. ~ **leyici**, captivating, entrancing. ~ **lü**, under a spell; having magical powers: ~ **fener**, magic lantern.

büyül·te¹çᶜⁱ (*cin.*) Enlarger. ~ **tme**, *vn.* (*cin.*) enlarging, enlargement; (*phys.*) amplification. ~ **tmek** (**-i**), extend, make larger; (*cin.*) enlarge; (*phys.*) amplify; (*fig.*) exaggerate.

büyü·me *vn.* Growth, development. ~ **mek**, *vi.* grow large; dilate; grow up; increase in importance: **büyümüş de küçülmüş**, appearing older than he is,

precocious. ~ **msemek**, see/regard as larger than in reality, exaggerate. ~ **sel**, magical. ~ **te¹çᶜⁱ**, (*phys.*) magnifying lens; burning-glass; (*el.*) amplifier. ~ **tken**, producing growth: ~ **doku**, (*bot.*) cambium. ~ **tme**, *vn.* making bigger; enlarging; exaggeration: ~ **gücü**, (*phys.*) magnification. ~ **tmek** (**-i**), make big/great; enlarge; amplify; magnify; exaggerate; (*soc.*) nourish and cherish; bring up. ~ **tme(lik)**, (*soc.*) adopted/foster child.

büz (*eng.*) Concrete pipe.

büz·dürmek (**-i**) (*mod.*) Make narrower/smaller; cause to constrict. ~ **gen**, (*bio.*) sphincter. ~ **gü**, (*mod.*) pleat, gather, pucker. ~ **gülü**, pleated, gathered. ~ **me**, *vn.* constriction, contraction; drawing tight. ~ **mek**, *vi.* gather; constrict, contract, tighten; pucker. ~ **ücü**, astringent, constrictor. ~ **ük**, *a.* constricted, tightened: *n.* (*vulg.*) anus; (*sl.*) pluckiness. ~ **üktaş**, (*vulg.*) intimate friend. ~ **ülme**, *vn.* contraction; shrinkage: ~ **derzi**, (*eng.*) contraction joint: ~ **payı**, (*tex.*) shrinkage allowance. ~ **ülmek**, *vi.* contract; shrink; shrivel up; cower, crouch: **büzülüp oturmak**, retire shyly into a corner. ~ **üşmek**, *vi.* shrivel up; become wrinkled. ~ **üşük**, shrivelled; wrinkled.

by. = BİNYIL.

C

C, c [je] Third Tk. letter, C; third (in a class/series); (*mus.*) doh. ~ **vitamini**, (*bio.*) vitamin C.

C = CİLT; CUMHURİYET; (*ch.s.*) KARBON; (*phys.*) KULON; (*phys.*) SANTIGRAT; (*math.*) 100.

-c- Replaces ç before a vowel suffix [BURÇ + U = BURCU].

Ca. = (*ch.s.*) KALSİYUM.

-ca *suf.* = -CE[1, 2].

caba [196] Free, gratis; into the bargain, in addition. ~ **etm./vermek**, give gratis. ~ **cı**, sponger, parasite. ~ **dan**, gratis, for nothing.

cacı'k^{ğ_1} (*cul.*) Chopped cucumber/lettuce, with garlic, in AYRAN.

Cad(d). = CADDE(si).

cadaloz Spiteful old hag. ~ **laşmak**, *vi.* behave as a hag.

cadde Main road/street; thoroughfare; highway. ~ **yi tutmak**, close the street; (*fig.*) clear out, run away.

cadı Witch, hag; vampire. ~ **gibi**, sluttish woman: ~ **kazanı**, den of intrigue/gossip: ~ **maki**, (*zoo.*) tarsier.

cadı·laşmak *vi.* Become haglike/sluttish. ~ **lık**, bad-temper; sluttishness: ~ **etm.**, be bad-tempered; behave like a slut. ~ **süpürgesi**^{ni}, (*myc.*) witches' brooms.

cafcaf/cafcuf Pompous/pretentious speech; ostentation. ~ **etm.**, pontificate. ~ **lı**, pompous, pretentious; ostentatious, showy; elegant.

Caferi (*rel.*) (A member of) a Shiite sect.

cağ^1 *n.* Banister; spoke of a wheel.

cağ^2 *n.* Large bag; nose-bag.

cağ^3 *n.* Stone trough/pit for dirty water.

-cağız *n. suf.* [57] = -CEĞİZ [HAYVANCAĞIZ].

cahil Ignorant; uneducated; inexperienced; young. ~ **düşürmek**, show up s.o.'s ignorance. ~ **ane**, ignorantly. ~ **iye(t**^{i}**)**, (*rel.*) the (pre-Islamic) Age of Ignorance (= paganism). ~ **lik**, ignorance; inexperience; youth: ~ **etm.**, behave ignorantly/uncouthly; make mistakes (from inexperience).

caiz Lawful; permitted, admissible, allowable; possible. ~ **e**, (*his.*) reward, present (to a poet); (*pub.*) ditto marks; mark, dash, tick.

-cak *suf.* = -CEK [OYUNCAK].

caka (*sl.*) Ostentation, swagger. ~ **satmak/yapmak**, swagger, show off, cut a dash. ~ **cı(lık)**, swagger·er/ (-ing). ~ **lı**, ostentatious, swaggering.

caket = CEKET.

cali False; imitation; insincere.

calip Attracting; attractive; causing. ~ **olm.**, attract, draw; arouse.

cam Glass; glass-pane; made of glass; goblet, glass; (*phys.*) lens; (*cin.*) plate. ~ **balon**, carboy: ~ **bölüm**, showcase, shopwindow: ~ **çerçevesi**, window-

frame/-sash: ~ **dolap**, glass-fronted case (for books. etc.): ~ **ev/yuvası**, (*carp.*) rebate/ groove for glass: ~ **fabrikası**, glass-works: ~ **fitili**, (*mot.*) weather-seal: ~ GÖBEĞİ: ~ GÖZ: ~ **keseceği**, glass-cutter: ~ **krikosu**, (*mot.*) window-winder: ~ **lifi**, glass-fibre: ~ **liflerinden keçe** = ~ PAMUĞU: ~ **mozaik**, (*art.*) glass mosaic: ~ **resim**, (*art.*) stained-glass window: ~ **sileceği**, (*mot.*) windscreen wiper: ~ **üfleyici**, glass-blower.

camadan (*mod.*) Double-breasted waistcoat; clothes/linen chest; valise; (*naut.*) reef (in a sail). ~ **bağı**, reef-knot: ~ **bağlamak/vurmak**, reef, take in a reef: ~ **ı fora etm.**, shake out a reef.

cambaz Acrobat; circus-rider; (*cin.*) stunt-man; horse-coper; swindler. ~ **hane**, circus. ~ **lık**, acrobatics; horse-coping; swindling: ~ **uçuşları**, (*aer.*) aerobatics.

cambul cumbul (*cul.*) Very watery, sloppy.

cam·cı Glazier; glass-seller; (*sl.*) peeping Tom, voyeur: ~ **elması**, glass-cutter, diamond pencil: ~ **macunu**, putty. ~ **cılık**, glazier's work/trade. ~ **ekân**, shop-window; show-case, display-cabinet; garden-frame; dressing-room (of HAMAM). ~ **göbeği**^{ni}, glass-green. ~ **göz**, (*med.*) artificial eye; (*fig.*) avaricious, stingy: ~ **balığı**, (*ich.*) tope. ~ **gözgiller**, (*ich.*) spiny sharks. ~ **güzeli**^{ni}, (*bot.*) balsam, (?) busy Lizzie.

camız (*zoo.*) Water-buffalo; ox.

cami$^{i/si 1}$ *n.* Mosque; large mosque in which Friday prayers are said. ~ **ne kadar büyük olsa . . .** = CEMAAT: ~ **yıkılmış ama mihrap yerinde**, the essential part is unharmed; she's not young but still beautiful.

cami^2 *a.* Collecting; bringing together; containing. ~ **a**, assembly of people; community.

cami'it^{di} *a.* Lifeless, inorganic, mineral; solid; frozen. *n.* Solid; inorganic substance.

cam·kanatlılar (*ent.*) Clearwing moths. ~ **lamak** (-i), cover with glass; glaze. ~ **lanmak**, *vp.* be glazed. ~ **laşmak**, *vi.* become like glass/glassy. ~ **latmak** (-i, -e), have glass fitted. ~ **lı**, fitted with glass; glassed over; glazed: ~ **sünger**, (*zoo.*) glass-sponge. ~ **lık**, stg. covered with glass; shop-window; garden-frame. ~ **pamuğu**^{nu}/ ~ **yünü**^{nü}, glass-fibre/-wool. ~ **sı**, glass-like, vitreous. ~ **suyu**^{nu}, (*chem.*) soluble/ water glass.

camus (*zoo.*) Water-buffalo.

can *n.* Soul; life; a soul, a living person; darling, beloved friend; (*rel.*) member (of certain Muslim sects); force, vigour, zeal. *a.* Agreeable, pleasant. ~ **acısı**, terrible pain: ~ **alacak yer**, the most sensitive spot: ~ **alıcı**, crucial, critical, vital; fateful; = CANALICI: ~ **alıp** ~ **vermek**, be worn out with pain and trouble: ~ **atarcasına**, ardently: ~ **atma**, alacrity: ~ **atmak (-e)**, desire passionately to; be anxious to: ~ **baş üstüne**, very willingly: ~ **beslemek**, be a gourmet: ~ **boğazdan gelir**, one must eat to live: ~ **borcunu ödemek**, die: ~ ~**a baş başa**, each for himself (when in danger): ~CİĞER: ~ **cümleden aziz**, o.s. is most precious: ~ **çekişme**, death agony; ~ **çekişme hırıltısı**, death rattle: ~ **çekişmek**, be at death's door: ~ **çıkmayınca huy çıkmaz**, 'what's bred in the bone won't out of the flesh': ~ **damarı**, the vital spot; the most important point: ~ **damarına basmak (-in)**, touch the most sensitive spot: ~ **dayanmamak (-e)**, be unable to resist stg.: ~ **direği**, (*mus.*) sound-post of a violin: ~ **dostu**, a very sincere friend: ~ **düşmanı**, a mortal enemy: ~ERİĞİ: ~ **evi**, the heart; the pit of the stomach; any vital spot: ~ **evinden vurmak (-e)**, attack s.o. where most defenceless: ~ **feda/kurban**, stg. one would give one's life for; 'I'd be only too glad!': ~ **gelmek**, come to life; become active/lively: ~ **halatı**, (*naut.*) lifeline: ~ **havliyle**, in terror of one's life; desperately, in desperation: ~ **kalmamak**, have no life left in o.s., be utterly exhausted: ~ **kaygısı**, thought for one's own interests: ~ **kulağı ile dinlemek**, listen with rapt attention: ~ **kurban** = ~ FEDA: ~ **kurtaran yok mu?**, help!: ~KURTARAN: ~ **kurtarma**, life-saving: ~ **olsun dayansın!**, it's more than flesh and blood can stand!: ~ **oyun/pazarı**, a situation/venture where life is at stake: ~ **pahasına**, at the risk of one's life: ~ **sağlığı**, health: ~ **sevecek bir şey**, stg. pleasant: ~ **sıkıcı**, boring, dreary, 'dry-as-dust': ~ **sıkıntısı**, extreme boredom; 'the blues': ~ **sıkıntısından patlamak**, be consumed with boredom/ bored stiff: ~ **sıkıntısını geçirmek**, beguile the time: ~ **sıkmak**, bore: ~ **ve mal kaybı**, (*mil.*) casualties: ~ **vermek**, *vi.* die; (-e), strengthen s.o.'s morale; revive: ~ **yakmak**, treat cruelly/harshly; oppress; cause harm/loss: ~ **yoldaşı**, very intimate/faithful friend; s.o. to keep one company.

cana: ~ **can katmak**, make one feel more alive; refresh, delight: ~ **kıymak**, kill: ~ **yakın**, amiable, congenial: ~ **yakınlık**, amiability, congeniality.

candan, cordial(ly); sincere(ly): ~ **bağlı**, devoted: ~ **geçmek/gelmek**, die; (be ready to) sacrifice one's life: ~ **dost**, bosom friend: ~ **ve gönülden**, with all one's heart and soul: ~ **yürekten**, very sincerely.

canı: ~ **ağız/burnuna gelmek**, be half dead (with anxiety/fatigue): ~ **aziz**, one's own dear self: ~ **burnunda olm.**, be worn out/dead tired: ~ **cehenneme!**, damn him!: ~ **çekilmek**, feel extreme pain: ~ **çekmek**, long for stg.: ~ **çıkası(ca)!**, accursed!; curse him!: ~ **çıkmak**, die; be very tired; (clothes) be very worn: ~ **çıksın!**, curse him!: ~ **gelip gitmek**, faint: ~ **gelmek** = ~ YERİNE: ~ **ile oynamak**, take great risks, flirt with death: ~ **istemek**, feel like doing stg.: ~ **isterse!**, 'all right!', 'as you will!': ~ **pek**, stoical: ~ **sağ olsun!**, it doesn't matter: ~ **sevmek (-i)**, like: ~ **sıkılmak**, be bored; be bad-tempered: ~ **tatlı**, s.o. who avoids all personal discomfort/labour: ~ **tez**, hustler; energetic; impatient: ~ **yanmak**, suffer pain/loss:

~ **yerine gelmek**, gain health/strength: ~ **yok mu (-in)?**, he's only human, you know!

canım, *a.* [41] beloved; *n.* (*iron.*) 'my dear fellow!', 'my good man!': ~ **ciğerim!/** ~ **ın içi!**, my dearest!, my darling!: ~ **istemiyor!**, I don't feel like it: ~ **yandı**, I have suffered: ~**a minnet!**, so much the better!; I accept with pleasure (and relief): ~**ı sokakta bulmadım**, life is precious to me.

canına: ~ **acımamak**, live unselfishly/without thought of o.s.: ~ **değmek**, be enjoyable; be happy: ~ **düşkün**, s.o. who attends to his own needs/ comfort: ~ **ezan okumak**, (*sl.*) get the better of s.o.: ~ **geçmek/işlemek/kâr etm.**, hurt s.o.'s feelings/ affect s.o. painfully: ~ **kıymak**, kill pitilessly; kill o.s.; wear o.s. out: ~ **minnet (bilmek)**, (*expression of great pleasure, mingled with relief*): ~ **okumak**, harass; spoil, ruin: ~ **susamak**, be extremely foolhardy; court death; thirst for s.o.'s blood: ~ **tak demek/etm.**, (pain, etc.) become intolerable/ unbearable: ~ **tükürmek**, ill-treat s.o.: ~ **üfürmek**, ruin: ~ **yandığım(ın)**, (*sl.*) the cursed . . . (*sometimes in admiration*): ~ **yetmek**, become intolerable; have enough of stg.

canından: ~ **bezmek/bıkmak/usanmak**, be tired/ sick of life.

canını: ~ **acıtmak**, cause suffering, oppress: ~ **almak**, kill s.o.; please s.o. extremely: ~ **bağışlamak**, pardon/reprieve s.o.; spare s.o.'s life: ~ **cehenneme göndermek**, kill s.o.: ~ **çıkarmak**, exhaust, ruin, ill-treat: ~ **dar atmak (-e)**, manage to take refuge in: ~ **dişine almak/takmak**, take one's life in one's hands: ~ **sıkmak,** annoy, bother; disgust: ~ **sokakta bulmak**, fail to look after o.s.: ~ **sokakta bulmamış olm.**, take good care of o.s.: ~ **vermek**, sacrifice o.s.; not spare anything; be addicted to: ~ **yakmak**, punish; hurt (s.o.'s feelings).

canının: ~ **derdine düşmek**, one's vital interests be at stake: ~ **içine sokacağı gelmek**, be extremely fond of, adore.

can-: ~**la başla**, with heart and soul; making every effort: ~**ü gönülden**, most willingly.

can·alıcı (*rel.*) The Angel of Death, Azrail; = CAN. ~**an**, sweetheart. ~**atış**, passionate desire.

canavar Monster; brute; (*zoo.*) wild beast; wild boar; unruly child. ~ **düdüğü**, warning syren: ~ **gibi**, powerfully built; aggressive; excessive(ly): ~ **kesilmek**, become angry; behave like a beast.

canavar·balığı[n1] (*ich.*) White shark. ~**ca**, brutish; brutal; boarish. ~**casına**, like a monster: ~**laşmak**, *vi.* behave like a beast; go berserk. ~**lık**, barbarity, brutality, ferocity, savagery. ~**otu**[nu], (*bot.*) branched broomrapes. ~**otugiller**, (*bot.*) broomrapes, Orobanchaceae.

can-cağız (*Term of endearment*): ~**ı isterse**, well, it's his funeral. ~**canlı** = ŞANJANLI. ~ **ciğer**, close friend; intimate: ~ **kuzu sarması**, a very intimate relationship: ~ **olm.**, be very close friends. ~**dan** = CAN. ~ **dar**, (*obs.*) *n.* living creature; defender: *a.* alive; animated.

candarma = JANDARMA.

caneriğiⁿⁱ (*bot.*) Greengage.

canfes (*mod.*) (Made of) taffeta. ~ **gibi yaprak,** smooth/silky (vine) leaf.

canfeza (*mus.*) Compound Or. melody.

cangıl cungul Ding-dong; noisily.

canhıraş Harrowing; disagreeable; strident (sound).

cani *n.* Criminal; cut-throat. ~ **yane,** felonious.

cani'pᵇⁱ Side; direction; (*leg.*) party. ~ **inden,** on the part of . . .: ~ **ine,** towards . . . .

cankurtaran *a.* Life-saving. *n.* Ambulance. ~ **arabası,** ambulance: ~ **çanı,** (*naut.*) bell-buoy: ~ **düdüğü,** (*naut.*) whistling buoy: ~ **gemisi,** (*naut.*) lifeboat: ~ **kulübesi,** mountain refuge/shelter: ~ **simidi,** (*naut.*) life-buoy, lifebelt: ~ **yeleği,** (*naut., aer.*) life-jacket.

canlan·dırıcı *a.* Enlivening, bracing, refreshing: *n.* (*cin.*) animator; activator. ~ **dırım,** (*art., archaeol.*) reconstruction. ~ **dırma,** *vn.* bringing to life; activation; animation. ~ **dırmak (-i),** enliven, brace, refresh; vitalize; revive; vivify; personify; reconstruct; activate; animate; (*cin., th.*) 'bring to life', play the role of. ~ **ma,** *vn.* embodiment. ~ **mak,** *vi.* come to life; become active/lively; be relived; be personified.

can·lı Alive, living; lively; animated; active; vigorous; (*lit.*) colourful, vivid: ~ **cenaze,** s.o. very weak; skinny; haggard: ~ **film/resim,** (*cin.*) animated cartoon: ~ **madde,** (*bio.*) living tissue: ~ **model,** (*art.*) model: ~ **müzakere,** animated discussion: ~ **şema,** animated diagram: ~ **yayın,** (*rad.*) live broadcast: ~ **sı (-in),** . . . addict. ~ **lıcı(lık),** (*phil.*) anim·ist/(-ism). ~ **lılık,** liveliness, activity; animation; colour(fulness); (*fin.*) boom: ~ **ını yitirme,** (*bio.*) degeneration. ~ **sız,** lifeless; weak; ineffective; listless; (*fin.*) slack; (*lit.*) colourless, dull, uninteresting; inorganic: ~ **doğa,** (*art.*) still life: ~ **düşmek,** become very weak/exhausted. ~ **sızlaştırmak (-i),** weaken; devitalize; make ineffective; (*med.*) destroy living tissue. ~ **sızlık,** lifelessness; weakness, etc.; (*med.*) abiosis. ~ **siperane,** self-sacrificing (act).

cant¹ = JANT.

car¹ *n.* (*mod.*) Woman's cloak/shawl.

car² *adv.* ~ ~, loud and continuous noise/talk. ~ **car,** chatterbox. ~ **cur¹,** ~ **etm.,** talk at random.

carcur² *n.* (*col.*) = ŞARJÖR.

cari Running, flowing; current (money, etc.); in force, valid; occurring, present; usual. ~ **dil,** current language: ~ **fiyat,** market price: ~ **hesap,** (*fin.*) current account.

carih Wounding. ~ **a,** (*bio.*) limb, organ; (*zoo.*) beast of prey.

cariye Female slave; concubine. ~ **leri/** ~ **niz,** (*obs.*) 'my daughter'. ~ **lik,** concubinage.

carlamak *vi.* Talk loudly and incessantly; (-i), declare stg. publicly.

carse = JARSE.

cart (*ech.*) Sound of tearing. ~ ~ **ötmek,** sing one's own praises, brag: ~ **curt etm.,** use threatening words: ~ **kaba kâğıt,** (*sl.*) stop boasting!

carta (*vulg.*) Fart. ~ **yı çekmek,** (*sl.*) die.

carta·dak/ ~ **dan** Suddenly and noisily.

cartla'kᵍ¹ (*cul.*) Offal.

cascavlak Completely bare, naked; uncovered; bald as a coot. ~ **kalmak,** be left destitute/helpless.

-casına *adv./v. suf.* = -CESINE.

casus Spy. ~ **luk,** espionage: ~ **a karşı korunma,** counter-espionage.

cav = CAĞ.

Cava (*geo.*) Java. ~ **insanı,** (*ethn.*) Java man, apeman.

cavalacoz (*sl.*) Worthless, unimportant.

cavcav (*col.*) Bad coffee.

cavid·(an) Eternal; celestial. ~ **i,** eternity.

cavla'kᵍ¹ Naked, nude; bald; featherless, hairless. ~ **ı çekmek,** (*sl.*) die. ~ **laşmak,** *vi.* (*sl.*) flare up, become quarrelsome. ~ **lık,** nudity; baldness; utter destitution.

cav·lamak *vi.* (Arrow) miss the mark; talk irrelevantly; (*sl.*) die. ~ **mak,** *vi.* miss the mark; (fish) be elusive.

caydır·ıcı(lık) Causing to change; deterrent. ~ **ılmak,** *vi.* be forced to change. ~ **ma,** *vn.* dissuasion. ~ **mak (-i),** *vc.* = CAYMAK; deflect; dissuade; deter.

cayır ~ ~, furiously, willy-nilly; 'jolly well': ~ ~ **yanmak,** burn furiously. ~ **damak,** *vi.* crackle; creak. ~ **datmak (-i),** *vc.* ~ **tı,** (*ech.*) (sound of) tearing, creaking, crackling flames: ~ **vermek,** threaten noisily: ~ **yı basmak/koparmak,** start shouting noisily.

cay·ma *vn.* (*leg.*) Cancellation; renunciation. ~ **mak,** *vi.* swerve; deviate from one's purpose; change one's mind/purpose; 'cry off', renounce.

cayro- Giro-; = CİRO-.

caz (*mus.*) Jazz. ~ **(bant),** jazz-band. ~ **bantçı,** jazz-player. ~ **cı,** jazz-composer//-player. ~ **ırda(t)mak,** (cause to) rumble/make an unpleasant noise. ~ **ırtı,** rumbling.

cazgır (*sp.*) (Or. wrestling). Announcer, referee.

cazibe Attractiveness; attraction; affinity; fascination; (*phys.*) force of gravity. ~ **li,** attractive; charming, 'fetching', enticing.

cazip Attractive; attracting; appealing; alluring; catchy. ~ **fiyat,** (*fin.*) 'draw': ~ **mal,** (*fin.*) loss leader.

Cb. = (*ch.s.*) KOLUMBİYUM.

CBD, cbd = (*cash before delivery*).

CC = (*Corps Consulaire*).

Cd. = CADDE(Sİ); (*ch.s.*) KADMİYUM; (*phys.*) KANDELA. ~ **/m²** = (*phys.*) METREKARE MUM.

CD = (*Corps Diplomatique*).

ce¹ *n.* (*ling.*) The Tk. letter C, c.

ce² *int.* (*child.*) Boh! ~ **demeğe gelmek,** pop in, pay a very short visit.

Ce. = (*ch.s.*) SERYUM.

-ce¹/-ca dative *n. suf.* [31] = -Ç + (-E) [GENÇ, TAÇ].

-ce²/-ca/-çe/-ça *adj./adv./n./pron. suf.* [58, 194] = -ly [GÜZELCE]; like, in the manner of [ÇOCUKÇA, TÜRKÇE]; -wise [BOYUNCA]; according to [BENCE]; for [HAFTALARCA]; on the part of, by, through [HÜKÜMETÇE]; in respect of [MALLARCA]; quite, fairly, rather [SOĞUKÇA]; little [ÇEKMECE].

cebanetⁱ Cowardice, timidity.

cebbar *a.* Tyrannical; (*rel.*) omnipotent; (woman) resourceful. *n.* Tyrant.

cebe (*mil.*) Cuirass; armour; munitions. ~ci, (*his.*) armoured infantryman; armourer. ~li, (*his.*) man-at-arms; provincial mounted policeman.

cebel (*geo.*) Mountain. ~itarık, *pr.n.* Gibraltar.

cebelleşmek *vi.* Argue, dispute.

cebellezi (*sl.*) Appropriating what does not belong to one. ~ etm., pinch.

ceberutᵘ *n.* The majesty of God; (*fig.*) despotism, tyranny. *a.* Despotic, tyrannical.

ceb(h)- = CEP(H)-.

cebin¹ *a.* Cowardly.

cebin² *n.* (*obs.*) Forehead.

ceb'irʳⁱ ¹ *n.* Force, violence, compulsion, constraint. ~ kullanmak, use force.

ceb'irʳⁱ ² *n.* (*math.*) Algebra. ~ + / ~sel, algebraic(al).

cebire (*med.*) Splint.

Cebrail (*rel.*) Archangel Gabriel.

cebr·en By force: ~ ırza geçme, rape, indecent assault. ~ˡetmek^eder (-i, -e), force, compel. ~i¹, *a.* forced, compulsory: ~ yürüyüş, (*mil.*) forced march. ~inefs¹, self-control/-restraint: ~ etm. (-den), restrain o.s. from/one's desire to.

cebri² *a.* (*math.*) Algebraic(al).

cedd- = CET. ~ani, atavistic. ~e, grandmother; female ancestor.

cedel Dispute, argument, ~leşmek, *vi.* dispute, debate.

Cedi (*ast.*) Capricorn.

cedit (*his.*) New, modern.

cedre (*med.*) Goitre, Derbyshire neck. ~li, ~ ceylan, (*zoo.*) Persian/goitred gazelle.

cefa Ill-treatment, unkindness, cruelty. ~ çekmek/görmek, suffer cruelty, etc.: ~ etm., ill-treat, torment. ~kâr, (*obs.*) cruel; (*now*) who has suffered much. ~keş, suffering, tormented; long-suffering.

ceffelkalem Offhand, without reflection.

-ceğiz/-cağız *dim. n. suf.* [57] Little, poor [EVCEĞİZ]; dear [ADAMCAĞIZ].

cehaletⁱ Ignorance.

cehennem (*rel.*) Hell; the inferno; (*fig.*) abyss; hot/unpleasant place. ~ azabı, the tortures of hell; cruel treatment: ~ gibi, very hot: ~ havası, (*met.*) suffocating weather: ~ kütüğü, (*rel.*) a hardened sinner: ~ olm., clear out, go away: ~ ol!, get to hell!; go to the devil!; go to blazes!: ~ taşı, (*chem.*) lunar caustic: ~e kadar yolu var!, he can go to hell for all I care!: ~i boyalamak, die and go to hell: ~in bucak/dibi, remote/inaccessible place: ~in dibine gitmek, clear out, go to the ends of the earth.

cehennem·i Hellish, infernal. ~lik, *a.* fit for hell; *n.* HAMAM hypocaust//stoke-hole. ~taşıⁿ¹, (*chem.*) silver nitrate; = ~ TAŞI.

ceh'ilˡⁱ Ignorance, unawareness. ~i mürekkep, the ignorance of s.o. who is sure he knows.

cehre (*tex.*) Spindle; reel.

cehr·en/~i¹ *adv.* Loudly, clearly, publicly.

cehri² *n.* (*bot.*) Dyer's rocket. ~ (ağacı), (*bot.*) buckthorn. ~giller, buckthorn family, Rhamnaceae.

ceht Striving, endeavour. ~ (sarf) etm., strive, endeavour. ~siz, effortless.

-cek/-cak/-cuk *dim. suf.* [57] Small [OYUNCAK]; very [KÜÇÜCEK]; -ish [BÜYÜCEK].

ceketⁱ (*mod.*) Jacket, coat. ~atay, morning-suit.

celadetⁱ Sturdiness; intrepidity; moral courage.

celalⁱ Majesty (of God); glory; wrath. ~i, bandit, highwayman. ~lenmek, *vi.* get into a rage. ~li, quick-tempered, irascible.

celb- = CELP. ~e, hunter's game-bag.

celep(lik) (Work/trade of) drover, cattle-dealer.

celi Clear, evident. ~ yazı, large cursive style of Arabic calligraphy.

cella'tⁿ¹ *n.* Executioner. *a.* Hard-hearted, merciless. ~ gibi, pitiless. ~lık, execution; butchery; mercilessness.

cel'pᵇⁱ A procuring; attraction; (*leg.*) summons, citation; (*mil.*) call-up. ~ etm., attract, bring, procure; supply; drive, transport; (*leg.*) summon, cite; (*mil.*) call up. ~name, summons, citation, subpoena.

celse (*adm.*, *leg.*) Sitting, hearing; session. ~yi açmak//kapamak, open//close the hearing/session: ~yi tatil etm., adjourn the hearing/session.

Celsius (*phys.*) Celsius.

cemᵐⁱ Crowd. ~mi gafir, a great multitude.

cemaatⁱ Community; party; group; (*rel.*) congregation. ~ ne kadar çok olsa imam gene bildiğini okur, rules are rules; an influential person imposes his own will: ~e uymak, behave like everyone else, conform: ~le namaz kılmak, participate in the prayers.

cemalⁱ Beauty.

ceman In all; as a total.

cemaziyül-âhır (*ast.*) The sixth lunar month. ~evvel, the fifth lunar month: ~ini bilmek (-in), know all about s.o.'s (discreditable) past.

cembiye (*mil.*) Curved Arab dagger.

ceme'kᵍⁱ (*agr.*) Iron-shod pointed tool.

cem·'etmek^eder Bring together; collect; (*math.*) add up, total. ~'i'i¹, *n.* collecting, bringing together; (*math.*) adding, total; (*ling.*) plural. ~i², *a.* all; everyone; the whole.

cemil Beautiful; charming, gracious. ~e, kindly/gracious act; compliment. ~ekâr, kindly, courteous, attentive; complimentary.

cemiyetⁱ Assembly; meeting; society, association; community; corporation; (*rel.*) (circumcision//wedding) feast. ~ adabı, social conventions: ~ haberleri, (*pub.*) society page: ~ hürriyeti, (*pol.*) freedom of association: ~e karşı, anti-social: ~i Akvam, (*his.*) League of Nations. ~li, full of people, crowded; compact; comprehensive.

cemre (*met.*) Gradual rise in temperature (with Spring). ~ düşmek, (weather) get warmer.

cenabetⁱ (*rel.*) (A person in) a state of impurity; (*vulg.*) foul brute.

cenah (*bio.*) Wing; fin; (*mil.*) flank.

cena'pᵇ¹ Majesty; excellency. ~ı Hak, God.

cenaze Corpse; the deceased. ~ alayı, cortège, funeral procession: ~ arabası, hearse: ~ gibi, very pale: ~ levazımatçısı, undertaker: ~ marşı, (*mus.*) funeral march, dead march: ~ merasimi, burial service: ~ **namazı**, funeral prayers outside the mosque: ~ **sedyesi**, bier: ~ **servis işleri**, undertakers, funeral directors: ~**yi kaldırmak**, take for burial; bury.

cendere (*eng.*) Press; roller press; extractor; (*geo.*) narrow gorge; crowded place, squash. ~ **baklası**, (*bot.*) very thin bean: ~**ye koymak/sokmak**, oppress, torture.

-cene *adv. suf.* [195] (*col.*) Fairly, rather [İYİCENE].

ceneralya (*bot.*) Cineraria.

Cenev·iz (*his.*) Genoese republic. ~**izli** *a.*, *n.* Genoese; (*pej.*) artful, cunning. ~**re**, (*geo.*) Geneva.

ceng- = CENK. ~**âver(lik)**, warlike(ness); brave(ry).

cengel (*for.*) Jungle. ~**tavuğu**nu, (*orn.*) scrub hen. ~**tavukları**, (*orn.*) Megapodes.

cenin (*bio.*) Foetus, embryo. ~ +, *a.* Foetal. ~**i sakıt**, (*med.*) miscarriage.

cen'kgi War; battle; quarrel. ~**çi**, warlike; quarrelsome: ~ **kartal**, (*orn.*) crested hawk-eagle. ~**leşmek (-le)**, *vi.* make war; fight; struggle.

cenneti (*rel., fig.*) Paradise. ~ **balığı**, (*ich.*) paradise-fish: ~ **gibi**, beautiful, well cared for (place): ~ **öküzü**, good-hearted but simple, innocent: ~ **yatağı**, (*dom.*) insprung mattress.

cennet·kuşunu (*orn.*) Bird of paradise. ~**li**, belonging to paradise; the late . . . ; 'of happy memory'. ~**lik**, worthy of paradise. ~**mekân**, (s.o.) in paradise.

Cenova (*geo.*) Genoa.

centilmen Gentleman. ~ **anlaşması**, gentlemen's agreement: ~**e yakışmaz**, caddish. ~**ce**, like a gentleman, in a gentlemanly manner. ~**lik**, behaviour of a gentleman.

CENTO = (*Central Treaty Organization*).

cenu·bi (*geo.*) Southern. ~**lp**bu, the South.

ce'pbi Pocket; purse; (*mil.*) pocket; (*mot.*) lay-by, stopping-place. ~ **defteri**, small notebook: ~ **feneri**, (*el.*) torch: ~ **harçlığı**, pocket-/spending-money: ~KITABI: ~ **kruvazör//zırhlısı**, (*naut.*) pocket cruiser//battleship: ~ **saati**, pocket-watch: ~ **sıçanı**, (*zoo.*) pocket mouse: ~**i boş/delik**, penniless, broke: ~**i para görmek**, begin to earn money: ~**i yufka**, penniless: ~**inde para durmaz**, money burns a hole in his pocket: ~**inden çıkarmak (-i)**, out-do s.o.: ~**ine atmak/indirmek/koymak**, 'pocket' (money wrongfully): ~**ini doldurmak**, line one's pockets, profit from an opportunity: ~**leri şıkırdamak**, have plenty of money: ~**lerini aramak/yoklamak**, search (in) one's pockets for stg.: ~**ten vermek**, pay from one's own pocket.

cephane (*mil.*) Powder-magazine; ammunition; munitions; armament; (*sl.*) opium. ~ **deposu**, armament depot; dump: ~ **sandık/vagonu**, caisson. ~**lik**, ammunition store, arsenal.

cephastalığını (*myc.*) Pocket plums.

cephe (*bio.*) Forehead; (*arch.*) front, elevation; (*met., mil.*) front; (*adm.*) group, circle; (*fig.*) side; aspect. ~ **almak (-e karşı)**, take the field/sides against: ~ **bozulmak**, (*mil.*) (the front) collapse: ~ **gerisi**, (*mil.*) behind the lines: ~ **hattı**, (*mil.*) the front line: ~ **hizmeti**, (*mil.*) active service: ~**den**

hücuma geçmek, (*mil., fig.*) go straight into the attack: ~**lere ayrılmak**, (*adm.*) separate into groups: ~**ye sokmak**, (*mil.*) bring up to/push through the enemy lines: ~**yi yarmak**, (*mil.*) break through the enemy lines. ~**leşmek**, *vi.* (*pol.*) group together; form a coalition.

cepken (*mod.*) Short jacket with slit sleeves.

cepkitabını (*pub.*) Pocket-book.

cerri A pulling/drawing; haulage; traction; jack; crane; derrick. ~ **atölyesi**, (*rly.*) repair shop: ~ **dişlisi**, traction gear: ~ **kancası**, (*rly.*) coupling hook: ~**e çıkmak**, (*obs.*) (religious students) go and preach to earn money: ~**e karşı dayanıklık**, (*eng.*) tensile strength.

cerahati (*med.*) Pus. ~ **akmak**, discharge: ~ **bağlamak**, suppurate: ~ **çekme tübü**, drainage tube. ~ **lenmek**, *vi.* suppurate. ~**li**, suppurating.

cerbeze Quick-wittedness; readiness of speech; persuasiveness; push, go; wiliness. ~**li**, go-ahead; loquacious, having 'the gift of the gab', very persuasive.

cereme Penalty; compensation, amends. ~**sini çekmek (-in)**, pay the penalty for/of . . . .

ceren (*dial.*) = CEYLAN.

cereyan A flowing; circulation, movement; (*el./geo.*) current; (*el.*) circuit; draught; occurrence; course; tendency, trend. ~ **açılmış**, (*el.*) live: ~ **etm.**, happen, occur; flow; conform: ~ **kesici**, (*el.*) circuit-breaker: ~ **yapıyor!**, it's draughty!: ~**la sürüklenme(k)**, (*naut.*) drift. ~**lı**, flowing; draughty.

cerh A wounding; (*leg.*) refusal to accept evidence; confutation, disproof. ~ **etm.**, wound; (*leg.*) declare invalid; confute, disprove, refute.

ceride (*obs.*) Newspaper. ~**i çamur**, organ of the gutter press.

ceri·ha Wound. ~ **me** = CEREME.

Cermen (*his.*) Teuton. ~ +, *a.* Teutonic. ~**ce**, (*ling.*) Germanic language(s).

cerr- = CER. ~**letmek**eder, drag, pull.

cerrah (*med.*) Surgeon. ~ **maşası**, extractor. ~**i**, surgical: ~ **müdahale**, surgical intervention, operation. ~**lık**, surgery.

cerrar Importunate beggar, mendicant.

cesameti Largeness; hugeness; size; importance; grandeur. ~**li**, huge; grandiose.

cesareti Boldness, daring; courage(ousness). ~ **almak/bulmak (-den)**, take courage from stg.: ~ **etm. (-e)**, dare/venture stg.: ~ **edemedi**, his courage failed him: ~ **gelmek (-e)/~e gelmek**, take courage, buck o.s. up: ~ **gösterişi**, bravura: ~ **göstermek**, show courage/daring: ~ **kırıcı**, demoralizing: ~ **vermek (-e)**, encourage; buck s.o. up: ~**i kırılmış**, dispirited, downhearted, dismayed, demoralized: ~**ini kaybetme!**, never say die!: ~**ini kırmak (-in)**, dishearten, dismay, demoralize: ~**ini toplamak**, pluck up/muster up courage.

cesaret·lendirmek (-i) = ~ VERMEK. ~**lenmek**, *vi.* take courage. ~**li**, courageous, bold, daring; adventurous, venturesome. ~**lilik**, courageousness, daring, boldness. ~**siz(lik)**, timid(ity), shy(ness).

cese^lt^{di} Body; corpse, cadaver; carcass. ~ **gibi**, cadaverous.

cesim Enormous; grandiose; of great importance. **-cesine/-casına/-çesine/-çasına** *adv. suf.* [195] In the manner of, like a [DELİCESİNE; EŞEKÇESİNE]. *v. suf.* [188] As if . . . [BOŞANIRCASINA; TANIŞIRMIŞÇASINA; GİDECEKMİŞÇESİNE].

ceste ~ ~, little by little, gradually; in instalments.

cesur Bold, daring; doughty; courageous. ~**ane**, boldly. ~**luk**, boldness, daring, courageousness.

ce^lt^{ddi} Grandfather; ancestor, ascendant. ~ **becet**, from generation to generation. ~**i âlâ**, remote ancestor; founder of the family: ~**ine lanet!**, curse him!: ~**ine rahmet!**, bravo!, well done!

cetvel (*agr.*) Irrigation canal; (*pub.*) ruled paper; (*adm.*) tabulated form; table, list, schedule. ~ **kalemi**, drawing-pen: ~ **(tahtası)**, ruler; (*eng.*) straight-edge.

cevab- = CEVAP. ~**en**, in reply. ~**i**, replying: ~ **mektup**, letter in reply.

cevahir *pl.* = CEVHER. Jewellery; *s.* jewel. ~ **yumurtlamak**, say some pricelessly silly things. ~**ci**, jeweller.

ceva^lp^{bi} Reply, answer. ~ **olarak**, in answer: ~ **vermek**, answer/satisfy (needs/requirements); reply to (criticism): ~ **yazısı**, (*adm.*) memo in reply: ~**ı dikmek/yapıştırmak**, give a sharp/decisive reply.

cevap·landırmak (-i) Reply to. ~**lı**, with a reply/ answer: ~ **telgraf**, reply-paid telegram. ~**sız**, unanswered; unsatisfied.

cevaz A being permissible/lawful; permission, approval. ~ **vermek (-e)**, regard as permissible; approve.

cevelan Revolution; circuit; circulation; going for a stroll. ~ **etm.**, stroll up and down.

cevher (*min.*) Ore; jewel; (*art.*) damascening (of steel); (*phil.*) essence; substance; nature, disposition. ~ **yumurtlamak** = CEVAHİR: ~**ini tüketmek**, be at the end of one's tether.

cevher·i Relating to ores/jewels; (*fig.*) essential, innate. ~**li**, containing ore; set with jewels; damascened; talented, naturally capable. ~**siz**, incapable.

cev^lir^{ri} Injustice; oppression; tyranny.

ceviz (*bot.*) Walnut; (*carp.*) (made of) walnut wood; (*naut.*) knot. ~ **ağacı**, walnut-tree: ~ **içi**, (*cul.*) shelled walnuts: ~ **kabuğu**, nutshell: ~ **kabuğu doldurmaz**, unimportant, slight. ~**giller**, (*bot.*) walnut family, Juglandaceae. ~**lik**, walnut grove/ orchard.

cevvalⁱ Active, lively, energetic.

cevvi (*met.*) Atmospheric.

Cevza (*ast.*) Gemini.

ceylan (*zoo.*) Dorcas gazelle. ~ **bakışlı**, gentle/ pleasant looking: ~ **gibi**, slim, shapely.

ceza (*leg.*) Punishment; fine; penalty; sanction; retribution; (*ling.*) apodosis: (*sp.*) penalty. ~ +, *a.* Criminal; penal: ~ **alan/sahası**, (*sp.*) penalty area: ~ **almak**, (child) be punished; (*leg.*) fine: ~ **çekmek**, be imprisoned; serve a sentence: ~ **görmek**, be punished: ~ **hukuku**, criminal law: ~ **indirimi**, (*sp.*) reduction of penalty: ~ **kanun(name)/yasası**, criminal/penal code: ~ **kesmek/yazmak**, fine; (*sl.*)

stand a round of drinks: ~ **mahkemesi**, criminal court: ~ **reisi**, presiding judge: ~ **sahası**, (*sp.*) = ~ ALANI: ~ **türesi** = ~ HUKUKU: ~ **vermek**, punish; chastise; pay a fine: ~ **vuruşu**, (*sp.*) penalty kick: ~ **yemek**, receive punishment: ~**sını bulmak/ çekmek**, get one's deserts; complete one's sentence: ~**ya çarptırılmak**, be punished: ~**ya çarptırmak**, punish: ~**ya dikmek**, (*ed.*) stand (a pupil) in the corner: ~**ya kalmak** (*ed.*) be in detention: ~**yı ağırlatıcı sebepler**, (*leg.*) aggravating circumstances.

ceza·eviⁿⁱ Prison. ~**lan(dırıl)mak**, *vi.* be punished. ~**landırma**, *vn.* punishment. ~**landırmak (-i)**, punish. ~**lı**, punished; (child) in disgrace. ~**sız**, unpunished.

Cezayir (*geo.*) ~ +, *a.* Algerian. ~ **(memleketi)**, Algeria: ~ **(şehri)**, Algiers: ~ **dayısı**, (*his.*) Dey of Algiers: ~ **dayısı gibi kurulmak**, put on an air of importance: ~ **menekşesi**, (*bot.*) Madagascar periwinkle. ~**li**, *n.* (*ethn.*) Algerian.

cez·b- = CEZP. ~**be**, ecstasy, rapture; (*rel.*) mystical contemplation. ~**belenmek**, *vi.* be enraptured. ~**^lp**^{bi}, attraction, allurement: ~ **etm.**, attract, allure; charm; imbibe; draw in.

cez·^lir^{ri} (*math., ling., bot.*) Root; source; (*geo.*) ebb: ~ **hali**, ebb, low water: ~ **hareketi**, ebbing. ~**ire**, (*geo.*) island; Mesopotamia. ~**ri**, *a.* radical; thorough.

cezve (*cul.*) Long-handled pot (to make Tk. coffee).

Cf. = (*ch.s.*) KALİFORNİYUM.

C·F = (*cost and freight*) ~**GP** = CUMHURİYETÇİ GÜVEN PARTİSİ. ~**GS** = (*centimetre-gram-second*). ~**HP** = CUMHURİYET HALK PARTİSİ.

-cı *suf.* = -Cİ^{1,2}.

cıbıl (*dial.*) Naked.

cıcı^lk^{ği} (*mod.*) Stuffing, padding. ~**ı çıkmış**, worn out, in pieces: ~**ını çıkarmak**, damage by use, wear to pieces.

cıdağ·ı/ ~ u (*zoo.*) Withers (of a horse).

cıgara = SİGARA. ~**lık**, (*sl.*) hashish.

-cık *a., n. suf.* = -CİK.

cıkcık (*ech.*) Squeak.

-cıl *n. suf.* = -CİL.

-cılayın *adv., suf.* = -CİLEYİN.

cılgar = ÇIVGAR.

cılız Puny, weak; thin; delicate; badly formed (writing); (*min.*) low-grade. ~**laşmak**, *vi.* become weak, etc.; lose strength/value. ~**lık**, weakness, etc.

cılk¹ (*bio.*) Addled; rotten; (*med.*) inflamed, festered; (*fig.*) abortive. ~ **çıkmak**, be addled; come to nothing, be abortive: ~ **etm.**, spoil. ~**laşmak**, *vi.* become addled.

cılkava (*zoo.*) Type of wolf; (*mod.*) fur (from the neck of wolves/foxes).

cımbar (*tex.*) Stretcher (on a loom).

cım·bız/ ~ bıstra (*med.*) Tweezers; (*fig.*) hurtful/ bitter words. ~**bızlamak (-i)**, pluck with tweezers.

cıncı^lk^{ği} (*dom.*) Glassware, porcelain. ~ **boncuk**, costume jewellery.

cıngıl (*mod.*) Decoration of beads, coins etc.

cır ~ ~ **ötmek**, (*ech.*) chatter endlessly.

cırboğa (*zoo.*) Jerboa; (*fig.*) puny child.

cırcır Rattle; babbler; chirping/creaking sound; (*eng.*) ratchet spanner. ~ **delgi**//**tornavida**, (*eng.*) ratchet-drill//-screwdriver. ~**böceği**ⁿⁱ, (*ent.*) (field-)cricket. ~**lık**, chattering, loquacity.

cırdaval Long, iron-tipped cıRiT stick.

cırıl·damak *vi.* Chirp, squeak. ~**tı**, chirping/creaking sound.

cır·la¹kᵍ¹ *a.* Screeching (voice): *n.* (*ent.*) (field-) cricket: ~ **sıçan**, (*zoo.*) common hamster. ~**lamak**, *vi.* screech. ~**latmak (-i)**, *vc.* ~**layı¹k**ᵍ¹, (*orn.*) shrike.

cırna¹kᵍ¹ (*zoo.*) Talon, claw.

cırnı¹kᵍ¹ (*eng.*) Spillway (of a dam).

cırt (*ech.*) Tearing sound. ~**lak**, screeching. ~**lamak**, *vi.* screech.

cıs (*child.*) Fire.

cıva (*chem.*) Mercury, quicksilver. ~ **alaşımı**, amalgam: ~ **buharlı lamba**, (*el.*) mercury-vapour lamp: ~ **gibi**, agile; uncontrollable: ~ **haznesi**, thermometer bulb. ~**lı**, containing mercury; (*gamb.*) loaded (dice).

cıvadra (*naut.*) Bowsprit.

cıvata (*eng.*) Bolt. ~ **anahtarı**, spanner: ~ **ile bağlamak**, bolt.

cıvı¹kᵍ¹ *a.* Wet; sticky; viscid; clammy; (*fig.*) tiresome, importunate, silly and facetious. *n.* Viscid/sticky substance; over-familiar/facetious person.

cıvık·lamak (-i) Make soft/sticky. ~**lanmak**/ ~**laşmak**, *vi.* become viscid/sticky, etc. ~**lık**, viscidity, etc. ~**mantarlar**, (*myc.*) myxomycetes, slime moulds.

cıvıl ~ ~, (*ech.*) (birds) chirping and twittering. ~**damak**, *vi.* twitter, chirp. ~**daşmak**, *vi.* chirp all together. ~**tı**, cheeping, twittering; crowing.

cıvı·mak *vi.* Become soft/sticky; become insipid/ tiresome; (person) become over-familiar/ impertinent; (work) be 'done for'/hopelessly spoilt. ~**tılmak**, *vp.* ~**tmak (-i)**, *vc.* make soft/sticky; spoil: *vi.* become tiresome/over-familiar.

cıyak ~ ~, (*ech.*) cry of a kite/small child.

cıyır· = CAYIR-.

cız (*child.*) Fire; (*ech.*) sizzling. ~ **etm.**, sizzle; be deeply affected (by pain, etc.): ~ **sineği**, (*ent.*) gadfly.

cız·bız (*cul.*) Grilled minced meat; a kind of toffee. ~**ıktırmak** = ÇIZIKTIRMAK. ~**ıldamak**/~**ırdamak**, *vi.* sizzle. ~**ıltı(lı)**/~**ırtı(lı)**, (with a) sizzling noise. ~**ır**, ~ ~, (*ech.*) sizzling (meat), cut (glass), scratching (pen). ~**ırdatmak (-i)**, make sizzle. ~**lamak**, *vi.* burn with a sizzling sound.

cızlam ~**ı çekmek**, (*sl.*) go away.

Ci. = (*phys.*) CURIE.

-ci¹/-cı/-cu/-cü/-çi/-çı/-çu/-çü *n. suf.* [59] Agent [EMLAKÇI]; maker [SAATÇİ]; seller [PASTACI]; user [YOLCU]; worker [GEMİCİ]; keeper [OTELCİ]; professional [HUKUKÇU]; supporter [CUMHURİ-YETÇİ]; player [FUTBOLCU].

-ci²/-cı/-cu/-cü *accusative n. suf.* [31] = -ç + (-i) [GENÇ, TAÇ, UÇ, GÜÇ].

CİA = (*Central Intelligence Agency*).

cibayetⁱ (*adm.*) Collection (of rents/taxes).

cibilli Natural; innate, inborn. ~**yet**ⁱ, nature;

innate character: ~**i bozuk**/~**siz**, of base character/origins; ignoble.

cibin (*obs.*) Fly/mosquito. ~**lik**, (*dom.*) mosquito-net.

cibre (*cul.*) Pulp residue (after pressing fruit).

Cibril = CEBRAİL.

cici (*child.*) *a.* Good, pretty. *n.* Toy; trinket; trifle. ~ **el**, (*child.*) right hand; ~ **mama**, inexperienced youth's first relationship with women: ~**m**, my darling.

cici·anne Grandmother. ~**bici**, gaudy clothes/ ornaments; knick-knacks. ~**li**, ~ **bicili**, gaudily (dressed).

cici¹kᵍⁱ (*bio.*) Nipple.

cicim (*tex.*) Light rug (used as curtain/wall-hanging).

cicoz *int.* (*sl.*) Not a one!, nothing at all! ~**lamak**, *vi.* (*sl.*) run away.

cidalⁱ Fight; dispute. ~**ci**, fighter, s.o. quarrelsome.

cidar (*arch.*) Wall; edge; (*bio.*) paries, cell-wall.

Cidde (*geo.*) Jeddah.

cidd·en Seriously; in earnest; greatly; exceedingly. ~**i**, earnest; serious, not joking; strenuous; critical; important: ~**dir**, he means business: ~**ye almak**, take seriously. ~**ileşmek**, *vi.* become serious, etc. ~**ilik**/~**iyet**ⁱ, serious action; seriousness.

CİF, cif = (*cost, insurance, freight*).

cife *n.* Carcass; carrion. *a.* Disgusting.

cig·ara = SİGARA ~**lör**, (*mot.*) (carburettor) jet.

ciğer (*bio.*) Liver (= KARA~); lungs (= AK~); entrails; vitals; (*cul.*) offal; (*fig.*) affections. ~ **acısı**, bitter grief: ~ **ezmesi**, (*cul.*) liver pâté: ~ **hastalığı**, (*med.*) consumption: ~ **tavası**, (*cul.*) fried liver: ~**i ağzına gelmek**, one's heart come into one's mouth; be terribly frightened: ~**i beş para etmez**, worthless fellow: ~**i yanmak**, be greatly grieved/upset: ~**i sızlamak**, feel deep compassion: ~**imin köşesi**, my darling; my beloved child: ~**ine işlemek (-in)**, hurt, cause suffering to: ~**ini okumak (-in)**, read s.o.'s deepest/most secret thoughts: ~**leri bayram etm.**, (*sl.*) inhale tobacco smoke.

ciğer·ci Seller of liver/offal. ~**ot/yosunları**ⁿⁱ, (*bot.*) liverworts. ~**pare**, darling.

cihan World; universe. ~ **harbi**, (*his.*) World War (I). ~**dide**, who has seen the world; experienced. ~**gir**, *a.* all-conquering: *n.* world-conqueror. ~**girlik**, world conquest. ~**nüma**, (*geo.*) map of the world; (*arch.*) room/terrace with extensive view. ~**şümul**, world-embracing; universal, world-wide, global: ~ **şöhret**, world-wide reputation.

cihar (*gamb.*) Four (at dice). ~**ıdü**, four and two. ~**ıse**, four and three. ~**ıyek**ⁱ, four and one.

ciha¹tᵈ¹ Holy War (against non-Muslims); (*fig.*) fight (in any good cause); 'crusade'.

cihaz Apparatus, appliance, device; contrivance; trousseau; (*bio.*) system.

cihetⁱ Side; quarter; direction; (*naut.*) bearing; motive; consideration; (*rel.*) service in a VAKIF. ~ ~, from this side and that: ~ **tayini etm.**, (*naut.*) take one's bearings: ~**ine gitmek**, set out: ~**ten (bu)**, from this direction; from this point of view. ~**li (bir)**, one-sided.

-cik/-cık/-cuk/-cük/-çik/-çık/-çuk/-çük *dim*

suf. [57] Little [EVCİK, GÖLCÜK]; dear, beloved [ANNECİK, MEHMETÇİK]; the only [BİRİCİK]; very [ALÇACIK]; just [ŞİMDİCİK].

-cil/-cıl/-cul/-cül/-çil/-çıl/-çul/-çül *a., n. suf.* [66] Tending towards [AKÇIL]; accustomed to [EVCİL]; addicted to [KİTAPÇIL]; -ivorous [OTÇUL]; adapted to, tolerating [KUMCUL].

cila Polish; varnish; *(fig.)* brightness, lustre. ~ **çark//topu**, polishing wheel//ball: ~ **etm.**, polish, burnish: ~ **vurmak**, apply polish; varnish.

cila·cı(lık) (Work of) polisher, burnisher; varnisher. ~ **lamak (-i)**, apply polish; polish, burnish. ~ **lanmak**, *vp.* ~ **latmak (-i)**, *vc.* ~ **lı**, polished; varnished; shining, lustrous. ~ **sız**, unpolished, unvarnished; dull; lustreless.

cilasun Hero. ~ **gibi**, well-built; brave; dextrous.

cilben¹tᵈⁱ *(adm.)* File; *(art.)* portfolio.

cild- = CİLT. ~ **i**, pertaining to the skin; cutaneous. ~ **iye**, *(med.)* skin diseases; dermatology. ~ **iyeci**, dermatologist.

cilet = JİLET.

-cileyin/-cılayın *adv. suf.* [205] Like . . . [BENCİLEYİN]; in the manner of . . . [ADAMCILAYIN]; to the extent of . . . [BUNCILAYIN].

cil¹tᵈⁱ *(bio.)* Skin; dermis; complexion; hide; *(pub.)* binding; volume. ~ **+**, *a. (bio.)* cutaneous; dermatological: ~ **hastalıkları**, *(med.)* skin diseases.

cilt·çi(lik) *(pub.)* Bookbind·er/(-ing). ~ **evi**ⁿⁱ, bindery. ~ **lemek (-i)**, bind. ~ **lenmek**, *vp.* ~ **letmek (-i, -e)**, *vc.* ~ **li**, bound; in volumes. ~ **siz**, unbound.

cilve Grace; charm; coquetry; *(fig.)* tiresome accident. ~ **etm./**~ **yapmak/**~ **lenmek**, *vi.* behave coquettishly. ~ **kâr/**~ **li**, graceful, charming; coquettish, capricious. ~ **leşmek (-le)**, tease each other; be friendly; flirt.

cim *(ling.)* Arabic letter 'jim', *(now)* 'c'. ~ **karnında bir nokta**, nonentity; matter of no importance.

cima¹ *(bio.)* The sexual act.

cimbakuka Ill-shaped, deformed (person).

cimcime *(bot.)* Small and sweet melon; *(fig.)* small and dainty.

cimnastik = JİMNASTİK.

cimri Mean, miserly, close-fisted, cheese-paring. ~ **leşmek**, *vi.* behave meanly. ~ **lik**, meanness, etc.

cin¹ *n. (cul.)* Gin.

cin² *n. (myth.)* Genie, djinn, demon, sprite; *(fig.)* spirit; intelligent man. ~ **bakışlı**, looking maliciously cunning: ~ **baykuş**, *(orn.)* elf owl: ~ **çarpmak**, *(med.)* have a stroke, be paralysed: ~ **çarpması**, *(med.)* paralytic stroke, sudden attack of insanity: ~ **çarpmışa dönmek**, be in a terrible state for unknown reasons: ~ **fikirli**, astute, shrewd, ingenious: ~ **gibi**, clever and agile: ~**GÖZ**: ~ **ifrit kesilmek/olm.**, be terribly angry: ~ **taifesi**, *(myth.)* the family of demons and sprites: ~ **tutmak**, go. mad (driven by demons): ~**i tutmak**, (child) have tantrums: ~**ler cirit/top oynuyor (-de)**, it's a deserted/haunted place: ~**leri ayağa kalkmak**, become irritated: ~**(ler)i başına toplanmak/üşüşmek**, become angry: ~**leri kovmak**, *(rel.)* exorcize.

cinai *a.* Criminal.

cinas *(lit.)* Pun, play upon words; ambiguous statement.

cinayetⁱ Murder; serious crime. ~ **işlemek**, commit a murder: ~ **mi ecel mi?**, was it murder or natural causes?: ~ **teşebbüsü**, attempted murder. ~ **kâr**, *n.* criminal.

cin·ci Witch-doctor; spiritualist. ~ **darısı**ⁿⁱ, *(bot.)* popcorn: ~ **rastığı**, *(myc.)* corn smut.

cingil = ÇINGIL.

cin·göz Shrewd; crafty; sly. ~ **mısırı**ⁿⁱ, *(bot.)* small-grained Indian corn.

cinnetⁱ Madness, insanity, dementia. ~ **getirmek**, become insane.

cins *n.* Genus; species; class; denomination; race; kind, type, brand, variety; *(bio.)* sex; breed(ing); *(ling.)* gender. *a.* Pure bred, thoroughbred. ~ **adı**, *(ling.)* common noun: ~ **at**, blood horse: ~ **atlar**, bloodstock: ~ ~, of various kinds: ~ **ve nevi**, *(bio.)* genus and species: ~**i latif**, the gentler sex.

cinsaçıⁿⁱ *(bot.)* Dodder.

cins·el/~ **i** Generic; sexual: ~ **birleşme/yaklaşma**, copulation: ~ **cazibe/çekicilik**, sex-appeal. ~ **ellik**, sexuality. ~ **ibir**, of the same genus/kind. ~ **iyet/**~ **lik**, the belonging to a race/genus; characteristic of sex; sexuality. ~ **likbilim**, sexology. ~ **liksiz**, *(bio.)* nonsexual, asexual.

cipⁱ *(mot.)* Jeep.

ciranta *(fin.)* Endorser (of a bill).

cir·imᵐⁱ (Inorganic) body; volume, size.

ciri¹tᵈⁱ *(sp.)* Stick (used as a dart in 'jerid'); the game 'jerid'; javelin; dart. ~ **atma**, throwing the javelin: ~ **atmak/oynamak (-de)**, swarm and move about freely in . . . .

ciro *(fin.)* Endorsement. ~ **etm.**, endorse (bill/ cheque). ~ **lu**, negotiable. ~ **suz**, not negotiable.

cis·imᵐⁱ Body; substance; material object. ~ **cik**, tiny body; *(bio.)* corpuscle. ~ **lendirmek (-i)**, *(art.)* touch up. ~ **lenmek**, *vi.* materialize.

cismani Corporeal; material; bodily; carnal.

civan Handsome youth/young man. ~ **kaşı**ⁿⁱ, zig-zag motif for embroidery, etc. ~ **lık**, youth; adolescence. ~ **mert**, generous, munificent. ~ **mertlik**, generosity. ~ **perçemi**ⁿⁱ, *(bot.)* milfoil, yarrow.

civar *n.* Neighbourhood; environs; countryside; *(soc.)* environment; *(naut.)* approaches. *a.* Neighbouring. ~ **hısımlığı**, *(soc.)* collateral relationship: ~ **ında (-in)**, in the neighbourhood of . . ., near . . . .

civciv *(orn.)* Chick(en); *(ech.)* chirrupping, chatter, noise. ~ **ler**, brood. ~ **li**, noisy/lively/difficult (time).

civele¹kᵍⁱ *n.* Strong lively youth; *(his.)* Janissary recruit. *a.* Brisk, lively, playful. ~ **lik**, briskness; playfulness.

ciyak = CIYAK.

cizvitⁱ *(rel.)* Jesuit; *(fig.)* trouble-maker, conspirator; defeatist; Muslim lax in his religious duties.

cizye *(his.)* Poll-tax on non-Muslims.

CK = CEP KILAVUZU; CEZA KANUNNAMESİ. ~ **MP** = CUMHURİYETÇİ KÖYLÜ MİLLET PARTİSİ.

Cl. = *(ch.s.)* KLOR.

cm. = (*math.*) SANTİMETRE.
Cm. = (*ch.s.*) KÜRİYUM.
Cmh. = CUMHURİYET. ~ **Bşk.** = CUMHURBAŞKAN-(LIĞ)I.
CM·P = CUMHURİYETÇİ MİLLET PARTİSİ. ~ **UK** = CEZA MUHAKEMELERİ USULÜ KANUNU.
Co. = (*ch.s.*) KOBALT.
coğ(r). = COĞRAFYA.
coğraf·i *a.* Geographical. ~ **ya(cı)**, geograph·y/ (-er).
cokey(lik) (*sp.*) (Work, duties of) jockey.
Conkikirik (*sl.*) John Bull.
conta (*eng.*) Gasket, seal. ~ **lık,** ~ **pay,** space, gap.
cop[u] Truncheon. ~ **lamak** –(-i), strike with a truncheon. ~ **lanmak,** *vp.*
corum (*ich.*) Shoal/school of fish.
coş·ku Exuberance; excitement; ebullition: ~ **vurgusu,** (*ling.*) emotional accent, emotive stress: ~ **ya kapılmış,** excited. ~ **kulanmak,** *vi.* become excited. ~ **kulu,** exciting, emotive. ~ **kun,** ebullient, boiling over; overflowing; ardent, demonstrative, enthusiastic, exuberant; furious, anxious. ~ **kunluk,** ebullience; enthusiasm, etc.; exaltation; vehemence. ~ **mak,** *vi.* boil up; overflow; become exuberant; be enthusiastic; be carried away. ~ **turmak (-i),** *vc.* ~ **turucu(luk),** (action/work of) s.o. who causes ebullience/enthusiasm, etc. ~ **turulmak,** *vp.* ~ **u,** ecstasy, rapture. ~ **untu,** excitement.
cömert Generous, bounteous; charitable, big-hearted; (*fig.*) fertile. ~ **çe,** generously. ~ **leşmek,** *vi.* behave generously. ~ **lik,** generosity, bounteousness, bounty.
cönk[ü] (*naut.*) Junk; (*lit.*) manuscript anthology of folk poetry, miscellany; manuscript with lines parallel to the seam.
CP = CUMHURİYETÇİ PARTİ.
Cr. = (*ch.s.*) KROM.
Cs. = (*ch.s.*) SEZYUM.
CS = CUMHURİYET SAVCISI//SENATOSU. ~ **O** = CUMHURBAŞKANLIĞI SENFONİ ORKESTRASI.
Cu. = (*ch.s.*) BAKIR.
-cu *n. suf.* = -ci[1,2].
cudam Useless sort of person.
cuk = AŞIK; (*sl.*) hashish.
-cuk *dim. suf.* = -CİK.
Cum(h). = CUMHURİYET.
cuma Friday. ~ **alayı,** (*his.*) Sultan's procession to the mosque on Friday: ~ **sı eksik (bir),** foolish. ~ **rtesi**[yi], Saturday: ~ **çocuğu,** (*sl.*) bastard: ~ **kibarı gibi süslenmek,** dress very showily and without taste; ape one's betters.
cumba (*arch.*) Projection; corbel; bow-window; balcony, room projecting over the street.
cumbadak (*ech.*) Splash!, (*fig.*) suddenly. ~ **düşmek,** fall suddenly into water.
cumbalak[lk][g1] Somersault. ~ **ı atmak,** (*sl.*) die.
cumbul/cumbur ~ ~, (*ech.*) swishing of water (in a container); (*cul.*) sloppy (food). ~ **damak,** *vi.* (*ech.*) swish about. ~ **lop,** (*ech.*) plop!, splash! ~ **tu,** (*ech.*) plop, loud splash.
cumhur The mass of the people; populace; republic;

(*rel.*) hymn. ~ +, *a.* Republican: ~ **a muhalefet kuvvei hatadandır,** it's a mistake to go against the masses: ~ **a uymak,** follow the majority.
cumhur·başkan/ ~ **reis(liğ)i**[ni] (*adm.*) Presiden·t/ (-cy) of the Republic. ~ **iyet**[i], republic: ~ **Halk Partisi,** (*pol.*) Republican People's Party: ~ **Savcısı,** (*leg.*) attorney general: ~ **senatosu,** Tk. Senate. ~ **iyetçi,** *n.* supporter of the Republic; republican: *a.* republican. ~ **luk,** republic.
cunda (*naut.*) End of a gaff; peak.
cunta (*adm.*) Junta; ruling clique. ~ **cı,** member of a junta.
cup (*ech.*) Plop!, splash! ~ **padak** = CUMBADAK.
cura (*mus.*) Two-/three-stringed lute; (*orn.*) a small shrill hawk; (*sl.*) last puff from a cigarette. ~ **zurna,** (*mus.*) small shrill horn. ~ **cı,** lute-player.
curcuna (*mus.*) Fast melody; disorderly/drunken revel; orgy; brawl. ~ **ya çevirmek/döndürmek/ vermek (-i),** create a noisy brawl.
curnal = JURNAL.
curnata (*orn.*) Mass arrival of quails.
cuş(iş) Effervescence; commotion; enthusiasm. ~ **a** ~, full of excitement: ~ **u huruş,** commotion, excitement, enthusiasm.
-cü *n. suf.* = -ci[1,2].
cüce *n.* Dwarf; pygmy. *a.* Dwarf, pygmy, little, lesser. ~ **antilop,** (*zoo.*) royal antelope: ~ **balaban//balıkçıl,** (*orn.*) little bittern//heron: ~ **baykuş,** (*orn.*) Scops owl: ~ **bekasin,** (*orn.*) jack snipe: ~ **çekirge,** (*ent.*) grouse/pygmy grasshopper: ~ **geyik,** (*zoo.*) chevrotain: ~ **göstermek (-i),** dwarf: ~ **karabatak,** (*orn.*) pygmy cormorant: ~ **kartal** (*orn.*) booted eagle: ~ **papağan,** (*orn.*) pygmy parrot: ~ **peri,** (*myth.*) elf: ~ **sıçan,** (*zoo.*) harvest-mouse: ~ **sıvacı kuşu,** (*orn.*) Eurasian nuthatch: ~ **sinekyutan,** (*orn.*) red-breasted fly-catcher: ~ **yarasa,** (*zoo.*) common pipistrelle: ~ **yıldız,** (*ast.*) dwarf star. ~ **lik,** (*med.*) dwarfism; dwarfishness.
cücü[lk][gü] *n.* (*bot.*) Bud, shoot; heart (lettuce, onion, etc.); (*mod.*) tuft of beard, imperial; (*bio.*) embryo; (*orn.*) chick. *a.* Sweet, pleasant, tender. ~ **lenmek,** *vi.* (*bot.*) shoot, bud; (*zoo.*) form an embryo. ~ **lü,** embryonic.
cüda Separated, separate, alone. ~ **düşmek (-den),** *vi.* become separated from s.o.
cühela *pl.* = CAHİL. Ignoramuses.
-cük *dim. suf.* = -CİK.
cülus (*his.*) Accession to the throne.
cümbür cemaat[1] All together, the 'whole caboodle'.
cümbüş Amusement, entertainment; merry-making, revel, jollity, binge; (*mus.*) a metal mandolin. ~ **etm./yapmak,** make merry, enjoy o.s.: ~ **lere düşkün,** convivial. ~ **lü,** with jollity and amusement.
cümle A total, a whole; category, system; (*ling.*) phrase, sentence. ~ **âlem,** all the world, everybody: ~ **kapısı,** (*arch.*) main/front door (of a big house): ~ **yapısı,** (*ling.*) construction: ~ **miz,** all of us: ~ **nin maksudu bir amma rivayet muhtelif,** they all mean the same thing but call it by different names: ~ **si,** all of them. ~ **cik/** ~ **msi,** (*ling.*) clause. ~ **ten,** wholly, entirely, all together.

cümudiye (*geo.*) Glacier, iceberg.

cünha (*leg.*) Rather serious offence, crime.

cünun (*med.*) Insanity.

cünüp (*rel.*) (S.o.) unclean (after sexual relations).

cüppe (*mod.*) Robe (with full sleeves, long skirts); academic gown; cassock, cope. ~ **gibi**, long full (dress).

cüret[i] Boldness, daring, dash, audacity; impudence, insolence. ~ **etm. (-e)**, make bold to . . ., dare to . . ..

cüret·kâr Bold; insolent. ~ **kârlık**, insolence. ~ **lenmek**, *vi.* behave daringly. ~ **li**, daring, audacious.

cüruf (*min.*) Slag, dross, scoriae; breeze; cinders.

cür'üm[mü] Crime, felony; fault, sin. ~ +, *a.* Criminal: ~ **ü meşhut (halinde)**, *in flagrante*

delicto: ~ **ü meşhut halinde yakalanmak**, be caught red-handed/ in the act: ~ **ü meşhut yapmak**, lay a trap to catch s.o. red-handed.

cüsse Bulky body. ~ **li**, big-bodied; huge.

cüz'ü Part; section; piece, fragment; (*eng.*) component; (*rel.*) one of the thirty sections of the Koran; (*pub.*) section of a book, fascicule; pamphlet.

cüzam (*med.*) Leprosy. ~ **lı**, leprous.

cüzdan Pocket-book, wallet; portfolio; (*adm.*) certificate.

cüzi Trifling, insignificant; partial, fragmentary; (*phil.*) particular (not general). ~ **ce**, somewhat small. ~ **yet**[i], insignificance; partiality; (*phil.*) particularity.

Cy. = (*ch.s.*) SİYANOJEN.

Ç

Ç, ç [che] Fourth Tk. letter, Ç; fourth (in a class/ series).

Ç, ç. = (*geo.*) ÇAY; ÇOĞUL.

-ç *a.*, *n. suf.* [222] [KORKUNÇ; İNANÇ].

-ça[1] *fem. n. suf.* [25] = -İÇE [TANRIÇA].

-ça[2] *suf.* [194] = -CE[2] [ARAPÇA].

çaba Endeavour, striving; effort; energy. ~ **göstermek**, work, endeavour, strive (to do stg.). ~**lama**, *vn.* endeavour, striving; struggling. ~**lamak**, *vi.* endeavour; strive; make an effort; struggle: **çabalama kaptan ben gidemem**, I have no wish to continue. ~**lanmak**, *vi.* move one's limbs agitatedly; struggle. ~**layış**, struggle.

çabuca(cı)k Very quickly (and easily); apace.

çabuk *a.* Quick; agile. *adv.* Quickly; in a hurry; soon. ~ ~, quickly: ~ (**ol)!**, hurry up!; look alive!: ~ **olm.**, hurry; be quick: ~ **parlayan** ~ **söner**, easy come easy go.

çabuk·ça Fairly quickly. ~**laşmak**, *vi.* accelerate, gain speed, go faster. ~**laştırıcı**, (*chem.*) accelerator. ~**laştırılmak**, *vp.* be accelerated. ~**laştırma**, *vn.* acceleration. ~**laştırmak (-i)**, accelerate, expedite, speed up, hasten. ~**luk**, speed; agility; haste.

çaça (*naut.*) Old and experienced sailor; (*fig.*) brothel-keeper, madam; (*mus.*) cha-cha dance. ~ **balığı**[nı], (*ich.*) sprat.

çaçaron Talkative person; charlatan. ~**luk**, talkativeness.

çadır Tent. ~ **ağırşağı**, tent-pole cap: ~ **bezi**, (*tex.*) canvas: ~ **kurmak**, pitch tent.

çadır·cı(lık) (Work/ trade of) tent-maker/-seller. ~ **çiçeği**[ni], (*bot.*) bindweed; cornlily. ~**lı**, having/ living in a tent: ~ **kamp**, holiday camp: ~ **ordugâh**, (*mil.*) bivouac. ~**uşağı**[nı], (*bot.*) *Doraema ammoniacum*; (*med.*) gum ammoniacum.

çağ Time; age, period; epoch, era; stature. ~ **açmak**, open a period: ~ **dışı olm.**, (*mil.*) be over the age for military service: ~DIŞI: ~ **üstü**, ultramodern: ~**ında**, the right time (for stg.).

çağa Child, infant.

çağ(a)na[1]**k**[ğı] = ÇALGI; (*mus.*) castanets, tambourine.

çağanoz (*zoo.*) Common shore crab.

çağaşım(sal) Anachron·ism/(-istic).

Çağatay (*ethn.*) The Chagatay branch of the Turkish race. ~**ca**, (*ling.*) the Chagatay language.

çağ·bilimi Chronology. ~**cıl**, modern, up-to-date; contemporary; fashionable. ~**cıllaşma**, *vn.* modernization. ~**cıllaşmak**, *vi.* be(come) modernized. ~**cıllaştırmak (-i)**, modernize; contemporize. ~**cıllık**, modernness, fashionableness. ~**daş**, *a.* contemporary, contemporaneous; coeval; modern: *n.* contemporary. ~**daşlaş(tır)ma(k)** =

~CILLAŞ(TIR)MA(K). ~**daşlık**, contemporaneity. ~**dışı**, out-of-date, backward; (*mil.*) outside call-up period. ~**dışılık**, backwardness.

çağıl ~ ~, (*ech.*) babbling (of running water). ~**damak**, *vi.* (*ech.*) babble, burble, murmur. ~ **tı**, the murmur of running water. ~**tılı**, murmuring.

çağır·ıcı S.o. sent to invite s.o.; (*th.*) call-boy. ~**ış**, manner of calling. ~**ma**, *vn.* calling; inviting; summoning; appeal. ~ **mak (-i)**, call; (**-i, -e**), invite; (*leg.*) cite, summon; (*adm.*) convoke: *vi.* call out, sing. ~**tı**, calling, shouting. ~**tkan**, decoy bird; (*fin.*) barker. ~**tma**[ç][cı], town-crier. ~**tmak (-i, -e)**, *vc.*

çağla (*bot.*) Edible though unripe stone-fruit. ~ **bademi**, green almond: ~ **yeşili**, almond-green.

çağla·ma *vn.* Murmuring of falling water. ~**mak**, *vi.* (water) fall noisily and frothily. ~**r**/ ~**yan**, small waterfall, cascade. ~**yı**[ğı], bubbling spring; hot spring. ~**yış**, purling/falling (of water).

çağlık Fixed for a period; periodical.

çağmak (-e) (Sun's rays) strike.

çağna[ı]**k**[ğı] (*bio.*) Amniotic fluid. = ÇAĞANAK.

çağrı Invitation; (*leg.*) citation, summons; (*mil.*) call-up; (*rel.*) message; (*th.*) call; (*ling.*) vocative. ~ **belgesi**, written invitation.

çağrı·cı S.o. sent to invite/summon. ~**lı**, s.o. invited/summoned. ~**lık**, written invitation. ~**lmak**, *vp.* = ÇAĞIRMAK; be called out/shouted/ sung; be called/invited/ summoned. ~**m**, distance a shout can travel. ~**şım**, (*phil.*) association of ideas: ~ **yapmak (-e)**, (*lit.*) be based on. ~**şımcılık**, associationism. ~**şımsal(lık)**, (*phil.*) associative/ (-ness). ~**şmak**, *vi.* call one another; make a row: (**-le**), cry out together. ~**ştırmak (-i, -e)**, remind, call to mind.

çak[1] *int.* (*ech.*) (*of clashing metals*).

çak[1][2] *a.* Torn; cracked. ~ ~, full of rents/cracks; all in pieces.

çak[3] *adv.* Exactly, precisely. ~ **ortasında**, exactly in the middle of it.

çakal (*zoo.*) Jackal; (*sl.*) liar, trickster. ~**eriği**[ni], (*bot.*) wild plum, sloe, blackthorn.

çakaloz (*mil.*) Small cannon (firing pebbles).

çakar *n.* Large trawl-net. *v.* = ÇAKMAK[1].

çakı Pocket-knife. ~ **gibi**, keen and active.

çakıl Pebble; shingle; gravel; (*rly.*) ballast. ~ **döşemek**, pave with pebbles; (*rly.*) lay down ballast: ~ **kayaç**, (*geol.*) conglomerate: ~ **ocağı**, gravel pit: ~ **taşı**, pebble.

çakıl·da[ı]**k**[ğı] Ball of dried dung (under animal's tail); (*eng.*) mill clapper; rattle; endless talker. ~**damak**, *vi.* make a clattering noise. ~**datmak (-i, -e)**, *vc.*

çakılı Stuck; fastened, tethered; fixed.

çakıl·lı Pebbly, gravelly: ~ **kum**, aggregate. ~ **lık**, pebbly place; pebbled courtyard. ~ **tı**, (*ech.*) clattering/rattling noise.

çakıl·mak (-e) *vp.* = ÇAKMAK; be stuck (in a place); (*sl.*) notice, understand. ~ **madan**, (*sl.*) without anyone noticing.

çak·ım/ ~ **ın** Lightning; flash, spark. ~ **ıntı**, flash; (*sl.*) booze; booze-up.

çakır[1] *a.* Grey with blue streaks; greyish blue; = ~ DOĞAN.

çakır[2] *n.* (*obs.*) Wine.

çakır[3] *n.* ~ **çukur**, chewing noise; uneven/broken ground; full of potholes.

çakır·cı Falconer; (*obs.*) wine-merchant. ~ **diken**, (*bot.*) eryngo; burr; sea-holly. ~ **doğan**, (*orn.*) goshawk. ~ **kana¹t**[d1], (*orn.*) green-winged teal. ~ **keyf**, half-drunk, beery. ~ **pençe**, grasping, rapacious.

çakış·ık (*math.*) Coinciding; (*phys.*) degenerate. ~ **ıklık/** ~ **ma**, degeneracy. ~ **mak**, *vi.* fit into one another; be united: **(-le)**, coincide; collide with one another; (poets) compete impromptu with one another; (*math.*) (two figures) coincide exactly. ~ **tırmak**, *vc.* = ~ MAK: *vi.* drink, booze; make merry.

çakkal = BAKKAL.

çakma *vn.* = ÇAKMAK[1]; flash of lightning; (*min.*) stamping/embossing (silver, etc.); (*eng.*) drive: ~ **pabucu**, (*eng.*) drive shoe: ~ **deneyi**, (*eng.*) driving test.

çakmak[1] **(-i, -e)** *vt.* Drive in by blows; (*eng.*) drive (piles); stamp/emboss (metals); nail/fasten stg.; tether (by a peg); strike (a flint/match); snap (the teeth); palm off (false coins); fit (one thing into another); (*sl.*) strike s.o.; (*sl.*) be aware/conscious of: **(-den)**, (*sl.*) understand/know about stg.; (*sl.*, *ed.*) be 'ploughed' (in an exam). *vi.* Be ostentatiouslydeferential;(lightning,etc.)flash;(*sl.*) carouse. **çakar almaz**, that which misfires; useless; not working; (*jok.*) blunderbuss: **çakar lamba**, (*mot.*) flashing indicator lamp; (*cin.*) photoflash.

çakma¹k[ğ1 2] *n.* Steel (for striking on flint); pocket-/cigarette-lighter; trigger; (*med.*) a skin disease (pustules and scabs on the face).

çakmak·çı Flint-knapper; maker/repairer of flintlock guns//cigarette-lighters. ~ **lı**, flint-lock (gun). ~ **lık**, *a.* for use in a lighter. ~ **taşı**[n1], (*geol.*) flint; chert.

çakoz ~ **etm./** ~ **lamak**, (*sl.*) reconnoitre; understand.

çakşır (*mod.*) Trousers (broad band at waist, light leather boots attached at ankles); (*orn.*) leg feathers. ~ **lı**, (*mod.*) wearing such trousers; (*orn.*) with leg feathers: ~ **tavuk**, (*orn.*) bantam.

çaktır·ılmak *vp.* ~ **mak (-i, -e)**, *vc.* = ÇAKMAK[1]. ~ **madan**, without attracting anyone's attention; without being noticed.

çal (*geo.*) Escarpment, bare hill.

çal(a)- *v. pref.* [175] *Indicating repeated action of the verb* ÇALMAK ~ **a** ~ **a**, by keeping on at stg.

çalaca¹k[ğ1] *n.* (*cul.*) Ferment, yeast.

çalak Quick, agile.

çala·kalem *adv.* With flowing pen; scribbling

hastily. ~ **kamçı**, lashing out with a whip. ~ **kaşık**, (eat) greedily. ~ **kılıç**, raining down sword-blows. ~ **kürek**, rowing hard.

Çalap (*obs.*) God.

çalapa (*bot.*) Jalap; (*chem.*) purgative drug.

çala·paça Pushing and pulling/dragging s.o. ~ **pala**, with all one's strength.

çalar *n.* Striking mechanism (of a bell/clock). *v.* = ÇALMAK. ~ **saat**[i], striking clock; repeater (watch); alarm clock.

çalçene Chatterbox, babbler.

çaldır·ılmak *vp.* ~ **mak (-i, -e)**, *vc.* = ÇALMAK; cause to strike/steal/play, etc.; let s.o. steal; lose by theft.

çalgı (*mus.*) Instrument. ~ **çağanak**, noisy musical party: ~ **çalmak**, (*mus.*) play an instrument: ~ **orağı**, (*agr.*) scythe: ~ **takımı**, (*mus.*) orchestra; band; their instruments: ~ **zili**, cymbal: ~ **da düzenleme**, harmony.

çalgı·cı Musician, player: ~ **lar heyeti**, band, orchestra. ~ **cılık**, music (as art/profession). ~ **cıotu**[nu], (*bot.*) hedge-mustard. ~ **¹çc**[1], (*mus.*) plectrum. ~ **lı**, with music; done to music: ~ **kutu**, musical-box. ~ **sız**, without instrument//music: ~ **müzik**, synthetic music.

çalı (*bot.*) Bush, shrub; thicket. ~ **çırpı**, brushwood; firewood, kindling; sticks and thorns (for fencing): ~ **demeti**, faggot; (*eng.*) fascine: ~ **gibi**, tangled and stiff (hair, etc.): ~ **karidesi**, (*zoo.*) (brown) shrimp: ~ **süpürgesi**, (*dom.*) broom.

çalı·bülbülü[nü] (*orn.*) Orphean warbler; (?) whitethroat. ~ **bülbülleri**[ni], (*orn.*) warblers. ~ **dikeni**[ni], (*bot.*) blackthorn. ~ **fasulyesi**[ni], (*bot.*) climbing kidney beans; runner beans; string beans. ~ **horozu**[nu], (*orn.*) capercaillie.

çalı¹k[ğ1] *a.* Slanting, awry; walking sideways; tainted, spoilt; (*tex.*) faded, discoloured; (*adm.*) dismissed, expelled; dazed, deranged. *n.* (*med.*) Boil, abscess; sheep scab.

çalı·kava¹k[ğ1] (*bot.*) Pollarded poplar (used in basket-making). ~ **kuşu**[nu], (*orn.*) firecrest, goldcrest. ~ **lık**, (*bot.*) thicket: ~ **yangını**, brushfire.

çalım Swagger, gesture; reach, range, (gun)-shot; stroke, blow; (*sp.*) feint, trick; dribble. ~ **atmak/ yapmak** = ~ LAMAK: ~ **satmak**, swagger, cut a dash, give o.s. airs: ~ **ına getirmek**, find a suitable opportunity: ~ **ından geçilmemek**, be very arrogant.

çalım·lamak (-i) Feint, trick. ~ **lanmak**, *vi.* swagger; (*sp.*) be tricked. ~ **lı**, swaggering, arrogant; (*naut.*) (ship) with fast lines: ~ ~, swaggering(ly), arrogantly.

çalın·mak (-e) *vp.* = ÇALMAK; be struck/stolen, etc.: *vi.* (bells) ring, chime. ~ **tı**, stolen goods; (*lit.*) unacknowledged quotation; plagiarism: ~ **akma**, (*el.*, *geo.*) borrowed current.

çalış *vn.* = ~ MAK: ~ **a** ~ **a**, by dint of working. ~ **an**, *n.* worker: *a.* active: ~ **ortaklık**, (*fin.*) going concern. ~ **ılmak**, (*imp. v.*) (work) be done; (efforts) be made. ~ **ım**, (*sp.*) training. ~ **ır**, *a.* working. ~ **kan**, industrious, diligent, hard-working. ~ **kanlık**, industriousness, diligence. ~ **ma**, *vn.* work; working; production; study; attempt, endeavour;

(*sp.*) training; (*th.*) rehearsal; (*for.*) warping: ~ **arızası**, (*ind.*) breakdown: ~ **ataşesi**, (*adm.*) labour attaché: ~ **Bakan(lığ)ı**, (*adm.*) Minis·ter/(-try) of Labour: ~ **çizelgesi**, (*th.*) call-board: ~ **izni**, (*adm.*) work permit: ~ **saatleri**, working hours: ~ **topu**, (*sp.*) medicine-ball. ~**mak**, *vi.* work; attempt, endeavour, strive, try; study; (*for.*) warp: **çalışıp çabalamak**, strive hard, do one's best. ~**mama**, (*ind.*) failure. ~**mamazlık**, idleness. ~**man**, worker, employee. ~**tırıcı**, (*eng.*, *el.*) actuator; (*sp.*) trainer. ~**tırılmak**, *vp.* be made to work, etc. ~**tırma**, *vn.*, employment; training; (*eng.*) start-up; actuator. ~**tırmak (-i, -e)**, *vc.* make/let s.o. work/ try; set to work, employ; (*eng.*, *el.*) actuate, start up; (*sl.*) make fun of s.o. simple.

çal·kağı (*tex.*) = ÇALKAR. ~**kala(n)mak**/~**kalat-mak** = ~KAMAK.

çalka·ma *vn.* Agitation; (*cul.*) stg. made by beating/ shaking, etc.; omelette: ~ **cihazı**, (*cul.*) beater. ~**mak (-i)**, agitate; shake/toss about; disturb; wash out (mouth), gargle; beat (eggs); churn (milk); riddle (grain); (hen) turn its eggs; (food) turn the stomach. ~**nmak**, *vp.* be agitated/shaken about: *vi.* (ship) pitch, roll; (sea) become rough; sway about (while walking); (egg) become addled; fluctuate; (news) spread like wildfire. ~**ntı**, agitation; shaking; (sea) tossing about; (river) rapids; (ship) pitching, rolling; (*med.*) stomach disturbance. ~**r**, (*med.*) stg. upsetting the stomach; purgative; (*tex.*) cotton gin. ~**tmak (-i, -e)**, *vc.* ~**yıcı**, (*phys.*) agitator.

çal·ma *vn.* Theft; (*fin.*) defalcation; (*mus.*) playing; (*mod.*) head-scarf: *a.* stolen; (*min.*) chiselled. ~**macı**, (*min.*) one who chisels designs. ~**mak (-i, -e)**, *vt.* give a blow, strike; knock (on a door); ring (bell); (*mus.*) play (an instrument); beat (the drum); (*sp.*) blow the whistle (for a foul, etc.); (*cul.*) spread (butter, etc.); mix; have the flavour/smell of stg. else; border/verge on (another colour); (*min.*) carve, chisel; (*dom.*) clean, dust; misappropriate, steal; spoil, upset; (sun/wind) scorch; (*ling.*) have a certain accent: *vi.* (things) make a noise; (bell/ telephone) ring; (clock) strike: **çal kapı gelmek**, arrive uninvited/unannounced: **çalıp çırpmak**, pilfer: **çalmadan oynamak**, be over-cheerful; be gushing/officious: **çalmadığım kapı kalmadı**, I have left no stone unturned; I have made every effort.

çalpara (*mus.*) Castanet; (*zoo.*) swimming crab.

çalu·kᵍu Stuffed animal/bird. ~**çu**, taxidermist.

çalyaka Suddenly seizing s.o.'s collar. ~ **etm.**, seize s.o. by the collar.

çam (*bot.*) Pine. ~ **baştankarası**, (*orn.*) coal tit: ~ **devirmek**, drop a brick, put one's foot in it; show one's ignorance: ~FISTIĞI: ~ **kelebeği**, (*ent.*) nun moth: ~ **keseböceği**, (*ent.*) processionary moth: ~ **tahtası**, (*for.*) deal: ~ **yağı**, pine tar: ~ **yarması gibi**, strong and well-built (man).

çamaşır Underclothes, underwear; linen; dirty linen, the washing, the laundry. ~ **asmak**, hang out the washing: ~ **azgını**, dirty underwear; stg. too dirty to wash/clean: ~ **dağ taş yığıldı**, there's a regular pile of dirty linen: ~ **değiştirmek**, change one's underwear: ~ **dolabı**, chest-of-drawers, linen

cupboard: ~ **ipeği**, (*mod.*) silk thread: ~ **ipi**, clothesline: ~ **makinesi**, washing-machine: ~ **mandalı**, clothes-peg: ~ **sepeti**, clothes-/laundry-basket: ~ **sıkmak**, wring out the washing: ~ **sırığı**, clothes-prop: ~ **suyu**, chlorinated water: ~ **teknesi**, wash-tub: ~ **tozu**, bleaching powder: ~ **yıkamak**, do the laundry, wash the clothes.

çamaşır·cı Laundry(wo)man. ~**cılık**, laundering; (*dom.*) white goods. ~**hane**, laundry. ~**lık**, *n.* laundry(-room): *a.* used in laundering.

çam·ça/~**ça¹kᵍı 1** (*ich.*) Roach.

çam·ça¹kᵍı 2 Wooden vessel for water. ~**fıstığıⁿⁱ**, (*bot.*) pine kernel, pine nut. ~**giller**, (*bot.*) the pine family, Pinaceae. ~**lık**, *a.* covered with pines: *n.* pine grove. ~**sakızıⁿⁱ**, pine-resin; (*fig.*) a sticky mess: ~ **çoban armağanı**, (apologizing for) a small gift: ~ **gibi**, a bore one can't get rid of.

çamuka (*ich.*) Silverside, sandsmelt.

çamur Mud; liquid clay; ooze, sludge; dirt; (*fig.*) unmannerly person, 'a bad lot'. ~ **atmak/** **sıçratmak (-e)**, sling mud at; slander s.o.: ~ **hoplar**, (*ich.*) mudskipper: ~ **humması**, (*med.*) swamp fever: ~ **ığrıbı**, shallow-water fishing net: ~ **sıvamak**, cast aspersions: ~ **tahtakurusu**, (*ent.*) assassin/masked bug: ~**a bulamak**, cover with disgrace: ~**a bulaşmak**, get involved in dirty business/with bad people: ~**a taş atmak**, ask for trouble from s.o. aggressive/impudent: ~**a yatmak**, (*sl.*) not pay one's debts; break one's promise: ~**dan çekip çıkarmak (-i)**, help s.o. out of the mud/difficulties: ~**u karnında çiçeği burnunda**, very fresh.

çamur·cu¹kᵍu (*ich.*) Tench. ~**cun**, (*orn.*) teal. ~**lamak (-i)**, cover with mud; slander. ~**lanmak**, *vp.* ~**laşmak**, *vi.* become muddy; form sludge; (*fig.*) become aggressive. ~**latmak (-i, -e)**, *vc.* ~**lu**, muddy. ~**luk**, muddy place; (*mod.*) gaiters; spats; (*mot.*) mudguard; boot-scraper. ~**taşıⁿⁱ**, (*geol.*) mudstone. ~**yılanıⁿⁱ**, (*zoo.*) coral snake.

çan Bell; (*sp.*) bell (for the last lap); (*sp.*) gong. ~ **çalmak**, ring the bell; (*fig.*) trumpet abroad, tell everybody: ~ **etm.**, chatter endlessly: ~ÇIÇEĞI: ~ **dil/tokmağı**, bell clapper: ~ **eğrisi**, (*math.*) normal frequency distribution curve: ~ **kulesi**, (*arch.*) bell-tower, belfry: ~ **kuşu**, (*orn.*) bellbird: ~ **şamandırası**, (*naut.*) bell-buoy: ~ **şekli**, (*mod.*) cloche (hat): ~**ına ot tık(a)mak**, silence/confound an opponent; muzzle; render impotent.

çana¹kᵍı (*dom.*) Earthenware bowl/pan/pot; beggar's alms-bowl; (*bot.*) calyx; (*bio.*) calix, calicle. ~ **ağızlı**, big-mouthed; (*fig.*) who can't keep a secret: ~ **çömlek**, crockery, pots and pans: ~ **koltuk**, (*mot.*) bucket-seat: ~ **maytabı**, Bengal fire: ~ **tutmak**, beg; ask for trouble, bring trouble on o.s.: ~ **üzengi**, broad stirrup: ~ **yalamak**, fawn on s.o. ~ **yalayıcı**, lick-spittle, toady: ~ **yalayıcılık** **etm.**, toady.

çanak·çı Potter. ~**çılık**, making/selling of pottery. ~**kale**, *pr.n.* (*geo.*) Dardanelles (town): ~ **Boğazı**, the Dardanelles (Straits), Hellespont. ~**lık**, (*naut.*) top of the mast, crow's nest. ~**sı**, bowl-like; (*bio.*) calyciform. ~**yaprağıⁿⁱ**, (*bot.*) sepal.

çan·cı Maker/seller of bells; bell-ringer. ~**çan**, loud and continuous chatter: ~ **etm.**, chatter loudly. ~**çiçegi**ni, (*bot.*) campanula. ~**çiçeğigiller**, (*bot.*) Campanulaceae.

çandır (*live.*) A cross between DAĞLIÇ and KARAMAN breeds of sheep; its mutton; (*agr.*) hybrid plant.

çangal Branch, twig; bean-pole. ~**lı**, branched.

çangıl ~ **çungul**, (*ech.*) (*of harsh broken speech; foreign/provincial accent*).

çangır ~ **çungur**, (*ech.*) clink-clank, jingle-jangle, clatter. ~**damak**, *vi.* make a clanking/jingling noise. ~**tı**, clanking, jingling.

çanıltı (*ech.*) Sound of bells.

çanta Bag; case; suitcase; knapsack. ~ **çiçeği**, (*bot.*) calceolaria: ~**da keklik**, stg. safely secured, in the bag: ~**ya koymak**, bag stg. ~**cı(lık)**, (work of) maker/seller of bags//(*adm.*) messenger carrying official correspondence to ministers//(*sp.*) man carrying hunter's game-bag.

çap[1] (*math.*) Diameter; (*eng.*) bore, calibre; (*fig.*) calibre; (*arch.*) plan showing dimensions/ boundaries of buildings/plots of land. ~ **pergeli**, callipers: ~**ını bulmak**, calibrate: ~**tan düşmek**, (*fig.*) be undersized; be in a hopeless state.

çapa (*agr.*) Hoe, mattock; (*naut.*) anchor (with flukes). ~ **dipten ayrılmış!**, anchor(s) aweigh! ~**cı**, (*agr.*) hoer.

çapaçul Slovenly; untidy. ~ **olm.**, be out at elbows. ~**luk**, slovenliness.

çapalk[g1] 1 (*ich.*) Common/freshwater bream.

çapalk[g1] 2 (*bio.*) Crust round 'bleary' eyes; (*eng.*) beard, burr. ~ **almak**, (*eng.*) deburr. ~**lanmak**, *vi.* be crusted. ~**lı**, crusted; burred.

çapala·mak (-i) (*agr.*) Hoe. ~**nmak**, *vp.* ~**tmak (-i, -e)**, *vc.*

çapanoğlunu (*fig.*) Troublesome situation, snag. = işi KURCALAMA: ~**nun aptes suyu gibi**, weak and cloudy (drink).

çapar *n.* Courier, postman; (*naut.*) medium-sized Black Sea boat. *a.* Speckled; albino.

çaparı Multi-hooked fishing-line; lure.

çaparız *n.* Obstacle, entanglement. *a.* Perverse. ~ **etm./getirmek**, create difficulties, block the way.

çapçalk[g1] Wooden water bowl; open barrel.

çapcı Raider, marauder.

çapkın Vagabond; rascal, scamp; rake, dissolute, gay dog; swift horse. ~ **edalı**, coquettish. ~**laşmak**, *vi.* be a rake, etc. ~**lık**, profligacy, debauchery.

çapla (*min.*) Cold chisel.

çap·lama *vn.* Calibration. ~**lamak (-i)**, calibrate. ~**lı**, wide bored; (*arch.*) according to standards.

çapmak (-i) Gallop (a horse); (-e), pillage, raid: *vi.* ride fast, gallop.

çapralk[g1] Saddle-cloth.

çapraş·ık Crosswise; complicated, entangled; abstruse, complex. ~**ıklaşmak**, *vi.* become complicated/entangled. ~**ıklık**, being complicated, etc. ~**mak**, *vi.* be interlaced/ interconnected; be involved/difficult.

çapraz *a.* Crosswise, transverse; diagonal(ly), corner-wise; (*mod.*) double-breasted; on the bias. *n.* (*carp.*) Saw-set; (*mod.*) metal clasp; (*sp.*) clinch. ~ **atlayış**, (*sp.*) scissors jump: ~ **bulaşım**, (*med.*) cross

infection: ~ **çizgili**, criss-cross: ~ **dikiş**, (*mod.*) cross-stitch: ~ **hat**, (*math.*) diagonal: ~ **koymak**, (mark with a) cross: ~ **sahın**, (*arch.*) transept: ~ **tarama**, (*art.*) cross-hatching: ~ **tozlaşma**, (*bot.*) cross-pollination: ~**a sarmak** = ~**laşmak**: ~**da sürmek**, (*sp.*) force the opponent back in a clinch.

çapraz·gaga (*orn.*) Red crossbill. ~**lama**, *a.* crossed, crossing; (*naut.*) athwart: *n.* (*carp.*) setting of saw-teeth; (*bio.*) cross; (*ling.*) repetition of words in a different order: ~ **çizgili**, (*min.*) engine-turned. ~**lamak (-i)**, cross; (*zoo.*) cross-breed. ~**laşmak**, *vi.* become entangled/inextricably difficult. ~**lı**, (*mod.*) with a clasp. ~**lık**, being crossed, etc. ~**ölçer**, (*eng.*) tooth-angle meter. ~**vari**, crosswise.

çapul Raid; booty, plunder. ~ **etm.**, sack, pillage; go on a raid. ~**cu**, raider; pillager. ~**culuk**, raiding, pillaging. ~**lamak (-i)**, go raiding; pillage, sack.

çaputu Rag; patch; (*dial.*) cloth.

çar[1] (*his.*) Tsar.

çar[2] (*mod.*) Shawl.

çarçabuk Very quickly; in haste; in a flash.

çarçur In a wasteful/squandering manner. ~ **etm.**, squander: ~ **olm.**, be wasted.

çardalk[g1] Brushwood shelter; bower; trellis; pergola.

çare Remedy, antidote, cure; means; measure, step; help; expedient; way out (of difficulties). ~ **aramak**, cast about for a solution: ~ **bulmak**, find a remedy/means: ~**sine bakmak (-in)**, find a way/ solution.

çare·siz *a.* Irremediable; inevitable; necessary; helpless, without means: *adv.* inevitably: ~ **kalmak**, find no solution. ~**sizlik**, lack of means; desperation, urgency; poverty; helplessness.

çareviç (*his.*) Tsarevich.

çargâh (*mus.*) Or. melody. ~ **perdesi**, sound 'do'.

çarılk[g1] (*mod.*) Sandal of rawhide/rope (for peasants); shoe/drag (for cart-wheel); (*sl.*) wallet; (*sl.*) tyre. ~**çı(lık)**, (work of) maker/seller of sandals. ~**lı**, wearing sandals; (*fig.*) ignorant and illiterate but clever (peasant): ~ **bezirgân/ diplomat/erkânıharp**, (*jok.*) (peasant) shrewder than one suspects. ~**lık**, *a.* used in making sandals.

çariçe (*his.*) Tsarina.

çark[1] Wheel; stg. that revolves; disc; machinery; (*naut.*) paddle-wheel; (*eng.*) flywheel, gear-wheel; (*ast.*) the celestial sphere; fate, destiny. ~ **çevirmek**, wander about: ~ **dişi**, (*eng.*) cog, tooth: ~ **dişi kökü**, dedendum: ~ **etm.**, turn, revolve; (*mil.*) wheel: ~ **işi**, machinery; machine-made: ~ **işletmek**, operate machinery; (*fig.*) work a scheme to one's own advantage: ~ **kayışı**, drive-belt: ~**a çektirmek/vermek**, put (a tool) to the grindstone: ~**ına etm./okumak**, (*sl.*) spoil/ruin stg.

çark·çı (*naut.*) Engineer; knife-grinder. ~**çıbaşı**y1, (*naut.*) chief engineer. ~**çılık**, work of engineer// knife-grinder. ~**ıfele**lk[g1], the sphere of heaven; destiny; Catherine wheel firework; (*bot.*) passion-flower. ~**ıfelekgiller**, (*bot.*) Passifloraceae.

çarlılk[g1] (*his.*) Reign/government of a tsar. ~ **idaresi**, the Tsarist regime.

çarliston (*mus.*) Charleston dance; (*sl.*) dandy. ~ **marka**, (*sl.*) unique; rare.

çarmıh (*leg.*) Cross (of execution). ~**a germek,** crucify.

çarmı'kᵍ¹ (*naut.*) Shroud.

çarnaçar Willy-nilly.

çarpan (*math.*) Multiplier; factor.

çarpanbalığıⁿ¹ (*ich.*) Greater weever.

çarpı¹ (*math.*) Multiplication sign (×); 'times'.

çarpı² Whitewash.

çarpı³ (*eng.*) Impact; shock. ~ **deneyi,** impact test: ~ **direnci,** impact resistance. ~**cı,** striking: ~ **söz(ler),** (*pub.*) slogan.

çarpık Crooked, awry, askew; bent; warped; slanting; deviating; (*med.*) struck with madness/paralysis. ~ **bacaklı,** bandy-legged: ~ **çurpuk,** crooked; deformed; deviating in all directions. ~**lık,** crookedness, etc.

çarpıl·an (*math.*) Multiplicand. ~**ım,** (*med.*) shock. ~**ış/**~**ma,** *vn.* being multiplied; becoming crooked, etc. ~**mak,** *vp.* be multiplied; become crooked/warped, etc.; be offended; become mad/paralysed; (**-e**), be punished with . . ..

çarpım (*math.*) Product. ~ **tablosu,** multiplication table.

çarpın·'çᶜ¹ Sensation. ~**çlı,** sensational. ~**ık,** (*psy.*) disturbed, agitated. ~**ma,** *vn.* struggle, (*psy.*) agitation. ~**mak,** *vi.* struggle; wave one's limbs about; get flustered. ~**tı,** shock; (*med.*) palpitation(s).

çarpış·ılmak *imp. v.* Collision/conflict occur. ~**ma,** *vn.* bump; collision; conflict; clash; (*mil.*) action, engagement; (*sp.*) contest: ~ **kapı,** swing door: ~**ya girişmek,** (*mil.*) go into action. ~**mak (-le),** strike one another; bump; come into collision, collide; (*mil.*) fight with; do battle; engage; (*sp.*) contend. ~**tırmak (-i),** *vc.*; click (heels).

çarpıt·ma *vn.* (*psy.*) Distortion. ~**mak (-i),** *vc.* make crooked, awry, etc.; contort; distort.

çarp·ma *vn.* Blow; stroke; impact; (*aer.*) buffeting; (*math.*) multiplication; (*arch.*) rough-cast; five-pointed fishing-hook: *a.* beaten; (*min.*) embossed: ~ **deney//direnci,** (*eng.*) impact test//resistance: ~ **inişi,** (*aer.*) crash-landing: ~ **kapı,** swing-door: ~ **tamponu,** (*rly.*) buffer. ~**mak (-i, -e),** *vt.* strike; knock; carry off, burgle; hold up (to rob); pick s.o.'s pocket; (*math.*) multiply; (*med.*) make ill, strike mad; make angry: *vi.* bump, buffet; come into collision; (heart) palpitate; (wine) go to the head: **çarpa çarpa dolaşmak,** blunder about. ~**tırmak, (-i, -e, -le),** *vc.* cause to collide, etc.; allow to pillage; have one's pocket picked.

çarşaf (*dom.*) Sheet; (*mod.*) dress with veil (once worn by Tk. women in public). ~ **gibi,** smooth, calm (sea, etc.): ~ **kadar,** unnecessarily big/wide: ~**a girmek,** (*obs.*) (girl) begin to wear the ÇARŞAF.

çarşaf·lamak (-i) Cover YORGAN with a sheet. ~**lanmak,** *vp.* be covered with a sheet; wear the ÇARŞAF; (*sl.*) get into difficulties.

çarşamba Wednesday. ~**dır** ~ **demek,** insist that one is right: ~ **karısı gibi,** very untidy woman, a 'regular fright'; witch, hag: ~ **pazarı gibi,** very untidy place.

çarşı Market(-hall); bazaar; street with shops. ~ **arşını,** (*obs.*) a measure (0.68 m.): ~ **ağası,** (*his.*)

market controller: ~ **esnafı,** tradesmen: ~ **pazar,** shopping district/precinct: ~ **pazar dolaşmak/gezmek,** wander through the markets: ~**ya çıkarmak,** display for sale: ~**ya çıkmak,** go shopping. ~**lı,** tradesman.

çarter (*fin.*) Charter. ~ **sözleşmesi,** charter-party. **-çasına** *adv. suf.* [195] = -CESINE.

çaşı'tᵈ¹ Spy. ~**lamak (-i),** spy. ~**lık,** spying.

çat¹ (*ech.*) (*Sudden noise*). ~ **diye,** all of a sudden: ~ **etm.,** make a sudden noise: ~ **kapı,** a sudden knocking; suddenly, unexpectedly: ~ **orada** ~ **burada** ~ **kapı arkasında,** here there and everywhere: ~ **pat,** now and then; rarely; somewhat: ~ **Fransızca konuşmak,** have a smattering of French: ~ **konuşmak,** (child) be able to talk a little.

çat¹² Confluence (of rivers); junction (of roads). ~**a'k**ᵍ¹, *n.* point of intersection, junction; impenetrable thicket; defile: *a.* involved; twin (fruit, nuts); quarrelsome.

çatal *n.* Fork, branch, prong; (*agr.*) winnowing fork; (*bio.*) crotch; (*fig.*) dilemma. *a.* Forked; bifurcated; two-sided; (*ling.*) with a double meaning; ambiguous; difficult/delicate (matter); hoarse (voice). ~ **ateşi,** (*mil.*) cross-fire: ~ **bıçak takımı/bıçaklık,** cutlery: ~ **çekiç,** claw-hammer: ~ **çutal,** confused, all mixed up: ~ **dal,** crotch: ~ **görmek,** see double, not see clearly: ~ **iş,** a vexed question: ~ **kavşak,** (*mot.*) fork (junction): ~ **matal kaç** ~, (*child.*) a guessing game: ~ **ses,** vibrating sound: ~ **tırnak(lı),** cloven hoof(ed).

çatal·ağız (*geo.*) Delta. ~**kurt,** (*zoo.*) gapeworm. ~**kuyruk,** (*ent.*) puss-moth. ~**lanım,** (*bio.*) bifurcation. ~**lanmak,** *vi.* bifurcate. ~**laşma,** (*bio.*) dichotomy. ~**laşmak,** *vi.* (voice) crack; (*bio.*) divaricate; become ambiguous/complicated. ~**laştırmak (-i),** *vc.* ~**lı,** (*bio.*) bifid.

çatana (*naut.*) Small steamboat; pinnace.

çatapat Firework cracker.

çatı Framework; structure, skeleton; (*arch.*) roof; (*ling.*) extended verb stem, 'voice'. ~ **altı/arası/katı,** (*arch.*) attic: ~ **ekleri,** (*ling.*) verb-stem suffixes: ~ **kemiği,** (*bio.*) pubic bone: ~ **makası,** (*arch.*) roof truss: ~ **penceresi,** (*arch.*) dormer-window: ~**yı almak,** reach the roof.

çatık Touching; fitted together; intimate. ~ **kaşlı,** with eyebrows that touch; frowning, beetle-browed: ~ **yüzlü,** sulky, scowling. ~**laşmak,** *vi.* come close together.

çatılı With a roof, roofed; with a head bandage.

çatılmak *vp.* = ÇATMAK.

çatır (*ech.*) ~ ~**/çutur,** (*crackling/clashing noise*); willy-nilly; by force; without any effort: ~ ~ **çatlamak,** crack extensively: ~ ~ **etm.,** make a crackling noise: ~ ~ **sökmek,** pull out by force. ~**damak,** *vi.* make a chattering/clattering/crackling/crashing noise. ~**tı,** clattering/chattering/crackling noise.

çatış·ık Opposing, contradictory. ~**ılmak,** *imp. v.* opposition exist. ~**kı,** (*phil.*) contradiction, antinomy, paradox. ~**kılı,** contradictory. ~**ma,** *vn.* (*mil.*) first clash with the enemy; conflict; dispute, disagreement. ~**mak (-le),** *vi.* bump into one another, collide; (joints) fit into one another; (*zoo.*) mate; (ideas, interests) be in conflict, clash. ~ **tırmak (-i, -le)**, *vc.*

çatkı Bandage round the head; pile (of rifles); tripod; assembly, construction; (*eng.*) chassis, frame, carcass. ~ **bezi**, (*tex.*) canvas. ~ **cı**, (*eng.*) assembler. ~ **lık**, pole linking the yokes of two oxen.

çatkın Favourite, protégé; frowning; creased. ~ **lık**, intimacy; sulkiness.

çatla¹k^{ğı} *n.* Crevice, crack, fissure; crazed (pottery); cleft; chink; (*naut.*) breakers, surf. *a.* Split; cracked; chapped (skin); hoarse (voice); (*geol.*) diaclase; (*fig.*) 'cracked', crazy. ~ **izi**, (*min.*) crack pattern: ~ **kafalı**, 'crackers', crack-brained: ~ **ses**, rough/ harsh sound: ~ **zurna**, (*fig.*) garrulous person. ~ **lık**, cracking; (*fig.*) craziness.

çatla·ma *vn.* (*min.*) Cracking; (*bot.*) dehiscence; (*for.*) peeling off (bark, etc.); (*naut.*) breaking (of waves). ~ **mak**, *vi.* crack, split; (pottery) craze; (waves) break; (animal) die of exhaustion; (*bot.*) dehisce; (*fig.*) burst (with rage, etc.); weep/groan bitterly: **çatladın mı?**, (*vulg.*) aren't you terribly impatient!: **çatlasa da (patlasa da)**, however much he tries . . ., at the very most . . .. ~ **latmak (-i)**, *vc.* split, cleave, crack; make one's head ache; make s.o. nearly burst with rage; ride a horse to death; declare pompously/pedantically; (*sl.*) lose one's wits.

çat·ma *vn.* Assembly; construction, framework; parts temporarily put together (for (*eng.*) testing//(*mod.*) fitting); (*tex.*) thick silk upholstery material; (*naut.*) collision: *a.* assembled, put together, loosely sewn together: ~ **daire//kolu**, (*ind.*) assembly-room//-line: ~ **kaş** = ÇATIK KAŞ. ~ **mak (-i)**, assemble, fit together; build, construct; set up; pile (arms); load (an animal); (*tex.*) tack, sew coarsely: **(-e)**, bump up against, collide with; come up against (a difficulty); meet; have a lucky encounter (with s.o. influential/helpful); seek a quarrel with s.o.: *vi.* (time for stg. unwelcome) come round; become aggressive: **çattık!**, (*col.*) we're up against it!

çatra ~ **patra**, with a clatter: ~ **patra söylemek**, speak (a language) incorrectly/with difficulty.

çattırmak (-i, -e), *vc.* = ÇATMAK.

çatur ~ **çutur** (*ech.*) = ÇATIR.

çav¹ (*dial.*) Sound; fame; news.

çav² (*dial., zoo.*) Genitals of male horse/ donkey.

çav·alye/-ela Fisherman's basket, creel.

çavdar (*bot.*) Rye. ~ **sürmesi**, (*myc.*) rye bunt. ~ **mahmuzu**^{nu}, (*myc., med.*) ergot of rye: ~ **hastalığı**, (*med.*) ergotism.

çavlan (*geo.*) Waterfall. ~ **mak**, *vi.* (*obs.*) be noised abroad; become well-known.

çavlı (*orn.*) Untrained young falcon.

çavmak (-e) Deviate, go astray; spread out; = ÇAĞMAK.

çavşir (*bot.*) Opopanax; (*med.*) its resin.

çavun Raw-hide whip.

çavuş (*his.*) Messenger; (*mil.*) sergeant, = ASSUBAY; (*adm.*) doorkeeper, uniformed attendant (of ambassador/consul). ~ **dişlileri**, (*eng.*) gear-wheels.

çavuş·kuşu^{nu} (*orn.*) Hoopoe. ~ **kuşugiller**, (*orn.*) Upupidae. ~ **luk**, (*mil.*) rank/duties of a sergeant. ~ **üzümü**^{nü}, large sweet white grape.

çay¹ (*geo.*) Stream, creek, brook; tributary of a river. ~ **kenarında kuyu kazmak**, take unnecessary trouble: ~ **taşı**, pebble: ~ **üzümü**, (*bot.*) bilberry: ~ **dan geçip derede boğulmak**, after great success be beaten by little things: ~ **ı görmeden paçaları sıvama!**, don't count your chickens before they are hatched!; there's many a slip 'twixt the cup and the lip!

çay² (*bot.*) Tea-bush; its leaves; (*cul.*) tea (the drink); tea (the meal). ~ **arabası**, (*dom.*) tea-trolley: ~ **bahçesi**, tea-garden: ~ **demlemek**, steep/ brew the tea: ~ **vermek**, offer tea and cakes, etc.; give a tea-party.

çay·cı Tea-grower; waiter in a tea-shop; tea-addict. ~ **cılık**, growing//making/selling tea. ~ **danlık**, teapot. ~ **evi**^{ni}/~**hane**, tea-house, tea-room; tea-shop. ~ **giller**, (*bot.*) Theaceae.

çayır (*agr.*) Meadow, pasture; prairie; common/ (-land). ~ + , *a.* Field-, wild; (*sp.*) grass: ~ **(otu)**, (*bot.*) meadow-grass: ~ **adaçayı**, (*bot.*) meadow clary: ~ **atkuyruğu**, (*bot.*) shady horsetail: ~ **balabanı**, (*orn.*) stone-curlew: ~ **biçmek**, mow the hay: ~ **doğanı**, (*orn.*) Montagu's harrier: ~ **engereği**, (*zoo.*) field adder: ~ **incir kuşu**, (*orn.*) meadow pipit: ~ **kenesi**, (*ent.*) hard tick: ~ **kertenkelesi**, (*zoo.*) praticole lizard: ~ **köpeği**, (*zoo.*) prairie dog: ~ **kurbağası**, (*zoo.*) common frog: ~ **nergisi**, (*bot.*) daffodil, trumpet narcissus: ~ **taş kuşu**, (*orn.*) whinchat: ~ **tavuğu**, (*orn.*) prairie chicken: ~ **a çıkarmak/salmak (-i)**, (*live.*) put out to grass.

çayır·güzeli^{ni} (*bot.*) Bent(-grass). ~ **kuşu**^{nu}, (*orn.*) lark. ~ **lamak**, *vi.* graze; (animal) be ill from grazing. ~ **lanmak**, *vi.* graze. ~ **laşmak**, *vi.* (land) become pasture. ~ **latmak (-i)**, *vc.* pasture, put out to grass. ~ **lık**, pasture, meadowland. ~ **mantarı**^{nı}, (*myc.*) common/field mushroom. ~ **melikesi**^{ni}, (*bot.*) common meadowsweet. ~ **otu**^{nu}, (*bot.*) timothy grass. ~ **peyniri**^{ni}, (*cul.*) a cream cheese. ~ **sedefi**^{ni}, (*bot.*) meadow-rue. ~ **teresi**^{ni}, (*bot.*) lady's smock. ~ **tirfili**^{ni}, (*bot.*) red clover. ~ **yulafı**^{nı}, (*bot.*) common wild oat.

çayla¹k^{ğı} (*orn.*) Black kite; (*fig.*) s.o. avaricious/ grasping; (*sl.*) clumsy novice. ~ **fırtınası**, early winter storm. ~ **giller**, (*orn.*) kites.

çaylık *n.* (*agr.*) Tea-garden. *a.* Used for tea.

ÇB = ÇALIŞMA BAKANLIĞI.

-çe *suf.* [194] = -CE² [TÜRKÇE].

çe¹ç^{ci} (*agr.*) Heap of winnowed grain.

çeçe (*ent.*) ~ **(sineği)**, tsetse fly.

Çeçen (*ethn.*) Tchetchen tribe (in NE Caucasus); (*fig.*) s.o. talkative: ~ **Kazağı**, Don Cossack. ~ **ce**, (*ling.*) Tchetchen language.

çedi¹k^{ği} (*obs.*) Yellow shoe (worn over MEST¹).

çehiz = ÇEYİZ.

çehre Face; countenance; appearance; sour face. ~ **eğmek**, show disapproval: ~ **etm./~si atmak**, make a wry face; sulk: ~ **züğürdü**, ugly: ~**yi ekşilemek**, frown, look cross. ~**sel**, facial.

çeki 1 *n.* (*fin.*) Cheque. ~ **defter/karnesi**, cheque-book: ~**i bozmak**, cash a cheque.

Çeki 2 *n.* (*ethn.*) Czech. ~ +, *a.* Czech. ~**çe**, (*ling.*) Czech language.

ÇEK = ÇOCUK ESİRGEME KURUMU.

çekap (*med.*) Check-up.

çekçeᴵkği Small four-wheeled handcart.

çeke (*ling.*) Comma.

çekeceᴵkği Shoehorn.

çekeᴵkği (*naut.*) Slipway, hard (for beaching boats).

çekel (*dial.*, *agr.*) Small hoe; point of a goad.

çekelemek (-i) Pull repeatedly.

çekelez (*dial.*, *zoo.*) Small squirrel.

çekem (*bot.*) Mistletoe.

çekeme·mek (-i) Be unable to pull, etc.; be unable to tolerate; envy. ~**mezlik**, intolerance; envy.

çeker Weighing capacity; (*mot.*) tractor; (*cin.*) lens. ~**lik**, (*psy.*) affinity.

çeki A measure of weight (about 250 kgs.) (for wood, etc.); horse-load (of firewood). ~ **taşı**, counterweight for weighing one ÇEKİ: ~ **taşı gibi**, very heavy, ponderous; immovable: ~**ye gelmek**, be adaptable: ~**ye gelmez**, very heavy; unbearable, intolerable; unseemly.

çekici *n.* S.o. who draws/pulls; tractor. *a.* Attractive, eye-catching, alluring, appealing. ~ **kancası**, towing hook: ~ **kas**, (*bio.*) contractor: ~ **kılmak**, find attractive: ~ **tablası**, (*mot.*) trailer mounting: ~ **vasıtası**, (*mot.*) tractor. ~**lik**, attractiveness; (*phys.*) attraction, pull.

çekiᴵçci Hammer. ~ **atma**, (*sp.*) throwing the hammer: ~ **balığı(giller)**, (*ich.*) hammerhead shark(s).

çekiç·başlı (*zoo.*) Hammerhead(ed). ~**hane**, (*ind.*) steam-hammer mill. ~**kemiği**ni, (*bio.*) hammer/malleus (of the ear). ~**lemek (-i)**, hammer.

çekidüzen Orderliness, tidiness; toilet. ~ **vermek**, put in order; tidy up.

çekik Elongated; slanting; almond-eyed. ~ **çene**, receding chin: ~ **durum**, (*geo.*) low water.

çekil·gen (*bio.*) Recessive. ~**gi**, seclusion. ~**gin**, recluse. ~**ir**, trailing; endurable, tolerable; (*min.*) ductile. ~**iş**, draw (for a lottery). ~**me**, *vn.* withdrawal; retirement; self-effacement; recession; contraction, shrinkage; abandonment; (*geo.*) low water. ~**mek (-e, -den)**, *vp.* = ÇEKMEK: be pulled, etc.; *vi.* withdraw, retire, abdicate; absent o.s., abandon; draw back; shrink, contract; (water) recede; dry up; (*naut.*) stand clear: **çekil oradan!**, clear out of there!: **çekildiğini bildirmek**, give in one's notice: **çekilip dayanmak**, shut o.s. up in a fortress. ~**mez**, unendurable, intolerable. ~**miş**, drawn (sword): ~ **kahve**, ground coffee.

çekim Act of pulling; quantity pulled; strength; ratio; (*phys.*, *ast.*) attraction, pull; gravity; (*cin.*) shot, take; shooting, filming; (*ling.*) conjugation, declination; (*sl.*) pinch of heroin. ~ **açısı**, (*cin.*) shooting angle: ~ **eki**, (*ling.*) ending, inflection, termination: ~ **etkisi**, (*phys.*) gravitation: ~**ler bahsi**, (*ling.*) accidence.

çekim·ci Copyist; (*cin.*) cameraman. ~**leme**, *vn.*

(*ling.*) conjugating, declining; (*phys.*) attracting. ~**lemek (-i)**, (*ling.*) conjugate, decline; (*phys.*) attract. ~**li**, graceful, attractive: ~ **eylem**, (*ling.*) finite verb. ~**ölçer**, (*phys.*) attractionometer. ~**sel** (*phys.*) gravitational. ~**se(n)me**, *vn.* abstention. ~**se(n)mek (-den)**, withdraw from; abstain from. ~**ser**, abstainer: ~ **oy/~lik**, abstention. ~**siz** unattractive, ugly; (*ling.*) indeclinable; (*phys.*) weightless. ~**sizlik**, unattractiveness; (*phys.*) weightlessness.

çekin (*phys.*) Nucleus. ~ +, *a.* Nuclear: ~ **kopması** nuclear fission. ~**cik**, nucleon. ~**sel**, nuclear.

çekin·ce Danger; reserve; warning. ~**celi** dangerous; critical. ~ **ecek**, which is to be avoided, guarded against. ~**gen**, timid; cautious; bashful coy; shy, diffident, reserved, retiring; backward: ~ **davranmak**, behave timidly, etc. ~**genlik**, timidity shyness; diffidence, etc.: ~**i bırakmak**, be brave dare. ~**ik**, (*bio.*) recessive. ~**mek (-den)**, beware be wary of, take precautions; draw back; stand aloof; recoil (through fear/dislike); refrain from abstain; hesitate: **(-i)**, apply stg.: **çekinmeden** without restraint. ~**memek (-den)**, make no bones about stg. ~**mez**, fearless; unscrupulous. ~**ti**, hesitation.

çekir·deciᴵkği (*bio.*) Nucleolus. ~**de**ᴵkği, *n.* (*bot.*) pip, seed, stone, (coffee) bean; (*bio.*, *phys.*) nucleus (*chem.*, *el.*, *eng.*, *geol.*) core; (weight) grain (0.05 gr.): ~ +, *a.* nuclear: ~ **dizilme**, (*bio.*) karyo-typing: ~ **ekşiti**, (*chem.*) nucleic acid: ~ **fiziği** nuclear physics: ~ **içi**, (*bot.*) kernel: ~ **kahve**, coffee beans: ~ **özsuyu**, (*bio.*) karyolymph: ~ **plazması**, (*bio.*) nucleoplasm: ~ **tıbbı**, nuclear medicine: ~ **zarı**, (*bio.*) nuclear membrane: ~**ten** yetişmek, be accustomed/trained to stg. from childhood. ~**deklenme**, (*phys.*) nucleation. ~**deklenmek**, *vi.* form a pip/core/nucleus, etc. ~**dekli**, with/having a pip/core/nucleus. etc. ~**deksel**, (*phys.*) nuclear. ~**deksiz**, (*bot.*) seedless (raisins).

çekirge (*ent.*) Grasshopper, cricket; locust. ~ **ötleğeni**, (*orn.*) grasshopper warbler. ~**giller**, (*ent.*) Acrididae. ~**kuşu**nu, (*orn.*) common starling.

çekiş *vn.* = ÇEKMEK. (*aer.*) Thrust; (*eng.*) traction; draft. ~**im**, *vn.* mutual attraction. ~**me**, *vn.* bickering, quarrelling; contention, dissension; (*sp.*) tug-of-war: ~ **halatı**, (*sp.*) tug-of-war rope: ~ **konusu**, bone of contention. ~**mek (-le)**, pull one another about; struggle; scramble for stg.; bicker, quarrel, contend; litigate: **çekişe çekişe pazarlık etm.**, make a bargain after long haggling. ~**meli**, leading to quarrels, etc.; arguable; hard, difficult; (*leg.*) disputed. ~**tirici**, slanderous; critical. ~**tirme**, *vn.* ~**tirmek (-i)**, slander; criticise; reproach; curse.

çekiᴵtdi (*rly.*) Locomotive.

çekkin Withdrawn; **(-den)**, indifferent to; unconnected with.

çekme *vn.* = ÇEKMEK. Act of drawing, etc.; (*phys.*) pull, tension, traction; hauling, towing; sliding; (*dom.*) drawer; till; (*mod.*) overalls; (*carp.*) shrinkage; (*agr.*) tree-lopping shears. *a.* Tensile; smooth, shapely. ~ **akım**, (*el.*) derived current: ~

direnci, (*phys.*) tensile strength: ~ **demir**, (*min.*) wrought iron: ~ **deneyi**, (*min.*) tensile test: ~ **donatımı**, (*eng.*) hauling gear: ~ **gücü**, (*phys.*) tractive power: ~KAT: ~ **kolu**, (*eng.*) drag link. ~**ce**, (*dom.*) drawer; jewel-box; (*naut.*) inlet (for shelter). ~**celi**, ~ **dolap**, (*dom.*) chest-of-drawers.

ekmek (**-i**) Pull, draw, transport; attract; allure; pull on (clothes); hoist; tow; withdraw; draw/trace (a line); undergo, suffer, bear, endure, support; cause to support; (*ling.*) decline, conjugate; inhale; absorb; (*sl.*) drink; make a copy of; (*zoo.*) mate: *vi.* contract, shrink; weigh; last/take (time): (**-e**), resemble. **çek!**, go on! (to a driver): **çek arabanı!**, (*sl.*) clear out!: **çekeceği olm.**, be faced with piles of work; (**-le**), have one's work cut out with: **çekip almak**, tear away: **çekip çekiştirmek**, gossip maliciously about s.o.: **çekip çevirmek**, run (a house, etc.); know how to treat s.o.: **çekip çıkarmak**, pluck out, eradicate: **çekip gitmek**, slip away, disappear: **çekip kaldırmak**, draw up: **çekip uzatma**, prolixity: **çekiver kuyruğunu!**, (*sl.*) don't expect any good from him!: **çektiği su**, (*naut.*) draught: **çektiklerimi ben bilirim!**, you can't imagine what I suffered!

ek·mekat[1] (*arch.*) Penthouse flat. ~**meli**, ~ **anahtar**, (*el.*) pull-switch: ~ **basmalı anahtar**, (*el.*) push-pull switch. ~**men**, (*bio.*) sucker. ~**mez**, unable to bear; (*tex.*) shrink-resistant.

Çekoslovak·(yalı) (*ethn.*) Czechoslovak. ~**ya**, (*geo.*) Czechoslovakia.

ektir·i (*his.*) War-galley (sails and oars). ~**im**, (*leg.*) execution of sentence. ~ **me**, *vn.*; (*naut.*) large boat with sails and oars; (*his.*) = ~**i**: ~ **somunu**, (*eng.*) draw-nut. ~**mek** (**-i, -e**), *vc.* = ÇEKMEK; cause to draw, etc.; let s.o. withdraw.

ekül (*arch.*, *eng.*) Plumb-line, bob.

elebi *n.* (*obs.*) (Title of) royal prince/dervish saint; educated man, gentleman. *a.* Well-mannered, courteous. ~**lik**, being courteous; courteous behaviour.

elen·lçci (*sp.*) Challenge-cup (match).

elen·lkgi Wreath; garland, crown; plume; (*obs.*) bejewelled aigrette. ~ **koymak**, lay a wreath (on grave/monument).

elgi (*mod.*) Head-scarf (tied under the chin).

eli·lkgi 1 (*min.*) *n.*, *a.* Steel. ~ **başlık**, steel helmet: ~ **ciğer**, (*med.*) iron lung: ~ **gibi**, thin but strong: ~ **halat**, (*naut.*) cable: ~ **kalem**, chisel: ~ **kasa**, safe-deposit box: ~ **macunu**, priming: ~ **mavisi**, electric blue: ~ **metre**, (roll-up) metal rule(r).

eli·lkgi 2 *n.* Short cut branch; (*agr.*) cutting (for planting); (*child.*) tipcat; (*naut.*) belaying-pin, marlin-spike. *a.* Clipped; bevelled.

elik·baş ~ **alabalık**, (*ich.*) rainbow trout. ~**çoma·lk**gı, (*child.*) game of tipcat. ~**hane**, (*ind.*) steel foundry. ~**leme**, *vn.* (*agr.*) growth from cuttings. ~**lemek**, *vi.* (*agr.*) grow from cuttings. ~**leşmek**, *vi.* (*min.*) become (like) steel. ~**pamu·lk**gu/**yün**ü, (*eng.*) steel-wool.

elim Form, shape, body. ~**li**, well-built/-made. ~**siz**, misshapen; uncouth; scraggy; infirm, frail. ~**sizlik**, uncouthness; frailty.

eliş·ik (*phil.*) Contradictory; ambivalent: ~ **duygu**, ambivalence. ~**iklik**, contradiction. ~**ken**, opposed, contrasting. ~**ki**, contradiction, contrast, discrepancy. ~**kili**, contradictory. ~**me**, *vn.* (apparent) contradiction: ~ **ilkesi**, principle of contradiction. ~**mek** (**-le**), *vi.* be in contradiction with. ~**meli**, opposite. ~ **mezlik**, (*phil.*) lack of contradiction.

çello (*mus.*) Cello.

çel·me *vn.* Trip (with the foot): ~ **atmak/takmak**, trip up; (*fig.*) hinder developments. ~**mek** (**-i**), strike lightly; clip, lop; (*sp.*) trip; divert the mind; persuade; dissuade; confute/rebut (a statement). ~**melemek** (**-i**), trip with the foot. ~ **melenmek**, *vp.* be tripped.

çelmi·lkgi (*dial.*) Thick straw.

çelti·lkgi (*bot.*) Unhusked rice. ~ **kargası**, (*orn.*) glossy ibis: ~ **tarlası**, (*agr.*) rice-/paddy-field. ~**çi**, rice-grower. ~**çilik**, rice-growing.

çember *n.* (*math.*) Circle; circumference; hoop; (wooden/metal) ring; fillet; large kerchief; (*fig.*) vault of heaven; (*sp.*) basket-ring. *a.* Rounded; circular; cyclo-. ~ **içine almak**, (*mil.*) encircle: ~ **kayık**, (*naut.*) round-sterned boat: ~ **sakal**, rounded beard.

çember·imsi Circular. ~**lemek** (**-i**), fit with hoops; encircle. ~**lenmek**, *vp.* ~**li**, fitted with hoops. ~**sel**, circular. ~**si**, ~ **akım**, (*el.*) convection current.

çemen (*bot.*) Cummin; (*cul.*) cummin seed; (*cul.*) spiced coating on PASTIRMA. ~**lemek** (**-i**), sprinkle with cummin seed.

çemkirmek (**-e**) *vi.* Reply rudely.

çemre·(le)mek (**-i**) Tuck up (clothes); roll up (sleeves, etc.). ~**nmek**, *vi.* roll up one's own sleeves, etc.; (*fig.*) prepare for action.

çene (*bio.*) Jaw(-bone); maxilla; chin; (*eng.*) jaw (vice); (*naut.*) end of ship's keel; (*fig.*) loquacity. ~ **çalmak**, chatter; talk nineteen to the dozen: ~ **çukuru**, dimple on chin: ~ **kavafı**, chatterbox: ~ **kayışı**, (*mod.*) chinstrap: ~ **yarışı**, prolonged argument: ~ **yarıştırmak**, enter on a prolonged argument: ~ **yormak**, talk in vain, waste one's breath: ~**n tutulsun!**, curse your evil tongue!: ~**si açılmak**, talk endlessly: ~**si atmak**, jaws fall open; die: ~**si düşük**, talkative; chatterbox: ~**si kitlenmek**, be silent, say nothing: ~**si kuvvetli**, s.o. who never tires of talking: ~**si oynamak**, find stg. to eat: ~**sini açtırmak** (**-in**), (unwillingly) give s.o. the chance to speak: ~**sini bağlamak**, bind up a dead person's jaws; (*fig.*) desire s.o.'s death: ~**sini bıçak açmamak**, be tongue-tied from grief: ~**sini dağıtmak**, strike s.o. hard on the jaw: ~**sini tutmak**, hold one's tongue, keep silent; shut up like a clam: ~ **ye kuvvet**, by force of words, by dint of talking.

çene·altını The underside of the chin; dewlap. ~**ayağı**nı, (*zoo.*) maxillipede. ~**baz**, talkative, garrulous. ~**bazlık**, talkativeness. ~ **lk**gi, (*bot.*) cotyledon; (*zoo.*) mandible. ~**kemiği**ni, jawbone. ~**kirpikli**, (*zoo.*) spirotrich. ~**l**, (*bio.*) maxillary. ~**li**, talkative; (*bio.*) -gnathous. ~**siz**, (*bio.*) agnathous. ~**lt**di, (*bot.*) valve. ~**ucu**nu, (*bio.*) point of the chin.

çenge (*mus.*) Song welcoming the bride.

çengel *n.* Hook; claw; (*sp.*) tripping up. *a.* Hooked;

crooked. ∼ **imi**, (*pub.*) paragraph sign (¶): ∼ **takmak**, get one's claws into: ∼ **tavuğu** = CENGEL.

çengel·lemek (-i) Hook; hang on a hook. ∼ **lenmek**, *vp.* be hooked. ∼ **li**, hooked. ∼ **liiğne**, safety-pin. ∼ **sakızı**[m], chewing-gum.

çengi Public dancing-girl. ∼ **kolu**, troop of dancing-girls. ∼ **lik**, public dancing.

çenilemek *vi.* Howl (like a dog in pain).

çen[l]**k**[gi] (*mus.*) Type of harp. ∼ **gü çegane**, musical entertainment.

çenti[l]**k**[gi] *n.* Notch; dent; defect. *a.* Notched. ∼ **açma**, notching: ∼ **vadi**, (*geo.*) V-shaped valley.

çent·iklemek (-i) Notch. ∼ **iklenmek**, *vp.* ∼ **ikli**, notched: ∼ **somun**, (*eng.*) castle-nut. ∼ **ilmek**, *vp.* ∼ **mek (-i)**, notch, nick, chip, dent; (*cul.*) chop up (vegetables).

çep(e)çevre All around, entirely surrounding.

çepel *a.* Foul (weather); gloomy, dull; muddy; mixed, adulterated. *n.* Storm (wind, rain, etc.); muddy season; mud, dirt; (*eng.*) foreign body.

çepel·lenmek *vi.* Become foul/dirty, etc. ∼ **li**, foul, dirty; adulterated. ∼ **lilik**, dirtiness; adulteration.

çeper Wall, fence, vine-pole; (*bio.*) diaphragm, wall; (*fig.*) immoral, base. ∼ **kemiği**, (*bio.*) parietal bone.

çepi[l]**ç**[ci] (*live.*) Yearling goat.

çepin (*agr.*) Trowel.

çepken = CEPKEN.

çer ∼ **den çöpten**, flimsy.

çerçeve (*art.*) Frame; (*arch.*) frame; (*mot.*) chassis; (*th.*) architrave; (*sp.*) climbing-frame; (*fig.*) limits, confines. ∼ **anteni**, (*rad.*) loop aerial: ∼ **sine sığmaz (-in)**, not in accordance with.

çerçeve·ci Frame-maker; picture-framer. ∼ **leme**, (*cin.*) framing. ∼ **lemek (-i)**, frame. ∼ **lenmek**, *vp.* ∼ **li**, framed.

çerçi Pedlar, hawker; (*dial.*) draper. ∼ **lik**, peddling.

çerçöp[ü] Brushwood; kindling.

çerez (*cul.*) Appetizer; hors-d'œuvre; dainty; dried/fresh fruit. ∼ **ci(lik)**, (work of) seller of hors-d'œuvres. ∼ **lenmek**, *vi.* partake of hors-d'œuvres; (*fig.*) make some use of; nibble at.

çer·ge/ ∼ **gi** (Gypsy) tent; gypsy. ∼ **başı**, gypsy-leader. ∼ **ci**, stallholder in a market.

çeri (*obs.*) Soldier; military force. ∼ **başı**[yı] = ÇERGE BAŞI.

Çerkez (*ethn.*) Circassian. ∼ **tavuğu**, (*cul.*) chicken with walnuts. ∼ **ce**, (*ling.*) Circassian. ∼ **istan**, (*geo.*) Circassia.

çermi[l]**k**[gi] Thermal springs/waters.

çerviş (*cul.*) Cooking fat; suet; tallow; juicy part of a dish.

-çesine *adv. suf.* [195] = -CESINE.

çeşi[l]**t**[di] Sort, kind, variety; brand; sample; set (of cups, etc.). ∼ ∼, of various sorts: ∼ **düzmek**, buy various kinds of stg.

çeşit·gen (*bio.*) Pleomorphic. ∼ **kenar**, (*math.*) irregular (polygon): ∼ **üçgen**, scalene triangle. ∼ **leme**, *vn.* increased variety; (*mus.*) variation. ∼ **lemek (-i)**, increase the variety, diversify. ∼ **lenmek**, *vp.* ∼ **li**, various; assorted; miscellaneous; composite. ∼ **lilik**, assortment, variety, diversity.

çeşme (Public) fountain. ∼ **ye gitse** ∼ **kuruyacak** s.o. very unlucky.

çeşmibülbül (*art.*) Glassware with coloured decorations.

çeşni (*cul.*) Taste; flavour; morsel (for judging the flavour); (*min.*) assay. ∼ **tutmak**, take a sample of dough: ∼ **sine bakmak**, test the flavour of stg.

çeşni·ci Food-taster; (*min.*) assayer; municipal inspector of standards and samples. ∼ **cibaşı**[nı] chief food-taster; (*min.*) chief assayer; (*fig.*) man who changes wives frequently. ∼ **lenmek**, *vi.* (*cul.*) be properly flavoured. ∼ **li**, tasty; flavoured. ∼ **lik** (*cul.*) spices, flavouring.

çete Band (of brigands, rebels, etc.), gang. ∼ **savaşı** guerilla warfare: ∼ **ye çıkmak**, set out on a marauding raid. ∼ **ci**, brigand, guerilla, chetnik comitadji. ∼ **cilik**, being a brigand; marauding.

çetele (*obs.*) Tally(-stick). ∼ **çekmek/tutmak**, keep a tally, tot up: ∼ **ye dönmek**, (face, etc.) become scratched/scarred.

çeten (*agr.*) Large basket (for straw); sheep-pen.

çetin Hard; difficult; harsh; awkward, perverse obstinate; critical. ∼ **ceviz**, hard nut to crack; (*fig.*) a tough customer.

çetin·leşmek *vi.* Become hard, etc. ∼ **leştirmek (-i)** make hard, etc. ∼ **lik**, hardness; awkwardness toughness, etc.

çetrefil Badly spoken/mispronounced (language esp. Turkish); confused, complicated, difficult to understand. ∼ **leşmek**, *vi.* become confused, etc ∼ **lik**, bad speech; mispronunciation; confusion etc.

çev. = ÇEVİRİ; ÇEVİR(M)EN.

çevgen Stick; (*sp.*) polo(-stick).

çevik Quick, agile, active, adroit; sound. ∼ **leşmek** *vi.* become agile, etc. ∼ **lik**, alacrity, quickness agility; activity.

çevir·ge[l]**ç**[ci] (*el.*) Commutator; (*phys.*) cyclotror turnstile. ∼ **gi**, rotating switch/knob. ∼ **i**, (*lit.* translation. ∼ **ibilim**, art of translation. ∼ **ici(lik)** (work of) translator. ∼ **im**, (*cin.*) filming, shooting (*chem.*) conversion: ∼ **senaryosu**, (*cin.*) shooting script: ∼ **senaryocusu**, continuity man: ∼ **takımı** film unit.

çevir·me *vn.* Turning, rotation, etc.; (*cul.*) meat roasted on a spit/skewer, kebab; kind of thick jam; (*mil.*) turning movement/manœuvre; (*lit.* translation; translated; (*phil.*) inversion. ∼ **mek (-i -e, -le)**, turn, turn round; change *A* into *B*: (*lit.* translate; corral (animals); (*mil.*, *sp.*) corner encircle, surround; direct to a place; send back (*cin.*) film, shoot, take; (*naut.*) bring about; (*mil.* bring to bear on; (*el.*) commutate; (*chem.*, *math.* convert; (*mod.*) turn inside out; trick s.o.: **çevir kazı yanmasın!**, (*jok.*) change the subject. ∼ **men(lik)** (*lit.*) (work of) translator. ∼ **tim**, (*chem.*) con version. ∼ **tmek (-i, -e)**, *vc.*

çevre Circumference; circle, circuit, perimeter ambience; surroundings; environment; (*fig.* connections, interests; (*geo.*) contour; (*eng.*) rim (*mod.*) embroidered handkerchief/hand-towel ∼ **+**, *a.* Ambient, surrounding, environmental ecological: ∼ **çizgisi**, contour: ∼ **mühendislik**// **sağlığı**, environmental engineering//health: ∼ **tiyatrosu**, theatre in the round: ∼ **treni**, suburban train: ∼ **yolu**, bypass, ringroad; (*geo.*) contour: ∼**de**, close by; at hand: ∼**ler**, (*soc.*) circles: ∼**sinde**, *post.* [91] around, in the neighbourhood of: ∼**sinden**, from all around: ∼**sine**, around, to: ∼**sini dolaşmak**, go all round/compass a place: ∼**sini sarmak**, surround.

çevre·açı (*math.*) Inscribed angle. ∼**bilim**, environmental studies, ecology. ∼**bilimci**, environmentalist, ecologist. ∼**bilimsel**, ecological. ∼**cilik**, (*soc.*) environmentalism. ∼**l**, circumscribed; environmental; peripheral. ∼**le¹çᶜⁱ**, (*eng.*) muffle. ∼**lemek (-i)**, surround, encircle, enclose; circumscribe, limit. ∼**lenmek**, *vp.* ∼**m**, (*geo.*) contour; (*bot.*) whorl, verticil; cycle. ∼**n**, (*ast.*) horizon. ∼**sel**, circular, circumferential; peripheral. ∼**teker**, (*bot.*) pericycle.

çevri¹ (*geo.*) Whirlpool; (*met.*) whirlwind.

çevri² (*ling.*) Explaining away; allegorical interpretation. ∼**lemek (-i)**, explain away, interpret allegorically.

çevri·li Surrounded, encircled; turned round/away. ∼**lmek**, *vp.* = ÇEVİRMEK: *vi.* turn o.s. round; reverse. ∼**m**, (*phys.*) cycle; (*eng.*) turbulence. ∼**mli**, capable, efficient, resourceful. ∼**msel**, (*bio.*) periodic; (*chem.*) cyclic. ∼**nme**, ∼ **resmi**, panorama. ∼**nmek**, *vi.* go around. ∼**nti**, (*phys.*) rotation; (*geo.*) whirlpool; (*bot.*) mixture of grains. ∼**ş** = ÇERVİŞ. ∼ **yazı**ʸ¹, (*ling.*) transcription.

çeyiz Bride's trousseau; dowry. ∼ **çemen**, complete trousseau: ∼ **düzmek**, prepare the trousseau/ 'bottom drawer'.

çeyiz·lemek (-i) Provide with a trousseau. ∼**lenmek**, *vp.* ∼**li**, having a trousseau. ∼**lik**, suitable/prepared for a trousseau. ∼**siz**, ∼ **çemensiz**, without a dowry, without means.

çeync ∼ **işi**, (*fin.*) foreign exchange business.

çeyre¹kᵍⁱ Quarter; one fourth; [202] quarter of an hour; (*obs.*) five-piastre piece. ∼ **ses**, (*mus.*) quarter-tone: ∼ **son**, (*sp.*) quarter-final.

çeyrek·çi Itinerant butcher. ∼**lemek (-i)**, cross a baby's limbs and exercise it. ∼**lenmek**, *vp.*

-çı *n. suf.* [59] = -Ci¹ [EMLAKÇI].

çıban (*med.*) Boil, abscess; blain, carbuncle, pustule. ∼ **ağırşağı**, red and swollen part of a boil: ∼ **başı**, head of a boil; (*fig.*) a delicate situation; (*fig.*) source of evil/trouble: ∼ **işlemek**, drain a boil: ∼**ın başını koparmak**, burst the boil; (*fig.*) bring matters to a head. ∼**laşma**, pustulation.

çıda·m Patience. ∼**mak**, *vi.* be patient; (-e) endure.

çıfıt (*pej.*) Jew; mean, stingy. ∼ **çarşısı**, like a jumble-sale; bedlam. ∼**lık**, (*pej.*) Jewishness: ∼ **etm.**, behave like a Jew; engage in sharp practice.

çığ (*geo.*) Avalanche; (*dom.*) partition, screen.

çığa¹ (*ich.*) ∼ (**balığı**), sterlet.

çığa² (*orn.*) Longest and showiest tail feathers. ∼**lanmak**, *vi.* (*zoo.*) horse's tail stand up like a cock's comb.

çığıltı Confused noise of animal cries.

çığ·ırʳ¹ (*geo.*) Track left by an avalanche; path, rut; course; (*fig.*) way, line of action; (*art.*) calligraphic

style. ∼ **açmak**, start a new method, pioneer, break fresh ground, blaze a trail; (-e), open the way to ... ; give an opportunity to: ∼**ından çıkmak**, go off the rails, fall into disorder.

çığırt·ı Shouting. ∼**kan**, (*orn.*) decoy bird; (*fin.*) tout, barker; noisy fellow. ∼**kanlık**, tout's work. ∼**ma**, *vn.* = ∼MAK; (*mus.*) small fife. ∼**macı**, fife-player. ∼**mak (-i, -e)** = ÇAĞIRTMAK.

çığ·lık Cry, clamour, scream: ∼ **atmak/koparmak**, cry out: ∼ ∼**a**, crying and screaming. ∼**lıkçı(lık)**, (profession of) hired mourner. ∼**rış(ma)**, clamour, outcry. ∼**rışmak (-le)**, *vi.* cry out together/against each other.

-çık *dim. suf.* [57] = -CiK [KİTAPÇIK].

çıka·ca¹kᵍ¹ Towel used on leaving the HAMAM; match, equal. ∼**¹çᶜⁱ**, (*arch.*) stair riser. ∼**gelmek**, *vi.* appear suddenly, arrive on the scene, blow in. ∼**lkᵍ¹**, exit, outlet; origin; (*fin.*) market; (*ling.*) mouth cavity. ∼**n**, (*bio.*) ascendant; outgoing.

çıkar *n.* Profit, benefit, advantage; the way out. *a.* Leading to success; leading to another street. ∼ **sağlamak (-den)**, profit from: ∼ **yol bulmak**, find a solution/way out: ∼ **yolu yok**, there's no way out of it: ∼**ı olm. (-de)**, have an axe to grind.

çıkar·an *n.* Publisher. ∼**cı**, s.o. who thinks only of his own advantage. ∼**cıl**, self-seeking. ∼**cılık**, thinking only of one's own advantage, self-interest. ∼**ılmak (-den, -e)**, *vp.* = ∼MAK. ∼**ım**, (*med.*) removal, -ectomy; (*phil.*) inference. ∼**lanmak**, *vi.* ensure one's own interests. ∼**ma**, *vn.* = ∼MAK; withdrawal; removal; dismissal; (*math.*) subtraction; (*min.*) extraction; (*bio.*) elimination; (*mil.*) landing on enemy beaches/territory: ∼ **gemisi**, (*naut.*) landing-craft: ∼ **plaj/sahili**, (*mil.*) landing-beach, beachhead.

çıkarmak (-i, -e, -den) Take out, abstract, extract; (*math.*) deduct, subtract; divest, remove; throw out, withdraw; eliminate; expel; export; extract; take off (clothes), doff (hat); (*mod.*) bring out (a fashion); launch, publish; (*ind.*) raise, produce; (*dom.*) bring out and offer (food, etc.); (*med.*) certify (unfit, etc.); (*sp.*) disqualify; make out, get the sense of; derive, deduce; last/serve (for a period): (-den), vent anger on s.o. **çıkarıp atmak**, (*naut.*) cast off.

çıkar·sama (*phil.*) Deduction, inference. ∼**sever**, self-interested. ∼**severlik**, self-interest. ∼**tı**, waste; (*bio.*) excrement. ∼**tım**, (*med.*) extraction. ∼**tma**, *vn.*; transfer (of a coloured print). ∼**tmabaskı**, (*pub.*) offset. ∼**tmak (-i, -e, -den)**, *vc.* = ∼MAK; cause/let remove, etc.; dismiss. ∼ **yol**, road leading to another; (*fig.*) the right way of doing stg.

çıka·tᵈ¹ Origin, source.

çıkı Small bundle. ∼**lamak (-i)**, make into a bundle. ∼**lanmak**, *vp.*

çıkı·kᵍ¹ Projecting; (*med.*) dislocated (limb); emergent; dislocation. ∼ **diş**, (*bio.*) bucktooth. ∼**çı**, bone-setter; osteopath.

çıkılmak *imp. v.* Go out; go up.

çıkın Stg. (esp. money) wrapped in a cloth; small bundle; hoard of money. ∼**lamak (-i)**, tie up in a bundle.

çıkıntı Projection; protrusion; (*arch.*) projecting

balcony; (*bot.*) emergence; (*bio.*) process(us); (*eng.*) boss; (*mil.*) salient; (*pub.*) marginal note; (*sl.*) cigarette. ~ **lı işaret**, (*pub.*) caret (˅).
çıkış Method of going out/up; exit, outlet; (*ind.*) output; ascent; (*sp.*) start (of a race); (*mil.*) sortie; (*fin.*) disbursements; scolding. ~ **barınağı**, (*naut.*) port of departure: ~ **borusu**, (*mot.*) exhaust manifold/pipe: ~ **deliği**, (*naut.*) escape hatch: ~ **izni**, (*fin.*) export licence: ~ **kapısı**, (*adm.*) exit customs barrier: ~ **noktası**, starting point: ~ **sözü**, (*th.*) exit line: ~ **seskesicisi**, (*mot.*) exhaust silencer: ~ **vergisi**, (*fin.*) export duty: ~ **vizesi**, (*adm.*) exit visa: ~ **yapmak**, scold.
çıkış·çı (*sp.*) Starter. ~ **lı**, (*ed.*) school-leaver; who has completed a course. ~ **ma**, *vn.*; scolding. ~ **mak**, *vi.* enter into competition/rivalry with s.o.; undertake stg. beyond one's power; reach; suffice: **(-e)**, burst out angrily, reproach, scold. ~ **tırmak** **(-i)**, make stg. suffice (for stg.); procure; cause to reach.
çıkı'tᵈ¹ Exit, outlet; source.
çık·ma *vn.* Act of going out/up, etc.; exit; (*geo.*) promontory; (*arch.*) cantilever; balcony, bow-window; invention; (*pub.*) marginal note/word; (*mod.*) loin-cloth worn on emerging from a HAMAM: *a.* newly appeared/invented: ~ **durumu**, (*ling.*) ablative case: ~ **köprü**, cantilever bridge: ~ **takımı**, bath linen. ~ **mak (-den, -e)**, come/go out, leave; issue; appear; come into existence; come to pass, happen; emerge, result; turn out to be; jut out, be prominent; (period) pass, be over; set forth, start; come/go up, ascend, climb, rise; make/suffice for stg.; (rumour) get about; (joint) be dislocated; leave (work), resign from; (*ed.*) pass out from, leave (school, etc.); amount to; fall to the lot of; start on (journey); compete with s.o.: **(-e)**, (*adm.*) be received in audience by s.o.; (*th.*) play the part of s.o.: **çık bakalım!**, (*sl.*) fork out, pay up: **çıkmadık candan ümit kesilmez**, while there's life there's hope. ~ **malı**, *a.* (*ling.*) ablative. ~ **maz**, stg. that does not come out, indelible; blind alley, cul-de-sac, dead-end; dilemma, impasse: ~ **ayın son çarşambasına kadar . . .**, until the cows come home, never: ~ **a gelmek**, be stumped: ~ **a girmek/ sap(lan)mak**, reach a dead-lock.
çıkra (*for.*) Thick brushwood/undergrowth. ~ **lık**, thicket.
çıkrı'kᵏ¹ Winding-wheel (well); (*naut.*) cathead, windlass; pulley; (*eng.*) reel; lathe; mandrel; (*tex.*) spinning-wheel. ~ **çı(lık)**, (work of) maker of pulleys, etc.//lathe operator.
çıktı (*ind.*) Output; expenditure.
-çıl *n. suf.* [66] = -CİL [AKÇIL].
çılan (*bot.*) Large kind of jujube; = ÇİĞDE.
çılbır¹ (*cul.*) Dish made of yoghurt and eggs.
çılbır² (*dial.*) Leading-rein, lunge.
çıldır·asıya Madly; dotingly: ~ ~, with bright staring eyes: ~ ~ **bakmak**, gaze about distractedly: ~ ~ **etm.**, (eyes) flash. ~ **ı**, (*psy.*) psychosis. ~ **mak**, *vi.* go mad; go off one's head: **(için)**, be crazy about/over. ~ **mış**, bereft of his senses. ~ **tmak (-i)**, drive mad/crazy.
çılgın Mad, insane; distraught; raging. ~ **ca(sına)**,

madly, like mad. ~ **laşmak**, *vi.* behave madly/ wildly. ~ **lık**, craziness; (*psy.*) delirium.
çıma (*naut.*) Hawser; cable; fall (of a tackle); rope's end. ~ **dikişi**, short splice: ~ **vermek**, lengthen a rope. ~ **cı(lık)**, (work of) quayside hand. ~ **riva**, ceremonial manning of the yards/decks.
çımkır·ık (*orn.*) Bird's faeces; (*dom.*) watering-can. ~ **mak**, *vi.* (*orn.*) evacuate, soil.
çın True, real. ~ ~, (*ech.*) (tinkling glass, etc.); *int.* cheers!; chin-chin!: ~ ~ **inletmek**, make pleasant noises: ~ ~ **ötmek**, make an empty/ringing sound; be empty/deserted: ~ **sabah**, early in the morning: ~ **tutmak**, state stg. to be true.
çınar (*bot.*) Plane-tree, Oriental plane. ~ **gıller**, plane family, Platanaceae. ~ **ımsı**, ~ **akçaağaç/ isfendan**, sycamore-tree. ~ **lık**, grove of plane-trees.
çıngar (*sl.*) Quarrel; dispute; law-suit. ~ **çıkarmak**, pick a quarrel.
çıngı (*dial.*) Small spark; tiny piece; metal pot.
çıngıl (*bot.*) Small bunch of grapes.
çıngır ~ ~, (*ech.*) tinkle tinkle. ~ **a'kᵏ¹**, small bell; (*mus.*) maraca: ~ **ı çekmek**, (*sl.*) die. ~ **aklı**, wearing a small bell. ~ **aklıyılan**, (*zoo.*) timber rattle-snake. ~ **da'kᵏ¹**, small bell (as child's toy). ~ **damak**, *vi.* give out a ringing sound, tinkle. ~ **tı**, ringing/clinking/tinkling sound.
çın·lak (Place) full of ringing/tinkling/echoing sounds. ~ **lamak**, *vi.* give out a ringing/tinkling sound; have a buzzing/singing in the ears; echo. ~ **larca**, (*med.*) tinnitis. ~ **latmak (-i)**, *vc.*
çıpı ~ ~, (*child.*) washing. ~ **ldak**, naked (baby).
çıplak Naked, bare; stripped; (*fig.*) destitute; empty; bleak, bald. ~ **bırakmak**, denude: ~ **gözle**, with the naked eye: ~ **olarak**, nude, 'in the altogether': ~ **sümüklü**, (*zoo.*) slug: ~ **yarasa**, (*zoo.*) naked bat.
çıplak·laşmak *vi.* Become naked/bare. ~ **laştır-mak/~latmak (-i)**, strip bare; denude. ~ **lık**, nudity, bareness; nudism; bleakness: ~ **ıyla (bütün)**, in all its details, with nothing concealed/ untold. ~ **tohumlular**, (*bot.*) gymnosperms.
çıra (*for.*) Resinous wood; kindling wood; torch.
çırağ Lamp, light, torch; (*fig.*) teacher, guide.
çıra'kᵏ¹ Apprentice; assistant; pupil; (*obs.*) pensioner, retainer; favourite. ~ **çıkmak/edilmek**, be pensioned off: ~ **çıkarmak/etm.**, pension off; support s.o. ~ **lık**, apprenticeship; fee paid by an apprentice; allowance from a patron: ~ **etm.**, work as an apprentice: ~ **sözleşmesi**, apprenticeship contract, articles.
çıra·kma Candlestick. ~ **kman**, beacon (to attract fish by night); lighthouse. ~ **lı**, used for kindling; resinous. ~ **moz**, torch-holder (for night fishing).
çır(ıl)çıplak Stark naked; absolutely destitute. ~ **lık**, nakedness; destitution.
çırçır (*tex.*) Cotton-gin, carding machine; (*geo.*) rivulet, spring; (*ent.*) field-cricket.
çırnı'kᵏ¹ (*naut.*) Fishing/grain boat; (*sl.*) stg. worthless.
çırpı Twig; chip; clipping; (*carp.*) chalk-line. ~ **ipi**, (*carp.*) chalk-line for marking: ~ **vurmak**, (*carp.*) mark straight lines: ~ **dan çıkmak**, get out of line:

~ya getirmek, put into line; make straight. **~cı,** beater; (*cul.*) mixer; (*tex.*) fuller; s.o. who washes printed stuffs in the sea (to fix the colours).

çırp·ılmak *vp.* **~ına¹kᵍ¹,** (*med.*) convulsion; eclampsia. **~ınım,** (*med.*) fibrillation. **~ınma,** *vn.* **~ınmak,** *vi.* flutter; struggle; have convulsions; fuss about; be all in a fluster. **~ıntı,** agitation; palpitation. **~ıntılı,** (*naut.*) choppy (sea). **~ışmak,** *vi.* flutter. **~ıştırılmak,** *vp.* **~ıştırma,** *vn.*; *a.* done hurriedly and carelessly. **~ıştırmak (-i),** strike lightly with a stick; do stg. hurriedly and carelessly; scribble. **~ma,** *vn.* (*aer.*) flapping; (*tex.*) type of hem-stitch. **~mak (-i),** strike lightly and repeatedly, tap, pat; beat (carpet); clap (hands); flutter (wings); (*cul.*) beat, whip; (*tex.*) rinse; bleach; trim the ends; (*fig.*) steal. **~tırmak (-i, -e),** *vc.*

çırt¹ (*agr.*) Leather irrigation bucket (raised and lowered by an animal).

çıt¹ (*ech.*) Crack! **~ ardıcı,** (*orn.*) sedge warbler; **~ çıkarmak/etm.,** make a sound: **~ çıkmamak,** no sound be made: **~ kuşu,** (*orn.*) wren: **~ yok,** there's not a sound to be heard: **~ı çıkmadı,** (*col.*) he did not say a word/express an opinion.

çıta (*carp.*) Border, moulding; long narrow strip of wood; (*sp.*) cross-bar. **~lı geçme,** (*carp.*) tongue and groove joint.

çıta¹kᵍ¹ Foreign(er); speaking (Tk.) with a broken/foreign accent; swashbuckler.

çıtçıt¹ (*mod.*) Press-stud; snap-fastener.

çıtı ~ pıtı, graceful; pretty; dainty.

çıtır ~ ~, (*ech.*) crackling: **~ pıtır konuşmak,** speak pleasantly (like a child). **~damak,** *vi.* crackle; crepitate. **~datmak (-i),** *vc.* **~tı,** slight sound.

çıtkırıldım Fragile; timid; effeminate; snob. **~lık,** fragility; timidity.

çıt·lamak *vi.* (*ech.*) Make a slight crackling sound. **~latılmak,** *vp.* **~latmak (-i),** *vc.*; hint at stg.; break news gently. **~lı, ~ engel,** (*sp.*) hurdle. **~ pıt¹,** percussion cap (exploding when trodden on).

çıv·dırmak (-i) *vc.* **~gar,** additional animal (for ploughing, etc.). **~gın,** (*met.*) sleet. **~lamak,** *vi.* rush off. **~mak,** *vi.* deviate; change direction.

çıyan (*zoo.*) Centipede. **~ gibi,** unpleasant blond person: **~ gözlü,** with cold reptilian eyes. **~cı¹kᵍ¹,** (*zoo.*) little centipede; (*bot.*) bistort. **~lık,** unpleasantness; treachery: **~ etm.,** betray.

çızıktırmak (-i) Scribble; scrawl.

-çi *n. suf.* [59] = -ci¹ [SAATÇİ].

çiçe¹kᵍ¹ (*bot.*) Flower; bloom; flowering plant; (*chem.*) flower; (*med.*) smallpox; (*fig.*) s.o. fickle, tricky. **~ açmak,** produce flowers, bloom; burst into bloom: **~ açmış,** blooming: **~ aşısı,** (*med.*) vaccination: **~ biti,** (*ent.*) aphid; plant-louse: **~ çıkarmak,** (*med.*) catch smallpox: **~ demeti,** bouquet: **~ durumu,** (*bot.*) inflorescence: **~ dürbünü,** (*phys.*) kaleidoscope: **~ düzenleme,** flower arrangement: **~ gibi,** attractively dressed (female): **~ olm.,** (*fig.*) be a know-all: **~ sapçığı,** (*bot.*) pedicel: **~ sapı,** (*bot.*) peduncle: **~ soğanı,** (*bot.*) corm, bulb: **~ suyu,** neroli; orange flower essence: **~ tacı,** (*bot.*) corolla: **~ tarhı,** (*agr.*) flower-bed: **~ TOZU:** **~ zarfı,** (*bot.*) calyx: **~ı**

burnunda (çamuru karnında), just happened, very fresh, brand new: **~ te,** in bloom.

çiçek·bozuğu^{nu} (*med.*) Pock-mark(ed). **~çi(lik),** (work of) flower-grower/-seller, florist. **~gagalayangiller,** (*orn.*) flower-peckers. **~lemek (-i),** plant flowers; decorate with flowers. **~lenme,** *vn.*; blooming; blossom-time; (*chem.*) efflorescence. **~lenmek,** *vi.* come into flower, blossom; effloresce. **~li,** in bloom; decorated with flowers; (*tex.*) with a flowery pattern; (*med.*) suffering from smallpox: **~ bitkiler,** (*bot.*) phanerogams: **~ dişbudak,** (*bot.*) flowering ash. **~lik,** flower garden; flower vase; conservatory; (*bot.*) flower-head; receptacle. **~sime,** *vn.* (*chem.*) efflorescence; (*med.*) eruption. **~simek,** *vi.* flower; (*chem.*) effloresce; (*med.*) erupt. **~sineğiⁿⁱ,** (*ent.*) root-maggot/flower-fly. **~siz,** without flowers; (*bot.*) cryptogamous: **~ bitkiler,** cryptogams. **~tozu^{nu},** (*bot.*) pollen: **~ kesesi,** pollen sac. **~tutar,** flower-holder. **~yaprağı^{nı},** (*bot.*) perianth.

çif- *pref.* = ÇİFT(E). **~akciğerliler,** (*zoo.*) dipneumones. **~ayaklılar,** (*zoo.*) Diplopoda, millipedes. **~desimetre,** (*math.*) 20 cm. ruler. **~dişliler,** (*zoo.*) Duplicidentata. **~kanatlılar,** (*ent.*) diptera. **~kapı,** (*arch.*) double-doors. **~küme,** (*ast.*) double cluster. **~parmaklılar,** (*zoo.*) even-toed ungulates. **~pencere,** (*arch.*) double window. **~sayı,** (*math.*) even number.

çiftⁱ = ÇİF(TE). *n.* Pair; couple; mate; brace (of birds); yoke (of oxen); pair of pincers, etc.); (*math.*) dyad. *a.* Even (number); double; dual; duplicate; (*math.*) binary; bi-; di-; (*bio.*) diplo-. **~ ağız anahtarı,** (*eng.*) monkey-wrench: **~ ağızlı,** double-edged (axe, etc.): **~ altı ~ beş,** double six double five (telephone number): **~ atış,** (*sp.*) double-shot (for false start): **~ atomlu,** (*phys.*) diatomic: **~ bazlı,** (*chem.*) dibasic: **~ biçimli,** (*chem.*) dimorphous: **~ camlı pencere,** (*arch.*) double-glazed window: **~ cidarlı,** (*eng.*) double-sleeved: **~ çeneli kepçe,** (*zoo.*) clamshell: **~ çubuk,** (*agr.*) farm equipment; general work of the farm/vineyard; agriculture: **~ çubuk sahibi,** owner of an estate, wealthy property owner: **~ değer ilkesi,** (*fin.*) bimetallism: **~ dikiş** (*tex.*) double-stitch: **~ dirsek,** (*eng.*) return bend: **~ görmek,** see double: **~ gözlü dürbün,** binoculars: **~ hece(li),** (*ling.*) disyllab·le/(-ic): **~ hörgüçlü deve,** (*zoo.*) Bactrian camel: **~ isimli,** (*bio.*) binominal (system): **~ kabuklu,** (*zoo.*) bivalve: **~ kale oynamak,** (*sp.*) play a proper game of football; = TEK KALE: **~ kanatlı,** (*arch.*) folding door: **~ kanat/yüzeyli uçak,** (*aer.*) biplane: **~ koşmak,** (*live.*) harness to the plough: **~ kulaç yüzmek,** (*sp.*) swim double overarm: **~ maden/metalli,** (*min.*) bimetallic: **~ makineli,** twin-engined: **~ meclisli,** (*adm.*) bicameral: **~ mi tek mi?,** (*gamb.*) odd or even?: **~ odaklı,** (*phys.*) bifocal: **~ öğecikli,** diatomic: **~ pistli anayol,** (*mot.*) dual carriageway: **~ renkli,** (*cin.*) two-colour (system); dichromatism: **~ sürat,** (*mil.*) double-quick time: **~ sürmek,** (*agr.*) plough, cultivate: **~ uçlu,** (*bio.*) bicuspid (tooth): **~ ücret,** (*ind.*) double-time (pay): **~ yapraklı,** (*bot.*) bifoliate: **~ yönlü,** (*eng.*) two-way: **~ yüzlü,** (*math.*) dihedral: **~i**

zamanı, (*agr.*) ploughing-time: ~**e gitmek,** go ploughing: ~**e koşmak,** transfer animals to ploughing: ~**i bozmak,** give up farm-work: ~**in birisi,** (*bio.*) doublet: ~**ine çubuğuna bakmak,** look after one's farm: ~**ler,** (*sp.*) doubles.

çiftçi Ploughman; cultivator, farmer. ~ **eğitim kampı,** agricultural training camp. ~**lik,** ploughing; farming; agriculture.

çifte = ÇİF(T). *a.* Paired; double; bi-; di-. *n.* (*sp.*) Double-barrelled shot-gun; pair-oared boat; animal's kick with both hind legs; double whorl on horse's forehead (considered unlucky). ~ **atmak,** (animal) lash out with both hind legs: ~ **çalışan,** (*eng.*) double-acting: ~ **dalmak,** (*sp.*) try to grab both legs: ~ **dikiş,** (*ed. sl.*) pupil who repeats his class: ~ **dip,** false bottom (suitcase): ~ **dürbün,** (*phys.*) field-glasses: ~ **gerdanlı,** (*bio.*) double-chinned: ~ **kavrulmuş,** (*cul.*) double-roasted; a very hard Tk. delight; (*sl.*) = ~ DİKİŞ: ~ **koşum,** (*live.*) double-harness: ~ **kumrular,** (*fig.*) a pair of inseparable friends: ~ **namlu,** double-barrelled (shot-gun): ~ **tasma,** (*eng.*) couple. ~**hane,** (*live.*) cage for rearing birds.

çifteker Bicycle. ~**ci,** cyclist. ~**ci¹k** ˢⁱ, mini-cycle. ~**cilik,** cycling.

çifte·lemek (-i) (Animal) lash out with hind legs; (*naut.*) drop a second anchor. ~**leşmek,** *vi.* (animals) lash out at each other. ~**li,** kicking horse; horse with double whorl on forehead; (*fig.*) ill-omened; treacherous, deceitful. ~**nağra,** (*mus.*) double-drum. ~**r,** ~ ~, having a pair each; always double; in large numbers. ~**telli,** (*mus.*) belly-dance.

çift·görme (*med.*) Diplopia. ~**lemek (-i),** (*live.*) mate animals. ~**lenmek,** *vp.* be mated. ~**leşme,** *vn.* coitus, copulation, mating. ~**leşmek (-le),** *vi.* become a pair; (*bio.*) copulate; (*zoo.*) cover, mate; (*bot.*) (cells) combine. ~**leştirmek (-i, -le),** make a pair; (*bio.*) cause to mate. ~**li,** (*phys.*) doublet. ~**lik,** farm: ~ **avlusu,** farmyard, barnyard: ~ **hayvanları,** livestock: ~ **kâhyası,** farm bailiff. ~**lilik,** duality. ~**ucay,** (*phys.*) dipole. ~**yıldız,** (*ast.*) double star.

çiğ¹ *n.* = ÇİY.

çiğ² *a.* (*cul.*) Raw, uncooked; unripe; (*fig.*) crude, hard, inexperienced. ~ ~ **bakmak,** look around in an uncouth/boorish manner: ~ ~ **yemek,** tear s.o. to pieces; (*fig.*) nourish a bitter enmity against s.o.: ~ **düşmek,** seem crude: ~ **ışık,** harsh light: ~ **iplik,** single-ply thread: ~ **kaçmak,** be out of place/unsuitable: ~ **köfte,** (*cul.*) a rissole eaten raw: ~ **renk,** startling/flashy colour: ~ **toprak,** unploughed/fallow land: ~ **yemedim ki karnım ağrısın!,** I've done nothing that I should be blamed!: ~**den vermek,** (*mil.*) pay a food allowance.

çiğ·de (*bot.*) Common jujube tree; its fruit. ~**dem(giller),** (*bot.*) autumn crocus, colchicum; (Colchicaceae).

çiğden (*for.*) Piece of resinous pinewood.

çiğin (*dial.*) Shoulder. ~**diri¹k** ˢⁱ, yoke (for buckets).

çiği¹t ᵈⁱ (*bot.*) Seed; cottonseed. ~ **küspesi,** cotton-cake.

çiğ·lenme = ÇİY-. ~**leşmek,** *vi.* (colours, light) be striking; behave crudely. ~**lik,** crudeness; crude behaviour. ~**nek,** much trodden (path). ~**nem** a chew; a quid (tobacco). ~**neme,** *vn.* chewing mastication: ~ **kası,** (*bio.*) masseter: ~ **tütünü** chewing tobacco: ~**den yutmak,** bolt (food) ~**nemek (-i),** masticate, chew, crunch; trample on crush; (*fig.*) ignore, show disrespect to s.o ~**nemi¹k** ˢⁱ, masticated food (fed to a baby) ~**nenmek,** *vp.* ~**nenmiş,** beaten (track). ~**netmek (-i),** *vc.* ~**neyici,** (*ent.*) chewing (insect) ~**renkçi(lik),** (*art.*) fauv·ist(-ism).

çihar (*gamb.*) = CİHAR.

-çik *dim. suf.* [57] = -CİK [MEHMETÇİK].

çik·let ⁱ (*cul.*) Chewing-gum. ~**olata,** chocolate.

çil¹ *n.* (*orn.*) Hazel grouse. ~ **ardıcı,** (*orn.*) grea reed-warbler: ~ **kuşu,** (*orn.*) = TURAÇ: ~ **yavrusı gibi dağılmak,** scatter in all directions, be utterl routed.

çil² *n.* (*bio.*) Freckle, spot; stain (on mirrors); (*bot.* fine hairy roots. *a.* Freckled, speckled; bright, shin (coin).

-çil *n. suf.* [66] = -CİL [ETÇİL].

çile¹ *n.* (*tex.*) Hank/skein; bowstring.

çile² *n.* (*rel.*) Forty days' retreat and fasting; perioc of penitence; (*fig.*) trial; suffering. ~ **çekmek, çıkarmak/doldurmak,** pass through a severe trial undergo suffering: ~**den çıkarmak (-i),** infuriate s.o.: ~**den çıkmak,** be exasperated: ~**ye girmek** begin the period of fasting. ~**ci(lik),** ascetic(ism).

çile¹k ˢⁱ (*bot.*) Strawberry.

çile·keş Suffering; (*rel.*) dervish in retreat/fasting ~**li,** (causing) suffering. ~**siz,** carefree.

çilemek *vi.* (*orn.*) (Nightingale) sing loudly.

çilenti (*met.*) Drizzle.

çilingir Locksmith; (*sl.*) picklock. ~ **sofrası,** (*sl.* small table/tray with drinks and hors-d'œuvres ~**lik,** making/repairing of locks.

çil·lenmek *vi.* Become freckled. ~**li,** freckled.

çim (*bot.*) Garden grass(-seed); grass-plot, turf. ~ **göbek,** (*sp.*) centre of arena (turfed): ~ **şeridi,** grass verge.

çimbal·i/ ~ o (*mus.*) Large cymbals.

çimçe¹k ˢⁱ (*orn.*) A small species of sparrow.

çim çim Unwillingly; without appetite.

çimdi¹k ˢⁱ Pinch; pinch of stg.; (*fig.*) unkind words (*cul.*) = TATARBÖREĞİ. ~ **atmak/basmak/~lemek (-i),** pinch s.o.; break into small pieces. ~**lenmek** *vp.*

çime¹k ˢⁱ (*dial.*) Bathing place.

çimen (*bot.*) Meadow; lawn; turf; = ÇEMEN. ~**lik** grassy spot; expanse of lawn; meadow.

çimento Cement. ~**lamak (-i),** spread/cover with cement. ~**lanmak,** *vp.* ~ **laşma,** (*eng.*) cementation.

çimerlik (*geo.*) Beach.

çimle·mek (-i) (*agr.*) Sow grass. ~**ndirmek (-i)** cause to grow. ~**nmek,** *vi.* (*bot.*) germinate, sprout become grassy; have a nibble; (*fin.*) get perquisites pickings.

çimmek *vi.* Plunge into water; bathe.

Çin (*geo.*) China. ~ +, *a.* Chinese: ~ **ayvası,** (*bot.* japonica: ~ **feneri,** Chinese lantern: ~ **geyiği,**

(*zoo.*) Chinese water-deer: ~ **Halk//Milliyetçi Cumhuriyeti**, (*adm.*) Chinese People's//Nationalist Republic: ~ **işi**, (*art.*) chinoiserie: ~ **mürekkebi**, (*pub.*) Indian ink: ~ **ördeği**, (*orn.*) mandarin duck: ~ **Seddi**, Great Wall of China.

-çin *suf.* [87] (*obs.*) = İÇİN [BİZİMÇİN].

çinakop[u] (*ich.*) Medium-sized bluefish.

çinanasonu[nu] (*bot.*) Aniseed tree.

Çince (*ling.*) Chinese.

çinçilya (*zoo.*) Chinchilla.

Çing. = ÇİNGENECE.

Çingene *n.* (*ethn.*) Gypsy; Bohemian. *a.* (*pej.*) Mean, cunning. ~ **borcu**, (*fin.*) a debt difficult to recover; petty debts: ~ **çalar Kürt oynar**, it's six of one and half a dozen of the other; a disorderly party: ~ **çergesi**, a dirty deserted spot: ~ **çergesinden musandıra ne arar?**, what do you expect from a destitute person?: ~ **düğünü**, a disorderly/riotous assembly: ~ **gibi**, *a.* Bohemian: ~ **pembe//sarısı**, bright pink//yellow: ~ **yengeci**, (*zoo.*) common shore crab.

Çingene·ce *n.* (*ling.*) Gypsy language, Romany: *a.* gypsy-like. ~ **leşmek**, *vi.* (*pej.*) behave meanly. ~ **lik**, gypsy way of life/habits; meanness, shabbiness: ~ **etm.**, behave in a mean/miserly way. ~ **palamudu**[nu], (*ich.*) young of bonito.

çingülü[nü] (*bot.*) Camellia.

Çinhindi *pr. n.* (*geo.*) Indochina.

çini *n.* Porcelain; encaustic tile; china, enamel ware. *a.* Tiled; made of porcelain. ~ **döşemek**, (*arch.*) tile: ~ **mavi**, bright blue: ~ **mürekkebi**, (*pub.*) Indian ink.

çini·ci Tile-maker/-seller. ~ **cilik**, art of tile-making. ~ **li**, (*arch.*) decorated with painted tiles.

çinko *n.* Zinc; (*pub.*) zinc plate. *a.* Made of zinc. ~ **kaplama**, (*min.*) galvanizing, zinc-plating: ~ **örtülü**, zinc-coated. ~ **graf(i)**, (*pub.*) zincograph·er/(-y).

çinleylağı[nı] (*bot.*) Persian lilac, bead-tree.

Çinli (*ethn.*) Chinese.

çintan (*mod.*) (Tk. peasant-woman's) baggy trousers.

çip ~ **patates**, (*cul.*) potato chips.

çipil Blear-eyed; dirty (weather). ~ ~, in a bleary manner. ~ **leşmek**, *vi.* (eyes) become bleary.

çipo (*naut.*) Anchor stock.

çipura (*ich.*) Gilt-head bream.

çir (*dial.*) Dried apricot/plum, etc.

çiriş Shoemaker/bookbinder's paste; size; (*aer.*) dope. ~ (**çanağı**) **gibi**, sticky and bitter. ~ **lemek** (-i), smear with paste/size. ~ **lenmek**, *vp.* ~ **li**, coated with paste/size. ~ **otu**[nu], (*bot.*) asphodel.

çirkef Filthy/dirty water; sink, sewer; (*fig.*) ill-bred/uncouth person. ~ **e taş atmak/~i üzerine sıçratmak**, do stg. to invite an insolent person's abuse. ~ **lik**, filthiness.

çirkin Ugly; deformed; ill-favoured; unseemly; unpleasant. ~ **leşmek**, *vi.* become ugly/disfigured. ~ **leştirmek** (-i), disfigure; deface. ~ **lik**, ugliness; disfigurement; nasty habit/behaviour. ~ **semek** (-i), consider ugly/unpleasant.

çiroz (*cul.*) Sun-dried thin mackerel; Bombay duck; (*fig.*) s.o. all skin and bone. ~ **laşmak**, *vi.*

(mackerel) become thin after spawning; (*fig.*) become very thin. ~ **luk**, mackerel suitable for drying; (*fig.*) thinness; dryness.

çis (*myc.*) Honeydew; manna. ~ **e(le)mek**, *vi.* (*met.*) drizzle. ~ **enti**, very fine rain, drizzle. ~ **kin**, (damp from) drizzle.

çiş (*child.*) Urine. ~ **bezi**, baby's nappy/diaper: ~ **etm.**, urinate, make water: ~ **i gelmek**, want to make water.

çişi·l·k[ği] (*zoo.*) Leveret.

çiş·inmek (*phys.*) *vi.* Condense. ~ **inir**, condensable. ~ **inti/~kin**, condensate.

çit[i] [1] *n.* (*tex.*) Printed cotton, chintz; (*mod.*) headkerchief.

çit[i] [2] *n.* (*agr.*) Fence (of hurdles/brushwood); barrier; grill. ~ **kuşu**, (*orn.*) common wren: ~ **ötleğeni**, (*orn.*) lesser whitethroat: ~ SARMAŞIĞI: ~ **serçesi**, (*orn.*) dunnock, hedge-sparrow.

çita (*zoo.*) Cheetah.

çitari (*tex.*) A silk and cotton cloth; (*ich.*) a Mediterranean sea-bream, (?) goldline.

çiten Wicker basket.

çiti Act of putting together; (*tex.*) darning. ~ **yapmak**, use a very fine-tooth comb. ~ **lemek** (-i), (*dom.*) squeeze/rub stg. while washing it. ~ **lenmek**, *vp.* ~ **li**, squeezed. ~ **lmek**, *vp.* = ÇİTMEK. ~ **şmek**, *vi.* become tangled/interlaced.

çitlembi·l·k[ği] (*bot.*) Terebinth berry. ~ **ağacı**, (*bot.*) terebinth/turpentine tree: ~ **gibi**, small and dark (girl).

çit·leme (*agr.*) Fencing in. ~ **lemek** (-i), (*agr.*) fence in; (*cul.*) shell and eat (seeds, nuts, etc.). ~ **lik**, branches for fencing. ~ **mek** (-i), put together; darn; = İLEMEK. ~ **mi·l·k**[ği], (*bot.*) small stalk in a bunch of grapes; small quantity/pinch of stg. ~ **sarmaşığı**[nı], (*bot.*) convolvulus, greater bindweed.

çivi (*carp.*) Nail; (*ich.*) bony tubercle (on turbot). ~ **çıkar ama yeri kalır**, a wounded heart heals but the scar remains: ~ **yi söker**, set a thief to catch a thief; another little drink won't do us any harm!: ~ **gibi**, brisk, alert: ~ **gibi olm.**, (hands, feet) be very cold/freezing: ~ **kesmek**, be bitterly cold; freeze: ~ **yukarı**, (*sp.*) throwing your opponent head over heels: ~ **ye ilişmek**, (clothing) be caught on a nail: ~ (**yi**) **çakmak**, drive in a nail. ~ **ci**, nail-maker/-seller: (*sp.*) player who drives the ball right into the other half.

çivid- = ÇİVİT. ~ **i**, *a.* indigo blue.

çivi-dişi[ni] (*bio.*) Canine tooth. ~ **leme**, *vn.* nailing; (*sp.*) dive (feet first); (*sp.*) smash. ~ **lemek** (-i, -e), nail stg. to stg.; (*sl.*) stab s.o.; (*sl.*) copulate; (*fig.*) fix s.o. to the spot. ~ **lenmek**, *vp.* be nailed; (*fig.*) be glued to the spot. ~ **letmek** (-i), *vc.* ~ **li**, with nails, nailed; nailed to the wall: ~ **ayakkabı**, (*sp.*) athlete's spiked shoes, 'spikes': ~ **duy**, (*el.*) bayonet socket. ~ **siz**, without nails: ~ **kalkan** (**balığı**), (*ich.*) brill.

çivi·l·t[di] Indigo; (*dom.*) laundering-blue. ~ **ağacı**[nı], (*bot.*) indigo plant. ~ **lemek** (-i), (*tex.*) dye with indigo; (*dom.*) use blue in the laundry. ~ **lenmek**, *vp.* ~ **li**, 'blued' (laundry). ~ **otu**[nu], (*bot.*)

indigo-plant; woad. ~**siz**, (washed) without blue.

çiviyazısı[ni] (*ling.*) Cuneiform writing.

çivmek *vi.* Miss the mark, go astray.

çiy (*met.*) Dew. ~ **damlası**, dewdrop: ~ **noktası**, dew-point: ~ **ölçeği**, drosometer: ~ **suyu**, (*phys.*) condensate. ~**lenmek**, *vi.* condense. ~**lendirmek** (**-i**), *vc.* condense. ~**semek**, *vi.* drizzle.

çiz·dirmek (**-i, -e**) *vc.* = ÇİZMEK. ~**ece**[l]k[ği], (*carp.*) scriber. ~**elge**, (*math.*, *etc.*) table, chart. ~**em**, scheme, diagram. ~**emsel**, schematic. ~**ene**[l]k[ği], diagram. ~**er**, draughtsman, artist. ~**eylem(leme)**, computer program/(-ming). ~**ge**, (*adm.*) chart, diagram; graph; (*art.*) graphics. ~**ge**[l]ç[ci], eraser. ~ **gelemek** (**-i**), trace, plot.

çizgi Line; mark; stroke; scratch; trace; drawing; stripe; (*bio.*) wrinkle; (*bio.*) stria; (*ling.*) dash (—); (*rad.*) (Morse) dash; (*child.*) hopscotch. ~ **çekmek/ çizmek**, draw a line: ~ **kalemi**, (*th.*) make-up pencil.

çizgi·l (*phys.*) Linear. ~**lemek** (**-i**), draw lines. ~**li**, lined; barred; striped; ruled (paper); (*bio.*) striate(d); (*geol.*) striated; (*mod.*) corded: ~ **baykuş**, (*orn.*) barred owl: ~ **çek**, (*fin.*) crossed cheque: ~ **kas**, (*bio.*) striated muscle: ~ **kertenkele//sırtlan**, (*zoo.*) striped lizard//hyena: ~ **ötleğen kuşu**, (*orn.*) barred warbler: ~ **sinek**, (*ent.*) yellow-fever//dengue mosquito: ~ **sinekkapan**, (*orn.*) spotted flycatcher. ~**lik**, drawing ruler. ~**sel**, (*math.*) linear; diagrammatic, graphic. ~**siz**, without lines: ~ **çek**, (*fin.*) uncrossed cheque.

çiz·i = ÇİZGİ; (*agr.*) furrow. ~**ici**, *a.* drawing; *n.* (*agr.*) s.o. who slits the opium-poppy capsules; (*phys.*) tracer. ~**i**[l]k[ği], *a.* drawn; striated; *n.* = ÇİZGİ: ~ ~, full of lines. ~**ikli**, lined, scored, scratched. ~**iktirmek** (**-i**), scrawl, scribble; dash off a letter. ~**ili**, drawn, lined; furrowed. ~**ilmek**, *vp.* = ÇİZMEK. ~**im**, (*math.*) construction, drawing: ~ **ressamı**, draughtsman: ~ **tahtası**, (*arch.*) drawing-board. ~**inti**, abrasion. ~**i**[l]t[di], (*math.*) graph; (*art.*) design. ~**itçi**, designer.

çizme[1] *n.* (*mod.*) Top-boot; Wellington boot. ~ **çekeceği**, boot-jack: ~ **kalıbı**, boot-tree: ~**den yukarı çıkmak**, meddle with things one doesn't understand. ~**ci(lik)**, (work of) boot-maker/ -seller.

çiz·me[2] *vn.* ~**mek** (**-i**), draw (a line/mark); construct; plot, sketch; design; describe; rule with lines; scratch; erase, cancel.

çoban Shepherd; rustic; boor. ~ +, *a.* Rustic; pastoral: ~ **armağanı çam sakızı** = ÇAMSAKIZI: ~ **değneği**, shepherd's crook: ~ **etm.**, shepherd; (*iron.*) look after children: ~ **kebabı**, (*cul.*) meat dish with yoghurt: ~ **kılıklı**, dressed like a shepherd: ~ **kızı**, shepherd·ess/-girl: ~ **kulübesinde padışah rüyası görmek**, build castles in Spain: ~ **salatası**, (*cul.*) onion salad with chopped cucumber and tomatoes.

çoban·aldatan (*orn.*) Eurasian nightjar/ goatsucker. ~**aldatangiller**, (*orn.*) goatsuckers, nightjars. ~**çantası**[ni], (*bot.*) shepherd's purse. ~ **dağarcığı**[ni], (*bot.*) field pennycress. ~ **değneği**[ni], (*bot.*) knot-grass. ~ **düdüğü**[nü], (*bot.*) asarbacca.

~ **iğnesi**[ni], (*bot.*) a perfumed geranium. ~ **köpeği**[ni], (*zoo.*) sheepdog. ~ **kuşu**[nu], (*orn.*) northern screamer. ~ **lama**, (*lit.*) pastoral, eclogue. ~ **lık**, shepherding; shepherd's wage: ~ **etm.**, work as a shepherd, drive animals to pasture. ~ **mayası**[ni], (*bot.*) milkwort. ~ **merhemi**[ni], (*med.*) turpentine and wax ointment. ~ **minaresi**[ni], (*bot.*) a type of grass. ~ **püskülü**[nü], (*bot.*) holly. ~ **püskülügiller**, (*bot.*) holly family, Aguifoliaceae. ~ **süzgeci**[ni], (*bot.*) goosegrass, cleavers. ~ **tarağı**[ni], (*bot.*) shepherd's needle; wild teasel. ~ **tuzluğu**[nu], (*bot.*) common barberry. ~ **yıldızı**[ni], (*ast.*) Venus.

çoc. = ÇOCUK (DİLİ).

çocuğumsu Childish, childlike.

çocu[l]k[ğu] Infant; child; boy; person; s.o. behaving childishly. ~ +, *a.* Children's: ~ **aklı**, a simple mind: ~ **aldırmak**, (*med.*) procure an abortion: ~ **almak**, (*med.*) perform an abortion: ~ **arabası**, perambulator, pram: ~ **bahçesi**, children's park/ playground: ~ **beyin inmesi**, (*med.*) cerebral palsy: ~ **bezi**, nappy, diaper: ~ **bir hikmet!**, the child is hopeless; there's stg. wrong with the child!: ~ **değiş olmuş**, the child must be a changeling: ~ **dili**, (*ling.*) nursery/children's language: ~ **doğurma**, childbirth: ~ **doğurmak**, (*med.*) be confined, give birth: ~ **düşüren**, (*med.*) abortive: ~ **düşürme(k)**, (*med.*) (have an) abortion/miscarriage: ~ **dünyaya getirmek**, give birth: ~ **emzirme oda/yeri**, (*ind.*) crèche: ~ **esirgeme**, (*soc.*) child welfare: ~ **Esirgeme Kurumu**, Society for the Protection of Children: ~ **ezmesi**, (*cul.*) mild kind of marzipan: ~ **gibi**, childlike; childish; credulous: ~ **gibi sevinmek**, be much loved: ~ **gözetimi**, (*soc.*) baby-sitting: ~ **imlaya gelmez!/lakırdı anlamıyor!**, the child is incorrigible!: ~ **işi**, easy, unimportant: ~ **mahkemeleri**, (*leg.*) juvenile courts: ~ **maması**, baby food: ~ **olm.**, be childish: ~ **oynamadan etmez**, a child must be allowed to play: ~ **oyuncağı**, a toy; (*fig.*) child's play: ~ **oyuncağı haline getirmek**, be spoilt by incapable people: ~ **peydahlamak**, (unmarried woman) become pregnant: ~ **tiyatrosu**, children's theatre: ~ **yapmak**, have a child: ~ **yardım/zammı**, (*adm.*) children's/family allowance: ~ **yatağı**, cot, crib: ~ **yetiştirmek**, bring up/train a child: ~ **yuvası**, (*ind.*) crèche; (*ed.*) playschool: ~**lar!**, (*col.*) friends!: ~**larının hayrını görmedi**, his children turned out badly/brought him no joy: ~ **tan al haberi!**, 'out of the mouths of babes and sucklings!'; 'little pitchers have long ears': ~ **tur**, he's only a child (what more do you expect?): ~ **tur yapacak**, boys will be boys: ~**u almak**, (*med.*) deliver a child: ~**u olm.**, give birth: ~**u olmaz**, (*med.*) barren, sterile.

çocuk·bilim(ci) (*ed.*) Pedago·gy/(-gue). ~**cağız**, poor wee child. ~**ça**, childish(ly), in a childlike manner. ~**ken**, as a child. ~**laşmak**, *vi.* be(come) childish. ~**lu**, having children. ~**luk**, childhood; childishness; folly: ~ **çağı**, boy-/child-/girlhood: ~ **etm.**, behave childishly/thoughtlessly: ~**u tutmak**, behave childishly: ~**una vermek** (**-i**), overlook stg. as being due to his youth: ~**undanberi**, from a boy, from childhood: ~**su**, childlike; childish.

çoğ- = ÇOK.
çoğal·an *a.* Increasing. ~ ım/~ ma, *vn.* increase; proliferation; (*bio.*) reproduction; (*fin.*) accrual. ~ mak, *vi.* increase, multiply; accrue; (*bio.*) breed, reproduce. ~ tım, increase; (*cin.*) duplication; duplicate. ~ tma, *vn.* increase; augmentation; reproduction: ~ hakkı, *n.* copyright: ~ hakkını almak, *vt.* copyright: ~ makinesi, duplicator. ~ tmak (-i), *vt.* increase, augment; multiply; copy, reproduce; (*bio.*) breed.
çoğan = ÇÖVEN.
çoğu *pron.* [75] The greater part/majority; most. *adv.* Many times; usually. = ÇOK. ~ gitti az kaldı, it won't be long before . . .; the end is near; the worst is over: ~ kez, often, frequently: ~ kimse, most people: ~ zaman, most times: ~muz, most of us: ~nuz, most of you.
çoğul (*ling.*) Plural. ~ ekleri, (*ling.*) plural endings/ suffixes. ~cu, *a.* majority: *n.* (*phil.*) pluralist. ~culuk, pluralism. ~laştırmak (-i), (*ling.*) make plural. ~luk, (*ling.*) the plural.
çoğ·umsamak (-i) Consider stg. excessive; deem too many/much. ~un(ca), many times, usually; maximum. ~unluk, (*adm.*) majority: ~la, by/with a majority; as often happens, most of the time: ~tan ayrılma, dissent, dissidence.
çoğurcu¹kᵍᵘ (*orn.*) Common starling.
çoğuz (*chem.*) Polymer. ~laşma, polymerization.
ço¹kᵍᵘ *a., adv.* [75, 197] Much; many; a great deal; too much/many; considerably; very. *pref.* Multi-; poly-; ultra-. ~ alçak gerilim, (*el.*) very low tension: ~ amaçlı, multi-purpose: ~ büyük, colossal: ~ çalıştırmak (-i), drive s.o.: ~ ~, at the most; in the end: ~ daha fazla, by far: ~ defa, often: ~ değerli, rare: ~ düşünüyor, it's very thoughtful (of an animal that seems ill): ~ fazla, far too much: ~ geçmeden, before long, very soon: ~ gelmek, be more than sufficient; be intolerable: ~ gerekli, obligatory: ~ görmek, deem too much; regard as undeserved; (-i, -e), grudge s.o. stg.: ~ güzel!, very good!; bewitching beauty: ~ içer, he drinks a lot, he's a toper: ~ işeme, (*med.*) polyuria: ~ kademeli, (*eng.*) multi-stage: ~ katlı, (*arch.*) multi-storey: ~KATLI: ~ kırıklı, (*geol.*) cataclastic: ~ kısa dalgalar, (*phys.*) ultra-short waves: ~ naz âşık usandırır, 'oh well, if you don't want to, don't!': ~ olm., go too far, bore s.o.: ~ ömür adamdır, he's an odd fellow (but likeable): ~ önemli, crucial: ~ rağbette olm., be in great demand: ~ sayıda, in large quantities; on a large scale: ~ sıcak!, (*met.*) it's boiling!: ~ söylemek, be talkative: ~ sürmedi, it didn't last long; it was not long before . . .: ~ şekerli, (*cul.*) very sweet: ~ şey!, really!; how odd!; you don't say so!: ~ şükür olsun ki, I bless my stars that . . .: ~ tembel, bone-idle: ~ üzmek, overpower: ~ veren maldan az veren candan, it's not the gift but the thought that counts; the widow's mite: ~YILLIK: ~ yorgun, worn-out, all in: ~ yüksek frekans, (*rad.*) very high frequency: ~ zaman ister, it will take a long time: ~a kalmaz, it won't be long before . . .: ~a varmak, cost a lot: ~ları, many (of them): ~larınca, according to/by/through many people: ~ tanberi/

~tan(dır), [201] for a long time, since long ago.
çokal (*his.*) (Suit of) armour, coat of mail.
çok·anlamlı(lık) (*ling.*) Polysem·ic/(-y). ~ayak/ bacaklılar, (*zoo.*) myriapods. ~ basamaklı, (*math., eng.*) multi-stage. ~ biçimli(lik), (*bio.*) poly- morph·ous/(-ism). ~ bilmiş, precocious (child); cunning (man). ~ cücük/embryonlu(luk), (*zoo.*) polyembryon·ic/(-y). ~ça, a good many; a good deal; somewhat. ~ çiçekli, (*bot.*) multi- florous. ~ çu(luk), (*phil.*) plural·ist/(-ism). ~ dişlilik, (*zoo.*) Polyodontia. ~ düzlemli, (*math.*) polyhedral. ~ eşli, ~ evlilik, polygamy. ~ eşlilik, polygamy. ~ evli, (*soc.*) polygamous; polygynous (man); polyandrous (woman). ~ evlilik, polygyny; polyandry. ~ fazlı, (*phys.*) polyphase, multi-phase. ~ gen, (*math.*) polygon. ~ göze/hücreli, (*bio.*) multicellular. ~ gözeliler, (*bot.*) metaphytes; (*zoo.*) Metazoa. ~ gözlü, (*zoo.*) multilocular. ~ karılı/ (-lık), (*soc.*) polygyn·ous(-y). ~ katlı(lık), multi·ple/ (-plicity). ~ kaynaklı, (*geol.*) polygene(tic). ~ kıllı- lar, (*zoo.*) Polychaetes. ~ kocalı(lık), polyandr·ous/ (-y). ~ kutuplu, (*phys.*) multipolar. ~ laşmak, *vi.* multiply, become numerous. ~ lu, multiple; poly-. ~ luk, *n.* abundance; multiplicity; (*med.*) excess; crowd, multitude; commonness: *adv.* often, frequently. ~ öğecikli, (*phys.*) polyatomic.
çokra·ğan (*geo.*) Bubbling spring. ~mak, *vi.* boil with much bubbling.
çok·samak (-i) Consider excessive. ~ satar, (*pub.*) best-seller. ~ sesli(lik), (*mus.*) polyphon·ic/(-y). ~ sıralı, (*bio.*) stratified. ~ şekilli, (*chem.*) polymorphous. ~ tan = ÇOK. ~ tanrıcı(lık), (*rel.*) polythe·ist/(-ism); pagan(ism). ~ taraflı, (*adm.*) multilateral. ~ tasım, (*phil.*) polysyllogism. ~ terimli/~üyeli, (*math.*) polynomial. ~ türel, (*phys.*) heterogeneous. ~ uluslu, (*adm.*) multi- national. ~ yanlı, multilateral. ~ yapımlı- (lık), (*min.*) heterogene·ous/(-ity). ~ yıllık, (*bot.*) perennial. ~ yönlü, multi-directional; (*ed.*) poly- math.
çolak(lık) (Being) with one arm/hand missing/ paralysed.
çolpa With one leg damaged; awkward, clumsy; untidy. ~ lık, clumsiness; untidiness; canter.
çolu¹kᵍᵘ ~ çocuk, wife and children; all the family; young and unimportant people: ~ çocuk sahibi, a family man: ~a çocuğa karışmak, become a family man.
çolum (*dial.*) Calf of the leg.
çolun (*dial.*) Fisherman's long-handled net.
çoma¹kᵍ¹ Club; cudgel; baton. ~ gibi, (*bot.*) clavate: ~ gözesi, (*bio.*) rod (in the retina). ~can(kıran), bacteri·a/(-cide). ~göz, (*zoo.*) ommatidium. ~ kurtlar, (*zoo.*) Rhabditidae.
çomar Big watchdog; mastiff; (*sl.*) old publican.
çoook (*col.*) Much too much.
çopra (*ich.*) Fish-bone; (*for.*) thick brushwood. ~ balığıⁿ¹, (*ich.*) spined loach.
çopur (*med.*) Pock-mark(ed). ~ ina, (*ich.*) type of sea-bream. ~ luk, being pock-marked.
çor Illness; worry; (*dial.*) cattle disease.
çora¹kᵍ¹ *a.* Arid, bare, barren; desert; bitter,

undrinkable; (*fig.*) bald. *n.* (*geol.*) Impervious clay; saltpetre bed.

çorak·laşmak *vi.* Become barren. ~ **laştırmak (-i),** make barren (through neglect). ~ **lık,** aridity, barrenness, infertility; (water) bitterness.

çora¹pᵇ¹ Stocking, sock. ~ **kaçmak,** (stocking) ladder: ~ **örmek** = BAŞINA: ~ **söküğü gibi gelmek/ gitmek,** proceed easily/quickly/in rapid succession. ~ **çı(lık),** (work of) maker/seller of stockings. ~ **sız,** barelegged.

çorba (*cul.*) Soup; (*fig.*) medley, mess. ~ **etm./ ~ ya döndürmek (-i),** make a mess of stg., turn stg. upside down: ~ **gibi,** muddy; sloppy; in disorder: ~ **içmeye çağırmak,** invite to a meal: ~ **kaplumbağası,** (*zoo.*) green turtle: ~ **da maydanoz/ tuzu bulunmak,** participate in a small way: ~ **dan ağzı yanan . . .** = SÜTTEN: ~ **ya dönmek,** be(come) a mess.

çorba·cı Maker/seller of soup; (*his.*) Christian notable; (*jok.*) a non-Muslim; (*his.*) colonel of Janissaries; (*naut.*) master; (*sl.*) boss. ~ **cılık,** making and selling soup. ~ **lık,** *a.* (*cul.*) suitable for soup.

çotira ~ **balığı,** (*ich.*) grey triggerfish. ~ **giller,** (*ich.*) triggerfish; filefish.

çotra Wooden mug/cup.

çotu¹kᵍᵘ (*for.*) Root above ground; tree-/vine-stump.

çov-çov (*zoo.*) Chow (dog).

çöğ·mek (Ball, etc.) spin off. ~ **önce¹k**ᵍⁱ, see-saw. ~ **ünmek,** *vi.* tip up. ~ **ür¹,** (*bot.*) eryngium; any seed-grown bush. ~ **ür²,** (*mus.*) type of lute. ~ **ürcü,** (*mus.*) lute-player.

çök·e¹kᵍⁱ (*geo.*) Depression; swamp. ~ **el,** deposit, dregs, sediment. ~ **ele¹k**ᵍⁱ, (*cul.*) skim-milk cheese; (*chem.*) precipitate. ~ **elge,** (*agr.*) alluvium-covered land. ~ **elme,** *vn.* (*chem.*) precipitation; (*geol.*) sedimentation. ~ **elmek,** *vi.* (*chem.*) settle, be deposited/precipitated. ~ **elti,** (*chem.*) sediment, precipitate. ~ **eltilmek,** *vp.* ~ **eltme,** *vn.* precipitation. ~ **eltmek (-i),** *vc.* (*chem.*) precipitate; deposit.

çök·ermek (-i) Make (a camel) kneel; cause to collapse, break the morale. ~ **erti,** (*geo.*) sediment, deposit. ~ **ertme,** *vn.* (*mil.*) breakthrough; draw-net (fish). ~ **ertmek (-i)** = ~ ERMEK. ~ **ken,** collapsed; settled. ~ **kün,** collapsed; (*fig.*) depressed. ~ **künlük,** collapse; (*psy.*) depression: ~ **giderici,** (*med.*) anti-depressant. ~ **me,** *vn.* collapse, decline, downfall; (*med.*) breakdown; (*geol.*) settlement, subsidence, sinking; (*ast.*) descent: ~ **metabolizma,** (*bio.*) catabolism: ~ **si yakın,** about to collapse. ~ **mek,** *vi.* collapse; cave in; fall down; give way; crumple up; (*chem.*) settle, be deposited; (*geol.*) settle, sink; (*ast.*) descend; (*fig.*) be prostrated (by age/fatigue): ~ **(-e),** (darkness, fog, sorrow, etc.) descend upon one. ~ **türme,** *vn.*: ~ **havuzu,** (*eng.*) settling-tank. ~ **türmek (-i),** *vc.* ~ **ük,** collapsed; broken-down; fallen down; caved-in; sunk, depressed; precipitated. ~ **üklük,** collapse, etc. ~ **üm,** decline; degradation; (*med.*) collapse. ~ **üntü,** collapse; (*geol.*) sediment, deposit; debris, dilapidation; wreckage; (*med.*) depression; (*geol.*)

subsidence. ~ **üş,** collapse, ruins; (camel) kneeling down; (*fig.*) decline, ruin. ~ **üşmek (-e),** fall down/ descend all together; rush upon stg. from all sides. ~ **üvermek,** *vi.* collapse (unexpectedly).

çöl Desert; wilderness. ~ **agaması,** (*zoo.*) desert agama: ~ **gibi,** silent and deserted: ~ **koşarı,** (*orn.*) cream-coloured courser: ~ **tavukları,** (*orn.*) sandgrouse: ~ **tilkisi,** (*zoo.*) fennec: ~ **varanı,** (*zoo.*) desert monitor: ~ **e dönmek,** become a wilderness.

çöl·leşmek *vi.* (*geol.*) Become a desert. ~ **leştirmek (-i),** create/turn into a desert. ~ **lük,** *a.* having much desert; bare, arid. ~ **ümsü,** desert-like, semi-desert.

çömçe (*dial.*) Wooden ladle.

çömel·me *vn.* Crouching, squatting: ~ **helataşı,** (*dom.*) pan closet. ~ **mek,** *vi.* crouch down; squat on one's heels. ~ **tmek (-i),** *vc.*

çömez Boy working for board and lodging; hodja's assistant; follower, disciple; (*ed. sl.*) swot. ~ **lik,** being such a boy; following; discipleship.

çömle¹kᵍⁱ Earthenware pot. ~ **hesabı,** clumsy work; accounts by an illiterate: ~ **kebabı,** (*cul.*) meat roasted in a pot.

çömlek·çi Potter; pot-seller: ~ **kuşu(giller),** (*orn.*) rufous hornero; (ovenbirds). ~ **çilik,** *n.* earthenware; the potter's art; ceramics: *a.* suitable for pottery.

çöngül (*geo.*) Small swamp, muddy lake.

çöpᵘ Fragment of vegetable matter; chip; straw; sweepings, litter, rubbish, garbage; (*min.*) dross. ~ **arabası,** dust-cart: ~ **atlamamak,** let nothing escape one, pay the utmost attention; be very particular: ~ ~ **üstüne koymamak,** not do a stroke of work: ~ **gibi,** very thin and dry: ~ **kebabı,** (*cul.*) small bits of meat grilled on tiny wooden skewers: ~ **tenekesi,** rubbish-bin, ash-can: ~ **yakma fırını,** refuse destructor: ~ **e dönmek,** become very thin/ weak.

çöp·atlamaz Punctilious, meticulous, pernickety. ~ **çatan,** predestination (as to marriage); marriage go-between. ~ **çatanlık,** work of the go-between. ~ **çatmak (-i),** arrange a marriage. ~ **çü(lük),** (work of) dustman; scavenger. ~ **leme,** (*bot.*) hellebore, Christmas rose. ~ **lenmek,** *vi.* pick up scraps of a meal; (*fig.*) make a profit (from others' business, etc.). ~ **lük,** rubbish-dump/-heap; dustbin: ~ **horozu,** s.o. with low tastes. ~ **süz,** (*bot.*) without a stalk: ~ **üzüm,** useful and without defects; (*fig.*) s.o. without relatives (and therefore desirable in marriage).

çör = ÇER.

çörçil (*mil.*) Soldier's boots. ~ **vari,** Churchillian.

çörde¹kᵍⁱ (*naut.*) Halyard. ~ **yakası,** head of a sail.

çördü¹kᵍᵘ (*bot.*) Hyssop; (*dial.*) wild pear.

çöre¹kᵍⁱ (*cul.*) Ring-shaped shortbread/cake; anything ring-shaped; (*zoo.*) snake's coil. ~ **otu** = ÇÖREOTU. ~ **çi(lik),** (work of a) maker/seller of such cake. ~ **lenmek,** *vi.* (snake) be coiled up; coil o.s. up; (*fig.*) settle down (in a place).

çöreotuⁿᵘ (*bot.*) Nigella, Damascus fennel-flower; its seeds (used to flavour ÇÖREK).

çörkü (*math.*) Abacus.

çörten (*arch.*) Projecting gutter, gargoyle.

çörtü (*agr.*) Corn-hopper pipe (in a mill).

çöven (*bot.*) Soapwort; = ÇEVGEN.
çöz (*cul.*) Suet (from round the intestines).
çöz·dürmek (-i, -e) *vc.* = ÇÖZMEK; catalyse.
çöz·elti (*chem.*) Solution; dip. ～**(g)en**, (*chem.*) solvent. ～**gü**, (*tex.*) warp; spun sheep's wool; (*math.*) problem. ～**gün(lük)**, (state of being) untied; disentangled; (*chem.*) dissolved, decomposed. ～**me**, *vn.*; solution; (*tex.*) hand-woven fine sheeting. ～**mek** (-i), untie; detach; unravel, disentangle, undo; (*eng.*) disengage; (*chem.*) dissolve; (*math.*) solve (an equation); (*fig.*) solve (a problem, cipher); decipher. ～**ücü**, solving; (*chem.*) dissolving; (*geol.*) dispersing/ deflocculating (agent). ～**ük**, dissolved; melted; dispersed. ～**ülme**, *vn.*; (*mil.*) withdrawal/ disengagement; (*ling.*) off-glide. ～**ülmek**, *vp.* be untied, etc.; *vi.* (*mil.*) withdraw/disengage one's troops; (*phys.*) melt, thaw; (*chem.*) decompose, be dispersed, break up; become weak, collapse; (*sl.*) run away, disappear. ～**ülüm**, break-up, dispersal; (*mil.*) rout; (*psy.*) dissociation. ～**ülüş**, being undone, etc.; thaw; (*fig.*) rout, destruction, collapse; (*lit.*) dénouement.
çözüm Solution (of a problem/equation). ～ **yolu**, solution, formula. ～**le·çi**, (*chem.*) analyser. ～**leme**, *vn.* (*chem.*, *ling.*, *phil.*) analysis. ～**lemek** (-i), analyse. ～**lemeli**, analytic. ～**lenmek**, *vp.* be analysed. ～**leyici**, analyser, analyst. ～**sel**, analytic(al).
çözün·dürme *vn.* (*chem.*) Solution. ～**dürmek** (-i), *vc.* dissolve. ～**en**, *n.* (*chem.*) solute. ～**me**, *vn.* decomposition; dissolution; ～**mek**, *vi.* (*chem.*) dissolve; be dispersed; (*phys.*) melt, thaw. ～**mez**, insoluble. ～**müş**, dissolved. ～**tü**, disintegration, break-up; remains. ～**ük**, dissolved. ～**üm**, (*psy.*) dissociation. ～**ür**, *a.* soluble. ～**ürlük**, solubility.
çözüş·me *vn.* (*chem.*) Dissociation, disintegration. ～**mek**, *vi.* break-up, disintegrate, dissociate. ～**ük**, dissociated. ～**üm**, (*psy.*) dissociation.
ÇS = ÇİMENTO SANAYİİ.
-çu *n. suf.* [59] = -Cİ [HUKUKÇU].
çubu·k·gu (*bot.*) Shoot; twig; sapling; stick, staff; (*eng.*) metal rod, bar, pipe; tobacco pipe, chibouk; (*tex.*) rib, stripe; (*naut.*) topmast. ～**unu tellendirmek**, take things easy; ～**unu tüttürmek**, smoke one's pipe; be lazy and indifferent.
çubuk·ağacı·nı (*bot.*) Hollow-branched *Euphorbia mabea*. ～**böceği·ni**, (*ent.*) dixippus, stick insect. ～**çu**, chibouk-maker/-seller. ～**lamak** (-i), beat (a carpet). ～**lu**, barred; (*tex.*) striped; ～ **kilit**, door-bolt. ～**luk**, (*obs.*) chibouk cupboard.
çuha (*tex.*) Broadcloth. ～**cı**, draper. ～**cılık**, (*tex.*) weaving of broadcloth. ～**çiçeği·ni**, (*bot.*) primrose. ～**çiçeğigiller**, (*bot.*) primulas. ～**dar(lık)**, (*obs.*) (work of) footman/lackey.
çuhçuh (*child.*) Chuff-chuff, puff-puff.
-çuk *dim. n. suf.* [57] = -CİK [KURTÇUK].
çuka (*ich.*) = ÇIĞA BALIĞI.
çukur *n.* Hole; dip; hollow; cavity; (*agr.*) ditch; (*fig.*) grave; (*bio.*) dimple; (*geo.*) abyss; crater; (*sl.*) backside. *a.* Hollowed out; sunk(en); (*phys.*) concave. ～ **açmak**, (*agr.*) dig, ditch: ～ **göz**, deep-set eyes: ～**a düşmek**, meet with misfortune: ～**unu**

kazmak (-in), (*fig.*) dig s.o.'s grave, prepare s.o.'s ruin.
çukur·el (*geo.*) Lowlands. ～**iz**, (*eng.*) indentation. ～**izaçar**, (*eng.*) indenter. ～**lanmak**/～**laşmak**, *vi.* be(come) hollow, etc. ～**laştırma**, hollowing out. ～**latmak** (-i), make hollow, etc. ～**lu**, pitted, hollow; dented. ～**luk**, hollow(ness); (*geo.*) depression; (*phys.*) concavity; (*agr.*) place full of hollows/ditches.
çul (*tex.*) Hair-cloth; horse-cloth; badly-made clothes. ～ **çaput**, woven cloths; clothes: ～ **tutmaz**, spendthrift; shiftless, improvident: ～**u düz(elt)mek**, renew one's clothes, become well-dressed: ～**u tutmak**, become rich, come into property.
-çul *n. suf.* [66] = -CİL [OTÇUL].
çul·ha Weaver; (*dial.*) loom. ～**hakuşu·nu**, (*orn.*) penduline tit. ～**lama**, *vn.* (*cul.*) food covered with dough and baked. ～**lamak** (-i), cover (a horse) with a rug; (waves) break right over a ship. ～**lanmak**, *vp.* be covered with a horse-cloth; put on new clothes; become rich; (-e), hurl o.s. upon s.o.; fall upon, pester s.o.
çullu·k·gu (*orn.*) Eurasian woodcock. ～ **balığı**, (*ich.*) trumpet-fish: ～ **tersi**, woodcock trail. ～**giller**, (*orn.*) Scolopacidae.
Çulpan (*ast.*) Venus, evening-star.
çul·suz Without horse-cloth; (*fig.*) destitute. ～**tar(ı)**, quilted saddle-cloth.
çurçur (*ich.*) Small inedible wrasse; (*fig.*) worthless.
çuval Sack; (*sl.*) s.o. fat. ～ **ağzı açmak**, (*sl.*) pay attention; be awake: ～ **bezi**, hessian, sacking: ～ **gibi**, coarse (cloth); baggy (clothes).
çuval·cı Maker/seller of sacks; (*agr.*) s.o. who puts crops into sacks. ～**dız**, packing-needle. ～**lamak** (-i), fill into sacks: (-den), (*ed. sl.*) fail (one's class) in . . . . ～**lık**, sacking.
Çuvaş (*ethn.*) Tk. tribe on the Volga. ～**ça**, (*ling.*) their language.
-çü *n. suf.* [59] = -Cİ [SÜTÇÜ].
çük·ü (*bio.*) (Little boy's) penis.
-çük *dim. n. suf.* [57] = -CİK [KÖKÇÜK].
çükündür (*bot.*, *dial.*) Beet.
çükür (*agr.*, *dial.*) Combined axe and hoe.
-çül *n. suf.* [66] = -CİL [ÇÜRÜKÇÜL].
-çün *suf.* [87] (*obs.*) = İÇİN [ONUNÇÜN].
çün·ki·kü *conj.* [215] Because, for.
çürü·k·gü *a.* Rotten; carious (tooth); unsound; broken; spoilt; corrupt; worthless; (*phil.*) unsound (argument); (*mil.*) unfit for service. *n.* Bruise, contusion. ～ **buhar**, (*eng.*) waste steam: ～ **çarık**, utterly rotten; (*art.*) arty-crafty: ～ **çıkmak**, turn out rotten; prove to be unsound/false: ～ **gaz**, (*mot.*) exhaust (gases): ～ **iple kuyuya inilmez/ merdivenle dama çıkılmaz**, don't undertake work with s.o. unreliable: ～ **para**, (*his.*) unsound/ debased money: ～ **tahta**, risky business: ～ **tahtaya basmak**, suffer loss, be cheated (because of one's imprudence): ～ **tekne**, (*naut.*) coffin-ship: ～ **yumurta**, bad/rotten egg: ～**e çıkarmak**, (*mil.*) invalid out: ～**e çıkmak**, turn out rotten; (*mil.*) be invalided out.
çürük·çe (*med.*) Gangrene. ～**çeleşmek**, *vi.* become

gangrenous. ~çül, (*zoo.*) saprophile; (*myc.*) saprophyte. ~lük, rottenness; putrefaction; (*med.*) ecchymosis; garbage pit; (*agr.*) compost-heap; common grave, charnel pit; (*fig.*) cemetery. çürü·me *vn.* Rot; decay, putrefaction, decomposition; corrosion; corruption, depravation. ~mek, *vi.* rot; decay; spoil; be bruised; (*fin.*) become worthless/unsound/ uncreditworthy; (*leg.*) (case, etc.) be refuted/ unsound; (*mil.*) be rejected (as unfit). ~tme, *vn.*

decay; corruption; (*chem.*) corrosion; (*leg.*) refutation, rebuttal: ~ çukuru, cess-pit/-pool, septic tank. ~tmek (-i), *vc.* cause to rot, etc.; bruise, contuse; corrupt; (*chem.*) decompose, corrode; (*leg.*) disprove, refute, rebut. ~tücü, cankerous; corrosive. ~tülmek, *vp.*
çüş (*ech.*) Sound made to stop an ass//deride s.o. behaving like one.
çütre = ÇOTİRA.
Çvş = ÇAVUŞ.

D

D, d [de] Fifth Tk. letter, D; fifth (in a class/series); (*mus.*) re; (*math.*) 500. ~ **kat/tabakası**, (*aer.*) D-layer: ~ **vitamini**, (*bio.*) vitamin D.

D, d. = DAİRE; DAKİKA; (*bio.*) DAL; (*geo.*) DERE; (*geo.*) DOĞU; DOĞUM; (*ch.s.*) DEUTERİUM.

-d- *Replaces* **t** *before a vowel suffix* [DAMAT + A = DAMADA].

da[1] *conj.* [206] = DE[2].

da[2] *n.* (*med.*, *obs.*) Illness; disease.

Da. = (*geo.*) DAĞ.

-da *n. suf.* [28] = -DE [OKULDA].

-da- *v. suf.* [231] = -DE- [ÇITIRDAMAK].

DAC = DEMOKRATİK ALMAN CUMHURİYETİ.

Dadacı(lık) (*art.*) Dada·ist/(-ism).

dadan·dırmak (-i, -e) *vc.* ~ **mak (-e)**, acquire a taste for, affect; get fond of; visit frequently, frequent; make free use of, abuse.

dadaş (*dial.*) Brother; youth, stout fellow; pal.

dadı(lık) (Status/work of) children's nurse.

dafi[i] Repelling, warding-off; anti-.

dağ[1] *n.* (*agr.*) Brand; mark; (*med.*) cautery, scar. ~ **basmak**, brand: ~ **ı dil**, (*obs.*) great sorrow.

dağ[2] *n.* Mountain. ~ +, *a.* Mountain-; (*bot.*) wild; (*fig.*) huge, rough. ~ **adamı**, mountaineer; rough fellow: ~ **ardında olsun da, yer altında olmasın**, parting is preferable to death: ~ **ayısı**, (*zoo.*) mountain bear; (*fig.*) uncouth/boorish fellow: ~ **babaları**, (*orn.*) brambling: ~ **başı**, mountain top; wild/remote spot: ~ ~ **üstüne olur, ev ev üstüne olmaz**, two families can't live together in one house: ~ ~**a kavuşmaz/ulaşmaz insan insana kavuşur/ulaşır**, you'll meet him again some day: ~ **deviren**, coarse and clumsy, a bull in a china-shop: ~ **doğura doğura fare doğurmuş**, great expectations with little result: ~ **elması**, (*bot.*) crab-apple: ~ **eteği**, (*geo.*) lower slopes of a mountain, foothills: ~**(lar) gibi**, huge; a great amount of stg., mountains of stg.: ~ **ispinozu**, (*orn.*) brambling: ~ **kar tavuğu**, (*orn.*) rock ptarmigan: ~ **kargası**, (*orn.*) chough: ~ **kırlangıcı**, (*orn.*) sand-martin: ~ **koyunu**, (*zoo.*) moufflon: ~ **kulübesi**, (*arch.*) chalet: ~ **kuyruksallayanı**, (*orn.*) grey wagtail: ~ **mersini**, (*bot.*) bilberry: ~ **ötleğeni**, (*orn.*) Bonelli's warbler: ~ **serçesi**, (*orn.*) tree sparrow: ~ **sıçanı**, (*zoo.*) Alpine marmot: ~ **silsilesi**, (*geo.*) mountain chain/range: ~ **taş**, all around; in great quantities, mountains of; greatly: ~ **tavuğu**, (*orn.*) hazel grouse: ~ **topu**, (*mil.*) gun carried on mule-back: ~ **yağmur kuşu**, (*orn.*) dotterel: ~ **yalımı**, (*geo.*) bluff: ~ **yürümezse, aptal yürür**, if the mountain won't go to Muhammad, Muhammad must go to the mountain: ~**a çıkmak**, climb a mountain; (brigands, rebels) take to the mountains: ~**a kaldırmak (-i)**, abduct s.o.: ~**da**

bağın var, yüreğinde dağın var, those with property or children are never carefree: ~**da büyümüş**, bucolic; a country bumpkin: ~**dan gelip bağdakini kovmak**, (newcomer) treat the inhabitants with contempt; (upstart official) treat the old hands cavalierly: ~ **lar anası**, a huge woman: ~ **lar kadar**, excessively big; great quantities of: ~ **lara düşmek**, be destitute: ~ **lara taşlara**, God preserve us from it (a calamity): ~ **ların gelin anası/şenliği**, (*jok.*) bear: ~ **ların misafir aldığı mevsim**, (*jok.*) summer-time.

dağ·ağzı[nı] (*geo.*) Crater. ~ **alası**[nı], (*ich.*) mountain-trout. ~ **arası**, (*geo.*) gorge, defile.

dağar Wide-mouthed earthen pot. ~ **cı**[lk][ğı], (shepherd's) leather bag/wallet; (*th.*) repertory: ~ **ı yüklü**, he has great knowledge: ~ **ındakini çıkarmak**, bring out a well-prepared remark: ~ **ta bir şey kalmamak**, everything be exhausted/used up.

dağ·bilgisi[ni] Orography. ~ **cı(lık)**, (*sp.*) mountaineer(ing). ~ **çamı**[nı], (*bot.*) mountain pine.

dağdağa Trouble and turmoil; confusion; noise. ~ **lı**, noisy; confused; troublesome.

dağ·ı (*phys.*) Entropy. ~ **ılım**, distribution; dispersion; (*chem.*) dissolution; (*psy.*) nervous breakdown, dissociation. ~ **ılış**, distribution; dispersion; (*adm.*) collapse. ~ **ılma**, *vn.* distribution; dispersal; disintegration; decomposition; scattering. ~ **ılmak**, *vi.* disperse, separate, scatter; disband, break away; disintegrate, fall to pieces; be spread; be disseminated; be distributed; (room, etc.) be untidy. ~ **ınık**, scattered; dispersed; wide apart; irregular; (*adm.*) disorganized; unorganized; untidy; (*fin.*) retail: ~ **ışık**, (*cin.*) broad/diffused light: ~ **nizam**, (*mil.*) open order. ~ **ınıkçı(lık)**, (*fin.*) retail·er/ (-trade). ~ **ınıklık**, dispersion; disorganization, etc. ~ **ınım**, dispersion. ~ **ınmak** = ~ ILMAK.

Dağıstan(lı) (*geo.*) (Inhabitant of) Daghestan.

dağıt·ıcı *n.* (*pub.*) Distributor; postman; newspaper seller; (*cin.*) broad light projector. *a.* Scattering, breaking up. ~ **ıcılık**, (*phil.*) distributivity; (*pub.*) distribution. ~ **ılmak**, *vp.* ~ **ım**, (*cin.*, *pub.*) distribution; diffusion: ~ **ımcı(lık)**, (*cin.*) (work of) distributor/renter. ~ **ımevi**, (*pub.*, *cin.*) distribution agency; renting company. ~ **ma**, *vn.*: ~ **çubuğu**, (*el.*) busbar. ~ **mak (-i)**, scatter, disband, disperse; (*phys.*) dissipate; dissolve; diffuse; allocate, deal out, dispense, distribute; break to pieces; disarrange, disturb.

dağ·i (*mus.*) Melody (from mountain regions). ~ **kazması**[nı], (*sp.*) ice-axe. ~ **keçisi**[ni], (*zoo.*) chamois. ~ **lalesi**[ni], (*bot.*) (?) Turkestan tulip.

dağ·lağı Branding iron. ~ **lama**, branding; cauterizing; (*min.*) etching; (*met.*) scorching. ~ **lamak (-i)**, brand; cauterize; (*min.*) etch; (*met.*) scorch; (*fig.*)

wound/grieve s.o. ~**lanık**, etched. ~**lanmak**, *vp.*
~**latmak (-i, -e)**, *vc.* ~**layan**, branding; wounding;
cauterizing. ~**lı**[1], *a.* branded; scarred; sore at
heart.
dağ·lı[2] *n.* Mountaineer; (*gamb.*) king: *a.* uncouth,
bucolic. ~**lı'ç**[c1], (*live.*) kind of sheep; its mutton.
~**lık**, mountainous (country). ~**oluş**, (*geol.*) *n.*
orogenesis: ~ +, *a.* orogenic. ~**servisi**[ni], (*bot.*)
cedar of Lebanon.
dah *int.* = DEH. ~ **etm.**, drive (animals); put, throw
in.
daha *a.* More; a greater quantity. *adv.* [203]
Already, so far; (not) yet, still; further; more, again,
besides; (*math.*) plus. *It forms the comparative*
degree of adjectives/adverbs [54] [~ **iyi**, better: ~
çabuk, more quickly]. ~ **az**, less: ~ **bu sabah geldi**,
he only arrived this morning: ~ **(bundan) aşağısı**
kurtarmaz, I can't sell it for less; (*iron.*) nothing
less/only the best will do for him: ~ ~**?**, and then
what happened?: ~ **doğrusu**, or to be more exact:
~ **dün**, only yesterday: ~ **erken**, earlier; it is still
early: ~ **iyisi can sağlığı**, health is best: ~ **neler!**,
what next!; how absurd!: ~ **öte**, farther still: ~ **son**
kozunu oynamadı, he still has a card up his sleeve:
~ **sonraki**, later, subsequent: ~ **şimdiden**, already:
~**sı var**, that's not all; (*pub.*) to be continued.
dahame (*med.*) Enlargement, hypertrophy.
dahdah (*child.*) Gee-gee.
dahi *conj.* [207] And; also; furthermore; too; even.
dâhi A genius. ~**nin dehası mektepte keşfedilmez**,
the genius of a genius is not recognized at school.
~**ce**/~**yane**, (a work) of genius. ~**lik**, state/
quality of a genius.
dah'il[li 1] *n.* Entry; interference; participation. ~**i**
olm. (-de), have a finger in, be implicated.
dahil[2] *n.* Interior; inside. *adv.* Inside; inner; included, inclusive. *post.* [91] In(side). ~ **etm.**,
include: ~ **edilmek/olm.**, be included: ~ **olm. (-e)**,
participate in: ~ **inde**, inside.
dahil·en Internally; in the interior (of a country).
~**i**, internal; inner; domestic: ~ **dekorasyon**,
interior decoration: ~ **harp**, (*mil.*) civil war: ~
muhabere, intercommunications. ~**iye**, (*adm.*,
obs.) Internal Affairs; (*med.*) clinic/ward for
internal diseases: ~ **subayı**, (*mil.*) administrative
officer in mil. colleges: ~ **Vekâleti**, (*obs.*) Ministry
of the Interior. ~**iyeci**, (*med.*) internist; (*adm.*)
professional official attached to the Ministry of the
Interior.
dahl- = DAHİL[1]. ~**letmek**[eder] **(-e)**, participate in;
interfere in.
daim (*obs.*) Enduring, permanent; continuous. ~
etm., make continuous; perpetuate: ~ **olm.**, continue, endure. ~ **a**, always; constantly; perpetually.
~**i**, constant; permanent; confirmed (habit, etc.);
perpetual: ~ **aza**, (*adm.*) permanent member: ~
cereyan, (*el.*) direct current: ~ **heyet**, (*adm.*) standing committee.
dair *a.* Revolving. *post.* (-e)[88] Concerning; about;
relating to; connected with. ~**e**, (*math.*) circle;
(*phys.*) cycle; (*arch.*) block; apartments; (*adm.*)
bureau, board, division, department; (*naut.*) compartment, room; (*leg.*) limit (of jurisdiction), com-

petence; range; (*mus.*) tambourine: ~ **kesitli**,
annular: ~ **kesme**//**parçası**, (*math.*) sector//
segment of a circle. ~**eli**, ~ **ev**, apartment house.
~**esel**/~**evi**, circular; rotational.
-daki *n. suf.* = -DEKİ [OKULDAKİ].
dakik[1] *a.* Minute; delicate; subtle, accurate, precise. *n.* (*obs.*) Flour. ~**a**, *n.* minute: ~**sı** ~**sına**, to
the very minute, on the dot, very punctually: ~**sı**
~**sına uymaz**, his mood is constantly changing:
difficult to get on with: ~**sında**, at that very
moment. ~ **alama**, (*cin.*) timing.
dak(k)or *int.* Agreed!
daktilo Typist, secretary; typewriting. ~ **etm.**, type:
~ **(makinesi)**, typewriter. ~**graf**, typist. ~**grafi**/
~**luk**, typing. ~**skopi**, (*leg.*) study of fingerprints.
dal[1] *n.* (*for.*) Branch, bough, twig; (*ed.*) branch;
(*zoo.*) clade. ~ **budak**, ramifications: ~ **budak**
salmak, send out ramifications; grow in size/
importance: ~ **gibi**, graceful, slender: ~ **gibi**
kalmak, become very thin/weak: ~**dan** ~**a**
atlamak/konmak, jump from one subject to
another: ~**ında satış**, (*fin.*) sale for delivery.
dal[2] *n.* (*bio.*) Shoulder, back. ~**ına basmak**, irritate
s.o.: ~ **ına binmek**, put pressure on s.o.; pester s.o.
dal- *pref.* Bare, naked [DALTABAN].
dala'k[ğı] (*bio.*) Spleen; honeycomb. ~ **olm.**, (*med.*)
have an inflamed spleen. ~**otu**[nu], (*bot.*) germander.
dalalet[i] A going astray; aberration, deviation, error.
~**e düşmek**, go astray; deviate.
dala·ma *vn.* Irritation. ~**mak (-i)**, (animal) bite;
(insect/plant) sting, prick; irritate.
dalan (*arch.*) (Entrance-)hall, lobby; waiting-room.
dalaş Quarrel. ~**mak**, *vi.* (dogs) bite each other;
(*fig.*) quarrel, wrangle, bicker.
dalavere Trick; deceit; intrigue. ~ **çevirmek/**
döndürmek, plot, intrigue. ~**ci**, trickster, crook,
intriguer. ~**cilik**, trickery, intrigue.
dalayıcı (*bio.*) Irritant.
dalbastı ~ **kiraz!**, fine and large cherries!
daldır·a'k[ğı] (*med.*) Catheter. ~**ık**, *a.* (*min.*) submerged; immersion. ~**ılmak**, *vp.* be dipped/
immersed/submerged. ~**ım**, (*med.*) catheteriza-
tion. ~**ma**, dipping, immersion; (*agr.*) layering;
layered shoot. ~**mak (-i, -e)**, plunge stg. into stg.;
dip/immerse/submerge stg. in stg.; (*agr.*) layer (a
shoot).
dalga (*geo., phys., etc.*) Wave; undulation; (*tex.*)
watering; (*sl.*) trick, deceit; (*sl.*) drug-addict's trip;
(*sl.*) absent-mindedness. ~ **boyu**, (*phys.*) wave-
length: ~ ~, light and dark (colours): ~ **devimi**,
(*phys.*) wave motion: ~ **geçmek**, (*sl.*) pull s.o.'s leg;
make fun of s.o. covertly: ~ **geçmek**/~**ya gelmek**,
(*sl.*) day-dream, be wool-gathering/lost in reverie;
pretend to be working; amuse o.s.: ~ **genliği**,
(*phys.*) wave amplitude: ~ **gibi gelmek**, come one
after the other and plentifully: ~ **ışınçekim**, (*med.*)
electrokymography: ~**sı olm. (-le)**, have a love-
affair with s.o.: ~**ya düşmek/gelmek**, (*sl.*) happen
in a moment of distraction: ~**ya düşürmek**, (*sl.*)
benefit from s.o.'s distraction to do stg.: ~**ya**
gelmek = ~ GEÇMEK: ~**ya getirmek**, (*sl.*) persuade,
deceive: ~**yı başa almak**, (*naut.*) meet the waves
head on; breast the waves; (*fig.*) face up to troubles.

dalga·cı (*sl.*) Day-dreamer, wool-gatherer; s.o. who pretends to work; tricky fellow: ~ **Mahmut**, (*col.*) a lazy chap. ~ **cık**, ripple. ~ **cılık**, day-dreaming, absent-mindedness. ~ **kıran**, (*naut.*) breakwater. ~ **landırmak (-i)**, cause to undulate, etc. ~ **lanım**, (*med.*) fluctuation. ~ **lanma**, *vn.* roughness; undulation; (*fin.*) fluctuation; (*chem.*) cycling. ~ **lanmak**, *vi.* (sea) become rough; (flag) wave; undulate; become corrugated; (*fin.*) fluctuate; (*fin.*) (currency) float. ~ **lı**, covered with waves; rough/choppy (sea); undulating; turbulent; corrugated (paper); (*tex.*) watered (silk): ~ **akım**, (*el.*) alternating current: ~ **akım dinamo/üretecisi**, (*el.*) alternator.
dalgı Inattention; dreaminess. ~ **lı**, inattentive, unwary.
dalgı'çᶜ¹ (*naut.*) Diver; (*orn.*) loon. ~ **elbisesi**, (*naut.*) diving-suit; ~ **hücresi**, diving-bell. ~ **böcekleri**ⁿⁱ, (*ent.*) large water-beetles. ~ **kuşları**ⁿⁱ, (*orn.*) grebes and loons. ~ **lık**, diving.
dalgın Plunged in thought; absent-minded, in the clouds, dreamy; somnolent. ~ **laşmak**, *vi.* become absent-minded/dreamy. ~ **lık**, reverie, dreaminess; absent-mindedness; distraction. ~ **lıkla**, in a fit of aberration.
dalgır (*tex.*) Watering (of silk).
dalıcı Diver. ~ **fırtına kuşu**, (*orn.*) diving petrel: ~ **papağan**, (*orn.*) puffin. ~ **martıgiller**, (*orn.*) Alcidae, divers.
dalın'çᶜ¹ Entrancement, ecstasy.
dalış *vn.* = DALMAK; (*sp.*) dive towards the goal. ~ **uçuşu**, (*aer.*) dive.
dalız (*bio.*) Vestibule (of the ear).
dalkavu'kᵍᵘ Toady; flatterer; sycophant; parasite. ~ **laşmak**, *vi.* become a toady, etc. ~ **luk**, sycophancy; flattery; fawning.
dal·kılı'çᶜ¹ Who has bared his sword; with drawn sword; (*fig.*) warrior, swashbuckler. ~ **kıran**, (*ent.*) shot-hole borer (ambrosia beetle). ~ **kurutan**, (*ent.*) lesser ash-bark beetle.
dal·landırmak (-i) Cause to ramify; complicate; render difficult; exaggerate. ~ **lanma**, *vn.* branching. ~ **lanmak**, *vi.* become branched, ramify; become complicated. ~ **budaklanmak**, spread out in all directions; have far-reaching effects. ~ **lantı(lı)**, (*min.*) dendri·te/(-tic). ~ **lı**, branched: ~ **budaklı**, complicated, intricate.
dalma *vn.* = DALMAK; dive, etc.
Dalmaçya (*geo.*) Dalmatia. ~ +, *a.* Dalmatian. ~ **lı**, (*ethn.*) Dalmatian.
dalmak (-e) Plunge, dive; be lost in thought; be absorbed in (work); (*med.*) lose consciousness; doze, drop off to sleep. **dalıp çıkmak**, sink in and rise again; take a dip; slip in and out of places.
daltaban Bare-footed; destitute; vagabond.
Dalton ~ **hastalığı/**~ **izm**, (*med.*) daltonism, colour-blindness.
daluyku Deep sleep.
dalya¹ *n.* Tally. ~ **beş!**, that makes five!
dalya² *n.* (*bot.*) Dahlia.
dalyan Fishing-nets (strung on poles); fishpond; fishgarth; reserved fishery. ~ **gibi**, well set-up: ~

tarlası, area enclosed by the nets. ~ **cı**, look-out (at the entrance to the nets).
dalyarak(lık) (*vulg.*) Stupid(ity); foolish(ness).
dalyasan (*mod.*, *obs.*) Part of a turban hanging down.
dam¹ *n.* Lady partner (for dancing); (*gamb.*) queen.
dam² *n.* (Flat) roof; roofed shed; small house; outhouse; stable; (*col.*) prison. ~ **aktarma**, repairing the roof: ~ **altı**, any roofed space; loft, garret: ~ **penceresi**, dormer window: ~ **saçağı**, eaves: ~ **üstünde saksağan, beline vurdum kazmaylan/vur beline kazmayı**, (*jok.*) what's that got to do with it?; what nonsense you are talking!: ~ **dan çardağa atlamak**, jump from one subject to another: ~ **dan düşen halden bilir**, only those who have suffered a similar mishap can sympathize with s.o.'s misfortunes: ~ **dan düşer gibi**, suddenly, out of the blue; untimely; out-of-place (remark, etc.).
dam. = DEKAMETRE.
dama Game of draughts. ~ **demek**, give up, accept defeat; (drink, etc.) be finished: ~ **tahtası**, draughtsboard: ~ **taşı**, draughtsman: ~ **taşı gibi**, s.o. constantly on the move: ~ **taşı gibi oynatmak**, constantly send s.o. from place to place; replace one official by another. ~ **cı**, draughts-player.
damacana Demijohn; carboy.
damad- = DAMAT.
dama'kᵍ¹ (*bio.*) Palate. ~ **eteği**, roof of the mouth: ~ **kemiği**, palatine bone: ~ **ünsüzü**, (*ling.*) guttural consonant: ~ **yarığı**, (*bio.*) cleft palate: ~ **ını kaldırmak**, reassure (s.o. frightened).
damak·lı Having a palate: ~ **diş**, dental plate with artificial palate. ~ **sıl**, (*ling.*) palatalized. ~ **sıllaşma**, (*ling.*) palatalization.
damalı (*tex.*) Having a check pattern.
damar (*bio.*) Vein; (*min.*) vein, lode, seam; duct; (*fig.*) disposition, character, vein; bad humour; (*fig.*) origins. ~ +, *a.* (*bio.*) Vascular, haemal; angio-: ~ **atmak**, (*bio.*) pulsate: ~ ~, full of veins; layered: ~ **iltihabı**, (*med.*) phlebitis: ~ **kat/tabaka**, (*bio.*) choroid: ~ **katılık/sertliği**, (*med.*) arteriosclerosis: ~ **tıkanıklığı**, (*med.*) embolism: ~ **ı çatlak**, brazen-faced, shameless: ~ **ı kurusun!**, curse his temper, etc.!: ~ **ı tutmak**, have a fit of bad temper; be capricious/obstinate: ~ **ına basmak**, tread on s.o.'s corns, exasperate s.o.: ~ **ına çekmek**, take after s.o.: ~ **ına girmek**, ingratiate o.s. with s.o.; coax s.o.: ~ **ını bulmak**, take advantage of s.o.'s weak spot: ~ **lar**, (*bio.*) vascular system: ~ **ları kabarmak**, make one's feelings clear: ~ **larına işlemek**, penetrate (s.o.'s feelings, etc.).
damar·bilimi (*med.*) Angiology. ~ **ca**, (*med.*) angiopathy. ~ **daraltan**, (*bio.*) vaso-constrictor. ~ **genişleten**, (*bio.*) vaso-dilator. ~ **içi**, (*bio.*) intravenous. ~ **lı**, (*bio.*) veined, vascular; (*geol.*) clouded (marble); multi-core telephone cable. ~ **lıdişliler**, (*zoo.*) aardvarks. ~ **sal**, vascular. ~ **sız**, veinless; (*fig.*) shameless.
damasko (*tex.*) Damask.
dama' tᵈ¹ Son-in-law; bridegroom; (*his.*) son-in-law of the Sultan. ~ **lık**, status of//gift for a son-in-law.
damdazlak Completely bald; bald as a coot.
damga Instrument for stamping (letters); die; (*live.*)

brand; stamp; cachet, mark; disgrace, stigma. ~
basmak/vurmak, stamp: ~ **kanunu**, *(leg.)* law on
the use of revenue stamps: ~ **pulu**, revenue stamp:
~ **resmi**, stamp duty: ~ **yemek**, *(fig.)* be stig-
matized; get a bad name: ~ **sını vurmak (-e)**,
condemn s.o. as . . ..

damga·cı Stamper. ~ **lama**, *(eng.)* stamping.
~ **lamak (-i)**, stamp; *(fig.)* stigmatize. ~ **lanmak**,
vp. be marked/stamped; be disgraced. ~ **lı**,
stamped, marked: ~ **eşek**, *(pej.)* s.o. ill-famed.
~ **sız**, unstamped, unmarked.

damıt·ıcı *(chem.)* Retort, still. ~ **ık**, distilled.
~ **ılmak**, be distilled. ~ **ım/ ~ ma**, *vn.* distillation.
~ **mak (-i)**, distil.

damız *(agr.)* Breeding-shed/establishment. ~ **lık**,
(live.) animal for breeding; stallion; *(bot.)* plant for
propagation: ~ **kısrak**, brood-mare.

dam·korkuluğu[nu] *(arch.)* Parapet. ~ **koruğu**[nu],
(bot.) sedum, stonecrop. ~ **koruğugiller**,
Crassulaceae.

damla Drop; medicine taken with a dropper; *(med.)*
paralytic stroke; gout. ~ ~, drop by drop: ~ ~
akmak, dribble: ~ ~ *(med.)* **beslemek/**/*(eng.)*
yağlamak, drip-feed: ~ **inmek (-e)**, *(med.)* have a
stroke/an attack of gout: ~ **ölçeği**, *(eng.)* dosi-
meter: ~ **şekli**, streamlined: ~ **yakut**, *(min.)* ruby
of the finest water.

damla·cı[k][ğı] Droplet. ~ **lanmak**, *vi.* condense.
~ **lık**, *(med.)* dropper; *(arch.)* window-sill, coping;
dripstone; space between houses where the gutters
drip; *(dom.)* draining-board. ~ **ma**, dripping; *(bot.)*
guttation. ~ **mak (-e)**, drip; dribble; fall in drops;
(fig.) appear suddenly; turn up unwanted; frequent:
damlaya damlaya göl olur, take care of the pennies
and the pounds will take care of themselves.
~ **sakızı**[m], *(bot.)* best quality mastic. ~ **tılmak**, *vp.*
~ **tmak**, *vc.* pour out drop by drop; distil. ~ **taş**,
(min.) drop-shaped gem, cabochon; *(geol.)* stalactite. ~ **taşı**, *(arch.)* boss.

dam·lı *(arch.)* Roofed: ~ **yer**, building. ~ **örtüsü**[nü],
(arch.) roofing (material). ~ **taşı**[m], *(geol.)* slate.

damp·er *(mot.)* Dumper(-truck). ~ **erli**, with
dumper. ~ **ing**, *(fin.)* dumping.

dan ~ **dun**, *(ech.)* bang-bang!

-dan[1] *n. suf.* [28] = -DEN [OKULDAN].

-dan[2] *n. suf.* Case, receptacle, container [ŞAMDAN].

daN. = DEKANEWTON.

dana Calf. ~ **derisi**, calf-leather: ~ **(eti)**, calf
meat, veal: ~ **paçası**, *(cul.)* calves' foot: ~ **nın
kuyruğu kopmak**, for the crucial moment to
come, for the worst to happen.

dana·ayağı[m] *(bot.)* Cuckoo-pint, lords-and-
ladies. ~ **burnu**[nu], *(ent.)* mole-cricket; *(bot.)*
purple snapdragon. ~ **kıranotu**[nu], *(bot.)* common
helleborine.

Danca *(ling.)* Danish.

dandini *int. (ech.)* Hup!, down! *(dangling a
baby)*. *a.* In a mess, untidy. ~ **bebek**, childish
person, effeminate dandy.

dane = TANE. *(geol.)* Grain. ~ **çapı**, grain-size: ~
dağılımı ölçümü, granulometry; particle-size distribution: ~ **ler arası**, inter-granular. ~ **leşme**,
granulation.

dang[1] *(med.)* Dengue-fever.

dangalak Loutish, boorish, stupid. ~ **lık**,
stupidity, etc.

dangıl ~ **dungul**, boorish: ~ **dungul konuşmak/**
~ **damak**, *vi.* speak roughly/coarsely/with a
provincial accent.

danış Consultation; conference. ~ **ı**[k][ğı], consultation; collusion. ~ **ıklı**, consultative: ~ **döviş**, plan
concocted to deceive s.o.; put-up job; *(sp.)* rigged
game: ~ **iş**, collusion; put-up job. ~ **ık(lı)lık**, collusion. ~ **ılmak**, *vp.* ~ **ım/ ~ ma**, consultation, conference; inquiry; advice; counsel; information: ~
bürosu, *(adm.)* information/public relations office:
~ **kitaplığı**, reference library: ~ **kurulu**, *(adm.)*
consultative committee, working-party. ~ **mak (-i,
-e)**, consult, take counsel with, ask advice of;
inquire; confer. ~ **man**, advisor, consultant: ~
mühendis/ölçmeni, consulting engineer. ~ **manlık**,
consultancy. ~ **tay**, *(leg.)* council of state; court
hearing cases between individuals and the
Government.

Danimarka *(geo.)* Denmark. ~ + , *a.* Danish. ~ **lı**,
(ethn.) Dane.

daniska The best of everything. ~ **sını bilir (-in)**, he
knows it better than anyone else; he knows all the
ins and outs.

dank ~ **demek/etm.(kafasına)**, suddenly understand
stg. (that had puzzled one); for the penny to drop.

dans *(mus.)* Dance. ~ **düzenleme**, choreography: ~
düzenlemecisi, choreographer: ~ **etm./yapmak**,
dance: ~ **salonu**, ball-room, dance-hall: ~ **a
kaldırmak**, invite (a lady) to dance.

dansimetre *(phys.)* Densimeter.

dans·ing Dance-hall. ~ **ör**, male (ballet) dancer.
~ **öz**, female (ballet) dancer, ballerina; *(th.)* artiste.

dantel(a) *(tex.)* Lace. ~ **ağacı**[m], *(bot.)* lace-tree.
~ **böceği**[ni], *(ent.)* lacebug.

Dantesel *(lit.)* Dantean.

dapdar(acık) Very narrow/tight/scanty.

dar[1] *n. (obs.)* House; habitation; country.

dar[2] *a.* Narrow; tight; scanty; reduced (size); difficult; short (of time); close; limited, restricted. ~
açı, *(math.)* acute angle: ~ **atmak (kendini)**, make
hastily for; run away: ~ **boğaz/geçit**, bottle-neck;
(fig.) critical period: ~ **burunlu maymunlar**, *(zoo.)*
Old-World apes: ~ ~ **ına**, with difficulty; hardly:
~ **fikirli/kafalı**, bigoted, narrow-minded: ~
geçirmek/kaçmak/kurtulmak, have a close shave,
narrowly escape: ~ **gelirli**, *(fin.)* having a restricted
income: ~ **hat**, *(rly.)* narrow-gauge (line): ~
köprü, *(eng.)* catwalk: ~ **ünlü**, *(ling.)* close/narrow
vowel: ~ **yetişmek**, reach with difficulty: ~ **a
boğmak**, take advantage of s.o.'s difficulties: ~ **a** ~,
[195] with difficulty; hardly; just: ~ **a
düşmek**, *(fin.)* get into difficulties: ~ **a gelememek**,
not be rushed: ~ **a gelmek**, be pressed for time; be
forced by circumstances: ~ **a getirmek**, hurry/ rush
s.o. (into doing stg.): ~ **da bulunmak/kalmak**, *(fin.)*
be in difficulties: ~ **da kalmak**, *(fig.)* be in difficulties: ~ **ı** ~ **ına** = ~ **A** ~.

dar- *pref. obs.* House/place of . . . [DARÜLHARP].

-dar/-tar *n. suf.* Holding . . . [BAYRAKTAR]; possessing . . . [HİSSEDAR]; working at . . . [TEZGÂHTAR].

dara Tare (weight). ~**sını almak**, weigh the container: ~**sını düşmek**, deduct the tare: ~**ya atmak/ çıkarmak**, regard as unimportant; take no notice of.

daraban (*bio.*) Pulsation, palpitation.

dar·acık Very narrow. ~**aç**, narrow. ~**ağacı**ⁿⁱ, (*leg.*) gallows; (*eng.*) sheer-legs.

daral·an Tapering. ~**ma**, contraction; narrowing; shrinkage; constriction; restriction; depression. ~**mak**, become narrow/tight; shrink, contract; become scanty; become difficult; be restricted. ~**tıcı**, reducing, limiting; (*eng.*) reduction-joint. ~**tılmak**, *vp.* ~**tım/~tma**, *vn.* contraction; narrowing; shrinking; constriction; restriction; reduction. ~**tmak (-i)**, *vc.* contract; narrow; restrict; reduce.

darasız Without tare (weight).

darb- = DARP. ~**e**, blow, stroke; coup; turn of fortune; chance; (*mus.*) percussion. ~**¹etmek**ᵉᵈᵉʳ **(-i)**, strike, mint (coins); (*math.*) multiply.

darbımesel (*obs.*) Proverb.

darbuka(cı) (*mus.*) Earthenware kettle-drum (player).

darçık·arır (*eng.*) Extrusion press. ~**armak(-i)**, extrude. ~**ık**, extruded. ~**im**, extrusion.

dardağan *a.* Scattered; in utter confusion. *n.* (*bot.*) Terebinth tree.

dargın Angry; irritated; offended. ~ **olm.**, be angry, etc.; pretend not to care about stg. ~**lık**, anger, irritability; 'bad blood'.

darı (*bot.*) Millet; (*dial.*) maize. ~ **güvesi**, (*ent.*) corn moth: ~ **rastığı**, (*myc.*) sorghum smut: ~**sı başına!**, may you/he follow suit!; may your/his turn (for good luck) come next!

darıdünya (*col.*) This world; = DAR¹.

darıl·gan Easily hurt/offended; sensitive. ~**ganlık**, sensitiveness. ~**maca**, ~ **yok**, you must not get angry; no offence meant! ~**mak (-e)**, scold s.o.: *vi.* be irritated; get angry/cross. ~**tmak (-i)**, *vc.*

dar·lanmak/~laşmak *vi.* Become narrow/confined; be in straits. ~**latmak/~laştırmak (-i)**, make narrow; restrict; oppress. ~**lık**, narrowness; narrow place; trouble; poverty.

darmadağın In utter confusion; cluttered; all over the place. ~ **etm.**, rout. ~**ık**, confused mass.

dar¹pᵇⁱ Blow, stroke; minting (coins); (*math.*) multiplication; (*mus.*) beat. ~**hane**, the mint.

dar·ülaceze (*soc.*, *obs.*) Alms-house (in Istanbul), poor-house, infirmary. ~**ülfünun**, (*ed.*) university. ~**ülharp**, (*rel.*, *mil.*) 'the house of war', the non-Muslim world, the theatre of war. ~**ülislam**, (*rel.*) the Muslim world. ~**üşşafaka**, (*soc.*) school for orphans (in Istanbul). ~**üşşifa**, (*med.*) mental hospital.

Darvin·cilik/~izm (*bio.*) Darwinism.

dasitⁱ (*min.*) Dacite.

dasitan (*lit.*) Story; legend; ballad; epic; adventure; spell. ~**i**, legendary, epic.

-daş/-deş/-taş/-teş *n. suf.* [64] Fellow- [YOLDAŞ]; co- [DİNDAŞ]; colleague [MESLEKTAŞ]; -mate [SINIFTAŞ]; GÖNÜLDEŞ; İŞTEŞ].

da·ülkel¹pᵇⁱ (*med.*, *obs.*) Hydrophobia. ~**ülmerak**¹, hypochondria. ~**üsseher**, insomnia. ~**üssıla**, nostalgia.

dav (*zoo.*) Burchell's zebra.

dava (*leg.*) Lawsuit; trial; claim; petition; problem; thesis; matter; question. ~ **açmak (-e)/etm. (-i)**, (*leg.*) bring an action/suit against s.o.: ~ **başı**, the main argument: ~ **dosyası**, (*leg.*) brief: ~ **etm.** = ~ AÇMAK; (*obs.*) claim, pretend to: ~ **ikame etm. (-e)**, bring an action against s.o.: ~**sında bulunmak**, claim that . . .: ~**sını tutmak (-in)**, take the side of/ support s.o.

dava·cı Claimant, suitor, petitioner, plaintiff: ~**yım!**, I'll have the law on you!, I'll sue you! ~**lı**, what is claimed; who/which is the subject of a lawsuit; accused; defendant; (*fig.*) pretentious; tendentious (book). ~**lık**, appropriate for a lawsuit. ~**vekili**ⁿⁱ, advocate, barrister, attorney.

davar (*zoo.*, *live.*) (Flock of) sheep/goats.

davetⁱ (*leg.*) Summons, citation; (*soc.*) invitation; feast. ~ **etm.**, (*soc.*) invite; (*adm.*) convene; (*leg.*) incite, cause: ~ **yapmak**, arrange a celebration/ party.

davet·çi The inviter. ~**iye**, (*soc.*) invitation-card; (*leg.*) notice, summons. ~**li**, person invited, guest. ~**name**, invitation. ~**siz**, uninvited: ~ **misafir**, gate-crasher; unexpected guest.

davlumbaz (*naut.*) Paddle-box (of a steamer); (*eng.*) hood (of a forge/stove).

davran·dırmak (-i, -e) Rouse s.o. to do stg. ~**ım/ ~ış**, behaviour, conduct; attitude, comportment; action. ~**ışçı(lık)**, (*phil.*, *psy.*) behaviour·ist/(-izm). ~**ma**, *vn.* action, behaviour: ~ **eylemi**, (*ling.*) verb of future action: ~ **töresi**, rules of behaviour. ~**mak**, *vi.* bestir o.s.; prepare for action; resist; act, behave; take pains: **davranma!**, don't stir!

davudi (*mus.*) Bass/baritone voice; fine manly voice.

davul (*mus.*) Drum; (*sl.*) backside. ~ **çalmak**, play the drum; (*fig.*) let everyone hear the news: ~ **çaldık**, we announced it everywhere (so don't pretend you don't know): ~ **dövmek**, beat/play the drum: ~ **(gibi)**, fat and swollen: ~ **onun boynunda tokmak başkasının elinde**, he's only a figure-head; s.o. else calls the tune: ~ **tokmağı**, drumstick: ~ **zurna ile**, publicly, ostentatiously: ~**u biz çaldık parsayı başkası/el topladı**, we did the work but others got the benefit: ~**un sesi uzaktan hoş gelir**, oh! the brave music of a distant drum! ~**cu(luk)**, (work of a) drummer.

davya Dental forceps.

daya·¹kᵍⁱ Prop; support; beating (esp. the bastinado). ~ **arsızı**, fearless, brazen-faced: ~ **atmak**, beat, give a thrashing: ~ **cennetten çıkmış**, spare the rod and spoil the child: ~ **düşkünü**, s.o. deserving a thrashing: ~ **kaçkını**, s.o. who deserves (but didn't get) a thrashing: ~ **vurmak (-e)**, prop up (a wall, etc.): ~ **yemek**, get a thrashing: ~ **yemek için kaşınıyor**, he's just asking for a beating: ~ **yemiş gibi**, very cowed: ~ **yoksulu**, s.o. deserving a beating: ~**a susamak**, 'ask' for a beating. ~**lamak (-i)**, (*arch.*) shore/prop up. ~**lık**, suitable as a prop; deserving a beating.

daya·lı Propped up; leaning against; **(-e)**, (*cin.*) based on: ~ **döşeli**, fully furnished (house). ~**mak (-i, -e)**, prop up; support; lean against (to support it); benefit (from a situation); bring near, stretch out (threateningly); give/do stg. without wasting time: **dayayıp döşemek**, furnish completely. ~ **na¹k&¹**, support, base; butment, bracket; (*phil.*) basis, substratum. ~ **naksız**, unfounded, baseless. ~ **narak (-e)**, relying on, based on. ~ **nca** = ~ NAK. ~ **ncalı**, strong. ~ **n¹ç**ᶜ¹, (*phys.*) strength, resistance; patience: ~ **alıştırmaları**, (*sp.*) body-building exercises. ~ **nçlı**, patient. ~ **nçsız(lık)**, impat·ient/(-ience). ~ **ndırmak (-i)**, *vc.* = ~ NMAK. ~ **nga**, (*mil.*) trench. ~ **nga¹ç**ᶜ¹, support, prop.

dayanık *a.* Leaning on, resting against; relying on. ~ **lı**, lasting, enduring; strong; **(-e)**, resistant to, -proof: ~ **lastik**, crepe rubber. ~ **lılaştırma**, (*eng.*) reinforcement; strengthening. ~ **lılık**, permanence; endurance, strength, resistance: ~ **deneme//sınırı**, (*phys.*) endurance test//limit. ~ **sız**, not lasting; temporary; weak; (*chem.*) unstable. ~ **sızlık**, temporariness; weakness; (*rad.*) fading.

dayan·ılmak *vp.* = ~ MAK. ~ **ıl(a)maz**, irresistible; compelling. ~ **ım**, resistance, endurance. ~ **ırlık**, strength, resistance.

dayanış (*sp.*) Endurance. ~ **çılık**, (*soc.*) mutual support/solidarity. ~ **ık**, mutually supporting. ~ **ma**, *vn.* (*soc.*) mutual aid/support, cooperation; solidarity: ~ **mesaji**, (*soc.*) message of support/cooperation. ~ **macılık**, cooperation, mutual support. ~ **mak**, *vi.* support each other; co-operate. ~ **malı**, in a continuous series; (*fin.*, *leg.*) joint.

dayan·ma *vn.* Endurance; resistance; support; (*sp.*) resting: ~ **kemeri**, (*arch.*) flying buttress: ~ **uçuşu**, (*aer.*) endurance flight. ~ **mak (-e)**, bear, endure, last, hold out; lean on, prop o.s. up; rely on; confide in; resist; support; push; (road) end at; succeed in reaching. ~ **malık**, (*arch.*) window-sill. ~ **tı**, (*phil.*) hypostasis.

dayat·ma Insistence. ~ **mak (-i, -e)**, *vc.* = DAYAMAK: make lean against/prop up; fling (an accusation/refusal) in s.o.'s face: *vi.* be obstinate in refusing to do stg.

dayı Maternal uncle; (*naut.*) captain of a ship; (*his.*) dey (of Algiers); (*col.*) a good fellow; (*col.*) protector, patron. ~ **sı dümende**, he has influential protectors. ~ **lık**, being an uncle. ~ **zade**, cousin.

daz *a.* Bald(headed); bare (countryside). *n.* Baldness; (*med.*) alopecia.

dazara ~ **dazar/dazır**, hurring and scurrying.

dazlak Bald. ~ **kartal**, (*orn.*) bald eagle. ~ **lık**, baldness.

dazlamak Find fault.

dB. = (*phys.*) DESİBEL.

DB = DENİZCİLİK BANKASI; DIŞİŞLERİ BAKANLIĞI. ~ **YKP** = DÖRDÜNCÜ BEŞ YILLIK KALKINMA PLANI.

DC = (*phys.*) (*direct current*).

DÇM = (*fin.*) DÖVİZE ÇEVRİLEBİLİR MEVDUAT.

DD = (*pub.*) DERLEMELER DERGİSİ. ~ **T** = (*dichlor-diphenyl-trichlorethane*). ~ **Y** = DEVLET DEMİR YOLLARI.

de¹ *n.* The Tk. letter D, d.

de²/da/te/ta *conj.* [206] And; also, too; but; and

then; so, therefore. ... ~ ... ~ , both ... and ...; ~ **cabası**, and into the bargain ....

-de/-da/-te/-ta *n. suf.* [28] *Forming the locative case*, or equivalent to a preposition. At [EVDE]; in [MEKTUPTA]; during [BAYRAMDA]; on [TABAKTA]. **-de hali**, (*ling.*) locative case: **-de'li tümleç alan eylem**, (*ling.*) verb taking a locative construction.

-de-/-da- *v. suf.* [231] *Forming denominal verbs with onomatopoeic words* [KÜTÜRDEMEK; HORULDAMAK].

de·bagat¹ Tanning. ~ **bağ**, tanner.

debbe (*dom.*) Copper vessel (with handles and lid).

debdebe Noise, clamour; pomp, display. ~ **li**, noisy; magnificent, resplendent, showy.

debelenmek *vi.* Struggle and kick; (*fig.*) struggle in vain.

de·bi (*ind.*) Output, flow. ~ **breyaj**, (*mot.*) clutch (pedal); declutching: ~ **yapmak**, declutch; let out the clutch.

Deccal¹ (*rel.*) The Antichrist.

dede Grandfather, ancestor; old man; (*rel.*) saintly dervish; (*ed. sl.*) very old pupil. ~ **koruk yer, torunun dişi kamaşır**, the sins of the fathers are visited upon the children. ~ **lik**, grandfatherhood; grandfatherly action.

dedektif = DETEKTİF.

dedi¹k&¹ = DEMEK *n.* Statement. ~ **lerini almak**, take down a statement.

dedikodu Tittle-tattle, gossip. ~ **cu**, a gossip. ~ **culuk**, gossiping.

dedir(t)mek *vc.* = DEMEK. Make/let say; cause, stg. to be said.

dedveyt ~ **tonluk**, (*naut.*) deadweight tonnage.

def = TEF.

defa Time; turn. ~ **ten**, all at once; (*fin.*) in a lump sum.

defans Defence. ~ **if**, defensive.

def·¹etmekᵉᵈᵉʳ **(-i)** Drive away; repel; expel; eject; abolish. ~ **¹i'¹**, repelling; expulsion; removal; refutation: ~ **'i bela kabilinden**, as a precaution against possible evil/trouble: ~ **'i hacet etm.**, relieve nature.

defile (*mod.*) Fashion parade.

def¹inⁿⁱ (*rel.*) Burial. ~ **e**, buried treasure; unexpected wealth; 'a real treasure' (of a servant). ~ **eci**, treasure-hunter; (*fig.*) impostor, confidence trickster. ~ **ecilik**, treasure-hunting.

de·finisyon (*cin.*) Definition. ~ **flasyon**, (*fin.*) deflation. ~ **flektör**, (*aer.*) baffle, cascade.

deflemek (-i) = DEFETMEK.

defne (*bot.*) Laurel, sweet bay. ~ **ağacı**, bay-tree: ~ **yaprağı**, (*cul.*) bay-leaf. ~ **giller**, (*bot.*) Lauraceae. ~ **yaprağı**ⁿ¹, (*ich.*) very small bluefish.

defn·edilmek Be buried. ~ **¹etmek**ᵉᵈᵉʳ **(-i)**, bury.

defo (*ind.*) Defect. ~ **lar**, defective goods, seconds. ~ **lu**, defective.

def¹olmakᵒˡᵘʳ Be removed; be off, go away. ~ **ol!**, buzz off!, get out!, go to blazes!

defor·masyon (*eng.*) Deformation; strain, stress. ~ **me**, deformed, misshapen; distorted.

defter Register; account book; classbook; notebook; list; catalogue. ~ **açmak**, open a list (of subscriptions, etc.): ~ **emini**, (*his.*) director of the Registry of Landed Property: ~ **tutma**, (*fin.*)

bookkeeping: ~ **tutmak**, keep books: ~ **den silmek (-i)**, (*fig.*) forget s.o., no longer consider s.o. as a friend: ~ **e çekmek/geçirmek**, copy down, record: ~ **e kaydetmek**, enrol: ~ **i dürülmek**, (*fig.*) die, be killed: ~ **i Hakani**, (*his.*) directorate of the Registry of Landed Property: ~ **i kapamak**, (*fin.*) close the books; (*fig.*) cease to do stg.; lose interest in stg.
defter·dar (*his.*) Finance Minister; (*adm.*) head of the fin. department of a vilayet; (*fin.*) bookkeeper, accountant. ~ **darlık**, (*adm.*) work/status/office of a DEFTERDAR. ~ **hane**, (*his.*) office of the Land Registry.
degajman (*sp.*) Clearance.
değdirmek (-i, -e) *vc.* = DEĞMEK. Cause/allow to touch/reach, etc.; cause to be worth; have stg. valued.
değe¹çci (*chem.*) Ligand.
değer *a.* Worth; worthy; suitable. *n.* (*fin.*) Value, worth, price; (*chem.*) valence; calibre; talent. ~ **alanı**, range of values: ~ **artışı**, (*fin.*) appreciation: ~ **azalması**, depreciation: ~ **biçici**, appraiser, valuer: ~ **biçmek**, appraise, evaluate: ~ **düşü(rü)mü**, devaluation: ~ **kâgıdı**, (*fin.*) securities: ~ **kuramı**, (*phil.*) theory of values: ~ **öğretisi**, (*phil.*) axiology: ~ **payı**, (*fin.*) premium: ~ **takdiri**, evaluation: ~ **üzerinden**, *ad valorem*: ~ **vermek**, esteem, appreciate, value: ~ **yargısı**, evaluation, appraisal: ~ **den düşme karşılığı**, (*fin.*) sinking fund: ~ **den düşürmek**, detract from; (*fin.*) devalue, demonetize (currency): ~ **den düşürüm**, devaluation: ~ **e göre**, (*fin.*) *ad valorem*: ~ **inde**, in the nature of, like . . .: ~ **ini anlamak**, appreciate, value: ~ **ini bozmak**, alloy: ~ **ini düşürme**, devaluation: ~ **ini düşürmek**, devalue, cheapen: ~ **ini küçültmek**, depreciate: ~ **ini yükseltmek**, revalue: ~ **ler**, assets.
değer·bilir(lik) Appreciative(ness). ~ **bilmez**, unappreciative. ~ **düşürümü**ⁿü, (*fin.*) devaluation. ~ **leme**, (*fin.*) appraisal, valuation, assessment. ~ **lendirme**, (*vn.*) assessment; valuation; appreciation. ~ **lendirmek (-i, -e)**, appreciate, increase the value of; realize; assess; evaluate; put to good use; take advantage of. ~ **lenmek**, increase in value; become valuable. ~ **li**, valuable; costly; estimable/deserving (person); (*chem.*) -valent: ~ **belgeler**, securities: ~ **madenler**, (*min.*) precious metals: ~ **para**, (*fin.*) hard currency: ~ **taş**, (*min.*) gemstone. ~ **lik**, (*chem.*) valency. ~ **siz**, valueless; cheap; (*fig.*) insignificant; humble: ~ **alacaklar**, small debts: ~ **para**, soft currency.
değgin (-e) Concerning, related to, connected with. ~ **lik**, connection.
değil *neg. particle* [103]. *Alone or with the appropriate endings of* OLMAK [-iM, -DiR, -MiŞ, -SE, etc.). Not; not only; not so [**Hasan'ı değil, Orhan'ı görmedim**, it wasn't Hasan but Orhan that I didn't see]. ~ **a**, let alone: ~ **mi?**, [106] is it not so? (*but notice the usual Eng. construction*: you do . . ., don't you?; you can . . ., can't you?; you will . . ., won't you?, *etc.*): ~ **mi ki**, [211] since, as. ~ **leme**, negation. ~ **lemeli**, negative(ly). ~ **leyici**, negative.
değim Value, merit, worth. ~ **li**, worthy. ~ **sız**, worthless.
değin¹ (-e) *post.* [88, 180] Up to, until; as far as.

değin² *n.* (*zoo.*) Squirrel.
değin·im/ ~ **me** Contact; discussion. ~ **mek (-e)**, make contact with; touch upon/discuss stg. ~ **ti**, inclusiveness.
değirmek (-i, -e) *vc.* = **değmek**; pass on a message.
değirmen Mill; (*col.*) wall-clock, pocket-watch. ~ **taşı**, mill-stone: ~ **unu**, (*cul.*) wholemeal flour: ~ **de sakal ağartmak**, be inexperienced/immature; not have learned from experience: ~ **in suyu nereden geliyor?**, who's paying for/financing all this?
değirmen·ci Miller. ~ **cilik**, miller's work; milling. ~ **lik**, a place full of mills. ~ **taşı**ⁿ¹, (*geol.*) millstone grit.
değirmi *a.* Round, circular. *n.* (*tex.*) Square (of cloth.). ~ **sakal**, round-trimmed beard. ~ **lemek (-i)**, make round. ~ **lik**, roundness.
değiş Exchange. ~ **tokuş**, (*fin.*) exchange, barter; (*math.*) permutation: ~ **(tokuş) etm.**, exchange, barter; permutate.
değiş·ebilir (Ex)changeable. ~ **ebilme**, variability. ~ **en**, changing; (*ast.*) variable (star); (*met.*) choppy (wind). ~ **ik**, *a.* changed, different, modified; varied, diverse; alternative, alternating; (*mod.*) new, unusual; (*phys.*) aniso-; hetero-: *n.* sickly child, weakling: ~ **akım**, (*el.*) alternating current. ~ **iklik**, adjustment, alteration, change, modification: ~ **yapmak**, alter, modify. ~ **im**, (ex)change; (*math.*) variation; (*met.*) backing (of the wind); alteration: ~ **yuvarı**, (*ast.*) troposphere. ~ **(in)im**, exchange; (*bio.*) mutation. ~ **(in)imcilik**, (*bio.*) mutationism. ~ **ir**, convertible: ~ **odaklı mercek**, (*cin.*) zoom lens. ~ **ke**, (*zoo.*) modification. ~ **kemek**, (*zoo.*) modify. ~ **ken**, *a.* very variable, changeable: *n.* (*math.*) factor, variable. ~ **kenlik**, variability, changeability. ~ **kin**, modified. ~ **me**, *vn.*, change, variation, etc.; exchange; (*sp.*) relay. ~ **mek**, *vi.* change; fluctuate; (-i, -e), exchange for; substitute (-i, -le), exchange with. ~ **mez**, fixed, invariable, constant; static; stable; permanent.
değiştir·ge (*adm., eng.*) Draft modification. ~ **ge¹çci**, (*min., phys.*) converter; (cycle) gearchange. ~ **gen**, (*math.*) parameter. ~ **i**, modification. ~ **ici**, (*eng.*) exchanger. ~ **ilebilir**, interchangeable; convertible. ~ **ilmek**, *vp.* ~ **im**, deformation, distortion; substitution. ~ **me**, act of changing. ~ **mece**, variation; (*sp.*) replacement, transfer. ~ **mek (-i)**, change, convert; amend, modify; alter; substitute; (*phys.*) commutate. ~ **meksizin**, literally, word for word.
değme¹ *a.* Ordinary; chance; any; every; the very best, 'super'; + *neg.* hardly any; not just any. ~ **de**, (*col.*) probably not, unlikely.
değ·me² *vn.* Touch; contact; application. ~ **mek (-e)**, touch; reach; attain; be worth; be worthwhile: **değme gitsin** = DEMEK (DEME . . .): **değme keyfine!**, now he should be happy!: **değmez!**, it isn't worthwhile. ~ **meli**, (*cin.*) contact.
değne¹kᵍⁱ Stick; cane, rod; (*fig.*) beating. ~ **çekirgesi**, (*ent.*) stick-insect: ~ **gibi**, slim: ~ **yemek**, get a beating. ~ **çi(lik)**, (*ind.*) (work/position of a) foreman/guild official/parking attendant. ~ **lemek (-i)**, beat with a stick.
değşincilik (*bio.*) Mutation.

deh *int.* Giddap! (to an animal).

deha Great ability; genius.

dehalet[i] Seeking refuge. ~ **etm.**, take refuge; (rebel) give o.s. up.

dehle·mek (-i) Urge on (an animal). ~ **nmek**, *vp.*

dehliz (*arch.*) Entrance-hall; vestibule, lobby; corridor; (*bio.*) vestibule.

dehşet[i] Terror. ~ **filmi,** (*cin.*) horror film: ~ **içinde,** aghast: ~ **saçmak/salmak,** spread terror: ~ **veren,** awesome. ~ **li,** dire, fearsome, terrible: ~ **sıcak,** 'terribly' hot.

dejene·rasyon Degeneration. ~ **re,** degenerate: ~ **etm.//olm.,** make//be degenerate. ~ **releşmek,** *vi.* become degenerate. ~ **resans,** (*bio.*) degeneration; weakening.

dek[1] **(-e)** *post.* [88] As far as, until.

dek[2] *n.* Trick.

dek[3] = TEK.

dekadan (*art.*) Decadent. ~ **lık,** decadence. ~ **s,** (*soc.*) decadence.

deka- *pref.* (*math.*) Deca-. ~ **gram//** ~ **litre//** ~ **metre,** decagram//decalitre//decametre.

de·kalkomani (*art.*) Decal(comania), transfer. ~ **kalsifiye,** (*chem.*) decalcified.

dekan (*ed.*) Dean, head of faculty. ~ **lık,** deanship; dean's office.

dekar (*math.*) One-tenth hectare.

dekartçılık, (*phil.*) Cartesianism.

dekaster (*math.*) Ten cubic metres.

-deki/-daki *n. suf.* The one at/in/of [EVDEKİ; OKULDAKİ].

de·klanşör (*cin.*) Burton, trigger. ~ **klarasyon,** (*adm.*) declaration. ~ **kolte,** (*mod.*) *n.* low-cut dress, etc.: *a.* open: ~ **konuşmak,** (*col.*) speak immodestly. ~ **kont,** (*fin.*) discount.

dekor (*th.*) Scenery; (*cin.*) set(ting); decoration. ~ **asyon,** (*th.*) scene-making; decoration. ~ **atif,** decorative. ~ **atör/** ~ **cu,** (*th.*) set-designer; (*dom.*) internal decorator. ~ **atörlük,** set-designing; decorating. ~ **e,** decorated.

de·kovil (*rly.*) ~ **hattı,** narrow-gauge railway. ~ **kreşendo,** (*mus.*) decrescendo.

deks·trin (*chem.*) Dextrin. ~ **tro-,** right-handed. ~ **trorotasyon,** clockwise rotation. ~ **troz,** dextrose.

delalet[i] Acting as guide/pilot; guidance; indication; agency. ~ **etm.,** guide; (**-e**), indicate, show; signify, denote; be an intermediary/help.

del·dirmek (-i, -e) *vc.* = DELMEK. ~ **er,** piercing.

dele·gasyon (*adm.*) Delegation. ~ **ge(lik),** (duties of) delegate.

del·ge[ci]**ç** Perforator, perforating machine. ~ **gi,** (*carp., eng.*) auger, bit, drill, punch.

deli *a.* Mad; insane; crazy; foolish, rash; (*bot., fig.*) wild; violently addicted to, mad about/on. *n.* Madman; (*sp.*) fan. ~ **alacası,** crude/clashing colours: ~ **bal,** honey gathered from poisonous flowers: ~ **balkabağından olmaz ya!,** he must be off his head!: ~ **baş,** pig-headed; = ~ BAŞ: ~ **bayrağı açmak,** (*jok.*) be in love: ~ **canlı,** restless, capricious: ~ **çıkmak,** go mad; (*fig.*) be very irritable: ~ ~ **den hoşlanır, imam ölüden,** everyone is wrapped up in his own concerns: ~ **divane olm.,** be utterly mad: ~ **etm.,** drive mad; ~ **gibi,** as if mad; like

mad, wildly: ~ **gömleği,** (*med.*) strait-jacket/-waistcoat: ~ **ırmak,** turbulent river: ~ **kızın çeyizi gibi,** in wild disorder: ~ **olm. (-e, için),** be mad on stg.; be very irritable: ~ **orman,** vast and dense forest: ~ **Raziye,** woman behaving wildly; strangely dressed/ eccentric woman: ~ **saçması,** absolute nonsense; utter rot: ~ **saraylı gibi,** very strangely dressed: ~ **nin eline değnek vermek,** give an opportunity to s.o. able to do harm: ~ **nin zoruna bak!,** what an extraordinary idea: ~ **si (-in),** fan of, mad about: ~ **ye dönmek,** be very pleased; be in a rage: ~ **ye her gün bayram,** (*pej.*) to a fool every day is a holiday: ~ **ye pösteki saydırmak,** give s.o. a tiresome and useless job.

deli·balta Cruel person. ~ **baş,** (*live.*) staggers. ~ **bozuk,** erratic, unstable, eccentric. ~ **ce,** *a.* slightly mad, foolish; (*bot.*) poisonous: *adv.* madly: *n.* (*bot.*) common darnel: ~ **doğan,** (*orn.*) hobby. ~ **cesine,** like a madman; exceedingly. ~ **ci,** piercing, penetrating. ~ **ci**[ği]**k** = DELİKÇİK. ~ **dolu,** s.o. who talks at random and without reflection. ~ **duman,** foolhardy, reckless; crazy, good-fornothing. ~ **fişe**[ği]**k,** unbalanced, flippant.

deli[i]**k** *n.* Hole; opening; aperture; (*bio.*) fenestra; bore; (*sl.*) prison. *a.* Bored; pierced. ~ **açmak/ delmek,** bore, broach, drill: ~ **büyük yama küçük,** the means do not meet the requirements: ~ **deşik,** full of holes: ~ **deşik etm.,** riddle with holes: ~ **deşik olm.,** be riddled with holes: ~ **kapamak,** fill the breach; make good a deficiency: ~ **kazmak,** burrow: ~ **kutru,** (*eng.*) calibre: ~ **mastarı,** (*eng.*) centre-punch: ~ **e girmek,** (*sl.*) go to prison: ~ **e tıkmak,** (*sl.*) put in 'clink', imprison.

delikanlı *n.* Youth; young man, adolescent. *a.* Young; sprightly. ~ **lık,** youth; youthfulness; adolescence.

delik·çi[ği]**k** (*bio.*) Pore. ~ **li** *a.* having holes; hollow; perforated; punched: *n.* (*cul.*) perforated skimmer: ~ **işleme,** (*tex.*) openwork embroidery. ~ **liler,** (*zoo.*) Foraminifera. ~ **siz,** without holes; unperforated; sound; (*arch.*) blind (wall): ~ **uyku,** sound sleep.

delil Guide, pilot; (*leg.*) proof, evidence; indication; sign. ~ **i olarak (-in),** as an earnest of . . .: ~ **ler,** (*fig.*) ammunition.

deli·lenmek Behave like a madman. ~ **lik,** craziness, madness: ~ **ine vurmak,** feign madness.

del·im (*med.*) Puncture. ~ **inme,** perforation. ~ **inmek,** *vp.* be pierced/perforated; be worn through; (*min.*) be drilled.

deli·otu[nu] (*bot.*) Golden alyssum, madwort. ~ **rmek,** *vi.* go mad; become insane; be furiously angry; be mad (with love/desire). ~ **rtmek (-i),** drive mad. ~ **şmen,** a bit crazy; wild (youth). ~ **şmenlik,** craziness; crazy behaviour; wildness: ~ **etm.,** behave crazily.

delk[i] Rubbing; (*phys.*) friction.

del·me *vn.* Piercing; boring, drilling; perforation: *a.* perforated, holed: ~ **kulesi,** (*min.*) drilling rig, derrick. ~ **mek (-i),** pierce; hole; drill; bore: **delip geçmek,** drill a hole right through.

delta (*geo.*) Delta. ~ **kası**[nı], (*bio.*) deltoid muscle. ~ **msı,** (*bio.*) deltoid.

dem[1] *n. (bio.)* Blood. ~ **dökmek**, lose much blood during menstruation.

dem[2] *n.* Breath; vapour; alcoholic drink; moment, time. ~ **çekmek**, (birds) sing sweetly; (*jok.*) drink wine, etc.: ~ **tutmak**, accompany music: ~ **vurmak** (-**den**), talk airily/vaguely/at random about stg.; claim stg. **dem.** = DEMİRYOLLARI.

dema·gog (*pol.*) Demagogue. ~ **goji**, demagogy: ~ **etm.**, appeal to the mob.

dema·rör (*mot.*) Starter. ~ **rş**, (*adm.*) action, step, *démarche.*

de·me *vn.* Saying; telling; meaning; (*lit.*) Shiite mystical poem: ~ **m o** ~ **değil**, that's not what I meant to say. ~ **me¹çci**, declaration, statement; words, speech.

demek (**der, diyor, diyecek, diyen**). Say; tell; mean; call, give a name to; think, intend, hope (to do stg.). ~ **...**, [215] that is to say, it means; so?: ~ **istiyorsunuz**, you mean to say: ~ **ki**, [216] that is to say; therefore: ~ **olm.**, mean: ~ **oluyor ki**, in that case: ~ **le maruf**, known as ...:... ~ **ten maksat**, ... means ...: **dediği çıkmak**, come true, be realized: **dediği dedik olm.**, abide by what one says; be obstinate: **dediği dedik düdüğü/öttürdüğü düdük**, s.o. whose every whim is satisfied, a spoilt child: **dediğinden (dışarı) çıkmak**, not pay attention to stg.: **dediğine gelmek**, finally agree with what was said: **deme!**, you don't say so!: **deme gitsin**, indescribable; unbounded: **demem ...** = DEME: **demeye getirmek**, tell stg. in a roundabout manner: ~ **ye kalmamak**, be no sooner said than done: **der demez**, immediately, straight away: **derken**, *adv.* [204] even as he spoke; just then, at that precise moment; all at once: **deyip de geçmemek**, not underestimate/underrate: **... deyip işin içinden çıktı**, he avoided further discussion by saying ...: DİYE: **diyor da başka bir şey demiyor**, he thinks of nothing but ....

demet[i] Sheaf; bunch; cluster, faggot; bundle; (*phys.*) beam; (*pub.*) fascicle. ~ **lemek (-i)**, tie up in a bunch, etc. ~ **lenmek**, *vp.*

demevi Connected with blood; full-blooded, sanguine.

demin Just now; not long ago. ~ **cek**, a moment ago. ~ **den**, just now, recently. ~ **ki**, what was done just now.

demir *n.* (*chem.*) Iron; (*naut.*) anchor; iron part (of stg.); barrel (of a gun); blade (of a knife). *a.* Made of iron, iron: (*chem.*) ferrous, ferric. ~ **almak**, (*naut.*) weigh anchor: ~ **atmak**, (*naut.*) cast anchor, anchor; (*fig.*) settle down (in a place): ~ **boku**, (*min.*) iron slag: ~ **cevheri**, (*min.*) iron ore: ~ **fıçı**, (*ind.*) drum: ~ **gibi**, healthy; strong: ~ **hindi**, (*sl.*) greedy, stingy: = ~ HİNDİ: ~ **leblebi**, a very difficult task; a tough nut to crack: ~ **mataforası**, (*naut.*) anchor davit: ~ **oksidi**, ferric oxide: ~ **pası**, rust colour: ~ **resmi**, (*naut.*) anchorage dues: ~ **taramak**, (*naut.*) drag the anchor: ~ **tavında, dilber çağında**, strike while the iron is hot, marry off the girl when she's young: ~ **üzerinde**, (*naut.*) ready to sail: ~ **yeri**, (*naut.*) anchorage, berth: ~ **e vurmak (-i)**, clap s.o. in irons/chains: ~ **i laçka etm.**, drop anchor: ~ **i grivaya almak**, (*naut.*) cat the anchor: ~ **i vira etm.**, weigh anchor.

demir·ağacı[n1] (*bot.*) Ironwood tree. ~ **baş**, ~ (**eşya**), (*leg.*) movable stock; furnishing, fixtures and equipment; (*fig.*) obstinate old man; (s.o.) always there, inevitable: ~ **defteri**, inventory: ~ **erzak**, (*mil.*) iron rations: ~ **yemek**, (*cul.*) standing dish. ~ **ci**, blacksmith: ~ **mengenesi**, iron vice. ~ **cilik**, hardware, ironmongery; blacksmith's trade/art. ~ **hane**, ironworks. ~ **hindi**, (*bot.*) tamarind tree: = ~ HINDI. ~ **kapan**, (*phys.*) magnet. ~ **kapı**, (*geo.*) gorge of a river; fortified defile. ~ **kazık**, (*ast.*) the Pole Star. ~ **kırı**, iron-grey. ~ **leme**, *vn.* (*naut.*) anchoring: ~ **yeri**, anchorage. ~ **lemek (-i)**, (*dom.*) bar (door/window, etc.); (*naut.*) drop anchor. ~ **leşmek**, *vi.* become (like) iron. ~ **li**, *a.* made of iron; ferrous; (*naut.*) anchored, at anchor; (*dom.*) barred. ~ **libeton**, (*arch.*) reinforced concrete. ~ **perde**, (*pol.*) the Iron Curtain. ~ **siz**, (*chem.*) non-ferrous. ~ **yolcu**, railwayman. ~ **yolunu**, railway.

demiurgos (*phil.*) Demiurge.

dem·lemek/ ~ **lendirmek (-i)** (*cul.*) Steam; brew (tea). ~ **lenmek**, be brewed; (*jok.*) drink alcoholic drinks. ~ **li**, brewed (tea). ~ **lik**, teapot.

demode Out of fashion.

demo·grafi (*soc.*) Demography. ~ **krasi**, democracy. ~ **krat**[1], democrat. ~ **kratik**, democratic. ~ **kratlaşmak**, become democratic. ~ **kratlaştırmak**, democratize. ~ **kratlık**, being a democrat.

demon·strasyon (*pol.*) Demonstration. ~ **taj**, (*ind.*) disassembly. ~ **te**, disassembled, knocked-down: ~ **etm.**, disassemble; dismantle.

den Tact.

den. = DENİZ(CİLİK).

-den/-dan/-ten/-tan *n. suf.* [28] *Forming the ablative case, or equivalent to a preposition.* From [EVDEN]; out of [TABAKTAN]; on [TELEFONDAN]; made of [YÜNDEN]; belonging to [HEYETTEN]; because/on account of [YAĞMURDAN]; through, by [GEÇİTTEN]. ~ (**az//daha**), *construction forming the comparative degree of an adj./adv.*, less//more than, -er than [**benden iyi bilirsin**, you know better than I: **ondan az büyük//daha küçük**, less big//smaller than it]. ~ **başka**, except, apart from: ~ **başlayarak**, starting with: ~ **beri**, since: ~ **çok**, exceeding: ~ **dolayı**, due to, on account of: ~ **geçmek**, do without: ~ **hali**, (*ling.*) ablative case: ~ **oluş**, relationship: ~ **oluşan**, consisting of: ~ **ötürü**, on account of: ~ **sonra**, after, subsequent to: ~ **yana** (**olm.**), (be) in favour of: ~ **'li tümleç alan eylem**, (*ling.*) verb taking an ablative construction.

denaet[i] Mean/low-down action; meanness.

denden (*pub.*) Ditto marks („) (in a table).

dendrit[i] (*geol., bio.*) Dendrite.

dene·l[kği] *a.* Proved, tried. *n.* Test subject, 'guinea-pig'. ~ **taşı**, (*min.*) touchstone.

dene·l Experimental. ~ **m**, (*med.*) test. ~ **me**, *vn.* trial, test(ing); (*min.*) assay; (*lit.*) essay: ~ **çekimi**, (*cin.*) test-shot: ~ **havuzu**, (*naut.*) test tank: ~ **kuruluşu**, (*ind.*) pilot plant: ~ **oynatımı**, (*cin.*) preview: ~ **tahtası**, (*med.*) guinea-pig, test-subject: (*eng.*) test-piece. ~ **meci(lik)**, (*lit.*) (art/work of an)

essayist. ~ **mek (-i)**, try, test, experiment on; (*min.*) assay. ~ **msel**, empirical. ~ **nce**, hypothesis. ~ **nme**, (*mod.*) fitting, trial. ~ **nmek**, *vp.* be tested, etc.
denet Control, inspection, supervision; checking, examination. ~ **raporu**, (*adm.*) inspection report. ~ **çi(lik)**, (office/work of) auditor, controller, checker, examiner, inspector, supervisor; (*fin.*) auditor; (*sp.*) scorer. ~ **ici**, (*phys.*) control device. ~ **im**, control, check, test; (*fin.*) audit: ~ **aygıtları**, test equipment. ~ **imsiz**, uncontrolled. ~ **imsizlik**, lack of control. ~ **le¹çᶜⁱ**, (*eng.*) control(ler). ~ **leme**, *vn.* inspection; testing; auditing; (*cin.*) censorship: ~ **belgesi**, (*cin.*) censor's certificate: ~ **kurulu**, (*cin.*) board of censors. ~ **lemek (-i)**, check, control, examine, inspect, supervise; (*fin.*) audit; (*cin.*) censor. ~ **lenmek**, *vp.* be checked, etc. ~ **leyici**, (*cin.*) censor. ~ **men**, inspector. ~ **mek (-i, -e)**, *vc.* = DENEMEK.
deney Experiment, test. ~ **bilimleri**, experimental sciences: ~ **nümune/örneği**, test-piece, specimen: ~ **yapma** = ~ LEME: ~ **yükü**, (*phys.*) proof load. ~ **ci(lik)**, experiment·er/(-ing). ~ **im**, (*phil.*) experimentation. ~ **(im)cilik**, empiricism. ~ **imli**, experienced. ~ **imsel**, empirical. ~ **ka¹pᵇⁱ**, (*chem.*) test-tube. ~ **leme**, experimentation. ~ **lemeli**, experimental. ~ **li**, experimental; demonstrable. ~ **sel**, experimental. ~ **selci(lik)**, experimental·ist/ (-ism). ~ **sellik**, experimentation. ~ **üstü**, transcendental. ~ **üstücü(lük)**, transcendental·ist/ (-ism), beyond the possibility of experimentation.
deng- = DENK.
denge (*phys.*) Balance, equilibrium; (*fig.*) aplomb; (*sp.*) balancing. ~ **araçları**, (*sp.*) balancing equipment: ~ **kalası**, (*sp.*) balance beam: ~ **kurmak**, create equilibrium: ~ **organı**, (*bio.*) organ of equilibrium: ~ **profili**, (*geo.*) river section: ~ **taşı**, (*bio.*) otolith: ~ **tozu**, (*bio.*) statolith: ~ **unsuru**, counterpoise: ~ **sini kaybetmek//korumak**, lose// keep one's balance.
denge·lem (*fin.*) Balance-sheet. ~ **leme**, *vn.* stabilization; (*fin.*) equalizing. ~ **lemek (-i)**, (*phys.*) balance, compensate; equalize; (*naut.*) ballast. ~ **lenme**, (*geol.*) isostasy. ~ **lenmek**, *vp.* ~ **leştirici**, (*min.*) stabilizer. ~ **leştirme**, (*min.*) stabilization. ~ **leyici**, ~ **özdek**, (*naut.*) ballast. ~ **li**, balanced; stable; (*fig.*) moderate, well-balanced. ~ **lilik**, stability. ~ **siz**, off balance; unbalanced; abnormal; unstable; (*fig.*) immoderate. ~ **sizlik**, instability, abnormality; (*med.*) ataxia.
deni Mean, low; vile, despicable.
denilmek (-e) Be named; be said.
denim (*tex.*) Denim(s).
deniye (*tex.*) Denier.
deniz *n.* Sea; wave; storm; (*fig.*) wide expanse, sea (of ...). ~ +, Sea-, aqua-; marine-: ~ **aslanı**, (*zoo.*) sea-lion: ~ **ataşesi**, (*adm.*) naval attaché: ~ **banyosu**, sea-bathe: ~ **baskını**, high tide; tidal wave: ~ **basması**, sea-flood: ~ **bindirmek**, become rough: ~ **buzulu**, (*geo.*) pack-ice: ~ **depremi**, (*geol.*) seaquake: ~ **derya ayak altında**, having a fine view of the sea: ~ **dibi**, sea-bottom: ~ **dokuncaları**, perils of the sea: ~ **durmak**, (storm) die down: ~ **düzey/seviyesi**, (*geo.*) sea-level: ~ **eri**,

sailor, blue-jacket: ~ **feneri**, lighthouse, etc. ~ **fizalya/kesesi**, (*zoo.*) Portuguese man-o'-war: ~ **gezintisi**, pleasure-cruise: ~ **giderleri**, (*fin.*) off-loading expenses: ~ **gülü**, (*zoo.*) sea-anemone: ~ **güvencesi**, (*fin.*) maritime insurance: ~ **güzeli**, (*ich.*) Atlantic shade-fish: ~ **haklar/hukuku**, (*leg.*) maritime law: ~ **haritası**, (*geo.*) chart: ~ **haydutluğu**, (*leg.*) piracy: ~ **(inşaatı) mühendis(liğ)i**, naval architect(ure): ~ **kargası**, (*ich.*) corb: ~ **kartalı**, (*orn.*) sea eagle: ~ **kazası**, accident at sea, shipwreck: ~ **kenarı**, shore, coast: ~ **kulübü**, yacht club: ~ **kurdu**, (*fig.*) old sea-dog: ~ **kuvvetleri**, (*naut.*) naval force(s); ~ **mili**, (*geo.*) sea mile: ~ **motoru**, (*naut.*) motorboat: ~ **nakliyatı**, shipping: ~ **okulu gemisi**, (*naut.*) training-ship: ~ **okulu öğrencisi**, naval cadet: ~ **onbaşısı**, able-bodied seaman: ~ **ödüncü**, (*fin.*) bottomry: ~ **pisti**, (*geo.*) channel: ~ **piyadeleri**, (*naut.*) marines: ~ **saksağanı**, (*orn.*) oyster-catcher: ~ **sathı**, (*geo.*) sea-level: ~ **sathından irtifa/rakım/yükseklik**, height above sea-level: ~ **sigortası**, (*fin.*) marine/maritime insurance: ~ **şeytanı**, (*ich.*) devilfish: ~ **şıpırtısı**, (*naut.*) choppiness: ~ **tarağı**, (*zoo.*) clam: ~ **taşemeni**, (*zoo.*) lamprey: ~ **taşıt belgesi**, (*fin.*) bill of lading: ~ **taşıtları**, (*naut.*) sea-going vessels, ships: ~ **ticaret kanunu**, maritime mercantile law: ~ **tutmak**, be sea-sick: ~ **uçağı**, (*aer.*) seaplane, hydroplane: ~ **üssü**, (*naut.*) naval base: ~ **yatağı**, (*geo.*) sea-bed: ~ **yayını**, (*ich.*) sheatfish: ~ **yeli**, İMBAT: ~ **yılan balığı**, (*ich.*) conger-eel: ~ **yitircesi**, (*fin.*) average: ~ **yolları**, (*fin.*) shipping lines: ~ **yoluyla**, by sea: ~ **yosunu**, (*bot.*) seaweed: ~ **yükü belgesi**, (*fin.*) bill of lading: ~ **yüzeyi** = ~ SATHI.
deniz-: ~ **de**, afloat: ~ **de kum onda para**, (*jok.*) he has money to burn: ~ **deki balığın pazarlığı olmaz/ balığa tava hazırlanmaz**, first catch your fish then eat it: ~ **den**, by sea: ~ **den bir avuç su gibi**, only a very small part of it: ~ **den çıkmış balığa dönmek**, be like a fish out of water: ~ **den geçip çayda/kıyıda boğulmak**, solve the big problem and stumble at the small one: ~ **e dökülmek**, (river) run into the sea: ~ **e düşen yılana sarılır**, a drowning man will clutch at a straw: ~ **e elverişli**, seaworthy: ~ **e indirmek**, (*naut.*) launch (boat/ship): ~ **e karşı**, facing the sea: ~ **e mecburi iniş**, (*aer.*) ditching: ~ **e nazır**, overlooking the sea: ~ **e su götürmek/taşımak**, carry coals to Newcastle; make a small gift to a rich man: ~ **i doldurmak**, reclaim land from the sea: ~ **i ötesi**, overseas: ~ **lerin özgürlüğü**, (*leg.*) freedom of the seas.
deniz·alasıⁿⁱ (*ich.*) Sea-trout. ~ **altı**ⁿⁱ, *a.* submarine, undersea; open to the sea, exposed: *n.* (*naut.*) submarine: ~ **kablosu**, (*el.*) submarine cable: ~ **lar detektörü**, asdic: ~ **lara karşı**, anti-submarine. ~ **anası**ⁿⁱ, (*zoo.*) jelly-fish. ~ **aşırı**, beyond the sea, overseas. ~ **at/aygırı**ⁿⁱ, (*zoo.*) seahorse. ~ **ayısı**ⁿⁱ, (*zoo.*) fur-seal, sea-bear. ~ **bilim(ci)**, oceanograph·y/(-er). ~ **ci**, sailor, seaman. ~ **cilik**, seamanship: ~ +, *a.* maritime, nautical. ~ **çakısı**ⁿⁱ, (*zoo.*) razor fish. ~ **çulluğu**ⁿᵘ, (*orn.*) sanderling. ~ **danteli**ⁿⁱ, (*zoo.*) millepore. ~ **dişi**ⁿⁱ, (*zoo.*) tooth-shell. ~ **el**, (*geol.*) marine. ~ **gergedanı**ⁿⁱ, (*zoo.*) narwhal. ~ **han**, (*ast.*) Nep-

tune. ~ **hıyarı**^{nı}, (*zoo.*) sea-cucumber. ~ **ısırganları**^{nı}, (*zoo.*) jelly-fishes. ~ **iğnesi**^{ni}, (*ich.*) great pipefish. ~ **ineği**^{ni}, (*zoo.*) sea-cow. ~ **kadayıfı**^{nı}, (*bot.*) bladderwrack. ~ **kaplumbağaları**^{nı}, (*zoo.*) turtles. ~ **kazı**^{nı}, (*orn.*) brent goose. ~ **kedisi**^{ni}, (*ich.*) rabbit-fish. ~ **kestanesi**^{ni}, (*zoo.*) sea-urchin. ~ **kırlangıcı**^{nı}, (*orn.*) common tern. ~ **kırlangıcıgiller**, (*orn.*) terns. ~ **kızı**^{nı}, (*myth.*) siren, mermaid; (*zoo.*) siren. ~ **kozalağı**^{nı}, (*zoo.*) cone-shell. ~ **köpüğü**^{nü}, (*geol.*) meerschaum. ~ **kulağı**^{nı}, (*geo.*) lagoon; (*zoo.*) ormer, sea-ear. ~ **laleleri**^{ni}, (*zoo.*) crinoids. ~ **li**, marine, maritime. ~ **lik**, (*naut., arch.*) weather-board. ~ **marulu**^{nu}, (*bot.*) sea-lettuce. ~ **maymunu**^{nu}, (*zoo.*) rabbit-fish; thornback-ray. ~ **menekşesi**^{ni}, (*bot.*) a campanula. ~ **minaresi**^{ni}, (*zoo.*) a conical mollusc. ~ **ördeği**^{ni}, (*orn.*) a petrel. ~ **örümceği**^{ni}, (*zoo.*) sea-spider. ~ **palamudu/peliti**^{ni}, (*zoo.*) acorn barnacle. ~ **perçemi**^{ni}, (*bot.*) seaweed. ~ **perisi**^{ni}, (*zoo.*) manatee. ~ **pırasası**^{nı}, (*bot.*) an edible seaweed. ~ **rezenesi**^{ni}, (*bot.*) samphire. ~ **salkımı**^{nı}, (*zoo.*) mollusc. ~ **sel**, marine, maritime. ~ **serçesi**^{ni}, (*orn.*) a small plover. ~ **şakayıkı**^{nı}, (*zoo.*) sea-anemone. ~ **tarağı**^{nı}, (*zoo.*) cockle. ~ **tavşanı**^{nı}, (*ich.*) lumpfish; (*zoo.*) sea-hare. ~ **tavşancılı**^{nı}, (*orn.*) osprey. ~ **yılanıgiller**, (*zoo.*) sea-serpents. ~ **yıldız(lar)ı**^{nı}, (*zoo.*) star-fish(es). ~ **yolu**^{nu}, (*naut.*) sea-lane/-way; shipping line.

den^{l}**k**^{gi} *n.* Bale; half a horse-load; (*phys.*) balance, equilibrium; counterpoise; (*naut.*) trim. *a.* In proper balance; equal; equivalent. ~ **ağırlık**, counterpoise, counterweight: ~ **bağlamak**, bale up: ~ **etm.**, make into bales; pack up; balance; (*naut.*) trim: ~ **gelmek**, *vi.* balance: ~ **getirmek**, *vt.* balance: ~ **ine getirmek (-i)**, choose the psychological moment for stg.: ~ **iyle karşılamak**, pay s.o. in his own coin, retaliate.

denk·lem (*math.*) Equation: ~ **ler sistemi**, simultaneous equations. ~ **lemek (-i)**, balance stg. ~ **lenmek**, *vp.* be baled up. ~ **lenti**, compensation. ~ **leşim**, (*geol.*) isostasy; equilibrium. ~ **leşme**, *vn.* being/becoming equal; equivalence. ~ **leşmek (-le)**, *vi.* be(come) equal with stg.; be balanced/in equilibrium; (*naut.*) be trimmed. ~ **leştirici**, (*fin.*) balancing, off-setting. ~ **leştirim**, (*psy.*) compensation. ~ **leştirmek (-i -e, -le)**, *vc.* make equal; equate; balance; compensate; trim; manage to find balance; compensate; trim; manage to find balance. ~ **lik**, balance, equilibrium; equivalence; equality; trim. ~ **ser**, just, equitable, fair. ~ **serlik**, (*phil.*) (natural) justice. ~ **siz**, unbalanced; unstable. ~ **sizlik**, imbalance; instability. ~ **teş**, balanced; equal.

denli^{1} *adv.* Of (such a) kind/manner; thus; of (such a) degree, to (that) extent; so.

denli^{2} *a.* Good-tempered, tractable; tactful; careful. ~ **densiz söz söylemek**, be tactless/disrespectful. ~ **lik**, tact.

denmek = DENİLMEK.

densiz Bad-tempered, peevish; inconsiderate; intractable. ~ **lenmek**, be bad-tempered. ~ **leşmek**, become bad-tempered, etc. ~ **lik**, bad-temper; lack of consideration.

denşir·ik (*chem.*) Denatured. ~ **mek (-i)**, denature.

den·tin (*bio.*) Dentine. ~ **ye** = DENİYE.

deontoloji (*soc.*) Deontology, ethics.

depar (*sp.*) Start; departure. ~ **tman**, (*adm.*) department.

deplasman (*sp.*) Change of position; shift; travelling: ~ **maçı**, away match.

depo (*ind.*) Depot; store; warehouse; (liquids) tank, reservoir; (coal) bunker; depository; (*ed. sl.*) very knowledgeable teacher. ~ **etm.**, make a stock of stg.

depo·cu(luk) (Work of) store-operator. ~ **lama**, storage. ~ **lamak (-i)**, store. ~ **zit(o)**, (*fin.*) deposit; security.

deppoy (*mil.*) Store, depot.

deprem (*geol.*) Earthquake; tremor. ~ **+**, *a.* Seismic; seismo-. ~ **bölgesi**, seismic region: ~ **çizisi**, seismogram: ~ **ocak/odağı**, hypocentre: ~ **özeği**, epicentre: ~ **yeğinlik ölçeği**, intensity scale: ~ **e dayanıklı**, (*arch.*) earthquake resistant.

deprem·bilim Seismology. ~ **çizer/ ~ yazar**, seismograph. ~ **ölçer**, seismometer. ~ **sel**, seismic: ~ **deniz dalgası**, tidal wave, tsunami. ~ **siz**, aseismic.

deprenmek *vi.* Move; be stirred; rise.

depresyon (*psy.*) Depression.

depreş·mek Be renewed; (*med.*) recur. ~ **tirmek (-i)**, *vc.*

der (*obs.*) Gate; door. ~ **saadet**, (*his.*) Istanbul.

derakap Immediately afterwards.

derbeder *n.* Vagrant, vagabond, tramp; Bohemian. *a.* Living an irregular life, careless, slovenly. ~ **lik**, vagrancy; slovenliness.

derben^{l}**t**^{di} (*geo.*) Defile, pass.

der^{l}**ç**^{ci} (*pub.*) Insertion. ~ **etm.**, insert, inscribe: ~ **olm.**, be inserted.

derd- = DERT.

derdest^{i} *a.* In hand; in possession; in course of being made/done. *n.* (*leg.*) Arrest. ~ **etm.**, (*leg.*) arrest; take possession of; sequestrate.

dere (*geo.*) Valley; brook, stream; (*arch.*) gutter. ~ **alabalığı**, (*ich.*) brook trout: ~ **burada boy vermez**, the river is out of one's depth here: ~ **gibi akmak**, (blood) pour out: ~ **iskorpiti**, (*ich.*) bullhead, miller's thumb: ~ **kayabalığı**, (*ich.*) gudgeon; ~ **kumrusu**, (*orn.*) collared turtle dove: ~ **pisisi**, (*ich.*) flounder: ~ **tepe**, hills and valleys: ~ **tepe demedik yürüdük gittik**, we stopped at no obstacle: ~ **tepe dolaşmak**, wander over hill and dale: ~ **den tepeden konuşmak**, have a long chat about all sorts of things; (*adm.*) explore every avenue.

dere·beyi^{ni} (*his.*) Feudal chieftain; despot; (*fig.*) bully. ~ **beylik**, (*his.*) feudalism; fief; despotism: ~ **devrinde**, in the feudal age.

derece *n.* (*arch.*) Step, stair; (*math.*) degree; (alcohol) degree, strength; extent; (*soc.*) rank, grade; (*phys.*) (clinical) thermometer. *adv.* So, to such an extent. ~ **~**, gradually, by degrees: ~ **koymak**, (*med.*) take s.o.'s temperature. ~ **lemek (-i)**, calibrate. ~ **lenme**, gradation. ~ **li**, graduated; in stages.

dereke The lowest stratum; descending degree; (*phys.*) degree below zero.

dereotu^{nu} (*bot.*) Dill; (fennel).

dergâh (*rel.*) Dervish convent.
dergi (*lit. obs.*) Collection of poems; (*pub.*) review, journal, magazine; digest, compendium. ~**ci(lik)**, (*pub.*) magazine publish·er(-ing) ~**lemek**, (*leg.*) codify; (*pub.*) edit, compile. ~**lik**, *a.* (*pub.*) suitable for magazines, etc.: *n.* magazine-rack. ~**n**, codified; compiled. ~**nlemek**, compile and produce in book form.
derhal Immediately; at once.
deri *n.* (*bio.*) Skin; derm(a); hide; leather. ~ +, *a.* Derma(to)-; cutaneous. ~ **değişimi**, (*zoo.*) (snake, etc.) moulting, sloughing: ~ **ile parlatmak**, (*ind.*) buff: ~ **kınkanatlısı**, (*ent.*) skin beetle: ~ **mantarı**, (*myc.*) skin fungus: ~ **yangısı**, (*med.*) dermatitis: ~**si kemiklerine yapışmış**, just skin and bone; skinny: ~**sine sığmaz**, too big for his boots: ~**sini soymak/yüzmek**, skin, flay; torture to death; (*fig.*) despoil.
deri·altıⁿⁱ (*bio.*) Subcutaneous layer. ~**bilim**, (*med.*) dermatology. ~**ce**, dermatosis. ~**ci(lik)**, (work of a) dealer in skins. ~**ci**ⁱ**k**ᵍⁱ, (*bio.*) cuticle; dandruff. ~**içi**, intradermal. ~**lenmek**, (*med.*) heal over.
der·ilgen Collected. ~**ilmek**, *vp.* = DERMEK; be collected; collect o.s. ~**im**, (*lit.*) anthology.
derin *a.* Deep; profound; abstruse; bathy-. *n.* Deep place; pit; abyss. ~ **baygınlık**, (*med.*) coma: ~ **deniz**, (*geo.*) abyss: ~ ~, deeply: ~ ~ **düşünmek**, think deeply (about stg.); be lost in thought: ~ **etek**, (*geo.*) continental shelf: ~ **helataşı**, WC.: ~ **kaynaklı**, (*geol.*) hypogene: ~ **uykuda**, fast asleep: ~**den**, from far off; not very clear: ~**den** ~**e**, from far away; minutely, profoundly: ~**ine gitmek**, get to the bottom of stg.
derin·leme(sine) Very deeply; in depth. ~**leşmek**, *vi.* become deep; obtain deep knowledge; (sound) become faint. ~**leştirmek (-i)**, deepen; study deeply. ~**letmek (-i)**, deepen. ~**lik**, *n.* depth; depths (of time); profundity; hollow; (*mil.*) field, range: ~ +, *a.* (*phys.*) bath(y)-; (*geol.*) intrusive: ~ **kayaçları**, (*geol.*) plutonic rocks: ~ **ölçeği**, (*phys.*) bathometer: ~ **ölçme cihazı**, (*naut.*) depth-sounder.
derinti Scraps, odds and ends.
derisidikenliler (*zoo.*) Echinoderms.
deriş·ik(lik) (*phys., chem.*) Concentra·ted/(-tion). ~**im**/~**me**, *vn.* concentration. ~**mek**, *vi.* gather around; be(come) concentrated. ~**tirmek (-i)**, concentrate.
derk ~ **etm.**, understand, comprehend.
derken = DEMEK.
derkenar (*lit.*) Marginal note; postscript.
derle·m Collection. ~**mci**, collector. ~**me**, *vn.* collecting; collection, compilation: *a.* collected. ~**mek (-i)**, gather together, collect; (*lit.*) compile; edit: **derleyip toplamak**, (*dom.*) tidy up, clear away. ~**nce**, (*lit.*) anthology. ~**nmek**, *vp.*: **derlenip top(ar)lanmak**, pull o.s. together. ~**yici(lik)**, (work of) collector//(*lit.*) compiler/editor.
derli ~ **toplu**, orderly, tidy; compact.
derman Strength, energy; (*med.*) medicine; cure, remedy. ~ **bulmak**, find a remedy: ~**ım yok**, I'm exhausted; (*fin.*) I haven't the means.
dermansız Feeble, decrepit, debilitated; exhausted.

~ **dert**, (*med.*) incurable disease: ~ **düş(ür)mek**, *vi.*, (*vc.*) atrophy. ~**laşmak**, be(come) weak/ exhausted. ~**lık**, weakness, exhaustion, atrophy.
dermatoloji (*med.*) Dermatology.
der·me *vn.* Collecting; collection: *a.* gathered together; collected: ~ **çatma**, hastily collected and put together; (*arch.*) jerry-built; (*mil.*) soldiers collected at random, scratch unit: ~ **devşirme**, collected at random, rubbish. ~ **meci(lik)**, (*phil.*) eclectic(ism). ~**mek (-i)**, collect, gather; pick (flowers).
dermeyan Under discussion. ~ **etm.**, put forward (for discussion); produce.
der·neⁱ**k**ᵍⁱ Gathering, assembly, party; (*soc.*) club, association, society; (*fin.*) corporation: ~ **kurma özgürlüğü**, (*pol.*) freedom of association. ~**nekevi**ⁿⁱ, premises, club-room. ~**neşik**, gathered together, in a crowd.
derpiş ~ **etm.**, take into consideration, suggest.
derris (*agr.*) Derris-powder.
ders Lecture; lesson; schoolwork; lesson-time; (*fig.*) lesson, example. ~ **almak (-den)**, take lessons from s.o.; learn/profit from (experience): ~ **filmi**, (*cin., ed.*) film-strip: ~ **halkası**, (*obs.*) class of students: ~ **kesimi**, end of term: ~ **odası**, classroom: ~ **olm. (-e)**, be a lesson/example to s.o.: ~ **vermek**, give a lesson; (*fig.*) give s.o. a lesson: ~ **yapmak**, teach: ~**e kaldırmak**, (teacher) hear a pupil say his lesson: ~**i asmak**, cut a lesson, play truant: ~**ler**, a course (of lessons).
ders·hane Classroom. ~**iam**, (*obs.*) religious teacher. ~**lik**, *n.* classroom: *a.* suitable for a lesson.
der·tᵈⁱ Pain; suffering; affliction; grief; trouble; grievance; obsession; (*med.*) chronic disease; boil. ~ **dökmek**, pour out one's grief, etc.: ~ **edinmek/ etm.**, let stg. prey on one's mind: ~ **olm. (-e)**, become a worry to s.o.: ~ **ortağı**, fellow-sufferer; confidant: ~ **yanmak**, pour out one's sorrows: ~**e girmek**, fall into trouble: ~**i günü (-in)**, one's pet grievance; obsession: ~**i ne imiş?**, what's his trouble?, what's he want?: ~**ine düşmek**, be quite absorbed in stg.: ~**ine yanmak**, complain: ~**ini dökmek (-e)**, pour out one's troubles to s.o.: ~**ini Marko Paşa'ya anlat!**, nobody wants to hear about your troubles: ~**ini ortaya dökmek**, air one's grievances.
dert·lenmek *vi.* Ache; be pained; be sorrowful. ~**leşmek (-le)**, pour out one's grief to each other; sympathize with each other. ~**li**, pained; sorrowful; aggrieved. ~**lilik**, being pained, etc.
dertop ~ **etm.**, (*sl.*) round up, catch: ~ **olm.**, curl o.s. up.
dert·siz Free of pain/sorrow; carefree: ~ **başa dert almak**, bring unnecessary trouble on o.s. ~**sizlik**, freedom from pain, etc. ~**taş**, confidant, sympathizer.
deruhte Undertaken; assumed. ~ **etm.**, undertake, take upon o.s., assume.
deruni Internal; intrinsic; cordial, sincere.
derviş *n.* Poor man, pauper; beggar; (*rel.*) dervish. *a.* Simple; contented; humble. ~ **meşrep**, unconventional: ~ **in fikri neyse zikri odur**, he has a bee in his bonnet about that. ~**lik**, being a dervish; modesty,

contentment: ~ **hırka ile olmaz**, the cowl does not make the monk.

derya (*geo.*) Sea, ocean; (*fig.*) very learned man. ~ **dil**, large-hearted, magnanimous; always looking at the best side of things.

derz (*tex.*) Seam; (*med.*) suture; (*arch.*) pointing (of a wall).

desen (*tex.*) Design; (*art.*) drawing, illustration. ~ **li**, with a design.

desi- (*math.*) Deci-. ~ **bel**, (*phys.*) decibel. ~ **gram**, (*math.*) decigram. ~ **katör**, (*ind.*) desiccator, dryer. ~ **litre**, (*math.*) decilitre. ~ **mal**, decimal. ~ **metre**, decimetre. ~ **natör**, (*art.*) artist, designer; (*ind.*) draughtsman. ~ **ster**, one tenth of a cubic metre.

desise Artifice, trick, ruse; intrigue. ~ **ci**, s.o. cunning; intriguer. ~ **kâr**, intriguing, plotting.

desman (*zoo.*) Desman.

despot[u] (*rel.*) Greek Orthodox bishop; (*adm.*) despot; (*fig.*) tyrant. ~ **ik**, despotic. ~ **izm**, despotism; tyranny. ~ **luk**, bishop's office/duties.

dessas Intriguing; deceitful.

destan (*lit.*) Story; legend; ballad; epic; adventure; spell. ~ **gibi**, long-winded (story/letter, etc.) ~ **laşmak**, win fame, become a legend. ~ **sı**, *a.* epic.

deste Bunch, bouquet; sheaf; packet; (*pub.*) quire. ~ **başı**, choice (fruit, etc.) on the top of the pile: ~ , in bunches/heaps, by dozens. ~ **ci**, (*agr.*) harvester who collects the sheaves.

deste[l]**k**[ği] Support; stand; frame; (*arch.*) beam; brace; prop; buttress; cantilever; (*fin.*) backing; (*fig.*) aid. ~ **akça**, grant, subsidy: ~ **muylusu**, (*eng.*) bearing: ~ **müfrezesi**, (*mil.*) covering party.

destek·doku[nu] (*bio.*) Supporting tissue. ~ **leme**, *vn.* supporting; bracing, etc.; (*fin.*) backing: ~ **alımı**, (*fin.*) support buying: ~ **belgiti**, (*fin.*) accommodation bill. ~ **lemek** (-i), support; brace; prop/shore up; buttress (up); aid; (*fin.*) back; (*ind.*) boost. ~ **lenmek**, *vp.* ~ **leyici**, supporting.

deste·lemek (-i) Make into a bundle, etc. ~ **lenmek**, *vp.* ~ **leyici**, (*agr.*) s.o. who ties the sheaves.

destroyer (*naut.*) Destroyer, torpedo-boat.

destur Formula; code; permission. ~ **!**, *int.* by your leave!, make way!: ~ **var mı?**, have I your permission?: ~ **un!**, *int.* [137] pardon the expression! ~ **suz**, without permission.

-deş *n. suf.* = -DAŞ [GÖNÜLDEŞ].

deşarj (*el.*) Discharge. ~ **olm.**, be discharged/run down; (*fig.*) unburden o.s.

deşelemek (-i) (Animals) scratch up stg.

deşifre Deciphering. ~ **etm.**, decipher: ~ **olm.**, (*sl.*) (spy) be blown.

deş·i[l]**k**[ği] *n.* Hole. *a.* Pierced. ~ **ilmek**, be pierced; (*med.*) (abscess) be opened up; burst (of itself). ~ **mek** (-i), open by incision, lay open; unearth; exhume; (*fig.*) open up (a sore point, etc.).

de·tantör (*leg.*) Holder. ~ **tay**, detail(s); (*cin.*) close-up. ~ **taylı**, detailed; in detail.

DETÇA = DEVLET TİYATROLARINDA ÇALIŞANLAR DERNEĞİ.

detek·siyon (*rad.*) Detection. ~ **tif**, detective. ~ **tör**, (*rad.*) detector. ~ **tris**, (*rad.*) detector lamp.

deter·jan (*chem.*) Detergent. ~ **minant**, (*math.*)

determinant. ~ **minist**, (*phil.*) determinist. ~ **minizm**, determinism.

deuter·ium (*chem.*) Deuterium. ~ **on**, deuteron.

dev *n., a.* Giant. ~ **adımlarıyla ilerlemek**, advance by leaps and bounds: ~ **balıkçıl**, (*orn.*) goliath heron: ~ **boylu kuş**, (*orn.*) moa: ~ **gibi**, huge, cyclopean, colossal: ~ **kanguru**, (*zoo.*) giant hopper: ~ **kolibri**, (*orn.*) giant humming bird: ~ **köpek-balığıgiller**, (*ich.*) porbeagle sharks: ~ **kulağı**, (*zoo.*) great green conch, giant's ear: ~ **yırtıcı martı**, (*orn.*) skua.

deva (*med.*) Medicine, remedy. ~ **yı kül**, panacea. ~ **i**, medicinal. ~ **imisk**[i], (*cul.*) a pleasant-smelling HELVA.

devalü·asyon (*fin.*) Devaluation. ~ **e**, ~ **etm.**, devalue: ~ **olm.**, be devalued.

devam A continuing; continuation; continuance; permanence; assiduity; regular attendance (at work). ~ **!**, *int.* continue!, don't stop!: ~ **etm.**, continue, carry on, go on, last; persevere; (-e), continue stg.; frequent (a place); (*ed.*) attend/ follow (lectures, etc.): ~ **etmemek**, discontinue; interrupt: ~ **ı var**, (*pub.*) to be continued/ concluded.

devam·lı Continuous; continual; uninterrupted; constant; permanent, enduring; assiduous, hardworking. ~ **lılık**, continuity; permanence; durability; constancy; assiduity. ~ **sız**, discontinuous; interrupted; neglectful; (*ind.*) absentee; (*math.*) discrete. ~ **sızlık**, discontinuity; impermanence; neglect; (*ind.*) absenteeism.

dev·anası[nı] Giantess; huge woman. ~ **aynası**[nı], (*phys.*) magnifying mirror: ~ **nda görmek (kendini)**, be too big for one's boots; exaggerate one's own importance.

deve Camel. ~ **bir akçeye** ~ **bin akçeye**, it all depends on the quality you want: ~ **gibi**, tall and clumsy: ~ **hamuru!**, (*cul., iron.*) indigestible food!: ~ **hörgücü**, (*bio.*) camel's hump: ~ **kini**, rancour; the nourishing of a grudge: ~ **kolu**, (*mil.*) camel corps: ~ **nalbanda bakar gibi**, (*jok.*) a look of sheer surprise/blank astonishment: ~ **olm.**, (money, etc.) disappear: ~ **yapmak**, (*jok.*) acquire stg. by deceit: ~ **de kulak**, just a drop in the ocean; a mere trifle: ~ **den büyük fil var**, there's always s.o. more important: ~ **nin baş/pabucu**, (*col.*) it's greatly exaggerated: ~ **ye binmek**, (*sl.*) smoke hashish: ~ **ye hendek atlatmak (gibi)**, it's quite impossible, out of the question: ~ **yi düze çıkarmak**, overcome all difficulties: ~ **yi hamut/havutuyla yutmak**, gobble up the lot: ~ **yi yardan uçuran bir tutam ottur**, greed/stg. insignificant can cause a great disaster.

deve·bağırtan (*fig.*) A steep and stony road. ~ **boynu**[nu], curved like a camel's neck; (*geo.*) saddle between hills; (*eng.*) S-/U-bend pipe, gooseneck. ~ **ci**, cameleer, camel-driver; camel-owner: ~ **ile görüşen kapısını yüksek açmalı**, when dealing with important people beware of what it entails. ~ **cilik**, camel breeding; camel transport. ~ **dikeni**[ni], (*bot.*) creeping thistle. ~ **dişi**[ni], (*bot.*) with large grains (wheat)//seeds (pomegranates), etc. ~ **döşlü**, thin-loined (horse). ~ **elması**[nı], (*bot.*)

= ÇAKIRDİKEN. ~ **giller**, (*zoo.*) camels and llamas.
~ **kuşu**[nu], (*orn.*) ostrich: ~ **gibi yüke gelince kuşum der, uçmaya gelince deveyim der**, he always has a suitable excuse.
develop·e ~ **etm.**, (*cin.*) develop. ~ **man**, development.
dever (*rly.*) Superelevation.
deveran Revolution, rotation; circulation; circuit. ~ **etm.**, circulate. ~ **ıdem**, (*bio.*, *obs.*) circulation of the blood.
deve·tabanı[nı] (*bot.*) Coltsfoot. ~ **tımarı**[nı], hastily and negligently performed job. ~ **tüyü**[nü], camel's hair; light brown colour.
DEVGENÇ = DEVRİMCİ GENÇLİK DERNEĞİ.
deviatör Deviatory. ~ **gerilme**, (*eng.*) deviator stress.
devim (*phys.*) Movement, motion. ~ **niceliği**, momentum. ~ **bilim**, (*phys.*) dynamics, kinematics. ~ **bilimsel**, dynamic. ~ **duyum** = DEVİNDUYUM. ~ **li**, dynamic, moving: ~ **resim**, (*art.*) kinetic picture. ~ **lilik**, mobility. ~ **sel**, dynamic, kinetic; (*bio.*) motor. ~ **selcilik**, (*phil.*) dynamism. ~ **sellik**, dynamic state. ~ **siz**, (*phys.*) static.
devin·dirme *vn.* Moving; impelling. ~ **dirmek (-i)**, *vc.* move/impel stg. ~ **duyum**, (*psy.*) kinesthesia. ~ **gen**, (*phys.*) moving, in motion, in transit; dynamic. ~ **genlik**, movement, mobility; dynamism. ~ **gi**, dynamic. ~ **im**, motion, movement. ~ **imli**, moving, mobile, dynamic. ~ **imlilik**, dynamism. ~ **imsiz**, motionless, immobile. ~ **imsizlik**, immobility. ~ **irlik**, (*phys.*) momentum. ~ **iş/** ~ **me**, *vn.* movement; (*ast.*) precession. ~ **mek**, *vi.* move. ~ **sel**, mobile.
dev'ir[ri 1] *n.* (*his.*) Age, period, epoch, era. ~ **açmak**, open an era: ~ **i saadet**, the Golden Age, the period of the Prophet Muhammad: ~ **i sabık**, the old régime: ~ **in valisi**, the then governor.
dev'ir[ri 2] *n.* (*phys.*) Rotation; revolution; cycle; circuit; (*geo.*) tour; transfer (from one container to another); (*adm.*) transfer; (*leg.*) cession. ~ **hatimi**, (*rel.*) simultaneous reading of different surahs: ~ **saati**, (*eng.*) rev(olution)-counter; tachometer: ~ **ve temlik**, (*leg.*) assignation, conveyancing.
devir·li (*phys.*) Periodic; (*pub.*) periodical. ~ **mek (-i)**, overturn, capsize; (wind) blow stg. over; knock down; pull down; reverse; (*adm.*) overthrow; drink (to the last drop); read (a book) from cover to cover. ~ **tmek (-i, -e)**, *vc.* ~ **siz**, (*phys.*) aperiodic.
devit·ken *a.* (*phil.*) Motive, motor. ~ **kenlik**, motivity. ~ **mek (-i)**, set in motion, move, put into action.
dev·kazanı[nı] (*geol.*) Pot-hole. ~ **leşmek**, *vi.* grow enormous, become huge; (*fig.*) show great development. ~ **leştirmek (-i)**, *vc.*
devlet[i] (*adm.*) State; government; kingdom; (*fig.*) prosperity, success, good luck. ~ +, *a.* State; public, official: ~ **adamı**, statesman: ~ **bakan(lığ)ı**, (duties/office of) Secretary of State: ~ **bankası**, (*fin.*) central/national bank: ~ **başkanı**, head of state, president: ~ **borçları**, (*fin.*) national/public debt: ~ **davası**, (*leg.*) public prosecution: ~ **düşkünü**, who has fallen on hard times: ~ **emlaki**, public property: ~ **hazinesi**, (*fin.*) treasury, ex-

chequer: ~ **hizmeti**, public/civil service: ~ **kuşu**, stroke of luck, windfall: ~ **memuru**, government official: ~ **memurluğu**, civil service: ~ **merkezi**, centre of government, capital: ~ **reisi**, the head of state: ~ **sektörü**, (*fin.*) the public sector: ~ **Şurası**, Council of State; = DANIŞTAY: ~ **tekeli**, state monopoly: ~ **tekelinden çıkarmak**, denationalize: ~ **le**, *int.* (*obs.*) goodbye!; good luck!; fare you well!!: ~ **ler birliği**, confederation.
devlet·çe By/on the part of/through the government/state. ~ **çi**, supporter of state control. ~ **çilik**, *étatisme*, policy of state control. ~ **hane**, (*obs.*) (respectfully) 'your house'. ~ **lerarası**, intergovernmental, international: ~ **İstişari Denizcilik Teşkilatı**, (*naut.*) IMCO: ~ **ticaret hukuku**, (*leg.*) international mercantile law. ~ **leştirmek (-i)**, nationalize; put under state control. ~ **li**, prosperous, wealthy. ~ **lû**, (*his.*) (title of high officials).
devon·ik (*geol.*) Devonian period. ~ **yen (dönemi)**, Devonian (period).
devr- = DEVİR[1, 2]. ~ **almak (-i)**, take over (a duty) in turn. ~ **an**, time, period; wheel of fortune; fate: ~ **sürmek**, live happily and prosperously. ~ **e**, cycle; generation; period; stage; (*adm.*) session; (*el.*) circuit: ~ **açıcı**, (*el.*) cut-out switch: ~ **den çıkmak**, cut out: ~ **ye girmek**, cut in. ~ **en**, (*leg.*) by cession/transfer: ~ **kiralık**, sub-letting. ~ **esel**, periodic. ~ **esiz**, (*chem.*) acyclic. ~ **letmek**[eder] **(-i, -e)**, revolve; circulate; turn upside down; (*leg.*) alienate, assign, cede, transfer.
devri (*phys.*) Periodic; (*chem.*) cyclic; rotatory. ~ **daim**, perpetual motion; recirculating (pump). ~ **hindi**, (*Or. mus.*) rhythm (of singing).
devr·ik Turned back on itself: ~ **cümle/tümce**, [241] (*ling.*) sentence with inverted word order: ~ **kıvrım**, (*geol.*) reversed fold: ~ **yaka**, turneddown collar. ~ **ilmek**, *vp.* = DEVİRMEK; be overturned; capsize; collapse.
devrim (*adm.*) Revolution; reform. ~ **ci**, *n.* revolutionary. ~ **cilik**, revolutionary spirit. ~ **sel(lik)**, *a.* revolutionary (state).
devri·revan (*Or. mus.*) Fast rhythm. ~ **si**, (*col.*) the next/following (day, etc.). ~ **ye**, (*mil.*) patrol; police round, policeman's beat: ~ **gezmek**, patrol.
devşir·ilmek *vp.* Be gathered, etc. ~ **im**, collecting, picking. ~ **imli**, tidy. ~ **imsiz**, untidy; scattered, in confusion. ~ **me**, *vn.* act of gathering/collecting; (*his.*) levy/recruitment of Christian boys to be trained as Janissaries; such a recruit: *a.* collected together. ~ **mek (-i)**, gather, pick, roll up (carpet, etc.); collect o.s.; (*his.*) levy, recruit. ~ **tmek (-i, -e)**, *vc.*
devvar Revolving continuously; (*fig.*) fickle: ~ **mengene//tulumba**, rotary press//pump.
dey. = DEYİM.
deyi (*psy.*) Ability to express o.s.; language; (*phil.*) logos.
deyim Expression; term; idiom; phrase. ~ **leşmek**, *vi.* become an accepted term.
dey·ip = DEMEK. ~ **iş**, (*lit.*) folk poetry; (*mus.*) folksong; (*ling.*) saying, style of speech; statement. ~ **işbilim**, (*lit.*) stylistics. ~ **ivermek**, say quickly.
deyyus Cuckold; pander.

dez·avantaj Disadvantage. ∼**enfektan**, (*med.*) disinfectant. ∼**enfekte**, disinfected: ∼ **edici**, disinfectant: ∼ **etm.**, disinfect.

DGSA = DEVLET GÜZEL SANATLAR AKADEMİSİ.

DH = DEVLETLERARASI HUKUKU. ∼**Mİ** = DEVLET HAVA MEYDANLARI İŞLETMESİ. ∼**Y** = DEVLET HAVA YOLLARI.

-dı *v. suf.* = -Dİ.

dığdığı (*ling.*) S.o. who pronounces 'r' like 'ğ'.

-dığı *v. suf.* = -DİĞİ.

-dık *v. suf.* = -DİK. ∼**ça** = -DİKÇE. ∼**ta(n)** = -DİKTE(N).

dıla¹k^{g1} (*bio.*) Clitoris.

dı¹lı¹'¹ (*bio.*) Rib; (*math.*) side.

dımdızlak Stark naked; bald as a coot; (*fig.*) destitute, stony-broke.

Dımışk (*obs.*) Damascus. ∼**i**, damascene.

-dır¹ *v. suf.* = -DİR¹.

-dır-² *v. suf.* = -DİR-².

dır·dır *n.* Continuous tiresome chatter/grumbling: *adv.* continuously. ∼**dırcı**, chatterer; grumbler; nag. ∼**dırlanmak (-le)**, murmur, mumble. ∼**ıltı**, continuous annoying chatter; slight squabble: ∼ **çıkarmak**, have a slight quarrel. ∼**la(n)mak**, *vi.* babble tiresomely; make annoying noises; nag. ∼**laşmak**, *vi.* squabble in undertones.

dış *a.* Outer, outside; exterior, external; foreign; (*cin.*) outdoor; (*bio.*) ecto-; exo-; peri-. *n.* Outside, exterior; outward appearance. *post.* [91] Outside. ∼ **açı**, (*math.*) external angle: ∼ **astarı**, (*mod.*) facing: ∼ **bölge**, outlying district: ∼ **çap** = ∼ KUTUR: ∼ **çokgen**, (*math.*) circumscribed polygon: ∼ **döllenme**, (*bio.*) external fertilization: ∼ **gezegen**, (*ast.*) superior planet: ∼ **görünüş**, external appearance, configuration: ∼ **haberler**, foreign news: ∼ **hat**, (*aer.*) external line/flight: ∼ **ilişkiler**, (*pol.*) foreign relations: ∼ **kabuk**, (*bot.*) exocarp: ∼ **kalıp**, (*eng.*) external mould: ∼ **kambiyo**, (*fin.*) foreign exchange: ∼ **kapak**, outer cover; slip-case; (*cul.*) outer part of a leg of mutton: ∼ **kapı**, outer/ street door: ∼ **kapının (∼) mandalı**, (*col.*) very distant relation: ∼ **kulak**, (*bio.*) external ear: ∼ **kutur**, (*eng.*) external/outer diameter (O.D.): ∼ **lastik**, (*mot.*) outer tyre: ∼ **özek**, (*geol.*) = ∼ MERKEZ: ∼ **pazar**, (*fin.*) foreign market: ∼ **salgı**, (*bio.*) external secretion: ∼ **sayrılıkları**, (*med.*) external diseases: ∼ **Seyahat Harcamaları (Vergisi)**, (*fin.*) foreign-travel allowance (tax): ∼ **ticaret**, (*fin.*) foreign trade: ∼ **yürekzarı**, (*bio.*) pericardium: ∼**ı**, outside of . . .; extra-: ∼**ı eli yakar, içi beni yakar**, don't be taken in by outward appearances: ∼**ına**, to the outside of: ∼**ında**, on the outside of; besides, apart from . . .: ∼**ından**, from the outside of.

dış·açeken (*bio.*) Abductor. ∼**adönük**, connected with the outside; outward-looking; (*psy.*) extrovert. ∼**adönüklük**, extroversion. ∼**alım**, import(ation). ∼**alımcı(lık)**, importer('s business). ∼**alımlamak (-i)**, import.

dışarda(n) = DIŞARIDA(N).

dışarı *n.* Outside, exterior; the provinces; the country (*not* town); abroad. *adv.* [198] Out; outside; abroad. ∼ **çıkmak**, go out(side); go to the lavatory:

∼ **satmak**, export: ∼ **uğramak**, (eyes) protrude; rush outside: ∼ **vurmak**, show; reflect; (illness) become manifest: ∼**da**, out of doors, outside; abroad: ∼**dan**, from outside; from abroad: ∼**dan evlenme**, (*soc.*) exogamy: ∼**dan getir(t)mek**, import: ∼**ya fırlamak**, rush outside: ∼**ya götürmek**, bear/take outside.

dışar·ısı^{n1} The outside: ∼ **seni yakar içerisi beni yakar** = DIŞI ELİ YAKAR . . .. ∼**lık**, (*geo.*) the provinces. ∼**lıklı**, a provincial; county, country.

dış·asalak (*bio.*) Ectoparasite. ∼**avurumcu(luk)**, (*art.*) expression·ist/(-ism). ∼**başkalaşım**, (*geol.*) exomorphism. ∼**beslenen**, (*bio.*) heterotrophic. ∼**bükey(lik)**, (*phys.*) convex(ity). ∼**değer**, ∼ **bulma(k)**, (*math.*) extrapol·ation/(-ate). ∼**deri**, (*bio.*) ectoderm. ∼**dünya**, (*phil.*) external world. ∼**evlilik**, (*soc.*) exogamy. ∼**ık**, (*min.*) slag; (*geol.*) scoria, cinder. ∼**ıl**, external; foreign. ∼**ındalık**, exception. ∼**ınlı**, (*phil.*) extrinsic. ∼**işleri^{ni}**, (*adm.*) foreign affairs: ∼ **Bakan(lığ)ı**, Minis·ter/(-try) of Foreign Affairs: ∼ **görevlisi**, Foreign Affairs official, diplomat. ∼**kı**, (*bio.*) faeces, excrement. ∼**kılama**. (*bio.*) defecation. ∼**kılık**, (*bio.*) cloaca. ∼**kula¹k^{g1}**, (*bio.*) external ear. ∼**kutsal**, (*phil.*) extra-religious. ∼**lak**, (*phil.*) external. ∼**lamak (-i)**, (*phil.*) externalize. ∼**lı**, relating to the outside: = İÇLİDIŞLI. ∼**merkez**, (*geol.*) epicentre. ∼**merkezli(lik)**, (*math.*) eccentric(ity). ∼**odun**, (*bot.*) sapwood. ∼**özekli(lik)**, (*eng.*) eccentric(ity). ∼**plazma**, (*bio.*) ectoplasm. ∼**rak**, (*phil.*) exoteric. ∼**satım**, (*fin.*) export(ation). ∼**satımcı(lık)**, exporter('s business). ∼**satımlamak (-i)**, export. ∼**tan**, externally: ∼ **takma motoru**, (*naut.*) outboard motor. ∼**tecim**, (*fin.*) foreign trade. ∼**ters**, ∼ **açı**, (*math.*) alternate external angle. ∼**yapı**, (*phil.*) macro-. ∼**yaprak**, (*bio.*) ectoderm. ∼**yarıçap¹**, (*math.*) external radius (of a regular polygon). ∼**yüz**, exterior, outer surface; appearance. ∼**zar**, (*bot.*) exosporium; (*bio.*) epidermis.

dızdı¹k^{g1} (*col.*) ∼**mın** ∼**ı**, a distant relative.

dız·dız (*ech.*) Buzzing; whizzing; (*ent.*) gadfly. ∼**dızcı**, (*sl.*) pickpocket. ∼**dızcılık**, pickpocketing (by a group in a crowd). ∼**gal**, (*sl.*) beard. ∼**ıltı**, humming, buzzing. ∼**lamak**, *vi.* hum, buzz; (*sl.*) cheat.

dızlak Naked; bald. = DAZLAK.

di- *pref.* (*chem.*) Di-; bi-.

-di/-dı/-du/-dü, -ti, *etc.*, **-ydi**, *etc. v. suf.* 1. [99] = İDİ. 2. *3rd pers. sing. past tense* [127] [gördü, he saw/has seen]. ∼ **-eli**, since [beni gördü göreli, since he saw me]: ∼ **gitti**, [192] *expresses finality* [kullandı gitti, used up and done with]: ∼'**li geçmiş**, (*ling.*) past definite tense: ∼**yse**, if . . . did/has done.

dia- *pref.* Dia-. = DİYA-.

dial·dehit (*chem.*) Dialdehyde. ∼**kol**, glycol.

dia·(pozitiv) (*cin.*) Transparency; slide. ∼**tomik**, (*chem.*) diatomic. ∼**zo**, diazo.

dib- = DİP.

DİB = DIŞİŞLERİ BAKANLIĞI.

diba (*tex.*) Flower-patterned silk tissue.

dibata (*ethn.*) Our earliest ancestors.

dibe'k^{ği} Large stone/wooden mortar. ~ **kahvesi**, mortar-ground coffee.

Dicle (*geo.*) River Tigris.

didakti'k^{ği} *a.* Didactic. *n.* Didactics.

-dide *n. suf.* Who has seen/experienced [CİHANDİDE].

didik ~ ~, (*tex.*) teased out; pulled to shreds. ~ **lemek (-i)**, (*tex.*) tease out; (*fig.*) pick to pieces, cut to shreds. ~ **lenmek**, *vp.*

didinmek *vi.* Wear o.s. out; toil; be over-eager/ -anxious; fret.

didiş·imcilik (*phil.*) Eristic. ~ **ken**, quarrelsome. ~ **me**, *vn.* quarrel. ~ **mek (-le)**, push each other about; quarrel; struggle.

didon (*obs.*) Frenchman; (*col.*) fop. ~ **sakallı**, with an imperial beard.

DİE = DEVLET İSTATİSTİK ENSTİTÜSÜ.

di·elektrik (*el.*) Dielectric. ~ **fana**, double/ triple fishing-net. ~ **fazlı**, (*el.*) diphase. ~ **feransiyel**, (*math.*) differential; (*mot.*) differential gear: ~ **hesap**, (*math.*) differential calculus. ~ **fraksiyon**, (*phys.*) diffraction.

dif·teri (*med.*) Diphtheria. ~ **tong**, (*ling.*) diphthong.

difüz·e (*cin.*) Diffused. ~ **yon**, (*phys.*) diffusion. ~ **yonist**, (*ethn.*) diffusionist.

diğer *pron.* [76] Other; another. *a.* Altered, different; next (day). ~ **biri**, another of them: ~ **taraftan**, moreover, at the same time: ~ **leri**, others. ~ **endiş**/ ~ **kâm**, altruistic.

-diği/-dığı/-duğu/-düğü/-tiği, *etc. v. suf.* [163, 184, 254] *Inflected form of* -DİK². ~ **bir sırada**, at a time when: ~ **gibi**, [187] as (soon as) he does/did: ~ **halde**, [186] in a state of doing; although he does/ did: ~ **için**, [186] as/because of doing: ~ **kadar**, [186] as much/long as doing: ~ **müddetçe/sürece**, [185] as long as doing: ~ **nispette**, [186] in proportion to doing: ~ **takdirde**, [186] in the event of doing; if doing: ~ **vakit/zaman**, [185] when doing: ~ **vehminde**, under the delusion that . . .: ~ **nce**, [183] to the extent of doing; since/because of doing: ~ **nden**, [186] because of doing: ~ **nden başka**, [184] apart from doing: ~ **ne göre**, [165] in view of doing.

dihedral (*math.*) Dihedral.

dijital (*eng.*) Digital. ~ **in**, (*med.*) digitalin. ~ **is**, (*med.*) digitalis.

dikⁱ Perpendicular; upright; vertical; straight; steep; (*fig.*) uncompromising, opinionated, bluff. ~ **açı**, (*math.*) right angle: ~ **adam**, uncompromising man: ~ **âlâsı**, the very utmost/worst: ~ **başlı**, pig-headed, obstinate; rebellious: ~ **biçme**, (*math.*) right prism: ~ ~ **bakmak (-e)**, glare at, look daggers at: ~ **dörtgen**, (*math.*) rectangle: ~ **durmak**, stand upright: ~ **düzlemler**, (*math.*) perpendicular planes: ~ **kafalı**, obstinate, pig-headed, uncompromising: ~ **katman**, (*geol.*) upturned stratum: ~ **kayalık**, escarpment: ~ **kırık**, (*geol.*) steep fault: ~ **rüzgâr**, (*naut.*) headwind: ~ **ses**, harsh/loud voice: ~ **silindir**, (*math.*) right cylinder: ~ **sözlü**, who does not mince his words: ~ **üçgen//yamuk**, (*math.*) right-angled triangle// trapezium: ~ İNE: ~ **ine dalış**, (*aer.*) nose-dive: ~ **ine gitmek**, do just the opposite (of what is asked); be pig-headed: ~ **ine kalkış ve iniş**, (*aer.*) vertical

take-off and landing: ~ **ine kırık**, (*geol.*) transverse fault: ~ **ine tıraş**, shaving against the bristles; (*fig.*) rubbing s.o. the wrong way; utterly boring talk.

-dik¹/**-dık/-duk/-dük/-tik**, *etc. v. suf.* [99, 127] *1st pers. pl. past tense.* [gördük, we saw/have seen].

-di'k^{ği 2}/**-dık/-duk/-dük/-tik**, *etc. v. suf.* [162] *Participle representing an action considered as completed.* [gördük, seen]. *With possessive suffixes* [gördüklerim, what I see/have seen: **gittiğini sana söyledim**, I told you he has/had gone]. ~ **çe**, [183] as long as; every time that, the more. ~ **te**, [183] on doing; at the moment of doing. ~ **ten**, from doing: ~ **başka**, [184] apart from/in addition to doing: ~ **sonra**, [183] after doing.

dik·çe (*tex.*) Spindle. ~ e'ç^{ci}, (*chem.*) column.

dikel (*agr.*) Long-handled fork. ~ e'ç^{ci}, dibber.

dikelmek *vi.* Become upright; wait on foot; (**-e**) defy s.o.

diken (*bot.*) Thorn; (*ent.*) sting; (*zoo.*) barb, spike, spine, bristle; obstacle. ~ ~ **olm.**, (hair, etc.) stand on end: ~ **kanatlı**, (*orn.*) spur-winged: ~ **kuyruklu ördek**, (*orn.*) ruddy shelduck: ~ **üstünde olm.**/ **oturmak**, be like a cat on hot bricks.

diken·(c)e (*ich.*) Ten-spined stickleback. ~ **dudu**^{nu}, (*bot.*) blackberry. ~ **li**, (*bio.*) aculeate; (*bot.*) thorny; (*zoo.*) spiked; barbed, prickly: ~ **balık/ (-giller)**, (*ich.*) stickleback(s): ~ **kurt**, (*zoo.*) spiny bollworm: ~ **salyangoz**, (*zoo.*) murex, sting winkle: ~ **tel (engeli)**, (*agr.*, *mil.*) barbed wire (entanglement): ~ **uyuşturan balık**, (*ich.*) common sting-ray: ~ **yüzgeçligiller**, (*ich.*) loaches. ~ **lik**, (*agr.*) thicket of brambles and thornbushes. ~ **liyılan**, (*zoo.*) death adder. ~ **si**, thornlike: ~ **çıkıntı**, (*bio.*) thornlike process of bone. ~ **siz**, thornless: ~ **gül olmaz**, there's no rose without a thorn.

dik·ey (*math.*) Perpendicular, orthogonal: ~ **kesit**, (*arch.*) elevation. ~ **gen**, rectangular.

dikici Cobbler; tailor. ~ **lik**, cobbling, shoe-repairing; tailoring.

dikili (*tex.*) Sewn; stitched; (*for.*) planted; (*arch.*) set up. ~ **ağacı olmamak**, have no property at all: ~ **taş**, obelisk, stone monument.

dikilmek *vp.* (*tex.*) Be sewn; (*for.*) be planted: (**-e**) (eyes) be intently fixed on: *vi.* (horse) jib; (*bio.*) become tumescent. **dikilip durmak**, stand stiff and immobile: **dikilir**, *a.* erectile.

dikim (*for.*) Planting; (*tex.*) sewing, stitching. ~ **evi**ⁿⁱ/ ~ **hane**, sewing/tailoring workshop.

dikine In the perpendicular: = DİK.

dikiş (*tex.*) Sewing; stitch(ing); seam; (*naut.*) splice; (*med.*) suture; (*for.*) planting. ~ **dikmek**, sew: ~ **kaldı (-e)**, almost/nearly (do): ~ **kaynağı**, (*min.*) seam welding: ~ **okuması**, rigmarole of quarrelsome words: ~ **payı**, (*tex.*) seam allowance; (*fig.*) that little bit extra: ~ **tutmak (-de)**, take root/settle down in a place: ~ **tutturamamak**, be unable to settle down: ~ **ini almak**, (*med.*) remove the stitches.

dikiş·çi Seamstress, sewing woman. ~ **li**, sewn; seamed; (*min.*) seam-welded. ~ **siz**, seamless.

diki't^{di} (*geol.*) Stalagmite.

dikiz *n.* (*sl.*) Roguish look; observation. *int.* Watch out! ~ **aynası**, (*mot.*) rear-view/observation mirror: ~ **etm./** ~ **geçmek/** ~ **lemek (-i),** (*sl.*) watch intently. ~ **ci,** (*sl.*) (thieves') look-out.

dikkat[i] *n.* Attention; attentiveness, care(fulness); consideration; accuracy, fineness; subtlety. *int.* Attention!, beware!; (*sp.*) get set! ~ **çekici,** arresting, striking; ~**(i) çekmek,** attract/engage attention; arouse: ~ **etm.,** pay attention; be careful; attract attention: ~ **kesilmek,** be all ears/eyes; pay great attention: ~**e almak,** take into consideration; ~**i celbetmek,** attract attention: ~**le,** with care, attentively.

dikkat·li Attentive; calculating; careful; carefully made. ~**siz,** inattentive, careless; casual; absentminded. ~**sizlik,** inattention, carelessness: ~ **etm.,** be inattentive; be clumsy.

dik·leme Perpendicular. ~**lemesine,** perpendicularly. ~**lenmek/**~**leşmek,** *vi.* become perpendicular/upright; (*fig.*) oppose s.o. ~**leştirmek (-i),** make perpendicular; make hard/rigid, stiffen. ~**lik,** being perpendicular, etc. = DİK.

diklor- *pref.* (*chem.*) Dichlor-. ~**it,** dichloride.

dik·me *vn.* Act of sewing, etc.; (*math.*) upright, vertical (line); (*agr.*) young plant; (*fig.*) only child, scion; (*arch.*) pillar, prop; strut; (*naut.*) derrick. *a.* Sewn; stitched; spliced. ~**mek (-i, -e),** (*tex.*) sew; stitch; splice; set up; (*agr.*) plant; (*arch.*) erect; drain (a cup, etc.); fix (the eyes on stg.); stick stg. into stg.; prick up (the ears), pay attention; (hair) stand on end; (*mil.*) post (sentry); (*sp.*) place (the ball); toss into the air. ~**men,** (*geo.*) conical hill; peak, summit. ~**sıra,** (*math.*) (matrix) column.

dikromat (*chem.*) Dichromate.

dikse Tree covered with birdlime, set up on the plain, to catch migrating birds.

diksiyon (*ling.*) Diction, elocution. ~**er,** dictionary.

dik·ta (*adm.*) Dictate, authoritarian ruling. ~**tacı/** (**-lık**), supporter of/(support for) absolute rule. ~**tafon,** dictaphone. ~**tatör(lük),** dictator(ship). ~**te,** (*ling.*) dictation: ~ **etm.,** (*ling., adm.*) dictate. **-dikte(n)** = -DİK[2].

diktirmek (-i), *vc.* = DİKMEK.

diktograf Dictograph.

dil (*bio.*) Tongue; (*ling.*) language; (*geo.*) spit of land; pointer, index (of a balance); (*naut.*) sheave (of a block); bolt (of a lock); (*mus.*) reed (of oboe, etc.); (*min.*) scab; (*mil.*) prisoner captured for information. ~ +, *a.* Linguistic: ~ **ağzı vermemek,** (*med.*) be unconscious: ~ **akrabalığı,** (*ling.*) relationship between languages: ~ **avcısı,** spy: ~ **bilmez,** he doesn't know Turkish//foreign languages: ~ **bir karış (-de),** s.o. speaking disrespectfully: ~ **bozuntusu,** jargon: ~ **çıkarmak (-e),** put out one's tongue at s.o.; mock: ~ **dökmek,** blandish, talk s.o. round: ~ **dönmez,** crackjaw (word): ~ **duygusu,** (*ling.*) a feeling for language: ~ **ebesi,** chatterbox; garrulous person; s.o. quick at repartee: ~ **kavgası,** quarrel, slanging match: ~ **kemiği,** (*bio.*) hyoid bone: ~ **Kurumu,** Philological Society, Language Academy: ~ **oğlanı,** (*his.*) student interpreter: ~ **pası,** (*med.*) fur on the tongue: ~ **pelesengi,** oily/unctuous speech: ~ **tutmak,** (*mil.*) capture an informer: ~ **tutukluğu,** inability to articulate words: ~ **ucu,** the tip of the tongue: ~

uzatmak (-e), speak ill of, malign: ~ **yakmak,** (pepper, etc.) burn the tongue: ~ **yarası,** feelings wounded by bitter words.

dile: ~ **düşmek,** become the subject of scandal: ~ **düşürmek,** make public, divulge: ~ **gelmek,** become the subject of scandal; find one's tongue: ~ **getirmek,** cause to be talked about; mention, speak about; get s.o. to speak: ~ **kolay,** easier said than done: ~ **vermek,** talk openly of stg. secret.

dili: ~ **açılmak/çözülmek,** the tongue to be loosened; (a silent person) begin to talk: ~ **ağırlaşmak,** speak incoherently (ill, drunk): ~ **bağlı,** silent, raising no objections: ~ **bir karış dışarı çıkmak,** get very tired from walking, etc. in the heat: ~ **bozuk,** unable to speak well: ~ **çalmak,** speak with a (strange) accent: ~ **çözülmek,** recover one's speech: ~ **damağına yapışmak,** the mouth to be dried up: ~ **dolaşmak,** talk confusedly (from drink, fear, etc.): ~ **döndüğü kadar,** (explain) as well as one can: ~ **dönmemek,** be unable to pronounce a word: ~ **durmamak,** talk endlessly; say what one shouldn't: ~ **ensesinden çekilsin!,** (*curse*) may his tongue be pulled out!: ~ **kurusun!,** let it not be said!, curse your tongue!: ~ **pabuç kadar,** he is impertinent/tactless in speech: ~ **tutuk,** unable to speak easily: ~ **tutulmak,** be speechless (from fear, etc.): ~ **uzun,** cheeky, insolent: ~ **varmak,** agree/bring o.s. to say stg.: ~ **yatkın,** who learns a language easily: ~ **zifir,** foulmouthed.

dilin: ~ **kemiği yok,** one can say what one likes: ~ **kurusun!,** (*curse*) may his/your tongue wither! ~**de tüy bitmek,** be sick and tired of repeating stg.: ~**den anlamak,** understand what is said; (*fig.*) be a specialist in the matter: ~**den düşürmemek,** never stop talking about stg.: ~**den kurtulamamak,** be unable to avoid s.o.'s reproaches/scolding: ~**e dolamak/pelesenk etm./virt etm.,** harp on a subject: ~**e sağlam olm.,** not use bad language; be discreet.

dilini: ~ **bağlamak,** silence s.o.: ~ **eşek arısı soksun!,** (*vulg.*) curse his tongue!: ~ **kesmek,** be silent: ~ **tut(ama)mak,** (be unable to) hold one's tongue: ~ **yutmak,** be overcome (by surprise/fear); appear to have lost one's tongue.

dilinin: ~ **altında bir şey olm.,** keep stg. back; hesitate to say stg.: ~ **belasını bulmak/çekmek,** one's tongue get one into trouble: ~ **ucuna gelmek,** be on the tip of one's tongue.

dil-: ~**iyle sokmak,** wound s.o. with words: ~**lerde dolaşmak/gezmek,** be talked about everywhere: ~**lere destan olm.,** be on everyone's tongue: ~**lere düşmek** = ~E DÜŞMEK.

dil(b). = DİLBİLGİSİ; DİLBİLİM.

dil·altı[ni] (*med.*) Pip (disease in fowls); pustule under the tongue: ~ **bağı,** (*bio.*) frenulum: ~ **bezleri,** (*bio.*) salivary glands. ~**balığı**[ni], (*ich.*) sole. ~**basan,** (*med.*) tongue-depressor. ~**baz,** talkative, coquettish; woman who can always persuade men.

dil·ber *a.* Captivating, charming. *n.* sweetheart, darling. ~**berdudağı**[ni], (*cul.*) sweet(heart's) lips. ~**beste,** attached to; in love.

dil·bilgisel (*ling.*) Grammatical. ∼**bilgisi**^{ni}, (*ling.*) grammar. ∼**bilim**, linguistics. ∼**bilimci**, linguistician. ∼**bilimsel**, linguistic. ∼**ce**, linguistically. ∼**ci**, linguist; language specialist. ∼**ci**^{l}**k**^{ği}, little tongue; (*bio.*) clitoris; (*bot.*) ligula. ∼**cilik**, linguistic studies.

dile^l**k**^{ği} Wish, desire; request; (*ast.*) Mercury. ∼ **şart kipi**, [271] (*ling.*) conditional mood: ∼**i gerçekleşmek**, achieve/realize one's desires.

dilek·çe (*adm.*) Petition, application, formal request. ∼**çi**, petitioner, applicant.

dilem Dilemma.

dilemek (-**i**) Wish for, desire; ask for, beg.

dilen·ci Beggar, mendicant; (*fig.*) shameless complainer: ∼ **çanağı gibi**, full of odds and ends: ∼ **değneğine dönmek**, become very thin: ∼ **vapuru**, ship stopping at every port of call: ∼**ye hıyar vermişler de eğri diye beğenmemiş**, beggars can't be choosers. ∼**cilik**, mendicancy, begging; beggary; shamelessness. ∼**dirmek** (-**i**), make s.o. beg; reduce s.o. to begging. ∼**mek** (-**den**), beg, ask for alms; cadge.

dilim Slice; strip; sector, section; (*mod.*) gore. ∼ ∼, in slices: ∼ ∼ **etm.**/∼**lemek**, cut/separate into slices. ∼**lenmek**, *vp.* ∼**li**, ∼ **ısıtıcı**, radiator.

dilin·im (*geol.*) Cleavage. ∼**me**, fissility.

dil·lendirme Causing/enabling to speak. ∼**lenge**^{l}**ç**^{ci}, repeated saying. ∼**lenmek**, *vi.* find one's tongue; (child) begin to talk; become chatty; grumble; talk indiscreetly/rudely; be the object of talk, be criticised. ∼**leşmek** (-**le**), talk pleasantly. ∼**li**, having a tongue, etc. = **DİL**; who chatters pleasantly: ∼ **dişli**, sharp-tongued. ∼**lidüdü**^{l}**k**^{ğü}, (*mus.*) a reed whistle; (*col.*) chatter-box: ∼ **etm.** (-**i**), spread the news. ∼**lilik**, chattering. ∼**ma**^{l}**ç**^{ci}, interpreter; (*his.*) dragoman. ∼**maçlık**, interpreting.

dil·me *vn.* Slicing; square pole. ∼**mek** (-**i**), cut into slices.

dil·mi^l**k**^{ği} (*bio.*) Lobe. ∼**mikçi**^{l}**k**^{ği}, lobule. ∼**peyniri**^{ni} (*cul.*) a cheese made in long strips. ∼**sel**, verbal; linguistic. ∼**sever**, talkative. ∼**siz**, *a.*, *n.* (a) mute, dumb (person); (*fig.*) silent, taciturn: ∼ **sağır**, deaf and dumb; a deaf mute. ∼**sizlik**, dumbness.

dilüviyum (*geol.*) Diluvium.

dimağ (*bio.*) Brain; encephalon; (*fig.*) intelligence. ∼**çe**, (*bio.*) cerebellum.

dimdik Bolt upright; quite perpendicular; very steep. ∼ **ayakta durmak**, not yield/collapse: ∼ **durmak**, stand bolt upright; not change one's conduct.

dimi (*tex.*) Close-woven cotton cloth, dimity.

diminuendo (*mus.*) Diminuendo.

Dimyat (*geo.*) Damietta; (*bot.*) a round white juicy grape. ∼**a pirince giderken evdeki bulgurdan olm.**, lose what one has in an effort to get more/better.

din^1 *n.* Religion, faith (esp. Islam). ∼ **bezirgânı**, s.o. who exploits religion for his own ends: ∼ **kardeşi**, co-religionist: ∼ **lideri**, apostle: ∼**den imandan çıkmak**, lose all patience, become exasperated: ∼**i bir uğruna**, for the sake of Islam: ∼**i bütün**, sincerely religious, devout, good and honest: ∼**i imanı para**, who thinks only of money: ∼**im hakkı**

için, (I swear) by my religion: ∼**ince dinlensin!**, (*col.*) may he (non-Muslim) rest in peace!: ∼**inden dönme**, apostasy: ∼**ine yandığım**, (*sl.*) the cursed.

din^2 *n.* (*phys.*) Dyne.

din^3 *n.* ∼ **doruk/tepesi**, a far-away place.

din. = **DİN·İ/SEL**.

DIN = (*Deutsche Industrie Norm*) German Industrial Standard.

dina·mik *n.* (*phys.*) Dynamics: *a.* (*phil.*) dynamic; (*phys.*) mobile; forceful: ∼ **bilimi**, dynamics. ∼**mikleşmek**, *vi.* become dynamic. ∼**mist**, (*phil.*) dynamist. ∼**mit**^{i}, (*chem.*) dynamite: ∼ **barut**// **lokumu**, blasting powder//gelatine: ∼**le atmak**/ ∼**lemek** (-**i**), blow up, blast; destroy; (*fig.*) oppose, sabotage. ∼**mitlenmek**, *vp.* ∼**mizm**, dynamism. ∼**mo**, (*el.*) dynamo. ∼**mometre**, (*phys.*) dynamometer. ∼**tron**, dynatron.

dinar Ancient gold coin; Iranian//Iraqi//Yugoslav currency.

dinbaşkan(lığ)ı (*rel.*) Caliph(ate).

dincelmek Become vigorous, recover one's strength.

dincierki^{ni} (*rel.*) Theocracy. ∼**l**, theocratic.

din^l**ç**^{ci} Vigorous, robust; free from care, light-hearted. ∼**leşmek**, *vi.* become strong; feel refreshed. ∼**lik**, robustness; good health.

din·dar Religious; devout, pious. ∼**darlık**, devotion, piety. ∼**daş**, co-religionist. ∼**dışı**, lay.

dindir·ici Making light/easy. ∼**mek** (-**i**), *vc.* = **DİNMEK**; cause to cease; quench; stop (bleeding, etc.); calm, quieten; silence.

dinelmek *vi.* (*col.*) Stand; stand up; be clear, appear; be obstinate; (-**e**), (*fig.*) oppose, resist.

dineri (*gamb.*) Diamonds.

ding (*cul.*) Mortar; (*tex.*) device for beating cloth.

dingi (*naut.*) Pair-oared ship's boat, dinghy.

dingil Axle, arbor. ∼ **açıklığı**, (*mot.*) wheelbase: ∼ **ağırlığı**, (*mot.*) axle weight. ∼**demek**, rattle, wobble.

dingin (*phys.*) Inert, motionless, static, stationary; (*chem.*) passive; (animal) exhausted. ∼**cilik**, (*phil.*) quietism. ∼**leşme**, (*chem.*) passivation. ∼**leşmek**, *vi.* (*phys.*) become inert/motionless/exhausted. ∼**leştirici**, (*chem.*) passivator. ∼**leştirmek**, (*chem.*) passivate. ∼**lik**, (*phys.*) inertia, rest; (*chem.*) passivity: ∼ **bilimi/dinimbilim**, (*phys.*) statics.

dini Religious. ∼ **hukuk**, canon law.

din·leme *vn.* Listening; (*leg.*) hearing; (*med.*) auscultation; (*th.*) audition: ∼ **merkezi**, (*mil.*, *rad.*) listening-post: ∼ **ve ses alma aleti**, audio surveillance equipment. ∼**lemek** (-**i**), listen to; hear; heed, pay attention to; obey; (*med.*) auscult. ∼**lemelikseyirlik**, audio-visual. ∼**lence**, holiday. ∼**lendirici**, relaxing, restful; calming. ∼**lendirmek** (-**i**), *vc.* make/let rest; calm; (*agr.*) leave fallow; leave (liquids) to settle; put out (light, fire, etc.) ∼**lenebilir**, *a.* (*leg.*) admissible. ∼**lene**^{l}**k**^{ği}, holiday camp. ∼**lenme**, *vn.* rest: ∼ **evi**, convalescent home: ∼ **fırsatı**, breathing space: ∼ **günü**, holiday: ∼ **odası**, rest-room: ∼ **yeri**, holiday camp. ∼**lenmek**, *vi.* rest; become quiet; be heard; be listened to; (*cul.*) hang, stand (to improve taste); (*agr.*) lie fallow. ∼**leti**, (*mus.*) recital, concert. ∼**letim**, (*mus.*)

master-class. ~**letmek (-i)**, cause to hear; make listen; bore; recount (a tale); sing (a song, etc.) well. ~**leyici**, listener: ~ **salonu**, auditorium: ~**ler**, the audience. ~**leyicilik**, being a listener.

din·me *vn.* Calm, quiet. ~**mek**, *vi.* cease; leave off (rain, bleeding, etc.); calm down.

dinozor (*zoo.*) Dinosaur.

din·öncesi[ni] (*soc.*) Pre-religious state. ~**perver**, pious. ~**sel**, religious: ~ **tören**, service. ~**siz**, without religion; atheist; irreligious, impious; cruel: ~**in hakkından imansız gelir**, 'diamond cut diamond', be worsted by a bigger villain. ~**sizlik**, irreligion, atheism; impiety. ~**yayar**/~**yayıcı**, missionary.

di·oksi·t[di] (*chem.*) Dioxide. ~**o(y)ik**, (*zoo.*) dioecius.

di·p[bi] Bottom; lowest part; base; foot (tree, cliff, etc.); far end (room, tunnel, etc.); background; (*bio.*) anus; (*geol.*) ground. ~ **doruk**, from top to bottom: ~ **gürültüsü**, (*rad.*) background noise: ~ **kaya**, (*geol.*) bedrock: ~ **kirişi**, (*naut.*) keelson: ~ **koymak**, bottom: ~ **oyulması**, (*geol.*) undercutting: ~**e çökmek**, (deposit) sink to the bottom: ~**e dokunmak/ulaşmak**, reach/touch bottom: ~**i düz**, flat-bottomed: ~**i görünmek (kabın)**, be drained to the dregs: ~**i kırmızı balmumuyla çağırmadım ya**, you came of your own free will: ~**ine darı ekmek**, squander, consume; utterly exterminate: ~**ine gelmek/inmek (kabın)**, drink to the dregs.

DİP = DEMOKRAT İŞÇİ PARTİSİ.

dip·çi·k[ği] Rifle-butt: ~ **kuvvetiyle**, by force. ~**çiklemek (-i)**, strike with a rifle-butt. ~**çiklenmek**, *vp.* ~**diri**, full of life; very robust; safe and sound. ~**koçanı**[nı], (*fin.*) counterfoil, voucher.

dipfriz Deep-freeze.

dipl. = DİPLOMA(LI).

diplarya (*ich.*) Small dab.

diplik (*art.*, *cin.*, *th.*) Background; (*cin.*) backing.

diploma (*ed.*) Diploma, certificate. ~**lı**, having a diploma, certificated. ~**sız**, not having a diploma, uncertificated. ~**si**, diplomacy. ~**t**[ı], diplomat. ~**tça**, diplomatically. ~**tik**, diplomatic: ~**dokunulmazlık**, diplomatic inviolability: ~ **münasebetler(in kesilmesi)**, (severance of) diplomatic relations: ~ **kurye**, (*adm.*) courier, Queen's messenger. ~**tlık**, status/work of a diplomat; diplomatic action.

di·plo(y)i·t[di] (*bio.*) Diploid. ~**pol**, (*el.*) dipole.

dip·not[u] (*pub.*) Footnote. ~**siz**, bottomless; fathomless; abysmal; (*geo.*) batho-; (*fig.*) unfounded, baseless, false; inconstant: ~ **çukur**, the bottomless pit, hell: ~ **kile boş ambar**, having not a penny to his name: ~ **testi**, spendthrift. ~**yüzey**, bottom; background.

-dir[1]/**-dır/-dur/-dür/-tir**, *etc.* *v.* *suf.* [96] *3rd sing.* *pres.* Is. ~**ler**, *3rd.* *pl.* *pres.* are. = OLMAK.

-dir-[2]/**-dır-/-dur-/-dür-/-tir-**, *etc.* *vc.* *suf.* [144] Make/cause/allow/let (do); have (done). [YEDİRMEK; YAZDIRMAK].

dirahmi = DRAHMİ.

dirayet[i] Comprehension, understanding; intelligence; ability. ~**li**, comprehending; intelligent;

capable. ~**siz**, stupid; unintelligent; unintellectual; incapable. ~**sizlik**, stupidity; unintelligence; incapacity.

dire·k[ği] Pole; (*arch.*) pillar; column; (*naut.*) mast; post; (*bio.*) septum; (*jok.*) very tall man; (*fig.*) foundation, support. ~ ~ **bağırmak**, shout at the top of one's voice: ~ **ıskaçası**, (*naut.*) mast step: ~ **sapanı**, (*naut.*) strop: ~**e çıkmak**, (*naut.*) go aloft: ~**ler arası**, (*arch.*) arcade. ~**si**, (*geol.*) columnar.

direk·siyon (*mot.*) Steering-gear/-wheel: ~ **simiti**, steering-wheel. ~**t**, *a.*, *adv.* direct. ~**tif**, (*adm.*) directive: ~ **vermek**, issue a directive. ~**tör(lük)**, (position/work of) director.

dir·emek (-i, -e) Take the weight of stg.; be obstinate; resist. ~**en**, (*agr.*) large (winnowing) fork; (*eng.*) drainage; = DREN. ~**en·ç**[ci], (*med.*, *phys.*) resistance. ~**ençli**, resistant; robust. ~**engen**, obstinate, resistant, unyielding. ~**engenlik**, obstinacy. ~**engi**, (*phil.*) inertia. ~**enim**, obstinacy, persistence. ~**eniş**, boycott; resistance. ~**enlemek (-i)**, (*agr.*) winnow. ~**enme**, *vn.* resisting; persisting; (*psy.*) perseveration. ~**enmek**, *vi.* disagree; demur; dissent emphatically; insist; dig one's toes in. ~**enti**, resisting. ~**eşim**, perseverance. ~**eşken**, enduring, persistent. ~**eşkenlik**, persistence: ~ **göstermek**, persevere. ~**eşme**, *vn.* persevering. ~**eşmek**, *vi.* persevere. ~**letmek**[eder], *vi.* persist.

direy (*zoo.*) Fauna.

dirgen = DİREN.

dirhem (*obs.*) 400th part of an OKKA (3 grams); ancient Arab coin; shot (in a sporting gun). ~ ~, little by little: ~ **kadar**, a very small quantity.

diri Alive; fresh, not faded (salad, leaf, etc.); energetic, lively; sharp (words); (*cul.*) not sufficiently cooked. ~ **açımı**, (*med.*) operation: ~ ~, alive; (*cul.*) not well cooked: ~ ~ **yanmak**, be burned alive: ~ **örtü**, (*bot.*) plants covering the ground. ~**cikkıran**, (*med.*) antibiotic.

diriğ Refusal; reluctance; regret, sorrow. ~ **etm. (-i, -den)**, refuse, withhold, grudge.

dirijan (*pol.*) Director, leader.

diriksel *a.* (*bio.*) Connected with life, animal. ~ **ısı**, animal heat.

diril *a.* = DİRİKSEL. *n.* (*tex.*) Drill, twill.

diril·çoğuz (*chem.*) Biopolymer. ~**fizik**, biophysics. ~**kimya**, biochemistry.

diri·lik Being alive; vitality; brusqueness. ~**liş**, coming to life. ~**lmek**, *vi.* come to life; be resuscitated/revived. ~**ltme**, resuscitation; (*chem.*) regeneration. ~**ltmek (-i)**, bring to life, resuscitate; reinvigorate; enliven.

dirim Life. ~ **konisi**, (*bot.*) cone of vegetation. ~**bilim(ci)**, biolo·gy/(-gist). ~**bilimsel**, biological. ~**li**, living, alive. ~**lik**, *a.* living, vital. ~**lilik**, being alive. ~**sel**, biological; vital. ~**selcilik**, (*phil.*) vitalism. ~**sellik**, vitality. ~**siz**, inanimate, lifeless. ~**sizlik**, inanimation. ~**yuvarı**[nı], (*geol.*) biosphere.

dirlik Living in amity; (*his.*) living, fief. ~ **düzenlik**, harmonious life, good fellowship: ~ **yüzü görmemek**, not find rest/tranquillity. ~**siz**, inharmonious (life); cantankerous (person).

dirse·k[ği] (*bio.*) Elbow; (*mot.*) bend; (*carp.*) knee;

bend; crank, bracket; cantilever; (*naut.*) outrigger.
~ **çevirmek (-e)**, take a dislike to; 'drop' s.o. (who is
of no further use): ~ **çıkıntısı**, (*bio.*) olecranon: ~
çürütmek, (*tex.*) wear out the elbows with study: ~
kemiği, (*bio.*) ulna: ~**leri delinmek**, (*mod.*) be out at
elbow.

dirsek·lemek (-i) Elbow s.o. ~**lenmek**, *vi.* be elbow-
shaped; be elbowed. ~**li**, elbowed, jointed: ~
kavşak, (*mot.*) staggered junction: ~ **mil**, (*eng.*)
crankshaft. ~**lik**, *a.* (*eng.*) usable as an elbow: *n.*
(*tex.*) elbow-patch/leather; (*sp.*) elbow-guard.

-dirt-/-dırt-/-durt-/-dürt- *v. suf.* [146] *Forming
double causative* [ÖLDÜRTMEK, cause to kill].

disimilasyon (*ling.*) Dissimilation.

disiplin Discipline. ~+, *a.* Disciplinary. ~**li**,
disciplined; having good discipline. ~**siz**, undisciplined; having bad discipline.

disjonktör (*el.*) Current-/circuit-breaker; cut-out
switch.

disk[i] Disc, disk; (*sp.*) discus; (*mus.*) record. ~ **atan**,
discobolus; discus-thrower: ~ **atma**, throwing the
discus: ~ **pulluğu**, (*agr.*) disc-harrow: ~ **şeklinde**,
discoid.

DİSK = DEVRİMCİ İŞÇİ SENDİKALARI KON-
FEDERASYONU.

diskalifiye (*sp.*) ~ **etm.**, disqualify: ~ **olm.**, be
disqualified.

disk·jokey (*mus.*) Disc-jockey. ~**li**, ~ **fren**, (*mot.*)
disk-brake: ~ **sürgü**, (*agr.*) disc-harrow. ~**otek**,
(*mus.*) discothèque.

dis·kur Discourse, speech: ~ **çekmek/geçmek**,
(*iron.*) make a speech. ~**panser**, (*med.*) dispensary,
out-patients' hospital: ~ **eczacısı**, dispenser.
~**pe¹çci**, (*fin.*) average adjustment, appraisal.
~**peççi**, (*fin.*) average adjuster, appraiser.
~**persiyon**, (*bio.*) dispersion.

disprosyum (*chem.*) Dysprosium.

dis·tile (*chem.*) Distilled. ~**torsiyon**, (*min., rad.*)
distortion. ~**tribütör**, (*fin.*) distributor, agent;
(*mot.*) distributor. ~**tribütörlük**, agency.

distrofi (*med.*) Dystrophy.

diş (*bio.*) Tooth; (*eng.*) tooth, cog; screw-thread;
(*bot.*) clove (of garlic, etc.); any tooth-shaped thing;
(*sl.*) a pinch of hashish. ~ +, *a.* Dental; denti-: ~
aralığı, (*eng.*) backlash, play: ~ **bilemek (-e)**,
cherish a grudge against s.o.; await a chance for
revenge against s.o.: ~ **çekmek**, pull a tooth out: ~
çıkarmak, cut a tooth: ~ **çukuru**, (*bio.*) dental alveolus: ~**çürüğü/çürümesi**, (*bio.*) caries, tooth decay:
~ **damak ünsüzü**, (*ling.*) palatalised dental consonant: ~ ~ **kar**, (*met.*) snow where each flake
stands out separately: ~ **doktoru**, dentist: ~ **doldurmak**, fill a tooth: ~ **dudak ünsüzü**, (*ling.*) labio-
dental consonant:~ **düzeltimi**, (*med.*) orthodontics:
~ **fırçası**, toothbrush: ~ **geçirememek (-e)**, be
unable to influence/harm s.o.: ~ **geçirmek (-e)**, be
able to influence s.o.: ~ **gıcırdatmak**, gnash one's
teeth (in anger): ~ **göstermek**, threaten: ~ **hekim/
tabibi**, (*med.*) dental surgeon: ~ **hekimlik/tababeti**,
(*med.*) dental surgery: ~ **kabukları**, (*zoo.*) scapho-
pods, tusk shells: ~ **kamaştırmak**, set the teeth on
edge: ~ **kemiği**, (*bio.*) dentine: ~ **kırmak**, (*sl.*) lace
a cigarette with hashish: ~ **kirası**, (*his.*) gift given

to guests at banquets in great houses; (*now sl.*)
salary for a sinecure: ~ **kökü**, (*bio.*) root, fang: ~
macunu, dentifrice, toothpaste: ~ **minesi**, tooth
enamel: ~ **sarmısak (bir)**, a clove of garlic: ~
sıkmak, set one's teeth (in perseverance): ~ **yarası**,
bite.

diş-: ~**e dokunur**, stg. profitable/worth while/
enjoyable: ~**i açmak**, (*eng.*) cut screw threads: ~**i
körleştirmek**, (*eng.*) burr the threads: ~**inden
tırnağından artırmak**, save money by skimping on
essentials: ~**ine değmemek**, (food) be very little:
~**ine göre**, to one's taste; within one's ability: ~**ini
sıkmak**, endure; take one's courage in both hands:
~**ini sökmek (-in)**, (*fig.*) draw s.o.'s teeth: ~**ini
tırnağına takmak**, make every effort: ~**inin
kovuğuna bile gitmedi**, a very minute portion of
food: ~**leri çatırdamak**, (one's teeth) chatter: ~**leri
dökülmek**, grow old: ~**ten artırmak**, live frugally.

diş. = DİŞÇİLİK; DİŞİL.

diş·bademi[ni] (*cul.*) Soft-shelled macaroon.
~**buda¹k**[ğı], (*bot.*) common ash. ~**buğdayı**[nı], (*soc.*)
sweetened wheat distributed when a child cuts its
first tooth. ~**çi**, dentist; dental surgeon; (*sl.*) s.o.
who removes and sells gold teeth from corpses: ~
koltuğu, dentist's chair. ~**çilik**, dentistry; dental
surgery. ~**eği**, device for setting saws/roughening
millstones. ~**emek (-i)**, set the teeth (of saws, etc.);
roughen millstones. ~**eti**[ni], (*bio.*) gums, gingiva: ~
ünsüzü, (*ling.*) alveolar consonant.

dişi *a.* Female; (*zoo.*) cow-, doe-, she-, -ess; (*orn.*)
hen-; (*eng.*) female; (*fig.*) soft, yielding. ~ **aslan**,
(*bio.*) lioness: ~ **bakır//demir**, (*min.*) soft copper//
iron: ~ **geyik (derisi)**, (*bio.*) doe(-skin): ~ **kaplan**,
(*bio.*) tigress: ~ **klişe**, (*pub.*) etched cliché/plate: ~
kopça, (*mod.*) eye (with a hook): ~ **koyun**, (*bio.*)
ewe: ~ **kurt**, (*bio.*) she-wolf: ~ **manda**, (*live.*)
buffalo-cow: ~ **tavşan**, doe: ~ **tazı**, brach.

dişi·ci¹k[ği] (*bot.*) Pistil: ~ **başı**, stigma. ~**kalı¹p**[bı],
(*art.*) matrix. ~**l**, connected with women; feminine,
womanish; (*ling.*) feminine. ~**li**, ~ **çark**, (*eng.*)
gear-wheel: ~ **erkekli**, (*bio.*) having a mate. ~**lik**,
being a woman/female. ~**lleşmek**, behave like/
become a woman. ~**lleştirmek (-i)**, (*ling.*) make
feminine. ~**llik**, (*ling.*) being feminine. ~**mastar**,
(*art.*) stencil. ~**organ**, (*bot.*) pistil.

dişindirik Halter, bit on lower jaw (of horse).

diş·lek Having protruding teeth. ~**leme**, (*arch.*)
(dog-)toothed ornamentation. ~**lemek (-i)**, take a
bite out of stg. ~**lenmek**, *vi.* (*fig.*) become s.o. to
reckon with; be strengthened. ~**letmek (-i)**, cause
to bite; (*eng.*) set saw-teeth.

dişli (*bio.*) Toothed, having (sharp) teeth; (*eng.*)
toothed, geared, cogged; serrated, jagged; crenate;
(*fig.*) formidable, influential; hustling, who gets
things done. ~ **(çark)**, (*eng.*) cog-wheel, gear-
wheel: ~ **dil**, (*bio.*) radula: ~ **güvercin**, (*orn.*)
tooth-billed pigeon: ~ **kutusu**, (*mot.*) gear-box: ~
olm., 'show one's teeth': ~ **makara**, (*eng.*)
sprocket: ~ **sazangiller**, (*ich.*) toothed carps: ~
tırnaklı, with tooth and nail: ~ **tirsi**, (*ich.*) twaite
shad: ~ **tren**, (*rly.*) rack railway.

diş·otu[nu] (*bot.*) Plumbago, leadwort. ~**otugiller**,
(*bot.*) Plumbaginaceae. ~**özü**[nü], (*bio.*) dental pulp.

~**sel**, (*bio*., *ling*.) dental. ~**siz**, toothless; (*zoo*.) edentate: ~ **balinalar**, (*zoo*.) whalebone whales. ~**tacı**ⁿ¹, (*bio*.) dental crown. ~**yuvası**ⁿ¹, (*bio*.) dental alveolus.

ditiramˡ**p**ᵇ¹ (*lit*.) Dithyramb.

ditmek (-i) (*tex*.) Pick into fibres; tease; card; (*zoo*.) tear (prey) to pieces.

dival (*tex*.) Gold/silver thread embroidery (on cardboard).

divan¹ *n*. (*dom*.) Divan, sofa, couch. ~ **halısı**, rug.

divan² *n*. (*his*., *adm*.) Council of state; public sitting (of a council); (*lit*.) collection of one classical poet's poems. ~ **durmak**, stand in a respectful position (with hands joined in front): ~ **edebiyatı**, (*lit*.) classical Turkish literature: ~ **taburu**, (*mil*.) parade for inspection: ~**a çekmek**, (*adm*.) summon into one's presence.

divane Crazy, insane. ~**si olm**., be crazy about stg. ~**lik**, insanity; crazy behaviour.

divan·hane (*adm*.) Council-chamber; (*arch*.) hall. ~**ıâli**, (*leg*.) supreme court (to try ministers and high officials). ~**ıhar**ˡ**p**ᵇ¹, (*leg*.) military court, court martial. ~**ımuhasebat**¹, (*adm*.) audit-office. ~**i**, a large style of Arabic script (used for FERMAN): ~ **kırması**, a smaller style of this script.

diviˡ**k**ᵍⁱ (*ent*.) White ant, termite.

divil ~ ~, uninterruptedly.

divitⁱ Case for reed pens and ink (for Arabic script).

divitin (*tex*.) Cotton/wool material with pile on one surface.

divizör (*eng*., *el*.) Divider.

divleˡ**k**ᵍⁱ (*bot*.) Unripe melon.

diya- *pref*. Dia-. = DİA. ~**baz**, (*geol*.) diabase. ~**bet**ⁱ, (*med*.) diabetes. ~**betik**, diabetic. ~**betli**, diabetic person. ~**bolo**, (*child*.) diabolo. ~**fram**, (*bio*., *eng*.) diaphragm; ~ **kası**, (*bio*.) phrenic muscle. ~**framlı**, ~ **ayırıcı**, (*med*.) dialyser. ~**gonal**, (*math*.) diagonal. ~**gram**, (*math*., *etc*.) diagram, chart, table: ~ **kâğıdı**, graph-paper. ~**klaz**, (*geol*.) diaclase. ~**kon**/~**koz**, (*rel*.) deacon. ~**kroni(k)**, (*ling*.) diachro·ny/(-nic). ~**laj**, (*geol*.) diallage. ~**lekt**ⁱ, (*ling*.) dialect. ~**lekti**ˡ**k**ᵍⁱ, (*phil*.) dialectics. ~**lektoloji**, (*ling*.) dialectology. ~**liz**, (*chem*.) dialysis. ~**log**, (*lit*.) dialogue; (*cin*.) script: ~ **kurmak (-le)**, establish a dialogue with s.o.: ~ **yazarı**, (*cin*.) scriptwriter. ~**magnetizm**, (*el*.) diamagnetism.

diyan·etⁱ (*rel*.) Piety: ~ **İşleri**, Religious Affairs. ~**i**, religious.

diya·pazon (*phys*.) Diapason, pitch; tuning-fork. ~ **pozitif**, (*cin*.) photographic plate, slide.

diyar *pl*. = DAR. Houses, countries. *s*. Country, district.

diya·re (*med*.) Diarrhoea. ~**staz**, (*bio*.) diastase, enzyme. ~**tome**, (*bot*.) diatom. ~**tomeli**, (*bot*.) diatomaceous. ~ **tonik**, (*mus*.) diatonic.

diye *Gerund of* DEMEK. [175] Saying; in order to; (*col*.) named, called. *Used after direct speech, it is best rendered by inverted commas; otherwise it expresses intention, purpose, reason, hope, supposition, etc. It often represents what a person says to himself when doing stg.* ~**ce**ˡ**k**ᵍⁱ, what will be

said: ~**ceği olmamak**, have nothing to say about stg!: ~**lim ki**, for example.

diyeleˡ**k**ᵍⁱ (*ling*.) Dialect.

diyesi Desire. ~**ni anlatmak**, express one's desires.

diyetⁱ ¹ *n*. (*leg*.) Blood-money, ransom. ~ **istemek**, demand retaliation.

diyetⁱ ² *n*. (*med*.) Diet. ~**etik**, dietetics.

Diyetⁱ ³ *n*. (*his*.) The German//Swiss, etc. Diet.

diyez (*mus*.) Sharp.

diyo- *pref*. Dio-. ~**pter**, (*phys*.) diopter. ~**ptri**, (*phys*.) dioptrics. ~**rama**, (*art*.) diorama. ~**rit**ⁱ, (*geol*.) diorite. ~ˡ**t**ᵈᵘ, (*el*.) diode.

diz (*bio*.) Knee. ~ **ağırşağı**, (*bio*.) knee-cap: ~ **boyu**, knee-deep/-high; all-pervading: ~ **çöker(t)mek**, make (a camel) kneel; cause to collapse: ~ **çökmek**, kneel, crouch: ~ **çukuru**, (*mil*.) shallow rifle-pit, fox-hole: ~ ~ **e oturmak**, sit close together: ~ **üstü**, on the knees, kneeling: ~**e gelmek**, surrender: ~**e getirmek**, bring to his knees: ~**e varmak**, kneel in entreaty: ~**ini dövmek**, be very repentant: ~**inin dibi**, close by: ~**leri kesilmek**, give way at the knees (from fatigue): ~**lerine kapanmak**, embrace s.o.'s knees in supplication: ~**lerinin bağı çözülmek**, give way at the knees (from fear, etc.).

dizanteri (*med*.) Dysentery.

dizayn (*art*., *ind*.) Design.

dizbağıⁿ¹ (*bio*.) Tendons of the knee; (*mod*.) garter.

dizdar (*his*.) Warden/constable of a castle.

dizdirmek (-i, -e) *vc*. = DİZMEK.

dize (*lit*.) Line of poetry. ~ˡ**ç**ᶜ¹, (*adm*.) file.

dizel Diesel. ~ **motor**//**yağı**, diesel-engine//-oil: ~ **çekit**, (*rly*.) diesel locomotive. ~ **elektrik(li)**, diesel-electric(al).

diz·elge List, schedule. ~**elgelemek (-i)**, list. ~**em**, (*mus*.) rhythm. ~**emli**/~**emsel**, rhythmic. ~**ey**, (*math*.) matrix.

dizge System, arrangement. ~**leştirme**, *vn*. systematization. ~**leştirmek (-i)**, systematize. ~**li**/ ~**sel**, systematic, classified. ~**siz**, unsystematic.

dizgi (*pub*.) Composition, type-setting; (*math*.) co-ordinate; arrangement, order. ~ **hatası**, printer's error: ~ **makinesi**, (*pub*.) type-setting machine: ~ **yanlışı**, printer's error. ~**ci**, compositor, type-setter. ~ **cilik**, type-setting.

dizgin Reins, bridle. ~ **takmak/vurmak**, put on the reins: ~**ini çekmek**, draw rein, stop, call a halt: ~**ini kısmak (-in)**, put pressure on s.o., restrain s.o.: ~**leri ele almak**, take full control: ~**leri ele vermek**, hand over the reins to s.o. else, let another take control: ~**leri salıvermek**, give the horse his head; (*fig*.) let things go; give s.o. a free hand: ~**leri toplamak**, rein in, curb.

dizgin·lemek (-i) Put on the reins; (*fig*.) restrain s.o. ~**lenmek**, *vp*. ~**siz**, (*fig*.) uncontrolled, unbridled, unlimited.

dizi Line, row, series; configuration; string (of beads); (*mil*.) file (of soldiers); (*math*.) sequence; progression; (*mus*.) notes of an octave; scale; (*phys*.)·catena; (*rad*.) array. ~ ~, set out in a row, etc.: ~ **filmi**, (*cin*.) serial/series film: ~ **reaksiyonu**, (*phys*.) chain reaction: ~ **röportajı**, (*pub*.) series-writing: ~ **sayısı**, serial number.

dizi·ci Arranger; (*pub*.) compositor. ~**leme**, (*cin*.)

assembly; (*rly.*) marshalling. ~**lemek (-i)**, arrange in a row, etc.; assemble. ~**li**, arranged in a row, etc.; (beads) on a string; (meat) on a skewer; (type) set up. ~**lim**, (*phil.*) concatenation. ~**liş**, *vn.* arrangement. ~**lme**, *vn.* arrangement, assembly, alignment. ~**lmek**, *vp.* be arranged/threaded, etc. ~**m**, arrangement; (*adm.*) file. ~**mbilim**, (*ling.*, *phil.*) syntax. ~**mlemek (-i)**, file. ~**msel**, syntactic(al): ~ **tutar·lı/(-sız)**, (in)consistent. ~**n**, (*pub.*) index.

diz·kapağı[ni] (*bio.*) Knee-cap: ~ **kemiği**, patella. ~**leme**, *a.* knee-deep/-high. ~**lemek (-i)**, sink knee-deep; press with the knee; fall to one's knees. ~**lik**, covering for the knees; knee-guard; (*mod.*) drawers reaching to the knees, knee-breeches.

diz·mek (-i) Arrange in a row; align; string (beads, etc.); (*pub.*) compose, set up type. ~ **men(lik)**, (*pub.*) (work of) type-setter/compositor.

dizüstü Kneeling. ~ **oturmak**, kneel.

dk. = DAKİKA.

DK = DENİZ KUVVETLERİ. ~**İ** = (*aer.*) DİKİNE KALKIŞ VE İNİŞ.

dl. = DESİLİTRE.

dm. = DESİMETRE.

DM = DEUTSCHE MARK (German mark). ~**MA** = DEVLET MİMARLIK VE MÜHENDİSLİK AKADEMİSİ. ~**O** = DEVLET MALZEME OFİSİ.

do (*mus.*) Doh. ~**anahtarı**[ni], key of C.

Do. = DOĞU.

DOB = DEVLET OPERA VE BALESİ.

dobra ~ ~, bluntly, frankly, without beating about the bush.

Doç. = **doçent**[i], (*ed.*) lecturer, assistant professor. ~**lik**, position/duties of a lecturer, etc.

Dodekanez (*geo.*) Dodecanese.

dogma (*phil.*) Dogma. ~**cılık**, (*phil.*) dogmatism. ~**tik**, dogmatic: ~ **felsefe**, dogmatic philosophy. ~**tist**, dogmatist. ~**tizm**, dogmatism.

doğ. = DOĞRAMACILIK; DOĞUM.

doğa Nature; natural law; natural/innate quality, nature of stg. ~ **bilimleri**, (*ed.*) natural sciences: ~ **yasası**, natural law: ~**ya aykırı(lık)**, abnormal(ity).

doğa·cı Naturist; nature-worshipper. ~**cılık**, nature-worship; naturism. ~**ı**[cı], inspiration; brain-wave: ~**tan**, extempore. ~**çlama**, improvisation. ~**dışı**, unnatural.

doğal Found in nature; natural; normal; inherent, innate. ~ **amfiteatr**, (*geo.*) cirque: ~ **anıt**, natural wonder: ~ **ayıkla(n)ma/seçme/seçim**, (*bio.*) natural selection: ~ **cam**, (*geol.*) obsidian: ~ **durum**, (*phil.*) state of nature: ~ **gaz/uçun**, natural gas: ~ **kaynaklar**, (*min.*) natural resources: ~ **kıran/ yıkım**, natural disaster: ~ **liman**, natural harbour: ~ **olarak**, naturally: ~ **savunma**, (*bio.*) defence mechanism: ~ **yaşlanma**, (*min.*) natural ageing.

doğal·cı Naturalist. ~**cılık**, (*phil.*, *art.*) naturalism. ~**lık**, naturalness: ~**ını bozmak**, (*chem.*) denature.

doğan (*orn.*) Peregrine falcon. ~**cı**, falconer.

doğa·ötesi[ni] *n.* (*phil.*) Metaphysics: *a.* metaphysical. ~**sal(lık)**, natural(ness). ~**üstü**[nü], *n.* supernatural: ~ **güç**, morale.

doğay (*bio.*) Fauna.

doğ·durmak (-i) *vc.* = ~MAK. ~**ma**, *vn.* birth; (*ast.*)

rising: *a.* born, by birth: ~ **büyüme buralıyım**, I was born and bred here. ~**maca**, (*th.*) improvisation. ~ **mak**, *vi.* be born; (sun, etc.) rise; (**-e**), (idea) come to; come to pass, arise, happen; (**-den**), be created/ born from; originate from; arise from: **doğduğuna pişman**, 'who wishes he had never been born', 'tired of life'; 'born tired': **doğmus**, born.

doğra·m Slice: ~ **kesilmek**, cut up in slices. ~**ma**, *vn.* slicing; things made by a carpenter. ~**macı(lık)**, joiner(y), carpen·ter/(-try). ~**mak (-i)**, chop/cut up into slices/pieces; (*fig.*) decimate; butcher stg. ~**nmak**, *vp.* be cut/sliced; (*fig.*) hurt as if cut. ~**tmak (-i, -e)**, *vc.*

doğru *a.* Straight; upright; level; direct; accurate; right; true; authentic; honest, faithful, straightforward. *adv.* Straight. *n.* The right; the truth; (*math.*) straight line. *post.* (**-e**) [87] Straight to; towards, in the direction of; (time) towards, close to. ~ **akım**, (*el.*) direct current: ~ **atılmak (-e)**, make a bolt for: ~ **bulmak (-i)**, approve of stg.: ~ **çıkmak**, come true; prove to be right: ~ **çizgi**, (*math.*) straight line: ~ ~ **dosdoğru**, (*col.*) the truth of the matter: ~ **durmak**, stand still; behave o.s.: ~ **dürüst**, properly: ~ **gitmek (-e)**, make a bee-line for: ~ **kokusu var**, there's an air of truth about it: ~ **köye**, straight to the village [köye ~, towards the village]: ~ **olmayan**, baseless: ~ **orantılı**, directly proportional: ~ **oturmak**, sit still, be quiet: ~ **söyleyeni dokuz köyden kovarlar**, home-truths are never welcome: ~ **yol**, the straight and narrow path.

doğru ~ (~**ya**), [195] direct(ly), without intermediary: ~**dan**, direct(ly): ~**dan ayrılmak**, swerve from the path of right: ~**su**, honestly, to tell the truth, in all conscience: ~**sunu ileri sürmek**, aver: ~**sunu isterseniz**, in reality, essentially: ~**sunu öğrenmek**, ascertain stg.: ~**ya** ~ **eğriye eğri**, good for good evil for evil: ~**yu araştırmak**, verify; investigate.

doğru·ca *a.* More or less straight: *adv.* direct(ly) ~**cu**, truthful: ~ **Davut**, a very meticulous person. ~**culuk**, veracity. ~**lam**, (*phil.*) model. ~**lama**, corroboration, confirmation: ~ **belgesi**, certificate. ~**lamak (-i)**, confirm, corroborate; attest, certify; endorse, verify. ~**lanmak**, *vp.* ~**layıcı**, confirmatory: ~ **mektup**, covering letter. ~**lmak**, *vi* become straight/level/true; sit up; come true; be realized; (*fin.*) be earned; (**-e**), set out for, go towards. ~**ltma**, (*min.*) rectification. ~**ltma**[lçı], (*el.*) rectifier. ~**ltmak (-i)**, put straight/right; adjust; correct; (*chem.*) rectify; (*sl.*) manage to earn. ~**ltman**, (*math.*) directrix. ~**ltu**, line; direction. ~**ltucu**, (*chem.*) rectifier. ~**ltulu**, directional. ~**lu**, (*math.*) straight, rectilinear. ~**luk**, straightness; accuracy; honesty; authenticity; rectitude, truth. ~**lukla**, justly. ~**lum**, (*bio.*) tropism. ~**sal**, (*math.*) (recti)linear; (*phil.*) truth-functional: ~ **denklem**, linear equation.

doğu (*geo.*) The East; the Orient; the eastern provinces of Turkey. ~ +, *a.* East(ern), Oriental ~ **Almanya**, (*geo.*) East Germany: ~ **atmacası** (*orn.*) Levant sparrow-hawk: ~ **çınar//gürgen**, **kayınağacı//ladini**, (*bot.*) oriental plane(-tree)/

hornbeam//beech//spruce: ~ **kerte poyraz//keşiş-leme**, (*geo.*) east-by-north//-south: ~ **poyraz//keşişleme**, (*geo.*) east-north-east//-south-east: ~ **yarımyuvarı**, (*geo.*) eastern hemisphere.
doğu·bilim Orientalism, oriental studies. ~ **bilimci**, orientalist. ~ **lu**, (*ethn.*) Oriental; Eastern Anatolian. ~ **luca**, in the Tk. manner. ~ **luluk**, being an Oriental; Oriental mentality.
doğum (*bio.*) Birth; (*med.*) confinement; delivery; year of birth. ~ **durumu**, (*chem.*) nascency: ~ **gün/yıldönümü**, birthday: ~ **kâğıdı**, (*adm.*) birth certificate: ~ **kontrolü**, (*med.*) birth control: ~ **oranı**, birth-rate: ~ **öncesi**, (*med.*) ante-natal: ~ **sancısı**, (*med.*) labour pains, travail: ~ **sonrası**, (*med.*) postnatal: ~ **tarihi**, date of birth: ~ **yapmak**, give birth: ~ **yardımı**, maternity benefit: ~ **yeri**, birthplace.
doğum·evi[ni] Maternity home. ~ **lu**, born in . . . (year): **1960** ~, (*mil.*) class of 1960. ~ **sal**, connected with birth; congenital.
doğur·anlar (*zoo.*) Viviparous animals. ~ **gan**, fecund, prolific. ~ **ganlık**, fecundity. ~ **mak (-i)**, give birth (to); bear a child, have a baby; bring forth; breed; (animals) drop, cast; (*fig.*) give rise to, cause, engender. ~ **tmak (-i, -e)**, *vc.* deliver (child). ~ **tuculuk**, (*phil.*) maieutics. ~ **ucu**, (*zoo.*) viviparous.
doğusal Oriental, Eastern.
doğuş Birth; origin; (*ast.*) sunrise. ~ **tan**, from birth; congenital; innate; a born . . .: ~ **tan alık**, cretin. ~ **lu**, by birth; well-born. ~ **tancı(lık)**, (*phil.*) nativ·ist/(-ism).
dok[u 1] *n.* (*naut.*) Dock.
dok[u 2] *n.* (*tex.*) Duck.
dok. = DOKUMACILIK.
doksan Ninety. ~ **dokuz babalık**, (*sl.*) real bastard: ~ **dokuzluk tespih**, rosary of 99 beads. ~ **ar**, ninety each/at a time. ~ **ıncı (90.)**, ninetieth. ~ **lık**, *a.* containing ninety items/parts; ninety-year-old. [*For further phrases* = KIRK.]
doktor (*med.*, *ed.*) Doctor. ~ **balığı**, (*ich.*) surgeon fish: ~ **muayene/sınaması**, medical examination: ~ **termometresi**, clinical thermometer: ~ **a sormak**, take medical advice. ~ **a**, (*ed.*) doctorate (examination): ~ **öğrenimi**, doctoral studies: ~ **tezi**, doctoral thesis. ~ **lu**, ~ **kâğıt**, (*gamb. sl.*) marked card. ~ **luk**, rank/work of a doctor; profession of medicine.
doktrin (*pol.*, *rel.*) Doctrine.
doku (*bio.*) Tissue; (*geol.*) texture, fabric; (*min.*) case. ~ **aşısı**, (*med.*) tissue transplant: ~ **sertleştirme**, (*min.*) case hardening: ~ **nu** ~ **nu vermek**, (*sl.*) hit repeatedly. ~ **bilim**, (*med.*) histology. ~ **m**, (*bio.*) texture.
doku·ma *vn.* (*tex.*) Weaving; woven tissue; cotton fabric; *a.* woven: ~ **tarağı**, carding machine. ~ **macı**, (*tex.*) weaver: ~ **kuşu**, (*orn.*) weaver-bird. ~ **macılık**, weaving; textile industry. ~ **mak (-i)**, weave; (*agr.*) knock fruit from trees with a pole.
dokun·a[l]**ç**[c1] (*bio.*) Tentacle. ~ **a**[l]**k**[g1], consequence; damage; (*mus.*) key. ~ **aklı**, (*fig.*) touching, moving; pathetic; (*cul.*) biting, piquant; caustic, harmful, strong (tobacco, etc): ~ **söz**, an unkind cut. ~ **aklılık**, touchingness, etc. ~ **ca**, harm,

injury; damage, loss; (*naut.*) average: ~ **ve eksime**, (*leg.*) damages: ~ **da boşaltma**, jettison. ~ **calı**, hazardous, risky: ~ **para bolluğu**, (*fin.*) runaway inflation. ~ **durma**, *vn.* allusion, hint. ~ **durmak (-i, -e)**, *vc.* make/let touch; allude to, hint at. ~ **durucu**, suggestive; alluding to.
dokun·ma *vn.* Contact, touch; (*bio.*) sense of touch: ~ **+**, *a.* tactile: ~ **mayın/bombası**, (*mil.*) contact-mine. ~ **mak**[1] **(-e)**, touch, be in contact with; (fish) bite; affect, concern; have an evil effect on; (*med.*) disagree with; injure; assault (a woman); meddle with; vex.
dokunmak[2] *vp.* Be woven.
dokun·sal (*bio.*) Tactile. ~ **tu**, contact. ~ **ulmak**, *vp.* be touched, etc. ~ **ulmamış**, untouched; virgin. ~ **ulmaz**, untouchable; immune. ~ **ulmazlık**, (*leg.*) immunity; inviolability. ~ **um**, (*bio.*) sense of touch. ~ **ur**, touching, affecting, harming: ~ **dokunmaz**, scarcely touching.
dokurcun (*agr.*) Hay/corn stack; (*child.*) game of nine stones, merels.
dokusal(lık) *a.* (*n.*) Textile.
dokutmak (-i -e) *vc.* Make/let weave.
dokuz Nine. ~ **ayın çarşambası bir araya gelmek**, a great accumulation of work to arise: ~ **babalı**, whose father is unknown, bastard: ~ **canlı**, sturdy and strong: ~ **doğurmak**, fret with impatience; suffer hardship: ~ **doğurtmak**, hustle s.o.: ~ **körün bir değneği**, the sole support for many people: ~ **köyden kovulmuş**, driven away from every side: ~ **yorgan eksitmek/paralamak**, live to a great age: ~ **da bir**, (*math.*) one ninth. [*For further phrases* = BEŞ.]
dokuz·ar Nine each; nine at a time. ~ **lu**, containing nine items/parts; (*gamb.*) nine (at cards); (*lit.*) nine-lined stanza. ~ **taş**, (*child.*) nine men's morris, merels. ~ **uncu (9.)**, ninth. [*For further phrases* = BEŞ.]
doküman Document. ~ **tasyon**, documentation. ~ **ter**, documentary (film, etc.).
dolab- = DOLAP.
dola·[l]**k**[g1] (*mod.*) Puttee. ~ **m**, one turn (of stg. coiled); fold (of a turban); (*phys.*) ring. ~ **ma**, *vn.* winding; (*mod.*) kind of wrap, dolman; (*bio.*) whitlow. ~ **mak (-i, -e)**, twist; wind round, encircle; bandage. ~ **maotu**[nu], (*bot.*) nail-wort, whitlow-wort. ~ **maotugiller**, (*bot.*) Paronychiae.
dolam·ba[l]**ç**[c1] *a.* Winding; sinuous; flexible; twisting (road). *n.* Tortuosity; labyrinth, maze; (*bio.*) internal ear. ~ **baçlı**, not straightforward; circuitous; zig-zag, tortuous: ~ **söz**, (*lit.*) circumlocution; euphuism: ~ **yer**, labyrinth. ~ **ı**[l]**k**[g1], hunter's net, snare. ~ **sız**, (*phys.*) acyclic.
dolan Deceit. ~ **dırıcı**, cheat, confidence-trickster, swindler. ~ **dırıcılık**, swindling; a swindle. ~ **dırılmak**, *vp.* ~ **dırmak (-i, -e)**, make go round; rotate; surround; cheat, swindle; obtain by fraud. ~ **ga**[l]**ç**[c1], labyrinth. ~ **ım**, revolution. ~ **ma**, *vn.* rotation. (*ast.*) revolution. ~ **mak**, *vi.* rotate, revolve; circulate; saunter about; (-e), surround. ~ **tı**, (*lit.*, *th.*) plot, intrigue. ~ **taşı**[n1], (*geol.*) dolerite.
dola[l]**p**[b1] (*dom.*) Cupboard; cabinet; wardrobe; anything that revolves; (*eng.*) water-wheel; treadmill;

turnstile; merry-go-round; shop (in the BEDESTEN); (*fig.*) trick, plot. ~ **beygiri gibi dönüp durmak**, turn around in small circles (like the miller's horse): ~ **çevirmek/kurmak**, set a snare, lay a trap: ~ **çivisi**, (*carp.*) medium-sized nail: ~**a girmek**, fall into a trap; be cheated.

dolap·çı (*carp.*) Cupboard maker; (*fig.*) plotter, intriguer. ~**lı**, (*dom.*) fitted with cupboards; (*fig.*) tricky, deceitful: ~ **saat**, grandfather clock.

dolar (*fin.*) Dollar. ~ **bölge/sahası**, (*fin.*) dollar area: ~ **kuşu**, (*orn.*) broad-billed rail: ~ **sıkıntısı**, (*fin.*) dollar (trade) gap.

dolaş *n*. Tangle; obstacle. *a*. Tangled; involved. ~**ı**, tour; promenade. ~**ık**, tortuous; devious; intricate; confused; turbulent. ~**ıklık**, tortuosity; intricacy; (*lit.*) obscurity of style, etc. ~**ıksız**, going straight; uninvolved. ~**ılmak**, *imp. v.* be walked over. ~**ım**, going round; (*geo.*) cycle; (*bio., etc.*) circulation: ~ **sistemi**, circulatory system. ~**mak (-i)**, go around, circulate; walk about; cruise; go a round (of visits, etc.); make a tour; become tangled/confused; get jammed; (street/river) wind in and out. ~**tırılmak**, *vp.* be taken for a walk, etc. ~**tırmak (-i, -e)**, *vc.* take for a walk, etc.

dolay *n*. Surroundings; outskirts; suburbs; road bend. ~**ı (-den)**, *post.* [89] on account/because of; due to: ~**ında**, approximately: ~**ısıyla**; on account of; in connection with; as regards; indirectly; consequently.

dolay·kutupsal (*ast.*) Close to the pole; circumpolar. ~**lama**, (*lit.*) metaphorical speech. ~**lı**, indirect: ~ **anlatmak**, hint at, suggest: ~ **özne**, (*ling.*) logical subject: ~ **tümleç**, (*ling.*) indirect object, adverbial complement. ~**lık**, suburbs. ~**lılık**, indirectness. ~**sız(lık)**, direct(ness).

dolaz (*cul.*) Jelly(-like substance).

doldur·ma *vn.* Action of filling; (*phys.*) loading; packing: ~ **anlatım**, over-wordy explanation. ~**mak (-i)**, fill; complete; stuff; load (a gun); (*cin.*) expose (a film); prime (a person); fill up (a hole); charge (an accumulator); (child) foul its clothes. ~**tmak (-i, -e)**, *vc.* ~**ulmak**, *vp.*

dolfin (*eng.*) Dolphin.

dol·gu (*med.*) Filling/stopping (of a tooth); (*geol.*) gangue; (*eng.*) embankment, bank, ramp; (*min.*) fill, pack: ~ **gereç/maddesi**, fill; packing. ~**gun**, full, filled; stuffed; plump; abundant; high (wages); (*fig.*) spiteful, full of wrath: ~ **maaş**, a fat salary. ~**gunlaşmak**, *vi.* become full/plump. ~**gunluk**, fullness, plenitude: a being overfull; anger, spite.

dolikosefal[i] (*bio.*) Dolichocephalic.

dolin (*geol.*) Doline, sink.

dol·ma *vn.* Filling, stuffing; anything filled/stuffed; (*cul.*) meat/vegetables stuffed with rice and forcemeat; (*eng.*) reclaimed land, embankment; (*fig.*) lie, invention: *a.* stuffed; filled (with earth/stones): ~ **lastik tekerlek**, (*mot.*) rubber tyre: ~ **yutmak**, (*sl.*) swallow a lie; be deceived. ~**mak**, *vi.* fill, become full; swell; be completed; be full of anger/spite: **dolup dolup boşalmak**, (place) be thronged with people. ~**makalem**, fountain-pen. ~**malık**, *a.* (*cul.*) (tomatoes, etc.) suitable for stuffing.

dolmen (*archaeol.*) Dolmen, cromlech.

dolmuş *a.* Filled, stuffed. *n.* Vehicle/boat that only starts when all the seats are filled/taken. ~ **yapmak**, take passengers in this way. ~**çu(luk)**, (work of) DOLMUŞ operator.

dolomit[i] (*geol.*) Dolomite.

dolu[1] *n*. (*met.*) Hail. ~ **yağmak**, hail.

dolu[2] *a.* Full; crowded; solid (*i.e.* not hollow); loaded (gun). *n.* Contents (of a bottle, etc.); charge/ load (of a gun). ~ **film**, (*cin.*) exposed film: ~ **tüfek**, a loaded gun; (*fig.*) an angry person: ~ **zar**, (*gamb. sl.*) loaded dice: ~**su (-in)**, contents, fill, -ful: ~**ya koydum almadı, boşa koydum dolmadı**, I couldn't find any solution to the problem.

dolu·dizgin At full speed. ~**k**, hide (used as waterbottle/float). ~**luk**, being full, fullness. ~**m**, *n.* filling. ~**nay**, (*ast.*) full moon. ~**nmak**, (*ast.*) (sun) set; (moon) be full. ~**şmak (-e)**, (people) gather together in a place; (place) become crowded.

dom·alan (*bio.*) Tumour, abscess; (*myc.*) Périgord truffle. ~**alı**[c][ı], protuberance; protruding (eyes). ~**almak (-e)**, project as a hump; bend down with the back protruding; (animal) lie humped up. ~**altmak (-e)**, *vc.*

domates (*bot.*) Tomato. ~ **salça//suyu**, (*cul.*) tomato sauce//juice: ~ **yaprak küfü**, (*myc.*) tomato leaf mould.

dombay (*zoo., dial.*) (Female) buffalo.

domin·ant (*bio.*) Dominant. ~**ik**, *pr.n.*: ~ **adası** / ~**a** (*geo.*) Dominica. ~**o**, (*gamb.*) game of dominoes; (*mod.*) domino: ~ **demek**, win the game by holding the last domino: ~ **taşı**, a domino. ~**yon**, (*adm.*) dominion.

domur Small bubble; (*bot.*) bud. ~ ~, like beads; swollen, blistered.

domuz (*zoo.*) Pig; swine; boar; (*fig.*) obstinate/ disagreeable man. ~ **arabası**, low four-wheeled cart: ~ **avı**, (*sp.*) boar-hunt: ~ **ayrıkotu**, (*bot.*) Bermuda grass: ~ **derisi**, pigskin: ~ **eti**, (*cul.*) pork: ~ **gibi**, swinish; boorish; malicious, obstinate; strong and healthy: ~ **gibi çalışmak**, work like a slave: ~ **herif**, stout fellow; obstinate/disagreeable fellow: ~ **pastırması**, (*cul.*) bacon: ~ **tenyası** (*bio.*) human tapeworm (from pork): ~**dan kıl koparmak**, succeed in getting money from a miser: ~**una**, (do stg.) like the devil; just to be bloody-minded.

domuz·ayağı[ı] (*mil.*) Caltrop; wormer for removing the charge from a gun; (*bot.*) small caltrops. ~**balığı**[ı], (*zoo.*) porpoise. ~**budu**[u], (*cul.*) leg of pork, ham. ~**damı**[ı], (*min.*) reinforced gallery-roof. ~**giller**, (*zoo.*) pigs, swine. ~**lan** (*ent.*) great diving beetle. ~**laşmak**, be malicious, obstinate. ~**luk**, pigsty; (*eng.*) site of wheel in a water-mill; (*fig.*) swinish behaviour; malice, obstinacy: ~ **etm.**, be treacherous/obstinate. ~**tırnağı**[ı], crowbar, jemmy.

don[1] *n.* (*obs.*) Clothes; (*mod.*) (under-)pants; colour of horse's hair. ~**una doldurmak/etm./kaçırmak/ yapmak**, soil one's clothes, wet one's pants; (*fig.*) be very frightened.

don[2] *n.* (*met.*) Frost. ~ **çözülmek**, thaw: ~ **tutmak** freeze: ~**a çekmek**, (weather) become very cold.

donakal·an (*bio.*) Cataleptic. ~**ım**, (*psy.*) catatonia

~ **tutması**, catalepsy. ~ **ımlı**, catatonic. ~ **mak**, *vi.* be petrified (with horror/fear): **donakalmış**, struck dumb.
dona·ma *vn.* Decoration. ~ **mak**, decorate.
donan·ım (*naut.*) Rigging. ~ **ma**, *vn.* being decked out with flags, etc.; illuminations; (*naut.*) fleet, navy. ~ **mak**, *vp.* = DONAMAK; be decked out/ illuminated/equipped/rigged. ~ **tı**, accessory.
donat·ı Equipment; fittings; (*eng.*) reinforcement. ~ **ıcı**, shipowner. ~ **ılmak**, *vp.* ~ **ım**, equipping; fitting out; (*mil.*) supplying; (*cin.*, *th.*) properties (*sp.*) food, etc. (for a long race). ~ **ımcı**, (*cin.*, *th.*) properties manager, props man. ~ **ımlık**, accessory. ~ **mak** (**-i**), deck out, ornament; equip, rig; illuminate; (*naut.*) dress ship; (*sl.*) abuse. ~ **tan** = ~ ICI. ~ **tırmak** (**-i, -e**), *vc.*
dondur·ma *vn.* Freezing; (*cul.*) water-ice, ice-cream; (*arch.*) concrete: *a.* frozen; set. ~ **macı(lık)**, (work of) ice-cream maker/vendor. ~ **mak** (**-i**), freeze; congeal; solidify; (*fin.*) freeze (prices, etc.). ~ **ucu**, *a.* freezing. ~ **ulmak**, *vp.* be frozen; be very cold. ~ **ulmuş**, *a.* frozen; frozen hard. ~ **umlu**, (*phys.*) cryogenic.
done (*ed.*) Details; data.
donjuan (*lit.*) Don Juan; rake; libertine.
donki (*naut.*) Donkey-engine.
donkişotluk Quixotism.
don·ma *vn.* Freezing; congelation; concretion: ~ **noktası**, (*phys.*) freezing-point. ~ **mak**, *vi.* freeze; become frozen; congeal; curdle; freeze to death; be very cold; (concrete, etc.) solidify, set hard; (*fig.*) be stunned (with surprise, etc.): **donup kalmak**, stand aghast. ~ **maönler**, (*mot.*) anti-freeze. ~ **ra¹**, *n.* frozen swamp/marshland.
donra² *n.* (*bio.*) Dandruff; layer of dirt on the body.
donsuz (*mod.*) Without pants; (*fig.*) destitute; vagabond.
donuk Frozen; frosted (glass); opaque; cold (colour); matt, dull, dim; torpid, frigid. ~ **gözlü**, blear-eyed. ~ **laşmak**, *vi.* become frozen/dull/dim, etc. ~ **laştırmak** (**-i**), make dull; dim. ~ **luk**, dullness, dimness; opacity.
donyağıⁿⁱ Tallow. ~ **gibi**, cold, unattractive (person): ~ **yla pekmez**, incompatible.
dopdolu Full up, chock-full, cram-full.
doping (*sp.*) Doping.
Dorik ~ **üslup**, (*arch.*) Doric (style).
dormi (*sp.*) Dormy (golf).
doru Bay (horse).
doruˡᵏᵘ *n.* (*geo.*) Summit, peak, crest; (*math.*) maximum; apex; (*phys.*) apogee; (*fig.*) climax, culmination. *a.* Piled up into a cone. ~ **çizgisi**, (*geo.*) watershed: ~ **üretim**, (*ind.*) peak production. ~ **lama**, *vn.* heap(ing): *adv.* in a heap, piled up. ~ **lamak** (**-i**), pile up, make a heap. ~ **laşmak**, *vi.* pile up, rise up.
dorum (*zoo.*) Camel colt.
dosa (*naut.*) Gangway; gangplank.
dosdoğru Absolutely straight; straight ahead; as the crow flies; straight as a die; perfectly correct.
dostᵘ *n.* Friend; lover; mistress; (*adm.*) ally. *a.* Friendly. ~ **ağlatır**, **düşman güldürür**, friends criticize but enemies only flatter: ~ **başa, düşman**

ayağa bakar, a friend looks at you, a critical person at your clothes: ~ **düşman**, everyone: ~ **edinmek**, become/win friends: ~ **kara günde belli olur**, a friend in need is a friend indeed: ~ **olm.**, become friends: ~ **tutmak**, gain a friend; have extramarital relations: ~ **a düşmana karşı**, publicly, for all to see: ~ **lar alışverişte görsün** (**diye**), for the sake of appearances: ~ **lar başından ırak!**, may a disaster be far from our friends!: ~ **lar şehit, biz gazi**, let them burn their fingers and we'll profit: ~ **un attığı taş baş yarmaz**, friendly criticism hurts no one.
dost·ane *adv.* In a friendly manner. ~ **ça**, *adv.* in a friendly manner: *a.* friendly, amicable. ~ **luk**, *n.* amity, companionship, friendship; cordiality; friendly act; favour: *a.* friendly: ~ **etm.**, become/ behave like friends: ~ **kantarla, alışveriş miskalle**, don't mix business with friendship: ~ **kurmak**, create a friendship.
dosya (*adm.*) Dossier; file. ~ **lamak** (**-i**), put in a file; start a dossier. ~ **lanmak**, be filed away.
doy (*obs.*) Feast. ~ **a** ~ **a**, until satisfied: ~ **a** ~ **a ağlamak**, have a good cry. ~ **asıya**, until satiated; plentiful. ~ **gu**, daily food, sustenance. ~ **gun**, satiated; with all one's needs satisfied; of independent means. ~ **gunluk**, satiation; saturation; being satisfied; contentedness. ~ **ma**, *vn.* being satiated; (*phys.*) saturation: ~ **noktası**, (*phys.*) saturation point. ~ **mak** (**-e**), be satiated (with), be full of; be sick of stg.; (*phys.*) be saturated: ~ **bilmez**, insatiable. ~ **mamış**, (*phys.*) unsaturated. ~ **maz**, insatiable, avid, greedy. ~ **mazlık**, greed; (*phys.*) non-saturation. ~ **muş**, (*phys.*) saturated. ~ **ulmak** (**-e**), *imp. v.* ~ **um**, satiety: ~ **olmamak** (**-e**), never have enough/get tired of s.o./stg. ~ **umlanmak**/ ~ **umsamak**, *vi.* be satisfied. ~ **umsatmak** (**-i**), satisfy. ~ **umevi**ⁿⁱ, small restaurant, eating-house. ~ **umluk**, amount sufficient to satiate; plunder, booty. ~ **una**ˡᵏᵍ*ⁱ*, restaurant. ~ **unmak**, have sufficient food, be full. ~ **uran**, (*phys.*) saturant. ~ **urma**, *vn.* reassurance; saturation. ~ **urmak** (**-i, -e**), satiate; (*phys.*) saturate; satisfy; nourish; be beneficial; corrupt by generosity. ~ **urucu**, filling; saturating. ~ **urulmak**, *vp.*
doz (*chem.*) Dose. ~ **miktarı**, dosage: ~ **unu kaçırmak**, accidentally mix the medicine too strong; (*fig.*) overdo things: ~ **unu vermek**, dose. ~ **aj**, dosage.
dozer (*eng.*) Bull-dozer.
döğ- = DÖV-.
dök·er (*mot.*) Dumper. ~ **me**, *vn.* act of pouring/ casting; (*min.*) metal casting; (*med.*) eruption: *a.* (*min.*) cast; (wheat, etc.) poured out in a heap (liquids) in bulk: ~ **demir**, cast iron: ~ **mal/yük**, bulk cargo, loose goods: ~ **su ile değirmen dönmez**, a job requires the proper means to carry it out. ~ **meci**, founder, moulder, metal worker. ~ **mecilik**, founding, metal working. ~ **mek** (**-i, -e**), pour; scatter; throw away; (*min.*) cast; shed (tears); (*bot.*) shed (leaves); (*orn.*) moult; (med.) (skin) erupt (measles, small-pox); reject; (*ed.*) fail (a pupil); change, turn into; pour out (complaints). ~ **türmek** (**-i, -e**), *vc.*; (*sl.*) write/speak well and easily. ~ **ük**,

hanging down; worn out: ~ **saçık**, dishevelled, unkempt. ~**ülme**, *vn.* (*med.*) desquamation. ~**ülmek**, *vp.* be poured, etc.; fall into decay; crumble, disintegrate, go to pieces; (*bot.*) (leaves) drop off, fall; (*bio.*) (teeth/hair) fall out; (*ed.*) be failed: **dökülüp saçılmak**, unburden o.s., tell everything; throw off one's clothes (when undressing); spend lavishly. ~**ülür**, *a.* (*bot.*) deciduous. **döküm** A pouring out; (*min.*) a casting/moulding; (*fin.*, *cin.*) breakdown, analysis; inventory. ~ **ocağı**, cupola furnace; ~ **potası**, crucible. **döküm·cü** (*min.*) Founder, metal-worker. ~**cülük**, founding, metal-working. ~**evi**ⁿⁱ/ ~**hane**, foundry. ~**lü**, (*mod.*) well-fitting.

dökün·mek Pour (water) over o.s. ~**tü**, waste; debris, remnants; (*geol.*) detritus; (*geo.*) reef; stones thrown into the sea (to make breakwater); (*phys.*) fall-out; (*soc.*) dregs of the population; (*med.*) skin eruption: ~ **yelpazesi**, (*geol.*) scree, talus. ~**tülü**, (*geol.*) detrital.

döl (*bio.*) Foetus; semen; germ; race, stock. ~ **almak**, breed thoroughbreds: ~ **döş**, progeny, descendants.

dölek (*dial.*) Serious, steady, quiet; smooth.

döl·eşiⁿⁱ (*bio.*) Placenta, afterbirth. ~**et(bilim)**, (*med.*) embryo(logy). ~**leme**, *vn.* fertilization. ~**lemek (-i)**, fertilize; inseminate. ~**lenim**, conception. ~**lenme**, *vn.* fertilization. ~**lenmek**, *vp.* fertilized. ~**lenmesiz**, parthenogenic. ~**lenmiş**, *a.* fertilized: ~ **yumurta**, zygote. ~**üt**ü, foetus: ~ **torbası**, amnion. ~**ütsel**, foetal. ~**yatağı**ⁿⁱ, womb, uterus: ~ **boynu**, cervix. ~**yolu**ⁿᵘ, vagina: ~ +, *a.* colpo-.

dön·baba (*bot.*) Crane's-bill. ~**dürme**, *vn.* turning back/round; rotating; (*sp.*) turning (the body). ~**dürmek (-i, -e)**, *vc.* turn back/round; rotate; spin; turn inside out; reverse; (*ed.*) fail. ~**dürücü**, (*eng.*) driving. ~**dürülmek**, *vp.* ~**dürüm**, (*fin.*) endorsement. ~**dürümlemek (-i)**, endorse.

döne (*sp.*) Tournament. ~**lç**ᶜⁱ, (*el.*) rotor.

dönek Untrustworthy; who never keeps his word; (*ed. sl.*) always failing in examinations. ~**lik**, untrustworthiness.

dönel (*math.*) Rotatory, rotational, axial; (*phys.*) gyratory; (*fin.*) returnable. ~ **alındılı**, (letter) with recorded delivery: ~ **karşılaşma**, (*sp.*) tournament: ~ **kavşak**, (*mot.*) roundabout. ~**mek**, *vi.* (*adm.*) be demoted from the highest rank; begin to decline.

dönem (*his.*) Period, age, era; (*phys.*) cycle; (*adm.*) life (of a parliament); (*ed.*) term; (*sp.*) round; set. ~**eç**ᶜⁱ, (*mot.*) curve, corner, bend: ~ **yüksekliği**, banking. ~**eçli**, ~ **yol**, winding road. ~**li/~sel**, periodic, cyclic. ~**lilik/~sellik**, periodicity.

dönen·ce Turning-point; (*ast.*) tropic. ~**cel**, (*ast.*) tropical: ~ **ay**//**yıl**, tropical month//year. ~**mek**, *vi.* continually search around.

döner *a.* Turning, rotating; rotary; circulating; gyro-. ~ **kanat**, (*aer.*) rotor: ~ **kapı**, revolving door: ~ **kebap**, (*cul.*) meat wrapped round and roasted on a vertical rotating spit: ~ **kemik**, (*bio.*) radius: ~ **köprü**, swing-bridge: ~ **punta**, (*carp.*) live centre: ~ **saç**, (*rly.*) turntable: ~ **sermaye**, (*fin.*) trading capital: ~ **uyak**, (*lit.*) repeated word.

döner·basar (*pub.*) Rotary press. ~**boyun(giller)**, (*orn.*) wryneck(s). ~**geçi**'**t**ᵈⁱ, turnstile. ~**im**, (*leg.*) dismissal (of case).

döngel (*bot.*) Medlar. ~**orucu**ⁿᵘ, prolonged fasting

döngü Rotation; (*met.*) cyclone; (*phil.*) vicious circle. ~ **atlama**, (*sp.*) bye; seeding.

dön·me *vn.* Act of turning, rotation; torsion; (*rel.*) conversion; convert to Islam; *pr. n.* member of a Jewish sect converted in 17th century: *a.* convert, renegade: ~ **dolap**, revolving cupboard (in a wall); merry-go-round. ~ **mek**, *vi.* turn; rotate; turn back; return; change; be transformed; (*rel.*) change, be converted; (*pol.*) defect; swerve (from a course); fail to keep (a promise); (*ed.*) fail (an examination); (*ed.*) fail to be promoted: **döne döne çıkmak**, ascend in a spiral: **dönemiyecek kadar yürüdük**, we reached the point of no return: DÖNER: **dönmez punta** (*carp.*) dead centre: **dönüp dolaşıp**, in the long run after all: **dönüp dolaşmak**, wander about, meander.

dön·ü Repentance; (*med.*) rotation; (*phys.*) spin (*th.*) run (of a play); tour; (*sp.*) lap. ~ **ük**, with the back turned; facing; changed; aimed at. ~**ülmek (-e)**, *imp. v.* ~ **üm**, (*math.*) an area forty ARŞIN square (approx. 900 sq. m., 1/4 acre); turn, revolution; anniversary; a time: ~ **noktası**, climacteric, turning-point. ~**ümlük**, quantity sufficient for one DÖNÜM; area measured in DÖNÜM.

dönüş Act of turning/returning; return journey, pivot: (*fin.*) turnover. ~ **ekseni**, (*math.*) axis of rotation: ~ **ve yatış**, (*aer.*) turn and bank. ~**lü**, rotational; (*ling.*) reflexive: ~ **adıl**//**eylem**, reflexive pronoun//verb: ~ **çatı**, reflexive form of the verb: ~ **günü**, date due (for return). ~ **me**, modification, transformation; (*ling.*) phonetic modification: ~ **mek (-e)**, change/be transformed (into). ~**ölçer**, tachometer. ~**türgeç/~türücü**, (*el.*) transformer: ~ **türme**, *vn.* transformation. ~ **türmek (-i, -e)**, *vc.* transform, convert. ~ **(tür)üm**, (*math.*) transformation, conversion: ~ **endüstrisi**, (*ind.*) processing industry. ~ **ül**, (*phys.*) critical. ~ **üm**, transformation, radical change. ~**ümce**, (*psy.*) hysteria. ~**ümcü(lük)**, (*phil.*) transform·ist/(-ism). ~ **ün**, on the return journey/way back.

döpiyes (*mod.*) Two-piece suit/costume.

dörd- = DÖRT. ~ **er**, four each; four at a time: ~ ~ in fours. ~ **ül**, *n., a.* (*math.*) square. ~ **ültaş**, (*gamb.*) diamond. ~ **ün**, (*ast.*) quarter (of moon, etc.). ~**üncü (4.)**, fourth: ~ **zaman**, (*geol.*) quaternary. ~**üz**, (*bio.*) quadruplet: ~ **tümsecikler/yum rucuklar**, (*bio.*) corpora quadrigemina (of the brain). ~**üzleme**, (*th.*) tetralogy. [*For further phrases* = BEŞ.]

dör'**t**ᵈü Four; (*used to express totality*) all, every. ~ **ayak üzerine düşmek**, land on all fours, get out of the difficulty, be lucky: ~ **başı mamur**, prosperous, flourishing; well-appointed: ~ **bir tarafı/yanı**, in every direction: ~ **bir yöreden**, from all quarters: ~ **bucak**, in all quarters: ~ **dolaşmak**, be in a quandary: ~ **dönmek**, turn a place upside down, search everywhere; think of every possible mean (to do stg.): ~ **duvar arasında kalmak**, be forced to stay at home: ~ **el ile**, with the greatest energy: **elle sarılmak/yapışmak (-e)**, give one's utmost to

..., show the greatest zeal in ...: ∼ **göz,** s.o. wearing spectacles: ∼ **göz bir evlat için,** all the parents' care is for the child: ∼ **gözle beklemek,** await with the greatest impatience: ∼ **gün sıtması,** (*med.*) quartan (fever): ∼ **işlem,** (*math.*) the four operations (+, −, ×, ÷): ∼ **kolluya binmek,** (*sl.*) go to the grave: ∼ **köşeli,** four-cornered/-sided, square: ∼ **taraftan,** all around, from every quarter: ∼ **ucunu bırakmak/koyuvermek,** lose heart about stg., give stg. up: ∼ **üstü murat üstü,** prosperous; in perfect condition: ∼ **yanı deniz kesilmek,** be in a hopeless plight: ∼ **yan(ın)a bakmak,** look in every direction: ∼ **yüz dirhem adamdır!,** he's a brick!: ∼ **te bir,** one fourth, one quarter. [*For further phrases* = BEŞ.]

dört·ayak *n.* Quadruped: *adv.* on all fours. ∼ **cihar,** (*gamb.*) double-four (at backgammon). ∼ **dişli/ (-giller),** (*ich.*) globe-fish(es). ∼ **gen/** ∼ **kenar,** (*math.*) quadrilateral. ∼ **kaşlı,** with bushy eyebrows; with a budding moustache. ∼ **leme,** *vn.* quartering; (*lit.*) quatrain. ∼ **lemek (-i),** increase to four; (*agr.*) plough four times. ∼ **lü,** having four ...; (*gamb.*) the four; (*lit.*) having four lines; (*mus.*) quartette. ∼ **lük,** that is worth four (units); that weighs four (units); (*lit.*) quatrain; (*mus.*) a quarternote; crotchet; (*ast.*) quadrature. ∼ **nal,** gallop: ∼ **a,** at a gallop, at full speed: ∼ **a kaldırmak,** gallop away. ∼ **yol,** crossroads: ∼ **ağzı,** crossroads, junction. ∼ **yüz,** (*gamb. sl.*) poker. ∼ **yüzlü,** (*math.*) tetrahedron.

döş (*bio.*) Flank; breast; withers; (*cul.*) brisket. ∼ **tarafından et,** scrag end of meat.

döşe¹kᵍⁱ Mattress; bed. ∼ **döşemek,** spread a bed (on the floor); make a bed: ∼ **e düşmek,** (*med.*) be ill in bed. ∼ **li,** having a bed; broad-based, fixed; broad and shallow-draughted (boat).

döşeli Spread out; laid down (carpet, etc.): furnished; ornamented. ∼ **dayalı,** fully furnished.

döşe·m Installation ∼ **mci(lik),** (work of) installer, fitter. ∼ **me,** floor; floor covering; carpet; furniture; upholstery; (*eng.*) roadway. ∼ **meci,** furnituredealer, upholsterer. ∼ **mecilik,** furniture and upholstery making/dealing. ∼ **mek (-i),** lay down/ spread (carpets, etc.); carpet; furnish; pave: **döşeyip dayamak,** fully furnish. ∼ **melik,** *a.* flooring; upholstery. ∼ **nmek,** *vi.* be spread out/laid down; 'let o.s. go', dilate upon stg.; give vent to one's feelings; (*col.*) take to one's bed, be bedridden. ∼ **tilmek (-e),** *vp.* ∼ **tmek (-i, -e),** *vc.* ∼ **yici,** installer, fitter.

döteriyum = DEUTERİUM.

döv·dü (*carp.*) Hammer; mallet; back of an axe. ∼ **dür(t)mek (-i, -e),** *vc.;* ∼ **dür(t)ülmek,** *vp.* = DÖVMEK, ∼ **e¹çᶜⁱ,** (*cul.*) wooden mortar. ∼ **en,** (*agr.*) flail; threshing sledge.

döviz (*fin.*) Foreign bills; foreign exchange; (*his.*) motto; banner.

dövlek = DİVLEK.

döv·me *vn.* Beating, battering; (*min.*) forging; (*agr.*) threshing; threshed corn; tattooing: *a.* (*min.*) wrought, beaten. ∼ **meci(lik),** (*min.*) (work of) forger. ∼ **me¹çᶜⁱ,** (*min.*) forging-press. ∼ **mek (-i),** beat; hammer, forge; (*agr.*) thresh; chastise, thrash; (*mil.*) bombard; (*cul.*) grind, pound: **dövüp yassıltmak,** (*min.*) beat out. ∼ **ülgen(lik),** (*min.*) malle·able/

(-ability). ∼ **ülmek,** *vp.* ∼ **ünmek,** *vi.* beat/scourge o.s.; beat one's breast, lament. ∼ **üm,** (*min.*) forging.

dövüş *vn.* = DÖVMEK; fight, conflict: ∼ **yeri,** cockpit. ∼ **çü,** fighter. ∼ **ken,** warlike, combative, bellicose: ∼ **horoz,** (*orn.*) fighting cock. ∼ **kenlik,** bellicosity. ∼ **me,** *vn.* fighting; affray, brawl. ∼ **mek (-le),** fight against each other; brawl; clash; struggle; (*sp.*) box. ∼ **türmek (-i),** *vc.*

DP = DEMOKRAT PARTİ. ∼ **T** = DEVLET PLANLAMA TEŞKİLATI.

Dr. = DOKTOR.

dragline (*eng.*) Dragline.

dragon (*mil.*) Dragoon; (*sl.*) penniless.

drah·mi (*fin.*) Drachma. ∼ **oma,** dower, dowry.

draje (*cul.*) Dragée.

dram (*th.*) Drama; tragedy. ∼ **yapıtı,** drama, play: ∼ **yapıtı kişileri,** dramatis personae: ∼ **yazarı,** dramatist. ∼ **atik,** dramatic; exciting. ∼ **atize,** ∼ **etm.,** (*th., fig.*) dramatise. ∼ **aturg,** dramatist, dramaturge. ∼ **aturgi,** dramaturgy.

drayer (*ind.*) Dryer.

dren (*agr.*) Drain. ∼ **aj,** drainage. ∼ **ajsız,** undrained. ∼ **e,** ∼ **etm.,** drain.

dresaj (*sp.*) Dressage.

dretnotᵘ (*naut.*) Dreadnought.

drezin (*rly.*) Plate-layer's trolley.

dripling (*sp.*) Dribbling.

droseragiller (*bot.*) Drosera, insectivorous plants.

drumlin (*geol.*) Drumlin.

DS = DERLEME SÖZLÜĞÜ. ∼ **H** = DIŞ SEYAHAT HARCI. ∼ **İ** = DEVLET SU İŞLERİ. ∼ **Ö** = DÜNYA SAĞLIK ÖRGÜTÜ.

DŞK = DEVLET ŞURASI KANUNU.

DTCF = DİL VE TARİH-COĞRAFYA FAKÜLTESİ.

-du *v. suf.* = -Dİ.

dua (*rel.*) Prayer; devotions; blessing; desire, wish. ∼ **etm.,** pray; bless; ask for a blessing on: ∼ **(sını) almak,** receive s.o.'s blessing.

dua·cı One who prays for another: ∼ **nız,** (*obs.*) your humble servant. ∼ **han,** prayer-reader: ∼ **olm.,** pray.

duayen Senior member (of a profession), doyen, dean.

duba (*naut.*) Barge, pontoon; floating bridge; (*eng.*) caisson. ∼ **gibi,** very fat. ∼ **cı,** bargee.

dubar (*ich.*) Common/striped grey mullet.

dubara (*gamb.*) Double-two (at backgammon); (*sl.*) fraud, trick. ∼ **cı,** gambler, trickster.

dubl·aj (*cin.*) Doubling. ∼ **e,** double; (*mod.*) lining. ∼ **etm.,** line. ∼ **eks,** (*arch.*) duplex, maisonette. ∼ **fas,** (*tex.*) double-faced cloth. ∼ **ör,** (*th.*) stand-in, understudy. ∼ **ür,** (*mod.*) lining.

duçar Subject to; afflicted with; exposed to. ∼ **etme,** exposure: ∼ **olm. (-e),** be subject/exposed to; (*med.*) contract (a disease); be afflicted by.

duda¹kᵍⁱ (*bio.*) Lip. ∼ +, *a.* Labial; cheilo-. ∼ **benzeşmesi,** (*ling.*) labial attraction: ∼ **boyası,** (*mod.*) rouge: ∼ **burmak,** screw up the lips: ∼ **bükmek,** curl one's lips (in disdain/contempt): ∼ **çukuru,** groove in the upper lip: ∼ **a gelmek,** kiss each other: ∼ **eşlemesi,** (*cin.*) lip synchronization: ∼ **kıpırdatmak,** open the lips, say a word: ∼ **payı bırakmak,** not fill a glass, etc. right up to the brim: ~ **sarkıtmak**, sulk: ~ **ünsüzü**, (*ling.*) labial (consonant).

dudak·lı Lipped: ~ **ayı**, (*zoo.*) sloth bear. ~**sıl**, (*ling.*) labial (sound). ~**sıllaşma**, (*ling.*) labialization.

dudu (*obs.*) Woman's title; old Armenian woman. ~ (**kuşu**), (*orn.*) parrot.

duetto (*mus.*) Duetto.

-duğu *v. suf.* = -DİĞİ.

duhul Entering, entrance; inclusion; penetration. ~ **etm.**, enter; be included; begin; be imported; (*bio.*) consummate the sexual act. ~**iye**, entrance-fee; admission(-ticket).

-duk *v. suf.* = -DİK. ~**ça** = -DİKÇE. ~**ta(n)** = -DİKTE(N).

duka Duke; ducat. ~**lık**, duchy.

dul *n.* (*fem.*) Widow; (*mas.*) widower. *a.* Widowed. ~ **kalmak**, be left a widow(er): ~ **karı enciği**, (*sl.*) double-chinned woman. ~**aptalotu**[nu], (*bot.*) daphne, mezereon. ~**aptalotugiller**, (*bot.*) daphnes. ~**avratotu**[nu], (*bot.*) great burdock.

dulda Shelter, refuge. ~**lamak (-i)**, give shelter to. ~**lanmak**, be sheltered.

dulluk Widowhood.

dulu·k[ğu] (*bio.*) Temple; cheek.

dumağı (*med.*) Cold in the head.

duman Smoke; mist; condensation (on cold glass, etc.); bloom (on fruit); (*sl.*) hopeless state. ~ **attırmak (-e)**, (*sl.*) defeat s.o. utterly; have s.o. at one's mercy: ~ **borusu**, (*arch.*) flue: ~ **etm.**, (*sl.*) spoil, scatter, defeat: ~ **olm.**, be very bad: ~ **yapmak**, (*gamb. sl.*) win much with little money: ~ı **doğru çıksın**, no matter as long as the result is good: ~ı **üstünde**, (food) very fresh; (book, *etc.*) brand new.

duman·cı (*gamb. sl.*) S.o. winning much with little capital. ~**lamak (-i)**, give out smoke; cover with mist; render turbid; cure (fish). ~**lanmak**, *vi.* be filled with smoke/mist; (fish, etc.) be smoked/cured; become confused in mind/fuddled. ~**lı**, smoky; (*chem.*) fuming; (*met.*) misty; tipsy. ~**rengi**, smoke-coloured. ~**sız**, smokeless.

dumdum (*mil.*) Dum-dum bullet.

dumur (*med.*) Atrophy. ~**a uğramak**, be(come) atrophied; disappear; (*mil.*) abort.

dun Low; base; lower; inferior.

duo (*mus.*) Duet.

dupduru Very clear, crystal clear.

dur = DURMAK. ~**a**, (*ling.*) full-stop (.)

-dur[1] *v. suf.* = -DİR[1].

-dur-[2] *v. suf.* = -DİR-[2].

dura·ç[cı 1] *n.* (*orn.*) Francolin.

dura·ç[cı 2] *n.* (*art.*) Pedestal, base.

durağan Fixed, stable, stationary; (*phys.*) permanent. ~ **değer**, (*fin.*) property: ~ **giderler**, overheads: ~ **mallar**, real estate. ~**laşmak**, *vi.* become fixed/permanent. ~**lık**, stability, fixity.

dura·k[ğı] *n.* Stopping-place; halt; pause; (*ling.*) pause; (*obs.*) full-stop; (*lit.*) caesura. *a.* Stationary. ~ **su**, stagnant water: ~ **yeri**, (*mot.*) hard standing.

durakalmak *vi.* Be bewildered/aghast.

durakı (*bot.*) Nectarine.

durak·lama Stand-still; (*mil.*) sudden halt. ~**lamak**, *vi.* halt, come to a stop, break off; hesitate. ~**latmak (-i)**, *vc.* ~**lı**, stationary. ~**sama**, hesitation. ~**samak**, *vi.* hesitate. ~**samalı**, hesitant. ~**sız**, direct, non-stop.

dural (*phil.*) Static. ~**ama**, pause; hesitation. ~**amak**, *vi.* pause, come to a halt; hesitate, baulk at. ~**andırma**, (*ling.*) punctuation. ~**ga**, terminal, station. ~**lı**, ~ **çeke**, (*ling.*) semi-colon. ~**lık**, calm.

duran (*ast.*) Fixed star.

dur·dinlen ~ **yok**, without a stop/interruption. ~**dura·**[cı], (*mot.*) brake: ~**a basmak**, brake, put on the brake. ~**durma**, *vn.* stopping; (*ind.*) shutdown; (*leg.*) injunction: ~ **düzeni**, (*aer.*) arrester-gear. ~ **durmak (-i)**, stop, make stand still; cause to wait; put out of action; dampen. ~ **durucu**, (*eng.*) arrester; brakesman. ~**durulmak**, *vp.*

durendiş(lik) Far-sighted(ness); pruden·t/(-ce).

durgu Pause, interval; interruption. ~**luk**, carpark. ~ **n**, stationary; stagnant; calm; dull; fatigued; perplexed; at a standstill: ~ **bir halde**, in a backwater: ~ **hava**, (*met.*) still air: ~ **olm.**, (*fin.*) be in the doldrums: ~ **su**, stagnant water: ~**lar**, (*geo.*) doldrums. ~**nlaşmak**, *vi.* become quiet/calm; (*fig.*) become depressed; (brain) cease to function, be perplexed. ~**nluk**, being stationary; stagnation; (*fin.*) depression; quiet; heaviness; prostration; anxiety; amazement.

dur·ma *vn.* Stopping, staying; cessation; (*phys.*) repose. ~**dan**, without cease. ~**mak**, *vi.* stop; cease; stand; wait; remain; endure; continue; dwell on stg.: *aux. v.* [191] *expresses continuous action* [bakadurmak/bakıp ~, keep on looking]: **dur!**, *int.* halt!, stop!; (*naut.*) avast!: **dur durak yok/dur otur yok**, no respite, not a moment's peace: **durduğu yerde**, without any effort; unnecessarily: **durmuş et**, (*cul.*) meat kept for a few days: **durmuş oturmuş bir hal**, a settled mature state; a being too old for one's years; seeming very experienced: **durundu!**, hey, stop!: **durup dinlenmeden**, unceasingly, continuously: **durup durma!**, don't keep standing there: **durup dururken**, [179] suddenly; without any reason; without provocation: **durur**, *a.* stationary. ~**maksızın**, unceasingly. ~**malı**, ~ **çıkış** (*sp.*) standing start. ~**maz**, unceasing; perpetual (motion). ~**sayı**, (*math.*) constant.

duru[1] *a.* Clear, limpid, crystalline.

duru[2] *n.* State, condition. ~**cu**, stationary; stable. ~**lk**[ğu], *a.* static: *n.* (*el.*) stator. ~**kluk**, steadiness. ~**ksamak**, *vi.* hesitate. ~**ksun**, (*col.*) hesitant; irresolute: ~ **şişkinlik**, (*fin.*) stagflation.

duru·lamak (-i) Rinse in clear cold water. ~**lanmak**, *vp.* be rinsed; rinse o.s. ~**lașmak**, *vi.* become clear/bright. ~**lmak**[1], *vi.* clarify, become clear; (*chem.*) settle; become quiet/well-behaved. ~**ltmak**, *vc.* make clear. ~**ltucu**, (*el.*) ballast. ~**luk**, clarity.

durulmak[2] *imp. v.* Stop. **durulmaz!**, no stopping!

durum Condition, case, state; position; status; circumstance; (*ling.*) case; attitude: (*sp.*) score. ~ **belgesi**, (*adm.*) identity papers: ~ **belirteci**, (*ling.*) adverb of manner: ~ **böyle değil**, that's not the

case: ~ **eki**, (*ling*.) case ending: ~ **ortacı**, (*ling*.) present participle: ~ **ulacı**, (*ling*.) gerund of state: ~**u açıklamak**, clear the air: ~**u değiştirmek**, turn the balance: ~**unda (-in)**, in the form/shape of a ....
duruş *vn*. Posture; attitude; type; aspect; behaviour; (*cin*.) pose; exposure. ~**ma**, *vn*. (*leg*.) court sitting/ hearing/session. ~**mak**, confront one another.
duş (*dom*.) Douche, shower; shower-bath. ~ **yapmak**, take a shower.
duşa¹kᵍ¹ Hobble; fetter. ~**lamak (-i)**, hobble, fetter (animal).
dutᵘ (*bot*.) Mulberry; (*sl*.) s.o. very drunk. ~ **ağacı**, mulberry tree: ~ **gibi olm.**, be very drunk; be ashamed: ~ **kurusu**, dried mulberries: ~ **yemiş Bulgar götü gibi**, (*sl. vulg*.) very talkative: ~ **yemiş bülbül gibi/(bulbüle dönmek)**, (become) taciturn.
dut-çu(luk) (Work of) mulberry-grower/-seller. ~**giller**, (*bot*.) Moraceae. ~**luk**, mulberry garden; full of mulberry trees.
duv. = DUVARCILIK.
duva¹kᵍ¹ (*mod*.) Veil (worn by brides); (*dom*.) stone/ earthenware lid. ~ **düşkünü**, bride who shortly becomes a widow: ~ **ına doymamak**, (bride) die, be divorced, be widowed. ~**lamak (-i)**, cover with a veil. ~**lanmak**, *vp*.; (*fig*.) become a bride. ~**lı**, veiled.
duvar Wall; dike; (*fig*.) obstacle; (*sp*.) blocking (the ball). ~ +, *a*. Wall-; mural: ~ **arısı**, (*ent*.) mason bee: ~ **arkası dolgusu**, (*eng*.) backfill: ~ **askısı**, (*dom*.) coat-hanger: ~ **ayağı**, foot of a wall; (*arch*.) footings: ~ **bölmesi**, (*arch*.) bay: ~ **çekmek**, divide by/surround with a wall: ~ **dayağı**, (*arch*.) buttress: ~ **dirseği**, (*arch*.) flying buttress: ~ **dişi**, (*arch*.) keying (for extending a wall): ~ **gibi**, very solid: ~ **gibi sağır**, as deaf as a post: ~ **haritası**, (*geo*.) wall-map: ~ **kâğıdı**, (*dom*.) wallpaper: ~ **kara sağanı**, (*orn*.) common swift: ~ **örgüsü**, (*arch*.) bond: ~ **resmi**, (*art*.) mural painting, etc.: ~ **saati**, wall-clock: ~ **sarmaşığı**, (*bot*.) common ivy: ~ **tırmaşık kuşu**, (*orn*.) wall-creeper: ~**a yazıyorum**, don't forget I've told you this; some day you will learn that I was right.
duvar-cı Bricklayer, stonemason; (*sl*.) burglar. ~**cılık**, bricklaying. ~**lamak (-i)**, wall in. ~**lı**, walled.
duy (*el*.) Lamp-socket, holder. ~ **priz**, lamp-holder-cum-socket.
duyar Sensitive. ~**ca(lı)**, (*bio*.) aller·gy/(-gic). ~**ga**, (*ent*., *zoo*.) antenna, feeler. ~**gan**, (*chem*.) allergen. ~**kat**, (*cin*.) emulsion. ~**lı**, able to feel, sensitive. ~**(lı)lık**, (*bio*., *phys*.) sensitivity. ~**lıkölçer**, (*cin*.) sensitometer. ~**sız(lık)**, insensitiv·e/(-ity). ~**sızlaş(tır)ma**, (*med*.) desensitization.
-duydu *v. suf.* = -DI¹.
duygan(lık) Sensitiv·e/(-ity).
duygu Perception; feeling; sense; sensation; stg. heard/perceived; information, knowledge; sentiment. ~ **organları**, (*bio*.) sense organs: ~ **ünlemi**, (*ling*.) emotional interjection.
duygu-daş (*psy*.) Sympathizer, empathist. ~**daşlık**, (*psy*.) sympathy; empathy. ~**lamak (-i)**, affect, arouse sympathy. ~**landırmak (-ı)**, move/touch s.o. ~**lanım**/~**lanma**, *vn*. emotion; (*psy*.) affectivity.

~**lanmak**, be affected/moved/touched. ~**lu**, sensitive; touchy; impressionable; perceptive, intelligent. ~**luluk**, sensitivity. ~**n(luk)**, sensitiv·e/ (-ity). ~**sal**, sensual; emotional, sentimental; romantic; (*psy*.) affective. ~**sallık**, sensuality, sensibility, feeling; romanticism. ~**suz**, insensitive, apathetic, heartless; ignorant. ~**suzluk**, insensitivity, apathy.
duy-ma *vn*. Feeling; hearing; etc. ~**mak (-i)**, feel; perceive; hear; get information about: **duyar gibi oldum**, I thought (I heard ...). ~**maz**, *a*. who does not perceive; imperceptive; insensitive. ~**mazlık**, insensitivity: ~**tan gelmek**, pretend not to have heard; ignore all entreaties. ~**sal**, sensory.
duyu (*psy*.) Sense. ~ **organları**, sense organs: ~ **yitimi**, (*med*.) anaesthesia. ~**dışı**, (*psy*.) extrasensory. ~**lkᵍu**, news. ~**lanma**, (*bio*.) sensation. ~**lma**, *vn*. being heard: ~ +, *a*. audio: ~ **frekansı**, (*phys*.) audio frequency. ~**lmadık**, unheard of, strange. ~**lmak**, *vp*. be heard/felt; be heard of; be known; be made public. ~**ltu**, story, rumour. ~**ltucu**, story-teller. ~**ltulamak (-i)**, tell, relate. ~**lur**, perceptible; noticeable. ~**lürüstü**, extrasensory.
duyum *vn*. Sensation. ~ **eşiği**, (*psy*.) threshold of sensation: ~ **ikiliği**, (*psy*.) synaesthesia: ~ **yitimi**, (*psy*.) anaesthesia.
duyum-cu(luk) (*psy*.) Sensual·ist/(-ism). ~**lamak (-i)**, sense stg. ~**ölçer**, (*phys*.) sensitivity-meter. ~**sal**, sensory. ~**samak**, *vi*. feel. ~**satmak (-i)**, cause to feel. ~**samazlık**, apathy, insensitivity. ~**suz**, without feeling, insensitive. ~**suzlaştırıcı**, (*med*.) anaesthetic. ~**suzlaştırma**, *vn*. anaesthesia. ~**suzlaştırmak (-i)**, anaesthetize.
duyun¹çᶜu Conscience. ~**lu(luk)**, conscientious/ (-ness). ~**suz(luk)**, unconscientious(ness).
duyur-ca (*pub*.) Poster. ~**mak (-i, -e)**, make heard/felt/perceived; make known, announce, divulge. ~**u**, notice, announcement; invitation; publication: ~ **tahtası**, notice-board: ~ **yoluyla**, by advertising. ~**ucu**, making known. ~**ulmak**, *vp*. ~**umluk**, (*pub*.) placard.
duyu-sal Affective, sensory; (*psy*.) sensitive. ~**ş**, (manner of) hearing/feeling; (*cin*.) contrasting: ~ **titrem**/**vurgusu**, (*ling*.) affective intonation//accent.
duziko (*cul*.) (Greek) RAKI.
-dü *v. suf.* = -DI.
DÜ = DİYARBAKIR ÜNİVERSİTESİ.
düalizm (*phil*.) Dualism.
Dübbü-asgar (*ast*.) Little Bear. ~**ekber**, Great Bear.
dübeş (*gamb*.) Double five (at backgammon).
düden (*geo*.) Chasm, pot-hole, swallow-hole.
düdü¹kᵍü *n*. (*mus*.) Whistle, pipe, flute; long hollow tube; (*sl*.) silly fellow. ~ **gibi kalmak**, be left alone and helpless (through one's own fault): ~ **gibi kıyafet**, (*mod*.) too small/tight clothes: ~ **makarnası**, (*cul*.) macaroni; (*sl*.) stupid.
düdük-çü (*mus*.) Piper, flautist. ~**lemek (-i)**, (*vulg*.) have sexual relations. ~**lü**, with a whistle: ~ **tencere**, (*cul*.) pressure-cooker.
düello Duel; single combat. ~**ya davet etm.**, challenge s.o.

düet (*mus.*) Duet. ~**to**, short duet.

dügâh (*Or. mus.*) A compound melody.

düğme (*mod.*) Button; knob; (*bio.*) pimple; (*el.*) (push-)button, switch; (*bot.*) bud. ~ **çengeli**, (*mod.*) button-hook.

düğme·ci Button-maker/-seller. ~**k** (-**i**), knot. ~**lemek** (-**i**), button (up). ~**lenmek**, *vp.* ~**li**, with buttons; buttoned: ~ **Afrika domuzu**, (*zoo.*) warthog.

düğmük Knot.

düğü (*cul.*) Fine-grained cracked wheat.

-**düğü** *v. suf.* = -DİĞİ.

düğün Knot; bow; knotty problem; (*bio.*) ganglion; (*math.*) node; (*lit.*) crisis, crux. ~ **atmak/vurmak**, knot, tie a knot: ~ ~, tightly knotted: ~ **noktası**, crucial/vital point: ~**ünü çözmek**, untie the knot; (*fig.*) solve the problem.

düğüm·cük (*bio.*) Nodule. ~**lemek** (-**i**), knot. ~**lenmek**, *vp.* ~**lü**, knotted; knotty.

düğün Feast (for a wedding//circumcision). ~ + , *a.* Bridal. ~ **bayram etm.**, feast, make merry: ~ **dayısı**, bridegroom's adviser/supporter/benefactor: ~ **dernek**, wedding ceremony/feast; festival: ~ **dernek hep bir örnek**, all of the same quality; always same old thing: ~ **evi gibi**, (place) over-illuminated/full of merrymakers: ~ **pastası** wedding-cake: ~ **pilavıyla dost ağırlamak** (-**i**), entertain s.o. at another's expense; take credit for what others have done: ~**e okumak** (-**i**), (*dial.*) invite s.o. to a wedding: ~**ün** **25.**//**50.**//**60. yıldönümü**, silver-//golden-//diamond-wedding (anniversary).

düğün·cü Wedding-guest. ~**çiçeği**ⁿⁱ, (*bot.*) ranunculus; buttercup, crowfoot. ~**çiçeğigiller**, (*bot.*) Ranunculaceae. ~**çorbası**ⁿⁱ, (*cul.*) soup (made with meat-stock, flour and yoghurt).

dükü Duke, ~ + , *a.* Ducal. ~**alık**, dukedom.

-**dük**ü *v. suf.* = -DİK.

dükkân Shop; (*sl.*) gambling-den. ~**cı**, shopkeeper. ~**lı**, ~ **pasaj**, arcade.

düldül (*jok.*) Old horse, jade, nag; (*fig.*) old motor-car, crock.

dülger Carpenter, builder. ~**balığı**ⁿⁱ, (*ich.*) John Dory. ~**lik**, carpentry.

dümbeleˡᵏᵍⁱ (*mus.*) Small drum; (*fig.*) idiot. ~**çi**, drum-player.

dümdar (*mil., his.*) Rearguard.

dümdüz Absolutely level/straight; as the crow flies.

dümen (*naut.*) Rudder; (*fig.*) management; (*sl.*) trick. ~ **bedeni**, (*naut.*) rudder-stock: ~ **çevirmek**, (*col.*) play a trick: ~ **kırmak**, change course; (*sl.*) manage well: ~ **kullanmak**, (*naut.*) cox/steer (the boat); (*sl.*) manage well: ~ **neferi**, helmsman; (*fig.*) last man in a file; s.o. who is left behind others; the laziest boy in the class: ~ **rüzgar**//**suyu**, (*aer.*// *naut.*) wake: ~ **suyundan gitmek**, (*fig.*) follow in s.o.'s steps, copy s.o.: ~ **tutmak**, (*naut.*) rudder work/have effect: ~ **yapmak** (-**e**), (*sl.*) try to deceive s.o.: ~**de dayısı var**, (*fig.*) he has powerful supporters, he has influence: ~**i dinlemek**, (*naut.*) answer the helm: ~**i eğri**, walking in a zigzag manner; acting aimlessly and without plan: ~**i elinde olm.** (-**in**), be in charge of stg.: ~**i kırmak**,

steer; (*sl.*) run off: ~**i sağ/sola kırmak**, (*naut.*) steer to starboard/port: ~**i viyasına!**, (*naut.*) helm amidships!

dümen·ci (*naut.*) Helmsman, coxswain; (*sl.*) last man; trickster. ~**cilik**, helmsmanship, steering; (*sl.*) always being last; trickery.

dümtek (*Or. mus.*) Tempo, rhythm. ~ **vurmak**, beat time (slapping the hands on the knees).

dün *n.* Yesterday; the past. *adv.* Yesterday. ~ **bir bugün iki**, only just arrived/happened: ~ **değil evvelki gün**, the day before yesterday. ~**den**, *adv.* (since) yesterday: ~ **bugüne**, in a short time: ~ **fit**/ **hazır/razı**, only too glad/willing/ready; just waiting for it: ~ **ölmüş**, with no desire to work. ~**kü**, of yesterday, yesterday's; (*fig.*) inexperienced: ~ **gün**, yesterday: ~ **çocuk**, only a beginner; young and inexperienced.

dünitⁱ (*geol.*) Dunite.

dünür (Relationship of) the parents-in-law of both bride and bridegroom. ~ **düşmek** (**bir kıza**), ask for a girl's hand on s.o. else's behalf: ~ **gezmek**, look for a bride for s.o.: ~ **gitmek**, go and ask for a girl's hand on s.o. else's behalf.

dünür·cü The person who looks, and asks, for the girl. ~**leşmek**, *vi.* become relations by marriage. ~**lük**, the relationship between the parents of both bride and bridegroom. ~**şü/dünüş**, mother-in-law.

dünya World; the Earth; this life; creation; worldly goods. ~ **ahret kardeşim olsun**, have only brotherly feelings for s.o.: ~ **âlem**, everybody; all the world: ~ **Bankası**, (*fin.*) World Bank: ~ **başına yıkılmak**/ **zindan olm.**, be terribly upset; feel very depressed: ~ **bir araya gelse**, under no circumstances, in no way: ~ **birinciliği**, (*sp.*) world championship: ~ **durdukça**, for ever and ever: ~ ~ **olalı**, since the world began: ~ **evi**, marriage: ~ **evine girmek**, begin married life: ~ **görüşü**, (*phil.*) conception of the world; *Weltanschauung*: ~ **gözüyle görmek** (-**i**), see stg. before one dies: ~ **güzeli**, extremely beautiful (woman): ~ **kadar**, a world of; very large: ~ **kelamı etm.**, talk (about things): ~ **kurulalıdan beri**, since the beginning of the world: ~ **malı**, wordly goods, possessions: ~ **malına düşkün**, acquisitive: ~ **penceresi**, (*fig.*) the eye: ~ **Sağlık Örgütü**, (*med.*) World Health Organization: ~ **varmış!**, (*int.*) (*relief, pleasure*) good!, that's better!: ~ **yüzü görmemek**, not find peace.

dünya-: ~**ca**, throughout the world: ~**ca meşhur**, world-famous: ~**da**, + *neg.* never: ~**dan çekmek**, withdraw from the world: ~**dan elini eteğini çekmek**, retire from active life; go into seclusion: ~**dan haberi olmamak**, not know what is happening: ~**lar kendisinin olmuş gibi sevinmek**, be overcome with joy: ~**lara bedel**, worth a fortune/ almost anything.

dünyanın: ~ **bir/öbür ucunda**, at the other end of the world: ~ **dört bucağı**, all four corners of the earth: ~ **kaç bucak olduğunu anlatmak/göstermek** (-**e**), teach s.o. a lesson, give s.o. 'what for'; make s.o. dance a different tune: ~ **parası**, a mint of money; all the money in the world: ~ **ucu uzundur**, the world is a very big place; all sorts of strange things can happen.

dünyasından (vaz)geçmek, give up all interest in things; neglect o.s.

dünyaya: ~ **gelmek,** be born: ~ **getirmek,** give birth to: ~ **gözlerini kapamak,** die: ~ **kazık kakmak,** live a very long life: ~ **kazık kakacak değil ya!**, he won't live for ever!: ~ **nam salmak/ vermek,** acquire a world-wide reputation.

dünyayı: ~ **anlamak,** understand how to live, be mature: ~ **başına dar etm./zindan etm.,** make life difficult for s.o.: ~ **gözü görmemek,** be overwhelmed by one's emotions; be irrational: ~ **toz pembe görmek,** see the world through rose-coloured spectacles.

dün·yalık Worldly goods, wealth; money. ~ **yaperest,** worldly-minded. ~ **yevi,** worldly, mundane; carnal.

düo (mus.) Duet.

düpedüz a. Absolutely flat; quite level; downright, simple. adv. Completely, utterly; patently; openly. ~ **delilik,** sheer madness.

dür(ler) v. suf. = -DİR(LER).

düralümin (min.) Duralumin.

dürbün (phys.) Telescope; field-glass; binoculars.

dür·me vn. (bot.) Cabbage; (cul.) cheese/meat pasty. ~ **mece,** (ent.) yellowish vineyard moth. ~ **mek (-i),** roll up; fold up.

dürt·mek (-i) Prod; goad; incite; instigate; stimulate. ~ **ü,** (live.) goad; (psy.) motive, stimulus. ~ **ücü,** s.o. who prods/goads; inciter; instigator. ~ **üklemek/~ üşlemek (-i),** keep on prodding s.o./ stg. ~ **ülmek,** vp. ~ **üş,** (sp.) hit. ~ **üşmek (-le),** prod each other. ~ **üştürmek (-i),** prod repeatedly at short intervals.

dür·ü Stg. rolled; wedding gift. ~ **ülmek,** be rolled. ~ **üm,** roll, fold; (mod.) pleat; (cul.) roll of bread with food: ~ ~, in folds/pleats: ~ ~ **dürzü,** (vulg.) double-dyed villain: ~ **ü bozulmamış,** (tex.) never unrolled, brand-new.

dürüst Straightforward, honest; above-board; conscientious; correct; accurate. ~ **olmayan,** dishonest. ~ **lük,** honesty; correctness, etc.

dürüşt Coarse; severe; brutal.

Dürzi (ethn., rel.) Druse, Druze.

dürzü Scoundrel; traitor.

düse (gamb.) Double three (at backgammon).

düstur Principle; formula; (leg.) code of laws; register; precedent; permission; authority; (med.) book of prescriptions.

düş Dream, fantasy; imagination; (lit.) fiction. ~ **azmak,** have a seminal emission during sleep: ~ **görmek,** dream: ~ **ile gerçek,** fact and fiction: ~ **kırıklığı,** disappointment. ~ **çü,** day-dreamer, visionary. ~ **çülük,** imagination.

düşelge (prov.) Share (of an inheritance).

düşerlik (fin.) Premium; bonus.

düşes (soc.) Duchess.

düşeş (gamb.) Double six (at backgammon); (fig.) happy chance.

düşey Vertical.

düşgel·e By chance/coincidence. ~ **im,** n. chance;

coincidence. ~ **imsel,** a. chance, fortuitous. ~ **me,** vn. hitting the mark. ~ **mek (-e),** meet by chance.

düş·görüntü Phantom, apparition. ~ **gücü,** imagination. ~ **kurucu,** visionary, dreamer.

düş·kü Calamitous misfortune; (phil.) incident; hobby. ~ **kün,** fallen; broken down, decayed; fallen on hard times, 'come down in the world'; (-e) addicted/a slave to: ~ **ler ev/yurdu,** poor-house, doss-house.

düşkün·ezen Tyrannical; oppressive. ~ **ezenlik,** tyranny; oppression: ~ **etm.,** oppress; 'hit a man when he's down'. ~ **leşmek,** vi. become poor/ addicted, etc.; fall on hard times. ~ **lük,** decay; poverty, adversity, misfortune; addiction.

düşle·m Fantasy. ~ **mek (-i),** imagine stg.

düşman Enemy, foe, antagonist; adversary; (fig.) wastrel; greedy person. ~ **ağzı,** calumny: ~ **çatlatmak,** make s.o. jealously angry: ~ ~ **a gazel/ Yasin okumaz,** expect only evil from an enemy: ~ ~ **ın halinden anlamaz,** one always thinks the enemy more powerful than he really is: ~ **etm.,** antagonize: ~ **kesilmek,** be(have like) an enemy: ~ **olm.,** begin to hate: ~ **tarafına geçmek,** (mil.) defect: ~ **ı savaş dışı bırakmak,** put the enemy out of action.

düşman·ca Like an enemy. ~ **lık,** enmity, antagonism; hatred, animosity: ~ **etm.,** behave like an enemy.

düş·me vn. Drop; fall; decline; downfall; (naut.) drift; (geol.) landfall; (ling.) disappearance; elision. ~ **mek (-e),** fall; fall down; fall (in price/ esteem/position); fall on evil days; become ill; (naut.) drift; befall, happen; fall to one's lot, devolve on; befit, become, be suitable; fall for, take to stg.; appear suddenly; give an impression of (oddity/ foolishness, etc.); (med.) be aborted: **düş önüme!,** come along with me!: **düşe kalka,** with great difficulty, after much effort: **düşmez kalkmaz bir Allah,** only God is not subject to the tricks of fate: **düşüp kalkmak (-le),** live/consort/associate with; be intimate with. ~ **meönler,** (ind.) arrester(-gear).

düş·sel Pertaining to dreams; oneiric; imaginary; (lit.) fictional. ~ **sellik,** (lit.) fiction. ~ **sever(lik)** = DÜŞÇÜ(LÜK).

düşük Fallen; drooping; low; sloping away; common; cheap (price); 'come down in the world'; (lit.) loose/disconnected (style); (med.) aborted; (phys.) low; (bio.) hypo-. ~ **lük,** fall; drop; commonness; (geo.) landfall; (met.) fall in pressure, depression.

düşüm vn. = DÜŞMEK; fall; gradient; large wooden stamp (used by tithe-collectors, etc.). ~ **devri,** period of decline. ~ **deşli,** (phil.) coincidence. ~ **deşmek (-le),** coincide (with).

düşün Thought. ~ **özgürlüğü,** (pol.) freedom of thought. ~ **ce,** thinking; a thought, conception; comment; reflection; anxiety: ~ **akımı,** current/ trend of thought: ~ **ler,** opinions: ~ **niz ne merkezdedir?,** what do you think about it?: ~ **ye dalmak,** meditate.

düşün·cel a. Ideal; expected, anticipated. ~ **celeme,** thinking, reflecting. ~ **celi,** thoughtful, pensive; considerate; circumspect; anxious. ~ **celilik,**

thoughtfulness; anxiety. ~ **cellik**, *n.* (*phil.*) ideality. ~ **cesiz**, thoughtless, unreflecting; brash; inconsiderate. ~ **cesizlik**, thoughtlessness: ~ **etm.**, be thoughtless/inconsiderate. ~ **deş**, having the same thoughts, like-minded. ~ **dürmek (-i)**, *vc.* give rise to thought; make think. ~ **dürücü**, giving rise to thought. ~ **gü(cü)**, ideolo·gy/(-gist). ~ **güsel**, ideological.

düşün·me *vn.* Thinking; (*phil.*) reflection, deliberation: ~ **özgürlüğü**, (*pol.*) freedom of thought: ~ **den**, unintentionally: ~ **den söylemek**, blurt stg. out. ~ **mek (-i)**, *vt.* think of/about; conceive; remember; consider, contemplate, ponder over; hesitate about doing; be reluctant to: *vi.* be pensive/thoughtful; reflect; be worried: **düşün bir kere!**, just think for a moment!: **düşünüp taşınmak**, cogitate over, ponder deeply over stg. ~ **sel**, mental, intellectual. ~ **sellik**, intellectuality. ~ **tü**, reflection: ~ **ler**, observations. ~ **ü**, thought: ~ **iyeliği**, (*leg.*) intellectual property. ~ **ücü**, thinker. ~ **ülmedik**, unthought of; inconceivable. ~ **ülmek**, *vp.* be thought about, etc. ~ **ülür**, intelligible. ~ **ür**, thinker, philosopher. ~ **ürlük**, thoughtfulness. ~ **üsel**, intellectual. ~ **üş**, mode/way of thinking; cerebration; reflection. ~ **yazı**, (*pub.*) article.

düşür·me *vn.* Act of dropping/causing to fall; (*leg.*) forfeiture; (*med.*) miscarriage: ~ **denemesi**, (*eng.*) drop-test. ~ **mek (-i, -e)**, *vc.* cause to fall; drop; beat down; bring/force down (aircraft); cause to meet; (*ling.*) elide; (*med.*) pass out of the body (worm, etc.); (*fin.*) obtain cheaply/easily; (*leg.*) gain possession of; (*gamb.*) cause to be played. ~ **tmek (-i, -e)**, *vc.* ~ **ülmek**, *vp.* ~ **üm**, (*fin.*) dumping.

düş·üş Fall; manner of falling: ~ **başlığı**, (*mot.*) crash helmet. ~ **üt**, (*med.*) miscarried/aborted foetus. ~ **yıkımı**, moral loss; frustration.

düttürü (*mod.*) *a.* Oddly/eccentrically dressed. *n.* Odd dress. ~ **leyla**, eccentrically-dressed woman; whose clothes are too tight/short.

düve (*zoo.*) Heifer. ~ **simek**, *vi.* (bull) seek out the cow.

düvel *pl.* = DEVLET.

düven (*agr.*) Threshing sledge. ~ **sürmek**, thresh.

düyek (*Or. mus.*) A rhythmic pattern.

düyun *pl.* (*fin.*) Debts. ~ **a kalmak**, (government debts) be postponed to the next financial year.

düz *a.* Flat; level; smooth; simple, plain; straight; uniform; (*geol.*) laminar. *n.* Flat/level place; unflavoured RAKI. ~ **ayna**, (*phys.*) plane mirror: ~ **geçiş**, transit: ~ **hat**, (*math.*) straight line: ~ **kaynak**, (*eng.*) butt weld: ~ **nefes etm.**, (*sl.*) be successful: ~ **tümleç**, (*ling.*) indefinite direct object: ~ **ünlü**, (*ling.*) unrounded vowel.

düz·aya¹kᵍ¹ (*arch.*) On a level with the street/ground; without stairs, on one floor. ~ **bağırsak**, (*bio.*) rectum. ~ **baskı**, (*pub.*) plate-making; typography. ~ **cam**, plate glass. ~ **ce**, quite flat, etc. ~ **cesi**, frankly, to tell the truth. ~ **çizer**, (*math.*) ruler. ~ **dizim**, level. ~ **döner**, (*phys.*) gyroscope. ~ **e¹çᶜ¹**, (*phys.*) (spirit-)level. ~ **eçleme**, (*eng.*) levelling.

düze (*chem.*) Dose; (*med.*) dosage; (*chem.*) order.

düzel·mek *vp.* Be arranged; be put in order; be improved; (*met.*) improve, clear; (*med.*) be/get better. ~ **ti**, improvement; (*pub.*) corrected proofs. ~ **tici**, *a.* improving, making better: *n.* (*pub.*) proofreader: ~ **jimnastik**, (*sp.*) remedial/corrective gymnastics. ~ **ticilik**, (*pub.*) proofreading. ~ **tilmek**, *vp.* ~ **tim**, improvement, reform. ~ **timci(lik)**, reform·er/(-ism). ~ **tme**, *vn.* correcting; proofreading; improvement, rectification; reform: ~ **cetveli**, (*pub.*) errata: ~ **hakkı**, errors and omissions excepted: ~ **im/işareti**, (*ling.*) circumflex accent (ˆ): ~ **işaretleri**, (*pub.*) proofreader's marks. ~ **tmek (-i)**, make smooth/level; put in order; adjust; arrange; coordinate; amend, correct; rectify; embellish, dress, set on the right road. ~ **tmen(lik)**, (*pub.*) proofread·er/(-ing).

düze·m (*chem.*) Dosage. ~ **mek (-i)**, prepare a dose.

düzen Order; regularity; harmony; device; plan, pattern, system; (*mus.*) tuning; tidiness; toilet; (*fig.*) invention, lie, trick. ~ **bağı**, discipline: ~ **kurmak**, set in working order; get organized; contrive; use cunning: ~ **verme**, (*sp.*) tactics: ~ **vermek/~e koymak/~e sokmak**, put in order; (*mus.*) tune: ~ **i bozuk**, out-of-order; out-of-tune: ~ **ine koymak**, adjust: ~ **ini bozmak**, spoil, disarrange, disorganize.

düzen·baz/~ci *a.* Tricky, calculating, deceitful. *n.* Trickster, cheat, impostor. ~ **ce**, discipline. ~ **cilik**, trickery. ~ **deş**, coordinate. ~ **e¹kᵍ¹**, coordinate; plan. ~ **ge¹çᶜ¹**, (*phys.*) regulator. ~ **le¹çᶜ¹**, programme. ~ **leme**, *vn.*: ~ **kurulu**, organizing committee. ~ **lemek (-i)**, tidy up, put in order; organize, coordinate; accommodate; plot; (*agr.*) clear land; (*phys.*) regulate; make, prepare, arrange for. ~ **leniş**, arrangement(s). ~ **lenmek**, *vp.* ~ **leşik**, *a.* coordinate. ~ **leşim**, coordination. ~ **leştirmek (-i)**, coordinate. ~ **leyici**, regulator, organizer: ~ **sayışım**, (*fin.*) suspense account. ~ **li**, in order; regular; systematic; orderly, neat, tidy; harmonious; (*fin.*) fraudulent. ~ **lik**, order; tidiness; harmony. ~ **lilik**, regularity. ~ **siz**, in disorder, chaotic; irregular; unsteady; untidy; off balance; (*fin.*) floating (debt); (*mus.*) out-of-tune, discordant; without guile, straightforward. ~ **sizlik**, disorder, disarray; untidiness; discord. ~ **teker**, (*phys.*) flywheel.

düzey *n.* Level; (*fig.*) importance, rank, value. ~ **çıta**, arris rail. ~ **siz**, unequal. ~ **sizlik**, inequality.

düzgü (*phil.*) Rule, norm, standard. ~ **leme**, (*min.*) normalizing. ~ **lü**, normal; (*min.*) normalized.

düzgün *a.* Smooth; level; laminar; in order; arranged; correct; in tune; in unison/harmony; (*math.*) regular; (*phys.*) uniform. *n.* (*obs.*) Make-up, cosmetics. ~ **duruş**, (*sp.*) good posture: ~ **sürmek**, make up (the face).

düzgün·cü Maker/seller of cosmetics. ~ **leme**, (*chem.*) levelling. ~ **lü**, made-up/painted (face). ~ **lük**, smoothness, orderliness, harmony, etc.; receptacle for cosmetics.

düzgü·sel Normative. ~ **süz**, abnormal.

düzine *n.* Dozen. *a.* Many, lots of.

düz·kanatlılar (*ent.*) Orthoptera. ~ **lem**, *a.* perfectly smooth: *n.* (*math.*) plane: ~ **geometri**, plane geometry. ~ **leme**, *vn.* levelling (of earth). ~ **lemek (-i)**, smooth, level, flatten, straighten. ~ **lemküre**,

(*geo.*) map of the world. ~**lemsel**, *a.* plane.
~**lenmek**, *vi.* become smooth/flat/level. ~**leşme**,
vn. smoothing, levelling; (*ling.*) 'unrounding' (of a
vowel). ~**leşmek**, *vi.* become smooth. ~**letmek (-i)**,
make smooth. ~**lük**, smoothness; flatness; uniformity; plainness; (*geo.*) plain; platform.
düz·me *vn.* Arranging, etc.: *a.* made up; false;
counterfeit; sham. ~**mece(lik)**, false(ness),
fraudu·lent/(-lence). ~**meci**, counterfeiter, forger;
trickster. ~**mecilik**, counterfeiting, forgery. ~**mek**
(-i), arrange, prepare, put in order; invent (a tale);
counterfeit, forge; have sexual relations with.
~**ülmek**, *vp.* be arranged, etc.

düz·taban *a.* (*bio.*) Flat-footed; (*fig.*) unlucky: *n.*
(*carp.*) narrow plane; (*med.*) flatfoot, fallen arch.
~**tabanlık**, being flat-footed. ~**ün(sel)**, rhythm(ic).
~**yazı**, (*lit.*) prose. ~**yazısal**, prosaic. ~**yuvar**, ~
haritası, (*geo.*) map of the world.
Dy. = (*ch.s.*) DİSPROSYUM.
DYO = DENİZCİLİK YÜKSEK OKULU.
Dz. = DENİZ: ~ **Ataş.** = DENİZ ATAŞESİ: ~ **HO** =
DENİZ HARP OKULU: ~ **Kuv.** (**Kom.**) = DENİZ
KUVVETLERİ (KOMUTAN(LIĞ)I): ~ **Ü** = DENİZ
ÜSSÜ.
Dza. = DENİZALTI.

E

E, e[1] [e] Sixth Tk. letter, E; sixth (in a class/series). ~ **vitamini,** (*bio.*) vitamin E.

e[2] *int.* Well! oh!; all right! ~ **mi?,** will you remember?; don't forget!

e. = (*ling.*) EDAT; ESAS.

-e[1]/**-a** *fem. n. suf.* [25] [AZIZE; REFİKA].

-e[2]/**-a** *dative n./pron. suf.* [28] To [ÖĞRETMENE, SİZE]; to(wards) [MEKTEBE]; on(to) [OTOMOBİLE]; in(to) [ŞİŞEYE]. ~ **hali,** (*ling.*) the dative case: ~ '**li tümleç alan eylem,** verb taking the dative construction.

-e[3]/**-a/-ye/-ya** *v. suf.* [174] Doing [DİYE]; doing repeatedly [GÜLE GÜLE]. = ~ DURMAK.

-e-[4]/**-a-** *v. suf.* [227] Forming denominal verbs [HARCAMAK].

(-e)[5] *Denotes a verb taking a dative construction.*

EB = ETİBANK.

ebabil (*orn.*) Manx shearwater, 'souls of the damned' or 'Bosphorus shearwater'; mountain swiftlet.

eba't[di] *pl.* = BUUT. Dimensions. ~ **ını almak,** measure.

ebced *Numerical mnemonic formula for the Arabic letters:* elif = 1, be = 2, etc. ~ **hesabı,** numeration by alphabetical letters.

ebe Midwife; (*child.*) captain/'he'. ~ **kurbağa,** (*zoo.*) midwife toad. ~ **bulguru**[nu], (*met.*) big and hard snowflakes.

ebed- = EBET. ~ **i,** deathless, eternal. ~ **ileşmek,** *vi.* become eternal/immortal. ~ **ileştirmek (-i)** make immortal, immortalize. ~ **ilik,** eternity. ~ **iyen,** for ever (and ever); eternally; + *neg.* never! ~ **iyet**[i], eternity (in the future).

ebe-gümeci[ni] (*bot.*) Mallow. ~ **gümecigiller,** (*bot.*) mallows. ~ **kuşağı**[nı], (*met.*) rainbow. ~ **lemek (-i),** (*child.*) make s.o. EBE. ~ **lik,** midwifery; obstetrics; (*child.*) being EBE.

ebe't[di] Eternity (in the future; = EZEL).

ebeveyn (*obs.*) Father and mother, parents.

-ebil-/-abil- *v. suf.* [151] Able to, can [GELEBİLİR].

EBK = ET VE BALIK KURUMU.

ebleh (*obs.*) Imbecile, stupid.

ebonit[i] Ebonite.

ebru Marbling; marbled (paper). ~ ~, waves of red (on cheeks). ~ **lamak (-i, -e),** marble (paper, etc.). ~ **li/** ~ **lu,** marbled; changing colour.

ebucehilkarpuzu[nu] (*bot.*) Colocynth, bitter apple.

Ebussuut ~ **Efendinin torunu,** very conservative.

ebülyosko'p[bu] (*phys.*) Ebullioscope.

ecda't[di] *pl.* = CET. Grandfathers, ancestors.

ece Queen; old man; (*vulg.*) elder brother/sister.

-eceği/-acağı *v. suf.,* inflected form of -ECEK. [163, 186] As an adj., that/which s.o. will (do/be done) [öğreneceğim ders, the lesson that I shall learn: yapabileceğim bir iş, a job within his capabilities].

As a noun, what s.o. will (do/be done) [**gideceğim belli değil,** it is not certain that I shall go: **bir diyeceği yok,** he has nothing to say]. ~ **gelmek,** [165] wish/long to do stg., feel like doing stg.: ~ **gibi,** [187] in such a way that . . . will . . .: ~ **kadar,** [186] as much as/the amount that will . . .: ~ **tutmak,** [166] have a sudden urge/feeling to do stg.: ~ **m,** [163] 1st., sing.: ~ **(mi)z,** 1st. pl.: ~ **n,** 2nd., sing.: ~ **ne,** [187] instead of (doing): ~ **niz,** 2nd., pl.

-ece'k[ği]/**-aca'k**[ğı] *v. suf.,* inflected. [113, 158] Shall, will [**geleceğim,** I shall come: **olacak,** it will be/ happen]. As an adj. [**öğrenecek bir ders,** a lesson to be learnt: **gidecek uçak,** the plane that will go]. As a noun [**gelecek,** the future: **içecek ve yiyecek,** food and drink]. ~ **iken,** while on the point of (doing), about to (do): ~ **kadar,** [160] sufficient for (doing): ~ **yerde,** [187] instead of (doing): ~ **ler,** 3rd pl.: ~ **se,** inflected, fut. conditional, if . . . about to (do). ~ **ti,** inflected, fut. past, [113] should/would/was about to (do).

ecektör (*eng.*) Ejector.

ecel The appointed hour of death; death. ~ **azabı çekmek,** die: ~ **beşiği,** (*ind.*) cradle on scaffolding, etc.; a regular death-trap (vehicle): ~ **perileri,** the Fates: ~ **teri dökmek,** be in mortal fear: ~ **den aman olursa,** if we live long enough: ~ **i gelen köpek cami duvarına işer/siyer,** s.o. who provokes his own ruin: ~ **i gelmek/yetişmek,** meet one's end, be about to die: ~ **i kaza ile ölmek,** die in one's boots: ~ **ine susamak,** knowingly face/court death; be foolhardy: ~ **iyle ölmek,** die a natural death/in one's bed.

ecinni (*col.*) Genie; evil spirit. ~ **ler top oynuyor,** deserted, empty.

ec'ir[ri] *n.* Reward, recompense; wages. *a.* Wage-earning. ~ **sabır dilemek,** offer one's condolences.

eciş ~ **bücüş,** shapeless; crooked; bent double with age: ~ **bücüş yazı,** scrawl, bad handwriting.

ecnebi *a.* Foreign. *n.* Foreigner, alien; stranger. ~ **parası,** (*fin.*) foreign exchange: ~ **nin memleketten çıkarılması,** deportation.

ecz. = ECZACI[LIK]; ECZANE.

ecza *pl.* = CÜZ. Parts, components; (*med.*) drugs, medicines, chemicals; (*pub.*) unbound sections of a book. ~ **çanta/kutusu,** first-aid kit.

ecza-cı Chemist, druggist, pharmacist: ~ **kalfası,** chemist's assistant: ~ **ölçüsü,** apothecaries' measure/weight. ~ **cılık,** (profession of) pharmacy. ~ **hane/** ~ **ne,** chemist's shop, pharmacy, drugstore. ~ **lamak (-i),** treat with chemicals; disinfect. ~ **lı,** containing chemicals; impregnated.

-eç/-aç/-ç *n. suf.* Denoting the instrument [KALDIRAÇ; KAZMAÇ].

eçhel Very ignorant.

ed- *v. pref.* = ETMEK.

ed. = (*ling.*) EDAT; EDEBİYAT.

eda Payment; performance (of a duty); air, tone, manner; affectation. ~ **etm.**, pay (debts); perform (duties). ~ **lı**, having an air of . . .; gracious, seductive, charming; affected: ~ **kız**, coquette.

edat[1] (*ling.*) Particle, postposition.

ede[1] *n.* Elder brother.

ede[2] *gerund* [176] = ETMEK. ~ ~, doing repeatedly.

edeb. = EDEBİYAT.

edeb- = EDEP. ~ **i**, literary. ~ **iyat**[1], literature; letters: ~ **eliştirmeni**, literary critic: ~ **Fakültesi**, (*ed.*) Arts Faculty: ~ **yapmak**, speak pompously. ~ **iyatçı(lık)**, (work/activities of) writer/student of literature/man of letters.

ede·durmak (-i) Continue/insist to do. ~ **memek** (-den, -le, -siz), be unable to manage with(out). ~ **n**, doer.

ede[1]**p**[bi] Breeding, manners, decency; ethics; education; (*ed.*) the science of letters; modesty, shame. ~ **dairesinde**, in a decent/polite manner: ~ **dışı**, obscene: ~ **erkân**, good manners: ~ **etm.**, be ashamed: ~ **göstermek/öğretmek/vermek**, teach s.o. manners; chastise: ~ **yahu!**, shame on you!: ~ **yeri**, (*bio.*) private parts: ~ **i kelâm**, euphemism: ~ **tir söylemesi**, pardon the expression.

edep·lenmek *vi.* Be(come) well-behaved. ~ **li**, well-behaved; with good manners; ethical; decent: ~, quietly. ~ **siz**, ill-mannered, rude; shameless; blackguard: ~ ~, very rude. ~ **sizce**, rudely. ~ **sizleşmek**, *vi.* behave rudely. ~ **sizlik**, bad manners, rudeness; impertinence; shameful act/ behaviour.

eder (*fin.*) Price, cost. ~ **çizelgesi/** ~ **lik**, price list.

edevat[1] *pl.* = EDAT. Tools, accessories.

Ed. F. = EDEBİYAT FAKÜLTESİ.

edi[1] *n.* (*prov.*) Operation, performance; act.

Edi[2] *n.* ~ **ile Büdü**, (Şakire dudu), (*col.*) like Darby and Joan.

-edici *a. suf.* Making, doing [mestedici, intoxicat-ing].

edi[1]**k**[gi] (*mod.*) Soft, unsoled house-shoe.

edil·gen (*ling.*) Passive: ~ **çatı**, passive voice: ~ **eylem**, passive verb: ~ **korunma**, (*mil.*) civil defence. ~ **genlik**, (*ling.*) a being passive. ~ **gi**, (*phil.*) effect, result. ~ **gin**, defensive; (*phil., bio.*) resulting, passive. ~ **ginlik**, passivity. ~ **mek**, *vp.* = ETMEK; be done; be made: *aux. v., forms the passive voice of compound verbs with* ETMEK [zannedilmek, be thought].

edim Act; action, deed; (*phil.*) actuality; (*mus.*) performance. ~ **li/** ~ **sel**, actual; active. ~ **selcilik**, (*phil.*) actualism. ~ **selleştirmek** (-i), actualize. ~ **sizlik**, (*med.*) apraxia.

edin·[1]**ç**[ci] Acquisition(s); attainment(s). ~ **ilmek**, *vp.* ~ **im**, acquisition. ~ **me**, *vn.* obtaining, acquiring; adoption: ~ **eğilimi**, acquisitiveness. ~ **mek** (-i), get, obtain, acquire, adopt, procure. ~ **sel/** ~ **tisel**, (*bio., etc.*) acquired. ~ **ti**, acquirement.

edi[1]**p**[bi] *n.* Literary man, scholar. *a.* (*obs.*) Polite, gentlemanly. ~ **lik**, scholarly work.

Edirne (*geo., his.*) Adrianople.

edisyon (*pub.*) Edition.

ediş Manner of doing/making.

editör (*pub.*) Editor, publisher, printer. ~ **lük**, print-ing, publishing.

-edurmak/-adurmak *v. suf.* [191] DURMAK *as aux. v.* Do continuously; keep on doing [çalışadurmak, keep on working].

edvar *pl.* = DEVİR. Revolutions, periods, etc. ~ **musikisi**, (*Or. mus.*) classical Tk. music.

ef. = EFENDİ; EFRAT.

EF = (*ed.*) EDEBİYAT FAKÜLTESİ.

efe ZEYBEK (leader); swashbuckler.

efedrin (*chem.*) Ephedrine.

efek·t[i] (*th., cin.*) (Sound/light) effects. ~ **tif**, (*fin.*) cash (in hand); ready money.

efele[1]**k**[gi] (*bot.*) Broad-leaved dock.

efe·lenmek Be obstinate/defiant. ~ **lik**, swagger, 'side': ~ **satmak**, swagger.

efemine Effeminate.

efendi Master; (*obs.*) Mr.; gentleman; (*col.*) husband. ~ **ahlakı**, gentlemanly behaviour; (*phil.*) master morality: ~ **baba**, (*obs.*) father!: ~ **çulluğu**, (*orn.*) snipe: ~ **daire/kapısı**, (*his.*) office dealing with the Janissaries: ~ ~, very well-behaved; like a gentleman: ~ **gibi yaşamak**, live like a gentleman; live quietly/at peace: ~ **den bir adam**, very polite person: ~ **m!**, *int.* Sir!; here!; I beg your pardon!; what did you say?: ~ **m nerede ben nerede**, (*iron.*) you don't understand my meaning: ~ **me söyliyeyim**, and then . . .; what was I going to say? ~ **lik**, gentlemanly behaviour: ~ **bende kalsın!**, I shall forget/ignore what you did!; I forgive you!

Efes (*geo., his.*) Ephesus. ~ **li**, (*ethn.*) Ephesian.

efil ~ ~ **esmek**, blow gently.

efkâr *n. pl.* = FİKİR. Opinions; ideas. *s.* Thinking; (*sl.*) anxiety. ~ **dağıtmak**, drown one's sorrows; enjoy o.s.: ~ **etm.**, be worried: ~ **ını bozmak**, pervert s.o.

efkâr·ıumumiye Pubic opinion. ~ **lanmak**, *vi.* (*sl.*) be(come) anxious. ~ **lı**, (*sl.*) thoughtful; worried; anxious.

eflak[i 1] *n. pl.* = FELEK. ~ **e ser çekmek**, be sky high.

Eflak[1 2] *n.* (*geo.*) Wallachia; (*ethn.*) Wallachian.

Eflatun[1] *pr. n.* Plato; learned man. ~ **i**[1], *a.* (*phil.*) platonic.

eflatun[2]**/** ~ **i**[2] *a.* Lilac-coloured.

efra[1]**t**[d1] *pl.* = FERT. Individuals; crew; (*mil.*) privates and NCO's. ~ **ını cami, ağyarını mani**, (descrip-tion) exact and precise in all its details.

efrenci European. = FRENK. ~ **takvimi**, (*ast.*) Gregorian calendar.

efriz (*arch.*) Frieze.

efsane Fable; idle tale. ~ **leşmek**, *vi.* become a fable. ~ **leştirmek** (-i), *vc.* ~ **vi**, fabled, legendary.

efsun = AFSUN.

eften ~ **püften**, jerry-built; rotten; worthless.

Ege[1] *pr. n.* (*geo.*) ~ (Denizi), the Aegean (Sea).

ege[2] *n.* Guardian. ~ **lik**, guardianship. ~ **men**, [221] sovereign, dominant. ~ **menlik**, sovereignty, domination: ~ **kurmak**, establish dominion, dominate.

-egelmek/-agelmek *v. suf.* [191] GELMEK *as aux. v.* Do continually/habitually [korkutagelmek, con-tinually frighten].

-egitmek/-agitmek v. suf. [191] GİTMEK as aux. v. Do continually; complete [**kaybolagitmek**, be lost for ever].

ego·ist[i] Egoist. ~**istik**, egoistic, calculating. ~**istlik**/~**izm**, egotism. ~**santrik**, egocentric. ~**santrizm**, egocentricity.

-egörmek/-agörmek v. suf. [191]. GÖRMEK as aux. v. Do continuously [**bakagörmek**, go on looking].

eg·zama (med.) Eczema. ~**zamalı**, eczematous. ~**zersiz**, (sp.) training, exercises. ~**zistansiyal·ist/(-izm)**, (phil.) existential·ist/(-ism). ~**zogami**, (soc.) exogamy. ~**zosfer**, (met.) exosphere. ~**zoterm**, (chem.) exothermal. ~**zot·ik/(-izm)**, exotic(ism). ~**zoz**, (mot.) exhaust (system/gases). ~**zozcu**, exhaust-system worker.

eğ- Also = EY-.

eğdirmek (-i) Bend, incline.

eğe[1] n. (bio.) ~ (**kemiği**), rib. ~**lerarası**, intercostal.

eğe[2] n. (min., carp.) File. ~ **talaşı**, filings. ~**lemek** (-i), file.

-eğen/-ağan a./n. suf. [223] Forming deverbal adjectives/nouns [OLAĞAN; GİDEĞEN].

eğer[1] n. Saddle. = EYER.

eğer[2] conj. [270] If; whether; but. ~**çi**, (obs.) although.

eği·lç[ci] Wooden hook (for gathering fruit, etc.).

eğik Oblique, inclined; slanting, sloping, raking, tilted. ~ **biçme//silindir**, (math.) oblique prism// cylinder: ~ **düzlem**, (phys.) inclined plane. ~**lik**, obliqueness; inclination; slant, rake; scarp.

eğil·im Inclination, aptitude, liking; bias, tendency; (psy.) urge: ~ **göstermek** (-e), be disposed to. ~**imli**, inclined, apt; biassed. ~**ir**, a. flexible. ~**me**, vn.; flexure; (math.) inclination; (phys.) bending, deflection, dip: ~ **ibre//pusulası**, (phys.) dipping needle//compass. ~**mek**, vi. bend; dip, incline; bow; lean out of (a window, etc.): **eğilen baş kesilmez**, one must submit to survive: **eğilip bükülmek**, bow and scrape. ~**miş**, a. (bot.) decumbent. ~**mez**, a. adamant; inflexible, rigid.

eğim (phys.) Dip; (math.) gradient, inclination; (geo.) incline, slope, gradient. ~ **açısı**, angle of dip/ gradient: ~ **eğrisi**, (geo.) river gradient. ~**li**, inclined, sloping; apt, skilled. ~**ölçer**, (phys., geol.) clinometer.

eği·in[ni] Back, shoulders. ~**e binmek**, bully s.o. ~**dirik**, (mod.) large turned-down collar.

eğin·ik Sloping, inclined. ~**im**, (psy.) inclination. ~**mek (-e)**, be inclined to, have a liking for.

eğinti (min., carp.) Filings; (geo.) bank, ramp.

eğir·ilmek vp.; vi. (tex.) twine. ~**me**, spinning. ~**mek (-i)**, spin, strand. ~**men**, spindle; spinning-wheel. ~ **tmek (-i, -e)** vc.

eğit. = EĞİTİM.

eğit·bilim(ci) Pedago·gy/(-gue). ~**ici**, n. tutor, instructor; trainer: a. educational. ~**icilik**, teaching, training. ~**ilmek**, vp. be taught.

eğitim Education; training. ~ +, a. Educational; training: ~ **Bakan(lığ)ı**, (adm.) Minis·ter/(-try) of Education: ~ **enstitüsü**, teachers' training college: ~ **uzmanı**, educationist: ~ **yeri**, training centre.

eğitim·ci Pedagogue, trainer, educationalist. ~**ci-**

lik, education, training. ~**li**, educated. ~**sel**, educational. ~**siz**, uneducated, untrained.

eğit·me vn. Educating; education. ~**mek (-i)**, educate, teach, train. ~**men**, instructor; village-institute teacher. ~**menlik**, teaching; instruction; teaching service. ~**meyurdu**, (leg.) reformatory. ~**sel**, educational.

eğle·lk[ği] Dwelling; rough shelter (for flocks).

eğlemek (-i) Stop; retard, delay.

eğlence Diversion, distraction; amusement; plaything; joke; useless/unimportant thing; very easy matter. ~ **düşkünlüğü**, dissipation: ~ **gezintisi**, pleasure-trip: ~ **yeri**, place of amusement (nightclub, park, etc.).

eğlen·celi Diverting, amusing. ~**celik**, (cul.) sweets, nuts, etc. (as tit-bits). ~**diri**, joke. ~**dirici**, diverting, amusing, humorous. ~**dirmek (-i)**, vc. amuse, divert; entertain. ~**i**, (lit.) humour; comedy. ~**ilmek**, vp. be amused. ~**me**, vn.; enjoyment; passing the time; joking. ~**mek**, vi. be diverted/amused; amuse o.s.; stop, pass the time: **(-le)**, make fun of s.o. ~**ti**, amusement; party, feast.

eğleş·ik Passing the time. ~**me**, vn. sojourn, stay. ~**mek**, vi. rest; reside, stay; amuse o.s.

eğ·me vn. Bending. ~**me·lç**[ci], bow; arc, curve. ~**meçli**, curved. ~**mek (-i)**, bend, curve; deflect; incline; persuade. ~**mel**, curved.

eğre Felt saddle-pad; saddle-cloth.

eğre·lk[ği] (dial.) Ditch; small watercourse; shelter (for flocks).

eğrelti·(otu[nu]**)** (bot.) Bracken, fern. ~**otugiller**, ferns.

eğreti Borrowed; makeshift, temporary; (med.) false, artificial; loose. ~ **almak**, borrow: ~ **ata binen tez iner**, borrowed things don't last long: ~ **kuyruk tez kopar**, a makeshift job doesn't last: ~ **tamirat**, emergency repairs: ~ **vermek**, lend: ~**ye almak**, prop up temporarily. ~**leme**, (lit.) metaphor. ~**lik**, impermanence; borrowed state.

eğri a. Crooked, bent; awry, sloping, slanting; oblique; askew; perverse; devious. n. (math.) Curve (of a graph); (naut.) curved timbers (of a ship); (phys.) non-linear. ~ **açı**, oblique angle: ~ **bacak(lı)**, bow-legged: ~ **büğrü**, twisted, gnarled: ~ **çizgi**, curve; (pub.) oblique stroke (/): ~ **gemi doğru sefer**, a good result in spite of the poor means: ~ **gitmek**, deviate; go astray/wrong: ~ **(gözle) bakmak**, look with unkind/evil intentions: ~ **harfler**, (pub.) italics: ~ **kalem**, (carp.) carving chisel: ~ **pergel**, (math.) bow compasses: ~ **söz**, malicious words: ~ **yüz**, embittered/harsh face: ~ **yüzey**, (math.) curved surface: ~ **de tok doğruda aç görülmez**, honesty is the best policy: ~ **si doğrusuna gelmek**, profit from one's mistakes; things turn out right.

Eğriboz = AĞRIBOZ.

eğri·ce a. Slightly bent: n. (bio.) Achilles tendon; (ent.) a big gadfly. ~**lce**, (med.) rickets. ~**li**, (math.) curvilinear. ~**lik**, crookedness; curvature; (eng.) camber; (fig.) perversity; dishonesty: ~ **yarıçapı**, (math.) radius of curvature. ~**lmek**, vi. become bent/curved; incline. ~**(l)tmek (~i)**, make crooked; bend, twist. ~ **m**, (*geo.*) whirlpool. ~ **sel**, (*math.*) curvilinear.

eğsi Wood with a burnt tip. ~ **nim**, (*psy.*) inclination.

eh *int.* All right!; very well!; well!; enough!

ehemmiyet[i] Importance; consideration, consequence. ~ **kazanmak/** ~ **lenmek**, *vi.* become important: ~ **vermek (-e)**, attach importance to: ~ **le**, carefully. ~ **li**, important. ~ **siz**, unimportant, minor, petty.

eh'il[li] *n.* People, community; family, household; friends; husband, wife; owner, possessor; expert, connoisseur. ~ **i idrak**, man of intelligence.

ehli *a.* (*live.*) Domestic(ated); tame.

ehli·beyt[i] The Prophet's family. ~ **dil**, wise; wise men. ~ **fesat**, conspirator(s), intriguer(s). ~ **hibre**, expert. ~ **irfan**, the learned. ~ **islam**, Muslims; a Muslim. ~ **keyif**, sensualist; *bon viveur:* ~ **ten**, one of the old boys. ~ **leşmek**, *vi.* (*live.*) become domesticated/tame. ~ **leştirmek (-i)**, domesticate, tame. ~ **marifet**, talented; able. ~ **nâr**, (*rel.*) the damned. ~ **rey**, a man of sound judgement. ~ **safa**, self-indulgent person. ~ **salip**, (*his.*) the Crusaders. ~ **sünnet**, (*rel.*) orthodox/Sunni Muslims. ~ **vukuf**, connoisseur, expert.

ehliyet[i] Ability, capacity; efficiency, competence; driving licence. ~ **li**, capable; competent; licensed; qualified, skilled. ~ **name**, licence, certificate of competence. ~ **nameli**, licensed. ~ **siz**, incapable, incompetent; unqualified. ~ **sizlik**, incompetence, incapacity; disability.

ehram (*arch.*) The Pyramids; a pyramid. ~ **uç(lu kalem)**, diamond-point. ~ **i**, (*math.*) pyramidal.

ehven Cheap, inexpensive; lesser (of evils); easiest. ~ **kurtulmak**, get off lightly, escape cheaply. ~ **işer**, the lesser of two evils. ~ **leştirmek (-i)**, cheapen. ~ **lik**, cheapness.

einsteinyum (*chem.*) Einsteinium.

ejder(ha) Monster; (*myth.*) chimera; dragon. ~ **gibi**, huge, monstrous: ~ **sineği**, (*ent.*) dragonfly, darter.

ejipto·log (*archaeol.*) Egyptologist. ~ **loji**, Egyptology.

ek[i] (*eng.*) Joint; patch; extension; addition; (*pub.*) appendix, annex, supplement; (*leg.*) codicil; (*ling.*) affix, suffix, particle; excess. ~ **+**, *a.* Additional, supplementary: ~ **bent olm.**, (*col.*) not know what to say: ~ **bileziği**, (*eng.*) coupling, sleeve(-joint): ~ **dirhem**, makeweight: ~ **dolaş olm.**, (*col.*) worry, pester: ~ EYLEM: ~ FİİL: ~ **görev**, (*adm.*) secondary/ additional duty: ~ **gün**, (*ast.*) intercalary day: ~ **inanca**, (*fin.*) collateral (security): ~ **kol**, extension arm: ~ **kök**, (*bot.*) subsidiary root: ~ **masraf**, (*fin.*) extras: ~ **olarak**, in addition; additionally: ~ OYLUM: ~ ÖDEME: ~ **ödenek**, (*fin.*) supplementary payment; perquisites, perks: ~ **parça**, extension piece: ~ **süre**, (*leg.*) period of grace: ~ **tekeri**, (*eng.*) flange: ~ **yapı**, (*arch.*) annexe: ~ **yetenek**, potential: ~ **ini belli etmemek**, dissimulate; not give o.s. away: hide the true state of affairs: ~ **ten pükten**, made up of odd pieces.

ek. = EKONOMİ.

-ek/-ak/-k *n./a. suf.* [223] *Forming deverbal nouns of*

place/instrument and adjectives [DURAK; ELEK; ÖLÇEK; AKSAK; ÜRKEK].

ekâbir *pl.* = EKBER. Great/important people, VIPs.

ekalliyet[i] (*ethn.*, *adm.*) Minority. ~ **te kalmak**, be in the minority.

-ekalmak/-akalmak [191] KALMAK *as aux. v.* Remain/be left (doing) [bakakalmak, remain staring].

ekbağırsa[l]**k**[ğı] (*bio.*) Appendix. ~ **yangısı**, (*med.*) appendicitis.

ekber Greater, greatest; elder, eldest.

ekçe Appendix, endorsement.

ekene[l]**k**[ği] (*agr.*) Arable land.

ek·eylem/ ~ **fiil** (*ling.*) Substantive/predicative verb [İRMEK].

EKG = ELEKTROKARDİYOGRAFİ.

ekici (*agr.*) Cultivator, farmer, planter, sower. ~ **lik**, agriculture, farming.

ekidne (*zoo.*) Spiny ant-eater.

eki·li (*agr.*) Sown, planted. ~ **lmek**, *vp.* be sown. ~ **l(me)miş**, *a.* (un)cultivated. ~ **m**, sowing; (*bio.*) culture: ~ **(ayı)**, October: ~ **biçim**, agricultural work. ~ **mlik**, plantation.

ekimoz (*med.*) Ecchymosis, bruise.

ekin (*agr.*) Sowing; cultivation; crops; corn; (*fig.*) culture. ~ **biçmek**, reap the harvest; harvest the crops: ~ **çekirgesi**, (*ent.*) locust: ~ **kazı**, (*orn.*) bean goose: ~ **savurmak**, winnow: ~ **tarlası**, cornfield: ~ **ürünleri borsası**, (*fin.*) corn exchange: ~ **vakti**, seed time: ~ **yelvesi**, (*orn.*) corn bunting.

ekin·biti[ni] (*ent.*) Grain weevil. ~ **ci**, harvester, cultivator. ~ **l**[çi], culture. ~ **çsel**, cultural. ~ **kargası**[m], (*orn.*) rook. ~ **li**, cultured. ~ **lik**, cornfield. ~ **sel**, *a.* harvest; (*fig.*) cultural. ~ **siz**, uncultured, boorish. ~ **sizlik**, lack of culture.

eki·nokok (*bio.*) Hydatid. ~ **noks**, (*ast.*) equinox. ~ **vok**, equivocal, ambiguous.

eki[l]**p**[bi] (*naut.*) Crew; (*ind.*) gang, shift; (*sp.*) team. ~ **man**, equipment, apparatus.

eklatör (*el.*) Spark-gap; spark-arrester.

eklek·tik (*phil.*) Eclectic. ~ **tizm**, eclecticism.

eklem (*bio.*) Joint, articulation; (*phil.*) connective. ~ **+**, *a.* Arthro-; articular: ~ **bağı**, (*bio.*) joint ligament: ~ **iltihap/yangısı**, (*med.*) arthritis: ~ **kaynaşım/sertleşmesi**, (*med.*) ankylosis. ~ **bacaklılar**, (*ent.*) arthropods.

ekle·me *vn.* Adding; addition; extension; *a.* added: ~ **dişi**, (*arch.*) keying. ~ **mek (-i, -e)**, add stg. (to stg.); extend; join stg. to stg.; append; attach; incorporate; join together; (*sl.*) deal a blow. ~ **meli**, (*ling.*) agglutinative.

eklem·lemek (-i, -e, -le) Join together; articulate. ~ **lenmek (-e, -le)**, *vp.* be joined to/with; be articulated. ~ **li**, jointed, articulated. ~ **sel**, (*bio.*) articular. ~ **si**, (*phil.*) connective.

eklen·mek (-e) *vp.* Be added (to stg.); be completed. ~ **ti**, addition; annex, accessory: ~ **ler**, fittings, fixtures.

ekler[1] *n. pl.* = EK. ~ [2], *v.* = EKLEMEK.

ekler[3] (*cul.*) Eclair. ~ [4], *n.* (*mod.*) zip-fastener.

ek·letmek (-i, -e) *vc.* = EKLEMEK. ~ **li**, added; annexed; attached; enclosed: ~ **püklü**, patched up: ~ **yıl**, (*ast.*) leap year.

ekliptiᵗkᵍⁱ (*ast.*) The ecliptic.
ekmek¹ (**-i, -e**) *v.* (*agr.*) Sow; scatter; drop (and lose); (*sl.*) deal (blows); (*sl.*) give s.o. the slip; (*sl.*) beat s.o. (in a race); (*sl.*) waste (money). **ekip biçmek**, (*agr.*) cultivate: **ekmeden biçilmez**, first sow and then reap: **ekmediğin yerde biter**, suddenly appears just to trouble s.o.: **ektiğini biçmek**, reap what one has sown.
ekmeᵗkᵍⁱ ² *n.* [170] Bread; food; livelihood, profession. ~ **aslanın ağzında**, it isn't easy to earn a living: ~ **bile çiğnenmeden yutulmaz**, there is no reward without effort: ~ **çarpsın**, so help me!: ~ **düşmanı**, (*sl.*) one who consumes without earning; (*sl.*) wife, children: ~ **elden su gölden**, live without working, get one's living free, sponge on s.o.: ~ **içi** = ~ UFAĞI: ~ **kabuğu**, (*cul.*) the crust of the loaf: ~ **kapısı**, the place where one earns one's living: ~ **kavgası**, the struggle for existence: ~ **kırıntısı** = ~ UFAĞI: ~ **kızartıcı**, bread toaster: ~ **küfü**, (*myc.*) bread mould; penicillium: ~ **mayası**, (*cul.*) yeast: ~ **parası**, the price of a meal; one's living/bread and butter: ~ **somunu**, loaf of bread: ~ **tatlısı**, (*cul.*) bread-and-butter pudding: ~ **ufağı**, crumbs.
ekmeğ-: ~ **e el basmak**, swear upon bread (as stg. sacred): ~ **inden etm. (-i)**, take the food out of s.o.'s mouth; cause s.o. to lose his job: ~ **inden olm.**, lose one's job: ~ **ine göz dikmek/koymak**, try to get s.o. else's job: ~ **ine koç**, hospitable: ~ **ine yağ sürmek**, help s.o. unintentionally and unwillingly; play into s.o.'s hand: ~ **ine yağ sürüldü**, that was an unexpected stroke of luck: ~ **ini çıkarmak**, earn one's livelihood: ~ **ini kana doğramak**, suffer terrible hardship: ~ **ini kazanmak**, earn one's living: ~ **ini taştan çıkarmak**, be capable of earning one's living anywhere: ~ **ini tuza banmak**, have to bear great difficulties: ~ **ini yemek**, owe one's bread-and-butter to s.o.; profit from s.o.'s help: ~ **iyle oynamak**, threaten s.o.'s livelihood/bread-and-butter.
ekmek·ağacıⁿ¹ (*bot.*) Bread-fruit tree. ~ **ayvası**ⁿ¹, (*bot.*) juicy kind of quince. ~ **çi**, baker: ~ **dükkânı**, baker's shop, bakery. ~ **çilik**, baking, the baker's trade. ~ **hane**, bakery. ~ **kadayıfı**ⁿ¹, (*cul.*) sweetmeat soaked in syrup and covered with clotted cream. ~ **lik**, *a.* suitable for making bread: *n.* breadbin; (*sl.*) a job one can live by; (*gamb.*) an habitual loser.
ekmel Most perfect/excellent. ~ **iyet**ⁱ, perfection.
eko Echo; (*rad.*) blip. ~ **lali**, (*psy.*) echolalia. ~ **lu**, echoing. ~ **praksi**, (*psy.*) echopraxia. ~ **suz**, echoless; without an echo.
ekol (*ed.*) Art-school.
eko·loji(k) Ecolo·gy/(-gical). ~ **nometri**, econometrics. ~ **nomi**, economics; economy; domestic economy: ~ **politik**, political economy. ~ **nomik**, economic; economical. ~ **nomist**ⁱ, economist.
ekose (*tex.*) Tartan (pattern).
ek·oylum (*arch.*) Ex(h)edra. ~ **ödeme**, (*fin.*) supplementary payment.
ek·ran (*cin., rad.*) Screen. ~ **remöz**, (*cul.*) cream-separator, creamer.
ek·santem, (*med.*) Exanthema. ~ **santrik**, (*eng.*) eccentric; (*fig.*) eccentric, crank, crackpot.

~ **santriklik**, eccentricity. ~ **selans**, (*adm.*) (His/Her) Excellency.
eksen (*math., eng.*) Axis; (*eng.*) axle. ~ +, *a.* Axial. ~ **birliği**, concentricity: ~ **kemiği**, (*bio.*) axis. ~ **el**, ~ **li**, axial. ~ **ter**, (*eng.*) cam. ~ **trik**, eccentric.
ekser (*carp.*) Big nail. ~ **ci**, nailer. ~ **lemek (-i)**, nail.
ekseri For the most part, most. ~ **ya**, generally; more frequently; for the most part. ~ **yet**ⁱ, the majority; greatest part; (*adm.*) quorum: ~ **le**, by/with a majority.
eksi (*math., etc.*) Negative; minus sign (−); minus [**beş eksi üç**, five minus three]; (*met.*) below zero. ~ **elektrik**, negative electricity: ~ **sayı**, negative number: ~ **uç**, (*el.*) cathode: ~ **yönde**, (*ast.*) clockwise: ~ **yönelim**, (*bio.*) negative tropism: ~ **yük(lü)**, negative(ly) charge(d).
eksibe *pl.* (*geo.*) Dunes.
eksi·ciᵗkᵍⁱ (*nuc.*) Electron. ~ **cil**, electrophilic.
eksiᵗkᵍⁱ *a.* Deficient; lacking; absent; amiss; defective, incomplete. *n.* Deficiency; short weight; (*fin.*) deficit. ~ **akçe**, short-weight coin: ~ **çıkmak**, be defective//short/underweight: ~ **doğmak**, be prematurely born: ~ **doldurmak**, fill up the gaps: ~ **etek**, (*col.*) woman, 'petticoats': ~ **etmemek**, not deprive s.o. of stg.; always have stg. in stock: ~ **gedik**, small deficiencies: ~ **gedik tamamlamak**, make up a deficiency; make everything good: ~ **gelmek**, fail; not be sufficient: ~ **olma!**, may you never be wanting! (*expressing gratitude*); thanks!: ~ **olmamak**, (s.o.) always turn up (at a party/meeting, etc.): ~ **olmasın!**, excuse me!: ~ **olsun!**, better without it!, I don't want it!: ~ **sıygalı**, (*ling.*) defective: ~ **tartı**, underweight: ~ **tutulum**, (*ast.*) partial eclipse: ~ **ine ne?**, what is there to complain of?: ~ **ini gediğini yoklamak**, inquire into the defects of stg.: ~ **ini tamamlamak**, make up, supplement.
eksik·lemek (-i) Render defective/deficient. ~ **li**, needy, in need; (*col.*) woman. ~ **lik**, deficiency; defectiveness/absence. ~ **siz**, without defect; complete; perfect; permanent, continuous.
eksil·en (*math.*) The greater number; minuend; decreasing. ~ **me**, *vn.* decrease; diminution; deficiency. ~ **mek**, *vi.* grow less, decrease: (**-den**), be absent from. ~ **ti(li)**, (*lit.*) ellip·sis/(-tical). ~ **tme**, *vn.* decrease; cut-back; (*fin.*) adjudication; putting up to tender; asking for the lowest contract terms. ~ **tmek (-i)**, *vt.* reduce, decrease, diminish; (*fin.*) adjudicate.
eksin *a.* Invalid; disabled; defective. *n.* (*phys.*) Anion. ~ **lik**, infirmity, defect. ~ **mek**, *vi.* be incapable.
eksistansiyal·ist/(-izm) (*phil.*) Existential·ist/(-ism).
eksiz Without an addition; in one piece; (*mod.*) seamless.
eks·kavatör (*ind.*) Excavator. ~ **oterm**, (*phys.*) exothermic. ~ **otik** = EGZOTİK. ~ **oz** = EGZOZ. ~ **pansiyon(ist)**, (*pol.*) expansion(ist). ~ **per**, expert; (*art.*) connoisseur. ~ **perimantal(ist/-izm)**, (*phil.*) experimental(ist/-ism). ~ **perimantasyon**, experimentation. ~ **perlik**, work/status of an expert. ~ **pertiz**, survey-report, appraisal: ~ **yapmak**,

assess. ~ **port(asyon)**, export; exportation. ~ **poze**, (*pol.*) exposé, statement. ~ **pozisyon**, (*art.*, *ind.*) exhibition; (*cin.*) exposure. ~ **pres**, *n.* express (train, etc.): *a.* express (letter, etc.): ~ **yol**, motorway. ~ **presif**, expressive. ~ **presyon(ist/-izm)**, (*art.*) expression(ist/-ism). ~ **tansiyometre**, (*phys.*) extensometer. ~ **tra**, *a.* extra; specially good, of the highest quality: *pref.* (*bio. etc.*) extra-; outside: ~ ~, the very best. ~ **trafor**, (*chem.*) extra/very strong. ~ **tre**, (*chem.*) extract. ~ **trem**, *n.* extremity, end: *a.* extreme, far: ~ **Oryan**, *pr.n.* (*geo.*) Far East. ~ **tremite**, (*bio.*) extremity. ~ **trüsif**, (*geol.*) extrusive. ~ **trüzyon**, (*min.*) extrusion.

ekşi *a.* Sour; acid; fermented; (*fig.*) sour-faced. *n.* Any sour substance; pickle. ~ **kiraz**, (*bot.*) morello cherry: ~ **surat/yüz**, a sour/bitter face: ~ **yapmak**, acidify.

ekşi-li Sour(-flavoured). ~ **lik**, sourness; acidity; (*fig.*) unfriendliness. ~ **me**, *vn.*; fermentation. ~ **mek**, become sour; ferment, acetify; become cross/disagreeable; (stomach) be upset; (style) become stale/hackneyed; (*sl.*) feel foolish/ashamed (when proved wrong). ~ **mi^lk^ği**, (*cul.*) cheese made from skim milk. ~ **msi**, sourish. ~ **mtırak**, slightly sour. ~ **t^i**, (*chem.*) acid: ~ **e dirençli**, acid-proof/ resistant; (*bio.*) acid-fast. ~ **tilmek**, *vp.* be made sour. ~ **tleme**, acid treatment. ~ **tlenim**, (*med.*) acidosis. ~ **tleş(tir)me**, acidification. ~ **tli**, acid. ~ **tlik**, acidity. ~ **tme**, *vn.*: ~ **kuyusu**, settling tank. ~ **tmek (-i)**, render sour; cause to ferment; (*fig.*) embitter; (*sl.*) make s.o. look foolish (by exposing his error). ~ **ttutar**, (*bio.*) acidophilic. ~ **yonca/ (-giller)**, (*bot.*) wood-sorrel(s).

ekti *a.* Parasitic; greedy. ~ **püktüler**, (*soc.*) hangers-on, parasites. ~ **lik**, parasitism.

ektirmek (-i, -e) *vc.* = EKMEK^1.

ekto- *pref.* (*bio.*) Ecto-; outside. ~ **derm**, ectoderm.

Ekva·dor (*geo.*) Ecuador. ~ **tor**, (*geo.*) Equator: ~ +, *a.* equatorial: ~ **frengisi**, (*med.*) yaws. ~ **toral**, *a.* (*geo.*) equatorial: *n.* (*ast.*) equatorial telescope.

ekyük (*phys.*) Overload.

ekz- = EGZ-; EKS-.

el^1 *n.* S.o. other than o.s.; people outside one's own family; stranger; people (in general); a people, tribe; the country (of a people/tribe); province. ~ **adamı**, stranger; ~ **arı düşman gayreti**, keeping up appearances; saving face: ~ **beğenmezse yel/yer beğensin**, an unpopular man is better dead: ~ ~ **in aynasıdır**, people reflect their background/surroundings: ~ **evi**, another's house: ~ **gün**, the world, the public; everybody: ~ **için içinde**, publicly: ~ **ile gelen düğün bayram**, a trouble shared is a trouble halved: ~ **kapısı**, an in-law's/a stranger's house: ~ **kazanıyla aş kaynatmak**, profit by others' preparations: ~ **mi yaman bey mi yaman?** ~ **yaman!**, the people are above the ruler: ~ **oğlu** = ELOĞLU. ~ **den vefa, zehirden şifa**, one doesn't expect kindness from strangers: ~ **e güne karşı**, in public; in the presence of others.

el^2 *n.* Hand; forefoot; handle; handful; (*gamb.*) hand/deal (at cards); one shot/discharge (of a pistol, etc.); means, assistance; capacity; posses-

sion; (*adm.*) control, oppression. ~ +, *a.* Hand-; hand-operated; portable; chiro-: ~ **açmak**, beg (for alms); (*gamb.*) show the trump card; (dummy) open his hand: ~ **alışkanlığı**, skill (resulting from practice): ~ **almak**, (*rel.*) (novice) receive permission to initiate others; (*ind.*) (apprentice) become a master craftsman; (*gamb.*) win a trick: ~ **altında**, ready, to hand: ~ **altında tutmak**, dominate, subjugate: ~ **altından** in an underhand way, secretly, clandestinely: ~ **altlığı**, writing-pad: ~ **arabası**, hand-cart, wheelbarrow: ~ **araçları**, (*sp.*) hand equipment: ~ **atma**, (*sp.*) infringement: ~ **atmak**, lay hands upon; (**-e**), start/tackle stg., put stg. in hand: ~ **ayak çabalamak**, make every effort: ~ **ayak çekilmek**, (streets at night) be deserted: ~ **ayak yürümek**, walk on all fours: ~ **ayası**, (*bio.*) palm of the hand: ~ **bagajı**, hand-luggage: ~ **bağlamak**, clasp one's hands in front (*out of respect*): ~ **basmak**, swear on a holy book, take an oath: ~ **bebek gül bebek**, coquettish, spoilt: ~ **bende**, (*child.*) game of tag: ~ **betiği**, handbook: ~ BEZİ: ~ BİLEĞİ: ~ BİRLİĞİ: ~ **bombası**, (*mil.*) hand grenade: ~ **bulmak**, find a helping hand: ~ **çabukluğu**, sleight of hand, dexterity, skill: ~ **çantası**, handbag: ~ **çekmek (-den)**, relinquish/ renounce/give up stg.: ~ **çevirme**, (*sp.*) hand circling/rotation: ~ **çırpmak**, applaud; clap the hands (to call s.o.): ~ **darlığı**, parsimony, carefulness: ~ **değirmeni**, (*cul.*) hand mill (to grind coffee, etc.): ~ **değiştirmek**, change hands: ~ **değmemiş**, untouched by hand; virgin; unused: ~ **dokumacılığı**, hand-weaving: ~ **de baş başta**, in great confusion; very embarrassed: ~ ~ **den üstündür (ta arşa çıkıncaya kadar)**, there is always one superior (right up to the throne of God): ~ ~ **e**, hand in hand; helping each other: ~ **emeği**, manual labour; elbow-grease; handwork, craftsmanship; wages: ~ **ense çekmek**, (*sp.*) throttle (in wrestling): ~ **erimi**, (*col.*) within reach: ~ **ermez güç yetmez**, an impossibility; hopelessness: ~ **etek çekilmek**, deserted: ~ **etek öpmek**, humbly beg a favour; toady: ~ **etm. (-e)**, point to; beckon s.o.: ~ **falı**, fortune told from the hand: ~ **falcılığı**, palmistry, chiromancy: ~ **feneri**, (*el.*) hand-torch: ~ **freni**, (*mot.*) hand-brake: ~ **gölgesi**, a letter of recommendation: ~ **ile**, by hand, manual(ly); hand-: ~ **ile tutulur**, clear and obvious: ~ **işçiliği**, handwork: ~ **işçisi**, handworker; craftsman, artisan: ~ **işi**: ~ **kadar**, tiny (baby): ~ **kaldırmak**, raise one's hand (to vote, etc.); (**-e**), show fight: ~ **katmak (-e)**, interfere in: ~ **kavuşturmak** = BAĞLAMAK: ~ **kesme**, (*sp.*) foul: ~ **kiri**, stg. non-essential: ~ KİTABI: ~ **koymak (-e)**, take action in/about stg.; commandeer, confiscate, seize: ~ **koyucu(luk)**, imperial·ist/(-ism): ~ **kumandasıyla**, by hand, hand-operated, manually: ~ **kumbarası**, (*mil.*) hand-grenade: ~ **lambası**, (*el.*) torch: ~ **öpmek**, kiss the back of s.o.'s hand and then raise it to one's forehead (in respect): ~ **pençe divan durmak**, stand respectfully (with right hand clasping the left): ~ **sanatları**, handicrafts: ~ **sıkmak**, clasp s.o.'s hand (in greeting); shake hands: ~ **silahları**, (*mil.*) small arms: ~ **silindiri**, garden roller: ~ **sokmak**, interfere; meddle: ~ **sürmek (-e)**, touch; meddle with: ~ **sürmemek (-e)**, not lift a finger (to do stg.); not interfere; show no interest in: ~ **şakası**, practical joke: ~ **tabancası**, (*mil.*) small-arms, hand-gun: ~ **tarağı**, (*bio.*) metacarpus: ~ TASI: ~ **tazelemek**, give the fingers a rest: ~ TOPU: ~ **üstünde gezmek**, be highly valued; be popular/beloved of the people: ~ **üstünde tutmak**, show great respect; treat s.o. with honour: ~ **uzatmak** = ~ ATMAK: ~ **uzluğu**, skill: ~ **vermek**, help s.o.; empower s.o.; (*gamb.*, *sp.*) give up, throw in one's hand; ~ VERMEK: ~ **vurmak**, clap one's hands to call s.o.: ~ **vurmamak** = ~ SÜRMEMEK: ~ **yatkınlığı**, dexterity, skill: ~ **yazısı**, handwriting, manuscript; codex: ~ **yazması**, a manuscript; writing: ~ **yordamı**, feeling with the hand, groping: ~ **yordamıyla**, by touch, groping: ~ **yummak**, be close-fisted/mean: ~ **yunağı**, washbasin.

elde, in possession; in hand; being done; (*math.*) (number) to be carried over: ~ **avuçta bir şey kalmamak**, have nothing left: ~ **bir**, a sure thing, a 'dead cert'; there's no doubt about it: ~ **bulunan**, existing, present, ready: ~ **edilmek**, be available: ~ **etm.**, obtain, acquire, get hold of; earn; take s.o. into one's service: ~ **kalmak**, be left over; remain unsold: ~ **olmamak**, be out of one's control; be unavailable: ~ **tutmak**, own, possess; keep in reserve: ~ **var**, (*math.*) and carry (five, *etc.*): ~ **yapmak**, do stg. easily/without effort: ~**ki**, ready; in stock, on hand; available.

elden, by hand (a letter, etc.); cash payment; directly, personally: ~ **ağza yaşamak**, live from hand to mouth: ~ **almak**, (*fin.*) deal directly with s.o.: ~ **ayaktan düşmek**, (*eng.*) be out of order; (*med.*) be crippled by illness/old age: ~ **bırakmak/ çıkarmak**, put down; relinquish; dispose of; surrender stg.; sell/get rid of stg.: ~ **çıkmak**, be lost, pass out of one's possession: ~ **düşme**, secondhand; a bargain: ~ **düşürmek**, get stg. cheap/a bargain: ~ **düşürmemek**, use continuously: ~ **ele**, from hand to hand: ~ **ele geçmek**, change hands/ ownership: ~ **geçirmek**, examine; clean, repair, overhaul: ~ **geçmek**, be examined; be overhauled: ~ **geldiğince**, as far as possible: ~ **gelmek**, be able to do; (-i) (*sl.*) cough up, pay: ~ **gelmemek**, be unable to do/bear stg.: ~ **gitmek**, be lost: ~ **hibe**, (*leg.*) executed gift: ~ **kaçırmak**, be unable to make use of: ~ **koymamak**, not grudge; not neglect: ~ **ne gelir**, what can one do?, what's to be done?

ele, to the hand: ~ **alınır**, serviceable; acceptable: ~ **alınmak**, (reason, excuse, etc.) be accepted: ~ **alınmaz**, very bad (quality); unacceptable: ~ **almak**, take in hand; tackle; begin to work on stg.; examine: ~ **avuca sığmamak**, be out of hand/ uncontrollable: ~ **bakmak**, read s.o.'s hand, tell s.o.'s fortune: ~ **geçirmek**, catch; get control of; obtain: ~ **geçmek**, be caught; come into one's possession; be accessible: ~ **geçmez**, not easily obtained/found: ~ **geçtiği yerde**, wherever one finds it: ~ **gelmek**, be useful, come in handy; (baby) be old enough to be carried in the arms: ~ **uygun**,

handy: ~ **verici**, correspondent: ~ **vermek**, deliver up; betray, 'give away'; communicate.

eli: ~ AÇIK: ~ **ağır**, slow worker; heavy-fisted: ~ **alışmak**, become skilful: ~ **altına almak**, keep occupied: ~ **altında bulunmak/olm.**, be at s.o.'s beck and call: ~ **armut devşirmiyor/toplamıyor ya!**, he can hit back; he can look after himself: ~ **ayağı bağlı**, he's bound hand and foot; he can't do as he wishes: ~ **ayağı düzgün**, he's strong and healthy: ~ **ayağı olm.**, be helpful/serviceable: ~ **ayağı kesilmek**, be weak/powerless: ~ **ayağı tutmak**, be sound in mind and limb: ~ **ayağı tutuşmak**, be in a great fright; be in desperation: ~ **bayraklı**, insolent, abusive: ~ **belde**, alert, ready for action: ~ **boş**, empty-handed; without work; at leisure: ~ **boş dönmek//gelmek**, return//come empty-handed: ~ **böğründe kalmak**, be discouraged/disheartened; be unable to do anything: ~ **çabuk**, dext(e)rous, quick-fingered: ~ **dar(da)**, close-fisted, mean; not having enough to live on: ~ **değmek**, have an opportunity/find time to do stg.: ~ **dursa ayağı durmaz**, always on the move: ~ **düzgün**, skilful: ~ **ekmek tutmak**, become able to earn one's own living: ~ **ermez**, incapable: ~ **geniş**, generous: ~ **genişlemek**, come into money, become rich: ~ **hafif**, (doctor, barber, etc.) having a delicate touch: ~ **işe yatmak**, be skilful: ~ **kalem tutmak**, able to write; able to express one's thoughts in writing: ~ **kırılmak (-e)**, become adept at stg.: ~ **kolu bağlı kalmak**, be tied hand and foot; be paralysed; cut the ground from under one's own feet (by one's words, etc.): ~ **koynunda** = ~ BÖĞRÜNDE: ~ **kulağında**, stg. that may happen any moment/ imminent: ~ **kurusun!**, (*curse*) may he have no work!: ~ **maşalı**, truculent, impudent, malevolent: ~ **olm. (-de)**, have a finger/participate in a matter: ~ **para görmek**, get some money: ~ **sıkı**, tight-fisted, mean: ~ **silah tutan**, able to defend himself: ~ **sopalı**, a man of violence, bully: ~ **şakağında**, thoughtful, pensive: ~ **tartısız**, inconsiderate, rash: ~ **uz**, skilful, adept: ~ **uzun**, light-fingered; pilferer, pickpocket: ~ **var(ma)mak**, (not) dare to do stg.: ~ **yatkin (-de)**, accustomed to, fairly skilled at: ~ **yatık**, skilful: ~ **yatmak (-e)**, be used to (work, etc.); be fairly skilful: ~ **yordamlı**, skilled/ suitable for: ~ **yüzü düzgün**, rather pretty (woman).

el-: ~ **im değmişken**, while I have the chance; whilst I am about it: ~ **imde değil**, it's not within my power: ~ **imden geldiği kadar**, as far as I can: ~ **imden geleni yaparım**, I will do what I can: ~ **ime kan oturdu**, my hand was severely bruised: ~ **imi sallasam ellisi, baş/kolumu sallasam tellisi**, I have only to wave my hand and people will come in crowds; there is no dearth of candidates: ~ **in dert görmesin!**, may you be free from trouble!

elinde (-in), under the care/control of s.o.: ~ **avucunda nesi varsa**, all his possessions: ~ **baziçe olm.**, be a mere tool of s.o.: ~ **bulundurmak**, have the use of: ~ **bulunmak**, be in one's possession: ~ **kalmak**, remain under s.o.'s control; remain undone/unsold; be spoilt by delay: ~ **olm.**, (work) be within one's powers: ~ **olmamak**, (work) be beyond one's powers; be unable to help (doing stg.): ~ **tutmak (-i)**, keep control of stg.; keep stg. in reserve: ~**ki kâğıt kaçlı?**, (*gamb.*) what's the value of the card you hold?

elinden, because of: ~ **almak**, deprive s.o. of stg.; remove/confiscate stg.: ~ **geleni ardına geri koymamak**, do one's damnedest/utmost: ~ **gelmek**, be able to do: ~ **gelse beni bir kaşık suda boğar**, he hates me like poison: ~ **hiç bir şey kurtulmamak**, be able to do everything: ~ **iş çıkmamak**, be slow at doing things: ~ **iş gelmek**, be capable/resourceful: ~ **kaza çıkmak**, cause an accident: ~ **kurtulmak**, escape from s.o.: ~ **tutmak**, protect s.o.; give s.o. a helping hand: ~ **yanmak**, suffer wrong at s.o.'s hands.

eline: ~ **ağır**, a slow worker: ~ **almak**, take delivery of stg.; assume (power, etc.); start doing stg.: ~ **ayağına düşmek/kapanmak/sarılmak**, beg s.o. fervently: ~ **ayağına üşenmemek**, work hard/ eagerly: ~ **bakmak (-in)**, depend on s.o. for one's living; watch s.o. carefully; read s.o.'s hand: ~ **bırakmak (-in)**, entrust to s.o.: ~ **çabuk**, a fast worker: ~ **dayamak (-i)**, thrust stg. into s.o.'s hand: ~ **doğmak**, (older person) know s.o. from childhood: ~ **düşmek**, fall into s.o.'s power; be captured; have need of s.o.; come into s.o.'s possession: ~ **eteğine doğru**, pure, chaste; decent: ~ **eteğine sarılmak**, beg s.o. fervently: ~ **fırsat geçmek**, have the ball at one's feet: ~ **geçmek**, come by, find; come into one's possession: ~ **girmek**, fall into s.o.'s hands; be caught: ~ **kalmak (-in)**, have no other helper: ~ **sağlık!**, well done!; thank you!: ~ **su dökemez (-in)**, he can't hold a candle to . . ..

elini: ~ **ayağını çekmek (-den)**, give up doing stg.; withdraw from . . .: ~ **ayağını öpeyim!**, I beg you!: ~ **belli etm./göstermek**, (*gamb.*) show one's hand: ~ **çabuk tutmak**, act quickly; get on with the work: ~ **eteğini çekmek**, retire from work, sever one's connections: ~ **göğüs/kalbine koymak**, lay one's hand on one's heart; search one's conscience: ~ **kana bula(ştır)mak**, kill s.o. in his own blood: ~ **kesmek (-den)**, cease from doing stg.: ~ **kolunu bağlamak**, tie s.o. up hand and foot: ~ **kolunu sallaya sallaya gelmek**, come empty-handed: ~ **kolunu sallaya sallaya gezmek**, wander about freely/ fearlessly: ~ **kulağına atıp gazele başladı**, (the attitude of an Or. singer with his hand to his ear): ~ **kulağının arkasına siper etm.**, put one's hand behind one's ear (to hear better): ~ **oynatmak**, spend freely: ~ **öpmek**, show gratitude: ~ **sıcak sudan soğuk suya sokmamak**, (a woman) be unwilling to do housework: ~ **siper etm.**, shade one's eyes with one's hand: ~ **sürmemek**, not touch; not deign to do stg.: ~ **veren kolunu alamaz (-e)**, give him an inch and he'll take a yard: ~ **(yüzünü) yıkamak (-den)**, wash one's hands of stg.

elinin: ~ **altında**, at one's disposal: ~ **hamuruyla erkek işine karışmak**, (woman) seek to do things beyond her power: ~ **körü**, you can go to hell!; stop your nagging!: ~ **tersiyle**, with the back of the hand.

el-: ~ **inle ver ayağınla ara**, (said of) s.o. slow to give back what he borrowed: ~ **iyle**, (letter) care of . . .: ~ **le**, by hand; hand-, manual: ~ **le çalışır**, hand-operated: ~ **le kesmek**, (*sp.*) handle the ball: ~ **le tutulacak taraf/yanı kalmamak**, have no sound/ tangible side to grasp: ~ **le tutulur**, tangible: ~ **ler yukarı!**, hands up!: ~ **lerde gezmek**, be a common object, pass from hand to hand: ~ **lerim yanıma gelecek**, I shall die one day (so I must tell you the truth): ~ **lerin dert görmesin!**, may your hands never see trouble! (thanking a helper).

-el[1]**/-al** *a. suf.* (*after* s/z) [65] = -SEL [ÖZEL].

-el[2]**/-al-/-l-** *v. suf.* Added *to adjectives*. [229] Become; make o.s. [YÖNELMEK].

ela Light-brown (eyes).

elâlem All the world, everybody; strangers.

elaman *int.* Enough. ~ **çağırmak**, cry for help: ~ **çekmek/demek**, have enough of; be sick of.

elan Now; at present; still.

elasti[1]**k**[ği] *n.* Elastic. ~ **i**, *a.* elastic; flexible; supple. ~ **iyet**[i], elasticity: ~ +, *a.* elastic. ~ **iyetsiz(lik)**, rigid(ity), inelastic(ity), inflexi·ble/(-bility).

elbecerisi (*med.*) Manipulation.

elbet(te) Most certainly; indeed; decidedly; of course.

el·bezi[ni] (*dom.*) Face-cloth, hand-towel. ~ **bileği**[ni], (*bio.*) wrist. ~ **birliği**[ni], cooperation, unity of action; communal work: ~ **etm.**, cooperate. ~ **birlikli**, shared, collective.

elbise Clothes, garments; clothing; costume; attire, apparel. ~ **asacak/askısı**, clothes-hanger/-peg/ -rack: ~ **çıkarmak**, undress: ~ **değiştirmek**, change clothes; undress: ~ **dolabı**, wardrobe: ~ **fırçası**, clothes-brush: ~ **kalıbı**, tailor's dummy: ~ **patronu**, pattern: ~ **ressamı**, dress-designer: ~ **yaptırmak**, have clothes made.

elbise·ci Clothier, costumier. ~ **kuşugiller**, (*orn.*) Hawaiian honeycreepers. ~ **li**, dressed. ~ **lik**, (cloth) suitable for clothes; suiting; suit-length. ~ **siz**, undressed.

el·ce[1]**k**[ği] (*sp.*) Handle. ~ **ci**[1]**k**[ği], (*mod.*) glove.

el·ci (*dial., ind.*) Foreman. ~ **cin**, (*dial., live.*) bell-wether. ~ **cil(lik)**, unselfish(ness).

elçi (*adm.*) Envoy; minister; ambassador; (*rel.*) prophet. ~ **eşi**, ambassadress: ~ **heyeti**, diplomatic corps; delegation: ~ **RNA**, (*bio.*) messenger RNA: ~ **vekili**, (*adm.*) chargé d'affaires: ~ **ye çıkmak**, go and see the ambassador: ~ **ye zeval olmaz**, an ambassador is sacrosanct; an envoy can not be blamed for his mission. ~ **lik**, embassy; mission: ~ **binası**, (*arch.*) embassy: ~ **etm.**, act as ambassador; act as a mediator: ~ **uzmanı**, embassy expert, attaché.

eldeci (*fin.*) Owner, possessor.

eldiven Glove. ~ **ci**, glover.

elebaşı[yı] Bandit-chief, gang-leader; ringleader; (*child.*) captain (in games). ~ **lık**, ringleadership.

eleğimsağma (*met.*) Rainbow.

ele[1]**k**[ği] Sieve; sifter. ~ **deliği**, mesh: ~ **ten geçirmek**, sieve, sift; (*fig.*) examine minutely. ~ **çi**, maker/ seller of sieves; (*fig.*) gypsy. ~ **çilik**, sieve-making/ -selling.

elek. = ELEKTRİK; ELEKTRONİK.

elektrifikasyon Electrification.
elektri¹kᵍⁱ *n.* Electricity. ~ +, *a.* Electric(al); electro-: ~ **akım/cereyanı**, electric current: ~ **anahtar/düğmesi**, electric switch/button: ~ **arkı**, electric arc: ~ **avizesi**, electric chandelier: ~ **çarpması**, electric shock, electrocution: ~ **devresi**, electric circuit: ~ **düzeyi**, current level: ~ **feneri**, hand-torch: ~ **geçirmez**, dielectric: ~ **gerilim//gücü**, electric potential//power: ~ **ışığı**, electric light: ~ **ile**, electric; electro-: ~ **kaynağı**, power source; (*min.*) electro-welding: ~ **kesilme/kısıntısı**, power-cut: ~ **kontağı**, short-circuit: ~ **merkezi**, power-station: ~ **mutfak ocağı**, (*dom.*) electric cooker: ~ **pili**, cell, battery: ~ **saati**, electricity meter: ~ **sandalyesi**, (*leg.*) electric chair: ~ **santralı**, power-station: ~ **sobası**, electric fire: ~ **süpürgesi**, vacuum-cleaner, hoover: ~ **tesisatçısı**, electrician: ~ **tablosu**, switch-board: ~ **üretici**, electric generator: ~ **ütüsü**, electric iron: ~ **verme**, electrification: ~ **yayı**, electric arc: ~ **yükü**, electrical charge/load: ~**e yöneltim**, (*bio.*) galvanotropism: ~**i yakmak**, switch on.
elektrik·çi(lik) (Work of) electrician. ~**i**, electrical. ~**le**, electrical, electro-: ~ **idam etm./öldürmek**, (*leg.*) electrocute: ~ **maden kaplamak**, (*min.*) electroplate. ~**lemek (-i)**, electrify, make live. ~**lendirme**, *vn.*; electrification. ~**lendirmek (-i)**, electrify; (*fig.*) electrify, excite. ~**lenmek**, *vi.* be electrified, become live; (*fig.*) be excitable. ~ **leştirmek (-i)**, electrify. ~**li**, electrical; having/operated by electricity; live (wire); electro-; galvanic; (*fig.*) electrified: ~ **buz dolabı**, electric refrigerator: ~ **delgi makinesi/matkap**, (*eng.*) electric drill: ~ **saat**, electric clock/watch: ~ **traş makinesi**, electric razor: ~ **yayın//yılan balığı**, (*ich.*) electric catfish//eel: ~ **yorgan**, (*dom.*) electric blanket. ~**sel**, electrical.
elektro- *pref.* Electro-. ~**d-** = ~**T**. ~**dinamik**, electrodynamic. ~**fizik**, electrophysics. ~**gitar**, (*mus.*) electric guitar. ~**ısılışı**, electroluminescence. ~**jen**, ~ **grubu**, electrogenerator. ~**kardiyograf(i)**, (*med.*) electrocardiograph(y). ~**kardiyogram**, (*med.*) electrocardiogram. ~**kimya(sal)**, electro-chemi·stry/(-cal). ~**lit**ⁱ, electrolyte. ~**litik**, electrolytic. ~**liz**, electrolysis. ~**manyetik**, electromagnetic. ~**manyetizm(a)**, electromagnetism. ~**mıknatıs**, electromagnet. ~**motor**, *n.* electro-motor: *a.* electromotive: ~ **kuvvet**, electromotive force.
elektron (*phys.*) Electron. ~**ik**, electronic: ~ **beyin**, electronic brain, computer: ~ **bilgisi**, electronics: ~ **çalgılar**, (*mus.*) electronic instruments: ~ **müzik**, electronic music.
elektro·negatif// ~ pozitif Electro-negative//-positive (poles, etc.). ~**skop**ᵘ, electroscope. ~**stati¹k**ᵍⁱ, electrostatic. ~**şimi(k)**, electrochemi·stry/(-cal). ~**şok**, (*med.*) electro-shock. ~**t**ᵘ, electrode. ~**teknik**, electrotechnical. ~**terapi**, (*med.*) electrotherapy. ~**termik**, electrothermic. ~**tip**, (*pub.*) electrotype.
elem Pain; suffering; illness; sorrow, distress; burden. ~ **çekmek**, suffer pain/grief.
eleman (*math.*) Element, component; (*adm.*)

personnel, employee, staff member. ~**sal/~ter**, elementary.
ele·me *n.* Screening, sifting; (*sp.*) elimination race, etc.: *a.* sieved; sifted; selected: ~ **maçı**, (*sp.*) elimination match, cup-tie: ~ **sınavı**, selection examination. ~**mek (-i)**, sift, sieve, screen; inspect, search carefully; grade, select; (*ed.*) examine; (*sp.*) eliminate, defeat; (*tex.*) wind yarn into hanks; (*sl.*) rob; consume, finish.
elemen¹tᵈⁱ (*chem.*) Element.
elemge (*tex.*) Spindle.
Elen·(ce) = YUNAN(CA). ~**ika**, (*ling.*) modern literary Greek: ~**sını bilmek (-in)**, know the best of stg.
elen·me *vn.* (*sp.*) Elimination. ~**mek**, *vp.* = ELEMEK ~**ti**, sifted/sieved material.
elerkiⁿⁱ (*adm.*) Democracy. ~**l**, democratic.
eleştir·el (*lit., art.*) Critical. ~**i**, criticism; critique review; examination. ~**ici**, *n.* critic: *a.* critical ~**icilik**, criticism. ~**ilmek**, *vp.* be criticised. ~**im** criticism. ~**imci**, *n.* critic: *a.* critical. ~**imcilik**, (art of) criticism. ~**isel**, critical. ~**me**, *vn.* ~**meci(lik)** critic(ism). ~**mek (-i)**, criticize, examine, comment on. ~**meli**, critical. ~**men(lik)**, (work of a) critic.
elezer Sadist. ~**lik**, sadism.
elgin *a.* Strange, foreign. *n.* Stranger. ~**lik** strangeness.
el·hak Truly, really, indeed. ~**hamdülillah**, int Thank God! ~**hasıl**, in short; in brief.
-eli/-alı *v. suf.* [181] ~ / ~ (den) beri, since [buradan gideli, since leaving here].
eliaçık Open-handed, generous, charitable.
elif The letter 'A' (in the Arabic alphabet); thin and straight vertically. ~ **gibi**, upright: ~**i bilmez** illiterate: ~**i** ~**ine**, exactly, on the dot: ~**i görse mertek/direk sanır**, he's quite illiterate. ~ **ba**, the (Arabic) alphabet.
eli¹kᵍⁱ (*zoo.*) Chamois.
elim Painful; grievous.
elimi·nasyon Elimination, defeat. ~**ne**, ~ **etm.** eliminate.
elindelik (*phil.*) Free will.
elinsaf *int.* Be fair/reasonable!
elip·s (*math.*) Ellipse. ~**soidal**ⁱ, ellipsoidal. ~**soi¹t**ᵈⁱ ellipsoid. ~**tik**, elliptical.
el·işiⁿⁱ *n.* Manual labour; handicraft; (*ed.*) hand work; artefact: *a.* hand-made: ~ **kâğıdı**, handwork paper. ~ **kitabı**ⁿⁱ, manual, handbook.
elit Elite, select. ~**ra**, (*ent.*) elytra.
elle·me *vn.* Handling; selecting; (*sp.*) handling hands: ~ **kömürü**, hand-picked/selected charcoal. ~**mek (-i)**, handle; feel with the hand; pick out select by hand; take by the hand. ~**nmek**, *vp.* be handled, etc.: **ellenmiş dillenmiş**, (woman's) lack of chastity be talked of. ~**şmek (-le)**, take each other by the hand; shake hands (on a bargain); come to blows; try each other's strength at hand grips.
el·li¹ *a.* Having hands; having a handle. ~**lik** hand-rest; glove.
elli² *a., n.* (*math.*) Fifty. ~ **de bir**, one fiftieth. ~**alt** (*sl.*) box on the ears. ~**lik**, containing fifty (parts) fifty years old; (money) worth fifty (units). ~**nc**

(50.), fiftieth. ∼ **şer**, fifty at a time; fifty each. [*For further phrases* = KIRK].

elma (*bot.*) Apple; round object. ∼ **ağacı**, apple-tree: ∼ **cenderesi**, cider press: ∼ **gibi**, red(-cheeked): ∼ **güvesi**, (*ent.*) codling moth: ∼ **şarabı**, (*cul.*) cider: ∼ **şekeri**, toffee apple: ∼ **nın yarısı o, yarısı bu**, as like as two peas in a pod.

elma·baş (*orn.*) Great-crested grebe. ∼ **cık**, (*bot.*) small apple; (*bio.*) hip-bone; high part of the cheek: ∼ **kemiği**, cheek-bone. ∼ **lı**, (*cul.*) apple-. ∼ **lık**, apple orchard. ∼ **siye**, (*cul.*) fruit-jelly.

elmas *n.* (*min.*) Diamond; diamond-cutter. *a.* Precious; beloved; decorated with diamonds. ∼ **gibi**, pure; valuable, precious: ∼ **havzası**, diamond field: ∼ **kakıcı**, diamond setter: ∼ **kaşlı**, diamond mounted (ring): ∼ **kırıntıları**, (*geol.*) bort: ∼ **kuşu**, (*orn.*) spotted pardalote: ∼ **parçası**, (*fig.*) enchanting (child, etc.): ∼ **pitonu**, (*zoo.*) diamond/Australian python: ∼ **ım**, my precious one.

elmas·çı(lık)(Work of) diamond-cutter/-merchant. ∼ **lı**, (*geol.*) diamantiferous; (*ind.*) diamond-. ∼ **tıraş**, cut glass, crystal; diamond glass-cutter; diamond cutter.

elmen Possessor, holder. ∼ **lik**, possession.

eloğluⁿᵘ Stranger; outsider; other people.

-elt-/-alt-/-lt- *v. suf.* [229] Cause/make/allow to become . . . [AZALTMAK; YÜKSELTMEK].

eltasıⁿⁱ (*dom.*) Finger-bowl.

elti Sister-in-law (as between brothers' wives).

el·topu (*sp.*) Handball. ∼ **ulagı**ⁿⁱ, stg. at hand; tool; servant; messenger, page. ∼ **üstü**, (*sp.*) on the hands.

elvan *pl.* Colours; multicoloured.

elveda Farewell!; goodbye! ∼ **etm.**, say goodbye.

elveriş·li Sufficient; suitable, apt, well-adapted; useful; convenient; efficient; profitable. ∼ **lilik**, suitability; usefulness; etc. ∼ **siz**, unsuitable; inconvenient; imperfect. ∼ **sizlik**, unsuitability.

elver·mek *vi.* Suffice; be suitable; be useful; be convenient; happen; be current: **elverir!**, that's enough. ∼ **memek**, *vi.* not suffice; not be suitable; not be possible. ∼ **mez**, *a.* unsuitable, inadequate.

elyaf *pl.* Fibres. ∼ **tahtası**, (*carp.*) hardboard.

elyevm Today, this very day.

elzem Most necessary; essential; indispensable.

em (*chem.*) Medicine, remedy. ∼ **e seme yaramaz**, useless; completely unsuitable: ∼ **le güçlendirme**, (*sp.*) doping.

Em. = EMEKLİ; EMNİYET.

EMA = (*European Monetary Association*).

emanetⁱ Anything entrusted to s.o.; deposit; (*his.*) government office receiving/paying out money; cloakroom. ∼ **bırakmak/etm./vermek (-i, -e)**, consign stg. to s.o., deposit stg. with s.o.: ∼ **eden**, consignor, depositor: ∼ **hesabı**, (*fin.*) deposit account: ∼ **yeri**, depository: ∼ **e hiyanet**, breach of trust.

emanet·çi(lik) (Work/position of a) consignee, depository, forwarding-agent. ∼ **en**, for safe keeping; on deposit/consignment.

emare Sign; token; (*leg.*) circumstantial evidence.

emaretⁱ (*adm.*) Chieftainship; emirate.

emaye *n.* Enamel(-ware); gloss. *a.* Enamelled.

∼ **leme**, enamelling. ∼ **li**, enamelled: ∼ **boya**, enamel paint: ∼ **kaplar**, (*dom.*) enamelware.

em·bilim Pharmacology. ∼ **boli**, (*med.*) embolism. ∼ **briyoloji**, (*bio.*) embryology. ∼ **briyon**, embryon: ∼ +, embryonic.

em·ci·lkᵍⁱ (*bio.*) Nipple; teat. ∼ **dirik**, (*chem.*) impregnated. ∼ **dirmek (-i, -e)**, *vc.* = EMMEK; (*bio.*) suckle, make/let suck; (*chem.*) impregnate, soak.

-eme-/-ama- *v. suf.* [151] Not able to . . . [GELEMEMEK].

eme·lçᶜⁱ (*myc.*) Mycelium.

eme·lkᵍⁱ Work; labour; manpower; trouble; fatigue. ∼ **çekmek/vermek**, become tired by working; take great pains: ∼ **harcamak**, work very hard, spare no pains: ∼ **olmadan yemek olmaz**, one must work to live: ∼ **i geçmek**, contribute great efforts to achieve stg.: ∼ **i geçmiş**, veteran: ∼ **i sağdıç** ∼ **ine dönmek**, one's efforts go for naught: ∼ **le ekmeğini kazanmak**, work for one's living.

emek·çi Worker; workman, labourer; s.o. who takes great pains: ∼ **altı kişiler**, riff-raff. ∼ **çilik**, state of a worker. ∼ **lemek**, *vi.* (baby) crawl; walk with difficulty; (*fig.*) be apprenticed. ∼ **li**, (*adm.*) retired; pensioner: ∼ **aylığı**, pension, allowance: **olm.**/ ∼ **ye ayrılmak**, be retired: ∼ **ödencesi**, superannuation: ∼ **profesör**, (*ed.*) professor emeritus: ∼ **sandığı fonu**, superannuation fund: ∼ **ye ayırmak/çıkarmak (-i)**, retire s.o.; pension s.o. off. ∼ **lik**, wages. ∼ **lilik**, retirement; pension, superannuation. ∼ **siz**, free from labour/fatigue; easy (life): ∼ **evlat**, stepchild. ∼ **tar**, old servant; veteran. ∼ **tarlık**, long service. ∼ **taş**, fellow workman.

emel Longing; desire; aim, ambition, aspiration; stg. desired; ideal. ∼ **beslemek**, aspire to: ∼ **etm. (-de)**, long for, aspire to.

emeroitⁱ (*med.*) Haemorrhoids.

emetik Emetic.

emfetamin (*chem.*) Amphetamine.

emge·lçᶜⁱ (*ind.*) Extractor.

emi *int.* Will you?

-emi *n. suf.* (*med.*) -aemia [ANEMİ].

emi·ci Sucking; absorbing; sucker; vacuum: ∼ **bit**, (*ent.*) sucking louse: ∼ **kıllar**, (*bot.*) root hairs: ∼ **tüp**, pneumatic tube: ∼ **yelvuran**, suction fan. ∼ **lk**ᵍⁱ, (*med.*) bruise caused by sucking. ∼ **lim**, absorption. ∼ **lmek**, *vp.* = EMMEK.

emin *a.* Safe; secure; sure, confident, certain; dependable, trustworthy. *n.* Steward; custodian; superintendent, controller. ∼ **olm. (-den)**, be sure/certain of; (-e) believe in.

Eminsu. = EMEKLİ İNKILAP SUBAYLARI.

emirⁱ ¹ *n.* Emir; chief; commander.

em·lirʳⁱ ² *n.* Order, command; matter, business; event, case; (*ling.*) imperative. ∼ **almak (-den)**, receive/take orders from: ∼ **atlısı**, (*mil.*) mounted orderly: ∼ **eri**, (*mil.*) orderly; batman: ∼ **hazır para**, (*fin.*) spot cash: ∼ **kipi**, (*ling.*) imperative mood: ∼ **kulu**, s.o. bound to obey orders: ∼ **subayı**, (*mil.*) adjutant, aide-de-camp: ∼ **şeklinde**, mandatory, obligatory: ∼ **vermek**, direct; order, command: ∼ **e amade**, at your service: ∼ **e hazır**, at hand for use, available; (*fin.*) on call: ∼ **e muharrer senet**, (*fin.*) promissory note: ∼ **e ödenir**, payable to order: ~e yazılı çek, (cheque) to order: ~i geri almak, countermand an order: ~inde olm., be under s.o.'s authority: ~ine girmek, accept s.o.'s authority: ~ine hazır bulunmak, be at s.o.'s beck and call: ~ine vermek, appoint to s.o.; allocate for s.o.: ~inize hazırım, I am at your disposal: ~leri üzerine, on the orders of . . . .

emir·ber (*mil.*) Bearer of an order; orderly. ~cik (kuşu), (*orn.*) kingfisher. ~name, (*adm.*) written command; decree; 'your letter'. ~ülhac, (*his.*) commander of the pilgrim caravan to Mecca. ~ülmüminin, (*his.*) 'Commander of the Faithful', Caliph.

emisyon (*fin.*) Issue; (*pub.*) publication; (*rad.*) broadcast.

emiş *vn.* = EMMEK. Suction.

emk = ELEKTROMOTOR KUVVET.

emlak¹ *pl.* = MÜLK. Lands; possessions; estate; property. ~ acentesi, estate agency: ~ bankası, (*fin.*) mortgage bank: ~ komisyoncu/simsar/tellalı, (real) estate agent: ~ vergisi, property-tax. ~çı-(lık), (work of an) estate-agent.

emlemek (-i) Apply/give a medicine; heal, cure.

em·me *vn.* Sucking; suction; vacuum; absorption: ~ basaç/tulumbası, suction pump: ~ basma tulumba, suction and force pump: ~ borusu, inlet manifold: ~ freni, (*rly.*) vacuum brake: ~ yüksekliği, suction head. ~me¹çᶜⁱ, aspirator; suction pump. ~mek (-i), suck; absorb; assimilate; 'drink in'; (*sl.*) suck dry.

emniyet¹ Security; safety; confidence; assurance; (*col.*) police; (*ind.*) safety device; (*el.*) fuse. ~ adası, traffic island: ~ amiri, (*adm.*) chief of police: ~ camı, safety glass: ~ cihaz/düzeni, safety device: ~ emsali, safety factor: ~ etm. (-e), trust/confide in s.o.: ~ kanadı, safety-catch (of a rifle): ~ kemeri, (*aer.*) safety-belt: ~ maşası, (*eng.*) split pin: ~ memuru, policeman: ~ müdürlüğü, (*adm.*) police headquarters: ~ müdürü, the Chief of Police: ~ nezareti, (*leg.*) police custody/supervision; probation: ~ payı, (*eng.*) safety margin: ~ sandığı, (*fin.*) loan institution: ~ somunu, (*eng.*) lock-nut: ~ tedbirleri, safety precautions: ~ tertibatı, (*ind.*) safety device: ~i umumiye, (*adm., obs.*) department of public security.

emniyet·li Safe; safety-; trustworthy; reliable. ~siz, untrustworthy; insecure; unsafe; distrustful. ~sizlik, untrustworthiness; insecurity; lack of confidence.

em·oglobin (*bio.*) Haemoglobin. ~oraji, (*med.*) haemorrhage. ~oroid, (*bio.*) haemorrhoids, piles.

em·pas Impasse. ~pedans, (*el.*) impedance. ~permeabl, *a.* waterproof: *n.* raincoat. ~peryalist¹, (*adm.*) imperialist. ~peryalizm, imperialism.

empir·ik/-izm (*phil.*) Empiri·cal/-cism.

em·poze ~ etm., impose on. ~prenye, impregnated: ~ etm., impregnate. ~presyon(ist/-izm), (*art.*) impression(ist/-ism). ~prime, (*tex.*) colourprinting; print, printed material.

emraz *pl.* = MARAZ. Illnesses; diseases.

emr- = EMİR. ~¹etmek^ᵉᵈᵉʳ (-i, -e), command, decree, order; dictate: **emretti patrik efendi!**, (*jok.*) it's an unreasonable order! ~ihak^ᵏ¹, God's will; death: ~

vaki olm., die. ~ivaki, *fait accompli*, accomplished fact. ~iyevmi, (*obs., mil.*) order of the day.

emsal¹ *pl.* = MESEL; MİSİL. Similars; the like; equals; (*lit.*) proverbs, tales; (*math.*) factors, coefficients. *s.* A like thing; an equal/peer; an example; precedent; (*math.*) coefficient. ~ olmamak şartıyle, provided it is not regarded as a precedent: ~ rakamı, coefficient: ~i var, there are precedents for it: ~i yok, there is no precedent; he has no equal: ~im misilli, like people in my condition. ~sîz, peerless, matchless; unequalled; unprecedented.

em·tia *pl.* = META: (*ind.*) goods; commodities: ~ borsası, (*fin.*) commodities market. ~val¹, *pl.* = MAL: goods; riches.

emülsi·fikasyon (*chem.*) Emulsification. ~yon, emulsion.

emzi¹k^ᵍ¹ (*bio.*) Nipple; teat; baby's bottle, feeder; dummy; spout; (*dial.*) cigarette-holder; narghile. ~ borusu, (*dom.*) pipe fitting onto a stove: ~ şişesi, (*med.*) feeding-bottle.

em·zikçi Wet nurse. ~ziklemek (-i), fit with a spout. ~zikli, having a spout//teat: ~ kadın, nursing mother. ~zirmek (-i), [146] suckle; (*sl.*) syphon off.

en¹ *n.* Width; breadth; (*live.*) brand. ~ boy oranı, (*aer.*) aspect ratio: ~ kirişi, (*arch.*) cross-member: ~i sonu, the long and the short of it: ~ince, according to/across its width; crosswise: ~inde sonunda, in the end, at last: ~ine, in width; breadthwise: (*naut.*) athwart(ships); lateral, crosswise, transverse: ~ine boyuna, breadthwise and lengthwise; fully; tall/well-built (man): ~ine çekmiş, boyuna çekmiş, buna karar verdi, he studied it from all angles and then selected this: ~ine kesit, transverse section: ~ine rıhtım, pier, mole.

en² *adv.* [55, 197] *Forming the superlative degree of a./adv.* Most; -est [~ küçük, smallest: ~ çabuk, fastest: ~ güzel, most beautiful]. ~ aşağı, lowest; bottom-most; minimum; at least: ~ az, the least; minimum: ~ aza indirmek, minimize: ~ azdan, least: ~ azından, minimum: ~ başta, in the first place: ~ baştan, from the very beginning: ~ büyük, biggest; greatest; maximum; maximal; arch-: ~ civcivli = ~ SIKIŞIK: ~ çoğu, for the most part: ~ çok, the most; at most: ~ çok kayrılan ulus, (*fin.*) most-favoured nation: ~ çok satılan, (*pub.*) best-seller: ~ dış, outermost: ~ düşük, lowest, minimum; rock-bottom: ~ fazla, maximum, peak: ~ fecii, the unkindest/most tragic cut of all: ~ güçlü, super: ~ güzel, choice, finest: ~ imtiyazlı millet, (*fin.*) most-favoured nation: ~ iyi, best, optimum: ~ iyisi, the best, the finest: ~ kabadayısı, (*col.*) at the most: ~ kenar(da), extreme: ~ kıçta, (*naut.*) sternmost, aftermost: ~ küçük, minimum, minimal: ~ sıkışık (zaman), peak (time): ~ son, the last, the latest; ultimate, final: ~ son baskı, (*pub.*) late night final: ~ son haberler, (*pub.*) stop-press: ~ son moda, the latest fashion; the 'last word': ~ sonra, at the very end; last of all; extreme: ~ ucuz, cheapest: ~ uygun, optimum; best: ~ uzak, farthest, most distant; extreme: ~ üst, topmost, uppermost; peak; supreme: ~ üstün, highest, supreme; maximum: ~ÜSTÜNLÜK: ~ yakın, next, nearest, closest: ~ yaşlı, elder, eldest: ~ yıkıcı, (*geol.*)

catastrophic: ~ **yukarı/yüksek**, highest, maximum: ~ **ziyade mazharı müsaade millet kaydı**, (*fin.*) most-favoured nation clause.

-en[1]**/-an** *adv. suf.* [196] [KAZAEN; ŞER'AN].

-en[2]**/-an** *v. suf.* [158, 180] *The present participle used as adjective/noun.* -ing, the person/thing performing//receiving the action [**gidenler**, those going: **gösterilen film**, the film being shown]. ~ ~ **e**, [248] many people rushing to do the same thing [**denize koşan koşana**, everyone running to the sea]: ~ **e değin/** ~ **e dek/** ~ **e kadar**, [180] until [**büyüne gelene kadar**, until today]. **En. ve Ta. Kay. B.** = ENERJİ VE TABİİ KAYNAKLAR BAKANLIĞI.

enam (*rel.*) Collection of passages from the Koran.

enayi (*sl.*) *a.* Credulous; conceited. *n.* Fool. ~ **dümbeleği**, a prize idiot. ~ **ce(sine)**, like a fool. ~ **lik**, stupidity; stupid action.

enberi (*ast.*) ~ **(nokta)**, periastron.

enbiya *pl.* = NEBİ. (*rel.*) Prophets.

encam End, result. ~ **bulmak**, end, result: ~ **vermek**, bring to an end, conclude: ~ **a varmak**, come to an end: ~ **ı kâr**, (*obs.*) the end of the matter. ~ **kâr**, finally.

en·cek/ ~ **cik(lemek)** = ENİK.

encümen (*adm.*) Meeting; council, committee, corporation; commission.

end. = ENDÜSTRİ.

endam Body; shape; figure; symmetry; stature. ~ **aynası**, full-length mirror, cheval-glass. ~ **lı**, well-proportioned, shapely; graceful.

endaze Measure; proportion; (*obs.*) measurement of length, ell (65 cms.). ~ **si bozuk**, out of proportion: ~ **sini almak**, measure up; (*fig.*) estimate s.o.'s ability: ~ **ye gelmemek**, be immeasurable: ~ **ye vurmak**, measure. ~ **hane**, (*naut.*) mould-loft.

endeks (*pub.*) Index.

endemik (*bio.*) Endemic.

ender More/most rare; rarely.

enderun (*obs.*) Women's quarters in a palace; interior.

en·determinizm (*phil.*) Indeterminism. ~ **direkt**, indirect. ~ **dividual** = İNDİVİDÜAL.

en·dikasyon Indication; (*med.*) symptom. ~ **dikatör**, indicator. ~ **dis** (*math.*) index.

endişe Thought; care, concern; anxiety, alarm; doubt. ~ **etm. (-den)**, be anxious/apprehensive about/whether: ~ **verici**, disturbing, disquieting: ~ **vermek**, disturb, worry.

endişe·lenmek *vi.* Be worried. ~ **li**, thoughtful; anxious, apprehensive; worried, agitated. ~ **siz**, carefree; calm.

endo- *pref.* (*bio.*) Endo-; internal. ~ **derm**, endoderm. ~ **gami**, (*soc.*) endogamy. ~ **krinoloji**, (*bio.*) endocrinology. ~ **skop**, endoscope.

Endonezya (*geo.*) Indonesia. ~ **lı, n.** Indonesian.

en·dui (*el.*) Armature. ~ **düksiyon**, (*el.*) induction.

endüstri Industry. ~ **+**, *a.* Industrial. ~ **leşme**, *vn.* industrialization. ~ **leşmek**, *vi.* become industrialized. ~ **leştirmek (-i)**, industrialize. ~ **yalize**, industrialized. ~ **yel**, industrial.

ene·k[gi] 1 *n.* (*bio.*) Lower cheek/jaw. ~ **çukuru**, dimple.

ene·k[2] *a.* (*live.*) Castrated, gelded. ~ **mek (-i)**, castrate, geld. ~ **nmek**, *vp.* ~ **nmiş**, *n.* eunuch; (*live.*) gelding.

enerji (*phys.*) Energy, power. ~ **almak**, absorb energy: ~ **bunalımı**, power/energy crisis: ~ **ve Tabii Kaynaklar Bakan(lığ)ı**, Minis·ter/(-try) for Power and Natural Resources: ~ **vermek**, energize: ~ **nin dönüşüm//korunum/sakınımı**, (*phys.*) transformation//conservation of energy. ~ **k**, energetic, forceful.

enez(e) Weak, feeble; incapable. ~ **eleşmek**, become weak. ~ **lik**, weakness; incapacity.

en·farktüs (*med.*) Infarction. ~ **feksiyon**, infection. ~ **fekte**, infected. ~ **feriyorite**, (*psy.*) inferiority.

enfes Most pleasing; choice; delightful, delicious.

enfiye Snuff. ~ **çekmek**, take snuff: ~ **kutusu**, snuffbox.

en·flamasyon (*med.*) Inflammation. ~ **flasyon(ist)**, (*fin.*) inflation(ary). ~ **flüanza**, (*med.*) influenza. ~ **formasyon**, information. ~ **formatik**, informatics. ~ **fraruj**, (*phys.*) infra-red. ~ **frastrüktür**, (*adm., ind.*) infrastructure.

enfüsi (*phil., obs.*) Subjective.

engebe (*geo.*) Unevenness; rough ground; broken ground. ~ **ler**, mountain chain/range. ~ **li**, uneven, hilly, steep, broken. ~ **lik**, unevenness; undulating ground, hilly terrain. ~ **siz**, unbroken, even.

engel Obstacle, barrier, barricade; difficulty; drawback, handicap; embarrassment; (*dial.*) rival; (*sp.*) hurdle; bunker (in golf). ~ **çıkarmak**, make things difficult, create obstacles: ~ **olm.**, hinder, obstruct; make difficult, handicap: ~ **sınavı**, (*ed.*) 'make-up' examination: ~ **den aşmak**, overcome/clear an obstacle: ~ **e rastlamak**, be hindered: ~ **i kaldırmak**, remove the obstacle, bulldoze one's way.

engel·balığı[nı] (*ich.*) Type of small mackerel. ~ **leme**, *vn.* hindrance, delaying action; (*fin.*) embargo; (*sp.*) obstruction, blocking. ~ **lemek (-i)**, hinder; (*phys.*) inhibit; (*sp.*) trip up (in wrestling). ~ **lenmek**, *vp.* be hindered/confined/restricted. ~ **leyici**, (*chem.*) inhibitor. ~ **leyim**, (*fin.*) embargo. ~ **li**, with obstacles: ~ **koşu**, (*sp.*) hurdle-race. ~ **siz**, clear, unhindered, unimpeded.

engere·k[gi] (*zoo.*) Adder, viper, asp-viper. ~ **giller**, vipers. ~ **otu**[nu], (*bot.*) viper's bugloss.

engin[1] *a.* Vast, boundless. *n.* The open sea; the high seas. ~ **den gitmek**, keep off shore: ~ **e çıkmak**, make for the open sea.

engin[2] *a.* Low; ordinary; cheap.

enginar (*bot.*) Globe artichoke.

engin·lik Being vast; vastness, boundlessness. ~ **sel**, (*bot.*) pelagic.

engizisyon (*his.*) The (Spanish) Inquisition.

eni·k[gi] (*bio.*) Young of mammals; puppy, kitten, whelp, cub, etc. ~ **lemek (-i)**, (animal) give birth, drop.

enikonu *adv.* Fully, at length. ~ **yoruldum**, I'm thoroughly tired.

eninci (*math.*) Nth (degree/power).

enir (*bot.*) Butcher's broom.

enişte Aunt/sister's husband; brother-in-law.

enjek·siyon (*med.*) Injection: ~ **natürel**, (*sl.*) sexual intercourse: ~ **yapma**, (*arch.*) grouting. ~**te**, ~ **etm.**, inject. ~**tör**, (*med.*) injector; needle, syringe.

enkaz Ruins; debris; wreck(age); carcass. ~ **arabası**, break-down lorry: ~ **şamandırası**, (*naut.*) wreck buoy: ~**ı kaldırmak**, bulldoze. ~**cı**, ship-breaker; house-breaker; wrecker.

en·kesit Cross-section. ~**lem**, (*ast.*) latitude. ~**leme(sine)**, transverse, cross. ~**lendirmek** (-i), enlarge, broaden. ~**li**, broad, wide. ~**lik**, breadth, width. ~**öte**, (*ast.*) apastron.

Ens(t). = ENSTİTÜ(SÜ).

ense (*bio.*) Back of the neck, nape; back; (*sl.*) buttocks. ~ **kökü**, base of the neck: ~ **kökünden gelmek**, be very close behind/on top of s.o.: ~ **sertliği**, (*med.*) stiff neck: ~ **yapmak**, lead a lazy/ comfortable life: ~**si kalın**, well-off; carefree; influential: ~**sinde boza pişirmek**, (*col.*) torment, pester (to finish work); inflict punishment on: ~**sinden gitmek**, follow s.o. closely: ~**sine binmek**, persecute, tyrannize, subject: ~**sine yapışmak**, seize/collar s.o.: ~**sine vur lokmasını al (elinden)**, he's a very mild person.

ense·lemek (-i) Seize by the neck (*sl.*) catch a fugitive. ~**lenmek**, *vp.* (*sl.*) be caught. ~**li**, (*orn.*) naped.

enser (*carp.*) A big nail.

ensiz Without width; narrow. ~**lik**, narrowness.

en·somni (*med.*) Insomnia. ~**spektör**, inspector. ~**stalasyon**, installation. ~**stantane**, (*cin.*) snapshot; stg. happening in a moment. ~**stenkt**[i], (*psy.*) instinct. ~**stitü**, (*ed.*) institute (of research/ higher education). ~**strüman**, (*mus.*) instrument. ~**strümantal(izm)**, (*phil.*) instrumental(ism). ~**strüman(tasyon)**, (*mus.*) instrument(ation). ~**sülin**, (*chem.*) insulin.

entari (*mod.*) Loose robe; dressing-gown. ~**lik**, material suitable for an ENTARİ.

entbent ~ **olm.**, be taken aback/shocked.

en·tegral (*math.*) Integral. ~**tegrasyon**, integration. ~**telektüalizm**, intellectualism. ~**telektüel**, *a.*, *n.* intellectual. ~**telekya**, (*phil.*) entelechy. ~**tere**, interest, advantage. ~**teresan**, interesting, attractive. ~**terese**, ~ **etm.**, interest. ~**terferans**, (*phys.*) interference. ~**terkonekte**, interconnected. ~**tern(lik)**, (*med.*) intern(ship). ~**ternasyonal/ (-izm)**, international(ism). ~**terne**, (*mil.*) interned: ~ **etm.**, intern. ~**tero-**, *pref.* (*med.*) entero-. ~**terpret**, (*ling.*) interpreter. ~**tertip**, (*pub.*) linotype. ~**terüptör**, (*el.*) cut-out switch. ~**timem**, (*phil.*) enthymeme.

entipüften (*sl.*) Insignificant; ridiculous; futile; flimsy.

ento·ksikasyon (*med.*) Intoxication. ~**molog**, entomologist. ~**moloji(k)**, entomolo·gy/(-gical). ~**nasyon**, (*ling.*, *mus.*) intonation.

entrika Intrigue; trick; cabal; (*lit.*) plot. ~ **çevirmek**, resort to tricks; intrigue: ~ **yolu**, (*pol.*) backstairs. ~**cı**, intriguer, plotter.

entropi (*phys.*) Entropy.

enüstünlük (*ling.*) Superlative (degree).

enva[1] *pl.* = NEVİ. Sorts, kinds.

en·vanter (*fin.*) Inventory (list). ~**versiyon**, in-

version. ~**vestisman**, investment. ~**zim**, (*bio.*) enzyme.

eo·gen (*geol.*) Nummulitic. ~**litik**, eolithic. ~**lyen**, (*geol.*) aeolian. ~ **sen**, (*geol.*) eocene.

epçet = EBCED.

epeğri Very crooked/curved.

epengle (*tex.*) Corded cloth; uncut fabric.

epey [56] Pretty good; pretty well; a good many; a good deal of. ~**ce**, considerably, fairly; to some extent; pretty well. ~**i**, very good.

epher (*bio.*) Aorta.

epi·demi(k) (*med.*) Epidemic. ~**diyaskop**[u], (*phys.*) epidiascope. ~**dot**[u], (*geol.*) epidote. ~**fit**, (*bot.*) epiphyte. ~**glotis**, (*bio.*) epiglottis. ~**grafi**, (*lit.*) epigraphy. ~**k**, (*lit.*) epic. ~**kerem**, (*phil.*) epicheirema. ~**kürcü(lük)**, (*phil.*) epicurean(ism). ~**lepsi**, (*med.*) epilepsy. ~**log**, (*th.*) epilogue. ~**santr**, (*geol.*) epicentre. ~**sikl**, (*eng.*) epicycle. ~**stemoloji**, (*phil.*) epistemology. ~**tel(yum)**, (*bio.*) epithelium.

epoksi (*chem.*) Epoxy. ~**t**[i], epoxide.

epope (*lit.*) Epic.

eprik Slightly dirty laundry water.

eprimek *vi.* Wear out; break up into pieces.

EPU = (*fin.*) (*European Payments Union*).

er[1] *n.* Man; male; husband; (*mil.*) private (soldier); hero; pawn (chess); (*fig.*) manly/capable man; (*ent.*) soldier (ant). ~ **azığı**, rations: ~ BEZİ: ~ **lokması** ~ **kursağında kalmaz**, a man repays good with good: ~ **meydanı**, (*sp.*) wrestling ring: ~ **oğlu** ~, hero: ~ **oyunu birdir**, once is enough: ~ **önbeze**, (*bio.*) prostate (gland): ~SIVI[L]: ~**e gitmek/varmak**, (woman) marry: ~**e vermek**, give a (woman) in marriage.

er[2] *adv.* Early, soon. ~ **geç**, sooner or later.

Er. = (*ch.s.*) ERBİYUM; (*ling.*) ERİL.

-er[1]/**-ar** *v. suf.* [116] = -R [DÖNER; YAPAR].

-er-[2]/**-ar-** *v. suf.* [145] *Forming a causative verb* [GİDERMEK; ÇIKARMAK].

-er-[3]/**-ar-** *v. suf.* [229] *Added to an adjective*, become . . . [AĞARMAK, YEŞERMEK]. *Added to a noun*, give; make [EVERMEK].

-er[4]/**-ar**/**-şer**/**-şar** *a. suf.* [83, 193] *Distributive.* Each; at a time [BİRER, ONAR, İKİŞER]. *Repeated*, *they become adverbs* [beşer beşer, in fives].

eradikasyon Eradication.

erat[1] (*mil.*) Privates and NCO's.

erbain (*math.*) Forty; (*met.*) forty days of severe winter (22 Dec.–30 Jan.); (*rel.*) forty days' penitence/retreat.

erba[1]**p**[bı] Expert. ~**ından sormalı**, ask the expert.

er·baş(lık) (*mil.*) (Rank of) non-commissioned officer, NCO. ~ **bezi**, (*bio.*) testicle.

erbi·n (*chem.*) Erbium (hydr)oxide. ~**yum**, erbium.

er·boğa (*myth.*, *ast.*) Centaur. ~**ci**[lk g i], (*bot.*) stamen. ~**ciksiz**, (*bot.*) andandrous.

erdem Virtue. ~**li**, virtuous. ~**lik**, virtue; ability. ~**lilik**, virtuosity. ~**siz**, without virtue/merit.

erden (*bio.*) Virgin, intact. ~**lik**, virginity.

erdirmek (-i, -e) *vc.* = ERMEK[2]; cause to reach/ attain.

erdişi *a.*, *n.* (*bio.*) Hermaphrodite. ~**lik**, hermaphroditism.

ere·kᵏᵍⁱ Aim, design, end, goal, purpose; (*ast.*) vertex. ~ **bilim**, (*phil.*) teleology. ~ **çi(lik)**, (*phil.*) final·ist/(-ism). ~ **li**, teleological. ~ **lik**, finality. ~ **sel**, final: ~ **neden**, final cause. ~ **siz(lik)**, aimless(ness).

-erek/-arak *v. suf.* [176] -ing(ly); by doing, with doing [**gülerek**, laughing(ly); **çalışarak**, by working].

ereksiyon (*bio.*) Erection.

eren (*rel.*) Saint; enlightened mystic. ~ **in sağı solu olmaz**, he is unpredictable: ~ **ler**, *int.* dervish term of address.

Erendiz (*ast.*) Jupiter.

erey (*phys.*) Limit.

ergⁱ (*geo.*) Sandy region (of Sahara); (*phys.*) erg.

erganun (*mus.*) Organ.

ergen Youth of marriageable age, adolescent bachelor, celibate. ~ **olm.**, reach marriageable age: ~ **e karı boşamak kolay**, it's easy for the spectator. ~ **lik**, maturity; (*med.*) acne.

ergene (*geol.*) Mine-field.

ergi Attainment, achievement.

ergi·me *vn.* (*phys.*) Melting: ~ **ısısı**, melting heat: ~ **noktası**, melting point. ~ **mek**, *vi.* melt.

ergin (*bot.*) Mature, ripe; (*bio.*, *leg.*) adult, senior. ~ **lemek (-i, -e)**, initiate; (*ed.*) teach s.o. a subject. ~ **lenmek**, *vp.* ~ **leşmek**, (become) mature. ~ **lik**, maturity, ripeness; adulthood: ~ **çağı**, age of discretion.

ergit·mek (-i) (*phys.*) Melt; (*min.*) fuse, smelt. ~ **meli**, *a.* fusion, melting.

ergo·metre (*phys.*) Ergometer. ~ **nomi**, (*ind.*) ergonomics.

erguvan (*bot.*) Judas-tree; purple colour. ~ **i**, purple: ~ **balıkçıl**, (*orn.*) purple heron: ~ **su tavuğu**, (*orn.*) purple gallinule.

erigen That easily melts; dissolving.

eri·kᵏᵍⁱ (*bot.*) Plum. ~ **ağacı**, (*bot.*) plum-tree: ~ **kurusu**, (*cul.*) prune. ~ **lik**, plum orchard.

eril (*ling.*) Masculine. ~ **lik**, masculineness.

erim¹ *n.* Range, reach; (eye-)sight; (gun)-shot; (*fin.*) term.

erim² *n.* (*dial.*) Good news/augury.

erim³ *adv.* ~ ~ **erimek**, be exhausted; waste away.

eri·me *vn.* (*phys.*) Melting; fusion; (*med.*) lysis. ~ **noktası**, melting point. ~ **mek**, *vi.* melt; dissolve; leach; fuse; (*tex.*) wear out; (*fig.*) pine away; become thin; be very ashamed: **eriyip bitmek**, (*med.*) waste away. ~ **mez**, *a.* (*phys.*) insoluble. ~ **miş**, *a.* molten; fused. ~ **mişlik**, (*med.*) cachexia.

erin (*bio.*) Mature, adult. ~ **cik**, lazy; bashful, timid. ~ **gen**, lazy. ~ **lik**, maturity, adulthood.

erin·çᶜⁱ Peace; rest. ~ **sizlik**, uneasiness.

er·inmek *vi.* Melt away; (*fig.*) flag. ~ **ir(lik)**, solu·ble/(-bility).

eristi·kᵏᵍⁱ (*phil.*) Eristics.

eriş Arrival. ~ **ilebilir**, *a.* accessible. ~ **ilebilme**, *vn.* accessibility. ~ **il(e)mez**, *a.* inaccessible, unattainable. ~ **ilmek**, *vi.* be reached; be attained. ~ **im**, *vn.*; (*geo.*) communications; (*sp.*) record; (*chem.*) liquation. ~ **kin**, adult, mature. ~ **kinlik**, adulthood, maturity. ~ **me**, *vn.*; attainment; access. ~ **mek (-e)**, arrive at; reach; attain, achieve; mature,

ripen; reach marriageable age; (season) arrive. ~ **men**, (*sp.*) record-holder. ~ **tirmek (-i, -e)**, *vc.*, give, grant.

erişte (*cul.*) Vermicelli, noodles.

eri·tem (*med.*) Erythema. ~ **tro-**, erythro-.

er·iten (*phys.*) Solvent. ~ **itici**, (*chem.*) solvent; melting. ~ **itilmek**, *vp.* be dissolved. ~ **itilmez**, *a.* insoluble. ~ **itken**, (*min.*) flux. ~ **itme**, *vn.* melting; fusion: ~ **kabı**, (*min.*) crucible: ~ **potası**, (*min.*) cupel. ~ **itmek (-i)**, *vc.* = ERİMEK; melt; dissolve; (*fig.*) cause to waste away; squander. ~ **iyi·k**ᵏᵍⁱ, (*chem.*) solution; dilution.

erkⁱ (*phys.*) Energy; (*adm.*) power; -ocracy; influence. ~ **e**, (*phys.*) energy, force, power: ~ **aktarımı//dağılımı**, transfer//diffusion of energy: ~ **nin korunması**, conservation of energy.

erkân *pl.* = RÜKUN. Important people; (*adm.*) senior officials; (*mil.*) senior officers; (*adm.*) rules, procedure. ~ **heyeti**, (*mil.*) staff: ~ **kürkü**, (*his.*) fur cloak given by the Sultan to s.o. promoted Vezir: ~ **ı harbiye(i umumiye)**, (*his.*, *mil.*) general staff: ~ **ı harp**, (*mil.*) staff.

erke·l·çᶜⁱ (*zoo.*) Male-/billy-goat. ~ **sakalı**ⁿ¹, (*bot.*) spiraea.

erke·kᵏᵍⁱ *n.* Man; male; husband; (*zoo.*) bull-, he-; (*orn.*) cock-; (*bio.*) andro-. *a.* Manly, virile; courageous; honest and true; (*eng.*, *zoo.*) male. ~ **adam**, a real man: ~ **ahçı**, chef, cook: ~ **akdiken**, (*bot.*) alder buckthorn: ~ **arı**, (*ent.*) drone: ~ **Ayşe/ Fatma**, a masculine type of woman: ~ **bakır// demir**, (*min.*) hard copper//iron: ~ **berberi**, barber: ~ **canlısı**, a woman always after men: ~ **çocuk**, boy: ~ **domuz**, (*zoo.*) boar: ~ **dul**, widower: ~ **e**, man to man: ~ **eşeylik organı**, (*bio.*) testis: ~ **geyik**, (*zoo.*) buck: ~ **gibi**, masculine, male, manly: ~ **hormonu**, (*bio.*) androgen: ~ **izci**, boy-scout: ~ **kardeş**, brother: ~ **kedi**, (*live.*) tomcat: ~ **kopça**, (*mod.*) hook (fitting the eye): ~ **kuğu**, (*orn.*) cob: ~ **olm.**, (woman) become a man; be manly: ~ **oyuncu**, actor: ~ **ördek**, (*orn.*) drake: ~ **tavşan**, (*zoo.*) buck rabbit/hare: ~ **tilki**, (*zoo.*) dog-fox: ~ **lere**, gentlemen's toilet/cloakroom.

erkek·çe Manly, manfully. ~ **çil**, (woman) interested in men. ~ **lenmek**, *vi.* behave in a manly way. ~ **leşmek**, *vi.* (woman) become like a man; (boy) grow into a man. ~ **li**, (*mod.*) dişili/kadınlı, comprising both men and women. ~ **lik**, manhood; masculinity; virility; manliness, courage: ~ **sende kalsın!**, behave like a man (whatever others do). ~ **organ**, (*bot.*) stamen. ~ **si**, tomboyish (girl), mannish (woman). ~ **siz**, (woman) husbandless, without support.

erkele·(ndir)mek (-i) (*chem.*) Energize. ~ **yici**, energizer.

erken Early; advanced, before time. ~ **bunama**, (*psy.*) (adolescent) schizophrenia: ~ **kaldırmak (-i)**, wake s.o. early: ~ **den**, (very) early. ~ **ce**, rather early. ~ **ci**, early-rising, 'early bird'; who comes early.

erketeci(lik) (*sl.*) (Work of) swindler/burglar's look-out man.

erkil Authoritarian.

erkin Free; autonomous; professional; liberal.

~ **inceleme,** (*phil.*) free-thinking. ~**lik,** freedom. ~**(lik)çi,** (*adm.*) liberal; independent. ~**(lik)çilik,** liberalism; independence; autonomy.

erk·li Powerful, influential; energetic. ~**lik,** powerfulness; influentiality; (*fin.*) penetration. ~**sizlik,** anarchy. ~**tekelci(lik),** (*pol.*) totalitarian(ism). ~**yurt,** state.

er·leşme (*bio.*) Virilization. ~**lik,** masculinity; virility; bravery; (*mil.*) soldierliness: ~ **içsalgısı,** (*bio.*) androgen.

Erm. = ERMENİ(STAN); ERMENİCE(DEN).

ermek[1] *vi.* (*obs.*) [96] Be. [*Exists in the inflected forms* İDİ; İKEN, İMİŞ, İSE.]

ermek[2] **(-e)** Reach; attain; arrive at maturity; (*rel.*) reach perfection: *vi.* become a saint; (*bot.*) become ripe. **erdiğine erer, ermediğine taş atar,** ill-mannered, quarrelsome.

Ermeni (*ethn.*) *n.* Armenian. ~ +, *a.* Armenian: ~ **gelini gibi kırıtmak,** hang back/be slow in doing stg.: ~ **Patriği,** (*rel.*) Armenian Catholicos.

Ermeni·ce (*ling.*) Armenian. ~**stan,** (*geo.*) (Soviet) Armenia. ~**stanlı,** (Soviet) Armenian.

ermiş(lik) (*rel.*) Saint(liness).

eroin (*chem.*) Heroin. ~**ci,** heroin seller/user.

Ero·s (*myth.*) Eros, God of Love; (*bio.*) sexual love; creative instinct. ~**sal/tik,** erotic. ~**sallık/**~**tizm,** eroticism. ~**sçu(luk),** (*lit./art.*) s.o. preoccupied/ (preoccupation) with sexuality.

erozyon (*geol.*) Erosion.

er·selik (*bio.*) Hermaphrodite; androgyne; hermaphroditism. ~**sıvı(l),** seminal. ~**siz,** (woman) husbandless; destitute. ~**sizlik,** husbandlessness; destitution. ~**suyu,** (*bio.*) seminal fluid.

erte The next day/month, etc.; the morrow. ~**leme,** *vn.* adjournment, postponement: ~ **maçı,** (*sp.*) postponed match. ~**lemek,** *vi.* remain till the next day; for the morrow to come: **(-i),** adjourn, defer, postpone. ~**lenme,** *vn.* postponement. ~**lenmek,** *vp.* ~**letmek (-i, -e),** *vc.* ~**si,** [202] the day, etc. after/following.

ertem Breeding; good manners.

ervah *pl.* = RUH. Spirits; souls. ~**ına yuf olsun!,** curse them!

erzak[1] *pl.* = RIZ(I)K. Provisions; food.

erzats Ersatz, artificial, substitute.

erze (*bot.*) Cedar(-tree).

es (*mus.*) Rest (sign). ~ **geçmek,** (*sl.*) pay no attention.

Es. (*ch.s.*) = AYNŞTAYNYUM. ~ **t.** = ESKİ TERİM.

ES = EMEKLİ SANDIĞI; (*phys.*) ERİME SICAKLIĞI.

esami *pl.* = isim. Names. ~**si okunmaz,** he is of no consequence.

esans (*chem.*) Essence, extract, perfume. ~**çı(lık),** perfumer(y). ~**iyel,** essential.

esaret[i] Captivity; slavery.

esas *n.* Foundation; base; principle; (*leg.*) case, suit; essence. *a.* Principal; main; original; basic. ~ **itibarıyla/olarak,** essentially: ~ **milliyet/soyu,** (*leg.*) nationality by birth: ~ **seviye,** (*geo.*) datum level: ~**a bağlamak,** base on a principle: ~**ı olmamak,** be unreal/untrue: ~**ı yok,** (rumour, etc.) it is without foundation: ~**ında,** fundamentally.

esas·en Fundamentally; essentially; in principle;

from the beginning; besides; anyhow. ~**i,** *a.* principal; basic. ~**lanmak,** *vi.* be established; be founded. ~**lı,** based; secure; true; sure; essential; principal; effectively. ~**sız,** baseless; unfounded; irrational. ~**sızlık,** baselessness; irrationality.

esatir *pl.* Legends; stories; myths; mythology.

esba'p[bi] *pl.* = SEBEP. Causes; reasons.

esef Regret. ~ **etm.,** regret; be sorry: ~ **verici,** worrying: ~**le,** regretfully. ~**lenmek,** *vi.* pity.

eselemek ~ **beselemek,** wheedle, get round s.o.

eseme (*phil.*) Logic.

esen Healthy; hearty, robust. ~**leme,** *vn.* greeting. ~**lemek (-i),** greet s.o. ~**leşmek (-le),** *vi.* greet each other. ~**leştirme,** (*med.*) rehabilitation. ~**lik,** health(iness).

eser Sign; mark; trace, remains; monument; (*art.*, *lit.*) work. ~ **bırakmak,** leave mark/trace: ~**i olarak,** as the result of . . ..: ~**icedit,** ~ **kâğıdı,** (*pub.*) foolscap paper.

esermek (-i) Look after; breed. ~ **besermek,** produce.

esham (*fin.*) Shares (of companies).

ESHOT = (İZMİR) ELEKTRİK, SU, HAVAGAZI, OTOBÜS, TRAMVAY İŞLETMELERİ.

-esi/-ası *v. suf. fut.* [115] ~ **gelmek,** feel like (do)ing. ~**(ce),** [161] *used only in curses,* may this/that happen! [**ipe gelesi,** may he hang!].

esi·ci Blower. ~**m,** blowing (of the wind).

esin (*met.*) Morning breeze; (*fig.*) inspiration. ~ **almak/**~**(len)mek,** be inspired by; (*lit.*) plagiarize: ~ **vermek/**~**dirmek/**~**lemek (-i, -e),** inspire s.o. ~**lenim,** inspiration. ~**ti,** (*met.*) light breeze.

esir[1] *n.* (*met./phys.*) The ether, atmosphere.

esir[2] *n.* Captive; prisoner of war; slave; (*fig.*) slave (by addiction to drink, etc.). ~ **almaca,** (*child.*) prisoner's base: ~ **almak,** take captive/prisoner: ~ **düşmek/olm.,** be captured/taken prisoner: ~ **etm.,** capture, (*fig.*) captivate: ~ **kampı,** (*mil.*) prison camp: ~ **pazarı,** slave market: ~ **ticareti,** (*his.*) slave-trade. ~**ci(lik),** slave-deal·er/(-ing). ~**lik,** captivity, bondage, slavery: ~**ten kurtarmak,** emancipate.

esirge·me *vn.* Protecting; mercy, compassion: ~**den vermek,** give unstintingly. ~**mek (-i, -den),** protect, guard; spare; grudge. ~**mez(lik),** self-sacri·ficing/ (-fice). ~**nmek,** *vi.* be protected; be spared. ~**yici,** who protects/spares; grudging, stingy; chary.

esirme (*psy.*) Ecstasy, rapture.

-esiye/-asıya *v. suf.* [180] To the point of . . . [DÜŞESİYE], ~ **kadar,** (*dial.*) until.

eskatologya (*phil.*) Eschatology.

esker (*geol.*) Esker.

eski Old; ancient; chronic; old-fashioned, out-of-date; worn; secondhand; the late, the former, the ex-. ~ **adet,** tradition: ~ **ağza yeni kaşık/taam,** (*said when eating the first fruit, etc. of the year*): ~ **ÇAĞ:** ~ **çamlar bardak oldu,** times have changed; things are not what they used to be: ~ **defterleri karıştırmak,** delve into the past; rely on past achievements: ~ **dost düşman olmaz,** only old friends are reliable: ~ **enayi biçimi,** (*mod.*) out-of-fashion: ~ **eserler,** (*archaeol.*) ancient monuments, etc.: ~ **göz ağrısı,** an old 'flame': ~ **hamam** ~ **tas,**

the same old thing; just the same as ever: ~ **hayratı berbat etm.**, by trying to improve stg. make it worse: ~ **kafalı**, (person) conservative, old-fashioned, behind the times, narrow-minded: ~ **köye yeni âdet!**, don't try to teach old dogs new tricks!: ~ **kurt**, old hand, old stager: ~ **kütük**, seasoned timber; experienced old man: ~ **maden**, genuine material; old china: ~ **moda**, old-fashioned: ~ **nüsha**, (*pub.*) back-number: ~ **politikaya saplı kaldılar**, they stuck to their old policy: ~ **püskü**, worn out; very old: ~ **talebe**, (*ed.*) old boy/girl: ~ **toprak**, s.o. old but strong: ~ **tüfek**, (*fig.*) s.o. experienced: ~ **den**, *adv.* [201] of old; in the old days: ~ **den beri**, from of old; for a long time past: ~ **ler**, (*his.*) the Ancients; (*col.*) old goods: ~ **si gibi**, as of old, as before: ~ **si kadar**, just as before: ~ **si olmayanın acarı olmaz**, don't throw away old things or the new ones will soon wear out: ~ **ye etkili**, (*leg.*) retrospective.

eski·ci Dealer in secondhand goods; old-clothes man; cobbler. ~ **cilik**, dealing in old clothes; cobbling. ~ **çağ**, (*his.*) prehistoric times: ~ **bilgisi**, archaeology. ~ **dünya**, (*geo.*) the Old World. ~ **l**, archaic. ~ **leralayımcı**, rag-and-bone man. ~ **leşme**, *vn.* obsolescence. ~ **leşmek**, *vi.* grow old; become obsolete; become worn/shabby. ~ **lik**, oldness; shabbiness; (*adm.*) seniority; ancientness; antiquity. ~ **llik**, (*ling.*) archaism. ~ **mek**, *vi.* be worn out; grow old in service; become obsolete; age. ~ **miş**, *a.* antiquated; archaic.

Eskimo (*ethn.*) Eskimo. ~ **ca**, (*ling.*) Eskimo.

eski·şehirtaşı (*geol.*) Meerschaum. ~ **tilmek**, *vi.* be made old; be aged; be worn out. ~ **tmek (-i)**, wear out; cause to grow old; (*ind.*) age; (*fig.*) exhaust. ~ **varlıkbilim**, (*geol.*) palaeontology. ~ **yazı**, ~ **bilimi**, palaeography.

es·kiz (*art.*) Sketch, draft. ~ **krim**, (*sp.*) fencing: ~ **etm.**, fence. ~ **krimci**, fencer.

es·laf *pl.* = SELEF. Predecessors. ~ **lek**, obedient.

eslemek (-i) Hear; listen to; (*mus.*) pause.

esma *pl.* = ISIM. Names; (*ling.*) nouns; (*rel.*) attributes of God. ~ **yı üstüne sıçratmak**, bring trouble upon o.s.

es·me *vn.* Blowing; happening; (*med.*) aura. ~ **mek**, *vi.* (wind, etc.) blow; come by chance; (unexpected good fortune) befall; come to mind: **esip savurmak**, shout and bluster.

esmer Dark-complexioned; dusky; brunette. ~ **akbaba**, (*orn.*) European black vulture: ~ **ekmek**, (*cul.*) brown bread: ~ **güzeli**, brunette: ~ **pelikan**, (*orn.*) brown pelican: ~ **suyosunları**, (*bot.*) brown seaweeds: ~ **şeker**, (*cul.*) brown sugar.

esmer·amber (*zoo.*) Ambergris. ~ **ce**/~ **imsi**, brownish. ~ **küf(ler)**, (*myc.*) mucor(aceae). ~ **leşmek**, *vi.* become brown. ~ **letmek (-i)**, make brown. ~ **lik**, brownness.

esna Course, duration; interval; time. ~ **da**, at the time; meanwhile: ~ **sında**, *post.* [94] in the course of ..., during ....

esnaf *pl.* = SINIF. Classes; kinds; trades; guilds. *s.* Tradesman, artisan, (*sl.*) prostitute; professional gambler. ~ **cemiyet/derneği**, trade association: ~ **zihniyeti**, shopkeeper's mentality; being

commercially-minded. ~ **ça**, mercenary; utilitarian. ~ **lık**, work of a tradesman, etc.

esnek (*phys.*) Elastic; flexible; (*fig.*) flexible, changeable. ~ **lik**, *n.* elasticity; resilience; flexibility: *a.* elastic.

esne·me *vn.* Yawn(ing); bending; resilience; expansion. ~ **mek**, *vi.* yawn; stretch and recover shape; bend; yield. ~ **mez(lik)**, rigid(ity). ~ **r(lik)** = ESNEK(LİK). ~ **tme**, *vn.*; (*sp.*) stretching the muscles. ~ **tmek (-i)**, cause to yawn; stretch; bend; (*fig.*) bore. ~ **yiş**, yawn; elasticity.

es·pas(e) (*pub.*) Space(d). ~ **peranto**, (*ling.*) Esperanto.

esperi (*orn.*) Hobby.

es·pressivo (*mus.*) Expressively. ~ **pri**, witticism: ~ **yapmak**, make jokes; say stg. witty. ~ **prili**, witty.

esrar[1] *n. pl.* = SIR[2]. Secrets; mysteries. ~ **kutu/küpü**, a man of mystery: ~ **kumkuması**, full of secrets: ~ **perdesi**, veil of secrecy. ~ **engiz**, mysterious; enigmatic(al); veiled in secrecy. ~ **engizlik**, secrecy, mystery. ~ **lı**, mysterious; cryptic; full of secrets.

esrar[2] *n.* (*bot.*, *chem.*) Hashish; drug. ~ **tekkesi**, hashish den. ~ **cı**, hashish-dealer/-smoker. ~ **keş** (-lik), hashish addict(ion). ~ **otu**nu, (*bot.*) cannabis, hemp.

esre (*ling.*) (Arabic) vowel-point indicating the sound of 'i'.

esri·(k) Drunk; over-excited. ~ **(k)lik**, drunkenness. ~ **me**, *vn.* faintness; being drunk; ecstasy. ~ **mek**, *vi.* swoon; become very excited; become drunk. ~ **tici**, intoxicating; exciting. ~ **tme**, *vn.* intoxication. ~ **tmek (-i)**, intoxicate; excite.

est. = ESTETİK.

estağfurullah *int.* You're too kind!; don't mention it! (*in reply to a compliment/polite expression*).

estek ~ **(etm.) köstek etm.**, make all sorts of excuses to avoid doing stg.

ester (*chem.*) Ester. ~ **leşme**, *vn.* esterification. ~ **leştirmek (-i)**, esterify.

este·ti[1]k[gi] Aesthetic(s): ~ **ameliyatı**, (*med.*) cosmetic surgery, (*col.*) face-lift. ~ **tikçi(lik)**, aesthe·te/ (-ticism). ~ **tisyen**, aesthete. ~ **tizm**, aestheticism.

estir·ilmek *vp.* ~ **mek (-i)**, *vc.* = ESMEK; cause to blow.

estomp (*art.*) Stump (drawing).

Estonya (*geo.*) Estonia. ~ **ca** (*ling.*) Estonian. ~ **lı**, (*ethn.*) Estonian.

esva[1]p[bı] (*mod.*) Clothes; clothing. ~ **çı**, ready-made clothes merchant; second-hand clothes dealer. ~ **lık**, (*tex.*) suitable for making clothes.

eş[1] *n.* One of a pair; a similar/matching thing; double; match; colleague, mate; fellow; husband, wife; (*math.*) analog(ue). ~ **dost**, one's friends and acquaintances: ~ **etm. (-i)**, match stg.: ~ **olm.**, be a match: ~ **olmıyan**, unequal; aniso-: ~ **tutmak**, choose a partner: ~ **yapmak**, couple: ~ **i benzeri yok**, unequalled, unique: ~ **i emsali görülmemiş**, unprecedented: ~ **i yok,** peerless; unmatched: ~ **ini yapmak**, copy, model, duplicate.

eş·[2] *pref.* Equal; uniform; equi-; homo-; iso-; syn-; co-. ~ **ad(lı)**, (*ling.*) homonym(ous). ~ **anlam(lı)**, (*ling.*) synonym(ous). ~ **anlamlılık**, synonymy.

eş·anjör (*phys.*) (Heat-)exchanger. ~**antiyon**, (*fin.*) sample. ~**apman**, (*mot.*) exhaust. ~**ar'p**ʰⁱ, (*mod.*) scarf, sash; cravat.

eş·ayak/bacaklılar (*zoo.*) Isopods. ~**aydınlık**, (*el.*) isophot. ~**bası(nç)**, (*geo.*, *phys.*) having equal atmospheric pressure: ~ **eğrisi**, isobar. ~**basınçlı**, (*bio.*) isotonic. ~**baskı**, (*pub.*) reprint. ~**biçim(li)**, isomorph(ous). ~**biçimlik**, isomorphism. ~**cinsel/ (-lik)**, homosexual(ity). ~**çoğuz**, (*chem.*) copolymer. ~**dağoluş**, (*geol.*) synorogenic. ~**değer(li)**, equival·ence/(-ent). ~**değerlik**, equivalence; equality. ~**deprem**, (*geol.*) isoseismal. ~**derinlik**, (*geo.*) isobath. ~**düzey**, (*carp.*) flush.

eşe'kᵍⁱ Donkey; ass; (*fig.*) dolt, ass. ~ **başı mısın?,** (*vulg.*) 'why don't you use your authority?': ~ **başı mıyım?,** (*vulg.*) why don't you ask my opinion?: ~ **büyüdü semeri küçüldü,** he has outgrown his clothes: ~ **çiçeği,** (*bot.*) evening primrose: ~ **derisi gibi,** thick-skinned; insensitive: ~ **gibi,** (*vulg.*) coarse, rough, thoughtless: ~ **hoşaftan ne anlar,** (*vulg.*) 'it's casting pearls before swine': ~ **inadı,** (*vulg.*) very stubborn: ~ **kadar oldu,** (*vulg.*) s.o. full-grown but not very bright: ~ **kafalı,** (*fig.*) thick-headed, stupid: ~ **kuyruğu gibi ne uzar ne kısalır,** s.o. who makes no progress: ~ **oğlu** ~**!,** (*vulg.*) dolt!, blockhead!: ~ **oyunu,** horse-play: ~ **sıpası,** (*vulg.*) (*term of affection or abuse*): ~ **sudan gelinceye kadar dövmek,** thrash soundly: ~ **şakası,** coarse practical joke: ~**e gücü yetmeyen semerini döver,** people avenge themselves on a strong man's followers: ~**e ters bindirmek (-i),** pillory s.o.; show s.o. up: ~**i düğüne çağırmışlar, 'ya su lazımdır ya odun' demiş,** some people always suspect others' motives: ~**in kulağı kesmekle küheylan olmaz,** physical changes do not alter the spirit/nature: ~**ten düşmüş karpuza dönmek,** be very surprised/ shocked.

eşek·arısıⁿⁱ (*ent.*) Hornet; wasp. ~**çe(sine),** like a donkey, asinine. ~**çi,** donkey-driver. ~**davası**ⁿⁱ, (*math.*) *pons asinorum.* ~**dikeni**ⁿⁱ, (*bot.*) cardoon. ~**hıyarı**ⁿⁱ, (*bot.*) squirting cucumber. ~**kulağı**ⁿⁱ, (*bot.*) comfrey. ~**lenmek,** *vi.* make a fool of o.s. ~**leşmek,** *vi.* (*vulg.*) behave very stupidly/coarsely. ~**lik,** (*fig.*, *vulg.*) stupidity; coarseness. ~**otu**ⁿᵘ, (*bot.*) sainfoin. ~ **sırtı**ⁿⁱ, (*arch.*) gable roof; saddlebacked.

eş·eksenli (*math.*) Equiaxial; concentric. ~**eksicikli,** (*phys.*) isoelectronic.

eşele'kᵍⁱ (*bot.*) Core (of apples, etc.).

eşelemek (-i) Stir up, scratch about, hunt for; rummage about; try to understand; inquire.

eşelmobil (*fin.*) Sliding scale.

eş·etkenlik Synergism. ~**evreli,** (*phys.*) coherent. ~**evresiz,** incoherent.

eşey (*bio.*) Sex. ~**li,** sexed; sexual: ~ **üreme,** sexual reproduction. ~**lik,** *a.* sexual; genital. ~**lilik,** sexuality. ~**sel,** sexual: ~ **seçim,** sexual selection. ~**siz,** asexual, agamous.

eş·gamet (*bio.*) Isogamete. ~**geçerli,** (*phil.*) equipollent. ~**güçlü,** equipotential. ~**güdüm,** (*adm.*) coordination; coordinating (committee, etc.). ~**güdümcü,** coordinator. ~**güdümsel,** co-ordinated.

eşhas *pl.* = ŞAHIS. Persons; individuals; (*th.*) characters.

eşısıl (*met.*). Isotherm(al).

eşi'kᵍⁱ (*arch.*) Threshold, door-step; entrance; (*phys.*) threshold; (*mus.*) bridge (violin, etc.). ~**ine gelmek/**~**ine yüz sürmek,** petition/importune s.o.: ~**ini aşındırmak,** frequent a place constantly.

eşil·me *vn.* Digging over; (*geol.*) landslide. ~**mek,** *vp.* = EŞMEK; be dug.

eşin·eğitim (*ed.*) Mixed education. ~**zaman,** synchronous.

eşinmek *vi.* (Animals) scratch up the ground.

eşitⁱ Equal; equivalent; the same; equi-, iso-, co-; (*sp.*) draw, tie. ~ **işareti,** (*math.*) 'equals' sign (=): ~ **işlem,** (*soc.*) non-discrimination: ~ **kılmak,** balance, equalize: ~ **yapmak,** equate: ~ **yarışım,** (*fin.*) fair competition.

eşit·çe Equally. ~**çenetli,** (*zoo.*) bivalves. ~**çi(lik),** (*phil.*) egalitarian(ism). ~**leme,** *vn.* equation; (*min.*) soaking. ~**lemek (-i),** make equal; equalize. ~**lenmek,** *vp.* ~**leşmek,** *vi.* become equal. ~**leyici,** ~ **bilgisayar,** analogue computer. ~**lik,** equality; identity; parity: ~ **derecesi,** (*ling.*) equative degree: ~ **eki,** (*ling.*) equative suffix [-CE, -sİ]: ~ **etm.,** (*mus.*) accompany. ~**likçi(lik)** = ~**çi**(LİK). ~**siz,** unequal; without equal, extraordinary. ~**sizlik,** inequality, disparity.

eşiz (*chem.*) Isomer. ~**lenme,** isomerization.

eşkâlⁱ *pl.* = ŞEKİL. Forms; figures; appearance. ~**ine uymak,** answer to/fit s.o.'s description: ~**ini tarif et!,** describe his appearance!

eş·kanatlı(lar) (*ent.*) Homopter·ous/(-a). ~**kaynar,** (*phys.*) azeotrope. ~**kenar(lı),** (*math.*) equilateral (triangle, etc.); rhomboid.

eşkbar Tearful, lachrymose.

eşkıya *pl.* = ŞAKİ. Rebels; brigands. *s.* Brigand. ~**lık,** rebellion; brigandage.

eşkin Canter(ing). ~ **gitmek,** canter.

eşkin·a/ ~ **e** = İŞKİNE.

eş·koşmak (-e) (*rel.*) Attribute a partner to God; be a polytheist. ~**le'k**ᵍⁱ, (*ast.*) equator: ~ +, *a.* equatorial. ~**leme,** copy; parity. ~**leme,** *vn.* matching; (*cin.*) synchronization; (*phil.*) correspondence. ~**lemek (-i),** match; (*cin.*) synchronize. ~**lemeli,** (*cin.*) synchronized. ~**lemesiz,** (*cin.*) unsynchronized. ~**lenik,** (*math.*) conjugate. ~**leşmek,** *vi.* be(come) equal; become a pair. ~**leyici,** (*cin.*) synchronizer. ~**li,** (*sp.*) in pairs, with partner. ~**lik,** equality; symmetry; companionship; (*mus.*) accompaniment.

eş·me *vn.* Digging; (*geo.*) shallow spring, waterhole. ~**mek (-i),** dig lightly; scratch up: (-e), get stuck into (work, etc.).

eşmerkezli Concentric.

eşofman (*sp.*) Warming up; (*mod.*) warms.

eşoğlu ~ **eşek,** (*vulg.*) thickhead, dolt, ass.

eş·oluşumlu (*geol.*) Syngenetic. ~**oylum,** (*rad.*) isochronous. ~**öğecikli,** (*phys.*) homonuclear. ~**ölçülü,** (*min.*) isometric. ~**özde'k**ᵍⁱ, allotrope. ~**özdekli(lik),** (*min.*) allotrop·ic/(-y).

eş·raf *pl.* = ŞERİF. Notables; rich people. ~**ref,** more/most noble/eminent: ~ **saati gelmek,** the propitious moment arrive.

ş·sesli (*ling.*) Homonym; equivocal. ~ **sıcak**, (*met.*) isotherm(al). ~ **sıralı**, (*math.*) coordinate. ~ **siz**, matchless, peerless, beyond compare; without a mate. ~ **sizlik**, matchlessness. ~ **söz**, (*ling.*) tautology. ~ **titrem**, (*ling.*) isotonic.

şşoğlu = EŞOĞLU.

ştirmek (-i) *vc.* = EŞMEK.

şya *pl.* = ŞEY. Things; objects; furniture; luggage; goods; merchandise; belongings. ~ **laşmak**, *vi.* objectivize. ~ **lı**, furnished. ~ **sız**, unfurnished.

ş·yatımlı (*geol.*) Isoclinal. ~ **yönelim**, (*geol.*) isotropy. ~ **yönlü(lük)**, (*min.*) isotrop·ic/(-y). ~ **yönsüz**, (*min.*) anisotropic. ~ **yükseklik/** ~ **yükselti**, (*geo.*) of equal altitude: ~ **eğrisi**, contour-line. ~ **zamanlı**, (*phys.*) synchronous; (*his.*) contemporaneous. ~ **zamanlılık**, synchrony; contemporaneity.

tⁱ (*zoo.*) Flesh; (*cul.*) meat; (*bot.*) pulp; skin. ~ **bağlamak**, get fat; (*med.*) (wound) begin to heal up: ~ **beni**, (*bio.*) pimple: ~ **bezi**, (*bio.*) gland: ~ **çalığı**, (*med.*) botulism: ~ **düşmanı**, (*cul.*) vegetarian: ~ **kafalı**, thick-headed: ~ KESİMİ: ~ KIRIMI: ~ **lokması**, (*cul.*) meat dish: ~ OBURLAR: ~ **özü**, meat essence: ~ SİNEĞİ: ~ **suyu**, (*cul.*) consommé, broth, stock; gravy: ~ ŞEFTALİSİ: ~ **tahtası**, (*cul.*) chopping-board: ~ **tırnak olm.**, (*fig.*) be a close-knit family: ~ **tırnaktan ayırmak**, separate s.o. from his family: ~ TOPRAK: ~ **tutmak**, get fat: ~ **tutmamak**, not put on flesh: ~ **yemeği**, (*cul.*) meat dish: ~ **i budu yerinde/** ~ **ine dolgun**, plump but not fat: ~ **i ne budu ne?**, what's the use of him; he's a poor creature: ~ **i senin kemiği benim!**, (*to schoolmaster*) don't spare the rod!: ~ **inden** ~ **kesmek/ koparmak**, cause great pain: ~ **le tırnak arasına girilmez**, don't meddle in others' family affairs: ~ **le tırnak gibi**, a very near relation.

tabli Established; resident. ~ **meselesi**, (*pol.*) questions regarding the interpretation of *établi* in the Treaty of Lausanne, 1923: ~ **Rumlar**, (*soc.*) Greeks settled in Istanbul (and exempt from exchange in 1924).

ta·jer (*carp.*) Shelves. ~ **lon**, (*math.*) standard. ~ **min**, (*tex.*) coarse muslin, cheesecloth. ~ **n**, (*chem.*) ethane. ~ **ıpᵇ¹**, (*sp.*) lap. ~ **tizm**, (*pol.*) étatisme.

t·çi Meat-seller, butcher. ~ **çiᵘkᵍⁱ**, (*bio.*) carbuncle. ~ **çil**, carnivorous. ~ **çiller**, (*zoo.*) carnivores.

te¹kᵍⁱ (*mod.*) Skirt; fringe; (*geo.*) foot(hill); (*arch.*) flashing; (*bio.*) private parts. ~ **bezi**, cover for baby's legs: ~ **dolusu/** ~ ~, plentiful, in abundance: ~ **kiri**, illicit relationship: ~ **öpmek**, flatter: ~ **i belinde**, industrious/active (woman): ~ **i düşük**, slovenly, slatternly: ~ **i kirlenmek**, (woman) be unchaste: ~ **i temiz**, chaste, honest: ~ **ine düşmek/ sarılmak**, entreat s.o.; turn to s.o. for help: ~ **ine yapışmak**, seek s.o.'s protection: ~ **ini göstermez**, chaste, modest: ~ **leri tutuşmak**, be exceedingly alarmed: ~ **leri zil çalmak**, be frightfully pleased.

tek·lemek (-i) Kiss s.o.'s skirt (in respect); flatter s.o. ~ **li**, skirted. ~ **lik**, skirt; skirt-length; skirt-material.

ten¹ *n.* (*bot.*) Edible part of fruit. ~ **li**, succulent.

eten²/ ~ **e** *n.* (*bio.*) Placenta. ~ **eli**, placental. ~ **esiz**, without placenta.

eten³ *n.* (*chem.*) Ethene, ethylene.

eter (*chem.*) Ether. ~ **lemek (-i)**, (*med.*) anaesthetize. ~ **leşmek**, *vi.* (*chem.*) become ether, vaporize.

etezyen (*met.*) Etesian (winds).

etıbba *pl.* = TABİP. Physicians. ~ **odası**, medical council.

Eti *a.*, *n.* (*his.*) Hittite.

etiᵘkᵍⁱ *n.* Ethics. *a.* Ethical.

etiketⁱ Label, ticket; (*soc.*) etiquette. ~ **çi**, labeller; authority on etiquette. ~ **lemek (-i)**, label. ~ **lenmek**, *vp.* ~ **letmek (-i, -e)**, *vc.* ~ **li**, labelled; (*soc.*) a matter of etiquette.

etil (*chem.*) Ethyl. ~ **en**, ethylene.

eti·moloji(k) (*ling.*) Etymolo·gy/(-gical). ~ **oloji**, (*phil.*) aetiology.

Etiyop·ik (*ethn.*) Ethiopic. ~ **ça**, (*ling.*) Ethiopian. ~ **ya**, (*geo.*) Ethiopia. ~ **yalı**, (*ethn.*) Ethiopian.

etkana¹tᵈ¹ (*zoo.*) Long-eared bat.

ETKB = ENERJİ VE TABİİ KAYNAKLAR BAKANLIĞI.

etken *n.* Agent, factor. *a.* (*chem.*) Active; effective; (*ling.*) active. ~ **eylem**, (*ling.*) active verb. ~ **lik**, activity; (*chem.*) actinism.

et·kesimiⁿⁱ/ ~ **kırımı**ⁿ¹ (*rel.*) Carnival before Lent.

etki *n.* Effect, influence. ~ **etm.** = ~ LEMEK: ~ **tepki**, cause and effect, action and reaction.

etki·ci (*cin.*) Effects-man. ~ **lemek (-i)**, affect, influence. ~ **lenirlik**, susceptibility. ~ **lenmek**, *vp.* ~ **leşim**, interaction, mutual effect. ~ **leşmek**, affect each other. ~ **li**, effective, influential; cutting: ~ **eylem**, (*leg.*) assault and battery: ~ **olm.**, be effective. ~ **lilik**, effectiveness. ~ **me**, *vn.* (*chem.*, *phys.*) action. ~ **mek (-e)**, (*chem.*, *phys.*) act on.

etkin Active; effective; dynamic; (*min.*) activated. ~ **ci**, (*phil.*) activist: ~ **okul**, (*ed.*) teaching by activities. ~ **cilik**, (*phil.*) activism. ~ **lemek (-i)**, activate. ~ **lenim/** ~ **leşim**, (*chem.*) activation. ~ **leştirmek (-i)**, make active, activate. ~ **leyici**, activator. ~ **lik**, activity; (*phys.*) efficiency.

etkisiz Without effect; ineffective; inactive. ~ **kalmak**, be ineffective, 'cut no ice'. ~ **leştirmek (-i)**, render ineffective; neutralize. ~ **lik**, ineffectiveness.

et·leç Fleshy; obese, corpulent. ~ **lenmek**, *vi.* grow fat; put on weight. ~ **li**, (*cul.*) with meat; (*bio.*) fleshy, plump: ~ **bitki/gövdeler**, (*bot.*) cacti, succulents: ~ **butlu**, plump: ~ **meyve**, (*bot.*) fleshy fruits: ~ **ye sütlüye karışmamak**, not interfere in matters that don't concern one. ~ **lik**, (*live.*) being fattened up; (*dom.*) meat-safe; meat-store.

etm. = ETMEK.

etme *vn.* = ETMEK. ~ **bulma dünyası**, one gets one's deserts: ~ **yahu!**, *int.* is it really so?

etmek (eder, ediyor, edecek, *etc.*) *vt.* [154] Do; make; cost, be worth; fetch (a price): (+*neg. adv.*) live, exist, manage: (-i), reach, find: (-den), do without; deprive of: (-e), do to; make; (*child.*) relieve o.s. *As aux. v. it is used with adjectives and nouns, combining with monosyllables* [BERBAT ETM., ZANNETMEK].

eden bulur, one pays for what one does: **etmediğini bırakmamak**, do as much evil/harm as possible; leave no stone unturned: **ettiği fenalık ayağına dolaştı**, he paid for his mistakes; his misdeeds were visited upon him: **ettiği hayır ürküttüğü kurbağaya değmez,** he does more harm than good: **ettiği ile kalmak,** be left only with the shame (of one's evil actions): **ettiğini bulmak/çekmek,** get one's deserts: **ettiğini yanına bırakmamak,** pay for one's evil deeds.

etmen Agent; doer; (*math.*) factor.

et·nik Ethnic. ~**nograf,** ethnographer. ~**nografik,** ethnographical. ~**nografya,** ethnography. ~**nolog,** ethnologist. ~**noloji(k),** ethnolo·gy/(-gical).

etobur (*zoo.*) Carnivorous, meat-eating. ~ **dişi,** (*bio.*) molar tooth, tusk: ~**lar,** (*zoo.*) carnivores. ~**luk,** being a meat-eater.

etolü (*mod.*) Stole.

etraf *pl.* = TARAF. Sides; ends; directions; regions; surroundings; environment; the world around; relatives; details; circumstances. ~ +, *a.* Surrounding, ambient: ~ **ahalisi,** the people of the district: ~**a atmak,** cast about: ~**a haber vermek,** give general/public notice: ~**ı çevrilmiş,** enclosed, confined: ~**ına (-in),** (movement) around . . .: ~**ına toplanmak,** gather around: ~**ında (-in),** *post.* [91] around . . .; about, concerning: ~**ında çırpınmak,** dance attendance on: ~**ında dört/fır dönmek,** dance attendance on s.o., hover around s.o.: ~**ını almak (-in),** surround: ~**ını çizmek,** circumscribe: ~**ını dönmek,** circle stg.: ~**ını kuşatmak,** (*mil.*) besiege, blockade: ~**ıyla,** in all its detail: ~**ta,** in the neighbourhood, around: ~**tan,** from all around; from all directions. ~**lı,** detailed, comprehensive; long-winded. ~**lıca,** fully, with all details.

et·sineğini (*ent.*) Grey flesh-fly. ~**siz,** meatless; without flesh; thin: ~ **cansız,** all skin and bone. ~**şeftalisi**ni, (*bot.*) clingstone peach.

ettir·gen (*ling.*) Causative: ~ **çatı,** causative voice/ structure: ~ **eylem,** causative verb. ~**genlik,** causation. ~**mek (-i, -e),** *vc.* = ETMEK; cause to do; get/have stg. done.

ettopraık**ğı** (*geol.*) Soft, red fertile soil.

etüıt**dü** (*art.*) Study, design; (*ed.*) inquiry, investigation, survey, research; (*ed.*) study-room//-time. ~ **etm.,** study; investigate, research.

etüv Stove, oven; sterilizer.

etvar (*obs.*) Manners, attitudes.

etyaran (*bio.*) Deep-seated whitlow/felon.

Eu. (*ch.s.*) = EVROPİYUM.

E·U = ERKÂNİ HARBİYEİ UMUMİYE. ~**Ü** = EGE ÜNİVERSİTESİ

eV = ELEKTRON-VOLT.

ev House; dwelling; home, household; family; (*adm.*) compartment, pigeon-hole. ~ +, *a.* Domestic; home-; household; family: ~ **açmak,** set up house: ~ **adamı,** family man: ~ **alma komşu al,** study the neighbours when buying a house: ~ **aşırı,** next door but one: ~ **bark,** house and family: ~ **bark sahibi,** a family man: ~ **basmak,** (*leg.*) raid a house: ~ **bekçiliği etm.,** have to stay at home: ~ **bozmak,** be divorced/separated: ~ **çıt kuşu,** (*orn.*) house wren: ~ **çıyanı,** (*zoo.*) scutiger: ~ **ekmeği,** (*cul.*) home-made bread: ~ **ekonomisi,** domestic economy: ~ **eşyası,** household effects: ~ **halkı,** household (family and servants): ~ **gailesi,**

domestic worries: ~ **hayatı,** domestic life domesticity: ~ **hayvanı,** domestic animal: ~ **içi** interior; indoors: ~ **işi,** housework; (*ed.*) homework: ~ **işletmek,** operate a brothel: ~ **kadını** housewife; houseproud woman: ~ **kemesi,** (*zoo.* black/ship rat: ~ **kızılkuyruğu,** (*orn.*) black redstart: ~ **kira/parası,** (*fin.*) rent: ~ **ocak kurmak** set up house: ~ **ödevi,** (*ed.*) homework: ~ **reisi** head of the family: ~ **sahibi,** master/mistress of the house; householder; proprietor of the house, landlord: ~ **sırası,** (*arch.*) terrace: ~ **sineği,** (*ent.* house-fly: ~ **süngeri,** (*myc.*) dry rot: ~ **takım** (*sp.*) home-team: ~ **takımı,** household: ~ **tutmak** rent a house: ~ **yapıcı,** bringing domestic happiness: ~ **yapımı,** home industry: ~ **yemeği** home-cooked/-made food: ~ **yıkmak,** bring ruin to a home; sow domestic discord, break up a home.

ev-: ~**de kalmak,** (girl) be on the shelf: ~**de ol(ma)mak,** (not) be at home: ~**deki hesap/pazar çarşıya uymaz,** things don't work out as one calculates; don't count your chickens before they are hatched: ~**den çıkmak,** leave a house (for good): ~**i sırtında,** a homeless wanderer: ~**in yıkılası!,** may your house be destroyed!: ~**ine doğru,** homeward bound: ~**ini başına geçiririm,** (*threat*) I'll bring the house down about his ears: ~**inin kadını olm.,** be a good housewife ~**lerden ırak/~lere şenlik!,** may Heaven save you from such a disaster! (as is talked of): ~**lerini iki-/üç·ledi,** he has bought a second/third house.

ev. = EVCİL.

-ev/-v *n. suf.* [226] *Forming deverbal nouns* [GÖREV; SINAV].

evaporatör (*phys.*) Evaporator.

evaze (*ind.*) Bell-mouthed; (*mod.*) flared.

ev·baş The lower classes, rabble. ~**ce(k),** all the family (together). ~**ci,** (*ed.*) weekly boarder; (*mil.*) soldier living out of barracks: ~ **çıkmak,** (*ed.*) come home for the weekend. ~**cik,** little house; (*bio.*) protective sheath. ~**cil,** (*live.*) domestic(ated), tame: ~ **serçe,** (*orn.*) house sparrow: ~ **tavuk,** (*orn.*) hen. ~**cilik,** ~ **oyunu,** (*child.*) playing at families. ~**cilleşmek,** *vi.* (*live.*) become domesticated/tame. ~**cilleştirmek (-i),** domesticate, tame. ~**cimen,** home-lover; domesticated; thrifty. ~**deş,** fellow-inhabitant of the house.

evıc**ci** Acme; (*ast.*) apogee; summit.

evdemonizm (*phil.*) Eudemonism.

ev·dirmek, ~**ecen,** ~**edi** = iv-.

eveğen (*med.*) Acute (illness).

evelemek ~ **gevelemek,** half mumble one's words.

evermek (-i) Give in marriage, marry off.

eveti Yes. ~ **efendim!,** yes!, certainly! ~ **efendimci,** yes-man. ~**çe,** permit. ~**leme,** affirmation. ~**lemek,** *vi.* say/keep saying 'yes'; affirm. ~**leyici,** affirmative.

evgin Hurried; urgent; in a hurry. ~**lik,** urgency; haste.

evham *pl.* = VEHİM. (*psy.*) Apprehensions, doubts; illusions; hypochondria. ~ **getirmek/~lanmak,** *vi.* become a hypochondriac, have a nervous breakdown. ~**lı**, full of false apprehensions, hypochondriac.

evi¹çᶜⁱ (*Or. mus.*) A compound melody.

vin Essence; (*bio.*) marrow; (*bot.*) kernel, grain (of corn). ~**li**, full, ripe. ~**siz**, empty, hollow.

virgen Knowledgeable; well-versed; practical.

evir·im (*cin.*) Version. ~**me**, *vn.*; (*phil.*) conversion. ~**mek (-i)**, change, convert; rotate; turn inside out: ~ **çevirmek**, turn stg. over and over; look about one in hesitation; explain in the wrong way: **evire çevire**, thoroughly, soundly. ~**melik**, (*math.*) circle; (*adm.*) office. ~**tik**, (*chem.*) converted. ~**tim**, (*chem.*) conversion; (*math.*) inversion. ~**tmek (-i)**, (*chem.*) convert; (*math.*) invert.

evkaf *pl.* = VAKIF. (*rel.*) Pious foundations; estates in mortmain; (*adm.*) department controlling such estates.

evla Most suitable; best; **(-den)**, better (than).

ev·ladiyelik Heirloom; stg. that will last for years. ~**la¹t**ᵈ¹, *pl.* = VELET; children, descendants; *s.* child, son: ~ **acısı**, grief for the loss of a child: ~ **ını dövmeyen** . . . = KIZINI: ~ **ının mürüvvetini görmek**, see one's child grow up and get married: ~**ü ıyal**, wife and children, family. ~**latlık**, (*leg.*) adopted child; foster-child (often a girl working as a servant): ~**a kabul etm.**, adopt. ~**latsız(lık)**, childless(ness).

evle¹kᵍⁱ (*agr.*) Furrow; quarter of a DÖNÜM (230m²); ditch draining a field.

evlen·dirilmek (-le) Be married off to s.o. ~**dirme**, *vn.* marriage: ~ **memuru**, (*adm.*) registrar. ~**dirmek (-i)**, marry s.o. off, give in marriage. ~**me**, wedding, marriage: ~ **akti**, marriage vow: ~ **cüzdanı**, marriage certificate: ~ **dairesi**, (*adm.*) registry office (for civil marriages): ~ **mukavelenamesi**, marriage contract: ~ **tellalı**, marriage broker/go-between: ~ **vaadi**, engagement. ~**mek (-le)**, marry s.o.; espouse stg.: ~ **barklanmak**, marry and set up house.

evleviyetⁱ Preference. ~**le**, all the more, so much the sooner, *a fortiori*.

ev·li Married; having . . . houses: ~ **barklı**, married and having a family: ~ **evine köylü köyüne dağıldı**, everyone dispersed and went home: ~ **kadın**, married woman. ~**lik**, domestic. ~**lilik**, being married, conjugality: ~ **birliğinin sıyaneti**, preservation of marital unity: ~ **dışı birleşmeler**, extramarital unions: ~ **içi**, marital: ~ **iptali davası**, (*leg.*) suit for nullity.

evliya *pl.* = VELİ. Guardians; relatives; saints. *sing.* Saint. ~ **devesi**, (*zoo.*) woodlouse: ~ **gibi**, pious, saintly. ~**lık**, *n.* saintliness: *a.* innocent. ~**otu**ⁿᵘ, (*bot.*) sainfoin.

evmek = İVMEK.

evolü·syon (*bio.*) Evolution. ~**t**, evolute.

evrak¹ *pl.* = VARAK. Leaves; (*adm.*) documents, papers, archives. ~ **çantası**, attaché-/brief-case: ~ **hazinesi**, archives: ~ **kutusu**, deed-box: ~ **memuru**, archivist.

evra¹tᵈ¹ (*rel.*) Scriptures recited at specific times. ~ **çekmek**, recite these verses.

evre Stage, phase.

evren *n.* Universe; surroundings; (*ast.*) firma-

ment, cosmos; time; (*bot.*) kingdom; monster. ~ +, *a.* Universal, cosmic: ~ **gemici(liğ)i**, cosmonaut(ics): ~ **ışını**, (*phys.*) cosmic rays.

evren·bilim(sel) Cosmolo·gy/(-gical). ~ **değer**, (*math.*) parameter. ~ **deş**, cosmopolitan. ~ **doğum**, cosmogony. ~ **doğumsal**, cosmogonical. ~ **pulu**ⁿᵘ, (*geol.*) mica. ~ **sel**, universal; cosmic. ~ **sellik**, universality.

evri·k (*phil.*) Inverted; inverse; converse. ~ **lir**, (*phil.*) convertible; (*cin.*) reversible. ~ **lme**, *vn.*; inversion. ~ **lmek**, *vp.* be transformed. ~ **şik**, converse.

evrim Development; (*bio.*) evolution; transformation. ~ **kuramı**, (*bio.*) theory of evolution. ~**ci(lik)**, (*phil.*) evolution·ist/(-ism). ~ **-devrim**, evolution-revolution. ~ **sel**, evolutionary.

evropiyum (*chem.*) Europium.

evsaf *pl.* = VASIF. Qualities; characteristics; qualifications; specification. ~ **ını bozmak**, (*chem.*) denature.

evsemek *vi.* Be homesick; feel nostalgia.

evsin (Hunter's) hide; (watchman's) hut.

evvel *a.* First; former; foremost; initial. *n.* The first part; beginning; antecedent. *post.* [89] Before. *adv.* [203] Before; first; ago; formerly. ~ **Allah**, with God's help: ~ **Allah, sonra** . . ., firstly God, then . . .: ~ **Allah sonra sayenizde** . . ., it is solely due to you (after God) . . .: ~ **davranmak (-den)**, anticipate stg.: ~ **hesap sonra kasap**, count your money before you go shopping: ~ **selam//taam sonra kelam**, first greet//eat and then talk: ~ **ve ahir**, formerly; on several occasions: ~ **ve ahirini bilirim**, I know him well; I know all about him: ~ **zaman**, in olden times; long ago: ~ **zaman içinde kalbur saman içinde** . . ., (*child. lit.*) once upon a time . . .: ~DEN: ~**e etkili**, (*leg.*) retrospective: ~**ine kadar**, [203] until: ~**leri**, in the past.

evvel·a *adv.* [196] Firstly; first of all: ~ **can sonra canan**, number one comes first; everyone considers his own interests first. ~**ce**, a little time before; previously; a little way in front. ~**den**, from former times; beforehand; previously: ~ **beri**, always. ~**emirde**, before anything else, first of all. ~**i**, *a.* the previous: *adv.* of old. ~**iyat**¹, origins; rudiments; first principles; preamble. ~**iyet**ⁱ, (*phil.*) primacy. ~**ki/**~**si**, [202] the previous, the one before: ~ **durumuna getirmek**, renovate: ~ **gün**, the previous day; the day before yesterday: ~ **yıl**, the previous year; the year before last. ~**lik**, antecedence.

ey *int.* O!; well!; hi!; eh! ~ **artık çok oluyorsun!**, that's enough of you!: ~ **gaziler, yol göründü!**, it's about time we were going!

ey- *Also* = EĞ-.

ey. = (*ling.*) EYLEM.

-ey/-ay *n./a. suf.* [226] *Forming deverbal nouns/adjectives* [DENEY; OLAY; DİKEY].

eyaletⁱ (*adm.*) Province; principality; Land (in Germany); State (in U.S.A.).

-eyazmak *aux. v. suf.* [191] = YAZMAK.

eyer Saddle. ~ **boşaltmak**, (*sp.*) (in CİRİT) lean out of the saddle: ~ **kaltağı**, saddletree: ~ **kapa(t)mak/ vurmak (-e)**, saddle (animal): ~ **kaşı**, pommel of

the saddle: ~**e de gelir semere de**, it will serve all purposes: ~**i boş kalmak**, (rider) die.
eyer·ci(lik) Saddler(y). ~**gagalı**, (*orn.*) saddlebill(ed). ~**lemek (-i)**, saddle. ~**lenmek**, *vp.* ~**letmek (-i, -e)**, *vc.* ~**li**, saddled. ~**siz**, saddleless; unsaddled; bareback.
eyi(ce) = iyi(CE).
eyitmek (*obs.*) Say.
eylem Action; activity; (*ling.*) verb. ~ **adamı**, man of action: ~ **çekim eki**, (*ling.*) verbal ending/ termination: ~ **çekimi**, conjugation of a verb: ~ **gövdesi**, verbal stem: ~ **kökü**, verbal root: ~ **tümcesi**, [239] verbal sentence: ~ **yeteneği**, ability to act: ~**de karşıt görünüm**, 'apparent opposite' [GELSEYDİ = GELMEDİ]: ~**den türeme ad**, [220] deverbal noun: ~**den türeme** ~, [143] deverbal verb: ~**e geçmek**, go into/take action.
eylem·ce (*mil.*) Operation. ~ **ci(lik)**, activ·ist/(-ism).
eylemek *aux. v.* [154] = ETMEK. Make, do; act, operate.
eylem·li Active; (*ed.*) full. ~**lik**, (*ling.*) infinitive. ~**lilik**, activeness. ~**sel**, active. ~**si**, (*ling.*) quasiverb. ~**siz**, passive; inert; (*ed.*) acting. ~**sizlik**, passiveness; inertia: ~ **kütlesi**, (*phys.*) inertial mass: ~ **momenti**, (*phys.*) moment of inertia.
eylülü September.
eytam *pl.* = YETİM. Orphans. ~ **maaşı**, orphan's allowance.
eytiş·im (*phil.*) Dialectic(s). ~**imsel**, dialectical: ~ **özdekçilik**, dialectical materialism. ~**mek**, *vi.* discuss.
eyvah *int.* Alas!, alack! ~ **çekmek**, sigh, moan.
eyvallah *int.* Yes, so be it!; goodbye!; thanks! ~ **demek**, accept, agree with: ~ **etmemek**, accept no one's favours: ~**ı olmamak**, be obliged to no one.
eyvan (*arch.*) Vaulted recess/antechamber.
eyyam *pl.* = YEVM. Days; (*met.*) favourable wind. ~ **ağa/efendisi**, time-server: ~ **reisi**, (*naut.*) fairweather sailor: ~ **görmüş/sürmüş**, that has seen better days: ~ **ola!**, (*naut.*) may the weather be kind to you! ~**cı(lık)**, opportun·ist/(-ism).
eza Vexation; torment. ~ **çekmek/görmek**, suffer.
ezan (*rel.*) Call to prayer by the MÜEZZİN. ~**i saat**, (*rel.*) the time reckoned from sunset.

ezber By heart. ~ **etm.**, learn by heart: ~ **okumak** recite from memory: ~**den**, by heart: ~**den çalmak** (*mus.*) play by ear: ~**e**, by heart, parrot-fashion ~**e bilmek**, know thoroughly: ~**e gitmek**, procee(blindly: ~**e iş görmek**, do stg. by rote/ignorantly ~**e konuşmak**, talk without understanding: ~**inde** in the mind, remembered.
ezber·ci S.o. who learns parrot-fashion/easily b heart. ~**cilik**, learning parrot-fashion. ~**leme** (-i), learn by heart; commit to memory. ~**lenmek** *vp.* ~**letmek (-i)**, *vc.*
ezcümle Chiefly; for instance, among other things
ezdir(t)mek (-i, -e), *vc.* = EZMEK.
ezel Eternity (in the past; = EBET). ~**den**, from eternity. ~**i**, eternal (no beginning); (*fig.*) old ~**iyet**ⁱ, eternity.
ezgi (*mus.*) Tune, melody; song. ~**sel**, melodic.
ez·gin Crushed; trampled on; oppressed. ~**ginlik** crushing; oppression; restlessness, upset; worry ~**ici**, crushing; (*fig.*) devastating: ~ **çoğunluk** (*adm.*) overwhelming majority. ~**ik**, crushed squashed: ~ **büzük**, (fruit) spoilt by crushing i transit. ~**iklik**, being crushed. ~**ilgen**, easil crushed (to powder). ~**ilmek**, *vp.* = EZMEK; b crushed/oppressed, etc.; feel a sinking sensation i the stomach: **ezile büzüle**, shamefacedly; humbly apologetically: **ezilip büzülmek**, be embarrassed.
ezim ~ ~ **ezmek**, crush thoroughly. ~**evi**ⁿ, (*agr.* seed-crushing mill.
ezin·ıççⁱ Suffering; pain. ~**mek** = EZİLMEK. ~**ti** weakness, faintness; breakdown.
eziyetⁱ Injury; ill-treatment; pain; vexation; torture ~ **çekmek**, suffer pain, etc.: ~ **etm.**, torment torture: ~ **vermek**, cause suffering, etc.
eziyet·çi(lik) (Work of) tormentor, torturer. ~**li** painful; vexatious, trying; tiring. ~**siz**, painless etc.
ezkaza By chance/hazard; accidentally.
ez·me *vn.* Crushing, etc.; (*min.*) peening; stg crushed; (*cul.*) purée; paste. ~**mek (-i)**, crush pound; peen; mash; triturate; bruise; (*fig.*) reduc(to poverty/impotence; defeat; (*sl.*) spend: **ez (ez) d** **suyunu iç**, it's totally useless.
Ezrail = AZRAİL.

F

F, f [fe] Seventh Tk. letter, F; seventh (in a class/ series). ~ **vitamini,** (*bio.*) vitamin F.

F, f. = (*mus.*) FA; FAHRENHAYT; (*ed.*) FAKÜLTE; (*bio.*) FAMİLYA; (*el.*) FARAD; (*adm.*) FEDERAL; FEDERE; (*pub.*) FIKRA; (*ling.*) FİİL; FİL (chess); FİYAT; (*ch.s.*) FLÜOR; FRANSA; FRANSIZ; FRANSIZCA[DAN]; (*rad.*) FREKANS.

fa (*mus.*) ~ **notası,** fah, F.

faal[i] Active; energetic, brisk; busy, industrious. ~ **idare,** (*adm.*) executive: ~ **(olmayan) ortak,** (*fin.*) active/(sleeping) partner: ~ **üye,** active member; (*ind.*) executive. ~ **iyet**[i], activity; energy; business, industry: ~ **raporu,** (*fin.*) director's report: ~ **sahası,** field of activity/business; arena: ~ **e geçmek,** go into action, begin to operate.

faanahtarı[n1] (*mus.*) Bass clef.

fabrika Factory, works, mill, plant. ~ +, *a.* Factory; industrial: ~ **fiyatı,** ex-works price: ~ **işi,** machine-made goods: ~ **markası,** trade-mark: ~ **masrafları,** (*fin.*) production overheads: ~ **da teslim,** ex-works.

fabrika-cı Manufacturer; mill-owner. ~ **cılık,** factory management. ~ **syon,** manufacture. ~ **tör,** manufacturer; builder. ~ **törlük,** manufacturing, production.

facia Tragedy; drama; calamity, catastrophe, disaster. ~ **lı,** tragic; terrible; catastrophic, disastrous.

faça (*naut.*) Going about; (*fig.*) volte-face; (*gamb.*) bottom card of the pack; (*sl.*) face. ~ **sını almak,** (*sl.*) disconcert, shame.

façeta Facet (of a diamond).

façuna (*naut.*) Serving/whipping (of a rope).

fagosit[i] (*bio.*) Phagocyte. ~ **oz,** phagocytosis.

fagot[u] (*mus.*) Bassoon. ~ **çu,** bassoonist.

fağfur (*his.*) Emperor of China; (*art.*) porcelain.

fah·ir[ri] Glory; pride; excellence. ~ **i âlem,** the Prophet Muhammad.

fahiş Immoral, obscene; excessive. ~ **fiyat//kâr,** (*fin.*) exorbitant price//profit. ~ **e,** harlot, courtesan, prostitute. ~ **elik,** prostitution.

fah·iz[zi] (*bio.*) Thigh.

fahrenhayt[i] (*phys.*) Fahrenheit. ~ **derece/kertesi,** degree F.

fah·ri Honorary, unpaid: ~ **doktorluk,** honorary doctorate: ~ **konsolos,** (*adm.*) honorary consul. ~ **riye,** (*lit.*) verse(s) praising the poet himself. ~ **riyyen,** as a volunteer. ~ **ur,** boasting, self-glorifying; = FERİH.

faide = FAYDA.

faik[i] Superior; preferable; excellent. ~ **gelmek,** overcome. ~ **iyet**[i], superiority; excellence.

fail[i] *n.* Who does/acts; author; agent; maker; (*ling.*)

---

subject. *a.* Efficient; (*bio.*) effective. ~ **i muhtar,** (*leg.*) free agent.

faiz (*fin.*) Interest. ~ **fiyat/oranı,** interest rate: ~ **getirmek,** earn interest: ~ **e vermek,** lend at interest: ~ **e yatırmak,** invest at interest: ~ **i işlemek,** bear interest: ~ **ini ödemek,** service a debt.

faiz·ci Usurer, moneylender. ~ **cilik,** usury, money-lending. ~ **lenmek,** *vi.* bear interest. ~ **li,** at/with interest. ~ **siz,** free of interest.

fak[1] ~ **a basmak,** (*sl.*) make a false step; be deceived. ~ **a bastırmak,** deceive, trick.

Fak. = FAKÜLTE.

fakat[1] [210] But; only; exclusively. ~ **ı makatı yok!,** but me no buts!

fakfon (*min.*) German silver.

fak·ır[ri] Poverty; destitution; need.

fakih Muslim jurist; learned.

fakir *a.* Poor. *n.* Pauper; 'your humble servant'; (*rel.*) Indian beggar, fakir. ~ **eczanesi,** (*med.*) dispensary: ~ **mahlut,** (*aer.*) weak mixture.

fakir·ane Poor, humble. ~ **hane,** old people's home; 'the poor man's house' = my house. ~ **izm,** (*rel.*) fakirism. ~ **leşmek,** *vi.* become poor. ~ **leştirmek** (-i), make poor, ruin. ~ **lik,** poverty.

fak·simile (*pub.*) Facsimile, copy. ~ **tör,** factor. ~ **ül,** (*ast.*) sun-spot, facula. ~ **ültatif,** optional.

fakülte (*ed.*) Faculty. ~ **başkanı,** dean: ~ **mezunu,** bachelor. ~ **li,** faculty student.

fal Omen, augury; fortune; (*pub.*) horoscope. ~ **açıcı,** soothsayer, fortune-teller: ~ **açmak/~a bakmak,** tell s.o.'s fortune: ~ **atmak,** cast lots: ~ **tutmak,** take an omen; draw a lot.

falaka Board to which the feet of the bastinado victim were tied; (*agr.*) swingletree. ~ **ya çekmek/ yatırmak,** bastinado s.o.

falan [77] So and so; such and such; and so on, or thereabouts; approximately. ~ **festekiz/feşmekân,** this that and the other: ~ **fıstık,** this and that; and so forth: ~ **filan,** and so on and so forth. ~ **ca,** so and so; s.o. or other. ~ **ıncı,** [82] numbered so-and-so, the 'so manyeth'.

falarop[u] (*orn.*) Phalarope.

falcı(lık) Fortune-tell·er/(-ing), soothsay·er/(-ing).

falçete Curved shoemaker's knife.

falez (*geo.*) Cliff.

falıhay·ır[ri] Good omen.

Fallop ~ **borusu,** (*bio.*) Fallopean tube.

falso (*mus.*) False note; (*naut.*) jury; (*fig.*) error, blunder. ~ **vermek/yapmak,** make a slip; fall into error. ~ **lu,** unharmonious; erroneous; false: ~ **vuruş,** (*sp.*) feint.

faltaşı[n1] Pebble, *etc.* used for telling fortunes. ~ **gibi,** (eyes) wide open.

falya (*mil.*) Touch-hole (of muzzle-loading gun). ~ çivilemek/tıkamak, spike a gun.

falyanos (*zoo.*) Whale; large dolphin.

familya (*bio.*) Family; (*soc.*) family; (*col.*) wife.

fan (*cin.*, *sp.*) Fan. ~ atik, fanatic. ~ atizm, fanaticism.

fanfan (*col.*) Unintelligible speech. ~ böceği, (*ent.*) bombardier beetle.

fanfar (*mus.*) Brass instruments; fanfare.

fanfin Foreign-sounding talk. ~ etm., talk gibberish.

fani Transitory, fleeting; decaying; mortal. ~ lik, being transitory/perishable.

fanila (*tex.*) Flannel; (*mod.*) knitted vest; blanket.

fan·klab¹/ ~ klü¹pbü (*sp.*) Fan-club.

fanta (*orn.*) Blue tit.

fan·tasma (*psy.*) Phantasm. ~ tastik, fantastic. ~ taziye, fantasy. ~ tezi, *n.* fancy, whim; fantasy; (*fin.*) fancy goods; (*mus.*) fantasia: *a.* fancy; extravagant: ~ eşya dükkânı, milliner's shop: ~ süs, fancy work.

fanti (*gamb.*) Knave, jack.

fanus Lantern; glass cover; (*chem.*) bell-jar.

fanya Wide-meshed fishing-net.

FAO = (*Food and Agriculture Organization*).

far (*mot.*) Headlamp; (*el.*) projector, beacon; (*mod.*) eye-liner/-shadow; (*sl.*) breast.

Far. = FARS; FARSÇA(DAN).

farad (*el.*) Farad.

faraş Dust-pan. ~ gibi/kadar, big(-mouthed).

faraz·a Hypothetically; supposing that, for argument's sake. ~ i, hypothetical; imaginary; assumed. ~ iyat¹, *pl.* hypotheses. ~ iye, hypothesis, assumption.

farba(la) (*mod.*) Flounce; fringe. ~ lı, frilled.

fare (*zoo.*) Mouse; rat. ~ deliğe sığmamış bir de kuyruğuna kabak bağlamış, (*describes*) an additional complication to a difficult situation; a guest who brings an uninvited friend with him: ~ deliği, mouse-hole; hiding-place: ~ düşse başı yarılır, an empty/deserted place: ~ kapanı, mouse-trap: ~ kuyruğu eğe//testere, (*carp.*) taper-file// keyhole-saw: ~ ler cirit oynuyor, (*describes*) a deserted place.

fare·başlı ~ iskorpit (*ich.*) Short-spined sea-scorpion. ~ kulağı¹¹, (*bot.*) mouse-ear hawkweed; (?) chickweed. ~ kulaklı, ~ yarasa, (*zoo.*) mouse-eared bat. ~ kuşugiller, (*orn.*) mouse-birds, colies. ~ otunu, (*bot.*) (?) castor-oil plant. ~ tifüsünü, (*med.*) murine/rat typhus.

faren·jit¹ (*med.*) Pharyngitis. ~ ks, (*bio.*) pharynx.

farfara Noisy, boasting. ~ cı, braggart; windbag. ~ lik, boasting.

farımak Grow old; become weak; wear out.

fariğ (*leg.*) Assignor, transferor; free from work, at leisure; exempt from. ~ olm., cede, renounce, transfer; cease from work.

farika Characteristic; distinguishing mark.

faril Goat's-hair rope used in fishing-nets.

farinks (*bio.*) Pharynx.

Faris (*geo.*) Fars; Persia. ~ i, (*ling.*) = FARSÇA.

fariza Religious duty; binding obligation.

fark¹ Difference, distinction; divergence; differen-

tial; discrepancy; discrimination. ~ etm. (-i), *vt.* distinguish, differentiate, discern; notice, perceive, detect; differ; alter: ~ etmez, it makes no difference; it's unimportant: ~ gözetmeden, without distinction: ~ gözetmek, discriminate; differentiate; treat differently: ~ olunmak, be differentiated; be agreed: ~ ölçeği, (*el.*) potentiometer: ~ ına varmak, become aware of, perceive; realize, understand: ~ ında olm., be aware of, know about; not overlook.

fark·lı Different, diverse; dissimilar; changed; better; (*math.*, *phys.*) differential: ~ farksız, hardly distinguishable: ~ tutmak, discriminate. ~ lıca, slightly changed; (*med.*) improved. ~ lılaşma, differentiation. ~ lılaşmak, *vi.* change, become different. ~ lılık, disparity. ~ sız, indistinguishable; without difference; equal. ~ sızlık, resemblance; equality.

farma·kolog/ ~ kolojist Pharmacologist. ~ koloji, pharmacology. ~ kope, pharmacopoeia. ~ sötik, pharmaceutical.

farmason Freemason; (*col.*) atheist.

fars¹ *n.* (*th.*) Farce, comedy.

Fars² *n.* (*ethn.*) People of SW Iran. ~ ça, (*ling.*) Persian, Farsi.

fart ~ furt, (*col.*) talking nonsense.

farta ~ furta, bragging; empty threats.

farz (*rel.*) Religious precept; binding duty; (*fig.*) hypothesis, conjecture, supposition. ~ etm., suppose, assume: ~ olm., be necessary; be a 'must'. ~ ımuhali, supposing the impossible; in the improbable event of.

Fas (*geo.*) Morocco; Fez. ~ +, *a.* Moorish; (*art.*) Moresque.

FAS = (*free alongside ship*).

fasa ~ fiso, (*sl.*) unimportant. ~ rya, (*sl.*) nonsense.

fa·sad (*arch.*) Façade. ~ set(a), (*min.*) facet, bezel.

fas¹ıl¹¹ Subdivision; chapter; section; (*Or. mus.*) performance; work. ~ heyeti, (*Or. mus.*) orchestra: ~ ı kapatmak, close the subject.

fasıla Separation; interval; break; interruption. ~ vermek, interrupt. ~ lı, with intervals/interruptions; intermittent, periodic; (*ind.*) part-time. ~ sız, uninterrupted, continuous.

fasih Correct, distinct (speech); eloquent.

fasikül (*pub.*) Fascic(u)le; part.

fasile (*bot.*) Family, order; classification.

fasit Vicious; perverse; false; mischievous, trouble-making. ~ daire, (*phil.*) vicious circle: ~ olm., (religious duties, etc.) be invalidated/spoilt. ~ lik, viciousness.

fasiyes (*geol.*) Facies.

faska Swaddling-band.

fasl- = FASIL. ~ letmekeder, settle.

fasla ~ ~, in places.

Faslı (*ethn.*) Moroccan, Morisco.

fason (*mod.*) Cut, style. ~ e, (*tex.*) striped woollen cloth.

fasulye (*bot.*) Bean; French/kidney bean. ~ böceği, (*ent.*) bean weevil: ~ gibi kendini nimetten saymak, think o.s. very important: ~ mi dedin?, (*jok.*) what nonsense!: ~ piyazı, (*cul.*) boiled bean salad with onions, eggs, etc.: ~ plakisi, (*cul.*) cold white bean stew in olive oil: ~ **sırığı (gibi)**, (as thin as a) bean pole.

faş Divulged; commonly talked about. ~ **etm.**, divulge; betray/reveal (a secret).

faşır (*ech.*) ~ ~, (water) splashing, rushing. ~ **tı**, splashing noise.

faş·ist[i] (*pol.*) Fascist. ~ **istlik/** ~ **izm**, Fascism. ~ **izan**, pro-Fascist.

fatal·ist Fatalist. ~ **izm**, fatalism.

fatih Conqueror; *pr. n.* Sultan Mehmet II. ~ **a**, (*rel.*) opening chapter of the Koran: ~ **demek (-e)**, 'say goodbye' to s.o./stg.: give up as lost: ~ **okumak (-e)**, recite this chapter; pray for s.o.'s soul; give up as lost.

fatin (*obs.*) Intelligent. ~ **Efendi/Hoca**, *pr.n.* former head of Kandilli Observatory; (*col.*) weather prophet.

fatura (*fin.*) Invoice; book of samples; (*carp.*) rabbet. ~ **lamak (-i)**, invoice stg.

fauna (*zoo.*) Fauna.

fava (*cul.*) Mashed broad beans (eaten cold).

favl (*sp.*) Foul.

favori *n.* (*mod.*) Whiskers, sideburns; (*sp.*) favourite. *a.* Favourite, preferred.

fay (*geol.*) Fault. ~ **ans**, (*art.*) faience, porcelain.

fayda Use; profit; gain; advantage. ~ **çıkarmak**, turn to advantage: ~ **etm./vermek**, be useful; serve a purpose: ~ **yok**, it's no use; there's nothing to be done: ~ **sı dokunur (-in)**, it's useful/profitable: ~ **sı olm.**, have an effect; be useful.

fayda·cıl(ık) (*phil.*) Utilitarian(ism). ~ **lanma**, *vn.* gain, advantage; utility. ~ **lanmak (-den)**, derive a profit from; profit by; make use of; take advantage of. ~ **lı**, useful; effective; profitable; advantageous; beneficial: ~ **yük**, (*mot.*) useful load. ~ **lılık**, use/ (-fulness), profitability. ~ **sız**, useless, unprofitable; in vain. ~ **sızlık**, uselessness.

faylanma (*geol.*) Faulting.

fayrap (*naut.*) Fire up! ~ **etm.**, stoke up; (*fig.*) get to work quickly on stg.; (*sl.*) open; remove.

fayton Phaeton, carriage; (*orn.*) tropic-bird. ~ **cu/** (-**luk**), (work of) phaeton-driver.

fayvoklok[u] (*cul.*, *soc.*) Afternoon-tea.

faz (*el.*) Phase.

faz·ıl *a.* Virtuous; eminent; learned. ~ **ilet**[i], merit; excellence; superiority. ~ **iletli**, virtuous, excellent. ~ **iletsiz**, vicious; mean.

fazla Excessive; excess, superfluous, too much; very much; beside; more than; further; over-; super-; additional. ~ **akım/cereyan**, (*el.*) overload: ~ **çalışma**, (*ind.*) overtime: ~ **gelmek/gitmek/kaçmak**, be too much; overdo: ~ **hız düzeni**, (*mot.*) over-drive: ~ **kaçırmak**, eat/drink excessively/more than usual; pour out more than intended: ~ **kurcalama**, let well alone: ~ **mal göz çıkarmaz**, you can't have too much of a good thing: ~ **olm.**, be excessive: ~ **olarak**, moreover, furthermore: ~ **söze ne hacet?**, enough said!: ~ **üsteleme!**, don't insist/press the matter!: ~ **viraj almak**, (*sl.*) tell many lies: ~ **yağlı**, (*chem.*) superfatted: ~ **dan**, plenty, heaps of: ~ **sı (-in)**, excess of: ~ **sıyla kâfi**, more than enough.

fazla·ca Excessively. ~ **laşmak**, *vi.* increase.

~ **lık**, plenty; excess: ~ **etm.**, be too much/ unnecessary.

faz·lı (*el.*) In . . . phase. ~ **metre**, phase-meter.

Fb. = FABRİKA.

FB = FENERBAHÇE (SPOR KLÜBÜ). ~ **I** = (*Federal Bureau of Investigation*).

fe The Tk. letter F, f.

Fe. = (*ch.s.*) DEMİR.

fec·aat[i] Calamity, tragedy. ~ **i**, painful; tragic; disastrous. ~ **ia** = FACİA.

fec·lir[ri] Dawn. ~ +, *a.* Crepuscular. ~ **ikâzip**, false dawn. ~ **isadık**, true dawn.

feda Sacrifice. ~ **etm.**, sacrifice: ~ **olm.**, be sacrificed: ~ **olsun!**, I'll gladly make this sacrifice!

feda·i Who sacrifices himself for a cause; (*pol.*) patriot; revolutionary: ~ **ler**, fedayeen; commandos. ~ **ilik**, self-sacrifice; devotion. ~ **kâr**, self-sacrificing; self-denying; devoted. ~ **kârlık**, self-sacrifice; abnegation; devotion: ~ **a katlanmak**, suffer for a cause.

feder (*aer.*) Feathering.

feder·al(izm) (*pol.*) Federal(ism). ~ **asyon**, federation. ~ **atif**, federated. ~ **e**, federated.

feding (*rad.*) Fading (effect).

fehamet·li/-lû (*his.*) His Excellency/Highness.

fehva Import, meaning. ~ **sınca**, as the saying goes; with the meaning of . . . .

fek[ki] Dislocation; breaking; removal; separation.

fekül (*chem.*) Fecula.

fel. = FELSEFE.

felah Prosperity; security; deliverance. ~ **bulmak**, be relieved/saved: ~ **bulmaz**, hopeless (drunkard, etc.).

felaket[i] Disaster, calamity, catastrophe; adversity. ~ **li**, disastrous, catastrophic. ~ **zede**, disaster victim.

fel·lç[ci] (*med.*) Apoplexy; paralysis. ~ **nöbeti**, apoplectic fit: ~ **olm.**, be paralysed: (*fig.*) (traffic) come to a halt: ~ **e uğramak**, have a stroke; (*fig.*) grind to a halt, be paralysed. ~ **li**, paralysed.

feldispat[i] (*geol.*) Feldspar. ~ **sı**, feldspathoid.

feldmareşal[i] (*mil.*) Field-marshal.

fele·lk[ği] (*ast.*) The firmament; the heavens; (*fig.*) fortune, destiny. ~ **bunu da çok gördü**, fate has denied me this too: ~ **kimine kavun yedirir kimine kelek**, fate treats us all differently: ~ **in çemberinden geçmiş**, who has suffered the ups and downs of fortune; who has seen life: ~ **in sillesine uğramak/ sillesini yemek**, suffer the buffetings of fate: ~ **ten bir gün aşırmak/çalmak**, pass a very enjoyable day: ~ **ten kâm almak**, have a very good time.

felek·i Astronomical; celestial. ~ **iyat**[ı], astronomy. ~ **zede**, unlucky, unfortunate.

Felemenk[i] Holland. ~ +, *a.* Dutch, Flemish. ~ **çe**, (*ling.*) Dutch. ~ **li**, (*ethn.*) Dutch(man). ~ **taşı**[nı], (*min.*) rose diamond.

felenk = FİLENK.

felfelek (*bot.*) Betel-nut; (*ent.*) a small butterfly.

felfellemek *vi.* (Bird) drop from tiredness; (top) stop spinning.

fellah Egyptian peasant; (*fig.*) Negro.

fellek/fellik ~ ~, running confusedly in all directions: ~ ~ **aramak**, search high and low.

felse·fe Philosophy: ~ **mantığı**, philosophical logic. ~ **feci**, philosopher. ~ **fi**, philosophical.
femin·ist[i] Feminist. ~ **izm**, feminism.
fen[ni] Science; branch of science; technology; engineering. ~ +, *a*. Scientific, technical: ~ **adamı**, scientist: ~ **bilgisi**, technology: ~ **subayı**, (*mil.*) engineer.
fena[1] *a*. Bad; poor; ill; awkward; unpleasant. *n*. Bad thing. ~ **bakmak**, glare angrily: ~ **değil/sayılmaz**, not bad, fairly good: ~ **etm.**, *vi*. behave badly, do harm: ~ **etm. (-i)**, upset s.o.: ~ **gözle bakmak**, look daggers at: ~ **halde**, badly, unpleasantly; (very) much, excessively: ~ **kalpli**, wicked, evil: ~ **koku**, stink, stench: ~ **kontakt**, (*el.*) poor contact: ~ **kullanmak**, maltreat, misuse: ~ **olm.**, feel bad/ill; feel like fainting; be very worried: ~ **yerine vurmak**, strike in a dangerous place: ~ **sına gitmek**, upset/exasperate s.o.: ~ **ya çekmek**, take stg. in a bad sense: ~ **ya sarmak**, take a turn for the worse: ~ **ya varmak**, turn out badly.
fena[2] *n*. Death, dissolution, extinction. ~ **bulmak**, come to an end; die (out); become extinct.
fena·laşmak *vi*. Become worse; deteriorate; be aggravated; go bad. ~ **laştırmak (-i)**, make worse, aggravate. ~ **lık**, evil; bad action; injury: ~ **etm.**, do harm/evil; behave badly: ~ **geçirmek/gelmek**, (*med.*) faint; feel ill.
fenci Scientist; science-teacher.
fener Lantern; street-lamp; (*naut.*) lighthouse; signal-lamp; (*eng.*) pinion (of shaft); *pr.n.* (*his.*) Greek quarter of Istanbul, Phanar. ~ **alayı**, torch-light procession: ~ **(askı)**, (*dom.*) coffee-tray (with handle on top): ~ **bekçisi**, lighthouse-keeper: ~ **çekmek**, light the way with a lantern, etc.; (*fig.*) lead the crowd: ~ **çiçeği**, (*bot.*) red-hot-poker: ~ **direği**, lamp-post: ~ **duba/gemisi**, (*naut.*) light-ship: ~ **gövdesi**, (*eng.*) headstock (of lathe): ~ **kasnak**, cone-pulley: ~ **mili**, spindle (of lathe); mandrel: ~ **punta**, live centre (of lathe): ~ **şamandırası**, (*naut.*) beacon buoy: ~ **i nerede söndürdün?**, (*jok.*) where have you been so late?: ~ **siz yakalanmak**, be caught in an awkward situation.
fener·balığı[nı] (*ich.*) All-mouth angler-fish, monk-fish; lantern-fish. ~ **böceği**[ni], (*ent.*) (?) glow-worm. ~ **ci**, lantern-maker/-seller; lighthouse-keeper; lamp-lighter. ~ **li**, having a lantern; *pr.n.* (*his.*) Phanariot (member of old Greek aristocracy); (*sp.*) member of FENERBAHÇE Sports Club. ~ **sineği/ (-giller)**, (*ent.*) lantern fly/(plant hoppers).
fenik[1] 'Pfennig'; penny.
fen·ik[2] (*chem.*) Phenic. ~ **il**, phenyl.
Fenike (*his.*) Phoenicia. ~ **li**, (*ethn.*) Phoenician.
fen·lenmiş (Child) knowing more than it should (for its age). ~ **n-** = FEN. ~ **ni**, *a*. scientific; technical: ~ **çiftçi(lik)**, agronom·ist/(-ics): ~ **tabir**, technical term.
fenol[ü] (*chem.*) Phenol, carbolic acid. ~ **lü**, phenolic.
feno·men (*phil.*) Phenomenon. ~ **men(al)izm**, phenomenalism. ~ **menoloji**, phenomenology. ~ **tip**, (*bio.*) phenotype.
fen·t[di] Trick, ruse.
feodal·(ite) (*his.*) Feudal(ism). ~ **izm**, feudalism.
fer Pomp, display; splendour, radiance; lustre.

ferace (*mod.*) Coverall (worn outdoors by Tk. women); cloak (worn by ULEMA). ~ **li**, wearing a FERACE. ~ **lik**, material for FERACE.
feragat[1] Abandonment (of work, etc.); renunciation; self-sacrifice; a being free from care/work. ~ **etm.**, abdicate; disclaim, renounce, give up; be at ease: ~ **göstermek**, renounce one's rights: ~ **sahibi**, contented, satisfied. ~ **li**, free from care.
ferağ (*leg.*) Renunciation; cession; (*fig.*) leisure. ~ **etm.**, renounce; cede: ~ **muamelesi**, conveyancing.
ferah *a*. Spacious; open; roomy; cheerful; untroubled. *adv*. Easily, with room to spare. *n*. Cheerfulness, joy, pleasure. ~ ~, amply; at least: ~ **fahur** = FERİH. ~ **feza**, pleasant; (*Or. mus.*) a compound melody.
ferahi (*his.*) Metal disc (on soldier's fez); metal plate (on military policeman's collar).
ferah·la(n)ma *vn*. ~ **la(n)mak**, *vi*. become spacious/ airy; become cheerful; enjoy o.s. ~ **landırmak (-i)**, *vc*. ~ **lık**, comfort; spaciousness, airiness; cheer-fulness, enjoyment; distraction, relief. ~ **nak**[i], cheerful, gay; (*Or. mus.*) a compound melody.
feraset[i] Sagacity, intuition, acumen. ~ **li**, sagacious, discerning.
ferat[1] (*chem.*) Ferrate.
fer·ç[ci] (*bio.*) Vulva.
ferd- = FERT.
ferda The morrow; the next day; the future.
ferde Small bale, bag.
ferd·en Individually. ~ **i**, *a*. private, personal; (*phil.*) individual; single-handed. ~ **iyet**[i], individuality. ~ **iyetçi(lik)**, (*phil.*) individual·ist/(-ism).
fer'i Derived; secondary; supplementary.
feribot[u] (*naut.*) Ferryboat.
ferih Cheerful. ~ **fahur**, in abundance; in comfort.
ferik[i 1] *n*. (*mil.*, *obs.*) Divisional general.
feri·k[ği 2] *n*. (*orn.*) Young game bird; young cock; (*bot.*) crisp apple.
ferli Bright, luminous, brilliant.
ferma ~ **etm.**, (game dog) point, set.
ferman Command; (imperial) decree, firman. ~ **çıkmak**, (*his.*) order be issued (by the Sultan): ~ **dinlememek**, ignore the Law: ~ **sizin!**, with pleasure!; as you wish! ~ **lı**, outlawed; (*fig.*) doing as he pleases.
fermantasyon (*chem.*) Fermentation.
fermejüp[ü] (*mod.*) Snap-fastener.
fermene(ci) (*mod.*) (Maker/seller of) braided waistcoat.
ferment (*bio.*) Ferment.
fermiyum (*chem.*) Fermium.
fermuar (*mod.*) Zip-fastener. ~ **sürgüsü**, sliding clip.
ferr·it (*chem.*) Ferrite. ~ **itli**, ferritic. ~ **o-**, ferro-.
fersah (*obs.*) League, five kilometres; an hour's journey. ~ ~, far and away, greatly, 'miles' (better): ~ ~ **geçmek (-i)**, be miles ahead of: ~ **larca uzaktan**, far/miles away. ~ **lık**, a distance of . . . leagues.
fersiz Lifeless; dull. ~ **gözler**, lack-lustre eyes. ~ **leşmek**, *vi*. become dull. ~ **lik**, dullness.
fersude Worn out, old. ~ **leşmek**, *vi*. become worn out.

fer¹tᵈⁱ *n.* Person, individual; (*math.*) odd number. *a.* Single, unique; peerless; odd.

ferti¹kᵍⁱ (*sl.*) Ready. ~ **çekmek/** ~**i kırmak**, sneak away.

ferya¹tᵈ¹ Cry (for help); wail. ~ **etm.**, cry out; call for help; (*fig.*) be in great difficulties: ~ **a yetişmek**, go to the rescue (of s.o. calling): ~**ı basmak**, begin to cry out.

ferz Queen (at chess). ~ **çıkarmak**, give the queen (as handicap): ~ **çıkmak**, (pawn) queen.

fes (*mod.*) Fez. ~ **tarağı**, (*bot.*) fuller's teasel: ~**ini havaya atmak**, be very happy/cheerful.

fesahatⁱ Eloquence.

fesa¹tᵈ¹ Depravity; corruption; duplicity; malice; (*pol.*) intrigue; sedition; disorder. ~ **çıkarmak/ karıştırmak**, intrigue: ~ **kazanını kurmak**, start a mutiny/sedition: ~ **kazanları kaynamak**, mischief/ trouble be brewing: ~ **kurmak**, plot mischief: ~ **kumkuma/kutusu**, mischief-maker. conspirator: ~ **a vermek**, intrigue.

fesat·çı Mischief-maker; conspirator; firebrand, activist, militant. ~**çılık**, conspiracy, intrigue, activism. ~**lık**, sedition, disorder.

fesh¹etmekᵉᵈᵉʳ (-i) Abolish, annul, abrogate; dissolve (Parliament, etc.); (*naut.*) salvage; (*mil.*) defuse.

fes¹ihʰⁱ (*leg.*) Abolition; cancellation; dissolution.

fesleğen (*bot.*) Sweet basil.

fesrengiⁿⁱ Deep red, crimson.

festekiz/feşmekân [77] = FALAN.

festivalⁱ (*art.*) Festival; (*sl.*) revelry, brawl. ~ **dışı**, (*th.*) fringe events.

fesuphanallah *int.* Good God alive!

fetha (*bio.*) Opening, orifice.

fet·h- = FETİH. ~**h¹etmek**ᵉᵈᵉʳ (-i), conquer. ~ ¹ihʰⁱ, conquest: ~ **hakkı**, right of conquest. ~**ihname**, declaration/poem of victory.

fetiş (*rel.*) Fetish. ~**ist//**~**izm**, fetish·ist//-ism.

fetretⁱ (*adm.*) Interregnum.

fettan Alluring, cunning, seducing. ~ **civelek**, coquettish rascal, scoundrel. ~**laşmak**, *vi.* grow cunning, etc.

fetva (*rel.*) Opinion/decision on a matter of Canon Law (given by a MUFTİ) ~**hane**, (*his.*) office of the ŞEYHÜLİSLAM.

fev¹çᵉⁱ Troop, crowd. ~ ~, in groups/troops/ hordes.

feveran Boiling; effervescence; eruption; anger. ~ **etm.**, (volcano) erupt; (*fig.*) boil over with anger.

fevk¹ Top, upper part. ~**ında**, *post.* [92] on the top; over; above. ~**alade**, *a.* extraordinary; very unusual; special; exceptional: *adv.* extraordinarily; exceptionally; specially: ~ **murahhas**, (*adm.*) ambassador extraordinary: ~ **nüsha**, (*pub.*) special edition/number: ~ **ucuz**, absurdly cheap. ~**aladelik**, singularity; being extraordinary. ~**albeşer**, superhuman. ~**ani**, upper, superior. ~**attabia**, supernatural.

fevri Sudden; speedy; impulsive. ~**lik**, suddenness.

fevtⁱ Irreparable loss; death. ~ **etm.**, lose (opportunity, etc.): ~ **olm.**, die; be lost.

feyezan Overflowing; flood; inundation; abundance.

feyizli Abundant; prosperous; successful.

feylesof Philosopher.

feyyaz Overflowing; abounding; flourishing.

feyz Abundance; munificence; progress. ~**li**, prosperous.

feza (*ast.*) Space. ~ **adamı**, (*aer.*) astronaut; spaceman: ~ **gemisi**, spaceship: ~ **şuaları**, cosmic rays: ~ **uçuş bilgisi**, astronautics.

fezleke Summary; précis; police report.

ff. (*mus.*) = FORTİSSİMO.

fg. (*phys.*) = FRİGORİ.

fıçı Cask, barrel; drum; vat; tub. ~ **balığı**, salted fish in barrels: ~ **birası**, draught/keg beer: ~ **deliği**, bunghole: ~ **dibi**, (*sl.*) low public-house: ~ **firesi**, ullage: ~ **gibi**, very fat: ~ **tapası**, bung. ~**cı(lık)**, cooper(age). ~**lamak** (-i), put in barrels.

fıkdan Absence; need; privation.

fıkı = SIKI.

fık¹ihʰ¹ (*leg.*) Muslim jurisprudence.

fıkır ~ ~, with a bubbling noise; boiling; coquettishly: ~ ~ **kaynamak**, bubble and boil; (*fig.*) be full of, be swarming with.

fıkır·dak Coquettish. ~**damak**, *vi.* boil noisily; skip about; flirt. ~**daşmak**, (girls) giggle and chatter together. ~**datmak** (-i), *vc.* ~**tı**, bubbling noise.

fıkra (*pub.*) Sentence; paragraph; newspaper-article; anecdote; (*leg.*) clause, sub-section; (*bio.*) vertebra. ~ **yazarı/**~**cı**, columnist; story-teller. ~**cılık**, article-writing; story-telling.

fıkramak *vi.* Ferment; become acid.

fıldır ~ ~, skipping about; rolling the eyes: ~ ~ **aramak**, hunt feverishly for stg.

fındı¹kᵍ¹ (*bot.*) Hazel-nut, pea-nut; (*sl.*) loaded dice. ~ **altını**, (*his.*) a gold coin; (*fig.*) stg. small but valuable: ~ **çiçeği**, (*bot.*) catkin: ~ **içi**, kernel: ~ **kabuğunu doldurmaz**, unimportant, valueless: ~ **kömür**, (*min.*) nut coal: ~ **yuvası**, dimple on the back of hands.

fındık·ağacıⁿ¹ (*bot.*) Hazel-nut tree. ~**biti**ⁿⁱ, (*ent.*) nut-weevil. ~**çı**, hazel-nut grower/seller; (*col.*) wily/coquettish woman. ~**çılık**, hazel-nut growing/ selling; coquettishness. ~**faresi**ⁿⁱ/~**sıçanı**ⁿ¹, (*zoo.*) common dormouse. ~**i**, nut-brown. ~**kıran**, nutcrackers. ~**kurdu**ⁿᵘ, (*ent.*) nut maggot: ~ **gibi**, plump and lively. ~**lık**, hazel-nut grove. ~**midyesi**ⁿⁱ, (*zoo.*) nut-shell. ~**tavuğu**ⁿᵘ, (*orn.*) hazel grouse.

fır (*ech.*) Whirr. ~ ~ **dolaşmak**, go whirring round: ~ ~ **dönmek**, hover around s.o.

Fırat¹ (*geo.*) River Euphrates.

fırça Brush. ~ **çekmek**, (*sl.*) scold severely: ~ **gibi**, bushy: ~ **ile sürtmek**, scrub: ~ **işi**, (*art.*) brush-work: ~ **kuyruk**, (*ent.*) bristle-tail.

fırça·cı(lık) (Work of) brush-maker/-seller. ~**dilligiller**, (*orn.*) lories. ~**lamak** (-i), brush/scrub stg. ~**lanmak**, *vp.* ~**latmak**, *vc.* ~**lı**, bushy.

fır·dolayı All around. ~**döndü**, (*eng.*) swivel; dog; lathe-carrier; (*gamb.*) top.

fır fır (*mod.*) Frill.

fırıl ~ ~, turning/rotating quickly: ~ ~ **aramak**, search high and low.

fırıl·da¹kᵍ¹ Weather-cock/-vane; ventilator; spinning top; whirligig; deception, ruse: ~ **böceği**,

fırıldakçı (*ent.*) whirligig beetle: ~ **çevirmek**, intrigue; be up to mischief: ~ **gibi**, scatter-brained. ~**dakçı**, trickster, rogue. ~**dakçiçeği**[ni], (*bot.*) passionflower. ~**daklı**, rotating. ~**danmak**, *vi.* spin round; move around hurriedly/anxiously. ~**datmak (-i)**, spin stg. round.

fırın Large oven; baker's oven; bake-house, bakery; incinerator; (*min.*) furnace; kiln. ~ **ekmek yemesi lazım (bu kadar)**, you will need a lot of practice: ~ **gibi**, very hot (place): ~ **kapağı gibi**, experienced, imperturbable: ~**a sürmek**, put in the oven: ~**da piş(ir)mek**, *vi.*/(*vt.*) bake.

fırın·cı(lık) (Work of) baker; (*min.*) furnaceminder. ~**kapağı**[nı], oven-door; (*fig.*) thickskinned; unruffled. ~**lamak (-i)**, (*cul.*) put/dry in the oven; bake; (*min.*) fire (bricks). ~**lanmak**, *vp.* be dried in the oven; be baked. ~**latmak (-i, -e)**, dry in the oven.

fırka Group; (*pol.*) party; faction; (*mil.*) division; (*naut.*) squadron. ~ ~, in separate parties. ~**cılık**, partisanship. ~**ta**, (*naut.*) frigate.

fırlak Protruding. ~ **çene**, (*bio.*) prognathism: ~ **göz**, exophthalmia.

fırla·ma *vn.* Act of flying off; ejection; (*sl.*) bastard. ~**mak**, *vi.* fly off into space; fly out; be ejected; leap up; dart, rush; (prices) soar. ~**tıcı**, (*aer.*) launcher. ~**tış**, launching. ~**tma**, *vn.* launching; impulsion; ballistic: ~ **kapsülü**, (*aer.*) ejection capsule. ~**tmak (-ı)**, *vc.* hurl; launch; eject. ~**yış**, *vn.* leaping up; rush; (prices) upward rush.

fırsat[1] Opportunity; chance; bargain. ~ **beklemek**, choose the right moment: ~ **bilip (-i)**, profiting by, taking advantage of: ~ **bilmek (-i)**, seize the opportunity: ~ **bulmak**, find an opportunity: ~ **çıktığında**, should the occasion arise: ~ **düşkünü**, opportunist; who has his eye on the main chance; profiteer: ~ **düşmek**, opportunity occur: ~ **elvermemek**, not have an opportunity: ~ **eşitliği**, (*leg.*) equality of opportunity: ~ **kollamak**, watch for an opportunity: ~ **vermek (-e)**, give s.o. an opportunity/break: ~ **yoksulu**, s.o. always seeking a chance to do evil: ~**ı ganimet bilmek**, seize an opportunity: ~**ı kaçırmak**, miss an opportunity: ~**ı tepmek**, spurn the opportunity: ~**ını beklemek**, bide one's time: ~**ını düşürmek**, seize an opportunity. ~**çı(lık)**, opportun-ist/(-ism).

fırt ~ ~ **girip çıkmak**, go in and out continuously.

fırtına (*met.*) Gale, storm; (*fig.*) difficult situation; anxiety. ~ **çapası**, (*naut.*) sea-anchor, drogue: ~ **gibi**, quickly; excitedly; noisily: ~ **kopmak/ patlamak**, (storm) break; (*fig.*) (quarrel) break out: ~ **var**, it's blowing a gale: ~ **yelkeni**, (*naut.*) storm sail: ~**nın hükmü geçti**, the worst of the storm is over. ~**lı**, stormy, (*orn.*) storm-petrel. ~**lı**, blowy; (*fig.*) quarrelsome.

fı(r)ttırmak (*col.*) Go mad, become insane.

fıs (*ech.*) ~ ~, in whispers: ~ **geçmek**, whisper. ~**ıl** ~**ıl**, whispering; in whispers. ~**ıldamak (-i)**, whisper. ~**ıldaşmak (-i, -le)**, whisper stg. to each other. ~**ıldayıcı**, (*th.*) prompter. ~**ıltı**, whisper: ~ **gazetesi**, gossip.

fısır (*ech.*) ~ ~, hiss (of burning//running water).

fıskıye Jet of water; fountain; sprinkler; atomizer.

~**li**, sprinkling, spraying: ~ **çeşme**, drinking fountain.

fısla·mak (-i, -e) Whisper; tell secretly; prompt. ~**nmak**, *vp.* ~**yıcı**, (*th.*) prompter.

fıstı[1]**k**[ğ1] (*bot.*) Pistachio nut; (*in general*) nut; ground-nut; pea-nut; pine-kernel. ~ **ağacı**, pistachio: ~ **gibi**, plump and healthy; very beautiful; who has a beautiful body.

fıstık·çamı[nı] Stone pine, umbrella pine. ~**çı(lık)**, (work of) pistachio grower/seller. ~**i**, light/ pistachio green: ~ **makam**, (*jok.*) ponderous. ~**lık**, pistachio grove.

fış (*ech.*) ~ (**ır**) ~ (**ır**), splashing; rustling. ~**ırdamak**, *vi.* splash; rustle. ~**ırdatmak (-i)**, splash; rustle. ~**ırtı**, splash; rustle.

fışkı Horse-dung; manure. ~ **şerbeti**, liquid manure.

fışkın (*bot.*) Sucker; shoot.

fışkır·dak (*chem.*) Wash-bottle. ~**ık**, squirt, syringe; (*child.*) water-pistol. ~**ma**, *vn.*; jet; gush; (*ast.*) protuberance. ~**mak**, *vi.* gush out, spurt out; burst forth; (*bot.*) spring up. ~**tı**, (*ech.*) hiss. ~**tıcı**, (*med.*) ejector. ~**tılmak**, *vp.* ~**tmak (-i)**, *vc.* ~**tmalı**, jet.

fış·lamak/ ~ namak *vi.* Ferment; go sour.

fıtı[1]**k**[ğ1] (*med.*) Hernia, rupture. ~ **bağı**, truss: ~ **olm.**, (*col.*) dislike s.o.

fıtr·at[1] Creation; nature; natural character. ~**aten**, naturally. ~**i**, natural; innate; congenital.

fi *prep.* In. ~ **tarihinde**, in days of yore, long ago.

fi. = FİYAT. ~ **at** = FİYAT.

fib·er Fibre. ~**erglas**, fibreglass. ~**rin(ojen)**, (*bio.*) fibrin(ogen). ~**ro-**, fibro-. ~**rosit**, (*med.*) fibrositis.

fidan (*bot.*) Plant; bush; sapling; shoot. ~ **boylu/ gibi**, straight, well-set. ~**bitini**, (*ent.*) aphis. ~**lık**, nursery-garden; plantation; newly-planted vineyard.

fide (*bot.*) Seedling plant (for bedding out). ~ **kazığı**, dibber. ~**ci(lik)**, (work of) plant-grower/ -seller. ~**lemek (-i)**, plant out, bed. ~**lik**, *n.* seed-/ nursery-bed; propagator: *a.* suitable for seedling.

fider (*el.*) Feeder.

fidye(inecat[1]**)** Ransom.

FİFA = (*Fédération Internationale de Football Association*).

fifre (*mus.*) Fife.

figan Cry of distress, wail.

figür (*art.*) Figure, figurine; (*math.*) shape. ~**an(lık)**, (*cin.*) (work of) extra, crowd-artist, stand-in. ~**atif**, figurative. ~**in**, statuette.

fiğ (*bot.*) Common vetch.

fihrist[i] Index; catalogue; list. ~ **yapmak/ ~ e almak**, index. ~**li**, indexed.

fiil Act; action, deed; (*ling.*) verb. ~**e gelmek**, become a fact; be done: ~**e getirmek**, execute, put into effect: ~**i çekmek**, (*ling.*) conjugate a verb.

fiil·en Actually, really. ~**i**, actual; real; (*pol.*) *de facto*; (*phys.*) effective. ~**imsi**, (*ling.*) quasi-verbal. ~**iyat**[1], deeds.

fik[1]**ir**[ri] Thought; concept; idea; opinion; mind; memory; advice, counsel. ~ **adamı**, man of ideas; brain-worker: ~**(ini) almak**, borrow s.o.'s ideas: ~ **edinmek**, get an idea: ~ **hürriyeti**, freedom of thought: ~ **ileri sürmek**, argue stg.: ~ **işçisi**, (*leg.*)

non-manual worker: ~ **işi**, brainwork: ~ **vermek**, make known one's opinion; communicate one's beliefs; advise: ~ **yormak**, think hard: ~ **yürütmek**, put forward one's opinion: ~**e getirmek**, call to mind: ~**e varmak**, ponder: ~**i bacadan aşmış**, peculiar, eccentric: ~**i başka olm.**, disagree: ~**i sabit**, *idée fixe*: ~**imce**, if you ask me, in my opinion: ~**inde saklamak**, bear in mind: ~**ine gelmek**, come into one's mind: ~**ine koymak (-i)**, decide to do stg.

fikir·li Having ideas; intelligent; thoughtful. ~**siz/ (-lik)**, thoughtless(ness); unintelligent (lack of intelligence).

fikr- = FİKİR. ~**¹etmek**ᵉᵈᵉʳ **(-i)**, ponder over, think about. ~**i**, intellectual; mental.

fiks ~ **menü**, (*cul.*) *table d'hôte*. ~**atif**, (*chem.*) fixative. ~ **tür**, (*sp.*) fixture(-list).

fik·siyon (*lit.*) Fiction. ~**tif**, (*lit.*) fictitious, imaginary.

fil (*zoo.*) Elephant; (chess) bishop. ~**Dİşİ**: ~**ELMASI**: ~ **faresi**, (*zoo.*) jumping shrew: ~ **gibi**, fat and greedy: ~ **hastalığı**, (*med.*) elephantiasis: ~ **hortumu**, elephant's trunk: ~ **yavrusu**, (*zoo.*) elephant calf: ~ **yürüyüşü**, (*sp.*) walking on all-fours.

fil. (*bio.*) = FİLUM.
fil- *Also* = FL-.
filaman (*el.*) Filament.
filan(-) = FALAN(-).
filantrop Philanthropist. ~**i(k)**, philanthrop·y/ (-ic).
filariz (*tex.*) Mallet for beating out flax. ~**lemek (-i)**, beat out the flax.
fil·armoni (*mus.*) Philharmonic society. ~**armonik**, philharmonic (orchestra). ~**atelist**, philatelist.
fila·to (*cul.*) Fillet; (*mod.*) gimp. ~**tür**, (*tex.*) spinning-mill.
filbah·ar/~**ri** (*bot.*) Clematis, virgin's bower.
fildekoz (*tex.*) Lisle thread.
fildişiⁿⁱ (*bio.*) Ivory; matt white (colour). ~ **gibi**, matt white: ~ **karası**, ivory black (oil-paint): ~ **Kıyısı**, *pr.n.* (*geo.*) Ivory Coast.
file (*tex.*) Net; netting; net-/string-bag.
filelmasıⁿⁱ (*bot.*) Elephant-apple.
fil·en¹çᶜⁱ (*eng.*) Pipe-flange. ~**en¹k**ᵍⁱ, (*naut.*) roller/ crosspiece (on slipway); boat-chock.
fil·er (*eng.*) Feeler. ~**et**ⁱ, (*naut.*) shallows. ~**eto**, (*cul.*) beefsteak, fillet.
filhakika In truth; really, truly.
filigran (*pub.*) Watermark; (*min.*) filigree.
filika (*naut.*) Cutter; pinnace; lifeboat. ~ **demiri**, grapnel: ~ **güvertesi**, boat-deck. ~**cı**, boatman.
filim = FİLM.
filint (*geol.*) Flint. ~**a**, (*mil.*) carbine: ~ **gibi**, (*sl.*) smart, handsome.
Filipin·ler (*geo.*) The Philippines. ~**li**, (*ethn.*) Filipino.
filispit 'Full speed' (bicycle); (*sl.*) dead drunk.
Filistin (*geo.*) Palestine. ~**li**, (*ethn.*) Palestinian.
filiz¹ *n.* (*geol.*) Ore. ~**lenme**, recrystallization.
filiz² *n.* (*bot.*) Tendril; bud; young shoot; cutting. ~ **gibi**, slender, well-shaped: ~ **vermek**, burgeon forth.

filiz·i Bright green. ~**kıran**, (*met.*) cold East wind (in May). ~**küf**, (*myc.*) budding fungus. ~**küflüce**, (*med.*) blastomycosis. ~**lemek (-i)**, prune. ~**lenmek**, (*bot.*) send forth shoots; sprout; (*fig.*) begin to develop. ~**li**, having shoots/tendrils.
film (*cin.*) Film. ~ **çekmek**, film, take a film; X-ray: ~ **çevirmek**, make a film; (*sl.*) amuse o.s.; show off: ~ **makinesi (ekipi)**, camera (crew): ~ **meraklısı**, film-fan: ~ **oynamak**, (film) be shown: ~ **oynatmak**, show a film: ~ **şenliği**, film festival: ~ **yıldızı**, film-star: ~**e almak**, make a film of stg: ~**leri yakmak**, (*sl.*) mess things up. ~**ci(lik)**, film-maker/(-making).
filo (*naut.*) Fleet; squadron; (*aer.*) squadron. ~ **etm.**, spill the wind (from sails): ~ **komutanı**, squadron-leader.
filoksera (*ent.*) Phylloxera.
filo·logᵘ (*ling.*) Philologist. ~**loji**, philology.
filotilla (*naut.*) Flotilla (torpedo-boats): ~ **kumandanı**, flotilla leader.
filoz (*naut.*) Fishing-net buoy (gourd, etc.).
filozof Philosopher. ~ **taşı**, philosophers' stone. ~**ça**, philosophically. ~**laşmak**, *vi.* philosophize. ~**luk**, philosophizing.
filtre (*eng.*) Filter; filter-tip. ~ **elemanı**, cartridge: ~ **etm.**, filter; percolate: ~ **kuyusu**, (*min.*) bleeder well. ~**li**, cork-/filter-tipped (cigarette).
filum (*bio.*) Phylum.
filvakiⁱ In fact, actually. ~ **... ama**, however.
filyal (*fin.*) Subsidiary (company).
Fin (*ethn.*) Finn. ~ **balinası**, (*zoo.*) rorqual, fin-whale: ~ **hamamı**, sauna bath.
finalⁱ (*sp.*) Final; (*mus.*) finale. ~**e katmak**, get into the finals. ~**ite**, finality. ~**izm**, (*phil.*) finalism.
finans (*fin.*) Finance. ~**al**, financial. ~**e**, ~ **etm.**, finance. ~**man**, finance, financing: ~ **kaynakları**, resources.
fincan (*dom.*) Cup; (*el.*) porcelain insulator. ~ **çiçeği**, (*bot.*) gloxinia: ~ **dolusu**, cupful: ~ **gibi (göz)**, saucer-eyed: ~ **oyunu**, (*child.*) hunt the thimble: ~ **tabağı**, saucer.
fincan·böreğiⁿⁱ (*cul.*) A round BÖREK. ~**cı**, pottery seller: ~ **katırlarını ürkütmek**, stir up a hornet's nest; irritate/provoke the authorities. ~**lık**, cupful.
Fince (*ling.*) Finnish.
fines (*gamb.*) Finesse.
fingir ~ ~, with a swaying motion; coquettishly: ~ ~ **etm.**, walk thus. ~ **dek**, frivolous, coquettish. ~**de(ş)mek**, *vi.* behave frivolously/coquettishly (with each other).
fini·saj ~ **boyası**, finishing coat (of paint). ~ **ş**, (*sp.*) finish.
fink ~ **atmak**, saunter about enjoying o.s.
Fin·landiya (*geo.*) Finland. ~**li**, (*ethn.*) Finn; Finnish.
fino (*live.*) Pet-dog; lap-dog.
firak¹ (Sorrow at) separation. ~**lı**, sad, melancholy.
firar Flight; escape; desertion. ~ **etm.**, fly; escape; desert: ~ **kenarı**, (*aer.*) trailing edge: ~ **noktası**, (*art.*) vanishing point. ~**i**, (*mil.*) deserter; (*pol.*) refugee; (*ed.*) truant.
firavun (*his.*) Pharaoh; (*fig.*) cruel/obstinate man. ~**faresi**ⁿⁱ, (*zoo.*) ichneumon. ~**inciri**ⁿⁱ, (*bot.*)

Indian fig, prickly pear. ~**laşmak**, *vi.* behave cruelly/pitilessly. ~**luk**, obstinacy.

firdevs Garden (of Paradise).

fire (*fin.*) Ullage; wastage; shrinkage. ~ **vermek**, suffer wastage, etc.

firengi = FRENGİ.

firez (*agr.*) Stubble.

firfiri Purple.

firi'kᵍⁱ (*dial.*, *cul.*) Roasted unripe wheat.

firkatⁱ Separation; absence; nostalgia.

firkateyn (*naut.*, *his.*) Frigate.

firkete Hairpin. ~**lemek** (-i), pin up (hair).

firma (*fin.*) Firm, business, concern. ~ **elemanları**, personnel: ~ **sahibi**, owner.

firuze (*min.*) Turquoise. ~ **rengi**, turquoise blue/green.

Fisagor *pr.n.* Pythagoras.

fisebilillah Free, gratis, for nothing.

fisk ~(**u fücur**), (*obs.*) wickedness.

fiske Flick; flip; pinch (of stg.); small bruise. ~ **dokundurmamak**, protect s.o. from the least harm: ~ ~ **kabarmak**, be covered with small bruises. ~**lemek** (-i), flick, flip; reproach lightly.

fisketⁱ (*naut.*) Bo's'n's pipe. ~ **çalmak**, pipe s.o. on board.

fiskos Whispering; insinuation. ~ **etm.**, whisper insinuations; plot secretly.

fistan (*mod.*) Clothes; kilt; skirt, petticoat. ~**lı**, wearing a kilt, etc. ~**lık**, cloth (for kilt, etc.).

fis·to (*mod.*) Braiding. ~**tül**, (*bio.*) fistula.

fisür (*geol.*) Crack, fissure. ~ **açılması**, fissuring; cracking. ~**lü**, cracked, fissured.

fisyon (*nuc.*) Fission. ~ **artıkları**, nuclear waste.

fiş (*gamb.*) Counter, chip; (*pub.*) docket, receipt; index-card; (*el.*) plug. ~ **açmak**, begin an index: ~ **katalogu**, card-catalogue: ~ **kutusu**, card cabinet/tray: ~ **usulü indeks**, card-index: ~**ini tutmak**, keep a record of s.o.

fişe'kᵍⁱ Cartridge; bullet; rocket; fireworks; roll of coins. ~ **atmak**, (*fig.*) drop a bombshell: ~ **gibi**, like lightning: ~ **salıvermek**, spread discontent.

fişek·çi Cartridge-maker/-seller. ~**çilik**, pyrotechnics. ~**hane**, cartridge factory. ~**lik**, cartridge belt; bandolier; ammunition pouch.

fişka (*naut.*) Cathead. ~ **etm.**, cat (the anchor).

fiş·lemek (-i) Write on a card; start a card index. ~**lenmek**, *vp.* be entered on a card: *vi.* have a record (with the police). ~**li**, entered on a card; having a (police) record. ~**lik**, filing cabinet, etc.; used for cards.

fitⁱ ¹ *n.* (*gamb.*) Equivalent gain/loss. ~ **olm.**, (*sl.*) be quits; (-e), agree on a price; consent.

fit² *n.* ~ **tulumbası**, feed-pump.

fitⁱ ³ *n.* Instigation; incitement. ~ **sokmak/vermek**, instigate, incite; spread discontent. ~**çi(lik)**, mischief-mak·er/(-ing).

fitil Wick; weather strip; draught excluder; (*med.*) pad; suppository; (*mod.*) piping; (*mil.*) fuse. ~ **gibi**, drunk as a lord: ~ **olm.**, (*sl.*) be very drunk: ~ **vermek**, excite, incite: ~**i almak**, get into a rage, flare up; become alarmed.

fitil·ci (*sl.*) Drunkard. ~**lemek** (-i), (*mil.*) light a fuse; (*fig.*) enrage; incite. ~**lenmek**, *vp.* be enraged.

fitle·mek (-i) Denounce; incite; instigate. ~**nmek**, *vp.* ~**yici**, inciting, instigating.

fitne (*pol.*) Instigation; disorder; sedition; mischief-making. ~ **fücur**, dangerous trouble-maker: ~ **kopmak**, disorders break out: ~ **sokmak/vermek**, make trouble.

fitne·ci(lik) (*pol.*) Activ·ist/(-ism); trouble-mak·er/(-ing). ~**lemek**, *vi.* instigate trouble/disorder; make mischievous remarks. ~**lik**, intrigue, mischief.

fito- *pref.* (*bot.*) Phyto-. ~**fag**, phytophagous.

fitre (*rel.*) Alms given at the end of Ramadan.

fiyaka Showing-off; ostentation. ~ **satmak/yapmak**, show off; put on an act: ~**sı bozulmak**, look sheepish when ridiculed. ~**cı**, swaggerer. ~**lı**, swaggering, ostentatious.

fiyasko Fiasco. ~ **vermek**, be unsuccessful; fail.

fiyat¹ (*fin.*) Price; cost. ~ **ayarlamak**, proportion/determine the prices: ~ **biçmek/vermek**, fix/set the price: ~ **kırmak/~ını düşürmek**, lower the price: ~ **teklifi**, bid, offer: ~**a satmak**, sell at a price: ~**ı yükselmek**, appreciate/rise in value: ~**lar arasındaki makas ağzı**, a very small difference in price: ~**ları dondurmak**, freeze prices. ~**lanmak**, *vi.* (price) rise.

fiyon'kᵍᵘ (*mod.*) Bow; bow-tie.

fiyor'tᵈᵘ (*geo.*) Fjord.

fiz. = FİZİK.

fizalya (*zoo.*) Portuguese man-of-war.

fizibilite (*fin.*) Feasibility.

fizi'kᵍⁱ Physics. ~ +, *a.* Physical: ~ **ötesi**, (*phil.*) metaphysics: ~ **tedavisi**, (*med.*) physiotherapy: ~ **yapısı**, (*bio.*) physical constitution, physique.

fizik·bilimler Physical sciences. ~**çi**, physicist; physics teacher. ~**i**, physical. ~**okimya**, physico-chemistry. ~**oterapi**, physiotherapy. ~**ötesi**ⁿⁱ, *n.* metaphysics: *a.* metaphysical. ~**sel**, physical: ~ **kimya**, physical chemistry.

fizy. = FİZYOLOJİ.

fizyo·grafya (*geo.*) Physiography. ~**krat(lık)**, (*adm.*) physio·crat/(-cracy). ~**log**, (*med.*) physiologist. ~**loji**, physiology. ~**lojik/~lojisel**, physiological: ~ **eriyik**, (*bio.*) physiological salt solution. ~**lojist**, physiologist. ~**nomi**, physiognomy. ~**terapi**, (*med.*) physiotherapy.

FK·B = FİZİK, KİMYA, BİYOLOJİ. ~**O//Ö** = FİLİSTİN KURTULUŞ ORDUSU//ÖRGÜTÜ.

fl- *Also* = FİL-.

flama (*mil.*) Pennant; small flag; (*eng.*) surveyor's pole. ~**cı**, pennant-bearer; signaller.

Flaman (*ethn.*) Fleming. ~**ca**, (*ling.*) Flemish. ~**kuşu**ⁿᵘ/**flamingo**, (*orn.*) flamingo.

flandra (*naut.*) Ship's pennant. ~**balığı**ⁿⁱ, (*ich.*) red bandfish.

flanel (*tex.*) Flannel.

flanş(lı) (*eng.*) Flange(d).

flap (*aer.*) Flap.

flaş (*cin.*) Projector, studio lamp; flash-bulb/-gun; flash (of light).

flater (*aer.*) Flutter.

flavta (*mus.*) Flute. ~**cı**, flautist.

fle·bit (*med.*) Phlebitis. ~**gmon**, (*med.*) phlegmon, cellulitis.

fle·ksibl (*eng.*) Hose-pipe. ~ **ol**ü, (*bot.*) Timothy grass, cat's-tail. ~ **tner**, (*aer.*) tab.

fliti 'Flit' insecticide/spray.

float (*ind.*) Float (method for plate-glass).

floku (*naut.*) Jibsail.

flok·aj (*tex.*) Flocking. ~ **ülasyon**, flocculation.

flora (*bot.*) Flora.

flor(esan(s)) = FLÜOR(ESAN(S)).

flor·i (*obs.*) Gold coin. ~ **in**, Dutch florin.

florya = FLURYA.

floş (*tex.*) Floss silk; (*gamb.*) flush (hand).

flöre (*sp.*) Foil.

flörtü Flirt. ~ **etm.**, flirt.

flu (*cin.*) Blurred.

flur·cun (*orn.*) Hawfinch. ~ **ya**, (*orn.*) greenfinch.

fluviyal (*geol.*) Fluvial.

flüi·tdi (*phys.*) Fluid.

flüor (*chem.*) Fluorine. ~ **spat**, (*geol.*) fluospar, fluorite. ~ **esan/** ~ **ışıl**, fluorescent. ~ **esans/** ~ **ışı**, (*phys.*) fluorescence. ~ **ik**, (*chem.*) fluoric (acid). ~ **in**, (*geol.*) fluorite. ~ **ür**, (*chem.*) fluoride.

flütü (*mus.*) Flute. ~ **çü**, flautist, flute-player.

Fm. (*ch.s.*) = FERMİYUM.

FOA = (*Foreign Operations Administration*).

f.o.b./fob = (*free on board*).

fo·bi (*psy.*) Phobia. ~ **depar**, (*sp.*) false start.

fodla (*cul.*, *obs.*) Flat round loaf (given as alms). ~ **cı**, (*obs.*) alms distributor; (*fig.*) s.o. taking a job just to get food; scrounger. ~ **cılık**, a sinecure.

fodra (*mod.*) Lining/padding (of a coat).

fodul Vain; presumptuous; egotistical. ~ **ca**, presumptuously. ~ **luk**, presumption.

foku (*zoo.*) Seal.

foks·terye (*live.*) Fox-terrier. ~ **trot**, (*mus.*) foxtrot.

fokur ~ ~ , (*ech.*) bubbling: ~ ~ **içmek**, smoke a narghile noisily. ~ **dak**, bubbling. ~ **damak**, *vi.* bubble noisily, boil up. ~ **datmak (-i)**, *vc.* ~ **tu**, bubbling noise.

Fol. = (*folio*).

fol Nest-egg. ~ **yok yumurta yok**, there's nothing as yet; a mere fancy. ~ **luk**, nesting-box.

folk. = **folk·lor**u, *n.* folklore. ~ **lorcu**, folklorist. ~ **lorik**, folkloric; folk-; country-.

fon (*fin.*) Fund(s); capital; (*art.*) background. ~ **müziği**, background music.

fonda (*naut.*) Let go the anchor! ~ **etm.**, anchor.

fon·dan (*cul.*) Fondant. ~ **dasyon**, foundation. ~ **döten**, (*mod.*) face-cream, pancake make-up.

fon·em (*ling.*) Phoneme: ~ **düşmesi**, elision. ~ **emik**, phonemic. ~ **eti·k**ği, *a.* phonetic: *n.* phonetics.

fonksiyon Work, duty; (*math.*) function. ~ **göstergesi**, (*el.*) indicator/pilot light. ~ **al·ist/(-izm)**, functional·ist/(-ism). ~ **el**, functional.

fono·graf(i) (*phys.*) Phonograph(y). ~ **jenik**, (*mus.*) phonogenic. ~ **lit**, (*geol.*) phonolite, clinkstone. ~ **loji**, (*ling.*) phonology. ~ **telgraf**, telephoned telegram.

font (*min.*) Cast-iron.

FOR = (*free on rail*).

fora (*naut.*) Out!, open!, unfurl (sails)! ~ **etm.**, (*eng.*) strip down, dismantle; (*naut.*) unfurl/set (sails); draw (sword, etc.). ~ **kürek!**, ship oars!

for·aj/ ~ **e** (*min.*) Drilling, boring.

Foreyn ~ **Ofis**, *pr. n.* Foreign Office.

forhen·tdi (*sp.*) Forehand.

form Form, shape. ~ **a**, form, shape; (*mod.*) school uniform; sportsgear; work-clothes; (*adm.*) form; (*pub.*) form(at).

formal·dehiti (*chem.*) Formaldehyde. ~ **in**, formalin.

formalık *a.* (*mod.*) Suitable for uniforms, etc.; (*pub.*) having . . . forms.

formal·ist Formalist. ~ **ite**, formality; red tape: ~ **düşkünü/** ~ **ci**, formalist. ~ **izm**, formalism.

for·masyon (*phys.*) Formation; (*soc.*) education, training. ~ **me**, ~ **etm.**, form, shape; train. ~ **mel**, formal.

formen (*ind.*) Foreman.

for·mika (*carp.*) Formica. ~ **mikasit**, (*chem.*) formic acid. ~ **mol**ü, formaldehyde, formalin.

for·mülü (*adm.*) Form; (*chem.*, *math.*) formula, equation: ~ **bulmak**, find a way (to do stg.). ~ **müle**, ~ **etm.**, formulate (ideas). ~ **müler**, formulary.

foroz The catch with one casting of a net. ~ **kayığı**, boat used to take fish from DALYAN.

fors (President/admiral's) personal flag; (*fig.*) power, prestige, influence. ~ **u olm.**, be influential. ~ **lu**, flying a pennant; (*fig.*) influential.

for·sa (*leg.*) Convict, galley-slave. ~ **seps**, (*med.*) forceps. ~ **smajör**, (*leg.*) force-majeure.

for·te(piano) (*mus.*) Forte(piano). ~ **tissimo**, fortissimo

forum (*arch.*) Forum; (*adm.*) meeting, debate, discussion.

forveti (*sp.*) Forward, striker: ~ **hattı**, forward-line.

fos (*sl.*) False, bad, rotten, empty. ~ **çıkmak**, come to nothing.

fos·fat¹ (*chem.*) Phosphate. ~ **fatlamak (-i)**, phosphatize. ~ **fit**, phosphite. ~ **for**, phosphorus. ~ **forışı**, (*phys.*) phosphorescence. ~ **forışıl**, phosphorescent. ~ **forik**, (*chem.*) phosphoric. ~ **forlanma**, phosphorescence. ~ **forlu**, *a.* phosphorous, phosphoric; bright; (*sl.*) showy; brightly coloured. ~ **gen**, phosgene.

fosil (*geol.*) Fossil. ~ **leşmek**, *vi.* become fossilized; (*fig.*) regress; become old.

fosla·mak *vi.* Fail, be disconcerted; be ashamed; come to nothing. ~ **tmak (-i)**, deflate; (*sl.*) disconcert s.o., put s.o. to shame.

fossepti·kği (*arch.*) Septic tank.

fosur (*ech.*) ~ ~ **içmek**, smoke (a cigarette) noisily. ~ **damak**, *vi.* breathe noisily. ~ **datmak (-i)**, smoke noisily. ~ **tu**, puffing sound; (*fig.*) pride.

fot. = FOTOĞRAFÇILIK.

fota Type of wine barrel, vat.

fotin = POTİN.

foto·elektrik Photoelectric: ~ **hücre/lamba**, photoelectric cell. ~ **grametri**, aerial survey(ing). ~ **gravür**, (*pub.*) photogravure.

foto(ğraf) Photograph. ~ **çekmek**, take a photograph: ~ **çıkarmak**, (*sl.*) crash one's car: ~ **kitabı**, album: ~ **lambası**, photoflood lamp: ~ **makinesi**, camera: ~ **ını almak**, be photographed.

fotoğraf·çı Photographer; photographer's shop/ studio. ~ **çılık**, photography. ~ **evi**/ ~ **hane**, photographer's shop/studio. ~ **ik**, photographic.

foto·jenik Photogenic. ~ **kopi**, photocopy. ~ **liz**, (*chem.*) photolysis. ~ **metre**, photometer, exposuremetre. ~ **metri**, (*phys.*) photometry. ~ **model**, photographer's model. ~ **modellik**, modelling. ~ **montaj**, photo-montage. ~ **morfoz**, (*bio.*) photomorphosis. ~ **n**, (*phys.*) photon. ~ **roman**, (*pub.*) story told in photographs, photonovel. ~ **sel**, (*phys.*, *cin.*) photocell. ~ **sentez**, (*bot.*) photosynthesis. ~ **sfer**, (*phys.*) photosphere. ~ **skop**, photo-telescope. ~ **stat**, photostat. ~ **taksi**, (*bot.*) phototaxis. ~ **terapi**, (*med.*) phototherapy. ~ **tropizm**, (*bot.*) phototropism.

fovizm (*art.*) Fauvism.

FOW/f.o.w = (*free on wagon*).

foya Foil (for a gem); (*fig.*) fraud. ~ **vermek**, give o.s. away: ~ **sı meydan/ortaya çıkmak**, (one's bad qualities) be show up.

fön (*met.*) Föhn.

fötr (*tex.*) Felt; (*mod.*) felt hat.

föy Sheet of paper; form.

Fr. = FRANSA; FRANSIZ; FRANSIZCA(DAN); (*ch.s.*) FRANSİYUM.

fragman Piece, part; (*cin.*) trailer.

frak[1] (*mod.*) (Evening-)dress coat; tail-coat. ~ **gömleği**, dress-shirt. ~ **siyon**, (*math.*) fraction; (*pol.*) splinter-group.

francala (*cul.*) French bread, white bread. ~ **cı**, French-bread baker. ~ **lık**, suitable for making white bread.

fran·kg[i] (*fin.*) (Belgian/French/Swiss) franc.

Fran·sa (*geo.*) France. ~ **salı**/ ~ **sız**, (*ethn.*) Frenchman: ~ **+**, *a.* French: ~ **salatası**, (*gamb.*, *sl.*) well-shuffled cards. ~ **sızca**, (*ling.*) French; in French. ~ **siyum**, (*chem.*) francium.

frapan Striking; imposing. ~ **lık**, being imposing.

fregat[1] (*naut.*) Frigate. ~ **kuşu**, (*orn.*) frigate-bird.

frekans (*phys.*) Frequency. ~ **bandı**, (*rad.*) channel. ~ **metre**, frequency-metre.

fren Brake. ~ **beygir gücü**, (*phys.*) brake-horsepower: ~ **izi**, brake-/skid-mark: ~ **kasnak/makarası**, brake-drum: ~ **patiği**, brake-block: ~ **roketi**, (*aer.*) retro-rocket: ~ **vagonu**, (*rly.*) brake-van: ~ **yapmak**, (put on the) brake. ~ **ci**, (*rly.*) brake-man.

frengi[1] *n.* (*naut.*) ~ **(deliği)**, scuppers.

frengi[2] *n.* (*med.*) Syphilis. ~ **çıban/yeniği**, chancre: ~ **şişi**, bubo. ~ **li**, syphilitic.

Frengi[3] *a.* (*obs.*) European(ized). ~ **stan**, (*obs.*) Europe.

Fren·kg[i] *n.* European. ~ **arpası**, (*cul.*) pearl barley. ~ **asması**[ni], (*bot.*) Japanese ivy, ornamental vine, virginia creeper. ~ **çe**, (*ling.*) European (esp. French) language. ~ **çileği**[ni], (*bot.*) large strawberry. ~ **elması**[ni], (*bot.*) loquat. ~ **gömleği**[ni], (*mod.*) man's shirt; stiff shirt. ~ **inciri**[ni], (*bot.*) Indian fig, prickly pear. ~ **lahanası**[ni], (*bot.*) Brussels sprouts. ~ **leşmek**, *vi.* be(have) like a European. ~ **maydanozu**[nu], (*bot.*) chervil. ~ **menekşesi**[ni], (*bot.*) rocket. ~ **salatası**[nı], (*bot.*)

endive. ~ **sarmısağı**[nı], (*bot.*) chives. ~ **üzümü**[nü], (*bot.*) red-currant.

frenle·me *vn.* Braking. ~ **mek (-i)**, brake; apply/put on the brake. ~ **nmek**, *vp.* ~ **yici**, brake-man.

frenoloji Phrenology.

freon (*chem.*) Freon.

fresk[1] (*art.*) Fresco.

freze·(ci) (*eng.*) Milling-cutter (operator): ~ **makinesi**, milling machine. ~ **lemek (-i)**, mill.

fri·bord (*naut.*) Freeboard. ~ **kik**, (*sp.*) free-kick.

fri·go (*cul.*) Ice-cream. ~ **gori**, (*phys.*) negative kilocalorie. ~ **gorifik**, *a.* refrigerating; refrigerated. ~ **jider**, refrigerator. ~ **jidite**, (*psy.*) frigidity.

friksiyon (*med.*) Friction; massage: ~ **yapmak**, massage.

fri·sa (*cul.*) Fried herring. ~ **şka**, (*met.*, *naut.*) fresh breeze; cat's-paw.

früktoz (*chem.*) Fructose.

ft. = (*foot*).

fu·ar Trade-fair; exhibition. ~ **aye**, (*arch.*) foyer.

fuh'uş[şu] Immorality; indecency; prostitution. ~ **yapmak**, be/act as a prostitute.

fujer (*bot.*) Fern; bracken.

fukara *a.* Poor; destitute; unfortunate. *n.* Dervish. ~ **babası**, charitable person. ~ **lık**, poverty.

fukusgiller (*bot.*) Brown seaweeds.

ful[ü] (*bot.*) Arabian jasmine.

ful·ar (*tex.*) Foulard. ~ **taym**, (*ind.*) full-time (work).

fulya (*bot.*) Jonquil. ~ **balığı**[nı], (*ich.*) eagle-ray.

funda[1] *int.* (*naut.*) Cast anchor! ~ **etm.**, anchor.

funda[2] *n.* (*bot.*) Heather. ~ **tavşanı**, (*zoo.*) cotton-tail rabbit: ~ **tavuğu**, (*orn.*) brush turkey: ~ **toprağı**, (*agr.*) heather humus. ~ **giller**, heathers, Ericaceae. ~ **lar**, heaths and heathers. ~ **lık**, heathland.

funya (*mil.*) Detonator, primer.

furgon (*rly.*) Luggage van; goods van.

furta = FARTA.

furya Rush; glut.

futa[1] *n.* (*dom.*) Apron; bath towel.

futa[2] *n.* (*naut.*) Light boat, skiff.

futbol[u] (*sp.*) Football. ~ **alan/sahası**, football field/ pitch: ~ **budalası**, s.o. mad on football: ~ **meraklısı**, football fan: ~ **takımı**, football team. ~ **cu**, footballer.

fuzuli Unnecessary, excessive, superfluous. ~ **işgal**, (*leg.*) unlawful squatting.

FÜ = FIRAT ÜNİVERSİTESİ.

fücceten Suddenly.

fücur Immorality. = FİTNE.

füg (*mus.*) Fugue.

fülüs Money. ~ **ü ahmere muhtaç olm.**, not have a 'red cent' to one's name.

füme (*cul.*) Smoked; (*art.*, *mod.*) smoke-coloured. ~ **rol**, (*geol.*) fumerole.

fünun *pl.* = FEN. Sciences.

Fürs (*his.*) Persian.

füru[u] *pl.* Branches; subdivisions; (*soc.*) distant relations. ~ **maye**, ignoble; low-down; ill-bred.

füsun Attraction, charm; magic. ~ **kâr**, enchanting, charming.

fütuhat[1] *pl.* = FETİH. Conquests, victories.

fütur Languor; abatement. ∼ **etmemek**, not care, not think important: ∼ **gelmek**, be languid/ lukewarm; be discouraged: ∼ **getirmek**, lose zeal/interest/energy. ∼**suz**, indifferent; regardless of public opinion; undeterred. ∼**suzca**, indifferently.

fütür·ist[i] Futurist. ∼**izm**, futurism. ∼**olog**, futurologist. ∼**oloji**, futurology.

füze (*mil.*) Rocket; missile. ∼**atar**, rocket-launcher. ∼**savar**, anti-missile.

füzen (*art.*) Charcoal pencil (drawing).

füzyon (*phys.*) Fusion.

G

G, g [ge] Eighth Tk. letter, G; eighth (in a class/ series); (*mus.*) soh. ~ **elbisesi,** (*aer.*) G-suit: ~ **katsayısı,** (*phys.*) g-factor.
G, g. = (*el.*) GAUSS; GEÇİCİ; GÖL; GRAD; GÜNEY.
Ga. = (*ch.s.*) GALYUM.
gabardin (*tex.*) Gabardine.
gabari (*eng.*) Template; (*rly.*) gauge; clearance.
gab·avetⁱ Stupidity; obtuseness. ~**i(lik),** stupid/ (-ity); obtuse(ness).
gab¹inⁿⁱ (*fin.*) Overcharge; (*leg.*) fraud(ulence); (*sl.*) swindle.
gab·ro (*geol.*) Gabbro. ~**ya,** (*naut.*) topmast.
gacır ~ **gucur,** (*ech.*) creaking.
gaco (*sl.*) Sweetheart; (*ich.*) very small PALAMUT. ~ **oskisi,** (*sl.*) pound sterling.
-gaç *n. suf.* [225] = -GEÇ [PATLANGAÇ].
gada¹kᵍ¹ Spike. ~**lı,** ~ **ayakkabı,** (*sp.*) spiked-shoes.
gaddar Cruel; barbarous; perfidious; exorbitant. ~ **olm.,** behave pitilessly.
gaddar·ca Cruelly. ~**e,** (*mil.*) heavy double-edged scimitar. ~**lık,** cruelty; atrocity; perfidy; selling at exorbitant prices; ~ **etm.,** behave cruelly.
gad¹irʳⁱ/ ~**lik** Cruelty; tyranny, injustice; perfidy; breach of trust.
gadolinyum (*chem.*) Gadolinium.
gadr- = GADİR. ~¹**etmek**ᵉᵈᵉʳ **(-e),** do s.o. a wrong; act unjustly; commit a breach of trust. ~**olmak,** *vi.* suffer a wrong. ~**olunmak,** *vp.* be wronged.
gaf Gaffe; blunder. ~ **yapmak,** make a blunder; put one's foot in it.
gaffar (*rel.*) Forgiving, indulgent (God).
gafil Careless; inattentive; unwary. ~ **avlamak,** catch s.o. unawares; take by surprise; cheat the unwary: ~ **avlanmak,** be caught unawares: ~ **olm.,** take no heed; pay no attention; be unaware.
gafletⁱ Heedlessness; inattention; somnolence; delusion. ~ **basmak/**~**e düşmek,** be heedless/ unaware: ~ **etm.,** be negligent/absent-minded: ~**ten,** inadvertently; absent-mindedly.
gafur (*rel.*) All-forgiving (God).
gaga (*orn.*) *n.* Beak, bill. ~ **burun,** aquiline, hook-nosed: ~**sından yakalamak,** settle s.o.'s hash.
gaga·lamak (-i) (*orn.*) Peck; eat; (*fig.*) scold. ~**lanmak,** *vp.* ~**laşmak,** peck each other; caress each other with their bills. ~**lı,** (*orn.*) beaked; billed; (*naut.*) Black-Sea sailing boat (high prow and stern): ~ **balina,** (*zoo.*) bottle-nosed whale: ~ **memeli,** (*zoo.*) duck-billed platypus. ~**msı,** beak-shaped, coronoid.
Gagavuz (*ethn.*) Orthodox Christian Turks in the Balkans. ~**ca,** (*ling.*) their language.
gâh Some time; a moment. ~ ~, at times, now and then.

-gâh *n. suf.* Place of . . . [ORDUGÂH].
gaile Anxiety, trouble, difficulty. ~**li,** troubled, worried; troublesome. ~**siz,** trouble-free; carefree. ~**sizlik,** freedom from anxiety.
gai¹pᵇⁱ *a.* Absent; invisible, hidden; lost. *n.* The invisible world; (*ling.*) the third person. ~**i gören,** clairvoyant: ~**lere karışmak,** disappear: ~**tedir,** he has disappeared: ~**ten haber almak/vermek,** practise divination; foretell the future. ~**lik,** (*leg.*) disappearance: ~ **kararı,** declaration of presumed death.
gaita (*bio.*) Human excrement.
GAK = (*mil.*) GÜNEY AVRUPA KOMUTANLIĞI.
gaklamak *vi.* (*orn.*) Croak, caw.
gal¹ *n.* (*phys.*) Gal. ~ⁱ², *pr. n.* (*geo.*) Wales. ~**a,** gala; (*th.*) gala performance. ~**ago,** (*zoo.*) bush-baby. ~**aksi,** (*ast.*) galaxy. ~**akto-,** *pref.* (*chem.*) galacto-.
galat¹ Error; (*ling.*) erroneous expression; barbarism. ~**ıhilkat**ⁱ, freak of nature, monster. ~**ıhis**ˢⁱ, illusion. ~**ımeşhur,** (*ling.*) commonly accepted error/solecism. ~**ırüyet**ⁱ, optical illusion.
galebe Victory; superiority; predominance; uncontrolled ferocity. ~ **çalmak/etm. (-e),** conquer, overcome; be superior.
galen (*geol.*) Galena, lead sulphide.
galeri (*arch., art., min.*) Gallery.
galeta (*cul.*) Hard biscuit; dried bread, rusk.
galeyan (*phys.*) Ebullition, bubbling; effervescence; (*fig.*) rage; excitement. ~ **etm.,** boil, effervesce; boil with rage: ~**a gelmek,** become angry: ~**a getirmek,** enrage.
gali (*naut.*) Galley.
galiba Probably; presumably.
galibarda Bright scarlet colour.
gali·biyetⁱ Victory; superiority. ~**p,** victorious; superior; dominant; prevailing; most usual; probable: ~ **gelmek/olm.,** be victorious, win; surpass.
galiz Coarse; thick; rude; crass. ~**lik,** coarseness.
Galler (*ethn.*) Welsh. ~ **Memleketi,** (*geo.*) Wales.
galon (*math.*) Gallon (= 4.5 litres); cylindrical metal container, drum.
galoş (*mod.*) Galoshes, overshoes.
galsama (*ich., obs.*) Gills.
galtavlama (*min.*) Galvannealing.
galvan·iz (*phys.*) Galvanization: ~ **banyosu,** galvanizing bath. ~**ize/**~**izli,** galvanized. ~**izleme,** *vn.* galvanizing. ~**izlemek (-i),** galvanize. ~**izlenmek,** *vp.* ~**izm,** galvanism. ~**o,** (*pub.*) electrotype. ~**okoter,** (*med.*) galvanocautery. ~**ometre,** (*el.*) galvanometer. ~**oplasti,** galvanoplasty.
gal·yotᵘ (*naut.*) Galliot, galley. ~**yum,** (*chem.*) gallium.

gam[1] *n.* (*mus.*) Gamut; scale.

gam[2] *n.* Care, anxiety; grief. ~ **çekmek**, be anxious: ~ **dağıtmak**, drive one's cares away: ~ **değil**, it's not important: ~ **yemek**, be oppressed with anxiety/sorrow.

gama = GAMMA. ~ **lı**, ~ **haç**, swastika.

gambot[u] (*naut.*) Gunboat; (*ich.*) small mullet.

gamet (*bio.*) Gamete. ~ +, *a.* Gametic.

gam·lanmak (-e) Be grieved; fret. ~ **lı**, grieved; anxious.

gamma (*ling.*) Greek letter 'gamma' (*Γ, γ*). ~ **ışınları**, (*phys.*) gamma rays.

gammaz Tell-tale, sneak, informer. ~ **lamak** (-i, -e), tell tales; (*pol.*) inform against, denounce. ~ **lık**, tale-bearing, informing.

gamsele (*mod.*) Mackintosh; oilskins.

gamsız(lık) (Being) free from grief; carefree.

gamz·e Wink; significant look; twinkle; dimple. ~ **'etmek**[eder], wink; inform against.

-gan *a. suf.* [223] = -GEN [SOKULGAN].

Gana (*geo.*) Ghana. ~ **lı**, (*ethn.*) Ghanaian.

gang (*geol.*) Gangue. ~ **liyon**, (*bio.*) ganglion. ~ **ren**, (*med.*) gangrene. ~ **ster(lik)**, gangster(ism).

gani Wealthy; independent; abundant; plentiful. ~ ~, abundantly, freely: ~ **gön(ül)lü**, generous: ~ **si** olm., want for nothing. ~ **lik**, abundance.

ganimet[i] Booty, plunder; (*fig.*) windfall; godsend.

Ganj (*geo.*) River Ganges.

gapar (*zoo.*) Type of wild cat; cheetah.

gar (*rly.*) Station. ~ **şefi**, station-master.

garabet[i] Being a stranger; exile; strangeness.

garai·'p[bi] *pl.* = GARİBE. Strange things, etc. ~ **ten**, very strange.

garaj Garage. ~ **a çekmek**/~ **lamak** (-i), garage: ~ **lar**, intercity bus-station. ~ **lı**, having a garage.

garam Passionate love.

garamet[i] (*fin.*) Debt, liability. ~ **en**, ~ **tevzi**, pro rata distribution.

garami (*lit.*) Emotional, lyrical. ~ **yat**[ı], lyricism.

garan·ti (*fin.*) Guarantee; warranty: ~ **etm.** (-i), guarantee stg. ~ **tilemek** (-i), guarantee stg.; make certain of stg. ~ **tili**, guaranteed; reliable. ~ **tisiz**, uncertain. ~ **tör**, guarantor.

garaz Selfish aim/motive; spite, rancour, grudge. ~ **bağlamak** (-e), nourish a spite against s.o.: ~ **olm.**/ **tutmak**, bear a grudge.

garaz·kâr Malicious; spiteful, selfish. ~ **kârlık**, malice; spite(fulness); evil intent. ~ **sız**, disinterested: ~ **ivazsız**, without ulterior motive.

garb- = GARP. ~ **i**, western.

garden·parti Garden-party. ~ **ya**, (*bot.*) gardenia.

gard·ıfren (*rly.*) Brakeman, guard. ~ **ıro·'p**[bu], (*dom.*) wardrobe; (*th., etc.*) cloakroom. ~ **iyan(lık)**, (duties of) prison-warder.

garez = GARAZ.

gargar (*dom.*) Porous bottle.

gargara Gargling; (*med.*) gargle. ~ **etm.**/**yapmak**, gargle: ~ **ilacı**, gargle, mouthwash: ~ **ya getirmek**, (*sl.*) soften the effect of a word/action.

garibe Strange thing, oddity; freak of nature; marvel.

gari·'p[bi] *a.* Strange, curious, fantastic, droll; lonely; poor, needy. *n.* Stranger; s.o. in a foreign land. ~

~, extraordinary: ~ **kuşun yuvasını Allah yapar**, God looks after the homeless/destitute: ~ **yiğidi**, youth fresh from his village: ~ **i şu ki**, curiously enough . . .: ~ **ine gitmek**, seem strange/odd.

garip·leşmek *vi.* Grow/become strange. ~ **lik**, strangeness; poverty. ~ **semek**, *vi.* feel strange/lonely: (-i), find stg. strange.

gark[ı] A being submerged; drowning; being overwhelmed. ~ **etm.** (-i, -e), submerge; overwhelm s.o. with gifts, etc.: ~ **olm.**, be submerged/drowned/buried/overwhelmed.

garnitür (*mod.*) Trimmings; decoration; (*cul.*) garnishing, trimmings.

garnizon (*mil.*) Garrison(-town).

gar·'p[bı] The West; Occident; Europe. ~ +, *a.* European, western. ~ **çı**, westernizer; Europeanizer. ~ **lı**, westerner; Occidental; European. ~ **lılaşmak**, *vi.* be(come) westernized. ~ **lılık**, westernization; behaving like a European.

garson Waiter; barman. ~ **iyer**, bachelor flat. ~ **luk**, duties/position of a waiter.

gaseyan (*med.*) Stomach upset; vomiting.

gas·'ıp[pı] *n.* Violent/wrongful seizure; usurpation. *a.* Seizing; usurping.

gas·'il[li] (Ritual) washing of the dead. ~ **ilhane**, mortuary. ~ **letmek** (-i), wash (the dead). ~ **sal**[i], corpse-washer.

gasp·'etmek[eder] (-i) Seize by force; usurp.

gastr·al (*bio.*) Gastral. ~ **alji**, (*med.*) gastralgia. ~ **it**[i], gastritis. ~ **o-**, gastro-. ~ **oentrolog**, gastroenterologist. ~ **oentroloji**, gastroenterology. ~ **ula**, (*bio.*) gastrula.

gaş·'iy[yi] Fainting, swoon; ecstasy. ~ **y·'etmek**[eder] (-i), cause to faint; (*fig.*) enrapture. ~ **yolmak**, *vi.* faint, swoon; (*fig.*) be in ecstasy.

GATT = (*General Agreement on Tariffs and Trade*).

gauss (*el.*) Gauss.

gavamız *pl.* Obscure matters; niceties; fine points. ~ **ına aşına olm.** (-in), know stg. in detail.

gavot[u] (*mus.*) Gavotte.

gâvur (*rel.*) Non-Muslim; ghiaour; infidel; atheist; cruel/heartless wretch. ~ **bozuntusu**, (*sl.*) stammering: ~ **etm.** (-i), waste utterly; ruin: ~ **eziyeti**, deliberately making s.o.'s task harder: ~ **gibi inat** etm., refuse obstinately: ~ **inadı**, obstinate refusal: ~ **olm.**, be a Christian; be wasted: ~ **orucu gibi** uzamak, be endless; be prolonged unnecessarily: ~ **ölüsü gibi (ortada kalmak)**, heavy, bulky/(be left unattended): ~ **a kızıp oruç bozmak/yemek**, hurt o.s. to spite others: ~ **un eniği!**, (*pej.*) son of an infidel!

gâvur·ca Like an infidel; heartlessly; (*ling.*) in a European language (usually French). ~ **casına**, pitilessly. ~ **laşmak**, *vi.* become cruel. ~ **luk**, being a non-Muslim; irreligion; fanaticism; cruelty: ~ **etm.**/~ **u tutmak**, behave cruelly.

gayakol (*med.*) Guaiacum resin.

gaybubet[i] (*obs.*) Absence; disappearance. ~ **etm.**, be absent; disappear: ~ **inde**, in his absence.

gayda (*mus.*) A type of bagpipes. ~ **cı**, piper.

gaye Aim, object, purpose. ~ **li**, with an objective; purposeful. ~ **siz**, aimless.

gayet Very much; really. ~**le**, extremely. ~**siz**, endless.

Gayger ~ **sayacı**, (*phys.*) Geiger counter.

gayr[i] Another person; = GAYRİ.

gayret[i] Zeal; eagerness; ardour; energy; endeavour, perseverance; protective feeling. ~ **almak**, take courage: ~ **dayıya düştü**, if no one else will I must do it!: ~ **etm.**, aim at; endeavour: ~ **göstermek**, do one's best: ~ **sarfetmek**, exert o.s.: ~ **vermek**, inspire; encourage: ~**e gelmek**, become active/ enthusiastic: ~**e getirme**, incentive: ~**ine dokunmak**, goad s.o. on to do his duty: ~**iyle**, in an endeavour to . . . .

gayret·keş Zealous; partisan. ~**keşlik**, zeal. ~**lenmek**, *vi.* be zealous. ~**li**, zealous, persevering, eager. ~**siz**, unenthusiastic; slack. ~**sizlik**, slackness.

gayrı *adv.* [203] Henceforth; at length, finally. +*neg.*, not any more.

gayri *a.* (*col.*) Other; different. *post.* [89] Other than, apart from. *Negative particle* (*sometimes prefixed to the adjective*). Dis-, in-, non-, un-, etc.: ~ **ahlaki**, immoral: ~ **askeri**, non-military; demilitarized: ~ **caiz**, illicit: ~ **cinsi**, (*bio.*) asexual: ~ **hukuki**, illegal: ~ **ihtiyari**, unwilling(ly); involuntary, willy-nilly; automatic: ~ **ilmi**, unscientific: ~ **iradi**, involuntary: ~ **kabil**, impossible: ~ **kabili itiraz//kıyas//şifa//tahammül//tahmin//telafi//tezelzül**, unobjectionable//incomparable//incurable//unbearable//unpredictable; incalculable//irreplaceable//unshakeable: ~ **kâfi**, insufficient: ~ **kâmil**, imperfect: ~ **kanuni**, illegal: ~ **kıyasi**, (*ling.*) irregular: ~ **layık**, unsuitable: ~ **maddi**, intangible, incorporeal: ~ **mahdut**, indefinite, unlimited: ~ **mahsus**, imperceptible: ~ **makul**, unreasonable: ~ **malum**, unknown: ~ **mefruş** unfurnished; bare: ~ **memnun**, discontented, displeased: ~ **memul**, unexpected: ~ **menkul**, immovable; (*leg.*) real estate: ~ **menus**, unfamiliar, strange: ~ **meskûn**, uninhabited, deserted, empty: ~ **mesul**, not responsible: ~ **meşru**, illegal, illicit; 'black'; illegitimate, bastard: ~ **meşur**, unconscious: ~ **mezru**, (*agr.*) unsown, uncultivated: ~ **muayyen**, indefinite: ~ **muharip**, non-belligerent, non-combatant: ~ **muhtemel**, impossible: ~ **muktedir**, incapable; impotent: ~ **muntazam**, irregular; disorderly: ~ **mutabık**, unsuitable: ~ **mübadil**, not subject to exchange; established: ~ **mümkün**, impossible: ~ **münasip**, unsuitable: ~ **münbit**, infertile, desert: ~ **müsait**, disadvantageous: ~ **müsellah**, (*mil.*) unarmed; non-combatant: ~ **müslim**, non-Muslim: ~ **mütecanis**, heterogeneous; unmixed: ~ **resmi**, unofficial: ~ **sabit**, (*el.*) astatic: ~ **safi**, (*fin.*) gross (weight, etc.): ~ **samimi**, insincere; disloyal: ~ **şahsi**, impersonal: ~ **şuuri**, unconscious: ~ **tabii**, unnatural; abnormal; strange: ~ **uzvi**, (*chem.*) inorganic: ~ **vakıf**, unaware: ~ **vaki**, that did not happen: ~ **varit**, not true/possible: ~ **vazıh**, incomprehensible; obscure; vague.

gayur Hard-working, industrious.

Gayya 'The bottomless pit'; abyss. ~ **kuyusu**, (*col.*) impasse, quandary.

gayz Anger, wrath.

gayzer (*geol.*) Geyser.

gaz[1] *n.* ~ **bezi**, (*tex.*) gauze; (*med.*) surgical gauze.

gaz[2] *n.* (*phys.*) Gas; (*chem.*) oil, paraffin; (*bio.*) wind; = HAVAGAZI. ~ +, *a.* Gas; gaseous: ~ **dolgulu**, gas-filled: ~ **fırını**, gas-oven/-furnace: ~ **gemisi**, (*naut.*) gas tanker: ~ **kaçırmaz**, gastight: ~ **kömürü**, (*min.*) gas coal, coking coal: ~ **lambası**, oil-lamp: ~ **maskesi**, gas mask; respirator: ~ **memesi**, burner: ~ **ocağı**, oil-stove: ~ **pedalı**, (*mot.*) accelerator: ~ **sayacı**, gas-meter: ~ **sızması**, (*bio.*) osmosis: ~ **sobası**, gas heater, paraffin stove: ~ **türbini**, (*eng.*) gas-turbine: ~ **üretici**, gas producer/generator: ~**a basmak**, (*mot.*) accelerate: (*sl.*) slip away: ~**ı kesmek**, (*mot.*) decelerate; (*sl.*) shut up.

gaza (*mil.*) Holy war. ~**nız mübarek olsun!**, well done!; congratulations!

gazal[i] (*zoo.*) Gazelle, antelope.

gaza'p[b1] Wrath. ~ **etm.**/~**a gelmek**, get angry: ~**a getirmek**, make angry: ~**a uğramak**, suffer s.o.'s wrath. ~**lanmak**, *vi.* become infuriated. ~**lı**, angry.

gazel[1] *n.* (*lit.*) Lyric poem; (*mus.*) extempore tune. ~ **boynuzu**, (*bot.*) bacon-and-eggs: ~ **okumak** give a recital; (*fig.*) tell lies. ~**han**, singer. ~**iyat**[1] collection of lyric poems.

gazel[2] *n.* (*bot.*) Withered leaves. ~ **vakti**, autumn fall. ~**lermek**, *vi.* (leaves) wither; (tree) shed its leaves.

gazete (*pub.*) Newspaper. ~ +, *a.* Press: ~ **çıkarmak**, publish a newspaper: ~ **kâğıdı**, newsprint: ~ **kapatmak**, (*pol.*) close down a newspaper ~ **kesik/maktuası**, cutting: ~ **toplantısı**, press conference: ~ **toplatmak**, (*pol.*) seize newspapers.

gazete·ci Newspaper publisher; journalist; news agent. ~**cilik**, journalism. ~**cisel**, journalistic ~**lik**, newspaper rack/stand.

gaz·hane Gas-works. ~**ışı(l)**, (*phys.*) luminescence/(-t).

gazi[1] *n.* (*mil.*) Warrior for the Faith/Islam; wounded soldier; war-veteran; title of a victorious Muslim leader, ghazi; *pr.n.* Atatürk; title of an heroic town [GAZİANTEP]. ~ **olm.**, return alive from the wars ~ **ler helvası**, (*cul.*) a type of HELVA. ~**lik**, quality rank of GAZİ.

gaz·i[2] *a.* Gaseous. ~**ibiği**, gas-burner.

gazino Large coffee-house/refreshment-bar; restaurant; casino (*not* for gambling). ~**cu(luk)**, (work of) GAZİNO-operator.

gaziye (*bot.*) Silver-wattle, mimosa.

gaz·küre (*phys.*) Atmosphere. ~**lamak (-i)**, smear with paraffin; gas; (*mot.*) accelerate; (*sl.*) run away ~**lanmak**, *vi.* (*bio.*) be windy. ~**laştırmak (-i)** gasify. ~**lı**, mixed with/operated by gas/paraffin gaseous, gas-. ~**oil/~oyl**, gas-oil. ~**ojen**, gas producer/-generator. ~**olin**, gasolene. ~**ometre** gasometer. ~**oz**, (*cul.*) fizzy lemonade/ginger-beer ~**ozcu(luk)**, (work of) maker/seller of fizzy drinks ~**ölçer**, gas-meter. ~**taşı**, whetstone. ~**yakıt** fuel-gas.

gazup Irritable; passionate, angry.

gazve = GAZA.

gaz·yağı[n1] (*chem.*) Paraffin; kerosene. ~**yuvarı** (*phys.*) atmosphere.

G·B = GÖK BİRİMİ; (*Great Britain*); GÜNEYBATI. **~CA** = (*aer.*) (*ground control apparatus*). **~D** = GÜNEYDOĞU.

Gd. = (*ch.s.*) GADOLİNYUM.

ge The Tk. letter G. **yumuşak ~**, the Tk. letter Ğ, soft G.

Ge. = (*ch.s.*) GERMANYUM.

gebe (*bio.*) Pregnant. **~ kadın**, expectant mother: **~ kalmak**, conceive, be pregnant: **~ zar**, (*gamb. sl.*) loaded dice. **~lik**, pregnancy: **~ testi**, pregnancy test: **~i önleme**/**~ten korunma**, contraception: **~i önleyici**, contraceptive.

geber·ik (*pej.*) Dead. **~mek**, *vi.* die (like a dog). **~tmek (-i)**, kill; butcher, slaughter.

gebeş Short and fat; ill at ease, awkward, uncouth; (*sl.*) fool. **~lik**, shortness; awkwardness, uncouthness.

gebre¹ *n.* Hair-cloth glove (for grooming horses). **~lemek (-i)**, groom with this. **~lenmek**, *vp.*

gebre² *n.* (*bot.*) Caper-bush; (*cul.*) caper. **~otu**ⁿᵘ, (*bot.*) caper. **~otugiller**, caper family.

gece *n.* Night; night-time. **~ +**, *a.* Night; nocturnal. *adv.* Last night; tonight; by night. **~ atmacası**, (*orn.*) common nighthawk: **~ aydınlığı**, (*ast.*) nightglow: **~ balıkçılı**, (*orn.*) black-crowned nightheron: **~ baskını**, (burglar's) night raid; (*mil.*) night attack: **~ bekçisi**, night-watchman: **~ çalıştırma**, (*ind.*) night work: **~ döneyi**, (*ind.*) night shift: **~ elbisesi**, (*mod.*) (man's) dress-suit; (woman's) evening-dress: **~ göğü**, (*ast.*) night sky: **~ gösterisi**, evening entertainment: **~ gözü kör gözü**, fine workmanship needs daylight: **~ gündüz**, day and night; continuously, uninterruptedly: **~ gündüz dememek**, not choose one's time: **~ işçiliği**, (*ind.*) night-work; (*sl.*) burglary by night: **~ kelebekleri**, (*ent.*) moths: **~ klübü**, night-club: **~ körlüğü**, (*med.*) night-blindness: **~ kuşu**, (*orn.*) owl; (*zoo.*) bat; (*fig.*) night-bird, prowler: **~ nöbeti**, night-duty: **~ okulu**, (*ed.*) night-school; evening-class(es): **~ oyunu**, (*th.*) evening performance: **~ SEFASI: ~ silahlı gündüz külahlı**, leading a double life: **~ vakti**, night-time: **~ vardiyası**, (*ind.*) night-shift: **~ yarısı**, midnight: **~ yatısı**, overnight stay; hospitality for the night: **~ yatısına buyurun!**, come and stay the night with us!: **~ yayı**, (*ast.*) nocturnal arc: **~ yırtıcıları**, (*orn.*) owls: **~ler gebedir!**, wait, things may be better tomorrow!: **~ler hayrolsun**/**~niz hayırlı olsun!**, goodnight!: **~ye kalmış**, benighted: **~yi gündüze katmak**, work day and night; make great efforts: **~yi sabah etm.**, spend a wakeful night.

gece·ci Night-worker; night-watchman; (*bio.*) vespertine. **~ki**, at night, by night.

gecekondu Squatter's house (put up illegally in one night and so allowed to remain). **~cu**, such a squatter; s.o. dealing in such houses. **~culuk**, living/dealing in such houses; jerry-building. **~laşma**, squatter development.

gece·lemek (-de) Spend the night in/at; become dark, (night) fall. **~leyin**, at/by night. **~li, ~ gündüzlü**, night and day; without a stop. **~lik**, pertaining to/used at night: **~ entari**, (*mod.*) nightdress/-gown: **~ külahıma anlat!**, tell me another!

~sefasıⁿ¹, (*bot.*) morning glory; marvel of Peru. **~yanığı**ⁿ¹, (*med.*) night skin disorders.

gecik·en Delayed, retarded. **~me**, *vn.* delay; timelag; lateness: **~den**, immediately. **~mek**, *vi.* be late; (*fin.*) fall into arrears. **~meli**, (*eng.*) delayed. **~miş**, behindhand, belated. **~tirilemez**, hasty; urgent; prompt. **~tirim**, (*cin.*) suspense. **~tirme**, *vn.* postponement, delay, adjournment: **~den**, promptly; urgently. **~tirmek (-i)**, delay, postpone, adjourn; leave in suspense.

geç Late. **~ ateşli**, (*mil.*) delayed-action: **~ kalmak**, be late: **~ oldu!**, it's late!: **~ olsun da güç olmasın!**, better late than never: **~ uçan yarasa**, (*zoo.*) serotine bat.

-geç/-gaç/-giç/-gıç *n. suf.* [225] *Denoting agent/instrument* [DALGIÇ; ŞİŞİRGEÇ].

geçe¹ *adv.* [174] Past (of time) [**beşi beş ~**, (at) five past five].

geçe² *n.* Side; flank.

geçe·ğen Temporary. **~ ¹k**ᵍⁱ, place of passage; ford; footbridge.

geçen *v.* = GEÇMEK. *a.* Passing; past; last. **~ gün**, the other day; not long ago: **~ günkü (gazete)**, (the paper) of a few days ago: **~ sefer**, last time: **~ yıl**, last year: **~(ler)de**, recently. **~e¹k**ᵍⁱ, corridor.

geçer *v.* = GEÇMEK. *a.* (*fin.*) Current; acceptable; valid; available; saleable: **(-e)**, (*med.*) contagious. **~ akçe**, currency; genuine; (*fig.*) sought after/valued by all: **~ olm.**, be valid.

geçer·li Current, in use; valid. **~(li)lik**, validity; being current; being in demand. **~siz**, not current; null; invalid: **~ kılmak**, cancel, nullify. **~sizlik**, nullity.

geç·ici Temporary, transient; provisional; (*bio.*) adventitious: **~ giderler**, (*fin.*) incidental expenses: **~ inanca**, (*fin.*) caution money: **~ iş(çi)**, casual labour(er): **~ madde**, (*leg.*) temporary clause: **~ olarak**, temporarily, *ad interim*: **~ satak**, (*fin.*) fair. **~ilir(lik)**, via·ble/(-bility). **~ilmek**, *vp.* = GEÇMEK; be passed; be passable; be given up/renounced. **~ilmemek (-den)**, be plentiful/too much. **~ilmez**, *a.* impassable; not to be given up; inevitable; impasse: *int.* no passage!, no thoroughfare!

geçim Living together in agreement; 'getting on' together; compatibility; (*fin.*) current value, currency; 'daily bread', livelihood. **~ aracı**, breadwinner: **~ derdi**, the daily struggle for existence, the 'rat race': **~ dünyası bu!**, 'one's got to live!': **~ genişliği**, comfort, luxury: **~ kapısı**, place of work: **~ masrafı**, (*fin.*) cost of living: **~ seviyesi**, standard of living: **~ yolu**, subsistence, 'bread and butter'.

geçim·li Easy to get on with; affable. **~lik**, subsistence, livelihood. **~siz**, quarrelsome, difficult, incompatible. **~sizlik**, incompatibility.

geçin·dirmek (-i) *vc.* Sustain; feed. **~ ¹k**ᵍⁱ, livelihood, income. **~ge**, (*fin.*) budget. **~im/~me**, *vn.*; existence; daily bread. **~mek**, *vi.* live; exist; subsist; make a living; pass for; have the reputation of: **(-le)**, get on well with others; (*dial.*) die: **geçinip gitmek**, subsist, just manage. **~melik**, subsistence.

geçir·ebilme (*phys.*) Conductance. **~gen**, (*phys.*) conductive, permeable. **~genlik**, (*phys.*) conductivity; permeability; (*ast.*) transmission. **~ici**, (*phys.*) conducting, transmitting. ~ **icilik**, (*phys.*) conduction, conductivity, transmissivity. ~ **ilmek** **(-e)**, *vp.* = ~ MEK. ~ **im**, transfer; transport. ~ **imli(lik)**, (*geol.*) permea·ble/(-bility); pervious(ness). ~ **imsiz(lik)**, (*geol.*) impermea·ble/ (-bility); impervious(ness). **geçir·me** *vn.* Passing; permeability; (*art.*) tracing. ~ **mek (-i, -e, -den)**, *vc.* make/let pass; transport over stg.; get rid of (pain, etc.); go through, experience; spend/pass (time); (*adm.*) appoint s.o.; see off (a friend, etc.); draw/pull on (clothes); insert, fit into; pass off as good/current; cause to renounce; (*med.*) pass stg. to s.o.; (*fin.*) enter (in an account). ~ **mez(lik)**, impervious(ness); -proof. ~ **tilmek**, *vp.* ~ **tmek (-i, -e, -den)**, *vc.*

geçiş Moving (house); passing; transfer; transit; (*phil.*) occurrence; (*art.*) transition; (*mus.*) transposition; (*leg.*) inheritance. ~ **belgesi**, (*adm.*) *laissez-passer*, passport: ~ **dönemi**, transition period: ~ **hakkı**, right of way: ~ **resmi**, (*fin.*) transit duty: ~ **üstünlüğü**, (priority) right of way: ~ **yüzeyi**, (*ind.*) interface.

geçiş·im/ ~ **me** *vn.* Interaction; (*min.*) transition; (*chem.*) osmosis: ~ +, *a.* osmotic. ~ **li**, (*ling.*) transitive. ~ **mek (-le)**, mix in with each other. ~ **siz**, (*ling.*) intransitive. ~ **tirilmek**, *vp.* ~ **tirmek (-i)**, *vc.*; attach no importance to stg.; (*med.*) get over (illness); escape/survive (accident).

geçi·t^{di} Place of passage; corridor; passage-way; cross-over; (*geo.*) pass, ford; (*naut.*) channel, fairway, sealane; (*min.*) drift; (*adm.*) transit; act of passing; parade; (*ast.*) transit. ~ **hakkı**, (*pol.*) right of transit: ~ **kalası**, (*eng.*) cat-walk: ~ **parası**, toll: ~ **parmaklığı**, (traffic) barrier: ~ **resmi**, (*mil.*) review, parade, march past: ~ **vermek**, (*geo.*) (river) be fordable; (pass) be open; (*adm.*) allow transit.

geçki Location, alignment, route.

geçkin Over-ripe; over-mature (wood); (*fig.*) past the prime; not so young; past (a certain age); (*adm.*) former, previous, ex-. ~ **leşmek** *vi.* pass one's prime; become over-ripe. ~ **lik**, over-ripeness; being past one's prime, etc.

geç·me *vn.* Passage (of person); lapse (of time); transmission; fitting (into stg. else); made in sections, 'knock-down'; change-over: ~ **hakkı**, right of way: ~ **parçası**, (*eng.*) adaptor. ~ **mek (-den, -e)**, *vi.* pass; pass along/by/into/over/through, etc.; pass away, come to an end, expire; elapse; deteriorate; fade; (fruit) be over-ripe; be transferred; move, pass as current/fashionable; be in vogue; (infection/inheritance) pass from A to B; be beyond s.o.; abandon/renounce/give up stg.; undertake stg.; take over (work/position): **(-i)**, *vt.* pass, overtake, go beyond; skip, leave out, omit; (*sl.*) denounce, tell tales about; talk about: **geç (efendim)!**, don't take any notice!, ignore that!: **geçelim!**, let's not talk about that: GECEN: GEÇER: **geçme namert köprüsünden ko aparsın su seni**, better to die than be indebted to a mean man: GEÇMEZ: GEÇMİŞ: **geçti Bor'un pazarı (sür eşeğini Niğde'ye)**, it's gone too far for you to do anything about it: **geçtim olsun!**, I'll drop the idea!; God forbid!

geç·melik (*fin.*) Toll. ~ **mez**, that does not pass; -proof; not current/fashionable; (*med.*) incurable; (*med.*) non-infectious; (*adm.*) invalid. ~ **mezlik**, invalidity.

geçmiş *v.* = GEÇMEK. *a.* Past; bygone; passed away; deceased; over-ripe. ~ **ola!**, [134] (illness) may it soon be past!; you've missed the opportunity/'the boat': ~ **olsun!**, may it soon be past!: ~ **zaman**, (*ling.*) past (in)definite tense: ~ **zaman görünümü**, (*ling.*) past aspect: ~ **zaman ortacı**, (*ling.*) past participle: ~ **zaman şekli**, (*ling.*) past tense conjugation: ~ **e mazi yenmişe kuzu derler**, that was a long time ago; let bygones be bygones: ~ **e etkili**, (*leg.*) retrospective: ~ **i kandilli/kınalı/tenekeli!**, (*vulg.*) damn the fellow!, that scoundrel!: ~ **i olm.** **(-le)**, have had occasion for dispute with s.o.: ~ **i unutalım!**, let bygones be bygones!: ~ **leri (-in)**, s.o.'s dead parents/ancestors: ~ **lerini karıştırmak (-in)**, abuse/curse s.o.'s ancestors: ~ **te suç**, (*leg.*) previous conviction.

gedele·l_{çci} (*sp.*) Quiver.

gedi·k^{ği} Breach; crevice; notch; (*geo.*) lacuna; gap; fault; (teeth) missing; (*leg.*) warrant; leasehold; licence; prerogative; (*mil.*) breakthrough. ~ **açılmak**, serious breach/fault appear: ~ **açmak (-de)**, (*mil.*) make a breach in: ~ **kapamak**, fill a gap: ~ **leri tıkamak**, block up the gaps.

gedik·li *a.* Breached; notched; holding a GEDİK warrant, etc. *n.* Regular customer/visitor, habitué; (*mil.*) regular NCO. ~ **siz**, junior (officer).

ged·ilmek *vi.* Become notched/jagged; have a gap. ~ **mek (-i)**, make a breach.

geğir·mek *vi.* Burp, belch. ~ **ti**, *n.* burp, belch.

geğre·lk^{ği} (*bio.*) Lower rib; false rib. ~ **ağrı/ batması**, (*med.*) pain in the side, stitch.

geko (*zoo.*) Gecko.

gelberi Iron rake (for furnace); (*ind.*) tool (for mixing mortar); (*agr.*) fruit-picking pole. ~ **etm.**, (*sl.*) steal.

geldiri (*leg.*) Warrant, summons.

gele (*gamb.*) Blank throw (in backgammon).

gelece·lk^{ği} *v.* = GELMEK. *a.* Future; about to come/ happen. *n.* The future. ~ **ay**, next month; (*fin.*) proximo: ~ **kuşaklar**, future generations: ~ **salı**, next Tuesday (after this coming one): ~ **sefer**, next time: ~ **zaman**, (*ling.*) future tense: ~ **zaman görünümü**, (*ling.*) future aspect: ~ **zaman ortacı**, (*ling.*) future participle: ~ **i açık adam**, an up and coming man: ~ **i varsa göreceği de var!**, let him try it on and see what he will get!: ~ **i yok**, with no future; in a backwater: ~ **te**, in times to come: ~ **teki**, future.

gelecek·bilim(ci) (*soc.*) Futurolo·gy/(-gist). ~ **çi(lik)**, (*art.*) futur·ist/(-ism).

geleğen (*geo.*) Tributary (river, etc.).

gelembe Sheepfold.

gelen *v.* = GELMEK. *a.* Coming, arriving; reaching; imminent; (*phys.*) incident. *n.* Comer. ~ **ağam giden paşam**, let them all come, they're all the same to me: ~ **evrak (defteri)**, (*adm.*) (register of) incoming documents: ~ **geçen/giden**, passers-by, visitors: ~ **gidene rahmet okutur/gideni aratır**, the newcomer makes you long for his predecessor.

gelenek[1]k[gi] Tradition, custom. ~ +, *a*. Traditional. ~ çi(lik), traditional·ist/(-ism). ~ li/ ~ sel, traditional. ~ selleşmek, *vi*. become a tradition. ~ sellik, traditionalism.

geleni (*zoo*.) Vole rat.

gel·geç Fickle, inconstant; impatient: ~ hanı, place where people come and go: ~ istek, (*phil*.) velleity. ~ gel, attractiveness. ~ gelelim, all the same; and yet; but; however. ~ gelli, attractive. ~ git[i], coming and going empty-handed, fruitless journey; (*geo*.) tides.

Gelibolu (*geo*.) Gallipoli. ~ Yarımadası, Gallipoli Peninsula; (*his*.) Thracian Chersonese.

gelici ~ geçici, transient, passing.

gelim (*geo*.) Flow, rising tide. ~ hali, high tide.

gelin Bride; daughter-in-law. ~ +, *a*. Bridal: ~ alayı, bridal procession to bridegroom's house: ~ alıcı, person sent to fetch the bride; (*sl*.) raiding police: ~ dul, young widow: ~ güvey olm., be highhanded; overlook the essentials: ~ odası gibi, neat, attractive: ~ olm., (girl) get married. ~ boğan, (*bot*.) type of wild pear. ~ böceği[ni], (*ent*.) ladybird.

gelince (-e) [180] Regarding; as for; as far as concerns.

gelinci[1]k[gi] (*bot*.) Corn-poppy; (*zoo*.) weasel; (*ich*.) three-bearded rockling. ~ illeti, (*med*.) dropsy, etc. (causing swollen legs). ~ böceği[ni], (*ent*.) ladybird. ~ giller, (*bot*.) poppy family, Papaveraceae.

gelin·çiçeği[ni] (*bot*.) Celosia, cockscomb. ~ feneri[ni], (*bot*.) gean, mazzard, wild cherry. ~ havası[nı], (*met*.) fine calm weather; (*mus*.) wedding music. ~ kuşu[nu], (*orn*.) type of lark. ~ lik, (*soc*.) *n*. being a bride; bridal/wedding-dress: *a*. marriageable/nubile (girl); suitable for bridal items: ~ etm., give away one's daughter as a bride; teach a daughter-in-law her duties. ~ otu[nu], (*bot*.) bladder cherry, Chinese lantern. ~ parmağı[nı], (*bot*.) type of long grape. ~ saçı[nı], (*bot*.) dodder.

gelin·mek (-e, -den) *imp. v.* Reach, arrive at; be reached. ~ ti, newcomer, immigrant.

gelir *v.* = GELMEK. *n.* (*fin*.) Income, revenue; (*th*., *etc*.) box-office receipts. ~ bildirimi, annual tax-return: ~ dağılımı, distribution of wealth: ~ gider, income and expenses: ~ sağlamak, endow: ~ sağlarlık, profitability: ~ vergisi, income-tax: ~ ler, revenues; income. ~ ci, *rentier*. ~ li, having so much income; having a fixed income; profitable.

geliş *vn*. Manner/act of coming; gait; arrival; the way stg. comes/happens; (*med*.) presentation (at birth); (*phys*.) incidence.

geliş·ici Progressive. ~ igüzel, by chance, at random; cursory, haphazard. ~ im, evolution, development, growth. ~ me, *vn*. growth, expansion, development; evolution; (*sp*.) approach; (*lit*.) development of plot: ~ doğrultusu, trend, tendency: ~ vitamini, (*bio*.) vitamin E. ~ mek, *vi*. grow up; develop, evolve; grow healthy//fat; progress; blossom out, bloom. ~ memiş, backward; underdeveloped. ~ tirilmek, *vp*. ~ tirim, (*cin*.) treatment (of subject). ~ tirmek (-i), *vc*. develop; improve; (*med*.) build up/strengthen (patient).

gelme *vn*. Act of coming; advent; arrival; (*phys*.) incidence. *a*. Come/arrived/risen from; imported.

gelmek (-den, -e) *vi*. Come; arrive; reach; come down/from/in/into/through/to, etc.; assure, provide; develop from; seem, appear; suit, fit, answer (a purpose), be suitable; affect, influence, touch; get at; amount to; be added; need; feel the need for; be the result of, come from; survive from; sham, pretend; endure, bear, suffer. *aux.v.* Happen habitually [= -EGELMEK]; want to [= -ECEĞİ GELMEK]; pretend not to [= -MEMEZLİKTEN GELMEK]. **gel de kızma!**, how could anyone not be angry?: **gel de ona bir daha yardımı et!**, how could one help him again (after the way he behaved last time)?: **gel gelelim** = GELGELELİM: **gel keyfim gel!**, how pleasant!, lovely!: **gel zaman git zaman**, a long time afterwards: **geldi geleli**, ever since he came: **geldiği gibi**, as soon as he came/comes: **geldiğine geleceğine pişman etm.**, give s.o. a hot reception: GELECEK: GELEN: GELİNCE: **gelip çatmak**, come, arrive, be near: **gelip geçici**, temporary; transient: **gelip gitmek**, come and go; go to and fro: GELİR, *n*.: **gelir gelmez (o)**, as soon as he comes: **gelmez (-e)**, it doesn't do to . . .: **gelmiş geçmiş**, what has happened so far: **gelmesi ile gitmesi bir oldu**, he no sooner came than he went: **gelmiye görsün!**, wait till he comes (and then you'll see!): **gelsin . . . (, gitsin . . .)**: it was only . . .: **gelsin yemek gitsin yemek**, there was heaps of food.

gelmi[1]ç[ei] (*ich*.) Large sword-like bone.

gem (Horse's) bit. ~ almak, submit to: ~ almamak, pay no heed: ~ almaz, uncontrollable: ~ vurmak (-e), fit the bit: (*fig*.) curb s.o.: ~ zinciri, curb: ~ i azıya almak, take the bit between one's teeth; get out of control: ~ ini kısmak, increase the pressure on s.o.: ~ ini ısırmak, champ the bit.

gemi (*naut*.) Ship; boat; craft, vessel. ~ acentesi, shipping office: ~ adamı, crewman, sailor, seaman: ~ ambarı, hold: ~ aslanı, ship's figurehead; (*fig*.) good-looking but useless: ~ başı, prow; bow(s): ~ belgeler/vesikaları, ship's papers: ~ bildirgesi, ship's manifest: ~ bordası, ship's side; freeboard: ~ bordasında teslim, (*fin*.) free alongside ship, f.a.s.: ~ boyunca, fore and aft: ~ demiri, anchor: ~ direğinde, aloft: ~ enkazı, wreck(age): ~ filosu, squadron: ~ havuzu, (wet) dock, basin: ~ hizmeti, service afloat: ~ ızgarası, stocks: ~ içbarınağı, port of registry, home port: ~ inşaatı, naval architecture, ship-building: ~ işleme, navigate: ~ işleticisi, ship-operator: ~ iye/sahibi, shipowner: ~ jurnalı, log-book: ~ kafilesi, convoy: ~ kalkışı, sailing: ~ kaptanı, ship's master: ~ karaya oturmak, run aground; be beached: ~ kızağı, cradle: ~ kirası, freight(age): ~ kirası sözleşmesi, charter-party: ~ levazımatçısı, ship's chandler: ~ leşi, wreck(age): ~ mühendis(liğ)i, marine engineer(ing): ~ ortaklığı, shipping company: ~ petrolu, bunker oil: ~ tayfası, crew, ship's company: ~ temsilcisi, ship-broker: ~ topu, naval gun: ~ yatağı, ship's berth; port of refuge: ~ zabitleri, ship's officers.

gemi-: ~ de teslim (satış), free on board, f.o.b.: ~ den hayır yoktu, the ship couldn't be saved: ~ ler, shipping: ~ nin akıntısı, ship's wake, backwash: ~ nin çektiği su, the ship's draught: ~ nin enine, abeam: ~**si şapa oturmak**, (*fig.*) suffer irreparable losses: ~**sini kurtaran kaptan(dır)**, he who succeeds is acknowledged: ~**ye bin(dir)mek**, *vi.*/(*vt.*) embark: ~**yi sapıtmak**, alter the ship's course.

gemi·ci Sailor, seaman; mariner; ship-owner: ~ **nuru**, (*met.*) St. Elmo's fire: ~ **pirinç**//**topmetali**, admiralty brass//gun-metal: ~ **pusulası**, mariner's compass: ~ **sandığı**, sea-chest. ~**cilik**, seafaring; seamanship; navigation. ~**lik**, dockyard, shipyard.

gem·lemek (**-i**) Fit the bit (horse); curb s.o. ~**lenmek**, *vp.*

gen[1] *a.* Broad; vast; abundant; (*agr.*) unploughed.

gen[2] *n.* (*bio.*) Gene.

gen- *Also* = JEN-.

Gen., gen. = GENEL(LİKLE); GENERAL.

-gen[1] *a.*/*n. suf.* -angle(d), angular, -side(d), -lateral [DÖRTGEN].

-gen[2]/**-gan/-ken/-kan** *a. suf.* [223] *Forming an intensifying deverbal adjective* [ÇEKİNGEN; UNUTKAN].

gen·belirti (*med.*) Syndrome. ~**birlik**, (*pol.*) confederation.

gence·cik Very young. ~**lmek**, *vi.* become youthful.

gen[1]**çci** *a.* Young; youthful, juvenile, adolescent; junior. *n.* Young man; adolescent, juvenile. ~ **delikanlı**, young blood: ~ **irisi**, tall and strong: ~ **izci**, cub: ~ **nesli bir varlık diye tanımıyanlar**, those who ignore the existence of the young generation: ~ **takım**, (*sp.*) junior team: ~ **yapılı**, of youthful build: ~**ten**, young.

genç·çe Quite young. ~**leşmek**, *vi.* become youthful/vigorous; be rejuvenated; take on a new lease of life. ~**leştirilmek**, *vp.* ~**leştirmek**, *vc.* ~**li**, ~ **yaşlı**, young and old alike. ~**lik**, youth; adolescence; youthful folly: ~ **ve Spor Bakan(lığ)ı**, (*adm.*) Minis·ter/(-try) for Youth and Sport: ~**ine bağışlamak**, put stg. down to one's youth and so forgive: ~**ine doyamamak**, die young: ~**ini kütah etm.**, not have enjoyed one's youth.

gene [204] Again; moreover; still. ~ **başladı**, he's at it again: ~ **de**, even so: ~ **görüşürüz inşaallah!**, I hope we shall meet again! ~**leme**, repetition; (*phil.*) tautology; (*lit.*) pleonasm.

genel *a.* General; public; collective; global, universal. ~ **af**, (*leg.*) general amnesty/pardon: ~ **alıcı**, (*bio.*) universal (blood) donee: ~ **arazi**, common land: ~ **bağışlama**, (*leg.*) general amnesty: ~ **bakış**, conspectus: ~ **başkan**, (*adm.*) general manager, chairman: ~ **çekim**, (*phys.*) gravitation; (*cin.*) long shot: ~ **durum**, general situation: ~EV: ~ **giderler**, (*fin.*) general expenses, overheads: ~ **görüşme**, (*adm.*) general discussion: ~ **gövdebilim**, (*bio., med.*) general anatomy: ~ **güvenlik**, public security: ~ **kadın**, prostitute: ~ **kanı**, general/public opinion: ~ **konsolos**, (*adm.*) consul-general: ~KURMAY: ~ **kural**, formula: ~ **kurul**, (*adm.*) general assembly/meeting; = KURULTAY: ~ **müdür**, (*adm.*) general manager: ~ **olarak**, generally: ~ **oy**, public opinion: ~ **oya başvurma**, (*pol.*) referendum: ~ **oynatım**, (*cin.*) general release: ~ **ödence**, (*fin.*) general average: ~ **satak**, market: ~ **sekreter/yazman**, general secretary: ~ **sözleşme**, collective agreement: ~ **suç bağışı**, (*leg.*)

general amnesty: ~ **taşıt**, public-service vehicle: ~ **tatil günleri**, public/bank holidays: ~ **türe**, common law: ~ **verici**, (*bio.*) universal (blood) donor: ~ **yetki**, (*adm.*) blanket powers.

genel·ev Brothel, bordello. ~**ge**, (*adm.*) circular/(-letter), general instruction. ~**geçer**, generally acceptable. ~**geçerlik**, general acceptability. ~**gelemek** (**-i, -e**), (*adm.*) circulate, circularize. ~**kurmay (başkanı)**, (*mil.*) (Chief of the) General Staff. ~**leme**, *vn.* (*phil.*) generalization. ~**lemek** (**-i**), generalize. ~**leşmek**, *vi.* become general. ~**leştirilmek**, *vp.* ~**leştirme**, *vn.* generalization. ~**leştirmek** (**-i**), make general. ~**lik**, a being general; generality. ~**likle**, generally; in general, on the whole.

genelmek *vi.* Become wide/spacious; be at ease.

general[i]**(lik)** (Rank/duties of) (*mil.*) general//(*aer.*) air-marshal.

generatör (*el.*) Generator, dynamo.

geneti[i]**k**[gi] (*bio.*) Genetics. ~ +, *a.* Genetic.

gen·görü Farsightedness. ~**güdüm(sel)**, (*mil.*) strate·gy/(-gic).

geniş Wide, broad; capacious; vast; extensive; abundant; comprehensive, cyclopaedic; generous, magnanimous; at ease, free from care. ~ **açı**, (*math.*) obtuse angle: ~ **açılı**, (*cin.*) wide-angle (lens): ~ **alan/kapsamlı**, comprehensive; all-inclusive: ~ **bir nefes almak**, breathe a sigh of relief: ~ **fikirli(lik)**, broad-minded(ness): ~ **gagalar**, (*orn.*) broadbills: ~ **gönüllü**, not easily upset, well-balanced: ~ **hat**, (*rly.*) broad gauge: ~ **kulaklı yarasa**, (*zoo.*) barbastelle: ~ **mezhepli**, having broad principles: ~ **omuzlu**, broad-shouldered: ~ **perde**, (*cin.*) wide screen: ~ **ünlü**, (*ling.*) open vowel: ~ **yürekli**, generous: ~ **yüzlü harf**, (*pub.*) bold face: ~ **zaman**, (*ling.*) [115] aorist tense: ~ **zaman görünümü**, (*ling.*) aorist/inchoative aspect: ~ **zaman ortacı**, (*ling.*) aorist participle.

geniş·görüş Farsightedness. ~**leme**, *vn.* becoming wide; (*phys.*) expansion; (*bio.*) dilation. ~**lemek**, *vi.* widen, extend, ease; expand; (*bio.*) dilate; become wide/broad//extensive/spacious; be at ease, be in easy circumstances. ~**lenim**, (*med.*) dilatation, ectasia. ~**letici**, *a.* broadening; amplifying: *n.* (*med.*) dilator. ~**letilmek**, *vp.* ~**letmek** (**-i**), *vc.* widen, broaden; enlarge, develop; (*phys.*) expand; amplify; (*med.*) dilate. ~**lik**, width, breadth; amplitude; spaciousness; abundance, ease of mind; easy circumstances: ~**ine**, across, crosswise.

gen[i]**iz**[zi] Nasal passages, nostrils. ~ +, *a.* Nasal. ~**den söylemek**, speak through the nose: ~**e kaçmak**, (food) go down the wrong way: ~**i tıkanmak**, have a stuffy nose. ~**si**, nasal. ~**sileşme**, (*ling.*) nasalization.

genleş·irlik (*phys.*) Expansivity. ~**me**, *vn.* dilation, expansion. ~**mek**, *vi.* dilate, expand, extend. ~**meölçer**, dilatometer.

gen·li Comfortable; prosperous. ~**lik**, spaciousness; abundance; (*phys.*) amplitude. ~**lileşmek**, *vi.* become prosperous.

geno·m (*bio.*) Genome. ~**sit**[i], (*pol.*, *ethn.*) genocide. ~**tip**[i], genotype.

gen·ortaklık (*fin.*) Holding company. ~**örgüt**

(*adm.*) bureaucracy. ~**örgütçü,** bureaucrat. ~**örgütsel,** bureaucratic. ~**soru,** (*pol.*) questions by MPs to Ministers.

genz- = GENİZ. ~**ek,** who speaks through the nose. ~**el,** (*ling.*) nasal (sound).

geo·fizik(sel) Geophysic·s/(-al). ~**i¹t**ᵈⁱ, (*geo.*) geoid. ~**metre,** (*ent.*) geometer, earth-measurer, inchworm. ~**metri,** (*math.*) geometry. ~**metricilik,** (*art.*) cubism. ~**metrik,** (*math.*) geometric(al): ~ **dizi,** geometrical progression. ~**teknik,** (*eng.*) geotechnical. ~**termik,** geothermal.

gepe·genç Very young. ~**geniş,** very wide.

-ger *n. suf.* Maker, doer [KİMYAGER].

gerçe¹kᵍⁱ *a.* True; real; factual; original; actual, effective; authentic, genuine; truthful; in the right. *adv.* In truth; in earnest; really. *int.* Truly!, really! *n.* Truth; fact. ~ **balinagiller,** (*zoo.*) right whales: ~ **boyutlu,** (*art.*) full scale/size: ~ **dolu,** (*met.*) hard hail: ~ **kişi,** (*leg.*) natural person: ~ **mantarlar,** (*myc.*) eumycetes, true fungi: ~ **maymunlar,** (*zoo.*) apes: ~ **medüzler,** (*zoo.*) jellyfishes: ~ **odun,** (*for.*) heart-wood: ~ **ol(ma)mak,** be (un)real: ~ **olmayan,** fictitious, sham, unreal: ~ **payı,** amount of truth: ~ **sanmak,** take seriously; believe in: ~**e aykırı,** contrary to the truth: ~**i gizlemek** (**-den**), hide the truth from s.o., throw dust in s.o.'s eyes: ~**ini söylemek,** tell the truth of stg.: ~**te,** in fact, really: ~ TEN.

gerçek·çi (*phil.*, *art.*) Realist; realistic. ~**çilik,** realism. ~**dışı(lık),** unreal(ity). ~**leme,** *vn.* confirmation, satisfaction. ~**lemek (-i),** confirm, verify; say stg. is true. ~**lenmek,** *vp.* ~**leşmek,** *vi.* prove to be true; materialize. ~**leştirilmek,** *vp.* ~**leştirmek** (**-i**), *vc.* realise, achieve; make real. ~**li,** real. ~**lik,** actuality, reality. ~**ten,** truly, really; in truth. ~**üstü,** (*art.*) surreal. ~**üstücü(lük),** surreal·ist/ (-ism).

gerçel (*ast.*, *math.*) Real.

gerçi [216] Although; granted that; it's true that ....

gerdan (*bio.*) Throat, neck; double-chin. ~ **kırmak,** bow; swing the head; put on coquettish airs.

gerdaniye (buselik) (*Or. mus.*) Compound melodies.

gerdan·kıran (*orn.*) Wryneck; (*live.*) stumbling (horse). ~**lı,** -throated. ~**lık,** necklace; neckband: ~ **tanesi,** bead.

gerde¹kᵍⁱ Bridal chamber. ~ **gecesi,** wedding night: ~ **uçuşu,** (*ent.*) mating flight: ~**e girmek,** groom go to his bride.

gerdel (*dom.*) Wooden/leather bucket; (*chem.*) tank.

gerdir·ilmek *vp.* ~**mek (-i, -e),** *vc.* = GERMEK.

gere¹çᶜⁱ Material(s), equipment. ~ **ambarı,** warehouse: ~**ler,** supplies; (*mil.*) munitions.

gereğince As far as is necessary; as required; if need be; in accordance with.

gerek¹ *conj.* [209] ~ ... ~**(se)** ..., whether ... or ...; both ... and ....

gere¹kᵍⁱ ² *a.* [127] Necessary; needed; fitting, proper, due; *with a conditional tense* probable. *n.* Necessity; requisite; requirement. ~**i düşünülmek,** think a problem through: ~**i gibi,** as is due, properly: ~ İNCE: ~**inde,** in case of need: ~**inden fazla,** more than necessary: ~**ini yerine getirmek,**

do what is necessary: ~**se,** if it be necessary; if it be proper: ~**tir,** it is necessary; it is right.

gerek·çe Motive, reason; covering letter; (*leg.*) ground; (*phil.*) corollary. ~**çeli,** motivated. ~**çesiz,** unmotivated. ~**en,** required, necessary. ~**irci(lik),** (*phil.*) determin·ist/(-ism). ~**li,** necessary: ~ **kılmak,** prefer, uphold: ~ **say(ma)mak,** consider (un)necessary. ~**(li)lik,** necessity; fitness; (*ling.*) necessitative. ~**mek,** *vi.* [127] be essential/ needful/necessary; be lacking; be fitting/suitable; be worthy of: **gerektiğinde,** in case of need. ~**seme/** ~**sinmek/** ~**sinme,** *vn.* need, necessity, requirement: ~**yi karşılamak,** meet a need. ~**semek/**~**sinmek** (**-i**), consider necessary; feel the need of. ~**siz(lik),** (being) unnecessary; inappropriate. ~ **tiren,** necessitating. ~**tirici,** causing, motivating. ~**tirim,** (*phil.*) determination. ~**tirmek (-i),** require, consider necessary; determine.

gerelti (*dial.*) Obstacle, hindrance.

geren (*geol.*) Stiff clay soil; (*agr.*) fallow land.

gergedan (*zoo.*) Rhinoceros. ~ **böceği,** (*ent.*) European rhinoceros beetle.

gergef (*tex.*) Embroiderer's frame. ~ **işi,** embroidery: ~ **işlemek,** embroider (on frame).

gergi Stretching device; brace; weaver's bar; (*bio.*) tone. ~ **çubuğu,** (*eng.*) tie-rod: ~ **yitimi,** (*bio.*) atony.

gergi·ce¹kᵍⁱ (Chair/boat) stretcher. ~**li,** braced. ~**n,** taut, stretched; (*fig.*) strained (nerves/ relations): ~ **dönem/evre,** limit/final stage. ~**nleşmek,** *vi.* become stretched/strained. ~**nleştirmek (-i),** *vc.* stretch, strain. ~**nlik,** tension, strain. ~**siz,** unsupported.

geri¹ *n.* (*agr.*) Sack for straw (on a cart).

geri² *n.* Hinder part; rear; background; remainder; rest. *a.* Hinder; posterior; back; (*fig.*) retrograde; backward; (clock) slow; (*sl.*) stupid. *adv.* [198] Behind; back(ward); retro-; again, re-. *int.* Back! ~ **akış,** back-flow: ~ **alınamaz,** irrevocable: ~ **almak,** repossess/take back (stg. given); lead back: ~ **ateşleme,** backfire: ~ **baskı,** back pressure: ~ **basmak,** reverse (car): ~ **bırakmak,** postpone; (*adm.*) adjourn: ~ **çağırmak,** recall (diplomat, etc.): ~ **çekilmek,** withdraw; retreat; not interfere: ~ **çevirmek,** give back, return; reject: ~ **dönmek,** turn back; double back: ~ **dönüş,** return: ~ **dönüşlü,** retrospective: ~ **durmak (-den),** abstain, refrain; not interfere: ~ **gelmek,** come back, return: ~ ~ **çekilmek,** withdraw, go back: ~ **gitmek,** go back, recede; (*naut.*) go astern; (*med.*) get worse, decline: ~ **gönderilemez,** non-returnable: ~ **göndermek,** send back: ~ **hizmet,** (*mil.*) support services: ~ **kafalı,** reactionary: ~ **kalmak,** stay behind; be late: ~ **kalan,** the rest, remainder; arrears (of work): ~ **kalmış,** backward: ~ **komak,** put back; leave undone; postpone: ~ **olm.,** (clock) be slow: ~ **perdesi,** (*th.*) backcloth: ~ **sürükleme,** (*phys.*) drag: ~ **tepmek,** kick back; (*phys.*) react: (*mil.*) recoil: ~ **tuşu,** (typing) back-spacer: ~ **verme,** *vn.* (*fin.*) reimbursement, draw-back; feedback: ~ **vermek (-i),** return, give back: ~ **verilmez,** non-returnable.

geri-: ~**de bırakmak,** leave behind; outstrip;

(*naut.*) leave astern: ~**de mevki almak**, take stations astern: ~**deki**, rear: ~**den aydınlatma**, (*cin.*) back lighting: ~**den** ~**ye**, secretly: ~**den gösterim**, (*cin.*) back-projection: ~**sin** ~**ye gitmek/ yürümek**, go/walk backwards: ~**sİNGERİYE**: ~**sine kalmak**, (*naut.*) fall astern: ~**ye**, *adv.* backwards; retro-; inversely: ~**ye!**, *int.* (*mil.*) about turn!: ~**ye atmak**, delay, postpone: ~**ye çağrılmak**, be recalled; (*adm.*) be removed from office: ~**ye doğru**, backward; retrogressive: ~**ye doğru sayma**, (*aer.*) count-down: ~**ye dönüş**, (*cin.*) flashback: ~**ye sarım**, (*cin.*) rewind: ~**ye yürüme**, (*leg.*) retroaction.

geriatri (*med.*) Geriatrics.
geri·ci (*pol.*) Reactionary. ~**cilik**, reaction. ~**çevrim**, (*chem.*) recycling.
geridon (*dom.*) Round pedestal table.
geri·lek (*phil.*) Regressive. ~**leme**, *vn.* regression; recession; (*mil.*) withdrawal. ~**lemek**, *vi.* regress; recede; be slow/late; remain behind; make no progress; worsen. ~**letmek (-i)**, leave behind; hinder. ~**leyici**, regressive: ~ **benzeşme**, (*ling.*) regressive assimilation. ~**leyiş**, retreat. ~**lik**, backwardness.
geril·i Stretched; tight, taut, ~**im**, (*phys.*) tension; (*el.*) voltage; (*fig.*) tension; (*min.*) stress: ~ **çizgesi**, stress diagram: ~ **giderme**, stress relieving. ~**imli**, stressed; strained; (*el.*) live; under tension. ~**imölçer**, (*el.*) potentiometer, voltmeter. ~**imsiz**, unstressed.
gerilla (*mil.*) ~ (**savaşı**), guerrilla warfare, bush-fighting. ~**cı**, guerrilla.
ger·ilme *vn.* Stress; stretching. ~**ilmek**, *vp.* be stretched/stressed/tightened: **gerile gerile**, self-importantly. ~**inim**, (*min.*) strain. ~**inmek**, *vi.* stretch (o.s.): **gerine gerine**, stretching. ~**iniş**, stretching.
gerisingeriye (*col.*) Going back(wards); returning.
geriz Sewer; drain. ~**e taş atmak**, provoke s.o. to rudeness, etc.
germanyum (*chem.*) Germanium.
ger·me *vn.* (*phys.*) Tension; stretching; strain; (*eng.*) brace: ~ **ölçeği**, extensometer: ~ **somunu**, turn-buckle. ~**mek (-i)**, stretch; tighten; stretch over, cover. ~ **meli**, braced.
germen[1] *n.* (*mil.*) Fortress, castle.
germen[2] *n.* (*bot.*) Germen.
germi Warmth; ardour; eagerness. ~ **vermek**, redouble (one's efforts); intensify (stg.)
geştalt (*phil.*) Gestalt; the whole.
get¹ir[ri] (*mod.*) Gaiters, spats.
getir·gen/ ~**ici** (*bio.*) Afferent. ~**ilmek**, *vp.* ~**mek (-i, -den, -e)**, *vc.* [146] = GELMEK; bring; carry; produce, cause; import; reach; put forward (ideas). ~**tme**, *vn.*: ~ **belgesi**, (*leg.*) citation, summons, subpoena. ~**tmek (-i, -e)**, *vc.* cause to bring/ appear/import; order (books, etc.).
getr (*mod.*) Spats.
getto (*soc.*) Ghetto.
gevele·me *vn.* ~**mek (-i)**, (*live.*) chew; (*fig.*) chew over, hum and haw, beat about the bush.
geven (*bot.*) Gum-tragacanth, goat's thorn.
geveze Talkative; chattering; gossiping; indiscreet,

unable to keep a secret. ~**lenmek**, *vi.* chatter; gossip. ~**lik**, chattering; babbling; gossip; indiscreet talk: ~ **etm.**, chatter; gossip; be indiscreet.
gevher = CEVHER.
gev·iş Chewing the cud; rumination: ~ **getirmek**, chew the cud, ruminate. ~**işgetirenler**, (*zoo.*) ruminants. ~**mek (-i)**, chew, masticate.
gevre·k *a.* Friable; brittle; crisp, crusty, crackly: *n.* (*cul.*) biscuit, cracker: ~ ~ **gülmek**, laugh in an easy/self-satisfied way: ~ **söğüt**, (*bot.*) crack willow. ~**kçi**, biscuit-maker/-seller. ~**klik**, brittleness; crispness. ~**mek**, *vi.* become brittle/crisp. ~**tilmek**, *vp.* ~**tmek (-i)**, *vc.*
gevşe·k Loose; baggy; slack; lax; soft; feeble; weak in health; lukewarm, lacking zeal: ~ **ağızlı**, gossip: ~ ~ **gülmek**, laugh too freely/vulgarly. ~**klik**, looseness; slackness; laxity, negligence; sluggishness; weakness; lethargy. ~**m**, (*bio.*) diastole. ~**me**, *vn.*; slackening; (*phys.*, *sp.*) relaxation; (*geol.*) loosening. ~**mek**, *vi.* slacken; become loose; relax. ~**mli**, (*bio.*) diastolic. ~**tici**, (*med.*) relaxant; slackening. ~**tilmek**, *vp.* ~**tmek (-i)**, *vc.* slacken, loosen; relax; enervate.
geyi¹k[ği] (*zoo.*) Deer; stag; red-deer. ~ **avcısı**, deer-stalker: ~ **boynuz/çatalı**, antlers: ~ **eti**, (*cul.*) venison: ~ **etine girmek**, (girl) reach puberty, become nubile: ~ **yavrusu**, (*zoo.*) fawn: ~**ler kırkımında**, never.
geyik·böceği[ni] (*ent.*) Stag-beetle. ~**dikeni**[ni], (*bot.*) hart's tongue fern. ~**domuzu**[nu], (*zoo.*) babiroussa. ~**giller**, (*zoo.*) deer family. ~**otu**[nu], (*bot.*) burning-bush, dittany; (?) savory.
geym (*sp.*) Game.
geyzer (*geol.*) Geyser.
gez (*sp.*) Notch (in arrow); (*mil.*) backsight (of gun); (*math.*) knotted rope (for measuring); (*arch.*) plumb-line.
gez·dirmek (-i, -e) *vc.* = GEZMEK; cause to walk/ travel; show s.o. round stg.; (*cul.*) sprinkle/spread stg. over stg. ~**egen**, *n.* (*ast.*) planet: ~ +, *a.* planetary: ~**ler arası**, interplanetary. ~**elemek**, *vi.* wander about; hesitate. ~**ente/** ~**enti**, who loves travelling. ~**er**, mobile, travelling: ~ **ev**, caravan: ~ **kaldırga**, (*eng.*) gantry crane: ~ **punta**, (*eng.*) back centre: ~ **punta gövdesi**, tailstock, poppet. ~**ge**, (*mil.*) patrol. ~**gin**, widely travelled, wandering; tourist; (*med.*) ambulatory: ~ **albatros**, (*orn.*) wandering albatross: ~ **balina köpekbalığı**, (*zoo.*) basking shark: ~ **kelime**, international word: ~ **satıcı**, pedlar. ~**ginci**, itinerant, pedlar. ~**gincilik**, itinerancy.
gezi[1] *n.* (*tex.*) Mixed silk and cotton cloth.
gezi[2] *n.* Journey; excursion; promenade. ~ **çeki**, (*fin.*) traveller's cheque: ~ **hürriyeti**, (*pol.*) freedom to travel: ~ **yazısı**, (*lit.*) travel-book.
gezi·ci Itinerant; mobile, travelling, touring. ~**cilik**, itinerancy. ~**lmek**, *vp.* be gone around; be visited/inspected. ~**m**, tourism. ~**mci**, tourist. ~**mcilik**, tourism; (*phil.*) peripateticism. ~**msel**, touristic. ~**ne¹k**[ği], (*arch.*) hall. ~**nme**, *vn.* wandering; strolling; (*mus.*) modulation. ~**nmek**, *vi.* wander about aimlessly; stroll; (*mus.*) trill the notes. ~**nti**, excursion; walk, promenade, stroll;

ambulatory; (*arch.*) passage, corridor; (*mil.*) walk on battlements; (*mus.*) trill: ~ **güvertesi**, (*naut.*) promenade deck: ~ **tozuntu**, stroll, excursion.

gezlemek (-i) Notch (arrows); measure (ground); adjust, set straight; aim a weapon.

gezlik Curved sword(-blade); pocket-knife.

gez·me *vn.* Walking; patrol; watchman. ~ **mek**, *vi.* go about; travel; tour, visit; walk about (for pleasure); go about and inspect: **gezip tozmak**, travel widely; saunter about and enjoy o.s. ~ **men**, traveller, tourist.

-gı *n. suf.* [222] = -GI [ÇALGI].

gıcı·k^{ğı} Tickling sensation (in throat); mistrust. ~ **almak/olm.**, be annoyed with s.o./stg.: ~ **tutmak**, have tickling sensation, want to cough: ~ **vermek**, make cough. ~ **lamak** (-i), cause irritation (in throat); (*mec.*) make suspicious. ~ **lanmak**, *vi.* feel irritation; (*fig.*) be suspicious.

gıcır Substance used in chewing-gum; mastic. ~ ~, (*ech.*) creaking; grinding/gnashing (of teeth); very white/clean, brand new: ~ **ı bükme**, done hastily/by force.

gıcır·dama *vn.* ~ **damak**, *vi.* creak, rustle; (teeth) chatter, gnash; (snow) crunch. ~ **datmak** (-i), *vc.* make creak; gnash/chatter (teeth). ~ **tı**, grinding/gnashing/creaking sound.

-gıç *n. suf.* [225] = -GEÇ [DALGIÇ].

gıda Food; nourishment; normal diet. ~ **ile rejim bilgini**, dietician: ~ **yedekleri**, reserves of food.

gıdaklamak *vi.* (Hen) cackle.

gıda·lanmak *vp.* Be fed/nourished. ~ **lı**, nutritious. ~ **sız**, not nutritious; without food: ~ **kalan**, undernourished. ~ **sızlık**, lack of food; undernourishment.

gıdı·k^{ğı} Tickling; (*child.*) under part of chin. ~ **lamak** (-i), tickle. ~ **lanmak**, *vp.* be tickled: ~ **lanırmısın?**, are you ticklish?

gıgı (*child.*) Under part of chin.

gık ~ **bile dememek/** ~ **ı çıkmamak**, not make a murmur: ~ **dedirtmemek** not give s.o. a chance to speak; listen to no objections.

gıldır ~ ~, (*ech.*) roaring sound (of machines).

gıllügiş (*obs.*) Malice, rancour; treachery. ~ **li**, malicious; treacherous. ~ **siz**, sincere.

-gın *a./n. suf.* [223] = -GİN [KIZGIN].

gına Wealth; contentment; sufficiency; satiety; disgust. ~ **gelmek**, have enough; be surfeited: ~ **getirmek**, satiate; disgust.

gıpta Longing; envy. ~ **etm./** ~ **lanmak** (-e), envy.

gır (*sl.*) ~ **atmak**, talk: ~ **geçmek**, chatter; be inattentive: ~ ~ **geçmek (ile)**, pull s.o.'s leg: ~ ~ **konuşmak**, talk nineteen to the dozen: ~ ~ **a almak**, make fun of: ~ **kaynatmak**, (group) converse.

gırgır (*ech.*) Snoring; snarling; (*dom.*) porous bottle; zip-fastener; (*naut.*) drag-/trawl-net; (*dom.*) carpet-beater/-sweeper. ~ **ile taramak**, trawl. ~ **lamak** (-i), sweep a carpet.

gırıl (*ech.*) ~ ~, creakingly: ~ ~ **işlemek**, work ceaselessly.

gırla Abundantly; incessantly; too much. ~ **gitmek**, go far; be too much.

gırnata(cı) (*mus.*, *col.*) Clarinet(-player).

gırt¹ (*ech.*) Cutting sound.

gırt·la¹**k**^{ğı} (*bio.*) Throat; gullet; larynx, windpipe; (*fig.*) eating, drinking: ~ +, *a.* laryngic: ~ **çıkıntı/kemiği**, (*bio.*) thyroid cartilage, Adam's apple: ~ ~ **a gelmek**, (*fig.*) be at each other's throats: ~ **gözgüsü**, (*med.*) laryngoscope: ~ **kapağı**, (*bio.*) epiglottis: ~ **yangısı**, (*med.*) laryngitis: ~ **ına basmak**, force s.o. to do stg.: ~ **ına düşkün**, greedy: ~ **ına kadar borcu olm.**, be up to one's ears in debt: ~ **ına sarılmak**, choke s.o.; pester/dun s.o.: ~ **ından kesmek**, eat sparingly, save by eating less. ~ **lamak** (-i), strangle s.o. ~ **laşmak**, throttle each other.

gışa (*bio.*) Membrane; (*mod.*) covering, veil.

gıt ~ ~ **gıdak**, (*ech.*) cackling of a hen.

gıvıl ~ ~, all together; in a rush.

gıya·ben (*leg.*) By default; in the absence of s.o.: ~ **tanımak**, know by name/hearsay. ~ **bi**, defaulting; absent from court; (*col.*) from a distance: ~ **hüküm/karar**, judgement given in default. ~ ^ı**p**^{bı}, absence; default: ~ **ında**, in his absence; behind his back: ~ **ında zemm·etmek**^{eder}, backbite.

gıybetⁱ Speaking ill of s.o. in his absence; backbiting. ~ **etm.**, slander, backbite. ~ **çi**, slanderer, backbiter.

-gi/-gı/-gu/-gü/-ki/-kı *n. suf.* [222] *Forming deverbal nouns indicating the action, its result/means* [SEVGİ; GÖRÜNGÜ; İÇKİ].

gibi *n.* The similar; the like. *post.* [86] Similar to, like; -ish. *conj.* As; as soon as; just as; as though. ~ **gelmek**, think, suppose: ~ **görünmek**, seem as if . . .: ~ **ler**, the likes of . . .: ~ **lerden**, as if to say: ~ **me geliyor**, I have a feeling that: ~ **sine gelmek**, seem to s.o. as if: ~ **sine getirmek**, (*col.*) suggest, insinuate.

-giç *n. suf.* [225] = -GEÇ [BİLGİÇ].

gid- = GİTMEK.

gideğen (*geo.*) Outflow (from lake).

gider *v. pres.* = GİTMEK. *n.* (*fin.*) Outgoings, expenses; expenditure; charge, appropriation. ~ **vergisi**, turnover tax.

gider·ayak At the last moment, just when going. ~ **ek**, slowly, gradually. ~ **ici**, removing, eliminating; (*med.*) analgesic. ~ **ilmek**, *vp.* ~ **im**, reparations, compensation. ~ **lik**, (*phys.*) mobility. ~ **me**, *vn.* removal; elimination. ~ **mek** (-i), *vt.* remove, eliminate, get rid of; satisfy (needs): *vc.* = GİTMEK; induce to go. ~ **siz**, without expense, free of charge.

gidi *n.* Pander. *int.* (*of abuse/affection*): ~ . . . **seni!**, you scoundrel!, you little rascal!

gid·ici S.o. about to go/depart/die: ~ **değilim**, I don't intend to go, I mean to stay. ~ **ilecek**, *a.* destination. ~ **ilmek**, *vp. imp.* be visited. ~ **ilmez**, prohibited, out of bounds. ~ **im**, (*geo.*) ebb (tide): (*phys.*) range. ~ **imizi**, (*phys.*) trajectory. ~ **imli**, (*phil.*) argumentative, discursive. ~ **ip** = GİTMEK.

gidiş *vn.* Going, departure; course; movement, gait; conduct. ~ ~ **o** ~, that was the last that was seen of him: ~ **ini beğenmiyorum**, I don't like his conduct.

gidiş·at^ı *pl.* Goings-on; affairs; situation. ~ **dönüş**, return (journey/ticket). ~ **geliş**, comings and goings, traffic: ~ **yolları**, lines of communication. ~ **mek**, *vi.* itch.

gidon (*naut.*) Burgee; (*sp.*) (bicycle) handlebar.

-gil *n. suf.* [65] Belonging to the house/family of . . . [HASANGİL(LER)]. ~**ler,** (*bio.*) . . . family [FLAMAN-GİLLER]; (*zoo.*) -(i)dae [AYIGİLLER]; (*bot.*) -ae [TURP-GİLLER], -aceae [SALEPGİLLER].

-gin/gın/-gun/-gün/-kin/-kın/-kun/-kün *a./n. suf.* [223] *Forming deverbal adjectives/nouns* [GİRGİN; SIKKIN].

Gine (*geo.*) Guinea. ~**li,** (*ethn.*) Guinean.

-gir *n. suf.* That takes/seizes [CİHANGİR].

girçık ~ **belgesi,** (*fin.*) triptyque.

girda¹p^(bı) Whirlpool; turbulence; vortex; dangerous place.

gir·di *v.* = GİRMEK: *n.* (*ind., el.*) input: ~**ler,** formalities: ~**si çıktısı,** the ins and outs of stg.: ~**si çıktısı var (-in),** it has its complications: ~**sini çıktısını bilmek (-in),** know all its ins and outs. ~**dirmek (-i),** introduce, insert. ~**gin,** ingratiating; pushing; intimate. ~**ginlik,** ingratiation; pushfulness; intimacy.

girift^i *a.* Interlaced (writing); involved; intricate. *n.* (*Or. mus.*) Small flute. ~ **tezyinat,** arabesque.

giriftar Captive; (**-e**) afflicted with; subject to; exposed to. ~ **olm.,** be exposed to; (*med.*) be struck down (by illness).

gir·ilir Entrance, way in. ~**ilmek,** *imp. v.* be entered. ~**ilmez!,** *int.* no admittance/entry! ~**im,** *vn.* Entrance, admission. ~**imlik,** admission-card. ~**inim,** (*min.*) penetration. ~**inti,** intrusion; indentation; (*geo.*) depression; (*arch.*) recess; alcove. ~**intili,** recessed; indented: ~ **çıkıntılı,** wavy, zigzag, indented.

girinus (*ent.*) Whirligig beetle.

giriş *vn.* Entry; entrance; admittance; importation; (*eng.*) input, inlet, intake; (*el.*) primary; (*lit.*) introduction. ~ **deliği,** (*eng.*) manhole: ~ **galerisi,** (*min.*) adit: ~ **hakkı,** right of entry: ~ **kapısı,** (*adm.*) entry customs-barrier: ~ **katı,** ground-floor: ~ **sınavı,** (*th.*) audition; (*ed.*) entrance examination: ~ **ücreti,** entrance fee: ~ **vergisi,** (*fin.*) import duty.

giriş·ik Complex, involved: ~ **bezeme,** (*art.*) arabesque: ~ **tümce,** (*ling.*) complex sentence. ~**ilmek,** *imp. v.* be entered. ~**im,** (*fin.*) enterprise, undertaking; (*phys.*) interference: ~ **aracı,** interferometer. ~**imci(lik),** (work of) contractor. ~**imgücü,** initiative. ~**imölçer,** (*phys.*) interferometer. ~**imölçme,** (*phys.*) measurement of interference. ~**ken,** enterprising, pushful. ~**kenlik,** enterprise, initiative. ~**lik,** (*lit.*) introduction. ~**me,** *vn.* undertaking. ~**mek (-e),** penetrate; mix o.s. in/with, meddle, interfere; set about; (*fin.*) undertake.

Giri¹t^(di) (*geo.*) Crete. ~ **+,** *a.* Cretan. ~ **otu,** (*bot.*) Cretan dittany: ~ **şakayıkı,** (*bot.*) wood anemone. ~**lalesi**^(ni), (*bot.*) ranunculus. ~**li,** *n.* (*ethn.*) Cretan.

girizgâh (*lit.*) Introduction; introductory part.

gir·me *vn.* Act of entering; admission; breaking into/through. ~**mek (-e),** enter; go into; be contained by; enter upon, begin; change to; come into; join/participate in: **girip çıkmak,** stay for a short while; be in and out of: **girmiş çıkmış,** (in and out of asylum) a bit queer, with a screw loose. ~**meli,** having an entrance/recess: ~ **çıkmalı,** with

entrances and exits; indented; zigzag. ~**melik,** admission/entrance-fee//-ticket.

Girne (*geo.*) Kyrenia.

gişe Guichet; ticket-window; grille; pay-desk; (*th.*) box-office. ~ **oyunu,** (*th.*) box-office attraction.

gitar (*mus.*) Guitar. ~**cı/~ist**^i, guitarist.

git·gide Gradually; with time. ~**me,** *vn.* going; departure: ~ **ücreti,** (*rly.*) single fare.

gi¹tmek^(der) **(-den, -e)** *vi.* Go; depart, go away; go on/ continue (doing stg.); fade; perish, die; **(-e),** suit, fit; be sufficient for: **(-le),** accompany; last, pass; wear out; (*mot.*) work. *aux. v.* Do continually; complete [= -EGİTMEK]; *with another verb it expresses finality/certainty* [**anlıyamadım gitti,** I just couldn't understand: **yaralı ölüp gidecek,** the wounded man will certainly die]. **gide gele,** by continually going and returning, with great insistence: **gidecek olm.,** be destined to/for . . .: **gidene ağam gelene paşam,** (of a toady) you say 'Sir!' to your outgoing superior but 'My Lord!' to his successor: **gidip gelme,** return journey//ticket: **gitti (de) geldi,** (said of s.o. who has survived a 'fatal' illness): **gitti gider (dahi gider),** he/ she/it is gone for ever: **gitti ha!,** he's gone, has he?

gittikçe *adv.* [183] By degrees, gradually; more and more; every day. ~ **azalarak,** decreasingly: ~ **kötüleşmek,** go from bad to worse.

giy·dirici (*cin., th.*) Dresser; wardrobe mistress. ~**dir(il)me,** *vn.* (*eng.*) cladding. ~**dirilmek,** *vp.* ~**dirmek (-i, -e),** put on (clothes); clothe/dress s.o.; (*fig.*) abuse, reproach. ~**ece¹k**^(ği), clothing; garment, dress. ~**ilmek,** *vp.* (clothes) be put on/worn.

giyim Clothing, apparel, garment, dress. ~ **kuşam,** (best) clothes, finery; (*mil.*) supplies: ~**i kuşamı yerinde,** well-dressed.

giyim·biti^(ni) (*ent.*) Body louse. ~**evi**^(ni), (*mod.*) clothes-shop, clothier's. ~**güvesi**^(ni), (*ent.*) common clothes moth. ~**li,** dressed: ~**kuşamlı,** well turned out, smartly dressed.

giy·inik Dressed, clothed. ~**inim/~iniş,** mode of dress. ~**inme,** *vn.* dressing: ~ **odası,** dressing-room. ~**inmek,** *vi.* dress o.s.; **(-i),** put on, wear; (*fig.*) be silently angry: **giyinip kuşanmak,** dress o.s. up; put on one's best clothes: **giyinmiş kuşanmış,** all dressed up. ~**i¹t**^(di), clothes. ~**mek (-i, -e),** wear, put on clothes; (*fig.*) listen silently; 'wear' insults: **giydiğini yakıştırır,** he dresses well.

giyotin (*leg.*) Guillotine; paper-knife.

giysi Clothes, costume. ~ **denemesi,** (*th.*) dress-rehearsal: ~ **dolabı,** (*dom.*) wardrobe: ~ **gösterisi,** (*mod.*) fashion-parade. ~**ci,** costumier; (*cin., th.*) wardrobe mistress. ~**li,** ~ **film,** costume film. ~**lik,** (*th.*) wardrobe.

giz¹ *n.* (*naut.*) Jack-staff.

giz² *n.* Secret. ~ **toplamak,** (*mil.*) collect intelligence. ~**açım/~döküm,** confession. ~**ci,** spy. ~**düzen(ci),** (*pol.*) plot(ter). ~**em,** secret; mystery. ~**emci(lik),** (*phil.*) mystic(ism). ~**emli/~emsel,** mysterious; mystical. ~**emlilik,** mystery. ~**il,** (*phys.*) potential, latent. ~**ilgü¹ç**^(cü), (*phys.*) potential; latent force; (*phil.*) potentiality. ~**leme,** *vn.* concealment; camouflage. ~**lemeden,** publicly. ~**lemek (-i, -den),** conceal, hide, secrete; camouflage, disguise. ~**lenilmek,** *imp. v.* be concealed; be kept secret.

~lenme, *vn.* hiding, concealment: ~ **çadırı,** *(orn.)* hide (for bird-watching). **~lenmek,** *vi.* hide/ conceal o.s.; dissimulate; be kept secret.

gizli Hidden, concealed; secret; esoteric; unknown; clandestine, covert; *(adm.)* classified, confidential; *(bio.)* crypto-; *(phys.)* latent. ~ **alay,** *(lit.)* irony, sarcasm: ~ **anlaşma,** *(leg.)* collusion; *(pol.)* conspiracy: ~ **araştırma,** *(mil.)* intelligence: ~ **celse/ oturum,** *(adm.)* secret session; *(leg.)* hearing *in camera*: ~ **din taşımak,** have a secret religion/ conviction: ~ **diplomasi,** *(pol.)* secret diplomacy: ~ **düşünce,** *arrière pensée*: ~ **görevli,** secret agent: ~ **kapaklı,** very secret, clandestine: ~ **maksat,** *arrière pensée*: ~ **oturum** = ~ CELSE: ~ **oy,** *(adm.)* secret vote/ballot: ~ **sorak,** curiosity: ~ **sıtma,** *(med.)* dormant· malaria; *(fig.)* sly/underhand person: ~ **toplaşım,** *(pol.)* secret group/network: ~ **tutmak,** keep secret: ~ **uyuşma,** collusion: ~**den** ~**ye,** secretly: ~**si kapaklısı olmamak,** lay/put one's cards on the table: ~**siz kapaklısız,** openly, frankly.

gizli·ce Secretly, furtively: ~ **bakma,** curiosity, wonder. ~**lik,** secrecy; confidentiality. ~ **yazı** = GİZYAZI.

giz·men Secret agent. ~**sömürü(cü),** blackmail(er). ~ **yazı,** *(mil.)* cipher, code. ~**yazılamak,** encipher, encode. ~ **yazılı,** in cipher/code.

gladyatör *(his.)* Gladiator.

glase *(mod.)* Patent leather.

glasye *(geo.)* Glacier. ~ +, *a.* Glacial.

glayöl *(bot.)* Gladiolus.

gli·kojen *(chem.)* Glycogen. ~**kol,** glycol. ~**koz,** glucose. ~**kozit**[i], glycoside. ~**kozüri,** *(med.)* glycosuria. ~**serin,** *(chem.)* glycerine.

glisiyer *(eng.)* Groove, slide.

glo·bal ~ **olarak,** as a whole, globally. ~**bül,** globule; pill.

glokoni *(geol.)* Glauconite.

glotis *(bio.)* Glottis.

glüten *(chem.)* Gluten. ~ **ekmeği,** *(cul.)* gluten-bread.

GM = GENEL MÜDÜR·LÜK/-LÜĞÜ. ~**T** = (*Greenwich Mean Time*).

Gmr. = GÜMRÜK.

Gn. = GENEL. ~ **Kur.** = GENELKURMAY. ~**l** = GENERAL.

gnays *(geol.)* Gneiss.

gnostikler *(phil.)* Gnostics.

gnu *(zoo.)* Gnu.

goblen *(tex.)* Gobelin tapestry (stitch).

gocu[l]**k**[ğu] *(mod.)* Sheepskin cloak; monkey-jacket.

gocun·durmak (-i) *vc.* Scare. ~**mak,** *vi.* take offence; sulk; be scared.

gode *(mod.)* Flare, gore; *(eng.)* bucket. ~**li,** bucket-.

gofret[i] *(cul.)* Waffle.

gol[ü] *(sp.)* Goal. ~ **atmak/kaydetmek/yapmak,** score a goal: ~ **yemek,** give away a goal: ~ **e çevirmek,** convert (penalty). ~**cü,** goal-scorer. ~**lük,** capable of being a goal.

golf *(sp.)* Golf. ~ **(pantolonu),** *(mod.)* plus-fours.

golf(i)strim *(geo.)* Gulf Stream.

golyan ~ **balığı,** *(ich.)* minnow.

golyat ~ **böceği,** *(ent.)* goliath beetle.

gom *(chem.)* Gum. ~**ala**[l]**k**[ğı], shellac. ~**ba,** *(bot.)* coir rope.

gomene *(naut.)* Ship's cable; cable's length (185 metres).

gonca *(bot.)* Bud. ~ **vermek,** bud: ~ **yaprağı,** bract.

gondol[ü] *(naut.)* Gondola. ~**cü,** gondolier.

gon[l]**k**[ğu] Gong.

gonokok[u] *(bio.)* Gonococcus.

gonyometre *(naut.)* Direction-finder.

goril *(zoo.)* Gorilla.

goşist[i] *(pol.)* Leftist.

got·ik *(his.)* Gothic: ~ **harfler,** *(pub.)* gothic type: ~ **sanat,** gothic art. ~**lar,** *(ethn.)* Goths.

goygoycu(luk) *(rel.)* (Work of) blind beggar collecting alms for 10 MUHARREM; *(sl.)* yes-man, toady.

göbe[l]**k**[ği] *(bio.)* Navel, umbilicus; belly; paunch; *(soc.)* generation; *(min.)* core; *(el.)* armature; *(eng.)* hub (wheel); *(fig.)* heart, centre; *(bot.)* hilum; core, heart; *(art.)* central ornament, boss. ~ **adı,** name given at birth: ~ **atmak/çalka(la)mak,** dance the belly-dance; *(fig.)* be wild with joy: ~ **bağı,** *(bio.)* umbilical cord; *(bot.)* funicle: ~ **bağlamak/ salıvermek,** develop a paunch: ~ **havası,** belly-dance music; *(fig.)* joyfulness: ~ **taşı,** central massage platform in HAMAM: ~**i bağlı/beraber kesilmiş,** inseparable friends: ~**i çatlamak,** exert o.s. to the utmost: ~**i düşmek,** *(med.)* develop umbilical hernia; carry heavy weights: ~**i sokakta kesilmiş,** s.o. always out and about; gadabout: ~**i yağ bağlamış,** bloated: ~**ini kesmek,** cut the infant's navel cord. ~**ten,** radiating.

göbek·boyu Radial. ~**çi,** *(col.)* guzzler. ~**lenmek,** *vi.* become paunchy; (plants) develop a heart. ~**li,** having a paunch; *(arch.)* with a central boss; *(min.)* cored; *(bot.)* with a heart.

göbel Orphan; *(fig.)* bastard; cairn, mound. ~**e**[l]**k**[ği], *(myc.)* edible mushroom. ~ **ez,** *(live.)* small hunting dog.

göce *(agr.)* Threshed wheat; split cereal.

göcen *(zoo.)* Young animal, *esp.* leveret.

göç[ü] Migration; emigration; immigration; change of abode, removal; goods being removed. ~ **etm.,** migrate; emigrate; move house; strike tents; die. ~ **ettirmek (-i),** force to migrate.

göç·ebe Nomad; wanderer. ~ **ebeleşmek,** *vi.* become a nomad/wanderer. ~**ebelik,** nomadism; *(fig.)* always changing house. ~**elge,** place for migration, new home. ~**er,** nomadic, migratory. ~**erevli,** nomad. ~**eri,** nomadic by preference. ~**erkonar,** nomadic, wandering.

göçer·mek (-i, -e) Pass/transfer stg. to s.o. ~**tmek (-i),** cause to collapse/cave in.

göçken *(zoo.)* Leveret; stoat.

göç·kün Nomadic. ~**me,** *vn. (geol.)* failure, rupture; migration; emigration. ~**mek (-e),** migrate; emigrate; strike tents and move on; move house; *(fig.)* die; (house, etc.) collapse, cave in. ~**men,** *n.* immigrant: ~ +, *a.* migratory; immigration; *(ast.)* erratic; *(geol.)* shifting: ~ **çekirge,** *(ent.)* old-world locust: ~ **keme,** *(zoo.)* brown rat: ~ **kotası,** *(adm.)* immigration quota: ~ **kuşu,** *(orn.)* bird of passage. ~**menlik,** immigration.

göç·ü Emigration; (*geo.*) landslide. ~ **ük**, collapsed; caved in; in ruins. ~ **üm**, (*bio.*) taxis. ~ **ümsüz**, immovable. ~ **ünmek**, *vi.* die. ~ **ürmek (-i, -e)**, *vc.* cause to migrate/move; deport; cause to collapse; (*col.*) finish off (food). ~ **ürtmek (-i)**, cause to migrate. ~ **ürülmek**, *vp.* be forced to migrate. ~ **üş**, *vn.* migration; collapse. ~ **üşme**, (*ling.*) metathesis.
göden (*bio.*) Large intestine, rectum. ~ **yangısı**, (*med.*) proctitis.
göğ- *Also* = GÖV-.
göğ·em Greenish purple. ~ **ermek** = GÖVERMEK.
göğ·üsᵘ (*bio.*) Thorax, breast, chest; bust, bosom; (*naut.*) (flare of) bows. ~ **+**, *a.* Thoracic, pectoral: ~ **anjini**, (*med.*) angina pectoris: ~ **bağı**, (*mod.*) brassière: ~ **bağır açık**, (*mod.*) bare-chested, carelessly dressed: ~ **boşluk/çukur/kovuğu**, thoracic cavity: ~ **boyu**, breast-high: ~ **cerrahisi**, (*med.*) thoracic surgery: ~ **çaprazı**, (*sp.*) wrestling hold: ~ **çekimi**, (*cin.*) close-up, close shot: ~ **darlığı**, (*med.*) asthma: ~ **geçirmek**, sigh, groan: ~ **germek (-e)**, face/stand up to, breast, resist: ~ **gırtlağı**, (*orn.*) syrinx: ~ ~**e gelmek**, come to hand-to-hand fighting: ~ ~**e savaş**, hand-to-hand fighting: ~ ~**e vermek**, embrace each other: ~ **hastalıkları**, (*med.*) chest infections: ~ **hizası**, breast-high: ~ **ingini**, chest catarrh; influenza: ~ **illeti**, tuberculosis, consumption; asthma: ~ **kafesi**, (*bio.*) thorax, chest, rib-cage: ~ **kanalı**, thoracic canal: ~ **kemiği**, sternum, breast-bone: ~ **sesi**, (*mus.*) full deep sound: ~ **siperi**, (*mil.*) breastwork: ~ **tahtası**, (*bio.*) breastbone; (*mus.*) sounding-board: ~ **yüksekliğinde**, breast-high: ~ **yüzgeci**, (*ich.*) pectoral fin: ~ **zarı**, (*bio.*) pleura: ~ **zırhı**, (*mil.*) breast-plate, cuirass: ~ **ü daralmak**, have difficulty in breathing: ~ **ü kabarmak**, swell with pride: ~ **ünü gere gere**, with pride/confidence: ~ **ünü germek**, stand up to confidently.
göğüs·leme *vn.* (*eng.*) Breast-board, walings. ~ **lemek (-i)**, stand up to, resist; breast (waves, etc.). ~ **lü**, broad-chested (man); big-breasted (woman); (*zoo.*) -breasted, -chested, -fronted; (*naut.*) having flared bows. ~ **lük**, (*mod.*) apron, bib, pinafore; (*sp.*) plastron; (*mil.*) breast-plate; chest-protector; breast harness (of horse). ~ **sel**, (*bio.*) thoracic, pectoral.
göl·kᵍᵘ ¹ *a.* Blue, sky-blue, greenish blue. ~ **ardıç**, (*orn.*) blue rock-thrush: ~ **balina**, (*zoo.*) great blue whale: ~ **baştankara**, (*orn.*) blue tit: ~ **bayraklı cennet kuşu**, (*orn.*) King of Saxony bird of paradise: ~ **beyaz-göz**, (*orn.*) bridled white-eye: ~ **cennet kuşu**, (*orn.*) blue bird of paradise: ~ **çamur**, (*geol.*) blue clay: ~ **doğan**, (*orn.*) marsh hawk: ~ **ela**, bluish grey: ~ **etsineği**, (*ent.*) blowfly, bluebottle: ~ **gözlü**, greenish-blue eyed; (*fig.*) mischievous; treacherous: ~ **gurami**, (*ich.*) blue gourami: ~ **güvercin**, (*orn.*) stock dove: ~ **kandil**, (*sl.*) dead drunk: ~ **köpekbalığı**, (*ich.*) blue shark: ~ **kubbe**, blue vault of heaven: ~ **kuzgun**, (*orn.*) blue roller: ~ **kuzgungiller**, (*orn.*) rollers: ~ **sinekler**, (*ent.*) blowflies: ~ **tilki**, (*zoo.*) blue/arctic fox: ~ **zümrüt**, (*geol.*) beryl, aquamarine.
göl·kᵍᵘ ² *n.* (*ast.*) Sky; heavens, ~ **+**, *a.* Celestial, heavenly; astronomical; aerial; star; coelo-: ~

atlası, star atlas: ~ **aydınlığı**, air-glow: ~ **birimi**, astronomical unit: ~ **bulutludur**, things look black: ~ DELEN: ~ **dürbünü**, astronomical binoculars: ~ **eşleği**, celestial equator: ~ **fiziği**, astrophysics: ~ **gürlemek**, *vi.* thunder: ~ **gürleme/gürültüsü**, *n.* (clap of) thunder: ~ **haritası**, star map: ~ **ırakgörürü**, astronomical telescope: ~ **katoloğu**, star catalogue: ~ **kubbe(si)**, vault of heaven: ~ KUŞAĞI: ~ **manzarası**, (*art.*) skyscape: ~ **mavisi**, azure blue: ~ **perdesi**, (*ast.*) cyclorama: ~ YOLU: ~ **yuvarlağı**, celestial globe.
gök-: ~ **lerde**, above: ~ **lere çıkarmak**, laud to the skies: ~ **lere çıkmak**, get into a towering rage; pass away, die: ~ **te ararken yerde bulmak**, meet/find/obtain stg. easily/unexpectedly: ~ **te yıldız ararken yerdeki çukuru görmemek**, with one's eyes on the stars fail to see the pit at one's feet: ~ **ten inme!**, heaven-sent!: ~ **ten ne yağar da yer kabul etmez**, one must submit to the decrees of Providence: ~ **ten zembille inmemiş ya!**, he's nothing out of the ordinary; he's just like anyone else: ~ **ten zembille insen bile!**, no matter what you do/who you are!: ~ **ün direkleri alındı**, utter ruin ensued.
gök(b). = GÖKBİLİM.
gök·ada (*ast.*) Galaxy: ~ **+**, *a.* galactic. ~ **bilim**, astronomy: ~ **+**, *a.* astronomical. ~ **bilimci**, astronomer. ~ **bilimsel**, astronomical. ~ **cismi**ⁿⁱ, heavenly body. ~ **çe**, celestial, heavenly; sky-blue; pleasant; (*orn.*) rock-dove; (*dial.*) angel: ~ **ağaç**, (*bot.*) willow-tree: ~ **yazın**, (*lit.*) literature. ~ **çek/** ~**çen**, pretty, pleasant. ~ **çül**, inclining to blue; celestial. ~ **delen**, (*arch.*) skyscraper, high-rise building. ~ **dere** = ~ YOLU. ~ **ekseni**ⁿⁱ, (*ast.*) celestial axis. ~ **evi**, (*arch.*) planetarium. ~ **fiziği**, astrophysics. ~ **han**, Uranus. ~ **kır**, blue-grey, ashen. ~ **kumu**, (*geol.*) meteoritic granules. ~ **kuşağı**ⁿⁱ, (*met.*) rainbow. ~ **kuşaklı**, ~ **alabalık**, (*ich.*) (?) rainbow trout. ~ **kutbu**, (*ast.*) celestial pole. ~ **küresi**ⁿⁱ, celestial sphere. ~ **lük**, blue colour. ~ **men**, blue-eyed blonde. ~ **ölçümü**, astrometry. ~ **sel**, celestial. ~ **taşı**ⁿⁱ, (*ast.*) meteorite, aerolite; (*min.*) turquoise: ~ **+**, *a.* meteoric. ~ **türk(çe)**, (language of) ancient Tk. people in Central Asia. ~ **yakut**, (*min.*) sapphire (blue). ~ **yolu**ⁿᵘ, (*ast.*) Milky Way. ~ **yüzü**ⁿᵘ, sky.
göl (*geo.*) Lake. ~ **+**, *a.* Lake-; lacustrine: ~ **ayağı**, outlet from lake: ~ **beyaz balığı**, (*ich.*) lake whitefish: ~ **kurbağası**, (*zoo.*) marsh frog: ~ **midyesi**, (*zoo.*) swan mussel: ~ **olm.**, lake be formed: ~ **toy**, (*orn.*) (?) curlew.
göl·alasıⁿⁱ (*ich.*) Lake trout. ~ **başı**ⁿⁱ, (*geo.*) head of lake; stream feeding lake. ~ **bilim**, limnology. ~ **cü**ᶥ**k**ᵍᵘ ¹/~**e**ᶥ**k**ᵍⁱ/~**et**ᶦ, small lake; pool; pond; puddle. ~ **cül**, lake-dwelling/-growing.
gölge Shadow; shade; silhouette; (*art.*) shading; (*fig.*) protection, patronage. ~ **çalışması**, (*sp.*) shadow-boxing: ~ **düşmek**, (stg. bright) become clouded: ~ **düşürmek (-e)**, (*fig.*) denigrate; overshadow: ~ **etm.**, make/cast a shadow; (*fig.*) trouble s.o.; become an obstacle: ~ **filmi**, (*cin.*) silhouette film: ~ **gibi**, shadowy: ~ **görüntü/resmi**, silhouette: ~ **kuşu**, (*orn.*) hammerhead stork: ~ **oyunu//tiyatrosu**, (*th.*) shadow-puppet play//

theatre: ~ **salmak** = ~ ETM.: ~ **de bırakmak**, overshadow, surpass: ~ **den çıkma**, (*ast.*) emersion: ~ **sinden korkmak**, be very cowardly: ~ **ye girme**, (*ast.*) immersion.

gölge·altını Shade; shady place. ~ **balığı**nı, (*ich.*) grayling; corb. ~ **cil**, shadow-loving; living in shade. ~ **lemek (-i)**, leave in the shade; (*fig.*) overshadow. ~ **lendirmek (-i)**, shade; give shade. ~ **lenmek**, *vi.* sit in the shade; become shady. ~ **li**, shady; shaded; blurred: ~ **resim**, (*art.*) sciagraphy. ~ **lik**, shady spot; arbour; awning, canopy. ~ **olay(cılık)**, (*phil.*) epiphenomenon(alism).

göl·kestanesinı (*bot.*) Water chestnut. ~ **le(n)mek**, *vi.* lake be formed. ~ **lük**, lakeland. ~ **otu**nu, (*bot.*) water-lily. ~ **sel**, lacustrine.

gölü'kgü (*live.*) Beast of burden.

gömdür·mek (-i, -e) *vc.* ~ **ülmek**, *vp.* = GÖMMEK.

gömeç = GÜMEÇ.

gömgök Intensely blue; dark blue.

gömle'kgi (*mod.*) Shirt; tunic; layer; cover; (*eng.*) sleeve; housing; gas-mantle; (*zoo.*) snake's slough; (*bio.*) tunic; (*soc.*) generation; (*pub.*) book-jacket/-wrapper; (*mus.*) record-sleeve; (*fig.*) degree, shade (of colour), step, certain amount. ~ **değiştirmek**, (snake) slough its skin; (*fig.*) change one's opinions, etc.: ~ **değiştirir gibi**, turncoat, inconstant; unstable: ~ **eskitmek**, live a long life; be very experienced: ~ **inden**/~ **ten geçirmek**, adopt a child.

gömlek·çi(lik) (Work of) shirt-maker//-seller. ~ **li**, with a shirt; (*pub.*) jacketed. ~ **lik**, suitable for shirts, shirting. ~ **liler**, (*zoo.*) tunicates.

göm·me *vn.* Act of burying, committal, burial: *a.* buried; (*ind.*) let-in, countersunk, recessed, inlaid, flush: ~ **banyo**, panelled/sunken bath: ~ **çeliği**, (*art.*) damask steel: ~ **dolap**, built-in wardrobe: ~ **kilit**, flush lock. ~ **mek (-i, -e)**, bury; hide by burying; let in, recess, inlay. ~ **ü** (*archaeol.*) buried treasure; (*fig.*) hidden qualities. ~ **ücü**, burying. ~ **ük**, buried.

gömüldürü'kgü Bow of ox-yoke; breast-band.

göm·ülmek *vi.* Be buried; bury o.s. (in stg.); sink deeply/be lost in; disappear. ~ **ültü**, hunter's hide. ~ **ülü**, buried; hidden; underground; flush, ~ **üt**, grave. ~ **ütçü**, grave-digger. ~ **ütlük**, cemetery.

gön Tanned hide; coarse leather. ~ **cü**, leather-seller//-worker, saddler.

gön. = GÖNDEREN.

gönç Rich; prosperous; (*bot.*) luxuriant.

gönder Pole; boom; gaff; goad; flag-staff.

gönder·en/~ **ici** Consignor, sender; dispatcher, forwarding agent: ~ **posta**, (*rad.*) emitter. ~ **i**, ~ **etm.**, see s.o. off. ~ **ilen**, addressee, consignee. ~ **ilmek (-e)**, *vp.* be sent/consigned. ~ **im**, (*fin.*) transfer. ~ **işme**, *vn.* correspondence. ~ **işmek (-i, -le)**, exchange; correspond. ~ **me**, *vn.* dispatching, sending; consignment; (*lit.*) reference; (*leg.*) remand: ~ **belgesi**/~ **melik**, dispatch/shipping documents. ~ **mek (-i, -e)**, send, dispatch, consign, forward; see s.o. off. ~ **tmek (-i, -e)**, *vc.*

gönen *a.*, (*n.*) Damp(ness), humid(ity), moist(ure).

gönen·ce(li) Comfort(able). ~ **¹çci**, prosperity. ~ **çli**, prosperous. ~ **dirilmek**, *vp.* ~ **dirmek (-i)**, make

prosperous/happy. ~ **mek**, *vi.* prosper; rejoice, be happy.

gön'üllü Heart; soul; feelings; (amorous) affection; mind; inclination; courage. ~ **açıklığı**, peace of mind, happiness: ~ **açmak**, give pleasure: ~ **alıcı**, conciliatory: ~ **almak**, please, content; make up to a child (after being severe): ~ **avcısı**, flirt, philanderer: ~ **avlamak**, attract: ~ **bağı**, affection: ~ **bağlamak (-e)**, set one's heart on, long for: ~ **belası**, troubles of love: ~ **birliği**, harmony: ~ **borcu**, gratitude, moral obligation: ~ **borçlusu**, grateful: ~ **bolluğu**, generosity: ~ **budalası**, hopelessly in love: ~ **bulandırmak**, nauseate; arouse suspicions: ~ **çekmek**, be madly in love: ~ **çelen**, captivating: ~ **çöküşü**, breakdown of morale: ~ **darlığı**, foreboding, anxiety: ~ **delisi**, s.o. who keeps falling in love; madly in love: ~ **dilencisi**, s.o. who will do/submit to anything to stay with his love: ~ **eğlencesi**, pleasure; solace: ~ **eğlendirmek**, amuse o.s.: ~ **eri**, wise, experienced: ~ **esenliği**, repose, quiet: ~ **ferahlığı**, carefreeness: ~ **ferman dinlemez**, the heart will never change: ~ **gezdirmek**, think things over (before choosing): ~ **gözü**, perception; ability to see the truth: ~ **hoşluğu**, willingness, consent: ~ **hoşluğu ile**, willingly, eagerly: ~ **indirmek**, demean o.s./condescend (to do stg.): ~ **isteği**, desire (to help others): ~ **işi**, an affair of the heart: ~ **kırmak**, hurt s.o.'s feelings: ~ **kimi severse güzel odur**, beauty is in the eye of the beholder: ~ **koymak**, be offended/hurt: ~ **maskarası**, s.o. who behaves foolishly because of his passion: ~ **okşamak**, treat kindly: ~ **rahatlığı**, inner calm: ~ **tokluğu**, content: ~ **vermek**, give one's heart, fall in love: ~ **yapmak**, content, satisfy: ~ **yarası**, heartfelt wound/pain: ~ **yatırmış**, inclined (to do stg.): ~ **yıkmak**, hurt s.o. deeply. [*Also* = iç; YÜREK].

gönülden: ~ **çıkar(ma)mak (-i)**, (never) give up/ forget s.o.: ~ **ırak olm.**, be free from love (affairs): ~ **kopmak**, (deed) proceed from kind-heartedness: ~ **ne koparsa**, whatever one feels inclined to give.

gönlü: ~ **açılmak**, feel at ease/serene; be cheered up: ~ **akmak**, feel attracted by, fall in love with: ~ **bulanmak**, feel sick/nauseated; be suspicious about stg./s.o.: ~ **çekmek**, desire: ~ **çelinmek**, be captivated: ~ **çökmek**, have a breakdown (in morale): ~ **(gözü) gani**, generous: ~ **ile oynamak (-in)**, trifle with s.o.'s feelings: ~ **kalmak**, hanker after stg.; feel resentment/hurt: ~ **kanmak**, stop worrying; become calm: ~ **kara**, malevolent: ~ **kararmak**, become pessimistic; be tired of life: ~ **olm. (-de)**, be in love with: ~ **olm. (-e)**, agree to: ~ **rahat**, with a quiet conscience: ~ **razı olmamak (-e)**, not be able to agree to: ~ **takılmak (-e)**, be interested in: ~ **tok**, satisfied: ~ **var/(yok)**, he is (un)willing; he is (not) in love: ~ **yatmak**, approve of, agree to: ~ **zengin**, s.o. always trying to be generous.

gönlün-: ~ **ce**, after one's heart; as desired: ~ **de bir aslan yatar**, each has high hopes of himself: ~ **den geçirmek**, contemplate (doing stg.); entertain (an idea): ~ **den kopmak**, (present/tip) be given gladly; do stg. gladly/freely: ~ **e danışmak**, ponder over stg.: ~ **e doğmak**, have a feeling/presentiment: ~ **e göre**, as you wish: ~ **e su serpilmek**, enjoy o.s.

gönlünü: ~ **almak**, conciliate, appease: ~ **avlamak/çelmek/kapmak**, captivate: ~ **etm.**, coax, console, satisfy: ~ **geniş tut!**, don't worry/take it seriously!: ~ **hoş etm.**, please s.o. (by doing stg.): ~ **hoş tutmak**, try to forget some trouble; not worry: ~ **okşamak**, favour: ~ **pazara çıkarmak**, fall in love with s.o. just for the sake of it: ~ **yapmak,** console; satisfy: ~**n dümeni bozuk,** (*col.*) s.o. not serious in his love affairs.

gönül·deş Sympathizer. ~**deşlik**, empathy. ~**gücü**, morale. ~**lenmek**, *vi.* be hurt/upset. ~**lü**, *a.* willing; disinterested; voluntary; self-assertive: *n.* volunteer; lover; beloved: ~ **kıtası**, (*mil.*) volunteer force. ~**lülük**, willingness. ~**süz**, without pride, modest; affable; unwilling, disinclined: ~ **köpek av avlamaz**, you can't force people against their will: ~ **namaz göğe çıkmaz**, stg. done unwillingly brings no good. ~**süzlük**, disinclination, unwillingness; modesty.

gönye (*math.*) Set-square. ~**sinde olm.**, be at right angles. ~**burun**, (*carp.*) mitre-block. ~**lemek (-i)**, set out with a set-square.

görde¹k^{gi} (*ich.*) Bitterling.

gördürmek (-i, -e) *vc.* Make s.o. undertake some work.

göre (-e) *post.* [87] According to; in view of; respecting; about; after; considering; suitable for; (just) right for; in comparison with.

göre·ce (*phil.*) Relative. ~**ceci(lik)**, relativ·ist/(-ism). ~**celik**, relativity. ~**cilik**, relativism. ~¹**çci**, comparator. ~¹**k**^{gi}, view, appearance. ~**kli**, showy. ~**li**, relative. ~**lik**, relation. ~**lilik**, relativity.

göremez (*cul.*) Sour curds mixed with fresh milk.

görene¹k^{gi} Custom, tradition; usage; fashion. ~**e göre**, conventional. ~**çi(lik)**, traditional·ist/(-ism). ~**li/ ~ sel**, traditional, customary; routine.

göresi ~ **gelmek**, long to see, miss. ~**mek(-i)**, long for.

görev Duty; work; function; commission; (*leg.*) jurisdiction. ~ **dışı**, beyond one's duties: ~ **uyuşmazlığı**, conflict of duties: ~ **yapmak**, do one's duty: ~ **yeri**, office: ~**de eski**//**yeni**, (*adm.*) senior// junior: ~**den alınmak**, (*adm.*) be dismissed/ discharged: ~**den almak/çıkarmak (-i)**, dismiss s.o.: ~**den ötürü**, by reason of duty: ~ **e alınmak**, be appointed: ~**inde kusur etm.**, fail in one's duty: ~**ler**, affairs.

görev·ci(lik) Functional(ism). ~**deş(lik)**, (*bio.*) syner·gic/(-gism). ~**lendirilmek (-e)**, be given work/special task. ~**lendirmek (-i, -le)**, give work to s.o. ~**lenmek**, *vi.* take on work. ~**li**, *a.* having work/duty/function: *n.* official: ~**ler**, personnel, staff. ~**lilik**, official's qualities/duties; official work; function. ~**sel**, connected with work; professional; (*adm., leg.*) official. ~**selci(lik)**, (*phil.*) functional·ist/(-ism). ~**sever(lik)**, conscientious/ (-ness), relia·ble/(-bility). ~**siz**, having no function/duty. ~**sizlik**, being without a position.

gör·ge¹ç^{ci} (*cin.*) Slide. ~**-işit**, (*ed.*) audio-visual.

görgü Experience; breeding; etiquette, good manners. ~ **tanığı**, eye-witness. ~**cü(lük)**, (*phil.*) empiric·ist/(-ism). ~**l**, empirical. ~**lendirmek**, *vc.* ~**lenmek**, *vi.* gain experience; learn by seeing/ practice. ~**lü**, experienced; well-bred/-mannered. ~**süz**, inexperienced; ill-bred/-mannered: ~ **akraba**, country-cousin. ~**süzlük**, inexperience; bad behaviour.

görk^{ü} Beauty; showiness. ~**em**, appearance; pomp, splendour. ~**emli**, attractive, splendid, magnificent; well-built. ~**lü**, beautiful; showy.

görme *vn.* Act of seeing; sight, vision. *a.* Seeing; seen; visual; optical. ~ **açısı**, (*phys.*) angle of vision: ~ **alanı**, field of vision: ~ **gezisi**, sightseeing tour: ~ **siniri**, (*bio.*) optic nerve. ~**ce**, (*fin.*) subject to being seen; estimate by sight only.

gör¹mek^{ür} **(-i)** See; deem, appreciate; understand; visit, speak to; experience; attend to, do; perform (duty); have/take (lessons); value; take care of; (house) look at/onto; undergo (cure, etc.); (*sp.*) mark (ball/opponent), anticipate. *aux. v.* Do continuously; go on doing [= -EGÖRMEK]. ~ **istemek (-i)**, ask for/to see s.o.: **gör bak!**, look and you will see!: ~**dün mü ya!**, there, you see what happens!: **göreceği gelmek**, long to see: **gören Allah için söylesin!**, I swear it's true!: **görerek atış**, (*mil.*) direct fire: **göreyim seni!**, beware!; let's see what you're made of!: **görmediğe dönmek**, (s.o. ill) be fully recovered: **görmiyerek atış**, (*mil.*) indirect fire: **görmüş geçirmiş**, very experienced: **görsün!**, let him see!: **görüp geçirmek**, experience: **görüp göreceği rahmet bu**, this is all he will ever get/have: **görüp gözetmek**, watch over, protect.

gör·melik (*th.*) Show, entertainment, spectacle. ~**(me)mezlik**, feigning not to see; indifference; connivance: ~**ten gelmek**, pretend not to see, turn a blind eye. ~**memiş(lik)**, (being a) parvenu/ upstart; inexperienced: ~**in oğlu olmuş**, a parvenu who spoils what he can't appreciate. ~**mez(lik)** blind(ness). ~**müşlük**, a having already seen: ~ **duygusu**, (*psy.*) feeling of *déjà vu*.

gör·sel Visual: ~**-işitsel**, audio-visual: ~ **sanatlar**, visual arts. ~**sellik**, visuality. ~**sü**, imagination. ~**ü**, sight; view. ~**ücü**, seer, viewer; (*soc.*) woman sent to find/inspect a prospective bride: ~ **gitmek**, go and inspect the girl: ~**ye çıkmak**, (girl) be inspected. ~**ücülük**, inspection of the girl.

görül·mek *vi.* Be seen/witnessed; appear; be evident. ~**dü**, (*adm.*) seen, approved: *n.* approval visa. ~**düğünde**, (*fin.*) at sight. ~**egelen**, ordinary normal. ~**medik/ ~ memiş**, (as yet) unseen, extraordinary; completely new. ~**mez**, invisible. ~**müş** seen, witnessed. ~**ür**, visible.

görüm Sight; look. ~**ce**, husband's sister, sister-in-law. ~**celik**, being a sister-in-law: ~ **yapmak** interfere in all the bride's affairs. ~**lük**, stg. worth seeing; fee for seeing stg.; (*med.*) fees for house-visit.

görün¹ç^{cü} (*th.*) Spectacle, show. ~**lemek (-i)**, look on, enjoy (the show). ~**lük**, stage: ~**e koyma**, *mise en scène*: ~**e koymak**, stage.

görün·ge (*art.*) Perspective; representation. ~**gü** (*phil.*) phenomenon, observable fact. ~**gücülük** phenomenalism. ~**me**, *vn.* appearance; apparition

~mek, *vi.* show o.s.; appear; seem; be visible: **göründü Sivas'ın bağları,** it's happening as I feared: **görünen,** (*phys.*) apparent; virtual: **görünen köy kılavuz istemez,** it's obvious; you don't need any explanation. **~mez,** concealed; invisible; unforeseen; unexpected: **~ kaza,** completely unforeseen accident: **~ olm.,** disappear: **~ yerde,** out of sight. **~tü,** spectre, phantom; (*phys., cin.*) image; (*cin.*) frame, picture, scene. **~tülemek (-i),** produce as an image. **~tülük,** (*cin.*) screen. **~üm,** appearance, view; (*ling.*) aspect. **~ür,** apparent; visible; predictable; (*min.*) proved: **~de,** apparently; in sight: **~lerde,** in sight. **~ürlük,** visibility. **~üş,** appearance, complexion; show, parade; exterior; (*arch.*) aspect, façade, elevation: **~ etm.,** make a show: **~e bakılırsa/göre,** probably; outwardly: **~te,** apparently: **~ten,** in appearance: **~ü kurtarmak,** save 'face'/appearances.

görüş Manner/act of seeing; (*met.*) visibility; (*fig.*) interpretation, opinion, view. **~ +,** *a.* Optical: **~ açısı,** opinion; angle of vision: **~ alanı,** field of view: **~ noktası,** viewpoint: **~ tarzı,** mentality. **görüş·me** *vn.* Meeting, interview; consultation; conversation; discussion, negotiations. **~meci,** (*pub.*) interviewer; negotiator. **~mek (-le),** meet, confer; have contact with; **(-i),** discuss stg.: **görüşeni karışanı olmamak,** be free from interference; be independent. **~türmek (-i, -le),** introduce. **~türülmek,** *vp.* be introduced; be allowed to see/meet. **~ü,** (*pub.*) interview. **~ücü,** interviewer; (*pol.*) negotiator. **~ülmek,** *vp.* be discussed: *imp. v.* meet. **~üm,** opinion, view; (*pub.*) reportage.

göster·ge (*phys.*) Indicator, pointer, needle; (*phil.*) sign; (*math.*) index. **~gebilim,** (*phil.*) semiology, semiotics; (*med.*) symptomatology. **~ge¹çci = ~GE. ~i,** demonstration, display; (*cin., th.*) show, performance; (*pol.*) demonstration, protest: **~ yürüyüşü,** protest march. **~ici,** indicator, (*cin.*) projector; (*pol.*) demonstrator. **~ilmek (-e),** be shown/demonstrated. **~im,** (*cin.*) projection; (*psy.*) manifestation. **~imcilik,** (*psy.*) exhibitionism. **~iş,** appearance; aspect; show, affectation, ostentation; display; eyewash; (*sp.*) feint; demonstration: **~ yapmak,** show off, cut a dash: **~e kaçmak,** be prone/given to ostentation/luxury. **~işçi(lik),** showman(ship). **~işli,** of striking appearance; showy; stately, imposing. **~işsiz,** unimposing, unimpressive; reserved, abstemious. **~işsizlik,** modesty; unimpressiveness. **~me,** *vn.* showing; demonstrating: **~ adıl//belirteç//sıfatı,** (*ling.*) demonstrative pronoun//adverb//adjective. **~mecilik,** (*psy.*) exhibitionism. **~mek (-i, -e),** *vc.* [146] show, display; demonstrate; denote, indicate; exhibit; show off; expose (to sun, etc.): *vi.* appear: **göstere göstere,** openly, publicly. **~melik,** (*fin.*) sample, for show only: stg. worth exhibiting: **~ şahıs,** (*cin.*) extra, walk-on part. **~meparmağı¹ı,** index-finger. **~tmek (-i, -e),** *vc.*

göt¹ü (*bio., vulg.*) Anus, arse; (*fig.*) pluck, spunk. **~ içi kadar,** very narrow: **~ üstü oturmak,** be in a fix: **~ten bacaklı,** s.o. very short: **~ün ~ün,** (*obs.*) backwards.

götür·me *vn.* Carriage, transport, removal. **~mek**

(-i, -den, -e), take s.o./stg. from A to B; deliver; take away; carry off; lead/conduct to; kill; bear, support, put up with; accompany to/as far as; (*leg.*) arrest. **~tmek (-i, -den, -e),** *vc.*

götürü (*fin.*) Approximately, in round figures; in a lump sum; in bulk. **~ almak,** buy in bulk, contract at a lump price: **~ bina,** building put up by contract; badly built house: **~ iş(çi),** (*ind.*) piece work(er): **~ pazarlık,** bargain for the whole lot: **~ satış,** bulk sale: **~ ücret,** piece rate.

götür·ücü Transporting, conveying; (*fin.*) subcontractor; (*bio.*) efferent. **~ücülük,** sub-contracting. **~ülme,** *vn.* carriage. **~ülmek (-den, -e),** *vp.* = GÖTÜRMEK. **~ülür,** transportable. **~üm,** endurance, patience. **~ümlü,** patient. **~ümsüz,** impatient. **~ümsüzlük,** impatience.

gövde Main part; whole structure; frame; (*bio.*) body, trunk; (*live.*) carcass; (*aer.*) fuselage; (*carp.*) handle; (*ling.*) stem. **~ gösterisi,** (*pol.*) show of strength: **~ heykeli,** (*art.*) torso: **~ yapısı,** (*bio.*) anatomy: **~ye atmak/indirmek,** eat greedily; gobble up.

gövde·bilim (*bio., med.*) Anatomy. **~bilimci,** anatomist, anatomy student. **~bilimsel,** anatomical. **~lenmek,** *vi.* become corpulent; (*bot.*) (trunk) develop. **~li,** bulky; corpulent. **~sel,** structural.

göve¹kᵍⁱ (*bot.*) Green shell (of walnut).

gövem (*ent.*) Horsefly. **~eriği¹ⁱ,** (*bot.*) buckthorn.

göver·i/~ti (*cul.*) Greenstuffs, vegetables, salads. **~mek,** *vi.* turn green/purple; (*bot.*) sprout; (*med.*) (bruise) become black and blue.

göya [216] = GÜYA.

göy·dergi (*med.*) Boil; abscess. **~mek (-i),** burn. **~nük,** burnt; sunburnt; (*bot.*) (fruit) quite ripe; (*fig.*) painful. **~nümek/~ünmek,** *vi.* be burnt/ scorched/spoilt. **~ük,** *a.* burnt: *n.* (*med.*) fever.

göz Eye; seeing; looking; look; hole; mesh; opening; aperture; drawer; compartment, pigeon-hole; tray (of balance); (*geo.*) water-spring; (*arch.*) arch (of bridge); room; (*bio.*) alveolus; (*bot.*) bud; (*fig.*) affection, favour; evil eye. **~ +,** *a.* Eye-; ocular; optical: **~ açamamak,** not find the time/opportunity: **~ açıp kapayıncaya kadar,** in the twinkling of an eye: **~ açtırmamak,** give s.o. no respite// chance to recover/take action: **~AĞRISI: ~ ahbabı,** nodding acquaintance; s.o. known by sight: **~AKI: ~ alabildiğine kadar,** as far as the eye can reach/ see: **~ alıcı,** striking, dazzling, attractive: **~ alımı,** range of view: **~ almak,** dazzle: **~ALTI: ~ aşinalığı,** knowing s.o. only by sight: **~ aşısı,** (*bot.*) bud grafting: **~ atmak (-e),** glance at: **~ aydına gitmek,** go for a visit of congratulations: **~ ayırmamak (-den),** not take one's eyes off: **~BAĞCI: ~BAĞI: ~ bağmak,** bewitch; hoodwink: **~BANKASI,** (*med.*) eye-bank: **~ banyosu,** (*med.*) eye-bath; (*sl.*) enjoying watching beautiful people: **~BEBEĞİ: ~ boncuğu,** charm against the evil eye: **~ boyama,** (*fig.*) eyewash, window-dressing: **~ boyamak,** hoodwink, deceive: **~ boyası,** (*mod.*) eye-liner/-shadow: **~ çukuru = ~EVİ: ~DAĞI: ~ değmek,** be affected by the evil eye: **~DEMİRİ: ~DİKEĞİ: ~ dikmek,** set one's eye on stg.: **~DİŞİ: ~ doldurmak,** prove one's competence to s.o; make a good impression: ~ **doyurmak**, have a great effect on: ~ **erimi**, horizon: ~ **etm.**, wink: ~EVİ: ~ **gezdirmek (-e)**, examine stg.; cast an eye over: ~ **göre göre**, what is obvious to all; openly, blatantly, knowingly: ~ **görmeyince gönül katlanır**, what the eye doesn't see the heart doesn't grieve: ~ ~, full of holes; porous; cellular: ~ ~**e gelmek**, catch each other's eye; looks meet: ~ ~**ü görmemek**, be unable to see anything; be pitch dark: ~ **hakkı**, small share given to onlooker to ward off evil eye: ~ **hapsi**, (*mil.*) surveillance, house/open arrest: ~ **hapsine almak**, keep under observation/open arrest: ~ **hekimi**, oculist, ophthalmic optician: ~ **ilacı**, (*med.*) eyewash: ~ **ile görülür**, (*min.*) macro-structure: ~ **ile görülmez**, (*min.*) microstructure: ~ **kadehi**, glass used as eye-bath: ~ **kalemi**, (*mod.*) eye-liner pencil: ~ **kamaşması**, glare: ~ **kamaştırmak**, dazzle; astonish: ~KAPAĞI: ~ **kararı**, measuring by the eye; guessing; roughly speaking: ~ **kararması**, dizziness: ~ **karası**, blindness: ~ **kesilmek**, watch attentively: ~ **kırpmadan**, without a thought/batting an eyelid: ~ **kırpmak**, blink; wink: ~ **kırpmamak**, not get a wink of sleep: ~ **korkutma**, threat: ~ **koymak**, cast covetous eyes on stg.: ~ **kulak kesilmek**, be all eyes and ears: ~ **kulak olm.**, be alert; keep an eye open: ~ **kuyruğu**, the corner of the eye: ~ **küresi**, (*bio.*) eyeball: ~ **merceği**, (*ast.*) eyepiece: ~ **muayenesi**, (*med.*) optometry: ~ **nuru**, ability to see, sight; eye-straining work: ~ **nuru dökmek**, strain the eyes with work: ~ **otu**, (*bot.*) euphrasy: ~ **ölçüsü**, estimate made by eye: ~ **önünde bulundurmak/ tutmak**, bear in mind; take into consideration; make allowances for: ~ **önüne almak/getirmek**, consider, plan: ~ **önüne sermek**, display: ~ **pekliği**, bravery, boldness: ~ **perdesi**, (*med.*) cataract: ~PINARI: ~ **sevdası**, love at (first) sight: ~ **siniri**, (*bio.*) oculomotor nerve: ~ **siperi**, eye-shade; (horse) blinkers: ~ **süzmek**, look amorously through half-closed eyes: ~TAŞI: ~ **ucuyla bakmak**, cast a sideways glance; take askance: ~ **yaşartıcı**, lachrymatory (gas); (*fig.*) very emotional/tragic (event): ~YAŞI: ~ **yaylası**, field of vision: ~ **yıldırmak,** destroy morale: ~ **yummak**, close the eyes; turn a blind eye to, condone, overlook: ~ **yummamak**, not condone; not sleep at all: ~ **yuvarlağı**, (*bio.*) eyeball: ~ **yuvası**, (*bio.*) eye socket.

gözde: ~ **olm.**, be popular, in favour: ~ **tutmak**, hold in favour. [*Also* = GÖZDE.]

gözden: ~ **çıkarmak (için)**, be prepared to sacrifice/ spend for stg.: ~ **çıkmak**, fall from favour/in esteem: ~ **düşmek**, lose affection/esteem; be disgraced: ~ **düşmüş olm.**, be in the dog-house: ~ **geçirmek**, examine, scrutinize; (*lit.*) revise: ~ **ırak olan gönülden de ırak olur**, out of sight out of mind: ~ **kaçmak**, escape detection; not be noticed: ~ **kaybolmak**, disappear; dissolve: ~ **sürmeyi çalmak/çekmek**, be extremely skilful (as a thief): ~ **uzaklaşmak**, go far away; be lost sight of.

göze: ~ **almak**, envisage; bring/resign o.s. to: ~ **batmak**, (*pej.*) be unfavourably conspicuous/ striking: ~ **çarpmak**, be noticeable, attract atten-

tion: ~ **diken olm.**, make people jealous: ~ **gelmek** = GÖZ DEĞMEK: ~ **girmek**, curry favour, gain importance: ~ **görünmek**, be visible/clear; seem to exist: ~ **göz, dişe diş**, an eye for an eye a tooth for a tooth: ~ **mil çekmek**, blind (with a tool): ~ **özsuyu**, (*bio.*) rheum, mucus from the eye-ducts: ~ **yasak olmaz**, even the cat may look at the queen. [*Also* = GÖZE.]

gözle: ~ **görülür**, visible: ~ **görülmez**, invisible: ~ **yemek**, devour with the eyes; put the evil eye on.

gözleri: ~ **bağlamak**, blindfold: ~ **bayılmak**, become languid: ~ **buğulanmak/bulanmak**, eyes fill with tears; be about to cry: ~ **büyümüş bir halde**, with eyes starting out of his head (from fear, etc.): ~ **çakmak çakmak olm.**, (*med.*) eyes be red/bright with fever: ~ **çekik**, with slanting eyes: ~ **çukura gitmek**, (*med.*) eyes become sunken: ~ **dışarıya uğramış** = ~ LOKMA . . .: ~ **dolmak/dolu dolu olm.**, be on the brink of tears: ~ **dönmek**, the eyes turn up (at death); be very angry: ~ **evinden fırlamak/ oynamak**, eyes pop out (with anger, etc.): ~ **fal taşı gibi açılmak**, be wide open with surprise: ~ **kan çanağına dönmek**, eyes be very red: ~ **kapanmak**, die; be very sleepy: ~ **kararmak**, eyes not see clearly: ~ **lokma gibi fırlamış**, his eyes started out of his head: ~ **parlamak**, eyes be bright with love/desire: ~ **sulanmak**, eyes water: ~ **süzülmek**, eyes begin to close: ~ **uyku tutmamak**, be unable to sleep: ~ **velfecri okuyor**, give the impression of being very astute/alert: ~ **yollarda kalmak**, wait impatiently for a loved one. [*Also* = GÖZÜ.]

gözlerine: ~ **inanamamak**, not be able to believe one's eyes: ~ **mil çekmek**, burn s.o.'s eyes out: ~ **uyku girmemek**, not be able to sleep. [*Also* = GÖZÜNE.]

gözlerini: ~ **açmak**, wake up: ~ **belertmek**, open eyes wide (surprise, etc.): ~ **devirmek (-e)**, look daggers at s.o.: ~ **dikmek (-e)**, look at stg. carefully: ~ **kaçırmak**, turn one's eyes away; avoid s.o.: ~ **kapamamak**, not sleep: ~ **kaydırmak**, squint the eyes: ~**n içi gülmek**, one's eyes shine with joy: ~**n içine kadar kızarmak**, become red with shame: ~**zden öperim**, (*in a letter*) I send you my love. [*Also* = GÖZÜNÜ(N).]

gözü: ~ **aç**, insatiable; greedy: ~ **açık**, alert; shrewd: ~ **açık gitmek**, die disappointed: ~ **açılmak**, become experienced/shrewd: ~ **akmak**, be blinded (accidentally): ~ **almamak**, be unable to trust: ~ **arkada kalmak**, leave things unfinished: ~ **bağlı**, blindfolded; inattentive, unsuspecting; bewitched; stupid, inexperienced: ~ **bulanmak**, eyes film over/become opaque: ~ **büyükte olm.**, have great ideas/intentions; be ambitious: ~ **çıkasıca!**, curse you!: ~ **çıkmak**, lose an eye: ~ **dalmak**, gaze at; stare: ~ **dışarıda**, discontented and looking for another job; with eyes straying (to other women): ~ **doymak**, have had enough (of stg.): ~ **doymaz**, greedy; avaricious: ~ **dönesi!**, curse him!: ~ **dönmek**, (so angry) not know what one is doing: ~ **dumanlanmak**, be blinded with hate: ~ **faltaşı**

gibi açılmak, learn by bitter experience: ∼ gibi sakınmak (-i), be over-interested in stg.: ∼ gibi sevmek (-i), be very fond of stg.: ∼ gitmek (-e), catch sight of by chance: ∼ gönlü açılmak, become cheerful: ∼ gönlü tok, contented: ∼ görmemek, not see anything; have eyes for only one thing: ∼ görmez, pitch dark: ∼ görmez olm. (-i), cease to value: ∼ hiç bir şey görmemek, be too excited to deal with anything: ∼ ısırmak, seem to know s.o.: ∼ ilişmek, become aware of: ∼ kalmak, hanker after stg.; envy stg. (owned by s.o. else): ∼ kapalı, without hesitation/a thought; inexperienced: ∼ kara, desperate, beside himself: ∼ kararmak, lose self-control; feel dizzy: ∼ kaymak, glance unwillingly; look surprised: ∼ keskin, sharp-eyed/-sighted: ∼ kesmek, think o.s. able (to do stg.); like, think suitable: ∼ kızmak, see red: ∼ korkmak, go in fear, be deterred: ∼ kör olsun (-in)!, curse it!: ∼ ol(ma)mak (-de), desire stg. strongly/(not at all): ∼ pek, bold, courageous; unyielding: ∼ sönmek, become blind: ∼ sidikli/sulu, (vulg.) blubberer: ∼ takılmak (-e), fix one's eyes on stg.: ∼ tok, contented: ∼ toprağa bakmak, be about to die: ∼ tutmak (-i), take a fancy to; trust: ∼ yaşartmak, make the eyes water: ∼ yaşlı, tearful: ∼ yememek, not dare to: ∼ yılmak, go in fear: ∼ yol(lar)da kalmak, wait expectantly for s.o.: ∼ yüksekte, ambitious. [Also = GÖZLERİ.]

gözüm: ∼!, darling, dearest: ∼ çıksın/kör olsun!, may I be struck blind if it is not so!: ∼ görmesin, I don't want to see him: ∼ ısırıyor (-i), I feel I know him: ∼den uyku su gibi akıyor, I'm terribly sleepy: ∼e uyku girmedi, I haven't slept a wink: ∼e toz kaçtı, dust got into my eye: ∼le, with my own eyes: ∼ün nuru!, my darling!

gözün: ∼ alabildiği kadar, as far as the eye can see: ∼ aydın!, bless you!; congratulations: ∼ kör olsun!, curse you!: ∼ önünde gibi, in the mind's eye: ∼ ucuyla, out of the corner of one's eye.

gözünde: ∼ büyümek, seem big/important to s.o.: ∼ büyütmek, exaggerate the importance of: ∼ ol(ma)mak, be in s.o.'s good/(bad) books: ∼ tütmek, long for, ardently desire. [Also = GÖZ-LERİNDE.]

gözünden: ∼ kaçır(ma)mak, (not) lose track of: ∼ kıskanmak, be very jealous of; regard as the apple of one's eye: ∼ sürmeyi çalar (-in), he's very crafty: ∼ uyku akmak, be very sleepy: ∼ yaşlar boşanmak, burst into tears.

gözüne: ∼ bakmak, look s.o. straight in the eye: ∼ çarpmak, catch one's attention: ∼ dizine dursun!, may it choke him (s.o. ungrateful)!: ∼ girmek, ingratiate o.s./curry favour with o.s.: ∼ ilişmek, happen to see: ∼ kestirmek, think o.s. capable (of doing stg.); pick out stg. as suitable/desirable: ∼ sokmak, thrust stg. under s.o.'s eyes by way of reproof/accusation: ∼ uyku girmemek, be unable to sleep: ∼ yedirmek, dare to do stg. [Also = GÖZLERİNE.]

gözünü: ∼ açmak, wake o.s. up; become alert; disillusion s.o.: ∼ ayır(ma)mak (-den), (not) take

one's eyes off stg.: ∼ bağlamak, blindfold s.o.; deceive s.o.: ∼ budak/çöpten sakınmaz, intrepid, dare-devil: ∼ çöpten sakınmamak/daldan budaktan esirgememek, be fearless, disregard dangers: ∼ dikmek, stare fixedly at: ∼ doyurmak, give freely: ∼ dört açmak, be very alert: ∼ fal taşı gibi açmak, stare in amazement: ∼ gözüne dikmek, stare fixedly at s.o.: ∼ kan bürümek, see red; be angry enough to kill: ∼ kırpmadan, without batting an eyelid/turning a hair: ∼ korkutmak, threaten/frighten s.o: ∼ morartmak, give s.o. a black eye: ∼ sevdiğim, my dearest: ∼ seveyim!, please!; well done!: ∼ toprak doyursun, he won't be satisfied till he's dead (s.o. very rapacious)!: ∼ yummak, die; (-e), pretend not to see. [Also = GÖZLERİNİ.]

gözünün: ∼ bebeği gibi sevmek, be very fond of, adore: ∼ çapağını silmeden, still bleary-eyed; just woken up: ∼ içine baka baka, boldly and calmly: ∼ içine bakmak, cherish dearly; be at s.o.'s beck and call; look entreatingly at s.o.: ∼ kuyruk/ucuyla bakmak, look at furtively: ∼ nuru, the light of one's eyes, darling: ∼ önünden gitmemek, be unable to forget: ∼ üstünde kaşın var dememek (-e), raise not the slightest objection: ∼ yaşına bakmamak (-in), be pitiless. [Also == GÖZLERİNİN.]

gözüyle: ∼ bakmak, look at with the eye of . . .: ∼ görmek, witness.

göz·ağrısı[ni] (med.) Eye-ache; (col.) 'flame'. ∼akı[ni], (bio.) sclera, white of the eye. ∼altı[ni], (leg.) house-arrest: ∼ etm./∼ na almak, put under house-arrest; intern. ∼aşısı[ni], (bot.) bud-grafting. ∼bağcı(lık), (work of) magician/conjurer. ∼bağı[ni], magic, conjuring; deception. ∼bebeği[ni], (bio.) pupil of the eye; (fig.) apple of one's eye. ∼bilim, ophthalmology. ∼cü, sentinel, watchman; spy; picket; (med.) oculist, ophthalmic optician: ∼ uçağı, (mil.) reconnaissance plane: ∼ yeri, observation post. ∼cük, (bio.) alveolus; (el.) cell. ∼cülük, sentinel-duty; watching; ophthalmology. ∼dağı[ni], intimidation, threats; fright: ∼ vermek, intimidate; act as a deterrent. ∼de, favourite; mistress; pet. ∼demiri[ni], (naut.) bower anchor. ∼dikeği[ni], (psy.) obsession: ∼ olm., be the envy of all. ∼dişi[ni], (bio.) eye-tooth.

göze (bio.) Cell; -cyte; (geo.) spring of water. ∼ +, (bio.) Cellular; cyto-: ∼ arası, intercellular: ∼ bölünmesi, cell division: ∼ çekirdeği ekşiti, (chem.) nucleic acid: ∼ dışı, extracellular: ∼ içi, intracellular: ∼ plazması, cytoplasm.

göze·bilim (bio.) Cytology. ∼lerarası[ni], intercellular space; (bot.) lacuna. ∼li, cellular. ∼mek (-i), (tex.) mend; silk-embroider. ∼meli, embroidered. ∼ne, beekeeper's mask. ∼ne'k[gi], (bio.) pore. ∼nekli(lik), (phys.) por·ous/(-osity). ∼nmek, vp. (tex.) be mended/embroidered. ∼r, widemeshed sieve/riddle, screen.

gözerimi[ni] (ast.) Horizon. ∼ +, a. Horizontal.

gözet·ici a. Watching; protecting; guarding: n. (sp.) observer. ∼ilmek, vp. ∼im, supervision, surveillance; watching: ∼ katı, (adm.) supervisory rank. ∼le'ç[ci], (phys.) microscope. ∼leçbilim, microscopy. ∼leçli, microscopic. ∼leme, vn. watching;

observing, observation; spying on: ~ **kulesi**, (*mil.*) block-house, watch-tower. ~**lemek (-i)**, watch, observe secretly, spy on. ~**lenmek**, *imp. v.* be observed. ~**letmek (-i, -e)**, *vc.* ~**leyici**, guard, protector. ~**mek (-i)**, mind, look after, take care of; watch; pay regard to; observe (duty); keep under observation; envisage. ~**men**, (*ind.*) supervisor. ~**tirmek (-i)**, *vc.*
gözevini (*bio.*) Eye-socket, orbit.
gözeyutarlığını (*bio.*) Phagocytis.
gözgöz Cellular, meshed; porous. ~**lük**, porosity.
göz·gü Mirror. ~**kapağı**nı, (*bio.*) eyelid. ~**kapaksız**, ~ **kertenkele**, (*zoo.*) lidless skink. ~**korkutum(cu)**, blackmail(er). ~**legörü**, (*med.*) autopsy. ~**leği**/ ~**lek**, observation post; hunter's hide. ~**lem**, (*ast.*, *etc.*) observation. ~**lemci(lik)**, (*ast.*, *etc.*) (work of) observer, watcher: ~ **merceği**, (*phys.*) ocular, eyepiece: ~ **tutanağı**, observer's report. ~**leme**[1], *vn.* observing; eyeing; watching for. ~**leme**[2], *n.* (*cul.*) 'glad eyes', fritter; pancake. ~**lemek (-i)**, watch for, wait for; keep an eye on; (*ast.*, *etc.*) observe. ~**lemen**, (*ast.*) observer. ~**lemevi**ni, observatory. ~**lemlemek (-i)**, (*phil.*) study, observe. ~**lenmek**, *vp.* be observed, etc. ~**letmek (-i)**, *vc.* ~**leyici**, witness; observer. ~**lü**, (*bio.*) having eyes; -eyed; (*arch.*) having arches/holes/openings; meshed; perforated; (*carp.*) having drawers/pigeon-holes; (*fig.*) having eyes for . . .: ~ **cıvata**, (*eng.*) eyebolt.
gözlük Eyeglasses; spectacles; (horse) blinkers. ~ **camı**, crown glass; ~ **kullanmak**, wear glasses: ~ **otu**, (*bot.*) honesty: ~ **takmak**, (*sl.*) see well, pay attention.
gözlük·çü Optician('s shop). ~**çülük**, selling/ repairing spectacles. ~**lü**, wearing glasses, bespectacled: ~ **çalı bülbülü**, (*orn.*) spectacled warbler: ~ **penguen**, (*orn.*) jackass penguin. ~**lüyılan**, (*zoo.*) hooded snake.
göz·pınarını Inner corner of the eye. ~**sel**, ocular. ~**süz**, without eyes, blind; eyeless; without holes/ openings. ~**taşı**nı, (*chem.*) copper sulphate crystal, bluestone. ~**ükmek**, *vi.* appear; be seen. ~**yaşı**nı, *n.* tears: *a.* lachrymal: ~ **bezi**, (*bio.*) lachrymal gland: ~ **dökmek**, weep: ~ **etçiği**, (*bio.*) lachrymal carbuncle: ~ **kesesi**, tear sac: ~ **nı silmek**, wipe one's tears. ~**yeri**, (*ast.*) eyepiece.
GP = GÜVEN PARTİSİ.
Gr., gr. = GRAM; GRAMER; GREKÇE.
grado (*phys.*) Degree (of alcohol, etc.).
graf·iikgi (*math.*) Graph, diagram, chart; (*art.*) graphics: ~**ini çıkarmak**, chart stg. ~**it**i, (*chem.*) graphite. ~**itleme**, (*min.*) graphitizing. ~**olog**u, graphologist. ~**oloji**, graphology. ~**ometre**, (*geo.*) graphometer.
gram (*math.*) Gram. ~**aj**/~**lık**, weight in grams. ~**kuvvet**i, (*phys.*) gram-force. ~**santimetre**, gram-centimetre.
gram·atikal (*ling.*) Grammatical. ~**er**, grammar. ~ **ofon**, (*mus.*) gramophone.
granaıtdı (*min.*) Garnet.
gran·di (*naut.*) Mainmast. ~**dük**ü, (*his.*) grandduke.
graniti (*geol.*) Granite. ~ **gibi**, hard, strong, resistant. ~**leşmek**, *vi.* be(come) like granite.

granül (*geol.*) Granule. ~**er**, granular. ~**it**i, (*geo* granulite. ~**ometri**, granulometry. ~**oz**, gran lose.
gratsiyel (*arch.*) Skyscraper.
gravimetre (*phys.*) Gravimeter.
gravür (*art.*) Engraving, etching.
gravyer (*cul.*) Gruyère cheese.
gre (*min.*) Sandstone.
gref (*med.*) Transplantation.
greger (*zoo.*) Gregarious.
gregoriyen ~ **takvimi**, (*ast.*) Gregorian calendar.
Grek (*ethn.*) Ancient Greek. ~**çe**, (*ling.*) classic Greek. ~**oromen**, (*sp.*) Graeco-Roman wrestling
grena (*min.*) Garnet.
gres (*mot.*) Grease. ~**lemek (-i)**, grease.
grev (*ind.*) Strike. ~ **bozmak/kırmak**, break a strik ~ **ilan etm.**, call a strike: ~ **kasası**, strike funds: **postası**, strike picket: ~ **ücreti**, strike pay: **yapmak**, go on strike, down tools: ~**e katılmaya** blackleg. ~**ci**, striker.
greyder (*eng.*) Grader.
greyfrut (*bot.*) Grapefruit.
gri Grey; (*fig.*) neutral. ~ **balıkçıl**, (*orn.*) grey hero ~ **renkli yalıçapkını**, (*orn.*) lesser pied kingfishe ~**msi**, greyish.
Griniiçei (*geo.*) Greenwich.
griipbi (*med.*) Influenza.
griitdi (*el.*) Electric (mains) grid.
griva (*naut.*) Cat-head. ~**ya almak**, cat (anchor): ~ **mataforası**, cat-davit.
grizu (*chem.*) Fire-damp.
Grk. = GREKÇE.
grosa (*math.*) Gross, twelve dozen.
grotesk (*th.*) Grotesque.
Grönland (*geo.*) Greenland.
gruipbu (*soc.*, *etc.*) Group, assembly, circle, bev cluster; (*sp.*) team, crew. ~ **halinde**, in groups.
grup·başı (*aer.*) (Parachutist) dispatcher. ~**la** **dırmak (-i)**, form into groups. ~**laşmak**, *vi.* for groups. ~**luk**, grouping.
GS·B = (*adm.*) GENÇLİK VE SPOR BAKAN(LIĞ)I. ~ = GÜZEL SANATLAR FAKÜLTESİ. ~**K** = GALAT SARAYI SPOR KULÜBÜ. ~**MH** = (*fin.*) GAYRİ SA MİLLİ HASILA.
GTB = (*adm.*) GÜMRÜK VE TEKEL BAKAN(LIĞ)I.
-gu *n. suf.* [222] = -GI [OLGU].
guano (*orn.*, *geol.*) Guano.
guatr (*med.*) Goitre, Derbyshire neck.
gudd·e (*bio.*) Gland. ~**i**, glandular.
gudubeti Impossibly ugly (face). ~ **bozuntusı** hideously ugly.
gufran (*rel.*) Mercy (of God).
guguçiçeğini (*bot.*) Sweet William.
guguikgu *n.* (*orn.*) Cuckoo. *int.* Cuckoo! ~ **gi** **kalmak/oturmak**, stay all alone: ~ **örümcek kuşı** (*orn.*) cuckoo shrike: ~ **yapmak**, mock by callin 'cuckoo!'. ~**lu**, making cuckoo-like sounds: ~ **saat**, cuckoo-clock.
gul (*myth.*) Ghoul; ogre. ~**yabani**, ogre.
guleti (*naut.*) Schooner, brigantine.
guluklamak *vi.* (*ech.*) (Hen) cluck, chuck.
gumena = GOMENE.
-gun *a./n. suf.* [223] = -GİN [OLGUN].

pilya (*eng.*) Cotter-pin.

rami (*ich.*) Gourami.

rbet[i] Foreign land; abroad; absence from home; xile. ~ **çekmek,** feel homesick: ~ **etm.,** emigrate: ~ **e/** ~ **ellere düşmek,** emigrate, go far from home. ~ **çi(lik),** (being) a wanderer/stranger//(*ind.*) guest-vorker, 'Gastarbeiter'.

reba *pl.* = GARİP. Strangers; paupers. ~ **astanesi,** infirmary.

rk[u] (*orn.*) Broody hen; turkey-cock. ~ ~ **etm.,** ech.) cluck; gobble: ~ **olm.**/~**lamak,** *vi.* be roody: ~ **a yatmak,** sit on/hatch eggs.

r·lamak/ ~**uldamak** (Stomach) rumble. ~**ultu,** umbling.

ru[l]**p**[bu 1] *n.* (*ast.*) Sunset; setting. ~ **etm.,** *vi.* set.

rup[2] = GRUP.

rur Pride, vanity; conceit; arrogance. ~ **gelmek/** etirmek, be puffed up; give o.s. airs: ~ **vermek,** late: ~**unu okşamak,** flatter s.o.'s pride. ~**lu,** roud, vain; conceited; arrogant.

sletmek *vi.* (*rel.*) Perform ritual ablutions.

sto Taste, gusto.

s[l]**ül**[lü] (*rel.*) Ritual ablution (of the whole body). ~**hane,** bath for ritual washing.

şa (*med.*) Goitre.

t[u] (*med.*) Gout.

vaş (*art.*) Gouache.

ü. = GÜMRÜK; GÜNEY.

ü *n. suf.* [222] = -Gİ [GÖRÜNGÜ].

ibre (*zoo.*) Dung, manure; (*bot.*) compost; ferti-izer, dressing. ~ +, *a.* Copro-. ~ **böceği,** (*ent.*) lung-beetle: ~ **şerbeti,** liquid manure: ~ **saçmak,** pread manure.

ibre·leme *vn.* Manuring. ~**lemek (-i),** (*agr.*) nanure, compost; fertilize, dress. ~**lenmek,** p. ~**li,** manured, composted. ~**lik,** dunghill, ompost-heap.

ic- = GÜÇ.

icem Force. ~ **salmak/**~**lemek (-i),** force, com-el: ~**le,** by force. ~**li,** obligatory, compulsory. ~**sel,** compelling, coercive: ~ **alım,** confiscation.

icen·dirmek (-i) Offend, displease, hurt, anger. ~**dirici,** harsh, offensive. ~**ik,** annoyed, dis-leased. ~**iklik,** annoyance, offence, anger. ~**ilmek,** *imp. v.* get annoyed. ~**mek,** *vi.* be offended/hurt/angry: (için) take exception to.

icü (*tex.*) Weaver's reed, sley.

icük Small; (*zoo.*) tailless. ~ **ay,** (*ast.*) February.

ic·ümsemek (-i) Find/consider difficult. ~ **ün,** with difficulty; by force.

ü[l]**ç**[cü 1] *n.* Strength; (*phys.*, *el.*) power; ability, capacity; influence; business, occupation. ~ **bilgisi,** energetics; ~ **birliği,** union of forces; cooperation; alliance: ~ **katımı,** (*sp.*) doping: ~ **kaybı,** (*el.*) ower loss: ~ **kullanmak,** use force: ~ **kümesi,** phil.) power set: ~ **özek/santralı,** (*el.*) power station: ~ **üretimi,** power production: ~**lerin** ayrılığı//birleşmesi, (*adm.*) separation//concentra-ion of powers: ~**ten düşmek,** become weak/owerless: ~**ü** ~ **ü yetene,** might is right, law of the ungle: ~**ü yeter,** capable: ~**ü yetmek,** be strong nough, be able: ~**ü yüksek,** powerful: ~**ün** eşitleşmesi//sakımı, (*phys.*) equalization//conserva-

tion of energy: ~**üne gitmek,** offend, annoy; hurt s.o.'s feelings: ~**ünü yenmek,** control one's emotions.

güç[2] *a.* Hard, difficult, arduous. *adv.* With difficulty. ~ **beğenen,** difficult to please: ~ **gelmek,** present difficulties; prove difficult: ~ **halle/**~**bela,** with great difficulty.

güç·lendirmek (-i) Make strong; lend credit/support to; (*sp.*) dope. ~**lenmek,** *vi.* become strong. ~**leşmek,** *vi.* grow difficult. ~**leştirmek (-i),** make difficult. ~**lü,** strong, powerful; dynamic; violent; influential; (*mot.*) powered: ~ **kuvvetli,** very strong and healthy: ~ **patlayıcı,** (*min.*) high explosive. ~**lük,** difficulty, arduousness; hardship: ~ **çekmek,** meet with difficulties: ~ **çıkarmak,** put forward difficulties: ~**lerle kaplı,** bristling with difficulties: ~**ü yenmek,** overcome difficulties. ~**lülük,** difficult situation; (*el.*) capacitance. ~**süz,** weak; powerless; incapable: ~ **kuvvetsiz,** without any strength. ~**süzlük,** weakness; impotence; slackness; unemployment.

güde[l]**k**[gi] Aim, motive. ~**siz,** aimless.

güdelemek (-i) Lag behind; wait for.

güdem (*leg.*) Intention.

güder- = GÜTMEK.

güderi Buckskin, deerskin; chamois leather.

güdü Drive; motive, incentive; aim, objective. ~ **cü,** who drives/aims at; (*ast.*) guiding; (*eng.*) driving.

güdük Stumpy, short; incomplete; under-; (*zoo.*) tailless, docked. ~ **kalmak,** remain small/unfinished/incomplete. ~**leşmek,** *vi.* become small/incomplete.

güdü·leme/ ~ **lenim** *vn.* (*psy.*) Motivation. ~**lenme,** being motivated. ~**leyici,** motive; incentive. ~**lmek,** *vp.* = GÜTMEK.

güdüm Driving; leading; guidance; control, management. ~**bilim(ci),** (specialist in) cybernetics. ~**ce,** tactics. ~**cü,** (*adm.*) planner; supporter of planning. ~**cülük,** (*adm.*, *fin.*) planning, control, management. ~**lemek (-i),** drive; urge. ~**lü,** (*adm.*) (government)-controlled; managed; directed, guided: ~ **balon,** (*aer.*) dirigible: ~ **mermi,** (*mil.*) ballistic/guided missile: ~ **sanat,** politically aligned art. ~**lülük,** being controlled, etc.

güfte (*mus.*) The lyric of a song.

güğüm (*dom.*) Copper vessel (with handle, spout, lid).

güher = CEVHER. ~**çile,** (*chem.*) saltpetre.

gül (*bot.*) Rose; (*ast.*) compass rose. ~ **ağacı,** rosetree; (*carp.*) rosewood: ~ **biti,** (*ent.*) rose aphis: ~ **böceği,** (*ent.*) rose chafer: ~ **gibi,** *a.* neat, charming; *adv.* finely, 'swimmingly': ~ **gibi bakmak,** ensure comfortable life; take care of, look after: ~ **gibi geçinmek,** be on very good terms with; (*fin.*) live comfortably: ~ **pası,** (*myc.*) rose rust: ~ **pembesi,** rose pink: ~ **reçeli** = BEŞEKER: ~ **üstüne** ~ **koklamamak,** not dream of making love to anyone else: ~ **yanaklı,** pink-cheeked: ~**ü** **seven dikenine katlanır,** no rose without its thorns: ~**ü tarife ne hacet ne çiçektir biliriz!,** you needn't tell me, I know all about the fellow!

gül·ab(dan) (Flask for sprinkling) rose-water. ~**bank**[1], prayer/song uttered in unison; chant;

slogan; war-cry. ~ **beşeker**, (*cul.*) rose-petal preserve. ~ **bezek**, (*arch.*) rose-window. ~ **çehreli**, rosy-cheeked. ~ **dan**, flower-vase/-bowl. ~ **deste**, (*lit.*) anthology.

güldür ~ ~ , very noisily. ~ **mek (-i)**, *vc.* = GÜLMEK; make laugh, amuse. ~ **men**, (*th.*) comic actor. ~ **ü**, (*lit.*, *th.*) comic; comedy. ~ **ücü**, laughter-making, comic(al), amusing: ~ **gaz**, (*chem.*) laughing-gas.

gül·e(cek) = GÜLMEK. ~ **eç**, always smiling, happy-faced. ~ **eçlik**, happiness. ~ **ence¹k^{gi}**, (*lit.*) anecdote. ~ **er (yüz)** = GÜLMEK.

gül·giller (*bot.*) Rosaceae, rose family. ~ **gün**, rosy, rose-coloured. ~ **hane/** ~ **istan**, rose-garden. ~ **hatmi**, (*bot.*) hollyhock. ~ **kurusu^{nu}**, (*cul.*) dried pink rose-petals (for GÜLBEŞEKER); their colour.

güllabi·(ci) (*obs.*) Warden in an asylum; flatterer. ~ **cilik**, ~ **etm.**, put up with s.o.'s whims; flatter.

gülla¹ç^{cı} (*cul.*) Sweet (starch wafers with cream and rose-water); (*med.*) sugared pill.

gülle (*mil.*) Cannon-ball; shell; (*sp.*) shot. ~ **atma**, (*sp.*) shot-put: ~ **atmak**, (*sp.*) put the shot: ~ **gibi**, very heavy: ~ **jimnastiği**, (*sp.*) training with weights. ~ **ci**, (*sp.*) shot-putter.

gül·lü Surrounded/decorated with roses. ~ **lük**, rose-garden: ~ **gülistanlık**, place of comfort and plenty.

gül·me *vn.* Laughing, laughter. ~ **mece**, humour, farce. ~ **mek**, *vi.* laugh; smile; be pleased; enjoy o.s.: **güle güle!**, [176] goodbye and good luck!: **güle güle + verb**, do stg. happily/with success [**güle güle giyiniz/kullanınız!**, may you be happy wearing/using (stg. new)!: **güle güle kirleniniz!**, (after a bath) may you get dirty again happily!]: **güle oynaya**, with pleasure: **gülece¹k^{gi}**, laughable, ridiculous: **güleceği tutmak**, feel like laughing: **güleceğim geldi**, I wanted to laugh: **gülen kumru**, (*orn.*) collared turtledove: **güler**, smiling, given to laughter: **güler ardıç kuşlari**, (*orn.*) laughing thrushes: **güler eşeği**, (*orn.*) laughing kookaburra: **güler martı**, (*orn.*) black-headed gull: **güler misin ağlar mısın!**, it makes you laugh and cry at the same time!: **güler yüz**, a smiling cheerful face: **güler yüz göstermek**, look cheerful/friendly; receive in a friendly manner: **güler yüz tatlı söz yılanı deliğinden çıkarır**, a smiling face and sweet words are very persuasive: **güler yüzlü**, merry, cheerful; affable: **gülerek**, laughingly: **gülerken ısırır**, beware of appearances!: **güleyim bari!**, don't make me laugh!: **gülme komşuna gelir başına**, don't laugh at your neighbour's misfortune, it may happen to you: **gülmeden bayılmak**, be exhausted with laughter: **gülmeden kırılmak**, one's sides ache with laughter: **gülmeden yapamadım**, I couldn't help laughing: **gülmekten katılmak/kırılmak**, split one's sides with laughing: **gülmemek**, keep one's countenance: **gülmez**, sullen; sour-faced; severe: **gülüp geçmek**, ignore/not worry about stg.: **gülüp oynamak**, laugh and be merry.

gül·pası^{nı} (*myc.*) Blackspot. ~ **rengi^{ni}**, rose-colour, roseate. ~ **suyu^{nu}**, (*cul.*) (distilled) rose-water.

gülücü¹k^{gü} (*child.*) Smile.

gülü¹k^{gü} (*live.*) Beast of burden; herd of horses.

gülümse·me *vn.* Smile. ~ **mek**, *vi.* smile.

gülünç Laughable; ridiculous, derisory. ~ **düşme**,

(*lit.*) anticlimax. ~ **leme**, (*lit.*) parody. ~ **leşmek**, ı become laughable/comic. ~ **leştirmek (-i)**, carica ture; make fun of. ~ **lü**, amusing, comic, funny grotesque. ~ **lük**, ridiculousness, absurdity.

gülün·mek *vi.* Laugh to o.s.; be laughabl gülünecek, laughable, comic. ~ **mez**, no laughin matter. ~ **tüçizim**, (*art.*) caricature.

gül·üş Way of laughing; laughter. ~ **üşmek**, ı laugh together/at each other. ~ **üşülmek**, *vp.* ~ **ü** (*cin.*, *th.*) gag, comic situation. ~ **ütçü**, gag-man.

gülyağ·cı(lık) (Work of) maker/seller of GÜLYAĞ ~ **ı^{nı}**, attar of roses.

Güm. = GÜMRÜK.

güm (*ech.*) Hollow/booming noise. ~ **atmak**, (s lie, deceive: ~ **etm.**, make a booming noise: ~ etm., make an echoing noise: ~ **e gitmek**, (s go for nothing, be wasted; die for nothin unnecessarily.

güm·bedek Noisily; suddenly. ~ **bür**, ~ ~ , (ech with a great clatter. ~ **bürdemek**, *vi.* boom, r verberate; (*sl.*) 'pop off', die. ~ **bürdetilmek**, v ~ **bürdetmek (-i)**, *vc.* ~ **bürtü**, booming noise.

güme¹ç^{cı} Honeycomb. ~ **balı**, comb-honey.

gümle Hunter's hut.

gümle(t)(il)mek = GÜMBÜRDE(T)(İL)MEK.

gümrah Dense; copious, abundant; luxurian ~ **lık**, abundance; luxuriance.

gümrü¹k^{gü} (*adm.*) Customs; customs-house. antreposu, bonded warehouse: ~ **bağışıklığı**, e emption from duty: ~ **beyanname/bildirges** customs declaration: ~ **deneti**, customs control: duvarı, customs barrier, tariff wall: ~ **gemis** revenue cutter: ~ **görevli/memuru**, customs office ~ **işgüder/komisyoncusu**, customs-agent/-brok ~ **makbuzu**, clearance: ~ **muayene/yoklama** customs inspection: ~ **resim/vergisi**, customs du duty: ~ **savaşı**, tariff war: ~ **tarifesi**, custor tariff: ~ **ve Tekel Bakan(lığ)ı**, Minis·ter(-try) f Customs and Monopolies: ~ **e tabi olm.**, be liab for duty: ~ **te bulunmak**, be in bond: ~ **ten bağışı** muaf, exempt from duty, duty-free: ~ **ten çekme** çıkarmak, clear through customs; take out of bon ~ **ten mal kaçırır gibi**, unnecessarily flustere hurried.

gümrük·çü(lük) (Work of) customs-office -agent. ~ **lemek (-i)**, clear through custom ~ **lenmek**, *vp.* ~ **lü**, dutiable; duty paid. ~ **s** duty-free: ~ **bölge**, free zone.

Güm. Ta. = GÜMRÜK TARİFESİ.

gümüş *n.* Silver. *a.* Made of silver; silvery. balıkçık, (*ent.*) bristle-tail: ~ **çınlayışlı**, silv (voice): ~ **dövme**, silver-beating: ~ **kaplam** silver-plating; silver-plated: ~ **kaplı**, silver-plat ~ **sağ olsun altın gide kosun**, a bird in the hand worth two in the bush: ~ **sepet**, (*bot.*) Alpine roc cress: ~ **takımı**, (*dom.*) silver-plate; set of silver: sülün/tavuskuşu, (*orn.*) silver pheasant: ~ **vara** (*min.*) silver foil.

gümüş·balığı^{nı} (*ich.*) Atherine, sand-sm ~ **çü(lük)**, (work of) silversmith. ~ **çün**, (*ent.*) silv fish. ~ **i/** ~ **ü**, silver grey; silvery: ~ **jibon**, (zo silver gibbon: ~ **martı**, (*orn.*) herring gull. ~ **lem (-i)**, plate with silver. ~ **lenmek**, *vp.* be silver-plat *vi.* (*fig.*) shine like silver. ~**letmek (-i),** plate/ decorate with silver. ~**lü,** (*geol.*) argentiferous; silver-plated; silvery: ~ **balık,** (*ich.*) dace. ~**sel,** *a.* silver: ~ **martı,** (*orn.*) herring gull. ~**servi,** moon's reflection on water. ~**suyu**ⁿᵘ, crystal-clear water. ~**ü** = ~**i.**

gün Day; day-time; time; date; sun; light; feast-day; at-home day. ~ **ağarmak,** (day) dawn: ~ **ağarması,** dawn: ~ **almak (-den),** make an appointment with: ~**AŞIRI:** ~ **aşırmak,** get through a bad day: ~**AYDIN:** ~**BALI:** ~**BALIĞI:** ~**BATISI:** ~ **batması,** sunset: ~**BERİ:** ~ **bilgisi,** calendar: ~ **bugün,** this is the day for it; an opportunity not to be missed: ~ **bugündür (o),** ever since, from that day to this: ~ **değmemiş,** (*geol.*) juvenile: ~ **dikilmesi,** midday: ~ **doğmadan kemliği söylenmez,** don't prejudge things: ~ **doğmadan (meşimei şebden) neler doğar,** before the day dawns what strange things may be born (in the womb of night): ~ **doğmak,** day break; **(-e),** s.o.'s day/luck/opportunity come: ~ **doğması,** sunrise: ~**DOĞRUSU:** ~**DÖNÜMÜ:** ~ **durumu,** (*ast.*) solstice, longest/shortest day: ~ **eğişmesi,** early afternoon: ~ **geçmek,** *vi.* (day) pass; **(-e),** (sun) scorch/tan s.o.: ~ **geçmez ki . . .,** not a day passes but . . .: ~ **gibi meydanda,** crystal-clear: ~ **görmek,** live in plenty/happiness: ~ **görmemek,** live in trouble: ~ **görmemiş,** s.o. of no importance/ standing; inexperienced: ~ **görmez,** sunless (place): ~ **görmüş,** who has seen better days; who has been important/of consequence; experienced: ~ ~**den,** daily; a little every day: ~ **ışığı,** daylight: ~ **kararması,** dusk, evening twilight: ~ **kavuşmak,** (sun) set, (night) fall: ~ **koymak,** fix a day: ~ **tün eşitliği,** (*ast.*) equinox: ~ **yapmak,** (women) be at home to guests: ~ **yayı,** (*ast.*) diurnal arc.

gün-: ~**den** ~**e,** [195] from day to day: ~**ler kısalıyor//uzuyor,** the days are drawing in//out: ~**lerden bir gün,** once upon a time: ~**leri gece olm.,** suffer great sadness: ~**leri sayılı olm.,** one's days are numbered: ~**lerini saymak,** be on one's deathbed.

günü: ~ **geçmiş,** outdated, outmoded; back-number: ~ **gelmiş,** due: ~ ~**ne,** [195] to the very day: ~ ~**ne uymaz,** be inconstant/changeable: ~ **yetmek,** (*fin.*) fall due; (*fig.*) death be near: ~**müz,** contemporary. [*Also* = GÜNÜ.]

günün: ~ **adamı,** subject of conversation; s.o. much talked about; a man for all seasons: ~ **birinde,** one of these fine days, some day: ~ **günü var,** the day may come (when we shall need it).

gününü: ~ **doldurmak,** (*fin.*) fall due; complete the period: ~ **görmek,** come to a sticky end; (woman) have her periods: ~ **görürsün!,** you'll pay for this!: ~ **göstermek,** give s.o. his deserts: ~ **gün etm.,** pass the day pleasantly: ~ **ikmal etm./tamamlamak,** (*leg.*) complete one's sentence: ~ **saymak** = ~**LERİNİ.**

·gün *a./n. suf.* [223] = -GİN [SÜRGÜN].

günah Sin; fault; blame. ~ **benden gitti,** I've done *my* duty!: ~ **çıkarmak,** (*rel.*) hear confession: ~ **çıkartmak,** (*rel.*) confess one's sins: ~ **işlemek,** commit a sin: ~ **olm.,** be shameful: ~ **vebali,** the

whole responsibility for an evil deed: ~**a girmek,** sin: ~**a sokmak,** make s.o. sin; drive s.o. to do evil: ~**ı boynuna!,** *you* must take the consequences!: ~**ına (bile) değmez,** the game is not worth the candle: ~**ına girmek/**~**ını almak,** accuse s.o. wrongfully; wrong s.o.: ~**ından geçmek,** overlook s.o.'s sin, forgive s.o.: ~**ını çekmek,** suffer/pay for s.o.'s sins: ~**ını vermez,** very mean.

günah·kâr *n.* Sinner; wrongdoer. *a.* Sinful; culpable, guilty. ~**kârlık,** sinfulness; guiltiness. ~**lı,** culpable, sinful. ~**sız(lık),** blameless(ness); sinless(ness).

gün·aşırı Every other day, on alternate days. ~**aydın,** *int.* good-morning! ~**balı**ⁿ¹, (*cul.*) grape-juice condensed by sunlight. ~**balığı**ⁿ¹, (*ich.*) rainbow wrasse. ~**batısı**ⁿ¹, (*ast.*) sunset; (*geo.*) West; (*met.*) west wind. ~**begün,** [196] day by day. ~**beri,** (*ast.*) perihelion. ~**ce,** (*lit.*) memoirs; news-paper. ~**ce¹k**ᵍⁱ, umbrella. ~**cel/**~**cül,** actual, current, today's; daily: ~ **olaylar,** current events. ~**celik,** diary. ~**celleşmek,** *vi.* become the topic of the day. ~**cellik,** actuality; up-to-dateness. ~**çiçeği**ⁿⁱ, (*bot.*) sunflower. ~**değişme,** ~ **çizgisi,** (*ast.*) international date line. ~**deleşmek,** become daily (habit, etc.). ~**delik,** *a.* daily; everyday; ephemeral: *n.* daily wage//newspaper. ~**delikçi,** day-worker; charwoman. ~**delikçilik,** day labour; thinking only of today. ~**dem,** [225] (*adm.*) agenda. ~**deş,** on the same day; contemporary. ~**doğ(r)usu**ⁿᵘ, (*geo.*) East; Orient; (*met.*) east wind. ~ **keşişleme,** east-south-east, ESE: ~ **poyraz,** east-north-east, ENE. ~**döndü,** (*bot.*) sunflower. ~**dönümü**ⁿᵘ, (*ast.*) solstice. ~**düşkün(lüğ)ü,** ambi·tious(-tion).

gündüz Daytime; by day; daylight. ~ **döneyi,** (*ind.*) day shift: ~ **gösterisi,** (*th.*) matinée: ~ **gözüyle,** by the light of day: ~ **feneri,** (*jok.*) Negro: ~ **külahlı gece silahlı,** not as good as he appears: ~ **oyunu,** (*th.*) matinée: ~ **tavus kelebeği,** (*ent.*) peacock butterfly: ~ **yırtıcıları,** (*orn.*) accipiters, hawks.

gündüz·cü (*ind.*) Day-worker; (*ed.*) day-student; daytime toper: ~**ki,** daytime: ~**lü,** (*ed.*) day pupil; day-student; [= GECELİ]. ~**lük,** day. ~**sefası**ⁿ¹, (*bot.*) field bindweed. ~**ün,** by day; in the daytime.

güne·bakan (*bot.*) Sunflower. ~**lçci,** sunny side. ~**doğrulum,** (*bot.*) phototropism. ~**ği¹k**ᵍⁱ, (*bot.*) chicory, wild succory. ~**r,** dawn. ~**re¹k**ᵍⁱ, (*ast.*) apex.

güneş (*ast.*) Sun; sunlight; sunshine. ~ **+,** *a.* Sun-; solar: ~ **açmak,** sun appear from clouds: ~ **almak,** get/receive sunlight; be in the sun: ~ **balçıkla sıvanmaz,** the truth can't be hidden: ~ **balığı,** (*ich.*) (?) redbreast sunfish: ~ **banyosu,** sun-bathing: ~ **başımızda kaynıyordu,** the sun beat down upon our heads: ~ **batmak,** sun set: ~ **çarpmak,** (*med.*) sun cause sunstroke: ~ **çiçeği,** (*bot.*) heliotrope: ~ **Dil teorisi,** (*ling.*) 'Sun Language' theory: ~ **dizgesi,** (*ast.*) solar system: ~ **doğmak,** sun rise: ~ **girmiyen eve hekim girer,** the physician enters where the sun does not: ~ **görmek** = ~ ALMAK: ~ **gözlüğü,** sunglasses: ~ **gücü,** (*phys.*) solar energy/power: ~ **gülü,** (*bot.*) common sundew: ~ **günü,** (*ast.*) solar day: ~ **ışığı,** sunlight:

~ **lekesi**, (*ast.*) sunspot: ~ **perdesi**, (*dom.*) sunblind: ~ **saati**, (*ast.*) solar time; sundial: ~ **sistemi** = ~ DİZGESİ: ~ **taç//takvimi**, (*ast.*) solar corona//calendar: ~ **tavuğu**, (*orn.*) sunbittern: ~ **teker//tutulma//yılı**, (*ast.*) solar disc//eclipse//year: ~ **vurmak** = ~ ÇARPMAK: ~ **e karşı işemek**, (*vulg.*) show great disrespect: ~ **e sermek**, air (clothes): ~ **in alnında/altında**, under the sun's burning rays: ~ **te kurumuş//yanmış**, sun-dried//-burnt, tanned.

güneş·le(n)mek *vi.* Bask in the sun; sunbathe; be spread in the sun to dry. ~ **letmek (-i)**, expose to the sun, air. ~ **li**, sunny; sunlit. ~ **lik**, awning, sunshade; sun curtains; (*cin.*) lens hood; (*mod.*) peak (of cap); sunny place. ~ **siz**, sunless; dark, cloudy. ~ **sizlik**, sunlessness. ~ **topu**[nu], (*bot.*) Californian poppy.

güney (*geo.*) South; (*met.*) south wind. ~ +, *a.* Southern; austral: ~ **açısı**, (*ast.*) azimuth: ~ **Africa (Birlik/Cumhuriyeti)**, (*geo.*) (Union/ Republic of) South Africa: ~ **Amerika**, (*geo.*) South America: ~ **Amerika kondor/tepeli akbabası**, (*orn.*) Andean condor: ~ **ışığı**, (*ast.*) aurora australis: ~ **kum kuşu**, (*orn.*) dunlin: ~ **kutbu**, (*geo.*) south pole: ~ **kutup dairesi**, Antarctic circle: ~ **e bakan**, south-facing.

güney·batı South-west. ~ **doğu**, south-east: ~ **Asya Ortak Savunma Antlaşması**, (*pol.*) SE Asia Treaty Organization. ~ **li**, southern; southerner. ~ **sel**, southern.

gün·indi (*dial.*) West. ~ **kü**, of the day. ~ **leme**[lçⁱ], date. ~ **lemeçli**, dated. ~ **lemek (-de)**, *vi.* pass the day at/in. ~ **lü**, dated.

günlük [1] *a.* Diurnal; daily; sufficient for ... days; ... days old. *n.* Calendar; memoirs, diary; daily (paper). ~ **böcek**, (*ent.*) mayfly: ~ **emir**, (*mil.*) order of the day: ~ **güneşlik**, bright sunny weather/ place: ~ **olaylar**, news: ~ **ücret**, daily wage: ~ **yaşantı**, daily life: ~ **yazılık**, (*fin.*) ledger, journal: ~ **yumurta**, new-laid egg: ~ **zaman**, (*ast.*) civil time. ~ **çü**, (*lit.*) diarist.

günlük [2] *n.* Incense, frankincense. ~ **ağacı**, (*bot.*) liquidambar tree, sweet gum: ~ **ardıcı**, (*bot.*) Spanish juniper: ~ **yakmak**, burn incense.

gün·merkezli (*ast.*) Heliocentric. ~ **oğlu**, opportunist. ~ **ortası**, (*geo.*) meridian. ~ **öte**, (*ast.*) aphelion. ~ **süler**, (*zoo.*) heliozoa, sun animalcules. ~ **tün** = GÜN. ~ **übirlik**, one-day.

günü Envy, jealousy. [*Also* = GÜN.] ~ **cü**, envious, jealous. ~ **lemek (-i)**, envy, be jealous of s.o.

güpegündüz In broad daylight.

gür Abundant, dense, rank. ~ ~ = GÜRÜL GÜRÜL: ~ **saç**, thick-growing hair: ~ **sesli**, with a fine strong voice.

gürbüz Sturdy, robust; bouncing (baby). ~ **lenmek**, *vi.* develop sturdily. ~ **lük**, sturdiness, healthiness.

Gürc·istan (*geo.*) Georgia. ~ **ü**, (*ethn.*) Georgian. ~ **üce**, (*ling.*) Georgian.

güre [1] *n.* (*live.*) Colt (1–3 years).

güre [2] *n.* Energy, strength. ~ **l**, (*phil.*) dynamic. ~ **lci(lik)**, (*phil.*) dynam·ist/(-ism). ~ **li**, energetic. ~ **llik**, dynamic state.

güreş (*sp.*) Wrestling. ~ **tutmak**, wrestle. ~ **çi**, wrestler: ~ **köprüsü**, on all fours with arched back.

~ **çilik**, wrestling. ~ **ilmek**, *imp. v.* be wrestled. ~ **mek (-le)**, wrestle. ~ **tirmek (-i)**, *vc.*

gürgen ~ **(ağacı)** (*bot.*) hornbeam; (*carp.*) made of hornbeam; (*commercially also used for* beechwood). ~ **giller**, hornbeams and beeches.

gürle·me Booming, roaring, thundering. ~ **mek**, *vi.* boom, roar, thunder; roar with anger; (*sl.*) die.

gür·leşmek *vi.* Become abundant. ~ **leştirici**, (*rad.*) amplifier. ~ **leştirme**, *vn.* amplification. ~ **leştirmek (-i)**, amplify. ~ **lük**, abundance.

güruh (*pej.*) Class, group, tribe, horde.

gürül ~ ~, (*ech.*) bubbling, gurgling; in a loud rich voice. ~ **demek**, *vi.* make a loud noise; roar, thunder; (cattle) low.

gürültü Loud noise, din; uproar, confusion, clamour; (*th.*) sound effects. ~ **çıkarmak/etm./ yapmak**, make a din; cause disturbance: ~ **efekti** (*th.*) sound effects: ~ **ye gelmek**, be lost in the confusion: ~ **ye getirmek**, bring about loss in the confusion: ~ **ye gitmek**, be lost in the confusion; perish; suffer innocently: ~ **ye pabuç bırakmamak**, not be intimidated by threats: ~ **yü azaltma// bastırma**, noise reduction//suppression.

gürültü·cü Noisy; boisterous. ~ **lü**, noisy, tumultuous, crowded. ~ **süz**, noiseless, quiet, calm.

gürz (*mil.*) Iron club; mace.

gütaperka (*ind.*) Guttapercha.

gü·tmek[der] Drive before one; drive (animals) to pasture; cherish; nurse (project, etc.); be at the controls; manage, direct.

güve (*ent.*) Moth; case-making clothes moth. ~ **(msi) sineği**, (*ent.*) moth fly: ~ **tozu**, moth-powder: ~ **yeniği**, (*tex.*) moth-eaten spot. ~ **lenmek**, *vp.* eaten by moths.

güve[lçⁱ] (*cul.*) Earthenware cooking pot; (meat and) vegetable casserole.

güven Confidence, reliance, trust; safety, security. ~ **altında**, safeguarded, assured: ~ **beslemek**, feel confidence: ~ **kapağı**, (*ind.*) safety-valve: ~ **mektubu**, (*adm.*) credentials: ~ **olmaz**, unreliable: ~ **oyu**: ~ **i kötüye kullanma**, (*leg.*) breach of trust: ~ **i olm. (-e)**, trust, believe: ~ **i sarsılmak**, distrust: ~ **ini kazanmak**, win s.o.'s confidence.

güvence (*fin.*) Insurance; guarantee. ~ **ödek// ödentisi**, insurance policy//premium. ~ **ci**, guarantor. ~ **li**, insured: ~ **yardımlar**, social assistance. ~ **lik**, guarantee.

güven·[lçⁱ] Trust, reliance. ~ **ışığı**[nı], (*cin.*) safety light. ~ **ilir**, reliable, trustworthy. ~ **ilmek**, *vp.* be trusted. ~ **irlik**, guarantee. ~ **li**, safe; trustworthy. ~ **lik**, security; safety; public order; trust: ~ **ağı** (*sp.*) safety-net: ~ **düzeni**, (*eng.*) safety appliance, device: ~ **kemer/kuşağı**, (*aer.*, *mot.*) safety-belt: ~ **Konsey/Meclisi**, (*pol.*) Security Council: ~ **vanası** (*ind.*) safety valve. ~ **me**, *vn.* reliance. ~ **mek (-e)** trust, rely on; be confident; dare: **güvendiği dağlara kar yağmak/dal elinde kalmak**, be let down; be sadly disappointed. ~ **oyu**[nu], (*adm.*) vote of confidence: ~ **almak//vermek**, obtain//give a vote of confidence. ~ **siz**, distrustful; shy, insecure ~ **sizlik**, distrust; discredit; (*pol.*) 'no confidence'.

güvercin (*orn.*) Pigeon. ~ **doğanı**, (*orn.*) merlin: ~ **ötüşü**, cooing: ~ **salması**, pigeon-loft: ~ **yuvası**

(*carp.*) pigeon-hole: ~**ler**, (*orn.*) Columbidae, pigeons and doves.

güvercin·boynu^{nu}/~**göğsü**^{nü} (*tex.*) Multicoloured, shot. ~**lik**, dove-cote, pigeon-loft; (*naut.*) pigeon-holed cupboard; (*mil.*) small fort. ~**otu**^{nu}, (*bot.*) verbena, vervain.

güverte (*naut.*) Deck. ~ **altı**, belowdecks: ~ **kamarası**, deckhouse: ~ **yolcusu**, deck-passenger: ~**yi neta etm.**, clear the decks (for action). ~**li**, decked; -decker.

güvey^{i/si} Bridegroom; son-in-law. ~ **girmek**, (man) marry; live with his in-laws: ~ **olmadık ama kapı dışında bekledik**, (*jok.*) we're not exactly unfamiliar with the matter: ~ **otu**, (*bot.*) marjoram: ~ **yemeği**, (*soc.*) wedding-supper (given by bridegroom's family). ~**feneri**ⁿⁱ, (*bot.*) bladder cherry. ~**i**^{si} = GÜVEY. ~**lik**, being/used by a bridegroom.

güvez Dark red, violet.

güya [216] As if, as though; it seemed that; one would think that; supposedly, allegedly.

güz (*ast.*) Autumn, fall. ~ +, *a.* Autumnal: ~ **ılım/ noktası**, autumnal equinox. ~**çiğdemi**ⁿⁱ, (*bot.*) meadow saffron, autumn crocus.

güzaf Idle talk; boasting.

güzel *a.* Beautiful; pretty; artistic; good, nice. *n.* A beauty. ~ **görünümlü**, picturesque: ~ ~, beautifully: ~ **hava**, fine weather: ~ **koku(lu)**, perfume(d), aroma(tic): ~ **sanatlar (Akademisi)**, (*art.*)

(Academy of) fine arts: ~ **sesli ardıçkuşu**, (*orn.*) song thrush: ~ **yazı sanatı**, calligraphy, penmanship: ~**e ne yakışmaz/yaraşmaz**, beauty looks well in any clothes: ~**im**, [41] beautiful (person/thing); *int.* my darling!: ~**ler geçidi**, beauty parade.

güzel·avratotu^{nu} (*bot.*) Deadly nightshade, belladonna. ~**ce**, beautifully; properly, thoroughly. ~**hatunçiçeği**ⁿⁱ, (*bot.*) belladonna lily. ~**leme**, (*lit.*) folk-song. ~**leşmek**, *vi.* become beautiful. ~**leştirici**, cosmetic. ~**leştirilmek**, *vp.* ~**leştirmek** (-**i**), make beautiful; beautify, adorn, embellish, decorate. ~**lik**, beauty; cosmetics; goodness; agreeableness; fragrance; happiness: ~ **eczaları**, cosmetics, cosmetic materials: ~ **ile**, gently, without using force: ~ **ilmi**, aesthetics: ~ **kraliçesi**, beauty queen: ~ **yarışması**, beauty contest: ~**ine de güzel hani!**, [249] there's no question about her beauty. ~**likçi**, beautician.

güzergâh Route; passage; ford; ferry; alignment; location.

güzey Shade; shady side; (*geo.*) lee.

güzi·de Select; choice; elect: ~**ler**, (*soc.*) élite. ~**delik**, choice/best part. ~**n**, chosen, choice.

güz·lek Autumnal rain; autumn house. ~**lemek** (-**de**), spend the autumn at/in. ~**lük**, autumn-sown (crops). ~**ün**, in the autumn.

GV(K) = GELİR VERGİSİ (KANUNU).

g.z.(o.) = GEÇMİŞ ZAMAN (ORTACI).

Ğ

Ğ, ğ [**yumuşak ge**] Ninth Tk. letter, 'soft' G; ninth (in a class/series). [4–5] *Never an initial letter; it lengthens the preceding vowel* [AĞIZ] *or is pronounced as a weak 'y'* [MEĞER].

-ğe/-ğa *n. suf. Forming the dative of* -K *words* [KÜTÜĞE; DAYAĞA].

-ği/-ğı/-ğu/-ğü *n. suf. Forming the accusative of* -K *words* [MELEĞİ; BARDAĞI; DORUĞU; BÜYÜĞÜ].

-ğin/-ğın/-ğun/-ğün *n. suf. Forming the genitive of* -K *words* [ÖRDEĞİN; TABAĞIN; TOPUĞUN; SÜLÜĞÜN].

H

H, h [he] Tenth Tk. letter, H; tenth (in a class/series).
H = (*el.*) HENRY; HİCRİ; (*ch. s.*) HİDROJEN.
ha *int.* Ah!, aha!; ha!; hi!; has he?, did he?, etc. *adv.*
Before long. *conj.* ~ ... ~ ..., both ... and ...;
either ... or .... ~ **babam** ~!, *int.* (*encouragement/
emphasis*): ~ **babam konuşuyor!**, he talks and
talks!: ~ **bire!**, and how!, endlessly!: ~ **bugün** ~
yarın, either today or tomorrow, before long,
shortly: ~ **çıktı** ~ **çıkacak**, it will start/come out
very soon: ~ **deyince bulunmaz**, you can't find it
just on the spur of the moment: ~ **hoca Ali** ~ **Ali
hoca**, they're much of a muchness: ~ **şunu bileydin**,
you should have known long ago; you've said it: =
HAH.
HA = HABER AJANSI; HARP AKADEMİSİ.
habanera (*mus.*) Habanera dance.
habaset[i] Wickedness; vice; act of villainy.
habbe (*bot.*) Grain; seed; (*phys.*) particle. ~
değmez, worthless: ~**si kalmadı/yok**, there is
nothing left: ~**yi kubbe yapmak**, make a mountain
out of a molehill.
habe (*sl.*) Bread. ~ **etm./kaymak**, eat, gobble up:
~**den**, for nothing. ~**ci**, stupid.
haber Knowledge; information; news, the press;
anecdote; (*fin.*) acknowledgement, receipt; (*ling.*)
predicate. ~ **ajansı**, news/press agency: ~ **alma**,
(*mil.*) intelligence: ~ **almak**, receive information,
learn; make an inquiry: ~ **atlamak**, (*pub.*) fail to
report a news item: ~ **atlatmak**, get an exclusive
story: ~ **bülteni**, news bulletin: ~ **çık(ma)mak**,
news (not) break: ~ **etm.**, inform, give notice: ~
filmi, newsreel: ~ **göndermek/salmak**, inform, send
news: ~ **güvercini**, (*orn.*) carrier pigeon: ~ **işareti**,
warning signal: ~ **kurumu**, news agency: ~ **merkezi**,
information centre: ~ **sızdırmak**, (*adm., pub.*) leak
information: ~ **teber**, news: ~ **vermek**, acquaint,
inform, tell, make known; announce, communicate:
~**i olm.** (-den), know about: ~**im var**, I know,
I am aware: ~**im yok**, I know nothing about it; I
have not heard: ~**ler**, (*mil.*) intelligence.
haber·ci Messenger, courier; (*rad.*) announcer;
informant; (*mil.*) dispatch-rider. ~**dar**, knowing,
aware of: ~ **etm.**, inform: ~ **olm.**, be informed.
~**leşme**, *vn.* communication; correspondence; (*mil.*)
signals; (*rad.*) telecommunications: ~ **uydusu**,
telstar. ~**leşmek (-le)**, communicate with; correspond with. ~**li**, knowing; informed; knowingly.
~**siz**, not knowing; uninformed; unannounced.
~**sizce**, unwittingly; secretly.
Habeş·(i) (*ethn.*) Abyssinian; dark-olive coloured.
~**çe**, (*ling.*) Abyssinian. ~**istan**, (*geo.*) Abyssinia:
~ **maymunu**, (*zoo.*) sacred baboon: ~ **muzculu**,
(*orn.*) go-away bird.
habis *a.* Wicked; abominable; diabolical; vicious;

(*med.*) malignant. *n.* Wretch; scoundrel. ~ **ruh**,
devil; evil spirit.
hac[c1] (*rel.*) Pilgrimage (to Mecca). ~**ca gitmek/
varmak/~cetmek**, *vi.* make the pilgrimage.
hacamat[1] (*med.*) Bleeding; cupping; (*sl.*) slight
wound. ~ **baltası**, lancet: ~ **şişesi**, cupping-glass.
~**çı**, cupper. ~**lamak (-i)**, bleed, cup; (*sl.*) stab.
hacet[i] Need; necessity; requirement, want; (*rel.*)
prayer, supplication; ritual ablution. ~ **dilemek**,
pray for fulfilment of stg.: ~ **görmek**, feel/consider
necessary; go to the toilet: ~ **kalmak**, be needed:
~ **kapı/penceresi**, door/window of a saint's tomb
(where such prayers are made): ~ **namazı**, (*rel.*)
prayer of supplication: ~ **tepesi**, hill where prayers
are made: ~ **yeri**, toilet: ~ **yok**, there's no need
for it: ~**i olm.**, need to go to the toilet: ~**ini
yapmak**, perform ablutions.
hacı (*rel.*) S.o. who has made pilgrimage to Mecca;
Hadji; pilgrim. ~ **ağa**, (*jok.*) provincial *nouveau
riche*: ~ **ağalık etm.**, spend unnecessarily for effect:
~ **baba**, venerable old pilgrim: ~ **bekler gibi
beklemek (-i)**, wait impatiently for s.o.: ~ **çekirge**,
(*ent.*) desert locust: ~ **fışfış**, (*jok.*) Arabs: ~ **olm.**,
perform the duties of pilgrimage: ~ **tehniyesi**,
solemn congratulations to returning pilgrims: ~**lar
bayramı** = KURBAN BAYRAMI: ~**m!**, my dear
fellow!: ~**sı hocası**, all the (Muslim) people.
hacı·bektaştaşı[n1] (*geol.*) Type of alabaster. ~**kadın**,
Muslim woman who has made the pilgrimage to
Mecca. ~**larkuşağı**[n1], (*ast.*) rainbow. ~**(lar)yolu**[nu],
(*ast.*) Milky Way. ~**lık**, being a pilgrim. ~**yağı**[n1],
kind of cheap perfume. ~**yatmaz**, (*child.*) tumbler
(toy); (*fig.*) restless/mischievous child; s.o. who
manages: ~ **kınkanatlı**, (*ent.*) click beetle.
hac[im]mi Volume, bulk; tonnage, displacement. ~ +, *a.* Volumetric: ~**i istiabı**, cubic
capacity (of container). ~**li**, bulky; solid. ~**sel**,
volumetric.
hac[ir]ri (*leg.*) Prohibition; interdiction. ~ **altına
almak**, put under restraint (s.o. legally incompetent).
Haciva[t]d1 (*th.*) The typical official in KARAGÖZ;
(*fig.*) officious bureaucrat.
hac[iz]zi (*leg.*) Sequestration; attachment; distraint.
~ **koymak (-e)**, sequestrate. ~**li**, sequestered.
hacm- = HACİM.
hacr- = HACİR. ~**'etmek**[eder] **(-i)**, put under restraint.
hacz- = HACİZ. ~**'etmek**[eder] **(-i)**, sequestrate.
haç[ı] (*rel.*) Cross; crucifix. ~ **çıkarmak**, cross o.s.:
~ **şekli**, cruciform; (*bot.*) cruciate: ~ **işareti**,
(*pub.*) obelisk: ~**a germek**, crucify: ~**ı suya atma**,
(casting the cross into the water at) Epiphany.
haç·lamak (-i) Crucify. ~**lı**, having a cross; (*his.*)
Crusader: ~ **bahçe örümceği**, (*zoo.*) garden spider:
~ **kara kurbağası**, (*zoo.*) natterjack, rush toad: ~

seferi, (*his.*) Crusade. ~ **tonoz**, (*arch.*) cross-vault. ~ **vari**, crosswise.

haddi *n.* Boundary; limit; degree, rank; (*phil.*, *math.*) term. ~ **çizmek (-e)**, set limits to stg.: ~ **i geçmek**, overstep the bounds, go beyond the limit: ~ **i hesabı yok**, unlimited: ~ **i kifayeyi bulmak**, be sufficient: ~ **i mi/~ ine mi düşmüs?**, he wouldn't dare!: ~ **i olmamak**, not be s.o.'s business: ~ **i varsa**, let him try: ~ **i zatında**, in itself, essentially: ~ **im değil**, it's not for me to (do/say): ~ **im olmıyarak**, if I may be so presumptuous; although it is not for me to say: ~ **im yok**, I dare not; I have no right: ~ **inden fazla/ziyade**, beyond the limit, excessively: ~ **ini aşmak**, overstep the mark, go too far: ~ **ini bildirmek (-e)**, put s.o. in his place; teach s.o. how to behave: ~ **ini bilmek**, know one's place: ~ **ini bilmemek**, be above o.s., presume: ~ **ini geçmek**, exceed: ~ **ini tecavüz etm.**, go too far; be insolent.

hâddi Sharp, pointed; (*med.*, *phys.*) acute; critical. ~ **safhaya girmek**, reach a critical stage.

hadd- = HAD.

hadde (*eng.*) Wire-drawer's plate; roll(er); rolling-mill. ~ **fabrikası** = ~ HANE: ~ **den çıkarmak**, extrude: ~ **den geçirmek**, roll metals; (*fig.*) examine minutely.

hadde·hane Rolling-mill. ~ **leme**, *vn.* rolling. ~ **lemek (-i)**, draw, mill, roll, extrude. ~ **lenmiş**, rolled, extruded.

hadem *pl.* ~ **ve haşem**, servants and retinue. ~ **e(lik)**, (duties of) manservant (in offices, etc.).

hadım Eunuch. ~ **etm./~ laştırmak**, castrate. ~ **ağası**nı, chief eunuch (in palace, etc.); black eunuch.

hadi(sene) = HAYDİ.

hadim *a.* Serving; serviceable, useful.

hadis (*rel.*) (Study of) traditions of the Prophet Muhammad's deeds/sayings; (*lit.*) tradition.

hadise Event, incident; circumstance; accident, mishap. ~ **çıkarmak**, provoke an incident. ~ **li**, (*pej.*) eventful, disturbed by incidents. ~ **siz**, uneventful; quiet, peaceful.

hadsiz Unbounded; unlimited. ~ **hesapsız**, innumerable.

haf (*sp.*) Half-back.

hafakan (*med.*) Palpitation. ~ **lar basmak/boğmak**, (*fig.*) be/feel exasperated.

hafazanallah *int.* May God preserve us! (from disaster).

hafız Keeper; protector; who has learned the Koran by heart; (*sl.*) stupid; (*sl.*) very studious; (*sl.*) who learns parrot-fashion.

hafız·a Memory; woman HAFIZ: ~ **sını yoklamak**, draw on one's memory. ~ **alı**, (*bot.*) type of large grape. ~ **lamak (-i)**, (*sl.*) be very studious. ~ **lık**, being a HAFIZ; (*sl.*) learning parrot-fashion; stupidity.

hafi Hidden; secret. ~ **celse**, (*adm.*) secret session.

hafid- = HAFİT. ~ **e**, granddaughter.

hafif Light, buoyant; easy; mild; flighty; dim; weak, dilute; slight, little; unimportant; (*sl.*) stony-broke. ~ **atlatmak**, escape lightly: ~ **giyinmek**, dress lightly: ~ **hapis cezası**, (*leg.*) normal imprisonment: ~ **kahvaltı**, (*cul.*) snack: ~ **makineli tüfek**, (*mil.*)

sub-machine-gun: ~ **para cezası**, (*leg.*) light fine: ~ **rüzgâr**, (*met.*) slight breeze: ~ **sanayi**, (*ind.*) light/consumer industry: ~ **tertip**, slightly; just a little: ~ **uyku**, nap, snooze: ~ **yapılı**, slightly built: ~ **e almak**, take lightly: ~ **ten almak**, make light of; not take seriously.

hafif·çe Lightly; gently; slightly. ~ **le(n)mek**, *vi.* lose weight; diminish; attenuate; relax; become less/lighter. ~ **leşmek**, *vi.* become light-headed. ~ **leştirmek/~ letmek (-i)**, lighten, lessen; attenuate; ease, alleviate; minimize; (*leg.*) commute. ~ **letici**, lightening, reducing; (*leg.*) extenuating. ~ **lik**, lightness; calm; flightiness; relief, ease of mind: ~ **etm.**, be flighty. ~ **meşrep**, flighty, frivolous; dissolute. ~ **meşreplik**, levity, frivolity; looseness of morals. ~ **semek (-i)**, despise; consider unimportant. ~ **sıklet**, (*sp.*) lightweight. ~ **ten**, lightly; gently.

hafi·tdi Descendant; grandson.

hafiye Detective; spy; secret agent. ~ **lik**, detection; spying.

hafniyum (*chem.*) Hafnium.

hafr·ıetmekeder **(-i)** Excavate. ~ **iyat**ı, excavation, earthwork; (*archaeol.*) 'dig': ~ **makinesi**, (*eng.*) excavator. ~ **iyatçı**, excavator.

hafta Week. ~ **+**, *a.* Weekly: ~ **arası**, midweek: ~ **arasında/içinde**, within/during the week: ~ **başı**, first day/beginning of the week: ~ **ortası**, midweek: ~ **sekiz gün dokuz**, very/too frequently: ~ **sonu**, end of the week; weekend: ~ **tatili**, weekly holiday, Saturday afternoon and Sunday: ~ **larca**, for weeks on end: ~ **sına**, the same day the following week: ~ **sına kalmaz**, within a week: ~ **ya**, a week today, today week.

haftalık *a.* Weekly; per week; lasting . . . weeks. *n.* Weekly wages. ~ **dergi**, (*pub.*) weekly. ~ **çı/~ lı**, weekly-paid worker.

haftaym (*sp.*) Half-time.

hah *int.* Hah!, there!; now! ~ **şöyle!**, that's right!, exactly! ~ ~, hah-hah!

haham (*rel.*) Rabbi. ~ **başı**, chief rabbi. ~ **hane**, chief rabbi's office.

hail[1] *a.* Interposing. *n.* Obstacle; (*arch.*) partition.

hail[2] *a.* Tragic; terrible. ~ **e**, (*fig.*, *lit.*) tragedy.

hain *n.* Traitor. *a.* Treacherous; disloyal; false, deceitful; ungrateful; mischievous. ~ ~, treacherously. ~ **leşmek**, *vi.* become a traitor; behave treacherously. ~ **lik**, treachery; perfidy; ingratitude.

haiz Possessing; obtaining; furnished with; endowed with; fulfilling, conforming to. ~ **olm.**, possess.

Hakkı [1] *n.* God. ~ **getire**, nil; nothing more; finished; that's all!: ~ **saklıya!**, God forbid!: ~ **yoluna**, for God!: ~ **a erenler**, men of God; devout people: ~ **ın rahmetine kavuşmak**, die.

hakki [2] (*min.*) Engraving; erasing. ~ **etm.**, engrave; erase.

haki [3] *n.* Earth, ground. ~ **ile yeksan etm.//olm.**, raze//be razed to the ground: ~ **i helake sermek**, exterminate.

hakkı [4] *n.* Truth; justice; due; respect; relation. *a.* Right; true; proper; equitable. ~ **aşığı**, platonic love(r); disinterested person: ~ **ediş**, merit: ~ **etm.**, be entitled to, deserve: ~ **iddia etm.**, claim:

~ **istemi**, claim: ~ **iye/sahibi**, person entitled: ~ **kazanmak**, be proved right; deserve; earn the right: ~ **üzere**, according to equity; by rights: ~ **vermek (-e)**, acknowledge s.o. to be right: ~ **yerini bulur/yerde kalmaz**, justice will prevail: ~ **yolu**, the right way/path.

hakk-: ~ **ı geçmek**, right be transferred; work hard for: ~ **ı için**, for the sake of: ~ **ı istemek**, demand one's rights/dues: ~ **ı olm.**, have a share in; be in the right; be due to: ~ **ı ödenmez**, he can never be repaid: ~ **ı tarik**, right of way; ~ **ı var**, he is right: ~ **ı yerine getirmek**, make right prevail; do justice: ~ **ın düşmesi**, (*leg.*) forfeiture, foreclosure: ~ **ında** = HAKKINDA: ~ **ından gelinmek**, be defeated/ overcome: ~ **ından gelmek (-in)**, get the better of s.o.; defeat, punish; avenge o.s.: ~ **ından vazgeçmek**, abdicate: ~ **ını almak**, get one's due/fair share: ~ **ını saklı tutmak**, reserve one's rights: ~ **ını tanımak**, admit, concede: ~ **ını vermek**, do what is necessary; do one's duty: ~ **ını yemek (-in)**, wrong s.o.; cheat s.o. of his rights: ~ **ınız var!**, you're right!; exactly!: ~ **ıyla**, duly; rightfully, properly.

hakan (*adm.*) Oriental potentate; Sultan. ~ **sinekkapanları**, (*orn.*) monarch flycatchers. ~ **i**, royal, imperial. ~ **lık**, sultanate, empire.

hakaret[i] Insult, affront; defamation; contempt. ~ **etm.**, insult; defame: ~ **görmek**, be insulted: ~ **yollu söylenir**, (*ling.*) pejorative: ~ **e uğramak**, suffer an affront. ~ **amiz**, pejorative.

hakça Rightly. ~ **sı**, the truth of it.

hakem (*leg.*) Arbitrator, adjudicator; (*leg.*, *sp.*) referee, umpire. ~ **heyeti**, panel of arbitrators: ~ **kararı**, arbitrament, arbitration award: ~ **mahkemesi**, board of arbitration. ~ **lik**, arbitration; refereeing: ~ **etm.**, arbitrate.

hakeza Thus, in this manner; similarly, ditto.

haki Earth-coloured; (*mod.*) khaki.

hakikat[i] *n.* Truth; reality; sincerity. *adv.* Truly; really. ~ **olm.**, be realized, come true: ~ **e kulaklarını tıkamak**, close one's ears to the truth: ~ **e tıpatıp uygun**, exactly in accordance with the truth: ~ **i şüpheli**, a doubtful story, apocryphal: ~ **in ta kendisidir**, that's the very truth: ~ **te**, in truth, at bottom.

hakikat-en In truth; really; actually. ~ **li**, true; sincere; faithful. ~ **perest**, who worships the truth. ~ **siz**, false, insincere.

hakiki True; actual, real, genuine; original; authentic; sincere; (*phys.*) effective. ~ **cilt**, (*bil.*) corium, dermis: ~ **kılmak**, actualize: ~ **mermi**, (*mil.*) live cartridge: ~ **şahıs**, (*leg.*) natural person.

hakim Sage; philosopher. ~ **ane**, wisely; prudently.

hâkim *n.* (*adm.*) Ruler; governor; (*leg.*) judge. *a.* Ruling; dominating; overlooking. ~ **muavin/ müşaviri**, (*leg.*) assessor: ~ **olm. (-e)**, dominate; rule over; overlook.

hâkim·iyet[i] Sovereignty; domination; -ocracy, rule. ~ **lik**, office of judge/ruler; jurisdiction; domination.

hakir Despicable; of no account; unimportant; (*fig.*) I, me. ~ **görmek**, despise. ~ **ane**, humbly.

hakk- = HAK[1, 2, 4]

hakkâk[i] Engraver. ~ **kalemi**, burin. ~ **lik**, engraving.

hakkaniyet[i] Justice; equity. ~ **li**, just, equitable.

hakk·etmek[eder] **(-i, -e)** Engrave; erase.

hakkı·hıyar Right of choice. ~ **huzur**, attendance fee/allowance. ~ **sükût**[u], hush-money. ~ **telif**, copyright.

hakkında *post.* [93] Concerning, regarding, about. ~ **bir dediği bir dediğine uymamak**, blow hot and cold about stg.: ~ **hüküm vermek**, decide about stg.

hak·lamak (-i) Destroy; finish off; eat up. ~ **laşmak**, settle mutual accounts; be quits.

hak·lı Right; cogent; who is right; having a right: ~ **bulmak**, consider to be right: ~ **çıkarmak (-i)**, prove s.o. right; maintain s.o. is right: ~ **çıkmak**, be proved right: ~ **imiş gibi cesaret takınmak**, put a bold face on it: ~ **olm.**, be right: ~ **savaş**, just war. ~ **lılık**, a being right. ~ **perest**/~ **sever**, honest, just. ~ **sız**, unjust; wrong; illicit; having no rights: ~ **yere**, unjustly. ~ **sızlık**, injustice; wrong. ~ **şinas**, who knows the truth; just; (*sp.*) fair. ~ **tanır**, respecting the rights of others; just, fair.

hakuran (*orn.*) A type of dove. ~ **kafesi gibi**, tumbledown (house).

hal[i 1] *n.* Covered market-place, fruit-market.

hal[li 2] *n.* Solution (of problem, etc.); untying (of knot, etc.); melting. ~ **çaresi**, method of solution: ~ **li hamur olm.**, satisfy all the conditions.

hal[i 3] *n.* Condition; situation, state, circumstance; strength; quality; attribute; ecstasy; trouble; the present time; (*ling.*) present; (*ling.*) case. ~ **almak (bir)**, take a turn, become: ~ **böyle iken**, yet, in spite of this situation: ~ **değişikliği**, (*chem.*) allotropy, metamorphosis; (*ast.*) transition: ~ **eki**, (*ling.*) case ending: ~ **hatır sormak**, ask formal questions (showing interest in s.o./his family): ~ **ile** consequently; as a matter of course: ~ **olm.**, (*rel.*) be in a trance; (*med.*) be in convulsions; (*fig.*) be in a state: ~ **ortacı**, (*ling.*) present participle: ~ **tercümesi**, biography; *curriculum vitae*: ~ **ulacı**, (*ling.*) gerund of state.

hal-: ~ **de** (*following a participle*) [186] although: ~ **den anlamak**, show understanding/sympathy: ~ **e bak!**, what cheek!; look at the result!: ~ **e yola koymak**, put to rights/in order: ~ **i duman olm.**, be in great trouble: ~ **i harap**, he's ruined; he's in a bad way: ~ **i inşada**, in course of construction: ~ **i kalmamak/olmamak**, have no strength left; be very tired: ~ **i tavrı yerinde**, worthy; well-behaved: ~ **i uygun/vakti yerinde**, in easy circumstances, comfortably off: ~ **in neye varacak!**, what will become of you I don't know!: ~ **inde**, in case of . . .: ~ **inden memnun**, contented; self-complacent: ~ **ine bakmamak**, have no regard to one's circumstances/abilities: ~ **ine köpekler gülüyor**, be in a very miserable/pitiful state: ~ **ine sokmak**, bring to (such) a condition: ~ **ine yanmak**, complain of one's circumstances: ~ **ine yoluna koymak** = ~ E YOLA: ~ **ini almak**, assume an attitude: ~ **ini sormak (-in)**, inquire as to s.o.'s health, etc.: ~ **lerini beğenmiyorum (-in)**, I don't like the way he carries on.

hala (*soc.*) Paternal aunt. ~ çocuğu, cousin.

hâlâ [203] At present time; now; just; up till now; still; yet. ~ daha, still!

halas Deliverance; salvation; safety. ~ bulmak/olm., be saved: ~ etm., save. ~kâr, saving; saviour, deliverer.

halat¹ Rope; hawser, cable. ~ bedeni, bight: ~ cevizi, knot: ~ çek(iş)me, (*sp.*) tug-of-war: ~ kangalı, (*naut.*) fake: ~a tırmanma, rope-climbing: ~la tırmanma, rock-climbing (roped together).

halaveti Sweetness; agreeableness.

halay (*mus.*) Anatolian folk-dance.

halayıˡkğı(lık) (Position of) female servant/slave.

halaza (*agr.*) Plant self-sown at harvest time.

halazade (*soc.*) Paternal aunt's child, cousin.

halbuki *conj.* [215] However; nevertheless; whereas.

haldır ~ ~, (*ech.*) hurriedly and noisily.

hale (*ast.*) Halo, aureola, corona.

halecan(lanmak) = HELECAN.

halef Successor; posterity; substitute, replacement. ~ selef olm., (*adm.*) succeed/replace one another.

halel Defect; injury; prejudice. ~ gelmek, injury, etc. occur: ~ getirmek/vermek, damage, disturb; cause harm/prejudice. ~dar, harmful, prejudicial: ~ etm., spoil, destroy.

halelenmek *vi.* (*ast.*) Have a halo.

halen Now; at present.

Haleˡpbi (*geo.*) Aleppo. ~ çamı, (*bot.*) Aleppo pine: ~ çıbanı, (*med.*) Aleppo button/boil: ~ orada ise arşın burada, well, prove it!; let's put it to the test!

haleti Situation; state, condition. ~i nezi, (*obs.*) death agony: ~i ruhiye, state of mind.

halˡetmekeder (-i) (*pol.*) Depose, dethrone.

halfa ~ (otu), (*bot.*) esparto grass.

halhali Anklet/bangle (worn by women).

halı Carpet. ~ böceği, (*ent.*) carpet beetle: ~ dokumak, weave a carpet: ~ döşmek, carpet, lay a carpet: ~ güvesi, (*ent.*) carpet moth: ~ süpürgesi, carpet-sweeper.

halı-cı Carpet-weaver/-seller. ~cılık, carpet-weaving. ~resim, tapestry.

halˡiʼi¹ *n.* (*pol.*) Deposition, dethronement.

hali² *a.* Vacant, empty; unoccupied; deserted. ~ (-den), exempt from: ~ arazi, waste land: ~ etm., quit; empty; leave vacant.

halibut (*ich.*) Halibut.

haliˡçei (*geo.*) Strait, estuary, gulf, canal; *pr.n.* the Golden Horn.

halife (*his.*) Caliph; Commander of the Faithful; (*rel.*) sheikh's assistant; (*adm.*) clerk; successor. ~lik, (*his.*) Caliphate.

hali-harˡpbı State of war. ~hazır, present state of things; status quo: ~da, at the present time.

halik¹ (*rel.*) Creator, God.

halim Mild; gentle; patient. ~ selim, quiet and good-tempered.

halis Pure, unadulterated; genuine; sincere. ~ muhlis, authentic, true. ~ane, sincere (words, etc.); sincerely; without ulterior motive.

halita (*chem.*) Mixed substance; (*min.*) alloy. ~ yapmak, alloy. ~lı, alloyed.

haliyle Consequently; as a matter of course.

halk¹ ¹ *n.* Creation.

halk¹ ² *n.* People; crowd; populace; common people; community. ~ +, *a.* Popular; folk-; colloquial; public; demo-. ~ ağzı, rumour, canard: ~ ağzından, (*ling.*) vernacular: ~ bilimi, sociology: ~ bilimcisi, sociologist: ~ çalgısı, popular music: ~ dili, (*ling.*) demotic, vernacular: ~ edebiyatı, folk literature: ~ hükümeti, (*pol.*) democracy: ~ kitaplığı, public library: ~ malı, public property: ~ münasebet/temasları, (*adm.*) public relations: ~OYU: ~ oyunu, folk-dance: ~ tavlayıcısı, (*pol.*) demagogue: ~ yığını, the masses: ~ yollara düştü, the people poured out into the streets: ~ zümresi, the common people.

halk-: ~a açık, public: ~a dönük, aimed at the people: ~a inmek, come down to the common level; condescend: ~a mal etm., socialize: ~a verir talkın/telkini kendi yutar salkımı, he preaches one thing and practises another: ~ın diline düşmek, be gossiped about: ~ın gözünde olm., be in the public eye: ~la ilişkiler, (*adm.*) public relations: ~tan saklamak, (*pol.*) conceal from the people.

halka Ring; hoop; circle; door-knocker; bangle; link (of chain); (*eng.*) collet; (*naut.*) clew; (*bio.*) annulus, segment. ~ +, *a.* Round; annular: ~ adası, (*geo.*) atoll: ~ ~ olan, (*ast.*) armillary: ~ olm., form a ring: ~ oyunları, (*sp.*) round games.

halka-dizilişli Arranged in a ring. ~lanmak, *vi.* form a ring. ~lı, ringed; linked; in coils; (*ast.*) annular; (*zoo.*) segmented; cyclic(al): ~ boyunlu sülün, (*orn.*) ring-necked pheasant: ~ defter, loose-leaf notebook: ~ delik, grommet: ~ gözler, tired eyes (with dark rings). ~lıdamar, (*bot.*) annular vessel. ~lıkurtlar, (*zoo.*) segmented worms. ~lılar, (*zoo.*) annelids. ~msı/~vi, annular.

halkavcı-lığı (*pol.*) Demagogy. ~sı, demagogue.

halkayay (*eng.*) Helical spring.

halk-bilgisini Study of folklore. ~bilim(ci), folklor·e/(-ist). ~ça, by the people. ~çı, (*pol.*) populist; supporter of CHP. ~çılık, populism. ~devinbilim, demography. ~erki, democracy. ~evini, People's House, community centre. ~odasını, People's Room, community centre. ~oylaması/~oyunu, public opinion; (*pol.*) referendum, plebiscite.

hallaˡçeı (*tex.*) Cotton/wool fluffer. ~ pamuğu gibi atmak/dağıtmak, scatter about in all directions. ~lık, fluffing the cotton/wool.

hal·lenmek *vi.* Acquire a new shape/condition; feel faint; (-e), manifest interest in/desire for: hallenip küllenmek, manage on one's own. ~leşmek (-le), confide troubles to each other; have a good talk.

hall·ˡetmekeder (-i) Undo; dispose of; solve (problems); explain; (*chem.*) dissolve; analyse. ~i¹ = HAL². ~olunmak, *vp.* be solved, etc. ~olunmaz, insoluble.

halli² Of/in a certain condition. ~ce, slightly better; quite well off. ~ hamur (ile), of the same substance; one with; part and parcel of.

halojen (*chem.*) Halogen. ~li, halogenic.

halsiz Weak; exhausted, tired out. ~lik, exhaustion.

halt¹ Impertinence; stupid/improper speech/deed. ~ etm., do/say stg. stupid/out-of-place: ~

karıştırmak, behave stupidly, make a blunder, put one's foot in it: ~ **yemek**, behave badly.
halter (*sp.*) Dumb-bell; weights. ~**ci**, weight-lifter.
halukᵘ Of good character; well-disposed; decent.
halüsinasyon (*psy.*) Hallucination.
halvetⁱ Solitude; retirement, privacy; lonely place, wilderness; private room; (*rel.*) cell, hermitage; private sweat-room in HAMAM. ~ **etm.**, make room private by turning others out; retire to a private room: ~ **gibi**, (room) hot and stuffy: ~ **olm.**, be closeted with s.o.: ~**e dönmek**, (room) become hot and stuffy. ~**gâh**, secluded place. ~**i**, (*rel.*) (member of) Halveti dervish order.
ham Unripe; green; immature; (*ind.*) raw, crude, untreated, unrefined; (*fig.*) inexperienced, tyro; (*sp.*) out of training; vain, useless; unreasonable. ~ **besisuyu**, (*bot.*) rising sap: ~ **demir**, (*min.*) bloom: ~ **elmas**, uncut/rough diamond: ~ **ervah**, coarse-minded: ~ **madde**, raw material: ~ **pamuk**, cotton wool: ~ **petrol**, crude oil: ~ **sofu**, intolerant bigot: ~ **şeker**, brown sugar: ~ **toprak**, uncultivated land: ~ **yol**, dirt road.
ham·ail/~**aylı** (*mil.*) Shoulder-belt (for sword, etc.); ribbon (of an order); amulet, charm.
hamaⁱ**k**ᵍⁱ Hammock.
hamakatⁱ Stupidity; folly.
hamal Porter; carrier; coolie; common/coarse fellow. ~ **camal**, low-class people: ~ **sırığı**, porter's stick: ~ **ücreti**, porterage: ~**a semeri yük olmaz**, one's own work is never difficult.
hamal·başıⁿⁱ Foreman porter. ~**iye**, porterage. ~**lık**, porter's work; coarse behaviour; toiling and slaving; unnecessary burden: ~**ını etm.**, do the donkey work.
hamam Bath; *esp.* Turkish bath. ~ **gibi**, very hot/steamy: ~ **kubbesi**, (echoing) domed chamber of a Turkish bath; noisy talker: ~ **takımı**, towels/equipment (for the bath): ~ **yapmak**, bath o.s.: ~**a giren terler**, with the job you accept its problems and rewards: ~**da deli var**, 'a sudden commotion': ~**ın namusunu kurtarmak**, gloss over an awkward situation, paper over the cracks.
hamam·anasıⁿⁱ Chief women's bath-attendant; (*fig.*) huge woman. ~**böceği**ⁿⁱ, (*ent.*) common cockroach, (?) American/German cockroach. ~**böcekleri**, (*ent.*) cockroaches. ~**cı**, public-bath proprietor: ~ **olm.**, (*rel.*) be canonically unclean, need ritual ablutions. ~**cılık**, operating a public-bath. ~**lık**, washroom. ~**otu**ⁿᵘ, depilatory. ~**tası**ⁿⁱ, metal bowl (used in washing o.s.).
hamaratⁱ (Woman) hard working, industrious. ~ **taze**, (woman/girl) hardworking, capable. ~**lık**, industry, activity.
hamas·etⁱ Heroism. ~**i**, epic. ~**iyat**ⁱ, epic poem.
Hambeli (*rel.*) (Member of) Hanbali school.
hamd- = HAMT.
Hamel (*ast.*) Aries, the Ram.
hamhalatⁱ Coarse, loutish, boorish.
hamhum Humming and hawing. ~ **etm.**, hum and haw: ~ **şaralop**, (*sl.*) a lot of nonsense; swindle.
hamız (*chem.*) Acid; sour. ~**iyet**ⁱ, acidity.
hami *a.* Protecting, guarding. *n.* Protector, patron.
hamil *a.* Bearing, bringing. *n.* Support. ~ **olm.**,

carry, bring: ~**ine yazılı**, (*fin.*) 'to bearer'; bearer. ~**e**, (*bio*) pregnant woman: ~ **kalmak (-den)**, be pregnant by . . .. ~**elik**, pregnancy.
haminne 'Grannie'.
hamiş Marginal note; footnote; postscript.
hamiyetⁱ Zeal; public spirit; patriotism. ~**li**, public-spirited; philanthropic. ~**siz**, lacking public spirit. ~**sizlik**, lack of public spirit.
hamla (*naut.*) Stroke. ~**cı**, stroke; chief oarsman.
hamlaⁱ**ç**ᶜⁱ (*min.*) Blowpipe; torch; nozzle; small bellows.
ham·lama *vn.* Being out of condition; (*art.*) first firing (of pots). ~**la(ş)mak**, *vi.* get out of condition/practice; become soft from lack of work.
hamle Attack, onslaught; effort; dash; *élan*; move (chess, etc.). ~ **etm./yapmak**, attack; make a great effort. ~**ci**, s.o. making great efforts. ~ⁱ**tmek**ᵈᵉʳ (-i, -e), load; attribute/impute to.
ham·lık Unripeness; crudeness; rawness; inexperience; lack of condition. ~**madde**, (*ind.*) raw material(s). ~**payı**, (*carp.*) mortise (for tenon).
hamsi (*ich.*) Anchovy (fresh); brisling, sprat. ~ **kuşu**, (*cul.*) mouthful of fried anchovy. ~**giller**, (*ich.*) herring family.
hamsin (*met.*) Last fifty days of winter.
hamster (*zoo.*) Hamster.
hamⁱ**t**ᵈⁱ (*rel.*) Giving thanks/praise to God. ~ **etm.**, give thanks/praise to God: ~ **olsun!**, thank God!; thanks be!
hamule (*phys.*) Load; charge; (*naut.*) cargo. ~**li**, laden.
hamur *n.* (*cul.*) Dough; leaven; paste; pulp; (*pub.*) quality (of paper); (*fig.*) essence, nature. *a.* Half-baked (bread). ~ **açmak**, roll out the dough: ~ **gibi**, limp, flabby: ~ **işi**, pastry: ~ **kâğıt**, first quality paper: ~ **tahtası**, pastry-board: ~ **tutmak/yogurmak**, knead the dough.
hamur·boya (*art.*) Impasto. ~**cu**/~**kâr**, baker's assistant. ~**lamak (-i)**, cover with dough; seal with dough, lute. ~**lanmak**, *vp.* ~**laşmak**, *vi.* become dough-like; become limp. ~**lu**, covered/made with dough; leavened; fermented. ~**su**, half-baked. ~**suz**, unleavened (bread). ~**umsu**, dough-like; half-baked.
hamutᵘ Collar (of draught horse).
han¹ *n.* (*adm.*) Sovereign; Khan; prince.
han² *n.* (*arch.*) Inn; caravanserai; merchants' lodgings; large office building. ~ **gibi**, vast: ~ **hamam sahibi**, a man of property.
han·ay Large room, hall; tall building. ~**cı**, inn-keeper: ~ **sarhoş yolcu sarhoş**, six of one and half-a-dozen of the other. ~**cılık**, inn-keeping.
hançer (*mil.*) Dagger. ~**lemek (-i)**, stab (to death). ~**lenmek**, *vp.*
hançere (*bio.*) Larynx.
handikap (*sp.*) Handicap; (*fig.*) disability, handicap.
hane House; dwelling; family; household; compartment; subdivision; (*fin.*) column (for figures); square (of chessboard). ~ ~, in separate compartments.
-hane/-ane/-ne *n. suf.* [66] House/building of/for . . .
[HAPİSHANE; KUŞANE; ECZANE].

ıanedan *n.* Great family; dynasty. *a.* Of illustrious descent, noble; courteous; hospitable. ~ **dan**, blue-blooded. ~ **lık**, nobility; (gentleman's) courteous hospitality.

Hanefi (*rel.*) (Member of) Hanafi school; orthodox Muslim. ~ **lik**, Hanafi school.

ıane·li Having . . . houses/compartments/columns; (*tex.*) chequered. ~ **lik**, containing houses.

ıanende (*Or. mus.*) Singer. ~ **lik**, singing.

ıangar (*ind.*) Large store; (*aer.*) hangar.

ıangi [74] Which?; whichever. ~ **akla hizmet ediyor?**, what does he think he's doing?: ~ **biri?**, which one?: ~ **dağda kurt öldü?**, what a pleasant surprise!: ~ **daire karışır (-e)?**, (*adm.*) which department deals with . . .?: ~ **peygambere kulluk edeceğini şaşırmak**, not know whose orders to follow/whom to please: ~ **rüzgâr attı?**, what brought you here?: ~ **taş pekse başını ona vur!**, you got yourself into the mess so get yourself out of it!: ~ **taşı kaldırsan altından çıkar**, he always turns up everywhere; he has a finger in every pie: ~ **miz**// ~ **niz**// ~ **si?**, which one of us//you//them?

ıanım *n.* Lady; mistress (of house); wife; lady-companion/-help. *a.* Feminine; ladylike. ~ **evladı**, mollycoddle, mother's darling: ~ **hanımcık**, model housewife; proper little lady (by *old* Turkish standards): ~ **kız**, shy little girl: ~ **teyze**, (*polite address to elderly lady*).

ıanım·böceğini (*ent.*) Ladybird. ~ **efendi**, Madam!, my lady! ~ **efendilik**, status/qualities of a lady. ~ **eli**yi, (*bot.*) honeysuckle. ~ **eligiller**, (*bot.*) honeysuckle family, Caprifoliaceae. ~ **göbeği**ni, (*cul.*) sweet dish (flour and eggs). ~ **lık**, status of a lady. ~ **ördeği**ni, (*orn.*) shelduck. ~ **parmağı**nı, (*cul.*) finger-shaped pastry.

ıani1 *n.* (*ich.*) Comber. ~ **giller**, sea bass.

ıani2 *adv.* [216] ~ (**ya**), where?; well?; you know!; and then; and in addition: ~ **bana?**, what about me?; where do I come in?: ~ **dir**, it's a long time now since . . .: ~ **dün bize gelecektin!**, I thought you were coming to see us yesterday!: ~ **o günler**, ah, those were the days!; I only wish we could!; (*iron.*) what an idea!; out of the question!: ~ **yok mu?**, you know what I mean.

ıanlık Title/territory of a Khan; khanate.

ıanos (*ich.*) Comber.

ıant ~ ~ **ötmek**, long for stg.

ıantal Big; bulky; cumbersome; clumsy; badly made; coarse; clownish; boorish. ~ **laşmak**, *vi.* become clumsy, etc. ~ **lık**, clumsiness, etc.

ıanut Shop. ~ **çu(luk)**, shopkeep·er/(-ing).

ıanüman Home; family and belongings. ~ **ı harap**, whose home is ruined.

Ianya (*geo.*) Canea/Khania (Crete). ~ **'yı Konya'yı anlamak/öğrenmek**, learn by bitter experience: ~ **'yı Konya'yı göstermek (-e)**, teach s.o. a lesson (*threat*).

ıap1 (*med.*) Pill, tablet, cachet. ~ **kutusu**, pill box: ~ **yutmak**, swallow the pill; (*fig.*) be 'done for', be 'in the soup'. ~ **ıcık**, ~ **yapmak**, catch a sweet, etc. in the mouth.

ıapır ~ ~ / ~ **hupur yemek**, gulp down noisily: ~ **sa da köpürse de**, no matter what happens I shall . . ..

hap·lissi *n.* Confinement; imprisonment; prison, gaol. *a.* Imprisoned; detained. ~ **cezası**, imprisonment: ~ **giymek**, be sentenced to prison: ~ **kalmak**, remain imprisoned: ~ **yatmak**, serve one's term of imprisonment: ~ **e mahkûm etm.**, commit to prison: ~ **e tıkmak**, clap into gaol.

hapis·(h)ane Prison: ~ **kaçkını**, criminal deserving imprisonment; (*fig.*) scoundrel. ~ **lik**, imprisonment

haps- = HAPİS. ~ **edilme**, *vn.* imprisonment. ~ **edilmek**, be imprisoned. ~ **etmek**eder (-i), imprison, gaol, incarcerate; trap; confine, shut up; (*fig.*) detain, keep waiting.

hapş·ırı·lkğı *n.* Sneeze. ~ **ırmak**, *vi.* sneeze. ~ **ırtmak** (-i), *vc.* ~ **u**, *int.* atishoo!

hapt1 ~ **etm.** (-i), get the better of s.o. in an argument; reduce to silence: ~ **olm.**, be reduced to silence.

har ~ ~, in plenty, fully: ~ **hur**, confusion: ~ **vurup harman savurmak**, spend money prodigally; 'blue' one's money: ~ **ı başına vurmak**, become furious: ~ **ı geçmek**, cool down/off.

hara1 *n.* (*live.*) Stud farm; stock farm.

hara2 *n.* (*geol.*) Marble; moiré, watering (silk, etc.).

harab- = HARAP. ~ **at**1, *pl.* (*arch.*) ruins: *s.* tavern. ~ **ati**, drunkard; careless and unconventional, bohemian. ~ **atilik**, bohemianism. ~ **e**, (*archaeol.*) ruins; tumble-down town//house. ~ **elik**, (site of) ruins; destruction.

haracı(lık) (*live.*) Stud-//stock-farm·er/(-ing).

hara·lçc1 Tax; tribute; public auction; (*his.*) land-tax and tax paid by non-Muslims instead of military service. ~ ~!, (at auction) going, going!: ~ **mezat satmak**, sell at auction: ~ **yemek**, (*sl.*) sponge on s.o.: ~ **a bağlamak**, force s.o. to pay taxes: ~ **a çıkarmak**, put up to auction: ~ **a kesmek (-i)**, levy tribute on; extort heavy taxes; oppress. ~ **çı(lık)**, (work of) tax/tribute collector.

harakiri (Japanese) harakiri.

haram *a.* (*rel.*) Forbidden; unlawful; sacred; inviolable. *n.* Forbidden deed. ~ **etm. (-i, -e)**, forbid s.o. the use/enjoyment of stg.: ~ **mal**, unlawfully acquired property; ill-gotten gains: ~ **olm.**, be unlawful/illicit; (pleasure, etc.) be spoiled: ~ **olsun!**, may you get no joy of it!: ~ **yemek**, enrich o.s. unlawfully: ~ **a uçkur çözmek**, have sexual relations outside marriage.

haram·i (*lit.*) Brigand, thief. ~ **ilik**, brigandage. ~ **zade**, bastard; scoundrel.

hara·lpb1 *n.* Ruining; destroying. *a.* Ruined; devastated; decayed; desolate. ~ **ender** ~, utterly ruined: ~ **etm.**, destroy, devastate: ~ **olm.**, be devastated; fall into ruin; (*fig.*) be impoverished; be desperately in love. ~ **laşmak**, *vi.* fall into ruins; become devastated. ~ **lık**, devastation.

harar Large sack made of haircloth.

harar·eti Heat; (*med.*) fever, temperature; thirst; fervour, exaltation. ~ **basmak**, feel thirsty: ~ **kesmek/söndürmek**, quench one's thirst: ~ **vermek**, make thirsty.

hararet·lenmek Get excited/angry. ~ **li**, feverish; irascible; heated (argument); enthusiastic.

haraza1 *n.* (*sl.*) Noisy argument/quarrel.

haraza² *n.* (*bio.*) Ox's gallstone.

harb- = HARP². ~**e**, (*mil.*) javelin, pike. ~**en**, by war/force of arms. ~**ˈetmek**ᵉᵈᵉʳ, go to war, fight.

harbi *n.* Ramrod. *a.* Straight; honest. ~ **bas**, (*col.*) fast walk: ~ **konuşmak**, (*col.*) speak forthrightly: ~ **zar**, (*gamb.*) 'honest' dice.

harbiye War Academy, Military College: ~ **Nezareti**, (*his.*) War Ministry. ~**li**, military college student, cadet.

harc- = HARÇ¹, ². ~**ama**, *vn.* spending; expenses; expenditure; consumption. ~**amak (-i)**, expend, spend; consume, use; put s.o. in danger intentionally; (*sl.*) get rid of, kill. ~**anmak**, *vp.* ~**ˈetmek**ᵉᵈᵉʳ **(-i)**, spend, disburse. ~**ı**, cheap. ~**ıâlem**, within everyone's means; in common use, ordinary; general-purpose. ~**ırah**, travelling expenses/ allowance.

harˈçᶜⁱ ¹ *n.* (*fin.*) Expenditure, expenses, outlay, cost; (*adm.*) fees (to government offices); stg. within one's means/power. ~**ı olm. (-in)**, be within one's means/capacity: ~**ını görmek**, meet/defray the expenses for stg.

harˈçᶜⁱ ² *n.* (*arch.*) Mortar, plaster; (*agr.*) soil mixture, compost; raw material; ingredients; (*mod.*) trimmings, braid, etc.

harç·lı (1) By paying fees; expensive: (2) made with mortar/compost; trimmed. ~**lık**, pocket-money. ~**sız**, without mortar: ~ **duvar**, dry-stone wall.

hardal (*bot.*, *cul.*) Mustard. ~ **sarısı**, mustard-coloured: ~ **tane/tohumu**, mustard seed: ~ **tozu**, mustard powder: ~ **yakısı**, (*med.*) mustard plaster: ~**la kızartmak**, (*cul.*) devil. ~**iye**, mustard-flavoured grape-juice. ~**lık**, mustard-pot.

hardun (*zoo.*) Starred lizard, hardun.

hare (*tex.*) Moiré; watering (of silk, etc.).

harekât¹ *pl.* Actions; (*mil.*) operations, manœuvres; (*ling.*) vowel-points. ~ **araştırması**, operational research: ~ **saha//üssü**, (*mil.*) field//base of operations.

hareke (*ling.*) (In Arabic) vowel-point. ~**lemek (-i)**, insert the vowel-points. ~**li**, with vowel-points inserted, vocalized.

hareket¹ Movement; act; action; activity; behaviour; departure; excitement; (*eng.*) migration; (*sp.*) muscular exercises. ~ **bilgisi**, (*phys.*) kinematics: ~ **dairesi**, (*rly.*) traffic department; movements control: ~ **değiştirme**, (*mot.*) gear-change: ~ **dingili**, (*eng.*) drive-axle: ~ **etm.**, move, act; set out, start; conduct o.s.: ~ **flaması**, (*naut.*) blue peter: ~ **halinde**, astir: ~ **kolu**, (*eng.*) con(necting) rod: ~ **limanı**, (*naut.*) port of departure: ~ **noktası**, departure; starting-point (of discussion): ~ **tarzı**, behaviour, conduct, deportment: ~ **üssü**, (*mil.*) base of operations: ~**e geçmek**, start work, go into action: ~**e gelmek**, begin to move, come into play: ~**e getirmek**, actuate, set in motion: ~**e hazır**, 'all booted and spurred', ready for action.

hareket·lenmek *vi.* Go into action. ~**li**, in action/ motion; sliding; mobile; animated, moving; active: ~ **açıölçer**, (*math.*) cursor. ~**lilik**, dynamism. ~**siz**, motionless, static; inactive; (*bot.*) dormant; stagnant. ~**sizlik**, inactivity; dormancy; stagnation.

hare·lenmek *vi.* Be rippled; (*tex.*) be watered. ~**li**, watered, moiré: ~ **kumaş**, tabby.

harem (*rel.*) Sacred territory (Mecca, Medina); (*soc.*) women's quarters (in Muslim house), harem; wife. ~ **ağası**, (*his.*) (black) eunuch in charge of harem: ~ **kâhyası**, steward of harem. ~**lik**, harem: ~ **selamlık olm.**, (*soc.*) men and women form separate groups.

harf¹ Letter (of alphabet); (*ling.*) particle; word, speech, language. ~ **arası**, (*pub.*) spacer: ~ **atmak**, make insulting remarks: ~ **çerçevesi**, (*pub.*) chase: ~ **çevirisi**, (*ling.*) transliteration: ~ **inkılabı**, reform of the Tk. alphabet (Arabic to Latin script, 1928): ~ **kasası**, (*pub.*) case(-cabinet): ~ **yüzü**, type-face: ~**i** ~**ine**, to the very letter, word for word, exactly.

harf·endaz(lık) (Action of) s.o. who uses insulting words (to women in the street). ~ **itarif**// ~ **itenkir**, (*ling.*, *obs.*) definite//indefinite article. ~**iyen**, literally, word by word.

harharyas (*ich.*) Porbeagle. ~**giller**, sharks.

harıl ~ ~, assiduously: ~ ~ **yanmak**, burn furiously/continuously. ~**tı**, loud/continuous (burning) noise.

harın Bad-tempered (animal); (*fig.*) obstinate. ~**lanmak**, *vi.* be bad-tempered.

haric- = HARİÇ. ~**en**, externally; in appearance. ~**i**, external; outer; foreign; heretic. ~**ilik**, (*phil.*) externalism. ~**iye**, (*pol.*) foreign affairs: (*med.*) external diseases: ~ **hizmeti**, (*adm.*) foreign/ diplomatic service: ~ **Nazır/Vekili**, (*obs.*) Minister of Foreign Affairs: ~ **Nezaret/Vekâleti**, (*obs.*) Ministry of Foreign Affairs. ~**iyeci(lik)**, (work of) (*adm.*) member of the Foreign Service//(*med.*) expert in external diseases.

hariˈçᶜⁱ *n.* The outside; exterior; abroad; foreign country. *a.* External; outside. *adv.* Apart from, not including. *post.* **(-den)** [90] Outside; extra. ~ **etm./tutmak**, exclude; except: ~ **olm.**, be excluded: ~**(in)den**, from abroad: ~**te**, abroad: ~**ten gazel atmak/okumak**, talk without authority on stg. burst into a conversation.

harik·a *n.* Wonder; miracle. *a.* marvellous, extraordinary: ~**lar yaratmak**, be very successful ~**ulade**, extraordinary; marvellous; wonderful: ~ **gözlü sülün**, (*orn.*) crested argus.

harim Most intimate/private place; place that must be defended against intrusion.

haris Greedy; avaricious; covetous; ambitious; eager.

harita (*geo.*) Map; plan; (*naut.*) chart. ~ **çizmek** (*fig.*) weave in and out drunkenly: ~ **dairesi** ordnance survey: ~ **kamarası**, (*naut.*) chart-room ~ **ressamı**, cartographer: ~**da olm.**, be expected planned: ~**dan silinmek**, be wiped off the map; be conquered; be destroyed: ~**ya almak**, chart stg ~**cı(lık)**, cartograph·er/(-y).

har·lamak *vi.* Be in flames; burn fiercely; (*fig.*) burst into anger. ~**latmak (-i)**, stir up (fire). ~**lı** burning furiously.

harman (*agr.*) Threshing; grain for threshing threshing-floor; harvest-time; blend (of tea/tobacco etc.); batch (of loaves/bricks); (*pub.*) sheets fo making a fascicle. ~ **çevirmek**, go round in circles: ~ **çorman**, (*sl.*) in confusion: ~ **döveni**, threshing-sledge driven over the grain: ~ **dövmek**, thresh: ~ **savurmak**, winnow: ~ **sonu**, residue of grain (left after threshing); (*fig.*) remnants of a fortune/business: ~ **sonu dervişlerin**, patience will be rewarded: ~ **yeri**, threshing-floor.

harman·cı(lık) (Work of) thresher//blender. ~ **dalı**, (*mus.*) Aegean folk-dance. ~ **i(ye)**, (*mod.*) long cloak, cape. ~ **lama**, *vn.*, blending. ~ **lamak (-i)**, blend (tobacco, etc.); (*pub.*) collate; (horse) run in a circle; (*naut.*) turn in a wide circle. ~ **lanmak**, *vp.* be blended; (*ast.*) (moon) have a halo.

harmon·i *etc.* = ARMONİ. ~ **yum**, harmonium.

harnu¹pᵇᵘ (*bot.*) Carob, locust-bean. ~ **iye**, drink made from the beans.

harp¹¹ *n.* (*mus.*) Harp.

har¹pᵇⁱ² *n.* (*mil.*) War. ~ **açmak (-e)**, go to war against: ~ **başlığı**, (*naut.*) (torpedo) war-head: ~ **cürümleri**, (*leg.*) war-crimes: ~ **dairesi**, military supplies department: ~ **divanı**, military court, court-martial: ~ **ertesi**, post-war: ~ **esiri**, prisoner-of-war: ~ **etm.**, make war: ~ **gemisi**, (*naut.*) warship; battleship: ~ **hali**, state of war: ~ **harici kalmak**, be non-belligerent: ~ **ilanı**, declaration of war: ~ **limanı**, (*naut.*) naval port: ~ **malulü**, wounded soldier, war casualty: ~ **meydanı**, battle-field: ~ **mıntıkası**, war-zone: ~ **Okulu**, military college: ~ **oyunu**, (*mil.*) war games, manœuvres: ~ **rizikosu**, (*fin.*) war risk: ~ **sonrası**, aftermath of war: ~ **suçu**, (*leg.*) war-crime: ~ **tazminatı**, (*fin.*) reparations: ~ **zamanı**, wartime: ~ **zengini**, (*fin.*) war profiteer: ~ **te hayli vurmuştu**, (*fin.*) they say he made a pile of money during the war. ~ **çi**, warlike; warmonger.

harrangürra In a disorderly/noisy manner.

hars Culture. ~ **i**, cultural.

hart ~ ~, (*ech.*) scratch, scratch: ~ **hurt**, (*ech.*) munch crunch. ~ **a¹**, ~ **sı hurtası olmamak**, behave badly. ~ **adak**/~ **adan**, (*ech.*) (sound of stg. suddenly bitten/seized).

harta² = HARİTA.

hartu¹çᶜᵘ (*mil.*) Cartridge (for cannon).

Hartum (*geo.*) Khartoum.

haru¹pᵇᵘ = HARNUP.

has⁵¹ *a.* Special; peculiar to; personal; private; (*cul.*) pure, unmixed, unadulterated. *n.* (*his.*) Fief of over 100,000 AKÇE. ~ **altın**, (*min.*) fine gold: ~ **boya**, (*tex.*) fast dye: ~ **ipek**, real silk: ~ **kefal**, (*ich.*) grey mullet: ~ **tımar**, (*his.*) apanage: ~ **un**, (*cul.*) fine/white flour.

hasar Damage; loss; devastation; (*naut.*) average. ~ **a uğramak**, *vi.* suffer loss/damage. ~ **lı**, damaged.

hasa¹tᵈ¹ (*agr.*) Reaping; harvest; crop. ~ **etm.**, reap. ~ **çı(lık)**, (work of) reaper.

hasbahçe (*his.*) Palace garden.

hasbıhal¹ Private/friendly chat. ~ **etm.**, converse, chat.

hasbi Disinterested; gratuitous; without reason. ~ **geçmek**, (*sl.*) not care; pay no attention. ~ **lik**, disinterestedness.

ha·seb- = HASEP. ~ **sed-** = HASET.

haseki (*his.*) One of Sultan's personal bodyguard;

(*his.*) Sultan's favourite wife. ~ **küpesi**ⁿⁱ, (*bot.*) columbine, aquilegia.

hasenat¹ Good works; pious deeds.

hase¹pᵇⁱ Personal qualities; merit. ~ **i nesebi**, of noble birth: ~ **iyle**, by reason of . . ., in conformity with . . ..

hase¹tᵈⁱ Envy, jealousy, covetousness. ~ **etm.**, envy. ~ **çi**, envious; jealous; covetous. ~ **lenmek**, *vi.* be jealous. ~ **lik**, covetousness.

hasıl (*agr.*) Barley cut green for fodder.

hâsıl Resulting; happening; produced; growing. ~ **etm.**, produce; obtain; bring about; acquire: ~ **olm.**, result, ensue; be produced/obtained: ~ **ı tahsil etm.**, waste one's time/energy (on what has been done).

hâsıl·a Produce; result. ~ **at¹**, produce; products; revenue; profit. ~ **ı**, *adv.* in short, to sum up.

has¹ımᵐ¹ Enemy; adversary. ~ **taraf**, (*leg.*) defendant. ~ **lık**, enmity, hostility.

has¹ırʳ¹¹ *n.* Restraint; restriction.

hasır² *n.* Rush mat/matting; wicker; straw. ~ **altı etm.**, hide; leave unanswered; shelve stg.; hush up stg.: ~ **gibi serilmek**, be scattered over the ground: ~ **halat**, (*naut.*) copra rope: ~ **iskemle**, cane-bottomed chair: ~ **işi**, basket-work: ~ **olm.**, (*sl.*) be defeated: ~ **örgü**, matting; (*arch.*) basket-weave pattern: ~ **sazı**, (*bot.*) bulrush: ~ **sepet**, wicker basket: ~ **şapka**, straw hat.

hasır·cı(lık) Basket-weav·er/(-ing). ~ **lamak (-i)**, cover with matting. ~ **lanmak**, *vp.* ~ **lı**, covered with matting; made of wicker-work: ~ **şişe**, carboy. ~ **otu**ⁿᵘ, (*bot.*) flowering rush. ~ **otugiller**, (*bot.*) rush family.

hasis Stingy; vile; mean, petty. ~ **lik**, stinginess; vileness; meanness: ~ **etm.**, be mean, etc.

hasiyet¹ Special quality/virtue; good effect on the body. ~ **li**, having a special quality; beneficial to health; (*cul.*) savoury.

haslet¹ Moral quality; character.

hasm- = HASIM. ~ **ane**, *a.* hostile.

haspa Minx; rascal (*used affectionately of girls*).

haspetenlillah *adv.* For God's sake.

hasr- = HASIR¹. ~ **¹etmek**ᵉᵈᵉʳ **(-i, -e)**, restrict; restrain; appropriate; devote/consecrate to one thing.

hasret¹ Regret (stg. lost); longing (for stg./s.o.). ~ **çekmek**, long for: ~ **gitmek**, die disappointed: ~ **kalmak (-e)**, feel loss/absence of: ~ **ini çekmek (-in)**, long to see again. ~ **li**/~ **keş**, suffering from separation; longing for s.o./stg. ~ **lik**, deprivation.

hassa Quality; property; peculiarity. ~ **alayı**, (*his.*) brigade of guards: ~ **askeri**, ruler's bodyguard.

hassas Very sensitive; delicate in feeling; scrupulous; conscientious; (*eng.*) precision. ~ **teline dokunmak**, touch s.o. on his tender spot: ~ **terazi**, (*phys.*) balance.

hassas·iyet¹ Sensitivity; perceptivity; touchiness; care and interest in stg. done: ~ **ini gidermek**, blunt one's feelings/sensitivity; (*chem.*) densensitize. ~ **laştırmak (-i)**, (*chem.*) sensitize. ~ **lık**, sensitivity; precision.

hassaten Specially; particularly.

hasse Each of the five senses; (*tex.*) fine cambric.

hasta *a.* Sick; ill; (*sl.*) moneyless. *n.* Patient. ~

düşmek/olm., fall/become ill: ~ **etm.**, make ill: ~ **gene daldı**, the patient is unconscious again: ~ **nakliye gemisi**, hospital ship: ~ **otomobili**, motor ambulance: ~ **yatmak**, be ill in bed: ~**sı olm.** (-in), be very fond of/crazy about: ~**yı kırklamak**, cure s.o. by spells: ~**yı kurtarmak**, bring a patient through.

hasta·bakıcı(lık) Nurs·e/(-ing). ~**hane** = ~NE. ~**landırmak (-i)**, make ill. ~**lanmak**, *vi*. be taken ill. ~**lık**, illness, sickness; disease; (*fig*.) craze (for stg.): ~ **almak/kapmak**, catch a disease: ~ **izni**, sick leave: ~ **sigortası**, (*fin*.) health insurance: ~**a tutulmak**, be taken ill, fall sick: ~ı **geçirdim**, I've got over that illness: ~ı **bana geçirdiniz**, you've given/passed on this illness to me: ~ı **kendine kondurmuyor**, he'll never admit that he's ill. ~**lıklı**, sick, ailing; in ill health. ~**ne/**~**hane**, hospital, infirmary, clinic: ~ **gemisi**, hospital ship: ~ **termometresi**, clinical thermometer. ~**nelik**, hospital-case: ~ **etm.**, cause to need hospital; beat to death: ~ **olm.**, need/be fit for hospital; be beaten up.

hasuˡtᵈᵘ Jealous; envious.

haşa (*mil*.) Saddle-cloth. ~ **örtmek**, caparison (horse).

hâşa *int*. God forbid! ~ **huzur(unuz)dan**, with all due respect!, saving your presence!

haşar·at¹ *pl*. = HAŞERE: (*ent*.) insects; (*zoo*.) reptiles; vermin; (*fig*.) mob; blackguards: ~ **öldürücü/yok edici ilaç**, insecticide. ~ı, wild; dissolute; out-of-hand; (child) naughty. ~**ılaşmak**, *vi*. become wild/unruly. ~**ılık**, unruly behaviour; wild prank.

haşefe (*bio*.) Glans penis.

haşere (*ent*.) Insect; creeping thing.

haşhaş (*bot*.) Poppy. ~**giller/**~**iye**, poppy family, Papaveraceae. ~**yağıⁿⁱ**, (*chem*.) poppy-seed oil.

haşıl (*tex*.) Sizing, starch. ~**lamak (-i)**, dip in/dress with size/starch.

haşım ~ **haşlanmak**, get thoroughly cooked.

haşır ~ ~/~ **huşur**, (*ech*.) crunching/crushing (sound).

haşin Harsh; rough; bad-tempered, brusque; acrimonious; acerbic. ~**lik**, harshness; roughness; acrimony, asperity.

haşˡirʳⁱ (*rel*.) Day of Judgement. ~ **neşir olm. (-le)**, be in close contact with; rub shoulders with.

haşiş (*chem*.) Hashish.

haşˡivᵛⁱ (*lit*.) Redundant word; parenthesis; padding.

haşiye (*lit*.) Marginal note; annotation, explanation, comment; postscript. ~ **yazmak**, annotate.

haşla·ma (*cul*.) Boiled (meat): ~ **tenceresi**, stewpan. ~**mak (-i)**, boil; scald; (insect) sting; (frost) nip; (*fig*.) scold severely, berate. ~**nmak**, *vp*. ~**nmış**, hard-boiled (egg). ~**tmak (-i)**, *vc*. ~**yıcı**, boiling, scalding.

haşlamlılar (*zoo*.) Infusoria.

haşmet¹ Majesty, pomp. ~**li**, majestic; (*pol*.) Her/His Majesty.

haşv- = HAŞiv. ~**iyat¹**, (*lit*.) redundant words, padding, verbiage.

haşyet¹ Fear, awe, consternation.

hatᵗⁱ ¹ *n*. Scratch; line; route; (*rly*.) line; cordon; mark; writing; (*his*.) decree; features. ~ **bakıcı/bekçisi**, (*rly*. *etc*.) linesman: ~ **çekmek**, lay (telephone) lines: ~ı **divani//rik'a//talik**, engrossing// ordinary cursive//Persian style (for writing OSMANLICA): ~ı **humayun/şerif**, (*his*.) Sultan's mandate to Grand Vizier.

hat² = HAD.

hat. = HATTATLIK.

hata Mistake, error; fault; defect; offence. ~ **etm.**, make a mistake, err; (*sp*.) miss: ~ **savap cetveli**, (*pub*.) list of corrections, errata: ~**sını kabul etm.**, stand corrected: ~**ya düşmek**, fall into error, be mistaken.

hata·en Mistakenly; by mistake. ~**lı**, mistaken, erroneous. ~**sız**, correct.

Hatay (*geo*.) Hatay; (*his*.) Sanjak of Alexandretta.

hatıl (*arch*.) Reinforcing beam, baulk of timber.

hatır¹ *a*. ~ ~, (*ech*.) crunching; (*fig*.) raw, crude: ~ **hutur**, (*ech*.) harsh crunching; (*fig*.) coarse, unpolished.

hatır² *n*. Thought; idea; memory; mind; feelings; influence; (*fin*.) accommodation; (*soc*.) consideration (expected from/shown to others). ~ **almak**, please, content: ~ **bilir**, considerate: ~ **gönül bilmemek/saymamak/tanımamak**, take no account of others' feelings: ~ **gözetmek**, respect s.o.'s feelings: ~ **için**, as a favour: ~ **için çiğ tavuk yenir**, one must stop at nothing for friendship's sake: ~ **kıran**, disobliging: ~ **saymak**, take s.o.'s feelings into account; esteem: ~ **senedi**, (*fin*.) accommodation bill: ~ **sormak**, inquire about s.o.'s health: ~ **yapmak**, satisfy, content.

hatır-: ~**a gelmemek**, not think of the future: ~**a (ve hayale) getirmek**, remember, think of: ~**a gönüle bakmamak**, act independently; be impartial: ~**a varit olm.**, come to mind: ~**da tutmak**, bear in mind: ~**dan çıkarmak**, forget: ~ı **için (-i)**, for the sake of . . ., out of regard for . . .: ~ı **kalmak**, feel hurt, be offended: ~ı **olm.**, be of account, be considered: ~ı **sayılmak**, have one's feelings respected; have influence: ~ı **sayılır**, important; considerable: ~**ım yokmu?**, don't I count for anything?: ~**ına bir şey gelmesin**, don't think I bear you a grudge: ~**ına** don't misunderstand me: ~**ına gelmek**, occur to one's mind, remember: ~**ına getirmek**, remind s.o. (of stg.): ~**ında kalmak/tutmak**, remember: ~**ında olm.**, not be forgotten: ~**ından çıkarmamak (-in)**, not refuse stg. for s.o.'s sake: ~**ından çıkmak**, pass out of one's mind; be forgotten: ~**ından (ve hayalinden) geçmek**, pass through one's mind: ~**ını almak**, content s.o., have a friendly thought for s.o.: ~**ını hoş etm.**, please s.o.: ~**ını hoş tutmak**, keep one's mind at ease over stg.; keep s.o. satisfied ~**ını kırmak**, offend s.o.: ~**ını saymak (-in)**, have consideration/respect for s.o.: ~**ını sormak (-in)**, inquire about s.o.'s health, ask news of s.o.: ~**ını yapmak**, placate s.o., make amends to s.o.: ~**ınız kalmasın/**~**ınıza toz konmasın (amma . . .)**, don't be offended (but . . .); present company excepted!: ~**larda olm.**, be in everyone's mind; be generally remembered.

hatır·a Memory; remembrance; souvenir: ~ **defteri**,

diary: ~ sı olarak, in memory of: ~ sını kutlamak, commemorate. ~ alık, souvenir, keepsake. ~ at¹, memories; memoirs; autobiography. ~ lama, vn. ~ lamak (-i), remember. ~ lanmak, be remembered. ~ latıcı, reminiscent. ~ latma, vn. reminder. ~ latmak (-i, -e), remind. ~ layış, reminiscence. ~ lı, influential; who must be considered; esteemed. ~ şinas, considerate, obliging, courteous.

hatif Mysterious voice; echo. ~ ten gelmek, (a voice) come from nowhere.

hat'imᵐⁱ (rel.) Reading/reciting the Koran from end to end. ~ duası, prayer said after so doing: ~ indirmek, finish reading the Koran: ~ sürmek, continue reading the Koran so as to finish it.

hatime (lit.) End, conclusion; epilogue; peroration; (pub.) colophon. ~ çekmek, conclude.

hati'pᵇⁱ (rel.) Preacher; (pol.) orator. ~ lik, preaching; oratory; elocution.

hatm- = HATİM. ~ 'etmek^eder (-i), conclude; complete; read through from end to end; read again and again.

hatmi (bot.) Marsh mallow; hollyhock.

hatt- = HAT¹.

hatta conj. [197] Even; so much so that . . .; to the extent that . . . .

hattat¹ (art.) Calligrapher. ~ lık, calligraphy, penmanship.

hattıhareketⁱ Line of conduct; method of proceeding.

Hattiler (his.) Hattians.

hatun Lady; woman; (after name) Madam; (his.) ruler's wife; wife. ~ kişi, woman.

hatve (aer.) Pitch. ~ kaçıklığı, being out of pitch.

hav (orn.) Down; (tex.) nap, pile; (bot.) down. ~ tüyü, down feather.

hav. = HAVACILIK.

hava n. (met.) Air; weather; wind; atmosphere; climate; (mus.) air, tune; (fig.) liking, desire, whim, fancy; hobby. ~ +, a. Aerial; atmospheric; pneumatic; overhead; aero-; (mil.) Air-, Flight-. ~ aç(ıl)mak, the sky become clear: ~ akım/ cereyanı, air current, draught: ~ akını, (mil.) air-raid: ~ALANI: ~ almak, take the air, go for an airing; let in air; (sl.) get nothing; be unsuccessful: ~ amortisörü, (naut.) air cushion: ~ ataşesi, (adm.) air attaché: ~ atmak/basmak, (sl.) boast, put on airs: ~ Bakan(lığ)ı, (adm.) Air Minis·ter/ (-try): ~ basıncı, (phys.) atmospheric pressure: ~ bilgisi, meteorology: ~ boşluğu, (phys.) vacuum, air-pocket: ~ bozmak, (met.) the weather show signs of rain, etc.: ~ bölgesi, (leg.) air space: ~ bulanmak, be about to rain: ~ bülteni, (met.) weather report/forecast: ~ cambaz(lığ)ı, aerobat(ics): ~ çalmak, (mus.) play a tune: ~ çarpmak, weather affect s.o. badly: ~ çeliği, (min.) air-hardening steel: ~ değişimi, (met.) change/break in the weather; (fig.) change in surroundings: ~ değiştirmek, change one's surroundings: ~ deliği, (eng.) air-hole, vent, breather; blow-hole: ~ (deneme) tüneli, (phys.) wind tunnel: ~ denkliği, (phys.) aerostatics: ~ devinim/dinamiği, (phys.) aerodynamics: ~ durumu, (met.) weather report/ forecast: ~ durum-

ları, weather conditions: ~ düzenleyici, air-conditioner: ~ fena//iyi esmek, things go badly//well: ~GAZI: ~ geçidi, (aer.) air lane: ~ geçirmiyen, airtight: ~ geçmez, air-proof: ~ gemisi, (aer.) dirigible; airship: ~ girişi, air inlet/intake: ~ göçümü, (bot.) aerotaxis: ~ haritası, (met.) weather-map/-chart: ~ hattı = ~YOLU: ~ hızı, (aer.) air speed: ~ hızölçeri, (met.) anemometer: ~ hoş olm. (-e göre), be all the same, not matter: ~ hücumu, (mil.) air-raid/-assault/-strike: ~ ile, air-, pneumatic: ~ işletmesi, (aer.) aerial navigation: ~ kabarcığı, bubble: ~ kaçırmak, leak air: ~ kanalı, (ind.) air-duct/-pipe: ~ kapağı, (eng.) damper: ~ kapanmak, sky become cloudy/cloud over: ~ kararmak, sky become dark; night fall: ~ kesesi, (zoo.) air sac/bladder: ~ keşfi, (mil.) aerial reconnaissance: ~ kıtaları, (mil.) air-borne troops: ~ kirlenmesi, (ind.) air-pollution: ~ kompartımanı, (naut.) air-lock: ~ korsanlığı, (aer.) air-piracy: ~ köprüsü, (aer.) air bridge/lift: ~ kuvvetleri, (mil.) air force; air-arm: ~ kuyusu, (arch.) air shaft: ~LİMANI: ~ matkabı, pneumatic drill: ~ meydanı, aerodrome, airport: ~ meydanı personeli, ground-crew/-staff: ~ mıntıkası, (leg.) air-space: ~ mihaniği, aeromechanics: ~ motoru, wind machine: ~ navlunu, (aer.) air freight: ~ oyunu, (fin.) speculation (on Stock Exchange): ~ parası, (fin.) key money; good-will; improvement levy: ~ parazitleri, (rad.) atmospherics: ~ payı, safety margin: ~ payı bırakmak, (fig.) leave a loophole: ~ pisti, (aer.) air-strip/ runway, taxiway: ~ postası, air mail: ~ raporu, weather report: ~ rasat bilgisi, (met.) aero-graphy: ~ rasat bürosu, weather bureau: ~ sahası, (leg.) air-space: ~ sız(dır)maz, airtight: ~ tahmini, (met.) weather forecast: ~ taşıtları, (aer.) aircraft: ~ trafiği, air traffic: ~ tutması, (med.) air-sickness: ~ üssü, (mil.) air base: ~ ve heves, fancies; pleasures: ~ vermek, ventilate: (med.) aerate: ~ yastığı, air-cushion: ~YOLLARI: ~ yutma, (med.) aerophagy: ~ yükü, air-freight.

hava-: ~ da, airborne: ~ da bulut sen onu unut!, you'll never see it again: ~ da kalmak, remain in the air; (fig.) remain unfinished: ~ da kuru(tul)muş, (ind.) air-dried: ~ dan, by air, aerial; (fig.) for nothing, gratis; as a windfall; empty, worthless: ~ dan foto alımı, aerial survey: ~ dan sudan mevzular, subjects of no importance: ~ nın gözü yaşlı, it's going to rain!: ~ nın keyfine tabidir, it depends on the weather: ~ nın muhalefeti yüzünden, on account of the bad weather: ~ sı olm. (-in), have the air of/resemble s.o.: ~ sına uymak, adapt o.s. to, fit in with: ~ sını bulmak, enjoy o.s.: ~ ya, for nothing: ~ ya kılıç/pala sallamak, make efforts to no purpose: ~ ya savurmak, spend unnecessarily: ~ yı bozmak, (fig.) spoil the atmosphere/pleasure: ~ yı yaratmak, (fig.) create an atmosphere: ~ yla, air . . . .

hava·alanıⁿⁱ (aer.) Airfield, aerodrome. ~ altı^nı, (bio.) living in the atmosphere. ~ cı, aviator, airman, pilot. ~ cıl, (bio.) aerobe. ~ cılık, aviation; aeronautics; airmanship: ~ +, a. aeronautical.

~**cıva**, (*bot.*) dyer's alkanet; (*sl.*) trifles; nothing. ~**dar**, airy, breezy; in love. **havadis** *pl.* = HADİSE. Events; news. **hava·fişeği**[n1] (*mil.*) Rocket. ~**gazı**[n1], coal-gas, town-gas: ~ **ocağı**[n1], gas-stove. **Havai**[1] *pr.n.* (*geo.*) Hawaii. **hava·i**[2] *a.* Sky-blue; aerial; fanciful, flighty: ~ **fişek**, firework, rocket: ~ **hat**, aerial railway: ~ **meşrep**, not serious, frivolous. ~**ilik**, flightiness; frivolity. ~**iyat**[1], empty words; trifles. ~**küre**, (*phys.*) atmosphere; unit of atmospheric pressure. ~**landırma**, *vn.* ventilation, aeration; air-conditioning; airing: ~ **havuzu**, (*ind.*) aeration tank: ~ **kuyusu**, (*ind.*) ventilation shaft: ~ **penceresi**, (*arch.*) casement window: ~ **tertibatı**, air-conditioning system. ~**landırmak (-i)**, ventilate; aerate; air-condition; (*aer.*) fly, cause to take off; make restless. ~**lanmak**, take the air; stroll; be aired; be ventilated/aerated; (*aer.*) take to the air, fly, be airborne; (*fig.*) (girl) become flighty/frivolous. **havale** (*leg.*) Assignment; referring/transfer (of a matter); (*fin.*) bill of exchange, draft, money-order; (*med.*) infantile convulsions, eclampsia; (*arch.*) palisade; overhang. ~ **etm.**, transfer (debt/business, etc.); refer (stg. to s.o.); send; point stg. towards s.o.: ~ **gelmek**, money arrive; (*med.*) have convulsions: ~ **göndermek/yollamak**, send money: ~ **illeti**, (*med.*) eclampsia: ~ TEN. **havale·li** Unwieldy, bulky, cumbersome, top-heavy; (*naut.*) with high superstructure; (*arch.*) surrounded by a palisade; (*med.*) subject to convulsions. ~**name**, (*fin.*) order for payment; bill of exchange; money-order. ~ **ten**, by bill of exchange; **(-e)**, being referred (to s.o.). **havalı** Airy; having a . . . climate; (*fig.*) in the clouds; restless; attractive; (*med.*) pneumo-; (*ind.*) pneumatic. ~ **yatak**, (*eng.*) air bearing. **havali** Environs, neighbourhood, district. **havalimanı** (*aer.*) Airport. **havan** (*cul.*) Mortar; (*obs.*) tobacco-cutting machine. ~ **dövücünün hınk deyicisi**, toady, yes-man: ~ **topu**, (*mil.*) mortar, howitzer: ~**da su dövmek**, engage in useless discussion/fruitless labour. ~**eli**[n1], (*cul.*) pestle. **havaölçer** (*phy.*) Pressure-gauge, manometer. **havari** (*rel.*) Apostle; assistant; (*fig.*) disciple. **havas**[1] *pl.* = HAS; HASSA. Special qualities; (*his.*) upper classes, people of distinction. **havas**[s1 2] *pl.* = HASSE. Senses. **hava·sız** Airless, close, stuffy; badly ventilated. ~**sızlık**, airlessness; poor ventilation. ~**sızyaşar(lık)**, (*bio.*) anaero·be/(-biosis). ~**taşı**[n1], (*ast.*) meteorite, bolide. ~**ylayaşar**, (*bio.*) aerobic. ~**yolları**[n1], (*fin.*) air-line(s), airway(s). ~**yolu**[nu], (*aer.*) air-route/-line/-way. ~**yuvarı**[n1], (*ast.*) atmosphere: ~ +, *a.* atmospheric. **havhav** (*child.*) Bow-wow, doggie; barking. **havi (-i)** Containing. ~ **olm.**, contain; include. **hav**[l]**il**[li] Horror, terror. = CAN. **havlamak** *vi.* Bark, howl. **havlı** *a.* Downy; (*tex.*) having nap/pile. *n.* Towel. ~**can**, (*bot./cul.*) galingale. ~**lık**, downiness.

havlu Towel. ~**cu(luk)**, (work of) towel-weaver/-seller. ~**luk**, towel-rail/-cupboard; (*tex.* towelling. **havra** (*rel.*) Synagogue; (*fig.*) 'bedlam'. ~**y** **dönmek**, become very noisy/crowded. **havruz** (*vulg.*) Chamber-pot; urinal. **havsala** (*bio.*) Pelvis; (*orn.*) gizzard, crop; (*fig.* comprehension, intelligence. ~**sı alamamak** **kavrıyamamak**, be unable to comprehend/gras stg.: ~**sı geniş**, broad-minded: ~**sına sığmaz** incomprehensible. **havşa** (*carp.*) Counter-bore/-sink. ~ **açmak** counter-bore, countersink. ~**lı**, countersunk. **havu·ç**[cu] (*bot.*) Carrot; (*geol., min.*) core. ~ **delmesi**, core drilling: ~ **koparıcı**, core extractor ~ **örneği**, (*min.*) core-sample: ~ **özü**, (*chem.* carotene: ~ **sineği**, (*ent.*) carrot-fly. **havu·t**[du] Camel's pack-saddle. **havuz** Artificial basin/pond; (*sp.*) (swimming-)poo (*naut.*) dock, dry-dock. ~ **balıkları**, (*ich.*) goldfish ~ **müdürü**, dock-master: ~**a girmek//sokmak (-i)** go//take into dry-dock. ~**cuk**, (*bio.*) calyx ~**lamak, (-i)**, (*naut.*) take into dry-dock. ~**lanmak** *vp.* **Havva** (*rel.*) Eve. **havya** (*min.*) Soldering-iron. **havyar** (*ich.*) Caviare. ~ **kesmek**, (*sl.*) swing th lead. **havza** (*geo.*) River-basin; catchment area; (*pol.* sphere, domain, territory. **hay** *int.* Hey!, alas! ~**dan gelen huya gider**, (money 'easy come easy go!' **haya** (*bio.*) Testicle. **hayâ** Shame, modesty; bashfulness. **hayal**[i] Spectre, phantom; (*phys.*) reflection, image abstraction; fancy, imagination; (*psy.*) delusion ~ **etm.**, imagine stg.: ~ **gibi**, imaginary, spectral ~ **güç/kuvveti**, power of imagination; lively imagination, fancy: ~ **kırıklığı**, disappointment disillusion, disenchantment: ~ **kurmak**, buil castles in Spain/the air: ~ **mahsulü**, figment of th imagination: ~ **meyal**, dim(ly); like a spectre hardly perceptible: ~ **meyal görmek**, be hardl able to see: ~ **meyal hatırlamak**, only vaguel remember: ~ **oyunu**, (*th.*) shadow pantomime KARAGÖZ: ~ **sukutu**, disappointment: ~ **yapmak** create a vision: ~**den uyandırmak**, disillusion: ~**e** **dalmak**, be lost in a dream-world: ~**e kapılmak** build high hopes: ~**imde bile yoktu**, little did **I** dream . . .: ~**inde**, in the mind's eye: ~**inde** **geçirmek**, think of, consider. **hayal·at**[i] Vain imaginings: ~**a kapılmak**, be fed on illusions. ~**ci**, shadow-puppeteer; visionary, day-dreamer. ~**et**[i], phantom, ghost, apparition: ~ **kotinga**, (*orn.*) snowy cotinga: ~ **sinek**, (*ent.* phantom gnat: ~ **yazarı**, (*lit.*) ghost-writer. ~**hane** imagination, fancy. **hayâlı** Bashful, modest, shy. **hayal·i** *a.* Fantastic, imaginary: *n.* shadow-puppet operator. ~**ifener**, (*cin.*) magic lantern; (*fig.*) a mere skeleton. ~**perest**, visionary; builde of castles in Spain. ~**perver**, nourishing vain hopes.

hayâsız Shameless, impudent, bare-faced. ~lık, impudence.

hayat[1] 1 *n.* (*arch.*) Covered courtyard; vestibule.

hayat[1] 2 *n.* Life; existence; living; biography; fate; living creature. ~ + , *a.* Life, living; bio-: ~ **adamı**, man for all seasons; adaptable; resourceful: ~ **arkadaşı**, husband, wife: ~ **baremi**, cost of living (index): ~ **bu!**, life's like that!; that's life for you!: ~ **geçirmek**, live, spend one's life: ~ **halinde sigorta**, (*fin.*) endowment insurance: ~ **kadını**, prostitute: ~ **kavga/mücadele/savaşı**, struggle for existence: ~ **memat meselesi**, a matter of life and death: ~ **pahalılığı (zammı)**, cost-of-living (bonus): ~ **sahası**, *Lebensraum*: ~ **sigortası**, (*fin.*) life insurance: ~ **sigortası uzmanı**, actuary: ~ **süresi**, lifetime: ~ **ukdesi**, (*bio., fig.*) nerve centre: ~ **verici**, life-giving: ~ **vermek (-e)**, give life to; bring to life.

hayat-: ~**a atılmak**, begin to work (for one's living): ~**a gözlerini kapamak/yummak**, die: ~**a küsmek**, be pessimistic/tired of life: ~**ı gidip bayatı kalmak**, be overcome with enthusiasm about stg.: ~**ı kaymak**, (*sl.*) everything go wrong; be ruined: ~**ı pahasına**, at the cost of one's life: ~**ım**, my darling!: ~**ın baharı**, youth: ~**ına girmek**, have an affair with, marry: ~**ına kasdetmek**, made an attempt on s.o.'s life: ~**ını borçlu olm. (-e)**, owe one's (way of) life to: ~**ını kazanmak**, earn one's living: ~**ını yaşamak**, live freely: ~**ta olm.**, be alive.

hayat·ağacı[n1] (*bot.*) White cedar; American arbor-vitae; (*bio.*) arbor vitae (of brain); (*soc.*) genealogical tree. ~**bilim**, biology. ~**i**, living; essential, vital; (*obs.*) biological: ~ **bır mahiyet**, a matter of vital concern: ~ **zaruretler**, necessities of life. ~**iyat**[1], (*obs.*) biology. ~**iyet**[i], vitality; activities. ~**sal**, *a.* life. ~**sız**, lifeless; (*geol.*) azoic.

hayda *int.* (*Call when driving animals; exclamation of surprise*). ~**(la)mak**[1] **(-i)**, drive animals (with loud shouts); (*sl.*) dismiss s.o. ~**ma**[1]**k**[gı 2], *n.* (*his.*) cattle-thief, marauder; vagabond.

haydar Lion; courageous man.

haydari(ye) (*mod.*) Dervish's sleeveless jacket. ~ **yaka**, V-neck.

haydi/hadi *int.* [137] Come (along)!; be off! ~ **bakalım!**, come, come!: ~ **canım!**, come along!: ~ **gidelim!**, come along!; let's be going!: ~ **git!**, clear out!: ~ ~, all the more; at the most; easily: ~ **hayırlısı!**, let's hope for the best!; good luck to it!: ~ **oradan**, get along: ~ **yandı!**, time's up! (on roundabout, etc.): ~**n!**, *pl.* ~**sene!**, come along!

haydu·t[du] Brigand, bandit. ~ **yatağı**, brigands' den. ~**luk**, brigandage, banditry.

hay·hay *int.* Certainly!; by all means!; right ho! ~**huy**, loud/continuous noise; confusion; tumult; worries and troubles.

hay·ıf[f1] *int.* Alas!; what a pity! *n.* Injustice; trouble; worry. ~**lanmak (-e)**, bemoan; lament.

hayır[1] *adv.* No; on the contrary. ~ **demek**, say 'No'.

hay·ır[r1 2] *n.* Good; prosperity; health; excellence; profit; advantage; charity, benefaction. *a.* Good; advantageous; beneficial; auspicious. ~ **beklemek**, expect/hope for benefit: ~ **dua etm.**, bless: ~ **etm.**,

be useful/serviceable: ~ **gelmek**, be helpful: ~ **görmek (-den)**, receive benefit (from), serve a purpose: ~ **işlemek**, help s.o.; do good; be charitable: ~ **kalmamak (-de)**, no longer be of use/service: ~ **kurum/müessesesi**, pious foundation, charitable institution: ~ **ola!**, good news, I hope!: ~ **sahibi**, philanthropist, benefactor: ~ **yok (-den)**, he's of no use.

hayır-: ~**dır inşallah**, I hope all is well!; I hope there is nothing the matter!: ~**lar!**, all's well!

hayr-: ~**a alâmet (değil)**, it's a good/(bad) sign/omen; it augurs well/(ill): ~**a karşı**, may it do good: ~**a yormak**, (dream, etc.) interpret favourably; consider auspicious: ~**ı dokunmak**, be of use; serve a useful purpose: ~**ı yok**, you can't expect any good of him: ~**ını görmek**, enjoy the advantages/profit of stg.: ~**ını gör!**, (to purchaser) may it bring you good luck!: ~**ını görme!**, bad luck to you!

hayır·dua (*rel.*) Blessing; benediction. ~**hah**, benevolent, kindly. ~**hahlık**, benevolence. ~**laşmak (-le)**, conclude a sale by wishing each other HAYRINI GÖR. ~**lı**, good; advantageous; auspicious: ~ **olsun!**, good luck!; congratulations!: ~**sı olsun!**, let's hope for the best! ~**perver/**~**sever**, philanthropic, charitable. ~**sız**, useless; good-for-nothing; unproductive; ill-omened. ~**sızlık**, uselessness, etc.

hayı·t[d1] (*bot.*) Chaste tree, tree of chastity.

hay·ız[z1] (*bio.*) Menstruation.

haykır·ı Shout; (*ling.*) exclamation, interjection. ~**ış**, shouting, bawling. ~**ışmak (-le)**, shout all together. ~**mak**, *vi.* shout, bawl; cry out, protest ~**tı**, screaming. ~**tmak (-i)**, *vc.*

haylaz *a.* Idle, lazy. *n.* Idler, loafer; vagabond. ~**laşmak**, *vi.* become lazy. ~**lık**, laziness, idleness: ~ **etm.**, be lazy.

hayli Much; many; very; fairly. ~**den** ~**ye**, a lot of; very much. ~**ce**, considerably.

haymana Large open plain for grazing. ~ **beygiri gibi dolaşmak** wander about aimlessly: ~ **manda/öküzü**, (*fig.*) big and lazy.

hayr- = HAYIR.

hayran Astonished; perplexed; filled with admiration; (*sp.*) fan. ~ **bırakmak/etm.**, entrance: ~ **kalmak/olm.**, admire; be moved/impressed. ~**lık**, amazement; enthusiasm; admiration: ~**ını çekmek**, be admired: ~**ını ifade etm.**, admire.

hayrat[1] *pl.* Pious deeds/foundations.

hayret[i] Amazement; stupor; wonder, admiration. ~ **etm.**, be perplexed; **(-e)**, be lost in admiration/astonishment at: ~ **verici**, amazing; fabulous: ~**e düşmek/**~**te kalmak**, be lost in amazement: ~**e düşürmek/**~**te bırakmak**, amaze; astound: ~**ten donmak/taş kesilmek**, be struck dumb: ~**ten küçük dilimi yuttum**, you could have knocked me down with a feather.

haysiyet[i] Personal dignity; self-respect, *amour propre*. ~ **divanı**, (professional) court of honour: ~**e yakışmaz**, degrading: ~**ini kırmak**, dishonour: ~**iyle**, because of.

haysiyet·li Jealous of one's honour; self-respecting. ~**siz**, having no self-respect, undignified. ~**sizlik**, dishonour. ~**şiken**, that hurts one's self-respect.

hayta (*his.*) Mounted guard (escorting caravans); mounted brigand; (*col.*) young hooligan. ~ **lık**, hooliganism: ~ **etm.**, behave like a hooligan.
hayvan (*zoo.*) Living creature; animal; beast of burden; (*fig.*) stupid fool. ~ **ayağı**, paw, hoof: ~ **âlem/evreni**, animal kingdom: ~ **gibi**, stupidly; roughly: ~ **hırsızlığı**, cattle-stealing: ~ **koklaşa koklaşa insan konuşa konuşa**, men get on better by talking: ~ **yavrusu**, cub, foal, fawn, etc.: ~ **a yük vurmak**, load an animal: ~ **ın alacası dışında insanın alacası içinde**, you judge a horse by appearances but a man by his character: ~ **lar**, livestock.
hayvan·at[1] *pl.* Animals: ~ **bahçesi**, zoological garden. ~ **bilim**, zoology. ~ **ca(sına)**, like an animal; bestially; stupidly. ~ **cağız**, the poor little creature. ~ **cı**, cattle-breeder/-dealer. ~ **cılık**, cattle-breeding/-dealing. ~ **i**, *a.* animal; bestial. ~ **kömürü**[nü], (*med.*) animal charcoal. ~ **laşmak**, *vi.* become bestial/brutish. ~ **laştırmak (-i)**, bestialize, brutalize. ~ **lık**, quality of an animal; (*fig.*) bestiality; stupidity; stupid/brutish action: ~ **etm.**, behave brutishly. ~ **sal**, *a.* animal.
haz[21] Pleasure; contentment; enjoyment. ~ **duymak**, feel pleasure: ~ **vermek**, charm.
haz. = HAZIRLAYAN.
hazakat[i] (*med.*) Skill, ability. ~ **li**, skilful.
hazan Autumn. ~ **yaprağı gibi titremek**, tremble like an aspen leaf.
Hazar[1] *n.* (*ethn.*) Khazar. ~ **denizi**, (*geo.*) Caspian Sea: ~ **denizi martısı**, (*orn.*) Caspian tern. ~ **ca**, (*ling.*) Khazar language.
hazar[2] *n.* Peace. ~ **kuvveti**, (*mil.*) peacetime strength. ~ **i**, peaceful.
hazcı(lık) (*phil.*) Hedon·ist/(-ism).
Hazer[1] = HAZAR[1].
hazer[2] Precaution. ~ **etm. (-den)**, be on guard against.
hazf'etmek[eder] **(-i)** (*ling.*) Elide; suppress, leave out, omit.
hazık[1] (*med.*) Skilful (doctor).
hâzım *a.* Digestive; patient, long-suffering.
haz'ım[mı] Digestion; assimilation; (*fig.*) patience (under insults). ~ **cihazı**, (*bio.*) digestive system.
hazım·lı Patient, long-suffering, tolerant. ~ **sız**, indigestible; (*fig.*) impatient, intolerant; irritable. ~ **sızlık**, (*med.*) indigestion, dyspepsia.
hazır Present (not absent); present (time); ready; prepared; ready-made; 'all cut and dried'; opportunity. ~ **bulunmak (-de)**, attend, be present; be ready (to do stg.): ~ **bulunmamak**, be absent; default: ~ **ekmek yemek**, live without working: ~ **elbise/giyim**, ready-made clothes; clothes 'off the peg': ~ **elbiseci/giyimci**, ready-made clothes dealer: ~ **etm.**, prepare, make ready: ~ **evin has kadını**, 'cuckoo in the nest': ~ **mezarın ölüsü**, (*jok.*) s.o. who is waited on hand and foot: ~ **mısınız?**, (*sp.*) ready!: ~ **ol!**, (*mil.*) attention!; get ready!: ~ **ol duruşu**, (*mil.*) standing at attention: ~ **olm.**, be ready; be present: ~ **para**, (*fin.*) ready money, cash; available wealth: ~ **paraya dağlar dayanmaz**, one can't live long on one's capital: ~ **sokağa giderken**, since you are just going out . . .: ~ **ve nazır**, ever-present and all-seeing (God): ~ **yemek**,

food already prepared; tinned food; take-away food: ~ **yiyici**, one who lives on his capital: ~ **a konmak**, enjoy what is already prepared; enjoy the fruits of others' labours: ~ **dan yemek**, live on one's capital.
hazır·ceva[i]**p**[bı] Quick at reply/repartee. ~ **cı**, dealer in ready-made clothes; s.o. who likes good things when they are prepared for him. ~ **cılık**, liking to find things all ready/prepared. ~ **lama**, *vn.* preparation. ~ **lamak (-i)**, prepare; design; (*ind.*) dress. ~ **lanmak**, *vi.* be ready, prepare o.s.; be prepared. ~ **latmak (-i, -e)**, *vc.* make ready. ~ **layan**, (*pub.*) compositor; (*lit.*) editor. ~ **lık**, readiness; development; preparedness; preparation: ~ **çalışması**, training: ~ **görmek**, make preparations. ~ **lıklı**, prepared, prearranged: ~ **bulunmak/olm.**, be prepared. ~ **lıksız**, unprepared; extempore. ~ **lop**[u], hard-boiled (egg); (*fig.*) lucky find; stg. got without effort.
hazin Sad; melancholy.
hazine (Buried) treasure; (*fin.*) treasury; coffers; storehouse; reservoir; cistern; chamber (of gun); source (of knowledge); womb. ~ **bonosu**, (*fin.*) treasury bond: ~ **li tüfek**, magazine rifle: ~ **ye irat kaydedilmek/yazılmak**, (deposit, etc.) be forfeited to the Treasury. ~ **dar(lık)**, (*adm.*) (duties/post of) treasurer.
haziran June. ~ **böceği**[ni], (*ent.*) summer chafer.
hazire Enclosed graveyard (in a mosque); (*live.*) cattle-pen, sheepfold.
hazm- = HAZIM. ~ **'etmek**[eder] **(-i)**, (*bio.*) digest; (*fig.*) assimilate; swallow (insults).
hazne Tank, reservoir; bunker; (*bio.*) vagina. ~ **yi doldurmak**, (*naut.*) bunker. = HAZİNE.
hazret[i] Excellency (title of early Caliphs); (*col.*) old fellow!, old man! ~ **i Nuh'tan kalma**, ancient, very old: ~ **i Peygamber**, the Prophet Muhammad: ~ **leri**, (*obs.*) (*after name/title*) His Excellency.
hazz- = HAZ. ~ **'etmek**[eder], *vi.* rejoice; be pleased; **(-den)**, be fond of.
h.d. = HALK DİLİ.
he[1] *n.* (*ling.*) The Tk. letter H.
he[2] *adv.* (*col.*) Yes. ~ **demek**, agree.
He. (*ch.s.*) = HELYUM.
heba Waste; loss. ~ **etm.**, waste; spoil: ~ **olm.**, be wasted/spoiled; be sacrificed in vain.
hebenneka Fool (who thinks himself clever).
heccav (*lit.*) Satirist.
hece (*ling.*) Syllable. ~ **+**, *a.* Syllabic. ~ **düş(ür)-mesi**, elision: ~ **ölçü/vezni**, (*lit.*) syllabic metre: ~ **yutumu**, (*ling.*) haplology, syncope.
hece·ci Ballad-monger. ~ **leme**, *vn.* (*ling.*) articulation. ~ **lemek (-i)**, articulate; spell out by syllables. ~ **li**, having . . . syllables.
hecin (*zoo.*) Dromedary. ~ **süvar**, (*mil.*) member of the Camel Corps.
hedef (*mil.*) Target; mark; butt; (*fig.*) aim, objective. ~ **almak (-i)**, take aim at; direct: ~ **gütmek**, pursue an aim: ~ **olm.**, be the target for: ~ **e çevirmek**, concentrate on: ~ **e isabet etm.**, hit the target; achieve one's aim: ~ **i sarma kabiliyeti**, pattern made by a shot-gun.
heder Waste; loss. ~ **etm.**, waste; spend for nothing: ~ **olm.**, go for nothing, be wasted; be a pity.

hedi'k^{ği} (*cul.*) Boiled wheat.

hediye Present, gift; price (of holy books). ~
etm., give, make a gift of: ~ **olarak**, complimentary,
as a gift, gratis. ~**lik**, suitable for a gift; stg.
choice.

hedonizm (*phil.*) Hedonism.

hegemonya (*pol.*) Hegemony.

hek. = HEKİMLİK.

hekim Doctor; physician. ~ **taslağı**, incompetent/
bungling doctor. ~**başı**^{nı}, (*his.*) Sultan's chief
physician. ~**lik**, profession of doctor; medical
science; medicine: ~ **satan**, charlatan.

hek·tar (*math.*) Hectare. ~**togram**// ~**tolitre**//
~**tometre**, hecto·gram//-litre//-metre.

hekz- (*chem.*) Hex-.

hela Closet, privy; public convenience.

helakⁱ Destruction; death; exhaustion. ~ **etm.**, kill;
destroy; (*fig.*) wear out with fatigue: ~ **olm.**, die;
be destroyed; (*fig.*) be worn out.

helalⁱ *n.* Permitted/legitimate act/person; lawful
spouse. *a.* Lawful; legitimate. ~ **etm.**, declare stg.
lawful; transfer a legitimate claim to s.o.: ~ **olsun!**,
may it be your lawful right and property! (on
selling/giving stg.): ~ **süt emmiş**, entirely trustworthy: ~ **ü hoş olsun!**, it was a pleasure! (of a
sacrifice): ~**inden**, legitimately; honestly earned; as
a gift.

helal·laşmak/ ~**leşmek** *vi.* Mutually agree with/
forgive (before a parting). ~**li**, lawful spouse.
~**lik**, (*obs.*) lawful spouse: ~ **dilemek**, ask
forgiveness for an unlawful act: ~**e almak**, take as
one's lawful wife. ~**zade**, legitimate offspring;
(*fig.*) honest man.

hele *adv.* [217] Above all, especially; at least; at last.
int. Hi!, listen to me! ~ **bak!**, now just look here!: ~
bir...!, now just you...!: ~ **bunu yapma!**, don't you
dare do it!: ~ ~, come on now, tell me truly!: ~
şükür!, thank goodness for that!

helecan (*bio.*) Palpitation; heart-beat; (*fig.*)
anxiety, agitation. ~**lanmak**, *vi.* be agitated.

Helenistik (*art.*) Hellenistic.

helezon (*math.*) Spiral; helix; (*aer.*) propeller;
convolution. ~**i**, helical; spiral. ~**lanmak**, *vi.* form
a spiral. ~**lu**, coiled, spiral.

heli'k^{ği} (*arch.*) Rubble infill (of wall).

heli·koi'i^{di} (*math.*) Helicoid. ~**kon**, (*mus.*) helicon.
~**kopter**, (*aer.*) helicopter. ~**s**, (*math.*) helix.
~**sel**, helical.

helke Pail, bucket.

helme (*cul.*) Thick liquid/paste (from starch),
gelatinous fluid. ~ **dökmek**/ ~**lenmek**, form a jelly/
paste: ~ **gibi**, well-cooked: ~ ~ **olm.**, become like
a paste.

helva (*cul.*) Sweetmeat (of sesame flour, butter,
honey, etc.), halva. ~ **demesini de bilirim halva
demesini de**, I can adjust myself to all circumstances:
~ **sohbeti**, (*soc.*) gathering (where halva is offered).

helva·cı(lık) (Work of) halva maker/seller.
~**cıkabağı**^{nı}, (*bot.*) autumn-and-winter squash.
~**cıkökü**^{nü}, (*bot.*) soapwort. ~**hane**, (*cul.*) large
shallow pan (for making halva).

hel·yograf (*pub.*) Heliograph: ~ **kopya**, blue-print.
~**yosta**, (*mil.*) signal-lamp. ~**yostacı**, signaller.

~**yoterapi**, (*med.*) heliotherapy. ~ **yum**, (*chem.*)
helium.

hem *conj.* [209] And also; in fact. ~ ... ~ ..., both
... and ...; as ... as ...: ~ **ağlarım** ~ **giderim**, be
keen on stg. but pretend reluctance: ~ **de**, besides:
~ **de nasıl!**, and how!, etc. (*emphasizing the
previous statement*); with great care: ~ **faydalı** ~
istifadeli, both useful (to others) and profitable (to
o.s.): ~ **İsa'yı** ~ **de Musa'yı memnum etm.**, try to
please everybody: ~ **kaçmak** ~ **davul çalmak**,
pretend not to like stg. but go on doing it: ~
karada ~ **de suda**, amphibian: ~ **kel** ~ **fodul**,
proud but with nothing to be proud of; in the wrong
but proud of it: ~ **nalına** ~ **mıhına**, regardless;
without respect of persons; impartially: ~ **sağır** ~
sığır, both stupid and obstinate: ~ **suçlu** ~ **güçlü**,
not only at fault but offensive about it: ~ **ziyaret**
~ **ticaret**, combining business with pleasure.

hemahenk Harmonious. ~ **olm.** (**ile**), be in accord
with, match.

hema·l (*bio.*) Haemal. ~**tit**ⁱ, (*geol.*) haematite.
~**toloji**, (*med.*) haematology.

hemame (*cul.*) Cardamom.

hem·asır Contemporary. ~**ayar**, of the same
standard/class; similar; alike. ~**cins**, of the same
kind/race; fellow-being. ~**civar**, neighbour(ing).
~**dem**, constant companion; crony. ~**dert**, fellow-
sufferer.

hemen *adv.* [204] At once; straight away; just; just
about; just now; continually; about, nearly; only
just; only. ~ ~, almost; barely; very nearly/soon;
just about to ...: ~ **yok denecek kadar az**, so few
one might almost say none: ~ **hepsi**, almost all: ~
sonra, immediately after; subsequently. ~**cecik**/
~**cek**, at once, instantly.

hem·fiil (*leg.*) Accomplice. ~**fik'ir**^{ri}, like-minded.
~**hal**ⁱ, in the same condition; fellow-sufferer.
~**hudut**, having the same boundary/frontier;
adjacent, contiguous. ~**meşreb**, alike in character.

hemo·fili (*med.*) Haemophilia. ~**globin**, (*bio.*)
haemoglobin. ~**liz**, haemolysis.

hem·pa Accomplice, confederate. ~**paye**, of equal
rank/standing. ~**şeri(lik)**, (being a) fellow-
townsman/-citizen; compatriot(ism). ~**şire**, sister;
(*med.*) trained nurse. ~**şirelik**, sister-relationship;
trained nurse status/work. ~**şirezade**, sister's
child; nephew, niece. ~**zaman**, contemporaneous,
simultaneous, synchronized. ~**zemin**, on the same
level: ~ **geçit**, (*rly.*) level-crossing.

hemze (*ling.*) Glottal stop, hamza.

hende'k^{ği} Ditch; dike; trench; moat. ~ **açmak**,
ditch. ~**li**, ~ **engel koşusu**, (*sp.*) steeplechase.

hendes·e (*math.*) Geometry. ~**i**, geometric.

hengâme Uproar; tumult.

hentbol^u (*sp.*) Handball.

henüz *adv.* [203] Yet, still; just now; a little while
ago; (+ *neg.*) not yet.

hepⁱ *pron.* [75] All; the whole. *adv.* Wholly; entirely,
altogether; always. ~ **altındır**, it is all gold: ~
beraber, all together: ~ **bir**, in unison: ~ **birlikte**,
with one accord: ~ **bir ağız olm.**, speak with one
voice: ~ **bir ağızdan**, all together: ~**imiz**, all of us:
~**imiz insanız**, even a cat may look at the queen:

~**ini yuttu!**, (*fig.*) he swallowed it all!: ~**iniz**, all of you: ~**le hiç ilkesi**, (*phil.*) principle of all or nothing.

hep·çil (*zoo.*) Omnivorous; grass- and meat-eating. ~**si**[ni], the whole of it; all of it//them; everyone: ~ **bir mal**, one's as bad as the other: ~ **birden**, all together: ~ **iyi hoş!**, bob's your uncle!, all is well!: ~**nden ziyade**, above all: ~**nin köküne kibrit suyu!**, to hell with the lot of them! ~**ten**, entirely, completely. ~**yek**, (*gamb.*) double-one (at backgammon).

her *adj.* [75, 164] Every; each. ~ **an**, always, at any moment: ~ **aşın kaşığı**, busybody, meddler: ~ **bakımdan**, from every viewpoint; all-round: ~ **biri**, every one: ~ **birimiz**, each one of us: ~ **biriniz**, each one of you: ~ **boyadan boyadı fıstıkisi kaldı!**, (*iron.*) he never gets anything right!: ~ **canipten**, from all quarters: ~ **çekiye gelir**, very adaptable, opportunist: ~ **daim**, always: ~ **dem**, every moment, continually. ~ **dem taze**, ageless; (*bot.*) evergreen: ~ **derde deva**, a panacea: ~ **-dikçe**, whenever: ~ **durumda**, in any case: ~ **firavunun bir Musa'sı çıkar**, a freedom-lover/liberator will arise against every tyrant: ~ **geçen gün**, with every day that passes: ~ **giz**, always; (+ *neg.*) never: ~ **gördüğü sakallıyı babası sanmak**, be misled by appearances: ~ **gördüğünden göz kirası istemek**, wish to imitate everything one sees: ~ **gün**, every day: ~ **gün papaz pilav yemez**, you can't expect good things to go on for ever; don't take things for granted: ~ **günkü**, common, everyday: ~ **günlük**, everyday clothes: ~ **güzelin bir kusuru var**, no beauty is perfect: ~ **hakkı saklıdır**, (*leg.*) all rights reserved: ~ **halde**, at all events; HERHALDE: ~ **hali sinirime dokunuyor** (-in), everything about him gets on my nerves: ~ **halli turhalli**, everyone is as badly off as his neighbour; all in confusion: ~ **halükârda**, in all circumstances: ~ **horoz kendi çöplüğünde öter**, everyone is boss in his own house: ~ **iki**, both: ~ **iki halde**, in both cases: ~ **ikinci**, every second/alternate: ~ **ikisi (de)**, both of them: ~ **işe burnu sokan**, busybody, meddler: ~ **işe mahsus/yarıyan**, all-purpose; universal: ~ **işi erbabından sormalı**, you should always get the expert's advice: ~ **işte bir hayır vardır**, every cloud has a silver lining: ~ **kaça**, at whatever price: ~ **kafadan bir ses çıkmak**, each give his own opinion: ~ **kez**, always: ~ **kim**, who(so)ever: ~ **koyun kendi bacağından asılır**, everyone must answer for his own misdeeds: ~ **kuşun eti yenmez**, everyone is not at your service: ~ **makamdan söylemek**, talk on all kinds of subjects: ~ **nasıl**, in whatever way: ~ **nasılsa**, in whatever way may be; somehow or other: ~ **ne**, whatever: ~ **ne hal ise**, well anyhow, anyway: ~ **ne ise**, whatever happens; anyhow: ~ **ne olursa olsun**, whatever may happen: ~ **ne pahasına olursa olsun**, at whatever cost: ~ **ne türlü**, of whatever kind; in whatever way: ~ **ne vakit**, whenever; every time that . . .: ~ **nedense**, for some reason or other; I don't know why: ~ **nekadar**, however much: ~ **nerede**, wherever: ~ **neyse**, whatever/however it be; anyhow: ~ **sakallıyı baban mı sandın?**, people

are not always what you think they are: ~ **şey**, everything: ~ **şey bitti**, it's all up/over: ~ **şey bitti, işimiz bir leğen örtüsüne kaldı!**, (*iron.*) only the essentials are missing!: ~ **şey olur biter kösenin sakalı bitmez**, all things come to an end: ~ **şeye baş sallamak**, agree to everything; raise no objections: ~ **şeye eyvallah demek**, agree with everything that is said: ~ **şeye tüy dikti**, this was the last straw: ~ **şeyi göze almak** (-için), go through fire and water for: ~ **şeyi havi/kapsayan**, all-inclusive: ~ **şeyi ihtiva eden**, across the board, blanket: ~ **şeyin başı sağlık**, health above all!: ~ **şeyin fazlası fazla**, enough is as good as a feast: ~ **şeyin yenisi dostun eskisi**, friendship grows with age: ~ **taraf insanın yüzüne gülüyor**, everything is tidy and clean: ~ **tarafta(n)**, all over, all around: ~ **telden çalmak**, know a bit of everything; be a jack-of-all-trades: ~ **türlü**, every sort of . . .: ~ **üçümüz**, all three of us: ~ **vadiden**, on every subject: ~ **vakit/zaman**, every time, always: ~ **yerde**, everywhere: ~ **yıl döken**, (*bot.*) deciduous: ~ **yiğidin bir yoğurt yiyişi vardır**, everyone has his own way of doing things: ~ **yiğidin gönlünde bir aslan yatar**, everyone has ambitions: ~ **yiğidin kârı değil**, it's not a thing everybody can do; it's not as easy as all that: ~ **yokuşun bir inişi her inişin yokuşu vardır**, life has its ups and downs: ~ **zaman**, always: ~ **zamanki**, accustomed.

hercai Ubiquitous; roving; inconstant. ~**lik**, inconstancy. ~**menekşe**, (*bot.*) wild pansy, heartsease.

hercümer[ç][ci] Confusion, turmoil.

herek[gi] (*agr.*) Prop (for vines, etc.); espalier fence; platform (for drying figs, etc.). ~**lemek** (-i), prop up.

hergele Unbroken horse; herd of animals; (*fig.*) street urchin, rough fellow. ~**ci**, herdsman. ~**lik**, coarse behaviour.

her·halde *adv.* [217] In any case; at any rate; under any circumstances; certainly, surely; I dare say; apparently. ~**hangi**, whoever; whatever; whichever: ~ **biri**, any one: ~ **bir sebeple**, for some reason or other.

herif (*pej.*) Fellow; scoundrel. ~**in biri**, some fellow or other. ~**cioğlu**[nu], (*vulg.*) the fellow!; the blighter!

herk[i] (*agr.*) Fallow land.

herkes *pron.* [75] Everyone, everbody. ~ **bir hava çalıyor**, everyone expresses a different opinion: ~ **gider Mersin'e biz gideriz tersine**, we should be doing just the opposite: ~ **kaşık yapar ama sapını ortaya getiremez**, it's not as easy as it looks: ~ **sakızı çiğner amma çatlamasını beceremez**, anyone can do this but few can do it properly: ~**e şan vermek**, become known to all; acquire fame: ~**in ağzı torba değil ki büzesin**, you can't stop people talking: ~**in arşınına göre bez vermezler**, rules are not made to be broken for each one's convenience: ~**in düt dediği keçi olmaz**, one doesn't get all one wants in life: ~**in geçtiği köprüden sen de geç**, follow the crowd: ~**in maksudu bir amma rivayet muhtelif**, everyone has the same aim but their approach is different: ~**in tenceresi kapalı kaynar**, only we know our own needs: ~in yorulduğu yere han yapılmaz = ~İN ARŞININA . . . .

herm·afrodit[i] (bio.) Hermaphrodite. ~etik, (phys.) hermetic.

Herse[ˈkᵍⁱ] (geo.) Herzegovina.

heryerdelik (rel.) God's omnipresence.

herze Nonsense. ~ yemek, talk nonsense. ~vekil, busybody.

hesab- = HESAP. ~i, pertaining to accounts; who calculates; economical; stingy, cheese-paring: ~ seyrüsefer, (naut.) dead reckoning.

hesa[ˈpᵇ¹] Counting; reckoning; calculation; computation; (fin.) account; bill; analysis; accounts; (math.) arithmetic; calculus; (fig.) plan. ~ açmak, open an account: ~ cetveli, slide-rule: ~ cüzdanı, bank pass-book: ~ çıkarmak, work out a sum/ account: ~ etm., calculate, compute; allow for, take into consideration; plan: ~ etmek kitap etmek, think carefully: ~ farkı, (fin.) balance: ~ görmek, have a reckoning, settle up: ~ günü, (rel.) day of judgement: ~ işi, embroidery done not by guesswork but by counting the threads before inserting the needle: ~ kitap, after full consideration: ~ makinesi, adding/calculating machine: ~ memuru, book-keeper ~ meydanda, it's quite clear: ~ müfettişi, auditor, comptroller: ~ sormak (-den), hold responsible; interrogate: ~ tutmak, keep (the) accounts: ~ vermek, make a report: ~ yapmak, vi. calculate: ~ yekûnu nakletmek, (fin.) bring/carry forward: ~ yılı, financial year.

hesaba: ~ almak/katmak (-i), take into consideration; include. ~ almamak/katmamak, attach no importance to; exclude: ~ çekmek, call to account, hold responsible: ~ dökmek, write out the account: ~ geçirmek, (fin.) enter to an account: ~ gelmez, countless; unbounded: ~ kitaba uygun, suitable to one's means: ~ saymak, reckon, calculate.

hesabı: ~ kapa(t)mak, close the books; settle an account: ~ kesmek, settle an account; (-le), sever relations with: ~ kitabı bilmez/yok, uncontrolled; unlimited: ~ tahrif etm., falsify accounts; 'cook the books': ~ tespit etm., make up an account: ~ temizlemek, pay one's debts: ~ yok, countless.

hesabına, for the account of . . .: ~ geçirmek, credit to the account of: ~ gelmek, suit, be convenient: ~ koymak, attribute to.

hesabını: ~ almak, get one's due: ~ bilmek, be careful/economical: ~ görmek, settle s.o.'s account; (fig.) eliminate s.o.

hesap-: ~ları tasfiye etm., wind up accounts: ~lı hareket etm., act with great care: ~tan düşmek (-i), be deducted from the account.

hesap·ça According to the reckoning; normally; properly speaking. ~çı, a. calculating; careful; miserly: n. accountant. ~çılık, accountancy. ~lamak (-i), reckon, calculate, compute; take into account: ~ kitaplamak, consider very carefully, give great thought to. ~lanmak, vp. ~laşmak (-le), (fin., fig.) settle accounts with. ~lı, profitable; calculated; economical; carefully considered; well-balanced. ~sız, countless, innumerable; un-

economical; uncertain, problematical; without reflection: ~ kitapsız, (fin.) uncontrolled; excessive; (fig.) casually, at random, without thought. ~sızlık, casualness.

hetero- pref. (bio.) Hetero-. ~gamet, heterogamete. ~gen, heterogeneous. ~kromozom, heterochromosome. ~nom, heteronomous. ~pati, heteropathy. ~siklik, heterocyclic.

heven[ˈkᵍⁱ] Bunch of fruit hung up.

heves Desire; inclination; mania; zeal. ~ etm., desire, fancy: ~i içinde/kursağında kalmak, one's desire remain unsatisfied: ~ini almak, satisfy a desire: ~ini kırmak, damp s.o.'s ardour.

heves·kâr/~li a. Desirous; curious; eager; having aspirations. n. Dilettante, amateur. ~kârlık, desire; longing; amateurship. ~lendirmek (-i, -e), arouse desire in s.o. to do stg. ~lenmek (-e), long for, desire. ~siz, disinclined; uninterested.

hey int. Hi!; ahoy!; look here!; O!; oh dear! ~ gemidekiler!, boat ahoy!: ~ gidi günler!, oh, for the good old days!

hey. = HEYKELTIRAŞLIK.

heyamola (naut.) Heave ho!; all together! ~ ile, with much difficulty and fuss: ~ ile iş görmek, only work when forced/hustled: ~ şarkısı, sea-shanty.

heybe Saddle-bag. ~liada, pr.n. (geo.) one of the Princes' Islands, Khalki.

heybet[i] Awe; majesty; imposing air. ~li, imposing, majestic; awe-inspiring.

heyecan Excitement; enthusiasm; ardour; agitation; emotion; (th.) suspense; (med.) affect. ~ bulmak/ duymak, be excited; be enthusiastic: ~a gelmek, get excited.

heyecan·landırılmak vp. Be (made) excited. ~landırmak (-i), excite; electrify; agitate. ~lanmak, vi. be/feel excited. ~lı, excited; dramatic; exciting; agitated; enthusiastic. ~sız, unexcited; unexciting; dull; without interest.

heyelan (geo.) Landslide; avalanche.

heyet[i] (adm.) Assembly, commission, board, committee; astronomy. ~iyle, completely; all at once.

heyhat int. Alas!; alack!

heyhey ~ler geçirmek/~leri tutmak, be very agitated; have a fit of nerves: ~leri üstünde, very agitated/disturbed; in a black mood.

heykel (art.) Statue. ~ gibi, motionless. ~ci/ ~tıraş, sculptor. ~ kalemi, chisel. ~cilik/ ~tıraşlık, sculpture. ~sütun, (arch.) caryatid.

heyula (phil.) Chaos; spectre, apparition. ~ gibi, huge; spectral.

hezaren (bot.) Delphinium; larkspur; cane, rattan, bentwood, bamboo.

hezel Joke; jest, comedy; comic tale; indecent story/verse. ~iyat[¹], jests; pleasantries; comic stories.

hezen ~ arısı, (ent.) bumble-bee.

hezeyan Talking nonsense; (psy.) delirium. ~ etm., talk nonsense. ~lı, (psy.) delirious.

hezimet[i] Utter defeat; rout. ~e uğramak, suffer a defeat; be routed.

Hf. = (ch.s.) HAFNİYUM.

H·F = HUKUK FAKÜLTESİ. ~H = HUSUSİ HUKUK.

Hg. = (ch.s.) CIVA.

hıçkır·a ~ ~, sobbing. ~ı'k^{ğı}, hiccup; sob: ~ tutmak, have the hiccups. ~mak, vi. sob. ~tmak (-i), vc.

hıdiv (his.) Khedive (of Egypt). ~i, Khedivial. ~iyetⁱ, Khediviate.

hıdrellez The summer months; beginning of summer (6 May).

hıf'ız^{zı} Guarding, protecting; committing (the Koran) to memory. ~a çalışmak, learn the Koran by heart.

hıfz·'etmek^{eder} (-i) Protect; preserve; commit to memory. ~ıssıhha, hygiene.

hık ~ demiş burnundan düşmüş, he is the very spit and image of . . .: ~ mık etm., hum and haw: ~ da dese mık da dese faydası yok, whatever he said it was no use: ~ tutmak, have the hiccups.

hımbıl Silly; slow. ~lık, silliness; slowness.

hımhım (ling.) Speaking through the nose. ~lık, nasal speech.

hımış (arch.) Timber-framed with brick infill.

hınc- = HINÇ. ~ahınç, full up, chock-a-block.

hın'ç^{cı} Rancour; hatred; revenge. ~ almak, take revenge: ~ beslemek, nourish a grudge: ~ını çıkarmak (-den), take revenge on; vent one's spleen on; (-in), take revenge for.

hınk ~ deyici, s.o. who makes much noise pretending to help; yes-man.

hınzır (pej.) n. Swine, beast; (fig.) cunning foul fellow. a. Swinish. ~lık, beastliness; a dirty trick: ~ etm., be spiteful; oppose s.o.

hır (sl.) Row, quarrel. ~ çıkarmak, start a quarrel.

hıra (prov.) Thin, weak; greedy.

hırbo (sl.) Loutish; boorish. ~luk, loutishness.

hırçın Ill-tempered; (sea) angry. ~laşmak, vi. become bad-tempered; grow obstinate. ~lık, bad temper; obstinacy: ~ etm., be bad-tempered// obstinate.

hırdavat^ı pl. Small wares; hardware, ironmongery. ~çı, pedlar; ironmonger. ~çılık, ironmongery.

hırgür (ech.) Snarling; noisy quarrel. ~ çıkarmak, (start a) quarrel.

hırıl (ech.) Growling ~damak, vi. growl, purr; (med.) have a râle (in chest/throat). ~daşmak (-le), snarl at each other; quarrel without reason. ~tı, growling, snarling; squabble; (med.) râle; death rattle. ~tıcı, (fig.) noisy, squabbling. ~tılı, growling; with a râle.

hırızma (Animal's) nose-ring. ~sı çıkmış, all skin and bone.

Hıristiyan n. (rel.) Christian. ~ +, a. Christian. ~ olm./~laşmak, vi. become a Christian; accept Christianity. ~laştırmak (-i), convert to Christianity. ~lık, Christianity; Christendom.

hırka (mod.) Short (quilted) cloak; dervish's coat. ~i Şerif, the Prophet's Mantle (preserved in Istanbul).

hır·lamak vi. Growl, snarl. ~lanmak, (person) growl, snarl. ~laşmak, snarl at each other; squabble noisily.

hırlı ~ mıdır hırsız mıdır?, is he honest or a thief?

hırpa·lamak (-i) Ill-treat; misuse. ~lanmak, vp. ~latmak (-i, -e), vc.

hırpani Ruffled; untidy, unkempt. ~lik, untidiness.

hırs Avarice, greed, inordinate desire; blind ambition; anger. ~ına mağlup olarak, losing his temper: ~ından çatlamak, be ready to burst with anger: ~ını alamamak, be unable to control one's anger: ~ını çıkarmak (-den), vent one's spleen on . . .: ~ını yenmek, control o.s.

hırsız Thief, burglar; thieving. ~ anahtarı, skeleton key: ~ feneri, dark-lantern: ~ gibi, secretly: ~ girmez, burglar-proof: ~ malı, stolen goods: ~ yatağı, thieves' den; receiver of stolen goods, fence: ~a yol göstermek, inadvertently help a wrongdoer.

hırsız·lama n. Stealing; adv. furtively; stealthily; surreptitiously. ~lık, theft, stealing, thieving: ~ etm./yapmak, steal, rob: ~a karşı alarm, burglar-alarm.

hırs·landırmak (-i) Make angry. ~lanmak, vi. become angry. ~lı, angry; desirous, greedy, avaricious.

hırt^ı Coarse and vulgar but conceited. ~lık, coarse conceit.

hırtıpırtı Trifles, rubbish; old clothes.

hırtlamba Poorly/untidily clothed; (med.) sickly person. ~ gibi giyinmek, be untidily dressed with too many clothes: ~sı çıkmak, be in rags and tatters; be thin and bony.

hırva (bot.) Castor-oil plant.

Hırvat^ı (ethn.) Croat. ~ +, a. Croatian. ~ça, n. (ling.) Croatian. ~istan, Croatia.

hısım (soc.) Relative, relation. ~ akraba, kith and 'kin. ~lık, relationship.

hış ~ ~, adv. rustling. ~ıldamak, vi. rustle. ~ıltı, n. rustling.

hış'ım^{mı} Anger; indignation. ~ına uğramak, be the object of s.o.'s anger.

hışır n. (bot.) Unripe melon; melon rind. a. (sl.) Stupid, gullible. ~ etm., (ech.) make a harsh/ grating noise: ~ ~, adv. rustling.

hışır·damak vi. (ech.) Rustle continuously (like leaves, etc.). ~datmak (-i), vc. ~lık, (sl.) stupidity, coarseness. ~tı, n. rustling.

hışlamak = HIŞILDAMAK.

hışm- = HIŞIM.

hıyaban (obs.) Alley; avenue.

hıyanetⁱ n. Treachery; perfidy. a. Treacherous; perfidious; basely ungrateful. ~lik, malicious act.

hıyar¹ n. (leg.) Option; right of choice.

hıyar² n. (bot.) Cucumber; (sl.) dolt, lout. ~ ağa, lout. ~cık/~cıl, (med.) bubo; tumour. ~laşmak, vi. become loutish; behave stupidly. ~lık, loutishness; stupidity. ~şembe, (bot.) cassia, pudding-pipe tree.

hız Speed; rate; (phys.) velocity; drive, impetus; (sp.) sprint. ~ almak, vi. get up speed; accelerate: ~ göstergesi, tachometer: ~ kesmek, decelerate: ~ kutusu, (mot.) gear-box: ~ ölçeği, chronograph, stop-watch: ~ saati, (mot.) speed indicator: ~ vermek, vt. increase the speed, accelerate: ~ yolu, motorway: ~ yöneyi, velocity: ~ını alamamak, be unable to slow down; be unable to stop o.s.: ~ını almak, slow down; take it easy: ~la, (fig.) flying.

hızar Big timber-cutting saw(-mill). ~cı(lık), (work of) sawyer, timber-cutter.

hız·bilim (*phys.*) Kinetics. ~**cı**, (*sp.*) sprinter.
Hızır (*myth.*) Help in trouble. ~ **gibi yetişmek**, be a timely help; come as a godsend.
hız·keser (*eng.*) Brake. ~**landırıcı**, (*chem.*) accelerator. ~**landırılmak**, *vp.* ~**landırılmış**, (*chem.*) speeded up, accelerated. ~**landırma**, *vn.* acceleration. ~**landırmak (-i)**, accelerate, speed up. ~**lanmak**, *vi.* gain speed/impetus; go faster. ~**lı**, fast, rapid; express; violent; loud: ~ **koşuş**, (*sp.*) dash, sprint: ~ **sağanak tez geçer**, violent storms soon pass: ~ **yaşamak**, live a life of pleasure. ~**lılık**, speed. ~**ölçer**, (*met.*) anemometer.
h.i. = (*ling.*) HAS İSİM.
hibe Gift, donation. ~ **eden**, donor: ~ **edilen**, donee: ~ **etm.**, give, donate: ~ **olarak**, as a gift, gratuitously.
hibri·ltᵈⁱ (*bio.*) Hybrid.
hica·lpᵇⁱ Modesty; shame. ~**lı**, veiled; modest, bashful.
Hicaz¹ *pr.n.* (*geo.*) Hedjaz.
hicaz²/ ~kâr *n.* (*Or. mus.*) Types of melodies.
hic·livᵛⁱ (*lit.*) Satire; lampoon.
hicran Separation; absence from the family; (*psy.*) pain; bitterness of heart.
hicr·etⁱ Abandoning one's country, emigration; (*rel.*) the Hegira (AD 622) (Muhammad's flight from Mecca to Medina): ~ **etm. (-den)**, emigrate. ~**i**, (date) reckoned from the Hegira.
hicv- = HİCİV. ~**letmek**ᵉᵈᵉʳ, (*lit.*) satirize. ~**i**, satirical. ~**iye**, satire, satirical verse.
hiçⁱ *a.* [77] No. *adv.* Not at all; never; (*without neg. v.*, ever). *n.* Nothing; (*math.*) zero. ~ **abartmadan**, without exaggeration: ~BİR: ~ **de**, in no way: ~ **değil**, not at all: ~ **değilse**, at least; at any rate; if nothing else: ~ **durmadan**, uninterruptedly; ceaselessly; without a moment's hesitation: ~ **fark yok**, alike as two peas: ~ **kimse**, nobody: ~ **kimse ayranım ekşi/yoğurdum kara demez**, no one runs down his own goods; no one cries 'stinking fish': ~ **kuşkusuz**, without a doubt: ~ **meteliği yok**, he hasn't a bean to his name: ~ **mi** ~, not in the least; absolutely nothing: ~ **olmaz mı?**, does it never happen?: ~ **olmazsa** = ~ DEĞİLSE: ~ **olur mu?**, can such a thing be (done)?; does it ever happen?; is it possible?: ~ **sallamamak**, (*sl.*) pay no attention; not care a brass farthing: ~ **sıkılma yok (-de)**, he has no sense of shame; he's very thick-skinned: ~ **şüphe yok**, without a doubt, it's a dead cert: ~ **te** = ~ DE: ~ **vazife etmemek (-i)**, not trouble/worry about stg.: ~ **yoktan**, for no reason: ~ **yoktan azı hoş görmeli**, 'half a loaf is better than no bread at all': ~ **yoktansa ona da razı olduk**, we agreed to that as better than nothing: ~**e saymak**, account as nothing; consider as of no importance: ~ TEN.
hiç·bir No . . . at all: ~ **kimse**, no one, nobody: ~ **suretle**, in no way at all: ~ **şey**, nothing (at all): ~ **şey anlamamak (-den)**, understand nothing of; not appreciate; think little of: ~ **vakit/zaman**, never: ~ **vechile**, in no way; by no means: ~ **yerim tutmuyor**, I feel rotten all over. ~**biri**, not one; no one. ~**çi(lik)**, (*pol.*) nihil·ist(/(-ism). ~**lik**, nothing(ness); nullity. ~**ten**, *a.* sprung from nothing, parvenu;

useless; got for nothing; trifling, insignificant: *adv.* unnecessarily, for no reason: ~ **bir mesele çıkarmak**, make a fuss about nothing; make a mountain out of a molehill: ~ **sebeplerle**, under absurd pretexts.
hidayetⁱ (*rel.*) The right way (to Islam); searching for the right way. ~**e ermek**, become a Muslim.
hiddetⁱ Violence; impetuosity; anger, fury. ~**e gelmek**, fly into a passion: ~**e kapılmak**, cut up nasty/rough: ~**i beynine sıçramak**, become angry: ~**ini tutmak**, curb o.s.: ~**ten kudurmak/köpürmek**, boil over with rage: ~**ten tepinmek**, dance with rage.
hiddet·lendirilmek *vp.* ~**lendirmek (-i)**, make angry, anger. ~**lenmek**, become angry. ~**li**, angry; violent.
hidra (*zoo.*) Hydra, hydropolip. ~**sitⁱ**, (*chem.*) hydracid. ~**tⁱ**, hydrate. ~**te**, ~ **etm.**, hydrate. ~**vyon**, (*aer.*) hydroplane, seaplane.
hidro- *pref.* Hydro-. ~**dinamik**, hydrodynamics. ~**elektrik**, hydroelectric. ~**fil**, hydrophilic; absorbent. ~**for**, hydrophoric; (*eng.*) gravity tank. ~**grafi**, (*geo.*) hydrography. ~**jen**, (*chem.*) hydrogen: ~ **bombası**, (*mil.*) hydrogen bomb. ~**jenlenme**, (*chem.*) hydrogenation. ~**karbon**, (*chem.*) hydrocarbon. ~**karbür**, hydrogen carbide. ~**klorik (asit)**, hydrochloric (acid). ~**ksil**, hydroxyl. ~**ksitⁱ**, hydroxide. ~**lik**, (*phys.*) *a.* hydraulic: *n.* hydraulics. ~**liz**, (*chem.*) hydrolysis. ~**loji**, (*phys.*) hydrology. ~**metre**, (*phys.*) hydrometer; (*ent.*) water measurer. ~**sfer**, (*geo.*) hydrosphere. ~**skopi**, hydroscopy; water-divining. ~**statik**, (*phys.*) hydrostatics. ~**terapi**, (*med.*) hydrotherapy. ~**termal**, hydrothermal. ~**zolü**, (*chem.*) hydrosol.
hiffetⁱ Levity, frivolity; idiocy.
higro·metre (*phys.*) Hygrometer. ~**skopᵘ**, hygroscope. ~**stat**, hygrostat.
hij(i)yen Hygiene. ~**ik**, hygienic.
hikâye (*lit.*) Narration, story-telling; anecdote, story; novel. ~ **birleşik zamanı**, (*ling.*) pluperfect tense, imperfect tense: ~ **etm.**, tell, narrate. ~**ci**, narrator, story-teller. ~**cilik/~leme**, narration, story-telling.
hikmetⁱ (*rel.*) The ultimate hidden cause; the Divine Wisdom; (*phil.*) wisdom; philosophy; wise saying, aphorism; reason; (*obs.*) physics. ~**inden sual olunmaz!**, Heaven only knows why! ~**amiz**, (*obs.*) mixed with wise sayings.
hilaf The contrary, opposite; contravention; opposition; (*col.*) lie. ~ **olmasın**, if I am not mistaken: ~**ı hakikat**, contrary to the truth: ~**ına**, contrary to . . .; contravening. ~**sız**, truly.
hilafetⁱ (*rel.*) The Caliphate.
hilalⁱ (*ast.*) Crescent, new moon; (*bio.*) arched eyebrow; lunula; tooth-pick; ear-pick; (*ed.*) pointer. ~ **gibi**, slim, fine. ~**i**, crescent-shaped: ~**i Ahmer**, (*obs.*) = KIZILAY. ~**iye**, (*bot.*) greater celandine.
hilatⁱ (*his.*) Robe of honour (given by Sultans).
hile Trick; wile; device, stratagem; cunning; fraud. ~ **çevirmek**, be up to some mischief: ~ **etm./ yapmak**, make use of a trick; swindle; cheat: ~ **hurda bilmez**, honest: ~ **sezmek (-den)**, suspect s.o.

of laying a trap: ~ **i şeriye**, legal device: ~ **si hurdası yok**, there's no guile in him: ~ **sini bozmak**, circumvent s.o.'s tricks.

hile·baz/ ~ **ci**/ ~ **kâr** *a.* Wily; deceitful; crafty, cunning; fraudulent: *n.* cheat, fraud, trickster. ~ **cilik**/ ~ **kârlık**, deceit; fraud; cunning; trickery. ~ **li**, tricky, false, dishonest; (*leg.*) fraudulent; (*cin.*) trick: ~ **benzeticilik**, (*art.*) forgery: ~ **iflas**, (*fin.*) fraudulent bankruptcy: ~ **zar**, (*gamb.*) loaded dice. ~ **siz**, straightforward, honest; genuine; unadulterated.

hilkat[1] Creation; natural form/disposition. ~ **en**, by nature. ~ **i**, natural; inborn, congenital.

hilozoizm (*phil.*) Hylozoism.

Himalaya (*geo.*) Himalayas. ~ **bal guguğu**, (*orn.*) Indian honeyguide: ~ **çamı**, (*bot.*) Bhutan pine: ~ **sediri**, (*bot.*) deodar.

himaye Protection; conservation; defence; patronage, auspices. ~ **etm.**, defend, protect: ~ **usulü**/ ~ **cilik**, (*fin.*) protectionist system: ~ **si altında** (**-in**), under the auspices/patronage of . . .. ~ **kâr**, protective. ~ **li**, escorted (convoy, etc.).

himmet[1] Effort, zeal, endeavour; influence; moral support; benevolence. ~ **etm.**, exert o.s., take trouble: ~ **etmemek**, be unwilling to help; make no effort: ~ **i hazır nazır olsun!**, may he long be at hand to help us!, (*said of a holy man*): ~ **in var olsun!**, thank you!

Hind- = HİNT. ~ **i**[1], *a.* Indian.

hindi[2] *n.* (*orn.*) Turkey. ~ **akbabası**, (*orn.*) turkey vulture: ~ **gibi kabarmak**, swell up with pride. ~ **ba**, (*bot.*) chicory; endive.

Hindistan (*geo.*) India. ~ +, *a.* Indian: ~ **sülünü**, (*orn.*) Malay peacock-pheasant. ~ **cevizi**[ni], (*bot.*) (**büyük**), coconut (palm): (**küçük**), nutmeg (tree): ~ **lifi**, coir.

Hind·olog// ~ **oloji** (*ling.*) Student//study of Indian languages. ~ **u**, Hindu.

hinoğluhin Scoundrel; very crafty fellow.

Hin[t][di] (*geo.*) India. ~ +, *a.* Indian: ~ **Adaları**, (*geo.*) East Indies, Malay Archipelago: ~ **ceylanı**, (*zoo.*) mountain gazelle: ~ DARISI: ~ **gergedanı**, (*zoo.*) great Indian/one-horned rhinoceros: ~ **kâğıdı**, (*pub.*) India paper: ~ **kobrası**, (*zoo.*) Indian cobra: ~ **kumaşı**, (*tex.*) Indian silk; (*jok.*) stg. very rare/precious: ~ **mandası**, (*zoo.*) water-buffalo: ~ **Okyanusu**, (*geo.*) Indian Ocean: ~ **timsahı**, (*zoo.*) marsh crocodile, mugger.

Hint. = HİNDİSTAN.

hint·armudu[nu] (*bot.*) Guava (tree). ~ **bademi**[ni], (*bot.*) cocoa bean. ~ **bezelyesi**[ni], (*bot.*) nonavist, hyacinth bean. ~ **darısı**[nı], (*bot.*) pearl millet, sorghum. ~ **domuzu**[nu], (*zoo.*) guinea-pig; Babyrusas pig.

hinterlant[1] (*geo.*) Hinterland.

hint·fıstığı[nı] (*bot.*) Physic nut. ~ **fulü**[nü], (*bot.*) lotus of the Nile; water-lily. ~ **güreşi**[ni], (*sp.*) Indian-style wrestling. ~ **hıyarı**[nı], (*bot.*) = HIYARŞEMBE. ~ **hurması**[nı], (*bot.*) tamarind tree; Palmyra palm. ~ **inciri**[ni], (*bot.*) prickly pear. ~ **ırmığı**[nı], (*bot.*) sago. ~ **kamışı**[nı], (*bot.*) bamboo. ~ **keneviri**[ni], (*bot.*) Indian hemp. ~ **kertenkelesi**[ni], (*zoo.*) flying dragon. ~ **kestanesi**[ni], (*bot.*) horse-

chestnut (tree). ~ **kirazı**[nı], (*bot.*) mango (tree). ~ **li**, (*ethn.*) Indian. ~ **pamuğu**[nu], (*tex.*) kapok. ~ **pirinci**[ni], (*bot.*) (?) a rice substitute. ~ **safranı**[nı], (*bot.*) turmeric. ~ **sarısı**[nı], amber-yellow paint. ~ **yağı**[nı], (*med.*) castor-oil.

hiperbol[ü] (*math.*) Hyperbola. ~ **ik**, hyperbolic. ~ **oidal**[i], hyperboloidal. ~ **oi**[t][di], hyperboloid.

hiper·metrop[u] (*med.*) Hypermetropic. ~ **tansiyon**, hypertension. ~ **trofi**, hypertrophy.

hipno- = İPNO-.

hipo·drom Hippodrome. ~ **potam**, (*zoo.*) hippopotamus.

hipo- *pref.* Hypo-. ~ **dermis**, (*bio.*) hypodermis. ~ **fosfit**, (*chem.*) hypophosphite. ~ **glisemi**, (*med.*) hypoglycaemia. ~ **staz**, (*phil.*) hypostasis. ~ **tenüs**, (*math.*) hypotenuse. ~ **tetik**, hypothetical. ~ **tez**, (*phil.*) hypothesis.

hippi (*soc.*) Hippie. ~ **lik**, being a hippie.

hipsometre (*phys.*) Hypsometer.

his[si] Sense; perception; consciousness; faculty; feeling, sensation; sentiment. ~ **ini vermek**, seem, give the appearance of: ~ **lerine kapılmak**, be swayed by one's feelings: ~ **lerini gizlemek**, dissimulate.

hisa (*naut.*) ~ **etm.**, hoist (flag, etc.); clew (sail).

hisar (*mil.*) Castle; fortress; stronghold; citadel. ~ **lık**, *pr.n.* (*his.*) Ilium, Troy.

his·lenmek *vi.* Be affected/moved. ~ **li(lik)**, sensitive(ness).

hisse Share; allotted portion; dole; (*fin.*) share, stock. ~ **çıkarmak**, assume some of the credit/ blame; take personally: ~ **kapmak** (**-den**), learn a lesson from: ~ **senedi**, (*fin.*) share certificate: ~ **lere ayırmak/taksim etm.**, divide up, allot. ~ **dar**, participator; (*fin.*) shareholder.

hissedilmek *vp.* Be felt; be noticed.

hisse-işayia (*leg.*) Co-ownership, joint ownership. ~ **işayialı**, jointly owned. ~ **li**, having shares; divided into portions; owned by several people.

hisset[i] Avarice; stinginess; stingy person.

hiss·etmek[eder] (**-i**) Feel; perceive. ~ **ettirilmek**, *vp.* ~ **ettirmek** (**-i**, **-e**), cause to feel/perceive. ~ **i**, perceptible; that can be felt; sensory; sentimental. ~ **ikablelvuku**[u], premonition, presentiment. ~ **iselim**, common sense. ~ **iyat**[1], *pl.* sensations; feelings; sentiment.

hissiz Insensitive; unfeeling; callous; apathetic. ~ **lik**, insensitivity; apathy.

histamin (*med.*) Histamine. ~ **karşıtı**, antihistaminic.

histerezis (*phys.*) Hysteresis.

histeri (*psy.*) Hysteria.

histol·iz (*bio.*) Histolysis. ~ **oji**, (*med.*) histology.

hiş(t) *int.* Hist! ~ **piş etm.**, call out 'hist!'; call out to a girl.

hitab- = HİTAP. ~ **e**, address, speech, discourse, ~ **en**, *adv.* addressing. ~ **et**[i], oratory.

hitam Conclusion; completion. ~ **bulmak**, come to an end: ~ **vermek** (**-e**), bring to an end.

hitan Act of circumcision.

hita[i][p][bı] An addressing a person; address; allocution. ~ **etm.** (**-e**), address; make a remark to: ~ **şekli**, form of address.

Hitit (*ethn.*) Hittite. ~**çe**. (*ling.*) Hittite. ~**olog**, (*archaeol.*) Hittite specialist. ~**oloji**, Hittite studies.
hiyalin (*bio.*) Hyalin. ~ +, *a.* Hyaline.
hiy·anet = HIYANET. ~**ar** = HIYAR.
hiyer·arşı (*adm.*) Hierarchy. ~**atik**, hieratic. ~**oglif**, (*ling.*) hieroglyphics.
hiza (*math.*) The point opposite/on the same level; line; level; alignment. ~**da**, in line; on the level; abreast: ~**dan çıkmış**, out of line/alignment: ~**sına** (-in), on a level with; in line with: ~**sına kadar (-in)**, up to the level of . . .: ~**sında (-in)**, at the level of; (*naut.*) in way of: ~**sını almak**, take the bearing/level of . . .: ~**ya gelmek**, get into line: ~**ya getirmek**, (*mil.*) dress ranks: ~**ya sokmak**, align. ~**lamak**, *vi.* be(come) level with; be in line with: (-i), *vt.* arrange in a line; collimate.
hiz¹ipᵇⁱ (*pol.*) Clique, faction; party. ~**çi**, member of a clique. ~**çilik**, formation of a clique; factionalism. ~**leşmek**, form into cliques/factions.
hizmetⁱ Service; duty; employment; function; attention, care. ~ **akti** (*ind.*) service contract: ~ **etm.** (-e), render service to s.o.: ~ **görmek**, serve; see service; render service: ~ **işletmeleri**, service organizations: ~ **sözleşmesi**, (*naut.*) ship's articles: ~**e girmek**, come into operation; (*ind.*) be commissioned; take up one's duties: ~**e koymak**, (*ind.*) commission: ~**inde bulunmak (-in)**, be in the service of s.o.: ~**ine almak (-i)**, engage s.o.: ~**ini görmek**, serve for; take the place of: ~**te**, in service: ~**ten çıkarmak**, (*ind.*) decommission; take out of service; dismiss from service; (*mil.*) cashier.
hizmet·çi Servant; domestic; attendant: ~ **dedikodusu**, backstairs gossip: ~ **gailesi var**, there is the servant problem. ~**çilik**, position/duties of a servant: ~ **etm.**, be a servant (with s.o.) ~**kâr(lık)**, (position/duties of) male servant. ~**li**, assistant.
HK = HAVA KUVVETLERİ.
hkr. = HAKARET YOLLU SÖYLENİR.
hlk = HALK AĞZINDA.
hm. = HEKTOMETRE.
HMUK = HUKUK MUHAKEMELERİ USULÜ KANUNU.
Ho. = (*ch.s.*) HOLMİYUM.
HO = HARP OKULU.
hobi Hobby, pastime.
hoca (*rel.*) Muslim leader; hodja; (*ed.*) schoolmaster, teacher. ~ **hakkı**, debt owed to one's teacher. ~**lık**, qualities/profession of a hodja// teacher: ~ **etm.**, teach; (*fig.*) give advice.
hodan (*bot.*) Borage.
hod·behot Of one's own accord, off one's own bat. ~**bin**, egotistical, selfish; conceited. ~**binlik**, self-conceit; selfishness. ~**füruş**, braggart. ~**kâm(lık)**, selfish(ness); wilful(ness). ~**pesent** self-satisfied; conceited.
hodri *int.* ~ **meydan!**, come and try (your ability/strength)!; (*th.*) fringe events.
hohlamak (-e) Breathe upon; blow on to.
hokey (*sp.*) Hockey.
hokka Ink-pot//-well. ~ **ağızlı**, with a small/pretty mouth: ~ **gibi**, small and pretty: ~ **gibi oturmak**, (*mod.*) (clothes) fit well.

hokkabaz Juggler, conjurer; (*fig.*) cheat, knave. ~**lık**, conjuring, juggling; trickery.
hokko (*orn.*) Black curassow.
holü (*arch.*) Hall.
holding (*fin.*) Holding company.
Hollanda (*geo.*) Holland. ~ +, *a.* Dutch: ~ **tipi**, (*cul.*) Dutch-type cheese. ~**ca**, (*ling.*) Dutch. ~**lı**, (*ethn.*) Dutch(man).
holmiyum (*chem.*) Holmium.
holo- *pref.* Holo-. ~**krin**, (*bio.*) holocryne. ~**sen**, (*geol.*) holocene. ~**türitler**, (*zoo.*) holothurians, sea-cucumbers.
homo- *pref.* Homo-. ~**gen**/~**jen**, (*bio., math.*) homogeneous. ~**log**, (*bio.*) *n.* homologue: *a.* homologous. ~**nükleer**, (*phys.*) homonuclear. ~**seksüel(lik)**, homosexual(ity). ~**teti**, (*math.*) similarity. ~**tetik**, homothetic.
homur ~ ~, *adv.* (*ech.*) muttering, grumbling. ~**danmak (-e)**, mutter, grumble. ~**tu**, *n.* muttering, grumbling.
hopᵘ *int.* Now then!; up!; jump! ~ ~!, stop!: ~ **oturup** ~ **kalkmak**, keep on jumping up and down (from rage).
hoparlör (*rad.*) Loudspeaker. ~ **ekranı**, baffle.
hopla·mak *vi.* Jump up and down (with pleasure, etc.). ~**tılmak**, *vp.* ~**tmak (-i)**, dandle (child).
hoppa Volatile, flighty, flippant (woman). ~ **adam**, coxcomb. ~**la**, *int.* 'up he goes!' (when dandling a child); well I never!: ~ **bebek**, childish person. ~**lık**, levity, flightiness.
hopurdatmak (-i) Drink noisily.
hor Contemptible. ~ **bakmak (-e)/görmek (-i)**, despise, look down on, hold in contempt: ~ **kullanmak**, misuse; use for the commonest purposes: ~ **tutmak**, treat contemptuously: ~**a geçmek**, be liked/appreciated.
hora (*mus.*) 'Cyclic' dance; (*fig.*) noisy party. ~ **tepmek**, dance the HORA; (*fig.*) dance about noisily/ clumsily/drunkenly. ~**n**, round dance. ~**nta**, (*soc.*) family circle.
Horasan (*geo.*) Khorasan; (*arch.*) brickdust-and-lime mortar. ~**i**, native of Khorasan; (*mod.*) turban once worn by clerks/teachers. ~**lı**, citizen of Khorasan.
horda (*soc.*) Aggressive nomadic people.
horgörü Contempt.
horhor Noisily flowing water.
horlamak¹ *vi.* Snore.
hor·lamak² (-i) *vt.* Treat with contempt; ill-treat. ~**lanmak**, *vp.* ~**luk**, contemptibility.
hormon (*bio.*) Hormone. ~**al**, hormonal.
hornblen¹tᵈⁱ (*geol.*) Hornblende.
horoz (*orn.*) Cock; (*mil.*) hammer (of a gun). ~ **akıllı/kafalı**, hare-brained: ~ **dövüşü**, cock-fight; (*sp.*) fighting while squatting: ~ **evlenir tavuk tellenir**, join in s.o. else's pleasure without any special reason: ~ **kuyruğu**, (*orn.*) cock's tail; (*bot.*) French bean: ~ **mahmuzu**, (*orn.*) cock's spur: ~ **ölmüş gözü çöplükte kalmış**, s.o. who looks back regretfully on what is now lost to him: ~ **ötüşü**, cock's crowing: ~ **şekeri**, (*cul.*) cock-shaped sweet (on a stick): ~ **yumurtası**, (*jok.*) a very small egg, pullet's egg: ~**dan kaçmak**, (girl) be very

shy/bashful//overdo the custom of veiling o.s.: ~ u **bile yumurtlar**, everything succeeds with him: ~ u **çok olan köyde sabah geç olur**, too many cooks spoil the broth: ~ u **tetiğe almak**, cock (a gun). **horoz·ağırlık/** ~ **sıklet** (*sp.*) Bantam-weight. ~ **ayağı**ⁿ¹, (*mil.*) cartridge-extractor. ~ **bina**, (*ich.*) blenny. ~ **cu**ᶦ**k**ᵍ**ᵘ**, (*orn.*) little cock; youth; (*bot.*) pepperwort. ~ **gözü**ⁿᵘ, (?) horse-fennel. ~ **ibiği**ⁿⁱ, (*orn.*) cockscomb; (*bot.*) celosia, cockscomb. ~ **ibiğigiller**, (*bot.*) Amaranthaceae. ~ **lanmak**, *vi.* give o.s. airs; strut about. ~ **luk**, self-importance. ~ **mantarı**ⁿ¹, (*myc.*) chanterelle.

hort·laᶦ**k**ᵍ¹ Ghost; spook; vampire. ~ **lamak**, *vi.* rise from the grave and haunt people.

hortum (*zoo.*) Elephant's trunk; (*met.*) water-spout; (*ind.*) hose-pipe. ~ **gibi**, very long (nose): ~ **rüzgârı**, (*met.*) whirlwind: ~ **sıkmak**, turn a hose-pipe (on a fire). ~ **lu** having a trunk/hose: ~ **böcekler**, (*ent.*) rhyncites: ~ **kınkanatlılar**, (*ent.*) snout beetles. ~ **lular**, (*zoo.*) elephants.

horul (*ech.*) Snoring. ~ ~ **horlamak**, snore noisily: ~ ~ **uyumak**, sleep soundly. ~ **damak**, *vi.* snore ~ **tu**, snoring.

hostes(lik) (*aer.*) (Duties/status of) air-hostess.

hoş *a.* Pleasant, amiable, agreeable; desirable; quaint; congenial. *conj.* Well; even. ~ **ben gitmiyecektim ya!**, well, I shouldn't have gone anyhow!: ~ **geçinmek (-le)**, get on well with s.o.: ~ **gelmek (-e)**, be agreeable; be liked: ~ **geldiniz!**, 'You are welcome!' (*greeting to s.o. arriving; the reply is:* ~ **bulduk!**, 'I am pleased to be here!'): ~ **gelse ne faydası var?**, even if he does come, what use will it be?: ~ **görmek**, condone, overlook, tolerate: ~ **görürlük**, tolerance: ~ **tutmak (-i)**, treat s.o. well: ~ **a gitmek**, be liked: ~ **uma gitmez!**, it's not my cup of tea!: ~ **una gitmek**, be agreeable to/appeal to/please s.o.

hoşaf (*cul.*) Fruit in syrup. ~ **gibi**, very tired: ~ **ın yağı kesilmek (-de)**, be dumbfounded: ~ **ına gitmek**, (*jok.*) please. ~ **lık**, (*cul.*) suitable for making HOŞAF; (*fig.*) weakness, exhaustion.

hoş·beş Friendly greeting; friendly chat: ~ **etm.**, pass the time chatting. ~ **ça**, pleasantly, agreeably: ~ **kal(ın)!**, goodbye! ~ **görü**, indulgence, tolerance; (*sp.*) allowance. ~ **görücü**, broad-minded, tolerant. ~ **görülü**, indulgent. ~ **görür(lük)**, toler·ant/(-ance). ~ **görüsüz(lük)**, intoler·ant/ (-ance). ~ ~, (*child.*) dog. ~ **lanmak (-den)**, like, be pleased with. ~ **lanmayış**, *vn.* dislike, distaste, aversion. ~ **laşmak (-den)**, get to like; feel well; (*col.*) like one another. ~ **luk**, pleasantness; happiness; comfort; quaintness: ~ **um var (bir)**, I'm feeling rather queer/unwell.

hoşnut (-den) Pleased, contented (with). ~ **etm.**, please. ~ **luk**, contentment. ~ **suz**, discontented; displeased. ~ **suzluk**, displeasure, dissatisfaction.

hoşsohbetⁱ Good company; conversationalist.

hoşt (*ech.*) (*Noise to drive away a dog.*)

hoşur Worthless; rough; vulgar.

hotoz (*orn.*) Crest; (*mod., obs.*) woman's headgear; topknot (of hair). ~ **lu**, ~ **ispinoz**, (*orn.*) plush-capped finch.

hov (*obs.*) Hawking, falconry. ~ **lamak**, throw a hawk.

hovarda Dissolute; rakish; spendthrift. ~ **ca**, wastefully. ~ **laşmak**, *vi.* behave like a rake, etc. ~ **lık**, dissoluteness; rakishness; wasting one's money.

hoverkraft (*naut.*) Hovercraft.

hoyrat¹ Vulgar; rough; coarse and clumsy. ~ **şakası**, practical joke. ~ **lık**, roughness; coarseness: ~ **etm.**, be vulgar/coarse; behave vulgarly, etc.

hödük *a.* Boorish; clumsy. *n.* Lout; bumpkin, clodhopper; clown. ~ **lük**, boorishness; boorish behaviour: ~ **etm.**, behave boorishly, be boorish.

höl Dampness; wetness ~ **lük**, (*prov.*) porous earth used instead of baby's nappies.

höpürdetmek (-i) Drink stg. noisily.

hörgüç Hump (of camel); any protuberance. ~ **kaya**, (*geol.*) roche moutonnée. ~ **lü**, humped: ~ **deve**, (*zoo.*) dromedary. ~ **lük**, humpiness.

höst *int.* (*Call for stopping animals//wakening s.o.*)

höşmerim (*cul.*) Dish made of fresh unsalted cheese with flour and honey.

höt *int.* (*To frighten; draw attention.*) ~ **demek**, arrive suddenly and be unpleasant: ~ **zöt**, harsh behaviour.

höykürmek *vi.* (*rel.*) (Dervishes) intone together.

höyüᶦ**k**ᵍᵘ Artificial hill/mound; (*archaeol.*) tumulus.

HP = (*mot.*) BEYGİR GÜCÜ; (*pol.*) HÜRRİYET PARTİSİ.

Hrk. Bşk. = (*mil.*) HAREKÂT BAŞKAN(LIĞ)I.

Hrp. T. D. Bşk. = (*mil.*) HARP TARİH DAİRESİ BAŞKAN(LIĞ)I.

Hs. Uz. = (*fin.*) HESAP UZMANI.

Hst. = HASTANE. ~ **Bş. Hek.** = HASTANE BAŞ HEKİM(LİĞ)İ.

hu *int.* Hi!; I say!; (*rel.*) a dervish salutation. ~ **çekmek/demek**, (dervishes) utter a prolonged ritual HU.

Hu. = HUKUK.

hububat¹ (*agr.*) Cereals; corn-crops. ~ **kabuğu**, chaff: ~ **taciri**, corn-merchant.

Huda (*rel.*) God. ~ **nekerde!**, God forbid!

hud'a Fraud; deceit.

hudayinabitⁱ Growing on its own, self-seeded.

huduᶦ**t**ᵈᵘ *pl.* = HAT²/(HAD) Boundaries; limits. *s.* Frontier, border; end. ~ **dışı etm.**, expel from a country: ~ **kapısı**, (*adm.*) frontier-post.

hudut·landırmak (-i) Limit; draw boundaries. ~ **lanmak**, *vi.* be limited. ~ **lu**, limited. ~ **suz**, unlimited.

huğ Mud and reed hut.

huk. = HUKUK; HUKUKİ.

hukukᵘ *pl.* = HAK. Rights; dues. *s.* Law, jurisprudence. ~ +, *a.* Legal: ~ **davası**, civil action: ~ **dışı**, illegal: ~ **fakültesi**, law faculty: ~ **mahkemesi**, civil court.

hukuk·an Legally. ~ **çu**, jurist. ~ **i**/~ **sal**, legal: ~ **şahıs**, body corporate. ~ **lu**, law-student.

hulasa *n.* Abstract, précis, summary; digest; quintessence. (*chem.*) extract. *adv.* In short; fine. ~ **etm.**, summarize, précis; compress. ~ **ten**, in short.

hulliyat¹ (*mod.*) Ornaments, jewellery.

hululü Entry; penetration; appearance; (*phys.*) osmosis. ~ **etm.**, enter, penetrate; occur.

hulus Sincerity; devotion; esteem; flattery (of superiors). ~ **çakmak (-e)**, court, flatter. ~**kâr**, sincere; (*fig.*) sycophantic. ~**kârlık**, sincerity; (*fig.*) sycophancy.

hulya Daydream. ~ **bu ya**, if by any possible chance . . .; supposing . . .: ~**ya dalmak**, daydream. ~**lı**, daydreamer.

humar Drunken headache; 'hangover'.

humma (*med.*) Fever. ~**lı**, feverish.

humor Humour.

humus[1] *n.* (*agr.*) Humus.

humus[2] *n.* (*cul.*) Seasoned mashed chick-peas.

hun·har/ ~**riz** Blood-thirsty.

huni (*dom.*) Funnel. ~**leme**, (*fin.*) funnelling.

hunnak[1] (*med.*) Inflammation of throat, quinsy, croup.

hurafe Silly tale; superstition, myth.

hur¹çcu Large leather saddle-bag.

hurda Small, tiny; (*fig.*) old (iron), scrap (metal); (*sl.*) hashish. ~ **demir**, scrap iron, junk: ~ **fiyatına**, at scrap price; for the value of the metal: ~**sı çıkmak**, be ruined beyond repair.

hurda·cı(lık) (Work/trade of) scrap merchant/ secondhand-metal dealer. ~**haş**, in rags and tatters: ~ **etm.**, tear to shreds: ~ **olm.**, be in shreds.

huri Houri. ~ **gibi**, very beautiful (girl).

hurma (*bot.*) Date. ~ **ağacı**, date-palm: ~ **dorusu**, brown bay colour (horse): ~ **kayası**, (*ich.*) common goby: ~ **rakısı**, (*cul.*) arrack: ~ **tatlısı**, (*cul.*) date-shaped sweet: ~ **yağı**, palm oil: ~**lar**, (*bot.*) palm family. ~**lık**, date-palm grove.

hur(r)a *int.* Hurrah!

hurrem Happy, gay.

huru¹çcu Exit; (*mil.*) sortie.

huruf *pl.* = HARF. Letters. ~**at¹**, (*pub.*) type; type-face. ~**ilik**, (*rel.*) Hurufi sect (seeing cabalistic meaning in the letters of the Koran).

husuf (*ast.*) Eclipse of the moon. ~**a uğratmak**, eclipse.

husulü An occurring/happening; a being produced/ attainment. ~ **bulmak/** ~**e gelmek**, happen, occur; be accomplished: ~**e getirmek**, accomplish, achieve.

husumet[1] Enmity, hostility. ~ **beslemek**, become an enemy.

husus [93] Particularity; peculiarity; matter; connection; particular. ~**ta (bu)**, in (this) matter/ connection: ~**unda**, with reference to.

husus·i Special, particular, private, personal: ~ **af**, (*leg.*) pardon: ~ **koltuklar** (*th.*) dress circle: ~ **mahkeme**, (*leg.*) special court: ~ **şirket**, (*fin.*) private company: ~ **teşebbüs(çülük)**, (*fin.*) private enterprise/sector. ~ **iyet¹**, characteristic; peculiarity; speciality; intimacy. ~**uyla**, especially.

husye (*bio.*) Testicle.

huş (*bot.*) Birch(-tree). ~**ağacıgiller**, birch family.

huşu Awe, deep/humble reverence. ~ **duymak**, stand in awe of: ~ **telkin etm.**, strike with awe/ wonder.

huşunet[1] Harshness; roughness; coarseness.

hutbe (*rel.*) Prayers/sermon delivered by the official preacher in a mosque on Fridays.

huy Disposition, character; temper; habit; bad habit. ~ **canın altındadır**, 'what's bred in the bone will out in the flesh': ~ **edinmek**, acquire a habit: ~ **etm./kapmak**, contract a bad habit: ~ **u** ~**uma suyu suyuma uygun**, we get on very well together: ~**u suyu**, disposition: ~**una suyuna gitmek**, treat s.o. very tactfully.

huy·landırmak (-i) Upset/disturb s.o.; annoy s.o. for no reason. ~**lanmak**, *vi.* get upset; become touchy/nervous; (animal) become restive/obstinate. ~**lu**, having (such a) disposition; suspicious, touchy, bad-tempered, fractious: ~ **huyundan vazgeçmez**, it's difficult to break a bad habit. ~**suz**, bad-tempered, disagreeable; cantankerous; malicious: ~ **densiz**, cross-patch. ~**suzlanmak**, *vi.* be(come) bad-tempered. ~**suzlaşmak**, grow into bad habits. ~**suzluk**, bad temper; obstinacy: ~ **etm.**, behave badly.

huzme Bundle, bunch, packet; (*phys.*) beam.

huzur Presence; attendance; repose, quiet, freedom. ~ **hakkı**, (*adm.*) attendance fee: ~ **içinde**, at ease: ~ **vermek**, calm s.o.; relax: ~**a kabul**, (*his.*) audience: ~**una çıkmak (-in)**, enter the presence of; have an audience with: ~**unda**, face to face: ~**unu kaçırmak**, disquieten s.o.

huzur·evini Old people's home. ~**lu**, at ease; comfortable; tranquil. ~**suz**, uneasy, troubled. ~**suzluk**, disquiet; discontent.

HÜ = HACETTEPE ÜNİVERSİTESİ.

hüccet[1] Argument; proof; (*leg.*) title-deed.

hücre *n.* (*bio.*) Cell; (*arch.*) small room, cell; niche, alcove; (*eng.*) cell, chamber; (*fig.*) (political) cell. ~ +, *a.* Cellular. ~ **bilimi** = BİLİM: ~ **hapsi**, (*leg.*) solitary confinement.

hücre·bilim (*bio.*) Cytology. ~**cik**, cellule. ~**li**, cellular, honeycombed. ~**lerarası**nı/ ~ **yutarlığı**nı = GÖZE-.

hücum (*mil.*) Attack, assault; (*aer.*) incidence; (*med.*) rush (of blood); (*lit.*) harsh criticism. ~ **açısı**, (*aer.*) angle of attack: ~ **etm. (-e)**, attack: ~ **edip girmek**, (*naut.*) board (ship): ~ **kenarı**, (*aer.*) leading edge: ~**a kalkmak**, (*mil.*) charge (enemy). ~**bot**, (*naut.*) assault-boat.

Hüda = HUDA.

hükm- = HÜKÜM. ~**en**, by judge's decision; legally; *de jure*; in accordance with the rules. ~**¹etmek**eder **(-e)**, decide on; judge; exert influence; master; rule; command: *vi.* assume. ~**i**, judicial; nominal: ~ **şahıs(lık)**, juridical person(ality), corporate body.

hük¹ümmü (*adm.*) Rule; authority; government; provision, condition; command, edict; (*leg.*) judicial sentence/decision; judgement, verdict; (*fig.*) tenor, import; effect, influence; importance. ~ **giydirmek**, (*leg.*) pass sentence: ~ **giymek**, be condemned; lose one's case: ~ **ifade etm.**, be valid: ~ **sürmek**, reign; prevail: ~ **vermek**, adjudge, adjudicate: ~**den düşmek**, (*adm.*) cease to be valid.

hükmü: ~ **geçmek**, (person) have authority, be important, one's word carry weight; (*adm.*) have ceased to be valid: ~ **kesinleşmek**, decree become final: ~ **olm.**, be of importance//valid/effective: ~ **parasına geçmek** one's authority be limited by

one's wealth: ~ **nde olm.**, be equivalent to, have the same effect as: ~ **nü geçirmek**, assert one's authority.
hükümdar Monarch, ruler. ~ **lık**, sovereignty.
hükümet[i] Government; administration; state; authority, dominion. ~ **darbesi**, *coup d'état*: ~ **etm.**/**sürmek**, rule, govern: ~ **kapısı**, the seat of government: ~ **kapısına düşmek**, have dealings with the government: ~ **konağı**, (provincial) governor's office: ~ **merkezi**, capital: ~ **nezdinde**, in the view of the government: ~ **i devirmek**, overthrow the government: ~ **i kurmak**, form a government. ~ **çe**, by/through the government.
hüküm·lü (*leg.*) Condemned. ~ **ran**, ruler, sovereign. ~ **ranlık**, dominion, sovereignty. ~ **süz**, no longer in force; invalid, null: ~ **kılmak**, cancel, invalidate. ~ **süzlük**, invalidity.
hülle (*obs.*) Pseudo-marriage (enabling a divorced woman to return later to her first husband). ~ **ci**, the second husband (who immediately divorces her).
hüman·ist[i] (*phil.*) Humanist. ~ **izm(a)**, humanism.
hümayun Felicitous; imperial.
hüner Skill, dexterity, ability; art, craft; talent. ~ **göstermek**, show one's skill; outdo others. ~ **li**, skilful, talented; cleverly made. ~ **siz**, without talent; inartistic; clumsily made.
hüngür ~ ~ **ağlamak**, weep bitterly; cry one's heart out. ~ **demek**, *vi*. sob. ~ **tü**, sobbing.
hünkâr Sultan. ~ **imamı gibi**, with an air of great importance: ~ **mahfili**, (*arch.*) royal gallery (in mosques). ~ **beğendi**, (*cul.*) Sultan's delight (aubergine purée and cheese).
hünnap (*bot.*) Common jujube. ~ **giller**, buckthorn family, Rhamnaceae.
hünsa (*bio.*) Hermaphrodite; (*bot.*) androgynous.
hür Free, at liberty. ~ **irade**, free will.
hürle (*bot.*) Field pea.

hürmet[i] Respect, veneration. ~ **etm.** (-e), respect, honour: ~ **lerimle**, with my respects/compliments; 'yours faithfully'.
hürmet·en (-e) Out of respect for s.o. ~ **kâr**, respectful. ~ **li**, venerable; respectable; (*iron.*) big. ~ **siz**, irreverent, disrespectful. ~ **sizlik**, disrespect.
hürriyet[i] Freedom, liberty; emancipation; (*jok.*) divorce. ~ **i seçmek**, (*pol.*) choose freedom/a free life. ~ **çi**, s.o. favouring democracy: freedom-fighter.
hürya All together; in a rush. ~ **etm.**, (crowd) rush in/out.
hüseyni (*Or. mus.*) A simple melody/mode.
hüsn- = HÜSÜN.
hüsnü- *pref.* Good. ~ **ahlak**[1], morality; good character. ~ **hal**[i], good character: ~ **kâğıdı**, certificate of good conduct, character reference. ~ **hat**[tı], (*art.*) calligraphy. ~ **kabul**[ü], friendly welcome. ~ **kuruntu**, fond imagination; wishful thinking. ~ **niyet**[i], good intention; goodwill: ~ **le**, in good faith. ~ **telakki**, favourable interpretation. ~ **tesadüf**, happy coincidence. ~ **yusuf**, (*bot.*) Sweet William.
hüsran Disappointment; frustration. ~ **a uğramak**, suffer a disappointment.
hüs'ün[nü] Goodness; beauty; agreeableness. ~ **halde**, in good condition/repair: ~ **surette**, in a proper manner.
Hüt ~ **dağı gibi kabarmak/şişmek**, be very swollen.
hüthüt (*orn.*) Hoopoe.
hüviyet[i] Identity. ~ **cüzdan/varakası**, identity papers: ~ **i meçhul**, identity unknown.
hüz'ün[nü] Sadness, melancholy, grief. ~ **lenmek**, *vi*. be grieved/sad. ~ **lü**, sad; dreary, cheerless.
hüzzam (*Or. mus.*) A compound melody.
Hv. = HAVA. ~ **Dur.** = HAVA DURUMU: ~ **Kuv.** = HAVA KUVVETLERİ.
Hz. = (*rel.*) HAZRETİ; (*el.*) HERTZ.

I

I, ı [ə] Eleventh Tk. letter, (undotted) I.
I = (*ch.s.*) İYOT; (*math.*) BİR(İNCİ).
-ı¹ *n. suf.* [28] = -i¹ [KIZI].
-ı² *n. suf.* [39] = -i² [KİTABI].
-ı³ *a./n. suf.* [221] = -i³ [YAPI].
I·AS = (*aer.*) (*indicated air speed*). ∼ **BRD** = (*International Bank for Reconstruction and Development*).
∼ **CAO** = (*International Civil Aviation Organization*).
ıblı'kᵍ¹ (*live.*) Capon.
-ıcı *a./n. suf.* [220] = -ici [YAZICI].
ıcık = icik.
-(ı)ça *fem. n. suf.* [25] = -içe [TANRIÇA].
IFR = (*aer.*) (*instrument flight rules*).
ığıl Still/currentless (water). ∼ ∼, gurgling; flowing gently.
ığrı'pᵇ¹ Large trawl/seine net. ∼ **çekmek,** draw up the net: ∼ **çevirmek,** (*fig.*) make use of, deceive.
ıh *int.* (*Cry used to make camels kneel.*) ∼ **lamak,** *vi.* cry 'IH' to make camels kneel; breathe noisily.
ıhlamur (*bot.*) Lime/linden (tree); (*carp.*) limewood; (*cul.*) infusion of lime-flowers, lime-tea.
-giller, lime family, Tiliaceae.
ıh·mak *vi.* (Camel) kneel. ∼ **tırmak (-i),** make a camel kneel (by crying IH).
-ık *a./n. suf.* [221] = -ik [ÇIKIK].
ıkıl ∼ ∼ **nefes almak,** gasp for breath.
ıkın·dırmak (-i) *vc.* ∼ **mak,** *vi.* hold one's breath when making great efforts: **ıkına sıkına,** grunting and groaning, with great effort: **ıkınıp sıkınmak,** make great efforts. ∼ **tı,** great effort.
ıkla·mak *vi.* Breathe with difficulty; sigh, groan. ∼ **ya sıklaya,** with great effort.
ıklım ∼ **tıklım,** chock-full.
-ıl- *vp. suf.* [149] = -il- [YAZILMAK].
ıldırgı'çᶜ¹ (*prov.*) Deceit, swindle.
ılga·mak (-i) Gallop one's horse. ∼ **r,** gallop; (*mil.*) cavalry charge; foray, raid: ∼ **etm./** ∼ **lamak,** (*mil.*) make a raid. ∼ **rcı,** raider.
ılgım(salgım) (*phys.*) Mirage.
ılgın (*bot.*) Tamarisk(-tree). ∼ **car,** (*bot.*) wild cherry, gean, mazzard. ∼ **giller,** tamarisks and false tamarisks.
ılgıt ∼ ∼, (blow/flow) gently.
ılı Tepid, lukewarm. ∼ **ca,** hot spring. ∼ **cak/** ∼ **k,** tepid, lukewarm. ∼ **klaşmak,** *vi.* become tepid. ∼ **klaştırmak (-i),** *vc.* ∼ **klık,** tepidness.
ılım (*psy.*) Moderation; temperance. ∼ **layıcı,** (*chem.*) moderator. ∼ **lı,** moderate, equable, temperate; avoiding extremes. ∼ **lılık,** moderation, mildness.
ılı·mak *vi.* Become tepid/lukewarm. ∼ **man,** (*geo.*) temperate; (*met.*) mild. ∼ **ndırmak/** ∼ **ştırmak/**

∼ **tmak (-i),** make tepid/lukewarm, ∼ **nmak,** *vi.* be(come) tepid.
ılın (*chem.*) Neutral. ∼ **cık,** (*phys.*) neutron. ∼ **lama,** *vn.* (*chem.*) neutralization. ∼ **lamak (-i),** neutralize.
IL·O = (*International Labour Organization*). ∼ **S** = (*aer.*) (*instrument landing system*).
-ıltı *n. suf.* (*ech.*) = -İLTİ [ÇANILTI; VIZILTI].
-ım *a./n./v. suf.* [39, 96, 224] = -im¹˒²˒³.
IM·C = (*International Materials Commission*). ∼ **CO** = (*Intergovernmental Maritime Consultative Organization*). ∼ **F** = (*International Monetary Fund*).
-ımız *n. suf.* [39] = -imiz [KİTABIMIZ].
ımızgan·ma *vn.* Dozing: ∼ **halleri,** (*psy.*) semi-hypnotic state. ∼ **mak,** *vi.* doze; (fire) be almost out; (*fig.*) hesitate.
-ımsa- *v. suf.* [230] = -imse-.
-(ı)msı *a. suf.* (*after consonant*) [58] = -(i)msi [BEYAZIMSI].
-(ı)mt(ı)rak *a. suf.* (*after consonant*) [58] = -(i)mt(ı)rak [BEYAZIMTIRAK].
In. = (*ch.s.*) İNDİYUM.
-ın¹ *n. suf.* [28] = -in¹ [KIZIN].
-ın² *n. suf.* [39] = -in² [ADAMIN].
-ın³ *n. suf.* [225] = -in³ [BASIN].
-ın⁴ *adv. suf.* [22, 201] = -in⁴ [YAZIN].
-ın-⁵ *v. suf.* [149] = -in-⁵ [ALINMAK].
-ınca¹ *adv. suf.* [94, 194] = -ince¹ [ARDINCA].
-ınca² *v. suf.* [179] = -ince² [ALINCA].
ıncalız (*bot., cul.*) Wild onion (used for pickles).
-ıncı *a. suf.* [82] = -inci [ALTMIŞINCI].
-ınç *a./n. suf.* [222] = -inç [BASINÇ].
-ınız *n. suf.* [39] = -iniz [PAYINIZ].
INS = (*International News Service*).
-ıntı *n. suf.* [222] = -inti, -ti [IKINTI].
IOC = (*International Olympic Committee*).
-ıp *v. suf.* [177] = -ip [IKINIP].
Ir. = (*ch.s.*) İRİDYUM.
-ır¹ *v. suf.* [116] = -ir¹ [ALIR].
-ır² *vc. suf.* [145] = -dir-² [KAÇIRMAK].
ıra (*bio.*) Character. ∼ **bilim,** (*psy.*) characterology.
Irak¹¹ *pr. n.* (*geo.*) Iraq; Mesopotamia. ∼ **çıbanı,** (*med.*) Baghdad/Aleppo boil. ∼ **lı,** (*ethn.*) Iraqi.
ırak² *a.* Far, distant. ∼ **görür,** (*ast.*) telescope. ∼ **laşmak (-den),** *vi.* become distant/remote; recede. ∼ **lık,** distance, remoteness: ∼ **açısı,** (*ast.*) parallax. ∼ **sak,** (*phys.*) divergent. ∼ **sama,** divergence. ∼ **samak (-i),** consider stg. unlikely. ∼ **sınmak (-i),** consider stg. far.
ıra·lamak (-i) (*phil.*) Characterize. ∼ **sal,** characteristic.
ıramak *vi.* Retire, withdraw, recede.
ırga·(la)mak (-i) Move; shake; (*sl.*) concern,

~ (la)nmak, *vi.* move; be moved; vibrate; be shaken. **~ tmak**, *vc.*

ırgat¹ Labourer, workman; bricklayer; (*naut.*) capstan, windlass. **~ başı**, foreman; (*naut.*) capstan head: **~ gibi çalışmak**, work very hard: **~ pazarı**, place for hiring labourers: **~ pazarına döndürmek** (i), turn a place upside down. **~ lık**, labouring; labourer's daily wage.

ırıp = ıĞRIP.

ırk¹ (*ethn.*) Race; (*soc.*) lineage. **~ bilim**, ethnology. **~ çı**, racist, racialist. **~ çılık**, racialism. **~ i/ ~ sal**, racial(ist); ethnic. **~ iyAt¹**, ethnology. **~ taş**, of the same race.

ırlamak (-i) Sing.

ırma¹k⁸¹ (*geo.*) Large river. **~ ardıcı**, (*orn.*) great reed warbler: **~ dalgıcı**, (*orn.*) little grebe: **~ domuzu**, (*zoo.*) bush pig: **~ inci midyesi**, (*zoo.*) pearl mussel: **~ kırlangıcı**, (*orn.*) river tern: **~ midyesi**, (*zoo.*) river mussel: **~ ötleğeni**, (*orn.*) river warbler: **~ taşemeni**, (*zoo.*) lampern, river lamprey.

IRO = (*International Refugee Organization*).

ırz Honour; modesty; chastity. **~ düşmanı**, vicious rake: **~ ehli**, honest; virtuous/chaste (woman): **~ ına dokunmak**, dishonour: **~ ına geçmek/tecavüz etm.**, abuse, violate; dishonour; ravish (a woman).

ıs (*obs.*) Master; owner; sign of habitation. **ıs-** *Also* = ız-.

ısdar (*tex.*) Carpet-weaver's loom.

Isfahan (*geo.*) Isfahan; (*Or. mus.*) compound melody.

ısı *n.* (*phys.*) Heat. *a.* Warm. **~ alıcı**, (*phys.*) heat sink: **~ dam**, hammam, Turkish bath: **~ değiştirgeci**, (*phys.*) heat exchanger: **~ dengesi**, heat equilibrium: **~ dirençli**, heat-resistant: **~ ışınımı**, thermal radiation: **~ iletimi**, thermal conduction: **~ iletkeni**, thermal conductor: **~ kuşak**, (*geo.*) tropics: **~ ot**, (*bot.*) pepper: **~ sığası**, (*phys.*) thermal flow: **~ yalıtımı**, (*phys.*) heat insulation: **~ yayılması**, heat convection.

ısı·alan (*chem.*) Heat-absorbent; endothermic. **~ denetir**, (*phys.*) thermostat.

ısıl (*phys.*) Calorific, thermal; heat-conducting. **~ erke**, thermal energy: **~ işlem**, (*min.*) heat-treatment: **~ sertleşmesi**, (plastic) thermosetting: **~ verimlilik**, thermal efficiency.

ısıl·çekinsel (*phys.*) Thermonuclear. **~ çift**, thermocouple. **~ değer**, calorific value. **~ devim-bilim**, thermodynamics. **~ devingen**, thermodynamic. **~ ışıma**, thermal radiation. **~ kesim**, (*nuc.*) pyrolysis. **~ kimya**, thermochemistry.

ısın (*phys.*) Calorie. **~ a¹k⁸¹**, (*dom.*) stove, heater. **~ dırmak (-i, -e)**, warm, heat; cause to like. **~ ılmak**, *vp.* be heated. **~ ma**, *vn.* heating: **~ ısısı**, (*phys.*) specific heat: **~ koşusu**, (*sp.*) jog-trot, warming-up run. **~ mak**, *vi.* grow warm, warm up: **(-e)**, (*fig.*) have an affection for; grow to like; get accustomed to. **~ ölçer**, (*phys.*) calorimeter.

ısıölçer (*med.*) Thermometer.

ısır·gan (*bot.*) Nettle. **~ gangiller**, (*bot.*) nettle family, Urticaceae. **~ gın**, (*med.*) heat-spots, rash. **~ ıcı**, biting: **~ bitler**, (*ent.*) biting lice. **~ ık**, mark/ wound from a bite. **~ ılmak**, *vp.* be bitten. **~ mak (-i, -den)**, bite s.o./stg. (on . . .): **ısıran bit**, (*ent.*) biting louse: **ısıran it dişini göstermez**, you get no warning of an evil deed. **~ tmak (-i, -e)**, *vc.*

ısı-sağıtım (*med.*) Diathermy. **~ salan**, (*phys.*) exothermic. **~ savar**, (*mot.*) radiator. **~ sever**, (*bot.*) thermophile. **~ ta¹çᶜ¹**, central-heating, radiator. **~ taççı**, central-heating engineer. **~ tıcı**, *a.* heating; calorific: *n.* (*dom.*) (water-)heater. **~ tılmak**, *vp.* be heated. **~ tma**, *vn.* heating; (*med.*) malaria: **~ döşemi**, central heating system. **~ tma¹çᶜ¹**, (*dom.*) water-heater. **~ tmak (-i)**, heat: **ısıtıp ısıtıp önüne koymak**, rehash, serve up an old problem as new. **~ veren** = **~ SALAN**. **~ yayar**, (*mot.*) radiator. **~ yuvarı**, (*ast.*) thermosphere.

ısk- *Also* = ısK-.

ıska Miss; failure. **~ geçme**, (*sp.*) miskick: **~ geçmek**, (*sp.*) miss the ball; (*sl.*) miss the mark; fail.

ıskaça (*naut.*) Step (of a mast).

ıskala (*mus.*) Scale. **~ yapmak**, play a scale.

ıskalar(y)a (*naut.*) Ratlines; port gangway.

ıskara = ızGARA.

ıskarça (*naut.*) Berthed close together; tightly stowed; crowded.

ıskarmoz (*naut.*) Rib frame; rowlock, thole-pin; (*ich.*) barracuda.

ıskarta (*gamb.*) *n.* Discard. *a.* Discarded, scrapped. **~ ya çıkarmak**, discard; scrap.

ıskat¹ ¹ Throwing down. **~ etm.**, throw down; overthrow; dispossess; annul; reject: **~ ı cenin**, (*bio.*) miscarriage.

ıskat¹ ² (*rel.*) Alms (given on behalf of the dead to compensate for their neglected duties). **~ çı**, priest/ beggar receiving such alms.

ıskonto (*fin.*) Discount. **~ etm.**, discount; reduce. **~ lu**, at a discount.

ıskota (*naut.*) Sheet (of a sail). **~ bağı**, sheet-bend: **~ yakası**, clew.

ıskuna (*naut.*) Schooner.

ıslah Improvement; reform, correction. **~ edici**, corrective: **~ etm.**, improve, put to rights, reform: **~ olmaz**, incorrigible: **~ ı beyn etm.**, promote good relations.

ıslah·at¹ Improvements; reforms. **~ atçı**, reformer. **~ atçılık**, reform. **~ eviⁿⁱ/ ~ hane**, (*leg.*) approved school, reformatory; house of correction.

ıs·lak Wet. **~ bez**, (*med.*) compress: **~ karga**, (*sl.*) chicken-hearted fellow: **~ kazı**, (*min.*) etching. **~ laklık**, wetness. **~ lamak (-i)**, wet. **~ lanmak**, *vi.* become wet; be wetted. **~ latıcı**, (*ind.*) wetting agent. **~ latılmak**, *vp.* **~ latmak (-i)**, wet; bathe, drench; (*sl.*) punish, flog; (*jok.*) drink to.

ıslı¹k⁸¹ Whistle. **~ çalan ördek**, (*orn.*) Eurasian wigeon: **~ çalmak**, whistle. **~ lamak (-i)**, hoot, boo. **~ lanmak**, *vi.* be booed. **~ lı**, whistling: **~ kuğu**, (*orn.*) whistling swan: **~ ünsüz**, (*ling.*) sibilant.

ısmarla·ma *vn.* (*fin.*) Ordering. *a.* Ordered; bespoke; made to measure/order; custom-built: **~ kalıntısı**, backlog of orders: **~ terzilik**, bespoke tailoring. **~ mak (-e)**, order; bespeak; (-i, -e), command; entrust; recommend. **~ nmak (-e)**, *vp.* **~ tmak (-i, -e)**, *vc.*

ısp- *Also* = ısP-; sP-.

ıspana¹k⁸¹ (*bot.*) Spinach; (*sl.*) dolt, blockhead.

~ **bastısı**, (*cul.*) spinach with rice. ~ **giller**, Chenopodiaceae.

ıspaŗçana (*naut.*) Serving of a cable. ~ **etm.**, serve.

ıspaŗmaça (*naut.*) Fouled cables.

ıspavlı (*naut.*) Twine.

ıspazmoz (*med.*) Spasm.

ısrar Insistence. ~ **etm.**, insist (on stg.); assert. ~ **lı**, insistent.

ıssız Lonely/desolate (place); without an owner; without signs of habitation, derelict, deserted; (*phys.*) adiabatic. ~ **laşmak**, *vi.* become deserted/desolate. ~ **lık**, desolation; loneliness.

ıstakoz (*zoo.*) Lobster.

ıstampa (*pub.*) Stamp; inking-pad.

ıstavroz (*rel.*) Cross; sign of the cross. ~ **çıkarmak**, cross o.s.

ıstıfa Choosing; (natural) selection. ~ **etm.**, choose.

ıstılah Technical term. ~ **paralamak**, use scientific jargon.

ıstıra'pᵇ¹ Distress; anxiety; pain. ~ **lı**, painful.

ıstırar Need; compulsion. ~ **i**, forced; involuntary.

ış. = IŞIK.

ış¹ *vn. suf.* [172] = -iş¹ [ALIŞ]

ış² *v. suf.* [143] = -iş² [YAZIŞMAK].

ışığ- = IŞIK. ~ **adoğrulum/** ~ **ayönelim**, (*bot.*) phototropism.

ışı'kᵍ¹ *n.* Light; lamp. ~ +, *a.* Light; optical; luminous; photo-: ~ **akısı**, (*phys.*) luminous flux: ~ **araçları**, optical instruments: ~ **aylası**, (*ast.*) aureola: ~ **baskısı**, (*pub.*) collotype: ~ **bükülmesi**, (*phys.*) diffraction: ~ **dağılması**, diffusion/dispersion of light: ~ **demeti**, beam, pencil of light: ~ **direği**, (*th.*) boom: ~ **erkesi**, (*phys.*) light energy: ~ **geçirmez**, light-proof; opaque: ~ **gözü**, photocell: ~ **ışını**, light ray: ~ **kaynağı**, light source: ~ **kesmek**, dim: ~ **kırıcı**, refractor: ~ **saçmak**, beam: ~ **titremesi**, flicker: ~ **titreşimi**, scintillation; twinkling: ~ **tutmak**, throw light on; light the way: ~ **veren**, luminous: ~ **yayı**, arc: ~ **yılı**, light-year: ~ **a tutulmuş**, (*cin.*) exposed: ~ **ı altında (-in)**, in the light of . . ..

ışık·bilgisiⁿⁱ (*phys.*) Optics. ~ **çı**, (*cin.*) electrician. ~ **çıl**, (*bio.*) photophilic. ~ **elektrik**, (*phys.*) photoelectric. ~ **göçüm**, (*bot.*) phototaxis. ~ **gözü**, (*el.*) photocell. ~ **kesen**, dimmer switch. ~ **küre** (*ast.*) photosphere. ~ **lama**, *vn.* lighting; (*cin.*) exposure: ~ **uzmanı**, (*cin.*) electrician. ~ **landırmak**, *vi.* (*cin.*) be exposed. ~ **landırma**, *vn.* illumination; (*cin.*) exposure. ~ **landırmak (-i)**, expose; illuminate. ~ **lı**, exposed; luminous; lit up. ~ **lık**, light fitting. ~ **lılık**, luminosity. ~ **ölçer**, photometer, exposuremeter. ~ **ölçme/** ~ **ölçümü**, photometry. ~ **özü**, photon. ~ **sal**, optical; luminous; photo-. ~ **yuvarı**, photocell; = ~ KÜRE.

ışıl ~ ~, shining brightly; sparkling. ~ **amak/** ~ **damak**, *vi.* shine, sparkle, flash. ~ **atmak/** ~ **datmak (-i)**, make shine/flash.

ışıl·da'kᵍ¹ (*phys.*) Projector; floodlight. ~ **dama**,

luminescence. ~ **dar**, luminescent. ~ **duygun**, photosensitive. ~ **eksici'kᵍⁱ**, photo-electron. ~ **ışı**, luminescence. ~ **kesim**, photolysis. ~ **kimya**, photochemistry. ~ **küf**, (*myc.*) actinomycete, ray fungus. ~ **küflüce**, (*med.*) actinomycosis. ~ **tı**, brightness; shining; flash; glow. ~ **tılı**, flashing, scintillating; glowing.

ışı·ma *vn.* (*phys.*) Radiation. ~ **mak**, *vi.* radiate; fluoresce; shine.

ışın Gleam; flash; (*phys.*) ray; (*math.*) radius. ~ **demeti**, beam of light.

ışın·cı'kᵍ¹ Photon. ~ **çekim**, (*med.*) radiography. ~ **etki(nlik)**, (*phys.*) radioactivity. ~ **etkin**, radioactive. ~ **ım**, radiation: ~ +, *a.* radiant. ~ **ımlama**, irradiation. ~ **ımölçer**, bolometer. ~ **ır(lık)**, fluores·cent/(-cence). ~ **kıvıl**, photoelectric. ~ **lama/** ~ **lanım**, (*med.*) radiation. ~ **lı**, actinic. ~ **lılar**, (*zoo.*) Radiolaria. ~ **mantar**, (*myc.*) actinomyces: ~ **sayrılığı**, (*med.*) actinomycosis. ~ **ölçer**, (*phys.*) radiometer. ~ **sal**, (*bio.*) radial: ~ **simetri**, (*math.*) radial symmetry.

ışıta'lçᶜ¹ (*min.*) Lamp. ~ **çı**, lampman. ~ **evi**, lamphouse.

ışı·tmak (-i) Illuminate. ~ **yan**, (*el.*) radiant. ~ **yıcı**, radiator.

ışkı Two-handled curved knife.

ışkın (*bot.*) Type of rhubarb.

ışkırla'kᵍ¹ (*th.*) Pointed cap worn by KARAGÖZ.

ıştın Earthenware lamp.

ıştır (*bot.*) Wild beet, (?) strawberry spinach.

-ıt¹ *a./n. suf.* [224] = -iT [KARŞIT; YAKIT].

-ıt-² *v. suf.* [145] = -DİR- [AKITMAK].

ıt'ırʳ¹ Perfume, aroma; fragrant plant. ~ **çiçeği**, (*bot.*) rose-scented geranium.

ıtır·lı Perfumed, sweet-smelling. ~ **şahı**ⁿⁱ, (*bot.*) sweet-pea. ~ **yağı**ⁿⁱ, attar of roses.

ıtlak¹ Liberation; generalization; naming. ~ **etm.**, set free; name: ~ **olunmak**, be named.

ıtna'pᵇ¹ (*lit.*) Verbosity, prolixity; pleonasm. ~ **etm.**, be verbose.

IT·O = (*International Trade Organization*). ~ **U** = (*International Telecommunications Union*).

ıtr- = ITIR. ~ **i**, perfumed; aromatic. ~ **iyat'**, perfumes; perfumery. ~ **iyatçı**, perfumer; perfumeseller.

ıttıla¹ Information; cognizance. ~ **kesbetmek**, acquire knowledge.

-ıvermek *v. suf.* [191] = -İVERMEK [ÇIKIVERMEK].

ıvır ~ **zıvır**, rubbish, nonsense; unimportant things; nonsensical.

-ıyla *n. suf.* [85] = iLE [KARIYLA].

ız- *Also* = ıs-.

-ız *v. suf.* [96] = -iz²; OLMAK [FRANSIZIZ].

ızbandu'tᵈᵘ Bandit, brigand; huge terrifying man.

ızgara Gridiron; grill; grate; grating; (*cul.*) grilled meat/fish, etc.; (*sp.*) boot-stud.

ızrar Harming, harm. ~ **etm.**, harm; prejudice.

ıztıra'pᵇ¹ Distress, anxiety, pain.

İ

İ, i [i] Twelfth Tk. letter, (dotted) İ.

İ, i. = İNGİLİZCE; İNGİLTERE; İSİM; İSTANBUL; İŞLERİ; (*ch.s.*) İYOT; İZMİR.

(-i) = -i'Lİ TÜMLEÇ ALAN EYLEM.

-i[1]**/-ı/-u/-ü/(-yi**, *etc. after vowels). n. suf.* [28] *Forming the accusative case.* Him, her, it [**kızı gördüm**, I saw the girl]. ~ **hali**, (*ling*.) accusative case: ~ **'li tümleç alan eylem**, (*ling*.) transitive verb.

-i[2]**/-ı/-u/-ü/(-si**, *etc. after vowels). n. suf.* [39] *Third person possessive ending of the element possessed.* His, her, its [**oğlu**, his son; **kitabı**, her book; **Mehmed'in parası**, Mehmet's money; **İstanbul camileri**, the mosques of Istanbul].

-i[3]**/-ı/-u/-ü** *a./n. suffix* [221] *Denoting action or result of an action* [**dolu**, full; **yapı**, building].

-i[4]**/-î** *a. suf.* [65] [TARİHİ].

iade Restoration; giving back; repetition. ~ **edilmez**, non-returnable; disposable (bottles, etc.): ~ **etm.**, give back, return; restore (peace); retrocede. ~ **li**, with return: ~ **satış**, sale or return: ~ **taahhütlü mektup**, registered letter with record of delivery returned to sender.

iane Help; subsidy; donation; (charitable) subscription. ~ **etm.**, contribute: ~ **toplamak**, collect subscriptions. ~ **ten**, as a donation.

iare Loan. ~ **etm.**, lend.

İAST = İSTANBUL ANKARA SANAT TİYATROSU.

iaşe Subsistence: feeding; (*adm.*) food supplies, victualling. ~ **etm.**, sustain, feed; ~ **ve ibate**, board and lodging.

İB = İÇİŞLERİ BAKAN(LIĞ)I; İŞ BANKASI.

ibadet[i] (*rel.*) Worship, prayer; cult. ~ **etm.**, worship. ~ **gâh/~hane**, place of worship.

ibadullah (*rel.*) Servants of God; (*col.*) a lot of, an abundance of, heaps of.

ibare (*ling.*) Sentence, clause; (*pub.*) title.

ibaret Consisting (of/in); composed (of). ~ **olm.** (-den), consist of/in; comprise; be equivalent to: ~ **olm. (bundan)**, be nothing but (this).

ibate Lodging, shelter. ~ **etm.**, lodge, house; shelter.

ibda[1] Creating; invention.

İberi(y)a (*geo.*) Iberia. ~ **çiçeği**, (*bot.*) candytuft.

ibibi[1]**k**[ği] (*orn.*) Hoopoe.

ibi[1]**k**[ği] (*orn.*) Comb, crest; (*bio.*) crest, crista; gasburner. ~ **ini kaldırmak**, be obstinate. ~ **li**, cristate; crested.

ibis (*orn.*) Glossy ibis. ~ **giller**, ibises.

ibiş (*th.*) Comic role (in TULUAT TİYATROSU); (*sl.*) blockhead. ~ **gibi**, comic(al).

iblağ Sending; communicating. ~ **etm.**, cause to reach; cause to amount to; communicate (to).

iblis Satan; devil; demon; devilish man.

ibne Catamite. ~ **lik**, catamite tendencies/behaviour.

İbr. = İBRANCA(DAN).

ibra (*leg.*) Discharge. ~ **etm.**, discharge (debts); free from claim; pass (accounts): ~ **kâğıdı/~name**, certificate of receipt/discharge.

İbran·ca/~ice (*ling.*) Hebrew. ~ **i**, (*ethn.*) Hebrew.

ibraz Manifestation; display (feelings, etc.); presentation (documents). ~ **etm.**, manifest, display, show; present: ~ **ında**, at sight.

ibre (*phys.*) Pointer, indicator; hand of clock/watch; magnetic needle; (*bot.*) style; pine-needle; (*ent.*) sting.

ibret[i] Example; warning, admonition. ~ **almak**, take warning: ~ **gözüyle bakmak (-e)**, look at s.t. to get a lesson/warning from it: ~ **olm. (-e)**, be lesson/warning to s.o.: ~ **verici**, exemplary: ~ **kudreti**, odd and ugly. ~ **en**, as an example/warning.

ibri[1]**k**[ği] (*dom.*) Vessel with handle and spout; kettle; coffee-pot; ewer. ~ **gagalı**, (*orn.*) boat-billed heron. ~ **otu**, (*bot.*) nepenthes, pitcher-plant. ~ **tar**, (*his.*) official superintending the Sultan's ablutions.

ibrişim (*tex.*) (Made of) silk thread. ~ **kurdu**, (*ent.*) silkworm.

ibt- = İPT-.

ibzal[i] ~ **etm.**, give without stint.

icab- = İCAP.

icabet[i] Acceptance; favourable answer. ~ **etm.**, accept (invitations); accede to (requests): ~ **etmemek**, ignore.

icad- = İCAT.

ica[1]**p**[bı] A rendering necessary; a requiring; exigency; necessity. ~ **etm.**, render necessary; require; be necessary: ~ **eden tedbirler almak**, take the necessary steps/precautions: ~ **ederse**, should the occasion arise: ~ **ettirmek**, necessitate: ~ **ve kabul** (*leg.*) proposal and acceptance: ~ **ı (-in)**, through, on account of; as required by: ~ **ı hale göre**, as required by circumstances: ~ **ı var**, it's needed, necessary: ~ **ına bakmak**, do what is necessary: ~ **ına bakarım!**, I'll soon settle that/his hash: ~ **ında**, in case of need.

icar Letting, leasing. ~ **bedeli**, rental: ~ **etm./~ vermek**, let out (on lease), rent out. ~ **e**, rent(al).

ica[1]**t**[dı] Invention; contrivance; fabrication. ~ **çıkarmak**, start a new (bad) trend; abandon good habits; raise unnecessary problems: ~ **etm.**, invent, devise; fabricate, trump up.

icaz (*lit.*) Abridgement; conciseness, terseness. ~ **etm.**, render concise; compress (speech, etc.). ~ **tarikiyle**, concisely, laconically.

icazet[i] Authorization; formal permission; (*ed.*

certificate, diploma. ~ **name,** (*ed., obs.*) diploma (to each).

bar Compulsion, constraint. ~ **etm.**, force, ompel.

ci-/-ıcı/-ucu/-ücü *a./n. suf.* [220] *Denoting regular ction* [yok edici, destroying; **uyuşturucu,** narcotic]. **i'k**ᵍⁱ ~**ini ciciğini bilmek,** know stg. inside out: ~**ini ciciğini çıkarmak,** examine very carefully. **mal**ⁱ Summary; résumé. ~ **etm.**, summarize; pitomize. ~**en,** briefly.

ra (*adm.*) Execution; (*leg., mus.*) performance; ccomplishment. ~ **dairesi,** court-bailiff's office: ~ **etm.**, carry out, perform, execute; enforce: ~ **eyeti,** committee executing judicial decisions: ~ **kuvveti,** executive power: ~ **memuru,** (*adm.*) xecutive officer; (*leg.*) court-bailiff: ~ **satışı,** orced sale: ~ **vekili,** (*adm.*) minister: ~**ya vermek,** efer a matter to the court-bailiff.

ra·at¹ Operations; performances; judicial acts; ffairs. ~**cı,** (*mus.*) performer.

t- = İÇT-.

i *n.* Inside; interior; (*bio.*) stomach; heart; (*eng.*) hamber; (*fig.*) core. *a.* Inner; interior; internal; nside (*geo.*) central; (*adm.*) domestic, home; *math.*) inscribed; (*bio.*) endo-. [**iç** *is often used nstead of a personal pronoun*: ~**im sıkıldı,** I was ored]. ~ **açı,** (*math.*) internal angle: ~ **açıcı,** heering (news, etc.): ~ **açmak (-i),** cheer up; set at ase: ~ **bağlamak,** inside of fruit become ripe: ~ **akla//bezelye,** shelled beans//peas: ~ **bölge,** (*geo.*) interland, interior: ~ **bükün,** (*ling.*) modification f medial sound; internal flexion: ~ **çamaşırı,** *mod.*) underclothing: ~ **çap,** (*eng.*) bore, inner diameter: ~ **çekmek,** sigh: ~ **çokgen,** (*math.*) nscribed polygon: ~ **deniz,** (*geo.*) inland/landocked sea: ~ **donu,** (*mod.*) underpants: ~ **etm.**, *col.*) appropriate stg. borrowed/found: ~ **gezegen,** *ast.*) inner planet: ~ **gıcıklamak,** tickle one's ancy: ~ **göbek,** chalaza: ~ **göçmen,** nomad in a country: ~ **gömleği,** (*mod.*) petticoat: ~GÜDÜ: ~GÜVEY(İ): ~ **harp,** (*mil.*) civil war: ~ **hastalıklar,** *med.*) internal diseases: ~ **hat,** internal communications; telephone extension; (*aer.*) domestic line: ~ ~**e,** one within the other; one opening into another (room); (*math.*) coaxial: ~ ~**e giren,** telescopic: ~ **işlemler,** (*adm.*) internal services: ~ **kabuk,** (*bot.*) endocarp: ~ **kale,** (*mil.*) citadel: ~ **karartıcı,** depressing: ~ **koşak,** (*sp.*) inner lane: ~ **kutur,** (*math.*) internal diameter: ~ **lastiği,** *mot.*) inner tube; (*sp.*) bladder: ~ **merkez,** *geol.*) (earthquake) hypocentre: ~ **omurga,** *naut.*) keelson: ~ **organlar,** (*bio.*) viscera; *cul.*) offal: ~ **oyuncu,** (*sp.*) inside forward: ~ **pazar,** (*fin.*) home market: ~ **pilav,** (*cul.*) pilaff with liver and raisins: ~PLAZMA: ~ **savaş,** (*mil.*) civil war: ~ **sayrılıklar,** (*med.*) internal diseases: ~ **sıkıcı,** (*psy.*) oppressive: ~ **sıkıntısı,** anima; ennui, boredom: ~ **sular,** (*geo.*) inland waterways: ~TEPİ: ~TERS: ~ **türeme,** (*ling.*) epenthesis: ~ **tüzük,** (*adm.*) regulations, by-laws: ~ **yakım,** *mot.*) internal combustion: ~YARIÇAP: ~ **yükümü,** sense of indebtedness. [*Also* = GÖNÜL, YÜREK.]

içe: ~ **geçmeli,** (*eng.*) telescopic: ~ **oynamak,** (*sp.*) keep losing; (*sl.*) be lost in o.s.

içi: ~ **açılmak,** be cheered up: ~ **almamak,** feel an aversion to (food): ~ **bayılmak,** feel faint (from hunger, etc.); be very hungry: ~ **beni yakar dışı eli yakar,** attractive to those that know nothing about it/him: ~ **boş,** hollow: ~ **bulanmak,** feel nauseated; wish to vomit: ~ **bulantısı,** nausea: ~ **burkulmak,** feel pangs of (remorse, etc.): ~ **çekmek,** long for: ~ **çıfıt çarşısı,** evil-minded, malevolent: ~ **dar,** impatient, hasty: ~ **daralmak,** be annoyed: ~ **dışı bir,** uniform; consistent; sincere: ~ **dışına çıkmak,** one's clothes become dishevelled; one's stomach be upset: ~ **dönmek,** be nauseated: ~ **durmamak,** feel uncomfortable until stg. is done; feel bound to do stg.: ~ **erimek,** be very upset: ~ **ezilmek,** have a sinking feeling in the stomach (from hunger, etc.): ~ **geçirmek,** sigh: ~ **geçmek,** doze; (*col.*) become unserviceable; (fruit) become overripe: ~ **geçmiş,** lethargic: ~ **geniş,** easy-going, phlegmatic: ~ **gitmek,** desire stg. strongly; (*med.*) have diarrhoea: ~ **götürmemek,** be unable to bear the misfortunes of others: ~ **götürememek,** not have the heart (to do stg.): ~ ~**ne geçmek,** be discontented: ~ ~**ne sığmamak,** be unable to contain o.s. (for joy, etc.): ~ ~**ni kemirmek/yemek,** be consumed with impatience/anxiety: ~ **kabarmak,** become bilious, feel sick: ~ **kabul etmemek** (-**i**), be sick from stg.: ~ **kalkmak,** the gorge to rise/have a feeling of nausea (from disgust): ~ **kan ağlamak,** grieve bitterly, pine away from grief: ~ **kanmak,** be certain: ~ **kapanmak,** feel depressed: ~ **kararmak,** despair: ~ **kazınmak,** feel very hungry: ~ **par(ç)alanmak,** one's heart ache for s.o.: ~ **rahat etm.,** gladden the heart: ~ **rahat olm.,** feel at ease (about stg.): ~ **sıkılmak,** be bored: ~ **sızlamak** = ~ BURKULMAK: ~ **sürmek,** have diarrhoea: ~ **tez,** energetic, impatient, hustling: ~ **titremek,** have a great desire for: ~ **yağ bağlamak,** feel pleased and relieved: ~ **yanmak,** suffer.

içim: ~ **götürmedi,** I couldn't find it in my heart to ... : ~ ~**i yiyordu (-den),** I was bursting with ... : ~ **de,** within me: ~**e heyheyler geliyor,** I can't stand it any longer; I shall have a nervous breakdown: ~**e öyle geliyor ki,** it seems to me that: ~**e zehir/ zemberek oldu,** it spoilt my enjoyment: ~**izde,** among(st) us.

için: [*also* = İÇİN¹] ~ ~, inwardly; internally; secretly: ~**de** (-**in**), inside; among; included; within (of time): ~**de yüzmek,** (*fig.*) be swimming/rolling in: ~**dekiler,** (*pub.*) contents.

içinden: from inside; spontaneously: ~ **çıkmak** (-**in**), be able to get at the root of stg.; be able to settle stg.; come from a certain place, etc.: ~ **çıkılmaz bir mesele,** an insoluble problem; an incomprehensible matter: ~ **doğmak,** have a sudden impulse (to do good): ~ **geçirmek,** review stg. in one's mind: ~ **geçmek,** pass through one's mind, occur to one: ~ **gelmek,** feel like doing, be disposed to do: ~ **gülmek (-e),** laugh at s.o. secretly: ~ **kan gitmek,** suffer secretly: ~ **okumak,** read to o.s./silently; (*sl.*)

curse s.o. mentally: ~ **pazarlıklı**, cunning, insincere, hypocritical.

içine: ~ **almak**, *vi.* contain; comprise; include: ~ **atmak**, endure in silence: ~ **bir kurt düşmek**, be full of misgivings: ~ **biriktirmek**, bury (insults/sorrows, etc.) in one's heart: ~ **çekmek/emmek**, aspirate; breathe in: ~ **dert olm.**, be a thorn in one's side; cause regret/remorse: ~ **doğmak**, have a feeling/presentiment (that stg. will happen): ~ **etm./sıçmak (-in)**, (*vulg.*) befoul/spoil things: ~ **geçmek**, penetrate; influence: ~ **işlemek**, hurt one's feelings; affect one painfully: ~ **kapanık**, keeping one's feelings to o.s.: ~ **kapanmak**, conceal one's feelings: ~ **koymak**, enclose: ~ **kurt düşmek**, have misgivings/doubts: ~ **öyle doğmak/gelmek**, have a presentiment that . . . : ~ **sığdıramamak**, be unable to cope with/accept: ~ **sığdırma**, capacity: ~ **sindirmemek**, spoil one's pleasure: ~ **sinmek**, feel at ease/happy; **(-in)**, permeate: ~ **sokacağı gelmek**, suddenly be very pleased: ~ **su serpilmek**, become happy: ~ **ukde olm. (-in)**, rankle; be stg. one can't get over.

içini: ~ **açmak**, cheer s.o. up; unburden o.s.: ~ **bayıltmak**, (food) be sickly, cause slight nausea; (*fig.*) bore, disgust: ~ **boşaltmak/dökmek**, unburden o.s. to s.o.; get stg. off one's chest; make a clean breast of stg.: ~ **çekmek**, sigh: ~ **kapatmak**, depress s.o.: ~ **kemirmek**, be worried by stg.: ~ **kurt yemek**, be in a continual state of anxiety: ~ **rahat ettirmek**, set s.o.('s mind) at ease.

iç-: ~ **inin yağı erimek**, be prostrate with grief: ~ **ler acısı**, heart-rending: ~ **ten**, *adv.* from within; honestly, sincerely; (*ind.*) internally; = İÇTEN: ~ **ten** ~ **e**, secretly.

iç·ağı (*med.*) Endotoxin. ~ **akkan**, (*bio.*) endolymph. ~ **alım**, (*fin.*) import(ation). ~ **asalak(lık)**, (*zoo.*) endoparasit·e/(-ism). ~ **atım**, (*geol.*) injection. ~ **avlu**, (*arch.*) inner courtyard. ~ **ayrılma**, (*geol.*) segregation. ~ **basınç**, (*phys.*) internal pressure. ~ **başkalaşım**, (*geol.*) endomorphism. ~ **bükey(lik)**, (*phys.*) concav·e/(-ity). ~ **cümle**, (*ling.*) clause. ~ **çelişmesiz**, (*phys.*) self-consistent. ~ **daralması**, (*psy.*) anguish. ~ **deri**, (*bio.*) endoderm. ~ **duyu**, (*phil.*) inner meaning. ~ **dünya**, (*psy.*) inner world. ~ **düzey**, (*min.*) matrix. ~ **ebakış**, (*psy.*) introspection, auto-observation.

-içe/-(ı)ça *fem. n. suf.* [25] [KRALİÇE; TANRIÇA].
içece¹kᵍⁱ *a.* Drinkable. *n.* (Non-alcoholic) drink, beverage.
içe·çeken (*bio.*) Adductor. ~ **doğma**, inspiration. ~ **dönük(lük)**, (*psy.*) introver·t/(-sion).
içekⁱ (*ling.*) Infix.
içekapan·ık (*psy.*) Autistic. ~ **ım**, ~ **sayrılığı**, schizophrenia. ~ **ış**/ ~ **ma**, autism.
içerde(n) [199] = İÇERİDE(N).
içeri(siⁿⁱ) *n.* The inside; interior; (*bio.*) stomach. *a.* Inside; inner. *adv.* In; to the inside. ~ **almak**, admit: ~ **atmak/tıkmak**, (*fig.*) imprison: ~ **dalmak**, insinuate o.s. unexpectedly into a place: ~ **düşmek**, (*sl.*) go to prison: ~ **getirmek**, bring in: ~ **girmek**, enter; (*sl.*) suffer (financial) loss: ~ **götüren**, (*bio.*) afferent: ~ **vurmak**, (*med.*) (illness) strike

internally: ~ **de**, within; inside: ~ **de olm.**, (*sl.*) hav suffered loss: ~ **den**, from the inside: ~ **si**, her/his its interior: ~ **ye**, to the inside: ~ **ye almak/çekmel** retract: ~ **(ye) buyurun!**, please come in!
içeri¹kᵍⁱ *n.* Content; meaning; (*lit.*) contents. *c* Implicit, implied. ~ **siz**, meaningless, empt**y** ~ **sizlik**, meaninglessness, emptiness.
içer·lek (House) standing back (from the road` secluded. ~ **lemek**, *vi.* be grieved; be annoyed; b angry (without showing it). ~ **me**, implicatioı ~ **mek (-i)**, imply, suggest; comprise, include; (*sl* beat s.o. ~ **si** = İÇERİSİ.
içevlilik (*soc.*) Endogamy.
içeyerleş·im/ ~ **tirim** (*med.*) Implantation.
iç·geçi¹tᵈⁱ (*min.*) Tunnel. ~ **gerilim**, (*phys.*) interna stress. ~ **göre¹çᶜⁱ**, (*med.*) endoscope. ~ **görü**, (*psy* insight. ~ **gözlem(sel)**, (*psy.*) introspec·tion/(-tive` ~ **gözleyim**, (*bio.*) chalaza. ~ **gücü**, (*psy.*) moralе ~ **güdü(lü/-sel)**, (*psy.*) instinct(ive). ~ **gümrül** (*fin.*) internal/inland customs. ~ **güvey(i)ˢⁱ**, son-iɪ law living with his wife's parents: ~ **isinden hallicе** (*jok.*) so so; not too well.
içi·ci (Heavy) drinker. ~ **lir**, drinkable. ~ **lmek**, *v*ɪ be drunk. ~ **m**, draught, drink, sip; taste. ~ **ml** having taste; tasty, pleasant.
için¹ [85] For; on account of; in order to; abou**t** concerning.
için², ~ **de**, ~ **deki**, ~ **den**, ~ **e** = İÇ.
içinde·leme (*phil.*) Inclusion. ~ **lik**, spontaneity.
içir·ilmek *vp.* ~ **me**, (*geol.*) impregnation. ~ **me** **(-i)**, cause to drink; impregnate. ~ **tmek (-e)**, *vc.*
içişleri (*adm.*) Internal/home affairs. ~ **Bakan(lığ)** Minis·ter/(-try) for Internal Affairs.
içitⁱ Drinks, beverages.
içit·er (*med.*) Injector. ~ **im**, (*med.*, *eng.*) injectioɪ ~ **me**, *vn.* injection. ~ **mek (-i)**, inject.
içkapa¹kᵍⁱ (*pub.*) Title-page.
iç·ken *a.* Drunken. ~ **ki**, alcoholic drink: ~ **âlem** drinking session, carousal: ~ **azgısı**, (*med* dipsomania: ~ **içmek**, drink (alcohol): ~ **ikra**ı **etm. (-e)**, stand s.o. a drink: ~ **insanın mihengidiı** drink shows a man's true nature: ~ **kaçakçılığ** bootlegging: ~ **müptelası**, an alcoholic: ~ **tuı** **kun(luğ)u**, (*med.*) alcohol·ic/(-ism): ~ **de yüzmeı** drink like a fish: ~ **ler fabrikası**, distillery: ~ **cümbüş**, drinking party: ~ **ye düşkünlük**, alcc holism: ~ **ye tövbeli**, total abstainer. ~ **kici**, makeı seller of alcoholic drinks; heavy drinker. ~ **kicilil** making/selling alcoholic drinks; heavy drinkinğ ~ **kili**, drunk; (restaurant) selling alcoholic drinkȿ ~ **kisiz**, sober; not licensed.
iç·kin(lik) (*phil.*) Immanen·t/(-ce); inheren·t/(-ce` ~ **kula¹kᵍⁱ**, (*bio.*) internal ear. ~ **kusur**, (*ind* internal/hidden defect. ~ **lek**, spiritual, mora ~ **lem**, (*phil.*) comprehension; intention, sensе ~ **lemsel**, intentional. ~ **lemsiz**, unintentiona ~ **lenmek**, *vi.* be affected emotionally/distressed.
içli (*bot.*) Having an inside/kernel/pulp, etc.; (*fig* reticent; sensitive; touching; emotional; sad, hur**t** ~ **köfte**, (*cul.*) KÖFTE stuffed with fried onioɪ ~ **dışlı**, familiar, intimate: ~ **olm.**, be on familia terms; two families intermarry their sons aɪ daughters. ~ **lik**, closeness, familiarity, intimacy.

çlik *a.* Internal; inner. *n.* Underclothes.

ç·me *vn.* Drinking: ~ **suyu**, drinking water: ~**den sarhoş**, 'drunk without drinking', behaving oddly: ~**(ler)**/~**ce**, mineral-water spring. ~**mek (-i)**, drink; inhale, smoke (cigarette, etc.); absorb: *vi.* drink (alcoholic drinks): **içtikleri su ayrı gitmez**, they are very intimate friends.

ç·mimar(lık) *(arch.)* Interior decora·tor/(-tion). ~**oğlanı**[ni], *(his.)* page (training for palace service). ~**örtü**, *(bio.)* endothelium. ~**plazma**, *(bio.)* endoplasm. ~**re**, *(obs.)* within; interior. ~**rek**, hidden, esoteric. ~**salgı**, *(bio.)* internal secretion, hormone: ~ **bezi**, endocrine gland. ~**salgıbilim**, *(med.)* endocrinology. ~**sel**, internal; moral, spiritual. ~**ses**, *(ling.)* median sound: ~ **düşmesi**, *(ling.)* syncope. ~**solunum**, *(bio.)* cellular respiration. ~**sürdürücü**, *(med.)* purgative. ~**tecim**, *(fin.)* internal commerce, home trade. ~**ten**, *a.* sincere, candid; intimate; = iç: ~ **pazarlık**, mental reservation: ~ **yanma(lı motor)**, *(mot.)* internal combustion (engine). ~**tenlik**, sincerity. ~**tenliksiz(lik)**, insincer·e/(-ity). ~**tepi**, *(psy.)* compulsion, constraint. ~**ters (açı)**, *(math.)* internal opposite (angle).

çtiha[ı]t[d1] *(leg.)* Interpretation, ruling; opinion, conviction. ~ **kapısı kapandı**, the last word has been said on that matter: ~**ında bulunmak**, be of the opinion that . . . .

çtima[1] Assembly, gathering, meeting. ~ **etm.**, assemble, meet: ~ **hakkı**/**hürriyeti**, *(pol.)* right// freedom of assembly. ~**i**, social. ~**ileşmek**, *vi.* be social/sociable. ~**iyat**[1], social sciences; sociology. ~**iyatçı**, sociologist.

çtina[ı]p[b1] Avoidance, abstention. ~ **etm.**, avoid; **(-den)** abstain (from).

ç·tümce *(ling.)* Clause. ~**tüzü**[ı]k[gü], *(adm.)* internal regulations, standing orders. ~**yağı**[ni], *(cul.)* suet. ~ **yapı**, internal structure; microstructure. ~**yapışkanlık**, *(phys., geol.)* cohesion. ~**yapra**[ı]k[g1], *(bio.)* endoderm. ~**yarıçap**[1], *(math.)* apothem. ~**yarık**, *(min.)* internal crack. ~**yürekzarı**, *(bio.)* endocardium. ~**yüz**, the inside of a matter; the 'inside story'; inner meaning; real truth: ~**ünü anlamak**, get at the back of stg. ~**zar**, *(bot.)* intine.

d. = İDARECİLİK.

dadi *(ed., obs.)* Secondary school.

dam *(leg.)* Capital punishment, execution. ~ **cezası**, death sentence: ~ **etm.**, put to death, execute: ~ **manga/takımı**, *(mil.)* firing squad: ~**ına karar vermek**, condemn to death. ~**lık**, (crime) meriting execution; (person) condemned to death.

dame Continuance. ~ **etm.**, prolong; extend; preserve.

dare Management, direction, superintendence; *(adm.)* administration; *(fin.)* economizing. ~ +, *a.* Managing, controlling: ~ **eden**, manager, director, controller, *(mus.)* conductor; *(mot.)* driver: ~ **etm.**, administer, manage, direct, control; *(fin.)* economize, make ends meet, suffice; *(mot.)* drive; *(naut.)* con (ship): ~ **etm. (-le)**, make do with; *(col.)* solve a problem somewhat illegally/improperly: ~ **heyeti**, *(adm.)* executive committee: ~ **hukuku**, *(leg.)* administrative law: ~ **kandil/lambası**, *(dom.)*

nightlight: ~ **meclisi**, *(fin.)* board of directors: ~ **müdürü**, *(fin.)* managing director: ~ **teşkilatı**, administration: ~ **üyesi**, *(fin.)* director: ~ **yolu**, diplomacy.

idare·ce By management. ~**ci**, administrator; director; organizer; executive; good manager, tactful person; *(fin.)* economizer; *(leg.)* specialist in administrative law. ~**cilik**, administration, management; economy. ~**hane**, office(s); administration. ~**imaslahat**[1], making do (with what one has): ~ **politikası**, policy of calming things down. ~**li**, good at managing; efficient; economical. ~**siz**, bad at managing, weak, inefficient; wasteful. ~**ten**, administratively.

idari Connected with administration; administrative. ~ **bilimler**, *(ed.)* management sciences: ~ **makamlar**, the authorities: ~ **örgüt**, administration.

idbar Adversity; falling into disgrace.

iddia Claim; pretension; allegation; assertion; bet. ~ **etm.**, claim; contend; allege, affirm, assert: ~ **varit olamaz**, the claim can not be accepted: ~**sından vazgeçmek**, give up one's claim, back down: ~**ya girişmek/tutuşmak**, put forward a counter-claim; enter a waiver.

iddia·cı Obstinate; assertive; dogmatic. ~**cılık**, obstinacy; assertiveness. ~**lı**, disputed; pretentious, arrogant. ~**name**, *(leg.)* formal charge/ accusation. ~**sız(lık)**, unpretentious(ness).

ide Idea, thought. ~**al(ist)**[i], ideal(ist). ~**alize** ~ **etm.**, idealize. ~**alism**, idealism. ~**fiks**, *(psy.)* *idée fixe*, monomania.

iden·tik Identical, exactly similar. ~**tite**, identity.

ideo·log *(phil.)* Ideologist. ~**loji(k)**, ideolo·gy/ (-gical).

idi[1] [99] He/she/it was. ~**k**, we were: ~**m**, I was: ~**n(iz)**, you were: ~**ler**, they were: ~**yse**, (+ *personal suf.*) if he, etc., was/were. = ERMEK[1].

idi[2]/**-di**/**-dı**/**-ti**, *etc. post.* Such as this . . . that . . . the other; whether it be . . . [**çaydi, kahvedi, süttü, ne istersen al**, tea, coffee, milk, take what you will].

idil *(lit.)* Idyll.

idiopati *(med.)* Idiopathy.

idiş = iğDİŞ.

idman *(sp.)* Physical exercise; training; sport; *(fig.)* practice, familiarity. ~ **yapmak**, train, exercise. ~**cı**, sportsman; trainer; gymnastics teacher. ~**lı**, in training, fit, in good condition; well-trained; accustomed.

İDOB = İSTANBUL DEVLET OPERA VE BALESİ.

idrak[i] Perception, comprehension, intelligence; gathering, collection; *(agr.)* getting-in (harvest). ~ **etm.**, catch up, overtake, reach; perceive, comprehend.

idrak·li Intelligent, perceptive. ~**siz**, dense, unintelligent. ~**sizlik**, lack of intelligence.

idrar *(bio.)* Urine. ~ **söktüren**, diuretic: ~ **yolu**, urethra: ~ **zorluğu**, retention of urine.

idris·ağacı[n1] *(bot.)* St. Lucie cherry. ~**otu**[nu], *(bot.)* andropogon.

idro- = HİDRO-.

İ·DSO = İSTANBUL DEVLET SENFONİ ORKESTRASI.

~ **DT** = İSTANBUL DEVLET TİYATROSU. ~ **EE** = İSTANBUL EĞİTİM ENSTİTÜSÜ. ~ **EF** = İZMİR ENTERNASYONAL FUARI. ~ **ETT** = İSTANBUL ELEKTRİK TÜNEL TRAMVAY İŞLETMESİ. ~ **F** = İLAHİYAT FAKÜLTESİ.

ifa (*leg.*) Performance, execution, fulfilment; payment. ~ **etm.**, execute, fulfil; pay: ~ **yer//zamanı**, place//time of performance.

ifade Explanation; expression; connotation; (*leg.*) deposition (of evidence), testimony, affidavit. ~ **etm.**, express, explain; depose, instruct: ~ **vermek**, give evidence: ~ **si tamam olm.**, be 'done for': ~ **sini almak**, investigate; receive (and take down) statements; (*sl.*) have a reckoning. ~ **lendirmek (-i)**, cause to make a statement.

iffet[i] Chastity; honesty, uprightness. ~ **ini bozmak**, defile. ~ **li**, chaste; virtuous; loyal. ~ **siz**, unchaste; dissolute, dishonest.

ifildemek *vi.* Tremble slightly.

iflah Salvation. ~ **olm.**, improve: ~ **olmaz**, incorrigible: ~ **ı kesilmek/** ~ **ını kesmek**, be exhausted.

iflas (*fin.*) Bankruptcy, insolvency. ~ **etm.**, go bankrupt, crash; (*fig.*) fail.

ifna Destruction. ~ **etm.**, destroy, annihilate.

ifrağ Transforming; moulding, shaping; (*bio.*) excretion. ~ **etm.**, transform, convert; excrete.

ifrat[1] Excess; doing too much. ~ **etm.**, overdo, go to excess: ~ **a kaçmak**, go far ahead: ~ **tan tefrite**, from one extreme to the other. ~ **çı(lık)**, extrem·ist/ (-ism). ~ **la**, excessively.

ifraz Separation; (*bio.*) secretion. ~ **etm.**, set aside, allot; secrete. ~ **at**[1], (*bio.*) secretions.

ifrit[i] *n.* Demon; afreet. *a.* Malicious, devilish. ~ **kesilmek/olm.**, be mad with fury.

ifsa[1]**t**[d1] *n.* Spoiling, contaminating, corrupting, inciting. ~ **etm.**, corrupt, seduce, incite; contaminate. ~ **çı**, (*pol.*) agitator, militant.

ifşa[1] *n.* Divulgence; disclosure, revelation. ~ **etm.**, divulge, disclose, reveal. ~ **at**[1], revelations.

iftar (*rel.*) Breaking a fast; meal at sundown (during Ramadan). ~ **etm.**, break one's fast: ~ **topu**, gun fired at sunset (during Ramadan).

iftar·lık *n.* Hors d'œuvres, etc. eaten at İFTAR: *a.* suitable for eating at İFTAR; (*fig.*) very little. ~ **iye**, light food for//gift to guests at İFTAR.

iftihar Laudable pride. ~ **etm.** (-le), glory in, be proud of: ~ **a geçmek**, (*ed.*) be the model pupil.

iftira Slander, calumny; fabrication, forgery. ~ **atmak/etm. (-e)**, slander, cast aspersions on. ~ **cı**, slanderer. ~ **lı**, defamatory.

iguana (*zoo.*) Iguana.

iğ- *Also* = EĞ-.

iğ (*tex.*) Spindle. ~ **biçim**, fusiform: ~ **taşı**, upper millstone. ~ **ağacı**[n1], (*bot.*) euonymus, spindle-tree. ~ **ci**, spindle maker.

iğbirar Annoyance, disappointment, chagrin, displeasure.

iğde (*bot.*) Elaeagnus, oleaster. ~ **giller**, oleaster family.

iğdemir (*carp.*) Chisel.

iğdiş *a.* Castrated, emasculated. *n.* (*live.*) Gelding. ~ **etm.**, geld, castrate. ~ **leme/** ~ **lenme**, castration.

iğfal[i] Deception; seduction. ~ **etm.**, deceive delude; seduce.

iğlik *a.* (*ind.*) Having so many spindles.

iğne (*tex.*) Needle, pin; (*ind.*) needle; (*bot.*) thorn (*zoo.*) spicule, sting; (*naut.*) pintle; fish-hook (*med.*) hypodermic needle/injection; (*fig.*) pin prick. ~ **atsan yere düşmez**, very crowded: ~ **delik**, göz/yurdu, eye of a needle: ~ **deliğine kaçmak**, hide o.s. in confusion: ~ **ile kuyu kazmak**, do stg. in a very unpractical manner; undertake stg. requiring much care/time: ~ **ile sağaltım**, (*med.*) acu puncture: ~ **ile vermek**, inject: ~ **iplik**, all skin and bone: ~ **ipliğe dönmek**, become very thin: ~ **işi** (*tex.*) needlework: ~ **kazısı**, (*art.*) drypoint: ~ **mahfazası**, book of needles: ~ **vurma/yapma** (*med.*) injection: ~ **vurmak/yapmak**, (*med.*) give an injection: ~ **yastığı**, (*dom.*) pincushion: ~ **yemek** (*med.*) have an injection: ~ **yutmuş köpek** maymuna dönmek, (*jok.*) become exhausted/upset ~ **den iplik/sürmeye kadar**, everything required with full details, in a circumstantial way: ~ **y** (önce) kendine batır (sonra) çuvaldızı başkasına/ele make sure you are not to blame before blaming others.

iğne·ardı[n1] (*tex.*) Backstitch. ~ **balığı**[n1], (*ich.*) needlefish. ~ **ci(lik)**, (*med.*) (work of) s.o. giving injections. ~ **cik**, (*naut.*) pintle, rudder-brace; (*ent.*) dragonfly. ~ **denlik**, (*tex.*) needlecase. ~ **kurdu** (*zoo.*) pinworm. ~ **lemek (-i)**, fasten with pins; pin up; prick; give an injection; wound with words ~ **lenmek**, *vp.* ~ **leyici**, pricking, stinging. ~ **li** having pins/needle; (*bio.*) aculeate; having a sting ~ **fıçı**, troublesome situation: ~ **pergel**, (*math.* dividers: ~ **söz**, biting/cutting words, epigram ~ **lik**, pincushion. ~ **liler**, (*ent.*) terebrantes ~ **yapraklılar**, (*bot.*) conifers.

iğren·l[ç][ci] *n.* Disgust, loathing. *a.* Disgusting loathsome; beastly, repulsive. ~ **çlik**, loathsome ness, beastliness. ~ **dirmek (-i)**, disgust. ~ **ecek** disgusting. ~ **erek**, with repugnance; unwillingly ~ **gen**, disgusted at everything. ~ **ilmek (-den)**, imp be disgusted. ~ **me**, *vn.*; hate. ~ **mek (-den)**, b disgusted; feel aversion/revulsion; abominate. ~ **ti** disgust.

iğr·eti = EĞRETİ. ~ **i** = EĞRİ.

ihale (*adm.*) Referring; delegating; (*fin.*) adjud cation, award. ~ **etm.**, hand over, delegate; (*fin.* adjudicate, award (contracts): ~ **kazanmak**, b awarded the contract: ~ **ye çıkarmak/koymak**, pu out to tender.

iham (*ling.*) Ambiguity; amphibology.

ihanet[i] Treason; betrayal; infidelity.

ihata Surrounding; embracing; comprehension understanding. ~ **etm.**, surround; embrace comprehend. ~ **lı**, broad, vast; widely read, erudite

ihbar Communication; advice, notification; warn ing; denunciation. ~ **etm.**, communicate; conve (news); inform; denounce: ~ **süresi**, period o notice.

ihbar·cı Notifier, declarer; denouncer. ~ **iye**, publi notice, declaration; reward for information denunciation. ~ **lı**, made known; person-to-perso (telephone call). ~ **name**, notification, declaratio

ihdas An inventing/creating. ~ **etm.**, produce; invent; raise (difficulty); introduce (stg. new); create (a post).

İHF = İSTANBUL HUKUK FAKÜLTESİ.

ihlal[i] *n.* Spoiling, disturbing; breach (of law, etc.); non-observance. ~ **etm.**, spoil; contravene, break, violate.

ihlil (*bio.*) Urethra.

ihmal[i] Negligence, carelessness, inattention. ~ **etm.**, neglect; act negligently, be careless. ~ **ci**/ ~ **kâr(lık)**, careless(ness), negligen·t/(-ce).

ihrac- = İHRAÇ. ~ **at**[ı], (*fin.*) exportation. ~ **atçı**, exporter. ~ **atçılık**, export business/trade.

ihra[ı]**çc**[ı] Extraction; exportation; expulsion; emission; issue; disembarkation. ~ **bankası**, (*fin.*) issuing bank: ~ **etm.**, extract; export; expel; emit; disembark: ~ **limanı**, port of export.

ihram (*mod.*) Woollen cloak (worn by Arabs/ pilgrims at Mecca); (*dom.*) sofa cover.

ihraz ~ **etm.**, obtain; attain.

ihsan Kindness; favour; benevolence. ~ **etm.**, do a kindness; extend/bestow a favour; make a gift.

ihsas Insinuation; (*bio.*) sensation. ~ **etm.**, cause to feel/perceive; inspire; insinuate.

ihtar Reminder; warning, caution, admonition. ~ **name**, written/official warning; protest.

ihtibas Imprisonment; (*bio.*) retention (of urine); (*psy.*) repression.

ihtida (*rel.*) Conversion to Islam.

ihtifal[i] Commemoration (ceremony).

ihtikâr (*fin.*) Profiteering; cornering the market.

ihtila[ı]**çc**[ı] Agitation; convulsion.

ihtilaf Difference; controversy; disagreement, dispute. ~ **a düşmek**, fall out, quarrel, disagree. ~ **lı**, controversial.

ihtilal[i] Riot; rebellion; revolution. ~ **çıkarmak**, revolt. ~ **ci**, revolutionary.

ihtilam (*bio.*) Nocturnal emission.

ihtilas (*fin.*) Embezzlement; misappropriation of funds.

ihtilat[ı] Confusion; (*med.*) complication. ~ **etm.**, mix, mingle; (*med.*) cause complications.

ihtimal[i] *n.* Probability; possibility; contingency; hypothesis. *a.* Probable; possible. *adv.* Probably; most likely. ~ **i**, probable. ~ **iyet**[i], probability.

ihtimam Care; carefulness; taking pains; solicitude. ~ **etm.**, take pains; work carefully.

ihtira[ı] Invention. ~ **beratı**, patent: ~ **etm.**, invent.

ihtirak[ı] Combustion.

ihtiram Respect.

ihtiras Passionate desire; greed; ambition. ~ **lı**, greedy, desirous.

ihtiraz Avoidance, abstention. ~ **kaydı**, reservation.

ihtisar Abbreviation; abridgement; conciseness.

ihtisas[1] *n.* Sensation; impression.

ihtisas[2] *n.* (*ed.*) Specialization. ~ **yapmak**, specialize.

ihtişam Pomp; magnificence; splendour.

ihtiva ~ **etm.**, hold, contain; include, comprise.

ihtiya[ı]**çc**[ı] Want; requirement; necessity; poverty, need. ~ **messetmek**, become necessary: ~ **a cevap vermek**/ ~ **ı karşılamak**, meet/satisfy a need.

ihtiyar[1] *n.* Choice; selection; option. ~ **etm.**, choose; prefer. ~ **i**, arbitrary, discretionary; optional, voluntary: ~ **durak**, (bus, etc.) request stop.

ihtiyar[2] *a.* Old; aged. *n.* Old man. ~ **heyet/meclisi**, (*adm.*) village council of elders. ~ **lamak**, *vi.* grow old. ~ **lamaz**, ageless. ~ **latmak (-i)**, *vc.* age; make old. ~ **lık**, old age.

ihtiyat[1] Precaution; (*fin.*, *mil.*) reserve. ~ **akçesi**, (*fin.*) reserve fund: ~ **kaydı ile**, with reservations: ~ **ordusu**, (*mil.*) reserve forces/troops: ~ **payı**, margin for safety.

ihtiyat·en As a precaution; in reserve. ~ **i**, precautionary: ~ **tedbirler**, precautionary measures. ~ **kâr**/ ~ **lı**, cautious, discreet, prudent. ~ **sız**, imprudent; improvident; incautious. ~ **sızlık**, imprudence; improvidence.

ihtizaz (*phys.*) Vibration.

ihvan Brothers; friends; colleagues.

ihya Bringing back to life, resuscitation; (*fig.*) invigoration, enlivening. ~ **etm.**, invigorate, enliven; bring good fortune: ~ **olm.**, be fortunate.

ihzar Preparation. ~ **i**, preparatory.

İİ·B = İMAR VE İSKAN BAKAN(LIĞI)I. ~ **K** = İCRA İFLAS KANUNU. ~ **KT** = İKTİSADİ İŞBİRLİĞİ VE KALKINMA TEŞKİLATI. ~ **Tİ(A)** = İSTANBUL İKTİSADİ VE TİCARİ İLİMLER (AKADEMİSİ).

-ik/-ık/-uk/-ük *a./n. suf.* [221]. *Denoting the result of action.* [EZİK BÜZÜK; SAPIK; BURUŞUK; PÜSKÜRÜK].

ika[1] ~ **etm.**, cause; bring about; commit (crimes).

ikame Setting up; establishing; substitution. ~ **etm.**, set up; (*mil.*) post (sentinels); substitute.

ikamet[i] Residence; dwelling; staying at a place. ~ **etm.**, dwell, reside, stay: ~ **tezkeresi**, residence permit: ~ **e memur edilmek (-de)**, be ordered to stay at; be exiled to. ~ **gâh**, residence, domicile: ~ **kâğıdı**, residence papers/permit.

ikaz Warning, caution; awakening. ~ **etm.**, caution, warn; arouse: ~ **işaret/sistemi**, warning signal//system.

ikbal[i] Good fortune; success, prosperity; (*his.*) Sultan's concubine. ~ **düşkünü**, one who has fallen on evil times: ~ **e tapan**/ ~ **perest**, ambitious.

iken [190] While being; while; though. *After a consonant it is suffixed as* -ken [GİDERKEN; ÇOCUKKEN], *after a vowel as* -yken [TALEBEYKEN; ÜZEREYKEN].

ikenemon ~ **sinekleri**, (*ent.*) ichneumon flies.

İKH = İNGİLİZ KÜLTÜR HEYETİ.

iki Two; double; couple; pair; brace (birds); ambi-; bi-; di-. ~ **AĞIZLI:** ~ **ahbap çavuşlar**, (*jok.*) very close friends: ~ **anlamlı**, equivocal, ambiguous: ~ **aşamalı**, (*eng.*) two-stage: ~ **atomlu**, (*phys.*) dyad: ~ **ayağını bir pabuca sokmak**, hustle, confuse, fluster: ~ **ayaklı hayvan**, (*zoo.*) biped: ~ **ayda bir**/ ~ **aylık**, (*pub.*) bimonthly: ~ **bacağından tutup ayırıveririm!**, I'll make mincemeat of you!: ~ **baş (soğan)**, a couple of (onions): ~ BAŞLI: ~ **baştan olm.**, require goodwill from both parties: ~ **boyutlu**, two-dimensional: ~ **büklüm**, bent double (with age): ~ **cambaz bir ipte oynamaz**, cunning people can't deceive each other: ~ **cami**

arasında (kalmış) beynamaz, he who hesitates is lost: ~CANLI: ~ cihanda, in this world and the next: ~CİNSLİLİK: ~ÇENEKLİLER: ~ÇENETLİ: ~ çıplak bir hamamda yakışır, two poor people can't make a happy marriage: ~ çift laf/söz, just a couple of words: ~ çifte (kayık), double pair-oared ·boat: ~ defa, twice; *bis*: ~ dirhem bir çekirdek, over-elegantly dressed; dressed up to the nines: ~ dünya, this world and the next: ~DÜZLEMLİ: ~ el bir baş için, each one must look after himself: ~ eli böğründe kalmak, be discouraged; not know what to do: ~ eli kanda olsa, no matter how overworked he is: ~ eli şakaklarında düşünmek, think deeply, ponder over: ~ eli yakasında olm., insist on one's claims: ~ elim yanıma gelecek, I swear I'm not lying: ~ eş, (married) couple: ~ etkili, (*eng.*) double-acting: ~EVCİKLİ: ~ evli, having two wives and families: ~ geçeli, in two rows facing each other: ~ gönül bir olm., two hearts beat as one; be in full agreement: ~ gönül bir olunca samanlık seyran olur, when two hearts beat as one surroundings/difficulties make no difference; love conquers all!: ~ göz arasında, in the twinkling of an eye: ~ gözü ~ çeşme, in floods of tears: ~ gözüm, my darling: ~ günde bir, every other day; frequently; every now and then: ~ haftalık, (*pub.*) biweekly: ~ işi birden görmek, kill two birds with one stone: ~ kanatlılar, (*ent.*) Diptera: ~ kaptan bir gemiyi batırır, too many cooks spoil the broth: ~ karpuz bir koltuğa sığmaz, you can't do two things at the same time: ~ kat, double; folded double; bent double with age; (*arch.*) two stories: ~ kat olm., bow to the ground: ~ katlı, (*arch.*) two-storied; duplex: ~ keçeli, on both sides: ~ kere ~ dört eder gibi, it's as clear as two and two makes four: ~ kişilik bir oda//yatak, a double room//bed: ~ kişinin arasını soğutmak, sow discord between two people: ~ kulak bir dil için, very attentive and saying little: ~ kutuplu, (*phys.*) bipolar: ~laf/lakırdı/sözü bir araya getirememek, be unable to explain one's thoughts clearly: ~ misli, (the) double, twice as much: ~ nokta (üstüste), (*ling.*) colon (:): ~ nokta (yanyana), diaeresis, umlaut (¨): ~ odalı, (*adm.*) bicameral: ~ paralık etm. (-i), vilify, ruin s.o.'s reputation: ~ parça etm., tear asunder: ~ rahmetten biri, (s.o. very ill) he'll die or get better: ~ renkli, pied (bird); dichromatic: ~ satır yazmak (-e), drop s.o. a line: ~ seksen uzanmak, (*sl.*) enjoy o.s.: ~ soluklugiller, (*zoo.*) Amphiumidae: ~ söz bir pazar, without a lot of bargaining: ~ sözü ... = ~ LAF: ~ŞEKİLLİ: ~ taç yapraklı, (*bot.*) bipetalous: ~ takdirde, in either case: ~ tarafı dışbükey//içbükey, (*phys.*) convexo-convex//concavo-concave: ~TARAFLI: ~TERİMLİ: ~ ucunu bir araya getirmek, make both ends meet; make a success of a business, etc.: ~ üç..., two or three: ~ yakası bir araya gelmemek, fail to get on; (*fin.*) make a mess of things: ~YANLI: ~YAŞAYIŞLI; ~ yılda bir, (*pub.*) biennial: ~ yönlü yöntem, (*fin.*) double-entry system: ~YÖNLÜ: ~YÜZLÜ: ~de bir(de), at frequent intervals, frequently, constantly: ~si de bir, they are identical: ~si ortası, the middle/mean between the two: ~si

ortası olmaz, there is no middle course; you can't have it both ways: ~sinden biri, either: ~sini bir kazana koysalar kaynamazlar, there's no way of bringing them together/making them agree: ~ye ayırmak, tear apart: ~ye biçmek, bisect: ~ye bölmek, divide into two: ~ye bükmek, double up [*For further phrases* = BEŞ].

iki·ağızlı Double-/two-edged (sword). ~anlamlı(lık), ambigu·ous/(-ity). ~bakışımlı, (*bot.*) bisymmetrical. ~başlı, ~ kas, (*bio.*) biceps. ~bazlı (*chem.*) dibasic. ~bir, (*gamb.*) two-one (in back gammon). ~boynuzlu, ~ kuş, (*orn.*) great pied hornbill. ~canlı, pregnant. ~ci, (*phil.*) dualist. ~cil(ik), dualism. ~cinsli, (*bio.*) bisexual, androgynous, hermaphrodite. ~cinslilik bisexuality, androgyny, hermaphroditism ~çenekliler, (*bot.*) dicotyledons. ~çenetli, (*bio.* bivalve. ~değerli(lik), (*chem.*) divalen·t/(-ce) (*phil.*) ambivalen·t/(-ce). ~dilli, (*ling.*) bilingual ~düzlemli, (*math.*) dihedral. ~eksenli, (*math. eng.*) biaxial. ~eşeyli = ~CİNSLİ. ~evcikli, (*bot.* dioecious. ~fazlı, (*phys.*) diphase. ~hörgüçlü, ~ deve, (*zoo.*) bactrian camel. ~kanatlılar, (*ent.* Diptera. ~karınlı, (*bio.*) digastric, biventral ~katlı, (*arch.*) duplex, maisonette. ~kollu, (*bot.* dichotomous. ~kutuplu, (*phys.*) *a.* dipolar: ~ dipole. ~l, dual. ~lem, (*phil.*) dilemma. ~leme *vn.*, (*ling.*) reduplication. ~lemek (-i), make two double; get a second one. ~leşmek, *vi.* become two/double.

ikili Double, dual, twin-; pair; having two (units parts, etc.); (*gamb.*) deuce, the two (dice, cards etc.); (*adm.*) bilateral, bipartite; (*math.*) binary (*phil.*) dichotomic; (*phys.*) stereo-; (*mus.*) duo. ~ bisiklet/çifteker, (*sp.*) tandem: ~ çatı, syncretism ~ dans, (*mus.*) pas de deux: ~ kapacık/kapakçık (*bio.*) bicuspid/mitral valve: ~ konuşma, (*th.* dialogue: ~ kök, (*ling.*) root for both noun and verb: ~ oynamak, play a double game; run with the hare and hunt with the hounds: ~ oyun, (*th.* duologue: ~ ünlü, (*ling.*) diphthong.

iki-lik Consisting of two (units); costing two (units) division, difference; duality; (*mus.*) half-note ~llik, duality.

ikinci (2.) Second; secondary. ~ balkon, (*th.*) upper circle: ~ basım/baskı, (*pub.*) second edition: ~ dizinden, secondary: ~ pilot, (*aer.*) co-pilot: ~ rol (*th.*) secondary part: ~ üstenci, subcontractor.

ikinci·l Secondary; subsidiary; (*ind.*) by(e): ~ yapı secondary structure: ~ yapımlılar, by-products: ~ yarı (*sp.*) second half. ~zar, (*bot.*) endocarp.

ikindi Afternoon (prayer time). ~ kahvaltısı, ligh afternoon refreshment: ~den sonra dükkân açmak undertake stg. when it is too late. ~yin, in the afternoon.

ikiodaklı (*phys.*) Bifocal.

ikir·cik/ ~cim(lik) Hesitation. ~ciklenmek, *vi* hesitate. ~cikli/~cimli, hesitant. ~cil, (*phil.* equivocal, ambiguous.

ikişekilli(lik) (*chem.*) Dimorph·ous/(-ism).

ikişer Two each; two at a time. ~ ~, two by two: ~ koşmak, harness a pair of horses/oxen (to cart): ~ ~ yürümek, march two abreast: ~ olm.

be in twos: ~ **üçer**, in twos and threes. ~ **li**, (*phys.*) pairwise.

iki·taraflı/ ~ **yanlı/** ~ **yönlü** (*adm.*) Bilateral. ~ **telli**, (*mus.*) two-stringed (instrument). ~ **terimli**, (*math.*) binomial. ~ **valanslı**, (*chem.*) bi-/di·valent. ~ **yaşayışlı**, (*zoo.*) amphibian. ~ **yıllık**, (*bot.*) biennial. ~ **yüzlü**, having two faces; (*tex.*) double-faced; (*fig.*) double-faced, double-dealer, hypocrite: ~ **bir kılıçtır**, it cuts both ways. ~ **yüzlüce**, ~ **söz**, cant, hypocrisy. ~ **yüzlülük**, (*fig.*) double-dealing, hypocrisy.

ikiz *n.* Twin(s). ~ + , *a.* Twin; twinned; (*eng.*) dual: ~ **doğuran**, (*bio.*) biparous: ~ **doğurmak**, give birth to twins; (*fig.*) meet with much trouble: ~ **ler (burcu)**, (*ast.*) Gemini.

ikiz·anlam (*phil.*) Amphibology, ambiguity. ~ **kenar**, (*math.*) equilateral: ~ **üçgen**, isosceles triangle: ~ **yamuk**, equilateral trapezium. ~ **leme** = İKİLEME. ~ **leşme**, gemination. ~ **li**, having twins; double; having two handles; (*phil.*) ambiguous. ~ **lilik**, ambiguity. ~ **uzay**, (*phys.*) dual.

iklim (*geo.*) Region, country; climate. ~ **e alış(tır)ma**, acclimatization. ~ **bilim**, climatology. ~ **leme**, ~ **aygıtı**, air-conditioning system: ~ **çalkantısı**, fluctuation in climate: ~ **kuşakları**, (*geo.*) climatic zones. ~ **sel**, climatic.

ikmali Completion. ~ **efradı**, (*mil.*) draft, replacements: ~ **etm.**, complete, finish: ~ **hatları**, (*mil.*) reinforcement/supply lines: ~ **imtihanı**, (*ed.*) repeat examination: ~ **inşaatı**, (*arch.*) extension: ~ **kolları**, (*mil.*) supply columns: ~ **e kalmak**, (*ed.*) have to repeat an examination. ~ **ci**, pupil who must repeat an examination.

ikna¹ ~ **etm.**, convince, satisfy, persuade: ~ **olm.**, be convinced/satisfied.

ikon (*rel.*, *art.*) Icon.

ikrah Disgust, loathing. ~ **etm.**, loathe. ~ **lık**, (*col.*) loathing: ~ **getirmek**, begin to loathe.

ikram Showing honour/respect (to guests); kindness; gift; (*fin.*) discount, reduction. ~ **etm.**, show honour to; give (gifts); offer stg.; (*fin.*) make a reduction.

ikram·cı Bountiful, generous; hospitable. ~ **iye**, bonus, gratuity; premium; lottery prize.

ikrar Declaration; confession; acknowledgement. ~ **etm.**, confess, acknowledge: ~ **vermek**, (*obs.*) join a TARİKAT.

ikraz Loan. ~ **etm.**, lend money.

iksa (*arch.*) Cladding; braced structure.

iksir Elixir; magical substance; (*med.*) cordial.

ikt. = İKTİSAT.

iktibas (*lit.*) Quotation; extract; adaptation. ~ **etm.**, quote; adapt.

iktidar Ability, capacity; power, control. ~ **mevkii**, (*pol.*) position of power: ~ **olm.**, (*pol.*) come to power: ~ **(partisi)**, (*pol.*) party in power, government: ~ **vermek**, enable: ~ **da bulunmak/olm.**, (*pol.*) be in power: ~ **ı olm.**, be capable of; be able to do.

iktidar·lı Capable; competent. ~ **sız**, incapable; (*bio.*) impotent. ~ **sızlık**, incapacity; impotence.

iktifa ~ **etm. (-le)**, content o.s. with; be satisfied.

iktiran A coming together, being joined; (*ast.*) conjunction.

iktisad- = İKTİSAT. ~ **i**, economic; financial; economical: ~ **İşbirliği ve Gelişme/Kalkınma Teşkilatı**, (*fin.*) Organization for Economic Cooperation and Development. ~ **iyat**¹, economic state (of a country).

iktisaᵖᵇ¹ Acquisition. ~ **etm.**, acquire.

iktisaᵗᵈ¹ Economy; political economy. ~ **bilimi**, economics: ~ **etm./yapmak**, economise. ~ **çı**, economist.

iktiyoloji Ichthyology.

iktiza Necessity, requirement. ~ **etm.**, be requisite.

İKTÖK = İNGİLTERE KIBRIS TÜRK ÖRGÜTLERİ KONSEYİ.

il (*geo.*) Country; province; people; (*adm.*) vilayet. ~ + , *a.* Provincial: ~ **meclis//merkezi**, provincial council//capital.

il. = İLGEÇ.

-il-/-ıl-/-ul-/-ül- *v. suf.* [149] *Forming the passive voice* [SEVİLMEK; SATILMAK; BOZULMAK; GÖRÜLMEK].

ila *prep.* [95] To, up to; until. ~ **ahiri**, and so on; et cetera: ~ **nihaye**, to the end.

ila¹çᶜ¹ (*med.*) Remedy, cure; medicine, drug; chemical (substance); (*fig.*) means, device. ~ **dolap/sandığı**, medicine chest: ~ **için** . . . **yok**, nothing at all: ~ **kapsülü**, capsule: ~ **kılavuz/ kitabı**, pharmacopeia: ~ **vermek**, administer medicine: ~ **tutkunu/** ~ **lara tutkun**, drug addict.

ilaç·bilim Pharmacology. ~ **lamak (-i)**, treat/spray with chemicals; medicate; disinfect. ~ **lanmak**, *vp.* ~ **lı**, containing medicine/chemical; medicated; disinfected. ~ **sız**, incurable.

ilah (*rel.*, *myth.*) God; deity. ~ **e**, goddess. ~ **i**¹, *n.* hymn, chant: *int.* strange!, wonderful! ~ **i**², *a.* divine. ~ **iyat**¹, theology. ~ **iyatçı**, theologian. ~ **laştırmak (-i)**, deify.

ilam (*leg.*) Sentence; judicial decree; (*adm.*) official decision. ~ **etm.**, notify officially.

ilamaşallah *adv.* For ever. *int.* = MAŞALLAH.

ilan Declaration, notice, announcement; proclamation; (*pub.*) advertisement; (*med.*) bulletin. ~ **acentesi**, advertising agency: ~ **etm.**, declare, proclaim, announce; advertise: ~ **tahtası**, notice-/ billboard: ~ **yapıştırmak yasaktır!**, stick no bills!: ~ **yazarı**, copy-writer: ~ **ı aşk etm. (-e)**, declare one's love to s.o. ~ **cılık**, publicity, advertising.

ilarya (*ich.*) Fry of grey mullet.

ilave Addition; excess; extra; (*pub.*) appendix; supplement; postscript. ~ **etm. (-e)**, add to: ~ **olarak/** ~ **ten**, in addition. ~ **li**, having an addition/ supplement.

il·bay (*adm.*) Governor; = VALİ. ~ **çe**, administrative district. ~ **çebay** = KAYMAKAM. ~ **deş**, fellow-countryman.

ile/ilen/-le/-la/-yle/-yla [85, 90] With [KALEMLE]; by [UÇAKLA]; for [PARA İLE]; by [KİLO İLE]; and [BENİMLE REFİKAM]. *With an abstract noun it forms an adverb* [korkuyla, fearfully; tereddütle, hesitantly]. ~ **beraber**, at the moment when; apart from; although; ~ **birlikte**, including . . . .

ilelebet For ever.

ilen·¹çᶜ¹ Curse. ~ **me**, *vn.* cursing. ~ **mek (-e)**, curse s.o.

ilerde(n) = İLERİ.

ileri *n.* Forward part; front; future. *a.* Advanced; progressive; in advance; forward; in front; future; fast (clock). *adv.* Forward; to the front. ~!, (*mil.*) at them!, charge!: ~ **almak**, (*adm.*) promote s.o.; put forward (clock): ~ **araştırmalar**, (*ed.*) advanced studies/research: ~ **bak!**, (*mil.*) eyes front!: ~ **geçmek**, pass forward; move to the front: ~ **gelenler**, leaders, notables, important people: ~ **gelmek**, come forward; make progress, surpass; **(-den)**, arise/result from, be caused by: ~ **geri**, back and forth: ~ **geri konuşmak/laflar etm.**, talk aggressively/out of place: ~ **geri sözler**, unseemly/ inappropriate words: ~ **gitmek/varmak**, go too far, say too much: ~ **sürmek**, drive forward; promote s.o.; assert, put forward (proposal/excuse/ reason); insist obstinately: ~ **de**, in front; in the future: ~ **sine gitmek (-in)**, follow up a matter; go deeply into stg.: ~ **sini gerisini düşünmek/ hesaplamak**, take everything into consideration; weigh up all the consequences.

iler·ici(lik) Progressiv·ist/(-ism). ~ **lek**, progressive. ~ **leme**, *vn.*; progress; (*min.*) heading. ~ **lemek**, *vi.* advance, proceed, go ahead; progress; be promoted. ~ **lemiş**, *a.* advanced; (*med.*) acute. ~ **letmek (-i)**, *vc.* ~ **leyici**, advancing; progressive: ~ **benzeşme**, (*ling.*) progressive assimilation (of sounds).

ilet·i Message; (*adm.*) announcement; declaration. ~ **ici(lik)**, (*el.*) conduct·ing/(-ance). ~ **ilmek**, *vp.* be conducted/transmitted/transferred. ~ **im**, (*el.*, *bio.*) conduction; (*ling.*) one-sided communication. ~ **işim**, (*rad.*) communication, transmission. ~ **ken**, conductive; conductor; conducting; trans- mitting: ~ **damarlar**, (*bot.*) conductor ducts: ~ **doku**, (*bot.*) conductive tissue. ~ **kenlik**, con- ductance; conduction; conductivity. ~ **ki**, (*math.*) protractor. ~ **me**, *vn.*: ~ **kuşağı**, (*ind.*) conveyor belt: ~ **teli**, (*el.*) lead-in wire. ~ **mek (-i, -e)**, send; carry off; conduct; transmit, transfer. ~ **mez**, (*el.*) non-conducting.

ilga (*leg.*) Abolition, annulment. ~ **etm.**, abolish, annul, extinguish.

ilge¹çᶜⁱ (*ling.*) Postposition, particle. ~ **ten ad//sıfat**, postposition/particle as noun//adjective. ~ **li**, con- taining a postposition: ~ **tümleç**, complement containing a postposition.

ilgi Relation, reference; connection, attachment; interest; (*chem.*) affinity. ~ **çekici/değer**, attractive, interesting: ~ **çekmek**, draw attention: ~ **duymak**, give/attach importance to: ~ **eki**, (*ling.*) pro- nominal/'mixed' suffix (-Kİ): ~ **fişi**, reference card: ~ **göstermek**, show interest in: ~ **kurmak**, connect; establish relations: ~ **toplamak**, attract attention: ~ **de**, in reference: ~ **si olmuş**, involved: ~ **sini çekmek (-in)**, attract s.o.'s attention: ~ **sini kesmek (-le)**, break one's connection with: ~ **ye değer**, worthy of attention.

ilgi·çliiğne (*dial.*) Thumb-tack, ~ **lendirmek (-i, -e)**, be of interest to; concern. ~ **lenmek (-le)**, be(come) interested; pay/show attention to. ~ **li**, interested; connected with; concerning, reference . . .: ~ **ler**, (*leg.*) interested parties: ~ **lere**, to whom it may concern: ~ **ye danışmaksızın**, on one's own initiative. ~ **lilik**, interest; connection. ~ **nç**,

interesting, picturesque; engrossing. ~ **nlik**, (*phys.*) affinity. ~ **siz**, apathetic, indifferent. ~ **sizlik** apathy, indifference.

ilhak¹ Annexation. ~ **etm.**, annex.

ilham Inspiration, brainwave. ~ **etm.**, inspire.

ilhan (*his.*) Prince, subordinate ruler (to the Great Khan). ~ **lık**, Ilkhanate.

ili¹kᵍⁱ ¹ *n.* (*bio.*) Marrow. *a.* Delicious. ~ **gibi**, tasty, appetizing: ~ **ine geçmek/işlemek**, (cold, etc.) penetrate to the marrow; (*fig.*) make a great impression: ~ **ine kadar ıslanmak**, be soaked to the skin: ~ **ini kurutmak**, wear s.o. out. ~ **balığı**ⁿⁱ (*ich.*) bitterling. ~ **li¹**, containing marrow. ~ **siz¹**, without marrow.

ili¹kᵍⁱ ² (*mod.*) Loop (for hook, etc.); buttonhole: ~ **lemek (-i)**, button stg. (up); fasten with a hook: ~ **lenmek**, *vp.* be buttoned//hooked up. ~ **li²**, buttoned; hooked. ~ **siz²**, unbuttoned.

il¹imᵐⁱ Knowledge, science. ~ **başka sanat başka**, science and art are two different things: ~ **ve amel**, theory and practice; ~ **yaymak**, spread knowledge: ~ **ini almak**, learn stg. thoroughly.

iline¹kᵍⁱ (*phil.*) Accident. ~ **li**/~ **sel**, accidental.

ilin·ge (*math.*) Topology. ~ **ti**, connection, relation; (*tex.*) tacking; knot; anxiety. ~ **tili**, connected; related; anxious.

ilişi¹kᵍⁱ *n.* Connection, relation, bond; impediment; obligation. *a.* Connected; relative; related; attached; enclosed (herewith). ~ **i bulunmak/olm.**, be con- nected: ~ **i kalmamak**, (matter) be settled; **(-le)** sever one's connection with, have no further interest in: ~ **ini kesmek (-le)**, sever one's connec- tion with; discharge/dismiss s.o.

ilişik·li Connected, related. ~ **lik**, relationship. ~ **siz**, unconnected, unrelated; unattached, free.

iliş·ilmek (-e) *vp.* ~ **ki**, relation, connection; con- tact; affinity, bond: ~ **kurmak**, connect; make contact: ~ **leri kesmek (-le)**, break with, boycott. ~ **kili**, related, connected. ~ **kin**, belonging to, connected with. ~ **kinlik**, a belonging; connection ~ **kisiz**, unrelated, unconnected. ~ **mek (-e)**, *vt.* touch; interfere with: *vi.* be fastened to; be caught on; hold on lightly to; sit uncomfortably (on the edge of stg.); stay a short while; disagree, quarrel. ~ **tirilmek (-e)**, *vp.* ~ **tirmek (-i, -e)**, *vc.* attach, affix; (*tex.*) baste.

ilk¹ First, initial; (*ed.*) primary; beginning. ~ **ağızda**, at the first attempt; at the first shot: ~ **baskı**, (*pub.*) first edition: ~ ÇAĞ: ~ **çıkış**, (*th.*, *etc.*) début: ~ **defa (olarak)**, (for) the first time: ~ DEVRE: ~ **eğitim**, primary education: ~ **elde**, in the first place: ~ **giren son çıkar kaidesi**, (*adm.*) first in last out principle: ~ **giriş**, (*soc.*) début: ~ **görünüş**, (*ast.*) apparition: ~ **görüşte**, at first sight: ~ **göz ağrısı**, one's first child//love//interest: ~ **hamlede**, at the first onslaught; at the first 'go': ~ **madde/özdek**, primary/raw material: ~ OKUL: ~ **oynatım/oyun**, (*cin.*) gala performance; première. ~ ÖĞRETİM: ~ **önce**, first of all; to begin with: ~ **soruşturma/ tahkikat**, (*leg.*) preliminary examination, inquiry: ~ **yardım**, (*med.*) first-aid (station): ~ **yargılık**, (*leg.*) court of first instance: ~ **yarı**, (*sp.*) first half: ~ **yayım** = ~ BASKI.

ilka Throwing/dropping into; suggestion. ~ **etm.**, suggest.

ilkah (*bio.*) Fertilization; insemination.

ilk·ağız (*zoo.*) Blastopore. ~**bahar**, (*ast.*) spring: ~ **ılımı**, vernal equinox. ~**çağ**, (*his.*) antiquity. ~**devre**, (*bio.*) prophase. ~**dördün**, (*ast.*) (moon's) first quarter.

ilke Element; principle, basis.

ilkel Elementary, primary; fundamental; initial; primitive. ~ **fonksiyon**, (*math.*) integral function: ~ **hız**, (*phys.*) initial speed: ~ **memeliler**, (*zoo.*) monotremes: ~ **renkler**, (*phys.*) primary colours: ~ **toplum**, (*soc.*) non-literate/primitive society: ~**ler**, (*art.*) primitives.

ilkel·ciler (*art.*) Modern primitives. ~**cilik**, (*art.*) primitivism. ~**kuş**, (*geol.*, *orn.*) archaeopteryx. ~**leşmek**, *vi.* return to its primary state. ~**leştirmek** (-i), *vc.* ~**lik**, primitiveness.

ilk·girişim Initiative. ~**in**, the first; in the first place. ~**kânun**, (*obs.*) December. ~**okul**, (*ed.*) primary school. ~**öğretim**, (*ed.*) primary education. ~**önce**, first of all, first. ~**örnek**, (*phil.*) archetype; (*ind.*) prototype. ~**sav(lı)**, (*phil.*) axiom(atic). ~**sezi**, (*phil.*) apprehension; first impression. ~**sizlik**, (*phil.*) eternity in the past. ~**söz**, (*pub.*) foreword, preface. ~**teşrin**, (*obs.*) October. ~**yaz**, (*ast.*) spring. ~**yazı**, (*leg.*) original (document).

illa/illaki/ille In any case, whatever happens; or else, if not; absolutely, especially. ~ **ve lakin**, but on the other hand.

illallah *int.* (*Annoyance, disgust.*) That will do! ~ (-den), I'm sick to death of . . .!

illet[i] (*med.*) Disease, illness; defect; (*phil.*) cause, reason. ~ **edinmek**, acquire an annoying habit. ~**li**, ill, diseased; defective; with annoying habits. ~**siz**, without cause.

illi Causal. ~**yet**, reason; causality.

ilme'k[gi 1] *n.* = İLMİK.

ilmek[2] (-i, -e) *v.* Tie loosely; tie knots (of carpet); touch. **iler tutar yeri kalmamak/olmamak**, be done for; be in a bad state.

ilm- = İLİM. ~**en**, scientifically; in scholarly fashion. ~**i**, scientific; connected with knowledge. ~ **ihal**[i], (*rel.*, *ed.*) book for teaching the elements of religion. ~ **iye**, Muslim religious teachers.

ilmi'k[gi] Knot, loop, bow; noose; slip-knot. ~ **atmak**, make a loop/knot. ~**lemek** (-i), tie loosely; make a loop. ~**lenmek**, *imp. v.* be tied up. ~**li**, loosely tied.

ilmühaber Identity papers; certificate; receipt.

-ilti/-ıltı/-ultu/-ültü *n. suf.* (*ech.*) The sound of . . . [İNİLTİ; VIZILTI; UĞULTU; GÜRÜLTÜ].

iltibas Confusion of one word, etc., with another; ambiguity. ~**a mahal kalmamak için**, to avoid all ambiguity. ~**a yol açmak**, cause confusion. ~**lı**, equivocal.

iltica Refuge. ~ **etm.** (-e), take refuge in.

iltifat[i] Courteous/kind treatment; favour; (*ling.*) apostrophe. ~ **etm.**, take notice of; greet; treat with kindness. ~**çı**, kind; affable.

iltihak[i] Joining; attaching o.s. ~ **etm.**, join; connect o.s. with; adhere to.

iltiha'p[bı] (*bio.*) Inflammation. ~**lanmak**, *vi.* become inflamed. ~**lı**, (*med.*) inflamed, angry.

iltimas Favouritism, patronage. ~ **etm.**, look after, protect: ~**ı olm.**, be favoured/protected. ~**çı**, protector, patron, backer. ~**çılık**, favouritism. ~**lı**, having a backer, favoured.

iltisak[i] Junction; contiguity; adhesion. ~ **noktası**, (*eng.*) junction. ~**i**, (*ling.*) agglutinative.

iltizam Looking after s.o.'s interests; favour; (*fin.*) farming of public revenues. ~ **cı**, s.o. who farms the revenues. ~**i**, intentionally, knowingly.

ilzam Silencing s.o. by argument.

im Meaningful sign/action; letter, symbol; (*ling.*) diacritical mark. ~ **lambası**, signal lamp: ~ **yorumlaması**, sign interpretation.

-im[1]/-ım/-um/-üm *a./n. suf.* [39] *1st pers. sing. possessive* [BENİM KİTABIM].

-im[2]/-ım/-um/-üm *v. suf.* [96] *1st pers. sing.* [GELİRİM; GELİYORUM].

-im[3]/-ım/-um/-üm *n. suf.* [224] *Often denoting a single action* [GÖZETİM; YATIRIM; ÖLÜM].

ima Allusion, hint, suggestion. ~ **etm.**, allude to, hint at.

imaj (*cin.*) Image; photograph, picture.

imal[i] Manufacture, production, making. ~ **etm.**, make, manufacture, produce, prepare. ~**at**[ı], manufactured goods; production: ~ **malzemesi**, capital goods; production: ~ **sanayii**, production industry. ~**atçı**, manufacturer, producer. ~**athane**, factory, workshop.

imale Bending, inclining; (*lit.*) pronouncing short vowels as long. ~ **etm.**, incline; persuade, convince.

imalı Alluding to; hinting at, implying.

imam (*rel.*) Leader (in public worship); imam. ~ **evinden aş ölü gözünden yaş**, as well expect tears from a corpse as food from an imam (reputedly very stingy): ~ **kayığı**, (*sl.*) coffin: ~ **nikâhı**, religious wedding ceremony (not recognized by Tk. law): ~ **osurursa cemaat sıçar**, (*vulg.*) leaders must avoid setting a bad example: ~ **suyu**, (*sl.*) raki.

imam·bayıldı (*cul.*) Stuffed aubergines cooked in oil. ~**e**, (*rel.*) stem of a rosary; pipe mouthpiece; turban. ~**et**[i]/ ~ **lık**, (*rel.*) qualities/office/duties of imam. ~**evi**[ni], (*col.*) woman's prison. ~ **zade**, son of an imam.

iman (*rel.*) Belief, faith, creed, religion. ~ **etm.**, have faith in God/Muslim tenets: ~ **getirmek** (-e), believe in: ~ **ikrarı**, confession of faith: ~ **tahtası**, (*col.*) breastbone: ~**a gelmek**, (*rel.*) be converted to Islam; (*fig.*) see reason: ~**a getirmek**, (*rel.*) convert to Islam; (*fig.*) make s.o. see reason: ~**ı ağlamak/ gevremek**, (*sl.*) suffer, undergo hardship: ~**ı yok**, (*term of abuse*): ~ **ım!**, *int.* (*sl.*) hey!; mate!: ~**ına kadar**, (*col.*) to the utmost degree.

iman·lı Having faith, religious; believer. ~**sız**, unbelieving, atheist; cruel, inhuman: ~ **gitmek**, die an unbeliever: ~ **peynir**, (*cul.*) fatless cheese. ~**sızlık**, disbelief, atheism.

imar Improvement by cultivation/building. ~ **Bakan(lığ)ı**, (*adm.*) Minis·ter/(-try) of Public Works: ~ **etm.**, improve, develop; render prosperous: ~ **ve İskân Bakan(lığ)ı,** (*adm.*) Minis·ter/(-try) of Construction and Housing.

imar·et(hane) Hospice; kitchen distributing food to the poor: ~ **çorbası,** soup so distributed; stg. for nothing. ~ **lık,** property development.

imbat¹ (*met.*) Cool Aegean summer sea-breeze.

im·biçimi (*phil.*) Sign-type. ~ **bilim,** semiotics.

imbiˡkᵍⁱ (*chem.*) Retort, still; condenser. ~ **etm./** ~ **ten çekmek,** distil.

imbisat¹ Act of spreading/expanding; dilatation. ~ **etm.,** be dilated/expanded/spread out; open out; be at one's ease: ~ **kabı,** (*phys.*) expansion chamber.

imdaˡtᵈ¹ Help, assistance, reinforcement. ~ +, *a.* Emergency-; distress-; breakdown-: ~ **çağırış//frekansı,** (*rad.*) distress call//frequency: ~ **etm./** ~ **a yetişmek,** come to s.o.'s help; reinforce: ~ **freni,** (*rly.*) communication cord, emergency brake: ~ **işareti,** (*rad.*) distress signal: ~ **motorbotu,** (*naut.*) crashboat.

imdi Now; in a short time; thus; and so.

imece (*soc.*) Work done by and for the community.

imek = ERMEK¹.

imge (*psy.*) Image; imagination; (*lit.*) fiction. ~ **gücü,** imaginative power: ~ **den,** imaginative.

imge·ci(lik) (*lit.*) Imag·ist/(-ism). ~ **lem(e),** imagination; imagining. ~ **lemek (-i),** imagine stg. ~ **sel,** imaginary; (*lit.*) fictional.

imha Destruction; annihilation; effacement. ~ **ateşi,** (*mil.*) annihilating fire: ~ **etm.,** destroy; annihilate; obliterate, cancel.

imiˡkᵍⁱ (*bio.*) Soft point on baby's skull, fontanel.

imiş/-ymiş/-ymış/-ymuş/-ymüş [101, 122] *Inferential present//past tense, with personal suffixes.* Am/is/are/was/were said//supposed to be. = ERMEK¹.

-imiz/-ımız/-umuz/-ümüz *n. suf.* [39] Our [EVİMİZ].

imkân Possibility; practicability. ~ **dahil/nispetinde,** within the bounds of possibility, as far as possible: ~ **vermek,** make possible; give s.o. a chance: ~ ı **yok,** it is impossible: ~ **lar,** means, facilities. ~ **lı,** possible. ~ **sız(lık),** impossi·ble/(-bility).

imla Action of filling; (*eng.*) fill, embankment; (*ling.*) spelling, orthography; (*ed.*) dictation. ~ **etm.,** fill; dictate: ~ **ya gelmemek,** *vi.* be unintelligible; (*fig.*) be incorrigible.

im·leˡçᶜⁱ (*phys.*) Auto-recording device. ~ **lemek (-i),** make a mark; hint at.

immoral(izm) Immoral(ity).

imparator (*adm.*) Emperor. ~ **içe,** empress. ~ **luk,** empire. ~ **otuⁿᵘ,** (*bot.*) masterwort.

im·pedans (*el.*) Impedance. ~ **pregnasyon,** (*geol.*) impregnation. ~ **presario** (*th.*) impresario.

imren Desire, envy, covetousness. ~ **ce,** stg. coveted; s.o. envied. ~ **dirmek (-i, -e),** arouse s.o.'s envy for stg. ~ **ilmek (-e),** *imp. v.* be desired. ~ **me/** ~ **ti,** *vn.* desire, envy. ~ **mek (-e),** desire/covet stg.

İmroz (*geo.*) Island of Imbros.

imsakⁱ (*rel.*) Fasting; abstention; abstinence; hour at which Ramadan fast begins each day. ~ **iye,** time-table for Ramadan fasting.

-imse-/-ımsa-/-umsa-/-ümse- *v. suf.* [230] Regard/consider [ÇOĞUMSAMAK].

imsel Semiotic. ~ **mantık,** (*phil.*) symbolic logic.

-(i)msi/-(ı)msı/-(u)msu/-(ü)msü *a./n. suf.* [58] Like, resembling; somewhat, -ish [ESMERİMSİ; MAVİMSİ; ÇINARIMSI].

-(i)mt(ı)rak/-(ı)mt(ı)rak *a. suf.* [58] Like, resembling; -ish [MAVİMTRAK; EKŞİMTRAK; BEYAZIMT(I)RAK].

imtihan (*ed.*) Exam(ination); trial, test. ~ **etm.,** examine s.o.: ~ **olm.,** be examined: ~ **vermek,** pass an exam; survive a test: ~ **a çekmek,** examine s.o. thoroughly: ~ **a girmek,** sit for an exam: ~ **a hazırlamak,** prepare/coach s.o. for an exam.

imtina¹ Avoidance; refusal. ~ **etm.,** avoid; refuse.

imtisal Conforming; complying. ~ **etm.,** conform to; comply with.

imtisas Sucking, absorption. ~ **etm.,** be absorbed.

imtiyaz Distinction; (*leg.*) privilege; (*fin.*) franchise, concession; (*adm.*) autonomy. ~ **sahibi,** (*fin.*) concessionaire; privileged person.

imtizaˡçᶜⁱ Blending; fitting together; combining. ~ **etm. (-le),** blend with, get on well with. ~ **sızlık,** (*leg.*) incompatibility.

imyaz·ar Stenographer. ~ **ım,** stenography.

imza Signature; autograph; (*pub.*) by-line. ~ **atmak (-e)/etm. (-i),** sign stg.: ~ **basmak,** append a signature: ~ **günü,** (*pub.*) autographing day: ~ **sahibi,** signatory; (*pub.*) author of a signed article/having a by-line: ~ **toplamak,** (*pol.*) collect signatures (for petitions): ~ **sını yalamak,** dishonour one's signature.

imza·lamak (-i) Sign, autograph; (*leg.*) endorse. ~ **lanmak,** *vp.* ~ **latmak (-i, -e),** *vc.* ~ **layan,** signatory. ~ **lı,** signed; autographed. ~ **sız,** unsigned; (*pub.*) anonymous.

in¹ *n.* (Animal's) den/lair; cave. ~ **açmak,** burrow: ~ **balığı,** (*ich.*) cave fish: ~ **gibi,** dark and narrow: ~ **ine girmek,** (fox) go to earth.

in² *n.* Human being. ~ **cin top oynuyor/yok,** there's not a soul there; a deserted place: ~ **misin cin misin nesin!,** whatever you are — man or spirit!

İn. = (*ch.s.*) İNDİYUM. ~ **Eml. D.** = İNŞAAT VE EMLAK DAİRESİ.

-in¹/-ın/-un/-ün *n. suf.* [28] *Forming the genitive case.* Of; -'s; -s': [kızın eli, the girl's hand; adamların işi, the men's work; evin bahçesi, the garden of the house]. ~ **hali,** (*ling.*) genitive/possessive case.

-in²/-ın/-un/-ün *n. suf.* [39] *2nd. pers. sing. possessive.* Thy; your: [kızın, your daughter; evin, your house].

-in³/-ın/-un/-ün *n. suf.* [225] *Forming deverbal nouns* [EKİN; BASIN].

-in⁴/-ın/-un/-ün *adv. suf.* [22, 201] *Forming adverbs from nouns* [ÖRNEĞİN; YAZIN; GÜZÜN; GECELEYİN].

-in-⁵/-ın-/-un-/-ün-/-n- *v. suf.* [149] *Forming* (1) *the reflexive verb, actions done to or for o.s.* [EDİNMEK; GİYİNMEK; YIKANMAK]: (2) *the passive voice* [KAPANMAK; YIKANMAK].

inad- = İNAT. ~ **ına,** out of obstinacy/contrariness; it would just happen that . . .; as luck would have it . . .: ~ **yapmak (-in),** do stg. just to spite s.o.

inaˡkᵍⁱ Dogma. ~ **çı(lık),** dogmat·ist/(-ism). ~ **sal,** dogmatic.

inal S.o. who is trusted; confidant(e).

inam Stg. left in trust for safe-keeping.

inambu (*orn.*) Red-winged tinamou.

inan Belief; faith, trust. ~ **bağı**, belief: ~ **olsun!**, believe me!; rest assured that . . .!

inan·ca (*fin.*) Guarantee, security, bond-note. ~**calı** (**-i**), guarantee. ~**calı**, guaranteed, confirmed. ~**cılık**, (*phil.*) fideism. ~**'çcı**, belief, confidence, trust. ~**çlı**, believing, trusting: ~ **işlem**, (*fin.*) credit operation. ~**çsız**, unbelieving, sceptical. ~**çsızlık**, disbelief, scepticism. ~**dırıcı**, convincing, persuasive. ~**dırıcılık**, persuasiveness. ~**dırım**, (*psy.*) suggestion. ~**dırmak** (**-i, -e**), *vc.* convince; persuade. ~**ılmak** (**-e**), *imp. v.* be believable: ~**ılır**, *a.* credible; authentic: ~**ıl(a)maz**, *a.* far-fetched; incredible. ~**ış**, belief; credulity. ~**lı**, believing, faithful. ~**lılık**, a believing. ~**mak** (**-e**), believe; trust; (*rel.*) believe in; give credit to stg.: **inanma dostuna saman doldurur postuna!**, my friend has betrayed me! ~**sız**, unbelieving. ~**sızlık**, unbelief.

ina'td¹ Obstinacy; stubbornness; persistence; obstinate person. ~ **etm.**, be obstinate; persist in stg.: ~ **tuğlası**, (*ind.*) firebrick: ~**ı tutmak**, be suddenly obstinate. ~INA.

inat·çı Obstinate; pig-headed. ~**çılık**, obstinacy. ~**laşmak** (**-le**), be obstinate with each other; reach a stalemate.

inayetⁱ Kindness; favour; grace; care, effort. ~ **ola!**, may God give (you alms)!

inbilim (*geol.*) Speleology.

ince Slender; thin; fine; slight; subtle; delicate; attractive; (*phys.*) net. ~AĞRI: ~BAĞIRSAK: ~ **çalımlı**, gracious, attractive: ~ **çamur**, (*min.*) slurry: ~ **donanma**, (*his.*) light fleet: ~ **elek**, (*min.*) fine sieve: ~ **elemek**, pass through a fine sieve: ~ **eleyip sık dokumak**, be too particular; be very meticulous: ~ **ezgi fıstıkı makam**, (*mus.*) in slow time; (*fig.*) lazily and slowly, taking one's time over it: ~ **gagalı kervan çulluğu//martı**, (*orn.*) slender-billed curlew//gull: ~ **görüşlü**, sagacious: ~HASTALIK: ~, vaguely; almost imperceptibly: ~ **kesim**, (*bio.*) with finely-structured bones: ~ **kömür**, (*min.*) small coal: ~SAZ: ~ **ses**, thin/shrill voice; (*mus.*) treble voice: ~ **tabakalı**, laminated: ~ **tane(li)**, (*geol. etc.*) fine grain(ed): ~ **toz şeker**, (*cul.*) castor sugar: ~ **tutkal**, thinned glue: ~TÜY: ~ **ünlü**, (*ling.*) front vowel: ~ **yaprak**, (*bot.*) blade: ~ **zar**, film; (*bio.*) pia mater; ~**den** ~ **ye**, in fine detail, meticulously.

ince¹/-ınca/-unca/-ünce *adv. suf.* [94, 194] Along, throughout; -ways, -wise, on the part of [ENİNCE; BOYUNCA; KENDİSİNCE].

ince²/-ınca/-unca/-ünce *v. suf.* [179] *Denoting just prior action.* When; as; as soon as; (*obs.*) until. ~ **ye değin//~ye kadar//~ye dek**, until: ~**ye kadar bir hal oldum**, I had quite a job to . . ..

ince·ağrı (*med.*) Slight intermittent pain. ~**bağırsak**, (*bio.*) small intestine. ~**cik**, very fine/slender, etc.; minutely, finely. ~**hastalık**, (*med.*) tuberculosis. ~**leme**, *vn.*; examination; review; survey; exploration. ~**lemek** (**-i**), examine minutely; go into stg. thoroughly; analyse; survey; explore. ~**lenmek**, *vp.* ~**letmek** (**-i, -e**), *vc.* ~**leyici**, researcher, investigator. ~**lik**, fineness; delicacy;

accuracy; refinement, detail; subtlety; ingenuity; affability. ~**likli**, distinguished. ~**lmek**, *vi.* become fine/thin; taper; be refined/delicate; be too subtle, quibble. ~**ltici**, (paint) thinner, solvent. ~**ltmek** (**-i**), make fine/slender; refine; thin; attenuate; make fine distinctions. ~**rek**, slender, elegant; rather thin. ~**saz**, (*Or. mus.*) orchestra of stringed instruments. ~**tüy**, (*orn.*) down. ~**yağ**, (*min.*) refined oil.

inci Pearl. ~ **dizisi**, (*mod.*) string of pearls: ~ **gibi**, small, neat; very pretty (girl); very white (teeth); clean: ~ **saçmak**, speak fine words.

-(i)nci/-(ı)ncı/-uncu/-üncü *a. suf.* [82] *Forming the ordinal numbers.* -st, -nd, -rd, -th [BİRİNCİ, ALTINCI; DOKUZUNCU; YÜZÜNCÜ].

inci·balığıⁿ¹ (*ich.*) Bleak. ~**çiçeği**ⁿⁱ, (*bot.*) lily-of-the-valley.

inci'kᵍⁱ ¹ *n.* (*bio.*) Shin (bone). ~ **kemiği sıyrılmak**, bark one's shins.

inci'kᵍⁱ ² *a.* Slightly bruised/broken. *n.* Sprain; bruise.

inci'kᵍⁱ ³ *a.* ~ **boncuk**, (*pej.*) cheap costume jewellery.

İncil (*rel.*) The Gospel; the New Testament.

incinmek *vi.* Be hurt/bruised/sprained: (**-den**), be offended (at).

incir (*bot.*) Fig(-tree). ~ **çekirdeğini doldurmaz**, trifling, insignificant: ~ **dolması**, (*sl.*) testicle: ~ **eşek arısı**, (*ent.*) fig chalcid/wasp.

incir·ağacıⁿ¹ (*bot.*) Fig-tree. ~**kuşları**ⁿ¹, (*orn.*) pipits. ~**kuşu**ⁿᵘ, (*orn.*) tree pipit, beccafico. ~**lik**, fig orchard.

incitaşıⁿ¹ (*geol.*) Perlite.

incit·ici Harmful; hurtful; offending; (*fig.*) barbed. ~**me**, *vn.* hurting; offending. ~**mebeni**, (*col.*) cancer. ~**mek** (**-i**), hurt; touch; offend, vex, aggrieve.

inçⁱ (*math.*) Inch.

-inç/-ınç/-unç/ünç/-nç *a./n. suf.* [222] *Forming abstract nouns, or corresponding adjectives* [SEVİNÇ; BASINÇ; KORKUNÇ; GÜLÜNÇ; ÜŞENÇ].

inde·ks Index. ~**terminizm**, (*phil.*) indeterminism.

indi Personal; subjective; arbitrary. ~**nde**, in his opinion.

indifa¹ (*geol., med.*) Eruption. ~ **etm.**, erupt.

indigo (*chem.*) Indigo.

indikatör (*phys.*) Indicator.

indirge·'çᶜⁱ (*chem.*) Reducer. ~**me**, *vn.* (*math. chem.*) reduction. ~**mek** (**-i, -e**), reduce. ~**n**, (*chem.*) reducing (agent). ~**nir**, reducible. ~**nmek**, *vp.* ~**nmez**, irreducible. ~**yici**, reducing.

indir·ilmek *vp.* ~**im**, (*fin.*) discount, reduction, allowance: ~ **yapmak** (**-den**), give a discount. ~**imli**, reduced, at a discount. ~**imsiz**, without discount, net. ~**me**, *vn.* act of lowering; unloading (from ship, etc.); (*aer.*) landing (troops); (*fin.*) cutting, reducing. ~**mek** (**-i**), cause to descend; bring down, lower; abate; calm; give (a blow); (*fin.*) cut/lower/reduce (prices). ~**tmek** (**-i, -e**), *vc.*

indis (*math.*) Index.

individüalizm (*phil.*) Individualism.

indiyum (*chem.*) Indium.

İndonezya(lı) = ENDONEZYA(LI).

indük·le·'çᶜⁱ (*el.*) Inductor. ~**lem(e)/~siyon**,

induction: ~ **akımı**, induction current. ~ **lemek (i)**, induce. ~ **lenmek**, *vp.*

ine'çᶜⁱ (*geol.*) Syncline.

ine'kᵍⁱ (*zoo.*) Cow; (*ed. sl.*) swot; (*sl.*) motor-car; (*sl.*) loose woman; catamite. ~ **ağılı**, cowpen: ~ **ahırı**, cowshed: ~ **antilopu**, (*zoo.*) hartebeest: ~ **balığı**, (*ich.*) cowfish: ~ **çıngırağı**, cowbell: ~ **kuşları**, (*orn.*) cowbirds: ~ **tezeği**, (*agr.*) cowdung: ~ **yavrusu**, (*zoo.*) calf.

inek·ağacıⁿⁱ (*bot.*) Cow-/milk-tree. ~**çi(lik)**, dairy-farm·er/(-ing). ~**lemek**, *vi.* (*ed. sl.*) work very hard. ~**lik**, cowshed, byre; (*fig.*) stupid.

in·en = İNMEK; (*bio.*) descending. ~**er-çıkar**, (*eng.*) lift.

ineze = ENEZE.

infaz (*leg.*) Execution (of an order), enforcement. ~ **etm.**, carry out, enforce, execute.

infeksiyon (*med.*) Infection.

infialⁱ Annoyance; anger, indignation.

infilakⁱ Explosion, blast. ~ **etm.**, *vi.* burst, explode, blow up, detonate: ~**i önleyici**, explosion inhibitor.

infinitezimalⁱ (*math.*) Infinitesimal.

infira'tᵈ¹ (*pol.*) Isolation. ~ **etm.**, isolate. ~**çı**, isolationist.

infisah Disintegration; (*adm.*) dissolution. ~ **etm.**, be dissolved.

İng. = İNGİLİZ; İNGİLİZCE(DEN); İNGİLTERE.

İngiliz *n.* Englishman. ~ +, *a.* English; British: ~ **altını**, (*fin.*) gold sovereign: ~ **açkı/anahtarı**, (*eng.*) wrench: ~ **arması**, (*sl.*) scolding: ~ **borusu**, (*mus.*) cor anglais: ~ **çimi**, (*bot.*) rye-grass: ~ **dostu**, Anglophile: ~ **düşmanı**, Anglophobe: ~ **kaymağı**, (*cul.*) clotted cream: ~ **Kültür Heyeti**, the British Council: ~ **(lirası)**, (*fin.*) pound sterling: ~ **madeni**, (*min.*) britannia metal: ~ **mili**, (*math.*) mile: ~ **sicimi**, very strong string: ~ **tuzu**, (*med.*) Epsom salts: ~ **yakısı**, (*med.*) court plaster.

İngiliz·ce (*ling.*) English language: ~ **bildiği vehmindedir**, he is under the illusion that he knows English: ~ **konuşan**, (*ling.*) Anglophone: ~ **olarak**, in English: ~ **öğretmeni**, English-language teacher: ~ **söylemek**, say stg. in English: ~**yi vermek**, give English lessons; teach English (in a school, etc.): ~**yi yutmuş**, he knows English perfectly. ~**leştirmek (-i)**, anglicize.

İngiltere (*geo.*) England; (*pol.*) Britain.

ingin¹ *n.* (*med.*) Catarrh.

ingin² *a.* Low; not high. ~**lik**, lowness; (*fig.*) decline; (*fin.*) deflation.

inha (*adm.*) Recommendation for appointment/promotion. ~ **etm.**, recommend for appointment; promote.

inhidam (*arch.*) Falling down, collapse; demolishing.

inhilalⁱ Being undone/solved/dissolved; disintegration; (*adm.*) being vacant; (*psy.*) dissociation. ~ **etm.**, be dissolved/decomposed; (*adm.*) become vacant.

inhimakⁱ Addiction. ~ **etm.**, become addicted to stg.

inhina Curvature, bending; (*aer.*) sweep; (*fig.*) abasement.

inhiraf Deviation, aberration. ~ **etm.**, deviate.

inhisar Limitation, restriction; (*fin.*) monopoly. ~ **etm. (-e)**, be restricted to: ~**a almak (-i)**, monopolize: ~**ında olm.**, be monopolized by, be the monopoly of: ~**lar idaresi**, (*adm.*) monopolies directorate.

inhitatⁱ Decline; degradation; degeneration.

ini'kᵍⁱ¹ *n.* (*zoo.*) Cub, pup; (*col.*) = ENİK.

ini'kᵍⁱ² *a.* Pulled down, lowered (blind); deflated; downcast (eyes). ~ **deniz**, (*geo.*) low tide: ~ **olm.**, (eyes) droop.

inikâs (*phys.*) Reflection; echo; (*fin.*) reaction. ~ **etm.**, be reflected.

inika'tᵈ¹ (*leg.*) Conclusion (of agreement); (*adm.*) setting up, assembly.

inil·demek *vi.* Echo; resound; moan. ~**detmek (-i)**, *vc.* ~**emek**, *vi.* (*obs.*) moan.

inilmek *imp. v.* One go down, descend.

in·ilti Moaning. ~**im**: ~ ~, with groans and laments: ~ ~ **inlemek**, groan and moan continuously.

inisiyal ~ **harf**, (*pub.*) initial letter.

inisiyatif Initiative, enterprise.

inisiye Initiated.

iniş Descent; slope; decline; (*aer.*) landing; (*sp.*) jumping down/off. ~ **alanı**, (*aer.*) landing field: ~ **aşağı**, straight down; downwards, downhill: ~ **çıkışlar**, ups and downs: (*fin.*) fluctuations; contours: ~ **pist/yolu**, (*aer.*) airstrip: ~ **takımları**, (*sl.*) a woman's legs: ~ **tekerleği**, (*aer.*) undercarriage: ~ **tertibatı**, landing-gear.

iniş·li Sloping down, downhill: ~ **yokuşlu**, undulating, uneven, uphill and downhill. ~**lik**, (*aer.*) airstrip.

-iniz/-ınız/-unuz/-ünüz *n. suf.* [39] *2nd pers. pl. possessive.* Your [**eviniz**, your house; **gözünüz**, your eye].

inkâr Denial; refusal. ~ **etm./~dan gelmek**, deny; refuse.

inkıbaz (*med.*) Constipation. ~**a uğramak**, be constipated. ~**lık**, being constipated.

inkıla'pᵇ¹ (*pol.*) Radical change; revolution; reform; transformation. ~ **etm. (-e)**, turn/be transformed into: ~ **geçirmek**, undergo a transformation. ~**çı(lık)**, *n.* revolutionary (spirit).

inkıraz (*his.*, *soc.*) Decline; extinction. ~ **bulmak**, become extinct.

inkısam A being divided; splitting up.

inkıtaⁱ Cessation; interruption. ~**a uğramak**, cease; be interrupted.

inkıya'tᵈ¹ Submission; obedience. ~ **etm.**, submit.

inkisar Breaking; (*phys.*) refraction; (*fig.*) vexation; curse. ~ **etm./~da bulunmak**, curse: ~**ı tutmak**, one's curse take effect.

inkişaf A being discovered; development. ~ **etm.**, be discovered; develop.

inle·mek *vi.* Moan, groan; hum: **inliye sıklıya**, aches and pains. ~**tmek (-i)**, cause to moan; oppress; make resound.

in·me *vn.* Descending; (*aer.*) landing; (*naut.*) launching; fall; (*med.*) apoplexy, paralysis, stroke; (*geo.*) ebb: *a.* fallen; dropped: ~ **inmek (-i)**, (*med.*) have a stroke. ~**mek (-den, -e)**, *vi.* descend; dismount; fall down; alight; (*aer.*) land; (*geol.*) subside, go down; (*geo.*) ebb; (*fin.*) drop, lower; stay at (hotel, etc.); be knocked over; be destroyed; (*med.*) (apoplexy) attack, strike; (*sl.*) strike, hit: **inip çıkma**, (*fin.*) fluctuation. ~ **meli**, (*med.*) paralysed.

inorganik (*chem.*) Inorganic.

insaf Justice; moderation; equity, fairness; reasonableness. ~ **!**, *int.* be reasonable!; be fair!: ~ **etm.**, act justly/fairly: ~ **namına**, in all fairness: ~ **a gelmek**, come to (see) reason; be fair; show moderation/pity: ~ **ı elden bırakma!**, don't be unreasonable.

insaf·lı Just, equitable; humane; considerate; reasonable, fair. ~ **sız**, unjust; unfair; without conscience; cruel. ~ **sızlık**, injustice; inhumanity; unfairness.

insan *n.* Human being; man; fine type of man. *imp. pron.* [77] One. *a.* Human; humane; upright. ~ **bitleri**, (*ent.*) human lice: ~ **eti yemek**, (*fig.*) reproach; criticise; slander: ~ **evladı**, upright/ noble person: ~ **gibi**, like a human being; decently, properly: ~ **gönlünün artığını söyler**, there's many a true word spoken in jest: ~ **gülmekten bayılır**, it's enough to make a cat laugh: ~ **hakları**, (*pol.*) human rights, civil liberties: ~ **hali**, it's only human (nature): ~ ~ **ın şeytanıdır**, one man leads another into evil ways: ~ **kaybı**, loss of life: ~ **kıtlığında**, in default of any better; as they couldn't find anyone else: ~ **konuşa konuşa hayvan koklaşa koklaşa**, men get to understand each other by talking: ~ **modeli**, effigy: ~ **müsveddesi**, an apology for a man: ~ **olan**, decent fellow; real man: ~ **piresi**, (*ent.*) human flea: ~ **sarrafı**, a good judge of men/character: ~ **(su)suz nasıl edebilir?**, how can a man live without (water)?: ~ **ticareti**, slave-trade: ~ **yapısı**, man-induced/produced: ~ **a benzer**, anthropoid: ~ **lar**, humanity, mankind.

insan·biçimcilik (*phil.*) Anthropomorphism. ~ **bilim(ci)**, anthropolo·gy/(-gist). ~ **bilimsel**, anthropological. ~ **ca**, humanely, as a man should; in human terms. ~ **cı**, *n.* humanist. ~ **cıl**, *a.* humanist; domestic (animal). ~ **cılık**, humanism. ~ **giller**, (*zoo.*) hominids. ~ **gücü**, (*ind.*) manpower. ~ **(ım)sılar**, (*zoo.*) anthropoids. ~ **i**, humane. ~ **içinci(lik)**, (*phil.*) anthropocentr·ic/(-ism). ~ **iyet**[i], humanity, mankind; kindness. ~ **iyetli**, humane. ~ **iyetsiz**, inhumane, cruel. ~ **lık**, humanity; mankind; kindness: ~ **a karşı suçlar**, crimes against humanity: ~ **tan çıkmak**, become very weak; become beastly: ~ **tan nasibi yok**, there is nothing human about him. ~ **oğlu**[nu], man, mankind, human race: ~ **çiğ süt emmiş**, to err is human. ~ **ölçüm**, (*ethn.*) anthropometry. ~ **sımaymungiller**, (*zoo.*) anthropoid apes. ~ **üstü**[nü], *a.* superhuman.

insıraf (*Arab ling.*) Being declinable. ~ **lı**, declinable.

insicam Coherence (of expression); harmony; regularity. ~ **lı**, coherent. ~ **sız**, incoherent, discursive. ~ **sızlık**, incoherence.

insiyak[i] Instinct. ~ **i**, instinctive.

insülin (*chem.*) = ENSÜLİN.

inş. = İNŞAAT(ÇILIK).

inşa (*arch.*) Construction; creation; (*lit.*) composition. ~ **etm.**, construct, build, engineer.

inşaat[1] *pl.* (*arch.*) Building (being constructed); construction; buildings, works. ~ **alanı**, work(s) site: ~ **mühendis(liğ)i**, civil engineer(ing): ~ **müteahhidi**, building contactor: ~ **sanayii**, construction industry. ~ **çı**, builder; foreman. ~ **çılık**, building (profession).

inşallah *int.* God willing!; I hope (so)!; it is to be hoped (that . . .).

inşa[t][d1] (*lit.*) Recitation. ~ **etm.**, recite.

inşirah Cheerfulness; exhilaration. ~ **bulmak**, be cheered up/comforted: ~ **vermek**, exhilarate.

inta[c][c1] Conclusion; ending. ~ **etm.**, conclude; bring to an end.

intak[1] (*lit.*) Endowing with speech; making speak.

intan (*med.*) Internal microbic infection. ~ **i**, infectious. ~ **iye**, infectious diseases.

integral (*math.*) Integral.

intelek·t[i] (*psy.*) Intellect. ~ **tüalizm**, (*phil.*) intellectualism.

inter- = ENTER-.

-inti/-ıntı/-untu/-üntü *n. suf.* [222] *Denoting (result of) action* [ESİNTİ; İVİNTİ; KIRPINTI; GÖRÜNTÜ].

intiba[1] Impression; feeling; suitability.

intibah Awakening; vigilance.

intibak[1] Adaptation; adjustment. ~ **etm.**, be adapted; adapt/adjust o.s. ~ **sız(lık)**, unadapt·able/ (-ability).

intifa[1] Gain, advantage; benefit.

intiha End, limit.

intihabat[1] *pl.* Elections.

intihal[i] (*lit.*) Plagiarism.

intiha[p][b1] Selection, choice; (*pol.*) election.

intihar Suicide. ~ **etm.**, commit suicide; (*sl.*) get married: ~ **uçakları**, kamikaze.

intikal[i] Transition; passage; transfer (of property); understanding; (*phil.*) inference. ~ **devresi**, transition(al) period: ~ **etm.**, pass to; move, transfer; understand; be inherited: ~ **vergisi**, (*fin.*) estate duty.

intikam Revenge. ~ **almak (-den)**, revenge o.s. on s.o. ~ **cı**, vengeful, vindictive.

intisa[p][b1] Relation(ship); attachment.

intişar Publication; appearance; dissemination. ~ **etm.**, be spread; spread out.

intizam Regularity; order; arrangement. ~ **lı**, orderly, regular. ~ **sız**, irregular; disordered. ~ **sızlık**, irregularity; confusion, disorder.

intizar Waiting, expectation; (*sl.*) abuse, curse.

inzibat[1] Discipline. ~ **memuru**, (*mil.*) military policeman. ~ **i**, disciplinary.

inzimam Being added/joined to. ~ **etm.**, be added.

inziva (*soc.*) Becoming a recluse/hermit.

ion (*phys.*) = İYON.

İÖ = İSA'DAN ÖNCE.

ip[i] Rope; cord; string. ~ **atlamak**, (*sp.*) skip: ~ **cambazı**, tight-rope walker: ~ **halkası**, (*naut.*) becket: ~ **kaçkını**, gaol-/gallows-bird: ~ **takmak (-e)**, gossip maliciously about s.o.: ~ **ucu**, rope's end: = ~ **UCU**.

ipe: ~ **çekmek**, hang s.o.: ~ **gelesi(ce)!**, may he hang!: ~ **gelmek**, come to the gallows, be hanged: ~ **kazığa vurmak**, (*his.*) execute by hanging or impaling: ~ **sapa gelmez**, incoherent, irrelevant: ~ **un sermek**, make vain excuses; offer empty assurances.

ipi: ~ **çözmek (-le)**, (*col.*) break relations with: ~ **çürük**, unreliable, not dependable: ~ **kırık**, (*sl.*) vagabond: ~ **kırmak**, slip away: ~ **koparmak (-le)**, break off relations with: ~ **sapı yok**, without connections, vagabond.

ipin: ~ **ucunu kaçırmak/kaybetmek**, lose the thread of stg.; lose control of stg.: ~**i çekmek (-in)**, keep s.o. under control: ~**i çözmek (-le)**, sever one's relations with stg.: ~**i kesmek/koparmak**, make off, slip away: ~**i kırmak**, get out of hand, become unmanageable: ~**i sürümek**, lead a life of crime (deserving the gallows): ~**i üstüne atmak**, (*sl.*) give s.o. his head, leave s.o. to his own devices.

ip-: ~**iyle kuyuya inilmez (-in)**, he is not reliable: ~**le çekmek (-i)**, await stg. anxiously: ~**leri birinin elinde olm. (-in)**, have control of stg.: ~**ten kazıktan kurtulmuş**, gallows-bird: ~**ten kuşak kuşanmak**, be in dire poverty.

-ip/-ıp/-up/-üp *v. suf.* [177] 1. *Replacing the first of two identical suffixes of different verbs* [**göremez ve işitemez = görüp işitemez**, he can neither see nor hear]. 2. *Replacing the first of two similar suffixes of one verb* [**onu tanıdığım veya tanımadığım önemli = onu tanıyıp tanımadığım önemli**, whether I know him or not is important]. ~ **de**, and (after that) [**kitabı okuyup da bana verin**, read the book and then give it to me].

ipçi¹kᵍⁱ (*bot.*) Filament (of stamen).

ipe¹kᵍⁱ (*tex.*) Silk. ~ BÖCEĞİ: ~ ÇİÇEĞİ: ~ **gibi**, silken: ~ **kâğıdı**, crêpe paper: ~ **kozası**, (*ent.*) silk cocoon: ~ **kurdu**, (*ent.*) silkworm: ~ **kuşu**, (*orn.*) hoopoe: ~ **kuyruk kuşu**, (*orn.*) waxwing: ~ **tüylü maymun**, (*zoo.*) marmoset: ~ **sinekkapanlar**, (*orn.*) silky fly-catchers: ~ **şarabı**, (*cul.*) mulberry wine: ~ **taşı**, (*min.*) asbestos: ~ **tül**, (*tex.*) chiffon: ~ **Yolu**, (*his.*) the Silk Road.

ipeka (*bot.*) Ipecacuanha.

ipek·ağacıⁿ¹ (*bot.*) Satinwood tree, yellow-wood tree. ~ **baskı**, (*pub.*) silkscreen printing. ~**böceği**ⁿⁱ, (*ent.*) silkworm. ~**çi(lik)**, (work of) silkworm-breeder/silk seller. ~**çiçeği**ⁿⁱ, (*bot.*) sun plant, rose moss, purslane. ~**hane**, silk factory, filature. ~**li**, made of silk; silken; silky: ~ **çardak kuşu**, (*orn.*) satin bowerbird. ~**matı**, (*carp.*) silk finish.

ipham Obscurity; (*lit.*) ambiguity.

ipince Very thin/slender.

ipipullah ~ **sivri külah**, stony-broke, destitute.

ipka (*adm.*) Making permanent; (*ed.*) keeping down (in class). ~ **etm.**, (*adm.*) maintain in office; (*ed.*) keep down: ~ **kalmak**, (*ed.*) repeat a class.

iplemek (-i) Bind (with rope); (*sl.*) respect, pay attention to.

ip·li Corded. ~**lici¹kᵍⁱ**, (*zoo.*) cattle lungworm.

ipli¹kᵍⁱ (*tex.*) Thread, cord; (*bot.*) filament. ~ **çekmek**, (*tex.*) draw threads; do drawn-thread work; spin thread: ~ ~, thread by thread: ~ **olm.**, become frayed/threadbare: ~**i pazara çıkmak**, get a bad name, be shown up.

iplik·çi(lik) (Work of) thread maker/seller. ~**çik**, filament. ~**hane**, spinning-mill. ~**kurdu**, (*zoo.*) nematode. ~**lenmek**, *vi.* become unravelled. ~**peyniri**ⁿⁱ, (*cul.*) cheese showing marks of the cheese-cloth. ~ **solucanlar**, (*zoo.*) nematodes.

ipno·tize Hypnotized: ~ **etm.**, hypnotize. ~**tizma(cı)**, hypnot·ism/(-ist). ~**z**, hypnosis.

ipote¹kᵍⁱ (*fin.*) Mortgage. ~**li**, mortgaged.

ipote·tik Hypothetical. ~**z**, hypothesis.

ip·si Threadlike; (*fig.*) lazy, vagabond: ~ **solucanlar**, (*zoo.*) roundworms: ~**ler**, (*zoo.*) nematodes. ~**siz**, without rope; (*fig.*) having no connections; (*sl.*) vagabond: ~ **kuşaksız**, vagabond: ~ **sapsız**, without house or home; irrelevant, incoherent.

iptalⁱ (*leg.*) Rendering null and void; cancellation. ~ **etm.**, annul, cancel; void.

iptida *n.* Beginning; start. *adv.* As a beginning. ~**i**, primary, primitive, elementary: ~ **mektep**, (*ed.*, *obs.*) primary school.

iptila Addiction. ~ **etm.**, be addicted.

iptizal Becoming commonplace; depreciation.

ipucuⁿᵘ Clue, motive. = **ip**.

İr. = (*ch.s.*) İRİDYUM.

-ir¹/-ır/-ur/-ür *v. suf.* [116] *3rd pers. sing. aorist tense.* ~ **-mez**, [182] directly, as soon as [**o gelir gelmez**, as soon as he comes].

-ir-²/-ır-/-ur-/-ür- *vc. suf.* [145] = -DİR-² [KAÇIR-MAK].

irade Will, will-power; (*adm.*) command, decree. ~ **beyanı**, (*leg.*) declaration of intention: ~ **yitimi**, (*psy.*) loss of will-power, aboulia: ~**si elden gitmek/~sine hâkim olmamak**, lose one's self-control: ~**si haricinde**, out of his control.

irade·cilik (*phil.*) Voluntarism. ~**dışı**, (*psy.*) involuntary. ~**li**, strong-willed; voluntary. ~**siz**, weak-willed; involuntary.

iradi Voluntary. ~ **şart**, (*leg.*) proviso.

İran (*geo.*) Iran, Persia. ~ **ceylanı**, (*zoo.*) Persian goitred gazelle. ~**lı**, (*ethn.*) Iranian, Persian.

ira¹pᵇ¹ ~ **ta mahalli yok**, unimportant, insignificant.

ira¹tᵈ¹ (*fin.*) Income, revenue. ~ **vergisi**, income tax.

irca¹ Sending back; (*chem.*) reduction.

irdele·me *vn.* Studying, observation; (*math.*) discussion. ~**mek (-i)**, examine, study; (*sp.*) inspect.

irfan Knowledge; culture; refinement.

irgitim (*el.*) Induction.

iri Huge; voluminous; coarse. ~ **ağızlı siyah levrek**, (*ich.*) largemouth/black bass: ~ **ayaklıgiller**, (*orn.*) megapodes: ~ **BAŞ**: ~ **blok**, (*geol.*) boulder: ~ **çakıl**, cobblestone; (*geol.*) boulder: ~ **çiçekli**, (*bot.*) grandiflora: ~ **fındık**, (*bot.*) cobnut: ~ **kalınbacak**, (*orn.*) great stone-curlew: ~ **KIYIM**: ~ **KULAKLI**: ~ **kumtaşı**, (*geol.*) gritstone: ~ **malzeme**, (*geol.*) aggregates: ~ **otsu tavuğu**, (*orn.*) barred rail: ~ **parça**, chunk: ~ **tane(li)**, (*geol.*, *etc.*) coarse grain(ed): ~ YARI.

iri·baş (*zoo.*) Tadpole. ~**ce**, medium-built.

iridyum (*chem.*) Iridium.

iri·kıyım Large-grained; well-built. ~**kulaklıgiller**, (*zoo.*) eared seals. ~**kum**, (*geol.*) gravel. ~**leşim**, (*med.*) hypertrophy. ~**leşme**, *vn.* becoming large; coarsening; (*med.*) hypertrophy, enlargement.

~ **leşmek**, *vi.* become large; coarsen. ~ **li**, ~ **ufaklı**, large and small; fine and coarse. ~ **lik**, largeness; coarseness; size.

rin (*bio.*) Pus; filth. ~ **lenim**, purulence. ~ **lenmek**, *vi.* suppurate; fester. ~ **li**, purulent. ~ **şiş**, abscess.

ri·ölçekte (*nuc.*) Macroscopic. ~ **özdecik**, macromolecule.

ris (*bio.*) Iris.

riş = ARIŞ.

riyarı Big/powerfully built (man); burly.

r·kilmek *vi.* (Water) collect; become stagnant; (*bio.*) become irritated, inflamed; (*fig.*) be startled; draw back in fear. ~ **kilten**, (*bio.*) irritant. ~ **kiltmek** (-i), *vc.* ~ **kinti**, stagnant pool.

İrlanda (*geo.*) Ireland. ~ +, *a.* Irish: ~ **Cumhuriyeti**, (*pol.*) Irish Republic, Eire. ~ **ca**, (*ling.*) Erse, Irish. ~ **lı**, (*ethn.*) Irish(man).

irmek *aux. v.* (*obs.*) = ERMEK[1].

irmi¹kᵍⁱ (*cul.*) Farina; semolina. ~ **helvası**, a semolina HELVA.

ir·rasyonel (*phil.*) Irrational. ~ **redantizm**, (*pol.*) irredentism.

irs Inheritance; (*bio.*) hereditary quality. ~ **en**, by inheritance. ~ **i**, hereditary. ~ **iyet**ⁱ, (*bio.*) heredity.

irsalⁱ Act of sending, dispatch. ~ **iye**, dispatch list, waybill.

irşa¹tᵈ¹ Act of guiding/directing; stimulation. ~ **etm.**, direct; guide; stimulate.

İrt. Sb. = (*mil.*) İRTİBAT SUBAYI.

irtibat¹ Connection, tie; (*mil.*) communications; liaison. ~ **subayı**, (*mil.*) liaison officer.

irtica¹ (*pol.*) Reaction. ~ **i**, reactionary.

irtical Speaking extempore; improvisation. ~ **en**, extempore, 'off the cuff'.

irtida¹tᵈ¹ (*rel.*) Apostasy.

irtifa¹ Elevation; (*aer., geo.*) height, altitude. ~ **dümeni**, (*aer.*) elevator: ~ **saati**, (*aer.*) altimeter.

irtifak¹ ~ **hakkı**, (*leg.*) easement.

irtihalⁱ Passing away, dying. ~ **etm.**, pass away, die.

irtikâ¹pᵇ¹ Corruption, dishonesty; committing (crimes).

irtisam (*geo.*) Projection.

irtişa Corruption; taking bribes.

is Soot. ~ **kokmak**, smell of soot; (*cul.*) be slightly burnt: ~ **kokusu**, (*cul.*) burnt smell: ~ **e tutmak**, blacken/cover with soot.

is. = isim.

İS = İSA'DAN SONRA.

İsa Jesus. ~ **'dan önce**, before Christ, BC: ~ **'dan sonra**, after Christ; Anno Domini, AD: ~ **'yı darılttın Muhammed'e de yaranamadın/küstürdü Muhammed'i de memnun edemedi**, between two fires; satisfying nobody.

isabetⁱ Falling to; hitting the mark; touching, striking; stg. said/done just right. ~ **!**, *int.* well done!, capital!: ~ **almak**, be hit/struck: ~ **etm.**, hit the mark; say/do just the right thing; guess rightly; win (in lottery, etc.): ~ **oldu da (ki)**, it was just right; (it was a good thing that). ~ **li**, on the mark. ~ **siz**, wide of the mark.

is'af (*adm.*) Granting (of a petition).

isalⁱ Causing to arrive/reach.

ise/-se/-sa *v. suf.* [99] *Forming the basis of the conditional tenses* = ERMEK[1]. *conj.* [217] However; whereas; with regard to . . ., as for . . .; if. ~ **de**, although.

İsevi (*rel.*) Christian. ~ **lik**, Christianity.

isfendan (*bot.*) Maple(-tree).

is·fenks (*myth.*) Sphinx. ~ **filt**ⁱ, (*geo.*) icefield.

ishakkuşuⁿᵘ (*orn.*) Short-eared owl.

ishalⁱ (*med.*) Purging, (*bio.*) catharsis; diarrhoea.

isilik (*bio.*) Heat spots, rash.

is¹imᵐⁱ Name; appellation; (*ling.*) noun. ~ **cümlesi**, (*ling.*) noun clause: ~ **hali**, (*ling.*) case: ~ **levhası**, name-plate: ~ **takımı**, (*ling.*) possessive construction: ~ **vermek**, call, name; baptize: ~ **i geçen**, the above, the afore-mentioned: ~ **i var cismi yok**, known by name but non-existent. ~ **lendirmek (-i)**, name, call.

isk- *Also* = ISK-.

iskalarya (*naut.*) Rope-ladder.

iskambilⁱ (*gamb.*) Card-game. ~ **kâğıdı**, playing-card: ~ **(kâğıdı) gibi dağıtmak (-i)**, scatter in all directions: ~ **masası**, card-table: ~ **oyunu**, game of cards: ~ **oyuncusu**, card-player.

iskân Causing to settle/inhabit; inhabiting; settling.

iskandil (*naut.*) Sounding (lead); (*fig.*) inquiry, soundings. ~ **atmak**, (*naut.*) cast/heave the lead: ~ **etm.**, (*naut.*) take soundings; (*fig.*) sound, probe, throw out feelers.

İskandinav (*ethn.*) *n./a.* Scandinavian. ~ **ya**, (*geo.*) Scandinavia. ~ **yalı**, *n.* (*ethn.*) Scandinavian.

iskar·mos = ISKARMOZ. ~ **pela**, (*carp.*) woodworking chisel. ~ **pin**, (*mod.*) woman's shoe. ~ **to**, (*tex.*) woollen waste.

iskele (*naut.*) Landing-place; quay; wharf; gangway; port of call; port(-side); ladder; (*arch.*) scaffolding; (*ind.*) cat-walk. ~ **almak**, (*naut.*) prepare to sail; (-e), (*sl.*) pester (a woman): ~ **babası**, (*naut.*) bollard; (*fig.*) father who has lost his authority: ~ **tarafında**, (*naut.*) on the port beam: ~ **verilmek**, gangway be attached to a ship. ~ **kuşu**ⁿᵘ, (*orn.*) common kingfisher.

iskeletⁱ (*bio.*) Skeleton; (*ind.*) skeleton, carcass, framework. ~ **gibi**, very thin: ~ **i çıkmak**, be(come) very thin. ~ **li**, (*eng.*) rigid.

iskemle Stool; coffee-table. ~ **kavgası**, (*adm.*) struggle for position/seniority.

İskender *pr.n.* Alexander. ~ **kebabı**, (*cul.*) kebab with yoghurt. ~ **iye**, (*geo.*) Alexandria. ~ **un**, (*geo.*) Iskenderun, (*obs.*) Alexandretta.

iskerletⁱ (*zoo.*) Murex.

İsketⁱ (*his.*) Scythian.

iskete (*orn.*) Coal-tit.

İskoçᵘ Scotch. ~ **çoban köpeği**, (*zoo.*) collie. ~ **ya**, (*geo.*) Scotland: ~ +, *a.* Scottish. ~ **yalı**, (*ethn.*) Scot(sman), Scotch(man).

iskorbütü (*med.*) Scurvy.

iskorçina (*bot.*) Scorzonera, viper's grass, black salsify.

iskorpitⁱ (*ich.*) Large-scaled scorpion-fish. ~ **giller**, (*ich.*) scorpion-fishes.

iskota (*naut.*) Sheet. ~ **bağı**, sheet-bend: ~ **yakası**, clew.

İsl. = İSLAM; İSLAV; İSLAVCA(DAN).

İslam (*rel.*) Islam; Muslim. ~ **gizemciliği**, mysticism, sufism: ~ **takvimi**, Muslim calendar, AH: ~ **a gelmek**, become a Muslim. ~ **cılık**, Pan-Islamism. ~ **iyet**[i], the religion of Islam; the Muslim world.

İslanda (*geo.*) Iceland. ~ +, *a.* Icelandic. ~ **ca**, (*ling.*) Icelandic. ~ **lı**, (*ethn.*) Icelander.

İslav *n.* (*ethn.*) Slav. ~ +, *a.* Slav. ~ **alfabesi**, (*ling.*) Cyrillic alphabet. ~ **ca**, (*ling.*) Slav language(s).

is·lemek (-i) Make black with soot. ~ **lenmek**, *vp.* be made/become sooty. ~ **li**, sooty. ~ **liküf**, (*myc.*) smut (fig/date), black mould (cotton).

islim (*ind.*) Steam. ~ /**istim arkadan gelsin**, we'll bother about the details later.

İsloven(li) *pr. n.* (*geo.*) Slovenia(n).

ismen By name; nominally.

ismet[i] Chastity; honour; innocence.

isna·t[dı] Imputation; calumny.

iso- *pref.* = EŞ-; İZO-.

isp- *Also* = ISP-; SP-.

İsp. = İSPANYA; İSPANYOL; İSPANYOLCA(DAN).

ispalya (*agr.*) Espalier-fence.

ispanya[1] *n.* (*tex.*) Chalk dust (used in fulling).

İspan·ya[2] *pr. n.* (*geo.*) Spain: ~ **ardıcı**, (*bot.*) Spanish juniper. ~ **yol**, *n.* (*ethn.*) Spaniard: ~ +, *a.* Spanish. ~ **yolca**, (*ling.*) Spanish, Castilian. ~ **yolet**, (*arch.*) window bolt/latch.

ispaolo (*tex.*) Double-twist linen thread.

ispari (*ich.*) (?) Annular sea-bream/gilthead.

İsparta (*geo.*, *his.*) Sparta. ~ **lı**, (*ethn.*) Spartan.

ispat[1] Proof; confirmation; demonstration. ~ **etm.**, prove; confirm; demonstrate: ~ **yükü**, (*leg.*) burden of proof: ~ **ı vücut etm.**, (*leg.*) put in an appearance, appear in person: ~ **lı şahitli**, with full proof.

ispati (*gamb.*) Club suit (cards).

ispatla·mak (-i) Bear witness, testify. ~ **nmak**, *vp.*

ispazmos (*med.*) Spasm, convulsion.

ispen·l ç[ci] (*orn.*) Bantam. ~ **horozu**, (*fig.*) small self-important person: ~ **horozu gibi**, 'cocky'.

ispençiyar (*obs.*) Apothecary, pharmacist. ~ **i**, pharmaceutical.

ispendi·l k[ği] (*ich.*) Bass fry.

ispermeçet[i] (*zoo.*) Spermaceti. ~ **balinası**, (*zoo.*) cachalot/sperm whale.

ispinoz (*orn.*) Chaffinch; (*sl.*) chatterbox. ~ **giller**, (*orn.*) finches.

ispir (Horse, carriage) groom.

ispiralya (*naut.*) Skylight; porthole.

ispirto (*chem.*) Alcohol; *aqua vitae*; (*med.*) spirit. ~ **çekmek**, distil alcohol. ~ **lu**, alcoholic. ~ **luk**, spirit stove.

ispit[i] Felloe (of wheel).

ispiyon (*pol.*) Spy.

ispritizma (*rel.*) Spiritualism.

israf Wasteful expenditure; extravagance; prodigality. ~ **etm.**, waste, squander, dissipate.

İsrail (*geo.*) Israel. ~ **li**, (*ethn.*) Israeli.

İst. = İSTANBUL; İSTASYON; İSTATİSTİK.

istadya Theodolite.

ista·lagmit[i] (*geol.*) Stalagmite. ~ **laktit**[i], stalactite.

istalya (*fin.*) ~ (**ücreti**), demurrage.

İstanbul (*geo.*) Istanbul; (*his.*) Byzantium, Constantinople. ~ **kaldırımı çiğnemiş**, experienced, knowing: ~ **kazan, ben kepçe araştırdım**, I have Istanbul thoroughly searched: ~ **burnunda tüttü** he longed for Istanbul: ~ **u göreceğim geldi**, long(ed) to see Istanbul: ~ **un kışı yaza doğrudur** Istanbul winters are (often) very late: ~ **un** **göbeğinde**, in the heart of Istanbul. ~ **in**, (*mod.*, *his.* stambouline, kind of frock-coat. ~ **lu**, citizen inhabitant of Istanbul.

İstanköy ~ **Adası**, (*geo.*) Cos.

istasyon Station; research station; (*fin.*) sales out let. ~ **şef(liğ)i**, (*rly.*) stationmaster('s office): ~ **girmek**, (train) draw into the station.

istatisti·l k[ği] Statistics. ~ +, *a.* Statistical: ~ **cetvel** **grafiği**, chart. ~ **çi**, statistician.

istavrit[i] (*ich.*) Horse mackerel. ~ **azmanı**, (*wrongly* tunny.

istavroz = İSTAVROZ.

istear·ik (*chem.*) Stearic. ~ **in**, stearin.

iste·l k[ği] Wish; will, intent; desire, longing; appetite (*ling.*) optative (mood). ~ **duymak**, long for: ~ **göstermek**, wish for: ~ **kâğıdı**, written request: ~ **yutumu**, (*ling.*) elision of the optative -E- [İSTEYİM = İSTEYEYİM]: ~ **e bağlı**, voluntary, optional: ~ **in** **kaçırmak**, make s.o. disinclined to . . .: ~ **ini** **üzerine**, at your request: ~ **iyle yanmak**, be bitte with a desire to . . ..

isteka (*sp.*) Billiard-cue; (*pub.*) bone folder. = İSTİKA.

istek·lendirmek (-i) *vc.* Make desirous; incite encourage. ~ **lenmek**, *vi.* become desirous. ~ **li** desirous; anxious (for stg.); bidder (at auction) ~ **siz**, unwilling, reluctant, apathetic; (*med.*) without appetite, anorexic. ~ **sizlik**, unwillingness reluctance; (*med.*) anorexia.

istem Demand, request; (*psy.*) volition. ~ **belgesi** written request: ~ **bildirimi**, (*leg.*) declaration o intention: ~ **de bulunmak**, request.

iste·me *vn.* Wishing; wanting; needing: ~ **kipleri** (*ling.*) subjunctive mood(s). ~ **mek (-den, -i)**, wisl for, desire; order (in restaurant); ask for (a girl ir marriage); require, need: **istediği gibi at koşturmak** **oynatmak**, do just as one pleases: **istediğin oldu ya!** after all you got what you wanted: **istemem yar** **cebime koy!**, (s)he is pretending not to want it **istemeyerek**, unwillingly; by chance: **istemez!**, it's not necessary: İSTER: **ister istemez**, whether he will or not; willingly or unwillingly, willy nilly: **iste misin şimdi gelsin!**, I'm afraid he may come now!; o what a pleasant surprise it would be if he came now!: **istersen!**, (*to s.o. being difficult*) well have i your own way!: **isteyenin bir yüzü kara, vermeyenin iki yüzü kara**, it is more embarrasing to refuse than to ask: **isteyerek**, intentionally. ~ **meksizin** obligatorily. ~ **melik**, written request.

istem·li Voluntary; facultative, optional; willing ~ **seme**, (*psy.*) velleity; uncertain wish. ~ **siz(lik)** involunt·ary/(-ariness).

istence Requirement, stg. needed; (*pub.*) slogan.

isten·l ç[ci] (*psy.*) Will-power. ~ **yitimi**, aboulia. ~ **dışı**, involuntary. ~ **sel**, voluntary.

isten·(il)mek *vp.* = İSTEMEK. ~ **irlik**, desirability.

istep (*geo.*) Steppe.

ister *n.* Requirement; necessity. *conj.* [209] Whether

... or ... : ~ **gelsin** ~ **gelmesin**, (I don't care) whether he comes or not: ~ **inan** ~ **inanma**, believe it or not, just as you wish. *v.* = İSTEMEK.

steri (*psy.*) Hysteria. ~ **nöbeti**, attack of hysterics. ~**k**, hysterical: ~ **akım**, (*soc.*) wave of hysteria.

stiane Asking for help.

stia'p[b1] (Containing/carrying) capacity.

stiare Borrowing; (*lit.*) metaphor.

stib'a'ı[d1] Considering stg. far off/unlikely.

stibda't[d1] Despotism; autocracy; absolute rule.

stical[i] Haste. ~ **etm.**, make haste, hurry.

sticar (*fin.*) Hiring, renting. ~ **etm.**, hire.

sticva'p[b1] Interrogation.

stida (*adm.*) Petition, application, demand. ~ **name**, written petition.

stida't[d1] Aptitude; talent. ~**lı**, promising, talented.

stidlal[i] Deduction, inference. ~ **etm.**, deduce.

stif Stowage; storage; stacking, arrangement of goods. ~ **etm.**, pack, stow, arrange: ~**i bozmak**, break bulk: ~**ini bozmadan**, (*fig.*) without being upset, undisturbed: ~**ini bozmak**, disturb, disconcert: ~**ini bozmamak**, be unperturbed; watch with indifference.

stifa (*adm.*) Resignation; abdication. ~ **etm.**, resign; abdicate. ~**name**, letter of resignation.

stifade Benefit, advantage. ~ **etm. (-den)**, avail o.s. of, benefit by, profit from. ~**li**, profitable, advantageous.

stif·çi Stevedore, packer; (*fig.*) hoarder. ~**çilik**, stowage, packing; (*fig.*) hoarding (for profit). ~**leme**, *vn.* stowing, packing; hoarding. ~**lemek** (-i), stow, pack; hoard. ~**lenmek**, *vp.*

stifham Questioning.

stifrağ Vomiting. ~ **etm.**, vomit.

stifsar Asking for an explanation. ~**ı hatır etm.**, inquire after s.o.'s health, etc.

stiğfar (*rel.*) Asking God's pardon.

stiğna Disdain; being able to do without.

stiğrak[1] (*fig.*) Contemplation; rapture. ~**a dalmak**, commune with o.s.

stihale Transformation; (*bio., etc.*) metamorphosis. ~ **etm.**, be transformed/metamorphosed.

stihare Divination by dreams, oneiromancy.

stihbar Asking for information. ~ **etm.**, get information. ~ **at**[1], *pl.* news, information: ~ **dairesi**, (*mil.*) intelligence department: ~ **hizmet//subayı**, (*mil.*) intelligence service//officer.

stihdaf Aiming at. ~ **etm.**, aim at, pursue an object.

stihdam Employing. ~ **etm.**, employ.

stihfaf Contempt, disdain. ~ **etm.**, despise: ~**a değer**, beneath contempt.

stihkak[1] Merit, right, entitlement; fee; ration.

stihkâm (*mil.*) Fortification; engineering. ~ **subayı**, engineer, sapper. ~**cılık**, (*mil.*) engineering.

stihkar Scorn, contempt. ~ **etm.**, scorn, despise.

stihlak[i] Consumption, using up. ~ **etm.**, consume.

stihra'ç[c1] Deduction; (*lit.*) acrostic. ~ **etm.**, deduce.

stihsal[i] Acquiring; producing, production. ~ **etm.**, acquire; produce.

stihza Ridicule; irony, sarcasm. ~ **etm. (-le)**, ridicule, mock.

istihzar Preparation.

istika Bone used for polishing undersoles of shoes.

istikamet[i] Direction; uprightness, integrity. ~ **dümeni**, (*aer.*) rudder: ~ **tekerleği**, (*mot.*) steering-wheel: ~ **vermek**, direct, guide.

istikbal[i] A going to meet s.o.; the future. ~ **etm.**/ ~ **e çıkmak**, (*pol.*) go forth to meet s.o.: ~ **de**, in times to come.

istiklal[i] (*pol.*) Independence. ~ **savaşı**, (*his.*) Tk. War of Independence, 1922: ~ **marşı**, (*mus.*) Tk. national anthem.

istikra (*phil.*) Inductive reasoning.

istikrah Aversion, loathing. ~ **etm.**, loathe.

istikrar Becoming established; stabilization. ~ **bulmak**, become established. ~**sız**. unstable.

istikraz Borrowing. ~ **etm.**, borrow.

istikşaf Reconnaissance.

istila Invasion; covering completely. ~ **etm.**, invade; spread over, flood. ~**cı**, invader, invading army.

istilzam Rendering necessary/inevitable. ~ **etm.**, render necessary; involve.

istim = İSLİM. Steam; (*fig.*) force; (*sl.*) alcoholic drink. ~ **boşaltmak**, (*eng.*) blow (boiler): ~ **kısma cihazı**, throttle: ~ **salıvermek**, blow off steam: ~**ini tutmak**, have steam up; (*fig.*) boil over (with anger); (*sl.*) be drunk. ~**bot**[u], (*naut.*) small steamboat.

istimal[i] A making use of. ~ **etm.**, make use of, employ.

istima·ra Estimating volume/contents of a container, appraising. ~**tor**, estimator, appraiser.

istimda't[d1] Asking for help. ~ **etm.**, ask for help.

istimlak[i] (*leg.*) Expropriation, (*fin.*) nationalization. ~ **etm.**, expropriate; nationalize.

istimna Self-abuse, masturbation.

istimrar Continuation.

istimza'ç[c1] Polite inquiry (as to health, etc.). ~ **etm.**, inquire.

istinabe (*leg.*) Taking evidence by commission.

istinaden Based on, relying on; supported by.

istinaf (*leg.*) Appeal. ~ **mahkemesi**, court of appeal.

istinas Being friendly/familiar; tameness; practice.

istina't[d1] Relying upon; being supported. ~ **duvarı**, (*arch.*) retaining wall. ~**gâh**, point of support.

istinga (*naut.*) Brail.

istinkâf Rejection, refusal; abstention. ~ **etm.**, draw back. refuse, abstain.

istinsah Copying. ~ **etm.**, make a copy: ~ **hatası**, clerical error.

istinta'ç[c1] Assumption, conclusion, inference.

istintak[1] Interrogation, cross-examination. ~ **etm.**, interrogate.

istirahat[1] Rest, repose. ~ **etm.**, rest, take one's ease. ~**gâh**, resting-place; grave.

istirda't[d1] Taking back, recovery of stg.

istirham Begging (for mercy); asking a favour. ~ **etm.**, beg; petition.

istiridye (*zoo.*) Common oyster. ~ **avcı/kuşu**, (*orn.*) oyster-catcher.

istiska (*med.*) Dropsy.

istiskal[i] Showing one's dislike of s.o. ~ **etm.**, be unwelcoming/disagreeable.

istismar Profiting from; exploitation. ~**cı**, selfish exploiter.

istisna Exception; anomaly. ~ **etm.**, except, exclude. ~**i**, exceptional, abnormal; special; unique. ~**sız**, without exception, bar none.

istişare Consultation. ~ **etm.**, consult.

istitra'ı tᵈ¹ (*lit.*) Digression, parenthesis.

istiva ~ **hattı**, (*geo.*) equator.

istizah Asking for an explanation; = GENSORU.

istizan Asking for permission. ~ **etm./eylemek**, ask for permission.

istokᵘ = STOK.

istor (*dom.*) Roller blind. ~**lu**, ~ **kapak**, roll-top (desk).

istralya (*naut.*) Stay (of a mast).

istrongilos (*ich.*) Kind of sea-bream.

İsve'çᶜⁱ (*geo.*) Sweden. ~ +, *a.* Swedish. ~**çe**, (*ling.*) Swedish. ~**li**, *n.* (*ethn.*) Swede, Swedish.

İsviçre (*geo.*) Switzerland. ~ +, *a.* Swiss. ~**li**, *n.* (*ethn.*) Swiss.

isyan (*pol.*) Rebellion, revolt, insurrection, riot. ~ **bayrağını açmak**, unfurl the flag of revolt: ~ **etm.**, rebel, revolt. ~**cı**, rebel. ~ **kâr**, rebellious; riotous; disorderly.

iş *n.* Work; action; business; occupation; profession; affair, matter, concern; profit, benefit; (*phys.*) force; (*sl.*) trick. ~ +, *a.* Working, industrial, business. ~ **açmak**, (*fig.*) cause problems: ~ **anlaşmazlıkları**, industrial unrest/strife: ~ **ayağa düşmek**, business fall into the hands of incapable people: ~ **bakımından**, practical: ~ **başa düşmek/ gelmek**, stg. have to be done personally: ~ **başa gelince çaresiz katlanılır**, you can't escape a job you must do yourself: ~ **başarı belgesi**, (*ind.*) reference: ~ **BAŞI:** ~ **başkadır**, business is business: ~ **becerenin/bilenin kılıç kuşananın**, success comes to those who know their job: ~ **bin liranın kapısıdır**, the business will cost a thousand pounds: ~ **bilmek**, know one's job, be skilful: ~ BİRLİĞİ: ~ **birlikli**, joint, done cooperatively: ~ **bitirici yalan**, a lie for a good purpose, a white lie: ~ **bitirmek**, bring to a successful conclusion: ~ **bitmek (-den)**, depend on s.o. for work: ~ **bölgesi**, business quarter: ~ BÖLÜMÜ: ~ **bulma bürosu**, employment agency: ~ **çatallanmak**, meet with difficulties: ~ **çevirmek**, be up to some mischief: ~ **çıkarmak**, raise (unnecessary) difficulties; do much work: ~ **deme değil**, it's an easy matter; it's a mere nothing: ~ **dayıya düştü**, I shall have to do it myself: ~ **donu** = ŞALVAR: ~ **düşmek**, be one's duty: ~ **düzlemi**, work(ing) surface: ~ **edinmek**, take on the job: ~ **elinde ekşimek**, let a matter drag on, neglect a matter: ~ **eri**, a good man for the job: ~ **fenama gitti**, the business has exasperated me; I was hurt: ~ **fenaya bindi**, the affair has taken a bad turn: ~ **garantısı**, (*ind.*) security of employment: ~ **geçiştirme**, makeshift: ~ **gömleği**, (*mod.*) dustcoat: ~ **görememezlik**, incapacity for work: ~ **göremez**, lazy: ~ **göremezlik**, (*ind.*) unemployment: ~ **görevlisi**, agent: ~ **görme**, function; operation: ~ **görmek**, work, perform a service; be suitable: ~ **görmez(lik)**, defective(ness): ~ **göstermek (-e)**, give s.o. a job of work: ~ **güç**, business, occupation; =

işGÜCÜ: ~ **güvenliği**, (*ind.*) industrial safety: ~ **hukuku**, (*leg.*) industrial law: ~ **inada binmek**, be a matter of sheer obstinacy; see who can hold out longest: ~ ~**ten geçmek**, be all over now; be too late to do anything: ~ **kapatımı**, (*ind.*) lock-out ~ **karıştırmak**, plot mischief/trouble: ~ **kazası** (*ind.*) industrial accident: ~ **mahkemesi**, (*leg.*) industrial/labour court: ~ **nöbeti**, service: ~ **neye varacak?**, what will be the end of it?: ~ **ola/olsun diye**, (*pej.*) (doing stg.) unnecessarily/officiously, in order to seem busy: ~ **olacağına varır**, things must take their course: ~ **öğretimi**, (*ed.*) professional training: ~ **ölçüsü bilimi**, (*ind.*) ergomatics ~ **sahibi**, employer: ~ **sarpa sarmak**, things become complicated: ~ **sendikası**, trade union: ~ **şaka götürmez**, it's not a joking matter: ~ **tanımı** (*ind.*) job description: ~ **tulumu**, work-bag, kitbag: ~ **tutmak**, work, have a job: ~ **uyuşmazlığı** (*ind.*) industrial dispute: ~ **üç nalla bir ata kaldı** (*jok.*) (*of stg. just begun*) 'all that is needed now is three shoes and a horse': ~ **üstünde**, practical: ~ **ve işçi bulma kurumu**, (*ind.*) employment bureau/ exchange: ~ VEREN: ~ **verimi**, productivity: ~ **vermek**, give s.o. work, employ s.o.: ~ **yapımı** business: ~ **yapmak**, do business, deal with: ~ **yavaşlatma**, (*ind.*) go-slow: ~ **yeni bir kalıba döküldü**, the affair has taken a new turn: ~ YERİ: ~ **yok (-de)**, (*sl.*) there's no profit in it: ~ **yükü**, (*ind.*) work load.

işde = İŞTE (*used to avoid confusion with* İŞTE²).

işe: ~ **bakmak**, attend to one's job, get on with one's work: ~ **devamsızlık**, irregular attendance: ~ **el atmak**, start/take up a matter: ~ **el vurmamak** not lift a finger to do stg.: ~ **elverişli**, businesslike; suitable for work: ~ **gelmek**, be suitable for the job: ~ **girişmek**, get busy, undertake work: ~ **girmek**, start a (new) job: ~ **kapak vurmak**, hush up a matter: ~ **koşmak**, rush to work; (-i), put s.o. to work: ~ **parmak sokmak**, meddle in a matter: ~ **sarmak**, work assiduously on a matter: ~ **sokmak** (-i), put s.o. into a job: ~ **yaramak**, be suitable, serviceable: ~ **yaramaz**, useless, dud: ~ **yarar**, serviceable, useful for the purpose in hand.

işi: ~ **alaya dökme!**, don't turn the matter into a joke: ~ **Allah'a kalmak**, not expect any help: ~ **azıtmak**, overdo, overstep the mark: ~ **başından aşkın olm./aşmak**, be up to one's ears in work: ~ **bir çırpıda çıkarmak**, make light of a job, do it easily: ~ **bırakmak**, interrupt stg.: ~ **bitmek**, be worn out; be done for: ~ **bozulmak**, work prove unprofitable: ~ **çıkarmak**, finish a job: ~ **dökmek** (-e), work turn into stg. else: ~ **duman**, (*col.*) he's in a bad state/ruined: ~ **düşmek (-e)**, be obliged to apply to s.o. for help, etc.; one's work take one to ... : ~ **geniş tutmak**, do stg. on a broad scale: ~ **gevşek tutmak**, not take the matter seriously: ~ **gücü yok**, he has no occupation: ~ **iş olm.**, work, etc. progress well: ~ **kalenderliğe vurmak**, take things philosophically: ~ **kime danışmalı?**, whom should one consult about the matter?: ~ **kitaba uydurmak**, manage an affair cleverly: ~ **kökünden kesip atmak**, reject/settle a matter once and for all:

~ **kurcalama!**, better not meddle in the matter (there's a snag somewhere)!: ~ **olm.**, have stg. to do, be busy; be settled/finished; be stg. one can do; have to deal with: ~ **oluruna bırakmak**, leave things to take their course: ~ **pişirmek**, (*col.*) reach a secret agreement: ~ **resmiyete dökmek**, become formal, adopt an official manner: ~ **tıkırında gidiyor**, it's going well.

işim: ~ **çiriş**, (*sl.*) I'm in a mess: ~ **mi yok?**, I've better things to do!: ~ **uygun**, my affairs are all right.

işin: ~ **alayında**, taking stg. too lightly: ~ **arasını soğutmak**, neglect an affair: ~ **başı**, most important point of a matter: ~ **bir çok boku püsürü var**, (*vulg.*) there are a lot of complications in this business: ~ **çoğunu bitirmek**, break the back of the work: ~ **daha bir çok girdisi çıktısı var**, there are a lot more complications in this matter: ~ **elifini dahi bilmiyor**, he doesn't know the rudiments of the business: ~ **fenası şu ki**, the worst of it is that . . . : ~ **garibi**, strangely enough: ~ **girdisi çıktısını bilmek**, know the ins and outs of a matter: ~ **içinde iş var**, there's stg. fishy about the job; there's stg. behind it all: ~ **içinden çıkmak**, get out of a difficulty; extricate o.s.; be successful: ~ **içinden iş çıkarmak**, keep raising difficulties: ~ **mi yok?**, what a ridiculous idea!: ~ **sakalı bitti**, the matter is getting tedious: ~ **sonu**, end, result: ~ **şüphe götürür yeri yok**, the matter leaves no room for doubt: ~ **tuhafı . . .**, the odd thing about it is . . .: ~ **tuzu biberidir bu!**, this is an essential addition!: ~ **ucu birine dokunmak**, be hurt because of a business: ~ **ucu ortası belli değil**, it's not clear how to tackle this matter: ~ **ucunda para var**, there's money to be made out of it: ~ **üstesinden gelmek**, succeed, cope with a matter: ~ **üstüne düşmek**, persist in/be very keen on stg.: ~ **vazifedarı kimdir?**, (*adm.*) who is responsible for attending to this matter?: ~**den çıkarmak (-i)**, (*adm.*) dismiss s.o.: ~**den olm.**, lose one's job.

işine: ~ **bak!**, mind your own business!: ~ **gelmek**, suit one's purpose/wish: ~ **gelmemek**, be unsuitable: ~ **göre**, according to his work/skill; according to its workmanship/quality: ~ **gücüne bakmak**, attend to one's work: ~ **karışmamak**, not interfere, leave s.o. to his own devices: ~ **yaramak**, be useful, come in handy.

işini: ~ **bilmek**, be good at/have a head for business: ~ **bitirmek**, finish s.o.'s business; (*fig.*) kill s.o.: ~ **bozmak**, upset s.o.'s plans: ~ **görmek**, do s.o.'s job; (*fig.*) kill s.o.: ~**n adamı**, man who knows his job: ~**z ne dir?**, what's your job?; what do you do?

işler, *n.* (*adm.*) affairs: *v.* = iŞLEMEK: ~ **açılmak**, (*fin.*) market become active: ~ **ayaz gitti**, (*sl.*) things have gone to pot: ~ **becermek**, do things clumsily: ~ **duruyor**, (*fin.*) the market is stagnant: ~ **kesat**, there's nothing doing (here): ~ **tıkırına girdi**, the matter is going well; things have taken a turn for the better: ~ **tıkırında gidiyor**, business is going well: ~ **yürümez olm.**, (*fig.*) (services)

become paralysed: ~ **i biraz kıpırdattık**, (*col.*) we've got a move on: ~ **inin erbabı**, masters of their craft.

işte, at work, on service: ~ **bir bityeneği var!**, there's stg. rotten in the state of Denmark!: ~ **çıkarı olm.**, have an axe to grind: ~ **kimse ona çıkamaz**, nobody can compete with him in the work. = iŞTE².

işten: ~ **alıkoymak (-i)**, keep s.o. from his work: ~ **anlamak**, be an expert: ~ **artmaz, dişten artar**, it's better to be economical than try to earn lots of money: ~ **atmak**, dismiss, discharge: ~ **başını kaşıyacak vakti olmamak**, be up to one's eyes in work: ~ **(bile) değil**, it's (mere) child's play: ~ **çıkarılmak**, be dismissed, get one's cards: ~ **çıkarma**, (*ind.*) lock-out; dismissal: ~ **çıkarmak (-i)**, dismiss s.o.: ~ **el çektirmek**, (*adm.*) dismiss/ suspend s.o. from office: ~ **iş çıkarmak**, raise unnecessary difficulties: ~ **kaçmak**, avoid work; be work-shy: ~ **yan çizmek**, shirk one's work: ~ **yüzümün akıyla çıktım**, I have come out of the affair without a stain on my honour.

-iş¹/-ış/-uş/-üş *vn. suf.* [172] *Denoting an action or manner of acting*. [GELİŞ; ÇIKIŞ].

-iş-²/-ış-/-uş-/-üş-/-ş- *v. suf.* [143] *Denoting a reciprocal or cooperative action*. [GÖRÜŞMEK; YAZIŞMAK; BİTİŞMEK].

işadamıⁿ¹ Businessman; s.o. successful in business.

iş'ar A making known. ~ **etm.**, notify.

işaretⁱ Sign; gesture; signal; mark; badge; (*ling.*) punctuation mark; (*th.*) cue. ~ **ateşi**, (*mil.*) beacon: ~ **bilimi**, semiotics: ~ **borusu**, (*mil.*) bugle: ~ **cihazı**, (*el.*) annunciator, indicator: ~ **çekmek**, (*naut.*) hoist a signal: ~ **değnek/kolu**, (*mot.*) traffic indicator: ~ **etm.**, make a sign/signal; beckon: make a mark: ~ **geçmek**, make signs: ~ **kulesi**, signal/watch tower: ~ **memuru**, (*mot.*) traffic policeman: ~ **sıfatı//zamiri**, (*ling.*) demonstrative adjective//pronoun: ~ **vermek**, give/make a signal; (**-e**), (*th.*) give s.o. the cue: ~ **yapmak**, make a mark.

işaret·çi (*mot.*) Traffic policeman. ~**lemek (-i)**, point to stg. ~**lenmek**, *vp.* ~**leşmek (-le)**, make (furtive/flirtatious) signs to each other. ~**parmağı**ⁿ¹, first/index finger.

işba¹ Saturation. ~ **etm.**, satiate; saturate.

iş·başıⁿ¹ Head of business; foreman; hour at which work begins; place of work: ~**na gelmek**, (*pol.*) come to power: ~**nda**, on the job, at work; on site: ~**nda ölmek**, die in harness: ~**ndan aşkın**, up to the ears/eyes in work. ~**bırakımcı**, (*ind.*) striker. ~**bırakımı**, (*ind.*) strike. ~**bıraktırımı**, (*ind.*) lock-out. ~**bilim**, ergonomy. ~**birliği**ⁿⁱ, cooperation; (*fin.*) collective/cooperative organization: ~ **yapmak (-le)**, collaborate (with). ~**birlikçi(lik)**, (*fin.*) partner(ship); (*pej.*) collabora·tor/(-tion). ~**birlikli**, collective. ~**bölümü**ⁿü, (*soc.*) division of labour; cooperation.

işbu (*obs.*) This; the present (year, etc.).

işçi Workman; worker; employee; labourer; work-woman; (*sl.*) cheat, trickster. ~ **arı**, (*ent.*) worker bee: ~ **Bayramı**, workers' festival, Labour Day (24 July): ~ **birliği**, trade-union: ~ **bulma kurumu**, employment agency: ~ **gömleği,** (*mod.*) blouse: ~ **kadın,** working woman; charwoman: ~ **Partisi,** (*pol.*) Labour Party: ~ **sendikası,** (*ind.*) trade-union: ~ **sınıfı,** (*soc.*) working class, proletariat: ~ **sigortası,** workers' insurance: ~ **temsilcisi,** (*ind.*) shop steward: ~ **ücreti,** wages. ~**leşmek,** *vi.* obtain worker's status; be considered a worker. ~**lik,** occupation/pay of a workman; labour; workmanship.

işe·mek *vi.* (*bio.*) Urinate; make water. ~**nmek,** *imp. v.* ~**tici,** (*med.*) diuretic. ~**tmek (-i),** *vc.*

işevi[ni] (*fin.*) Office; bureau.

işgal[i] Causing to be occupied; (*mil.*) occupation. ~ **etm.,** keep busy; engage the attention of; keep s.o. from his work; (*mil.*) occupy. ~**ci,** (*mil.*) occupier.

iş·gücü[nü] Workforce, manpower: ~ **bozum/yitimi,** (*psy.*) demoralization. ~**güder(lik),** (*adm.*) (office/rank/work of) chargé d'affaires. ~**günü**[nü], working-day. ~**güzar,** efficient; busybody. ~**güzarlık,** efficiency; (*fig.*) excessive zeal/officiousness.

işit·ilmek *vp.* Be heard/audible. ~**im,** (*bio.*) (sense of) hearing. ~**me,** *vn.* hearing: ~ +, *a.* auditory; acoustic; audio-: ~ **cihazı,** (*med.*) hearing-aid: ~ **kesesi,** (*bio.*) otocyst: ~**konuşma,** audio-lingual: ~ **taşı,** (*bio.*) otolith. ~**mek (-i),** hear; listen; catch (a name, etc.): **işitmedi ki cevap versin!,** how can he answer since he didn't hear? ~**melik,** (*phys.*) acoustics. ~**memezlik,** a not hearing: ~**e getirmek/** ~**ten gelmek,** pretend not to hear, feign deafness. ~**ölçer,** (*med.*) audiometer. ~**ölçümü,** audiometry. ~**sel,** aural, auditory, audio-. ~**tirmek (-i, -e),** *vc.* cause to hear/be heard; announce; communicate.

işkembe (*bio.*) Stomach; paunch; (*cul.*) tripe. ~ **çorbası,** (*cul.*) tripe soup: ~ **çorbası hikâyesi,** one mustn't expect too much of stg./s.o. inferior: ~ **suratlı,** (*vulg.*) pockmarked (face): ~**den atmak/** **söylemek,** invent a story, etc.; exaggerate; embroider a tale: ~**sini düşünmek,** think only of one's stomach/(*fig.*) interests: ~**sini şişirmek,** eat greedily. ~**ci(lik),** (work of) tripe(-soup) seller.

işkence Torture; pain; (*carp.*) clamp. ~ **etm.,** torture: ~ **görmek,** agonize: ~**ye sokmak (-i),** cause pain/suffering to s.o.

işkil Doubt; suspicion; anxiety. ~**lendirmek (-i),** *vc.* ~**lenme,** *vn.* ~**lenmek,** *vi.* be dubious/suspicious; be anxious. ~**li,** suspicious, anxiously doubtful. ~**lik,** dubiousness; mistrust. ~**siz,** without a doubt, sure, certain. ~**sizlik,** certainty; trust.

işkine (*ich.*) Corb.

iş·kolu[nu] *n.* Branch of industry: *a.* industry-wide; across-the-board. ~**lek,** hard-working; busy, bustling; experienced: ~ **ekler,** (*ling.*) frequently-used suffixes: ~ **yazı,** hurried but legible handwriting. ~**leklik,** business.

işlem Action; (*math.*) operation; (*fin.*) transaction; (*ind.*) operation, process, treatment. ~ **devresi,** (*chem.*) cycling: ~ **yapmak,** process, treat: ~**lerden geçirmek,** (*chem.*) cycle. ~**ce,** (*med.*) operation. ~**ci,** (*fin.*) drawer.

işle·me *vn.* Work; processing; workmanship; handi-

work; (*math.*) computation, calculation; (*tex.*) embroidery; (*art.*) carving; engraving; (*cin.*) processing: ~ +, *a.* working: ~ **gemisi,** factory ship. ~**meci(lik),** (*tex.*) embroider·er/(-ing). ~**mek (-i),** work (up), process; manipulate; (*tex.*) embroider; carve; engrave; dress (leather); commit (crime): **(-e),** (*chem.*) penetrate, act on: *vi.* work, function; take effect; (road, etc.) be frequented/much used; (ship, etc.) ply; (*med.*) (boil) suppurate, discharge: **işlemez,** (*ind.*) idle: **işLER.** ~**meli,** (*tex.*) embroidered; decorated with needlework.

işlem·lemek (-i) Calculate, compute; process. ~**lenmek,** *vp.* ~**leyici,** algorithm. ~**siz,** idle.

işlen·ge Decoration. ~**ir,** (*eng.*) workable, machinable. ~**mek,** *vp.* be worked; be embroidered. ~**memiş,** (*ind.*) untreated, unprocessed, crude, raw. ~**miş,** (*ind.*) processed, treated; (*agr.*) cultivated, worked.

işler *a.* Working. *n.* (*math.*) Operator. ~**ge,** (*chem.*) mechanism.

işlet *int.* (*ind.*) Switch on!, start! ~**ici,** (*fin.*) operator. ~**me,** *n.* working/exploiting (railway, mine, etc.); running (business, hotel, etc.); (*agr.*) cultivation; (*fin.*) undertaking, enterprise; establishment: *a.* (*eng.*) driving; operational; working: ~ **Bakan(lığ)ı,** (*adm.*) Minis·ter/(-try) of Industry: ~ **basıncı,** working pressure: ~ **dairesi,** (*rly.*) traffic department: ~ **iyesi,** (*leg.*) patentee: ~ **ölçütü,** operational parameter: ~ **malzemesi,** (*rly.*) rolling-stock: ~ **sermayesi,** (*fin.*) working capital: ~ **vergisi,** (*fin.*) turnover tax. ~**meci,** businessman; executive, manager; operator. ~**mecilik,** operation, service (of national enterprise). ~**mek (-i, -e),** work, run, operate, exploit; process; (*sl.*) deceive, make fun of. ~**men,** operator.

işlev Function; duty, role. ~ +, *a.* Functional: ~ **yitimi,** (*psy.*) apraxia. ~**bilim(sel),** (*med.*) physi·olo·gy/(-gical). ~**ci(lik),** (*phil.*) functional·ist/ (-ism). ~**sel,** functional. ~**siz,** without function.

iş·leyici (*chem.*) Penetrating. ~**leyim,** industry. ~**leyimsel,** industrial. ~**leyiş,** action. ~**lik,** (*art.*) workshop, studio.

işmar Sign; nod; wink.

işporta Large basket. ~ **malı,** shoddy goods. ~**cı,** pedlar, hawker. ~**cılık,** peddling, hawking.

işra[b1] (*obs.*) Insinuation; imputation.

işret[i] Drinking, carousal, festival. ~ **etm.,** drink; make merry.

işsiz Without work, unemployed. ~ **güçsüz,** idle; unemployable: ~**lerin değnekçisi miyim!,** am I responsible for looking after the unemployed? ~**lik,** unemployment.

iştah Appetite; desire; greed. ~ **açan,** (*cul.*) appetizer, apéritif: ~ **açmak,** whet the appetite: ~ **kapamak/kesmek,** satisfy the appetite: ~**ı açılmak,** be hungry: ~**ı kesilmek,** lose one's appetite: ~**ı tıkamak,** spoil one's appetite: ~**ım yok,** I have no appetite.

iştah·landırmak (-i) *vc.* ~**lanmak (-e),** *vi.* have an appetite; have a craving for; desire. ~**lı,** having an appetite, hungry; desirous; (*fig.*) over-zealous/ -officious. ~**sız,** without appetite/desire. ~**sızlık,** lack of appetite; (*psy.*) anorexia.

işte¹ = iş.

işte² *int.* Look!; here!; now!; exactly, precisely; thus. ~ **bu kadar!**, and that's an end to it!: ~ **şimdi bir şeye benzedi**, now it's beginning to look like stg., it's all right *but*: ~ **şimdi kıyamet kopacak**, now the fat's in the fire: ~ **şimdi oldu!**, that's better now!: ~ **şimdi tam benzedi**, look at the mess it's in now.

işteş Fellow-worker, workmate. ~ **çatı**, *(ling.)* reciprocal form: ~ **eylem**, *(ling.)* reciprocal verb. ~ **lik**, reciprocity, cooperation.

iştialⁱ Catching fire; blazing up; conflagration: ~ **etm.**, burst into flames.

iştigalⁱ Being busy/occupied. ~ **etm. (-le)**, occupy o.s. with.

iştihar Becoming famous; fame; notoriety.

iştikak¹ *(ling.)* Derivation; etymology.

-iştir-/-ıştır-/-uştur-/-üştür-/-ştir-, *etc. v. suf.* [148] *Denoting a repetitive/intensive action* [ARAŞ-TIRMAK; ÇEKİŞTİRMEK].

iştira Purchase.

iştirakⁱ Participation; association; assistance; sharing. ~ **etm. (-e)**, participate in; assist in; share. ~ **çi**, participator; associate.

iştiyak¹ Longing. ~ **çekmek/duymak**, long for.

işve Coquetry, flirting. ~ **baz/~li**, coquettish, amorous.

iş·veren Employer. ~ **yar**, functionary. ~ **yarlık**, official duty, office. ~ **yazar**, *(phys.)* recording instrument (of muscular activity). ~ **yeri**ⁿⁱ, place of work, work-site.

itⁱ Dog. ~ **canlı**, insupportable (person): ~ **dişi domuz derisi**, it's pleasant to see one's enemies quarrel: ~ **elli**, (animal) knock-kneed and splay-footed: ~ **gibi çalışmak**, work untiringly: ~ ~ **e** ~ **de kuyruğuna**, everyone trying to get s.o. else to do the job: ~ **izi at izine karışmak**, things get very involved: ~ **menekşesi**, *(bot.)* heath dog-violet: ~ **nişanı**, *(zoo.)* growth on a horse's fetlock: ~ **oğlu** ~, scoundrel, foul brute: ~ **sürüsü**, pack of dogs; rabble: ~ **sürüsü kadar**, *(col.)* more than necessary, very crowded: ~ **ürür kervan yürür**, get on with the job and pay no attention to others: ~ **e atsan yemez**, very nasty: ~ **e bulaşmaktansa çalıyı dolaşmak**, go out of one's way to avoid unpleasantness: ~ **i öldürenler sürütürler**, one must clear up the mess one has made: ~ **in duası kabul olunsa gökten ekmek/kemik yağar**, if wishes were horses then beggars would ride: ~ **in göt/kıçına sokmak**, *(vulg.)* disgrace/shame s.o.: ~ **in kuyruğunda**, *(col.)* plentiful.

İt. = İTALYA(N); İTALYANCA(DAN).

-it¹/**-ıt/-ut/-üt/-t** *n./a. suf.* [224] [ANIT; TAŞIT; EŞİT; SOMUT]

-it-²/**-ıt-/-ut-/-üt-/-t-** *v. suf.* [145] *Forming the causative verb* = -DİR- [KORKUTMAK; ÜRKÜTMEK; DÜZELTMEK].

ita Giving, paying. ~ **amiri**, *(adm.)* authority approving payments: ~ **emri**, *(adm.)* order for payment.

itaatⁱ Obedience. ~ **etm.**, obey: ~ **ettirmek/~e zorlamak**, enforce obedience. ~ **li**, obedient. ~ **siz**, disobedient; disorderly; a law to o.s. ~ **sizlik**, disobedience: ~ **etm.**, be disobedient.

ital·ik *(pub.)* Italic(s). ~ **ya**, *pr.n.* *(geo.)* Italy: ~ +, *a.* Italian. ~ **yan**, *(ethn.)* Italian: ~ **çekirgesi**, *(ent.)* Italian locust: ~ **çimi**, *(bot.)* Italian rye-grass: ~ **malmignati**, *(ent.)* European black widow. ~ **yanca**, *(ling.)* Italian.

itaⁱ**p**ᵇⁱ Reproof; reprimand. ~ **etm.**, reprove, reproach.

it·boğan *(bot.)* Colchicum, meadow saffron, autumn crocus. ~ **burnu**ⁿᵘ, *(bot.)* hip of wild rose; dog rose. ~ **dirseği**ⁿⁱ, *(med.)* sty(e) on eyelid.

İTC = İTTİHAT VE TERAKKİ CEMİYETİ.

ite·klemek (-i) *(col.)* Push roughly; manhandle. ~ **lemek (-i)**, push repeatedly; *(phys.)* repel. ~ **lenmek**, *vp.* ~ **ne**ⁱ**k**ᵍⁱ, *(eng.)* piston: ~ **li ayırıcı**, jig.

iterbiyum *(chem.)* Ytterbium.

İTF = *(ed.)* İSTANBUL TIP FAKÜLTESİ.

itfa Extinguishing; *(phys.)* damping; *(fin.)* redemption, amortization. ~ **etm.**, extinguish; *(fin.)* pay off, redeem. ~ **iye**, fire-brigade. ~ **iyeci**, fireman.

ithaf Presentation; *(art.)* dedication. ~ **etm.**, dedicate; autograph.

ithalⁱ Introducing; importing; inserting. ~ **etm.**, import: ~ **malı**, import. ~ **at**¹, imports. ~ **atçı**, importer. ~ **atçılık**, importation, importing.

itham Imputation; accusation. ~ **etm.**, suspect, accuse. ~ **name**, *(leg.)* indictment: ~ **maddeleri**, counts.

ithıyarıⁿ¹ *(bot.)* Colocynth, bitter apple.

itibar Esteem; dignity; consideration; regard; *(fin.)* credit; *(fin.)* nominal value; hypothesis. ~ **etm.**, esteem, regard; consider, deem; credit: ~ **görmek**, be respected; be in demand: ~ **kırıcı**, derogatory: ~ **mektubu**, *(fin.)* letter of credit: ~ **a almak**, keep in mind, take account of: ~ **dan düşmek**, be discredited: ~ **dan düşürmek (-i)**, discredit s.o.: ~ **ını düşürmek (-i)** debase: ~ **ıyla**, reckoning from (date); as regards.

itibar·en (-den) From, dating from, with effect from, as from. ~ **i**, theoretical, conventional; *(fin.)* nominal: ~ **kıymet**, face-value.

itici *a.* Pushing. *n.* Pusher. ~ **güç**, *(aer.)* thrust.

itidalⁱ Moderation; temperance; equilibrium. ~ **dairesinde**, on conservative lines: ~ **sahibi**, (s.o.) calm/self-possessed/cool: ~ **ini kaybetmek**, lose one's self-control/temper: ~ **ini muhafaza etm.**, control o.s., keep calm. ~ **siz**, extreme; extravagant.

itikâf *(rel.)* Becoming a recluse.

itikâlⁱ *(geol.)* Corrosion.

itikaⁱ**t**ᵈ¹ Belief, creed.

itila Ascending; being elevated; progress.

itilaf Agreement; *entente*; understanding. ~ **Devletleri**, *(his.)* Entente (*Cordiale*) Powers.

it·ilim/ ~ **ilme** *vn.* *(psy.)* Repression; *(geol.)* thrust. ~ **ilmek**, *vp.* be pushed; be repressed. ~ **im**, *(phys.)* repulsion.

itimaⁱ**t**ᵈ¹ Confidence, reliance; trust, credit. ~ **etm. (-e)**, have confidence in, rely on: ~ **reyi**, *(pol.)* vote of confidence: ~ **telkin etm.**, inspire confidence. ~ **lı**, confidently. ~ **name**, *(adm.)* credentials. ~ **sızlık**, distrust.

itina Care, attention. ~ **etm.**, pay great attention, be very careful. ~ **lı**, careful. ~ **sız(lık)**, careless(ness).

itiraf Confession, admission. ~ **etm.**, confess, admit, acknowledge.

itiraz Objection, protest; disapproval. ~ **etm.**, object to, dispute, contest; protest. ~**cı**, s.o. always objecting; protester.

itiş·li (*phys.*) Repulsive. ~**mek (-le)**, repel/push each other; brawl; skylark: **itişe kakışa**, pushing and shoving each other. ~ **tirmek (-i, -le)**, *vc.*; push lightly but steadily.

itiya'ı'^{dı} Habit, custom. ~ **etm.**, make a habit of: ~ **üzere**, habitually.

itizar Excuse, apology. ~ **etm.**, make excuses, apologise.

itki (*psy.*) Instinct; impulse.

itlaf Killing, destruction. ~ **etm.**, kill, destroy.

itlik (*fig.*) Villainy, vileness.

itmam Completing, perfecting. ~ **etm.**, complete, finish.

itmek (-i) Push; thrust; lead into; depress, immerse. **ite kaka**, pushing: **itip kakmak**, push and shove, elbow one's way.

itminan Tranquillity; confidence; certainty.

itriyum (*chem.*) Yttrium.

ittıra'ı'^{dı} Regularity; rhythm. ~**sız**, irregular; variable.

ittifak[1] Harmony; alliance; agreement; coincidence. ~ **etm.**, reach agreement; ally with. ~**la**, unanimously.

ittiha'ı'^{dı} Union; being united. ~ **etm.**, unite: ~ **ve Terakki Cemiyeti**, (*his.*) Committee of Union and Progress. ~**çı**, member of the CUP.

ittihaz Procurement; (*adm.*) adoption (of proposals).

ittisal'ⁱ Contiguity. ~**inde**, touching, contiguous.

İ·TÜ = İSTANBUL TEKNİK ÜNİVERSİTESİ. ~**Ü** = İSTANBUL ÜNİVERSİTESİ.

itüzümü^{nü} (*bot.*) Black nightshade.

ivaz (*leg., obs.*) Consideration; exchanging. ~**sız**, without expecting any return, disinterested.

iv·dire'ç'^{ci}/~ **dirici** (*phys., chem., etc.*) Accelerator. ~**dirme**, *vn.*; acceleration. ~**dirmek (-i)**, *vc.* = İVMEK; hurry s.o.

ive·cen Impatient, hasty. ~**cenlik**, hastiness. ~**di**, *n.* haste: *a.* hasty, hurried; urgent: ~ **yardım**, emergency assistance, first-aid. ~**dilenmek**, *imp. v.* one make haste, hurry. ~**dileşmek**, *vi.* become urgent. ~**dili**, urgent. ~**dilik**, urgency: ~**le**, urgently. ~**gen**, (*med.*) acute.

-ivermek/-ıvermek, *etc. v. suf.* VERMEK *as aux. v.* [191] Do suddenly/rapidly [**çöküvermek**, suddenly collapse].

ivgi (*for.*) Axe/hatchet (for splitting wood).

iv·inti Speed, haste: ~ **yeri**, (*geo.*) (current) race; rapids. ~**me**, *vn.* hurry; (*phys.*) acceleration. ~**mek**, *vi.* be in a hurry. ~**meli**, accelerated.

iye Owner, possessor; landlord, proprietor. ~**lendirme**, (*leg.*) conveyancing. ~**lenmek**, possess. ~**lik**, ownership, possession: ~ +, *a.* (*ling.*) possessive: ~ **düşmesi**, (*ling.*) elision of the possessive suffix: ~ **eki**, (*ling.*) possessive suffix.

-iyet'ⁱ *n. suf. Denoting an abstract noun* [KETUMİYET].

iyi *a.* Good; plentiful; well, healthy, in good health; suitable. *n.* The good (side of stg.). ~ **bilmek**, have

a good opinion about s.o.: ~ **dilek**, goodwill, blessing: ~ **dilekli**, well-disposed: ~ **durum belgesi/ hal kâğıdı**, (*adm.*) certificate of good conduct: ~ **etm.**, make well, cure; do well; (*sl.*) rob: ~ **evsaflı**, in good condition: ~ **gelmek**, be useful/suitable: ~ **gitmek**, go well: ~ **gözle bakmamak (-e)**, have a bad opinion of: ~ **gün dostu**, fair-weather friend: ~ **gün görmemek**, live a troubled/anxious life: ~ **hazım**, (*med.*) eupepsia: ~ **huylu**, good-tempered, well-behaved: ~ **kalpli**, benign, kind-hearted: ~ **ki . . .**, it's a good thing that: ~ **konuşan**, fluent speaker: ~ **kötü**, mediocre; more or less; so so: ~ **kötü işi başarmak**, blunder through: ~ **misiniz hoş musunuz?**/~ **siniz inşallah!**, I hope you are well!: ~ **muamele etm. (-e)**, treat s.o. well/fairly: ~ **niyet**, good intention: ~ **niyet heyeti**, (*pol.*) goodwill mission: ~ **oldu ki . . .**; thank goodness that . . .: ~ **olm.**, be better/well; be suitable: ~ **saatte olsunlar**, (*myth.*) spirits, jinns; the unseen: ~ **söylemek (biri için)**, praise s.o.: ~ **ün**, respectability: (*fin.*) goodwill: ~ **den** ~ **ye**, properly, thoroughly: ~ **si**, the right (thing to do): ~ **si mi**, the best thing to do is . . .: ~ **ye çekme**, good faith: ~ **ye** ~ **kötüye kötü demek**, speak one's mind/without fear or favour.

iyi·ce *a.* Fair; rather good; (*med.*) convalescent: *adv.* fully, thoroughly. ~ **celik**, (*med.*) convalescence. ~**cene**, (*col.*) properly. ~**cil**, philanthropic, benevolent. ~**leşmek**, *vi.* improve, get better; (*med.*) recover. ~**leştirici**, curative. ~**leştirmek (-i)**, cure; correct, reform. ~**lik**, goodness; good deed, kindness, charity; good health; good part/side: ~ **bilmek**, be grateful: ~ **bilmez**, ungrateful: ~ **görmek**, receive kindness/favour: ~ **sağlık!**, we're well!: ~ **yap, denize at, balık bilmezse Halik bilir**, cast your bread upon the waters . . ., a good deed is never in vain: ~ **e yüz tutmak**, change for the better: ~ **ini söylemek**, speak well of: ~ **le**, soft-spoken. ~**likbilir**, grateful, appreciative. ~**likçi**/~ **liksever**, benevolent, philanthropic. ~**mser**, optimist(ic): ~ **piyasa**, (*fin.*) bull market. ~**mserlik**, optimism.

-iyle *n. suf.* [85] = İLE [BİSİKLETİYLE].

iyod- = İYOT. ~**oform**, (*chem.*) iodoform. ~ **ür**, iodide.

iyon (*phys.*) Ion. ~ +, *a.* (*phys.*) ionic; (*art.*) Ionic: ~ **düzeni**, (*art.*) Ionic order. ~**ik**, ionic. ~**lanma**/ ~**laşma**, *vn.* (*phys.*) ionization. ~**osfer**/~ **yuvarı**, (*ast.*) ionosphere.

iyo'ı'^{du} (*chem.*) Iodine.

iz Footprint; track; badge; (*math.*) path, trace; (*fig.*) sign, proof, trace. ~ **bırakmamak**, escape detection: ~ **toz**, s.o.'s tracks: ~ **i belirsiz olm.**, disappear without leaving a trace: ~ **i silinmek**, disappear completely, be forgotten: ~ **inde olm.**, be on s.o.'s track: ~ **inden yürümek (-in)**, follow in s.o.'s footsteps; (*fig.*) imitate, copy: ~ **ine basmak/sürmek (-in)**, observe s.o. till he is out of sight: ~ **ine dönmek**, retrace one's steps; (*fig.*) go back on one's word/decision: ~ **ine uymak**, follow in s.o.'s footsteps: ~ **ini düşürmek (bir cismin)**, (*math.*) project: ~ **ini kaybetmek**, lose track of: ~ **ini takip etm.**, follow s.o.'s tracks.

İz. = İZMİR.

-iz[1]**/-uz/-üz/-z** *a./n. suf.* [84] *Forming collectives from numerals* [İKİZ; BEŞİZ].

-iz[2]**/-ız/-uz/-üz** *v. suf.* [96] (We) are. = OLMAK [ZENGİNİZ].

izabe (*phys.*) Melting; fusion. ∼ **fırını**, (*min.*) blast furnace.

iza'ç[c1] Vexation, worry.

izafe Attaching, joining. ∼**t**[i], (*ling.*) [41, 50] the linking of two nouns by i/ı [**okul(un) öğretmeni**, the school('s) teacher: **Babıâli**, the Sublime Porte]; (*phil.*) relativity. ∼ **ten**, referring, attributing.

izafi Relative; (*phil.*) nominal. ∼ **sıklet**, (*phys.*) specific gravity. ∼ **lik**, relativeness. ∼ **yet**[i], (*phys.*) relativity.

izah Explanation. ∼ **etm.**, explain. ∼ **at**[1], explanations.

izale Removing, making disappear. ∼ **etm.**, remove, destroy.

izam[1] Sending.

izam[2] Enlarging, exaggerating. ∼ **etm.**, exaggerate.

izan Understanding; consideration. ∼ **etm.**, be considerate; think. ∼ **lı**, intelligent; considerate. ∼ **sız(lık)**, inconsiderate(ness).

izaz Honour, respect.

izbarço (*naut.*) ∼ **bağı**, bowline.

izbe *n.* Hovel, hut. *a.* Dark and dirty.

izbiro Sling (for lifting goods).

iz·ci Tracker; boy-scout. ∼ **cilik**, tracking; scouting. ∼ **dem**, (*art.*, *mus.*) theme. ∼ **deş**, (*rel.*) disciple.

izdiham Crowd; (traffic) congestion.

izdiva'ç[c1] Marrying; marriage. ∼ **etm.**, marry.

izdiya't[d1] Augmentation.

İz. DSO = İZMİR DEVLET SENFONİ ORKESTRASI.

izdüş·üm(ü) (*phys.*, *math.*) Projection. ∼ **ümsel**, (*math.*) projective. ∼ **üren**, (*math.*) projecting. ∼ **ürmek (-i)**, project.

izerge (*phil.*) Function, correspondence.

izge (*phys.*) Spectrum. ∼ **bilim**, spectroscopy. ∼ **çizer**, spectograph. ∼ **ölçer**, spectroscope.

izhar Manifestation. ∼ **etm.**, manifest, display.

iz'in[ni] Permission; consent; leave (of absence), day off; discharge. ∼ **almak**, take leave (to do stg.); take a holiday: ∼ **belgesi**, authorization, permit: ∼ **koparmak**, manage to get leave: ∼ **vermek**, grant, leave; allow, give permission; dismiss.

izin·li On leave. ∼ **name**, (*obs.*) permit, (marriage) licence. ∼ **siz**, without permission, unauthorized; absent without leave; (*ed.*) (punishment of being) 'kept in'/'gated': ∼ **almak**, be so punished: ∼ **kalmak**, be 'kept in'. ∼ **sizlik**, being unauthorized// 'kept in'.

iz·lem Tracking; pursuing; observing. ∼ **emci(lik)**, (work of) detective. ∼ **emek (-i)**, trace, track; pursue; follow; observe; watch; (*fig.*) follow (events), keep to (programme). ∼ **ence**, programme. ∼ **endirmek (-i)**, (*psy.*) impress. ∼ **enim**, (*psy.*) impression. ∼ **enimci(lik)**, (*art.*) impression·ist/(-ism). ∼ **enmek**, *vp.* (*psy.*) be impressed. ∼ **eyici**, *a.* following: *n.* (*phys.*) tracer.

İzm. = İZMİR.

izmarit[i] (*ich.*) Blotched picarel; (*col.*) cigarette-end. ∼ **giller**, sea-breams.

izmihlal (*obs.*) Collapse, disappearance.

izmineral (*chem.*) Trace element.

İzmir (*geo.*) İzmir; (*his.*) Smyrna; (*sl.*) type of dice. ∼ **köftesi**, (*cul.*) meatballs in tomato sauce: ∼ **yalı çapkını**, (*orn.*) white-breasted kingfisher. ∼ **li**, (*ethn.*) Smyrniote.

İzmit (*geo.*) İzmit; (*his.*) Nicomedia.

izn- = İZİN.

İznik (*geo.*) İznik; (*his.*) Nicaea.

izo- *pref.* Iso-; = EŞ-. ∼ **bar**, (*met.*) isobar. ∼ **hips**, (*geo.*) contour-line.

izo·lasyon (*el.*) Insulation; (*soc.*) isolation. ∼ **latör**, insulator. ∼ **le**, insulated: ∼ **etm.**, insulate; isolate.

izo·mer *a.* (*chem.*) Isomeric. ∼ **meri**, *n.* isomer. ∼ **merili**, *a.* isomeric. ∼ **morf**, (*chem.*) isomorphous. ∼ **term**, (*met.*) isotherm. ∼ **top**[u], (*phys.*) isotope. ∼ **trop**, (*phys.*) isotropic.

izzet[i] Might; honour; glory; dignity. ∼ **inef'is**[si], self-respect; amour-propre.

J

J, j [je; (zhe)] Thirteenth Tk. letter, J.
J = JANDARMA; JUL.
ja·guar (zoo.) Jaguar. ~**kamar(lar)**, (orn.) jacamar(s).
jakar (tex.) Jacquard loom.
jaketatay (mod.) Morning-coat.
jako (orn.) Grey parrot.
jale (met.) Dew; (fig.) tears.
jaluzi (dom.) Venetian blind.
Jamayka (geo.) Jamaica; (cul.) rum.
jambon (cul.) Ham.
jandarma (adm.) Gendarmerie; gendarme. ~**lık**, gendarme's duties; (jok.) trying to get stg. by force.
janjanlı = ŞANJANLI.
janr Type.
jant[i] Rim, felloe (of wheel).
Japon (ethn.) Japanese. ~ +, a. Japanese: ~ **tavuskuşu**, (orn.) green peafowl. ~**ca**, (ling.) Japanese. ~**gülü**[nü], (bot.) camelia. ~**ya**, (geo.) Japan.
jarse (tex., mod.) Jersey.
jartiyer, (mod.) Garter.
je (ling.) The Tk. letter J.
jelada (zoo.) Gelada monkey.
jelatin (chem.) Gelatine. ~**li benzin bombası**, (mil.) napalm bomb.
jeloz (bot.) Agar.
jene·ralize Generalized: ~ **etm.**, generalize. ~**rasyon**, (soc.) generation. ~**ratör**, (el.) generator; (ind.) steam generator. ~**rik**, (cin.) credits.
jenet[i] (zoo.) Genet(te).
je·netik (bio.) Genetic. ~**nosi**[t][di], (soc.) genocide.
jeo- pref. Geo-. ~**dezi**, geodesy. ~**fizik**, geophysical. ~**log**, geologist. ~**loji**, geology. ~**lojik**, geological. ~**morfoloji**, geomorphology. ~**sismik**, geoseismic. ~**termal**, geothermal.
jest[i] Gesture.

jet (aer.) Jet. ~ **motoru**, jet engine: ~ (**uçağı**), jet aircraft: ~ **yakıtı**, jet-fuel.
jeton (gamb.) Counter, chip, check.
JGK = JANDARMA GENEL KOMUTAN(LIĞ)I.
jibon (zoo.) Gibbon.
jiga- (math.) Giga-.
jigolo Gigolo.
jikle (mot.) Choke, throttle.
jile (mod.) Waistcoat.
jilet[i] Safety-razor. ~ **bıçağı**, razor-blade.
jimnastik (sp.) Gymnastics. ~ **adımla**, at the double: ~ **gülle**, dumb-bell: ~ **külotu**, (mod.) bloomers. ~**çi**, gymnast.
jinekolo·g (med.) Gynaecologist. ~**ji**, gynaecology.
jip (mot.) Jeep.
jips (geol.) Gypsum.
jir·asyon (phys.) Gyration. ~**oskop**[u], gyroscope.
jiujitsu (sp.) Jujitsu.
jiyan (obs.) Angry.
jokey (sp.) Jockey. ~ **klübü**, riding school.
jorjet (tex.) Georgette.
jöle (cul.) Jelly.
jön·prömiye (th.) Juvenile lead. ~**türk**, (his.) Young Turk.
judo (sp.) Judo. ~**cu**, judoist.
jul (phys.) Joule.
jurnal (pub.) Journal, diary; (adm.) report of police-informer, denunciation. ~ **etm.**, inform against, denounce. ~**cı(lık)**, (work of) informer.
jübile Jubilee.
jülide Disorganized; in confusion; scattered.
jülyen (ast.) ~ **takvimi**, Julian calendar.
jüp (mod.) Skirt. ~ **on**, petticoat, slip.
Jüpiter (myth., ast.) Jupiter.
jüri (leg.) Jury; committee of examiners/experts.
jüt (tex.) Jute.

K

K, k [ka/ke] Fourteenth Tk. letter, K. ~ **vitamini**, (*bio.*) vitamin K.

K, k. = (*chess*) KALE; (*aer.*) KALKIŞ; (*leg.*) KANUN; KARA; KARAR; KARŞILAŞTIRINIZ; KARŞIT; (*phys.*) KELVİN; KİLO; (*ling.*) KİŞİ; (*mil.*) KOMUTAN/ (-LIK); (*adm.*) KURUM³; (*fin.*) KURUŞ; (*geo.*) KUZEY; KÜÇÜK; (*ch.s.*) POTASYUM.

-k *a./n. suf.* [233] = -EK [TARAK].

ka/ke The Tk. letter K.

kA = KİLOAMPER.

kaa- *These words are now generally written* KA-.

kab- = KAP².

kaba Rough, coarse; ugly; common, boorish, crude, vulgar, = ~ KONUŞMADA; rough (estimate/ guess, etc.); gross; large but not heavy, puffed up, spongy. ~ **çakıl**, (*geol.*) coarse gravel, cobble/ (-stone): ~ **çini**, glazed earthenware: ~ **döşek**, soft downy mattress: ~ **et**, (*bio.*) buttocks; brawn: ~ **iş**, botched-up job; heavy-duty: ~ **kâğıt**, coarse wrapping paper: ~ **konuşmada**, (*ling.*) in vulgar speech: ~ KULAK: ~ **kum**, coarse sand: ~ **kumpas**, (*naut.*) dead-reckoning: ~ **olarak**, roughly: ~ **saba**, coarse; rough; common: ~ SAKAL: ~ **sesli**, gruff-voiced: ~ **sofu**, (*rel.*) fanatic, bigot: ~ SOĞAN: ~ SORTA: ~ **şiş** = ~ KULAK: ~ TASLAK: ~ **telaffuz**, (*ling.*) broad accent: ~ **toprak**, (*agr.*) freshly dug soil: ~ **Türkçe**, (*ling.*) simple Turkish (*originally as opposed to flowery literary language*): ~ YEL: ~ YONCA: ~ YONTU: ~ **sını almak**, tidy up roughly; get rid of the worst (dirt, etc.); (*carp.*) trim roughly, rough-hew.

kaba·bulut (*met.*) Alto-cumulus. ~ **burun**, (*ich.*) nase. ~ **ca**, roughly; coarsely, crudely; rather bigger/older. ~ **dayı**, bully, blusterer, 'tough guy'; (*fig.*) brave, generous; the best/most of . . .. ~ **dayılık**, bluster, bullying: ~ **taslamak**, bluster, show off.

kabahatⁱ Unseemly act; fault; offence. ~ **bende**, it's my fault; I am to blame: ~ **bulmak**, criticise, find fault: ~ **etm./işlemek**, commit an offence: ~ **kimde?**, whose fault is it?, who is to blame?: ~**i başkasında arama!**, you've only yourself to blame!: ~**i kendi üzerinden atmak**, exculpate o.s.: ~**i üzerine almak**, take the blame: ~**i üzerine atmak** (-nin), throw the blame on s.o. ~ **li**, guilty; at fault, to blame. ~ **siz**, innocent; blameless.

kabaⁱkᵍ¹ *n.* (*bot.*) Marrow; courgette, zucchini; pumpkin, squash; hashish pipe; (*mus.*) gourd-shaped guitar. *a.* Unripe, tasteless (melon); (*fig.*) ignorant, vulgar; bald, bare, close-shaven (head). ~ **başına patlamak** (-in), suffer a disaster: ~ **böceği**, (*ent.*) squash-bug: ~ **çekmek**, smoke hashish: ~ **çiçeği gibi açılmak**, (newcomer) be too forward; suddenly become too free and easy: ~

dolması, (*cul.*) stuffed vegetable marrow: ~ **gibi**, hairless, bald, bare: ~ **kafalı**, quite bald; close-shaven (head); (*fig.*) stupid: ~ **tadı vermek**, become a bore: ~**ı başka yerde patlatmak**, cause trouble to break out elsewhere.

kabak·çı (*mus.*) Gourd-shaped-guitar player. ~**giller**, (*bot.*) Cucurbitaceae, gourd family, marrows and pumpkins. ~**lamak** (-i), (*for.*) pollard. ~**laşmak**, *vi.* grow bald. ~**lık**, (melon) unripeness; (*fig.*) ignorance, coarseness; baldness.

kabakulaⁱkᵍ¹ (*med.*) Mumps.

kabala (*rel.*) Cabbala; spiritualism.

kabalaⁱkᵍ¹ (*mil.*) Ottoman soldier's hat (World War I).

kaba·laşmak *vi.* Become coarse/vulgar. ~**laştırmak** (-i), *vc.* make coarse. ~**lık**, coarseness, vulgarity.

kaballama (*min.*) Shoring up a gallery with pit-props.

kaban (*mod.*) Hooded overcoat, donkey-jacket.

kabara Hob-nail; (*dom.*) ornamental brass-headed stud. ~**lı**, so nailed.

kabarcıⁱkᵍ¹ Bubble; bladder; (*bio.*) pimple, blister. ~**lı**, ~ **düzeç**, (*arch., carp.*) spirit-level.

kabare (*mus.*) Cabaret.

kabarıⁱkᵍ¹ *a.* Swollen, blistered; convex; loose (in texture). *n.* Blister, swelling. ~ **deniz**, (*naut.*) high tide. ~**lık**, swelling; (*mot.*) camber (of road).

kabar·ma *vn.* Swelling; (*min.*) blistering; buckling; (*tex.*) bulking; (*fig.*) upheaval; heaving; (*geo.*) swell, flood tide: ~ **alçalma**, ebb and flow (of tides). ~**mak**, *vi.* swell; be puffed out; become fluffy; blister; be raised; be increased; (*cul.*) rise when boiling; (*geo.*) (tide) flow; (sea) become rough; (*fig.*) be puffed up, swell with importance. ~**tı**, swelling; puffiness; camber (of road). ~ **tma**, *vn.*; embossed (design); raised, in relief: ~ **harita**, (*geo.*) relief map. ~**tmak** (-i), *vc.* ~**tmalı**, with a raised/relief design, embossed.

kaba·sakal Having a bushy beard. ~ **soğan**, 'rotter', coward at heart. ~ **sorta**, (*naut.*) square-rigged. ~ **taslak**, roughly drawn, only in outline; crude. ~ **yel**, (*met.*) south wind. ~ **yonca**, (*bot.*) lucerne, alfalfa. ~ **yontu**, (*art.*) rough carving.

Kâbe (*rel.*) Kaaba (at Mecca); (*sl.*) drinking place. ~ **toprağı**, Üsküdar and beyond (from Istanbul).

kabız¹ *a.* Astringent.

kabⁱız^{z1 2} *n.* (*med.*) Constipation; grasping (with the hand). ~ **olm.**, be constipated; (*sl.*) be out of work; (*sl.*) be struck dumb: ~ **olunmak**, be grasped/ taken: ~ **verici**, constipating: ~ **vermek/yapmak**, constipate. ~**lık**, being constipated.

kabil¹ *a.* Capable, possible. ~**i**+*n.*, capable of, admitting [~ **istifade**, profitable: ~ **taksim**, divisible].

kabil² *n.* Sort, category. ~**den (bu)**, of this sort, like this: ~**inden**, on the lines of, stg. like.
Kâbil (*geo.*) Kabul.
kabile¹ *n.* (*med.*) Midwife. ~**lik**, midwifery.
kabile² *n.* (*soc.*) Tribe, clan; (*bot.*) genus. ~ **başkanı**, chieftain: ~ **harpleri**, (*mil.*) tribal warfare: ~ **teşkilatını bozmak/kaldırmak**, detribalize: ~ **üyesi**, tribesman, clansman.
kabili = KABİL¹.
kabiliyet¹ Capability; possibility; ability. ~**li**, capable, skilful; intelligent. ~**siz**, incapable; unintelligent. ~**sizlik**, incapability, incapacity.
kabin (*naut., aer.*) Cabin; booth. ~ **memuru**, (*aer.*) steward, hostess: ~ **yatağı**, bunk.
kabine (*pol.*) Cabinet; (*arch.*) small room; (*med.*) surgery (room); beach-hut; toilet, water-closet. ~ **çekilmek**, (*pol.*) (cabinet) resign: ~ **düşmek**, fall, be defeated.
kab'ir^ri Grave, tomb. ~ **azabı çekmek**, be greatly troubled: ~ **suali**, endless questioning.
kabl- *pref.* Before. ~**elmilat**, before Christ, BC. ~**elvuku**, before the event. ~**ettarih**, prehistoric. ~**ettufan**, before the Flood, antediluvian. ~**ezzeval**, before noon.
kab·laj (*el.*) Cabling, wiring. ~**lo**, cable, wire; conductor: ~ **başlığı**, terminal: ~ **döşemek**, lay a cable: ~ **gemisi**, (*naut.*) cable ship: ~ **işareti**, (*naut.*) cable sign.
kabotaj (*naut.*) Coastal trade; cabotage.
kabr- = KABİR. ~**istan**, cemetery.
kabu'k^gu Outer covering; (*bio.*) cortex, scale; (*bot.*) bark, rind, peel, shell, skin; (*zoo.*) skin, scale, shell, carapace; scab; (*geol.*) crust; (*min.*) scale; (*eng.*) casing, tubing. ~ **bağlamak**, form a skin/crust; (*med.*) (wound) heal over, cicatrize: ~ **böcekleri**, (*ent.*) bark beetles: ~ **reçinesi**, balsam: ~ **zarı**, (*bot.*) cuticle: ~**una çekilmek**, (*fig.*) retire into one's shell: ~**unu soymak**, remove the skin, etc.; (*bot.*) decorticate.
kabuk·lanmak *vi.* Form a skin, etc. ~**lu**, having a shell/skin, etc.; (*col.*) uncircumcised; (*bot.*) corticate; (*zoo.*) crustacean: ~ **bit**, (*ent.*) cochineal/scale insect: ~ **bitler**, (*ent.*) Coccidae, scale insects: ~ **yıldız**, (*ast.*) shell star. ~**lular**, (*zoo.*) Crustacea. ~**sal**, cortical. ~**su**, scaly. ~**suz**, without any skin/shell, etc.: ~ **sümüklüböcek**, (*zoo.*) slug. ~**suzlaştırma**, (*min.*) descaling.
kabul^ü *n.* Acceptance; acknowledgement; approbation, approval; (*soc.*) reception; admittance; consent. ~**!**, agreed!, done!: ~ **edilir**, acceptable, admissible: ~ **etm.**, accept, approve; acknowledge; receive; admit; consent: ~ **etmemek**, disapprove; decline; disallow: ~ **görmek**, (*soc.*) be received: ~ **günü**, (*soc.*) 'at-home' day: ~ **odası**, reception-room; drawing-room: ~ **olunur**, admissible: ~ **resmi**, court/state reception: ~ **salonu**, (*adm.*) audience-chamber: ~ **tecrübesi**, (*ind.*) acceptance trial/test: ~**e şayan**, (*fin.*) acceptable: ~**e sunmak**, present for acceptance.
kabul·cü (*fin.*) Acceptor. ~**lenme**, *vn.*; acceptance, acknowledgement. ~**lenmek (-i)**, accept, etc.; seize for o.s., appropriate.
kaburga (*bio.*) The ribs, a rib; (*naut.*) frame (of a

ship). + ~, *a.* Costal: ~**lar arası**, (*bio.*) intercostal: ~**ları çıkmak/sayılmak**, be very thin. ~**lı**, costate.
kâbus Nightmare.
kabz- = KABIZ. ~**a**, handle; hilt. ~**ımal(lık)**, (work of) middleman/wholesaler in fruit and vegetables.
kacak = KAP².
kaç¹ How many?; (+*sing.*) how much?; how many; how much. ~ **kere/kez?**, how many times?, how often?: ~ **para eder?**, what's it worth?, what use is it?; it's too late now!: ~ **paralık . . .**, useless . . .; in vain: ~ **parça olayım?**, which shall I do first?; I can't do everything at once!: ~ **tane?**, how many?: ~ **yaşındasın?**, how old are you?: ~**a?**, (for) how much?: ~**ın kur'asıyım**, I'm too old a bird for that trick.
kaçaburu'k^gu (*carp.*) Bradawl; shoemaker's awl.
kaça'k^g¹ *n.* (*leg.*) Fugitive; (*mil.*) deserter; (*fin.*) smuggled goods, contraband; leakage. *a.* Illegal; smuggled. ~ **arama**, (*ind.*) leak detection: ~ **inşaat**, (*arch.*) unlicensed building.
kaçak·çı Smuggler; tax evader. ~**çılık**, smuggling; tax evasion. ~**lık**, being illegal/smuggled; (*mil.*) desertion.
kaçama'k^g¹ ¹ *n.* (*cul.*) Maize flour and oil hasty-pudding.
kaçama'k^g¹ ² *n.* Flight; evasion; subterfuge; refuge; shelter. ~ **yapmak**, evade, dodge; try to escape: ~ **yolu**, excuse/trick/subterfuge (to avoid doing stg.). ~**lı**, evasive: ~ **söz**, equivocation.
kaçan¹ *adv.* (*prov.*) When; at the time that . . ..
kaçan² *a., n.* Running away; escapee.
Kaçar¹ *n.* (*ethn.*) Kajar. ~ **hanedanı**, (*his.*) Kajar dynasty (Persia).
kaçar² *n.* Fugitive. ~**lık**, (*phys.*) fugacity.
kaçar³ *a.* How many each? ~ ~, how many at a mouthful/time, etc.?: ~**a**, for how much each?
kaçarula (*cul.*) Casserole.
kaçgöç^ü (*soc.*) Muslim practice of women veiling their faces in the presence of men//of separating men from women in the home.
kaçık *a.* Receding; (*fig.*) eccentric, crazy, daft; (stocking) laddered. *n.* Ladder (in stocking). ~**lık**, eccentricity, craziness. ~**öz**, (*bot.*) eccentric growth.
kaç·ılmak *imp.v.* Be avoided; (*col.*) draw back, be reluctant. ~**ımsamak (-den)**, make excuses not to do stg. ~**ımsar**, evasive.
kaçıncı 'How manyeth?', which (in order)?: ~ **katta?**, (*arch.*) on which floor?
kaçın·gan Shy, unsociable. ~**ık**, recluse; (*rel.*) anchorite. ~**ılmaz**, inescapable, unavoidable, inevitable. ~**ım**, (*phys.*) correlation. ~**ımlı**, ~ **giderler**, (*fin.*) incidental expenses. ~**ma**, *vn.* avoidance; abstinence. ~**mak (-den)**, abstain (from), be reluctant; avoid, keep away from. ~**tı**, leak(age).
kaçır·ılmak *vp.* ~**mak (-i, -den)**, make/let escape; drive away; smuggle; abduct, kidnap: elope with; hide (possession, etc.); lose (opportunity, etc.); let slip (remark): **(-e)**, be incontinent; (child) mess its clothes: *vi.* go off one's head. ~**maz**, *a.* tight; that cannot slip.
kaçış *vn.* = KAÇMAK; fleeing; (*sp.*) outdistancing

(other competitors). ~ **noktası**, (*phys.*) infinity.
~**mak**, *vi.* disperse, flee in confusion.
kaçkın Fugitive, absconder; (*mil.*) deserter; (*ed.*)
truant; (*fig.*) crazy.
kaç·lı Having how many?; worth how much?:
~**sınız?**, (*mil.*) what is your year of birth/call-up
class? ~**lık**, worth how many (pounds, etc.); at
which price?
kaç·ma *vn.* (*mil.*) Desertion; absence without leave;
escape: ~ **kuşkusu**, (*leg.*) suspicion of (debtor's)
flight. ~**mak (-den)**, *vi.* flee, run away; avoid;
escape; leak; (*mil.*) desert; (*ed.*) play truant;
(woman) veil herself before men; seem (good/
inopportune, etc.); (stocking) ladder: **(-e)**, slip into;
approach, become; be prone/given to; verge on:
kaçacak delik aramak, seek somewhere to hide:
kaçanın anası ağlamamış, safety lies in being
cautious: **kaçıp kurtulmak**, break away, escape:
kaçmaktan kovalamaya vakit olmamak, have no
time for the less important matters.
kaçsız ~ **göçsüz**, (*soc.*) (woman) not observing the
rule about veiling in the presence of men.
kadana[1] *n.* (Prisoner's) fetters.
kadana[2] *n.* Heavy horse; artillery horse. ~ **gibi**,
huge (woman).
kadar *n.* [86] Quantity, amount, degree. *post.* [88]
As much as; as big as; about: **(-e)**, as far as; by,
until; down/up to, as far as. *Used to form the
equative degree* [**kaplan kadar büyük**, as big as a
tiger: **taş kadar sert**, as hard as stone]. ~ **sarkmak
(-e)**, go as far as. ~**cık**, a small amount.
kadastro Land survey/registry. ~ +, *a.* Cadastral.
kadavra (*bio.*) Corpse; carcass.
kadayıf (*cul.*) Name of various types of sweet
pastry. ~**çı(lık)**, (work of) KADAYIF maker/seller.
kadeh Glass; cup; wine-glass. ~ **kaldırmak**, raise
one's glass to: ~ **tokuşturmak**, clink glasses. ~**çik**,
(*bio.*) cupule; (*bot.*) acorn-cup.
kadem (*bio.*) Foot; (*math.*) foot (38 cm); pace; good
luck. ~ **basmak (-e)**, set foot in, enter: ~ **getirmek/
~i yaramak**, bring good luck.
kademe Step, stair; rung (of ladder); (*adm.*) grade,
rank; (*eng.*) stage. ~ ~, step by step, steadily;
(*mil.*) in echelon. ~**li**, in stage(s): ~ **dizi**, (*el.*)
cascade.
kadem·hane (*obs.*) Latrine. ~**li**, lucky, auspicious.
~**siz**, unlucky, inauspicious. ~**sizlik**, unluckiness.
kader Destiny, fate; doom; providence. ~ **darbesi**,
blow of fate: ~**de varmış/~i olduğu gibi**, it was
fated thus/inevitable: ~**in küs!**, it's a bit of bad
luck!; you're not to blame! ~**ci(lik)**, (*phil.*)
fatal·ist/(-ism). ~**iye**, (*rel.*) (Muslim sect believing
in) free will.
kadı (*leg.*) Muslim judge; cadi. ~**köy**, *pr.n.* (*geo.*)
Kadıköy; (*his.*) Chalcedon. ~**köytaşı**, (*geol.*) chalcedony.
kadın *n.* (*bio.*) Woman; (*soc.*) married woman;
lady; (*fig.*) servant. ~ +, *a.* Women's. *a.* Woman,
female: ~ **avcısı**, womaniser, woman-chaser: ~
berberi, hairdresser: ~ **büyükelçi**, (*adm.*) lady
ambassador, ambassadress: ~ **cimnastiği**, (*sp.*)
callisthenics: ~ **doktor**, female/woman doctor: ~
doktoru, (*med.*) gynaecologist: ~ **düşmanı**, miso-

gynist: ~ **elçi**, ambassadress: ~ **gibi**, effeminate:
~ **güzellikçisi**, beautician: ~ ~**a**, only amongst
women: ~ **kadıncık**, domestic-minded/homely
woman: ~ **kısmı**, the female sex, womenfolk: ~
nine, grandmother; elderly woman: ~ **olm.**, (*bio.*)
lose one's virginity; (*fig.*) be a good housewife:
~ **oyuncu**, (*th.*) actress: ~ **öğretmen**, school-
mistress: ~ **polis**, policewoman: ~ **sayfası**, (*pub.*)
women's page: ~ **sayrılıkları (uzmanı)**, (*med.*)
gynaecolo·gy/(-gist): ~ **terzi(liğ)i**, dress-mak·er/
(-ing): ~ **velinimet**, fairy godmother: ~ **yönetmen**,
manageress: ~**ın fendi erkeği yendi**, a woman's
wiles are too much for a man: ~**ın yüzünün karası
erkeğin elinin kınası**, illicit relations shame a
woman but men boast of them: ~**lar hamamı**,
women's Turkish bath; (*fig.*) very noisy place:
~**lara**, ladies' cloakroom, powder-room.
kadın·budu[nu] (*cul.*) Meat-and-rice rissoles fried in
egg batter. ~**cılk**[ğı] = KADIN ~. ~**cıl**, woman-
chaser. ~**göbeği**[ni], (*cul.*) doughnut-like sweet of
semolina and eggs. ~**lık**, qualities of a lady; ladylike behaviour. ~**sı**, ladylike, feminine; effeminate.
~**tuzluğu**[nu], (*bot.*) barberry.
kadırga (*naut.*) Galley; ancient warship. ~**balığı**[nı],
(*zoo.*) cachalot, sperm whale.
kadid- = KADİT.
kadife (*tex.*) Velvet. ~ **çiçeği**, (*bot.*) amaranth;
French marigold: ~ **gibi**, soft and bright.
kadim *a.* Old, ancient. *n.* Olden times. ~ **teamül
kanun gibidir**, custom has the force of law: ~ **yol**,
(*leg.*) ancient right-of-way.
kadinne (*col.*) Grandmother, old woman.
kadir[1] *a.* Mighty, powerful, strong. *pr.n.* God
Almighty.
kad'ir[ri 2] *n.* Worth; personal value; rank; dignity;
(*ast.*) magnitude. ~ **gecesi**, (*rel.*) Night of Power
(27 Ramadan) (when the Koran was revealed): ~
gecesi doğmuş, very lucky (in marriage): ~**ini
bilmek**, know the value of, appreciate: ~**ini sengi
musallada bilmek**, recognize s.o.'s worth only after
his death. ~**bilir/~şinas**, who appreciates merit/
value; appreciative. ~**bilirlik/~şinaslık**, appreciation.
Kadiri (*rel.*) Member of the Muslim ~LIK sect.
kadi't[di] *a.* Very thin. *n.* Skeleton; skin and bone;
sun-dried meat. ~**i çıkmak**, be all skin and bone.
kadmiyum (*chem.*) Cadmium.
kadran Face/dial (of clock, etc.).
kadril (*mus.*) Quadrille.
kadro (*adm.*) Staff; workforce; payroll; establishment; framework. ~ **harici**, not employed, on half-
pay: ~**ya dahil/~ lu**, on the permanent staff. ~**suz**,
unestablished, having no permanent position.
kaf (*ling.*) Arabic letter 'kaf'; (*myth.*) a fabulous
mountain. ~**tan ~a**, from one end of the world to
the other. = ~**DAĞI**.
kafa (*bio.*) Head; back of the head; nape; (*fig.*)
intelligence; mentality; (*child.*) big marble. ~ +, *a.*
(*bio.*) Cephalo-; cephalic ~ **değiştirmek**, change
one's mentality: ~ **dengi bir insan**, a man of one's
own kind, kindred spirit: ~ **duman olm.**, be
befuddled: ~ **göz yaran**, breakneck (speed): ~ **göz
yarmak**, be very quarrelsome/tactless: ~ ~**ya**

vermek, put their heads together (to discuss stg.): ~ KÂĞIDI: ~ **patlatmak**, work very hard (mentally); cudgel/rack one's brains over stg.: ~ **sallamak**, say 'yes' to everything; flatter s.o.: ~ **şişirmek**, give s.o. a headache by noise/worrying: ~ TASÇI: ~ TASI: ~ **tutmak**, be obstinate/defiant: ~ **ütülemek**, (*sl.*) bore s.o. stiff: ~ **vuruşu**, (*sp.*) heading: ~ **yağı**, (*sl.*) sperm: ~ **yormak**, ponder, think hard: ~ **yorucu**, head-splitting.

kafadan: ~ BACAKLI: ~ **gayrimüsellâh**, (*jok.*) off his head, 'having a screw loose': ~ **kontak**, (*col.*) unthinking, acting illogically: ~ **sakat**, weak in the head.

kafası: ~ **almamak**, not understand; be unable to take stg. in; be incomprehensible: ~ **boş**, empty-headed, stupid: ~ **bozulmak/kızmak**, get angry: ~ **dönmek**, be stupefied: ~ **dumanlı**, slightly tipsy; fuddled with too many different ideas: ~ **durmak**, be too tired to think: ~ **işlemek**, one's brain work well/'be in the right place': ~ **kazan olm./şişmek**, be distraught/dazed (by noise, work, etc.): ~ **kopasıca!**, damn him!: ~ **taşa çarpmak**, suffer for one's mistakes: ~ **yerinde olmamak**, lose one's head; be preoccupied: ~ **yerine gelmek**, collect one's thoughts, pull o.s. together.

kafasına: ~ **dank demek/etm.**, the truth suddenly dawn; learn one's lesson: ~ **koymak (-i)**, definitely decide to do stg.; make up one's mind: ~ **kurt sokmak**, put an idea into s.o.'s head: ~ **sığmamak**, be unable to understand: ~ **söz girmez**, he is stupid/obstinate: ~ **vur, ekmeğini elinden al**, (said of) s.o. very quiet and easy-going: ~ **vura vura**, by force: ~ **vurmak**, (strong drink) go to one's head.

kafasında: ~ **bir sual çengellenmek**, a query arise in one's mind: ~ **büyütmek**, exaggerate: ~ **şimşek çakmak**, suddenly have an idea/inspiration: ~ **n ayrılmamak**, follow s.o. wherever he goes.

kafasını: ~ **dinlemek**, rest one's brain: ~ **dinlendirmek**, rest o.s.: ~ **kullanmak**, act/behave intelligently: ~ **kurcalamak**, make s.o. think: ~ **patlatmak**, dig away at some problem: ~ **taştan taşa çarpmak**, repent bitterly: ~ **n dikine gitmek**, be self-willed; go one's way regardless.

kafayı: ~ **bulmak**, (*sl.*) become very drunk: ~ **çekmek**, (*sl.*) drink heavily: ~ **dumanlamak**, become fuddled: ~ **tütsülemek**, (*sl.*) become tipsy: ~ **(yere) vurmak**, be ill and take to one's bed.

kafa·danbacaklılar (*zoo.*) Cephalopods. ~ **dar**, *n.* intimate friend, crony: *a.* intimate; likeminded. ~ **darlık**, intimacy; likemindedness. ~ **içi**ni, (*bio.*) skull. ~ **kâğıdı**nı (*adm., col.*) identity card. ~ **lı**, having (a certain) head; intelligent, brainy. ~ **sız/(-lık)**, stupid(ity). ~ **tasçı(lık)**, (*jok.*) racial·ist/(ism). ~ **tası**nı, (*bio.*) skull, cranium.

Kafdağını *pr.n.* (*myth.*) Mountain inhabited by djinns; (*fig.*) great obstacle; (*geo.*) Caucasus. ~ **na kadar**, to the end of the world.

kafein (*chem.*) Caffeine.

kafes Cage; lattice; grating, grill; (*arch.*) framework (of wooden house); (*eng.*) carcass; (*sl.*) prison; (*his.*) compulsory isolation of Ottoman princes. ~ **devresi**, (*el.*) grid circuit: ~ **gibi**, a mere skeleton: ~ ~, full of holes: ~ **oyma**, (*arch.*) openwork; (*carp.*) fretwork: ~ **tamiri**, (*arch.*) repairs to building framework (without major changes): ~ **e almak**, (*sl.*) bore s.o. stiff: ~ **e girmek**, be duped: ~ **e koymak**, cage; (*fig.*) dupe, deceive, take in: ~ **te oturmak**, live in solitude.

kafes·çi Maker/seller of cages; (*sl.*) cheat, deceiver, money-grubber. ~ **lemek (-i)**, (*sl.*) cheat, deceive; get by cheating. ~ **lenmek**, *vp.* (*sl.*) be cheated. ~ **li**, having a cage; cage-shaped; reticulated: ~ **piton**, (*zoo.*) reticulated python. ~ **lik**, wire-netting.

kafeterya Cafeteria.

kaffe The whole, all, everyone. ~ **ten**, wholly, entirely.

kâfi Sufficient, enough; competent. ~ **gelmek**, be sufficient: ~ **ve vafi**, enough and more than enough.

kafile Caravan; convoy; group, gang.

kâfir *n.* (*rel.*) Unbeliever; non-Muslim, infidel. *int.* (*Expresses surprised admiration.*) ~ **istan**, (*obs.*) land of infidels, Europe. ~ **lik**, disbelief; irreligion.

kafiye (*lit.*) Rhyme. ~ **ci**, composer of rhymed verse. ~ **li**, rhyming. ~ **siz**, blank (verse), unrhymed.

Kafkas ~ **dağları/** ~ **lar**, (*geo.*) Caucasus Mountains: ~ **semenderi**, (*zoo.*) Caucasian salamander. ~ **ya**, (*geo.*) Caucasia; (*carp.*) dark walnut wood: ~ **köknarı**, (*bot.*) Caucasian pine. ~ **yalı**, (*ethn.*) Caucasian.

kaftan (*mod.*) Robe (of honour), caftan. ~ **böceği**ni, (*ent.*) ladybird.

kâfur (*chem.*) Camphor; (*fig.*) stg. very white. ~ **lu**, camphorated. ~ **u**, spirits of camphor.

kâgir (*arch.*) Built of brick/stone.

kağan (*his.*) Khan; ruler. ~ **lık**, khanate.

kağıştı Clashing/clanking noise.

kâğı·tdı *n.* Paper; letter; playing-card; (*sl.*) lira-note. *a.* Paper: ~ **açmak**, (*gamb.*) select trumps: ~ **balığı**, (*cul.*) fish cooked in paper/foil: ~ BALIĞI: ~ **gibi olm.**, become very pale (faced): ~ **hamuru**, cellulose: ~ **kavafı**, (*col.*) petty official: ~ **oyunu**, (*gamb.*) card game: ~ **para**, (*fin.*) paper money/currency, banknote: ~ **sepeti**, waste-paper basket: ~ **üzerinde kalmak**, (plan) remain on paper only, be hypothetical: ~ **a çekmek**, copy out (on paper): ~ **a dökmek**, commit to paper, write down: ~ **ta**, (*cul.*) cooked in grease-proof paper/foil.

kâğıt·ağacını/ ~ **dutu**nu (*bot.*) Paper mulberry (tree). ~ **balığı**nı, (*ich.*) dealfish. ~ **çı(lık)**, (work of) paper-maker/stationer. ~ **hane**, paper-mill; *pr.n.* (*geo.*) Sweet Waters of Europe. ~ **helvası**nı, (*cul.*) pastry in thin layers. ~ **lamak (-i)**, cover with paper. ~ **lanmak**, *vp.* ~ **lı**, wrapped in paper; (*pub.*) with wrapper. ~ **lık**, *n.* card-box: *a.* suitable for paper.

kağnı Two-wheeled ox-cart.

kağşa·k (*carp.*) Dry and cracking; about to collapse; decrepit; (*min.*) fatigued. ~ **ma**, (*min.*) fatigue: ~ **çatlağı**, fatigue crack. ~ **mak**, *vi.* (*carp.*) crack with dryness; be about to collapse; (*min.*) show fatigue; (*fig.*) become old and wizened.

kâh *n.* A time, moment; place. *adv.* At one time, sometimes. ~ ... ~ ..., at one time ... and at another ....

kah'ır[r1] An overpowering, subjugation; anxiety, distress. ~ **çekememek**, be unable to bear s.o.'s (oppressive) behaviour: ~ **çekmek**, suffer for a long time: ~ **yüzünden lütfa uğramak**, have good fortune arise from misfortune: ~ı **çekilir**, bearable, tolerable: ~ı **çekilmez**, unbearable, intolerable: ~ **ından ölmek**, die of a broken heart: ~ **ını çekmek** (-in), suffer anxiety/trouble on account of s.o. ~ **lanmak**, *vi.* be grieved/distressed. ~ **lı**, suffering deeply.

kâhil Adult; mature. ~ **lik**, adulthood; maturity.

kâhin Soothsayer; seer; diviner; oracle. ~ **lik**, soothsaying; prophecy.

kahir Overpowering, dominant, irresistible. ~ **ekseriyet**, crushing majority: ~ **kuvvet**, overwhelming force.

Kahire (*geo.*) Cairo. ~ **li**, (*ethn.*) Cairene.

kahkaha Loud laughter. ~ **atmak**, laugh noisily: ~ **ile gülmek**, roar with laughter: ~ **yı basmak/ koparmak/salıvermek**, burst out laughing. ~ **çiçeği**[ni], (*bot.*) convolvulus, bindweed.

kahpe *n.* Prostitute. *a.* (*vulg.*) Perfidious, deceitful. ~ **ın dölü**, (*vulg.*) bastard. ~ **lik**, prostitution; dirty trick, perfidious behaviour: ~ **etm.**, deceive/trick s.o. ~ **oğlu**[nu], (*vulg.*) 'son of a bitch'; low-down/ treacherous fellow.

kahraman Hero; champion; gallant fellow; (*lit.*) hero. ~ **ca**, heroically. ~ **lık**, heroism, bravery.

kahr- = KAHIR. ~ **ı etmek**[eder] (-i), overpower; crush, subdue: (-e), curse s.o.: *vi.* be distressed/anxious; fret. ~ **olmak**, *vi.* be worried. ~ **olsun!**, *int.* damn him!, curse him!; down with ...!

kaht[1] Drought; famine. ~ **zede**, drought-stricken.

kahvaltı (*cul.*) Light meal with coffee; breakfast. ~ **etm.**, partake of breakfast. ~ **lık**, food, etc. for breakfast.

kahve (*bot.*) Coffee-tree; coffee-bean; (*cul.*) coffee; coffee-house, café. ~ **çekirdeği**, coffee-bean: ~ **çekmek**, grind coffee: ~ **değirmeni**, coffee-mill/ -grinder: ~ **dolabı**, coffee-roaster: ~ **dövücünün hınk deyicisi** = HAVAN . . .: ~ **ibriği**, pot for Tk. coffee: ~ **ocağı**, room where coffee is made: ~ **parası**, tip: ~ **telvesi**, coffee grounds.

kahve·ci(lik) (Work of) coffee-seller/-maker// coffee-house owner. ~ **hane**, coffee-house. ~ **rengi**[ni/yi], coffee-colour; brown: ~ **kıçlı megapod**, (*orn.*) wattled brush turkey: ~ **köryılan(sı)**, (*zoo.*) slow-worm.

kâhya (*obs.*) Steward; butler, major-domo, bailiff; warden of a trade-guild; (*ind.*) union official; foreman; (*fig.*) busybody. ~ **kadın**, housekeeper: ~ **kesilmek**, set o.s. up as adviser to others; interfere in other people's affairs: ~ **sı yok**, he can do as he likes. ~ **lık**, post/duties/fees of steward, etc.: ~ **etm.**, act as steward, etc.; (-e), meddle in the affairs of ....

kaide Base, pedestal; (*fig.*) rule, principle, custom; (*eng.*) bearer. ~ **ye uymıyan**, anomalous: ~ **yi çiğnemek**, ignore a rule. ~ **ten**, according to rule; in principle.

kail Saying; consenting, agreeing. ~ **etm.**, persuade: ~ **olm.** (-e), consent/agree to.

kaim Standing; lasting; taking the place of; perpendicular. ~ **olm.** (-le), exist thanks to . . .; be dependent on . . .: ~ **olm.** (**yerine**), act for . . ., take the place of . . .. ~ **e**, (*adm.*) official paper; (*obs.*) bank-note.

kâin Existing, being. ~ **olm.**, exist; be situated. ~ **at**[1], cosmos, the universe; everybody: ~ **ilmi**, cosmography.

kak[i 1] *a.* Dried up, shrivelled. *n.* Dried fruit.

kak[i 2] *n.* (*geol.*) Cavity where rainwater collects.

kaka (*child.*) *a.* Bad. *n.* Excrement. ~ **yapmak**, excrete.

kaka'ç[c1 1] *n.* (*cul.*) Salted and dried food; dried buffalo meat.

kaka'ç[c1 2] *n.* (*orn.*) Beak, bill; (*min.*) embossing tool. ~ **ına**, (*orn.*) snipe.

kakadu (*orn.*) Cockatoo.

kakalamak[1] (-i) Keep on pushing.

kakala·mak[2] (-e) *vi.* (*child*) Excrete. ~ **nmak**, *vi.* be fouled with excrement.

kakan (*orn.*) Woodpecker; = AĞAÇKAKAN.

kakao (*bot.*) Cacao tree; cacao/cocoa bean; (*cul.*) cocoa. ~ **yağı**[nı], (*cul.*) cocoa butter.

kakavan Tiresome, peevish and old. ~ **lık**, peevishness: ~ **etm.**, be peevish.

kakı'ç[c1] Fisherman's gaff.

kakılı Nailed; driven in.

kakım (*zoo.*) Ermine; stoat.

kakı·mak (-i) Rail at, scold, reproach. ~ **n'ç**[c1], railing, scolding.

kakırca (*zoo.*) Dormouse.

kakır·dak (*ech.*) *a.* Making a crackling noise: *n.* (*cul.*) skin, etc., of suet/sheep's tail fat after melting down the fat. ~ **damak**, *vi.* rattle, rustle, crackle; become dry and hard; be lifeless; (*sl.*) die, croak. ~ **datmak** (-i), *vc.*; (*sl.*) kill. ~ **tı**, (*ech.*) crackling noise (from dry things).

kakış·mak (-le) Push/shove one another about. ~ **tırmak** (-i), push lightly but continuously.

kak·ma *vn.* (*art.*) Relief/repoussé work; marquetry, inlay: *a.* worked in relief, repoussé: ~ **işi**, damascening. ~ **macı**, (*art.*) relief-/inlay-/marquetry-worker. ~ **macılık**, relief-work, inlay, marquetry, damascening. ~ **mak** (-i), push; prod; tap; nail; (*art.*) strike metal to raise relief on other side; inlay; encrust (with jewels, etc.); (*tex.*) embroider with a raised pattern (of gold/silver/mother-of-pearl). ~ **malı**, *a.* covered with inlay, etc.

kaknem Dry, thin and weak; (*sl.*) very ugly.

kako- *pref.* Caco-. ~ **foni**, cacophony.

kaktüs (*bot.*) Cactus. ~ **çit kuşu**, (*orn.*) cactus wren. ~ **giller**, (*bot.*) Cactaceae.

kakule (*bot., cul.*) Cardamom.

kâkül (Side-)lock of hair. ~ **lü**, with pendant locks: ~ **bela**, a damned nuisance.

kal[i 1] *n.* Speech; talk. ~ **e almak**, take into consideration: ~ **e gelmek**, be discussed/considered.

kal[i 2] *n.* (*min.*) Operation of refining metals; cupellation. ~ **potası**, cupel.

kal. = KALORİ.

kala *gerund* [176] = KALMAK; (time) before . . .,

remaining to . . ., wanting to . . .; (place) distant from . . ., short of . . .: = BEŞ; SAAT: ~ ~ . . . **kaldı,** only . . . remains; all that is left is . . . .

kalaazar (*med.*) Tropical fever, kala-azar.

kalaba(lık) *n.* Crowd, throng; (traffic) congestion; confused mass; mass of furniture/belongings. *a.* Crowded, thronged; bustling: ~ **etm.,** be in the way: ~ **halinde girmek,** crowd in: ~ı **kaldırmak,** tidy up: ~**lar,** unnecessary things, junk. ~**laşmak,** *vi.* form a crowd.

kalafat[1] (*naut.*) Caulking; (*carp.*) false decoration to hide repairs; trick; (*his.*) Janissary helmet. ~ **yeri,** (*naut.*) repair yard: ~**a çekmek,** beach for repairs; (*fig.*) put s.o. where he can't use his abilities.

kalafat·çı(lık) Caulk·er/(ing). ~**lamak (-i),** caulk; (*fig.*) repair like new. ~**lanmak,** *vp.*

kala'k[gı] (*zoo.*) Nose tip, nostril.

kalakalmak *vi.* Stand petrified (with fear/surprise).

kalamar (*zoo.*) Common squid, calamary, cuttle-fish.

kalamış Reed-bed, marsh (on sea-shore).

kalamin (*chem.*) Calamine.

kalan *a.* Remaining; residual. *n.* (*math.*) Remainder. ~**ca,** remainder, balance.

kalantor (*sl.*) Seemingly well-to-do/important person.

kalao (*orn.*) Rhinoceros hornbill.

kalas (*carp.*) Beam; rafter.

kalastra (*naut.*) Boat-chocks.

kalay (*chem.*) Tin; tinsel; (*sl.*) scolding, cursing. ~ **atmak/vermek,** scold: ~ **kaplama,** tin-plating: ~ **kaplı,** tin-plated: ~ı **basmak,** abuse, curse, swear.

kalay·cı(lık) Tinsmith('s work); (*fig.*) fraud, impostor. ~**la'ç**[cı], tinning machine. ~**lama,** *vn.* tinning. ~**lamak (-i),** tin; adorn superficially; (*sl.*) abuse. ~**lanmak,** *vp.* ~**latmak (-i, -e),** *vc.* ~**lı,** tinned; containing tin; tinsel; sham. ~**sız,** untinned; without tin.

kalb- = KALP[2, 3]. ~**en,** *adv.* from the heart, sincerely. ~**i,** *a.* from the heart, cordial.

kalbur Sieve, riddle, screen. ~ **gibi,** full of holes, riddled with holes: ~ **kemiği,** (*bio.*) ethmoid bone: ~**a dönmek,** be riddled (with holes): ~**dan geçirmek,** sieve, riddle, screen: ~**la su taşımak,** make futile efforts.

kalbur·cu Maker/seller of sieves and riddles; s.o. who riddles/sieves things. ~**lamak (-i),** riddle, sieve. ~**lanmak,** *vp.* ~**latmak (-i, -e),** *vc.* ~**üstü**[nü], the 'cream', the choicest/most distinguished: ~ **nde kalmak/~ne gelmek,** be selected/chosen.

kalcı (*min.*) Smelter; refiner.

kalça (*bio.*) Hip. ~ **kemeri,** hip-girdle: ~ **kemiği,** hip-bone. ~**lı,** with broad hips.

kalçete (*naut.*) Gasket; packing.

kalçın Coarse felt/leather inside a boot.

kaldır·a'ç[cı] (*phys.*) Lever: ~ **kolu,** lever arm. ~**an,** *a.* lifting. ~**ga,** winch, crane. ~**ıcı,** *n.* (*bio.*) elevating muscle; (*eng.*) jack: ~ **kuvvet,** (*aer.*) lift. ~**ılma,** *vn.* cancellation, abolition. ~**ılmak,** *vp.* = KALDIR-MAK.

kaldırım Pavement; causeway. ~ **çiğnemek,** (*fig.*) increase one's experience (by living in towns): ~

karga/yaması, (*sl.*) loose woman: ~ **mühendisi,** (*jok.*) loafer, tramp, ne'er-do-well: ~ **süpürge/ yosması,** (*fig.*) street-walker: ~ **taşı,** paving-stone.

kaldırım·cı Paver; (*sl.*) loafer; pickpocket, purse-snatcher. ~**cılık,** paving the streets; (*sl.*) pocket-picking. ~**lı,** paved. ~**sı,** (*bio.*) pavement (epithelium). ~**sız,** unpaved.

kaldır·ma *vn.* Lifting; carrying; removal; cancellation; repeal: ~ **kuvveti,** (*phys.*) lift, thrust. ~**ma'ç**[cı], (*ind.*) fork-lift. ~**mak (-i),** *vc.* = KALKMAK (*not* KALMAK!): raise, erect; lift; carry; take away, remove; kidnap, carry away; (*leg.*) abolish, abrogate, cancel; tolerate, bear; let start/ sail; cause to get up; (*med.*) cause to recover; (*sl.*) steal, pinch. ~**tmak (-i, -e),** *vc.*

kale (*mil.*) Fortress, castle; citadel; castle walls; (chess) castle, rook; (*sp.*) goal. ~ **burcu,** bastion: ~ **gibi,** as firm as a rock: ~ **vuruşu,** (*sp.*) goal-kick: ~**yi içinden fethetmek,** capture/win by betrayal. ~**bent(lik),** (*pol.*) confine·d/(-ment) in a fortress. ~**ci(lik),** (*sp.*) goalkeep·er/(-ing).

Kaledonya (*geo.*) Caledonia.

kalem (*bot.*) Reed; pen; paint-brush; (*agr.*) plant-cutting; (*carp.*) fine chisel, turning tool; (*adm.*) office, department; (*fin.*) item/entry (in accounts); category, class; style; (*med.*) vaccination tube. ~ **açmak,** sharpen a pen(cil): ~ **çekmek (üstüne),** draw a line through, cancel: ~ **efendisi,** (*adm.*) clerk: ~ **işi,** work done with a pen//chisel: ~ **kaşlı,** having slender eyebrows: ~ **kömürü,** high quality charcoal: ~ **kulaklı,** (animal) with small upright ears: ~ **oynatmak,** write; correct; spoil by altering: ~ **parmaklı,** with long delicate fingers: ~ **sahibi,** (*lit.*) good writer: ~ **tartışması,** polemics: ~**e almak,** write; draw up, edit: ~**e gelmez,** indescribable; unreasonable: ~**i olm.,** write (in such a way): ~**inden çıkmak,** be written by . . .: ~**inden kan damlamak,** (*col.*) write movingly; have a brilliant style. ~**aşısı**[nı], (*agr.*) grafting with a cutting.

kalembe'k[gi] (*bot.*) Aloes wood; type of maize.

kalem·dan Pen-case. ~**en,** in writing.

kalemis (*zoo.*) Civet-cat.

kalem·kâr (*tex.*) Painter of designs (on muslin, etc.); engraver (on gold/silver). ~**lik,** pen(cil) case. ~**şor,** (*lit.*) hack-writer, ghost-writer. ~**tıraş,** pen-knife; pencil-sharpener.

kalender Wandering mendicant/dervish; s.o. living the simple life; unconventional person, bohemian. ~**ane,** unconventional; free and easy. ~**hane/~ yurdu,** hospice for wandering dervishes. ~**i,** ballad sung to SAZ accompaniment. ~**leşmek,** *vi.* behave/ live like a wandering dervish. ~**lik,** wandering/ unconventional life.

kalensöve (*mod.*, *obs.*) Peaked headgear; (*bot.*) calyptra.

kaleska Small open carriage.

kaleta (*cul.*) Type of biscuit.

kalevi (*chem.*) Alkaline.

kaleydosko'p[bu] Kaleidoscope.

kalfa Master-builder, contractor; qualified workman, charge-hand; (*obs.*) head of female servants; (*ed.*, *obs.*) usher. ~**lık,** work/position/fees of KALFA.

kalgımak vi. (dial.) Give a slight jump/start; prance, run.

kalhane (met.) Refinery; smelting works.

kalıcı Continuing, lasting, permanent; residual. ~lık, continuance, permanence; (phys.) permanent magnetism; (phil.) subsistence.

kalı¹çᶜ¹ (agr.) Sickle.

kalı¹kᵍ¹ a. Defective, lacking, incomplete; missed. n. Elderly spinster, 'left on the shelf'.

kalım Life, survival. ~lı, permanent, lasting; perennial; stable; immortal. ~lılık, permanence; stability; immortality. ~sız, impermanent, transient; mortal. ~sızlık, transience; mortality.

kalın¹ n. Present/settlement from bridegroom to bride.

kalın² a. Thick; stout; coarse; dense; (sl.) rich. ~ halat, (naut.) cable: ~ harf, (pub.) bold face/type: ~ kafa(lı), thick-head(ed): ~ ses, deep voice: ~ sıra, (ling.) back vowels (A, I, O, U): ~ ünlü, (ling.) back vowel: ~YAĞ.

kalın·bacaklı(lar) (orn.) Stone-curlew; (thick-knees). ~bağırsak, (bio.) large intestine, colon: ~ yangısı, (med.) colitis. ~laşmak, vi. become thick, etc.; (ling.) become a back vowel. ~laştır-mak/~latmak (-i), vc. make thick, etc. ~lık, thickness; depth; coarseness; stupidity.

kalın·mak imp. v. Remain, stay. ~tı, residue; (fin.) remainder, balance, arrears; (tex.) remnant; ruins, debris.

kalınyağ (min.) Heavy oil; (eng.) lubricating oil.

kalı¹pᵇ¹ Mould; form; die; model; last, shoe-tree; block; cake/bar (soap, etc.); (phil.) schema; (fig.) appearance; shape. ~ dökümü, (min.) cast(ing): ~ gibi serilmek, lie stretched out: ~ gibi uyumak, sleep like a log: ~ gibi yatmak, lie in bed, etc., from laziness: ~ kesilmek, be petrified: ~ kıyafet, appearance: ~ kıyafet yerinde amma yürek Selanik, he looks all right but at heart he's a coward: ~ sabun (bir), a bar/cake of soap: ~ sigarası, freshly-rolled cigarette: ~a dökmek, (min.) pour into the mould, cast: ~a vurmak, put (hat) on block for reshaping: ~ı değiştirmek/ dinlendirmek, (sl.) die: ~ı kıyafeti yerinde, very showy appearance: ~ını basmak, guarantee stg.: ~ının adamı olmamak, appearances deceive: ~tan ~a girmek, make any changes needed for profit.

kalıp·çı (eng.) Maker/seller of moulds, dies, etc.; (fig.) knave, trickster. ~çılık, making/selling moulds, etc.; die-sinking. ~lamak (-i), make in a mould; block (hats). ~lanmak, vp. ~laşmak, vi. take on a particular shape. ~laşmış, a. having a permanent shape; (fig.) unchanging; (ling.) stereotyped, cliché: ~ iyelik, (ling.) frozen forms with the 3rd possessive suffix [ÇOĞU]. ~latmak (-i, -e), vc. ~lı, moulded; having shape: ~ dövme, (min.) drop-forging.

kalıt¹ (leg.) Inheritance. ~ almak, inherit. ~ bırakan, testator. ~çı, inheritor, heir(ess). ~ım, inheritance; (bio.) hereditary quality/characteristic; heritage: ~ belgesi, (leg.) will, testament: ~ bilimi, (bio.) genetics: ~ iplikçiği, (bio.) chromosome: ~ vergisi, (fin.) death/estate duty. ~ımcı(lık), heir/

(heredity). ~ımsal, hereditary. ~sal, inherited, hereditary.

kali·brasyon Calibration. ~bratör, calibrator. ~bre, bore, calibre (of guns): ~ etm., calibrate. ~breli, calibrated.

kalifiye Qualified, competent.

kaliforniyum (chem.) Californium.

kaliks (bot.) Calyx.

kalinis (orn.) Dotterel.

kalinos (ich.) Common perch.

kalite Quality. ~ denetimi, (ind.) quality control: ~si bozuk, good-for-nothing, degenerate: ~sini düşürmek, adulterate. ~li, of good quality. ~siz, of poor quality. ~sizlik, poor quality.

kalk v. = KALKMAK. ~ borusu, (mil.) reveille.

kalkan (mil.) Shield; (arch.) gable. ~ (balığı), (ich.) turbot. ~bezi ⁿⁱ, (bio.) thyroid gland: ~ alıklığı, (med.) cretinism. ~böcekleri, (ent.) tortoise beetles. ~lı, bearing a shield: ~ böcek, (ent.) shield bug.

kalker (geol.) Limestone, chalk. ~leşmek, vi. calcify. ~li, calcareous.

kalk·ık Raised; lifted; erect, on end. ~ımak = KALGIMAK. ~ındırma, vn. bringing progress. ~ındırmak (-i), vc. ~ınma, (fin., soc.) recovery; development, progress: ~ Bakan(lığ)ı, (adm.) Minis·ter/(-try) for Development: ~ hızı, rate of development/progress: ~ programı, development programme: ~ınmak, vi. (med.) improve, recover; (fin.) make material progress, develop. ~ış, (aer.) take-off; departure; (rly.) departure; (fig.) venture: ~-varış (çizelgesi), (rly. etc.) timetable. ~ışan, presumptuous, audacious. ~ışma, vn. attempt. ~ışmak (-e), attempt stg. beyond one's ability; pretend to be able to do stg.

kalkmak vi. Rise; get up; start (to do stg.); decide (to do stg.); set out (on journeys); start from; (aer.) take off; (naut.) (set) sail; (rly.) depart; (adm.) be annulled/cancelled; be removed/done away with; disappear; stand up, rise; (pol.) rise in rebellion. **kalk gidelim olm.**, (sl.) disappear, get lost; be stolen: **kalkar köprü**, (eng.) bascule bridge: **kalkıp oturmak**, show one's anger by one's movements: **kalkmış**, afoot.

kalko- pref. (geol.) Chalco-.

Kalküta (geo.) Calcutta; (tex.) calico.

kallavi n. (his.) Ceremonial turban; (dom.) large coffee-cup. a. Huge; weighty.

kalleş Unreliable, untrustworthy; mean, caddish. ~çe, treacherously. ~lik, unreliability; dirty trick: ~ etm. (-e), play a dirty trick on s.o.

kalma vn. Act of remaining; spending time at a place. a. Remaining (from); dating (from): ~ (-den), inherited from: ~ durumu, (ling.) locative case.

kalmak vi. Remain; be left; be left over; be, become; survive; halt; cease; be abandoned; be postponed; spend (time at a place), stay the night; (wind) drop. aux. v. denoting continuation of an action [bakakalmak, keep on looking]. ~ (-den), be prevented from/remain without (doing stg.); be inherited from: KALA: **kala kala**, there only remains; all that is left: **kala ~**, suddenly find o.s. in difficulties; be left in the lurch; be disconcerted: **kaldı ki**, there remains the fact that . . .; it only remains to say . . .; and moreover: **kalır yeri yok (-den)**, he/she/it is not much better than . . .: **kal(ır)sa (-e)**, in the opinion of . . .; if it's left to . . .: **kalsın!**, leave it!; it doesn't matter.

kalmalı *a.* Remaining; surviving. ~ **tümleç**, (*ling.*) locative phrase.

kaloma (*naut.*) Slack (of rope/anchor-chain). ~ **etm.**, pay out (rope).

kalomel (*chem.*) Calomel, mercurous chloride.

kalori (*phys.*) Calorie; (*cul.*) calorie. ~**fer**, (*dom.*) radiator; central heating. ~**ferci(lik)**, (work of) heating-system engineer/boilerman. ~**fik**, calorific. ~**metre**/~**ölçer**, (*phys.*) calorimeter.

kaloş (*mod.*) Galosh(es).

kalp[1] [1] *a.* False; counterfeit, spurious; adulterated; (*fig.*) blustering; insincere, untrustworthy. ~ **akçe sürmek**, pass counterfeit money.

kal'p[bi] [2] *n.* Conversion; transformation; transposition. ~ **etm.**, convert; transform; transpose.

kal'p[bi] [3] *n.* (*bio.*) Heart; (*med.*) heart disease; (*phys.*) core, nucleus; (*fig.*) feeling, sentiment. ~ +, *a.* Cardiac; cardio-: ~ **bilimi**, (*med.*) cardiology: ~ ~**e karşıdır**, friendship is mutual: ~ **kırmak**, hurt s.o.'s feelings: ~ **olmamak (-de)**, be heartless/pitiless: ~ **sektesi**, (*med.*) heart attack: ~ **soğutma sistemi**, (*phys.*) core-cooling system: ~**i çarpmak**, (heart) palpitate, throb; beat fast: ~**i dinleme**, (*med.*) auscultation: ~**i kırık**, heartbroken, hurt: ~**i kırılmak**, be offended/hurt: ~**ine doğmak**, have a presentiment: ~**ine girmek**, win s.o.'s affections: ~**ine göre**, according to one's feelings for others: ~**ten bağlı**, affectionate: ~**ten rahatsız olm.**, (*med.*) have heart trouble: ~**ten yaralı**, afflicted, grieved.

kalpa'k[ğ] [1] (*mod.*) (Fez-like) headgear of fur/astrakhan. ~**çı**, KALPAK maker/seller. ~**lı**, wearing KALPAK.

kalpazan False-coiner, counterfeiter; (*fig.*) liar, cheat. ~**lık**, counterfeiting.

kalp·laşmak *vi.* Lose one's skill/ability. ~**lık**, falseness; being good for nothing.

kalp·li Having a weak heart; -hearted. ~**siz**, unkind, insensitive; pitiless. ~**sizlik**, pitilessness.

kalseduan (*geol.*) Chalcedony.

kal·sine ~ **etm.**, (*chem.*) calcinate. ~**sit**[i], (*geol.*) calcite. ~**siyum**, (*chem.*) calcium.

kaltaban(lık) (State/work of) pander//cuckold//charlatan.

kalta'k[ğ] [1] Saddle(-tree); (*fig.*) whore. ~**lık**, (woman's) dishonourable behaviour.

kalubela ~**dan beri**, from time immemorial.

kalya (*cul.*) Vegetable stew.

kalyon (*his.*) Galleon. ~**cu**, sailor; (*sl.*) old sea-dog.

kam[1] (*eng.*) Cam.

kam[2] (*rel.*) Shaman.

kâm Desire, wish. ~ **almak (-den)**, enjoy stg. to the full.

kama Wedge; dagger; (*mil.*) breech-block; (*eng.*) key; (*naut.*) chock; (*sp.*) scoring mark. ~**cı**, gun-repairer. ~**msı**, wedge-shaped: ~ **kertenkele**, (*zoo.*) wall lizard.

kama·ra (*naut.*) Cabin; (*adm.*) chamber, house: ~ **iskelesi**, companion-way. ~**rilla**, (*pol.*) camarilla. ~**rot(luk)**, (*naut.*) (duties of) steward.

kamaş·mak *vi.* Be dazzled; (teeth) be set on edge. ~**tırmak (-i)**, dazzle; set on edge.

kamber ~**siz düğün olmaz!**, of course he must come!

kambiyo (*fin.*) Foreign exchange (operations). ~ **rayici**, rate of exchange: ~ **senedi**, bill of exchange: ~ **tellalı**, broker. ~**cu**, money changer.

kambriyum (*geol.*) Cambrian (system).

kambur Hunchback(ed); round-back(ed); crooked, warped. ~ **balina**, (*zoo.*) humpback whale: ~ **felek**, cruel fate: ~ ~ **üstüne**/~ **üstüne** ~, one trouble after another: ~ **kumbur/zambur**, bumpy, uneven: ~**u çıkmak**/~**laşmak**, *vi.* become hunchbacked: ~**unu çıkartmak**/~**laştırmak**, make hunchbacked. ~**luk**, being hunchbacked; protuberance.

kamçı Whip; (*naut.*) pendant, tail; (*bio.*) flagellum. ~ **başı**, (*tex.*) coarse silk: ~ **kuyruk**, (*live.*) fine type of KIVIRCIK.

kamçı·lamak (-i) Whip; (rain) beat down; (*fig.*) excite, stimulate. ~**lanmak**, *vp.* ~**latmak (-i, -e)**, *vc.* ~**lı**, having a whip; (*fig.*) using force: ~ **kırbaç**, cat-of-nine-tails. ~**lılar**, (*zoo.*) flagellates.

kamelya (*bot.*) Camellia.

kamer (*ast.*) Moon. ~ **takvimi**, (*ast.*) lunar calendar. ~**balığı**[n] [1], (*ich.*) sunfish.

kamera (*cin.*) Cinema camera. ~**man**, cameraman

kameriye Arbour, small garden pavilion.

kamet[i] [1] Stature. ~**i artırmak**, become insolent.

kamet[i] [2] ~ **getirmek**, (*rel.*) announce the beginning of NAMAZ.

kamga Chip (of wood).

kamış (*bot.*) Reed; (sugar-)cane; fishing-rod; (*bio.*) penis. ~ **atmak (-e)**, (*sl.*) play a trick on s.o. ~ **başı**, (*bio.*) glans penis: ~ **böceği**, (*ent.*) reed-beetle: ~ **iskemle**, cane(-bottomed) chair: ~ **kemiği**, (*bio.*) fibula: ~ **koymak (arasına)**, (*sl.*) create a rift between.

kamış·çık (Jeweller's) blowpipe; nozzle of bellows (*bio.*) clitoris. ~**kalem**, reed-pen. ~**kulak**, (*zoo.*) horse with long pointed ears. ~**lı**, having a reed etc.; large-stemmed. ~**lık**, reed-bed, cane-brake ~**sı**, reed-like.

kâmil Perfect; complete; mature; of mature years well-educated; well-behaved. ~**ce**, in a quiet and good-mannered way. ~**en**, perfectly; fully; entirely ~**lenmek**, *vi.* become mature. ~**lik**, perfection.

kamineto Small spirit lamp.

kamlı (*eng.*) Having a cam. ~ **mil**, camshaft.

kamp[1] Camp; camping; (*pol.*) concentration camp ~ **kurmak**, set up camp: ~**ı dağıtmak**, break camp.

kampana Bell; (*sl.*) testicle. ~**cı**, (*sl.*) charlatan.

kampanya (*agr.*) Cropping-season; (*pol.*) campaign.

kamp·çı Camper. ~**ing**, camp-site. ~**us**, (*ed.*) campus.

kamu *a.* (*obs.*) All; the whole. *n.* The people; the public. ~ +, *a.* Public, civil, state: ~ **borcu**, (*fin.*) public debt: ~ **davası**, (*leg.*) public prosecution

~ **düzeni,** public order/safety: ~ **duyuruları,** (*pub.*) public notices/information: ~ **gelirleri,** (*fin.*) public income, state revenue: ~ **giderleri,** public expenditure: ~ **görevi,** (*adm.*) public service; civil service: ~ **hakları,** political rights: ~ **hizmeti,** public service: ~ **hukuku,** public law: ~ **iktisadi teşekkülü,** (*com.*) state enterprise: ~ **işletmeleri,** state enterprises; public utilities: ~ **malları,** public property: ~ OYU: ~ **personeli,** (*adm.*) public/civil servants: ~ **sağlığı,** public welfare: ~ **sektörü,** (*fin.*) public sector: ~ TANRICI: ~ TAY: ~ **toprağı,** public domain, common land: ~ **türesi,** (*leg.*) public law: ~ **tüzel kişiliği,** public corporation: ~ **yararı,** public interest, common good: ~ **yönetimi,** public management: ~ **ya sunmak,** publish.

kamu·flaj (*mil.*) Camouflage. ~ **fle,** camouflaged: ~ **etm.,** camouflage.

kamu·laştır(ıl)ma *vn.* (*leg.*) Expropriation; nationalization. ~ **laştırılmak,** *vp.* ~ **laştırmak (-i),** expropriate; collectivize; nationalize. ~ oyu^{nu}, public opinion: ~ **na duyurmak,** (*pol.*) make known to the public: ~ **nu yoklamak,** (*pol.*) put to the vote.

kamus (*ling.*) Large dictionary, lexicon.

kamu·sal Public, official; communal; collective; state. ~ **sallaşma,** *vn.* ~ **sallaşmak,** *vi.* become public/state property. ~ **tanrıcı(lık),** (*rel.*) pan-the·ist/(-ism). ~ **tay,** (*adm.*) Tk. Grand National Assembly.

kamyon (*mot.*) Lorry, truck, large van; (*sl.*) immoral woman. ~ **cu,** transport-lorry operator; lorry-driver. ~ **culuk,** transport-lorry operation; lorry-driving. ~ **etⁱ,** small lorry, van.

kan (*bio.*) Blood; (*soc.*) descent, family, relationship; breed; bloodshed; vendetta. ~ **ağlamak,** weep bitterly; be in deep distress: ~ **akçesi,** (*obs.*) blood money: ~ **akıtma,** blood-letting: ~ **akıtmak,** shed blood; sacrifice: ~ **akmak,** (blood) be shed, flow: ~ **aktarımı** = ~ AKTARIM: ~ **aktarmak,** give a blood transfusion: ~ **almak,** take blood; shed blood; bleed s.o.: ~ **azlığı,** (*bio.*) ischaemia: ~ **bağı her şeyden kuvvetlidir,** blood is thicker than water: ~ **bankası,** (*med.*) blood-bank: ~ **basınç/baskısı,** (*bio.*) blood-pressure: ~ **basıncı yüksekliği,** (*med.*) hypertension: ~ **başına sıçramak/beynine çıkmak,** get very angry: ~ **birikmesi,** (*med.*) congestion: ~ **boğmak (-i),** (*med.*) s.o. die of cerebral haemorrhage: ~ **çanağı,** (*obs.*) barber's bleeding basin: ~ **çanağı gibi,** with blood-shot eyes: ~ **çıbanı,** (*med.*) boil, furuncle: ~ **çıkmak,** blood be spilt: ~ **damarı,** (*bio.*) blood-vessel: ~ **davası,** blood-feud, vendetta: ~ DOKU: ~ **dolaşımı,** blood circulation: ~ **dökme,** carnage: ~ **dökmeden,** bloodless: ~ **dökmek,** shed blood; wound, kill; be wounded, die: ~ **dökücü,** blood-thirsty: ~ **emici yarasa,** (*zoo.*) vampire bat: ~ **gelmek,** *vi.* bleed: ~ **gitmek (-den),** (*med.*) bleed profusely (esp. during defecation/menstruation): ~ **gövdeyi götürmek,** there's a regular massacre going on; 'there's a hell of a mess': ~ **gözesi,** (*bio.*) blood-cell: ~ **grubu,** (*bio.*) blood-group: ~ **gütmek,** cherish a vendetta: ~ **hısımlık/karabeti,** consanguinity, blood-relationship: ~ **istemek,** (*leg.*) demand the death penalty: ~ **kanseri,** (*med.*)

leukaemia: ~ **kardeşi,** blood-brother; intimate friend: ~ **kırmızı,** blood-red; (*fig.*) evil: ~ KURU-TAN: ~ **kusmak,** vomit blood; be in great pain, suffer greatly: ~ **kusup kızılcık şerbeti içtim der,** (*said of*) s.o. who is too proud to reveal his real trouble: ~ **kusturmak,** cause great pain: ~ **nakli,** (*med.*) blood transfusion: ~ **olm.,** be bloodstained; be killed; cause bloodshed: ~ **olm. (aralarında),** be a blood-feud between them: ~ **oturmak,** blood be effused (in bruise, etc.): ~ **pıhtısı,** (*bio.*) clot of blood; embolus: ~ **plazması,** blood plasma: ~ **portakalı,** (*bot.*) blood orange: ~ **rengi,** blood-red: ~ **revan içinde,** covered in blood; bleeding freely: ~ **sağlantısı,** (*bio.*) blood supply: ~ **serumu,** (*bio.*) blood serum: ~ **sülünü,** (*orn.*) blood pheasant: ~ TAŞI: ~ **ter,** profuse sweat: ~ **ter içinde kalmak/tere batmak,** be in a profuse sweat; make great exertions: ~ **tipi,** (*bio.*) blood type/group: ~ **tutmak,** faint at the sight of blood; (victim) haunt a murderer: ~ **uyuşmazlığı,** (*med.*) blood incompatibility: ~ **verici,** blood-donor: ~ **vermek,** transfuse blood; give blood for transfusion: ~ **yürümesi,** (*bio.*) blood congestion: ~ **zehirlenmesi,** blood-poisoning.

kana: ~ **boyamak,** cause bloodshed: ~ **boyanmak/bulanmak,** be blood-stained: ~ **bulamak,** stain with blood; cause a massacre: ~ **kan istemek,** demand the killer's death: ~ **kanmak,** shed blood unsparingly: ~ KANMAK: ~ **susamak,** be out for blood: ~ **susamış,** bloodthirsty.

kanı: = KANI: ~ **bozuk,** (*med.*) suffering from unhealthy blood/indigestion; (*fig.*) degenerate, base: ~ **donmak,** be petrified: ~ **ısınmak (-e),** warm to s.o.: ~ **içine akmak,** keep one's troubles to o.s.: ~ **kaynamak,** be very lively/restless; (-e), take to/grow fond of s.o.: ~ **kurumak,** be beside o.s. with anxiety/suffering: ~ **pahasına,** at the cost of one's life: ~ **sıcak,** warm-hearted, sympathetic, lovable: ~ **soğuk,** cold-mannered; antipathetic: ~ **sulanmak,** (*med.*) be(come) anaemic.

kanına: ~ **dokunmak,** make one's blood boil; hurt one's pride: ~ **ekmek doğramak (-in),** rejoice openly in s.o.'s afflictions: ~ **girmek,** have s.o.'s blood on one's hands; have raped a woman: ~ **susamak,** thirst for s.o.'s blood.

kanında: ~ **var,** inborn, innate; inherited.

kanını: ~ **emmek (-in),** suck s.o.'s blood; exhaust, exploit pitilessly: ~ **içine akıtmak,** conceal one's resentment/anxieties: ~ **kurutmak (-in),** persecute s.o.; vex/exasperate s.o.

kanıyla: ~ **ödemek,** pay for stg. with one's life.

-kan a. suf. [223] = -GEN [UNUTKAN].

kana[1] *n.* (*naut.*) Waterline/draught marks (stem and stern).

kana[2] = *n.* KAN; *v.* KANMAK.

kanaat[1] Contentment; conviction; opinion. ~ **etm.,** be satisfied: ~ **getirmek,** be convinced/persuaded: ~ **notu,** (*ed.*) mark based on teacher's opinion: ~ **sahibi,** contented with what he has: ~ **indeyim,** I am of the opinion that . . .: ~ **ine varmak,** reach an opinion: ~ **lerine bağlı kalmak,** stick to one's

opinions/'guns'. ~**kâr**/~**li**, contented; satisfied with little, abstemious, ~**kârlık**, contentment.
kanaçiçeğini (*bot.*) Canna.
kanad- = KANAT.
Kanada (*geo.*) Canada. ~ +, *a.* Canadian: ~ **geyiği,** (*zoo.*) moose, wapiti: ~ **kazı,** (*orn.*) Canada goose: ~ **koyunu,** (*zoo.*) bighorn/Rocky Mountains sheep: ~ **kunduzu,** N. Amer. beaver. ~**lı,** (*ethn.*) Canadian.
kanağan (*psy.*) Credulous. ~**lık,** credulity.
kanaktarım (*med.*) Blood transfusion.
kanal (*geo.*) Canal; (*bio.*) canal, duct; (*el., rad.*) channel; (*eng.*) conduit, culvert; (*carp.*) dovetail slot.
kanal·cıᵏᵏᵍ¹ (*bio.*) Canaliculus. ~**izasyon,** drainage. ~**ize,** ~ **etm.,** channel. ~**lı,** ducted. ~**sız,** ductless.
kana·ma *vn.* Bleeding; (*med.*) haemorrhage. ~**mak,** *vi.* bleed. ~**malı,** with bleeding.
kanara (*obs.*) Slaughterhouse, abattoir.
kanarya (*orn.*) Canary. ~ **Adaları,** *pr.n.* (*geo.*) Canary Islands: ~ **çiçeği,** (*bot.*) garden nasturtium, Indian cress: ~ **otu,** (*bot.*) canary grass: ~ **sarısı,** canary yellow. ~**lık,** canary-breeding cage.
kana·tᵈ¹ (*orn., aer., mil.*) Wing; (*aer.*) aerofoil; (*ich.*) fin, flipper; blade; (door) leaf; (screen) fold; (tent) flap; (windmill) sail; (waterwheel) paddle. ~ **açısı,** (*aer.*) dihedral angle: ~ **alıştırmak,** try to get used to a job: ~ **boyu,** (*aer.*) wing span: ~ **germek (üstüne)**/~**ı altına almak,** take under one's protection: ~ **şekli,** aliform: ~ **şeklinde,** alar: ~**ı altına sığınmak,** be under s.o.'s protection.
kanata Earthenware/tin goblet (for measuring fluids).
kanat·ayaklıgiller (*zoo.*) Fruit-bats. ~**çı**ᵏᵏᵍ¹, (*eng.*) flange; vane; (*aer.*) aileron. ~**lanmak,** *vi.* be fledged; take wing; fly away; (*fig.*) become strong. ~**lı,** (*orn.*) winged, alate; (*ich.*) finned; folding, folded: ~ **at,** (*myth., ast.*) Pegasus: ~ **bomba,** (*mil.*) flying bomb: ~ **keseli,** (*zoo.*) flying phalanger: ~ **sıtması,** (*orn.*) bird malaria: ~ **somun,** (*eng.*) butterfly/wing nut: ~**lar,** (*ent.*) winged insects. ~**sız,** (*orn.*) wingless, flightless, apterous; (*ich.*) apodal: ~**lar,** (*ent.*) flightless insects.
kanatmak (-i) (*med.*) Bleed s.o.; make bleed; draw blood.
kan·ava/~**aviçe** (*tex.*) Coarsely-woven linen, canvas.
kanb- *pref.* = KAMB-.
kanca Large hook; meat-hook; (*naut.*) boathook; (*dom.*) tongs; (*pub.*) staple. ~**yı atmak/takmak (-e),** make a grab at stg.; (*fig.*) 'have one's knife into' s.o., 'have a down on' s.o.
kanca·lamak (-i) Grapple with a hook; put on a hook; connect, couple; (*fig.*) 'have a down on' s.o. ~**lı,** hooked, barbed: ~ **dişli engerek,** (*zoo.*) moccasin: ~ **iğne,** safety-pin: ~ **kurt,** (*zoo., med.*) hookworm.
kancı·kᵍ¹ (*zoo.*) Bitch; any female animal; (*fig.*) perverse/treacherous person. ~**ça,** treacherously. ~**lık,** treachery; deceit: ~ **etm.,** be treacherous/deceitful.
kançıl (*zoo.*) Chevrotain.

kançılar (*adm.*) Consular assistant, chancellery clerk. ~**lık**/~**ya,** chancellery (office, work).
kandaş One of the same blood, blood-brother. ~**lık,** consanguinity, kinship.
kandela (*phys.*) Candle-power, candela.
kandıra(otu) (*bot.*) Small reed, calamagrostis.
kandır·ıcı *a.* Convincing; deceiving; satisfying. ~**ıcılık,** a convincing, persuasion; deceit. ~**ılmak,** *vp.* ~**ma,** *vn.* persuasion. ~**maca,** bluff. ~**mak (-i),** convince, persuade, cajole; deceive, trick, cheat; satisfy, satiate.
kandil *n.* (*obs.*) Oil-lamp. *a.* (*sl.*) Drunk. ~ **çöreği,** (*cul.*) cake for KANDİL GÜNÜ feast: ~ **gecesi,** (*rel.*) night of a Muslim feast (when minarets are illuminated): ~ **günü,** day before KANDİL GECESİ: ~ **yağı,** poor quality olive-oil: ~**in yağı tükenmek,** one's life draw to a close.
kandil·ci Lamplighter of mosque. ~**leşmek (-le),** greet each other on KANDİL GÜNÜ. ~**li,** decorated with lamps, illuminated; (*sl.*) very drunk; = GEÇ-MİŞİ/ÖLÜSÜ: ~ **küfür,** coarse swearing: ~ **selam**/**temenna,** bowing and scraping: ~ **sümbül,** (*bot.*) grape hyacinth. ~**lik,** oil-lamp store.
Kandiya (*geo.*) Candia/Herakleion (Crete).
kandoku (*bio.*) Blood plasma and cells.
kanepe¹ *n.* (*dom.*) Couch, sofa; bench. ~-**yatak,** divan.
kanepe² *n.* (*cul.*) Canapé.
kangal Coil, loop; skein. ~ **etm.**/~**lamak (-i),** coil, wind in a skein. ~**lanmak,** *vi.* coil up: *vp.* be coiled.
kangren (*bio.*) Gangrene. ~ **olm.**/~**leşmek,** *vi.* be affected with gangrene; (*fig.*) become hopeless, insoluble.
kanguru (*zoo.*) Kangaroo. ~ **faresi,** kangaroo rat.
kanı Opinion. ~**sınca,** according to his opinion.
kanık Contented, satisfied. ~**lamak (-le),** be contented with. ~**lık,** contentment, satisfaction ~**mak (-e),** become satiated with. ~**samak (-e)** be inured to; be sick of/satiated with. ~**satmak** cloy. ~**sıcak,** pleasant, well-liked.
kanır·mak (-i) Force back; bend; break off; try to force open. ~**tma**ᵏᶜ¹, lever, crowbar. ~**tmak (-i)** remove by force/bending.
kanış Opinion, conviction.
kanıt¹ Proof, evidence, argument. ~**lama,** *vn.* proving; argumentation: ~ **yükümü,** burden of proof ~**lamak (-i),** prove stg. ~**lanım,** proof. ~**lanmak** *vp.* ~**lı,** supported by evidence. ~**samak (-i),** consider as proof of . . ... ~**sav,** (*phil.*) theorem.
kani Contented; satisfied; convinced.
kaniş (*zoo.*) Poodle(-dog).
kankan (*mus.*) Cancan dance.
kan·kurutan (*bot.*) Mandrake. ~**lamak (-i),** stain with blood. ~**landırmak (-i),** *vc.* ~**lanmak,** *vi.* be stained with blood; become bloodshot; become healthy. ~**lı,** bloody; (*cul.*) underdone, rare guilty of murder; full-blooded: ~ **basur/sürgün** (*med.*) dysentery: ~ **bıçaklı olm.,** fight to wound (*fig.*) be at daggers drawn: ~ **canlı,** full of health robust: ~ **gömleğini giymek (-in),** be after s.o. blood: ~ **katil,** savage killer: ~ **kavga,** murderou affray: ~ **yaş dökmek,** weep bitterly.
kanmak (-e) Be persuaded/convinced; be deceive

by; be content with; be satiated/satisfied. **kana kana**, to repletion: **kana kana dinlemek**, drink in (ideas).
kano (*naut.*) Canoe. ~**tye**, (*mod.*) straw-hat, boater.
kansa = KONSA.
kanser (*med.*) Cancer. ~**li**, cancered, cancerous.
kansız Bloodless; without shedding blood; (*med.*) anaemic; (*fig.*) weak, cowardly. ~ **cansız**, weak and anaemic. ~**laşmak**, *vi.* become anaemic. ~**lık**, (*med.*) anaemia. ~**su**, (*bio.*) plasma.
kanş (*bot.*) Hair-grass.
kant (*cul.*) Hot drink with lemon and sugar.
kantar Weighing-machine, balance, steelyard; (*obs.*) weight of 44 okes (56 kg.). ~ **ağası**, (*his.*) weights and measures controller: ~ **topu**, ball of a steelyard: ~**a çekmek/vurmak**, weigh stg.; (*fig.*) weigh up in one's mind: ~**ı belinde**, wide awake, acute: ~**ın topunu kaçırmak**, go too far, overdo stg.
kantar·cı(lık) (Work of) weighing-machine maker/ seller//public weighing official. ~**iye**, fee for weighing. ~**lı**, (*sl.*) curse: ~ **atmak**, curse, abuse: ~ **küfür**, violent abuse.
kantar·ma Curb-rein (on horse). ~**mak (-i)**, pull up/curb (horse).
kantaron (*bot.*) Common centaury.
kantaşıⁿ¹ (*geol.*) Agate, blood-stone, haematite.
kantat¹ (*mus.*) Cantata.
kantin Canteen. ~**ci(lik)** (work of) canteen-operator.
kanti·tatif Quantitative. ~**te**, quantity.
kanto (*mus.*) Canto; song (in cabaret, etc.) ~**cu(luk)**, (work of) cabaret-singer.
kanton (*adm.*) Canton. ~ +, *a.* Cantonal.
kanun¹ *n.* (*mus.*) Dulcimer. ~**i**¹, dulcimer player.
kanun² *n.* (*leg.*) Rule, law, code of laws. ~ **dışı**, outside the law, outlaw: ~ **hükmünde olm.**, have the force of law: ~ **tasarısı**, draft law: ~ **vazetmek**, lay down a law: ~ **yapıcı**, lawmaker: ~ **yolları**, legal channels: ~**a rağmen**, in defiance of the law: ~**dan kaçmak**, abscond: ~**ların çatışması**, conflict of laws: ~**u çıkmak**, law be promulgated: ~**u çiğnemek**, ignore the law: ~**un çerçevesine sığmaz**, it is not in accordance with the law.
kânun = BİRİNCİ/İKİNCİ ~; ~**u-**.
kanun·en According to law; legally. ~**i**², *a.* legal; legislative: *pr.n.* Lawgiver (Süleyman I). ~**iyet**¹, force of law; legality: ~ **kesp etm.**, become legal. ~**laşmak**, *vi.* become law. ~**laştırmak (-i)**, *vc.* ~**name**, code of laws. ~**suz**, without law; illegal; lawless. ~**suzluk**, illegality; lawlessness.
kânunu·evvel (*obs.*) December. ~**sani**, (*obs.*) January.
kanut ~ **kuşu** (*orn.*) red knot.
kanül (*med.*) Cannula.
kanyak (*cul.*) Cognac, brandy.
kanyon (*geo.*) Canyon.
kanyotᵘ (*gamb.*) Pool, pot.
kaolin (*geol.*) Kaolin, china-clay.
kaon (*phys.*) Kaon.
kaos (*phil.*) Chaos.
kap¹ ¹ *n.* (*mod.*) Cape; mantle.
kap¹**p**ᵇ¹ ² *n.* Cover; envelope; vessel; receptacle, con-

tainer; (*cul.*) dish, portion (of food); parcel, package. ~ **geçirmek (-e)**, put a cover on; bind (books): ~ **kacak**, pots and pans; household goods: ~ **yok kacak yok**, bare of the simplest necessities: ~**ına sığmamak**, be uncontrollably impatient/ambitious, etc.
Kap³ *pr.n.* (*geo.*) ~ (**şehri**), Cape Town: ~ **dokumacı kuşu**, (*orn.*) Cape weaver: ~ **muzculu**, (*orn.*) violet turaco.
kâ¹**p**ᵇ¹ (*bio.*, *obs.*) Knuckle-bone; (*gamb.*) dice. ~**ına varılmaz**, unrivalled, peerless: ~**ına varamamak**/ ~**ında olmamak (-e)**, not reach the standard of . . . .
kapa·cı¹**k**ᵍ¹ Small cover; (*bio.*) valve, valvula. ~¹**ç**ᶜ¹, valve.
Kapadokya (*geo.*) Cappadocia.
kapa¹**k**ᵍ¹ Cover; lid; cap; (*pub.*) cover; (*naut.*) hatch; (*aer.*) canopy. ~ **kâğıdı**, (*pub.*) endpaper: ~ **taşı**, broad flat stone; coping-stone: ~**ı (dar) atmak (-e)**, take refuge in a place; succeed in reaching a place.
kapak·çık = KAPACIK; (*bio.*) valve. ~**lanmak**, *vi.* stumble and fall on one's face; overturn; (*naut.*) capsize. ~**lı**, having a lid/cover; (*fig.*) concealed; clandestine. ~**lık**, (*arch.*) coping stone.
kapalı Shut; covered; closed; shut-in, secluded, out-of-the-world; indoor; (*adm.*) secret, closed; covert; obscure. ~ **alan**, (*sp.*) indoor arena: ~ **bez**, (*bio.*) ductless gland: ~ **celse/oturum**, (*adm.*, *leg.*) secret session, in camera: ~ **çarşı**, (*fin.*) covered market: ~ **devre**, (*el.*, *rad.*) closed circuit: ~ **eksiltme**, (*adm.*) sealed tender: ~ **fonksiyon**, (*math.*) implicit function: ~ **gişe**, (*th.*) house full: ~ **hece**, (*ling.*) closed syllable: ~ **kalp ameliyatı**, (*med.*) heart-operation (without stopping the heart): ~ **kutu**, a closed box; a secret; inscrutable (man): ~ **salon** +, (*sp.*) indoor-: ~ **sekilik**, (*sp.*) covered stand: ~ **tekne**, (*geol.*) closed basin: ~ **yer korkusu**, (*psy.*) claustrophobia: ~ **yetişmek**, grow up in seclusion/on one's own: ~ **zarf (usulü)**, (*adm.*) sealed envelope (tender).
kapalı·ca Vague, indefinite. ~**lık**, a being covered, etc.; vagueness. ~**tohumlular**, (*bot.*) flowering plants.
kapa·ma *vn.* Act of shutting, etc.; (*soc.*) mistress; (*mod.*, *obs.*) complete ready-made suit; (*ind.*) masking; (*cul.*) stew of lamb, onions and lettuce. ~**macı**, (*obs.*) dealer in ready-made clothes. ~**mak (-i)**, shut, close; shut up; confine; cover up; hush up (scandal, etc.); turn off (tap, etc.); fill up (hole, etc.); (*fin.*) close (an account); (*el.*) make (a circuit).
kapan¹ *v.* = KAPMAK. *a.* Who seizes/grabs. ~ **da kaçan mı?**, (*dial.*) nothing doing!, no you don't!: ~ ~**a**, a general scramble: ~**ın elinde kalmak**, be in great demand.
kapan² *n.* Trap (for animals); (*agr.*) wicker cover for tobacco plants. ~ **kurmak**, set a trap: ~**a düşmek/girmek/tutulmak/yakalanmak**, (*fig.*) get into difficulties: ~**a düşürmek**, catch by deceit: ~**a kısılmak**, fall into a trap.
kapan·ca Small trap; small wicker cover. ~**ık**, shut in/confined (place); (*met.*) cloudy, overcast; (*psy.*) unsociable, shy, introspective, gloomy. ~**ıklık**, a

being shut in; shyness. ~ **ım**, (*adm.*) enclave. ~ **ış**, closure; (*ind.*) shut-down: ~ **tarihi**, (*adm.*) closing date. ~ **kaplumbağa**, (*zoo.*) snapping turtle. ~ **tı**, (*ling.*) stop, occlusion.

kapanmak *vp.* Be shut/closed; be shut up/confined; be covered; (*met.*) be dull and cloudy; (subject, etc.) be closed; shut o.s. up, not go out; (woman) veil herself before men; (*ind.*) cease work, close down; fall down, stumble; (*med.*) (wound) heal up; (*soc.*) (family) die out; (*naut.*) (ship) broach to: (**-e**), be absorbed/engrossed in.

kapari (*bot.*, *cul.*) Caper.

kaparo (*fin.*) Earnest/key money.

kaparoz (*sl.*) Illicit gain; bribe. ~ **etm.**, (strive to) obtain stg.: ~ **a gezmek**, be on the look out for pickings. ~ **cu**, s.o. who lives by his wits. ~ **lamak** (**-i**), obtain stg. illicitly/by force.

kapasi·te Capacity, volume; (*el.*) capacitance; (*fig.*) capacity, ability. ~ **tör**, (*el.*) capacitor.

kapat·ılmak *vp.* Be abrogated. ~ **ım**, closing. ~ **ımlı**, prisoner. ~ **ma**, *vn.* shut-down, closure; cut-off (tap); (*sp.*) blocking (a player); (*soc.*) kept mistress: *a.* confined; obtained illicitly/by deceit. ~ **mak** (**-i**), *vc.* = KAPAMAK *and often used with the same meanings*; acquire by deceit; get stg. cheaply; keep (a mistress); (*pub.*) forbid publication, close down.

kapça·ˡkᵍ¹ Long-handled large hook.

kapçıˡkᵍ¹ Small container; (*bot.*) husk, shell; (*min.*) cap, detonator. ~ **meyve**, (*bot.*) achene.

kapelan (*ich.*) Capelin.

kapı Door; gate; (*fin.*) situation, employment; place of employment; cause for expenditure; (*col.*) the Government; (*gamb.*) point (in backgammon). ~ **açmak** (**-den**), prepare the way for stg., hint at stg.: ~ **ağası**, (*his.*) chief white eunuch: ~ **almak**, (*gamb.*) make a block (in backgammon): ~ **aralığı**, (*sl.*) bastard: ~ **baca açık**, open to all; unguarded, unprotected: ~ **boşluğu**, door opening/aperture: ~ **çuhadarı**, (*his.*) courier, messenger: ~ **dayağı**, prop to keep a door shut: ~ **dışarı etm.**, show s.o. the door, eject, chuck out: ~ **dikmesi**, (*arch.*) door-post: ~ **duvar**, no one opened the door (to ringing/knocking): ~ **gibi**, (s.o.) large, powerful: ~ **halkı**, (*his.*) household (of great persons): ~ **kadar**, long and broad: ~ **kâhya/kethüdası**, (*his.*) provincial governor's agent with central government: ~ **kapamaca**, everyone in the house, the whole household: ~ ~ **dolaşmak**, go from door to door; (*adm.*) apply to every government office: ~ **kol/kulpu**, door-handle/-latch: ~ **komşusu**, next-door-neighbour: ~ KULE: ~ KULU: ~ **mandalı**, door-latch; (*fig.*) unimportant person: ~ **mapı**, doors and the like: ~ **oğlanı**, (*his.*) agent of embassy/Patriarchate conducting business with the Government: ~ **sundurması**, awning: ~ **tamponu**, door-stop: ~ **topuzu**, door-knob: ~ **yapmak**, prepare the way for stg. one wants/will say; (backgammon) capture a point: ~ **yavrusu**, wicket-gate: ~ **yeri**, doorway: ~ **yoldaşı**, fellow-servant; colleague.

kapı-: ~ **dan kovsan bacadan düşer**, one can't get away from such a bore: ~ **nın ipini çekmek**, call at so many houses: ~ **sı açık**, hospitable, welcoming:

~ **sı bacası yok**, tumble-down/jerry-built building: ~ **sı olm.**, be a matter of so much money: ~ **sına kilit vurmak**, lock up a place; (*ind.*) close down: ~ **sından olm.**, (servant) lose his job: ~ **sını aşındırmak**, be always visiting s.o., pester s.o. with visits: ~ **sını çalmak**, appeal/apply to s.o.: ~ **ya dayanmak**, burst (in) upon: ~ **yı açmak**, open the door; start stg.; set an example: ~ **yı büyük açmak**, start an expensive business; spend money prodigally: ~ **yı çekmek**, close the door: ~ **yı kırıp girmek**, force an entry.

kapı·cı(lık) (Work/position of) door-keeper/care-taker/porter/concierge. ~ **cıˡk**ᵍ¹, small door; (*bot.*) micropyle. ~ **kule**, (*mil.*) fortified main gate. ~ **kulu**, (*his.*) Janissary guard; palace servant.

kapılan·dırmak (**-i**, **-e**) Arrange employment for s.o. ~ **mak** (**-e**), secure employment; enter the service of . . . .

kapıl·anduygu (*psy.*) Heteropathy. ~ **gan**, easily misled/carried away (by emotions). ~ **gı**, caprice, whim. ~ **gın**, capricious. ~ **mak**, *vp.* = KAPMAK: be seized with: (**-e**), be deceived by; be overwhelmed by.

kapısız Without a door; without employment.

kapış Manner of seizing; looting; scramble. ~ ~ **gitmek**, sell like hot cakes: ~ ~ **yemek**, eat greedily.

kapış·ılmak *vp.* ~ **mak** (**-i**), snatch stg. from one another; scramble for stg.: (**-le**), quarrel, wrestle, get to grips with; (*sl.*) embrace: **kapışan kapışana** they are selling like hot cakes. ~ **tırmak**, (**-i**, **-le**), *vc*

kapik (*fin.*) Russian copeck.

kapi·larite (*phys.*) Capillarity. ~ **ler**, capillary.

kapital·(ist)ⁱ (*fin.*) Capital(ist). ~ **izasyon**, capitalization. ~ **izm**, capitalism.

kapitone (*dom.*) Padded, upholstered; quilted.

kapitülasyonlar (*his.*) Capitulations.

kapka·ˡçᶜ¹ Stealing by snatching. ~ **çı(lık)**, (being a) snatch thief; trickster; s.o. living by his wits.

kapkara Exceedingly black; coal-black, pitch-dark. ~ **nlık**, deep blackness/darkness.

kapla·ˡkᵍ¹ (*med.*) Capsule.

kaplam Comprehensiveness, extent; extension.

kapla·ma *vn.* Act of covering, etc.; covering, coating, (*min.*) plate, plating; (tooth) crowning; (*carp.*) veneer, plywood; (*arch.*) casing, cladding; (*naut.*) skin (of boats): *a.* covered; lined; faced; plated; veneered. ~ **macı**, silver-plated. ~ **mak** (**-i**, **-e**, **-le**), cover over; line; coat; face; (*min.*) plate; bind (books); (*arch.*) case, clad; (*carp.*) veneer; encrust with (jewels); envelop, surround; include, comprise. ~ **malı**, covered, coated; plated; veneered, bound.

kaplam·daş Co-extensive. ~ **lı**, inclusive, comprehensive.

kaplan (*zoo.*) Tiger. ~ **atlaması**, (*sp.*) diving vault ~ **kedisi**, (*zoo.*) margay: ~ **köpekbalığı**, (*ich.*) tiger shark: ~ **pitonu**, (*zoo.*) Indian python: ~ **sazan** (*ich.*) tiger barb. ~ **boğan**, (*bot.*) common monks hood, aconitum. ~ **böcek**, (*ent.*) green tiger-beetle ~ **ler**, tiger-beetles.

kap·lanmak (**-le**) *vp.* = KAPLAMAK. ~ **laşım**, (*phys.*) overlap. ~ **laşma**, (*ind.*) containerization. ~ **latma**

(-i, -e, -le), *vc.* = KAPLAMAK. ~lı = KAPLAMALI; coated; plated; sheathed: ~ **tel**, (*el.*) cable.
kaplıca[1] *n.* (*geol.*) Thermal spring.
kaplıca[2] *n.* (*bot.*) Small-grained wheat; spelt.
kaplık (*dom.*) Rack, etc. for pots and pans; (book) binding material.
kaplin (*eng.*) Sleeve.
kaplumbağa (*zoo.*) Turtle; tortoise. ~ **kınkanatlısı**, (*ent.*) tortoise beetle: ~ **yürüyüşü**, snail's pace: ~**lar**, (*zoo.*) Chelonia.
kap·ma *vn.* Act of seizing; (*geo.*) capture: *a.* seized: ~ **dirseği**, (*geo.*) ox-bow: ~ **havzası**, (*geo.*) catchment-area/-basin. ~**maca**, (*child.*) puss-in-the-corner. ~**mak (-i)**, snatch; seize; carry off; acquire; capture; scramble for stg.; learn quickly, pick up; (*med.*) get infected.
kapon (*naut.*) Cat-tackle. ~ **çengeli**, cathook.
kaporta (*naut.*) Skylight; companion-hatch; (*aer.*) fairing, cowling; (*mot.*) bonnet. ~ **iskelesi**, (*naut.*) companion-ladder. ~**cı(lık)**, (*mot.*) (work of) coachwork repairer.
kap·rin (*chem.*) Capric. ~**ron**, caproic.
kapris Caprice, whim. ~ **yapmak**, be capricious. ~**li**, capricious.
kapsa·m Comprehensiveness, scope, range, coverage: ~**ı içinde (-in)**, within the scope of . . . ~**ma**, *vn.* inclusion. ~**mak (-i)**, comprise, include, cover. ~**mlı**, comprehensive; (*fin.*) blanket (order, etc.). ~**tmak (-i, -e)**, *vc.* ~**yıcı**, comprehensive.
kapsol[u] (*mil.*) Percussion cap, detonator.
kapsül[ü] Dish; (*med.*) capsule, cachet; (*bot.*) shell.
kaptan (*naut.*) Captain, master; (*sp.*) captain. ~ **köprüsü**, (*naut.*) bridge: ~ **paşa/~ı derya**, (*his.*) head of the Ottoman Navy: ~ **pilot**, (*aer.*) chief pilot; (*mot.*) inter-city bus-driver. ~**lık**, captaincy: ~ **etm.**, captain.
kaptıkaçtı (*mot.*) Minibus; (*gamb.*) a card-game; sneak-thief.
kaptır·ma *vn.*; (*carp.*) small hand-saw. ~**mak (-i, -e)**, *vc.* = KAPMAK; give o.s. up to (drink, etc.); be crushed/broken (in an accident).
kapuska(lık) (*cul.*) (Materials for) cabbage stew.
kapuşon (*mod.*) Hood.
kaput[u] (*mod.*) Military cloak; (*med.*) contraceptive, French letter; (*mot.*) opening part of bonnet; (*gamb.*) losing all the tricks in a game: ~ **etm.**, (*gamb.*) win all the tricks: ~ **gitmek**, (*ed. sl.*) fail all one's exams: ~ **olm.**, (*gamb.*) lose all the tricks: ~**u kesmek**, (*gamb.*) win only one trick; (*ed. sl.*) pass just one exam. ~**bezi**[ni], (*tex.*) coarse calico. ~**luk**, used in making cloaks.
kapuz (*geo.*) Mountain pass, gorge; dense forest.
kar (*met.*) Snow. ~ **fırtınası**, snowstorm, blizzard: ~ **gibi**, clean, white: ~ **helvası**, (*cul.*) snow mixed with PEKMEZ: ~ **kazı**, (*orn.*) snow goose: ~ **kuyusu**, snowpit (for keeping snow for summer use): ~ **piresi**, (*ent.*) snowflea: ~ **sineği**, (*ent.*) snow-fly: ~ **siperi**, snow-fence: ~ **tarak makinesi**, snowplough: ~ **tavşanı**, (*zoo.*) mountain hare: ~ **tavuğu**, (*orn.*) ptarmigan: ~ **topu**, snowball; (*fig.*) white and round; = ~ TOPU: ~ **tut(ma)mak**, snow (not) lie: ~ **yağmak**, snow: ~ **yığıntısı**, snow-drift:

~ **zinciri**, (*mot.*) snow-chains: ~**da gezip izini belli etmez**, s.o. very cunning/furtive in his work.
kar. = KARŞILIK.
kâr (*fin.*) Gain, profit; earnings; revenue; advantage, benefit, use. ~ **belgiti**, (*fin.*) dividend warrant: ~ **bırakmak**, bring/show profit: ~ **çıkarmak (-den)**, make a profit from, profit by: ~ **etm.**, win; (make a) profit; have an effect; be useful: ~ **etmez**, it's no good; it's useless: ~ **haddi**, (*fin.*) limit on profits: ~ **payı**, interest, dividend, bonus: ~**dan zarar**, get stg. but not all one hoped for: ~**ı ol(ma)mak**, be stg. one can(not) do: ~**ını tamam etm.**, kill.
-kâr *n. suf.* Who does . . ./makes . . . [HİLEKÂR, SANATKÂR].
kara[1] *n.* Land; mainland; shore; dry land. ~ +, *a.* Terrestrial, land-, continental-; road-; military: ~ **Ataşesi**, (*adm.*) Military Attaché: ~ **düzlük/platformu**, (*geo.*) continental shelf/platform: ~ **gümrüğü**, (*fin.*) customs-house at land frontier: ~ **harp/savaşı** (*mil.*) land warfare: ~ **iklimi**, continental climate: ~ **kaplumbağası**, (*zoo.*) tortoise: ~ **kurbağası**, (*zoo.*) toad: ~ **Kuvvetleri**, (*mil.*) Land Forces; = KARA[2]: ~ **nakli**, road/land transport: ~OLUŞ: ~ **suları**, (*naut.*) territorial waters: ~ **suları hakkı**, (*naut., aer.*) cabotage: ~ **vapuru**, (*col.*) railway: ~ **yeli**, (*met.*) off-shore wind: ~ YOLU: ~ YOSUNLARI.

kara-: ~**da**, ashore, on land: ~**dan gitmek**, go by land: ~**lar arası**, intercontinental: ~**ların kayması**, (*geol.*) continental drift: ~**ya ayak basmak**, step on to land: ~**ya çekmek/oturtmak**, (*naut.*) beach: ~**ya çıkarmak (-i)**, disembark: ~**ya çıkmak**, go ashore: ~**ya düşmek/oturmak**, (*naut.*) run aground, be stranded: ~**ya vurmak**, (fish, etc.) be driven ashore: ~**ya vurmuş balık gibi**, like a fish out of water.

kara[2] *a.* Black; dark; gloomy; ill-omened. ~ **ağaçkakan**, (*orn.*) black woodpecker: ~ **alınlı örümcek kuşu**, (*orn.*) lesser grey shrike: ~ **antılop**, (*zoo.*) blackbuck: ~ **ardıç**, (*bot.*) savin: ~ **asma**, (*bot.*) birthwort: ~ **balık**, (*ich.*) type of carp; tench: ~ **balina**, (*zoo.*) pilot whale: ~ **bayram**, day of mourning: ~BİBER: ~BORSA: ~BOYA: ~BOYUNLU: ~BÖCEKLER: ~BUĞDAY: ~BULUT: ~BURÇAK: ~ **burun**, (*ich.*) nase: ~ **cahil**, utterly ignorant: ~ **camgöz**, (*ich.*) lantern shark: ~ **cehalet**, crass ignorance: ~CEVİZ: ~CİĞER: ~ **cisim**, (*phys.*) black body: ~ **cümle**, (*jok.*) simple arithmetic: ~ **cümlesi bozuk**, half illiterate, very ignorant: ~ **çalı**, s.o. who causes bad blood among others: ~ÇALI: ~ **çalmak**, slander: ~ÇAM: ~ÇAYIR: ~ **çayla**[l]**k**[ğı], (*orn.*) black kite: ~DAĞ: ~ **damaklı**, obstinate, awkward: ~ **davar**, cattle: ~DEMİR: ~DENİZ: ~ **denizkırlangıcı**, (*orn.*) black tern: ~DİKEN: ~ **domalan**, (*myc.*) French truffle: ~DUL: ~ **eğleni**, (*lit.*) black comedy/humour: ~ELMAS: ~ **et**, (*cul.*) lean/sinewy meat: ~FATMA: ~GAGALI: ~GERDANLI: ~GÖVDE: ~GÖZ: ~ **gözlü**, black-eyed: ~GÜL: ~ **gün**, time of trouble/need: ~ **gün dostu**, a friend in need: ~ **güne karşı**, against a rainy day: ~ **gürgen**, (*bot.*) common beech: ~ **haber**, news of death/disaster: ~HİNDİBA: ~HORASAN: ~HUMMA: ~İĞNE: ~KABARCIK: ~KAFES: ~KALEM: ~ **kan**, (*bio.*) venous blood: ~ **kaplı kitap**, (*rel.*) orthodox/ formal/traditional way; the law: ~ ~ **düşünmek**, brood over stg.: ~ **karga**, (*orn.*) raven: ~ **kaş**, black eyebrows, beetle brows: ~KAVAK: ~KAVZA: ~KEÇİ: ~ **kedi geçmek**, feel a shiver down one's spine: ~KEHRİBAR: ~KIŞ: ~KOCA: ~KOL: ~KON-COLOS: ~ **kuğu**, (*orn.*) black swan: ~KUL: ~KULAK(LI): ~ **kuru**, dark and skinny: ~KUŞ(İ): ~ **kutu**, (*aer.*) flight recorder, black box: ~ **kuvvet**, (*rel.*) force of bigotry/fanaticism; = KARA[1]: ~LAHANA: ~LEYLEK: ~ **liste**, (*adm., ind.*) black list: ~ **maça**, (*gamb.*) spades: ~ **martı**, (*orn.*) lesser black-backed gull: ~ **maşa**, slim and dark female: ~ **mika**, (*geol.*) biotite mica: ~ **mizah** = ~ EĞLENİ: ~ **molinezya**, (*ich.*) sail-fin molly: ~ **okka**, old OKKA: ~ **ördek**, (*orn.*) black duck/scoter: ~ **pazı**, (*bot.*) orach(e), mountain spinach: ~SABAN: ~ **sağan**, (*orn.*) common swift: ~ **sakız**, (*geol.*) bitumen, pitch; (*bot.*) colophony: ~ **samankapan**, (*geol.*) jet: ~SEVDA: ~ **sıcaklık**, (*min.*) black heat: ~ **sığır**, (*zoo.*) water-buffalo: ~ **sığırcık**, (*orn.*) spotless starling: ~SİNEK: ~ **sinekkapan**, (*orn.*) pied fly-catcher: ~SU: ~ **sürmek**, (*fig.*) blacken, calumniate: ~TABAN: ~ **tahta (sehpası)**, (*ed.*) blackboard(-easel): ~ **tarlakuşu**, (*orn.*) black lark: ~TAVUK: ~ **tepeli baştankara**, (*orn.*) black-capped chickadee: ~ **tespihböceği**, (*zoo.*) pill-bug: ~ **toprak**, (*geol.*) chernozem; (*fig.*) the grave: ~TURP: ~ **yağız**, deep black: ~ **yazı**, tragic destiny: ~YEL: ~YEMİŞ: ~ **yüz**, disgrace, shame: ~**lar**, (*mod.*) mourning clothes: ~**sı elinde**, habitual backbiter: ~**yı seçmek**, be in a predicament; have great difficulty (in doing stg.). [*Also* = SİYAH.]

kara·ağa¹çᶜ¹ (*bot.*) Elm-tree. ~**ağaçgiller**, (*bot.*) elm family, *Ulmus*. ~**baca¹k**ᵍ¹, (*myc.*) beet fungus and disease. ~**baldır**, (*bot.*) maidenhair fern. ~**ballık**, (*myc.*) sooty mould. ~**basan**, nightmare; (*psy.*) depression. ~**baskı**, blackmail. ~**baş**, (*rel.*) priest, monk; (*fig.*) confirmed bachelor; (*bot.*) French lavender; (*zoo.*) Anatolian sheep-dog; (*orn.*) black-head (in turkeys). ~**başlı**, black-headed: ~ **iskete**, (*orn.*) Eurasian siskin: ~ **martı**, (*orn.*) Mediterranean gull: ~ **ötleğeni**, (*orn.*) Sardinian warbler: ~ **yalı bülbülü**, (*orn.*) blackcap. ~**bata¹k**ᵍ¹, (*orn.*) great cormorant. ~**benek**, (*myc.*) blackspot. **karabet**ⁱ (*soc.*) blood relationship.

kara·biber (*bot.*) Pepper plant; (*cul.*) black pepper; (*fig.*) charming/darkly handsome. ~**bibergiller**, (*bot.*) Piperaceae.

karabin·a (*mil.*) Carbine; blunderbuss. ~**yer**, Italian carabiniere.

kara·borsa (*fin.*) Black market. ~**borsacı(lık)**, black-marketeer(ing). ~**boya**, (*chem.*) sulphate of iron; sulphuric acid; lamp-black. ~**boyunlu**, black-necked: ~ **dalgıç**, (*orn.*) black-necked grebe: ~ **kıyı koşarı**, (*orn.*) black-winged stilt. ~**böcekler**, (*ent.*) darkling beetles. ~**buğday**, (*bot.*) buckwheat. ~**buğdaygiller**, (*bot.*) Polygonaceae. ~**bulut**ᵘ, (*met.*) nimbus cloud. ~**bulutsu**, (*ast.*) dark nebula. ~**burça¹k**ᵍ¹, (*bot.*) type of vetch, smooth tare.

karaca¹ *n*. (*zoo.*) Roe-deer.
karaca² *n*. (*bio.*) Upper arm. ~ **kemiği**, humerus.
karaca³ *a*. Somewhat black, swarthy. ~**darısı**ⁿ¹,

(*bot.*) type of buckwheat. ~**ot**ᵘ, (*bot.*) Christmas rose.

karaceviz (*bot./carp.*) Black walnut (tree/wood).
karacı¹ *n*. (*mil.*) Member of land forces; (*col.*) brigand, highwayman; gypsy.
karacı² *n*. Backbiter; slanderer. ~**lık**, slander.
karaciğer (*bio.*) Liver. ~ +, *a*. Hepatic: ~ **kelebeği**, (*zoo.*) liver fluke.
kara¹çᶜ¹ (*mot.*) Carburettor.
kara·çalı (*bot.*) Blackthorn, sloe; (*ich.*) type of red mullet. ~**çam**, (*bot.*) Austrian pine. ~**çayır**, (*bot.*) rye-grass. ~**çıban**, (*med.*) carbuncle. ~**damga(lı)**, stain(ed), defect(ive).
Kara·dağ *pr.n.* (*geo.*) Montenegro. ~**dağlı**, (*ethn.*) Montenegrin. ~**deniz**, (*geo.*) Black Sea: ~ **levreği**, (*ich.*) Black-Sea bass: ~ **de gemilerin mi battı?**, why so worried?
kara·demir (*min.*) Wrought iron. ~**diken**, (*bot.*) blackthorn. ~**dul**, (*zoo.*) black widow (spider). ~**duygu(luk)**, (*psy.*) melancholy; melancholia. ~**duygulu**, *a*. melancholy. ~**elmas**, (*min.*) bort, carbonado; (*fig.*) coal.
karafa(ki) (Small) raki carafe.
kara·fatma (*ent.*) Carabus ground beetle; (*col.*) common cockroach, black beetle. ~**gagalı**, (*orn.*) black-beaked/-billed: ~ **yelkovan**, Manx shearwater. ~**gerdanlı**, (*orn.*) black-necked/-throated: ~ **dalgıç**, black-throated diver, arctic loon. ~**gövde**, (*phys.*) black body. ~**göz**, black-eyed person; gypsy; (*th.*) Tk. Punch; Tk. shadow-theatre: ~ **(balığı)**, (*ich.*) sea-bream: ~ **oynatmak**, (*th.*) present the shadow-play; (*fig.*) create an amusing situation. ~**gözcü(lük)**, (*th.*) (work of) shadowplay operator//shadow-figure maker. ~**gül**, (*zoo.*) broadtail sheep (from lambs of which astrakhan fur comes). ~**günlü**, unlucky.
karağı¹ Fire-rake; crook. ~² Blindness.
Karahan (*ast.*) Pluto. ~**lı**, (*his.*) a Tk. dynasty.
kara·hindiba (*bot.*) Dandelion. ~**horasan**, (*min.*) finest Damascus steel. ~**humma**, (*med.*) typhus; black death. ~**iğne**, (*ent.*) black stinging ant.
Karaim (*ethn.*) Jewish people of Tk. origin in Poland. ~**ce**, (*ling.*) their language.
kara·kabarcık (*med.*) Anthrax. ~**kafes**, (*bot.*) comfrey. ~**kalem**, (*art.*) charcoal-pencil (sketch). ~**kava¹k**ᵍ¹, (*bot.*) black poplar. ~**kavza**, (*bot.*) wild carrot. ~**kaygı**, melancholy. ~**keçi**, (*ich.*) barbel. ~**kehribar**, (*geol.*) jet. ~**kış**, severe winter; the depths of winter. ~**koca**, white-haired old man. ~**kol**, (*adm., mil.*) patrol; guard; sentry; guardroom; police-station. ~**kolluk**, *a*. who should be locked up: ~ **olm.**, end up in the police-station. ~**koncolos**, bogy, vampire; (*fig.*) s.o. very ugly.
karakter (*psy.*) Character; moral character; (*pub.*) letter; (*lit.*) character; (*th.*) part, role. ~**istik**, *n*. characteristic. ~**ize**, ~**etm.**, characterize. ~**oloji**, (*psy.*) characterology. ~**siz**, having weak character, unreliable. ~**sizlik**, unreliability.
kara·kul = ~GÜL. ~**kula¹k**ᵍ¹¹, (*zoo.*) caracal, lynx, bobcat. ~**kula¹k**ᵍ¹², (*adm., obs.*) confidential messenger of the Grand Vizier. ~**kulaklı**, blackeared: ~ **kuyrukkakan**, (*orn.*) black-eared wheatear. ~**kuş¹**, (*orn.*) type of eagle. ~**kuş²**, (*live.*

swelling on horse's hoof. ~**kuşi**, arbitrary, despotic. ~**kuşku**, suspicion. ~**lahana**, (*bot.*) savoy cabbage; field kale.

kara·lama *vn.* Act of blackening; writing exercise; (*lit.*) draft text: ~ **defteri**, copybook. ~**lamak (-i)**, blacken; make dirty; scribble; black/cross out; censor; (*lit.*) draft (speech, etc.); (*fig.*) sully (reputation, etc.). ~**lanmak**, *vi.* be made dirty; become black; (*fig.*) be sullied. ~**laştırma**, (*min.*) blackening. ~**latmak (-i)**, *vc.*

kara·leylek (*orn.*) Black stork. ~**lı**, having black (spots, etc.): ~ **beyazlı**, black and white. ~**lık**, blackness. ~**ltı**, indistinct figure; silhouette; small stain.

karamak¹ **(-i)** Slander, sully.

karamak² **(-i)** (*obs.*) Look at, watch, observe.

Karaman (*his.*) Principality in Anatolia; (*live.*) fat-tailed sheep; (*cul.*) its mutton; (*fig.*) swarthy-complexioned man. ~**ın koyunu sonra çıkar oyunu**, not so innocent as he looks. ~**lamak**, *vi.* (*naut.*) (sail) flap wildly. ~**oğlu**, (*his.*) Karamanid, prince of Karaman.

karamandola (*tex.*) Prunella.

karamaru (*ich.*) S. American lungfish.

karambol (*sp.*) Cannon (at billiards).

karamela (*cul.*) Caramel.

karamsar Pessimistic. ~**lık**, pessimism.

karamuk (*bot.*) Corn cockle; (*med.*) (baby) rash.

karamusal (*naut.*) Mooring swivel. ~ **sepeti**, small, weak, flimsy: ~**a vurmak**, moor.

karanfil (*bot.*) Clove pink, carnation; clove tree; (*cul.*) clove. ~**giller**, pink family. ~**yağı**ⁿⁱ, (*cul.*) oil of cloves.

karanlık *n.* Darkness; a dark place. *a.* Dark; obscure; bad, dangerous. ~ **basmak/olm.**, become dark; night fall: ~ **kınkanatlılar**, (*ent.*) meal-worm beetles: ~ **oda**, (*cin.*) dark-room: ~ **perdesi altında**, under cover of darkness: ~**a çıkmak**, go out in the dark: ~**a kalmak**, be caught out in the dark: ~**ta göz kırptığını ne bileyim?**, how was I to know? ~**çı(lık)**, (*phil.*) obscurant·ist/ (-ism).

karantina Quarantine. ~ **hududu**, (*med.*, *fig.*) cordon sanitaire: ~ **koymak/vazetmek**, (*adm.*) impose quarantine.

karaoluş (*geol.*) Epeirogeny.

karar Decision; (*leg.*) judgement, sentence; (*adm.*) resolution, decree; agreement; constancy; stability; firmness; customary state/degree; estimation; right amount, reasonable degree; (*Or. mus.*) pause. ~ **almak**, take a decision: ~ **bulmak (-de)**, become settled; be decided: ~ **kılmak (-de)**, decide on; settle down to stg.: ~ **vermek (-e)**, decide (to do stg.): ~**a varmak**, reach a decision: ~**ı iptal etm.**, set aside a decision.

karargâh (*mil.*) Headquarters.

karar·lama *vn.* An estimating; approximation: *a.* estimated: *adv.* by rule of thumb. ~**lamadan**, by calculation/estimation/guesswork. ~**lamak (-i)**, estimate (by eye); calculate. ~**laşmak**, *vi.* be agreed upon; be decided. ~**laştırmak (-i)**, *vc.* decide on stg.; arrange. ~**layıcı**, determinant. ~**lı**, fixed; stable; stationary; settled; decided: ~ **dalga**,

(*phys.*) stationary wave: ~ **denge**, (*phys.*) stable equilibrium. ~**lılık**, stability; decisiveness.

karar·ma *vn.* (*cin.*) Fade-out; (*min.*) tarnishing. ~**mak**, *vi.* become black; become dark; be indistinctly perceived; (*met.*) become overclouded/misty; (*min.*) be tarnished.

karar·name Decree; legal decision. ~**sız**, unstable; undecided; changeable; restless; hesitating: ~ **denge**, unstable equilibrium. ~**sızlık**, instability; indecision; fickleness; restlessness.

karart·ı Blackness; darkness; shadow(y figure). ~**ma**, *vn.*; (*mil.*) black-out; ~**mak (-i)**, blacken; black out, dim.

karasaban (*agr.*) Primitive plough.

karasal = KARA¹; continental; terrestrial; (*geol.*) terrigenous. ~ **kumul**, (*geo.*) inland dune: ~ **oluşuk**, (*geol.*) land/strata formation: ~**lar**, terrestrial animals.

kara·sevda (*psy.*) Hypochondria; depression; melancholy, melancholia. ~**sinek**, (*ent.*) common house-fly; stable-fly. ~**su**, deep/slow-flowing water; (*med.*) glaucoma; = KARA¹: ~ **humması**, (*med.*) blackwater fever. ~**suluk**, sewage water. ~**şın**, dark-complexioned/-haired. ~**taban**, (*ent.*) *pébrine.* ~**tavu**ⁱkᵍᵘ, (*orn.*) blackbird. ~**tavukgiller**, (*orn.*) thrushes. ~**turp**ᵘ, (*bot.*) horseradish.

karate (*sp.*) ~ **dövüşü**, karate (unarmed combat).

karavan (*mot.*) Caravan.

karavana (*mil.*) Mess-tin, dixie; (*mil.*) food, rations; (*min.*) flat type of diamond; (*mil., sl.*) miss (in target shooting). ~**cı**, (*mil.*) mess carrier; (*sl.*) soldier who misses a shot.

karavela (*naut., his.*) Caravelle; (*now*) unseaworthiness.

karavide (*zoo.*) Freshwater crayfish.

kara·yandıⁱkᵍⁱ (*bot.*) Creeping thistle; camel's thorn. ~**yanı**ⁱkᵍⁱ, (*med.*) anthrax. ~**yazı**, evil fate, bad luck. ~**yazılı**, unlucky; fated.

kara·yel (*met.*) North-west wind; (*geo.*) north-west. ~**yemiş**, (*bot.*) cherry-/common laurel. ~**yıkım**, disaster. ~**yılan**, (*zoo.*) (?) European whip-snake. ~**yolu**ⁿᵘ, main road, highway. ~**yosunları**ⁿⁱ, (*bot.*) bryophytes.

Karayib (*geo.*) ~ **denizi**, the Caribbean.

karbo- *pref.* (*chem.*) Carbo-. ~**ksil**, carboxyl(ic).

karbon (*chem.*) Carbon. ~ +, *a.* Carbon(ic): ~ **biroksit/monoksit**, carbon monoxide: ~ **çeliği**, (*min.*) carbon steel: ~ **devri**, (*geol.*) carboniferous age: ~ **dioksit/ikioksit**, carbon dioxide; liquid CO_2: ~ **kâğıdı**, (*pub.*) carbon paper: ~ **siyahı**, (*pub.*) carbon black.

karbon·ado (*min.*) Carbonado. ~**at**¹, (*chem.*) carbonate; (*cul.*) baking powder. ~**atlama**, (*chem.*) carbonation. ~**atlaşma**, carbonization. ~**hidrat**¹, carbohydrate. ~**ik**, carbonic: ~ **asit**, carbonic acid. ~**il**, carbonyl. ~**lama**, *vn.* (*min.*) carburizing. ~**lamak (-i)**, carburize. ~**lanma**, carburation. ~**lanmış**, carburized. ~**laşma**, carbonization. ~**layıcı**, carburizer. ~**lu**, (*chem., min.*) carbonaceous; (*geol.*) carboniferous; carbon-. ~**suzlaşma**, decarbonizing; decarburizing.

karborundum (*chem.*) Carborundum.

karbür Carbide. ~**asyon,** carburation. ~**atör,** (*mot.*) carburettor.

karcığar (*Or. mus.*) A famous melody.

kardelen (*bot.*) Snowdrop.

kardeş Brother; sister; fellow-; co-; like; comrade. ~ **kat(i)li,** fratricide: ~ **payı,** equally, half and half: ~**im!,** my friend!

kardeş·çe Brotherly; sisterly; fraternal. ~**kanı**[n1], (*bot.*) dragon's blood: ~ **ağacı,** dragon gum tree. ~**lenme,** *vn.* (*bot.*) shoots, suckers. ~**lenmek,** *vi.* (*bot.*) produce shoots/suckers, tiller. ~**lik,** brotherhood; fraternity; friendship.

kardırmak (-i, -e) *vc.* = KARMAK.

kardinal[i] (*rel.*) Cardinal. ~ **kuşu,** (*orn.*) cardinal. ~**lik,** rank/duties of a cardinal.

kardiyo- *pref.* (*med.*) Cardio-. ~**graf(i),** cardiograph(y). ~**gram,** cardiogram. ~**log,** cardiologist. ~**loji,** cardiology.

kare (*math.*) Square; (*gamb.*) group of four players. ~ **bulmaca,** crossword puzzle: ~**ler,** (*tex.*) chequers: ~**ye yükseltmek,** (*math.*) square. ~**kök,** (*math.*) square root. ~**li,** in squares; chequered; (*tex.*) check(ed), tartan.

karfiçe (*carp.*) Small-headed nail, brad.

karga[1] *n.* (*orn.*) Raven; (*col.*) crow, rook. ~ +, *a.* Corvine: ~ **akbabası,** (*orn.*) black vulture: ~ **bok(unu) yemeden,** (*vulg.*) very early in the morning: ~BURUN: ~ **derneği,** gang of ruffians; den of thieves: ~ **döleği,** (*bot.*) bitter apple/cucumber: ~ **gibi,** very thin: ~ **karakuş,** (*orn.*) common grackle: ~ **taşlamak,** (*sl.*) pester women at bus-stops: ~TULUMBA: ~ **yürüyüşü,** (*sp.*) leap forward with knees bent.

karga[2] *adv.* (*naut.*) Upside down. ~ **etm.,** top (yards); prime (pump).

karga·burnu[nu] (*carp.*) Round pliers; (*med.*) curved forceps; (*sp.*) crampon. ~**burun,** *a.* having a Roman nose: ~ **çıkıntısı,** (*bio.*) coracoid (process). ~**büken,** (*bot., med.*) nux vomica. ~**cık,** ~ **burgacık,** little misshapen thing; scrawl; crooked, twisted. ~**delen,** (*bot.*) soft-shelled almond. ~**giller,** (*orn.*) crows, etc., Corvidae.

kargaşa·(lık) Confusion; anarchy; disorder; tumult: ~ **çıkarmak,** create confusion; raise Cain. ~**cı(lık),** (*pol.*) anarch·ist/(-ism).

kargatulumba ~ **etm.,** frogmarch s.o.

kargı (*mil., obs.*) Pike, javelin, lance; (*bot.*) reed. ~**lık,** cartridge bag/belt.

kargı·ma *vn.* Cursing. ~**mak (-i),** curse s.o.

kargın (*carp.*) Large plane.

kargış *vn.* Cursing; vituperation. ~ **etm.**/~**lamak (-i),** curse. ~**lanmak,** *vp.* ~**lı**/~**lık,** cursed.

kârgir = KÂGİR.

kargo Cargo.

karha (*med.*) Ulcer; canker.

karı Wife; (*vulg.*) woman. ~ **almak,** marry: ~ **kızan,** wives and children; the whole population: ~ **koca,** wife and husband; married couple: ~ **koca kavgası,** domestic quarrel: ~ **koca malları,** marital estate: ~ **kocalık,** married state; conjugality: ~**sı ağızlı,** mouthpiece for his wife's thoughts: ~**sının üstüne evlenmek,** take a second wife.

karı·k[g1 1] *n.* (*agr.*) Irrigation ditch; plot of land between ditches; furrow.

karı·k[g1 2] *n.* Snow-blindness. *a.* Snow-blind(ed). ~**mak,** *vi.* be dazzled.

karı·laşmak *vi.* Become womanish/effeminate. ~**lı,** having one (or more) wives: ~ **kocalı,** several couples together. ~**lık,** womanhood; wifehood: ~ **etm.,** play a dirty trick. ~**mak,** *vi.* (*obs.*) grow old.

kar·ın[n1] (*bio.*) Belly; abdomen; stomach; womb; inside of stg.; protuberant part; (*naut.*) bulge of hull; (*fig.*) brains. ~ +, *a.* Abdominal, ventral: ~ **ağrısı,** (*med.*) stomach-ache; (*fig.*) stg. unpleasant/incomprehensible, a 'headache'; pest, troublesome child: ~ **deşmek,** disembowel: ~ **yüzgeci,** (*ich.*) ventral fin: ~ZARI: ~**ı acıkmak,** be hungry: ~**ı aç,** hungry; ~**ı ağrımak,** have stomach-ache: ~**ı burnunda,** in the last stages of pregnancy: ~**ı geniş,** carefree, light-hearted: ~**ı göçmek,** belly sink in from starvation: ~**ı tok,** not hungry, satisfied: ~**ı tok sırtı pek,** well fed and clothed, in easy circumstances: ~IYARIK: ~**ı zil çalmak,** be very hungry/starving: ~**ım tok (-e),** (*fig.*) I'm not deceived by stg.: ~**ındakini ne bileyim?,** how do I know what's on your mind?: ~**ından konuşan,** ventriloquist: ~**ından söylemek,** (*col.*) invent things.

karınca (*ent.*) Ant; (*min.*) blow-hole (in moulding); pitting (from rust). ~ **ardıçları,** (*orn.*) ant-thrushes: ~ **arslanı,** (*ent.*) ant-lion: ~ **asidi,** (*chem.*) formic acid: ~ **belli,** narrow-waisted: ~ **çıt kuşu,** (*orn.*) ant-wren: ~ **duası,** a written charm: ~ **duası gibi,** small and illegible (writing): ~ **eşekarısı,** (*ent.*) velvet ant (a cuckoo wasp): ~ **incirkuşları,** (*orn.*) gnateaters: ~ **kaderince/kararınca,** as a modest contribution; as much as I can afford: ~ **örümcek-kuşları,** (*orn.*) antshrikes: ~ **yuvası,** ant-heap/-hill: ~ **yuvası gibi kaynamak,** swarm with activity: ~**lar,** (*ent.*) ants, Formicidae: ~**yı bile ezmemek/incitmemek,** not hurt a fly; be very kind/sensitive.

karınca·böceği (*ent.*) Lomechusa. ~**kuşugiller,** (*orn.*) antbirds. ~**lanmak,** *vi.* (ants) swarm; (*bio.*) have pins and needles; feel benumbed; (*min.*) be full of blisters/blow-holes; be pitted (with rust): ~**lı,** infested with ants; (*min.*) full of blow-holes; pitted with rust. ~ **yiyen,** (*zoo.*) echidna, spiny anteater. ~**yiyengiller,** (*zoo.*) anteaters.

karın·cı·k[g1] (*bio.*) Ventricle; cavity, chamber. ~**cıl,** coeliac. ~**çatlağı,** abdominal rupture. ~**danbacaklılar,** (*zoo.*) gastropods. ~**daş** = KARDEŞ. ~**lamak (-e),** (*naut.*) come alongside. ~**lı,** having a paunch; pot-bellied. ~**zarı**[n1], (*bio.*) peritoneum: ~ **yangısı,** (*med.*) peritonitis.

karın·mak (-i) *vt.* Mix; (birds) mate. ~**sa,** moulting (of birds). ~**tı,** vortex; eddy.

karış[1] *n.* (*math.*) Span (22 cm.); a third of an ARŞIN. ~ ~ **aramak**//**bilmek,** search//know every inch of a place: ~ ~ **ölçmek,** measure/calculate very carefully. ~**lamak (-i),** measure in spans.

karış[2] *n.* Confusion, turmoil. ~ ~ **etm.,** throw into utter confusion. ~**gın,** complicated. ~**ık,** mixed, compound; (*bot.*) composite; (*chem.*) adulterated, complicated; confused, in disorder; (*sp.*) mixed doubles; (*myth.*) connected with djinns/fairies: ~ **bir adam**, s.o. about whom one has doubts: ~ **meyve**, (*bot.*) multiple fruit. ~**ıklık**, confusion, disorder; tumult, riot: ~**ın daniskası**, confusion worse confounded. ~**ılmak (-e)**, *imp. v.* interfere. ~**ım**, (*phys.*) mixture; (*med.*) complication. ~**ma**, *vn.* mixing; interference, meddling; confusion; (*mot.*) weaving. ~**mak (-le)**, mix/be involved with; become confused/disordered: (**-e**), interfere/ meddle with; exercise control over: **karışanı görüşeni yok**, he is free from interference, he can act independently: **karışır**, (*chem.*) miscible: **karışma!**, don't interfere!: **karışmaz**, immiscible: **karışmış olm.**, be involved. ~**malı**, ~ **cücüklenme**, (*bio.*) amphimixis. ~**mama**, (*pol.*) non-intervention. ~**masız**, ~ **cücüklenme**, (*bio.*) apomixis.

karıştır·ıcı *a.* Causing confusion/tumult; agitating: *n.* mixer. ~**ıcılık**, confusion, discord. ~**ılmak (-e, -le)**, *vp.* ~**ma**, *vn.* confusion, interference; mixing. ~**mak (-i, -e, -le)**, mix, blend; (*bio.*) cross; stir up, agitate; confuse with; disarrange, disorder; complicate; allow to interfere (with); add (to).

kari (*obs.*) Reader.

-kâri *suf.* Worked in . . .; in the style of . . . [TELKÂRİ].

karibu (*zoo.*) Caribou.

karides (*zoo.*) Shrimp.

kariha Fertile mind; imaginative power.

karikatür (*art.*) Caricature, cartoon; (*fig.*) caricature of. ~**cü**/~**ist**, caricaturist, cartoonist. ~**cülük**, caricaturist's art. ~**ize**, caricatured. ~**leştirmek (-i)**, caricature.

karina (*naut.*) Bilge, underwater hull, bottom; (*orn.*) carina. ~ **başlı**, (*zoo.*) blunthead (snake): ~ **etm.**/~**ya basmak**, (*naut.*) careen. ~**lı**, (*orn.*) carinate. ~**sız**, (*orn.*) ratite.

karine (*phil.*) Context; deduction. ~ **ile anlamak**, deduce/infer from circumstances/context.

kariyama (*orn.*) (Red-legged) seriema.

karkara (*orn.*) Demoiselle crane.

karkas (*arch.*) Ferro-concrete frame; (*med.*) corpse.

kar·kuşuⁿᵘ (*orn.*) (?) Snow-bunting. ~**lamak**, *vi.* snow. ~**lı**, covered with snow; (*met.*) likely to snow; snowy. ~**lık**, snow-pit; vessel cooled with snow.

kârlı Profiting; profitable, advantageous. ~ **çıkmak**, come out a winner; turn out profitably.

kar·ma *vn.* Mixing, etc.: *a.* mixed; compound, composite; (*leg.*) joint: ~ **eğitim**, (*ed.*) mixed/co-education: ~ **ekonomi**, (*fin.*) mixed economy: ~ **eşeyli(lik)**, (*bio.*) gynandromorph(ism): ~ **hükümet**, (*pol.*) coalition: ~ **komisyon**, (*adm.*) mixed commission: ~ **makinesi**, (*cul.*) blender: ~ **okul**, (*ed.*) mixed school: ~ **takım**, (*sp.*) mixed team: ~ **tamlama**, (*ling.*) adjectival possessive construction. ~**macı**, mixer; blender. ~**macılık**, mixing; combining. ~**ma'ç**ᶜ¹, (*chem.*) mixer, agitator; (*arch.*) mud-and-straw filler. ~**mak (-i)**, (*cul.*) make a mash of; knead; (*arch.*) mix (cement, etc.); (*gamb.*) shuffle (cards). ~**makarış(ık)**/~**mançor-man**, all mixed up; in complete disorder. ~ **etm.**, mix things up; complicate; create disorder. ~ **olm.**, be all mixed up; fall into confusion.

karmanyola A night attack (by robbers). ~ **etm.**, attack and rob by night. ~**cı**, robber; mugger.

karmaş·a Complexity; (*psy.*) complex. ~**ık**, complex: ~ **sayı**, (*math.*) complex number. ~**ıklaşma**, *vn.* ~**ıklaşmak**, become complex/complicated. ~**ıklık**, complexity. ~**mak**, *vi.* mix, mingle; blend. ~**tırmak (-i)**, *vc.*

karmı'kᵏ¹ Weir at river-mouth for catching fish.

karmu'kᵏᵘ Large hook, grappling iron.

karn- = KARIN.

karna·bahar/~**bit** (*bot.*) Cauliflower.

karnaval (*rel.*) Carnival; (*soc.*) masked ball.

karne Book of tickets, etc.; (*ed.*) report, list of marks; note-book. ~**li yolcu**, commuter.

karnıyarı'kᵏ¹ (*bot.*) Seeds of fleawort; (*cul.*) split and stuffed aubergines; type of LAKERDA; (*naut.*) snatchblock.

karni (*chem.*) Retort. ~**ye**, (*bio.*) cornea.

karo (*gamb.*) Diamonds; (*arch.*) square flagstone.

karoser(i) (*mot.*) Coachwork, bodywork.

karotᵘ (*geol.*) Core. ~ **tübü**/~**iye**, core barrel.

karoten (*chem.*) Carotene.

karotis (*bio.*) Carotid (artery).

Karpatlar (*geo.*) Carpathian Mountains.

karpi'tᵈ¹ (*chem.*) Calcium carbide. ~ **ışıtacı**, acetylene lamp.

karpuz (*bot.*) Water-melon; (*col.*) anything round; (*el.*) lamp-bulb. ~ **fener**, Chinese lantern; ~ **kabak çıktı**, the melon proved tasteless. ~ **cu(luk)**, (work of) water-melon grower/seller.

karsa'kᵏ¹ (*zoo.*) Corsac, Tartar fox.

kârsız Unprofitable.

karst (*geol.*) Karst. ~**ik**, cavernous.

karş. = KARŞILAŞTIRINIZ!

karşı *n.* Opposite side/direction. *a.* Opposite; contrary; opposed; counter. *adv.* [198] Opposite; in any opposite way/direction. *post.* (**-e**) [88, 91] Against; towards; facing; in reply to; opposite to. ~ **açılar**, (*math.*) reverse angles: ~ **ağırlık**, counter·poise/-weight: ~ **basınç** (*min.*) back-pressure: ~ **çıkmak (-e)**, go to meet s.o.; prepare to oppose stg.: ~ **durmak (-e)**, oppose, resist; be at cross purposes: ~ **etki**, counter-effect, counter-poise: ~ **gelme**, objection, protest: ~ **gelmek (-e)**, confront, oppose; answer back (impertinently): ~ **hareket**, (*mil.*) counteraction: ~ **hücum(a geçmek)**, counter-attack: ~ **kafa tutmak (-e)**, resist obstinately: ~ ~**ya**, face to face; exactly opposite: ~ **konum**, (*ast.*) opposition: ~ **ko(y)mak (-e)**, make a stand against; resist: ~ **olm.**, face; be against; oppose: ~ **oy**, (*adm.*) negative vote: ~ **saldırı**, (*mil., sp.*) counter-attack: ~ **söylemek (-e)**, speak against, oppose: ~ **tazyik**, (*eng.*) back-pressure: ~ **yaka**, (*geo.*) opposite side/shore.

karşı-: ~**dan** ~**ya**, from one side to the other; across: ~**nızda**, opposite you; against you: ~**sına çıkmak**, appear suddenly before s.o.: ~ **sına getirmek**/~**sında durmak**, confront: ~ **sında yutkunmak**, resign o.s. to doing without stg.: ~**ya**, to the opposite side/bank: ~**ya geçmek**, cross over.

karşı·cı *n.* Opponent: *a.* opposed. ~ **devrim(cilik)**, (*pol.*) counter-revolution. ~**devrimci**, counter-revolutionary. ~**döngü**, (*met.*) anti-cyclone.

~**duygu**, antipathy. ~**gelim**, (*bio.*) antagonism, opposition. ~**gün**, (*ast.*) after-glow. ~**haberalma**, (*mil.*) counter-intelligence. ~**köpürme**, (*ind.*) antifoaming.

karşı·lama *vn.* Going to meet, welcoming; (*leg.*) indemnity, compensation; (*sp.*) return (stroke). ~**lamak (-i)**, go out to meet/welcome s.o.; oppose, balance, counter(act); reply to; meet (a need, etc.), cover (an expense); guarantee; (*sp.*) block; (*med.*) prevent. ~**lanmak**, *vp.* be met; be paid; come opposite. ~**laşma**, *vn.* confrontation, meeting; (*sp.*) match, bout, fight, encounter: ~ **derecesi**, (*ling.*) comparative degree: ~**lar**, (*sp.*) competition, tournament. ~**laşmak**, *vi.* confront one another; meet face to face; balance, be equivalent: (**-le**), encounter (difficulties, etc.); come across s.o.; (*sp.*) fight. ~**laştırma**, *vn.*; comparison; verification: ~ **derecesi**, (*ling.*) comparative degree. ~**laştırmak (-i, -le)**, *vc.* make meet/balance; confront *A* with *B*; compare. ~**laştırmalı**, comparative: ~ **anatomi**, (*bio.*) comparative anatomy: ~ **basım**, (*lit.*) critical edition: ~ **dilbilgisi**, (*ling.*) comparative grammar: ~ **dilbilim**, comparative linguistics/philology. ~**layan**, (*sp.*) receiver: ~ **ilerde**, advantage out/receiver. ~**layıcı**, *n.* (*soc.*) receiver, welcomer: *a.* preventive; meeting, fulfilling; (*fin.*) compensatory, countervailing.

karşılık Equivalent, counterpart; reciprocity; converse; reply, retort; (*fin.*) recompense, compensation, allowance, collateral, cover. ~ **istemez!**, no backchat!: ~ **olarak**, in consideration of; by way of acknowledgement: ~ **vermek**, answer back (to s.o. bigger); respond: ~**ı yok**, it has no equivalent: ~**ında**, in return for: ~**ını yapmak**, give the equivalent, recompense; reciprocate.

karşılık·lı Equivalent; reciprocal, mutual; alternate; corresponding; balanced; done in return; in reply; facing one another: ~ **açılar**, (*math.*) corresponding angles: ~ **asalaklık**, (*zoo.*) mutualism: ~ **benzeşme**, (*ling.*) reciprocal assimilation (of sounds): ~ **çıkar**, mutual benefit: ~ **dava**, (*leg.*) counterclaim: ~ **konuşma**, (*th.*) dialogue: ~ **taraf**, (*leg.*) other party: ~ **yapraklar**, (*bot.*) opposite leaves: ~ **yardım**, mutual assistance. ~**lıoluş**, reciprocity. ~**sız**, disinterested; honorary, unpaid; (*fin.*) overdrawn (account); fiduciary (issue): ~ **çek**, dud/worthless cheque.

karşı·ma (*ast.*) Opposition. ~**n (-e)**, *post.* [88] in spite of. ~**nlık**, opposition. ~**ntan**, (*bio.*) antibody. ~**olum**, (*phil.*) opposition. ~**sav**, (*phil.*) antithesis. ~**sürtünme**, (*ind.*) anti-friction. ~**sürüm**, (*mus.*) counterpoint.

karşıt[1] Opposite, contrary; (*math.*) reciprocal; contradictory; (*art.*) contrasting; anti-, contra-, counter-. ~ **anlamlı**, (*ling.*) antonym: ~ **durum**, (*leg.*) opposite case: ~ **etki**, (*adm.*) backlash: ~ **özdek**, (*phys.*) anti-matter.

karşıt·ağı (*med.*) Antidote. ~**çı(lık)**, oppo·nent/(-sition). ~**değerlilik**, (*psy.*) ambivalence. ~**duygu**, (*psy.*) antipathy. ~**etkinlik**, (*psy.*) antagonism. ~**lama**, *vn.* reprisals; (*leg.*) counter-claim, complaint. ~**lamak (-i)**, put forward an opposite theory. ~**laşma**, *vn.* ~**laşmak (-le)**, be opposed to

each other. ~**lık**, contrast; (*math.*) reciprocity; contradiction; (*leg.*) objection; (*bio.*) antagonism. ~**ten**, (*bio.*) antibody. ~**yenim**, (*min.*) anticorrosion.

kart[1][1] *a.* Dry; hard; tough; wizened; old.

kart[1][2] *n.* Card; board; visiting-card; post-card; entrance-/identity-card.

Kartaca (*his.*) Carthage. ~**lı**, (*ethn.*) Carthaginian.

kartal (*orn.*) Eagle. ~ **ağacı**, (*bot.*) aloes wood, eagle wood: ~ **bakışıyla**, with an eagle eye: ~ **(gagası) gibi**, aquiline: ~ **örgesi**, (*his.*) double-headed eagle: ~**a kaçmak**, (*sl.*) grow old/shrivelled: ~**lar**, (*orn.*) birds of prey. ~**giller**, (*orn.*) hawks and falcons. ~**lı**, having eagles: ~ **eğreltiotu**, (*bot.*) bracken.

kart·almak/~**lanmak**/~**laşmak** *vi.* Become dry/tough/shrivelled/old. ~**aloş**/~**aloz**, (*sl.*) old, shrivelled.

kartel[1] (*fin.*) Cartel, combine.

kartel[2] (*naut.*) Fresh-water barrel.

karter (*eng.*) Casing; crankcase; gearcase; sump.

kartezyen *a./n.* (*phil.*) Cartesian.

kartlık Dryness; toughness; loss of youth.

karto·graf(çı) Cartographer. ~**grafi(k)**, carto-graph·y/(-ic).

karton (Card)board, pasteboard. ~**pat**, millboard. ~**piyer**, thick cardboard.

kartopu[nu] (*bot.*) Guelder-rose. = KAR TOPU.

kart·ote[l][k][ği] (*adm.*) Card-index/-catalogue; filing-box/-cabinet. ~**postal**, postcard(-size photograph). ~**vizit**, visiting-card: ~ **bırakmak**, (*sl.*) vomit.

kartu[l][k][ğu] (*agr.*) Large rake.

kartuş (*mil.*) Cartridge.

Karun Very rich person; a regular Croesus. ~ **kadar malı olsa kimseye koklatmaz**, however rich he were he would give nothing away: ~ **kadar zengin**, fabulously rich.

Karya (*his.*) Caria.

karyağdı(lı) Speckled, spotted, 'pepper and salt'.

karye (*obs.*) Village.

karyo·kinez (*bio.*) Karyokinesis. ~**lenf**, karyo-lymph.

karyola (*dom.*) Bedstead; bed.

kas (*bio.*) Muscle, cord. ~ **+**, *a.* Muscular: ~ **distrofisi**, (*med.*) muscular dystrophy: ~**DOKU**: ~ **kopması**, tearing a muscle: ~ **teli**, muscle fibre: ~ **tutulması**, cramp.

kasa Cash-box; strong-box; coffers; safe; box, chest; (*fin.*) till; cashier's office; (*mot.*) cab, bodywork; (*gamb.*) banker; (*fin.*) cash; (*pub.*) case; (*naut.*) spliced eye/loop (of rope); (*arch.*) door-/window-frame; (*sp.*) box. ~ **açığı**, (*fin.*) cash deficit: ~ **dairesi**, safe-deposit: ~ **defteri**, cashbook: ~ **etm.**, (*naut.*) pull taut; haul: ~ **mevcudu**, cash in hand.

kasab- = KASAP.

kasaba Small town, borough. ~**lı**, town-dweller.

kasadar Cashier; treasurer.

kasa[l][p][bı] Butcher('s shop); slaughterer; (*sl.*) wild car-driver. ~ **kuş(lar)ı**, (*orn.*) butcher-bird(s): ~**a yağ kaygısı, keçiye can kaygısı**, everyone thinks of his own interests.

kasap·hane Slaughter-house. ~**lık**, butcher's trade; fee for slaughtering; (animal) fit for

slaughter; (*fig.*) butchery, massacre: ~ **koyun gibi**, 'like a lamb to the slaughter', meek, uncomplaining.
asara (*naut.*) Deck-cabin.
asatura (*mil.*) Sword-bayonet.
asavet[i] Depression; melancholy; gloom; oppressiveness. ~ **basmak**, become dejected: ~ **çekmek**, be anxious/distressed: ~ **vermek**, depress. ~ **lenmek** (**-e**), be worried. ~ **li**, oppressive, gloomy, dreary, drab, dismal.
as·bilim (*bio.*) Myology. ~ **doku**, muscular tissue.
asd- = KASIT; KAST(EN).
âse Bowl; basin; (*sl.*) buttocks. ~ **lis**, sponger, toady.
asem Oath.
aset[i] (*cin.*, *mus.*) Cassette.
ası·k[ğı] (*bio.*) Groin. ~ **fıtık/yarığı** = ~ ÇATLAĞI. ~ **bağcı**, truss-maker/-seller. ~ **bağı**[nı], (*med.*) truss. ~ **biti**[ni], (*ent.*) crab/pubic louse. ~ **çatlağı**[nı], (*med.*) rupture, hernia. ~ **otu**[nu], (*bot.*) agrimony. ~ **sal**, (*bio.*) inguinal.
asıl (*bio.*) Muscular. ~ **duyumlar**, (*psy.*) muscular sensations. ~ **ım**, (*bio.*) contraction, spasm. ~ **ımlı**, spastic. ~ **mak**, *vi.* be stretched tight; contract; decrease, diminish; (*fig.*) pose, swagger.
asım[1] *n.* (*ast.*) November; 8 November (start of winter).
asım[2] *n.* (*bio.*) Systole. ~ **lı**, systolic.
Kasımpaşa (*geo.*) Naval arsenal, Istanbul. ~ **ağzı**, (*ling.*) 'Billingsgate'. ~ **lı**, foul-mouthed.
asımpatı[nı] (*bot.*) Chrysanthemum.
asın·ıç[cı] (*bio.*) Cramp, spasm. ~ **ma**, *vn.*; (*bio.*) spasmodic contraction; (*fig.*) self-importance. ~ **mak**, *vi.* shrink, contract; (*fig.*) be self-important. ~ **tı**, (*mod.*) tacking (for shortening a garment); (*fig.*) swagger. ~ **tılı**, proud.
as·ır[rı] Castle; summer-house, pavilion.
asırga (*met.*) Cyclone, hurricane. ~ +, *a.* Cyclonic.
as·ıt[tı] (Evil) intention; endeavour; premeditation; attempt on s.o.'s life. ~ (**-den**), what is meant by . . .: ~ **ı olm.** (**-e**), have evil intentions against s.o. ~ **lı**, purposeful, deliberate.
aside (*lit.*) Eulogy, commemorative poem. ~ **ci(lik)**, (work of) writer of such poems.
asis (*eng.*) Trench (across road); dip, hole; ford.
asiyer Cashier, teller.
aska·t[dı] (*geo.*) Cascade.
askatı Very hard; rigid; benumbed; petrified.
asket[i] (*mod.*) Cap. ~ **li**, wearing a cap.
asko (*naut.*) Hull; (*mot.*) motor-vehicle. ~ **kazası**, motor accident.
aslı Muscular, well-built.
asmak (**-i**) Stretch tight; tighten; (*mod.*) take in (a garment); curtail; dominate s.o. **kasıp kavurmak**, turn topsy-turvy; plague, torment, tyrannize; damage, destroy.
asna·k[ğı] Rim/hoop (of sieve, etc.); embroidery-frame; (*eng.*) belt pulley; (*arch.*) drum (of cupola); (*pub.*) chase, form; (*sp.*) wheel-rim. ~ **işlemek**, embroider on a frame: ~ **ı sıkmak**, (*pub.*) lock up a form.
asnak·çı Sieve-/hoop-/frame-maker. ~ **lamak** (**-i**), fit a hoop round stg.; pinion s.o.'s arms.

kasnı (*bot.*) Galbanum (resinous gum).
kasr- = KASIR.
kast[1] (*soc.*) Caste.
kast- = KASIT.
kastan·yet[i] (*mus.*) Castanets. ~ **yola**, (*eng.*) pawl, dog; (*naut.*) cleat: ~ **yuvası**, pawl-slot.
kastar (*tex.*) Bleaching. ~ **lamak** (**-i**), bleach. ~ **lı**, bleached.
kast·en Intentionally, deliberately; (*leg.*) with malice aforethought. ~ **ıetmek**[eder] (**-i**), purpose, intend, aim at/for; have a design against s.o.; mean, express. ~ **i**, premeditated, deliberate, intentional: ~ **mahsus**, with a special intention.
Kastilli (*ling.*) Castilian (Spanish).
kastor (*zoo.*) Beaver.
kastrasyon (*med.*) Castration.
kasvet(li) = KASAVET(Lİ).
kaş (*bio.*) Eyebrow; stg. curved (and projecting); collet (of ring, etc.); (*mus.*) accolade ({); (*pub.*) brace. ~ **boyası**, (*mod.*) eyebrow pencil: ~ **göz etm.**, wink, make signs with eye and brow: ~ **yapayım derken göz çıkarmak**, try to help a little but spoil everything: ~ **ı çatılmak**, cloud the brow: ~ **la göz arasında**, in the twinkling of an eye: ~ **larını çatmak**, frown.
kaş·ağı/~ **ak** (*live.*) Curry-comb; back-scratcher. ~ **ağılamak**/~ **amak** (**-i**), curry, groom. ~ **ağılanmak**, *vp.*
kaşalot *n.* (*zoo.*) Cachalot, sperm whale. *a.* (*sl.*) Stupid.
kaşan Urine (of horses). ~ **yeri**, stopping-place (for horses): ~ **ı gelmek**, (horse) need to urinate. ~ **dirmak** (**-i**), *vc.* ~ **mak**, *vi.* urinate.
kâşane Luxurious dwelling; mansion.
kaşar/kaşer/~ **peyniri**[ni] (*cul.*) Flat (cheddar-type) cheese; (*sl.*) s.o. cunning.
kaşar·lanmak *vi.* Become old/worn out; become experienced/callous. ~ **lanmış**/~ **lı**, *a.* experienced, hardened, callous, cunning; insensitive; old, worn-out.
kaşbastı (*mod.*) Band(age) round the head.
kaşe (*med.*) Capsule, cachet; (*mod.*) cachet.
kaşeksi (*med.*) Cachexia.
kaşı·k[ğı] Spoon; spoonful; (*min.*) boring-bit; (*mus.*) wooden spoon (used as castanet). ~ **atmak/çalmak**, eat heartily/greedily: ~ **dolusu**, spoonful: ~ **düşmanı**, (*jok.*) one's wife: ~ **oyunu**, (*mus.*) dance to rattling spoons: ~ **la karıştırmak** (**-i**), stir stg.: ~ **la yedirip sapıyla gözünü çıkarmak**, spoil a good deed by a bad one.
kaşık·ağızlı ~ **mersin balığı**, (*ich.*) paddlefish. ~ **çı**, spoonmaker. ~ **çıkuşu**[nu], (*orn.*) European white pelican. ~ **çılık**, spoon-making/-selling. ~ **çın**/~ **gaga (ördeği)**, (*orn.*) northern shoveler. ~ **lamak** (**-i**), eat spoonfuls (from a dish); (*fig.*) hasten to avail o.s. of stg. ~ **lanmak**, *vp.* ~ **lı**, *ich.* **balıkçıl**, (*orn.*) white spoonbill. ~ **lık**, case, etc. for spoons; suitable for making spoons; spoonful. ~ **otu**[nu], (*bot.*) scurvy-grass.
kaş·ımak (**-i**) Scratch. ~ **ındırmak** (**-i**), make scratch; itch. ~ **ınmak**, *vi.* scratch o.s., itch; (*fig.*) ask/look for trouble. ~ **ıntı**, itching.
kâşif Discoverer; explorer; revealer.

kaşkariko (*sl.*) Trick; deceit; buffoonery.

kaşkaval (*cul.*) Round sheep's cheese; (*sl.*) stupid.

kaş·kol (*mod.*) Scarf. ~ **korse**, (*mod.*) camisole.

kaşlı Having eyebrows; having . . . mounted (as a ring). ~ **gözlü**, s.o. complete in every way; pretty.

kaşmer(lik) Buffoon(ery), clown(ing).

Kaşmir (*geo.*) Kashmir; (*tex.*) = KAZMİR.

katı¹ Fold; crease; layer; coating; (*arch.*) storey; quantity; stage; time (of repetition); multiple; (*tex.*) ply; opinion. ~ **çıkmak**, (*arch.*) add a storey: ~ **etm.**, fold; stow in layers/tiers: ~ ~, in layers; time after time; many times more; much more: ~ ~ **daha (iyi)**, far and away the (best): ~ ~ **üstündür (-den)**, that beats . . . .

kat(a)- *pref.* Cat(a)- ~ **basis**, (*th.*) anticlimax. ~ **batik**, (*met.*) katabatic. ~ **bolizm**, (*bio.*) catabolism. ~ **drom**, (*ich.*) catadromous. ~ **falk¹**, (*rel.*) catafalque. ~ **fot**ᵘ, (*phys.*) cat's eye. ~ **klastik**, (*geol.*) cataclastic. ~ **komp**ᵘ, (*rel.*) catacomb.

katakulli (*sl.*) Act of cheating; hoax. ~ **ye gelmek**, be swindled.

kata·lepsi (*med.*) Catalepsy. ~ **litik**, (*chem.*) catalytic. ~ **liz**, catalysis. ~ **lizlemek (-i)**, catalyse. ~ **lizör**, catalyst. ~ **lo¹g**ᵍᵘ, (*pub.*) catalogue. ~ **loglama**, cataloguing.

katalpa (*bot.*) Catalpa, Indian bean.

kata·na = KADANA². ~ **pult** (*aer.*) catapult.

katar Train/file of camels, etc.; convoy; railway train. ~ ~, in long lines: ~ **kılavuzu**, donkey leading the camels; (*rly.*) pilot-engine. ~ **lamak (-i)**, make a train/file of camels, etc. ~ **lanmak**, *vp.*

katarakt (*med.*) Cataract.

katarsis (*th.*) Catharsis.

katavasya (*ich.*) Catabasis, winter migration (Black Sea to Aegean).

katbek¹ (*chem., eng.*) Cutback.

katbilim (*geol.*) Stratigraphy.

kate·dral (*arch.*) Cathedral. ~ **gori**, category. ~ **gorik**, categorical. ~ **şizm**, (*rel.*) catechism.

katem (*chem.*) Additive.

kat¹etmekᵉᵈᵉʳ **(-i)** Cut; interrupt; terminate; travel over, traverse.

katev (*arch.*) Flat, apartment.

katgüt (*bio.*) Catgut.

katı¹ *n.* (*orn.*) Gizzard.

katı² *a.* Hard; violent, cruel; (*phys.*) solid. *adv.* Very. ~ **hal**, (*phys.*) solid state: ~ **söz**, harsh words: ~ YAKIT: ~ **yürekli**, hard-hearted. ~ **cıl**, (*chem.*) solidus.

katı¹kᵍ¹ (*cul.*) Stg. eaten with one's bread; stg. added. ~ **etm.**, eat stg. with one's bread. ~ **sız**, unmixed, unadulterated; (*fin.*) net: ~ **ekmek**, dry bread: ~ **hapis**, (*mil.*) detention on bread and water.

katı·lama (*min.*) Cementation. ~ **laşma**, *vn.* hardening; congealing; solidification. ~ **laşmak**, *vi.* become hard/heavy; solidify, cake, congeal, coagulate; (*fig.*) become concrete. ~ **laştırmak (-i)**, *vc.*

katılgan (*bio.*) Conjunctive. ~ **doku**, conjunctive/connective tissue.

katı·lık Hardness; rigidity; dryness; severity.

katıl·ma *vn.* Addition; mixing; participation; collaboration; (*leg.*) intervention; (*fin.*) fusion, merger, amalgamation. ~ **mak¹ (-e)**, *vp.* = KATMAK: be added; be mixed; be driven along; be included in; collaborate/participate with others; (*mus.*) accompany; intervene in; contribute/share/ adopt (ideas, etc.). ~ **maz**, excluded.

katıl·mak² *vi.* Become hard; get out of breath (from laughing/crying, etc.). ~ **tmak (-i)**, *vc.*

kat·ım Adding; joining; mixing; (*chem.*) additive. ~ **ımlık**, amount to be added. ~ **ıntı**, *n.* mixture: *a.* added, mixed.

katır¹ ~ **kutur** = HATIR¹.

katır² *n.* (*live.*) Mule; (*fig.*) obstinate/ungrateful/ malicious person. ~ **kuyruğu gibi kalmak**, make no progress: ~ (**yemeni**), (*mod.*) rough shoe with iron heel tips, clog.

katır·boncuğuⁿᵘ Blue bead/talisman (hung round animal's neck); (*zoo.*) cowrie shell. ~ **cı(lık)**, (work of) muleteer. ~ **kuyruğu**ⁿᵘ, (*bot.*) horseshoe vetch. ~ **tırnağı**ⁿ¹, (*bot.*) common/Scots broom. ~ **yılanı**ⁿ¹, (*zoo.*) type of viper.

katış·ık Mixed; impure. ~ **ıklama**, (*ling.*) hybridization. ~ **ıksız**, pure, unadulterated. ~ **kı**, impurity. ~ **ma¹ç**ᶜ¹, (*phil.*) aggregate. ~ **mak (-e)**, add o.s. to; introduce o.s. into. ~ **tırmak (-i, -e)**, *vc.* introduce into; adulterate.

katı·yağ Solid grease; tallow; paraffin wax: ~ **giderme**, (*min.*) degreasing: ~ **sürme**, greasing: ~ **tabancası**, grease-gun. ~ **yakıt**, solid fuel. ~ **yuvar**, (*min.*) ball. ~ **yuvarlı**, ~ **fıçılama**, burnishing: ~ **yatak**, (*eng.*) ball-bearing.

kati Definite, certain, distinct, decisive, absolute. ~ **olarak**, definitely.

kâtib- = KÂTİP. ~ **e**, female secretary. ~ **iadil**, (*leg., obs.*) notary.

katil¹ ¹ *n.* Murderer; assassin, butcher, cut-throat. *a.* Murderous. ~ **böceği**, (*ent.*) assassin bug.

kat¹ilˡ¹ ² *n.* Killing; assassination; murder.

kati·leşmek *vi.* Become definite/certain. ~ **leştirmek (-i)**, *vc.* confirm stg. ~ **lik**, definiteness.

katillik Being a murderer; murder.

kâti¹pᵇ¹ Clerk; secretary. ~ **parçası**, (*pej.*) some sort of clerk, very ordinary clerk. ~ **lik**, quality/profession of clerk/secretary; clerkship, secretaryship.

kati·yen Definitely, absolutely; finally. ~ **yet¹**, definiteness; precision, certitude.

katkı Participation, share; assistance; addition; (*chem.*) additive; thickener. ~ **da bulunmak**, participate/assist (in some way); contribute.

katkı·lı Adulterated, impure; (*fin.*) gross (weight/ income, etc.). ~ **sız**, unadulterated, pure; (*fin.*) net (weight/income, etc.).

katkonutᵘ (*arch.*) Flat, apartment.

katla·¹kᵍ¹ (*med.*) Chart. ~ **mak (-i)**, bend; fold; pleat; put layer upon layer; repeat. ~ **ndırmak (-i, -e)**, *vc.* = NMAK. ~ **nılmak (-e)**, *imp. v.* endure, accept. ~ **nır**, *a.* collapsible/folding (table, etc.). ~ **nıvermek**, accept. ~ **nmak**, *vi.* bend, fold; be folded; become stratified: **(-e)**, undergo, suffer, endure; acquiesce in. ~ **ntı**, patience; (*min.*) fold. ~ **ntılı**, patient. ~ **ntısız**, impatient. ~ **tmak (-i, -e)**, *vc.* = MAK.

katl- = KATİL². ~ **¹etmek**ᵉᵈᵉʳ **(-i)**, kill, assassinate. ~ **iam**, general massacre, butchery, blood-bath.

katlı *a.* In layers; multiple; (*arch.*) having . . . storeys. *n.* (*adm.*) File, dossier. ~ **kavşak**, (*mot.*) interchange junction.

kat·ma *n.* Addition; admixture; appendage: *a.* joined on, annexed; additional, supplementary: ~ **bütçe**, (*fin.*) supplementary budget: ~ **vergi**, surtax. ~ **mak (-i, -e)**, add; join, annex; mix; send together; embroil: **katıp karıştırmak**, admix. ~ **malı**, (*cin.*, *chem.*) additive.

katman Layer; (*geol.*) bed, stratum. ~ +, *a.* Stratigraphic: ~ **karabulut**, (*met.*) nimbo-stratus: ~ **doku**, (*bot.*) cambium. ~ **bilgisi**, (*geol.*) stratigraphy. ~ **bulut**ᵘ, (*met.*) stratus. ~ **laşma**, *vn.* (*geol.*) layering, stratification. ~ **laşmak**, *vi.* stratify, form layers. ~ **lı**, (*geol.*) stratified; (*min.*) lamellar; (*phys.*) laminar. ~ **yazar**, chromatograph.

katmer *n.* A having folds; (*bot.*) double flower; (*cul.*) flaky pastry. *a.* Folded. ~ ~, in folds, in layers.

katmer·ci (*cul.*) Maker/seller of flaky pastry. ~ **leşmek**, *vi.* become folded/double. ~ **li**, having many folds; manifold; multiple; (*bot.*) double, many-petalled; (*cul.*) flaky: ~ **birleşik zaman**, (*ling.*) secondary compound tense: ~ **iyelik**, (*ling.*) double possessive suffix: ~ **yalan**, one lie after another. ~ **libadem**, (*bot.*) almond with a double kernel.

Katoli·kᵍⁱ (*rel.*) Catholic. ~ **lik**, (Roman) catholicism.

kat·optrik (*phys.*) Catoptrics. ~ **'ot**ᵈᵘ, (*el.*) cathode: ~ **ışınları**, cathode rays. ~ **otsal**, cathodic.

katra Drop. ~ ~, drop by drop: ~ **sı kalmadı/yok**, there's nothing (left) at all.

katran Tar, coal-tar; bitumen. ~ **ağacı**, (*bot.*) cedar of Lebanon; terebinth, turpentine tree: ~ **çamı**, (*bot.*) Scots pine, pitch pine: ~ **suyu**, (*med.*) tar-water.

katran·ardıcıⁿ¹ (*bot.*) Prickly juniper. ~ **köpüğü**ⁿᵘ, (*myc.*) false tinder fungus; amadou. ~ **lamak (-i)**, cover with tar. ~ **lanmak**, *vp.* ~ **lı**, tarred, tarry; bituminous; covered/mixed with tar. ~ **ruhu**ⁿᵘ, (*chem.*) creosote. ~ **taşı**ⁿⁱ, (*geol.*) bitumen.

katrat¹ (*pub.*) Quadrat; pica (type-size); em.

katrilyon (*math.*) Quadrillion (10¹⁵).

kat·sayı (*math.*) Coefficient, factor. ~ **yapı**, (*phys.*) build-up.

katyon (*phys.*) Cation.

katyuvarı (*ast.*) Stratosphere.

kauçu·kᵍᵘ Caoutchouc, unvulcanized rubber; (*bot.*) Indiarubber tree. ~ **kaplı**, rubberized.

kav Tinder, touchwood. ~ **çakmak**, tinder and flint: ~ **gibi**, soft and inflammable.

kavaf Dealer in ready-made shoes. ~ **işi**, coarsely/shoddily made: ~ **malı**, fraudulent rubbish. ~ **hane**, shoe workshop. ~ **lık**, cheap-shoe trade.

kava·kᵍ¹ (*bot.*) Poplar. ~ **ağacı**, poplar-tree; cottonwood. ~ **çılık**, poplar culture. ~ **inciri**ⁿⁱ, purple fig. ~ **lık**, poplar grove. ~ **oyan**, (*ent.*) poplar longhorn.

kaval (*mus.*) Shepherd's pipe; any hollow pipe. ~ **kemiği**, (*bio.*) tibia [= BALDIR KEMİĞİ]: ~ **tüfek**, (*mil.*) smoothbore (gun). ~ **lanmak**, (*sl.*) bore, annoy.

kavalye(lik) (*mus.*) (Duties of) male dancing-partner.

kavanço (*naut.*) Transhipment (of goods); transfer; handing over; (*sl.*) passing the buck; (*sl.*) making a switch.

kavanoz Glass/earthenware jar; pot. ~ **dipli dünya**, this inconstant/treacherous world. ~ **balığı**, (*ich.*) glassfish.

kavara Emptied honeycomb; honey left to feed bees; (*fig.*) loud noise, uproar.

kavas(lık) (Duties of) embassy/consular guard.

kavasya (*bot.*) Quassia, bitterwood.

kavata (*bot.*) Bitter tomato (for pickling); (*dom.*) wooden bowl.

kavela (*carp.*) Dowel, plug.

kavga Tumult; affray, brawl, quarrel; (*obs.*) fight, battle. ~ **bizim yorganın başına imiş**, (said of) s.o. who suffers to end others' quarrels: ~ **elinin köründen çıkar**, a mere trifle may start a quarrel: ~ **etm.**, quarrel, fight: ~ **kaşağısı**, trouble-maker; pretext for a quarrel: ~ **mis gibi kokuyor/tütüyor**, a quarrel seems certain: ~ **ya kaşınmak**, be itching for a fight: ~ **ya tutuşmak**, quarrel; come to blows.

kavga·cı Quarrelsome, combative: ~ **balık**, (*ich.*) fighting fish. ~ **laşmak**, *vi.* quarrel. ~ **lı**, quarrelling, angry: ~ **yer**, disputed site.

kavgımak (-le) *vi.* Run; walk fast.

kavi Strong, robust, forceful. ~ **leşmek**, *vi.* become strong/robust. ~ **leştirmek (-i)**, *vc.*

kav'ilˡⁱ Word; assertion; agreement. ~ **etm.**, agree; promise. ~ **ince**, according to s.o.'s assertion. ~ **leşmek (-le)**, reach an agreement (with s.o.).

kav'imᵐⁱ (*ethn.*) Tribe; people; nation.

kav'isˢⁱ Bow; arc, curve; (*ast.*) Sagittarius. ~ +, *a.* Curved, curvi-: ~ **çizmek**, curve. ~ **lenme**, curvature. ~ **li**, curved: ~ **pencere**, bow-window.

kavi·tasyon (*phys.*) Cavitation. ~ **te**, cavity.

kavkı (*zoo.*) Shell (of shellfish, etc.). ~ **lı**, full of shells.

kavl- = KAVİL.

kavla·k Having the (*bio.*) skin//(*bot.*) bark peeled off: ~ **süngüsü**, crowbar. ~ **kçı**, (*min.*) ripper, stripper. ~ **mak**, *vi.* become dry and peel off. ~ **nma**, (*bio.*) desquamation. ~ **nmak**, *vp.* ~ **şmak**, *vi.* become dry (like tinder). ~ **tmak (-i)**, *vc.*

kavlı·çᶜ¹ (*med.*) Rupture(d); swelling.

kavmantarıⁿ¹ (*myc.*) Tinder fungus; amadou.

kavm- = KAVİM. ~ **i**, ethnic; tribal; national. ~ **iyat**¹, ethnography. ~ **iyet**ⁱ, nationality.

kavra·içᶜ¹ Large tongs for lifting stones).

kavram¹ *n.* (*bio.*) Omentum, peritoneum.

kavra·m² *n.* (*phil.*) Concept; idea, notion; (*eng.*) coupling. ~ **ma**, *vn.* understanding; conception; (*arch.*) tie beam; (*mot.*) clutch-pedal: ~ **tertibatı**, coupling system. ~ **mak (-i)**, seize; grasp; understand, comprehend, fathom. ~ **mcı(lık)**, (*phil.*) conceptual·ist(-ism). ~ **msal**, conceptual. ~ **n(ıl)mak**, *vp.* be seized; be conceived/understood. ~ **nılmaz**, inconceivable. ~ **tmak (-i)**, *vc.* ~ **yıcı**, comprehending/absorbing (thought). ~ **yış**, comprehension. ~ **yışlı**, quick at understanding. ~ **yışsız**, unintelligent.

kavru·k Scorched; dried up; arid; (*fig.*) stunted.

~**kluk,** dryness; being stunted. ~**lmak,** *vp.* = KAVURMAK; (*cul.*) be roasted/fried; be scorched; be withered/stunted. ~**lmuş,** *a.* dried up; blighted; (*cul., min.*) roasted.

kavs- = KAVİS.

kavşa¹k^{ğı} (*mot.*) Junction; confluence; cross-roads, intersection.

kavu¹k^{ğu} *n.* (*mod., obs.*) Large padded headgear; (*bio.*) bladder. *a.* Hollow; rotten. ~ **giydirmek,** cheat, deceive: ~ **sallamak,** acquiesce unhesitatingly; toady: ~**uma anlat/dinlet!,** tell that to the Marines!

kavuk·çu Toady; hypocrite. ~**lu,** wearing a KAVUK; (*th.*) character in ORTA OYUN. ~**luk,** (*dom.*) shelf for KAVUK.

kavun (*bot.*) Melon. ~**ağacı^{nı},** pawpaw tree; passion-flower. ~**içiⁿⁱ,** flesh of the melon; pinkish dark yellow.

kavur·ga (*cul.*) Dried/roasted corn, etc. ~**ma,** *vn.* roasting; frying; broiled/fried meat: *a.* fried; roast (coffee). ~**ma¹ç^{cı},** parched wheat. ~**mak (-i),** fry; sautée; roast (coffee, etc.); (wind, etc.) scorch, blast, blight. ~**malık,** suitable/selected for roasting/frying. ~**tmak (-i, -e),** *vc.*

kavuş·a¹k^{ğı} Junction. ~**ma,** *vn.* coming together; union; (*ast.*) conjunction; (*bio.*) conjugation. ~**mak (-e),** *vi.* come together; reach; attain; obtain; join; touch; meet (after long separation); (*bio.*) conjugate: **kavuşur,** *a.* (*bot.*) conjugate: **kavuşmaz,** (*math.*) asymptote. ~**turmak (-i, -e),** *vc.* bring together; write; join; cause to meet. ~**uk,** joining, touching. ~**ulmak,** *vp.* ~**um,** (*ast.*) conjunction. ~**umdevriⁿⁱ,** (*ast.*) synodic period.

kavu¹t^{du} (*cul.*) Dish of roast wheat and dried pear.

kavuz (*bot.*) Glume. ~**lu,** glumaceous. ~**lular,** Glumiferae.

kavzamak (-i) Hold tightly; guard, protect; arrange.

kay^{yı} Vomiting.

kaya Rock; rocky cliff/hill. ~ **antilopu,** (*zoo.*) klipspringer: ~ **ardıcı,** (*orn.*) rock thrush: ~ **döküntüsü,** (*geol.*) detritus: ~ **gibi,** rock-hard: ~ **güvercini,** (*orn.*) rock dove: ~ HOROZU: ~ **kangurusu,** (*zoo.*) rock wallaby: ~ **kara sağan,** (*orn.*) Alpine swift: ~ **kartalı,** (*orn.*) golden eagle: ~ **kırlangıcı,** (*orn.*) crag martin: ~ÖRÜMCEĞİ: ~ **parçası,** boulder: ~ **sansarı,** (*zoo.*) beech-marten: ~ **sıvacı kuşu,** (*orn.*) Neumayer's rock nuthatch: ~ **suyu,** (*geol.*) rock spring: ~TUZU: ~ **uçması,** rock-fall: ~ **yelvesi,** (*orn.*) rock bunting.

kaya·balığı^{nı} (*ich.*) Goby. ~**balığıgiller,** (*ich.*) gobies. ~**başı^{nı},** (*mus.*) Anatolian tune; (*lit.*) rustic ballad. ~**cık,** small rock; (*bot.*) hop-hornbeam.

kaya¹ç^{cı} (*geol.*) Rocks. ~ +, *a.* Litho-, petro-: ~ **örneği,** rock sample. ~**bilgisiⁿⁱ,** petrography. ~**bilim,** petrology.

kayağan·(lık) Slipper·y/(-iness). ~**taş,** (*geol.*) laminated rock; slate.

kaya·hanisiⁿⁱ (*ich.*) Type of grouper. ~**horozu^{nu},** (*orn.*) cock-of-the-rock.

kaya¹k^{ğı} (*sp.*) Ski; skiing. ~**ça/~kabı,** skate: ~ **ile kaymak,** skate. ~**çı,** skier. ~**çılık,** skiing.

kaya·keleriⁿⁱ (*zoo.*) Chameleon. ~**koruğu^{nu},**

(*bot.*) stone-crop. ~**lık,** *a.* rocky: *n.* rocky place, crag, cliff: ~ **serçesi,** (*orn.*) rock sparrow. ~**lifiⁿⁱ,** (*min.*) asbestos. ~**meşesiⁿⁱ,** (*bot.*) English oak. ~**örümceğiⁿⁱ,** (*zoo.*) rock-spider, drassodes.

kayan *n.* Mountain torrent/flood. *a.* Swift; violent. ~ **yıldız,** (*ast.*) falling star.

kayar¹ *v.* = KAYMAK¹. *a.* Sliding.

kayar² *n.* Footpath; reusing old horseshoes; trimming hoofs. ~**lama,** *vn.* refitting/renewing old horseshoes. ~**lamak (-i),** (*sl.*) swear.

kayatuzu^{nu} (*min.*) Rock-salt.

kayb- = KAYIP. ~**¹etmek^{eder} (-i),** lose; forfeit. ~**olmak,** *vi.* be lost/missing; disappear.

kayd- = KAYIT. ~**edici,** ~ **(cihaz),** recording (apparatus). ~**¹etmek^{eder} (-i, -e),** enrol; register; record; notice; note down; (*sp.*) score. ~**ıhayat¹:** ~**la/**~ **şartıyla,** (*fin., leg.*) for life, during one's lifetime.

kaydır·a¹k^{ğı} Flat round stone; (*child.*) hopscotch; slide. ~**ılmak (-e),** *vp.* ~**ım/**~**ma,** *vn.* sliding; (*phys.*) displacement; (*cin.*) tracking, travelling; (*sp.*) sudden change of fortune. ~**mak (-i, -e),** *vc.* = KAYMAK¹; cause to slip, etc.; graze; (*adm.*) cause s.o. to lose his position. ~**tmak (-i),** *vc.*

kayd·iye (*adm.*) Registration fee. ~**olmak** *vp.* = KAYDETMEK; be registered, etc. ~**olunmak (-de),** check in at.

kaygan Slippery; polished; (*fig.*) fickle. ~ **derili köpek balığı,** (*ich.*) smooth hound. ~**lık,** slipperiness.

kaygana (*cul.*) Omelette; dessert made with eggs.

kaygı Care; anxiety; grief. ~**landırmak (-i),** *vc.* ~**lanmak,** *vi.* be anxious; grieve. ~**lı,** anxious; worried; causing anxiety. ~**lılık,** anxiousness; anxiety. ~**sız,** carefree. ~**sızlık,** freedom from care.

kaygın Slippery; polished; (*zoo.*) pregnant.

kayı¹k^{ğı} *a.* Inclined to one side. *n.* Boat, caique. ~ **dolusu,** boatful: ~ **salıncak,** (*child.*) swing-boat: ~ **tabak,** (*dom.*) oval dish: ~ **tığı,** cutwater.

kayık·çı Boatman. ~**çık,** (*bio.*) carina. ~**çılık,** building/selling boats; operating/sailing boats. ~**hane,** boathouse.

kayın¹ *n.* (*bot.*) Beech. ~ **ağacı,** beech tree: ~ **palamudu,** beech-mast/-nut: ~ **tavuğu (erkeği),** (*orn.*) black grouse/(blackcock). ~**giller,** (*bot.*) beech family, Fagus.

kayı¹n^{nı ²} *n.* (*soc.*) In-law. ~ **hısımlığı,** relationship by marriage. ~**baba/**~**peder,** father-in-law. ~**(birader),** (brother)-in-law. ~**ço,** (*col.*) brother-in-law's child. ~**valide,** mother-in-law.

kay¹ıp^{bı} *n.* Loss; (*mil.*) casualties. *a.* Lost. ~ **listesi,** (*mil.*) casualty-list: ~**lara karışmak,** disappear; vanish into thin air; abscond.

kayır (*geo.*) Sandbank.

kayır·ıcı Protector; supporter; guardian. ~**ıcılık,** favouritism. ~**ılmak (-e),** be favoured/protected. ~**ış/**~**ma,** *vn.* protection, backing. ~**mak (-i),** look after, take care of; protect; back; support; employ. ~**tmak (-i, -e),** *vc.*

kayısı (*bot.*) Apricot. ~ **ağacı,** apricot tree: ~ **sineği,** (*ent.*) Mediterranean fruit-fly.

kayış¹ *vn.* Act of slipping.

kayış[2] *n.* Strap; (razor-)strop; belt; band. ~ **besleyici,** (*ind.*) belt/conveyor feed: ~ **çemberi,** (*eng.*) drum/pulley (of belt-drive): ~ **gibi,** tough, (*cul.*) like leather: ~ **testeresi,** band-saw: ~ **a çekmek (-i),** strop a razor; (*fig.*) cheat/deceive s.o.: ~ **la işletme,** (*eng.*) belt-drive.

kayış·balığı[nı] (*ich.*) Cusk eel. ~ **çı,** *n.* maker/seller of belts, etc.: *a.* (*fig.*) deceitful. ~ **dili**[ni], (*ling.*) coarse/vulgar speech; slang. ~ **kıran,** (*bot.*) restharrow. ~ **lı,** with a belt; belted: ~ **taşıyıcı,** belt conveyor.

kay¹ıt[dı 1] *n.* Any part of a frame.

kay¹ıt[dı 2] *n.* Restriction; reservation; enrolment; registration; entry, record; caring, paying attention; brooding over stg. ~ **altına girememek,** refuse to be limited by restrictions; be independent: ~ **cihazı,** (*phys., etc.*) recording instrument: ~ **hatası,** clerical error: ~ **muamelesi,** registration formalities: ~ **ücreti,** registration fee: ~ **a geçirmek,** enter/ record in a register: ~ IHAYAT: ~ **ını silmek,** annul, cancel: ~ **ıyla,** with the reservation that; provided that: ~ **lar,** (*adm.*) records: ~ **tan düşmek (-i),** cancel an entry.

kayıt·ım (*phil.*) Recurrence. ~ **lamak (-i),** limit/ restrict with conditions. ~ **layıcı,** restrictive. ~ **lı,** restricted; with reservations; careful; recorded, registered. ~ **mak (-den),** withdraw; retract. ~ **sız,** unregistered; careless, indifferent; carefree: ~ **şartsız,** unconditionally. ~ **sızlık,** indifference, complacency, carelessness; freedom from care; not being registered.

kaykılmak (-e) Lean; lean back.

kay·ma *vn.* Slipping; sliding; (*sp.*) glide; skating; (*geol.*) drift; shear; (*phys.*) distortion, shift. ~ **maç,** slanting (eyes). ~ **mak**[1], *vi.* slip; slide; glide; skate; (*geol.*) subside; become awry; (*fig.*) do stg. unintentionally: **(-e),** (*ling.*) change meaning.

kayma¹k[gı 1 2] *n.* (*cul.*) Cream, (*esp.*) clotted cream; (*fig.*) the cream of stg.; essence; (*geo.*) hard crust (after rain). ~ **ağzı,** (*cul.*) crust of clotted cream: ~ **altı,** skim milk: ~ **bağlamak/tutmak,** form cream: ~ **gibi,** very white; sweet and soft.

kaymakam (*adm.*) Governor of a KAZA/İLÇE; acting representative; (*mil., obs.*) lieutenant-colonel. ~ **lık,** his position/district.

kaymak·çı Cream maker/seller: ~ **dükkânı,** creamery. ~ **kâğıdı**[nı], (*pub.*) art-paper, surface-coated paper. ~ **lanmak,** *vi.* form cream. ~ **lı,** creamy, made with cream: ~ **dondurma,** (*cul.*) milk-based ice-cream. ~ **taşı**[nı], (*geol.*) alabaster. ~ **yağı**[nı], fresh butter.

kay·man (*zoo.*) Caiman. ~ **me,** (*col.*) paper money.

kaymaoluşum (*geol.*) Tectonics. ~ **sal,** tectonic.

kayna¹ç[cı] (*min.*) Welding press; (*geol.*) geyser.

kayna¹k[gı] Spring, fountain; place of origin; (*phys., lit.*) source; place where two things join; (*bio.*) buttocks; (*min.*) weld(ing). ~ **pirinci,** (*min.*) hard solder, welding brass: ~ **suyu,** (*geol.*) spring water: ~ **tozu,** (*min.*) welding powder, flux: ~ **üfleci,** welding torch: ~ **yapma,** welding: ~ **yapmak,** weld: ~ **ında,** (*fin.*) at source.

kaynak·ça(sal) (*pub.*) Bibliography/(-ical). ~ **çı,**

(*min.*) welder. ~ **çılık,** welding. ~ **lama,** welding. ~ **lı,** welded.

kayna·ma *vn.* Boiling; welding; teeming: *a.* boiled: ~ **nokta/sıcaklığı,** (*phys.*) boiling-point. ~ **mak,** *vi.* boil; be boiled; bubble, effervesce; (stomach) burn; join; be welded; (bones) knit; (trouble) be brewing; swarm, teem; be perpetually moving; (*naut.*) founder; (*sl.*) be 'pinched'; be lost (in the confusion); (*sl.*) disappear.

kayn- = KAYIN[2]. ~ **ana,** mother-in-law. ~ **anadili**[ni], (*bot.*) prickly pear. ~ **analık,** status of mother-in-law; behaving like a bad mother-in-law. ~ **anazırıltısı**[nı], (*child.*) rattle.

kaynar Boiling; (*sl.*) hashish. ~ **ca,** (*geol.*) hot spring.

kaynaş·ık Restless, changing; (*min.*) fused. ~ **ma,** *vn.*; restless movement (in crowd); (*min.*) fusion. ~ **mak (-le),** *vi.* unite; (*chem.*) combine; coalesce; be welded/joined; unite in friendship; (crowd) swarm; (*mod.*) match. ~ **tırma,** *vn.:* ~ **harf//sesi,** (*ling.*) letter (-N-/-S-/-Ş-/-Y-) linking two vowels [EVİNİN; ALTIŞAR]//elision of vowel between two syllables [CUMA(E)RTESİ]. ~ **tırmak (-i, -le),** *vc.* cause to unite; weld together.

kaynata(lık) (Status of) father-in-law.

kaynat·ılmak *vp.* ~ **mak (-i),** cause to boil; boil stg.; weld; (*naut.*) cause to founder; plot (trouble); (*col.*) have a long chat; (*sl.*) 'pinch', pilfer; (*sl.*) welsh on a debt.

kaypak Slippery; (*fig.*) unreliable, shifty. ~ **mal,** stolen/smuggled goods. ~ **çı,** thief; smuggler; receiver (of stolen goods). ~ **lık,** slipperiness; unreliability.

kaypamak *vi.* Slip away (unnoticed).

kayra Kindness, charity; grace, benevolence. ~ **bileti,** (*th.*) complimentary ticket. ~ **cı(lık),** (*phil.*) providential·ist/(-ism).

kayr·a¹k[gı] *n.* Slippery place; (*sp.*) ski slope; flat round stone; (*geol.*) slate. *a.* Shifting, sliding (earth). ~ **almak,** *vi.* (river) form sandbanks, become choked.

kayran (*agr.*) Forest clearing.

kayrılmak *vp.* = KAYIRMAK.

kayser (*his.*) Caesar; emperor; kaiser. ~ **i,** *pr.n.* (*geo.*) Kayseri; (*his.*) Caesarea.

kayşa (*geol.*) Avalanche. ~ **mak,** *vi.* (avalanche) slide down. ~ **t**[1], debris, detritus.

kaytak Sheltered; (*fig.*) fickle.

kaytan (*tex.*) Cotton/silk cord; braid. ~ **bıyıklı,** with thin curling moustache.

kaytar·ıcı Dodger; work-shy person. ~ **mak (-i),** return, give back; refuse; avoid/dodge work.

kayyım Mosque caretaker/attendant; (*leg.*) administrator, trustee.

kaz (*orn.*) Goose; (*fig.*) silly fool. ~ AYAĞI: ~ BOKU: ~ **gelen yerden tavuk esirgenmez,** don't grudge a penny where you may get a pound: ~ **gibi,** (*orn.*) anserine: ~ **kafalı,** unintelligent, stupid: ~ KANADI: ~ **karabatağı,** (*orn.*) African darter: ~ **ı gibi bakmak (Agop'un),** stare stupidly: ~ **ı koz anlamak,** misunderstand out of ignorance: ~ **ın ayağı (öyle değil),** the truth of the matter (is really quite different).

kaza Accident, mischance; casualty; chance; (*leg.*) office/functions of a judge; (*adm.*) district governed by a KAYMAKAM; (*rel.*) performance of a duty previously omitted; performance of an act; (*fin.*) payment of a debt. ~ **bela savmak kabilinden**, as a wise precaution: ~ **geçirmek**, have an accident: ~ **güvence/sigortası**, (*fin.*) accident insurance: ~ **hakkı**, (*leg.*) right to judge: ~ **idare heyeti**, (*adm.*) district council: ~ **kurşunu**, stray bullet: ~ **kuvveti**, power to judge; judiciary power: ~ **süsü vermek** (**-e**), pass stg. off as an accident: ~ **ve kader**, fate and destiny: ~**ya karşı sigorta**, (*fin.*) accident insurance: ~**ya rıza!**, it can't be helped!: ~**ya rıza göstermek**, resign o.s. to one's fate: ~**ya uğramak**, have an accident. ~**en** = ~RA.

kazağı Digging tool, shovel; scraper.

kaza¹k^{ğ11} *n.* (*mod.*) Jersey, pullover; jockey's multicoloured shirt.

kaza¹k^{ğ12} *n.* (*mil.*) Cossack soldier. ~ (**koca**), masterful husband. ~**lık**, being a masterful husband.

Kaza¹k^{ğ13} *n.* (*ethn.*) Kazakh; Cossack. ~ **çömelmesi**, (*mus.*) Cossack dance. ~**ça**, (*ling.*) Kazakh language. ~**istan**, (*geo.*) Kazakhstan.

kazalı Causing accidents; dangerous; (*adm.*) having . . . districts.

kazamat¹ (*mil.*) Casemate.

kazan (*dom.*) Cauldron, big soup-kettle; (*ind.*) boiler. ~ **bölüm/dairesi**, boiler-house: ~ **devirmek/ kaldırmak**, (*his.*) signs of mutiny among Janissaries; (*fig.*) revolt, mutiny: ~ **kaynamayan yerde maymun oynamaz**, no work gets done for nothing: ~ . . . **kepçe** = İSTANBUL: ~**da kaynamak** (**bir**), be in complete agreement; get on well together: ~**ı kapalı kaynamak** (**-in**), keep one's affairs secret.

kazan·cı Boiler-maker/-repairer. ~**dibi**^{ni}, (*cul.*) sweet made from burnt milk (in bottom of pot).

kazan¹ç^{c1} (*fin.*) Gain; profits, yield; earnings; assets; advantage. ~ **ortak(lığ)ı**, co-partner(ship): ~ **payı**, dividend: ~ **sağlamak**, ensure a profit/ benefit: ~ **vergisi**, profits tax: ~**-yitirce**, profit and loss.

kazanç·bilim (*fin.*) Economics. ~**çı**, (*sp.*) professional. ~**lı**, who has earned/won; profitable; economical. ~**sal**, (*fin.*) economical. ~**sız**, at cost.

kazan·dırmak (**-i, -e**) *vc.* ~**ılmak**, *vp.* ~**ılmış**, *a.* (*bio.*) acquired. ~**ım/**~**ma**, *vn.*, gain. ~**mak** (**-i**), earn; acquire; attain, win; gain; (*pol.*) persuade, win over; carry off (prize). ~**malık**, (*sp.*) prize.

kazantaşı^{n1} (*chem.*) Scale (in boiler).

kazar (*min.*) Scraper. ~**atar**, excavator.

kazara By chance; accidentally.

kazaska (*mus.*) A Caucasian folk-dance.

kazasker (*his.*) Chief military judge; senior judge.

kazayağı^{n1} (*bot.*) Goosefoot, good King Henry; (*zoo.*) goose-foot stag; (*naut.*) multi-pronged hook; branching halyard, three-ended rope, crowfoot; shearlegs; (*tex.*) cross-stitching; light orange (colour).

kazaz (*tex., obs.*) Silk manufacturer.

kazazede *n.* Accident victim; injured party. *a.* Struck down by misfortune; ruined; shipwrecked.

kaz·beyinli Stupid; idiot. ~**boku**^{nu}, (*col.*) dirty greenish yellow (colour).

kazdırmak (**-i, -e**) *vc.* = KAZMAK.

kazein (*chem.*) Casein. ~ **tutkalı**, (*carp.*) casein adhesive.

kazevi^{ni} (*dom.*) Receptacle made of palm-leaves/ reeds.

kazı Excavation; excavating; (*archaeol.*) dig; (*art.*) carving, engraving. ~ **makinesi**, (*mot.*) excavator, digger. ~**bilim(ci)**, archaeolo·gy/(-gist). ~**bilimsel**, archaeological. ~**cı**, excavator, digger.

kazı¹k^{ğ1} Stake, peg; (*eng.*) pile; impalement; (*fig.*) trick, swindle; (*sp.*) grabbing the opponent's shorts. ~**!**, *int.* what a fraud!: ~ **atmak**, stake out; (**-e**), (*sl.*) cheat: ~ **bağı**, (*naut.*) clove hitch: ~ **başı**, (*eng.*) butt end (of pile): ~ **çakma**, pile-driving: ~ **gibi**, straight and hard: ~ **kadar**, (*pej.*) huge (man): ~ **kakmak**, drive in a stake; (*fig.*) establish o.s. firmly: ~ **kesilmek**, be petrified: ~ **kök**, (*bot.*) tap-root: ~ **marka**, (*sl.*) stg. exorbitantly expensive: ~ **yemek**, (*his.*) be impaled; (*fig.*) be cheated: ~ **yutmuş gibi**, as stiff as a poker: ~**a oturtmak/ vurmak**, (*his.*) impale s.o.: ~**ını koparmak**, make one's escape; (animal) get loose.

kazık·çı (*sl.*) Swindler. ~**hane**, (*sl.*) clip-joint. ~**lamak** (**-i**), stake out (land); impale s.o.: (*sl.*) cheat s.o. ~**lanmak**, *vp.* be impaled; (*sl.*) be cheated. ~**lı**, having piles/stakes, etc.; impaled; swindling. ~**lıhumma**, (*med.*) tetanus.

kaz·ılı Excavated. ~**ılmak**, *vp.* = KAZMAK. ~**ım**, excavation.

kazı·ma *vn.* Scratching, etc.; (*med.*) curettage: ~ **yapmak**, (*med.*) perform an abortion. ~**mak** (**-i**), delete, erase by scraping; scratch; shave off completely; eradicate; (*med.*) curette; (*min.*) engrave. ~**mı¹k**^{ğ1}, (*cul.*) scrapings (from dish/pan). ~**nmak**, *vi.* scratch o.s.; be scratched/shaved off, etc. ~**ntı**, scrapings; erasure. ~**ntılı**, scraped; erased. ~**tmak** (**-i, -e**), *vc.* ~**yacak**, scraper (tool). ~**yıcı**, scraper (person/tool).

kaziye Question, matter; (*leg.*) decision; (*phil.*) theorem, assertion, proposition.

kazkanadı^{n1} (*sp.*) Arm-lock, nelson.

kaz·ma *n.* (*agr.*) Digging; (*art.*) engraving; pickaxe, mattock: *a.* dug; excavated; engraved: ~ **kürek**, digging implements: ~ **resim**, (*art.*) engraving. ~**macı**, (*mil.*) sapper. ~**ma¹ç**^{c1}, (*eng.*) excavator, digger. ~**madiş**, (s.o.) with long projecting teeth. ~**mak** (**-i**), dig, excavate; engrave: **kazdığı çukura kendisi düşmek**, be hoist by one's own petard: **kazıp çıkarmak**, dig out: **kazıp delmek**, dig into/through.

kazmir (*tex.*) Cashmere wool, kerseymere.

kazsılar (*orn.*) Anatidae.

kazulet^{i} (*col.*) Ugly/coarse fellow.

kazurat¹ (*bio.*) Faeces, excrement.

KB (*geo.*) KUZEY-BATI.

k.ç. (*ling.*) = KİŞİ ÇOĞUL.

Kd. (*mil.*) = KIDEMLİ.

KD (*geo.*) = KARA DENİZ; KUZEY-DOĞU. ~ **TÜ** = KARA DENİZ TEKNİK ÜNİVERSİTESİ.

ke/ka (*ling.*) The Tk. letter K.

keba¹p^{b1} (*cul.*) Roast meat; kebab; anything roasted. ~ **kestane**, roast chestnut: ~ **şişi**, skewer, broach.

~çı, maker/seller of roast meats; proprietor of small eating-house: ~ dükkânı, chophouse. ~çılık, cooking/selling roast meats.

kebe (*tex.*) Thick felt; felt cloak//carpet.

kebir Great; important; old. ~e, (*rel.*) great sin.

kebise (*ast.*) Leap-year.

kebze (*bio.*) Shoulder-blade; (*obs.*) soothsaying. ~ci, fortune-teller.

keçⁱ (*naut.*) Ketch.

keççapⁱ (*cul.*) Ketchup.

keçe *n.* (*tex.*) Felt; (*dom.*) mat, carpet. *a.* Made of felt; felt. ~sini sudan çıkarmak, get out of difficulties skilfully; manage things cleverly.

keçe·ci(lik) (Work of) maker/seller of felt. ~lenmek/~leşmek, *vi.* become matted; (*fig.*) become numb, be benumbed. ~leştirmek (-i), *vc.* ~li, made of felt.

keçi *n.* (*live.*) Goat. *a.* (*fig.*) Obstinate. ~ derisi, goatskin; kid leather: ~ yavrusu, kid: ~leri kaçırmak, become mad: ~ye can kaygısı . . ., = KASAP. **keçi·ayağı**ⁿⁱ (*bot.*) Goatweed, ground elder; (*eng.*) sheep-foot roller. ~boynuzuⁿᵘ, (*bot.*) carob, locust-tree: ~ gibi, insipid. ~leşmek, *vi.* (*fig.*) become pig-headed/obstinate. ~lik, (*fig.*) obstinacy. ~mantarıⁿⁱ, (*myc.*) field mushroom. ~sağan, (*orn.*) goatsucker, nightjar. ~sakal, goatee (beard). ~sakalıⁿⁱ, (*bot.*) wood goatsbeard; goat's rue; rock-rose. ~tırnağıⁿⁱ, (*carp.*) triangular-shaped chisel. ~yemişiⁿⁱ, (*bot.*) bilberry, whortleberry; cowberry. ~yoluⁿᵘ, narrow footpath.

keder Grief; care; affliction. ~ etm. (-e), be troubled/grieved (at stg.): ~e kapılmış, broken-hearted: ~i önleyici, (*psy.*) anti-depressant: ~ini gömmek/saklamak, bury one's sorrows.

keder·lenmek *vi.* Be sorrowful/anxious. ~li, sorrowful; grieved; anxious, depressed. ~siz, untroubled.

kedi (*zoo.*) Cat. ~ ciğere bakar gibi bakmak, look with intense longing: ~ gibi, (*fig.*) cattish: ~ gibi her zaman dört ayak üstüne düşmek, always fall on one's feet: ~ gözleri, (*mot.*) cat's eyes: ~ ile harara girmek, join up with a useless partner: ~ ile köpek gibi, (squabbling) like cats and dogs: ~ kuşu, (*orn.*) catbird: ~ ne budu ne?, well, what can you expect from such a poor creature?; you've nothing to fear from him!: ~ olalı bir fare tuttu, at last he has achieved stg.: ~ payı, cat's meat: ~ uzanamadığı/yetişemediği ciğere pis dermiş, it's a case of sour grapes: ~ yavrusu, kitten: ~ yavrusunu yerken sıçana benzetir, make excuses for knowingly doing stg. wrong: ~nin bacağı ikinci gece ayıran damat, taking a wise step too late: ~ye ciğer/peynir ısmarlamak, entrust stg. to s.o. unreliable.

kedi·ayasıⁿⁱ (*bot.*) Lesser celandine. ~balıⁿⁱ, (*bot.*) resin from plum-trees, etc. ~balığıⁿⁱ, (*ich.*) dogfish, shark; lesser spotted dogfish. ~bastı, action of dabbing on glue. ~diliⁿⁱ, (*cul.*) finger biscuit. ~gözüⁿᵘ, (*mot.*) red rear-light. ~msi, catlike, feline. ~nanesiⁿⁱ, (*bot.*) catmint. ~otuⁿᵘ, (*bot.*) valerian.

keenlemyekûn As if it had never been.

kefaf Sufficiency. ~ınefs etm., have just enough to eat.

kefal (*ich.*) Lesser grey mullet. ~giller, mullets.

kefaletⁱ (*leg.*) Bail, surety; (*fin.*) security, bond. ~ parası, caution money: ~ senedi, bail(bond): ~le (bırakma), (release) on bail. ~name, written guarantee; agreement to stand as surety.

kefaretⁱ Atonement; penance; indemnity. ~ keçisi, scapegoat: ~ini ödemek (-in), atone for stg.

kefe¹ *n.* Scale (of a balance).

kefe² *n.* Hair glove (for grooming horses). ~lemek (-i), groom.

kefeki (*med.*) Tartar (on teeth). ~ye dönmek, be all in holes. ~taşıⁿⁱ, (*geol.*) coarse sandstone.

kefen Shroud, winding-sheet. ~ kumaşı, (*tex.*) domet: ~i yırtmak, cheat death; return from death's door.

kefen·ci Maker/seller of shrouds; stealer of grave-clothes; (*fig.*) extortioner. ~lemek (-i), wrap in a shroud; (*cul.*) cover in batter, etc. before roasting. ~lik, shroud material.

kefere *pl.* = KÂFİR. Unbelievers.

kefil Surety; security; bail. ~ olm. (-e), go bail for s.o. ~lik, guarantee; security.

kefir (*cul.*) Alcoholic drink made from milk.

kefiye (*mod.*) Head-shawl (worn by Arabs).

kefne Sailmaker's palm.

kehanetⁱ Soothsaying; divination; augury. ~ etm., predict the future.

kehkeşan (*ast.*) The Milky Way.

kehle (*ent.*) Louse. ~lenmek, *vn.* become lousy. ~li, lousy.

keh·libar/~ribar Amber: ~ balı, clear yellow honey. ~ribarcı, worker in amber.

kekⁱ (*cul.*) Fruit-cake.

kekâ(h) *int.* (Expression of comfort.)

keke *a.* Stammering, stuttering. ~lemek, *vi.* stammer, stutter; falter in one's words. ~lik, *n.* stammer, stutter. ~me, *a.* having a stammer. ~meleşmek, start to stammer. ~melik, *n.* stammer, stutter; speech defect; incoherence.

keki¹kᵍⁱ (*bot.*) Thyme. ~li, (*cul.*) coated/flavoured with thyme. ~yağıⁿⁱ, oil of thyme.

kekli¹kᵍⁱ (*orn.*) Gray partridge. ~ sürüsü, covey.

kekre Acrid; pungent; setting the teeth on edge. ~lik, acridity; pungency. ~msi, slightly acrid, etc. ~msilik, slight acridity/pungency. ~si, as if acrid.

kel *n.* (*med.*) Ringworm; bald spot. *a.* Bald; bare of vegetation; scabby; mangy; poor, miserable. ~AYNAK: ~ başa şimşir tarak, an unnecessary luxury: ~ kâhya, busybody: ~ ölür . . ., = KÖR ÖLÜR . . .: ~ tavuk ~ horozla, birds of a feather: ~ turna balığı, (*ich.*) bowfin: ~den köseye yardım olur mu?, can the blind lead the blind?: ~i görünmek (-in), a defect be shown up: ~i kızmak, (s.o very even-tempered) lose his temper: ~i körü toplamak, select incompetent people (for a job): ~in melhemi olsa kendi başına sürer, don't expect help from s.o. who needs it himself.

kelam Word; speech; language; the Scriptures. ~ıkadim, the Koran. ~ıkibar, saying of a wise man.

kelayna¹kᵍⁱ (*orn.*) Hermit ibis.

kelbiye (*phil.*) Cynicism.

kele (*zoo.*) Young bull; (*fig.*) robust youth.

kelebe'kᵍⁱ (*ent.*) Butterfly; (*fig.*) gaily-dressed girl; (*zoo.*) liver-fluke; (*eng.*) wings (of screws, etc.), throttle. ~ **balıkları,** (*ich.*) butterfly fishes: ~ **cam,** (*mot.*) front quarter-light: ~ **gözlük,** pince-nez (glasses): ~ **izci,** (*soc.*) Brownie: ~ **somun,** (*eng.*) butterfly nut: ~ **vida,** thumbscrew. ~**otu**ⁿᵘ, (*bot.*) black medick.

kele'kᵍⁱ ¹ *n.* Raft (of inflated sheepskins).
kele'kᵍⁱ ² *n.* (*bot.*) Unripe melon. *a.* Partly bald; hairless; (*fig.*) immature; (*sl.*) stupid.
kelem (*bot.*) Cabbage; (*cul.*) cabbage stew.
kele'pᵇⁱ (*tex.*) Large skein of thread.
kelepçe Handcuffs; (*eng.*) clamp, bracket, toggle. ~ **vurmak (-e)**/~**lemek (-i),** handcuff s.o. ~**lenmek,** *vp.* ~**li,** handcuffed: ~ **saat,** wristwatch.
kelepir Stg. acquired for little or nothing; bargain; (*pej.*) bad bargain; (*fig.*) step-child. ~ **kaçırmak,** miss a bargain/opportunity: ~ **koca,** a good catch: ~ **mağazası,** cut-price shop. ~**ci,** bargain-hunter; opportunist.
kelepser Martingale (for horse).
keler (*zoo.*) Lizard; reptile. ~**ler,** reptiles. ~**balığı**ⁿⁱ, (*ich.*) angel shark, monkfish. ~**bilim,** (*zoo.*) herpetology. ~**derisi**ⁿⁱ, (*carp.*) shark-skin (used as abrasive); (*mod.*) shagreen.
keleş Handsome; attractive; ringwormy, bald; dirty. ~**lik,** handsomeness.
kelime Word. ~ **bulamıyorum!,** words fail me!: ~ **karışıklığı,** (*med.*) paraphasia: ~ **oyunu,** word-game: ~ **türü,** (*ling.*) part of speech.
kelle (*pej.*) Head; sheep's head; (sugar) loaf, cake (of cheese); ear (of corn). ~ **götürür gibi,** with unnecessary haste/fuss: ~ **koşturmak,** hurry unnecessarily: ~ **kulak yerinde,** robust and handsome (man): ~**sini koltuğuna almak,** take one's life in one's hands: ~**sini uçurmak (-in),** cut off s.o.'s head: ~**yi vermek,** (*col.*) sacrifice o.s.
kelli ¹ **(-den)** *post.* (*dial.*) Since, because; as; after.
kel·li ² *a.* Having ringworm. ~**lik,** baldness; (*med.*) favus; (*agr.*) bare waste land.
kellifelli Well-dressed; serious, dignified; showy.
keloğlan (*myth.*) 'Dick Whittington'; (*col.*) poor child adopted/apprenticed.
kelpe (*agr.*) Vine-prop.
Kelt (*ethn.*) Celt, Kelt. ~ +, *a.* Celtic. ~**çe,** (*ling.*) Celtic.
Kelvin (*phys.*) Kelvin.
kem Bad; evil; deficient, short (change, weight). ~**GÖZ:** ~ **nazarla bakmak,** look at s.o. with evil intent: ~ **sanmak,** think ill of: ~ **söz,** calumny: ~ **söz** ~ **akçe sahibinindir,** evil words reflect on the speaker.
kemalⁱ Perfection; maturity; cultural attainment; moral quality; worth, value, price; the most that can be said of . . .. ~**e ermek/gelmek,** reach perfection/maturity: ~**i beş lira,** five pence at most: ~**i ne?,** well after all it's not a great expense!
Kemal·ist (*pol., soc.*) Supporter of Kemal Atatürk. ~**izm,** his principles, Kemalism.
keman (*mus.*) Violin; (*mil.*) bow. ~ **kaşlı,** with arched eyebrows: ~ **kirişi** = KEMENT: ~ **sapı,** fingerboard.
keman·cı(lık) (Work of) violin maker/violinist.

~**e,** (*mus.*) bow; (*carp.*) bow (for small lathe): ~ **çekme,** (*sp.*) a wrestling hold. ~**i,** (*Or. mus.*) violinist. ~**keş,** archer; bowyer.
kemayar Of low standard/poor quality.
keme (*zoo.*) Small rat.
kemen·çe (*Or. mus.*) Small three-stringed violin; (*agr.*) instrument for spreading fertilizer. ~**'t**ᵈⁱ, lasso; halter; snare; (*his. mil.*) bowstring (used for executions). ~**tlemek (-i),** (*sl.*) trick s.o. out of his money.
kemer *n.* (*mod.*) Belt, girdle; waist(-line); (*arch.*) arch, vault; (*bio.*) arch; (*geol.*) anticline. *a.* Arched, hooked. ~ **bağlama,** (*soc.*) ceremony of putting a gold/silver belt round the bride: ~ **gözü,** (*arch.*) bay, archway: ~ **kuşağı,** (*mod.*) cummerbund: ~ **taşı,** (*arch.*) keystone: ~**ini sıkmak,** (*fig.*) tighten one's belt, be economical.
kemer·altıⁿⁱ (*arch.*) Covered way; arcade; vaulted bazaar. ~**e,** (*naut.*) deck-beam. ~**leme,** (*pub.*) rounding of book spine. ~**lenme,** arching. ~**li,** (*mod.*) belted, girdled; (*arch.*) arched, vaulted: ~ **burun,** aquiline nose: ~ **hayvangiller,** (*zoo.*) armadillos; Dasypodidae: ~ **pencere,** (*arch.*) bow-window: ~ **yol,** cloister. ~**lik,** belt with compartments to hold glasses/tools, etc. ~**patlıcan,** (*bot.*) long thin aubergine.
kemgöz The evil eye.
kemha (*tex.*) Brocade.
kemi'kᵍⁱ *n.* (*bio.*) Bone. ~ +, *a.* Made of bone; bone-: ~ **atmak (-e),** throw a bone (to a dog); (*fig.*) appease s.o. (with a favour): ~ **bilimi,** (*med.*) osteology: ~ **boşluk,** (*bio.*) bony labyrinth: ~ **çıkıntısı,** apophysis: ~ **gibi,** as hard/dry as a bone: ~ **gövdesi,** (*bio.*) diaphysis: ~ **gübre,** (*agr.*) bone-meal: ~ **hastalığı,** (*med.*) rickets: ~ **iliği,** (*bio.*) bone marrow: ~ **kapmak,** (*pej.*) get stg. out of it, profit by it: ~ **kömürü (tozu),** (*chem.*) bone-black: ~ **ucu,** (*bio.*) epiphysis: ~ **yalayıcı,** toady: ~ **zarı,** (*bio.*) periosteum: ~**i çıkmak,** have a bone dislocated: ~**leri çıkık,** barebones: ~**leri ayrılmış,** (*cul.*) boned (fish, etc.): ~**leri sayılmak,** be all skin and bone: ~**lerini kırmak,** beat s.o. mercilessly.
kemik·çe (*med.*) Osteopathy. ~**doku**ⁿᵘ, (*bio.*) bony tissue. ~**leşme,** ossification. ~**leşmek,** *vi.* ossify; become solid. ~**li,** having bones; -boned; bony: ~ **balıklar,** (*ich.*) bony fishes: ~ **turnabalığı (-giller),** (*ich.*) longnose garfish(es). ~**si,** bonelike; osteoid. ~**siz,** (*bio.*) boneless; (*cul.*) boned; (*fig.*) flexible.
kemir·ci'kᵍⁱ (*bio.*) Small cartilage. ~**de'k**ᵍⁱ, tail skeleton. ~**gen,** *a., n.* (*zoo.*) rodent: ~ **gagalılar,** (*orn.*) trogons: ~**ler,** rodents. ~**ici,** gnawing, rodent; corrosive: ~**ler,** (*zoo.*) gnawing animals, rodents. ~**mek (-i),** gnaw, nibble; corrode; (*fig.*) (grief, etc.) consume.
kemiyetⁱ Quantity; (*ling.*) number.
kemküm Hesitantly; confusedly (of speech). ~ **etm.,** hum and haw.
kemlik Evil; malice.
kemmi Quantitative.
kemo- (*med.*) Chemo-.
kemre (*agr.*) Fertilizer, manure.

-ken[1] *v. suf.* [190] = İKEN; while (doing) [GELİRKEN].
~ **denberi,** [191] since while being.
-ken[2] *a. suf.* [223] = -GEN [DÖVÜŞKEN].
kenar *n.* Edge, brim, border; boundary; brink; bank, shore; (*pub.*) marginal note, postscript; remote place, nook, corner; suburb. *a.* Remote; bordering, peripheral, marginal. ~ **çekmek (-e),** (*mod.*) hem, edge: ~ **kırması,** (*eng.*) chamfer: ~ **mahalle,** (*soc.*) distant (and poor) suburb: ~ **pürüzü,** (*eng.*) burr: ~ **tiyatrosu,** (*th.*) fringe theatre: ~**a çekilmek,** withdraw, not interfere at all: ~**a kalmak,** remain in an inferior position/in a backwater: ~**da köşede,** in unlikely places: ~**ın dilberi (nazik de olsa nazenin olamaz),** unpolished beauty (however polite she can never be refined): ~**ına bak bezini al . . .** = ANASINA . . .: ~**ını kırmak,** (*eng.*) chamfer.
kenar·cı Fisherman fishing from the shore. ~ **lı,** edged; rimmed; with a decorated edge; having a marginal note. ~**lık,** (*mod.*) edging. ~**ortay,** (*math.*) median. ~**suyu,** (*mod.*) border decoration.
kendi *a.* [70] Own [~ **evimiz,** our own house]. *pron.* [70] -self, -selves; *emphatic* [**ben** ~**m,** I myself]; *reflexive* [~ ~**ni eleştirdi,** he criticized himself]. ~ **ağzıyla tutulmak,** be given away by one's own words; contradict o.s.: ~ **alanında (oynanan maç),** (*sp.*) at-home (match): ~ **aleminde olm.,** be busy with one's own affairs; live quietly/contentedly: ~ **ayağıyla gelmek,** come of one's own accord; be obtained without effort: ~ **başına,** all by o.s.; on one's own, independently; of one's own accord: ~ **başına getirmek,** bring it on o.s.: ~ **başından,** on his own account: ~ **bildiğini okumak,** go one's own way: ~ **bilir!,** just as he wishes!; it's up to him!; on his head be it!: ~ **çapında,** simple, unpretentious: ~ **çıkarına bakmak,** seek one's personal advantage; 'look after number one': ~ **derdine düşmek,** be preoccupied with one's own problems: ~ **düşen ağlamaz,** one must accept the consequences of one's own deeds: ~ **elyazısı,** autograph: ~ **evim,** my own home: ~ **gelen,** a godsend: ~ **göbeğini** ~ **kesmek,** rely only on o.s. for everything: ~ **halinde,** occupied with one's own affairs; quiet, inoffensive: ~ **haline bırak!,** let him be!; leave him alone!: ~ **havasına gitmek/havasında olm.,** follow one's own whims and fancies; think only of o.s.: ~ **hesabına çalışmak,** be in business for o.s.: ~ **ile,** personally: ~ **kanına susamak,** seem anxious to sacrifice one's own life: ~ ~**me,** to myself; by myself: ~ ~**ne,** on one's own, by o.s.; all alone; (*th.*) aside; auto-: ~ ~**ne düzelir,** that will take care of itself; things will straighten themselves out: ~ ~**ne gelin güvey olm.,** try to settle matters without the authority/competence to do so; be ridiculously self-important; reckon without one's host: ~ ~**ne hak almak,** take the law into one's own hands: ~ ~**ne yetmek,** be self-sufficient: ~ ~**ni idare eden,** autonomous: ~ ~**ni yemek,** worry o.s. to death: ~ ~**sine,** to himself; by himself; all alone: ~ **payıma,** for my part; in my opinion: ~ **resmi,** (*art.*) self-portrait: ~ **sahada** = ~ ALANINDA: ~ **söylediğine göre,** according to his statement: ~ **söyler** ~ **dinler,** he's incompre-

hensible; he's talking to himself: ~ **taksiri haricinde,** through no fault of his own: ~ **yağıyla kavrulmak,** manage by o.s.; fend for o.s.; live very modestly: ~ **yaptığını çekmeli,** as you make your bed so must you lie on it.
kendimi: ~ **bildim bileli,** from the time I was capable of thinking: ~ **tutmadım,** I could not restrain myself; I could not help . . .: ~**zi küçük düşürmiyelim,** do not let us demean ourselves.
kendin, thyself, yourself: ~ **seç,** (*fin.*) self-service: ~**ce,** by o.s., on one's own; personally: ~**de bulunmak,** possess: ~**de olmamak,** be incapable of clear thought.
kendinden, from itself; automatically; naturally: ~ **aşağıda olan,** inferior, subordinate: ~ **geçmek,** lose consciousness; be beside o.s. (with anger/joy, etc.); become slack: ~ **geçmiş,** (man) no longer of any use: ~ **menkul,** that which (according to him) he possesses: ~ **pay biç!,** what would *you* do in the circumstances?, put yourself in his place!: ~ **yana yontmak,** turn stg. to one's own advantage; 'look after number one'. [*Also* = KENDİLİĞİNDEN.]
kendine: ~ **bağlamak,** fascinate: ~ **çekidüzen vermek,** tidy o.s. up; (*fig.*) put one's house in order: ~ **çekmek,** attract: ~ **etm.,** harm o.s.: ~ **gelmek,** regain consciousness; come to one's senses; things come right: ~ **gel!,** pull yourself together!: ~ **güvenme,** self-reliance: ~ **kıyma,** suicide: ~ **mahsus,** his alone: ~ **malik olmamak,** be unconscious; lose one's self-control: ~ **özgü,** peculiar to o.s.: ~ **. . . süsü(nü) vermek,** play the part/role of . . .: ~ **yedirememek,** be unable to bring o.s. (to do stg.): ~ **yontmak,** only look after o.s.; (ignoring others) profit from everything.
kendini: ~ **ağır satmak,** sell o.s. high: ~ **alamamak (-den),** be unable to resist stg.; be unable to restrain o.s. from (doing stg.): ~ **âleme güldürmek,** be a laughing-stock: ~ **alıştırmak,** adapt/adjust o.s.; conform: ~ **atmak (-e),** rush off to (a place): ~ **beğenmek,** think a lot of o.s.; be conceited/presumptuous/complacent; be too big for one's boots: ~ **bırakmak,** neglect o.s.: ~ **bilmek,** be conscious; have self-respect: ~ **bilen/bilir,** s.o. reasonable; who knows his own place: ~ **bilmez,** unconscious; confused; arrogant, insolent: ~ **bir yerde bulmak,** arrive somewhere (without noticing it): ~ **büyük satmak,** make great claims for o.s.: ~ **dar atmak (-e),** just manage to take refuge in: ~ **destekleyen,** self-supporting/-sustaining: ~ **devaynasında görmek,** exaggerate one's own importance: ~ **dinlemek,** worry about one's health; fuss about o.s.: ~ **dirhem dirhem satmak,** give o.s. airs: ~ **fasulya gibi nimetten saymak,** consider o.s. very important: ~ **fazla üzme!,** care killed the cat!: ~ **göstermek,** prove one's worth; assert o.s.: ~ **hiç bozmadan,** with complete composure: ~ **idare etm.,** manage for o.s.: ~ **idareden âciz,** utterly incapable: ~ **iyice vermek,** concentrate: ~ **kapıp koyuvermek,** lose interest in o.s./one's business, etc.; become pessimistic; put all one's efforts into a job: ~ **(eğlence/**

içkiye) kaptırmak, give o.s. up (to amusement/ drink, etc.): ~ **kasmak**, draw o.s. up in a superior manner: ~ **kaybetmek**, lose consciousness; lose one's head, lose control of o.s.: ~ **naza çekmek**, behave affectedly/coquettishly; show contempt: ~ **okut!**, 'get yourself exorcized', you're crazy!: ~ **öldürmek**, commit suicide: ~ **sakatlamak**, inflict injury on o.s.: ~ **satmak**, give o.s. airs: ~ . . . **satmak**, set o.s. up as . . .: ~ **satmasını bilmek**, know how to make the best of o.s.; be able to display one's abilities: ~ . . . **saymak**, count/ consider o.s. . . .: ~ **tartmak**, weigh up one's own position: ~ **temize çıkarmak**, clear o.s. (of some accusation): ~ **toparlamak**, pull o.s. together: ~ **toplamak**, recover (from illness): ~ **tutmak**, restrain o.s.: ~ **üzmek**, be upset (about stg.): ~ **vermek (-e)**, dedicate o.s. to stg.: ~ **yerden yere vurmak**, roll on the ground in agony: ~ **yenilemek**, renew o.s., take on a new lease of life: ~ **zorlamak**, force o.s.; exert o.s.: ~**n bulunması**, (*leg.*) personal appearance/attendance.

kendiniz, yourself, yourselves: ~ **yapınız!**, do-it-yourself.

kendi-: ~**si**, himself, herself, itself: ~**since**, according to him/her: ~**sinden**/~**sine**/~**sini** = KENDİN·DEN/~E/~İ: ~**yle zevklendirmek (-i)**, be the object of s.o.'s amusement/derision.
kendi·beslek (*bio.*) Autotrophic organism. ~**işler**, automatic.
kendili¹k^{ği} Entity; one's own personality; initiative. ~**inden**, automatic(ally); of one's own accord; intrinsically; spontaneous(ly): ~**inden çoğalma**, (*bio.*) autogenesis: ~**inden doğma/türeme**, abiogenesis; spontaneous generation: ~**inden tutuşma**, (*min.*) spontaneous combustion: ~**indenlik**, spontaneity.
kendin- = KENDİ-.
kendir (*bot.*) Hemp. ~**cilik**, hemp growing. ~**giller**, (*bot.*) Cannabaceae.
kene (*zoo.*) Tick, acarid. ~ **gibi yapışmak**, stick like a burr: ~**ler**, mites and ticks. ~**ci**, (*live.*) charlatan tick-remover.
kenef *n.* (*vulg.*) Toilet, WC. *a.* Very dirty, filthy. ~ **sazlığı**, straggly moustache.
kene·göz Small-eyed. ~**otu**^{nu}, (*bot.*) castor-oil plant.
kenet (*carp., eng.*) Metal clamp; cramping iron. ~ **demiri**, clevis: ~ **mili**, tie-bolt. ~**lemek (-i)**, clamp together; fasten together. ~**lenmek**, *vi.* be clamped together; be clamped tight. ~**li**, clamped.
kenevir (*bot.*) Hemp; hempseed. ~ **halat**, hempen rope: ~ **kuşu**, (*orn.*) linnet. ~**cilik**, hemp growing.
kengel/kenger (*bot.*) Cardoon; globe artichoke. ~**sakızı**^{nı}, resin from milk-thistle. ~**yaprağı**^{nı}, (*arch.*) acanthus(-leaf).
kentⁱ Town, city; (*dial.*) village. ~ **bölgesi**, quarter.
ken·tal (*math.*) Quintal (100 kg.). ~**tet**ⁱ, (*mus.*) quintet. ~**tilyon**, (*math.*) quintillion (10^{18}).
kent·er *n.* Citizen: *a.* municipal. ~**işleri**, municipality. ~**leşme**, urbanization. ~**leşmek (-i)**, urbanize. ~**li**, citizen, town-dweller. ~**mimarlığı**, town-planning. ~**sel**, urban, municipal. ~**soylu(luk)**, bourgeois (quality); bourgeoisie.

kepⁱ (*mod.*) Cap; academic cap, 'mortar-board'.
kepaze *a.* Vile; contemptible; worthless; laughable, scoffed at. *n.* Ridiculous/contemptible person.
kepaze·lemek/~**letmek (-i)** Render vile/contemptible; render worthless, cheapen. ~**lik**, vileness; degradation; ignominy: ~**in düz pembesi**, this is absolutely scandalous.
kepbastı Double-layered net (used at DALYAN).
kepçe (*dom.*) Skimmer; ladle; (*ich.*) landing-net; (*ent.*) butterfly-net; (*sp.*) a wrestling hold.
kepçe·kulak With large prominent ears. ~**kuyruk**, (*sl.*) sponger, parasite. ~**lemek (-i)**, (*sp.*) grab the ball before it touches the ground. ~**li**, with a ladle, etc.: ~ **ekskavatör**, (*eng.*) bucket excavator.
kepe¹k^{ği} (*cul.*) Bran; (*med.*) scurf, dandruff. ~**çi**, bran-seller. ~**lenmek**, *vi.* have dandruff; (apple) be dry and tasteless. ~**li**, containing bran; scurvy, having dandruff; dry and tasteless.
kepene¹k^{ği 1} *n.* (*ent.*) Moth.
kepene¹k^{ği 2} *n.* (*mod.*) Shepherd's coarse felt cloak.
kepen¹k^{ği} Large pull-down shutter; wooden cover.
kepez Rocks (on sea-shore).
kepir Arid/infertile land.
kepmek *vi.* Collapse; fall down.
ker. = KERAMİK.
kerahetⁱ A being abominable; repugnance, aversion. ~ **etm.**, abominate, detest: ~ **vakti**, (*jok.*) (evening) drinking time.
kerametⁱ Miracle; providentially opportune word/ deed. ~ **buyurdunuz**/~**te bulundunuz!**, (*iron.*) how right you are!: ~ **göstermek**, work a miracle: ~ **sahibi**, prophet; miracle-worker: ~**im yok ya!**, how was I to know!: ~**ine yormak (-i)**, attribute stg. to s.o.'s miraculous powers.
keramik Ceramics.
kerata (*pej.*) Cuckold; pander; scoundrel; (*affectionately*) little rascal; shoehorn. ~**lık**, cuckoldry, etc.; villainy.
keratin (*bio.*) Keratin. ~**li**, keratose; horny.
keraviye (*bot.*) Caraway; (*cul.*) caraway seed.
Kerbela (*geo.*) Kerbela (Iraq). ~ **sıkıntısı**, lack of water.
kere One time; (*math.*) times (×).
kerem (*obs.*) Nobility, kindness. ~ **buyurun!**, please, I beg you!
kerempe (*geo.*) Rocky spit/headland.
keres (*dom.*) Large bowl.
kereste (*arch.*) Timber (for building); any kind of material; (*sl.*) stupid. ~ **örgü**, timber frame; (*min.*) crib. ~**ci(lik)**, (work of) timber-merchant. ~**li**, strongly built (man). ~**lik**, (tree) suitable for timber.
kerevetⁱ Wooden bedstead; couch; (*cin.*) rostrum.
kerevides (*zoo.*) Freshwater crayfish.
kereviz (*bot.*) Celery.
kerhane Brothel. ~**ci**, brothel-keeper; pimp.
ker·hen With repugnance; involuntarily, against one's will. ~**ih**, disgusting, detestable.
kerim Noble; generous; honoured, illustrious. ~**e**, (*obs.*) daughter (*term of respect*).
keriz¹ *n.* = GERİZ. Drain, sewer.

keriz[2] *a.* Credulous, easily duped. *n.* (*sl.*) Gambling. ~ **alayı**, troupe of gypsy musicians: ~**e bayılmak**//**etm.**, lose//cheat at gambling. ~**ci**, musician. ~**lemek**, (*mus.*) play.

kerkenez (*orn.*) Common kestrel; Egyptian vulture.

kerki (*for.*) Large axe.

kerliferli = KELLİFELLİ.

kermen (*mil.*) Fortress.

kermes Village festival, fair; charitable function.

kermez ~ **meşesi**, (*bot.*) kermes oak.

kerpeten (*carp.*) Pincers.

kerpi'ç[ci] *n.* Sun-dried brick; adobe. *a.* Made of sun-dried bricks. ~ **gibi**, hard, dry; ~ **kesilmek**, be petrified (with fear, etc.).

kerrake (*mod., obs.*) Light cloak.

kerrat[1] *pl.* = KERE. Times. ~ **cetveli**, (*math.*) multiplication table: ~**la**, repeatedly.

kerte (*naut.*) Rhumb; one of 32 compass-points; point; degree; grade; mark, sign; best state/quality; right moment. ~ ~, gradual: ~**sine gelmek**, come to the right degree/point of perfection: ~**sine getirmek**, find the appropriate moment: ~**sini almak**, (*naut.*) take the bearing of stg.: ~**sini geçmek**, pass the exact degree; be overdone: ~**ye gelmek**, come to such a point/degree that . . ..

kerte·leme Gradualness; grading; (*th.*) gradation: ~ **gediği**, anticlimax. ~**leyici**, grader. ~**li**, gradual.

kertenkele (*zoo.*) Lizard. ~**ler**, reptiles, Lacertilia; lizards, Lacertidae. ~**msigiller**, Caecilians.

kerteriz (*ast./naut.*) Bearing. ~ **almak**, take a bearing: ~ **gülü**, pelorus: ~ **noktası**, reference bearing.

kerti = KERTE.

kert·i'k[gi] *a.* Notched. *n.* Notch; gash; tally; fraction. ~**iklemek (-i)**, cut a notch. ~**ilmek**, *vp.* ~**mek (-i)**, notch; scratch; gash; scrape against.

kervan Caravan. ~ **çulluğu**, (*orn.*) Eurasian curlew; slender-billed curlew: ~**a katılmak**, join the procession, go with the crowd.

kervan·başı/~**cı** Caravan leader. ~**kıran/**~**yıldızı**, (*ast.*) Venus (when a morning star); ~**saray**, caravanserai; inn with large courtyard; ~**motel**.

kes[1] *n.* (*agr.*) Thick straw for burning.

kes[2] *n.* (*sp.*) Gymnast's ankle-length shoes.

-kes *pron. suf.* Person [HERKES].

kesafet[i] (*phys.*) Density; consistency; thickness; opacity; coarseness.

kesa·t[d1] (*fin.*) A not being saleable; dullness (of market). ~**lık**, stagnation (of market); time of scarcity/unemployment.

kese[1] *n.* Short cut.

kese[2] *n.* Small bag; case; (bath-)glove (for washing the body); money-bag, purse; (*obs.*) sum of 500 piastres; wealth, power of the purse; (*med.*) capsule; (*bio.*) cyst, bladder; (*bio., zoo.*) pouch. ~ **sürmek**, rub the body with a bath-glove: ~ **yangısı**, (*med.*) bursitis: ~**den eklemek**, be out of pocket: ~**nin ağzını açmak**, prepare to spend money: ~**nin dibini görmek**, run out of money: ~**nize bereket!**, blessings on your purse! (when s.o. else pays): ~**sinde Halil İbrahim bereketi var**, he knows how to make his money last: ~**sine güvenmek**, be able to

afford: ~**sine hiç bir şey girmemek**, bring no benefit/profit: ~**ye elvermemek**, be beyond one's means.

kese·ci'k[gi] (*bio.*) Bursa. ~ **iltihabı**, (*med.*) bursitis. ~**dar**, treasurer. ~**kâgıdı**[ni], paper-bag.

kese'k[gi] Clod; a turf; turf of peat.

kese·le'k[gi] (*eng.*) Block-diagram. ~**lemek (-i)**, rub the body with a bath-glove. ~**lenmek**, *vi.* rub o.s.; be rubbed. ~**letmek (-i, -e)**, *vc.*

keseli Having a bag; (*zoo.*) pouched, marsupial. ~ **antilop**, springbok: ~ **ayı**, koala bear: ~ **fare**, jerboa: ~ **kurt**, bladder-worm: ~ **memeliler**, marsupials: ~ **porsuk**, bandicoot: ~ **sansar**, dasyure: ~ **sıçan**, opossum: ~ **şeytan**, Tasmanian devil: ~**ler**, marsupials.

kesen That cuts; (*math.*) secant line.

kesene Agreement; subscription; payment, wage.

kesene'k[gi] (*fin.*) Farming of revenues; premium; deduction. ~**e almak**, farm revenues. ~**çi**, revenue-farmer.

kesenkes Decisively, categorically, definitely.

keser (*carp.*) Adze.

kesi (*math.*) Interceptor. ~**ci**, *n.* that/who cuts; (*cin., mod.*) cutter; animal-slaughterer: *a.* cutting: ~ **ağız**, (*carp.*) cutting edge: ~ **kılıç**, (*sp.*) sabre: ~ **parça**, (*ind.*) cutter. ~**cidiş**, (*bio.*) incisor tooth.

kesif (*phys.*) Dense; thick; opaque; (*geo.*) densely populated.

kesi'k[gi] *a.* Cut; broken; spoilt; (*bio.*) castrated; (*cul.*) curdled; (*ling.*) clipped; (*sp.*) sliced/chopped (ball); weary. *n.* (*pub.*) Newspaper clipping/cutting; (*cul.*) skim-milk cheese. ~ ~, intermittently: ~ ~ **parıldamak**, blink: ~ **koni**, (*math.*) truncated cone: ~ **kuyruk**, bobtail: ~ **sözcük**, (*ling.*) abbreviated word.

kesik·li Intermittent; discontinuous: ~ **akım**, (*el.*) alternating current. ~**lik**, a being cut/broken; lassitude. ~**siz**, uncut; uninterrupted, continuous; (*pub.*) uncensored.

kesilmek *vp.* = KESMEK. Be cut, etc.; be cut off; cease; be exhausted; be turned into, become; pretend to be: **(-e)**, be pleased about: (*cul.*) be curdled, clot; coagulate: **(-den)**, cease from; be unable to do; lose. ~**sizin**, uninterruptedly.

kesim Act of cutting; slaughter (animals); cut, shape, form; make; (*mod.*) cut, fashion; (*lit.*) stanza; abstention; vacation; agreed price/rent; (*fin.*) sector; (*geo.*) zone, region. ~ **ayırım**, (*med.*) dissection: ~ **noktası**, (*math.*) point of intersection: ~ **vakti**, agreed time for payment: ~**e vermek**, put up for rent.

kesim·ci Contractor who farms revenues. ~**evi**[ni], slaughterhouse. ~**leme**, (*geol.*) fragmentation; segmentation; (*chem.*) fractionation. ~**lemek (-i)**, fragment; segment. ~**li**, partial; (*chem.*) fractional. ~**lik**, (animal) ready for slaughter. ~**sel**, (*met.*) zonal.

kesin Definite; certain; accurate; distinct; (*leg.*) binding, final, conclusive; categorical; crucial. ~ **bilgi**, (*phil.*) definite knowledge: ~ **eder**, (*fin.*) list/fixed price: ~ **kabul**, final acceptance: ~ **karar vermek**, determine: ~ **olarak**, definitely; for certain: ~ **öneri**, firm offer: ~ **süre**, definite period.

kesin·bilgi (*phil.*) Certitude. ~**leme**, *vn.* statement. ~**lemek (-i)**, state precisely, specify. ~**leşmek**, *vi.* become definite/final, etc. ~**leştirmek (-i)**, *vc.* ~**lik**, certainty; finality; conclusiveness, etc. ~**likle**, certainly; definitely. ~**siz(lik)**, uncertain(ty); inconclusive(ness).

kesin·mek (-i) (*mod.*) Cut stg./have stg. cut for o.s. ~**ti**, clipping; cutting; chip; (*pub.*) press-cutting; (*th.*) cut; (*math.*) deduction. ~**tili**, interrupted, discontinuous; (*ind.*) step-, stage-; (*fin.*) net, with deduction(s). ~**tisiz**, continuous, uninterrupted; (*fin.*) gross, without deduction.

kesˈirʳⁱ A breaking; (*med.*) fracture; (*math.*) fraction; fragment. ~**li**, (*math.*) fractional: ~ **sayı**, (improper) fraction.

kesiş·en (*math.*) Intersecting. ~**im**, intersection. ~**me**, *vn.*: ~ **noktası**, point of intersection. ~**mek (-le)**, cut each other; intersect; (*fin.*) conclude (agreement); settle (accounts); fix (price); (*sp.*) draw (game).

kesit̄ⁱ (*math.*) Section; profile. ~ **alan**, cross-section. ~**li**, sectional.

kesitaşıⁿ¹ Flat stone (by river, for beating out the laundry).

keskenmek (-i) Threaten s.o. (with the fist).

keski (*carp.*) Cutter; chisel; small axe; (*agr.*) billhook, coulter. ~ **kalemi**, (*min.*) cold chisel; parting-tool (lathe): ~ **uç**, drilling bit.

keskin Sharp; acute; biting, keen; pungent; shrill (sound); severe; decided; peremptory; (*fig.*) incisive; shrewd; (*carp.*) edged (tool); (*bio.*) aculeate. ~ **bakışlı/gözlü**, keen eyed: ~**-gaga**, (*orn.*) sharpbill: ~ **hatlı**, clear-cut: ~ **sirke küpüne zarar (verir)**, s.o. whose bad temper only hurts himself: ~ **viraj**, sharp bend.

keskin·leşmek *vi.* Become sharp, etc. ~**leştirmek (-i)**, *vc.* ~**lik**, sharpness; acuteness, acuity; pungency; incisiveness; shrewdness; cutting edge: ~**ine**, edgeways: ~**ine koymak**, set stg. edgewise.

kes·me *vn.* (*min.*) Shearing; shears; (*cul.*) Turkish delight; type of flat macaroni; (*math.*) sector; (*cin.*) cutting; (*mod.*) openwork embroidery. *a.* Cut; that can be cut; decided, definite. ~ **akımı**, (*el.*) breaking current: ~ **im/işareti**, (*ling.*) apostrophe: ~ **kaya**, (*geol.*) soft rock (suitable for foundations): ~ **kutusu**, (*min.*) shear apparatus: ~ **makarna**, (*cul.*) macaroni: ~ **makinesi**, cutter: ~ŞEKER: ~ **takımı**, (*eng.*) cutting tools. ~**mece**, with the right to cut and examine (when buying melons, etc.); (bought) in a job-lot/for a lump sum. ~**meˈçᶜⁱ**, (*el.*) telegraph key.

kesmek (-i) Cut; cut off; cut down; interrupt; stop; intercept; deduct; reduce, diminish; determine, decide, agree upon; cut (animal's) throat, kill; (*med.*) amputate; castrate; (*fin.*) mint (money); (*gamb.*) cut (cards); (*adm.*) issue (document). *vi.* Cut well, be sharp; (wind) bite; cost; (*sl.*) talk boringly; exaggerate: **(-den)**, cut o.s. off/dissociate o.s. from. **kes (sesini)!**, (*sl.*) shut up!, dry up!: **kesip atmak**, decide (without much discussion); settle once and for all; destroy root and branch: **kesip biçmek**, try to frighten with threats: **kesip çıkarmak**, cut out, remove: **kesip devirmek**, cut down: **kesip koparmak**, cut off.

kes·melik Quarry for building-stone. ~ **meşeker**, (*cul.*) cube/lump sugar. ~**mez**, *a.* blunt. ~**mik**, (*agr.*) chaff mixed with straw; (*cul.*) milk curds.

keson (*eng.*) Caisson; bulkhead.

kesˈpᵇⁱ Acquisition, gain. ~ˈ**etmek**ᵉᵈᵉʳ, acquire.

kesr- = KESİR. ~ˈ**etmek**ᵉᵈᵉʳ, break; subdue; abate.

kesre = ESRE.

kesretⁱ Multitude; great quantity; superabundance, excess. ~**li**, abundant.

kestane (*bot.*) Chestnut; light-brown colour. ~ **ağacı**, (*bot.*) Spanish/sweet chestnut-tree: ~ **dorusu**, chestnut-bay (colour/horse): ~ **kabuğundan çıkmış da kabuğunu beğenmemiş**, s.o. who is ashamed of his family/origins: ~ **kargası**, (*orn.*) Eurasian jay.

kestane-ci¹kᵍⁱ (*bio.*) Prostate gland; fetlock. ~**fişeği**ⁿⁱ, cracker (firework). ~**kabağı**ⁿ¹, (*bot.*) squash, pumpkin. ~**lik**, chestnut grove. ~**rengi**ⁿⁱ, (chestnut) brown, auburn. ~**şekeri**ⁿⁱ, (*cul.*) marron glacé.

kestere = KİTRE.

kestir·ilmiş *a.* Fixed, regular. ~**im**, prediction; estimate. ~**me**, *vn.* estimate; snooze: *a.* definite; decisive; approximate; practical: ~ **cihazı**, (*mil., naut.*) direction-finder: ~ **yol**, short cut: ~**den gelmek**, cut (the corners). ~**mece**, approximate. ~**mek (-i, -e)**, *vc.* = KESMEK; cause to cut, etc. shorten; cause to cease; (*fin.*) appreciate; estimate; (*cul.*) cause to curdle, turn milk, etc. sour; decide; perceive; clearly understand; (*mil., naut.*) take a bearing: *vi.* snooze, doze: **kestirip atmak**, destroy utterly.

keş¹ *n.* (*cul.*) Skim-milk cheese. *a.* (*sl.*) Gullible; foolish. ~ **etm.**, (*sl.*) shame: ~ **ten gelmek**, not care, be indifferent.

keş² (*chess*) Check. ~ **demek**, check(-mate).

-keş *a./n. suf.* Drawing, bearing, suffering, withdrawing; drinking; addicted to [AFYONKEŞ, CEFAKEŞ].

keşen Chain bridle/fetters.

keşf- = KEŞİF. ~ˈ**etmek**ᵉᵈᵉʳ, uncover; dig out; discover, reconnoitre; examine carefully and evaluate; guess; divine.

keşide Drawing (cheque/lottery, etc.); hyphen; dash. ~ **etm.**, draw (line/cheque/lot, etc.); send (telegram).

keşˈifᶠⁱ Exposure; discovery; scrutiny, investigation; valuation, estimate; reconnaissance; divination. ~ **kolu**, (*mil.*) reconnoitring patrol: ~ **seferi** (*geo.*) expedition: ~ **uçağı**, (*aer.*) reconnaissance plane: ~ **ve takdir etm.**, assess, writter estimate (of costs).

keşi¹kᵍⁱ Turn of duty, watch, shift. ~**çi**, duty man, watch(man). ~**leme**, alternation. ~**leşe**, in turn/shifts. ~**leşmek (-le)**, work in shifts.

keşiş (*rel.*) Christian priest/monk. ~**dağı**ⁿ¹, *pr.n* (*geo.*) Mount Olympus (near Bursa). ~**hane** monastery. ~**leme**, (*geo.*) south-east; (*met.*) south east wind (in Istanbul); sirocco (in Mediterranean).

keşke/keşki Would that . . .!, if only . . .! ~ **bilsem//bilseydim!**, if only I knew//had known!

keşke'k^{ği} (*cul.*) Wheat boiled with minced meat.
keşkül Begging-bowl. ~ (**üfukara**), (*cul.*) almond custard.
keşlemek (**-i**) (*sl.*) Attach no importance to; ignore.
keşmekeş Great confusion.
Keşmir (*geo.*) Kashmir. ~ **şalı**, (*mod.*) cashmere shawl.
keşşaf Investigator, discoverer; (*mil.*) scout.
ket$^{i 1}$ Obstacle. ~ **vurmak** (**-e**), hinder.
ket$^{i 2}$ (*cul.*) Starch. ~ **al**, (*tex.*) starched and glazed cotton/linen.
ketçap = KEÇÇAP.
kete (*cul.*) Cake made of rice-flour.
keten (*bot.*) Flax; (*tex.*) linen. ~ **ci(lik)**, (work/trade of) linen-weaver/-seller. ~ **ci'k**^{ği}, (*bot.*) eel-grass, grass-wrack; gold-of-pleasure. ~ **giller**, (*bot.*) Linaceae. ~ **helvacı**, maker/seller of candy-floss. ~ **helvası**, (*cul.*) candy-floss. ~ **kuşu**^{nu}, (*orn.*) linnet. ~ **tohumu**^{nu}, (*bot.*) linseed. ~ **yağı**^{nı}, linseed oil.
kethüda (*his.*) Steward. ~ **bey**, (*his.*) home affairs minister.
keton (*chem.*) Ketone.
ketum Tight-lipped, reticent, discreet. ~ **iyet**^{i}, discretion.
keven = GEVEN.
kevgir (*dom.*) Perforated ladle/bowl; strainer.
Kevser (*rel.*) River in Paradise. ~ **gibi**, like nectar.
keyf- = KEYİF. ~ '**etmek**^{eder}, *vi.* amuse/enjoy o.s. ~ **i**, arbitrary, despotic; capricious; ~ **olarak**, arbitrarily. ~ **ince**, as one pleases; arbitrarily. ~ **iyet**^{i}, condition; quality; circumstance; affair: ~ **böyle böyle!**, well, that's how things are!
key'lif^{fi} *n.* Health; bodily/mental condition; merriment, fun, good spirits; pleasure, amusement; inclination, whim, fancy; slight intoxication. *a.* Hilarious, tipsy. ~ **benim köy Mehmet ağanın**, it's my business so no one else need interfere: ~ **çatmak**, make merry: ~ **halinde**, tipsy, intoxicated: ~ **olm.**, be tipsy: ~ **sormak**, inquire after s.o.'s health; say 'how are you?': ~ **sürmek**, live in clover: ~ **vermek**, intoxicate: ~ **yetiştirmek**, make merry with drink.

keyfi: ~ **bilmek**, do as one pleases: ~ **bozuk**, in bad health: ~ **bozulmak**, become ill; be bored/restless: ~ **gelmek**, be delighted; feel in a good humour: ~ **iyi/yerinde ol(ma)mak**, feel (un)well: ~ **kaçmak**, become dispirited/gloomy: ~ **oluncaya kadar**, to his heart's content: ~ **sıra**, arbitrarily, as he pleases: ~ **tıkırında**, in the best of spirits: ~ **min kâhyası mısın?**, what right have you to interfere in my affairs?: ~ **nden dört köşe olm.**, feel very pleased/proud about stg.: ~ **ne bakmak**, have a pleasant time: ~ **ne gitmek**, arrange to enjoy o.s.: ~ **ni bozmak/kaçırmak**, treat harshly: ~ **ni çıkarmak** (**-in**), get great pleasure from stg.: ~ **niz nasıl?**, how are you?
keyif·lenmek *vi.* Enjoy o.s.; be tipsy. ~ **li**, merry; happy; comfortable; tipsy. ~ **siz**, off colour, indisposed; gloomy. ~ **sizlenmek**, *vi.* become slightly ill. ~ **sizlik**, indisposition; ailment; depression.
keyk^i = KEK.
key·lüs = KİLÜS. ~ **müs** = KİMÜS.

kez Time. ~ (**bu**), this time.
keza(lik) Thus; similarly; also, too.
kezza'p^{bı} (*chem.*) Nitric acid, *aqua fortis*.
kg(r). = KİLOGRAM.
Kh. = KARARGÂH.
kHz. = KİLOHERTZ.
-kı *n. suf.* [222] = -Gİ [ASKI].
kıble (*rel.*) Direction to face when praying (towards Mecca); (*geo.*) south; (*met.*) south wind; (*fig.*) place to which/person to whom everyone turns. ~ **gâh**, direction of Mecca. ~ **nüma**, compass for determining KIBLE.
Kıbrıs (*geo.*) Cyprus. ~ +, *a.* Cypriot. ~ **lı**, (*ethn.*) Cypriot. ~ **taşı**^{nı}, (*min.*) diamond-cut rock-crystal; paste.
kıç^1 Hind part; (*col.*) behind, buttocks, rump; (*naut.*) stern. ~ **atmak**, (horse) lash out with both hoofs; (*fig., sl.*) long for, desire: ~ **attırmak** (**-e**), (*sl.*) get the better of s.o.: ~ **bodoslaması**, (*naut.*) stern-post: ~ **çıkıntısı**, counter: ~ **güverte/kasarası**, quarter-deck: ~ **oturaklar**, stern sheets: ~ **tarafın(d)a**, abaft; astern: ~ **topu**, stern-chaser: ~ **üstü oturmak**, squat on the ground; (*fig.*) squander one's possessions; be helpless: ~ **ı kırık**, (*sl.*) worthless, unimportant: ~ **ına tekmeyi atmak**, (*vulg.*) kick s.o. out: ~ **ına baka baka/bakarak**, failing in one's expectations: ~ **ını yırtmak**, (*vulg.*) shout out excitedly: ~ **tan bacaklı**, short-legged (person): ~ **tan kara etm.**, (*naut.*) moor by the stern. ~ **ın**, ~ ~, backwards; astern. ~ **lı**, down by the stern.
kıdem Antiquity; priority, precedence, seniority. ~ **hakkı**, birthright: ~ **zammı**, (*ind.*) seniority bonus: ~ **e göre**, by seniority.
kıdem·li Earliest; senior. ~ **lilik**, seniority. ~ **siz**, without seniority; junior.
kığ (*live.*) Dung (in pellets). ~ **lamak**, *vi.* excrete.
kıh (*child.*) Dirt(y).
kıkır ~ ~, giggling: ~ ~ **gülmek**, giggle.
kıkırda'k^{ğı} (*bio.*) Cartilage; gristle; (*cul.*) crackling. ~ +, *a.* Chondr-; cartilaginous. ~ **doku**, cartilaginous tissue. ~ **lı**, cartilaginous; gristly.
kıkır·damak *vi.* Make a crackling noise; (*sl.*) die. ~ **datmak** (**-i**), *vc.* ~ **tı**, giggling.
kıl *n.* (*bio.*) Hair; bristle; goat's hair; (*fig.*) hair's breadth. *a.* Made of hair; hair-. ~ **biti**, (*ent.*) crab/pubic louse: ~ **çadır**, horsehair/felt tent (of nomads): ~ **çatlağı**, (*eng.*) hair crack: ~ **çekmek**, (*sl.*) toady: ~ **dökümü**, (*med.*) alopecia: ~ **gibi**, very fine/thin: ~ **kadar**, the smallest degree/quantity: ~ **kalem**, (*art.*) camel-hair brush: ~ **kalmak** (**-e**), be within an ace/a hair's breadth of stg.; be on the brink of stg.: ~ **keseciği**, (*bio.*) follicle: ~ **payı kalmak**, be very little left: ~ **payı kurtulmak**, escape by a hair's breadth: ~ **şaşmadan**, with scrupulous care: ~ **testere**, (*carp.*) fretsaw: ~ **yılanı**, (*zoo.*) hair-worm: ~ **ı kırk yarmak**, split hairs: ~ **ına bile dokunmamak**, not hurt a single hair of s.o.'s head: ~ **ını bile kıpırdatmamak**, not turn a hair; remain indifferent: ~ **ları gidermek**, depilate.
kılağı (*min.*) Burr/wire-edge (from grindstone). ~ **lamak** (**-i**), give a keen edge (to razor, etc.). ~ **lı**, keen, sharp. ~ **sız**, blunt, dull.
kılaptan (*tex.*) Gilt copper thread; gold wire

wound on silk; imitation gold thread. ~ **işleme**, brocade.

kılavuz Guide, leader; (*naut.*) pilot; (*soc.*) go-between (in arranged marriages); (*eng.*) gimlet, screw-tap; threader; (*cin.*) leader-strip; (*pub.*) directory; (*min.*) adit. ~ +, *a.* Guiding; key-; characteristic: ~ **kitap**, directory; guide-book: ~ **ücreti**, (*naut.*) pilotage (fee): ~**u karga olanın (burnu boktan ayrılmaz)**, if you take bad advice you will regret it.

kılavuz·lu With a guide; guided; (*eng.*) threaded: ~ **gezinti**, conducted tour. ~**luk**, profession of guide/pilot; (*psy.*) guidance: ~ **etm.**, act as guide/pilot. ~**suz**, without a pilot; (*eng.*) unthreaded.

kıl·bara'kᵍ¹ (*zoo.*) Type of Tk. Shetland pony; shaggy dog. ~**baz**, (*sl.*) toady. ~**burun**, (*geo.*) narrow promontory. ~**cal**, *a.* (*phys.*) capillary; (*bio.*) very fine. ~**calkurt**, (*zoo.*) capillary worm. ~**callık**, capillarity. ~**can**, bird-net (of horse-hair). ~**çı'k**ᵍ¹, (*ich.*) fish-bone; (*bot.*) awn, beard; (bean) string; thorn: ~**larını ayıklamak**, bone (fish). ~**çıklı**, (*ich.*) bony; (*bot.*) awned; stringy; (*fig.*) confused, complicated. ~**çıksı**, (*geol.*) feathery. ~**çıksız**, (*ich.*) boneless; (*bot.*) awnless: ~ **buğday**, spelt.

kıldırmak (-i, -e) *vc.* = KILMAK.

kılgı *n.* (*phil.*) Practice, action, application. ~**lı**/~**sal**, practical, applied. ~**n**, practicable, applicable.

kılıbı'kᵍ¹ Man ruled by his wife; henpecked husband. ~**laşmak**, *vi.* become henpecked. ~**lık**, being henpecked.

kılı'çᶜ¹ *n.* (*mil.*) Sword; blade. *a.* Curved. ~ **kaşı**, sword-guard: ~ **kırlangıcı**, (*orn.*) common swift: ~ **oynatmak**, be the ruler, dominate: ~ **pabucu**, (*mil.*) ferrule of scabbard: ~ **şiş**, (*cul.*) skewered swordfish: ~**ı (Demokles'in)**, the sword of Damocles, ever-present danger: ~**ın hakkı olarak**, by right of conquest: ~**ına**, on (its) edge: ~**tan geçmek**, *vp.* be put to the sword: ~**tan geçirmek (-i)**, put to the sword.

kılıç·bacak Bandy-/bow-legged. ~**balığı**ⁿ¹, (*ich.*) swordfish. ~**gagalı**, (*orn.*) avocet. ~**hane**, sword-workshop. ~**kuyruğu**ⁿᵘ, (*ich.*) swordtail. ~**lama**, *adv.* edgewise; set on edge; slung from the shoulder, crosswise. ~ **lamak (-i)**, put to the sword, massacre. ~**lı**, sword-bearing. ~**oyuncusu**ⁿᵘ, (*sp.*) fencer. ~**oyunu**ⁿᵘ, (*sp.*) fencing.

kılıf Sheath; case, casing; cover; (*bio.*) tunic. ~ **geçirmek/**~**lamak (-i)**, sheath; cover. ~**lı**, sheathed; covered: ~ **yatak**, (*eng.*) bearing.

kılı'kᵍ¹ Shape; appearance; aspect; cut, fashion; costume; (*phil.*) form; (*sp.*) dress, uniform. ~ **kıyafet**, one's dress/appearance: ~ **kıyafet köpeklere ziyafet**, very dirty and untidy: ~ **kıyafeti düzmek**, renew one's clothes.

kılık·landırmak (-i) Imagine stg. ~**lı**, having . . . appearance/dress; well-shaped: ~ **kıyafetli**, well-dressed. ~**sız**, shabby, dowdy; untidy, bedraggled. ~**sızlaşmak**, *vi.* (let o.s.) become shabby. ~**sızlık**, shabbiness, untidiness.

kılınmak *vp.* = KILMAK. Be done/performed/celebrated.

kıl·kıran (*med.*) Alopecia, baldness. ~**kök**, hair root. ~**kuyruk**, (*orn.*) pintail (duck); (*fig.*) tatterdemalion; shifty-looking fellow. ~**lanmak**, *vi.* become hairy; (youth) begin to grow a beard. ~**lı**, hairy; bristly; (*bio.*) crinite, barbate, chaeto-. ~**sız**, hairless; beardless. ~**yakı**, (*med.*) seton.

kılmak *aux. v.* [154] Do; perform; celebrate.

kımıl¹ *n.* (*ent.*) (?) Bishop's mitre bug.

kımıl² ~ ~, always moving, astir. ~**danış**, movement. ~**da(n)mak**, *vi.* move; shake, stir. ~**datma**, (*pol.*) agitation. ~**datmak (-i)**, *vt.* move; shake; (*pol.*) stir up, agitate. ~**tı**, motion, movement; mimicry.

kımız (*cul.*) Koumiss (fermented mare's milk).

kın (*mil.*) Sheath (of sword); (*bio.*) sheath; (*ent.*) elytron.

-kın *a./n. suf.* [223] = -GİN [ŞAŞKIN].

kına Henna (dye). ~ **ağacı**, (*bot.*) henna bush: ~ **gibi**, very fine, powdery: ~ **koymak/sürmek/vurmak/yakmak**, dye with henna: ~**lar yakmak**, be overjoyed (at s.o.'s misfortune).

kına·cı'kᵍ¹ (*myc.*) Black/stem rust (on cereals). ~**çiçeği**ⁿⁱ, (*bot.*) balsam. ~**çiçeğigiller**, (*bot.*) Balsaminaceae. ~**gecesi**ⁿⁱ, women's celebration on eve of wedding (when bride's fingers/toes were dyed with henna). ~**kına**, (*bot.*) cinchona tree (source of cinchona bark and quinine). ~**lamak (-i)**, apply/dye with henna. ~**lanmak**, *vp.* ~**lı**, dyed with henna; *pr.n.* (*geo.*) island of Kınalı/Proti: ~ **kaz**, (*orn., col.*) flamingo: ~ **keklik**, (*orn.*) rock partridge.

kına·ma *vn.* Blame, reproach. ~**mak (-i)**, blame, condemn; reproach; be sarcastic to; mock, taunt. ~**nmak**, *vp.*

kınam·sık Hypercritical; sarcastic. ~**sımak (-i)**, find fault with everything.

kındıra'çᶜ¹ (*carp.*) Spokeshave; chisel.

kın·kanat (*ent.*) Elytron. ~**kanatlı(lar)**, beetle/ (Coleoptera). ~**lamak (-i)**, sheathe (sword).

kınna'pᵇ¹ String, twine, yarn.

Kıpça'kᵍ¹ (*ethn.*) Tk. tribe in the Ukraine. ~**ça**, (*ling.*) their language.

kıpı Moment.

kıpık Half-closed; winking. ~ **gözlü**, with half-closed eyes.

kıpır ~ ~, constantly moving. ~**dak**, active, lively. ~**damak/**~**danmak/**~**daşmak**, *vi.* move slightly; start; quiver; vibrate. ~**datmak (-i)**, cause to move quickly; agitate. ~**tı**, slight quick movement; start; quiver; unsteadiness.

kıpıştırmak (-i) Wink/blink (the eyes).

kıp·kırmızı/~**kızıl** Bright red; very red.

kıp·ma Twinkling. ~**mak (-i)**, wink/blink (an eye).

Kıpti (*ethn.*) Copt; gypsy. ~**ce**, (*ling.*) Coptic; Romany.

kır¹ *a.* Grey. *n.* Greyness; grey horse. ~ **düşmek (-e)**, (hair/beard) turn grey.

kır² *n.* Country(side); uncultivated land; prairie; wilderness. ~ **akçaağacı**, (*bot.*) hedge/field maple: ~ **bekçisi**, village watchman: ~ **eğlenceleri**, field sports: ~ **evi**, (*arch.*) bungalow, cottage: ~ **gezisi**, picnic: ~ **incir kuşu**, (*orn.*) tawny pipit: ~ **kırlangıcı**, (*orn.*) barn swallow: ~ **koşusu**, (*sp.*)

cross-country race: ~ **kurdu**, (*zoo.*) coyote: ~ **resmi**, (*art.*) idyll: ~ **dan kestirme gitmek**, cut across country.

kıraat¹ Reading; reading-book. ~ **hane**, public reading-room; coffee-house providing newspapers.

kıraca'kᵍ¹ (*dom.*) Nut-crackers.

kıra'çᶜ¹ *n.* (*agr.*) Uncultivated/barren land. *a.* Parched; barren; sterile. ~ **lık**, barrenness.

kıraça (*ich.*) Small horse-mackerel.

kırağı (*met.*) Hoar-frost. ~ **çalmak (-i)**, (*agr.*) be damaged by frost: ~ **düşmek/yağmak**, have a frost.

kıral- = KRAL.

kıran¹ *n.* Edge; shore; horizon; hillside, mountain top.

kıran² *a.* Breaking; destructive. *n.* (*med.*) Epidemic; (*zoo.*) murrain, epidemic. ~ **girmek (-e)**, many die; be struck by epidemic.

-kıran *n. suf.* Breaking-, destroying- [DALGAKIRAN]; -cide [ASALAKKIRAN].

kıranta S.o. elderly with hair turning grey.

kırat¹ Carat (weight); (*fig.*) quality.

kırba Water-skin; leather bottle; (*med.*) swollen stomach. ~ **olm.**, (child) be potbellied and rickety.

kırba'çᶜ¹ Whip; scourge. ~ **cezası**, flogging: ~ **kurdu**, (*zoo.*) whipworm. ~ **lamak (-i)**, whip, flog. ~ **lanmak**, *vp.*

kırcın (*zoo.*) Murrain.

kır'çᶜ¹ (*met.*) Heavy snow-like frost.

kır-çıl/ ~ **çoz** Greying, grizzled. ~ **çıllaşmak**, *vi.* turn grey. ~ **donlu**, greycoated (horse).

kırdır·mak (-i, -e) *vc.* = KIRMAK; (*fin.*) discount (bills).

kırgı (*geo.*) ~ **bayır**, badlands.

kırgın Disappointed, hurt. ~ **lık**, disappointment; resentment.

Kırgız (*ethn.*) Kirghiz. ~ **ca**, (*ling.*) Kirghiz. ~ **istan**, (*geo.*) Kirghizistan.

kırıcı *a.* Breaking; crushing; harsh; unkind. *n.* (*min.*) Breaker; crusher; (*fin.*) broker. ~ **lık**, harshness.

kırı'kᵍ¹ ¹ *n.* Woman's lover.

kırı'kᵍ¹ ² *a.* Broken; cracked; (*met.*) milder; (*zoo.*) mongrel. *n.* Break; fragment; splinter; (*med.*) fracture; (*geol.*) fault. ~ **dökük**, scrap (metal); odds-and-ends; broken down; (*ling.*) broken (French): ~ **dökük değeri**, scrap value: ~ **numara almak**, (*ed.*) get bad marks: ~ **tahtası**, (*med.*) splint.

kırık-çı(lık) (*med.*) (Work of) bone-setter. ~ **kırak**, (*cul.*) cracker-stick. ~ **lık**, state of being broken; breakage; physical weakness/weariness.

kırıl·acak Breakable, fragile. ~ **ayazmak**, be almost broken. ~ **ca**, (*chem.*) crystal. ~ **cal**, crystalline. ~ **calaşma**, crystallization. ~ **cayazım**, crystallography. ~ **gan**, easily broken, fragile; (*geol.*) friable. ~ **ım**/ ~ **ma**, *vn.* breaking; failure; (*med.*) rupture; (*phys.*) refraction; (*fig.*) coquettishness: ~ **açısı**, angle of refraction: ~ **dayancı**, breaking resistance. ~ **mak**, *vi.* break; *vp.* be broken; (*phys.*) be refracted; be ruined/killed; (*mil.*) suffer heavy casualties; be hurt/offended; be mitigated, become milder; (*fig.*) die of laughter: **kırılıp dökülmek**, be constantly broken; (woman) be coquettish. ~ **maz**, unbreakable; ~ **cam**, safety glass.

kırım¹ *n.* Massacre; wholesale slaughter; carnage; (*fin.*) discount.

kırım² *adv.* ~ ~, coquettishly.

Kırım³ *pr.n.* (*geo.*) The Crimea. ~ +, *a.* Crimean: ~ **kertenkelesi**, (*zoo.*) Crimean lizard: ~ **Savaşı**, the Crimean War. ~ **lı**, (*ethn.*) Crimean Tartar.

kırımtartar (*chem.*) Cream of tartar.

kırın·ım/ ~ **ma** (*phys.*) Diffraction. ~ **tı**, fragment; crumb; crushed stone; chip; debris; garbage: ~ +, *a.* (*geol.*) clastic: ~ **değirmeni**, garbage disposer.

kırış·ık *a.* Wrinkled; crinkly; *n.* wrinkle; crack, small fissure. ~ **ıklık**, wrinkledness; wrinkling. ~ **ma**, *vn.* (chess) reciprocal elimination of pawns, etc. ~ **mak**, *vi.* become wrinkled: (-le), kill one another; (*gamb.*) bet with each other: *vt.* (-i, -le), mutually break stg.; (*fin.*) balance (two accounts). ~ **tırıcı**, ~ **kas**, (*bio.*) corrugator. ~ **tırmak (-i, -e)**, *vc.*; (*col.*) flirt with each other.

kırıt·ış Coquetry. ~ **kan**, coquettish; flighty. ~ **kanlık**, coquettishness. ~ **mak (-e)**, behave coquettishly: **kırıta kırıta**, being coquettish/flighty.

kırk¹ Forty; large indefinite number/quantity. ~ **anahtarlı**, very wealthy; man of property: ~ **Arabın aklı bir incir çekirdeğini doldurmaz**, (*pej.*) forty Negroes haven't enough wits to stuff a fig-seed: ~ **baş sığır**, forty head of cattle: ~ **bir** *etc.*, forty-one, etc.: ~ **bir kere maşallah**, say MAŞALLAH repeatedly in admiration: ~ **bir buçuk maşallah!**, (*jok.*) may God preserve it!: ~ **defa**, time after time; countless times: ~ **derece yatık**, (*naut.*) with a 40° list: ~ **dereden su getirmek**, make endless excuses: ~ **ekmek yemesi lazım**, you will need a lot of practice: ~ **evin kedisi**, s.o. always in and out of other people's houses: ~ **ev/haneli köy**, a village of some forty houses: ~ **ikindi**, season of afternoon rains (in parts of Anatolia): ~ **kadar kişi**, some forty people: ~ **kapının ipini çekmek**, knock at many doors: ~ **kapının mandalı**, s.o. who goes everywhere poking his nose into everything: ~ **kişiyiz birbirimizi biliriz**, we know too much about you/ him to be taken in: ~ **lira kazanırsan yağ bala ver!**, count yourself lucky if you earn forty liras: ~ **liraya düşürdüm (-i)**, I was lucky to get the price down to forty liras: ~ **lirayı gözden çıkarmak lazım**, you will have to be prepared to pay forty liras: ~ MERDİVEN: ~ **oda//yataklı**, (hotel) with forty rooms//beds: ~ **paraya dokuz takla atar**, he'd do anything for money: ~ **şahit lazım**, it's unbelievable: ~ **tarakta bezi olm.**, have many irons in the fire; have a finger in every pie: ~ **yaşına girdi**, he is in his fortieth year: ~ **yaşını aşkın**, over forty (years old): ~ **yıl görmesem aramam**, I wouldn't touch it with a barge-pole: ~ **yıl kıran olmuş eceli gelen ölmüş**, we only die at the appointed time: ~ **yılda bir**, once in a lifetime/blue moon: ~ **yılın başında**, just for once: ~ **yıllık bir adam**, a forty-year-old man: ~ **yıllık pala çalmış kalem**, the pen I have wielded for forty years: ~ **yıllık Yani olur mu Kâni?**, can the leopard change his spots?

kırk-: ~ **ı boylamak**, be getting on for forty: ~ **ı çıkmak**, complete forty days (after childbirth/a death): ~ **ı tutmak**, be in one's forties: ~ **ına doğru olm./merdiven dayamak**, be nearing forty (years of age): ~ında var yok, he must be about forty: ~ından sonra azmak, behave in a manner unseemly for one's age: ~ından sonra saz çalmak, start on a new job late in life: ~ını geçkin, in his forties: ~LAR: ~ları karışmış olm., be born in the same period of forty days.

kırk·ambar General store; general dealer; (*naut.*) mixed cargo; (*fig.*) s.o. with encyclopaedic knowledge. ~ar, forty each; forty at a time. ~aya[lk][ğ1], (*zoo.*) centipede; myriapod. ~ayaklar, (*zoo.*) centipedes, Chilopoda; Myriapoda. ~bayır, (*zoo.*) third stomach of ruminants. ~geçi[lt][di], (*geo.*) very winding river.

kırk·ı Shears; shearing. ~ıcı, sheep-shearer. ~ılmak, *vp.* = KIRKMAK. ~ım, shearing (season); clip (of wool). ~ıntı, clippings.

kırk·ıncı (40.) Fortieth. ~lamak, *vi.* complete forty days (after an event); reach the age of forty: (-i), do stg. forty times; make forty. ~lanma, *vn.* ~lanmak, *vp.* ~lar, *pr.n.* (*rel.*) forty saints of Islam: ~a karışmak, disappear; make o.s. scarce. ~lı, having forty parts; born within forty days of each other: ~ olm. (-le) be born soon after s.o. else. ~lık, containing forty units; forty years old; (money) worth forty units; forty para coin; clothes for a newborn child; (*dial.*) shears: ~ bir adam, a man of forty.

kırk·ma *vn.* Clipping; shearing; hair cut so as to cover the forehead; (*min.*) grit. ~mak (-i), clip; shear.

kırk·merak Very interested/curious. ~merdiven, very steep slope/climb.

kırlağan (*med.*) Epidemic, fatal illness; plague, typhus.

kırlangı[lç][c1] (*orn.*) Swallow; martin; itinerant charlatan eye-doctor; (*naut.*, *his.*) light fast galley. ~balığı[n1], (*ich.*) gurnard. ~dönümü[nü], first days of October. ~fırtınası[n1], (*met.*) storm in early April. ~giller, (*orn.*) swallows and martins. ~kuyruğu[nu], (*carp.*) dovetail. ~otu[nu], (*bot.*) greater celandine.

kırlaşmak *vi.* Become/turn grey.

kırlık (*geo.*) Countryside.

kır·ma *vn.* (*mod.*) Fold, pleat, crease; (*cul.*) coarse flour, crushed barley; (*zoo.*) half-breed, mongrel; (*fin.*) discount; (*chem.*) cracking: *a.* broken; folding (gun, etc.); (*phys.*) hybrid: ~ makinesi, crusher. ~macı, corn-merchant; (*pub.*) folder (bookbinding). ~mak (-i), break, crush, split; kibble (corn); fold, pleat, crease; kill, destroy; offend; dash (hopes); (*fin.*) discount (bill), change (money), lower (price); (*gamb.*) take (in backgammon); (*naut.*) turn (rudder); (*phys.*) diffract: **kır boynunu!**, get out!: **kıran kırana**, pitilessly, to the death: **kırdığı ceviz/koz bin/kırkı aşmak**, commit endless blunders/stupidities: **kırıp açmak**, burst open: **kırıp dökmek**, keep on breaking; destroy: **kırıp geçirmek**, destroy, exterminate; tyrannize. ~malı, (*mod.*) pleated; creased. ~mataş, (*eng.*) ballast.

kırmız (*chem.*) Cochineal. ~ madeni, (*min.*) kermes mineral (antimony trisulphide). ~böceği[ni], (*ent.*) cochineal scale-insect.

kırmızı Red; blood-red; crimson-red. ~ akik, (*min.*) cornelian: ~ ayaklı, (*orn.*) red-footed

(falcon, etc.): ~ balık, (*ich.*) goldfish: ~ boyunlu, (*orn.*) red-necked (grebe, etc.): ~ çaylak, (*orn.*) sparrowhawk: ~ dipli mumla davet etmedim!, (*iron.*) nobody asked you to come!: ~ doğan, (*orn.*) marsh harrier: ~ farekulağı, (*bot.*) scarlet pimpernel: ~ fener, (*sl.*) brothel: ~ gagalı, (*orn.*) red-billed (chough, etc.): ~ gerdanlı, (*orn.*) red-breasted (goose, etc.): ~ gömlek, (*fig.*) stg. that can never be hidden/kept secret: ~ ısırgan otu, (*bot.*) red deadnettle: ~ ilik, (*bio.*) bone marrow: ~ keklik, (*orn.*) rock partridge: ~ kuyruklu, (*orn.*) red-tailed: ~ kuyruklu şakrakkuşu, (*orn.*) great rosefinch: ~ kürecik, (*bio.*) erythrocyte: ~ orman karıncası, (*ent.*) wood ant: ~ oy, (*adm.*) vote against: ~ sakız, (*bot.*) dragon's blood: ~ sırtlı, (*orn.*) red-backed (shrike, etc.): ~ sögüt, (*bot.*) purple osier: ~ şebboy, (*bot.*) stock: ~ yaban mersini, (*bot.*) cowberry: ~ yüksükotu, (*bot.*) foxglove: ~ zambak, (*bot.*) martagon/Turk's cap lily: ~ya kayma, (*ast.*) red-shift. [*Also* = AL; KIZIL.]

kırmızı·ağa[lç][c1] (*bot.*) Burmese rosewood. ~biber, (*bot.*, *cul.*) cayenne/red pepper; chilli. ~laşmak, *vi.* become red; turn red; blush. ~lı, partially red; dressed in red. ~lık, redness; ruddiness. ~msı/ ~mtırak, reddish. ~turp, (*bot.*) radish.

kırna[lk][ğ1] (*obs.*) Slave girl; (*sl.*) pretty woman.

kırp·ık Clipped. ~ılmak, *vp.* ~ıntı, clippings; waste. ~ışmak, *vi.* flicker. ~ıştırmak (-i), blink (eyes). ~ma, *vn.* ~mak (-i), clip; trim; shear; (*fin.*) cut down (expenses); (*lit.*) abridge; wink. ~tırmak, *vc.*

kırsal Rural, rustic; country-; village-.

kırsıçanımsı (*zoo.*) Daman.

kırtasiye Stationery; (*adm.*) 'red tape'. ~ci, stationer; (*adm.*) bureaucrat; s.o. given to 'red tape'. ~cilik, stationer's trade; (*adm.*) bureaucracy; 'red tape'.

kırtıpil (*col.*) Wearing old clothes; shabby; common; insignificant.

kıs (*ech.*) ~ ~ gülmek, laugh under one's breath; snigger.

kıs. = KISALTMA.

kısa Short; brief; curt; compact; concise; (*zoo.*) brachy-. ~ başlı = ~KAFALI: ~ boylu, short, not tall: ~ çizgi, (*ling.*) hyphen (-): ~ dalgalar, (*phys.*) short waves: ~ devre, (*el.*) short-circuit: ~ devre cereyanı, transient peak current: ~ geçmek, refer briefly to a subject: ~ görüşlü, short-sighted: narrow-minded: ~ haberler, (*pub.*) news in brief: ~ hapis, (*mil.*) confinement to barracks: ~KAFALI: ~ kanatlı kınkanatlı, (*zoo.*) rove beetle: ~ kesilmiş, close-cropped/-cut: ~ kesmek, cut short; be brief; bob (hair); dock (tail): ~ kuyruklu, (*zoo.*) short-tailed: ~ kuyruklu piyano, (*mus.*) baby grand: ~ ömürlü, ephemeral, short-lived: ~ pantolon, (*mod.*) shorts: ~ parmaklı, (*orn.*) short-toed (lark, etc.): ~ süre/vadeli, (*fin.*) short-term: ~ tutmak, make too short: ~ ünlü, (*ling.*) short vowel: ~ ve anlatımlı, brief but to the point, pithy: ~ vuruş, (*sp.*) jab: ~ yargılama yöntemi, (*leg.*) summary procedure: ~ yoldan, briefly.

kısa·ca *a.* Quite short: *adv.* shortly, briefly: ~sı, in short. ~cık, very short.

kısa'ç[c1] (*carp.*) Pliers, pincers; (*zoo.*) crab's claws.

kısa·kafalı (*bio.*) Brachycephalic. ~ **lık**, shortness; conciseness; brevity. ~ **lmak**, *vi.* become short; contract; shrink. ~ **ltıcı**, shortening. ~ **ltma**, *vn.*; (*ling.*) abbreviation; acronym. ~ **ltmak (-i)**, shorten; curtail; contract; summarize; (*lit.*) edit, compress, abridge; (*ling.*) abbreviate; (*tex.*) shrink. ~ **ltmalı**, shortened, abbreviated. ~ **sözcük**, (*ling.*) acronym.

kısas (*leg.*) Retaliation. ~ **etm.**, retaliate: ~ **usulü/** ~ **a** ~, an eye for an eye. ~ **en**, in retaliation.

kısı·cı (*cin.*) Fader, sound-control. ~ **k**, *a.* pinched; squeezed up; screwed up (eyes); hoarse/choked (voice); (*math.*) irreducible: *n.* narrow place/passage; (*bio.*) groin. ~ **klı**, flowing in a mere trickle. ~ **klık**, hoarseness. ~ **lma**, *vn.*; (*rad.*) attenuation, fading; (*bio.*) systole. ~ **lmak**, *vi.* be pinched/squeezed; be attenuated/reduced/diminished; fade; be in difficulties; (voice) become hoarse; (limb) be cramped/numbed.

kıs'ım[m1] Part; portion; piece; kind, sort; (*adm.*) department, division, section; handful. ~ ~, in groups/sections. ~ **lamak (-i)**, take a handful.

kısın·mak (-e) Be moderate; avoid excess. ~ **tı**, restriction, limitation. ~ **tılı**, restricted, limited.

kısır Barren, sterile, infertile; (*fig.*) unproductive, unprofitable. ~ **etm.**, make sterile, etc.

kısır·döngü[nü] Vicious circle. ~ **ganmak (-i, -den)**, grudge s.o. stg.; be chary of doing stg. ~ **laşmak**, *vi.* become infertile/sterile/unproductive. ~ **laştırma**, (*bio.*) *vn.*; sterilization; castration. ~ **laştırmak (-i)**, render infertile/sterile; castrate. ~ **lık**, sterility.

kısı'ı[d1] Restriction, limitation; (*leg.*) incapacity; disability. ~ **lama**, *vn.* ~ **lamak (-i)**, restrict, limit; put under restraint. ~ **layıcı**, restricting. ~ **lı**, restrictive; restricted, limited; (*leg.*) under legal disability. ~ **sız**, unrestricted; (*fin.*) free, liberalized.

kıska'ç[c1] (*dom.*) Folding steps; (*carp.*) clamp, vice; pincers; (*zoo.*) chela, claw. ~ **gözlük**, pince-nez.

kıskan·ç Envious, jealous. ~ **çlık**, envy, jealousy: ~ **tan içi içini yemek**, be consumed with envy. ~ **dırmak (-i)**, make jealous. ~ **ılmak (-den)**, *vp.* be envied. ~ **mak (-i, -den)**, envy, be jealous of; be jealous for (one's honour, etc.); be jealous about (one's partner).

kıs·kı (*eng.*) Wedge. ~ **kıvrak**, tightly bound/ squeezed; tightly coiled up; neat and tidy: ~ **bağlamak//yakalamak**, bind//hold tightly.

kısım- = KISIM. ~ **en**, partly, partially.

kıs·ma *vn.*: ~ **kangalı**, (*el.*) choke coil: ~ **sürgüsü**, (*mot.*) choke throttle. ~ **mak (-i)**, squeeze; tighten; pinch; cut down, reduce, diminish; (*eng.*) choke, throttle.

kısmet[i] *n.* Destiny; lot; fate; luck, chance; (for girl) chance to marry. *int.* God knows!; if fate wills it! ~ **kapısı**, one's place of work: ~ **olm.**, be fated: ~ **i açık**, fortunate; (girl) sought after: ~ **i açılmak**, be possible; be successful; be in luck; (girl) be sought after: ~ **i ayağına gelmek**, have unexpected luck/success: ~ **i çıkmak**, (girl) be asked for in marriage: ~ **inde olan kaşığında çıkar**, you get what Fate brings you: ~ **ine mani olm.**, spoil s.o.'s chances; make impossible: ~ **ini bağlamak**, hinder

s.o.'s marriage (by magic). ~ **li**, fortunate, lucky. ~ **siz**, unlucky; (girl) who does not marry.

kısmık Miserly, stingy.

kısmi Partial. ~ **körlük**, (*med.*) amblyopia: ~ **seçim**, (*adm.*) by-election: ~ **tutulma**, (*ast.*) partial eclipse.

kısra'k[g1] (*live.*) Mare.

kıssa (*lit.*) Story, tale, fable. ~ **dan hisse**, the moral of the story. ~ **han**, storyteller.

kısta'k[g1] (*geo.*) Isthmus.

kıstas Measure(ment); criterion.

kıstelyevm (*ind.*) Deduction for absence/lateness.

kıstır·ılmak *vp.* ~ **mak (-i, -e)**, *vc.* = KISMAK; cause to be pinched, etc.; crush (finger); catch (by driving into a corner); corner.

kış[1] *int.* Shoo! (to scare birds). ~ **alamak (-i)**, shoo away birds, etc.

kış[2] *n.* Winter; winter cold. ~ **basmak**, winter set in: ~ **çıkmak**, winter be over: ~ **çıt kuşu**, (*orn.*) common wren: ~ **dönencesi**, (*ast.*) winter solstice: ~ **kıyamet**, intense cold; depths of winter: ~ **uykusu**, (*zoo.*) hibernation: ~ **üstü**, at the coming of winter: ~ **a çıkarmak**, make stg. last till winter: ~ **ı çıkarmak (-de)**, spend the winter at/in . . .; last the winter: ~ **ı etm.**, reach the winter; stay until winter comes. ~ **ın**, in the winter.

kış'ır[r1] Peel, rind; skin; shell; crust. ~ **dimağı**, (*bio.*) cerebral cortex.

kışkırt·ı (*pol.*) Incitement. ~ **ıcı**, *a.* stimulating, provocative, inciting: *n.* agitator, inciter, instigator, *agent-provocateur*. ~ **ıcılık**, provocation, agitation. ~ **ılmak**, *vp.* ~ **ma**, incitement, instigation, provocation. ~ **mak (-i)**, excite, frighten; (*pol.*) incite, instigate, provoke.

kış·la (*mil.*) Barracks: ~ **hapsi**, confinement to barracks. ~ **la'k**[g1], winter quarters (animals/ nomads/army). ~ **lamak**, *vi.* become wintry/cold; pass/spend the winter. ~ **latmak (-i)**, *vc.* ~ **lık**, suitable for the winter; winter residence.

kışr- = KIŞIR.

kıt[1] *a.* Little, few; scarce; deficient. *adv.* Scarcely, rarely. ~ **kanaat**, having to be satisfied with little; in scarcity; barely: ~ **kanaat geçinmek**, eke out a living: ~ **ı** ~ **ına hesaplamak**, cut it fine: ~ **ı** ~ **ına idare etm.**, just be able to manage: ~ **ı** ~ **ına yaşamak**, just keep body and soul together: ~ **ı** ~ **ına yetişmek**, be barely sufficient.

kıta Portion, piece; (*geo.*) dry land, continent; district; (*mil.*) detachment (of troops); segment; size, dimension; (*lit.*) four-lined verse. ~ **+**, *a.* Continental: ~ **platform/sahanlık/şelfi**, continental shelf. ~ **at**[1], *pl.* (*mil.*) forces.

kıtal[i] A killing; battle; massacre, carnage.

kıtı'k[g1] (*tex.*) Flax waste; tow; stuffing (of mattress, etc.)

kıtıpiyos (*sl.*) Common, poor, trifling, insignificant.

kıtır (*cul.*) Maize grains cracked over a fire; (*col.*) lie. ~ **atmak**, tell a lie; make an impudent exaggeration: ~ ~, (*ech.*) crackling, crunching, gnashing: ~ ~ **kesmek**, kill in cold blood: ~ ~ **yemek**, crunch.

kıtır·cı (*sl.*) Liar. ~ **damak**, *vi.* make a crackling/

crunching sound. ~**datmak (-i)**, make stg. crackle/ crunch. ~**tı**, crackle, crunch.
kıt·lama Drinking tea (with lump of sugar in the mouth). ~**laşmak**, *vi.* become scarce. ~**lık**, scarcity; dearth; famine: ~**ına kıran girmek (-in)**, be a shortage of . . ..
kıvam Proper degree of consistency/maturity; propitious moment to do stg.; (*sp.*) fitness, form. ~**ına gelmek/ ~ ını bulmak**, come to the right consistency/ degree; be at the best possible moment (for some action): ~**ında olm.**, be in its prime.
kıvam·lanmak *vi.* Reach its prime/maturity. ~**lı**// (~**sız**), (not) having reached the proper degree of consistency/maturity.
kıvan·'ç[c1] Pleasure, content(edness); proper pride: ~ **duymak**, feel proud. ~**çlı**, pleased, happy. ~**mak (-le)**, be proud of: **(-e)**, be pleased with.
kıvıl *a.* Electric. ~ ~, constantly moving. ~**cım**, spark. ~**cımlanmak**, *vi.* catch fire, burn giving off sparks. ~**devimbilim**, electrodynamics. ~**dinimbilim**, electrostatics. ~**iter**, electromotive. ~**kesilgen**, electrolyte. ~**kesim(sel)**, electroly·sis/(-tic). ~**landırma**, electrification. ~**lık**, electricity. ~**mıknatıslık**, electromagnetism. ~**uç**, electrode.
kıvır ~ ~, in curls; wriggling, writhing: ~ **zıvır**, trifling, insignificant. ~**cı'k**[g1], *a.* curly, wavy; crisp: *n.* (*live.*) small-tailed curly-fleeced sheep; (*cul.*) its mutton: ~ **lahana**, (*bot.*) curly kale: ~ **marul/ salata**, (*bot.*) crisp curly-leaved cabbage-lettuce: ~ **saçlı**, curly-head: ~ **solungaç balığı**, (*ich.*) frill shark. ~**mak (-i)**, curl; twist; coil; (*tex.*) turn in and hem; crumple; make wavy, crimp, crinkle; invent a lie; put in order, do stg. successfully; (*sl.*) eat greedily: *vi.* succeed; turn; dance gracefully. ~**tma'ç**[c1], (*mod.*) hair-curler. ~**tmak (-i, -e)**, *vc.*
kıvra·cık Compact, easy to operate. ~**k**, supple; brisk; agile; tidy, orderly. ~**klık**, suppleness, agility, etc. ~**mak**, *vi.* become crushed/curly/ tangled. ~**nmak**, *vi.* writhe (with pain); be agitated; suffer. ~**tmak (-i)**, = KIVIRMAK; curl, etc. thoroughly.
kıvr·ık Curled, twisted; curly; dog-eared; convoluted; (*tex.*) hemmed, folded; (*min.*) lap: ~ **bacaklı**, (*zoo.*) cirripede: ~ **bağırsak**, (*bio.*) ileum: ~ **dal**, (*art.*) scrollwork: ~ **yapraklı**, (*bot.*) circinate. ~**ıklık**, curvature. ~**ılma**, *vn.*; (*geol.*) folding. ~**ılmak**, *vp.* = KIVRIMAK; be twisted, etc.; be curly; become rounded; writhe; (*fig.*) shrink into a narrow space: **kıvrıla kıvrıla gitmek**, (*aer.*) corkscrew. ~**ım**, twist; bend; curl; fold; (*geol.*) folding: ~ **kanadı**, (*geol.*) flank: ~ ~, curly; wavy: ~ ~ **kıvranmak**, (*med.*) writhe convulsively, be doubled up with pain: ~ **menteşesi**, (*geol.*) bend: ~ **süs**, (*art.*) fret, key-pattern. ~**ımlı**, (*geol.*) folded. ~**ıntı**, twist; bend; (*min.*) hook.
kıya (*leg.*) Murder; manslaughter. ~**bilim(ci)**, criminolo·gy/(-gist). ~**cı**, criminal.
kıyafet[i] General appearance/dress; costume; aspect; physiognomy. ~ **balosu**, fancy-dress ball: ~ **düşkünü**, wretchedly dressed: ~ **tebdili**, disguise: ~**ine düşkün**, particular about one's dress: ~**ini değiştirmek**, disguise o.s.
kıyafet·li In . . . dress/shape. ~**name**, (*lit.*) book

about costume; book on physiognomy. ~**siz**, badly-dressed; shabby, untidy. ~**sizlik**, shabbiness, etc.
kıyak (*col.*) Nice, pretty; smart, elegant. ~**çı**, (*sl.*) reckless gambler. ~**laşmak**, *vi.* become pretty/ smart, etc. ~**lık**, prettiness; smartness, elegance.
kıyam Act of rising/starting; standing up; (*pol.*) rebellion. ~ **etm.**, stand up; rebel; **(-e)**, prepare to, set about: ~ **flaması**, (*naut.*) Blue Peter.
kıyamet[i] (*rel.*) Resurrection of the Dead; end of the world; (*fig.*) great disaster; tumult. ~ **alameti!**, how dreadful!: ~ **gibi/kadar**, very much, lots, heaps of: ~ **günü**, (*rel.*) Day of Judgement, doomsday: ~ **kopmak**, (*rel.*) the dead rise again; (*fig.*) be very noisy: ~ **koptu**, a great disaster has occurred; all hell broke loose: ~ **mi kopar?**, what's it matter?; is it important?: ~ **mi koptu?**, what the dickens has happened?; what the devil does it matter?: ~**e kadar**, for ever and ever: ~ **(ler)i koparmak**, create an uproar; 'raise hell'.
kıyas Comparison, analogy; (*math.*) reference; (*phil.*) reasoning, syllogism; rule; opinion. ~ **etm.**, compare: ~ **hat/kot/noktası**, (*math.*) datum: ~ **ile**, by analogy: ~ **kabul etmez**, incomparable: ~ **üzere (bu)**, by analogy with this; at this rate: ~**a muhalefet**, (*ling.*) irregularity. ~**en**, by comparison/ analogy/rule.
kıya·sal (*leg.*) ~ **düşük**, criminal abortion. ~**sıya**, murderous; merciless; (*fin.*) cut-throat (competition).
kıyas·i In accordance with the rule; (*ling.*) regular; (*phil.*) analogous. ~**lama**, *vn.* comparison; analogy. ~**lamak (-i, -le)**, compare *A* with *B*.
kıydırmak (-i, -e) *vc.* = KIYMAK.
kıygı Injustice; cruelty. ~**n**, unjustly treated; wronged; (*leg.*) injured party. ~**nlık**, being unjustly treated; oppression: ~**a uğratmak**, treat unjustly.
kıyı Edge; coast, shore, littoral; bank; corner; extremity. ~ +, *a.* Coastal: ~ **boyunca**, coastwise: ~ **çizgisi**, coastline: ~ **çukuru**, ditch, palisade: ~ **çulluğu**, (*orn.*) bar-tailed godwit: ~ **dili**, sandbar, spit: ~ **kırlangıcı**, (*orn.*) arctic tern: ~ **koşarı**, (*orn.*) black-winged stilt: ~ **resifi**, (*geo.*) barrier reef: ~ **sıra(da)**, along the shore: ~ **süsü**, border, edging: ~**da bucak/köşede**, in out-of-the-way places: ~**dan** ~**dan**, along the shore; (*fig.*) very cautiously: ~**dan gitmek**, (*naut.*) stand in close to land: ~**sına bucağına kadar bilmek (-in)**, know stg. inside out.
kıyı·cı[1] *n.* Shore-fisherman; beachcomber. ~**lamak**, *vi.* go along the shore. ~**sal**, coastal.
kıyı·cı[2] *n.* Who cuts up; tobacco cutter. *a.* Cruel, pitiless. ~**cılık**, cruelty: ~ **etm.**, treat cruelly. ~**k**, minced; chopped up. ~**lmak**, *vp.* = KIYMAK; (*fig.*) feel weak, ache all over. ~**m**, *n.* act of mincing/chopping; cut; cruelty; massacre. ~**mlık**, amount minced/chopped/cut. ~**n**, cruelty. ~**ncı**, cruel. ~**n'ç**[c1], torture. ~**nmak**, *vi.* feel weak, ache. ~**ntı**, stg. chopped up; griping (of stomach); aching (of limbs); languor.
kıyışmak (-le) Come to an agreement with s.o.; (*sp.*) compete with, race against.

kıy·ma *vn. (cul.)* Minced meat. ~**mak (-i)**, *(cul.)* mince, chop up finely; slaughter, massacre; decide on: **(-e)**, bring o.s. to injure s.o.; not spare (expense); sacrifice: **kıyamamak**, spare s.o.'s life; have pity on; grudge (expense); not have the heart (to do stg.). ~**malı**, *(cul.)* containing minced meat. ~**malık**, *(cul.)* suitable for mincing.

kıymet[i] Value, worth; price; esteem. ~ **biçmek**, evaluate, assess: ~ **bilmek**, appreciate the value of; show gratitude for: ~ **üzerinden**, *(fin.)* ad valorem: ~**i artmak**, *vi.* appreciate, increase in value: ~**ini düşürmek**, *vt.* depreciate: ~**ler**, assets: ~**ten düşmek**, *vi.* depreciate.

kıymet·lendirme *vn.* Valuation, assessment. ~**lendirmek (-i)**, utilize; value, assess; increase the value of. ~**lenmek**, *vi.* increase in value; be worth. ~**li**/ ~**tar**, valuable; precious. ~**siz**, valueless, worthless.

kıymı¹k[ğı] *(carp.)* Splinter, sliver.

kız *n.* Girl; daughter; virgin; *(ast.)* Virgo; *(gamb.)* queen. *a.* Girl-; female-. ~ **alıp vermek**, intermarry: ~ **almak (-den)**, marry into a family: ~**BÖCEĞİ**: ~ **gibi**, new, untouched; beautiful: ~ **ismi**, maiden name: ~ **istemek**, ask for a girl in marriage: ~ **kaçırmak**, elope with a girl: ~ **kardeş**, (younger) sister (= ABLA): ~ **kilimi**, KİLİM made by a nomad girl for her trousseau: ~ KUŞU: ~ **lisesi**, *(ed.)* girls' high school: ~ **o gencin dengi değil**, the girl is not a good match for the young man: ~ **oğlan** ~, young virgin: ~ **tarafı**, the bride's family: ~ **vermek**, give one's daughter in marriage: ~**a dünür düşmek**, ask for a girl in marriage for s.o. else: ~**ı kısrağı (-in)**, one's womenfolk: ~**ım sana söylüyorum gelinim sen anla!**, make remarks to *A* but intended for *B*: ~**ın kısmeti bağlandı**, somehow she never found a husband: ~**ın kısmeti çıktı**, s.o. has asked to marry the girl: ~**ını (evladını) dövmeyen dizini döver**, spare the rod and spoil the child: ~**ını vermek (-e)**, accept s.o. as son-in-law: ~**lar ağası**, *(his.)* chief black eunuch (in the palace).

kıza¹k[ğı] Sledge, toboggan; slide; *(naut.)* slipway, launching ways; *(carp.)* stiffener; *(eng.)* carriage, slide, chute. ~ **kaymak**, slide on ice; sledge: ~ **yapmak**, slide; *(mot.)* skid: ~**a çekmek**, *(naut.)* draw up on the slipway; *(fig.)* withdraw from use; retire s.o.

kızak·lamak *vi.(mot.)* Skid. ~**lı**, ~ **masa**, expanding table. ~**lık**, *(carp.)* joist.

kızala¹k[ğı] *(bot.)* Corn poppy.

kızamı¹k[ğı] *(med.)* Measles. ~ **çıkarmak**, have measles. ~**çık**, German measles. ~**lı**, child with measles.

kızan Youth, lad; sturdy country lad. ~**lık**, youth.

kızar·mak *vi.* Turn red; blush; *(bot.)* ripen; *(cul.)* be roasted/toasted: **kızarıp bozarmak**, grow red and pale by turns (from shame, etc.): **kızarmış patates**, *(cul.)* chips. ~**tı**, red/roasted part; *(med.)* erythema. ~**tılı**, roasted. ~**tma**, *vn.; (cul.)* roasted; roast meat, etc. ~**tmak (-i)**, make red; cause to blush; *(cul.)* roast, grill, fry.

kız·böceği[ni] *(ent.)* Broad-bodied libellula/darter. ~**böcekleri**, *(ent.)* dragonflies. ~**cağız**, the dear little girl.

kızdır·ılmak *vp.* ~**ma**, *vn.; (mot.)* ignition. ~**mak (-i)**, heat; anger, annoy; = KIZMAK.

kızgın Hot; red-hot; ablaze; angry, excited, feverish; *(zoo.)* on heat, in rut. ~ **bulut**, *(geol.)* ash cloud (of volcano): ~ **demir**, brand(ing iron). ~**laşmak**, *vi.* become hot/angry, etc. ~**lık**, great heat; fury; feverish excitement; sexual excitement.

kızıl *a.* Red; red-hot; crimson; golden; *(fig.)* Communist, Red. *adv.* Utterly, completely. *n.* *(med.)* Scarlet fever. ~ **akbaba**, *(orn.)* griffon vulture: ~ **akçe**, gold coins: ~ **aşı boyası**, *(geol.)* red ochre: ~ **başlı örümcek kuşu**, *(orn.)* woodchat-shrike: ~ **buğday**, *(bot.)* spelt: ~ **cahil** utterly ignorant: ~ **çam**, *(bot.)* Calabrian pine: ~ **deli/divane**, raving lunatic: ~ **deniz**, *pr.n. (geo.)* Red Sea: ~ **dilbalığı**, *(ich.)* lemon sole: ~ **doğan**, *(orn.)* marsh harrier: ~ **gerdan (kuşu)**, *(orn.)* Eurasian robin (redbreast): ~ **gerdanlı incirkuşu**, *(orn.)* red-throated pipit: ~ **geyik**, *(zoo.)* red deer: ~ **gürgen**, *(bot.)* copper beech: ~ **iblis**, s.o. very evil/malicious: ~ **kantaron**, *(bot.)* gentian: ~ **keklik** = KINALI: ~ **kırlangıç**, *(orn.)* red-rumped swallow: ~ **kuyruklu**, *(orn.)* red-tailed: ~ **orkinos**, *(ich.)* bluefin tuna: ~ **saçlı**, red-head, carrot-top: ~ **su tavuğu**, *(orn.)* corncrake: ~ **suyosunları**, *(bot.)* red algae: ~ **şahin**, *(orn.)* long-legged buzzard: ~ **yılan**, *(zoo.)* Oriental pipe snake: ~ **yüksükotu**, *(bot.)* foxglove: ~**a kayma**, *(ast.)* red slip. [*Also* = AL; KIRMIZI].

kızıl·ağa¹ç[cı] *(bot.)* Common alder; *(carp.)* Brazil wood. ~**ay**, *pr.n. (soc.)* Red Crescent. ~**altı** = ~ÖTESİ. ~**bacak**, *(orn.)* redshank. ~**baş**, *pr.n. (rel.)* (member of) Shiite sect; *(pej.)* person of loose morals: ~ **ördek**, *(orn.)* red-crested pochard. ~**başlık**, *(rel.)* being a Shiite. ~**ca**, reddish: **kıyamet kopmak**, a 'hell of a row' break out. ~**cı¹k**[ğı], *(bot.)* cornelian cherry (tree); cornel wood: ~ **sopası**, caning, birching. ~**cıkgiller**, *(bot.)* dogwood family, Cornaceae. ~**derili**, *pr.n. (ethn.)* Red Indian, Redskin. ~**elma**, *(myth.)* ideal land; promised land; Rome; utopia for Panturkists. ~**ha¹ç**[cı], *pr.n. (soc.)* Red Cross. ~**ımsı**, reddish. ~**ısı**, *(met.)* hot days at end of July. ~**kanat**, *(ich.)* rudd. ~**kantaron**, *(bot.)* purple gentian. ~**kantarongiller**, *(bot.)* gentian family, Gentianaceae. ~**kök**[ü] = KÖKBOYASI. ~**kuyruk**, *(orn.)* redstart. ~**laşmak**, *vi.* become red; *(pol.)* turn Communist. ~**lık**, redness; red colour; glow; *(mod.)* rouge; *(met.)* red sky: ~ **otu**, *(bot.)* common centaury.

kızılmak *imp. v.* Get angry.

kızıl·ötesi[ni] *(phys.)* Infra-red (rays). ~**şap**, light purple. ~**tı**, redness; red spot. ~**yaprak**, *(bot.)* agrimony. ~**yara**, *(med.)* carbuncle; anthrax. ~**yörük**, *(med.)* erysipelas.

kızış·ık Angry; excited. ~**mak**, *vi.* get angry/ excited; become heated; increase in fury/violence; *(zoo.)* be on heat; *(agr.)* rot down and become hot. ~**tırıcı**, subversive, provocative. ~**tırmak (-i)**, *vc.*; encourage; incite, provoke.

kız·kuşu[nu] *(orn.)* Lapwing, peewit. ~**lık**, maidenhood; virginity: ~ **zarı**, *(bio.)* hymen: ~**ını bozmak**, deflower. ~**memesi**[ni], *(col.)* grapefruit.

kızmabirader A party game (with dice).

kızmak vi. Get hot; glow; get red-hot; get angry; get excited; (zoo.) be on heat; (orn.) become broody. **kızmaya görsün!**, beware lest he gets angry!: **kızmış**, angry; disgusted.

ki conj. [211] That; as; so that, in order that; seeing that, since [**gelmedi** ~ **bilsin**, how can he know since he didn't come?]. int. (of surprise) Then!, behold!, see! [**geldim** ~ **kimseler yok**, I came but found no one!; **baktım** ~ **sandık bomboş**, behold the box was empty!]. relative pron. [72] Who, which, that [**bir çocuk** ~ **çalışmaz**, a child who does not work]. Expressing stg. left unsaid [**öyle şaştım** ~!, I was so surprised that . . .!]. Used with BİLMEK [**bilmem** ~ **ne yapmalı**, I don't know what one should do!].

-ki¹/-kü a./n. suf. [69] Forming possessive pronouns [**benimki**, mine; **çocuklarınki**, those of the children]; also adjectives [**bugünkü ders**, today's lesson; **Londra'daki Türkler**, the Turks in London].

-ki² n. suf. [222] = -Gİ [İÇKİ].

KİB = KÖY İŞLERİ BAKAN(LIĞ)I.

kibar Noble, distinguished; cultured, refined, polite; rich. ~ **bir adam**, a real gentleman: ~ **düşkünüdür**, he has seen better days.

kibar·ca Nobly; politely. ~**laşmak**, vi. become more refined; (pej.) assume superior airs. ~**lık**, greatness; nobility; gentle birth; culture, refinement: ~ **akmak** = PAÇA: ~ **budalası**, self-important: ~ **düşkünü**, s.o. attaching too much importance to nobility, etc.: ~ **etm.**, behave like a gentleman: ~ **taslamak**, give o.s. airs, play the fine gentleman: ~ı **tutmak**, behave pretentiously.

kiberneti·kᵍⁱ (phys., bio.) Cybernetics.

kib·irʳⁱ Pride, conceit; disdain; arrogance. ~**den kabarmak**, be blown up with conceit. ~**lenmek**, vi. behave disdainfully/arrogantly. ~**li**, proud, conceited; disdainful; arrogant, contemptuous.

kibritⁱ Match; (obs.) sulphur. ~ **çakmak**, strike a match: ~ **suyu**, (chem.) dilute sulphuric acid. ~**çi**, matchseller; (fig.) stingy person.

kifaf·ınefs = KEFAF. ~**lanmak (-le)**, make do with whatever food one finds.

kifayetⁱ Adequacy, sufficiency; competence; ability, capacity. ~ **etm.**, suffice: **(-le)**, be content with. ~**li**, competent; adequate. ~**siz(lik)**, inadequa·te/(-cy): ~ **kararı**, (adm.) referring back (for further information).

kikⁱ (naut.) Gig; skiff.

kikirik Slim, tall; (col.) John Bull.

kikla (ich.) Ballan wrasse.

kiklo·n (met.) Cyclone. ~**p**, (myth.) Cyclops. ~**tron**, (phys.) cyclotron.

kil (geol.) Clay; argil; fuller's earth. ~ **taşı**, shale, claystone: ~ **yapraktaşı**, slate.

kile (math.) Bushel (36.5 kg.).

kiler Pantry, larder; store-cupboard. ~ **kınkanatlısı**, (ent.) bacon beetle. ~**ci**, (obs.) steward, butler.

kilermeni (geol.) Red clay; (med.) bole armeniac.

Kilikya (geo.) Cilicia. ~ **köknarı**, (bot.) Cilician fir.

kilim (dom.) Woven matting; pileless carpet. ~**i kebeyi sermek**, settle down in a place. ~**ci(lik)**, (work of) KİLİM-weaver/-seller.

kilise Church. ~ **hukuku**, canon law. ~**cik**, chapel.

kili·tᵈⁱ Lock; (naut.) shackle. ~ **açmak**, unlock: ~ **ağızlığı**, keyhole: ~ **altına almak**, lock stg. away: ~ **altında**, under lock and key: ~ **aynası**, finger-plate: ~ **dili**, bolt (of lock): ~ **gibi (ağız)**, tight-lipped, discreet: ~ **gibi olm.**, be close and loyal friends: ~ **kürek olm.**, protect (a place): ~ **nokta/yeri**, (fig.) keypoint: ~ **taşı**, (arch.) keystone: ~ **vurmak (-i)**, lock (up): ~**i küreği olmamak**, be left unlocked/unprotected.

kilit·lemek (-i) Lock; (eng.) lock into each other. ~**lenme**, vn.; interlocking. ~**lenmek**, vp. be locked; (teeth) be clenched: vi. interlock. ~**letmek (-i, -e)**, vc. ~**li**, having a lock; lock-up; locked. ~**siz**, without a lock; unlocked: ~ **küreksiz**, open, unlocked.

kiliz (bot.) Reed. ~**balığı**ⁿⁱ, (ich.) tench. ~**man**, reed-bed.

killi (geol.) Argillaceous; clayey. ~ **şist**, shale.

kilo (math.) Kilo(gram). ~ **almak//vermek**, put on//lose weight: ~ **ile**, by the kilo. ~**amper**, (el.) kiloampere. ~**gram**, kilogram. ~**gramkuvvet**, (phys.) kilogram-force. ~**grammetre**, (phys.) kilogram-metre. ~**hertz**, (el.) kilohertz. ~**jul**, (el.) kilojoule. ~**kalori**, (phys.) kilocalorie. ~**litre**, (math.) kilolitre. ~**luk**, weighing . . . kilos. ~**metre**, (math.) kilometre: ~ **kare**, square kilometre: ~ **küp**, cubic kilometre. ~**parsek**, (ast.) kiloparsec. ~**sikl**, (el.) kilocycle. ~**ton**, (math.) kilotonne. ~**vat**, (el.) kilowatt: ~ **saati**, kilowatt-hour.

kils (geol.) Chalk, limestone. ~**i**, calcareous.

kilükal Gossip, tittle-tattle.

kilüs (bio.) Chyle.

kim¹ pron. [72, 85] Who?; whoever. ~ **bilir?**, who knows?: ~ **e, (dum duma)**, nobody will notice it; nobody knows anything about it: ~ ~ **inle o da benimle**, everyone has his bête noire and I am his: ~ **o?**, who's there?, who's that?: ~ **oluyor?**, who does he think he is?: ~ **vurduya gitti**, whoever killed him is not known: ~**e?**, to whom?: ~**e ne?**, what does it matter to anyone?: ~**e rastgelsem beğenirsiniz/iyi!**, guess whom I met!: ~**i**, whom; some: ~**i . . . ~i . . .**, some . . . others . . .: ~**i enine çeker ~ı boyuna**, everyone has a right to his own opinion: ~**i kez**, sometimes: ~**i kimsesi**, the members of his family: ~**i köprü bulamaz geçmeye**, ~**i su bulamaz içmeye**, our lives/fates are all different: ~**i zaman . . ., ~i zaman . . .**, sometimes . . . sometimes . . .: ~**in(?)**, whose(?): ~**in arabasına binerse, onun türküsünü çağırır**, he changes the tune to suit the boss/occasion: ~**in haddine?**, who would dare?: ~**ine hayhay**, ~**ine vay vay**, some are lucky and others are not: ~**iniz**, some of you: ~**i(si)**, some people: ~**miş?**, who is he supposed to be?

kim² conj. (obs.) = Kİ.

kim. = KİMYA. ~ **s.** = KİMYA SİMGESİ.

kim·denlik Generic. ~**esne**, n. (obs.) = KİMSE. ~**lik**, identity; credentials: ~ **belge/cüzdanı**, birth certificate; identity papers: ~ **kartı**, identity card: ~ **simgesi**, bookplate: ~**i açığa anlaşılmak/çıkmak**, be identified; have one's cover blown.

kimono (mod.) Kimono; dressing-gown.

kimse pron. [78] Somebody, someone; anybody;

anyone; a person; (+ *neg.*) nobody, no one. ~
çakmadan, (*sl.*) without anybody noticing: ~ **halin
nedir demedi**, no one took any interest in me: ~
kendi memleketinde peygamber olmaz, no one is a
prophet in his own country: ~ **üstüne alınmasın**,
let no one think this refers to him: ~ **nin burnu
kanamadan**, without hurting anyone; bloodlessly:
~ **si olmamak**, be alone in the world: ~ **ye danış-
madan**, on one's own initiative: ~ **ye eyvallah
etmezdi**, he sought nobody's favour: ~ **ye söyleme
emi!**, don't tell anyone, will you!: ~ **ye uymaz**, he
goes his own way heeding no one.
kimse·cik *pron.* [78] ~ **ler kalmamış//yok**, there's
not a soul left//to be seen. ~ **siz**, alone; orphaned;
destitute; desolate. ~ **sizlik**, a being alone/uncared
for; destitution.
kimüs (*bio.*) Chyme.
kimya Chemistry; (*fig.*) rare and precious thing.
~ **ca**, chemically. ~ **cı(lık)/**~ **ger(lik)**, (work of)
chemist. ~ **doğrulumu**[nu], (*bot.*) chemotropism.
~ **göçümü**[nü], (*bio.*) chemotaxis. ~ **sal/kimyevi**,
chemical; chemo-: ~ **aşın(dır)ma**, corrosion: ~ **bireşim**, (*bio.*) chemosynthesis: ~ **maddeler**,
chemicals: ~ **sağı(l)tım**, (*med.*) chemotherapy.
kimyon (*bot.*) Cummin. ~ **i**, sage-green.
kin Malice; grudge; hatred. ~ **bağlamak (-e)**, bear
a grudge against s.o.: ~ **beslemek/gütmek**, cherish
a grudge; **(için)**, be bitter about: ~ **tutmak**, nourish
a secret hatred.
-kin *a./n. suf.* [223] = -GİN [BİTKİN].
kinaye Allusion; hint; insinuation; (*lit.*) metaphor.
~ **li**, allusive; sarcastic; knowingly.
kin·ci/~ **dar/**~ **li** Vindictive; nourishing a grudge.
~ **cilik**, vindictiveness.
kine·mati[k][ği] (*phys.*) Kinematic(s). ~ **ti**[k][ği], kine-
tic(s).
kin·i[k][ği] (*phil.*) *n.* Cynic. *a.* Cynical. ~ **izm**,
cynicism.
kinin (*chem.*) Quinine.
kinistin ~ **valf**, (*naut.*) sea-cock.
kiniş (*carp.*) Slot; groove; mortise.
kip[i] Example; (*phil.*) temporary quality; (*phil.*)
mode; (*ling.*) mood; paradigm.
kipe (*sp.*) Sudden straightening of the body.
kipkirli Extremely dirty.
kip·lik Modality. ~ **örne**[l][k][ği], (*eng.*) template. ~ **sel**,
modal.
kir Dirt, filth; uncleanliness. ~ **götürmek**, *vi.*
(cloth) not show the dirt; **(-i)**, be very dirty: ~
tutmak, show the dirt.
kira A hiring; hire; rent; rental. ~ **arabası**, cab:
~ **ile tutmak**, rent, hire: ~ **karşılık/parası**, rental:
~ **mukavele/sözleşmesi**, lease; (*naut., aer.*) charter:
~ **da olm.**, be hired/rented: ~ **ya vermek**, hire out,
let: ~ **ya veren**, lessor.
kira·cı Who rents/hires; tenant; carrier (of goods):
~ **nın kiralaması**, sub-letting. ~ **cılık**, renting,
hiring; tenancy; carriage (of goods). ~ **lama**, *vn.*
letting, hiring. ~ **lamak (-i, -e)**, hire out, let: **(-i,
-den)**, hire, rent; (*naut., aer.*) charter. ~ **lanmak**, *vp.*
~ **lı**, rented, let; hired. ~ **lık**, for hire, to let:
~ **kadın/kız**, prostitute: ~ **kasa**, (*fin.*) deposit-
box (in a bank).

kiraz (*bot.*) Cherry. ~ **ağacı**, cherry-tree: ~ **ayı**,
month of May: ~ **boncuğu**, (*geol.*) chrysoprase: ~
çekirdeği, cherry pit/stone: ~ **dudaklı**, full red-
lipped: ~ **kuşu**, (*orn.*) black-headed bunting: ~
rengi, cherry-red, cerise: ~ **sineği**, (*ent.*) cherry
fly. ~ **elması**[nı], (*bot.*) lady-apple. ~ **lık**, cherry
orchard.
kirde (*cul.*) Type of maize bread.
kire[l]**ç**[ci] (*chem.*) Lime. ~ +, *a.* Lime-; calc-: ~ **gibi
olm.**, be very white/pale: ~ **kuyusu**, lime-pit: ~
ocağı, lime-kiln: ~ **söndürmek**, slake lime: ~ **suyu**,
(*chem.*) lime water: ~ **taşı**, (*geol.*) limestone,
marble.
kireç·çi Lime-burner/-seller. ~ **çil**, (*bot.*) lime-
tolerant. ~ **kaymağı**[nı], (*chem.*) slaked lime.
~ **lemek (-i)**, put in lime; add lime; whitewash.
~ **lenme**, *vn.*; calcination; scaling; (*med.*) calcification. ~ **lenmek**, *vi.* calcify; form scale. ~ **leşme**, *vn.*;
calcification. ~ **leşmek**, *vi.* calcify. ~ **li**, calcareous;
containing lime; whitewashed. ~ **lik**, *n.* limestone:
a. containing much lime. ~ **silemek**, (*chem.*) calcinate; dry out. ~ **sizleş(tir)me**, decalcification.
~ **sütü**[nü], whitewash. ~ **taşı**[nı], (*geol.*) limestone.
~ **yeren**, (*bot.*) lime-intolerant.
kiremi[l]**t**[di] Tile. ~ **kırmızı**, brick-red. ~ **çi(lik)**,
(work of) tiler. ~ **li**, tiled: ~ **kaplumbağa**, (*zoo.*)
hawkbill turtle.
kirez = KİRAZ.
kirgiderici (*chem.*) Detergent.
Kiril ~ +, *a.* (*ling.*) Cyrillic.
kiriş (*bio.*) Catgut; tendon; (*mil.*) bowstring; (*mus.*)
violin string; (*arch.*) beam, joist, girder, rafter;
(*math.*) chord. ~ **i kırmak**, (*sl.*) run away.
kiriş·leme *vn.: adv.* set on edge. ~ **lemek (-i)**, string
a bow. ~ **li**, (*arch.*) having joists: ~ **köprü**, girder
bridge. ~ **lik**, (*carp.*) suitable for beams.
kirizma (*agr.*) Trenching of land. ~ **etm./**~ **lamak
(-i)**, double-trench.
kirkit[i] (*tex.*) Carpet-weaver's comb.
kir·lenmek *vi.* Become dirty; be dirtied; be polluted;
become morally soiled; (*rel.*) be(come) unclean;
(woman) menstruate; (girl) be defiled. ~ **letmek
(-i)**, make dirty, soil; pollute; slander, calumniate;
rape. ~ **li**, dirty, soiled; dirty linen, laundry;
(woman) menstruating: ~ **çamaşırlarını ortaya
çıkarmak/dökmek (-in)**, show up s.o.'s misdeeds:
~ **çıkı(n)**, s.o. rich by stinginess: ~ **hanım peyniri**,
(*cul.*) soft rich white cheese: ~ **su**, waste (water):
~ **ye atmak**, put aside to be washed. ~ **likan**, (*bio.*)
venous blood. ~ **lilik**, dirtiness; pollution; (*rel.*)
uncleanness. ~ **loz**, (*pej.*) dirty, slovenly.
kirman (*mil.*) Fortress.
kirmen (*tex.*) Distaff.
kirpi (*zoo.*) Hedgehog. ~ **balığı**[nı], (*ich.*) porcupine-
fish.
kirpi[l]**k**[ği] (*bio.*) Eyelash; cilium. ~ **imi kırpmadım**,
I didn't sleep a wink. ~ **kanatlı(lar)**, (*ent.*) thrips.
~ **li(ler)**, (*zoo.*) ciliate(s). ~ **si**, ciliary.
kirtil Fishing-basket.
kirve (*rel.*) Sponsor of boy being circumcised.
kisbi Acquired (not natural).
kispet[i] (*sp.*) Tk. wrestler's tights. ~ **çıkarılması**,
being debagged/ignominiously defeated.

kist[i] (*med.*) Cyst. ~ **iltihabı,** cystitis.
kisve(t[i]**)** (*mod.*) Garment; special costume, uniform.
kiş Check (in chess). ~ **etm.,** put in check.
kişi *n.* Person; human being; entity; (*th.*) character; (*ling.*) person. *indef. pron.* One, you; man. ~ +, *a.* Personal: ~ **adı,** forename, first/given name: ~ **adıl/zamiri,** (*ling.*) personal pronoun: ~ **bilmediğinin düşmanıdır,** man hates what he does not understand: ~ **dokunulmazlığı,** (*leg.*) personal inviolability: ~ **eki,** (*ling.*) personal ending, declination: ~ **ektiğini biçer/ettiğini bulur,** as you sow so shall you reap: ~ **kapasitesi,** (*th.*) seating capacity: ~ **refikinden azar,** evil communications corrupt good manners: ~**de yanılma,** mistaken identity: ~**ler kütüğü,** state register of persons.
kişi·ce Personally. ~**leştirme,** (*lit.*) personification; (*th.*) characterization. ~**lik,** *n.* personality; individuality; humanity; (*mod.*) best clothes: *a.* special to/suitable for . . . persons: ~ **kazanmak,** develop one's personality. ~**likdışı**[nı], impersonal. ~**liksiz,** having no character/personality. ~**oğlu,** of gentle birth/good family. ~**sel,** personal, individual, private: ~ **dava,** (*leg.*) civil action: ~ **denklem,** personal equation: ~ **durum,** personal/civil status: ~ **girişim,** (*fin.*) individual enterprise: ~ **iyelik,** private property: ~ **varlık,** private fortune. ~**zade** = ~OĞLU.
kişmiş (*bot.*) Small black seedless grape/raisin.
kişnemek *vi.* (Horse) neigh.
kişniş (*bot.*) Coriander. ~ **şekeri,** (*cul.*) sweet containing a coriander seed.
KİT = KAMU İKTİSADİ TEŞEKKÜLÜ.
kitab- = KİTAP. ~**e,** inscription. ~**eli,** with an inscription; with an ornamental pattern. ~**elik,** (*art.*) inscription panel. ~**et**[i], art of writing; writing lesson; (*lit.*) essay writing; literary style; office/ duties of a clerk/secretary. ~**evi**[ni], bookshop; publishing-house. ~**i,** connected with books; bookish.
kita[i]**p**[bı] Books; (*rel.*) sacred book. ~ **açacağı,** paperknife: ~ **biti,** (*ent.*) book louse: ~ **desteği,** book-end/-rest: ~ **dolabı,** bookcase: ~ **ehli,** (*rel.*) people of the Book (Jews and Christians): ~ **eleştiri/tenkidi,** (*pub.*) book-review: ~ **etiketi,** book-plate: ~ **gibi,** (*sl.*) very pretty (girl): ~ **gömleği,** book-jacket, dust-wrapper: ~ **hakları,** (*leg.*) royalties: ~ **imi,** (*pub.*) imprint: ~ **kurdu,** (*zoo., fig.*) book-worm: ~ **rafı,** bookshelf: ~ **rahlesi,** book-rest/-stand: ~ **resmi,** illustration: ~SARAYI: ~ **sergisi,** bookstall: ~ **yazısı,** printed letters: ~**a el basmak,** take an oath (on a sacred book); be quite certain about stg.: ~**a kapanmak,** be absorbed in a book: ~**a/**~**ına uydurmak,** do stg. illegal in what seems a legal way; get round the law: ~**ı gözden geçirmek/karıştırmak,** dip into/glance through a book: ~**ı kapmak,** cease to read.
kitap·ça Pamphlet. ~**çı,** book-printer/-seller. ~**çı**[i]**k**[ğı], pamphlet, brochure. ~**çıl,** bookish. ~**çılık,** printing, publishing; book-selling; the book trade. ~**deliliği**[ni], bibliomania. ~**lık,** *n.* bookcase; library, reading-room; library (of

books): *a.* suitable for books. ~**lıkbilim,** librarianship. ~**sarayı**[nı], large public library. ~**sever,** bibliophile. ~**sız,** without books; (*rel.*) pagan.
kitara (*mus.*) Kithara; guitar.
kitin (*zoo.*) Chitin.
kitle = KÜTLE.
kitonlar (*zoo.*) Chitons.
kitre (*bot.*) Gum tragacanth.
kivi (*orn.*) Kiwi, apteryx.
kiyanus (*chem.*) Cyanogen. ~**lu,** cyanic.
kiyaset[i] Shrewdness, sagacity.
kizir (*adm.*) Assistant to village headman.
kkal. = KİLOKALORİ.
K·K = KIZILAY KURUMU. ~**Kİ** = (*aer.*) KISA KALKIŞ VE İNİŞ. ~**KK** = KARA KUVVETLERİ KOMUTAN(LIĞ)I. ~**Kuv.** = KARA KUVVETLERİ.
kladus (*zoo.*) Branch, clade.
klaket[i] (*cin.*) Clacker.
klakson (*mot.*) Horn, klaxon.
klan (*ethn.*) Clan.
klapa (*mod.*) Point of collar.
klarnet(çi) (*mus.*) Clarinet(tist).
klasifikasyon Classification.
kla·sik (*art./lit.*) *n.* Classic. *a.* Classic(al); typical, standard. ~**sikçi,** (*ed.*) classical scholar. ~**sikçilik,** (*th.*) classicism. ~**sikleşmek,** *vi.* become a classic. ~**sisizm,** classicism.
klasör Filing cabinet.
klastik (*geol.*) Clastic.
klav·sen (*mus.*) Clavichord. ~**ye,** clavier, keyboard.
kleptoman Kleptomaniac. ~**i,** kleptomania.
klik (*soc.*) Clique; (*pol.*) caucus.
kliket[i] (*mot.*) Pinking. ~**leşmek,** *vi.* pink, knock.
klima Climate. ~ **cihazı,** air-conditioning apparatus. ~**tize,** air-conditioned: ~ **etm.,** air-condition. ~**toloji,** climatology.
klini[i]**k**[ği] (*med.*) Clinic. ~ +, *a.* Clinical.
klips (*mod.*) Brooch, etc. held with a spring clip.
kliring (*fin.*) Clearing. ~ **odası,** clearing house.
klişe (*pub.*) Cliché; block; engraving; (*fig.*) cliché. ~**leşmek,** *vi.* become a cliché.
klm. = (*ling.*) KULLANILMIYOR.
klor (*chem.*) Chlorine. ~**al,** chloral. ~**at,** chlorate. ~**hidrik,** hydrochloric. ~**ik,** chloric. ~**it,** chlorite. ~**lama,** *vn.* (*med.*) chlorination. ~**lamak (-i),** (*med.*) chlorinate; (*mil.*) spray with chlorine. ~**lanmak,** *vp.* ~**ofil,** (*bot.*) chlorophyll. ~**oform,** (*chem.*) chloroform. ~**omisetin,** (*med.*) chloromycetine. ~**oplast**[i], (*bot.*) chloroplast. ~**oz,** (*med., bot.*) chlorosis. ~**ölçer,** (*chem.*) chlorimeter. ~**ür,** chloride.
kloş (*mod.*) Bell-shaped shirt; (*agr.*) cloche.
klü[i]**p**[bü] = KULÜP.
klüz (*geo.*) Gorge.
km. = KİLOMETRE.
koala (*zoo.*) Koala bear.
koalisyon (*pol.*) Coalition. ~ **kabinesi,** coalition government.
koati (*zoo.*) Coati.
kobalt[i] (*chem.*) Cobalt. ~ **bombası,** cobalt bomb.
kobar (*ich.*) Leaping grey mullet.
ko·bay (*zoo.*) Guinea-pig, cavy. ~**bra,** cobra.

koca[1] *n.* Husband. ~ **bulmak**, find a husband: ~ **ya varmak**, (woman) marry: ~ **ya vermek**, marry off (daughter).

koca[2] *a.* Old, ancient; large, great; important, famous. *n.* Old man, elder. ~ **albacak**, (*orn.*) redshank: ~ **baş**, cattle: ~ BAŞ: ~ **herif olm.**, (*vulg.*) (child) grow like a man: ~ **oğlan**, (*jok.*) bear.

koca·baş (*orn.*) Hawfinch; (*bot.*) large beet. ~ **başı**, (*adm.*) village headman. ~ **göz**, (*orn.*) stone curlew. ~ **karı**, old woman: ~ **ilacı**, (*med.*) folk remedy: ~ **lakırdısı**, old wives' tales; silly nonsense: ~ **soğuğu**, (*met.*) cold spell (at end of March): ~ **zırıltısı**, cackle of old women. ~ **la**[l]**k**[ğı], (*orn.*) (?) red kite. ~ **lı**, married (woman). ~ **lık**, husbandhood; old age. ~ **(l)mak**, *vi.* age, grow old. ~ **(l)tmak (-i)**, *vc.* ~ **man**, very big, bulky. ~ **manca**, quite big, biggish. ~ **sız(lık)**, (a being) unmarried// widowed. ~ **yemiş**, (*bot.*) strawberry tree.

kocunmak *vi.* Take offence; sulk; be scared.

kocuşmak (-le) Embrace one another.

koç[u] (*live.*) Ram; (*ast.*) Aries. ~ BAŞI: ~ BOYNUZU: ~ **burunlu**, Roman-nosed: ~ **katımı**, (*live.*) (time for) putting ram to the ewes: ~ **yiğit**, sturdy/plucky young man: ~ YUMURTASI.

koçak Brave; generous. ~ **lama**, (*lit.*) heroic folksong/ballad; boasting. ~ **lamalı**, epic. ~ **lık**, bravery.

koçan (*bot.*) Corncob; stump; heart; (*adm.*) (stump of) counterfoils.

koç·başı[nı] (*mil.*) Battering-ram. ~ **boynuzu**[nu], (*naut.*) cleat. ~ **kar**, (*live.*) ram bred for fighting. ~ **lanmak**, *vi.* become brave/plucky. ~ **yumurtası**[nı], (*bio.*) ram's testicles.

koçmak (-i) Embrace; finish.

koçu Granary; cattle-shed; bullock-cart.

kod[u] Code. ~ **anahtar/pedalı**, (*mot.*) dip-switch: ~ **lambaları**, dipping headlamps.

kodaman (*jok.*) Large; clumsy; slow-moving; influential. ~ **lar**, magnates, 'big-wigs'. ~ **lık**, bigness; superiority.

kodein (*med.*) Codeine.

kodeks (*pub.*) Codex; (*med.*) pharmacopoeia.

kodes (*sl.*) Prison, 'clink'. ~ **e tıkmak**, put in clink.

ko·deş/ ~ doş (*sl.*) Pimp.

kof Hollow; rotten; weak; stupid, ignorant.

kofa (*bot.*) Flowering rush. ~ **na**, (*ich.*) large bluefish.

koferdam (*eng.*) Cofferdam.

kof·laşmak *vi.* Become hollow/worthless. ~ **luk**, hollowness; a hollow; ignorance. ~ **ul**, (*bio.*) vacuole.

koğ- = KOV-. ~ **uş**, (*arch.*) large room; (*ed.*) dormitory; (*med.*) ward. ~ **uşağacı**[nı], (*carp.*) baulk of timber; beam, joist.

kohe·ran Coherent. ~ **zyon**, cohesion. ~ **zyonlu**, cohesive.

kok[u] (*min.*) Coke. ~ **fırını**, coke furnace/oven: ~ **kömürü**, coking coal.

koka (*bot.*) Coca. ~ **in(oman)**, (*med.*) cocaine (addict). ~ **kola**, (*cul.*) Coca-Cola.

kokana Elderly Greek woman. ~ **gibi**, overdressed elderly woman.

kokar That smells; fetid, stinking. ~ **ardı**[ı]**ç**[cı], (*bot.*) Phoenician juniper. ~ **ca**, (*zoo.*) skunk; (?) polecat.

kokar[lı]**t**[dı] (*mil.*, *mod.*) Cockade.

koket[i] Coquette; coquettish. ~ **lik**, coquetry.

kokil ~ **dökümü**, (*min.*) die-casting.

kok·lam (*bio.*) Sense of smell; olfaction. ~ **lama**, *vn.* = ~ LAM: ~ +, *a.* olfactory. ~ **lamak (-i)**, smell; nuzzle; (*fig.*) get wind of stg.: **koklayanın burnu düşmek**, smell unpleasant, stink. ~ **laşmak (-le)**, smell each other; caress each other; (*fig.*) reach an understanding. ~ **latmak (-i, -e)**, *vc.*; *neg.* (*sl.*) not give s.o. even a sniff of stg. ~ **mak**, *vi.* smell; stink; go bad; be about to happen. ~ **muş**, *a.* putrid, stinking; rotten (egg); (*fig.*) very lazy/ dirty.

koklea (*bio.*) Cochlea.

koko (*bot.*) Coconut. ~ **ipliği**, coir: ~ **paspas**, (*dom.*) coconut doormat.

kokona = KOKANA.

kokore[l]**ç**[ci] (*cul.*) Sheep's chitterlings cooked on a spit.

kokoriko (*ech.*) Cock-a-doodle-do!

kokoroz (*bot.*) Maize plant, ear of maize; (*fig.*) stg. long and pointed; (*sl.*) ugly person. ~ **lanmak**, *vi.* be defiant/threatening.

kokot[u] Prostitute.

kokoz (*sl.*) Penniless; hard up. ~ **lamak**, *vi.* become penniless/'broke'. ~ **luk**, destitution.

kok·pit (*aer.*) Cockpit. ~ **teyl**, (*cul.*) cocktail/ (-party): ~ **barı**, cocktail-bar.

koksa (*bio.*) Coxa, hip.

koksiks (*bio.*) Coccyx.

koku Smell; odour, scent; perfume; trace; (*fig.*) indication/inkling of stg.; (*sl.*) cocaine. ~ **almak**, (*pub.*) have a nose for news: ~ **almazlık**, (*med.*) anosmia: ~ **giderici**, deodorizer: ~ **su çıkmak**, (*fig.*) be divulged (a secret); signs be given of stg.'s approach: ~ **sunu almak**, perceive the smell of; (*fig.*) get an inkling of/presentiment about stg.: ~ **sunu gidermek**, deodorize stg.

koku·lu Having a . . . smell; perfumed: ~ **alabalık**, (*ich.*) smelt: ~ **böcek**, (*ent.*) shield-bug: ~ ~ **çayırotu**, (*bot.*) sweet violet: ~ **sülün**, (*orn.*) hoatzin. ~ **nuk(luk)**, (*chem.*) aromatic(ity). ~ **sal**, olfactory. ~ **suz**, without smell. ~ **şma**, *vn.* putrefaction. ~ **şmak**, *vi.* putrefy, go bad. ~ **şuk**, bad, putrid. ~ **tmak (-i)**, give off a smell; smell (badly); make a place smell; cause s.o. to smell; sicken, disgust.

kol[u] (*bio.*) Arm; (*zoo.*) foreleg; (*cul.*) shoulder; (*bot.*) stolon; (*mod.*) sleeve; (*bot.*) branch; (*eng.*) bar, handle, crank, lever; bracket; (*tex.*) twist (of thread); (*naut.*) strand (of rope); (*geo.*) arm, branch; col; (*adm.*) branch, (sub)division; (*mil.*) wing (of army); column (of troops); (*ind.*) team, gang; (*th.*) troupe. ~ +, *a.* Brachio-; brachial: ~ **akımı**, (*el.*) derived current: ~ **atmak**, send forth branches, ramify; extend, develop: ~ **bastı**, (*sp.*) wrestling match ending in a draw: ~ **boyu**, arm's length, cubit: ~ **demiri**, cross-bar (for securing a door): ~ **düğmesi**, (*mod.*) cuff-links: ~ **emeği**, manual labour: ~ **gezmek**, go the rounds, patrol; (*fig.*) (criminals) swagger about: ~ **güreşi**, (*sp.*) arm wrestling: ~ **kayığı**, patrol-boat: ~ **kemiği**, (*bio.*) humerus: ~ **a (yürümek)**, (walk) arm-in-arm: ~ **nizamı**, (*mil.*) column: ~ **saati**, wrist-watch: ~ **uzatmak**, ramify, extend: ~ **vurmak**, patrol: ~ **yürütmek**, (*naut.*) splice a rope.

kol-: ~**ları kavuşturmak**, fold one's arms: ~**larını açmak (-e)**, welcome s.o. with open arms: ~**larını sallaya sallaya gelmek**, come empty-handed: ~**larını sıvamak**, roll up one's sleeves (for work): ~**u kanadı kırılmak**, be broken down; be dismayed: ~**u uzun**, influential: ~**una girmek (-in)**, take s.o. by the arm: ~**unda altın bileziği olm.**, have the means of earning one's living: ~**unu bükmek**, twist s.o.'s arm; break s.o.'s power.

kola[1] *n.* (*bot.*) Cola (tree, nut). ~**giller**, cola trees.

kola[2] *n.* Starch (paste). ~**cı(lık)**, (work of) s.o. who starches and irons laundry.

kolaçan Walking about (with intent to pilfer, etc.). ~ **etm.**, rummage/poke about: ~**a çıkmak**, wander about (to pilfer, etc.).

kolağası (*mil.*) Adjutant-major.

kolaj (*art.*) Collage. ~**en**, (*bio.*) collagen.

kola·lamak (-i) Starch stg. ~**lanmak**, *vp.* ~**latmak (-i, -e)**, *vc.* ~**lı**, starched.

kolan[1] *n.* (*zoo.*) Young foal; wild ass.

kolan[2] *n.* Broad band/belt; (horse's) girth; binding; (*child.*) swing-rope. ~ **takımı**, harness: ~ **vurmak**, girth a horse; swing standing up.

kolateral (*fin.*) Collateral.

kolay *a.* Easy. *n.* Easy way to do stg.; means to do stg. ~ **gele/gelsin!**, (*greeting*) may it be easy! (for you to do): ~ **kanmaz**, (*fig.*) hard-boiled: ~ **kırılır**, brittle, fragile: ~ ~, easily: ~**da**, just to hand; handy: ~**ı var**, there's a solution/an easy way out: ~**ına bakmak (-in)**, look about for the easiest way to do stg.: ~**ına gelmek (öyle)**, find the easy way in such a manner: ~**ına kaçmak**, take the easy way out: ~**ını bulmak**, find the easy way.

kolay·ca *a.* Fairly/quite easy; *adv.* easily. ~**cacık**, very easily. ~**erir**, (*phys.*) eutectic. ~**lamak (-i)**, facilitate; have nearly finished (work, etc.); break the back (of a task). ~**lanmak**/~**laşmak**, *vi.* become easy; be nearly finished. ~**laştırmak (-i)**, facilitate; expedite; bring near to finishing. ~**lık**, easiness; facility in working; convenience, means; easy circumstances, comfort: ~ **göstermek (-e)**, give facilities, make things easy: ~**la**, with ease, easily.

kol·başı[nı]**(lık)** (Work of) foreman. ~**böreği**[ni], (*cul.*) type of long BÖREK. ~**cu(luk)**, (work of) watchman//customs-house guard//agent for supplying servants. ~**cuk**, (*phys.*) moment. ~**çal**[kgı], (*mod.*) gauntlet; mittens; cuff-protector; armlet. ~**daş(lık)**, (status of) colleague/associate/mate.

kold ~ **cilt kremi**, cold-cream.

koledok ~ **kanalı**, (*bio.*) biliary duct.

kolej (*ed.*) Private school/college (at lycée level). ~ **alanı**, campus: ~ **mezunu**, former pupil. ~**li**, college student.

kolek·siyon Collection (of objects). ~**siyoncu(luk)**, collect·or/(-ing). ~**tif**, collective, collecting: ~ **emniyet/güvenlik**, (*pol.*) collective security: ~ **ortaklık**, (*fin.*) collective/mutual partnership. ~**tivist**, (*soc.*) collectivist. ~**tivizm**, collectivism. ~**tör**, (*el.*) collector; (*eng.*) manifold.

kol·era (*med.*) Cholera. ~**eralı**, cholera victim. ~**esterin**/~**esterol**, (*bio.*) cholesterol.

koli Parcel; package; case. ~ **listesi**, packing-list.

kolibasil (*bio.*) Colibacillus.

kolibri(giller) (*orn.*) Hummingbird(s).

kol·ik (*med.*) Colic. ~**it**, colitis.

kolla·mak (-i) Search; keep under observation; look after, protect; watch for (an opportunity). ~**nmak**, *vp.* ~**yıcı**, guard, watchman.

kol·lu Having arms/sleeves/handles; (*mil.*) having . . . contingents; (rope) having . . . strands: ~ **pergel**, beam compass: ~ **şamdan**, candelabra: ~ **testere**, (*carp.*) hacksaw. ~**luk**, (*mod.*) cuff-(protector); armband; (*adm.*) police: ~ **kuvveti**, police/gendarmerie force.

kol·odion/~**odyum** (*chem.*) Collodion.

kolofon (*pub.*) Colophon.

kolofonyum (*chem.*) Colophony, rosin.

kol·oidal (*chem.*) Colloidal. ~**oi**[tdi], colloid.

kolokyum (*ed.*) Colloquium, conference.

Kol·ombiya(lı) *pr.n.* (*geo.*) Colombia(n). ~**ombiyum**, (*chem.*) columbium, niobium.

kolon (*pub.*) Column; (*arch.*) main services duct; (*naut.*) bollard; (*bio.*) colon.

koloni (*adm.*) Colony. ~ **yalizm**, (*pol.*) colonialism. ~**zatör**, colonizer.

kolon·lu Columned. ~**su**, columnar.

kolonya ~ **(suyu)**, eau-de-Cologne.

kolordu (*mil.*) Army-corps.

koloridye (*ich.*) Small Spanish mackerel.

kolorime·tre Colorimeter. ~**tri**, colorimetry.

Kol. Ort./Şrt = KOLEKTİF ORTAKLIK/ŞİRKET.

kolsuayaklılar (*zoo.*) Brachiopods.

koltuk (*bio.*) Armpit; (*bot.*) axil; (*dom.*) armchair; (*cin.*) stalls; (*soc.*, *obs.*) bride and groom walking arm-in-arm; support; dark/out-of-the-way place; small shop; (*col.*) official position; (*sl.*) brothel; (*fig.*) support, protection. ~ **altı**, (*bio.*) armpit axilla; (*fig.*) protection: ~ **değneği**, crutch: ~ **değneğiyle**, (*fig.*) with s.o.'s support/backing: ~ **halatı**, (*naut.*) mooring-rope: ~ **kapısı**, servants'/ tradesmen's entrance: ~ **kapmaca**, children's game; (*fig.*) rat-race: ~ **kapmak**, (*adm.*) get a post by devious means: ~ **meyhanesi**, small wine-shop/ tavern: ~ **sarrafı**, (*fin.*) street money-changer: ~ **vermek (-e)**, flatter s.o.: ~**a girmek**, marry s.o.: ~**ları kabarmak**, swell with pride: ~**ta olm.**, be s.o.'s guest; be entertained at s.o.'s expense: ~**una girmek**, give one's arm to s.o.; put one's arm through s.o.'s; show close relationship: ~**una sığınmak (-in)**, be under the protection/wing of s.o.

koltuk·çu Chairmaker; second-hand furniture dealer; tavern-keeper; (*fig.*) flatterer, hypocrite. ~**çuluk**, chairmaking; furniture dealing; flattery. ~**lama**, *vn.*; compliment. ~**lamak (-i)**, support by the arm; take stg. under one's arm; (*fig.*) flatter s.o. ~**lanmak**, *vi.* feel flattered. ~**lu**, having arms: ~ **sandalye**, armchair. ~**luk**, (*mod.*) under-arm gusset; dress-shield.

kolye Necklace. ~**li**, ~ **ardıçkuşu**, (*orn.*) ring ouzel.

kolyoz (*ich.*) Spanish mackerel.

kolza (*bot.*) Rape, swede.

Kom. = KOMİSYON. ~ Ort. = KOMANDİT ORTAK-
LIĞI.
koma (med.) Coma. ~ halinde, comatose: ~ dan
çıkmak, come out of a coma, revive: ~ ya girmek,
go/sink into a coma; (sl.) be amazed.
komak = KOYMAK.
kom·andit[i] ~ (ortaklığı), (fin.) mixed liability company. ~ anditer, (fin.) sleeping partner. ~ ando,
(mil.) commando-group; commando soldier.
~ bina, (fin.) combine. ~ bine, combined, composite. ~ binezon, arrangement, combination; (mod.)
petticoat.
komed·i/ ~ ya (th.) Comedy: ~ aktörü, comedian:
~ aktrisi, comedienne: ~ den ibaret, mere play-
acting. ~ yacı, comic. ~ yen, comedi·an/-enne.
komi Agent; assistant-waiter; bell-boy.
komik Comic(al); laughable, farcical. ~ leşmek, vi.
become comical. ~ lik, comical behaviour/situa-
tion; farce.
Komin·form (pol.) Cominform. ~ tern, Comin-
tern.
komis·er(lik) (Rank, duties of) superintendent of
police; commissioner. ~ yon, (adm.) commission;
committee; (fin.) commission, percentage, brokerage: ~ işi, work on commission. ~ yoncu, agent,
broker. ~ yonculuk, agency, brokering.
kom·ita (pol.) Secret society; resistance movement.
~ itacı(lık), (work of) comitadji/resistance-fighter.
~ ite, (adm.) committee. ~ mansalizm, (bio.) commensalism. ~ odin, (dom.) bedside table, com-
mode. ~ odor, (naut.) commodore. ~ o[l]t[du], (dom.)
chest-of-drawers.
kom·paksiyon (geol.) Compaction. ~ pansatör,
(phys.) compensator, balance. ~ partıman, (rly.)
compartment. ~ pas, (math.) dividers. ~ pavnd,
compound. ~ petan, specialist, expert. ~ ple, a.
full; all-: adv. completely: n. (mod.) suit. ~ pleks,
complicated; (arch., psy.) complex. ~ plikasyon,
complication. ~ plike, complicated. ~ pliman,
compliment, flattery: ~ yapmak, pay a compliment; flatter. ~ plo, (pol.) plot: ~ kurmak, weave a
plot. ~ ponent, (eng.) component. ~ posto, (cul.)
stewed fruit, compote. ~ poze, composite, mixed.
~ pozisyon, (ed., lit.) composition. ~ pozitör, (mus.)
composer. ~ prador, (fin.) agent, factor; (pej.)
local agent of Westerners; collaborationist. ~ pres,
(med.) compress. ~ presiyon, (phys.) compression.
~ presör, compressor. ~ prime, (med.) pill, tablet.
~ promi, (pol.) compromise. ~ pütür, (math.) computer.
komşu n. Neighbour. a. Neighbouring. ~ açı,
(math.) adjacent angle: ~ kapısı, next-door; somewhere near: ~ kapısı yapmak/kapısına çevirmek,
frequent a distant place unnecessarily: ~ da pişer
bize de düşer, we hope to benefit from our neighbours: ~ nun tavuğu ~ ya kaz görünür, the grass
grows greener on the other side. ~ luk, being a
neighbour; neighbourly deed: ~ etm., visit each
other.
komut[u] (mil.) Order. ~ vermek, give an order. ~ a,
(mil.) command: ~ etm., be in command, direct.
~ an, (mil.) commander; commandant. ~ anlık,
rank/duties of commander; a command.

komü·nal (soc.) Communal. ~ nikasyon, com-
munication(s). ~ nike, (pol.) communiqué. ~ nist,
(pol.) communist. ~ nistlik/ ~ nizm, communism.
~ tatör, (el.) commutator, switch.
kon. = KONUŞMA DİLİ.
kona[l]k[ğı 1] n. (bio.) Scurf (on the head).
kona[l]k[ğı 2] n. Halting-place; stage, day's journey;
(arch.) mansion; large town house, (adm.) government house; (bio.) = ~ çı. ~ etm., make a halt (on
journey): ~ gibi, big and impressive (house): ~
yavrusu, small mansion.
konak·çı (mil., etc.) Billeting officer; (bio.) host.
~ lamak, vi. stay for the night; (mil.) be billeted.
~ lı, who lives in a big house; gentleman.
kon·alga Position: ~ ya girmek/ ~ lanmak, vi. be
positioned. ~ biçim, (phys.) configuration.
konc·a (bot.) = GONCA. ~ olos = KARAKONCOLOS.
kon[l]ç[cu] (mod.) Leg (of boot/stocking). ~ lu, having
a (long) leg. ~ suz, having no/a short leg.
kon·çerto (mus.) Concerto. ~ dansatör, (el.) capacitor. ~ dansör, (phys.) condenser.
kondil (bio.) Condyl.
kon·disyon (leg., sp.) Condition. ~ dominyum,
(pol.) condominium.
kondor (orn.) Condor.
kondr(o)- pref. (bio.) Chondr(o)-.
kondurmak (-i, -e) vc. = KONMAK. Find lodgings
for s.o.; (mil.) billet/quarter (troops); put/place stg.
on stg.; attribute stg. to s.o.; accuse s.o. of stg.;
suddenly do stg.
kon·düksiyon (phys.) Conduction. ~ düktör(lük),
(rly.) (work of) guard. ~ düvit, (th.) call-boy.
~ federasyon, (pol.) confederation. ~ federatif, a.
confederate. ~ federe, (con)federated. ~ feksiyon/
(-culuk), (mod.) ready-made clothes (trade).
~ ferans, (ed.) lecture; (adm.) conference: ~ salonu,
auditorium, lecture/conference hall: ~ vermek,
give a lecture; (sl.) vomit. ~ feransçı/ ~ feransiye,
lecturer. ~ feti, confetti. ~ figürasyon, configuration. ~ for, comfort, ease. ~ forlu, comfortable.
~ forsuzluk, discomfort.
Konfüçyüs pr.n. Confucius.
konglomera (geol.) Conglomerate.
Kongo(lu) pr.n. (geo.) Congo(lese).
kongövde (bot.) Trunk (of palms).
kongre (adm., ed.) Congress.
kon·i (math.) Cone; (geol.) fan: ~ şeklinde, coni-
form, conoid. ~ ik, conical; (carp.) bevelled: ~
çadır, (mil.) bell-tent: ~ dişli, (eng.) bevel(led) gear.
kon·işmento = KONŞİMENTO. ~ jonktür, (fin.) con-
juncture. ~ kasör, (eng.) crusher. ~ kav, (phys.)
concave. ~ korda(to), (pol.) concordat; (fin.) composition (with creditors). ~ kre, (art.) concrete.
~ kresyon, concretion. ~ kur, race, competition.
~ kur(h)ipik, horse-show/-race.
kon·mak (-e) vi. Alight; perch; settle; camp; make
a night's halt; have a piece of good luck; vp. =
KOYMAK; be put: konup göçmek, lead a nomadic
life. ~ malı, complex. ~ oluşum, (phys.) conformation.
konsa (orn.) Bird's gizzard.
kon·santrasyon Concentration. ~ santre, concentrated: ~ olm. (-de), concentrate into. ~ santrik,

concentric. ~ **sayı**, (*math.*) coordinate. ~ **sept(ualizm)**, (*phil.*) concept(ualism). ~ **ser**, (*mus.*) concert: ~ **salonu**, concert-hall: ~ **vermek**, give a concert. ~ **serto** = ~ ÇERTO. ~ **servatör**, preservationist. ~ **servatuar**, (*mus.*) academy of music, *conservatoire*. ~ **serve**, (*cul.*) *a.* preserved, bottled, tinned: *n.* preserves, bottled/canned foods: ~ **müzik**, recorded music. ~ **servecilik**, canning of foods. ~ **sey**, (*adm.*) council. ~ **sinyasyon**, (*fin.*) consignment. ~ **sol**, (*dom.*) chest-of-drawers; (*el.*) console; (*carp.*) bracket, support; (*eng.*) cantilever: ~ **köprü**, cantilever bridge: ~ **saati**, bracket clock. ~ **solidasyon**, (*fin., geol.*) consolidation. ~ **solide**, (*fin.*) consolidated. ~ **solit**, (*fin.*) undated government stock. ~ **solitçi**, stockbroker. ~ **solos**, (*adm.*) consul: ~ +, *a.* consular: ~ **muavini**, vice-consul. ~ **soloshane**, (*arch.*) consulate. ~ **solosluk**, rank/ duties of consul; (*adm.*) consulate: ~ +, *a.* consular: ~ **vergisi**, consular fees. ~ **somasyon**, (*cul.*) drinks, snacks. ~ **somatris**, hostess (in a bar). ~ **some**, (*cul.*) *consommé*, clear meat soup. ~ **son**, (*ling.*) consonant. ~ **sorsiyum**, (*fin.*) consortium. ~ **stant**, (*phys.*) constant. ~ **stantan**, (*min.*) constantan alloy. ~ **strüksiyon**, construction. ~ **strüktivizm**, (*art.*) constructivism. ~ **sulto**/ ~ **sültasyon**, (*med.*) consultation. ~ **sül**, (*his.*) consul. ~ **şimento**, (*fin.*) bill of lading.

kontᵘ (*soc.*) Count. ~ **gibi**, well-dressed (man): ~ **gibi yaşamak**, live like a lord.

kon·tak (*el.*) Contact; short-circuit; (*sl.*) 'a screw loose': ~ **adesesi**, (*med.*) contact lens: ~ **anahtarı**, (*mot.*) starter key: ~ **kurmak**, establish relations: ~ **yapmak**, (*el.*) short-circuit. ~ **tekst**, (*lit.*) context. ~ **tenjan**, contingency; (*fin.*) quota, share; (*adm.*) quota: ~ **senatörü**, (*adm.*) senator selected by the President.

kontes (*soc.*) Countess; (*ed. sl.*) school-mistress.

konteyner (*fin., ind.*) Container.

kontluk County.

kontör Meter, counter.

kontr·a *adv.* Against: *n.* (*naut.*) top-gallant, royal: ~ **flok**, flying jib: ~ **gitmek**, oppose s.o.: ~ **mizana**, after-mast: ~ **omurga**, false keel; centre-board. ~ **aktil**, (*bio.*) contractile. ~ **alize**, (*met.*) anti-tradewinds. ~ **alto**, (*mus.*) contralto. ~ **asomun**, (*eng.*) lock-nut. ~ **ast**, (*cin.*) contrast.

kontrat (*leg.*) Contract. ~ **briç(oyunu)**, (*gamb.*) contract bridge. ~ **lı**, let/sold by contract.

kontr·atabla (*carp.*) Plywood. ~ **atak**, (*sp.*) counter-attack/-offensive. ~ **bas(çı)**, (*mus.*) double-bass (player). ~ **file**, (*cul.*) beefsteak.

kontrolᵘ Control, check; comparison; inspection, testing. ~ **etm.**, keep check of, control; test: ~ **kalemi**, (*el.*) neon tester: ~ **kulesi**, (*aer.*) control tower: ~ **memuru**, (*adm.*) censor: ~ **saati**, master clock.

kontrol·cu/ ~ **ör** Controller, auditor, checker, inspector. ~ **lu**, controlled. ~ **suz**, uncontrolled; unchecked.

kontr·plak (*carp.*) Laminated wood, three-/four-plywood. ~ **puvan**, (*mus.*) counterpoint.

konu[1] *n.* Theme, subject(-matter). ~ **dan ayrılmak**,

digress: ~ **sunda**, concerning: ~ **ya dönmek**, get (back) to the point.

konu[2] *n.* ~ **komşu**, the neighbours; all the neighbourhood.

konu[1]**k**ᵍᵘ (*soc.*) Guest; (*bio.*) parasite. ~ **bitki**, (*bot.*) epiphyte: ~ **oyuncu/sanatçı**, (*th.*) guest-artist: ~ **topluluk**, invited audience.

konuk·çu Host(ess), guide. ~ **evi**ⁿⁱ, guest-house. ~ **lamak (-i)**, entertain/put up (guests); give a feast. ~ **luk**, being a guest; guest-house. ~ **sever(lik)**, hospita·ble/(-bility).

konulmak (-e) *vp.* = KONMAK; KOYMAK. Be put/ placed/set.

konum Position, situation; orientation; site, location; (*aer.*) attitude. ~ **luk**, base.

konur Swarthy; (*fig.*) brave, proud. ~ **al**, light brown.

konuş *vn.* = KONMAK; manner of placing; (*geo.*) situation, location; (*mil.*) disposition (of forces).

konuş·kan Talkative, loquacious. ~ **kanlık**, talkativeness. ~ **ma**, *vn.* talking; lecture, talk; (*th.*) dialogue; diction; discussion: ~ **aygıtı**, (*bio.*) organs of speech: ~ **dili**, (*ling.*) colloquial speech, demotic: ~ **kuralları**, (*ling.*) rules of diction: ~ **odası**, (*th.*) green room: ~ **özrü**, (*med.*) speech defect: ~ **sanatı**, (*th.*) elocution: ~ **tarzı**, (*th.*) enunciation: ~ **yazarı**, (*th.*) dialogue-writer. ~ **macı**, lecturer, speaker. ~ **mak**, *vi.* converse, talk: **(-i, -le)**, discuss stg. with s.o.; talk about stg.

konuşur babam konuşur, he just talks and talks. ~ **mamak (-le)**, not be on speaking terms with s.o. ~ **turmak (-i, -le)**, *vc.* ~ **u**, lecture. ~ **ucu**, speaker. ~ **ulmak (-le)**, *vp.* be discussed: *imp. v.* talk, speak.

konuşulan dil, (*ling.*) colloquial speech, spoken language, vernacular.

konutᵘ ¹ *n.* (*phil.*) Postulate.

konutᵘ ² *n.* Dwelling, residence, domicile; house flat; housing. ~ **belgesi**, (*adm.*) residence papers. ~ **bölgesi**, residential area: ~ **dokunulmazlığı**, (*leg.*) inviolability of one's dwelling: ~ **sıkıntısı**, housing shortage: ~ **sorunu**, housing problem: ~ **tasarımı**, house-planning. ~ **lu**, domiciled.

kon·vansiyon (*adm.*) Convention. ~ **veks**, (*phys.*) convex. ~ **veksiyon**, (*phys.*) convection. ~ **vektör**, (*dom.*) convector heater. ~ **vertibilite**, (*fin.*) convertibility. ~ **vertisör**, (*el.*) converter. ~ **veyör**, (*ind.*) conveyor. ~ **voy**, (*mil., naut.*) convoy.

Konya (*geo.*) Konya; (*his.*) Iconium.

konyak¹ (*cul.*) Cognac, brandy.

kooperatif *n.* Cooperative, association. ~ **çi**, cooperative member/manager. ~ **çilik**, formation, operation of cooperatives. ~ **leşmek**, *vi.* (*fin.*) be based on cooperatives.

koordi·nasyon (*adm.*) Coordination. ~ **nat**¹, (*math.*) coordinate. ~ **natör**, coordinator. ~ **ne** coordinated: ~ **etm.**, coordinate.

kopal (*bot.*) Copal resin.

kopanaki (*tex.*) Bobbin-lace.

kopar·ılmak *vp.* ~ **mak (-i)**, break off/in two; pluck, gather; detach; burst (into pieces); take by force, get stg. out of s.o.; set up an outcry; (*sp.*) pass, overtake s.o. ~ **tmak (-i)**, *vc.*

kopça (*mod.*) Hook (and eye). ~ **iliği**, eye(let). ~ **lamak (-i)**, fasten with hooks and eyes. ~ **lanmak**, *vp.* ~ **lı**, having/fastened with hooks and eyes.

Kopenhag (*geo.*) Copenhagen.

kopil (*sl.*) Rascal; street urchin.

kop·ma *vn.* Break; rupture; (*phys.*) fission: ~ **dayanç/mukavemeti**, (*min.*) rupture/tensile strength. ~ **mak**, *vi.* break in two; snap; set out on an action; (disturbance, etc.) break out, begin; ache violently; (*dial.*) run.

kopoy (*live.*) Sporting dog; hound.

kopra (*bot.*) Copra.

kop·uk *a.* Broken off, torn; penniless, vagabond. ~ **untu**, piece broken off.

kopuz(cu) (*mus.*) One-stringed guitar (player).

kopülasyon (*bio.*) Copulation.

kopya Copy; copying; (*ed.*) cheating, cribbing. ~ **defteri**, copybook: ~ **etm.**, copy; duplicate: ~ **kâğıdı**, carbon paper: ~ **kalem//mürekkebi**, copying pen//ink: ~ **makinesi**, cyclostyle, duplicator: ~ **sını çıkarmak**, make a copy of stg., reproduce stg. ~ **cı**, (*art.*) copyist; (*ed.*) s.o. who copies/ cribs. ~ **cılık**, copying.

kopye = KOPYA.

kor Red-hot cinder, ember. ~ **dökmek**, burn for a long time: ~ **kayaç**, (*geol.*) igneous rock.

Kor. = KOLORDU. ~ **a.** = KORAMİRAL.

kora (*med.*) Chorea. ~ **lⁱ**, (*mus.*) chorale.

koram (*adm.*) Hierarchy.

koramiralⁱ(lik) (*naut.*) (Rank/duties of) (junior) admiral.

korangle (*mus.*) Cor anglais.

kord ~ **bezi**, (*mot.*) cord fabric (of tyres).

kordalılar (*zoo.*) Chordates.

kordiplomatik (*pol.*) Diplomatic corps.

kordon (*tex.*) Cord; (medal) ribbon; watch-chain; (*el.*) cord, cable; strand of rope, (*arch.*) string-course; (*geo.*) line of jetsam.

Kore (*geo.*) Korea. ~ +, *a.* Korean. ~ **li**, (*ethn.*) Korean.

korek·siyon (*ling.*, etc.) Correction. ~ **t**, correct.

koreograf(i) (*mus.*) Choreograph·er/(-y).

korgeneralⁱ(lik) (*mil.*) (Rank/duties of) lieutenant-general/corps commander.

koridor (*arch.*) Corridor; (*aer.*) gate.

korindon (*geol.*) Corundum.

Korint (*geo.*) Corinth. ~ **li**, (*ethn.*) Corinthian.

kork·ak *a.* Cowardly, timid; *n.* coward: ~ **karga**, cowardly fellow. ~ **akça**, cravenly. ~ **aklık**, cowardice, timidity. ~ **ma**, *vn.*: ~ **dan**, fearlessly. ~ **mak**, *vi.* be afraid; be anxious: (-**den**), be afraid of, fear; stand in awe of: (-**e**), be afraid to (do stg.): **korktuğu başına gelmek**, one's fears be realized.

korku Fear, dread; alarm, anxiety; danger. ~ **dağları bekler**, of course you are/he is, etc. afraid: ~ **düşürmek (-e)**, dismay s.o.: ~ **salmak**, frighten: ~ **dan sinmek**, cower.

kork·ulmak (-den) *imp. v.* Be feared/afraid of: ~ **ulur bir şey**, stg. to be afraid of. ~ **ulu**, frightening, dreadful; critical, dangerous: ~ **rüya**, nightmare: ~ **rüya görmektense uyanık yatmak hayırlı/ yeğdir**, better to be safe than sorry. ~ **uluk**, (*agr.*) scarecrow; (*arch.*) banister; parapet; barrier;

balustrade, (*fig.*) mere figurehead. ~ **unç**, terrible, dreadful, fearful: ~ **ayı**, (*zoo.*) grizzly bear. ~ **unçluk**, terror, dreadfulness. ~ **untu**, (*psy.*) phobia. ~ **usuz(luk)**, fearless(ness); intrepid(ity), safe(ty). ~ **usuzca**, fearlessly. ~ **utma**, *vn.*; terror. ~ **utmak (-i)**, *vc.* frighten; worry; threaten, bully. ~ **utucu**, frightening, threatening: ~ **ceza**, (*leg.*) deterrent punishment.

kor·lanmak *vi.* Become red-hot. ~ **laşma**, (*min.*) coking. ~ **luk**, fire of red-hot embers; brazier.

kor·na (*mot.*) Horn. ~ **nea**, (*bio.*) cornea.

korner (*sp.*) Corner. ~ **vurmak**, take a corner: ~ **atış/vuruşu**, corner-kick.

kornetⁱ (*mus.*) Cornet.

korniş (*dom.*) Curtain-rod; (*arch.*) cornice.

korno (*mus.*) Horn; (*mil.*) powder-horn; (*mot.*) oil-can.

koro (*mus.*) Choir; chorus.

kor·ozif (*min.*) Corrosive. ~ **ozyon**, corrosion.

korporasyon (*fin.*) Corporation.

kor·sa/ ~ se (*mod.*) Corset. ~ **sacı(lık)**, (work of) corset-maker/-seller. ~ **saj**, (*mod.*) bodice.

korsan (*naut.*) Pirate, corsair. ~ **lık**, piracy.

kortᵘ (*sp.*) Tennis-court.

korte Flirting. ~ **etm.**, flirt.

kortej Procession; cortège, funeral procession.

kor·teks (*bio.*) Cortex. ~ **tizon**, (*med.*) cortisone.

koru·(luk) (*for.*) Small wood, copse, covert. ~ **cu(luk)**, (work of) rural guard/forester.

koruⁱkᵍᵘ (*bot.*) Unripe grape. ~ **lüferi**, (*ich.*) medium-sized LÜFER (caught in August).

koru·ma *vn.* Protection; conservation; patronage; custody; (*med.*) prevention, prophylaxy: ~ **memuru**, (*adm.*) waterguard officer: ~ **seddesi**, (*eng.*) levee: ~ **ünsüzü**, (*ling.*) intervocalic euphonic consonant. ~ **mak (-i, -den)**, defend; support; protect (from); conserve; (*fin.*) balance, meet. ~ **malık**, protection, mask, shield. ~ **man(lık)**, (*leg.*) trustee(ship).

korun (*bio.*) Stratum corneum. ~ **aⁱkᵍ¹**, shelter, refuge. ~ **aklı**, sheltered, protected. ~ **caⁱkᵍ¹**, protective case/sheath; (*ind.*) warehouse: ~ **tan çıkma**, (*ent.*) eclosion. ~ **ⁱçᶜᵘ**, (*fin.*) insurance. ~ **dokusuⁿᵘ**, (*bio.*) epidermal tissue.

korunga (*bot.*) Sainfoin. ~ **lık**, (*agr.*) sainfoin meadow.

koru·nma *vn.* Defence; protection; preservation; precautions; (*med.*) prevention. ~ **nmak**, *vi.* defend/protect o.s.; take shelter: *vp.* be protected: (-**den**), avoid/beware of stg. ~ **nuk**, creature. ~ **num**, (*phys.*) conservation. ~ **yucu**, *a.* protecting; protective; safety; (*med.*) contraceptive; prophylactic: ~ **engel**, protective barrier: ~ **hekimlik**, preventive medicine. ~ **yuculuk**, (*fin.*) protection/ (-ism). ~ **yum**, (*fin.*) consignment. ~ **yumcu**, depository; consignee.

korvetⁱ (*naut.*) Corvette; escort-vessel.

korza (*naut.*) Fouling (of two cables, etc.).

Kos (*geo.*) Island of Cos.

kos- *pref.* = KOZ-.

ko·sekant (*math.*) Cosec(ant). ~ **sinüs**, cosine.

koskoca Enormous; very eminent. ~ **man**, very big, huge.

kostak Slender; refined; well-dressed.

Kostarika(lı) (*geo.*) Costa Rica(n).

kostüm (*mod.*) Suit, costume. ~**lük**, (*tex.*) suit-length.

koşa Contemporary; parallel; (*phil.*) concomitant; double. ~ˡçᶜ¹, (*ling.*) copula. ~ˡkᵍ¹, (*sp.*) lane. ~**lık**, a being parallel. ~**ltı**, two animals harnessed/yoked together. ~**m**, (*cul.*) handful (two hands together).

koşar *v.* = KOŞMAK. *a.* Running. ~ **adım**, (*mil.*) at the double; (*sp.*) jog-trot: ~ **guguk kuşu**, (*orn.*) roadrunner. ~**giller**, (*orn.*) coursers.

koşarmak (-i, -e) (*live.*) Foster a lamb, etc. on a second ewe, etc.

koş·ma *vn.* Harnessing; running; (*lit.*) musical ballad; (*naut.*) stiffener, stay. ~**maca**, (*child.*) game of tag. ~**mak**, *vi.* run: (-i, -e), *vt.* harness, yoke; give as escort/companion; put to work; attribute; lay down conditions; hasten to do stg.

koşnil (*ent.*) Cochineal scale insect; (*chem.*) cochineal dye.

koş·turmak (-i, -e) *vc.* Make run; dispatch; run about in a panic. ~**u**, (*sp.*) running race: ~ **alanı**, race-track: ~ **atı**, (*live.*) racehorse: ~ **yer/yolu**, (*sp.*) running track; racecourse. ~**ucu**, (*sp.*) runner: ~ **devekuşu**, (*orn.*) emu. ~**ulu**, harnessed, yoked; (*mil.*) horse-drawn.

koşuˡkᵍᵘ (*lit.*) Ballad; folk-song.

koşul Condition; reservation; (*leg.*) condition, clause. ~ **bildirimliği**, (*eng.*) specification; (*leg.*) contract: ~ **birleşik zaman**, (*ling.*) conditional tense: ~**la**, (*leg.*) conditional (release, etc.).

koşul·landırılma *vn.* (*psy.*) Conditioning (passive). ~**landırılmak**, *vi.* be conditioned/accustomed (to stg.). ~**landırma**, *vn.* conditioning (active). ~**landırmak** (-i, -e), condition/habituate s.o. to stg. ~**lanma**, *vn.* becoming conditioned/accustomed. ~**lanmak**, *vi.* become conditioned/accustomed. ~**lu**, conditional; hypothetical; conditioned, accustomed: ~ **olgu**, (*phil.*) conditioned event: ~ **tasım**, conditional comparison: ~ **yantümce**, (*ling.*) conditional clause: ~ **yarış**, (*sp.*) handicap race. ~**luluk**, conditionality. ~**suz**, unconditional, absolute, categorical. ~**suzluk**, independence.

koş·ulmak (-e) *vp.* Be harnessed/yoked to: *imp. v.* be run (after); run: **koşulan ad**, (*ling.*) noun in apposition. ~**um**, act of harnessing; harness; (*eng.*) engaging, coupling: ~ **at/hayvanı**, carriage-/draught-horse: ~ **kayışı**, trace: ~ **yüreği**, (*eng.*) thimble. ~**un**, row, rank, line: ~ **bağlamak**, get into line: ~ ~, in rows/ranks. ~**uşmak** (-le), run together; run in all directions. ~**ut(luk)**, parallel/(-ism).

kotᵘ (*math.*) Altitude; height; code. ~**a**, (*fin.*) quota.

kotan (*agr.*) Large plough.

kotanjan (*math.*) Cotangent.

kotarize ~ **etm.**, (*med.*) cauterize.

kotarmak (-i) (*cul.*) Dish up; serve out; (*fig.*) settle stg.

kotiledon (*bot.*) Cotyledon.

kotinga(giller) (*orn.*) Cotinga(s).

kotiyon (*mus.*) Cotillion dance. ~ **dansı**, formal ball.

kotlamak (-i) (*geo.*) Mark in altitudes (on maps, etc.); encode, classify.

kotletⁱ (*cul.*) Cutlet, chop. ~**pane**, (*cul.*) cutlet in breadcrumbs.

koton (*tex.*) Cotton. ~**perle**, corded cotton.

kotra (*naut.*) Cutter; small racing yacht. ~ **omur-gası**, finkeel.

kov Scandal, gossip. ~ **etm.**, slander.

kova Bucket; (*naut.*) bailer; *pr.n.* (*ast.*) Aquarius. ~**lı**, ~ **tarak**, (*eng.*) bucket-dredger.

kovala·ma *vn.* Chase, hunt. ~**maca**, (*child.*) game of 'touch last'/'catch'. ~**mak** (-i), pursue, chase, chivvy; endeavour to obtain; wait for; (*sp.*) try to catch up with.

kovan (*ent.*) Hive; (*mil.*) cartridge-/shell-case; (*eng.*) hole (to receive handle). ~**lı**, with a case: ~ **anahtarı**, (*eng.*) box-spanner. ~**lık**, apiary.

kovboy Cowboy.

kov·durmak (-i) *vc.* ~**lamak** (-i), denounce; slander. ~**mak** (-i), drive away; banish; turn back; eject; repel; persecute; denounce, slander. ~(**u**)**cu**, informer; slanderer. ~(**u**)**culuk**, denunciation; slander.

kovu·cuk (*bot.*) Lentical. ~ˡkᵍᵘ, *a.* hollow: *n.* cavity; (*phys.*) black body. ~**klaşma**, (*phys.*) cavitation.

kov·ulmak *vp.* = KOVMAK. ~**umsama**, *vn.*; in-hospitability. ~**umsamak** (-i), be disagreeable/inhospitable to. ~**untu**, s.o. driven away, banished. ~**uş**, *vn.* = KOVMAK. ~**uşturma**, *vn.*; legal proceedings, prosecution: ~ **açmak**, open proceedings: ~ **yapmak**, proceed with prosecution. ~**uşturmak** (-i), prosecute. ~**uşturmazlık**, (*ling.*) anacoluthon.

koy (*geo.*) Small bay, inlet, cove, creek; nook.

koyacaˡkᵍ¹ Receptacle, container.

koy·aˡkᵍ¹ (*geo.*) Valley; hollow. ~**ar**, confluence (two streams).

koydurmak (-i, -e) *vc.* = KOYMAK.

koygun Tragic; touching, moving.

koy·ma *vn.* (*med.*) Application. ~**mak/komak** (-i, -e), put, place; employ; settle, plant, install; insert; let go, leave, put down; permit; add to; write/put (date, address, etc.); hurt; (*fin.*) allocate: **koyduğum yerde otluyor**, (*col.*) they're making no progress: **koydunsa bul!**, I can't find him/it anywhere!

koyn- = KOYUN¹.

koyu Thick; dense (liquid, darkness); hyper-; deep; dark (colour); (*fig.*) genuine, fervent, extreme. ~ **renkli baştankara**, (*orn.*) sombre tit: ~ **yeşil**, bottle green.

koyu·laşma *vn.* ~**laşmak**, *vi.* become dense; coagulate; become deep/dark. ~**laştırma**, *vn.*; condensation; intensification. ~**laştırmak** (-i), condense; concentrate; deepen. ~**lmak**¹, *vi.* become dense, etc. ~**ltmak** (-i), *vc.* render dense; (*cul.*) thicken (soup); darken/intensify (colour). ~**luk**, density, consistence; darkness/deepness (of colour).

koyulmak² *vp.* = KOYMAK. Be put, etc.; be poured: (-e), be busied with; set to work, etc.; begin; fall on; attack.

koy·unⁿᵘ¹ *n.* Bosom; arms, embrace; (*mod.*) breast-pocket; (*fig.*) pleasant surroundings. ~ ~**a**, in each other's arms: ~ **saati**, pocket-watch: ~**una**

almak, take to bed with one: ~ **una girmek (-in)**, go to bed with s.o.

koyunu 2 *n.* Sheep; (*fig.*) s.o. mild/spiritless; simpleton; (*sp.*) buck, vaulting horse. ~ **bakışlı**, sheepish; stupid-looking: ~ **başlı**, 'mutton-head': ~ **dede**, imbecile: ~ **eti**, (*cul.*) mutton: ~ **gibi**, stupid: ~ **gibi takip etm. (-i)**, follow s.o. unquestioningly: ~ **kaval dinler gibi dinlemek**, listen uncomprehendingly: ~ **kenesi**, (*ent.*) sheep ked/tick: ~ **otu**, (*bot.*) agrimony; hemp agrimony: ~ **saman yemez**, only the best will do: ~ **yatırma**, folding (sheep): ~ **un bulunmadığı yerde keçiye Abdurrahman Çelebi derler**, (have to) make the best of what you have. ~ **gözü**nü, (*bot.*) feverfew; daisy.

koyuntu Grief, sorrow; pain.

koyutu (*phil.*) Postulate.

koy(u)vermek (-i) Let go; just put down; allow.

koz (*bot.*) Walnut; (*gamb.*) master-card, trumps; (*fig.*) opportunity. ~ **helvası**, (*cul.*) nougat: ~ **kabuğuna girmek**, creep into any hole to hide o.s.: ~ **kırmak**, (*gamb.*) play a trump; (*fig.*) commit an indiscretion/*faux pas*: ~ **oynamak**, (*gamb.*) play trumps: ~ **paylaşmak**, go shares, reach an agreement: ~ **u kaybetmek**, lose one's case (at law//in argument): ~ **umuzu kendimiz paylaşırız!**, we'll settle our differences without your help!: ~ **unu oynamak**, play one's trump card, seize one's opportunity: ~ **unu pay etm.**, reach a settlement: ~ **unu paylaşmak (-le)**, (*fig.*) settle accounts with s.o.

koza (*ent.*) Cocoon; silk cocoon; (*bot.*) seed-capsule/-vessel. ~ **cı(lık)**, (work of) dealer in silk cocoons. ~ lkğı, (*bot.*) cone; round object. ~ **la**lkğı, (*bot.*) cone, cypress cone; small stunted object. ~ **laklı**, (*bot.*) coniferous. ~ **laklılar**, (*bot.*) conifers. ~ **laksı**, cone-shaped: ~ **bez**, (*bio.*) pineal gland.

koz·metik Cosmetic(s). ~ **mik**, cosmic. ~ **mogoni**, (*geol.*) cosmogony. ~ **mograf**, (*ast.*) cosmographer. ~ **mografya**, cosmography. ~ **moloji**, (*geol.*) cosmology. ~ **monot**u, (*aer.*) cosmonaut. ~ **mopolit(izm)**, cosmopolitan(ism). ~ **mos**, cosmos.

köçelkği (*zoo.*) Camel foal; (*obs.*) dancing boy; (*fig.*) s.o. frivolous/inconsequent. ~ **çe**, (*mus.*) dance tune. ~ **lik**, dancing; (*fig.*) inconsequence, frivolity.

köfte (*cul.*) Meatball, croquette, rissole. ~ **ci(lik)**, (work of) meatball maker/seller. ~ **hor**, *n.* cunning rogue: *int.* lucky fellow!

köfter (*cul.*) Sweets made from boiled grape-juice.

köftün Oil-cake (fed to cattle).

köhne Old; worn; dilapidated; old-fashioned; secondhand. ~ (**leş)mek**, *vi.* wear out; become old/old-fashioned; (*fig.*) become depressed. ~ **lik**, disrepair; being worn out; being old-fashioned.

kökü (*bot.*) Root; (*bio.*) root, fang (of tooth); (*bot.*) one (plant); (*fig.*) base, basis; source, origin, derivation; (*mus.*) tuning-key (of violins, etc.); (*ling.*) root, etymon; (*math.*) root; (*chem.*) radical. ~ **almış**, (*fig.*) confirmed: ~ **işareti**, (*math.*) radical sign: ~ **kurdu**, (*ent.*) mole cricket: ~ **salmak**, be deeply rooted: ~ **sökmek**, do very difficult work: ~ **söktürmek**, force s.o. (to do stg.): ~ **taslağı**, (*bot.*) radicle: ~ TEN: ~ **ü kazınmak**, disappear:

~ **ünden**, basically: ~ **ünden kesip atmak**, reject// settle once and for all: ~ **ünden koparmak**, eradicate: ~ **ünden sökmek**, eradicate: ~ **üne kibrit suyu dökmek**/~ **ünü kurutmak**, exterminate: ~ **ünü kazımak**, dig up, root out, destroy, exterminate.

kök·anlam (*ling.*) Semanteme. ~ **bacaklılar**, (*zoo.*) rhizopods. ~ **bilgisi**ni, (*ling.*) etymology. ~ **boyası**nı, (*bot.*) dyer's madder; (*chem.*) madder. ~ **boyasıgiller**, (*bot.*) Rubiaceae. ~ **boynu**, (*myc.*) collar. ~ **çe**, *n.* (*math.*) radical. ~ **çü**, herbalist. ~ **çü**lkğü, (*bot.*) radicle, rootlet. ~ **el**, *a.* radical. ~ **en**, (*bot.*) branch of melon-plant, etc.; plant-bed; (*fig.*) root, basis, origin; (*ling.*) etymon: ~ **belgesi**, (*adm.*) certificate of origin: ~ **ülkesi**, (*adm.*) country of origin: ~ **inde büyümüş**, who has not seen the world. ~ **ertme (-i)**, plant and grow (shoots). ~ **kırmızısı**nı, madder-red. ~ **lemek (-i)**, (*agr.*) uproot; clear roots from the ground; (*dom.*) stitch buttons (to cushions, etc.). ~ **lenmek**/~ **leş-mek**, *vi.* take root; become firmly established. ~ **leşik**, classic. ~ **leştirme**, *vn.* (*ling.*) paronomasia. ~ **leştirmek (-i)**, root; establish. ~ **lü**, having roots; rooted; (*fig.*) deep-seated, fundamental, basic: ~ **aile**, long-established/historic family. ~ **mantar**, (*myc.*) mycorrhiza, fungus root. ~ **nar**, (*bot.*) fir-tree: ~ **baştankarası**, (*orn.*) coal-tit: ~ **kargası**, (*orn.*) nutcracker. ~ **sap**ı, (*bot.*) rhyzome. ~ **sel**, *a.* rootlike. ~ **sü**, (*bot.*) root-hair (of moss). ~ **süz**, rootless; (*fig.*) baseless, transient. ~ **ten**, radical, thorough, fundamental: ~ **sürme**, inherited quality: ~ **sürme (ressam)dır**, he's an (artist) by birth. ~ **tenci(lik)**, (*phil.*) radical(ism). ~ **teş**, (*ling.*) cognate. ~ **tümleç**, cognate object. ~ **türkçe** = GÖKTÜRKÇE.

kölçer (*myc.*) Wheat smut.

köle Slave, bondsman. ~ **doyuran**, a filling food: ~ **n olayım!**, *int.* I beg you!: ~ **niz**, your very humble servant.

köle·leşmek *vi.* Become a slave. ~ **leştirmek (-i)**, enslave; treat as a slave. ~ **lik**, slavery, bondage. ~ **men**, (*his.*) Mameluke; (*mil.*) slave corps.

kömelçci (*bot.*) Capitulum, flower-head.

kömür *n.* Charcoal; coal. *a.* Coal-black. ~ **alnı**, (*min.*) coal-face: ~ **başa vurmak**/~ **çarpmak**, (*med.*) be affected by charcoal fumes: ~ **cürufu**, (*min.*) clinker: ~ **damarı**, (*min.*) coal measure/seam: ~ **gibi**, black as coal: ~ **havzası**, (*geol.*) coalfield: ~ **işçisi**, collier, miner: ~ **işleri**, (*naut.*) coaling: ~ **iyi kor döker**, the charcoal burns well: ~ **kalem**, (*art.*) charcoal pencil: ~ **kazmacısı**, collier, face-worker: ~ **mucuru**, (*min.*) breeze: ~ **ocağı**, (*min.*) colliery, coal-mine/-pit: ~ **şilebi**, (*naut.*) collier: ~ **uçunu**, coal-gas: ~ **yatağı**, (*geol.*) coal measure: ~ **yayı lambası**, (*el.*) carbon arc lamp.

kömür·cin ~ **kayası**, (*ich.*) black goby. ~ **cü**, charcoal burner/seller; coal-merchant; (*naut.*) stoker: ~ **çırağına dönmek**, get black all over. ~ **cülük**, charcoal-burning; (*naut.*) stoking. ~ **leşme**, *vn.* carbonization: ~ **leşmek**, *vi.* become carbonized: ~ **leştirmek (-i)**, carbonize. ~ **lük**, coal-hole; coal-cellar; (*naut.*) bunker.

köpe·cilkği Little dog; puppy. ~ **ğimsi**, dog-like.

köpe¹k^{gi} (*zoo.*) Dog; (*fig.*) vile man. ~ **biti**, (*ent.*) dog-louse: ~ **gibi**, always begging: ~ **kulübesi**, dog-kennel: ~ **muamelesi yapmak (-e)**, treat s.o. like dirt/a dog: ~ **soyu**, degenerate, good-for-nothing: ~ **piresi**, (*ent.*) dog flea: ~ **tenyası**, (*zoo.*) dog tapeworm: ~ **yayını**, (*ich.*) catfish: ~**le yatan pire ile kalkar**, if you touch pitch your hands get dirty: ~**in ağzına kemik atmak**, give s.o. a sop to quieten him.

köpek·ayası^{nı} (*bot.*) White horsehound. ~**balığı**^{nı}, (*ich.*) smooth hound. ~**dili**^{ni}, (*ich.*) flounder. ~**dişi**^{ni}, (*bio.*) canine tooth. ~**giller**, (*zoo.*) dog family, Canidae. ~**kuyruğu**^{nu}, (*sp.*) a wrestling hold. ~**lemek**, *vi.* get very tired; regret stg. ~**lenmek/~leşmek**, *vi.* become like a dog; cringe. ~**lik**, low-down behaviour; baseness. ~**memesi**^{ni}, (*bio.*) tumour under the armpit. ~**üzümü**^{nü}, (*bot.*) black nightshade.

köpoğlu^{nu} Scoundrel; s.o. very cunning. ~ **köpek!**, you dog, son of a dog! (*violent abuse*). ~**luk**, dirty trick.

köprü (*eng.*) Bridge; hasp (of lock); (*naut.*) bridge; (*sp.*) various bridge-like wrestling holds/positions. ~ **ayağı**, abutment: ~ **başı**, (*mil.*) bridge-head; (*fig.*) small success: ~ **kantar**, weigh-bridge: ~ **vinci**, (*eng.*) gantry-crane: ~**den geçinceye kadar ayıya dayı derler**, treat people with respect as long as they can harm//help you: ~**ye gelmek**, (*sp.*) (wrestling) be held in a bridgelike position.

köprü·cü (*eng.*) Bridge-builder; (*mil.*) pontoon builder. ~**cü¹k**^{gü}, small bridge. ~**cükkemiği**^{ni}, (*bio.*) clavicle, collar-bone. ~**cülük**, bridge-building. ~**gözü**^{nü}, arch of a bridge. ~**lü**, bridged: ~ **kavşak**, (*mot.*) multilevel interchange.

köpü¹k^{gü} Froth; foam; scum; lather; foam-rubber. ~**lenmek**, *vi.* be covered with foam, etc. ~**lü**, fizzy, frothy, bubbly: ~ **kaymak**, (*cul.*) whipped cream: ~ **şarap**, (*cul.*) sparkling wine.

köpüle·mek (-i) (*tex.*) Quilt. ~**nmiş**, *a.* quilted.

kö·pürmek *vi.* Froth; foam; lather; bubble; (*fig.*) foam at the mouth, be very angry. ~**pürtmek (-i)**, *vc.* ~**pürtücü**, (*chem.*) foaming. ~**püz**, scum.

kör Blind; dim, dark; blank; blunt (knife, etc.); small-meshed (net); (*fig.*) without foresight; careless. ~ **baca**, (*fig.*) dead-end, cul-de-sac: ~ **baskı**, (*pub.*) blind stamping/tooling: ~ **boğaz**, (*pej.*) appetite: ~ **çapa**, (*agr.*) shovel: ~ **değneğini bellemiş gibi**, he does it as a matter of course// without reflection: ~ **dövüşü**, confusion, muddle: ~ **duman**, (*bot.*) bloom (on fruit): ~ **fare**, (*zoo.*) lesser mole rat: ~ **hat**, (*rly.*) dead end: ~ **kadı**, outspoken, forthright: ~ **kadıya** ~**sün demek**, 'call a spade a spade': ~KANDİL: ~ **kapak**, (*naut.*) dead-light: ~KAYA: ~ ~ **parmağım gözüne**, as plain as a pikestaff: ~KÖSTEBEK: ~KUYU: ~ **kütük**, blind/dead drunk: ~ **mağara balığı**, (*ich.*) blind cave-fish: ~ **nişancılık**, aiming at random: ~ **nokta**, blind spot: ~OCAK: ~OĞLU: ~ **olası herif**, the cursed fellow: ~ **ölür badem gözlü olur, kel ölür sırma saçlı olur**, exaggerated praise of the dead//the past//stg. missing: ~ **sıçan**, (*zoo.*) mole; ~ **talih**, bad luck, evil destiny: ~ **tane**, (*myc.*) bunted grain; smut-ball: ~ **tapa**, (*eng.*) blanking-

off plug: ~ **topal**, incompletely; somehow: ~ **uçuş**, (*aer.*) blind flying: ~YILAN: ~**le yatan şaşı kalkar**, evil communications corrupt good manners: ~**ü** ~**üne**, blindly; like lightning; at random; carelessly: ~**ün taşı rast geldi**, a lucky shot: ~**ünü kırmak**, humble s.o.'s pride: ~**ünü öldürmek**, control one's temper: ~**ünü öldürmez**, he will not give way.

Kör. = (*geo.*) KÖRFEZ.

kör·ağa¹ç^{cı} (*carp.*) Middle sheet of plywood. ~**bağırsa¹k**^{gı}, (*bio.*) caecum; appendix: ~ **yangısı**, (*med.*) appendicitis. ~**düğüm**, knot that can't be untied; tangle; deadlock. ~**ebe**, (*child.*) blind man's buff; the blindfolded player. ~**elim/~elme**, (*bio.*) atrophy. ~**elmek**, *vi.* (fire) die down, go out; (spring) dry up; (*bio.*) atrophy; disappear; (knives) become blunt. ~**eltici**, blinding. ~**eşe**, frozen crust on snow.

körfez (*geo.*) Gulf; inlet, cove; (*fig.*) sheltered (spot).

kör·kandil Blind drunk. ~**kaya**, (*geo.*) submerged rock. ~**kemer**, (*arch.*) blind arch(way). ~**köstebe¹k**^{gi}, (*zoo.*) Mediterranean mole. ~**kuyu**, dried-up well. ~**lemeden/~lemesine**, blindly, at random. ~**lenmek/~leşmek**, *vi.* become blind; become blunt; (*fig.*) get rusty/stale; become useless. ~**leştirmek/~letmek (-i)**, blind; blunt; deaden; extinguish; (*fig.*) damp, discourage; bring to nought. ~**lük**, blindness; bluntness; lack of foresight; blundering. ~**oca¹k**^{gı}, childless home. ~**oğlu**^{nu}, (*myth.*) popular hero; (*col.*) 'the missus': ~**nun ayvazı**, inseparable companion.

körpe Fresh; tender; young and fresh. ~**lik**, freshness; tenderness; youth.

köruzantı (*bio.*) Diverticulum.

körü¹k^{gü} Bellows, blower; (*mot.*) folding hood. ~**çü**, bellows-maker; s.o. who fans the flames; (*pol.*) instigator, agitator. ~**lemek (-i)**, fan the flames, blow with bellows; (*pol.*) encourage, incite, instigate. ~**lenmek**, *vp.* ~**leyici**, (*pol.*) instigator, agitator. ~**lü**, having a bellows: ~ **barometre**, aneroid barometer: ~ **tampon**, bellows shock-absorber.

kör·yılan (*zoo.*) Blindworm; blind snake. ~**yol**, dead-end, cul-de-sac.

kös^1 *n.* (*mil.*) Big drum. ~ **dinlemiş (davulun sesi vız gelir)**, too sophisticated to be impressed; callous, insensitive.

kös^2 *adv.* ~ ~, walk in a pensive/dejected manner.

köse With little or no beard; (*for.*) sparsely timbered. ~**lik**, beardlessness.

köseği Poker; stick charred at tip.

kösele Stout leather (for soles, etc.). ~ **gibi**, very tough: ~ **suratı**, shameless. ~**taşı**^{nı}, sharpening/grinding tool; sandstone (for polishing marble).

köse·m/~men (*live.*) Ram/goat leading the flock; bellwether; ram/billy-goat trained to fight; (*fig.*) daredevil. ~**menlik**, ~ **etm.**, act as guide.

köskötürüm (*med.*) Completely paralysed.

kösnü Sexual desire; eroticism; lust; sensuality. ~**cül**, sensual, lustful. ~**k**, (*zoo.*) on heat. ~**l**, erotic; desirous; lustful. ~**llük**, eroticism; lust. ~**mek**, *vi.* (*zoo.*) be on heat. ~**yazı**, pornography.

köstebe'kᵍⁱ (*zoo.*) European mole. ~ (illeti), (*med.*) scrofula.
köste'kᵍⁱ Hobble, tether; fetter(s); watch-/keychain; brake; = ESTEK. ~ olm., be a hindrance: ~ vurmak, (*sp.*) squeeze opponent's legs (wrestling): ~i kırmak, break one's fetters, run away.
köstek·lemek (-i) Hobble/tether (animal); (*fig.*) inhibit; bring work to a halt. ~lenmek, *vp.* be hobbled/tethered; be fettered; (*fig.*) grind to a halt. ~li, hobbled, fettered, tethered.
Köstence (*geo.*) Constantsa.
köşe Corner; angle; nook; retreat; (*bot.*) axil. ~ atışı, (*sp.*) corner-kick: ~ başı, street corner; corner (shop, etc.): ~ bucak, every hole and corner: ~ dikmesi, (*arch.*) corner-post: ~ kadısı, stay-at-home: ~ kapmaca, (*child.*) puss-in-thecorner: ~ kırması, (*eng.*, *carp.*) chamfer, bevel: ~ ~ = ~ BUCAK: ~ sarrafı, street-corner moneychanger: ~ taşı, (*arch.*) corner-stone: ~ye çekilmek, withdraw into o.s., participate in nothing: ~ye oturmak, (girl) get married: ~yi dönmek, succeed, 'make it': ~yi dönünce, round the corner. ~bent, (*eng.*) brace clamp; angle-iron. ~gen, (*math.*) diagonal.
köşe'kᵍⁱ (*zoo.*) Camel foal. ~lemek (-i), (camel) drop its foal.
köşe·leme Obliquely, diagonally. ~li, having corners; angled; elbowed; square: ~ ayraç/parantez, (*pub.*) square brackets []: ~ mesnet, (*carp.*) angle-bracket: ~ sıyırcı, (*eng.*) angledozer: ~ yığışım, (*geol.*) breccia. ~lik, (*arch.*) cornerstone; (*dom.*) corner-piece (furniture).
köşkü Pavilion; summer-house; villa, chalet. ~lü, (*obs.*) lookout to give warning of fires.
köt. = KÖTÜLEYİCİ.
köte'kᵍⁱ Beating (with stick). ~ yemek, get a beating.
kötü Bad; abominable; evil. ~ ad, bad name, evil reputation: ~ adam, (*cin.*) the 'baddie': ~ anlaşılmak, be misunderstood: ~ beslenme, (*med.*) malnutrition: ~ davranış/işlem, (*leg.*) misconduct: ~ düşünce/niyet, evil intention: ~ hareketler, evil courses: ~ kadın, prostitute: ~ kişi olm. (-le), incur s.o.'s enmity: ~ ~ düşünmek, be anxious/worried: ~ nitelikli, second-rate: ~ söylemek, speak evil of s.o.: ~ şöhret, disrepute; notoriety: ~ yola düşmek, become a prostitute: ~ yönetim, mismanagement: ~ yürekli, ill-disposed: ~ye almak, misunderstand: ~ye kullanmak, misuse one's powers; abuse s.o.'s kindness, etc.
kötü·cü *a.* Evil, bad. ~cül, malevolent, malicious; evil-doing; (*med.*) pernicious; malignant: ~ ur, (*med.*) carcinoma, cancer: ~ ur yapan, (*bio.*) carcinogen(ic). ~leme, *vn.* slander. ~lemek (-i), slander, speak ill of, denigrate; censure: *vi.* become a wreck (from illness). ~lenmek, *vi.* evil be spoken of s.o. ~leşim, *vn.* deterioration. ~leşmek, *vi.* become bad; deteriorate. ~leştirmek (-i), *vc.* ~leyici, derogatory. ~lük, badness; bad action; harm; evil, wickedness: ~e yüz tutmak, change for the worse. ~lükçü, evil, wicked; malevolent. ~msemek (-i), think ill of s.o. ~mser, pessimistic; derogatory: ~ piyasa, (*fin.*) bear market. ~mserlik, pessimism.

kötürüm (*med.*) Paralysed; crippled; (*fig.*) unworkable. ~leşmek, *vi.* become paralysed. ~lük, paralysis.
köy Village; country(-side). ~ ağa/muhtarı, village headman: ~ İşleri Bakan(lığ)ı, (*adm.*) Minis·ter/ (-try) for Rural Affairs: ~ kurulu, council of (village) elders: ~ü bugün çıkarırız, we'll reach the village today: ~ün kabadayısı, young blood.
köy·cü(lük) (Work of) s.o. involved in village affairs/rural development. ~deş, fellow-villager. ~kentⁱ, independent rural centre. ~lü, *n.* villager; peasant; village people: *a.* rough; bucolic. ~lük, site of a village. ~lülük, being a villager. ~odasıⁿ¹, guesthouse for travellers; community centre. ~sü, rustic.
köz Embers, cinders. ~leme, *vn.*; (*cul.*) meat, etc. grilled on the embers. ~lemek (-i), grill/cook on the embers.
Kr. = (*adm.*) KRALLIĞI; (*ch.s.*) KRİPTON; (*fin.*) KURUŞ.
kraft Kraft wrapping paper.
kraking (*chem.*) Cracking.
kral (*adm.*) King; (*fig.*) most important person; very successful businessman. ~ cennet kuşu, (*orn.*) king bird of paradise: ~ kolibri, (*orn.*) crimson topaz: ~ kuş, (*orn.*) eastern kingbird: ~ naibi, (*adm.*) regent: ~ olm., become king, ascend the throne: ~ penguen, (*orn.*) king penguin: ~ yengeç, (*zoo.*) horse-shoe crab.
kral·ağacıⁿ¹ (*bot.*) Madagascar rosewood. ~cı(lık), royal·ist/(-ism). ~içe, queen; queen-consort; (*ent.*) queen; (*fig.*) first woman (in a contest): ~ gibi, beautiful and splendidly dressed (woman). ~ içelik, (*adm.*) queendom; (*fig.*) queenship; queenliness. ~iyetⁱ/~lık, (*adm.*) kingdom; (*fig.*) kingship.
krampⁱ (*med.*, *sp.*) Cramp. ~ girmek, get cramp. ~on, (*sp.*) crampon.
krankⁱ (*eng.*) Crank(shaft). ~ kol/mili, con(nect-ing)-rod.
kran(y)oloji (*med.*) Craniology.
-kra·si *n. suf.* -cracy [PLUTOKRASİ]. -~t, *n. suf.* -crat [BÜROKRAT]. -~tik, *a. suf.* [OTOKRATİK].
krater (*geol.*) Crater.
kravat¹ (*mod.*) Cravat, tie.
kre·asyon(izm) Creation(ism). ~atör, creator.
kredi (*fin.*) Credit; loan; (*fig.*) trust. ~ açan, creditor: ~ açmak (-e), give credit: ~ ile, credit-; on account: ~ kartı, credit card: ~ mektubu, letter of credit: ~si düşmek, lose credit.
krem Face-/hand-cream; cream (colour). ~ karamel, (*cul.*) crème brûlée: ~ kraker, (*cul.*) cream cracker: ~ renkli, cream-coloured: ~ şantiyi, (*cul.*) whipped cream: ~ tartar = KIRIMTARTAR.
krem·a (*cul.*) Cream; custard. ~alı, creamy. ~lemek (-i), spread cream on stg.
krematoryum Crematorium.
kreol (*ethn.*) Creole.
kreozotᵘ (*chem.*) Creosote.
krepⁱ (*tex.*) Crêpe silk; (*cul.*) pancake; (*chem.*) crêpe rubber. ~ sol, crêpe sole (of shoes). ~döşin, (*tex.*) crêpe de Chine. ~on, crêpe paper.
kreş (*soc.*) Crèche, day nursery.

kreşendo (*mus.*) Crescendo.
kretase (*geol.*) Cretaceous.
kreten(izm) (*med.*) Cretin(ism).
kreton (*tex.*) Cretonne.
kriket[i] (*sp.*) Cricket.
krik-krak (*cul.*) Bread sticks.
kriko (*eng.*) Jack(ing device).
kriminoloji Criminology.
krinolin (*mod.*) Crinoline.
krip ~ etm., (*geol.*) creep.
krip·to (*pol.*) Crypto. ~ton, (*chem.*) krypton.
kristal[i] (*chem.*) Crystal; (*dom.*) cut-glass. ~ bilgisi = ~OGRAFİ: ~ gibi = ~Lİ. ~leşme, *vn.* crystallization. ~leşmek, *vi.* crystallize. ~leştirmek (-i), crystallize. ~li, crystalline. ~ografi, crystallography. ~oit, crystalloid.
kri·ter Criterion. ~tik, (*lit.*, *phys.*) critical; (*lit.*) review; (*fig.*) critical, dangerous. ~tisizm, criticism.
kriyo- *pref.* Cryo-. ~lit[i], (*geol.*) cryolite. ~loji, (*phys.*) cryology. ~skopi, cryoscopy.
kriz Crisis; turning-point; (*fin.*) depression; (*med.*) acme, crisis, attack. ~ geçirmek, pass through a crisis; (*med.*) have an attack of . . ..
kriz- *pref.* Chrys-. ~alit[i], (*ent.*) chrysalis. ~antem, (*bot.*) chrysanthemum. ~olit[i], (*geol.*) chrysolite. ~opraz, (*geol.*) chrysoprase, green chalcedony.
kroke (*sp.*) Croquet.
kroket[i] (*cul.*) Croquette.
kroki Drawing, sketch.
krol ~ yüzme, (*sp.*) crawl stroke: ~ yüzmek, crawl.
krom (*chem.*) Chromium. ~ kap(lama)lı, (*min.*) chromium-plated: ~ sarısı, chrome yellow. ~at[i], chromate. ~atik, chromatic. ~atin, (*bio.*) chromatin. ~atofor, chromatophore. ~atografi, (*chem.*) chromatography. ~e, ~ kapak, (*pub.*) colour-printed jacket. ~ik, (*chem.*) chromic. ~lamak (-i), (*min.*) chromium-plate. ~oplast[i], (*bio.*) chromoplast. ~osfer, (*ast.*) chromosphere. ~ozom, (*bio.*) chromosome.
kron (*fin.*) Crown, kroner.
kron·aksi (*bio.*) Chronaxia. ~ik, (*med.*) chronic. ~ikleşmek, *vi.* become chronic. ~ograf, (*phys.*) chronograph. ~oloji, (*his.*) chronology. ~ometre, (*phys.*) chronometer.
kropi ~ bağı, (*naut.*) figure-of-eight knot.
kros (*sp.*) Cross-country running.
kroşe ~ örgüsü, (*tex.*) crochet(-work).
krş. = KARŞILAŞTIRINIZ; KURUŞ. ~ d. = (*ling.*) KARŞILAŞTIRMA DERECESİ.
krupiye(lik) (*gamb.*) (Work of) croupier.
kruvasan (*cul.*) Croissant.
kruvaze (*mod.*) Double-breasted.
kruvaziyer Pleasure-cruise.
kruvazman (Street-)crossing; cross-over.
kruvazör (*naut.*) Cruiser, light battleship.
ks. = KİLOSİKL.
ksantofil (*bot.*) Xantophyll.
ksenon (*chem.*) Xenon.
ksilofon (*mus.*) Xylophone.
ksilol (*chem.*) Xylol, xylene.
KT, kt. = (*ling.*) KİŞİ TEK. ~C = KIBRIS TÜRK CEMİYETİ. ~FD = KIBRIS TÜRK FEDERE DEVLETİ.

~HY = KIBRIS TÜRK HAVA YOLLARI. ~p = KİTAPLIK. ~Ü = KARADENİZ TEKNİK ÜNİVERSİTESİ.
ku (*sp.*) Blow, hit.
Ku. = (*ch.s.*) KURÇATOVYUM; (*geo.*) KUZEY.
kuaför Hairdresser.
kuars (*geol.*) Quartz. ~it[i], quartzite.
kuartet[i] (*mus.*) Quartet.
kuasar (*ast.*) Quasar.
kuaterner (*geol.*) Quaternary.
kubaşmak (-le) Share/be partners in doing stg.
kubat[i] Vulgar, coarse; common (accent). ~lık, coarseness, vulgarity.
kubbe (*arch.*) Dome; cupola; vault; canopy; (*ast.*) vault of heaven. ~ bileziği, (*arch.*) drum: ~leri çınlatmak, make the welkin ring. ~altı[m], (*his.*) council chamber. ~li, domed; dome-shaped.
kubur Holster; quiver; horse-pistol; waste-pipe of latrine. ~ sıkmak, fire (pistol). ~luk, powder flask; pistol-holster.
kuca[lk][ğı] Breast; bosom; embrace; armful; lap. ~ açmak (-e), welcome with open arms: ~ çocuğu/ ~ta, babe-in-arms: ~ dolusu, armful: ~ ~, in armfuls, plentifully: ~ ~a, in one another's arms: ~ına almak, embrace; take on one's lap: ~ına düşmek, fall into (stg. evil): ~ına oturmak (-in), sit on s.o.'s knee. ~lamak (-i), embrace; surround; include. ~laşmak (-le), embrace each other.
kuçukuçu (*child.*) Bow-wow, doggie.
kudas (*rel.*) Holy Communion, Mass.
kudret[i] Power; energy; strength; capacity; (*rel.*) God's omnipotence; (*fig.*) wealth; nature. ~ hamamı, thermal spring: ~ helvası, (*bot.*) manna: ~im yetişmez, I am not strong enough; I can't afford it. ~li, powerful; capable. ~siz(lik), powerless(ness); feeble(ness); incapa·ble/(-city).
kudur·gan Furious; wild. ~ganlık, ferocity; wildness. ~mak, *vi.* (*med.*) be attacked by rabies; (*fig.*) go mad/berserk. ~muş, *a.* mad/rabid (animal): ~ gibi etrafa saldırmak, run amok. ~tmak (-i), enrage, infuriate. ~uk, rabid (person/animal); furious.
kuduz *n.* (*med.*) Hydrophobia, rabies. *a.* Rabid; furious. ~böceği[ni], (*ent.*) Spanish blister fly. ~böcekleri, (*ent.*) soldier beetles, Cantharidae. ~otu[nu], (*bot.*) golden alyssum.
kudüm (*Or. mus.*) Small kettle-drum.
Kudüs (*geo.*) Jerusalem. ~ şehri, the Holy City.
kufa Round wickerwork coracle (on Tigris), gufa.
kufi (*art.*) Cufic script for Arabic.
kuğu (*orn.*) Mute swan; (*col.*) swan. ~ yavrusu, cygnet. ~rmak, *vi.* coo (dove).
kuintet[i] (*mus.*) Quintet.
kuka (*tex.*) Ball of lace-thread; (*bot.*) coconut wood.
kukla Doll; (*th.*) puppet; (*mod.*) dummy; (*fig.*) puppet. ~ gibi oynatmak (-i), control/use s.o. (like a puppet): ~ hükümet, (*pol.*) puppet government: ~ oyunu, (*th.*) puppet-show.
kukla·baz/~cı (*th.*) Puppeteer. ~cılık, puppetry. ~lık, puppet-like behaviour.
kuku (*orn.*) Cuckoo.
kuku[lç][cu] (*bot.*) Shell of peach-stone, etc.
kukulete (*mod.*) Hood, cowl.

kukulya (*ent.*) Silkworm cocoon. ~**cı**, gypsy fortune-teller: ~ **fırtınası**, mid-April storm.
kukumav (*orn.*) Little owl. ~ **gibi**, sitting all alone: ~ **gibi düşünup durmak**, be very thoughtful and anxious.
kul Slave; creature; (*rel.*) man; (*his.*) Janissary. ~ **cinsi**, slave-born: ~ **daralmayınca/sıkışmayınca Hızır yetişmez**, *said when unexpected help arrives*: ~ **hakkı**, one's duty to one's fellowman: ~ **kâhyası**, (*his.*) Janissary officer: ~ **köle/kurban olm.** (**-e**), be devoted to s.o.: ~ **oğlu**, (*his.*) Janissary son of a Janissary: ~ **olm.**, be s.o.'s slave; do everything asked of one: ~ **taksimi**, equal shares: ~ **yapısı**, man-made, perishable: ~**unuz**, (*obs.*) your servant, I.
kula Russet; dun (horse). ~**cık** = KULAKÇIK.
kula¹çc¹ (*naut.*) Fathom. ~ **atmak**, take soundings; swim overarm: ~ ~, in full measure, freely. ~**lamak (-i)**, fathom; measure with arms extended; swim swiftly.
kulağakaçan (*ent.*) Earwig.
kula¹kğ¹ (*bio.*) Ear; (*ich.*) gill; (*fig.*) attention; ear-shaped handle, etc.; flap; (*mus.*) peg (of violin, etc.); (*mus.*) pitch recognition; (*cul.*) forcemeat ball (in soup). ~ + , *a.* Aural; auditory: ~ **ağrısı**, (*med.*) ear-ache; ~ **asmak**, lend an ear; pay attention: ~ **asma!**, pay no heed!: ~ **çınlaması**, (*med.*) tinnitus: ~ **çukuru**, (*bio.*) concha: ~ **delmek**, make an ear-splitting noise: ~ **dolgunluğu**, hearsay; knowledge acquired by listening: ~ **erimi**, range of hearing: ~ **kabartmak**, prick up one's ears; eavesdrop, listen furtively: ~ **kepçesi**, (*bio.*) auricle: ~ **kesilmek**, listen attentively, be all ears: ~ **kiri**, (*med.*) cerumen, ear-wax: ~ **misafiri olm.**, overhear others' conversation; eavesdrop: ~ **tıkamak**, pretend not to hear; shut one's ears: ~ **tutmak**, listen: ~ **vermek (-e)**, listen attentively, pay heed to: ~ **yumuşağı**, (*bio.*) ear-lobe.
kulağı: ~ **ağır**, hard of hearing: ~ **ağır işitmek**, hear with difficulty: ~ **bunda/şunda olm.**, pay attention: ~ **çınlasın!**, may his ears burn: ~ **delik**, who keeps his ears open, wide awake, alert: ~ **dolgun**, well-informed: ~ **kirişte (olm.)**, wide awake/(listen very hard): ~ **okşamak**, be pleasant to the ears: ~ **tıkalı**, deaf, hard of hearing: ~**ma küpe oldu**, that was a lesson to me; I never forgot it: ~**n dış çukuru**, (*bio.*) concha.
kulağına: ~ **çalınmak**, overhear stg.: ~ **çan çalmak**, din stg. into s.o.'s ears: ~ **davul mu çalınıyor?**, are you deaf?: ~ **girmek**, pay attention: ~ **kar suyu kaçmak**, be in a difficult situation: ~ **koymak/solmak**, prime s.o., drop s.o. a hint; force s.o. to hear stg.: ~ **küpe olsun**, let that be a warning to you, take that piece of advice: ~ **söylemek**, whisper.
kulağını: ~ **bükmek**, warn s.o. secretly of stg.: ~ **çekmek**, pull s.o.'s ear; punish as a warning: ~ **çınlatmak (-in)**, think of/remember s.o.: ~ **doldurmak**, prime s.o.; persuade s.o.: ~ **ensesinden göstermek**, do stg. clumsily.
kulak-: ~**la duyulur**, audible: ~**ları ağırlaşmak**, become hard of hearing: ~**ları çınlasın** = KULAĞI:

~**ları dolmak**, get tired of hearing stg. repeatedly: ~**ları kirişte**, all ears: ~**ları paslanmak**, not have heard good music for a long time: ~ **ları patlatan**, ear-splitting (noise): ~**larına kadar kızarmak**, blush to the roots of one's hair: ~**larını dikmek**, cock one's ears: ~**larını tıkamak (-e)**, shut one's ears to stg.: ~**larının pasını gidermek**, hear good music again: ~**tan dolma**, hearsay; knowledge gained here and there: ~**tan ~a**, (news, etc.) passed on secretly: ~**tan pamuğunu çıkarmak**, take the cottonwool out of one's ears; become attentive.
kulak·altı (*bio.*) Parotid: ~ **bezi yangısı**, (*med.*) parotitis. ~**burunboğazbilimi**, otorhinolaryngology. ~**çı**, (*med.*) ear nose and throat specialist. ~**çı¹kğ¹**, (*bio.*) auricle (of heart). ~**çın**, (*mod.*) ear-flaps. ~**davulu**, (*bio.*) tympanum. ~**demiri**ⁿⁱ, (*agr.*) mouldboard (of plough). ~**lı**, having ears; eared; double-edged knife: ~ **dalgıç kuşu**, (*orn.*) horned grebe: ~ **fok**, (*zoo.*) fur-seal: ~ **orman baykuşu**, (*orn.*) long-eared owl: ~ **somun**, (*eng.*) wing-nut: ~ **tarla kuşu//yumurta piçi**, (*orn.*) horned lark// grebe. ~**lık**, (*mod.*) ear-flaps; (*rad.*) ear-piece, headphone; (*med.*) hearing-aid. ~**memesi**ⁿⁱ, (*bio.*) ear-lobe. ~**mumu**ⁿᵘ, cerumen, wax. ~**sız**, earless. ~**tozu**ⁿᵘ, (*bio.*) sensitive spot behind the ear. ~**zarı**ⁿⁱ, (*bio.*) ear-drum membrane.
kulampara(lık) Pederast(y), bugger(y).
kulan (*zoo.*) Asiatic wild ass.
kulas (*mot.*) Cylinder-head.
kule Tower, turret. ~ **kara sağan**, (*orn.*) swift. ~**li**, (*arch.*) castellated.
kulis (*th.*) Coulisses, wings, backstage; (*fin.*) street broker; (*adm.*) corridors of power; inner workings, secret machinations. ~ **faaliyeti**, behind-the-scenes activity: ~ **gürültüsu**, (*th.*) noises off: ~ **yapmak**, work behind the scenes.
kullan·dırmak (-i, -e) *vc.* ~**ılmak**, *vp.* ~**ılmama**, abeyance, desuetude. ~**ılmış**, used, worn; second-hand. ~**ık**, used, spent. ~**ım**, use; economy: ~**dan düşmüş** (*ling.*) obsolete. ~**ımbilim**, (*phil.*) pragmatics. ~**ımsal**, pragmatic. ~**ış**, manner of use. ~**ışlı**, in use; serviceable; handy; practical; easily run/used. ~**ışsız**, not in use; difficult to run/use. ~**ma**, *vn.* using; use; operating; driving (car): ~ **hakkı**, (*leg.*) easement. ~**mak (-i)**, use; employ; treat; direct; operate, drive (car), steer (ship); exercise, make use of, avail o.s. of; take habitually (food, drink, tobacco, etc.); deal tactfully with s.o., humour s.o.
kulla¹pb¹ (*tex.*) Device for winding gold thread on silk.
kulluk Slavery, servitude; (*his.*) guard-house; devotion. ~ **etm.**, be a slave: ~ **kölelik**, being at s.o.'s beck and call. ~**çu**, (*his.*) Janissary on duty in the guard-house; (*adm.*) official.
kulm (*geol.*) Culm.
kulom(b) (*el.*) Coulomb.
kulör Colour.
kulpᵘ Handle (of jug, etc.); pommel; pretext, excuse. ~ **takmak**, invent a pretext; find an excuse (to blame/ridicule s.o.): ~**una getirmek**, seize the opportunity (to say stg.): ~**unu bulmak**, find an excuse/a way of settling a matter: ~**unu**

kaybetmek, be at a loss to know what to do. ~lu, having a handle.

kuluçka (*live.*) Broody hen; incubation. ~ **devri**, incubation period (eggs, microbes): ~ **makinesi**, incubator, hatching machine: ~ **olm.**, become broody: ~**ya oturmak/yatmak**, brood, sit, incubate.

kulun (*zoo.*) New-born foal. ~ **atmak**, (*live.*) abort a foal. ~**lamak (-i)**, drop a foal. ~**luk**, (*zoo.*) womb.

kulun¹çᶜᵘ (*med.*) Sharp pain; colic; lumbago, stiff neck. ~ **kırmak**, massage away the pain.

kulübe Hut; shed, booth; cabin; (*mil.*) sentry-box.

kulü¹pᵇᵘ Club; club-house. ~ **değiştirme**, (*sp.*) transfer: ~-**otel**, apartment-hotel, service flats.

kulvar (*sp.*) Lane.

kum Sand; grain; gravel; (*med.*) stone, gravel. ~ **alanı**, (*sp.*) arena: ~ **bağırtlağı**, (*orn.*) black-bellied sandgrouse: ~BALIĞI: ~ **başı**, sandy beach: ~ **engereği**, (*zoo.*) sand viper: ~ **fırtınası**, (*met.*) sandstorm: ~ **gibi**, countless, innumerable: ~ **gibi kaynamak**, swarm in countless numbers: ~ **kırlangıcı**, (*orn.*) bank swallow: ~ **lirası**, (*zoo.*) lyre urchin: ~ **piresi**, (*ent.*) sand-hopper; jigger, sand-flea: ~ **püskürtme**, (*min.*) sandblasting: ~ **saati**, hourglass: ~ **seti**, (*geo.*) sandbar: ~ **tepeciği**, sand-dune: ~ **torbası**, sandbag: ~ **turnası**, (*orn.*) sandhill grouse: ~ **yılanı**, (*zoo.*) sand boa: ~**a oturmak**, (*naut.*) run on a sandbank: ~**da oynamak**, remain emptyhanded.

kuma (*obs.*) Fellow-wife; second/third/fourth wife.

Kuman (*his.*, *ethn.*) Tk. tribe in the Ukraine.

kumanda (*mil.*) Command, order; command, authority; control. ~ **etm.**, command; give an order; (*aer.*) be at the controls: ~ **kulesi**, (*naut.*) conning tower: ~ **masası**, (*aer.*) console: ~ **modülü**, (*aer.*) command module.

kuman·dalı (*eng.*) Robot. ~**dan**, (*mil.*) commander, commandant. ~**danlık**, (*mil.*) command. ~**darya**, (*cul.*) Comanderia wine of Cyprus.

Kumandı (*ethn.*) Shamanist Tk. tribe in Altay region.

kumanya (*aer.*, *naut.*) Provisions; (*mil.*) portable rations; (*naut.*) stern locker. ~**cı**, ship's chandler; caterer.

kumar Gambling. ~ **müptelası/**~**a düşkün**, addicted to gambling: ~**a yüzü yok**, he can't resist a gamble: ~**da yemek (-i)**, gamble stg. away. ~**baz/**~**cı**, gambler. ~**bazlık**, gambling. ~**hane**, gambling-den.

kumaş (*tex.*) Tissue; fabric; material; cloth; texture; quality. ~ **mengenesi**, mangle, roller: ~ **topu**, bolt of cloth: ~ **ütü tutmuyor**, the cloth won't iron well: ~ **yıkamağa gelmez boyası çıkar**, the cloth won't wash as its colour runs: ~**ı asmak**, drape: ~**tan bir palto çıkmak**, cloth suffice for an overcoat.

kumbalığıⁿ¹ (*ich.*) Sandeel. ~**giller**, sandeels.

kumbara Money-box; (*mil.*) mortar-bomb. ~ **çivisi**, hobnail. ~**cı**, (*his.*) bombardier. ~**hane**, (*obs.*) bomb factory.

kum·cu Building-sand dealer. ~**cul**, (*bot.*) arenaceous.

kumkuma Narrow-necked vase/bottle; collector// collection of things.

kum·la Sandy place; beach; bathing-beach. ~**lama**, sand-blasting. ~**lu**, sandy, arenaceous; gravelly; gritty; (*tex.*) speckled: ~ **göktaşı**, (*geol.*) chondrite. ~**luk**, sandy (place); sands. ~**otu**ⁿᵘ, (*bot.*) scabious; sandwort.

kumpanya (*fin.*) (Foreign) company; (*th.*) troupe; (*fig.*) gang.

kumpas (*math.*) Callipers; (*pub.*) composing-stick; (*fig.*) calculation; trick, plot. ~ **kurmak**, calculate; plot: ~ **sallamak**, (*sl.*) daydream; be heedless: ~**ı iyi kurdu**, he laid his plans well. ~**lı**, arranged, concerted; plotted, planned.

kumral Reddish-yellow; auburn (hair); light-chestnut (horse); darkish (complexion).

kumru (*orn.*) Turtle dove. ~ **ötüşü**, cooing. ~**giller**, doves.

kum·sal Sandy (beach). ~**sallık**, sandiness; sand-pit. ~**taşı**ⁿ¹, (*geol.*) sandstone.

kumu¹çᶜᵘ (*ent.*) Type of swarming crop-damaging fly.

Kumuk (*ethn.*) Tk. tribe in Daghestan.

kumul (*geo.*) Sand-dune; down(s).

kumulus (*met.*) Cumulus.

-kun *a./n. suf.* [223] = -GİN [COŞKUN].

kunda (*zoo.*) A large poisonous spider.

kunda¹kᵍ¹ Bundle of rags; swaddling clothes; headscarf; bundle of oily rags (for incendiarism); stock (of gun); gun-carriage. ~ **bombası**, (*mil.*) fire-/incendiary-bomb: ~ **sokmak (-e)**, set fire to; sabotage: ~**taki çocuk**, babe-in-arms: ~**tan beri**, from the cradle.

kundak·çı Gun-stock maker; incendiary, arsonist; firebrand, saboteur, wrecker. ~**çılık/**~**lama**, arson; sabotage. ~**lamak (-i)**, swaddle; set fire to; (*fig.*) wreck, sabotage; tie hair in a headscarf. ~**lanmak**, *vp.*

kundura (Rough) shoe. ~ **bağı**, shoelace: ~ **boyası**, boot-polish. ~**cı**, shoemaker, cobbler. ~**cılık**, shoemaking; cobbling.

kunduz (*zoo.*) Beaver; (*col.*) otter. ~ **böceği** = KUDUZ-: ~ **hayası**, castor sac.

kuntᵘ Strong; thick; solid.

kuntrat = KONTRAT.

kup (*mod.*) Cut.

kupa¹ Metal cup/vase; (*sp.*) cup; (*gamb.*) hearts. ~ **birincisi**, (*sp.*) cup-winner: ~ **final/sonu**, (*sp.*) cup-final.

kupa² Brougham, coupé.

kupes (*ich.*) Bogue.

kupkuru Bone-dry; dry as dust.

kup·laj (*eng.*) Coupling. ~**ol**, (*min.*, *naut.*) cupola ~**on**, (*fin.*) coupon; (*mod.*) suitlength; remnant ~**ür**, (*pub.*) cutting.

kur¹ *n.* (*fin.*) Rate of exchange; (*ed.*) course.

kur² *n.* Courting, flirting. ~ **yapma**, courtship: ~ **yapmak (-e)**, court, pay one's addresses to.

Kur. = (*mil.*) KURMAY. ~ **Bşk.** = KURMAY BAŞ KAN(LIĞ)I.

kura¹/**kur'a** Drawing of lots; ballot; (*mil.*) conscription (by lots); year/class of conscripts. ~ **asker eri**, conscript: ~ **çekmek**, draw lots; ballot: ~

efradı, raw conscripts: ~ **sı olm. (. . . yılın)**, belong to such a year/class (of conscripts).

kura² (*obs.*) Villages. = KARYE.

kurabiye (*cul.*) Cake with almonds/nuts, short-bread.

kuracı (*mil.*) Officer in charge of conscripting.

kurada Shrivelled; decrepit; worn out, broken down.

kurak (*geo.*) Dry, arid, rainless; desert. ~ **çıl**, (*bot.*) xerophilous; xerophyte. ~ **lık**, drought, aridity; dustbowl.

kural Rule; (*leg.*) code; basis; standard, system; (*ling.*) rule, harmony. ~ **bozmak**, break/violate a rule.

kural·cı(lık) Norma·tive/(-lcy). ~ **dışı**, (*ling.*) irregular; anomalous; exceptional. ~ **dışılık**, irregularity; anomaly; exception. ~ **laşma**, *vn.* becoming a rule. ~ **laşmak**, *vi.* become a rule. ~ **laştırmak (-i)**, make into a rule. ~ **lı**, in accordance with rules; fair; (*ling.*) regular. ~ **sız**, (*ling.*) irregular, exceptional, anomalous; unfair, foul.

kuram (*phil.*) Theory. ~ **cı**, theoretician, theorist. ~ **cılık**, theoretics. ~ **sal**, theoretical; abstract. ~ **sız**, lacking theory.

Kur'an/Kuran¹ *n.* (*rel.*) Koran. ~ **çarpmak (-e)**, for the Koran to punish a profane act.

kuran² *n.* (*arch.*) Constructor, builder; founder.

kuran³ *n.* Current. ~ **der**, draught.

kurbağa (*zoo.*) Frog. ~ **adam**, (*naut.*) frogman: ~ **ağızlıgiller**, (*orn.*) frogmouths: ~ **balığı**, (*ich.*) stargazer: ~ **hoplar**, (*ent.*) frog-hopper.

kurbağa·cık (*zoo.*) Little frog; (*med.*) tumour on the tongue; (*eng.*) adjustable wrench; spanner; (*arch.*) handle of window-frame. ~ **giller**, (*zoo.*) Amphibia; batrachians. ~ **lama**, (*sp.*) climbing frogwise; breast-stroke (swimming). ~ **lık**, grill on water-pipes. ~ **otu**ⁿᵘ, (*bot.*) buttercup. ~ **zehiri-giller**, (*bot.*) frog-bit family, Hydrocharidaceae.

kurban (*rel.*) Sacrifice; victim; (*fig.*) fall-guy. ~ **Bayramı**, Muslim Festival of Sacrifices: ~ **etm. (-i, -e)**, sacrifice: ~ **gitmek (-e)**, fall a victim to: ~ **kesmek**, kill as a sacrifice: ~ **olm.**, sacrifice o.s.: be a victim: ~ **olayım!**, I beseech you!: ~ **payı**, part of sacrificed sheep given to the poor: ~ **vermek**, suffer casualties. ~ **lık**, sacrificial sheep; (*fig.*) mild inoffensive man: ~ **koyun gibi**, knowing nothing of the (unpleasant) future.

kurca Irritation; itching. ~ **çıbanı**, irritable ulcer. ~ **lama**, *vn.*; irritation. ~ **lamak (-i)**, scratch, rub; irritate; (*fig.*) meddle with; fiddle about with; tamper with. ~ **lanmak**, *vp.*

kurçatovyum (*chem.*) Kurchatovium.

kurd- = KURT.

kurdele (*mod.*) Ribbon, sash, tape. ~ **sini kesmek**, (*mot. sl.*) be given a ticket. ~ **balığı**ⁿ¹, (*ich.*) red bandfish.

kurdeşen (*med.*) Rash (as in measles); nettle-rash.

kurdur(t)mak (-i, -e) *vc.* = KURMAK.

kurgan Fortress; (*archaeol.*) sepulchre; tumulus.

kurgu Winder/key (of watch); winding up; (*arch.*) assembly, construction; (*phil.*) speculation; (*cin.*) montage, editing.

kurgu·bilim (*lit.*) Science-fiction. ~ **cu(luk)**, (*cin.*)

(work of) editor. ~ **lamak (-i)**, edit. ~ **sal**, (*phil.*) speculative.

kuriye = KURYE.

kurkᵘ (*orn.*) Broody hen.

kurlağan (*med.*) Whitlow.

kur·ma *vn.* Erecting, installation; winding, etc.; creation, formation, etc.: *a.* portable; (toy) that winds up: ~ **suç**, (*leg.*) premeditated crime. ~ **macılık**, (*art.*) constructivism. ~ **mak (-i)**, set up; constitute, establish; organize, create, form, found; (*th.*) produce; plan, devise; set one's heart on; set (trap); cock (gun); pitch (tent); wind (clock, toy, etc.); prime s.o.; egg s.o. on; brood over stg.: **kura kura**, by brooding over stg.: **kurup takma**, assembly: **kurup takmak**, assemble.

kurmay (*mil.*) Staff. ~ **başkan(lığ)ı**, (rank/post/duties of) chief of staff. ~ **lık**, staff duties.

kurna Basin (of bath/fountain); sink.

kurnaz Cunning, shrewd; astute, artful, crafty. ~ **ca**, cunningly, etc. ~ **lık**, cunning, shrewdness; astuteness; trick; sharp practice.

kuron (*med.*) Crown (of tooth); (*fin.*) crown, kroner. ~ **takmak**, crown a tooth.

kurs¹ *n.* Disc; (*med.*) lozenge; pastille of incense.

kurs² *n.* (*ed.*) Course; seminar. ~ **iyer**, s.o. taking a course.

kursaˡk**ᵍ¹** (*orn.*) Crop; (*zoo.*) stomach; dried bladder/membrane. ~ **lı**, greedy; 'full of guts'; (*med.*) goitrous.

kurşun (*chem.*) Lead; (*mil.*) bullet; (*adm.*) lead seal. ~ **atmak**, fire (rifle, etc.): ~ **dökmek**, (*med.*) (*superstitious 'cure'*) pour molten lead into cold water over a sick person's head (*performed by* KURŞUNCU KADIN): ~ **erimi**, (*mil.*) range of a bullet: ~ **geçmez/ işlemez**, bullet-proof: ~ **gibi**, very heavy: ~ **kâğıdı**, leadfoil, tinfoil: ~ **tavası**, ladle for melting lead: ~ **tozu**, blacklead, blacking: ~ **yarası**, (*med.*) bullet wound: ~ **a dizmek (-i)**, (*mil.*) condemn to be shot.

kurşun·cu ~ **kadın** = = DÖKMEK. ~ **i**, lead-coloured, dark grey. ~ **kalem**, lead-pencil. ~ **lamak (-i)**, (*arch.*) roof with lead; (*adm.*) apply lead seals; (*mil.*) shoot s.o. ~ **lanmak**, *vp.* ~ **lu**, containing lead; sealed; roofed with lead: ~ **akümülatör**, (*el.*) lead-acid battery. ~ **rengi**, dark grey. ~ **suz**, ~ **fişek**, (*mil.*) blank cartridge.

kurˡ**t**ᵈᵘ (*zoo.*) Wolf, grey wolf; worm, maggot; (*fig.*) s.o. cunning/experienced. ~ **BAĞRI**: ~ **balığı**, (*ich.*) wolf-fish: ~ **BOĞAN**: ~ **dökmek**, (*med.*) pass a worm: ~ **dumanlı havayı sever**, evil-doers shun the light: ~ **düşürmek**, worm (animals): ~ **gibi**, cunning: ~ KAPANI: ~ **kuş yuvasına döndü**, everybody has gone home: ~ **kuyusu**, wolf-pit/-trap: ~ MASALI: ~ PENÇESI: ~ TIRNAĞI: ~ **larını dökmek**, sow one's wild oats; fulfil a long-desired wish: ~ **u olm. (-in)**, be an old hand at . . .; be a hard-bitten . . .: ~ **unu kırmak**, satisfy one's whims.

kurtağzıⁿ¹ (*carp.*) Dovetail; (*naut.*) fairlead.

kurtak (*ind.*) Assembly. ~ **çı**, assembler.

kurtar·ıcı Rescuer, saviour. ~ **ılmak**, *vp.* ~ **ış**, deliverance; rescue. ~ **ma**, *vn.*; rescue; (*naut.*) salvage. ~ **mak (-i)**, save, deliver, rescue; salvage; redeem (stg. pawned); (*gamb.*) recover (one's

losses); (*fin.*) (price) be acceptable. ~**malık**, ransom.
kurt·ayağıⁿ¹ (*bot.*) Clubmoss. ~**bağrı**ⁿ¹, (*bot.*) common privet. ~**bilim**, (*zoo.*) helminthology. ~**boğan**, wolfsbane aconite, common monkshood. ~**çu¹kᵍu**, (*ent.*) grub, larva. ~**döken**, (*med.*) worming (powder). ~**kapanı**ⁿ¹, wolf-pit; (*sp.*) wrestling hold. ~**kıyan**, (*orn.*) oxpecker. ~**köpeği**ⁿ¹, (*zoo.*) wolf-dog, Alsatian. ~**landırmak (-i)**, *vc.* ~**lanmak**, become maggoty/worm-eaten; (*fig.*) become agitated/impatient; fidget. ~**lu**, maggoty, wormy; uneasy, suspicious; fidgety: ~ **kaşar/peynir**, maggoty cheese; (*fig.*) fidgety child. ~**luca**, (*bot.*) germander, (?) birthwort. ~**mantarı**ⁿ¹, (*myc.*) puffball. ~**masalı**ⁿ¹, 'the same old story/excuse!' ~**pençesi/** ~**tırnağı**ⁿ¹, (*bot.*) bistort, snake-root.
kurtul·ma *vn.* Escape. ~**mak**, *vi.* escape; be saved; slip away/out; (woman) be delivered, give birth; be finished: **(-den)**, be rid of, be free from; avoid; evade; get out of; lose one's grip of. ~**malık**, ransom. ~**uş**, liberation; escape; way of escape: ~ **Savaşı**, (*his.*) Tk. War of Liberation, 1919-23: ~ **yolu**, remedy, solution.
kuru *a.* Dry; dried; arid; withered; emaciated; bare; mere; curt; empty (promise, etc.); ineffective. *n.* Dry land; dry part (of stg.). ~ **barometre**, (*phys.*) aneroid barometer: ~ **başına kalmak**, live/be left all alone: ~ **buz**, (*chem.*) dry ice, solid carbon dioxide: ~ **çaylarda boğulmak**, toil without reward: ~ **duvar**, (*arch.*) dry-stone wall: ~ **ekmek**, crust: ~ **erik**, (*cul.*) prune: ~ **fasulye**, (*cul.*) haricot/white bean: ~ **filtre**, dry air-filter: ~ **gösteriş**, mere show: ~ **gürültü**, mere clamour; just a rumour: ~ **hava**, low-humidity/dry air: ~ **iftira**, sheer calumny: ~ **incir**, (*cul.*) dried fig(s): ~ **kadit**, a mere skeleton: ~ **kafa kalmak**, (widow) be left all alone: ~KAFA: ~KAHVE(Cİ): ~ **kalabalık**, aimless crowd: ~ **kalabalık etm.**, hang around and do nothing: ~ **kazı**, (*art.*) dry-point (engraving): ~ **köfte**, (*cul.*) rissole: ~KÖPRÜ: ~ ~**ya**, uselessly, in vain; for no good reason; mere: ~ **kuyu**, cess-pit: ~ **laf**, nonsense; idle promises: ~ **meyve**, (*cul.*) dried fruit: ~ **oda**, unfurnished room: ~ **ot**, (*agr.*) hay: ~ **pil**, (*el.*) dry cell/battery: ~ **poğaça**, (*cul.*) crisp pasty: ~SIKI: ~ **soğuk**, (*met.*) dry cold weather: ~ **şişe**, (*med.*) cupping-glass: ~ **tahtada kalmak**, lose one's furniture; be destitute: ~ **tarım**, (*agr.*) dry farming: ~ **tekne**, (*naut.*) bare hull: ~ **temizle·me/-yici**, (*mod.*) dry-clean·ing/(-er): ~ **toprak/yerde**, on the bare ground: ~ **ün**, a mere name; an empty sound: ~ **üzüm**, (*cul.*) raisin(s): ~ **yanında yaş ta yanar**, the innocent suffer with the guilty: ~YEMİŞ: ~**da kalmak**, (*naut.*) be beached.
kurucu *a.* Founding, establishing; formative. *n.* Founder, promoter; organizer; founder-member. ~ **Meclis**, (*adm.*) Constituent Assembly.
kuru·çekim (*cin.*) Photocopy. ~**kafa**, (*bio.*) skull; (*fig.*) stupid person; (*ent.*) death's head hawk moth; = KURU. ~**kahve(ci)**, (seller of) roasted/ground coffee-beans. ~**köprü**, (*arch.*) viaduct. ~**lamak (-i)**, dry; dry up; wipe dry. ~**lanmak**, *vp.* be dried: *vi.* dry o.s. ~**luk**, dryness.
kurul (*adm.*) Council, committee, board; assembly.

~**lar birliği**, (*adm.*) federation. ~**mak**, *vp.* = KURMAK; be wound; be founded/established, etc. pose, swagger; settle o.s. comfortably. ~**tay** (*adm.*) assembly; congress. ~**uş**, (*adm.*) formatioı foundation, establishment; institution, organiza tion, enterprise.
kurum¹ *n.* Soot. ~ **boyası**, bistre: ~ **tutmak** ~**lanmak¹**, be full of soot. ~**laşma¹**, soot forma tion. ~**lu¹**, sooty.
kurum² *n.* Pose, conceit. ~ ~ **kurulmak**, be exceed ingly puffed up: ~ **satmak/**~**lanmak²**, give o.s airs: ~**undan geçilmiyor**, his conceit is intolerable ~**lu²**, conceited, immodest. ~**suz**, modest.
kurum³ *n.* (*soc.*) Association, society, institutioı (*fin.*) establishment, corporation. ~**lar birliği** (*adm.*) federation: ~**lar vergisi**, corporation tax ~**laşma²**, *vn.* formation of an association, etc ~**laşmak**, *vi.* become an association, etc. ~**laştır mak (-i)**, form an association, etc. ~**sal**, institu tional.
kuru·ma *vn.* Drying; withering; (*ind.*) desiccatioı ~**mak**, *vi.* become dry; dry up; run dry; (*bot.*) wither; (*fig.*) become thin; (*med.*) become para lysed. ~**muş**, *a.* dried up; desiccated.
kuruntu Strange fancy; apprehension, forebodinı illusion, melancholy. ~ **etm.**, be apprehensive: ~ **görmek**, daydream. ~**cu**, apprehensive, sus picious. ~**lanmak (-i)**, forebode; surmise. ~**lu**, fuı of imaginary fears, etc.
kurusıkı (*mil.*) Blank cartridge; (*fig.*) idle threat bluff. ~ **atmak**, fire a blank cartridge; (*fig.*) bluff utter empty threats: ~ **kabadayılık**, bravado.
kuruş (*fin.*) Tk. kurush/piastre. ~ ~, countinı every penny: ~**u** ~**una**, down to the last penny ~**landırmak (-i)**, set out the prices (in lists). ~**luk** piastre-piece; piastre's worth.
kurutᵘ (*cul.*) Dried milk (powder). ~**a¹ç**ᶜ¹, autoı clave; desiccator. ~**ma**, *vn.* drying; (*ind.*) deı hydration, desiccation; (*agr.*) drainage; (*geol.* exsiccation: ~ **dolabı**, (*dom.*) airing cupboardı (*ind.*) autoclave: ~ **kâğıdı**, blotting papeı ~**ma¹ç**ᶜ¹, blotter; blotting paper. ~**mak (-i)**, drʏ dry out; (*ind.*) dehydrate, desiccate; (*geol.* exsiccate; (*agr.*) drain. ~**malık**, (fruit) suitable fo drying. ~**ucu**, (*ind.*) desiccant; drier. ~**ulmak**, *vp* **kuruyemiş** (*cul.*) Dried fruit (nuts, etc.).
kurye Courier; (*adm.*) diplomatic/queen's mes senger. ~ **çantası**, diplomatic bag. ~**lik**, courier' work/status.
kuskun (Horse's) crupper strap; (*naut.*) stern-cableı ~**u düşük**, broken-down (horse); (*fig.*) s.o. dowı and out; s.o. too wretched to care about appear ances. ~**suz**, without a crupper strap; wretchedı in disorder.
kuskus (*cul.*) Pellets of dough for pilaff; semolinaı ~**giller**, (*zoo.*) opossums.
kus·mak (-i) Vomit; disgorge; (*tex.*) show an olı stain (after cleaning/dyeing): **kusacağım geliyor**, feel sick; I am utterly disgusted. ~ **muk/**~**untu**, *n* vomit. ~**turmak (-i, -e)**, *vc.* ~**turucu**, (*med.* emetic.
kusur Failure to do one's duty; defect, fauli deficiency; (*fin.*) remainder. ~ **bulmak**, carȷ

criticise: ~ **etm.**, be at fault; fail in one's duty: ~ **etmemek**, spare no effort: ~ **işlemek**, behave badly; be at fault: ~ **sigortası**, (*fin.*) third-party liability insurance: ~**a bakmamak**, overlook an offence; forgive: ~**u (-in)**, apology for a .... ~**lu**, at fault, responsible; defective, faulty. ~**suz**, without defect; perfect, complete; blameless, innocent.

uş (*orn.*) Bird. ~ +, *a.* Bird-; birdlike; avi-: ~ BAKIŞI: ~ BAŞI: ~ **beyinli**, of limited intelligence; feather-brained: ~ BURNU: ~ **çorbası**, (*cul.*) lark soup: ~ DİLİ: ~ EKMEĞİ: ~ **fiği**, (*bot.*) false sainfoin: ~ **gibi**, birdlike; very light/agile: ~ **gibi uçup gitmek**, die after a very short illness: ~ **gibi yemek**, eat very little: ~ **gözlemi**, (*orn.*) bird-watching: ~ **gözlemcisi**, bird-watcher: ~ GÖMÜ: ~ **kafesi**, bird-cage: ~ **kafesi gibi**, small but attractive (house): ~ KANADI: ~ **kanadıyla gitmek**, fly, hasten: ~ **kenesi**, (*ent.*) fowl tick: ~ KİRAZI: ~ KONMAZ: ~ LOKUMU: ~ **markalaması**, (*orn.*) bird-marking/-ringing: ~ **mu konduracak?**, what's so special about his work?: ~ **örümceği**, (*zoo.*) bird(-catching) spider: ~ **ötüşü**, bird-song; bird-call: ~ PALAZI: ~ **piresi**, (*ent.*) bird flea: ~ SÜTÜ: ~ **uçmaz kervan geçmez**, desolate/deserted spot: ~ **uçurmamak**, be very vigilant/alert/capable: ~ **uykusu**, very light sleep: ~ ÜZÜMÜ: ~ YEMİ: ~ **yetiştirme**, aviculture: ~ **yuvası**, bird's nest; (*cul.*) bird's nest pastry: ~**a benzetmek (-i)**, spoil stg. by trying to improve it: ~**lar**, avifauna, birds: ~**larla çarpışma**, (*aer.*) bird-strike.

uşa¹kᵍ¹ (*mod.*) Sash; girdle; band; (*arch.*) diagonal beam, brace; (*cin.*) band, track; (*math.*, *geo.*) zone; (*ast.*) aureola; Saturn; (*soc.*) generation; (*mil.*) class/year.

uşak·lama *a.* Diagonal; bracing: *vn.* brace. ~**lamak (-i)**, brace, support. ~**lı**, ~ **ördek**, (*orn.*) shelduck. ~**lık**, for . . . generations. ~**taş(lık)**, (being) of the same generation.

uşam(lı) = GİYİM(Lİ).

uşan·ık (*eng.*) Armoured (pipe, etc.). ~**ılmak**, *vp.* ~**mak (-i)**, (*mod.*) gird o.s. (with stg.); put on a sash; dress: = GİYİNMEK. ~**tı** = GİYİM.

uşat·ılmak *vp.* ~**ım**/~**ma**, *vn.* winding; environ-ment; (*mil.*) siege, blockade. ~**mak (-i)**, (*mod.*) wind round the waist; gird stg. on; (*mil.*) besiege, blockade; (*live.*) corral; confine, envelop.

uş·bakışıⁿ¹ Bird's-eye view. ~**başı**, in small pieces; (snow) in big flakes: ~ **et**, (*cul.*) stewing meat. ~**baz**, (*orn.*) bird-fancier; bird-catcher. ~**bilim(ci)**, ornitholo·gy/(-gist). ~**burnu**ⁿᵘ, (*orn.*) beak; (*bot.*) dog-rose and its hips. ~**çu**, bird-breeder; falconer. ~**çuluk**, bird-breeding; falconry. ~**dili**ⁿⁱ, children's (secret) language; thieves' slang; (*bot.*) type of ash-tree.

uşekâğıdıⁿ¹ (*pub.*) White laid paper; art paper.

uşekmeğiⁿⁱ (*bot.*) Common mallow.

uşetⁱ (*rly.*, *naut.*) Berth, bunk, couchette. ~**li**, with couchettes/bunks.

uş·gömüⁿᵘ (*cul.*) Fillet of meat/PASTIRMA. ~ **gözü**, ~ **akçaağaç**, (*bot.*) sugar maple. ~**hane**, (*orn.*) aviary (*esp.* for hawks); (*cul.*) small saucepan. ~**kanadı**ⁿ¹, (*orn.*) bird's wing: (*med.*) type of eye

sore. ~**kirazı**ⁿ¹, (*bot.*) bird cherry (tree). ~**konmaz**, (*bot.*) asparagus; asparagus fern.

kuşku Doubt, suspicion; nervousness; anxiety. ~ **etm.**, become suspicious: ~ **perdesi**, (*psy.*) wall of suspicion. **kuşku·cu** S.o. suspicious; (*phil.*) sceptic. ~**culuk**, scepticism. ~**landırmak (-i)**, *vc.* ~ **lanmak**, *vi.* feel nervous/suspicious; be doubtful. ~**lu**, nervous, suspicious, doubtful. ~**luluk**, suspicion. ~**suz**, *a.* unsuspecting: *adv.* without a doubt, certainly.

kuş·la¹kᵍ¹ (*orn.*) Place full of game-birds. ~**lamak**, *vi.* (*ed. sl.*) work very hard. ~**lokumu**ⁿᵘ, (*cul.*) type of sweetish cake. ~**luk**¹, aviary. ~**luk**², forenoon, morning: ~ **yemeği**, (*cul.*) early lunch, brunch, 'elevenses'. ~**mar**, (*orn.*) bird-trap. ~**palazı**ⁿ¹, (*med.*) diphtheria. ~**sütü**ⁿᵘ, stg. non-existent/unobtainable: ~ **ile beslemek**, cherish, coddle, look after very carefully: ~**nden gayrı her şey vardı**, there was every conceivable thing to eat. ~**tüyü**ⁿᵘ, *n.* (*orn.*) feather, down: *a.* filled with down; down-: ~ **gibi**, very soft: ~ **yorgan**, (*dom.*) eiderdown. ~**uçuşu**, distance as the crow flies. ~**üvezi**ⁿⁱ, (*bot.*) whitebeam (tree). ~**üzümü**ⁿᵘ, (*bot.*) currant. ~**yemi**ⁿⁱ, (*bot.*) canary grass; (*orn.*) bird-/canary-seed, chicken-feed.

kutᵘ Luck, prosperity, happiness. **kuta¹k**ᵍ¹ (*arch.*/*rel.*) Sanctuary.

kutan (*agr.*) Large plough. ~ (**kuşu**), (*orn.*) (?) steamer duck.

kutb- = KUTUP.

kutikula (*bio.*) Cuticle.

kutla·ma *vn.* Celebration; congratulation. ~**mak (-i)**, congratulate s.o.; celebrate stg. ~**nmak**, *vp.*

kutlu Lucky, auspicious, happy. ~**lamak (-i)**, offer congratulations to s.o. ~**luk**, luckiness; happiness.

kutnu (*tex.*) Mixed cotton-silk cloth.

kutr- = KUTUR.

kut·sal Sacred, holy: ~ **hap yuvarlayıcı**, (*ent.*) dung beetle: ~ **ibis**, (*orn.*) sacred ibis: ~ **inanç**, (*rel.*) belief: ~ **verim**, blessing. ~**salcı**, exploiter of religious feelings. ~**sallaşmak**, *vi.* become sacred/holy. ~**sallık**, holiness. ~**sama**, *vn.* consecra-tion; blessing. ~**samak (-i)**, consecrate, sanctify; venerate. ~**si**, sacred, holy. ~**siyet**ⁱ, holiness. ~**tören(sel)**, (*rel.*) ceremon·y/(-ial).

kutsuz Unlucky; unhappy. ~**luk**, bad luck; unhap-piness.

kutu Small box/case (with lid); chest; (*el.*) junction-box; (*fig.*) s.o. endowed with . . . qualities [AKIL KUTUSU]. ~ **gibi**, small but pleasant/convenient. ~**cuk**, capsule; (*rad.*) cassette. ~**cuklu**, sesalıcı, cassette tape-recorder.

kut¹upᵇᵘ (*geo.*) Pole; (*el.*) pole; (*fig.*) axis of activity; most important person. ~ +, *a.* Polar: ~ **fırtına kuşu**, (*orn.*) northern fulmar: ~ **kazı**, (*orn.*) snow goose: ~ **tilkisi**, (*zoo.*) arctic/blue fox.

kutup·ayısıⁿ¹ (*zoo.*) Polar bear. ~**engel**, (*el.*) de-polarizer. ~**lamak (-i)**, (*phys.*) polarize. ~**lanma**, (*phys.*) polarization. ~**lanmış**, polarized. ~**laş-mak**, *vi.* (*soc.*) polarize. ~**laştırmak (-i)**, (*el.*/*soc.*) polarize. ~**ölçer**, (*el.*) polarimeter. ~**sal**, polar. ~**yıldızı**ⁿ¹, (*ast.*) Pole Star.

kut¹urʳᵘ (*math.*) Diameter; region.

Kuv. = KUVVET(LER).

kuva- = KUA-.

kuvars (*geol.*) Quartz.

kuver (*pub.*) Jacket, dust-wrapper. ~**li**, with dust-wrapper. ~**tür**, (*fin.*) cover(age).

Kuveytⁱ (*geo.*) Kuweit.

kuvve Faculty; quality; potency; possibility; (*mil.*) muster-roll; logistic requirements. ~**de kalmak**, remain merely a project: ~**de olm.**, be a possibility; exist as a project: ~**de olarak**, potentially: ~**den fiile çıkarmak/getirmek**, execute a project: ~**den fiile çıkmak/geçmek**, be put into practice: ~**i hafıza**, memory.

kuvvetⁱ Strength; force; power; vigour; (*math.*) power; (*phys.*) force. ~ **(-e)!**, let us try . . .!: thanks to . . .!; there's no other remedy but to . . .: ~ **almak**, increase one's strength: ~ **çifti**, (*phys.*) torque: ~ **dengesi**, (*pol.*) balance of power: ~ **ilacı**, (*med.*) tonic, restorative: ~ **komutanları**, (*mil.*) commanders-in-chief of armed forces: ~ **merkezi**, (*el.*) power-station: ~ **vermek (-e)**, attach importance to: ~**ini artırmak**, (*eng.*) boost; (*el.*) amplify: ~**iyle (-in)**, by dint of . . .: ~**le**, strongly: ~**ler ayrılığı**, (*adm.*) separation of powers: ~**ler birliği**, (*adm.*) concentration of power: ~**ten düşmek**, *vi.* weaken, lose strength: ~**ten düşürmek**, *vt.* (*med.*) weaken, debilitate: ~**ten kesilmek**, be exhausted.

kuvvet·lendirmek (-i) Strengthen; (*chem.*) enrich. ~**lenmek**, *vi.* become strong; be strengthened. ~**li**, strong, powerful, forceful; concentrated; brawny (person). ~**ölçer**, (*phys.*) dynamometer. ~**siz**, weak, without strength; (*med.*) asthenic. ~**sizlik**, weakness; (*med.*) asthenia.

kuyru¹kᵍᵘ (*bio.*) Tail; appendix; (*jok.*) follower; queue; (*mod.*) train; corner (of eye); (*mil.*) breech (of gun). ~ +, *a.* (*bio.*) Caudal: ~ **acısı**, rancour; desire for revenge: ~ **kakık**, (*orn.*) white-headed duck: ~ **mili**, (*eng.*) tail shaft: ~ **sallamak**, wag one's tail; fawn and flatter: ~ **rotoru**, (*aer.*) tail rotor: ~ **takımı**, (*aer.*) empennage: ~ **yüzgeci**, (*ich.*) caudal fin: ~**tan dolma**, (*mil.*) breech-loading (gun): ~**u kapana kısılmak/sıkışmak**, be caught by the tail; be in great straits: ~**u titremek**, (*sl.*) die: ~**una baka baka**, very dejectedly: ~**una basmak (-in)**, tread on s.o.'s toes, provoke s.o.: ~**una teneke bağlamak (-in)**, make a laughing-stock of s.o.: ~**unu kesmek**, dock (a horse's) tail: ~**unu kısmak**, (*fig.*) put one's tail between one's legs: ~**unu kıstırmak**, put s.o. in a very difficult position; have s.o. by the short hairs: ~**unu tava sapına çevirmek**, thrash s.o. soundly.

kuyruk·ışığıⁿⁱ (*mot.*) Rear-/tail-light. ~**kakan**, (*orn.*) wheatear. ~**kemiği**ⁿⁱ, (*bio.*) coccyx. ~**lu**, having a tail; -tailed; caudate; (*zoo.*) scorpion: ~ **kelebek**, (*ent.*) swallow-tail (butterfly): ~ **piyano**, (*mus.*) grand piano: ~ **saat**, grandfather clock: ~ **sürme**, (*mod.*) eyelid-shadow overdone: ~ **yalan**, a 'whopping' lie. ~**luyıldız**, (*ast.*) comet: ~ **saçı**, coma. ~**sallayan(giller)**, (*orn.*) wagtail(s, Motacillidae). ~**sokumu**ⁿᵘ, (*bio.*) sacrum. ~**suz**, tailless, acaudal: ~**lar**, (*zoo.*) tailless frogs. ~ **yağı**ⁿⁱ, (*cul.*) fat (rendered down from tail of fat-tailed sheep).

kuytu *a.* Sheltered from the wind; cosy, snug; dar hidden. *n.* Sheltered nook; remote place. ~ **ya** lee side.

kuyu Well; pit; (*min.*) bore-hole; mine-shaft. **bileziği**, crown/parapet of well: ~ **fındığı**, (*cu* type of hazel-nut buried to give it special flavou ~ **kafesi**, (*min.*) pit-cage: ~**sunu kazmak (-in)**, lay trap for s.o. ~**cu(luk)**, (work of) well-sinker.

kuyudat¹ (*fin.*) Registrations.

kuyum Gold/silver trinkets, jewellery. ~**cu(luk** (work of) jeweller/goldsmith.

kuz Remaining in shadow, sunless (side).

kuzen (*soc.*) Male cousin.

kuzey *n.* (*geo.*) North. *a.* North(ern); Arctic; Nord ~ **Atlantik Antlaşması Teşkilatı/Paktı/Örgü** (*pol.*) North Atlantic Treaty Organization: **balinası**, (*zoo.*) sei whale: ~ **Buz denizi**, (*gea* Arctic Ocean: ~ **büyük dalgıcı**, (*orn.*) commo loon: ~ **fecir/ışığı**, (*ast.*) northern lights, auro borealis: ~ **kutbu/yerucu**, (*geo.*) North Pole: **kutbu deniz kırlangıcı**, (*orn.*) arctic tern: ~ **kut** **dairesi**, Arctic Circle: ~ **noktası**, (*ast.*) north poir

kuzey·batı (*geo.*) North-west. ~**doğu**, north-eas ~**li**, (*soc.*) northerner. ~**sel**, northern.

kuzgun (*orn.*) Raven. ~**a** yavrusu **anka/şah** görünür, 'all his geese are swans'. ~**cuk**, grille prison-doors. ~**i**, raven black. ~**kılıcı**ⁿⁱ, (*bot.*) eastern) gladiolus.

kuzin (*soc.*) Female cousin.

kuzu (*zoo.*) Lamb; (*bot.*) small fruit (next to a b one); (*cul.*) lamb. ~ **budu**, (*cul.*) leg of lamb: **çevirmek**, roast a lamb on a spit: ~ **doldurma** stuff a lamb (for roasting): ~ **gibi**, (*fig.*) very mil gentle (person): ~ **güveci**, (*cul.*) lamb cassero ~ **haşlaması**, boiled lamb: ~ **kartalı**, (*orn* bearded vulture: ~ **pirzolası**, (*cul.*) lamb cho ~ **postuna bürünmek**, be a wolf in sheep's clothin ~ **sarması**, (*cul.*) lamb chitterlings: ~**m!**, my de fellow!

kuzu·cu¹kᵍᵘ Little/pet lamb. ~**çıbanı**ⁿⁱ, (*mea* small boil. ~**dişi**ⁿⁱ, (*bio.*) milk-tooth. ~**göbeği** (*myc.*) common/field mushroom. ~**kestanesi** (*bot.*) small chestnut eaten raw. ~**kulağı**ⁿⁱ, (*bot* sheep's sorrel: ~ **asidi**, (*chem.*) oxalic acid. ~**lam** *vn.* (*bio.*) lambing; (*child.*) crawling. ~**lamak**, l lamb; crawl. ~**laşmak**, *vi.* become mild/harmles ~**lu**, (*live.*) (sheep) big with lamb; with lamb a its side. ~**luk**, sheepfold; (*fig.*) mildness: ~ **kapıs** (*arch.*) wicket gate (of a khan). ~**mantarı**ⁿⁱ, (*myc* saffron milk-cap; morel.

Kü. = KÜÇÜK.

-kü *a./n. suf.* [69] = -Kı¹ [DÜNKÜ].

küb- = KÜP¹.

Küba (*geo.*) Cuba. ~ +, *a.* Cuban. ~**lı**, (*ethn* Cuban.

küb·ik (*math., art.*) Cubic; (*bio.*) cuboidal. ~**is** (*art.*) cubist. ~**izm**, cubism.

küç. = KÜÇÜLTME.

küçücük Very small, tiny; (*fig.*) darling little.

küçük *a.* Small, little; (*bio.*) lesser, dwarf; dimin tive; low; (*soc.*) minor; younger, baby; insignif cant, paltry; (*fin.*) inferior, low-grade; (*adm* low-ranking, junior. *n.* Child; (*leg.*) minor; youn

animal/bird. ~ **akbalıkçıl**, (*orn.*) little egret: ~
alaca ağaçkakan, (*orn.*) lesser spotted woodpecker:
~ **aptes**, urination: ~ **araba**, (*eng.*) top slide-rest:
~ **avarya**, (*fin.*) particular average: ~ **ay**, Feb-
uary: ~ **aysberk**, (*geo.*) calf: ~ **bağırgan kartal**,
(*orn.*) lesser spotted eagle: ~ **baldıran**, (*bot.*) fool's
parsley: ~ **cennetkuşu**, (*orn.*) lesser bird of paradise: ~ **cezayirmenekşesi**, (*bot.*) lesser periwinkle:
~ **çekirdek**, (*zoo.*) micronucleus: ~ **çil keklik**,
(*orn.*) see-see partridge: ~ **çinçilya**, (*zoo.*) (true)
chinchilla: ~ **çizme**, (*mod.*) bootees: ~ **dağları ben
yarattım demek**, be incredibly conceited: ~
dolaşım, (*bio.*) pulmonary circulation: ~ **dudaklar**,
bio.) nymphae: ~ **düşmek**, *vi.* look small; feel
ashamed/foolish: ~ **düşürmek (-i)**, make s.o. look
small/foolish: ~ **gezegen**, (*ast.*) minor planet,
asteroid: ~ **görmek (-i)**, belittle, hold in contempt:
~ **güneşlik**, (*bot.*) umbel: ~ **harf**, (*pub.*) minuscule,
lower case: ~ **Hindistan cevizi**, (*bot.*, *cul.*) nutmeg:
~ **ısın/kalori**, (*phys.*) (small) calorie: ~ **ilanlar**,
pub.) classified/small ad(vertisement)s: ~ **kabak**,
bot.) courgette: ~ **kalkanbezi**, (*bio.*) parathyroid
gland: ~ **karaciğer kelebeği**, (*bio.*) lesser liver
fluke: ~ **kardeş**, (*soc.*) younger brother/sister,
cadet: ~ **karga**, (*orn.*) jackdaw: ~ **karides**, (*zoo.*)
prawn: ~ **kasa**, (*fin.*) petty cash: ~ **kedibalığı**,
ich.) lesser spotted dogfish: ~ **kerkenez**, (*orn.*)
lesser kestrel: ~ **köprü**, on hands and knees: ~
köyün büyük ağası, 'a big frog in a little pond'; self-
important person: ~ **kumru**, (*orn.*) laughing dove:
~ ~ **doğramak/kesmek**, (*cul.*) cube, dice: ~
lahana, (*bot.*) Brussels sprouts: ~ **mağara kara
sağan**, (*orn.*) edible-nest swiftlet: ~ **martı**, (*orn.*)
common gull: ~ **mevlut ayı** = REBİYÜLÂHİR: ~ **Nil
aygırı**, (*zoo.*) pygmy hippo(potamus): ~ **oda sineği**,
(*ent.*) lesser house-fly: ~ **oynamak**, (*gamb.*) play
for small stakes: ~ **önerme**, (*phil.*) subordinate
proposition: ~ PARMAK: ~ **penguen**, (*orn.*) little
blue penguin: ~ **sakızlevreği**, (*ich.*) = ~ KEDİ-
BALIĞI: ~ **şalgam**, (*bot.*) rape, swede: ~ **tarla kuşu**,
(*orn.*) lesser short-toed lark: ~ **tavuk her gün piliç**, a
small woman always looks young: ~ **tavus kelebeği**, (*ent.*) emperor moth: ~ **terim**, (*phil.*) conclusion (of a syllogism): ~ **testere gagalı ördek**, (*orn.*)
smew: ~ **tövbe ayı** = CEMAZİYÜLÂHIR: ~ **ünlü
uyumu**, (*ling.*) labial harmony: ~ **yarasalar**, (*zoo.*)
Microchiroptera: ~ **ten beri**, from childhood.
üçük·ayı *pr.n.* (*ast.*) Little Bear. ~ **ayıgiller**, (*zoo.*)
raccoons. ~ **baş**, (*live.*) sheep and goats. ~ **dil**,
(*bio.*) uvula: ~ **ini yutmak**, be overcome with
surprise/fear. ~ **lemek (-i)**, despise, slight.
~ **leşmek**, *vi.* grow smaller; behave like children.
~ **lü**, intermixed with small ones: ~ **büyüklü**, some
big some small; young and old. ~ **lük**, smallness;
childhood; pettiness; indignity. ~ **parma¹kᵍⁱ**, (*bio.*)
little finger/toe. ~ **semek (-i)** = KÜÇÜMSEMEK.
üçül·me *vn.* Decrease; reduction. ~ **mek**, *vi.* become small; be reduced; wane; feel insignificant.
~ **tme**, *vn.* a making smaller; reducing; (*eng.*)
reduction; diminution; (*ling.*) diminutive: ~ **eki**,
(*ling.*) diminutive suffix. ~ **tmek (-i)**, make
small(er); diminish; reduce; belittle. ~ **tücü**,
humiliating, derogatory.

küçü·men/~**rek** Smallish; tiny. ~**msemek (-i)**,
belittle, disdain; humiliate. ~**msenmek**, *vi.* be
humiliated.
küesal (*orn.*) Quetzal.
küf (*myc.*) Mould; mouldiness. ~ **bağlamak**/
tutmak, become mouldy: ~ **kokmak**, smell mouldy/
unaired: ~ **tadı**, mouldy taste.
küfe Large deep basket (for carrying on the back);
(*sl.*) buttocks. ~**ci(lik)**, (work of) porter//basket-
maker. ~**li**, porter. ~**lik**, basketful; (*fig.*) blind-/
dead-drunk.
küff- = KÜFÜV.
küf·lendirmek/~**letmek (-i)** Cause to/let become
mouldy. ~**lenmek**, *vi.* become mouldy; (*fig.*) suffer
from neglect; lose the ability to work. ~**lü**,
mouldy; (*fig.*) perished from neglect; out-of-date:
~ **para**, (*jok.*) hoarded money. ~**lüce**, (*med.*)
mycosis. ~**mantarı**, (*myc.*) aspergillus.
küfran Ingratitude.
küfr- = KÜFÜR². ~ **ᴵetmek**ᵉᵈᵉʳ **(-e)**, curse/abuse s.o.
küfür¹ *adv.* ~ ~, (*ech.*) rustling (of wind).
küf·ürʳü **²** *n.* (*rel.*) Denial, disbelief; blasphemy.
küfürü **³** *n.* Curse, oath, swear-word. ~ **etm.**/~**ü
basmak**, curse and swear; blaspheme: ~ **savurmak**,
let out an oath. ~**baz**, swearing; foul-mouthed.
~**bazlık**, swearing.
küf·ᴵüvᵛü An equal in social status (for marriage).
küheylan (*live.*) Pure-bred Arab horse.
kükre (Animal) in a state of excessive rage/sexual
desire. ~**mek**, *vi.* bellow with rage/sexual desire;
foam at the mouth; (lion) roar.
kükür·ᴵtᵈü (*chem.*) Sulphur. ~**atar**, (*geol.*) solfa-
tara. ~**çiçeği**ⁿⁱ, (*chem.*) flowers of sulphur.
~**lemek (-i)**, (*agr.*) spray with sulphur. ~**lenmek**,
vp. ~**lü**, sulphurous: ~ **hidrojen**, hydrogen sulphide: ~ **tütenler** = ~ATAR.
külˡü **¹** *n.* The whole; all. ~ **halinde**, as a whole:
~ **öksüz**, completely orphaned (neither father nor
mother).
külü **²** *n.* Ash(es), cinders. *a.* Ash-coloured, ashen;
ruined. ~ **etm.**, ruin, destroy: ~ **gibi**, pale, ashen:
~KEDİsi = **kesilmek**, turn pale: ~ (**kömür) olm.**,
(s.o.) be utterly ruined: ~ **olm.**, be reduced to
ashes: ~RENGİ: ~ **yemek**, (*sl.*) miscalculate: ~
yutmak, (*sl.*) be tricked/deceived: ~**ünü savurmak**,
completely destroy stg.; (*fig.*) ruin s.o.
külah (*mod.*) Conical hat; cone-shaped container;
(*arch.*) spire; (*fig.*) trick, deceit. ~ **giydirmek**, (*his.*)
deprive of office; play a trick on s.o.: ~ **kapmak**,
secure an advantage by trickery: ~ **peşinde**, s.o.
trying to secure an advantage by trickery: ~ **sallamak**, toady, flatter: ~**ıma anlat/dinlet!**, tell me
another!; tell that to the Marines!: ~**ını havaya
atmak**, throw one's hat in the air for joy: ~**ını
ters giydirmek**, make s.o. sorry for his deeds: ~**ları
değiş(tir)mek (-le)**, (*col.*) fall out/quarrel with s.o.
(a threat): = ALİ. ~**çı**, trickster.
külbastı (*cul.*) Grilled cutlet/meat.
külbütör (*eng.*) Rocker. ~ **manivelası**, rocker arm.
külçe (*min.*) Metal ingot, bullion; pile; bunch of
keys. ~ **gibi oturmak**, collapse from fatigue: ~
kalıbı, (*min.*) mould.
küldür = PALDIR.

küle⁺kᵍⁱ (*dom.*) Tub with handles, shallow pail.
külfetⁱ Trouble; inconvenience; great expense; ceremonious behaviour. ~ **etm.**, put o.s. to inconvenience.
külfet·li Troublesome; laborious; expensive; ceremonious; forced, unnatural. ~**siz**, easy; convenient; unceremonious; natural, spontaneous; informal; not expensive.
külhan Stoke-hole (of HAMAM). ~**beyi**ⁿⁱ, a rough, a rowdy; a layabout: ~ **ağzı**, (*ling.*) slang: ~ **kılıklı**, disreputable. ~**cı**, stoker, boilerman. ~**i**, urchin; young scamp; merry fellow.
kül·kedisiⁿⁱ S.o. who feels the cold/who likes the fire. ~**leme**, *vn.*; (*myc.*) mildew. ~**lemek (-i)**, cover with ashes. ~**lenmek**, *vi.* be turned to ashes; smoulder; cool down, die down; (*fig.*) (pain/trouble) be forgotten.
külli Total; universal; abundant. ~**yat**ⁱ, (*lit.*) complete works of an author. ~**ye**, (*arch.*) complex of buildings (round a mosque). ~**yen**, totally; entirely; (+ *neg.*) not at all, absolutely not. ~**yet**ⁱ, totality; entirety; abundance: ~**le**, in great quantity. ~**yetli**, plentiful, abundant.
kül·lü Containing/mixed with ashes: ~ **su**, lye. ~**lük**, ashpit; ashtray.
külotᵘ (*mod.*) Riding-breeches; underpants, knickers.
külrengiⁿⁱ Ash-coloured, ashen, grey: ~ **ağaçkakan**, (*orn.*) grey-headed woodpecker: ~ **balıkçıl**, (*orn.*) common/grey heron: ~ **etsineği**, (*ent.*) fleshfly: ~ **guguk**, (*orn.*) cuckoo: ~ **karga**, (*orn.*) carrion/hooded crow: ~ **kaşıklı balıkçıl**, (*orn.*) roseate spoonbill: ~ **köryılan**, (*zoo.*) glass snake: ~ **ötleğen**, (*orn.*) white-throat: ~ **sağan**, (*orn.*) pallid swift: ~ **yelve**, (*orn.*) ashy-headed bunting.
kültü (*pol., rel.*) Cult.
külte Metal ingot; bunch; (*geol.*) rock.
kültivatör (*agr.*) Cultivator.
kültür (*ed.*) Culture; (*bio.*) culture. ~ **Bakan(lığ)ı**, (*adm.*) Minis·ter/(-try) of Culture/(*obs.*) Education: ~ **bakımından**, culturally: ~ **dili**, (*ling.*) literary language: ~ **vasatı**, (*bio.*) culture medium.
kültür·el Cultural. ~**fizik**, (*sp.*) physical culture/education. ~**lü**, cultured, well-educated. ~**süz**, uncultured, uneducated.
külün⁺kᵍü Pick; mace; crowbar.
külüstür (*sl.*) Shabby; out-of-date; of poor quality, useless. ~**leşmek**, *vi.* become shabby, etc.
küm Small heap, pile; small sheepfold.
kümbetⁱ (*arch.*) Vault, dome; conical roof(-ed tomb); projection; (*sl.*) the behind. ~**li**, projecting.
küme Heap; mass; mound; hillock; straw/reed hut; (*agr.*) clamp; (*bot.*) clump; (*ast.*) cluster; (*soc.*) group; (*math.*) set; (*sp.*) league. ~ **haline gelmek**, cluster together: ~ ~, in heaps/piles/groups: ~**den düşmek**, (*sp.*) be relegated.
küme·bulutᵘ (*met.*) Cumulus cloud. ~⁺**ç**ᶜⁱ, (*bio.*) colony. ~**leme**, *vn.*; (*cin.*) grouping of shots; (*min.*) grading. ~**lemek (-i)**, heap/group together. ~**lenmek**, *vp.* ~**leşim**, (*bio.*) agglutination. ~**leşmek**, *vi.* come together in heaps/groups, etc.
kümes (*live.*) Poultry-house; farmyard; hatchery; coop; (*fig.*) hut. ~ **hayvanları**, poultry.

kümül·atif Cumulative. ~**o-nimbüs**//-**stratü**s (*met.*) cumulo-nimbus//-stratus. ~**üs**, cumulus.
kümültü (Keeper's) small hut; (hunter's) hide.
-kün *a./n. suf.* [223] = -GİN [KÜSKÜN].
küncü (*bot.*) Sesame (seeds).
künde Fetter, hobble; trap, ambush. ~**den atmak** (*fig.*) trip s.o. up: ~**ye almak/düşürmek**, (*sp.* throw by a trick (in wrestling).
küney (*geo.*) South-facing side.
künh Essence; reality. ~**üne varmak**, get to th bottom of stg.; learn thoroughly.
kün⁺kᵍü (*arch.*) Earthenware/cement waterpipe. ~ **döşemek**, lay down water/drainage pipes.
künye Personal record; identity disc. ~ (**defteri**, register of names; Army list: ~**si bozuk**, s.o. with bad record: ~**sini okumak**, throw s.o.'s record in his face; curse s.o.: ~**sini silmek**, (*sl.*) banish.
kü⁺pᵇü 1 *n.* (*math.*) Cube. ~ +, *a.* Cubic: ~ **kap**a **sitesi**, cubic capacity: ~ **şeklinde**, cuboid.
küpü 2 *n.* Large earthenware jar. ~ **gibi**, enormousl stout: ~ **yıkamak**, (*sl.*) be dissolute: ~ **lere binme**k get into a rage: ~ **ünü doldurmak**, grow rich; feathe one's nest.
küpe (*mod.*) Ear-ring; (*bio.*) dewlap. ~**çiçeği**ⁿ (*bot.*) fuchsia. ~**çiçeğigiller**, (*bot.*) willow-her family, Onagraceae. ~**li**, wearing ear-rings; (*bio* having a dewlap.
küpeşte (*naut.*) Gunwale; bulwark; guard-rai (*arch.*) banister.
küpleği (*carp.*) Hole in tools for the haft.
küpleme (*med.*) Excess fluid in the abdomen.
küplü S.o. fat; (*fig.*) wineshop; (*sl.*) drunkard.
kür (*med.*) Cure; a cure, special treatment; (*chem* curing. ~**ar**, (*chem.*) curare. ~**dan(lık)**, (cup t hold) toothpick.
Kürd- = KÜRT. ~**i**, (*Or. mus.*) a simple melod⁺ ~**istan**, (*geo.*) land of the Kurds.
küre¹ *n.* (*geo., math.*) Globe; sphere. ~ **kuşağ** (*geo.*) zone of sphere.
küre² *n.* (*min.*) Smelting furnace.
küre⁺kᵍⁱ (*agr.*) Shovel; (*naut.*) oar; (*leg.*) har labour, penal servitude. ~ **cezası**, (*his.*) condem nation to the galleys; (*leg.*) hard labour: ~ **çekme**k row: ~ **kemiği**, (*bio.*) shoulder-blade: ~ ~, b the shovel(ful): ~ **mahkûmu**, (*his.*) convict: ~ **palası**, blade (of oar): ~ **sırası**, bank of oars: ~ **mahkûm olm.**, be condemned to hard labour: ~**le**s **sıya etm.**, back water.
kürek·ayaklılar (*orn.*) Web-footed birds. ~**ç** maker/seller of oars//shovels; worker with shovel. oarsman, rower: ~ **böcek**, (*ent.*) lesser wate boatman. ~**çilik**, making/selling of oars//shovel. shovelling; rowing.
küre(le)mek (-i) Shovel up; clear away.
küre·msi/~sel/~vi (*math.*) Spherical; globula ~ **gökbilim**, spherical astronomy: ~ **üçgen**, (*math* spherical triangle. ~**yve**, (*bio.*) globule.
kür·etⁱ (*med.*) Curette. ~**iyum**, (*chem.*) curium.
kürkü (*zoo.*) Fur; (*mod.*) fur-coat; fur-lined. ~ **böceği**, (*ent.*) common hide/black carpet beetl ~ **güvesi**, (*ent.*) clothes moth.
kürkas (*bot.*) Physic nut.
kürk·çü(lük) Furrier('s business). ~**lü**, (*mod.*) (

fur; adorned with fur; wearing a fur-coat; (*zoo.*) fur-bearing (animal).

kürnemek *vi.* Gather together socially.

kürsü (*rel.*) Pulpit; (*pol.*) dais, platform; rostrum; (*ed.*) desk, 'chair'; (*fig.*) professorship. ~ **hoca/ şeyhi,** (*rel.*) preacher.

Kür¹tᵈᵘ (*ethn.*) Kurd; (*pej.*) uncivilized person. ~ +, *a.* Kurdish. ~ **çe,** (*ling.*) Kurdish. ~ **çülük,** Kurdish nationalism.

kürtaj (*med.*) Curettage; abortion. ~ **traşı,** (*col.*) clumsy hair-cut.

kürtün Large/clumsy pack-saddle; (*met.*) snow-drift.

kürümek (-i) Shovel up; clear away.

küs (*child.*) Easily offended; sulky. ~ ~, dejectedly, forlorn. ~ **eğen,** easily offended; (*bot.*) = KÜSTÜM-OTU.

küskü Crow-bar; fire-dog; iron wedge/poker. ~ **lük,** ~ **kaya,** (*geol.*) loose rock.

küskün Disgruntled, sulky; offended; (*bot.*) = KÜSTÜMOTU. ~ **lük,** vexation; a being in the sulks.

küsküt (*bot.*) Dodder.

küskütük Stiff/motionless (like a log); (*fig.*) drunk as a lord.

küsmek (-e) Be offended (by s.o./stg.): *vi.* be cross; sulk.

küspe (*agr.*) Residue of crushed seeds; oilcake.

küstah Insolent; brazen-faced; audacious, arrogant. ~ **ça,** insolently. ~ **laşmak,** *vi.* behave insolently. ~ **lık,** insolence, arrogance: ~ **(bu ne)!,** how dare you!: ~ **etm.,** behave insolently.

küstere (*carp.*) Jack-plane; (stone for) grindstone/whetstone.

küstümotuⁿᵘ (*bot.*) Mimosa, 'sensitive/humble plant'.

küstürmek (-i) *vc.* Offend s.o.; = İSA.

küsuf (*ast.*) Eclipse of the sun.

küsur *pl.* = KESİR. (*math.*) Fractions; (*with a round figure*) some . . ., . . . and a bit; = BEŞ. ~ **at¹,** groups of fractions.

küsü Vexation; sulkiness. ~ **lü,** on bad terms. ~ **şmek (-le),** be vexed/on bad terms with each other.

küşa·de Open; cheerful. ~ **¹t**ᵈ¹, opening; inauguration; (*gamb.*) opening move (in backgammon, etc.): ~ **etm.,** open, inaugurate: ~ **merasimi,** inaugural ceremony. ~ **yiş,** opening; serenity.

küşne (*bot.*) Type of vetch.

küşüm = KUŞKU.

küt *a.* Short and thick; blunt; (*ech.*) sound of knocking//heart beating. ~ **diye vurdu,** he gave it a sharp blow: ~ ~, several sharp knocks.

küt. = KÜTÜPHANE(CİLİK).

küti·kül (*bot.*) Cuticle. ~ **n,** (*chem.*) cutin.

kütle Heap; block; mass; great quantity; aggregate; (*phys.*) mass; (*soc.*) group, social body. ~ **eğitimi,** mass education: ~ **haberleşmesi,** (*pub.*) mass communication: ~ **haberleşme araçları,** mass media: ~ **halinde,** in a crowd: ~ **hareketi,** (*soc.*) mass movement: ~ **kültürü,** (*ed.*) mass culture.

küt·lemek *vi.* Give out a thudding noise. ~ **leşmek,** *vi.* become blunt. ~ **letmek (-i),** knock/strike with a thud. ~ **tedek,** with a bang/thud.

kütü·kᵍᵘ Tree-stump; baulk; log; chopping-block; (*bot.*) vine-stock; (*adm.*) ledger, register; (*mil.*) cartridge pouch; (*min.*) billet, bloom. ~ **gibi,** very fat; very drunk: ~ **horozu,** (*orn.*) pileated woodpecker: ~ **e geçirmek,** record, register: ~ **e yazım/** ~ **leme,** registration. ~ **lük,** (*mil.*) cartridge-pouches on a belt.

kütüphane Library; bookshop. ~ **ci(lik),** librarian/(-ship).

kütür (Fruit) crisp, fresh. ~ ~, (*ech.*) (eating) with a crunch; (fruit) fresh, appetizing. ~ **demek,** *vi.* make a cracking/crunching sound. ~ **detmek (-i),** *vc.* ~ **tü,** (*ech.*) crack; crunch.

küvet¹ (*dom.*) Wash-hand basin; (*cin.*) developing dish/tank.

k·V = KİLOVOLT. ~ **W** = KİLOVAT.

L

L, l [le] Fifteenth Tk. letter, L. ~ **demiri**, (*eng.*) angle-bar.

L, l. = LATİNCE; LİTRE; (*math.*) ELLİ.

-l- *v. suf.* [229] = -EL- [SİVRİLMEK].

la[1] ~ **(notası)**, (*mus.*) la, A.

la(-)[2] *neg. particle.* ~ **ilaç**, (*obs.*) through sheer necessity, there being no other remedy.

La. = (*ch.s.*) LANTAN.

-la[1] *n./pron. suf.* [86] = İLE [VAPURLA].

-la-[2] *v. suf.* [227] = -LE-[3] [KUZULAMAK].

lab. = LABORANT.

labada (*bot.*) Dock.

labirent[i] (*arch.*) Labyrinth, maze.

labo·rant[i] Laboratory assistant/worker. ~ **ratuvar**, laboratory.

labrador (*geol.*) Type of feldspar, labradorite.

labros (*ich.*) Type of large wrasse.

lacivert Deep blue, navy blue. ~ **taşı**, (*geol.*) lapis lazuli.

laçka (*naut.*) Let go!, slacken off!; (*eng.*) play, backlash. ~ **etm.**, (*naut.*) slacken//cast off (a rope): ~ **olm.**, (*eng.*) be loose, have excessive play; (*fig.*) (plan) not work well; (person) be slack/idle. ~ **laşmak**, *vi.* work loose; (*fig.*) be badly managed.

laden (*bot.*) Cistus; ladanum resin.

lades (*gamb.*) Game/bet with the wishbone. ~ **tutuşmak (-le)**, bet by pulling a wishbone with each other. ~ **kemiği**[ni], (*bio.*) wishbone.

ladin (*bot.*) Spruce. ~ **tavuğu**, (*orn.*) spruce grouse.

ladini Not connected with religion; lay.

laedri (*obs.*) Anonymous author. ~ **ye**, (*phil.*) agnosticism.

laf Word, talk; empty words; boasting; = SÖZ. ~ **ağzında kalmak**, have no time to say stg.: ~ **altında kalmamak**, be quick to retort; give as good as one gets: ~ **anlamaz**, stupid, unintelligent; obstinate: ~ **anlayan beri gelsin**, no one seems to see the point (of what I say): ~ **aramızda**, we'll keep it to ourselves: ~ **atmak**, chatter; make insolent remarks to/about s.o.: ~ **çıkmak**, a rumour go about: ~ **değil**, it's no trifle; it's important: ~ **dinlemek**, listen: ~ **dokundurmak**, try to explain in other words: ~EBESİ: ~ **etm. (-i)**, gossip about (unfavourably); (-le), (*col.*) talk to s.o.: ~ **işitmek**, get a scolding, be rebuked: ~ **kıtlığında asmalar budayayım/söyledi balkabağı!**, don't talk nonsense!; what's that got to do with it?: ~ **ı açar**, one topic leads to another: ~ **olm.**, be talked about: ~ **ola!**, what nonsense!: ~ **ola beri gele**, that's beside the point: ~ **olsun diye**, just for stg. to say; for the sake of talking: ~ **taşımak**, repeat gossip to create friction.

laf-: ~**a boğmak**, drown with words: ~**a tutmak (-i)**, detain s.o. by talking to him: ~**a yekûn çek!**,

enough of that!; oh, shut up!: ~**a yekûn tutmak**, put an end to a conversation: ~**ı mı olur?**, what's the importance of it?: ~**ı uzatmak**, go into unnecessary details: ~**ını(zı) balla kestim!**, (*col.*) forgive me for interrupting: ~**ını bilmek**, weigh one's words: ~**ını etm. (-in)**, talk about stg.: ~**ını sakınmaz**, s.o. outspoken: ~**ını şaşırmak**, not know what to say: ~**la peynir gemisi yürümez!**, fine words will get you nowhere!: ~**ü güzaf**, empty words, boasting.

laf·azan Braggart; windbag. ~ **azanlık**, chatter; boasting. ~ **çı**, talkative, chatterbox. ~ **çılık**, talkativeness; (*lit.*) padding. ~ **ebesi**[ni], great talker; s.o. quick at repartee. ~ **ız**[zı], word: ~ **ı murat**, said but not meant; s.o./stg. of no account. ~ **lamak**, *vi.* boast. ~ **zan**, literally.

la·gos = LAKOZ. ~ **ğap**, (*col.*) = LAKAP.

lağar Thin and weak; (animal) weedy.

lağım Underground tunnel; sewer, drain; (*mil.*) mine; adit. ~ **açmak**, dig a drain; (*mil.*) tunnel for a mine: ~ **atma**, blasting: ~ **atmak**, fire a mine; blast: ~ **barutu**, blasting powder: ~ **çukuru**, cesspit: ~ **mili**, borer: ~ **sineği**, (*ent.*) lesser house-fly: ~**la atmak**, blow up, blast. ~ **cı(lık)**, (work of) sewerman//(*mil.*) sapper.

lağ·ıv[vı] Cancellation; annulment; suppression. ~ **vetmek**[eder] **(-i)**, abrogate, cancel; abolish. ~ **volmak**, be cancelled/abolished.

lahana (*bot.*) Cabbage. ~ **güvesi**, (*ent.*) diamondback moth: ~ **kelebekleri**, (*ent.*) pierids: ~ **turşusu**, (*cul.*) pickled cabbage: ~ **(yaprak)biti**, (*ent.*) cabbage aphis.

lahavle ~ **çekmek/okumak**, be annoyed/impatient.

Lahey (*geo.*) The Hague.

lahika Appendix; suffix; codicil.

lah·it[ti] Tomb.

lahmacun (*cul.*) Type of meat pizza.

lahos (*ich.*) Type of grouper.

lahuri (*mod.*) Indian (Lahore) shawl.

lahuti (*rel.*) Divine; spiritual.

lahza Instant; a split second; the twinkling of an eye. ~ **da**, instantly, immediately.

laik[i] Laic, lay. ~ **leştirmek (-i)**, laicize. ~ **lik**, laicism.

lak·(a) Lacquer. ~ **acı**, lacquer-worker; polished. ~ **e**/~ **lı**, lacquered.

laka·p[bı] Family name; surname; nickname. ~ **lı**, nicknamed.

lakay·dane Indifferently: ~ **geçiştirmek**, pass over stg. with indifference. ~ **di**, indifference, nonchalance. ~ **t**[di], indifferent; nonchalant: ~ **kalmak**, behave indifferently.

lakerda (*ich., cul.*) Salted tunny.

lakırdı Word; talk; promise. ~ **ağzından dökülmek**,

lie fluently; talk unwillingly: ~ **altında kalmamak,** answer back, retort promptly: ~ **etm.**, talk; gossip: ~ **kaldırmamak,** be easily offended; be susceptible to criticism: ~ **karıştırmak,** draw a red herring across the trail: ~ **kavafı,** chatterbox; great talker: ~ **taşımak,** repeat to s.o. other people's gossip about him: ~ **yakası açmak,** bring up again an old/ unpleasant subject: ~ **yetiştirmek,** always have a ready answer: ~**sı ağzında kalmak,** stg. be left half said: ~**sı anlaşılır,** *a.* articulate: ~ **sı mı olur?,** is it the time/place to talk about it?: ~**sını etm. (-in),** mention/talk about stg.: ~**ya boğmak (-i),** purposely obscure/divert the discussion with irrelevances: ~**yı tutmak,** engage s.o. in conversation: ~**yı ağza tıkmak,** cram s.o.'s words down his throat: ~**yı ağzına tıkamak,** silence s.o. abruptly: ~**yı çiğnemek,** mumble, chew one's words: ~**yı ezip büzmek,** hum and haw, be unable to express o.s. ~**cı,** loquacious; chatterbox.

lakin But; nevertheless.

laklak[1] *(ech.)* Clacking noise made by storks; senseless chatter. ~ **etm.,** chatter. ~**a,** idle chatter. ~**ıyat**[1], twaddle, nonsense.

lakoz *(ich.)* Large grey mullet.

lak·tik *(chem.)* Lactic. ~**toz,** lactose, milk sugar.

lal[1] *n. (geol.)* Ruby, garnet; red ink; *(fig.)* red lips. *a.* Bright red, carmine, ruby-coloured. ~ **yakut,** garnet.

lâl[1] *(obs.)* Dumb.

lala *(obs.)* Servant in charge of a boy; tutor, pedagogue. ~ **paşa eğlendirmek,** keep people amused/ flattered. ~**lık,** tutorship.

lalanga *(cul.)* Type of pancake.

lale *(bot.)* Tulip; *(agr.)* forked pole (for picking fruit); *(his.)* iron ring (round a convict's neck). ~ **devri,** *(his.)* Tulip Age (1718–1730): ~ **soğanı,** *(bot.)* tulip bulb. ~**ağacı**[n], *(bot.)* tulip tree. ~**gün,** red. ~**zar,** tulip garden.

lalettayin At random, accidentally.

lam[1] *n. (ling.)* Arabic letter 'L'. ~ **elif çevirmek/ çizmek,** take a stroll: ~**ı cimi yok!,** it must be done!; I'll take no denial!; it's all up!; it's no joke.

lam[2] *n.* Thin plate; microscope slide.

lama[1] *n. (zoo.)* Llama.

lama[2] *n. (rel.)* Lama, Buddhist monk.

lama[3] *n. (min.)* Sheet of metal. ~ **demiri,** sheet metal.

lamba Lamp; *(el.)* bulb; *(rad.)* valve; *(carp.)* long narrow slot/housing. ~ **gömleği,** incandescent (gas) mantle: ~ **karpuzu,** globe (of lamp): ~ **pır pır edip söndü,** the lamp spluttered and went out: ~ **şişesi,** lamp chimney: ~**yı açmak,** turn up the wick (of paraffin-lamp).

lamba·lamak (-i) Examine by lamp-light; *(carp.)* open a slot. ~**lı,** having bulbs/valves; *(carp.)* morticed. ~**lık,** lamp-bracket; lamp-shade; oil for a lamp.

lam·e *(tex.)* Lamé. ~**el,** *(phys.)* cover-glass (of microscope). ~**inarya,** *(bot.)* type of seaweed. ~**iner,** *(phys.)* laminar. ~**ise,** *(bio.)* sense of touch; *(ent.)* antenna.

lan *int. (vulg.)* Hey fellow!, hey son!

-lan- *v. suf.* [228] = -LEN- [CANLANMAK].

-landır- *v. suf.* [228] = -LENDİR- [CANLANDIRMAK].

lando(n) Landau.

lanet[i] *n.* Curse, imprecation. *a.* Damnable; peevish; cross-grained. ~ **etm./okumak (-e),** curse s.o.: ~ **olsun!,** a curse upon him, etc.

lanet·leme *vn.* Act of cursing/anathematizing; *a.* accursed. ~**lemek (-i),** curse; *(rel.)* anathematize. ~**li,** cursed.

langır ~ **lungur,** random/tactless (talk); in a loud voice, with a vulgar accent.

langırt Pin-ball game.

langust[u] *(zoo.)* Crawfish, spiny-/rock-lobster.

lanolin *(chem.)* Lanolin.

lanse ~ **etm.,** bring out (fashion).

lantan *(chem.)* Lanthanum. ~**it**[i], lanthanide.

lap *(ech.)* Flop!, flap! ~ ~ **içmek/yemek,** drink/eat greedily (smacking the lips).

lapa *(cul.)* Rice pudding; any moist dish; invalid food; *(med.)* poultice. ~ **gibi,** soft, sloppy: ~ ~ **(kar yağmak),** (snow) with large flakes: ~ **vurmak,** *(med.)* apply a poultice.

lapa·cı *(cul.)* Fond of sloppy dishes; *(fig.)* languid, flabby; effeminate, milksop. ~**msı,** flabby.

lapçın *(mod.)* Indoor boot.

lapilli *(geol.)* Type of volcanic ash.

lapina(giller) *(ich.)* Wrasse(s).

Lapon *(ethn.)* Lapp. ~**ca,** *(ling.)* Lapp language. ~**ya(lı),** *(geo.)* Lapland(er).

lappadak = LARPADAK.

-lar *n./pron./v. suf.* [25, 29, 107] = -LER [KİTAPLAR; ALIRLAR]. ~**a/ ~ca/ ~da/ ~dan/ ~ı/ ~ın** = -LER.

larenjit[i] *(med.)* Laryngitis.

lar·getto *(mus.)* Larghetto. ~**go,** *(mus.)* largo.

larmo ~ **yakası,** *(naut.)* luff of a sail.

larp[j]**(adak)** Suddenly, sharply; with a flop.

larva *(ent.)* Larva.

laser = LAZER.

laskine *(gamb.)* Type of card-game.

laso Lasso.

lasta *(naut.)* Maximum load for a ship.

las·teks *(tex.)* Lastex. ~ **tik**[i], *n. (bot.)* rubber; *(mod.)* galoshes; eraser, rubber; *(mot.)* pneumatic tyre: *a.* made of rubber: ~ **tutkalı,** *(mot.)* rubber bonding material. ~**tikağacı**[n], *(bot.)* rubber tree. ~**tikli,** made of rubber; elastic; *(fig.)* flexible: ~ **sapan,** *(child.)* catapult: ~ **söz,** *(ling.)* pun.

-laş- *v. suf.* [228] = -LEŞ- [KARŞILAŞMAK].

laşe Corpse, carcass; carrion; *(fig.)* stg. past repair.

-laştır- *v. suf.* [229] = -LEŞTİR- [TANRILAŞTIRMAK].

Lat. = LATİNCE(DEN).

-lat- *v. suf.* [228] = -LET- [SULATMAK].

lata *(carp.)* Lath, batten; *(mod.)* (hodja's) gown.

latanya *(bot.)* Latania, Bourbon-palm.

lat·arna/ ~erna *(mus.)* Barrel-organ; *(sl.)* worn-out car. ~ **arnacı,** organ-grinder.

lateks *(bot., chem.)* Latex.

laterit[i] *(geol.)* Laterite.

latif Fine; slender; pleasant; elegant; light; subtle; witty. ~ **e,** joke; witticism; anecdote: ~ **etm.,** make jokes: ~ **latif gerek,** a joke should be refined. ~ **eci,** fond of telling jokes/stories. ~**lik,** amenity.

latilokum *(cul.)* Turkish delight.

Latin *(ethn.)* Latin (language-speaking people);

(*rel.*) Eastern Catholic. ~ **yelkeni**, (*naut.*) lateen sail. ~ **ce**, (*ling.*) Latin. ~ **çiçek(ler)i**, (*bot.*) nasturtium (family).

laubali Free-and-easy; informal; too familiar/intimate; careless; offhand. ~ **leşmek**, *vi.* be too free-and-easy; take liberties. ~ **lik**, informal behaviour; offhand manner.

lav (*geol.*) Lava.

lava *int.* (*naut.*) Pull!; hoist away! ~ **etm.**, pull (boat, etc.).

lav·abo (*dom.*) Wash(-hand) basin. ~ **aj**, (*min.*) separation by washing; (*med.*) lavage.

lavanta Lavender water, perfume. ~ **çiçeği**ni, (*bot.*) lavender: ~ **mavisi**, lavender blue.

lavaş (*cul.*) Flat bread.

lav·danom (*med.*) Laudanum. ~ **man**, (*med.*) clyster, enema. ~ **rensiyum** = LORENTİYUM.

lavta (*mus.*) Lute; (*med.*) obstetrical forceps; (*obs.*) obstetrician. ~ **cı**, (*mus.*) lute-player.

layemut Undying; immortal.

-layıcı *a./n. suf.* = -LEYİCİ [DOĞRULAYICI].

layı¹kğı *a.* Suitable; deserving, worthy. *n.* That which is deserved. ~ **görmek**, deem worthy/suitable: ~ **olm.** (-e), be worthy of, deserve, merit: ~ ı **veçhile/** ~ ıyla, as it should be; in a worthy manner: ~ ını **bulmak**, get one's deserts.

layiha Explanatory document; project; (*leg.*) bill.

layiki = LAİK.

laytmotif (*mus.*) Leitmotiv.

layuhti (*obs.*) Infallible, unerring.

Laz (*ethn.*) Laz people (of SE Black Sea coast). ~ **ca**, *n.* (*ling.*) Laz language; *adv.* in the Laz manner.

laza Tray; small trough.

lazer (*phys.*) Laser.

lazım Necessary; requisite; (*ling.*) intransitive (verb). ~ **gelmek**, be necessary; be a necessary consequence: ~ **gelenlere**, to whom it may concern: ~ **olm.**, be necessary; be needed. ~ **lı**, (*col.*) necessary; unavoidable. ~ **lık**, chamber-pot.

le (*ling.*) The Tk. letter L.

(-le)¹ = (*ling.*) -LE'Lİ TÜMLEÇ ALAN EYLEM.

-le²/-la/-yle/-yla *n./pron. suf.* [86] = İLE [TRENLE; VAPURLA; GÖZÜYLE; BABASIYLA]. ~ '**li tümleç alan eylem**, (*ling.*) verb taking a -LE construction.

-le-³/-la- *v. suf.* [227] *Forming a verb from a noun/ adjective* [GÖZLEMEK; SULAMAK; TEMİZLEMEK].

leb·aleb Full to the edge, brim-full. ~ **iderya**, sea-shore.

lebistes (*ich.*) Guppy.

leblebi (*cul.*) Roasted chick-peas; (*sl.*) bullet. ~ **ci(lik)**, (work of) seller of roasted chick-peas.

led¹ünnü (*rel.*) Consciousness of God. ~ **ilmi**, knowledge of God's nature.

leffi A wrapping up; an enclosing. ~ **ü neşir**, (*lit.*) series of subjects followed by their respective attributes. ~ **fen**, enclosed (in a letter, etc.). ~ **f¹etmek**eder (-i, -e), wrap up; enclose in stg. else.

Lefkoş·a/ ~ **e** (*geo.*) Nicosia (Cyprus).

legato (*mus.*) Legato.

legorn (*live.*) Leghorn fowl.

leğen (*dom.*) Bowl, basin; (*bio.*) pelvis. ~ **başından almak (kızı)**, choose a girl for being hard-working:

~ **ibrik**, bowl and ewer (for washing the hands at table): ~ **örtüsü**, stg. unnecessary (when essentials are missing). ~ **kemiği**ni, (*bio.*) hip bones (ilium, etc.).

leh¹ *post.* [94] For him, etc.; in favour of him, etc. ~ **ve aleyh**, for and against: ~ **imde**, in my favour: ~ **inde bulunmak/söylemek**, speak on behalf of: ~ **inde olm.**, be for/pro/in favour of: ~ **ine olm.**, be in favour of; support: ~ **te olm.**, support: ~ **te ve aleyhte**, pro and con.

leh.² = **lehçe**¹, (*ling.*) dialect.

Leh³ *n.* (*ethn.*) Pole, Polish. ~ **çe**², (*ling.*) Polish. ~ **istan**, (*geo.*) Poland. ~ **li**, Polish, Pole.

lehim (*min.*) Solder. ~ +, *a.* Soldering. ~ **eritkeni**, flux: ~ **lambası**, blow-lamp. ~ **ci**, solderer, plumber. ~ **cilik/** ~ **leme**, soldering. ~ **lemek** (-i), solder. ~ **lenmek**, *vp.* ~ **li**, soldered.

leh·tar Supporter; in favour of. ~ **te** = LEH¹.

leke Spot; stain; blemish; mark; (*ast.*) sunspot; (*fig.*) fault, defect. ~ **çıkarmak**, remove a stain: ~ **etm.** (-e), make a stain: ~ **etkinliği**, (*ast.*) sunspot activity: ~ **getirmek (-e)**, bring dishonour to; stain the character of: ~ **olm.**, become stained/spotted: ~ **sürmek (-e)**, (*fig.*) besmirch s.o.'s name: ~ **tozu**, (*chem.*) bleaching powder.

leke·baskı (*art.*, *pub.*) Aquatint. ~ **ci**, cleaner of clothes: ~ **kil/toprağı**, fuller's earth. ~ **cilik**, (*art.*) tachism. ~ **dar**, who is dishonoured. ~ **lemek** (-i), stain, blot; (*fig.*) besmirch, defile, dishonour, cast aspersions. ~ **lenmek**, *vp.* ~ **li**, spotted; stained; dishonoured. ~ **lihumma**, (*med.*) typhus fever; spotted fever. ~ **siz**, spotless, stainless; (*fig.*) immaculate; blameless.

leken (*sp.*) Type of snow-shoe. ~ **de**, (*tex.*) roughly-tacked edge.

leksiko·graf (*ling.*) Lexicographer. ~ **log**, lexicologist. ~ **loji**, lexicology.

lektör (*ed.*) Foreign-language assistant/lecturer.

lem (*geol.*) Loam.

lemha Furtive glance; flash.

lem¹issi Touching, feeling.

-len-/-lan- *v. suf.* [228] *Forming the reflexive and passive (of* -LE- *verbs).* Make o.s.; become, be made [LEKELENMEK; CANLANMAK].

-lendir-/-landır- *v. suf.* [228] *Forming the causative of* -LEN- *verbs.* Cause to become/be made [LEKELENDİRMEK; CANLANDIRMAK].

lenduha Enormous; clumsy.

lenf·(a) (*bio.*) Lymph: ~ **boğum/düğme/düğümleri**, lymph nodes: ~ **damarları**, lymph vessels. ~ **atik**, lymphatic. ~ **osit**i, (*zoo.*) lymphocyte.

lenger (*dom.*) Large deep copper dish; (*naut.*) anchor.

lengüist(ik) (*ling.*) Linguist(ics).

lenk (*med.*) Lame (*his.* = TİMURLENK).

lens (*med.*) Contact lens.

lento (*mus.*) Lento; (*arch.*) lintel.

leopar (*zoo.*) Leopard.

lep ~ **demeden leblebiyi anlamak**, understand instantly.

lepiska (*tex.*) Leipzig silk. ~ **(saçlı)**, flaxen(-haired).

-ler/-lar *n./pron./v. suf.* [25, 29, 107] *Sign of the plural* [EVLER; BİZİMKİLER; GİDİYORLAR]. ~ **ce**, according to them [HOCALARCA]; in their . . . [BİNLERCE]: ~**de**, at/on them [OKULLARDA]: ~**den**, from/by them [TRENLERDEN]: ~**e**, to them [ONLARA]: ~**i**, them; their [ANNELERİ]: ~**in**, of them, their(s) [KIZLARIN].

lerci (*zoo.*) Type of musk deer.

lesepase (*adm.*) *Laissez-passer.*

leş (*zoo.*) Carcass. ~ **akbabası**, (*orn.*) Egyptian vulture: ~ **böceği**, (*ent.*) carrion/burying beetle: ~ **gibi**, foul-smelling, putrid: ~ **gibi serilmek**, lie with the limbs stretched out: ~ **kargası**, (*orn.*) carrion crow: ~ **yapmak**, crush, kill: ~**ini çıkarmak (-in)**, beat s.o. soundly: ~**ini sermek**, kill s.o. (as a warning).

-leş-/-laş- *v. suf.* [228] *Forming the reciprocal of* -LE- *verbs.* Do to each other/one another [DERTLEŞMEK; KARŞILAŞMAK]. *Also means* become, -fy, -ize [ÖLMEZLEŞMEK; BİRLEŞMEK].

-leştir-/-laştır- *v. suf.* [229] *Forming the causative of* -LEŞ- *verbs.* Make do to each other [KARŞILAŞ- TIRMAK]; cause to become [BİRLEŞTİRMEK].

-let-/-lat- *v. suf.* [228] *Forming the causative of* -LE- *verbs.* Cause/make do [KİRLETMEK; SULATMAK].

letafet[i] Charm; grace; elegance; amiability.

let·al Lethal. ~ **arji**, (*med.*) lethargy, stupor, coma.

leva (*fin.*) Bulgarian lev. ~**nten**, *pr.n.* (*ethn.*) Levan- tine.

levazım/ ~ **at**[1] *pl.* Necessities; requirements; equip- ment; materials; (*mil.*) munitions; supplies, pro- visions. ~ **dairesi**, (*mil.*) commissariat/Quarter- master-General's department: ~ **sınıfı**, supply corps. ~**cı(lık)**, (work of) member of the supply corps.

leve (*gamb.*) Trick (at cards).

leven[t]**k**[di] (*his.*) Irregular military force; marines; (*fig.*) fine/well-built lad.

levha Signboard; (*min.*) plate, sheet; (*carp.*) board. ~ **halinde**, laminar: ~ **resmi**, (*fin.*) tax on bill- boards.

lev·iye (*mot.*) Gear-lever. ~**orotasyon**, (*chem.*) anti- clockwise rotation. ~ **üloz**, levulose.

levre[l]**k**[gi] (*ich.*) (Sea-)bass. ~**giller**, perches.

ley (*fin.*) Romanian leu.

-leyici/-layıcı *a./n. suf. Forming adjectives/nouns from* -LEMEK *verbs. a.* Doing, making. *n.* Doer, maker [OKSİTSİZLEYİCİ; DOĞRULAYICI].

-leyin *invariable adv. suf.* [201] *Forming adverbs of time from nouns.* At . . .; in the . . . [AKŞAMLEYİN].

leyla[l]**k**[gi] (*bot.*) Lilac. ~ **ağacı**, lilac-tree. ~**i**, lilac- colour.

leyle[l]**k**[gi] (*orn.*) White stork. ~ **gibi**, tall and thin: ~**i havada görmek**, (*jok.*) be s.o. much travelled: ~**in attığı yavru**, s.o. abandoned/shut out: ~**in ömrü laklak ile geçer**, he talks much but does nothing.

leylek·gagası[nı] (*math.*) Pantograph. ~**giller**, (*orn.*) stork family ~**siler**, (*orn.*) stork-like birds (herons, etc.).

leyli *a.* Nocturnal. *n.* (*ed.*) Boarder. ~ **mektep**, boarding-school.

Leymosun *pr.n.* (*geo.*) Limassol (Cyprus).

leziz Tasty, delicious; delightful.

lezzet**[i]** Taste, flavour; pleasure, enjoyment. ~

almak/duymak, enjoy the taste; (*fig.*) find pleasure in stg.

lezzet·lendirmek (**-i**) Make tasty//enjoyable. ~**lenmek**, *vi.* become tasty//enjoyable. ~**li**, tasty; enjoyable, delightful. ~**siz**, tasteless; insipid.

-lı *a./n. suf.* [44, 60] = -Lİ [HIZLI; KIBRISLI].

lığ (*geol.*) Alluvion, alluvium. ~**lanmak**, *vi.* become covered with alluvion. ~**lı**, alluvial.

-lık[1,2] *n. suf.* [62] = -LİK[1,2] [AŞAĞILIK].

lıkır ~ ~, (*ech.*) with a gurgling sound. ~**damak**, *vi.* gurgle, bubble. ~**lık**, gurgling.

Li. = (*ch.s.*) LİTYUM.

-li/-lı/-lu/-lü *a./n. suf.* [44, 60, 84, 200, 234] *Forming:* (1) *nouns of nationality* [ÇİNLİ; KIBRISLI]: (2) *nouns of place or institution* [HP'Lİ; İSTANBULLU; KÖYLÜ; OSMANLI]: (3) *adjectives indicating quality* [AKILLI; RESİMLİ; UMUTLU]: (4) *card-game numbers* [BİRLİ; ONLU]: (5) *compound adjectives* [DELİKANLI; UZUNBOYLU].

liba·de (*mod.*) Short quilted coat. ~**s**, garment.

liber·al[i] (*soc.*) Liberal. ~ **alizm/** ~ **allik**, liberalism. ~ **asyon**, (*pol.*) liberation; (*fin.*) freeing, unblock- ing: ~ **listesi**, schedule of permitted imports.

libido (*psy.*) Libido.

libre (*math.*) Pound (weight).

libretto (*mus.*) Libretto.

Libya (*geo.*) Libya. ~**lı**, (*ethn.*) Libyan.

lider (*pol., soc.*) Leader. ~**lik**, leadership.

lied (*mus.*) Lied, song.

lif (*bio., bot.*) Fibre; loofah; bunch of fibres (for scrubbing o.s. in the bath); (*el., tex.*) filament. ~ ~, fibrous.

lif·cam (*ind.*) Fibreglass. ~**lemek (-i)**, scrub with loofah/fibres. ~**lenmek**, *vi.* become fibrous; be scrubbed. ~**li**, fibrous. ~**sel/** ~ **si**, fibrous; (*zoo.*) filarial.

lig/lik (*sp.*) League. ~**den düşme**, relegation.

-lik[1]**/-lık/-luk/-lük** *n. suf.* [62] *Forming:* (1) *abstract nouns*, -age, -(al)ity, -(an)cy, -dom, -hood, -ing, -ism, -ness, -ship, -tion, -ty [KRALLIK; ANNELİK; İNCELİK; ARKADAŞLIK; GÜZELLİK]: (2) *nouns show- ing rank, duties, place of work* [BİNBAŞILIK; MÜHENDİSLİK; BAKANLIK].

-lik[2]**/-lık/-luk/-lük** *a./n. suf.* [62] *Forming:* (1) *adjectives and nouns showing intention/suitability* [DOLMALIK; ELBİSELİK; LİMANLIK; SATILIK]: (2) *adjectives and nouns with numerical content* [ONDALIK; İKİ HAFTALIK; SEKSENLİK].

lika (*tex.*) Raw silk; (*ind.*) lacquer, priming coat.

liken (*bot.*) Lichen; (*med.*) papular skin disease.

lik·idasyon (*fin.*) Liquidation. ~**i**[t]**t**[di], liquid.

likorinoz (*cul.*) Smoked mullet, etc.

likör (*cul.*) Liqueur.

liman Harbour, port; (air-)port. ~ **amelesi**, docker: ~ **kenti**, port, harbour town: ~ **maniası**, boom: ~ **odası**, harbour-master's office: ~ **reisi**, harbour- master: ~ **rüsum/vergisi**, harbour dues: ~ **sığlığı**, (*geol.*) harbour-bar.

liman·lamak *vi.* (*naut.*) Come into harbour, berth; (*met.*) (wind/sea) die down. ~**lık**, place serving as/ suitable for a harbour; (*met.*) calm (sea); windless.

limb·a/ ~ **o** (*naut.*) Barge; lighter.

lime Strip. ~ ~, in strips, in tatters.

limit[i] (*math.*) Limit. ~**et**[i], (*fin.*) limited (company).

Limni (*geo.*) Island of Lemnos.

limon (*bot.*) Lemon. ~ +, *a.* Citric, citrous: ~ **ağacı**, lemon-tree: ~ **çiçeği**, lemon-blossom: ~ **gibi (sararmak)**, (turn) very pale: ~ **kabuğu**, lemon-peel/-rind: ~ **kabuğu gibi**, (*col.*) small/shapeless (hat): ~ **salçası**, (*cul.*) lemon sauce: ~ **suyu**, lemon-juice.

limon·ata (*cul.*) Lemonade: ~ **gibi**, (*met.*) light summer (breeze). ~**atacı**, lemonade-seller. ~**i**, lemon-coloured, pale yellow; (*fig.*) touchy, capricious; (relationship) upset: ~ **hava**, (*met.*) likely to rain. ~**it**[i], (*geol.*) limonite. ~**küfü**[nü], greenish blue. ~**lu**, (*cul.*) flavoured with lemon-juice; sour. ~**luk**, (*agr.*) greenhouse, hothouse; (*cul.*) lemon-squeezer; (*arch.*) parapet, windbreak. ~**tozu**/~**tuzu**[nu], (*chem.*) citric acid.

linç[i] Lynching. ~ **etm.**, lynch: ~ **usulü**, lynch law.

lin·eer (*math.*) Linear. ~**in**, (*tex.*) linen.

link[i] (Horse's) trot. ~ **etm.**, trot.

lin·ol ~ **oyma**, (*art.*) lino-cut. ~**olyum**, (*dom.*) linoleum. ~**otip**[i], (*pub.*) linotype.

linyit[i] (*geol.*) Lignite.

lipari (*ich.*) Fat mackerel.

liparit[i] (*geol.*) Type of talc, liparite.

lipaz (*bio.*) Lipase.

lipitler (*chem.*) Lipids.

lipsos (*ich.*) Small-scaled scorpion-fish.

lir (*mus.*) Lyre. ~ **kuşları**, (*orn.*) lyre-birds.

lir·a (*fin.*) Tk. pound, lira; gold coin. ~**alık**, worth . . . liras. ~**et**[i], Italian lira.

lir·ik (*lit.*) Lyrical: ~ **şiir**, lyric(al poem). ~**izm**, lyricism.

lisan Tongue; language; dialect; talk. ~**a almak (-i)**, talk about stg.: ~**a gelmek**, become talked about; (inanimate things) begin to talk.

lisan·aşina Linguist. ~**en**, verbally. ~**i**, linguistic. ~**iyat**[i], linguistics, philology.

lisans (*ed.*) Diploma; degree; (*fin.*) licence. ~ **öğrencisi**, undergraduate: ~ **öğrenimi**, degree studies: ~ **sahibi**, (*fin.*) licensee; licence-holder: ~ **üstü öğrenimi**, (post-)graduate studies.

lisans·iye (*ed.*) Holder of degree/diploma. ~**lı**, (*fin.*) licensed. ~**üstü**, post-graduate (studies).

lise (*ed.*) Lycée, high school, grammar school. ~**li**, lycée pupil.

liste List, schedule; bill; (*cul.*) menu.

literatür Literature.

lito·grafya/~**grafi** (*pub.*) Lithography: ~ **taşı**, (*geol.*) lithographic stone. ~**grafyacı**, lithographer. ~**loji(k)**, litholo·gy/(-gical). ~**sfer**, (*geol.*) lithosphere.

litre (*math.*) Litre. ~**lik**, holding/amounting to . . . litre(s).

liturya (*rel.*) = KUDAS; Christian liturgy.

lityum (*chem.*) Lithium.

liva Flag; (*mil.*) brigade; brigadier-general; (*adm.*, *obs.*) administrative district, sub-province. ~**lık**, rank/duties of a brigadier.

livar (*ich.*) Sea-pool for keeping live fish.

livret (*mus.*) Libretto.

liyakat[i] Merit; suitability; capacity. ~**li**, meritori-

ous; efficient, capable. ~**siz**, inefficient, incapable. ~**sizlik**, inefficiency; incapacity.

liynet[i] (*med.*) Looseness of the bowels, slight diarrhoea.

lizol[ü] (*med.*) Lysol, disinfectant, antiseptic.

lm. = LÜMEN.

lobelya (*bot.*) Lobelia.

lobi (*arch.*, *pol.*) Lobby.

lobut[u] Cudgel; beam; (*sp.*) Indian club; (*tex.*) wool-fluffer's mallet.

loca (*th.*) Box; (*soc.*) Masonic lodge.

loça (*naut.*) Hawse-pipe.

loda (*agr.*) Clamp (for storing straw, etc.).

loder (*aer.*) Cargo-loader.

lodos (*geo.*) South(-west); (*met.*) S(-W) wind/gale. ~ **poyraz**, (*fig.*) blowing hot and cold, capricious: ~**a tutulmak**, sway about like a drunkard: ~**un** gözü yaşlıdır, the SW wind brings rain. ~**lamak**, *vi.* (wind) blow from the S(-W); (weather) become mild. ~**luk**, south-facing side; exposed to the S(-W).

logaritma (*math.*) Logarithm. ~ **tablosu**, logarithmic tables.

log·istik (*phil.*) Symbolic logic. ~**os**, (*rel.*) Logos.

loğ Stone roller (for flat mud-roofs, etc.). ~**lamak** (-i), roll and flatten.

loğusa (*med.*) Woman after childbirth. ~ **olm.**, be confined: ~ **şekeri**, (*cul.*) red spiced sugar used in: ~ **şerbeti**, drink offered to visitors after childbirth. ~**lık**, confinement, childbirth. ~**otu**[nu], (bot.) aristolochia, birthwort.

lojisti·k[gi] (*mil.*) Logistics.

lojman (*ind.*) Lodging, living-quarters.

lokal[i] *n.* Premises. *a.* Local. ~**ize**, (*med.*) localized.

lokanta Restaurant. ~ **vagonu**, (*rly.*) dining-car, diner. ~**cı(lık)**, (work of) restaurant-keeper.

lokatif (*ling.*) Locative.

lokavt[i] (*ind.*) Lock-out.

lokma (*cul.*) Mouthful; morsel; type of sweet fritter; (*bio.*) condyle; (*eng.*) screw-die. ~ **başlığı**, (*eng.*) die-stock: ~ **çiğnemeden yutulmaz**, every job requires some effort: ~ **dökmek**, (*cul.*) make fritters: ~ **gözlü**, with bulging eyes: ~ ~, piece by piece: ~ **doğramak**, (*cul.*) cube, dice: ~ **sade**, (*cul.*) sweet mouthfuls: ~**sını dökmek**, distribute fritters (to the poor *in memoriam*). ~**cı**, maker/seller of fritters. ~ **göz**, pop-eyed.

Lokman (*myth.*) Name of two sages (father of medicine//storyteller). ~ **hekimin ye dediği!**, just what the doctor ordered (attractive woman// delicious food)! ~**ruhu**[nu], (*chem.*) ether.

lokomo·bil Steam engine. ~**tif**, (*rly.*) locomotive, engine: ~ **garajı**, engine-shed.

lokum (*cul.*) Turkish delight; (*gamb.*) diamonds; (*min.*) blasting cartridge; (*ed. sl.*) soft-hearted teacher.

lolo (*sl.*) Showing off, putting on airs.

lom·bar (*naut.*) Port (side). ~**boz**, port-hole; dead-light; air-scuttle.

lonca Tradesmen's guild/corporation; their meeting-place.

Londra (*geo.*) London. ~**'da yok yok**, there is nothing that can't be found in London. ~**lı**, Londoner.

longpley (*mus.*) Long-playing record.
longuz Abrupt deep spot (sea/river).
lonjeron (*aer.*) Longeron.
lop[u] *a.* Round and soft (mouthful). *n.* (*bio.*) Lobe.
~ **et,** (*cul.*) boneless meat: ~ **inciri,** (*bot.*) green fig:
~ ~, in lumps: ~ ~ **yutmak** = ~LATMAK: ~
yumurta, (*cul.*) hard-boiled egg.
lop·çu[l]**k**[ğu] (*bio.*) Lobule. ~**latmak (-i),** bolt one's
food. ~**padak,** (*ech.*) flop! ~**ur,** ~ ~, gobbling,
eating noisily.
Lor[1] *n.* (*ethn.*) Lur people (of S. Persia).
lor[2] *n.* (*cul.*) Goat's milk curd. ~ **peyniri,** goat's
cheese.
loran (*rad.*) Loran tracking system.
lorentiyum/lavrensiyum (*chem.*) Lawrencium.
lori(giller) (*zoo.*) Lori(s).
lor[l]**t**[du] (*soc.*) Lord; (*fig.*) s.o. very rich. ~ **gibi,** like
a lord, in luxury: ~**lar Kamarası,** (*adm.*) Eng.
House of Lords.
lorta Shoemaker's last; last size.
lostra Shoe-polish. ~ **salonu,** shoe-black's booth.
~**cı,** bootblack.
lostromo (*naut.*) Boatswain, bo'sun.
losyon (*chem.*) Lotion; eau-de-cologne.
loş Dark, dismal, gloomy; dusky; slack, weak.
~**laşmak,** *vi.* become dim/gloomy/slack. ~**laştırmak (-i),** *vc.* ~**luk,** darkness; slackness.
lota (*ich.*) Burbot.
lotarya (*gamb.*) Lottery. ~**cı,** (*fin.*) s.o. who goes in
for lotteries.
loyi[l]**t**[di] (*fin., naut.*) Lloyd's (marine insurance
organization).
Lozan (*geo.*) Lausanne. ~ **(Sulh) Antlaşması,** (*his.*)
Treaty of Lausanne, 1923.
lök[ü] *a.* Awkward; clumsy; sluggish. *n.* Male camel.
~ **gibi oturmak,** sit down awkwardly/heavily.
lök·oplast[1] (*bot.*) Leucoplastid. ~**osit**[i], (*bio.*) leucocyte. ~**ün,** putty.
löpür = LOPUR.
lös (*geol.*) Loess. ~**emi,** (*med.*) leukaemia.
löviye (*aer.*) Control column.
LPG = LİKİT PETROL GAZ.
lt(.) = LİTRE. ~**d** = (*limited*) LİMİTET.
-lt- *v. suf.* [229] = -ELT- [SİVRİLTMEK].
Lu. = (*ch.s.*) LÜTESYUM.
-luk[1,2] *a./n. suf.* [62] = -LİK[1,2] [BOŞLUK; SOYUTLUK].
lum·bago (*med.*) Lumbago. ~**bar** = LOMBAR.
lumpen Riff-raff, scoundrel. ~**dil,** slang. ~**leşmek,**
vi. become riff-raff.
lun (*orn.*) Loon. ~**ula,** (*bio.*) lunula.
lup (*phys.*) Magnifying-glass. ~**ing,** (*aer.*) looping-
the-loop.

lut[1] *n.* (*mus.*) Lute.
Lut[2] *pr.n.* ~ **deniz/gölü,** (*geo.*) Dead Sea.
luti Pederast.
lutr (*zoo.*) Otter; otterskin.
Lübnan (*geo.*) The Lebanon. ~ +, *a.* Lebanese:
~ **sediri,** (*bot.*) cedar of Lebanon. ~**lı,** (*ethn.*)
Lebanese.
lüfer (*ich.*) Blue-fish.
lügat[1] Word; dictionary. ~ **paralamak,** use learned/
foreign words. ~**çe,** vocabulary; glossary. ~**çı(lık),**
lexicograph·er/(-y).
-lük[1,2] *a./n. suf.* [62] = -LİK[1,2] [KÖTÜLÜK; ÖNLÜK].
lükata (*leg.*) Unclaimed property.
lüks[1] *n.* Luxury; ostentation. *a.* Luxurious, *de luxe*;
costly; ostentatious. ~ /**lüküs hayatı,** life of luxury:
~ **koltuk,** (*th.*) best seats: ~ **lambası,** vaporized oil
lamp: ~ **vergisi,** (*fin.*) luxury tax: ~ **yaşamak,** live
expensively: ~**e kaçmak,** be given to ostentation/
luxury.
lüks[2] *n.* (*phys.*) Lux.
lüle Pipe; (*obs.*) bowl of tobacco pipe; spout; paper
cone; curl, fold; (*obs.*) water measure. ~**ci,** maker
of pipe-bowls: ~ **çamuru,** (*geol.*) pipe clay. ~**cilik,**
making pipe bowls. ~**taşı**[nı], (*geol.*) meerschaum.
lüm·en (*phys.*) Lumen. ~**ifor,** luminous (paint).
~**inesans,** luminescence.
lüp[ü] (*col.*) Stg. got without cost/trouble; (*ech.*) gulping; essence/heart of stg. ~ **diye yutmak,** gulp
down: ~**e konmak,** get stg. free/without effort.
~**çü,** s.o. who lives by his wits; parasite. ~**çülük,**
parasitism.
lütein (*bio.*) Lutein.
Lüteriyen (*rel.*) Lutheran Christian.
lütesyum (*chem.*) Lutetium.
lüt·fen As a favour!, please! ~**f**[l]**etmek**[eder]/ ~**feyle-
mek,** do the favour; have the kindness to; kindly
(do stg.). ~**l**[uf][fu], kindness, goodness; favour: ~
süresi, period of grace: ~**unda bulunmak (-mek),** be
so kind as to . . .: ~**uyla (-in),** with the permission
of, by the grace of . . .. ~**ufkâr,** kind, affable,
gracious. ~**ufname,** 'your letter'.
lüzuc·et[i] Viscosity. ~**i,** viscous.
lüzum Necessity, need. ~ **görüldüğü takdirde,** in
case of need. ~**lu,** necessary; needed; useful: ~
lüzumsuz yere, even when not needed. ~**suz,**
unnecessary; useless. ~**suzluk,** a being unnecessary.
Lv. = LEVAZIM. ~**A.** = LEVAZIM AMİRLİĞİ. ~ **Sa.
Al. Ko.** = LEVAZIM SATIN ALMA KOMİSYONU.
Lw. = (*ch.s.*) LAVRENSİYUM.
lx. = LÜKS[2].

M

M, m [me] Sixteenth Tk. letter, M.
M, m. = MAHALLE; METRE; MİKTAR; MİLAT; MİLADİ; (*Monsieur*).
m- (*col.*) *Initial letter of the second, invented word in a doublet.* [237] And so on, and such-like; anything/anyone like [AĞAÇ MAĞAÇ; FAKATI MAKATI].
-m[1] *n. suf.* [39] *1st person possessive suffix after a vowel-stem.* = -İM [BABAM; ÇEHREM].
-m[2] *v. suf.* [106] *1st person suffix after a vowel-stem* [İDİM; ALIRSAM].
-m[3] *n. suf.* [225] *Denoting the action of the verb.* [ANLAM; GÖZLEM].
mA = MİLİAMPER.
-ma[1] *vn. suf.* [170] = -ME[1] [ALMA; SORMA].
-ma-[2] *v. suf.*, *negative.* [110] = -ME-[2] [ALAMAM; SORMADI].
maada (-den) *post.* [89] Besides; apart from; except.
ma·aile Together with the family. ~ **alesef**, unfortunately; with regret; I'm afraid . . . not. ~ **almemnuniye**, with pleasure. ~ **amafih**, = MAMAFİH.
maarif *pl.* = MARİFET. Branches of science; education; culture. ~ **Vekâleti**, (*obs.*) Ministry of Education. ~ **çi**, educationalist.
maaş (*fin.*) Salary; (*soc.*) (widows', etc.) allowance. ~ **almak**, receive a salary: ~ **bağlamak**, earn a salary: ~ **cüzdanı**, (*soc.*) pension-/family-allowance-book, etc.: ~ **kırdırmak**, borrow money against salary due but not yet paid: ~ **vermek**, pay a salary: ~ **zammı**, increase in salary. ~ **lı**, receiving a salary/allowance, etc.: ~ **memur**, (*adm.*) established official.
maatteessüf Unfortunately; with regret.
maba·lt[di] (*lit.*) Sequence; continuation; remainder. ~ **ı var**, to be continued.
mabe·lt[di] (*rel.*) Place of worship, temple.
mabey·lin[ni] Interval; (*soc.*) relations between two people; (*arch.*) room between HAREM and SELÂMLIK; (*his.*) the Palace; the Sultan's private apartments. ~ **de**, between them: ~ **imizde**, between us: ~ **leri bozuk**, they are on bad terms, relations are strained. ~ **ci**, (*his.*) court chamberlain.
mabla·lk[ğı] (*carp.*) Putty knife; (*cul.*) spatula, wooden spoon.
mabu·de (*rel.*) Goddess. ~ **lt**[du], *a.* worshipped: *n.* god; idol.
Mac. = MACAR(İSTAN); MACARCA(DAN).
-maca *n. suf.* [57-8] = -MECE [SORMACA].
Macar (*ethn.*) Hungarian; (*sl., pej.*) louse. ~ **ördeği**, (*orn.*) red-crested pochard. ~ **ca**, (*ling.*) Hungarian. ~ **istan**, (*geo.*) Hungary.
-macasına *vn. suf.* [189] = -MECESİNE [KOŞ-MACASINA].

macera Event; adventure. ~ **cı**, adventurer. ~ **lı**, adventurous; eventful; hazardous. ~ **perest**[i], adventurous, venturesome.
macun (*ind.*) Putty; paste; plasticine; (*aer.*) dope; cement; (*med.*) electuary; (*cul.*) fruit paste. ~ **cu**, seller of coloured/spiced toffee. ~ **lamak (-i)**, stop up/fill with putty/cement. ~ **lanmak**, *vp.* ~ **laşmak**, *vi.* become like putty/paste.
maç[1] (*sp.*) Match; fight; contest.
maça (*gamb.*) Spades (at cards); (*min.*) core (of a mould). ~ **beyi**, knave of spades; ostentatious/conceited person: ~ **beyi gibi kurulmak**, sit in a sprawling/indecorous manner.
maçuna (*naut.*) Crane, derrick, winch. ~ **gemisi**, sheer-hulk: ~ **ücreti**, cranage.
mad. = (*leg.*) MADDE; MADENCİLİK.
madal·ya Medal: ~ **nın ters tarafı**, the reverse of the medal. ~ **yon**, medallion.
madam Madame; Mrs.
madampol[ü] (*tex.*) Calico.
-madan *vn. suf.* [181] = -MEDEN [ALMADAN].
madde Matter; substance; material; subject; (*leg.*) article, paragraph, clause; (*fin.*) entry; (*chem.*) agent. ~ ~, divided into articles; item by item: ~ **ismi**, (*ling.*) concrete noun: ~ **nin sakınımı**, (*chem.*) conservation of matter.
madd·eci(lik) (*phil.*) Material·ist/(-ism). ~ **esel**, *a.* material. ~ **eten**, materially; physically. ~ **i**, *a.* material; physical; tangible; substantial. ~ **ileşmek**, *vi.* become material/physical. ~ **ilik**, materiality. ~ **iyat**[1], material things; materialism.
madem(ki) While; since; as.
maden *n.* (*min.*) Mine; mineral; metal; (*fig.*) a mine of (learning, etc.). ~ +, *a.* Metal; mining: ~ **araştırma**, prospecting: ~ **cevher/filizi**, (*geol.*) ore: ~ **damarı**, lode, vein: ~ **direği**, pit-prop: ~ **işlemeciliği**, metal working: ~ **katranı**, (*chem.*) coal-tar: ~ **ocağı**, (coal, etc.) mine: ~ **posası**, slag: ~ **yatağı**, (*geol.*) mineral stratum: ~ **yerbilimi**, mining geology.
maden·bilim Mineralogy. ~ **ci**, miner; mining expert; metallurgist; mine-owner: ~ **ışıtaç/lambası**, Davy lamp: ~ **kuyusu**, mine-shaft. ~ **cilik**, mining: ~ **okulu**, school of mining(-engineering). ~ **i**, *a.* metal; mineral: ~ **para**, (*fin.*) specie: ~ **yağlar(ın parçalanması)**, (*chem.*) (cracking of) mineral oils: ~ **zıvana**, (*eng.*) bush. ~ **kırmız**, (*min.*) kermesite, native red antimony. ~ **kömürü**[nü], coal. ~ **leşme**, (*bot.*) mineralization. ~ **sel**, *a.* metal, mineral: ~ **boyaözü**, pigment. ~ **si**, *a.* metallic: *n.* (*chem.*) semi-metal. ~ **suyu**[nu], mineral water. ~ **yünü**[nü], mineral wool.
mader *n.* (*obs.*) Mother. ~ **ane**, maternal. ~ **şahi**, matriarchal. ~ **şahilik**, matriarchy; matriarchate.

madi·kᵍⁱ (*sl.*) Trick, ruse. ~ **atmak/etm./oynamak,** cheat. ~**çi,** trickster, cheat.

madrabaz (*obs.*) Middleman (dealing in foodstuffs); (*col.*) cheat, impostor. ~**lık,** cheating: ~**la elde etm.,** cadge.

Madras (*geo.*) Madras. ~ **humması,** (*med.*) dumdum fever.

madrepor ~ **plağı,** (*bio.*) madrepore.

madru·ı**p**ᵇᵘ (*obs.*) *a.* Beaten, struck. *n.* (*math.*) Multiplicand.

madun *a.* Inferior, lower; subordinate. *n.* Subordinate.

maes·toso (*mus.*) *Maestoso.* ~**tro,** (*mus.*) n.aestro; conductor.

mafevkⁱ That which is above; a superior.

mafiş *n.* (*cul.*) Type of light fritter. *int.* Finished!; nothing left!

mafsal (*bio., eng.*) Joint; articulation. ~ **ile birleştirmek,** articulate: ~ **iltihabı,** (*med.*) arthritis: ~ **romatizması,** rheumatoid arthritis. ~**lı,** articulated: ~ **mihengir,** (*carp.*) scribing-block.

mag·azin (*pub.*) Magazine. ~**ma(sal),** (*geol.*) magma(tic). ~**nalyum,** (*min.*) magnalium. ~**netik,** *etc.* = MANYETİK. ~**nezyum,** (*chem.*) magnesium. ~**nitüd,** (*math.*) magnitude. ~**ri,** (*ich.*) conger eel.

mağ (*orn.*) Type of pigeon. **-mağa** *vn. suf., dative.* [168] = -MEĞE [BAKMAĞA].

mağara (*geo.*) Cave; pit. ~ **adamı,** (*ethn.*) caveman: ~ **semenderi(giller),** (*zoo.*) olm/(Proteidae). ~**msı,** cavernous.

mağaza Large store, shop; storehouse, warehouse.

mağdur *a.* Unjustly treated; wronged. *n.* Sufferer, victim. ~**e,** female victim. ~**iyet**ⁱ/~**luk,** a being unjustly treated; oppression; suffering loss.

mağ·firetⁱ (*rel.*) Forgiveness (of sins); grace. ~**fur,** forgiven, pardoned. **-mağı** *vn. suf., accusative.* [168] = -MEĞİ [BAKMAĞI].

mağlu·biyetⁱ Defeat. ~**p,** defeated, overcome.

mağmum Sad, anxious; gloomy, overclouded.

Mağosa (*geo.*) Famagusta (Cyprus).

Mağri·bi (*ethn.*) Moroccan; Moor. ~**ı**p**ᵇⁱ,** (*geo.*) West; sunset; *pr.n.* (*geo.*) Morocco: ~ **kurbağası,** (*zoo.*) moor frog.

mağrur Self-confident; proud; conceited. ~**en,** proudly; confidently. ~**iyet**ⁱ/~**luk,** conceit; over-confidence. ~**lanmak,** *vi.* become foolishly conceited.

mağşuş Alloyed; adulterated; base (coin).

Mah. = MAHALLE(Sİ); MAHKEME(Sİ).

mahalˡⁱ Place; premises; post; occasion, cause. ~ **bırakmamak/vermemek (-e),** not give occasion for stg.: ~ **kalmamak,** be no longer necessary: ~**linde,** at his post; opportune(ly). ~**siz,** inopportune; out of place.

mahalle Quarter/district (of a town); ward, parish; street(-corner). ~ **çapkını,** inept womanizer: ~ **çocuğu,** street urchin, guttersnipe: ~ **kahvesi gibi,** stuffy/noisy/crowded (place): ~ **kahvesine dönmek,** become disorderly/slack: ~ **karısı,** common/quarrelsome woman: ~ **tavrı,** vulgar manners: ~**yi ayağa kaldırmak,** set the neighbourhood in an uproar.

mahallebi (*cul.*) Sweet dish of rice and milk.

~**ci(lik),** (work of) maker/seller of milk dishes: ~ **çocuğu,** mother's darling; milksop.

mahall·eli *a.* Belonging to the same district: *n.* people of the district; neighbour. ~**i,** local, district: ~ **idare,** local government: ~ **örf,** local custom/ tradition: ~ **özellik/renk,** (*lit.*) local colour. ~**ileşmek,** *vi.* reflect local customs, etc.; be assimilated.

maharetⁱ Skill, ability, proficiency; diplomacy. ~ **kazanmak,** gain proficiency, become skilled. ~**li,** skilful, capable, proficient; diplomatic; cunning. ~**siz,** unskilful; clumsy.

mah·cubiyetⁱ Bashfulness; shame; modesty. ~**cup,** ashamed; bashful, coy; confused: ~ **etm.,** put to confusion; shame: ~ **olm.,** be confused//ashamed. ~**cupluk,** shame, confusion.

mahcur (*leg.*) Not allowed to dispose of his property.

mahcuz (*leg.*) Sequestrated.

mahdum (*obs.*) Son.

mahdut Bounded, surrounded; definite; limited; few.

mahfaza Case; casket; sheath. ~**lı,** having/kept in a case.

mahfe Twin basket-seats on a camel.

mahfil (*soc.*) Meeting-place, club, circle; gathering; (*rel.*) private gallery/pew (in a mosque); (*soc.*) masonic lodge.

mahfuz Protected, looked after, conserved; memorized. ~**en,** under guard; in custody.

mah·ııv**ᵛⁱ Destruction; annihilation; abolition.

mahir Skilful. ~**lik,** skill.

mahiye Monthly, per month.

mahiyetⁱ Reality; true nature of stg.; character/ (-istic). ~ **almak,** assume . . . form/character. ~**li,** having the nature/character of . . ..

mahkeme (*leg.*) Lawcourt, court of justice. ~ **duvarı** = YÜZ²: ~ **heyeti,** the Court: ~ **kapısı,** court-house (door): ~ **masrafları,** legal costs: ~ **de dayısı olm.,** have a protector/patron: ~**i asliye,** court of first instance: ~ **nin hükmünü giymek,** be condemned by a court: ~**ye dayanmışlar,** they ended up in court: ~**yi boylamak,** have to appear in court.

mahkeme·li (*leg.*) The subject of a lawsuit; defendant. ~**lik,** a matter for the courts: ~ **olm.,** have a dispute only to be settled in court.

mahkûkᵘ Engraved; scratched; erased. ~**at**ı, engravings; inscriptions.

mahkûm *a.* (*leg.*) Sentenced; condemned; judged; (*fig.*) obliged, forced. *n.* The condemned. ~ **etm.,** condemn, convict: ~ **olm.,** be condemned; (*fig.*) be obliged (to do stg.). ~**iyet**ⁱ, condemnation; sentence.

mahlas Surname; (*lit.*) pseudonym, pen-name.

mahle·ı**p**ᵇⁱ (*bot.*) St. Lucie/mahaleb cherry(-tree); (*cul.*) spice from its dried fruit.

mahlukᵘ *a.* Created. *n.* Creature. ~**at**ı, creatures; all creation.

mahlulᵘ̈ *a.* Dissolved; vacant; (*leg.*) escheated. *n.* Solution. ~**at**ı, (*leg.*) escheated property.

mahlutᵘ *a.* Mixed; adulterated. *n.* (*chem.*) Compound.

mahmude (*bot.*) Scammony; (*med.*) its purgative resin.

mahmudiye (*fin.*) Gold coin of Mahmud II.

mahmulü *a.* Borne; loaded (on animals); (*phil.*) attributed, imputed; (*lit.*) heavy (style). *n.* (*phil.*) Predicate, attribute.

mahmur Sleepy; languid; torpid; lackadaisical. ~ **bakış**, soft/tender look. ~ **çiçeği**ni, (*bot.*) autumn crocus, meadow saffron. ~ **laşmak**, *vi.* become sleepy/languid, etc. ~ **luk**, sleepiness; dreaminess; 'hang-over': ~ **bozmak**, take stg. to cure a 'hang-over'.

mahmuz (*sp.*) Spur; (*orn.*) cock's spur; (*naut.*) (ship's) ram, beak, cutwater; (*arch.*) (bridge) fender. ~ **lamak (-i)**, spur. ~ **lanmak**, *vp.* ~ **lu**, spurred: ~ **camgöz**, (*ich.*) spiny dogfish: ~ **incir kuşu**, (*orn.*) Richard's pipit.

mahpus *a.* Imprisoned. *n.* Prisoner, convict. ~ **hane**, prison. ~ **luk**, imprisonment.

mahra Wooden case for carrying grapes.

mahrama (*mod.*) Woman's shawl worn over a coat.

mahre¹çci Outlet; channel; origin, source; (*math.*) denominator.

mahreki (*ast.*) Orbit (of planet, etc.); trajectory.

mahrem *a.* Confidential; secret; intimate; within the relationships forbidden for marriage (*thus having access to the harem*). *n.* Confidant(e). ~ **tutmak**, keep stg. secret. ~ **iyet**i, secrecy; confidentiality.

mahruk Burnt. ~ **at**ı, combustibles; fuel.

mahrum Deprived, destitute; disappointed. ~ **etm.**, deprive: ~ **kalmak**, be disappointed; **(-den)**, remain deprived of. ~ **iyet**i, deprivation; destitution: ~ **e katlanmak**, suffer privation; do without.

mahrutu (*math.*) Cone. ~ **i**, conic(al); conoid: ~ **çadır**, bell tent. ~ **iyet**i, conicity.

mahsub- = MAHSUP. ~ **en**, (*fin.*) on account; **(-e)**, to the account of.

mahsulü Product; produce; (*agr.*) crop; (*fig.*) result; return; profit. ~ **at**ı, products; (*agr.*) crops. ~ **dar**/ ~ **lü**, productive, fertile.

mahsu¹pbu Counted; calculated. ~ **etm.**/~ **unu yapmak**, count; reckon in an account.

mahsur Confined; limited; besieged; cut off (by floods, etc.).

mahsus¹ *a.* Special; peculiar to; proper to; particular, private; reserved. *adv.* Specially; expressly, on purpose.

mahsus² *a.* Felt, perceived. ~ **bir suretle**, perceptibly. ~ **at**ı, sensations.

mahşer (*rel.*) The Last Judgement; (*fig.*) great crowd; great confusion. ~ **gibi**, crowded: ~ **midillisi**, (*fig.*) little trouble-maker. ~ **i**, crowded.

mahun (*bot.*, *carp.*) Mahogany. ~ **ya**, (*bot.*) mahonia.

mahur (buselik) (*Or. mus.*) A melody.

mahut Well-known; notorious; (*pej.*) your.

mahv·¹etmekeder Destroy; devastate; abolish. ~ **iyet**i, humility, modesty. ~ **olma**, destruction; bankruptcy. ~ **olmak**, *vp.* be destroyed/ruined/ abolished: **mahvolduğumuzun resmidir**, our ruin is certain.

mahya (*rel.*) Illuminated texts/figures strung be-

tween minarets (during Ramadan); (*arch.*) roof-ridge; ridge-tiles. ~ **cı**, MAHYA maker; tiler.

mahzar (*adm.*) Multi-signature petition; round robin.

mahzen (*arch.*) Underground storehouse; granary; cellar. ~ **mezar**, undercroft, crypt.

mahzun Sad; grieved. ~ **baştankara**, (*orn.*) sombre tit: ~ **olm.**, be grieved/depressed. ~ **iyet**i/~ **luk**, grief, sadness.

mahzur Stg. to be guarded against; objection; inconvenience; danger. ~ **görmek**, see objections. ~ **lu**, to be avoided.

mai Light blue.

mail Leaning; inclined; oblique: **(-e)**, (*fig.*) inclined to; tending towards. ~ **e**, slope.

main (*math.*) Rhombus; lozenge.

maişeti Means of subsistence; livelihood, daily bread.

maiyeti Suite, following, attendants. ~ **alayı**, (*mil.*) escort: ~ **memuru**, (*adm.*) governor's assistant (in training): ~ **vapuru**, (*naut.*) ambassador's *stationnaire*: ~ **inde**, accompanying; in his suite.

maj·olika (*art.*) Majolica. ~ **ör**, *a.* major, important: *n.* (*mus.*) major key, etc.; (*phil.*) major premiss. ~ **üskül**, (*pub.*) capital (letter).

mak (*aer.*) Mach. ~ **sayısı**, Mach number.

mak. = MAKİNE.

-mak¹ *v. suf.* [96] = -MEK [OLMAK].

-mak² *vn. suf.* [167] = -MEK [BULMAK].

makab¹illi That which goes before. ~ **(in)e şamil olm.**, (*leg.*) be retrospective.

makadam (*eng.*) Macadamized road.

makak¹ (*zoo.*) Macaque.

makale (*pub.*) Article (in newspapers, etc.).

makam Place; abode; (*adm.*) post; rank; department, authority, office; (*Or. mus.*) mode, melody, tune. ~ **araba/otomobili**, official car: ~ **tutturmak**, strike up a tune; annoy by constant repetition: ~ **ında**, in token of; after the manner of: ~ **lar**, (*adm.*) the authorities: ~ **lı**, (*mus.*) harmonious. ~ **sız**, inharmonious, discordant.

makara (*eng.*, *naut.*) Pulley, block; reel, bobbin, spool; roller; drum; castor; (*sp.*) indoor training-cycle. ~ **çekmek**, (*orn.*) (songbird) sing different notes: ~ **dili**, (*naut.*) sheave: ~ **evi**, (*naut.*) pulley block: ~ **gibi söylemek**, chatter endlessly: ~ **ları koyuvermek/salıvermek**, (*col.*) burst into peals of laughter: ~ **ları zaptedememek**, be unable to control one's laughter: ~ **yı takmak**, tease s.o. ~ **lı**, fitted with a pulley, etc.: ~ **kuş**, bird with varied song: ~ **yatak**, (*eng.*) roller-bearing.

makarna (*cul.*) Macaroni, spaghetti. ~ **cı**, macaroni maker; s.o. partial to macaroni; (*jok.*) Italian.

makas *n.* Scissors; shears; (*zoo.*) claws (of lobster, etc.); (*rly.*) switch, points; (*mot.*) steering-rods; suspension springs; anything scissor-shaped; (*sp.*) cross-legged wrestling-hold. *int.* (*sl.*) Enough! ~ **almak**, tweak with the fingers: ~ **ateşi**, (*mil.*) cross-fire: ~ **gagalılar**, (*orn.*) skimmers: ~ **gülle**, (*mil.*) chain-shot: ~ **hak/payı**, remnants after cutting out a suit; (*fig.*) remainder, margin: ~ **kavşak**, (*mot.*) scissors junction: ~ **kolu**, (*rly.*) points lever: ~ **kulakları**, scissors handles: ~ **payı**, (*mod.*) cutting line: ~ **yaprakları**, (*mot.*) leaves of suspension springs: ~**ı kapa!**, (*sl.*) shut up!

makas·çı (*rly.*) Pointsman. ~**çılık**, (*rly.*) points switching; (*pub.*) (newspapers) plagiarism. ~**lama**, *a.* crosswise; *vn.*; (*min.*) shear(ing); (*sp.*) scissors kick/vault. ~**lamak (-i)**, cut with scissors; tweak with the fingers; rob; (*pub.*) plagiarize. ~**lanmak**, *vp.* be cut; be shortened. ~**lı**, scissor-shaped: ~ **dürbün**, stereo-telescope. ~**lıböcek**, (*ent.*) stagbeetle. ~**tar**, (*mod.*) tailor's cutter.

makat¹ (*dom.*) Covering (of sofa, etc.); cushion; sofa; (*bio.*) the posterior.

makber Tomb; grave; cemetery.

makbulü Accepted; acceptable; eligible; liked. ~**e geçmek**, be received with pleasure: ~ **ümdür**, it's my pleasure; I gladly accept.

makbuz (*fin.*) *a.* Received. *n.* Receipt; voucher. ~ **mukabilinde**, against receipt: ~**um olmuştur**, I acknowledge receipt.

Makedon·ca (*ling.*) Macedonian. ~**ya**, (*geo.*) Macedonia: ~ +, *a.* Macedonian. ~**yalı**, (*ethn.*) Macedonian.

maketⁱ (*art.*) Sketch; outline; model; (*pub.*) layout; (*mod.*) dummy. ~**çi**, model-maker.

makferlan (*mod.*) Inverness cape.

maki (*for.*) Undergrowth, scrub; *maquis*; (*zoo.*) lemur.

makin·a/~**e** Machine; machinery; engine; mechanism; clockwork; (*col.*) motor-car. ~ **adamı**, robot: ~ **dairesi**, (*naut.*) engine-room; (*pub.*) pressroom: ~ **dili**, (*el.*) machine language: ~ **gibi**, very quick; repetitive: ~ **gibi adam**, very regular/hardworking man: ~ **gücü**, (*eng.*) (horse-)power of a machine: ~ **kumanda telegrafı**, (*naut.*) engineroom telegraph: ~ **subay/zabıtı**, (*naut.*) engineerofficer: ~ **uzmanı**, (*eng.*) mechanic: ~ **ye verilirken**, (*pub.*) 'Stop press!': ~**yi bozmak**, (*jok.*) have an upset stomach.

makine·ci Mechanic; machinist; (*rly.*) enginedriver. ~**leşme**, *vn.* mechanization; automation. ~**leşmek**, *vi.* be(come) mechanized; become mechanical. ~**leştirmek (-i)**, mechanize. ~**li**, mechanical; driven by/fitted with a machine: ~ **şahmerdan**, (*eng.*) drop-hammer: ~ **tabanca**, (*mil.*) machine-pistol: ~ **tüfek**, machine-gun. ~ **yağı**ⁿⁱ, (*chem.*) engine/lubricating oil.

makinist(lik) (Work of) (*rly.*) engine-driver// (*naut.*) engineer; mechanic. ~ **yeri**, (*rly.*) cab.

mak·iyaj = MAKYAJ. ~**rama** = MAHRAMA.

-makla *v. suf.* [187] = -MEKLE [KOŞMAKLA].

-maklık *vn. suf.* [170] = -MEKLİK [BULUNMAK-LIĞINIZ].

makmetre (*phys.*) Mach-meter.

makro- *pref.* Macro-.

maksa·tᵈ¹ Aim; purpose; intention. ~ **gütmek**, have a secret aim: ~**ınız nedir?**, what are you driving at?: ~**ıyla**, with a view to/the intention of. ~ **lı**, having an aim; tendentious; intentional. ~**sız**, desultory.

-maksızın *v. suf.* [188] = -MEKSİZİN [ALMAKSIZIN].

maksi Long. ~ **etek**, (*mod.*) maxi-skirt. ~**l**, (*bio.*) maxilliped. ~**m**, (*phil.*) maxim. ~**mum**, (*math.*) maximum; peak.

maksure (*rel.*) Private pew (in mosque); private grounds.

maksu·tᵈᵘ *a.* Intended; wished for. *n.* Aim; intention.

makta¹ (*carp.*) Cutting; (cross-)section; end-grain: (*fig.*) pause.

-mak·ta *vn. suf.* [111] = -MEKTE [OKUMAKTA]. ~ **tan**, *vn. suf.* [168] = -MEKTEN [ALMAKTAN]. ~**tansa**, *v. suf.* [188] = -MEKTENSE [KALMAKTANSA].

maktuᵘ (*fin.*) Fixed value; sold as a lot. ~ **fiyat**, fixed price.

maktua (*pub.*) Cutting.

maktulü Killed. ~ **düşmek**, die from a blow.

makulü Conceivable; reasonable; wise, prudent. ~ **görmek**, approve, consider reasonable.

makule Kind, sort, type; (*phil.*) category.

makûs Inverted; reverse; opposed.

makyaj (*th.*, *mod.*) Make-up. ~ **aynası**, adjustable three-section mirror: ~ **eksperi**, cosmetician; beautician: ~ **malzemesi**, cosmetics. ~**cı**, (*th.*) make-up artist.

Makyavel·ce (*pol.*) Machiavellian. ~**izm**, Machiavellianism.

mal¹ *n.* (*live.*) Cattle; herd of cattle.

mal² *n.* Property; possession(s); effects; wealth; commodity; merchandise, goods; (*fig.*) scoundrel; loose woman. ~ **aktarımı**, trans-shipment: ~ **ayrılığı//birliği//ortaklığı**, (*leg.*) (husband and wife) separate//common//joint ownership of property: ~ **beyan/bildirimi**, (*fin.*) declaration: ~ **borsası**, (*fin.*) commodity exchange: ~ **bulmuş Mağribi gibi**, grasping, mean: ~ **bulmuş Mağribiye dönmüş**, overjoyed: ~ **canın yongasıdır**, it is hard to part with any of one's possessions: ~ **canlısı**, covetous, avaricious, greedy: ~ **çıkışı**, (*fin.*) export: ~ **değişimi**, (*fin.*) clearing: ~ **edilmek**, *vp.* be appropriated: ~ **edinmek**, become rich; appropriate: ~ **edinmemek**, take no account of; not worry about: ~ **etm.**, take possession of, appropriate; buy up: ~ **iyesi**, owner of a property; proprietor; rich man: ~ **meydanda**, the proof is here; it's obviously bad: ~**MÜDÜRÜ**: ~ **mülk (yığmak)**, (amass) riches/wealth: ~ **olm. (-e)**, cost; pay dearly for stg.: ~ **oluş eder**, cost price: ~ **sahibi** = İYESİ: ~ **sandığı**, (*adm.*) financial department; cashbox: ~ **sayışımı**, (*fin.*) stock account: ~ **ücret yöntemi**, truck system: ~**ı kapışıyorlar**, there's a rush on the goods: ~**ı piyasadan kaldırmak**, corner goods: ~**ın gözü**, (*sl.*) rascal, ne'er-do-well: ~**ın kadar zekâtın olsun!**, you are mean!; (*iron.*) can you afford it?: ~**lar**, (*fin.*) assets: ~**ların geri alınması**, repossession.

mal. = MALİYE.

mala Bricklayer's trowel. ~**lamak (-i)**, work/ smooth with a trowel.

malafa (*eng.*) Arbor; mandrel.

malaka (*live.*) Buffalo calf.

malakitⁱ (*min.*) Malachite.

malarya (*med.*) Malaria.

malayani Meaningless; nonsense.

malaz Fallow//flooded land.

Malazgirt *pr.n.* (*his.*) Manzikert.

mal·ca Financially; property-wise. ~**dar**, wealthy.

malgama (*chem.*) Amalgam.

-malı-[1] *v. suf.* [125] = -MELİ-[1] [KULLANMALIYIM].

-malı[2] *vn. suf.* [172] = -MELİ[2] [ASMALI].

malıtaşı[nı] (*naut.*) Large stone used as anchor.

mali Financial. ~ **denge vergisi**, fiscal balance tax: ~ **durum**, circumstances: ~ **yıl**, financial year.

malihulya Melancholy; whim, fancy.

malik[i] *a.* Owning, possessing. *n.* Owner. ~ **olm.** (-e), possess, own. ~ **ane**, state lands (held in fief); large estate. ~**i**, *pr.n.* (member of) Maliki sect. ~**iyet**[i], ownership.

maliye *a.* Financial. *n.* Finance. ~ **Bakan(lığ)ı**, (*adm.*) Minis·ter/(-try) of Finance: ~ **hazinesi**, (*adm.*) treasury. ~**ci(lik)**, (work of) financier// finance official. ~**t**[i], cost: ~ **fiyatı**, cost price.

malkıran (*med.*) Cattle plague, murrain.

malkoç (*his.*) AKINCILAR leader. ~**oğlu**, swindler.

mal·lanmak *vi.* Become rich. ~**müdürü**[nü], (*adm.*) İLÇE financial director. ~**perest**, avaricious.

malt[1] (*cul.*) Malt (for brewing).

Malta (*geo.*) Malta. ~ +, *a.* Maltese. ~ **gibi**, very expensive (place): ~ **haçı**, Maltese cross.

Malta·ca (*ling.*) Maltese. ~**eriğin**[i], (*bot.*) loquat. ~**humması**[nı], (*med.*) Malta/Mediterranean fever, brucellosis. ~**palamudu**[nu], (*ich.*) pilot fish. ~**taşı**[nı], (*geol.*) soft building stone.

mal·taz (*bio.*) Maltase. ~**toz**, (*chem.*) maltose.

maltız (*dom.*) Brazier; *pr.n.* (*ethn.*) Maltese. ~**keçisi**[ni], (*live.*) short-haired milk-producing goat.

malul[ü] *a.* (*med.*) Ill; invalid; disabled. *n.* Cripple. ~ **arabası**, (*med.*) wheel-chair: ~ **gazi**, (*mil.*) disabled soldier. ~**en**, as an invalid. ~**iyet**[i], illness; disablement.

malum *a.* Known; (*ling.*) active (verb). *int.* Yes!; true! ~ **olm.**, be(come) known; (-e), be sensed/ revealed: ~**u ilam**, telling stg. that is known to all: ~**unuzdur ki**, you know that . . ..

malumat[1] Information; data; knowledge. ~ **almak**, get information/learn about: ~ **kumkuması**, a mine of information: ~ **sahibi**, man of learning, knowledgeable man: ~**ım yok (-den)**, I have no knowledge of/information about: ~**ına müracaat etm.**, ask for information about.

malumat·furuş (*obs.*) Who poses as learned; pedant. ~**lı**, learned; educated; well-informed. ~**sız**, ignorant; uneducated. ~**tar**, informed.

malzeme Necessaries; materials. ~ **ocağı**, (*eng.*) borrow pit.

mama (*child.*) Food; baby food. ~ **bezi**, bib.

mamafih [211] Nevertheless; however.

-mamazlık *vn. suf.* [173] = -MEZLİK [ANLAŞIL-MAMAZLIK].

mambo (*mus.*) Mambo dance.

mamelek[i] All that one possesses.

mamul[ü] Made; manufactured: (-den), made of. ~ **şey**, finished product. ~**at**[1], manufactured goods; products.

mamur Prosperous; flourishing; built-up (town). ~**e**, prosperous/cultivated place. ~**iyet**[i]/~**luk**, prosperity.

mamut[u] (*zoo.*) Mammoth.

-man[1] *a. suf.* [220]. *With intensifying effect* [KOCAMAN].

-man[2] *n. suf.* [220] = -MEN [SAYMAN; VATMAN].

mana Meaning; sense; motive; essence. ~ **çıkarmak** (-den), put a false interpretation on stg.: ~ **dolu**, expressive, meaningful: ~ **vermek**, explain; interpret: ~ **verememek (-e)**, be unable to explain stg.; be suspicious about stg.

mana·lı Meaningful; significant; suggestive. ~**sız** (-lık), senseless(ness); meaningless(ness); absurd, (-ity).

manas (*ent.*) Fuller cockchafer.

manastır (*rel.*) Monastery; abbey; convent. ~ **odası**, cell.

manati(giller) (*zoo.*) Manatee(s).

manav Fruiterer/greengrocer('s shop). ~ **kayığı**, bumboat. ~**lık**, selling fruit/vegetables.

manca (*col.*) Food; pet-food. ~**na**, (*naut.*) water-tank.

mancını'k[ğı] (*mil.*) Catapult; ballista; (*tex.*) spinning wheel. ~ **işi**, reeling silk from cocoons: ~**la atmak**, (*aer.*) catapult. ~**çı**, silk-reeler.

Mançu (*ethn.*) Manchurian. ~**ca**, (*ling.*) Manchu(rian). ~**rya**, (*geo.*) Manchuria.

manda[1] *n.* (*adm.*) Mandate.

manda[2] *n.* (*live.*) Water-buffalo; (*fig.*) very fat person. ~ **gibi**, big and clumsy. ~**göz**, ~ **mercan balığı**, (*ich.*) type of red sea-bream. ~**gözü**[nü], (*col. obs.*) twenty-five piastre nickel coin.

mandal (*dom.*) Latch; catch; clothes-peg; (*eng.*) tumbler; pawl; (*naut.*) cleat; (*mus.*) tuning-peg. ~**lamak (-i)**, fasten with latch, etc. ~**lanmak**, *vp.*

mandalina (*bot.*) Mandarin(e)/tangerine (orange).

mandapost[u] (*fin.*) Postal money-order.

mandar (*naut.*) Small pulley block.

manda·rin (*adm.*) Chinese mandarin; (*bot.*) = ~LİNA.

mandater (*adm.*) Mandatary.

mandepsi (*sl.*) Trick, trap. ~**ye basmak/düşmek**, be taken in/cheated/tricked: ~**ye bastırmak**, cheat.

mandıra (*live.*) Small cow-shed; sheep-pen; dairy farm; cheese dairy. ~ **köpeği**, cattle dog; (*fig.*) hatchet man. ~**cı**, dairy farmer.

mandibula (*bio.*) Mandible.

mandolin (*mus.*) Mandolin(e).

mandoz (*naut.*) Block, pulley.

mandren (*eng.*) (Drill) chuck.

mandril (*zoo.*) Mandrill.

manej (*live.*) Horsemanship; riding-school.

man·en In sense; virtually; indirectly; morally: ~ **ve maddeten**, morally and physically. ~**ent**, resembling.

manevi Moral; spiritual. ~ **cebir**, moral pressure, force: ~ **evlat**, child treated as one's own; adopted child: ~ **zarar**, moral injury. ~**yat**[1], spiritual and moral matters; morale: ~**nı bozmak/kırmak**, demoralize.

manevra Manœuvre; (*naut.*) manœuvring; handling; (*rly.*) shunting; (*mil.*) manœuvres; (*fig.*) trick. ~ **çevirmek**, manœuvre: ~ **fişeği**, (*mil.*) blank cartridge: ~ **kemer/kayışı**, (*mil.*) belt: ~ **sandığı**, (*mil.*) officer's kit-box: ~ **yapmak**, manœuvre; (*rly.*) shunt: ~ **yeteneği**, manœuvrability.

manga (*mil.*) Platoon; (*naut.*) mess.

mangal Charcoal brazier. ~ **kenarı kış gününün lalezarıdır**, the fireside is the best place in winter: ~ **da kül bırakmak**, be self-assertive; boast. ~ **kömürü**nü, charcoal.

mangan(ez) (*chem.*) Manganese.

mangır (*obs.*) Copper coin; (*jok.*) money; charcoal disc (used to light a narghile).

mangiz (*sl.*) 'Brass', money.

mangrov (*bot.*) Mangrove.

mani[1] *n.* (*psy.*) Mania; passion.

mani[2] *n.* (*lit.*) Song, ballad.

mânii/yi *n.* Obstacle; impediment. *a.* Preventing, hindering. ~ **olm.** (-e), prevent, hinder: ~ **tedbirler**, preventive precautions.

mania Obstacle; barrier; difficulty. ~ **lı**, presenting obstacles/difficulties: ~ **yarış**, (*sp.*) obstacle/hurdle race.

manidar Meaningful, significant; expressive.

mani·fatura (*tex.*) Textiles, cloths: ~ **eşyası**, dry goods. ~ **faturacı(lık)**, draper(y business). ~ **festo**, (*naut.*) ship's manifest; (*pol.*) manifesto.

maniheizm (*rel.*) Manichaeism.

manika (*naut.*) Windsail.

manikür (*mod.*) Manicure. ~ **cü(lük)**, (work of) manicurist.

manila ~ **kendiri**, (*bot.*, *tex.*) abaca.

mani·ple (*rad.*) Signalling key. ~ **pülatör**, signaller; key.

Manisa (*geo.*) Manisa; (*his.*) Magnesia. ~ **lalesi**, (*bot.*) wood anemone.

manişka (*naut.*) Tackle with two double-sheaved blocks.

manita Swindle. ~ **cı**, swindler; pickpocket. ~ **cılık**, swindling; collaborative pocket-picking.

nanivela (*phys.*) Lever; (*eng.*) lever-arm, crank. ~ **ile işletmek**, crank: ~ **kolu**, crowbar.

nankafa Stupid; dazed; awkward; big; (*live.*) (horse) suffering from glanders. ~ **lık**, stupidity; thick-headedness; (*med.*) glanders.

nanke (*sp.*) Miss.

nanken (*art.*) Wooden model; (*mod.*) tailor's dummy; (*mod.*) mannequin; (*agr.*) scarecrow. ~ **lik**, mannequin's work.

nanolya(giller) (*bot.*) Magnolia/(Magnoliaceae).

nanometre (*phys.*) Manometer.

nansa'pbi (*geo.*) River-mouth; downstream; (*ind.*) outlet.

nansı'pbi (*adm.*) High office.

nansiyon Mention (award).

nanş Sleeve. ~ **denizi**, *pr.n.* (*geo.*) the (English) Channel: ~ **tulumu**, (*aer.*) drogue. ~ **et**, (*pub.*) banner headline; (*mod.*) cuff. ~ **on**, (*mod.*) muff; (*eng.*) sleeve coupling.

nant. = MANTIK.

nantar (*myc.*) Mushroom, fungus; (*bot.*) cork; cork (bottle); inner sole (shoe); (*child.*) cap (of pop-gun); (*live.*) (animal's) nose-tip; (*fig.*) lie, invention. ~ **atmak**, tell lies: ~ **burgusu**, corkscrew: ~ **gibi yerden bitmek**, spring up like mushrooms: ~ **hastalığı**, (*med.*) mycosis: ~ **kavı**, (*myc.*) amadou: ~ **meşesi**, (*bot.*) cork-oak tree: ~ **özü**, (*bot.*) suberin: ~ **pabuç**, (*mod.*) shoes with cork soles/ heels: ~ **tabakası**, (*bot.*) cork (layer): ~ **tabancası**,

(*child.*) pop-gun: ~ **a basmak**, be duped; fall into the trap: ~ **la tıkamak**, cork (bottle): ~ **lar**, (*myc.*) mushrooms, fungi.

mantar·ağacını (*bot.*) Cork tree; cork oak. ~ **bilim**, (*ed.*) mycology: ~ **uzmanı**, mycologist. ~ **cı**, mushroom-seller; (*fig.*) swindler; liar. ~ **cılık**, swindling; lying. ~ **doğuran**, (*bot.*) phellogen, cork cambium. ~ **lamak (-i)**, swindle. ~ **laşma**, *vn.* (*bot.*) suberization; dry-rot. ~ **laşmak**, *vi.* suberize, become corklike. ~ **lı**, (*ind.*) cork-lined; corked (bottle); cork-tipped (cigarette); (*cul.*) prepared with mushrooms. ~ **sı**, ~ **kayaç**, (*geol.*) laccolith.

mantı[1] *n.* (*naut.*) Large pulley-block.

mantı[2] *n.* (*cul.*) Meat pasty.

mantı'kgı (*phil.*) Logic, reasoning power; logicality. ~ **ça**, logically. ~ **çı**, logician; dialectician. ~ **çılık**, reasoning. ~ **dışı**nı, alogical. ~ **i**/ ~ **lı**/ ~ **sal**, logical; reasonable; plausible. ~ **laştırıcılık**, logicism. ~ **öncesi**ni, prelogical. ~ **sız(lık)**, illogical(ity); unreasonable(ness).

mantin (*tex.*) Thick silk tissue.

mantis (*math.*) Mantissa.

manto (*mod.*) (Woman's) overcoat; cloak; mantle. ~ **luk**, (*tex.*) cloth for a cloak.

mantol (*chem.*) Menthol.

manual Manual. ~ **olarak**, manually.

man·ya (*psy.*) Mania. ~ **yak**, maniac(al). ~ **yaklık**, maniacal state.

manyat[1] (*naut.*) Small fishing-boat//-net.

manye·tik (*phys.*) Magnetic: ~ **akı**, magnetic flux: ~ **alan**, magnetic field: ~ **teyp**, magnetic tape. ~ **tit**i, (*geol.*) magnetite. ~ **tize**, mesmerized; magnetized. ~ **tizma**, (*psy.*) mesmerism, hypnosis; (*phys.*) magnetism. ~ **tizmacı(lık)**, hypnot·ist/ (-ism). ~ **to**, (*el.*) magneto. ~ **zi**, (*chem.*) magnesia. ~ **zit**i, (*geol.*) magnesite; meerschaum.

manyoku (*bot.*) Manioc, cassava; tapioca.

manzara View; landscape; panorama; perspective. ~ **da** ~ **ha!**, what a wonderful view! ~ **lı**, having a fine view.

manzum (*lit.*) Written in rhyme and metre. ~ **e**, (*lit.*) poem; series, row.

Mao'cu (*pol.*) Maoist. ~ **luk**, Maoism.

mapa (*eng.*) Eye-bolt; hooded lantern.

mar (*zoo.*) Snake.

mar. = MARANGOZLUK.

marabu (*orn.*) Marabou.

maral (*zoo.*) Doe.

marangoz (*carp.*) Joiner, carpenter; cabinet-maker. ~ **kalemi**, chisel: ~ **mengenesi**, clamp, vice. ~ **balığı**nı, (*ich.*) sawfish. ~ **luk**, joinery, carpentry; cabinet-making.

maranta (*bot.*) Arrowroot.

maraton ~ **(koşusu)**, (*sp.*) marathon race.

maraz (*med.*) Disease, illness; worry, pain. ~ **i**, pertaining to disease; pathological; diseased; morbid. ~ **lı**, diseased, ill, sick.

maraza Controversy, misunderstanding; (*sl.*) quarrel.

marda Discarded goods; rubbish.

maregraf (*geo.*) Marigraph, recording tide-gauge.

mareşali (*mil.*) Field Marshal. ~ **lik**, Field-Marshal's rank/duties: ~ **asası**, his baton.

marga·rik ~ **asit**, (*chem.*) margaric acid. ~**rin**, (*cul.*) margarine.
margarit[i] (*bot.*) Daisy.
margarita ~ **bağı**, (*naut.*) sheepshank.
Mari ~ **banyosu**, (*cul.*) double-saucepan, *bain-marie*.
marifet Knowledge; skill; ability, talent; craft; skilled trade; clever thing; contrivance; device; means, intervention; (*jok.*) mess. ~**iyle**, by means of, through. ~**li**, skilful, talented; cleverly done/made.
marina (*sp.*) (Yachting) marina.
mariz Sick, ailing; depressed; (*sl.*) beating. ~ **atmak**/~**ine kaymak**/~**lemek**, (*sl.*) beat. ~**lenmek**, *vp.*
marj (*pub.*) Margin.
mark (*fin.*) German mark.
marka Mark; (*fin.*) trademark; make, brand; (*mod.*) initials (on clothes, etc.); counter, ticket; (*sp.*) marking (opponent), foul.
marka·cı Swindler. ~**lamak (-i)**, mark stg. ~**lanmak**, *vp.* ~**lı**, marked; bearing the mark of. ~**sız**, unmarked. ~**to**, (*mus.*) marcato.
markazit[i] (*geol.*) Marcasite.
mark·i Marquis. ~**iz**, marquise; (*dom.*) backless armchair. ~**izet**, (*tex.*) marquisette.
Marks·çı/~**ist** (*pol.*) Marxist. ~**çılık**/~**izm**, Marxism.
Marmara ~ **(Denizi)**, (*geo.*) Sea of Marmara: ~ **çırası gibi yanmak**, suffer greatly.
marmelat[i] (*cul.*) Jam; marmalade.
marmenevişleme (*min.*) Martempering.
marmoset[i] (*zoo.*) Marmoset.
marmot (*zoo.*) Marmot.
marn (*geol.*) Marl.
maroken Morocco (leather).
marpu·ç[cu] Narghile tube. ~**çu**, tube maker/seller.
mars[1] *n.* (*gamb.*) (Bridge) grand slam; (backgammon) a win without losing one piece. ~ **etm.**, win completely: ~ **olm.**, be badly beaten; be dumbfounded.
Mars[2] *n.* (*myth.*, *ast.*) Mars.
marsı·k[ğı] Incompletely burnt charcoal (giving off fumes). ~ **gibi**, black and ugly (woman).
marsıvan (*his.*) Marcher lord; (*zoo.*) ass. ~ **eşeği**, (*fig.*) stupid, backward. ~**otu**[nu], (*bot.*) tanacetum, tansy.
Marsilya (*geo.*) Marseilles.
marş (*mil.*) March; (*mus.*) march tune; (*mot.*) starter. ~**!**, (*mil.*) quick march!: ~ ~**!**, at the double!: ~**a basmak**, (*mot.*) press the starter-button.
marşandiz Merchandise; goods; (*rly.*) goods-train.
mart[1] Month of March. ~ **dokuzu**, (Gregorian calendar) vernal equinox; (*met.*) storm (during 3rd week of March): ~ **havası**, changeable weather: ~ **içeri pire dışarı**, s.o. leaves because another arrives: ~ **kapıdan baktırır kazma kürek yaktırır**, March is too cold to go out and you burn your tools to keep warm.
martaval (*sl.*) Nonsense, lies, cock-and-bull story. ~ **atmak/okumak**, talk nonsense; tell lies. ~**cı**, liar, boaster. ~**cılık**, lying, boasting.

martensit[i] (*min.*) Martensite.
martı (*orn.*) Seagull. ~**giller**, gulls.
martin (*mil.*) Martini rifle. ~**i**, (*cul.*) martini cocktail.
maruf Known; well-known; proper; usual.
marul (*bot.*) Cos lettuce. ~**cu**, lettuce grower/selle ~**cu·k**[ğu], (*bot.*) Christmas rose.
Maruni (*rel.*) Maronite Christian (sect).
maruz Presented, submitted: **(-e)**, exposed to. **bırakmak**, expose: ~ **kalmak**, be exposed. ~**at** (*adm.*) representations, submissions.
marya (*zoo.*) Ewe, female animal; (*ich.*) fry. ~ **ağ** type of fishing-net.
mas[sı] *n.* Sucking; absorbing.
masa Table; board; office desk; (*adm.*) departmen section; (*fin.*) bankrupt's effects; (*sp.*) jumpin, table. ~ **başında**, at/around the (conference) tabl ~ **ışıklığı**, (*dom.*) table-lamp: ~ **örtüsü**, tableclot ~ **yalpalığı**, (*naut.*) fiddle.
masaj (*med.*) Massage. ~**cı**, masseur.
masal Story; tale; fable, myth; silly tale. ~ **kabilinden**, fabulous: ~ **okumak**, read/tell a tale: ~ **saati**, (*rad.*) story-time: ~ **söylemek**, tell idle tale ~**cı**, storyteller.
masarif *pl.* = MASRAF. Expenses; disbursements.
masarika (*bio.*) Mesentery.
masa·t[dı] Sharpening steel (knives).
masa·tenisi/~**topu**[nu] (*sp.*) Table-tennis; pin, pong.
-ması·na *vn. suf.* [249] = -MESİNE. ~**yla**, *vn. suf.* -MESİYLE.
masif (*geo.*) Massif.
mask (*art.*) Mask.
maskara *n.* Buffoon; laughing-stock; droll chil mask; (*mod.*) mascara. *a.* Ridiculous; amusing. **etm.**, make a laughing-stock of s.o.: ~ **olm.**, loo foolish: ~**sını çıkarmak**//~**ya almak/çevirme** ridicule.
maskara·lanmak Play the fool; make o.s. laughing-stock. ~**laşmak**, become ridiculou ~**lık**, buffoonery; making o.s. ridiculous; sham disgrace: ~ **etm.**, play the fool.
maskarata Toe-cap (of a shoe).
maske Mask; (*fig.*) deceptive appearance. ~ **düşmek**, real quality be revealed: ~**sini atma (kendi)**, reveal o.s.: ~**sini indirmek/kaldırmak (-in** unmask s.o.
maske·lemek (-i) Mask; camouflage, concea ~**lenmek**, *vp.* ~**li**, masked: ~ **balo**, masked ba ~ **örümcek kuşu**, (*orn.*) masked shrike: ~ **ötleğen** (*orn.*) Ruppell's warbler.
maskot[u] Mascot, talisman.
maslahat[1] Business; affair; the proper cours ~**güzar(lık)**, (*adm.*) (rank, duties of) charg d'affaires.
masla·k[ğı] Stone trough; running tap; wate tower.
maslu·ben By hanging. ~**p**, hanged.
masmavi Very blue; deep blue.
mason(luk) (*soc.*) Freemason(ry).
ma·sör (*med.*) Masseur. ~**söz**, masseuse.
masraf Expense; cost; outlay; disbursement; (*ina* ingredients, raw materials. ~ **etm.**, spend:

görmek, be in charge of buying/spending; incur expense: ~ **ihtiyar etm.**, go to the expense of (doing stg.): ~ **kaldırmak**, bear an expense: ~ **kapısı**, much expense; (*fin.*) debit side: ~ **kapısı açmak**, cause expenditure: ~ **a aldırma!**, blow the expense!: ~ **a bakılmaz**, money is no consideration: ~ **a girmek**, spend a great deal: ~ **a sokmak (-i)**, put s.o. to great expense: ~ **ı çekmek**, bear the expense, meet the bills: ~ **ını çıkarmak**, recover one's expenses: ~ **tan çıkmak**, suddenly have expenses: ~ **tan kaçmak**, avoid expenditure. ~ **lı**, expensive.

asruf *a.* Spent; expended. *n.* Expense.

ass·edici Absorbent. ~ **ᶦetmek**ᵉᵈᵉʳ **(-i)**, suck; absorb.

astar (*ling.*) Infinitive; deverbal noun; (*carp.*) ruler, straight edge; gauge. ~ **usulü**, gauging.

astara, (*math.*) Index (of sextant); cursor; slidade.

aster ~ **planı**, (*fin.*) master plan.

astı (*zoo.*) Spaniel. ~ **çiçeği/öküzü**ⁿᵘ, (*bot.*) arnica.

astika (*bot.*) Mastic (resin); (*cul.*) mastic-flavoured raki.

astur (*sl.*) Drunk; drowsy. ~ **i**, (*naut.*) broadest beam. ~ **laşmak**, (*sl.*) get drunk.

astürbasyon (*med.*) Masturbation.

asum *a.* Innocent; blameless. *n.* Child. ~ **yüzlü**, cherub(ic). ~ **ane**, innocently. ~ **iyet**ⁱ, innocence; infancy.

asun Preserved; protected; guarded; safe, inviolable. ~ **iyet**ⁱ, security; inviolability; immunity.

asura (*tex.*) Shuttle; bobbin; fountain spout; duct. ~ **kamışı**, (*bot.*) giant reed, arundo.

aş (*bot.*) Tongs; pincers; clip, peg; (bicycle) fork; (*fig.*) s.o.'s tool. ~ **gibi**, (s.o.) thin, dried up: ~ **gibi kullanmak (-i)**, make use of s.o.: ~ **kadar**, very small (baby): ~ **varken elini yakmak**, do stg. in an unnecessarily difficult way: ~ **sı olm. (-in)**, be s.o.'s tool, be used by s.o.

aşallah *int.* Wonderful! (*said to ward off the evil eye*). ~ **ı var**, he is unusually good, etc. today.

aşatlık (*rel.*) Non-Muslim (esp. Jewish) cemetery.

aşer (*soc.*) Company, community, assembly. ~ **i**, collective.

aşlah (*mod.*) Sleeveless cloak.

aşrapa (*dom.*) Metal pot/mug.

aşrık¹ (*geo.*) East.

aşukᵘ Beloved. ~ **a**, *fem.* darling.

at¹ ¹ (Chess) checkmate. ~ **etm.**, checkmate: ~ **olm.**, be checkmated.

at¹ ² (*cin.*, *pub.*) Matt (finish).

at. = MATEMATİK.

ata·dor (*sp.*) Matador. ~ **fora**, (*naut.*) davit. ~ **fyon**, (*naut.*) eyelet.

atah (*pej.*) Goods. ~ **değil ya!**, it's not as precious as all that!

atara Leather waterbottle. ~ **cı**, watercarrier (of caravan).

atb. = MATBAACILIK.

at·baa Printing-house; printing-press. ~ **baa-cı(lık)**, print·er/(-ing). ~ **bu**ᵘ, printed. ~ **bua**, printed form; printed matter. ~ **buat**¹, the papers;

the Press: ~ **hukuku**, Press law: ~ **hürriyeti**, freedom of the Press.

matem *n.* Mourning; bereavement. ~ **ayı**, (*obs.*) MUHARREM: ~ **etm./tutmak**, mourn; go into mourning: ~ **marşı**, (*mus.*) funeral march. ~ **li**, *a.* mourning; in mourning: ~ **kumru**, (*orn.*) mourning dove.

matemati·kᵍⁱ (*ed.*) Mathematics. ~ **çi**, mathematician. ~ **sel**, mathematical.

mater·yalist (*phil.*) Materialist. ~ **yalizm**, materialism. ~ **yel**, materials.

matine (*cin.*, *th.*) Matinée.

matiz *n.* (*naut.*) Long splice. *a.* (*sl.*) Dead drunk. ~ **olm.**, be 'dead to the world'. ~ **lik**, drunkenness.

matka·pᵇⁱ (*carp.*) Borer; bit; drill. ~ **kolu**, brace: ~ **mandreni**, drill chuck: ~ **tezgâhı**, drill.

matla (*lit.*) Opening couplet (of poem).

matlaşmak *vi.* (*cin.*) Become matt.

matlu·pᵇᵘ *a.* Desired; demanded. *n.* (*fin.*) Debt due; credit; asset. ~ **bakiyesi**, credit balance: ~ **a kaydetmek**, credit s.o.'s account: ~ **a muvafık çıkmadı**, it was not up to standard.

matmazel (*soc.*) Mademoiselle, Miss (non-Turk).

matrah (*fin.*) Category (for taxation); assessment (for tax).

matrak¹ *n.* Joke, amusement; cosh, cudgel. *a.* Amusing: ~ **geçmek/** ~ **a almak**, joke, amuse o.s.

matriarkalⁱ (*soc.*) Matriarchal.

matris (*math.*) Matrix; (*eng.*) die.

matruş Shaved, shaven.

matrut Banished; expelled.

matuf Directed.

matuh Doddering; in one's dotage.

maun (*bot.*, *carp.*) Mahogany.

maval Lie, story. ~ **okumak**, tell lies.

mavera The beyond. ~ **yı Ürdün**, (*his.*) Transjordania. ~ **ünnehir**, (*geo.*) Transoxania.

mavi Blue. ~ **baştankara**, (*orn.*) blue tit: ~ **boncuk**, blue bead (against the evil eye): ~ **boncuk dağıtmak**, please both/all parties: ~ **boncuk illeti**, (*med.*) infantile convulsions: ~ **cincile**, (*myc.*) blewit: ~ **doğan**, (*orn.*) marsh hawk: ~ **gerdanlı**, (*orn.*) bluethroat: ~ **güvercin**, (*orn.*) stock-dove: ~ **kâğıt almak//vermek**, (*sl.*) be dismissed//dismiss: ~ **kantaron**, (*bot.*) cornflower: ~ **kaz**, (*orn.*) snow goose: ~ **kuzgun**, (*orn.*) blue roller: ~ **küf**, (*myc.*) tobacco mildew: ~ **sıvacıkuşu**, (*orn.*) Eurasian nuthatch: ~ **suyosunları**, (*bot.*) cyanophyta: ~ **yolculuk**, a boat-tour of the SW Anatolian coast: ~ **yüzgeçli ton balığı**, (*ich.*) bluefin tuna.

mavi·leşmek *vi.* Become/turn blue. ~ **leştirme**, *vn.* (*min.*) blueing. ~ **lik**, blueness, blue colour. ~ **msi/** ~ **mtırak**, bluish. ~ **ş**, blue-eyed blonde.

mavna (*naut.*) Barge; lighter. ~ **ücreti**, lighterage. ~ **cı**, bargee; lighterman.

mavzer (*mil.*) Mauser rifle/pistol.

maya¹ *n.* (*live.*) She-camel; brood mare.

maya² *n.* (*myc.*) Yeast; ferment; activator; (*fig.*) essence, essential; origin; stock; talent. ~ **tozu**, (*cul.*) baking-powder: ~ **sı bozuk!**, a bad lot!

-maya *vn. suf.* [168] = -MEĞE [ALMAYA].

maya·ağacıⁿⁱ (*bot.*) (?) Oil-palm. ~ **bozan**, (*bio.*) antiferment. ~ **lama**, *vn.* fermentation. ~ **lamak**

(-i), *vt.* ferment, leaven; activate. ~**lanma**, *vn.* fermentation. ~**lanmak**, *vi.* ferment; (*fig.*) increase; be accumulated. ~**lı**, fermented, leavened. ~**lık**, ferment(-ing agent), leaven. ~**sız**, unfermented, unleavened; characterless.

mayasıl (*med.*) Chilblain; eczema; (*col.*) haemorrhoids, piles. ~ **otu**, (*bot.*) (?) scrophularia, germander.

maydanoz (*bot.*) Parsley. ~**lu**, (*cul.*) served with parsley. ~ **giller**, (*bot.*) Umbelliferae.

mayhoş Slightly acid; tart; (*fig.*) bitter-sweet; slightly strained (relations). ~**luk**, slightly sour taste.

-mayı *vn. suf.* [168] = -MEĞI [ALMAYI].

mayın (*mil.*) Mine. ~ **salma**, (*naut.*) mine-laying: ~ **tarayıcı**, (*naut.*) mine-hunter/-sweeper: ~ **tarlası**, minefield. ~**lamak (-i)**, mine, lay mines. ~**lanmak**, *vp.* be mined.

mayıs[1] *n.* (*agr.*) Fresh stable manure.

mayıs[2] *n.* Month of May. ~**böceği**[ni], (*ent.*) cockchafer, May bug. ~**böcekleri**, (*ent.*) chafers.

mayışmak *vi.* Become too friendly; (*col.*) get sleepy.

mayi[i] Liquid; fluid. ~ **mahruk**, liquid fuel. ~**at**, liquids.

mayistra (*naut.*) Mainsail. ~ **sereni**, mainyard.

maymun *n.* (*zoo.*) Monkey. *a.* (*fig.*) Ugly, laughable. ~ **ekmeği ağacı**, (*bot.*) baobab tree: ~ **gözünü açtı**, 'we shan't be caught napping again!': ~ **iştahlı**, inconstant, capricious: ~ **saltası**, ill-fitting clothes: ~ **suratlı**, hideous, repulsive: ~ **yiyen kartal**, (*orn.*) monkey-eating eagle: ~**a benzetmek/çevirmek**, make a mockery of: ~**a dönmek**, become ugly/ laughable; come to one's senses: ~**lar**, (*zoo.*) primates: ~**lar kafesi**, apery.

maymun-balığı[nı] (*ich.*) Monkfish, angel shark. ~**cu**[k]**k**[ğu], picklock; (*zoo.*) little monkey; (*ent.*) vine-weevil. ~**luk**, drollery; buffoonery. ~**sular**, (*zoo.*) lemurs.

mayna (*naut.*) Down sails! ~ **etm.**, down sails; (*fig.*) cease work: ~ **olm.**, come to a stop; calm down.

mayo (*mod.*) Bathing costume. ~**lu**, wearing a bathing costume: ~ **çorap**, body stocking.

mayonez(li) (*cul.*) (Served with) mayonnaise.

mayoz (*bio.*) Meiosis.

mayta[l]**p**[bı] Small fireworks; Bengal fire. ~**a almak/ etm.**, make fun of.

maza[l]**k**[ğı] (*ich.*) Streaked gurnard.

mazarrat[ı] Injury; harm; detriment.

mazbata (*adm.*) Official report; minutes. ~ **muharriri**, secretary/spokesman (of a commission).

mazbut[u] Well-protected (against rain, etc.); solid well-built (house); neat, compact; correct (style); fixed (in the mind); decided; recorded; level-headed; decent.

-mazdan *vn. suf.* [181] = -MEDEN [ALMAZDAN].

mazeret[i] Excuse; reason; apology. ~ **beyan etm.**, make an apology, excuse o.s. ~**li**, having an excuse/reason. ~**siz**, without excuse.

mazgal (*mil.*) Embrasure; loop-hole; slit (in gun-shield). = MISKALA. ~**lı**, embrasured; castellated: ~ **siper**, casemate, battlement.

mazhar Who acquires; honoured; distinguished.

mazı (*bot.*) Chinese thuja. ~ **böceği**, (*ent.*) gall-

wasp: ~ **meşesi**, (*bot.*) gall-bearing oak: ~ **tuzı** tannin: ~ (**uru**), gall-nut.

mazi *a.* Past, bygone. *n.* The past; (*ling.*) definit past tense. ~**ye karışmak**, belong to/be a thing c the past: ~**yi kurcalamak**, rake up the pas ~**perest**, who worships the past.

-mazlık *vn. suf.* [173] = -MEZLİK [ANLAŞMAZLIK].

mazlum Victim of cruelty; oppressed; (*fig.*) milc inoffensive.

mazmun Signification; implication; tenor.

maznun (-den, -le) Suspected (of); accused (of).

mazoşizm (*psy.*) Masochism.

mazot/mazut[u] (*chem.*) Diesel oil; fuel oil; (*sl* liquor; cigarette. ~ **almak**, (*sl.*) eat.

mazruf In an envelope. ~**en**, under cover; enclose¢

mazur Excused; excusable. ~ **görmek (-i)**, pardo stg.: ~ **tutmak (-i)**, hold s.o. excused.

mazurka (*mus.*) Mazurka dance/tune.

MB = MALİYE BAKAN(LIĞ)I. ~ **K** = MİLLİ BİRLİ KOMİTESİ.

MC = MİLLİ(YETÇİ) CEPHE(Sİ) (PARTİSİ).

Md. = MADDE; MÜDÜR(LÜK); MÜDÜR(LÜĞ)Ü. ~**lüğ** = MÜDÜRLÜĞÜ.

me The Tk. letter M.

-me[1]**/-ma** *v. suf.* [170] *Forming a verbal nou denoting the action* [**dolma**, filling, becoming fu¶ **dönme**, turning; **yazma**, writing]. *These may becon common nouns showing the result of the actic* [**dolma**, stuffed vine-leaf; **dolma kalem**, fountai¶ pen; **dönme**, religious convert; **yazma**, han¢ painted kerchief; **el yazması**, manuscript].

-me[2]**/-ma-** *v. suf.* [110] *Denoting a negative actic* [**gelmedi**, he did not come; **almam**, I do not tak¢ *Before a 'Y-' syllable, it is modified to* '**-mi-/-m▪ -mu-/-mü-**' [**gelmiyecek**, he will not com **almıyorum**, I am not taking].

meal[i] Meaning; purport. ~**en**, as regards t¶ meaning.

MEB = MİLLİ Eğitim BAKAN(LIĞ)I.

mebde[i] Beginning; origin; (first) principle.

mebiz (*bio.*) Ovary.

meblağ Sum of money; amount.

mebni (-e) *post.* On account of.

mebus(luk) (*adm.*) (Position/work of) deput member of parliament.

mebzul[ü] Abundant, lavish; cheap. ~**iyet**[i], abu¶ dance, plenty.

mec. = MECAZ OLARAK.

mecaz (*lit.*) Metaphor; figure of speech. ~ **olara¶** ~**en**, figuratively. ~**i**, figurative, metaphorical.

mecbur Compelled. ~ **etm.**, compel: ~ **olm.**, ▮ compelled. ~**en**, by force, compulsorily. ~ compulsory, mandatory, obligatory, (en)forced: **durak**, regular (tram-)stop: ~ **hizmet**, (*mil.*) con pulsory service, conscription: ~**iyet**[i], compulsio obligation, force; necessity.

meccan-en Gratis; freely. ~**i**, gratuitous.

meccele Volume; book; (*leg.*) Ottoman Civil Coc

-mece/-maca *n. suf.* [57–8] [BİLMECE; SORMACA].

-mecesine/-macasına *vn. suf.* [189] On condition (doing) [**müdürü görmecesine**, on condition that₄ we can see the director].

meci-diye/~ t (*fin.*, *obs.*) 20 piastre silver coin.

meclis (*adm.*) Sitting; assembly; convention; council; (*soc.*) gathering; (*th.*) scene. ~ **kurmak**, sit in council: ~ **soruşturması**, (*pol.*) parliamentary inquiry.

meclup Affected by; attracted by.

mecmuᵘ *a.* Assembled, gathered together. *n.* Collection; heap; total. ~**u (-in)**, all of . . .. ~**a**, collection; (*pub.*) periodical, magazine, bulletin, digest, volume.

mecnun Mad; madly in love.

necra Watercourse; conduit; canal.

necruh Wounded; confuted.

Mecusi (*rel.*) Pagan; fireworshipper. ~ **lik**, fireworship; Zoroastrianism; paganism.

meczup (*rel.*) Possessed; ecstatic (dervish); (*fig.*) crazy (fellow).

neçi ¹ (*sp.*) Rapier.

neçi ² (*mod.*) Hair-piece.

neçhulü Unknown; (*ling.*) passive (verb). ~ **at**¹, unknown matters.

nedar (*phil.*) Point on which a question turns; centre of movement; (*ast.*) orbit; (*geo.*) tropic; (*fig.*) support, help. ~ **olm. (-e)**, help: ~ **ı iftihar**, object of pride.

nedd- = MET. ~ **ücez**ᵗ**ir**ʳⁱ, (*geo.*) tide, ebb and flow.

neddah Eulogist; public story-teller. ~ **lık**, storytelling; eulogizing; flattering.

meden/-madan/-mezden/-mazdan. *vn. suf.* [181]. *Not ablative.* Before, without [**beni görmeden çıktı**, he left before/without seeing me; **acı duyurmadan**, without causing pain]. ~ **evvel/önce**, before [**beni görmeden evvel çıktı**, he left before seeing me]. ~ **se** = -MEK TENSE.

nedeni Civilized; civil; civic. ~ **cesaret**, moral courage: ~ **evlenme**, civil marriage: ~ **haklar**, civil rights: ~ **hal**, civil status: ~ **hukuk/kanun**, (*leg.*) civil law/code.

nedeni·leşmek *vi.* Become civilized. ~ **leştirmek (-i)**, civilize. ~ **lik/** ~ **yet**ⁱ, civilization: ~ **in nimetleri**, the blessings of civilization. ~ **yetsiz**, uncivilized; backward.

nedeᵗ**t**ᵈⁱ *n.* Help, aid. ~ **!**, *int.* Help! ~ **Allah!**, only God can help (me, us, etc.): ~ **ummak**, expect s.o.'s help.

ned·f- = METF-. ~ **h-** = ~ **ıH**; METH-. ~ **ᵗih**ʰⁱ, praise.

medik/-madık *v. suf.* [162] *Negative past participle used as an adjective/with passive meaning* [**görülmedik**, unseen, extraordinary; **satılmadık**, unsold].

nediko-(farmasötik) Medico-(pharmaceutical).

nedine *n.* Town, city. *pr.n.* (*geo.*) Medina. ~ **fukarası**, in rags and tatters. ~ **kurdu**ⁿᵘ, (*zoo.*) Medina worm.

nediyastin (*bio.*) Mediastinum.

nedlulü *a.* Inferred, understood. *n.* Sense, meaning.

nedrese (*ed.*) Muslim theological school. ~ **kaçkını**, fanatic; reactionary: ~ **ye düşmek**, become the subject of futile discussion. ~ **li**, MEDRESE pupil.

nedülla (*bio.*) Medulla.

nedüz (*zoo.*) Jellyfish.

nedyum(luk) (*psy.*) Medium(ism).

nedyun Indebted; in debt; debtor.

nef·ahir *pl.* = ~ **haret**ⁱ, cause/object of glory; pride.

nefhum Sense; significance, concept; idea.

mefkûre Ideal.

mefluç (*med.*) Paralysed.

mefruş, Spread (carpet); furnished. ~ **at**, carpets, etc.; furniture. ~ **atçı**, furniture-dealer; decorator.

mefsuh (*leg.*) Annulled; abrogated; void.

meftun (-e) Madly in love with; admiring. ~ **iyet**ⁱ**/** ~ **luk**, being madly in love; intense admiration.

mefulü (*ling., obs.*) Object, complement.

mega- *pref.* Mega-. ~ **fon**, (*phys.*) megaphone. ~ **kalori**, (*phys.*) therm. ~ **loman(i)**, (*psy.*) megaloman·iac/(-ia). ~ **metre**, (*naut.*) instrument for determining longitude; (*math.*) thousand kilometres. ~ **vat**, (*el.*) megawatt.

-meğe/-mağa/-meye/-maya *vn. suf.* [168] *Forming the dative case of* -ME¹/-MEK. To; and; in order to [**görmeğe gelmek**, come to/and see; **almağa çıktı**, he went out (in order) to buy]. ~ **gelmemek**, not do to . . . ; not be suitable for . . .: ~ **halim yok**, I don't feel like . . .: ~ **salahiyeti yok**, he has no authority to . . .: ~ **savaşmak**, work hard/struggle to . . .: ~ **yüzüm tutmaz**, I can't bring myself to . . ..

meğer(se) *conj.* [211] But; however; only; it seems that; apparently. ~ **ki**, *conj.* [214] unless.

-meği/-mağı/-meyi/-mayı *vn. suf.* [168] *Forming the accusative case of* -ME¹/-MEK [**görmeği beklemek**, expect to see].

mehabetⁱ Awe; majesty.

mehaz (*lit.*) Source; authorities.

Mehdi *pr.n.* (*rel.*) Muslim Messiah, Mahdi.

mehil (*fin.*) Term; permitted delay. ~ **vermek**, allow a delay.

mehle (*cul.*) Neck end PASTIRMA.

Mehmetçik *pr.n.* (*mil.*) Tk. 'Tommy Atkins'; (*orn.*) Eurasian robin.

mehtaᵗ**p**ᵇ¹ Moonlight. ~ **a çıkmak**, go for a walk in the moonlight.

mehter (*his., mus.*) Military band; bandsman. ~ **başı**, chief bandsman. ~ **hane**, band('s quarters).

-mek/-mak *v. suf.* [96] *The sign of the infinitive* [**görmek**, to see; **almak**, to take], *which is also* [167] *a verbal noun that can be:* 1. *subject//object of another verb* [**bulunmak yetmez**, just to be present is not enough; **gelmek istemez**, he doesn't want to come]: 2. *object of the postpositions* İÇİN *and* ÜZERE [*see below*]: 3. *qualifier in izafet groups* [**yazmak görevi**, the duty of writing]. *Note the few common nouns* [169] [**yemek**, food; **çakmak**, lighter]. ~ **için**, in order to (do stg.) [**yaşamak için**, in order to live] ~ **istememek**, be averse to . . .: ~ **lutfunda bulunmak**, be so kind as to . . .: ~ **üzere olm.**, [168] be about to . . .: ~ **üzere iken**, just as/when . . ..

mek. = MEKANİK.

mekân Place; site; dwelling; (*aer.*) space. ~ **tutmak**, establish o.s.

mekan·iᵗ**k**ᵍⁱ *n.* (*phys.*) Mechanics *a.* Mechanical; mechanized; automatic; clockwork. ~ **ikçilik/** ~ **izm**, (*phil.*) mechanism. ~ **izma**, mechanism, 'works'; operation.

mekiᵗ**k**ᵍⁱ (*tex.*) Shuttle. ~ **atmak**, throw the shuttle; (*fig.*) always on the move: ~ **dokumak**, shuttle backwards and forwards; (*fig.*) be moved from pillar to post: ~ **gibi**, always moving; restless.

mekkâre (Hired) beast of burden, pack-animal;

goods so carried; (*mil.*) pack-animal. ~ci, s.o. hiring out/soldier in charge of pack-animals.

Mekke (*geo.*) Mecca. ~ **ayrıkotu**, (*bot.*) andropogon.

-mekle/-makla *v. suf.* [187] *Forming a gerund.* With/by (do)ing [**koşmakla**, by running; **yemekle**, with eating]. ~ **beraber/birlikte**, together with (do)ing; although; while [**içmekle beraber**, although he drinks].

-meklik/-maklık *vn. suf.* + *possessive suf.* [170] *Forming an unambiguous noun, replacing* -ME¹ [**gelmekliğim imkân yok**, I cannot possibly come].

mek·nuz Stored away; hidden; buried. ~**ruh**, abominable; disgusting; (*rel.*) disapproved of. ~**sefe**, (*el.*) condenser.

Meksi·ka (*geo.*) Mexico (state): ~ +, *a.* Mexican: ~ **yıldızı**, (*orn.*) lucifer hummingbird. ~**kalı**, (*ethn.*) Mexican. ~**ko**, Mexico City.

-meksizin/-maksızın *v. suf.* [188] *Forming a gerund.* Without (do)ing [**görmeksizin**, without seeing/ sight of].

-mekte-/-makta- *vn. suf.* [111]. *The locative case of* -MEK, *used in forming tenses of uncompleted action.* Be in the act of doing [**bakmaktayım**, I am in the act of/just looking; **öğrenmekteydi**, he was in the middle of learning].

-mekten/-maktan *vn. suf.* [168] *Forming the ablative case of* -MEK. From; than [**ödemekten kaçınmak**, escape from/avoid paying; **ağlamaktan gülmek yeğdir**, laughing is better than crying]. ~ **çekinmek**, be averse to (do)ing: ~ **ise** = -MEK TENSE: ~ **kendisi almak**, restrain o.s. from (do)ing.

-mektense/-maktansa *v. suf.* [188] *Forming a gerund.* Rather than . . .(ing) [**kalmaktansa**, rather than stay].

mekte¹pᵇⁱ School. ~ **görmüş**, educated (at school): ~ **kaçkını**, uneducated, ignorant: ~ **ücreti**, school fees: ~**i asmak**, play truant. ~**li**, school-child; educated at school; having a school diploma; (*mil.*) officer from a military academy.

mektu¹pᵇᵘ Letter. ~ **gelse de meraktan kurtulsak**, if only a letter would come and relieve our anxiety. ~**çu(luk)**, (*adm.*) (office, duties of) chief secretary of a ministry/provincial governorate. ~**laşmak (-le)**, *vi.* correspond (with).

melaike *pl.* = MELEK.

melal¹ (*psy.*) Melancholy, depression.

melanet¹ Execrable act.

melanin (*bio.*) Melanin.

melankoli *n.* (*psy.*) Melancholy, hypochondria. ~**k**, *a.* melancholy, depressed.

melanurya (*ich.*) Blacktail.

melas (*cul.*) Molasses.

melbusat¹ Clothes, clothing.

melce Asylum, refuge. ~ **hakkı**, (*pol.*) right of asylum.

mele¹kᵍⁱ Angel; cherub. ~ **balığı**, (*ich.*) angelfish: ~ **gibi/**~**si**, angelic. ~**otu**ⁿᵘ, (*bot., cul.*) angelica.

meleke Proficiency, skill; natural faculty.

mele·me *vn.* Bleating. *a.* Incapable; shy. ~**mek**, bleat. ~**ngiç** = MERLENGEÇ.

mel·es (*live.*) Swaybacked horse. ~**eş**, ewe with two lambs.

melez (*bio.*) *a.* Cross-bred; half-bred; hybrid. *n.* Cross-breed; half-breed; hybrid; mulatto. ~ (**ağacı**), (*bot.*) larch: ~ **yetiştirme**, allogamy, hybridization. ~**lemek (-i)**, cross-breed. ~**leşmek**, *vi.* hybridize. ~**leştirmek (-i)**, *vt.* hybridize.

mel·hem = MERHEM. ~**huz**, expected; probable.

-meli-¹/-malı- *v. suf.* [125] *Forming the necessitative tenses.* Must, ought to, have to [**görmeliyim**, I ought to see; **yapmalıydım**, I had to do].

-meli²/-malı *vn. suf.* [172] *Forming an adjective* [**asmalı**, having/with vines].

melih Pretty; gentle.

melik¹ (*adm.*) King; ruler. ~**ane**, kingly. ~**e**, queen(-consort).

melinit¹ (*chem.*) Melinite.

melisa (*bot.*) Balm.

melo·di (*mus.*) Melody. ~**dram**, (*th.*) melodrama.

melon ~ (**şapka**), (*mod.*) bowler-hat.

meltem (*met.*) Summer offshore breeze.

melun Accursed (man). ~**ca**, devilish, diabolical.

melülᵘ Low-spirited; weak. ~ ~ **bakmak**, wear a piteous expression.

memat Death.

memba (*geo.*) Inlet; source, spring; (*fig.*) origin.

meme (*bio.*) Teat; nipple; udder; breast; lobe (of ear); (*med.*) tumour; (*eng.*) nozzle; (*naut.*) anchor crown; (*dom.*) burner (of lamp). ~ **bez/süngeri** mammary gland: ~ **vermek**, suckle: ~ **de olm.**, be breast-fed: ~**den kesmek (-i)**, wean.

meme·başı (*bio.*) Nipple; papilla. ~**başı** papillary. ~**li**, having teats; mammiferous: ~ **deniz hayvanı**, cetacean: ~ **hayvan**, mammal: ~**ler** mammals: ~**ler bilimi**, (*ed.*) mammalogy. ~**lik** teat cover. ~**msi**, teat-like, mamillary.

memeş Ox's saliva.

-memezlik *vn. suf.* [173] = -MEZLİK.

memişhane Privy, toilet.

memleha Salt-pit; salt-pan; saltings.

memleket¹ Dominion; country; town; one's home district. ~ **dışı**, abroad; (*leg.*) extraterritorial (rights): ~**ler arası**, borderland. ~**li**, inhabitant fellow-countryman.

memlukᵘ Slave; *pr.n.* (*his.*) Mameluke. ~**iyet** (*obs.*) slavery.

memnu Forbidden, prohibited. ~ **mıntıka**, (*mil.*) prohibited zone: ~ **silah**, forbidden weapon ~**iyet¹**, prohibition.

memnun Pleased; glad; content, happy; grateful under an obligation. ~ **etm.**, please; make happy ~ **olm.**, be pleased, etc.

memnun·en Gladly, with pleasure. ~**iyet¹/**~**luk** pleasure; happiness; gratitude. ~**iyetle**, with pleasure. ~**iyetsizlik**, dissatisfaction.

memorandum (*adm.*) Memorandum.

memulᵘ *a.* Hoped; expected; desired. ~ **etm.** hope.

memur (*adm.*) *a.* Charged with; ordered to. *n.* Official; agent; employee; bureaucrat. ~ **etm. (-e)** charge with (a duty): ~ **olm.**, be charged with. ~ **in** *pl.* officials. ~**iyet¹/**~**luk**, official duty; appoint ment; office; charge; post: ~**ten çıkarılma**, dis missal.

men ~ **dakka dukka**, the biter bit(ten).

men/-man *n. suf.* [221] *Forming nouns of occupation* [seçmen, elector; sayman, accountant].

nenafi *pl.* = MENFAAT. Benefits, advantages.

nenajer (*fin., sp.*) Manager.

nendebur Worthless; repulsive; slovenly. ~**luk**, worthlessness; repulsiveness.

nendel·cilik (*bio.*) Mendelism. ~**evyum**, (*chem.*) mendelevium.

nenderes (*geo.*) Winding river; *pr.n.* R. Maeander.

nendil Handkerchief. ~ **kadar**, very small (field, etc.): ~ **sallamak**, wave a handkerchief (in greeting, etc.).

nendire'kᵍⁱ (*naut.*) Breakwater.

nenecer (*sp.*) Manager.

nenedilmek *vp.* Be forbidden.

nenekşe (*bot.*) Violet; (*sl.*) anus. ~**giller**, violet family, Violaceae. ~**gülü**ⁿᵘ, China rose.

nen·emen (*cul.*) Vegetable omelette. ~**engiç** = MERLENGİÇ.

nenenjitⁱ (*med.*) Meningitis.

nen'etmekᵉᵈᵉʳ (-i) Forbid, prevent, check, embargo.

neneviş (*bot.*) Seed of terebinth tree; (*tex.*) 'shot silk' effect; (*min.*) blueing (of steel); temper. ~**leme**, *vn.* (*min.*) tempering; damascening. ~**lemek** (-i), temper. ~**lenmek**, *vi.* (*min.*) be tempered; be damascened; (*tex.*) be watered. ~**li**, wavy; (*min.*) blued (steel), tempered; (*tex.*) watered: ~ **çelik**, tempered/damask steel.

nenfa (*adm.*) Place of exile.

nenfaatⁱ Use; advantage, benefit; profit. ~ **görmek**, receive a benefit: ~ **temin etm.**, ensure an advantage. ~ **perest**ⁱ, self-seeking; always looking for profit.

nenfez (*eng.*) Air-hole; vent; doorway; culvert.

nenfi Exiled; (*ling.*) negative.

nenfur Beneath contempt; loathed, abhorred.

nenge'lç**ⁱ (*tex.*) Large wool-shuttle.

nengel Anklet, bangle.

nengene (*ind.*) Press; (*carp.*) vice; clamp; (*dom.*) mangle.

nenhiyatⁱ (*rel.*) Forbidden things.

nenholü (*eng.*) Manhole.

nenhus Ill-omened; unlucky.

neni (*bio.*) Semen, sperm.

nenisk (*phys., bio.*) Meniscus, disc.

nenkıbe (*lit.*) Epic, saga; legend.

nen·kubiyetⁱ Disgrace. ~**kûp**, unfortunate; disgraced.

nenkul Transported; conveyed; traditional. ~ **eşya**, goods and chattels: ~ **mallar**, (*fin.*) personal assets: ~ **dur ki**, it is traditionally related that . . . .

nenolunmak *vi.* Be prevented/forbidden.

nenopoz (*bio.*) Menopause.

nens. = MENSUCAT.

nensubiyetⁱ (*soc.*) Relationship; membership.

nensucatⁱ Textiles; dry goods.

nensu'pᵇᵘ (-e) Related to; belonging to, connected with. ~ **olm.** (-e), belong to; (*fig.*) be a supporter of.

nensur (*lit.*) In prose.

nenşe Place of origin; source; basis. ~ **memleketi**, (*adm.*) country of origin: ~ **şahadetnamesi**, (*adm.*) certificate of origin. ~**li**, originating from; exported from.

menşur (*math.*) Prism; (*his.*) firman.

menteşe (*carp.*) Hinge. ~ **mili**, gudgeon (pin). ~**li**, hinged: ~ **pencere**, casement (window).

mentol (*chem.*) Menthol.

menus Accustomed; familiar; current.

menzil Halting-place; stage, day's journey; inn; (*mil.*) range (of gun); army transport corps. ~ **açısı**, (gun) elevation: ~ **uçuşu**, (*aer.*) direct flight.

menzil·ci (*his.*) Courier (with relays of horses). ~**e**, (low) rank; social status. ~**hane**, posting-house. ~**li**, having a range of . . . .

mepsuten (*math.*) Directly.

mer. = MERİYETSİZ.

mera (*agr.*) Pasture.

merak¹ Curiosity; whim; passion (for stg.); great interest (in stg.); anxiety; (*psy.*) depression, melancholy. ~ **etm.** (-e), have a passion for/be greatly interested in stg.; (-i), be very curious about stg.; be very anxious about s.o.: ~ **etme!**, don't worry!: ~ **getirmek**, (*psy.*) have melancholia, be hypochondriac: ~ **halini almak**, (stg.) become a passion: ~ **olm.** (-i), want to learn about/understand stg.; be anxious about stg.: ~ **sarmak** (-e), have a passion for stg.; make a hobby of stg.: ~**a değmek**, be worthy of wonder: ~**ı kalkmak**, be sad at the memory of stg.: ~**la beklemek** (-i), await stg. impatiently: ~**ta bırakmak**, cause s.o. anxiety.

merak·i Whimsical; hypochondriac. ~**landırmak** (-i), *vc.* ~**lanmak** (-e), be anxious about stg.; be curious about/interested in stg. ~**lı**, *a.* curious; interested in, fond of; anxious: *n.* (*art.*) amateur; connoisseur; (*sp.*) fan, devotee: ~**sı** (-in), -fancier. ~**sız**, carefree; uninterested; indifferent. ~**sızlık**, indifference.

mer·alⁱ = MARAL. ~**alık**, (*agr.*) pasturage.

meram Desire; intention; aim. ~ **anlamaz**, unreasonable; who can't be made to understand: ~ **anlıyan beri gelsin!**, what's the use of talking—nobody takes any notice!: ~ **etm.**, wish; intend; strive: ~ **etmiye görsün**, he gets whatever he wants: ~**ına nail olm.**, attain one's object: ~**ını anlatmak**, be able to express one's wishes.

meramet Temporary repairs. ~ **etm.**, patch up. ~ **çi**, tinker, cobbler; (*naut.*) net-mender.

merasim *pl.* Ceremonies; customs. *s.* Ceremony; commemoration. ~ **elbisesi**, (*mod.*) full/court-dress: ~ **geçişi**, (*mil.*) ceremonial march-past: ~**le karşılamak**, give a ceremonial welcome to. ~**li**, ceremonial.

merbutᵘ Attached; dependent; (*aer.*) captive (balloon). ~**iyet**ⁱ, dependence.

mercan (*zoo.*) Coral. ~ **ağaç/çiçeği**, (*bot.*) erythrina, coral-tree: ~ **gibi/rengi**, coralline: ~ **kıyı/resifi**, (*geo.*) coral reef; atoll: ~ **terliği**, (*mod.*) red leather slippers: ~**lar**, corals.

mercan·ada (*geo.*) Coral island. ~**balığı**ⁿⁱ, (*ich.*) pandora; red sea-bream. ~**köşk**ü, (*bot.*) sweet marjoram. ~**otu**ⁿᵘ, (*bot.*) pearlwort. ~**yılanı**ⁿⁱ, (*zoo.*) coral snake.

merce'kᵍⁱ (*phys.*) Lens. ~ **tekeri**, (*cin.*) lens turret. ~**si**, lenticular.

merci Recourse; source; reference; competent authority.

mercime¹kᵍⁱ (*bot., cul.*) Lentil. ~ **başlı**, (*eng.*) rounded-headed (screw): ~ **böceği**, (*ent.*) lentil weevil: ~ **gibi**, lacking self-confidence: ~**i fırına vermek (-le)**, flirt with; come to terms with.

merd- = MERT. ~**ane**¹, *a.* manly, virile.

merdane² *n.* (*pub.*) Inking cylinder; (*cul.*) rolling-pin.

merdiven Ladder; steps; stairs. ~ **dayamak (-e)**, be nearing (an age) = KIRK: ~ **kovası**, staircase well: ~**den çıkmak**, go up-/downstairs. ~**ci**, (*arch.*) concrete-step moulder.

merdüm Man. ~**ek**, little man; manikin. ~**giriz**, misanthropic; unsociable. ~**perest**ⁱ, hero-worshipper.

meretⁱ *vulg.* Damned (fellow)!; cursed (thing)!

mergup Longed for; sought after; desirable.

merhaba *int.* Good day!; how are you?; (*col.*) hello! ~**sı olm. (-le)**, be on nodding terms with s.o.: ~**yı kesmek (-le)**, sever relations with s.o. ~**laşmak (-le)**, *vi.* greet each other.

merhale Day's journey (45 kms.); stage; (*adm.*) rank. ~ ~, by stages.

merhametⁱ Mercy; pity, compassion. ~ **etm. (-e)**, pity s.o.: ~**e gelmek**, become merciful: ~**ten maraz çıkar**, misplaced pity may bring trouble.

merhamet·li Merciful; compassionate, tender-hearted. ~**siz**, merciless, cruel: ~**den merhamet beklemek**, try to get blood out of a stone. ~**sizlik**, mercilessness, cruelty.

merhem (*med.*) Ointment; salve.

merhum Deceased; 'the late'. ~ **olm.**, die. ~**cu**, (*his.*) supporter of the late Prime Minister Menderes. ~**e**, *fem.* deceased.

meri¹ *a.* (*leg.*) Observed; in force. ~ **olm.**, (*adm.*) take effect.

meri² *n.* (*bio.*) Gullet; oesophagus.

Meri¹çᶜⁱ *pr.n.* (*geo.*) River Maritsa.

meridyen (*ast.*) Meridian. ~ **düzlemi**, meridian plane.

Merih (*ast.*) Mars.

merinos (*live.*) Merino sheep.

meriyet Being valid/in force. ~**e geçmek/girmek**, come into force: ~**ten çıkmak**, (*ling.*) disappear, become obsolete. ~**siz**, invalid; (*ling.*) obsolete.

merka¹tᵈ¹ Resting-place; grave.

merkep(çi) Donkey(man).

merkez Centre; (*adm.*) administrative centre; central/head office; main police-station; (*fig.*) matter, condition. ~ **Bankası**, *pr.n.* (*fin.*) Central Bank: ~ **birliği**, concentricity: ~**de (bu)**, on these lines: ~**den**, central: ~**den uzak**, (*bio.*) distal.

merkez·ci (*adm.*) Centralist. ~**cil**/~**gel (kuvvet)**, (*phys.*) centripetal (force). ~**cilik**, (*adm.*) centralism. ~**i**, central; centralized; centred; centro-: ~ **Antlaşma Örgütü**, (*pol.*) Central Treaty Organization. ~**ileşmek**, *vi.* concentrate; gather together; be centralized. ~**ileştirmek (-i)**, concentrate; centralize. ~**iyet**ⁱ, centralization; being central. ~**iyetçi**, centralist; bureaucrat. ~**iyetçilik**, centralism; bureaucracy. ~**kaç (kuvvet)**, (*phys.*) centrifugal (force). ~**leme**, *vn.* (*eng.*) centering. ~**lenmek**, *vp.* (*adm.*) be centralized; (*phys.*) be

concentrated. ~**leyici**, (*eng.*) workholder, center-ing device. ~**sel**, central.

merkum (*pej.*) The said, the above-mentioned.

Merkür *pr.n.* (*ast., myth.*) Mercury.

merlanos (*ich.*) Whiting.

merlenge¹çᶜⁱ (*bot.*) Mastic tree, lentisc.

merlin (*orn.*) Merlin.

mermer (*geol.*) Marble. ~ **ocağı**, marble quarry: ~ **kaymağı**, alabaster: ~ **kireci**, lime (from burn¹ marble). ~**ci(lik)**, (work of) marble-cutter; stone-mason. ~**lik**, marble paving. ~**şahı**, ~ **tülbendi** (*tex.*) book muslin.

mermi (*mil.*) Projectile; shell; bullet; bombshell.

merserize (*tex.*) Mercerized.

mersi *int.* Thanks!

mersin (*bot.*) Myrtle. ~ **balığı**, (*ich.*) sturgeon: ~ **morinası**, (*ich.*) beluga: ~**ler**, (*ich.*) sturgeons ~**giller**, (*bot.*) myrtle family, Myrtaceae.

mersiye (*lit.*) Elegy. ~ +, *a.* Elegiac.

mer¹tᵈⁱ *n.* Man; brave/manly man. *a.* Manly; brave fine. ~**çe**, bravely; as becomes a man. ~**lik** manliness, courage.

mertebe (*adm.*) Rank; grade; stage. ~**ler silsilesi** hierarchy.

merte¹kᵍⁱ (*carp.*) Baulk; beam.

Meryemana *pr.n.* (*rel.*) Virgin Mary. ~ **kandili gibi**, (light) burning dimly. ~**asması**ⁿ¹, (*bot.*) clematis. ~**eldiveni**ⁿⁱ, (*bot.*) type of bellflower ~**pelesengi**ⁿⁱ, (*bot.*) Santa Maria tree, calaba.

mes. = MESELA.

mesabe Quality; nature. ~**sinde**, of the nature of ... like . . ..

mesafe Distance, space; (*mil.*) range. ~ **almak** **kapatmak**, cover a distance.

mesaha Measurement; area. ~ **şeridi**, tape-measure: ~ **zinciri**, surveyor's chain.

mesai Efforts; pains. ~ **saatleri**, (*ind.*) working hours.

mesaj Message; (*fig.*) news. ~**eri**, transport service.

mesa·mat¹ *pl.* (*bio.*) Pores. *s.* Porosity. ~**me**, (*bio.*) pore. ~**ne**, (*bio.*) bladder: ~ **taşı**, calculus.

mesci¹tᵈⁱ (*arch.*) (A small) mosque (without a pulpi¹ for the Friday sermon; or minaret).

mesel (*lit.*) Proverb; parable; instance. ~**a**, fo¹ instance/example.

mesele Question; affair; problem; matter o¹ concern. ~ **çıkarmak**, make a fuss; raise difficulties: ~ **ne sularda?**, how does the matte¹ stand?: ~ **su götürür**, it's an open question. ~ **yapmak (-i)**, make an ado about stg. ~**nin alt ucu**, purpose/consequence of a¹ matter: ~**yi eşelemek**, rake up/inquire into a¹ matter.

meserret Joy; rejoicing.

mesh¹etmekᵉᵈᵉʳ **(-e)** Stroke, rub lightly; (*rel.*) per-form ritual ablution.

Mesih *pr.n.* (*rel.*) Messiah, Jesus Christ.

-mesine/-masına *vn. suf.* [249] As far as it goes, fo¹ what it's worth. ~ **kalmadan**, before he could . . .. ~ **ramak kaldı**, it almost/all but . . ..

mesire(lik) Promenade; excursion-spot; picnic-site.

-mesiyle/-masıyla *vn. suf.* ~ **beraber**, just as he had . . .; hardly had he . . ..

mesken Dwelling; domicile.
meskenet[i] Poverty; sluggishness.
meskûkât[1] Coins.
meskûn Inhabited. ~ **kılmak**, populate.
meskût Silenced; passed over in silence. ~ **geçmek**, keep silent about: ~ **kalmak**, say nothing.
mesle·lk[gi/ki] Career; profession; trade; mode of acting/thinking; moral character. ~ **ahlakı**, professional ethics: ~ **dayanışması**, professional solidarity: ~ **hastalıkları**, industrial diseases: ~ **hayatı**, professional career: ~ **okulu**, (*ed.*) training college: ~ **sahibi**, who has a profession; man of sound principles: ~ **sırrı**, professional secret: ~ **iniz nedir?**, what do you do?: ~ **ten**, by profession: ~ **ten yetişme**, (*adm.*) professional; career-.
meslek·i/~**sel** Professional: ~ **öğretim**, professional education. ~ **siz**, without a career; unprincipled. ~ **taş**, of the same profession; colleague.
mesne·lt[di] Support; (*phys.*) fulcrum; (*arch.*) abutment; (*eng.*) carrier, bearing; (*adm.*) office of dignity.
mesnevi (*lit.*) Poem in rhymed couplets.
meson (*nuc.*) Meson.
mesrur Glad; contented.
mest[i 1] *n.* (*mod.*) Light thin-soled house-shoe. ~ **çi**, shoe-maker.
mest[i 2] *a.* Drunk. ~ **etm.**, intoxicate; (*fig.*) enchant: ~ **olm.**, be drunk/intoxicated; (*fig.*) be enraptured. ~ **ane**, drunkenly. ~ **edici**, intoxicating.
mestur Covered; veiled; secret. ~ **e**, (*fin.*) secret funds.
mesul (-**den**) Responsible; answerable (for). ~ **tutulmak**, be held responsible/accountable. ~ **iyet**[i], responsibility. ~ **iyetli**, involving responsibility.
mesu·lt[du] Happy; fortunate. ~ **iyet**[i], happiness.
meşakkat[i] Hardship; trouble.
meşale Torch. ~ **olm.**, be the pioneer.
meşbu[u] Full, satiated; (*chem.*) saturated.
meşe *n.* (*bot.*) Oak-tree. *a.* Oaken; made of oak. ~ **odunu**, (*fig.*) blockhead: ~ **palamudu**, (*bot.*) acorn: ~ **palamudu ağaçkakan**, (*orn.*) acorn woodpecker.
meşe·büken (*sl.*) Tough guy. ~ **cik**, (*bot.*) water germander. ~ **lik**, oak-grove/forest.
meş·gale Business; occupation; preoccupation. ~ **gul**[ü], occupied; busy; preoccupied; (telephone) engaged: ~ **etm.**, take up time, occupy: ~ **olm.**, be busy/engaged/occupied. ~ **guliyet**[i], preoccupation; occupation; being busy.
meşher Exhibition.
meşhe·lt[di] Place of martyrdom; battlefield; martyr's tomb.
meşhur Famous; well-known. ~ **olm.**, be(come) famous. ~ **luk**, fame.
meşhu·lt[du] (*leg.*) Seen, witnessed. ~ **cürümler mahkemesi**, court examining witnessed crimes: ~ **suç**, witnessed/flagrant crime.
meşihat[1] (*rel.*) Office of the Sheikh-ul-Islam.
meşime (*bio.*) Placenta, afterbirth.
meşin Leather. ~ **gibi**, (one's skin) dark and hardened: ~ **suratlı**, (*fig.*) thick-skinned.
meşk[i] (*ed.*) Copy-book; musical exercise; writing/music lesson.

meşkûk[ü] Doubtful; suspicious.
meşkûr Worthy of thanks/praise.
meşre·lp[bi] Natural disposition; character.
meşru[u] Legal; legitimate; permissible.
meşrubat[1] (Soft) drinks.
meşruhat[1] Marginal notes, comments, explanations.
meşrut[u] (*leg.*) Stipulated; bound by conditions. ~ **a**, inalienable legacy/trust. ~ **en**, conditional. ~ **i**, constitutional. ~ **iyet**[i], constitution; constitutional government: ~ **devri**, (*his.*) constitutional period.
meşum Ill-omened; fatal.
meşveret[i] Consultation.
me·lt[ddi] (*geo.*) (Flow of) the tide; high tide. ~ **ve cezir**, ebb and flow.
met. = METEOROLOJİ.
meta[1] (*fin.*) Merchandise; goods.
meta- *pref.* Meta-. ~ **bolizma**, (*bio.*) metabolism. ~ **faz**, (*bio.*) metaphase. ~ **fizik**, (*phil.*) metaphysics. ~ **fora** = MATAFORA. ~ **genez**, (*bio.*) metagenesis.
metal[i] (*min.*) *n.* Metal. *a.* Metal(lic). ~ **bilim**/~ **ürji**, metallurgy. ~ **bilimsel**, metallurgical. ~ **lemek** (-**i**), metallize. ~ **ografi**/~ **yapıbilim**, metallography. ~ **sel**, metallic. ~ **siz**, non-metallic.
meta·morfik (*geol.*) Metamorphic. ~ **morfoz**, metamorphosis.
metan (*chem.*) Methane.
metanet[i] Firmness, solidity; tenacity; resistance. ~ **li**, firm; solid; tenacious; resistant.
metanol (*chem.*) Methanol.
metapsişik (*psy.*) Metapsychic(al).
metatez (*ling.*) Metathesis.
metazoa (*bio.*) Metazoa.
metazori (*col.*) By force and threats.
metbu *a.* Followed; obeyed. *n.* Leader; sovereign.
meteli·lk[gi] (*obs.*) Ten-PARA coin; (*col.*) farthing, cent, sou. ~ **etmez**, not worth a brass farthing: ~ **vermemek** (-**e**), not care a damn for . . .: ~ **e kuruşun atmak**, be penniless. ~ **siz(lik)**, (being) penniless/broke.
meteor (*ast.*) Meteor; (*met.*) (?) weather, atmospheric conditions. ~ **it**, (*ast.*) meteorite. ~ **oloji**, meteorology. ~ **olojik**, meteorological; (*ast.*) meteor-like. ~ **taşı**, meteorite, aerolite.
metfen Tomb; burial-place.
methal[i] (*arch.*) Entrance; (*pub.*) introduction. ~ **i olm.** (-**le**), be connected/have to do with. ~ **dar**, participating; involved in.
meth·letmek[eder] (-**i**) Praise, commend. ~ **iye**, eulogy.
metil (*chem.*) Methyl. ~ **en**, methylene. ~ **etil**, methylethyl. ~ **ik**, methylic.
met·lin[ni 1] *n.* (*lit.*) Text; copy.
metin[2] *a.* (*psy.*) Solid; firm; tough; trustworthy.
metis (*ethn.*) Half-breed; of mixed blood; metis.
met·odoloji (*phil.*) Methodology. ~ **o·lt**[du], method. ~ **otlu**, methodical, systematic. ~ **otsuz**, unmethodical.
metrdotel(lik) (Work of) *maître d'hôtel*, headwaiter.
metre (*math.*) Metre. ~ **kare**, square metre: ~ **küp**, cubic metre: ~ **sistem**/**yöntemi**, metric system.

metres (*soc.*) Mistress, concubine. ~ **tutmak**, keep a mistress.

metrik (*math.*) Metric.

metris (*mil.*) Trench.

metro (*rly.*) Underground.

metronom (*mus.*) Metronome.

metropol Metropolis; homeland. ~ **it(lik)**, (*rel.*) (title/duties of) Greek Orthodox bishop, Metropolitan.

metrukü Abandoned; deserted; neglected; obsolete. ~ **ât**ı, (*leg.*) deceased's effects. ~ **iyet**i, being abandoned/neglected.

mevcu·datı All existing things; creation. ~ **diyet**i, existence; presence. ~ **lt**du, *a.* existing; available; present: *n.* (*soc.*) total number of those present; (*fin.*) stock; (*mil.*) available force.

mevduu Entrusted. ~ **at**ı, things entrusted; (*fin.*) deposits; investments.

mevhibe Gift; talent.

mevhum Imaginary, fancied; fictitious.

mevkii Place; position; situation; post; (*th.*) seat; (*rly.*, *etc.*) class. ~ **olm.**, have an important position: ~ **ine göre**, according to circumstances.

mevki·ce ~ **emsaller**, (*soc.*) people of equal station/ status. ~ **i**, local: ~ **olarak**, locally.

mevkuf Arrested; detained: **(-e)**, dependent (on).

mevkut Fixed for a period; periodical. ~ **e**, (*pub.*) periodical, magazine.

mevla Owner; master: *pr.n.* God. ~ **sını bulmak**, get what one deserves. ~ **na**, (*rel. title*) 'our lord'.

Mevlevi (*rel.*) Mevlevi. ~ **lik**, Mevlevi dervish sect, the Whirling Dervishes.

mevli·ltdi (*rel.*) Night of the Prophet Muhammad's birth; (*lit.*) poem celebrating this birth; (*rel.*) ceremony when this poem is read.

mevrus Inherited; hereditary.

mevru·ltdu Arrived; coming.

mevsim Season; proper time (for stg.); spring, autumn. ~ **li**, in season: ~ **mevsimsiz konuşmak**, speak out of turn/unnecessarily. ~ **lik**, (*mod.*) spring/autumn clothes; for one season; seasonal. ~ **siz**, inopportunely; before time, out of season.

mevsuf Endowed; (*ling.*) qualified (by an adjective).

mevsuku Trusted; reliable; authentic.

mev·ti Death. ~ **ta**, the dead.

mevu·ltdu Promised; predestined.

mev·zii Place; position. ~ **zii**, local(ized). ~ **zilenmek**, *vp.* (*mil.*) be billeted.

mevzuu *n.* Subject; (*phil.*) proposition. *a.* Placed; situated; conventional, customary. ~ **at**ı, subjects; rules; regulations; legislation; (*fin.*) containers. ~ **bah·lis**si, subject under discussion.

mevzun Weighted; balanced; symmetrical. ~ **yürüyüş**, (*mil.*) marching in step.

mey (*cul.*) Wine; (*mus.*) small pipe.

Mey. = MEYDAN(I).

meyan[1] *n.* Middle; interval. ~ **da (bu)**, among these; including . . .; in the meantime: ~ **larında**, among them. ~ **cı**, go-between.

meyan[2] *n.* (*bot.*) Liquorice plant. ~ **balı**nı, (*cul.*) liquorice. ~ **kökü**nü, (*bot.*) root of liquorice plant.

meyane *n.* Middle; interval; (*cul.*) correct degree of cooking (jam, etc.). *a.* Middling; moderate. ~ **de**,

between us/them, etc.: ~ **si gelmek**, reach the right moment; (*cul.*) reach the right consistency: ~ **sini bulmak**, find the means; reconcile; reach just the right moment (for stg. to be done): ~ **ye girmek**, get between as an obstacle/mediator. ~ **ci**, middleman.

meydan Open space; public square; (*sp.*) arena, ring, ground; the open; (*rel.*) place for Bektashi ceremonial; (*fig.*) opportunity; being apparent; condition. ~ **almak**, (stg. unwanted) be plenty of; take advantage of every opportunity: ~ **aramak**, seek space; seek an opportunity: ~ **bulmak**, find an opportunity: ~ **dayağı**, (*leg.*) public flogging: ~ **korkusu**, (*psy.*) agoraphobia: ~ **muharebe/savaşı**, (*mil.*) pitched battle: ~ **okumak**, challenge, defy: ~ **saati**, big public clock: ~ **vermek**, give an opportunity/encouragement: ~ **vermemek**, get out of an awkward situation: ~ **a atılmak**, be brought into the open; rush headlong into stg.: ~ **a atmak**, put forward, suggest: ~ **a çıkarmak**, show; expose to view; publish; elicit, bring into the open; discover; bring up (a child) to maturity: ~ **a çıkmak**, come into the open; appear; show o.s.; (secret, etc.) be revealed; (child) grow up: ~ **a düşmek**, mix with everyone: ~ **a gelmek**, occur, happen; come into the open; reach maturity: ~ **a getirmek**, bring into existence, create; cause; accomplish: ~ **a koymak**, bring out, produce; put forward (reason, etc.); prove: ~ **a vurmak**, show openly; make clear; make public: ~ **da**, in the open; homeless; exposed; manifest, obvious, 'evidently': ~ **ı boş bulmak**, seize an opportunity when rivals are absent.

meydan·cı Cleaner of public places; caretaker; bank messenger; (*rel.*) supervisor of Mevlevi dances; (*leg.*) convict leader in prison. ~ **lık**, wide open space. ~ **sazı**nı, (*Or. mus.*) large 12-stringed guitar.

-meye *vn. suf.* [168] = -MEĞE [GELMEYE].

meyhane Wine-shop; tavern. ~ **ci(lik)**, (work of) tavern-keeper, publican. ~ **ciotu**nu, (*bot.*) asarabacca.

-meyi *vn. suf.* [168] = -MEĞİ [GÖRMEYİ].

mey·lilli Inclination; slope; rake; tilt; (*ast.*) declination; propensity; bias; affection, liking. ~ **göstermek (-e)**, have an inclination for stg.; desire stg. ~ **li**, inclined, sloping. ~ **siz**, aclinic.

meyl- = MEYİL. ~ **letmek**eder **(-e)**, be inclined; have a propensity/liking for stg.

meymeneti Being lucky/auspicious. ~ **li**, lucky, auspicious, prosperous. ~ **siz**, unlucky; disagreeable.

meyus Hopeless, despairing, pessimistic. ~ **olm.**, despair, be despondent. ~ **iyet**i/ ~ **luk**, hopelessness, despair, pessimism.

meyva/meyve (*bot.*) Fruit; product; (*fin.*) profit. ~ +, *a.* Fruit-; fruiting; carpo-: ~ **bilimi**, (*ed.*) carpology: ~ **dalı**, fruiting branch: ~ **dumanı**, bloom (on fruit): ~ **şekeri**, (*chem.*) fructose, laevulose: ~ **şekerlemesi**, (*cul.*) candied fruit: ~ **tatlısı**, (*cul.*) (quince, etc.) cheese: ~ **tüyü**, down, bloom: ~ **yarasası**, (*zoo.*) fruit-bat.

meyva-/meyve- *pref.* ~ **ci**, fruit-grower/-seller. ~ **cilik**, fruit-growing/-selling. ~ **dar**, fruit-bearing; fruitful. ~ **dışı**, (*bot.*) exocarp. ~ **hoş**, fruit-market.

~içi, (*bot.*) endocarp. ~li, made of/containing fruit. ~ortası^{nı}, (*bot.*) mesocarp. ~siz, infertile. ~yapra^ık^{ğı}, fruit-bud.

meyyalⁱ (-e) Very inclined towards/fond of.

mezalim Cruelties.

mezamir (*rel.*) Psalms.

mezar Grave, tomb. ~ **bozan**, grave-robber: ~ **eşmek**, rob a grave: ~ **kaçkını**, s.o. with one foot in the grave: ~ **kazmak**, dig a grave: ~ **kitabesi**, tombstone inscription; epitaph: ~ **tümseği**, (*archaeol.*) barrow: ~**a koymak**, entomb, inter: ~**dan çıkarmak**, exhume, disinter; (*med.*) bring back to life: ~**ına nur inmek/yağmak**, (*fig.*) be very holy: ~**ını kazmak**, (*fig.*) dig one's own grave.

mezar·cı Grave-digger, sexton: ~ **böceği**, (*ent.*) sexton/burying beetle. ~**istan**/~**lık**, graveyard, cemetery.

mezarna (*naut.*) Coaming(s).

meza^ıt^{dı} (*fin.*) Auction; auction-room, etc. ~ **malı**, goods bought at auction; cheap trifles; bargain; cheap/tawdry goods: ~ **olm.**, be sold at auction: ~**a çıkarmak/koymak/vermek**, put up for/sell by auction: ~**ta artırma**, bidding: ~**ta kırmak (-i)**, make a successful bid for stg. ~**çı(lık)**, auctioneer/ (-ing).

mezbaha Slaughter-house, abattoir.

mezbele Rubbish-heap.

mezc^ıetmek^{eder} (-i, -e, -le) Mix, combine, amalgamate, blend (stg. with stg.).

-mezden *vn. suf.* [181] = -MEDEN [GELMEZDEN].

meze (*cul.*) Appetizer, snack, hors-d'œuvre, 'starters'. ~**ci(lik)**, (work of) maker/seller of snacks. ~**lik**, suitable for/used as snacks.

meze·borda (*naut.*) Broadside. ~**stre**, half-mast. ~**volta**, half-hitch.

mezelletⁱ Abjectness; baseness.

mez(g)i^ıt^{di} (*ich.*) Whiting. ~**giller**, codfishes.

mezhe^ıp^{bi} (*rel.*) Religion; creed; doctrine; sect; (*phil.*) school of thought. ~**i geniş**, lax/over-tolerant in morals.

meziyetⁱ Excellence; virtue; talent; ability; value. ~**li**, excellent; virtuous; capable.

mezkûr Mentioned; above-mentioned; the said ....

-mezlik/-mazlık *vn. suf.* [173] *Forming a negative abstract noun* [gelmezlik, non-attendance; dokunulmazlık, immunity]. *The negative can be reduplicated in emphasis* [bakmamazlık, repeated inattention; öğrenememezlik, inability to learn]. *The ablative of this form is used with* GELMEK [işitmemezlikten geldim, I pretended not to hear].

mezo- *pref.* Meso-. ~**derm**, (*bio.*) mesoderm. ~**potamya**, *pr.n.* (*geo.*) Mesopotamia. ~**zoik**, (*geol.*) Mesozoic.

mez·raa (*agr.*) Arable field. ~**ru**, sown.

mezun (*adm.*) Authorized; on leave; (*ed.*) having a school diploma; graduate; excused (some duty). ~ **olm.**, finish school. ~**iyetⁱ**, (*adm.*) permission, authorization; (*ed.*) finishing (class); leave, furlough.

mez·ura/~**ür** (*math.*) Metre-ruler; measurement.

mezzo·forte// ~**soprano** (*mus.*) Mezzo·forte// -soprano.

Mf. = (*adm.*) MÜFETTİŞ(LİĞİ).

MF = (*ed.*) MALİYE FAKÜLTESİ; (*mus.*) MEZZOFORTE.

Mg. = (*ch.s.*) MAGNEZYUM.

MGK = (*adm.*) MİLLİ GÜVENLİK KONSEYİ.

MHP = (*pol.*) MİLLİYETÇİ HAREKET PARTİSİ.

MHz = (*el.*) MEGAHERTZ.

mı *particle* [105] = Mİ¹ [YAPILIR MI?].

-mı- *v. suf. neg.* [110] = -ME-² [ALMIYACAK].

mıh (*carp.*) Nail. ~ **gibi kapalı**, tightly shut. ~**ladız**, (*col.*) = MIKNATIS. ~**lamak (-i, -e)**, nail; fasten down; (*fig.*) fix securely; nail s.o. down. ~**lanmak**, *vp.* be nailed; (*fig.*) be nailed to the spot. ~**lı**, nailed. ~**sıçtı**, (*sl.*) mean, tight-fisted.

mıkna·tın (*phys.*) Magneton. ~**tıs(i)**, magnet(ic). ~**tısiyetⁱ**, magnetism. ~**tıslamak (-i)**, magnetize stg. ~**tıslanmak**, *vp.* ~**tıslanmaz**, non-magnetic. ~**tıslı**/~**tıssal**, magnetized; magnetic: ~ **iğne**, magnetic needle. ~**tıslık**, magnetism: ~**ını gidermek**, demagnetize.

mıncık ~ ~, spoilt, messed about. ~**lamak (-i)**, mess about; handle stg.; ill-treat; tease apart.

mıntıka Zone, district; region.

mırıl ~ ~, *adv.* (*ech.*) muttering; grumbling. ~**da(n)mak (-i)**, mutter (stg.) to o.s.; grumble. ~**tı**, *n.* muttering; grumbling.

mırın ~ **kırın etm.**, show vague disapproval; appear unwilling; boggle at stg.

mır·mır (*ech.*) Murmuring. ~**nav**, (*ech.*) miaow.

mısdak¹ Criterion; proof; authority.

Mısır¹ *pr.n.* (*geo.*) Egypt. ~ +, *a.* Egyptian: ~ **buğdayı**, (*bot.*) maize: ~ **Çarşısı**, *pr.n.* Egyptian/ Spice Bazaar (Istanbul): ~ **çaylağı**, (*orn.*) Egyptian black kite: ~ **çekirgesi**, (*ent.*) Egyptian locust: ~ **kutnusu**, (*tex.*) fustian: ~ **tavuğu**, (*orn.*) turkey: ~ **yılanı**, (*zoo.*) asp: ~**daki sağır sultan bile bunu işitti**, it's notorious.

mısır² *n.* (*bot.*) Maize, Indian corn; parched maize. ~ **gevreği**, (*cul.*) cornflakes: ~ **kalburu**, (*cul.*) griddle used for parching maize: ~ **koçanı**, corn-cob: ~ **püskülü**, (*bot.*) maize tassel: ~ **püskülü gibi**, scant/lifeless (hair): ~ **rastığı**, (*myc.*) corn smut: ~ **unu**, (*cul.*) cornflour.

mısır·cı Maize-seller. ~**fulü**^{nü}, (*bot.*) lotus. ~**lı**, *pr.n.* (*ethn.*) Egyptian. ~**lık**, (*agr.*) maize-field. ~**özü**^{nü}, (*bot.*) grain of maize. ~**turnası**^{nı}, (*orn.*) sacred ibis. ~ **yağı**^{nı}, (*cul.*) cornseed oil.

mıskal¹ (*mus.*) Panpipe. ~ **kamışı gibi**, close together.

mıskala Burnisher. ~ **vurmak**, burnish.

mısra (*lit.*) Line of poetry. ~ **vurgusu**, accent, stress.

mıs·tak = MISDAK. ~**tar** = MASTAR.

-mış *v. suf.* [122, 162] = -Mİş [ALMIŞ]. ~**çasına** *v. suf.* [188] = -MİŞÇESİNE.

mışıl ~ ~ **uyumak**, sleep soundly.

mışmış (*bot.*) Apricot.

-mıya- *v. suf.* = -MİYE-² [ALMIYACAK].

mıymıntı(lık) Weak(ness); slack(ness); useless/ (-ness).

mızıka (*mus.*) Brass band; mouth-organ. ~**cı**, bandsman.

mızık·çı S.o. unreliable/untrustworthy; (*sp.*) s.o. who does not obey the rules; cheat. ~**çılık**, unreliability; cheating: ~ **etmez**, (*sp.*) fair. ~**lanmak**, *vi.* (*sp.*) spoil a game by breaking the rules.

mızırdanmak *vi.* Speak in a grumbling manner.

mızmız Hesitant; shilly-shallying; lazy; querulous. ~**lanmak**, *vi.* be hesitant, etc. ~**lık**, hesitancy, etc.

mızra'kᵍ¹ (*mil.*) Lance, spear. ~ **çuvala girmez/ sığmaz**, 'it's an obvious falsehood': ~ **kuyruklu**, (*zoo.*) with a sharp/pointed tail. ~**lı**, s.o. bearing a lance.

mızra'pᵇ¹ (*mus.*) Instrument for striking; plectrum.

mi¹/**mı/mu/mü** 1. *Interrogative particle* [105] [**gelir** ~?, does he come?: **değil** ~?, is it not so?: **olur** ~?, is it possible?]. 2. *Emphatic particle, between repeated words* [235] Certainly!, and how!; definitely; very [**çirkin** ~ **çirkin**, horribly ugly].

mi² *n.* (*mus.*) Me/mi, E.

-mi- *v. suf. neg.* [110] = -ME-² [GELMİYECEK].

mia'ttᵈ¹ Fixed place/time; rendezvous; (*fin.*) fixed period/term.

mibzer (*agr.*) Drill for sowing.

miço = MUÇO.

mide (*bio.*) Stomach; (*fig.*) good taste. ~ +, *a.* Stomach; entero-: ~ **baygınlığı**, (*psy.*) sinking sensation in the stomach: ~ **bezleri**, (*bio.*) gastric glands: ~ **bulandırmak (-i)**, make sick, nauseate; make suspicious: ~ **dolgunluğu**, indigestion; heavy feeling in the stomach: ~ **ezikliği**, hunger: ~ **fesadına uğramak**, suffer stomach disorder after eating too much: ~ **kapısı**, (*bio.*) pylorus: ~ **kelebeği**, (*zoo.*) stomach fluke: ~ **sancısı**, (*med.*) colic: ~ **sineği**, (*ent.*) botfly: ~ **suyu**, (*bio.*) gastric juice(s): ~ **yangısı**, (*med.*) gastritis: ~**si almamak**, have no appetite: ~**si bulanmak**, be nauseated; be disgusted; (*fig.*) feel suspicious: ~**si ekşimek**, have an acid taste in the mouth: ~**si kabarmak**, feel bilious: ~**si kaldırmak**, feel like eating stg.: swallow an insult: ~**si kazınmak**, feel empty from hunger: ~**ye durmak/oturmak**, lie heavy on the stomach; be indigestible.

mide-ağzı (*bio.*) Cardia: ~ +, *a.* cardio-. ~**ci**, s.o. who thinks only of food; (*fig.*) self-seeker. ~**cilik**, thinking only of food. ~**siz**, s.o. who eats/can eat everything; (*fig.*) who has bad taste. ~**sizlik**, bad taste. ~**vi**, connected with// good for the stomach; digestive.

midi Medium. ~ **etek**, (*mod.*) midi skirt.

Midilli (*geo.*) Mytelene, Lesbos; (*zoo.*) shaggy pony.

midye (*zoo.*) Mussel. ~ **dolma**// **tavası**, (*cul.*) stuffed// fried mussels. ~**ci**, mussel-catcher/-seller.

migren (*med.*) Migraine.

miğfer (*mil.*) Helmet. ~**li kakadu**, (*orn.*) cockatoo.

mihaniki (*fig.*) Mechanical (work).

mihen'kᵍⁱ Touchstone; criterion; test; standard. ~**e vurmak**, test. ~**çi**, (silver, etc.) assayer.

mihman Guest. ~**dar(lık)**, (duties of) host// official accompanying a foreign visitor.

mihnetⁱ Trouble; affliction. ~**keş**/ ~**zede**, afflicted.

mihrace (*soc.*) Maharajah.

mihrak¹ (*phys.*) Focus.

mihra'pᵇ¹ (*rel.*) Niche in a mosque (indicating the direction of Mecca).

mihver Pivot; axle; axis. ~ +, *a.* Axial.

mika (*geol.*) Mica. ~ **şist**ⁱ, mica schist.

mikado (*soc.*) Mikado; (*gamb.*) mahjong.

mikâ'pᵇ¹ (*math.*) Cube. ~ **şeklinde**, cubic(al).

mikro- *pref.* Micro-. ~**biyoloji**, (*ed.*) microbiology. ~**film**, (*cin.*) microfilm. ~**fon(ik)**, (*phys.*) microphon·e/(-ic): ~ **kolu**, (*cin.*) boom. ~**kok**ᵘ, (*bio.*) micrococcus. ~**lit**ⁱ, (*geol.*) microlith. ~ **metre**, (*eng.*) micrometer. ~**n**, (*math.*) micron. ~**organizm** = MİKROP.

mikro'pᵇᵘ (*bio.*) Microbe. ~ **öldürücü**, (*chem.*) germicide: ~**tan arınmış**, (*med.*) sterile. ~**lanmak**, become infected. ~**lu**, having microbes, septic. ~**suz**, free from microbes, sterile, aseptic. ~**suzluk**, asepsis. ~**suzlandırmak**/ ~**suzlaştırmak (-i)**, disinfect, sterilize.

mikro·sefal (*bio.*) Microcephalous. ~**sinema**, (*med.*) microcinema. ~**skobik**, microscopic. ~**sko'p**ᵇᵘ, (*phys.*) microscope.

miktar Quantity; amount; extent; value; content. ~ **analizi**, quantitative analysis: ~ **tayini**, dosage.

mikyas (*math.*) Measuring instrument; proportion; scale; standard.

mil *n.* 1. (*geol.*) Silt, alluvium. 2. (*math.*) Mile (1609 metres). 3. (*eng.*) Pivot; axle; pin; probe; (*arch.*) obelisk.

mila·di ~ **tarih**, Christian era: ~ **yıl**, year AD. ~**t**ᵈ¹, birth of Christ: ~**tan önce**, before Christ, BC: ~**tan sonra**, Anno Domini, AD.

mildiyu (*myc.*) Mildew, blight.

milföy (*cul.*) *Mille-feuille*, puff-pastry.

mili- *pref.* (*math.*) Milli-. ~**amper**, (*el.*) milliampere. ~**bar**, (*met.*) millibar. ~**gram**, milligram. ~**litre**, millilitre. ~**m**/~**metre**, millimetre. ~**metrik**, ~ **kâğıdı**, graph paper. ~**mikron**, millimicron.

mili·s (*mil.*) Militia. ~**tan**, (*pol.*) militant. ~**tarist**, militarist. ~**tarizm**, militarism.

milletⁱ (*pol.*) Nation; people; (*rel.*) people of one faith; (*soc.*) class of people; crowd. ~ +, *a.* National: ~ **meclisi**, (*adm.*) chamber of deputies, national assembly: ~ **reis(liğ)i**, (*pol.*) ethnarch(y): ~**ler Cemiyeti**, (*his.*) League of Nations.

millet·lerarası International: ~ **Adalet Divanı**, Int. Court of Justice: ~ **Çalışma Teşkilatı**, Int. Labour Organization: ~ **hukuk**, int. law: ~ **İmar ve Kalkınma Bankası**, Int. Bank for Reconstruction and Development: ~ **Para Fonu**, Int. Monetary Fund: ~ **Posta Birliği**, Universal Postal Union: ~ **ticaret hukuku**, int. mercantile law. ~**vekili**ⁿⁱ, (*pol.*) deputy, member of the Tk. Parliament. ~**vekilliği**ⁿⁱ, duties/position of a deputy: ~ **dokunulmazlığı**, parliamentary immunity/privilege.

milli National; ethnic. ~ **bayram**, national holiday: ~ **benlik**, national pride// character: ~ **Cephe**, (*pol.*) National Front: ~ **Eğitim Bakan(lığ)ı**, (*adm.*) Minis·ter/(-try) of (National) Education: ~ **güvenlik**, (*mil.*) national security: ~ **itibar**, (*fin.*) national credit: ~ **korunma mahkemesi**, (*leg.*) special tribunal for emergencies: ~ **marş**, (*mus.*) national anthem: ~ **Müdafaa/Savunma Bakan-(lığ)ı**, (*adm.*) Minis·ter/(-try) of National Defence: ~ **numara**, identity/registration number.

milli·leşmek *vi.* Become a nation. ~**leştirmek (-i)**, (*adm., fin.*) nationalize. ~**yet**ⁱ, nationality; religious community. ~**yetçi(lik)**, (*soc., pol.*)

national·ist/(-ism): ~ **Cephesi**, Conservative Front. ~**yetperver**, patriotic, nationalist. ~**yetsiz**, non-nationalist; unpatriotic.

nil·yar *n.* Thousand million (10^9), billion. ~**yarder**, billionaire. ~**yarlık**, *a.* billion. ~**yon**, *n.* million (10^6). ~**yoner(lik)**, (being a) millionaire. ~**yonluk**, *a.* million. ~**yonuncu**, millionth.

nilyö (*soc.*) Surroundings, ambience.

nim[1] *n.* (*ling.*) Arabic letter M; (*col.*) tick, mark. ~ **koymak**, tick/mark off; blacklist.

nim[2] *n.* (*th.*) Panto(mime). ~**ik**, mimicry.

nim. = MİMARLIK.

nimar Architect. ~**başı**, (*his.*) Chief Architect. ~**i**, architectural. ~**lık**, architecture.

nim·lemek (-i) Tick/mark off; blacklist. ~**lenmek**, *vp.* ~**li**, marked off; black-listed; (*pol.*) suspect; marked man.

nimoza (*bot.*) Mimosa.

ninakop[u] (*ich.*) Corb.

ninare (*arch.*) Minaret. ~ **boyu**, 10 to 20 metres high: ~ **gibi**, very tall (person): ~ **kırması**, very tall person: ~ **külahı**, (*arch.*) spire of the minaret: ~**yı çalan kılıfını hazırlar**, in a risky business you prepare for the consequences.

ninber (*rel.*) Pulpit in a mosque.

ninder (*dom.*) Cushion; mat, mattress; divan; (*sp.*) mat, wrestling ring. ~ **altı etm.**, (*fig.*) hide, cover up; sweep under the carpet: ~ **çürütmek**, sit about endlessly; (visitor) show no sign of leaving.

nine (*art.*) Enamel; (clock) dial; shiny decoration; (*med.*) tooth-filling. ~ **işlemek**, enamel. ~**ci**, enamelist. ~**çiçeği**[ni], (*bot.*) vervain; verbena. ~**çiçeğigiller**, verbena family, Verbenaceae. ~**lemek (-i)**, enamel. ~**li**, enamelled: ~ **balık**, (*ich.*) large dragonet: ~ **iş**, enamelware.

nineral[i] (*chem.*) Mineral. ~ **yağlar**, mineral oils. ~**bilim**, mineralogy. ~**ize**, ~ **etm.**, mineralize. ~**leştirmek (-i)**, (*chem.*) mineralize. ~**og**[u], mineralogist. ~**oji**, mineralogy.

nini Small. ~ **etek**, (*mod.*) miniskirt. ~**büs**, (*mot.*) minibus. ~**büsçü(lük)**, minibus opera·tor/(-tion). ~**cik**, very very small, tiny. ~**göre**[l]**ç**[ci], (*phys.*) microscope. ~**k**, small and sweet. ~**l**, micro. ~ **mini**, tiny. ~**mum**, minimum.

nink[i] (*zoo.*, *mod.*) Mink.

ninkale (*math.*) Protractor.

ninnacık (*col.*) Very small, tiny.

ninnet[i] Obligation (for favour received); indebtedness; favour; taunt (about former kindness). ~ **altında kalmamak**, feel no obligation (having returned the favour): ~ **etm.**, put o.s. under an obligation; ask a favour; beg. ~**tar**, grateful; indebted. ~**tarlık**, gratitude.

ninnoş *int.* (*col.*) Little darling!

nino (*orn.*) Myna-bird.

Minos *pr.n.* (*his.*) Minos.

ninör (*mus.*) Minor.

nintan (*mod.*) Waistcoat with sleeves; shirt. ~**lık**, cloth for waistcoat.

ninü·skül (*pub.*) Minuscule; lower case. ~ **tye**, (*eng.*) timer.

ninval[i] Method; manner. ~ **üzere (bir)**, in the same way; regularly: ~ **üzere (bu)**, in this manner.

minyatür (*art.*) Illumination; miniature. ~ **motor**, clockwork motor. ~**cü**, illuminator; miniaturist. ~**cülük**, miniature-painting.

minyon Slender, small, delicate.

mira (*geo.*) Surveyor's rod, levelling staff.

mira[l]**ç**[ci] (*rel.*) Ascension. ~ **gecesi**, Muhammad's ascension.

mir·ahor (*his.*) Master of the Horse. ~**alay**, (*his.*, *mil.*) colonel; (*naut.*) captain.

miras Inheritance. ~ **vergisi**, inheritance/capital transfer tax: ~ **yemek**/~**a konmak**, come into an inheritance: ~ **tan mahrum etm.**, disinherit.

miras·çı Inheritor. ~**yedi**, spendthrift. ~**yedilik**, extravagance, squandering.

miri (*adm.*) Belonging to the State. ~ **ambarı**, government storehouse: ~ **için**, on government account: ~ **malı**, public money/property.

mirliva (*his.*) Brigadier(-general).

mirza (*his.*) Prince; son of a lord; gentleman.

mis[1] *n.* (*soc.*) (English) Miss.

mis[2] *n.* = MİSK. ~ **sabunu**, perfumed soap.

misafir Guest; visitor; company; traveller; speck in the eye. ~ **kabulü**, at-home; reception: ~ **konağı**, village guest-house for travellers: ~ **odası**, guest-room; reception-room: ~ **tohumu**, natural child: ~ **umduğunu değil bulduğunu yer**, one must put up with what one finds: ~**leri eksik olmaz**, they entertain a lot.

misafir·hane Public guest-house; hotel; motel. ~**lik**, being a guest; visit: ~**e gitmek**, pay a visit: ~**e kabul etm.**, entertain s.o. ~**perver**, hospitable. ~**perverlik**, hospitality.

misak[1] Compact; solemn promise; pact. ~**ımilli**, *pr.n.* (*his.*) National Pact, 1920.

misal[i] Mode; precedent; the like; match. ~ **getirmek**, give an example.

misel (*chem.*) Micelle. ~**yum**, (*myc.*) mycelium.

misil[i 1] *n.* (*mil.*) Missile. ~ **savar**, anti-missile.

mis[l]**il**[li 2] *n.* A similar one; an equal amount; as much again. ~**i yok**, peerless, matchless. ~**leme**, (*leg.*) retaliation. ~**li**, like, similar.

misina Line (of fishing-rod).

misis (*soc.*) (English) Mrs., missis.

misk[i] Musk. ~ **çiçeği**, (*bot.*) field scabious: ~ **faresi**, (*zoo.*) musk rat: ~ **geyik/keçisi**, (*zoo.*) musk deer: ~ **gibi**, sweetly scented; delicious; in a perfect manner: ~ **kedisi**, (*zoo.*) civet-cat: ~ **otu**, (*bot.*) musk plant: ~ **öküz/sığırı**, (*zoo.*) musk-ox.

MİSK = MİLLİYETÇİ İŞÇİ SENDİKALARI KONFEDE-RASYONU.

miskal[i] Weight of 1.5 drams (for jewels). ~ **ile**, in tiny quantities.

misket[i 1] *n.* (*bot.*) Scented fruit. ~ **limonu**, lime: ~ **şarabı**, muscatel wine: ~ (**üzümü**) muscatel grape.

misket[i 2] *n.* (*mil.*) Musket; grape-shot.

miskin Poor; wretched; lazy; abject; poor-spirited; (*med.*) leprous. ~ **hastalık/illeti**, (*med.*) leprosy: ~**ler tekkesi**, (*pej.*) place of idleness.

miskin·hane (*med.*) Leper hospital. ~**lenmek/ ~leşmek**, *vi.* become poor/wretched; become idle. ~**lik**, poverty; abjectness; incompetence; (*med.*) leprosy.

miskliler (*zoo.*) Musk-producing animals.

misl- = MİSİL².
mister (*soc.*) (English) Mr., mister.
misti·kⁱ (*rel.*) Mystic. ~ **sizm**, mysticism.
misvak¹ Fibrous wood used as toothbrush.
misyon (*adm.*) Mission. ~ **er(lik)**, (*rel.*) (work of) missionary.
-miş/-mış/-muş/-müş *v. suf.* [122] *Forming:* 1. *inferential past tense*, [122] it is said/thought/reported that; one gathers that [**gitmiş diyorlar**, they say he has gone; **gitmemişse**, if (you find that) he has not gone]: 2. *the past participle* [162] [**gitmiş**, gone; **satılmış**, sold]. ~ **gibi**, as if/though; it seemed that: ~ **ler muşlar**, (*col.*) gossip: ~ **'li geçmiş**, (*ling.*) the indefinite/inferential past: ~ **se de**, although, while. ~ **çesine/** ~ **çasına** [188], as if [GÖRMÜŞÇESİNE, as if seen].
mitⁱ Myth.
MİT = (*adm.*) MİLLİ İSTİHBARAT TEŞKİLATI.
mitil (*dom.*) Type of light quilt.
miting (*pol.*) Meeting. ~ **çi**, organizer of/participant in meetings.
mitoloji(k) Mytholo·gy/(-gical).
mitoz (*bio.*) Mitosis.
mitralyöz (*mil.*) Machine-gun.
MİTT = MİLLETLERARASI İKTİSADİ İŞBİRLİĞİ TEŞKİLATI.
miyar (*math.*) Standard (of measurement); (*chem.*) reagent.
miyasma (*med.*) Miasma.
miyavla·mak *vi.* Miaow, caterwaul. ~ **tmak** (**-i**), *vc.*
-miye¹ *vn. suf.* [168] = -MEĞE.
-miye-²/**-mıya-** *v. suf.* = -Mİ-+-E- [GİDECEK—GİT-MİYECEK]. ~ **gör!** [191] mind you don't . . .!; beware lest . . .! [**onunla konuşmıyagör**, mind you don't speak to him!].
miyop (*med.*) *a.* Myopic; short-sighted. *n.* Myope. ~ **luk**, myopia; short-sightedness.
miyosen (*geol.*) Miocene period.
miza (*gamb.*) Kitty, pool; stakes.
miza'çᶜ¹ Temperament; disposition; state of health; mood. ~ **lı**, having . . . temperament/mood. ~ **sız**, unwell. ~ **sızlık**, indisposition.
mizah Humour; joke. ~ **çı**, humorist. ~ **i**, humorous.
mizan (*math.*) Balance, scales; (*fin.*) trial balance.
miz·ana (*naut.*) Mizzen. ~ **anpaj**, (*pub.*) page-setting. ~ **anpli**, (*mod.*) setting (hair). ~ **ansen**, (*th.*) staging, production; setting. ~ **arna**, (*naut.*) hatch-coamings.
MK = MEDENİ KANUN. ~ **E(K)** = MAKİNE KİMYA ENDÜSTRİSİ (KURUMU). ~ **S** = (*math.*) METRE-KİLOGRAM-SANİYE.
Mlle = (*mademoiselle*).
mm. = MİLİMETRE.
MM = MİLLET MECLİSİ. ~ **B** = MİLLİ MÜDAFAA BAKANLIĞI.
Mme = (*Madame*).
Mn. = (*ch.s.*) MANGAN(EZ).
mnemotekni (*psy.*) Mnemonics, mnemotechny.
MNP = (*pol.*) MİLLİ NİZAM PARTİSİ.
Mo. = (*ch.s.*) MOLİBDEN.
moa (*orn.*) Moa. ~ **giller**, moas.

mobilya Furniture. ~ **cı**, furniture-maker/-dealer('. shop). ~ **cılık**, furniture-making/-selling.
moda *n.* Fashion. *a.* Fashionable, modern; i(fashion. ~ **çabuk tutundu**, the fashion caught o(quickly: ~ **çıkarmak**, set the fashion: ~ **çizim** resimleri, fashion-plate: ~ **dergisi**, (*pub.*) fashio(magazine: ~ **olm.**, be the fashion: ~ **da**, in th(fashion: ~ **sı aldı yürüdü**, the fashion for . . . ha(grown: ~ **sı geçmek**, be/go out of fashion; b(out-of-date/old-fashioned. ~ **cı**, fashion-designer modiste.
model (*art.*) Model; pattern; style, fashion; (*pub.* fashion-magazine; (*mot.*) model, type; copy. ~ **a(** modelling. ~ **ci(lik)**, model-maker/(-making).
moderato (*mus.*) Moderato.
modern Modern. ~ **ize**, modernized: ~ **etm.** modernize. ~ **leşme**, *vn.*; modernization. ~ **leşmek** *vi.* become modern/up-to-date/contemporary ~ **leştirmek** (-i), *vc.* ~ **lik**, modernism.
mod·istra (*mod.*) Dressmaker. ~ **ül**, (*math., ind.* module. ~ **ülasyon**, (*mus.*) modulation. ~ **üle** (*phys.*) modulated.
Moğol (*ethn.*) Mongol(ian): ~ **ırkı**, yellow race ~ **ca**, (*ling.*) Mongolian. ~ **istan**, (*geo.*) Mongolia.
mokamp Mɔ(toring-)camp.
mokasen (*mod.*) Moccasin.
mola Rest; pause; time out; (*naut.*) act of letting g(slacking off. ~ **etm.**, ease off; slacken; rest o.s.: ~ **taşı**, block on which HAMAL can rest his load ~ **vermek**, break one's journey; take things easy.
molas (*geol.*) Molasse, sandstone.
Moldavya, *pr.n.* (*geo.*) Moldavia.
molekül (*chem.*) Molecule. ~ +, *a.* Molecular: ~ **derişmesi**, molecular concentration. ~ **er**, mole(cular.
molibden (*chem.*) Molybdenum.
molla (*rel.*) Theological student; mulla(h); (*leg.* chief judge; doctor of Muslim law. ~ **lık**, position(duties of a mullah.
molotofkokteyl (*mil.*) Molotov cocktail.
moloz (*geol.*) Aggregate; rubble; (*fig.*) stg./s.c(useless. ~ **laşmak**, *vi.* become shrivelled/ugly.
momentⁱ (*phys.*) Moment, torque.
monarşi (*adm.*) Monarchy.
monat(çılık) (*phil.*) Monad(ism).
monden Mundane; worldly.
mongoloit (*psy.*) Mongoloid.
mongos (*zoo.*) Mongoose.
mon·ist (*phil.*) Monist. ~ **izm**, monism.
mono·blok (*arch.*) Monobloc. ~ **gam(i)**, (*soc.* monoga·mous/(-my). ~ **graf(i)**, (*lit.*) monograph ~ **kl**ü, monocle. ~ **kok**, (*naut.*) monohull. ~ **ksit** (*chem.*) monoxide. ~ **log**, (*th.*) monologue ~ **pol**, (*fin.*) monopoly. ~ **teist**, (*rel.*) monotheist ~ **teizm**, monotheism. ~ **tip**, (*pub.*) monotype ~ **ton(luk)**, monoto·nous/(-ny).
monsenyör (*soc., rel.*) Monseigneur.
monsun (*met.*) Monsoon.
mon·taj (*eng.*) Assembly; erection; fitting: ~ **dairesi**, assembly-shop: ~ **hattı**, assembly-line: ~ **odası**, (*cin.*) cutting-room. ~ **tajcı(lık)**, (work of assembler, fitter. ~ **te**, ~ **etm.**, assemble, moun(fit; (*th.*) produce.

montgomeri (*mod.*) Short zip-up jacket, duffel coat.

montör Assembler, erector.

monüman(tal) Monument(al).

mor Purple, violet. ~ **salkım**, (*bot.*) wistaria: ~ **tavuk**, (*orn.*) purple gallinule: ~ **taş/yakut**, (*geol.*) amethyst.

moral (*psy.*) Morale. ~ **eğitimi**, moral training: ~ **kırıcı**, disheartening. ~ **ist**/~**izm**, (*phil.*) moral·ist/(-ism). ~ **man**, morally.

mor·amık (*med.*) Purpura. ~ **arım**/~ **arma**, *vn.*; (*med.*) cyanosis. ~ **armak**, *vi.* become purple; (*med.*) become bruised; be red with weeping. ~ **artı**, (*med.*) bruise. ~ **artmak** (**-i**), *vc.*

moratoryum (*fin.*) Moratorium.

moray (*ich.*) Moray (eel).

mordan (*chem.*) Corrosive. ~ **boyası**, mordant paint.

moren (*geol.*) Morraine.

morfem (*ling.*) Morpheme.

morfin (*chem.*) Morphine. ~ **lenmek**, *vp.* be drugged with morphine. ~ **oman**, morphine addict.

morfoloji (*bio.*, *ling.*) Morphology.

morg (*med.*) Morgue.

morina (*ich.*) Cod.

mor·laşmak *vi.* Become/turn purple. ~ **luk**, being purple/violet. ~ **ötesi**/~ **üstü**, (*phys.*) ultra-violet. ~ **umsu**/~ **umtırak**, purplish.

mors[1] *n.* (*zoo.*) Walrus.

mors[2] *n.* ~ **alfabe/şifresi**, (*rad.*) morse-code.

morto (*sl.*) Dead. ~ **yu çekmek**, die. ~ **cu/mortucu**, coffin-bearer; hearse-driver; imam; professional mourner.

mortutar(lık) (*bio.*) Basophi·le/(-lia).

moru'kᵍᵘ (*sl.*) Dotard; old fogy; 'the old man'. ~ **laşmak**, *vi.* grow old.

morula (*bio.*) Blastula.

Mos·kof (*his.*) Musco·vite/-vy; Russian; (*fig.*) ruth-less: ~ **ördeği**, (*orn.*) Muscovy duck. ~ **kofcamı**ⁿ¹, (*geol.*) muscovite. ~ **koftoprağı**ⁿ¹, (*geol.*) rotten-stone, diatomite, tripoli. ~ **kova**, (*geo.*) Moscow.

mosmor Bright purple.

mostra (*ind.*) Pattern; sample; (*geol.*) outcrop (of rock). ~ **olm.**, (*sl.*) make an exhibition of o.s. ~ **lık**, stg. only a sample (not for sale); (*fig.*) s.o. who is present but does nothing.

motel Motel. ~ **ci(lik)**, (work of) motel operator.

motif (*art.*) Motif; design; (*mod.*) ornament. ~ **li**, with a motif.

moto·pomp (*eng.*) Motor-driven pump. ~ **r**, (*eng.*) motor, engine; (*aer.*) power-plant; (*naut.*) motorboat; (*mot.*) motor-cyle; (*bio.*) motor (nerve, etc.): ~ **kapağı**, (*mot.*) bonnet; (*aer.*) cowling. ~ **rbot**ᵘ, (*naut.*) motorboat. ~ **rin**, engine oil. ~ **rize**, motor-ized. ~ **rlu**, motorized; having an engine: ~ **bisiklet**, auto-cycle, moped: ~ **taşıt**, motor-vehicle: ~ **tren** = ~ **TREN**. ~ **siklet**ⁱ, motor-cycle. ~**tren**, (*rly.*) diesel-electric train.

motris (*rly.*) Diesel-electric motor-carriage.

mozaik (*art.*) Mosaic. ~ **çi**, mosaic-dealer/-worker.

moza'kᵍ¹ (*live.*) Young pig, piglet.

mozole (*arch.*) Mausoleum.

MÖ = MİLATTAN ÖNCE.

möble Furniture.

mönü (*cul.*) Menu.

mösyö Monsieur.

MP = (*pol.*) MİLLET PARTİSİ.

Mrşl = (*mil.*) MAREŞAL.

MS = MİLATTAN SONRA. ~ **P** = (*pol.*) MİLLİ SELAMET PARTİSİ.

-msi/-msı/-mtırak/-mtrak *a.* *suf.* [58] = -iMSİ/ -İMTIRAK [SARIMSI].

MT·A = MADEN TETKİK VE ARAMA (ENSTİTÜSÜ). ~ **TB** = MİLLİ TÜRK TALEBE BİRLİĞİ.

mu *particle* [105] = Mİ¹ [OLUR MU?]

Mu. = (*adm.*) MUHABERE.

mu- *pref.* Also = MÜ-.

-mu- *v.* *suf.* *neg.* [110] = -ME-² [BULMUYORDUK].

muaccel Paid down/in advance/in cash. ~ **e**, deposit.

muad·del Corrected; modified. ~ **dil**, modifying.

muad·ele (*math.*) Equation; (*fig.*, *obs.*) incompre-hensible work. ~ **elet**ⁱ, equivalence. ~ **il**, *a.* equiva-lent: *n.* equivalent, similar one; (*math.*) parameter.

muaf Pardoned; excused: (**-den**), exempt (from); immune (to). ~ **tutmak**, excuse, exonerate. ~ **iyet**ⁱ/ ~ **lık**, being excused; exemption; immunity.

muahede(name) Pact; treaty; convention.

muaheze Censure; criticism.

muahhar Later; deferred; subsequent.

muahi'lᵗᵈⁱ (*leg.*) Signatory; contracting party.

muakki'lpᵇⁱ Follower; pursuer; (*ind.*) progress chaser.

muallak¹ (*adm.*) Suspended; in suspense; depen-dent. ~ **bırakmak**, postpone: ~ **kalmak**, hang in the balance: ~ **ta kalan sorunlar**, outstanding questions: ~ **ta olm.**, be undecided.

muallel Defective; incomplete; unsound.

muallim (*ed.*) Teacher. ~ **e**, female teacher.

muamel·at¹ *pl.* Dealings; procedures. ~ **e**, dealing; treatment; conduct; transaction; procedure; (*chem.*) reaction: ~ **etm.**, behave; treat; deal with: ~ **vergisi**, (*fin.*) turnover tax: ~ **yi elden takip etm.**, follow up the matter personally. ~ **eci**, broker. ~ **eli**, under consideration; 'for action'.

muamma Enigma, riddle. ~ **lı**, cryptic.

muammer Long-lived.

muannit Obstinate; unyielding.

muaraza Controversy.

muarefe Acquaintance(ship). ~ **m var hukukum yok (-le)**, I am acquainted with . . . but not on close terms.

muarız Opposing, hostile.

muasır Contemporaneous. ~ **olan**, contemporary.

muaşaka Mutual affection; love-making.

muaşeretⁱ Social intercourse. ~ **adabı**, etiquette: ~ **etm.**, live together.

muattal Abandoned; disused; (factory) idle.

muattar Perfumed.

muavaza Exchange.

mua·venetⁱ Help; assistance: ~ **etm.** (**-e**), help s.o. ~ **vin**, (*adm.*) assistant; deputy; (*sp.*) half-back: ~ **yakıcı**, (*eng.*) after-burner.

muayede (*soc.*) Reciprocal visit/congratulations on a feast-day.

muayene Inspection; scrutiny; (*med.*) examination, check-up. ~ **etm.**, inspect, examine, scrutinize: ~

kaçağı, (*mil.*) that has escaped/avoided (medical) inspection: ~ **penceresi,** (*eng.*) inspection port: ~ **saatleri,** (*med.*) consulting hours. ~**ci,** (*adm.*) customs inspector. ~**hane,** (*med.*) consulting-room, surgery.

muayyen Definite; determined; known. ~**iyet¹,** definiteness; (*phil.*) determinism.

muazzam Great; esteemed; important.

muazzep Tormented, pained. ~ **etm.,** torment: ~ **olm.,** be tormented.

muazzez Cherished; honoured; esteemed.

mubah (*rel.*) Lawful; permissible.

mubassır (*ed.*) Usher.

mubayaa (*fin.*) Purchase; transaction; wholesale buying. ~ **etm.,** buy (wholesale). ~**cı,** buyer; wholesaler.

muci·bince According to regulations//requirements; as necessary; (*adm.*) approved. ~¹**p**bi, cause; motive; requirement; approval: ~ **çekmek,** approve: ~ **olm.,** cause; require: ~ **sebep,** reason, motive: ~**ten çıkmak,** be approved.

mucir Who lets/hires out stg.

muci¹tdi Inventor; inventing.

muciz Overpowering; perplexing. ~**e,** miracle; wonder.

mucu¹kgu (*ent.*) Small fly.

mucur (*min.*) Slack; slag; dross.

muço (*naut.*) Cabin-boy; boy-waiter.

mudi¹ (*fin.*) Depositor; investor.

mudil Difficult; complex.

mufassal Detailed; lengthy.

mufla (*eng.*) Muffle.

mugaddi Nutritious.

mugalata Misleading statement; fallacy.

muganni(ye) (Female) singer.

mugayeret¹ Difference; apposition.

mugayir Opposed; contrary; adverse.

muğber Hurt; offended. ~ **olm.,** be hurt.

muğlak¹ Obscure; complicated; incomprehensible.

muhabbet¹ Love; affection; friendship; friendly chat. ~ **etm.,** have a friendly chat: ~ **tellalı,** (*soc.*) procurer, pimp. ~**çiçeği**ni, (*bot.*) mignonette. ~**kuşu**nu, (*orn.*) budgerigar. ~**li,** affectionate.

muha·bere Correspondence; communications; (*mil.*) signals service: ~ **etm.,** correspond: ~ **sınıfı,** (*mil.*) signals corps: ~ **vermek (-e),** communicate with s.o. ~ **bereci,** (*mil.*) signaller. ~**bir(lik),** (duties of) correspondent.

muhaceret¹ Emigration.

muhacim Assailant; raider; (*sp.*) striker.

muhacir Emigrant; (*pol.*) (Muslim) refugee. ~ **arabası,** covered four-wheeled wagon. ~**lik,** emigrant status.

muhaddep (*phys.*) Convex.

muha·faza Protection; conservation; preservation: ~ **altında,** (*mil.*) under escort: ~ **etm.,** protect; take care of, keep; preserve. ~**fazakâr(lık),** conservativ·e/(-ism). ~**fız,** *a.* guarding, defending, protecting: *n.* (*mil.*) escort, guard; (*adm.*) custodian: ~ **av uçakları,** (*aer.*) fighter escort: ~ **kıtası,** bodyguard.

muhak·eme (*leg.*) Hearing; trial; judgement: ~ **etm.,** try: ~ **masrafları,** legal costs. ~**kak¹,** *a.*

certain; well-known: *adv.* certainly, without doubt. ~**kık¹,** who verifies/scrutinizes.

muhal¹ Impossible; inconceivable.

muhal·efet¹ Opposition; contrariness: ~ **etm. (-e),** oppose, contest; disagree with: ~ **partisi,** (*pol.*) the Opposition: ~ **şerhi,** counter-statement: ~**ten dolayı (-e),** for contravention of . . .. ~**if,** *a.* opposing; contrary; conflicting; contradictory: *n.* opponent, adversary.

muhallebi = MAHALLEBI.

Muhammed (*rel.*) Prophet Muhammad. ~**i,** Muhammadan, Muslim.

muham·men Estimated. ~**min,** assessor, valuer.

muhammes (*math.*) Pentagon(al); (*lit.*) five-line stanza.

muhar·ebe (*mil.*) Battle; war. ~**i¹p**bi, warrior, combatant.

muharrem (*ast.*) The first lunar month, Muharrem.

muharrer Written.

muharrik¹ (*phys.*) Motor, propulsive; (*fig.*) instigating, agitating.

muharrir Writer, author. ~**lik,** writing, authorship.

muharriş Irritating; itching.

muhasamat¹ Hostilities; war.

muhasara Siege. ~ **etm.,** besiege.

muhas·ebat¹ (*fin.*) Accounts. ~**ebe,** book-keeping, accountancy: ~ **makinesi,** calculator. ~**ebeci(lik),** account·ant/(-ancy).

muhasım Opponent; adversary.

muhasır Besieging; surrounding.

muhasip(lik) Account·ant/(-ancy).

muhassala Result; (*phys.*) resultant.

muhassas (-e), (*fin.*) Assigned/appropriated to. ~ **at¹,** appropriations.

muhassenat¹ Good things; virtues; benefits.

muhat¹ Surrounded; contained.

muhata¹pbi (*ling.*) Person addressed.

muhatara Danger. ~**lı,** dangerous.

muhav·ere Conversation; dialogue: ~ **etm.,** converse. ~**vile,** (*el.*) transformer.

muhay·yel Imagined; imaginary. ~**yile,** imagination; fancy.

muhayyer Choice; optional; on approval. ~ **bırakmak,** leave optional.

muhbir(lik) (Work of) correspondent/reporter/ informant.

muhikki True; right.

muhilli Troubling, spoiling.

muhi¹pbbi Loving, friendly.

muhit¹ *a.* Surrounding; ambient; including. *n.* Circumference; surrounds; atmosphere; circle, milieu; (*med.*) practice. ~ **yapmak,** get to know people.

muh·kem Firm; sound; strong. ~**lis** = HALİS.

muhrik¹ Burning; heart-rending (sound).

muhri¹pbi (*naut.*) Destroyer.

muhtaç In need; indigent.

muhtar *a.* Independent, autonomous. *n.* (*adm.*) Village headman. ~**iyet¹,** independence, autonomy. ~**lık,** headman's post/duties.

muhtasar Concise; abridged. ~ **beyanname,** (*fin.*) monthly tax declaration. ~**an,** in brief.

muhtekir (*fin.*) Speculator, profiteer.
muhtel[i] Spoilt; disturbed.
muhtelif Diverse, various, miscellaneous.
muhtelis Embezzler, pilferer.
muhtelit[i] Mixed; composite. ~ **mahkeme**, (*leg.*, *his.*) mixed court.
muhtemel Possible; probable. ~ **kılmak**, expect: ~ **olm.**, be 'on the cards'/possible: ~**dir ki**, the chances are that . . .. ~**en**, possibly.
muhterem Respected; honoured.
muhteri Inventor.
muhteris Covetous, desirous.
muhteriz Cautious; reserved, timid.
muhteşem Magnificent; majestic.
muhte·va Contents. ~**vi**, containing. ~**viyat**[i], contents.
muhtıra Note; memorandum. ~ **(defteri)**, note-book, diary.
muhzır (*leg.*) Process-server; court-bailiff.
muin Helping, assisting. ~**li**, (*mil.*) recruit with s.o. looking after his family. ~**siz**, having no such helper.
muit[i] (*ed.*, *obs.*) Usher; supervisor.
mujik[i] Russian peasant, moujik.
mukabele Confrontation; reciprocation; reward; retaliation; retort, reply; (*lit.*) collating, comparing; (*rel.*) recitation of the Koran. ~ **etm.**, confront; counter(act); retaliate; reciprocate; retort; collate; resist: ~ **görmek (-le)**, be received with (applause, etc.): ~ **okumak**, recite the Koran: ~**de bulunmak**, return (an act); retort, reply.
mukabele·bilmis[l]**il**[l]i Reprisal; tit-for-tat. ~**ci**, (*adm.*) collator of documents; (*rel.*) Koran reciter. ~**ten**, in return; reciprocally.
mukabil *a.* Facing; opposite; equivalent. *post.* [89] **(-e)** In return for. *n.* Opposite; equivalent; stg. in return; compensation. ~ **hücum**, (*mil.*) counter-attack: ~ **sıklet**, counterweight: ~**inde**, in return.
mukad·dem Previous, before. ~**dema**, previously; in the past. ~**deme**, (*lit.*) preface, introduction.
mukadder Predestined, fated, inevitable. ~**at**[l], destiny; fate: ~**ın istihzası**, the irony of fate.
mukaddes (*rel.*) Holy, sacred. ~ **Kitap**, Bible. ~**at**[l], sacred objects.
mukaffa (*lit.*) Rhymed.
mukallit Imitating.
mukannen Fixed; regular.
mukarenet[i] Drawing near; association; (*ast.*) conjunction.
mukarrer Established; decided; due. ~ **bulunmak**, be decided. ~**at**[l], decisions.
mukassi Oppressive, stuffy.
mukataalı Subject to EVKAF rent.
mukattar (*chem.*) Distilled.
mukavele (*leg.*) Agreement; contract. ~ **yapmak**, sign a contract: ~**ye bağlamak (-i)**, make a contract about stg. ~**li**, settled by agreement. ~**name**, contract document.
mukav·emet[i] Endurance, opposition; (*aer.*) drag; (*phys.*) resistance; strength; (*phil.*) opposition: ~ **etm.**, endure; resist: ~ **koşusu**, (*sp.*) long-distance race. ~**emetçi**, (*mil.*, *pol.*) resistance-fighter.

~**emetli**/ ~**im**, resisting; resistant; enduring; fast (colour).
mukavva Cardboard.
mukavves Curved.
mukavvi (*med.*) Strengthening.
mukay·ese Comparison; (*fin.*) adjudication (of tenders): ~ **etm.**, compare; adjudicate. ~**eseli**, comparative. ~**yet**, written; registered. ~**yit**, (*adm.*) registrar; (*phys.*) recorder.
mukim Who dwells/stays.
mukni[i] Convincing; satisfying.
muk·oza (*bio.*) ~ **(zarı)**, mucous membrane. ~**us**, mucous.
mukta·za Need; requirement. ~**zi**, necessary, required.
muktebes Acquired; borrowed.
muktedir Capable, powerful. ~ **kılmak**, enable: ~ **olm.** **(-e)**, be able to, be capable of.
muktesit (*fin.*) Careful, economical.
mulaj (*art.*, *min.*) Mould; moulding.
mum Candle; wax; (*phys.*) candela, candle(-power). ~ **ağacı**, (*bot.*) candleberry myrtle; wax palm: ~ **dibine ışık vermez**, s.o. influential who neglects to help his relatives: ~ **direk**, upright: ~ **duruşu**, (*sp.*) 'standing' on one's shoulders: ~ **gibi**, very upright; stiff; like new; docile: ~ **ışığı**, candle-light: ~ **kuvveti**, candle-power: ~ **olm.**, become disciplined/ compliant: ~ **söndü**, (*reference to Bektashi rites*) immoral, improper: ~ **yakmak**, (*rel.*) light a candle (in a holy place): ~ **yapıştırmak**, seal with wax; (*fig.*) keep stg. important in mind: ~**a çevirmek**/ **döndürmek**, render disciplined/obedient: ~**a dönmek** = ~ **OLM.**: ~**la aramak**, search diligently for; crave for; miss bitterly.
mum·boyası Wax paint. ~**cilası**, wax-polish. ~**cu**, tallow-chandler; (*mil.*) matchlock-gunman; (*his.*) Janissary officer. ~**çiçeği**[ni], (*bot.*) honeywort. ~**lamak (-i)**, wax; wax-polish; attach a seal to stg. ~**laşım**, (*med.*) cirrhosis. ~**laşmak**, *vi.* become like wax. ~**layıcı**, (*cin.*) waxing machine. ~**lu**, having a candle; waxed: ~ **bez**, cerecloth: ~ **kâğıt**, wax-paper: ~ **kil**, plasticine. ~**lubit**[i], (*ent.*) wax scale. ~**luk**, (*el.*) candle-power; candelabra. ~**yağı**[nı], tallow.
mumya (*rel.*) Mummy; (*fig.*) shrivelled/sallow person. ~**lar müzesi**, waxworks. ~**lamak (-i)**, embalm; mummify. ~**laşmak**, *vi.* be(come) embalmed/mummified.
munafık(lık) Trouble-mak·er/(-ing).
munça[l]**k**[ğı] (*zoo.*) Barking deer.
mundar = MURDAR.
munfasıl Separated.
munhasır Restricted, limited.
munis Familiar; friendly; tame; (*fig.*) suitable.
munkabız Shrivelled; constipated; tongue-tied.
munkalip Changed, transformed.
munsif Just; equitable.
muntazam Regular; tidy; orderly. ~**an**, regularly.
muntazır Waiting expectantly.
munzam Added; additional. ~ **vergi**, (*fin.*) surtax.
murabaha (*fin.*) Usury. ~**cı(lık)**, usurer('s work).
murabba[1] *n.* (*cul.*) Fruit preserve; jam.
murabba[2] (*math.*) Square; (*lit.*) quatrain.

murabutᵘ *(rel.)* Muslim monk/hermit, marabout. ~ **kuşu**ⁿᵘ, *(orn.)* marabou (stork).
murafaa *(leg.)* Trial, hearing.
murahhas(lık) Envoy/delegate('s work/status).
mura·kabe Vigilance; control, supervision; *(rel.)* contemplation: ~ **etm.**, control: ~ **ye dalmak**, meditate. ~ **kı'p**ᵇ¹, controller, supervisor. ~ **kıplık**, supervision.
murana *(ich.)* Moray (eel).
murassa Bejewelled.
mura'tᵈ¹ Wish; intention; aim. ~ **edinmek**, hope, desire: ~ **etm.**, desire; suggest to o.s.: ~ **ta o!**, that's just what is needed: ~ **ına ermek**, attain one's desire.
mur'çᶜᵘ Cold chisel.
murdar Dirty; unclean. ~**ili'k**ᵍ¹, *(bio.)* spinal marrow. ~**lık**, dirt; filth.
muris *(leg.)* Who bequeaths; testator.
Musa Moses. ~ **ağacı**, *(bot.)* fire thorn.
musaffa Purified; clean.
musahabe Conversation.
musahhih(lik) *(pub.)* Proofread·er/(-ing).
musahi'pᵇ¹ *(his.)* Companion, gentleman-in-waiting.
musakka *(cul.)* Mousaka.
musal·la *(rel.)* Place of prayer: ~ **taşı**, stone on which the coffin is placed during the funeral service. ~**li**, *(rel.)* who prays regularly; devout.
musallat¹ Worrying; attacking. ~ **etm. (-i, -e)**, cause to worry: ~ **olm. (-e)**, worry, pester s.o.; attack s.o.
musandıra *(dom.)* Large wardrobe; sideboard.
musanna False; skilfully/artistically made.
musannif *(lit.)* Author; compiler; classifier.
musa'pᵇ¹ Stricken by illness.
musavver Illustrated.
Musevi *(rel.)* *n.* Jew. *a.* Jewish. ~**lik**, Jewishness; Judaism.
Mushaf *(rel.)* A (copy of the) Koran.
musırʳ¹ Insistent; obstinate.
musibet¹ *n.* Calamity; evil. *a.* Ill-omened, unlucky.
musik·ar *(myth.)* A bird that produced music; *(mus.)* pan-pipe. ~**i**, music (in general); *also* = MIZIKA, MÜZİK, SAZ. ~**işinas**, music-lover; musician.
muska Amulet, charm. ~**cı(lık)**, (work of) charm-maker.
muslihane By peaceful means.
muslin *(tex.)* Muslin.
musluk Tap, faucet, cock, spigot; *(sl.)* penis. ~ **taşı**, stone basin under a tap. ~**çu(luk)**, (work of) tap-seller/-repairer; *(sl.)* thief, pickpocket.
muson *(met.)* Monsoon.
mustar Forced, compelled. ~ **kalmak**, be obliged to do stg.
mustarip Agitated; careworn: **(-den)**, suffering from.
mustatil *(math.)* Rectangle.
Musul *pr.n.* *(geo.)* Mosul.
muş *(naut.)* Steam-launch.
-muş *v. suf.* [122, 162] = -Mİş [BULUNMUŞ].
muşamba *(tex.)* Oiled silk; tarpaulin; linoleum; *(mod.)* waterproof, mackintosh. ~ **gibi**, filthy (clothes, etc.).

muşmula *(bot.)* Medlar. ~ **gibi/suratlı**, shrivelleı thing; wrinkled face; 'old fogy'.
muşta Fist; blow with the fist; knuckleduster; (shoeı maker's) iron ball. ~**lamak (-i)**, thump, pound.
muştu Good news. ~**cu**, bearer of good newsı ~**lamak (-i, -e)**, bring good news. ~**luk**, gift tı MUŞTUCU.
mutᵘ Luck; good fortune; happiness.
muta Given; data, information.
mutaassı'pᵇ¹ *a.* Fanatical; bigoted. *n.* Fanatic.
muta·bakat¹ Conformity, agreement; approvaı *(bio.)* accommodation (of eye). ~**bık**¹, conformı ing; agreeing: ~ **kalmak**, agree.
mutaf *(tex.)* Goat's-hair weaver.
mutallaka Divorced woman.
mutant *(bio.)* Mutant.
mutantan Ostentatious.
mutarıza *(pub.)* Parentheses.
mutasarrıf *a.* Owning. *n.* *(his.)* Governor of SANCAK. ~**lık**, his post/jurisdiction.
mutasavver Imagined.
mutasavvıf *(rel.)* Sufi; mystic.
mutasyon(izm) *(bio.)* (Theory of) mutation.
muta'tᵈ¹ Customary; usual. ~ **ım değil**, it's not mʏ habit.
mutatabbi'pᵇ¹ *(med.)* Quack.
mutavaat¹ Submission. ~ **eylemi**, *(ling.)* reflexivı verb.
mutavassıt¹ *n.* Mediator. *a.* Medium; middle.
mutazarrır Injured; suffering loss.
mutçuluk *(phil.)* Eudemonism.
muteber Reputable; *(fin.)* solvent; *(leg.)* valid. ~ **olm.**, be valid. ~**lik**, validity, etc.
mutedil Temperate; moderate; *(phys.)* neutral.
mutekit *(rel.)* Believing; religious.
muteme'tᵈ¹ S.o. reliable/trustworthy; *(adm.)* iı charge of finances. ~ **eli**, 'safe' hand.
mutena Carefully done; select; refined.
muteriz Objecting, opposing.
mutezile *(rel.)* Schismatic Muslim sect.
mutfa'kᵍ¹ Kitchen; cuisine.
mutlak¹ *a.* Absolute; autocratic; unconditional *adv.* Absolutely; certainly; as sure as fate. ~ **ekseriyet**, *(adm.)* absolute majority: ~ **gelecek**, hı is sure to come: ~ **gelmeli**, he *must* come: ~ **hâkimiyet**, autarchy. ~**a**, absolutely; without faiı certainly. ~**iyet**¹, absolutism; autocracy.
mut·lu Lucky, fortunate; happy. ~**luluk**, luck, gooı fortune; happiness: ~ **vermek**, invigorate, enliven ~**main**, tranquil; contented. ~**suz**, unfortunateı unhappy. ~**suzluk**, misfortune.
muttali (-e) Informed; aware (of).
muttarit Regular; uniform.
muttasıf Endowed (with some quality).
muttasıl *a.* Connected; joined. *adv.* Continuously.
muvacehe Confrontation. ~**sinde**, in the presence of; with regard to.
muvafakat¹ Agreement, consent. ~ **etm.** agree/consent to; comply with.
muvaffak Successful. ~ **olm. (-e)**, succeed (in doingı stg.): ~ **olmamak**, fail. ~**iyet**¹, success. ~**ıyetli** successful. ~**ıyetsiz**, unsuccessful. ~**ıyetsizlik** failure.

nuvafık Agreeable; suitable; favourable; like-minded.

nuvahhit Monotheist.

nuvak·kat[i] Temporary; (*ind.*) casual (worker). ~**katen**, temporarily. ~**kit**[i], (*rel.*) mosque time-keeper.

nuvasa·la Communication. ~**lat**[1], arrival.

nuvazaa Collusion; dissimulation. ~**lı**, simulated.

nuvazene Equilibrium, balance. ~**li**, balanced; (*fig.*) equable; level-headed; reliable. ~**siz**, un-balanced; (*fig.*) hesitant; unreliable. ~**sizlik**, im-balance.

nuvazi Parallel; collateral.

nuvazzaf Having a duty; salaried. ~ **hizmet**, (*mil.*) regular service: ~ **kadro**, active list: ~ **subay**, officer on the active list.

nuylu (*mil.*) Trunnion; (*mot.*) hub. ~ **yatağı**, trunnion seating.

nuymul (*orn.*) Marsh-harrier.

nuz (*bot.*) Banana. ~ **gibi olm.**, (*sl.*) be ashamed. ~**giller**, bananas, plantains, Musaceae. ~**culgiller**, (*orn.*) plantain-eaters.

nuzaffer Victorious. ~**iyet**[i], victory.

nuzır Harmful. ~**lık**, harm.

nuzip Tormenting, teasing. ~**leşmek**, *vi.* be teased. ~**lik**, teasing; mischief; practical joke: ~ **etm.**, tease.

nuzlim Dark, gloomy.

nuzmahil[li] Dispersed; annihilated.

nü *particle* [105] = **mi**[1] [GÖRÜLÜR MÜ?]

MÜ = MARMARA ÜNİVERSİTESİ.

nü- *pref. Also* = MU-.

mü- *v. suf. neg.* [110] = -ME-[2] [GÖRMÜYORUM].

nüba·dele Exchange; (*fin.*) barter. ~**dil**, exchang-ing; subject to exchange; (*his.*) Tk. immigrant from Greece settled on land of an exchanged Greek, after 1921-2 war.

nüba·hase Discussion. ~**hat**[1], boasting, glorying.

nübalağa Exaggeration; (*ling.*) superlative. ~ **edatı**, (*ling.*) augmentative: ~ **etm.**, exaggerate. ~**cı**, exaggerator. ~**lı**, exaggerated.

nübarek *a.* Blessed; bountiful; auspicious. *int.* Bless it! ~ **ağzını açmak**, (*iron.*) start speaking evil: ~ **herif!**, (*iron.*) blessed fellow!: ~ **olsun!**, con-gratulations. ~**otu**[nu], (*bot.*) geum, avens.

nüba·reze Single combat; duel. ~**rız**, champion; dueller.

nübaşeret[i] Beginning.

nübaşir(lik) (*leg.*) (Work of) process-server.

nübayenet[i] Divergence, disagreement.

nübeccel Honoured.

nübeddile (*el.*) Transformer.

nüberri[tdi] Refrigerator.

nübeşşir Bringing good news.

nübeyyiz Clerk (making fair copies).

nübrem Inevitable; exigent.

nüca·dele Dispute; struggle; fight: ~ **etm.**, struggle; fight. ~**deleci**, combatant; contestant. ~**hede**, fighting for Islam. ~**hi**[tdi], champion of Islam.

nücamaa (*bio.*) Copulation.

nücavir Neighbour.

nücazat[1] Punishment.

mücbir Compelling. ~ **sebep**, reason of *force majeure*, act of God.

mücehhez Equipped; furnished. ~ **olm.**, carry.

mücella Polished, bright.

mücellit(lik) Book-bind·er/(-ing).

mücerrep Proved, tested.

mücerret *a.* Stripped, bare; simple; abstract; un-married; (*ling.*) nominative. *adv.* Alone; simply.

mücessem Solid.

mücevher·(at[1]**)** Jewel(lery). ~ **balığı**, (*ich.*) jewel-fish: ~ **tarih**, (*obs.*) Arabic chronogram; = EBCET. ~**ci**, jeweller.

mücmel Brief, concise.

mücrim, *a.* Guilty. *n.* Criminal.

mücver (*cul.*) Croquette.

müçtehi[tdi] (*rel.*) Expounder of Islamic law.

müda·faa Defence; resistance: ~ **etm.**, defend. ~**fi**, defender; (*leg.*) defence counsel: (*sp.*) back.

müdahale Interference; intervention. ~ **etm.**, inter-fere; intervene.

müdana (*col.*) Obligation.

müdara Dissimulation; pretended friendship.

müdavele ~ **etm.**, consult: ~**i efkâr**, exchange of views.

müdavi (*med.*) Treating, curing.

müdavim Frequenter, regular visitor.

müddei (*leg.*) *a.* Asserting; claiming. *n.* Claimant; plaintiff; prosecutor. ~**umumi(lik)**, (duties/post/ office of) public prosecutor.

müddet[i] Space of time; period, interval. ~ **tayin etm.**, fix a time/period of delay: ~**i bitmek**, (*fin.*) fall due: ~**in hitamı**, end of the period; expiry. ~**çe**, during the period. ~**siz**, ~ **olarak**, indefinitely.

müdebbir Prudent; far-sighted.

müdekkik[i] Investigating.

müdellel Proved.

müderris Professor; MEDRESE teacher.

müdevven(at[1]**)** (*lit.*) Collected (works).

müdevver Round, circular: (**-den, -e**), transferred.

müdir(lik) = MÜDÜR(LÜK).

müdrik[i] *a.* Understanding; perceiving.

müdrir (*med.*) Diuretic.

müdür (*adm.*) Director; administrator; official in charge of BUCAK; (*ed.*) headmaster. ~ **muavini**, assistant/deputy director: ~**ü çiğneyip umum müdüre çıkmış**, ignoring the director he went straight to the Director-General. ~**e**, woman administrator/director. ~**üyet**[i]/~**lük**, office/ functions of MÜDÜR; directorate; head office.

müebbet Eternal, perpetual; life-long.

müeccel Postponed; adjourned.

müeddep Well-behaved; modest.

müel·lefat[1] (*lit.*) Works, compositions. ~**lif**, author; compiler: ~ **hakkı**, author's rights.

müemmen Assured, safeguarded.

müennes (*ling.*) Feminine.

müesses Founded; established. ~**e**, foundation; establishment; institution; organization.

müessif Sad; regrettable.

müessir Touching, moving; effective, influential; (*chem.*) agent.

müessis Founder, organizer.

müeyyide Corroboration; sanction.

müezzin (*rel.*) Muezzin.
müfekkire (*psy.*) Ability to think.
müferrih Gladdening, exhilarating.
müfessir (*rel.*) Commentator on the Koran.
müfettiş(lik) (Post/duties of) inspector/controller.
müfit Useful; explanatory.
müflis *a.* (*fin.*) Bankrupt; penniless.
müflon (*zoo.*) Moufflon; (*mod.*) loose overcoat lining. ~**lu**, (*tex.*) mohair cloth.
müfredat[1] Details; particulars; detailed inventory. ~ **programı**, (*ed.*) curriculum.
müfret (*ling.*) Singular.
müfrez Separated; detached. ~**e**, (*mil.*) detachment, brigade.
müfrit Excessive; exaggerated.
müfsit Seditious; trouble-maker.
müftehir (-le) Glorying in, proud of.
müfteri Slanderer.
müftü(lük) (*rel.*) (Post/duties of) Muslim jurist; mufti; Muslim religious leader; (*adm.*) provincial director of religious affairs.
müh. = MÜHENDİS(LİK).
mühendis Engineer. ~**hane**, (*mil.*, *his.*) school of gunnery; (*ed.*) school of engineering. ~**lik**, engineering (profession).
müheyya Ready, prepared.
müheyyiç Exciting.
mühim[mi] Important; urgent. ~**mat**[1], (*mil.*) munitions; ammunition. ~**semek** (-i), consider important.
mühlet[i] (*fin.*) Term; respite; delay. ~ **vermek**, grant a delay.
mühlik Dangerous; deadly.
mühmel Neglected; abandoned.
mühr- = MÜHÜR.
mühre Burnisher; ball for polishing paper; (*zoo.*) crawfish shell; (hunter's) decoy. ~**lemek** (-i), polish (paper). ~**li**, polished. ~**senk**[i], (*geol.*) onyx.
mührüsüleyman (*bot.*) Solomon's seal.
mühtedi (*rel.*) Convert (to Islam).
müh·ür[rü] Seal; signet-ring; impression (of seal). ~ **açılması**, (*leg.*) removal of seals: ~ **kazmak**, engrave a seal: ~ **kimde ise Süleyman odur**, whoever is empowered has the authority: ~ **mumu**, sealing wax: ~**ü kaldırmak**, remove the seals: ~**ünü basmak**, affix one's seal; (*fig.*) guarantee the truth of stg.: ~**ünü yalamak**, go back on one's word; not keep an agreement.
mühür·cü(lük) Seal-engrav·er/(-ing). ~**dar**, (*his.*) seal-keeper. ~**lemek** (-i), affix a seal; seal stg. ~**lenmek**, *vp.* ~**letmek** (-i), *vc.* ~**lü**, with a seal; sealed. ~**süz**, without a seal; unsealed.
müjde Good news; gift to MÜJDECİ. ~**ci**, bearer/announcer of good news. ~**lemek** (-i, -e), bring/announce good news. ~**lenmek** (-e), *vp.*
mükâfat[1] Reward; prize. ~ **etm.**, reward. ~**landırmak** (-i), cause to be rewarded.
mükâleme Conversation; (*pol.*) negotiation.
mükedder Sad, grieved. ~ **olm.**, be sad.
mükellef *a.* Adorned, sumptuous, costly; (*fin.*) obliged, liable, taxed. *n.* Tax-payer. ~**iyet**[i], tax liability.

mükemmel *a.* Complete; perfect; excellent. *int* Splendid! ~**en**, perfectly. ~**iyet**[i], perfection.
mükerrer(en) Repeated(ly).
mükevvenat[1] Creatures.
mükeyyifat[1] (*med.*) Intoxicants; stimulants; narcotics.
mükrim Hospitable; kind.
mükte·sebat[1] Acquisitions; attainments. ~**sep**, acquired; earned: ~ **hak**, vested interest; privilege.
mülahaza Thought; observation. ~**sındayım**, I am of the opinion that . . .: ~**sıyla**, in consideration of . . .. ~**t**[1], thoughts; comments: ~ **hanesi**, column for remarks/observations: ~ **hanesini açık bırakmak**, have no definite opinion about s.o.
mülahham Fat; fleshy.
müla·kat[1] *n.* Meeting; interview. ~**ki**, *a.* meeting; interviewing: ~ **olm.** (-e), meet/have an interview with s.o.
mü·layemet[i]/ ~**layimlik** Mildness, docility; softness; (*med.*) looseness of the bowels. ~**layim** suitable; mild; gentle; soft; pliant; (*med.*) loose: ~ **gelmek**, seem reasonable; appeal to s.o.
mülazim Novice; apprentice; (*mil.*, *obs.*) lieutenant.
mülemma *a.* Smeared with. *n.* (*lit.*) Macaronic poem.
mülevves Soiled, dirty.
müleyyin (*med.*) Laxative.
mülga Suppressed; abolished.
mülhak *a.* Added; annexed: (-e), dependent. *n.* (*mil.*) Officer's assistant. ~**at**[1], (*adm.*) dependent districts/regions.
mülhem Inspired; suggested. ~ **olm.** (-den), be inspired by.
mülhit (*rel.*) Atheist; irreligious; heretic.
mülk[ü] Possession; real estate; property; (*adm.*) dominion. ~ **sahibi**, landed proprietor. ~**i**, civil(ian). ~**iye**, (*adm.*) civil service: ~ **mektebi**, (*obs.*) school for civil servants. ~**iyeli**, graduate of such a school. ~**iyet**[i], ownership (of property): freehold.
mülteci Refugee, exile.
mültefit[i] Courteous, kind.
mültezim (*adm.*) Tax-farmer.
mülti·milyoner Multimillionaire. ~**pleks**, multiplex telegraphy.
mümanaat[1] Opposition; prevention. ~ **etm.**, oppose; prevent.
mümarese Skill, dexterity; practice.
mümas (*math.*) Tangent.
mümasil Similar.
mümbit Fertile; fruitful, productive.
mümessil Representative; agent. ~**lik**, representation; agency.
mümeyyiz *a.* Distinguishing; distinctive. *n.* (*ed.*) Examining official; (*adm.*) chief clerk. ~ **lik**, duties/post of MÜMEYYİZ.
mümin (*rel.*) *a.* Believing. *n.* Muslim.
mümkün Possible. ~ **mertebe/olduğu kadar**, as far as possible: ~**se bir an önce**, at your earliest convenience.
mümtaz Distinguished; privileged.
mümteni[i] Impossible; unattainable; (*phil.*) absurd.
münacat[1] (*rel.*) (Silent) prayer/supplication.

münadi Public crier; herald.

müna·kalat[1] Transport; communications. ~ **kale**, transport; transfer.

münakasa (*fin.*) Tendering; adjudication.

münakaşa Dispute; argument. ~ **etm.**, argue; dispute: ~ **etmeğe gelmez (-le)**, it doesn't do to argue with . . .: ~ **götürmez**, indisputable.

münakis Reflected; reflex.

münase·bat[1] (*pol.*) Relations. ~ **bet**[i], suitability; relation, connection; reason, motive; opportunity: ~ **almak**, be suitable/opportune: ~ **almaz**, it is not seemly: ~ **aramak**, seek an opportunity: ~ **düşürmek**, find a suitable occasion: ~ **e girmek**, enter into relations with: ~ **i düşmek**, occur (suitably): ~ **ini getirmek**, arrange (for stg. to happen): ~ **iyle**, in connection with, apropos of: ~ **leri kes(me)mek**, break off//(maintain) connections: ~ **te bulunmak**, be in touch. ~ **betli**, reasonable; suitable; opportune: ~ **münasebetsiz**, take it or leave it! ~ **betsiz**, inopportune; unsuitable; unreasonable; unseemly. ~ **betsizlik**, unseemly/inopportune action.

münasip Suitable; proper; opportune. ~ **görmek**, consider appropriate.

münavebe Alternation; alternating; taking turns; rotation. ~ **ile**, in turn; alternately.

münazaa Dispute; quarrel. ~ **lı**, controversial.

münazara Discussion; argument. ~ **etm.**, debate: ~ **ilmi**, (*phil.*) dialectics.

müncer[ri] Drawn; attracted. ~ **olm.**, result in.

münde·miç Contained in; underlying. ~ **recat**[1], contents. ~ **riç**, inserted; included.

münebbih Rousing, stimulating.

müneccim(lik) Astrolo·ger/(-gy); (*obs.*) astrono·mer/(-my).

münekki·t[di] Critic.

münevver Enlightened; educated; intellectual.

münfe·riden Separately; singly. ~ **rit**, separated; isolated; single, individual: ~ **hapis**, solitary confinement.

münfesih Annulled, abolished.

münhal[i] Soluble.

münhani *a.* Curved. *n.* Curve.

münharif Deviating.

münhasır Restricted: (-e), limited to; confined to. ~ **an**, exclusively.

münhat[tı] (*geo.*) Low-lying.

münhezim Routed; defeated.

Münih *pr.n.* (*geo.*) Munich.

münkariz (*soc.*) Extinct; exterminated.

münkesif (*ast.*) Eclipsed.

münkesir Broken; broken-hearted.

münkir Denying; rejecting; (*rel.*) disbelieving.

münşeat[1] (*lit.*) Compositions, works; letters. ~ **çı**, (*obs.*) letter-writer.

münta·habat[1] (*lit.*) Anthology. ~ **hap**, select; selected. ~ **hi**[1]**p**[bi], (*pol.*) elector.

münte·ha End; limit. ~ **hi**, final; last: ~ **olm.** (-e), end in.

müntehir S.o. who commits suicide.

müntesip (-e) Connected with; belonging to.

müntesir Diffused; published.

münzevi Recluse, hermit.

müon (*phys.*) Muon.

müphem Vague; confused. ~ **iyet**[i], vagueness.

müptedi Beginner; novice.

müptela (-e) Addicted to; in love with. ~ **olm.**, be addicted.

müptezel Common; banal.

müracaat[i] Recourse; application; reference. ~ **etm.** (-e), have recourse/apply/refer to. ~ **çi**, applicant.

müradif (*ling.*) Synonym.

mürai(lik) Hypocri·tical/(-sy).

mürdesen[i]**k**[gi] (*chem.*) Litharge.

mürdolmak (*zoo.*) Die.

mürdüm(eriği[ni]**)** (*bot.*) Damson.

mürebbi (*ed.*) Tutor, trainer. ~ **ye(lik)**, (duties of) (foreign) governess.

müreccah Preferable.

müreffeh(en) Prosperous(ly).

mürekke[i]**p**[bi] 1 *n.* Compound. *a.* Compound; complex, composite. ~ **olm.** (-den), consist of.

mürekke[i]**p**[bi] 2 *n.* Ink. ~ **kesesi**, (*zoo.*) ink sac: ~ **yalamış**, more or less educated: ~ **i kurumadan bozmak**, break (an agreement) very soon.

mürekkep·balığı[nı] (*zoo.*) Cuttlefish. ~ **çı**, (*obs.*) ink-maker/-seller. ~ **lemek (-i)**, ink in; cover with ink. ~ **lenmek**, *vp.* ~ **li**, inky; filled with ink.

müret·tebat[1] (*naut.*) Crew, complement; allocation. ~ **tep**, prepared; invented, concocted; allocated; earmarked for. ~ **ti**[1]**p**[bi], (*pub.*) compositor; typesetter: ~ **hatası**, misprint. ~ **tiphane**, (*pub.*) composing-room. ~ **tiplik**, composing, typesetting.

mürevviç Supporting/publishing (ideas).

müri[i]**t**[di] (*rel.*) Novice; disciple. ~ **lik**, novitiate.

mürşi[i]**t**[di] (*rel.*) Spiritual guide/teacher.

mürteci[i] Reactionary.

mürtefi[i] Elevated, high.

mürtekip Corrupt; taking bribes.

mürtesem (*math.*) Projection.

mürte[i]**t**[ddi] (*rel.*) Apostate (from Islam).

mürur Passage. ~ **iye**, toll. ~ **uzaman**, (*leg.*) prescription, (time) limitation.

müruvvet[i] Generosity; charity; humanity. ~ **e endaze olmaz**, give all you can. ~ **li**, generous, charitable; humane. ~ **siz**, mean; inhumane, cruel.

mürver (*bot.*) Elderberry. ~ **ağacı**, elder-tree.

müsaade Permission; consent; favour; (*aer.*) clearance. ~ **belgesi**, licence. ~ **etm.** (-e), permit; consent to. ~ **kâr**, tolerant.

müsa·baka Competition; contest; race: ~ +, *a.* competitive: ~ **ya girmek**, compete. ~ **bık**, competitor.

müsademe Collision; skirmish. ~ **tamponu**, (*mot.*) bumper: ~ **yayı**, (*rly.*) buffer.

müsadere (*leg.*) Confiscation. ~ **etm.**, confiscate.

müsadif Coinciding.

müsait Permitting; favourable; convenient.

müsakkafat[1] Roofed buildings.

müsamaha(kârlık) Indulgence; tolerance; forbearance. ~ **kâr**, indulgent; tolerant.

müsamere (*soc.*) Evening gathering/entertainment.

müsa·vat[1] Equality. ~ **vi**, equal; equivalent.

müsebbip Causing.

müseccel (*adm.*) Registered.
müseddes (*math.*) Hexagon(al); (*lit.*) six-line stanza.
müsekkin Sedative, calming.
müsellem Incontestable.
müselles (*math.*) Trian·gle/(-gular). ~at¹ (*math.*) trigonometry.
müselsel Consecutive; linked.
müsemma Named.
müsemmen (*lit.*) Eight-line stanza.
müshil (*med.*) Purgative, aperient.
müskirat¹ Intoxicants; drinks.
Müs·lim (*rel.*) Muslim. ~lüman, Muslim: ~ adam, pious; honest: ~ mahallesinde salyangoz satmak, do stg. that 'isn't done'. ~lümanca, in a Muslim way; honestly; honourably. ~lümanlık, Islam; Muslim world.
müs·mir Fruitful; productive; successful.
müspetⁱ Proved; established; (*ling., phys.*) positive. ~ iyon, (*el.*) cation.
müsrif(lik) Extrava·gant/(-gance).
müstacel·(en) Urgent(ly). ~iyetⁱ, urgency.
müstafi Resigned, retired.
müstağni Satisfied; disdainful. ~ olm. (-den), have no need of.
müstahakᵏ¹ Due, merited. ~ olm. (-e), deserve: ~kını bulmak, get one's deserts.
müstahdem *a.* Employed. *n.* Employee.
müstahkem (*mil.*) Fortified.
müstahsil (*ind.*) Producer.
müstahzar *a.* Ready-made. *n.* Patent medicine.
müstai¹tᵈᵈⁱ Clever, capable.
müstakarʳ¹ Settled, fixed.
müstakbel *a.* Future.
müstakil(en) Independent(ly).
müstakim Straight; upright, honest.
müstamel Used; not new.
müstantikⁱ (*leg.*) Examining magistrate.
müstear Temporary, borrowed. ~ ad, (*lit.*) pseudonym.
müstebat Remote; improbable.
müstebit Despotic, tyrranical. ~lik, despotism, tyranny.
müstecir Tenant, renter.
müstefit Profiting. ~ olm. (-den), profit by/from.
müstefreşe Concubine.
müstehase (*geol.*) Fossil.
müstehcen Loathsome; obscene, bawdy. ~ neşriyat, pornography.
müstehlikⁱ Consumer.
müstehzi Cynical, mocking.
müstekreh Disgusting.
müstelzim Requiring; involving.
müstemirren Continuously, perpetually.
müstemleke Dependency, colony. ~ci(lik), colon·ist/(-ialism).
müste·niden Relying on. ~nit (-e), relying/based on.
müstenkif Abstaining.
müstensih *a.* Copying. *n.* Duplicator.
müsterih Content, at ease. ~ etm., set at ease: ~ olm., be at ease.
müstesna Exceptional; excepted.
müsteşar(lık) (*adm.*) (Rank/duties of) councillor; under-secretary; secretary of state.

müsteşrik¹ (*ed.*) Orientalist.
müstevi *a., n.* (*math., obs.*) Plane.
müstevli Invading; predominant; prevalent.
müsteza¹tᵈ¹ (*lit.*) Rhymed addition to each half-line.
müsvedde(lik) (Paper for) rough copy/draft.
-müş *v. suf.* [122, 162] = -mİş [GÖRÜLMÜŞ].
müşa·behetⁱ Resemblance; similarity. ~bih, resembling; similar.
müşahede Observation.
müşahhas Personified; concrete.
müşahi¹tᵈⁱ Observer.
müşareketⁱ Partnership; association. ~ eylemi, (*ling.*) reciprocal verb.
müşarünileyh Aforementioned; the said.
müşa·vere Consultation; counsel. ~vir(lik), (*adm.*) (rank/duties of) counsellor; (*med.*) consultant: ~ mühendis, consulting engineer.
müşebbeh Compared.
müşekkel Huge; imposing.
müşerref Honoured. ~ olm., be honoured; feel it an honour: ~ oldum!, I am honoured to meet you!
müşevves Confused; dubious.
müşevvik Inciting; encouraging.
müşfik Compassionate.
müşir = MÜŞÜR.
müş'ir *a.* Indicating. *n.* (*phys.*) Index, pointer.
müşkül *a.* Difficult. *n.* Difficulty; obstacle. ~ü atlatmak, (*fig.*) turn the corner. ~at¹, difficulties; obstacles: ~ çekmek, meet with difficulties: ~ çıkarmak, raise difficulties. ~e, (*bot.*) type of late-ripening grape. ~ pesent, hard to please; fastidious; exigent.
müşrikⁱ (*rel.*) Polytheist; pagan.
müştakᵏ¹ ¹ *a.* Derived. *n.* Derivative.
müştak¹ ² (-e) *a.* Filled with desire for/to.
müşteki Complaining; disgruntled.
müştemilat¹ Annexes; (*arch.*) extensions.
müşterekⁱ Common; communal, cooperative; collective; joint. ~ bahis, (*gamb.*) tote-betting: ~ borçlu, co-debtor: ~ emniyet, collective security: ~ hakimiyet, condominium: ~ kiracı, co-tenant: ~ merkezli, (*math.*) concentric: ~ mihverli, (*phys.*) coaxial: ~ mülkiyet, joint ownership: ~ nehirler, international rivers. ~en, jointly; mutually; collectively.
müşteri¹ *n.* (*fin.*) Customer; buyer; client. ~ tutmak, attract customers.
Müşteri² *pr.n.* (*ast.*) Jupiter.
müşür(lük) (*mil.*) (Rank/duties of) Field Marshal.
müt'a Benefit; (*soc.*) Shiite temporary marriage.
mütaa- = MÜTEA-.
mütalaa Studying; observation; thought, opinion. ~ etm., study, read: ~sında bulunmak, be of the opinion that.
mütareke (*mil.*) Armistice.
müteaddit Many; several.
müteaffin Putrid; stinking.
müteahhi¹tᵈⁱ (*fin.*) Contractor; purveyor. ~e vermek, put out to contract.
müte·akıben Subsequently. ~akıp, following, subsequent; successive.
müteallik¹ Related to; concerning.

müteammim General; in common use.
mütearife Axiom.
mütebahhir Very erudite, learned.
mütebaki *a.* Remaining. *n.* Remainder; balance.
mütebasbıs Flattering; fawning, cringing.
mütebeddil Changeable; undecided.
mütebessim Smiling.
mütecanis Of the same kind; homogeneous.
mütecasir Daring; presumptuous.
mütecaviz *a.* Exceeding; exorbitant: (**-den, -i**), more than. *n.* (*pol.*) Aggressor.
mütecessis Curious; inquisitive.
mütedair Concerning.
mütedavil (*fin.*) Current; valid. ~ **para**, currency: ~ **sermaye**, working capital.
mütedeyyin Religious.
müteessif Grieved; sorry, regretful. ~ **olm.** (**-e**), be sad about.
müteessir (**-den**) Affected by; hurt by. ~ **etm.**, affect: ~ **olm.**, regret.
mütefekkir Thinker.
mütefennin Scientist.
müteferrik[1] Separated; miscellaneous. ~ **a**, (*fin.*) petty cash; sundries; (*adm.*) police department for petty offenders.
mütegallibe Oppressors; usurpers.
mütehakkim Despotic; domineering.
mütehammil (**-e**) Supporting.
müteharrik[i] Moving; portable; (*eng.*) drive, driving: (**-le**), working with.
mütehassıs(lık) (Work of) specialist; consultant; connoisseur.
mütehassis Moved (by emotion).
mütehavvil Changing; variable.
mütehayyir Amazed; bewildered.
mütehevvir Impetuous; furious.
müteheyyiç Excited.
mütekabil Reciprocal; mutual. ~ **iyet**[i], reciprocity: ~ **esası üzerine**, on a reciprocal basis.
mütekait Retired; pensioner.
mütekâmil Perfect(ed); developed.
mütekâsif Thick; condensed; concentrated.
mütekebbir Proud, haughty.
mütekellim *a.* Speaking. *n.* (*ling.*) First person.
mütemadi(yen) Continuous(ly); continual(ly). ~ **cereyan**, (*el.*) direct current.
mütemayil Inclined; apt.
mütemayiz (**-le**) Distinguished for.
mütemeddin Civilized.
mütemekkin Settled; established.
mütemerkiz Concentrated; assembled.
mütemmim *a.* (*math.*) Supplementary/complementary (angle); (*phil.*) complementary. *n.* (*ling.*) Complement.
mütenakız Contradictory.
mütenasip Proportional; symmetrical.
mütenavip Alternating. ~ **cereyan**, (*el.*) alternating current.
mütenazır Corresponding; symmetrical.
mütenebbih Vigilant; on one's guard.
müteneffir (**-den**) Disgusted with.
mütenekkiren *adv.* Incognito.
mütenevvi[i] Of various kinds.

müteradif (*ling.*) Synonymous.
müterafik Concurrent.
müterakim Accumulated.
müterakki Progressive.
mütercim (*ling.*) Translator.
mütereddi Degenerate; depraved.
mütereddit Hesitant; undecided.
mütesanit Mutually supporting; joint (responsibility).
müteselli Comforted. ~ **olm.**, console.
müteselsil In continuous succession; uninterrupted.
müteşebbis Enterprising; with initiative.
müteşekkil Formed.
müteşekkir Thankful, grateful.
mütetebbi Investigating, researching.
mütevakkıf (**-e**) Dependent on.
mütevali Consecutive.
mütevaris Inherited, hereditary.
mütevazı Humble, modest.
mütevazi Parallel.
mütevazin Balancing.
müteveccih (**-e**) Turned towards, facing; aimed at; favourable to. ~ **en**, towards.
müteveffa Deceased; the late.
mütevehhim Imagining (fears, etc.).
mütevekkil Believing in Providence, resigned.
mütevelli Administering a VAKIF.
mütevellit Born; caused; resulting.
müteverrim (*med.*) Consumptive, tuberculous.
müteyakkız Vigilant.
mütezayit Increasing.
müthiş Terrible, catastrophic; enormous; excessive. *int.* Extraordinary!
müttefik[i] *a.* Agreeing; allied. *n.* Ally. ~ **an**, unanimously.
mütte·hiden Unitedly, unanimously. ~ **hit**, united; unanimous; corporate.
müvekkil Client.
müvellidülhumuza (*obs.*) Oxygen.
müvellidülma (*obs.*) Hydrogen.
müvellit Begetting; generating.
müverrih Historian, chronicler.
müvesvis Apprehensive, suspicious.
müvezzi[i] Distributor.
müyesser Facilitated; practicable; helped by God.
müz ~ **ler**, (*myth.*) the Muses.
müz. = MÜZİK.
müza·heret[i] Help, support. ~ **hir**, helping, assisting.
müzahrefat[i] Filth.
müza·kerat[i] (*fin.*) Negotiations. ~ **kere**, discussion, conference: ~ **etm.**, talk over, discuss. ~ **kereci**, (*ed.*) tutor.
müzayaka Hardship; straits. ~ **ile geçinmek**, subsist with difficulty.
müzayede Auction.
müze Museum; gallery. ~ **müdürü**, curator. ~ **ci**, museum founder//attendant. ~ **cilik**, museology. ~ **lik**, museum-piece; (*fig.*) queer; antiquated.
müzebzep In utter confusion.
müzehhep Gilded; gilt.
müzekker (*ling.*) Masculine.
müzekkere (*adm.*) Memorandum, note; (*leg.*) warrant.

müzevir Mischief-maker. ~**lik**, knavery: ~ **etm.**, make trouble.

müzeyyen Decorated.

müziç Annoying, vexatious.

müzi¹kᵍⁱ (Western style) music; concert. ~ +, *a.* Music(al): ~ **okulu**, *conservatoire*, school of music: ~ **yönetmeni**, (*cin.*, *th.*) musical director.

müzik·al *a.* Musical: *n.* (*th.*) musical comedy; (*cin.*) musical film. ~**bilimci(lik)**, musicolo·gist/(-gy).

~**çi/müzisyen**, music-lover; musician. ~**hol**, (*th.*) music-hall. ~**li**, ~ **güldürü**, (*th.*) musical comedy. ~**sever**, music-loving.

müzmin (*med.*) Chronic. ~**leşmek**, *vi.* become chronic.

Mv. = (*ch.s.*) MENDELEVYUM; (*adm.*) MUAVİN. ~ **Hst.** = MEVKİ HASTANESİ.

MV = MOTOR VAPURU.

N

N, n [ne] Seventeenth Tk. letter, N.

N, n. = (ch.s.) AZOT; (geo.) NEHİR; (phys.) NEWTON; (ling.) NİDA; (geo.) (north).

-n¹ v. suf. [106] 2nd sing. of İDİ/İSE [İDİN; İSEN].

-n² n. suf. [39] = -İN² [BABAN; KUTUN].

-n-³ v. suf. [149] = -İN-⁵ [BELLENMEK; ÇALKANMAK].

-n-⁴ buffer letter in n. suf. [29, 40] = -NDE(N); -NİN [BABASINDAN; ANNENİN].

na int. (vulg.) There!; there it is!; take it! ~ kafa!, what a fool I/he was!; what am I thinking about!: ~ sana!, so much for you!; there, take that!

na- neg. pref. Dis-, mis-, un- [NAHOŞ].

Na. = (ch.s.) SODYUM.

naˡaşᵃˑşı Corpse; bier.

naˡatᵃˑtı (lit.) Eulogy (of the Prophet Muhammad).

nabe·ca Inopportune. ~ dit, invisible. ~ kâr, useless. ~ mahal, untimely. ~ mevsim, premature.

nabˡızᶻ¹ (bio.) Pulse. ~ yoklamak, (fig.) check on s.o.'s aims/feelings: ~ ına bakmak/~ ını yoklamak, (med.) feel s.o.'s pulse: ~ ına girmek, win s.o.'s favour: ~ (ın)a göre şerbet vermek, handle s.o. with tact: ~ ını tutmak, take s.o.'s wrist (to feel the pulse). ~ gir, tactful, diplomatic.

na·caˡkᵍ¹ (carp.) Small axe. ~ car, carpenter.

na·çar Without a remedy; of necessity; helpless. ~ çiz, insignificant; modest, humble. ~ çizane, humbly. ~ dan, rude, uncouth; ignorant. ~ danlık, rudeness; ignorance.

nadas (agr.) Field ploughed and left fallow. ~ a bırakmak, leave fallow. ~ lık, a. fallow.

na·dide Never seen before; rare; curious. ~ dim, regretful, contrite: ~ olm. (-e), regret stg. done. ~ dir¹, n. (ast.) nadir. ~ dir², a. rare, unusual: ~ toprak madeni, (geol.) rare earth mineral. ~ dire, rarity; witty anecdote. ~ diren, rarely.

nafaka Subsistence; livelihood; (leg.) maintenance allowance; alimony. ~ bağlamak (-e), assign a subsistence allowance: ~ sını temin etm., earn one's living. ~ lanmak, vp. be ensured a living.

nafıa Public works. ~ mühendis(liğ)i, civil engineer/ (-ing): ~ Vekâleti, (obs.) Ministry of Public Works.

nafiⁱ Useful; profitable; beneficial.

nafile Useless; in vain, to no purpose. int. It's no use!; don't persist! ~ yere, uselessly, in vain.

nafiz Penetrating; (fig.) influential.

naftalin (chem.) Naphthalene. ~ lemek (-i), sprinkle/ protect with naphthalene. ~ lenmek, vp.

nagana (live.) Nagana.

nağme (mus.) Tune, song; note; (fig.) affected words. ~ yi değiştirmek, (fig.) change one's tune.

nah int. (vulg.) = NA.

na·hakᵏ¹ Unjust; iniquitous: ~ yere, unjustly, unfairly. ~ hif, thin, emaciated; weak, fragile.

nahˡivᵛⁱ (ling.) Syntax.

nahiye (adm.) Region; sub-district. ~ +, a. Regional; local.

nahoş Disagreeable; unpleasant; unwell. ~ luk, unpleasantness.

nail Who attains/obtains. ~ olm. (-e), attain; obtain: ~ i şeref olm., have the honour of . . . .

naiˡpᵇⁱ (adm.) Substitute; regent. ~ lik, regency.

nakarat¹ (mus.) Refrain; (fig.) harping, nagging.

nakavt (sp.) Knock-out. ~ olm., be counted out.

nakd- = NAKİT. ~ en, in cash; for ready money. ~ i, cash; in ready money.

nakıs a. Deficient; defective; (math.) minus; below zero. n. Minus sign (–). ~ a, deficiency, defect.

nakˡışşı (art.) Design; drawing; picture; (tex.) embroidery; decoration. ~ işlemek, embroider. ~ çı(lık), embroider·er/(-y). ~ lamak (-i), embroider.

nakˡızᶻ¹ (leg.) Annulment; violation.

nakˡilˡⁱ Transport; removal; (adm.) transfer; (el.) conduction; (lit.) narration; translation. ~ kafilesi, (mil.) convoy: ~ sandığı, container: ~ tekerleği, castor wheel: ~ vasıtaları, means of transport.

nâkil a. Transporting; (adm.) transferring; (el.) conducting; (lit.) narrating. n. (el.) Conductor; (lit.) narrator. ~ iyetⁱ, (el.) conductivity.

nakˡitᵈⁱ Cash; money; ready money.

nak·kare (mil., Or. mus.) Large kettle-drum. ~ karhane, (his.) ruler's band.

nakkaş Artist; illuminator of manuscripts; decorator. ~ lık, decoration; illumination.

nakl·en By tradition; by transfer: ~ yayın, (rad.) live broadcast. ~ ˡetmekᵉᵈᵉʳ (-i), carry, transport; transfer; (el.) conduct; (lit.) relate, narrate; translate: vi. move, change one's abode. ~ i¹ n. = NAKİL. ~ i², a. related to transport; traditional: ~ mazi, (ling.) past indefinite: ~ yekûn, (fin.) brought/ carried forward. ~ iyat¹, means of transport; (mil.) transport; (lit.) traditional knowledge. ~ iye, means of transport; transport expenses, carriage: ~ gemi/uçağı, (mil.) transport ship/plane: ~ ödenecek, (fin.) carriage forward: ~ ödenmiş, carriage paid: ~ senedi, bill of lading, way-bill: ~ ücreti, fare. ~ iyeci(lik), (work of) transporter/ carrier/shipper/forwarding agent. ~ iyesiz, carriage free.

nakş- = NAKIŞ. ~ ˡetmekᵉᵈᵉʳ (-i, -e), decorate; design.

Nakşibendi(lik) (rel.) Nakshibendi dervish/(sect).

nakz- = NAKIZ. ~ en, (leg.) by annulment; in violation. ~ ˡetmekᵉᵈᵉʳ (-i), annul, quash; violate; contradict.

nal Horseshoe. ~ ları atmak/dikmek, (sl.) die.

nal·banˡtᵈⁱ Shoeing-smith, farrier. ~ bantlık,

horse-shoeing, farriery. ~**bur**, hardware-dealer, ironmonger. ~**burunlu**, ~ **yarasagiller**, (*zoo.*) horseshoe bats. ~**ça**, iron tip/heel (on boots). ~**döken**, stony road.

nâlet = LÂNET. Cross-grained, peevish. ~ **olsun!**, damn him!

Na.lı = NUMARALI.

nalın Pair of pattens/clogs. ~**cı**, patten-/clog-maker: ~ **keseri**, adze; (*fig.*) egoist: ~ **keseri gibi kendine yontmak**, think only of one's own advantage. ~**sı**, ~ **kas**, (*bio.*) soleus muscle.

nalla·mak (**-i**) Shoe (a horse); (*sl.*) kill. ~**nmak**, *vp.*

nam Name; renown; reputation; quality. ~ **almak/ kazanmak**, become famous, make a name for o.s.: ~ **salmak/vermek**, acquire a reputation: ~**a muharrer/yazılı**, (*fin.*) to the order of . . .; registered in the name of . . .: ~**ı diğer**, pseudonym; alias: ~**ı nişanı kalmamak**, leave no trace; perish utterly: ~**ı ve hesabına**, in the name and for the account of . . .: ~**ına**, in the name of; *post.* [93], by/in the way of: ~**ına kızarmak**, blush for s.o.: ~**ına söz söylemek**, answer for s.o.: ~**ıyla**, under the name of . . .: ~**ıyla maruf**, known as . . . .

na·mağlup Invincible. ~**mahdut**, boundless. ~**mahrem**, not related (and so able to marry); not having access to the harem. ~**makul**, unwise. ~**malum**, unknown.

namaz (*rel.*) Ritual worship; prayer. ~ **bezi**, head-cover worn by women when praying: ~ **kıldırmak**, conduct the prayers: ~ **kıl(ın)mak**, perform the ritual prayers of Islam: ~ **seccadesi**, prayer rug: ~ **vakti**, prayer-time: ~**ı kılındı**, his burial service has been read; (*sl.*) he's as good as dead.

namaz·gâh Open-air place for public prayers. ~**lık**, prayer-rug, etc. ~**sız**, (woman) menstruating, canonically unclean.

namdar Famous, celebrated.

name *n.* Letter; love-letter; document.

-name *n. suf.* Written (*esp. leg.*) document [KANUN-NAME].

namer·t·di *a.* Unmanly; cowardly; cruel; vile. *n.* S.o. despicable; coward. ~**e muhtaç olm.**, be forced to rely on s.o. one despises: ~**e muhtaç olmamak**, depend on/be under an obligation to no one. ~**çe**, cowardly, unmanly; contemptible. ~**lik**, cowardice; vileness; cruelty.

namlı Renowned; famous.

namlu (Gun-)barrel; (sword-)blade. ~ **matkabı**, (*eng.*) D-bit.

namus Honour; good name; rectitude; honesty. ~ **belası**, need to consider one's reputation: ~ **sahibi**, a man of honour: ~ **yoksulu**, devoid of honour: ~**um hakkı için**, upon my honour: ~**una dokunmak**, dishonour; hurt one's pride; violate (a woman): ~**unu lekelemek**, stain one's honour.

namus·kâr/ ~**lu** Honourable; honest, upright: ~ **olm.**, have clean hands. ~**luluk**, honourableness; uprightness. ~**suz**, dishonest; dishonourable. ~**suzca**, dishonourably. ~**suzluk**, dishonourableness.

na·müsait Unfavourable. ~**mütenahi**, endless, un-ending; infinite.

namze·t·di Candidate; betrothed person; (*mil.*) cadet. ~**lik**, candidacy.

nan Bread; livelihood. ~**ı aziz**, one's daily bread.

nanay (*sl.*) There isn't (any).

nane (*bot.*) Mint; peppermint. ~ **likörü**, (*cul.*) crème de menthe: ~ **suyu**, peppermint water: ~ **yemek**, commit a blunder/indiscretion.

nane·li (*cul.*) Containing/tasting of peppermint. ~**molla**, timid/useless fop. ~**ruhu·nu**, (*cul.*) oil of peppermint. ~**şekeri·ni**, peppermint (sweet).

nani·k·gi Long nose, snook. ~ **yapmak**, cock a snook.

nankör Ungrateful. ~**lük**, ingratitude.

nano- (*math.*) Nano-.

nanpare Piece of bread; livelihood. ~**ye muhtaç olm.**, be destitute.

nansu·k·gu (*tex.*) Fine soft cotton fabric, nainsook.

nap (*geol.*) Nappe.

nar (*bot.*) Pomegranate. ~ **ağacı**, pomegranate tree: ~ **bülbülü**, (*orn.*) Eurasian robin: ~**çiçeği**: ~ **gibi**, (*cul.*) well-roasted.

nâr Fire; hell-fire; pain, injury. ~ **opali**, (*geol.*) fire opal: ~**a yakmak**, injure s.o.: ~**ına yanmak** (**-in**), suffer for s.o.'s misdeeds.

nara Cry, shout. ~ **atmak**, yell, shout out.

nar·cıl (*bot.*) Coconut. ~**çiçeği·ni**, bright scarlet, vermillion: ~ **kotinga**, (*orn.*) Guianan cock-of-the-rock. ~**denk**, (*cul.*) pomegranate/damson syrup.

nardin (*bot.*) Nardus, mat-grass.

narenc (*bot.*) Seville orange. ~**iye**, citrus fruits. ~**iyecilik**, citriculture.

nargile Narghile, hookah, water-pipe.

nargiller (*bot.*) Pomegranate family.

narh (*fin.*) Officially-fixed price. ~ **koymak**, fix prices for essential goods.

nârıbeyza White heat, incandescence.

narin Slim, slender; tender, delicate. ~**lik**, slimness, slenderness; elegance, delicacy.

narko·tik *a., n.* (*med.*) Narcotic. ~**z**, narcosis: ~ **vermek/** ~**lamak** (**-i**), narcotize, anaesthetize. ~**zlayan**, narcotic. ~**zcu**, anaesthetist.

narsis·izm/ ~**lik** (*psy.*) Narcissism.

nartaş(lar)ı (*geol.*) Garnet (group of minerals).

nas·sı (*phil.*) Dogma. ~**laştırmak**, *vi.* dogmatize.

nasb- = NASIP. ~**edilmek**, *vp.* ~**ı etmek·eder** (**-i, -e**), (*adm.*) nominate, appoint.

nasıl [74] *a.* What kind/sort?; whatever sort. *adv.* How? *int.* What did you say?; how is it? ~ **isterseniz**, as you wish: ~ **ki**, *conj.* [215] however; just as; as a matter of fact: ~ **olup da . . .**, how is it that . . .: ~ **olursa olsun**, in any case: ~**sa**, in any case; somehow or other: ~**sam öyleyim**, I am what I am: ~**sın(ız)?**, how are you?

nas·ı·p·bı Nomination; appointment.

nasır (*bio.*) Wart; corn; callosity, callus. ~ **bağlamak**, get warts/corns; = ~ LAŞMAK.

nasır·cı(lık) Chiropod·ist/(**-y**). ~**lanmak**, *vi.* get warts/corns. ~**laşmak**, *vi.* become calloused; (*fig.*) become callous. ~**lı**, warty with corns; calloused; (*fig.*) callous.

nasihat·i Advice, counsel; admonition. ~ **etm.**, advise: ~ **yollu**, by way of advice: ~**ini tutmak** (**-in**), follow/take s.o.'s advice.

nasi·p·bi Lot, share, portion; one's lot in life. ~

almak, (*rel.*) be initiated (into the Bektashi dervish order): ~ **almak (-den),** enjoy: ~ **etm.,** destine s.o. for stg.: ~ **etmemek,** deny s.o. stg.: ~ **olm.,** be destined, happen, have the opportunity; achieve (stg. good), be blessed with: ~ **olursa,** if fate wills it: ~ **im olmadı,** I was not destined to . . .: ~ **ini almak/** ~ **lenmek,** *vi.* achieve one's destiny.

Nasrani *n.* Christian.

naş Corpse; bier/coffin with a corpse.

naşi (-den) *post.* Because of; on account of.

naşir *a.* Spreading; publishing. *n.* Publisher.

natamam Incomplete.

natıka Fluency; eloquence. ~ **lı,** eloquent, fluent.

natır(lık) (Work of) servant in the women's HAMAM.

nativizm (*phil.*) Nativism.

NATO = (*North Atlantic Treaty Organization*).

natron (*chem.*) Natron; native sodium bicarbonate.

natukᵘ Eloquent; fluent.

natura Nature; characteristics; constitution.

natür·alistⁱ Naturalist. ~ **alizm,** naturalism. ~ **el,** natural; inherent. ~ **ist**ⁱ, naturist. ~ **izm,** naturism. ~ **mort**ᵘ, (*art.*) still life.

navar (*aer.*) Flight control system.

navçağan (*bot.*) Type of thorn apple, Datura metel.

naviga·syon Navigation. ~ **tör,** navigator.

navlun (*naut.*) Charter fees; freight. ~ **sözleşmesi,** charter-party: ~ **ücreti,** freight(age).

naylon *n.* (*chem., tex.*) Nylon. *a.* (*fig.*) Artificial; fake(d). ~ **fatura,** (*fin.*) falsified invoice.

naz Coquetry; coyness; whims; disdain. ~ **etm./** **yapmak/** ~ **a çekmek,** be coy (about doing stg.); pretend not to be keen on stg.: ~ **niyaz ile yapmak,** do stg. only after much entreaty: ~ **ı geçmek (-e),** one's whims be tolerated; be *persona grata*: ~ **ını çekmek,** tolerate s.o., put up with s.o.'s peculiarities: ~ **la büyütmek,** spoil, coddle: ~ **ü naim içinde,** in comfort and luxury.

nazar Look; regard; consideration; the evil eye. ~ **atfetmek/atmak (-e),** glance at: ~ **boncuğu,** bead worn against the evil eye: ~ **değmek/** ~ **a gelmek,** the evil eye to strike one: ~ **değmesin!,** *int.* may God preserve it! (said when praising stg.); touch wood!; keep your fingers crossed!: ~ **a atmak,** take into account: ~ **da olm.,** be in (s.o.'s) favour: ~ **dan düşmek,** fall from favour: ~ **ı değmek (-e),** overlook s.o.; cause illness, etc. by the evil eye: ~ **ı dikkat/** **itibara almak (-e),** take into account/consideration: ~ **ı dikkati celbetmek (-e),** call attention to stg. ~ **ı dikkatini celbetmek (-in),** attract s.o.'s attention: ~ **ımda,** in my view, as for me: ~ **ında,** according to him, in his view: ~ **ıyla bakmak (-e),** look at it in a particular way.

nazaran (-e) *post.* [87] According to; in respect of, with regard to; in proportion to; seeing that.

nazari *a.* Theoretical; abstract; academic; doctrinaire. ~ **yat**ⁱ, theories. ~ **yatçı,** *n.* doctrinaire; theorist. ~ **ye,** theory, doctrine. ~ **yeci,** theorist.

nazarlık Stg. hung/worn against the evil eye.

naz·ende/ ~ **enin** Graceful; delicate; amiable; petted, spoilt; (*pej.*) whippersnapper.

nazⁱ**ım**ᵐⁱ (*lit.*) Versification; verse.

nâzım *a.* Arranging. *n.* (*eng.*) Regulator; (*lit.*) versifier, arranger. ~ **plan,** master plan.

nazır (-e) *a.* Overlooking; facing. *n.* Spectator; inspector; (*adm., obs.*) Minister. ~ **lık,** (*adm.*) Ministry.

Nazi (*pol.*) Nazi. ~ **zm,** National Socialism, Nazism.

nazikⁱ Delicate; easily damaged, critical; agreeable; affable; kind; polished, refined, courteous.

nazik·âne/ ~ **çe** Delicately; affably; courteously. ~ **leşmek,** *vi.* behave courteously; (*med.*) take a turn for the worse, become critical. ~ **lik,** delicacy; refinement; polished manner(s); courtesy.

nazil Descending; alighting. ~ **olm.,** descend; alight.

nazir Anything opposite/parallel; match, like, similar. ~ **e,** similar thing; (*lit.*) imitative poem.

naz·lanmak *vi.* Behave affectedly/coquettishly; be coy; show contempt; feign reluctance. ~ **lı,** coquettish; coy; spoilt; reluctant; ticklish (job); delicate (flower): ~ **davranmak,** be/show o.s. disinterested. ~ **lılık,** coquetry; coyness; reluctance, etc.

nazm- = NAZIM. ~ **en,** in verse.

Nb. = (*ch.s.*) NİYOPYUM.

-nce/-nca *adv. suf.* [194] = -CE [KENDİSİNCE, BUNCA].

-nci/-ncı *a. suf.* [82] = -İNCİ [ELLİNCİ; ALTINCI].

-nç *vn.* [222] = -İNÇ [ÜŞENÇ].

Nd. = (*ch.s.*) NEODİM.

-nde(n)/-nda(n) *n. suf.* [40] = -DE(N) [BABASINDA(N)].

ne¹ The Tk. letter N.

ne² *a., pron., adv.* [72] What?; which; whatever; how. ~ **aksilik,** how awkward/disappointing: ~ **âlâ,** what a good thing; (*iron.*) what a shame!: ~ **âlâ memleket!,** (*iron.*) how wonderful!: ~ **âlemdesiniz?,** how are you getting on?: ~ **alıp veremiyor,** what's the matter with him?; what's he after?: ~ **arar (-de),** there isn't any: ~ **arıyor (-de)?,** what does he want?: ~ **asıl** = NASIL: ~ **bahsine istersen girerim,** I'll bet you anything you like/my bottom dollar: ~ **biçim!,** how?: ~ **bu çehre?,** why do you make/pull such a face?: ~ **buyurdunuz?,** I beg your pardon, what did you say?: ~ **buyururlar?,** what is your opinion?; (*iron.*) what have you got to say about that?: ~ **çare?,** what can one do?: ~ **çare ki . . . ,** inevitably; it can't be helped but . . . .: ~ **çıkar!,** what does it matter!: ~ **çiçek olduğunu bilirim,** I know the sort of fellow he is: ~ **de olsa,** still; all the same; after all (is said and done): ~ **demek!,** what does it mean?; (disapproval) how so!; (politely) not at all!; certainly you may!: ~ **demek olsun?,** of course not!: ~ **dedim de . . .?,** why on earth did I . . .?: ~ **demeye?,** why?: ~ **denir/dersin?,** words fail me!: ~ **denli,** what/ (-ever) sort: ~ **desen kabulümüz,** I'll do whatever you say: ~ **devleti!,** what good luck!: ~ **diye?,** why?; what's the idea of . . .?: ~ **ekersen onu biçersin,** as you sow so shall you reap: ~ **ettiyse kendine etti,** whatever he did he only hurt himself: ~ **eylemek,** what to do?: ~ **fayda?,** what's the use?: ~ **gezer,** by no means, not at all; not likely!; out of the question: ~ **gibi?,** what sort of?; how?: ~ **gibi hallerde?,** under what conditions?: ~ **güne duruyor?,** why not use it?; why not do this?: ~ **günlere kaldık,** what (evil) times we live in:

~ **güzel!**, how lovely!: ~ **hacet?**, what's the need?: ~ **haddimize!**, how could I presume to do such a thing!; I wouldn't dare!: ~ **halin varsa gör!**, all right, go your own way!: ~ **halteder ağanın beygiri!**, what a mess!: ~ **haltediyorsun?**, what the devil are you doing?: ~ **haltetmeğe oraya gittin?**, what the devil did you go there for?: ~ **hikmetse . . .**, it's strange that . . .: ~ **için**, for what reason; why: = NİÇİN: ~ **idiği belirsiz bir adam**, a man of doubtful antecedents/no consequence: ~ **imiş!**, what does it matter!: ~ **inat!**, what obstinacy!: ~ **ise**, luckily!; well, never mind; anyway: ~ **iyi**, how nice!: ~ **kadar?**, how much?; however much; how!: ~ **kadar olsa**, after all: ~ **karın ağrısıdır . . .**, or whatever it's name is; or whatever he calls himself: ~ **karışıyorsunuz?**, what are you interfering for?: ~ **keyif, ~ cümbüş!**, how enjoyable!; this is the life for me!; (pej.) what a miserable show!: ~ **ki**, it is not that . . .: ~ **kumaş/mal/meta olduğu anlaşıldı**, it's clear now what a rogue he is: ~ **malum?**, how do you know?: ~ **mene**, (col.) what sort of thing: ~ **münasebet!**, by no means!; not a bit of it!; no fear!; not likely!; what's that got to do with it!: ~ . . . ~ . . . = NE . . . NE . . .: ~ **olacak!**, the inevitable has happened; it's no use worrying; we might as well; (pej.) what do you expect?; what of it!: ~ **oldu/olur ~ olmaz**, just in case: ~ **olduğumu bilemedim**, I lost control of myself: ~ **oldum delisi olmak**, be a parvenu: ~ **oldum dememeli ~ olacağım demeli**, don't boast of your present state unless you're sure of the future: ~ **olduysa bana oldu**, I got the brunt of it: ~ **olup bitiyor?**, what's happening?: ~ **olursa olsun**, come what may: ~ **olur(sun)!**, please!: ~ **oluyor?**, what's happening?: ~ **ömür şey!**, how wonderful!; how beautiful!: ~ **pahasına olursa olsun!**, whatever the cost may be!; for all the world!: ~ **satıyorsun?**, what are you prating about?: ~ **siktirir?**, (vulg.) what the hell's he after?: ~ **söylüyorsun**, be careful what you're saying!; is it true?: ~ **sularda?**, in what condition?: ~ **şekilde?**, how?, in what manner?: ~ **şüphe?**, what doubt can there be?; most certainly!: ~ **vakit?**, when?: ~ **var (ki)**, what . . .; however: ~ **var ~ yok**, whatever there is; whatever you possess: ~ **var ~ yok?**, what's the news?: ~ **veçhile olursa olsun**, in whatever way: ~ **verseler ona şakir ~ kılsalar ona şad**, whatever happens he is grateful and contented: ~ **yaparsın/ yapmalı ki**, it can't be helped but . . .: ~ **yapıp yapıp**, in some way or other; by fair means or foul: ~ **yazık!**, alas!: ~ **yazık ki**, what a pity that: ~ **yönden?**, in what respect?: ~ **yüzle geldin?**, how have you the face to come? ~ **yüzle söyleceğim?**, how shall I bring myself to tell him?: ~ **yüzünden**, for what reason?; on what pretext?: ~ **zaman?**, when?: ~ **zamandır . . .**, how long ago it is since . . .; for a long time past: ~ **zannettiniz!**, you bet!

ne-: ~**den(se)** = NEDEN: ~**ler**, many things: ~**ler çektiğimi bir ben bilirim (bir de Cenabı Hak)**, only (God and) I know what I suffered: ~**ler ~ler de maydanozlu köfteler**, ah, I could tell you a lot of stories; wouldn't you like to know!: ~**ler olmuş**, what happened!: ~**me gerek/lazım?**, what's that to me?; what do I care?: ~MELAZIMCI: ~**ne gerek/**

lazım?, why worry?, it doesn't concern you!: ~**niz var?**, what's ailing you?: ~**ye?**, to/for what?; why?; ~**yi?**, what (specific thing)?: ~**ylerseniz**, etc. = ~ EYLEMEK.

ne . . . ne (de) . . . conj. [207] Neither . . . nor . . .; not . . . either . . . or . . .. ~ **altını bırakmak ~ üstünü**, leave no stone unturned: ~ **izi belli ~ tozu**, he disappeared without a trace: ~ **kokar ~ bulaşır**, harmless but useless: ~ **od var ~ ocak**, in dire poverty: ~ **sakala minnet ~ bıyığa**, avoid being under obligations to anyone: ~ **sen sor ~ de ben söyleyim**, ask no questions and you'll be told no lies: ~ **selam ~ sebah**, without as much as saying good-morning; ignoring everyone: ~ **Şam'ın şekeri ~ Arab'ın yüzü**, in spite of its attractions I want nothing of it: ~ **şap ~ şeker**, neither one thing nor the other: ~ **şaşın ol basıl, ~ taşkın ol asıl!**, be moderate in all things: ~ **şiş yansın ~ kebap**, so that neither party suffers damage.

-ne n. suf. [66] = -HANE [ECZANE, POSTANE].

Ne. = (ch.s.) NEON.

nebat[1] (bot.) Plant; vegetation. ~**at**[1], pl. plants; botany: ~ **bahçesi**, botanical garden. ~**atçı**, botanist. ~**i**, vegetable; botanical.

neb·evi Concerning prophets; prophetical. ~**i**, prophet.

nebul·a (ast.) Nebula. ~**öz**, nebulous.

nebze Particle; bit. ~ **(bir)**, a little bit.

necabet[i] Nobility. ~**li**, noble.

necaset[i] (rel.) Impurity, canonical uncleanness; (bio.) excrement.

Necaşi, pr.n. (his.) Negus; Emperor of Abyssinia.

necat[1] Salvation; safety. ~ **bulmak**, escape.

nece In what language?

neceftaşı[n1] (geol.) Rock-crystal, Derbyshire spar.

neci Of what trade/profession? ~**dir?**, what is his trade?, what does he do (for a living)?

neci·p[bi] Noble, of high lineage. ~ **gaz**, (chem.) noble gas.

nedamet[i] Regret, remorse. ~ **duymak/getirmek**, regret.

nedbe (bio., med.) Scar, cicatrice.

neden n. Cause; reason. adv. Why?; for what reason? ~ **sonra**, quite a long time after: ~**ini açıklamak**, explain why: ~**iyle**, in connection with; on the occasion of: ~**le**, in . . . way: ~**ler**, (leg.) grounds: ~**se**, somehow or other; for some reason or other.

neden·bilim (phil.) Aetiology. ~**sel**, causal. ~**sellik**, (phil.) causation, causality. ~**si**, excuse. ~**siz(lik)**, causeless(ness).

nedim Boon companion; (his.) courtier; court jester.

nedret[i] Rarity. ~ **kesp etm.**, become infrequent.

nefaset[i] A being exquisite/beautiful/rare.

nefer Individual; person; (mil.) private soldier.

nefes Breath; moment; spell; (rel.) Bektashi hymn; (sl.) hashish. ~ **aldırmamak**, give no rest/respite: ~ **almak**, breathe, take a breath; rest; breathe freely again: ~ **borusu**, (bio.) air vessel: ~ **çekmek**, take a whiff (tobacco, etc.); smoke hashish: ~ **darlığı**, shortness of breath; (med.) asthma: ~ **darlığı çeken**, asthmatic: ~ **etm.**, cure by breathing on s.o. and casting a spell: ~ **kesilmesi**, asphyxia: ~ **(-tion)**: ~ ~ **e**, panting; out of breath: ~ **tüketmek**, talk o.s. hoarse: ~ **vermek**, expire, breathe out: ~**i daralmak**, be short of breath: ~**i kesilmek/ tutulmak**, be unable to breathe; (*med.*) have an attack of asthma: ~**i kesilmiş**, breathless, out of breath: ~**ine güvenen borazancı başı olur!**, by all means do it if you think you can!

nefes·lemek (-i) = ~ ETM. ~**lenmek**, *vi.* breathe; take a rest; breathe with relief. ~**leşmek**, (*sl.*) smoke hashish. ~**li**, (*mus.*) played by blowing; able to hold one's breath: ~ **alet/çalgı**, (*mus.*) wind instrument. ~**lik**, ventilator; vent-hole; blow-hole; time taken in breathing: ~ **canı kalmış (bir)**, he's quite worn out; he looks wretched.

nef ha Puff; breath; (trumpet) blast; pleasant smell.
nefir (*Or. mus.*) Trumpet; horn; (*med.*) tube; clamour; (*mil.*) battle-cry.
nefis[1] *a.* Excellent; exquisite; rare; (*cul.*) appetizing; dainty. ~**e**, exquisite/beautiful object.
nef 'is[si 2] *n.* Soul; life; self; essence; physical/sexual desire; (*bio.*) seminal fluid. ~ **genişlemek**, feel more at ease: ~ **körletmek**, take the edge off one's appetite/desires: ~**i emmare**, lusts of the flesh: ~**i İstanbul**, Istanbul proper (not the suburbs): ~**ine düşkün**, self-indulgent: ~**ine mağlup olm.**, be overcome by one's desires: ~**ine yediremememk**, be unable to bring o.s. (to do stg.): ~**ini beğenmek**, think a lot of o.s.: ~**ini öldürmez**, he will not give way: ~**ini tutma**, continence: ~**ini yenmek**, master o.s. ~**perest**, selfish.
nef 'iy[yi] (*adm.*) Banishment; exile; deportation; (*ling.*) negation; (*phil.*) denial.
nefret[i] Disgust; detestation; hate; abhorrence, loathing; animosity. ~ **duymak**, feel disgust, etc.: ~ **etm. (-den)**, detest, abhor, loathe; feel aversion for: ~ **verici**, detestable, loathsome, abominable.
nefr·idyum (*zoo.*) Nephridium. ~**it**[i], (*geol.*) nephrite; (*med.*) nephritis. ~**oloji**, (*med.*) nephrology.
nefs- = NEFİS[2].
nefsani Sensual, carnal; rancorous, malignant, spiteful. ~**yet**[i], spite, hatred; sensuality.
neft[i] (*geol., chem.*) Naphtha. ~**i**, dark blackish green. ~**yağı**[nı], naphtha.
nefy- = NEFİY. ~**edilmek**, *vp.* (*adm.*) be exiled; (*ling.*) be made negative. ~**'etmek**[eder] **(-i)**, (*adm.*) exile; deport; deny; (*ling.*) make negative.
negatif *a.* (*math.*) Minus; (*phys.*) negative. *n.* (*cin.*) Negative. ~ **elektrikli**, electro-negative: ~ **sayı**, minus number: ~ **yönelim**, (*bot.*) negative tropism.
nehar·en By day. ~**i**, (*ed.*) day-pupil//school.
neh'ir[ri] River. ~ **kuyruksallayanı**, (*orn.*) white wagtail: ~ **yatağı**, river bed/channel.
neh'iy[yi] Prohibition; obstacle, restraint.
nekadar = NE KADAR.
nekahet[i] (*med.*) Convalescence. ~ **evi**, convalescent home: ~**te olm.**, convalesce: ~**te olan**, convalescent.
nekbet[i] Misfortune; disgrace.
nekes Mean, stingy. ~**lik**, stinginess.
nekre S.o. who makes witty remarks.
nektar (*myth./bot.*) Nectar. ~ **emengiller**, (*orn.*) sunbirds: ~ **kuşu**, (*orn.*) bronze pygmy sunbird.
neli'k[ği] True nature of stg.
nem Moisture; damp(ness); humidity. ~ **geçmez**,

damp-proof: ~ **kapmak**, absorb moisture; get damp; (*fig.*) be easily offended: ~ **niceliği**, (*phys.*) moisture content: ~**e yönelim**, (*bot.*) hygrotropism.
nema Growth; increase; (*fin.*) interest; profit. ~**landırmak (-i)**, make profitable. ~**lanmak**, *vi.* (*fin.*) grow (with interest).
nemcil (*bot.*) Hygrophilous. ~ **bitki**, hygrophyte.
Nemçe (*geo., his.*) Austria(n).
nem·çeker (*chem.*) Hygroscopic. ~**denetir**, hygrostat. ~ **geçirmez**, moisture-proof.
nemelazımcı Indifferent. ~**lık**, indifference.
nemf (*bio.*) Nymph.
nem·lendirici Humidifier. ~**lendirmek (-i)**, humidify; moisten, damp(en). ~**lenmek**, *vi.* become humid/moist/damp; (*chem.*) deliquesce. ~**letmek (-i)**, make moist, etc. ~**li**, humid, moist, damp. ~**ölçer**, (*phys.*) hygrometer.
nemru'l[du] *pr. n.* (*his.*) Nimrod. *a.* Cruel; very obstinate/contrary. ~**luk**, cruelty, tyranny; obstinacy: ~**u tutmak**, have a fit of obstinacy.
Nemse = NEMÇE. ~ **arpası**, (*cul.*) pearl barley: ~ **böreği**, (*cul.*) meat pasty.
nen Thing; object. ~**sel**, material.
neo·dim (*chem.*) Neodymium. ~**gen**, (*geol.*) neocene. ~ **klasisizm**, (*art.*) neoclassicism. ~**litik**, (*his.*) neolithic. ~**lojizm**, (*ling.*) neologism. ~ **misin**, (*med.*) neomycin. ~ **n**, (*chem.*) neon: ~ **balığı**, (*ich.*) neon tetra: ~ **lamba//tübü**, (*el.*) neon lamp//tube. ~ **plazma**, (*med.*) neoplasm. ~**pren**, (*ind.*) neoprene. ~**realist**, (*art.*) neorealist. ~**realizm**, neorealism. ~**zoik**, (*geol.*) neozoic.
nep·tunyum (*chem.*) Neptunium. ~**tün**, *pr. n.* (*myth., ast.*) Neptune.
ner·de(yse) = NEREDE(YSE). ~**den** = NEREDEN.
nere *n.* [199] What place?; what part?; whatsoever place.

nerede, where?; where!; far from it!; not likely!: ~ **akşam orada sabah**, he'll sleep where he can: ~ **bu bolluk?**, that's a bit stiff, isn't it?: ~ **çokluk orada bokluk**, too many people spoil a party, etc.; too many cooks spoil the broth: ~ **hareket orada bereket**, activity brings prosperity: ~ **ise**, before long: ~ **kaldı!**, well, what about it!: ~ **kaldı ki . . .**, how much less . . .; let alone that . . .: ~ **. . . ~ . . .**, there is no comparison; they are poles apart: ~ **olursa olsun**, anywhere; wherever you like.

nereden, from where?; whence?; wheresoever; how?; why?: ~ **aklınıza geldi?**, why on earth did you . . .?: ~ **başıma sardın (-i)**, why did you saddle me with this?: ~ **bileyim!**, I'm blest if I know!: ~ **geldi?**, where did he come from?: ~ **geldi!**, why the devil did he have to come!: ~ **nereye**, for some reason or other; I don't quite know why: ~ **söyledim!**, why on earth did I say that!, how did I come to say that!

nere-: ~**deyse**, before long; as usual: ~**lerde geziyor!**, what on earth is he about: ~**li**, coming from what place: ~**lisiniz?**, where are you from?: ~**m**, what part of me?: ~**n**, what part of you?: ~**si**, what place?; which part?

nereye, to what place?; whither?; to whatever place. ~ **giderse gitsin**, let him go where he will; wherever he goes: ~ **gitsen okka dörtyüz dirhem**, certain things/people are the same everywhere.
nergis (*bot.*) Narcissus. ~ **zambağı**, belladonna lily. ~ **giller**, daffodil family, Amaryllidaceae.
neritel (*geo.*) Reclaimed land, polder.
nervür (*mod.*) Piping; (*eng.*) flange; (*aer.*) rib.
nese'p[bi] Family; ancestry; genealogy. ~ **esası**, (*leg.*) principle of heredity. ~ **i gayri sahih**, of uncertain parentage; illegitimate: ~ **i sahih**, legitimate: ~ **i tashih etm.**, legitimize. ~ **en**, by descent.
nes'iç[ci] (*tex.*) Weaving; web; tissue.
nes'ih[hi] Commonest form of Arabic script/type.
nes'il[li] Descendants; generation; family.
nes'ir[ri] (*lit.*) Prose. ~ **ci**, prose-writer.
nesne Thing; anything; product; (*phil.*) object; (*ling.*) direct object. ~ **merceği**, (*ast.*) object glass: ~ **öbeği**, (*ling.*) object phrase. ~ **leş(tir)me**, *vn.* (*phil.*) materialization. ~ **leş(tir)mek**, *vi./(vt.)* materialize.
nesnel *a.* Material; physical; (*phil.*) objective. ~ **ci/** (**-lik**), (*phil.*) objectiv·ist/(-ism). ~ **leş(tir)me**, *vn.* (*phil.*) objectivation. ~ **leşmek**, *vi.* be(come) objective. ~ **lik**, objectivity.
nesr- = NESİR. ~ **en**, in prose.
Nesturi (*rel.*) Nestorian Christian. ~ **lik**, Nestorianism.
neşe Slight intoxication; gaiety, merriment; joy. ~ **si yerinde**, he is in a good humour: ~ **sine payan yoktu**, his joy was unbounded: ~ **sini kırmak**, depress.
neşe·lendirmek (-i) Render merry; put in a good humour; slightly intoxicate. ~ **lenmek (-e, -den)**, grow merry; be in a good humour; be(come) slightly drunk. ~ **li**, cheerful; merry; in good humour. ~ **siz**, out of sorts; thoughtful; anxious. ~ **sizlik**, anxiety, worry; the blues.
neşet[i] A coming into existence; adolescence. ~ **etm.**, originate; grow up; (*ed.*) leave school. ~ **li**, appearing; starting; (*ed.*) graduating.
neşide (*lit.*) A popularly recited poem; verses.
neş'ir[ri] A spreading broadcast; (*pub.*) publishing; publication; promulgation, dissemination; (*rad.*) broadcasting. ~ **hürriyeti**, freedom of the press.
neşr- = NEŞİR. ~ **edilmek**, *vp.* ~ **en**, by way of publication. ~ **'etmek**[eder] (**-i**), spread abroad; publish; circulate; disseminate; (*rad.*) broadcast. ~ **iyat**[ı], *pl.* publications; (*rad.*) emission.
neşter (*med.*) Bistoury, lancet.
neşvünema Growth, development. ~ **bulmak**, grow and flourish.
net[i] *a.* (*phys.*) Clear, distinct, sharp; (*math.*) net. ~ **ağırlık**, net/tare weight: ~ **kazanç**, net/clear profit.
ne·tameli Ill-omened; sinister; best avoided; accident-prone. ~ **tekim** = NİTEKİM.
netice Consequence; effect; result; conclusion; (*math.*) corrollary. ~ **i kelam**, in short; in conclusion: ~ **si . . .**, it all adds up to . . .: ~ **si olarak**, as a result of . . .: ~ **ye iktiran etm.**, be brought to a conclusion: ~ **ye varmak**, reach a conclusion.
netice·lendirmek (-i) Bring to an end/conclusion; finish. ~ **lenme**, *vn.* ~ **lenmek**, *vi.* culminate; come

to an end; finish. ~ **siz**, unfinished; useless; inconclusive.
neuzübillah God help us!; God forbid!; a whited sepulchre.
neva (*Or. mus.*) Tune; melody.
nevale Portion; food; meal. ~ **yi düzmek**, prepare food. ~ **çin**, ~ **olm.**, (*obs.*) eat a snack. ~ **lenmek** (**-den**), *vi.* take a taste of stg.
nevazil (*med.*) Cold in the head. ~ **olm.**, have a cold.
nev·bahar Spring. ~ **civan**, youth. ~ **eser**, (*Or. mus.*) compound melody. ~ **ha**, lament. ~ **hager**, hired mourner.
nev'i[i] Species; sort, variety, kind. ~ **beşer**, the human race: ~ ~, of various kinds. ~ **'i şahsına münhasır**, of its own kind, *sui generis*.
nev'ir[ri] Complexion. ~ **i dönmek**, change one's mood; become moody/angry.
nevmi't[di] Without hope; in despair. ~ **i**, despair.
nev·ralji (*med.*) Neuralgia. ~ **rasteni**, neurasthenia. ~ **roloji**, neurology. ~ **ron**, neuron. ~ **ropat**[ı], neuropath. ~ **roz**, neurosis.
nevruz (*ast.*) Persian New Year's Day (22 March). ~ **iye**, (*cul.*) sweetmeat offered on that day. ~ **otu**[nu], (*bot.*) common toadflax.
Nevyork (*geo.*) New York.
nevza't[dı] Newly-born (child).
ney (*bot.*) Reed; (*Or. mus.*) flute. ~ **zen**, flute-player: ~ **bakışlı**, looking sidelong/askance.
ney·e = NE; NİYE. ~ **lemek** = NE EYLEMEK.
neza·fet[i] Cleanliness. ~ **het**[i], purity; decency.
nezaket[i] Delicacy; refinement; courtesy, good breeding; matter requiring delicate treatment. ~ **kesp etm.**, (matter) become delicate/critical: ~ **payısı olarak**, out of politeness: ~ **le**, courteously.
nezaket·en As a matter of courtesy. ~ **li**, refined, delicate. ~ **siz**, discourteous; curt. ~ **sizlik**, discourtesy; curtness.
nezaret[i] Prospect, view; inspection, supervision; superintendence; (*adm.*) administration; direction; (*obs.*) Ministry; (*leg.*) custody. ~ **altında**, under surveillance; on probation: ~ **etm. (-e)**, superintend, direct, inspect: ~ **e almak**, take into custody. ~ **hane**, (*leg.*) custodial/remand prison.
nezd- = NEZT.
nez'etmek[eder] (**-i**) Tear away; remove; withdraw.
nez'if[fi] (*med.*) Haemorrhage, bleeding.
nezih Decent, pure (in character); quiet/pleasant (place).
nez'ir[ri] (*rel.*) A vowing/devoting; vow; votive offering.
nezle (*med.*) Cold in the head; catarrh. ~ **olm.**, catch a cold. ~ **otu**[nu], (*bot.*) pyrethrum.
nezr- = NEZİR. ~ **'etmek**[eder], (*rel.*) vow; promise to give.
nez't[di] Vicinity of a person. ~ **inde**, in his/its view: ~ **inizde**, near you; in your opinion.
nıkris (*med.*) Gout.
-nıl- *vp. suf.* [150] = -NİL- [BAŞLANILMAK].
-nın *n. suf.* [29] = -NİN [BABANIN].
nısf- = NISIF. ~ **en**, half; in half. ~ **ınnehar**, (*ast.*) meridian; midday.
nısfiye (*Or. mus.*) Small flute.

nıs'ıf[f1] *a.* A half. ~ **daire**, semicircle: ~ **kutur**, radius: ~ **küre**, hemisphere.

nışadır (*chem.*) Salammoniac; ammonia. ~ **kaymağı**[n1], ammonium carbonate. ~ **ruhu**[nu], liquid ammonia.

-nız *n. suf.* [39] = -İNİZ [BABANIZ].

Ni. = (*ch.s.*) NİKEL.

nice *a., pron., adv.* [74] How many?; how many!; many a . . .; how?; however many; howsoever. ~ **adamlar**, how many men . . .!; many a man: ~ ~, very many: ~ **olur?**, how will it be?; what will happen?: ~ **senelere!**, many happy returns! (*greeting on feast-days*).

nice·l Quantitative: ~ **çözümleme**, (*chem.*) quantitative analysis. ~ **lemek (-i)**, quantify. ~ **leyici**, quantifier. ~ **lik**, quantity: content. ~ **(lik)sel**, quantitative. ~ **m**, (*nuc.*) quantum.

niçin *adv.* [74] For what?; why? ~ **ci**, s.o. always asking 'why?'.

nida Cry, shout; (*ling.*) interjection, exclamation. ~ **etm.**, shout, proclaim; exclaim.

nifak[1] Discord; enmity; strife; hypocrisy, insincerity. ~ **sokmak**, stir up trouble; make mischief.

niha·i Final, last, ultimate. ~ **le**, (*dom.*) mat (under plates). ~ **ven'**[t]di, (*Or. mus.*) a very old melody.

nihayet[i] *n.* End; extremity. *adv.* Finally; at last; at most. ~ **bulmak**, come to an end: ~ **derecede**, extremely: ~ **kafama dank dedi ki**, finally it dawned on me that . . .: ~ **vermek (-e)**, bring to an end; put an end to. ~ **siz**, endless; infinite; countless.

nihil·ist[i] (*pol.*) Nihilist. ~ **izm**, nihilism.

Nijerya (*geo.*) Nigeria. ~ +, *a.* Nigerian. ~ **lı**, *n.* (*ethn.*) Nigerian.

nikâh Betrothal; marriage; marriage portion (paid by bridegroom). [*It is the leg./rel. ceremony, making the couple* ~ LI; *it is followed by the soc.* DÜĞÜN *making them* EVLİ]. ~ **düşmek**, (*leg., rel.*) the marriage be possible: ~ **etm. (-e)**, betroth/marry (the woman): ~ **kıymak**, perform the marriage ceremony: ~ **ı kaçmak**, the marriage be annulled.

nikâh·lamak (-i) Marry (the woman). ~ **lanmak (-e, -le)**, *vi.* become betrothed/married. ~ **lı**, betrothed; (*leg., rel.*) married. ~ **sız**, unmarried: ~ **yaşamak**, cohabit (though unmarried).

nika'p[b1] (*mod.*) Veil with eyeholes; mask.

nikbet[i] Misfortune; disgrace.

nikbin *a.* Optimistic. *n.* Optimist. ~ **lik**, optimism.

nikel (*chem.*) Nickel. ~ **çelik//gümüşü**, (*min.*) nickel-steel//-silver: ~ **kaplama/~ aj**, nickel-plating: ~ **kaplı**, nickel-plated. ~ **lemek (-i)**, nickel(-plate).

nikotin (*chem.*) Nicotine. ~ **ik**, nicotinic.

nikriz (*Or. mus.*) Very old melody.

niktitant (*bio.*) ~ **zar**, nictitating membrane.

nil[1] *n.* Indigo; (*bot.*) indigo plant.

Nil[2] *pr.n.* (*geo.*) River Nile. ~ **balçık balığı**, (*ich.*) E. African lungfish: ~ **bülbülü**, (*orn.*) common Nile bulbul: ~ **timsahı**, (*zoo.*) Nile crocodile: ~ **turna balığı**, (*ich.*) sacredfish: ~ **varanı**, (*zoo.*) Nile monitor.

-nil-/-nıl- *vp. suf.* [150] *Forming the 'double' passive of certain verbs* [DENİLMEK].

nilsbohriyum (*chem.*) = HAFNİYUM.

nilüfer (*bot.*) Water-lily. ~ **giller**, water-lily family, Nymphaeceae.

nim Half; semi. ~ **resmi**, (*adm.*) semi-official.

nim·bostratus (*met.*) Nimbostratus. ~ **bus**, nimbus.

nimet[1] Blessing; good fortune; benefaction; favour; food. ~ **i (ayağıyla) tepmek**, spurn a piece of good luck. ~ **şinas**, grateful.

nimfa (*bio.*) = NEMF.

-nin/-nın/-nun/-nün *n. suf.* (*after a vowel*) [29] = -İN[1] [ANNENİN; ÖNCÜNÜN].

nine Grandmother, granny; 'mother'.

ninni (*mus.*) Lullaby, cradle-song.

nipel (*eng.*) Nipple; adaptor.

nirengi (*geo.*) Triangulation. ~ **noktası**, landmark; benchmark.

nisai Pertaining to women; womanish. ~ **ye(ci)**, (*med.*) gynaecolo·gy/(-gist).

nisan April. ~ **balığı**[m], April fool('s trick).

nisa'p[b1] (*adm.*) Quorum.

nispet[i] Relation; proportion, ratio; comparison; relationship; spite, defiance. ~ **eki**, (*ling.*) suffix of relationship [TARİHİ; KURŞUNİ]: ~ **etm.**, attribute; compare; act spitefully: ~ **kabul etmemek**, not be comparable: ~ **vermek**, say/do stg. out of spite: ~ **ine**, out of spite; in defiance: ~ **le**, in comparison with.

nis·petçi Spiteful; defiant. ~ **peten (-e)**, *post.* [88] in proportion to; in comparison with: *adv.* relatively; out of spite, spitefully. ~ **petli**, proportional, in proportion; symmetrical. ~ **petsiz**, out of proportion; asymmetrical. ~ **petsizlik**, disproportion. ~ **pi**, proportionate; proportional; comparative; relative: ~ **temsil**, (*pol.*) proportional representation. ~ **piyet**[i], relativity.

niş (*arch.*) Niche.

nişaburek (*Or. mus.*) Old compound melody.

nişan Sign; mark; indication; (*med.*) scar; (*mil.*) target; (*soc.*) order, decoration, medal; distinction; (token of) engagement/betrothal. ~ **almak**, (*mil.*) take aim; be awarded a medal, etc.: ~ **atmak**, shoot, fire: ~ **halka/yüzüğü**, engagement ring: ~ **koymak**, make a mark: ~ **takmak**, confer a medal: ~ **vermek (-den)**, bear a resemblance to; (-e) award a medal to: ~ **yapmak**, arrange an engagement: ~ **a atmak**, shoot at a target: ~ **dan dönmek/~ ı bozmak**, break off an engagement.

nişan·cı (*mil.*) Marksman; a good shot; (*his.*) official who affixed the Sultan's TUĞRA to documents; (*ast.*) Sagittarius. ~ **cılık**, marksmanship. ~ **e**, sign, mark. ~ **gâh**, butt, target; sighting device (of gun): ~ **dürbünü**, telescopic sight. ~ **ge'l**[ç]ci, device for drawing parallel lines. ~ **lamak (-i, -le)**, sign, mark; aim at; betroth/engage s.o. to s.o. ~ **lanmak**, *vi.* become engaged; be betrothed. ~ **lı**, fiancé(e), betrothed. ~ **lılık**, engagement. ~ **taşı**[m], stone used as a target/marking a great shot.

nişasta (*chem., cul.*) Starch; cornflour; farina. ~ **buğdayı**, small-grained wheat with high starch content. ~ **lı**, farinaceous.

nite *adv.* (*obs.*) [215n.] How. ~ **kim/netekim**, *conj.* [214] just so/as; in just the same way.

nite·l Qualitative: ~ **çözümleme**, (*chem.*) qualitative analysis. ~ **leme**, *vn.* qualification; description:

~ +, *a.* qualificatory: ~ **belirteci**, (*ling.*) adverb of manner: ~ **sıfatı**, (*ling.*) descriptive adjective, adjective of quality. ~ **lemek (-i)**, qualify, limit; describe. ~ **lendirme**, *vn.* (*adm.*) description; qualification. ~ **lendirmek (-i)**, qualify; describe; give the quality. ~ **lenmek**, *vp.* be qualified/described: *vi.* assume the quality. ~ **leyici**, qualifying; specific. ~ **lik**, quality, grade; status, position, capacity; characteristic: ~ **denetimi**, (*ind.*) quality control. ~ **likli**, qualified; having the quality. ~ **liklilik**, superiority, superlative quality. ~ **(lik)sel**, qualitative. ~ **liksiz**, lacking quality; defective, faulty. ~ **liksizlik**, defectiveness.

nitr·asyon (*chem.*) Nitration. ~ **at¹**, *n.* nitrate: ~ +, *a.* nitro-. ~ **atlaşma**, nitrification. ~ **ik**, nitric. ~ **ikasi¹t**ᵈⁱ, nitric acid. ~ **il**, nitrile. ~ **i¹t**ᵈⁱ, nitrite.

nitro- (*chem.*) Nitro-. ~ **gliserin**, nitro-glycerine. ~ **jen**, nitrogen. ~ **selüloz**, nitro-cellulose.

nitrür (*chem.*) Nitride. ~ **leme**, *n.* nitriding. ~ **leyici**, *a.* nitriding.

ni·velman Levelling; surveying. ~ **vo**, surveyor's level.

niyabet¹ Acting as substitute; regency.

niye Why?; for what reason?

niyet¹ Resolve; intention; (*rel.*) vow; slip of paper with s.o.'s 'fortune' on it. ~ **çekmek**, have one's fortune told (by drawing slips of paper): ~ **etm.**, resolve; intend, contemplate: ~ **kuyusu**, wishing-well: ~ **tutmak**, when consulting a fortune-teller concentrate on some problem: ~ **i bozmak**, change one's mind: ~ **i bozuk**, with evil intention: ~ **inde bulunmak**, have the intention.

niyet·çi Fortune-teller (with slips of paper). ~ **lenmek (-e)**, intend. ~ **li**, having . . . intention(s); (*rel.*) fasting: ~ **yim**, I'm fasting.

niyopyum (*chem.*) Niobium, columbium.

-niz¹ *v. suf.* [107] *2nd pl. of* İDİ *and* İSE [İDİNİZ, İSENİZ].

-niz² *n. suf.* [39] = -İNİZ [ANNENİZ].

niza¹ Quarrel, dispute. ~ **etm.**, contend, dispute. ~ **cı**, contentious; quarrelsome. ~ **lı**, disputed (matter).

nizam Order; regularity; law; regulation; system. ~ **a getirmek/koymak**, put in order. ~ **en**, according to law; legally. ~ **i**, legal; regularized. ~ **iye**, (*his.*, *mil.*) Regular Army: ~ **kapısı**, main entrance of barracks. ~ **lı**, in order; regular; legal. ~ **name**, (*adm.*) regulation(s); (*leg.*) code. ~ **sız**, in disorder; irregular; illegal. ~ **sızlık**, disorder; irregularity; illegality.

No. = (*ch.s.*) NOBELYUM; NUMARA(LI).

Nobel ~ **ödülü**, Nobel prize. ~ **yum**, (*chem.*) nobelium.

nobran Arrogant; discourteous, churlish, ill-bred. ~ **lık**, arrogance; discourtesy.

noda (*agr.*) Clamp (of straw).

nodul Spike (on a goad). ~ **lamak (-i)**, goad; (*fig.*) goad, incite. ~ **lanmak**, *vp.*

Noel (*rel.*) Christmas. ~ **ağacı**, Christmas tree: ~ **baba**, Father Christmas, Santa Claus: ~ **gecesi**, Christmas Eve.

Nogay (*ethn.*) Tk. tribe in N. Caucasia. ~ **ca**, (*ling.*) their language.

no·hudi Chick-pea colour. ~ **hu¹t**ᵈᵘ, (*bot.*, *cul.*)

chick-pea: ~ **oda bakla sofa**, a small-roomed house.

nokra (*live.*) Warble, tumour (in cattle). ~ **sineği**, (*ent.*) warble fly.

noksan *a.* Deficient; defective; missing. *n.* Deficiency; defect; shortcoming. ~ **ı ikmal etm.**, make good a deficiency. ~ **lık**, deficiency, etc.

nokta Point; dot; spot; speck; subject, point; place; (*ling.*) full stop; point; (Morse) dot; (*mil.*) isolated sentry; military/police post. ~ **biraz karanlık (bu)**, this point/matter is rather obscure: ~ **kaynağı**, (*eng.*) spot weld: ~ **koymak**, bring to an end, finish: ~ **olm.**, (*sl.*) get lost: ~ **(zımbası)**, (*eng.*) centre-punch: ~ **i nazar**, point of view: ~ **i nazardan (bu)**, from this point of view: ~ **sı** ~ **sına**, exactly, in every way: ~ **sını koymak**, dot: ~ **yı kapalı geçmek**, pass over a point without discussion.

nokta·cı(lık) (*art.*) Pointill·ist/(-ism). ~ **lama**, *vn.* (*ling.*) punctuation: ~ **imleri**, punctuation marks. ~ **lamak (-i)**, dot; (*ling.*) punctuate, point. ~ **lı**, dotted; (*ling.*) punctuated, pointed; speckled: ~ **virgül**, (*ling.*) semi-colon. ~ **sel**, point. ~ **sız**, un-punctuated, unpointed.

No.lu = NUMARALI.

nom·anklatür (*ling.*) Nomenclature. ~ **inal**, (*fin.*) nominal. ~ **inal·ist/(-izm)**, (*phil.*) nominal·ist/(-ism). ~ **inatif**, (*ling.*) nominative.

nomsuzluk Lawlessness, disorganization, anarchy.

nonoş (*child.*) Little darling, little pet.

norm Norm, model, rule.

normal *a.* Normal. *n.* (*math.*) Perpendicular; normal. ~ **akım**, (*el.*) steady-state (current). ~ **altı**ⁿ¹, (*math.*) sub-normal. ~ **ize**, (*min.*) normalized. ~ **leşmek**, *vi.* become normal.

normatif *a.* Normative.

Norve¹çᶜⁱ (*geo.*) Norway. ~ +, *a.* Norwegian: ~ **uyuzu**, (*med.*) Norwegian scabies. ~ **çe**, *n.* (*ling.*) Norwegian. ~ **li**, *n.* (*ethn.*) Norwegian.

nostalji (*psy.*) Nostalgia.

No.su = NUMARASI.

nosyon Notion, idea.

notᵘ Note; memorandum; (*ed.*) mark; opinion. ~ **almak**, record a note; (*ed.*) obtain a mark: ~ **atmak**, write down a mark: ~ **baremi**, evaluation: ~ **defteri**, copybook: ~ **düşmek**, write a note: ~ **etm.**, make a note of stg.: ~ **kırmak**, (*ed.*) give a low mark: ~ **tutmak**, make/take notes of stg.: ~ **vermek (-e)**, give an opinion of stg.; evaluate; (*ed.*) give a mark: ~ **unu vermek**, reach a bad opinion about s.o.

nota (*mus.*) Note; (*adm.*) (diplomatic) note. ~ **yazısı**, (*mus.*) notation.

noter(lik) (*leg.*) (Position/duties of) notary.

notilus (*zoo.*) Nautilus.

nova (*ast.*) Nova.

nozül (*aer.*) Nozzle.

Nö. Amr. = (*mil.*) NÖBETÇİ AMİRİ.

nöbet¹ (*adm.*) Turn (of duty, etc.); (*mil.*) watch (of sentry); (*med.*) access (of fever), attack, bout. ~ **başında**, on duty: ~ **beklemek/tutmak**, (*mil.*) mount guard; await one's turn: ~ **çalmak**, (*mus.*) (band) play at specific times: ~ **yeri**, (policeman) beat; (*naut.*) action station: ~ **e çıkmak/girmek**, (*mil.*) mount guard; go on sentry duty: ~**ini savmak**, have done one's duty/turn/'one's bit': ~**te olm.**, be on duty.

öbet·çi *a.* On guard/duty: *n.* sentry; (night-) watchman: ~ **dikmek**, (*mil.*) post sentries: ~ **eczane**, pharmacy on late-/all-night duty: ~ **subayı**, (*mil.*) officer of the watch; duty/orderly officer. ~**çilik**, duties of sentry, etc.; being on duty. ~**leşe**, *adv.* in turn, alternately: ~ **değiş(tir)mek**, alternate. ~**leşme**, *vn.* taking turns; (*agr.*) rotation (of crops). ~**leşmek**, *vi.* take turns. ~**şekeri**ni, (*cul.*) sugar candy.

öro- *pref.* Neuro-. ~**gliya**, (*bio.*) neuroglia. ~**loji**, (*med.*) neurology. ~**-motor**, (*bio.*) nervimotor. ~**n**, neuron.

ötr Neutral. ~**alist**, (*pol.*) neutralist. ~**alizasyon**, neutralization. ~**alize**, ~ **etm.**, neutralize. ~**alizm**, neutralism, neutrality. ~**ino**, (*phys.*) neutrino. ~**lemek (-i)**, (*chem.*) neutralize. ~**leşmek**, *vi.* become neutral. ~**on**, (*nuc.*) neutron.

Np. = (*ch.s.*) NEPTUNYUM.

Nr. = NUMARA.

ısz. = (*ling.*) NESNESİZ; NESNE/TÜMLEÇ ALMAYAN EYLEM.

Nuh (*rel.*) Noah. ~ **der peygamber demez**, he's very obstinate: ~ **nebiden kalma**, antediluvian; ancient: ~ **teknesi**, (*bio.*) wishbone: ~**'un gemisi**, Noah's Ark; (*zoo.*) small bivalve.

ıuhuseti A being unlucky; evil omen.

ıuku·tdu *pl.* Moneys.

ıuman ~ **çiçeği**, (*bot.*) red anemone/peony.

ıumara Number; (*ed.*) marks; size (of goods); trick; performance; (*th.*) number, item, event; (*fig.*, *pej.*) a caution. ~ **levhası**, dial: ~ **on**, (*ed.*) full marks: ~ **plakası**, (*mot.*) number/registration plate: ~ **vermek**, give marks: ~ **yapmak**, (*sl.*) play a part, act up; give o.s. airs: ~**larını çevirmek**, dial s.o.'s (telephone) number: ~**sını kırmak**, (*ed.*) give s.o. a bad mark: ~**sını vermek (-e)**, size s.o. up; reach an opinion about s.o.

ıumara·cı Charlatan; tall-talker, actor. ~**lamak (-i)**, number stg.; (en)code. ~**lanmak**, *vp.* ~**lı**, numbered. ~**sız**, unnumbered; plain (glasses). ~**tör**, numbering machine.

ıumen (*phil.*) Noumenon.

ıumune Sample; pattern; instance; example; model. ~ **alıcı**, (*ind.*) sampler: ~ **almak**, sample: ~ **çiftliği**, model farm. ~**lik**, *a.* sample; (*sl.*) ridiculous.

·nun *n. suf.* [29] = -NİN [ANADOLU'NUN].

ıur Light; brilliance; (*rel.*) halo; light of holiness; glory. ~ **aylası**, halo: ~ **damla/topu**, a lovely child: ~ **gibi**, bright, shining: ~ **içinde yatsın!**, may he rest in 'radiance'/peace!: ~ **inmek/yağmak**, (*rel.*) divine light descend (on a holy place); be very holy: ~ **ol!**, bravo!: ~ **yüzlü**, benevolent looking (old person). ~**ani**/~**lu**, luminous, shining.

Nusayri (*rel.*) Turk of the (N. Syrian) Nusayriye sect.

nut·ukku Faculty of speech; speech; discourse. ~ **söylemek**, make a speech: ~**a gelmek**, begin to speak: ~**u tutulmak**, be tongue-tied; be confused and silent.

nüans (*lit.*, *mus.*) Nuance; (*art.*) shade, tinge; (*min.*) grade.

nübüvveti Quality of a prophet; gift of prophecy.

nüfus *pl.* = NEFİS. People; souls; inhabitants: *s.* person; inhabitant. ~ **(cüzdan/kâğit/tezkeresi)**, (*adm.*) identity book/papers; birth certificate: ~ **dağılımı**, distribution of population: ~ **kütüğü**, state register of persons: ~ **memurluğu**, Registry of Births, etc.: ~ **patlaması**, population explosion: ~ **sayımı**, census: ~ **yoğunluğu**, density of population.

nüfus·bilim Demography. ~**ça**, as regards people; in terms of population. ~**lanmış**, populated, inhabited. ~**lu**, having . . . inhabitants.

nüfuz Penetration; permeation; insight; ascendancy; dominance; influence. ~ **etm.**, penetrate; go into; influence: ~ **kazanmak**, gain influence: ~ **sahası**, sphere of influence: ~ **sahibi**, influential person: ~ **sahibi olm.**, have authority: ~ **ticareti**, using one's influence/position for selfish profit. ~**lu**, influential; dominant. ~**suz**, without influence.

nühüft (*Or. mus.*) A compound melody.

nük. = NÜKLEER (FİZİK).

nükle·er *a.* Nuclear: ~ **etkinlik**, nuclear activity: ~ **fizik**, nuclear physics: ~ **santral**, (*el.*) nuclear power station: ~ **silah**, (*mil.*) nuclear weapon, atom bomb. ~**ik**, (*chem.*) nucleic. ~**on**, (*nuc.*) nucleon. ~**us**, (*bio.*) nucleus.

nüks·etmekeder *vi.* (*med.*) (Disease) return and cause a relapse.

nükte Subtle point; (*ling.*) nicety; witticism; epigram. ~ **saçmak/yapmak**, make witty remarks; crack jokes.

nükte·ci/~**dan** Witty. ~**cilik**/~**danlık**, wittiness. ~**li**, witty; facetious; subtle (speech).

nük·ullü A withdrawing/abstaining; withdrawal. ~ **etm.**, withdraw; retract; recant; cancel.

nümayiş Show; pomp; simulation; (*pol.*) demonstration. ~**çi**, (*pol.*) demonstrator. ~ **kâr**, demonstrative/showy (person). ~ **kârane**, demonstrative/showy (manner); affected (manner).

nümune = NUMUNE.

-nün *n. suf.* [29] = -NİN [SÜRÜCÜNÜN].

nüsha (*pub.*) Copy, reproduction; issue, number.

nütasyon (*ast.*) Nutation.

nüve (*phys.*) Focus; centre; (*bio.*) nucleus.

nüzulü (*med.*) Apoplexy, stroke.

Nz. = NİZAMNAME.

O

O, o[1] [o] The eighteenth Tk. letter, O.
O[2] *int.* O!; ah!; oh!
o[nu][3] *pron.* [67] He; she; it; [71] that (one, over there).
a. That; those [~ **adam**, that man: **o adamlar**, those men]. ~ **balık başka bir balık!**, that's a different kettle of fish!: ~ **bir**, that other one, the other: ~ **bir âlem!**, he's quite a character!: ~ **bir gün**, the other day; several days ago: ~ **bu**, whether this or that: ~ **denli**, thus; so: ~ **duvar senin bu duvar benim**, (drunkard) rolling from side to side: ~ **gün bu gün(dür)**, ever since that day: ~ **halde**, in that case: ~ **kadar**, so, so much: ~ **melun . . .!**, that abomination of a . . .: ~ **mesele başka**, that's quite a different matter: ~ **saat**, at that very moment, straight away: ~ **sokak senin bu sokak benim gezip duruyor**, he spends all his time wandering about the streets: ~ **takdirde**, in that case: ~ **taraflı olmamak**, attach no importance to; show no interest in: ~ **tarakta bezi olmamak**, have no connection with: ~ **tasa bu tasa**, we've got enough to worry about as it is: ~ **yolda**, thus; in that way: ~ **yolun yolcusu**, he leads a miserable life; he's about to die: ~ **zaman**, then; in that case . . .: ~ **zaman durum değişir**, that puts a different complexion on the matter: ~ **zamandan beri/itibaren**, ever since: ~ **zamandan bu yana**, since that time, until now.

ona, to him/her/it; to that: ~ **buna dil uzatmak**, malign everybody: ~ **halt düşer!**, he has no right at all to interfere; it's nothing to do with him!: ~ **kuşum kondu**, I took to him: ~ **sebep**, on account of that: ~ **vergidir**, only he can do it.

onda, at//by//with him/her/it/that.

ondan, from him/her/it/that; for that reason: ~ **dolayı**, on account of that: ~ **gayri**, other than that; moreover; besides: ~ **sonra**, after him, etc.; after that; then: ~ **yana**, in favour of.

onlar, *pl.* they: ~ **ermiş muradına biz çıkalım kerevetine**, (*child.*) and they all lived happily ever after: ~**a**, to them: ~**da**, at/with them: ~**dan**, from them: ~**ı**, them: ~**ın(ki)**, their(s).

onsuz, without him/her/it/that.

onu, him, her, it; that: ~ **son görüşüm oldu**, that was the last time I saw him.

onun, his, her, its: ~ **gayri**, a different one: ~ **gibi**, like him, etc.: ~ **görmediği yok**, he has eyes at the back of his head: ~ **için**, for him, etc.; for his sake; because/on account of him/that: ~ **yerine**, in default of . . .: ~**ki**, *pron.* his, hers, its: ~ **la beraber**, with him, etc.; for all that; at the same time: ~**la göbeğiniz bitişik değil ya!**, must you always do everything together?; can't you do this by yourself?: ~ **la kırklıyım**, I was born soon after him.

O. = (*ch.s.*) OKSİJEN; (*geo.*) ORTA; (*fin.*) ORTAÇ; (*sp.* OYUN.

oba Large compartmented nomad tent; noma[c] family; nomad camping site; beach-hut; Boy Scou[ ] pack.

obart·ı(cı) = ABARTI(CI). ~**(ıl)ma(k)** = ABART(IL) MA(K).

obelisk[i] (*arch.*) Obelisk.

obelya (*zoo.*) Obelia.

obesite (*med.*) Obesity.

ob·je (*ling.*) Object. ~**jektif**, *a.* objective, detache[d] *n.* (*phys.*) object lens. ~**jektivizm**, (*phil.*) objectivit[y]

obligasyon Obligation; (*fin.*) bond; bonded/funde[ ] debt.

obru[l]**k**[ğu] *a.* Steep; precipitous; concave. *n.* Pit pothole; abyss. ~**luk**, concavity.

obser·vasyon Observation. ~**vatör**, observe[r] ~**vatuar**, (*ast.*) observatory.

obstrüksiyon (*pol.*, *sp.*) Obstruction.

obtüratör (*cin.*) Shutter.

obua(cı) (*mus.*) Oboe (player).

obur Gluttonous, greedy. ~**ca**, gross. ~**laşmak**, v[a] become greedy. ~**luk**, gluttony.

obüs (*mil.*) Shell; howitzer.

oca[l]**k**[ğ1] (*ind.*) Furnace, kiln, (*dom.*) hearth, fire place, cooker, oven, range; (*min.*) quarry, min[e] (garden) bed; (*soc.*) fraternity, chamber, guild club; family, dynasty, home. ~ **(ayı)**, January: ~ **balıkçığı**, (*ent.*) silverfish: ~ **başı**, fireside, chimney corner: ~ **bucak**, every corner of the house; th whole house: ~ **çekirgesi**, (*ent.*) house-cricket: ~ **direği**, (*min.*) pit-prop: ~ **halkı**, (*his.*) the Corps o Janissaries: ~ **kaşı**, stone hob for pans: ~ **külah**[ ] (*arch.*) hood-shaped chimney breast: ~ **nişi**, heart[ ] (place): ~ **süngüsü**, poker: ~**ı daim yanan**, family dynasty that will never die out: ~**ı söndü**, his lin[ ] has died out: ~**ına düşmek (-in)**, seek s.o.'s protec tion; implore; be at s.o.'s mercy: ~**ına incir dikmek** break up s.o.'s home; ruin, exterminate: ~**ını söndürmek**, destroy s.o.'s family; ruin s.o.

ocak·çı(lık) (Work of) chimney-sweep; tea-/coffee maker (in offices); (*eng.*) stoker; member of TÜR[K] OCAĞI. ~**lı**, having a fireplace; being a member o a club, etc. ~**lık**, fireplace; hearthstone; chimney (*leg.*) entailed family estate: ~ **demiri**, (*naut.*) she[ ] anchor.

od Fire; poison. ~ **ocak temin etm.**, secure a home ~ **taşı**, (*geol.*) coarse sandstone: ~ **yok ocak yok** in dire poverty.

oda Room; office; chamber; (*his.*) Janissary bar racks. ~ **hapsi**, (*mil.*) confinement to quarters: ~ **müziği**, chamber music: ~ **orkestrası**, chambe orchestra: ~ **sıcaklığı(nda)**, (at) room temperature ~ **ücreti**, room price.

oda·başı[n1] Man in charge of rooms (inn, karavanserai); (*his.*) Janissary officer. ~ **cı**, cleaner/watchman in public buildings; inn servant. ~ **cık**, booth, cabin, carrel. ~ **lık**, (*his.*) concubine, odalisque.

oda'k[g1] (*phys.*) Focus, focal-point; centre. ~ **ayarı**, (*cin.*) focusing: ~ **düzlem**//**nokta**//**uzunluğu**, *phys.*) focal plane//point//length: ~ **ta**, in focus.

odak·lama *vn.* Focusing. ~ **laşmak (-de)**, become focused on; be centred/centralized. ~ **laştırmak** (-i), *vc.* focus. ~ **layıcı**, (*cin.*) assistant cameraman. ~ **sal**, focal.

odeon (*th.*) Odeum. ~ **itoryum**, auditorium; lecture-/concert-hall.

odsuz Without fire. ~ **ocaksız**, very poor.

ODTÜ = ORTA DOĞU TEKNİK ÜNİVERSİTESİ.

odun Firewood; cudgel; stupid/coarse fellow. ~ **ağa**, (*pej.*) blockhead: ~ **arısı**, (*ent.*) wood-wasp: ~ **çekmek**, weigh wood: ~ **gibi**, very hard; unripe (fruit); (*fig.*) stupid: ~ **kesiciler**, (*orn.*) wood-creepers: ~ **ruhu**, (*chem.*) methanol.

odun·cu Wood-cutter; seller of firewood. ~ **culuk**, wood-cutting/-selling. ~ **kömürü**[nü], charcoal. ~ **laşma**, (*bot.*) lignification. ~ **laşmak**, *vi.* lignify; *vulg.*) become coarse/stupid. ~ **luk**, wood-shed/pile. ~ **özü**, (*bot.*) lignin. ~ **su**, ligneous.

ODÜ = ORTA DOĞU ÜNİVERSİTESİ.

odyometre (*chem.*) Eudiometer.

OECD = (*Organization for Economic Cooperation and Development*). ~ **EC** = (*Organization for European Economic Cooperation*). ~ **ED** = *Organization for European Economic Development*).

of *int.* (*of disgust, grief, annoyance*) Ugh!

ofis (*adm.*) Office, chamber.

oflamak *vi.* Exclaim 'ugh!' ~ **puflamak**, huff and puff (from heat/weariness).

oforoz Exquisite, beautiful, attractive.

ofris (*bot.*) Ophrys, bee-/fly-spider orchid.

ofsayt (*sp.*) Offside. ~ **set**, (*pub.*) offset (printing).

oftalmo·loji (*med.*) Ophthalmology. ~ **sko'p**[bu], ophthalmoscope.

OĞ. = OĞULLARI; OĞLU.

oğa- = OVA-.

Oğan (*rel., obs.*) God, the Almighty.

oğla'k[g1] (*zoo.*) Kid. ~ (**burcu**), (*ast.*) Capricorn: ~ **önencesi**, (*geo.*) tropic of Capricorn.

oğlan Boy; servant; catamite; (*carp.*) tongue; gamb.) jack, knave. ~ **cı(lık)**, pederast(y), bugger(y).

oğm- = OVM-.

oğul[lu] Son; male child; son of a ...; (*ent.*) swarm of bees. ~ **arısı**, (*ent.*) young bee: ~ **balı**, white honey (from a fresh swarm): ~ **döl**, offspring: ~ **edinmek**, adopt a son: ~ **göze**, (*bio.*) daughter-cell: ~ **ermek**, (*ent.*) swarm: ~ **ları**, *n. suf.* [233] sons of, dynasty of [OSMANOĞULLARI]: ~ **u**, *n. suf.* [43], son of, -son (*in family names*) [HEKİMOĞLU]: ~ **um bina kur döner döner yine okur**, of s.o. always harping on the same subject; of stg. that doesn't progress: ~ **unu kestirmek**, (*med., rel.*) have one's son circumcised.

oğul·cu'k[ğu] Young son; (*bio., bot.*) embryo. ~ **du-**

ru'k[ğu], (*bio.*) womb. ~ **luk**, status/duties of a son; adopted son. ~ **otu**[nu], (*bot.*) balm.

oğulmak, *etc.* = ovulmak, *etc.*

oğuz[1] *n.* Robust lad; simple fellow; peasant; good fellow.

Oğuz[2] *pr. n.* (*ethn.*) Tk. tribes of S.W. Asia. ~ **ca**, their language.

oh! *int.* (*of* (*malignant*) *satisfaction*) Oh!; ah!; ha! ~ **çekmek**, gloat over s.o.'s misfortunes: ~ **demek**, breathe a sigh of relief; rest: ~ **olsun!**, serve you right!; I'm so glad!

oha *int.* (*vulg.*) Hey you!; stop that!

ohm (*el.*) Ohm.

oj·e (*mod.*) Nail-polish. ~ **it**[i], (*geol.*) augite.

ok[u] Arrow; dart; (*zoo.*) quill; (carriage, plough, etc.) beam, pole; (*math.*) sagitta. ~ **atım/menzili**, bow-shot: ~ **balığı**, (*ich.*) hagfish: ~ **gibi fırlamak**, dart off: ~ **meydanı**, archery field: ~ **meydanında buhardan yakmak**, expect too much from inadequate means: ~ **yayından fırlamış**, the die is cast: ~ **ucu**, barb: ~ YILANI.

ok. = OKUNUŞU.

okaliptüs (*bot.*) Eucalyptus tree.

okapi (*zoo.*) Okapi.

okazyon (*fin.*) Bargain; opportunity.

okçu Bowyer; bowman, archer. ~ **balığı**, (*ich.*) archer fish. ~ **luk**, bowmaking; archery.

okka (*math.*) Oke (= 400 DİRHEM = 1.28 kg.); = YENİ OKKA. ~ **çekmek**, weigh heavy//heavier than expected: ~ **dört yüz dirhem**, facts are facts; it's obvious: ~ **her yerde dört yüz dirhem**, men/things are the same everywhere: ~ **tutmak**, be heavy: ~ **nın altına gitmek**, bear the brunt; be the chief victim.

okka·lamak (-i) Estimate weight with the hands; (*fig.*) applaud. ~ **lı**, weighing . . . okes; heavy, weighty; important: ~ **kahve**, large cup of coffee.

ok·lamak *vi.* Fly like an arrow: *vt.* (-i), shoot with an arrow. ~ **lava**, (*cul.*) long thin rolling-pin for YUFKA. ~ **lu**, barbed; quilled. ~ **luk**, quiver. ~ **lukirpi**, (*zoo.*) porcupine.

okramak *vi.* (Horse) whinny for water.

ok·salat[1] (*chem.*) Oxalate. ~ **salik**, oxalic. ~ **siasetilen**, oxy-acetylene. ~ **sidasyon**, oxidation. ~ **sijen**, oxygen: ~ **azlığı**, (*med.*) anox(aem)ia: ~ **ini gidermek**, deoxidize. ~ **sijenlendirmek (-i)**, oxygenate. ~ **sijensizlik**, (*med.*) anoxia. ~ **si'tdi**, oxide. ~ **sitlemek (-i)**, oxidize. ~ **sitlenmek**, *vp.* ~ **sitsizleş(tir)mek**, *vi.*/(*vt.*) deoxidize. ~ **sitsizleyici**, (*min.*) deoxidizer.

oksu (*bio.*) Sagittal; (*phys.*) jet.

okşa·mak (-i) Caress, fondle; flatter; faintly resemble, remind one of; (*sl.*) ill-treat, strike. ~ **nmak**, *vp.* ~ **ntı**/~ **yış**, caress. ~ **rövgü(lemek)**, *n.*/(*vt.*) compliment. ~ **ş**, (*obs.*) resemblance. ~ **tmak (-i, -e)**, *vc.*

okşın ~ **briç**, (*gamb.*) auction-bridge.

ok·tan (*chem.*) Octane. ~ **sayısı**, fuel grade. ~ **tant**[1], (*ast.*) octant. ~ **tav**, (*mus.*) octave.

oktruva (*fin.*) Octroi.

okul (*ed., art., phil.*) School. ~ **aile birliği**, (*ed.*) parent–teacher association: ~ **defteri**, exercise-book: ~ **gemisi**, (*naut.*) cadet-/training-ship: ~

mezunu, old-boy; school-leaver: ~ **sırası,** school desk/bench: ~ **taburu,** (*mil.*) cadet corps: ~ **vasıtası,** school-bus: ~ **a devam etm.,** attend school.
okul·daş School-mate. ~ **içi,** in school; intra-school. ~ **lu,** school-pupil; educated. ~ **öncesiⁿⁱ,** ~ **eğitim,** pre-school/nursery-school education. ~ **sonrasıⁿⁱ,** post-school.
oku·ma *vn.* Reading: ~ **kitabı,** (*ed.*) reading-book: ~ **saati,** (*phys.*) meter: ~ **yazma,** reading and writing: ~ **yazma bilmiyen,** analphabetic, illiterate: ~ **yitimi,** (*med.*) alexia, dyslexia. ~ **mak (-i),** read; learn; study; sing; recite; (*rel.*) say a prayer; exorcise; invite, call; (*sl.*) curse: **(-den),** understand: **(-e),** (*sl.*) harass, ruin. ~ **mamış,** *a.* illiterate; uneducated. ~ **muş,** *a.* literate; educated. ~ **muşluk,** literacy.
okun·acak For reading; to be read. ~ **aklı,** legible. ~ **aksız,** illegible. ~ **mak,** *vp.* = OKUMAK; be read, etc.; (*rel.*) be prayed over/exorcised: **okunmuş su,** holy water. ~ **tu,** invitation. ~ **ulmak,** *imp. v.* read; be read. ~ **ur,** reader. ~ **urluk,** readability. ~ **uş,** manner of reading, delivery.
okur Reader. ~ **yazar(lık),** liter·ate/(-acy).
okut·a¹çᶜ¹ Reading machine. ~ **mak (-i, -e),** *vc.* cause to read/learn; instruct; educate; (*sl.*) sell. ~ **man,** (*ed.*) lector. ~ **turmak (-i, -e),** *vc.* cause to be taught; have educated; (*sl.*) cause to be sold. ~ **ulmak,** *vp.*
oku·yanlar (*pub.*) Readers, audience. ~ **yucu,** reader; inviter; singer; exorcist: ~ **mektupları,** (*pub.*) letters to the editor: ~ **larla başbaşa,** (*pub.*) to our readers. ~ **yuş** = ~ NUŞ.
oküler (*phys.*) *n.* Eye-piece. *a.* Ocular.
okyanus (*geo.*) *n.* Ocean. ~ +, *a.* Oceanic: ~ **fırtına kuşu,** (*orn.*) Leach's storm-petrel. ~ **al,** oceanic. ~ **ya,** (*geo.*) Oceania.
okyılanı (*zoo.*) Horn-viper.
ol *pron.* (*obs.*) [67] = O³.
olabil·ir *a.* Possible: ~ **ki,** probably. ~ **irlik,** possibility. ~ **mek,** *vi.* be possible/probable.
olaca¹kᵏᵍ¹ *int.* So fate has willed! *a.* [160] Supposed to be; so-called; confounded! [**otel olacak şu gecekondu,** that shanty of a so-called hotel]. ~ **gibi değil,** impossible: ~ **iş değil!,** that's impossible!; it's absurd: ~ **olur,** what is fated will happen: ~ı **nedir?,** what's its lowest price?: ~ **ına varır,** it must take its course.
ola·gelmek *vi.* Happen now and again; occur frequently ~ **gelen,** ordinary; usual.
olağan Usual, normal; common, ordinary, every-day; frequent. ~ **dışı(lık),** abnormal(ity); unusual/(-ness). ~ **laşmak,** *vi.* become normal/usual. ~ **lık,** normality, usualness, ordinariness. ~ **üstü,** extra-ordinary; abnormal, unnatural; extreme: ~ **baskı,** (*pub.*) extra: ~ **durum,** emergency. ~ **üstülük,** extraordinariness; unnaturalness.
olamak (*agr.*) Remove suckers (from a vine).
olamaz *a.* Impossible; improbable. ~ **lık,** impossibility.
olana¹kᵏᵍ¹ Possibility; facility. ~ **sağlamak/vermek,** make possible, facilitate; ensure: ~ı **olm.,** be possible. ~ **lı,** possible. ~ **sız(lık),** impossi·ble/(-bility). ~ **sızlaşmak,** *vi.* become impossible. ~ **sızlaştırmak (-i, -e),** *vc.* make impossible.

olanca *a.* Utmost; all possible; the whole of. ~ **kurumuyla,** out of pure conceit: ~ **kuvvetiyle,** wit all his strength: ~ **malını kaybetti,** he lost his who fortune.
olarak *With an adjective/noun it forms an adverbi phrase* [177] [**kesin** ~, definitely; **sarhoş** ~ drunkenly; **netice** ~, consequently: **ilk defa** ~, fc the first time].
olası *a.* That/which may be; possible, probabl ~ **yanılgı,** (*ast.*) probable error. ~ **cılık,** (*phil* probabilism. ~ **lı,** *a.* probable, contingent. ~ **lı** potential, probability; risk.
olay Event; fact; incident; circumstance; phenc menon; (*ast.*) effect. ~ **çıkarmak,** create an ur pleasant situation: ~ **ın yankılar/tortusu,** (*fig* backwash: ~ **lar dizisi,** (*th.*) plot.
olay·anlatım Explanation. ~ **cılık,** (*phil.*) ph nomenonalism. ~ **lı,** eventful. ~ **sız,** uneventful.
olçum (*med.*) Charlatan.
ol·dubitti *n.* An accomplished fact, *fait accompl* ~ **dukça,** *adv.* rather, quite, fairly; -ish: ~ **mürekkep yalamış,** somewhat educated. ~ **dulama (-i),** approve, okay. ~ **durgan,** (*ling.*) causative: ~ **çatı//eylem,** causative mood//verb. ~ **durmak (-i** *vc.* = OLMAK; cause to be(come); cause to riper mature; bring to perfection; (*agr.*) raise (plants).
ole·fin (*chem.*) Olefin(e). ~ **ik,** oleic. ~ **in,** oleine.
OLEYİŞ = OTEL LOKANTA VE EĞLENCE YERLE İŞÇI SENDIKASI.
olgu Fact; event; (*th.*, *cin.*) plot; (*cin.*) actio ~ **cu(luk),** (*phil.*) positiv·ist/(-ism). ~ **sal,** factual.
olgun Mature; adult; ripe (fruit); experienced, a complished; cultured. ~ **odun,** close-texture timber. ~ **laşma,** *vn.* maturation; ripening; (*chem* ageing. ~ **laşmak,** *vi.* mature; ripen; (*chem.*) ag ~ **laştırmak (-i),** mature; perfect; ripen; (*chem* age, cure. ~ **luk,** maturity; ripeness; accomplis ment; culture: ~ **sınavı,** (*ed.*, *obs.*) universi entrance examination.
oli·garşi (*pol.*) Oligarchy. ~ **goklaz,** (*geol.*) olig clase. ~ **gosen,** (*geol.*) Oligocene. ~ **jist,** (*geo* haematite.
olim·pik, (*sp.*) Olympic. ~ **piyat¹,** (*sp.*) Olympia ~ **oyunları,** Olympic games.
olivin (*geol.*) Olivine.
ol·ma *vn.* = OLMAK. Being; existing; becomin event. ~ **madık,** *a.* that has not happened; u precedented; unacceptable: ~ **bahaneler ile sürmek,** put forward all sorts of excuses: ~ **bir ş değil,** it may well happen; it is not uncommon: ~ **olmaz,** anything may happen; nothing is in possible.
ol¹makᵘʳ *vi.* [141] *This verb is so important and i parts so frequently used in idiomatic expressions th the 'non-verbal' forms are also treated separatel* = OLACAK; OLDUKÇA; OLMAMIŞ, *etc.* Be; exist; t present; become; happen; grow; ripen; mature; t cooked/prepared; have, possess; catch/get/hav (an illness); undergo, suffer: **(-den),** lose, be depriv of: **(-e),** be suitable for, fit: **(-e),** happen to s.o.: **(-e** be stg. to s.o.: **(-e),** cause/lead to stg. for s.o.; ~ get drunk. *aux. v.* [156] *Replaces* EDILMEK *to for the passive of* ETMEK [KAYDOLMAK; TIRAŞ OLM

~ **bitmek** (*both verbs declined*), happen, occur: ~ **üzere**, [167] being, as being.

ol *imperative* [142] Be! ~ **a**, *optative*: ~ **ki**, it may be/happen that . . .. ~ **abilir**, it can/may be: *a.* = OLABİLİR. ~ **acak**, *fut.* it will be: *a.* = OLACAK. ~ **amaz**, it can not be: *a.* = OLAMAZ. ~ **an**, *pres. part.* being; becoming; having, possessing; the one that is: ~ **biten**, happening: ~ **oldu**, what's done is done!; it's too late now!: ~ **lar**, events. OLANCA. ~ **arak**, *gerund* [177] being; as: *adv.* = OLARAK. ~ **ası**, may it be! ~ **aydı**, if only/would to God he had.

oldu *past tense* Became, has become: *int.*, OK!: ~ **bitti**, it's happened: OLDUBİTTİ: ~ **da bitti maşallah!**, well that's done the trick!; don't worry—it's all over now!: ~ **ne olmaz**, just in case: ~ **olacak**, the inevitable has happened; so one may as well . . .; it's no use worrying any more: ~ **olacak kırıldı nacak**, there's nothing more to be done about it; the die is cast: ~ **olanlar**, the fat's in the fire: ~ **olmadı**, it is scarcely: ~ **m olası(ya)**, [181] ever since the beginning of things; for as long as one can remember.

olduğu *part.* Being, existing. ~ **gibi**, as it is/was; as often happens: ~ **yerde kakılı kaldı**, he stood rooted to the spot.

ol·mamış *neg.* = OLMUŞ. That did not happen: *a.* = OLMAMIŞ. ~ **masa**, *neg.* = OLSA: ~ **da olur**, we could very well do without it; it's not essential: ~ **(ydı)**, if it were not for, but for. ~ **masına**, [249], he is . . . for what it's worth. ~ **maya**, ~ **ki** . . ., beware lest . . .. ~ **mayacak**, *neg.* = OLACAK: *a.* = OLMAYACAK. ~ **mayan**, *neg.* = OLAN; the one that is not; non-. ~ **mayarak**, *neg. gerund =* OLARAK. ~ **maz**, *neg. aorist* [118] that does not happen; it's impossible!; certainly not!; it's not done!: ~ **mı**, won't it be all right?: ~ ~, anything may happen. ~ MAZ·LI/-LIK. ~ **muş**, *past. part.* that has happened: *a.* = OLMUŞ.

ol·sa *conditional* It would happen: ~ **bile pek az**, there is little if any: ~ **da olur olmasa da**, it's all the same whatever happens: ~ **fena olmaz**, it wouldn't come amiss: ~ **gerek**, [273] it must be!: ~ ~, [272] at the very most; in the last resort: ~ **olabilir**, the worst that can happen is . . .. ~ **sun**, *imperative* [142] let him/it be; so be it!; all right!, I don't mind!; so much the better!: ~ ~, at the very most: *conj.* = OLSUN.

ol·up: ~ **bitmek**, [179] happen. ~ **bitti**, event; happening: ~ BİTTİ: ~ **olacağı**, that's all. ~ **ur**, *aorist* [117] it is, it becomes; it may be; all right!, OK!; you may do it!: *a.* = OLUR: ~ **mu?**, is it all right?: ~ **mu böyle?**, can such things happen?: ~ **mu** ~!, of course it's possible!; it may happen so!; one never knows!

•mamış *a.* Unripe; immature. ~ **mayacak**, *a.* unlikely; unseemly; unsuitable: ~ **duaya âmin demem**, I can't agree with such unpractical ideas. ~ **mazlı**, (*phil.*) impossible. ~ **mazlık**, impossibility. ~ **muş**, *a.* completed; ripe; mature: ~ **armut gibi eline düşmek**, obtain stg. without any effort: ~ **bitmiş iş**, *fait accompli*.

olsun *conj.* [210] If only. ~ **olmasın**, whether or not: ~ . . . ~ . . ., [209] both . . . and . . .; whether . . . or . . ..

olta Fishing-line. ~ **iğnesi**, fish-hook: ~ **yemi**, bait: ~ **ya vurmak**, (fish) bite.

oltu ~ **taşı**, (*geol.*) jet.

olu (*phil.*) A becoming; a changing of state/condition.

olu·kᵍᵘ Open pipe; channel, conduit; gutter-pipe; chute; groove; furrow; cleft; (*bio.*) sulcus; (*met.*) trough; (*min.*) corrugation. ~ **açmak**, (*min.*) chase: ~ **gibi akmak**, flood down: ~ ~, in streams: ~ **rendesi**, (*carp.*) fillister.

oluk·çu·kᵍᵘ (*bio.*) Sulcus. ~ **lu**, grooved: ~ **kâğıt//saç**, corrugated paper//iron: ~ **kalem**, (*carp.*) gouge: ~ **zehirdişi**, (*bio.*) fang.

olum·lama (*phil.*) Affirmation. ~ **lamak (-i)**, affirm. ~ **lu**, affirmative, positive; constructive: ~ **bilim(ler)**, science(s): ~ **eylem//tümce**, (*ling.*) positive verb//sentence: ~ **koşaç**, (*ling.*) copula. ~ **luk**, biography, *curriculum vitae.* ~ **lulaşmak**, *vi.* become positive. ~ **luluk**, positivity. ~ **sal(lık)**, possi·ble/(-bility); contin·gent/(-gency). ~ **suz**, negative: ~ **eylem** *etc.*, (*ling.*) negative verb, etc. ~ **suzlaşmak**, *vi.* become negative. ~ **suzluk**, negation; negativity: ~ **eki**, (*ling.*) affix of negation.

olun·mak *imp. v.* [150] Become. *aux. v.* [151] *forming the passive of Arabic verbal nouns conjugated with* ETMEK [TENKİDOLUNMAK; ZİKROLUNMAK]. ~ **tu**, fact.

olupbitti Accomplished fact. ~ **ye getirmek**, make it difficult to turn back.

olur *a.* Possible; permissible; all right!; done! ~ **olmaz**, [182] ordinary, chosen at random; any; whatever; anybody; whoever: ~ **şey**, common, ordinary: ~ **şey değil!**, it's incredible!: ~ **u ile iktifa etm./yetinmek**, make the best of things: ~ **u ile yetinmeli**, beggars can't be choosers: ~ **una bağlamak (-i)**, make the best of a matter: ~ **una bırakmak (-i)**, leave things to take their own course. ~ **lu**, possible. ~ **luk**, requirement. ~ **suz**, impossible.

oluş *vn.* = OLMAK. State/manner of being//becoming; entity; nature; condition; occurrence; event; formation; coming into existence. *n. suf.* -genesis [dağoluş, orogenesis]. ~ **unda**, in itself, in reality. ~ **ma**, *vn.* forming, formation. ~ **mak**, *vi.* come into existence; originate; arise; take shape; be formed: (**-den**), consist of. ~ **turmak (-i)**, form; produce; create. ~ **turulmak**, *vp.* **u·k**ᵍᵘ, (*geol.*) a formation. ~ **um**, (*ast.*, *geol.*) formation, generation, development: ~ **+**, tectonic: ~ **çöküntü koyağı**, rift valley.

olu·tᵈᵘ (*phil.*) Fact.

om¹ *n.* (*el.*) Ohm.

om² *n.* (*bio.*) Rounded prominence (bone, *etc.*); protuberance. ~ **aca**, (*bio.*) rounded bone-end; (*bot.*) tree-stump. ~ **ça**, (*bot.*) vine-stock.

ombra (*geol.*) Umber.

omega (*ling.*) Omega (Ω, ω).

omletⁱ (*cul.*) Omelette.

omnibüs Horse-drawn bus.

omur (*bio.*) Vertebra. ~ **deliği**, spinal canal. ~ **al**, vertebral. ~ **ga**, (*bio.*) backbone, spine; (*orn.*) carina; (*naut.*) keel: ~ **sını kırmak**, (*naut.*) break its back. ~ galı(lar), (*zoo.*) vertebrate(s). ~ gasız(lar), (*zoo.*) invertebrate(s). ~ ilik, (*bio.*) spinal cord.

om**¹uz**ᶻᵘ (*bio.*) Shoulder. ~ atkısı, (*mod.*) stole: ~ çevirmek (-e), cold-shoulder s.o.: ~ kaldırmak/silkmek, shrug one's shoulders; (*fig.*) attach no importance to stg.: ~ kayışı, (*mil.*) bandolier, shoulder-strap: ~ ~ a, shoulder to shoulder, very close together; (*fig.*) together: ~ öpüşmek, be (almost) equal to; be neck and neck: ~ vermek, push/hold with the shoulder; (-e), give s.o. a shoulder up; (*sl.*) consider unimportant: ~ da taşımak, honour, hold in high esteem: ~ una almak/vurmak, shoulder, undertake.

omuz·başı**ⁿ¹** Point of the shoulder. ~ daş, (*col.*) companion, colleague, pal. ~ daşlık, companionship. ~ lamak (-i), shoulder; undertake; give a shoulder to, assist; (*sl.*) carry off, steal. ~ lu, having . . . shoulders. ~ luk, (*mod.*) epaulette; (*naut.*) quarter; yoke (for carrying).

on (*math.*) Ten. ~ altı(ncı), sixteen(th): ~ beş(inci), fifteen(th): ~ beş günlük, (*pub.*) fortnightly: ~ bir(er), eleven (each): ~ birinci, eleventh: ~ dokuz(uncu), nineteen(th): ~ dördüncü, fourteenth: ~ dört, fourteen: ~ iki(nci), twel·ve/(-fth); = ~ iki: ~ İki Ada, *pr.n.* (*geo.*) Dodecanese: ~ ikide bir, one twelfth: ~ kaidesi, (*math.*) decimal system: ~ para etmez, not worth a brass farthing: ~ paralık etm., disgrace s.o.; treat badly: ~ parmak, the two hands: ~ parmağında ~ kara, s.o. slanderous: ~ parmağında ~ marifet, s.o. very skilful: ~ sekiz(inci), eighteen(th): ~ üç(üncü), thirteen(th): ~ yedi(nci), seventeen(th): ~ yıl(lık), decade: ~ DA¹·²: ~ da bir, one tenth. [*For further phrases* = KIRK].

ona *pron.* = o³. To him/her/it.

onaltılık (*mus.*) Semi-quaver.

ona·ma *vn.* Approval; preference. ~ mak (-i), approve; prefer; choose. ~ nılır, suitable. ~ nmak, *vp.* be chosen, etc.

onanizm (*psy.*) Onanism, masturbation.

onar Ten each; ten at a time. ~ ~, by tens.

onar·ılmak *vp.* ~ ım, repair, reparation; (*art.*) restoration; reconstruction: ~ bakım, repair and maintenance: ~ cerrahisi, (*med.*) neoplasty. ~ ımcı, repairer; restorer. ~ ma, *vn.*; repairs: ~ macunu, (*carp.*) plastic wood. ~ mak (-i), repair; restore; reconstruct; (*fig.*) heal. ~ tmak (-i), *vc.*

onaş·ım/ma *vn.* Consent; approval. ~ mak, *vi.* consent.

onay *a.* Suitable; convenient. *n.* Approval; acknowledgement. ~ belgesi, certificate, attestation: ~ ını almak, get stg. approved.

onayaklılar (*zoo.*) Decapods.

onay·lamak (-i) Approve, ratify; certify. ~ lamalık, certificate. ~ lanmak, *vp.* ~ latmak, *vc.* ~ lı, approved; certified. ~ lılık, approval. ~ sız, not approved.

Onb. = onbaşı**ʸ¹**(lık), (*mil.*) (rank of) corporal.

on·ca According to him/her; in his/her opinion; as far as he/she is concerned. ~ culayın, like him/her; according to him/her. ~ da¹; ~ dan, *pron.* = o³.

onda² *n.* (*math.*) One tenth. ~ lık, *n.* a tenth part; ten percent (commission); (*fin.*, *obs.*) tithe: *a.* (*math.*) decimal: ~ kesir//sayı, decimal fraction//number. ~ lıkçı, ten-percent commission-agent.

ondurmak (-i) *vc.* = ONMAK. Cure, heal; improve.

ondü·lasyon (*mod.*) Permanent wave (of hair). ~ latör, (*rad.*) undulator. ~ le, curly, wavy; waved (hair).

ongen (*math.*) Decagon.

ongun Flourishing; prosperous; developed; happy. *n.* (*rel.*) Totem; heraldic arms. ~ besisuyu, (*bot.*) flowing sap: ~ heykeli, totem (pole). ~ culuk, (*rel.*) totemism. ~ luk, fruitfulness; prosperity; happiness.

oniki = ON İKİ. ~ gen, (*math.*) dodecagon. ~ lik, dozen. ~ parmak, ~ yarası, (*med.*) duodenal ulcer. ~ parmakbarsağı**ⁿ¹**, (*bio.*) duodenum. ~ şer, twelve each; twelve at a time; (*math.*) duodecimal. ~ telli, (*mus.*) 12-stringed guitar.

onik·ofaji (*psy.*) Onychophagy. ~ s, (*geol.*) onyx.

onkoloji (*med.*) Oncology.

onlar *pron. pl.* = o³.

on·lu *a.* Having ten parts: *n.* (*gamb.*) ten (of a suit): ~ yarış, (*sp.*) decathlon. ~ luk, of ten parts; worth ten (units); ten-unit coin/note, 'tenner': ~ birimler bölüğü, (*math.*) numbers from 10 to 99: ~ lar, tens: ~ lar basamağı, tens column.

on·mak *vi.* Heal up; mend; improve; prosper. ~ madık, *a.* not healed/cured; unfortunate. ~ maz, *a.* that will not heal.

onomatope (*lit.*) Onomatopoeia.

ons (*math.*) Ounce (28.3 grs).

onsuz Without him/her/it/that.

ontoloji (*phil.*) Ontology. ~ +, *a.* Ontological.

on·u// ~ un(ki)// ~ unla *pron.* = o³.

on·ulmak *vi.* Heal up; recover; *vp.* be healed/cured. ~ ulmaz, incurable. ~ um, deliverance, recovery; prosperity.

onuncu (10.) Tenth (in order).

onur Dignity; honour; self-respect; *amour-propre* ~ duymak, be/feel honoured: ~ kırıcı, discreditable: ~ konuğu, guest of honour: ~ kupası, (*sp.*) challenge cup: ~ kurulu, (*adm.*) disciplinary ethical committee: ~ üyesi, honorary member ~ una, in honour of . . .: ~ una dokunmak, hurt s.o.'s pride: ~ una yedirememek, defend one's honour.

onur·landırmak (-i) *vc.* ~ lanmak, *vi.* be honoured acquire honour. ~ lu, honoured, esteemed. ~ luluk honour; self-respect. ~ sal, honorary. ~ suz without honour; dishonourable; lacking self respect. ~ suzluk, dishonour.

OO = YÜZNUMARA.

oo·lit**ⁱ** (*geol.*) Oolite. ~ sfer, (*bot.*) oosphere. ~ sit**ⁱ** (*bio.*) oocyte.

op *int.* ~ ~ !, stop!

opal**ⁱ** (*geol.*) Opal. ~ imsi, (*phys.*) opalescent.

OPEC = (*Organization of Petroleum Exporting Countries*).

oper·a (*mus.*) Opera; (*arch.*) opera-house. ~ a komik, comic opera. ~ asyon, (*adm.*, *med.*) operation. ~ atör, operator; (*med.*) surgeon. ~ et**ⁱ**, (*mus.* operetta.

oportün·ist**ⁱ** Opportunist. ~ izm, opportunism.

opossum (*zoo.*) Opossum.

psiyon (*fin.*) Option.

pt. = OPERATÖR; OPTİK.

ptik *n.* (*phys.*) Optics. *a.* (*cin.*) Optical: ~ **hile**, optical illusion: ~ **kaydırma**, (*cin.*) zoom(ing).

ptim·ist[i] Optimist. ~**izm**, optimism. ~**um**, optimum (of conditions).

pus (*mus.*) Opus.

Or. = ORDU. ~ **Gn. Kh.** = ORDU GENEL KARAR-GÂHI. ~**a.** = ORAMİRAL.

ra [199] That place. ~**ca**, by/on the part of that place/organization: ~**cıkta**, just over there: ~**da**, there: ~**dan**, from there; thence: ~**larda**, in those parts; thereabouts; in that region: ~**larda olmamak**, pay no attention; pretend not to notice: ~**ları**, those places/parts; those circumstances: ~**lı**, (native) of that place: ~**lı olmamak**, pay no attention; feign indifference: ~**sı**[nı], that place; that affair; that aspect of the matter: ~**sı ne yana düşer?**, whereabouts is that?: ~**sı öyle**, that is so: ~**sı senin burası benim dolaşmak**, saunter about: ~**ya**, to that place; thither; there: ~**ya gidilmez!**, you can't go there!: ~**yacak**, all that way.

ra·lk[ğ1] (*agr.*) Sickle; reaping-hook; harvest. ~ **çekirgesi**, (*ent.*) cicada: ~ **makinesi**, (*agr.*) harvester: ~ **mevsimi**, harvest-time: ~ **şeklinde**, (*bio.*) falcate: ~**a gelmek**, be ripe (for harvesting): ~**a gitmek**, go reaping.

rak·böceği[ni] (*ent.*) Grasshopper. ~**çı**, reaper, harvester. ~**çılık**, reaping. ~**-gagalı**, (*orn.*) sickle-bill. ~**lamak** (**-i**), reap.

ral Oral.

ra·lar// ~**lı** = ORA.

ramiral[i] (*naut.*) Admiral (senior).

ran Measure; scale; proportion; ratio; factor; rate; estimate. ~ **birimi**, module. ~**dışı**, (*math.*) irrational.

rangutan (*zoo.*) Orangutan.

ran·lama *vn.* Evaluation; approximation. ~**lamak** (**-i**), calculate; estimate, forecast. ~**layıcı**, appraiser, estimator. ~**lı**, proportional. ~**sal**, (*math.*) rational. ~**sız**, out of proportion; disproportionate; asymmetrical. ~**sızlık**, asymmetry; disproportion. ~**tı(lı)**, proportion(al).

ra·sı[nı]// ~**ya** = ORA.

Ord. Prof. = ORDİNARYÜS PROFESÖR.

ordi·naryüs ~ (**profesör**), (*ed.*) senior professor holding a university 'chair'. ~**nat**[ı], (*math.*) ordinate. ~**natör**, computer. ~**no**, (*fin.*) certificate of ownership; delivery order.

ordonat = ORDU DONATIM İŞLERİ.

ordövr (*cul.*) Hors-d'œuvres.

rdu (*mil.*) Army; army corps; armed forces; camp. ~ **ağırlığı**, baggage: ~ **aşamaları**, Tk. army ranks (MAREŞAL; ORGENERAL; KORGENERAL; TÜM-GENERAL; TUĞGENERAL; ALBAY; YARBAY; BİNBAŞI; YÜZBAŞI; ÜSTEĞMEN; TEĞMEN): ~ **emri**, order of the day, general order: ~ **kaldırmak**, break camp: ~ **kurmak**, encamp.

ordu·bozan[1] (*col., med.*) Varicose veins. ~**bozan**[2]/ (**-lık**) = OYUNBOZAN(LIK). ~**evi**[ni], (*mil.*) officers' club/mess. ~**gâh**, camp: ~ **bozmak**, break camp. ~**güdüm(sel)**, strate·gy/(-gic).

reomisin (*chem.*) Aureomycin.

orfeus ~ **ötleğeni**, (*orn.*) Orphean warbler.

org (*mus.*) Organ. ~ **klaviyesi**, console.

Org. = ORGENERAL.

organ (*bio.*) Organ; (*pub.*) organ; publication. ~**cık**, (*bio.*) cell organ. ~**ik**, (*chem.*) organic: ~ **külte**, (*geol.*) organic rock: ~ **olmayan**, inorganic. ~**izasyon**, organization. ~**izatör**, organizer. ~**ize**, ~ **etm.**, organize. ~**izma**, (*bio.*) organism. ~**laş-mak**, *vi.* become a living organism. ~**ze**, (*tex.*) organdy.

orgeneral[i] (*mil.*) Full general; Army Commander; (*aer.*) Air Chief Marshal.

orijin Origin. ~**al**[i], original; different. ~**alite**/ ~**allik**, originality.

orkestra (*mus.*) Orchestra; (*th.*) stalls. ~ **çukuru**, orchestra pit: ~ **şefi**, conductor.

orkide (*bot.*) Orchid.

orkinos (*ich.*) Tuna/tunny.

orkit[i] (*med.*) Orchitis.

orlon (*tex.*) Orlon; nylon.

orman Forest; wood. ~ **asması**, (*bot.*) purple clematis: ~ **atkuyruğu**, (*bot.*) wood horsetail: ~ **çileği**, (*bot.*) wild strawberry: ~ **çulluğu**, (*orn.*) Eurasian woodcock: ~ **dağ ezmek**, walk over hill and dale/straight across country: ~ **Fakültesi**, (*ed.*) School of Forestry: ~ **horozu**, (*orn.*) blackcock; capercaillie: ~ **ibisi**, (*orn.*) wood stork: ~ **karıncası**, (*ent.*) red ant: ~ **kebabı**, (*cul.*) stewed mutton chops: ~ **kırlangıç**//**kızılbacağı**, (*orn.*) wood swallow//sandpiper: ~ **kibarı**, (*jok.*) bear; (*fig.*) bull in a china shop: ~ **kurmak**, afforest: ~ **menekşesi**, (*bot.*) common dog violet: ~ **mühendisi**, forestry engineer: ~ **ördek**//**ötleğeni**, (*orn.*) wood duck//warbler: ~ **perisi**, (*myth.*) dryad: ~ **sıçanı**, (*zoo.*) field/wood mouse: ~ **soreksi**, (*zoo.*) common shrew: ~ **söğüt bülbülü**, (*orn.*) yellow-browed warbler: ~ **su tavuğu**, (*orn.*) banded crake: ~ **tarla kuşu** (*orn.*) woodlark: ~ **taşlamak**, pry indirectly into s.o.'s thoughts: ~ **tavuğugiller**, (*orn.*) grouse family: ~ **tırmaşık kuşu**, (*orn.*) common tree-creeper: ~ **yasaları**, law of the jungle: ~ **a vurmak**, take the forest road: ~ **ı kes(tir)mek**, disafforest.

orman·cı Forester; forest guard; forest engineer. ~**cı·lk**[ğ1], little wood, copse. ~**cılık**, forestry: ~ **Fakültesi**, (*ed.*) School of Forestry. ~**laşmak**, *vi.* become wooded. ~**laştırmak** (**-i**), afforest. ~**lı**, forested. ~**lık**, *a.* thickly wooded: *n.* woodland.

ornat·ık (*chem.*) Substituent. ~**ma**, *vn.* substitution. ~**mak**, substitute (A for B).

ornito·log Ornithologist. ~**loji**, ornithology. ~**ren·lk**[ği], (*orn.*) duck-billed platypus, ornitho-rhynchus.

orojeni (*geol.*) Orogenesis, orogeny. ~**k**, orogenic.

oros·pu Prostitute, harlot, whore. ~**puluk**, prostitution, harlotry; (*fig., vulg.*) dishonesty. ~**topolluk**, (*sl.*) trickery.

orsa (*naut.*) Windward side. ~ **alabanda!**, down with the helm!: ~ **alabanda eğlendirmek/yatmak**, be hove to: ~ **boca etm.**, tack and veer; cruise about: (*fig.*) struggle along: ~ **etm.**/~**lamak**, luff: ~ **giden**, close-hauled: ~**dan düşmek**, fall off: ~ **sına gitmek/seyretmek**, be close-hauled; hug the wind.

Ort. = ORTAKLIK. ~ **O.** = ORTAOYUNU.
orta¹ *n.* (*mil.*, *his.*) Janissary regiment.
orta² *n.* Middle; centre; mean; the space around
one; (*naut.*) the high seas. *a.* Middle; central;
medium; average; middling; public; (*bio.*) meso-. ~
Afrika//Amerika//Asya//Avrupa, (*geo.*) Central
Africa//America//Asia//Europe: ~ AĞIRLIK: ~
akıncı, (*sp.*) centre-forward: ~ **avlu,** (*arch.*) central
courtyard, atrium: ~ **beyin,** (*bio.*) mesencephalon,
midbrain: ~ **boy,** medium size; (*pub.*) quarto: ~
boylu, of medium height: ~ÇAĞ: ~ **çizgi,** (*sp.*)
centre-line: ~DAMAR: ~DERİ: ~ **dikme,** (*math.*)
mid-perpendicular: ~ **Doğu/Şark,** (*geo.*) Middle
East: ~ELÇİ: ~ **hakemi,** (*sp.*) referee: ~ **halli,** *a.*
(*fin.*) not too well off; lower middle class: ~ **hece**
yutumu, (*ling.*) syncopation: ~ **hesapla,** taking one
thing with another: ~ **hizmetçisi,** housemaid:
~ **işi,** housework: ~ **karar,** medium (degree): ~
katmanlar/tabakalar, (*soc.*) middle classes: ~KU-
LAK: ~ **kuşak,** (*geo.*) temperate zone: ~ **malı,**
common to all; common possession; prostitute: ~
müdafi/oyun kurucu, (*sp.*) centre-half(back):
~OKUL: ~OYUNU: ~ÖĞRETİM: ~PARMAK: ~
röfüj, (*mot.*) central reserve: ~SIKLET: ~ **şekerli,**
(*cul.*) medium-sweet (coffee): ~ **terim,** (*phil.*)
middle term: ~ **vuruşu,** (*sp.*) centre kick: ~ **yaşlı,**
middle-aged: ~ **yolcu,** middle-of-the-road man,
moderate: ~YUVAR: ~ **yuvarlak,** (*sp.*) centre circle.

ortada, in the middle; in sight; in full view: ~ **bir**
çok sözler geçti, much was said by those present: ~
bir şey yok, there's nothing to be seen: ~ **bir şeyler**
dönüyor, there's stg. brewing/in the air: ~
bırakmak, leave in the lurch: ~ **fol yok yumurta**
yok, there's nothing on which to base a claim/prove
anything; there's nothing in it yet: ~ **kalmak,** be
left destitute; be stranded; be caught between two
fires: ~ **olm.,** be manifest.

ortadan, from the centre/middle; from view: ~
gidermek/kaldırmak, remove; do away with; hide
away; (*fig.*) kill: ~ **kalkmak,** be removed; be
hidden; disappear; be destroyed: ~ **kaybolmak,** be
lost to view; disappear.

ortanın: ~**sağı//solu,** (*pol.*) right//left of centre.

ortası, the middle; the mean; compromise: ~**na,**
[91] towards the middle: ~**nda,** in the middle;
amid(st): ~**ndan,** from the middle; across;
through: ~**nı almak/bulmak,** take/find the average;
find a middle course; reach a compromise: ~**nı**
çıkarmak, strike an average.

ortaya, to(wards) the centre/middle; into view: ~
almak, put in the middle; surround: ~ **atmak,**
make a suggestion; put forward (ideas): ~ **bir**
balgam atma, (*vulg.*) throw a spanner in the
works: ~ **çağırmak,** call forth: ~ **çeken,** (*phys.*)
centripetal: ~ **çıkarmak/dökmek,** produce; divulge;
bring to light: ~ **çıkmak,** arise; emerge; appear;
come into being: ~ **dökülmek,** be revealed: ~
düşmek, (woman) become a prostitute: ~ **koymak,**
produce; display; put forward; bring into action;
prove; expose.

orta·ağırlık (*sp.*) Middleweight (71-75 kg.). ~**cık**
(*phys.*) meson.
orta¹çᶜ¹ (*ling.*) Participle; (*math.*) median.
orta·çağ (*his.*) Middle Ages. ~**damar,** (*bot.*) mid
rib/-vein. ~**deri,** (*bio.*) mesoderm. ~**elçi,** (*adm.*
Minister (of a legation).
orta¹kᵏ¹ *n.* (*fin.*) Partner; associate; shareholder,
stockholder; (*soc.*) fellow-wife (in polygamy); (*leg.*
accessory, accomplice. *a.* Common; communal
collective; cooperative; joint; co-; (*chem.*) covalent
~ **bahis,** (*gamb.*) tote-betting: ~ **bildiri,** (*adm.*
joint communiqué: ~ **borç,** (*fin.*) joint liability: ~
çarpan, (*math.*) common ratio: ~ **duyu,** commor
sense: ~ **fark,** (*math.*) common difference: ~
gemisi yürür elti gemisi yürümez, fellow wives car
live in harmony but not brothers' wives/sisters-in-
law: ~ **girişim,** (*fin.*) joint venture: ~ **güvenlik**
(*pol.*) collective security: ~ **hakimiyet,** (*pol.*
condominium: ~KAT: ~ **merkezli,** (*math.*) concentric: ~ **olm. (-le),** be in partnership//league
with; associate with: ~ **ölçülmez sayılar,** (*math.*
irrational numbers: ~ **özne,** (*ling.*) commor
subject: ~ **Pazar,** *pr.n.* (*fin.*) Common Market: ~
pazarlık, (*ind.*)collective bargaining: ~ **sorumluluk**/
sözleşme, (*fin.*) joint liability//agreement: ~ **(tam**
bölen, (*math.*) common factor: ~ **tümleç.** (*ling.*
common object: ~YAPIM: ~YAŞAMA: ~YAŞAR: ~
yazar, (*lit.*) joint author: ~ **yüklem,** (*ling.*) commor
predicate.
ortak·çı (*agr.*) Share-cropper; (*bio.*) commensal
~**çılık,** share-cropping; commensalism. ~**kat**
(*math.*) common multiple. ~**laşa,** *adv.* jointly; ir
common; as a partner; collectively: *a.* (*phil.*) collective; (*fin.*) joint. ~**laşacı(lık),** (*soc.*) collectiv·ist
(-ism). ~**laşalık,** community; mutualism. ~ **laşma**
vn. participation; partnership. ~**laşmak,** *vi.* ente
into partnership; work together. ~**laştırmak (-i)**
collectivize. ~**lık,** partnership, association; co
operative; company, corporation: ~ **sözleşmesi**
deed of partnership; articles of incorporation: ~**ıı**
dağılımı//düşmesi, (*fin.*) dissolution of the com
pany//partnership.
ortakula¹kᵏ¹ (*bio.*) Middle ear.
ortak·yapım (*cin.*) Coproduction. ~**yaşama,** (*bot.*
symbiosis. ~**yaşar,** (*bot.*) symbiont. ~**yönetim**
(*pol.*) coalition.
orta·lama *vn.:* *a.* Medium; average; (*ast.*) mean
middle: *adv.* through the middle: ~ **bir hesapla**
olarak, on an average: ~ **zamanı,** mean time
~**lamak(-i),** divide in the middle; split the dif
ference; reach the middle ; (*sp.*) centre.
ortalık One's immediate suroundings; the worlc
around; the face of nature; people, the public. ~
ağarmak, dawn break: ~ **dandini,** everything's in a
mess: ~ **durulmak,** become quiet: ~ **düzelmek,** be
straightened out: ~ **kararmak,** get dark; night fall
~ **karışmak,** (*pol.*) rebellion/disturbance break
out: ~ **pahalılık!,** everything is expensive: ~
süpürmek, sweep up: ~ **sütliman!,** everything i
perfectly quiet; (*fig.*) the coast is clear!: ~ **vıcık,** the
whole place was a quagmire: ~ **yatışmak,** quarre
come to an end: ~**ı birbirine katmak,** make a mess
turn the place upside down; cause alarm anc

confusion: ∼ı . . . **götürmek**, be covered with . . .: ∼ı **toz pembe görmek**, see the world through rose-coloured spectacles: ∼ **ta**, in front of one's nose; publicly: ∼ **ta kimse yok**, there's no one about: ∼ **tan kaybolmak**, disappear.

orta·m Surroundings; environment; ambience; atmosphere; space; (*bio.*) medium. ∼ **nca**[1], *a.* medium; middle: *n.* the one in the middle (of 3).

ortanca[2] (*bot.*) Hydrangea.

orta·okul[u] (*ed.*) Middle school, intermediate/comprehensive school. ∼ **oyunu**[nu], (*th.*) Tk. folk theatre with set plots (performed among the crowd). ∼ **öğrenim**// ∼ **öğretim**, intermediate education. ∼ **parma**[l]**k**[ğı], second/middle finger. ∼ **sıklet**[i], (*sp.*) middle-weight. ∼ **şım**, (*phil.*) association. ∼ **yaprak**, (*bio.*) mesoderm. ∼ **yuvar**, (*ast.*) mesosphere.

orto- *pref.* Ortho-. ∼ **doks(luk)**, (*rel.*) Greek Orthodox (Church). ∼ **genez**, (*bio.*) orthogenesis. ∼ **graf**, (*ling.*) orthography. ∼ **klaz**, (*geol.*) orthoclase. ∼ **pedi**, (*med.*) orthopaedics.

ortolan (*orn.*) Ortolan bunting.

oru·ç[cu] Fasting; fast. ∼ **açmak/bozmak**, break/violate one's fast: ∼ **çizelgesi**, diet sheet: ∼ **günü**, fast day: ∼ **tutmak**, fast: ∼ **yemek**, purposely not observe the fast. ∼ **lu**, fasting. ∼ **suz**, not fasting.

orun Place, spot, site; (*adm.*) office, post, position.

orya (*gamb.*) Diamonds.

oryan(tal) (*geo., etc.*) Orient(al); East(ern). ∼ **ist**[i], (*ling., lit.*) Orientalist.

Os. = (*ling.*) OSMANLICA; (*ch.s.*) OSMİYUM.

osilo·graf (*phys.*) Oscillograph. ∼ **sko**[l]**p**[bu], oscilloscope.

Osm. = (*his.*) OSMANLI; (*ling.*) OSMANLICA.

Osman·lı (*his.*) Ottoman: ∼ **hanedanı**, Ottoman dynasty: ∼ **imparatorluğu**, Ottoman Empire. ∼ **lıca**, (*ling.*) Ottoman Turkish. ∼ **lılık**, quality of being an Ottoman; the Ottomans. ∼ **oğulları**, Ottoman Dynasty.

osmiyum (*chem.*) Osmium.

os·motik (*bio.*) Osmotic. ∼ **moz**, osmosis.

ossaat = O SAAT. Straight away.

ostenit(li) (*min.*) Austen·ite/(-itic).

os·teo- (*bio.*) Osteo-. ∼ **tiyum**, ostium.

osur·gan (*vulg.*) Always breaking wind. ∼ **ganböceği**, (*ent.*) bombardier beetle. ∼ **mak**, *vi.* break wind, fart. ∼ **u**[l]**k**[gu], fart: ∼ **u cinli**, easily provoked.

ot[u] *n.* (*agr.*) Grass; small plant/herb; weed; fodder; medicine; depilatory; poison; (*sl.*) dope, hashish. *a.* Made of grass/straw, etc. ∼ **çekirgesi**, (*ent.*) bush cricket: ∼ **tutunmak**, remove hair with a depilatory: ∼ **yiyenler**, (*zoo.*) herbivores: ∼ **yemek**, (*sl.*) smoke hashish: ∼ **yoldurmak (-e)**, oppress s.o.

otacı Physician; doctor. ∼ **lık**, medicine.

ota·ğ Large sumptuous tent: ∼ **kurmak**, settle, establish o.s. ∼ **kçı**, tent-maker/-seller; (*mil.*) tent erector.

ota·lamak (-i) Poison s.o.; treat with medicine. ∼ **mak (-i)**, try to cure s.o.; treat with medicine.

otarmak (-i) = OTLATMAK.

otarşi (*fin.*) Sufficiency; (*adm.*) autarchy.

ot·çu Village medicine-man. ∼ **çul**, (*zoo.*) herbivorous.

otel Hotel. ∼ **ci**, hotel-keeper/-manager. ∼ **cilik**, hotel management.

otizm (*psy.*) Autism.

otla[l]**k**[ğı] *n.* (*agr.*) Pasture; grazing-land. *a.* (*sl.*) Cushy. ∼ **lüferi**, (*ich.*) medium-sized bluefish (caught in August). ∼ **çı(lık)**, (*sl.*) spong·er/(-ing). ∼ **ıye**, tax for using common pasture-land.

otla·mak *vi.* Be out to pasture; graze; (*fig.*) lead a bovine existence, vegetate; (*sl.*) cadge, sponge. ∼ **nmak**, *vi.* be out at pasture; be grazed; be overgrown (with grass). ∼ **tılmak**, *vp.* ∼ **tmak (-i)**, pasture/graze (animals).

ot·lubağa (*zoo.*) Toad. ∼ **luk**, (*agr.*) pasture; hayrick; barn.

oto *pref.* Auto-. *n.* (Motor-)car. ∼ **kazası**, car-accident. ∼ **ban**, motorway. ∼ **biyografi**, (*lit.*) autobiography.

otobur(luk) (*zoo.*) Herbivorous (state).

oto·büs (*mot.*) (Omni)bus. ∼ **büscü**, bus-operator; bus-driver. ∼ **büsçülük**, bus-management. ∼ **didakt**, (*ed.*) self-taught person. ∼ **din**, (*aer.*) autodyne. ∼ **erotizm**, (*psy.*) auto-eroticism. ∼ **gami**, (*bio.*) autogamy. ∼ **gar**, (*mot.*) coach station. ∼ **jiro**, (*aer.*) autogiro. ∼ **kar**, motor-coach. ∼ **klav**, (*bio.*) autoclave. ∼ **krasi**, (*adm.*) autocracy. ∼ **krat**[ı], autocrat. ∼ **kritik**, self-criticism. ∼ **lit**[i], (*bio.*) otolith. ∼ **masyon**, (*ind.*) automation. ∼ **mat**[ı], automaton, robot; (*ind.*) automatic device. ∼ **matik**, *a.* automatic (device); instinctive (action) ∼ **gibi**, (*sl.*) very active/talkative: ∼ **olarak**/ ∼ **man**, automatically. ∼ **matikleşmek**, *vi.* become automatic. ∼ **matizm**, (*psy.*) automatism. ∼ **mobil**, motor-car: ∼ **idare etm./kullanmak**, drive a car: ∼ **plakası**, car registration/number plate: ∼ **tahsisi**, (*fin.*) car allowance. ∼ **mobilcilik**, dealing in cars. ∼ **motiv**, automotive. ∼ **nom(i)**, (*adm.*) autono·mous/(-my). ∼ **park**, car-park. ∼ **pilot**, (*aer.*) autopilot. ∼ **plasti**, (*med.*) autoplasty. ∼ **portre**, (*art./lit.*) self-portrait. ∼ **psi**, (*med.*) autopsy. ∼ **ray**, (*rly.*) rail-car. ∼ **rite**, authority. ∼ **riter**, authoritative; authoritarian. ∼ **rotasyon**, autorotation. ∼ **sist**[i], (*bio.*) otocyst. ∼ **stop(çu)**, (s.o.) thumbing a lift. ∼ **yolu**, motorway.

otsu(l) Vegetal; herbaceous; plant-like.

otur·aca[l]**k**[ğı] Seat. ∼ **a**[l]**k**[ğı], *n.* low chair; seat; (*naut.*) thwart; bottom of stg.; base; posterior; chamberpot; (*eng.*) seating; housing: *a.* seated; resting; sedentary; house-bound: ∼ **(âlemi)**, drinking party (with dancing women). ∼ **aklı**, well settled; solidly based; imposing looking (man); dignified (language). ∼ **aklılık**, sound/serious behaviour. ∼ **anlar**, inhabitants.

otur·ma *vn.* Sitting; staying (as a guest); (*geol.*) settlement; (*eng.*) settling: ∼ **belgesi**, (*adm.*) residence permit: ∼ **helataşı**, W.C.: ∼ **odası**, sitting-room: ∼ **ya gitmek (-e)**, go to visit s.o. ∼ **mak (-e)**, sit down; be seated; sit and enjoy o.s.; rest; live; fit well; (ship) be stranded, run aground; (building) settle, collapse; (liquid) settle: **otur oturduğun yerde/oturmana bak!**, don't meddle!, mind your own business!: **oturduğu mevkiin eri oldu**, he was the right man for the post he held: **oturup kalkmak**, be restless, move about. ∼ **muş**, *a.* settled.

oturt·ma *vn.* Seating, placing; set/mounted (gem); (*cul.*) minced meat with vegetables. ~ **maç**, (*ind.*) non-slip. ~ **mak** (**-i, -e**), *vc.* = OTURMAK; cause/ allow to sit; seat; place; (*naut.*) run aground, beach; embed; set/mount (gem). ~ **malık**, (*arch.*) foundation wall. ~ **ulmak**, *vp.*

otur·ulmak *imp. v.* Sit; live. ~ **um**, (*adm.*) sitting, session; (*leg.*) hearing; ~ **yerli**, (*fin.*) domiciled. ~ **uş**, sitting position. ~ **uşlu**, liveable. ~ **uşmak**, *vi.* become calm/pacified; reduce speed.

otuz Thirty. ~ **bir**, thirty-one; (*gamb.*) a card game: ~ **bir çekmek**, (*vulg.*) masturbate. ~ **ar**, thirty each; thirty at a time. ~ **luk**, of thirty . . .; worth thirty units; thirty years old. ~ **uncu**, thirtieth. [*For further phrases* = KIRK].

ov- *pref. Also* = OĞ-.

ova (*agr.*) Grassy plain; meadow. ~ **akçaağacı**, (*bot.*) hedge/field maple; ~ **karaağacı**, (*bot.*) smooth-leaved elm.

oval[1] Oval.

ova·lamak (**-i**) Crush; make into small pieces. ~ **lanma**, *vn.* crushing. ~ **lanmak**, *vp.* ~ **latmak** (**-i, -e**), *vc.*

ova·lı S.o. from the plains. ~ **lık**, grass-land; plain.

ovdur(t)mak (**-i, -e**) *vc.* = OVMAK.

over·ley (*pub.*) Overlay. ~ **lokçu**, (*ind.*) overseer, foreman.

ovma'ç[ci] (*cul.*) Soup with bread-crumbs; fresh TARHANA.

ovmak (**-i**) Rub (with the hands); (*med.*) apply friction, massage; wipe (clean).

ovo- *pref.* Oo-. ~ **gon**, (*myc.*) oogonium: ~ **dağarcığı**, (*bot.*) conceptacle. ~ **lit**[i], (*geol.*) oolite.

ov·ucu Masseur. ~ **ulmak**, *vp.* be rubbed. ~ **unmak**, *vi.* rub, chafe. ~ **uşturmak** (**-i**), rub against each other.

oy Opinion; (*adm.*) vote. ~ **birliği**, unanimity; consensus; unanimous vote: ~ **çokluğu**, majority vote: ~ **hakkından mahrum etm.**, disfranchise: ~ **ile seçmek**, ballot for: ~ **kâğıt//sandığı**, ballot-paper//-box: ~ **vermek/~unu kullanmak**, vote (for): ~ **vermemek**, abstain: ~ **a koymak**, put to the vote.

oy. = OYMACILIK.

oya (*mod.*) Pinking; embroidery (on edges of garment). ~ **gibi**, pretty, delicate. ~ **cı**, embroiderer; embroidery seller.

oyaca'k[ğı] (*eng.*) Drill.

OYAK = ORDU YARDIMLAŞMA KURUMU.

oyala·mak[1] (**-i**) Put s.o. off to gain time; divert/ distract s.o.'s attention; waste s.o.'s time; keep a child quiet. ~ **ndırmak** (**-i**), *vc.* ~ **nmak**, *vi.* be distracted; be put off; waste one's time, dilly-dally. ~ **yıcı**, amusing, distracting.

oya·lamak[2] (**-i**) (*mod.*) Pink; embroider. ~ **lı**, pinked; embroidered (along the edges).

oyan (*eng.*) Borer; driller.

oy·cu(luk) (*adm.*) Vote-seek·er/(-ing) (by any means). ~ **daş**, s.o. of the same opinion. ~ **durmak** (**-i**), cause to vote.

oygu (*bio.*) Sinus. ~ **yangısı**, (*med.*) sinusitis.

oyla'k[ğı] (*ind.*) Ball-joint.

oy·lama *vn.* Voting. ~ **lamak** (**-i**), vote; put to the vote. ~ **lanma**, *vn.* voting. ~ **lanmak**, *vp.* be voted. ~ **laşım**, discussion; (*phil.*) deliberation. ~ **laşlık**, deliberative. ~ **laşmak** (**-i, -le**), discuss.

oylu'k[ğu] (*bio.*) Thigh; (*math.*) minimum.

oylum *n.* Excavation; volume, bulk; (*art.*) depth, pit; (*bio.*) pock-mark. *a.* Hollowed out; carved. ~ ~, curving, serrated; curling (smoke). ~ **lama**, shaping, modelling. ~ **lu/~sal**, volumetric; by volume.

oyma (*art.*) Decoration by hollowing out; sculpture, carving, engraving, etc. ~ **ressamı**, engraver: ~ **testeresi**, compass saw. ~ **baskı**, engraving; etching. ~ **cı(lık)**, (art of) sculptor, carver, engraver. ~ **lı**, carved, sculptured; (*bot.*) lobate.

oymak[1] (**-i**) *vt.* Excavate; scoop out; scour; carve; etch, engrave; cut out (paper, etc.) in decorative patterns.

oyma'k[ğı][2] *n.* Tribe; boy-scout troop; (*bot.*) subfamily; (*soc.*) association. ~ **beyi**, scoutmaster.

oyna'k[ğı] *a.* Playful; frisky; mobile, unstable; flirtatious; (*eng.*) loose, with much play, shifting. *n.* (*bio.*) Joint, articulation. ~ **kemiği**, (*bio.*) knee-cap: ~ **ölçü**, (*fin.*) sliding scale: ~ **yeri**, articulation.

oynak·lı (*mot.*) Articulated (lorry). ~ **lık**, playfulness; mobility; coquetry; frivolity; (*eng.*) play, looseness; ~ **sayrılığı**, (*med.*) chorea.

oyna·ma *vn.* Playing; acting; movement; (*geol.*) dislocation; (*fin.*) fluctuation: ~ **payı**, (*ind.*) tolerance. ~ **mak**, *vi.* play; move; dance; skip; jump about; (*eng.*) be loose, have too much play; play (a game); amuse o.s.: (**-i**), (*th.*) produce, present; enact (role); (*cin.*) be shown: (**-le**), tamper with; pass the time with; endanger stg.: **oynama!**, don't joke!, be serious!; don't dawdle!: **oynaya oynaya**, joyfully. ~ **maz**, *a.* fixed, immovable. ~ **nmak**, *vp.* be played, etc.: *imp. v.* play. ~ **ş**, playfellow; sweetheart, lover. ~ **şmak** (**-le**), play with each other; joke together. ~ **tılmak**, *vp.* ~ **tım(cı)**, (*cin.*) exhibi·tion/(-tor). ~ **tmak** (**-i**), *vc.* cause to play/ dance, etc.; move; (*cin.*) exhibit; (*th.*) produce, perform; (*fig.*) dupe; trifle with; (*carp.*) warp; (*med.*) dislocate. ~ **yış**, *vn.* production, presentation.

oysa(ki) *conj.* [215] Whereas, though; yet, however, but.

oyu'k[ğu] *a.* Hollowed out; gouged out. *n.* Hollow part of stg.; cavity; pit; cave(rn); (*bio.*) antrum. ~ **laşma**, (*min.*) pitting.

oyulga (*mod.*) Tacking; loose sewing. ~ **(la)mak** (**-i**), tack together, baste. ~ **n**, (*med.*) ulcer. ~ **nmak**, *vp.*: **oyulgana oyulgana gelmek**, creep up like a toady.

oy·ulma *vn.* Scouring, erosion. ~ **ulmak**, *vp.* = OYMAK. ~ **um**, excavating; digging out; excavation, pit, hollow; (*bot.*) tap-root. ~ **umlamak**, *vi.* take root.

oyun (*sp.*) Game; (*th.*) drama, play; spectacle; jest; dance; trick, dodge; device, artifice. ~ **alanı**, arena, sportsfield, court, etc.: ~ **almak**, win a game: ~ **çıkarmak**, (*sp.*) play: ~ **çizelgesi**, (*th.*) repertory: ~ **dışı etm.**, (*sp.*) knock out: ~ **ebesi**, (*child.*) leader, captain: ~ **etm./oynamak/yapmak**, play a trick, deceive: ~ **fişi**, (*gamb.*) chip, counter: ~ **havası**, (*mus.*) dance-tune; folk-music: ~ **kâğıdı**, (*gamb.*) playing-card(s): ~ **kurucu**, (*sp.*) half-back:

oyuncak, an easy matter: ~ **sahası** = ~ ALANI: ~ **uzatma**, (*sp.*) extra time: ~ **vermek**, (*th.*) present (a play); (*sp.*) lose: ~ **yasaklaması**, (*th.*) stage censorship: ~ **yazarı**, (*lit.*) dramatist, playwright: ~ **zar(lar)ı**, (*gamb.*) dice: ~**a çıkmak**, (*th.*) appear on stage: ~**a gelmek**, be deceived/taken in: ~**a getirmek**, trap s.o.; deceive s.o.: ~**da**, (*sp.*) in play: ~**u almak**, win the game.

oyun·baz *a.* Playful; (*fig.*) deceitful: *n.* swindler. ~**bazlık**, deceit. ~**bozan(lık)**, (action of) spoilsport, etc.: ~ **etm.**, create difficulties. ~**ca¹k^gı**, plaything, toy; trifle, easy job; (*fig.*) laughingstock; tool. ~**cakçı(lık)**, (work of) toy-maker/ -seller. ~**cu**, player; (*th.*) artist, actor; dancer;

comedian; sportsman; gambler; trickster: ~ **yönetmen**, (*th.*) actor-manager. ~**culuk**, playing; acting; sportsmanship; trickery. ~**laştırmak**, (*lit.*) adapt (for the theatre). ~**luk**, (*th.*) stage; dancefloor. ~**suz**, artless.

oyuntu Opening, hole; part carved out.

oz- *pref. Also* = os-.

ozalit¹ ~ **kâğıdı**, (*pub.*) blue-print.

ozan (*lit.*) Wandering minstrel; bard; poet. ~**ca**, poetically. ~**ımsı**, poetaster. ~**lık**, poet's nature/ quality. ~**sı(lık)**, poetic (nature).

ozon (*chem.*) Ozone. ~**osfer**/~**yuvarı**ⁿ¹, (*ast.*) ozonosphere.

Ö

Ö, ö [ö] The nineteenth Tk. letter, Ö
ö *int. (Of boredom/disgust).* Ugh!
ö.a. = (*phys.*) ÖZGÜL AĞIRLIK.
öbe**¹k**ᵍⁱ Heap; mound; group; (*ling.*) phrase, clause; (*soc.*) class; (*ast.*) population. ~ ~, in heaps/groups.
öbek·lemek *vi.* (*art.*) Form a group. ~lendirmek (-i), classify. ~leyici, (*phil.*) classifier.
öbür *a.* [76] The other; the next. ~ (gün), the (day) after next: ~ dünya (bilgisi), (*rel.*) the next world/ (eschatology): ~ tarafta, on the other side: ~ ucunda, at the far end: ~(k)ü, *pron.* the other one; that one.
öcü (*child.*) Ogre; bogy man.
ö**¹ç**ᶜü Revenge. ~ almak/çıkarmak (-den), take revenge on: ~ güdücü, vindictive: ~ünü almak, avenge.
öd**ü** ¹ (*bio.*) Gall; bile; (*fig.*) courage, 'guts'. ~ +, *a.* Biliary, chole-: ~ boya/sarısı, bilirubin: ~KESESİ: ~TAŞI: ~ yeşili, biliverdin: ~YOLU: ~ü kopmak/patlamak, be frightened to death.
öd**ü** ² (*bot.*) Aloes. ~agacıⁿ, (*bot.*) aloes-wood tree.
öde**¹k**ᵍⁱ (*fin.*) Bill of exchange; indemnity; (*sp.*) suspension; penalty. ~ alanı, (*sp.*) penalty area: ~ kabulü, (*fin.*) acceptance: ~i kabul eden, acceptor.
ödem (*med.*) Oedema.
öde·me *vn.* (*fin.*) Payment; disbursement; (*leg.*) performance: ~ dengesi, balance of payments: ~ güç(süzlüğ)ü, (in)solvency: ~ vakti, due date: ~leri kesmek, stop payments. ~mek (-i), pay; repay; indemnify; reimburse. ~meli, (*fin.*) COD; (telephone) reverse charges: ~ alım, cash on delivery: ~ isteme, cash with order. ~melik, fee; salary. ~mesiz, free, gratis. ~nce, indemnity; benefit. ~n**¹ç**ᶜⁱ, credit; loan. ~ne**¹k**ᵍⁱ, *n.* appropriation; allocation; indemnity; subsidy: ~ +, *a.* financial: ~ yılı, financial year. ~nekli, subsidized (theatre, etc.). ~neklik, budget: ~ +, *a.* budgetary. ~neksiz, unsubsidized. ~nili, cash: ~ eder, spot price. ~nme, *vn.* payment: ~si gecikmiş aylık, back-pay. ~nmek, *vp.* ~nmeme, non-payment. ~nmemiş, *a.* unpaid; dishonoured (cheque); outstanding. ~nmiş, *a.* paid; paid up (share). ~nti, dues; subscription. ~ş, exchange, barter; clearing: ~ gödeş olm./~mek (-le), pay one another; settle accounts: ödeştik!, we're all square! ~tici, (*adm.*) official who authorizes payment. ~timci, payee's proxy. ~tmek (-i, -e) *vc.* let/make pay.
ödev Duty; obligation. ~ bilgisi/~bilim, (*phil.*) deontology; ethics. ~cil, dutiful, conscientious. ~lendirmek (-i), entrust; appoint. ~li, having an (official) duty; on duty. ~sel, (*phil.*) deontic.
öd·kesesiⁿⁱ (*bio.*) Gall-bladder: ~ yangısı, (*med.*) cholecystitis. ~lek, cowardly.

ödometre (*phys.*) Eudiometer; (*eng.*) consolidometer.
öd·süz(lük) (*bio.*) Acho·lic/(-lia). ~taşıⁿ, gallstone.
ödül**ü** Reward; prize; (*fin.*) premium. ~ vermek, adjudge; award. ~lemek (-i), reward, gratify. ~lendirmek (-i), award a prize.
ödün Concession; compensation. ~cülük, policy based on concessions. ~**¹ç**ᶜü, *adv.* as a loan: *a.* borrowed: *n.* (*eng.*) borrow: ~ almak, borrow: ~ para, loan: ~ verme ve kiralama, (*pol.*) lendlease: ~ vermek, lend, loan: ~ yeri, (*eng.*) borrow pit. ~çü, lender. ~leme, *vn.* compensation; concession. ~lemek (-i), compensate; concede. ~lendirmek (-i), *vc.* ~lü, compensatory; concessionary.
ödyoluⁿᵘ (*bio.*) Biliary/biliferous duct.
öf *int.* Ugh!
öfke Anger; rage. ~ baldan tatlıdır, it's so easy to get angry: ~ ile kalkan zarar/ziyanla oturur, losing one's temper only leads to trouble: ~ topuklarına çıkmak (-in), fly into a rage: ~den köpürmek, boil over with rage: ~den kudurmak, champ at the bit: ~sini yenmek, control/curb one's anger: ~yle, full of rage.
öfke·ci Irascible. ~lendirmek (-i), anger s.o. ~lenmek (-e), grow angry, get into a rage. ~li, angry, choleric; hot-headed; impetuous.
öfonyum (*mus.*) Baritone tuba, euphonium.
öğ- *pref. Also* = öv-.
öğ. = ÖĞRETMEN.
öğe *n.* (*phil.*) Element; item; member; (*ling.*) part. *a.* Elementary. ~ci**¹k**ᵍⁱ, (*phys.*) atom. ~cikleşme, atomization. ~ciksel, atomic. ~lik, (*phil.*) membership.
öğle Noon, midday. ~ yemeği, midday meal, lunch: ~den önce, (in the) forenoon: ~den sonra, (in the) afternoon. ~n, (*col.*) noon; (*ast.*) meridian. ~nci, (*ed.*) afternoon student (in double-shift school). ~nde/~ yin, at noon; about midday.
öğren·ce Lesson. ~ci(lik), (status/duties of) pupil; student. ~dik, news. ~e**¹k**ᵍⁱ, lesson, example; (*fig.*) eye-opener. ~ilmek, *vp.* be learned. ~im, education; (course of) study: ~ görmek, be educated. ~imli, educated. ~imlik/~melik, bursary; scholarship. ~imsiz, uneducated. ~mek (-i), study; learn; get familiar with/accustomed to. ~miş, *a.* informed, educated.
öğret·i Creed, doctrine; teaching. ~ici, didactic; instructive; educational. ~icilik, instruction; teaching; pedagogy. ~ilmek, *vp.* be taught. ~im, education; ~ bilgisi, pedagogics: ~ görevlisi, lecturer: ~ izlence/programı, curriculum: ~üyesi, staff member: ~ yardımcıları, assistant-lecturers:

~ **yılı**, educational/school year. ~**mek (-i, -e)**, teach; instruct; suggest; admonish. ~**men(lik)**, (profession/duties of) teacher, instructor.

öğün[1] Share, portion; meal. ~**lük**, sufficient for ... meals.

öğün-[2] = ÖVÜN-.

öğür Of the same age; (horse) broken in; quiet; used to, accustomed to. ~ **olm.**/~**leşmek**, be(come) accustomed to each other. ~**lük**, being accustomed/familiar. ~**mek**, *vi.* retch; sob; bellow, low: **öğüreceği gelmek**, be disgusted. ~**tlemek (-i)**, choose; appoint. ~**tmek (-i)**, *vc.* ~**tü**, retching (sound): ~ **gelmek**, begin to retch.

öğüt[dü] Advice; admonition; warning. ~ **vermek**, advise; admonish. ~**çü**, advisor; preacher. ~**lemek (-i, -e)**, advise, counsel. ~**lenmek**, *vi.* take heed/warning. ~**örne**[k][gi], admonition, warning.

öğüt·mek (-i) Grind; crunch, chew. ~**ücü**, grinding: ~ **dişler**, (*bio.*) molar teeth. ~**ülmek**, *vp.*

öhö *int.* (*of contempt/derision*).

ö.ı. = (*phys.*) ÖZGÜL ISI.

öjeni[k][gi] (*bio.*) Eugenics.

ökçe Heel (of shoes). ~ **kemiği**, (*bio.*) heel bone. ~**çene**, (*eng.*) fixed arm of a wrench. ~**li**, with heels. ~**siz**, heelless (shoe); (*sl.*) cowardly.

öke(lik) (Quality of) genius.

Ökli[t][di] Euclid. ~ +, *a.* Euclidian.

ökse Birdlime. ~ **ardıç kuşu**, (*orn.*) mistle thrush: ~ **çubuğu**, birdlimed stick: ~**ye basmak**, get into difficulties through inattention. ~**otu**[nu], (*bot.*) mistletoe: ~ **kuşu**, (*orn.*) mistletoe flowerpecker. ~ **otugiller**, (*bot.*) mistletoe family, Loranthaceae.

öksü Half-burnt piece of wood.

öksür·mek *vi.* Cough; (*med.*) have a cough. ~**tmek (-i)**, *vc.* ~ **ü**[l][k][gü], cough; fit of coughing: ~ **pastili**, cough drop/lozenge. ~**üklü**, having a cough: ~ **tıksırıklı**, in poor health. ~**ükotu**[nu], (*bot.*) coltsfoot.

öksüz Motherless child; orphan; (*fig.*) without friends or relations. ~ **oğlan kırk yılda bir hırsızlığa çıkmış, ay akşamdan doğmuş**, if you're born unlucky there's nothing to be done about it: ~ **sevindiren**, common/tawdry thing: ~ **ler anası// babası**, foster-mother//-father; charitable woman// man. ~**balığı**[nı], (*ich.*) piper.

öküz (*zoo.*) Ox; (*fig.*) heavy/stupid person; (*sl.*) loaded dice. ~ **arabası**, ox-cart; ~ **arabası gibi**, very slowly: ~ **balıkçıl**, (*orn.*) cattle egret: ~ **damı**, ox-stall, cow-shed: ~ **dönüşü**, (*art.*) boustrophedon: ~ **gibi (bakmak)**, (look) stupidly/without understanding: ~ **kurbağası**, (*zoo.*) bull-frog: ~ **öldü, ortaklık bitti/bozuldu**, there's nothing to keep them together now: ~**e boynuzu ağır gelmez/yük olmaz**, to help one's own friends and family is no burden: ~**ü bacaya çıkarmak**, undertake stg. impossible: ~**ü bıçağın yanına götürmek**, make things unduly difficult: ~**ün altında buzağı aramak**, (*iron.*) hunt for stg. in the most unlikely place!

öküz·balığı[nı] (*zoo.*) Walrus. ~**burnu**[nu], (*orn.*) rhinoceros hornbill. ~**dili**[ni], (*bot.*) alkanet. ~**gözü**[nü], (*bot.*) arnica. ~**lük**, bovineness; (*fig.*) dullness, stupidity. ~**soğuğu**[nu], (*met.*) storm at the end of April.

öl Wetness; wet and muddy place.

ölçe[k][gi] Corn measure (9 kg.); (*math.*) measure; (*geo.*) scale. ~ **çizgisi**, (*geo.*) scale indicator. ~**lemek (-i)**, scale (up/down). ~**li**, measured.

ölçer Poker; fire-rake.

ölç·me *vn.* ~ **zinciri**, surveyor's chain. ~**mek (-i)**, measure; survey; (*fig.*) behave moderately: **ölçüp biçmek/tartmak**, take in stg. at a glance; decide after full consideration; plan carefully. ~**men**, engineer. ~ **mengüve**, (*ent.*) geometer.

ölçü Measure; measurement; dimensions; quantity; (*lit.*) metre; (*mus.*) measure, bar. ~ **belirteci**, (*ling.*) adverb of degree: ~**sünde (-in)**, all over the (country, etc.): ~**sünü almak**, measure stg. ~**dışı** Excessive. ~**lemek (-i)**, calibrate. ~**lmek**, *vp.* = ÖLÇMEK. ~**lü**, measured; temperate, moderate, well-balanced: ~ **davranmak**, behave prudently. ~**lülük**, moderation; equanimity. ~**m**, the measure of stg.; appraisal; estimate; air, manner. ~**mleme**, *vn.* evaluation. ~**mlemek (-i)**, evaluate; measure/consider carefully. ~**n**, statistic; standard. ~**nlemek (-i)**, standardize. ~**nlü**, standard, normal. ~**nmek (-i)**, calculate stg. ~**süz**, unmeasured; immeasurable; excessive(ly). ~**şmek (-le)**, measure against each other; compete with each other. ~**ştürmek (-i)**, *vc.*; compare; match. ~**ştürmeli**, comparative. ~ [t][dü/tü], criterion, standard; parameter, measurement.

öldür·esiye With the intention of killing; ruthlessly; to the death. ~**mek (-i)**, *vc.* = ÖLMEK; kill; (*cul.*) tenderize; kill time; dry off (plants); make ill; (*fig.*) destroy, ruin. ~**men**, (*leg.*) executioner. ~**menlik**, execution. ~**tmek (-i, -e)**, *vc.* make/let kill. ~ **ü**, *n.* killing. ~**ücü**, *a.* killing, lethal, mortal, fatal, deadly; -cide: ~ **balina**, (*zoo.*) killer whale. ~**ülmek**, *vp.* be killed. ~**üm**, murder, killing.

öle·siye To the death. ~ **t**[i], epidemic. ~ **yazmak**, *vi.* be about to die; feel like death.

ölgün Faded; withered; enervated; calm (sea). ~**lük**, fading, etc.

ölker (*tex.*) Nap, pile; (*bot.*) down. ~**siz**, pileless; smooth: ~ **şeftali**, (*bot.*) nectarine.

ölm. = ÖLÜMÜ.

ölmek *vi.* Die; expire; fade, wither, lose freshness; suffer great grief/anxiety. ~ **var dönmek yok**, to have burnt one's boats; the die is cast: **ölme eşeğim ölme, keep going!, there are better times ahead: ölmeğe üzere olm.**, be at death's door: **ölsem de gam yemem**, I don't care what happens: **ölünceye kadar**, till death: **ölüp ölüp dirilmek**, go through very hard times: **ölür müsün öldürür müsün?**, (*expression of extreme exasperation*).

öl·mez Undying, deathless, immortal; hard-wearing, resistant; everlasting. ~**mezleşmek**, become immortal. ~**mezlik**, immortality. ~**mezoğlu**[nu], *a.* hard-wearing, resistant. ~**müş**, *a.* dead: *n.* the dead: ~ **gitmiş**, as dead as a doornail.

ölü *a.* Dead; feeble, lifeless; faded, withered. *n.* Corpse; carcass; (*gamb. sl.*) loaded dice, marked card. ~ **açımı**, (*med.*) autopsy: ~ **dalga**, (*naut.*) spent wave: ~ **deniz**, swell; *pr.n.* (*geo.*) Dead Sea: ~ **dil**, (*ling.*) dead language: ~ **doğa**, (*art.*) still-life: ~ **doğmuş**, (*med.*) still-born: ~ **el**, (*gamb.*) dummy:

~ **fiyatına**, very cheaply, dead cheap: ~ **gibi**, cadaverous, dead-alive: ~ **gömmek**, bury the dead: ~ **gövde**, corpse: ~ **gözü gibi**, lifeless: ~ **kafası**, (*ent.*) death's head moth: ~ **kalıp**, death mask: ~ **katılığı**, (*med.*) rigor mortis: ~ **mevsim**, (*fin.*) dead/ slack season: ~ **nokta**, (*eng.*) dead-centre; (*fin.*) break-even point: ~ **örtü**, (*bot.*) covering of dead leaves: ~ **salı**, washing a corpse for burial: ~ **top**, (*sp.*) dead ball: ~ **ya da diri**, dead or alive: ~**sü kandil/kınalı**, (*vulg.*) the cursed fellow: ~**sü ortada kalmak**, be no one to conduct the funeral: ~**sünü öpmek (-in)**, swear by s.o.'s corpse: ~**yü güldürür**, very funny: ~**yü yakmak**, cremate s.o.

ölü·cü Mortal. ~**k**, *a.* lifeless: *n.* corpse. ~**lük**, morgue. ~**yük**, (*eng.*) dead weight.

ölüm Death, decease. ~ **Allah'ın emri**, even if I die!: ~ **cezası**, (*leg.*) death penalty: ~ **dirim/kalım meselesi**, matter of life and death: ~ **döşeği(nde)**, (on one's) death-bed: ~ **haberleri**, (*pub.*) obituaries: ~ **hak miras helal**, there's nothing wrong with coming into an inheritance: ~ **halinde**, dying: ~ **kâğıdı**, death certificate: ~ **oranı**, death rate: ~ **sessizliği**, a deathly hush: ~ **sıklığı**, mortality (rate): ~ **sigortası**, (*fin.*) life insurance: ~ **tezkeresi**, death certificate: ~ **var dirim var**, beware!, take care!; prepare for all eventualities!: ~**den acı**, worse than death: ~**le burun buruna gelmek**, come face to face with death/danger: ~**le öç alınmaz**, do not rejoice at your enemy's death: ~**ü göze almak**, risk one's life: ~**ün ötesi kolay**, it's a hard world!: ~**ünden sonra**, posthumous: ~**üne susamak**, be foolhardy, court death.

ölüm·cül Mortal, fatal; dying, moribund. ~**lü**, mortal, transitory: ~ **dünya**, this mortal world. ~**lük**, money saved for one's funeral expenses. ~**lülük**, mortality. ~**sek**, very weak, at death's door. ~**sü**, deathlike, deathly. ~**süz(lük)**, death-less(ness); immortal(ity).

ölünmek *imp. v.* Die; be mortal.

öm·'**ür**ʳü *n.* Life; existence; enjoyment of life, hap-piness; age. *a.* Odd, amusing. ~ **adam**, a very pleasant man: ~ **boyu**, lifetime: ~ **boyunca**, during one's lifetime, for life, as long as one lives: ~ **boyunca gelir**, (*fin.*) life annuity: ~ **çürütmek**, waste one's life: ~ **geçirmek**, live: ~ **sürmek**, live a good life: ~ **törpüsü**, an exhausting task; a trying person: ~**e bedel**, worth a life: ~**ler olsun!**, may you live long! (*to s.o. younger kissing one's hand in respect*): ~**ü billah!**, it has always/never been so!: ~**ü oldukça**, for the rest of one's life, as long as one lives: ~**ü uzamak**, live long: ~**ü vefa etmemek (-e)**, not live long enough to . . .: ~**ümün varı!**, my treasure!: ~**ünde**, never: ~**üne bereket!**, long may you live: ~**ünü kütah etm.**, not to have enjoyed one's life: ~**ünüz çok olsun!**, may you live long/be rewarded! (*reply to* AFİYET OLSUN!). ~**lü**, having a long life. ~**süz**, short-lived.

ön *n.* [90] Front; space in front; foreground; face; (*bio.*) breast, chest; the future. *a.* Front; foremost; advance; prior; preparatory, preliminary; (*bio.*) anterior, frontal. *pref.* Fore-; front-; pre-; (*ling.*) initial. ~ **ad**, first/fore/given/Christian name: ~ **ayak**, (*bio.*) forefoot; (*fig.*) pioneer; promoter;

ringleader: ~ **ayarlı**, pre-set/-timed: ~ **cam**, (*mot.*) windscreen: ~ **çalışma**, preparatory study: ~ **denetim**, (*th.*, *cin.*) censor(ship): ~ **fener**, (*mot.*) headlamp: ~ **gösteri**, (*th.*) curtain-raiser: ~ **müzik**, overture: ~ **oynatım**, (*cin.*) première: ~ **ödeme**, ödence, (*fin.*) earnest money, deposit: ~ **plan**, foreground: ~ **planda gelmek**, be(come) very important: ~ **son değişimi**, (*phil.*) transposition: ~ **soruşturma**, (*leg.*) preliminary interrogation: ~ **sözleşme**, (*adm.*) draft treaty/contract: ~ **suç**, (*leg.*) previous conviction: ~ **şart**, pre-condition: ~ **ünlü**, (*ling.*) front vowel: ~ **yazı**, (*lit.*) preface; introductory note: ~ **yükleme**, (*eng.*) precom-pression.

ön-: ~**de**, at the front; before: ~**den**, in advance; anterior; frontal: ~**den gitmek**, go ahead: ~**e almak**, take precedence: ~**e düşmek**, walk in front of s.o.: ~**e sunmak**, put forward, propose: ~**e sürmek**, use as a shield; put forward (excuses, etc.): ~**lerinde**, in front of them: ~**ü alınmak**, be pre-vented: ~**ü ardı**, the beginning and the end: ~**ü sıra**, just in front of s.o.: ~**ümde**, in front of me: ~**ümüzde**, in front of us: ~**ümüzdeki (hafta)**, this coming (week).

önün-: ~**ce**, a little before: ~**de**, in/at the front of: ~**de amana gelmek**, be helpless in the face of: ~**de perende atmak**, dupe; play tricks on: ~**de sonunda**, sooner or later: ~**den**, (passing) in front of; by, from, through.

önüne: ~ **arkasına bakmadan**, thoughtlessly; without regard to the consequences: ~ **bak!**, look out!, mind!; mind your own business: ~ **bakmak**, hang one's head (in shame): ~ **dikilmek**, stand up to, oppose: ~ **durulmaz**, it's irresistible: ~ **düşmek**, place o.s. at the head of/in front of: ~ **geçmek**, avoid, prevent; discourage; combat; (*naut.*) cross the bows of: ~ **gelmek**, come before . . .; present o.s. to . . .: ~ **gelene (kavga eder)**, (he quarrels) with everyone he meets: ~ **katmak**, drive in front of one: ~ **kavuşturmak**, button up one's coat.

önünü: ~ **almak**, prevent stg.: ~ **ardını bilmek**, be tactful and considerate: ~ **ardını düşünmek**, think well before acting; act circumspectly: ~ **kesmek**, bar s.o.'s way; hinder s.o.; waylay s.o.

ön. = (*ling.*) ÖNEK.

ön·alım (*leg.*) Pre-emption. ~**atım**, (*cin.*) projection. ~**avurt**, ~ **ünsüzü**, (*ling.*) alveolar lateral con-sonant. ~**başlık**, (*pub.*) banner headline. ~**belirti**, (*med.*) early symptom, prodrome; premonitory warning. ~**besi**, (*chem.*) protein. ~**bileşen**, antecedent. ~**bilgi**, (*ed.*) necessary prior know-ledge. ~**bili**, foreknowledge, soothsaying.

önce *adv.* [89] In front; in advance; first; early: (-den), before, ago; prior to; in front of. ~ **can sonra canan**, charity begins at home: ~ **davranmak**, anticipate: ~ **gelmek**, precede: ~ DEN: ~ LERİ: ~ **si**, origin: ~ **ye etkili**, (*leg.*) retrospective.

önce·bilim (*phil.*) Predestination. ~**den**, *adv.* at first; initially; in advance, beforehand; prior: ~ **görmek**, anticipate: ~ **hesaplı**, in cold blood. ~**ki**, the previous, the former; first; ex-. ~**l**, *n.* predecessor; antecedent: ~ **düzen**, (*phil.*)

pre-ordained order. ~ **leme,** ~ **filmi,** (*cin.*) science-fiction film. ~ **lemek (-i),** present, introduce. ~ **leri,** *adv.* at the beginning; at first; formerly, previously. ~ **lik,** (*adm.*) precedence, priority; preference: ~ **hakkı,** exclusive rights: ~ **li,** privileged; (*fin.*) preferential, preferred. ~ **likle,** *adv.* taking precedence. ~ **lim,** (*ast.*) precession. ~ **siz,** eternal (without beginning). ~ **sizlik,** eternity in the past.
öncü Leader; (*mil.*) advance-guard; (*art.*) avantgardist. ~ **l,** (*phil.*) premiss. ~ **lük,** leadership; (*art.*) avant-gardism.
ön·çim (*bot.*) Prothallus. ~ **dama¹kᵍ¹,** (*bio.*) front palate: ~ **ünsüzü,** (*ling.*) prepalatal guttural consonant. ~ **damaksı,** (*ling.*) prepalatal. ~ **de¹çᶜⁱ,** (*math.*) commutator. ~ **delemek,** *vi.* commute. ~ **delik,** (*fin.*) credit; advance. ~ **der(lik),** leader/(-ship). ~ **deyiş,** (*th.*) prologue. ~ **dölütü,** (*bio.*) embryo. ~ **döşem,** viability. ~ **duyu,** premonition. ~ **ekⁱ,** (*ling.*) prefix. ~ **el,** (*fin.*) term, period; permitted delay. ~ **elci¹kᵍⁱ,** (*phys.*) proton.
önem Importance; calibre; consideration; consequence. ~ **vermek,** value, consider important; emphasize: ~ **i yok,** it's of no consequence: ~ **ini anlamak,** appreciate, value: ~ **le,** earnestly.
önem·li Important; considerable: ~ **yol,** arterial road. ~ **semek (-i),** consider important. ~ **senmek,** *vp.* ~ **siz,** unimportant; of no account. ~ **sizlik,** unimportance.
öner·ge (*adm.*) Proposal, motion. ~ **gi,** (*adm.*) recommendation for promotion. ~ **i,** (*adm.*) proposal, project. ~ **ili,** (*fin.*) pro forma. ~ **me,** *vn.*; proposal; recommendation; (*phil.*) assertion; (*ling.*) proposition; sentence. ~ **mek (-i),** propose; suggest; recommend. ~ **mesel,** declarative, assertive. ~ **ti,** (*phil.*) premiss.
öne·sürüm (*phil.*) Claim, thesis. ~ **sürüş,** statement.
öneze Hunter's hide.
ön·gelme Precedence, priority; (*mus.*) anticipation. ~ **gerilmeli,** (*eng.*) prestressed. ~ **görme,** *vn.* foreseeing. ~ **görmek (-i),** envisage, foresee; provide for. ~ **görü,** foresight, prudence. ~ **görülmek,** *vp.* ~ **görülü,** farsighted; prudent.
ön·gün The day before; the eve. ~ **günleme,** backdating. ~ **ısıtım,** pre-heating. ~ **işlem,** (*eng.*) pretreatment. ~ **işleri,** preliminaries. ~ **kayıt,** (*ed.*) enrolment, registration. ~ **kol,** (*bio.*) forearm: ~ **kemiği,** ulna. ~ **le¹çᶜⁱ,** buffer, stopper.
ön·lem Precaution, disposition; measure; procedure: ~ **almak,** take precautions: ~ **kararı,** (*leg.*) temporary injunction. ~ **leme,** *vn.* ~ **lemek (-i),** prevent, prohibit; intercept; check, inhibit, counter(act); anticipate, avert; avoid. ~ **lemli,** provident, cautious. ~ **lemsiz,** incautious. ~ **lenmek,** *vp.* ~ **leyici,** *a.* preventive, restrictive; deterrent: *n.* preventative; inhibitor; deterrent, damper. ~ **leyimevi,** (*med.*) observation sanatorium.
önlü Pertaining to the front; frontal. ~ **ve arkalı bir sayfa,** a page with writing on both sides.
ön·lük (*mod.*) Apron; pinafore. ~ **oda,** (*bio.*) anterior chamber (of eye). ~ **oluş(um),** (*phil.*) preformation. ~ **örgü,** (*art.*) skeleton, framework; (*lit.*) main plot. ~ **sahne,** (*th.*) apron stage. ~ **sayı,** (*pub.*) advance copy. ~ **seçim,** (*adm.*) primary

election; (*rad.*) preselection. ~ **sel,** (*phil.*) *a priori.* ~ **ses,** (*ling.*) initial sound: ~ **düşmesi,** aphaeresis. ~ **sezi,** premonition. ~ **söz,** (*pub.*) foreword, preface. ~ **tasar,** draft plan. ~ **tasım,** (*phil.*) presupposition. ~ **tasla¹kᵍ¹,** rough draft. ~ **türeme,** (*ling.*) prosthesis. ~ **yargı,** prejudice; bias. ~ **yargı¹çᶜ¹,** (*leg.*) magistrate, justice of the peace. ~ **yargılı,** prejudiced; biased. ~ **yargısız,** unprejudiced. ~ **yüz,** (*mil.*) front; (*pub.*) recto. ~ **yüzbaşıʸ¹,** (*naut.*) lieutenant-commander.
öp·me *vn.* ~ **mek (-i, -den),** kiss; caress: **öp babanın elini!,** well this is a mess!; what's to be done now?: **öperken ısırır,** he's not to be trusted: **öp(üp) de başına koymak,** be thankful for small mercies. ~ **türmek (-i, -e),** *vc.* let/make kiss. ~ **ücü¹kᵍü,** a kiss: ~ **böceği,** (*ent.*) assassin bug: ~ **göndermek (-e),** blow s.o. a kiss. ~ **ülmek,** *vp.* ~ **üş,** act/manner of kissing; kiss. ~ **üşmek (-le),** kiss each other.
ör Fence, barrier. ~ **cin,** rope ladder.
Ör. = ÖRNEĞIN.
örde¹kᵍⁱ (*orn.*) Duck; (*med.*) bed-pan, urinal; (*sl.*) (taxi) passenger picked-up en route. ~ **avlamak,** (*sl.*) look for clients: ~ **gagalı platipüs,** (*zoo.*) duck-billed platypus: ~ **midyesi,** (*zoo.*) barnacle: ~ **tuzağı,** decoy: ~ **yavrusu,** (*orn.*) duckling: ~ **yürüyüşü,** waddling.
ördek·balığıⁿ¹ (*ich.*) Striped wrasse. ~ **başı**ⁿ¹, greenish blue. ~ **gagası**ⁿ¹, light orange.
ördürmek (-i, -e) *vc.* = ÖRMEK.
öre¹kᵍⁱ (*bio.*) Network of a tissue; (*arch.*) build(ing work). ~ **e,** (*tex.*) distaff.
ören Ruin. ~ **gülü,** (*bot.*) bryony. ~ **yerler,** ruins.
örf (*leg.*) Common usage; custom; tyranny. ~ **ve âdet,** usage and custom. ~ **i,** customary; arbitrary: ~ **idare,** (*adm.*) martial law.
örge (*art.*) Motif, subject.
örgen (*bio.*) Organ; limb. ~ **ci(lik),** (*phil.*) organi-cist/(-cism). ~ **lemek (-i),** (*phil.*) arrange, organize. ~ **leşmek,** *vi.* (*bio.*) become living organs. ~ **lik,** organism. ~ **sel,** organic.
örgü Plaited/knitted thing; plait; tress of hair; strand (of rope); (*bio.*) plexus; (*chem.*) lattice; (*arch.*) bond (of bricks). ~ **iğne/yumurtası,** darning-needle//-ball. ~ **cü,** plaiter; knitter. ~ **lü,** plaited; braided. ~ **n,** (*phil.*) organized.
örgütü Organization, association; office. ~ **toplantısı,** (*pol.*) demo(nstration). ~ **çü/~leyici,** organizer. ~ **çülük,** organizing work/ability. ~ **le-(ndir)mek (-i),** organize. ~ **lenmek,** *vp.* be(come) organized. ~ **lü,** organized. ~ **sel,** (*fin.*) organic; organizational. ~ **süz,** unorganized; disorganized.
ör·me *vn.* Knitting; plaiting. ~ **mecilik,** knitting. ~ **mek (-i),** (*tex.*) knit; plait; weave; interlace; darn; (*arch.*) lay (bricks), build (a wall); block up (a door); (*sp.*) weave.
örn. = ÖRNEĞIN; ÖRNEK.
örneğin *adv.* [195] For example.
örne¹kᵍⁱ *n.* Specimen, sample; copy; model, type, pattern; example; (*sp.*) classic (race). *a.* Model; typical. ~ **alma,** (*ind.*) sampling: ~ **almak,** copy, adopt; (-**den**), take an example from; sample: ~ **çıkarmak,** take copies from: ~ **olarak,** for instance:

~ **olay,** typical event, example: ~ **olm.,** be/set an example: ~ **in** = ÖRNEĞİN: ~ **ini almak (-in),** draw stg. in outline: ~ **ini çıkarmak (-in),** make a copy of stg.
örnek·dışı Atypical, abnormal. ~ **lem,** example. ~ **leme,** *vn.*; (*math.*) type selection; sampling. ~ **le(ndir)mek (-i),** set an example. ~ **lik,** example; (*fin.*) sample. ~ **se,** for example. ~ **seme,** *vn.*; (*ling.*) comparison, analogy. ~ **semek (-i),** compare.
öropiyum (*chem.*) Europium.
örs (*ind.*) Anvil; shoemaker's last. ~ **kemiği,** (*bio.*) anvil, incus.
örse·lemek (-i) Handle roughly, misuse; wear out; spoil; rumple; (*med.*) exhaust, weaken; disturb. ~ **lenme,** *vn.*; disturbance. ~ **lenmek,** *vp.* ~ **nti,** (*med.*) lesion.
ört·bas Hushing up, concealment; dissimulation: ~ **etm.,** cover up, conceal. ~ **ene^lk^{ği},** (*bio.*) mantle, sheath. ~ **kal,** (*med.*) plaster. ~ **me,** *vn.*; coating, covering; (*phys.*) screening; (*mil.*) camouflage. ~ **mece/** ~ **mecilik,** (*ling.*) euphemism. ~ **mek (-i),** cover; wrap; clothe; cloak, veil; shut, close; (*fig.*) conceal; eclipse. ~ **türmek (-i, -e),** *vc.* ~ **ü,** cover; wrap; roof; carpet; blanket. ~ **üalım,** (*chem.*) pickling, stripping. ~ **ücü,** covering; concealing; (*cin.*) shutter. ~ **ük,** covered; closed; implicit: ~ **tasım,** (*phil.*) enthymeme. ~ **ülme,** *vn.*; (*ast.*) occultation. ~ **ülmek,** *vp.* be covered; be closed, etc. ~ **ülü,** coated; covered; wrapped up; concealed; shut; roofed; obscure (of speech): ~ **ödenek,** (*adm.*) discretionary fund. ~ **ünmek (-le),** cover/conceal o.s. (with stg.). ~ **üsüz,** uncovered; open; bare; obscene. ~ **üşme,** coincidence.
örü Texture; network; web; darn; (*arch.*) wall, building; barrier, division; enclosed space. ~ **cü,** mender, darner. ~ **cülük,** mending, darning. ~ **l-mek,** *vp.* = ÖRMEK. ~ **lü,** plaited, knitted; enclosed (by a wall, etc.).
örüm·ce (*ent.*) (?) Fig moth. ~ **ceğimsiler,** (*zoo.*) Arachnidae. ~ **ce^lk^{ği},** (*zoo.*) spider: ~ **(ağı),** spider's web, cobweb; ~ **almak,** sweep away cobwebs: ~ **bağlamak,** be covered in cobwebs; (*fig.*) be neglected: ~ **kafalı,** old-fashioned, 'square'; reactionary: ~ **kuşu,** (*orn.*) shrike: ~ **maymunu,** (*zoo.*) spider monkey: ~ **sarmak/ tutmak,** be full of cobwebs: ~ **ler,** spiders, Araneae.
örümcek·lenmek *vi.* Become covered with cobwebs; (*med.*) when feverish feel eyes/mouth covered with cobwebs. ~ **li,** covered with cobwebs: ~ **kafa,** old-fashioned; reactionary. ~ **si,** (*bio.*) arachnoid/ weblike (membrane).
örüntü Pattern; example. ~ **cü(lük),** (*phil.*) pattern·ist/(-ism).
örüt (*ling.*) Text; (*phys.*) network. ~ **bilim,** philology.
östaki (*bio.*) ~ **borusu,** Eustachian tube.
ösz. = (*ling.*) ÖZNESİZ; ÖZNE ALMAYAN EYLEM.
öşür = AŞAR.
öt = ÖD.
öte *n.* The farther side; what is on the farther side; the beyond; the other side. *a.* Other; farther; being on the other side. ~ **gün,** the other day, recently: ~ **yaka,** the other side/shore: ~ **yandan,** from the other side; moreover: ~ **de,** over there; farther on:

~ **de beride,** here and there, around: ~ **den,** on the other hand: ~ **den beri,** from of old; heretofore: ~ **den beriden,** from here and there: ~ **si berisi,** things; various things/places: ~ **si var mı?,** have you any more to say?: ~ **sini beri etm. (-in),** study a matter from all sides: ~ **ye,** over there: ~ **ye beriye,** in various places: ~ **ye geçme,** oppression.
öte·beri This and that; various things; this side and that; here and there; = ÖTE. ~ **devim,** (*psy.*) telekinesis. ~ **duyum,** telepathy. ~ **kiⁿⁱ,** the other (one); the farther (one); the one over there: ~ **beriki,** this one and that; anybody and everybody: ~ **gün,** (*dial.*) the day before yesterday; the other day. ~ **le(n)me,** (*phys.*) transition; (*math.*) translation. ~ **lenmeli,** transitional.
ötek·ti^lk^{ği} (*min.*) Eutectic. ~ **toid,** eutectoid.
ötle·ğen (*orn.*) Whitethroat; warbler. ~ **ğengiller,** warblers. ~ **ği,** (*orn.*) bearded vulture.
ötmek *vi.* (Birds) sing; (cock) crow; (bell) ring; resound, echo; (*sl.*) talk foolishly, chatter; (*sl.*) (drunkard) vomit.
ötre Arabic vowel sign for O/Ö/U/Ü.
öt·türmek (-i) *vc.* Cause to sing: *vi.* talk airily; swank. ~ **ücü,** singing well: ~ **ardıç kuşu,** (*orn.*) song-thrush: ~ **kuğu,** (*orn.*) whooper swan: ~ **kuş,** song-bird. ~ **ülmek,** *imp. v.* sing.
ötüm·lü (*ling.*) Voiced. ~ **süz,** voiceless, unvoiced.
ötür·mek (*med.*) Have diarrhoea. ~ **ü^lk^ü,** diarrhoea.
ötürü (-den) *post.* [89] Because of, on account of.
ötüş Singing (of birds); (*phys.*) resonance. ~ **mek,** *vi.* sing/chirp together; sound together.
öv- *pref. Also* = ÖĞ-.
öv·e^lç^{ci} (*live.*) Two-/three-year-old ram. ~ **endire,** (*live.*) goad.
övgü Praise, commendation; compliment. ~ **belgesi,** certificate of commendation: ~ **ye değer,** with distinction; commendable. ~ **değerlik,** commendation, distinction, honourable mention. ~ **lemek (-i),** compliment s.o.
öv·me *vn.* ~ **mek (-i),** praise, commend; compliment. ~ **ücü,** commendatory, praising. ~ **ülmek,** *vp.* ~ **ünce,** cause/object of pride. ~ **ün^lç^{cü},** pride. ~ **ünçlü,** proud. ~ **üngen,** boastful; vainglorious. ~ **üngenlik,** boastfulness; vainglory. ~ **ünmek (-le),** be proud of: *vi.* praise o.s., boast: ~ **gibi olmasın,** without wishing to boast. ~ **üş,** eulogy.
öykü (*lit.*) (Short) story; folk tale. ~ **ce/** ~ **cük,** fable, myth, story. ~ **cü,** story-teller; narrator; short-story writer. ~ **cülük,** story-telling; story-teller's art; short-story writing. ~ **leme,** (*cin., etc.*) narration. ~ **nme,** *vn.*; (*art.*) imitation. ~ **nmek (-e),** imitate, copy. ~ **nmeli,** imitative. ~ **ntü,** (*lit.*) pastiche. ~ **nücü,** imitator. ~ **nüm,** simulation. ~ **sel,** narrative.
öyle *a.* [72] Such; that kind of, like that. *adv.* So; in that manner. ~ **bir adam,** such a man: ~ **bir ... ki deme/sorma gitsin!,** you never saw such a ...: ~ **de battık böyle de!,** we're done for anyhow!: ~ **gelmek (-e),** seem: ~ **gelmek ki,** feel a desire to: ~ **gibime geliyor ki,** it seems to me that: ~ **ise/** ~ **yse,** if so, in that case: ~ **mi?,** is that so?: ~ **olsun,** so be it; as you wish: ~ **şey/yağma yok,** that sort of

thing's not done; no you don't!: ~ **ya!**, yes, indeed!; naturally!: ~ **yse** = ~ **iSE.**

öyle·ce *adv.* [195] Just like that; in that manner/way: ~ **tutmak**, prolong; preserve. ~ **lik**, that manner; such a way: ~ **le**, in such a manner. ~ **(me)sine**, to such an extent; excessively. ~ **si**, *adv.* such.

öz *n.* Self; content; essence; element; (*bot.*) pith; kernel; (*zoo.*) marrow; cream; (*geo.*) brook, valley. *a.* Own; proper; essential; main; real, genuine; intrinsic; self-; auto-. ~ **ad**, first/fore/given name: ~ **kardeş**, full brother: ~ **konuşmak**, speak to the point: ~ **olmayan**, (*phil.*) improper: ~ **saygısı**, self-respect: ~ **Türkçe**, [xxi] (*ling.*) pure Turkish: ~ **ü** sözü bir, genuine, sincere; reliable.

öz. = ÖZEL. ~ **a./i.** = (*ling.*) ÖZEL AD/iSİM.

öz·ağırlık (*phys.*) Specific weight. ~ **anamal**, (*fin.*) net assets/capital.

Özbe¹kᵍⁱ (*ethn.*) Uzbek. ~ **çe**, (*ling.*) Uzbek. ~ **istan**, (*geo.*) Uzbekistan.

öz·belirlenim (*phil.*) Self-determination. ~ **beöz**, (*col.*) *a.* real; true, 100 per cent genuine: *adv.* essentially. ~ **beslenme**, (*zoo.*) autotrophy. ~ **birey**, individual. ~ **decik(sel)**, (*phys.*) molecu·le/(-lar). ~ **decik·içi/-lerarası**, intermolecular. ~ **de¹kᵍⁱ**, *n.* substance, matter; (*fin.*) goods, merchandise; (*phil.*) material. ~ **dekçe**, materially. ~ **dekçi(lik)**, (*phil.*) material·ist/(-ism). ~ **deksel**, *a.* material; materialist; (*leg.*) factual; (*fin.*) real. ~ **dem**, (*chem.*) mole. ~ **demli(lik)**, molar(ity). ~ **den**, (*bio.*) thymus. ~ **denlik**, (*phil.*) aseity. ~ **denlikle**, sincerely. ~ **deş**, same, synonymous, identical. ~ **deşbaskı**, (*pub.*) reproduction. ~ **deşleme**, *vn.* identification. ~ **deşlemek (-i)**, make/accept as identical; identify. ~ **deşleşmek**, *vi.* become identical. ~ **deşlik**, a being identical; (*math.*, *phil.*) identity. ~ **devekuşları**ⁿⁱ, (*orn.*) ostriches. ~ **devim**, (*phil.*) automatism; (*ast.*) proper motion. ~ **devim·li/-sel**, automatic. ~ **devimsellik**, auto-maticity. ~ **devinim**, automation. ~ **deyiş**, adage, maxim, aphorism. ~ **dışı**ⁿⁱ, (*phil.*) extrinsic. ~ **diren¹ç**ᶜⁱ, (*el.*) resistivity.

öze Proper, special (to).

öze¹kᵍⁱ Centre; (*bio.*) cyst. ~ **çek**, (*phys.*) centri-petal. ~ **doku**, (*bio.*) parenchyma. ~ **kaç**, centri-fugal. ~ **leşme** = ODAKLAŞMA. ~ **lik**, centre. ~ **sel**, central.

özel Personal; private; distinctive; particular; special; specific. ~ **af**, (*ling.*) proper noun: ~ **af**, (*leg.*) pardon: ~ **avarya/dokunca**, (*fin.*) particular average: ~ **daire**, private/special office: ~ **deyiş**, (*ling.*) idiom: ~ **dil**, (*ling.*) professional slang, jargon: ~ **doktor**, medical attendant: ~ **düşünce**, personal opinion: ~ **erdem**, (*psy.*) charisma: ~ **girişim(cilik)**, (*fin.*) private enterprise; (*pol.*) liberalism: ~ **girişimci**, private contractor; (*pol.*) liberal: ~ **görüs**, interpretation: ~ **haber**, (*pub.*) exclusive story, scoop: ~ **hakem**, (*leg.*) arbitrator: ~ **izin (hakkı)**, (*leg.*) licence//(royalty): ~ **kesim**, (*fin.*) private sector: ~ **kuriye**, special messenger: ~ **muhabir**, (*pub.*) special correspondent: ~ **okul**, (*ed.*) private school: ~ **ortaklık**, (*fin.*) private partnership: ~ **sayı**, (*pub.*) special edition/number: ~ **sektör** = ~ KESİM. ~ **tertibat**, contrivance,

device: ~ **ulak**, courier; special delivery (letter): ~ **uygulamalık**, (*ind.*) special-purpose: ~ **yol**, accommodation road. ~ **ci**, (*fin.*) supporter of private enterprise.

öz·eleştiri Self-criticism. ~ **elik**, characteristic, property.

özel·leştirmek (-i) Make personal/private/special. ~ **lik**, peculiarity, characteristic; property, special feature: ~ **lerini kaybetme**, degradation. ~ **likle**, in particular, specially.

özen Care, attention; pains; taking pains. ~ **bezen**, trinkets, ornaments; ceremony: ~ **göstermek**/~ **le bakmak**, take great care.

özen·ce (*fin.*) Bonus, premium. ~ **ci**, non-professional, amateur. ~ **cilik**, amateurism. ~ **çli**, capricious. ~ **dirim**/~ **dirme**, *vn.*; encouragement, support: ~ **ödülü**, consolation prize. ~ **dirmek (-i, -e)**, *vc.*; encourage; support. ~ **gen**, (*sp.*, *th.*) amateur. ~ **ilmek**, *vp.* ~ **ilmiş**, elaborate. ~ **iş**, taking great pains. ~ **li**, painstaking, careful: ~ **çeviri**, (*lit.*) literal translation. ~ **me**, *vn.* ~ **mek**, *vi.* take pains, be painstaking, try hard: **(-e)**, take pains over stg.; elaborate on stg.; desire ardently; try to imitate s.o.: **özene bezene**, painstaking, with particular care: **özene özene**, paying great attention: **özenip bezenmek**, take great pains, go to great trouble. ~ **siz**, negligent; careless. ~ **sizlik**, negligence, carelessness. ~ **ti**, care, attention; affectation; pseudo-, counterfeit; mock: ~ **şair**, pseudo-poet. ~ **tili**, careful. ~ **tisiz**, careless.

özerk(lik) Autono·mous/(-my); indepen·dent/ (-dence).

özetⁱ (*lit.*) Summary, précis; digest, synopsis; epi-tome; (*chem.*) extract. ~ **i budur**, it all boils down to this: ~ **le**, in detail.

özet·çe (*pub.*) Abstract: ~ **çıkarmak**, abstract. ~ **kitap**, abridgement. ~ **lem**/~ **leyim**, (*mil.*) brief-ing. ~ **lemek (-i)**, summarize; abridge, condense; extract. ~ **lenmek**, *vp.* ~ **li**, concise, succinct.

özezer (*psy.*) Masochist(ic). ~ **lik**, masochism.

özge *a.* Other; another; different; uncommon. *n.* Stranger. ~ **ci(l)**, altruist(ic). ~ **cilik**, altruism. ~ **lik**, characteristic.

özgeç·i Self-sacrifice. ~ **ili**, self-sacrificing. ~ **ilik**, altruism. ~ **miş**, (*lit.*) autobiography: ~ **ler**, cur-riculum vitae. ~ **mişsel**, autobiographical.

öz·gen (*chem.*) Enzyme. ~ **gü**, particular, peculiar, special; specific, characteristic. ~ **gü¹ç**ᶜᵘ, ability, capacity. ~ **güdüm(lü)** (*mil.*) self-guid·ance/(-ed), homing. ~ **gül**, specific: ~ **ağırlık**, (*phys.*) specific gravity, density, buoyancy: ~ **ısı**, (*phys.*) specific heat. ~ **gülemek (-i, -e)**, assign/allocate to. ~ **gülen-mek**, *vp.* ~ **güllük**, specificity. ~ **gülük**, particu-larity; specificness; property. ~ **gün**, original; own; unique. ~ **günleşmek**, *vi.* become unique. ~ **günlük**, originality. ~ **gür**, free, independent, autonomous, private: ~ **bırakmak**, release, set free: ~ **girişimci**, (*fin.*) private contractor: ~ **istenç**, free will. ~ **gürlük**, freedom, independence. ~ **gürlükçü**, freedom lover. ~ **gürlüksüz**, lacking freedom. ~ **güveni**, self-reliance.

öz·ısı (*phys.*) Specific heat. ~ **ışın**, (*bot.*) medullary

ray. ~ **iletkenlik**, (*phys.*) conductivity. ~ **inandırım**, (*psy.*) auto-suggestion. ~ **indükleme**, (*el.*) self-induction. ~ **kertenkelegiller**, (*zoo.*) lizards. ~ **kesi⋅t**^{di}, (*carp.*) radial cross-section. ~ **köpekbalığı**^{nı}, (*ich.*) smoothhound. **öz⋅lem** *n.* Longing (for stg.); aspiration (to stg.). ~ **leme**, *vn.* longing. ~ **lemek** (-i), long for; wish for; aspire to. ~ **lemli**, *a.* longing. ~ **lenmek**, *vp.* ~ **leşmek**, (*bot.*) acquire pith/kernel; become pasty; (*bio.*) coagulate; become pure/unadulterated. ~ **leştirme**, *vn.* (*ling.*) purifying, simplifying. ~ **leştirmeci(lik)**, (*ling.*) purifi⋅er/(-cation). ~ **leştirmek** (-i), *vc.* purify, refine; render authentic and unadulterated. ~ **letmek** (-i, -e), *vc.* make long for. ~ **leyiş**, longing; homesickness. ~ **lü**, (*bot.*) having kernel/pith, etc.; sappy, pulpy; sticky, pasty; (*fig.*) pithy, concise, terse; substantial; fertile: ~ **çamur**, sticky mud: ~ **söz**, (*lit.*) aphorism: ~ **toprak**, potter's clay; fertile soil: ~ **ün**, (*cul.*) flour making a sticky paste. ~ **lük**, *a.* personal: *n.* substance; essence; conciseness; (*bot.*) pith, etc.; self, identity, personal relationship; egoism, selfishness: ~ **işleri**, (*ind.*) personnel affairs/management.
öz⋅mayabilim (*bio.*) Enzymology. ~ **memeliler**, (*zoo.*) higher mammals. ~ **menevişleme**, (*min.*) self-tempering.
öz⋅ne (*ling.*, *phil.*) Subject; ego. ~ **nel**, subjective; moral. ~ **nelci(lik)**, subjectiv⋅ist/(-ism). ~ **nellik**, subjectivity. ~ **nitelik**, attribute.

öz⋅odun (*for.*) Heartwood. ~ **öğrenim**, (*ed.*) self-teaching; private study. ~ **öğrenimli**, self-taught. ~ **saygı**, self-respect. ~ **saygılı**, self-respecting. ~ **sel**, of the self; essential; real. ~ **sevi**, self-respect. ~ **su**, (*bot.*) sap. ~ **suverilme**, (*min.*) self-quenching. ~ **tavlama**, (*min.*) self-annealing. ~ **ton**, (*lit.*) local colour.
özüm⋅leme/ ~ seme *vn.* Assimilation. ~ **lemedokusu**^{nu}, (*bot.*) assimilation tissue. ~ **lemek/ ~ semek** (-i), assimilate. ~ **lenmek/ ~ senmek**, *vp.*
özün⋅erosluk (*psy.*) Auto-eroticism. ~ **lü**, intrinsic.
öz⋅lür^{rü} Defect; impediment; excuse, apology, pardon. ~ **dilemek**, apologise, ask pardon: ~ **dilerim!**, I beg your pardon!: ~ **ü kabahatinden büyük**, his excuse is worse than his fault: ~ **ü meşru**, (*obs.*) legitimate excuse.
özür⋅lü Defective; having an excuse. ~ **süz**, faultless; without excuse: ~ **pürüzsüz**, free from any defect.
öz⋅üştürüm (*chem.*) Metabolism. ~ **ü⋅t**^{dü}, extract. ~ **ütleme**, extraction. ~ **varlık**, (*phil.*) soul; self; essence. ~ **veren/ ~ verili**, self-sacrificing, unselfish. ~ **veri**, self-sacrifice: ~ **istiyen iş**, a very demanding job. ~ **yapı(sal)**, character(istic). ~ **yaşam**, personal/private life: ~ **romanı**, (*lit.*) autobiographical novel. ~ **yaşamöyküsü**, (*lit.*) autobiography. ~ **yaşlanma**, (*min.*) self-ageing. ~ **yazı**, (*lit.*) aphorism. ~ **yiti**, (*psy.*) absence.

P

P, p [pe] The twentieth Tk. letter, P. ~ **vitamini**, (*bio.*) vitamin P.

P, p. = (*ch.s.*) FOSFOR; (*mus.*) PİYANO.

Pa. = (*phys.*) PASKAL; (*ch.s.*) PROTAKTİNYUM.

pabu¹çᶜᵘ Shoe; slipper; (*el.*) tag (of a wire); (*eng.*) dog. ~ **bırakmamak (-e)**, not be intimidated by stg.: ~ **eskitmek/paralamak**, display great energy in pursuing a matter: ~ **kadar dili var**, he answers back rudely: ~ **pahalı**, recognize when you're outmatched, 'time to quit'; it's a dangerous situation: ~ **larını çevirmek**, give s.o. a hint that he should go: ~ **tan aşağı**, contemptible, shameful: ~ **u başına giydirmek**, make s.o. do the wrong thing: ~ **u büyük!**, (*jok.*) hodja: ~ **u büyüğe okut (kendini)!**, you must be crazy!: ~ **u dama atılmak**, lose favour; fall into discredit: ~ **u eline verilmek**, be dismissed, 'get the boot': ~ **uma alırsın!**, nothing doing!: ~ **umda değil**, it doesn't concern/matter to me: ~ **unu eline vermek**, send s.o. away; give s.o. the sack, dismiss s.o.: ~ **unu ters giydirmek (-e)**, cause s.o. to escape hurriedly; play a trick on s.o.; teach s.o. a lesson.

pabuç·çu Shoe-maker/-seller; attendant looking after people's shoes at a mosque, etc.: ~ **kölesi**, shoemaker's iron last. ~ **çuluk**, shoemaking. ~ **gagalı**, (*orn.*) whale-headed stork. ~ **lu**, having/ wearing shoes. ~ **luk**, place for keeping shoes/ slippers near the front door. ~ **suz**, shoeless: ~ **kaçmak**, rush away; be routed.

paça (*live.*) (Sheep's, etc.) trotters; (*cul.*) dish made from trotters; (*mod.*) lower part of trouser-leg. ~ **kasnağı**, (*sp.*) a wrestling hold: ~ **ları sıvamak**, tuck up one's trousers; 'roll up one's sleeves', get down to work: ~ **larından kibarlık akmak**, be over-polite: ~ **sı düşük**, slovenly, untidy: ~ **sından tutup atmak**, drive s.o. out contemptuously: ~ **sını çekecek hali olmamak**, be hopelessly clumsy and incapable: ~ **sını/ ~ yı kurtarmak**, escape, save one's skin.

paça·cı(lık) (Work of) s.o. who sells trotters. ~ **günü**, the day after a wedding (when a dish of trotters is eaten). ~ **lı**, (*mod.*) having trouser legs; (*cul.*) made of trotter jelly; (*orn.*) having feathered legs: ~ **şahin**, (*orn.*) rough-legged hawk. ~ **lık**, (*mod.*) 'ankle' of trouser-leg; (*cul.*) food served// (*mod.*) bridal dress worn on the day after the wedding.

paçal (*cul.*) The proportion of various grains legally permitted for making bread. ~ **fiyat**, (*fin.*) satisfactory price for a tender.

paçavra Rag(s); (*fig.*) worthless and disgusting; (*pub.*) the gutter/yellow press. ~ **etm./ ~ sını çıkarmak/ ~ ya çevirmek**, botch, make a mess of stg.: ~ **hastalığı**, (*med.*) influenza. ~ **cı(lık)**, (work of) ragman. ~ **lıkurbağagiller**, (*zoo.*) flying frogs.

paç·oz (*sl.*) Prostitute. ~ **uz**, (*ich.*) grey mullet.

padavra (*arch.*) Shingle; thin board (under tiles). ~ **gibi/ ~ sı çıkmış**, so thin that his ribs stick out: ~ **tahtası**, clapboard.

padişah (*adm.*) Ruler; (*esp.*) the Ottoman Sultan. ~ **lık**, the Sultanate; sovereignty; reign.

pafta Horse-brass; screw-plate; (*pub.*) each section of a large map, etc.; (*eng.*) thread-cutter; (*bio.*) large coloured spot. ~ **kolu**, (*eng.*) die stock: ~ **lokması**, die: ~ ~, covered/stained with spots.

pagan(izm) (*rel.*) Pagan(ism).

pagoda (*arch.*) Pagoda.

pağur(ya) = PAVURYA.

pah (*carp., eng.*) Bevel, chamfer; (*arch.*) coving.

paha (*fin.*) Price; cost; value. ~ **biçilmez**, priceless, invaluable: ~ **biçmek/kesmek**, estimate/evaluate/ fix a price: ~ **dan düşmek**, fall in price: ~ **sını**, at the cost of . . .: ~ **ya çıkarmak**, raise in price: ~ **ya çıkmak**, rise in price.

paha·cı S.o. who sells at a high price. ~ **lanmak/ ~ lılaşmak**, *vi.* become expensive. ~ **lı**, dear, high-priced, expensive: ~ **dır hikmeti var ucuzdur illeti var**, it always pays to buy the best: ~ **ya oturmak**, be very expensive. ~ **lılık**, expensiveness, costliness.

pahlamak (-i) (*carp., eng.*) Bevel, chamfer; (*arch.*) cove.

pak Clean; pure, untarnished; holy.

paka (*zoo.*) Paca.

paket¹ Packet; parcel; small box; (*adm.*) package deal. ~ **etm.**, wrap up, make a parcel: ~ **program**, (*rad.*) package programme: ~ **taşı**, rectangular paving-stone.

paketle·me *vn.*: ~ **makinesi**, wrapping machine. ~ **mek (-i)**, make into a parcel; pack/wrap up. ~ **nmek**, *vp.*

Pakistan (*geo.*) Pakistan. ~ **+**, *a.* Pakistani. ~ **lı**, *n.* (*ethn.*) Pakistani.

pak·lak (*min.*) Pickler (machine). ~ **lama**, *vn.*; (*min.*) pickling. ~ **lamak (-i)**, clean; (*min.*) pickle; (*leg.*) clear, acquit; take away, use up. ~ **lık**, purity; cleanliness.

pakt¹ (*adm.*) Pact, treaty, agreement.

pal (*orn.*) A species of pigeon.

pala (*mil.*) Scimitar; (*naut.*) oar-blade, paddle; (*aer.*) blade; (*carp.*) thin wide plank set on edge. ~ **çalmak/sallamak**, brandish a scimitar; (*fig.*) swagger about; strive (to do stg.): ~ **çekmek**, draw one's sword: ~ **çevirmek**, feather an oar.

pala·bıyı¹kᵏ¹ Large curved moustache. ~ **lık**, edge of a rafter: ~ **ına**, edgeways: ~ **ına koymak**, set up on edge.

palamar (*naut.*) Cable. ~ **boyu**, 120 fathoms: ~ **parası**, mooring fee: ~ **ı çözmek/koparmak**, slip the cable; (*fig.*) make off. ~ **gözü**ⁿᵘ, hawse-hole.

palamu'tᵈᵘ¹ *n.* (*ich.*) Short-finned tunny, bonito. ~ **pastırması**, (*cul.*) salted bonito.
palamutᵘ² (*bot.*) Valonia oak; its (dried) acorn. ~**lular**, (*bot.*) beech family, Fagaceae.
palan Broad soft saddle without frame. ~**ga**, (*naut.*) tackle, pulley-block: ~ **çımaları**, falls. ~**ka**, (*mil.*, *arch.*) redoubt.
palas Luxury hotel; any large building; (*sl.*) easy life.
palaska (*mil.*) Cartridge belt; bandolier.
palaspandıras Hastily, abruptly, brusquely.
palavra (*naut.*) Main deck (of warship); (*sl.*) idle talk, claptrap, boasting, bravado. ~ **altında**, below decks: ~ **atmak/savurmak/sıkmak**, boast: ~ **haber**, (*pub.*) canard, hoax. ~**cı(lık)**, (*sl.*) boast·er/(-ing).
palaz (*orn.*) Duckling, gosling, etc. ~**la(n)mak**, *vi.* grow plump; (*fig.*) (child) grow up; (*fig.*, *pej.*) become noticeably richer: **(-e)**, (*sl.*) defy, oppose.
paldım Crupper. ~**ı aşmak**, meddle in things beyond one's ability.
paldır küldür (*ech.*) With great noise and clatter. ~ **düşmek**, come clattering down: ~ **girmek**, dash in.
paleo- *pref.* Palaeo-. ~**grafi**, (*his.*) palaeography. ~**ntolog**, (*geol.*) palaeontologist. ~**ntoloji**, palaeontology. ~**zoik**, palaeozoic.
paletⁱ (*art.*) Palette; (*ind.*) plate, baffle; blade, vane; (*mot.*) articulated track. ~ **pabucu**, tractor shoe. ~**li**, caterpillar/tracked (vehicle): ~ **traktör**, crawler.
palikarya Greek youth; (*pej.*) Greek rowdy.
palisa'tᵈ¹ (*bot.*) ~ **katmanı**, assimilation layer.
palladyum (*chem.*) Palladium.
palm (*bot.*) Palm. ~ **yağı**, palm-oil. ~**itikⁱ**, (*chem.*) palmitic (acid). ~**iye**, (*bot.*) palm-tree.
palplanş (*eng.*) Sheet-pile.
palto (*mod.*) Overcoat.
paluze (*cul.*) Blancmange. ~ **gibi**, pale and flabby.
palyaço (*th.*) Harlequin, clown, buffoon. ~ **gibi**, clowning, clownlike. ~**luk**, clowning, buffoonery.
palyoş (*mil.*) Short double-edged sword; dagger.
pama (*zoo.*) Krait.
pampa (*geo.*) Pampas. ~**tavşanıⁿⁱ**, (*zoo.*) viscacha.
pamu'kᵏᵍᵘ (*bot.*, *tex.*) Cotton. ~ **atmak**, card cotton: ~ **balı**, (*cul.*) white honey: ~ **barutu**, (*mil.*) guncotton: ~ **bezi**, (*tex.*) cotton cloth, calico: ~ **böceği**, (*ent.*) cotton-boll weevil: ~ **çırçırı**, (*tex.*) cotton gin: ~ **döküntüsü**, cotton waste: ~ **gibi**, very soft: ~ **iği**, bobbin: ~ **ipliği**, (*tex.*) cotton thread: ~ **ipliğine bağlı olm.**, hang on by the skin of one's teeth: ~ **ipliğiyle bağlamak (bir işi)**, make a temporary//unsatisfactory arrangement: ~ **kozası**, (*bot.*) cotton boll.
pamuk·aki (*tex.*) Embroidery thread. ~**balığıⁿⁱ**, (*ich.*) blue shark. ~**çu**, cotton-grower/-seller. ~**çu'kᵏᵍᵘ**, (*med.*) aphtha, thrush. ~**çuluk**, cotton-growing/-selling. ~**elmasıⁿⁱ**, (*bot.*) cotton boll. ~ **kale**, *pr.n.* (*geo.*, *his.*) Hierapolis. ~**lanmak**, *vi.* be covered with thin layer of mildew/dust. ~**lu**, made of cotton; padded, quilted: ~ **bez fabrikası**, cotton mill: ~ **bit**, (*ent.*) woolly aphis: ~ **kadife**, (*tex.*) corduroy: ~ **kumaş**, cotton fabric. ~**taş**, (*geol.*) travertine. ~**umsu**, ~ **pullu böcek**, (*ent.*) cottony scale. ~**yağıⁿⁱ**, cotton-seed oil.

pan (*eng.*, *mot.*) Breakdown.
Panama (*geo.*) Panama; (*mod.*) panama hat. ~ **tiranı**, (*orn.*) piratic flycatcher. ~**lı**, (*ethn.*) Panamanian.
panayır (*fin.*, *soc.*) Fair, market. ~**cı**, showman.
pancar (*bot.*) Beet(root). ~ **kesilmek**, turn red in the face. ~**cı(lık)**, (work of) beet-grower/-seller.
pancur (*col.*) = PANJUR.
panda (*zoo.*) Panda.
pandantif (*mod.*) Pendant (necklace).
pandispanya (*cul.*) Sponge-like cake. ~ **gazetesi**, (*sl.*) pack of lies.
pandomim(a) (*th.*) Pantomime. ~ **çıkmak**, an amusing quarrel break out.
pandül Pendulum.
pane (*cul.*) Coated with breadcrumbs. ~ **yapmak**, crumb.
panel (*rad.*) Panel (of speakers).
pan'ikᵍⁱ Panic. ~ **kırmak**, (*sl.*) run away: ~ **olm.**, panic break out: ~ **yaratmak**, create/start a panic: ~**e kapılmak/vermek**, panic.
panislamizm (*rel.*) Pan-Islamic movement.
panjur (*arch.*) Outer window blind, Venetian shutter.
pankart¹ (*pub.*) Placard; poster.
pankras (*sp.*) Pancratium.
pankreas (*bio.*) Pancreas. ~ **suyu**, pancreatic juice.
pano Panel; notice-board; (*mot.*) dashboard. ~ **lambası**, (*mot.*) dashlamp.
panorama Panorama.
pansiyon Accommodation; board (and lodging); boarding-house, guest-house; students' hostel. ~**cu(luk)**, (work of) guest-house keeper. ~**er**, paying-guest, lodger.
pansuman (*med.*) Dressing; bandage. ~ **yapmak**, dress a wound. ~**cı**, (*med.*) dresser.
pan·teist (*rel.*) Pantheist. ~**teizm**, pantheism. ~**teon**, (*arch.*, *rel.*) pantheon.
panter (*zoo.*) Panther.
pan·tograf (*eng.*) Pantograph. ~**tol**, (*col.*) trousers. ~**tolon**, (*mod.*) trousers, breeches: ~ **askısı**, braces: ~ **kıvrığı**, trouser-leg turn-up: ~ **ütüsü**, crease (of trousers). ~**tomim** = ~DOMİMA. ~**tufla**, (*mod.*) felt slipper; (*sl.*) trick. ~**turanizm**, (*his.*) Panturanianism. ~**türkizm**, (*his.*) Panturkism. ~**ya**, (*naut.*) stern painter.
panzehir (*med.*) Antidote, panacea, catholicon. ~ **taşı**, (*zoo.*) bezoar, panacea; (*geol.*) opal.
papa (*rel.*) Pope. ~**lık**, Papacy.
papağan (*orn.*) Parrot. ~ **anahtarı**, (*eng.*) adjustable spanner/wrench: ~ **gagalar**, (*orn.*) parrotbills/-finches: ~ **gibi ezberlemek**, (*ed.*) learn parrot-fashion.
papağan·balığıᵐ (*ich.*) Parrot-wrasse. ~**giller**, (*orn.*) parrots, Psittacidae. ~**lık**, repeating everything heard. ~**yemiⁿⁱ**, safflower (seeds).
papa'kᵍ¹ (*mod.*) Tall Persian-lambskin cap.
papara (*cul.*) Cheese soup; anything insipid; (*col.*) scolding. ~ **yemek**, get a severe scolding: ~**yı yiyeceksin!**, you'll catch it!
papatya (*bot.*) Camomile; daisy. ~ **çelengi**, daisy chain: ~ **falı**, '(s)he loves me, (s)he loves me not!'
papaz Priest, clergyman; monk; (*gamb.*) king (at

cards). ~ **çömezi**, (*rel.*) novice: ~ **hergün/herzaman pilav yemez** = HERGÜN: ~ **uçurmak**, (*sl.*) have a drinking party: ~ **a dönmek**, let one's hair grow; need a hair-cut: ~ **a kızıp oruç/perhiz bozmak**, cut off one's nose to spite one's face.
papaz·balığı[ni] (*ich.*) Small type of goby. ~ **i**, (*tex.*) fine shirt material. ~ **kaçtı**, (*gamb.*) a card-game. ~ **lık**, priest's office/duties; priesthood. ~ **yahnisi**[ni], (*cul.*) mutton stewed in wine/vinegar.
papel (*sl.*, *obs.*) Tk. lira note; (*gamb.*) playing-card. ~ **ci(lik)**, cardsharp·er/(-ing).
papirüs (*bot.*) Papyrus plant; papyrus. ~ **giller**, Cyperaceae.
papuç = PABUÇ.
papura (*agr.*) Heavy plough (two yoke of oxen).
papye·büvar (*pub.*) Blotting-paper. ~ **kuşe**, art/ coated paper.
papyon ~ **kravat**, (*mod.*) bow-tie: ~ **somunu**, (*eng.*) wing-nut: ~ **vidası**, thumb-screw.
PAR = (*aer.*) (*precision approach radar*).
para Money; coin; cash; currency; (*obs.*) a para ($\frac{1}{40}$th of a piastre). ~ +, *a.* Monetary; financial: ~ **aktarımı**, (*fin.*) transfer: ~ **alımı**, collection: ~ **almak**, be paid/subsidized; take a bribe: ~ **aşırmak**, pilfer: ~ **atış**, (*sp.*) tossing the coin: ~ **babası**, s.o. very rich: ~ **basmak**, mint/coin money; print money; (*gamb.*) stake money: ~ **basımevi**, mint: ~ **batmak**, (money) be lost; burn a hole in one's pocket: ~ **bolluğu**, inflation: ~ **bozmak**, change money: ~ **canlısı**, a lover of money: ~ **cezası**, (*leg.*) fine: ~ **cicoz!**, not a penny left!: ~ **çalmak**, embezzle, steal: ~ **çantası**, purse: ~ **çekmek**, withdraw money (from a bank); squeeze money out of s.o.: ~ **çıkarmak**, issue money: ~ **darlığı**, deflation: ~ **dökmek**, pour out money, spend money like water: ~ **etm.**, be worth stg.: ~ **etmemek**, be worthless; (*fig.*) be in vain, have no effect: ~ **farkı**, rate of exchange; agio: ~ **gönderim/ havalesi**, remittance, money order: ~ GÖZ: ~ **hırsı**, avarice: ~ **ile değil**, cheap: ~ **inanca**, security, guarantee: ~ **kesmek**, mint money; become rich: ~ **kırmak**, become rich: ~ **koparmak/sızdırmak**, squeeze money out of s.o.: ~ **kutusu**, money-/cash-box: ~ **küt cebe**, he popped the money into his pocket: ~ **mevzubahis değil**, it's not a question of money: ~ **nam bir şey yok**, I haven't a brass farthing: ~ **olarak**, in cash: ~ **ödeme**, payment: ~ ~ **yı çeker**, money breeds money: ~ **pul**, money: ~ **sistemi**, coinage, currency: ~ **şişkinliği**, (*fin.*) inflation: ~ **toplama**, collection: ~ **tutarı**, (*math.*) total: ~ **tutmak**, have money; save money: ~ **vurmak**, steal by pickpocketing; make money by dubious means, profiteer: ~ **yapmak**, make money: ~ **yardımı**, assistance: ~ **yatırmak**, deposit/ invest money: ~ **yedirmek**, spend unnecessarily; bribe: ~ **yeme**, corruption: ~ **yemek**, spend money unnecessarily/on pleasure; take bribes: ~ **yöntemi**, monetary system: ~ **yüzü görmek**, get a little money.

para-: ~ **dan çıkmak**, be obliged to spend money: ~ **m var//yok**, I have some//no money: ~ **na geçer hükmün**, you can't have your cake and eat it: ~ **nın üstü**, change (from payment): ~ **nın yüzü sıcaktır**,

money talks: ~ **sı pulu yok**: he has no money: ~ **sını çarçur etm.**, blue one's money: ~ **sını çıkarmak**, save one's capital: ~ **sını sokağa atmak**, throw one's money down the drain: ~ **sını sızdırmak**, bleed s.o.: ~ **sını son santimine kadar almak/ kurutmak**, drain s.o. dry: ~ **sını vermek**, pay one's BEDEL: ~ **sını yemek**, do s.o. out of his money: ~ **sıyla rezil olm.**, pay a lot for a bad job: ~ **ya çevirmek**, cash; convert into money: ~ **ya haris**, avaricious: ~ **ya kanmamak**, have an insatiable desire for money: ~ **ya kıyamamak**, avoid spending where due: ~ **ya kuvvet muvaffak oldu**, he succeeded thanks to money: ~ **ya pul dememek**, make much money: ~ **yı araya değil** ~ **ya vermeli**, money must be well spent: ~ **yı bayılmak**, pay up, hand over the cash: ~ **yı deniz/sokağa atmak**, squander money: ~ **yı mülk haline sokmak**, invest in real estate: ~ **yı veren düdüğü çalar**, he who pays the piper calls the tune: ~ **yla değil**, very cheap: ~ **yla değil sırayla**, money won't help so wait your turn.
para·bellum (*mil.*) Automatic pistol. ~ **bol**[ü], (*math.*) parabola. ~ **bolik**, parabolic. ~ **boloi**[t][di], paraboloid.
paraca In cash.
para·çol (*arch.*, *naut.*) Bracket, knee; = ~ ŞOL. ~ **di** (*th.*) gallery, the 'gods'. ~ **doks(al)**, (*phil.*) para-dox(ical). ~ **f**, (*adm.*) paraph. ~ **fazi**, (*psy.*) paraphasia. ~ **fe**, initialled: ~ **etm.**, initial (an agreement). ~ **fin**, (*chem.*) paraffin wax: ~ **likit**, liquid paraffin. ~ **fudr**, (*el.*) spark-gap arrester.
paragöz(lü) Money-grubber.
para·graf (*lit.*) Paragraph; (*leg.*) section; paragraph sign (§). ~ **ka**, multi-hooked fishing line. ~ **kete**, (*naut.*) ship's log (instrument); = PARAKA: ~ **hesabı**, dead-reckoning. ~ **laks**, (*phys.*) parallax.
para·lamak (-i) Tear/cut to pieces; (*fig.*) use learned words to show off. ~ **lanmak**, *vp.* be torn to pieces; *vi.* become rich; strain every nerve; do one's utmost (to help s.o.). ~ **latmak** (-i, -e), *vc.*
paralel (*math.*) Parallel, collateral. *n.* (*geo.*) Parallel (of latitude). ~ **kaidesi**, principle of parallel lines. ~ **kenar**, parallelogram. ~ **lik**, parallelism; similarity. ~ **yüz**, parallelepiped.
para·lı Having money; rich; fee-paying (school); (*sp.*) professional: ~ **yol**, toll-road, turnpike. ~ **lık**, (*obs.*) of so many PARA.
para·litik (*med.*) Paralytic. ~ **lizi**, paralysis. ~ **lojizm**, (*phil.*) paralogism. ~ **metre(li)**, (*math.*) parame·ter/(-tric).
paramparça All in bits. ~ **etm.**, tear to pieces, break to bits.
para·nkima (*bio.*) Parenchyma. ~ **noya(k)**, (*psy.*) paranoia(c). ~ **ntez**, (*pub.*) (round) brackets. ~ **pet**[i], (*naut.*) guard-rail; (*arch.*) parapet.
para·sal Monetary, financial; in cash. ~ **sıkıntısı**[ni], financial difficulties. ~ **sız**, penniless, without money; free, gratis, complimentary: ~ **olarak**, gratis, for nothing: ~ **pulsuz**, destitute: ~ **tellal**, s.o. who blazes abroad news that doesn't concern him: ~ **yatılı**, (*ed.*) free boarder. ~ **sızlık**, penniless-ness, destitution.
para·şol Open-sided roofed one-horse carriage. ~ **şüt**[ü], (*aer.*) parachute: ~ **le atlamak**, parachute,

bail out. ~ **şütçü(lük)**, (work/skill of) parachutist.
~ **toner**, (*el.*) lightning conductor. ~ **van**, ~ **şirketi**,
(*fin.*) subsidiary company used for risky business.
~ **vana**, (*dom.*) folding screen: ~ **yapmak (-i)**,
secretly make use of s.o.'s influence. ~ **zit**[i], (*bio.*)
parasite; (*rad.*) atmospherics, interference, static.
~ **zitlik**, (*bio.*) parasitism. ~ **zitoloji**, (*bio.*) parasitology.

parça Piece; bit; fragment; (*eng.*) component; section; (*tex.*) length (of cloth); (*lit.*) passage; (*mus.*)
piece, work; (*sl.*) attractive girl. ~ **almak**, (*med.*)
take a specimen (for biopsy): ~ **başına**, per piece;
(*ind.*) piece-work: ~ **bohçası**, rag-bag: ~ **halinde**,
(*ind.*) knocked-down: ~ **mal**, piece goods: ~ ~, in
bits, in pieces; by instalments: ~ ~ **etm.**, break/
dash/tear to pieces: ~ **tesirli bomba**, (*mil.*) fragmentation bomb: ~ **lar halinde**, in pieces, in ruins:
~ **sı**, (*pej.*) (*of a type of person*) a very ordinary ...,
some sort of ... [**kâtip** ~ **sı**, some sort of clerk]: ~ **sı**,
(*of things*) like, resembling [**elmas** ~ **sı**, enchanting
(child, etc.)].

parça·cı (*tex.*) Seller of piece goods/remnants;
(*eng.*) spare-parts dealer. ~ **cık**, (*phys.*) particle;
(*bio.*) corpuscle. ~ **k**, ~ **purçak**, in rags and tatters.
~ **lama**, *vn.* ~ **lamak (-i)**, break/cut into pieces;
(*fig.*) dismember, break up. ~ **lanma**, *vn.* break-
up; disintegration. ~ **lanmak**, *vi.* break up; disintegrate; (*phys.*) decay; (iceberg) calve; (*fig.*) wear
o.s. out. ~ **latmak (-i)**, *vc.* ~ **layıcı**, destructive,
breaking up. ~ **lı**, in pieces; patched; (*fig.*) sarcastic: ~ **bohça**, patchwork BOHÇA: ~ **bohça gibi**,
made of ill-assorted pieces: ~ **tutulma**, (*ast.*)
partial eclipse.

pardon *int.* Pardon!, excuse me!; (*iron.*) well done!
pardösü (*mod.*) Light overcoat.
pare *n.* Piece. *suf.* Piece. ~ ~, in pieces.
par·ekete = PARAKETE. ~ **füm**, perfume. ~ **fümeri**,
cosmetics; perfume-seller's shop.
parıl ~ ~, ablaze; very brightly; brilliantly; flashing. ~ **damak**, *vi.* gleam, glitter; twinkle; flash;
blaze. ~ **datmak (-i)**, *vc.* ~ **tı**, glitter, gleam; luminosity; flash; glow. ~ **tılı**, glittering, gleaming,
sparkling; (*ast.*) flaring.
parite (*fin.*) Par; parity.
park[1] Park, public garden; (*mil.*) dump; vehicle
pool; (*mot.*) parking-lot, car-park. ~ **etm./yapmak**,
park (a car): ~ **yeri**/~ **ing**, car-park. ~ **metre**,
parking metre.
par·ka (*mod.*) Parka, anorak. ~ **ke**, (*arch.*) parquet
(block/flooring); cobble-stone. ~ **keci(lik)**, (work
of) parquet-block maker/layer. ~ **kur**, (*sp.*) course,
track.
parlak Bright, brilliant; shining; luminous; (*cin.*)
glossy; beautiful; successful; influential; (*vulg.*)
good-looking (lad). ~ **ibis**, (*orn.*) glossy ibis: ~
kömür, (*geol.*) anthracite: ~ **kuş(giller)**, (*orn.*)
jacamar(s): ~ **tavuk**, (*orn.*) Himalayan monal
pheasant.
parlak·ça Brightly. ~ **laşmak**, *vi.* become bright,
etc. ~ **laştırmak (-i)**, make bright, brighten. ~ **lık**,
brilliance; beauty; influence; ability; (*ast.*) brightness, magnitude: ~ **birimi**, (*phys.*) candela.
~ **pullular**, (*ich.*) ganoids.

parla·ma *vn.* Shining: ~ **noktası**, (*phys.*) flash
point. ~ **mak**, *vi.* shine; blaze, burn and flare up;
(*fig.*) flare up in anger; become influential/dis-
tinguished: (-i), (*sp.*) fly a hawk at its prey. ~ **maz**,
(*cin.*) noninflammable (film).
parlamen·tarizm (*adm.*) Parliamentarianism. ~ **ter**,
n. member of parliament: *a.* parliamentary.
~ **to**, parliament: ~ +, *a.* parliamentary: ~ **nun**
dağıtılması, dissolution of parliament.
parla·ta[l]**ç**[c1] (*min.*) Polisher. ~ **tmak (-i)**, *vc.* cause to
shine, polish, etc.; (*sl.*) drink (too much). ~ **yan**,
shining, aglow. ~ **yıcı**, combustible, inflammable.
~ **yış**, brilliance; a shining.
parma[l]**k**[g1] (*bio.*) Finger; toe; digit; spoke (of wheel);
bar, rod, rail (of railing = ~ LIK); (*math.*) inch
(25.4 mm); finger-breadth; amount (of honey, etc.)
sticking to the finger. ~ +, *a.* Dactylo-. ~ **atmak**,
cause trouble, interfere: ~ **basmak (-e)**, put a finger
on stg.; (*leg.*) make one's mark: ~ **bozmak**, (*child.*)
quarrel: ~ **hesabı**, counting on the fingers; (*lit.*)
syllabic metre: ~ **ısırmak**, be surprised, marvel: ~
ısırtmak, surprise s.o.: ~ **izi**, fingerprint, dactylo-
gram: ~ **kadar**, tiny (child): ~ **kaldı**, almost,
nearly, just: ~ **kaldırmak**, raise one's hand (re-
questing permission to speak): ~ **karıştırmak**,
meddle: ~ **kemiği**, (*bio.*) phalanx: ~ **lekesi**, finger-
mark: ~ **lisanı**, deaf-and-dumb/sign language:
~ ~, finger-shaped: ~ **tatlısı**, (*cul.*) finger-like
pastries: ~ **üzümü**, (*bot.*) type of long grape:
~ **yalamak**, lick one's fingers; (*fig.*) make an
unexpected profit.

parmağı: ~ **ağzında kalmak**, be astounded; be lost
in admiration: ~ **olm. (içinde)**, have a finger in the
pie: ~ **var**, he's involved: ~ **na dolamak/sarmak**,
have a bee in one's bonnet about stg.: ~ **nda**
oynatmak (-i), twist s.o. around one's little finger:
~ **nı basmak**, take one's oath on stg.: ~ **nı bile**
kıpırdatamamak/oynatamamak, be unable to lift
even one's little finger, be worn out: ~ **nı koymak**
(-e), take a hand in stg.: ~ **nı sokmak (-e)**, meddle
with stg.: ~ **nı yaranın üzerine basmak**, put one's
finger on the spot/cause of the trouble: ~ **nın**
ucunda/üzerinde çevirmek, do stg. easily and skilfully.

parmak-: ~ **la gösterilmek**, be a person of distinction: ~ **la sayılmak**, be counted on the fingers
of one hand, be rare: ~ **larını yemek**, find a dish
delicious.
parmak·çı (*carp.*) Maker of banisters/spokes, etc.;
(*pol.*) inciter. ~ **lamak (-i)**, finger; eat with the
fingers; (*fig.*) meddle with; stir up, incite. ~ **lı**,
having fingers/toes; (*zoo.*) digitate. ~ **lık**, railing,
balustrade, banisters; grating, grill. ~ **lıklı**, barred.
par·mazan/~ **mıcan** (*cul.*) Parmesan cheese. ~ **odi**,
(*lit.*) parody. ~ **ola**, password, watchword, countersign: ~ **sormak**, (*mil.*) challenge s.o.
parpa (*ich.*) Turbot fry.
par par Brightly, gleamingly.
pars[1] *n.* (*zoo.*) Leopard; cheetah.
Pars[2] *n.* (*geo.*) Persia proper; the province of Shiraz.
parsa Collection of money. ~ **toplamak**, take a
collection; pass the hat round; (-den), profit by/

exploit s.o.: ~ yı başkası toplamak, s.o. else get the benefit.
parsek (*ast.*) Parsec.
parsel Plot of land. ~ lemek (-i), divide up into plots. ~ lenmek, *vp.* ~ li, divided up.
parşömen Parchment. ~ kâğıdı, high-grade paper.
partal *n.* Old worn clothes. *a.* In tatters.
partenogenez (*bio.*) Parthenogenesis.
parter (*th.*) Stalls.
parti (*fin.*) Consignment (of goods); (*pol.*) party; faction; (*soc.*) party; (*mus.*) part, melody; (*gamb.*) hand, game; (*sp.*) game, match; (*fig.*) bargain. ~ üyesi, party member, adherent: ~ vermek, give a party: ~ yi kaybetmek, (*fig.*) lose to one's opponent: ~ yi vurmak, get a bargain, do a good stroke of business.
parti·ci (*pol.*) Party member; partisan. ~ cilik, partisanship. ~ li, member of . . . party. ~ si¹pᵇⁱ, (*ling.*) participle. ~ syon, (*mus.*) score ~ zan(lık), (*pol.*) partisan(ship).
par·ya (*soc.*) Pariah, outcast. ~ yetal, (*bio.*) parietal.
pas¹ *n.* (*min.*) Rust; tarnish; dirt; (*med.*) fur (on tongue); (*myc.*) rust. ~ açmak, clean off rust; (*sl.*) have a drink: ~ bağlamak/tutmak, rust, become rusty: ~ giderici, rust remover: ~ önleyici, rust inhibitor: ~ rengi ardıç kuşu, (*orn.*) redwing: ~ rengi gerdanlı dalgıç, (*orn.*) red-throated loon: ~ rengi kızılbacak, (*orn.*) spotted redshank.
pas² *n.* (*sp.*) Pass. *int.* (*gamb.*) Pass! ~ geçmek, (*sl.*) give up, change one's mind: ~ vermek, (*sl.*) make a pass (at a man): ~ ını almak, (*sl.*) get the glad eye.
pasaj (*arch.*) Arcade, precinct; (*lit.*) passage.
pasak Dirty/untidy clothes. ~ lı, slovenly.
pasa·parola (*mil.*) Password. ~ portᵘ, (*adm.*) passport: ~ unu eline vermek (-in), (*fig.*) drive s.o. away. ~ van, (*adm.*) permit to cross the frontier regularly.
pasbaş (*orn.*) White-eyed pochard, ferruginous duck.
pasif *a.* (*ling.*) Passive; inactive. *n.* (*fin.*) Liabilities. ~ korunma, civil defence; air-raid precautions: ~ mukavemet, (*pol.*) passive resistance. ~ ik, pr.n. (*geo.*) the Pacific (Ocean). ~ ist, (*pol.*) pacifist. ~ istlik/~ izm, pacifism.
paskal *n.* 1. (*phys.*) Pascal. 2. (*th.*) Clown, buffoon; comic. ~ lik, clowning, buffoonery.
paskalya (*rel.*) Easter. ~ çöreği, (*cul.*) Easter cake: ~ yumurtası, painted Easter egg: ~ yumurtası gibi, red-faced (with make-up).
pas·landırıcı (*min.*) Corrosive. ~ landırma, vn. corrosion. ~ landırmak (-i), corrode. ~ lanma, vn.; oxidation; corrosion: ~ yı önleyici, anticorrosive. ~ lanmak, vi. be(come) rusty; (*med.*) be furred; (*fig.*) be rusty/out of practice. ~ lanmaz, non-corrosive, stainless. ~ laşmak¹, vi. = LANMAK. ~ latmak (-i), make rusty, corrode.
paslaşmak² (-le) (*sp.*) Pass to each other; (*sl.*) exchange amorous glances.
pas·lı Rusty; (*med.*) furred; dirty; dingy; faded. ~ mantarıgiller, (*myc.*) rust fungi, Uredinales. ~ sız, rustfree, rustless. ~ sızlaştırma, vn. (*min.*) derusting.
pas·o *n.* (*rly.*, *cin.*, *etc.*) Pass: *int.* (*sl.*) I'm not

interfering! ~ pal, (*cul.*) flour with much bran. ~ pas, (*dom.*) doormat.
pasta¹ *n.* (*cul.*) Sweet cake; pastry; tart; confectionery. ~ cı(lık), (work of) pastry-cook, confectioner. ~ ne, pastry-shop, café.
pasta² *n.* (*mod.*) Fold, pleat. ~ lı, pleated.
pas·tal (*agr.*) Bundle of tobacco leaves. ~ tav, (*tex.*) roll (of cloth): ~ la pazarlık, wholesale bargaining.
pastel *n.* (*art.*) Pastel (colours//crayons). *a.* Pale (colour).
pastırma (*cul.*) Pressed, cured, spiced meat. ~ yazı, (*met.*) Indian/St. Martin's summer (in mid-November): ~ sını çıkarmak, give s.o. a good thrashing; (*fig.*) beat s.o. into a cocked hat. ~ cı(lık), (work of) PASTIRMA curer/seller. ~ lık, (meat) suitable for curing.
pas·til (*cul.*, *med.*) Pastille. ~ tiş, (*art.*, *lit.*) pastiche. ~ toral, (*lit.*, *mus.*) pastoral. ~ törize, (*cul.*) pasteurized. ~ tra, (*gamb.*) a card game.
paşa *n.* (*adm.*) Pasha; (*mil.*) general. *a.* Serious. ~ bardağı, treasured object: ~ gibi yaşamak, live like a lord: ~ kapısı, (*his.*) provincial government office: ~ olm., (*col.*) be as drunk as a lord: ~ ~, calmly, without worrying. ~ m!, *int.* My Lord!; Your Excellency!
paşa·ağacıⁿⁱ (*bot.*) African satinwood. ~ çadırı ⁿⁱ, (*bot.*) Feast's begonia. ~ eli, (*his.*) European Turkey, Thrace. ~ lı, having influence. ~ lık, title/rank of pasha. ~ zade, son of a pasha.
paşmak(çı) = BAŞMAK(ÇI).
pat¹ ¹ *a.* Flat(tened).
pat¹ ² *n.* (*ech.*) Thud. *adv.* Suddenly. ~ ~, thudding.
pat¹ ³ *n.* (*bot.*) Aster; (*mod.*) star-like diamond pin.
pata (*sp.*) Drawn game; stalemate; deadlock; 'all square'. ~ çakmak, (*sl.*) salute: ~ gelmek, (*gamb.*) be all square.
pata·lıkᵍ¹ A whacking. ~ lamak (-i), give s.o. a whacking; beat (carpet); wash/dust hurriedly. ~ lanmak, *vp.*
patalya (*naut.*) Warship's small gig.
patates (*bot.*) Potato. ~ böceği, (*ent.*) Colorado beetle: ~ mildiyö/peronosporası, (*myc.*) potato blight.
patavatsız Who talks at random; thoughtless blundering. ~ lık, thoughtless behaviour; disrespect.
paten (*sp.*) Skate; roller-skate. ~ ci, skater. ~ cilik, skating. ~ li, ~ hokey, ice-hockey.
patent(a) (*ind.*) Patent; licence; (*adm.*) naturalization papers; (*naut.*) bill of health. ~ inin altına almak (-i), grant naturalization.
patır (*ech.*) Tapping sound. ~ kütür, with the noise of footsteps; noisily: ~ ~, sound of footsteps. ~ damak, vi. make a noise of footsteps/knocking. ~ datmak (-i), vc.; (*col.*) speak a foreign language a little.
patırtı Noise; clamour; row. ~ çıkarmak, make a row; cause a commotion: ~ kopmak, make a great noise; start a quarrel: ~ ya pabuç bırakmamak, not be scared off by the quarrelling: ~ ya vermek (-i), put to confusion; create a disturbance. ~ lı, noisy; quarrelling.

pati·lkᵍⁱ (*mod.*) Child's shoe. ~ **a**, footpath, track.
patinaj (*sp.*) Skating; (*mot.*) skid(ding). ~ **yapmak**, skate; slip, skid.
patis (*tex.*) Fine cambric. ~ **ka**, cambric.
patiyo (*arch.*) Patio.
patka (*orn.*) Tufted duck, northern shoveller.
pat küt (*ech.*) Sound of repeated blows.
patla·lkᵍⁱ *n.* Explosion; bursting. *a.* Burst; torn open. ~ **gözlü**, goggle-eyed: ~ **mısır**, (*cul.*) popcorn: ~ **vermek**, burst; (rebellion) burst out; be discovered/divulged.
patla·ma *vn.* Explosion; detonation; eruption. ~ **mak**, *vi.* burst; explode; erupt; burst open; (winter, etc.) arrive suddenly; react violently; (*col.*) cost, 'blow' (money): **patlama!**, be patient!, keep calm! ~ **nga·lç/ngı·lç**ᶜⁱ, (*child.*) pop-gun; fire-cracker. ~ **tmak (-i, -e)**, cause to burst/explode; detonate; blast; make s.o. furious. ~ **yıcı**, explosive: ~ **ünsüz**, (*ling.*) plosive.
patlıcan (*bot.*) Aubergine, egg-plant. ~ **burunlu**, (*zoo.*) bottle-nosed: ~ **inciri**, (*bot.*) large purple fig: ~ **karnıyarık**, (*cul.*) aubergine surprise: ~ **rengi**, aubergine: ~ **sız tarafından olsun!**, for goodness' sake let's have a change! ~ **giller**, Solanaceae.
pato·log (*med.*) Pathologist. ~ **loji(k)**, patholo·gy/ (-gical).
patri·arkal (*soc.*) Patriarchal. ~ **k**, (*rel.*) Patriarch. ~ **khane**, Patriarchate (building). ~ **klik**, rank/ office of Patriarch, Patriarchate. ~ **muan**, patrimony.
patron (*ind.*) Owner, boss; employer; (*fin.*) backer; (*mod.*) pattern, model. ~ **a**, (*naut., obs.*) viceadmiral. ~ **aj**, (*leg.*) after-care (for criminal). ~ **luk**, ownership.
patta·dak/ ~ dan All of a sudden.
pavkırmak *vi.* Bark (of fox/jackal).
pavurya (*zoo.*) Large edible crab; (*fig.*) s.o. lopsided.
pavyon (*arch.*) Detached building, pavilion; exhibition stand; night-club.
pay Share; quota; commission; lot, portion; reproach, scolding, blame; (*eng.*) margin, tolerance; (*math.*) numerator. ~ **belgiti**, (*fin.*) stock share: ~ **bırakmak**, leave a margin (for error): ~ **biçmek**, apportion/allot a share; **(-den)**, take as an example; judge/deduce from: ~ **etm./vermek**, allocate, share out: ~ **sahibi**, (*fin.*) shareholder: ~ **ını almak**, take one's share; be scolded.
payanda Prop, support; (*naut.*) stanchion, stay. ~ **vermek (-e)**, prop up: ~ **vurmak**, buttress: ~ **ları çözmek**, run away. ~ **lamak (-i)** = ~ VURMAK.
pay·da (*math.*) Denominator. ~ **daş**, partner, sharer; (*fin.*) shareholder ~ **daşlı**, having shareholders. ~ **daşlık**, participation, sharing.
paydos *n.* Cessation from work; break, rest. *int.* Knock off!, stop work!; enough! ~ **borusu çalmak**, leave one's work: ~ **demek**, give up some job: ~ **etm.**, cease work, knock off.
paye Grade, rank; degree; dignity. ~ **vermek (-e)**, show deference to; esteem unduly. ~ **dar**, having (a) rank.
paye·n (*rel.*) Pagan. ~ **t**, (*mod.*) spangle, paillette.

payi·dar Firm, stable; established, enduring. ~ **taht**¹, (*adm.*) sovereign's residence; capital.
payla·ma *vn.* Scolding. ~ **mak (-i)**, scold, reproach. ~ **nmak**, *vp.* ~ **tmak (-i, -e)**, *vc.*
paylaş·ım/ ~ ma *vn.* Dividing up, sharing out. ~ **mak (-i)**, share out, divide up; go shares. ~ **tırmak (-i, -e)**, allot, distribute; share out.
payplayn (*ind.*) Pipe-line.
payta·lkᵍⁱ *a.* Bowlegged, bandy-legged; knockkneed. *n.* Pawn (chess). ~ **lık**, being bowlegged.
payton Phaeton.
pazar Bazaar; market; market-place; bargaining; *pr.n.* Sunday. ~ **etm.**, bargain: ~ **günü**, Sunday; market-day: ~ **kayığı**, (*naut.*) large freight caique: ~ **kayığı gibi**, (vehicle) loaded down; very crowded: ~ **kesmek**, conclude a bargain; settle a price: ~ **ola!**, *int.* good luck/business! (*to tradesman*): ~ **tatili**, Sunday holiday: ~ **tavsamak**, market become dull: ~ **yeri**, street market-place: ~ **a çıkarmak (-i)**, put on sale.
pazar·başıⁿⁱ Market superintendent. ~ **cı**, market trader. ~ **lama**, *vn.* marketing: ~ **eğitimi**, (*ed.*) business studies. ~ **lamak (-i)**, market. ~ **laşmak (-le)**, *vi.* bargain; settle a price. ~ **lık**, bargaining; haggling; deal; price agreement: ~ **etm.**, bargain; do a deal: ~ **uymamak**, no agreement/bargain be reached: ~ **a oturmak**, agree to a bargain: ~ **uydurmak**, make a good bargain; clinch a bargain: ~ **ını bozmak**, break one's bargain: ~ **la indirmek**, beat down (the price). ~ **lıklı**, clever at bargaining. ~ **tesi**ʸⁱ, *pr.n.* Monday. ~ **yeri**ⁿⁱ, foreign market.
pazen (*tex.*) Cotton flannel; fustian.
pazı¹ (*bot.*) Spinach beet, chard; wild beet.
pazı² (*cul.*) Lump of dough; type of thin bread.
pazı³ (*bio.*) Muscles of upper arm, biceps; strength. ~ **kemiği**, funny-bone. ~ **ben·t**ᵈⁱ, armband; amulet worn on the arm.
paz·val Cobbler's strap (to hold shoes). ~ **vant**¹, market watchman.
Pb. = (*ch.s.*) KURŞUN.
Pd. = (*ch.s.*) PALADYUM.
pe (*ling.*) The Tk. letter P.
peçe (*mod.*) Black veil (worn by Muslim women); (*cin., ast.*) veil. ~ **lemek (-i)**, veil; disguise, camouflage. ~ **li**, veiled: ~ **baykuş(giller)**, (*orn.*) barn owl(s).
peçe·ta (*fin.*) Spanish peseta. ~ **te**, (*dom.*) serviette, napkin.
peçi·lçᶜⁱ Game played with sea-shells for dice.
peda·gog Pedagogue; educationalist. ~ **goji**, pedagogy.
pedal (*eng.*) Pedal; foot-operated machine.
pedan (*ed.*) Pedant.
peder Father. ~ **ane**, fatherly, paternal. ~ **şahi(lik)**, patriarchal(ism).
pedikür Pedicure. ~ **cü(lük)**, chiropo·dist/(-dy).
pedo·loji (*ed.*) Study of children. ~ **tekni**, child education.
pegmatitⁱ (*geol.*) Pegmatite.
pehlivan (*sp.*) Wrestler; strongman; (*fig.*) hero. ~ **çağlı/yapılı**, built like a wrestler; strong, robust: ~ **yakısı**, (*med.*) cautery (by burning/caustic

substance): ~ **yakısını açmak,** cause great pain.
~ **lık,** wrestling; bravery.
pehpeh *int.* Bravo!; my! my! ~ **lemek (-i),** applaud, flatter.
pejmürde Withered, faded; decayed; shabby.
pejoratif (*ling.*) Pejorative.
pek[i] *a.* Hard; firm; unyielding; violent; tight. *adv.* Very; very much; very often; violently; loudly. ~ **az,** rare(ly): ~ **başlı,** stubborn: ~ **bol,** very plentiful: ~ **canım istemiyor (-i),** I'm not very anxious to . . .: ~ **canlı,** strong, resistant: ~ **çirkin şey,** (*col.*) abomination, abortion: ~ **çok,** a great deal, many; much: ~ **de yanlış olmasa gerek,** and it's probably not far from the truth: ~ **değerli tutmak,** think no end of, esteem: ~ **eskiden,** for years: ~ **eskiden . . . -cesine,** as if . . . for years: ~ **etkili,** drastic: ~ **gerekli,** essential: ~ **gözlü,** bold, courageous: ~ **hoş,** delightful: ~ **kalabalık,** congested (area): ~ **ileride gezmek,** put forward great pretensions: ~ **iyi,** very good: ~ **iyi:** ~ **nadir,** few and far between: ~ **okumak,** read aloud; sing loudly: ~ ~, at most: ~ **seyrek,** rarely: ~ **söylemek,** speak out; speak loudly: ~ **yürekli,** hard-hearted: ~ **yüzlü,** brazen-faced; thick-skinned; callous; blunt; with no respect for others' feelings: ~ **ziyade,** excessively; extremely.
pekala *a.* As good as similar ones. *adv.* Very good; perfectly all right!; very well!
pek·doku (*bot.*) Collenchyma. ~**en**[i]**t**[di], (*geol.*) natural obstacle.
peki *adv.* All right!, very well!, certainly!; well then! ~**n(li),** (*phil.*) certain, definite. ~**nlik,** certainty, certitude.
Pekin (*geo.*) Peking. ~ **insanı** (*ethn.*) Pekin man. ~ **li,** (*ethn.*) Pekingese; (*zoo.*) pekinese dog.
pekiş·mek *vi.* Become hard/firm/tight; consolidate. ~**tirme,** *vn.* consolidation: ~ **ünlüsü,** (*ling.*) intensifying vowel [GÜPEGÜNDÜZ; YAPAYALNIZ]. ~**tirmek (-i),** consolidate; strengthen; intensify. ~**tirmeli,** (*ling.*) intensive; emphatic: ~ **belirteç,** intensive/emphatic adverb [ÇARÇABUK]: ~ **özne,** emphatic subject [BEN KENDİM]: ~ **sıfat,** intensive adjective [KUPKURU]: ~ **sözcük,** intensive word.
pekitmek (-i) Make hard/firm; strengthen.
pekiyi Very well; all right.
pek·leşme Consolidation; (*eng.*) strain-hardening. ~**lik,** (*med.*) constipation; ~ **vermek,** constipate.
pekmez (*cul.*) Boiled grape-juice; thin molasses. ~ **toprak,** (*geol.*) marl: ~**in olsun sineği Bağdat'tan gelir,** parasites soon gather round one who has money.
pekmez·ci(lik) (Work of) PEKMEZ maker/seller. ~ **li,** containing PEKMEZ; strongly flavoured. ~ **lik,** (suitable) for making PEKMEZ.
peksimet[i] (*cul.*) Hard biscuit; melba toast.
pektin (*chem.*) Pectin.
peleme (*naut.*) Flat-bottomed river boat; punt.
pelerin (*mod.*) Cloak, cape.
pelesen[i]**k**[gi] (*chem.*) Balsam; balm. ~ **ağacı**[nı], balsam-wood, Brazilian jacaranda.
pelikan (*orn.*) (European white) pelican.
pelikül (*cin.*) Film.
pelin(otu) (*bot.*) Wormwood; absinthe.

peli[i]**t**[di] (*bot.*) Acorn; valonia. ~ **ağacı,** valonia oak: ~ **yüksüğü,** cupule.
pelte (*cul.*) Jelly; (*chem.*) colloid. ~ **gibi,** jelly-like, flabby. ~**leşmek,** *vi.* become jellified/flabby, coagulate, congeal. ~**li,** (*chem.*) colloidal.
peltek *a.* Lisping. ~ **diş ünsüzü,** (*ling.*) interdental consonant. ~**leşmek,** *vi.* lisp. ~**lik,** lisp(ing).
pel·ür/ ~ **üş** (*tex.*) Plush; (*pub.*) stencil 'skin'.
pembe *n.* Rose colour. *a.* Rosy, pink. ~ **görmek,** be optimistic: ~ **sığırcık,** (*orn.*) rose-coloured starling. ~**leşmek,** *vi.* turn pink. ~**lik,** rosiness, pinkness. ~**msi,** rather rosy, pinkish: ~ **kurşuni,** dove-coloured.
pena (*sp.*) Triangular sail; (*mus.*) plectrum.
penaltı (*sp.*) Penalty.
Penca[i]**p**[bı] *pr.n.* (*geo.*) Punjab.
pencere (*arch.*) Window; (*cin.*) gate. ~ **boşluğu,** aperture: ~ **eteği,** wall below a window: ~ **kırlangıcı,** (*orn.*) house-martin. ~**li,** windowed: ~ **zarf,** window envelope.
pencü·dü// ~ **se//** ~ **yek** (*gamb.*) Five-two//-three// -one (dice).
pençe (*bio.*) Whole hand; paw; talon; (*his.*) = TUĞRA; (*fig.*) strength, violence; clutches; sole (of shoe); (*bot.*) tuber, crown (of asparagus, etc.). ~ **atmak (-e),** lay hands on, seize: ~ ~ **yanakları,** fresh pink cheeks (as if just slapped): ~ **vurmak,** resole (a shoe): ~**sine düşmek,** fall into s.o.'s clutches: ~**sine geçirmek (-i),** get control of stg.
pençe·lemek (-i) Grasp; seize; claw. ~**lenmek,** *vp.* ~**leşmek (-le),** *vi.* come to grips with; engage in contest. ~**li,** having claws; repaired/resoled (shoes); (*fig.*) formidable.
pene·plen (*geol.*) Peneplain. ~ **s** = PAYET. ~**trasyon** (*min.*) penetration. ~**trometre,** (*med.*) penetrometer.
penguen (*orn.*) Penguin; (*cul.*) chocolate-coated ice-cream.
pen·i (*fin.*) Penny, copper. ~ **s,** (*fin.*) pence.
penis (*bio.*) Penis.
penisilin (*myc., med.*) Penicillin.
pens(e) Tweezers, pliers; (*mod.*) pleat.
pent·(a)- *pref.* Pent(a)-. ~ **atlon** (*sp.*) pentathlon. ~**oksi**[i]**t**[di], (*chem.*) pentoxide.
pepe·(me) Stammer; stammerer. ~ **lemek,** *vi.* stammer, stutter. ~**melik,** stammer(ing).
pep·sin (*chem.*) Pepsin. ~**tidaz,** peptidase. ~**ton,** peptone.
perakende Dispersed, scattered; (*fin.*) retail. ~**ci(lik),** retail·er/(-selling).
perçem Tuft of hair; long lock of hair; (horse) forelock; mane.
perçin (*carp.*) Clenching a nail; (*min.*) riveting/ locking a bolt; rivet. ~ **etm./**~ **lemek (-i),** clench, rivet; (*fig.*) strengthen, make fast. ~**lenmek,** *vp.* ~**leşmek,** *vi.* become strong/rigid. ~**li,** riveted.
perdah Polish; gloss; burnish; finishing shave. ~ **vurmak,** polish. ~ **cı,** polisher. ~**lamak (-i),** polish, burnish; shave a second time; (*sl.*) seek to annoy s.o. ~**lanmak,** *vp.* ~**lı,** polished, glossy, shining; smooth-shaven. ~**sız,** unpolished; dull, matt.
perde (*dom.*) Curtain; screen; partition; (*eng.*) baffle; (*mod.*) veil; (*fig.*) veil, cloak; (*geol.*) (cut-off) wall;

(*bio.*) membrane; web; (*med.*) cataract (of eye); (*th.*) curtain; act; (*cin.*) screen; (*mus.*) fret; note; voice pitch; (*fig.*) modesty, chastity. ∼ **arası**, (*th.*) entr'acte, intermission: ∼ **arkası**, hidden/secret matter: ∼ **arkasında(n)**, secretly, furtively: ∼ **çekmek (-e)**, veil, conceal: ∼ **çubuğu**, curtain rod: ∼ **inmek**, (*med.*) cataract develop: ∼ **kurup şema yakmak**, (*th.*) prepare for a KARAGÖZ show; have all ready for the performance: ∼**lerini açmak**, (*th.*) open for a new season: ∼**nin ötesinde**, (*th.*) backstage: ∼**si yırtık**, shameless: ∼**si yırtılmak**, be shameless: ∼**yi çekmek**, draw the curtain.

perde·ayaklılar (*orn.*) Palmiped(e)s. ∼**ci**, curtain maker/seller; (*th.*) curtain-operator; (*obs.*) doorkeeper. ∼**leme**, *vn.* ∼**lemek (-i)**, curtain, veil; conceal; (chess) cover. ∼**lenme**, *vn.*; (*ling.*) change of pitch. ∼**lenmek**, *vp.* be veiled/curtained; (*med.*) have cataract. ∼**li**, veiled; curtained; screened; partitioned; (*bio.*) webbed; membraneous; having cataract; (*mus.*) fretted; (*fig.*) modest, chaste. ∼**siz**, unveiled; unscreened; (*fig.*) shameless, immodest. ∼**sizlik**, shamelessness, immodesty, unchastity.

pere (*arch.*) Retaining wall. ∼**me**, (*naut.*) two-oared boat.

perende (*sp.*) Somersault. ∼ **atamamak (yanında)**, not be able to challenge//dupe s.o. ∼**baz**, acrobat, tumbler.

perese (*arch.*) Plumb-line; level; (*naut.*) direction, bearing; (*fig.*) stage, state, condition. ∼**sine getirmek**, choose the right moment, find the opportunity: ∼**ye almak (-i)**, consider/weigh (a matter, etc.): ∼**ye gelmek ki**, come to such a point that . . . .

(-)perest *a. suf.* . . . -worshipping [PUTPEREST]. ∼**iş**, worshipping, adoration: ∼ **etm. (-e)**, worship. ∼**işkâr**, adoring, worshipping.

performans Performance, capability.

pergel (*math.*) (Pair of) compasses. ∼**leri açmak**, (*col.*) walk with long strides. ∼**lemek (-i)**, measure/ scribe with compasses; pace out; (*fig.*) think out.

perhiz (*med.*) Diet; regimen; abstinence, continence; (*rel.*) fasting. ∼**günü**, fast day. ∼**kâr**, abstinent. ∼**li**, on a diet; fasting.

peri Fairy; good genie/jinn(ee). ∼ **deniz kırlangıcı**, (*orn.*) white tern: ∼ **gibi**, very beautiful: ∼ **masalı**, (*lit.*) fairy tale: ∼**ler diyarı**, fairyland: ∼**leri bağdaşmak**, reach agreement: ∼**si hoşlanmamak (-den)**, dislike s.o.: ∼**si pis**, he's never clean.

peri·bacası/ ∼ **piramidi**^{ni} (*geol.*) (Capped) earth pillar, erosion column, chimney rock. ∼**ci**^{l}**k**^{ği}, little fairy; bolt of a door; (*med.*) epilepsy. ∼**hastalığı**^{nı}, (*med.*) epilepsy, hysteria, etc. ∼**li**, haunted; possessed. ∼**masası**^{nı}, (*geol.*) dolmenlike rock.

peri·dot(it) (*geol.*) Peridot(ite). ∼**kard**, (*bio.*) pericardium. ∼**patetizm**, (*phil.*) peripateticism. ∼**odi**^{l}**k**^{ği}, (*pub.*) periodical. ∼**skop**^{u}, (*naut.*) periscope.

perişan Scattered; disordered; routed; perplexed; ruined. ∼ **etm.**, scatter; ruin; rout: ∼ **olm.**, be scattered/routed; be in misery/ruin: ∼ **ve zaruret içinde**, in misery and want. ∼**lık**, being scattered; disorder; ruin, wretchedness.

peri·ton (*bio.*) Peritoneum. ∼**tonit**^{i}, (*med.*) peritonitis. ∼**yot** = PERYOT.

perki (*ich.*) Common perch. ∼**tmek** = PEKİTMEK.

perlon (*tex.*) Type of nylon.

per·m (*geol.*) Permian system. ∼**ma(nant)**, (*mod.*) permanent wave (hair). ∼**manganat**^{ı}, (*chem.*) permanganate. ∼**meabilite**, (*phys.*) permeability. ∼**meametre**, (*eng.*) permeameter. ∼**meçe**, (*naut.*) small hawser; tow-rope. ∼**mi**, (*fin.*) permit; (*rly.*) pass.

per·oksi^{l}**t**^{di} (*chem.*) Peroxide. ∼**on**, (*rly.*) platform. ∼**onospora**, (*myc.*) peronospora, mildews.

persenk^{i} Refrain; continually repeated words ('you know/see').

personel (*adm.*) Personnel. ∼**e karşı bomba**, (*mil.*) anti-personnel bomb.

perspek·tif/ ∼ **tiv** (*art.*) Perspective.

perşembe Thursday. ∼**nin gelişi çarşambadan belli olur**, it's as clear as that night follows the day; you can feel it coming.

pertavsız (*phys.*) Magnifying-glass; burning-glass.

Peru (*geo.*) Peru. ∼ **+**, *a.* Peruvian: ∼ **karabatak**, (*orn.*) guanay cormorant. ∼**lu**, (*ethn.*) Peruvian.

pe·ruk(a) (*mod.*) Wig. ∼**rükâr**, (*obs.*) barber.

perva Heed, attention; fear, anxiety; restraint. ∼**sız**, fearless; indifferent; blunt; unrestrained. ∼**sızlık**, fearlessness; indifference; lack of restraint.

pervane (*ent.*) Moth (round a candle); (*eng.*) flywheel; propeller; paddle-wheel; airscrew; windmill sails. ∼ **gibi**, continually rotating; (*fig.*) protective: ∼ **kanadı**, (*eng.*) blade: ∼ **olm. (-e)**, accompany, look after, protect: ∼ **rüzgârı**, (*aer.*) slipstream.

pervaz (*arch.*) Ornamental border; cornice; moulding; fringe.

-perver *a. suf.* Nourishing . . .; caring for . . .. ∼**lik**, caring nature [MİSAFİRPERVER(LİK)].

per·yodik *a.* Periodic. *n.* (*pub.*) periodical. ∼**yo**^{l}**t**^{du}, period.

peş^{1} *a.* Low, soft (voice). ∼ **perdeden konuşmak**, speak softly: ∼ **perdeli**, (*mus.*) bass.

peş^{2} *int.* Defeated, beaten. ∼ **dedir(t)mek**, make s.o. cry small: ∼ **demek**, give in, submit: ∼ **etm.**, accept defeat; cry small.

pese^{l}**k**^{ği} (*bio.*) Tartar (of the teeth).

pesi·mist^{i} Pessimist. ∼**mizm**, pessimism.

pes·paye(lik) Common(ness), vulgar(ity), cheap/ (-ness); ∼ **adam**, bounder. ∼**pembe**, very pink/rosy.

pest^{i} = PES^{1}.

pestenkerani Idiotic, nonsensical; (*arch.*) jerrybuilt, ramshackle.

pestil (*cul.*) Dried layers of fruit pulp. ∼ **gibi olm./ yatmak**, lie exhausted: ∼**i çıkmak**, be beaten/ crushed: ∼**ini çıkarmak**, beat s.o. to a jelly. ∼**leşmek**, *vi.* be worn out.

pestisi^{l}**t**^{di} (*chem.*) Pesticide.

pesüs Open earthenware oil-lamp.

peş^{1} *n.* (*mod.*) Edging; fullness (of a garment).

peş^{2} *n.* [90] Space behind; back. ∼ ∼ **e**, one after the other: ∼**i sıra**, behind/following him; afterwards: ∼**iN(EN)**: ∼**inde (-in)**, after/behind him; stg. much wanted: ∼**inde dolaşmak/gezmek**, follow s.o. with specific intention: ∼**inde olm.**, aspire to stg.

~inden gitmek (-in), follow s.o., adopt s.o.'s ideas: **~inden koşmak**, pursue a matter; chase after stg./ s.o.: **~inden sapan taşı yetişmez**, you won't catch him!: **~ine düşmek**, follow s.o.; work to achieve stg.: **~ine takılmak**, tack o.s. on to s.o.: **~ine takmak**, bring with one: **~ini bırakmak**, cease following.

peşin *a.* Former; first; paid in advance; ready (money). *adv.* First; in the first place; in advance. **~ almak**, buy for cash: **~ cevap**, answer prepared/given before the question is asked: **~ fiyat**, cash price: **~ hüküm/yargı**, prejudice, bias: **~ olarak**, in anticipation: **~ ödeme**, down-payment: **~ ödenen**, prepaid: **~ para**, ready money, cash; down payment: **~ pazarlık**, prior agreement: **~ satış**, cash sale: **~ söylemek**, foretell, prognosticate.

peşin·at[1] Down payment. **~atsız**, without down payment. **~ci**, 'cash-only' dealer; cash customer. **~en**, in advance.

peş·keş Gift; offering: **~ çekmek**, give stg. not belonging to o.s. **~kir**, (*dom.*) napkin. **~rev**, (*mus.*) overture, prelude; (*sp.*) preliminary movements in wrestling. **~tahta**, small desk; counter; money-changer's board.

peştamal Large bath-towel; large apron/waist-cloth. **~ kuşanmak**, finish one's apprenticeship; become master workman.

peştamal·cı Maker/dealer in bath-towels. **~lık**, fee paid for the goodwill of a business: **~ vermek**, purchase the goodwill.

Peştu (*ethn.*) Pathan. **~ca**, (*ling.*) Pushtu.

petalinis (*zoo.*) Limpet.

pete·k[gi] Honeycomb; a circular disc; clay jar; (*arch.*) uppermost cylindrical section of a minaret; (*eng.*) core. **~ gözü**, honeycomb cell; (*bio.*) alveolus: **~ güvesi**, (*ent.*) wax moth.

petek·göz (*ent.*) Compound eye. **~li**, honeycombed: **~ kurbağa**, (*zoo.*) Surinam toad. **~si**, (*bio.*) alveolar.

petro- *pref.* (*chem.*) Petro-. **~grafi**, (*geol.*) petrography. **~kimya +**, *a.* petro-chemical.

petrol[ü] Petroleum, oil. **~ araması**, oil-prospecting: **~ kuyusu**, oil well: **~ rafinerisi**, oil refinery: **~ sondajı**, oil-drilling.

petunya (*bot.*) Petunia.

pey (*fin.*) Earnest money; money on account; deposit; auction-bid. **~ akçesi**, earnest money: **~ sürmek**, bid: **~ vermek**, pay a deposit: **~ vurmak**, make a bid: **~i tutulmaz**, unreliable.

peycent[i] (*th.*) Pageant.

peyda *a.* Existent, manifest; born. **~ etm.**, procure; create; develop; acquire: **~ olm.**, come into being; appear. **~hlamak** = **~ ETM.**; have an illegitimate child.

peyderpey One after the other; steadily; slowly.

peygamber (*rel.*) Prophet; the Prophet Muhammad. **~ ağacı**[nı], (*bot.*) guaiacum, lignum vitae. **~ çiçeği**[ni], (*bot.*) cornflower, centaury. **~ devesi**[ni], (*ent.*) praying mantis. **~ kuşu**[nu], (*orn.*) white wagtail. **~lik**, prophethood.

peyk[i] Lackey, messenger, follower; (*ast., pol.*) satellite. **~lik**, being a lackey//satellite, etc.

peyke Wooden bench. **~ kurusu**, (*sl.*) who sleeps the night on a coffee-house bench.

pey·lemek (-i) Pay a deposit on stg.; book/engage/reserve (in advance). **~lenmek**, *vp.* **~leşmek (-le)**, conclude a bargain (paying a deposit).

peynir (*cul.*) Cheese. **~ akarı**, (*ent.*) cheese mite: **~ dişli**, toothless: **~ ekmekle yemek**, do stg. easily/as a matter of course: **~ gemisi** = LAFLA: **~ kurdu**, (*zoo.*) cheese maggot: **~ tekeri**, (*cul.*) whole cheese.

peynir·ağacı[nı] (*bot.*) Kapok tree. **~ci**, cheese-maker/-monger. **~cilik**, cheese-making. **~dişi**[ni], last remaining tooth of an old man. **~hane**, cheese factory. **~lenmek/~leşmek**, *vi.* (milk) coagulate; become cheesy; be flavoured with cheese. **~şekeri**[ni], soft white candy. **~tatlısı**[nı], cheese-cake.

peyrev Subordinate; follower; imitator.

peyzaj Landscape. **~ mimarisi**, landscape-gardening.

pez·eta (*fin.*) Spanish peseta. **~o**, Argentinian peso.

pezeven[k][gi] (*vulg.*) Pimp, procurer; (*fig.*) scoundrel. **~lik**, procuring.

Phil. = (*Philology*).

pıhtı Clot; coagulated liquid. **~lanmak**, *vi.* be clotted. **~laşma**, *vn.* coagulation, clotting. **~laşmak**, *vi.* coagulate, clot, congeal. **~laştırıcı**, (*med.*) coagulant. **~laştırmak (-i)**, *vc.*

pıl- *pref. Also* = PL-.

pılı pırtı Old rubbish; belongings, goods and chattels; (*naut.*) dunnage. **pılı(yı) pırtıyı toplamak**, pack up one's belongings.

pınar (*geol.*) Spring, source. **~ başı**[nı], fountain-head.

pır (*ech.*) Whizzing, whirring. **~ ~ etm.**, whiz, whirr.

pırasa (*bot.*) Leek. **~ bıyıklı**, with very long moustache: **~ olsa yemem!**, thank you, I'm not hungry!; I couldn't eat anything: **~ pide**, (*cul.*) leek pie.

pıratika (*naut.*) Pratique, clean bill of health.

pırazvana (*eng.*) Shank (of blade); metal socket, ferrule; (*bio.*) fang.

pırıl·da[k][gı] (*mil.*) Signal lamp; blinker. **~dakçı**, signaller. **~dama**, *vn.* flashing, gleaming. **~damak**, *vi.* flash, gleam, glitter. **~ ~**, very brightly, brilliantly, flashing; as clean as a new pin. **~tı**, glitter, gleam, flash.

pır·la[k][gı] Lure, decoy. **~lamak**, *vi.* flutter: **pırlayıp gitmek**, fly away. **~langı**[çı], (*child.*) whistling top. **~lanmak**, *vi.* (fledgling) flutter and try to fly.

pırlanta *n.* A brilliant. *a.* Set with brilliants. **~ gibi**, fine, valuable. **~ sülün**, (*orn.*) Lady Amherst's pheasant.

pırnal (*bot.*) Holm oak. **~lık**, oak grove.

pırpı (*geol.*) Serpentine; supposed antidote to snake-bite; (*bot.*) monkshood.

pırpır (*ech.*) Whirring (of wings); light aeroplane.

pırpırı (*sl.*) Shabbily dressed; dissolute, rake.

pırpıt[1] *n.* (*tex.*) Coarse homemade cloth; (*sp.*) wrestler's woven breeches. *a.* Worn-out, shabby.

pırtı = PILI PIRTI. **~k**, torn, ragged; = YIRTIK.

pırt·lak Bulging; easily peeled/skinned. **~lamak**, *vi.* bulge (out).

pısırık Shy, diffident; weak, incapable, clumsy.

~laşmak, *vi.* become shy, etc. ~lık, shyness, diffidence; clumsiness.
pıt[1] (*ech.*) Sound of dripping water. ~ ~ **atmak**, (heart) palpitate rapidly (from fear, etc.): ~ **yok**, there's not a sound.
pıtır (*ech.*) ~ ~, sound of rapid footsteps. ~**damak**, *vi.* make a tapping sound; crackle. ~**datmak (-i)**, *vc.* ~**tı**, light tapping/crackling sound.
pıtra'k[ğı] (*bot.*) Burr. ~ **gibi**, (tree) full of flowers/fruit.
pi (*math.*) Pi (π).
piç (*soc.*) Bastard; (*bot.*) offshoot, sucker; cuticle (of nail); small/defective replica; (*fig.*) naughty child. ~ **etm. (-i)**, spoil stg.: ~ **kurusu**, (*vulg.*) tiresome/naughty child: ~ **olm.**, be spoiled; be wasted; be incomplete. ~**leşmek**, *vi.* become spoiled. ~**lik**, bastardy; (*vulg.*) bad behaviour.
piçuta (*ich.*) Bonito.
pide (*cul.*) (Almost unleavened) flat bread. ~ **gibi**, completely flat. ~**ci**, PIDE baker/seller.
pigme (*zoo.*) Pygmy.
pigment (*chem.*) Pigment.
pijama (*mod.*) Pyjamas.
pik[i] (*naut.*) Gaff topsail; (*el.*) peak. ~ **demir**, (*min.*) pig iron.
pika (*gamb.*) Spades.
pikap (*rad.*) Pick-up gramophone; (*mot.*) small van.
pike[1] (*tex.*) Piqué; quilting.
pike[2] (*aer.*) Nose-dive. ~ **bombardımanı**, dive-bombing: ~ **etm./yapmak**, dive-bomb: ~ **uçağı**, dive-bomber.
piket[i] (*gamb.*) Piquet.
piketaj (*eng.*) Staking out.
pikflör (*dom.*) Flower-holder.
pikni'k[ği] Picnic. ~ **sahası**, picnic area: ~ **yapmak**, picnic.
piknometre (*phys.*) Pycnometer.
piko *n.* (*tex.*) Picot.
piko- *pref.* (*math.*) Pico- (10^{-12}). ~**lo**, (*mus.*) piccolo.
pikrik (*chem.*) Picric.
pil (*el.*) Battery, cell.
pil- *pref. Also* = PL-.
pila·ki (*cul.*) Fish/bean stew with oil and onions (eaten cold). ~**tika**, (*ich.*) pope(-fish).
pilav (*cul.*) Pilaff; boiled rice (with meat, pine kernels, raisins, etc.) ~**dan dönenin kaşığı kırılsın**, you can rely on me!; I'll abide by my decision. ~**lık**, suitable for making pilaff.
pili (*mod.*) Pleat. = PLİ.
pili'ç[ci] (*orn.*) Chick(en); (*cul.*) chicken; (*sl.*) pretty girl. ~ **çıkarmak**, hatch chicks: ~ **gibi**, young and pretty (girl).
pi·lon (*el.*) Pylon. ~**m**, (*eng.*) pin.
pilot[u] (*aer.*) Pilot; s.o./stg. acting as guide. ~ **balığı**, (*ich.*) pilot fish: ~ **bölge**, (*ind.*) development area: ~ **mahal/yeri**, (*aer.*) cockpit. ~**luk**, pilot's rank/duties. ~**suz**, pilotless: ~ **uçak**, drone.
pineklemek *vi.* Slumber, doze, take a nap.
pinel (*naut.*) Ship's weathervane.
pines (*zoo.*) Fan mussel.
pin(g)pon(g) (*sp.*) Ping-pong, table-tennis.

pin·pirik (*jok.*) Old and feeble. ~**pon**, (*sl.*) dotard.
pinti Miserly, stingy; shabby. ~**le(ş)mek**, *vi.* become dirty/shabby from miserliness. ~**lik**, miserliness.
pi·pet[i] (*chem.*) Pipette. ~**po**, tobacco pipe: ~ **balığı**, (*ich.*) flute-mouth.
pir *n.* Old man; (*rel.*) founder of a dervish order; patron saint. *adv.* Thoroughly; wisely. ~ **aşkına/yoluna**, just 'for love', disinterested(ly): ~ **ol**, (*jok.*) bravo!: ~ **yoluna gitmek**, die in vain; ~**i fani**, a decrepit old man.
pira·lis (*ent.*) Pyralid. ~**midal**, pyramidal. ~**mi'td**[i], (*arch., sp.*) pyramid. ~**ya**, (*ich.*) piranha, piraya.
Pire[1] *pr.n.* (*geo.*) Piraeus.
pire[2] *n.* (*ent.*) Flea; aphis. ~ **gibi**, very agile, lively: ~ **için**/~ **ye kızıp yorgan yakmak**, cut off one's nose to spite one's face: ~**yi deve yapmak**, greatly exaggerate; ~**yi gözünden vurmak**, be a good shot: ~**yi nallamak**, attempt the impossible; be very cunning.
pirekapan (*bot.*) Pyrethrum, fleabane.
pirekateşin (*carp., chem.*) Pyrocatechin.
pire·kıran Flea-powder, pulicide. ~**lendirmek (-i)**, (*fig.*) make suspicious/uneasy. ~**lenmek**, *vi.* become infested/flea-ridden; hunt for fleas on o.s.; (*fig.*) become suspicious/uneasy; be in a bad temper. ~**li**, infested with fleas; (*fig.*) suspicious, uneasy. ~**otu**[nu] = ~KAPAN.
pirina (*agr.*) Crushed-olive cake (oil extracted).
pirin'ç[ci] [1] *n.* (*min.*) Brass. ~**ten**, brazen.
pirin'ç[ci] [2] *n.* (*bot.*) Rice. ~ **biti**, (*ent.*) rice weevil: ~ **hamsteri**, (*zoo.*) grey hamster: ~ **kâğıdı**, (*pub.*) rice paper; tissue paper: ~ **kuşu**, (*orn.*) rice-bird, bobolink: ~ **örgüsü**, (*tex.*) moss-stitch: ~ **rakısı**, (*cul.*) arrack: ~ **su kaldırmamak**, rice not absorb much water: ~**e giderken Dimyat'a evdeki bulgurdan olm.**, lose what one has while trying to get more/better: ~**i su kaldırmaz**, be very touchy: ~**in taşını** = AYIKLAMAK.
pi·rit[i] (*geol.*) (Iron) pyrites. ~**roksen**, pyroxene. ~**rometre**, (*phys.*) pyrometer. ~**rop**[u], (*geol.*) pyrope. ~**rosfer**, pyrosphere.
piruhi (*cul.*) Stewed dough with cheese.
pirüpak[i] Spotlessly clean.
piryol Wide-bottomed cask. ~ **saati**, 'turnip' pocket-watch.
pirzola (*cul.*) Cutlet, chop. ~**lık**, cutlet (meat).
pis Dirty, filthy; disgusting, foul; obscene; (*fig.*) complicated. ~ **lakırdı**, obscene language: ~ ~ **düşünmek**, brood over stg.; appear distraught/worried: ~ ~ **gülmek**, laugh at s.o.'s discomfiture: ~**i** ~**ine**, uselessly, in vain.
pis·bıyık Drooping moustache. ~**boğaz**, greedy; s.o. who will eat anything at any time. ~**boğazlık**, greediness.
pisi (*child.*) Cat. ~ ~, puss! puss! ~**balığ**[nı], (*ich.*) dab. ~**pisi**, (*child.*) cat. ~**pisiotu**[nu], (*bot.*) wall barley.
piskopos (*rel.*) Bishop. ~**hane**, bishop's residence. ~**luk**, bishopric; diocese, see; bishop's rank/duties.
pis·lemek (-e) Dirty, soil; relieve o.s.; (animal) soil stg. ~**lenmek**/~**leşmek**, *vi.* become dirty; be soiled. ~**letmek (-i)**, make dirty; defile, soil. ~**lik**,

dirtiness; dirt; mess; faeces; obscenity: ～ **böceği**, (*ent.*) sacred beetle: ～ **götürmek (-i)**, become very dirty: ～ **parmak(lar)ından akmak**, be filthy. ～**likarkı**, drains, sewer. ～**su**, (*dom.*) waste water.
pist[i] [1] *int.* Psst! (*driving away the cat*).
pist[i] [2] *n.* (*sp.*) Race-course/-track; (*aer.*) runway.
pistole (Paint) spray-gun; (*art.*) French curve.
piston (*eng.*) Piston; (*fig.*) backing, influence. ～ **kırmak**, (*sl.*) go joy-riding: ～ **kolu**, (*eng.*) piston-rod: ～ **kolu başı**, big-end: ～ **mil/pimi**, gudgeon-pin: ～ **seyri**, piston stroke. ～**lu**, having a piston; reciprocating; (*fig.*) with backing, influential.
pisuar Urinal, lavatory bowl.
pişdar (*mil.*) Vanguard.
piş·eğen/ ～**ek** That cooks easily.
pişekâr (*Tk. th.*) A kind of clown.
piş·i¹k[ği] (*med.*) Sore in groin/armpit (inflamed by sweat). ～**im**, (*cul.*) act of being cooked; amount cooked at one time, batch. ～**irici**, *a.* cooking: *n.* baker, cook. ～**irilmek**, *vp.* be cooked. ～**irim(lik)**, amount cooked at one time, batch. ～**irmek (-i)**, cook, bake; ripen; cure (rubber); plan (action); hatch (plot); (sweat) cause a sore/**pişik**; (*fig.*) learn stg. extremely well: **pişirip kotarmak**, cook and serve up (food); settle (question); finish (job). ～**irtmek (-i, -e)**, *vc.* ～**kin**, well-cooked/-baked; ripe, mature; (*fig.*) 'hard-baked', hardened, experienced. ～**kinlik**, a being well-cooked; ripeness, maturity; assurance, experience, knowledge of the world: ～**e vurmak**, ignore evil words/action.
pişman Sorry; regretful; penitent, repentant, contrite. ～ **etm.**, make repent: ～ **olm. (-e)**, be sorry for; repent: ～ **papaz**, apostate priest. ～**iye**, (*cul.*) fibrous sweet. ～**lık**, regret, contrition, penitence: ～ **navlunu**, (*fin.*) dead freight.
piş·mek *vi.* Be cooked/baked; ripen, mature; be perfected; become experienced; be overcome by the heat; (skin) be chafed/inflamed (by heat/sweat). ～**memiş**, *a.* uncooked, raw; immature; inexperienced. ～**miş** *a.* cooked, done; ripe; mature: ～ **armut gibi eline düşmek**, obtain stg. with great ease: ～ **aşa soğuk su katmak**, spoil things at the last moment/when the job is already completed: ～ **kelle gibi sırıtmak**, be always grinning (without reason).
pişti (*sp.*) A ball game; (*gamb.*) a card game.
piştov (*mil.*) Pistol. ～**u dokuz patlar,** he's very irritable.
pito (*aer.*) Pitot (tube).
piton (*zoo.*) Python.
pitoresk Picturesque.
pitsikato (*mus.*) Pizzicato.
pitta (*orn.*) Pitta.
piyade (*mil.*) Foot-soldier, infantryman; pedestrian; (chess) pawn; single pair-oared boat; (*fig.*) s.o. of small capacity/knowledge.
piyan (*med.*) Yaws.
piyango Lottery, raffle. ～**da bana bin lira isabet etti,** I won a thousand liras in the lottery: ～**su çıkmak,** win a lottery.
piyan·issimo (*mus.*) Pianissimo. ～**ist**[i], pianist. ～**o**, piano.
piyasa Public place, open space; stroll; (*fin.*)

market; current price; rate of exchange. ～ **+**, *a.* Commercial, market: ～ **çöktü,** the bottom fell out of the market: ～ **etm.**, walk/stroll about: ～ **rayici,** market price, going rate: ～**da bulunmak,** be available/in circulation: ～**ya çıkmak,** go out for a walk; (goods) come on the market: ～**ya düşmek,** be plentiful; (woman) become a prostitute.
piyata (*dom.*) Dinner-plate. ～ **+**, *a.* Flat.
piyaz (*cul.*) White bean salad (with chopped onions); (*sl.*) flattery, back-slapping. ～**ı vermek/** ～**ları basmak,** applaud, flatter. ～**cı**, flatterer. ～**lamak (-i)**, (*cul.*) marinade; (*sl.*) sing s.o.'s praises, flatter s.o.
piyes (*th.*) Piece, drama, play. ～ **başlaması,** curtain-up!: ～ **e çevirmek,** adapt for the theatre, dramatize.
piyezometre (*phys.*) Piezometer.
piyon (*chess; fig.*) Pawn.
piyore (*med.*) Pyorrhoea.
pizolit[i] (*geol.*) Pisolitic.
PK = POSTA KUTUSU.
pl- *Also* = PIL-; PİL-.
plaçka Spoil, booty. ～**cı**, raider, freebooter.
plafon (*aer., fin.*) Ceiling.
plaj (Bathing-)beach.
plajiyoklaz (*geol.*) Plagioclastic.
pla¹k[ği] Plate, disc; (*cin.*) plate; (*mus.*) gramophone record; (*sp.*) clay pigeon. ～ **kalıbı,** master disc: ～**a almak (-i)**, make a recording of stg.
plaka Plate; badge; name-plate; (*mot.*) registration/ number-plate. ～ **No.,** registration number. ～**cı**, plate-maker/-seller. ～**lı**, (*mot.*) registered. ～**sız**, unregistered.
plak·çalar (*el.*) Record-player. ～**çı**, (*mus.*) record-dealer. ～**et**[i], plate, plaque; (*bio.*) platelet; name-plate. ～**etli**, (*geol.*) flaky.
plan Plan, scheme, intention; (*art.*) plan, design. ～**a düşmek (-inci)**, lose/cease to have importance: ～**da olm. (-inci)**, have . . . qualities/value: ～**da tutmak (-inci)**, attach . . . importance to stg.: ～**ını yapmak,** design stg.
plan·cı Planner. ～**çete**, (*geo.*) plane-table. ～**et(aryum)**, (*ast.*) planet(arium). ～**imetre**, (*math.*) planimeter. ～**kton**, (*zoo.*) plankton. ～**lama**, *vn.* planning. ～**lamak (-i)**, plan stg. ～**lı**, planned. ～**ör(cü)**, (*aer.*) glider(-pilot). ～**örcülük**, gliding. ～**sız**, unplanned, casual. ～**ş**, (*pub.*) plate, illustration. ～**tasyon**, (*agr.*) plantation. ～**ya**, (*carp.*) plane.
plasenta (*bio.*) Placenta, afterbirth.
plasiye (*fin.*) Commercial traveller, agent.
plasman (*fin.*) Investment.
plas·ter (*med.*) Adhesive plaster. ～**tifiyan**, (*chem.*) plastifier. ～**tik**, *a., n.* plastic (material): ～ **ameliyat**, (*med.*) plastic surgery: ～ **özdek**, plastic material: ～ **sanatlar**, (*art.*) plastic arts: ～ **tutkal**, (*carp.*) plastic bonding. ～**tisite**, plasticity. ～**tron**, (*sp.*) plastron.
platerina (*ich.*) Sand-smelt, atherine.
platform (*geo., etc.*) Platform; carriageway; (*pol.*) platform, programme.
platin (*chem.*) Platinum; (*mot.*) point(s).
plato (*geo.*) Plateau; (*cin.*) set.
platonik Platonic (love).

plazma (*bio., phys.*) Plasma. ~ **bozulması**, plasmolysis.
plebisit[i] (*adm.*) Plebiscite.
pleistosen (*geol.*) Pleistocene.
plevra (*med.*) Pleura.
pli (*mod.*) Fold, pleat, crease. ~ **se**, ~ **ütüsü**, (*mod.*) crimping iron.
plio·en (*geol.*) Pliocene.
plonjon (*sp.*) Dive (by goalkeeper).
Plt. = (*aer.*) PİLOT.
pluto·krasi (*adm.*) Plutocracy. ~ **nyum**, (*chem.*) plutonium.
Plüton (*myth., ast.*) Pluto.
Pm. = (*ch.s.*) PROMETYUM.
pnö·matik (*phys., eng.*) Pneumatic. ~ **moni**, (*med.*) pneumonia.
po- *pref. Also* = BO-.
Po. = (*ch.s.*) POLONYUM.
poca (*naut.*) = BOCA. ~ **alabanda!**, to leeward!: ~ **etm.**, bear/veer to leeward.
podüsüet[i] Suede leather.
podyum (*sp.*) Podium, dais.
pof (*ech.*) Puff! ~ **urdamak**, puff, snort (*with boredom*).
poğaça(cı) (*cul.*) (Maker/seller of) flaky cheese pastry.
pohpoh Applause; flattery. ~ **cu**, flatterer. ~ **lamak (-i)**, flatter.
poker (*gamb.*) Poker.
pol. = POLİTİKA.
polar·gı/ ~ **izör** (*phys.*) Polarizer. ~ **ılmak**, *vp.* ~ **izasyon** = ~ MA. ~ **ize**, polarized (light). ~ **ma**, *vn.* (*chem., phys.*) polarization. ~ **mak (-i)**, polarize. ~ **ölçer**, polarimeter.
polemi[i]**k**[ği] (*pol., pub.*) Polemics.
poli- *pref.* Poly-. ~ **asit**, (*chem.*) polyacid.
poliçe (*fin.*) Bill of exchange, draft; insurance policy. ~ **yi kabul et(me)mek/öde(me)mek**, (dis)honour a bill.
poli·ester (*chem.*) Polyester. ~ **etilen**, polyethylene. ~ **foni**, (*mus.*) polyphony. ~ **gam(i)**, (*soc.*) polyga·mous/(-my). ~ **gon**, (*mil.*) artillery-range; (*math.*) polygon. ~ **klinik**, (*med.*) polyclinic, general hospital. ~ **mer(izasyon)**, (*chem.*) polymer/ (-ization). ~ **nom**, (*math.*) polynomial. ~ **p**[i], (*zoo., med.*) polyp(us). ~ **propilen**, (*chem.*) polypropylene.
polis (*leg.*) Police; policeman. ~ **devleti**, (*pol.*) police-state: ~ **hafiyesi**, detective: ~ **komiseri**, police superintendent: ~ **memuru**, constable: ~ **merkezi**, police-station: ~ **nezareti altında**, under police observation. ~ **iye**, (*lit.*) detective story. ~ **lik**, police duties.
poli·stiren (*chem.*) Polystyrene. ~ **teist**, (*rel.*) polytheist. ~ **teizm**, polytheism. ~ **teknik**, (*ed.*) polytechnic.
politik Political. ~ **a**, politics; policy; (*fig.*) cunning, flattery: ~ **bezirgânı**, s.o. who exploits politics for his own ends: ~ **gütmek**, flatter: ~ **yapmak**, play politics to achieve an end. ~ **acı**, politician; flatterer. ~ **acılık**, politics.
poli·üretan (*chem.*) Polyurethane. ~ **vinil**, polyvinyl. ~ **yester**, polyester.
pol·ka (*mus.*) Polka. ~ **o**, (*sp.*) polo.

Polon·ez/ ~ **yalı** (*ethn.*) Pole. ~ **ya**, (*geo.*) Poland: ~ +, *a.* Polish. ~ **yum**, (*chem.*) polonium.
Poma[i]**k**[ğı] (*ethn.*) Pomak, Bulgarian Muslim. ~ **ça**, (*ling.*) their language.
poma[i]**t**[dı] Pomade, (hair-)cream.
pompa Pump. ~ **j**/ ~ **lama**, pumping. ~ **lamak (-i)**, pump. ~ **lanmak**, *vp.*
ponje (*tex.*) Pongee (silk).
ponk·siyon (*med.*) Puncture, injection. ~ **tüasyon**, (*ling.*) punctuation.
ponpon (*mod.*) Pompom.
ponton (*naut.*) Pontoon.
ponza (*geol.*) Pumice-stone. ~ **lamak (-i)**, pumice, rub down. ~ **lanmak**, *vp.*
pop[1] (*rel.*) Greek Orthodox priest.
pop[2] (*mus.*) Pop-music.
poplin (*tex.*) Poplin.
popo (*child.*) Buttock(s).
popüler (*art., lit.*) Popular.
porfir (*geol.*) Porphyry. ~ **it**[i], porphyrite. ~ **si**, porphyritic.
por·no(grafi) (*lit.*) Pornography. ~ **ozite**, (*geol.*) porosity. ~ **selen**, (*dom.*) porcelain, china. ~ **siyon**, (*cul.*) portion.
porsu[i]**k**[ğu 1] *n.* Badger. ~ **ağacı**[nı], (*bot.*) yew-tree. ~ **giller**, Taxaceae, yew family.
por·suk[2] *a.* Shrivelled (up), withered. ~ **sumak**, *vi.* = PÖRSÜMEK.
porsun (*naut.*) Boatswain, bo's'n. ~ **kuşu**, (*orn.*) tropic bird.
portakal (*bot.*) Orange; orange-tree. ~ **çiçeği suyu**, (*cul.*) orange-flower water: ~ **kabuğu**, orange-peel: ~ **rengi**, orange (colour): ~ **suyu**, orange juice. ~ **lık**, orange orchard.
port·atif Portable; collapsible. ~ **bagaj**, truck, trolley. ~ **e**, range, importance, field; (*mus.*) stave.
Portekiz (*geo.*) Portugal. ~ +, *a.* Portuguese. ~ **çe**, (*ling.*) Portuguese. ~ **li**, *n.* (*ethn.*) Portuguese.
port·föy Wallet, pocket-book. ~ **manto**, (*dom.*) hat-/coat-stand; coat-hanger. ~ **mone**, purse. ~ **o**, (*cul.*) port(-wine). ~ **olan**, (*naut.*) portolano, book of charts. ~ **re**, (*art.*) portrait.
pos ~ **bıyıklı**/ ~ **bıyık**, having a large bushy moustache.
posa Sediment, dregs. ~ **sını çıkarmak (-in)**, (*fig.*) drink to the very dregs.
pos·itif = POZİTİF. ~ **izyon** = POZİSYON.
post[u] (*zoo.*) Skin; hide; tanned fur-skin (used as rug, etc.); (*adm., pej.*) post, position, office; (*fig.*) 'skin', life. ~ **elden gitmek**, be killed, lose one's life; lose one's post: ~ **kalpak**, (*mod.*) sheepskin cap: ~ **kapmak**, (*adm., pej.*) get an office (by influence): ~ **kavgası**, struggle for power/position, rat-race: ~ **u kurtarmak**, save one's skin/life: ~ **u sermek**, settle down in a place/post (intending to stay); overstay one's welcome: ~ **una oturmak**, (*adm.*) take possession of one's office; (*fig.*) assume airs.
posta The post, mail; postal service; mail-coach/ -steamer/-train; (*mil.*) post, sentry; (*ind.*) shift, gang, relay; trip; journey. ~ **çeki**, (*fin.*) giro cheque: ~ **etm.**, take s.o. to the police-station: ~ **gemisi**, (*naut.*) mail-boat: ~ **gönderimi**, (*fin.*) money/postal order: ~ **güvercini**, (*orn.*) carrier

pigeon: ~ **koymak**, arrange things to trick s.o.: ~ **kutusu**, post-box: ~ **pulu**, postage stamp: ~ **tatarı**, (*his.*) post-rider; courier: ~ **yapmak**, make a return trip: ~**ya bırakmak**, post a letter: ~**yı kesmek**, cease frequenting a place/doing stg.

posta·cı Postman. ~**cılık**, postal service/operation; postman's work. ~**hane**/~**ne**, post-office. ~**l**[1], *a.* postal. ~**lamak (-i)**, post. ~**lanmak**, *vp.*

postal[2] *n.* (*mod.*) Heavy army boot; (*fig.*) loose woman.

poster (*pub.*) Poster.

postnişin (*rel.*) Head/sheikh of dervish order.

post·restant[1] Poste restante. ~**ulat**[1], (*phil.*) postulate.

poşu (*mod.*) Light military turban; kerchief worn round the head.

pot[u 1] *n.* (*naut.*) River-ferry punt/raft; (*agr.*) wooden cattle-shed floor. ~**başı**, river-ferry site.

pot[u 2] *n.* (*mod.*) Crease, fold, pleat. *a.* Puckered, too full. ~ **gelmek**, go wrong, turn out badly: ~ **kırmak**, make a *faux-pas*/blunder, 'drop a brick': ~ **yeri (-in)**, defect.

pota (*min.*) Crucible, converter, cupel. ~**da eritme/ tasfiye**, cupellation.

potansi·yel *a.*, *n.* (*phys.*, *phil.*) Potential: ~ **farkı**, (*phys.*) stress; (*el.*) potential difference. ~**yometre**, (*el.*) potentiometer.

pota·s (*chem.*) Potash. ~**syum**, potassium. ~**şe**, commercial potash.

potin (*mod.*) Buttoned/elastic-sided boots.

potkal (*naut.*) Bottle containing a message.

pot·lanmak (*mod.*) *vp.* Be creased/puckered. ~**lu**, puckered; in folds. ~**luk**, fullness.

potpuri (*mus.*) Selection, pot-pourri.

potu[l]**k**[ğu 1] *n.* (*live.*) Young camel.

pot·uk[2]/~ **ur** *a.* (*mod.*) Puckered, full; in pleats. *n.* Full-gathered knee-breeches.

poyra Hub (cart); axle-end (car). ~**lık**, hard-wood log for cutting hubs.

poyraz (*met.*) North-east wind; (*geo.*) NE point. ~ **kuşu**, (*orn.*) oyster-catcher: ~**a açmak**, be disappointed; get nothing. ~**lamak**, *vi.* (*met.*) veer to the NE.

poz (*art.*, *cin.*) Pose; (*cin.*) exposure. ~ **almak**, strike an attitude: ~ **ölçek**//**süresi**, (*cin.*) exposure meter// time: ~ **vermek**, pose. ~**cu**, (*fig.*) affected, artificial.

poz·isyon Position; item, heading: ~**u izlemek**, (*sp.*) mark the man. ~**itif**, (*math.*, *phil.*, *phys.*) positive: ~ **elektrikli**, electropositive: ~ **film**, (*cin.*) positive film: ~ **görüntü**, positive image. ~**itivist**, (*phil.*) positivist. ~**itivizm**, positivism. ~**itron**, (*phys.*) positron.

pöl'ç[cü] (*bio.*, *dial.*) Tail; coccyx.

pöf *int.* (*disgust*) Pugh!

pörçük pörçük In bits and pieces.

pör·sük Shrivelled, withered. ~**süklük**, shrivelling, withering. ~**sümek**, *vi.* shrivel up; become withered/wrinkled.

pösteki Sheepskin, goatskin; sheepskin rug (on divan). ~ **olm.**, become limp: ~ **saymak**, engage in a futile/tedious task: ~**sini saydırmak (-i)**, set s.o. a futile/tedious task: ~**sini sermek**, flay s.o.; give s.o. a severe thrashing.

pötikare (*mod.*) Small check design/material.

pp. = (*mus.*) PİYANİSSİMO.

pr- *Also* = PIR-.

Pr. = (*ch.s.*) PRASEODİM; (*soc.*) PRENS(LİĞİ).

prafa (*gamb.*) A card game (for three).

pragma·cı/~ **tist** (*phil.*) Pragmatist. ~**cılık**/~**tizm**, pragmatism.

pranga (Criminal's) leg-irons, fetters; penal servitude. ~ **cezası**, (*mil.*) in irons: ~ **kaçağı**, ferocious bandit: ~**ya vurmak**, clap in irons.

pras·a = PIRASA. ~**eodim**, (*chem.*) praseodymium. ~ **ya**, (*naut.*) brace.

prat·ik *n.* Practice; application: *a.* practical, applied; businesslike: ~ **bilgiler**, practical hints. ~**ika** = PIRATİKA. ~**ikleşmek**, *vi.* become practical/possible. ~ **isyen**, (*art.*) one who learns by practice, craftsman.

pre·fabrike (*arch.*) Prefabricated. ~**jüje**, prejudice. ~ **kambriyum**, (*geol.*) pre-Cambrian. ~**lüd**[ü], (*mus.*) prelude.

prens (*adm.*) Prince. ~**es(lik)**, (rank/title of) princess. ~**lik**, rank/title of a prince; princedom, principality.

prensi'p[bi] Principle; basis. ~ +, *a.* Theoretical. ~ **meselesidir!**, it's a matter of principle!: ~ **olarak**, in principle.

pres Press, crusher.

presbit[i] (*med.*) Long-sighted. ~**lik**, presbyopia, long-sightedness.

pres·döküm (*min.*) Casting, moulding. ~**e**, pressing device.

pre·sesyon (*ast.*) Precession. ~**sizyon**, precision.

pres·lendirmek (-i) Press, stamp. ~**tij**, (*soc.*) prestige. ~**to**, (*mus.*) presto.

pre·vantif (*med.*) Preventive. ~**vantoryum**, sanatorium (for tuberculosis suspects). ~**zantasyon**, presentation. ~**zante**, ~ **etm.**, present, show; introduce. ~**zervatif**, (*med.*) condom, contraceptive.

prim (*fin.*) Premium; bonus; insurance premium; lottery prize; (*ind.*) subsidy.

pri·madonna (*mus.*) Primadonna, diva. ~**mat**[1], (*zoo.*) primate. ~**mer**, primary. ~**mitif**, primitive.

priz (*el.*) Socket; (*eng.*) drive. ~**ma**, (*phys.*) prism. ~ **matik**, prismatic.

prob·abilizm (*phil.*) Probabilism. ~**lem**, *n.* problem: *a.* problem (child): ~**i çözmek**, solve a problem.

prodük·siyon (*th.*) Production. ~**tif**, productive. ~**tivite**, productivity. ~**tör**, (*th.*) producer.

Prof. = ~**esör(lük)**, (*ed.*) (post/duties of) professor, teacher. ~**esyonel(lik)**, (*sp.*, *th.*) professional(ism).

profil (*math.*) Profile, section. ~ **demiri**, (*min.*) angle/sectional iron: ~ **kesiti**, (*eng.*) contour.

pro·filaktik (*med.*) Prophylactic. ~**forma**, (*fin.*) pro forma (invoice).

program Programme. ~**cı**, programmer, planner; (*th.*) programme-seller. ~**lama**, *vn.* programming. ~**lamak**/~**laştırmak (-i)**, programme. ~**lı**, with a programme; programmed. ~**sız**, without a programme; unprogrammed.

proje (*eng.*) Project, design, plan; (*adm.*) draft.

~ **hız//kabul//koşul//yükü**, (*eng.*) design speed// approval//condition//load.

proje·ksiyon (*cin.*) Projection; slide. ~ **ktör**, projector; floodlight. ~ **lendirme**, *vn.* designing: ~ **ye dayanak**, design basis. ~ **lendirmek (-i)**, design stg. ~ **lenmek**, *vp.*

pro·ksimal Approximate; (*bio.*) proximal. ~ **letarya**, (*soc.*) proletariat. ~ **leter**, proletarian, worker. ~ **log**, (*lit.*) prologue. ~ **metyum**, (*chem.*) promethium.

propaganda Propaganda, publicity. ~ **cı**, propagandist, ad-man. ~ **cılık**, propagandism.

pro·pan (*chem.*) Propane. ~ **sedür**, procedure. ~ **ses**, process. ~ **sodi**, (*lit.*, *mus.*) prosody. ~ **spektüs**, (*fin.*, *ind.*) prospectus. ~ **stat¹**, (*bio.*) prostate (gland). ~ **stela**, (*dom.*) apron. ~ **taktinyum** (*chem.*) protactinium. ~ **tein**, (*bio.*) protein. ~ **tektora**, (*adm.*) protectorate.

protes·tan(lık) (*rel.*) Protestant(ism). ~ **to**, protest: ~ **etm.**, protest against, reject; send a protest: ~ **çekmek**, (*adm.*) issue a formal protest.

protez Artificial, false; (*mod. sl.*) falsies. ~ **dişler**, (*med.*) false teeth: ~ **organ**, artificial limb. ~ **ci**, maker of artificial items.

proto·jin (*geol.*) Protogine. ~ **kol**, (*adm.*) protocol, treaty, agreement; rules of diplomatic usage. ~ **n**, (*chem.*) proton. ~ **nema**, (*bot.*) protonema. ~ **plazma**, (*bio.*) protoplasm. ~ **tip**, (*ind.*) prototype. ~ **zoa**, (*bio.*) protozoa.

prova Trial, test; (*mod.*) fitting; (*th.*) rehearsal; (*pub.*) proof. ~ **etm.**, try on (clothes). = PRUVA.

pro·vidansializm (*phil.*) Providentialism. ~ **vokasyon**, (*pol.*) incitement, provocation. ~ **vokatör**, inciter, *agent-provocateur*.

prömiyer (*th.*, *etc.*) Première.

Prusya (*geo.*) Prussia. ~ +, *a.* Prussian: ~ **mavisi**, Prussian blue. ~ **lı**, *n.* (*ethn.*) Prussian.

pruva (*naut.*) Bow, stem. ~ **direği**, foremast: ~ **hattı**, line astern: ~ **topu**, bow-chaser.

psi·kanaliz (*psy.*) Psychoanalysis. ~ **kasteni**, psychasthenia. ~ **kiyatr**, psychiatrist. ~ **kiyatri**, psychiatry. ~ **kolog**, psychologist. ~ **koloji(k)**, psycholo·gy/(-gical). ~ **kometri**, psychometry. ~ **kopat(i)**, psychopath(y). ~ **koz**, psychosis. ~ **şiatri** = ~ KİYATRİ. ~ **takoz**, (*med.*) psittacosis.

Pt. = (*ch.s.*) PLATİN.

PTT = POSTA, TELGRAF VE TELEFON (İDARESİ): ~ **ile**, by post.

Pu. = (*ch.s.*) PLUTONYUM.

puan (*ling.*) Full-stop; (*ed.*) mark; (*sp.*) point. ~ **almak/kazanmak**, (*sp.*) score a point: ~ **hesabıyla yenmek**, (*sp.*) win on points: ~ **vermek**, give points/ marks.

puan·lamak (-i) Mark, correct. ~ **lı**, spotted. ~ **ter**, (*sp.*) pointer (dog). ~ **tiye**, dotted, spotted.

puding (*geol.*) Conglomerate; (*cul.*) pudding.

pudra Powder. ~ **lamak (-i)**, powder, cover with powder. ~ **lık/pudriyer**, powder-box; powder compact. ~ **şeker**, castor sugar.

pudu·ᵏkᵍᵘ (*live.*) Newly-born camel foal.

puf Puff; (*dom.*) pouffe. ~ **minderi**, pouffe, cushion-seat. ~ **böreği**ⁿⁱ, puff pastry stuffed with meat and cheese. ~ **la**, *n.* (*orn.*) common eider duck: *a.* puffed

out, soft; filled with eider-down. ~ **lamak**, *vi.* blow and puff; become puffed out/soft.

puhu ~ **kuşu**, (*orn.*) great eagle owl.

pul Thin round disc; (*zoo.*) (fish, etc.) scale; (*min.*) flake; (*mod.*) spangle; (*eng.*) washer, small nut; (postage, etc.) stamp; piece (in draughts/backgammon); (*obs.*) small coin. ~ **etmemek (bir)**, be worthless: ~ ~, covered with large spots/scales: ~ **şişe**, rough glass jar: ~ **vergisi**, (*adm.*) stamp duty: ~ **yapıştırmak**, affix a stamp.

pula·ᵗtᵈ¹ (*min.*) Steel.

pul·cu Revenue-stamp seller; stamp-collector; stamp-dealer. ~ **culuk**, stamp-dealing; stamp-collecting; philately. ~ **kanatlılar**, (*ent.*) butterflies and moths, Lepidoptera. ~ **lamak (-i)**, stick stamps on stg.; decorate. ~ **lanma**, (*min.*) flaking. ~ **lanmak**, *vp.* ~ **lu**, bearing stamps/scales; stamped; scaly; spangled; spotted: ~ **böcek**, (*ent.*) scale insect: ~ **hayvanlar**, (*zoo.*) scaly anteaters: ~ **memeligiller**, (*zoo.*) pangolins: ~ **sürüngenler**, (*zoo.*) Squamata, snakes and lizards. ~ **su**, flaky; imbricate. ~ **suz**, without stamps/scales, etc.

pul·luk (*agr.*) Heavy plough. ~ **man**, (*mot.*) long-distance coach. ~ **sar**, (*ast.*) pulsar.

puluç (*bio.*) Sexually impotent (man). ~ **luk**, impotence.

puma (*zoo.*) Puma, cougar.

pun·ᵗçᶜᵘ (*cul.*) Punch (drink).

pun·ᵗtᵈᵘ (*naut.*) Ship's position; appropriate time. ~ **una getirmek/** ~ **unu bulmak**, find a suitable opportunity to do stg.

punta (*eng.*) (Lathe) centre, centre-bit. ~ **aralığı**, between centres: ~ **tornası**, centre lathe. ~ **l**, (*naut.*) stanchion. ~ **lama**, centring.

punto (*pub.*) Type size, type face.

pupa¹ *n.* (*ent.*) Pupa.

pupa² *n.* (*naut.*) Poop, stern; following wind. *adv.* From the stern, aft. ~ **gitmek**, sail before the wind: ~ **seyri**, sailing with the wind: ~ **yelken açmak (-e)**, take advantage of, profit by.

puro Cigar.

pus¹ (*math.*) Inch.

pus² (*met.*) Mist, haze; condensation (on cold surface); bloom (on fruit); (*myc.*) blight, mildew; (*bot.*) moss (on trees, etc.); (*ent.*) web, cocoon (on leaves); (*live.*) crust (on ewe's nipples). ~ **arıᵏk**ᵍ¹, haze, hazy weather; mirage. ~ **armak**, *vi.* be hazy, etc.

pusat¹ Equipment; arms, instruments of war. ~ **çı**, (*th.*) 'soldier'-clown in ORTAOYUNU. ~ **landırmak (-i)**, arm, supply with weapons, equip. ~ **lanmak**, *vi.* be armed/equipped; (*his.*) put on armour. ~ **lı**, armed; (*his.*) wearing armour.

pus·etⁱ Baby's push-cart. ~ **la**, = PUSULA¹·².

pus·lanmak *vi.* Become hazy, be misted with condensation; (fruit) have a bloom. ~ **lu**, misty, hazy; having a bloom.

pusmak *vi.* Crouch down; lie in ambush; descend; become misty; be grieved/offended.

pusu Ambush. ~ **kurmak**, lay an ambush: ~ **ya düşürmek (-i)**, ambush s.o.: ~ **ya yatmak**, lie in wait.

pusula¹ *n.* (*naut.*) Compass. ~ **daire/gülü**, compass rose: ~ **dolabı**, binnacle: ~ **ibre/iğnesi**, compass needle: ~ **kertesi**, compass point: ~ **kertelerini saymak**, box the compass: ~ **nın sapması**, compass deviation: ~ **yı şaşırmak**, lose one's bearings; be bewildered.

usula[2] *n.* Note, chit; memorandum; list. ~ **etm.**, make a note/list of.

usval[i] Measure used by YEMENİCİ.

uşt[u] Catamite. ~ **luk**, being a catamite; (*vulg.*) behaving like one.

ut[u 1] *n.* (*tex.*) Three-ply silk thread.

ut[u 2] *n.* (*rel.*) Idol, god, fetish; crucifix. ~ **gibi**, silent, staring, motionless: ~ **heykeli**, idol, image, statue: ~ **kesilmek**, stand silent and motionless: ~ **ları kırmak**, (*col.*) debunk.

ut·hane Pagan temple. ~ **kıran**, iconoclast. ~ **laşmak**, *vi.* be idolized; be over-valued. ~ **laştırmak** (-i), idolize; value excessively. ~ **perest(lik)**, idola·ter/(-try).

u·trel (*arch.*) Iron beam/post; boom. ~ **van** = PUAN.

üf (*ech.*) Puff. ~ **desen uçacak**, as light as a feather: ~ **noktası** (-in), weak/vital spot. ~ **kürmek** (-i), scatter by puffing. ~ **lemek** (-i), blow out; blow to cool. ~ **ür** ~ **ür**, (*ech.*) gentle breeze. ~ **ürtü**, breath.

ülverizatör (*ind.*) Sprayer, atomizer.

ünez Drawing-pin.

ür·çek/ ~ **çük** Curl; (*bot.*) hairy root. ~ **çeklenmek**, *vi.* become curly. ~ **çekli**, curly.

üre (*cul.*) Purée. ~ **yapmak**, mash.

pürtü[l k][gü] Knob, small protuberance. ~ **lenmek**, *vi.* become knobby. ~ **lü**, knobby.

pürüz Shagginess, roughness; unevenness, irregularity; fluff; (*eng.*) beard; (*fig.*) hitch, difficulty.

pürüz·alır (*eng.*) Reamer. ~ **lemek** (-i), (*min.*) roughen. ~ **lenmek**, *vi.* become rough, etc. ~ **lü**, rough, etc. ~ **süz**, smooth.

püs = SÜS.

püskü = ESKİ ~.

püskül Tuft; tassel; (*bot.*) coma, beard; difficulties. ~ **kuyruklular**, (*ent.*) Thysanura, bristle-tails. ~ **lü**, tasselled; (*bot.*) comate, bearded: ~ **bela**, great calamity; thorough nuisance.

püskür·ge[l ç][ci]/ ~ **te**[l ç][ci] Atomizer, sprayer, spraygun. ~ **me**, *vn.* scattering, splashing; (*geol.*) volcanic activity, eruption: ~ **ben**, beauty spots (on face): ~ **memesi**, (*mot.*) injection nozzle: ~ **pompa**, fuel injection pump. ~ **mek** (-i), blow out liquid/powder from the mouth; spray/atomize (liquid); (*geol.*) extrude; erupt. ~ **tme**, *vn.*; spraying (paint, etc.): ~ **tabancası**, spray-gun. ~ **tmek** (-i, -e), *vc.*: (-i), force to turn back, scatter (enemy). ~ **tü**, (*geol.*) eruption. ~ **tücü**, atomizer. ~ **ük**, erupted (lava, etc.); extrusive (rock); sprayed.

püslü = SÜSLÜ.

püsür Filth, rubbish; unpleasant additions (children, relatives, etc.). ~ **lü**, full of complications/difficulties. ~ **süz**, simple, uncomplicated.

pütür pütür Rough/chapped (skin).

py·elit[i] (*med.*) Pyelitis. ~ **üri**, pyuria.

R

R, r [re] Twenty-first Tk. letter, R.
R = REİS(LİK); RESİM; (el.) REZİSTANS; RÖNTGEN.
-r v. suf. [116] Forming the aorist tense [ANLAR, DER].
Ra. = (ch.s.) RADYUM.
Rabᵇⁱ (rel.) The Lord God. ~ **bim**, my God. ~ **bani**, divine. ~ **bena**, our Lord, God: ~ **hakkı için**, (in oaths) By God!
ra'bıtᵖᵗ¹ A binding, bond; connection. ~ **(edatı)**, (ling.) conjunction: ~ **işareti**, (pub.) brace (}): ~ **sıygası**, gerund of time.
rabıta Tie, bond; connection; attachment; orderly arrangement; (ling.) copula: logical/grammatical conformity.
rabıta·lı In good order; regular; decorous, decent. ~ **sız**, disordered; disjointed; irregular; incoherent, desultory; disorderly. ~ **sızlık**, disorder; irregularity; bad behaviour.
rabi (obs.) Fourth.
raca (soc.) Rajah.
raciⁱ Returning; concerning, relating to. ~ **olm. (-e)**, concern; fall to s.o.
racon (sl.) Custom, rule; ostentation, showing off. ~ **kesmek**, show off; make a decision.
rad. = RADAR; RADYO.
radansa (naut.) Thimble/cringle (of a rope).
radar (rad.) Radar. ~ **aynası**, plan position indicator. ~ **cı(lık)**, (work of) radar-operator; (sl.) spy(ing).
radde Degree, point. ~ **sinde**, approximately: ~ **lerinde**, about (of time): ~ **lerine gelmek (-mek)**, come near to (doing stg.).
radikal Radical. ~ **ist**, radicalist. ~ **izm**, radicalism.
ra·dike (bot.) Dandelion. ~ **don**, (chem.) radon.
rad·yal Radial. ~ **yan**, (ast.) radian; (el.) radiant element (of fire). ~ **yasyon**, radiation. ~ **yatör**, (dom.) radiator; (mot.) cooling radiator: ~ **peteği**, radiator core. ~ **yatörcü**, maker/seller/fitter of radiators. ~ **ye**, (naut.) raft; mat.
radyo Radio, wireless; broadcasting station; receiver, set. ~ **alıcısı**, receiving set: ~ **farı**, radio beacon: ~ **gonyometresi**, radio direction-finder: ~ **gökbilimi**, radioastronomy: ~ **ırakgörürü**, radio telescope: ~ **istasyonu**, broadcasting station: ~ **spikeri**, broadcaster: ~ **vericisi**, transmitter: ~ **yayımı**, broadcast(ing).
radyo·aktif Radioactive: ~ **çökelek/tortu**, nuclear fall-out: ~ **izotop**, (med.) radioactive isotope. ~ **aktivite**, radioactivity: ~ **sini artırmak**, enrich. ~ **cu(luk)**, (work of) radio maker/seller/repairer. ~ **elektrik**, (ed.) radioelectricity. ~ **etkinliği**ⁿⁱ, irradiation effect/influence. ~ **evi**ⁿⁱ, broadcasting house. ~ **fonik**, radiophonic. ~ **foto**, radiophoto. ~ **grafi**, radiography. ~ **gram**, radiogram. ~ **izotop**, (med.) radioisotope. ~ **link**ⁱ, radio-link. ~ **loji(k)**,

radiolo·gy/(-gical). ~ **metre**, radiometer. ~ **skopi**, radioscopy. ~ **teknoloji**, radio-technology. ~ **telefon**, radio-telephone. ~ **telgraf**, radio-telegraph. ~ **terapi**, (med.) radiotherapy.
rad·yum (chem.) Radium. ~ **yus**, (orn.) barbule.
raf Shelf. ~ **a kaldırmak/koymak**, shelve (a matter), postpone: ~ **tan sünger düştü başı yarıldı**, an absurd exaggeration; 'much ado about nothing'.
rafadan (cul.) Very lightly boiled egg; (sl.) inexperienced.
Rafızi (rel.) Member of an extremist Shiite sect; heretic. ~ **lik**, a Shiite sect; its beliefs.
rafine (chem.) Refined. ~ **etm.**, refine. ~ **ri**, refinery
rafitⁱ (bot.) Raphide.
rafya (bot.) Raffia (tree/fibre).
rağbetⁱ Desire, inclination; craze, vogue: **(-e)**, wish (for stg.); demand (for goods). ~ **etm. (-e)**, wish for; esteem: ~ **görmek**, be in demand; be esteemed: ~ **i var//yok (-e)**, he has an//no inclination for: ~ **te**, in the fashion: ~ **ten düşmek**, fall from esteem; no longer be in demand; be out of favour/fashion.
rağbet·li Desirous, having an inclination for; in demand, sought after, liked: ~ **si var//yok**, there is great//no demand for stg. ~ **siz**, having no inclination for; unesteemed, unwanted. ~ **sizlik**, lack of inclination/esteem; not being in demand.
rağm Spite. ~ **ına (-in)**, out of spite for. ~ **en (-e)**, conj. [88] despite, in spite of.
rahat¹ n. Rest; ease; comfort; quiet. a. At ease; tranquil; comfortable; easy. int. (mil.) (Stand) at ease! ~ **batmak (-e)**, give up a comfortable position without reason: ~ **bırakmak**, leave in peace, let alone: ~ **bırakmamak/vermemek**, annoy, disturb: ~ **döşeği**, one's death-bed: ~ **döseğinde ölmek**, die in one's bed: ~ **(dur)!**, (mil.) at ease!: ~ **durmak**, keep quiet; not fidget: ~ **duruş**, (sp.) relaxed position: ~ **etm.**, be at ease; make o.s. comfortable, relax, rest: ~ **kıçına batmak**, not appreciate one's comfort/good fortune: ~ **yaşama**, life of ease: ~ **yüzü görmemek**, have no peace: ~ **ına bakmak** look after one's own comfort: ~ **ını bozmak/kaçırmak**, disturb s.o.'s peace, be a source of worry to s.o.: ~ **ınıza bakın!**, please don't worry, it really isn't important!; don't bring trouble on yourself by interfering.
rahat·lama vn. Relaxation. ~ **lamak**, vi. get comfortable; feel relieved; cease to worry. ~ **lanmak**, vi. relax, rest, take one's ease. ~ **latmak (-i)**, make comfortable; put at ease. ~ **lık**, ease; comfort; quiet. ~ **lıkla**, in comfort; comfortably. ~ **sız**, unquiet, disturbed; uneasy; indisposed; uncomfortable: ~ **etm.**, disturb, agitate: ~ **olm.**, be disturbed/ uneasy; worry. ~ **sızlık**, disquiet, uneasiness,

discomfort; (*psy.*) dysphoria; (*med.*) ailment, indisposition: ~ **vermek**, disturb, worry.

ahib- = RAHİP. ~ **e(lik)**, (*rel.*) (duties of) nun.

ah¹im^mi ¹ (*bio.*) Womb. ~ **borusu**, Fallopian tube.

ahim² Merciful.

ahi¹p^bi (*rel.*) Monk; priest. ~ **akbaba**, (*orn.*) European black vulture: ~ **ler**, clergy. ~ **lik**, duties/ position of monk/priest.

ahle Low reading-stand/writing-desk, faldstool.

ahm- = RAHİM¹.

ahman (*rel.*) Compassionate, merciful (of God). ~ **i**, divine.

ahmet^i Mercy; God's compassion; rain. ~ **okumak (-e)**, pray for s.o.'s soul; work for s.o.'s good/benefit; regret stg. lost: ~ **okutmak (-e)**, cause s.o. to regret stg.; make s.o. long for . . . (instead of . . .). ~ **li**/~ **lik**, the deceased, the late: ~ **olm.**, die.

ahne Rent, tear; breach, fissure; damage; (*fig.*) chasm.

ahvan *n.* Amble; ambling horse. *a.*, *adv.* Ambling.

rak *a. suf.* [57] = -REK [ALÇARAK].

akam Figure, number, numeral; a quantity. ~ **levhası**, dial: ~ **ları toplamak**, tot up the figures.

aket^i (*sp.*) Racket, bat.

akı (*cul.*) Raki, arrack. ~ **âlemi**, drinking party. ~ **cı**, raki distiller/seller; raki addict. ~ **cılık**, raki distilling; raki addiction.

akım (*geo.*) Altitude (above sea level). ~ **işareti**, bench-mark.

ak¹ıs^s1 Dance; dancing; (*phys.*) oscillation.

akik Slender, fine; tender, soft-hearted.

aki¹p^bi Rival; competitor; antagonist, enemy.

akit Calm, still (water).

ak·kas (*mus.*) Male dancer; (*phys.*) pendulum: ~ **çarkı**, balance-wheel (of watch). ~ **kase**, dancing-girl. ~ **s**, dance. ~ **s-** = RAKIS. ~ **s¹etmek**^eder, dance; (*phys.*) oscillate.

akor (*eng.*) Coupling, connection, union. ~ **lu**, connected.

akun (*zoo.*) Rac(c)oon.

alli (*sp.*) Rally.

am Tame, gentle; submissive. ~ **etm.**, subjugate; force to yield: ~ **olm.**, submit, yield.

amak^i Smallest possible quantity of stg.; just enough food to sustain life; the last spark of life. ~ **kaldı (-e)**, all but, almost, nearly: ~ **kalma politikası**, brinkmanship.

amazan (*rel.*) Ninth Muslim month, Ramadan; month of fasting. ~ **keyfi**, irritability of those who fast: ~ **tiryakisi**, quick-tempered person. ~ **lık**, suitable for Ramadan.

ami (*bot.*) Ramie, China grass.

ampa (*naut.*) Boarding; going alongside; (*eng.*) incline, slope, ramp; (*rly.*) loading platform; (*mil.*) firing ramp. ~ **etm.**, (*naut.*) board (an enemy ship); (*sl.*) accost (a woman); gate-crash (a party). ~ **cı**, (*his.*) boarder, boarding-party.

amus (*orn.*) Barb (of feather).

anda (*naut.*) Spanker (sail).

andevu Meeting, rendezvous; assignation. ~ **almak**, make an appointment: ~ **vermek**, give an appointment: ~ **su olm.**, have an appointment.

~ **cu(luk)**, (work of) brothel-keeper. ~ **evi**, clandestine brothel.

randıman Yield; profit; output. ~ **lı(lık)**, profit·able/(-ability). ~ **sız(lık)**, unprofit·able/(-ability).

ran·tabilite (*fin.*) Profitability. ~ **tabl**, profitable. ~ **tiye**, (*pej.*) rentier.

ranza (*naut.*, *rly.*) Berth, bunk.

rapor Report; dispatch; medical certificate. ~ **etm.**/ **yazmak**, make a report: ~ **vermek**, (*med.*) issue a certificate, certify.

rapor·cu Inspector, etc. (making a report). ~ **lu**, with a report; having a medical certificate; (*col.*) unbalanced, crazy. ~ **tör(lük)**, (*adm.*) (work of) rapporteur.

rap-rap (*ech.*) Sound of marching.

rapsodi (*mus.*) Rhapsody.

rapt- = RABIT. ~ **eden**, (*ling.*) copulative. ~ **¹etmek**^eder (-i, -e), bind; fasten (to); connect. ~ **iye**, paper-clip, fastener; drawing-pin; clamp. ~ **iyelemek (-i)**, clip together, fasten. ~ **iyelenmek**, *vp.*

rasa¹t^d1 A watching; (*ast.*, *met.*) observation. ~ **kulesi**, (*aer.*) blister. ~ **çı**, observer. ~ **hane**, observatory; meteorological station.

rasgele *adv.* By chance, haphazardly, at random. *a.* Chance, random; accidental. *int.* May it work out well!, good luck! ~ **ateş**, (*mil.*) scattered fire: ~ **değişken//devinim**, (*phys.*) random variable// motion: ~ **uğramak**, drop in. ~ **lik**, random, chance.

rası¹t^d1 (*ast.*) Observer.

raspa Scraper; scraping; (*sl.*) greedy. ~ **etm.**, scrape: ~ **taşı**, (*naut.*) pumice-stone, holystone. ~ **cı**, (*sl.*) greedy person. ~ **lamak (-i)**, scrape; (*sl.*) approach. ~ **lanmak**, *vp.*

rast Straight; right; proper; straightforward; in order; successful; (*Or. mus.*) a melody. ~ **gelinmek (-e)**, *imp. v.* s.o. be met by chance: ~ **geliş**, chance meeting/encounter; coincidence: ~ **gelmek (-e)**, meet by chance, come across; find; hit the mark/ target; turn out right, succeed: ~ **getirmek**, succeed in meeting; choose the appropriate moment; cause to succeed; cause to hit the mark: ~ **gitmek**, (business) go well, succeed.

rastı¹k^g1 (*mod.*) Black cosmetic for eyebrows; (*myc.*) smut (on wheat). ~ **çekmek**, blacken the eyebrows: ~ **mürekkep**, black indelible ink: ~ **taşı**, (*chem.*) antimony, kohl.

rast·lamak (-e) Come across, meet by chance; coincide. ~ **lanmak**, *vp.* be met by chance. ~ **lantı**, chance meeting/happening, coincidence: ~ **yla**, by chance/accident. ~ **laşmak (-le)**, *vt.* meet each other; *vi.* coincide. ~ **latmak (-i, -e)**, *vc.* ~ **sal**, coincidental, accidental.

rasyon·alist^i (*phil.*) Rationalist. ~ **alizm**, rationalism. ~ **el**, rational.

raşit·ik (*med.*) Having rickets. ~ **izm**, rickets.

ratanya (*bot.*, *med.*) Rhatany.

ratıp Damp, moist.

raunt/ravnt (*sp.*) Round.

raven¹t^di (*bot.*) Rhubarb.

ray (*rly.*) Rail. ~ **a**/~ **ına girmek**, be arranged satisfactorily: ~ **da teslim**, (*fin.*) free on rail: ~ **dan**/

~ **ından çıkmak,** go off the rails; (*fig.*) go wrong: ~ **ına oturmak,** stay on the rails: ~ **ına oturtmak,** put on the right track.
rayba (*eng.*) Reamer. ~ **lamak (-i),** ream.
rayi'çci *a.* Current; in demand; saleable. ~ **(fiyat),** market price; current value.
rayiha Smell, odour; bouquet (wine). ~ **lı,** scented.
razakı (*bot.*) Large white grape (producing the best raisins).
razı Satisfied, contented; willing; pleased. ~ **etm.,** satisfy s.o.; obtain s.o.'s approval: ~ **olm.,** be willing, consent; approve; be pleased.
Rb. = (*ch.s.*) RUBİDYUM.
RC = (*Red Cross*).
rd. = RADAR; RADYAN.
re (*ling.*) The Tk. letter R; (*mus.*) ray, re.
Re. = (*ch.s.*) RENYUM.
reak·siyon(er) (*pol.*) Reaction(ary). ~ **tans,** (*el.*) reactance. ~ **tif,** reactive. ~ **tör,** reactor.
real·isti (*phil.*) Realist. ~ **ite,** reality. ~ **ize,** ~ **etm.,** realize, bring true. ~ **izm,** realism.
reasürans (*fin.*) Re-insurance.
reaya (*his.*) Non-Muslim subjects of the Ottoman Empire; (*fig.*) Christian.
reba'pbı (*mus.*) Type of lyre. ~ **kuyruklu,** (*orn.*) lyre-tailed.
rebiyül·âhır// ~ **evvel** (*ast.*) Fourth//third lunar month.
rece'pbi (*ast.*) Seventh lunar month.
rec·'immi A pelting; a stoning to death. ~ **m'etmek**eder **(-i),** pelt; stone (to death).
reçel (*cul.*) Fruit conserve/preserve, jam. ~ **lik,** suitable for jam-making.
reçete (*med.*) Prescription; (*cul.*) recipe. ~ **ile,** (*med.*) on prescription.
reçine (*bot.*) Resin; (*chem.*) colophony; pitch. ~ **leştirmek,** (*chem.*) make resinous. ~ **li,** resinous.
redak·siyon (*pub.*) Writing, editing; publishing. ~ **tör,** editor; publisher. ~ **törlük,** editing; publishing.
redd- = RET. ~ **edilmek/** ~ **eylemek,** *vp.* ~ **'etmek**eder, reject; repel; retort; repudiate, disown; refute; disallow, disclaim. ~ **iye,** (*pub.*) refutation.
Redh. = (*ling.*) REDHOUSE SÖZLÜĞÜ(NDEN).
redif (*mil.*) Reserve, reservist; (*lit.*) repeated word (in poem).
redingotu (*mod.*) Frock coat, morning-dress.
re·dresör (*el.*) Rectifier, converter. ~ **düksiyon,** (*chem.*) reduction. ~ **düktör,** reducer. ~ **el,** real. ~ **eskont**u, (*fin.*) rediscount.
refah Easy circumstances; comfort; luxury. ~ **hissi,** euphoria: ~ **içinde,** affluent.
refakati Accompaniment; companionship. ~ **etm.,** accompany; (*naut.*) convoy: ~ **inde bulunmak,** attend on s.o.
referan·dum (*adm.*) Referendum. ~ **s,** (*ind.*) reference: ~ **lar,** (*pub.*) references, bibliography.
ref'etmekeder **(-i)** Raise, heighten; (*adm.*) promote; remove.
refiki Companion, associate; husband. ~ **a,** female companion; wife.
refle Reflection. ~ **yapmak,** reflect: ~ **yapmayan,**

non-reflecting. ~ **ks,** (*bio.*) reflex. ~ **ktif,** luminous (paint). ~ **ktör,** reflector.
reform (*adm.*) Reform, improvement. ~ **atör/** ~ **cu,** reformer. ~ **culuk,** reforming. ~ **ist,** reformist. ~ **izm,** reformism.
re·frakter (*phys.*) Refractory. ~ **füj** = RÖFÜJ. ~ **füze,** (*med.*), reject, refuse; send back.
regai'pbi (*rel.*) ~ **gecesi,** eve of first Friday of RECEP, conception of the Prophet Muhammad.
reg·laj (*eng.*) Adjustment. ~ **lan,** (*mod.*) raglan sleeve. ~ **ülatör,** (*eng.*) regulator. ~ **üle,** ~ **etm.,** regulate.
reha Escape; preservation. ~ **bulmak,** escape.
rehabilitasyon (*med.*) Rehabilitation.
rehaveti Softness; limpness; slackness, lethargy.
rehber Guide; guide-book; directory. ~ **öğretmen** (*ed.*) teacher giving personal guidance, tutor. ~ **lik,** guidance; guiding: ~ **etm.,** guide.
reh'inni (*fin.*) Pawn, pledge, collateral, security; (*pol.*) hostage. ~ **de olm.,** be pawned: ~ **e koymak,** pawn, pledge, give as security. ~ **e,** object pledged hostage. ~ **li,** pledged: ~ **borç,** bonded debt.
reis Head; chief; (*adm.*) president, chairman; (*naut.*) boatswain; master. ~ **efendi,** (*his.*) foreign minister. ~ **muavin/vekili,** vice-president, deputy-chairman
reis·icumhur (*adm.*) President (of the republic). ~ **lik,** chieftaincy; presidency, chairmanship. (*naut.*) captaincy: ~ **makamı,** (*adm.*) the Chair ~ **ülküttap** = ~ EFENDİ.
re·jans Regency. ~ **jeneratif,** regenerative. ~ **ji** (*fin., his.*) Régie, Tobacco Monopoly. ~ **jim,** (*pol.*) government, regime; (*med.*) course of treatment diet: ~ **yapmak,** diet. ~ **jisör(lük),** (*cin., th.*) (work of) director.
-rek/-rak *a. suf.* [57] *With diminutive effect* [KÜÇÜREK; BOZRAK].
rekabeti Rivalry, competition; antagonism. ~ **etm.,** (*fin.*) compete: ~ **fiyatı,** competitive price.
rekaketi Speech defect, stuttering; incoherence (*lit.*) defect in style.
rekatı (*rel.*) Complete Muslim act of worship in the prescribed postures.
reklam Advertisement; advertising, publicity. ~ **ajansı,** advertising agency: ~ **ını yapmak,** advertise stg. ~ **cı(lık),** advertis·er/(-ing).
re·kolte (*agr.*) Harvest. ~ **kor,** (*sp., etc.*) record: ~ **kırmak,** beat/break the record. ~ **korder,** (*med.* recording instrument. ~ **kortmen,** (*sp.*) record-breaker/-holder. ~ **kreasyon,** recreation, amusement.
rektör(lük) (*ed.*) (Position/duties of) university rector/vice-chancellor.
rektum (*bio.*) Rectum.
rela·tif (*phil.*) Relative. ~ **tivite,** relativity. ~ **tivist** relativist. ~ **tivizm,** relativism.
remayözcü (*mod.*) (Stocking) ladder-mender.
remel (*lit.*) A poetic metre; (*Or. mus.*) a style.
rem'illi Sand; geomancy. ~ **atmak,** foretell by geomancy.
rem·'izzi Sign, nod; symbol; abbreviation, logo (-type). ~ **izlendirmek(-i),** symbolize. ~ **z'etmek**eder make a sign; hint; symbolize, typify. ~ **zi,** symbolical; allegorical.

Ren (*geo.*) River Rhine.

encide Pained, hurt, annoyed. ~ **etm.**, hurt, annoy: ~ **olm.**, be heart-broken.

en¹çᶜⁱ (*rad.*) Range.

ençper Workman, (day-)labourer; farm-hand/ -labourer. ~ **başı**ⁿ¹, foreman. ~ **lik**, occupation of labourer/farm-hand.

ende (*carp.*) Plane; (*cul.*) grater; gratings. ~ **lemek** (**-i**), plane, shave; grate. ~ **lenmek** *vp.* ~ **li**, having a plane/grater; planed; grated.

eng- = RENK. ~ **ârenk**, multi-coloured; variegated.

engeyiğiⁿⁱ (*zoo.*) Reindeer.

en¹kᵍⁱ Colour; pigment; colour/complexion of stg.; (*fig.*) nature, quality. ~ +, *a.* Colour; chromatic; chrom(o)-: ~ **bilgisi**, chromatics: ~ **cümbüşü**, riot of colours: ~ **katmak/vermek**, colour; enliven: ~ **maddesi**, pigment: ~ **türü**, hue, tinge: ~ **uyarısı**, colour stimulus: ~ **uyumu**, colour harmony: ~ **vermemek**/~ **ini belli etmemek**, appear unmoved; conceal one's feelings.

rengi ~ **atmak**, lose colour, fade: ~ **atmaz/ uçmaz**, (*tex.*) fast, non-fading: ~ **belli değil**, of uncertain character: ~ **çalık/dönük**, discoloured, faded: ~ **kaçmak/uçmak**, turn pale; change colour: ~ **nde**, with the colour of . . .: ~ **ni belli** = RENK: ~ **ni bozmak**, discolour: ~ **ni gidermek**, bleach.

enk·çi (*art.*) Colourist. ~ **gideren**, (*chem.*) colour-dispersant, bleach. ~ **körlüğü**ⁿü, achromatopsia; colour-blindness, daltonism. ~ **körü**, colour-blind. ~ **küresi**, (*ast.*) chromosphere. ~ **lemek** (**-i**), colour. ~ **lemeli**, (*lit.*) picturesque. ~ **lendirmek** (**-i**), colour; enliven. ~ **lenmek**, *vp.* be(come) coloured; become lively. ~ **li**, coloured; colourful; of such a colour; chromo-; (*fig.*) lively, cheerful: ~ **badana**, (*dom.*) colourwash: ~ **basma**, (*pub.*) colour-process/ -printing: ~ **film/fotoğraf**, (*cin.*) colour-film/ -photograph: ~ **işitmesi**, (*psy.*) synaesthesia; colour hearing: ~ **kabartma**, (*art.*) cameo: ~ **kalem**, crayon. ~ **lilik**, chromaticity. ~ **ölçer**, (*phys.*) colorimeter. ~ **ölçme**/~ **ölçüm**, colorimetry. ~ **seçmezlik**, (*med.*) achromatopsia, defective colour discrimination. ~ **sel**, *a.* colour. ~ **sellik**, chromaticity. ~ **seme**, (*chem.*) chromatography. ~ **semez**, (*phys.*) achromatic. ~ **ser**, chromatic. ~ **seyici**, (*chem.*) chromatograph. ~ **siz**, (*med.*) achromatic; clear, drab; colourless; pale; (*fig.*) without character/personality. ~ **sizlenme**, (*chem.*) decolorization. ~ **sizlik**, colourlessness; paleness; lack of character. ~ **teş**, (*phys.*) isochrome. ~ **teşlik**, (*bot.*) homochromy. ~ **veren**, (*bio.*) chromophore. ~ **yuvarı** = ~ KÜRESİ.

enyum (*chem.*) Rhenium.

eomür (*phys.*) Réaumur scale.

eorganizasyon (*adm.*) Reorganization.

eosta (*el.*) Rheostat.

e·pertu(v)ar (*th.*) Repertory. ~ **plik**, (*th.*) retort. ~ **por**, (*fin.*) carry over, contango. ~ **prodüksiyon** = RÖPRODÜKSİYON.

es. = RESİM; RESSAM.

esen On one's own account/initiative; directly.

e·sepsiyon(ist) Reception(ist). ~ **septör**, (*phys.*) receiver. ~ **sidüel**, residual. ~ **sif**, (*geo.*) reef.

e'sikâr (*adm.*) Supreme direction; highest position.

res¹imᵐⁱ (*art.*) Design, drawing, picture; photograph; (*adm.*) ceremony; (*fin.*) due, tax, toll. ~ **almak**, make/draw a picture; collect a tax: ~ **bezi**, (*art.*) canvas: ~ **çekmek/çıkarmak**, (*cin.*) take a photograph: ~ **fırçası**, (*art.*) paintbrush: ~ **gibi**, very beautiful/pleasant: ~ **kalemi**, crayon: ~ **sanatı**, drawing, draughtsmanship: ~ **tahsil etm.**, (*ed.*) study art: ~ **ve heykeltraş okulu**, (*ed.*) art school: ~ **i**, *a.* = RESMİ: *n.* ~ **i geçit**, (*mil.*) review, parade: ~ **i kabul**, official reception: ~ **i küşat**, official inauguration: ~ **idir** (**-in**), it is certain/clear/ obvious: ~ **inden bağışık**, (*fin.*) duty-free: ~ **ini çıkarmak**, have one's photograph taken: ~ **ler**, (*pub.*) artwork.

resim·altıⁿ¹ (*pub.*) Caption. ~ **ci**, (*cin.*) photographer; (*ed.*) art-teacher; (*art.*) artist, decorator. ~ **hane**, drawing-office. ~ **lemek** (**-i**), (*pub.*) illustrate (book). ~ **lendirmek** (**-i**), explain/tell in pictures. ~ **li**, illustrated; figurative: ~ **öykü**, (*pub.*) strip-cartoon. ~ **lik**, picture-frame; album. ~ **yazı**, (*ling.*) pictography.

Res(i)mo/Retimnon (*geo.*) Rethymnon (Crete).

resital¹ (*mus.*) Recital; concert.

res·megider (*cin.*) Photogenic. ~ **men**, officially; ceremoniously; as a matter of form. ~ **m¹etmek**ᵉᵈᵉʳ (**-i**), draw; depict. ~ **mi**, *n.* = RESİM: *a.* official; authorized; ceremonious; formal; done as a matter of form: ~ **dil**, (*ling.*) official language (of a country): ~ **elbise**, uniform; dress suit: ~ **Gazete**, (*adm.*) Official Gazette: ~ **makam**, official position: ~ **tatil günü**, bank holiday: ~ **tebliğ**, official communiqué: ~ **temaslar**, official relations: ~ **ziyafet**, (state) banquet: ~ **dir!**, it's official/certain! ~ **milik**/~ **miyet**, official character/nature/status; formality: ~ **e dökmek**, make official.

ressam (*art.*) Artist, painter; designer; illustrator. ~ **sehpası**, easel. ~ **lık**, art; painting.

rest ~ **çekmek**, stake all; (*fig.*) act boldly, dare to do stg.: (**-e**), stake all on stg.

resto *int.* (Waiter) cancel the order!; (*sl.*) enough! ~ **ran** (*cul.*) restaurant. ~ **rasyon**, restoration. ~ **re**, (*art.*) restored: ~ **etm.**, restore.

resulü (*rel.*) Envoy; apostle; prophet.

resülmal¹ (*fin.*) Capital.

reşi¹tᵈⁱ Mature; adult. ~ **olm.**, arrive at years of discretion, come of age.

re¹tᵈᵈⁱ Rejection; expulsion; refutation; repudiation, denial, refusal. ~ **cevabı**, negative reply: ~ **di cevap etm.**, return an answer, retort: ~ **diyle cevap vermek**, answer with a refusal.

re·tiküler (*bio.*) Reticular. ~ **tina**, retina. ~ **torik** (*ling.*) rhetoric(al). ~ **tro-**, *pref.* backwards. ~ **trovizör**, (*mot.*) rear-view mirror. ~ **tuş(çu)** = RÖTUŞ(ÇU).

reva Lawful, permissible; proper, suitable. ~ **görmek** (**-i, -e**), deem lawful/proper/suitable.

reva¹çᶜ¹ A being current/in demand; currency.

revak¹ (*arch.*) Porch, portico, colonnade; arbour, pavilion. ~ **lı**, colonnaded: ~ **bahçe**, cloisters. ~ **iye**, (*phil.*) stoicism.

revalü·asyon (*fin.*) Revaluation. ~ **e**, ~ **etm.**, revalue.

revani (*cul.*) Sweet of baked semolina.

re·vanş = RÖVANŞ. ~**vendük**ü, (*tex.*) thick cotton cloth. ~**verans**, bow, curtsey. ~**vir**, (*ed., mil.*) infirmary, sick-bay.

revizyon Revision; (*eng.*) overhaul. ~**ist**, (*pol.*) revisionist. ~**izm**, revisionism.

revnak¹ Brightness, splendour; brilliance.

re·volver (*mil.*) Revolver: ~ **başlı torna**, (*eng.*) capstan lathe. ~**vü**, (*th.*) review, show.

rey Opinion, judgement; (*adm.*) vote. ~ **beyan etm.**, declare one's opinion: ~ **sandığı**, ballot box: ~ **vermek**, vote: ~**e koymak/vazetmek**, put to the vote.

re·ye (*tex.*) Striped. ~**yon**, (*adm.*) section; department.

reyhani (*art.*) Type of Arabic calligraphy.

rezalet¹ Vileness; baseness; scandal, disgrace; scandalous behaviour. ~ **çekmek**, suffer disgrace: ~ **çıkarmak**, cause a scandal.

reze (*carp.*) Hinge; door-bolt; fine shavings. ~**lemek (-i)**, fit with hinges; bolt. ~**lenmek**, *vp.*

reze·de (*bot.*) Dyer's rocket. ~**ne**, (*bot.*) fennel.

rezer·v(e) (*fin., geol.*) Reserve. ~**vasyon**, reservation, booking. ~**vuar**, reservoir.

rezil *a.* Vile, base, contemptible; disreputable; disgraced. *n.* Scoundrel, blackguard. ~ **etm (-i)**, disgrace s.o.: ~ **olm.**, be disgraced: ~ **rüsva olm.**, be publicly disgraced. ~**ce**, disgraceful. ~**lik**, infamy; scandal; disgrace.

re·zistans (*el.*) Resistor. ~**zistivite**, resistance. ~**zonans**, (*phys.*) resonance. ~**zonatör**, resonator. ~**züme**, (*lit.*) summary

Rf. = (*ch.s.*) RUTHERFORDYUM.

Rh. = (*ch.s.*) RODYUM.

rıh (*obs.*) Sand sprinkled to dry ink. ~**dan**, sand-sprinkler.

rıhtım (*naut.*) Quay, wharf; embankment. ~ **ücret/ vergisi**, dock dues: ~ **yanında**, alongside the quay: ~**a yanaşmak**, berth, dock.

rıka Cursive Arabic script (used chiefly by Tks.).

rıza Consent, acquiescence; resignation. ~ **göstermek (-e)**, accept; resign o.s. to: ~**sı olm.**, give consent, approve: ~**sını almak**, get consent/ approval.

rızk One's daily food; sustenance; necessities of life.

riayet¹ (*rel.*) Observance; respect, esteem; respectful treatment; consideration, regard, kind attention. ~**etm. (-e)**, treat with respect; pay attention to: ~**e mecbur olm.**, (*rel.*) be obliged to observe.

riayet·en (-e) Out of respect for; in consideration of. ~**kâr**, respectful, considerate. ~**kârlık**, consideration, respectfulness. ~**siz**, disrespectful; irreverent. ~**sizlik**, disrespect; breach, non-observance.

ribo·flavin (*chem.*) Riboflavin. ~**nükleik (asit)**, ribonucleic (acid).

rica Request; prayer. ~ **etm. (-den)/~da bulunmak (-e)**, request, desire: ~ **minnet**, after much beseeching: ~ **olunmak**, be requested. ~**cı**, one who makes a request; intercessor.

rical¹ *pl.* Men (of importance), high officials.

ricat¹ Return; retreat. ~ **etm.**, retreat, withdraw: ~ **emri vermek**, (*mil.*) beat the retreat.

ri·cit(lik)/~jit(lik) Rigid(ity).

rikkat¹ Slenderness, delicacy; tenderness, compassion. ~**e gelmek**, show compassion. ~**li**, compassionate, pitiful.

rimel (*mod.*) Cosmetic for eyelashes; mascara.

rina (*ich.*) Flapper skate.

ring (*sp.*) Boxing-ring. ~ **gezisi**, (*mot.*) circular trip.

ringa (balığı) (*ich.*) Herring.

rin'tᵈⁱ Jolly/unconventional/humorous man.

riper (*agr.*) Reaper.

risale (*pub.*) Dissertation; pamphlet, booklet, brochure.

risk¹ = RİZİKO; (*fin.*) risk. ~**e**, ~ **etm.**, venture.

rit·im (*mus.*) Rhythm. ~**mik**, rhythmic(al): ~ **jimnastik**, (*sp.*) eurhythmics. ~**üel**, (*rel.*) ritual.

rivayet¹ Narrative, tale; rumour. ~ **birleşik zaman**, (*ling.*) narrative tense: ~ **etm.**, tell, relate: ~ **olunmak**, be narrated//rumoured: ~ **yaymak**, spread a rumour: ~**ler dolaşıyor**, rumours are in the air.

riya Hypocrisy. ~**kâr**, hypocritical. ~**kârlık**, hypocrisy.

riyal (*fin.*) Spanish real. ~ **a**, (*his.*) sovereign's ship.

riyaset¹ (*adm.*) Presidency, chairmanship.

riyazet¹ Asceticism, abstinence.

riya·ziyat¹/~**ziye** (*obs.*) Mathematics. ~**ziyeci**, mathematician.

riyolit¹ (*geol.*) Rhyolite.

riziko (*fin.*) Risk. ~ **ikramiye**, danger money.

Rn. = (*ch.s.*) RADON.

rob- = ROP. ~**a**, dress. ~**alı**, dressed.

robotᵘ Robot, automaton. ~**luk**, automatism.

roda (*naut.*) Coil of rope.

Rod·ayland (*orn.*) Rhode Island red. ~**ezya(lı)**, *pr.n.* (*geo.*) Rhodesia(n). ~**os**, *pr.n.* (*geo.*) Rhodes. ~**oslu**, *pr.n.* (*ethn.*) Rhodian. ~**yum**, (*chem.*) rhodium.

rokᵘ (Chess) castling. ~ **yapmak**, castle.

ro·ka (*bot.*) Eruca, rocket (for salad). ~**ket**¹, (*aer., mil.*) rocket; ballistic missile. ~**ketatar**, rocket-launcher. ~**koko**, (*art.*) rococo. ~**kos**, (*ich.*) jewfish.

rolü (*th.*) Role, part, character; (*fig.*) show(iness). ~ **almak**, play a part: ~ **dağıtımı**, *dramatis personae*: ~ **dağıtma**, casting: ~ **kesme**, over-acting: ~ **oynamak**, act; (*fig.*) play an influential part: ~ **yapmak**, behave affectedly, be insincere: ~**ü olm.**, be influential: ~**üne çıkmak**, (*th.*) play the part of s.o.

rom (*cul.*) Rum.

Rom. = ROMANYA; ROMENCE(DEN).

Roma (*geo.*) Rome. ~**lı**, (*ethn.*) a Roman.

roman (*lit.*) Novel. ~**cı**, novelist. ~**cılık**, novel-writing. ~**esk**¹, romantic. ~**s**, romance. ~**tik**, romantic; romance-writer. ~**tiklik**, being romantic. ~**tizm**, romanticism.

Ro·manya (*geo.*) Romania: ~ +, *a.* Romanian ~**manyalı**, *n.* (*ethn.*) Romanian. ~**men**, (*his., ethn.*) Roman: ~ **rakamları**, Roman numerals. ~**mence** = RUMENCE.

roma·tizma (*med.*) Rheumatism: ~ +, *a.* rheumatic. ~**tizmalı**, having rheumatism. ~**toloji**, rheumatology.

ron·dela (*eng.*) Washer. ~**tgen** = RÖNTGEN.

o**'p**ᵇᵘ (*mod.*) Dress (of heavy material). ~ **döşambr**, dressing-gown.

osto (*cul.*) Roast meat. ~ **luk**, (meat for) roasting.

otᵘ (*mot.*) Rod; steering column. ~ **a**, (*naut.*) course, bearing: ~ **yı değiştirmek**, alter course. ~ **ari**, rotary. ~ **asyon**, rotation. ~ **atif**, (*pub.*) rotary press. ~ **atör**, (*bio.*) rotator. ~ **or**, (*el.*) rotor.

oz·a Rose-diamond. ~ **et**ⁱ, rosette; badge; (*eng.*) rivet washer.

ozbif (*cul.*) Roast beef.

ozvelt (*mod.*) Soldier's boots.

öfüj (*mot.*) Traffic island, refuge.

ölativ·ite (*phil.*) Relativity. ~ **izm**, relativism.

ö·le (*rad.*) Relay, tripping. ~ **lyef**, (*art.*) relief.

ömorkᵘ (*mot.*) Trailer (vehicle). ~ **aj**, towing. ~ **lu**, ~ **kamyon**, articulated lorry. ~ **ör**, (*mot.*) tractor; (*naut.*) tug.

tö·nesans (*art.*) Renaissance. ~ **nons**, (*gamb.*) revoke.

öntgen (*phys.*) ~ **ışınları**, X-rays. ~ **ci**, radiographer; (*sl.*) peeping Tom, voyeur. ~ **cilik**, radiography; (*sl.*) voyeurism.

ö·per (*geo.*) Reference point, landmark: ~ **noktası**, benchmark. ~ **portaj**, (*pub.*) feature story, article; (*rad.*) feature (programme/film). ~ **portajcı(lık)**, (work of) reporter, feature-writer. ~ **prezantan**, (*fin.*) representative, agent. ~ **prodüksiyon**, reproduction; copy; forgery. ~ **şüt**ᵘ, (*med.*) relapse.

ö·tar Delay. ~ **tarlı**, delayed; late. ~ **tre**, (*geol.*) retreat, shrinkage. ~ **tuş**, (*cin.*) retouch(ing). ~ **tuşçu**, retoucher. ~ **tuşlu**, retouched. ~ **vanş**, (*sp.*) revenge, return match.

tu. = (*ch.s.*) RUTENYUM.

uam (*med.*) Glanders.

uba (*obs.*) Clothing, clothes.

ubai (*lit.*) Quatrain.

ubidyum (*chem.*) Rubidium.

uble (*fin.*) Rouble.

u'buᵇ'ᵘ Quarter.

ubya (*fin.*) Rupee.

uf (*arch.*) Flat roof; roof floor/storey.

tufai (*rel.*) Rufaiyah dervish order, Howling Dervishes. ~ **ler karışır (-e)**, insoluble (problem, matter); what happens next is beyond our ken!

ug·an Patent leather. ~ **bi**, (*sp.*) rugby.

uh¹ *n.* (Chess) rook, castle.

uh² *n.* (*rel.*) Breath of life; soul; (*psy.*) spirit; essence; energy, activity. ~ **bilgini**, psychologist: ~ **çözümleme**, psychoanalysis: ~ **göç/sıçraması**, (*rel.*) metempsychosis, reincarnation: ~ **haleti**, morale; mood: ~ **hekim(liğ)i**, psychia-trist/(-try): ~ **ölçümü**, psychometry: ~ **sağaltım**, psychotherapy: ~ **yorgunluğu**, indecision: ~ **u (bile) duymamak**, not (even) notice: ~ **un şad olsun!**, bless his soul: ~ **unu teslim etm.**, die; give up the ghost.

uh(b). = RUHBİLİM.

uh·ani Spiritual; clerical; immaterial. ~ **aniyet**ⁱ, spirituality. ~ **ban**, (*rel.*) *pl.* = RAHİP; clergy. ~ **baniyet**ⁱ, monastic life.

uh·bilim/~iyatⁱ Psychology. ~ **bilimci**/~ **iyatçı**, psychologist. ~ **bilimsel**, psychological. ~ **çözümcü**, psychoanalyst. ~ **çözümsel**, psychoanalytic(al). ~ **çözümü**, psychoanalysis. ~ **en**, psychologically. ~ **i**, psychological; psychic: ~ **anormallik**, complex. ~ **ilik**, animism. ~ **lu**, lively, active. ~ **ötesi**ⁿⁱ, parapsychology. ~ **sal**, psychological: ~ **çözümleme**, psychoanalysis.

ruhsat¹ Permission; permit; leave; dismissal. ~ **iyesi**, licence-holder, concessionaire: ~ **vermek**, give leave; dismiss.

ruhsat·iye Licence. ~ **lı**, authorized; (*mil.*) on leave. ~ **name**, permit; (*adm.*) credentials.

ruh·suz Inanimate, lifeless; spiritless. ~ **suzluk**, lifelessness; lack of spirit. ~ **ulkud'üs**ʸü, (*rel.*) (Muslim) Archangel Gabriel; (Christian) Holy Spirit.

ruj (*mod.*) Rouge, lipstick.

rul·e (*aer.*) Taxiing: ~ **yapmak**, taxi. ~ **et**ⁱ, (*gamb.*) roulette. ~ **man**, (*eng.*) (ball-)bearing. ~ **o**, roll (of cloth); roller: ~ **halinde**, in rolls.

Rum (*his.*) Byzantine Greek; (*adm.*) Greek of Tk. nationality. ~ **diyarı**, (*his.*) Byzantine Empire; Ottoman Empire.

rumba (*mus.*) Rumba.

Rum·ca (*ling.*) Modern Greek. ~ **eli**, (*geo.*) Roumelia; (*his.*) Ottoman Balkans: ~ **yakası**, European shore of the Bosphorus. ~ **en**, *n.* (*ethn.*) Romanian: ~ **+**, *a.* Romanian. ~ **ence**, (*ling.*) Romanian. ~ **i**, (*his.*) belonging to Ancient Romans/Byzantine Greeks: ~ **takvim**, (*ast.*) modified Muslim Era based on solar years; adapted version of Gregorian calendar. ~ **laşmak** *vi.* become like a Greek. ~ **luk**, status of a Greek of Tk. nationality.

rumuz *pl.* = REMİZ. Signs; nods, etc. *s.* Symbol; abbreviation; initial.

rupi (*fin.*) Indian rupee.

Rus (*ethn.*) Russian; (*geo.*) Russia. ~ **+**, *a.* Russian. ~ **ça**, (*ling.*) Russian. ~ **laşmak**, *vi.* become Russian(-ized). ~ **laştırmak (-i)**, Russianize. ~ **ya**, (*geo.*) Russia.

Rus. = RUSÇA(DAN); RUSYA.

rusta Village; peasant. ~ **i**, rustic, pastoral; boorish.

ru·tenyum (*chem.*) Ruthenium. ~ **therfordyum**, (*chem.*) rutherfordium. ~ **tin**, routine.

rutubetⁱ Dampness; humidity. ~ **derecesi**, relative humidity. ~ **lendirmek (-i)**, make damp. ~ **lenmek** *vi.* become damp/humid. ~ **li**, damp, moist, humid.

ruzname Diary; calendar; journal; (*adm.*) agenda.

rübap = rebap.

rücuᵘ Return; going back on one's word; (*phil.*) reaction. ~ **etm. (-den)**, withdraw from stg.

rüçhan·(iyet) Preponderance; preference; advantage: ~ **hakkı**, precedence. ~ **lı**, preferential.

rüesa *pl.* = REİS. Leaders.

rüfeka *pl.* = REFİK. Companions; partners.

rükûᵘ (*rel.*) Bowing down in prayer.

rük'ünⁿü Influential person; 'bigwig'.

rüküş Comically dressed woman; frump.

rüsum *pl.* = RESİM. Taxes. ~ **tonajı**, (*naut.*) registered tonnage. ~ **at**¹, *pl.* dues, taxes; (*his.*) Customs Administration.

rüsu'pᵇᵘ Dregs; sediment.

rüsva(y) Publicly disgraced; scorned.

rüşeym (*bio.*) Embryo; germ.

rüştᵘ Maturity, adulthood. ~ **iye**, (*ed., obs.*) high/secondary school.

rüşvet[i] Bribe; bribery, corruption. ~ **almak/yemek,** take/accept bribes: ~ **vermek/yedirmek,** give a bribe. ~**çi,** bribe-taker. ~**çilik,** bribery.

rütbe Degree; grade; (*mil.*) rank. ~ **almak,** rise in rank: ~**sini indirmek,** demote. ~**li,** having (high) rank.

rüya Dream. ~ **çıkmak,** dream come true: ~ **görmek,** have a dream; dream: ~ **tabiri,** interpretation of dreams: ~**sında görememek,** be unable to envisage stg.: ~**sında görse hayra yormamak,** not imagine in one's wildest dreams.

rüyet[i] Seeing; visibility; perception; examination.

rüzgâr (*met.*) Wind. ~ +, *a.* Wind; aeolian: ~ **almak,** be exposed to much wind: ~ **altı,** the lee downwind: ~ **altıya düşme,** leeway: ~ **çorap tulumu,** (*aer.*) windsock: ~ **ekip fırtına biçmek,** sow the wind and reap the storm: ~ **gelecek delikleri tıkamak,** take every precaution: ~ **ile gitmek,** sail with the wind: ~ **kuvveti,** (*met.*) wind force: ~ **payı,** (*mil.*) wind allowance (in shooting): ~ **tüneli** (*phys.*) wind tunnel: ~ **üstü,** windward side: ~**a maruz,** bleak: ~**ı yaka almak,** (*naut.*) luff.

rüzgâr·gülü[nü] (*naut.*) Wind-rose. ~**lanmak,** v/i become windy; catch the breeze. ~**lı,** windy. ~**lık** shelter against the wind, windbreak.

S

S, s [se] Twenty-second Tk. letter, S.

S, s. = (*ch.s.*) KÜKÜRT; SABAH; SANİYE; (*ling.*) SIFAT (YERİNE); (*bio.*) SINIF; (*South*).

s- *buffer letter in n. suf.* [39] = -i² [ANNESİ].

sa *v. suf.* [100, etc.] = İSE [BAKARSA].

sa- *v. suf.* [230] = -SE- [SAYRIMSAMAK].

Sa., sa. = SAAT; SAVUNMA.

saadetⁱ Happiness; prosperity. ~ **asrı**, Prophet Muhammad's lifetime: ~ **devri**, the Golden Age: ~ **le**, goodbye! ~ **li**, happy, fortunate.

saatⁱ Hour; time; time of day; one hour's journey on foot; watch, clock. ~ **akrebi**, hour-hand of clock/watch: ~ **başı galiba!**, (*jok.*, at) a general pause in the conversation: ~ **başına**, for every hour; hourly: ~ **başında**, on the hour: ~ **besaat**, from hour to hour: ~ **beş (sularında)**, (about) five o'clock: ~ **beş buçuk**, half-past five: ~ **beşe kadar**, by five o'clock: ~ **beşte**, at five o'clock: ~ **bu ~!**, this is your chance/opportunity: ~ **çember/dairesi**, (*ast.*) hour-circle: ~ **dilimi**, (*geo.*) time zone: ~ **elifi elifine beş**, it is exactly five o'clock: ~ **farkı**, time difference/lag: ~ **gibi**, like clockwork, very regular(ly): ~ **gibi işlemek**, work uninterruptedly: ~ **hakemi**, (*sp.*) time-keeper: ~ **ibresi**, clock hand: ~ **kaç?**, what time is it?: ~ **kaçta?**, at what time?, when?: ~ **kadranı**, dial: ~ **kulesi**, clock tower: ~ **makinesi**, clock mechanism/works: ~ **maşası**, escapement: ~ **minesi**, dial of a clock: ~ **on bir buçuğu çalmak**, be getting old: ~ **rakkası**, balance-wheel: ~ **tutmak**, time (work/race, etc.): ~ **vurmak**, strike the hours: ~ **yelkovanının tersi**, anti-clockwise: ~ **yüzü**, clock-face: ~ **e karşı**, (*sp.*) against the clock: ~ **i çevirmek**, (*ind.*) clock in/out: ~ **i kurmak**, wind up a clock/watch: ~ **i ~ine**, at the right time, punctually: ~ **i sormak**, ask the time: ~ **i vurmak**, chime the hour: ~ **in dönüş yönünde**, clockwise: ~ **iniz var mı?**, have you/can you tell me the time?: ~ **ler olsun**, (*col.*) = SIHHATLER OLSUN: ~ **lerce**, for hours.

saat·çi(lik) (Trade of) watch-maker/-seller/-repairer. ~ **li**, *a.* clockwork. ~ **lik**, lasting . . . hours: ~ **bir yer**, a place . . . hours' journey away.

saba (*met.*) Gentle east wind; (*or. mus.*) old melody.

sabah *n.* Morning. *adv.* In the morning; tomorrow morning. ~ **akşam**, from morning till night, all day long: ~ **kahvaltısı**, (*cul.*) breakfast: ~ **karanlığında**, before daybreak/at cock-crow: ~ **kızıllığı**, (colours of) sunrise: ~ **ola hayır ola**, leave it till the morning (and it may straighten itself out): ~ ~, early in the morning: ~ **yıldızı**, (*ast.*) Venus (as morning star): ~ **a çık(ma)mak**, (*med.*) (not) live till the morning: ~ **a doğru/karşı**, towards morning: ~ **ı bulmak/etm.**, stay awake all night; work, etc. through the night: ~ **ı dar etm.**, wait impatiently for morning:

~ **ın köründe**, in the pre-dawn twilight: ~ **lar hayır olsun!**, good morning: ~ **ları**, in the morning, every morning.

sabah·çı Early riser; working, etc. till morning; (*ed.*) mornings-only pupil (in double-shift school): ~ **kahvesi**, all-night coffee-house. ~ **ki**, this morning's . . . . ~ **lamak**, *vi.* work/stay till morning; sit up all night; become morning. ~ **leyin**, in the morning, early. ~ **lı** = AKŞAMLI. ~ **lık**, *n.* (*mod.*) dressing-gown, house-coat: *a.* morning; for the morning.

saban (*agr.*) Plough. ~ **bıçak/keski/kılıcı**, coulter: ~ **izi**, furrow: ~ **kulağı**, mould-board: ~ **sürmek**, (*sp.*) drag face-down along the ground (in wrestling): ~ **uç demiri**, ploughshare.

saban·balığı//~ **kemiği** = SAPAN-. ~ **kıran**, (*bot.*) restharrow. ~ **otu**ⁿᵘ, (*bot.*) soapwort.

sabık Former, previous, preceding; foregoing. ~ **a**, (*leg.*) previous misdeed/conviction: ~ **alı**, previously convicted; habitual criminal, recidivist. ~ **asız**, without previous record.

sab'ırʳ¹ Patience; forbearance; endurance; (*bot.*) aloes. ~ **taşı**, s.o. very patient: ~ **ı taşmak/tükenmek**, one's patience be exhausted: ~ **ını tüketmek**, exasperate, exacerbate: ~ **la koruk helva, dut yaprağı atlas olur**, anything can be achieved with patience.

sabır·lı Patient. ~ **sız**, impatient. ~ **sızlanmak**, *vi.* become impatient: (-için), itch to do stg. ~ **sızlık**, impatience.

sabit Fixed; constant; stationary; captive; firm, enduring; proved, sure; valid. ~ **çarpan**, (*math.*) constant factor: ~ **gelir**, (*fin.*) fixed income: ~ **istikamet dümeni**, (*aer.*) fin: ~ **kadem**, steadfast: ~ **kalmak**, remain firm: ~ **mürekkep**, indelible ink: ~ **nokta**, fixed point: ~ **olm.**, be fixed, etc.: ~ **seviye kabı**, (*mot.*) float chamber: ~ **tartı istasyonu**, weighbridge: ~ **tutmak**, maintain: ~ **yağ**, standard quantity of oil.

sabit·e (*math.*) Coefficient, constant; (*ast.*) fixed star. ~ **leşmek**, *vi.* become fixed, etc. ~ **leştirmek** (-i), consolidate. ~ **lik**, constancy, fixity.

sabo·taj (*mil.*) Sabotage. ~ **tajcı**, saboteur. ~ **te**, ~ **etm.**, sabotage.

sabr- = SABIR. ~ **letmek**ᵉᵈᵉʳ, *vi.* be patient: (-e), endure stg.

sabuk = ABUK. ~ **lama**, (*psy.*) delirium.

sabun Soap. ~ **köpüğü**, soap bubble, foam: ~ **köpüğü gibi sönmek**, very showy but easily destroyed.

sabun·cu(luk) (Work of) soap-maker/-seller. ~ **hane**, soap-factory. ~ **iye**, (*cul.*) type of HELVA. ~ **lamak** (-i), soap; wash with soap. ~ **lanmak**, *vp.*; (*sl.*) lose all one's money gambling. ~ **laşmak**, *vi.* become soapy; (*chem.*) saponify. ~ **lu**, soapy.

~**luk**, *n.* soap-dish: *a.* for making soap. ~**otu**ⁿᵘ, (*bot.*) soapwort. ~**taşı**ⁿ¹, (*geol.*) soapstone, steatite; tailor's chalk.

sabur = SABIR. ~**a**, (*naut.*) ballast.

sac- = SAÇ². ~**ayağı**ⁿ¹, (*dom.*) trivet (for cooking).

saç¹ ¹ *n.* (*ast.*) Coma.

sa¹çᶜ¹ ² *n.* (*min.*) (Made of) sheet iron; iron plate; (*cul.*) girdle. ~ **levha**, plate.

saç¹ ³ (*bio.*) Hair. ~ **ağartmak**, live long and become grey-haired; (*fig.*) work long and hard: ~ **bağı**, hair-ribbon: ~ **buklesi**, coil of hair: ~ **dökülmesi**, (*med.*) alopecia: ~ **düzeni**, coiffure: ~ **kıvırma iğnesi**, curling-pin: ~ **makinesi**, hair-clippers: ~ **maşası**, curling-iron/-tongs: ~ ~**a baş başa gelmek**, come to blows: ~ ~**a gelmek**, (women) fight, tear each other's hair: ~ **sakal ağartmak (-te)**, toil over stg.: ~ **sakalına karışmış**, unkempt, dishevelled: ~ **topuzu**, chignon, 'bun': ~**ı başı ağarmak**, become old and grey: ~**ı bitmedik (yetim)**, (an orphan while still) an infant: ~**ına ak düşmek**, hair begin to turn grey: ~**ına sakalına bakmadan**, forgetting his age: ~**ını başını yolmak**, tear one's hair in despair: ~**ını süpürge etm.**, exert o.s. unstintingly: ~**ları dökülmüş**, bald: ~**ları iki türlü olm.**, be(come) partially grey.

saça¹kᵍ¹ (*arch.*) Eaves; canopy; (*mod.*) fringe. ~ **buzu**, icicle: ~ **kanatlı**, (*ent.*) thrips: ~ **kök**, (*bot.*) fibrous root: ~ **pervazı**, (*arch.*) bargeboard: ~ **silmesi**, cornice: ~ **yüzgeçliler**, (*ich.*) lobe-finned fish.

saçak·bulutᵘ (*met.*) Cirrus. ~**lanmak**, *vi.* develop a fringe. ~**lı**, (*arch.*) having eaves; (*bio.*) fimbriate, fringed; (*fig.*) dishevelled, unkempt.

saça·lamak (-i) Scatter; sprinkle. ~**lanmak**, *vp.* ~**n**, spreading, publishing.

saç·ı (*obs.*) Wedding present to the bride; coins/sweets/rice thrown over the bride; confetti: ~ **kılmak**, throw coins, etc. ~**ık**, disordered; scattered; = AÇIK ~. ~**ılmak**, *vp.* = SAÇMAK: **saçılıp dökülmek**, spend lavishly; (*fig.*) express all one's feelings. ~**ınım**, (*phys.*) scattering. ~**ıntı**, things scattered about. ~**ıştırmak (-i)**, sprinkle; scatter, sow.

saç·kıran (*med.*) Ringworm. ~**lı**, having hair; hairy; (*bio.*) crinite: ~ **sakallı adam**, man of mature age (and so wise).

saç·ma *vn.* Scattering; stg. scattered/sprinkled; (*mil.*) lead shot; (*ich.*) cast-net; (*fig.*) nonsense: *a.* nonsensical: ~ **lakırdı/söz**, drivel: ~ **sapan (konuşmak)**, (talk) a lot of nonsense. ~**macı**, talking nonsense. ~**mak (-i)**, scatter, sprinkle; sow broadcast; disseminate: **saçıp savurmak**, spend money prodigally. ~**malamak**, *vi.* talk nonsense/inconsequently. ~**malık**, place for the cast net; being out of place/nonsense. ~**mavıyat**, (*jok.*) stuff and nonsense.

saçsız(lık) Bald(ness); (*med.*) alopecia.

saçula (*min.*) Wooden mould (for castings).

sada/seda Echo; sound; voice.

sada¹kᵍ¹ (*mil.*) Quiver.

sadaka Alms, charity. ~**ya muhtaç olm.**, be reduced to penury.

sadakatⁱ Faithful friendship; fidelity; devotion;

(*pej.*) hypocritical friendship. ~**li**, loyal, faithful; devoted. ~**siz(lik)**, disloyal(ty); unfaithful(ness).

sadakor (*tex.*) Raw silk.

sada·lı Sonorous; echoing; voiced: ~ **harf**, (*ling.*) vowel. ~**sız**, silent: ~ **harf**, (*ling.*) consonant.

sadaretⁱ (*his.*) Grand Vizierate.

sade *a.* Mere; simple; unmixed; pure; simple-minded, ingenuous; (*lit.*) simple, unadorned (style): artless; (*bot.*) single (flower); (*mod.*) plain, unadorned; (*cul.*) unsweetened (coffee), plain/unstuffed (pastry). *adv.* Simply, merely, just. ~ **birimler bölüğü**, (*math.*) units column: ~ **göz**, (*bio.*) simple eye: ~ **güzel**, naturally beautiful; unadorned beauty: ~ **kahve**, unsweetened black coffee: ~ **öttürüyor**, he's only swanking: ~ **suya**, (*cul.*) without fat; (*fig.*) mere, plain; unimportant: ~ YAĞ.

sade·ce Simply; merely; just. ~**dil(lik)**, ingenuous/(-ness); naïve(ty). ~**leşme**, *vn.* simplification. ~**leşmek**, *vi.* become simple, etc. ~**leştirmek (-i)** simplify. ~**lik**, simpleness, plainness; simplicity. ~ **yağ**, (*cul.*) butter.

sade¹tᵈⁱ Point/object in view; intention; scope. ~**e gelmek**, come to the point (under discussion). ~**inde**, within the scope of: ~**inde bulunmak**, have the intention of . . .: ~**ten ayrılmak**, digress: ~**ten hariç**, extraneous, off the point.

sadık True, sincere; faithful; honest; loyal.

sad¹ırʳ¹ Breast; prominence; position of honour. ~**a geçmek**, (*adm.*, *obs.*) take the chief seat; (*his.*) become Grand Vizier: ~**a şifa vermek**, be satisfactory.

sâdır Happening; ~ **olm.**, happen, take place; (*adm.*) emanate.

sad·istⁱ (*psy.*) Sadist. ~**izm**, sadism.

sadme Collision; sudden blow/misfortune; explosion. ~**yi hafifletmek**, cushion/soften the blow

sadr- = SADIR. ~**azam(lık)**, (*his.*) Grand Vizier(ate).

safᶠ¹ ¹ *n.* Row; line; rank. ~ **dışı etm.**, leave out/(-side): ~ **düzmek**, (*mil.*) draw up in line of battle: ~ ~, in rows/ranks: ~**ı harp (gemisi)**, line of battle//(battleship): ~**ları sıkıştırmak**, close ranks: ~**tan ayrılan**, (*soc.*) drop-out: ~**tan hariç**, *hors de combat*.

saf ² *a.* Pure; unadulterated; homogeneous; limpid; cloudless; sincere, unfeigned; ingenuous, simple, naïve. ~ **bakışlı**, innocent(-looking): ~ **ırk**, (*ethn.*) pure race: ~ **ispirto**, (*chem.*) absolute alcohol ~ **su**, distilled water.

safa/sefa Freedom from anxiety; peace, ease; enjoyment, pleasure. ~ **bulduk!**, the pleasure is ours! ~ **geldine gitmek**, pay the first visit to a newcomer: ~ **geldiniz!**, welcome!: ~ **pezevengi**, (*sl.*) s.o addicted to pleasure: ~(**sını**)**sürmek**, live at ease/in comfort: ~ **vermek**, give pleasure: ~**yı hatır**, peace and quiet; ease and comfort: ~**yı hatırla kullanınız!** may you enjoy the use of it (gift, purchase, etc.)! ~**lı**, giving pleasure; pleasant.

safahat¹ *pl.* = SAFHA. Stages, phases.

saf·derun Simple, naïve; sincere. ~**derunluk**, simplicity; credulity. ~**dil**, ingenuous, naïve; credulous.

safer (*ast.*) Second lunar month.

affet[i] Purity; sincerity; ingenuousness.
afha Phase, stage; surface; page.
afi Clean; pure; sincere; (*fin.*, *math.*) net. ~ **yet**[i], purity.
afiha Thin leaf/sheet; plate, plaque; surface.
afir (*geol.*) Sapphire.
af·kan (*live.*) Thoroughbred, pure-blooded. ~ **lık**, simplicity; ingenuousness.
afra[1] *n.* (*naut.*) Ballast. ~ **atmak**, (*fig.*) get rid of s.o. embarrassing/stg. useless: ~ **koymak**, ballast: ~ **sarnıcı**, (*naut.*) ballast tank.
afra[2] *n.* (*bio.*) Bile, gall; choler. ~ +, *a.* Biliary: ~ **bastırmak**, have a snack: ~ **kesesi**, gall-bladder: ~ **sı bulanmak/kabarmak**, feel sick; be nauseated. ~ **lı**, bilious.
afran (*bot.*) Saffron.
afsata (*phil.*) False reasoning; fallacy; casuistry, quibbling; chicanery. ~ **ya düşmek**, use silly arguments. ~ **cı**, casuist, sophist. ~ **lamak**, *vi.* argue falsely, quibble. ~ **lı**, fallacious.
ago/sagu (*cul.*) Sago. ~ **ağacı**, (*bot.*) sago tree.
ağ[1] *a.* Right, right-hand. *n.* Right-hand side; (*pol.*) the right; conservative. ~ **elinin verdiğini sol elin görmesin**, let not your left hand know what your right hand does; conceal your charity: ~ **gözü sol gözünden kıskanmak**, be very jealous: ~ **iç**, (*sp.*) inside right: ~ **kol**, right arm; (*mil.*) right wing: ~ **kulağını sol eliyle göstermek**, do things the hard way: ~ **savunucu**, (*sp.*) right full-back: ~ **yap!**, (*mot.*) turn right!: ~ **a bak!**, (*mil.*) eyes right!: ~ **a bükülen**, (*bot.*) dextrorse: ~ **a dönen**, clockwise: ~ **a sola**, here and there: ~ **a sola bakmadan**, carelessly, inconsiderately: ~ **a sola çatmak**, seek a pretext for a quarrel: ~ **dan hizaya gel!**, (*mil.*) right dress!: ~ **dan sola**, counter-clockwise: ~ **dan sola değişmek**, (*met.*) (wind) back: ~ **ı solu yok**, tactless; eccentric; devil-may-care; unpredictable: ~ **ına soluna bakmak**, look about one: ~ **ına soluna bakmamak**, act without consideration: ~ **ını solunu bilmemek/şaşırmak**, be bewildered, not know what to do.
ağ[2] *a.* Alive; safe; sound; healthy; trustworthy; strong. ~ **akçe/para**, good money, genuine coin: ~ **bırakmamak**, kill: ~ **DUYU:** ~ **kalanlar**, (*mil.*) the survivors: ~ **kurtulmak**, escape with one's life; come out safe and sound: ~ **ol!**, thanks!, bravo!: ~ **olsun!**, forgive me, but . . . (criticizing a 3rd person): ~ **salim/selamet/** ~ **ve esen**, safe and sound. ~ **YAĞ.**
ağ. = SAĞLIK.
ağaçık (*sp.*) Outside right.
ağal·mak *vi.* (*med.*) Be cured; become well. ~ **tan** = ~ TIMCI. ~ **tıcı**, therapeutic; parasiticide. ~ **tım**, cure. ~ **tımcı**, medical attendant; healer, curer. ~ **tımevi**, sanatorium. ~ **tma**, *vn.* treatment: ~ **tmak (-i)**, make well; heal, cure. ~ **tsal**, medical.
ağan(giller) (*orn.*) Swift(s).
ağana[l]**k**[ğı] (*met.*) Heavy rainstorm, downpour; squall; (*fig.*) sudden loss/damage.
ağ·bek[i] (*sp.*) Right-back. ~ **beğeni**, (*art.*) good taste. ~ **cı** (*pol.*) rightist; conservative, reactionary. ~ **cılık**, conservatism, reaction. ~ **dı**[l]**ç**[cı], intimate

friend (of bride/groom), best man: ~ **emeği**, useless efforts.
sağdırmak (-i, -e), *vc.* = SAĞMAK.
sağ·duyu(lu) (Man of) common-sense. ~ **görü(lü)**, (possessing) perception, insight; foresight. ~ **görüsüz**, lacking perception.
sağı (*orn.*) Bird droppings/excrement.
sağılmak *vp.* = SAĞMAK; be milked, etc.; (*tex.*) become frayed; (snake, etc.) uncoil itself.
sağım (*live.*) Act of milking; quantity of milk/honey taken; dairy animal. ~ **lı**, kept for milking. ~ **lık**, dairy (animal); milch (cow, etc.).
sağın (*phil.*) True, exact, correct. ~ **bilimler**, exact sciences. ~ **ım/** ~ **ma**, (*bio.*) peristalsis.
sağır Deaf; muted; giving out a dull sound (full cask, etc.); sound-proof; opaque (glass); (*cul.*) slow-boiling/-cooking (vessel); (*arch.*) closed up, blind, sham (door, etc.). ~ **borusu**, ear-trumpet: ~ **dilsiz**, deaf and dumb, deaf mute: ~ **sultan bile duydu**, everyone has heard/knows that.
sağır·laşmak *vi.* Be(come) deaf; (*cul.*) be slow (in cooking). ~ **laştırmak (-i)**, deafen. ~ **lık**, deafness. ~ **yılan**, (*zoo.*) asp viper.
sağıtımsal (*med.*) Therapeutic.
sağ·iç (*sp.*) Inside right. ~ **istem**, good intention; goodwill.
sağlam *a.* Sound; whole; healthy; able-bodied; trustworthy; wholesome; (*fin.*) solvent; gilt-edged. *adv.* (*col.*) Certainly. ~ **ayakkabı değil**, unreliable, untrustworthy: ~ **kaba kotarmak (-i)**, make suitable: ~ **kazık**, sound foundation (for an enterprise): ~ **rüzgâr**, (*met.*) steady wind: ~ **temele oturmak**, be based on sound statements: ~ **tutmak (-i)**, start stg. on a sound basis: ~ **a/** ~ **kazığa bağlamak**, make safe/secure/sure.
sağla·ma *vn.* Making sure; acquisition, etc.; (*math.*) proof. ~ **mak**[1] **(-i)**, *vt.* make safe/secure/certain; ensure; put in working order; acquire; secure; guarantee, ensure; (*math.*) prove. ~ **mak**[2], *vi.* (*mot.*) keep to/drive on the right.
sağlam·cı Who checks/makes certain. ~ **lamak (-i)** = SAĞLAMAK[1]. ~ **laşmak**, *vi.* become sound/firm; be put right (machine, etc.); prove to be true; become safe, escape from danger. ~ **laştırmak (-i)**, make firm/safe; consolidate; put right; etc. ~ **lık**, soundness, wholeness; safety; health; tenacity; trustworthiness; wholesomeness; trueness.
sağ·lanca (*fin.*) Mortgage. ~ **lanmak**, *vp.* = SAĞLAMAK[1]. ~ **layıcı**, ensuring.
sağlı Right-handed. ~ **sollu**, ambidextrous.
sağlıcakla ~ **gidiniz!**, go in good health!, good journey!
sağlı[l]**k**[ğı] *n.* A being alive; life; good health; health, hygiene. ~ +, *a.* Health; sanitary. *int.* All is well! ~ **almak**, ask the way; have stg. recommended: ~ **evi**, hospital: ~ **görevlisi**, (*adm.*) health officer: ~ **koruyumu**, quarantine: ~ **muayenesi**, medical examination: ~ **ocağı**, (*med.*) rural health centre: ~ **olsun!**, never mind!: ~ **raporu**, medical report: ~ **selametle**, in health and safety: ~ **sigortası**, health insurance: ~ **topu**, (*sp.*) medicine-ball: ~ **ve Sosyal Yardım Bakan(lığ)ı**, (*adm.*) Minis·ter/ (-try) for Health and Social Security: ~ **vermek**,

recommend (shop, doctor, etc.): ~ **yazanağı**, medical report: ~ **yoklaması**, medical examination; check-up; health inspection: ~**ınca**, while living, during the lifetime of: ~**ında**, in his lifetime, while he was alive.

sağlık·bilim (*ed.*) Medicine. ~**bilimsel**, medical. ~**işleri**, (*adm.*) Health Department. ~**lı**, healthy; (*fig.*) in good order. ~**lılık**, good health. ~**sal(lık)**, hygie·nic/(-ne). ~**sız**, ill, unhealthy. ~**sızlık**, ill health.

sağ·ma *vn.*: ~ **makinesi**, milking machine. ~**mak** (-**i**), milk; collect honey; (*sl.*) fleece s.o.; (cloud) pour down rain; unwind (rope, etc.). ~**mal**/~**man**, giving milk; (*sl.*) source of income: ~ **inek**, (*live.*) milch cow; (*fig.*) s.o. who is continually exploited.

sağpay *n.* Right. ~**lı**, person entitled.

sağrı (*bio.*) Rump, crupper; (*geo.*) ridge. ~ **bölgesi**, (*bio.*) pelvis: ~ **kemiği**, sacrum.

sağu Lament(ation). ~**cu**, professional mourner.

sağyağ (*cul.*) Cooking butter.

sah[hı] (*adm.*) Mark/sign indicating 'examined'/ 'registered'. ~ **çekmek**, make such a mark.

saha Open space; courtyard; (*sp.*) field; arena; ground; (*fig.*) field, domain.

sahabe *pl.* Companions of the Prophet Muhammad.

sahabet[i] Support, protection, patronage. ~ **etm.**, protect.

sahaf(lık) (Work of) second-hand/antique bookseller.

sahan (*dom.*) Large copper dish; (*cul.*) dish of food. ~**da**, fried. ~**lık**, (*cul.*) dishful; (*dom.*) stand for dishes; (*arch.*) landing; (*mot.*) platform (of tram).

sahavet[i] Generosity, munificence.

sahi *int.* Really!, truly! ~ **mi?**, is that really so? ~**ci**, (*col.*) real, genuine, true. ~**den**, *adv.* really, truly.

sahib- = SAHİP. ~**e**, female owner.

sahife Page, leaf. = SAYFA.

sahih Sound; true; correct; authentic; legitimate.

sahil (*geo.*) Shore; coast; bank. ~ **boyunca**, along the shore: ~ **çizgisi**, coastline: ~ **muhafızı**, coastguard: ~**i selamet**, safety from danger. ~**hane**, house on sea-shore/river-bank. ~**topu**[nu], (*mil.*) coastal gun/battery.

sahileş·mek *vi.* Prove to be true; be confirmed. ~**tirmek** (-**i**), verify, show to be true; fulfil.

sahi'lp[bi] *a.* Possessing; endowed with. *n.* Owner; possessor; master; protector. ~ **çıkmak** (-**e**), claim ownership of stg.; stand as s.o.'s protector/patron; master stg.: ~ **kılmak**, put in possession: ~ **olm.**, possess, be the owner: ~ **şirketi**, (*fin.*) parent company: ~ **zuhur**, a man who rises from obscurity to power: ~**i değişmek**, change hands.

sahip·lik Ownership, possession; protection: ~ **etm. (-e)**, protect, champion s.o. ~**siz**, unowned; ownerless; without a protector, abandoned; anonymous.

sahne (*th.*) Stage; (*cin.*) main scene; (*fig.*) site, setting. ~ **+**, *a.* Stage-; theatrical: ~ **arkası**, backstage: ~ **dışı**, off-stage: ~ **donatımı**, stage-props: ~ **olm. (-e)**, be the scene/setting for stg.: ~**den çıkmak**, (*th.*) exit: ~**ye çıkarmak**/~**lemek (-i)**, stage: ~**ye çıkmak**, appear on stage, enter.

sahra (*geo.*) Open plain/country; wilderness, desert. (*mil.*) field. ~ **topları**, field artillery/guns.

sahre (*geol.*) Boulder, rock.

sahte False; artificial; spurious; counterfeit; sham. ~ **iddia**, false pretences: ~ **tavırlı**, deceitful.

sahte·ci/~**kâr** Counterfeiter, forger. ~**cilik**, ~**kârlık**, forgery, counterfeiting; false coining. ~**lik**, falsity; spuriousness.

sahtiyan Morocco leather.

sahur (*rel.*) Meal before dawn during the Ramadan fast. ~**luk**, (food) suitable for this meal.

saik[1] Cause (*phil.*) factor, motive. ~**a**[1], cause, motive, incentive.

saika[2] (*met.*) Lightning, thunderbolt.

sair That remains; the rest of; other. ~**e (ve)** etcetera. ~ **filmenam**, sleep-walker, somnambulist.

sak[kı 1] *n.* Shank; stem; trunk.

sak[2] *a.* (*dial.*) Awake; vigilant. *n.* Light sleeper. ~ **durmak**, be attentive/vigilant: ~ **yatmak**, sleep lightly.

-sak *v. suf.* [100, etc.] = İSE [ALIRSAK].

saka Water-carrier. ~ **beygiri**, water-carrier's horse; (*fig.*) sponger, parasite: ~ **beygiri gibi** running about on errands; (*fig.*) wandering about aimlessly: ~ **(takımıyıldızı)**, (*ast.*) Aquarius ~**kuşu**[nu], (*orn.*) Eurasian goldfinch.

sakağı (*live.*, *med.*) Glanders, farcy.

saka'lk[ğı] (*bio.*) Double chin; dewlap.

sakal Beard; whiskers. ~ **bırakmak/koyuvermek**, **salıvermek/uzatmak**, let one's beard grow: ~ **likeni**, (*myc.*) beard lichen: ~ **oynatmaz**, (fruit) that melts in the mouth: ~**ı bitmek (-in)**, (job) become tedious: ~**ı değirmende ağartmak**, grow old without becoming experienced: ~**ı ele vermek**, allow o.s. to be led by the nose; let all one's secrets be guessed: ~**ı saydırmak**, cease to be important, respected: ~**ımı uzatsam değecek**, very close: ~**ına gülmek (-in)**, mock s.o. to his face.

sakalık Water-carrier's work.

sakal·lanmak *vi.* Grow a beard. ~**lı**, bearded: ~ **akbaba**, (*orn.*) bearded vulture: ~ **bebek**, s.o. who behaves unsuitably for his years: ~ **guguk**, (*orn.*) puffbird: ~ **kuşlar**, barbets. ~**sız**, beardless.

sakamet[i] Defect; fault; harm.

sakamonya (*bot.*, *med.*) Scammony.

sakan-dırı'k[ğı] (*mod.*) Chin-strap. ~**gur**, (*zoo.*) skink; (*tex.*) coarse book-muslin.

sakar *n.* Horse's blaze. *a.* Ill-omened, unlucky (servant) who always breaks things, bull in a china shop.

sakar·ca (*orn.*) White-fronted goose. ~**laşmak**, *vi* be(come) very clumsy. ~**lı**, (horse) with a blaze unlucky, ill-omened; clumsy. ~**lık**, clumsiness ~**meki**, (*orn.*) coot.

sakar·in (*chem.*) Saccharine. ~**oz**, saccharose.

sakat[1] Unsound, defective; crippled, lame, disabled, invalid; broken, damaged.

sakat·at[1] *pl.* (*cul.*) Offal, giblets. ~**atçı(lık)**, (work of) offal-seller. ~**lamak (-i)**, injure, disable damage, mutilate. ~**lanmak**, *vp.* be injured; break down. ~**lık**, infirmity, disability; deficiency; defect mistake.

sakım (*phys.*) Conservation of energy/matter.

ı**akın** *int.* [218] Beware!, take care!, mind!, don't! ~ **ha!**, mind you don't!

akın·ca Objection; inconvenience; drawback: ~ **yaratmak**, raise objections. ~ **calı**, inconvenient, dangerous. ~ **gan(lık)**, timid(ity); cautious(ness); shy(ness). ~ **ıcı**, s.o. cautious/avoiding risks. ~ **ım**, self-possession; (*phys.*) conservation. ~ **ımlı**, self-possessed. ~ **ma**, *vn.* looking after o.s.; avoidance of risks: ~ **sı olmamak**, not care a straw/give a fig for anyone. ~ **mak**, *vi.* take care of o.s.; be cautious: (**-den**), guard o.s. from, guard against; avoid: (**-i**), protect: **sakınan göze çöp batar**, over-caution invites misfortune. ~ **malık**, (*fin.*) cover, collateral. ~ **masız**, fearless; carefree. ~ **maz**, fearless; unscrupulous. ~ **tı**, precaution. ~ **tılı**, cautious. ~ **tısız**, incautious.

ı**akır** ~ ~, shivering, trembling. ~ **damak**, *vi.* shiver, tremble. ~ **ga**, (*ent.*) tick. ~ **tı**, shivering (from cold/fear).

ı**akıt**[1] [1] *a.* Falling, dropping; fallen in esteem; aborted. ~ **olm.**, be(come) unimportant//void.

ı**akıt**[1] [2] *n.* (*ast.*) Mars.

ı**akız** (*bot.*) Mastic; (*cul.*) chewing-gum. ~ (**Adası**), (*geo.*) Chios: ~ **ağacı**, (*bot.*) mastic tree, lentisc: ~ **bademi**, soft-shelled Chiote almond: ~ **çiğnemek**, chew gum: ~ **gibi**, very white/clean; sticky; (*fig.*) clinging: ~ **leblebisi**, (*cul.*) roasted white chick-pea: ~ **rakısı**, mastic-flavoured raki.

ı**akız-kabağı**[n1] (*bot.*) Vegetable marrow. ~ **lanmak**, *vi.* become resinous//sticky. ~ **lı**, *a.* resinous: *pr. n.* (*ethn.*) Chiote.

ı**aki** (*his.*) Cup-bearer.

ı**akil** Heavy; wearisome; harsh (sound); ugly.

akim Faulty; defective; harmful; wrong.

akin *a.* Quiet; motionless, stationary; calm; in-habiting, dwelling. *n.* Inhabitant. ~ **lerden olm.**, 'belong'.

ı**akin·leşmek** *vi.* Become quiet; calm down. ~ **leştirmek** (**-i**), quieten; calm. ~ **lik**, quiet; stillness; calm.

ı**akit**[i] Silent; taciturn. ~ **kalmak**, remain silent.

akkaroz = SAKAROZ.

ı**ak·lam** Stg. deposited. ~ **lama**, *vn.*; protection; preservation. ~ **lamak** (**-i**), hide, conceal; keep/save/store up for future use; conserve, protect from danger: (**-i, -den**), keep stg. secret from s.o.: (**-i, -e**), set stg. aside for s.o.: **sakla samanı gelir zamanı**, one day it will come in useful (though useless now!) ~ **lamba**[ıç1], (*child.*) hide-and-seek. ~ **lamcı**, depositary. ~ **lamlık**, depository. ~ **lanca**, (*cul.*) preserve, tinned food. ~ **lancalık**, (*cul.*) suitable for preserving. ~ **lanılmak** (**-e**), be kept for s.o.: (**-den**), be kept secret from s.o.: *imp. v.* hide. ~ **lanmak**, *vi.* hide o.s.; go to earth. ~ **lantı**, object hidden/kept, etc. ~ **latmak** (**-i, -e**), *vc.* ~ **lı**, hidden; secret; put aside, reserved; preserved: ~ **resim**, (*ast.*) virtual image. ~ **lılık**, (*leg.*) reservation.

ı**aklık** (*dial.*) Wakefulness, vigilance.

ı**aksağan** (*orn.*) Common magpie.

ı**aksı** (*agr.*) Flower-pot; vase. ~ **güzeli**, (*bot.*) pennywort, navelwort. ~ **lık**, shelf for flowerpots; decorated pot-holder; winter-storage for flowers in pots.

sakso·fon(cu) (*mus.*) Saxophone(-player). ~ **nya**, (*dom.*) Dresden china.

sakulta (*mil.*) Case-shot.

sal (*naut.*) Raft; (*med.*) stretcher.

-sal *a. suf.* [65] = -SEL [KİMYASAL].

sala (*rel.*) Call to prayer/a funeral. ~ **etm.**, proclaim.

salabet[i] Hardness; toughness; firmness; solidity.

salaca[ık[g1]] (*rel.*) Slab on which corpses are washed.

salah Goodness, righteousness; peace; improvement. ~ **bulmak/kesbetmek**, improve, get better, mend: ~ **a doğru**, improving.

salahiyet[i] (*leg.*) Authority/right (to do stg.); competence. ~ **verme**, delegation of authority: ~ **vermek**, authorize, commission, delegate: ~ **i muteber kitap/yazar**, (*fig.*) authority: ~ **i yok**, he has no authority.

salahiyet·li Authorized; competent; (*adm.*) concerned. ~ **name**, (*adm.*) credentials; written authority; (*leg.*) letters of administration. ~ **siz**, unauthorized. ~ **tar**, authoritative, competent.

salak Silly, stupid. ~ **ça**, stupidly. ~ **laşmak**, *vi.* behave stupidly. ~ **lık**, silliness, stupidity.

sala·m (*cul.*) Salami (sausage). ~ **mandra**, (*dom.*) portable coke stove. ~ **manje**, dining-room.

salamura (*cul.*) Brine (for pickling); stg. pickled in brine. ~ **lık** suitable for brine//pickling.

sala·ngan (*orn.*) Edible-nest swiftlet. ~ **purya**, (*naut.*) small lighter, barge. ~ **ş**, booth; market-stall; shed. ~ **şpur**, (*tex.*) loosely-woven cotton (for linings).

-salar *v. suf.* [100, etc.] = İSE [TUTSALAR].

sala·t[1] (*rel.*) Muslim ritual prayer; prayer to the Prophet. ~ **vat**[1], *pl.* prayers.

salata (*cul.*) Salad; lettuce. ~ **lık**, *n.* cucumber: *a.* suitable for salads; (*ed. sl.*) old teacher.

salça (*cul.*) Tomato purée/sauce; sauce, dressing. ~ **lı**, with sauce. ~ **lık**, suitable for sauce-making.

saldır·gan *n.* Aggressor: *a.* aggressive. ~ **ganlık**, aggression. ~ **ı(m)**, aggression; offensive; attack: ~ **teknesi**, (*naut.*) assault craft. ~ **ıcı**, aggressive. ~ **ış**, assault. ~ **ma**, *vn.* attacking; large knife. ~ **mak** (**-i, -e**), *vc.* = SALMAK; rush s.o. to a place: (**-e**), hurl o.s. on; attack s.o.; (*chem.*) attack; (*naut.*) put to sea. ~ **mazlık**, (*pol.*) non-aggression.

sale[ıp[bi]] (*bot.*) Early purple orchid; (*cul.*) its powdered root; (*cul.*) hot drink made with the powder, salep. ~ **çi(lik)**, (work of) salep-seller. ~ **giller**, (*bot.*) orchids, Orchidaceae.

salgı (*bio.*) Glandular secretion; mucus; (*ast.*) ejection. ~ **bezi**, (*bio.*) secretory gland. ~ **lamak** (**-i**), secrete.

salgın *a.* Aggressive, savage (animal); (*med.*) contagious. *n.* (*med.*) Epidemic; contagion; (*fin.*) tax on a community; annual tribute; (*ent.*) plague, invasion; (*fig.*) craze, vogue. ~ **hastalık/sayrılık**, (*med.*) epidemic. ~ **cı**, (*fin.*) tax-gatherer. ~ **lıkbilim**, epidemiology.

salhane Slaughter-house, abattoir.

salı Tuesday.

salı[ık[g1]] Information; directions. ~ **almak**, get news from: ~ **vermek**, inform; advise; give directions. ~ **sız**, uninformed; ignorant of stg.

salım (*phys.*) Emission.

salın·ca¹k^{ğı} Swing; hammock: ~ **sandalye**, rocking-chair. ~**caklı**, swinging, rocking. ~**ım**, (*phys.*) oscillation; (*aer.*) hunting; (*eng.*) beat: (*ast.*) libration. ~**mak¹**, *vp.* = SALMAK; be thrown; be turned on, etc. ~**mak²**, *vi.* sway; oscillate: **salına salına**, swaying from side to side. ~**tı**, swaying; (*naut.*) swell. ~**tılı**, swaying, tottering; (sea) with a swell.

salıvermek (-i) Let go; set free, discharge, release; allow (beard, etc.) to grow; emit.

salih Good; serviceable; suitable, proper; pious.

salik^{i} Who follows/belongs to (a profession, sect, etc.); devotee.

salim Safe, sound; free from defects. ~**en**, safely; soundly.

sali¹p^{bi} (*rel.*) Cross. ~**iahmer**, (*obs.*) Red Cross.

salisi·lat¹ (*chem.*) Salicylate. ~**lik (asit)**, salicylic (acid).

salkım (*bot.*) Hanging bunch (grapes), raceme, cyme (flowers); tree bearing hanging flowers; wistaria; (*mil., obs.*) shrapnel. ~ **ağacı**, (*bot.*) false acacia: ~ **ateş**, (*mil.*) firework ending in a shower of sparks: ~ **saçak**, hanging about untidily/in rags: ~ ~ , in scattered groups: ~ **topu**, (*obs.*) machine-gun.

salkı·mak *vi.* Hang loosely. ~**mküflüce**, (*myc.*) botryomycosis. ~**msı**, (*bot.*) racemose; bunchlike. ~**msöğü¹t**^{dü}, (*bot.*) weeping-willow.

salla·baş (*med.*) Afflicted with involuntary shaking of the head. ~**ma**, *vn.* rocking, shaking. ~**mak (-i)**, swing; rock; shake; wag; (*fig.*) put off; leave in suspense. ~**mamak**, (*sl.*) attach no importance to.

sallan·dırmak (-i, -e), *vc.* Swing; shake; execute by hanging; put off, delay; put off with false promises. ~**mak**, *vi.* swing about; rock; oscillate; undulate; totter, be about to fall; loiter, lounge about, waste time: **sallana sallana yürümek**, amble: **sallanma!**, look alive! ~**malı**, undulatory. ~**tı**, *vn.* swinging, oscillation; putting off, delaying: ~**da bırakmak**, put off without reason. ~**tılı**, swinging, oscillating. ~**tısız**, (*phys.*) dead-beat.

salla·pati Without reflection; careless, tactless. ~**sırt¹**, ~ **etm.**, hoist on the shoulders, shoulder.

sallı Large and wide; (*arch.*) straggling, badly planned.

salma *vn.* = SALMAK. *n.* (*cul.*) Stew cooked with rice; (*his.*) policeman; (*fin.*) local rate levied on villagers; (*mod.*) long hanging sleeve; (*live.*) room for bird-breeding. *a.* (*live.*) Untethered; let out to pasture; continuously running (water). ~ **gezmek**, (*fig.*) saunter about: ~ **tomruğu**, (*his.*) police-cell.

salmak (-i, -e) *vt.* Set free, let go; send in haste; throw; spread out; let hang down; send forth (shoots, smoke); postpone; levy (tax); give out (shade), cast (shadow); (*ast.*) emit; (*arch.*) lay (foundation); (*cul.*) add/put into a saucepan. *vi.* Be aggressive: **(-e)**, attack; (*naut.*) swing at anchor.

salmalık (*agr.*) Pasture-land; (*cul.*) mussels for stewing.

salmastra (*naut.*) Anti-chafing cord; (*eng.*) gland, gasket; packing. ~ **kutusu**, stuffing box.

salname Almanac, calendar; year-book; directory.

salon (*arch.*) Lounge (for receiving guests); dining-room; hall, auditorium; (*art.*) small gallery, show-room. ~ **adamı**, socialite: ~ **general/sosyalisti**, (*pej.*) armchair general/socialist: ~ **zabiti**, (*pej.*) carpet-knight.

saloz (*sl.*) Fool, imbecile. ~**laşmak**, *vi.* behave foolishly. ~**luk**, foolishness, imbecility.

salpa(k) Loose; slack; untidy; slovenly.

salt¹ *adv.* Merely, solely; absolutely. *a.* Mere, simple; (*phil., phys.*) absolute, pure. ~ **bolluk**, (*ast.*) abundance: ~ **çoğunluk**, (*adm.*) absolute majority: ~ **doğa**, unspoilt nature: ~ **nem**, (*phys.*) absolute humidity: ~ **sıfır**, absolute zero.

salta *a.* (Dog) standing on hind legs; (*naut.*) slack (rope). *n.* (*mod.*) Short collarless jacket. ~ **durmak**, (dog) beg.

saltanat¹ (*adm.*) Sultanate; sovereignty, dominion; (*fig.*) pomp, magnificence. ~ **arabası//kayığı**, state coach//barge: ~ **sürmek**, rule as Sultan; live in great splendour. ~**lı**, splendid, magnificent. ~**sız**, without display.

salt·çılık (*adm.*) Absolutism. ~**ık**, (*phil.*) absolute. ~**ıkçı(lık)**, auto·crat/(-cracy), absolut·ist/(-ism). ~**ın**, absolutely, certainly.

salvo (*mil.*) Salvo, broadside, barrage.

sal·ya (*bio.*) Saliva; ~**sı akmak**, dribble; (*fig.*) drool. ~**yangoz**, (*zoo.*) snail; (*bio.*) cochlea: ~ **delgi**, (*carp.*) gimlet, auger.

sam^{m¹} (*met.*) Blighting. ~ YELİ.

-sam *v. suf.* [100, etc.] = İSE [BAKARSAM].

-samak *v. suf.* = -SEMEK [AÇINSAMAK].

saman (*agr.*) Straw. ~ **alevi**, flash in the pan: ~ **alevi gibi**, flaring up (and dying down) suddenly: ~ **altından su yürütmek**, do stg. in an underhand manner, intrigue secretly: ~ **bir kıtık**, straw mattress: ~ **çöp/tozu**, chaff: ~ **doldurur postuna!**, he has betrayed me!: ~ **gibi**, tasteless, insipid.

saman·i Straw-coloured, light yellow. ~**kâğıdı**^{n¹}, tracing-paper; wrapping-paper. ~**kapan**, amber. ~**lık**, straw-rick/-loft. ~**rengi**^{ni}, light yellow. ~**uğrusu/~yolu**^{nu}, (*ast.*) Milky Way: ~ +, *a.* galactic.

sam·aryum (*chem.*) Samarium. ~ **ba**, (*mus.*) samba. ~**i**, (*ling.*) Semitic.

samimi Sincere, cordial. ~ **olmamak (-le)**, keep s.o. at a distance. ~**lik/~yet**^{i}, sincerity, cordiality. ~ **yetsiz(lik)**, insince·re/(-rity).

samsa (*cul.*) A pastry sweetened with syrup.

samsun (*zoo.*) Mastiff, guard-dog. ~**cu**, (*mil., his.*) soldier in charge of assault-dogs.

samur (*zoo.*) Sable. ~ **kaşlı**, with thick dark eyebrows: ~ **kürk**, (*mod.*) sable skin coat: ~ **kürkü sırtına almak**, take the blame, bear the responsibility: ~ **kürkü birinin sırtına giydirmek**, lay the blame on s.o.

samyeli^{ni} (*met.*) Simoon, blighting wind. ~ **vurmuş mayıs çirozu**, (*sl.*) very thin; all skin and bone.

san Reputation, esteem; title; surname.

san. = SANAT; SANİYE.

-san *v. suf.* [100, etc.] = İSE [KONUŞURSAN].

sana *pron. dative* [67] = SEN. To thee/you. ~ **bir çift sözüm var**, I want a couple of words with you: ~ **bir hal olmuş!**, what's come over you?: ~ **gösteririm!**, I'll show you!, I'll teach you not to do that again!:

~ **Hanya'yı Konya'yı gösteririm!**, I'll teach you a lesson: ~ **şeşi beş gösteririm**, I'll knock stars out of you!

-sana *v. suf.* [271] = -SENE [OTURSANA].

sanal Conjectural, nominal. ~ **sayı**, imaginary number.

sanat[1] Art; skill, ability; = ZANAAT, trade, calling, craft. ~ **altın bileziktir**, a skilled man can always find work: ~ **enstitüsü**, (*ed.*) art school: ~ **eser/yapıtı**, work of art: ~ **filmi**, (*cin.*) art/noncommercial film: ~ **için** ~, art for art's sake: ~ **meraklısı**, dilettante: ~ **okulu**, trade school: ~ **şöleni**, art festival: ~ **züppesi**, (*pej.*) aesthete: ~**la**, artistically.

sanat·çı/ ~**kâr** Artist; author; craftsman: ~ **adı**, (*lit.*) *nom de plume*: ~ **simgesi**, monogram. ~**çılık/** ~**kârlık**, profession of art; artistic ability. ~**kârane**, artistically. ~**lı**, skilfully/artistically made. ~**sal**, artistic. ~**sever**, art-lover.

sanatoryum (*med.*) Sanatorium.

sanayi[i] *pl.* Industries. ~ **bitkileri işletmesi**, (*agr.*) plantation: ~ **devrimi**, (*his.*) Industrial Revolution: ~ **odası**, Chamber of Industry: ~ **ve Teknoloji Bakan(lığ)ı**, (*adm.*) Minis·ter/(-try) for Industry and Technology: ~**de kullanılan**, industrial (diamonds, etc.).

sanayi·ci *n.* Industrialist. ~**ci/**~**i**, *a.* industrial. ~**leşme**, industrialization. ~**leşmek**, *vi.* become industrialized. ~**leştirmek (-i)**, industrialize.

sanca[1]**k**[ği] Flag, banner; (*mil.*) standard; (*adm., obs.*) sub-vilayet, county; (*naut.*) starboard. ~ **tarafında**, on the starboard beam: ~**ı şerif**, the noble flag (of the Prophet, unfurled only for CİHAT). ~**tar**, standard-bearer.

sancı (*med.*) Stomach-ache, colic, gripes, stitch. ~**lanma**, *vn.* aching. ~**lanmak**, *vi.* have a stomach-ache/internal pain. ~**lı**, having/with internal pain. ~**mak**, *vi.* ache, be griped. ~**sız**, painless.

sançmak (-i) Thrust into; set up in the ground; plant.

sandal (*bot.*) Sandalwood(-tree); (*mod.*) sandals; (*naut.*) rowing-boat; (*tex.*) brocade. ~ **Bedesteni**, municipal auction-rooms (Istanbul): ~ **vinci**, (*naut.*) davit. ~**cı(lık)**, (work of) boatman.

sandalye (*dom.*) Chair; (*adm.*) office, post. ~ **kavgası**, struggle for a post: ~ **sazı**, (*bot.*) bulrush.

sandalye·ci(lik) (Work of) chair-maker/-seller. ~**siz**, without a chair: ~ **nazır**, (*adm.*) minister without portfolio.

sandı[1]**k**[ği] Chest, coffer, box; bin; (*eng.*) coffer-dam; (*fin.*) cash-box; bank; fund; (*adm.*) cash department; (*pol.*) ballot-box; old-fashioned fire-pump; (*arch.*) box for measuring sand, etc. ~ **düzmek**, (girl) prepare her bottom-drawer: ~ **emini**, cashier: ~ **eşyası**, clothes etc. as part of a bride's dowry: ~ **geçmesi**, (*carp.*) dovetail (joint): ~ **lekesi**, (*myc.*) stain on long-stored clothes: ~ **odası**, store-room, box-room: ~ **sepet**, bag and baggage: ~**ı sepeti kaldırmak**, take o.s. off lock stock and barrel: ~ **tan çıkmak**, (*pol.*) be elected, come to power.

sandık·balığı[nı] (*ich.*) Boxfish, trunkfish. ~**çe**, small box. ~**çı(lık)**, (work of) box-maker/-seller. ~**lamak (-i)**, put in a box, box. ~**lanmak**, *vp.* ~**lı**,

having a box; (*carp.*) thin board, veneer; (*his.*) gold coin for decoration. ~**sal**, (*pol.*) based on the ballot-box: ~ **demokrasi**, (*iron.*) pseudo-democracy.

sanduka Sarcophagus.

sandviç (*cul.*) Sandwich. ~ **deniz kırlangıcı**, (*orn.*) Sandwich tern.

sanem (*rel.*) Idol; (*fig.*) idol of one's heart.

sangı Confused, stupefied, dizzy. ~**lamak**, *vi.* be stupefied/confused.

sanı Idea; thought; surmise. ~**cı**, who thinks/imagines/surmises. ~**sal**, doxastic.

sanı[1]**k**[ği] (*leg.*) Suspected, accused; defendant. ~ **yeri**, dock. ~**lık**, a being accused.

-sanız *v. suf.* [100 etc.] = İSE [BAKARSANIZ].

-sanıza *v. suf.* [271] = -SENE [KULLANSANIZA].

sani·din (*geol.*) Sanidine. ~ **tasyon**, sanitation.

saniye (*ast.*) Second; (*fig.*) moment; seconds-hand; (*his.*) second grade of officials. ~ **si** ~ **sine**, dead on time, on the dot, to the very second. ~**li**, (watch) with seconds-hand: ~ **tapa**, (*eng.*) time-fuse. ~**lik**, lasting one second.

sanki *conj.* [218] As if, as though, supposing that; do you think...? ~ **iş yaptın değil mi?**, a fine lot of use you are!

sanlı Well-known, esteemed.

san·ma *vn.* (*phil.*) Belief; supposition. ~**mak (-i)**, think, suppose, imagine, deem.

sanrı (*psy.*) Hallucination. ~**lamak (-i)**, hallucinate.

sansar (*zoo.*) Beech-marten; (?) polecat.

Sanskrit[i]**(çe)** (*ling.*) Sanskrit.

sansür (*lit.*) Censorship. ~ **cü**, censor. ~**lemek (-i)**, censor. ~**lenmek**, *vp.*

santi·ar (*math.*) Centiare. ~**gram**, centigram(me). ~**gra**[1]**t**[dı], (*phys.*) Centigrade, Celsius. ~**litre**, (*math.*) centilitre. ~**m**, one-hundredth (of any unit): ~ **kaçırmamak**, be very careful/economical. ~**metre**, centimetre: ~ **kare/küp**, square//cubic centimetre. ~ **pua**, (*phys.*) centipoise.

san·tra(haf) (*sp.*) Centre(-half). ~**tral**[1], (*el.*) power-station; telephone exchange; (*ind.*) works site: ~ **personeli**, site personnel: ~ **yeri**, site. ~**tralcı**, station/exchange operator. ~**trfor**, (*sp.*) centre-forward. ~**trfüj**, *a.* (*phys.*) centrifugal. ~**trfujör**, centrifuge. ~**trozom**, (*bio.*) centrosome.

santur (*mus.*) Dulcimer. ~**cu/**~**i**, dulcimer player.

sanzatu (*gamb.*) No trumps.

sap[1] (*bot.*) Peduncle, stem, stalk; sheaf; (*carp.*) handle. ~ **çekmek**, take sheaves for threshing: ~ **demeden samanı anlamak**, be very 'quick in the uptake': ~ **derken saman demek**, talk twaddle: ~ **oyucusu**, (*ent.*) stem-borer: ~**ı silik**, vagabond, tramp: ~**ına kadar**, to the backbone/core, thoroughly, utterly.

sapa Off the road; out of the way, secluded; devious. ~ **düşmek**, be off the main road; be remote/inaccessible: ~ **yol/**~**ı**[1]**k**[ği], abnormal; entry to side-street, by-road. ~**klık**, (*phil.*) anomaly, deviation; defect, abnormality.

sapan (*mil.*) Sling, catapult; (*eng.*) hoisting sling; (*naut.*) strop; (*sp.*) crampon. ~**balığı**[nı], (*ich.*) fox/thresher shark. ~**kemiği**[ni], (*bio.*) vomer.

saparna (*bot.*) Smilax; (*chem.*) sarsaparilla.
saparta (*mil.*) Broadside; (*fig.*) scolding. ~ yı yemek, get a scolding.
sapasağlam Very healthy, sound, robust.
sapçılkᵍı (*bot.*) Small stalk, tigella.
sapeli ~ maun, (*bot.*, *carp.*) sapele (mahogany).
sapık *a.* Gone astray; perverted, eccentric; erratic, abnormal; crazy; (*ast.*) aberrant. *n.* Harmless lunatic; pervert. ~ laşmak, *vi.* become perverted, etc. ~ lık, perversion; abnormality; craziness.
sapılmak (-e) *imp. v.* One be diverted, turn away.
sapın¹çᶜı (*phil.*) Deviation; (*ast.*) aberration.
sapır sapır (*ech.*) Sound of continuous falling. ~ ~ dökülmek, (ripe fruit, etc.) fall/drop continuously.
sapıtmak *vi.* Go off one's head; (*fig.*) talk nonsense; go astray: (-i), *vt.* lead/send astray.
sap·kı (*phil.*) Perverseness, perversity; (*sp.*) foul. ~ kın, astray; abnormal; perverse, off the right road: ~ kaya/taş, (*geol.*) erratic block. ~ kınlık, perverseness; being astray; abnormality.
sapla·ma *vn.* (*eng.*) Stud-bolt; (*mot.*) (wheel) balancing weight: ~ kutusu, (*sp.*) pole-vault box. ~ mak (-i, -e), thrust into, pierce; skewer. ~ nmak (-e), stick into, penetrate; sink into; (*fig.*) get a fixed idea; get a handle/stem. ~ ntı, (*psy.*) *idée fixe*, obsession.
saplı *a.* Having a handle/stem, pedunculate; sticking into a thing. *n.* Bowl/pot with a handle; scoop; ladle. ~ meşe, (*bot.*) common/pedunculate oak: ~ tencere, (*dom.*) casserole.
sap·ma *vn.* (*phys.*) Deviation; declination; distortion; (*ast.*) aberrance; (*aer.*, *naut.*) yawing; (*ling.*) irregularity; sound shift: ~ ölçeği, (*ast.*) declinometer. ~ mak (-e), swerve; deviate; diverge; turn off in a new direction; (*fig.*) go astray; fall into error; have recourse to.
sa·potgiller (*bot.*) Myrtle family, Myrtaceae. ~ profitⁱ, (*myc.*) saprophyte, saprobe.
sap·sağlam Robustly healthy. ~ sarı, bright yellow; (*fig.*) deathly pale.
sapsız Handleless; (*bot.*) stalkless, stemless. ~ balta, s.o. without backing/influence; good-for-nothing: ~ meşe, (*bot.*) durmast/sessile oak.
sapta·ma *vn.* Fixing; deciding; establishing. ~ mak (-i), fix, establish; (*fig.*) determine, prove, confirm. ~ nca, (*fin.*) contingency, quota. ~ nım, fixity. ~ nımcılık, (*phil.*) predestination. ~ nma, *vn.*; (*psy.*) alienation; fixation. ~ nmak, *vp.* ~ yıcı, *a.* fixing, establishing; confirming: *n.* (*chem.*) fixative.
saptır·ılmak (-e) *vp.* ~ ım, (*pol.*) revision. ~ ımcı(lık), revision·ist/(-ism). ~ ma, *vn.* deflection; (*arch.*) broken-line moulding. ~ mak (-i, -e), *vc.* = SAPMAK; deflect; divert; refract.
sara (*med.*) Epilepsy, epileptic fit. ~ hastalığı, falling sickness: ~ sı var/tutuyor, he's having a fit.
sara¹çᶜı Saddler; leather-worker. ~ hane, saddlery workshop/market. ~ lık, saddlery.
sarahatⁱ Clarity; explicitness. ~ en, clearly, explicitly.
sara¹kᵍı (*arch.*) Low-relief moulding.
saraka (*his.*) Pillory (*sl.*) ridicule. ~ etm./~ ya almak, barrack, ridicule, mock, deride. ~ cı, *a.* mocking, jeering: *n.* mocker.

saralı (*med.*) Subject to epileptic fits.
sarar·mak *vi.* Turn yellow/pale; blanch. ~ tma, *vn.*: *a.* delicate, pale. ~ tmak (-i), *vc.* turn yellow: make pale.
saray Palace; mansion; (*adm.*) government house/ office; 'the Government'. ~ lokması, (*cul.*) sweetmeat of dough, eggs and sugar: ~ patı, (*bot.*) China aster.
Saray·bosna (*geo.*) Sarajevo. ~ burnu, Seraglio Point (Istanbul). ~ lı, (*his.*) attached to/brought up in a palace; palace servant/slave.
sardalye (*ich.*) Sardine, pilchard. ~ gibi istif olm., be packed in like sardines: ~ sarması, (*cul.*) sardines in vine leaves.
sardırmak (-i, -e) *vc.* = SARMAK; start to have a passion for . . ..
sardoğan (*orn.*) Type of hawk; (?) hobby.
sardun Type of fisherman's rope.
sardunya (*bot.*) Geranium, pelargonium. ~ giller, geranium family, Geraniaceae.
sarf (*fin.*) Expenditure, cost; (*ling.*) grammar. ~ etm., spend, expend; exert; consume, use. ~ iyat¹, *pl.* expenditure; consumption.
sarfınazar (-den) Putting aside; apart from. ~ etm., ignore, disregard; give up, relinquish.
sargı (*med.*) Bandage, dressing; (*el.*) winding, coil. ~ lamak (-i), bandage. ~ lı, bandaged, strapped up.
sarhoş *a.* Drunk. *n.* Drunkard. ~ edici, intoxicating: ~ olarak, in a drunken condition. ~ luk, drunkenness.
sarı *a.* Yellow; fair-haired; pale, haggard. *n.* Yellow colour; (*bio.*) yolk. ~ altın, pure gold; Tk. gold coin: ~ aşıboyası, (*geol.*) yellow ochre: ~ bakır, (*min.*) brass: ~ balık, (*ich.*) chub: ~ basın, (*pub.*) non-Marxist press: ~ basın kartı, journalist's press-card: ~ çam, (*bot.*) Scots pine: ~ çıyan, (*pej.*) fair-complexioned but unpleasant person: ~ çizmeli Mehmet Ağa, inadequately specified person/address (i.e. Mr. Smith of London): ~ çobanaldatan/~ kuyruk sallayan, (*orn.*) yellow wagtail: ~ gagalı, (*orn.*) yellow-beaked/-billed: ~ gagalı dağkargası//ketenkuşu//yelkovan, (*orn.*) Alpine chough//twite//Cory's shearwater: ~ hani, (*ich.*) jewfish: ~ HUMMA: ~ ırk, (*ethn.*) yellow/ Mongolian race: ~ ışık, (*mot.*) amber light: ~ kiraz kuşu/~ yelve, (*orn.*) yellowhammer: ~ kuyruk, (*ich.*) yellowtail: ~ maun, (*bot.*, *carp.*) limba wood: ~ menekşe, (*bot.*) mountain pansy: ~ mukallit, (*orn.*) icterine warbler: ~ nilüfer, (*bot.*) yellow water-lily: ~ papatya, (*bot.*) corn marigold: ~ pirinç, (*min.*) yellow brass: ~ sıcak, (*met.*) burning heat (of S.E. Turkey): ~ şebboy, (*bot.*) wallflower: ~ yakut, (*geol.*) topaz: ~ yonca, (*bot.*) kidney vetch.
sarı·ağız (*ich.*) Meagre, shadefish. ~ asma/~ cık, (*orn.*) golden oriole. ~ benek, (*bio.*) macula (lutea). ~ ca, yellowish; (*ent.*) wasp; (*his.*) militia. ~ çalı, (*bot.*) barberry. ~ göz, (*ich.*) type of sea-bream. ~ humma, (*med.*) yellow-fever.
sarı¹kᵍı Turban. ~ sarmak, put on/wear a turban: ~ ıburma, (*cul.*) type of sweet pastry, sultan's turbans. ~ lı, wearing a turban; (*fig.*) Muslim hodja.

sarı·kana'tᵈ¹ (*ich.*) Medium-sized LÜFER. ~**kız**, blonde girl; (*col.*) cow; (*sl.*) gold lira. ~**lı¹**, coloured yellow. ~**lık**, yellowness; (*med.*) jaundice; (*myc.*) blight; (*bot.*) chlorosis.
sarıl·gan (*bot.*) Creeping/climbing/entwining plant. ~**ı²**, wound; fastened; surrounded. ~**ıcı**, winding, intertwining; ~ **gövde**, (*bot.*) tendril, sucker. ~**ma**, *vn.* ~**mak**, *vp.* = SARMAK; be surrounded/enveloped/entangled/bandaged: (**-e**), be wound/wrapped round; be wound/wrapped up in; clasp, embrace; throw o.s. upon; be absorbed in, give o.s. up to; (*bot.*) entwine itself round, climb up. ~**mış**, convolute.
sar·ım *vn.* = SARMAK; single turn; (*el.*) helix, winding. ~**ımlık**, (*el.*) coil. ~**ımsak** = SARMISAK. ~**ınmak (-e)**, wrap o.s. in; gird o.s.; cocoon itself.
sarı·msı/ ~**mtırak** Yellowish. ~**ot**, (*carp.*) small pine plank. ~**sab'ır'ı**, (*bot.*) aloe; (*chem.*) best quality aloes. ~**salkım**, (*bot.*) laburnum. ~**şın**, fair-haired/-skinned, blond(e). ~**şınlık**, blondness, fairness.
sari (*mod.*) Indian sari.
sâri (*med.*) Contagious, catching. ~ **hastalık**, contagious disease.
sarig (*zoo.*) Sarigue, S. Am. opossum.
sarih Clear, explicit.
sark·a'ç'ı (*phys.*) Pendulum. ~**açlamak (-i)**, oscillate; (*sp.*) swing up and down. ~**an**, pendant. ~**ık**, pendulous; hanging loosely; flabby; (*mod.*) baggy; ~ **etli karga**, (*orn.*) wattlebird: ~ **kaşlı**, beetle-browed. ~**ıklık**, looseness, flabbiness. ~**ıl**, (*phys.*) pendulous, swinging, oscillating. ~**ıntı**, robbery, spoliation; molestation. ~**ıntılık**, aggression; molestation (of women). ~**ıt'**, (*geol.*) stalactite; (*arch.*) stalactitic decoration. ~**ıtmak (-i)**, *vc.* let hang down; suspend; hang (s.o.). ~**mak**, *vi.* hang down; droop: (**-den**), lean out of, hang from: (**-e**), come down on, attack suddenly.
sarko·m (*med.*) Sarcoma. ~**mer**, (*bio.*) sarcomere. ~ **plazma**, sarcoplasm.
sar·ma *vn.* Act of winding/enveloping/rolling up; embrace; thing wrapped up in stg. else; (*cul.*) stuffed; (*mil.*) siege; (*sp.*) a wrestling hold; (*min.*) sagging. ~**ma'ç'ı**, packing, wrapping; (*eng.*) winding drum. ~**maçlamak (-i)**, wrap up, pack. ~**mak (-i, -e)**, wind/wrap round; (*med.*) bandage, dress; embrace; cling to; envelop, surround; wind (wool, coils, etc.); (*fig.*) comprehend, take in; captivate, interest: *vi.* (*bot.*) twine, climb; (*fig.*) busy o.s. about stg.: **sarıp sarmalamak**, pack/wrap up tightly. ~**mal**, (*phys.*) helical; spiral: ~ **taşıyıcı**, (*eng.*) screw/worm conveyor: ~ **yapraklar**, (*bot.*) alternate leaves. ~**mala'ç'ı**, packaging. ~**malamak (-i)**, envelop; put in an envelope. ~**malanmak**, *vp.*
sarman Huge, enormous.
sarmaş ~ **dolaş**, in close embrace; inextricably intertwined: ~ **dolaş olm.**, embrace one another; be very close friends.
sarmaş·an (*bot.*) Intertwining, climbing. ~**ı'k'ı**, (*bot.*) ivy, hedera: ~ **bitki**, climber. ~**ıkgiller**, Araliaceae, ivy family. ~**mak (-le)**, embrace one another; be intertwined.
sarmısa'k'ı (*bot.*) Garlic. ~ **dişi**, (*cul.*) clove of

garlic: ~ **kurbağası**, (*zoo.*) spade-foot toad: ~**ı gelin etmişler de kırk gün kokusu çıkmamış**, people don't change easily/reveal themselves immediately. ~ **lı**, (*cul.*) flavoured with garlic.
sarnı'ç'ı (Rain-water) cistern; (*naut.*) freshwater tank. ~ **gemisi**, (*naut.*) tanker: ~ **vagonu**, (*mot.*) tanker; (*rly.*) tank-car. ~**lı**, ~ **kamyon**, (*mot.*) tanker, bowser.
sarp¹ Steep; hard, difficult; inaccessible; intractable. ~ **kayalık**, (*geo.*) bluff: ~**a sarmak/** ~**laşmak**, *vi.* become steep; become difficult/impracticable.
sarpa (*ich.*) Mediterranean/sea bream.
sarpın (*agr.*) Grain-pit, silo; (*cul.*) dough-tub.
sarraf (*fin.*) Money-changer, banker. ~**iye**, rate of exchange; money-changer's fee. ~**lık**, money-changing; money-changer's fee.
sar·sa'ç'ı (*eng.*) Vibrator. ~**sak**, shaking from feebleness; doddering; (*med.*) palsied; quivering, clumsy: ~ **sursak**, shakily, tremblingly. ~**saklık**, trembling, palsy; clumsiness: ~ **etm.**, be all of a dither.
sars·ı (*geol.*) Tremor. ~**ık**, shaken; quivering, shaky. ~**ılış**, a being shaken; shock, jolt; loss of balance; (*geol.*) earthquake. ~**ılma**, *vn.* ~**ılmak**, *vp.* be shaken, etc.; break down. ~**ılmazlık**, (*phil.*) ataraxia. ~**ım**, (*min.*) shock: ~ **dirençli**, shock resistant. ~**ıntı**, a being shaken; shock, bump; (*med.*) concussion; (*geol.*) tremor, earthquake. ~**ıntılı**, being shaken; jigging; (*fig.*) shaky, precarious, hazardous. ~**ıntısal**, (*geol.*) seismic. ~**ıntısız**, immobile; (*fig.*) sound, secure, safe. ~ **ma**, *vn.* shaking; shake. ~ **mak (-i)**, shake; agitate; give a shock to; upset; (*med.*) concuss.
Sart (*geo.*) Sardis.
sası Smelling mouldy, musty; putrefied. ~**mak**, *vi.* decay; putrefy.
sat. = SATIR.
sata = SATMAK. ~ **'k'ı**, market: ~ **ederi**, retail price.
sataş·ılmak *vp.* ~**kan**, aggressive; quarrelsome. ~**ma**, *vn.* attack. ~**mak (-e)**, become aggressive; seek a quarrel; annoy, tease; interfere with, molest.
saten (*tex.*) Satin.
sath- = SATIH. ~**i**, superficial, cursory. ~**ileşme**, *vn.* ~**ileşmek**, *vi.* be(come) superficial. ~**ileştirmek (-i)**, *vc.* ~**ilik**, superficiality.
satı Sale, selling. ~**ya çıkarmak**, put up for sale. ~**cı**, salesman; seller, vendor; hawker. ~**cılık**, selling, salesmanship.
sat'ıh'ʰ¹ Surface; plane; upper surface; face; (*aer.*) skin. ~ **sertleştirici**, (*min.*) case-hardening.
sat·ılık *a.* On sale; for sale: ~ **kadın**, prostitute. ~**ılmak**, *vp.* be sold; (*fig.*) sell o.s., secretly help the opposition: **satılacak!**, for sale!: **satıldı!**, sold! ~**ım**, sale; selling. ~**ımca**, invoice. ~**ımcı(lık)**, trad·er/ (-ing). ~**ımevi**, shop. ~**ımlık**, invoice; salesman's commission. ~**ın**, sale: ~ **alma**, buying, purchase: ~ **almak**, buy. ~**ınalıcı**, buyer, purchaser.
satır¹ *n.* (*pub.*) Line of writing. ~**başı'ʰ¹**, paragraph (inset).
satır² *n.* Large butcher's knife, chopper, cleaver; tobacco cutter; (*his.*) executioner's sword. ~ **atmak**, exterminate. ~**cı**, butcher's assistant.
satış Manner of selling; sale. ~ **bilimi**, marketing:

~ **ruhsatı**, sales permit (for monopoly goods): ~ **sonrası servis**, after-sales service: ~ **şefi**, (*pub.*) circulation manager; sales manager: ~ **a çıkarmak**, put up for sale. ~ **lık**, shop.
satir (*myth.*) Satyr; (*lit.*) satire.
satlıcan (*med.*) Pleurisy.
sat·ma *vn.* Selling. ~ **mak (-i, -e)**, sell; make a false show of; claim/pretend to be; (*sl.*) get rid of s.o.; exaggerate; betray s.o. to s.o. else: **sata/satıp savmak**, sell up/out: **sata sava geçinmek**, be reduced to selling one's possessions just to live.
satran¹çᶜ¹ Chess; (*mod.*) check pattern. ~ ~ / ~ **lı**, with a check pattern: ~ **tahta//taşları**, chess-board// -men.
satra¹pᵇ¹ (*his.*) Persian provincial governor, satrap.
sattırmak (-i, -e) *vc.* = SATMAK; let/force s.o. to sell.
Satürn (*ast.*) Saturn.
satvetⁱ Rush, spring; attack; force, vigour.
Saudi Arabistan (*geo.*) Saudi Arabia. = SUUDİ.
sauna (*med.*) Sauna bath.
sav Word; assertion, statement; (*leg.*) allegation; (*phil.*) thesis, proposition. ~ **ı kanıtlama**, proof.
sava Message; good news. ~ **cı**, messenger; bearer of good news.
sava¹kᵍ¹ (*agr.*) Distribution cistern; mill-pond sluice.
savana (*geo.*) Savanna(h).
-savar *suf.* Anti- [**uçaksavar**, anti-aircraft].
savaş Struggle, combat, fight; battle, war: *pr.n.* (*ast.*) Mars. ~ **açma**, start of hostilities: ~ **açmak**, fight; ~ **bölgesi**, war zone; front: ~ **divanı(na çıkarmak/vermek)**, *n.* court martial/(*vt.* court-martial): ~ **durumu**, state of war: ~ **esir/tutsağı**, prisoner of war: ~ **gemisi**, (*naut.*) battleship: ~ **gereçleri**, military supplies, munitions: ~ **giderimi**, (*fin.*) war reparations: ~ **hattı**, fighting-line: ~ **ilanı**, declaration of war: ~ **kazancı**, booty, pillage: ~ **meydanı**, battlefield: ~ **ödencesi**, (*fin.*) war reparations: ~ **parolası**, battle-cry: ~ **vurguncusu**, war-profiteer: ~ **vurgunu**, booty, pillage: ~ **a gidiş**, campaign: ~ **ta ölmek**, die in action, bite the dust.
savaş·çı *a.* Belligerent, bellicose: *n.* combatant, warrior: ~ **kadın**, (*myth.*) Amazon. ~ **çıl**, warlike; war-monger. ~ **çılık**, belligerence. ~ **ım**, struggle. ~ **kan**, fighting, warring; warlike. ~ **ma**, *vn.* fighting, combat: ~ **yı durdurma**, cease-fire. ~ **mak (-le)**, struggle, fight; dispute: **(-meğe)**, struggle/work hard/endeavour to do.
savat¹ (*art.*) Engraving in black on silver; niello. ~ **lamak (-i)**, engrave thus. ~ **lı**, engraved in black.
sav·ca (*leg.*) Accusation, charge. ~ **cı(lık)**, public prosecutor('s office), counsel for the prosecution. ~ **dırmak (-i, -e)**, *vc.* = SAVMAK.
savla (*naut.*) Signal halyards.
savla·mak (-i) Claim, put forward. ~ **yıcı**, claiming, prosecuting.
savletⁱ Impetuous assault; dash.
savlı (*lit.*) Tendentious.
sav·ma *vn.* ~ **mak (-i)**, drive away; dismiss; get rid of; avoid, evade; get over (illness): *vi.* pass away, come to an end, fade: **(-e)**, pass to. ~ **mış**, gone; come to an end; lost; past use.

savruk Awkward; clumsy; too hasty. ~ **lama**, (*th.*) burlesque. ~ **luk**, awkwardness, etc.
sav·rulmak *vp.* = SAVURMAK. ~ **runtu**, (*agr.*) chaff.
savsa Slow; gentle, calm.
savsak Negligent; dilatory. ~ ~, prowling about. ~ **lama**, *vn.*; delaying; making excuses. ~ **lamak (-i)**, put s.o. off with excuses/pretexts; put off doing stg. ~ **lık**, negligence; dilatoriness.
savsama(k) = SAVSAKLAMA(K).
savsöz (*lit.*, *pol.*) Slogan, cliché. ~ **cü**, s.o. always using slogans. ~ **cülük**, use of slogans/clichés.
savul *int.* Stand aside!, out of the way! ~ **mak**, *vi.* stand aside; get out of the way.
savun·an (*leg.*) Defendant. ~ **ca**, apology. ~ **ma**, (*leg.*, *mil.*) defence: ~ + , *a.* defensive, strategic: ~ **Bakan(lığ)ı**, Minis·ter/(-try) of Defence. ~ **mak (-i)**, defend. ~ **malı**, defensive. ~ **man**, (*leg.*) counsel, solicitor, barrister: ~ **lar kurumu**, bar. ~ **u**, defence. ~ **ucu(luk)**, (work of) defence counsel; (*sp.*) full-back. ~ **ulmayan**, (*mil.*) undefended, open (city).
savur·gan Spendthrift; extravagant; prodigal. ~ **ganlık**, extravagance; prodigality. ~ **ma**, *vn.*; (*sp.*) muscle-flexing: ~ **makinesi**, (*agr.*) winnowing machine. ~ **mak (-i)**, toss about; throw into the air; blow about; (*agr.*) winnow; (*mil.*) brandish (a sword); (*fin.*) spend extravagantly: *vi.* blow violently; boast, brag.
savuş·ma *vn.* ~ **mak**, *vi.* (illness, etc.) pass; cease; slip away. ~ **maz**, that will not pass/go away; (*med.*) incurable. ~ **turmak (-i)**, *vc.* cause to go away/cease; escape/avoid s.o./stg. disagreeable.
savutlar *pl.* (*mil.*) Arms, weapons; munitions.
say (*zoo.*) Capuchin (monkey).
say. = SAYGILI KONUŞMADA.
sây Effort; endeavour; exertion.
saya(cı) (Maker of) shoe-uppers.
say·a¹çᶜ¹ (Gas, etc.) meter, counter. ~ **al**, ~ **sayı**, (*math.*) cardinal number.
sayca (*fin.*) Credit; loan. ~ **belge/mektubu**, letter of credit: ~ **ile**, on credit.
saydam Transparent; clear; (*tex.*) diaphanous. ~ **boya**, glazing: ~ **kat/tabaka**, (*bio.*) cornea: ~ **resim**, (*cin.*) diapositive, transparency.
saydam·lama *vn.* (*cin.*) Lightening. ~ **lamak (-i)**, make lighter/transparent. ~ **laşmak**, *vi.* become transparent. ~ **lık**, transparency. ~ **sız**, opaque.
-saydı *v. suf.* [131] = -SEYDİ [BAKSAYDI].
saydırmak (-i, -e) *vc.* = SAYMAK.
saye Shadow; shade; protection; favour. ~ **de (bu)**, in this way/manner: ~ **nizde**, thanks to you: ~ **sinde (-in)**, *post.* [94] thanks to . . ., under the auspices of . . ., by means of . . ., due to . . . .
sayfa (*pub.*) Page; leaf. ~ **bağlamak**, set up in pages: ~ **düzeni**, page-setting. ~ **lık**, having . . . pages; making . . . pages.
sayfiye Summer house, villa; country-house. ~ **ye gitmek**, go to one's summer/country house.
saygı Respect, esteem; thoughtfulness, considera-tion. ~ **çoğulu**, editorial/royal 'we'; consideration: ~ **göstermek**, show consideration: ~ **larımı sunarım**, I present my respects, 'yours faithfully'.
saygı·değer Esteemed; excellent. ~ **lı**, respectful; dutiful; considerate; well-mannered: ~ **konuşma**,

polite conversation. ~n, esteemed; enjoying credit. ~nlaştırma, (*soc.*) rehabilitation. ~nlık, esteem, regard; prestige; (*fin.*) credit. ~sız, without regard; inconsiderate; brusque, disrespectful. ~sızlık, disrespect; lack of consideration; (*rel.*) blasphemy.
sayha Cry; clamour.
sayı (*math.*) Number; reckoning; (*pub.*) number, issue; (*sp.*) point, goal; handicap; score. ~ basamağı, (*math.*) order of numbers: ~ göstergesi, (*sp.*) score-board: ~ sıfatı, (*ling.*) numeral adjective: ~lar, (*sp.*) score: ~m suyum yok!, (*child.*) 'pax!'; count me out, I'm taking no part: ~sını Allah bilir/~ya gelmez, innumerable: ~sını hatırlamak, keep count of.
sayı·ca Numerical(ly). ~cı, *n.* (*adm.*) official teller (for animal tax); (*sp.*) lap-counter; points scorer: *a.* digital: ~ bilgisayar, digital computer.
sayıkla·ma *vn.* Delirium; talking in one's sleep; dreaming for stg. ~mak, *vi.* talk in one's sleep; be delirious; dream of stg. longed for; rave about stg.
sayı·lama (*adm.*) Statistics; (*math.*) counting: ~ +, *a.* statistical: ~ hesabı, points-scoring system. ~lamacı, statistician. ~layıcı, numbering machine. ~lı, counted; limited in number; numbered, marked; special, important: ~ gün, red-letter day. ~lma, *vn.* enumeration. ~lmak, *vp.* = SAYMAK; be counted/numbered; be esteemed; be taken into account. ~lmaz, of no account. ~m, a counting; (*adm.*) census: ~ çizelgesi, inventory: ~ dönüşü, stock turnover: ~ vergisi, (*fin.*) tax based on number of animals.
sayın Esteemed; excellent. ~ Bay..., Dear Mr....
sayı·sal Numerical; statistical. ~sız, innumerable.
sayış·ım (*fin.*) Account. ~ımcı/~man, book-keeper, accountant. ~ma, *vn.*; compensation, clearing. ~mak (-le), settle accounts with. ~tay, (*adm.*) Exchequer and Audit Department.
sayıtım Statistics. ~sal, statistical.
saykal Metal-polish. ~lamak (-i), polish/burnish (metal).
say·lamak (-i) Choose. ~lav, (*adm.*) deputy, MP.
~ma, *vn.* counting, etc. ~maca, *a.* (*fin.*) fiduciary, theoretical, nominal; rated: *adv.* by counting: ~ değer, face value. ~mak (-i), count; number; enumerate; calculate; (*fig.*) regard, assume, consider; esteem; respect; deem; suppose: saymakla bitmemek/tükenmemek, be countless/endless: sayıp dökmek, recount at length/in full detail; enumerate. ~(ma)mazlık, disrespect; irreverence. ~man, (*fin.*) accountant. ~manlık, accountancy, accounting: ~ uzmanı, chartered accountant.
saynsfikşin (*lit.*) Science-fiction.
sayrı (*med.*) Ill. ~bakıcı, nurse. ~l, morbid, pathologic. ~lanmak, vi. become ill. ~larevi, hospital. ~lı, connected with disease; pathological. ~lık, illness, disease; -pathy. ~lıkbilim, pathology. ~lıklı, morbid. ~msak, feigning illness, malingering. ~msamak, *vi.* pretend to be ill, malinger.
saystep (*sp.*) Sidestep.
sayvan (*dom.*) Awning, sunshade; canopy, tent; (*mod.*) fringe, frill; (*bio.*) auricle, external ear; (*bot.*) umbel.

saz[1] *n.* (*bot.*) Bulrush, reed. ~ ardıcı = SAZLIK: ~ benizli, pale(-faced): ~ kalem, reed-pen, calamus.
saz[2] (*Or. mus.*) Musical instrument; band, group; Oriental music. ~ çalmak, play an instrument: ~ semaisi, instrumental form: ~ söz, music and conversation; party: ~ şairi, minstrel; bard; improviser of words and music: ~ takımı, Or. music group.
sazan (*ich.*) Carp. ~giller, carps, Cyprinidae.
saz·cı (*mus.*) Instrument player; musician. ~ende, instrument player; lute-player. ~endelik, musical performance. ~lı, done to music: ~ sözlü, entertainment with music.
saz·lık (*bot.*) Reed-bed; place covered with rushes: ~ ardıcı, (*orn.*) reed warbler: ~ balıkçıl ördeği, (*orn.*) tufted duck: ~ yelvesi, (*orn.*) reed bunting. ~rengi, beige.
Sb. = (*ch.s.*) ANTIMON; (*mil.*) SUBAY.
SB = (*adm.*) SANAYİ BAKANLIĞI; (*cin.*) SİYAH-BEYAZ; SOVYETLER BİRLİĞİ; SÜMERBANK. ~F = SİYASAL BİLİMLER FAKÜLTESİ.
Sc. = (*ch.s.*) SKANDİYUM.
se (*gamb.*) Three (at dice).
Se. = (*ch.s.*) SELENYUM.
SE = SANAT ENSTİTÜSÜ.
-se *v. suf.* [130] = İSE [GELİRSE]. ~ beğenir sin(iz), you'll never guess what ....
-se-/-sa- *v. suf.* [230] Want, crave [SUSAMAK]; regard as, consider [GARİPSEMEK].
seans (*art.*) Sitting; (*adm.*) hearing, meeting; (*th.*) performance; (*gamb.*) game.
SEATO = (*South-East Asia Treaty Organization*).
Seba (*geo., his.*) Saba, Sheba.
sebat[1] Stability; firmness; determination, perseverance; constancy. ~kâr/~lı, enduring; stable; persevering, persistent. ~sız, unstable; erratic; fickle, capricious; lacking perseverance. ~ sızlık, instability; caprice.
sebayüdü (*gamb.*) Three-two (at backgammon).
sebeb- = SEBEP. ~iyet[i], ~ vermek (-e), cause, lead to, induce.
sebe[lp]b[i] Cause, factor; reason, motive; source; means; occasion. ~ aramak, search for a pretext: ~ göstermek, explain o.s.; show cause, argue: ~ olan ~siz kalsın!, curse those responsible!: ~ olm. (-e), cause, occasion, bring about/on; create: ~iyle, on account of: ~le (bu), for this reason, in consequence, therefore: ~ler, (*leg.*) grounds: ~ tendir ki (bu), it's because of this.
sebep·lenmek *vi.* Manage to earn one's living; make a small profit; get stg. out of it. ~li, having a reason/cause: ~ sebepsiz, without any reason. ~siz, without a reason/cause.
sebil Road; public fountain; free distribution of water. ~ etm., spend lavishly, squander: ~ini tahliye etm., (*obs.*) set free (a prisoner).
sebil·ci Man who distributes water gratis (but begs). ~hane, public fountain: ~ bardak/ibriği gibi, (*pej.*) people all in a row.
sebkihindi (*lit.*) A very flowery style.
sebze (*bot.*) Green plant; vegetable. ~ci(lik), (work of) greengrocer. ~lik, (*agr.*) vegetable garden;

(dom.) vegetable compartment. ~ **vat**[1], *pl.* vegetables.

sec·cade (*rel.*) Prayer-rug. ~ **cadeci**, weaver/seller of prayer rugs. ~ **de**, act of prostration in prayer: ~ **etm.**/~ **ye varmak**, perform the ritual prostrations: ~ **ye yatmak (-e)**, prostrate o.s., fall down and worship.

sec'i[i] (*lit.*) Rhyming prose.

seciye Moral quality; character; natural disposition. ~ **li**, good; reliable, trustworthy. ~ **siz**, vicious; unreliable.

seç·ene[i]k[gi] *n.* Alternative. ~ **i**, choosing, selection. ~ **ici**, selector; selective: ~ **ler kurulu**, (*adm.*) selection committee/jury/panel. ~ **icilik**, selection.

seçik (*phil.*) Clear; distinct; sharp; definite. ~ **lik**, distinctness, sharpness.

seçil·mek *vp.* = SEÇMEK. Be eligible/chosen/selected. ~ **men**, (*adm.*) delegate: ~ **ler (kurulu)**, delegation. ~ **miş**, picked, choice; left-over, second-class.

seçim Choice, selection; evaluation, perception; (*pol.*) election. ~ **bölge/çevre/dairesi**, constituency: ~ **dönemi**, period between elections: ~ **heyeti**, electoral college: ~ **kurulu**, electoral commission: ~ **kütüğü**, electoral roll/register: ~ **sandığı**, ballot-box: ~ **suçları**, electoral offences: ~ **tutanağı**, poll declaration: ~ **yapmak**, elect. ~ **li(lik)**, optional/(-ity).

seç·ki (*lit.*) Anthology. ~ **kin**, choice, select; exclusive; conspicuous, distinguished: ~ **konuşmak**, (*ling.*) articulate (clearly): ~ **ler**, élite. ~ **kinci(lik)**, (*soc.*) élit·ist/(-ism). ~ **kinleşmek**, *vi.* become select, etc. ~ **kinlik**, selectness, exclusivity, etc.

seç·me *vn.* Choosing; choice; election; perception: *a.* select, choice: ~ **hakkı**, right of choice; (*fin.*) option: ~ **yarış**, (*sp.*) qualifying race, etc.: ~ **ler**, (*lit.*) anthology; selections. ~ **mece**, (*fin.*) with the right to pick and choose. ~ **meci(lik)**, (*phil.*) eclectic(ism). ~ **mek (-i)**, choose, select; elect; perceive; distinguish, make out: **seçip toplamak**, compile. ~ **meli**, free to choose; optional, selective. ~ **men**, (*pol.*) elector: ~ **kütüğü**, register of electors: ~ **ler**, electorate; constituents. ~ **menlik**, elector's duty. ~ **mez**, neutral, non-selective. ~ **tirmek (-i, -e)**, *vc.*

sed = SET. ~ **a(lı)** = SADA(LI).

sedef (*bio.*) *n.* (Shell producing) mother-of-pearl. *a.* Made of mother-of-pearl. ~ **hastalığı**, (*med.*) psoriasis. ~ **çi**, worker in mother-of-pearl. ~ **li**, made of/decorated with mother-of-pearl. ~ **otu**[nu], (*bot.*) rue: ~ **giller**, Rutaceae, rue family.

sedi·l (*ling.*) ~ **işareti**, cedilla ( ). ~ **mantasyon**, (*bio.*) sedimentation,

sedir[1] *n.* (*dom.*) Divan, sofa.

sedir[2] *n.* (*bot.*) Cedar (tree).

sedye (*med.*) Stretcher; (*obs.*) sedan-chair. ~ **ci**, stretcher-bearer. ~ **lik**, stretcher-case.

sefa = SAFA. ~ **het**[i], dissipation, debauchery.

-sefal *suf.* (*bio.*) -cephal·ic/-ous.

sefalet[i] Poverty; misery; 'a dog's life'. ~ **çekmek**, suffer privation; ~ **içinde**, down and out, down at heel: ~ **e düşmek**, be reduced to poverty, 'go to the dogs'.

sefalo- *pref.* (*bio.*) Cephalo-.

sefaret[i] (*adm.*) Ambassadorship; embassy, legation. ~ **hane**, (*arch.*) embassy (building), legation.

sefer Journey, voyage, expedition; (*mil.*) campaign; state of war; time, occurrence. ~ **(bu)**, this time: ~ **açmak**, open hostilities, campaign: ~ **ayı** = SAFER: ~ **etm.**, go on a journey: ~ **heyeti**, (*mil.*) expedition: ~ **TASI**: ~ **e gitmek**, go to war, start a campaign.

sefer·ber Mobilized for war: ~ **etm.**, use all one's resources (to do stg.): ~ **olm.**, undertake stg. with all one's resources. ~ **berlik**, mobilization. ~ **i**, relating to travel/campaigns; (*rel.*) travelling and so exempt from fasting: ~ **kuvvet**, (*mil.*) expeditionary force. ~ **lik**, (related to) travel/campaigning. ~ **tası**[m], travelling food-box (with superimposed compartments): ~ **gibi**, (house) with one room on each floor.

sef·ih Spendthrift, prodigal; dissolute, abandoned. ~ **il**, poor, miserable; abject, destitute.

sefine Ship.

sefir (*adm.*) Ambassador. ~ **e**, ambassadress, lady ambassador; ambassador's wife.

segâh (*Or. mus.*) A typical melody.

seg·man (*mot.*) Piston-ring. ~ **mentasyon**, (*zoo.*) cleavage.

seğir·dim (*sp.*) Running race; (*mil.*) recoil (of a gun); incline of a mill-race: ~ **yapmak**, recoil: ~ **yolu**, narrow access-road. ~ **me**, *vn.* vibration; tremor; nervous twitch. ~ **mek**, *vi.* tremble; twitch nervously. ~ **tme**, *vn.*; fishing-line used without bait. ~ **tmek**, *vi.* dash, run; hasten.

seğmen Armed young man, in national costume, taking part in festivals/processions.

seher Time just before dawn; early morning.

seh'im[mi] Lot, share, portion; (*fin.*) treasury bond.

seh'iv[vi] Minor mistake; inadvertence; (*eng.*) sag.

sehpa Tripod; three-legged stool/table; (*art.*) easel; (*leg.*) gallows. ~ **ya çekmek**, hang s.o.

sehv- = SEHiv. ~ **en**, inadvertently, by mistake.

sek (*cul.*) Dry, *sec* (wine); champagne. ~ **ant**, (*math.*) secant.

-sek/-sak *v. suf.* [100, etc.] = isE [GELiRSEK].

sek·ban (*his.*) Type of Janissary; hunting-dogs keeper. ~ **endiz**, (*ast.*) Saturn.

sekene *pl.* = SAKiN. Inhabitants.

seki[1] *n.* Pedestal; platform; stone seat; (*agr., arch.*) terrace. ~ **lik**, (*sp.*) stand, terrace.

seki[2] *n.* (*zoo.*) White sock (of a horse). ~ **li**, with a sock.

sekincilik (*phil.*) Tranquility, perfection.

sekiz (*math.*) Eight. ~ **+**, *a.* Eight; figure-of-eight: ~ **de bir**, one eighth. ~ **er**, eight each; eight at a time. ~ **gen**, octagon(al). ~ **inci (8.)**, eighth. ~ **kollu**, (*zoo.*) octopod. ~ **li**, having eight (parts); (*gamb.*) eight (at cards); (*mus.*) octave, octet. ~ **lik**, containing eight parts; worth eight units; (*mus.*) quaver; (*ast.*) octant. ~ **yüzlü**, octahedron. [*Further phrases* = BEŞ].

sek·me *vn.* Hop; leap; ricochet. ~ **mek**, *vi.* hop; leap; run in a series of jumps; ricochet; miss. ~ **men**, (*dom.*) stool; step.

sekonder Secondary.

sekoya (*bot.*) Sequoia tree.

sekreter (*adm.*) Secretary. ~ **kuşu**, (*orn.*) secretary bird. ~**lik**, secretary's work/office; secretariat. ~**ya**, secretariat.

seks (*bio.*) Sex. ~**apel**, sex-appeal.

seksen (*math.*) Eighty. ~ **kapının ipini çekmek**, knock at many doors; try many possibilities: ~**de bir**, one eightieth: ~**ini bulmak**, reach the age of eighty. ~**er**, eighty each; eighty at a time. ~**inci** (80.), eightieth. ~**lik**, containing eighty parts; worth eighty units; octogenarian. [*Further phrases* = KIRK].

sek·siyoner (*el.*) Sector switch. ~**soloji**, sexology. ~**stant**, (*ast.*) sextant. ~**süel(ite)**, (*bio.*) sexual(ity).

sekte Pause; interval; stoppage; interruption; stagnation; (*med.*) apoplexy. ~ **vermek**, relax; give a respite: ~ **vurmak**, interrupt: ~**ye uğramak**, stop.

sekte·dar Defective; disturbed, interrupted; prejudiced. ~**ikalp**, (*med., obs.*) heart failure. ~**lenmek**, *vp.* be interrupted.

sektir·me *vn.* Causing to rebound/ricochet. ~**mek** (-**i**), *vc.* = SEKMEK; cause to hop/rebound; cause to miss. ~**memek**, be extremely careful, miss nothing.

sektör (*math.*) Sector; (*fin.*) sector.

selⁱ (*geo.*) Torrent, cataract; inundation, flood. ~ +, *a.* flood; (*geol.*) alluvial. ~ **basmak**, deluge: ~ **gider kum kalır**, don't rely on temporary circumstances: ~ **götürmek** (-**i**), rain very heavily; be flooded: ~ **kili**, (*geol.*) boulder-clay: ~ ~**i götürmek**, be inundated: ~ **yatağı**, flood-plain: ~**i suyu kalmamış**, (*cul.*) having no juice/liquid. -**sel**/-**sal**/-**sul**/-**sül** *a. suf.* [65] [MADENSEL].

selam Salutation; greeting; compliments; (*mil.*) salute. ~ **almak**, acknowledge a salute/greeting: ~ **dur!**, (*mil.*) present arms!: ~ **manga/takımı**, (*mil.*) firing party/squad: ~ **sabah!**, how are you?: ~ **söylemek/yollamak** (-**le**), send one's compliments/greetings (by s.o.): ~ **vermek**, greet, salute; (*rel.*) complete the NAMAZ: ~ **verip borçlu çıkmak**, get lumbered with a job just because you greet s.o.: ~**a durmak**, rise respectfully (to receive a superior's greeting); (*mil.*) salute: ~**ı sabahı kesmek** (-**le**), terminate relations with s.o.; ignore s.o. completely.

selametⁱ Safety, security; freedom from danger/illness; soundness; liberation; successful result; (*ling.*) free from defect/error. ~ **bulmak**/~**e çıkmak**, gain safety; turn out well: ~**le**, goodbye and good luck! ~**lemek** (-**i**), see s.o. off; wish s.o. a safe journey.

selam·lamak (-**i**) Salute; greet. ~**lanmak**, *vp.* ~**laşmak** (-**le**), greet each other; be on nodding terms. ~**lık**, (*dom.*) men's quarters (in a large Muslim house); (*his.*) Sultan's Friday procession to the mosque. ~**ünaleyküm!**, peace be on you!: ~ **demeden**, without so much as a by-your-leave; brusquely, tactlessly: ~ **kör kadı**, downright, forthright.

Selani'kᵍⁱ (*geo.*) Salonica, Thessaloniki. ~ **dönmesi**, (descendant of) Jewish convert to Islam in 17th century: ~ **Yahudisi**, a Salonica Jew; (*pej.*) coward. ~**li**, inhabitant of Salonica; Salonica Jew.

selasetⁱ (*ling.*) Fluency of speech; (*lit.*) smoothness of style. ~**le**, fluently.

selatin *pl.* = SULTAN. *n.* Sovereigns, sultans. *a.* Imperial; grand: ~ **camileri**, (*rel.*) mosques built by the sultans: ~ **meyhane**, (*his.*) type of large wine-shop.

Selçuk (*his.*) Seljuk; (*geo.*) Ephesus. ~**i**/~**lu**, (*ethn.*) a Seljuk.

sele¹ *n.* Flat wicker basket.

sele² (*sp.*) Bicycle saddle. ~ **altı çanta**, saddle-bag.

se·le³ *n.* = SERE. ~**lef**, predecessor. ~**lek**, (*dial.*) generous. ~**len**, sound. ~**lenli**, (*ling.*) voiced consonant.

selek·siyon Selection. ~**tör**, (*agr.*) winnowing device; (*el.*) selector; (*mot.*) dip-switch.

selentereler (*zoo.*) Coelenterata.

selenyum (*chem.*) Selenium.

selika (*lit.*) Innate ability to speak/write well.

selim Sound; honest; perfect; (*med.*) benignant.

selinti (Bed of//debris left by) small torrent.

selis (*ling.*) Fluent; (*lit.*) easy-flowing (style).

sellemehüsselam Without ceremony, rudely. ~ **girişmek**, butt in.

selo·fan Cellophane. ~**teyp**, Sellotape.

sel'pᵇ¹ Seizing; depriving. ~ **etm.** (-**i**), seize, deprive; ruin.

selülo·i'tᵈⁱ (*chem.*) Celluloid. ~**z(ik)**, cellu·lose/(-losic).

sel·va Rain-forest. ~**vi(lik)** = SERVİ.

selviçe (*naut.*) Flexible rope; running rigging.

semᵐⁱ (*chem.*) Poison. ~**dar**, poisonous.

sema¹ *n.* Sky; heaven. ~**vi**, celestial; heavenly.

sema¹·² *n.* Hearing; mention; (*rel.*) Mevlevi dervish dance. ~**hane**, (*rel.*) hall for dervish music/dancing.

Semadirek (*geo.*) Island of Samothrace.

semafor (*naut.*) Semaphore; (*mot.*) emergency road signs.

semahatⁱ Generosity, munificence; philanthropy.

semai (*Or. mus.*) Solemn folk tune. ~ **kahvesi**, coffee-house where folk-singers meet.

se·man (*bio.*) Cementum. ~**mantem**, (*ling.*) semanteme. ~**manti'k**ᵍⁱ, (*ling.*) semantics. ~**maver**, (*dom.*) samovar.

sembolü Symbol. ~**ik**, symbolic(al). ~**ist**, symbolist. ~**ize**, ~ **etm.**, symbolize. ~**izm**, symbolism. ~**leşmek**, *vi.* become a symbol.

seme Stupid, foolish; perplexed. ~ **tavuk**, stupidity. -**semek**/-**samak** *v. suf.* [230] Think/consider . . .; endeavour/try to . . . [YEĞNİSEMEK].

semen Stoutness. ~ **bağlamak/peyda etm.**, grow stout.

semen·der (*zoo.*) Salamander. ~**tasyon**, (*min.*) cementation. ~**tit**ⁱ, cementite.

semer Pack-saddle; HAMAL's pad; (*geol.*) anticline; (*sl.*) buttock. ~ **vurmak**, fasten on pack-saddle. ~**ci(lik)**, (work of) saddle-maker/-seller.

semere Fruit; profit, result. ~ **vermek**, be fruitful. ~**dar**/~**li**, fruitful; profitable.

Semerkant (*geo.*) Samarkand.

semer·lemek (-**i**) Saddle a pack-animal. ~**li**, (animal) with a pack-saddle; (porter) with a pad; with a hump; (*fig.*) coarse, vulgar. ~**otu**ⁿᵘ, (*bot.*) great reedmace.

sem'i'ⁱ Sense of hearing; listening, acoustics.

semih Liberal; generous.

seminer (*ed.*) Seminar; course; conference.
semir·gin Lazy because fat; fat because lazy. ~**mek**, *vi.* grow fat. ~**tmek (-i)**, *vc.* make fat; (*live.*) fatten; (*agr.*) manure.
semiz Fat, fleshy. ~**ce**, rather fat. ~**le(ş)mek**, *vi.* grow fat. ~**lik**, fatness. ~**otu**nu, (*bot.*) purslane. ~**otugiller**, (*bot.*) Portulaceae, purslane family.
sem·pati Sympathy; pleasantness: ~ **duymak**, find pleasant/congenial: ~ **sinirleri**, (*bio.*) sympathetic nerves. ~**patik**, *a.* pleasant, congenial: *n.* (*psy.*) sympathy: ~ **sinir sistemi**, autonomic nervous system. ~**patizan**, (*psy.*) sympathizer. ~**pozyum**, (*ed.*, *lit.*) symposium. ~**ptomatoloji**, (*med.*) symptomatology.
semti District, neighbourhood; quarter where s.o. lives. ~ ~, in certain places; in every quarter: ~**e gitmek**, go home: ~**i meçhule gitmiş**, 'address unknown': ~**ine uğramamak (-in)**, not go near . . .. ~**ikadem**, (*ast.*) nadir. ~**ürres**, (*ast.*) zenith.
sen *pron.* [67] Thou; *s.* you. ~ **ağa, ben ağa, koyunları kim sağa?**, we're both gentlemen, so who'll do the work?: ~ **beni aptal yerine koyuyorsun**, you take me for a fool: ~ **de, ben de**, both you and I: ~ **giderken ben geliyordum**, I've forgotten more than you ever knew; you can't take me in: ~ **işine bak!**, mind your own business!: ~ **kendini pabucu büyüğe okut!**, you must be crazy (to do such a thing)!: ~ **kim oluyorsun?**, who do you think you are to . . .?: ~ **misin . . .?**, so it's you . . ., is it?: ~ **olsan ne yaparsın?**, if it were you what would you do?: ~ **onu unut!**, you'll never see that again!, forget it!: ~ **onun bağırıp çağırmasına bakma!**, his bark is worse than his bite!: ~ **paşa ben paşa bu ineği kim sağa? =** AĞA: ~ **sağ ben selamet!**, well that's that!; well we've seen the last of that!: ~ ~ **ol!**, now don't forget!; be careful!: ~ **vız gelirsin!**, you be blowed!: = SANA.

sen-: ~**ce**, according to you; in your opinion: ~**de**, *locative*, on/with you: ~**den**, *ablative*, by/from/through you: ~**den illallah!**, I'm sick of/fed up with you!: ~**i**, *accusative*, thee, you: ~**i afacan** ~**i**, [68] you cheeky little urchin, you!: ~**i gidi** ~**i!**, you scoundrel!, you little rascal!: ~**i gören hacı olur!**, you're quite a stranger!: ~**i köftehor!**, you lucky blighter!: ~**in**, *possessive a.* thy, your: ~**in ağzında bir bakla var!**, you're keeping stg. back/hiding stg.: ~**in anlıyacağın**, you know what I mean; to cut a long story short: ~**in canın can da benimki patlıcan mı?**, why should you be treated better than me?: ~ **in eline su dökemez**, he can't hold a candle to you: ~**in ne üstüne lazım?**, what's that got to do with you?: ~**in olsun!**, keep it!: ~**inki**, *possessive pron.* thine, yours: ~**inki can . . .** = SENİN CANIN . . .: ~**inle**, with thee/you: ~**inle bir daha konuşursam iki olsun**, I'll never speak to you again: ~**inle paylaşacak kozum var**, I've got a bone to pick with you.
sena Praise, eulogy. ~ **etm.**, praise.
senaryo (*th.*, *cin.*) Scenario, screenplay, script. ~ **yazarı**, script-writer. ~**cu**, (*cin.*) continuity-man.
sena·to (*adm.*, *ed.*) Senate. ~**tör(lük)**, (rank/duties of) senator.
senbernar (*live.*) St. Bernard dog.

sen·ce/ ~**de/** ~**den** *pron.* [67] = SEN-.
sendelemek *vi.* Totter, stagger; (*fig.*) hesitate.
sendilkği (*fin.*) Official receiver, public trustee. ~**a**, (*soc.*) trade-union: ~ **temsilcisi**, union agent, shop-steward. ~**acı(lık)**, trade-union·ist/(-ism). ~**alı**, belonging to a union, card-carrying.
sene (*ast.*) Year. ~**i hicri**, year of the Hegira era: ~**i kameriye**, lunar year. ~**lik**, lasting . . . years; of . . . years. ~**vi**, annual.
-sene/-sana/-senize/-sanıza *v. suf.* [271] *Forming an emphatic imperative.* Do . . .!; if only you would . . .! [GELSENE].
senelkği (*dom.*) Pine-wood pitcher/jug.
seneltdi (*leg.*) Written proof, document; title-deed; (*fin.*) bond, voucher, receipt. ~ **etm.**, hold/put forward as proof: ~ **sepet**, by way of proof: ~ **iniz var mı?**, do you have positive proof that . . .?
senet·leşmek (-le) Exchange documents of proof. ~**li**, based on/accompanied by written proof: ~ **sepetli**, with absolute proof. ~**siz**, without written proof: ~ **sepetsiz**, without any receipt/proof.
senfo·ni (*mus.*) Symphony. ~**nik**, symphonic.
se·ni(n) *a.*, *pron.* [67] = SEN-. - ~**nize**, *v. suf.* [271] = -SENE.
sen·kop (*mus.*) Syncopation. ~**kron**, *a.* synchronous. ~**kronizasyon**, synchronization. ~**kronize**, synchronized. ~**kronizm**, synchronism.
senlibenli Hail-fellow-well-met; unpretentiously, informally. ~ **konuşmak**, have a confidential talk; be intimate.
sensen (*cul.*) Chewing-gum to remove breath smells.
sensiz Without thee/you.
sent (*math.*) Cent.
sen·taks (*ling.*) Syntax. ~**tetik**, (*chem.*) synthetic. ~**tez** synthesis.
sen·tro (*bio.*) Centro-. ~**trum**, (*bio.*) centrum.
separa·syon Separation. ~**tör** (*ind.*) separator.
sepelkği Pivot of a millstone.
sepe-lek/ ~**rek** = SERSEM.
sepeti Basket; (item made of) wickerwork; wicker fish-trap; ~ **dolusu**, basketful: ~ **havası çalmak (-e)**, (*sl.*) show s.o. he is not wanted; get rid of/dismiss s.o.: ~ **örgü(sü)**, basketry, basketwork: ~ **sandık**, leather-covered basketwork trunk: ~**e atmak**, throw away; (*sp.*) shoot: ~**te pamuk**, (*jok.*) knowledge.
sepet·çi Basket-maker/-seller: ~ **söğütü**, (*bot.*) common osier. ~**çilik**, basket-making/-selling. ~**kulpu**nu, (*arch.*) broad arch. ~**leme**, *vn.* ~**lemek (-i)**, put in a basket; (*sl.*) get rid of s.o. unpleasantly; dismiss, sack. ~**lenmek**, *vp.* (*sl.*) be dismissed. ~**li**, with a basket; = SENETLİ. ~**lik**, *a.* suitable for basket-making: *n.* (*bio.*) front of the abdomen. ~**topu**nu, (*sp.*) basketball.
sepi Dressing for hides; tanning; currying; dyeing of furs. ~ **yeri**, tannery.
sepi·ci Tanner, currier. ~**cilik**, tanning. ~**lemek (-i)**, tan; curry; prepare furs. ~**li**, tanned (hide); prepared and dyed (fur).
sepken Stg. sprinkled; rain-shower; (light) snowfall.
septi·k (*phil.*) Sceptical. ~**sizm**, (*phil.*) scepticism.
septisemi (*med.*) Septicaemia.
sepya (*art.*) Sepia (drawing).

ser[1] (*adm.*) Head; chief; top; end. ~ **vermek**, devote one's life to . . .: ~ **vermek sır vermemek**, better die than betray a secret: ~ **de . . . var**, well, after all . . .; what do you expect of . . .: ~ **den mi geçmeli yardan mı?**, which of two difficult alternatives to choose?

ser[2]/~ **a** (*agr.*) Greenhouse; hothouse. ~ **acı(lık)**, (work of) greenhouse-maker; greenhouse vegetable-grower. ~ **a**[l]**k**[ğı], (*geo.*) serac. ~ **ami**[l]**k**[ği], *n.* (*art.*) ceramics, pottery: *a.* ceramic. ~ **amikçi(lik)**, (work of) ceramist, potter.

sera[l]**p**[bı] Mirage.

serapa From head to foot; entirely, utterly.

serasker (*his.*) Commander-in-chief, Minister of War.

serbaz Bold, fearless.

serbest[i] Free; independent; free-lance; unreserved, frank; (*fin.*) competitive; (*eng.*) disengaged. ~ **askılı anten**, (*rad.*) whip aerial: ~ **atış**, (*sp.*) free shot: ~ **bırakmak**, release from: ~ **bölge**, (*fin.*) free zone: ~ **düşmeli tokmak**, (*eng.*) drop-hammer: ~ **girişim**, (*fin.*) free enterprise: ~ **güreş**, (*sp.*) all-in wrestling, catch-as-catch-can: ~ **İrlanda**, *pr.n.* (*geo.*) Irish Free State: ~ **liman**, (*fin.*) free port: ~ **su**, (*eng.*) free/gravitational water: ~ **vuruş**, (*sp.*) free kick: ~ **yürüyüş**, stroll.

serbest·çe Freely, without constraint. ~ **i**, freedom. ~ **lemek**, *vi.* be free of restraints. ~ **lik**, freedom, liberty; independence; frankness.

serçe (*orn.*) House-sparrow. ~ **den korkan darı ekmez**, s.o. too fearful to achieve his aims. ~ **giller**, (*orn.*) Passeridae. ~ **parma**[l]**k**[ğı], (*bio.*) little finger/toe.

serçin *n.* (*tex.*) Shuttle bobbin. *a.* Choice, select; the best.

serdar (*mil.*) Commander-in-chief; general; sirdar.

serdengeçti (*mil.*) Suicide squad; (*fig.*) dare-devil. ~ **lik**, mad enterprise, foolhardiness.

serd[l]**etmek**[eder] (-**i**) Put forward; expound.

serdirmek (-**i**, -**e**) *vc.* = SERMEK.

serdümen (*naut.*) Quartermaster, coxswain; chief petty-officer.

sere Span between thumb and first finger.

sere[l]**k**[ği] Display; stall.

sere·moni Ceremony. ~ **n**, (*naut.*) yard, boom, spar; (*arch.*) door-post. ~ **na**[l]**t**[dı] (*mus.*) serenade.

serencam Result; end; event.

serendi[l]**p**[bi] (*geo.*) Sri Lanka, Ceylon.

sergen (*dom.*) Shelf; display cabinet.

sergerde Chief; leader (of bandits, guerrillas). ~ **lik**, chieftainship.

sergi Stg. spread out; mat/rug (for displaying goods); temporary stall; shop-front; exhibition, display. ~ **sermek**, spread out (to dry/display).

sergi·ci Exhibitor. ~ **evi**, (*art.*) gallery; exhibition hall. ~ **leme**, *vn.*; exhibition; (*lit.*) presentation. ~ **lemek** (-**i**), exhibit, display, show; (*th.*) present. ~ **lenmek**, *vp.* be exhibited; be put on display. ~ **li**, ~ **satak**, fair. ~ **lik**, *a.* suitable for display: *n.* display-cabinet. ~ **n**, displayed; ill in bed: ~ **vermek**, (*med.*) take to one's bed. ~ **yeri**, gallery.

sergüzeşt[i] Adventure. ~ **çi**, adventurer.

seri[1] *n.* Series. ~ (**halinde**) **imalat**, (*ind.*) serial/mass production: ~ **ye açılım**, (*math.*) serial development.

seri[i 2] *a.* Quick, fast, swift. ~ **ateşli top**, (*mil.*) quick-firing gun. ~ **an**, quickly, swiftly, fast.

serigrafi (*pub.*) Silk-screen printing.

seril·i Stretched/spread out (on the ground). ~ **mek** (-**e**), *vp.* = SERMEK; lie at full length; fall ill; drop in a faint: **serilip serpilmek**, stretch o.s. out at full length; grow, develop: **serilip yatmak**, lie down limply.

serim (*th.*) Exposition.

serin (*met.*) Cool; chill. ~ **kanlı(lık)**, (*fig.*) calm/(-**ness**), cool-headed(ness). ~ **lemek**/ ~ **leşmek**, (*met.*) become cool; (*fig.*) console o.s., become calm. ~ **lenmek**, *vi.* feel cool. ~ **letici**, *a.* cooling: *n.* cooler. ~ **letmek** (-**i**), make cool; cool down. ~ **lik**, coolness; chilliness; calm: ~ **vermek**, make cool; (*fig.*) distract, console.

serkeş Unruly, rebellious. ~ **lik**, disobedience; rebelliousness.

serlevha (*pub.*) Title, heading, caption.

sermaye (*fin.*) Capital; stock; initial cost; (*ed.*) acquired knowledge; (*sl.*) prostitute. ~ **komak**, invest capital: ~ **ye çevirmek**, capitalize: ~ **yi kediye yükletmek**, (*jok.*) squander one's fortune, become bankrupt.

sermaye·ci (*fin.*) Investor, shareholder. ~ **cilik**, investment, capitalism. ~ **dar**, capitalist; investor: ~ **sistemi**, capitalism. ~ **li**, having a capital of . . .. ~ **siz**, without capital; (*fig.*) without attainments.

sermek (-**i**) Spread out on the ground, strew; spread over; beat down to the ground; (*fig.*) neglect. **sere serpe**, free and unrestrained; nonchalant.

sermest[i] Drunk; (*fig.*) intoxicated (with joy, etc.).

ser·muharrir (*pub.*, *obs.*) Editor-in-chief. ~ **müret-tip**, chief compositor.

ser·om = SERUM. ~ **pantin**, (*child.*) streamer; (*eng.*) pipe coil; (*geol.*) serpentine.

serp·elemek *vi.* Fall (like rain); be sprinkled. ~ **ici**, (water-)sprinkler. ~ **ilme**, *vn.* ~ **ilmek**, *vp.* be sprinkled: *vi.* stretch o.s. out to rest; (child) grow apace. ~ **inme**, dispersion. ~ **inti**, dispersion; drizzle; spray; traces of stg. left behind; after-effects, repercussions. ~ **iştirme**, *vn.* ~ **iştirmek** (-**i**, -**e**), sprinkle in small quantities; (*cul.*) dredge; distribute/scatter (money) in small amounts; (rain) just begin to fall. ~ **me**, *vn.*; a sprinkling: *a.* sprinkled about/with: ~ **ağ**, cast-net. ~ **mek** (-**i**, -**e**), sprinkle lightly; scatter by hand: *vi.* fall in a sprinkle. ~ **tirmek** (-**i**, -**e**), *vc.*

sersefil Very miserable/wretched.

sersem Stunned; bewildered; scatter-brained, dozy; foolish. ~ **sepelek/seperek**, dreamily, stupidly.

sersem·lemek/ ~ **leşmek** *vi.* Be stunned/stupefied; lose one's head; become silly/absent-minded/forgetful. ~ **letici**, astounding; bewildering. ~ **letmek** (-**i**), stupefy, daze; bewilder; astound; dope, drug. ~ **lik**, stupefaction; confusion; stupidity; 'wool-gathering'.

serseri *n.* Vagabond; tramp. *a.* Vague, aimless. ~ **ce**, like a vagabond. ~ **leşmek**, *vi.* be(come) a vagabond. ~ **lik**, vagabondage; vagrancy.

sert[i] Hard; stiff; harsh; severe, drastic; brusque,

sertdoku 416 **seve**

abrupt; violent; potent; (*bio.*) sclerotic; (*cin.*) contrasty. ~ **alçıtaşı**, (*geol.*) anhydrite: ~ **amir**, disciplinarian: ~ **banket**, (*mot.*) hard shoulder: ~ **buğday**, (*bot.*) macaroni wheat: ~ **çelik**, (*eng.*) tempered steel: ~ **damak**, (*bio.*) hard palate: ~ **esmek**, (wind) bluster: ~ **kabuk (bağlamak)**, (*cul.*) (form a) crust: ~ **kil tabakası**, (*geol.*) hardpan: ~ **lastik**, ebonite: ~ **lehim**, (*min.*) braze, hard solder: ~ **lehimleme**, brazing: ~ **pirinç**, (*min.*) hard brass: ~ **rüzgâr**, (*met.*) violent wind: ~ **ses**, harsh noise, blaring: ~ **su**, (*chem.*) hard water: ~ **tabaka**, (*bio.*) sclera, white of the eye: ~ **ünsüzler**, (*ling.*) hard consonants: ~ **yapraklı**, (*bot.*) sclerophyll: ~ **zar**, (*bio.*) dura mater. ~**doku**nu, (*bot.*) sclerenchyma. ~**elmek (-e)**, strengthen; behave harshly/severely; stand fast (against).
sertifika(syon) (*adm.*, *ed.*) Certifi·cate/(-cation).
sert·lenmek *vi.* Become hard, etc. ~**leşme**, *vn.*; (*ling.*) hardening: ~ **noktası**, (*phys.*) solidification point. ~**leşmek**, *vi.* become hard/severe/violent; harden. ~**leştirici**, (*min.*) hardener. ~**leştirme**, *vn.* hardening. ~ **leştirmek (-i)**, harden. ~**lik**, hardness; harshness; violence; potency: ~**i gidermek**, (*min.*) soften.
seru·m (*bio.*) Serum. ~**s**, serous.
serüven·(cilik) (Love of) adventure. ~**ci**, adventurer.
servet[i] Riches, wealth. ~ **beyanı**, (*fin.*) tax return: ~ **vergisi**, capital levy, wealth tax. ~**li**, wealthy.
servi (*bot.*) Cypress(-tree). ~ **boylu**, tall and slender, graceful. ~**giller**, Cupressaceae, cypress family. ~**lik**, cypress-grove.
servis Service; (*adm.*) operation, department; waiting (at table). ~ **bölgesi**, (*mot.*) service area: ~ **dışı yapmak**, put out of action/service: ~ **istasyonu**, (*mot.*) service-station, garage: ~ **kapısı**, service door, tradesmen's entrance: ~**e girmek**, come into operation/service; be commissioned: ~**i kaldırmak**, axe (a worker).
servo·fren (*mot.*) Servo-brake. ~**kumanda**, servo-control. ~**mekanizma**, servo-mechanism.
seryum (*chem.*) Cerium.
serzeniş Reproach; reprimand. ~**kâr**, reproachful.
ses Sound; noise; voice; cry; (*ling.*) phoneme. ~ +, *a.* Sound-; sonic-; acoustic; audio-: ~ **ahengi**, (*ling.*) euphony: ~ **aksettirmek**, echo: ~ **alma aygıtı**, (tape-)recorder: ~ **almak**, record: ~ALTI; ~ **bandı**, tape: ~BİLGİSİ: ~ **benzeyişi**, (*ling.*) assonance: ~ **bozulması**, (*rad.*) wow: ~ **büyüteci**, (*rad.*) amplifier: ~ **çıkarmadan**, without any fuss/ more ado: ~ **çıkarmak**, speak; blab: ~ **çıkarmamak (-e)**, say nothing; approve, condone: ~ **çıkmak**, be heard; become known; be rumoured: ~ **çıkmamak**, no news come: ~ **dağılımı**, (*phys.*) acoustics: ~ **değişmesi**, breaking (boy's voice): ~ **duvarı**, (*phys.*) sound barrier: ~ **düşmesi**, (*ling.*) elision: ~ **etm.**, call out: ~ **geçirmez**, soundproof: ~ **ikizlenmesi**, (*ling.*) gemination: ~ **iskandili**, (*naut.*) echo-sounder: ~ **kakışımı**, cacophony: ~ **karşılanması**, (*ling.*) phonetic substitution: ~ **kası**, (*bio.*) vocal cord: ~ **kaydedici**, recorder, dictaphone: ~ **kirişleri**, (*bio.*) vocal cords: ~ **kuşağı**, (*cin.*) sound-track; audiotape: ~ **makinesi**, tape-

recorder: ~ **olmamak**, be silent: ~ **oluşumu**, phonation: ~ **operatörü**, (*cin.*) sound technician: ~ **patlaması**, (*aer.*) sonic boom: ~ **sada çıkmamak**, no news emerge; get no reaction: ~ **sada yok**, not a sound to be heard: ~ **sapması**, (*phys.*) diacoustics: ~ **soluk**, sound, noise; news: ~ **türemesi**, (*ling.*) adventitious sound: ~ÜSTÜ: ~ **vermek**, give out a sound; say stg.: ~ **vermemek**, not answer (when called): ~ **yitimi**, loss of voice: ~ **yolu**, (*bio.*) voice passage; (*cin.*) sound track: ~**i çıkmamak**, keep silent: ~**i çıkmaz**, taciturn: ~**i kesilmek**, be reduced to silence: ~**i tutulmak**, become hoarse: ~**i yerleştirmek**, throw one's voice: ~**ine güvenen** borazancı başı olur, by all means do it if you think you can: ~**ini kes!**, shut up!: ~**ini kesmek**, cease speaking; become silent: ~**ini kısmak**, lower one's voice.
ses(b). = SESBİLİM.
ses·alıcı Tape-recorder. ~**altı**, (*phys.*) subsonic: ~**bilgisel**, (*ling.*) phonetic. ~**bilgisi**, phonetics: ~**bilim**, phonology; acoustics. ~**bilimci**, phonologist. ~**birim(sel)**, phone·me/(-mic). ~**borusu**, megaphone. ~**büyütür**, microphone. ~**çi**, (*rad.*) sound-technician. ~**çil**, (*ling.*) phonetic: ~ **alfabe** phonetic alphabet. ~**dağılımı** = SES. ~**elim** (*phys.*) resonance. ~**lem**, (*ling.*) syllable. ~**leme** *vn.* intonation. ~**lemek (-i)**, hearken, give ear: ~**lendirmek (-i)**, *vc.*; record (music, etc.). ~**lenme** *vn.*; remark: ~ **durumu**, (*ling.*) vocative case: ~**lenmek (-e)**, call out (to s.o.); reply (to s.o. calling). ~**li**, having a . . . voice; noisy: ~ **film** sinema, (*cin.*) talking film, talkie: ~ **harf**, (*ling.*) vowel. ~**litaş**, (*geol.*) phonolite. ~**siz**, dumb, voiceless; mute; quiet; silent; (*fig.*) meek; (*mus.*) having a poor tone: ~ **çıngıraklı yılan**, (*zoo.*) bushmaster: ~ **film**, (*cin.*) silent film: ~ **harf**, (*ling.*) consonant: ~ **kuğu (kuşu)**, (*orn.*) mute swan: ~ **oyun**, (*th.* mime: ~ **sadasız**, silently, stealthily. ~**sizleşmek** *vi.* be(come) silent. ~**sizlik**, quietness, silence tranquillity; (*fig.*) meekness. ~**teli**, (*bio.*) voca cord. ~**teş**, (*ling.*) homophone. ~**üstü**, (*phys.* ultrasonic, supersonic. ~**yayar**, loudspeaker: ~**yazar**, phonograph.
set[i] Barrier, obstacle; dam, bank; earthworks parapet; (*agr.*) terrace; (*geo.*) bar. ~ **çekmek** strengthen, bank up: ~ **gölü**, (*geo.*) barrier lake: ~ **resifi**, (*geo.*) barrier reef.
set·an (*chem.*) Cetane. ~**en**, (*tex.*) satin.
set·ir[ri] A covering, veiling, hiding.
setre (*mod.*) Old-fashioned frock-coat.
setr·letmekeder **(-i)** Cover; veil; hide, concea: ~**i avret**[i], covering one's privy parts.
seva[bbı] (*rel.*) Pious deed, meritorious act. ~ **etm.** do a good deed; live righteously: ~**a girmek** acquire merit. ~**lı**, meritorious.
sevda Melancholy; spleen; passion, love; intens longing, passionate desire; scheme, project. ~ **çekmek**, be deeply in love: ~**dan vazgeçmek**, giv up an idea: ~**sına düşmek**, long for: ~**ya düşmek** fall in love. ~**lanmak**, *vi.* fall in love. ~**lı**, madly i love; enamoured.
sev·diceğim My darling. ~**diği**, favourite. ~**dirme** **(-i, -e)**, *vc.* = SEVMEK; endear. ~**e**, ~ ~, lovingly

~**ecen**, compassionate. ~**ecenlik**, compassion. -~**er**, *suf.* -phile, -loving [BARIŞSEVER]. ~**gi**, love; affection; compassion. ~**gili**, *a.* loveable; beloved: *n.* darling; boy-/girl-friend.

sevi Love, passion. ~**ci(lik)**, lesbian(ism).

sevil·gen Popular. ~**ir**, lovable; amiable; desirable. ~**mek**, *vp.* = SEVMEK: *vi.* be lovable/amiable.

sevim Love; affection; affability. ~**li**, lovable; appealing, attractive; charming. ~**lileşmek**, *vi.* become lovable, etc. ~**lilik**, charm, affability. ~**siz**, unlovable, unattractive; unsympathetic, not likeable. ~**sizleşmek**, *vi.* become unattractive, etc. ~**sizlik**, unattractiveness.

sevin·¹çᶜⁱ Joy; delight; pleasure: ~**inden takla atmak**, dance for joy. ~**çli**, joyful. ~**dirmek (-i)**, please, make happy. ~**me**, *vn.* ~**mek**, *vi.* be pleased/happy; rejoice. ~**melik**, bribe.

Sev¹irʳⁱ (*ast.*) Constellation of Taurus.

seviş·me *vn.* ~**mek (-le)**, love/caress each other; make love.

seviye Equality; level; rank, degree; (*eng.*) head. ~**çubuk/göstergesi**, (*mot.*) dipstick: ~**sini gösterir cam**, (*eng.*) sight-glass. ~**li**, good quality; (*fig.*) high-ranking. ~**siz**, (*fig.*) low-ranking, common.

sevk¹ Drive, driving; impulse; urging, inciting; (*mil.*) dispatch (troops). ~ **çemberi**, (*eng.*) drive band: ~ **etm.**, drive, impel; urge, incite; convey, send: ~ **maddesi**, (*chem.*) propellant: ~ **mahalli**, destination: ~ **memuru**, dispatcher: ~ **tertibatı**, conveyor (belt): ~ **ücreti**, (*fin.*) carriage.

sevk·ıtabii (*psy.*) Instinct. ~**ıyat¹**, dispatch; consignment. ~**ulceyş**, (*mil.*) strategy.

sevmek (-i) Love; be fond of, like; caress, fondle; (*bot.*) grow well. **sevsinler!**, (*pej.*) how nice!

seyahat¹ Journey; travelling; (*ed.*) expedition; (*soc.*) cruising. ~ **çeki**, (*fin.*) travellers' cheque: ~ **hürriyeti**, (*pol.*) freedom of movement: ~ **irtifaı**, (*aer.*) cruising altitude. ~**name**, (*lit.*) book of travels.

seydi/-saydı *v. suf.* [131] *Forming the conditional past* [gitseydi, if (only) he had gone].

seyek (*gamb.*) Three-one (at backgammon).

seyelan A flowing; flood. ~ **etm.**, stream, pour.

sey¹irʳⁱ Movement, progress; travel; journey, excursion; (*naut.*) cruising; looking at stg.; spectacle. ~ **halinde**, in motion/flight: ~ **hızı**, (*naut.*) cruising speed: ~ **jurnalı**, logbook: ~ **kılavuz kitabı**, sailing directions: ~ **tecrübesi**, trials: ~ **süresi**, (*eng.*) running time: ~ **yeri**, (*th.*) auditorium: ~**e çıkmak**, go for a walk/ride; make an excursion.

seyir·ci Spectator; *pl.* audience; (mere) onlooker, bystander; cinema-/theatre-goer: ~ **araştırma**, audience research: ~ **kalmak**, be an onlooker, not participate: ~ **mektupları**, fanmail. ~**lik**, (for) watching.

seyis Groom. ~**lik**, horse-grooming.

seyi¹tᵈⁱ Master, lord; (*rel.*) descendant of the Prophet.

Seylan (*geo.*) Ceylon, Sri Lanka. ~ **baykuşu**, (*orn.*) brown fish-owl. ~**i/~taşıⁿⁱ**, (*geol.*) garnet. ~**lı**, (*ethn.*) Ceylonese, Cingalese, Sri Lankan.

seyla¹pᵇⁱ Flood, torrent.

seyran Outing, pleasure-trip, excursion. ~ **etm./~a çıkmak**, go for a trip, make an excursion.

seyrek Wide apart; few and far between; at infrequent intervals (time/space); rare; rarely; (*tex.*) loosely woven; sparse. ~**leşme**, *vn.* (*soc.*) depopulation. ~**leşmek**, *vi.* become infrequent; become rarefied/sparse; thin out; be at wide intervals. ~**leştirmek (-i)**, *vc.* ~**lik**, extent/frequency of intervals; rarity of occurrence, infrequency; (*tex.*) looseness of weave.

seyrel·mek *vi.* = SEYREKLEŞMEK. ~**tik**, diluted. ~**tmek (-i)** = SEYREKLEŞTİRMEK; (*phys.*) dilute.

seyr- = SEYİR. ~**¹etmekᵉᵈᵉʳ (-i)**, view, look at; look on at; contemplate: *vi.* move, go along; cruise: **seyret!**, now you'll see (what will happen)! ~**üsefer**, traffic (people/vehicles); (*naut.*) navigation(al): ~ **memuru**, traffic policeman.

sey·yah Traveller: ~ **çeki**, (*fin.*) traveller's cheque: ~ **şehri**, tourist city: ~ **vapuru**, (*naut.*) passenger ship, cruise-ship. ~**yal¹**, fluid; liquid. ~**yanen**, in equal parts; share and share alike. ~ **yar**, habitually moving; mobile, portable: ~ **çalgıcı**, (*th.*) busker: ~ **esnaf**, hawker: ~ **hastane**, (*mil.*) field hospital: ~ **satıcı**, barrow-boy, street hawker: ~ **sebzeci**, costermonger. ~**yare**, (*ast.*) planet. ~**yiat¹**, *pl.* (*rel.*) sins. ~**yibe**, widow. ~ **yie**, evil thing/deed/ consequence: ~**sini çekmek**, suffer the consequences of an evil deed.

seza (-e) Meet, fit, suitable (for); worthy (of).

sezaryen (*med.*) Caesarian (birth/operation).

sez·dirme *vn.* Allusion; hint. ~**dirmek (-i, -e)**, make clear; explain; make understand. ~**gi**, perception; discernment; (*phil.*) intuition. ~**gicilik**, (*phil.*) intuition(al)ism. ~**gili/~gisel**, intuitive; (*phil.*) intuitional. ~**gin**, discriminating. ~**i** = ~ Gİ; feeling, intuition. ~**ilmek**, *vp.* be felt. ~**ilmeyen**, imperceptible, unnoticeable; (*geol.*) (earthquake) only recorded on instruments. ~**inç(li)**, tact(ful). ~**indirmek (-i)**, make aware/understand. ~**inleme**, *vn.* ~**inlemek/~inmek/~insemek (-i)**, be aware of, be conscious of; have an inkling of. ~**inti/~iş**, perception; awareness; inkling. ~**mek (-i)**, perceive; feel; discern, make out; discriminate.

se·zon (*sp.*, *th.*) Season. ~**zü**, (*bot.*) cork oak. ~**zyum**, (*chem.*) caesium.

sf. = SAHİFE.

sf·agnum (*bot.*) Sphagnum (moss). ~**enks**, (*myth.*) sphinx. ~**ero-**, (*phys.*) sphero-.

SGB = SOSYAL GÜVENLİK BAKANLIĞI.

-sı¹ *n. suf.* (*after a vowel*) [39] = -si¹ [BABASI].

-sı² *a. suf.* (*after a consonant*) [58] = -si² [KADINSI].

sıcacık Comfortably warm, cosy.

sıca¹kᵏᵍ¹ *a.* Hot; warm (colour); (*fig.*) friendly, warm, sympathetic. *n.* Heat; hot place; hot bath. ~ **alın/cephe**, (*met.*) warm front: ~ **çıban**, (*med.*) abscess: ~ **ekmek**, (*cul.*) fresh bread: ~ **iklim**, (*met.*) tropical climate: ~ **kuşak**, (*geo.*) torrid zone: ~ **olm.**, become hot: ~ **su deposu**, (*eng.*) boiler: ~ **yastığı**, (*agr.*) hotbed: ~**a yüzüm yok**, I can't face the heat: ~**ı ~ına**, immediately; without wasting time; 'while the iron is hot': ~ **tan börtmek**, (*fig.*) be half broiled in the heat: ~**tan bükülmek**, (*min.*) buckle.

sıcak·çıl (*bio.*) Thermophile. ~**kanlı(lık)**, (*zoo.*) warm-blooded(ness); (*fig.*) warm-hearted(ness), amia·ble/(-bility). ~**lık**, heat; hotness; (*phys.*) temperature; hot room (of hammam): ~ **farkı**, temperature range: ~ **seviyesi**, temperature. ~**ölçer**, (*phys.*) thermometer.

sıçan (*zoo.*) Rat; mouse. ~ **başlı iskorpit**, (*ich.*) bull-trout: ~ **deliğine paha biçilmez olm.**, everyone be seeking a refuge: ~ **fiği**, (*bot.*) purple broad bean: ~ **kırı**, mouse-coloured (horse): ~ **kuşu**, (*orn.*) mousebird: ~ **piresi**, (*ent.*) Indian rat-flea: ~**a dönmek**, be soaking wet, look like a drowned rat: ~**ın geçtiğini aramam ama yol olur**, I don't mind it once but it might become a precedent.

sıçan·dişini (*mod.*) A fine edging on linen garments. ~**ımsı**, (*zoo.*) mouse-like. ~**kulağı**nı, (*bot.*) mouse-ear chickweed. ~**kuyruğu**nu, (*carp.*) rat-tailed file. ~**otu**nu, (*chem.*) arsenic. ~**tersi**ni, mouse excrement. ~**yolu**nu, (*mil.*) gallery for a landmine.

sıç·ılmak vp. (*vulg.*) Be fouled with one's own excrement; be filthy. ~**ırgan(lık)**, (*med.*) incontin·ent/(-ence). ~**mak**, vi. (*vulg.*) excrete, defecate, shit: **(-i)**, foul stg.: **sıçtı Cafer, bez getir**, he's done a filthy job.

sıçra·ma vn. (*sp.*) Leaping into the air: ~ **tahtası**, (*sp.*) springboard, take-off board. ~**mak (-e)**, jump, leap, spring; (give a) start; spurt out; spread out: **sıçrayıp kıç atmak**, (horse) buck. ~**tmak (-i, -e)**, vc. ~**yış**, vn. jumping, springing.

sıçtırmak (-i) (*vulg.*) = SIÇMAK. Cause to excrete; frighten to death.

sıd·lıkkı Truth; sincerity. ~**ı sıyrılmak (-den)**, lose confidence in s.o.

sıfatı Quality, attribute, title; (*col.*) appearance, mien, aspect; (*ling.*) adjective; epithet. ~ **eylem**, (*ling.*) participle: ~ **tamlaması**, (*ling.*) adjectival construction: ~**ından anladım**, I could see from his expression: ~**ıyla**, in the capacity of . . ., acting as . . . .

sıfır (*math.*) Zero; nought; cipher; (*fig.*) nothing; worth nothing, valueless, insignificant; (*sp.*) nil, duck('s egg). ~ **numara makine/traş**, Nº 0 barber's clippers; (*fig.*) cut as closely as possible; (*mil.*) get one's hair shaved (a punishment for cadets): ~**a** ~ **elde var bir**, (*fig.*) the barest minimum: ~**a** ~ **elde var** ~, (*fig.*) all that work comes to nothing: ~**ı tüketmek**, (*sl.*) exhaust one's patience; be on one's beam ends; be exhausted, die.

sıf·ıraltı (*phys.*) Sub-zero (temperature). ~**ırcı**, (*ed.*) teacher who always gives bad marks. ~**ırlı**, (*math.*) zero-place. ~**ramak (-i)**, (*math.*) reduce to zero.

sığ a. Shallow. n. (*geo.*) Shoal, sandbank. ~ **yayla**, continental shelf: ~**a oturmak**, (*naut.*) go aground.

sığa Capacity. ~**lık**, (*el.*) capacitance. ~**(n)mak** = SIVA(N)MAK². ~**msal**, ~ **devinim**, (*bio.*) vermicular movement, peristalsis.

sığdır·ılmak vp. ~**mak (-i, -e)** vc. = SIĞMAK; cram into.

sığın (*zoo.*) Fallow deer.

sığın·a·lkkı Refuge, shelter, bunker; (*his.*) citadel;

(*mil.*) dug-out; (*pol.*) asylum. ~**ık**, refugee. ~**ma**, vn.; (*sp.*) sheltering behind another competitor: ~ **barınağı**, (*naut.*) emergency port: ~ **hakkı**, (*pol.*) right of asylum. ~**mak (-e)**, vi. squeeze into stg.; take cover/shelter/refuge. ~**mış**, n. refugee. ~**tı**, (*pej.*) refugee, parasite.

sığır (*zoo., live.*) Ox; bull; cow; buffalo; beast; cattle. ~ **ağılı**, cattle-pen: ~ **budu**, (*cul.*) aitch bone: ~ **deri/köselesi**, cowhide: ~ **eti (suyu)**, (*cul.*) beef (-tea): ~ **otlağı**, cattle-range: ~ **paçası**, (*cul.*) cow's heel: ~ **sineği**, (*ent.*) gadfly: ~ **ve davar**, cattle: ~ **yüreği yutmadım!**, I'm sick and tired of telling you!

sığır·cı·lkkı (*orn.*) Common starling. ~**cıkgiller**, (*orn.*) starlings. ~**dili**ni, (*cul.*) ox-tongue; (*bot.*) alkanet, bugloss. ~**diligiller**, (*bot.*) Boraginaceae. ~**gözü**nü, arnica, corn marigold. ~**kuyruğu**nu, (*bot.*) motherwort. ~**lık**, (*fig.*) bovine stupidity; boorishness. ~**tenyası**nı, (*zoo.*) beef tapeworm. ~**tma·lç**cı, cowherd, herdsman, drover.

sığış·mak (-e) vi. Go/fit into (with difficulty). ~**tırmak (-i, -e)**, put/fit into (with difficulty).

sığ·laşmak vi. Become shallow. ~**lık**, shallowness: shallow place, sandbank.

sığmak (-e) vi. Go into; be contained by.

sıhhatı Health; truth. ~**ini tahkik etm.**, ascertain the truth of stg.: ~**inize!**, good health!, cheers!: ~**ler olsun!**, (after bath/shave) good health to you! ~**li**, healthy.

sıhhi Pertaining to health; hygienic. ~**ye**, (*adm.*) Health Department: ~ **memuru**, health officer: ~ **uçağı**, (*aer.*) ambulance plane. ~**yeci**, (*adm.*) health officer; (*mil.*) medical orderly; (*naut.*) sick-bay attendant.

sıhriyetı Relationship by marriage, in-laws.

sık a. Close together; dense; (*tex.*) closely woven; frequent; tight. adv. Frequently, often. ~ **çizgili**, (*bot.*) close-grained (tree): ~ ~, constantly; very frequently, continually: ~ **taneli**, (*min.*) fine-grained.

sık·a·lçcı (*eng.*) Compressor. ~**boğaz**, urgently: ~ **etm.**, take s.o. by the throat; force s.o. to do stg. keep on at s.o. to do stg. ~**ça**, fairly often.

sıkı¹ a. Tight; firmly driven in; fast; compact, dense; strict, severe; hurried; (*tex.*) close, fine; (*met.*) heavy (gale): (*fig.*) tight-fisted. ~ **basmak**, resist; stand up to: ~ **bas!**, hold tight!; stand firm!: ~ **dostlar** firm friends: ~ **durmak**, 'sit tight'; stick fast: ~ **esmek**, (*met.*) blow a gale: ~ **fıkı**, close together intimate: ~ **fıkı dostlar**, fast friends: ~ **ise!** (*vulg.*) if you dare!: ~ ~**ya**, very close, etc. thoroughly, severely: ~ **tutmak**, consider important: ~YÖNETİM: ~ **yürümek**, walk briskly.

sıkı² n. Pressing necessity; trouble, straits; severe threat/reprimand; (*mil.*) wad (for muzzle-loader) ~**ya dayanmak**, stand hard work; brave trouble ~**ya gelmek**, meet with great difficulty, be hard put to it: ~**ya koymak**, press s.o. hard; try to force s.o. (to do stg.): ~**yı görünce**, when pressed compelled/threatened: ~**yı yemek**, receive a severe threat/reprimand.

sıkı·cı Tiresome; boring. ~**denetim**, (*pub.*) censorship. ~**denetimci**, censor. ~**düzen**, orderliness discipline. ~ lamak (-i), tamp; (*mil.*) load (a muzzle-loader); (*fig.*) press; force.

sıkılgan Easily embarrassed; awkward, shy. ~ lık, awkwardness, shyness.

sıkılık Closeness; firmness; tightness; density, compactness; (*fig.*) meanness.

sıkıl·ma *vn.* A being bored//ashamed; sense of shame: ~ ya gelmemek, dislike hardship/taking trouble. ~ mak (-e), *vp.* = SIKMAK; be pressed/ squeezed; be in difficulties; be bored/annoyed; be uneasy/ashamed. ~ maz(lık), shameless(ness).

sıkım/ ~ lık A fistful; (*fig.*) very small quantity.

sıkın·mak *vi.* Restrain/constrain o.s. ~ tı, annoyance; boredom; embarrassment, discomfort; adversity, distress; weariness; financial straits: ~ çekmek, suffer annoyance/inconvenience: ~ vermek, cause vexation/inconvenience: ~ da olm., (*fin.*) be in difficulties/straits: ~ sı olm., be in difficulties; (*bio.*) need to relieve o.s.: ~ sını çekmek, bear the brunt of: ~ ya düşmek, (*fin.*) get into difficulties: ~ ya gelememek, be unable to cope with life. ~ tılı, annoying, boring, distressing, etc.; annoyed, bored, distressed, etc. ~ tısız, comfortable, carefree, relaxed.

sıkış·ık Compact; crowded; congested: ~ olm., feel cramped for room. ~ ma, *vn.*; (*phys.*) compression. ~ mak, *vi.* be closely pressed together; be crowded together; (*fin.*) be in straits; become urgent; 'be taken short'. ~ tırıcı, (*eng.*) compressor, compactor. ~ tırılmak, *vp.* ~ tırma, *vn.*; compaction, condensation; (*fig.*) duress. ~ tırmak (-i), press, constrict, squeeze; compress; condense; tighten; clamp together; force; oppress; interrogate; corner s.o.

sıkıt¹ ¹ (*chem.*) *a.* Compressed. *n.* Pill, tablet.

sıkıt¹ıt¹² (*med.*) Miscarriage.

sıkıyönetim (*mil.*) Martial law; state of siege.

sıkkın Annoyed; disgusted; in need. ~ lık, annoyance; disgust.

sıklaş·ılmak *vp.* ~ mak, *vi.* be frequent (in time/ space); be close together; (*tex.*) be closely woven. ~ tırmak (-i), bring close together; render frequent.

sıklet¹ Heaviness; weight; (*fig.*) uneasiness; languor. ~ çekmek, be bored: ~ merkezi, (*phys.*) centre of gravity: ~ vermek, annoy, bore.

sıklık Frequency (of occurrence), incidence; density (of arrangement//population).

sık·ma *vn.* A squeezing; (*mod.*) tight-fitting trousers; (*mod.*) brassière: *a.* (fruit) suitable for squeezing: ~ baş, (*mod.*) hair-band. ~ ma¹çcı, (*eng.*) compressor. ~ mak (-i), press; squeeze; tighten; put pressure on; (*fin.*) dun; cause annoyance/embarrassment/discomfort; (*mil.*) discharge/fire (a gun); clench (fist/ teeth). ~ sayı, (*phys.*) frequency.

sıla (*soc.*) Reunion; visiting one's native land. ~ hastalığı, (*psy.*) homesickness: ~ sıygası, (*ling.*) gerund: ~ sını çekmek (-in), feel homesick for stg.: ~ ya gitmek/varmak, visit one's native land, go home. ~ cı, s.o. returning home; (*mil.*) soldier on leave.

sımak (-i) (*obs.*) Break; spoil; demolish; annihilate.

sımsıkı Very tight; squeezed; narrow. ~ kapatmak, batten down: ~ sarılmak, *vi.* cling.

-sın *v. suf.* [96, 137] = -SİN¹· ² [FRANSIZSIN; BAKSIN].

sın. = SINAİ.

sınaat¹ Craft; handicraft.

sınai Connected with craftsmanship; industrial.

sına·¹k^gı Test. ~ lı, tested. ~ ma, *vn.*; (*ed.*) examination, test. ~ mak (-i), try, test; (*ed.*) examine. ~ nmak, *vp.* ~ sız, untested. ~ tmak (-i, -e), *vc.* ~ v, (*ed.*) examination: ~ vermek, take an examination; pass an examination: ~ a çekilmek, be examined thoroughly: ~ a girmek, enter for an examination: ~ dan geçirmek, examine. ~ vlamak (-i), examine. ~ vman, examiner.

sıncan (*bot.*) (?) Milk-vetch, wild lentil.

sındı Large cutting-out scissors.

-sındı *v. suf.* [138] = -SİNDİ [BAKSINDI].

sın·dırgı (*mil.*) Scene of a defeat: ~ yı sıyırmış karaağaca kandil asmış, brazen-faced; of ill repute. ~ dırılmak, *vp.* ~ dırmak (-i), utterly defeat, rout. ~ gın, broken; defeated, routed.

sınıf (*ed.*, *etc.*) Class; sort; category; classroom. ~ albümü, (*ed.*) class-/year-book: ~ çelişki/ mücadelesi, (*soc.*) class warfare: ~ tenzili, (*adm.*) demotion: ~ ı(nı) geçmek, (*ed.*) be promoted: ~ ta kalmak, (*ed.*) fail, stay down.

sınıf·la(ndır)ma *vn.* Classification. ~ la(ndır)mak (-i), classify; grade; categorize. ~ lanmak, *vp.* ~ lı, classified; graded. ~ sal, *a.* class. ~ taş, classmate; fellow-student.

sınık Broken; defeated; routed. ~ çı, (*med.*) bone-setter.

sınır (*geo.*) Frontier; border; boundary; limit; margin. ~ açı, (*math.*) limit angle: ~ bölgesi, frontier/border zone: ~ çekmek, define/draw the boundary: ~ değer, (*phys.*, *etc.*) limit value: ~ dışı etm., expel: ~ dışına çıkarmak, deport: ~ dışından, from abroad: ~ teşkil etm. (-e), border on: ~ ını çizmek, demarcate: ~ ları bir olm., abut, adjoin.

sınır·daş Having a common frontier; bordering; contiguous. ~ daşlık, contiguity. ~ lama, *vn.* restriction. ~ la(ndır)mak (-i), draw the boundary; set bounds, restrict; (*phil.*) define; compartmentalize. ~ lanma, *vn.* ~ lanmak, *vp.* be restricted; be surrounded. ~ layıcı, restrictive, limiting. ~ lı, close; limited, restricted; determinate; (*math.*) finite: ~ basım, (*pub.*) limited edition: ~ sayı, finite number: ~ sorumluluk, (*fin.*) limited liability. ~ sal, marginal. ~ sız, unlimited, boundless; (*math.*) infinite: ~ sayı, infinite number.

-sınız *v. suf.* [96] = -SİNİZ [OKULDASINIZ].

sınmak *vi.* Break; be scattered; be defeated/routed; (*fin.*) be bankrupt/'broke'.

sıpa (*zoo.*) Donkey-foal; fawn; = SEHPA.

sır¹ Glaze (on pottery); silvering (of mirror). ~ çatlağı, craze: ~ vermek, (give a) glaze; = SIR².

sır¹² ² Secret; mystery. ~ açmak, reveal/confide a secret: ~ kâtibi, (*his.*) confidential/private secretary: ~ küpü, s.o. who keeps secrets: ~ saklamak, keep secret: ~ söylemek (-e), confide in: ~ tutmak, keep secret; keep a secret: ~ vermek, betray/ divulge a secret; = SIR¹: ~ ra kadem basmak, (*jok.*) not be seen, disappear: ~ rı ağzından kaçırmak, let the cat out of the bag.

sıra Row; file; rank; category; order; sequence;

series; regularity; turn; opportune moment; (*ind.*) bench; (*ed.*) desk; (*pub.*) line; (*arch.*) course (of bricks); (*eng.*) in-line; (*geo.*) chain/range (mountains); (*agr.*) drill. ~ **beklemek**, wait one's turn, queue up: ~ **çekmek**, (*sp.*) draw lots: ~ **dayağı**, giving many people a beating in turn: ~ **düşürmek**, find a suitable opportunity: ~ **evler**, (*arch.*) terraced houses in rows: ~ **gözetmek/kollamak**, watch for a suitable opportunity: ~ **ile**, in rows; in turn; in order: ~ **(karpuzu)**, (melons) large and small as they come (not selected): ~ **malı**, ordinary/inferior goods: ~ **numarası**, (*adm.*) serial number: ~ **sayısı**, (*math.*) ordinal number: ~ **sayı sıfatı**, (*ling.*) ordinal numeral adjective: ~ ~, in rows/courses/layers; range on range: ~ ~ **ekmek**, (*agr.*) drill.

sıra-: ~**da**, in a row; [201] at the moment/time; [185] just when, as: ~**dan**, normal, ordinary (not specially selected).

sırası, his/her/its turn: ~ **düştü**, the right moment for it has come: ~ **gelince**, in due course: ~ **gelmek**, its turn come: ~ **gelmişken**, by the way, apropos: ~ **ile**, respectively: ~**na geçmek**, take one's turn; be counted (undeservedly) as . . .: ~**na getirmek**, await a favourable opportunity: ~**na göre**, according to circumstances; as required: ~**na koymak**, put in its proper place; set to rights: ~**nda**, in his/her/its turn; when necessary; in the course of . . .; during: ~**nı düşürmek**, seize an opportunity: ~**nı kaybetmek**, (child) miss its sleep/feeding-time: ~**nı savmak**, have done one's turn (of duty); have 'done one's bit'.

sıra-: ~**ya bakmak**, pay attention to time/one's turn: ~**ya girmek**, (*mil.*) fall in; join the queue: ~**ya koymak**, arrange, put in order: ~**ya toplamak**, (*pub.*) collate (pages): ~**yla(n)**, in turn, one after the other; respectively.

-sıra *adv. suf.* [92] *Forming postpositions* [**ardısıra**, after him].

sıraca (*med.*) Scrofula. ~**giller**, (*bot.*) Scrophulariaceae. ~**lı**, (*med.*) scrofulous. ~**otu**nu, scrophularia, figwort.

sıra·dağ(lar) (*geo.*) Moutain chain. ~**düzen**, (*adm.*) hierarchy. ~**l**, ~ **sayı**, (*math.*) ordinal number. ~**la¹ç**cı, (*adm.*) dossier, file. ~**la¹k**ğı, catalogue. ~**lama**, *vn.* classification; ordering; (*ind.*) routing, processing. ~**lamak (-i)**, arrange in a row: set up in order; enumerate (series of complaints, etc.); coordinate; (child) begin to walk (by holding on to things in turn). ~**lanış**, series. ~**lanmak**, *vp.*; *vi.* queue up. ~**lanmış**, ordered. ~**latmak (-i, -e)**, *vc.* ~**lı**, in a row; in due order, in sequence, consecutive; at the right moment: ~ **cümle/tümce**, (*ling.*) coordinate sentence: ~ **sırasız**, in and out of season; at all sorts of times. ~**lıoluş**, (*bio., phil.*) epigenesis. ~**sız**, out of order, without any order; ill-timed; improper.

sırat¹ Road, path. ~ **köprüsü**, (*rel.*) bridge on the road to heaven (that only the righteous will cross!).

Sırb- = **Sırp**. ~**istan**/~**iya**, (*geo.*) Serbia. ~**istanlı**, (*ethn.*) Serbian.

sırça Glass; glazed brick; paste (diamond); spun

glass; glass bead; rock crystal; (*zoo.*) long glossy fur hairs. ~ **köşkte oturan başka/komşusuna taş atmamalı**, people who live in glass houses shouldn't throw stones.

sırdaş Fellow holder of a secret; confidant(e); intimate. ~**lık**, sharing a secret; intimate friendship.

sırf Pure, mere; sheer, only, nothing but.

sırı¹kğı Pole; stick; (*agr.*) stake, cane. ~ **domates/ fasulyesi**, (*bot.*) type of tomato/bean requiring support: ~ **gibi**, (*pej.*) tall and thin: ~ **gibi boy büyütmek**, grow in size but not in sense: ~ **gibi durmak**, stand aside and do nothing: ~**la atlama**, (*sp.*) pole-vault. ~**lamak (-i)**, (*agr.*) stake out (plants); (*sl.*) carry off, steal.

sırılsıklam Sopping wet.

sırım Leather thong; strap. ~ **gibi**, wiry (person).

sırıt·kan Given to grinning. ~**kanlık**, continuous grinning. ~**ma**, *vn.* ~**mak**, *vi.* show one's teeth; grin; be frozen; (*fig.*) (defect) show up/through; become obvious; be a fiasco: **sırıta kalmak**, stay grinning like a corpse.

sır·lama *vn.* ~**lamak (-i)**, glaze (pottery); vitrify; silver (mirror). ~**lı**, glazed; vitrified; silvered.

sırma Silver(-gilt) (*tex.*) thread//(*mod.*) embroidery/ lace. ~ **saç**, golden hair. ~**keş**, maker of/embroiderer in gold/silver thread. ~**lı**, embroidered with gold/silver thread.

sırnaş·ık Worrying, tiresome; pertinacious; importunate, brazen-faced. ~**ıklık**, tiresomeness; importunity, etc. ~**mak (-e)**, worry, annoy. ~**tırmak (-i)**, *vc.*

Sır¹pbı (*ethn.*) Serb(ian). ~**ça**, (*ling.*) Serbian. ~**hırvat**, (*ethn.*) Serbo-Croat.

sırr- = **sır²**. ~**en**, secretly. ~**olmak**, disappear.

sırsıklam Soaking/sopping wet; wet through/to the skin. ~ **âşık**, madly in love: ~ **etm.**, drench.

sırt¹ (*bio.*) Back; (*geo., met.*) ridge. ~ +, *a.* (*bio.*) Dorsal: ~ **ağrısı**, (*med.*) backache: ~ **çevirmek (-e)**, turn one's back on s.o.: ~ ~**a**, back to back (*fig.*) co-operating, supporting each other: ~ **üstü** on one's back, face upwards: ~ **üstü yüzüş**, (*sp.*) back-stroke: ~**-üstü yüzen böcek**, (*ent.*) water boatman, back swimmer: ~ **yüzgeci**, (*ich.*) dorsal fin: ~**ı kaşınıyor**, he's itching for a beating: ~**ı pek** well clad: ~**ı sıra**, one after the other: ~**ı yere gelmek**, be defeated; be brought low: ~**ı yufka** scantily clad: ~**ına almak**, shoulder; undertake put on (extra) clothes: ~**ında yumurta küfesi yok ya!**, he thinks nothing of changing his mind/plans etc.: ~**ından atmak**, get rid of, free o.s. from ~**ından çıkarmak (-in)**, get stg. at s.o. else's expense: ~**ından geçinmek (-in)**, live at s.o. else's expense: ~**ını dayamak (-e)**, lean against stg. (*fig.*) rely on/trust in s.o.: ~**ını kamburlaştırmak** arch one's back: ~**ını yere getirmek (-in)**, (*sp.*) put s.o. on his back; (*fig.*) overcome, get the better of

sırtar (*zoo.*) Type of thick-skinned lizard. ~ **balığı** (*ich.*) fresh-water bream.

sırtarmak¹ *vi.* Grin.

sırt·armak² *vi.* (Cat) arch its back; (*met.*) (clouds) pile up; (*fig.*) set o.s. up in opposition to. ~**ıkara** (*ich.*) small bluefish; (*sl.*) double-six (at back gammon). ~ **lamak (-i)**, take on one's back; (*fig.*) back, support. ~ **lan**, (*zoo.*) hyena.

sıska (*med.*) Dropsical; rickety; thin and weak. ~ **lık**, dropsy; rickets.

sıtma (*med.*) Malaria, ague. ~ **ağacı**, (*bot.*) blue gum tree, eucalyptus(-tree): ~ **asalağı**, (*bio.*) plasmodium: ~ **görmemiş ses**, rich deep voice: ~ **sivrisineği**, (*ent.*) anopheles mosquito: ~ **tutmak/** ~ **ya tutulmak**, catch malaria.

sıtma·bilim (*med.*) Malariology: ~ **uzmanı**, malariologist. ~ **lı**, having malaria; malaria-infested, malarial. ~ **lık**, malarial swamp, etc.

sıva (*arch.*) Plaster. ~ **harcı**, stucco. ~ **cı**, plasterer: ~ **kuşu**, (*orn.*) Eurasian nuthatch: ~ **kuşugiller**, nuthatches. ~ **lamak (-i)**, plaster. ~ **lı**[1], plastered, stuccoed. ~ **ma**, *vn.*: *a.* laid on (like plaster); covered with; washed over with: *adv.* full (to the brim): ~ **kel**, bald all over. ~ **mak (-i)**[1], plaster; daub; cover over with; soil. ~ **nmak**[1], *vp.* be plastered with. ~ **şmak (-e)**, become sticky; adhere, stick to; be daubed. ~ **ştırmak (-i)**, daub, coat; make sticky. ~ **tmak (-i, -e)**, *vc.*

sıva·lı[2] With sleeves rolled up. ~ **mak (-i)**[2], tuck/ roll up (skirts/sleeves, etc.); rub with the hand; smooth; massage. ~ **nmak**[2], *vp.* (*fig.*) prepare for/ set to work. ~ **zlamak (-i)**, stroke, caress. ~ **zlatmak (-i)**, *vc.*

sıvı *n.* Liquid. ~ **azot**, (*chem.*) liquid nitrogen: ~ **YAĞ**. ~ **k**, semi-fluid; sticky; bedaubed. ~ **laş-(tır)ma**, *vn.* (*phys.*) condensation, liquefaction. ~ **laştırmak (-i)**, (*phys.*) liquefy. ~ **ndırmak (-i)**, (*phys.*) condense. ~ **nmak**, *vp.* be condensed/ liquefied. ~ **ölçer**, (*phys.*) hydrometer.

sıvırya (*fig.*) Continually; one after the other; in full swing; (*sl.*) brim-full.

sıvış·ık/ ~ **kan** Sticky; (*chem.*) colloid(al); (*fig.*) importunate; boring (person). ~ **ıklık**, stickiness; (*fig.*) importunity. ~ **mak (-e)**, become sticky: (**-den**), (*fig.*) clear off, abscond, do a bunk.

sıvıyağ (*chem.*) Liquid oil.

sıya ~ **kürek!**, (*naut.*) back water!

sıyanet[i] Preservation, protection. ~ **etm.**, preserve, protect: ~ **meleği**, guardian angel.

sıyga (*ling.*) Mood, tense. ~ **ya çekmek**, interrogate, cross-examine.

sıyır·ga (*agr.*) Shovel. ~ **ma**, *vn.*; abrasion; (*min.*) stripping; (*sp.*) disengagement. ~ **mak (-i)**, tear/ peel off; strip off; skim off; graze, abrade; draw (a sword, etc.); (*sp.*) smash (ball); finish up, polish off: (**-den**), (*fig.*) slip away, escape. ~ **tmak (-i, -e)**, *vc.*

-sıyla *post.* [87] = -SİYLE [BABASIYLA].

sıyr·ık *a.* Peeled; skinned; stripped; abraded, grazed; (*fig.*) brazen-faced, unashamed: *n.* Abrasion, graze. ~ **ılma**, *vn.*; detachment. ~ **ılmak**, *vp.* = SIYIRMAK; be skinned, etc.: (**-den**), be stripped off; get rid of; (*fig.*) slip off, sneak away; get out of a difficulty. ~ **ıntı**, (*cul.*) scrapings from a dish; peelings; scratch; torn-off strip.

-sız *a./pron. suf.* [62] = -siz [ŞAPKASIZ].

sız·a[1]**ğı**[1] Water oozing/trickling from the rocks. ~ **dırılmak**, *vp.* ~ **dırma**, *vn.*; filtering. ~ **dırmak (-i)**, *vc.* = SIZMAK; cause to ooze out; leak stg.; filter; (*sl.*) squeeze money out of; leak (news); (drink)

stupefy and put to sleep. ~ **dırmaz**, watertight, leakproof. ~ **dırmazlık**, tightness; leakproofing; (*eng.*) cut-off.

sızgıt (*cul.*, *dial.*) Minced/grilled meat.

sızı (*med.*) Ache, pain; (*fig.*) grief.

sızıcı Oozing, trickling. ~ **ünsüz**, (*ling.*) fricative, spirant.

sızıltı Lamentation; complaint; discontent. ~ **çıkarmak**, utter//cause mutterings of discontent: ~ **ya meydan vermemek**, give nobody cause to complain.

sızım Very gradual oozing/leakage. ~ ~ **sızla(n)mak**, suffer/complain bitterly.

-sızın *v. suf.* [188] = -SİZİN [OLMAKSIZIN].

sız·ınım (*nuc.*) Effusion. ~ **ıntı**, *n.* oozing, trickling; leak; (*fig.*) leaking (of secrets, etc.). ~ **ırmak (-i)**, strain, filter.

sızla·mak *vi.* Suffer sharp pain; ache all over; lament. ~ **nmak**, *vi.* moan with pain; lament, complain. ~ **tmak (-i)**, (give) pain, hurt; make groan/lament.

-sızlık *n. suf.* = -SİZLİK [PARASIZLIK].

sız·ma *vn.* Airing (a room); percolation, seepage; (*bio.*) transpiration; (*mil.*) infiltration. ~ **mak**, *vi.* ooze, seep, trickle, leak; (secret, etc.) leak out; (*mil.*) infiltrate; (*fig.*) drop into a drunken stupor.

si (*mus.*) Te; B.

Si. = SİGORTA; (*ch.s.*) SİLİSYUM; SİNEMA(CILIK).

-si[1]**/-sı/-su/-sü** *n. suf.* [39] *Third person sing. possessive, after vowels.* His, her, its [**babası**, his father: **penceresi**, its window].

-si[2]**/-sı/-su/-sü** *a. suf.* [58] *After consonants.* Resembling, like; -ish [**kadınsı**, womanish: **ölümsü**, deathlike].

sibak[1] (*phil.*) Preceding context; = SİYAK.

siberneti[1]**k**[gi] Cybernetics.

Sibirya (*geo.*) Siberia. ~ +, *a.* Siberian: ~ **kazı**, (*orn.*) red-breasted goose: ~ **sıçrıyan sıçanı**, (*zoo.*) jerboa. ~ **lı**, *n.* (*ethn.*) Siberian.

sicil[1]**i** (*adm.*) Register; record. ~ **etm./** ~ **le kaydetmek**, enter in the register, record: ~ **limanı**, (*naut.*) port of registration: ~ **memuru**, archivist. ~ **li**, registered, recorded; (*fig.*) with previous conviction(s).

Sicilya (*geo.*) Sicily. ~ **lı**, *n.* (*ethn.*) Sicilian.

sicim String; cord. ~ **gibi yağmur**, pelting rain.

sidi[1]**k**[gi] (*bio.*) Urine. ~ **asit**, uric acid: ~ **borusu**, ureter: ~ **damlaması**, urinary incontinence: ~ **söktürücü**, (*med.*) diuretic: ~ **torba yangısı**, cystitis: ~ **torbası**, (*bio.*) bladder: ~ **tutamaması**, (*med.*) enuresis; incontinence: ~ **tutulması**, urine retention: ~ **yarışı**, (*fig.*) futile rivalry; dispute about trifles: ~ **yarışına çıkmak/girmek (-le)**, enter into useless competition with s.o.

sidik·kavuğu[nu] (*bio.*) Bladder. ~ **li**, soiled with urine; suffering from urinary incontinence: ~ **meşe**, (*bot.*) an oak that 'bleeds' when burnt. ~ **şekeri**[ni], (*med.*) diabetes. ~ **yolu**[nu], (*bio.*) urethra. ~ **zoru**[nu], (*med.*) urine retention: ~ **na tutulmak**, retain one's urine.

sidr (*cul.*) Cider.

siena ~ **sarısı**, burnt sienna.

sif = (*fin.*) (c.i.f.; *cost, insurance, freight*).

sif·ilis (*med.*) Syphilis. ~**on**, (*phys.*) siphon. ~**ono-forlar**, (*zoo.*) siphonophores.

siftah *n.* (*fin.*) First stroke of business (of the day); first sale (of new commodity). *adv.* For the first time. ~ **etm.** (-e) = ~LAMAK: ~ **senden bereketi Allahtan,** I hope you will bring me good luck! (said to first customer of the day; *also fig.*). ~**lamak** (-i), make the first sale of the day; eat stg. for the first time that season; begin.

siftinmek *vi.* Wriggle about and scratch o.s.; approach s.o. fawningly; guzzle.

Sig. = SİGORTA.

sigar Cigar. ~**a**, cigarette: ~ **artığı**, cigarette-end, 'dog-end': ~ **içilmez!**, no smoking!: ~ **içmek,** smoke a cigarette: ~ **iskemlesi,** coffee-table: ~ **kâğıdı,** cigarette paper: ~ **kâğıdı gibi,** very thin/fine: ~ **kullan(ma)mak,** (not) smoke (as a habit): ~ **külü,** cigarette ash: ~ **tablası,** ash-tray.

sigara·böceği[ni] (*ent.*) Cigarette bettle, lasioderma. ~**böreği**[ni], (*cul.*) meat-/cheese-filled pastry roll. ~**lık,** cigarette-holder//-case.

sigma (*ling.*) Sigma (Σ, σ). ~ + / ~**msı,** (*bio.*) sigmoid.

sigorta (*fin.*) Insurance; insurance company; (*el.*) fuse; safety device. ~ **acentesi,** insurance agency: ~ **değeri,** insurable value: ~ **etm.,** insure stg.: ~ **kutusu,** (*el.*) fuse-box: ~ **olm.,** be insured: ~ **poliçesı,** insurance policy: ~ **prim/ücreti,** insurance premium.

sigorta·cı(lık) (Work of) insurance agent. ~**lamak** (-i), insure stg.; (*col.*) mortgage stg. ~**lı,** insured; (*fig.*) secured.

siğil (*med.*) Wart. ~**li,** covered with warts.

sih·ir[ri] Magic; sorcery, witchcraft; (*fig.*) charm, fascination. ~**baz,** who practises magic; magician, sorcerer. ~**bazlık,** magic, sorcery. ~**lemek** (-i), bewitch, enchant. ~**li,** bewitched: ~ **fener,** (*cin.*) magic lantern.

sik (*vulg.*) Penis. ~**işmek,** *vi.* copulate.

sika (*bot.*) Cycad. ~**lar,** Cycadaceae. ~**tif** (*art.*) siccative.

sikke[1] *n.* (*mod.*) Mevlevi dervish's cap.

sikke[2] *n.* (*fin.*) Coin. ~ **basmak,** coin money: ~ **ve hutbe,** (*his.*) the Sultan's right to mint coins and be prayed for in the HUTBE.

sikla·mat[1] (*chem.*) Cyclamate. ~**men,** (*bot.*) cyclamen (colour).

siklememek (-i) (*vulg.*) Consider unimportant.

sik·lik (*phys.*) Cyclic. ~**lo-,** *pref.* cyclo-. ~**lon,** (*met.*) cyclone. ~**lotron,** (*nuc.*) cyclotron.

sik·mek (-i) (*vulg.*) Have sexual intercourse with; injure; ruin. ~ **tirici,** (*vulg.*) base, low, worthless. ~**tirmek,** *vc.*; *vi.* (*vulg.*) clear out, go away: **siktir!,** get out!: **siktir et (-i)!,** ignore it!: **siktirip gitmek,** go away; leave s.o. alone.

silah (*mil.*) Weapon, arm. ~ **altına almak,** call up: ~ **başı,** call to arms, alarm: ~ **başı etm.,** call to arms: ~ **başına!,** to arms!: ~ **çatmak,** pile arms: ~ **deposu,** armoury: ~ **kurmak,** cock a gun, etc.: ~ **patlamak,** begin battle: ~ **vermek,** arm: ~**a davranmak,** take up and prepare to use arms: ~**a sarılmak,** take up arms; seize a weapon (intending to use it): ~**ı dikmek** (-e), cover with a

weapon: ~**ını almak,** disarm: ~**lar,** armament, weapons.

silah·çı (*his.*) Armourer. ~**endaz,** (*mil.*) marine. ~**hane,** armoury, arsenal. ~**la(ndır)mak (-i),** arm. ~**lanmak,** *vp.* ~**lı,** armed: ~ **kuvvetler,** armed forces: ~ **saldırı,** armed attack: ~ **tarafsızlık,** (*pol.*) armed neutrality. ~**lık,** weapon-belt; armoury. ~**sız,** unarmed: ~ **bırakmak,** disarm: ~ **direnme,** (*pol.*) passive resistance: ~**a ayırmak,** allocate to non-combatant duties. ~**sızlandırmak** (-i), disarm. ~**sızlanma,** disarmament. ~**sızlanmak,** *vp.* be disarmed. ~**şor,** (*his.*) warrior; knight; musketeer. ~**şorluk,** knighthood; skill in using weapons. ~**tar,** (*his.*) sword-bearer; weapons-keeper, armourer.

sil·dirilmek *vp.* ~**dirmek (-i, -e),** *vc.* = SİLMEK. ~**ece**[lkği], (*dom.*) large bath-towel; = ~GİÇ. ~**ge**[lçci], doormat. ~**gi,** (*dom.*) towel, sponge, duster; (*ed.*) blackboard-duster; eraser, rubber; = ~GEÇ; = ~GİÇ. ~**gi**[lçci], (*mot.*) windscreen-wiper.

sili Clean; (*fig.*) virtuous. ~**ci,** cleaner, polisher; (*carp.*) planer. ~**lik,** cleanness; (*fig.*) virtue.

silia (*bio.*) Cilia.

silik Rubbed out; worn; colourless; dim; indistinct; (*fig.*) insignificant, second-rate.

sili·ka (*geol.*) Silica. ~**kat**[1], (*chem.*) silicate. ~**kon,** silicon.

sil·ikleşmek *vi.* Become worn, etc. ~**iklik,** indistinctness, etc. ~**im,** cancellation.

silindir (*math., eng.*) Cylinder; (*ind.*) roller. ~ **gömleği,** (*eng.*) cylinder lining: ~ (**şapka**), (*mod.*) top-hat. ~**aj,** rolling. ~**ik/~sel,** cylindrical; columnar. ~**li,** with a roller: ~ **perdahlamak,** (*tex.*) calender.

silin·mek *vp.* = SİLMEK; be wiped; be scraped/rubbed down (for polishing); wipe/dry o.s. ~**ti,** erasure; stg. wiped off: ~ **yazı(m),** (*lit.*) palimpsest.

silis (*geol.*) Silica. ~**çil,** (*bot.*) silicicolous. ~**leşmek,** *vi.* silicify. ~**li,** silicic, siliceous, silico-. ~**yum,** (*chem.*) silicon.

silk·eleme *vn.* ~**elemek (-i),** shake off (dust, etc.); (*sl.*) drop s.o. at his destination. ~**elenme,** *vn.* ~**elenmek,** *vi., vp.*; shake o.s. ~**i,** convulsion/start (in sleep). ~**indirmek (-i),** *vc.* ~**inmek,** *vi.* shake o.s.: (-den), (*fig.*) shake o.s. free; shake off the effects of stg. ~**inti,** shake; shaking, trembling; stg. shaken off; (*bot.*) dropping of flowers. ~**me,** *vn.*; (*cul.*) meat dish with chopped aubergines, etc. ~**mek (-i),** shake; shake off; shake down (fruit, etc.). ~**tirmek (-i, -e),** *vc.*

sille Box on the ear; slap. ~ **atmak,** slap: ~ **tokat,** fisticuffs.

sil·me *vn.* (*arch.*) Moulding: *a.* brim-full: ~ **tahtası,** board for levelling off corn-measures. ~**mece,** *adv.* brim-full. ~**mek (-i),** wipe (clean/dry); scrub; (*carp.*) plane; rub down; polish; erase; remove the excess, level off: **silip süpürmek,** clean out thoroughly; (*fig.*) make a clean sweep of; destroy. ~**metaş(çı),** (*art.*) mosaic(-cutter).

silo (*agr.*) Silo, grain-store.

silsile Chain (of mountains, etc.); line, series; (*soc.*) genealogy, pedigree; (*his.*) dynasty; (*adm.*)

chain of promotion. ~ **name**, genealogical tree, pedigree.

sil·t (*geol.*) Silt. ~ **tlenme**, siltation. ~ **uet**[i], silhouette. ~ **ür**, (*geo.*) Silurian.

sim[1] *n.* Sign, symbol.

sim[2] *n.* (*chem.*) Silver. ~ **a**[1], *n.* (*geol.*) sima.

sima[2] *n.* Face, features; figure, personage.

simetri Symmetry. ~ **k**/~ **li**, symmetrical. ~ **siz**, asymmetrical.

simge Sign, symbol; notation; abbreviation. ~ **bilim**, (*phil.*) symbolics. ~ **ci(lik)**, (*art., phil.*) symbol·ist/(-ism). ~ **lemek** (-i), symbolize. ~ **leşmek**, *vi.* become a symbol. ~ **leştirme**, symbolization. ~ **lik**, system of symbols. ~ **sel(lik)**, symbolic(s).

simi[l]**t**[di] (*cul.*) Ring-shaped bread-roll; sesame ring; (*naut.*) lifebuoy; (*ed., sl.*) zero, nought. ~ **çi(lik)**, (work of) siMiT-maker/-seller.

simpozyum (*ed.*) Symposium.

simsar (*fin.*) Broker; middleman; commission-agent. ~ **iye**, brokerage, commission. ~ **lık**, profession of broker; brokerage.

simsiyah Jet black, black as coal.

simültane Simultaneous.

simya Alchemy. ~ **ger**, alchemist.

sin[i 1] *n.* (*obs.*) Grave, tomb.

sin[ni 2] *n.* (*obs.*) Age. ~ **ni temyiz**, age of discretion.

-sin[1]/**-sın/-sun/-sün** *v. suf.* [96] *Second person sing.* *pres.* = OLMAK. (Thou) art, (you) are [**annemsin**, you are my mother: **adamsın**, thou art a man].

-sin[2]/**-sın/-sun/-sün** *v. suf.* [137] *Third person sing. imperative* [**gitsin**, let him go; **görmesin**, let him not see]. ~ **için**, [139] (in order) for him to . . ..

sin. = SİNEMA(CILIK).

sinagog (*rel.*) Synagogue.

sina(g)ri[l]**t**[di] (*ich.*) Large-eyed dentex, sea-bream.

sinameki (*bot.*) Senna. ~ **gibi**, hesitant, slow; unattractive.

sinca[l]**p**[b1] (*zoo.*) (Fur of) red squirrel. ~ **balığı**, (*ich.*) squirrel/soldier fish: ~ **maymunu**, (*zoo.*) squirrel monkey. ~ **ımsı**, squirrel-like. ~ **i**, brownish grey.

-sindi/-sındı/-sundu/-sündü *v. suf.* [138] How/who/what should . . .? [**onu kim görsündü?**, who should see it?].

sindi[l]**k**[ği] = SENDİK.

sindir·ici (*rad.*) Attenuator. ~ **ilmek**, *vp.* ~ **im**, (*bio.*) digestion: ~ +, *a.* digestive; alimentary; gastro-: ~ **aygıt/sistemi**, digestive system: ~ **kanalı**, alimentary canal. ~ **imbilim(ci)**, gastroenterolo·gy/(-gist). ~ **imsel**, digestive. ~ **imsizlik**, (*med.*) dyspepsia. ~ **me**, *vn.* ~ **mek** (-i, -e), *vc.* = SİNMEK: (-i), digest; swallow; assimilate; (*rad.*) attenuate, dampen; (*fig.*) terrify, cow: **sindire sindire**, permeating; very thoroughly.

sine Bosom, breast: = SİNMEK. ~ **ye çekmek**, put up with, resign o.s. to.

sine[l]**k**[ği] (*ent.*) Fly. ~ **avlamak**, potter about, idle: ~ **raketi**, fly-swat: ~ **ufak ama mide bulandırır**, small causes can produce big results: ~ **in yağını hesap eder**, he's so mean he charges for the fat of a fly (in the butter): ~ **ler**, (*ent.*) Muscidae, flies: ~ **ten yağ çıkarmak**, profit from the smallest things.

sinek·ağırlık/ ~ **sıklet** (*sp.*) Flyweight. ~ **çil/**

~ **kuşu**[nu]/ ~ **yutan**, (*orn.*) flycatcher. ~ **kâğıdı**[nı], fly-paper. ~ **kapan**, (*bot.*) Venus's fly-trap. ~ **kapangiller**, (*orn.*) Old World flycatchers. ~ **kaydı**, ~ (**tıraş**), (*jok.*) a very smooth shave. ~ **lenmek**, *vi.* flies multiply; be covered with flies. ~ **lik**, fly-swat/-whisk; fly-paper. ~ **mantarı**, (*myc.*) fly agaric.

sinema Cinema; motion-picture. ~ +, *a.* Cinema/(-tographic): ~ **makinesi**, cinematograph: ~ **salgını**, craze for the cinema: ~ **sı oynanmak**, (book/play) be filmed.

sinema·cı Cinema-operator. ~ **cılık**, motion-picture industry; cinema-operation, cinematography. ~ **evi/** ~ **tek**, film library/club. ~ **sever**, cinema-goer, film-fan. ~ **tik**, (*phys.*) kinematics. ~ **tograf**, cinematograph.

sin·erji (*bio.*) Synergy. ~ **estezi**, (*psy.*) synaesthesia.

singin Shy; easily embarrassed; (*naut.*) low-built.

sini (*dom.*) Round metal tray (used as a table).

sini[l]**k**[ği 1] *a.* Crouching; cowed.

sinik[i 2] *n.* (*phil.*) Cynic. ~ **lik**, cynicism.

sinir (*bio.*) Sinew; nerve; fibre; (*bot.*) rib; (*fig.*) unusual sensitivity; (*psy.*) nervous habit. ~ **ağrı/hastalığı**, (*med.*) neuralgia: ~ **argınlık/bozukluk/zayıflığı**, (*psy.*) neurasthenia: ~ **çemberi**, (*bio.*) nerve ring: ~ **düğümü**, (*bio.*) ganglion: ~ **hücresi**, (*bio.*) neuron: ~ **olm.**, lose one's temper, become angry: ~ **savaşı**, (*psy.*) war of nerves: ~ **sistemi**, (*bio.*) nervous system: ~ **tabakası**, (*bio.*) optic nerve, retina: ~ **tutsaklığı**, (*psy.*) hysterics: ~ **tutulması**, (*med.*) cramp: ~ **ucu**, (*bio.*) nerve ending: ~ **i oynamak**, become angry and excitable: ~ **ine dokunmak** (-in), irritate, annoy; get on s.o.'s nerves: ~ **leri altüst olm.**, be upset/nervy: ~ **leri ayakta olm.**, one's nerves be on edge: ~ **leri boşanmak**, be unable to control o.s.; have a nervous fit: ~ **leri gerilmek**, be irritable: ~ **leri kuvvetli**, calm and collected: ~ **leri yatışmak**, calm down, become calm: ~ **leri zayıf**, easily irritated: ~ **lerine hakim olm.**, control o.s.; be quite calm.

sinir·ağı (*bio.*) Plexus. ~ **bilim**, (*med.*) neurology. ~ **ce**, (*psy.*) neurosis. ~ **doku**, (*bio.*) nervous tissue. ~ **kanatlılar**, (*ent.*) ant-lions. ~ **lemek** (-i), (*cul.*) remove the sinews (from); (*bio.*) hamstring. ~ **lendirmek** (-i), irritate, annoy; make nervous. ~ **lenme**, *vn.* ~ **lenmek** (-e), become irritated with: *vi.* have one's nerves set on edge; be hamstrung. ~ **li**, (*bio.*) sinewy; tough; wiry; (*psy.*) on edge, irritable, nervy. ~ **lilik**, wiriness; state of nerves, irritability. ~ **sel**, neural, neuro-; nervous.

-siniz/-sınız/-sunuz/-sünüz *v. suf.* [96] *Second person pl. pres.* = OLMAK. (You) are.

sin·izm (*phil.*) Cynicism. ~ **kretizm**, (*phil.*) syncretism. ~ **kronizm**, synchronism.

sinlik Cemetery.

sin·mek *vi.* Crouch down (to hide); (*fig.*) be humiliated/cowed, sing small: (-e), sink into, penetrate; be swallowed/digested. ~ **mez**, indigestible.

sinn- = SİN[2].

sino·log (*ethn., ling.*) Sinologue. ~ **loji**, sinology.

sin·onim (*ling.*) Synonym. ~ **opsis**, (*lit.*) synopsis.

sinsi Stealthy; slinking; sneaking; insidious. ~ **ce**, stealthily, etc. ~ **leşmek**, *vi.* become stealthy, etc. ~ **lik**, stealthiness; subtlety; underhand dealing.

sinsin (*Or. mus.*) Young people's dance round fire.

sintine (*naut.*) Bilges. ~ **tulumbası**, bilge pump.

sinü·s (*math.*) Sine; (*bio.*) sinus. ~**zi¹t**^{di}, (*med.*) sinusitis. ~**zoidal**^{i}, (*math.*) sinusoidal. ~**zoi¹t**^{di}, sinusoid.

sin·yal Signal. ~ **vermek**, (give a) signal. ~ **yalizasyon**, signalling system. ~**yor**, signor.

sipahi(lık) (*mil.*, *his.*) (Duties of) cavalry soldier.

sipariş (*fin.*) Order; commission; allotment of pay. ~ **almak**, take an order: ~ **etm.**, order stg.; transfer stg.: ~ **vermek**, give an order (to make/send stg.).

siper (*mil.*) Shield; shelter; trench; rampart; barricade; protecting item; (*mod.*) peak (of cap); (*mot.*) car-bumper; windscreen; (*eng.*) top-slide (lathe); (*fig.*) aegis, protection. ~ **almak**, parry a blow; take cover/shelter (behind stg.): ~ **etm.**, blank off: ~ **humması**, (*med.*) trench fever: ~ **kazmak**, (*mil.*) dig a trench; dig in.

siper·isaika (*obs.*) Lightning-conductor. ~**lenmek**, *vi.* take shelter. ~**lik**, stg. used as a shelter/protection; giving shelter; deflector.

sipolin (*geol.*) Cipolin.

sipsi (*naut.*) Boatswain's pipe; (*mus.*) reed (of clarinet, etc.); (*sl.*) cigarette.

sipsivri Sharply pointed. ~ **çıkagelmek**, appear unexpectedly (and unwanted): ~ **kalmak**, be suddenly deserted by all; be destitute.

sirayet^i Spreading/propagating itself; (*med.*) contagion, infection. ~ **etm.**, (*med.*) spread.

sir·en (*phys.*) Siren. ~**k**^{i}, (*geol.*, *th.*) circus.

sirkat^i Theft. ~ **etm.**, steal.

sirke^1 *n.* (*ent.*) Nit. ~**lenmek**, *vi.* be infested with nits.

sirke^2 *n.* (*cul.*) Vinegar; acetate. ~ **asidi**, (*chem.*) acetic acid; ~**yi savurmak**, brew vinegar.

sirke·ci(lik) (Work of) vinegar-maker/-seller. ~**leşmek**, *vi.* become vinegary/sour. ~**leştirmek** (-i), acetify. ~**ngebin**, (*med.*) oxymel, honey and vinegar. ~**sineği**, (*ent.*) vinegar fly, drosophila.

sirkü·lasyon (*pub.*) Circulation. ~**ler**, circular (-letter).

sir·oko (*met.*) Sirocco. ~**oz**, (*med.*) cirrhosis. ~**ro-kümülüs**//**-stratüs**, (*met.*) cirro·cumulus//-stratus. ~**rüs**, (*met.*) cirrus. ~**to**, (*mus.*) folk dance/tune.

sis (*met.*) Fog, mist, haze. ~ **bombası**, (*mil.*) smoke-bomb: ~ **farı**, (*mot.*) fog-lamp: ~ **odası**, (*chem.*) cloud chamber.

sisal (*bot.*) Sisal.

Sisam *pr.n.* (*geo.*) Samos. ~**lı**, *n.* (*ethn.*) Samian.

sis·lenmek *vi.* Become damp/foggy; (glass) be covered with dew, be misty. ~**li**, foggy, misty, hazy. ~**libalık**, (*ich.*) type of barbel.

sis·mik (*geol.*) Seismic. ~**mograf(i)**, seismograph(y). ~**molog**, seismologist. ~**moloji**, seismology.

sistem System. ~**atik**, *a.* systematic; classified; (*bio.*) taxonomical: *n.* systematics. ~**leşmek**, *vi.* become systematized. ~**leştirmek** (-i), systematize; classify. ~**li**, systematic, orderly; systematized, classified. ~**siz**, disordered.

sistire (*carp.*, *cul.*) Scraper. ~**lemek** (-i), scrape down, smooth.

sis·tit^i (*med.*) Cystitis. ~**tolit**, cystolith.

sit (*arch.*, *ind.*) Site.

-sit *n. suf.* (*bio.*) -cyte [LÖKOSİT].

sitayiş Eulogy. ~ **etm.**, eulogize. ~**kâr**, praising.

site (*archaeol.*) Lake-dwellers' village; (*his.*) city-state; quarter (of a city); (*ind.*) industrial estate; (*ed.*) university campus; (*soc.*) housing estate.

sitem Reproach. ~**kâr**/~**li**, reproachful.

sitil Large metal bucket; large pot.

sito·krom (*bio.*) Cytochrome. ~**loji**, cytology. ~**plazma**, cytoplasm.

sitr·at (*chem.*) Citrate. ~**ik**, citric. ~**in**, (*geol.*) citrine. ~**on**, (*bot.*) citron.

sitt·eisevir (*met.*) Period of six stormy days in April. ~**insene**, for sixty years, for a very long time.

sivil Civilian; in mufti; plain-clothes policeman; (*jok.*) naked. ~ **savunma**, civil defence: ~ **şahıs**, civilian: ~ **yıl**, (*ast.*) civil year. ~**lik**, civilian status; (*jok.*) nakedness.

sivilce (*bio.*) Pimple; (*med.*) acne.

sivişmek = SIVIŞMAK.

sivri Sharp-pointed; tapering; (*math.*) acute; peak; tall and thin. ~ **akıllı**, eccentric, odd and self-opinionated: ~ **burun(lu)**, (with a) pointed nose; (*ich.*) tuna: ~ **diş**, (*bio.*) fang: ~ **kafalı**, obstinate: ~ **uç**, (*bot.*) cusp.

sivri·biber (*bot.*) Long green pepper. ~**fare**, (*zoo.*) common shrew. ~**kuyruk**, (*zoo.*) pinworm. ~**leşmek**, *vi.* become pointed. ~**lik**, pointedness, acuteness. ~**lmek**, *vi.* become pointed/prominent; (*fig.*) make rapid progress in one's career, gain distinction: **sivrilen**, distinguished. ~**ltmek** (-i), make pointed/sharp. ~**sincapçık(giller)**, (*zoo.*) tree-shrew(s). ~**sine¹k**^{gi}, (*ent.*) mosquito: ~ **balığı**, (*ich.*) mosquito fish.

siy. = SİYASET.

siya (*naut.*) Reversing the oars and rowing backwards. ~**!**, back oars!: ~ ~ **gitmek**, go backwards.

siyah Black; (*pub.*) black-letter; (*sl.*) opium. ~ **ağaçkakan**, (*orn.*) black woodpecker. ~ **alınlı çekirgekuşu**, (*orn.*) lesser grey shrike: ~ **baştankara**, (*orn.*) coal tit: ~ **beyaz**, (*art.*) black and white drawing, etc.: ~ **beyaz dere kuşu**, (*orn.*) lesser pied kingfisher: ~ **beyaz (film)**, (*cin.*) black-and-white film: ~ **boyunlu**, (*orn.*) black-necked: ~ **çaylak**, (*orn.*) black kite: ~ **gagalı yelkovan**, (*orn.*) Manx shearwater: ~ **gerdanlı dalgıç**, (*orn.*) arctic loon, black-throated diver: ~ **göğüslü**, (*orn.*) black-bellied: ~ **ırk**, (*ethn.*) black race: ~ **kanatlı**, (*orn.*) black-winged: ~ **keklik**, (*orn.*) black-cock: ~ **krep**, (*tex.*) crêpe: ~ **sırtlı kuyrukkakan**, pied wheatear: ~ **sinekyutan**, red-breasted flycatcher: ~ **üzüm**, (*bot.*) black grape. [*Also* ~ KARA.]

siyah·ımsı/~**ımtırak** Blackish. ~**i**, (*ethn.*) Negro. ~**lanmak**/~**laşmak**, *vi.* become black. ~**latmak** (-i), make black, blacken. ~**lı**, dressed in black. ~**lık**, blackness; dark/black place.

siyak^1 (*phil.*) Subsequent context; = SİBAK. ~**u sibak**, context.

Siyam (*geo.*) Siam, Thailand. ~ + , *a.* Siamese. ~**lı**, *n.* (*ethn.*) Siamese, Thai.

siyan·amit (*chem.*) Cyanamide. ~**ojen**, cyanogen.

~**oz**, (*med.*) cyanosis. ~**ür**, (*chem.*) cyanide. ~**ürlü**, cyanide(d).

siyansfiksiyon (*lit.*) Science-fiction.

siya·sa Policy. ~**sacı(lık)**, (work of) politician. ~**sal**, political: ~ **amaçlı**, politically motivated: ~ **bilgiler**, (*ed.*) political science: ~ **suç**, (*leg.*) political offence. ~**sallaştırmak (-i)**, make political. ~**set**[i], politics; policy; diplomacy; (*leg.*, *obs.*) capital punishment: ~ +, *a.* political: ~ **meydanı**, place of execution. ~**setçi(lik)**, (work of) politician. ~**seten**, politically. ~**si**, *a.* political: *n.* politician: ~ **münasebetler**, diplomatic relations. ~**siyat**[i], politics; diplomacy.

siyati[i]**k**[gi] (*med.*) Sciatica.

siy·ek (*bio.*) Urethra. ~**mek**, *vi.* (cat, dog) urinate.

-siyle/-sıyla *post.* [87] = -si[1] + İLE [ANNESİYLE].

siyon·ist (*pol.*) Zionist. ~**izm**, Zionism.

siz *pron. sing./pl.* [67] You. ~ **bilirsiniz!**, you know best!, as you will!: ~ **olmadan**, [182] without you: ~ **sağ olun!**, it doesn't matter!; don't worry!

siz-: ~**ce**, according to you; in your opinion: ~**de**, *locative* on/with you: ~**de kalsın!**, keep the change!: ~**den**, *ablative* from/by/through you: ~**den iyi olmasın!**, (*col.*) present company excepted: ~**e**, *dative* to you: ~**e bir ricam var**, I have a request to make of you: ~**e doyum olmaz!**, (*jok.*) (to a parting guest) we can't have enough of you! [*the reply*: ~**e de inan olmaz!**, I don't believe you!]: ~**e gelince**, as for/to you: ~**e son bir zahmetim daha olacak!**, I'll trouble you for one last thing: ~**i**, *accusative* you: ~**in**, *possessive a.* your: ~**in kadar (zengin)**, as (rich) as you: ~**in neniz?**, what relation is he to you?: ~**inki**, *possessive pron.* yours: ~**inle**, with you: ~**inle paylaşacak bir kozum var**, I have a bone to pick with you: ~**ler**, (*col.*) [68] you (*plural*): ~**lere ömür!**, (s.o. has died but) may you have a long life!

-siz/-sız/-suz/-süz *a./pron. suf.* [62] Without; devoid of; -less, a(n)-; un- [**sonsuz**, without end, endless: **tarihsiz**, undated: **susuz**, anhydrous: **sensiz**, without you]. - ~**in** [188] = -MEKSİZİN. - ~**lik**, *n. suf.* lack of, non-existence of [**parasızlık**, lack of money, poverty: **susuzluk**, thirst, aridity].

skan·dal Scandal. ~**dinav** = İSKANDİNAV. ~**diyum**, (*chem.*) scandium.

sk·arab (*ent.*) Scarab beetle. ~**alar**, (*math.*) scalar. ~**avut**[u], (*naut.*) patrol-/scout-boat. ~**e**[i]**ç**[ci], (*rad.*, *th.*) sketch. ~**i**, (*sp.*) ski. ~**ink**, (*zoo.*) skink. ~**lero-**, *pref.* (*bio.*) sclero-. ~**olastik**, *n.* (*phil.*) scholasticism: *a.* scholastic. ~**or**, (*sp.*) score. ~**reyper**, (*eng.*) scraper. ~**uter**, (*mot.*) motor-scooter.

sl·ay[i]**t**[d1] (*cin.*) Slide. ~**ogan**, (*lit.*) slogan.

Slo·vak (*ethn.*) Slovak. ~**vakça**, (*ling.*) Slovak. ~**vakya**, (*geo.*) Slovakia. ~**ven**, (*ethn.*) Slovene. ~**vence**, (*ling.*) Slovene. ~**venya**, (*geo.*) Slovenia.

Sm., sm. = (*ch.s.*) SAMARYUM; (*math.*) SANTİMETRE.

smokin (*mod.*) Dinner-jacket. ~**li**, wearing a dinner-jacket; (*sl.*) well-dressed.

Sn. = SANİYE; SAYIN; (*ch.s.*) KALAY.

sno[i]**p**[bu] Snob.

SO = SANAYİ ODASI.

soba (*dom.*) Stove. ~ **borusu**, stove-pipe. ~**cı(lık)**,

(work of) stove-maker/-seller/-repairer. ~**lık**, suitable for (making) a stove; stoveful (wood, etc.).

sobe (*child.*) Home! ~**lemek (-i)**, call/reach 'home!'

sod·a (*chem.*) Sodium carbonate; (*dom.*) soda; (*cul.*) soda-water. ~**yum**, (*chem.*) sodium: ~ **klorür**, sodium chloride, common salt.

sof (*tex.*) Camlet, mohair, alpaca; (*mod.*) raw-silk lining.

sofa (*arch.*) Hall, anteroom; (*dom.*) sofa.

sofi (*rel.*) Sufi, mystic; devotee. ~**yane**, piously.

sofizm (*phil.*) Sophism.

sofra Dining-table; travellers' portable table; meal; mealtime; group of those eating; round pastry-board; (*bio.*) anus. ~ **başı**, around the table: ~ **başına geçmek**, sit down to a meal: ~ **bezi**, tablecloth: ~ **donatmak**, load the table with food: ~ **kurmak**, lay the table: ~ **örtüsü**, table cover: ~ **takımı**, table service (cutlery, crockery, etc.): ~**sı açık**, hospitable: ~**yı kaldırmak**, clear the table. ~**cı**, butler; waiter.

softa *n.* (*rel.*) Muslim theological student; (*pej.*) bigot, fanatic. *a.* Behind the times, old-fashioned. ~**laşmak**, *vi.* become very pious//bigoted. ~**lık**, bigotry, fanaticism.

sofu (*rel.*) Devotee; fanatic. ~**luk**, religious devotion; fanaticism.

Sofya (*geo.*) Sofia.

soğan (*bot.*) Bulb; onion; (thermometer) bulb. ~ **gibi**, bulbous. ~**cık**, (*bot.*) pickling onion, shallot; (*bio.*) medulla oblongata. ~**lı**, bulbous; (*cul.*) prepared with onions. ~**lık**, (*agr.*) onion-bed; onion-rack. ~**zarı**[m], onion-skin.

soğrumsama (*chem.*) Adsorption.

soğubilim (*phys.*) Cryogenics.

soğuk *a.* Cold; chilly, cool; (*med.*) algid; (*geo.*) polar, arctic; (*fig.*) frigid; unfriendly; bleak; out-of-place, in bad taste. *n.* Cold weather. ~ **algınlığı**, (*med.*) cold, chill: ~ **almak**, catch cold: ~ **apse**, (*med.*) cold abscess: ~ **bastı**, (*met.*) cold weather has set in: ~ **büfe**, (*cul.*) cold buffet: ~ **çekilmiş**, (*min.*) cold drawn: ~ **çıban**, (*med.*) boil: ~ **damga**, (*pub.*) embossed stamp: ~ **davranmak (-e)**, treat s.o. coldly, keep s.o. at a distance: ~ **dövmek**, (*min.*) cold-hammer: ~ **durmak**, look on coldly: ~ **düşmek/kaçmak**, (word/deed) be out of place/in bad taste: ~ **harp/savaş**, (*mil.*) cold war: ~ **hava deposu**, (*cul.*) cold store: ~ **ısırması**, (*med.*) chilblain: ~ **kanlı**, (*zoo.*) cold-blooded: ~ KANLI: ~ **keski**, (*arch.*) cold chisel: ~ **neva(lı)**, (*fig.*) cold, unfriendly: ~ **söz**, unfriendly word: ~ **terler döktürmek**, put s.o. in a cold sweat (from terror): ~ **yapmak**, (*met.*) be very cold: ~**lar**, (*met.*) the cold weather, winter: ~**tan (içi) katılmak**, be chilled to the marrow.

soğuk·alın (*met.*) Cold front. ~**altı**, (*phys.*) supercooled. ~**bez**, (*tex.*) cotton cloth, jaconet, gauze. ~**ça**, rather cold. ~**kanlı**, calm, coolheaded; cold, unsympathetic; (*zoo.*) cold-blooded. ~**kanlılık**, calmness; coldness, lack of sympathy. ~**lama**, *vn.*; (*med.*) chill, cold. ~**lamak**, *vi.* catch a chill. ~**laşmak**, *vi.* become cold; behave coldly. ~**luk**, cold, coldness; (*fig.*) antipathy; irritability; (*cul.*)

cold sweet, fruit; cold-store; cooling room (of hammam). ~taş, (*chem.*) cryolite.

soğulmak *vi.* (*cul.*) Be drained, become dry; (*geo.*) (river) disappear into the ground, dry up.

soğu·ma *vn.* Cooling. ~mak, *vi.* become cold; cool off; (*med.*) catch cold; (*fig.*) be chilly in one's relationships: (-den), cease to care for, take a dislike to.

soğur·gan (*phys.*) Absorbent. ~ma, absorption; adsorption. ~mak (-i), absorb; adsorb. ~tmak (-i), *vc.* ~tulmak, *vp.* ~um, adsorption.

soğuşmak *vi.* (*agr.*) (Ground) become moist and productive.

soğut·kan *a.* Cooling: *n.* (*cul.*) cooler, chiller; coolant. ~ma, *vn.* cooling; refrigeration; cryo-: ~ kulesi, (*ind.*) cooling tower: ~ odası, chilling room: ~ sıvı, refrigerant. ~ma'ç^{cı}, refrigerator. ~mak (-i), cool, refrigerate; (*fig.*) alienate. ~malı, frigorific. ~ucu, *a.* cooling: *n.* refrigerator: ~ karışım, (*phys.*) cryogen. ~ulmak, *vp.* ~um, refrigeration.

sohbetⁱ Friendly intercourse; chat, conversation. ~ etm., have a chat, converse: ~ meraklısı, chatty person.

sok. = SOKAK; SOKAĞI.

soka'k^{ğı} Road, street; (*fig.*) out of the house, outside. ~ çocuğu, street urchin: ~ kadın/kızı, woman of the streets, prostitute, street-walker: ~ kapısı, front-/street-door: ~ ~ sürtmek, lounge about through the streets: ~ süpürgesi, (woman) always gadding about: ~a atsan bin lira eder, it's worth at least 1000 lira anywhere: ~a çıkmak, go out, not be at home: ~a dökmek, spend unnecessarily: ~a dökülmek, (people) pour/rush into the streets: ~a düşmek, (woman) become a prostitute; (thing) lose its value: ~ları arşınlamak, walk the streets.

sok·ma *vn.* Introduced from outside; imported. ~mak (-i, -e), thrust into, insert; introduce (into); import; involve, entail; drive into; let in; (insect/snake) sting, bite; (*fig.*) injure, calumniate.

sokman (*mod.*) Type of long coarse boot.

sokra (*carp.*) Butt end (of a plank).

sokturmak (-i, -e) *vc.* = SOKMAK.

soku (*cul.*) Stone mortar.

sokul·gan Sociable; friendly; ingratiating. ~ganlık, sociability; friendliness. ~ma, *vn.*; (*geol.*) intrusion: ~ +, *a.* intrusive. ~mak, *vp.* = SOKMAK: (-e), insinuate o.s. into; push into; cultivate friendly relations with. ~mamak, *vi.* stand clear/aloof. ~maz, aloof.

sokum = KUYRUKSOKUMU; mouthful, morsel.

sokur *n.* (*zoo.*) Mole. *a.* Sunken; blind; one-eyed.

sokuş·mak (-e) *vi.* Push into gently/furtively; sneak in; infiltrate. ~turmak (-i, -e), *vc.*; (*fin.*) switch goods.

sol^ü *n.* 1. (*mus.*) Soh, sol. 2. (*chem.*) Sol.

sol³ *a.* Left. *n.* Left-hand side/direction; (*pol.*) leftist, socialist; socialism. ~AÇIK; ~BEK: ~ eğilimli, with leftist tendencies: ~ eli beklemek, (*jok.*) not wait for s.o. who is late for a meal: ~ haf/oyun kurucu, (*sp.*) left-half: ~ iç: ~ savunucu, (*sp.*) left-back: ~ tarafından kalkmak, get out of bed the

wrong side: ~ yap!, left turn!: ~a dönen, anticlockwise: ~da sıfır, a mere/complete cipher: ~dan geri dönmek, retreat, retire: ~una düşmek, be on the left side (of road).

sol·açı'k^{ğı} (*sp.*) Outside left. ~ak, left-handed, cack-handed; (*his.*) Sultan's guardsman. ~aklık, being left-handed. ~anahtarı^{nı}, (*mus.*) treble clef. ~bek, (*sp.*) left-back. ~cu, (*pol.*) left-winger, leftist, radical. ~culuk, left-wing/radical politics.

soldurmak (-i) *vc.* = SOLMAK; fade, discolour.

sol·enoi'^{tdi} (*el.*) Solenoid. ~fej, (*mus.*) solfeggio, sol-fa.

solgun Pale; (*tex.*) faded; (*bot.*) withered. ~luk, paleness.

soliçⁱ (*sp.*) Inside left.

soli·darite (*soc.*) Solidarity. ~darizm, (*soc.*) solidarism. ~psizm, (*phil.*) solipsism. ~stⁱ, (*mus.*) soloist; solo singer. ~ter, (*bio.*) solitary.

sol·lamak *vi.* (*mot.*) Keep to/drive on the left. ~lu = SAĞLI.

sol·mak *vi.* Become pale; (*tex.*) fade; (*bot.*) wither. ~maz, colour-fast, fadeless; (*bot.*) amaranthine.

solo (*mus.*) Solo.

solucan (*zoo.*) Worm. ~ gibi, pale, weak, thin; s.o. unpleasant. ~biçim, vermiform. ~otu^{nu}, (*bot.*) tansy. ~sı, wormlike.

soluğan *a.* Short of breath. *n.* (*naut.*) Swell.

soluk¹ *a.* Pale; colourless; (*tex.*) faded; (*bot.*) withered.

solu'k^{ğu 2} *n.* Breath; breathing; panting. ~ aldırmak, give s.o. time to take a breath; give a respite: ~ alma, (*bio.*) inspiration: ~ almak, breathe in, take a breath; recover o.s.: ~ borucuğu, (*bio.*) bronchia: ~ borusu, (*bio.*) trachea, windpipe: ~ darlığı, breathlessness: ~a, out of breath, panting: ~ tutmak, hold one's breath: ~ verme, (*bio.*) expiration: ~ vermek, breathe out: ~u (Bağdat)'ta almak, make a bee-line for (Baghdad); flee the country, escape: ~u kesilerek, with bated breath: ~u kesilmek, be unable to breathe; (horse) be blown; (*fig.*) have no strength left.

soluk·lanmak *vi.* Take a long deep breath; (*fig.*) take a 'breather'; have a rest. ~suz, without breath//respite.

solu·mak *vi.* Inhale; breathe heavily; pant, gasp; (horse) blow. ~nga'ç^{cı}, (*bio.*) gills. ~nmak, *vi.* breathe. ~num, *n.* breathing; respiration: ~ +, *a.* respiratory: ~ aygıtı, (*med.*) respirator: ~ dalcığı, (*bio.*) bronchiole: ~ dalı, bronchus: ~ dalı öykence//yangısı, (*med.*) bronchopneumonia// bronchitis: ~ jimnastiği, breathing exercises: ~ sistemi, (*bio.*) respiratory system. ~tmak (-i), make breathless.

solüsyon (*phys.*, *fig.*) Solution.

som¹ *a.* Solid (not hollow/veneered); massive; unadulterated. *n.* (*arch.*) Part of quay above water.

som² *n.* ~ balığı, (*ich.*) salmon.

soma¹ *n.* (*cul.*) Raki without aniseed.

soma² *n.* (*bio.*) Soma, body. ~tik, somatic.

soma'k^{ğı 1} *n.* (*bio.*) Muzzle.

soma'k^{ğı 2} *n.* (*bot.*) Sumach. ~i, (*geol.*) porphyry.

somata (*cul.*) Almond SÜBYE.

somru'k^{ğu} (*med.*) Dummy; sweet to suck.

omun[1] *n*. (*cul*.) Loaf of bread; stg. large and soft.
omun[2] *n*. (*eng*.) Nut. ~ **anahtarı**, spanner, wrench.
omur·danmak/~tmak *vi*. Pout; sulk; frown; grumble: **somurta somurta**, frowning, sulking. ~ **tkan(lık)**, sulk·y/(-iness).
omut[u] *a*. Concrete; tangible. ~ **ad**, (*ling*.) concrete noun. ~ **laşmak**, *vi*. become concrete. ~ **laştırmak** (-i), make concrete, concretize. ~ **luk**, concreteness.
omya (*dom*.) Spring mattress; sprung metal bedstead.
on *a*. Last; latter; final; ultimate; (*phys*.) critical. *n*. End; ending, close; result; (*sp*.) final; (*bio*.) afterbirth, placenta. ~ **bulmak**, come to an end, be exhausted: ~ **çalışma**, (*th*.) dress-rehearsal: ~ **dakika**, (*pub*.) stop press: ~ **defa**, last time: ~ **derece**, (to) the highest degree; the uttermost; (*col*.) awfully: ~ **derece bıkmış (-den)**, sick to death of . . .: ~ **dördün**, (*ast*.) moon's last quarter: ~ **gürlük**, ease and comfort in one's old age: ~ **istek**, last will/ wishes: ~ **kalıtçı**, (*leg*.) residual heir: ~ **konakçı**, (*bio*.) final host: ~ **kozunu oynamak**, play one's last trump: ~ **moda**, the latest fashion; craze: ~ **nefesi(ni vermek)**, (breathe) one's last breath: ~ **pişmanlık fayda vermez**, it's no good being sorry after the event/crying over spilt milk: ~ **sayı**, (*pub*.) current number: ~ SES: ~ **soruşturma**, (*leg*.) trial: ~ **terbi**, (*ast*.) moon's last quarter: ~ **turfanda**, (*agr*.) the last fruit/crop of the season: ~ **uyarı**, (*pol*.) ultimatum: ~ **vermek/~a erdirmek (-e)**, finish; put an end to; call off: ~ **yarış**, (*sp*.) final: ~ **a ermek**, finish; (come to an) end: ~ **a kalan dona kalır**, the Devil take the hindmost: ~ **dan bir evvelki**, penultimate, last but one: ~ **u dumandır**, he'll come to a bad/sticky end: ~ **u ne olacak?**, what will come of it?: ~ **unda**, in the end, finally, after all: ~ **unu düşünmek**, think of the result/consequences: ~ **unu getirememek (-in)**, fail to accomplish/ complete stg.: ~ **unu getirmek (-in)**, accomplish/ complete successfully.
son. = (*ling*.) SONEK.
on·ar (*naut*.) Sonar. ~ **at**[1] (*mus*.) sonata.
son·aşam(cı) (*sp*.) Record(-holder). ~ **aşamlamak**, break the record. ~ **bahar(da)**, (in) autumn. ~ **çağ**, (*his*.) recent times.
son·da Probe; (*geol*.) bore; (*med*.) catheter: ~ **çubuğu**, sounding rod: ~ **ipi**, (*naut*.) fathom line. ~ **daj**, (*geol*.) boring, drilling; (*fig*.) inquiry: ~ **aleti**, drill: ~ **delik/kuyusu**, borehole: ~ **döküntüsü**, chiselled soil: ~ **kulesi**, derrick: ~ **numunesi**, borehole/core sample: ~ **takımı**, drill-rig: ~ **yapmak**, drill, bore. ~ **dajcı**, borer, driller. ~ **dalama**, *vn*. sounding, probing; (*geol*.) drilling, prospecting. ~ **dalamak (-i)**, sound, probe; (*geol*.) drill, prospect. ~ **dör**, driller.
son·deyiş (*th*.) Epilogue. ~ **dördün** = SON. ~ **durmak** (-i), stretch.
sone (*lit*.) Sonnet.
son·ek[1] (*ling*.) Ending; suffix. ~ **lama**, (*sp*.) final. ~ **lu**, (*math*.) finite.
sonra *adv*. [203] In future; after, afterwards, later, by and by; otherwise. *n*. The future; a later time. ~ **(-den)**, *post*. [89] after, beyond. ~ **külahları**

değişiriz, otherwise we shall quarrel/fall out: ~ **dan/~ları**, [201] later, recently, subsequently: ~ **dan görme**, parvenu, upstart: ~ **dan olma**, comparatively recently: ~ **dan oluşum**, (*geol*., *chem*.) epigene: ~ **ki**, subsequent, later; ultimate: ~ **kiler**, successors; posterity; those that come/happen later: ~ **sı**, its result/consequence/sequel: ~ **sını soğan doğra!**, don't pursue the subject!: ~ **ya bırakmak**, put off, postpone. ~ **sız**, eternal, endless. ~ **sızlık**, eternity.
son·sal (*phil*.) A posteriori. ~ **ses**, (*ling*.) final sound: ~ **düşmesi**, (*ling*.) apocope. ~ **söz**, (*th*.) epilogue. ~ **suz**, (*math*., *phil*.) infinite; boundless, endless; eternal: ~ **kayış**, (*ind*.) endless belt: ~ **küçük**, (*math*.) infinitesimal: ~ **olarak**, infinitely; *ad infinitum*, endlessly: ~ **vida**, (*eng*.) worm screw: ~ **a değin**, eternally: ~ **a dek**, to the end. ~ **suzca**, for ever. ~ **suzluk**, infinity; eternity: ~ **a göçen**, deceased, the late . . . . ~ **takı**, (*ling*.) suffix. ~ **teşrin**, (*ast*., *obs*.) November.
sonu[1]**ç**[cu] Result, consequence; conclusion; aim, purpose: (*th*.) dénouement. ~ **almak**, finish; produce: ~ **lar**, (*adm*.) findings: ~ **unda (-in)**, in consequence/as a result of.
sonuç·lamak (-i) Produce, lead to. ~ **landırmak** (-i), finish, conclude. ~ **lanmak**, *vi*. be finished/ concluded, end. ~ **lu**, productive; successful. ~ **suz**, inconclusive; drawn (game/battle).
son·uncu The last/final (one). ~ **urgu** (*phil*.) logical/ semantic consequence. ~ **urtu**, (*phil*.) consequence. ~ **uşmaz**, (*math*.) asymptote. ~ **yargı**, (*leg*.) judgement.
sop[u] (*soc*.) Clan. = SOY.
sopa Thick stick, cudgel; (*sp*.) club, bat; (*tex*.) stripe; (*fig*.) beating; blow. ~ **atmak/çekmek**, beat with a stick: ~ **çekirgesi**, (*ent*.) stick insect: ~ **düşkünü**, deserving a beating: ~ **yemek**, get a beating.
sopa·cı[1]**k**[ğı] (*bio*.) Rod (of retina). ~ **lama**, *vn*. beating; (*cin*.) slapstick (comedy). ~ **lamak (-i)**, beat with a stick. ~ **lı**, armed with a stick; (*tex*.) with broad stripes.
soplu = SOYLU.
soprano (*mus*.) Soprano.
sor (*bot*.) Sorus. ~ **eks(giller)**, (*zoo*.) shrew(s).
sora[1]**k**[ğı] Anxiety; curiosity. ~ **ı**, (*psy*.) hypochondriac. ~ **landırmak (-i)**, *vc*. ~ **lanmak**, *vi*. be anxious; be curious. ~ **lı**, anxious, curious.
sordurmak (-i, -e) *vc*. = SORMAK[1].
sorgu Question; (*leg*.) examination, interrogation. ~ **avukatı**, (*mil*.) judge-advocate: ~ **hâkim/yargıcı**, (*leg*.) examining magistrate; coroner: ~ **sual**, investigation: ~ **su yapılmak/~ya çekilmek/ ~lanmak**, be questioned/interrogated/examined: ~ **ya çekmek/~lamak**, question, interrogate, examine: ~ **yu yanıtlamak**, testify.
sorgu[1]**ç**[cu] (*mod*.) Aigrette; (*bio*.) crest. ~ **lu**, (*orn*.) crested.
sor·gun / ~ **kun** (*bot*.) Ben-tree; common osier.
sor·maca Inquiry. ~ **mak**[1] (-i, -e, -den), ask; inquire; ask about: ~ **ayıp olmasın!**, excuse my asking!: **sora sora**, (**Bağdat bulunur**), (you can get anywhere) by asking: **sorma (gitsin!)**, don't ask me!, it was terrible/wonderful!

sormak[2] **(-i)** = EMMEK; SOĞURMAK; SORUMAK.
soru Question; interrogation. ~ **adıl//belirteci,**
(*ling.*) interrogative pronoun//adverb: ~ **eki,**
(*ling.*) interrogative particle/affix: ~ **imi,** question-
mark (?): ~ **sıfat//tümleci,** (*ling.*) interrogative
adjective//sentence: ~**lu görünüm,** (*ling.*) clause
(used conditionally). ~**lmak,** *vp.* = SORMAK[1].
sorum Responsibility; liability. ~ **alıcıya aittir,**
caveat emptor.
sorumak (-i) Suck/lap up noisily.
sorum·lu Responsible; accountable, answerable,
liable: ~ **olm.**, be liable for, answer for: ~ **sınırlı
ortaklık,** (*fin.*) limited liability company: ~
tutmak, hold responsible, blame: ~ **yazı işleri
müdürü,** (*pub.*) managing editor. ~**luluk,** responsibility; liability; blame: ~**undan kurtarmak,**
relieve of responsibility. ~**suz,** without responsibility; irresponsible. ~**suzluk,** being without responsibility; irresponsibility.
sorun Problem, question, concern. ~**a yanaş-
mamak,** blink the question, avoid the problem.
~**ca,** (*leg.*) suit, claim: ~ **açmak (-e),** bring a
suit against s.o. ~**cacı,** claimant; plaintiff. ~**calı,**
defendant. ~**lu/**~**sal,** problematic. ~**suz(luk),**
(being) without problems.
soruşmak[1] *vi.* Be sucked up, be drained away;
(*dom.*) (laundry) begin to dry.
soruş·mak[2] *vi.* Question each other. ~**turma,** *vn.*;
investigation; questionnaire; (*adm.*) inquiry: ~
açmak, open an inquiry into; investigate: ~
yargıcı, (*leg.*) examining magistrate: ~**turmak (-i,
-e),** make investigations/inquiries; ask s.o. about
stg. ~**turu,** (*adm.*) questionnaire.
sorut·kan Sulky; peevish; disdainful. ~**mak,** *vi.* be
cross/sulky/disdainful.
sos (*cul.*) Sauce. ~**is,** sausage.
sos. = SOSYAL; SOSYOLOJİ.
SOS = (*International distress call*).
sosyal[i] Social. ~ **bilimler,** (*ed.*) social sciences: ~
çevre, background, environment: ~ **devlet,** social-
welfare state: ~ **Güvenlik Bakan(lığ)ı,** (*adm.*)
Minis·ter/(-try) for Social Security: ~ **konut,**
council-house: ~ **sigorta(lar),** (national) health
insurance: ~ **yardım,** social assistance/welfare.
sosyal·ist[i] (*pol.*) Socialist. ~**izasyon,** socialization.
~**izm,** socialism. ~**leştirme,** *vn.* ~**leştirmek (-i),**
socialize, nationalize; train to be sociable.
sos·yete (*soc.*) Society; (*fig.*) high society. ~**yeti**[1]**k**[gi],
(*iron.*) belonging to high society. ~**yoekonomik,**
socio-economic. ~**yolog,** (*ed.*) sociologist.
~**yoloji(k),** sociolo·gy/(-gical). ~**yopolitik,** socio-
political.
sote (*cul.*) Sauté.
Sov. B. = SOVYETLER BİRLİĞİ.
Sovyet *a.*, *n.* (*pol.*) Soviet; (*fig.*) Russia(n). ~
Birliği, (*pol.*) Soviet Union: ~ **Sosyalist
Cumhuriyetleri Birliği,** (*geo.*) Union of Soviet
Socialist Republics.
soy *n.* Family; race; ancestry, lineage; ancestors;
descendants; breeding; kind, sort. *a.* Pure-blooded;
noble; select. ~ **ADI:** ~ **AĞACI:** ~ **at,** thoroughbred
horse: ~ **esası,** (*leg.*) according to nationality: ~
metal, (*chem.*) noble metal: ~ **sop,** one's family

and relations: ~ ~**a çeker,** heredity is strong
~**AÇEKİM:** ~**a çekmek,** take after one's family
~**u sopu belli,** he comes of a good family: ~**und**
vardır, it's in his blood.
soya ~ **fasulyesi,** (*bot.*) soya bean.
soy·açekim (*bio.*) Heredity. ~**adı,** surname, family
name. ~**ağacı**[m], family tree. ~**aktaran,** (*bio.*
chromosome. ~**ca,** as a family; as regards family
~**daş,** of the same kind/race; (*bio.*) consan
guineous. ~ **daşlık,** (*bio.*) consanguinity. ~**değişim**
mutation.
soydurmak (-i, -e) *vc.* = SOYMAK.
soyga (*orn.*) Small crow; (*sp.*) decoy.
soy·gun *n.* Pillage; spoliation; ill-gotten gains: *a*
undressed; stripped; robbed: ~ **vermek,** b
plundered. ~**guncu,** brigand, highwayman
plunderer, pillager. ~**gunculuk,** brigandage
plundering; fleecing. ~**ka,** clothes stripped from
a corpse/prisoner.
soy·kırım(ı) Genocide. ~**lu,** pure-bred; dis
tinguished: ~ **kişi,** aristocrat: ~ **soplu,** of well
known family. ~**luerki,** aristocracy. ~**luluk**
breeding; nobility.
soy·ma *vn.* ~**mak (-i),** strip, undress; (*cul.*) peel
skin, shell; flay; rob, sack, plunder: **soyup soğan**
çevirmek, pillage, strip; denude.
soymu[l]**k**[gu] (*bot.*) Edible inner bark of the pine.
soy·oluş (*bio.*) Phylogenesis. ~**sal,** *a.* family; (*med.*
hereditary (disease, etc.). ~**serim,** (*bio.*) pheno
type.
soysuz Of bad stock/family; base-born; degenerate
good-for-nothing. ~**laşma,** *vn.*, degeneracy. ~**laş**
mak, *vi.* degenerate. ~**laştırmak (-i),** *vc.* ~**luk**
degeneracy; worthlessness.
soytarı(lık) Clown(ing); buffoon(ery).
soy·ulma *vn.* Stripping; (*geol.*) desquamation
~**ulmak,** *vp.* be robbed/stripped. ~**unma,** *vn.*: ~
gösteri(ci)si, strip-tease (artist): ~ **odası,** (*sp.*
changing-room. ~**unmak,** *vi.* undress o.s.; chang
one's clothes; take off one's street-clothes: **soyunu**
dökünmek, change into more comfortable clothes
~**untu,** peel; bark; stg. stripped off.
soyut[u] (*phil.*) Abstract; intangible. ~ **ad,** (*ling.*
abstract noun: ~ **düşünce,** abstraction: ~ **say**
abstract number.
soyut·çuluk (*phil.*) Abstractionism. ~**lama,** *vn*
abstraction. ~**lamak (-i),** abstract, isolate. ~**laş**
mak, *vi.* become abstract. ~**luk,** abstractness.
soyyapı (*bio.*) Genotype.
sö·be/~**ğe** Oval, elliptical.
sögonder (*phys.*, *chem.*) Secondary.
söğ- *Also* = SÖV-.
söğüş (*cul.*) Boiled meat served cold.
söğüt (*bot.*) Willow(-tree). ~ **bülbülü,** (*orn.*) chiff
chaff: ~ **çiçeği,** (*bot.*) catkin: ~ **kar tavuğu,** (*orn.*
willow ptarmigan: ~ **ötleğeni,** (*orn.*) willow
warbler: ~ **serçesi,** (*orn.*) Spanish sparrow: ~
yaprağı, (*bot.*) willow leaf; (*mil.*) very thin dagge
~**giller,** (*bot.*) Salicaceae, willow family. ~**lük**
willow-grove.
sökel(lik) Infirm(ity), ill(ness).
sök·me *vn.* (*ind.*) Knock-down. ~**mek (-i),** pull/di
up; tear down; rip open; take apart; extract; (*adm*

decipher; (*eng.*) disassemble, dismantle, strip down; overcome/break through (obstacle); surmount (difficulty); (*agr.*) break up (land): *vi.* (*med.*) (purge) take effect; (mucus) flow; (dawn) break; appear, come out; succeed.

sök·türmek (-i, -e) *vc.* = SÖKMEK. ~**ücü**, dismantler; remover. ~**ük**, *a.* (*tex.*) unstitched; unravelled: *n.* dropped stitch: ~ **örmek**, repair a tear/rent. ~**ülmek**, *vp.*; (*sl.*) be forced to give/pay: **sökülüp atılmak**, be utterly eradicated: **sökülüp takılır**, portable. ~**üm**, *vn.* ~**ün**, ~ **etm.**, appear suddenly; burst in as a crowd; crop up; follow each other. ~**üntü**, sudden rush (of crowd), (*tex.*) rent (in seam); unravelled knitting. ~**üotu**^{nu}, (*bot.*) bird's foot trefoil.

ölom (*bio.*) Coelom. ~**lular**, (*zoo.*) coelomates.

ölpü·k Flabby; lax. ~**mek**, *vi.* hang flabbily; be flabby/sluggish.

sö·mel (*geol.*) Footing. ~**mestr**, (*ed.*) term. ~**mi-**, semi-. ~**mikok**, (*min.*) semi-coke, coalite. ~**mitreyler**, (*mot.*) semi-trailer.

sömürge (*adm.*) Colony, dependency. ~ +, *a.* colonial. ~**ci**, *a.* colonial: *n.* colonialist. ~**cilik**, colonialism, imperialism. ~**leşme**, *vn.* ~**leşmek**, *vi.* become a colony. ~**leştirmek (-i)**, colonize. ~**lik**, colonialism; exploitation. ~**n**, colonizer; exploiter. ~**nlik**, exploitation.

sömür·me *vn.* Exploiting; swallowing. ~**mek (-i)**, exploit (illegally); swallow down; devour. ~**ü**, exploitation. ~**ücü(lük)**, exploit·er/(-ation). ~**ülmek**, *vp.*

söndür·me *vn.* ~**mek (-i)**, extinguish; put out; douse; quench, slake; deflate. ~**ücü**, (fire-)extinguisher. ~**ülmek**, *vp.* ~**üm**, (*leg.*) extinction.

sön·me *vn.* ~**mek**, *vi.* be extinguished/put out; (fire, light) go out, die down; (balloon) be deflated; (*naut.*) (sail) become slack, flap; (*geol.*) (volcano) become extinct; (*fig.*) cease, die: **sönüp yanmak**, (*naut.*) occult. ~**müş**, put out, died down: ~ **kireç**, (*chem.*) slaked lime: ~ **yanardağ**, (*geol.*) extinct volcano. ~**ük**, extinguished; dim, dark; (*min.*) tarnished; (*naut.*) slack; deflated; washed out; (*fig.*) obscure, undistinguished. ~**üklük**, being extinguished, etc. ~**üm**, (*phys.*) damping (of pendulum); (*fin., phys.*) extinction (of debt, etc.): ~ **ayrımı**, (*fin.*) sinking fund. ~**ümlemek (-i)**, (*phys.*) damp (pendulum); (*fin.*) extinguish/ redeem/wipe out (debt). ~**ümlü**, (*phys.*) damped. ~**ümsüz**, (*phys.*) undamped, continuous.

sör (*rel.*) Nun, sister; (*med.*) sister; (*soc.*) sir.

sövdürmek (-i, -e) *vc.* = SÖVMEK.

söve (*arch.*) Door-post; (*agr.*) load-frame (of cart).

söv·gü Curse, swear-word. ~**mek (-e)**, curse, swear (at): **sövüp saymak**, curse and swear at s.o., abuse s.o. ~**ülmek**, *vi.* be sworn at. ~**üntü/** ~ **üş**, cursing, swearing. ~**üşlemek (-i)**, (*sl.*) get money from. ~**üşmek (-le)**, curse/swear at each other. ~ **üştürmek (-i, -e, -le)**, *vc.*

söyle·m Pronunciation; diction. ~**me**, *vn.* ~**mek (-i, -e)**, speak; say; tell; explain; suggest; ask s.o. to do stg.; recite; sing (song); write (poetry): **söyledi ya!**, he *did* say it!: **söylediklerimden şaşmam!**, I won't budge from what I've said: **söylemeğe dilim**

varmadı, I couldn't bring myself to say it: **söylemez olaydım!**, I wish to God I hadn't said it: **söyleyeceği olm.**, have stg. to say: **söyleyecekler**, comments: **söyleyip yazdırmak**, dictate.

söylen·ce Saying, proverb; myth. ~**cebilim(sel)**, mytholo·gy/(-gical). ~**celeşmek**, *vi.* become proverbial//a myth. ~**cesel**, proverbial; mythological. ~**ilmek**, *vp.* be said/pronounced. ~**iş**, (*ling.*) accentuation, pronunciation. ~**me**, *vn.* ~**mek**, *vp.* be spoken/said: *vi.* talk to o.s.; mutter, grumble: **söylendiğine göre**, according to what is being said. ~**ti**, rumour.

söy·leşi Conversation; discussion; (*rad.*) TV chat-show: ~ **gezisi**, (*pub.*) propaganda trip. ~**leşili**, ~ **sınav**, (*ed.*) colloquium. ~**leşmek (-le)**, talk over/ discuss with s.o. ~**letmek (-i, -e)**, *vc.* make/force/ allow to speak. ~**lev**, speech, discourse. ~**leyiş**, pronunciation, accent; manner of speaking: ~**ine göre**, from his manner of speaking. ~**leyivermek (-i)**, drop a remark/hint.

söz Word; expression; speech; talk; rumour, gossip; promise; agreement. ~ **açmak (-den)**, open a conversation/begin to speak about stg.: ~ **almak**, begin to speak, open the proceedings; obtain a promise: ~ **altında kal(ma)mak**, (not) remain silent when attacked/criticized/insulted: ~ **anlamak**, be reasonable/sensible: ~ **anlamaz**, he is unreasonable: ~ **anlatmak**, persuade: ~ **aramızda**, between you and me (and the bedpost): ~ **arasında**, in the course of conversation; by the way: ~ **atmak**, make biting/insulting remarks; make improper remarks (to a girl): ~ **ayağa düşmek**, 'anarchy rules': ~ **bir Allah bir**, I am a man of my word: ~ **bir etm.**, unite with others against s.o./stg.: ~ BİRLİĞİ: ~ **dinlemek**, listen to advice; be docile/ obedient: ~ **dinlemez**, disobedient: ~ **dinler**, obedient: ~ DİZİMİ: ~ **düellosu**, battle of words: ~ **ebesi**, quick at repartee; good talker: ~ **ehli**, eloquent: ~ **eri**, good talker; influential; whose word 'goes': ~ **eslemek**, be obedient: ~ **etm. (-den)**, talk about; gossip about: ~ **geçirmek**, make s.o. listen to one; make one's influence felt: ~ **geçme**, dominance: ~ GELİMİ: ~ GELİŞİ: ~ **götürmek**, lead to talk: ~ **götürmez**, it admits of no discussion; it is beyond question: ~ **gümüşten**, **sükût altından**, speech is silver, silence is golden: ~ **güreşi**, polemics: ~ **işitmek**, be admonished/'told off': ~ **kaldırmak**, not take offence (at stg.): ~ **kaldırmamak**, be easily offended; be unable to bear criticism: ~ **kaldırmaz**, s.o. who can't take a joke, etc.: ~ **kavafı**, chatterbox: ~ **kesimi**, agreement to marry, engagement: ~ **kesişmek (-le)**, come to an agreement: ~ **kesmek**, decide, agree; conclude a marriage agreement: ~ **kıtlığında asma budayayım**, in this dearth of conversation let me prune my vines (said when s.o. gets off the subject): ~ **konusu**, the matter in question/being discussed: ~ **konusu etm./ olm.**, be talked about/under discussion; be rumoured: ~ **konusu değildir**, it's a matter of course: ~ **olm.**, be discussed/talked about: ~ **olsun diye**, for the sake of talking; without meaning it: ~ **olur**, people will talk about it: ~ **onun**, he is right; it is his turn to speak: ~ **sahibi**, master of words, eloquent;

who has a say in matters: ~ **sahibi olm.**, be qualified to speak: ~ **satmak**, boast: ~ **sırası bende**, now it's my turn to speak: ~ **tatsız kaçtı**, the remark seemed out of place: ~ **temsili**, for example: ~ **tutmak**, listen to advice: ~ **vermek**, give one's word, promise: ~ **yitimi**, (*med.*) aphasia: ~ **yok!**, there's no answer to that!; it's true!: ~ **yöneltmek**, make a speech.

söz-: ~DE: ~**de kalmak**, not be realized: ~**den mana çıkarmak**, misinterpret a word/stg. said: ~**e girişmek**, broach a subject: ~**e kapılmak**, be deceived by fair words: ~**e karışmak**, chip in, put one's spoke in: ~**leri**, *etc.* = ~Ü, *etc.:* ~**lerin çelişmesi**, contradiction in terms: ~**leriniz birbirine uymuyor**, you're contradicting yourself.

sözü: ~ **açar**, one topic leads to another: ~ **açılmak**, get the opportunity to speak about stg.: ~ **ağzında bırakmak**, cut s.o. short, interrupt s.o.: ~ **bağlamak**, bring a speech to a conclusion: ~ **çevirmek**, express stg. in other words: ~ **geçen**, the aforesaid; dominant, the boss: ~ **geçmek**, one's word carry weight, be influential; be talked about/ mentioned: ~ **kesmek**, become silent; interrupt o.s.: ~ **mü olur?**, is it worth talking about?: ~ **özüne uymak**, be sincere; be consistent: ~ **sapıtmak**, lose the thread of an argument; change the subject: ~ **tartmak**, weigh one's words carefully: ~ **uzatmak**, talk too much: ~MONA: ~**m yabana!**, pardon the expression!

sözün: ~ **gelişi**, in the course of conversation: ~ **kısası**, it all boils down to this; in short: ~ **sırası**, (*phil.*) the context of a word: ~**de durmak**, keep one's word: ~**den çıkmak (-in)**, disregard s.o.'s advice; disobey s.o.: ~**den dönmek**, go back on one's word: ~**e gelmek**, approve what s.o. has said: ~**ü ağzına tıkamak**, interrupt and silence s.o.: ~**ü balla kesmek (-in)**, apologize for interrupting the conversation: ~**ü bilmek**, be tactful and considerate when speaking: ~**ü bilmez**, tactless, inconsiderate: ~**ü değiştirmek**, change one's tone: ~**ü dinletmek**, make o.s. heard/listened to; be obeyed: ~**ü doğrulmak/tasdik etm.**, bear s.o. out: ~**ü esirgememek/sakınmamak**, not mince one's words: ~**ü fenaya çekmek**, put a bad interpretation on s.o.'s words: ~**ü geri almak**, change one's mind; take back what one has said: ~**ü ihtiyatla kaydetmek**, accept what s.o. says with caution: ~**ü kesmek**, cut s.o. short, interrupt s.o.: ~**ü tutmak**, follow s.o.'s advice; keep one's word: ~**ünün eri**, a man of his word.

söz·avcılığı[nı] (*pol.*) Demagogy. ~**avcısı**[nı], demagogue. ~**başı**[nı], (*pub.*) (chapter, etc.) heading. ~**bilim**, (*th.*) rhetoric. ~**birliği**[ni], unanimity, agreement. ~**bölükleri**[ni], (*ling.*) parts of speech. ~**cü(lük)**, (*adm.*) (duties of) spokesman//public-relations officer//rapporteur. ~**cü**[l]k[gü], (*ling.*) word: ~ **dağarcık/hazinesi**, lexis, vocabulary: ~ **öbeği**, group of words: ~ **türü**, (*ling.*) part of speech: ~ **vurgusu**, (*ling.*) accent on a word. ~**cül**, verbal. ~**de**, *a.* so-called, pseudo: *adv.* as if/though; supposing that: ~ **neden**, excuse. ~**dinletir(lik)**, authoritarian(ism). ~**dizimi**[ni], (*ling.*) syntax.

~**dizimsel**, (*ling.*) syntactical. ~**el**, verbal. ~**geçme** effect. ~**gelimi/**~**gelişi**, for example; supposing that, for the sake of argument let's say. ~ KONUSU. ~**lendirici**, (*cin.*) dubber. ~**lendirme**, (*cin.*) dubbing. ~**lendirmek (-i)**, (*cin.*) dub (a film). ~**leşme** *vn.*; promise, bond; (*leg.*) agreement, contract. (*pol.*) convention. ~**leşmek (-le)**, agree together; enter into an agreement. ~**leşmeli**, contractual ~**lü**, verbal, in words, oral; agreed together; having promised; engaged to be married: ~ **(film)** (*cin.*) talking picture, talkie: ~ **olarak**, orally verbally: ~ **sınav**, (*ed.*) oral examination: ~ **soru** (*pol.*) question requiring an oral reply. ~**lük** (*ling.*) dictionary; lexicon, glossary: ~ +, *a.* (*pub.*) alphabetical (order). ~**lükbilgisi**[ni], (science of lexicography. ~**lükçü**, lexicographer. ~**lükçülük** lexicography, dictionary compilation. ~**öbeği**[ni] (*ling.*) word-group. ~**süz**, dumb; speechless ~**ügeçer(lik)**, influen·tial/(-ce). ~**ümona**, (*col.* so-called, alleged.

sp. = SPOR[2].

spatül (*med.*) Spatula. ~ **kuşu**, (*orn.*) white spoonbill.

spazm (*bio.*) Spasm. ~ **giderici**, (*med.*) anti spasmodic.

spek·taküler Spectacular. ~**tral**, (*phys.*) spectral ~**troskop**[u], (*phys.*) spectroscope. ~ **trum**, (*phys.* spectrum.

spekü·lasyon (*fin.*, *phil.*) Speculation. ~**latör**, (*fin.* speculator, 'bull'.

speleoloji (*geol.*) Speleology.

sperma (*bio.*) Semen. ~ **hayvancığı**, sperm (-atozoon).

spesi·fik Specific. ~**yalist**, specialist. ~**yalite** speciality.

spiker(lik) (Work of) (*rad.*) announcer//(*pol.*) speaker.

spi·ral Spiral. ~**ril**, (*bio.*) spirillum.

spiritualizm (*rel.*, *phil.*) Spiritualism.

spor[1] *n.* (*bio.*) Spore. ~**kesesi**[ni], (*bot.*) sporangium ~**lanma**, sporogenesis. ~**lu**, ~ **bitki**, (*bot.* sporophyte, cryptogam. ~**lar**, (*zoo.*) sporozoa.

spor[2] *n.* (*sp.*) Sports; athletics; games. ~ +, *a* Sports, sporting. ~ **alanı**, sports ground, playing field: ~ **antrenörü**, coach, trainer: ~ **malzemesi** sports equipment: ~ **meydanı**, arena.

spor·cu Sportsman, athlete, games-player ~**sever**, sports-lover, sports fan. ~**tif**, *a* sports, sporting. ~**tmen**, sportsman. ~**toto** (*gamb.*) football pools.

sprey Spray (liquid); spray(er), spraying device.

Sr. = SERİ; SIRA; (*ch.s.*) STRONSİYUM.

SS = SOSYAL SİGORTA. ~**CB** = SOVYET SOSYALİS CUMHURİYETLER BİRLİĞİ. ~**K** = SOSYAL SİGORTA LAR KURUMU. ~**YB** = SAĞLIK VE SOSYAL YARDI BAKANLIĞI.

st. = SAAT; (*math.*) STER.

stabi·l (*phys.*) Stable, fixed. ~**lite**, stability. ~**li zasyon**, stabilization. ~**lizatör**, stabilizer: ~ **kanadı**, (*naut.*) fin. ~**lize**, stabilized: ~ **etm.** stabilize: ~ **yol**, unmetalled road.

stad(yum) (*sp.*) Stadium.

stafilokok (*bio.*) Staphylococcus.

taj (*ed.*, *ind.*) Apprenticeship; course of instruction; probation. ~ **yer(lik)**, (status/work of) apprentice, probationer, trainee.
tand (*mus.*) Stand. ~ **ardizasyon**, standardization. ~ **ardize**, ~ **etm.**, (*ind.*) standardize. ~ **ar¹t**ᵈ¹, *a.*, *n.* standard.
ta·tik (*phys.*) *n.* Statics: *a.* static. ~ **tolit**ⁱ, (*bio.*) statolith. ~ **tor**, (*phys.*) stator. ~ **tosist**, (*bio.*) statocyst. ~ **toskop**ᵘ, (*phys.*) statoscope. ~ **tü**, (*adm.*) statute, regulation. ~ **tüko**, *status quo.* ~ **tükocu**, (*pol.*) conservative. ~ **tüs**, (*soc.*) status.
te·arikasi¹tᵈⁱ (*chem.*) Stearic acid. ~ **no(graf)**, stenographer, shorthand writer. ~ **no(grafi)**, stenography, shorthand. ~ **notip**ⁱ, shorthand typewriter. ~ **nsil**, stencil. ~ **p**, (*geo.*) steppe: ~ **doğanı**, (*orn.*) pallid harrier. ~ **r**, (*math.*) stere (1m³). ~ **reofonik**, (*phys.*) stereophonic. ~ **reografi**, (*phys.*) stereography. ~ **reoskop**ᵘ, (*phys.*) stereoscope. ~ **reotip**ⁱ, (*pub.*) stereotype. ~ **ril**, (*med.*) sterile; (*bio.*) sterile, infertile. ~ **rilizatör**, sterilizer. ~ **rilize**, sterilized: ~ **etm.**, sterilize. ~ **rlin**, (*fin.*) pound sterling: ~ **alan/sahası**, sterling area. ~ **rnum**, (*bio.*) sternum. ~ **rol**, (*chem.*) sterol. ~ **toskop**ᵘ, (*med.*) stethoscope.
til (*art.*, *lit.*) Style. ~ **o**, stylo, ball-point/fountain-pen.
toacılık (*phil.*) Stoicism.
tokᵘ (*ind.*) Stock, store. ~ **etm.**, buy in. ~ **çu**, stockist; hoarder.
top *int.* Stop!. ~ **etm.**, stop, halt: ~ **lambası**, (*mot.*) rear brake lamp. ~ **aj**. (*fin.*) stoppage, deduction. ~ **lazma** = SİTOPLAZMA.
tra·teji (*mil.*, *pol.*) Strategy. ~ **tejik**, strategic: ~ **silahların sınırlandırılması görüşmeleri**, (*pol.*) strategic arms limitation talks. ~ **tigrafi**, (*geol.*) stratigraphy. ~ **tokümülüs**, (*met.*) stratocumulus. ~ **tosfer**, (*met.*) stratosphere. ~ **tüs**, (*met.*) stratus.
strepto·kok (*bio.*) Streptococcus. ~ **misin**, (*med.*) streptomycin.
str·ey(n)gey¹lçᶜⁱ (*phys.*) Strain-gauge. ~ **iknin**, (*chem.*) strychnine. ~ **iptiz(ci)**, (*th.*) striptease (artist). ~ **oboskop**ᵘ, (*phys.*) stroboscope. ~ **onsiyum**, (*chem.*) strontium. ~ **üktür**, structure.
stüdyo (*art.*, *cin.*, *rad.*) Studio.
suʸᵘ Water; fluid; (*geo.*) stream; (*bot.*) sap; (*bot.*) juice, essence; (*cul.*) broth; (*min.*) temper; (*art.*) running pattern/decoration. ~ **+**, *a.* Water; hydraulic; aqua-; hydro-. ~ **ağzı**, hydrant: ~ **akrebi**, (*zoo.*) water scorpion: ~ **akümülatörü**, (*phys.*) hydraulic accumulator: ~ **alma ağzı**, water intake: ~ **almak**, (*naut.*) make water, leak: ~ **altında**, submerged: ~ **altında kalma**, (*geo.*) inundation: ~ ASKILARI: ~ **ardıcı**, (*orn.*) aquatic warbler: ~ AYGIRI: ~ BALDIRANI: ~ **basıncı**, (*phys.*) hydrostatic/water pressure: ~ **baskını**, flood: ~ **basmak**, (*agr.*) flood, drown: ~ **başı**, source; spring, fountain; waterside: ~ BAŞI: ~ **bendi**, (*eng.*) reservoir: ~ BİLGİSİ: ~ BİTİ: ~ **bombası**, (*naut.*) depth charge: ~ **böceği**, (*ent.*) scavenging water-beetle; (*zoo.*) crayfish: ~ **bölmeleri**, (*naut.*) watertight compartments: ~ **bölümü çizgisi**, (*geo.*) watershed: ~ BÖREĞİ: ~ BUĞUSU: ~ **bulaşımı**, water contamination/pollution: ~ **cenderesi**, (*eng.*)

hydraulic press: ~ **cismi**, (*bio.*) aqueous humour: ~ **çarpmak**, wash (the face) with water: ~ **çekimi** (**işaretleri**), (*naut.*) draught (marks): ~ **çekmek**, (*naut.*) draw water; take in water; pump up water: ~ **çeliği**, (*min.*) water-hardening steel: ~ **ÇİÇEĞİ**: ~ ÇULLUĞU: ~ **damgası**, (*pub.*) watermark: ~ **damlası**, drop of water; blob: ~ **değirmeni**, watermill: ~ **deposu**, cistern; reservoir; tank: ~ **dökmek**, make water, urinate: ~ **dökünmek**, wash o.s.; be washed: ~ **döşemcisi**, plumber: ~ **döşemi**, plumbing: ~ **düzey/seviyesi**, water-level; (*geol.*) water-table: ~ **etm./yapmak**, (*naut.*) make water, leak: ~ **emme**, (*geol.*) imbibition: ~ GEÇİRMEZ: ~ **gibi akmak**, (time) fly: ~ **gibi aziz ol!**, thanks! (for offering of water): ~ **gibi bilmek**, know perfectly: ~ **gibi ezberlemek**, be word perfect: ~ **gibi gitmek**, (money) be spent like water: ~ **gibi okumak**, read fluently: ~ **gibi terlemek**, be dripping with perspiration/sweat: ~ **götür(me)mek**, be (in)disputable: ~ **götürmez**, beyond doubt/controversy: ~ **götürür**, doubtful, suspect: ~ **güvesi**, (*ent.*) caddis fly: ~ **hattı**, (*naut.*) waterline: ~ **haznelerini boşaltmak**, (*naut.*) (submarine) blow its tanks: ~ **hendeği**, (*sp.*) water-jump: ~ **hızarı**, water-powered sawmill: ~ **hortumu**, (*met.*) waterspout: ~ **içinde**, (*fin.*) at the very least, easily, certainly: ~ **iktiza etm.**, (*rel.*) need to perform ablutions: ~ **incir kuşu**, (*orn.*) water pipit: ~ KABAĞI: ~ **kaçırmak**, leak; annoy: ~ **kaçırmaz**, watertight: ~ **kaldırmak**, absorb/take up water: ~ KAMIŞI: ~ **kanadı**, (*naut.*) hydrofoil: ~ **kapma**, (*med.*) blister: ~ **kapmak**, (*med.*) (blister) form; fester: ~ **-kara**, amphibious: ~ **karatavuğu(giller)**, (*orn.*) dipper(s): ~ **katılmamış**, pure, undiluted, unadulterated: ~ **katmak**, (*chem.*) dilute: ~ **kayağı**, (*sp.*) water-skiing: ~ KEMERİ: ~ **kerevizi**, (*bot.*) water-parsnip: ~ **kertenkelesi**, (*zoo.*) eft, newt: ~ **kesimi**, (*naut.*) waterline: ~ **kesmek**, become watery: ~ **kınkanatlısı**, (*ent.*) water-beetle: ~ **kireci**, (*chem.*) slaked lime: ~ KOBAYI: ~ **koşar**, (*ent.*) water-measurer: ~ **koyuvermek**, (*cul.*) drain off liquid: (*sl.*) become impudent/over-familiar: ~ **köstebeği**, (*zoo.*) water shrew: ~ **kurbağası**, (*zoo.*) frog: ~ **kuşu**, (*orn.*) moorhen: ~ MERCİMEĞİ: ~ MERMERİ: ~ **mokaseni**, (*zoo.*) water moccasin: ~ ÖRÜMCEĞİ: ~ **piresi**, (*ent.*) water-flea: ~ **saati**, water meter: (*ast.*) clepsydra: ~ **salmak**, (*cul.*) add water: ~ SAMURU: ~ **sayacı**, water meter: ~ **seti**, (*agr.*) dike: ~ **seviyesi** = ~ DÜZEYİ: ~ **seviyesinde**, (*naut.*) awash: ~ SIÇANI: ~ **sığırcığı**, (*orn.*) rose-coloured starling: ~ SIĞIRI: ~ **sızmak**, leak, drip: ~ SİNEĞİ: ~ **soğutmalı**, (*eng.*) water-cooled: ~ **dökmek**, (*naut.*) make water, pump ship: ~ **süpürmesi**, (*geo.*) denudation: ~ ŞERİDİ: ~ **taşır/taşıyan**, (*geol.*) aquifer(ous): ~ TAVUĞU: ~ TERAZİSİ: ~ TERESİ: ~ **testisi** = ~ **yolunda kırılır**, one must accept the risks of one's occupation: ~ **toplama sahası**, (*geo.*) catchment area/basin: ~ **topu**, (*sp.*) water-polo: ~ **uyur düşman uyumaz**, always be on your guard against the enemy: ~ **üzerinde**, afloat: ~ **vermek**, water (plants/animals): bring water to drink: (*min.*) quench; temper (steel): ~ **yarpuzu**, (*bot.*) water mint: ~ **yelvesi**, (*orn.*)

water-rail: ~ **yılanı**, (*zoo.*) grass snake: ~
yitimi, (*med.*) dehydration: ~YOLCU: ~YOLU:
~YOSUNLARI: ~YUVARI: ~ **yürümek**, (*bot.*) sap
begin to rise: ~ **yüzüne çıkmak (-e)**, become clear/
definite.

suda: ~ **balık satmak**, promise what cannot be
fulfilled: ~ **bırakmak**, (*cul.*) leave to soak: ~
boğulmak, be drowned: ~ **pişirmek**, (*cul.*) boil;
poach: ~ **pişmiş**, (*cul.*) boiled: ~ **yapılan/yaşıyan/
yetişen**, aquatic: ~ **yüzen**, floating; (*geo.*) drift (ice,
etc.).

sudan: = SUDAN[1]: ~ **çıkma**, emersion: ~ **çıkmış
balığa dönmek**, not know what to do, be like a fish
out of water: ~ **geçirmek**, wash (laundry) superficially: ~ **ucuz**, dirt cheap.

sular: ~ **kararmak**, darkness fall: ~ **kırılmak**,
weather become warmer: ~ **ında**, about, around (of
time).

suya: ~ **atlamak**, (*sp.*) dive: ~ **batırmak**, immerse;
(*min.*) chill: ~ **doygun**, (*chem.*) saturated: ~
düşmek, fail, come to nothing, collapse: ~
göstermek, wash stg. lightly: ~ **sabuna
dokunmamak**, avoid anything likely to cause
trouble: ~ **sabuna dokunmadan tarafsız kalmak**, sit
on the fence: ~ **salmak**, waste; throw away.

suyu: ~ **başından kesmek**, cut stg. off at its source;
nip in the bud: ~ **çekilmiş**, dry, dried up: ~
çekilmiş değirmene dönmek, be in a helpless/hope-
less position: ~ **görmeden paçaları sıvamak**, count
one's chickens before they are hatched: ~ **görünce
teyemmüm bozulur**, have to do/start stg. all over
again: ~ **mızrakla delmek**, make useless efforts: ~
mu çıktı (bir yerin), what's wrong with the place?,
why don't you like it?: ~ **seli kalmamak**, (*cul.*) be
boiled dry: ~ **sert**, (steel) hard tempered; (man)
harsh: ~ **tokmakla kesiyor**, (knife, etc.) is very
blunt/won't cut butter: ~ **yenemiyoruz**, (*naut.*) we
can't keep the water from pouring in.

suyun: ~ **başı**, (*geo.*) source, spring; (*fig.*) most
important part of (a business, etc.): ~ **içimi iyidir**,
the water has a good taste: ~ **kaldırma kuvveti**,
(*phys.*) uplift, buoyancy: ~**a/~ca gitmek**, treat
s.o. tactfully; flatter s.o. when necessary: ~**a tirit**,
perfunctory, careless; worthless: ~**a tirit geçinmek**,
live on next to nothing: ~**u akıtmak/almak**, (*cul.*)
drain, strain stg.; (*chem.*) dewater: ~**u boşaltmak**,
drain out; (*naut.*) bail out: ~**u çekmek**, (*cul.*) boil
down, render; (*fig.*) be exhausted/used up: ~**u
gidermek/kaybetmek**, (*chem.*) dehydrate: ~**un
suyu**, (*soc.*) a distant relationship/connection.

-su[1] *n. suf.* (*after a vowel*) [39] = -si[1] [BALOSU].
-su[2] *a. suf.* (*after a consonant*) [58] = -si[2] [ÇOÇUKSU].
sual[i] Question; inquiry; request. ~ **açmak**,
question; interrogate: ~ **etm./sormak**, ask/put
a question.
sualtı Underwater; bottom (of sea, etc.).
suare = SUVARE.
su·askıları[nı] (*bot.*) Characeae, type of seaweed.
~**aygırı[nı]**, (*zoo.*) hippopotamus. ~**baldıranı[nı]**,
(*bot.*) cowbane. ~**başı[nı]**, (*agr.*) water-superinten-
dent; farm bailiff; (*his.*) police superintendent.

subay(lık) (*mil.*) (Rank, duties of) officer.
su·bilgisi[ni] Hydrography. ~**bilim** (*phys.*) hydrology. ~**biti[ni]**, (*ent.*) daphnia, water-flea. ~**boyası[nı]**,
(*carp.*) wood stain. ~**böreği[ni]**, (*cul.*) pastry of pre-
boiled sheets of dough.
su·bra (*mod.*) Under-arm section; dress-shield.
~**bye**, (*mod.*) under-strap, trouser-strap.
su·buğulu With steam; steam-. ~**buğusu[nu]**, (*phys.*)
water-vapour, steam. ~**cu(luk)**, (work of) water-
seller/-distributor.
sucu[1]k[ğu] (*cul.*) (Garlic) sausage; sweetmeat of
grape-juice and nuts. ~ **bağırsağı**, sausage-casing.
~ **gibi ıslanmak/kesilmek/olm.**, be wet through.
~**unu çıkarmak**, tire out, exhaust; give s.o. a
thrashing. ~**çu(luk)**, (work of) sausage-maker,
-seller. ~**laşmak**, *vi.* (*sl.*) be full of money.
su·cul *a.* Water-loving; water-absorbent, hydro-
philous: ~ **böcekler**, (*ent.*) waterbeetles. ~**culuk** =
SUCU.
su[1]ç[u] Fault; offence; crime; sin. ~ + , *a.* Criminal:
alışkını, habitual criminal: ~ **atmak (-e)**, attribute
an offence to s.o.: ~ **etm./işlemek**, commit an
offence: ~ **ortağı**, accomplice, confederate: ~
ortaklığı, complicity: ~ÜSTÜ: ~ **yükletmek (-e)**
lay the blame on s.o.: ~**a katılma/~ta iştirak**
complicity: ~**u sabit görmek**, find guilty: ~**undan
geçmek/~unu bağışlamak**, overlook an offence:
~**unu ispat etm.**, convict. ~**bilim**, criminology.
su·çiçeği[ni] (*med.*) Chicken-pox. ~**çulluğu[nu]**, (*orn.*)
common snipe.
suç·lama (*leg.*) Accusation, charge: ~ **yazısı**, indictment. ~**lamak (-i, -le)**, accuse s.o. of stg.
charge s.o. with stg. ~**landırmak (-i)**, convict s.o.
find s.o. guilty. ~**lanmak**, *vp.* ~**lu**, culpable, guilty
(-**den**), accused of, charged with: ~ **çıkarmak**, find
guilty: ~ **durmak**, stand guiltily: ~ **olm.**, be found
guilty: ~**nun iade/verilmesi**, extradition. ~**lularevi**
prison. ~**luluk**, guilt(iness); criminality; culpa-
bility. ~**suz**, not guilty, innocent: ~ **çıkarmak**
find not guilty, acquit. ~**suzluk**, innocence. ~**üstü**
red-handed, in the act, *in flagrante delicto*: ~
yakalamak, catch red-handed.
suda[1]k[ğı] (*ich.*) Pikeperch.
sudan[1] *a.* Unimportant, nonsensical, insignificant
~ **cevap**, unsatisfactory answer: = SU(DAN).
Sudan[2] *n.* (*geo.*) Sudan. ~**lı**, (*ethn.*) Sudanese
~**tavuğu[nu]**, (*orn.*) type of guinea-fowl.
su·dolabı[nı] (*agr.*) Wheel for raising water. ~**dur**
emanation.
sufi (*rel.*) Muslim mystic. = SOFİ.
suflör (*th.*) Prompter. ~**lük**, prompting.
su·geç(ir)mez Impermeable; waterproof, watertight. ~**ibriği[ni](giller)**, (*bot.*) pitcher-plant(s
Repenthaceae).
sui· *pref.* Evil-. ~**ahlak[ı]**, immorality, vice. ~**hareket[i]**, misconduct. ~**idare**, mismanagement. ~**istimal[i]**, abuse, misuse: ~ **etm.**, abuse, misuse. ~**kast[ı]**
criminal attempt, conspiracy: ~ **kastçı**, conspirator. ~**misal[i]**, bad example. ~**niyet[i]**, evil intention. ~**talih**, misadventure; bad luck. ~**zan[nı]**
suspicion; distrust.
suit[i] (*arch.*) Suite (of rooms).
su·kabağı[nı] (*bot.*) Gourd; vegetable marrow

~**kamışı**ⁿⁱ(**giller**), (*bot.*) reedmace; (Typhaceae, reedmace family). ~**keleri**, (*zoo.*) (?) newt. ~**ke-meri**ⁿⁱ, (*arch.*) aqueduct. ~**kobayı**, (*zoo.*) capybara.

ı**ukut**ᵘ Fall, downfall; (*med.*) abortion. ~ **etm.**, fall: ~**u hayal**, disappointment.

ı**uküre** (*geo.*) Hydrosphere.

ı**sul** *a. suf.* [65] = -SEL [YOKSUL].

u·**lak** *a.* Watery; marshy: *n.* water-bowl/-trough. ~**laklık**, wateriness. ~**lama**, *vn.*; watering; irrigation: ~ **arabası**/~**lama**ⁱ**ç**ᶜ¹, water-cart. ~**lamak** (-i), water; irrigate; (*sl.*) spend money; pay in advance. ~**landırıcı**, (*chem.*) thinner, diluent. ~**landırılmış**, diluted. ~**landırma**, *vn.*; dilution. ~**landırmak** (-i), (*chem.*) dilute; (*cul.*) baste; (*bio.*) blear (eyes). ~**lanmak**, *vp.* be watered; be irrigated: *vi.* become wet/watery; (*chem.*) deliquesce; (*sl.*) flirt: (-e), manifest interest in stg. (one wants), envy. ~**latmak** (-i, -e). *vc.*

ı**ulfata** (*chem.*) Quinine sulphate.

ı**ulh** Peace; reconciliation; accord, harmony. ~ **etm.**, make peace; be reconciled: ~ **hâkim/yargıcı**, (*leg.*) justice of the peace; police-court magistrate: ~ **mahkemesi**, petty sessions, police-court: ~ **olm.**, settle for an amicable agreement: ~**a süphana yatmamak**, not become docile/amenable.

ı**ulh·çu** Peace-loving; pacifist. ~**en**, peaceably. ~**i**, peaceful. ~**name**, (*pol.*, *obs.*) peace treaty. ~**perver**, peace-loving; pacific.

ı**ul**ⁱ**p**ᵇᵘ *a.* Hard; solid; firm; tough. *n.* (*bio.*) Loins; (*fig.*) descendants. ~**ünden gelmek**, be descended from.

ı**ul·ta** (*adm.*) Power; authority; sovereignty. ~**tan**, ruler; sovereign; sultan: ~ . . ., Sultan . . .: . . . ~, Prince(ss) . . .. ~**tani**, *a.* relating to a sultan; imperial; (fruit, etc.) of fine quality: *n.* (*ed.*, *obs.*) secondary school; (*bot.*, *cul.*) sultana: ~ **tembel**, bone idle: ~ **yegâh**, (*Or. mus.*) a melody. ~**tanlık**, sovereignty; office of sultan; sultanate; (*fig.*) success, distinction: ~ **tembel**, remarkably lazy.

ı**su·lu** Watery; moist, juicy; (*fig.*) silly, too familiar, importunate: ~ **gözlü**, always bursting into tears: ~ **Halepçıbanı**, (*med.*) cutaneous leishmaniasis. ~**luboya**, (*art.*) water-colour (paint): ~ **resım**, water-colour, aquarelle. ~**luca**, rather watery. ~**luk**, birds' water-bowl; (*sp.*) water-bottle, canteen; (*med.*) skin disease (on baby's head). ~**luluk**, being importunate/too familiar. ~**lusepken**, (*met.*) sleet.

ı**umak** (*bot.*) Sumach.

ı**umen** (*pub.*) Blotting-/writing-pad.

ı**su·mercimeği**ⁿⁱ(**giller**) (*bot.*) Duckweed; (Lemnaceae, duckweed family). ~**mermeri**ⁿⁱ, (*geol.*) alabaster. ~**muhallebisi**ⁿⁱ, (*cul.*) rice-flour sweet.

-**sun**¹ *v. suf.* [96] = -SİN¹ [ÇOCUKSUN].

-**sun**² *v. suf.* [137] = -SİN² [BULUNSUN].

ı**una** (*orn.*) Drake; pheasant. ~ **gibi**, tall, handsome.

ı**una**ⁱ**k**ᵍ¹ (*rel.*) Altar. ~ **taşı**, altar stone: ~ **tepeliği**, baldachin.

SUNFED = (*Special United Nations Fund for Economic Development*).

ı**sundur·ma** Open shed; lean-to roof. ~**mak** = SONDURMAK.

sun·gu Gift to a superior; = ~U.

sungur (*orn.*) Falcon.

suni Artificial; false; affected. ~ **kalp**, (*med.*) artificial heart: ~ **kauçuk**, (*ind.*) buna: ~ **peyk**, (*ast.*) satellite: ~ **teneffüs**, (*med.*) artificial respiration. ~**lik**, artificiality; affectation; (*ling.*) euphuism.

sun·ma *vn.* ~**mak** (-i, -e), put forward; offer; (*rad.*) present.

sun·ta (*carp.*) Artificial wood, chipboard. ~**tıraç**/ ~**tıraş**, farrier's paring-iron.

suntur (*mus.*) Dulcimer; (*fig.*) hilarious noise. ~**lu**, severe (scolding); resounding (oath): ~ **bir . . . dir**, he's the deuce of a . . ..

su·nu (*fin.*) Offer, supply; (*pub.*) dedication; = SUNGU: ~ **ve istem**, supply and demand. ~**nucu(luk)**, (*rad.*) present·er/(-ation). ~**nulmak** (-e), *vp.* be offered/presented. ~**num**, supply. ~**numluk**, snack-bar. ~**nuş**, offer, presentation; (*adm.*) proposals (to a superior). ~**nutaksir**, wrongdoing; (*leg.*) culpable negligence.

-**sunuz** *v. suf.* [96] = -SİNİZ [COŞKUNSUNUZ].

su·odasıⁿⁱ Toilet. ~**oku**ⁿᵘ, (*bot.*) arrow-head. ~**örümceği**ⁿⁱ, (*zoo.*) water-spider.

supaⁱ**p**ᵇ¹ (*eng.*) Valve. ~ **şapkası**, valve head.

supara (*ed.*, *obs.*) Children's reading-book.

suphanallah *int.* Good heavens! oh my God!

sup·l Flexible, supple. ~**les**, suppleness, flexibility.

supya (*zoo.*) Cuttlefish, squid.

sur¹ *n.* (*mil.*) Wall, rampart. ~ **dahilinde**, within the city walls: ~ **dışında**, extramural.

sur² *n.* Good luck, success.

sur³ *n.* (*obs.*) Wedding; wedding/circumcision feast.

sur⁴ (*mus.*) Trumpet.

surat¹ Face; mien, sour face. ~ **asmak**, frown, pull a sour face: ~ **bir karış**, bad-tempered, sulky: ~ **düşkünü**, very ugly: ~ **etm.**, look sulky: ~ **mahkeme duvarı**, shameless, brazenfaced: ~**a bak süngüye davran**, (seeing s.o. ugly/disagreeable) prepare for the worst!: ~**ı değişmek**, change one's attitude, become harsh towards s.o.: ~**ı kasap süngeriyle silinmiş**, shameless, brazen-faced: ~**ı kaşık kadar kaldı**, emaciated: ~**ına indirmek**, slap s.o.: ~**ından düşen bin parça olur**, very bad-tempered: ~**ını ekşitmek**, look angry/sulky.

surat·lı Sulky; sullen; frowning. ~**sız**, sulky; ugly; awkward. ~**sızlık**, sulkiness; ugliness.

sure (*rel.*) Chapter of the Koran, sura(h).

suretⁱ Form, shape; appearance, aspect, manner; picture; copy; case; supposition. ~ **almak/ çıkarmak**, make a copy: ~**i haktan görünmek**, appear sincere: ~**ine girmek**, take the shape of: ~**iyle**, by (means of). ~**a**, outwardly; in appearance; as a matter of form; simulated. **surezenesi**ⁿⁱ (*bot.*) Cowbane.

Suriye (*geo.*) Syria. ~ +, *a.* Syrian: ~ **ayısı**, (*zoo.*) Syrian brown bear: ~ **damanı**, (*zoo.*) daman. ~**li**, (*ethn.*) Syrian: ~ **alaca agaçkakan**, (*orn.*) Syrian woodpecker.

su·saⁱ**k**ᵍ¹ *a.* Thirsty. *n.* Wooden/gourd drinking-cup. ~**sallar**, (*bot.*, *zoo.*) aquatic plants/animals.

Susam¹ = SİSAM.

susam² (*bot.*) Sesame; iris; (*cul.*) sesame (seed). ~**sı**, (*bio.*) sesamoid. ~**yağı**ⁿⁱ, (*chem.*) sesame/benne oil.

susa·mak *vi.* Be thirsty: **(-e)**, thirst after, long for. ~**mış**, thirsty; longing for. ~**tmak (-i)**, make thirsty; (*fig.*) create difficulties.
su·samuruⁿᵘ (*zoo.*) Otter. ~**sarmısağı**ⁿ¹, (*bot.*) water germander. ~**sıçanı**ⁿ¹, (*zoo.*) water rat. ~**sığırı**ⁿ¹, (*zoo.*) water-buffalo. ~**sineği**ⁿⁱ, (*ent.*) water beetle. ~**sinirotu**ⁿᵘ, (*bot.*) water plantain.
sus·ku Silence. ~**kun**, silent; taciturn: ~ **destekçi**, (*pol.*) silent supporter. ~**kunluk**, quiet, calm; taciturnity. ~**ma**, *vn.*; silence. ~**mak**, *vi.* be silent; stop speaking: **sus payı**/~**malık**, bribe, hush-money. ~**pus**, reduced to silence; silent and cowering.
susta Safety-catch. ~ **durmak**, (dog) stand on its hind legs; (*fig.*) be very obsequious: ~**ya kalkmak**, (animal) get on its hind legs. ~**lı**, with a safety catch: ~ **çakı**, clasp-knife.
sustur·mak (-i) Silence; crush. ~**ucu**, *a.* silencing, crushing: *n.* (*mot.*) silencer. ~**ulmak**, *vp.* be silenced. ~**untu**, silence, calm.
su·suz Waterless, arid; thirsty; (*chem.*) anhydrite, anhydrous. ~**suzluk**, aridity, drought; thirst: ~**tan yanmak**, be consumed with thirst. ~**şeridi**ⁿⁱ (*bot.*) lesser reedmace.
sut (*chem.*) Caustic soda.
sutaşıⁿ¹ (*mod.*) Braid, trimming. ~**lı**, braided.
su·tavuğuⁿᵘ (*orn.*) Coot. ~**terazisi**ⁿⁱ, (*carp.*) spirit-level; (*phys.*) water-balance (device for maintaining and distributing a head of water in Istanbul aqueducts). ~**teresi**ⁿⁱ, (*bot.*) watercress.
sutyen (*mod.*) Brassière.
Suudi Arabistan (*geo.*) Saudi Arabia.
suüstü Above-water, surface: ~ **hız**, (*naut.*) (submarine's) surface speed.
su·vare (*soc.*) Evening party; (*th.*) soirée. ~**ver**, (*dom.*) coaster.
su·varım (*agr.*) Amount of water for one irrigation. ~**varmak (-i)**, water (animals). ~**vat**¹, watering-place/trough. ~**verme**, (*min.*) quenching. ~**yılanı**ⁿ¹, (*zoo.*) water-snake. ~**ylakesim**, (*chem.*) hydrolysis. ~**yolcu**, man in charge of water-conduits. ~**yolu**ⁿᵘ, (*eng.*) water-conduit, duct; drain, culvert; (*bio.*) urethra; (*pub.*) watermark; (*mod.*) braid. ~**yosunları**, (*bot.*) algae, seaweeds: ~ **bilimi**, algology. ~**yu**ˡ**k**ᵍᵘ, (*bio.*) fluid/humour (of the body). ~**yuvarı**ⁿ¹, (*geo.*) hydrosphere.
-suz *a./pron. suf.* [62] = -siz [SONSUZ].
suz·inaˡ**k**ᵍ¹ *a.* Grieved; suffering: *n.* (*Or. mus.*) a sad mode. ~**iş**, *n.* burning; suffering; great sorrow. ~**işli**, *a.* burning; suffering; sorrowful.
-suzluk *n. suf.* = -SİZLİK [SUSUZLUK].
-sü¹ *n. suf.* (*after a vowel*) [39] = -si¹ [SÜRÜSÜ].
-sü² *a. suf.* (*after a consonant*) [58] = -si² [ÖLÜMSÜ].
sübeˡ**k**ᵍⁱ Urinal attached to a baby's cradle.
süb·jektif (*phil.*) Subjective. ~**jektivizm**, subjectivism. ~**lime**, (*chem.*) corrosive sublimate. ~**limleşmek**, *vi.* be sublimated. ~**limleştirmek (-i)**, sublimate. ~**vansiyon**, (*fin.*) subsidy.
sübutᵘ (*leg.*) A being proved; certainty; reality. ~ **bulmak**, be proved: ~ **delili**, certain proof.
sübye (*chem.*) Emulsion; (*cul.*) sweet drink (made with pounded almonds/melon seeds, etc.). ~**leştirmek**, emulsify.

sücuˡ**t**ᵈᵘ (*rel.*) Prostrating o.s. ~ **etm.**/~**a varmak** prostrate o.s.
südre·me *vn.* Getting drunk; slurring words like drunkard. ~**mek**, *vi.* get drunk.
süetⁱ (*tex.*) Suede.
süfli Low, inferior; common, low-down; menial; shabby. ~**leşmek**, *vi.* become inferior/common, shabby, etc. ~**lik**, lowness; inferiority; commonness; shabbiness.
süfrajetⁱ (*pol.*) Suffragette.
Süheyl (*ast.*) Canopus.
sühu·letⁱ Facility; comfort. ~**net**ⁱ, heat; temperature.
süklüm püklüm In a crestfallen manner; sheepishly.
sükse Success; ostentation. ~ **yapmak**, make/have a success.
sükûn(etⁱ**)** *n.* Calm, quiet; repose, rest. ~**et bulmak**, compose o.s.: ~**ette**, at rest. ~ **etli**, quiet; peaceful, calm.
sükûtᵘ Silence. ~ **etm.**, be silent: ~ **hakkı**, hush money: ~ **ikrardan gelir**, silence gives consent: ~**lı geçiştirmek**, pass over stg. in silence, make no comment: ~**u iltizam etm.**, prefer to keep silent.
sülale Family; line; descendants; dynasty.
sü·len/~**line** (*zoo.*) Grooved razor shell, solen.
sül·f (*chem.*) Sulphur. ~**fami**ˡ**t**ᵈⁱ, sulphanilamide. ~**fat**¹, sulphate. ~**fatlama**, (*agr.*) spraying with copper/iron sulphate. ~**für**, sulphide. ~**fürik asi**ˡ**t**ᵈⁱ, sulphuric acid.
sülûkᵘ Following a road//(*fig.*) a career//(*rel.*) a way.
sülüğen (*chem.*) Red lead paint.
sülükᵘ (*zoo.*) Leech, bloodsucker; (*bot.*) sucker, tendril; extortioner. ~ **gibi**, clinging; sticking like a leech: ~ **salyangozu**, (*zoo.*) common slug. ~**çü**, leech-seller; (*med.*) blood-letter. ~**dal**, (*bot.*) tendril. ~**giller**, (*zoo.*) Hirudinea.
sülümen (*chem.*) Corrosive sublimate.
sülün (*orn.*) (Ring-necked) pheasant. ~ **Bey**, brisk, lively little man: ~ **gibi**, tall and graceful. ~**giller**, (*orn.*) Phasianidae, pheasant family.
sül·üsˢᵘ One third; large-lettered Arabic script.
sülyen Anticorrosive primer paint.
sümbül (*bot.*) Hyacinth. ~**e**, (*Or. mus.*) a mode. (*ast.*) Virgo. ~**i**, hyacinth (colour); (*met.*) cloudy, overcast. ~ **teber**, (*bot.*) tuberose.
sümeˡ**k**ᵍⁱ (*tex.*) Ball of wool for the distaff.
Sümer (*his.*) Sumeria; (*ethn.*) Sumerian. ~**ce** (*ling.*) Sumerian. ~**olog**, Sumerologist. ~**oloji**, Sumerology.
sümkür·me *vn.* ~**mek**, *vi.* expel mucus from the nose, blow one's nose. ~**tmek (-i)**, *vc.*
sümmettedarik On the spur of the moment.
sümsüˡ**k**ᵍᵘ *a.* Imbecile; uncouth. ~ **kuşu**, (*orn.*) gannet. ~**giller**, (*orn.*) boobies. ~**leşmek**, *vi.* become uncouth.
sümter (*bot.*) A type of wheat.
sümüˡ**k**ᵍᵘ (*bio.*) Mucus; nasal mucus, snot. ~ **zarı**, ~**doku**, mucous membrane. ~**lü**, mucous; slimy; (*pej.*) snivelling, snotty. ~**lüböcek**, (*zoo.*) snail. ~**sel**, (*bio.*) mucous, conjunctive. ~**sü**, mucoid.
-sün¹ *v. suf.* [96] = -sin¹ [BÜYÜKSÜN].
-sün² *v. suf.* [137] = -sin² [GÖRSÜN].

ündüs (*mod.*) Fine silk brocade.

üne (*ent.*) Eurygaster, sun pest; (*orn.*) drake.

ünek (*min.*) Ductile. ~**lik**, ductility.

ünepe(lik) Sloven·ly/(-liness); sluggish(ness).

ünger (*zoo.*) Sponge. ~ **geçirmek (-den)**, pass the sponge over, cancel: ~ **kâğıdı**, blotting-paper: ~ **yapılı**, spongy: ~**le silmek**, wipe the slate clean.

ünger·ci Sponge-diver/-seller. ~**cilik**, sponge-diving/-selling. ~**doku**, (*bot.*) sponge-like tissue. ~**imsi**, porous. ~**kök**, (*bot.*) velamen. ~**ler**, (*zoo.*) sponges. ~**leştirmek (-i)**, make sponge-like. ~**leştir(il)miş kauçuk**, (*chem.*) foam rubber. ~**si**, sponge-like, spongy. ~**taşı**[n1], (*geol.*) pumice-stone.

üngü (*mil.*) Bayonet; (*eng.*) poker. ~ **dip**, (*el.*) bayonet cap: ~ **tak vaziyetinde**, with fixed bayonets: ~**sü ağır**, slow-moving: ~**sü düşük**, subdued, depressed, crestfallen: ~**sü depreşmesin!**, speak no evil of the dead!

üngü·lemek (-i) Bayonet. ~**lenmek**, *vp.* ~**leşmek (-le)**, attack each other with bayonets.

ünmek *vi.* Stretch; be(come) extended.

ünnet[i] (*rel.*) Muslim practices and rules (deduced from the Prophet's own habits/words); (*med.*) ritual circumcision. ~ **derisi**, (*bio.*) foreskin, prepuce: ~ **düğünü**, (*soc.*) circumcision feast: ~ **ehli**, (*rel.*) orthodox/Sunni Muslims: ~ **etm.**, (*med.*) circumcise: ~ **olm.**, *vi.* be circumcised.

ünnet·çi(lik) (*med.*) (Work of) circumciser. ~**leme**, short round beard (like the Prophet's). ~**lemek**, (*sl.*) eat up entirely; finish off. ~**li**, circumcised. ~**siz**, uncircumcised.

ünni (*rel.*) Orthodox; Sunnite. ~**lik**, Sunnite faith.

ünuhat[1] Thoughts occurring; inspiration.

sünüz *v. suf.* [96] = -siNiz [KÜÇÜKSÜNÜZ].

üper Super. ~**devlet**, (*pol.*) super-power. ~**market**, (*fin.*) supermarket, ~**vizör**, (*ind.*) supervisor.

üprüntü Sweepings, dross, rubbish; (*fig.*) rabble. ~ **sinekler**, (*ent.*) hover-flies. ~**cü**, street-sweeper; dustman, rubbish-collector; (*fig.*) collector of rubbish. ~**lük**, dust-heap, rubbish-heap.

üpürge (*dom.*) Broom, (sweeping-)brush. ~ **sapı**, broom-stick: ~ **sapı yemek**, get the stick.

üpürge·çalısı[n1]/~**otu**[nu] (*bot.*) Heather. ~**ci**, broom-maker/-seller; street-sweeper. ~**darısı**[n1], (*bot.*) sorghum. ~**lik**, (*arch.*) skirting-board.

üpür·me *vn.* ~**mek (-i)**, sweep, brush; sweep away, clear the table; (*fig.*) finish off. ~**tmek (-i, -e)**, *vc.* ~**ücü**, sweeper. ~**ülmek**, *vp.*

ürahi Decanter, carafe, water-bottle.

ürat[i] Speed; velocity; celerity; haste. ~ **katarı**, (*rly.*) express train: ~ **müşiri**, speed indicator: ~**le**, quickly.

ürat·lendirici (*mot.*) Accelerator. ~**lenmek**, *vi*, accelerate, go faster. ~**li**, fast; quick, hurried.

ür[l]**ç**[cü] Stumble; slip, mistake. ~**ü lisan**, slip of the tongue. ~**me**, *vn.* ~**mek**, *vi.* stumble, slip; make a mistake. ~**türmek (-i)**, *vc.*

ürdür·me *vn.* ~**mek (-i)**, *vc.* = SÜRMEK; continue with; ensure. ~**üm(cü)**, (*pub.*) sub·scription/ (-scriber). ~**ümletmek (-e)**, subscribe to.

üre Period; duration; extension; (*fin.*) term. ~ **aralığı**, period, interval: ~-AŞIMI: ~ **ölçen**/ **yargıcısı**, (*sp.*) time-keeper: ~ **ölçümü**, (*sp.*) time-

keeping: ~ **sonu**, (*fin.*) due date: ~ **üstü (boşaltma —yükleme)**, (*fin.*) demurrage: ~**si geçmek**, fall due: ~**si uzatımı**, renewal, extension: ~**sinde**, in due course.

süre·aşımı[n1] (*leg.*) Prescription. ~**bölüm**, (*el.*) time-sharing. ~**ce**, while. ~[l]**ç**[ci], way, path, manner; period, duration; (*ind.*) process. ~**çsel**, periodic; about a process. ~**dizin**, chronology. ~**duran**/ ~**durumlu**, (*phys.*) inert. ~**durum**, inertia. ~**gelmek**, *vi.* continue; happen frequently. ~**ğen(lik)**, (*med.*) chronic(ity). ~**ğenleşmek**, *vi.* become chronic.

süre[l]**k**[ği] Duration; (*live.*) drove of cattle; fast driver. ~ **avı**, (*sp.*) drive/beat (shooting).

sürek·li Lasting; prolonged; continuous, regular; perpetual: ~ **asalak**, (*bio.*) permanent parasite: ~ **film**, (*cin.*) serial: ~ **ısmarlama**, (*fin.*) standing order: ~ **olarak**, continuously, permanently: ~ **yayın**, (*pub.*) periodical. ~**lilik**, continuity; regularity; permanence. ~**siz**, discontinuous; irregular; short: ~ **sizlik**, discontinuity.

süre·l (*ind.*) Part-time. ~**li**, *a.* (*pub.*) periodical; (*fin.*) forward, for account: ~ **yarış**, (*sp.*) race against the clock: ~ **yayın**, (*pub.*) periodical, magazine. ~**m**, (*th.*) season. ~**ölçer**, (*ast., etc.*) chronometer; (*sp.*) stop-watch. ~**rdurum(cu)**, (*pol.*) (supporter of) *status quo.* ~**rlik**, ~ **eylemi**, (*ling.*) durative verb: ~ **görünüm**, (*ling.*) durative aspect. ~**siz**, indefinite; transitory; (*fin.*) at sight, on call. ~ **yazar**, chronograph.

Süreyya (*ast.*) The Pleiades.

sürfe (*zoo.*) Caterpillar; maggot; teredo.

sürgen (*med.*) Purgative. ~**doku**, (*bot.*) (permanent) meristem tissue.

sürgit Endlessly, for ever; stable. ~ **yapmak**, make last, prolong.

sürgü (*arch.*) Door-bolt; sliding-bar; (*agr.*) harrow, roller; (*arch.*) plasterer's trowel; (*phys.*) cursor; slide; (*med.*) bed-pan. ~ **kolu**, (*mil.*) rifle-bolt.

sürgü·lemek (-i) Bolt (door); harrow (field); roll (surface); smooth (plaster). ~**lenmek**, *vp.* ~**lü**, bolted; sliding: ~ **pergel**, beam-compasses.

sürgün (*pol.*) Banishment; (*leg.*) deportation; place of exile; an exile; (*bot.*) shoot, sucker, tiller; (*med.*) diarrhoea. ~ **cezasına çarpılmak**, (*pol.*) be banished: ~ **avı** = SÜREK: ~ **gitmek**, (*pol.*) go into exile, be banished; (*med.*) have diarrhoea: ~ **yeri**, place of exile: ~ **e göndermek**, (*pol.*) banish, exile.

sürme *vn.* Stg. drawn/pulled/driven, etc.; (door-) bolt; (*carp.*) drawer; (*med.*) aperient; application; (*mod.*) kohl, eye-liner; (*sp.*) move (chess, etc.); (*myc.*) smut/blight (wheat, etc.). *a.* Sliding; drawing in and out. ~ **cihazı**, (*med.*) applicator: ~ **kapı**, sliding door: ~ **pencere**, sash window; sliding window: ~ **taşı**, (*chem.*) antimony: ~ **dan**, pot for eye-salve.

sürmek (-i, -e) Drive (animals) in front; drive away; drive (vehicle); (*pol.*) banish; (*leg.*) deport; push along; (*bot.*) put forth (buds, etc.); (*med.*) apply, rub on, smear, spread; (*agr.*) plough; sell; pass (forgery); spend (time/life). *vi.* Push on, go on;

continue, extend; (time) last, pass; (*bot.*) germinate.
sürüp gitmek, continue: **sürüp sürüştürmek**, apply
make-up.
sürme·lemek (-i) Bolt (door); apply eye-salve. ~**li**,
with a bolt; bolted; sliding; tinged with eye-salve:
~ **çalı kuşu**, (*orn.*) firecrest; graceful prinia: ~ **kilit**,
dead-lock: ~ **kumpas**, slide gauge. ~**lik** = ~DAN.
~**mantarı(giller)**, (*myc.*) wheat bunt/(smut fungi).
sür·menaj (*med.*) Exhaustion (from overwork).
~**normal**, extraordinary, supernormal. ~**plüs**, ~
malzemesi, (*fin.*) government surplus. ~**priz**, surprise; gift.
sürre Purse; (*his.*) Sultan's annual gifts to Mecca/
Medina. ~ **alayı**, procession accompanying the
gifts: ~ **devesi**, an oddly-dressed person: ~ **devesi
gibi dolaşmak**, loaf about with an air of being busy:
~ **emini**, official entrusted with the SÜRRE (ALAYI).
sür·realist (*art.*) Surrealist. ~**realizm**, surrealism.
~**şarj**, (*pub.*) overprinting, (*adm.*) surcharge; (*el.*)
overload. ~**tansiyon**, (*el.*) excess voltage.
sürt·me *vn.* Rubbing, friction; ~ **ağı**, two-boat
trawl net. ~**mek (-i, -e)**, rub stg. against stg. else;
rub with the hand; wear down by friction, chafe: *vi.*
wander about aimlessly: **sürt Allah kerim!**, what a
vagabond!: **sürt Allah sürt!**, (*col.*) let's wander
around and pass the time!: **sürtüp durmak**, wander
about aimlessly. ~**ük(lük)**, (state of) (woman)
always gadding about. ~**ülmek**, *vp.*, be rubbed,
etc. ~**ünme**, *vn.*; friction. ~**ünmek**, *vi.* rub o.s.
against stg., chafe; drag o.s. along, creep; (*fig.*)
seek a quarrel, behave provocatively: **sürtünüp
durmak**, toady. ~**ünüm**, contact. ~**üşme**, *vn.*
~**üşmek (-le)**, rub against each other. ~**üştürmek
(-i, -e)**, rub two things against each other.
sürur Joy; pleasure.
sürü (*live.*) Herd, drove, flock; pack; (*ich.*) shoal;
(*ent.*) swarm; (*fig.*) crowd; gang; a lot of. ~ **sepet**,
all together, the lot; in great numbers: ~ ~, in
droves/flocks, etc.: ~**den ayrılanı kurt kapar**,
there's safety in numbers: ~**den ayrılmak**, (*fig.*) go
it alone, follow one's own ideas: ~**süne bereket!**,
(*sl.*) heaps of!, crowds of!: ~**ye katılmak**, (*fig.*) go
with the crowd, do as others do; (child) start to play
with others.
sürü·cü(lük) (Work of) drover; driver (of vehicles);
man in charge of post-horses. ~**cül**, (*zoo.*) living in
herds/packs, etc.
sürük·leme *vn.*: ~ **demiri**, (*naut.*) drift anchor: ~
kuvveti, (*aer.*) drag. ~**lemek (-i, -e)**, drag (along the
ground); drag s.o. (against his will); involve/lead
s.o. into; entail; (*th.*, *lit.*) carry one's audience/
readers with one. ~**lendirmek (-i, -e)**, *vc.* ~**lenmek
(-e)**, *vp.* be dragged: *vi.* drag o.s.; drag on, be
protracted. ~**letmek (-i, -e)**, *vc.* ~**leyici**, dragging;
fascinating; attractive.
sür·ülme *vn.* Introduction of stg.; (*cin.*) release.
~**ülmek (-e)**, *vp.* = SÜRMEK; be rubbed/driven, etc.:
sürülmüş toprak, arable land.
sürüm (*fin.*) Circulation, rapid sale, great demand.
~ **bankası**, bank of issue: ~ **romanı**, (*lit.*) popular novel: ~ ~ **sürünmek**, live in utter misery:
~**de**, in circulation: ~**den çekmek**, withdraw
from circulation: ~**den kazanmak**, profit from

the volume of sales: ~**e çıkarmak**, issue, put int
circulation.
sürüm·cü(lük) (*fin.*) Commercial travel·ler/(-ling
~**değer**, rate (of exchange).
sürümek (-i) Drag lightly: *vi.* procrastinate.
sürüm·lü (*fin.*) In great demand, selling well. ~**lü**
(*mod.*) cosmetics. ~**lüluk**, (*fin.*) brisk tradin
~**süz**, in little demand, hardly selling. ~**süzlük**
(*fin.*) stagnation.
sürün·ceme Delay; a dragging on: ~**de kalmak**
drag on, be long drawn out. ~**cemeli**, dilatory
~**dürmek (-i)**, bring into utter misery. ~**dürülmek**
vp. ~**gen**, (*zoo.*) reptile: ~ **bilimi**, herpetology:
sap, (*bot.*) creeper: ~**ler**, (*zoo.*) Reptilia. ~**genleş
mek**, *vi.* become sluggish. ~**me**, *vn.* creeping
crawling: ~ **pantolonu**, (*mod.*) (baby's) crawler
~**mek (-i)**, rub in/on o.s.: *vi.* drag o.s. along, cree
crawl; (*fig.*) grovel; live in misery.
sürür (*chem.*) Mercuric sulphide; vermilion varnis
sür·üşmek (-le) *vi.* Rub together/each other. ~**üş
türmek (-i, -e)**, rub together; rub in gently, massag
~**ütme**, (*naut.*) drag-net, trawl-net; trawl-lin
~**ütmek (-i, -e)**, *vc.* = SÜRÜMEK.
Süryani (*ethn.*) Syrian Christian. ~**ce**, (*ling*
Syriac.
süs (*art.*) Ornament, adornment, decoration; (*mod*
elegance of dress; toilet; luxury. ~ **eşyas**
ornament: ~ **kuşağı**, (*arch.*) frieze: ~ **ocağı**, fire
place: ~ **püs**, (*pej.*) fussy ornament: ~ **saltana**
great luxury: ~ **semizotu**, (*bot.*) sun plant, ros
moss: ~ **ü vermek (kendine)**, pretend to be.
süsen (*bot.*) Iris. ~ **kökü**, orris root. ~**gille**
Iridaceae, iris family.
süs·leme *vn.*: ~ **sanatları**, decorative arts. ~**leme
(-i)**, adorn, decorate; embellish; dress (up), dec
out; (*fig.*) recount s.o.'s shameful deeds: **süsley**
püslemek, decorate with care. ~**lemelik**, decor
tive. ~**lendirmek (-i)**, *vc.* ~**lenme**, *vn.* ~**lenmek**,
adorn o.s.; deck o.s. out: *vp.* be decorated. ~**len**
decoration. ~**letmek (-i, -e)**, *vc.* ~**leyici**, decor
tive. ~**lü**, ornamented, decorated; careful
dressed; luxurious: ~ **atmaca kartalı**, (*orn.*) ornat
hawk-eagle: ~ **başharf**, (*pub.*) illuminated initia
~ **destek**, (*dom.*) console: ~ **elbise**, (*mod.*) fin
clothes, array: ~ **püslü**, ornately dressed. ~**lü**
(*dom.*) ornament.
süsmek (-i) (Animal) butt, toss; gore.
süspan·s (*lit.*) Suspense. ~**siyon**, (*eng.*) suspensio
süssüz Bare, plain, undecorated. ~**lük**, barenes
lack of decoration.
süt[ü] *n.* (*zoo.*) Milk; (*bot.*) milk-like juice; milky sa
latex; (*bio.*) fish-sperm. ~ +, *a.* Milk-; dairy
(*chem.*) lactic; (*live.*) suckling. ~ **ağzı**, (*zoo.*) bees
ings, colostrum: ~ **asidi**, (*chem.*) lactic acid:
bezi, (*bio.*) mammary gland: ~ **çalmak**, milk mak
(the baby) ill: ~ **danası**, (*live.*) suckling calf; (*cul*
real veal: ~ **dökmüş kedi gibi**, in a crestfalle
manner: ~ **güğümü**, milk churn: ~ **kesilmek**, mil
turn sour: ~ **kesimi**, (*bio.*) weaning: ~ **koyun**
(*live.*) dairy sheep: ~ **kuzusu**, suckling lamb; (*fig*
baby; (*fig.*) pure-hearted: ~ **mahsul/ürünü**, dairy
produce: ~ **sağma makinesi**, milking machine: ~
vermek, (*bio.*) suckle: ~**ten ağzı yanan ayranı üfle**

de içer/yoğurdu üfliyerek yer, a burnt child fears the fire, a scalded cat fears cold water: ~ ten kesmek, wean: ~ ü bozuk, base; without character; unprincipled: ~ ü çekilmiş, (live.) dry (cow): ~ üne havale etm. (-in), leave stg. to s.o.'s sense of honour: ~ ünü kesmek, (live.) dry off (cow). süt·ağacı[n1] (bot.) Galactodendron. ~ ana/ ~ anne, wet-nurse; foster-mother. ~ baba, foster-father. ~ başı[n1], (cul.) cream, top of the milk. ~ beyaz, milk-white. ~ çü, milkman: dairyman. ~ çülük, milk-selling; making dairy produce. ~ dişi[ni], (bio.) milk-tooth. ~ hane, dairy. ~ kardeş, foster-brother/-sister. ~ kırı, milk-white horse. ~ kızı[n1], foster-daughter. ~ labi, (orn.) smew. ~ la[l]ç[c1], (cul.) rice-pudding. ~ leğen(giller), (bot.) Euphorbia/ (-ceae), spurge (family). ~ lenmek, vi. milk be produced. ~ liman, (met.) dead calm. ~ lü, (cul.) milky; with milk; (live.) milch; (bot.) almost ripe but soft grain: ~ kahve, (cul.) white coffee: ~ pelte, blancmange. ~ lüce, (bot.) petty spurge. ~ lüot, (bot.) sea milkwort. ~ (ni)ne, wet-nurse. ~ oğ[l]ul[lu], foster-son. ~ otu[nu], (bot.) milkwort, polygala. ~ ölçer, milk-density meter. ~ şekeri[ni], (chem.) lactose. ~ sü, (chem.) emulsion. ~ süz, (cul.) without milk; (live.) giving little milk, dry; (bot.) shrivelled (grain); (fig.) base, ignoble: ~ kahve, (cul.) black coffee. ~ süzlük, absence/lack of milk; (fig.) baseness, ignobility. ~ tozu[nu], (cul.) powdered milk. ~ vurgunu[nu], (med.) suffering from poor milk; rickety.
sütun (arch.) Column, pillar; (pub.) column; (phys.)

beam. ~ başlığı, (arch.) abacus, cap(ital): ~ gövdesi, drum: ~ kornişi, fascia: ~ teknesi, architrave. ~ lu, columnar; with columns: ~ giriş, portico.
süvari Horse-rider; (mil.) cavalryman; (chess) knight; (naut.) ship's master. ~ alayı, cavalcade. ~ lik, being on horseback; duties of cavalryman// ship's master; (mod.) leather patch on riding-breeches.
sü·ve = SÖVE. ~ veter, (mod.) sweater. ~ veyş, pr.n. (geo.) Suez: ~ Kanalı, Suez Canal. ~ ye, (med.) splint. ~ yüm, (tex.) first thread of new distaff.
-süz a./pron. suf. [62] = -siz [GÖZSÜZ].
süz·dürme vn. ~ dürmek (-i, -e), vc. = SÜZMEK. ~ dürüm, (med.) dialysis. ~ e[l]k[g1], (dom.) spray-head, rose; (tex.) net, gauze. ~ eni, (tex.) very fine embroidery. ~ ge[l]ç[ci]/ ~ gü, filter, strainer; (cul.) colander; (ind.) grill, grid: ~ ten geçirmek, strain, filter. ~ gün, grown thin/weak; languid; (eye) half-closed: ~ bakış, a looking with half-closed eyes. ~ günlük, weakness.
-süzlük n. suf. = -SİZLİK [GÖTÜRÜMSÜZLÜK].
süz·me vn.: a. Strained, filtered: ~ bal, (cul.) run honey: ~ çukuru, (eng.) cess-pit/-pool. ~ mek (-i), strain, drain, filter; look at carefully (through half-closed eyes); look languidly. ~ ücü, a. filtering: ~ tabaka, filter-bed. ~ ük, drawn/strained (face). ~ ülme, vn.; filtration. ~ ülmek, vp. be strained/ filtered; be closely examined: vi. become thin; become languorous; slip/creep away; glide along swiftly/silently. ~ üntü, filter-cake, dregs.

Ş

Ş, ş [she] Twenty-third Tk. letter, Ş.
Ş = ŞAH.
-ş- *v. suf. after a vowel* [143] = -iş- [KAYNAŞMAK].
şa *int.* = YAŞA(SIN). Long live . . .!; hurrah!
şaban *n.* (*ast.*) Eighth lunar month. *a.* Foolish, stupid.
şablon (*eng.*) Pattern, model, template; (*art.*) stencil.
şad Joyful, happy.
şadırvan Water-tank (with a fountain); (*rel.*) fountain for ritual ablutions.
şafa'kᵍ¹ Dawn, daybreak. ~ **atmak**, dawn break: ~ **atmak (-de)**, realize the difficulties facing one (and turn pale with fear): ~ **kelebeği**, (*ent.*) orange-tip butterfly: ~ **ötüşü**, (*orn.*) dawn chorus: ~ **serenadı**, (*mus.*) aubade: ~ **sökmek**, dawn break: ~ **sökmesi**, crack of dawn: ~ **la beraber/** ~ **ta**, at dawn/cock-crow.
şafi Health-giving; satisfactory; categorical (reply).
Şafii (*rel.*) (Member of) Shafi school of Islam. ~ **köpeği gibi titremek**, (*pej.*) tremble all over: ~ **köpeği(ne dönmek)**, (become) a dirty-faced fellow. ~ **lik**, Shafi school/doctrines.
şaft¹ (*eng.*) Shaft.
şaful Wooden tub (for honey).
şah¹ *n.* (Horse) front legs off the ground. ~ **a kalkmak**, rear up, curvet.
şah² *n.* Shah; monarch; (chess) king. ~ DAMARI: ~ **iken şahbaz olm.**, (*iron.*) finer and finer!; become worse and worse: ~ **kartal**, (*orn.*) imperial eagle: ~ **ımı bu kadar severim (ben)**, I can't risk any more; don't count on me further.
şah. = ŞAHIS.
şahadetⁱ (*leg.*) A witnessing; testimony, deposition; evidence; stg. witnessed; (*rel.*) testifying to Islam; (Muslim's) death in battle, martyrdom. ~ **etm. (-e)**, bear witness to stg.: ~ **getirmek**, (*rel.*) pronounce the formula 'there is no God but God and Muhammad is the messenger of God': ~ **e nail olm.**, die on the battlefield, achieve martyrdom: ~ **te bulunmak**, bear witness, testify. ~ **name**, testimonial; diploma; certificate. ~ **parmağı**ⁿ¹, index-finger.
şahane Royal; imperial; regal, magnificent.
şaha'pᵇ¹ (*ast.*) Meteor.
şah·baz *n.* (*orn.*) A royal falcon; (*fig.*) champion; hero: *a.* fine. ~ **damarı**ⁿ¹, (*bio.*) carotid artery. ~ **dere(otu)**, (*bot.*) common fumitory. ~ **eser**, masterpiece, *chef d'œuvre*.
şah'ımᵐ¹ (*bio.*) Fat.
şah'ısˢ¹ Person; individual; personal features; (*lit.*) character.
şâhıs (*geo.*) Surveyor's levelling staff.
şahika (*geo.*) Peak, summit.

şahin (*orn.*) Common buzzard; hawk. ~ **bakışlı**, hawk-eyed. ~ **ci**, falconer.
şahi'tᵈⁱ Witness; (*ling.*) example; (*bio.*, *etc.*) control (in an experiment). ~ **olm. (-e)**, attest, witness: ~ **tutmak**, call on s.o. to witness; accept as witness. ~ **lik**, giving evidence; testimony; being witness to stg.: ~ **etm.**, bear witness, testify.
şahlan·dırmak (-i) *vc.* ~ **mak**, *vi.* (horse) rear up; (*fig.*) get out of hand; become angry and threatening.
şahlık Rank/authority/government of a shah.
şahm- = ŞAHIM. ~ **ı**, adipose, fatty.
şah·meran (*zoo.*) Basilisk. ~ **merdan**, (*mil.*) battering-ram; (*eng.*) pile-driver, steam-hammer ~ **name** = ŞEHNAME. ~ **niş(in)**, (*arch.*) bay window (of enclosed balcony).
şahrem ~ ~ **çatlamak**, (skin) be covered with cracks: ~ ~ **yırtılmak**, (cloth) be badly torn.
şahs- = ŞAHIS. ~ **en**, personally; in person; by sight ~ **i**, personal, private: ~ **hal**, (*leg.*) civil status ~ **iyat**¹, personalities; personal matters: ~ **yapmak**, ~ **a dök(ül)mek**, descend to personalities. ~ **iyet**ⁱ personality; important person: ~ **sahibidir**, he has an air about him. ~ **iyetli**, important, individual. ~ **iyetsiz**, insignificant.
şah·süvar/ ~ **tane** = ŞEH-. ~ **tere** = ŞAHDERE ~ **tur**, (*naut.*) large river ferry-boat.
şaibe Dirt, stain; defect. ~ **li**, stained; defective.
şair Poet; minstrel; public singer. ~ **bozuntusu**, a mere parody of a poet. ~ **ane**, poetical(ly). ~ **lik** quality of a poet/minstrel: ~ **davasına düşmek**, set out/claim to be a poet.
şak¹¹ *n.* (*ech.*) Clacking noise; crack (of whip) ~ ~, clapping.
şakᵏ¹² *n.* Split, crack; fissure. *a.* Split, cracked. ~ **etm.**, (*eng.*) cannibalize.
şaka Fun; joke; jest. ~ **bertaraf**, joking apart: ~ **derken/iken kaka olm.**, a joke may easily turn into stg. serious: ~ **etm.**, joke; jest; banter: ~ **gibi gelmek**, be incredible/unbelievable: ~ **götürmez** it's no laughing matter: ~ **kaldırmak**, be able to stand a joke: ~ **maka (derken)**, by making light of stg. (it disappears): ~ **olarak**, jokingly: ~ **olmaktan çıkıyor**, it's beyond a joke: ~ **söylemek**, tell stg. not (meant to be) serious: ~ **yapmak**, do stg. as a joke ~ **yollu**, (*ling.*) jokingly: ~ **sı yok**, in earnest, not to be trifled with; serious: ~ **ya boğmak/bozmak** ridicule, make a jest/mockery of stg.: ~ **ya gelmek** take a joke: ~ **ya gelmemek**, not to be joked about not take a joke: ~ **ya getirmek**, tell stg. serious jokingly; turn stg. serious into a joke: ~ **ya vurmak** pretend to take stg. as a joke.
şaka·cı Joker; s.o. fond of joking. ~ **cıktan** (*child.*) as a joke; (do stg. serious) under pretence

of a joke; without noticing (difficulties). ~ dan, as a joke.

şaka¹kᵍ¹ (*bio.*) Temple. ~ **kemiği**, temporal bone.

şaka·laşmak (-le) Joke with each other. ~ **sız**, seriously.

şakayı¹kᵏ¹/ᵍ¹ (*bot.*) Peony.

şakımak *vi.* (Bird) sing loudly; speak pleasantly.

şakır ~ ~, (*ech.*) splashing, jingling, rattling: ~ ~ **oynamak**, dance in a very happy mood: ~ **şukur**, (*ech.*) rattling, banging. ~ **damak**, *vi.* (bird) sing loudly; rattle, jingle, splash. ~ **datmak (-i)**, *vc.* ~ **tı**, continuous clatter/rattle.

şakıt¹ (*ich.*) Moray eel; lamprey.

şaki Brigand; rebel, outlaw; bandit. ~ **lik**, brigandage, rebellion, banditry.

şakir¹tᵈⁱ (*ed.*) Pupil; apprentice; disciple.

şakkadak Suddenly; unexpectedly.

şaklaban Mimic; jester; buffoon; (*fig.*) toady; charlatan. ~ **lık**, mimicry; buffoonery.

şakla·mak *vi.* Make loud cracking noise. ~ **tmak (-i)**, *vc.*; crack (whip).

şak·rak Noisy; cheerful, vivacious; chatty. ~ **rak-kuşu**ⁿᵘ, (*orn.*) bullfinch. ~ **ramak**, *vi.* (bird) sing loudly.

şakşa¹kᵍ¹ Slap-stick; large castanet; (*cin.*) clapper; (*fig.*) applause; toadying. ~ **çı**, (*cin.*) clapper-boy; (*th.*) claqueur; (*fig.*) toady, 'yes-man'. ~ **çılık**, applause; base adulation.

şakulᵘ (*phys.*) Plumb-line; plummet. ~ **i**, (*math.*) perpendicular. ~ **lamak (-i)**, (*arch.*) set up with a plumb-line; (*fig.*) plan, measure.

şal (*tex.*) Fine woollen cloth, cashmere; (*mod.*) (cashmere) shawl. ~ **örneği**, cloth with shawl motifs.

şala¹kᵍ¹ (*bot.*) Small undeveloped water-melon.

şalgam (*bot.*) Turnip.

şali (*tex.*) Alpaca, camlet; bunting.

şalopa (*naut.*) Sloop.

şalt (*el.*) ~ **cihazı**, switching apparatus: ~ **sahası**, (*ind.*) switchyard. ~ **er**, (*el.*) cut-out switch, circuit-breaker.

şalvar (*mod.*) Tk. baggy trousers. ~ **gibi**, very full (trousers). ~ **lı**, wearing baggy trousers.

Şam (*geo.*) Damascus. ~ BABA: ~ **çeliği**, (*min.*) damask steel: ~ FISTIĞI: ~ **iş/kumaşı**, (*tex.*) damask: ~ **Trablusu**, (*geo.*) Tripoli (Lebanon).

şama Wax-taper. ~ **lı kibrit**, wax vesta.

şamama (*bot.*) Musk melon; (*fig.*) undersized, weak. ~ **gibi**, s.o. small but attractive.

Şaman (*rel.*) Shaman. ~ **izm**/ ~ **lık**, Shamanism.

şamandıra (*naut.*) Buoy; (*dom.*) float (for a wick), paraffin-lamp burner; ball (of ball-cock).

şamar Slap; box on the ear. ~ **oğlanı**, scapegoat: ~ **yemek**, get a slap. ~ **lamak (-i)**, slap.

şamata Great noise, din, uproar. ~ **cı**, noisy/ uproarious person. ~ **lı**, noisy; clamorous; blatant.

şam·babaˢ¹ (*cul.*) Type of pastry; (*fig.*) father lacking in authority. ~ **dan**, candlestick: ~ **külahı**, (candle) extinguisher. ~ **dancı**, (*obs.*) lamp-lighter. ~ **fıstığı**ⁿ¹, (*bot.*) pistachio-nut.

şamil Comprising; including; comprehensive. ~ **olm.**, contain, include, comprise.

şam·panya (*cul.*) Champagne. ~ **piyon**, (*sp.*) champion. ~ **piyona**/ ~ **piyonluk**, championship. ~ **puan**, (*dom.*) shampoo. ~ **ua**, (*zoo.*) chamois.

şan¹ *n.* (*mus.*) Song.

şan² *n.* Fame, renown, distinction; glory; reputation; state, quality, aspect; display; importance. ~ **vermek**, become known to all; acquire fame: ~ **ına düşmek**/ ~ **ından olm.**, befit one's reputation.

şangır (*ech.*) ~ **şungur**, with a crash. ~ **dama**, *vn.* crashing (sound). ~ **damak**, *vi.* (break with a) crash. ~ **tı**, crash (sound).

şan·jan (*tex.*) 'Shot' (silk, etc.). ~ **jman**, (*mot.*) gear-box. ~ **kr**, (*med.*) chancre.

şanlı Glorious; famous; good-looking. ~ **şöhretli**, fine and imposing.

şano (*th.*) Stage. ~ **ya çıkmak**, appear on stage.

şans Chance; luck; good fortune. ~ **getirsin diye**, for/to bring good luck: ~ **işi**, a matter of luck: ~ **tanımak**, give an opportunity: ~ **ı yaver gitmek**, be very lucky.

şansız Without renown, unknown; undistinguished. ~ **şöhretsiz**, insignificant in appearance.

şans·lı Lucky, fortunate. ~ **lılık**, luckiness. ~ **sız**, unlucky, unfortunate. ~ **sızlık**, misfortune.

şan·son (*mus.*) Solo song. ~ **sölye**, (*adm.*) chancellor. ~ **taj(cı)**, blackmail(er). ~ **tiye**, (*ind.*) worksite, yard: ~ **mühendisi**, resident engineer. ~ **tör**// ~ **töz**, (*th.*) male//female singer. ~ **z(ı)man** = ŞANJMAN.

şap¹ *n.* (*ech.*) Sound of kissing. ~ ~, continually kissing.

şap¹² *n.* (*chem.*) Alum; (*geo.*) coral reef. ~ **Denizi**, (*geo.*) Red Sea: ~ **gibi**, very salty: ~ **gibi donmak**/ **kalmak**, be embarrassed/disconcerted: ~ **hastalık**/ **illeti**, (*live.*) foot-and-mouth disease: ~ TAŞI: ~ **a dönmek/kesilmek**, become bitter: ~ **a oturmak**, (*naut.*) be grounded on a coral reef; (*fig.*) be in a hopeless dilemma; be greatly disconcerted. ~ **hane**, alum factory.

şapır ~ ~/ ~ **şupur**, (*ech.*) smacking of lips: ~ ~ **yemek**, gobble/guzzle one's food.

şapır·dama *vn.* ~ **damak**, *vi.* make a smacking noise (eating/kissing). ~ **datmak (-i)**, smack (one's lips). ~ **tı**, smacking noise (of lips).

şapka (*mod.*) Hat; (*naut.*) mast-truck; (*eng.*) chimney-cowl; (*myc.*) cap, pileus. ~ **giymek**, wear a hat; (*rel.*, *his.*) apostatize from Islam, serve a foreign power: ~ **ters giymek**/ ~ **yı yere vurmak**, show anger.

şapka·cı(lık) (Work of) hatter. ~ **lı**, hatted, wearing a hat; (*ling.*) with a circumflex; (*obs.*) European: ~ **mantar**, (*myc.*) basidiomycete: ~ **maymun**, (*zoo.*) bonnet monkey: ~ **vida**, (*eng.*) mirror screw. ~ **lık**, *n.* hatstand: *a.* suitable for hat-making. ~ **sız**, hatless; bare-headed.

şap·la¹kᵍ¹ Slap/smack on the face. ~ **lamak**, *vi.* make a smacking noise. ~ **latmak (-i)**, *vc.*; give a slap. ~ **padak**, suddenly, all at once.

şapra¹kᵍ¹ Saddle-cloth.

şap·şal Stupid; untidy, slovenly. ~ **şalak**, (*col.*) careless; slovenly. ~ **şallık**, untidiness.

şaptaşıⁿ¹ (*geol.*) Coral from the Red Sea.

şar = ŞARIL.

-şar *a. suf.* (*after vowels*) [83, 193] = -ER⁴ [ALTIŞAR].

şarab- = ŞARAP. ~ **i**, red-wine-coloured.
şarampol (*mil.*) Stockade; (*eng.*) roadside ditch.
sara¹pᵇ¹ Wine. ~ **mahzeni**, wine cellar: ~ **mayası**, (*chem.*) wine yeast: ~ **tortusu**, crude tartar: ~ **tortusu gibi**, Bordeaux red.
şarap·çı *n.* Wine-maker/-seller, vintner: *a.* fond of wine. ~ **çılık**, wine-making/-selling. ~ **hane**, wine factory; wine-cellars/store; wine shop.
şarapnel (*mil.*) Shrapnel, case-shot.
şarbon (*med.*) Anthrax; (*myc.*) smut.
şarıl ~ ~, (*ech.*) sound of running water: ~ ~ **akmak/** ~ **damak**, *vi.* flow with a splashing noise. ~ **tı**, gurgling; splashing.
şarj (*phys.*) Load; (*el.*) charge. ~ **edafer**, (*adm.*) chargé d'affaires. ~ **ör**, (*el.*) charger.
şark¹ *n.* (*geo.*) East; Orient. ~ +, Eastern, oriental: ~ **çıbanı**, (*med.*) Aleppo button.
şarkadak (*ech.*) Slap; noise of stg. falling. ~ **bayılmak**, fall down in a faint.
şarkı (*mus.*) Song, ballad. ~ **okumak/söylemek**, sing (a song). ~ **cı**, song-writer; singer: ~ **kuşu**, (*orn.*) accentor. ~ **cılık**, song-writing; singing.
şark·i (*geo.*) Eastern; oriental. ~ **iyat¹**, (*ed.*) orientalism; study of oriental languages/literature. ~ **iyatçı**, orientalist. ~ **lı**, eastern.
şar·küteri (*cul.*) (Shop selling) hors d'œuvres, cold meats, etc. ~ **latan(lık)**, charlatan(ry). ~ **pa**, (*mod.*) scarf. ~ **pi**, (*naut.*) sharpie.
şart¹ Condition, stipulation; (*leg.*) article/clause (of a contract). ~ **cümleciği**, (*ling.*) conditional clause: ~ **etm.**, swear saying ~ OLSUN!; invoke a divorce with conditions; lay down conditions: ~ **kipi**, (*ling.*) conditional mood: ~ **koşmak**, lay down conditions; covenant: ~ **olm.**, be necessary/ unavoidable: ~ **olsun!**, if it is not so may my wife be divorced!: ~ **şurt tanımaz**, recognizing no conditions: ~ **a bağlamak**, make stg. dependent on conditions: ~ **a bağlı**, conditional, contingent: ~ **ınca**, as necessary: ~ **ıyla**, on condition (that . . .).
şart·lamak (-i), (*rel.*) Wash stg. canonically. ~ **landırmak (-i)**, *vc.*; (*psy.*) condition s.o. ~ **lanmak**, *vp.*: *vi.* adapt to conditions, be conditioned. ~ **laşma**, *vn.*; contract. ~ **laşmak (-le)**, mutually agree conditions. ~ **lı**, with conditions attached, conditional; s.o. who has sworn ~ OLSUN!: ~ **refleks**, (*psy.*) conditioned reflex. ~ **name**, list of conditions; (*ind.*) specification; (*leg.*) contract. ~ **sız**, unconditional; categorical.
şar·tröz (*cul.*) Chartreuse liqueur. ~ **yo**, (*eng.*) carriage; trolley.
şasi (*cin.*, *arch.*) Frame; (*mot.*) chassis. ~ **ye bağlama**, (*el.*) earth-to-frame.
şaşaa Glitter, sparkle; splendour. ~ **lanmak**, *vi.* sparkle; be magnificent. ~ **lı**, sparkling; resplendent.
şaşa·kalmak (-e), *vi.* Be absolutely bewildered/ dumbfounded. ~ **lama**, *vn.* ~ **lamak**, *vi.* be bewildered/confused.
şaşı *a.* Squinting; squint-eyed. ~ **laşma**, *vn.* squinting. ~ **laşmak**, *vi.* become squint-eyed; squint. ~ **lık**, squint(ing).
şaşılmak *imp. v.* One be surprised; it be surprising. **şaşılacak/şaşılası**, surprising, wonderful.
şaşır·mak (-i) Be confused about stg.; lose the way,

etc.: *vi.* become bewildered/embarrassed; lose one': head: **şaşırıp duralamak**, dither: **şaşırmış**, abashed ~ **tı**, surprise. ~ **tıcı**, surprising. ~ **tma**, *vn.* mis leading/confusing act; zig-zag; (*lit.*) tongue-twister (*agr.*) transplanting: ~ **hareketi**, (*mil.*) diversion ~ **tmaca**, (*lit.*) tongue-twister; puzzle. ~ **tmak (-i)** confuse, bewilder; disorientate; mislead; (*agr.* transplant (seedlings, etc.).
şaş·kaloz (*sl.*) Cross-eyed; bewildered. ~ **kı**, sur prise, astonishment. ~ **kın**, bewildered, confused stupid; (*bio.*) wandering, stray: ~ ~, bewilderedly ~ **a çevirmek**, confuse: ~ **a dönmek/** ~ **laşmak**, *vi* become confused/bewildered. ~ **kınlık**, bewilder ment, confusion: ~ **tan serseme çevirmek**, astound ~ **mak (-e)**, be surprised/bewildered at stg.: **(-den)** be confused about stg.; go astray, deviate: **(-i)**, mis one's way. ~ **mamak (-den)**, keep/stick to stg ~ **maz**, (*fig.*) stop-watch.
şatafat¹ Luxury; ostentatious display. ~ **lı**, osten tatious, showy.
şathiyat¹ (*lit.*) Flippant/satirical writings.
şat·o Castle, château. ~ **ranç** = SATRANÇ.
şavk¹ (*col.*) Light. ~ **ımak**, *vi.* shine.
şaya¹kᵍ¹ (*tex.*) Homespun, serge.
şayan Fitting, suitable; worthy.
şayet *conj.* [270] If by any chance, if at all (possible)
şayiⁱ ~ **olm.**, be commonly known. ~ **a**, new spread around, rumour.
şayka (*naut.*) Large Black Sea boat.
şaz Exceptional; (*ling.*) irregular.
Şb. = ŞUBE.
şe (*ling.*) The Tk. letter Ş.
şeamet¹ Inauspiciousness; evil omen.
şebboy (*bot.*) (sarı) ~, wallflower: **(kırmızı)** ~, stock **şebe¹kᵍ¹** *n.* (*zoo.*) (Chacma) baboon. *a.* Ugly shameless; impudent. ~ **ler**, baboons.
şebeke Net; lattice-work; grating; (*el.*) circuit mains; (railway/telephone) network; band; gan; (of criminals); student's pass (on rly. etc.).
şebnem (*met.*, *obs.*) Dew.
şec·aat¹ Bravery, courage. ~ **aatli/** ~ **i** brave.
şecere Genealogy; family tree; pedigree. ~ **li**, o good family.
şed·d- = ŞET. ~ **dadi**, big, strong (building). ~ **de** (*ling.*) sign for a double consonant in Arabic ~ **deli**, doubled (consonant): ~ **eşek**, (*vulg.* complete/utter fool. ~ **it**, strong; violent.
şef (*adm.*) Chief, head; (*mus.*) conductor. ~ **kürsüsü**, conductor's stand.
şefaatⁱ (*leg.*) Intercession. ~ **çi**, intercessor.
şeffaf Transparent; clear, crystalline; (*tex.*) dia phanous, filmy. ~ **laşmak**, *vi.* become transparen ~ **lık**, transparency.
şef·ik Compassionate. ~ **kat¹/** ~ **katlilik**, compas sion, affection; concern, solicitude. ~ **katli**, com passionate; affectionate; solicitous. ~ **katsiz** callous, pitiless. ~ **katsizlik**, callousness.
şef·lik (*adm.*) Rank/duties/office of a chief/head ~ **tren**, (*rly.*) guard.
şeftali (*bot.*) Peach; a kiss. ~ **ağacı**, peach-tree ~ **güvesi**, (*ent.*) peach twig-borer.
şeh·adetⁱ = ŞAHADET. ~ **bender(lik)**, (*his.*) Tk. Iranian consul(ate). ~ **evi**, sensual, lustful.

şeh'irri Large town, borough, city. ~ **eşkiyası,** urban guerrilla: ~ **hatları,** city roads; urban communications: ~ **kırlangıcı,** (*orn.*) house-martin: ~ **planı,** town plan: ~ **planlaması,** town-planning: ~ **rehberi,** town-guide, street-atlas. **şehir·ci(lik)** Town-plan·ner/(-ning). ~**dışı**nı, suburb. ~**lerarası,** inter-urban, inter-city. ~**leşme,** *vn.* urbanization. ~**leşmek,** *vi.* develop into a town/city. ~**li,** townsman, city-dweller, citizen. ~**lileşmek,** *vi.* become a townsman.

şehi'ltdi (*rel.*) Martyr; (*pol.*) Muslim dying on duty/in battle/for his country. ~ **düşmek,** die in battle. ~**lik,** martyrdom; patriotic death; (*mil.*) cemetery.

şeh·la Having a slight squint. ~**name,** (*lit.*) poetical history, epic. ~**naz,** (*Or. mus.*) a mode. ~**nişin** = ŞAHNİŞ(İN).

şehr- = ŞEHİR. ~**emaneti**ni, (*obs.*) Istanbul/Ankara prefecture. ~**emini**ni, (*obs.*) prefect. ~**i,** urban; municipal.

şehriye (*cul.*) Various types of pasta, vermicelli.

şeh·süvar Fine horseman. ~**tane,** large lustrous pearl; largest bead of a rosary; (*bot.*) hempseed.

şeh·vani Carnal, erotic, sensual. ~**vaniyet**i/~**vet**i, lust, eroticism, sensuality: ~ **düşkünlüğü,** animalism. ~**vetengiz,** appetizing; exciting; aphrodisiac. ~**vetli**/~**vetperest,** sensual, lustful; voluptuous.

şehzade (*his.*) Prince; Sultan's son.

şekki Doubt, uncertainty. ~ **ve şüphe,** doubt and misgiving.

şek. = ŞEKİL.

şekaveti Brigandage.

şeker (*cul.*) Sugar; sweet; (*fig.*) darling. ~ **Bayramı,** (*rel.*) feast following Ramadan: ~ **hastalık/illeti,** (*med.*) diabetes: ~ **hastalıklı,** diabetic: ~ **hokkası,** (*dom.*) sugar-bowl: ~ **kuşları,** (*orn.*) honey-creepers: ~ **pancarı,** (*bot.*) sugar-beet: ~ **pekmezi,** (*cul.*) molasses: ~**i kestirmek,** (*chem.*) prevent recrystallization: ~**im!,** my darling.

şeker·ci Sugar-merchant; sweet-seller; confectioner. ~**ciboyası**nı, (*bot.*) virginian poke(weed). ~**ciboya-sığiller,** (*bot.*) pokeweeds, Phytolaccaceae. ~**cilik,** sugar-production; sweet-making/-selling. ~**fasul-yesi**ni, (*bot.*) type of bean. ~**kamışı**nı, (*bot.*) sugar-cane. ~**leme,** *vn.*; candied fruit; confectionery; sweets; (*fig.*) doze, nap. ~**lemeci,** confectioner. ~**lemek (-i),** sugar; preserve in sugar. ~**lenmek,** *vp.*; crystallize. ~**leşmek,** *vi.* (child) become pretty/pleasant. ~**li,** sugared; sweetened with sugar; (*med.*) diabetic. ~**lik,** sugar-bowl; suitable for sugar-/sweet-making. ~**pare,** (*bot.*) type of apricot; (*cul.*) a sweetmeat; lump of sugar; type of crackly PASTIRMA. ~**ren'lk**gi, whitish brown; (*fig.*) uncordial/cool (relationship). ~**si,** (*chem.*) saccharoid. ~**siz,** without sugar, unsweetened.

şek'illi Form; shape; figure, contour; figuration; plan; kind; manner; feature; (*math.*) diagram; (*lit.*) form. ~ **çizmek,** draw a diagram: ~ **değiştirmek,** deform, distort; disguise: ~ **vermek,** fashion, mould: ~**i** = ŞEKLİ: ~**inde,** -(i)form; in the shape of: ~**le girmek,** take form/shape: ~**le koymak/ sokmak,** put straight, adjust: ~**le riayeten,** for form's sake.

şekil·bilgisini (*ling.*) Morphology. ~**bilim,** (*bio.*) morphology. ~**ci,** (*phil.*) formalist. ~**cilik,** form, manner; (*phil.*) formalism. ~**değişimcilik,** (*phil.*) transformism. ~**değişimi,** transformation. ~**deş(lik),** homomor·phous/(-phism). ~**lendirmek (-i, -e),** give form/shape to; form, shape. ~**lenmek,** *vi.* take shape. ~**perest,** formalist. ~**siz,** amorphous; shapeless; without diagrams; (*fig.*) uncouth.

şekl- = ŞEKİL. ~**en,** in form/appearance. ~**i,** *a.* formal.

Şekspirvari (*lit.*) Shakespearian.

şekva Complaint.

şelale (*geo.*) Waterfall; cascade.

şele'kgi Load carried on the back.

şelf (*geol.*) Shelf-like rock. ~ **bölgesi,** (*geo.*) continental shelf.

şellak¹ (*chem.*) Shellac.

şema Outline; sketch; plan, diagram; scheme.

şemail Features; appearance.

şempanze (*zoo.*) Chimpanzee.

şems (*ast., obs.*) Sun. ~**e,** (*art.*) sun-burst/-disc; rosette. ~**i,** solar. ~**isiper,** (*mod.*) peak of cap. ~**iye,** parasol; umbrella; (*aer.*) canopy; (*bot.*) umbellifer: ~ **kuşu,** (*orn.*) umbrella bird. ~**iyeci(lik),** (work of) umbrella-maker/-seller. ~**iyeli,** carrying an umbrella; (*bot.*) umbelliferous. ~**iyelik,** umbrella stand; umbrella material.

şen Joyous, cheerful; inhabited; civilized.

şena·ati Foulness; wickedness. ~**yi,** shameful acts.

şendere (*carp.*) Thin board, veneer; stave (of cask); (*ich.*) surmullet, goatfish.

şenel·mek *vi.* (*col.*) Become inhabited/prosperous; (*bot.*) grow and spread. ~**tmek (-i),** populate.

şeni Disgraceful, vile, atrocious, immoral.

şenlen·dirilmek *vp.* ~**dirmek (-i),** *vc.* ~**me,** *vn.* ~**mek,** *vi.* become cheerful/gay/joyful; become inhabited/prosperous.

şenlik Gaiety, cheerfulness; public rejoicings; prosperity; (*art.*) festival. ~ **görmemiş,** ill-mannered, uncouth. ~**li,** prosperous; full of gaiety. ~**siz,** miserable; uninhabited; solitary, waste.

şerri *n.* Evil, wickedness. *a.* Evil. ~**rine lanet!,** a curse on his wickedness!

-şer/-şar *a. suf.* (*after vowels*) [83, 193] = -ER⁴ [YEDİŞER].

şeraiti *pl.* = ŞART. Conditions. ~**i haiz olanlar,** those who fulfil the conditions.

şer'an (*rel.*) In accordance with canon law.

şerare Spark.

şerbeti (*cul.*) Sweet drink; sherbet; drink for special occasions; infusion; (*med.*) aperient draught; (*ind.*) liquid (manure, etc.). ~ **almak,** take an aperient.

şerbet·çi(lik) (Work of) sherbet-maker/-seller. ~**çiotu**nu, (*bot.*) hop. ~**lemek (-i),** (*med.*) immunize (against snake-bite, etc.); (*agr.*) manure (with liquid). ~**lenmek,** *vp.* be immunized; be manured. ~**li,** (*cul.*) with sherbet; (*med.*) immune, immunized; (*fig.*) notorious, hardened. ~**lik,** suitable for sherbet. ~**siz,** without sherbet; (*med.*) not immune; (*agr.*) not manured.

şer'çci (*bio.*) Anus. ~**i,** anal.

şeref Honour; glory; credit; excellence; legitimate pride, exaltation; superiority, distinction. ~ **bulmak**, be honoured; (*fin.*) increase in value: ~ **divanı**, (*adm.*) court of honour: ~ **kazanmak** (**-den**), gain credit for stg.: ~ **meselesi**, question of honour: ~ **misafiri**, guest of honour: ~ **salonu**, reception hall: ~ **üyesi**, (*adm.*) honorary member: ~ **vermek** (**-e**), do credit to s.o.: ~ **yasası**, (*adm.*) code of ethics: ~ **yeri**, place/seat of honour: ~(**iniz**)**e!**, to your health!: ~**ine içmek**, drink to s.o.'s health: ~**ine rest çekmek**, stake one's honour.

şeref·e (*arch.*) Minaret balcony. ~**iye**, (*fin.*) capital gains tax, betterment levy. ~**lendirmek** (**-i**), (crown with) honour. ~**lenmek**, *vi.* acquire honour; be honoured; (*fin.*) increase in value. ~**li**, honoured, esteemed; creditable; favoured/ distinguished (place). ~**siz**(**lik**), (being) without honour. ~**yap**, ~ **olm.**, be honoured.

şergil Rebellious; malicious; naughty.

şerh (*lit.*) Explanation; commentary. ~ **etm.**, explain, comment: ~ **ve izah etm.**, annotate.

şerha Cut; split (on lips); wound; slice. ~ ~ **doğramak**, cut to pieces.

şeriat[1] (*rel.*) Muslim canonical obligations; religious law. ~**ın kestiği parmak acımaz**, just punishment is not resented. ~**çı**(**lık**), supporter of/(support for) the religious law.

şerif[1] (*soc.*) Noble; descendant of Muhammad.

şerif[2] (*leg.*) Sheriff.

şerik[i] (*fin.*) Partner; shareholder; companion.

şerir Scoundrel. ~**lik**, wickedness, evil.

şeri·t[di] (*tex.*) Ribbon; tape; (*ind.*) strip, band, lamina; belt; (*cin.*) film; (*zoo.*) tapeworm; (*mot.*) lane; (*arch.*) fascia. ~ **arşın/metre**, (*math.*) tapemeasure: ~ **çizgileri**, (*mot.*) lane markings: ~ **izge/tayfı**, (*phys.*) band spectrum: ~ **testere**, (*carp.*) band-saw: ~**ler**, (*zoo.*) tapeworms.

şerit·döken (*med.*) Teniafuge. ~**giller**, (*zoo.*) platyhelminths, tapeworms. ~**lemek** (**-i**), bind/ ornament with ribbon, etc. ~**li**, (*mot.*) . . . -lane (road); (*geol.*) varved.

şerr- = ŞER.

şeş (*gamb.*) Six (at backgammon). ~**i beş görmek**, squint; be mistaken/thoroughly confused: ~**i beş göstermek** (**-e**), 'knock stars out of s.o.' ~**beş**, (*gamb.*) six-five. ~ **cihar**, six-four. ~ **idü**, six-two. ~ **üse**, six-three. ~(**ü**)**yek**, six-one.

şe·t[ddi] (*Or. mus.*) Transposal of a scale. ~**aret**[i], merriment, gaiety. ~**im**[mi], abuse, invective.

şev *n.* Slope; glacis; bevel, bezel. *a.* Sloping. ~ **kayması**, slide.

şev·iot/~**yot** Cheviot (*live.*) sheep//(*tex.*) wool, tweed.

şevk[i] Desire; ardent longing; eagerness. ~**e gelmek**, become eager; grow merry: ~**ini kırmak**, chill.

şevket[i] Majesty, pomp. ~**li**, majestic (sultan).

şev·lenmek *vi.* Slope. ~**li**, sloping; bevelled.

şevval[i] (*ast.*) Tenth lunar month.

şey [77] Thing; object; (*col.*) what d'you call it; what's his name.

şeyh (*rel.*) Sheikh, head of an order; (*soc.*) sheikh, head of family/tribe. ~**in kerameti kendinden menkul**, I want further proof before I believe it.

şeyh·lik Office/rank of sheikh; sheikhdom. ~**ül-islam**, (*adm.*, *his.*) Sheikhulislam, minister for all religious matters: ~ **kapısı**, his ministry.

şeyl (*geol.*) Shale.

şeytan (*rel.*) Satan; devil; (*fig.*) crafty man; sharp child. ~ **azapta gerek!**, it serves you/him/her right!: (*jok.*) no peace for the wicked!: ~ **bezi**, (*tex.*) velveteen: ~ **boku** = ~ TERSİ: ~ **çekici**, very bright child: ~ **diyor ki**, I'm tempted (to do stg. foolish): ~ **dürtmek** (**-i**), be tempted to do stg. bad: ~ **feneri**, (*bot.*) chinese lantern: ~ **gibi**, very clever/cunning: ~ **kulağına kurşun!**, (*col.*) touch wood!: ~ **maymun**, (*zoo.*) saki: ~ **tüyü**, (talisman making one) very lovable: ~ **uçurtması**, toy-kite: ~ **külahı**(**nı**) **ters giydirmek**, be very cunning: ~**a uymak**, let o.s. be led astray; yield to temptation: ~**ı eşeğe ters bindirir/şişeye sokar**, as cunning as the devil: ~**ın art ayağı/kıç bacağı**, very cunning/ naughty child: ~**ın ayak/bacağını kırmak**, make an effort/bring o.s. to do stg.; overcome temptation: ~**ın işi yok!**, it was pure bad luck!: ~**ın yattığı yeri bilmek**, know the most unimaginable/ incredible things: ~**ları tepesine çıktı**, he lost his temper.

şeytan·arabası[nı] (*bot.*) Floating thistledown/ dandelion seeds; (*rly.*) linesman's trolley; (*col.*) bicycle. ~**başı**[nı], (*med.*) carbuncle. ~**ca**/~**i**, devilish, diabolical. ~**et**[i], act of devilry; malice; cunning. ~**kuşu**[nu], (*zoo.*) (?) noctule bat. ~**lık**, devilment; cunning. ~**masası**[nı], (*geol.*) dolmen-like rock. ~**minaresi**[ni], (*zoo.*) whelk('s shell). ~**otu**[nu], (*bot.*) scabious. ~**örümceği**[ni], (*zoo.*) gossamer. ~**saçı**[nı], (*bot.*) dodder. ~**şalgamı**[nı], (*bot.*) bryony. ~**tersi**[ni], (*bot.*) asafoetida. ~**tırnağı**[nı], (*bio.*) hang-nail; (*bot.*) devil's claw. ~**tükürüğü**[nü], (*ent.*) common frog-hopper, spittlebug.

şezlong Deck-chair, *chaise-longue*.

şık[1 1] *a.* Smart, fashionable; (*fig.*) fitting, apropos.

şık[kı 2] *n.* Alternative.

şıkır ~ ~, (*ech.*) clinking, jingling; dazzling: ~ ~ **oynamak**, dance with castanets; (*fig.*) be very pleased. ~**dama**, *vn.* ~**damak**, *vi.* rattle, jingle, clink. ~**datmak** (**-i**), *vt.* rattle, jingle: *vi.* (*col.*) give money. ~**tı**, jingling/clinking noise.

şık·laşmak *vi.* Be(come) smart. ~**lık**, smartness.

şıllık Gaudily dressed woman; (*fig.*) loose woman.

şımar·ık Spoilt (child); saucy, impertinent; stuck-up. ~**ıklık**, conceit; rudeness. ~**ma**, *vn.* ~**mak**, *vi.* be spoilt by indulgence; get above o.s.; lose one's self-control. ~**tılmak**, *vp.* ~**tmak** (**-i**), spoil (a child); cosset.

şıngıl (*bot.*) One of several small bunches forming a big one.

şıngır ~ ~, (*ech.*) crash (of breaking glass). ~**dama**, *vn.* ~**damak**, *vi.* crash. ~**tı**, sound of breaking glass.

şıp[1] (*ech.*) Plop; a sudden slight noise. ~ **diye**, suddenly: ~**ınişi**: ~ **sevdi**.

şıpıdık (*mod.*) Low-heeled shoe/slipper.

şıpıldamak *vi.* (Water) make a lapping sound; lap.

şıpınişi[ni] Stg. done very quickly and easily.

şıpır ~ ~, (*ech.*) falling in drops. ~**tılı**, splashing: ~ **hava**, rainy weather.

şıpka (*naut.*) Rope/wire net; torpedo-net.

şıp·padak Quickly, at once. ~**şak**, (*cin.*) snapshot. ~**sevdi**, (*sl.*) quick to fall in love, susceptible, impressionable. ~**sevdilik**, susceptibility. ~**şıp**, (*mod.*) slipper without any back.

şıra (*cul.*) Must, unfermented grape-juice. ~**cı**, grape-juice maker/seller. ~**lı**, juicy.

şırak (*ech.*) Sharp sudden sound. ~**kadak**, suddenly.

şırfıntı (*pej.*) Low/common woman; bitch.

şırıl ~ ~, (*ech.*) gently flowing (water). ~**damak**, *vi.* (water) flow gently. ~**tı**, sound of flowing water, splashing, gurgling.

şırınga (*med.*) Hypodermic syringe; injection; enema. ~ **yapmak**, inject.

şır·lağan Current; (*cul.*) oil of sesame. ~**lamak**, *vi.* flow gently.

Şia (*rel.*) Shiite sect of Muslims.

şiar Badge; sign; watchword; characteristic, trait.

şiddet[i] Hardness; strength; violence; severity; intensity. ~ **olayı**, act of violence: ~**le**, violently.

şiddet·lendirmek (-i) Make stronger/more violent; intensify; aggravate. ~**lenmek**, *vi.* become stronger; increase in violence. ~**li**, violent; vehement; drastic; (*med.*) acute, severe: ~ **acı**, agony: ~ **rüzgâr**, (*met.*) strong wind: ~ **sıcak**, boiling hot: ~ **soğuk**, bitterly cold: ~ **yağmur**, deluge.

şif (*bot.*) Cotton boll.

şifa (*med.*) Restoration to health; healing; cure. ~ **bulmak**, recover health, get well: ~ **olsun!**, may it (medicine, etc.) bring you health!: ~ **vermek**, restore health: ~**yı bulmak/kapmak**, (*iron.*) fall ill; turn out badly. ~**hane**/~**yurdu**, hospital, clinic.

şifah·en Orally, verbally. ~**i**, oral, verbal.

şiflemek (-i) (*ind.*) Gin cotton from the boll.

şifon (*tex.*) Chiffon. ~**iyer**, (*dom.*) chest of drawers.

şifre Cipher; code. ~ **açmak/çözmek**, decipher, decode: ~ **anahtarı**, cipher key: ~ **ile yazmak**, encipher, encode. ~**li**, in cipher/code: ~ **kilit**, combination lock.

Şii (*rel.*) Shiite. ~**lik**, Shiism.

şiir (*lit.*) Poetry; poem. ~**sel**, poetic.

Şikago (*geo.*) Chicago.

şikâr The chase; hunting; game (killed); prey, victim; rarity. ~ **bir şey mi?**, is it a rarity?: ~ **pazar**, cheap bargain.

şikâyet[i] Complaint. ~ **etm.**/~**te bulunmak**, complain: ~**i yok**, contented. ~**çi**, complainant. ~**name**, written complaint.

şike 'Put-up job'; (*sp.*) match with result faked for profit.

şikem (*bio.*) Belly; womb. ~**perver**, gluttonous.

şile (*bot.*) Sweet marjoram. ~**bezi**[ni], (*tex.*) type of cheesecloth (made in Şile).

şilem (*gamb.*) Slam (in bridge).

şile·p[bi] (*naut.*) Tramp steamer, cargo-boat. ~**çilik**, cargo-boat operation.

Şili (*geo.*) Chile. ~ **güherçilesi**, (*chem.*) Chile saltpetre.

şil·in (*fin.*) Shilling. ~**t**[di], (*sp.*) shield.

şilte Thin mattress/quilt; (*eng.*) blanket.

şim. = ŞİMAL; ŞİMDİ(Kİ ZAMAN).

şimal[i] *n.* (*geo.*) North. ~ **fecri**, (*ast.*) aurora borealis: ~ **yıldızı**, Pole Star. ~**en**, to/from the north. ~**i**, *a.* north(ern).

şimdi *adv.* [203] Now; currently. *conj.* Now, therefore, so. ~ **anlaşıldı**, now the matter is clear: ~ ~, very soon: ~ DEN: ~**den tezi yok**, with all speed, the sooner the better: ~**lerde**, nowadays: ~**ye değin/kadar**, so far, up till now, already: ~**ye kadar hoş**, so far so good.

şimdi·cik Just now; right away. ~**den**, already now: ~ **sonra**, from now on, henceforth. ~**ki**, *a.* present: ~ **durum/halde**, under present circumstances: ~ **hali eskisinden bir gömlek iyidir**, his present condition is hardly better than before: ~ **zaman**, (*ling.*) present tense: ~**ler**, (*soc.*) the younger generation, present-day youth. ~**lik**, for the present: ~ **bu kadar!**, that's all for now!: ~ **şu kadarını söyliyelim ki . . .**, for the present let us say this much about it, that . . . .

şimendifer Railway; train.

şimi Chemistry. ~**k**, chemical. ~**otaksi**, (*bio.*) chemotaxis. ~**oterapi(k)**, chemothera·py/(-peutic). ~**tropizm**, chemotropism.

şimşe·k[ği] (*met.*) Lightning flash; (*el.*) arc; (*fig.*) flash. ~ **ağacı**, (*bot.*) spiny broom: ~ **çakmak** = ~ LENMEK: ~ **çöreği**, (*cul.*) lightning buns: ~ **gibi**, like a flash: ~**leri üstüne çekmek**, be harshly criticised.

şimşek·lenmek *vi.* Flash, lighten. ~**li**, flashing: ~ **fener**, (*naut.*) occulting light(house). ~**taşı**[nı], (*geol.*) meteorite.

şimşir (*bot.*) ~ (**ağacı**), common box: ~ **tahtası**, boxwood. ~**giller**, Buxaceae, box family.

şinanay *int.* How lovely!; (*sl.*) damn all! *a.* Glaring, gaudy.

şini·k[ği] (*math.*) Peck (10 litres).

-şin(iz) *v. suf.* [103] = -(Mİ)ŞSİN(İZ).

şin·şile (*zoo.*) Chinchilla (fur). ~**yon**, (*mod.*) chignon.

şip·şak (*sl.*) Immediately. ~**şakçı**, street-photographer. ~**şirin**, very sweet/charming.

şiraze Order, regularity; (*pub.*) head-band (of bound book); (*sp.*) leg of wrestler's shorts; binding. ~**den çıkmak**, lose one's mental balance: ~**sinden çıkmak**, deteriorate beyond recovery.

şirden (*bio.*) Fourth/rennet stomach (of ruminants).

şirin Sweet, affable, charming. ~**lik**, sweetness; affability: ~ **muskası**, charm (worn by women) to attract a man.

şirk[i] (*rel.*) Polytheism.

şirket[i] (*fin.*) Partnership; joint ownership; (joint-stock) company. ~ **mukavele(name)/sözleşmesi**, articles of association/incorporation: ~ **sermayesi**, company capital: ~ **vapuru**, Bosphorus ferry steamer.

şirpençe (*med.*) Carbuncle; anthrax.

şirret[i] Malicious; quarrelsome. ~**leşmek**, *vi.* become malicious. ~**lik**, malice.

şirürji (*med.*) Surgery. ~**en**, surgeon.

şiryan (*bio.*) Artery. ~**i**, arterial.

şist[i] (*geol.*) Schist, shale. ∼**ozom(a)**, (*zoo.*) blood fluke.

şiş[1] *a.* Swollen. *n.* Swelling; tumour. ∼ **yapmak**, bulge, swell.

şiş[2] *n.* (*cul.*) Spit, skewer; (*mil.*) rapier; (*tex.*) knitting-needle. ∼KEBABI: ∼**te pişirmek**, cook on skewers.

şişe[1] *n.* (*carp.*) Planed/moulded lath.

şişe[2] *n.* Bottle; lamp-chimney; (*med.*) cupping-glass. *a.* Bottle(ful). ∼ **açacağı**, bottle-opener: ∼ **askısı**, bottle-rack: ∼ **boğazı**, bottle-neck: ∼ **çekmek**, (*med.*) cup: ∼ **kapağı**, capsule, crown-cork: ∼**ye koymak (-i)**, bottle stg.: ∼**yi dikmek**, drink straight from the bottle.

şişe·ci Bottle-maker/-seller. ∼**hane**, glass-works. ∼**lemek (-i)**, bottle.

şişe[l]**k**[ği] (*live.*) Year-old lamb, teg.

şişhane (*mil.*) Rifling; rifled gun.

şiş·ik Inflated. ∼**inmek**, be proud/overbearing. ∼**irge**[l]**ç**[ci], (*mot.*) pump. ∼**irilmek**, *vp.* ∼**irme**, *vn.*; careless work; (*lit.*) padding: ∼ **lastik**, (*mot.*) pneumatic tyre. ∼**irmek (-i)**, cause to swell; blow up, inflate; (*fig.*) exaggerate; (*sl.*) do stg. hastily/carelessly; stab; (*ed.*) 'cram' for an examination. ∼**irtmek (-i, -e)**, *vc.*

şiş·kebabı[nı] (*cul.*) Shish kebab, skewered lamb. ∼**köfte**, rissole (on skewer).

şiş·kin Swollen; puffed up. ∼**kinlik**, puffiness, swelling; inflation. ∼**ko**, (*jok.*) very fat (person). ∼**koluk**, fatness. ∼**lik**[1], *n.* (*med.*) oedema.

şiş·lemek (-i) (*cul.*) Spit, skewer; stab. ∼**lik**[2], *n.* stewing meat.

şişman Fat; obese. ∼**lamak**, *vi.* grow fat. ∼**latmak (-i)**, *vc.* ∼**lık**, fatness, obesity.

şiş·me Swelling; (*aer.*) development; (*bio.*) turgescence. ∼**mece**, (*med.*) emphysema. ∼**mek**, *vi.* swell; become inflated; expand; grow fat; become swollen; be distended; (clothes) bag; (*fig.*, *sp.*) be too tired to continue; (*sl.*) be ashamed: **şişen**, expanding: **şişen engerek**, (*zoo.*) puff adder: **şişti**, (*ed.*, *sl.*) he got a bad mark.

şiv = ŞEV.

şive (*ling.*) Accent; pronunciation; idiom; style. ∼**kâr**/∼**li**, graceful, elegant, stylish. ∼**siz**, with a bad accent/pronunciation; unidiomatic; without style.

şivester (*med.*) Nursing-sister.

şizofren(i) (*psy.*) Schizophre·nic/(-nia).

şof. = ŞOFÖR.

şof·aj (*dom.*) Heating. ∼**ben**, geyser, water-heater.

şoför (*mot.*) Chauffeur, driver. ∼ **okulu**, driving school: ∼ **mahal/yeri**, driver's cab. ∼**lük**, driving: ∼ **testi**, driving test.

şok[u] Shock. ∼ **dalgası**, (*aer.*) shock wave: ∼ **tedavisi**, (*psy.*) electro-shock treatment. ∼**e**, shocked: ∼ **etm.**, shock.

şol (*obs.*) [71] = ŞU.

şom *a.* Inauspicious, sinister. *n.* Evil omen. ∼ **ağızlı**, who always predicts misfortune.

şor·lamak *vi.* Flow with a splash. ∼**olop**, gulping greedily; (*sl.*) lying.

şort[u] (*mod.*) Shorts.

şos·e (*eng.*) Macadamized road, carriage-way.

∼**et**, (*mod.*) socks. ∼**on**, (*mod.*) galoshes, overshoes.

şov (*th.*) Show, spectacle.

şoven·(ce) (*pol.*) Chauvinist(ically). ∼**lik**, chauvinism.

şöhret[i] Fame; reputation, character; (*lit.*) pseudonym. ∼ **hastası**, one who seeks notoriety: ∼**i dünyayı tutmak**, become world-famous. ∼**li**, famous; notorious.

şölen Feast (in s.o.'s honour); (*rel.*) feast; (*art.*) exhibition; (*soc.*) gathering.

şö·mine (*arch.*) Fireplace. ∼**miz(li)**, (*pub.*) (with) dust-jacket/-wrapper. ∼**miziye**, (*mod.*) shirt-blouse. ∼ **vale**, (*art.*) easel. ∼**valye**, (*his.*) chevalier, knight: ∼ **yüzüğü**, signet ring. ∼**valyelik**, chivalry.

şöyle [72] *a.* Such; this/that kind of; of this/that sort. *adv.* Thus; in this/that way/manner; so; just. ∼ **bir**, just (a little): ∼ **bir bakmak**, just glance at; look at contemptuously: ∼ **böyle**, so so; after a fashion; roughly speaking; (*med.*) not too well: ∼ **böyledir**, he's all right (but . . .): ∼ **dursun**, *conj.* [218], let alone . . ., never mind about . . . [**oturmak** ∼ **dursun durmak imkânsızdı**, it was impossible to stand let alone sit]: ∼ **ki**, in such a way that; as follows; that is to say.

şöyle·ce *adv.* [195] Thus; in this way. ∼**lik**, this way/manner: ∼**le**, in this way. ∼**mesine**, in this way, just as I show you. ∼**si**, *pron.* [72] that sort of person. ∼**sine**, *adv.* to such a great extent.

Şrt./Şti. = ŞİRKET(İ).

-ştir-/-ştır-/-ştur-/-ştür- *v. suf. after a vowel* [148] = -İŞTİR- [UYUŞTURMAK].

şu[nu] [71] *a.* This, that, the following. *pron.* This one (*between* BU, this here *and* O, that over there). ∼ **bu**, this and/or that; any one of several: ∼ **demek ki**, that is to say: ∼**dur budur diyecek yok**, there's nothing to be said against it: ∼ **günlerde**, just recently: ∼ **halde**, in that case, if that is so: ∼ **kadar**, so much, so many; so; this much: ∼ **kadar ki**, to such an extent that: ∼ **kadar var ki**, moreover; it remains to be said: ∼ **sırada**, at present: ∼**na bak!**, (*pej.*) just look at him!: ∼**na buna**, to this person and that, to all and sundry: ∼**ndan bundan konuşmak**, talk about this and that: ∼**nlar**, these: ∼**nu bunu bilmemek**, not listen to excuses/objections: ∼**nun bunun** ∼**su busu ile alakadar olmıyan**, not interested in other people's private affairs: ∼**nun şurası**, (*col.*) this little place here: ∼**su busu (-in)**, s.o.'s private affairs.

şua[1] (*phys.*) Ray of light, beam.

şubat[1] February.

şube (*adm.*) Branch, department, section; subsidiary, affiliate; (*bio.*) phylum. ∼ **hattı**, (*el.*) feeder.

şuh Lively, full of fun, coquettish, pert.

şule Flame. ∼**li**, blazing; brilliant. ∼**lenmek**, blaze.

şun·a *dative* = ŞU. ∼**ca**, so much. ∼**cağız**, this little one. ∼**da**, *locative*‖ ∼**dan**, *ablative*‖ ∼**lar**, *pl.*‖ ∼**u**, *accusative* = ŞU.

şûra (*adm.*) Council. ∼**yı Devlet**, (*obs.*) Council of State.

şura *n.* [199] This/that place (close by) (*between*

BURA, this place here *and* ORA, that place there).
~**da**, there: ~**da burada**, here and there: ~**dan**, from there, thence: ~**dan buradan**, from here and there; of this and that: ~**larda**, in those parts: ~**ları**, those places; that region: ~**m**, that part of me: ~**ya**, to there, thither.

şura·cık(ta) Just there; close by. ~**lı**, belonging to/inhabitant of that place: ~ **buralı**, (people) from here and there. ~**sı**ⁿⁱ, that place; that fact: ~**nı unutmıyalım**, let us not forget that point.

şur·da// ~**dan** (*col.*) = ŞURA·DA// ~DAN.

şuru·l pᵇᵘ (*cul.*) Syrup; sweet medicine.

şutᵘ (*sp.*) Shoot, kick. ~ **çekmek**, shoot (the ball).

şuur Comprehension; intelligence; conscience, mind; consciousness. ~**u bozuk**, out of his senses: ~**u gitti**, he is out of his mind.

şuur·altı Subconscious. ~**lu**, intelligent; conscious (will, etc.); being conscious of; sensible. ~**suz**, unconscious (deed, etc.); callous; unreasonable. ~**suzluk**, unconsciousness.

şüheda *pl.* = ŞEHİT. Martyrs.

şükr- = ŞÜKÜR. ~**an**, thankfulness, gratitude. ~**ˡetmek**ᵉᵈᵉʳ (**-e**), feel thankful; be grateful for.

şükˡürʳü Thanks, gratitude. ~ **ki**, thanks to God. ~ **ünü bilmek** (**-in**), be grateful for stg.

şümulü An including/comprehending; comprehensiveness. ~**ü olm.**, include, cover, embrace. ~**lendirmek** (**-i**), amplify, extend, generalize. ~**lü**, comprehensive, inclusive.

şüphe Doubt; suspicion; ambiguity, uncertainty; distrust. ~ **altında olm.**, be under a cloud: ~ **bırakmak**, leave a doubt behind, instil a suspicion: ~ **etm.** (**-den**), suspect; challenge: ~ **götürmek**, cause doubt: ~ **götürmez**, beyond doubt: ~ **kurdu**, a nagging suspicion: ~**ye duşmek**, begin to suspect; have a suspicion: ~**ye düşürmek** (**-i**), throw suspicion on, discredit.

şüphe·ci Suspicious person; sceptic. ~**cilik**, (*phil.*) scepticism. ~**lenmek** (**-den**), have a suspicion/doubt about. ~**li**, doubtful; dubious; ambiguous; suspicious; suspecting: ~ **alacak**, (*fin.*) bad debt. ~**siz**, *a.* doubtless; sure; giving no reason for suspicion: *adv.* assuredly, of course, certainly.

şüreka *pl.* = ŞERİK. Partners, etc.

şüyuᵘ Publicity; divulgation. ~ **bulmak**, be rumoured: ~**u vukuundan beterdir** (**-in**), the news of stg. is often worse than the event itself.

T

T, t [te] The twenty-fourth Tk. letter, T. ~ **bağlan-tısı**, (*eng.*) T-joint: ~ **cetveli**, (*math.*) T-square: ~ **kavşağı**, (*mot.*) T-junction.

T, t. = (*bio.*) TAKIM; TEK; (*ling.*) TEKİL; TEKNİK; (*el.*) TESLA; (*ch.s.*) TRİTİUM; TÜRK[ÇE]; TÜRKİYE.

-t *n. suf.* [224] = -İT [AYIRT].

-t- *v. suf.* [145] *Forming the causative verb* [ANLAT-MAK; OTURTMAK].

ta¹ *conj.* [206] And; = DE.

ta² *adv.* Even; even as far as; even until. ~ ... 'de, way back in/at: ~ **kendisi**, his very self: ~ **kendisidir (-in)**, it is the very ... .: ~ **ki**, so that, in order that; so much so that: ~ **sabaha dek/kadar**, right until morning: ~ **sabahtan beri**, ever since morning: ~ **uzağa**, right into the distance, for miles and miles.

Ta. = (*ch.s.*) TANTAL.

-ta *n. suf.* [28] = -DE [BAŞTA].

taaccü¹pᵇᵘ Wonder, astonishment.

taaddü¹tᵈᵘ A multiplying, increase.

taaffün Putrefaction; stink. ~ **etm.**, stink.

taahhü¹tᵈᵘ Undertaking/engagement (to do stg.); registration (of letters, etc.). ~ **etm.**, undertake, engage: ~**e girmek**, contract. ~**lü**, registered (letter); (*sl.*) strong, healthy. ~**name**, written undertaking; contract.

taallukᵘ Connection; relation; attachment. ~ **etm.** (**-e**), have connections with, concern. ~**at**¹, (*soc.*) relations, family connections.

taam Food; meal. ~ **etm.**, have a meal.

taam·müden Intentionally; with malice afore-thought. ~**mü¹tᵈᵘ**, premeditation.

taammüm A becoming general. ~ **etm.**, become general; spread.

taannü¹tᵈᵘ Obstinacy; persistence.

taarruz Attack, assault; molestation. ~ **etm. (-e)**, attack, assault; molest/violate (a woman).

taassu¹pᵇᵘ (*rel.*) Bigotry; (*pol.*) fanaticism; zeal.

taayyün A being evident/clear. ~ **etm.**, become clear; be defined.

TAB = TÜRK AMELE BİRLİĞİ.

Tab. Kay. = TABİİ KAYNAKLAR.

taba Tobacco-coloured.

tabaat¹ Printing.

tababet¹ Medical profession.

taba¹kᵍ¹ ¹ (*dom.*) Plate; dish; (*cul.*) course. ~ **dolabı**, dresser, sideboard: ~ **gibi**, quite flat: ~ **salyangozu**, (*zoo.*) ramshorn.

taba¹kᵍ¹ ² Tanner, currier. ~ **sevdiği deriyi taştan taşa çalar**, one must be cruel to be kind.

tabaka¹ Tobacco/cigarette case.

tabaka² Sheet (of paper); fold; (*arch.*) course; (*geol.*) bed, layer, stratum; (*soc.*) class, category. ~ **halinde**, in sheets/layers. ~ **laşma**, (*eng.*) bedding.

tabak·çı¹kᵍ¹ (*dom.*) Small plate. ~**lık**¹, *n.* (*dom.*) plate-rack/shelf; dresser.

tabak·hane Tannery. ~**lamak (-i)**, tan, curry. ~**lanmak**, *vp.* ~**lık**², *n.* tanning.

taban (*bio.*) Sole (*also* of sh>e); heel; bottom (end); (*arch.*) floor; base, pedestal; (*geo.*) bed (of river); plateau; (*geol.*) subsoil; (*min.*) fine steel; (*math.*) base; (*fin.*) minimum; (*adm.*) lowest grade; (*eng.*) girder, wall-plate; (*naut.*) anchor fluke; (*cin.*) film-backing; (*fig.*) firmness, pluck. ~ **açısı**, (*math.*) base angle: ~ **astarı**, inner sole (of shoe): ~ **basma**, (*sp.*) a wrestling hold: ~ **boya**, (*ind.*) under-coat: ~ **çizgi**, baseline: ~ **döşeği**, (*arch.*) footings: ~ **fiyat**, (*fin.*) official minimum price: ~ **inciri**, (*bot.*) small sweet figs ripening last: ~ **karşısı**, (*geo.*) antipodes: ~ **kılıç**, (*mil.*) sword of Damascus steel: ~ **patlatmak/tepmek**, go a long journey on foot: ~**suyu**: ~ **sürtmek**, walk incessantly: ~ ~**a zıt**, diametrically opposed: ~**a kuvvet**, by dint of hard walking: ~**ları kaldırmak**, take to one's heels: ~**ları patlamak/sızlamak**, feet become blistered/ache from walking: ~**ları yağlamak**, (*jok.*) prepare for a long journey on foot.

tab'an Naturally.

tabanca (*mil.*) Pistol; (*ind.*) paint-gun; (*sl.*) bottle of raki, etc. ~ **boyası**, paint sprayed on with a gun.

taban-lı Soled; -bottomed; (*fig.*) brave. ~**lık**, (*rly.*) sleeper; sole-plate. ~ **sız**, soleless; (*fig.*) cowardly. ~**sızlık**, cowardliness. ~**suyu**, (*geol.*) phreatic/ground water: ~ **düzeyi**, water-table: ~ **yüzeyi**, hydrostatic level. ~**vayla**, (*jok.*) on foot.

tabasbus *n.* Cringing, fawning. ~ **etm. (-e)**, fawn, flatter.

tabela Shop-sign; (doctor's) plate; list of day's food (in institutions); (*med.*) treatment card (on patient's bed). ~**cı**, sign-painter.

tab-¹etmekᵉᵈᵉʳ **(-i)** (*pub.*) Print. ~**ı**, (*pub.*) printing, stamping; an edition; (*fig.*) disposition. ~**i**¹ ¹, *n.* (*pub.*) printer; editor; publisher.

tabiⁱ ² *a.* Following, consequent; dependent; subsidiary; subject; conforming; submissive. *n.* (*pol.*) Subject; (*geo.*) tributary. ~ **olm. (-e)**, follow; be dependent on; be subject to: ~ **tutmak**, subject.

tabiat¹ Nature; character, natural quality, disposi-tion; (*bio.*) regularity (of bowels); (*fig.*) taste, refinement. ~ **sahibi**, man of good taste: ~**ı saniye**, (*obs.*) second-nature.

tabiat·ıyla Naturally; by itself. ~**lı**, having ... character; having good taste. ~**sız**, devoid of good taste; unpleasant. ~**sızlık**, lack of good taste; un-pleasantness. ~**üstü**ⁿᵘ, supernatural.

tabib- = TABİP.

tabii *a.* Natural; normal. *adv.* Naturally; of course. ~ **afetler**, natural disasters: ~ **ilimler**, (*ed.*) natural

sciences: ∼ **olarak**, as a matter of course: ∼ **senatör**, (*adm.*) life senator.
tabii·lik Naturalness. ∼ **yat**¹, (*ed.*) natural sciences. ∼ **ye(ci)**, (*ed.*) (teacher of) natural history.
tabi·iyetⁱ/∼ **lik** Dependence; (*pol.*) nationality; ∼ **iyetsiz**, (*pol.*) *heimatlos*.
tabiⁱ**p**ᵇⁱ (*med.*) Doctor, physician.
tabir (*ling.*) Word, phrase, expression, idiom; (*psy.*) interpretation of dreams, oneiromancy. ∼ **etm.**, express in words; call, name; interpret (dream): ∼ **olunmak**, be called, have the name of. ∼ **ci**, interpreter of dreams. ∼ **name**, book on dream interpretation.
tabla Circular tray; ash-tray; flat surface; disc. ∼ **kâr**, itinerant vendor of foods (carried on a tray); (*his.*) servant bringing food-trays. ∼ **lı**, with a tray; flat-topped.
tabl·dotᵘ (*cul.*) Table-d'hôte. ∼ **et**ⁱ, (*med.*) tablet; (*archaeol.*) tablet. ∼ **o**, (*art.*) picture; scene, view; (*math.*) table; (*fin.*) schedule; (*th.*) scene, setting; (*aer.*) control panel, console; (*mot.*) panel, dashboard.
tabu (*soc.*) Taboo.
tabur (*mil.*) Battalion; (*soc.*) large group. ∼ **cu**, (*mil.*) soldier discharged from hospital: ∼ **etm.**, discharge (as fit for service): ∼ **olm.**, be discharged.
tabure (*dom.*) Stool; footstool.
tabutᵘ Coffin; large egg-box. ∼ **çivisi**, (*sl.*) cigarette: ∼ **sehpası**/∼ **luk**, bier; coffin-stand in mosque courtyard.
tabya (*mil.*) Bastion; redoubt; fort.
tac- = TAÇ.
tacil Acceleration; making haste. ∼ **etm.**, hasten; accelerate.
tacir Merchant.
taciz A disturbing. ∼ **etm.**, disturb, annoy; accost. ∼ **lik**, annoyance: ∼ **getirmek**, complain: ∼ **vermek**, annoy, harass.
taⁱ**ç**ᶜ¹ Crown; diadem; (*ast.*) corona; (*bot.*) corolla; (*arch.*) capital; (*orn.*) crest; (*pol.*) kingdom. ∼ **beyit**, (*lit.*) eulogy mentioning the poet's name: ∼ **giydirmek**, crown s.o.: ∼ **giymek** = ∼ LANMAK: ∼ **şeklinde**, (*med.*) coronary.
taç·çeker (*ast.*) Coronagraph. ∼ **damar**, (*bio.*) coronary artery. ∼ **dar**, (*pol.*) sovereign. ∼ **lanmak**, *vp.* be crowned; become king. ∼ **lı**, crowned; (*bio.*) coronate: ∼ **bağırtlak**, (*orn.*) coroneted sandgrouse: ∼ **pas**, (*myc.*) oat/crown rust: ∼ **yılan**, (*zoo.*) smooth snake. ∼ **sız**, (*bot.*) apetalous. ∼ **yaprak(lı)**, (*bot.*) petal(ous).
tad- = TAT¹.
tadaⁱ**t**ᵈ¹ A counting. ∼ **etm.**, count, enumerate.
tadım Faculty of taste. ∼ **cisimciği**, (*bio.*) tastebud. ∼ **lık**, just a taste (of stg.).
tadil(at¹) Adjustment; modification. ∼ **etm.**, adjust; modify; equate: ∼ **teklifi**, (*adm.*) amendment.
tafdil (*obs.*) Preference. ∼ **etm.**, prefer.
taflan (*bot.*) Common/cherry laurel.
tafra Conceit, pride. ∼ **satmak**, give o.s. airs. ∼ **cı**, conceited.
tafsil Detailed explanation. ∼ **at**¹, *pl.* details: ∼ **vermek**, explain in detail.

tafta (*tex.*) Taffeta. ∼ **angle**, (*med.*) sticking-plaster.
tagaddi Being fed; nutrition. ∼ **etm.**, be fed.
tagallüⁱ**p**ᵇᵘ (*pol.*) Usurpation, tyranny. ∼ **etm.**, usurp; subjugate.
taganni Singing. ∼ **etm.**, sing.
tagayyür Change; deterioration. ∼ **etm.**, change; deteriorate.
tağdiye Feeding; (*el.*) input. ∼ **etm.**, (*eng.*) feed.
tağşiş (*chem.*) Adulteration. ∼ **etm.**, adulterate, 'doctor'.
tahaccür (*geol.*) Petrifaction. ∼ **etm.**, become petrified.
tahaffuz Guarding o.s. ∼ **hane**, (*med.*) quarantine station.
tahakkukᵘ Proving to be true; realizing. ∼ **etm.**, prove true; be realized: ∼ **memuru**, assessor.
tahakküm Domination; tyranny. ∼ **etm.**, dominate, oppress.
tahammuz (*chem.*) Oxidization.
tahammül Endurance, patience, forbearance. ∼ **etm.**, endure; support; (*med.*) tolerate. ∼ **fersa**, intolerable.
tahammür (*chem.*) Fermentation. ∼ **etm.**, ferment.
taharetⁱ Cleanliness; (*rel.*) purification. ∼ **lenmek**, *vi.* cleanse/purify o.s.
taharri Investigation, (re)search. ∼ **etm.** (-i), seek: ∼ **memuru**, detective.
tahassür Regret; longing.
tahassüs Feeling; sensation.
tahaşşüⁱ**t**ᵈᵘ Collecting together.
tahattür Remembering. ∼ **etm.**, call to mind.
tahavvül Turning; hanging. ∼ **etm.**, turn; change.
tahayyül Imagination, fancy. ∼ **etm.**, imagine, fancy.
tahdi·dat¹ *pl.* Limitations. ∼ **ı**ᵗᵈⁱ, limitation; definition: ∼ **etm.**, limit; define; confine.
tah·ıl (*agr.*) Cereals, grain. ∼ **in**, (*cul.*) ground sesame seed. ∼ **inhelvası**ⁿ¹, (*cul.*) sweetmeat of sesame seed and sugar/molasses. ∼ **ini**, yellowish-grey colour.
tahkikⁱ Verification; investigation. ∼ **etm.**, verify; investigate. ∼ **at**¹, investigations, inquiries; research: ∼ **hakimi**, (*leg.*) investigating magistrate.
tahkim (*mil.*) Fortifying; (*leg.*) arbitration. ∼ **etm.**, fortify, strengthen. ∼ **at**¹, *pl.* fortifications: ∼ **name**, arbitration agreement.
tahkir Treating with contempt. ∼ **etm.**, abuse, insult; despise.
tahkiye (*lit.*) Narration, story-telling.
tahlif (*leg.*) Administering an oath.
tahlil (*chem.*) Analysis. ∼ **etm.**, analyse; (*ling.*) construe. ∼ **i**, analytical.
tahlisiye Life-saving.
tahliye Emptying; discharge (of cargo); setting free. ∼ **boruları**, (*naut.*) bilge-pipes: ∼ **etm.**, empty; discharge; set free.
tahmil Loading. ∼ **etm.**, load; impose a burden.
tahmin Estimate; conjecture, guess. ∼ **etm.**, estimate, reckon, calculate. ∼ **en**, *circa*; approximately. ∼ **i**, approximate; estimated.
tahmis¹ (*lit.*) Making verses up to five lines.
tahmis² (*cul.*) Coffee roasting. ∼ **çi**, coffee roaster/grinder.

tahnit[i] Embalming (the dead); stuffing (dead animals). ~çi, embalmer; taxidermist.

tahra (*agr.*) Pruning-hook/-knife.

Tahran *pr.n.* (*geo.*) Teheran.

tahrib- = TAHRİP. ~at[1], *pl.* destruction, depredation: ~sız muayene yöntemleri, (*ind.*) non-destructive testing methods.

tahrif Distortion; falsification. ~ etm., distort; falsify, 'doctor'. ~at[1], *pl.* alterations.

tahrik[i] A moving; (*pol.*) incitement, instigation; provocation. ~ etm., (*pol.*) incite, provoke; impel; (*eng.*) actuate, propel, drive; (*aer.*) disturb: ~ grubu, power unit. ~ât[1], *pl.* movements; subversive acts. ~çi, (*pol.*) agitator.

tahril Line. ~li, ~ göz, (*bio.*) iris with bands of colour.

tahri[1]**p**[bi] Destruction; devastation. ~ etm., destroy, demolish; devastate. ~kâr, destructive.

tahrir (*lit.*) A writing, composition; essay. ~ etm., write down; (*adm.*) draw up (documents). ~at[1], *pl.* official document(s): ~ kâtibi, (*adm.*) general secretary. ~en, in writing. ~i, written.

tahsil Production; (*fin.*) collection; (*ed.*) study, education. ~ etm., produce; (*fin.*) collect; (*ed.*) study: ~ görmek (-de), study (at): ~ görmüş, educated, cultivated. ~at[1], (*fin.*) money collected; taxes, etc. ~dar(lık), (*fin.*) (work of) tax-collector.

tahsis (*fin.*) Assignment; allocation. ~ etm. (-e), assign/allot/allocate (to); destine/earmark (for). ~at[1], appropriations; allowance: ~ı mesture, secret funds/payments.

tahşidat[1] (*mil.*) Concentration of troops.

tahşiye (*lit.*) Annotation; marginal note.

taht[1] (*pol.*) Throne. ~ tepeliği, canopy: ~a çıkmak, accede: ~a geçmek, succeed: ~a oturmak, ascend the throne: ~a oturtmak, enthrone: ~tan indirmek, dethrone, depose.

tahta *n.* (*carp.*) Piece of wood; board, plank; sheet (of metal); (*agr.*) garden-bed. *a.* Wooden. ~ bacak, (*med.*) wooden leg: ~ başı, top end of a board (or list); (*fig.*) chief man: ~ başına!, (*ed.*) to the blackboard!: ~ bezi, scrubbing cloth: ~ blok, (*art.*) wood block: ~ güvercini = ~LI: ~ işleri, woodwork; cabinet-making: ~ kaplı, boarded, planked over: ~ kiremit, (*arch.*) shingle: ~ perde, fence; partition; boarding: ~ top oyunu, (*sp.*) bowls: ~lar, (*mus.*) woodwinds: ~sı eksik, 'a screw loose': ~ya çamaşıra gitmek, go as a charwoman: ~ya kaldırmak, (*ed.*) call a pupil to the blackboard.

tahta·biti[ni]/~**kurusu**[nu] (*ent.*) Bed-bug. ~boş, (*arch.*) covered terrace (on roof for drying clothes). ~koz, (*sl.*) police. ~kurdu[nu], (*zoo.*) woodworm. ~kuruları, (*ent.*) bugs. ~lı, wooden; planked, boarded; (*orn.*) wood-pigeon: ~ köy, (*sl.*) cemetery: ~ köye gitmek, (*sl.*) die. ~pamuk, (*tex.*) upholstery material. ~yiyen, (*ent.*) termite.

taht·elbahir (*naut.*) Submarine. ~erevalli, (*child.*) see-saw. ~eşşuur, (*psy.*) subconscious. ~ırevan, litter; palanquin.

tahvil Transforming, converting; (*math.*) conversion; (*fin.*) changing; draft, security, debenture. ~ etm., convert; transform; change; (*leg.*) commute (sentence). ~at[1], (*fin.*) securities; debentures.

taife Gang of men; crew; = TAYFA.

tak[1 1] (*ech.*) Tack!, tock!

tak[1 2] *n.* (*arch.*) Arch; vault. ~IZAFER.

taka (*naut.*) Small sailing-boat. ~cı(lık), (work of) sailing-boat operator.

ta·kaddüm Precedence; priority. ~kanak = ~KINTI.

takarrü[1]**p**[bü] Approach; proximity.

takarrür A being established/decided.

takas (*fin.*) Setting off claims, clearing; (foreign) exchange, barter; compensation. ~ etm./olm., balance off (claims, debts, etc.): ~ odası, clearing-house: ~ tukas olm., (accounts, etc.) be all square. ~lamak (-i), compensate.

takat[1] Strength; power. ~ amplifikatörü, (*el.*) power amplifier: ~ getirmek (-e), have the strength to: ~ı kalmamak, have no strength to. ~lı, powerful, strong; (*eng.*) power-operated. ~sız, powerless, exhausted. ~sızlık, weakness, exhaustion.

takatuka (*ech.*) Noise; tumult; (*pub.*) printer's mallet; (*obs.*) ashtray.

ta·kayyü[1]**t**[dü] Care, attention. ~kaza, taunt.

takbih Disapproval; blame. ~ etm., disapprove; blame.

takdim Presentation, introduction; offer; giving precedence. ~ etm., present, introduce; offer; give precedence: ~ ve tehir, (*ling.*) transposition. ~ci(lik), (work of) presenter, master of ceremonies.

takdir (*rel.*) Predestination, fate; (*fin.*) appreciation, appraisal; (*eng.*) rating; understanding; supposition, case. ~ böyle imiş, it was so fated: ~ etm., (*rel.*) predestine, prearrange; (*fin.*) cost, appreciate (values), appraise; suppose: ~ tedbiri bozar, 'man proposes, God disposes': ~ ve tahmin etm., assess: ~ yetkisi, (*adm.*) discretionary power: ~de (o), in (that) case: ~e layik, admirable: ~ini kazanmak (-in), win the admiration of.

takdir·amiz Appreciative. ~en, virtually; in consideration of; appreciating the fact that. ~kâr, appreciative; admirer. ~name, letter of appreciation.

takdis Sanctification; hallowing; consecration; dedication. ~ etm., sanctify, consecrate; revere; celebrate the memory of

TAKE = TÜRK-ALMAN KÜLTÜR ENSTİTÜSÜ.

takeometre (*phys.*) Tachometer, tachymeter.

takı Gift of jewellery (to the bride); (*ling.*) suffix, case-ending. ~ sanatı, jewellery.

takıl·gan *a.* Teasing. ~ı, affixed, attached. ~ır, detachable. ~ış, banter, raillery. ~mak (-e), *vp.* = TAKMAK; be affixed; be stuck; be attracted to; enjoy o.s.; attach o.s. to: (-e), *vi.* deride, tease, ridicule; worry.

takım A set/lot/number (of things); (dinner, etc.) service; (*mod.*) suit (clothes); (*gamb.*) suit (cards); (*cul.*) offal, giblets; (*dom.*) suite (furniture); (*ling.*) compound (word); (*mil.*) platoon, squad; (*cin.*) crew; (*sp.*) team; (*ind.*) gang, shift; (*soc.*) class; (*bio.*) order; kind, type; system; cigarette-holder. ~ açmak, start running: ~ çeliği, (*min.*) tool steel: ~ değiştirme, (*sp.*) transfer: ~ elbise, (*mod.*) suit of

clothes: ~ ERKİ: ~ sandığı, (*carp.*) tool-box: ~ ~, in sets/lots/classes: ~ taklavat, in full detail; bag and baggage; the whole lot: ~ ı yatırmak, (*sl.*) let down one's friends.
takım·ada (*geo.*) Archipelago. ~erkiⁿⁱ, (*soc.*) oligarchy. ~ yıldız, (*ast.*) constellation.
takın·a¹k^{ğı} (*psy.*) Obsession. ~aklı, obsessed. ~mak (-i), put on, wear; assume/put on/affect (attitude). ~tı, connection (with s.o.), affair (with a woman); (*ed.*) second chance for an examination; (*fin.*) small debt; (*mod.*) jewellery. ~tılı, having a connection, etc.
takır ~ ~, (*ech.*) clippety clop: ~ tukur, (*ech.*) alternate tapping and knocking. ~damak, *vi.* make a tapping/knocking noise. ~datmak (-i), *vt.* make a tapping/knocking noise. ~dayan kuyrukkakan, (*orn.*) stonechat. ~ tı, tapping, knocking.
takış·mak (-i, -le) Tease each other; quarrel with each other. ~tırmak, *vi.* wear (much) jewellery; dress up.
takızafer (*arch.*) Triumphal arch.
takib- = TAKİP. ~at¹, (*leg.*) proceedings, prosecution.
takim (*med.*) Sterilization. ~ etm., sterilize.
takimetre (*mot.*) Tachymeter; speedometer.
taki¹p^{bi} Pursuit; follow-up; persecution; (*leg.*) prosecution. ~ etm., follow (up), pursue, chase; prosecute: ~ gemisi, (*naut.*) pursuit vessel. ~sizlik, (*leg.*) decision not to prosecute.
takke (*mod.*) Skull-cap; night-cap; (*arch.*) cupola. ~ düştü kel göründü, he was shown up: ~sini gök/ havaya atmak, throw one's cap in the air for joy.
takla/ ~ ¹k^{ğı} (*sp.*) Somersault. ~ atmak/kılmak, turn a somersault; (*fig.*) be very pleased; toady: ~ attırmak, (*fig.*) twist s.o. round one's little finger.
takla·baz Acrobat, tumbler. ~böceğiⁿⁱ, (*ent.*) lined click-beetle. ~böcekleri, (*ent.*) click-beetles. ~vat = TAKIM.
taklid- = TAKLİT. ~i, imitative: ~ ses, (*ling.*) onomatopoeia.
takli¹p^{bi} Inversion, reversal; overthrow.
takli¹t^{di} *n.* Copying; counterfeiting; imitation. *a.* Counterfeit, sham, artificial. ~ etm., follow blindly, imitate; feign, sham: ~ini yapmak (-in), mimic s.o. ~çi(lik), (*art.*, *etc.*) forger(y); (*th.*) mimic(ry).
tak·ma *vn.* Act of attaching, etc.: *a.* stuck on; attached; (*mod.*) artificial/false; (*ind.*) in kit form; prefabricated: ~ ad, (*leg.*) alias; (*lit.*) pseudonym, pen-name: ~ diş, denture: ~ meme, (*mod.*) falsie: ~ parça, (*eng.*) attachment: ~ saç, wig, postiche: ~ süs, (*art.*) appliqué. ~mak (-i, -e), affix, attach; put on; give (a name, etc.); give (jewellery, etc.); assemble/collect/bring s.o.; (*cin.*) load (film); (*sl.*) incur debts; (*sl.*) surpass; (*sl.*) attach importance to, take notice of: (-den), (*ed. sl.*) fail (in a subject); takıp takıştırmak, adorn o.s. elaborately.
takometre (*mot.*) Tachometer.
takoz (*carp.*) Wooden wedge; (*min.*) billet; (*naut.*) chock, slipway frames. ~dan ~a hız//müddet, (*aer.*) block speed//time. ~lamak (-i), wedge; shore up.
tak·rib- = TAKRİP. ~riben, *circa*; approximately,

about. ~ribi, approximate. ~ri¹p^{bi}, approximation; pretext; means: ~ etm., bring near; approximate.
takrir (*adm.*) Deposition, statement, memorandum, report; motion, proposal; official notification of conveyance of property. ~ etm., explain (lesson): ~ vermek, notify a conveyance; put forward a motion. ~lik, (*pub.*) foolscap.
takriz (*lit.*, *obs.*) Eulogy; favourable review; foreword.
taksa (*adm.*) Postage due. ~ pulu, postage-due stamp. ~lı, postage-due (letter).
taksi (*bio.*) Taxis; (*mot.*) taxi(-cab). ~ durağı, cabrank/-stand: ~ şoförü/~ci, cabman, taxidriver. ~metre, taximeter.
taksim (*math.*) A dividing into parts; division; partition; distribution; (*eng.*) reservoir for distributing water; (*Or. mus.*) improvisation, instrumental solo. ~ etm., (*math.*) divide (into parts); share out, distribute: (*Or. mus.*) play a solo. ~at¹, *pl.* divisions; (*arch.*) compartments. ~atlı, divided up; calibrated: ~ daire, dial.
taksir Abbreviation; failure in duty; fault. ~ etm., abbreviate; fail in one's duty. ~at¹, failings; (*col.*) destiny.
taksitⁱ (*fin.*) Instalment; annuity. ~ ödemek, pay an instalment: ~ ~ / ~le, by instalments. ~çi, s.o. doing hire-purchase business.
taksonomi (*bio.*) Taxonomy.
takt¹ Tact; good-temper. ~ sahibi, tactful.
tak·tak (*ech.*) Knock knock. ~tuk, (*ech.*) banging, knocking.
taktırmak (-i, -e) *vc.* = TAKMAK; (*sl.*) deceive one's husband.
takti A cutting up; (*lit.*) scanning a verse.
takti¹k^{ği} (*mil./sp.*) Tactics.
taktir (*chem.*) Distillation. ~ etm., distil. ~hane, distillery.
takunya (*mod.*) Clog; sabot. ~cı, clog-maker.
takva (*rel.*) Fear of God; piety.
takvim (*ast.*) Almanac, calendar. ~ ay//yılı, calendar month//year.
takviye Reinforcement; stiffener. ~ etm., reinforce, consolidate, strengthen; (*fig.*) lend colour/ credit to. ~li, reinforced, strengthened.
takyi¹t^{di} A binding; putting conditions/restrictions. ~ etm., bind; limit, restrict.
tal (*bot.*) Thallus. ~amus, (*bio.*) thalamus.
talak¹ (*leg.*, *obs.*) Divorce.
talakat¹ (*ling.*) Eloquence. ~lı, eloquent.
tala·mak (-i) Pillage, plunder; raid: ~ etm., pillage.
talaş (*carp.*) Wood-shavings, chips; sawdust; filings. ~ sirkesi, wood vinegar, acetic acid: ~ tahtası, chipboard. ~kebabı^{nı}, (*cul.*) lamb pasty. ~lamak (-i), scatter sawdust, etc. ~lanmak (-e), *vp.*
talaz (*geo.*) Wave, billow; (*tex.*) ruffling up (of silk). ~lanmak, *vi.* (sea) be rough; (silk) be ruffled up; (sheep) surge into a mass. ~lık, (*naut.*) washboard.
talebe(lik) (*ed.*) (Status of) student, pupil.
tale¹p^{bi} Request; demand; desire. ~ etm., request; ask for: ~ halinde, if required: ~ sahibi, applicant.

~**kâr**, *a.* desirous: *n.* applicant; suitor. ~**name**, written request.

taler (*fin.*) Thaler, Austrian dollar.

tali Secondary; subordinate; subsidiary; by(e). ~ **boru**, (*eng.*) bypass: ~ **hareket**, (*th.*) by-play: ~ **hasılat/mamul**, (*ind.*) by-products: ~ **hikâye/oyun**, (*th.*) by-plot: ~ **madde/mahsul/ürün**, (*ind.*) by-product: ~ **yol**, by-road.

talib- = TALIP.

talih Good fortune; luck, chance; one's star/destiny. ~ **eseri**, a piece of luck: ~ **küskünü**, unlucky: ~**e bağlı**, depending on luck/chance: ~**e küsmek**, be tired of life; curse one's fate: ~**ine bakmak**, cast s.o.'s horoscope, tell s.o.'s fortune: ~**ine küsmek**, curse one's luck: ~**ini denemek**, take one's chance.

talih·li Lucky: ~ **olm.**, be lucky/'in clover'. ~**siz**, unlucky. ~**sizlik**, misfortune; disaster: ~**e vermek (-i)**, put stg. down to bad luck.

talik[i] Dependency (on stg.); (*adm.*) postponement; suspension; (*art.*) Persian style of Arabic script. ~ **etm.**, make depend on; suspend; postpone.

talika Light four-wheeled carriage.

talim (*ed.*) Teaching; instruction; practice; (*mil.*) drill. ~ **etm.**, teach; drill; practise: ~ **fişeği**, (*mil.*) blank cartridge: ~ **ve terbiye**, instruction, training.

talimar (*naut.*) Cut-water.

talim·at[i] Instructions; exercises: ~ **vermek**, direct, instruct: ~**la hareket etm.**, act upon instructions. ~**atname**, book of instructions. ~**gâh**, (*mil.*) cadet training-ground. ~**hane**, parade-ground, drill-hall. ~**name**, drill-book.

tali[i]**p**[bi] *a.* Who requests; desirous. *n.* Applicant, candidate; customer; suitor. ~ **olm.**, aspire.

talk[i] (*chem.*) Talc; talcum powder.

tal·kım (*bot.*) Raceme, cyme. ~**kın**, (*col.*) advice.

tallahi *int.* ~ **vallahi!**, by God!

tallıbitkiler (*bot.*) Thallogens, thallophytes.

taltif A gratifying; kindness; favour; appreciation; recompense. ~ **etm.**, gratify; treat kindly; show favour to, reward; honour.

tal·veg (*geo.*) Thalweg. ~**yum**, (*chem.*) thalium.

tam *a.* Complete, entire, full; perfect; uniform; absolute. *adv.* Completely; fully; exactly; just. ~ **adamına çatmak/düşmek/** ~ **adamını bulmak**, strike upon the very man (to help//ruin one): ~ **ay tutulması**, (*ast.*) total eclipse of the moon: ~ **bakışımlı**, (*geol.*) holohedral: ~ **bölen**, (*math.*) aliquot: ~ **çoğunluk**, (*adm.*) clear/absolute majority: ~ **faaliyette olm.**, be in full blast: ~ **gün(eş) tutulması**, (*ast.*) total eclipse of the sun: ~ **(kalk)acağı sırada**, just as he was going to (get up): ~ **karar**, just right: ~ **kare**, (*math.*) perfect square: ~ **kayıp**, a dead loss: ~ **kısım**, (*math.*) characteristic: ~ **kıvamında**, (*bot.*) (tree) in full fruit: ~ **kopya**, facsimile: ~ **maaşla tekaüt**, (*jok.*) a sinecure: ~ **manasıyla hapı yuttuk!**, we're properly in the soup!; it's all up with us!: ~ **okka dört yüz dirhem bir adam**, a first-class/thoroughly reliable man: ~ **olarak**, in full, completely: ~ **ortasında**, dead centre: ~ **pansiyon**, (hotel) full board: ~ SAYI: ~ **takım**, complement: ~ TAKIR: ~ **teğet**, (*math.*) cotangent: ~ TERS: ~ **tersine**, on the contrary: ~ **tutulma**, (*ast.*) total eclipse: ~ **üstüne basmak**,

hit the nail on the head: ~ **yetkili (elçi)**, (*adm.*) plenipotentiary (ambassador): ~**ı** ~**ına** = TAMAMI.

tamah Greed; avarice; stinginess. ~ **etm. (-e)**, covet, desire. ~**kâr**, greedy; avaricious; stingy.

tamam *n.* The whole. *a.* Complete; finished; ready; just right, (*cul.*) done; true, correct. *int.* That's right!; that's it!; ready!; there you are—see what you've done! ~ **etm.**, complete; terminate: ~ **gelmek (-e)**, just suit: ~ **olm.**, be complete(d); be finished: ~ **yerine gelmek**, reach the point of perfection; get exactly into place: ~**ı** ~**ına**, complete; perfect.

tamam·en Completely; entirely: ~ **bitti**, it's all over. ~**ıyla**, wholly, in its entirety. ~**iyet**[i], completeness; wholeness; integrity. ~ **lama**, *vn.*; completion. ~**lamak (-i)**, complete, finish; make good (a defect). ~**lanmak**, *vp.* ~**latmak (-i, -e)**, *vc.* ~**layıcı**, complementary.

tam·asala[l]**k**[ği] (*bio.*) Total parasite. ~**bölen**, (*math.*) factor.

tambur (*Or. mus.*) Any instrument played with a plectron; type of guitar. ~**a(cı)**, small TAMBUR/ (-player). ~**i**, TAMBUR player.

tam·deyim (*phil.*) Formula. ~**durum**, (possible) world. ~**evirme**, inversion. ~**gün**, (*ind.*) full-time.

tamik[i] Profound investigation; (*ed.*) research.

tamim Generalization; (*adm.*) circular. ~ **etm.**, generalize; circulate.

tamir Repair; overhaul, maintenance; restoration. ~ **etm.**, repair, mend; overhaul: ~**e değmez**, not worth repairing: ~**e vermek (-i)**, give to be repaired.

tamir·at[i] *pl.* Repairs. ~**ci**, repairer; handyman. ~**hane**, repair workshop. ~**sizlik**, disrepair.

tamla·ma (*ling.*) Determinative construction/ group. ~**nan**, (*ling.*) determined, defined. ~**yan**, (*ling.*) determining, determinative, defining: ~ **durumu**, genitive/possessive case(-ending). ~**yıcı**, determinative.

tampon (*rly.*) Buffer; (*naut.*) fender; (*eng.*) dashpot; (*mot.*) bumper; cushion; (*med.*) wad, plug; (*sl.*) breast. ~ **bölge//devlet**, (*pol.*) buffer-zone//-state.

tam·sayı (*math.*) Whole number; (*adm.*) quorum. ~**takır**, absolutely empty. ~**tam**, (*mus.*) tom-tom. ~**ters**, the exact opposite, exactly the reverse.

tamu (*rel.*) Hell. ~**sal**, hellish, hell-like.

tan Dawn, daybreak; twilight. ~ **ağartısı**, daybreak: ~ **atmak**, (day) dawn/break: ~ YELİ: ~ YERİ.

-tan *n. suf.* [28] = -DEN [BAŞTAN].

tandır Oven (in a hole in the ground); brazier under a covered table (to warm those sitting round). ~ **başında oturmak**, (*soc.*) sit around a TANDIR: ~ **ekmeği**, (*cul.*) bread baked in a TANDIR: ~ **kebabı**, (*cul.*) dish of roast meat and onions: ~ **kebesi**, felt rug covering a TANDIR. ~**name**, old wives' tales.

tane (*bot.*) Grain; seed; pip; (*min.*) particle, grain; (*mil.*) bullet; (*gen.*) [80] piece; single thing, item. ~ **bağlamak/** ~**ye gelmek**, (*bot.*) form seeds/berries: ~ **büyüklüğü**, (*min.*) grain size: ~ **halinde**, granular: ~ **konumu**, (*min.*) grain orientation: ~ **ölçümü**, granulometry: ~ ~, in separate grains; one by

one, item by item: ~ ~ **söylemek**, (*ling.*) articulate clearly.
tane·ci¹kᵍⁱ (*bot.*) Granule; (*min.*) subgrain; (*nuc.*) particle; (*cin.*) grain. ~**cikli**, granular; pimply (face). ~**cil**, (*zoo.*) granivorous. ~**lemek (-i)**, separate into grains; granulate. ~**lenmek**, *vp.*; *vi.* produce grains/berries. ~**li**, having grains/berries; in separate grains; -grained.
tanen (*bot.*) Tannin.
tangır ~ ~/~ **tungur**, (*ech.*) loud clanging noise. ~**damak**, *vi.* clang. ~**datmak (-i)**, *vc.* clang. ~**tı**, clang, repeated clanging. ~**tılı**, very noisily.
tango (*mus.*) Tango; (*fig.*) loudly-dressed woman.
tanı (*med.*) Diagnosis. ~**dı¹k**ᵍⁱ, aquaintance: ~ **çıkmak (-le)**, have met s.o. before.
tanı¹kᵍⁱ Witness; (*fig.*) proof. ~ **göstermek**, call to testify: ~ **olm.**, see, witness: ~ **tepe**, (*geol.*) outlier, butte. ~**lamak (-i)**, (*leg.*) support with witnesses. ~**lık**, testimony, statement, deposition; evidence: ~ **etm.**, testify, depose.
tanı·lama *vn.* (*med.*) Diagnosis. ~**lamak (-i)**, diagnose. ~**lmak**, *vp.* = TANINMAK. ~**m**, definition, description.
tanı·ma *vn.* Recognition; acknowledgement; diagnosis: ~ **yitimi**, (*psy.*) agnosia. ~**mak (-i)**, recognize s.o.; be acquainted with, know s.o.; know about s.o.; identify stg.; diagnose; acknowledge/accept stg.; heed, listen to. ~**mamak (-i)**, disclaim, disown; pay no attention to, ignore. ~**mamazlık**, (*pol.*) non-recognition.
tanım·(lama) *vn.* Definition, description. ~**lamak (-i)**, define, describe. ~**lanma**, *vn.*; (*ling.*) definition. ~**lanmak**, *vp.* ~**lı**, (*phil.*) definite; limited. ~**sal**, descriptive.
tanın·ma *vn.* Recognition. ~**mak**, *vp.* be known/recognized; be acknowledged/recognized as. ~**mış**, well-known, recognized.
tanısızlık (*psy.*) Agnosia.
tanış (*col.*) Acquaintance. ~ **çıkmak**, have met s.o. before. ~**ık(lık)**, mutual acquaintance(ship). ~**ma**, *vn.* ~**mak (-i, -le)**, become acquainted; be acquaintances. ~**tırma**, *vn.* introduction. ~**tırmak (-i, -le)**, introduce (A to B).
tanı¹tᵈⁱ Proof, evidence. ~**ıcı**, *n.* introducer, presenter; advertiser: *a.* introductory; advertising. ~**ıcılık**, advertising. ~**ılmak**, *vp.* ~**ım**, introduction; advertisement. ~**lama**, *vn.*, demonstration; certainty. ~**lamak (-i)**, prove, demonstrate. ~**lanmak**, *vp.* ~**lı**, positive. ~**ma**, *vn.* introduction, presentation: *a.* introductory: ~ **belgesi**, (*adm.*) credentials: ~ **yazıları**, (*cin.*) credits. ~ **macı**, (*fin.*) agent; presenter. ~**mak (-i, -e)**. *vc.* make known, advertise; introduce (A to B). ~**malık**, (*fin.*) prospectus; (*ind.*) instructions (for use). ~**man**, introducer, presenter.
tanjan(t¹) (*math.*) Tangent.
tank¹ (*mil.*) Tank; (fuel/water, etc.) tank. ~ **çiftliği**, (*ind.*) tank farm: ~ **engel//tuzağı**, (*mil.*) tank obstacle//trap.
tank·çı (*mil.*) Tank soldier. ~**er**, (*mot., naut.*) tanker. ~**savar**, (*mil.*) anti-tank gun.
tan·lamak/ ~ mak (-e) Be amazed at stg.
tannan (*ech.*) Resounding; ringing.

Tanrı (*rel.*) God; deity; (*myth.*) god. ~ **dağı koyunu**, (*live.*) Marco Polo's sheep: ~ **dağları**, (*geo.*) Tien Shan Mountains: ~ **deveciği**, (*ent.*) woodlouse: ~ **esirgesin/korusun!**, God preserve us!: ~ **kayrası**, (*phil.*) providence: ~ **kulları**, men, people; (*col.*) a great many: ~ **misafiri**, an unexpected guest: ~**nın günü**, every (blessed) day: ~ **ya şirk koşmak**, be a polytheist: ~**'ya şükür!**, thank God!: ~**'yı yadsıyan**, unbeliever.
Tanrı·bilim(ci) Theolo·gy/(-gist). ~**bilimsel**, theological. ~**cı(lık)**, (*phil.*) the·ist/(-ism). ~**ça**, (*myth.*) goddess. ~**laşmak**, *vi.* become divine; be deified. ~**laştırma**, *vn.* apotheosis. ~**laştırmak (-i)**, deify. ~**lık**, divinity. ~**sal(lık)**, divi·ne/(-nity). ~**sız(lık)/ ~ tanımaz(lık)**, athe·ist/(-ism).
tansı¹kᵍⁱ (*rel.*) Miracle.
tansiyon (*med.*) Blood-pressure; (*el.*) voltage; (*fig.*) stress.
tantal¹ (*chem.*) Tantalum.
tantana Pomp, display; magnificence. ~**lı**, magnificent, grand.
tantun ~**a gitmek**, be killed/ruined/lost.
tan·yeliⁿⁱ (*met.*) Light wind at dawn. ~ **yeri**ⁿⁱ, (*geo.*) east(ern horizon): ~ **ağarmak**, (day) break/dawn.
tanzifat¹ (*adm.*) Highways and sewers service. ~ **amelesi**, roadsweeper.
tanzim A putting in order; organization. ~ **etm.**, put in order; organize; reorganize; (*lit.*) arrange, edit: ~ **satışı**, official sale of foodstuffs to control prices.
tanzimat¹ (*adm.*) Reforms, reorganization. *pr.n.* (*his.*) period of reforms, 1839- . ~**çı**, reformer.
TAO = TÜRK ANONİM ORTAKLIĞI.
tapa Stopper, bung, plug, cork; (*mil.*) fuse, detonator. ~ **çivi**, (*carp.*) dowel: ~ **takmak**, (*mil.*) arm (rocket, etc.): ~**sını çıkarmak**, (*el., mil.*) defuse. ~**lamak (-i)**, stop/plug (up); cork. ~**lanmak**, *vp.*
tapan (*agr.*) Harrow.
tapı (*rel.*) Idol. ~**na¹k**ᵍⁱ, temple. ~**nca¹k**ᵍⁱ, fetish. ~**ncakçı(lık)**, fetish·ist/(-ism). ~**n¹çç**ⁱ/~ **nı(ş)/ ~ nma**, worship, adoration; cult. ~ **nmak (-e)**, (*rel.*) worship; (*fig.*) worship, adore.
tapir (*zoo.*) Tapir.
tapisöri (*tex.*) Tapestry.
tap·ma *vn.* ~**mak (-e)**, worship.
tapon Discarded; common; second-rate; ugly.
taptaze Absolutely fresh.
taptırmak (-i, -e) *vc.* Cause to worship.
tapu (*leg.*) Title-deed. ~ **+**, *a.* Cadastral: ~ **dairesi**, land registry: ~ **kütüğü**, land register: ~ **ve kadastro**, (*adm.*) land registration and ownership. ~**lama**, *vn.* ~**lamak (-i)**, register (property).
tapyoka (*cul.*) Tapioca.
tar. = TARIM; TARİH.
-tar *n. suf.* = -DAR [TARAFTAR].
taraça (*arch.*) Terrace (of a house).
taraf Side; aspect; direction; district; part; end; (*leg.*) party; protector. ~ **çıkmak (-e)**, become s.o.'s protector: ~ ~, in various directions// places: ~ **tutmak**, take sides (in a dispute): ~ **tutmayan**, neutral: ~**a (o)**, in that direction: ~**ıma**, towards me: ~ **ına**, towards . . .: ~ **ında**, on . . . side: ~ **ından**, [93] on the part of . . ., by . . .; from the

direction of . . .; a kind/sort of . . .: ~ **ını tutmak**
(-in), take the part of, side with, champion: ~ **lar**,
(*leg.*) parties.
taraf·eyn (*leg., obs.*) The two parties/sides. ~ **gir**,
partisan; partial, biased. ~ **girlik**, partisanship. ~ **lı**,
having sides, -sided; having support; supporter.
~ **sız**, neutral, impartial; (*fig.*) dispassionate, detached: ~ **bayrak//bölge//sular**, (*pol.*) neutral flag//
zone//waters. ~ **sızlandırmak** (-i), declare/make
neutral; neutralize. ~ **sızlık**, neutrality, impartiality; detachment. ~ **tar**, partisan; adherent,
supporter. ~ **tarlık**, partiality, partisanship.
tara¹kᵍ¹ Comb; (*agr.*) rake, harrow; (*naut.*) drag;
(*tex.*) weaver's reed/comb; serrated pattern; (*bio.*)
hand bones; instep; (*zoo.*) scallop; (*ich.*) gills; (*arch.*)
stone-dressing axe. ~ **duba/gemisi**, (*naut.*) dredger:
~ **kabuğu**, (*zoo.*) scallop/cockle shell: ~ **makinesi**,
(*tex.*) carding machine: ~ **solungacı**, (*zoo.*) cockle.
tarak·çı Comb-maker/-seller. ~ **işi**ⁿⁱ, (*tex.*) serrated
embroidery. ~ **kemiği**ⁿⁱ, (*bio.*) bones of hand/foot.
~ **lama**, *vn.* ~ **lamak** (-i), comb; (*agr.*) rake, harrow; (*naut.*) dredge. ~ **lı**, (*mod.*) wearing a comb;
(*bio.*) crested; (*tex.*) with serrated embroidery;
(*bio.*) broad-footed. ~ **lıkuş**, (*orn.*) great bustard.
~ **lılar**, (*zoo.*) ctenophores. ~ **otu**ⁿᵘ, (*bot.*) teasel.
~ **si**, (*bio.*) pectinate.
tara·lı Combed. ~ **ma**, *vn.*; (*cul.*) red caviare; soft-
roe; (*art.*) hatching/shading (on maps, etc.): (*med.*)
scanning: (*rad.*) surveillance: ~ **ağı**, (*naut.*) drag
net: ~ **resim**, (*art.*) line drawing. ~ **mak** (-i), comb
(out); (*tex.*) tease, card; (*agr.*) rake, harrow; (*naut.*)
drag (anchor); dredge; (*arch.*) dress (stone); (*min.*)
trim; (*fig.*) search thoroughly; make inquiries
about; (*lit.*) prepare a glossary.
taranga (*ich.*) Common bream.
taran·mak *vp.* = TARAMAK: *vi.* comb o.s. ~ **tı**,
combings.
tarassu¹tᵈᵘ Watching; observation. ~ **altında**,
under observation: ~ **etm.**, watch; observe.
taratmak (-i, -e) *vc.* = TARAMAK.
tarator (*cul.*) Hazelnut sauce.
taravetⁱ Freshness; juiciness; bloom of youth. ~ **li**,
fresh; juicy; ruddy.
tarayıcı That combs/dredges; (*rad.*) scanner. ~
gemisi, (*naut.*) minesweeper.
tarbuş (*mod.*) Tarboosh, fez.
tarçın (*cul.*) Cinammon.
tard- = TART. ~ **iye**, (*lit.*) poem of five-lined verses.
taretⁱ (*arch.*) Turret; (*naut.*) gun-turret; (*zoo.*)
teredo.
tarh (*math.*) Subtraction; (*fin.*) imposition (of
taxes); (*agr.*) flower-bed, border. ~ **etm.**, subtract;
impose (tax); ~ **a koymak**, bed out (plants).
tar·hana (*cul.*) (Soup of) dried curds and flour.
~ **hanalık**, suitable for this soup. ~ **hun**, (*bot.*)
tarragon.
tarım Agriculture, cultivation. ~ +, Agricultural:
~ **Bakan(lığ)ı**, (*adm.*) Minis·ter/(-try) of Agriculture: ~ **işçisi**, farm-labourer: ~ **uzmanı**, agrono-
mist: ~ **ürünü**, agricultural produce.
tarım·cı(lık) Agricul·turalist/(-ture); farm·er/
(-ing). ~ **lık**, arable: ~ **toprak**, top soil. ~ **sal**,
agricultural.

tarif Description; definition. ~ **etm.**, describe;
define: ~ **e sığmaz**, it beggars description: ~ **e**
uymak, answer/fit the description. ~ **li**, descriptive.
tarife (*fin.*) Tariff; price-list; (*rly.*) timetable; (*med.*)
prescription, directions; (*cul.*) recipe; menu.
tarih Date; history; annals; chronicle; epoch. ~ +,
a. Historical: ~ **atmak/koymak**, put the date: ~
aykırılık/hatası, anachronism: ~ **başı**, epoch: ~
boyunca, in the course of history: ~ **çizgisi**, (*ast.*)
date-line: ~ **damgası**, date-stamp: ~ **düşürmek**,
give the date by EBCED: ~ **hesabı**, (*ast.*) era: ~
sıralaması, chronological order: ~ **yazmak**,
chronicle; write a history: ~ **e karışmak**, be out of
date, be a thing of the past: ~ **e karışmış**, as dead as
the dodo: . . . ~ **inde**, as of/on such a date: ~ **ten**
atmak, date (a letter, etc.): ~ **ten önce**, prehistoric.
tarih·çe Short history; chronicle. ~ **çi(lik)**, (work
of) historian. ~ **i**, historical. ~ **li**, dated: ~ **mektup**,
letter dated . . .. ~ **öncesi**, prehistory: ~ +, *a.* prehistoric. ~ **sel**, historic: ~ **anıt**, ancient monument:
~ **özdekçilik**, (*phil.*) historical materialism.
~ **selcilik**, (*phil.*) historicism. ~ **siz**, undated; without a history.
tarikⁱ Way, road. ~ **at**¹, (*rel.*) way; dervish order.
~ **atçı(lık)**, (life of) dervish; sectarian(ism).
tariz Allusion, hint, (criticism by) innuendo. ~
etm. (-e), censure by innuendo: ~ **de bulunmak**, *vt.*
criticize/censure.
tarla (*agr.*) Arable field; garden bed. ~ **açmak**,
bring under cultivation: ~ **cüce faresi**, (*zoo.*)
striped field mouse: ~ **kiraz kuşu**, (*orn.*) corn
bunting: ~ **sıçanı**, (*zoo.*) common vole: ~ **sincabı**,
(*zoo.*) European souslik: ~ **tırmığı**, (*agr.*) drag: ~
yaban kazı, (*orn.*) bean goose.
tarla·faresiⁿⁱ (*zoo.*) Common vole. ~ **koz**, small
fishing-net. ~ **kuşu**ⁿᵘ, (*orn.*) lark.
tarpan (*zoo.*) Tarpan, wild horse of Tartary.
tar¹tᵈ¹ ¹ Expulsion; driving away. ~ **etm.**, expel.
tart¹ ² (*cul.*) Fruit pie/tart.
tart·a¹çᶜ¹ (*phys.*) Balance, scales. ~ **ı**, weighing;
weight; balance, scales; (*naut.*) hoisting rope; (*lit.*)
poetic measure: ~ **ya gelmez**, imponderable: ~ **ya**
vurulmak, be pondered over. ~ **ıl**, (*chem.*) by
weight, gravimetric. ~ **ılı**, weighed; balanced; (*fig.*)
pondered over; (*lit.*) metric. ~ **ılmak**, *vp.*: *vi.* weigh
o.s. ~ **ım(lı/-sal)**, (*lit., mus.*) rhythm(ic). ~ **ısız**
unweighed; unbalanced; not well thought out.
tartak·lamak (-i) Pull to pieces; (*tex.*) tease; (*fig.*)
tease, worry, harass. ~ **lanmak**, *vp.*
tartış·ı Discussion, debate; polemics: ~ **lı oturum**
(*med.*) symposium. ~ **ılmak**, *vp.* ~ **ma**, *vn.*; discussion; dispute; argument. ~ **macı**, one who argues,
disputant. ~ **mak** (-le), weigh up; struggle; debate;
argue, dispute. ~ **malı**, controversial; debatable.
tart·ma *vn.* Act of weighing; gravimetry: *a.* by
weight. ~ **mak** (-i), weigh; shake; ponder well;
estimate, weigh up. ~ **tırmak** (-i, -e), *vc.*
tartura (*carp.*//*tex.*) Turner's//spinner's wheel.
tarumar Scattered, in disorder. ~ **etm.**, rout.
tarz Form, shape, appearance; manner, method;
style. ~ **ında**, in the style of, after.
tarziye Apology; (giving) satisfaction. ~ **vermek**,
give satisfaction, make an apology.

tas Bowl, cup; dipper. ~ **kebabı**, (*cul.*) braised lamb: ~**ı tarağı toplamak**, (*col.*) pack up and go.

TAS = (*aer.*) (*true air speed*).

tasa Worry, anxiety, grief. ~ **bu** ~ (**o**), we've got enough to worry about as it is: ~ **vermek**, cause anxiety: ~**mın on beşi!**, I don't care a hang!: ~**sı sana mı düştü?**, why worry, it doesn't concern you!: ~**sını çekmek**, suffer grief/regret for.

tasa·landırmak (**-i**) Cause to worry, make anxious. ~**lanmak** (**-e**), be anxious about stg. ~**lı**, anxious, grieved.

tasallutᵘ (*pol.*) Usurpation; aggression. ~ **etm.**, usurp power; (**-e**), attack s.o. violently.

tasallü'pᵇᵘ ~ **etm.**, become hard.

tasannuᵘ Feint, pretence; artifice.

tasar Project, plan; draft. ~**çizim(ci)**, design(er). ~**ı**, (*leg.*) draft law, bill: ~ **geometri**, descriptive geometry: ~**lar**, (*pol.*) platform. ~**ım**, (*psy.*) imagination; (*phil.*) representation; (*eng.*) design: ~ **yükü**, design load. ~**ımlamak** (**-i**), (*psy.*) imagine, conceive. ~**ımsız(lık)**, unimaginative/(lack of imagination). ~**ıvarlık**, (*lit.*) allegory. ~**lamak** (**-i**), plan, project; deliberate; premeditate; draft, sketch out. ~**lanmak**, *vp*.

tasarruf (*leg.*) Possession, use; (*fin.*) economy, saving. ~ **bankası**, savings bank: ~ **bonosu**, savings bond: ~ **etm.**, possess; save, economize: ~ **hesabı**, savings account: ~ **senedi**, (*leg.*) title-deed: ~ **sandığı**, (*fin.*) savings bank: ~ **yeteneği**, (*leg.*) power of disposal: ~**unda olm.** (**-in**), be possessed by and at the disposal of.

tasarsız Unplanned, extempore.

tasasız Care-free.

tasavvuf (*rel.*) Mysticism; sufism. ~**i**, mystical; sufic.

tasavvur Imagination; plan. ~ **etm.**, imagine; plan: ~**unda olm.**, contemplate.

tasdiⁱ ~ **etm.**, give a headache; (*fig.*) pay a visit to.

tasdikⁱ Confirmation, certification; ratification. ~ **etm.**, confirm, certify; acknowledge; ratify: ~ **imzası**, (*adm.*) counter-signature: ~ **memuru**, (*adm.*) registrar, notary.

tasdik·li Certified. ~**name**, letter of confirmation; certificate. ~**siz**, unconfirmed.

tasfiye A cleaning/clarifying; purification; (*chem.*) refining; (*fin.*) liquidation; clearance; elimination. ~ **bankası**, (*fin.*) clearing house: ~ **etm.**, clean, clarify; clear up (a matter); (*chem.*) refine; (*fin.*) liquidate; eliminate: ~ **memuru**, liquidator. ~**ci**, (*ling.*) supporter of a 'pure-language' policy. ~**hane**, (*chem.*) refinery.

tasgir Making smaller. ~ **etm.**, diminish, reduce.

tashih Correction; (*pub.*) proof-reading. ~ **etm.**, correct; (*pub.*) read proofs.

tasım (*phil.*) Syllogism. ~**lama**, *vn.* plan, programme. ~**lamak** (**-i**), plan, project. ~**sal**, (*phil.*) syllogistic.

tas-la'ıkᵍ¹ Rough state of stg.; draft; sketch; model; (*fig.*) poor specimen. ~**lam**, model. ~**lamak**, *vi.* affect/pretend to (be/have) stg. non-existent.

tasma *n.* Collar (of dog, etc.); strap (of clogs). *a.* (*sl.*) Credulous, simple.

tasmim Resolution; intention. ~ **etm.**, resolve upon.

tasni Falsehood; invention; (*phil.*) fiction.

tasnif (*adm.*) Classification. ~ **etm.**, classify. ~**li**, classified.

tasrif (*ling.*) Declension, conjugation. ~ **etm.**, decline, conjugate.

tasrih Clear expression/interpretation. ~ **etm.**, make clear, specify.

tastamam Quite complete, perfect.

tasvi'pᵇⁱ Approval. ~ **etm.**, approve.

tasvir Description; picture, design. ~ **etm.**, describe; depict: ~ **gibi**, pretty as a picture. ~**i**, descriptive: ~ **dilbilgisi**, (*ling.*) descriptive grammar.

taş *n.* (*geol.*) Stone; rock; precious stone; (*gamb.*) piece, man (chess, etc.); (*med.*) calculus, stone; (*fig.*) allusion, innuendo; (*sl.*) money. *a.* Stone; hard as stone: ~ **atımı (bir)**, a stone's throw away: ~ **atmak** (**-e**), throw a stone at; (*fig.*) allude to; have a dig at s.o.: ~ **attın da kolun mu yoruldu?**, (*iron.*) are you exhausted/worn out?: ~ BADEMİ: ~ BALIĞI: ~ BASMASI: ~ **bebek gibi**, a mere doll, pretty but cold (woman): ~ BİLİM: ~ **Çağ/Devri**, (*his.*) Stone Age: ~ **çatlasa**, whatever happens, under any circumstances: ~ **çıkarmak**, (*min.*) quarry stone: ~ **çıkartmak** (**-e**), give points/be greatly superior to s.o.: ~ **çeviren (yağmur kuşu)**, (*orn.*) ruddy turnstone: ~DOLGU: ~ **döküntüsü**, (*geol.*) detritus: ~ **döşeme**, (*arch.*) flag, stone pavement: ~ **düşürmek**, (*med.*) pass a gall-stone: ~ **evi (tırnağı)**, (claw of) jewel setting: ~ **gibi**, hard as stone; very hard: ~ **ısıran**, (*ich.*) spined loach: ~İLİĞİ: ~ **kadar sert**, as hard as stone: ~ **kalem**, (*ed.*) slate pencil: ~ **kesilmek**, be petrified/horrified: ~ **kırıcı**, (*min.*) stone crusher: ~KÖMÜR: ~ **kuşu**, (*orn.*) stonechat: ~MANTARI: ~ **mı taşıdın?**, what have you done to be so tired?: ~OCAĞI: ~PAMUĞU: ~ **parke**, paving stone: ~ **sektirme**, (*child.*) ducks and drakes: ~ **sineği**, (*ent.*) stone-fly: ~ **tahta**, slate (for writing on): ~ **üstünde bırakmamak**, raze to the ground: ~ **toprak**, rubble: ~ **tutmak**, (*sl.*) be rich: ~ **yağar kıyamet koparken**, it was a terrible disaster: ~YAĞI: ~ **yerinde ağırdır**, only his friends appreciate him: ~YOLU: ~ **yontmak**, (*min.*) cut/dress stone: ~ **yosunu**, (*myc.*) lichen: ~ **yuvarlamak** (**-e**), attack/inveigh against s.o.: ~YÜREKLİ.

taş-: ~**a çekmek** (**-i**), whet (knife): ~**a tutmak** (**-i**), pelt with stones, stone to death; (*carp.*) grind (a tool): ~**ı gediğine koymak**, give as good as one gets; make a clever retort: ~**ı ölçeyim!**, (*col.*) may God protect us! (when pointing at a wound, etc. on the body): ~**ı sıksa suyunu çıkarır**, he's terribly strong: ~**tan ekmeğini çıkarır**, he can make a living at anything.

-taş *a./n. suf.* [64] = -DAŞ [MESLEKTAŞ].

TAŞ = TÜRK ANONİM ŞİRKETİ.

taşa'ıkᵍ¹ (*bio.*) Testicle. ~ **torbası**, scrotum. ~**lı**, having testicles; (*fig.*) virile; bold. ~**sız**, without testicles; (*fig.*) weak, cowardly.

taş·bademiⁿⁱ (*bot.*) Wild almond. ~**balığı**ⁿⁱ, (*ich.*) non-migratory fish; stone-fish. ~**baskı**, (*pub.*) lithography. ~**basması**ⁿⁱ, (*pub.*) lithograph. ~**bilim**,

(*geol.*) lithology. ~ **böceği**ⁿⁱ, (*zoo.*) cowry. ~ **çı**, (*min.*) stone-cutter, mason: ~ **kalemi**, mason's chisel. ~ **çılık**, stone-cutting/-masonry. ~ **dolgu**, (*arch.*) stone-infill, rubble. ~ **emen**, (*ich.*) lamprey.
taşeron (*fin.*) Sub-contractor.
taşıl (*geol.*) Fossil. ~ **bilim**, palaeontology. ~ **laşma**, *vn.*, fossilization. ~ **laşmak**, *vi.* be(come) fossilized. ~ **sı**, sub-fossil.
taşım (*cul.*) A coming to the boil. ~ **lık**, (*adv.*) until it boils over.
taşı·ma *vn.* Transport; carriage, forwarding: ~ **gücü**, (*eng.*) bearing capacity/strength: ~ **kayışı**, conveyor belt: ~ **oranı**, (*eng.*) bearing ratio: ~ **sözleşmesi**, (*naut.*) charter-party: ~ **su ile değirmen dönmez**, an enterprise needs adequate means for success: ~ **ücreti**, (*fin.*) carriage; fare: ~ **vasıtası**, conveyance, vehicle. ~ **macı**, carrier, forwarding-agent. ~ **macılık**, carrying; forwarding (agency). ~ **mak** (-i), carry, transport; bear, wear; carry (news), spread (gossip). ~ **malık**, transport costs.
taşımsı Rocklike; strong.
taşın·ca Taxi; baggage: ~ **sayacı**, taximeter. ~ **cak**/ ~ **calık**, baggage. ~ **ım**, transportation. ~ **ır**, portable: ~ **değerler**, (*fin.*) securities, bearer-bonds: ~ **demirbaş**, furniture: ~ **mallar**, movable possessions/goods: ~ **silahlar**, (*mil.*) small-arms. ~ **ma**, *vn.* transport(ing); house moving; (*phys.*) convection: ~ **topraklar**, (*geol.*) weathered soils. ~ **mak**, *vp.* = TAŞIMAK; be carried, etc.: *vi.* move house, change one's dwelling; visit too often; ponder over. ~ **maz**, immovable: ~ **mal**, real estate.
taşır·ma *vn.*: ~ **(suyu)**, (*naut.*) displacement. ~ **mak** (-i), *vc.* = TAŞMAK; cause to overflow; (*naut.*) displace: *vi.* go beyond the bounds/too far.
taşıt¹ Vehicle; carrier. ~ **aracı**, means of transport: ~ **gemisi**, (*naut.*) ferryboat: ~ **gideri**, (*fin.*) carriage, transport costs. ~ **an**, consignor. ~ **çı**, driver, operator. ~ **mak**/~ **tırmak** (-i, -e), *vc.* = TAŞIMAK.
taşı·yan Transporter, carrier; (*fin.*) bearer, holder: ~ **ına yazılı**, to bearer. ~ **yıcı**, porter; (*eng.*) conveyor, transporter; (*phys.*, *med.*) carrier: ~ **bant**/ **kayış/kolanı**, (*eng.*) conveyor-belt: ~ **dalgası**, (*el.*) carrier-wave: ~ **sistemi**, transporter system.
taş·iliği (*geol.*) Veining (in rocks). ~ **kaldıran**, (*orn.*) ruddy turnstone.
taş·kı (*psy.*) Mania: ~ **-çökkü**, manic-depressive. ~ **kın**, *a.* overflowing; overlapping; excessive; boisterous: *n.* (*geo.*) flood. ~ **kınca**, sudden; impulsive. ~ **kınlık**, overflowing; flooding; excess; impetuosity; (*psy.*) mania.
taşkıran (*min.*) Stone-crusher. ~ **çiçeği**ⁿⁱ, (*bot.*) mountain saxifrage. ~ **giller**, Saxifragaceae. ~ **otu**ⁿᵘ, saxifrage.
taş·kırım (*med.*) Lithotomy. ~ **kömürü**ⁿᵘ, (*min.*) coal, anthracite: ~ **katranı**, coal-tar. ~ **küre** = ~ YUVARI.
taş·lama *vn.* Stoning; (*eng.*) grinding; (*lit.*) satire. ~ **lamacı(lık)**, (work of) grinder. ~ **lamak** (-i), stone, throw stones; remove stones (from stg.); (*min.*) grind; (*lit.*) satirize. ~ **lanmak**, *vp.* be stoned. ~ **laşma**, (*geol.*) diagenesis, petrification. ~ **laşmak**, *vi.* petrify. ~ **latmak** (-i, -e), cause to be stoned. ~ **levreği**ⁿⁱ, (*ich.*) corb. ~ **lı**, stony, rocky; set with

jewels. ~ **lık**, stony/rocky place; (*arch.*) paved courtyard; stone threshold; (*orn.*) gizzard.
taş·ma *vn.* Flood. ~ **mak**, *vi.* overflow; boil over; overlap; (*fig.*) lose one's patience; be in a ferment; go too far; get above o.s.; be insolent.
taş·mantarıⁿⁱ (*myc.*) Boletus, cep. ~ **ocağı**ⁿⁱ, (*min.*) stone quarry. ~ **oluş**, (*geol.*) diagenesis.
Taşoz (*geo.*) (Island of) Thasos.
taş·pamuğuⁿᵘ (*min.*) Asbestos. ~ **pudra**, (*mod.*) powder compact.
taşra (*geo.*) The country; the provinces. ~ +, *a.* Provincial: ~ **ağzı**, (*ling.*) provincialism, local dialect. ~ **lı**, *a.* living in the provinces: *n.* provincial, countryman. ~ **lık**, (conditions of life in) the provinces.
taş·sı (*bio.*) Callous. ~ **yağı**ⁿⁱ, (*min.*) kerosene. ~ **yolu**ⁿᵘ, carriage-way. ~ **yuvarı**ⁿⁱ, (*geol.*) lithosphere. ~ **yürekli**, stony-hearted, cruel.
ta·tᵈ¹ ¹ (*cul.*) Taste; flavour; relish; charm. ~ **alma cisimcik//organı**, (*bio.*) taste bud//organ: ~ **almak** (-den), taste; enjoy the taste of: ~ **vermek**, give taste to; flavour: ~ **ı damağında kalmak**, its flavour linger on one's palate; still hanker after it: ~ **ı tuzu kalmamak**, no longer give any pleasure: ~ **ı tuzu yok**, tasteless, insipid: ~ **ına bakmak (-in)**, taste, test the taste of: ~ **ına doyum olmamak**, never have too much of stg.: ~ **ına varmak**, get the full flavour of, enjoy: ~ **ında bırakmak**, not overdo stg.: ~ **ından yenmez**, delicious; (*iron.*) insipid: ~ **ını almak**, acquire a taste for; enjoy: ~ **ını bulmak**, have the right flavour/taste: ~ **ını çıkarmak**, get the utmost pleasure out of stg.: ~ **ını kaçırmak**, overdo stg.; spoil the enjoyment of stg.
Tat¹ ² (*ethn.*, *pej.*) Kurd/Persian; (*pej.*) poor wretch.
Tatar (*ethn.*) Tartar; (*adm.*) courier. ~ **akçaağacı**, (*bot.*) Tartarian maple: ~ **oku**, (*mil.*) cross-bow.
tatar·böreğiⁿⁱ (*cul.*) Lamb pie with yoghurt. ~ **ca**, (*ling.*) Tartar language. ~ **cık**ᵏᵍⁱ, (*ent.*) sandfly; midge: ~ **humması**, (*med.*) sandfly fever. ~ **ı**, (*cul.*) undercooked. ~ **ımsı**/~ **sı**, like a Tartar; (*cul.*) not well-cooked.
tatbikⁱ Adaptation; application; comparison. ~ **etm.**, apply (rules, etc.); adapt; compare; fit stg.; (*mus.*) arrange: ~ **edilmek**, (*adm.*) be brought into application, come into force: ~ **mührü**, (*adm.*) official seal: ~ **sahasına koymak**, put into practice.
tatbik·at¹ (*leg.*) Applications; putting into practice; (*mil.*) manœuvres. ~ **atçı**, one who applies. ~ **i**, practical, applied.
tatil *n.* Suspension of work; stoppage (of activity); holiday; rest. *a.* Closed for a holiday. ~ **beldesi**, holiday resort: ~ **etm.**, close; suspend; cause to cease: ~ **günü**, holiday, day off: ~ **köyü**, holiday camp/village: ~ **olm.**, be closed (for a holiday): ~ **yapmak**, take a holiday: ~ **e girmek**, close for a period.
tatlan·dırmak (-i) (*cul.*) Sweeten/flavour stg. ~ **mak**, *vi.* become sweet/tasty; get a flavour; become ripe.
tatlı *a.* Sweet; agreeable; drinkable (water); dulcet (sound); (*fig.*) sweet, pleasant. *n.* (*cul.*) Sweetmeat; confection; sweet. ~ **acı**, bitter-sweet: ~ **bakış**, a sweet glance: ~ **bela!**, sweet little devil!: ~ **boyan**,

(*bot.*) liquorice plant/root: ~ **dil**, soft words; pleasant way of speaking: ~ **dil yılanı deliğinden çıkarır**, sweet words work wonders: ~ **dilli**, pleasant-spoken: ~ **düş**, daydream: ~ **limon**, (*bot.*) sweet lime/lemon: ~ **sert**, kindly severe: ~ **su**, drinking water; (*geo.*) fresh water: ~ **su balığı**, (*ich.*) freshwater fish: ~ **su gelinciği**, (*ich.*) burbot: ~ **su Fransızcası**, (*pej.*) (poor) French spoken by Levantines: ~ **su Frengi**, (*pej.*) Levantine: ~ **su ıstakozu**, (*zoo.*) crayfish: ~ **su kaptanı**, (*pej.*) inexperienced sailor: ~ **su kayabalığı**, (*ich.*) tench: ~ **su kefalı**, (*ich.*) chub: ~ **su levreği**, (*ich.*) perch: ~ **su sardalyası**, (*ich.*) bleak: ~ **su yengeci**, (*zoo.*) river crab: ~ **(tabağı)**, (*cul.*) dessert, sweet course: ~ **yerinde bırakmak/kesmek**, bring stg. to a conclusion just in time: ~**sı**, (*cul.*) . . . cake: ~**ya bağlamak**, settle matters amicably.

tatlı·ca (Only) slightly sweet; sweetish; rather agreeable. ~**cı**, maker/seller of sweetmeats; (*fig.*) sweet-toothed. ~**cılık**, sweetmeat business. ~**laşmak**, *vi.* become sweet. ~**laştırmak (-i)**, sweeten. ~**lı**, (*cul.*) with sweetmeats. ~**lık**, sweetness, kindness, amiability: ~**la**, pleasantly. ~**msı**, sweetish. ~**sülümen**, (*chem.*) calomel. ~**yosun**, (*bot.*) sealeek.

ta'tmakᵈᵃʳ **(-i)** Taste; try; experience, suffer.

tatmin Tranquillizing reassurance. ~ **etm.**, satisfy (curiosity, desire, etc.); calm, reassure. ~ **kâr**, satisfactory. ~**sizlik**, unsatisfactoriness.

tat·sal *a.* (*bio.*) Relating to taste; gustatory. ~**sız**, tasteless; disagreeable; insipid: ~ **tuzsuz**, completely tasteless, insipid; (*fig.*) stupid, dull. ~**sızlaşma**, *vn.* ~**sızlaşmak**, *vi.* become insipid; behave disagreeably. ~**sızlık**, insipidity; dullness; disagreeableness. ~**tırmak (-i, -e)**, *vc.* = TATMAK.

tatula (*bot.*) Datura; thorn-apple; stg. evil-tasting.

taun (*med.*) Pest; plague; epidemic. ~**zede**, plague-stricken.

tav (*ind.*) Correct heat/humidity (for any process); (*min.*) annealing: (*fig.*) opportune moment; (*live.*) well-nourished condition/fatness; (*gamb.*) doubling the stakes. ~ **fırın/ocağı**, (*min.*) tempering furnace: ~ **sürmek**, (*gamb.*) double the stakes: ~ **vermek**, (*ind.*) ensure the correct humidity: ~**a getirmek/**~**ını vermek**, bring to the correct heat: ~**ı geçti/savdı**, (*fig.*) the best moment has passed: ~**ı kaçırmak**, miss the right moment, let slip a suitable opportunity: ~**ına getirmek**, bring to the right condition: ~**ını bulmak**, reach the right condition.

tava (*cul.*) Frying-pan; fried food; (*min.*) ladle (for melting metal); (*arch.*) trough (for slaking lime); (*chem.*) ditch (bringing sea-water to saltpans); (*naut.*) lower platform of gangway; (*agr.*) nursery-bed. ~**sı**, (*cul.*) fried . . . .

tavaf (*rel.*) Circumambulation of the Kaaba (during pilgrimage to Mecca). ~ **etm.**, circumambulate the Kaaba; (*fig.*) keep going round stg.

tavan (*arch.*) Ceiling; uppermost section; (*adm.*) highest grade; (*aer.*) ceiling; (*fin.*) maximum, limit, ceiling. ~ **arası**, (*arch.*) garret, attic: ~ **başına çökmek**, be crushed/ruined; be overcome by fear/shame: ~ **eder/fiyatı**, (*fin.*) (official) maximum

price: ~ **penceresi**, (*arch.*) dormer window: ~ **pervazı**, cornice.

tavassutᵘ Intervention; mediation. ~ **etm.**, intervene; mediate: ~**uyla**, by means of, through the agency of.

tavattun Settling; making one's home. ~ **etm.** **(-de)**, settle/make one's home in . . ..

tavazzuh Becoming clear. ~ **etm.**, become clear/ manifest.

tavcı(lık) (Work of) accomplice in a swindle; confidence-man.

taverna Tavern-cum-restaurant (with music).

tavhane (*agr.*) Glasshouse, greenhouse.

tav'ırʳⁱ Mode, manner; kind; air, attitude; arrogance. ~ **satmak**, give o.s. airs: ~ **ıyla**, with the air of . . .: ~**la**, affectedly.

tavikⁱ *n.* Hindering, delaying. ~ **etm.**, hinder, delay, prevent. ~**li**, delayed-action (bomb, etc.).

taviz Compensation; replacement; concession. ~ **vermek**, compensate. ~**ci(lik)**, (policy of) s.o. who achieves success by small concessions.

tavla¹ Stable. ~ **halatı**, tether: ~ **uşağı/**~**cı**, stable-boy.

tavla² (*gamb.*) Backgammon. ~ **atmak**, play backgammon: ~ **pul//tahtası**, backgammon piece// board: ~ **tiryakisi**, keen backgammon player.

tav·lama *vn.* Conditioning; (*min.*) annealing, case-hardening; (*fin.*) confidence-trick. ~**lamak (-i)**, bring stg. to its best condition (= TAV); (*ind.*) bring to correct heat/humidity; dampen; (*min.*) anneal, case-harden; (*fin.*) deceive, swindle (= TAVCI); (*col.*) flirt. ~**lanmak**, *vp.*: *vi.* (*live.*) get fat. ~**lı**, at its best condition (= TAV); (*ind.*) damped (tobacco, etc.); (*min.*) red-hot, annealed; (*live.*) in prime condition. ~**sama**, *vn.* ~**samak**, *vi.* lose its TAV; (*live.*) fall away from its prime; (*min.*) cool down; (*fig.*) decline, decay. ~**satmak (-i)**, make/let lose its TAV; cool down; slow up; let decline; lose the opportunity. ~**sız**, (*min.*) not heated sufficiently; not tempered; (*live.*) not in prime condition.

tav·sif Description; eulogy. ~ **etm.**, describe; eulogize. ~**siye**, recommendation, advice: ~ **etm.**, advise, recommend: ~**li**, recommended.

tavşan¹ (*carp.*) Joiner, cabinet-maker. ~**lık**, (*carp.*) fine joinery, cabinet-making.

tavşan² (*zoo.*) Hare. ~ **anahtarı**, picklock: ~ **bayırı aştı**, it's gone for ever; it will never be seen again: ~ **boku (gibi ne kokar ne bulaşır)**, harmless but useless: ~ **dağa küsmüş de dağın haberi olmamış** s.o. important is unaware of the effect of his actions: ~ **uykusu**, cat-nap: ~ **yuvası**, burrow: ~ **yürekli**, timid: ~**a kaç tazıyı tut demek**, run with the hare and hunt with the hounds: ~**ı araba ile avlamak**, do stg. calmly and easily: ~**ın suyunun suyu**, a very distant connection.

tavşan·bıyığıⁿⁱ (*bot.*) Type of trefoil. ~**cıl**, (*orn.*) eagle, vulture. ~**cılotu**ⁿᵘ, (*bot.*) hogweed. ~**cıltaşı**ⁿⁱ, (*geol.*) type of iron oxide. ~**dudağı**ⁿⁱ, (*bio.*) hare-lip. ~**ımsı**, (*zoo.*) hare-like. ~**kanı**ⁿⁱ, bright carmine. ~**kulağı**ⁿⁱ, (*bot.*) sowbread, cyclamen. ~**paçası**ⁿⁱ, (*bot.*) hare's-foot clover.

tavu'kᵍᵘ Hen. ~ **biti**, (*ent.*) poultry louse: ~ **gelen yerden yumurta esirgenmez**, set a sprat to catch a

mackerel: ~ **eti**, (*cul.*) chicken: ~ **götü tövbe tutmaz**, (*vulg.*) s.o. weak doesn't repent for long: ~ **kafesi**, hen-coop: ~ **kanadı**, wing-feathers; (*dom.*) fan (to fan a fire): ~ **kaza bakmış da kıçını yırtmış**, keeping up with the Joneses can prove expensive: ~ **yufka içinde**, (*cul.*) chicken in pastry.
tavuk·balığıⁿ¹ (*ich.*) Whiting. ~**çu**, poultry-rearer; poulterer. ~**çuluk**, rearing/selling poultry. ~**giller**, (*live.*) poultry. ~**göğsü**ⁿü, (*cul.*) sweet dish of milk and pounded chicken-breast. ~**götü**ⁿü, (*bio.*, *vulg.*) wart. ~**karası**ⁿ¹, (*med.*) night-blindness, nyctalopia. ~**lama**, (*min.*) hand-picking/-sorting.
tavulga (*bot.*) Goat//purple willow.
tavus (*orn.*) Peacock. ~ **kelebeği**, (*ent.*) hawk-moth: ~ **kuşu**, (*orn.*) peafowl (cock/hen): ~ **kuyruğu**, peacock's tail; (*sl.*) drunken vomiting: ~ **turnası**, (*orn.*) crowned crane: ~ **yeşili**, emerald green. ~**lanmak**, *vi.* strut about.
tavzif Entrusting, appointing. ~ **etm.**, entrust with a duty; appoint as an official.
tavzih Clarification; correction. ~ **etm.**, clarify; correct.
tay¹ *n.* (*live.*) Foal, colt.
tay² *a.* Balancing; equal. ~ **durmak**, (child) begin to stand up: ~ ~!, stand up!: ~ ~ **arabası**, baby-walker.
-tay *n. suf.* [226] Assembly, council [KURULTAY].
taya Child's nurse. ~ **çocuğu**, spoilt child.
taydaş Equal, peer; contemporary; companion.
tayf Ghost; (*phys.*) image; spectrum. ~ +, *a.* Spectral. ~**çeker**, (*phys.*) spectrograph. ~**ölçer**, spectrometer.
tayfa (*naut.*) Crew; sailor(s); gang, troop.
tay·fun (*met.*) Typhoon. ~**ga**, (*geo.*) taiga.
taygeldi Child(ren) of a woman's previous marriage.
tayın (*cul.*) Ration(s). ~ **bedeli**, (*mil.*) rations allowance: ~ **ekmeği**, (*cul.*) soldier's loaf.
tayin (*adm.*) Appointment, designation; assign; pointing out. ~ **etm.**, appoint, designate; decide; fix, settle, determine; assign.
tayi¹pᵇⁱ Finding fault; reproaching.
taylak (*live.*) Nearly full-grown foal.
Tay·land (*geo.*) Thailand. ~**lorculuk**, (*ind.*, *soc.*) Taylorism. ~**mis**, (*geo.*) Thames; (*pub.*) The Times. ~**van**, (*geo.*) Taiwan.
tayyar Flying; volatile. ~**e**, (*aer.*) aeroplane: ~ **böceği**, (*ent.*) dragon-fly: ~ **meydanı**, airfield. ~**eci**, (*aer.*) pilot, airman.
tayy¹etmekᵉᵈᵉʳ (-i) Delete; (*fin.*) write off.
tayyör (*mod.*) Coat and skirt, costume.
tazallüm Complaining of injustice. ~ **etm.**, complain.
tazammun Comprising; (*phil.*) comprehension; implication.
tazarruᵘ Supplication. ~ **etm.**/~**da bulunmak**, humbly beg.
taze *a.* Fresh; new, recent; young; tender. *n.* Young girl. ~ **bezelye**, (*cul.*) green peas: ~ **fasulye**, French beans: ~ **incir**, fresh figs: ~ **ot görmüş eşek gibi sırıtmak**, (*sl.*) become intoxicated/hilarious: ~ **soğan**, green onions: ~ **yaprak**, fresh vine-leaves.

taze·leme *vn.* ~**lemek** (-i), freshen up; renew ~**lenmek**, *vp.* ~**leşmek**, *vi.* become fresh/young; be renewed. ~**lik**, freshness; bloom; tenderness; youth.
tazı (*sp.*) Greyhound; (*fig.*) sleuth. ~ **gibi**, thin as a rake: ~**ya dönmek**, become very thin; get soaked. ~**laşmak**, *vi.* grow thin.
ta·zim Respect, reverence: ~ **etm.**, honour; respect. revere. ~**zimat**¹, honours; homage. ~**zi¹p**ᵇⁱ, *n.* torturing; tormenting. ~**ziye**, condolence: ~ **etm.**, ~ **de bulunmak (-e)**, condole with. ~**ziz**, honouring s.o.'s memory.
tazmin Compensation, indemnity. ~ **etm.**, compensate, indemnify. ~**at**¹, compensation; reparations; (*naut.*) average: ~ **davası**, (*leg.*) suit for damages.
tazyik¹ (*phys.*) Pressure; compression; (*fig.*) coercion, oppression. ~ **etm.**, compress; oppress, coerce. ~**li**, pressurized.
Tb. = (*mil.*) TABUR; (*ch.s.*) TERBİYUM. ~**b.** = TIBBİ. ~**p.** = TABİP.
TB = TARIM//TİCARET BAKANLIĞI. ~**B** = TİCARET BORSALARI BİRLİĞİ. ~**MM** = TÜRKİYE BÜYÜK MİLLET MECLİSİ. ~**P** = TÜRKİYE BİRLİK PARTİSİ. ~**TAK** = TÜBİTAK.
Tc. = (*ch.s.*) TEKNETYUM.
TC = TÜRKİYE CUMHURİYETİ. ~**DD** = TC DEVLET DEMİRYOLLARI. ~**K** = TÜRK CEZA KANUNU; TC KARAYOLLARI. ~**MB** = TC MERKEZ BANKASI. ~**Tİ** = TC TEKEL İDARESİ.
TÇEK = TÜRKİYE ÇOCUK ESİRGEME KURUMU.
TD = (*pub.*) TARAMA DERGİSİ(NDEN); (*ling.*) TÜRK DİLİ; TÜRKİYE DEMİRYOLLARI. ~**K** = TÜRK DİL KURUMU.
te¹ (*ling.*) Tk. letter T; (*eng.*) T-joint.
te² *conj.* [206] = DE.
Te. = (*ch.s.*) TELLÜR; (*phys.*) TERMİ.
-te *n. suf.* [28] = -DE [MEKTEPTE].
teadül (*obs.*) Equilibrium; balancing.
teakup Following one after the other. ~ **etm.**, follow in succession.
teali Elevation; loftiness.
teamül Custom, practice; (*chem.*) reaction.
tearuz Mutual opposition. ~ **etm.**, oppose.
teati Exchange. ~ **etm.**, exchange (gifts, etc.) bandy (words).
teavün Mutual aid. ~ **etm.**, help each other.
tebaa *pl.* = TABİ; subjects.
tebahhur Evaporation; vaporization. ~ **cihazı**, evaporator: ~ **etm.**, evaporate; vaporize.
tebaiyetⁱ Allegiance, submission, conformity.
tebarüz ~ **etm.**, become clear/prominent.
tebcil Veneration. ~ **etm.**, venerate, honour.
tebdil Change. ~ **etm.**, change; alter: ~ **gezmek**, go about in disguise. ~**ihava**, change of scene.
tebeddül ~ **etm.** be changed/altered.
tebelleş ~ **olm.**, pester, worry.
tebellüğ ~ **etm.**, be informed, receive a communication.
tebellür (*chem.*) Crystallization. ~ **etm.**, crystallize: (*fig.*) become crystal clear.
teber Small axe, hatchet; leather-cutting knife.
teberruᵘ Charitable gift, donation. ~ **etm.**, donate. ~**ken**, *adv.* counting stg. as a blessing/good omen

tebessüm Smile. ~ **etm.**, smile.

tebeşir (Piece of) chalk. ~ +, *a.* (*geol.*) Cretaceous. ~**leşme,** (*med.*) calcification. ~**li,** (*geol.*) cretaceous.

teb·ligat[1] (*adm.*) Communications; reports. ~**liğ,** communication; announcement; bulletin; notice: ~ **etm.**, communicate; notify.

tebrik[i] Congratulation. ~ **etm.**, congratulate.

tebriye (*leg.*) Acquittal. ~ **etm.**, acquit, absolve.

Tebriz *pr.n.* (*geo.*) Tabriz.

tebşir Glad tidings. ~ **etm.**, bring good news.

tebyiz ~ **etm.**, make a fair copy.

tecahül Feigned ignorance. ~ **etm.** (-**den**), pretend ignorance of: ~**ü arifane,** (*lit.*) using assumed ignorance for satire.

tecanüs Homogeneity.

tecavüz Transgression; excess; aggression. ~ **etm.**, attack; exceed; contravene; transgress: ~ **savaşı,** war of aggression: ~**i (ve tedafüi) ittifak,** (*pol.*) offensive (and defensive) alliance.

tecdi[t]di Renewal. ~ **etm.**, renew, renovate.

teceddü[t]dü Being renewed; renovation; reform.

tecelli Manifestation; fate, luck. ~ **etm.**, be shown; appear, happen.

tecemmu[u] *n.* Coming together; collecting.

tecennün ~ **etm.**, become insane.

tecerrü[t]dü ~ **etm.**, divest o.s. of; withdraw from.

tecessüm ~ **etm.**, appear; come to life; take shape.

tecessüs Inquisitiveness; curiosity.

tecezzi ~ **etm.**, *vi.* disintegrate, break into pieces; divide up.

techil ~ **etm.**, show up s.o.'s ignorance.

tecil Delay, postponement. ~ **etm.**, defer, postpone.

tecim Commerce, trade. ~ +, *a.* Commercial; trade: ~ **Bakan(lığ)ı,** (*adm.*) Minis·ter/(-try) of Commerce/for Trade: ~ **bankası,** commercial/merchant bank: ~ **birliği,** cartel: ~ **dengesi,** balance of trade: ~ **gemileri,** merchant marine: ~ **markası,** trademark: ~ **odası,** chamber of commerce/trade.

tecim·ci/~**en** Merchant, trader. ~**evi,** business, office. ~**lik**/~**sel,** commercial, trade. ~**yer(lik),** agen·t/(-cy).

tecri[t]di *n.* Separating; isolating; (*phys.*) insulating. ~ **etm.**, separate; isolate; insulate: ~ **tabakası,** (*arch.*) damp course.

tecrübe Trial, test; experiment; experience. ~ **etm.**, try, test, assay; experiment; experience: ~ **ile (satış),** (sale) on approval: ~ **müddeti,** trial period: ~ **sehpası,** (*eng.*) test-bed: ~ **tahtası,** guinea-pig: ~ **tahtasına görmek,** suffer a series of setbacks: ~**sini etm.**, try stg. out; experiment on: ~**yi göğe çekmediler ya!,** there's no reason why you shouldn't try!

tecrü·beli Experienced; tried and tested, proved. ~**besiz,** inexperienced; untried, untested. ~**bi,** experimental.

tecvi[t]di (*rel.*) Art of reading/reciting the Koran rhythmically.

tecviz *n.* Considering lawful; finding suitable.

tecziye Punishment. ~ **etm.**, punish.

teçhiz *n.* Fitting out, equipping. ~ **etm.**, equip, fit out; arm. ~**at**[1], equipment; apparatus; (*mil.*) armament.

ted- *pref. Also* = TET-.

tedafüi Defensive. ~ **ittifak,** defensive alliance.

tedai (*psy.*) Association.

tedarik[i] Preparation; provision. ~ **etm.**, obtain, procure; prepare; provide; (*cul.*) cater for: ~**te bulunmak,** make preparations. ~**li,** prepared. ~**siz,** unprepared.

tedavi (*med.*) Treatment; cure. ~ **etm.**, treat: ~ **yolu,** course of treatment.

tedavül (*fin.*) Circulation, currency. ~ **bankası,** bank of issue: ~ **etm.**, circulate: ~**de olm.**, be in circulation/current: ~**den kaldırmak,** demonetize.

tedbir Precaution; plan; disposition, measure; course of action; device. ~ **almak,** take precautions: ~**e takdir uymuyor,** man proposes, God disposes.

tedbir·li Provident; thoughtful; prudent; cautious. ~**siz,** improvident, thoughtless. ~**sizlik,** thoughtlessness, negligence.

tedenni Retrogression; decline; decadence. ~ **etm.**, decline; fall.

tedfin Burial. ~ **etm.**, bury.

tedhiş Terror(izing). ~ **etm.**, terrify. ~**çi(lik),** (*pol.*) terror·ist/(-ism).

tedi[p]bi A teaching manners. ~ **etm.**, correct, discipline.

tedir·gilemek (-i) (*nuc.*) Perturb. ~**gin,** grumbling, restless, discontented: ~ **etm.**, disturb, upset. ~**ginlik,** restlessness, discontent; (*ast.*) perturbation.

tediye (*fin.*) Payment. ~ **etm.**, pay: ~**ler muvazenesi,** balance of payments: ~**ler tatili,** moratorium.

ted·ricen By degrees, gradually. ~**rici,** gradual. ~**ri**[ç]ci, an advancing by degrees.

tedris (*ed.*) Instruction, teaching. ~ **bloku,** teaching unit: ~ **etm.**, teach by lessons. ~**at**[1], instruction; course of lessons.

tedvin ~ **etm.**, collect an author's works; codify.

tedvir A causing to revolve; (*fin.*) direction. ~ **etm.**, cause to revolve; direct (business).

teeddü[p]bü A showing good manners; a refraining from doing. ~ **etm.**, refrain (out of politeness).

teehhül A marrying. ~ **etm.**, marry.

teehhür Postponement, delay. ~ **etm.**, be postponed; be late.

teemmül Reflection; deliberation; caution. ~ **etm.**, reflect, deliberate.

teenni A being deliberate; discretion; composure.

teessüf Regret; a being sorry. ~ **etm.**, regret, sorry for: ~ **ederim!,** shame!

teessür Emotion; grief. ~ **etm.**, be affected; grieve.

teessüs A being founded/established.

teeyyü[t]dü A being strengthened/confirmed; support. ~ **etm.**, be strengthened/confirmed.

tef (*mus.*) Tambourine (with cymbals). ~ **çalmak,** play the tambourine: ~ **çalsan oynayacak!,** what a muddle!: ~**e koymak**/~**e koyup çalmak** (-i), hold up to public ridicule.

tefahür Boasting; arrogance. ~ **etm.** (-le), boast (about).

tefcir (*agr.*) Drainage.

tefe (*tex.*) Frame to hold weaver's reed. ~**li,** closely woven, close textured.

tefeci (*fin.*) Usurer. ~ **lik**, usury.
tefe·cik = UFACIK. ~ **k** = UFAK.
tefehhüm Understanding.
tefekkür Reflection; thought. ~ **etm.**, think: ~ **hürriyeti**, (*pol.*) freedom of thought: ~ **e dalmak**, be lost in thought.
teferruat[1] *pl.* Details; accessories. ~ **lı**, detailed.
teferrü'ç[cü] Pleasure trip, excursion.
teferrü't[dü] A standing apart; being distinguished.
tefessüh Decomposition, putrefaction. ~ **etm.**, decompose, putrefy.
tefevvuk Superiority. ~ **etm.** (**-e**), be superior to.
tefeyyüz Progress; prosperity. ~ **etm.**, make progress; prosper.
tefhim An explaining, communicating.
tefrik Separation; distinction. ~ **etm.**/**yapmak**, separate. distinguish (A from B), discriminate between. ~ **a**, discord; (*pub.*) supplement; newspaper serial.
tefriş A carpeting/furnishing. ~ **etm.**, carpet; furnish.
tefrit[i] Remissness; deficiency.
tefsir (*rel.*) Commentary; (*leg.*) interpretation. ~ **etm.**, comment.
teftiş Investigation; inspection; (*fin.*) audit. ~ **etm.**, investigate; inspect; audit.
tefviz Handing over (duties).
tegafül Feigned ignorance. ~ **etm.**, feign ignorance.
teğelti Saddle-pad, numnah.
teğet[i] (*math.*) Tangent. ~ **sel**, tangential.
teğmen(lik) (Rank/duties of) (*mil.*) second lieutenant//(*naut.*) sub-lieutenant//(*aer.*) pilot-officer.
tehacüm A rushing/crowding together; concerted attack.
tehalüf Difference. ~ **etm.**, differ.
tehalük[ü] Keenness, zeal; ardent desire. ~ **etm.**, desire ardently.
tehcir Deportation. ~ **etm.**, deport; cause to migrate.
tehdi't[di] Threat. ~ **etm.**, threaten: ~ **savurmak**, breathe forth threats: ~ **le almak**, extort: ~ **le zorlamak**, bully: ~ **leri hep kurusıkıdır**, his bark is worse than his bite. ~ **kâr**, threatening.
tehevvür Sudden anger, fury. ~ **etm.**, burst into anger.
teheyyüç[cü] Excitement; emotion.
tehir Delay, postponement. ~ **etm.**, delay, postpone.
tehlike Danger; emergency; risk. ~ **atlatmak**, escape from/avoid danger: ~ **çanları çalmak**, signs of disaster appear: ~ **geçti!**, (*mil.*) all clear!: ~ **den kurtulmuş**, out of danger: ~ **ye atılmak**, court danger: ~ **ye atmak/koymak**, risk; (*fin.*) venture: ~ **ye sokmak**, endanger: ~ **yi geçiştirmek**, turn the corner. ~ **li**, dangerous; risky; (*med.*) malignant; critical. ~ **siz**, safe; inoffensive; (*med.*) benign.
tehyi'ç[ci] Excitement. ~ **etm.**, excite.
tehzil Ridicule, mocking; (*lit.*) satire, parody, caricature.
tein (*chem.*) Caffeine (in tea), theine.
tek[i] *n.* Single thing; (*math.*) odd number; one of a pair, fellow, mate. *a.* Single; unique; alone, solitary;

(*math.*) odd; mono-; uni-. *adv.* Only; merely once; as long as, provided that. ~ **amaçlı**, single purpose(d): ~ **aşamalı**, (*eng.*) single stage: ~ **at** ~ **mızrağı**, all alone, without family: ~ **atmak** (**bir**), (*sl.*) have a drink (of liquor): ~ **başına** apart; alone; individually; on one's own: ~ **bir** just one; + *neg.*, not a single one: ~ **çare budur** there's no alternative: ~ **çekirdekli**, mono nuclear: ~ **durmak/oturmak**, sit alone; be quiet ~ **elden**, under one (*fin.*) management//(*mil.* command: ~ **etkili**, (*eng.*) single-acting: ~ **fırsatınız budur**, Christmas comes but once a year: ~ **gözlük**, monocle: ~ **heceli (dil)**, (*ling.* monosyllabic (language): ~ **hörgüçlü deve**, (*zoo.* dromedary: ~ **kademe(li)**, (*eng.*) single-stage: ~ **kale**, (*sp.*) single-goal play (for practice): ~ **kanatlı** (*aer.*) monoplane: ~ **kişilik**, for one person; single (room, etc.): ~ **kürekle mehtaba çıkmak**, under take stg. with insufficient means; make a feeble attempt to mock s.o.: ~ **parça(lı)**, integral: ~ **pistl** **anayol**, single carriageway: ~ RENKLİ: ~ **say** (*math.*) odd number: ~ **sefer**, (*naut.*) single journey (charter): ~ **taraf/yanlı**, unilateral ~ ~, odd ones, not a pair; (*eng.*) stop-start ~ **tığ**, (*tex.*) crochet-hook: ~ TÜK: ~ **yerden** (*adm.*) centralized: ~ **yönlü tepkime**, (*chem.* irreversible reaction: ~ **yönlü yol**, one-way street ~ **e** ~ **kavga**, single combat: ~ **ler**, (*sp.*) singles (match).
Tek. = (*adm.*) TEKEL; TEKNİK; TEKNİSYEN.
teka·bbül ~ **etm.**, receive willingly; undertake stg ~ **bül**, a meeting; (*phil.*) correspondence.
tekâlif (*fin.*) Dues, taxes.
tekâmül Evolution, development. ~ **etm.**, evolve. mature, develop.
tekâsüf Condensation; density. ~ **etm.**, *vi.* condense; become dense.
tekâsül Negligence; laziness.
tekâsür Becoming numerous; (*phys.*) diffraction.
teka·üdiye (*fin.*) (Deduction for) pension. ~ **ü't**[dü] *n.* retirement; pension: *a.* retired; pensioned: ~ **etm.**, pension off, retire s.o.: ~ **maaşı**, half-pay; pension: ~ **olm.**, be retired: ~ **sandığı**, pension fund. ~ **ütlü**, on a pension, retired. ~ **ütlük**, retirement on a pension.
tek·baskı (*pub.*) Monotype. ~ **bencilik**, (*phil.*) solipsism. ~ **biçim(li)**, *a.* standard, uniform.
tekbir (*rel.*) Proclaiming God's greatness in ALLAHU EKBER. ~ **getirmek**, pronounce this prayer.
tek·boynuz (*myth.*) Unicorn. ~ **cinsten**, homogeneous. ~ **çe**, individual. ~ **çi(lik)**, (*phil.*) mon-ist/ (**-ism**). ~ **çizge**, (*lit.*) monograph. ~ **delikliler**, (*zoo.*) monotremes.
tekdir Scolding; reprimand. ~ **etm.**, scold, reprimand: ~ **e layik**, blameworthy.
tek·dizer/~ **dizim** (*pub.*) Monotype. ~ **düşüncelik**, (*psy.*) monoideism. ~ **düze(lik)**, mono·tonous (**-tony**).
teke (*zoo.*) He-goat, billy-goat; prawn. ~ **böceği**[ni], (*ent.*) long-horned beetle. ~ SAKALI.
tekebbür Haughtiness.
tekeffül (*leg.*) Standing surety.

ekel (*fin.*) Monopoly. ~ +, *a.* Monopolistic: ~**ine almak**, get control of, monopolize. ~**ci**, monopolist. ~**cilik**, monopolism: ~**e karşı**, (*leg.*) anti-trust. ~**leşme**, *vn.* ~**leşmek**, *vi.* be monopolized. ~**leştirmek (-i)**, monopolize.

ekellüf Display; taking great pains.

ekellüm Speaking.

ekemmül Perfection, evolution.

eker[1] *n.* Wheel; circle; (*ast.*) disc. ~ **arası**, (*mot.*) wheel track: ~ **kavraması**, (*eng.*) coupling, gearing: ~ **meker yuvarlanmak**, roll along; go head over heels: ~ **tabanı**, cartwheel tyre.

ek·er[2] One at a time: ~ ~, [193] one by one. ~**erklik**, (*adm.*) monarchy.

ekerle[1]**k**[gi] *n.* Wheel; disc. *a.* Circular, round. ~ **aralığı**, wheel-track: ~ **çarığı**, cart-wheel drag: ~ **izi, rut**: ~ **kırıldıktan sonra yol gösteren çok olur**, it's easy/a bit much to give advice after the event: ~ **kampanası**, brake drum: ~ **pabucu**, brake-shoe: ~ **parmağı**, spoke: ~ **peynir (bir)**, (*cul.*) a whole cheese. ~**li**, wheeled: ~ **sandalye**, (*med.*) wheelchair.

eker·leme *vn.* Rotation; (*lit.*) rigmarole; cant phrase; verse competition; witty reply. ~**lemek (-i)**, roll/rotate stg. ~**lenmek**, *vp.* ~**li**, wheeled.

ekerrür Repetition. ~ **etm.**, be repeated; repeat itself.

ekesakalı[nı] (*bot.*) Goatsbeard.

ekessür Multiplication; increase.

ekevli (*soc.*) Monogamous. ~**lik**, monogamy.

ekevvün Origination; being created; birth.

ekfin Wrapping in a shroud.

ekfir (*rel.*) Accusation of heresy/blasphemy.

ekfur (*his.*) Prince (in Byzantine Empire).

ek·gövde (*pub.*) Monobloc. ~**il**, individual, isolated; (*ling.*) singular. ~**illeştirmek (-i)**, make singular. ~**illik**, singularity.

ekin Empty; deserted; lucky; (*psy.*) of sound mind. ~ **değil**, haunted by djinns; ill-omened; (*psy.*) of unsound mind. ~**siz**, taboo.

ekir *a.* Striped, spotted, tabby (cat). *n.* (*ich.*) Surmullet, striped red mullet. ~ **kayası**, (*ich.*) type of goby. ~**dağ**, *pr. n.* (*geo.*) Rodosto.

eki[1]**t**[di] Confirmation; corroboration. ~ **etm.**, confirm; certify; emphasize.

ek·iz (*chem.*) Monomer. ~**kaynakçılık**, (*ethn.*) monogeny; (*bot.*) monophyleticism.

ekke (*rel.*) Dervish lodge; (*sl.*) opium den.

ek·lemek (-i) (*agr.*) Plant/thin out (seedlings): *vi.* (*mot.*) fire on one cylinder; (*col.*) show signs of failure; (*sl.*) stammer. ~**leşme**, (*ling.*) elision of half a double consonant. ~**li**, *a.* individual: *n.* singleton: ~ **dizi**, Indian file.

eklif Proposal; offer: (*fin.*) bid, tender; (*adm.*) motion; (*soc.*) etiquette, ceremony, formality; (*fin.*) tax. ~ **etm./vermek**, propose, offer formally; (*fin.*) tender, bid; (*adm.*) move: ~ **mektubu**, (*fin.*) letter of tender: ~ **sahibi**, (*adm.*) proposer of a motion; (*fin.*) one submitting a tender: ~ **tekellüf**, the rules of etiquette and decorum; pomp and ceremony: ~ **(tekellüfe lüzum) yok**, there's no need to stand on ceremony.

eklif·at[1] Proposals; formalities. ~**li**, s.o. very

formal/etiquette-conscious. ~**name**, (*fin.*) proposal form. ~**siz**, without ceremony; informal, familiar; (*ling.*) colloquial: ~ **konuşmada**, in colloquial speech. ~**sizlik**, lack of ceremony; informality.

teklik (*phil.*) Oneness, singleness; uniqueness.

tekme Kick. ~ **atmak**, give a kick: ~ **yemek**, get a kick/blow; (*fig.*) fall into disgrace. ~**lemek (-i)**, kick. ~**lenmek**, *vp.* ~**lik**, (*sp.*) shin pad.

tekmil *n.* A completing/perfecting. *a.* All, the whole of; perfect. ~ **haberi**, (*mil.*) verbal report (to a senior); (*fig.*) news of completion: ~ **vermek**, (*mil.*) make a report (to a senior). ~**lemek (-i)**, complete, finish; perfect.

tekne (*dom., ind.*) Trough; sink, tub, basin, tank; bath; (*naut.*) hull; craft, ship; (*pub.*) galley; (*geol.*) basin, syncline; (*zoo.*) carapace. ~ **kazıntısı**, (*jok.*) the Benjamin of a large family; child of elderly parents: ~**li deniz uçağı**, (*aer.*) flying boat.

tek·netyum (*chem.*) Technetium. ~**nik**, *n.* technics, technology; technique; method: *a.* technical: ~ **adamı**, technician: ~ **ressam(lık)**, draughtsman/(-ship). ~**nikçi**/~ **niker**/~**nisyen**, technician. ~**nikokul**, (*ed.*) technical school/college. ~**niköğretimi**, (*ed.*) technical education. ~**nokrasi**, (*adm.*) technocracy. ~**nokrat**, technocrat. ~**noloji(k)**, technolo·gy/(-gical).

tek·örnek(li) *a.* Uniform. ~**parça**, (?) monobloc. ~ **parmaklı**, (*zoo.*) perissodactylate.

tekrar *adv.* Again, afresh; *bis. n.* Repetition; recurrence. ~ **etm.**, repeat: ~ **olm.**, happen again, recur: ~ ~, over and over again, time and again.

tekrar·lama *vn.*: ~ **işareti**, (*pub.*) ditto marks (,,). ~**lamak (-i)**, repeat, start again. ~**lanmak**, *vp.* ~**layici**, repeater. ~**lı**, repeated.

tekrenkli (*phys.*) Mono·chromatic/-chrome.

tekrir Repetition.

teksif Making dense. ~ **etm.**, condense; compress; (*phys.*) render opaque.

teksir A multiplying; (*pub.*) duplication. ~ **etm.**, multiply, duplicate: ~ **kâğıdı**, (*pub.*) stencil: ~ **makinesi**, duplicator.

teks·til (*tex.*) Textile (industry). ~ **türe**, texturized: ~ **etm.**, texturize.

tek·tanrıcı(lık) (*rel.*) Monothe·ist/(-ism). ~**taş**, (*arch.*) monolith. ~**ten(ci)**, (*fin.*) retail(er).

tektoni[1]**k**[gi] (*geol.*) Tectonic(s).

tek·tük Here and there; now and then. ~**türel**, (*chem.*) homogeneous. ~**türellemek**, homogenize. ~**uçay**/~**uçlu**, (*el.*) single-pole. ~**yapılı**, mono·bloc. ~**yazı(m)**, (*ed., lit.*) monograph.

tekvando (*sp.*) Type of karate.

tekvin Creation; production.

tekzi[1]**p**[bi] Contradiction. ~ **etm.**, contradict; deny.

tel *n.* (*bio.*) Fibre; (*min.*) wire; (*el.*) filament; single thread/hair; (*mus.*) string; (*tex.*) silver/gold thread; (*el.*) telegram, wire, cable. *a.* Made of/like wire. ~ **başlık**, (*sp.*) mask: ~ **boyu**, (*tex.*) staple: ~ **çekmek**, (*min.*) draw wire; enclose with wire; send a telegram; (*sl.*) urinate: ~ DOLAP: ~ **halat**, (*naut.*) wire rope, cable: ~ KADAYIF: ~ **kalınlığı**, (*ind.*) wire gauge: ~ **örgü**, barbed-wire (*agr.*) fence//(*mil.*) obstacle: ~ **süs**, filigree: ~ **şehriye**, (*cul.*) vermicelli:

~ ~, like wire; in fibres/single threads: ~ **yazısı**, (*el.*) telegram message: ~ **yol**, cable railway: ~ **ler takınmak**, be extremely happy: ~ **ler takınsın!**, let him rejoice (because I shan't)!

Tel. = TELEFON.

tela (*tex.*) Horsehair stiffening; buckram.

telaffuz (*ling.*) Pronunciation. ~ **etm.**, pronounce; enunciate: ~ **etmemek**, elide.

telafi Compensation. ~ **etm.**, make up for, compensate; counterbalance.

telaki A meeting; (*geo.*) confluence.

telakki Reception; interpretation, view. ~ **etm.**, receive (news); consider, interpret.

telaş Confusion, flurry; alarm; hurry; embarrassment; anxiety. ~ **etm.**/ ~ **a düşmek**, be confused/ alarmed, etc.: ~ **göstermek**, show one's anxiety: ~ **a düşürmek**, confuse, alarm; make anxious: ~ **a gelmek**, be hurried: ~ **a vermek**, bustle.

telaş·landırmak (-i) Alarm, confuse. ~ **lanmak**, *vi.* be alarmed/confused/anxious. ~ **lı**, confused; upset; anxious. ~ **sız**, calm, composed.

telatin (*mod.*) Russian leather.

tel·cik Thread; fibre; (*bio.*) fibril(la). ~ **çivi**, (*carp.*) wire nail. ~ **dolap**, (*cul.*) meat-safe.

telef Destruction; ruin; kill. ~ **etm.**, consume, destroy; ruin; kill: ~ **olm.**, be destroyed/ruined/ killed. ~ **at¹**, (*mil.*) casualties: ~ **ver(dir)mek**, suffer/(inflict) casualties.

tele·feri¹kᵍⁱ (*rly.*) Cable railway. ~ **film**, (*cin.*) TV film; video-tape recording. ~ **fon**, (*el.*) telephone: ~ **açmak**, lift the receiver, make a telephone call: ~ **etm.**, telephone s.o.: ~ **hücresi**, call-box: ~ **kapamak**, put down the receiver: ~ **rehberi**, (*pub.*) telephone directory: ~ **santralı**, telephone exchange. ~ **foncu(luk)**, (work of) telephone engineer//telephonist. ~ **fonlaşmak (-le)**, telephone each other. ~ **foto(grafi)**, (*rad.*) telephoto(graphy).

tele¹kᵍⁱ (*orn.*) Wing-/tail-feather. ~ **damarlı**, (*bot.*) pinnate. ~ **e**, quill, remex.

tele·kinezi (*psy.*) Telekinesis. ~ **komünikasyon**, (*rad.*) telecommunications. ~ **ks**, (*rad.*) telex.

teleli ~ **balıkçıl**, (*orn.*) little white heron.

teleme (*cul.*) Type of cottage-cheese. ~ **peyniri gibi**, soft white complexioned.

tele·metre (*cin.*, *mil.*) Range-finder; (*el.*) telemeter. ~ **objektif**, (*cin.*) telephoto lens. ~ **oloji**, (*phil.*) teleology. ~ **pati**, (*psy.*) telepathy. ~ **pirinter**, (*el.*) teleprinter. ~ **radyo**, (*med.*) teleradiography.

teles Threadbare. ~ **imek**, *vi.* become threadbare; pant, be out of breath; become thin/weak. ~ **mek**, *vi.* hasten.

tele·sinema (*cin.*) TV-film making; telephotography. ~ **sko¹pᵇᵘ**, (*phys.*) telescope. ~ **skopik**, telescopic: ~ **dikme**, (*aer.*) oleo (leg). ~ **vizyon**, (*rad.*) television: ~ **alıcısı**, TV receiver set : ~ **gazetesi**, TV news: ~ **vericisi**, TV transmitter. ~ **vizyoncu(luk)**, (work of) TV-set dealer/repairer//TV producer.

tel·f. = TELEFON. ~ **g.** = TELGRAF.

telgraf (*el.*) Telegraph; telegram, cable, wire. ~ **çekmek**, send a telegram: ~ **şifresi**, telegraphic code.

telgraf·çı(lık) Telegraph·ist/(-y). ~ **çiçeği**ⁿⁱ, (*bot.*)

tradescantia, wandering Jew. ~ **hane**, telegraph office. ~ **la**, by telegram; telegraphic.

telhane (*min.*) Wire-drawing mill.

telhis Abstract, summary. ~ **etm.**, summarize, abstract. ~ **çi**, (*his.*) official summarizing reports for the Sultan.

telif A reconciling; (*lit.*) composition, compilation. ~ **etm.**, reconcile; (*lit.*) compile, write: ~ **hakkı**, (*pub.*) copyright, author's rights: ~ **ücreti**, (*pub.*) royalty.

telin A cursing, denunciation. ~ **etm.**, curse.

tel·is Coarsely-woven sack. ~ **kadayıf**, (*cul.*) sweet dish (like Shredded Wheat). ~ **kâri**, filigree work.

telkih (*agr.*) Grafting; (*med.*) inoculation, vaccination.

telkin Suggestion; inspiration; (*rel.*) graveside prayers.

tel·kurduⁿᵘ (*zoo.*) Wireworm. ~ **küf**, (*myc.*) sporotrichum. ~ **küflüce**, (*med.*) sporotrichosis.

tellak¹ Hammam attendant; masseur.

tellal Town crier; (*fin.*) auctioneer; broker, middleman; estate agent. ~ **iye**, broker's fee. ~ **lık**, profession/fees of TELLAL.

tel·le Wired; telegraphic. ~ **lemek¹ (-i)**, telegraph. ~ **lemek² (-i)**, adorn with filigree; (*fig.*) praise extravagantly. ~ **lendirmek (-i)**, (*sl.*) enjoy a smoke. ~ **lenmek**, *vp.* ~ **li**, wired; fibrous; adorned with filigree; (*mus.*) stringed; (*fig.*) joyful: ~ **bebek**, gaudily dressed: ~ **cam**, (*arch.*) wire-reinforced glass: ~ **pullu**, decked out. ~ **liturna**, (*orn.*) demoiselle crane.

tellür (*chem.*) Tellurium.

telmih Allusion; hint.

tel·sel/ ~ **si** Wire-like; fibrous. ~ **siz**, *a.* without wires: *n.* (*rad.*) wireless, radio: ~ **anteni**, radio aerial: ~ **telefon**//**telgraf**, radio-telephone// -telegraph. ~ **sizci(lik)**, radio-telegraph·ist/(-y). ~ **solucanı**, (*zoo.*) hair worm.

telti¹kᵍⁱ Deficiency, defect; (*fin.*) small debt. ~ **i temizlemek**, settle a small debt. ~ **li**, with a small debt. ~ **siz**, complete, whole; round (number); fully paid.

telve (*cul.*) Coffee-grounds. ~ **falı**, fortune-telling by one's coffee-cup.

telvis Soiling; contamination; desecration. ~ **etm.**, soil, dirty; desecrate.

telzon (*bio.*) Telson.

tem(a) (*art.*) Subject; (*mus.*) theme. ~ +, *a.* Thematic. ~ **lı**, having a theme.

temadi Continuing uninterruptedly. ~ **etm.**, *vi.* continue.

temaruz Feigning sickness. ~ **etm.**, pretend to be ill; malinger.

temas Contact; relationship; dealing with; communications. ~ **etm. (-e)**, contact; touch on (subject): ~ **etm. (-le)**/ ~ **ta bulunmak (-le)**, be in contact with, get in touch with: ~ **sathi**, (*ind.*) interface: ~ **a geçmek**, get together to talk: ~ **a gelmek**, come together.

temaşa Walking about to see things; (*th.*) spectacle, show. ~ **etm.**, watch, enjoy: ~ **ya çıkmak**, stroll about to see things.

emayül Inclination; bias, tendency. ∼ **etm. (-e)**, have a tendency to/inclination towards.

emayüz Distinction. ∼ **etm.**, be distinguished/privileged: ∼ **etm. (-le)**, distinguish o.s. by.

embel *a.* Lazy. *n.* Lazy person. ∼ **dolma**, (*cul.*) dish of DOLMA-stuffing cooked without the leaves: ∼ **e iş buyur sana akıl öğretsin**, (said of/to) s.o. who tries to avoid work by suggesting stg. else.

embel·hane (*obs.*) Leper-house; (*col.*) place where lazy people gather/neglect their work. ∼ **hayvangiller**, (*zoo.*) true sloths. ∼ **leşmek**, *vi.* become lazy. ∼ **lik**, laziness; apathy, sluggishness.

embih A waking s.o.; injunction, reminder, warning; stimulation. ∼ **etm.**/∼ **lemek (-i)**, warn; enjoin; stimulate. ∼ **li**, warned.

embul (*bot.*) (Leaf of) betel pepper vine.

emci'tᵈⁱ (*rel.*) Glorification of God; (*cul.*) predawn meal during Ramadan. ∼ **pilavı**, (*cul.*) standing dish; (*fig.*) stg. that grows wearisome with repetition.

emdi'tᵈⁱ Prolongation; extension. ∼ **etm.**, prolong; extend; stretch.

emeddüh Boasting.

emeddün Becoming civilized.

eme'kᵍⁱ Stable window.

emel Foundation; base; basis; background. ∼ +, *a.* Fundamental, elementary; basic; master; principal: ∼ **atmak**, (*arch.*) lay a foundation; (*fig.*) start a job: ∼ **cümle/tümce**, (*ling.*) main clause: ∼ **çivisi çakmak/kakmak (-e)**, intend to settle down in a place: ∼ **duruş**, (*sp.*) basic position/stance: ∼ **eğitim**, (*ed.*) basic education: ∼ **kemiği**, (*bio.*) sphenoid bone: ∼ **neden**, (*leg.*) grounds: ∼ **örnek**, prototype: ∼ **taşı**, (*arch.*) foundation//cornerstone: ∼ **tutmak**, become firm/solid; settle down permanently, grow roots: ∼ **den**, radical, thorough: ∼ **inden**, basically.

emel·lenmek *vi.* Be firmly settled/based. ∼ **leşmek**, *vi.* become firmly settled; settle down permanently. ∼ **li**, well-founded; permanent; fundamental; (*chem.*) -based: ∼ **oturmak**, settle down permanently: ∼ **gitti**, he went for good. ∼ **siz**, without foundation; baseless.

emellükᵘ A taking possession.

emenna(h) Or. salute (fingers of the right hand to the lips and then forehead).

emenni Desire; wish. ∼ **etm.**, desire, request.

emerküz Concentration. ∼ **etm.**, concentrate; centralize: ∼ **kabinesi**, (*pol.*) coalition cabinet: ∼ **kampı**, (*pol.*) concentration camp.

emerrü'tᵈᵘ Obduracy. ∼ **etm.**, be obdurate.

emessül Assuming a likeness; (*bio.*) assimilation; (*soc.*) absorption into a foreign community.

emettüᵘ (*fin.*) Profit; advantage.

emevvül'çᶜᵘ Fluctuation, undulation.

emeyyüz Being distinguished; distinction.

emhir (*adm.*) Sealing. ∼ **etm.**, sign with/affix a seal.

emin Making safe/sure; assurance, confidence. ∼ **etm.**, assure; ensure; make secure; reassure, inspire confidence; cater for (wishes). ∼ **at¹**, *pl.*: *s.* security; deposit; guarantee: ∼ **akçesi**, (*fin.*) guarantee fund: ∼ **vermek**, inspire trust; give a guarantee. ∼ **atli**, guaranteed. ∼ **en**, *adv.* guaranteeing.

temiz *a.* Clean; pure; honourable; (*fin.*) clear, net. *adv.* Neatly; in good taste. ∼ **bir . . .**, a sound/thorough . . .: ∼ **çevirmek**, (*sl.*) play poker: ∼ **giyinmek**, dress neatly/respectably: ∼ KAN: ∼ **konuşmak**, talk in an educated/polished manner: ∼ **pak**, very clean: ∼ **para**, (*fin.*) net sum: ∼ **pratika**, (*naut.*) clean bill of health: ∼ **raporu**, (*med.*) certificate of good health: ∼ **tanıtmak**, clear s.o.'s character: ∼ **taş**, flawless jewel: ∼ **yemek**, eat good food in good places: ∼ **e çekmek**, make a fair copy of (writing): ∼ **e çıkarmak**, (*leg.*) clear s.o.: ∼ **e çıkmak**, (*leg.*) be cleared/proved innocent: ∼ **e havale etm.**, (*sl.*) clean up; kill.

temiz·ce *a.* Fairly clean: *adv.* cleanly; nicely. ∼ **kan**, (*bio.*) aerated/arterial blood; (*live.*) thoroughbred. ∼ **lek**, cleaning room. ∼ **leme**, *vn.;* cleaning; clearance: ∼ **işleri**, public cleaning services. ∼ **lemek (-i)**, clean; cleanse; decontaminate; clear away; clear up; rob; (*sl.*) kill. ∼ **lenmek**, *vp.* be cleaned; (*fig.*) be cleared away; (*bio.*) menstruation-cycle terminate. ∼ **letmek (-i)**, *vc.* ∼ **leyici**, *a.* cleansing: *n.* cleaner (person/material); detergent. ∼ **lik**, cleanliness; cleanness; purity; honesty; act of cleaning; (*med.*) purge: ∼ **işleri**, (*adm.*) cleansing department. ∼ **likçi**, cleaner.

temkin Self-possession; dignity; composure. ∼ **li**, dignified; serious; demure. ∼ **siz**, undignified; frivolous.

temlikⁱ Putting in possession (of property). ∼ **etm.**, (*leg.*) assign: ∼ **muamelesi**, conveyancing. ∼ **name**, conveyance, deed of transfer.

temmuz July.

tempo (*mus.*) Tempo; (*fig.*) manner, speed; (*sp.*) rhythm. ∼ **tutmak**, beat time.

temren Arrowhead.

temrin Exercise; practice.

temriye (*myc.*) Lichen; (*med.*) type of skin disease.

temsil (*fin.*) Representation, agency; (*th.*) acting, performance; a symbolizing; (*bio.*) assimilation; comparison. ∼ **etm.**, (*fin.*) represent; (*th.*) present; (*bio.*) assimilate; compare: ∼ **i resim**, (*art.*) likeness. ∼ **ci(lik)**, representa·tive/(-tion), agen·t/(-cy): ∼ **ler Meclisi**, (*pol.*) House of Representatives.

temyiz Separating, distinguishing; discernment; (*psy.*) discrimination; (*leg.*) appeal. ∼ **etm.**, distinguish; (*leg.*) appeal: ∼ **kudreti**, power of judgement/discernment: ∼ **mahkemesi**, supreme court of appeal.

ten (*obs.*) Body; (*bio.*) flesh, skin; complexion. ∼ **boyası**, base-cream: ∼ **fanilası**, (*mod.*) vest: ∼ **rengi**, flesh-coloured.

-ten *n. suf.* [28] = -DEN [MEKTEPTEN].

tenafür Mutual aversion; incompatibility; (*mus.*) cacophony.

tenakus Decrease; diminution.

tenakuz Contradiction, discrepancy.

tenasüh (*psy.*) Metempsychosis.

tenasül (*bio.*) Reproduction, generation. ∼ **aleti**, genitals.

tenasü'pᵇᵘ Proportion, symmetry.

tenazur Symmetricality.

tenbih = TEMBIH.

tencere (*dom.*) Saucepan. ~ **dibi**, (*cul.*) food adhering to saucepan bottom: ~ **dibin kara seninki benden kara**/~ ~**ye dibin kara demiş**, the pot calling the kettle black: ~ **kebabı**, (*cul.*) dish cooked in a stewpot with embers on the lid: ~ **kızartması**, (*cul.*) pot-roasted: ~ **tava herkeste hava**, everyone goes his own way; nobody cares a straw: ~ **yuvarlanmış kapağını bulmuş**, birds of a feather flock together: ~**de pişirip kapağında yemek**, live very economically: ~**si kaynarken maymunu oynarken**, when s.o. is comfortable and happy all around.

tender (*rly.*) Tender.

tendürüst Healthy, robust.

teneffüs Respiration; a 'breather'; recreation: ~ **etm.**, breathe; pause for breath. ~**hane**, recreation room.

teneke *n.* (*min.*) Tin; tinplate; (*ind.*) a tin/can (*esp.* paraffin/petrol can); a tinful. *a.* Made of tin. ~ **çalmak (arkasından)**, boo s.o. publicly: ~ **kaplı**, (*min.*) tin-plated; (*fig.*) brazen faced: ~ **mahallesi**, shanty-town (huts built of old petroleum tins): ~ **peyniri**, (*cul.*) type of sheep's milk cheese: ~**sini eline vermek**, give s.o. the sack. ~**ci(lik)**, (work of) tinsmith. ~**li**, tinned.

teneşir (*rel.*) Ritual washing of a corpse; bench on which it is washed. ~ **horoz/kargası**, s.o. very thin/skinny: ~**e gelesi!**, may he die!: ~**e sürmek**, (bad habit, etc.) last till death. ~**lik**, *a.* (*vulg.*) dying: *n.* place/bench where corpses are washed (in mosque courtyard).

tenevvü[ü] Variation; variety.

tenevvür Enlightenment; illumination.

tenezzüh Excursion, trip.

tenezzül Coming down; condescension. ~ **etm.**, diminish, reduce; condescend: ~ **etmez**, it's beneath him.

tenha *a.* Desolate, deserted (place). ~**laşmak**, *vi.* become deserted/empty. ~**lık**, solitude; deserted/lonely place.

tenis (*sp.*) Tennis. ~**çi**, tennis player.

tenkil (*pol.*) Repression.

tenkis Diminishing.

tenkit[i 1] (*ling.*) Punctuation; vocalization (of Arabic).

tenki[l]**t**[di 2] Criticism; censure. ~ **etm.**, criticize. ~**çi**, critic; critical.

tenkiye (*med.*) Enema.

tennure Mevlevi dervish's skirt.

tenor (*mus.*) Tenor.

ten·perver Fond of comfort. ~**rengi**[ni], flesh-coloured. ~**sel**, of the body, corporeal.

tensikat[ı] Reorganization; arrangement; (*adm.*) reduction of staff.

tensi[l]**p**[bi] Approval. ~ **etm.**, approve: ~**inize bırakıyorum (-i)**, I leave it to your discretion.

tente Awning. ~ **omurgası**, (*naut.*) ridge-pole.

tentene (*mod.*) Lace.

tentür(diyo[l]**t**[du]**)** (*chem.*) Tincture (of iodine).

tenvir Illumination. ~ **etm.**, illuminate; enlighten. ~**at**[ı], illumination; street lighting.

tenya (*zoo.*) Taenia, tapeworm.

tenzih (*rel.*) Absolving; finding no fault.

tenzil Lowering; (*fin.*) reduction. ~ **etm.**, lower; reduce (prices). ~**at**[ı], (*fin.*) reduction: ~ **yapmak**, make reductions. ~**atlı**, reduced: ~ **fiyat**, cut-price: ~ **satış**, bargain sale.

teodolit[i] (*ast.*) Theodolite.

teo·krasi (*adm.*) Theocracy. ~**kratik**, theocratic. ~**log**, (*rel.*) theologist. ~**loji**, theology.

teo·rem (*math.*) Theorem. ~**ri**, theory. ~**rik(man)**, theoretical(ly). ~**risyen**, theoretician.

tepe[1] = TEPMEK.

tepe[2] (*geo.*) Hill; summit, peak; top, tip; (*bio.*) crista; crown (of head); apex; (*orn.*) crest; (*math.*) vertex. ~ **aşağı gitmek**, fall headlong: ~ **noktası**, crown (of road); zenith: ~**den**, in a superior manner; condescendingly: ~**den bakmak (-e)**, look down on, despise: ~**den inme**, sudden, unexpected; from above; (*adm.*) from a higher authority: ~**den tırnağa (kadar)**, from head to foot/top to toe: ~**den tırnağa donatmak**, curse s.o. up and down: ~**m attı**, it made my blood boil: ~**si aşağı gitmek**, (business) go downhill, be ruined: ~**si atmak**, run amok: ~**si üstü**, upside down; headfirst, headlong. ~**sinde bitmek (-in)**, pester, worry: ~**sinde değirmen çevirmek/havan dövmek**, disturb those living below one: ~ **sinden kaynar su dökülmek**, feel great shame/embarrassment: ~**sine binmek**/ **çıkmak (-in)**, presume on s.o.'s kindness: ~**sine dikilmek**, worry, insist: ~**sine varmak**, reach the crest/peak.

tepe·camı[n1] (*arch.*) Skylight. ~**cik**, (*bot.*) stigma; (*geo.*) little hill. ~**damgası**[n1], (*bio.*) fontanelle. ~**göz**, narrow-browed; (*ich.*) stargazer; (*zoo.*) cyclops; (*myth.*) Cyclops. ~**gözler**, (*zoo.*) cyclopids. ~**leme**, *vn.* sound thrashing; killing mound: *adv.* brim-full. ~**lemek (-i)**, thrash mercilessly; (*fig.*) kill, repress, rout. ~**lenmek**, *vp* ~**letmek (-i, -e)**, *vc.* ~**li**, (*orn.*) crested: ~ **ağaçkakan**, pileated woodpecker: ~ **akbaba** condor: ~ **baştankara**, crested tit: ~ **bülbül**, red-whiskered bulbul: ~ **dalgıç**, great crested grebe: ~ **deve kuşu**, Australian cassowary: ~ **guguk**, great spotted cuckoo: ~ **karabatak**, shag: ~ **patka** tufted duck: ~ **pelikan**, Dalmatian pelican: ~ **tarla kuşu/toygar**, crested lark: ~ **tavuk**, hoatzin. ~**lik** (*mod.*) ornamental knob/button; crest; (*geo.*) hilly (country). ~**takla(k)**, on one's head, upside down.

tephir Vaporization; (*med.*) fumigation, disinfection. ~ **etm.**, vaporize; (*med.*) fumigate, disinfect. ~**evi**, fumigation station.

tepi (*psy.*) Reaction.

tep·ilmek *vp.* = TEPMEK. ~**indirmek (-i)**, *vc* ~**inmek**, *vi.* kick and stamp; dance with joy//rage. ~**işmek (-le)**, kick each other; quarrel violently.

tepir (*cul.*) Hair sieve. ~**lemek (-i)**, sieve finely.

tep·ke (*bio.*) Reflex. ~**ken**, (*chem.*) reactant. ~**ki** (*chem., etc.*) reaction; (*phys.*) recoil, thrust. ~**kici** (*pol.*) reactionary. ~**kili**, reactive, reacting; recoiling: ~ **motör/uçak**, (*aer.*) jet engine//aircraft ~**kime**, *vn.;* (*chem.*) reaction. ~**kimek**, *vi.* react recoil. ~**kin**, (*chem.*) reagent; reactive. ~**kir** (*chem., nuc.*) reactor. ~**kisel**, reactive. ~**kisiz** non-reacting.

tep·me *vn.* Kick; (*med.*) relapse: ~ **atmak**, kick

~mek (-i), *vt.* kick, boot; spurn; underestimate: *vi.* kick; (*mil.*) recoil; (*med.*) recur; burst out: **tepe tepe kullanmak**, (*mod.*) wear continuously and roughly: **teptim keçe oldu, sivrilttim külah oldu**, people interpret things to suit themselves.

epre- = DEPRE-.

epsi (*dom.*) Small tray; (*cul.*) baking tin/tray.

er Sweat, perspiration. **~ alıştırmak**, wait till one's sweat has dried: **~ basmak/boşanmak**, sweat from terror, etc.: **~ bezi**, (*bio.*) sweat gland: **~ dökmek**, sweat; (*fig.*) labour hard: **~ kebe**, thick horse-blanket: **~e batmak**, sweat heavily: **~e yatmak**, make o.s. sweat (by drinks/clothes): **~ini soğutmak**, sit and cool off.

er. = TERİM.

erahi (*obs.*) Lethargy; sluggishness.

erakki Advance, progress; increase. **~ etm.**, make progress, advance; increase. **~ perver**, progressive.

eraküm Accumulation. **~ etm.**, accumulate, collect.

erane (*mus.*) Tune; refrain; (*fig.*) boringly repeated story, etc.

erapi (*med.*) Therapy.

eras (*arch.*, *agr.*) Terrace. **~lamak (-i)**, (*agr.*) terrace (hill-side). **~lanmak**, *vp.*

eravi (*rel.*) Special evening prayer during Ramadan.

erazi Balance, pair of scales; tightrope-walker's pole; (*sp.*) balancing. **~ (burcu)**, (*ast.*) Libra. **~lemek (-i)**, weigh (in the hand); balance o.s.

erbiye Bringing up; breeding; education, training; decency, good manners; correction, punishment; (*cul.*) thickened-gravy, sauce; (*live.*) training; reins. **~ etm.**, educate; train; teach manners; discipline, correct; (*cul.*) flavour (with lemon and egg sauce): **~ görmek**, be educated: **~ yapmak**, make a sauce: **~ züğürdü**, uneducated: **~ni takın!**, behave yourself!: **~sini bozmak**, behave badly: **~sini vermek (-in)**, reprimand; teach s.o. his manners.

erbiye·ci Educator; pedagogue; trainer. **~li**, educated, cultured; civil, well-bred; (*cul.*) with a sauce. **~siz**, uneducated; ill-bred, boorish. **~sizlik**, rudeness; lack of education. **~vi**, educational.

erbiyum (*chem.*) Terbium.

ercih Preference, choice; priority. **~ etm.**, prefer, choose. **~an**, preferably. **~li ~ yol**, (*mot.*) 'buses only' lane.

erciibent (*lit.*) Poem where each stanza ends with the same couplet.

ercü·man Interpreter, translator; (*his.*) dragoman: **~ olm.**, explain (s.o's ideas). **~manlık**, work of interpreter: **~ etm.**, interpret. **~me**, translation: **~ etm. (-den, -e)**, translate from/into. **~meci**, translator. **~mehal**[i], (*lit.*) biography, memoirs: **~ yazan**, biographer.

erdöşeği[ni] (*med.*) Childbed.

ere (*bot.*) Dill, false fennel; garden cress. **~bentin**, (*chem.*) turpentine. **~ci**, seller of dill/herbs: **~ye tere satmak**, teach one's grandmother to suck eggs: **~ye tere satma!**, don't try to trick me!

ereddi Degeneration; deterioration. **~ etm.**, deteriorate.

tereddü[dü] Hesitation; indecision. **~ etm.**, hesitate; falter; demur.

tereke (*leg.*) Dead person's estate; heritage.

terekkü[bü] (*chem.*) Being composed/compounded. **~ etm.**, be composed.

terelelli Scatter-brained; frivolous.

terementi (*bot.*, *med.*) Turpentine.

terennüm Singing, warbling. **~ etm.**, sing, hum, warble.

teres (*vulg.*) Cuckold, pimp; scoundrel.

teressü[bü] Sediment, precipitation. **~ etm.**, be precipitated/deposited.

terettü[bü] **~ etm. (-e)**, be incumbent upon.

tereyağı[nı] Fresh butter; (*sl.*) fool. **~ balığı**, (*ich.*) butterfish: **~ gibi**, very soft (pear, etc.): **~ndan kıl çeker gibi**, skilfully and easily.

terfi (*adm.*) Promotion, advancement. **~ etm.**, be promoted.

terfih Ensuring s.o.'s prosperity. **~ etm.**, bring prosperity to.

terfik[i] Providing a companion. **~ etm.**, send as escort/companion.

tergal (*tex.*) French polyester thread, tergal.

terhin ~ etm., pawn, pledge.

terhis (*mil.*) Discharge. **~ etm.**, discharge, demobilize: **~ tezkeresi**, discharge papers.

terilen (*tex.*) Terylene.

terim (Technical) term. **~ler dizgesi**, terminology. **~sel**, terminological.

terk[i] Abandonment; cession. **~ etm.**, abandon, desert; relinquish.

terki Back of saddle. **~sine almak (-i)**, take as pillion rider.

terkib- = TERKİP. **~i**, compound, composite. **~iben**[di], (*lit.*) poem with stanzas linked by a refrain.

terkin Cancellation. **~ etm.**, cancel, erase.

terki[bi] (*chem.*) Composition, compound; (*ling.*) phrase. **~ etm.**, compose, compound; constitute.

Terkos *pr.n.* **~ suyu**, Istanbul municipal water supply.

ter·leme *vn.* Sweating, perspiration; (*min.*) sweating; (*eng.*) bleeding; (*med.*) diaphoresis; (*bot.*) transpiration: **~ ek**, (*eng.*) sweat joint: **~ önleyici**, anti-perspirant. **~lemek**, *vi.* sweat, perspire; be covered in condensation; (*min.*) weep, sweat; (moustache) begin to grow; (*fig.*) be very tired. **~letici**, (*med.*) diaphoretic, sudorific; (*fig.*) very fatiguing. **~letmek (-i)**, cause to sweat; (*fig.*) greatly fatigue. **~li**, sweating, perspiring. **~lik**, (*mod.*) house-slipper; sweat-band. **~likçi(lik)**, (work of) slipper-maker/-seller. **~liksi**, **~ hayvan**, (*zoo.*) paramecium.

termal *a.* Thermal. *n.* Thermal springs.

terme (*bot.*) Type of wild radish.

ter·mi (*phys.*) Thermie. **~mik**, thermic, thermal: **~ santral**, (*el.*) thermal power-station.

terminal Terminal station, terminus.

terminoloji Terminology.

termit[i] (*chem.*) Thermite; (*zoo.*) termite, white ant.

termo·dinamik (*phys.*) Thermodynamics. **~elektrik**, thermoelectricity: **~ çifti**, thermocouple: **~**

olayı, thermoelectric effect. ~**for**, (*med.*) thermophore. ~**kimya**, thermochemistry. ~**metre**, thermometer: ~ **çanağı**, thermometer bulb. ~**nükleer**, (*nuc.*) thermonuclear. ~**plastik**, thermoplastic. ~**s**, thermos flask. ~**sifon**, thermosyphon. ~**stat**, thermostat.

ternöv (*live.*) Newfoundland dog.

terör(cü) (*pol.*) Terror(ist).

ters *n.* Back/reverse (of stg.); wrong/reverse direction; (*bio.*) dung. *a.* Reverse, backward; inverse; wrong; opposite; inverted; back to front, inside out; (*fig.*) contrary, surly, churlish; unfortunate, ill-timed. ~ **açı**, (*math.*) alternate angle: ~ **akım/akıntı**, (*aer.*) turbulence: ~ **alizeler**, (*met.*) antitrades: ~ **bağlantı**, (*el.*) cross-connection: ~ **beşik**, (*sp.*) back-rocking exercise: ~ **damar**, (*carp.*) cross grain: ~ **düşmek (-e)**, be opposed to: ~ **gelmek**, be the wrong way round; be in the opposite direction: ~ **gitmek**, go wrong, turn out badly: ~ **kaş**, (*pub.*) sign of the 'soft g' (ğ): ~ **orantılı**, (*math.*) inversely proportional: ~ **pers**, all wrong; disconcerting; disappointed: ~ **pers olm.**, be completely upset: ~ **somun**, (*eng.*) locknut: ~ **tarafından kalkmış**, 'got out of bed on the wrong side', bad-tempered: ~ ~ **bakmak**, look sourly: ~ **vuruş**, (*sp.*) backstroke; backhand: ~ **yönelme**, reversibility: ~YÜZ: ~ **yüzü geri dönmek**, return empty-handed/disappointed: ~**i dönmek**, lose one's bearings: ~**inden okumak**, misunderstand: ~**ine**, backwards; on the contrary: ~**ine çevirmek** = TERSYÜZ: ~**ine olm.**, turn out wrongly: ~**ine yazmak**, write mirror-fashion.

tersane (*naut.*) Dockyard; naval arsenal. ~**li**, (*obs.*) naval officer/rating.

tersevirme (*phil.*) Contraposition.

tersi (*ich.*) Type of sardine.

tersim ~ **etm.**, picture; draw. ~**i**, (*math.*) descriptive.

tersi·ne On the contrary: ~ **kerteleme**, (*lit.*) bathos. ~**nir(lik)**, (*phys., etc.*) reversi·ble/(-bility). ~**nleme**, irony. ~**nmek**, go back, return; (*fig.*) be awkward. ~**nmez(lik)**, irreversi·ble/(-bility).

terslemek (-i) Scold; snub: **(-e)**, foul with dung.

ters·lik Contrariness; turning out wrong; reversal; inversion. ~ **yön**, (*ast.*) apparent direction of rotation. ~**yüz**, ~ **etm.**, (*mod.*) turn inside out. ~**yüzleme**, transposition.

tertemiz Absolutely/spotlessly clean.

tertibat[1] *pl.* Arrangements; dispositions; gear, apparatus, appliances.

terti·p[bi] Arrangement; order; series; disposition; plan, project; (*pub.*) type-setting, format; (*med.*) prescription; (*cul.*) recipe. ~ **etm.**, arrange, plan; prepare; (*pub.*) compose; (*med.*) prescribe: ~ **gönyesi**, (*pub.*) composing-stick: ~ **hatası**, printer's error.

tertip·çi Organizer, planner. ~**lemek (-i)**, organize, plan, arrange. ~**lenmek**, *vp.* ~**leyici**, organizer. ~**li**, planned, organized. ~**siz**, disorganized; ill-prepared. ~**sizlik**, lack of organization/planning/system.

terütaze Very fresh.

tervi·ç[ci] Encouragement; support. ~ **etm.**, encourage (ideas).

terzi Tailor. ~ **kendi söktüğünü dikemez**, the physician can not heal himself: ~ **kuşları**, (*orn.*) tailorbirds: ~ **sabunu**, French chalk. ~**hane**, tailor's workshop; clothing factory. ~**lik**, tailoring.

terzil ~ **etm.**, humiliate publicly; insult; ill-treat.

tesadüf Chance meeting/event; contingency; coincidence. ~ **etm. (-e)**, meet/happen by chance; coincide. ~**en**, by chance/coincidence. ~**i**, chance, fortuitous.

tesahu·p[bu] Becoming owner//patron/protector of. ~ **etm.**, take possession of; protect.

tesalü·p[bü] (*live.*) Cross-breeding. ~ **ettirmek**, crossbreed.

tesanü·t[dü] Mutual support; cooperation.

tesb- = TESP-.

tescil (*leg.*) Registration. ~ **etm.**, register.

tesdis Dividing by six; (*lit.*) making six-couplet stanzas.

teselli Consolation. ~ **bulmak**, console o.s.: ~ **etm./vermek (-e)**, comfort/console s.o.

tesellüm ~ **etm.**, take delivery of.

teselsül Continuous succession; continuity. ~ **etm.**, follow uninterruptedly.

tesemmüm Being poisoned.

tesettür Being veiled/hidden. ~ **etm.**, veil/conceal o.s.

teseyyü·p[bü] Negligence, slackness.

teshil Making easy. ~ **etm.**, facilitate.

teshin Heating. ~ **etm.**, heat.

teshir Fascination; enchantment. ~ **etm.**, enchant, fascinate.

tesir Effect; impression; influence. ~ **etm. (-e)**, affect, impress, influence: ~ **olunmak**, be influenced. ~**li**, effective; impressive; moving. ~**siz**, ineffective; without influence.

tesis Foundation, establishment; (*ind.*) plant. ~ **etm.**, found, establish; instal. ~**at**[1], (*ind.*) installation; plant. ~**atçı(lık)**, (work of) installer, fitter.

tesi·t[di] Celebration. ~ **etm.**, celebrate; commemorate.

teskere (*obs.*) Litter; stretcher; hand-barrow.

teskin ~ **etm.**, calm, comfort; alleviate, appease.

teslihat[1] (*mil.*) Armaments.

teslim Handing over, delivery; consignment; (*fin.*) payment; (*mil.*) surrender, submission; admission. ~ **almak**, take delivery of: ~ **etm.**, hand over, deliver; consign; pay over; surrender stg., submit; admit, accept: ~ **olm.**, capitulate; surrender o.s., yield: ~ **taşı**, (*rel.*) Bektashi 'stone of surrender': ~ **ve tesellüm**, a handing over and receipt: ~**de ödeme**, cash on delivery. ~**at**[1], instalments (of money, etc.). ~**iyet**[i], submission, surrender: ~ **göstermek**, submit to s.o.'s wishes.

teslis (*rel.*) Belief in the Trinity.

tesmiye Naming. ~ **etm.**, name.

tespih (*rel.*) Rosary, prayer-beads. ~ **çekmek**, tell one's rosary: ~ **çiçeği**, (*bot.*) canna: ~ **tanesi**, bead.

tespih·ağacı[nı] (*bot.*) Persian lilac/bead-tree//Chinaberry. ~**ağacıgiller**, (*bot.*) Meliaceae, mahogany family. ~**böceği**[ni], (*ent.*) pill-bug. ~**böcekleri**, (*ent.*) woodlice. ~**li**, having a rosary; (*arch.*, *carp.*) beading.

espi¹tᵈⁱ Establishing, fixing; stabilization. ~ **çubuğu**, (*carp.*) batten: ~ **davası**, (*leg.*) test-case: ~ **etm.**, establish, fix; stabilize.

esri Hastening; acceleration. ~ **etm.**, accelerate.

estⁱ (*ed.*, *med.*, *etc.*) Test.

estere (*carp.*) Saw. ~ **ağzı**, saw blade. ~**balığı**ⁿⁱ, (*ich.*) sawfish. ~**gagalı büyük**//**küçük ördek**, (*orn.*) common merganser//smew. ~**li**, saw-toothed, serrated.

esti Jug, pitcher. ~ **gibi**, large/pendulous (breast): ~ **kebabı**, (*cul.*) type of stewed meat: ~ **kırılsa da kulpu elde kalır**, the rich can cope with losses: ~**yi kıran da bir suyu getiren de**, the good and the wicked both go unrewarded. ~**ci(lik)**, (work of) jug-maker/-seller.

es·tis (*bio.*) Testis, testicle. ~**tosteron**, testosterone.

esviye Making even/level; grading; (*fin.*) payment, settlement; (*mil.*) travel warrant. ~ **aleti**, (*arch.*) level: ~ **atölyesi**, (*eng.*) fitting shop: ~ **eğrisi**, (*geo.*) contour line: ~ **etm.**, equalize; level; pay, settle; (*carp.*) smooth, plane: ~ **haritası**, (*geo.*) contour-map: ~ **hudut/sınırı**, (*geo.*) contour line. ~**ci**, fitter; leveller. ~**cilik**, fitting; levelling. ~**ruhu**ⁿᵘ, (*carp.*) spirit-level.

eş *a./n. suf.* [64] = -DAŞ [KÖKTEŞ].

eş·bih Comparison: ~**te hata olmaz**, only for the sake of a comparison; don't let it be misunderstood. ~**ci**ⁱ, encouragement: ~ **etm.**, encourage.

eşdi¹tᵈⁱ Intensification; (*ling.*) doubling a consonant.

eşebbüs Enterprise; effort; initiative; adventure. ~ **etm.**, set to work at; undertake; start stg.: ~**e geçmek**, go into business: ~**ü ele almak**, start to manage stg.

eşehhü¹tᵈᵘ (*rel.*) Prayer of praise to God. ~ **miktarı**, short moment.

eşekkül Formation; organization, institution, association. ~ **etm.**, be formed/constituted.

eşekkür (Giving) thanks. ~ **etm.**, thank: ~ **ederim!**, thank you!

eşerrüf Being honoured. ~ **etm.**, be honoured.

eşevvüş Confusion.

eşhir Making public; exhibition; (*adm.*) making a public example of; pillorying. ~ **cezası**, (*leg.*) pillory: ~ **etm.**, make public; expose to view, exhibit; pillory.

eşhis Recognition; identification; (*med.*) diagnosis. ~ **etm.**, recognize; identify; diagnose: ~ **uzmanı**, diagnostician: ~ **ve intak**, (*lit.*) personification.

eşkil Formation; organization. ~ **etm.**, form; organize; constitute. ~**at**ⁱ, *pl./s.* organization(s). ~**atçı(lık)**, organiz·er/(-ing). ~**atla(ndır)mak (-i)**, organize. ~**atlanmak**, *vp.* be organized. ~**atlı**, organized.

eşmil Extension; generalization. ~ **etm.**, extend to, include.

eşne Thirsty, parched; (*fig.*) longing for. ~ **olm.**, long for.

eşriⁱ Legislation.

eşrif Honouring. ~ **buyurmak**, do the honour of visiting: ~ **etm.**, honour (by one's presence). ~**at**ⁱ,

ceremonial; (*adm.*) etiquette, protocol. ~**atçı(lık)**, (rank/work of) director of protocol/master of ceremonies. ~**atlı**, ceremonial.

teşrih (*med.*) Dissection; anatomy; (*col.*) skeleton. ~ **etm.**, dissect. ~**hane**, dissecting room/laboratory.

teşrii Legislative. ~ **kuvvet**, legislative power: ~ **masuniyet**, (*leg.*) immunity of legislators.

teşrikⁱ (*fin.*) Making s.o. a partner. ~**i mesai**, cooperation.

teşrin (*obs.*) Tenth and eleventh months. ~**ievvel**, October. ~**isani**, November.

teştⁱ (*dial.*) Laundry bucket.

teşvikⁱ Encouragement; (*pol.*) incitement. ~ **etm.**, encourage; (*pol.*) incite. ~**kâr**, encouraging.

teşviş Confusion; disorder; complication.

teşyiⁱ Seeing s.o. off, saying goodbye.

tetabukᵘ Conformity; accord; (*ling.*) agreement.

tetanos (*med.*) Tetanus.

tetari (*zoo.*) Tadpole.

tetebbuᵘ Study; investigation; research. ~ **etm.**, study; investigate.

teti¹kᵍⁱ ¹ *n.* (*mil.*) Trigger.

teti¹kᵍⁱ ² *a.* Vigilant; agile, quick. ~ **durmak**, be ready and prepared: ~**ini bozmamak**, keep a cool head: ~**te beklemek/bulunmak/durmak/olm.**, be vigilant/on the *qui vive*. ~**dur**, alarm. ~**lik**, alertness, vigilance; agility.

tetir (*bot.*) Walnut's green bark/leaf; fruit stain.

tetkikⁱ Close examination, scrutiny. ~ **etm.**, investigate/examine thoroughly; go into a matter.

tet·re/ ~ **ri** (*bot.*) Sumach.

tevabiⁱ *pl.* = TABI; followers; dependants.

tevafukᵘ Agreement, conformity.

tevahhuş ~ **etm.**, be frightened/wild/timid.

tevakki ~ **etm.**, take care of o.s., be on one's guard.

tevakkuf ~ **etm.**, stop, stay; depend on. ~ **mahalli**, tram-/bus-stop.

tevali Uninterrupted succession. ~ **etm.**, follow uninterruptedly.

tevarüs ~ **etm.**, inherit.

tevarü¹tᵈᵘ Having the same thoughts; (*lit.*) identical verse/phrase written by coincidence by two authors.

tevatür Hearsay, general report.

tevazuᵘ Humility, modesty. ~ **göstermek**, condescend.

tevazün Equilibrium, balance.

tevbih Rebuke, reprimand.

tevcih ~ **etm. (-i)**, turn/direct towards; confer (office/rank); appoint.

tevdiⁱ ~ **etm.**, entrust; (*fin.*) deposit; tender. ~**at**ⁱ, deposits: ~ **ta bulunmak**, deposit.

teveccüh ~ **etm.**, *vi.* turn towards: ~ **göstermek**, show favour: ~**ünüz efendim!**, it's kind of you to say so!

tevehhüm Imagining, fancying.

teve¹kᵍⁱ (*bot.*) Tendril (of vine, etc.); vine-stock.

tevekkel Leaving to chance, resigned, fatalistic. ~**i**, by chance: + *neg.* it was not without reason/for nothing that . . . .

tevekkül Putting one's trust in God, resignation.

tevellü¹tᵈü Birth. ~ **etm.**, be born. ~**lü (-de)**, born in (year).

teverrüm (*med.*) Tuberculosis. ~ **etm.**, become consumptive.

tevessüü Extension, expansion. ~ **etm.**, expand.

tevessül ~ **etm.**, begin, undertake, proceed with.

tevettür Strain, stress; (*el.*) tension, voltage.

tevfikan (-e) In accordance/conformity with.

tevhi¹tᵈⁱ Unification; consolidation; (*rel.*) monotheism; (*lit.*) song praising God. ~ **etm.**, unite: ~ **ehli**, (*rel.*) monotheists.

tevki (*his.*) The Sultan's signature (TUĞRA); imperial rescript. ~**ci**, (*his.*) official who drew the TUĞRA.

tevkif Arrest, detention. ~ **ateşi**, (*mil.*) artillery barrage: ~ **etm.**, detain, arrest; (*fin.*) deduct. ~**at**, (*fin.*) deduction. ~**hane**, prison.

tevkil ~ **etm.**, appoint as representative.

tevli¹tᵈⁱ Giving birth; acting as midwife.

tevliyetⁱ Appointment of a VAKIF administrator.

tevrat¹ (*rel.*) The Pentateuch.

tevris (*leg.*) ~ **etm.**, appoint as heir.

tevriye (*lit.*) Use of ambiguous words.

tevsi Enlargement. ~ **etm.**, enlarge, extend.

tevsikⁱ ~ **etm.**, confirm, certify.

tevzi Distribution; delivery (letters, etc.). ~ **etm.**, distribute; deliver.

tevzin ~ **etm.**, counter-balance.

teyakkuz Being awake; vigilance.

teyel (*tex.*) Basting, tacking. ~ **dikişi**, backstitch. ~**lemek (-i)**, baste, tack. ~**lenmek**, *vp.* ~**li**, tacked.

teyemmüm (*rel.*) Ritual ablutions with sand, etc. (lacking water).

teyi¹tᵈⁱ Reinforcement; confirmation. ~ **etm.**, strengthen; confirm.

tey¹pᵇⁱ (*el.*) Tape-recorder, cassette-player. ~**e almak**, record (on tape).

teyze (*soc.*) Maternal aunt. ~**zade**, cousin.

tez¹ *a.* Quick. *adv.* Quickly, promptly. ~ **beri**, at once; easily: ~ **canlı**, impatient: ~ **elden**, without delay, in haste: ~ **mizaçlı**, hasty, passionate.

tez² *n.* (*ed.*) Thesis; question, argument.

tezahür Manifestation; appearance. ~**at**¹, (*pol.*) demonstration; (*med.*) symptoms.

teza¹tᵈⁱ Contrast, antithesis; contradiction; incompatibility. ~**a düşmek**, contradict.

tezayü¹tᵈü Increasing; growth. ~ **etm.**, *vi.* increase, multiply.

tez·dişilik (*bot.*) Protandry. ~**duyarca**, (*med.*) anaphylaxia. ~**erlik**, (*bot.*) protogyny.

teze¹kᵍⁱ Dried dung (as fuel).

tezekkür Discussion; consultation.

tezellül Abasement.

tezelzül Shock; quaking.

tezene (*mus.*) Plectrum.

tezevvü¹çᶜü Taking a wife. ~ **etm.**, *vi.* marry.

tezgâh (*carp.*) Work-bench; (*tex.*) loom; frame; (*fin.*) shop-counter; (*naut.*) ship-building yard; workshop; machine-tool. ~ **başında yapmak**, stand drinking at the bar: ~**ı kurmak**, set up a business/workshop, etc.

tezgâh·lamak (-i) Equip, set up a business, etc.; prepare a project to make it acceptable/'sellable';

make ready. ~**lanmak**, *vp.* ~**tar**, bar/counter server; shop-assistant. ~ **tarlık**, being a server/assistant: ~ **etm.**, (*fig.*) have a ready/persuasive tongue.

tezgen (*chem.*) Catalyst. ~**lemek (-i)**, catalyse ~**leştirme**, catalysis. ~**li**/~**sel**, catalytic.

tezhi¹pᵇⁱ (*art.*) Gilding, inlaying with gold, illumi nating.

tezkere Note; memorandum; official certificate licence; (*mil.*) discharge papers. ~ **almak**, (*mil.*) ge one's discharge papers: ~**sini eline vermek**, give s.o. the sack. ~**ci**, (*mil.*) discharged soldier, re servist; (*obs.*) memorandum writer.

tezkiye Purification; praise. ~**si bozuk**, with a bad reputation: ~**sini düzeltmek**, reform o.s.

tez·leşmek *vi.* Make haste; be impatient. ~**leştirmek (-i)**, *vt.* hasten; (*chem.*) catalyse. ~**lik**, speed; haste impatience: ~ **eylemi**, (*ling.*) verb of haste, = -İVERMEK.

tezlil Degradation, humiliation.

tezviç ~ **etm.**, join in matrimony.

tezvir Falsehood; malicious instigation.

tezyif Derision, mockery. ~ **etm.**, deride; hold in contempt.

tezyin (*art.*) Adorning; decoration. ~ **etm.**, adorn decorate, embellish. ~**at**¹, decoration(s). ~**i** decorative.

tezyi¹tᵈⁱ Increase. ~ **etm.**, *vt.* multiply, increase.

TF = TIP FAKÜLTESİ.

TGS = TÜRKİYE GAZETECİLERİ SENDİKASI. ~**S** = TÜRKİYE GAZETE SAHİPLERİ SENDİKASI. ~**YO** = TATBİKİ GÜZEL SANATLAR YÜKSEK OKULU.

Tğm. = (*mil.*) TEĞMEN.

Th. = (*ch.s.*) TORYUM.

TH·A = TÜRK HABERLER AJANSI. ~**K** = TÜRK HAVA KURUMU. ~**KP** = TÜRKİYE HALK KURTU LUŞ PARTİSİ. ~**Y** = TÜRK HAVA YOLLARI.

-tı¹ *v. suf.* [99, 127] = -Dİ² [YAPTI]; -İDİ² [SICAKTI].

-tı² *n. suf.* [222] = -Tİ² [ÇALKANTI].

tıb- = TIP. ~**bi**, medical. ~**biye**, (*ed.*) medica school/faculty. ~**biyeli**, medical student.

tıf¹ılˡⁱ Infant, child; young animal.

tıgala (*bot.*) Gum euphorbia.

tığ (*tex.*) Crochet-needle/-hook; knitting needle awl; (*carp.*) plane-iron. ~ **gibi**, slender but strong wiry: ~ **iş/örgüsü**, crochet work: ~ **kalem**, (*min.*) graving tool.

tık ~ ~, (*ech.*) ticking.

tıka ~ **basa**, crammed full: ~ **basa doldurmak** cram full: ~ **basa doymak**, eat one's fill. ~ ¹**çı** plug; stopper; gag; (*med.*) embolism. ~**çlamak (-i)** stop up; plug. ~**lı**, stopped up; plugged. ~**ma**, *vn* ~**mak (-i, -e, -le)**, block/stop up; plug; gag; (*med.* occlude. ~**nık**, stopped up; choked. ~**nıklık** being stopped up; (*med.*) choking, suffocation (*mil.*) interruption of communications. ~**nmak** *vp.* be stopped up; (*cul.*) lose one's appetite; (*med.* choke, be suffocated; engorge. ~**tmak (-i, -e)**, *vc.*

tık·ılmak *vp.* = TIKMAK: *vi.* stuff o.s. ~ **ım**, rea mouthful. ~**ınmak**, *vi.* (*vulg.*) stuff o.s.; eat in haste; gulp one's food.

tıkır (*ech.*) Clinking, rattling, tapping; (*sl.*) money 'chink'. ~ ~, with a clinking/rattling noise: ~ ~,

şlemek, (clock, etc.) work perfectly, go like clock-work: ~ı **yolunda,** doing well, prospering: ~ı **'olunda gitmek/olm.,** be well off: ~ını **yoluna ;oymak,** arrange one's affairs satisfactorily. **kır·damak** vi. (ech.) Clink, rattle. ~**datmak (-i),** *)c.;* (cul.) bring to the boil. ~**tı,** (ech.) clinking, 'attling.

kış Cram full. ~**lık,** congestion, crowding. ~**mak -le),** vi. be crammed/squeezed together. ~**tırmak -i, -e),** cram into a small space; gulp (food). **k·ız** a. Hard; compact; tightly packed (together): *ı.* (min.) briquette. ~**ızlık,** tightness; hardness. ~**lım,** ~ ~, brim-full; filled to overflowing. ~**mak -i, -e),** thrust/squeeze/cram into. ~**naz(lık),** ›lump(ness); stout(ness). ~**nefes,** (col.) short of ›reath; asthmatic. ~**sırık,** suppressed sneeze. ~**sırıklı,** (fig.) ill at ease. ~**sırmak,** vi. sneeze with he mouth shut.

lsım Talisman; charm, amulet; spell. ~ **bozmak,** ›reak the spell: ~ı **bozuldu,** the spell is broken; his nfluence has waned. ~**lı,** having a charm/spell; ›pell-binding.

mar (med.) Attention to sick man/beast; dressing vounds; (live.) grooming; (agr.) pruning; (his.) eudal fief. ~ **etm.,** (med.) dress (wound); (live.) ;room, curry: ~ **vermek,** (his.) enfeoff. **mar·cı** (his.) Fief-holder. ~**hane,** lunatic asylum: ~ **kaçkını,** escaped lunatic; (fig.) s.o. behaving nadly. ~**hanelik,** who ought to be put in an ısylum.

naz (agr.) Stack of hay/corn. ~ **gibi,** a whole ıeap of . . . .

ngadak (ech.) Falling with a clang. **ngır** a. (sl.) Destitute, stony-broke; empty. n. Money. ~ **elek** ~ **tas,** bare and empty: ~ **mıngır/** ~ ~, (ech.) clashing, clanging; (sl.) cash down: ~ı **yolunda,** with a fair profit. **ngır·dama** vn. ~**damak,** vi. tinkle, clink, clang; *sl.)* die. ~**datmak (-i),** vc. ~**tı,** clinking, clanking; ıoisy conviviality. **n·ı** (phys., mus.) Timbre. ~**ım,** (mus.) tonality. ~**lamak,** vi. tinkle, ring; etc. ~**mak,** vi. make a ›ound; reveal a secret. ~**mamak,** vi. not utter a ›ound; pretend not to notice. ~**maz,** who takes no ıotice: ~ **melaike,** (iron.) quiet, aloof; non-:ommittal. ~**net*,** (mus.) tone, timbre.

*pᵇᵇ¹ ¹ The science of medicine; therapeutics. ~ +, a. Medical; medicinal: ~ **gereçleri,** materia nedica: ~ **sülüğü,** (zoo.) medicinal leech: ~ **ve 5ağlık Bilimleri,** Science of Medicine and Health. **p²** ~ ~, (ech.) tap-tap; pit-a-pat. **p.** = TIBBİ **pa** = TAPA.

patıp Exactly; absolutely. ~ **yetişmek,** arrive :xactly on time: ~ **uygun (-e),** entirely in accor-dance with.

pır ~ ~, (ech.) drip-drip; pat-pat. ~ **damak,** vi. valk quietly; (drops) drip; (heart) go pit-a-pat. ~**datmak (-i),** vc. ~**tı,** dripping; pattering. **pış** ~ ~, (ech.) of a child's short steps: ~ ~ ;itmek/yürümek, walk with short steps; (fig.) go villy-nilly.

pkı [77] Exactly like; just like; in just the same way.

~ ~**sına,** being exactly the same: ~ **sı,** exactly like it; the very image of . . . . ~ **basım,** (pub.) facsimile, re-production. ~ **çekim,** photocopy. ~ **lık,** similarity. **tır** ~ ~ **titremek,** tremble like an aspen leaf. **-tır** v. suf. [96] = -DİR; OLMAK [BALIKTIR]. **-tır-** v. suf. [144] = -DİR- [ALIŞTIRMAK]. **TIR** = (International Road Transport). **tırabzan** (arch.) Hand-rail; banister. ~ **babası,** (knob of) newel post; (fig.) father with no influence over his children: ~ **parmaklığı,** balustrade. **tırak** (ech.) Crack, snap. **tıraş** Shaving; hair to be shaved; (sl.) boring talk, bragging; (lit.) padding. ~ **bıçağı,** razor blade: ~ **edilmiş elmas,** (min.) cut diamond: ~ **etm.,** shave; (sl.) bore; tell lies, take s.o. in: ~ **makinesi,** safety-razor; electric shaver: ~ **olm.,** shave o.s.; get a shave: ~ **sabunu,** shaving cream: ~**a tutmak,** (sl.) detain s.o. with idle talk; buttonhole s.o.: ~ı **gelmek/uzamak,** need a shave. **tıraş·çı** (sl.) Boring talker; braggart; swindler. ~**lamak (-i),** shave; pare; sharpen (pencil); (sl.) bore; try to swindle. ~**lı,** needing a shave, un-shaven; or shaved, clean-shaven; sharpened. ~ **sız,** unshaven; (arch.) undressed (stone). **tırhallı** ~ **hep bir hallı,** all in the same boat; all in confusion. **tırık** (ech.) Slam. ~ **tırak,** (ech.) rattling/slamming (of dice and backgammon pieces). ~**lamak,** (sl.) steal. **tırıl** Naked; thinly clad; (sl.) stony-broke, penniless. ~ ~, shivering. ~**lamak,** vi. shiver with cold; (sl.) be broke. ~**lık,** pennilessness. **tırıs** (live.) Trot. ~ **gitmek,** trot: ~**a kalkmak,** begin to trot. **tırkaz** Door-bolt/-bar. ~**lamak (-i),** bolt/bar (door); (sl.) run away! **tır·malamak (-i)** Scratch, claw; worry, annoy; offend (the senses). ~**malanmak,** vp. ~**mananlar,** (orn.) small climbing birds. ~**manış,** climb. ~**manma,** vn.; (sp.) climbing. ~**manmak (-e),** cling to (with claws, etc.); climb (tree, etc.). ~**maşık:** ~ **balık,** (ich.) climbing fish: ~ **kuşlar** (orn.) tree-creepers. ~**mık,** scratch; (agr.) rake, harrow. ~**mıklamak (-i),** scratch; (agr.) rake, harrow. ~**mıklanmak,** vp. **tırna*k**ᵍ¹ (bio.) Finger-nail; toe-nail; claw; hoof; (mil.) cartridge-ejector; (eng.) catch; dowel; (naut.) anchor fluke. ~ **çekici,** (carp.) claw-hammer: ~ **göstermek,** become angry: ~ **imişaretleri,** (ling.) inverted commas, quotation marks, quotes: ~ **sürüştürmek,** incite to quarrel: ~ **takmak (-e),** have one's knife into s.o.: ~ **yeri,** nail-slot (on knife-blade): ~**ına benzemez/** ~ **ının kiri bile olamaz (-in),** he's not fit to lick s.o.'s boots: ~**ını sökmek,** torture s.o.; (fig.) draw s.o.'s claws. **tırnak·çı** (sl.) Pickpocket. ~**lamak (-i),** scratch, claw. ~**lanmak,** vp. ~**lı,** having nails/claws; (eng.) spiked: ~ **kavrama,** dog-clutch. ~**lık,** nail-slot; notch (on gun-barrel). ~**sı,** nail-/claw-like: ~ **kemiği,** (bio.) lachrymal/nasal bone. ~**sız,** (sl.) opportunist. **tırpan** (agr.) Scythe; (med.) trepan. ~ **atmak (-e),** exterminate: ~**dan geçirmek,** (fig.) mow down.

tırpana (*ich.*) (Flapper) skate.

tırpan·cı (*agr.*) Mower, scythe-user. ~ **kurdu**, (*zoo.*) cutworm. ~ **lamak (-i)**, mow; (*fig.*) mow down. ~ **lanmak**, *vp.*

tırtı'kᵏᵍ¹ Unevenness; raw spot. ~ ~, uneven, jagged; (*met.*) fleecy (cloud).

tırtık·çı (*sl.*) Pickpocket; rogue. ~ **lamak (-i)**, pull to pieces; pluck; (*sl.*) rob. ~ **lı**, rough, uneven, jagged.

tırtıl (*ent.*) Caterpillar; knurl; (coin) milling; (stamp) perforation; (tank/tractor) track; crawler; (*sl.*) parasite. ~ **avcısı**, (*ent.*) caterpillar hunter: ~ **ipliği**, (*tex.*) silk thread; ~ **kesmek**, mill; perforate.

tırtıl·lanmak *vi.* (*ent.*) (Tree) swarm with caterpillars. ~ **lı**, having a milled/perforated edge: ~ **bıçak**, (*cul.*) vegetable knife: ~ **tekerlek**//**traktör**, (*mot.*) caterpillar wheel//tractor. ~ **sı**, (*bot.*) catkin-producing (trees). ~ **yiyen**, (*orn.*) cuckoo-shrike.

tırtır (*ent.*) Ichneumon fly; (*chem.*) tartar.

tıs (*ech.*) Goose's hiss. *int.* Hush! ~ **dememek**, make no sound; raise no objection: ~ **yok**, not a sound. ~ **lamak**, *vi.* (goose) hiss; (cat) spit.

tıynetⁱ Temperament; disposition. ~ **siz**, of base character.

ti ~ **işareti**, (*mil.*) bugle-call.

Ti. = (*ch.s.*) TİTAN(YUM); TİYATRO.

-ti¹/**-tı**/**-tu**/**-tü** *v. suf.* [99] = -iDi² [GELİŞTİ].

-ti²/**-tı**/**-tu**/**-tü** *n. suf.* [222] *Forming nouns of action or result* [BEKLENTİ; SIZINTI].

TİB = TÜRKİYE İŞ BANKASI.

Tibet (*geo.*) Tibet. ~ +, *a.* Tibetan: ~ **atı**, (*zoo.*) kiang: ~ **ayısı**, (*zoo.*) Asiatic black bear: ~ **sığırı**, (*zoo.*) yak. ~ **çe**, (*ling.*) Tibetan. ~ **li**, (*ethn.*) Tibetan.

tibya (*bio.*) Tibia.

tic. = TİCARET; TİCARİ.

ticaretⁱ (*fin.*) Trade; commerce; profit. ~ **açığı**, trade gap: ~ **ataşesi**, (*adm.*) commercial attaché: ~ **Bakan(lığ)ı**, (*adm.*) Minis·ter/(-try) for Trade/Commerce: ~ **bankası**, merchant bank: ~ **borsası**, commodities market: ~ **eşyası**, commodity: ~ **etm.**, trade, engage in commerce; make a profit: ~ **filosu**, (*naut.*) mercantile marine, merchant navy: ~ **hukuk/kanunu**, (*leg.*) commercial law: ~ **işletmesi**, business, commercial operation: ~ **limanı**, commercial port: ~ **mahkemesi**, (*leg.*) commercial court: ~ **merkezi**, *entrepôt*: ~ **muvazenesi**, balance of trade: ~ **okulu**, (*ed.*) commercial school: ~ **unvanı**, trading style: ~ (**ve sanayi**) **odası**, chamber of commerce (and industry): ~ **i bırakmak**, show a profit.

tica·retgâh Centre of commerce; business quarter. ~ **rethane**, business house; firm; offices. ~ **retli**, profitable. ~ **ri**, commercial; trading: ~ **anlaşma**, bargain: ~ **meta**, merchandise: ~ **yük**, payload. ~ **rileştirmek (-i)**, commercialize.

tifdruk (*pub.*) Photogravure printing.

ti·fo (*med.*) Typhoid fever. ~ **füs**, (*med.*) typhus.

tifti'kᵏᵍⁱ (*tex.*) Angora wool, mohair. ~ **gibi**, very soft: ~ **keçisi**, Angora goat: ~ ~ **etm.**, unravel, pull to threads: ~ ~ **olm.**/ ~ **lenmek**, *vi.* become unravelled/frayed.

tikⁱ 1 (*bio.*) Tic, twitching; mannerism.

tikⁱ 2 (*carp.*) Teak(wood). ~ **ağacı**ⁿⁱ, (*bot.*) teak tree.

tike (*cul.*) Small piece, crumb; mouthful. ~ ~ patched.

tikel (*phil.*) Partial, particular; existential ~ **-evetleme**, disjunction, alternation. ~ **lik**, particularity.

TİKKO = TÜRKİYE İŞÇİ KÖYLÜ KURTULU ORDUSU.

tiksin·ç Loathed, abhorred. ~ **çlik**, loathesome ness. ~ **dirici**, loathsome, abhorrent. ~ **dirmek (-i -den)**, disgust; sicken. ~ **ilmek (-den)**, *imp. v.* one b₍ disgusted with. ~ **me**, *vn.*; disgust, distaste. ~ **me** (**-den**), be disgusted with; loathe, abhor. ~ **ti** disgust; loathing.

tiksotropi (*phys.*) Thixotropy.

tik tak (*ech.*) Tick-tock.

tilavetⁱ (*rel.*) Reading/chanting (the Koran).

tilki (*zoo.*) Fox; (*fig.*) cunning fellow, smart Aleck ~ **ini**, fox's earth: ~ **tırnağı**, (*bot.*) early purpl₍ orchid (used for making SALEP): ~ ~ **liğin** **anlatıncaya kadar post elden gider**, one can have ₍ lot of trouble explaining the truth: ~ **nin dönü dolaşıp geleceği yer kürkçü dükkânıdır**, you/he wil end up there anyhow; you/he can't help comin₍ back here/to the same job.

tilki·kuyruğuⁿᵘ (*bot.*) Canadian fleabane; typ of long-bunched grape; (*sp.*) a wrestling hold ~ **leşmek**, *vi.* grow cunning/crafty. ~ **lik**, cunning craftiness.

tilmiz (*rel.*) Disciple, pupil.

tim (*adm.*, *sp.*) Team.

timalyakuşugiller (*orn.*) Babblers and wren-tits.

timbalⁱ (*mus.*) Kettle-drum.

timsah (*zoo.*) Crocodile. ~ **bekçisi**, (*orn.*) Egyptia₍ plover.

timsalⁱ Image, picture; symbol, example.

Timurlenk *pr.n.* (*his.*) Timurlenk, Tamberlane.

timüs (*bio.*) Thymus.

tin¹ ~ ~, silently: ~ ~ **yürümek**, (baby) toddl₍ (old man) move briskly.

tin² (*phil.*) Spirit, soul; mind. ~ **bilim**, psychology.

tin·amu (*orn.*) Tinamou. ~ **ka**, (*ich.*) tench.

tinsel (*phil.*) Spiritual, moral. ~ **bilimler**, mor₍ sciences. ~ **ci(lik)**, spiritual·ist/(-ism). ~ **lik** spirituality.

tipⁱ Type, sort; style; (*fig.*) queer specimen.

TİP = TÜRKİYE İŞÇİ PARTİSİ.

tipi (*met.*) Blizzard. ~ **lemek**, *vi.* blow a blizzard snow heavily.

tip·ik Typical. ~ **leme**, (*cin.*) type-casting. ~ **ograf** (*pub.*) typography.

tipula (*ent.*) ~ **kurdu**, leather-jacket: ~ **sineğ** crane-fly.

-tir *v. suf.* [96] = -DİR; OLMAK [TİCARETTİR].

-tir- *v. suf.* [144] = -DİR- [GELİŞTİRMEK].

tiraj (*pub.*) Circulation.

tiramola (*naut.*) *int.* Haul! *n.* Type of capstan. ~ **etm.**, tack; go about.

Tiran¹ *pr.n.* (*geo.*) Tirana.

tiran² (*pol.*, *fig.*) Tyrant. ~ **giller**, (*orn.*) tyran flycatchers.

tira'ıtᵈ¹ (*th.*) Tirade, soliloquy.

tirbuşon Corkscrew.

tire¹ *n.* (*tex.*) Sewing cotton. *a.* Cotton.

tire[2] (*ling.*) Dash (–).

tiren = TREN.

tirendaz *n.* Archer. *a.* (*fig.*) Skilful, dextrous; trim, well-dressed.

tirfil (*bot.*) Trefoil, clover. ~**lenmek**, *vi.* become threadbare.

tiril ~ ~, *adv.* tremblingly: *a.* very new (cloth); (*fig.*) clean as a new pin. ~**demek**, tremble.

tiri[l]t[di] (*cul.*) Bread soaked in gravy. ~ **gibi**, feeble old man: ~**i çıkmak**/~**leşmek**, *vi.* grow old and feeble.

tiriz (*arch.*) Lath, batten; moulding; (*mod.*) piping.

tiroi[l]t[di] (*bio.*) Thyroid gland.

tir·pidin/~**pit** (*agr.*) Small mattock.

tirsi ~ **balığı**, (*ich.*) allis shad, alewife.

tirşe *n.* Vellum, parchment. *a.* Pale green.

tiryak[1] (*med.*) Theriac; antidote to poison. ~**i**, *a.* addicted; (*fig.*) tiresome: *n.* addict; great smoker; keen player: ~**si olm.** (**-in**), be addicted to. ~**ilik**, a being addicted to stg.; the subject of addiction; obsession; smoking.

Tİ·SAN = TÜM TİYATRO SANATÇILARI BİRLİĞİ. ~**SK** = TÜRKİYE İŞVEREN SENDİKALARI KON-FEDERASYONU. ~**T** = TÜRKÇÜ İNTİKAM TUGAYI.

titan(yum) (*chem.*) Titanium.

titiz Peevish, captious, hard to please; fastidious, sensitive; meticulous, discriminating. ~**lenmek**/ ~**leşmek**, *vi.* be tiresome/hard to please; become annoyed. ~**lik**, peevishness, irritability; being over fastidious; pedantry; delicacy; sensitivity.

titre·k Trembling: ~ **kavak**, (*bot.*) aspen. ~**m**, tone; intonation. ~**me**, *vn.* ~**mek (-den)**, *vi.* shiver; tremble; be afraid of. ~**mesiz**, (*ast.*) aperiodic. ~**nti**, (*med.*) clonus. ~**rci**[l]k[ği], (*phys.*) phonon. ~**rsinek**, (*ent.*) midge. ~**şim**, (*phys.*) vibration; resonance; oscillation; (*rad.*) pulse: ~ **sayısı**, frequency. ~**şimli**/~**şimsel**, vibrating; oscillating; (*ling.*) voiced. ~**şimsiz**, (*ling.*) unvoiced. ~**şir**, (*phys.*) oscillator. ~**şmek**, *vi.* shiver/tremble/ vibrate together. ~**ştirmek (-i)**, *vc.* ~**tmek (-i)**, *vc.* = TİTREMEK.

titrilemek (*chem.*) Titrate.

tiy. = TİYATRO.

tiyatro Theatre. ~ +, *a.* Theatrical; drama-, stage-: ~ **sanatı**, drama: ~ **yazarı**, dramatist. ~**cu(luk)**, (work/art of) theatre-actor//-owner/-producer.

tiz (*phys.*) High-pitched (sound/voice). ~ **perdeden**, on a high note; violently: ~ **sesli söğüt bülbülü**, (*orn.*) wood warbler. ~**leşmek**, *vi.* become high-pitched.

Tk. = TÜRK; TÜRKÇE; TÜRKİYE.

TK = (*med.*) TÜRK KODEKSİ. ~**B** = TÜRK KADINLAR BİRLİĞİ. ~**İ** = TÜRKİYE KÖMÜR İŞLETMELERİ. ~**P** = (*pol.*) TÜRKİYE KOMÜNİST PARTİSİ; TÜRKİYE KÖYLÜ PARTİSİ.

tkz. = TEKLİFSİZ KONUŞMADA.

Tl. = (*ch.s.*) TALYUM.

TL = (*fin.*) TÜRK LİRASI.

Tm. = (*ch.s.*) TULYUM.

TM = (*fin.*) TÜRK MALI. ~**MOB** = TÜRK MÜHENDİS VE MİMAR ODALARI BİRLİĞİ. ~**O** = TOPRAK MAHSULLERİ OFİSİ. ~**TF** = TÜRKİYE MİLLİ TALEBE FEDERASYONU.

TO = TİCARET ODASI. ~**DAİE** = TÜRKİYE VE ORTA DOĞU AMME İDARESİ ENSTİTÜSÜ.

toğrul (*orn.*) Goshawk.

tohum (*bot.*) Seed; grain; (*bio.*) semen, sperm; (*ent.*) eggs. ~ **dağıtmak**, scatter seed; disseminate: ~ **ekme makinesi**, (*agr.*) drill: ~ **kargası**, (*orn.*) rook: ~ **yatağı**, (*agr.*) seed-bed, drill: ~**a bağlamak**/ **kaçmak**, (*bot.*) go to seed; (*fig.*) be aged/past one's prime.

tohum·cu(luk) (*agr.*) (Work of) seed-grower/ -merchant. ~**lamak (-i)**, (*live.*) inseminate artificially. ~**lanmak**, *vp.* ~**lu**, having seed, etc.; producing seed, etc.: ~ **bitki**, (*bot.*) phanerogam. ~**luk**, *a.* (*agr.*) suitable for seed; (*live.*) suitable for breeding: *n.* (*agr.*) seed-bed: ~ **buğday**, seed wheat.

tok[u] Satiated; full; deep (voice); (*tex.*) closely-woven, thick; (*min.*) tough. ~ **ağırlamak güç olur**, it's hard to please those who have everything: ~ **evin aç kedisi**, well-off but still envious: ~ GÖZLÜ: ~ **karnına**, on a full stomach: ~ **satıcı**, reluctant seller; one who does not need to sell: ~ **ses**, deep voice: ~ SÖZLÜ: ~ **tutmak**, (*cul.*) (food) be filling.

toka[1] (*mod.*) Buckle; clasp; fastener.

toka[2] Shaking hands; clinking glasses. ~ **etm.**, shake hands; clink glasses; (*naut.*) (two parts) support each other; (*sl.*) give, pay.

toka[i]ç[ci] (*dom.*) Bat (for beating laundry); (*carp.*) mallet; (*min.*) swage; (*sp.*) racket. ~**lamak (-i)**, beat, strike; (*min.*) swage. ~**lanmak**, *vp.*

toka·lamak (-i) (*mod.*) Buckle, fasten. ~**laşmak (-le)**, *vi.* shake hands. ~**lı**, buckled.

toka[l]t[dı] [1] (*live.*) Open sheep-fold.

toka[l]t[dı] [2] Cuff, box on the ears. ~ **atmak/indirmek**/ **yapıştırmak**/~**lamak (-i)**, cuff s.o.: ~ **şaplamak**, give a noisy slap: ~ **yemek**/~**lanmak**, be cuffed.

tok·gözlü Contented, satiated; not covetous. ~**gözlülük**, contentment, satiety. ~**laşmak**, (*tex.*) become closely woven. ~**laştırma**, (*min.*) toughening. ~**lu**, (*live.*) yearling lamb. ~**luk**, satiety; (*tex.*) thickness, density; (*min.*) toughness.

tokma[l]k[ğı] *n.* (*carp.*) Mallet, beetle; (door) knocker; (bell) clapper; (*cul.*) wooden pestle. ~ **gibi**, chubby, plump.

tokmak·baş ~ **kaya**, (*ich.*) goby. ~**böceği**, (*ent.*) rove beetle. ~**çı**, (*col.*) gigolo. ~**lamak (-i)**, beat with a mallet.

tok·semi (*med.*) Toxaemia. ~**sin**, toxin.

tok·sözlü Outspoken, not mincing his words. ~**sözlülük**, candour. ~**tağan**, everlasting, perennial: ~ **karlar**, (*geo.*) perennial snow.

tokur ~ **alınlı**, with a protruding forehead. ~**cun**, (*agr.*) stook. ~**damak**, *vi.* (*ech.*) bubble. ~**datmak (-i)**, make a narghile bubble. ~**tu**, bubbling sound.

tokuş = DEĞİŞ. ~**mak (-le)**, (glasses) clink; collide, butt each other. ~**turmak (-i, -le)**, clink glasses; cause to collide; (*sp.*) wrestle; cannon (billiards).

tokuz (*tex.*) Thick and closely woven.

tolerans (*soc.*) Tolerance; (*eng.*) tolerance, clearance, play.

tol·ga (*his.*) Helmet. ~**oz** = TONOZ.

tolüen (*chem.*) Toluene.

toma[l]k[ğı] Wooden ball; wooden club; (*mod.*) heavy boots.

tomar Roll/scroll (paper, etc.); (*mil.*) gun rammer/ swab.

tomba'kᵍ¹ (*min.*) Copper-zinc alloy.

tombala (*gamb.*) Tombola, lotto; big prize. ~ **çekmek**, play tombola. ~ **cı(lık)**, (work of) itinerant tombola ticket-seller.

tombalak Round; short and plump; stout.

tombaz (*naut.*) Barge; punt; pontoon.

tombul·(luk) Plump(ness). ~ **laşmak**, *vi.* grow plump.

tomru'kᵍᵘ (*carp.*) Felled tree-trunk, heavy log; (*min.*) block of stone (for dressing); boulder; ingot; (*obs.*) prison; (*bot.*) bud. ~ **vermek**/ ~ **lanmak**, put forth buds.

tomur (*bio.*) Papilla. ~ **cu'k**ᵍᵘ, (*bot.*) bud. ~ **cuklanmak**, *vi.* burst into bud.

ton¹ (*mus.*) Tone; (*art.*) tone, shade; (*fig.*) manner.

ton² (*math.*) Tonne, metric ton. ~ **la**, by the ton; (*fig.*) heaps of. ~ **aj**, tonnage.

ton³ (*cul.*) Tinned tuna(-fish). ~ **balığı**ⁿ¹, (*ich.*) tuna, tunny.

tonel = TÜNEL. ~ **geçmek**, (*sl.*) be absent-minded, go wool gathering.

tonga Rotten timber/board; (*sl.*) trap, trick. ~ **ya basmak/düşmek**, fall into a trap; be deceived.

tonik *a.*, *n.* (*med.*) Tonic.

tonilato (*naut.*) (Net register) tonnage. ~ **luk**, *a.* having a tonnage of . . . .

tonlama (*ling.*) Intonation.

tonluk *a.* Of . . . tons.

tono (*aer.*) Roll.

tonoz¹ (*arch.*) (Arched) vault.

tonoz² (*naut.*) ~ **demiri**, kedge anchor.

tontin (*fin.*) Tontine.

tonton Darling.

topᵘ *a.* Round; ball-shaped; in a mass. *n.* (*sp.*) Ball; any round object; (*mil.*) gun, cannon; cannon-ball; (*tex.*) roll (of cloth/paper); whole of stg.; all, the whole lot. ~ **arabası**, (*mil.*) gun-carriage: ~ **ateşi**, cannonade: ~ **atmak**, fire a gun; (*fin.*, *sl.*) go bankrupt; (*ed.*, *sl.*) fail a class: ~ **ensesi**, (*mod.*) hair grown full at the back: ~ **gibi**, willy-nilly, without question: ~ **gibi patlamak**, (bad news) burst upon one: ~ **güllesi**, (*mil.*) cannon-ball: ~ **kandil**, (*dom.*) round chandelier: ~ **kuyruğu**, (*mil.*) breech: ~ **mevzii**, (*mil.*) gun emplacement: ~ **sapması**, (*sp.*) break: ~ **siperi**, (*naut.*) barbette: ~ **sürmek**, (*sp.*) dribble: ~, in groups; in lumps/masses: ~ **olm.**, (blood) clot: ~ **toplayıcı**, (*sp.*) ball-boy: ~ **tüfek**, various weapons: ~ **yekûn**, in all, all together: ~ **yoluna gitmek**, be sacrificed in vain; perish miserably: ~ **a tutmak**, (*mil.*) bombard: ~ **a vuruş**, (*sp.*) drive: ~ **lar**, (*mil.*) artillery: ~ **TAN**: ~ **u atmak**, (*fin.*) go bankrupt; (*ed.*, *sl.*) fail (an exam.): ~ **u sürmek**, (*sp.*) dribble: ~ **u** ~ **u**, in all; all told: ~ **un ağzında**, the one most in danger: ~ **unu birden**, one and all: ~ **unuz**, all of you.

top. = TOPLUMBİLİM.

topa'çᶜ¹ (*child.*) Top, teetotum; (*phys.*) gyroscope; (*naut.*) thick rounded part of a Tk. oar; round basket. ~ **gibi**, chubby/sturdy (child).

topa'kᵍ¹ (*cul.*) Roundish lump of dough; clod, (*min.*) pellet; any lump; (*live.*) inner side of fetlock;

(*dial.*) glass, bottle. ~ **la'ç**ᶜ¹, (*min.*) pelletizer. ~ **lamak (-i)**, pelletize. ~ **lanma**, *vn.* ~ **lanmak**, *vi.* become round/lumpish. ~ **laşmak**, *vi.* coagulate; flocculate.

topal *a.* Lame; crippled; (*stg.*) with one leg short. ~ **eşekle kervana katılmak**, undertake stg. with inadequate means. ~ **lama**, *vn.* ~ **lamak**, *vi.* limp. ~ **lık**, lameness.

topa·la'kᵍ¹/ ~ **lan** (*bot.*) Type of buckthorn.

topaltıⁿ¹ (*mil.*) Terreplein (of a fort).

topar·cı'kᵍ¹ (*mil.*) (Small) shot; (*eng.*) ball(-bearing). ~ **la'k**ᵍ¹, *n.* sphere; (*mil.*) limber: *a.* round, spherical: ~ **hesap**, (*math.*) in round numbers: ~ **rakam/sayı**, round number. ~ **lama**, *vn.* ~ **lamak (-i)**, collect together; pack up; (*mil.*) roll up. ~ **lanmak**, *vp.* be collected together: *vi.* pull o.s. together; recover.

topatan (*bot.*, *cul.*) Oval, scented yellow melon.

topaz (*min.*) Topaz.

top·çeker *n.* (*naut.*) Gunboat: *a.* (*mil.*) gun-hauling (animal). ~ **çu**, (*mil.*) artilleryman; gunner; the artillery; (*sl.*) bankrupt; (*ed. sl.*) pupil likely to fail: ~ **barajı**, artillery barrage. ~ **çuluk**, artillery; gunnery. ~ **hane**, (*his.*) ordnance factory; (*mil.*) gunnery school.

topla (*agr.*) Three-pronged winnowing fork.

top·la'çᶜ¹ (*el.*) Accumulator; collector. ~ **la'k**ᵍ¹, aggregate; (*min.*) sinter. ~ **lam**, (*math.*) total, aggregate; overall: ~ **geçimi**, total brought/carried forward: ~ **olarak**, in all/total: ~ **lar** ~ **ı**, (*math.*) grand total. ~ **lama**, *vn.*; (*math.*) addition, plus; (*fin.*) collection: ~ **borusu**, (*eng.*) header: ~ **eser/ yapıtı**, (*lit.*) compilation: ~ **gücü**, (*el.*) capacitance: ~ **kampı**, (*pol.*) concentration camp: ~ **makinesi**, (*fin.*) adding machine. ~ **lamak (-i)**, add; collect together, accumulate; gather, pick; sum up; fold up (clothes); tidy up; clear away; (*fin.*) save, put aside; (*adm.*) convene: (*mil.*) mobilize; (*fin.*) collect (taxes): *vi.* put on weight.

toplan·a'kᵍ¹ (*soc.*) Camp. ~ **ca**, (*arch.*) complex. ~ **ık**, *a.* gathered, collected. ~ **ılmak**, *imp. v.* come together, meet. ~ **mak**, *vp.* = TOPLAMAK: *vi.* collect, assemble, come together; (*med.*) regain one's health; put on weight; (boil) come to a head. ~ **tı**, (*soc.*) assembly, gathering; (*adm.*) convention, meeting: ~ **başkan/reisi**, chairman: ~ **haberleri**, (*pub.*) society page: ~ **nisabı**, quorum: ~ **salonu**, assembly hall.

top·lardamar (*bio.*) Vein: ~ **yangısı**, (*med.*) phlebitis. ~ **laşık**, (*min.*) sintered. ~ **laşım**, (*phys.*) association. ~ **laşmak**, *vi.* gather together, assemble; (*cul.*) form hard lumps. ~ **laştırma**, (*min.*) sintering. ~ **latılmak**, *vp.* ~ **latmak (-i, -e)**, *vc.* = TOPLAMAK. ~ **layan**, collector, compiler. ~ **layıcı**, concentrating, storing, collecting: ~ **ışıldak**, (*el.*) spotlight.

toplb. = TOPLUMBİLİM.

toplu Having a knob/round head; compact; collected together, in a mass; well-arranged; tidy; buxom; plump; global, over-all, inclusive; (*adm.*) collective; cumulative; group-. ~ **anlaşma** = ~ **SÖZLEŞME**: ~ **ateşi**, (*mil.*) concentrated fire: ~ **İĞNE**: ~ **işletme**, (*fin.*) amalgamation: ~ **olarak**, collectively: ~ **pazarlık**, (*ind.*)

collective bargaining: ~ **sigorta**, group insurance: ~ SÖZLEŞME.
oplu·biçem (*art.*) Stylistic. ~ **ca**, *adv.* as a whole: *a.* collective; plumpish. ~ **çalışım**, (*ed.*) seminar. ~ **iğne**, (*mod.*) pin. ~ **luk**, collection; compactness; (*soc.*) community; society; gathering; (*bio.*) colony; (*th.*) company, troupe: ~ **adı**, (*ling.*) collective noun.
oplum (*soc.*) Community, society. ~ +, *a.* Social: ~ **çalışmanı**, social worker: ~ **çıkar/yararı**, communal advantage/benefit/interest: ~ **hayatı**, social life: ~ **töresi**, (*soc.*) public morals.
oplum·bilim(ci) Sociolo·gy/(-gist). ~ **bilimsel**, sociological. ~ **cu**, *a.*, *n.* socialist. ~ **culuk**, (*soc.*, *pol.*) socialism. ~ **daş**, fellow-member (of a society). ~ **dışı**, (*soc.*) banished; (*rel.*) excommunicated. ~ **durum**, (*soc.*) social status. ~ **laşmak**, *vi.* come together, form a society. ~ **laştırmak (-i)**, (*pol.*) socialize. ~ **lu/** ~ **sal**, social: ~ **bilim**, art of living. ~ **sallaştırma**, *vn.* socialization.
oplu·sözleşme (*ind.*) Collective agreement/ contract. ~ **tartışma**, collective bargaining.
opograf(ya) (*geo.*) Topograph·er/(-y).
opra'k^{ğı} *n.* Earth; ground; soil; land; country; (*el.*) earth; (*fig.*) the grave. *a.* Earthen; earthenware; made of clay; earth-coloured. ~ **aşınması**, (*geol.*) erosion: ~ ALTI: ~ **baraj**, earth dam: ~ **boya**, paint in powder-form: ~ BOYA: ~ **çekmek**, (*eng.*) move earth: ~ **esası**, (*leg.*) nationality by place of birth: ~ **işleri**, (*eng.*) earthworks: ~ **kaldırma işi**: earth movement: ~ **kayması**, (*geol.*) landslide: ~ **kazması**, (*agr.*) mattock: ~ **kirası**, (*fin.*) ground rent: ~ **Mahsulleri Ofisi**, (*adm.*) grain-/wheat-purchasing agency: ~ **piresi**, (*ent.*) flea beetle: ~ **rengi**, ochre: ~ **reformu**, (*pol.*) land reform: ~ **sahibi**, landowner: ~ **set**, (*eng.*) embankment, bund: ~ **sıçanı**, (*zoo.*) field vole: ~ **sürmek**, break up ground: ~ **tabya**, (*mil.*) earthworks: ~ **tırmaşık kuşları**, (*orn.*) earth-creepers: ~ **vergisi**, (*adm.*) land tax: ~ **yabanarısı**, (*ent.*) humble-bee: ~ **yapılar**, (*eng.*) earthworks: ~ **yıkanması**, (*geol.*) leaching: ~ **yol**, dirt road: ~ **a bağlamak**, (*el.*) earth: ~ **a bakmak**, one's death seem near: ~ **a karışmak**, be dead and buried: ~ **a vermek**, bury (the dead): ~ **ı bol olsun!**, *int.* may he (a non-Muslim) rest in peace!: ~ **ı işlemek**, (*agr.*) cultivate the land: ~ **ı kabartmak**, (*agr.*) break up/loosen the ground: ~ **ına ağır gelmesin!**, *int.* may my criticism not disturb his rest!: ~ **ta bahar tütüyordu**, the earth was seething with spring.
oprak·altı^{nı} *a.* Underground; buried: *n.* (*geol.*) subsoil. ~ **bastı**, (*fin.*, *obs.*) octroi. ~ **bilim**, (*geol.*) pedology. ~ **boya**, (*chem.*) mineral pigment. ~ **çıl**, (*zoo.*) terricolous. ~ **eşya**, (*art.*) ceramics. ~ **kazan**, (*zoo.*) mole-rat. ~ **lamak (-i)**, earth up/over; (*el.*) earth. ~ **landırmak (-i)**, grant land to s.o. (to live on). ~ **lı**, mixed with earth; earthy; (*soc.*) landed (peasant). ~ **sız**, without earth; (*soc.*) having no land. ~ **su**, (*adm.*) civil engineering office for rural areas. ~ **üstü**^{nü}, ground surface: ~ **suyu**, surface water.
optan (*fin.*) Wholesale; in the mass, in bulk; at one go, all at once. ~ **kiralama**, (hotel, etc.) block booking: ~ **ödeme**, lump-sum payment: ~ **öldürme**, massacre. ~ **cı**, wholesaler. ~ **cılık**, wholesale business.
topu'k^{ğu} (*bio.*) Heel; ankle; fetlock; (*geo.*) (river) bar; shallows; (*mod.*) (shoe) heel; (*naut.*) (mast) heel. ~ **-burun**, (*sp.*) heel-and-toe (walking): ~ **çalmak**, strike one heel against another (walking): ~ **kapmak**, (*sp.*) grab by the ankle: ~ **larına kadar**, up to the ankles: ~ **u çiğnenmiş**, down-at-heel (shoe).
topuk·demiri^{ni} (*carp.*) Hinge-pin. ~ **lamak (-i)**, prod with the heel. ~ **lu**, (*mod.*) high-heeled.
topur (*bot.*) Chestnut shell.
toput^{u} (*chem.*) Deposit.
topuz (*mil.*) Mace; knob (of stick); knot (of hair). ~ **gibi**, short and stout. ~ **cu'k**^{ğu}, (*bio.*) tubercle. ~ **lu**, with a knob/knot.
tor^{1} *n.* Fine-meshed net; tissue. *a.* Net-like. ~ **a düşmek**, be tricked/deceived.
tor^{2} *a.* (*live.*) Wild, unbroken; (*ind.*) raw, crude; (*fig.*) inexperienced, rough.
tora'k^{ğı} Charcoal-burner's pit; kiln; (*cul.*) dried skim milk.
toraks (*bio.*) Thorax.
toraman Robust (youth).
torba Bag; sack; (*bio.*) scrotum; cyst. ~ **yoğurdu**, (*cul.*) yoghurt strained in a bag: ~ **dakiler**, s.o.'s secret/unsuspected nature: ~ **ya koymak/** ~ **lamak (-i)**, (*col.*) ensure, get in the bag. ~ **lanmak**, *vi.* (*mod.*) become baggy. ~ **laşım**, (*med.*) aneurysm. ~ **lı**, cystic.
tori'k^{ği} (*ich.*) Atlantic bonito; (*sl.*) brains. ~ **ini çalıştırmak**, use one's brains: ~ **ini kaşımak**, think.
tor·lak *a.* Young, wild; (*live.*) unbroken: *n.* dervish. ~ **luk**, wildness; inexperience; = TORAK.
torna (*carp.*, *eng.*) Lathe. ~ **aynası**, lathe chuck; potter's wheel: ~ **etm.**, turn (on lathe): ~ **fırdöndüsü**, lathe carrier: ~ **kalemi**, lathe tool: ~ **tezgâhı**, machine-shop: ~ **dan çıkmış gibi**, exactly the same.
torna·cı (*carp.*, *eng.*) Lathe-operator, turner. ~ **cılık**, turning. ~ **do**, (*met.*) tornado. ~ **hit**, (*naut.*) ahead! ~ **lamak (-i)**, turn. ~ **lanmak**, *vp.* ~ **lı**, turned, machined. ~ **vida**, (*carp.*) screwdriver.
tornistan (*naut.*) Sternway. ~ **etm.**, go astern; (*mod.*) turn (clothes).
Toros ~ **dağları**, (*geo.*) Taurus Mountains: ~ **köknarı**, (*bot.*) Cilician fir: ~ **sediri**, (*bot.*) cedar of Lebanon: ~ **semenderi**, (*zoo.*) type of newt.
tor·pido (*naut.*) Torpedo: ~ (**bot**^{u}), torpedo-boat: ~ **kovanı**, torpedo tube. ~ **pil**, mine; torpedo; (*fig.*) backer, patron. ~ **pilbalığı**^{nı}, (*ich.*) electric ray. ~ **pillemek (-i)**, torpedo: *vi.* (*ed. sl.*) fail in class. ~ **pillenmek**, *vp.*
tortop^{u} Quite round.
tortu Deposit; dregs; grounds; sediment; (*fig.*) lowest section. ~ **l**, (*geol.*) sedimentary. ~ **lanmak/** ~ **laşmak**, *vi.* be deposited. ~ **lbilim**, sedimentology. ~ **lu**, with sediment; turbid.
torun Grandchild; descendant. ~ **torba/tosun sahibi olm.**, have children and grandchildren: ~ **lar**, progeny, descendants.
toryum (*chem.*) Thorium.

tos A blow with the head. ~ **vurmak,** butt. ~ **bağa,** (*zoo.*) tortoise. ~**lama,** *vn.* butting. ~**lamak (-i),** butt: **(-e),** (*naut.*) ram; (*sl.*) give (money); (*ed. sl.*) be lazy. ~**laşmak,** *vi.* butt each other.

tostᵘ (*cul.*) Toast.

tostoparlak Absolutely/perfectly round.

tosun (*live.*) Bullock. ~ **gibi,** plump, sturdy. ~**cuk,** (*med.*) overweight baby.

totaliter (*pol.*) Totalitarian.

totem (*rel.*) Totem. ~**cilik/**~**izm,** totemism.

toto (*sp.*) Football pools.

totoloji (*ling.*) Tautology.

toy¹ (*cul.*) Banquet, feast.

toy² (*orn.*) Great bustard. ~**dan,** (*orn.*) type of large bustard. ~**gar,** (*orn.*) lark.

toy³ Inexperienced, raw, amateur. ~**luk,** inexperience, rawness: ~ **etm.,** behave clumsily.

toyna¹kᵍ¹ (*bio.*) Hoof. ~**lılar,** (*zoo.*) ungulates.

toz *n.* Dust; powder; (*sl.*) heroin. *a.* Like dust; in powder form. ~ **almak,** (*dom.*) dust: ~ **bezi,** duster: ~ **etm.,** raise the dust; (*chem.*) atomize: ~ **fırtınası,** (*met.*) dust-storm: ~ **geçmez,** dustproof: ~ **halinde,** powdery: ~ **haline getirmek,** (*phys.*) atomize: ~ **hortumu,** (*met.*) dust-devil: ~ **kondurmamak (-e),** not allow/listen to any criticism of: ~ **koparmak,** raise much dust; kick up a dust: ~ **olm.,** (*sl.*) clear out: ~PEMBE: ~ **sayrılığı,** (*med.*) pneumoconiosis: ~ **silkmek,** beat out/shake off the dust: ~ŞEKER: ~**dan dumandan ferman okunmamak,** be in a state of complete confusion: ~**u dumana karışmak/katmak,** raise clouds of dust; make a great fuss; create confusion: ~**unu silkmek,** give s.o. a 'dusting'.

toz·ak Dust storm. ~**amak,** *vi.* raise the dust; run away. ~**an,** mote, particle. ~**armak,** *vi.* become dust; turn to powder. ~**boya,** (*chem.*) pigment powder. ~**koparan,** (*geo.*) very windy place; exposed to strong winds. ~**la,** (*geol.*) loess. ~**lamak (-i),** sprinkle/coat with dust. ~**lanmak,** *vi.* become dusty. ~**laşma,** *vn.;* (*bot.*) pollination. ~**laşmak,** *vi.* become dust; (*chem.*) effloresce. ~**layıcı,** pulverizer, atomizer. ~**lu,** dusty. ~**luk,** (*mod.*) gaiters; (*bot.*) theca. ~**mak,** *vi.* = GEZMEK. ~**pembe,** light pink: ~ **görmek,** see things through rose-coloured spectacles. ~**sabun,** (*dom.*) soap-powder. ~**şeker,** (*cul.*) granulated sugar. ~**umak,** *vi.* become dusty all around. ~**untu,** dusty atmosphere. ~**utmak (-i),** raise the dust, make the air dusty; (*fig.*) become unreasonable; talk nonsense.

Töbank = TÜRKİYE ÖĞRETMENLER BANKASI.

töhmetⁱ Crime, offence; guilt. ~ **altına girmek,** be unjustly blamed. ~**li,** under suspicion; guilty. ~**siz,** innocent.

tökez·lemek *vi.* Stumble, stagger; (*th.*) fluff one's lines. ~**lenmek,** *vi.* be knocked into.

tömbeki (*bot.*) Persian tobacco (smoked in narghiles).

töre (*soc., phil.*) Customs, traditions; rules, moral laws. ~ **gereği,** custom: ~ **komedyası,** (*th.*) comedy of manners: ~**ye aykırı,** immoral; illegitimate; illicit; unjust.

töre·bilim (*phil.*) Ethics, morals. ~**bilimci,** moralist. ~**bilimsel,** ethical, moral. ~**ce,** morally.

~**ci(lik),** moral·ist/(-ism). ~**dışçı(lik),** amoral·ist (-ity). ~**dışı,** amoral. ~**li,** legitimate.

törel (*phil.*) Ethical, moral. ~ **bilinç (özgürlüğü)** (freedom of) conscience. ~**cilik,** moralism. ~**lik** morality. ~**siz(cilik),** immoral(ity).

tören Ceremony; ceremonial; celebration. ~ **alayı** procession, cortège: ~ **borusu,** fanfare. ~**çağrı** reception. ~**düzen,** ceremonial, protocol. ~**li** ~**sel,** *a.* ceremonial.

töre·sel Moral. ~**tanımaz(lık),** immoral(ism) ~**siz(lik),** immoral(ity).

törpü (*carp.*) Rasp, file. ~ **balıkları,** (*ich.*) filefish ~**lemek (-i),** file. ~**lenmek,** *vp.* ~**leyici,** abrasive ~**lü,** filed.

tös *int.* (*live.*) Go back! ~**kürtmek (-i),** (*live.*) back drive back. ~**kürü,** backwards.

tövbe (*rel.*) *n.* Repentance; contrition; vow not to d again. *int.* Pax!; enough! ~ **ayları,** (*ast., rel.*) fift and sixth lunar months: ~ **etm. (-e),** repent o doing stg. and vow not to do it again: ~**ler olsun** ~**ler ~si!,** I'll never do it again!: ~**sini bozmak** break one's vow of repentance.

tövbe·kâr Penitent, contrite, repentant: ~ **(kadın)** reformed prostitute. ~**li** penitent; swearing to o.ₛ not to repeat stg. harmful. ~**siz,** impenitent.

töz *n.* Base, root; (*geol.*) ore, mineral; (*phil.*) sub stance, essence. ~**cülük,** substantialism. ~**e** (*phil.*) essential.

TPAO = TÜRK PETROLLERİ ANONİM ORTAKLIĞI.

Trablus (*geo.*) Tripoli. ~**gar¹p**ᵇ¹, Tripoli (Libya ~**şam,** Tripoli (Lebanon).

trabzan = TIRABZAN.

Trabzon (*geo.*) Trebizond. ~**hurması**ⁿ¹, (*bot.* Chinese persimmon.

trafi¹kᵍⁱ Traffic. ~ **kazası,** road-accident: ~ **memuru,** traffic policeman: ~ **şeridi,** traffic lane.

trafo (*el., col.*) Transformer.

tragedya (*th.*) Tragedy.

trahom (*med.*) Trachoma, conjunctivitis.

tra·jedi (*th.*) Tragedy. ~**jik,** tragic. ~**jikomik,** (*th* tragi-comic.

trak Funk; (*th.*) stage-fright.

tra·kea (*bio.*) Trachea. ~**keliler,** (*zoo.*) tracheate ~**kit**ⁱ, (*geol.*) trachyte.

traktör (*mot.*) Tractor. ~ **römorku,** tractor-traile

trakunya (*ich.*) Greater weever.

Trakya *pr.n.* (*geo.*) Thrace. ~**lı,** (*ethn.*) Thracian.

trampa (*fin.*) Barter; exchange. ~ **etm.,** exchang goods.

trampetⁱ (*mus.*) Side-drum. ~ **balığı,** (*ich.*) drum fish: ~ **sopası,** (*mus.*) drumstick. ~**çi,** drummer.

tramplen (*sp.*) Trampolene.

tramvay Tramcar.

trança (*ich.*) Type of sea-bream (in the Aegean).

trans·atlantik (*naut.*) Liner. ~**düser,** (*el.*) tran ducer. ~**fer,** (*fin., sp., etc.*) transfer. ~**formasyo** transformation. ~**formatör,** (*el.*) transforme ~**formizm,** (*phil.*) transformism. ~**istor,** (*el.*) tran sistor. ~**it**ⁱ, (*fin.*) transit: ~ **merkezi,** (*mil.*) trans camp: ~ **yolu,** through road. ~**kripsiyon,** (*pub* transcription. ~**literasyon,** (*ling.*) transliteratio ~**misyon,** (*eng.*) transmission, drive: ~**mili,** driv shaft. ~**plantasyon,** (*med.*) transplant. ~**por**

(*naut.*) cargo ship. ~ **portör**, (*ind.*) conveyor-belt.
~ **seksüel**, sex changing. ~ **sendental**, (*phil.*) transcendental.
trapez(ci) (*sp.*) Trapeze(-artist).
traş = TIRAŞ
travers (*rly.*) Sleeper.
travma(tik) (*med., psy.*) Trauma(tic).
tre·matodᵘ (*zoo.*) Trematode, fluke. ~ **molit**ⁱ,
(*geol.*) tremolite.
tren (*rly.*) Train. ~ **tutmak**, (*med.*) get train-
sickness: ~ **de teslim**, (*fin.*) free on board (train):
~ **e yetiş(me)mek**, catch//(miss) the train: ~ **i**
kaçırmak, miss the train/(*fig.*) the opportunity.
trençkotᵘ (*mod.*) Trenchcoat, raincoat.
trepan (*eng.*) Trepan, rock-bit.
treyler (*mot.*) Trailer, caravan.
tribün Platform, stage; (*sp.*) stand.
tri·faze (*el.*) Three-phase. ~ **gonometri(k)**, (*math.*)
trigonome·try/(-trical). ~ **kloretilen**, (*chem.*) tri-
chlorethylene.
triko (*mod.*) Knitted wear/fabric. ~ **sefal**¹, (*zoo.*)
trichocephalus. ~ **taj(cı)**, (*tex.*) knit·ting/(-ter).
tri·logya (*lit.*) Trilogy. ~ **lyon**, (*math.*) trillion
(10¹²). ~ **mestre**, (*ed.*) term.
trinketa (*naut.*) Foresail.
trioksitⁱ (*chem.*) Trioxide.
tripo (*sl.*) Gambling-den.
tripoli (*geol.*) Opal dust.
triportör (*mot.*) Three-wheeled van, tricycle.
trips (*ent.*) Thrips.
triptik (*adm.*) Triptyque.
trişin(ez) (*zoo.*) Trichi·na/(-nosis).
tri·ton (*phys.*) Triton. ~ **yas**, (*geol.*) Trias. ~ **yo**,
(*mus.*) trio.
tro·leybüs (*mot.*) Trolley-bus. ~ **li**, trolley.
trom·bin (*bio.*) Thrombin. ~ **bogen**, prothrombin.
trom·bon(cu) (*mus.*) Trombone(-player). ~ **pet(çi)**,
(*mus.*) trumpet(er).
tropik·a (*geo.*) Tropic; tropics. ~ **al**ⁱ, tropical: ~
kuşak, tropics. ~ **kuşugiller**, (*orn.*) tropicbirds.
tro·pizm (*bio.*) Tropism. ~ **plar**, (*phil.*) tropes.
~ **posfer**, (*met.*) troposphere.
tro·tinet (Child's) scooter. ~ **tuvar**, pavement.
tröstᵘ (*fin.*) Trust. ~ **ortaklığı**, trust company.
TRT(K) = TÜRKİYE RADYO VE TELEVİZYON
KURUMU.
trupᵘ (*th.*) Troupe, company.
Truva (*geo.*) Troy. ~ + , *a.* Trojan. ~ **lı**, (*ethn., his.*)
Trojan.
truvakar (*mod.*) Three-quarter length (dress, etc.).
trük Knack, trick; gadget.
TS = TÜRK STANDARDI; TÜRKÇE SÖZLÜK. ~ **E** =
TÜRK SANAT//STANDARTLARI ENSTİTÜSÜ. ~ **İP** =
TÜRKİYE SOSYALİST İŞÇİ PARTİSİ. ~ **O** = TİCARET
VE SANAYİ ODASI. ~ **YD** = TÜRKİYE SPOR YAZAR-
LARI DERNEĞİ.
TT·B = TURİZM VE TANITMA BAKANLIĞI. ~ **D** =
TALİM VE TERBİYE DAİRESİ. ~ **K** = TÜRK TARİH
KURUMU. ~ **OK** = TÜRKİYE TURİNG VE OTOMOBİL
KURUMU.
tu *int.* Ugh!
-tu¹ *v. suf.* [99] = -İDİ² [BULUŞTU].
-tu² *n. suf.* [222] = -Tİ² [BUYRULTU].

tual (*art.*) Canvas.
Tuba (*rel.*) Tree in Paradise; (*fig.*) happiness, good
fortune.
tufa·cı (*sl.*) Violent thief. ~ **cılık**, stealing. ~ **lamak**
(-i), (*sl.*) pinch, pilfer.
tufan (*rel.*) The Flood; (*met.*) violent rainstorm;
flood; cataclysm. ~ **çöküntü/tortusu**, (*geol.*)
diluvium: ~ **dan önceye ait**, antediluvian.
tufeyli (*bio.*) Parasite; drone; (*fig.*) sponger, toady.
~ **lik**, parasitism; toadying.
Tug. = **tugay**, (*mil.*) brigade.
tuğ (*mil.*) Horse-tail crest/plume (sign of rank).
~ **a.** = ~ **amiral**ⁱ(**lik**), (*naut.*) (rank/duties of) rear-
admiral. ~ **bay(lık)**, (*mil.*) (rank/duties of) brigadier. ~ **g.** = ~ **general**ⁱ(**lik**), (rank/duties of) (*mil.*)
brigadier-general//(*aer.*) air-commodore. ~ **lu**,
(*his.*) entitled to/bearing a TUĞ.
tuğla (*arch.*) Brick. ~ **harman/ocağı**, brick-field/
yard: ~ **işi**, brickwork: ~ **örgüsü**, brick bond.
~ **cı(lık)**, (work of) brick-maker/-seller. ~ **msı**,
(*min.*) refractory.
tuğra (*his.*) Sultan's monogram; imperial cipher.
~ **keş(lik)**, (*adm.*) (duties of) official applying the
cipher.
tuğyan Breaking bounds; overflowing, flooding;
(*fig.*) uprising, rebellion. ~ **etm.**, overflow; rebel.
tuh *int.* Oh dear!; what a pity/shame! ~ **sana!**,
shame on you!
tuhaf Uncommon, strange; curious, odd; comic,
amusing. ~ (**şey**)!, that's odd!, how curious!: ~
olm., be strange/curious, etc.: ~ **ına gitmek**, stg.
seem strange/odd to one.
tuhaf·iye (*mod.*) Millinery, drapery. ~ **iyeci(lik)**,
(work of) milliner/draper. ~ **laşmak**, *vi.* be(come)
strange/curious, etc.; become confused; change (in
manner). ~ **lık**, strangeness; curiousness; antics,
etc.: ~ **yapmak**, make funny remarks.
tukan (*zoo.*) Toucan.
tulᵘ Length; (*ast.*) longitude. ~ **dairesi**, meridian.
~ **ani**, lengthwise; longitudinal. ~ **u**ᵘ, (*ast.*) rising
(of sun, etc.); (*fig.*) birth (of ideas).
tuluat¹ *pl.* (*th.*) Improvisations. ~ **yapmak**, impro-
vise. ~ **çı**, actor who improvises. ~ **çılık**, impro-
vising.
tu·luk/ ~ **lum** Skin made into a bag; water-bottle;
(*naut.*) float (for a raft); (*ind.*) tube (for pastes);
(*mus.*) bag of GAYDA; (*mod.*) overalls; pair of fur
squares (making a cloak). ~ **çalgısı**, (*mus.*) bagpipes: ~ **çıkarmak**, (*live.*) remove the skin whole
(for a bag): ~ **çıkmak (-de)**, achieve one's purpose
fully: ~ **gibi**, as fat as a pig: ~ PEYNİRİ.
tulumba (*eng.*) Pump; (*his.*) fire-engine; (*geo.*)
water-spout. ~ **tatlısı**, (*cul.*) sweetmeat of dough
soaked in syrup. ~ **cı**, (*his.*) member of local fire-
brigade; (*fig.*) rowdy; unmannerly youth: ~ **ağzı**,
slang. ~ **cılık**, work of fireman; (*fig.*) rowdiness.
tulum·cuk (*bio.*) Utricle. ~ **lular**, (*zoo.*) tunicates,
sea-squirts. ~ **peyniri**ⁿⁱ, (*cul.*) type of white cheese
made in a skin-bag. ~ **su**, (*zoo.*) utricular.
tulyum (*chem.*) Thulium.
tumağı (*med.*) Catarrh, cold.
tuman (*mod.*) Long wide pants/trousers.
tum·ba (*naut.*) Turning upside down; (*child.*)

tumbling into bed. ~ **badız**, short and fat. ~ **şu¹k**ᵍᵘ, (*orn.*) curved beak. ~ **turak**, pompous/extravagant language. ~ **turaklı**, pompous, high-flown.

tun ~ **dan** ~ **a**, from place to place: ~ **dan** ~ **a atmak**, drive far away: ~ **dan** ~ **a düşmek**, wander far and wide.

Tuna (*geo.*) The Danube. ~ **havyarı**, (*cul.*) botargo: ~ **som balığı**, (*ich.*) huchen, Danube salmon.

tun¹çᶜᵘ (*min.*) Bronze. ~ **çağı**, (*his.*) Bronze Age: ~ **renkli guguk kuşu**, (*orn.*) golden bronze cuckoo: ~ **tan**, brazen.

tunç·laşmak *vi.* Turn bronze-coloured. ~ **laştırmak (-i)**, (*art.*) make a bronze statue of; make bronze-coloured. ~ **sulama**, *vn.* (*min.*) bronzing.

tun·d(u)ra (*geo.*) Tundra. ~ **gsten**, (*chem.*) tungsten.

Tunus (*geo.*) Tunis; Tunisia. ~ +, *a.* Tunisian: ~ **gediği**, opportunity not to be missed; rich woman married for her money. ~ **lu**, (*ethn.*) Tunisian.

tur Tour; promenade; (*sp.*) round (of golf). ~ **atmak**, wander about: ~ **operatörü**, tour operator.

-tur *v. suf.* [96] = -DİR; OLMAK [TURUNÇTUR].

-tur- *v. suf.* [144] = -DİR- [TUTTURMAK].

tura = TUĞRA; (*tex.*) skein (of silk, etc.); (*child.*) knotted handkerchief used in some games.

tura¹çᶜ¹ (*orn.*) Francolin; black partridge.

turala·ma *vn.* ~ **mak (-i)**, (*tex.*) make into skeins; (*child.*) strike with knotted handkerchief.

Turan (*geo.*) Turan, an ideal land where all Turks live. ~ **cı**, (*pol.*) supporter of Pan-Turanism. ~ **cılık**, (*pol.*) Pan-Turanism. ~ **i**/ ~ **lı**, (*ethn.*) Turanian.

tur·ba (*bot.*) Peat. ~ **balık**/ ~ **biyer**, peat-bog.

turfa Worthless; rotten; (*rel.*) unclean. ~ **olm.**, be despised. ~ **lamak (-i)**, despise.

turfanda (*agr.*) Early fruit/vegetables; stg. found out of season; (*jok.*) novice, new. ~ **cı(lık)**, (work of) producer/seller of early produce. ~ **lık**, field for growing early produce.

tur·gay (*orn.*) Type of lark. ~ **gor**, (*bio.*) swelling. ~ **gu** = VAKIF.

tur·istⁱ *n.* Tourist. ~ **istik**, *a.* tourist; touristic. ~ **izm**, tourism: ~ **ve Tanıtma Bakan(lığ)ı**, (*adm.*) Minis·ter/(-try) for Tourism and Information.

tur·kuaz = TÜRKUVAZ. ~ **malin**, (*geol.*) tourmaline.

turna (*orn.*) Crane. ~ **gözü gibi**, light yellow: ~ **katarı**, (*orn.*) flock of cranes; (*fig.*) procession of people: ~ **kırı**, ashen grey: ~ **sineği**, (*ent.*) cranefly: ~ **yı gözünden vurmak**, hit the mark; do a good stroke of business.

turna·ayağıⁿ¹ (*bot.*) Ranunculus, buttercup, crowfoot. ~ **balığı**ⁿ¹, (*ich.*) pike. ~ **cı**, (*his.*) type of Janissary. ~ **gagası**ⁿ¹, (*bot.*) geranium, cranesbill, herb robert. ~ **geçidi**ⁿ¹, (*met.*) spring storm.

tur·ne (*th.*, *mus.*) Tour. ~ **nike**, turnstile. ~ **no**, (*eng.*) single-sheaved block. ~ **nusol**ü, (*chem.*) litmus(-paper). ~ **nuva**, (*sp.*) tournament.

turpᵘ (*bot.*) Radish. ~ **gibi**, robust, fit as a fiddle: ~ **un sıkından seyreği iyidir**, it's best not to get too familiar (with s.o.). ~ **giller**, (*bot.*) Cruciferae, crucifers.

turşu *n.* (*cul.*) Pickle. *a.* Pickled; (*sl.*) very drunk. ~ **gibi**, very tired: ~ **kurmak**, pickle stg.: ~ **kesilmek**/ **olm.**, (*cul.*) turn sour; go bad: ~ **suratlı/yüzlü**, sour-

faced: ~ **su çıkmak**, be very tired; (*cul.*) be crushed: ~ **sunu kurmak**, (*cul.*) pickle stg.; (*fig.*) keep indefinitely; spoil by not using: ~ **sunu kur!/mu kuracaksın?**, keep it then (for all the good it may do you)!

turşu·cu(luk) (Work of) pickles-maker/-seller. ~ **laşmak**, *vi.* get crushed (and spoiled). ~ **luk**, (*cul.*) suitable for pickling.

turta (*cul.*) Fruit-tart/-pie; cake.

turun¹çᶜᵘ (*bot.*) Seville/bitter orange. ~ **likörü**, (*cul.*) curaçao. ~ **gil**, citrus. ~ **giller**, citrus fruits, Rutaceae. ~ **u**, orange-coloured. ~ **ulaşmak**, *vi.* turn orange.

TUS·İAD = TÜRK SANAYİCİLER VE İŞ ADAMLARI DERNEĞİ. ~ **LOG** = (*The US Logistics Group*).

tuş (Piano/typewriter) key; push-button; (*sp.*) touch; (*art.*) touch.

tu·ta (*fin.*) On account, down payment. ~ **taca¹k**ᵍ¹, (*dom.*) pot-holder. ~ **ta¹ç**ᶜ¹, pot-holder; (laboratory) tongs; forceps, tweezers. ~ **ta¹k**ᵍ¹, handle; pot-holder; arm (of tongs); (*mil.*) hilt; hostage. ~ **tam**, handful, pinch: ~ ~, in small quantities. ~ **tama¹ç**ᶜ¹, grip, handle. ~ **tama¹k**ᵍ¹, *n.* handle; (*pub.*) proof. ~ **tamlamak (-i)**, take a handful/pinch of stg. ~ **tana¹k**ᵍ¹, (*adm.*) minutes; written report; signed proceedings; protocol.

tutar Total, sum; sum of money. ~ **a¹k**ᵍ¹/ ~ **ga**/ ~ **ı¹k**ᵍ¹, (*med.*) seizure, fit; epilepsy: ~ **ı tutmak**, have a fit; (*fig.*) become obstinate. ~ **ıklı**, epileptic. ~ **lı**, coherent, consistent, balanced; (*phil.*) consequent. ~ **lık**, coherence; consistence; harmony; regularity. ~ **lılık**, coherency. ~ **sız**, incoherent; inconsistent. ~ **sızlık**, incoherence; irregularity; inconsistency.

tutaş (*math.*) Contiguous.

tutkal Glue; size; adhesive; bond(ing). ~ **boya**, distemper: ~ **gibi**, inseparable, unavoidable. ~ **lamak (-i)**, coat/stick with glue. ~ **lı**, gluey; glued. ~ **sı**, (*chem.*) colloidal.

tut·ku (*psy.*) Desire; passion; addiction: ~ **larına gem vurmak**, curb one's passions. ~ **kulu**, passionate; addicted. ~ **kun (-e)**, affected by; addicted to; in love with. ~ **kunluk**, passion; (*psy.*) -mania; love; harmony. ~ **kusal**, passionate.

tut·ma *vn.* = TUTMAK; (*leg.*) arrest; occupation; adhesion; support; hired labourer. ~ **ma¹ç**ᶜ¹, (*cul.*) dish of pastry squares, meat and yoghurt.

tutmak (-i, -e) *vt.* Hold; hold on to; keep, retain; preserve; take, take hold of, capture, catch, seize; control; stop, detain, arrest; attack s.o. with stg.; understand, esteem, account, reckon, suppose; contain, hold; (*mod.*) take to, like; agree with, tally with; take the part of, side with, favour; keep (one's word); listen to (advice, etc.); engage (labour); hire (property); book (seats, etc.); spread to/reach/ cover (a place); (*med.*) affect, make ill; (*naut.*) touch at (a port); (*sp.*) block; (*sl.*) have a wife. *vi.* Take root; (seeds/graft/vaccination, etc.) take; succeed; (curse) take effect; hold on, endure, last; (*fin.*) amount to, total, reach; stick, adhere; come into one's head, occur to one; (*met.*) (rain, etc.) begin; (*med.*) (pain, etc.) come on, attack one; take effect; (*cul.*) (wine, etc.) go to one's head; (*sl.*) be rich. **tut**

kelin perçeminden, he's a slippery customer: **tutalım ki**, let us suppose that . . .: **tutar kolu kanadı olmamak**, be helpless/broken: **tuttu, İstanbula gitti**, he suddenly decided to go to Istanbul: **tuttuğu dal elinde kalmak**, be let down: **tuttuğunu koparmak**, succeed in what one sets out to do; be resolute: **tutuyor musun?**, (*sl.*) have you any money?

tut·maz(lık) (*med.*) Incontin·ent/(-ence). ~**sa¹k^{ğ¹}**, (*mil.*) captive, prisoner. ~**saklık**, captivity, imprisonment. ~**su**, (*leg.*) legacy. ~**suluk**, will, testament.

tuttur·a¹ç^{c¹} Implement for holding stg.; holder. ~**ma**, *vn.*; (*min.*) bonding. ~**mak (-i, -e)**, *vc.* = TUTMAK; cause to hold, etc.; begin; cause to succeed: *vi.* begin and continue; hit the mark; keep pestering s.o. (to do stg.): **tutturabildiğine satmak**, sell at the maximum possible price. ~**malık**, fastening.

tutu (*fin.*) Mortgage, pledge. ~**su altında (-in)**, indebted to: ~**ya koymak**, mortgage, pawn. ~**cu(luk)**, conserva·tive/(-tism).

tutuk *a.* (*med.*) Paralysed; having had a stroke; (*eng.*) stopped up; broken down; embarrassed, tongue-tied, hesitant; (*sl.*) infatuated, 'gone on s.o.' ~ **su**, (*geol.*) captive water.

tutuk·eviⁿⁱ (*leg.*) Prison; detention-centre. ~**lama**, *vn.*, arrest, detention: ~ **yazısı**, warrant. ~**lamak (-i)**, arrest, take into custody; imprison. ~**lanmak**, *vp.* ~**larevi**, detention-centre. ~**lu**, *a.* arrested, imprisoned; (*fin.*) blocked, frozen: *n.* detainee, prisoner. ~**luk**, being paralysed, etc.; (*eng.*) breakdown, stoppage. ~ **(lu)luk**, imprisonment, detention.

tutul·ma *vn.* A falling in love; (*med.*) disease, complaint; (*ast.*) eclipse: ~ **evreleri**, phases of the eclipse. ~**mak**, *vp.* = TUTMAK; be held, etc.; be occupied/busy; fall in love with; be angered; (*mod.*) succeed, catch on; (*eng.*) be stopped up/closed; (*fin.*) be rented/hired; (*med.*) be taken ill; (*th.*) dry up, be tongue-tied; (*ast.*) be eclipsed: **tutulan**, popular: **tutulmuş**, booked; occupied, busy; (*med.*) affected, diseased. ~**maz**, elusive.

tutu·lu (*fin.*) Mortgaged, pawned. ~**lum**, (*ast.*) ecliptic.

tutum Manner, conduct; procedure; policy; (*fin.*) economy, thrift. ~**a elverişli/uygun**, economical. ~**bilim**, economy. ~**lu**, economical, thrifty, careful. ~**luluk**, thriftiness. ~**sal**, economic. ~**suz(luk)**, wasteful(ness), prodigal(ity).

tutun·mak (-i) *vt.* Apply to o.s.; wear: **(-e)**, *vi.* hold on(to); cling (to); take a hold; (*mod.*) catch on. ~**maz**, (*nuc.*) unstable. ~**mazlık**, instability. ~**ur**, stable, steady. ~**urluk**, steadiness, stability.

tuturu¹k^{ğu} Kindling, firewood.

tutuş Hand-hold; grip; catch. ~**kan(lık)**, inflamma·ble/(-bility). ~**ma**, *vn.*; combustion, ignition. ~**mak**, *vi.* catch hold of one another; quarrel; catch fire; ignite; flare up. ~**maz(lık)**, non-inflamma·ble/(-bility). ~**muş**, alight, ablaze. ~**turma**, *vn.*; ignition: ~ **alevi**, pilot light: ~ **sırası**, (*eng.*) firing sequence. ~**turmak (-i, -e)**, *vc.* set on fire/alight; ignite; set people quarrelling; suddenly give stg. (esp. a bribe) to s.o.

tutya (*chem.*) Zinc; (*mod.*) eye-liner. ~ **taşı**, calamine.

tuval = TUAL. ~**etⁱ**, articles of toilet; dressing-table; (*mod.*) evening-dress; (*dom.*) toilet, W.C.: ~ **kâğıdı**, toilet-paper: ~ **malzemesi**, toiletry. ~**etli**, in evening dress.

tuvenan (*min.*) Ungraded.

tuyug (*lit.*) Type of ballad.

tuz (*chem.*) Salt. ~ **atma**, (*chem.*) salting-out: ~ **biber ekmek (-e)**, stir up (quarrel); rub salt in s.o.'s wounds; be the last straw: ~ **biraz fazla kaçtı**, (*cul.*) it was rather too salty: ~ **ekmek hainliği**, base ingratitude: ~ **ekmek hakkı**, gratitude to a benefactor: ~ **püskürtme deneyi**, (*eng.*) salt-spray test: ~RUHU: ~**la buz etm.**, smash to smithereens: ~**la buz olm.**, be smashed to bits; (*fig.*) be utterly routed: ~**u biberidir (-in)**, it's a necessary addition: ~**u biberi yerinde**, (*cul.*) properly seasoned; (*fig.*) nothing lacking, all right: ~**u kuru**, well off, in easy circumstances; without worries: ~**unu çıkarmak/gidermek**, (*chem.*) desalinate.

tuza¹k^{ğ¹} Trap. ~ **kurmak (-e)**, set a trap for stg./ (*fig.*) s.o.: ~ **kuşu**, decoy, call-bird: ~**a düşmek**, fall into a trap: ~**a düşürmek**, trap, decoy. ~**çı**, trickster.

tuz·cu Salt-seller. ~**cul (bitki)**, (*bot.*) halo·phile/ (-phyte). ~**la(k)**, saltpan, saltern; salt-mine: ~ **tavası**, salt evaporator. ~**lama**, *vn.* salting: *a.* (*cul.*) salted; pickled in brine. ~**lamak (-i)**, (*cul.*) salt; pickle in brine: **tuzlayım da kokma(yasın)!**, stuff and nonsense!, you must be off your head! ~**lanmak**, *vp.* ~**lu**, (*cul.*) salt(y), saline; salted; pickled; (*fig.*) very expensive: ~ **su**, brine: ~ **ya mal olm.**, be very expensive: ~ **ya oturmak**, pay dearly for. ~**lubalgam**, (*med.*) scrofula/scurvy, etc. ~**luca**, (*cul.*) oversalted; (*fig.*) rather expensive. ~**luçubuk**, (*cul.*) *bâton salé.* ~**luk**, salt-cellar. ~**luluk**, saltiness; (*chem.*) salinity. ~**lumsu**, brackish. ~**ocağı^{nı}**, saltern. ~**ruhu^{nu}**, (*chem.*) spirit of salt; hydrochloric acid. ~**suz**, without (enough) salt; insipid. ~**suzlaşma**, (*chem.*) desalination. ~**ul**, (*chem.*) base. ~**ultutar(lık)**, (*med.*) basophil(ia). ~**veren**, (*geol., chem.*) halogen(ic).

tü *int.* Shame!

-tü¹ *v.suf.* [99] = İDİ² [GÖRÜŞTÜ].

-tü² *n.suf.* [222] = -Tİ [ÇÖKÜNTÜ].

TÜ = TEKNİK ÜNİVERSİTESİ. ~**BİTAK** = TÜRKİYE BİLİMSEL VE TEKNİK ARAŞTIRMALAR KURUMU.

tüberkül (*bio.*) Tubercle. ~**oz**, (*med.*) tuberculosis.

tüccar Merchant, businessman. ~ **malı**, goods, merchandise. ~**lık**, trade, business.

tüf (*geol.*) Tufa.

tüfe¹k^{ği} (*mil.*) Gun, rifle. ~ **çatmak**, pile arms: ~ **haznesi**, chamber: ~ **patlamaksızın**, peacefully: ~**i duvara dayamak**, be worn out/bankrupt/powerless.

tüfek·çi Gun-maker; armourer; (*his.*) type of Palace guard. ~**çilik**, gun-making/-repairing/-selling. ~**hane**, arsenal. ~**lik**, armoury; gun-bag/-stand.

tüh *int.* What a pity! ~ **sana!**, shame on you!

tükel Perfect; complete.

tük·enmek *vi.* Be exhausted; come to an end, die out; give out. ~**enmez**, inexhaustible; (*cul.*) type of

fruit-syrup (to which water is continually added). ~**enmezkalem**, (ball-point) pen with refills. ~**enmiş**, (*pub.*) out-of-print; finished; (*bio.*) extinct. ~**etici**, *a.* consuming; (*phil.*) exhaustive: *n.* (*fin.*) consumer. ~**etim**, consumption: ~ **eşyası**, consumer goods. ~**etmek (-i)**, (*fin.*) deplete, exhaust; use up; consume; drain; spend.
tükür·mek (-i) *vt.* Spit out: **(-e)**, *vi.* spit (at): ~ **yasaktır!**, it is forbidden to spit!; do not spit!: **tükürdüğünü yalamak**, (*col.*) eat one's words. ~**ü¹kᵍü/tükrü¹kᵍü**, spit(tle), saliva: ~ **bezleri**, (*bio.*) salivary glands: ~ **böceği**, (*ent.*) frog-hopper: ~ **hokkası**, cuspidor, spittoon: ~**ünü yutmak**, one's mouth water with longing. ~**üklemek (-i)**, wet with saliva. ~**üklenmek**, *vp.* ~**ükotu**ⁿᵘ, (*bot.*) ornithogallum, Star of Bethlehem.
tül (*tex.*) Tulle, fine silk. ~**ben¹t**ᵈⁱ, (*tex.*) muslin, gauze, cheese-cloth: ~ **kuruyuncaya kadar**, in a very short time. ~**bentçi**, muslin-seller. ~**bulut**, (*met.*) cirrostratus cloud. ~**yum** = TULYUM.
tüm *a.* Whole; entire; total, absolute. *n.* The whole of: = ~EN. ~ **cahil**, very ignorant: ~ **hakları korunmuştur**, (*leg.*) all rights reserved: ~ **ü**, in all, as a whole: ~**ü ile**, as a whole.
tüm·a. = ~**amiral**ⁱ**(lik)**, (*naut.*) (rank/duties of) vice-admiral. ~**bakış**, (*lit.*) synopsis. ~**başkalaşma**, (*ent.*) holometaboly, complete metamorphosis. ~**başlılar**, (*ich.*) Chimaeridae. ~**be¹k**ᵍⁱ, small round object; mound; = DÜMBELEK. ~**beyin**, (*bio.*) encephalon. ~**ce**, (*ling.*) sentence: ~ **öğeleri**, parts of a sentence: ~ **vurgusu**, sentence intonation/stress. ~**celeme**, *vn.*: ~ **kanunu**, (*phil.*) integration law. ~**celemek (-i)**, recreate. ~**cemsi**, (*ling.*) statement, proposition. ~**cül**, integral. ~**dengelim(li)**, (*phil.*) deduc·tion/(-tive). ~**değer**, (*fin.*) cost(-price).
TÜM-DER = TÜM MEMURLAR BİRLEŞME VE DANIŞMA DERNEĞİ.
tüm·el (*phil.*) Universal: ~**-evetleme**, conjunction: ~**ler**, universal concepts. ~**ellik**, universality. ~**en**, great quantity; great heap; (*mil.*) division; (*obs.*) force of ten thousand men: ~ **mahkemesi**, military court: ~ ~, in great numbers. ~**evarım**, (*phil.*) induction, inductive reasoning. ~**evarımlı**, inductive. ~**g.** = ~**general**ⁱ**(lik)**, (rank/duties of) (*mil.*) major-general//(*aer.*) air vice-marshal.
tüm·le¹çᶜⁱ That which perfects/completes; (*ling.*) [240] complement, modifier of the verb. ~**lem**, complex. ~**leme**, *vn.*; (*math.*) integrating. ~**lemek (-i)**, complete, perfect. ~**lenmek**, *vp.* ~**ler/**~**leyici**, supplementary, complementary: ~ **açı**, (*math.*) complementary angle. ~**lev**, (*math.*) integral: ~**ini almak**, integrate. ~**lük**, totality, entirety. ~**ortaklık**, (*fin.*) holding company. ~**sayı**, (*adm.*) total membership.
tüm·ör (*bio.*) Tumour. ~**seci¹k**ᵍⁱ, (*bio.*) tubercle. ~**se¹k**ᵍⁱ, (*geo.*) small mound; protuberance. ~**sekli**, (*phys.*) convex. ~**selmek**, *vi.* become round; be protuberant. ~**ülüs**, (*archaeol.*) tumulus. ~ **ür**, (*bio.*) intestinal villus.
tün (*obs.*) Night. ~**aydın**, *int.* good evening!
tün·e¹kᵍⁱ Perch (in hen-house). ~**e(kle)mek**, *vi.* perch. ~**emiş**, suspended, hanging.

tünel (*eng.*) Tunnel. ~ **açmak**, drive a tunnel: ~ **geçmek**, (*sl.*) be absent-minded/wool-gathering.
tü¹pᵇü Tube; (*chem.*) test-tube. ~ **gazı**, calor gas. ~**lük**, test-tube rack/holder.
tür (*bio.*) Species, genus; kind, sort, type, category; (*art.*) genre.
-tür *v. suf.* [96] = -DİR; OLMAK [TÜRK'TÜR].
-tür- *v. suf.* [144] = -DİR- [GÖRÜŞTÜRMEK].
türa¹pᵇ¹ Earth, dust.
türban (*mod.*) Turban, headscarf.
türbe (*arch.*) Tomb, mausoleum. ~**si gibi (Nasrettin Hoca'nın)**, place open on all sides but with one entrance. ~**dar**, tomb guardian. ~**eriği**ⁿⁱ, (*bot.*) type of plum.
tür·bin (*eng.*) Turbine. ~**bo-**. *pref.* turbo-. ~**bojeneratör**, turbo-generator. ~**bopomp**, turbo-pump. ~**bülans**, (*aer.*, *met.*) turbulence. ~**bün** = DÜRBÜN.
türdeş (*bio.*) Of the same kind/species; homogeneous; (*chem.*) homologous. ~**lik**, homogeneity; homology.
türe (*leg.*) Law; right. ~ +, *a.* Legal. ~**dışı**, illegal; (*bio.*) heteronomous. ~**l**, legal.
türe·di Upstart; parvenu. ~**m(e)**, *vn.*; invention: ~ **belgesi**, (*ind.*) patent: ~ **ünlü**, (*ling.*) anaptyctic vowel [HÜKÜM; GEPEGENÇ]: ~ **ünsüz**, (*ling.*) inserted consonant [YURMAK]. ~**mek**, *vi.* spring up suddenly; come into existence; appear: **(-den)**, (*ling.*) derive/be formed from. ~**miş**, (*ling.*) derived: ~ **ad//belirteç//eylem//sıfat//sözcük**, derived noun// adverb//verb//adjective//word. ~**ti**, invention. ~**tici**, derivative; forming, formative. ~**tilmek**, *vp.* ~**tim**, derivation, deduction. ~**tme**, *vn.* (*ling.*) (word-)formation/derivation; invention. ~**tmek (-i)**, create, invent; form, derive. ~**tmen**, inventor. ~**v**, (*ling.*) derivative; (*ind.*) by-product: ~ **boru**, (*eng.*) bypass. ~**vsel**, (*math.*) differential.
Türkü *n.* (*ethn.*) Turk. ~ +, *a.* Turkish: ~ **Dil Kurumu**, Turkish Linguistic Society: ~ **Dili Dergisi**, (*pub.*) Turkish Language Journal: ~ **iş**, [44] (*col.*) poor piece of work: ~ **kahvesi**, (*cul.*) Turkish coffee: ~ **kodeksi**, (*med.*) Turkish codex: ~ **mavisi**, turquoise blue: ~ **Ocağı**, (*pol.*) Turkish Nationalist Club: ~ **Parası Kıymetini Koruma Mevzuatı**, (*fin.*) Turkish currency control regulations.
Türkbank = TÜRK TİCARET BANKASI
Türkçe (*ling.*) Turkish language. ~ **bilmez**, slow-witted: ~ **bilmez Allahtan korkmaz**, barbarian: ~ **söylemek**, speak in Turkish; put things bluntly: ~**de buna ne dersiniz?**, what do you call this in Turkish?: ~**si**, the long and the short of it, in plain English: ~**ye çevirmek**, translate into Turkish: ~**yi kaybetmek**, be utterly bewildered: ~**yi pürüzsüz konuşmak**, speak Turkish fluently.
Türkçe·ci (*ling.*) Turkicist; (*ed.*) Turkish language teacher. ~**cilik**, (*ling.*) Turkicism. ~**leşmek**, *vi.* (*ling.*) become pure Turkish; be translated into Turkish. ~**leştirmek (-i)**, make pure Turkish; translate into Turkish.
Türk·çü (*pol.*) (Pan-)Turkist. ~**çülük**, (Pan-)Turkism. ~**istan**, (*geo.*) Turkestan: ~ **pilavı**, (*cul.*) carrot pilaff.

TÜRKİŞ = TÜRKİYE İŞÇİ SENDİKALARI KON-FEDERASYONU.

Türk·iyat[1] Turcology. ~**iye**, (*geo.*) Turkey: ~ **Büyük Millet Meclisi**, (*pol.*) Turkish National Assembly: ~ **Cumhuriyeti**, (*pol.*) Republic of Turkey: ~ **Türkçesi**, (*ling.*) Turkish as spoken in Turkey. ~**iyeli**, (*ethn.*) Turk; belonging to/ originating in Turkey. ~**izm**, (*ling.*) Turkish idiom, Turkicism. ~**leşmek**, *vi.* become Turkish/like a Turk; adopt Turkish habits. ~**leştirmek (-i)**, (*soc.*, *pol.*) Turkicize. ~**lük**, quality of being a Turk; Turkish community. ~**lükbilim(ci)**, Turcolo·gy/ (-gist). ~**men**, (*ethn.*) Turkoman. ~**mence**, (*ling.*) Turkoman. ~**menistan**, (*geo.*) Turkmen S.S.R. ~**olog**, (*ed.*) Turcologist. ~**oloji**, (*ed.*) Turcology. ~**uvaz**, *n.* (*geol.*) turquoise: *a.* turquoise-blue.

türkü (*mus.*) Folk-song. ~ **okuyucusu**, folk singer: ~ **söylemek**, sing: ~ **yakmak**, compose a song: ~**sünü çağırmak (-in)**, praise s.o.; speak to please s.o.

tür·lü Sort, kind, category, variety; (*cul.*) meat and vegetable casserole: ~ **güveç**, (*cul.*) casserole: ~ ~, of all sorts, various: ~**sü**, all kinds: ~**sünü görmek**, have varied experiences of stg. ~**sel(lik)**, specific(ity).

türüm (*geo.*) Genesis, creation; (*phil.*) emanation.

tüs = TÜY.

TÜTED = TÜM TEKNİK ELEMANLAR DERNEĞİ.

tüt·en (*geol.*) Fumarole. ~**me**, *vn.* ~**mek**, *vi.* (chimney, etc.) smoke.

tütsü (*chem.*) Fumigation; fumigant; incense. ~**leme**, *vn.* ~**lemek (-i)**, fumigate; (*cul.*) cure, smoke. ~**lenmek**, *vp.* ~**lenmiş**/ ~**lü**, (*cul.*) smoked, cured.

tüttürmek (-i) *vc.* = TÜTMEK.

tütün Smoke; (*bot.*) tobacco. ~ **içmek**, smoke/ inhale (tobacco): ~ **yuvası**, pipe-bowl. ~**balığı**[nı], (*cul.*) smoked fish. ~**cü(lük)**, (work of) tobacco-grower//tobacconist. ~**lemek**, (*cul.*) smoke. ~**lük**, (*cul.*) crispest PASTIRMA.

tüvan Power, strength. ~**a**, strong, robust.
tüvey[l]ç[ci] (*bot.*) Corolla.
tüvi[l]t[di] (*tex.*) Tweed.
tüy (*zoo.*) Feather; down; bristle, hair; (horse) coat; (*bot.*) down. ~ **atmak**, moult: ~ **bayrağı**, (*bio.*) vane: ~ **dikmek (-e)**, be the last straw for stg.: ~ **dökmek**, (*zoo.*) cast/shed its coat: ~ **düzmek**, (*orn.*) preen its feathers; (*fig.*) arrange one's clothes: ~ **gibi**, as light as a feather; agile: ~ **kalem**, quill pen: ~ **tüsü yok**, the hair has not sprouted on his cheeks: ~**ler ürpertici**, atrocious; blood-curdling: ~**leri diken diken olm.**/**ürpermek**, one's hair stand on end; (*fig.*) shudder: ~**lerini yolmak**, pluck its feathers.

tüy·ağırlık/ ~**sıklet** (*sp.*) Feather-weight. ~**bitleri**, (*ent.*) birdlice. ~**bulu**[l]t[du], (*met.*) cirrus cloud. ~**döken**, (*sl.*) razor. ~**dürmek (-i)**, *vc.* (*sl.*) steal. ~**lenmek**, *vi.* grow hair/feathers, etc.; (*fig.*) become rich. ~**lü**, feathered; downy: ~ **kuyruk**, (*zoo.*) brush: ~ **meşe**, (*bot.*) Turkey oak. ~**mek**, *vi.* (*sl.*) slip away. ~**sü**, (*bot.*) pennate. ~**süz**, (*zoo.*) hairless; (*orn.*) featherless, unfledged; (*fig.*) beardless, young: ~ **şeftali**, (*bot.*) nectarine.

tüz·e (*leg.*) Justice; equity; (*adm.*) courts: ~ **Bakan(lığ)ı**, (*adm.*) Minis·ter/(-try) of Justice: ~ **doktoru**, (*med.*) forensic pathologist: ~ **yargılığı**, (*leg.*) court of justice. ~**eci**, jurist. ~**el**, judicial: ~ **karar**, judgment, sentence: ~ **kişi**, juridical person: ~ **kütük**, criminal record: ~ **tıp**, forensic medicine: ~ **yardım**, legal aid. ~**elkişi**, legal entity, corporate body. ~**ü**[l]k[gü], (*leg.*) administrative law; (*adm.*) regulations, rules, bye-laws. ~**üksel**, administrative, regulatory.

TV = TELEVİZYON: ~'**la yayım**, television transmission/broadcast. ~**K** = TÜRK VATANDAŞLIĞI KANUNU.

TY·MB = TÜRKİYE YÜKSEK MÜHENDİSLER BİR-LİĞİ. ~**S** = TÜRKİYE YAZARLAR SENDİKASI.

TZB = TÜRKİYE ZİRAAT BANKASI.

U

U, u [u] Twenty-fifth Tk. letter, U. ~ **borusu**, (*eng*.) U-tube: ~ **demiri**, channel iron: ~ **dirseği**, U-bend.
U = (*ch.s.*) URANYUM.
-u[1] *n. suf.* [28] = -i[1] [BUZU].
-u[2] *n. suf.* [39] = -i[2] [ÇOCUĞU].
-u[3] *a./n. suf.* [221] = -i[3] [DOLU; KORKU].
UB = (*adm*.) ULAŞTIRMA BAKANLIĞI.
ubudiyet[i] Slavery, servitude.
uc- = UÇ. ~ **a**, (*bio*.) coccyx; (*fig*.) stump.
ucay (*phys*.) Pole. ~**la(n)ma**, polarization. ~**layıcı**, polarizer. ~**lık**, polarity. ~**sal**, polar. ~**sı**, polaroid.
ucra = ÜCRA.
-ucu *a./n. suf.* [220] = -ici [OKUYUCU].
ucube Strange thing; a wonder; curiosity; abortion; monstrosity.
ucun ~ ~, partially, bit by bit.
ucuz Cheap. ~ **atlatmak/kurtulmak**, get off lightly; escape cheaply: ~ **etin yahnisi tatsız/yavan olur**, you get what you pay for, cheap things are not worth much: ~ **satmak**, sell cheaply; think stg. easy to get/do; underestimate: ~**a çıkmak**, get stg. cheaply: ~**a dayanamamak**, be unable to resist stg. cheap/free: ~**dur illeti var**, there's a catch in it: ~**dur vardır illeti, pahalıdır vardır hikmeti**, don't despise cheapness or fear expense.
ucuz·cu S.o. who sells cheaply; bargain-hunter. ~**lamak**, *vi*. become cheap, go down in price; (*fig*.) be easy to get. ~**latılmak**, *vp*. ~**latmak** (-i), make cheap; dump; (*fig*.) cheapen. ~**luk**, cheapness; place where living is cheap: ~ **bölümü**, bargain basement.
u[l]**ç**[cu] *n.* Tip, point; extremity, end; top; (*his*.) frontier, march; course, direction; cause, motive; pen-nib; (*agr*.) ploughshare; (*el*.) terminal; (*eng*.) bit. ~ +, *a*. End, terminal: ~ **aralığı**, (*eng*.) end-clearance: ~ **bölüğü**, (*mil*.) advance party: ~ **demiri**, (*agr*.) ploughshare: ~ ~**a**, end to end, point to point; just enough: ~ ~**a gelmek**, be just enough: ~ ~**a karşılamak**, make both ends meet: ~ **vermek**, appear; (*bot*.) sprout; grow; (*med*.) (boil) come to a head: ~**tan** ~**a**, from one end/extreme to the other: ~**u bucağı olmamak**, be very wide/vast: ~**u dokunmak**, involve/affect one; entail: ~**u ortası belli olmamak**, not know how to tackle stg.: ~**u** ~**una**, a close thing: ~**u** ~**una getirmek**, just make both ends meet: ~**u uzundur (dünyanın)**, all sorts of strange things happen: ~**u buna/şuna dokunmak**, s.o. be hurt: ~**unda bir şey olm.** (-in), some secret purpose be behind stg.; ~**unda bu/şu olm.**, end this/that way: ~**unu altına kaçırmak**, be on the downward path (by mismanagement, etc.): ~**unu göstermek** (-in), drop a

hint (of stg. advantageous): ~**unu kaçırmak**, lose the thread of a matter: ~**unu (kulpunu) bulmak** (-in), find a clue to stg.; find a way to succeed in stg.: ~**unu kulpunu kaybetmek**, be at a loss what to do: ~**unu ortasını bulmak**, get to the bottom of stg.
uç·ağrısı[n1] (*med*.) Acrodynia. ~**irileşim**, acromegaly. ~**kesim**, amputation. ~**morarım**, acrocyanosis.
uça[l]**k**[g1] (*aer*.) Aeroplane. ~ +, *a*. Air; aircraft; aviation; aerial; aero-; avi-: ~ **adamı**, crew-member: ~ **bölüğü**, squadron: ~ **çatkısı**, airframe: ~ **çekimi**, photogrammetry: ~ **gemisi**, (*naut*.) aircraft-carrier: ~ **himaye/koruması**, (*aer*.) air cover/umbrella: ~ **hostesi**, air-hostess: ~ **kanadı**, aerofoil: ~ **kazası**, air-crash: ~ **personeli**, air-crew: ~ **saldırısı**, air-raid/-strike: ~ **şirketi**, airline: **trafiği**, air navigation: ~**a bin(dir)mek**, *vi./*(*vt*.) embark: ~**la**, by air(mail): ~**lar**, aircraft: ~**tan gemiye** // **uçağa** // **yere**, air-to-sea // -air // -ground (missile, etc.).
uçak·çı Aeronaut, aviator. ~**çılık**, aviation, aeronautics: ~ **elektroniği**, avionics: ~ **teknolojisi**, aerospace technology. ~ **savar**, anti-aircraft (gun).
uçan Flying; (*chem*.) vaporizing, volatile. ~ **bomba**, flying bomb: ~ **kuşa borçlu olm.**, be in debt all round/up to one's ears: ~ **kuştan medet ummak**, clutch at any straw for help. ~**top**[u], (*sp*.) volleyball.
uçar Flying; (*chem*.) volatile. ~ **balık**, (*ich*.) flying fish: ~ **gibi ilerlemek**, advance by leaps and bounds: ~ **kırlangıç balığı**, (*ich*.) flying gurnard: ~ **kurbağa/maki//tilki**, (*zoo*.) flying toad//lemur// fox. ~**a**, (*sp*.) volley: ~**a atmak**, shoot a bird on the wing. ~**ı**, (*pej*.) excessive; dissolute: ~ **çapkın**, debauchee, rake: ~ **takımından**, arrant scoundrel. ~**ılık**, debauchery. ~**kefal**[i], (*ich*.) Atlantic flying fish.
uçkun Flying spark. ~ **kül**, flue ash.
uçkur (*mod*.) Belt, threaded trouser-strap. ~ **çözmek**, (*fig*.) have sexual relations: ~**una gevşek**, (*col*.) a regular Don Juan: ~**una sağlam**, (*fig*., *col*.) chaste, virginal. ~**luk**, seam (for trouser-strap/ flag-halyard, etc.).
uçkurutan (*myc*.) Fungus attacking citrus plants.
uç·lanmak *vi*. Have a tip; become pointed; (*sl*.) give, pay, return. ~**laşma**, polarization. ~**lu**, pointed; tipped; (penholder) with a nib; filter-tipped cigarette.
uçma[l]**k**[g1 1] *n.* (*obs*.) Heaven, paradise. ~**lı**, heavenly.
uçmak[2] *vi*. Fly; (*sp*.) dive at; (*phys*.) evaporate, vaporize; turn pale; (*jok*.) disappear, fade away; fall (from cliff, etc.); (*fig*.) behave outrageously; be wild (with joy, etc.). = UÇAN; UÇAR.

uç·man(lık) (*aer.*) (Work of) airman, pilot. ~**maz**, (*orn.*) flightless.
Uçs. = UÇAKSAVAR.
uçsuz Without a point; untipped; endless; without a nib. ~ **bucaksız**, endless, vast.
uç·tuuçtu (*child.*) Game imitating flying objects. ~**ucu**, *a.* flying; (*chem.*) volatile: *n.* (*aer.*) pilot: ~ **mühendis**, flight engineer. ~**uculuk**, volatility. ~**uçböceği**ni, (*ent.*) ladybird.
uçuk[1] *a.* Pale; light (colour).
uçu·kgu [2] *n.* (*med.*) Blain (on lips); vesicle; herpes. ~**lamak**, *vi.* have vesicles break out on lips.
uçul (*aer.*) Rocket.
uçun (*chem., phys.*) Gas; (*naut.*) (flag) free edge. ~ **bulucu**, gas detector: ~ **kömürü**, (*geol.*) gas coal: ~ **yüzlüğü**, gas mask. ~**laştırma**, gasification. ~**lu**, gaseous. ~**ma**, (*phys.*) sublimation. ~**tu**, gas.
uçur·mak (**-i**) *vc.* = UÇMAK[2]. Cause to fly; fly (aeroplane); evaporate; cut off, chop off; (*sl.*) exaggerate, boast; (*sl.*) steal. ~**tma**, (*child.*) kite. ~**tmak** (**-i**), *vc.* ~**ucu**, (*phys.*) evaporator. ~**ulmak**, *vp.* ~**um**, (*geo.*) cliff, precipice, abyss; (*fig.*) tragic end.
uçuş Act/style of flying; flight. ~ **bilim/ilmi**, aeronautics: ~ **güvertesi**, flight deck: ~ **hızı**, cruising speed: ~ **meydanı**, landing-ground, aerodrome: ~ **ortalama hız//süresi**, block speed//time: ~ **planı**, flight plan: ~**a elverişli(lik)**, airworth·y/(-iness): ~**a gitmek**, (*sl.*) have sex. ~**mak**, *vi.* fly together/in a flock; fly about; flap the wings.
ud- = UT[1, 2]. ~**i**, (*mus.*) lute-player.
uf *int.* Oof!, ooh! ~ **puf demek**, sigh; express annoyance.
ufacık Very small, tiny. ~ **tefecik**, tiny, dainty.
ufak Small; miniature. ~ **akçe/para**, (*fin.*) small change: ~ **çapta**, on a small scale: ~ **göstermek**, look younger than one is: ~ **harf (kasası)**, (*pub.*) lower case: ~ **rol**, (*th., cin.*) extra, bit-part: ~ **tefek**, small, trifling; of no account; s.o. small and short; odds and ends, trifles: ~ **tefek görmek**, regard as unimportant.
ufak·ça Quite small. ~**dalga**, (*phys.*) microwave. ~**lı**, containing small pieces. ~**lık**, smallness; (*fin.*) small change; (*jok.*) lice. ~**ölçekte**, microscopic.
ufa·lamak (**-i**) Reduce in size; break into small pieces; crumble; break up; (*geol.*) comminute; weather. ~**lanma**, *vn.* weathering. ~**lanmak**, *vp.*: *vi.* disintegrate; crumble. ~**layıcı**, crusher. ~**lmak**, *vi.* become smaller; diminish. ~**ltmak** (**-i**), crush, crumble. ~**rak**, smallish, rather tiny.
ufk- = UFUK. ~**i**, horizontal.
uflamak *vi.* Say 'oof', complain (from boredom, etc.). **uflayıp puflamak**, complain continually.
uf'ukku (*geo.*) Horizon. ~**unu genişletmek**, broaden one's horizons, become more educated.
ufuneti Putrefaction; putrid smell; (*med.*) inflammation. ~**lenmek**, *vi.* putrefy; (*med.*) become inflamed and putrid. ~**li**, putrefying; putrid; stinking, fetid.
uğr- = UĞUR[1].
uğra (*cul.*) Flour sprinkled on dough to be kneaded. ~**lamak** (**-i**), sprinkle flour.

uğra·'kg1 Much frequented place. ~**mak** (**-e**), stop at/touch at/visit (place); meet with (accident); suffer (illness); call/drop in on s.o.; undergo (change, etc.): *vi.* be possessed by evil spirits: **uğramadan**, direct. ~**nmak**, *vp.* ~**ntı(sal)**, accident(al).
uğraş(ı) Struggle, fight; occupation, profession. ~ **vermek** (**-e**), work on stg. ~**ılmak**, *vp.* ~**macı**, fighter, one who struggles. ~**mak** (**-le**), struggle/fight with; strive hard; take great pains; endeavour. ~**man**, (*sp., th.*) professional. ~**taş**, professional colleague. ~**tırmak** (**-i**), *vc.* ~**sal**, professional.
uğratmak (**-i, -e**) *vc.* = UĞRAMAK; expose s.o. to stg.; send away.
uğru Thief. ~**lamak** (**-i**), steal. ~**luk**, theft.
uğrun ~ (~), secretly.
uğul·damak *vi.* Hum; buzz; (wind) howl. ~**tu**, humming/buzzing noise; (*med.*) tinnitus; (*cin.*) background noise.
uğunmak = UVUNMAK.
uğ'urru [1] *n.* Aim, end, goal.
uğur[2] *n.* Good luck; good omen; *pr.n.* (*ast.*) Jupiter. ~ **heykeli**, fetish: ~ **ola!**/~**lar olsun!**, good luck!: ~**u açık**, lucky, fortunate: ~**una**/ ~**unda** (**-in**), *post.* [94] for the sake of . . .; on account of . . ..
uğur·böceğini (*ent.*) Seven-spot ladybird. ~**böcekleri**, ladybirds, Coccinellidae. ~**lamak** (**-i**), wish s.o. good luck; bid s.o. godspeed; see s.o. off. ~**lanmak**, *vp.* ~**lu**, lucky, auspicious: ~ **kademli olsun**, may it be a good omen/bring good luck. ~**luk**, mascot, talisman. ~**samak** (**-i**), consider stg. a good omen, regard as lucky. ~**suz**, inauspicious; bringing bad luck; ill-omened; rascal: ~ **kadın**, vamp, *femme fatale.* ~**suzluk**, ill omen; being unlucky.
uhde Obligation; charge; duty; responsibility. ~**sinde olm.** (**-in**), be entrusted to . . .; be in the charge of . . .: ~**sinden gelmek** (**-in**), carry out the task of . . .; discharge the duty of . . .: ~**sine almak**, take on the duty of . . .: ~**sine geçirmek**, charge s.o. with the duty of . . ..
UHF = (*ultra high frequency*).
uhrevi (*rel.*) Pertaining to the next world.
uhuvveti (*obs.*) Brotherly feeling; brotherhood; affection.
-uk *a./n. suf.* [221] = -İK [BOZUK].
UK = (*United Kingdom*).
ukala *pl.* = AKIL. *s.* Wiseacre; know-all. ~ **dümbeleği**, pretentious quack, know-all. ~**lık**, pretended cleverness; conceitedness.
uk·de Knot; (*fig.*) sore point, stg. that sticks in the throat. ~**num**, root, basis; (*phil.*) hypostasis.
Ukrayna (*geo.*) Ukraine. ~**lı**, (*ethn.*) Ukrainian.
ukubeti *n.* Retribution, punishment. *a.* Ugly, wearisome.
-ul- *vp. suf.* [149] = -İL- [UNUTULMAK].
ula·'çc1 (*ling.*) Gerund. ~**lı**, ~ **birleşik eylem**, verb compounded with a gerund [YAPABİLMEK]. ~**lık**, gerundial.
Ulah (*ethn.*) Wallachian. ~**ça**, (*ling.*) Wallachian.
ula·'kg1 Courier, messenger.
ula·m Group; (*phil.*) category: ~ ~, in groups. ~**ma**, *vn.*; addition, appendix; (*ling.*) liaison.

~**mak (-i)**, add, join on; bring into contact. ~**nmak**, *vp.* ~**ntı**, addition.
ulan *int.* (*vulg.*) My good fellow!; man alive!; hey you!
ulaş·ık Reaching; touching, contiguous. ~**ılmak**, *vp.* ~**ım**/~**ma**, *vn.* access; communications; transport; connection, relation; contact. ~**mak (-e)**, reach, arrive at; climb (mountain); come into contact with; meet. ~**tırma**, *vn.* causing to reach; communications; (*mil.*) transport corps: ~ **araçları**, means of communication: ~ **Bakan(lığ)ı**, (*adm.*) Minis·ter/(-try) of Communications/ Transport. ~**tırmak (-i, -e)**, *vc.*
ulayıcı Linking, connecting.
ulema *pl.* = ÂLİM. Learned men; (*rel.*) ulema, doctors of Muslim theology. ~**lık**, learning, scholarship: ~ **taslamak**, make a parade of one's knowledge.
ult(.) = (*ultimo*). ~**ra** = ÜLTRA.
-ultu *n. suf.* [222] = -İLTİ [UĞULTU].
ulu Great; big; tall. ~ **doğan**, (*orn.*) saker falcon. ~**dağ**, *pr.n.* (*geo.*) Mount Olympus (Bithynia): ~**-köknarı**, (*bot.*) type of fir: ~**-yüksükotu**, (*bot.*) rusty foxglove. ~ORTA.
ulufe (*his.*) Soldier's pay. ~**ci**, (*his.*) member of cavalry corps.
ulu·lama *vn.* ~**lamak (-i)**, extol, honour. ~**lanmak**, *vp.* ~**luk**, greatness, honour.
ulum *pl.* = İLİM. Sciences. ~**u diniye**, (*obs.*) theology.
ulu·ma *vn.* (Dog's) howling. ~**mak**, *vi.* howl: **uluyan**, howling.
uluorta Openly; rashly, recklessly.
ulus (*his.*) Tribe; (*soc.*) people, nation. ~**al**, national: ~ **bayram**, National Holiday (29 October): ~ **saat**, local time. ~**allaştırmak (-i)**, nationalize. ~**allık**, nationality; territoriality. ~**çu(luk)**, national·ist/(-ism). ~**lararası**, international: ~ **Ayaktopu Birliği**, (*sp.*) FIFA: ~ **Gelişme Örgütü/Kalkınma Dairesi**, (*fin.*) Agency for International Development: ~ **hukuk**, international law: ~ **Olimpiyat Kurulu**, (*sp.*) International Olympic Committee: ~ **Para Fonu**, (*fin.*) International Monetary Fund: ~ **Tecim Odası**, (*fin.*) International Chamber of Commerce: ~ **yarış**, (*sp.*) international competition. ~**lararası·cılık**, internationalism. ~**laşmak**, *vi.* become a nation. ~**laştırmak (-i)**, create a nation. ~**sever(lik)**, patriot·ic/(-ism).
ulvi High, sublime, celestial. ~**yet**[i], superiority; loftiness; sublimity.
-um[1] *a./n. suf.* [39] = -İM[1] [ÇOCUĞUM].
-um[2] *v. suf.* [96] = -İM[2] [GELİYORUM].
-um[3] *n. suf.* [224] = -İM[3] [DOĞUM].
UM = (*adm.*) UMUMİ MÜDÜR(LÜK).
umacı Ogre, bogyman. ~ **gibi**, terrible, ugly.
umak [151] *obs.* Be powerful/able.
umar Remedy, solution; means; help. ~**sız**, irremediable; inevitable; helpless. ~**sızlık**, lack of means; helplessness.
umde Principle.
um·ma *vn.* Hope; expectation: ~**ya uğratmak (-i)**, disappoint. ~**madık**, *a.* unexpected. ~ **mak (-i)**,

hope; expect, anticipate: **ummadığın taş baş yarar**, small/unimportant things often have big effects.
umman (*geo.*) Ocean. *pr.n.* Oman. ~ **denizi**, Arabian Sea: ~ **körfezi**, Gulf of Oman.
umran = ÜMRAN.
-umsu *a. suf.* [58] = -İMSİ [PAMUĞUMSU].
umu Hope, desire. ~ **vermek**, hope. ~**d-** = UMUT. ~**lmadık**, *a.* unexpected. ~**lmak**, *vp.* = UMMAK; be hoped/expected. ~**lur**, *a.* contingent.
umum *a.* General, universal; all. *n.* The public, people. ~ **millet**, the whole nation: ~ **muvacehesinde**, publicly, before everyone: ~ **müdür**, (*fin.*) general manager; (*ed. sl.*) fat pupil: ~ **müdürlük**, general managership/manager's office.
umum·ca/~**en** Generally. ~**hane**, brothel. ~**i**, general; universal; public: ~ **af**, (*leg.*) general amnesty: ~ **efkâr**, (*pol.*) plebiscite: ~ **harp**, (*his.*) World War I. ~**iyet**[i], generality; universality. ~**iyetle**, in general.
umun[1]**ç**[cu] Longing; ambition; aim.
umur *pl.* = EMİR. Affairs, matters. *s.* Matter of importance; concern. ~ **et(me)mek**, (not) trouble about stg.: ~ **görmüş**, experienced: ~**umun teki**, I'm not the least interested in it: ~**unda bile olmamak**, not care, be indifferent.
umur·samak (-i) Care/be concerned about; consider important. ~**samaz(lık)**, careless(ness); callous/ (-ness); indiffer·ent/(-ence). ~**sanmak**, *vp.* become stg. important.
umu[1]**t**[du] Hope, expectation; hopefulness. ~ **bağlamak (-e)**, rely/pin one's hopes on: ~ **etm.**, hope, expect; contemplate: ~ **kırıklığı**, disappointment: ~ **vermek**, give hope: ~**a düşmek**, be hopeful: ~**unu kesme!**, never say die!: ~**unu kırmak**, discourage, disappoint. [*Also* = ÜMİT]
umut·landırmak (-i) Make hopeful, fill with hope. ~**lanmak**, *vi.* be hopeful. ~**lu(luk)**, hopeful(ness). ~**suz**, without hope; hopeless, despondent. ~**suzluk**, hopelessness, despondency: ~**a kapılmak**, be filled with despair.
-umuz *n. suf.* [39] = -İMİZ [OKULUMUZ].
un (*cul.*) Flour, meal, farina. ~ **böceği**, (*ent.*) meal-worm beetle: ~ **güvesi**, (*ent.*) Mediterranean flour moth: ~ **şekeri**, powdered sugar: ~ **ufak (etm.)**, (make) as fine as flour; (break) in pieces: ~**unu elemiş eleğini duvara asmış**, he's finished with, he's too old for that sort of thing.
-un[1] *n. suf.* [28] = -İN[1] [OKULUN].
-un[2] *n. suf.* [29] = -İN[2] [ÇOCUĞUN].
-un[3] *n. suf.* [225] = -İN[3] [SORUN].
-un-[4] *vp. suf.* [149] = -İN- [BULUNMAK].
UN = (*United Nations*).
-unca[1] *adv. suf.* = -İNCE[1] [BOYUNCA].
-unca[2] *v. suf.* [179] = -İNCE[2] [BOĞULUNCA].
uncu(luk) (Work of) flour-miller/-seller.
-uncu *a. suf.* [82] = -İNCİ [DOKUZUNCU].
-unç *a./n. suf.* [222] = -İNÇ [KORKUNÇ].
undurmak (-i) *vc.* = UNMAK.
UN·ESCO = (*United Nations Educational, Scientific and Cultural Organization*). ~**İCEF** = (*UN International Children's Emergency Fund*).
un·lamak (-i) (*cul.*) Sprinkle with flour. ~**lanmak**, *vp.* ~**lu**, made with flour; farinaceous; floury: ~

bit/böcek, (*ent.*) mealy bug. ~ **luk**, *a.* suitable for flour: *n.* (mill) hopper.

un·madık *a.* Incurable; that will not heal. *n.* Unlucky person. ~ **mak**, *vi.* heal; get well. ~ **maz**, *a.* that will not heal; incorrigible; unlucky.

UN·O = (*United Nations Organization*). ~ **RRA** = (*UN Relief and Rehabilitation Agency*).

unsur Element; root; component.

-untu *n. suf.* [222] = -İNTİ [KURUNTU].

unul·mak *imp. v.* One be healed/cured. ~ **maz**, incurable.

unut·kan Forgetful; absent-minded. ~ **kanlık**, forgetfulness; (*med.*) amnesia. ~ **mabeni**, (*bot.*) forget-me-not. ~ **mak (-i)**, forget: **unutma emi!**, now don't forget! ~ **turmak (-i, -e)**, *vc.* ~ **ulmak**, *vp.*

-unuz *n. suf.* [39] = -İNİZ [OKULUNUZ].

unvan Title; superscription; (letter) address; (*ed.*) degree; designation. ~ **grubu**, form of address [Profesör Doktor Toğrol]: ~ **sıfatı**, (*ling.*) adjective of rank/status, etc.: ~ **tezkeresi**, (*adm.*) trading licence. ~ **lı**, bearing the title . . .; entitled.

UP·F = ULUSLARARASI PARA FONU. ~ **U** = (*Universal Postal Union*).

up·uygun Quite adequate/suitable. ~ **uzun**, extremely long.

ur (*bio.*) Tumour, wen, neoplasm; (*bot.*) gall; excrescence. ~ **arı//sineği**, (*ent.*) gall wasp//fly: ~ **u**, (*med.*) -oma (carcinoma).

-ur[1] *v. suf.* [116] = -İR [BULUR].

-ur-[2] *vc. suf.* [145] = -DİR- [DOĞURMAK].

urağan (*met.*) Hurricane.

uran Industry.

uran·ötesi (*chem.*) Transuranic. ~ **us**, *pr.n.* (*ast.*) Uranus. ~ **yum**, (*chem.*) uranium.

uray (*obs.*) Municipality.

urba (*mod.*) Dress, robe.

Urban (*ethn.*) Bedouin Arabs.

urbilim (*med.*) Oncology.

Urduca (*ling.*) Urdu.

Urfa (*geo.*) Urfa; (*his.*) Edessa. ~ **yağı**, (*cul.*) cooking fat.

urgan Rope. ~ **cı**, rope-maker/-seller.

urmak (*obs.*) = VURMAK.

uruk[u] Tribe.

uru·p[bu] (*math., obs.*) Eighth part of ARŞIN (8 cms.).

uryapan (*bio.*) Oncoge·nic/-nous.

us (*psy.*) (Right state of) mind; reason; discretion. ~ **pahası**, (learning by) experience: ~ **sayrılıkları** (**evi**), (*psy.*) mental diseases/(hospital): ~ **a aykırı/** (**-lık**), unreasonable(ness); irrational(ism): ~ **a uygun/yatkın**, reasonable; rational: ~ AVURMA(K).

US·(A) = (*United States* (*of America*)). ~ **AF** = (*US Air Force*). ~ **IS** = (*US Information Service*).

usan[cı] Boredom, tedium; disgust. ~ **gelmek (-den)**, be bored by: ~ **getirmek**, get bored: ~ **vermek**, bore.

usan·dırıcı *a.* Boring. ~ **dırmak (-i)**, bore. ~ **ılmak (-den)**, *imp. v.* one get bored with. ~ **mak (-den)**, become sick of/bored/disgusted with.

usare (*bot.*) Sap; (*cul.*) squeezed juice.

us·avurma (*phil.*) Reasoning. ~ **avurmak**, *vi.* reason. ~ **çu(luk)**, rational·ist/(-ism). ~ **dışı(cılık)**, irrational(ism). ~ **gücü**, intelligence.

uskumru (*ich.*) Mackerel. ~ **turnası**, (*ich.*) Atlantic saury, skipper.

uskuna (*naut.*) Schooner.

uskur (*naut.*) Screw, propeller. ~ **u**, (*eng.*) screw-thread.

uskut *int.* Shut up! ~ **lamak**, *vi.* (*sl.*) be silent.

us·lamlamak (-i) Judge, decide. ~ **landırmak (-i)**, bring s.o. to his senses; make s.o. behave. ~ **lanmak**, *vi.* become sensible/discreet/well-behaved; come to one's senses. ~ **lu**, well-behaved; sensible; good (child); quiet (horse): ~ **dur!**, be a good child!: ~ **oturmak**, sit still, keep quiet. ~ **luluk**, being well-behaved, etc. ~ **sal**, rational; mental.

usta *n.* Master workman; craftsman; artisan; foreman; overseer; (*his.*) woman superintendent of servants/slaves. *a.* Skilled, deft, clever; experienced. ~ **çıkmak/olm.**, (apprentice) become a master workman.

usta·başı[nı] Foreman; charge-hand. ~ **ca**, skilfully; cunningly. ~ **laşmak**, *vi.* become skilled. ~ **laşmamış**, unskilled, novice. ~ **lık**, mastery (of craft); skill, proficiency; master-stroke: ~ **satmak**, pretend to ability: ~ **la**, skilfully; cunningly. ~ **lıklı**, skilfully done.

ustun[çu] (*med.*) Set of surgical instruments.

ustura *n.* Cut-throat razor. *a.* (*sl.*) Strong (drink); false (story). ~ **gagalı alk**, (*orn.*) razorbill: ~ **midyesi**, (*zoo.*) razor shell: ~ **taşı**, (*geol.*) fine gritstone: ~ **tutmak**, use a razor, shave: ~ **tutunmak**, shave body hair. ~ **cı**, barber; (*sl.*) gossip.

usturla[pbı] (*ast.*) Astrolabe.

ustur·maça (*naut.*) Fender; collision-mat. ~ **pa**, (*naut.*) swab of rope ends; scourge.

usturuplu (*col.*) Striking, impressive; just right; decent.

usul[ü 1] *n. pl.* = ASIL. (*obs.*) Origins; (*soc.*) ancestors.

usul[ü 2] *n.* Method; system; manner; procedure; (*Or. mus.*) tempo, time. ~ **erkân**, rules of good behaviour: ~ **tutmak/vurmak**, (*mus.*) beat time: ~ **/** ~ **la**, carefully, gently.

usul·ca Slowly, gently. ~ **cacık/lacık**, very slowly/ gently/quietly. ~ **en**, in the normal course of events. ~ **lü**, procedural. ~ **süz**, unmethodical; unsystematic; irregular; contrary to rules. ~ **süzlük**, lack of system; irregularity; anomaly. ~ **ünce**, according to the rules.

-uş[1] *vn. suf.* [172] = -İŞ [VURUŞ].

-uş-[2] *v. suf.* [143] = -İŞ-[2] [VURUŞMAK].

uşa·k[ğı] Boy, youth; male servant, shop assistant; (*soc.*) male from a certain region.

uşak·kapan (*orn.*) Lammergeier, bearded vulture. ~ **lık**, childhood; servant status: ~ **etm.**, serve, act as servant: ~ **tan gelme**, ex-servant.

uşkun (*bot.*) Edible rhubarb.

uşşa·k[ğı] (*Or. mus.*) A very common melody.

u·t[du 1] (*Or. mus.*) Six-pair stringed lute (with plectrum).

u·t[du 2] Shame(fulness). ~ **yeri**, (*bio.*) privy parts.

-ut[1] *a./n. suf.* [224] = -İT [SOYUT].

-ut-[2] *vc. suf.* [145] = -DİR- [KORKUTMAK].

ut·açıcılık (*psy.*) Tendency to expose o.s. indecently. ~ **açım**, perversion of indecent exposure. ~ **anacak**, shameful. ~**anca**, scandal. ~**an¹ç**ᶜ¹, shame; modesty, bashfulness: ~ **biti**, (*ent.*) crab-louse: ~**ından yere geçmek**, be thoroughly ashamed. ~**andırmak (-i)**, make ashamed; put to shame; cause to blush/look foolish. ~**angaç/**~**angan**, bashful, shy; shamefaced. ~**angaçlık**, shyness. ~**anış/anma**, *vn.* being ashamed. ~**anmak (-den, -e)**, be ashamed; be shy/bashful; blush with shame/embarrassment. ~**anmaz(lık)**, shameless(ness); impud·ent/(-ence).

Utari¹tᵈⁱ (*ast.*) Mercury.

utçu(luk) (*mus.*) (Work of) lute-maker/-seller/ -player.

ut·ku Victory, triumph. ~**kulu/**~**kun**, victorious. ~**mak (-i)**, (*mil.*) conquer; (*sp.*) defeat. ~**ulmak**, *vp.*

-uvermek *v. suf.* [191] = -İVERMEK [UÇUVERMEK].

uvertür (*mus.*) Overture.

uvunmak *vi.* Faint, lose consciousness.

uya¹kᵍ¹ (*lit.*) Rhyme. ~**lı**, rhyming. ~**sız**, un-rhymed, blank (verse).

uyan·dırıcı *a.* Awakening, arousing: ~ **saat**, alarm clock. ~**dırma**, *vn.* awakening. ~**dırmak (-i)**, awaken; arouse; revive (fire, etc.); set light to (fire, etc.); (*fig.*) stir into activity. ~**ık**, awake; vigilant, alert; wide awake, smart. ~**ıklık**, wakefulness; vigilance; smartness. ~**ış**, wakening: ~ **çağı**, (*his.*) Renaissance. ~**ma**, *vn.* ~**mak**, *vi.* awake; wake up; (fire) burn up; (*bot.*) start growth; (*fig.*) revive, come to life.

uyar Fitting, applicable; resembling; comfortable. ~**ı yok**, there's no comparison, incomparable.

uyar·an (*bio.*) Stimulant. ~**ga**, (*adm.*) note, memorandum. ~**ı**, *n.* caution, warning, reminder; (*bio.*) excitation, stimulus: ~ **eki**, (*ling.*) *nota bene*!: ~**da bulunmak**, warn; remind. ~**ıcı**, *a.* warning; exciting, stimulating. ~**ıcı¹k**ᵍ¹, (*phys.*) exciton. ~**ık**, excited. ~**ılgan(lık)**, (*bio.*) able/ (ability) to be aroused/stimulated. ~**ılmak**, *vp.* be aroused/excited/stimulated: **uyarılmış düşük**, (*med.*) induced abortion. ~**ım**, excitation, stimulation.

uyarınca *post.* As required by; in accordance with.

uyar·la¹çᶜ¹ (*lit.*) Adaptor. ~**lama**, *vn.* (*lit.*, *etc.*) adaptation: *a.* adapted. ~**lamak (-i, -e)**, adapt A to B; (*lit.*) adapt. ~**lanır**, adaptable. ~**lanma**, adaptation. ~**lanmak**, *vp.* ~**lanmış**, adapted. ~**layıcı**, adaptor. ~**lı**, suitable. ~**lık**, suitability.

uyar·ma *vn.* Warning, caution; reminder; (*bio.*) excitation: ~ **komutu**, (*sp.*, *mil.*) preparatory command. ~**mak (-i)**, (*dial.*) awaken; (*fig.*) warn, remind; (*bio.*) excite, stimulate. ~**tı**, word of warning; (*bio.*, *phys.*) stimulus. ~**tılı**, (*phys.*) stimulated. ~**tmak (-i)**, *vc.*

uydu (*ast.*) Moon, satellite; (*pol.*) satellite. ~**cu(luk)**, supporter of/(desire for) dependence. ~**laşmak**, *vi.* become a satellite. ~**luk**, being a satellite. ~**mcu(luk)**, (*soc.*) conform·ist/(-ism).

uydur·ma *vn.*: *a.* invented; false; made-up (story, etc.). ~**mak (-i, -e)**, *vc.* = UYMAK; cause to conform/agree; make to fit: **(-i)**, adapt; blend (colours); invent; make up, concoct; coin (words); fabricate; (*vulg.*) have sexual relations with. ~**masyon**, (*jok.*, *sl.*) [172] invention, fable, con-

coction, fabrication. ~**masyoncu**, (*sl.*) liar. ~**u**, (*lit.*) fiction. ~**uk**, invention, lie. ~**ukçu**, inventing, fabricating. ~**ulmak**, *vp.*

uygar Civilized; civil. ~**cı(lık)**, Western·izer/ (-ization). ~**laşma**, *vn.* ~**laşmak**, *vi.* become civilized. ~**laşmamış**, uncivilized. ~**laştırmak (-i)**, civilize. ~**lık**, civilization.

uygu Convenience, proportion; correspondence. ~**lama**, *vn.* practice, application; comparison. ~**lamak (-i, -e)**, apply; carry out; adapt; compare; (*th.*) produce. ~**lamalı**, applied, practical: ~ **araştırmalar//sanatlar**, applied research//arts. ~**laman**, technician. ~**lanabilirlik**, feasibility. ~**lanabilme**, (*phil.*) applicability. ~**lanış**, applica-tion. ~**lanmak**, *vp.* ~**layıcı**, one who practises/ applies; technician; adaptor; (*eng.*) actuator. ~**layım(bilim)**, tech·nique/(-nology). ~**layımcı/ (-erki)**, techno·crat/(-cracy). ~**layımsal**, technical. ~**lu**, corresponding.

uygun Conformable; in accord; fitting, suitable, appropriate; favourable, auspicious; (*mus.*) in tune; (*fin.*) cheap, reasonable (price); (*fig.*) just right. ~ **adım**, (*sp.*) keeping in step: ~ **bulmak/ görmek**, approve, permit, find satisfactory: ~ **düşmek/gelmek**, apply, be suitable; match, suit; correspond: ~ **katmanlaşma**, (*geol.*) concordant stratification.

uygun·luk Conformity; accord; suitability, appro-priateness; (*ling.*) agreement, concord. ~**suz**, not conforming; unsuitable; unseemly: ~ **kadın** immoral woman. ~**suzluk**, unsuitability; unseem-liness; impropriety; bad behaviour.

Uygur (*ethn.*) Uygur Turks. ~**ca**, Uygur Turkish.

uyku Sleep; sleepiness; dreamland; inattention. ~ **basmak**, be overcome by sleep: ~ **çekmek**, sleep well: ~ **durak yok**, unable to rest: ~ **gözünden akıyor**, looking very sleepy: ~ **hali**, (*bot.*) dormancy: ~ **hastalığı**, (*med.*) sleeping sickness: ~ **ilacı**, (*med.*) sleeping potion/pill: ~ **kestirmek**, have a nap: ~ **sersemliği**, drowsiness: ~ **tulumu**, sleeping-bag; (*fig.*) sleepy-head: ~ **yitimi**, (*med.*) insomnia: ~**da**, asleep: ~**da olm.**, (*fin.*) stagnate: ~**su açılmak/dağılmak**, one's sleepiness pass off: ~**su başına vurmak**, become drowsy/sleepy: ~**su gelmek**, feel sleepy: ~**su kaçmak**, be unable to get to sleep; (*fig.*) become anxious: ~**sunu açmak**, shake off one's sleepiness: ~**sunu almak**, have a good night's sleep: ~**ya dalmak/kalmak**, fall asleep: ~**ya varmak**, go to sleep: ~**ya yatmak**, go to bed, lie down to sleep.

uyku·cu Fond of sleep: ~ **kaya balığı**, (*ich.*) sleeper goby. ~**culuk**, sleepiness. ~**lu**, dozy, sleepy: ~ ~, sleepily. ~**luk**, (*bio.*, *cul.*) sweetbreads; (*med.*) scurf on baby's head/hands. ~**suz**, sleepless. ~**suzluk**, sleeplessness; (*med.*) insomnia.

uylaşım (*phil.*) Convention.

uylu¹kᵍᵘ (*bio.*) Thigh. ~**kemiği**ⁿⁱ, femur. ~**sal**, femoral.

uy·ma *vn.* Conformity, agreement; adaptation; compatibility. ~**maca**, adaptation. ~**mak (-e)**, *vi.* conform; agree; coincide; fit; suit; answer; har-monize; adapt to, comply with; follow; listen to; be fitting/seemly; be arranged/settled. ~**mama**, non-conformity. ~**maz**, opposed; contrary; adverse. ~**mazlık**, not conforming; difference; discrepancy; anomaly opposition.

uyruk (*soc.*) Citizen. ~**lu**, of . . . nationality. ~**luk**, *n.* nationality: *a.* national.

uysal Conciliatory; easy-going; acquiescent; compliant, docile; (*min.*) ductile. ~**laşmak**, *vi.* be(come) conciliatory, etc. ~**lık**, being conciliatory, etc.; conciliatory etc. behaviour; (*min.*) ductility.

uyukla·ma Lethargy. ~**mak**, *vi.* doze, keep dozing off; drowse.

uyum Harmony; observance; adaptation; (*bio.*) accommodation (of eye lens); (*ling.*) harmony.

uyu·ma *vn.* Sleeping; inattention. ~**mak**, *vi.* sleep; be asleep; go to sleep; (*fig.*) be negligent/slothful; come to a halt, stagnate, make no progress; (*bio.*) clot, coagulate: **uyuyan yılanın kuyruğuna basma!**, let sleeping dogs lie!

uyum·lu Harmonious; concordant; (*phys.*) harmonic. ~**ölçüm**, (*soc.*) sociometry. ~**suz**, inharmonious, discordant; (*phys.*) anharmonic. ~**suzluk**, lack of harmony, discord. ~**vuruş**, (*mus.*) tempo.

uyun·mak *imp. v.* One be able to sleep. ~**tu**, half-asleep; numbed; lazy.

uyur Sleeping; stagnant (water). ~**gezer(lik)**, (*med.*) sleep-walk·er/(-ing), somnambul·ist/(-ism). ~**su(luk)**, careless(ness).

uyuş·kan Easily fitting in with, harmonizing, conforming. ~**ma**, *vn.* ~**mak**[1] (-le), = UYMAK; come to a mutual understanding; concur; harmonize with: **uyuştuk!**, it's a bargain! ~**mazlık**, contention; disagreement, dispute; disharmony; (*ling.*) haplology. ~**turmak**[1] (-i, -le), ensure agreement/harmony. ~**um**, *vn.* blending, getting on well together; conformity; (*cin.*) matching.

uyuş·mak[2] *vi.* = UYUMAK; (*bio.*) become numb/insensible; (pain, etc.) relax, slacken. ~**turan**, benumbing. ~**turanbalığı**[nı], (*ich.*) electric ray. ~**turma**, *vn.*; (*med.*) anaesthesia. ~**turmak**[2] (-i), benumb; assuage/deaden (pain, etc.); (*med.*) anaesthetize. ~**turu**, narcosis. ~**turucu**, numbing, deadening; (*med.*) anaesthetic: ~ **maddeler**, (*med.*) anaesthetics, anodynes; narcotics, drugs. ~**turum**/ (-bilim), anaesthe·sia/(-siology). ~**turumlu**, ~ **çözümleme**, (*psy.*) narcoanalysis. ~**uk**, numbed; insensible; apathetic; indolent. ~**ukluk**, numbness; laziness.

uyut·ma *vn.* (*med.*) Narcosis. ~**maca**, (*psy.*) hypnotism. ~**mak** (-i), *vc.* = UYUMAK; send to sleep; (*med.*) anaesthetize; (*psy.*) hypnotize; (*fig.*) bore; keep s.o. quiet; put s.o. off; put stg. off indefinitely. ~**ucu**, soporific. ~**ulmak**, *vp.* ~**um**, (*psy.*) hypnosis.

uyuyakalmak *vi.* Fall fast asleep (involuntarily); be overcome by sleep.

uyuz (*med.*) Itch; (*live.*) mange, scab. ~ **olm.**, (*sl.*) be penniless: ~ **sayrılığı**, (*med.*) itch, scabies.

uyuz-böceği[ni] (*zoo.*) Itch mite. ~**böcekleri**, Sarcoptidae. ~**laşmak**, *vi.* (*zoo.*) look mangy; (*fig.*) become clumsy. ~**luk**, (*med.*) manginess; (*fig.*) clumsiness; poverty. ~**otu**[nu], (*bot.*) devil's bit scabious. ~**sineği**[ni], (*ent.*) (?) tiger beetle.

uz[1] *adv.* Far.
uz[2] *a.* Good; fitting, suitable; quiet, well-behaved.
-uz *v. suf.* [96] = -iz[2] [YORGUNUZ].

uza·duyum (*psy.*) Telepathy. ~**görüm**, (*med.*) long-sightedness.

uza·lk[ğı] *a.* Distant, remote, far-off (space/time); (*ling.*) incontiguous; improbable; incapable; contrary. *n.* Distant place; the distance. ~ **durmak** (-den), give a wide berth to: ~ **görmez**, *n.* (*med.*) myope; *a.* myopic: ~ **görüşlü**, far-sighted: ~ **olan**, (*bio.*) distal: ~**a düşmek**, be far (from each other): ~**a gitmek**, go far afield, travel far: ~**ı göremezlik**, short-sightedness: ~**ı görmek**, foresee: ~**lara gitmek**, deviate from the subject: ~**lara sürmek** (-i), banish: ~**larda**, in the far distance; far off: ~**ta**, at a distance: ~**tan**, from far off; in s.o.'s absence; (*eng., etc.*) remote-(controlled): ~**tan akraba**, (*soc.*) distant relative: ~**tan bakmak/seyirci kalmak**, be a mere spectator, take no part in: ~**tan davulun sesi hoş gelir**, distance lends enchantment to the view: ~**tan görmek**, have a distant view of: ~**tan gütme/idare/kumanda/yönetme(li)**, remote-control(led): ~**tan merhaba**, a cool/distant/formal greeting: ~**tan tanımak**, know s.o. by sight: ~**tan ~a**, only remotely connected; from far off.

uzak·ça Rather far off/distant. ~**çeker**, (*cin.*) telephoto lens. ~**doğu**, *pr.n.* (*geo.*) Far East. ~**laşılmak**, *vp.* ~**laşmak** (-den), drive/move away, retire to a distance; leave; retire from; become a stranger to. ~**laştırıcı**, (*bio.*) abductor. ~**laştırmak** (-den, -i), remove, take away; displace; drive away; banish. ~ **lık**, distance; remoteness; difference; ~ **aygıtı**, (*cin.*) focusing device. ~**lıkölçer**, telemeter, odometer, range-finder. ~**sal**, (*bio.*) distal. ~**samak** (-i), consider remote/unlikely. ~**tarım**, (*ind.*) telemechanics.

uza·m (*phil.*) Extent, extension; volume. ~**ma**, *vn.*; stretching; elongation; (*phys.*) linear expansion. ~**mak**, *vi.* grow longer, stretch, extend, lengthen; continue, be prolonged: **uzayıp gitmek**, continue. ~**mölçer** (*phys.*) extensometer. ~**msal**, extensive.

uzan·ılmak *vp.* ~**ım**, distance; (*phys.*) elongation; (*ast.*) elongation, digression. ~**ır**, *a.* extending. ~**mak**, *vi.* be prolonged/extended; stretch o.s. out, lie down (to rest); reach out (for stg.): **(-e)** extend to, go as far as. ~**tı**, extent, extension.

uzat·ıcı Extension (piece). ~**ılır**, extensible, expanding. ~**ım**/~**ma**, *vn.* extension; elongation; (*ling.*) lengthening (of syllable); (*fin.*) contango; (*fishing*) seine net; (*sp.*) extra time: ~ **işareti**, (*ling.*) circumflex accent (ˆ): ~ **ölçeği**, (*phys.*) extensometer: ~ **parçası**, (*eng.*) extension, adaptor. ~**mak** (-i), extend, elongate, stretch out; prolong; drag out, make tedious; allow (hair, etc.) to grow long; (*lit.*) pad out; (*fig.*) give, send: **uzatmıyalım!**, come to the point!; to cut a long story short! ~**malı**, (*mil.*) with voluntary extended service (*esp.* as sergeant): ~ **aday**, (*jok.*) a 'chronic' candidate: ~ **âşık**, (*jok.*) long-time lover.

uzay (*ast., maths., phys.*) Space. ~ +, *a.* Astro-, space-: ~ **açı**, (*math.*) solid angle: ~ **adamı**, (*aer.*) spaceman, astronaut: ~ **gemisi**, spacecraft: ~

geometrisi, (*math.*) solid geometry: ~ **gözetme kubbesi**, (*aer.*) astrodome: ~ **kapsülü**, space capsule: ~ **uçuş bilgisi**, astronautics: ~ **uçuşu**, space flight. ~ **cı(lık)**, astronaut(ics). ~ **lama**, (*math.*) extrapolation. ~ **sal**, *a.* space. **uz·bilim** (*ed.*) Authority; specialization (in science). ~ **çeker**/~ **çektirim**, telex. ~ **göre'ç**[ci], television. ~ **gören**/~ **görür**, far-sighted; prudent. ~ **iletişim**, telecommunications. **uzlaş·ılmak** *vp.* ~ **ım(cılık)**, (*phil.*) convention/ (-alism). ~ **ımsal**, conventional. ~ **ma**, *vn.*; agreement; understanding; compromise: ~ **ya varmak**, reach agreement. ~ **mak**, *vi.* come to an agreement/ understanding; compromise: ~ **malı**, agreeing; contractual. ~ **mazlık**, disagreement, difference of opinion. ~ **tırıcı**, *a.* conciliatory: *n.* (*leg.*) referee, conciliator. ~ **tırma**, *vn.* reconciling; conciliation. ~ **tırmak** (-i), reconcile, conciliate. **uzlet**[i] (*rel.*, *soc.*) Life of a recluse. **uz·luk** Ability, skill; shrewdness: ~ **belgesi**, (*ind.*) patent. ~ **m.** = ~ **man**, expert, specialist; connoisseur. ~ **manlaşmak**, *vi.* become an expert. ~ **manlık**, expertise; specialization. **uzun** Long; tall; (*fig.*) long-winded; in detail. ~ **atlama**, (*sp.*) long jump: ~ **beygir**, (*sp.*) vaulting horse: ~ **boylu**, tall, long; (*fig.*) lengthy: ~ **burun**, (*zoo.*) proboscis: ~ **çizgi**, (*pub.*) dash (—): ~ **dalga**, (*phys.*) long wave: ~ **dilli**, indiscreet in speech: ~ **EŞEK**: ~ **etm.**, hold forth at great length: ~ **etme!**, that's enough!; come off it!: ~ **gelmek**,

(*aer.*) overshoot: ~ **hava**, (*Or. mus.*) regional song: ~ **hayvan**, (*zoo.*) snake: ~ **hece**, (*ling.*) long syllable: ~ **hikâye**, a long(-drawn-out) story: ~ **ivdirici**, (*phys.*) linear accelerator: ~ **kulaklı**, (*zoo.*) long-eared; donkey: ~ **kulaktan haber almak**, get news indirectly/in a round-about way: ~ **kuyruk**, (*orn.*) type of finch: ~ **kuyruklu**, (*zoo.*) long-tailed: ~ **lafın kısası**, in short: ~ **levrek** (*ich.*) pikeperch: ~ **menzilli**, (*mil.*, *etc.*) long-range: ~ **metrajlı**, (*cin.*) full-length (film): ~ **oturmak**, (*col.*) sit with outstretched legs: ~ **süreli**, (*fin.*) long-term/-dated: ~ **uzadıya**, at great length, diffusely: ~ **uzadıya anlatmak** (-i), dilate upon stg.: ~ ~, lengthy; at length: ~ **ünlü**, (*ling.*) long vowel: ~ **vadeli**, (*fin.*) long-dated. **uzun·baca'k**[ğı] (*orn.*) Black-winged stilt. ~ **ca** somewhat long/tall. ~ **çalar**, (*mus.*) long-playing record. ~ **diş**, (*eng.*) screw-thread (long enough for joining pipes). ~ **eşe'k**[ği], (*child.*) type of leapfrog. ~ **kafalı**, (*ethn.*) dolycocephalic. ~ **kollumaymungiller**, (*zoo.*) gibbons. ~ **lamasına**, lengthwise, longitudinal. ~ **luk**, length; lengthiness; height ~ **oranı**, (*aer.*) aspect ratio: ~ **ölçüsü**, (*math.*) linear measurement: ~ **una**, lengthwise; along end·ways/-wise: ~ **unda**, . . . in length. **uz'uv**[vu] (*bio.*) Member; organ; limb; component. **uzv-** = UZUV. ~ **aniye**, (*phil.*) organicism. ~ **i** (*chem.*) organic; pertaining to a member. ~ **iyet**[i] organism. **uzyaz·dırım**/~ **ı** Telegraph, telegram.

Ü

Ü, ü [ü] Twenty-sixth Tk. letter, Ü.

ü *conj.* [206] And.

-ü[1] *n. suf.* [28] = -i[1] [ÖKÜZÜ].

-ü[2] *n. suf.* [39] = -i[2] [ÖKÜZÜ].

-ü[3] *a./n. suf.* [221] = -i[3] [ÜRKÜ].

Ü, ü. = ÜNİVERSİTE; ÜS; ÜST.

ücra Remote, out of the way, solitary.

ücret[i] (*fin.*) Pay; wage, salary; fee; (postage, etc.) cost; (ticket, etc.) price; charge; dues. ~ **baremi,** (*adm.*) scale of wages/salaries.

ücret·li Receiving pay: ~ **izin,** paid leave: ~ **memur,** (*adm.*) unestablished official. ~ **siz,** unpaid; without payment; free, gratis.

-ücü *a./n. suf.* [220] = -ici [ÖLDÜRÜCÜ].

üç[ü] (*math.*) Three. ~ **adım atlama,** (*sp.*) hop step and jump: ~ **aşağı beş yukarı,** approximately; a few: ~ **aşağı beş yukarı dolaşmak,** walk up and down aimlessly/anxiously: ~ **aşağı beş yukarı uyuşmak,** reach an agreement of sorts: ~ **ayaklı ayna,** (*eng.*) three-jaw chuck: ~ **ayda bir/aylık,** quarterly: ~ **aylar,** (*rel.*) the three (sacred) months, RECEP, ŞABAN, RAMAZAN: ~ **beş,** three or four: ~ **buçuk,** three and a half; small quantity: ~ **buçuk atmak (-den),** (*sl.*) be very frightened about: ~ **buçuk cahil/serseri,** a handful of ignoramuses/vagabonds, etc.: ~ **dikenli balık,** (*ich.*) three-spined stickleback: ~ **direkli,** (*naut.*) three-masted: ~ **eksenli,** (*math.*) triaxial: ~ **fazlı,** (*el.*) three-phase: ~ **gün sıtması,** (*med.*) tertian fever: ~ **hal kanunu,** (*phil.*) three-states law: ~ **keçili Kürt gibi kurulmak,** (*pej.*) give o.s. airs: ~ **nalla bir ata kaldı,** (*iron.*) we've almost succeeded!/achieved our goal!: ~ **otuzunda,** nonagenarian, very old: ~ **soklu pulluk,** (*agr.*) three-furrow plough: ~ **tekerlekli,** three-wheeler, three-wheeled vehicle: ~ **tuğ vermek,** (*his.*) confer the highest rank of pasha: ~ **tuğlu paşa,** (*his.*) pasha of the highest rank: ~ **yılda bir,** triennial: ~ **yollu,** three-way: ~ **e beşe bakmamak,** not haggle about the price: ~ **te bir,** one in three; one-third. [*For further phrases = * BEŞ.]

üç·ambarlı (*naut.*) Three-decker (man-of-war). ~ **aya**[l]**k**[ğı], tripod. ~ **başlı,** ~ **kas,** (*bio.*) triceps. ~ **boyutlu,** (*math., cin.*) three-dimensional: ~ **ses,** (*el.*) stereophony. ~ **düzlemli,** (*math.*) three-planed, trihedral. ~ **er,** three each; three at a time: ~ ~, three by three, in threes. ~ **ete**[l]**k**[ği], (*mod.*) three-layered skirt. ~ **gen,** (*math.*) triangle: ~ +, *a.* triangular. ~ **gül,** (*bot.*) hare's foot clover. ~ **kâğıtçı,** (*gamb.*) three-card trickster; (*col.*) lying, deceiving. ~ **kâğıtçılık,** lying, deceit; trickery. ~ **köşe,** (*aer.*) delta (wing). ~ **köşeli,** three-cornered, triangular; (*bio.*) deltoid: ~ **midye,** (*zoo.*) zebra mussel. ~ **leme,** making three; triple; threefold; (*naut.*) three-stranded rope; (*lit.*) three-lined stanza. ~ **lemek (-i),** make/increase to three; triple; divide by three; (*agr.*) let a farm for one-third of its produce; plough a field three times. ~ **leşmek,** *vi.* become/increase to three. ~ **lü,** *n.* (*gamb.*) three (at dice/cards); consisting of three; (*mus.*) trio; (*phys.*) triplet: *a.* triple; (*adm.*) tripartite: ~ **kapakçık,** (*bio.*) tricuspid: ~ **kuralı,** (*math.*) rule of three: ~ **ünlü,** (*ling.*) triphthong. ~ **lük,** consisting of/worth three units; for three persons; (*rel.*) Trinity. ~ **parmaklı,** (*zoo.*) three-toed. ~ **renksel,** (*phys.*) trichromatic. ~ **teker,** tricycle. ~ **üncü (3.),** third: ~ **derece denklem,** (*math.*) cubic equation: ~ **derece yanık,** (*med.*) third-degree burn: ~ **Dünya (Ülkeleri),** (*pol.*) Third-World (Countries): ~ **kişi,** (*ling.*) third person; (*leg.*) third party; (*leg.*) umpire. ~ **üncül,** (*chem.*) tertiary. ~ **üncülük,** being third; third place. ~ **üz(ler),** (*bio.*) triplet(s); tripartite, triple. ~ **üzlü,** (mother) having triplets; three-directional; three-branched: ~ **bir taret,** (*naut.*) three-gun turret.

Ü·çvş = (*mil.*) ÜSÇAVUŞ. ~ **.f.** = (*bio.*) ÜSTFAMİLYA.

üdeba *pl.* = EDİP. Literary people, men of letters.

üf·le[l]**ç**[ci] (*eng.*) Blow-pipe/-torch; aspirator, extractor-fan. ~ **leme,** *vn.* blowing: ~ **kalıbı,** (*eng.*) blow-mould. ~ **lemek (-i),** blow out (candle, etc.); blow upon; blow up (balloon); (*mus.*) blow/play (wind instrument): *vi.* blow, puff, pant. ~ **lemeli,** (*mus.*) wind (instrument). ~ **lenmek,** *vp.* ~ **leyici,** blower.

üful[ü] (*ast.*) Setting, sinking; extinction; (*fig., obs.*) death. ~ **ü nabehengâm,** untimely demise.

üfür·me *vn.* Blowing, blast: ~ **borusu,** blast-pipe. ~ **mek (-i),** blow/carry away; blow upon; blow up (with breath); cast a spell on/cure by breathing: *vi.* (wind/draught) blow. ~ **ü**[l]**k**[ü], breathing on a sick person to cure him; (*geol.*) exhalation. ~ **ükçü(lük),** (work of) one who claims to cure by such breathing. ~ **üm,** breath.

üğ- = ÜV-. ~ **rüm,** (*ast.*) nutation.

-ük *a./n. suf.* [221] = -ik [PÜSKÜRÜK].

-ül- *vp. suf.* [149] = -il- [GÖRÜLMEK].

üleş Portion, share. ~ **ilmek,** *vp.* ~ **mek (-i, -le),** divide with each other; go shares. ~ **tirilmek,** *vp.* ~ **tirimli,** (*phil.*) distributive. ~ **tirme,** *vn.* distributing: ~ **sıfatı,** (*ling.*) distributive adjective. ~ **tirmek (-i),** distribute; share out.

ülfet[i] Familiar habit/intercourse; familiarity.

ülger (*bot.*) Down (as on peach); (*tex.*) pile.

ülke Country; province; domain, territory. ~ +, *a.* Country: ~ **çapında,** countrywide: ~ **dışında egemenlik,** (*leg.*) extraterritoriality.

Ülker (*ast.*) The Pleiades.

ülkü *n.* Ideal. ~ **cü(lük),** (*phil.*) ideal·ist/(-ism).

~deş(lik), (state of) sharing the same ideals. ~l, ideal. ~leştirmek (-i), idealize. ~sel, *a.* ideal.
ülser (*bio.*) Ulcer.
ültimatom (*pol.*) Ultimatum. ~ mahiyetli bir nota, (*adm.*) a note in the nature of an ultimatum: ~ vermek, issue an ultimatum.
ültra- *pref.* Ultra-. ~marin, (*art.*) ultramarine. ~ruj, (*phys.*) infra-red. ~son, ultrasonics. ~viyole, (*phys.*) ultraviolet.
-ültü *n. suf.* [222] = -iLTi [GÜRÜLTÜ].
üluhiyeti (*rel.*) Divinity.
-üm1 *n. suf.* [39] = -iM1 [GÖZÜM].
-üm2 *v. suf.* [96] = -iM2 [GÖRÜRÜM].
-üm3 *n. suf.* [224] = -iM3 [ÖLÜM].
ümera *pl.* = EMİR. Chiefs; (*mil.*) staff officers.
ümi'tdi Hope; expectation, anticipation. ~ Burnu, *pr.n.* (*geo.*) Cape of Good Hope: ~ dünyası bu!, hope never dies: ~ etm., hope, expect: ~ etmediği felaket başına geldi, an unexpected catastrophe befell him: ~ kapısı!, if we're lucky!: ~ kesilecek bir hal, a hopeless state: ~im var, I hope: ~ini kesmek, give up/abandon hope of. [*Also* = UMUT.]
ümit·lendirmek (-i) Make hopeful, fill with hope. ~lenmek, *vi.* be hopeful, conceive hopes. ~li, hopeful. ~siz, without hope; hopeless; desperate. ~ sizlik, hopelessness; desperation. ~var, hopeful.
ümmeti (*rel.*) Community (of believers). ~i Muhammed, Muslims, Islam. ~çi(lik), (*pol.*) partisan(ship) of theocratic government.
ümmi (*ed.*) Illiterate. ~lik, illiteracy.
ümran A being in good condition/well-built; prosperity.
ümük = iMiK.
-ümüz *n. suf.* [39] = -iMiZ [SÜRGÜNÜMÜZ].
ün Voice; cry; fame, reputation. ~ almak/kazanmak/ salmak/yapmak, win fame, become famous.
-ün1 *n. suf.* [28] = -iN1 [GÖLÜN].
-ün2 *n. suf.* [39] = -iN2 [GÖZÜN].
-ün3 *n. suf.* [225] = -iN3 [TÜTÜN].
-ün4 *adv. suf.* [22, 201] = -iN4 [GÜZÜN].
-ün-5 *vp. suf.* [149] = -iN-5 [GÖRÜNMEK].
üna'kğ1 (*dial.*) Larynx.
-ünce *v. suf.* [179] = -iNCE2 [ÖLÜNCE].
-üncü *a. suf.* [82] = -iNCi [DÖRDÜNCÜ].
-ünç *a./n. suf.* [222] = -iNÇ [GÜLÜNÇ]
Üni. = ÜNiVERSiTE(si).
üni·form *a.* Uniform, even; (*geol.*) closely graded. ~forma, (*mod.*) uniform. ~te, (*math.*) unit. ~versel, universal. ~versite, (*ed.*) university; (*sl.*) place of amusement, bar, etc.: ~ başkanı, rector: ~ seçme/sıralama sınavı, university entrance examination. ~versiteli, undergraduate.
ün·l. = ÜNLEM. ~le'kği, (*bio.*) glottis. ~lem, (*ling.*) exclamation, interjection: ~ im/işareti, exclamation mark (!): ~ vurgusu, circumflex accent (^).
ün·lemek (-e) Cry out, call to; proclaim. ~lenmek, *vp.*
ünlü *a.* Famous, celebrated, honoured. *n.* (*ling.*) Vowel. ~ boşluğu, hiatus: ~ düşmesi, elision: ~ uyumu, vowel harmony. ~leşme, vocalization.
ünsiyeti Familiarity; being on friendly terms with s.o.
ünsüz *a.* Unknown; undistinguished. *n.* (*ling.*)

Consonant. ~ düşmesi, consonantal elision: ~ uyumu, consonant assimilation/harmony.
-üntü *n. suf.* [222] = -iNTi [GÖRÜNTÜ].
-ünüz *n. suf.* [39] = -iNiZ [GÖZÜNÜZ].
ünvan = UNVAN.
-ür1 *v. suf.* [116] = -iR [GÖRÜR].
-ür-2 *vc. suf.* [145] = -DiR-2 [DÜŞÜRMEK].
üra'tdi (*chem.*) Uric acid salt.
Ürdün (*geo.*) Jordan; (*his.*) Transjordan. ~lü, (*ethn.*) Jordanian.
üre (*chem.*) Urea. ~ plastikleri, urea resins.
üre·ğen Productive; prolific. ~m, increase; (*fin.*) interest: ~ oranı, interest rate. ~me, *vn.* (*bio.*) reproduction, procreation. ~mek, *vi.* (*bio.*) reproduce; multiply, increase.
üre·mi (*med.*) Uraemia. ~tan, (*chem.*) urethane.
üre·te'çci (*el.*) Generator: ~ gazı, (*chem.*) producer gas. ~tici, *n.* (*live.*) breeder; (*ind.*) producer: *a.* productive. ~tilmek, *vp.* ~tim, (*live.*) breeding; (*ind.*) production; generation: ~ organı, (*bio.*) genital organ. ~timlik, factory. ~timsel, productive; (*ling.*) generative. ~tken(lik), produc·tive/(-tivity). ~tme, *vn.* breeding; producing; culture. ~tmek (-i), (*live.*) breed; (*ind.*) produce. ~ tmen, (*live.*) breeder; (*ind.*) producer.
üretra (*bio.*) Urethra.
ürgün (*geo.*) Pond; back-stream/-water.
ürik (*chem.*) Uric. ~ asit, uric acid.
ürk·ek Timid, fearful. ~ekleşmek, *vi.* grow timid. ~eklik, timidity; (*orn.*) Caspian snowcock. ~me, *vn.* being frightened/timid. ~mek, *vi.* start with fear: (-den), be frightened of; (horse) shy; (*bot.*) produce no fruit. ~ü, panic; (*psy.*) phobia. ~ünç, frightening, terrifying. ~üntü, a being frightened/ timid. ~ütmek (-i), terrify, startle, scare.
ürodel (*zoo.*) Newt, salamander.
ürolog (*med.*) Urologist.
ürper·mek (Hair) stand on end; shiver; feel creepy. ~ti, shiver, shudder. ~tmek (-i), startle, scare.
ürümek *vi.* (Dog) bark, howl; bay the moon. **ürümesini bilmeyen köpek sürüye kurt getirir,** clumsy people do more harm than good: **ürüyen köpek ısırmaz,** his bark is worse than his bite.
ürün (*agr.*) Crop; produce, product; (*art.*) work.
üryan Naked, bare. ~i, (*bot.*) type of thin-skinned plum; (*cul.*) skinned and dried plum: ~ eriği likörü, (*cul.*) plum liqueur.
üsde/sü Base, basis, foundation; (*math.*) exponent, index; (*mil.*) base, installation; (*sp.*) base camp. ~se dönüş, homing.
üs- *pref.* = ÜST. Senior; upper.
ü.s. = (*bio.*) ÜSTSINIF.
üsçavuş (*mil.*) Company quarter-master sergeant.
Üsküdar (*geo.*) Üsküdar; (*his.*) Scutari (Istanbul).
üsküf (*mod., his.*) Knitted bonnet with tassel; (*sp.*) falcon's hood; wind-cover for a narghile.
üslenmek (-e) Choose and settle in a place.
üslu'pbu Manner; form; (*art., lit.*) style. ~unda, in the style of . . ., after . . . . ~çu, stylist. ~laştırma, *vn.* stylization. ~laştırmak (-i), stylize.
üslü (*math.*) Exponential.
üsmutu (*phil.*) Beatitude.
üss- = ÜS.

ÜSS = ÜNİVERSİTE SEÇME/SIRALAMA SINAVI.

üssubay (*mil.*) Senior officer (BİNBAŞI, YARBAY, ALBAY).

üst[ü] *also* = ÜZERİ. *n.* Upper/outside surface; top of stg.; space over stg.; clothing; (*adm.*) superior; (*fin.*) remainder, change; address (on letter). *a.* Upper; uppermost; superior; (*ast.*) super-; (*bio.*) epi-. *post.* [91] On; over; on the top of. ~ **baş,** (*mod.*) clothes, dress, attire: ~ **baş kalmamak,** have no clothes left: ~ **başlık,** (*pub.*) headline: ~ **çıkmak,** win: ~DERİ: ~DİL: ~ **direk,** (*sp.*) crossbar: ~ **düzey(deki),** top-level: ~ **fırçası,** clothesbrush: ~ **geçit,** (*mot.*) overpass: ~ **gelmek,** surpass; prevail; come out on top: ~ **hakkı,** prior right: ~ **katman bulut,** (*met.*) altostratus: ~ **köşeye çıkmak,** place o.s. in the seat of honour: ~ **perdeden,** (*mus.*) on a high note; in a high pitch: ~ **perdeden atıp tutmak/konuşmak,** talk big, give o.s. airs: ~ **perdeden başlamak,** start threatening/cursing: ~ **sahne,** (*th.*) balcony (scene): ~ **satıh,** (*aer.*) extrados: ~ **tabaka,** (*soc.*) upper class/'crust': ~ **tarafı (-in),** the rest/remainder of . . .: ~ **terim,** (*math.*) numerator: ~ ~ **e,** one after/on top of the other; continuously; in succession: ~ **yan,** (house) next door; a little further on.

üst-: = ÜSTE: ~ **e çıkmak,** pretend to be innocent: ~ **e vermek,** give in addition; (*fin.*) suffer a loss: ~ **e vurmak,** increase: ~ **ler,** (*adm.*) high officials: ~ **te,** above; on top: ~ **ten,** overhead; superficially: ~ **ten almak,** talk/behave in a superior manner.

üstü: ~ **açık,** open at the top; (*fig.*) obscene, smutty: ~ **başı dökülmek,** be in a pitiful state: ~ **kapalı/örtülü,** indirectly, secretly, furtively: ~ **örtülü söz,** equivocal/ambiguous speech: ~ **temiz,** he is cleanly dressed: ~ **mde para yok,** I have no money on me: ~ **me iyilik sağlık!,** that's the limit!; I've never heard of such a thing!; God forbid!: ~ **me varma!,** don't come near me!; don't keep on at me!, don't insist!: ~ **müzden ırak!,** may God save us from such a calamity!

üstün: = ÜSTÜN: ~ **de,** on; on the top of; over; above: ~ **de durmak (-in),** work hard at; insist on: ~ **de kalmak,** (at auction) fall to one's bid:

üstünden, from on top of: ~ **akmak,** a situation be very clear: ~ **atmak,** ignore/try to avoid (duty, etc.): ~ **dökülmek,** (clothes) be unsuitable/unbecoming: ~ **geçmek (-in),** violate (a woman): ~ **kibarlık akmak,** be very conceited: ~ . . . **zaman geçmek,** time elapse from . . ..

üstüne, onto; against; on the subject of: ~ **almak,** put on clothes; take (a duty, etc.) upon o.s.; be offended (by a remark); (*naut.*) row ahead: ~ **atmak,** impute stg. to s.o., accuse s.o. of stg.: ~ **basmak,** (*col.*) hit the nail on the head: ~ **başına etm. (-in),** (*vulg.*) abuse/curse s.o. violently: ~ **bırakmak,** quit, give up: ~ **bir bardak (soğuk) su içmek (-in),** (*jok.*) write stg. off, forget stg., never see stg. again: ~ **çevirmek,** (*leg.*) assign/transfer/turn over to s.o.: ~ **çıkmak,** come to the top; get the better of: ~ **düşmek,** be very interested in; work hard at: ~ **evlenmek (-in),** take a second wife: ~

geçirmek, coat/cover stg.; = ~ ÇEVİRMEK: ~ **geçirtmek,** cause (property) to be registered; adopt (child); marry (woman) officially: ~ **gelmek,** appear, turn up (bringing good/bad luck); overcome: ~ **gül koklamamak (-in),** not dream of making love to another woman: ~ **güneş doğ(ma)mak,** get up late/(early) in the morning: ~ **koymak,** add: ~ **mal etmemek,** take no interest in; not participate in: ~ **oturmak,** appropriate s.o. else's property; embezzle: ~ **perde çekmek,** draw a veil over, conceal: ~ **titremek,** be a-quiver with love for s.o.: ~ **toz kondurmamak,** not accept blame/criticism of: ~ **tuz biber ekmek,** rub salt into the wound: ~ ~ **gitmek (-in),** struggle with/face up to danger, not be daunted: ~ **varmak,** keep on at s.o.; (*fin.*) increase the price; bid higher for stg.; (*soc.*) (woman) marry a married man: ~ **yapmak,** transfer stg. to s.o.: ~ **yaptırmak,** have (property) registered: ~ **yaşamak (-in),** outlive s.o.: ~ **yatmak (-in),** misappropriate/ hang on to stg.: ~ **yok,** this is the best: ~ **yormak (kendi)** be offended: ~ **yürümek,** threaten/attack/go for s.o.

üstünü: ~ **görmek,** (woman) have her periods: ~ **kirletmek,** dirty one's clothes; (child) dirty itself.

üst- *pref. also* = ÜS-.

üst. = (*ling.*) ÜSTÜNLÜK DERECESİ.

usta[¹t][d¹] *n.* Master; teacher; expert. *a.* Adept, skilled. ~ **ve amatör,** (*art.*) professional and amateur: ~ **ım!,** (*col.*) hello, my friend! ~ **lık,** mastery, expertise.

üst·alize (*met.*) Anti-trade (winds). ~ **aydınlık,** (*arch.*) skylight. ~ **baş** = ÜST BAŞ. ~ **bitken,** (*bot.*) epiphyte. ~ **çene,** (*bio.*) upper jaw, maxilla. ~ **deri** (*bio.*) epidermis: ~ **altı,** corium. ~ **dil,** (*phil.*) meta-language.

üste Further; in addition. ~ **sinden gelmek (-in),** succeed in, cope with. ~ **cilik,** extra, additional item.

üsteğmen(lik) (Rank/duties of) (*mil.*) (first) lieutenant//(*aer.*) flying officer//(*naut.*) acting first-lieutenant.

üstel (*math.*) Exponential.

üste·leme *vn.* Confirmation; emphasis; repetition; (*med.*) relapse. ~ **lemek,** *vi.* increase, become dominant; (*med.*) recrudesce; dwell on stg., persist, insist: (-i), confirm; repeat: (-e), add to stg. ~ **lik,** in addition; furthermore, to boot; the beauty of it is . . .: ~ **bir de,** to add to my work.

üst·enci (*fin.*) Contractor. ~ **enme,** *vn.* undertaking. ~ **enmek (-i),** undertake. ~ **ermek (-i, -e),** hand over/delegate stg. to s.o.

üst·familya (*bio.*) Super-family. ~ **geçiş,** (*ast.*) upper culmination. ~ **geçi**[¹t][d¹], (*mot.*) overpass. ~ **havayuvarı,** (*geo.*) stratosphere.

Üstğm. = (*mil.*) ÜSTEĞMEN.

üst·insan (*soc.*) Superman. ~ **lenmek (-i),** undertake, take on. ~ **lük,** (*mod.*) overcoat. ~ **oluşumlu,** (*geol.*) epigenic. ~ **sınıf,** (*bio.*) superclass. ~ **takım,** (*bio.*) superorder.

üstübe[¹ç][ci] (*chem.*) Lead carbonate, white lead. ~ **macunu,** (*eng.*) filler paste.

üstün *a.* Superior; preferable; victorious; super-, ultra-. ~ **akışkanlık,** (*phys.*) superfluidity: ~

beslenme, (*bio.*) hypertrophy: ~ **çekiş gücü**, (*phys.*) high traction capacity (engine): ~ **gelmek**, come out on top; be victorious: ~ **ırk**, (*soc.*) master race: ~ KÖRÜ: ~ **olan**, ruling; superior: ~ **olm.**, excel: ~ **tutmak**, prefer: ~ **tutulmak**, be privileged: ~ **yapım**, (*cin.*) block-buster: ~ **ü kaplamak**, brood.

üstün·de// ~ **den//** ~ **e//** ~ **ü** = ÜST.

üstün·körü Superficial(ly); only on the surface. ~ **lük**, advantage; superiority: ~ **derecesi**, (*ling.*) superlative degree: ~ **kompleksi**, (*psy.*) superiority complex: ~ **sağlayan**, advantageous.

üstüpü (*naut.*) Oakum.

üstü·vane (*math.*) Cylinder. ~ **vani**, cylindrical.

üst·yapı(sal) (*arch.*, *phil.*) Superstruc·ture/(-tural). ~ **yargı**, ~ **yolu**, (*leg.*) appeal. ~ **yargılık**, court of appeal.

ÜSYS = ÜNİVERSİTE SEÇME VE YERLEŞTİRME SINAVI

-üş *vn.* *suf.* [172] = -iş[1] [GÖRÜŞ]

-üş- *v.* *suf.* [143] = -iş-[2] [GÖRÜŞMEK].

üşe·lk[ği] (*zoo.*) Type of small lynx.

üşen·lç[ci] Sloth, lassitude. ~ **geç/** ~ **gen**, lazy, slothful. ~ **geçlik/** ~ **genlik**, laziness, sloth, lassitude. ~ **mek** (-e), be too lazy (to do stg.); do reluctantly. ~ **mez**, zealous, persevering.

üşmek (-e) Come/gather/flock/swarm together.

üşniye *pl.* (*bot.*) Seaweeds, algae.

üşümek *vi.* Be/feel cold; (*med.*) catch cold. **üşüdüm de giyindim**, I was cold so I put on all my clothes.

üş·üntü (*obs.*) A flocking together; crowd, mob; (*ent.*) swarm; (*zoo.*) flock, pack: ~ **etm.**, crowd together: ~ **köpek mandayı paralar**, unity is strength. ~ **ürmek** (-i, -e), *vc.* = ÜŞMEK; collect together; gather into a crowd; cause to make a concerted attack, set on. ~ **üşmek** (-e), crowd together; make a concerted attack; descend on s.o.

üşütmek (-i) *vc.* = ÜŞÜMEK; cause to feel/catch cold; chill.

-üt- *vc.* *suf.* [145] = -DİR-[2] [ÜRKÜTMEK].

ü.t. = (*bio.*) ÜSTTAKIM.

Ütğm. = (*mil.*) ÜSTEĞMEN(LİK).

üt·me (*cul.*) Roasted fresh corn. ~ **mek**[1] (-i), heat strongly; (*cul.*) singe, roast.

ütmek[2] (-i) (*child.*) Win a game.

ütopya (*phil.*) Utopia. ~ **cı(lık)**, utopian(ism).

ütü Heating; (*dom.*) flat iron; ironing. ~ **masası**, ironing board: ~ **tutmamak**, not take the iron: ~ **sü bozulmak**, lose the crease; need ironing.

ütü·cü Ironer. ~ **lemek** (-i), iron; crease (intentionally); (*cul.*) singe. ~ **lenmek**, *vp.* ~ **lmek**, *vp.* = ÜTMEK[2], lose a game. ~ **lü**, ironed, well-creased; (*cul.*) singed. ~ **me**, (*cul.*) roasted fresh meat. ~ **süz**, unironed; needing ironing.

üvendire (*live.*) Ox-goad.

-üvermek *v.* *suf.* [191] = -İVERMEK [ÇÖKÜVERMEK].

üvey[i/si] *a.* Not blood-related. *pref.* Step-. ~ **ana// baba**, step·father//-mother: ~ **evlat**, stepchild: ~

evlat gibi tutulmak, be unfairly treated: ~ **kardeş**, half-brother/-sister. ~ **lik**, 'step'-relationship.

üvey·i'lk[ği] (*orn.*) Wood pigeon; stock dove. ~ **mek**, *vi.* coo.

üvez (*ent.*) Type of mosquito. ~ **ağacı**, (*bot.*) mountain ash, rowan.

üye (*pol.*, *soc.*) Member; (*bio.*) organ; (*phil.*) coordinate. ~ **kaydetmek**, enrol. ~ **lik**, membership: ~ **belgesi**, membership card.

ÜYS = ÜNİVERSİTE YERLEŞTİRME SINAVI.

-üz[1] *n.* *suf.* [84] = -iz[1] [DÖRDÜZ].

-üz[2] *v.* *suf.* [96] = -iz[2] [TÜRKÜZ].

üzengi Stirrup. ~ **kemiği**[ni], (*bio.*) stapes. ~ **lemek** (-i), spur with the stirrups. ~ **taşı**, (*arch.*) springer.

üzer- (*always with a personal suffix*) [91] Top. = ÜZERİ.

üzere, **üzre** *post.* [88, 167] On, upon; according to; about; on the subject of; on condition of; for the purpose of; on the point of, just about to. ~ **olm.**, be about to.

üzeri *n.* Upper/outer surface of stg.; space above stg.; (*fin.*) remainder, change. *post.* [91] On; over; about. ~ **nde**, on (the top of); over: ~ **nde durmak**, dwell upon (a subject): ~ **nden**, from (on top of): ~ **nden sünger geçirmek**, pass the sponge over; (*fig.*) erase, cancel: ~ **ne**, onto; against; on the subject of: ~ **ne atılmak**, dash at s.o.: ~ **ne bindirmek**, fall on; increase in violence; blame (wrongly): ~ **ne çullanmak**, hurl o.s. on s.o.: ~ **ne su serpmek**, douse: ~ **ne yemin etm.**, swear on/by stg. [*For other phrases* = ÜST, *with which it is interchangeable.*]

üzerlik (*bot.*) Harmala, wild rue.

üzge·lc[ci] Rope ladder.

üz·gü Oppression, cruelty. ~ **gülü**, oppressive. ~ **gün**, weak, ill; anxious, worried. ~ **günbalığı**[nı], (*ich.*) dragonet. ~ **günlük**, weakness; anxiety. ~ **güsel**, dramatic. ~ **güsüz**, benevolent.

üzlük (*dom.*) Small earthen bowl; type of fumigant.

üzmek (-i) Strain to breaking point; treat harshly, harass.

üzre = ÜZERE.

üz·ücü Worrying, harassing. ~ **ülme**, *vn.* ~ **ülmek** *vp.* = ÜZMEK: (-e), be anxious/worried about stg. **üzülme!**, cheer up!

üzüm (*bot.*) Grape. ~ **asması**, grape vine: ~ **kütüğü** vine stock: ~ **salkımı**, bunch of grapes: ~ **suyu** grape juice: ~ ~**e baka kararır**, evil communications corrupt good manners: ~ **zarı**, (*bot.* grape skin: ~ **ünü ye de bağını sorma**, enjoy your pleasure/benefit and don't ask where it came from.

üzüm·cü(lük) (Work of) vine-grower/grape-seller. ~ **sü**, (*bot.*) grape-like (fruit). ~ **şekeri**[ni], (*chem.* glucose.

üzün·lç[cü] Sadness, melancholy; drama. ~ **tü** anxiety, worry, dejection; fatigue. ~ **tülü**, anxious worried: ~ **iş**, bother(some work). ~ **tüsüz** carefree.

V

V, v [ve] Twenty-seventh Tk. letter, V. ~ **kayışı,** (*eng.*) V-belt: ~ **kesimi,** V-cut.

V, v. = (*ch.s.*) VANADYUM; VARAK; VARIŞ; VEKİL; VEZİR; VOLT.

-v *n. suf.* [226] = -EV [SINAV].

vaaˡtᵈⁱ Promise; commitment, engagement, undertaking. ~ **etm.,** undertake: ~ **koparmak (-den),** extort a promise from: ~ **lerle cezbetmek,** entice: ~ **te bulunmak,** promise.

vaaz¹ (*rel.*) Admonition, sermon. ~ **etm.,** preach.

vabeste (-e) (*obs.*) Dependent on, depending on.

vaciˡpᵇⁱ Incumbent; (*rel.*) necessary, obligatory. ~ **olm.,** become necessary.

vade (*fin.*) Fixed term/date; maturity. ~ **ile borç etm.,** borrow for a fixed term: ~ **tarihi,** expiry//due date: ~ **si geçmiş,** overdue, expired: ~ **si gelmek/ yetmek,** fall due; (*fig.*) one's hour of death arrive.

vade·li Maturing at a certain date; term: ~ **hesap,** deposit account (for a fixed period). ~ **siz,** unlimited: ~ **hesap,** current account: ~ **ödünç,** call-money.

vadi (*geo.*) Valley, vale; wadi; (*fig.*) sense, meaning, manner. ~ **de (bu),** in this sense; along these lines.

vaftiz (*rel.*) Baptism. ~ **ana/babası,** god·mother/ -father: ~ **etm.,** baptize.

vagon (*rly.*) Carriage, coach, car; truck. ~ **fabrikası,** carriage works: ~ **restoran,** dining-car.

vagon·etⁱ Small coach. ~ **li,** (*rly.*) sleeping-car. ~ **lu,** having ... carriages/trucks. ~ **luk,** truckload.

vah *int.* ~ ~ **!,** what a pity!; oh dear!

vaha (*geo.*) Oasis.

vahametⁱ Gravity, seriousness.

vahdaniyetⁱ (*rel.*) The unity of God. ~ **e inanmak,** be a monotheist.

vahdetⁱ Unity; uniqueness; solitariness.

vahi Futile, useless, silly.

vahim Grave, serious, dangerous, critical.

vahiˡtᵈⁱ *a.* One, single. *n.* Unit.

vahˡiyⁱ (*rel.*) Divine inspiration/revelation (to a prophet).

vahş·etⁱ Wildness, savageness; terror; melancholy; solitude. ~ **etgâh,** lonely/terrifying spot. ~ **i,** wild, savage; brutish; afraid of man. ~ **ice,** *a.,* (*adv.*) wild(ly), brutal(ly), savage(ly). ~ **ilik,** wildness, savageness; brutality.

va·ız = VAAZ. ~ **iˡtᵈⁱ** = VAAT. ~ **iz,** preacher.

vaka Event, occurrence; historical event. ~ **yı bütün çıplaklığıyla anlatmak,** recount the event in all its details. ~ **nüvis(lik),** (work of) chronicler. ~ **yi-name,** (*his.*) chronicle.

vakar Gravity; dignity. ~ **lı,** grave; dignified. ~ **sız,** undignified.

vaketa Fine calf-skin leather.

vakfe Stop; pause; interval.

vakf·ˡetmekᵉᵈᵉʳ **(-i, -e)** Dedicate (to a pious foundation; devote/dedicate o.s. to stg. ~ **iye,** trust deed of a pious foundation.

vakıa *n.* Fact; occurrence, event. *conj.* In fact, actually; it is true that; indeed.

vakˡıfᶠⁱ (*rel.*) Pious foundation; Wakf. ~ **name** = VAKFİYE.

vâkıf Aware, cognizant; wide awake. ~ **gözlerle,** with an expert's eye: ~ **olm. (-e),** be aware of, know.

vaki Happening, taking place; real, actual.

vakˡitᵗⁱ [33] Time; suitable occasion; appointed time; -time, season: (*with a participle,* -DİĞİ, -ECEĞİ) [185] when. ~ **daraldı,** there's not much time: ~ **geçirmek,** pass the time; occupy o.s.: ~ **kaybetmeden,** straight away, without losing any time: ~ **kazanmak,** save time; gain time: ~ **öldürmek,** idle away the time: ~ ~ **,** at times, from time to time: ~ **i boşuna geçirmek,** waste time: ~ **i dolu olm.,** be busy/occupied; be booked up: ~ **i gelmek,** one's time/the end/death come: ~ **i olm.,** have time, not need to hurry: ~ **i olmamak (-e),** have no time to: ~ **inde,** *à propos*; at the right time: ~ **inde ödenmemiş,** (*fin.*) in arrears: ~ **ini almak/yemek,** take up s.o.'s time: ~ **ini şaşmamak,** do stg. at the right time (not early, not late): ~ **iniz var mı?,** have you/can you afford the time?: ~ **ler hayrolsun!,** good day!

vak·itli Done at the right time; in due season: ~ **vakitsiz,** in season and out of season; at all sorts of times. ~ **itsiz,** unseasonable; inopportune; premature. ~ **taki,** *conj.* when, at the time that . . .. ~ **ti** = VAKİT. ~ **tihal,** financial circumstances: ~ **yerinde,** in easy circumstances. ~ **tiyle,** in its proper time; in times past; at one time: ~ **görmüs geçirmiş,** one who has seen better days.

vaks (*bio.*) Wax.

vakum (*phys.*) Vacuum.

vakur Grave, dignified, solemn.

vakvak (*ech.*) Croaking. ~ **etm.,** croak.

val·abi (*zoo.*) Wallaby. ~ **e,** (*gamb.*) jack, knave. ~ **f,** (*eng.*) valve.

vali (*adm.*) Vali; governor of a province. ~ **lik,** rank/ duties of a vali; province.

valide Mother. ~ **sultan,** (*his.*) 'princess-mother' (of a reigning sultan).

valiz Suit-case, attaché-case.

vallahi *int.* By God!; I swear it is so!

valör (*fin.*) Exchange rate.

vals (*mus.*) Waltz. ~ **lı,** ~ **pres,** (*eng.*) roller press.

vampir (*myth.*) Vampire; (*zoo.*) vampire bat.

van·a (*eng.*) (Water) valve. ~ **adyum,** (*chem.*) vanadium. ~ **dal(izm),** vandal(ism). ~ **ilya,** (*bot.*) vanilla; (*cul.*) vanilla essence/pod. ~ **tilatör,** fan, ventilator. ~**trilog**ᵘ, ventriloquist. ~**tuz**, (*med.*) cupping-glass; (*zoo.*) sucker: ~ **çekmek**, cup: ~**balığı**ⁿ¹, (*ich.*) slender suckerfish.

vap·orizatör Spray(-gun). ~**ur(culuk)**, (*naut.*) steamship (operation). ~**urda teslim**, (*fin.*) free on board. ~**urdumanı**, dark grey (colour).

var [142] *a.* Existent; present; at hand; available; (*med.*) positive. *n.* Belongings; possessions; wealth. *v.* There is; there are; *used with possessive suffixes*, have [**kitabım** ~/**bende kitap** ~, I have a book: **paranız** ~**mı?**, have you any money?]. ~ **etm.**, cause to be present, create: ~ **etm. (-den)**, make stg. out of stg.: ~ **kuvvetiyle**, with all possible force/his strength; . . . for dear life/like anything: ~ **oğlu** ~, everything was there: ~ **olm.**, be, exist: ~ **ol!**, well done!, bravo!: ~YEMEZ: ~ **yok**, about, barely, perhaps: ~**a yoğa karışmak**, meddle in everything: ~**ı yoğu**, all one's possessions: ~**ımı yoğumu kaybettim**, I lost all I possessed: ~**ını yoğunu elinden almak**, bleed s.o. white: ~**ını yoğunu ortaya atmak**, be ready to sacrifice everything: ~**sa** . . . **yoksa** . . ., he thinks of nothing else than . . . .

varagele (*eng.*) Shaper, work-tool. ~ **halatı**, continuous rope.

varak¹ (*bot.*) Leaf; petal; sheet of paper; (*min.*) leaf, foil. ~**a**, single leaf; paper; note, document. ~**çı**, gold-leaf worker; ~ **kursağı**, goldbeater's skin. ~**lamak (-i)**, decorate with gold-leaf. ~**lanmak**, *vp.* ~**lı**, ornamented with gold-leaf, gilded.

varan = VARMAK. Reaching, amounting to. ~ **beş!**, that makes five!; that's number five!

varangiller (*zoo.*) Monitor lizards.

varda *int.* Look out!, keep clear!; make way! ~ **bandıra**, (*naut.*) yeoman of signals. ~**kosta**, (*naut.*, *obs.*) coastguard vessel; (*sl.*) heavily-built and imposing (woman). ~**mana**, handrope. ~**topu**ⁿᵘ, signal gun. ~**vela**, ship's rail.

vardırmak (-i, -e) *vc.* = VARMAK. Allow to reach; cause to arrive.

vardiya (*naut.*) The watch (position); (*ind.*) shift.

vareste Free; exempt.

vargel Incline; = VARAGELE.

var·gı (*phil.*) Result, consequence; conclusion. ~**ılmak**, *imp. v.* = VARMAK, one reach. ~**ış**, *vn.* arrival, destination, etc.; (*sp.*) finish; (*fig.*) quickness of perception: ~ **çizgi**//**direk**//**ipi**, (*sp.*) finishing line//post//tape: ~ **noktası**, destination: ~**ına gelişim tarhanana bulgur aşım**, as you do to others so they do to you. ~**ışım**, (*phys.*) convection. ~**ışlı**, quick-witted.

-vari *a. suf.* [66] Similar to . . ., like . . .; -ian, -ish [HAÇVARİ; ÇÖRÇİLVARİ].

varid- = VARİT. ~**at**¹, (*fin.*) revenues, income. ~**e**, (*adm.*) incoming papers.

varil Small cask/barrel.

varis(li) (*med.*) (Suffering from) varicose veins.

vâris *a.* Inheriting. *n.* Heir.

vari·tᵈⁱ That which arrives/happens; probable; admissible. ~ **değildir**, it is unlikely to happen.

variyetⁱ (*col.*) Wealth, riches; income. ~**li**, wealthy.

varla·ma *vn.* Approval. ~**mak (-i)**, approve, accept.

varlı·kᵍ¹ Existence; being; presence; self, personality; possessions; assets, wealth; easy circum-

stances. ~ **göstermek**, make one's presence felt; achieve one's aims: ~ **içinde yaşamak**, live a life of luxury: ~ **vergisi**, (*fin.*) wealth tax, capital levy: ~**a darlık olmaz**, wealth overcomes all obstacles: ~**lar**, assets: ~**ta darlık çekmek**, be unable to use one's wealth.

varlık·bilim (*phil.*) Ontology. ~**lı**, (*fin.*) well-to-do. ~**lılaştırma**, capitalization. ~**sal**, (*phil.*) existential.

var·ma *vn.* Arrival: ~ **limanı**, (*naut.*) destination. ~**mak (-e)**, *vi.* go towards; arrive at; reach; attain; approach; succeed in understanding; result, end in; (woman) marry s.o.; give o.s. up to: **var istediğini yap!**, do as you wish/whatever you like!: ~ **kıyas et!**, draw your own conclusions!: VARAN: **varıncaya kadar**, up to, to: **varsın gelsin**, let him come if he wishes: **varsın gelmesin!**, [134] it doesn't matter whether he comes or not!: **varsın o da** . . ., well if he wants to . . . let him.

varoluş (*phil.*) Existence. ~**ça**/~**sal**, existential. ~**çu(luk)**, existential·ist/(-ism).

varoş (*geo.*) Suburbs, outskirts.

varsağı (*mil.*) Type of scimitar; (*mus.*) type of song.

varsam (*ich.*) Lesser weever, stingfish.

varsay·ılı/~**ımsal** (*phil.*) Hypothetical; nominal. ~**ım**/~**ış**, *vn.* hypothesis. ~**mak (-i)**, suppose, assume.

varsıl Rich, wealthy; (*min.*) high-grade. ~**erkçi**, (*pol.*) plutocrat. ~**erki**, plutocracy. ~**laşmak**, *vi.* become rich. ~**laştırmak (-i)**, make rich; enrich. ~**lık**, wealth.

Varşova (*geo.*) Warsaw.

varta Abyss; great peril. ~**yı atlatmak**, escape a great danger.

var·yant (*lit.*) Variant; (*mot.*) detour, loop-road, diversion. ~**yasyon**, (*mus.*) variation.

varyemez Miserly, skinflint.

varyete (*th.*) Variety-show.

varyos (*min.*) Sledgehammer.

vasat¹ *n.* Middle; average; ambience, milieu. *a.* Middling; mediocre. ~ **ını almak**/**bulmak**, average: ~**tan aşağı**//**yukarı**, below//above average. ~**i**, central, middle; mean, average.

vas·f- = VASIF. ~**f**¹**etmek**ᵉᵈᵉʳ, describe; qualify. ~**fi**, qualifying. ~**ıf**ᶠ¹, quality; qualification; characteristic; description; eulogy; epithet, adjective: ~**a gelmez**, indescribable.

vasıf·landırmak (-i) Qualify, describe. ~**lanmak**, *vp.* be qualified/described. ~**lı**, qualified; having . . . quality.

vasıl *a.* Arriving; joining. ~ **olm.**, arrive; join; attain.

vasıta Means; channel; agent, agency; intermediary, go-between; vehicle; appliance; apparatus. ~**sıyla (-in)**, by means of, through (the agency of). ~**lı**, indirect. ~**sız**, direct; without intermediary.

vâsi *a.* Extensive, capacious, wide; abundant. ~ **mikyasta**, on a large scale.

vasi (*leg.*) Executor; trustee; administrator; guardian. ~**lik**, executorship, etc.

vasistas (*arch.*) Opening window-frame; fanlight; louvre.

vasiyetⁱ (*leg.*) Will, testament; last request (of dying).

~ **etm.**, bequeath. ~ **name**, written will: ~ **zeyli**, codicil. ~ **siz**, intestate.

vaşa¹kᵍ¹ (*zoo.*) Lynx; bob-cat, karakul; (*mod.*) lynx-fur.

Vaşington (*geo.*) Washington. ~ **tipi**, (*sl.*) strange-looking; new-fangled; eccentric.

vat¹ (*el.*) Watt. ~ **-saat**, watt-hour.

vatan Native country, motherland, homeland. ~ **haini**, defector, traitor: ~ **yoluna**, for one's country's sake: ~ı **kurtarmak**, (*col.*) save the situation.

vatan·daş Compatriot, fellow-citizen: ~ **muamelesi**, procedure relating to citizens: ~ **muamelesi yapmak**, treat as a citizen. ~ **daşlık**, citizenship, nationality. ~ **i**, pertaining to one's homeland. ~ **perver/sever**, patriot(ic). ~ **perverlik**, patriotism. ~ **sız**, stateless, *heimatlos.* ~ **sızlık**, statelessness.

vatikan (*pol.*) Vatican.

vatka (*mod.*) Shoulder-padding.

vat·man Tram-driver. ~ **metre**, (*el.*) wattmeter.

vatoz (*ich.*) Thornback ray.

vaveyla *int.* (*of horror/sorrow*) Alas! ~ **yı koparmak**, cry with horror; lament.

vay *int.* (*of surprise/regret*) Oh!; alas! ~ **anam** ~!, oh, how strange!: ~ **anasını!**, why? for heaven's sake!; curse him!: ~ **başım!**, oh, my poor head!: ~ **başıma!**, woe is me!: ~ **benim köse sakalım!**, this is just a dream!, I'll have to wait for ever!: ~ **bize olanlar!**, how disappointing!: ~ **canıma**, amazing!: ~ **kâfir!**, lucky dog!; oh, well done!: ~ **sen misin!**, hullo, is that you! ~ **babacığımcılık**, (*sl.*) type of pick-pocketing.

vazelin (*chem.*) Vaseline.

vaz¹etmekᵉᵈᵉʳ **(-i)** Put; place; (*arch.*) lay; (*fin.*) impose.

vazgeç·irmek (-i, -den) *vc.* Dissuade, deter. ~ **ilmek**, *vp.* ~ **ilemez**, essential, necessary. ~ **me**, *vn.* (*leg.*) waiver. ~ **mek (-den)**, give up, discontinue; cease from; renounce; abandon (project); change one's mind. ~ **ti**, difference, dispute.

vazıh Clear, obvious; distinct.

vazıham¹ilˡⁱ (*bio.*) Birth, parturition.

vazıkanun (*adm.*) Legislator.

vazıye¹tᵈⁱ (*leg.*) Seizure, confiscation.

vazife Duty; obligation; task; business; charge; (*fin.*) salary. ~ **almak**, go on duty, take one's turn: ~ **başında**, on duty: ~ **damarı tuttu**, (*iron.*) his sense of duty called him!; he's very punctilious: ~ **etm.** (-i), care/trouble about; mind, be interested: ~ **görmek**, act, do one's duty: ~ **si mi?**, what does he care!: ~ **sinden olm.**, be retired: ~ **sini görmek**, act for s.o.: ~ **ye kayırılmak**, get a job by favour: ~ **yi ihmal etm.**, neglect one's duty.

vazife·dar (*adm.*) Responsible official, competent authority. ~ **lendirilmek**, *vp.* ~ **lendirmek (-i)**, charge with a duty. ~ **li**, in charge; on duty: ~ **şahıs**, (*adm.*) competent authority. ~ **siz**, without duties; careless, slack. ~ **şinas**, dutiful, conscientious.

vaziyetⁱ Position, situation; attitude; condition; state. ~ **almak**, (*mil.*) stand to attention; (*fig.*) take sides: ~ **meydanda!**, you know the situation very well!: ~ **planı**, (*th.*) booking plan.

vazo Flower-vase. ~ **motor**, (*bio.*) vasomotor.

vb. = VE BAŞKARLARI/BENZERLERİ; VE BUNUN GİBİ.

vd. = VE DEVAMI.

ve *conj.* [206] And. ~ **başkalari/benzerleri/saire**, etcetera: ~ **dahi duralar!**, and that was the end of it!: ~ **devamı**, and so on: ~/**veya**, and/or.

veba (*med.*) Bubonic plague; pestilence. ~ **şişi**, bubo. ~ **lı**, plague-stricken.

vebalⁱ (*rel.*) Sin; (*fig.*) evil consequence. ~ **i kendi boynuna**, his blood be on his own head.

veb·er (*el.*) Weber. ~ **-ofset**, (*pub.*) web-offset.

veca¹ (*med.*) Pain; colic. ~ **lı**, painful; in pain.

vecibe Duty, obligation.

ve¹cihᶜʰⁱ Face, surface; manner; means. ~ **ile**, in . . . way/manner.

vec¹itᵈⁱ Ecstasy, rapture. ~ **e gelmek**, become ecstatic: ~ **e getirmek**, entrance.

veciz Brief, concise, laconic, terse. ~ **e**, terse saying; slogan; aphorism; epigram.

veçh- = VECİH. ~ **e**, direction.

veda¹ Farewell; leave-taking. ~ **etm**, (-e), bid farewell to s.o./stg.: ~ **a gitmek (-e)**, pay s.o. a farewell visit. ~ **laşmak**, bid each other farewell; make one's adieux.

vedia Stg. deposited/given into safe keeping.

vefa Fidelity, loyalty, faithfulness. ~ **etm. (-e)**, be true to (one's word, etc.). ~ **dar/** ~ **kâr/** ~ **lı**, faithful, loyal, constant. ~ **sız(lık)**, faithless(ness); disloyal(ty).

vef·at¹ Death; decease: ~ **etm.**, die. ~ **iyat¹**, *pl.* deaths; *s.* mortality; (*obs.*) obituary.

veh¹imᵐⁱ Foreboding, anxiety; groundless fear; illusion, delusion.

vehleten For the first moment; just at first.

vehm- = VEHİM. ~ **¹etmek**ᵉᵈᵉʳ **(-i)**, forebode; fear; surmise, conjecture. ~ **i**, *a.* imaginary.

veje·talin (*chem., cul.*) Vegetable oil/fat. ~ **taryen**, vegetarian.

vekâletⁱ Being the agent/deputy/representative of; (*leg.*) attorney; (*adm., obs.*) Ministry. ~ **etm. (-e)**, act on behalf of, deputize for.

vekâlet·en As agent/deputy of . . .; by proxy. ~ **name**, (*leg.*) power of attorney, proxy. ~ **siz**, direct.

vekil Agent, representative; deputy; attorney; proxy; (*adm., obs.*) Minister. ~ **olan**, acting: ~ **tayin etm.**, depute: ~ **e çıkmak**, go and see the Minister: ~ **ler heyeti**, (*adm.*) Council of Ministers.

vekil·har¹çᶜ¹ (*obs.*) Steward, majordomo. ~ **lik**, status/duties of agent, etc.; agency; attorneyship: ~ **belgesi**, proxy, power of attorney.

vektör (*math.*) Vector.

vela·detⁱ Birth. ~ **yet**ⁱ, guardianship; trusteeship.

velense (*dom.*) Type of thick blanket; horse-rug.

velespitⁱ Bicycle.

vele¹tᵈⁱ Child; progeny. ~ **i zina**, bastard.

vel·ev(ki) *conj.* Even if; even though. ~ **fec¹ir**ʳⁱ = GÖZ. ~ **hasıl**, *conj.*, in brief/short.

veli (*leg.*) Guardian, trustee; (*rel.*) saint. ~ **ah¹t**ᵈ¹, (*adm.*) crown prince, heir apparent. ~ **lik**, qualities/duties of a guardian. ~ **nimet**ⁱ, benefactor, patron.

velodrom (*sp.*) Cycling-track.

velum (*bio.*) Velum.

velur (*tex.*) Velvet.

velut Productive; fruitful; prolific.

velvele Outcry; clamour, hubbub. ~**ye vermek**, make a great outcry. ~**ci**, noisy, clamorous.

Vene·di¹kği (*geo.*) Venice: ~ **dukası**, (*his.*) Doge. ~**dikli**, (*ethn.*) Venetian.

Venezüella (*geo.*) Venezuela.

ven·til (*eng.*) Valve, cock. ~**to**, (*naut.*) topping-lift.

Venüs (*myth.*, *ast.*) Venus. ~**çarığı**ⁿⁱ, (*bot.*) lady's slipper orchid. ~**kemeri**ⁿⁱ, (*zoo.*) Venus's girdle. ~**sepeti**ⁿⁱ, (*zoo.*) Venus's flower-basket.

veranda (*arch.*) Veranda(h).

verasetⁱ Inheritance; heritage. ~ **(ve intikal) vergisi**, (*fin.*) death-duty//(capital transfer tax).

verdi (*phys.*) Flow per second, output.

verdirmek (-i, -e) *vc.* = VERMEK.

vere (*mil.*) Surrender, capitulation. ~ **bayrağı**, white flag: ~ **vermek**, capitulate.

verece¹kği Debt. ~**li**, owing, debtor; indebted.

verem *n.* (*med.*) Tuberculosis, consumption. *a.* Tuberculous. ~**e tutulmak**, go into a decline. ~**li**, tuberculous, consumptive.

vere·ne¹kği (*fin.*) Credit. ~**se**, *pl.* = VARİS; heirs. ~**si(ye)**, [181] (*fin.*) on credit; (*fig.*) carelessly, inattentively: ~ **satış**, credit sale. ~**siyecilik**, credit trading.

verev Oblique, diagonal, slanting; (*tex.*) bias(sed).

vergi (*fin.*) Tax, contribution; (*fig.*) gift, talent; gift, present. ~ **beyanı**, tax declaration: ~ **çizelgesi**, tax tables: ~ **dairesi**, tax office: ~ **ile bağımlı**, taxable: ~ **kaçakçılığı**, tax evasion: ~ **kaldırmak**, be capable of paying tax: ~ **koymak/salmak**, impose taxes: ~ **muaflığı**, tax immunity: ~ **mükellef/yükümlüsü**, taxpayer: ~ **mültezimi**, tax farmer: ~ **nispet/oranı**, rate of tax: ~ **olm. (-e)**, be the speciality of: ~ **tahakkuku**, determination of tax: ~ **tahsili**, collection of tax: ~ **tahsildarı**, tax-collector: ~**ye bağlı**, taxable, dutiable.

vergi·ci(lik) (*fin.*) Tax-collect·or/(-ing). ~**lemek**, *vt.* impose taxes, tax. ~**lendirme**, *vn.* taxation; assessment. ~**lendirmek (-i)**, tax s.o./stg. ~**li**, generous; (*fin.*) taxed. ~**siz**, untalented; (*fin.*) untaxed.

veri Information, datum. ~**ler**, data: ~**ler bankası**, data bank. ~**ci**, giving; giver; (*med.*) donor; (*eng.*) feed; (*el.*) transformer; (*rad.*) transmitter. ~**le**, *int.* let it be given!: *n.* (*adm.*) order to pay. ~**lme**, *vn.* delivery. ~**lmek**, *vp.* = VERMEK: **(-e)**, be devoted to: **verilmiş sadakası varmış**, have a lucky escape.

verim Produce; output; return; profit; (*phys.*) delivery. ~ **gücü**, (*ind.*) output, yield, profitability. ~**li**, productive, fertile; fruitful; efficient; profitable; (*geol.*) pay-(dirt/sand, etc.). ~**lilik**, fruitfulness; profitability; (*phys.*) yield, efficiency. ~**siz/(-lik)**, unproductive(ness); barren(ness), steri·le/(-lity); unfruitful(ness).

veriş Act/manner of giving; grant. ~**im**, exchange. ~**mek (-i)**, give to each other; exchange. ~**tirmek (-i, -e)**, talk too much; utter abuse, swear at.

veri¹tᵈⁱ (*bio.*) Vein.

ver·ivermek (-i) Give immediately; hand over. ~**kaç**, (*sp.*) pass and run. ~**me**, *vn.* giving, etc.: ~ **hali**, (*ling.*) dative case. ~¹**mek**ⁱʳ **(-i, -e)**, give,

donate; award; leave; deliver; lean against; turn towards; give/arrange (concert, etc.); give in marriage; pay; offer; sell; produce; give off; attribute, ascribe; suffer (losses); teach. *As aux*, *v. it* implies (1) easiness/quickness [191] [**anlayıverdi**, he readily understood: **gelmeyiverdi**, he suddenly stopped coming]: (2) *a polite request* [**kapıyı açıver!**, would you mind opening the door?]. **ver elini bu/şu yer**, have pleasure in visiting: **verip veriştirmek**, speak one's mind: **vermedi mabut, ne yapsın Mahmut?**, man proposes, God disposes; it can't be helped.

ver·mikülitⁱ (*min.*) Vermiculite. ~**mut**ᵘ, (*cul.*) vermouth: ~ **otu**, (*bot.*) wormwood.

ver·ni¹kği Varnish. ~**niklemek (-i)**, varnish.

verniye (*eng.*) Vernier.

veronika (*bot.*) Common speedwell.

veryansın ~ **etm.**, destroy without mercy; (*fin.*) squander; (*fig.*) get excited; exaggerate.

vesaikⁱ *pl.* = VESİKA; documents.

vesaire Etcetera.

vesaitⁱ *pl.* = VASITA; means.

vesayetⁱ Trusteeship.

vesika Document; title-deed; certificate; credentials, identity-paper; ration-card. ~**lı**, having a document, etc.; certified; licensed/registered (prostitute).

vesile Means; cause; excuse, pretext; opportunity. ~ **buldukça**, on any pretext: ~ **ile (bir)**, by some means, on some pretext: ~ **olm.**, afford.

vesselam *int.* So that's that/an end to the matter!

vestiyer(ci) Cloakroom (attendant).

vesvese Anxiety; apprehension; scruple. ~ **etm.**, have misgivings. ~**li**, anxious, apprehensive.

vet. = VETERİNER.

veter (*mil.*) Bowstring; (*mus.*) (violin, etc.) string; (*bio.*) tendon, sinew; (*math.*) chord. ~**e**, (*bio.*) septum.

veteriner Veterinary surgeon. ~ **+**, *a.* Veterinary. ~**lik**, veterinary surgery.

vetire Path, track; mode, manner.

veto (*pol.*, *soc.*) Veto. ~ **etm.**, veto.

veya(hut) *conj.* [210] Or.

vezaretⁱ (*adm.*) Vizierate.

vez¹inⁿⁱ (*math.*) Weighing; weight; (*lit.*) metre. ~**li**, weighed; balanced. ~**siz**, unweighed; unbalanced.

vezir (*adm.*, *obs.*) Vizier, Minister; (chess) queen. ~**iazam**, Grand Vizier. ~**lik**, vizierate. ~**parmağı**ⁿⁱ, (*cul.*) a type of sweetmeat.

vezne (*adm.*) Treasury; pay-office; (*phys.*) balance, gauge. ~**ci//** ~**dar(lık)**, (duties/office of) treasurer// cashier.

V·FR = (*visual flight rules*). ~**HF** = (*very high frequency*).

vıcık Semi-fluid, viscid; sticky; dirty. ~ ~, (*ech.*) squelching: ~ ~ **etm.**, make very sticky. ~**lamak (-i)**, make sticky.

vıdı ~ ~, talkative: ~ ~ **etm.**, talk endlessly.

vık (*ech.*) Squeak (of distress). ~ **dememek**, not make a single squeak. ~**lamak**, *vi.* squeak.

vın (*ech.*) Humming, whirring. ~**lamak**, *vi.* hum; whirr. ~**layan kuyrukkakan**, (*orn.*) whinchat.

vır (*ech.*) ~ ~ **başının etini yemek**, keep on nagging at s.o. ~**ılda(n)mak**, *vi.* talk incessantly; keep on complaining querulously. ~ıltı, tiresome talk; nagging; querulousness. ~lamak, nag. ~vırcı, nagger.

ız (ech.) Buzz. ~ gelmek (-e), be a matter of indifference: ~ gelip tırıs gitmek, not care two hoots.

ız·ıldamak vi. Buzz, hum; complain endlessly. ~ıltı, buzzing/whirring sound. ~ır ~ır, (ech.) whirring; (fig.) stg. easily and quickly done. ~lamak, vi. = VIZILDAMAK.

vi a. suf. [65] = -i⁴ [ABİDEVİ].

i·brasyon (phys.) Vibration. ~bratör, (el., eng.) vibrator, buzzer. ~briyon, (bio.) vibrio. ~brofon, (mus.) vibraphone.

ica·hen adv. Face to face; in the presence of. ~hi, a. done in the presence of s.o.

icdan Conscience. ~ azabı, pangs of conscience: ~ hürriyeti, (pol.) freedom of conscience: ~ı müsterih olarak, with a clear conscience: ~ım razı olmaz (-e), I would not have the conscience to.

icdan·en In accordance with one's conscience. ~lı, conscientious; honest. ~sız(lık), unscrupulous/ (-ness).

ida (eng., carp.) Screw; screw-thread. ~ başı yuvası, countersink: ~ dişi, screw thread: ~ tarağı, chaser: ~ yatığı, nut.

idala/videle Box-calf; calfskin.

ida·lamak (-i) Screw; screw down/up. ~lanmak, vp. ~lı, having a screw; screwed; threaded: ~ cıvata, screw-bolt.

ideo (rad.) Video. ~ teybi, videotape.

'ietnam (geo.) Vietnam. ~lı, (ethn.) Vietnamese.

igla Look-out post of DALYAN. ~cı, look-out man.

ikaye Protection; (med.) prophylaxis.

ikontᵘ(es) (soc.) Viscount(ess).

ikunya (zoo.) Vicuna.

iladi From birth; innate, congenital.

ilayetⁱ (adm.) Province, vilayet; (arch.) gover-norate; (fig.) country. ~ konağı, provincial government offices. ~li, of/from . . . vilayet; fellow-countryman.

il·la (arch.) Villa. ~lüs, (bio.) villus.

in·çⁱ (naut., eng.) Winch, capstan; crane, derrick: ~ ücreti, cranage. ~il, (chem.) vinyl. ~ter, (naut.) trawl-net.

ira int. Haul! (a crane); (naut.) anchor aweigh! adv. continuously. ~j, (road) bend, curve: ~ almak, (sl.) tell lies: ~ yapmak, cut/take a corner: ~ yüksekliği, banking.

iran Devastated, ruined; desolate. ~e, ruin; ruined building: ~ ye çevirmek, reduce to ruins, devastate. ~elik, a place of ruins.

ire = VERE.

ir·gül (ling.) Comma; (math.) decimal point. ~il, (aer.) spin.

ir¹tᵈⁱ (rel.) Text recited daily; (fig.) oft repeated saying. ~ etm., repeat constantly.

irtüöz(lük) (mus.) (Being a) virtuoso.

irüs (bio.) Virus. ~ +, a. Viral.

isalⁱ Meeting; reunion; lovers' union.

isamiralⁱ (naut.) Vice-admiral.

iski (cul.) Whisk(e)y.

iskoz (chem.) Viscose. ~ite, viscosity.

vişne (bot.) Morello cherry. ~ ağacı, sour cherry: ~ likörü, (cul.) cherry brandy. ~çürüğünᵘ, carmine, purplish-brown colour.

vitamin (bio.) Vitamin. ~ eksikliği, vitamin deficiency. ~li, with vitamins. ~siz, without vitamins.

vitellüs (bio.) Vitellus, yolk.

vites (mot.) Gear (system). ~ değiştirmek, change gear/speed: ~ kolu, gear-lever: ~ kutusu, gear-box: ~i büyültmek//küçültmek, change up// down.

vit¹irʳⁱ (rel.) Act of worship between night and morning.

vi·tray (art.) Stained glass. ~trin, (dom.) display cabinet; shop-window.

viya (naut.) Steer ahead! ~dükᵘ, (arch.) viaduct.

viyak (ech.) ~ ~, squawking. ~lamak, vi. squawk, cry.

Viyana (geo.) Vienna.

viyol·a (mus.) Viola. ~on(ist), violin(-player). ~onsel, (violon)cello. ~onselci, (violon)cellist.

vize (adm.) Counter-signature, endorsement; visa. ~ almak, obtain a visa: ~ etm., countersign, endorse.

vizite (med.) Doctor's rounds; domiciliary visit; doctor's fee.

vizon (zoo.) Mink. ~ (kürkü), (mod.) mink fur.

viz·ör (cin.) Viewfinder. ~yon, (cin.) vision: ~a girmek, be shown.

vodvil (th.) Light comedy; vaudeville.

vokal a. Vocal. n. (ling.) Vowel. ~ müzik, vocal music.

vol·an (eng.) Flywheel; (mod.) flounce. ~e, (sp.) volley. ~eybolᵘ, (sp.) volleyball.

volfram (chem.) Wolfram, tungsten. ~ çeliği// karbür, tungsten steel//carbide.

voli (ich.) Cast of a net. ~ ağı, cast-net: ~ çevirmek, cast a net; (fig.) set a trap: ~ vurmak, (sl.) do a good stroke of business.

volkan(ik) (geol.) Volca·no/(-nic).

voltᵘ (el.) Volt. ~a, (naut.) a round turn/knot; tack: ~ atmak, walk up and down: ~ etm./vurmak, (naut.) come about, tack to windward; cruise about: ~sını almak, (col.) run away. ~aj, (el.) voltage: ~ ölçeği, electrometer. ~amper, volt-ampere. ~ metre, voltameter. ~ölçer, voltmeter.

vo·lüm (mus.) Volume. ~lümetri, (math.) cubic measure.

vombat (zoo.) Wombat.

vonoz (ich.) Young mackerel/bonito, etc.

votka (cul.) Vodka.

voyvo int. (sl.) My! bravo! ~da(lık), (his., adm.) (rank/duties/province of) governor (in Rumelia).

VP = VATAN PARTİSİ.

v.s. = VESAİR[E].

VUK = VERGİ USULÜ KANUNU.

vukuᵘ Occurrence, event, happening. ~ bulmak/ ~a gelmek, happen, occur, take place: ~a getirmek, bring about, cause to happen: ~u hal, the fact of the matter: ~u vardır (-in), this has happened. ~atᵗ, pl. events; (criminal) incidents.

vukuf Knowledge, information. ~u tammı var (-e), he has a thorough knowledge of. ~suz, ignorant;

badly informed. ~**suzluk**, lack of information, ignorance.

vulkani·zasyon (*chem.*) Vulcanization. ~**zatör**, vulcanizer; tyre repairer/remoulder. ~**ze**, vulcanized: ~ **etm.**, vulcanize, cure.

vur·a¹ç^{c1} (*sp.*) Racket. ~**dumduymaz**, insensitive; thick-skinned; blockhead: ~ **kör ayvaz olm.**, be insensitive. ~**dumduymazlık**, insensitivity. ~**durmak (-i, -e)**, *vc.* = VURMAK.

vurgu (*ling.*) Accent, stress; emphasis. ~ **almıyan**, enclitic: ~ **sözcük**, catchword, keyword. ~**lamak (-i)**, accentuate, stress; emphasize. ~**lu**, accented, stressed; accentuated; emphasized. ~**suz**, unaccented, unstressed, atonic.

vurgun *a.* Struck: **(-e)**, in love with, 'gone on'. *n.* Plunder; good stroke of business; profiteering, speculation; (*agr.*) blight; (*med.*) caisson disease, the bends. ~ **yemek**, (*med.*) (diver) die/be maimed.

vurgun·cu(luk) (*fin.*) Profiteer(ing), specula·tor/(-tion). ~**cul**/~**sal**, speculative. ~**luk**, love, passion.

vur·ma *vn.* Striking, etc.; hitting the mark; (*phys.*) percussion; jolt, shock. ~¹**mak**^{ur} **(-e)**, *vt.* strike, bang, hit, knock; take (road/direction); (sun) beat down on; (wind/rain, etc.) penetrate into; pretend to: **(-i)**, (clock) strike (the hours); rob s.o., steal stg.; hit the target; shoot (game); shoot and wound/kill s.o.; (*med.*) chafe, blister; make ill; (*agr.*) blight (crops); (*gamb.*) take a piece (backgammon): **(-i, -e)**, hit against; put on; apply to; turn into (stg. else); stick into: *vi.* (clock, etc.) strike, chime; appear; pretend to be: **vur abalıya**, attack the weak, blame the defenceless: **vur dedimse öldür demedim ya!**, gently, don't go too far!: **vur deyince öldürmek**,

exceed one's orders/advice: **vur kör ayvaz**, behave insensitively: **vur patlasın çal oynasın**, squandering money on pleasure; going on the spree: **vurdukça tozumak**, you'll get there if you persevere!: VUR-DUMDUYMAZ.

vur·tut A shooting quarrel; confusion, tumult; (*fin.*) hard bargaining. ~**u**, (*bio.*) pulse, heartbeat. ~**ucu**, (*mil.*) marksman; (*sp.*) kicker, striker: ~ **güç/kuvvet**, (*mil.*) fire-power. ~**uk(sal)**, (*psy.*) trauma(tic). ~**ulmak**, *vp.* = VURMAK; **(-e)**, be in love with: **vurularak çalınan çalgı**, (*mus.*) percussion instrument. ~**um**, (*bio.*) pulsation, beating. ~**uş**, *vn.* blow, stroke; impact; (*pol.*) coup; (*mus.*) tempo, beat; (*sp.*) kick. ~**uşma**, *vn.* (*sp.*) combat. ~**uşmacı**, combatant. ~**uşmak (-le)**, strike each other, fight. ~**uşturmak (-i)**, *vc.*; (*sl.*) drink together.

vuslat¹ Union (with one's beloved).

vus¹ul^{lü} Arrival. ~ **bulmak**, arrive: ~**ünde**, on his arrival.

vuzuh Clearness; (*lit.*) clarity. ~**suzluk**, obscurity.

vücu¹t^{du} Existence, being; (*bio.*) human body. ~ **bulmak**/~**a gelmek**, come into existence, arise: ~ **lekesi**, birthmark: ~ **vermek**/~**a getirmek**, bring into existence, create, produce: ~ **tan düşmek**, fail; become thin/weak: ~**um kırık**, I don't feel up to much: ~**unu ortadan kaldırmak**, kill.

vücut·ça Bodily; physically. ~**lu**, large in body; heavily built. ~**suz**, bodiless, non-existent; small, weak.

vükela *pl.* (*adm.*, *obs.*) Ministers.

vüru¹t^{du} Arrival, coming.

vüsat¹ Spaciousness; abundance; extent; means, capacity. ~**ine göre**, according to one's means.

W

W, w [vu] *Not a Tk. letter.*
W = (*el.*) VAT; (*ch.s.*) VOLFRAM; (*geo.*) (*West*).
Wb. = (*el.*) VEBER.
W·B = (*World Bank*). ~**C** = (*water-closet*). ~**HO**

= (*World Health Organization*). ~**MO** = (*World Meteorological Organization*).
Ws = (*el.*) VAT-SAAT.

X

X, x [ks] *Not a Tk. letter*; (*math.*) first unknown quantity. ~ **ekseni**, (*math.*) *x*-axis.

X = (*ch.s.*) KSENON. ~ **ışınları**, (*phys.*) X-rays.

Y

Y, y [ye] Twenty-eighth Tk. letter, Y; (*math.*) second unknown quantity. ∼ **borusu**, (*eng.*) Y-pipe: ∼ **ekseni**, (*math.*) *y*-axis: ∼ **kavşağı**, (*mot.*) Y-junction: ∼ **kromozomu**, (*bio.*) Y-chromosome.

Y, y. = (*ch.s.*) İTRİYUM; YANSIMA; YAPRAK; YARDIM(CI); YUNANCA(DAN); YÜKSEK. ∼ **ad.** = (*geo.*) YARIMADA(SI).

-y¹ *a./n. suf.* [226] = -EY [DENEY].

-y-² *buffer letter* [29, 96] = -N- [GELMİYECEĞİM].

ya¹ *int.* O . . .!; oh!; hi! ∼ **Rabbi!**, oh my God!: ∼ **Rabbi, sen bilirsin!**, *int.* (*of annoyance*): ∼ **sabır çekmek**, accept uncomplainingly.

ya² *int.* [218] Ah indeed!; oh!; then!; so!; especially!; don't forget . . .!; after all!; yes, of course!; you know . . .!; does one?; isn't that so?; and what about . . .? ∼ **ben ne yapayım?**, well then, what shall *I* do?: ∼ **duyarsa?**, yes, but what if he hears?: ∼ **gelmezse?**, and if he doesn't come?: ∼ **öyle mi?**, ah, is that so?

ya³ *conj.* [210] Or. ∼ **A** ∼ **B** (**veya/ya da/yahut C**), either A or B (or C): ∼ **bu deveyi gütmeli ya bu diyardan gitmeli**, if you wish to succeed you must adjust to your circumstances: ∼ **da**, or: ∼ **devlet başa** ∼ **kuzgun leşe**, either victory or death!: ∼ **harrü** ∼ **marrü!**, well, let's have a try, it may work!

yaba (*agr.*) Wooden winnowing fork. ∼**lamak (-i)**, winnow.

yaban *n.* Desert; wilderness. ∼ **+**, *a.* Wild: ∼ **ağaççileği**, (*bot.*) cloudberry: ∼ **eriği**, (*bot.*) bullace: ∼ **hayvanı**, (*zoo.*) wild animal: ∼ **kazı**, (*orn.*) greylag goose: ∼ **menekşesi**, (*bot.*) dog-violet: ∼ **sığırı**, (*zoo.*) gaur, wild ox: ∼**a atmak**, consider unimportant: ∼**a söylemek**, talk nonsense: ∼**ın köpeği**, an outcast.

yaban·arısıⁿ¹ (*ent.*) Common wasp. ∼**asması**ⁿ¹, (*bot.*) clematis. ∼**cı**, *a.* strange, exotic; alien, foreign: *n.* foreigner; stranger; interloper: ∼ **ayrıcalığı**, (*his.*) capitulations: ∼ **dil**, foreign language: ∼ **kazı**, (*orn.*) greylag goose: ∼ **kelime**, borrowed word: ∼ **kökenli**, of foreign origin: ∼ **madde/özdek**, (*chem.*) foreign body; impurity: ∼**sı (-in)**, a stranger to . . .. ∼**cıl**, exotic. ∼**cılaşma**, *vn.* ∼**cılaşmak**, *vi.* (*soc.*) become alien, opt out. ∼**cılaştırmak (-i)**, estrange. ∼**cılık**, being a stranger/foreigner: ∼ **çekmek**, suffer for being a stranger/foreigner. ∼**cıllık**, exoticism. ∼ **defnesi**ⁿ¹, (*bot.*) laurustinus, wild bay; daphne. ∼**domuzu**ⁿᵘ, (*zoo.*) wild boar. ∼**enginarı**ⁿ¹, (*bot.*) cardoon. ∼ **eşeği**ⁿ¹, (*zoo.*) wild ass. ∼**gülü**ⁿᵘ, (*bot.*) dog-rose. ∼**havucu**ⁿᵘ, (*bot.*) wild parsnip. ∼**ıl**, wild (plant/ animal); primitive (man). ∼**ıllık**, wildness; primitiveness.

yabani Belonging to the wilds; wild; untamed; timid; rough, unmannerly. ∼ **adaçayı**, (*bot.*) meadow clary: ∼ **akasya**, (*bot.*) common/false

acacia: ∼ **akdiken**, (*bot.*) alder buckthorn: ∼ **çuhaçiçeği**, (*bot.*) cowslip: ∼ **gül**, (*bot.*) eglantine: ∼ **hardal**, (*bot.*) charlock: ∼ **horoz**, (*orn.*) blackcock: ∼ **koç**, (*zoo.*) wild sheep: ∼ **ot**, (*bot.*) weed: ∼ **sardunya**, (*bot.*) crane's bill: ∼ **sümbül**, (*bot.*) bluebell: ∼ **zerrin**, (*bot.*) daffodil.

yabani·ıspanaˡ**k**ᵍ¹ (*bot.*) Chard. ∼**kimyon(giller)**, (*bot.*) bean-caper/(Zygophyllaceae). ∼**lahana**, (*bot.*) seakale. ∼**lik**, wildness; roughness. ∼**mercanköşk**, (*bot.*) marjoram. ∼**yasemin**, (*bot.*) bittersweet, woody nightshade.

yaban·inciriⁿ¹ (*bot.*) Wild fig. ∼**keçisi**ⁿ¹, (*zoo.*) wild goat; ibex. ∼**kedisi**ⁿ¹, (*zoo.*) wild cat. ∼**kekliği**ⁿ¹, (*bot.*) wild thyme. ∼**keteni**ⁿ¹, (*bot.*) dodder. ∼**lık**, (*mod.*) one's best (clothes, for visiting). ∼**maydanozu**ⁿᵘ, (*bot.*) cow parsley. ∼**mersini**ⁿ¹, (*bot.*) butcher's broom. ∼**ördeği**ⁿ¹, (*orn.*) mallard. ∼**pancarı**ⁿ¹, (*bot.*) chard. ∼**sı**, strange, unusual; cosmopolitan (city). ∼**sılık**, strangeness. ∼**sımak (-i)**, find/consider strange. ∼**sümbülü**ⁿᵘ, (*bot.*) catmint. ∼**tavşanı**ⁿ¹, (*zoo.*) rabbit. ∼**teresi**ⁿ¹, (*bot.*) pepperwort. ∼**tırak**, (*bot.*) dill, false fennel. ∼**turpu**ⁿᵘ, (*bot.*) horse-radish.

-yacak *v. suf.* [112, 158] = -ECEK [YAŞAYACAK].

yad *a.* Strange; alien; enemy. *n.* Stranger. ∼ **elde**, in a strange land; far from home: ∼ **eller**, strange lands: ∼ **ellere satmak**, sell to foreigners.

yâd Remembrance; mention. ∼**a getirmek**/∼**etmek (-i)**, call to mind, recollect; mention. ∼**igâr**, keepsake, souvenir; (*col.*) scoundrel; notorious.

yada ∼ **taşı**, (*geol.*) jade.

yad·el(ci) (*pol.*) Exile. ∼**erklik**, foreign domination/government; (*phil.*) heteronomy. ∼**estetik**, unaesthetic. ∼**gerekirci(lik)**, (*phil.*) indetermin·ist/(-ism). ∼**ımlamak**/∼**ımsamak (-i)**, (*bio.*) deassimilate, excrete. ∼**ınkurun**, (*phys.*) asynchronous. ∼**ırgamak (-i)**, regard as a stranger; find stg. strange/odd; (child) cry at a stranger. ∼**ırganmak**, *vp.* ∼**ırgatıcı**, making feel strange. ∼**ırgatmak (-i)**, *vc.* ∼**ırgı**, strange(r), foreign(er). ∼**sılı**, negative. ∼**sıma**, *vn.*, denial, rejection; (*phil.*) negation. ∼**sımacılık**, (*phil.*) negativism. ∼**sımak (-i)**, deny, reject.

Yafa (*geo.*) Jaffa. ∼ (**portakalı**), (*bot.*) Jaffa/navel orange.

yafta Label; placard; label (on a criminal).

yağ (*chem.*) Oil; fat; grease; lubricant; ointment; mineral/vegetable oil; (*bot.*) attar, essential oil. ∼ **bağlamak**, put on/become fat; (*fig.*) feel pleased: ∼ **bal olsun!**, (*cul.*) I hope you'll enjoy it!, *bon appétit*!: ∼ **basmak**, fill with oil; become fat: ∼ **çekmek**, (*sl.*) toady: ∼ **damlalığı**, (*eng.*) drip-pan: ∼ **gemisi**, (*naut.*) tanker: ∼ **gibi kaymak**, (vehicle) move fast/ smoothly: ∼ **gidermek**, degrease: ∼ **kuşu**, (*orn.*)

oilbird: ~ **sürmek**, (*cul.*) spread butter, rub on oil: ~ **tulumu**, (*jok.*) very fat person: ~ **yumrusu**, (*med.*) atheroma: ~ **yüzgeci**, (*ich.*) adipose fin: ~ **a bala batırmak**, feast s.o.: ~ **da**, (*cul.*) in oil; oil-.

yağ·bezini (*bio.*) Sebaceous gland. ~ **cı(lık)**, (trade of) maker/seller of butter/oil; (*sl.*) (action of) unctuous person, toady: ~ **etm.**, toady. ~ **dan(lık)**, (*eng.*) oil-can; grease-pot; (*cul.*) oil-bottle. ~ **doku**, (*bio.*) adipose/fatty tissue. ~ **göze**, (*bio.*) fat cell. ~ **hane**, (*ind.*) oil-mill; butter factory.

yağı Enemy; adversary; (*sp.*) opponent. ~ **laşmak (-le)**, be(come) enemies. ~ **lık**, enmity, hostility. ~ **sız**, ~ **yenme**, (*sp.*) walkover.

yağ·ımsı Oily. ~ **ır**, (*live.*) withers; saddle-gall.

yağış (*met.*) Raining; snowing; precipitation, rain-(fall); snow(fall). ~ **alanı**, catchment area. ~ **lı**, rainy; snowy. ~ **ölçer**, rain-gauge.

yağız Black (horse); dark-skinned (man); (*min.*) brown coal, lignite. ~ **doru**, (*live.*) brown bay.

yağla·ma *vn.* Lubrication, oiling. ~ **mak (-i)**, lubricate, oil, grease; (*fig.*) flatter: **yağlayıp ballamak**, overpraise; paint in glowing colours. ~ **nmak**, *vp.*; become oily/dirty with grease; (*fin.*) make a profit. ~ **tmak (-i, -e)**, *vc.* ~ **yıcı**, lubricant.

yağlı Fat; adipose; fatty; greasy; oily; dirty with grease; (*fig.*) rich, free-spending; profitable. ~ **ballı olm.**, be on the best of terms: ~ **cilt kremi**, (*mod.*) cold cream: ~ **güreş**, (*sp.*) wrestling (with opponents coated in oil): ~ **kâğıt**, (*cul.*) grease-proof paper: ~ **kalem**, (*art.*) chinagraph: ~ **kapı**, (*fig.*) rich employer: ~ **kuyruk**, (*live.*) sheep's fat tail; (*fig.*) milch cow; profitable business: ~ **lokma**, rich windfall: ~ **müşteri**, free-spending customer: ~ **peynir**, (*cul.*) cream cheese: ~ **sıvı**, (*aer.*) dope: ~ **taşkömürü**, (*min.*) bituminous coal.

yağ·lıboya Oil-paint; (*art.*) oil-painting. ~ **lık**, (*dom.*) napkin; large handkerchief. ~ **lıkçı**, draper; hirer of wedding garments.

yağma[1] *n.* Booty, loot; depredation. ~ **etm.**, plunder, pillage, despoil: ~ **Hasan'ın böreği**, irresponsible waste of others'/public money: ~ **yok!**, nothing doing!; you can't/get away with that!

yağ·ma[2] *vn.* Raining; downfall. ~ **mak**, *vi.* (*met.*) rain, snow; (*fig.*) rain down on, be poured out in abundance.

yağma·cı Plunderer, pillager. ~ **cılık**, plundering, pillage. ~ **lamak (-i)**, despoil, plunder, pillage. ~ **lanmak**, *vp.*

yağmur (*met.*) Rain; downpour. ~ **borusu**, (*arch.*) drainpipe: ~ **duası**, (*rel.*) prayer for rain: ~ **efekti**, (*th.*) drencher: ~ **içeriye vuruyor**, the rain is coming in: ~ **kanalı**, storm drain: ~ **kesildi**, the rain has stopped: ~ **olsa, kimsenin tarlasına düşmez/ yağmaz**, he's an uncharitable/disobliging person: ~ **yağmak**, rain: ~ **yağacak gibi görünüyor**, it looks like rain: ~ **yemek**, be caught in the rain: ~ **dan kaçarken doluya tutulmak**, be out of the frying-pan into the fire.

yağmur·ca (*zoo.*) Fallow deer; ibex. ~ **kervançulluğu**nu, (*orn.*) whimbrel. ~ **kuşağı**nı, (*met.*) rainbow. ~ **kuşu**nu, (*orn.*) plover, golden plover; water-rail. ~ **kuşugiller**, (*orn.*) waders. ~ **lama**, *vn.* ~ **lamak**, *vi.* become rainy; fall like rain. ~ **lu**,

rainy. ~ **luk**, (*mod.*) raincoat, trenchcoat, mackin tosh. ~ **luluk**, raininess. ~ **suz**, rainless, dry ~ **suzluk**, drought.

yağ·sız Without fat/oil; (*cul.*) skim (milk/cheese): ~ **taşkömürü**, (*min.*) lean coal. ~ **sızlık**, lack of fat/oil ~ **taşı**ni, (*eng.*) whetstone. ~ **yakıt**, (*chem.*) fuel-oil

yahey *int.* Ah, that's nice!

yahni (*cul.*) Meat stew with onions. ~ **lik**, (*sl.* simpleton.

yahşi Pretty; agreeable; good. ~ **lik**, prettiness goodness.

yahu *int.* Hey!, look here!; isn't it so?; please don't' why not?

Yahudi (*ethn.*) Jew; (*pej.*) coward; miser. ~ +, *a* Jewish: ~ **balığı**, (*ich.*) giant sea-bass: ~ **dönmesi** Jew converted to Islam: ~ **düşmanlığı**, (*soc.*) anti semitism: ~ **pazarlığı**, (*fin.*) hard bargaining: ~ **takvimi**, (*ast.*) Jewish calendar: ~ **züğürtleyince eski defter/hesapları karıştırırmış**, 'when a Jew i hard up he searches his old accounts'; s.o. wh relies on his past achievements/wealth: ~ **de dönme** = ~ DÖNMESİ.

yahudi·baklasını (*bot.*) Lupin. ~ **ce**, (*ling.*) Hebrew ~ **lik**, Jewishness; (*rel.*) Judaism; (*soc.*) Israel; (*fin. pej.*) Jewish business methods; stinginess.

yahut *conj.* [210] Or; or indeed; or else; alias.

yak (*zoo.*) Yak.

yaka (*mod.*) Collar; (*naut.*) edge/corner (of sail) (*geo.*) bank, shore; incline, slope; (*arch.* eaves lining. ~ **bir tarafta paça bir tarafta**, one' clothes all dishevelled: ~ **ısırmak**, express horror say 'God forbid!': ~ **kavramak**, make earnes entreaty: ~ **paça**, by force: ~ **paça etm.**, seize s.o by collar and trousers and chuck out: ~ **silkme (-den)**, be disgusted/fed up: ~ **ya gelmek**, come t blows: ~ **dan atmak**, get rid of: ~ **dan geçirmek** adopt (child): ~ **mı bırak!**, leave me alone/in peace! ~ **sı açılmadık**, unusual/unheard of (oath, etc.) ~ **sına asılmak/yapışmak**, hold responsible; forc s.o. to do stg.: ~ **sından/~sını tutmak**, keep hol of, not let escape; hold responsible: ~ **sını bırak mamak (-in)**, not let s.o. go; cling to s.o.: ~ **sın kaptırmak**, be under s.o.'s influence/thumb: ~ **sın kurtarmak (-den)**, elude: ~ **sını sıyırmak**, get out o a difficulty: ~ **yı ele vermek**, be caught/arrested ~ **yı kurtarmak/sıyırmak**, escape, abscond.

yakacak *v.* = YAKMAK. *n.* Fuel, combustible.

yaka·lama *vn.* (*leg.*) Arrest: ~ **belgesi**, warrant ~ **lamak (-i)**, collar, seize, capture; (*leg.*) arrest detain; find; have a hold on s.o.; hold responsible ~ **lanmak**, *vp.*: (-e), be caught by; (*med.*) be infecte by, be subject to. ~ **latmak (-i, -e)**, *vc.* ~ **lı**, (*mod.* with a collar; (*zoo.*) collared, frilled: ~ **kara sağan** (*orn.*) white-collared swift. ~ **lık**, (*tex.*) suitable fo collars; (*mod.*) loose collar (of shirt).

yakamoz (*naut.*) Phosphorescence (in the sea) fluorescence. ~ **lanmak**, *vi.* (sea) be phos phorescent; fluoresce.

yakar *v.* = YAKMAK. *a.* Burning. *n.* Burner. ~ **ağrı** (*med.*) causalgia. ~ **ca**, (*ent.*) sandfly.

yakar·ı ~ **ış** (*rel.*) Entreaty, prayer. ~ **ma**, *vn.* ~ **mak (-e)**, entreat, implore.

yakı (*med.*) Cautery; poultice; (adhesive) plaster. ~

açmak, open a blister; apply a cautery: ~ **ağacı,** (*bot.*) Mediterranean mezereon: ~OTU: ~ **vurmak,** apply a poultice.

yakı·cı *a.* Burning, smarting; (*cul.*) biting: *n.* caustic; cautery maker/seller; (*eng.*) burner: ~ **potas,** (*chem.*) caustic potash. ~ **cılık,** *n.* burning; cautery making. ~**lmak,** *vp.* = YAKMAK[1]; be burnt, etc.; pour out one's woes. ~**m,** combustion.

yakın *a.* Near (space/time); close, adjacent; contiguous; associated, allied. *n.* Nearby place, neighbourhood; recent time, near future. *adv.* From near at hand; closely, thoroughly. ~ **akraba,** (*soc.*) close relation: ~ **amir,** (*mil.*) immediate superior: ~ **anlamlı (sözcükler),** (*ling.*) (words) of similar meaning: ~ **benzeşme,** (*ling.*) assimilation (of adjacent consonants): ~ **benzeşmezlik,** (*ling.*) dissimilation: ~ **dost,** close friend, companion: ~ **görmez,** long-sighted, hypermetropic: ~ **ilişkili olan,** akin, related: ~ **muharebe,** (*mil.*) close action: ~ **olan,** (*bio.*) proximal: ~ **plan,** (*cin.*) close-up: ~ **zamanda,** not long ago, recently: ~**a getirmek,** bring near; (telescope) magnify: ~**da,** near by; recently; in the near future; about: ~**dan,** closely: ~**dan alakadar,** closely interested: ~**dan bilmek/ tanımak,** be closely acquainted with: ~**ımızda,** close to us, in our neighbourhood: ~**ında(n),** by: ~**lar,** (*soc.*) relatives: ~**larda** = ~DA.

yakın·cacık Very near. ~**çağ,** (*his.*) modern times. ~**daş,** (*soc.*) relative. ~**doğu,** *pr.n.* (*geo.*) Near East. ~**laşmak (-e),** draw near, approach; become close (friends, etc.). ~**laştırmak (-i, -e),** *vc.* bring close together. ~**lık,** closeness, nearness, proximity; affinity: ~ **duymak,** feel close to, have an affinity for: ~ **eylemi,** (*ling.*) approximative verb [= -EYAZ-]: ~ **göstermek,** show sympathy/concern.

yakın·ma *vn.* Complaint; petition. ~**mak**[1], *vi.* complain.

yakınmak[2] **(-i)** Apply stg. to the body.

yakın·sal (*med.*) Proximal. ~**sak(lık),** (*math., phys.*) conver·gent/(-gence). ~**samak (-i),** consider stg. about to happen; (*math.*) converge.

yakıotu[nu] (*bot.*) Rosebay willow-herb, fireweed.

yakışık Suitability; most suitable way, plausibility; beauty. ~ **almak,** be suitable/appropriate: ~ **alır,** becoming, suitable: ~ **almaz,** it's 'not done'.

yakış·ıklı Suitable, becoming; handsome (man); well set up. ~**ıksız,** unsuitable; unbecoming; ugly. ~**ıksızlık,** unsuitability; unbecoming appearance. ~**mak (-e),** be suitable/becoming; be fit/proper; (object) look well, be pretty: **yakışır,** *a.* suitable. ~ **tırma,** *vn.*; (*ling.*) attraction. ~**tırmaca,** attribution (of stg. said); invention. ~**tırmak (-i, -e),** *vc.* think stg. becoming to s.o.; expect stg. of s.o.; make up: **yakıştırıp uydurmak,** invent stg. suitable for the occasion.

yakıt[1] Fuel; combustible. ~**yağ,** fuel-oil.

yakin Certainty. ~**en,** for certain, positively.

yaklaş·ık Approximate: ~ **değer,** (*math.*) approximation: ~ **olarak,** approximately. ~**ılmak (-e),** *vp.* be approached; be approachable. ~**ım,** *vn.* approximation; approach (to a problem). ~**ma,** *vn.*; approximation; approach: ~ **çizgisi,** (*math.*) asymptote: ~ **eylemi** = YAKINLIK. ~**mak (-e),**

drawn near, approach; (*naut.*) close; approximate; resemble: **yaklaşma yakarım!,** stand still or I'll fire! ~**tırım,** (*math.*) approximation. ~**tırma,** *vn.*; (*phil.*) approximation. ~**tırmak (-i),** bring near; approximate; (*bio.*) adduct.

yak·ma *vn.* Burning: ~ **resim,** (*art.*) pyrogravure. ~**ma**[1]**çı,** burner. ~**mak**[1] **(-i),** burn; set on fire; scorch; light; (*med.*) cauterize; (*agr.*) blight; (*cul.*) bite, burn; (*met.*) (cold) sting, 'burn': **yakıp kaşındırma,** (physical) irritation: **yakıp kül etm.,** consume: **yakıp yıkmak,** burn down, devastate.

yakmak[2] **(-i)** Apply/spread on (ointment, etc.); (*mus.*) compose (songs).

yakşı = YAHŞi.

yaktırmak (-i, -e) *vc.* = YAKMAK[1].

Yakubi (*rel.*) Jacobite (Christian in Iraq).

yakut[u] [1] (*min.*) Ruby.

Yakut[u] [2] (*ethn.*) (Member of) Tk. tribe in Siberia. ~**ça,** (*ling.*) Yakut language.

yal (*live.*) Mash/gruel for dogs/cattle.

yala·bık *a.* Shining, glittering; *n.* brightness. ~**bımak,** *vi.* sparkle, glitter.

yala[l]**k**[ğı] (*live.*) Feeding-trough; (*arch.*) drinking-basin (of fountain).

yalaka (*col.*) Toady; tiresome, importunate. ~ **olm.,** be a toady.

yala·ma *vn.* (*live.*) Licking; sore; (*geol.*) erosion, abrasion; (*eng.*) wear, play: ~ **olm.,** be worn/ eroded: ~ **resim,** (*art.*) wash-drawing: ~ **yazı,** (*geo.*) peneplain. ~**macı,** (*sl.*) toady. ~**mak (-i),** (*live.*) lick; graze; (*mil.*) (gunfire, etc.) sweep over; (*naut.*) (waves) wash over: **yalayıp emici,** (*ent.*) sucker: **yalayıp yutmak,** devour. ~**mu**[l]**k**[ğu], (*dial.*) sweet pine resin; = SOYMUK.

yalan *n.* Lie, falsehood; hoax. *a.* Lying, false. ~ **ant,** (*leg.*) false oath, perjury: ~ **atmak/kıvırmak/ söylemek,** tell a lie: ~ **bayrak,** false colours: ~ **çıkmak,** turn out untrue, prove false: ~ **dolan,** lies, deceits, frauds: ~ **dünya** = YALANCI: ~ **yanlış,** false and erroneous; carelessly, superficially: ~ **yere yemin (etm.),** *n.* perjury/(*v.* perjure o.s.): ~**a sapmak/tevessül etm.,** have recourse to lies: ~**a şerbetli,** always ready to tell a lie: ~DAN: ~**ın kubbesini yapmak,** make a lie seem true by telling more lies: ~**ını çıkarmak,** show up s.o.'s lies: ~**ını tutmak/yakalamak,** catch s.o. out in a lie.

yalancı *n.* Liar, deceiver. *a.* False; deceitful; pseudo, imitation. ~ **akasya,** (*bot.*) false acacia; locust-tree: ~ **çıkmak,** tell a lie unknowingly: ~ **çıkarmak (-i),** make s.o. look a liar; claim/prove s.o. is a liar: ~DOLMA: ~ **dünya,** the false world, this transitory life: ~ **mermer,** (*arch.*) stucco: ~ **odun,** (*bot.*) sapwood: ~ **ödağacı,** (*bot.*) Indian aloe tree: ~ **pehlivan,** s.o. not what he claims to be, mock hero: ~ **servi,** (*bot.*) false cypress: ~ **şahit/ tanık(lık),** false witness/(evidence): ~ **taş,** imitation/costume jewel(lery): ~**nın mumu yatsıya kadar yanar,** a lie has only a short life: ~**sı olm.,** repeat s.o.'s lie unwittingly.

yalancı·ayak (*bio.*) Pseudopodium. ~**dolma,** (*cul.*) vine-leaves stuffed with rice. ~**ktan,** superficially; not intentionally; in pretence: ~ **ağlamak,** shed crocodile tears: ~ **yapmak,** affect. ~**lık,**

lying; mendacity; lies, deceit. ~**safran**, (*bot.*) safflower.

yalan·dan Not seriously, for appearance sake: ~ **hasta**, malingering: ~ **söylemek**, not mean what one says: ~ **yapmak**, feign, pretend: ~ **yıkamak**, wash superficially. ~**lama**, *vn.* contradiction; denial. ~**lamak (-i)**, contradict; deny. ~**lanmak**, *vp.*

yalanmak *vp.* = YALAMAK. *vi.* Lick o.s./one's chops; get a little profit from stg.

yalap ~ ~, in a sparkling manner. ~**şap**, half/badly/carelessly done.

yala·tmak (-i, -e) *vc.* = YALAMAK. ~**yıcı**, licking; eroding: ~ **ateş**, (*mil.*) flat-trajectory/grazing fire.

yalaz·(a) Flame. ~**lanmak**, *vi.* flame up, blaze. ~**lı**, flaming.

yalçın Rugged; steep; bare; slippery.

yaldırak Shining, brilliant, bright.

yaldız (*min.*) Gilding; foil; (*fig.*) superficial finish; false decoration; superficial achievement. ~ **işi**, gilding, inlaying with gold; ~**dan ibaret**, superficial.

yaldız·cı Gilder. ~**cılık**, *n.* gilding: *a.* (*fig.*) showy but valueless. ~**lamak (-i)**, gild; polish; (*fig.*) give stg. a false finish; be cuckolded. ~**lanmak**, *vp.* ~**latmak (-i, -e)**, *vc.* ~**lı**, gilt; lacquered; falsely adorned: ~ **pisibalığı**, (*ich.*) plaice.

yalelli (*mus.*) Arab song. ~ **gibi**, unending, monotonous, boring.

yalgın Glitter, glow; mirage.

yalı (*geo.*) Shore; beach; (*arch.*) waterside residence. ~ **ağası**, (*his.*) coastal commander: ~ **çamı**, (*bot.*) maritime pine: ~ **kazığı**, tall thin person: ~ **mevsimi**, summer season: ~ **uşağı**, s.o. born and bred by the seaside. ~**çapkını**[n], (*orn.*) common kingfisher.

yalım Flame; (sword, etc.) blade; (*fig.*) kind, nature. ~**ı alçak**, faint-hearted. ~**almaz**, flame-proof. ~**lamak (-i)**, set aflame. ~**lanmak**, *vi.* burst into flame.

yalın[1] *n.* Flame.

yalın[2] *a.* Simple; plain; single; bare, stripped; naked (sword). ~ **ad**//**belirteç**, (*ling.*) simple noun//adverb: ~ **durum/hal**, (*ling.*) nominative case: ~ **önerme**, (*phil.*) assertion: ~ **sıfat**//**sözcük**//**tümce**// **zaman**, (*ling.*) simple adjective//word//sentence// tense.

yalın·ayak Barefooted. ~ **başı kabak**, bareheaded and barefooted; (*fig.*) in rags. ~**cak**, all alone; bare, naked; poor. ~**cılık**, love of simplicity. ~**ç**, elementary, simple, plain; single. ~**çlık**, simplicity. ~**gaç**, (*bot.*) (tree) that sheds its bark naturally. ~**göz**, (*bio.*) without eyelids; (*zoo.*) type of lizard. ~**kat**, (*tex.*) single-fold; (*arch.*) single-storeyed; (*carp.*) veneered; (*fig.*) superficial, shallow. ~**kılıç**, (*mil.*) naked sword; with drawn sword. ~**laşmak**, *vi.* become simple/single/bare. ~**laştırmak (-i)**, *vc.* simplify. ~**lık**, simpleness, singleness; (*lit.*) simplicity.

yalıt·ık Isolated. ~ **ım**/~**ma**, *vn.* (*el.*) insulation: ~ **sargısı**, insulating tape. ~**kan**, *a.* insulating: *n.* insulator. ~**kanlık**, insulation. ~**mak (-i)**, insulate; (*fig.*) isolate.

yalıyar (*geo.*) Seaside cliff.

yalız(kas) (*bio.*) Smooth (muscle).

yallah *int.* Come!; go! ~ ~, at most.

yalman (Sword, etc.) pointed blade; (*geo.*) steep jagged end.

yalnız *a.* Alone; lonely, solitary. *adv.* Only, alone exclusively, solely. *conj.* [211] But, however. ~ **başına**, alone, by o.s.; single-handed: ~ ... **olm.**, b restricted to ....

yalnız·ca Alone, by o.s. ~**cı(lık)**, (*pol.*) isolation·ist (-ism). ~**göz**, (*arch.*) single-arch (bridge) ~**laşmak**, *vi.* become alone. ~**lık**, solitude loneliness.

Yalova (*geo.*) Yalova (thermal springs). ~ **kay makamı**, (*jok.*) self-important person.

yalpa (*naut.*) Rolling; (*phys.*) precession ~ **omurgası**, (*naut.*) bilge-keel: ~ **vurmak** ~**lamak**, *vi.* roll; (drunkard) sway about, lurch ~**lanmak**, *vp.* ~**lık**, bunk-rail.

yal·pak Friendly, intimate; ingratiating. ~**pık** broad, shallow; skew-cut. ~**pılı**, lopsided.

yaltak Fawning; sycophantic; cringing. ~**çı(lık)** toady(ing). ~**lanma**, *vn.* ~**lanmak**, *vi.* fawn cringe; adulate: (-e), bow and scrape to. ~**lık** fawning; cringing flattery: ~ **etm.**, fawn, cringe.

yalva·[c][1]**(lık)** (*rel.*) (Work of) messenger/prophet.

yalvar·ı Entreaty, prayer. ~**ıcı**, entreating, im ploring. ~**ılmak**, *vp.*; *imp. v.* one beg. ~**ışmak**, v (many) entreat, implore. ~**mak (-e)**, entreat, beg implore: **yalvarıp yakarmak**/**yakar olm.**, beseech entreat persistently. ~**tmak (-i, -e)**, *vc.*

yama (*tex.*, *etc.*) Patch; (*bio.*) blotch (on skin). ~ **gibi durmak**, look out of place/as if not belonging ~ **küçük delik büyük**, the means are insufficient fo the end: ~ **vurmak**, put on a patch. ~**cı**, patcher repairer; cobbler; (*fig.*) skinflint. ~**cılık**, patching cobbling.

yama·[c][1] (*geo.*) Slope of a hill; side. ~ **kaynağı** hillside spring.

yama·[k][ğı]**(lık)** (Work of) assistant, mate; (*leg.* *pub.*) devil; (*his.*) frontier guard.

yama·lak = YARIM. ~**lamak (-i)**, patch, repair ~**lanmak**, *vp.* ~**lı**, patched; (*bio.*) (skin) blotched scarred: ~ **bohça**, bits and pieces; patched together rag-bag. ~**ma**, *vn.* ~**mak (-i)**, patch, repair cobble: (-i, -e), dump stg. on s.o.

yaman Strong, violent; capable, dashing, smart efficient; remarkable; (*obs.*) bad, disagreeable. ~ **bilmek (-i)**, be a dab hand at.

yama·nmak *vp.* = YAMAMAK. Be patched: (-e), get a footing, settle down; foist o.s. on; be dumped on ~**tmak (-i, -e)**, *vc.*

yamçı (*tex.*) Thick rough cape; felt saddle-cover.

yampala ~ **zeydün**, at one's wits' end; nonplussed

yampiri Lopsided; distorted; crabwise.

yam·rı ~ **yumru**, uneven, lumpy; gnarled ~**rulmak**, be uneven, etc.

yam·u·[l][k][ğu] *a.* Inclined, oblique: *n.* (*math.*) trape zium. ~**ukluk**, obliqueness; ~**ulmak**, be inclined ~**ultma**, distortion.

yamyam Cannibal. ~**lık**, cannibalism, anthro pophagy.

yamyassı Quite flat; as flat as a pancake.

an *n.* Side; flank; (*bio.*) lateral; (*leg.*) party; (*met.*) quarter; vicinity (of stg.); presence (of s.o.); direction, bearing. *a.* Side; lateral; auxiliary, subsidiary. *post.* [90] Side. ~ **ateşi**, (*mil.*) flanking fire, enfilade: ~ **atmak**, enjoy o.s. lazily: ~ **bağlantı yolu**, (*mot.*) slip-road: ~ **bakmak**, look askance, cast unfriendly looks: ~ **baksam kabahat**, every little error is brought up against me: ~ **basınç**, (*phys.*) static pressure: ~ **basmak**, (*sl.*) have one's hopes dashed; come a cropper; be deceived: ~ **boşluğu**, (*pub.*) indentation: ~ **çizgisi**, (*sp.*) touch line: ~ **çizmek**, (*col.*) sneak off; pretend not to see; ignore; shirk: ~ **duruşu**, (*cin.*) side view, profile: ~ **etki**, (*med.*) side effect; complication: ~ **geçit**, (*mot.*) bypass: ~ **gelmek**, take one's ease, make o.s. comfortable: ~ **görünüş**, (*art.*) profile: ~ **gözle**, askance: ~ **gözle bakmak**, look out of the corner of one's eye; look at with evil intentions: ~ **iş yapmak**, (*fin.*) moonlight: ~ **kâğıdı**, (*pub.*) flyleaf: ~ **konumlu**, sideways: ~ **sallamak** = ~ ÇİZMEK: ~ **sanayi**, (*fin.*) side/subordinate industry: ~ **tutar/tutucu**, supporter: ~ **tutmak**, take sides: ~ **ürün**, (*ind.*) by-product: ~ **yamaç**, (*geo.*) flank: ~ ~, sideways, sidelong: ~ ~ **bakmak**, look treacherously at: ~ ~ **ilerlemek**, edge forwards: ~ ~ **yürümek**, walk sideways/crabwise: ~ ~**a**, side by side, abreast; alongside: ~ ~**a koyma**, juxtaposition: ~ ~**a olan**, adjacent: ~ **yargıcı**, (*sp.*) linesman: ~ **yatmak**, lean over to one side.

yan-: ~**a**, sideways; = YANA[1]: ~**a bırakmak**, leave/put to one side: ~**a doğru**, askew, aslant: ~**da**, (*naut.*) abeam: ~**daki kapı**, next door: ~**dan**, from the side; sideways; in profile: ~**dan bir** ~**a (bir)**, across; from one side to the other: ~**dan çarklı**, (*sl.*) (coffee/tea) with sugar in the saucer: ~**dan gelen**, (*naut.*) beam (wind): ~**dan görünüş**, (*arch.*) elevation: ~ IBAŞINDA: ~**ı sıra**, together, with; beside; side by side: ~**ıma**, to my side, towards me: ~**ımda**, at my side; by me; in my opinion: ~**ımdan**, from my side; from me.

yanın-: ~**a**, to the side of, beside, towards: ~**a almak**, take into one's service; take to live with one, house: ~**a bırakmamak/koymamak**, not leave unpunished: ~**a kalmak**, remain unpunished: ~**a kalmak için (-i)**, to save/avoid stg.: ~**a katmak**, take as a partner: ~**a salavatla varılır**, a proud/angry/cruel/unapproachable person: ~**a salavatla varılmaz**, terribly expensive: ~**a ulaşmak**, have access to: ~**a yanaşılmaz**, he's out for blood: ~**da**, at, on, with; at the side of, beside: ~**da (-in)**, in comparison with: ~**da bulunmak**, accompany: ~**da haltetmiş**, he's nothing by comparison: ~**da olm.**, support: ~**da onun lafı olur mu (-in)**, he can't be mentioned in the same breath as . . .: ~**da oturmak**, sit down beside s.o.; lodge with s.o.: ~**da pes demek**, recognize s.o.'s superiority: ~**dan**, from beside/the side: ~**dan bile geçmemiş (-in)**, having no connection with stg.

ana[1] *post.* [89] ~ **(bu)**, until now, since [**Noel'den bu** ~, since Christmas]: ~ **(-den)**, as regards, concerning; in favour/support of, on the side of [**yemekten yana**, as regards food: **hürriyetten yana**,

in support of liberty]: ~ **olm. (-den)**, be on the side of, take the part of. [*Also* = YAN.]

yana[2] *v.* = YANMAK. ~ ~/~ **yakıla**, in a moving way; pouring out one's sorrows; complaining bitterly.

yana[1]**k**[g1] (*bio.*) Cheek. ~ **çukuru**, dimple: ~**ından kan damlıyor**, he is ruddy with health. ~**lı**, -cheeked.

yanal *a.* (*math.*) Lateral; (*col.*) dappled.

yanar *v.* = YANMAK. *a.* Inflammable. ~**dağ**, (*geol.*) volcano: ~ +, *a.* volcanic: ~ **ağzı**, crater: ~ **püskürmesi**, volcanic activity/eruption. ~**dağbilim**, vulcanology. ~**döner**, (*tex.*) shot (silk).

yanaş·ık Adjacent; contiguous: ~ **nizam**, (*mil.*) close formation/order. ~**ılmak (-e)**, *imp. v.* one be approached, be approachable. ~**ılmaz**, unapproachable. ~**lık**, (*naut.*) pier; (*rly.*) platform. ~**ma**, *vn.* approaching; (*agr.*) casual labourer, hireling: ~ **yeri**, (*naut.*) pier. ~**mak (-e)**, *vi.* draw near, approach; accost; (*naut.*) come/go alongside; (*fig.*) accede (to requests); feel like doing; be willing. ~**tırmak (-i, -e)**, *vc.*

yanay (*math., etc.*) Vertical section, profile. ~ **doğruları**, section verticals.

yan·cümle (*ling.*) Subordinate clause. ~**dal**, (*soc.*) collateral. ~**dan** = YAN. ~**daş**, supporter, partisan. ~**daşlık**, partisanship.

yandı[1]**k**[g1] *v.* = YANMAK. *n.* (*bot.*) Camelthorn.

yan·dışı (*sp.*) Touch, out-of-play: ~ **atışı**, throw in. ~**eğrilik**, (*med.*) scoliosis. ~**geçi(ş)**, (*mot.*) bypass. ~**gelmek**, take it easy; ease off.

yangı (*med.*) Inflammation. ~**sı**, -itis [**mide yangısı**, gastritis]. ~**lanmak**, *vi.* be(come) inflamed. ~**lı**, inflamed; inflammatory. ~**sız**, ~ **şiş**, (*med.*) oedema.

yangın *n.* Conflagration, fire; (*med.*) high temperature, fever. *a.* Burning; suffering; in love. ~ **bombası**, (*mil.*) incendiary bomb: ~ **bulucu/detektörü**, fire-detector: ~ **kulesi**, (*arch.*) fire-watching tower: ~ **perdesi**, (*th.*) safety-curtain: ~ **söndürme alet//örgütü**, fire-extinguisher//-brigade: ~ **söndürümcü**, fireman: ~ **var!**, fire! fire!: ~**a gitmek**, go in great haste: ~**a körükle gitmek**, add fuel to the flames: ~**a vermek**, set fire to: ~**dan çıkmış gibi**, destitute: ~**dan mal kaçırır gibi**, in great excitement/haste. ~**cı**, fireman.

yanıbaşında By the side of, just beside, close by.

yanı[1]**k**[g1] *n.* Burn; scald; (*myc.*) blight, stinking smut, bunt. *a.* Burnt, scorched; tanned; blighted; (*el., etc.*) lighted, turned on; (*med.*) smarting, painful; piteous, pathetic. ~ **kokmak**, smell of burning; (*cul.*) have a burnt/smoky flavour: ~ **rüzgâr**, (*met.*) wind that subsides rapidly: ~ **ses**, piteous/doleful voice.

yanık·ara (*med.*) Anthrax. ~**çı**, complaining. ~**kara**, (*med.*) plague bubo. ~**mak**, *vi.* complain. ~**yağı**[n1], (*med.*) burn ointment.

yanıl·gı/ ~ **ma** *vn.* Mistake; error; defect; (*sp.*) foul. ~**mak**, *vi.* make a mistake; err; go wrong. ~**maz**, unerring; unfailing; faultless (worker, etc.). ~**sama**, (*psy.*) illusion. ~**tı**, minor error; illusion. ~**tıcı**, misleading. ~**tmaca**, (*phil.*) misleading argument; sophism, fallacy. ~**tma**[1]**ç**[c1], (*phil.*)

paradox; (*lit.*) tongue-twister. ~**tmak (-i)**, *vc.* lead into error; mislead.
yanım/yanış *vn.* = YANMAK. Combustion, burning. ~**ölçer**, pyrometer.
yanıt[1] Answer, reply. ~ **vermek/**~**lamak (-i)**, answer, reply. ~**lanmak**, *vp.* ~**sal**, in reply.
yani *conj.* That is to say; i.e.; namely; (*col.*) in short.
yankesici·(lik) (Operations of) pickpocket. ~**lerden sakınız!**, beware of pickpockets.
yankı (*phys.*) Echo; (*fig.*) reaction. ~ **uyandırmak/ yapmak**, (re)echo; have an effect. ~**bilim/** ~**düzeni/**~**lanım**, (*phys.*) acoustics. ~**ca**, (*psy.*) echolalia. ~**la(n)mak**, *vi.* (re)echo. ~**laşım**, (*phys.*) resonance. ~**sız**, (*phys.*) anechoic.
yan·lama(sına) Sideways; broadside on. ~**lamak (-i)**, pass stg. sideways: *vi.* move sideways; lie on one's side. ~**lı**, *n.* supporter: *a.* subjective.
yanlış *n.* Error, mistake; (*sp.*) fault. *a.* Wrong, mistaken, incorrect. ~ **açmışsınız!**, you've got the wrong (telephone) number!: ~ **besle(n)me**, (*med.*) dystrophy: ~ **çıkarmak**, prove false: ~ **çıkış**, (*sp.*) false start: ~ **çıkmak**, prove to be wrong: ~ **davranış**, blunder: ~**-doğru cetveli**, (*pub.*) list of corrigenda/errata: ~ **hamle**, false move: ~ **herif**, formidable person; s.o. not to be trifled with: ~ **hesap Bağdat'tan döner**, mistakes will always show up sometime: ~ **kapı çalmak**, be out in one's calculations; make a bad shot: ~ **olm.**, be mistaken: ~ **söz**, erroneous word/expression: ~ **ve unutma dışı**, errors and omissions excepted: ~ **yere**, wrongly, falsely: ~**ı çıkmak**, realize one's mistake: ~**ını çıkarmak**, find out one's mistakes. ~**lık**, error, erratum: ~ **olmasın diye**, for fear of making a mistake. ~**lıkla**, by mistake, in error.
yan·ma *vn.* Burning, combustion; (*chem.*) oxidation; (*bot.*) blight. ~**mak**, *vi.* burn; be alight; catch fire; (*cul.*) be burnt/over-roasted; (*bot.*) be blighted; (*med.*) be painful, burn, hurt; (*el.*) (fuse/lamp, etc.) blow; (*bio.*) become tanned/sunburnt; be very thirsty; (*adm.*) become invalid/forfeited; (*fin.*) be ruined/'done for'; (*fig.*) feel grieved/sorry; recount one's woes; (*sp.*) lose one's turn: YANA[2]: **yanıp kavrulmak (-e, için)**, have an obsession about; be very keen on: **yanıp kül olm./sönmek**, burn down/ out: **yanıp sönen**, flashing: **yanıp tutuşmak**, burn with passion: **yanıp tükenmek**, burn away: **yanıp yakılmak**, pour out one's woes. ~**makta**, *a.* alight, ablaze. ~**maz**, noninflammable: ~ **taş**, (*min.*) asbestos: ~**mış**, *a.* burnt: ~ **kireç**, caustic lime.
yanödeme (*fin.*) Secondary allowance; (*adm.*) supplementary pay.
yansı (*phys.*) Reflection; (*bio.*) reflex, reaction. ~**ca**, (*psy.*) echopraxia. ~**lama**, *vn.*; imitation. ~**lamak (-i)**, (*phys.*) reflect; (*fig.*) imitate. ~**layıcı**, mimic(king). ~**ma**, *vn.*; (*phys.*) reflection; (*ling.*) onomatopoeia. ~**mak**, *vi.* be reflected. ~**malı**, reflex. ~**ta'ç**[cı], (*phys.*) reflector; projector; epidiascope. ~**tıcı**, *a.* reflecting: *n.* reflector. ~**tıcılık**, reflectivity. ~**tım/**~**tma**, *vn.* projection; (*bio.*) mimesis. ~**tımca**, (*psy.*) paranoia. ~**tmak (-i)**, reflect; project. ~**tmalı**, reflecting.
yansız (*pol.*, *soc.*) Independent; objective; neutral; (*chem.*, *phys.*) neutral. ~ **aracı**, (*leg.*) arbitrator.

~**laşmak**, *vi.* become neutral(ized). ~**laştırmak (-i)**, neutralize. ~**layıcı**, neutralizing. ~**lık**, independence; neutrality; impartiality.
yan·şak(lık) Dull(ness), tedious(ness); talkative/ (-ness). ~**şamak**, *vi.* be talkative/tedious.
yan·tutmaz(lık) (*pol.*) Neutral(ity). ~**tümce**, (*ling.*) subordinate clause. ~**yan(a)** = YAN. ~**yol**, (*mot.*) minor road. ~**yüzer**, (*ich.*) flat-fish.
yapadurmak (-i) Keep on doing stg.
yapa·ğı/~[l]**k**[ğı] (*live.*) Spring-shorn fleece/wool [= YÜN]. ~**kçı**, wool-merchant. ~**klı**, well-fleeced.
yapala[l]**k**[ğı] (*orn.*) Great eagle owl.
yap·an *v.* = YAPMAK: *n.* doer, author, agent, maker. ~**ay**, artificial, synthetic; induced. ~**aylaşmak**, become artificial. ~**aylık**, artificiality.
yapayalnız Absolutely/quite alone.
yapı (*arch.*) Building, edifice; (*bio.*) build; (*ling.*, etc.) structure; construction; conformation, configuration. ~ +, *a.* Structural: ~ **alanı**, work-/building-site: ~ **işleri/kurma**, building: ~ **iyesi**, landlord, owner: ~ **kurucu**, builder: ~ **mühendis(liğ)i**, (*eng.*) civil engineer(ing): ~ **ve kredi müessese/ kooperatifi**, (*fin.*) building society: ~ **yapmak**, build, erect, construct.
yapı·bilgisi[ni]**/**~**bilim** (*bio.*, *ling.*) Morphology. ~**cı**, *n.* maker; builder; mason; constructor: *a.* creative, constructive; positive. ~**cılık**, making; building; construction.
yapı[l]**k**[ğı] (*live.*) Horse-blanket; (*mod.*) shaggy cape; (*arch.*) prefabricated (house).
yapıl Structural. ~**abilirlik**, feasibility. ~**ageliş**, habit, custom. ~**ı**, made; of . . . construction/ build; -morphic. ~**ış**, building structure, method of construction. ~**mak**, *vp.* = YAPMAK: *vi.* happen, occur: **yapılmış**, (*cul.*) ready-made.
yapım Construction; (*bio.*) anabolism; (*ind.*) manufacture, production; (*cin.*, *rad.*) production. ~ **eki**, (*ling.*) morpheme, constructive suffix: ~ **endüstrisi**, (*arch.*) construction/building industry: ~ **gizi**, (*ind.*) trade secret: ~ **hakları**, industrial rights: ~ **iyeliği**, (*leg.*) industrial/intellectual property; patent: ~ **öncüsü**, captain of industry: ~ **yeri**, workshop: ~**-yıkım**, (*bio.*) metabolism: ~ **yordamı**, (*ind.*) manufacturing process.
yapım·cı Manufacturer; (*cin.*) producer. ~**cılık**, manufacturing, production. ~**evi/**~**lık**, factory; (*cin.*) production company: ~ **ederi**, (*fin.*) works price. ~**sal**, industrial.
yapınca[l]**k**[ğı] (*bot.*) Type of white grape; = YAPIK.
yapın·ış Affected/hypocritical air. ~**mak (-i)**, make/have made for o.s.: (-e), strive/try to. ~**tı(lı)**, (*phil.*) fiction(al). ~**tıcılık**, (*phil.*) fictionalism. ~**tısal**, imaginary, fictitious.
yapırgan (*bot.*) Petal; floret.
yapı·sal *a.* Doing, making; founding; constituent; structural; (*geol.*) tectonic: ~ **bağ**, (*chem.*) structural bond: ~ **dilbilim**, (*ling.*) structural linguistics. ~**salcı(lık)**, (*phil.*) structural·ist/(-ism). ~**sallık**, structure. ~**ş**[1], *vn.* act/way of doing.
yapış[2] ~ ~, *a.* sticky. ~**ıcı**, sticky: ~ **sap**, (*bot.*) creeper, sucker. ~**ık**, adhesive; stuck on, attached; (*geol.*) cemented: ~ **kulaklı**, with closely adhering ears. ~**ıklık**, adhesion. ~**kan**, sticky, adhesive;

cohesive; (*chem.*) viscous; (*fig.*) clinging, pertinacious, importunate: ~ **balığı**, (*ich.*) slender suckerfish, remora: ~ **şerit**, adhesive tape: ~ **tohum**, (*bot.*) burr. ~ **kanlık**, stickiness; viscosity; adhesion; cohesion; (*fig.*) pertinacity; importunity. ~ **kanotu**nu, (*bot.*) pellitory-of-the-wall. ~ **ma**, *vn.* sticking; adhesion; (*chem.*) caking, bonding: ~ **adesesi**, (*med.*) contact lens. ~ **mak (-e)**, stick, adhere, bond; (*fig.*) cling, (bore) stick to one; set about (work). ~ **tırıcı**, sticky (material); adhesive, bond, binder. ~ **tırılmak**, *vp.* ~ **tırma**, *vn.* sticking on; stg. stuck on; (*pub.*) transfer; (*mod.*) ornaments stuck on bride's face: ~ **resim**, (*art.*) collage. ~ **tırmak (-i, -e)**, stick on, fasten down, attach; cement; strike s.o.; give a prompt reply: ~ **yasaktır!**, stick no bills!

apıt[1] (*art., lit., mus. etc.*) Work (of art), composition, creation. ~ **hakkı**, (*leg.*) copyright: ~ **kazanç/ücreti**, (*fin.*) royalty.

apıtaşıni (*arch.*) Building-stone.

apkın (*obs.*) Wealthy; (*chem.*) rich; (*fig.*) drunk.

apma *vn.* = YAPMAK. Act of doing/making. *a.* False; imitation, artificial (language). ~ **geçişli**, (*ling.*) derived transitive verb [UYUTMAK]: ~ **mıknatıs**, (*el.*) induced magnetism: ~ **seçim**, (*bio.*) artificial selection: ~ **sinek**, (*sp.*) dry fly: ~ **şey**, fake; dummy: ~ **uydu**, (*aer.*) artificial satellite.

apmacık *a.* Artificial, simulated, pretended. *n.* Affectation; mannerism. ~ **eylemi**, (*ling.*) artificial/ simulated verb: ~ **görünümü**, (*ling.*) simulation. ~ **çı(lık)**, (*art., lit.*) manner·ist/(-ism). ~ **lı**, mannered, affected. ~ **sız**, simple, unadorned.

apmak (-i) Do; make; create; give rise to; build, construct; constitute; arrange; repair; apply; set to rights; make ready. *aux. v.* [155] Make, do. **yap da göreyim!**, I defy you to do so!: **yapa yapa alışmak**, train o.s. to do stg.: **yapacağını ben bilirim!**, you just see what I'll do!: **yapacağını yap!**, do your worst!: **yapacağını yaptı!**, he did his worst!: **yapıp bitirmek**, achieve, accomplish: **yapıp bozmak**, constantly remake/reconstruct: **yapıp vermek**, (*med.*) dispense: YAPMA, *vn., a.*: **yapma!**, *int.* don't (do it)!; incredible!: **yapmadığını bırakmamak/koymamak**, do all the harm one can: **yapmağa düşünmek**, hesitate to do: **yapmağı düşünmek**, think of doing: **yaptığı hayır ürküttüğü kurbağaya değmemek**, make matters worse (when helping); be more trouble than it is worth: **yaptığını bilmemek**, not know what one is doing, be beside o.s.

apra[1]k**g**1 (*bot.*) Leaf; vine-leaf; sheet, foil, layer; flake. ~ **aşısı**, (*agr.*) bud-grafting: ~ **ayası**, (*bot.*) leaf lamina: ~ **böceği**, (*ent.*) leaf/capsid bug: ~ **çürüğü**, (*agr.*) leaf-mould: ~ **dolması**, (*cul.*) stuffed vine-leaves: ~ **dökümü**, leaf-fall; autumn: ~ **hoplar**, (*ent.*) leaf hopper: ~ **kayaç**, (*geol.*) schist: ~ **kınkanatlısı**, (*ent.*) leaf beetle: ~ **kurmak**, (*cul.*) pickle vine-leaves: ~ **sigarası**, cigar: ~ **tabanı**, (*bot.*) heel of a leaf: ~ **tütün**, leaf tobacco: ~ **larını döktürmek/koparmak**, defoliate.

aprak·arısıni (*ent.*) Sawfly. ~ **biti**ni, (*ent.*) aphis. ~ **çık**, (*bot.*) leaflet. ~ **lanmak**, *vi.* come into leaf; become flaky; (*geol.*) foliate; (flag, etc.) flap in the wind. ~ **lı**, leafed; leafy; having . . . leaves; flaky.

~ **piresi**ni, (*ent.*) plant-louse, leafhopper. ~ **sı**, (*geol.*) lamellar; laminar. ~ **sız**, leafless, aphyllous; bare. ~ **solucan**, (*zoo.*) fluke. ~ **taş**, (*geol.*) foliate rock.

yaptır·ım *vn.* (*leg.*) Sanction. ~ **mak (-i, -e)**, *vc.* = YAPMAK; get done, have made.

yapyalnız Absolutely alone; by o.s.

yar (*geo.*) Cliff, precipice; abyss. ~ **kırlangıcı**, (*orn.*) cliff swallow: ~ **dan atmak**, (*fig.*) lead into trouble, cause an accident: ~ **dan uçmak**, fall down a precipice; (*fig.*) get into serious trouble.

yar- *n. pref.* Deputy, assistant; sub- [YARBAY; YARKURUL].

yar. = YARDIMCI; (*ling.*) YARDIMCI EYLEM.

yâri Friend; lover. ~ **olm.**, help, assist: ~ **dan mı geçersin serden mi?**, have to choose between two difficult alternatives: ~ **ü ağyar**, friend and foe; all the world: ~ **ü ağyara karşı**, in the presence of others.

yara (*med.*) Wound, sore, cut; ulcer, boil; (*fig.*) trouble, anxiety. ~ **açmak**, wound; (*fig.*) cause great anxiety: ~ **bandı**, (*med.*) plaster: ~ **bere**, all wounds and bruises; rotten: ~ **işlemek**, (*med.*) discharge, suppurate: ~ **iz/kabuğu**, scar, eschar, cicatrix: ~ **kapanmak**, heal (up/over): ~ **toplamak**, (boil) come to a head: ~ **n yok ne gocunuyorsun?**, you've done nothing wrong, why are you scared?: ~ **sı olan gocunsun!**, if the cap fits wear it!: ~ **sına dokunmak**, touch s.o. on his sore spot: ~ **sını deşmek**, open up a wound; touch a sore spot: ~ **ya tuz biber ekmek**, rub salt into a wound: ~ **ya tuz saçmak**, add fuel to the flames.

yara·dan (*rel.*) The Creator: ~ **kurban olayım!**, my, what a beauty/wonder!: ~ **a sığınıp (bir iş yapmak)**, do stg. with all one's strength: ~ **dancılık**, (*phil.*) deism. ~ **dılış**, creation; nature, temperament, constitution. ~ **dılıştan**, from birth.

yara[1]k**g**1 Arms, weapon; (*vulg.*) penis.

yara·lamak (-i) Wound; hole (a ship). ~ **lanmak**, *vp.* be wounded/hit; (*fig.*) be offended. ~ **layıcı**, caustic (words). ~ **lı**, wounded; casualty; (*fig.*) anxious, troubled: ~ **kuşa kurşun sıkılmaz**, may don't hit s.o. when he's down.

yara·mak (-e) Be serviceable/useful; be of use/ suitable. ~ **mamak**, serve no purpose; be useless. ~ **maz**, unserviceable, useless; good-for-nothing; naughty. ~ **mazlaşmak**, *vi.* be naughty/disobedient. ~ **mazlık**, uselessness, unsuitability; naughtiness; escapade; bad behaviour: ~ **etm.**, be naughty.

yâran *pl.* = YÂR. Friends; lovers; (*his.*) allies.

yaran·ış/ ~ **ma** *vn.* Currying favour; polite attention. ~ **mak (-e)**, make o.s. agreeable; offer one's services; curry favour; pay polite attention.

yarar *a.* Serviceable, useful; capable, brave. *n.* Use, service; advantage, benefit. ~ **yitirme**, disadvantage: ~ **ına (-in)**, in aid of, for the benefit of.

yarar·cı(lık) (*phil.*) Pragmat·ist/(-ism); utilitarian/ (-ism). ~ **lanma**, *vn.*: ~ **hakkı**, usufruct. ~ **lanmak (-den)**, *vi.* make use of, benefit from; exploit. ~ **lı**, useful; beneficial, effective. ~ **lık**, utility; bravery: ~ **belgesi**, (*ind.*) reference. ~ **lılık**, usefulness; capability. ~ **sız**, useless, unprofitable; unsuitable; unpleasing. ~ **sızlık**, uselessness.

yarasa (*zoo.*) Bat. ~ **atmacası**, (*orn.*) bat hawk.
yaraş·ı¹kᵍ¹ Pleasing appearance; suitability: ~ **almak**, be suitable. ~ **ıklı**, suitable; pleasing, elegant. ~ **ıksız**, unsuitable; unpleasing. ~ **mak (-e)**, be suitable; be pleasing; harmonize, go well with. ~ **tırmak (-i, -e)**, *vc.* make suitable; deem suitable/ becoming.
yarat·an *a.* Creating: *n.* = YARADAN. ~ **ı**, created object; work (of art). ~ **ıcı**, *a.* creative, constructive: *n.* creator, designer. ~ **ıcılık**, creativity. ~ **ı¹kᵍ¹**, creature. ~ **ılış** = YARADILIŞ. ~ **ılmak**, *vp.* ~ **ım**, creation. ~ **ımcılık**, (*phil.*) creationism. ~ **ısal**, creative. ~ **ma**, *vn.* ~ **macı** = ~ **ICI**. ~ **mak (-i)**, create; compose, make, produce; (*fig.*) give rise to, produce.
yarbay(lık) (Rank/duties of) (*mil.*) lieutenant-colonel//(*naut.*) commander//(*aer.*) wing commander.
yarda (*math.*) Yard. ~ **lık**, . . . yards long.
yar·da¹kᵍ¹ Assistant; mate; accomplice; (*eng.*) booster. ~ **dakçı**, accomplice. ~ **dakçılık**, complicity. ~ **deneyci**, laboratory assistant.
yardım Help; assistance; backing, support; subsidy; contribution; influence. ~ **dilemek**, ask/call for help: ~ **etm. (-e)**, help, assist; support; contribute: ~ **görmek**, receive help: ~ **koşturmak**, send help: ~ **yürütüm birliği**, (*fin.*) consortium, syndicate: ~ **ına koşmak/yetişmek (-in)**, come to the aid/help of: ~ **ını temin etm.**, enlist the services of: ~ **ıyla**, thanks to.
yardım·cı Helper, assistant; associate; deputy; subsidiary; (*eng.*) auxiliary, booster: ~ **eylem**, (*ling.*) auxiliary verb: ~ **servis**, emergency service: ~ **teorem**, (*math.*) lemma: ~ **yargıcı**, (*sp.*) assistant referee. ~ **cılık**, quality of helper, etc.; assistance. ~ **cısız**, without any help(er). ~ **laşma**, *vn.* ~ **laşmak (-le)**, help each other. ~ **sal**, (*fin.*) subsidizing. ~ **samak (-den)**, ask for help. ~ **sever**, benevolent, philanthropic. ~ **sı**, (*adm.*) deputy-, assistant-.
yardırmak (-i, -e) *vc.* = YARMAK.
yaren Friend, companion. ~ **lik**, companionship; friendly conversation: ~ **etm.**, converse, chat; joke.
yarga (*live.*) Big chicken, pullet.
yargı (*leg.*) Jurisdiction; office/duties of a judge; decision, decree, judgement, sentence; (*phil.*) judgement. ~ + , *a.* Judicial, legal: ~ **gücü**, jurisdiction, competence: ~ **hakkı**, justice: ~ **sonucu**, judgement, sentence: ~ **yeri**, lawcourt: ~ **dan önceki karar**, precedent: ~ **yla kazanma**, (*sp.*) winning on points.
yargı·cı (*leg.*) Arbitrator, referee; (*sp.*) judge: ~ **kararı**, (*leg.*) arbitration award: ~ **lar kurulu**, jury. ~ **cılık**, arbitration. ~ **¹çᶜ¹(lık)**, (*leg.*) judge(ship). ~ **evi**ⁿⁱ, courthouse, lawcourt. ~ **lama**, *vn.* lawsuit, legal process; hearing, trial: ~ **giderleri**, costs. ~ **lamak (-i)**, hear a case, try; judge; decree. ~ **lanmak**, *vp.* ~ **lı**, condemned/convicted person. ~ **lık**, court. ~ **sal**, judicial: ~ **yardım**, legal aid. ~ **tay**, supreme court of appeal: ~ **a başvurmak/iletmek**, appeal.
yarı [81] *n.* Half. *a.* Half; partial; demi-; hemi-; semi-. *adv.* Half. ~ **açık**, ajar: ~ **ağır sıklet**, (*sp.*)

cruiserweight, light heavyweight: ~ **belden aşağı**//**yukarı**, from the waist down//up: ~ **bele kadar**, waist-high: ~ **bitirilmiş**, (*ind.*) semi-finished: ~ **buçuk**, small, inadequate, insufficient; only half a . . .: ~ **buçuk askerle**, with only a handful of soldiers: ~ **çekili bayrak**, half-masted flag: ~ **devre**, (*sp.*) half-time: ~ **gece**, midnight; at midnight: ~ **katrat**, (*pub.*) en: ~ **orta sıklet**, (*sp.*) light middleweight: ~ **ortadan hafif sıklet**, (*sp.*) welterweight: ~ **römork**, (*mot.*) semi-trailer: ~ SAYDAM: ~ **son(lama)**, (*sp.*) semi-final: ~ **üye**, (*adm.*) associate member: ~ **yapımlı**, (*ind.*) semi-finished: ~ ~ **ya**, on a fifty-fifty basis, taking equal shares: ~ **yolda**, half-way: ~ **yolda bırakmak**, leave half-finished; give up before completion; leave in the lurch: ~ **da bırakmak**, (*mil.*) abort: ~ **ya çekmek**, lower (flag) to half-mast. ~ **başkalaşma**, (*ent.*) hemimetabolism.
yarıcı *a.* Splitting. *n.* Wood-cutter; (*agr.*) sharecropper. ~ **lık**, wood-cutting; share-cropping.
yarı·çap (*math.*) Radius. ~ **çapsal**, radial. ~ **gölge** (*ast.*) penumbra. ~ **iletken**, (*el.*) semi-conductor.
yarı¹kᵍ¹ *a.* Split, cracked. *n.* Crack, slit; kerf; fissure, split; cleavage. ~ **ayaklılar**, (*zoo.*) cloven-hoofed ~ **damak**, (*bio.*) cleft palate: ~ **kuru bezelye**, (*cul.*) split pea. ~ **lı**, cracked, etc.
yarı·küre (*geo.*) Hemisphere. ~ **lamak (-i)**, be halfway through/to. ~ **lanmak**, *vp.*
yarıl·ım/ ~ **ma** *vn.* Cleavage; fission; (*nuc.*) splitting. ~ **mak**, *vp.* = YARMAK; be split; crack: **yarılabilir**, fissile.
yarım [81] A half; half a; demi-, hemi-, semi-; 12.30 p.m. ~ **adam**, cripple; poor specimen: ~ **ağız(la)** not seriously meant: ~ **doğru**, (*math.*) half line: ~ **elma, gönül alma**, a very small kindness may win a heart: ~ **elmanın yarısı o, yarısı bu**, as like as two peas in a pod: ~ **gün (çalışma)**, (*ind.*) part-time (work): ~ **kafiye**, (*lit.*) assonance: ~ **kalmak** remain unfinished/incomplete: ~ **kan**, (*live.*) half-bred: ~ **kârgir**, (*arch.*) half-timbered: ~ **kubbe** (*arch.*) apse: ~ **oturak**, stretcher (in rowing-boat): ~ **pabuç(lu)**, pauper; vagabond; prostitute: ~ **pansiyon**, (*dom.*) half-board: ~ **porsiyon**, (*sl.*) scraggy person: ~ **saat**, half an hour: ~ **sağ**//**sol**, (*mil.*) half right//left: ~ **ton tiz**, (*mus.*) sharp: ~ **yamalak**, perfunctory; half-done/-learnt, etc.; incompletely: ~ **yamalak bir Türkçe ile**, in broken Turkish.
yarım·ada (*geo.*) Peninsula, chersonese. ~ **ay**, (*ast.*) half-moon, crescent. ~ **ayak**, (*arch.*) pilaster. ~ **ca** (*med.*) stroke affecting one side; migraine. ~ **çember**, semicircular. ~ **dilli**, unable to express o.s. clearly ~ **kanatlılar**, (*ent.*) hemiptera, bugs. ~ **küre**, (*geo. math.*) hemisphere. ~ **lamak (-i)**, halve. ~ **lık**, (*col.*) hernia, rupture; being crippled. ~ **şar**, [83] half each.
yarın Tomorrow; the future. ~ **değil öbür gün**//**ertesi**, the day after tomorrow, sometime soon: ~ **olsun da hayrı beri gelsin**, let's wait till tomorrow and hope for the best: ~ **ziyaretinize geleceğim**, I'll come and see you tomorrow: ~ **dan tezi yok, işe başlamalı**, the work must begin tomorrow at latest. ~ **ki**, tomorrow's.

yarı·saydam(lık) Translu·cent/(-cency). ~ **son**, (*sp.*) semi-final.

yarış (*sp.*) Race; competition. ~ **atı**, racehorse: ~ **direği**, (*sp.*) greasy pole: ~ **etm.**, race, compete: ~ **pisti**, cinder-track; race-track: ~ **tabancası**, starting-pistol: ~ **tazısı**, (*live.*) greyhound: ~ **tan çıkarmak**, disqualify. **yarış·başı** (*sp.*) Champion. ~ **çı**, competitor, runner. ~ **dışı**, ~ **bırakmak**, disqualify. ~ **ıcı**, (*fin.*) competitor, rival. ~ **ım**, (*fin.*) competition: ~ **+**, *a.* competitive. ~ **ımcı(lık)**, (*sp.*) athle·te/(-tics). ~ **lık**, race-/running-track. ~ **ma**, *vn.* competition; contest; rivalry. ~ **macı**, competitor; contestant; rival. ~ **mak (-le)**, race, contend; compete; rival. ~ **tırmak (-i)**, *vc.* ~ **yolu**^{nu}, (*sp.*) circuit, course.

yarı·yaşam (*phys.*) Half-life. ~ **yıl**, (*ed.*) semester.

yarkurul (*adm.*) Commission; (sub-)committee.

yar·lıgamak (-i) (*rel.*) (God) show mercy, pardon sins. ~ **lığ**, (*his.*) command, edict, firman. ~ **lık**, (*phil.*) moral obligation.

yar·ma *vn.* Splitting; cleft, fissure; (*rly.*) cutting; (*mil.*) breakthrough: *a.* split; (*cul.*) coarsely ground (wheat): ~ **gibi**, big, coarse (man): ~ **kereste**, (*carp.*) timber split along the grain: ~ **şeftali**, (*bot.*) freestone peach. ~ **mak (-i)**, split, cleave; cut through; (*mil.*) break through. ~ **malamak (-i)**, split/tear lengthwise. ~ **malık**, (*cul.*) coarse-ground wheat. ~ **man**, (*med.*) surgeon.

yarpuz (*bot.*) Penny-royal.

yas Mourning. ~ **tutmak**, be in mourning.

yasa (*leg.*) Law; code of laws; natural law. ~ **çıkarmak/koymak/yapmak**, issue/promulgate a law: ~ **dışı**, illegal; optional: ~ **koyucu**, legislator: ~ **sözcüsü**, DANIŞTAY prosecutor: ~ **tasarısı**, draft law: ~ **yolu**, legal remedy/means: ~ **ya (aykırı)//uygun**, (un)lawful, (il)legal.

yasa·k^{ğı} *n.* Prohibition; ban; interdict. *a.* Prohibited, forbidden. ~ **bölge**, (*mil.*) prohibited/military zone: ~ **etm.**, ban; prohibit, forbid; (*ind.*) black; (*pub.*) censor: ~ **liste**, (*fin.*) black list: ~ **mevsim**, (*sp.*) close season: ~ **olm.**, be banned, etc.: ~ **savmak**, serve in case of need, 'do' when nothing better available; do stg. just to comply with a rule: ~ **savar**, that will do/serve for the time being: ~ **savutlar**, prohibited weapons: ~ **yere girmek**, (*mil.*) break bounds.

yasak·çı (*his.*) One who cleared the way for a great person; embassy/consular guard. ~ **lamak (-i)**, ban, embargo, forbid, prohibit. ~ **layıcı**, prohibitive. ~ **lık**, prohibition.

yasa·l Legal, lawful, legitimate; (*phys.*) canonical: ~ **konut**, domicile: ~ **para**, (*fin.*) legal tender. ~ **laşmak**, *vi.* become law, come into force. ~ **laştırmak (-i)**, make lawful; bring into force. ~ **lı(lık)**, legal(ity). ~ **ma**, *vn.* act of legislating; legislation: ~ **dokunulmazlığı**, parliamentary privilege/immunity: ~ **erki**, legislative power: ~ **kurulu**, legislature: ~ **meclisleri**, the legislative chambers. ~ **mak (-i)**, arrange; *vi.* legislate; govern, control. ~ **malı**, legislative. ~ **man**, legislator. ~ **sız**, arbitrary.

yasan (*phil.*) Intention, aim.

yasemin (*bot.*) Jasmine.

yas·lamak (-i) Support; bolster up. ~ **lanmak**^{1} **(-e)**, lean against; (*fig.*) rely on.

yas·lanmak^2 *imp. v.* Be in mourning. ~ **lı**, in mourning.

yasmak (-i) Spread, smooth out.

yasmı·k^{ğı} (*cul.*) Lentil.

yassı Flat and smooth. ~ **böceği**, (*ent.*) flatbug; ~ **burunlu**, (*zoo.*) flat-nosed: ~ **çakıl**, (*geol.*) pebble, cobble: ~ **çivi**, (*eng.*) cotter-pin: ~ **kadayıf**, (*cul.*) batter cakes soaked in syrup; crumpet: ~ **kurt**, (*zoo.*) flatworm: ~ **kütük**, (*min.*) slab.

yassı·lama *vn.* (*eng.*) Flattening. ~ **lamak (-i)**, flatten. ~ **lanmak**/ ~ **laşmak**/ ~ **lmak**, *vi.* be(come) flat and smooth. ~ **lık**, flatness, smoothness. ~ **solucanlar**, (*zoo.*) flatworms. ~ **solungaçlılar**, (*zoo.*) bivalves.

yastağa·l ç^{cı} (*ich.*) Bream; (*dom.*) pastry-board.

yastı·k^{ğı} (*dom.*) Bolster, pillow; cushion; pad; (*agr.*) nursery-bed; (*eng.*) bed, bearing. ~ **lı**, cushioned: ~ **hücre**, (*psy.*) padded cell.

yaş^1 *a.* Wet; damp; (*bot.*) fresh; (*sl.*) difficult. *n.* Wetness; moisture; tears. ~ **akıtmak/dökmek**, weep, shed tears: ~ **odun**, (*carp.*) green wood: ~ **odun ağır çeker**, wet wood weighs heavy: ~ **saçmak**, weep copiously: ~ **tahta/yere basmak**, be cheated/taken in: ~ **yemiş**, (*agr.*) unripe fruit: ~ **ını içine akıtmak**, hide one's grief: ~ **lara boğulmak**, weep copiously.

yaş^2 *n.* Age. ~ **günü**, birthday: ~ **haddi**, (*adm.*) age-limit: ~ **ı benzemesin**, may he not be so old (as to die): ~ **ı ne başı ne!**, he's too young!: ~ **ı toprak/yerde sayılası!**, may he die!: ~ **ına basmak**, reach the age of . . . : ~ **ına başına bakmadan**, regardless of your/his age: ~ **ında (değil)**, he's (not yet) one year old: ~ **ında (kırk)**, in his (fortieth) year, (forty) years old: ~ **ını almak**, be of mature years/advanced in age: ~ **ını bulmak**, become adult: ~ **ını doldurmak**, complete one's . . . year.

yaş·a *int.* Long live . . .!: ~ **sesi**, cheering. ~ **am**, life; living: ~ **düzeyi**, (*fin.*) standard of living: ~ **görüşü**, view of/attitude to life: ~ÖYKÜSÜ: ~ **süresi**, life-span, lifetime: ~ **a gözleri yummak**, die. ~ **ama**, *vn.* life, living: ~ **gücü**, vitality: ~ **kabiliyeti**, viability: ~ **uğraşı**, (*bio.*) the struggle for existence: ~ **amaca**, during one's lifetime. ~ **amak**, *vi.* live; dwell; exist; earn one's living; live in . . . way; (*fig.*) live on; know how to live, enjoy o.s.; be lucky: **yaşadığım kadar**, as long as I live: **yaşadıkça**, (*leg.*) for life: **yaşadınız çocuklar!**, you are in luck!: **yaşayan dil**, living language. ~ **ambilim(ci)**, biolo·gy/(-gist). ~ **ambilimsel**, biological. ~ **amöyküsel**, biographical. ~ **amöyküsü**^{nü}, (*lit.*) biography. ~ **amsal(lık)**, living; vital(ity). ~ **anabilir**, habitable. ~ **anamaz**, uninhabitable. ~ **an(ıl)mak**, *imp. v.* one live, exist. ~ **antı**, period of one's life. ~ **arlık**, viability: ~ **güvencesi**, (*fin.*) endowment policy.

yaşar·mak *vi.* Become wet; fill with tears. ~ **tmak (-i)**, *vc.* make wet; cause to weep.

yaş·atıcı Causing to live; keeping alive. ~ **atkan**, (*bot.*) vegetative. ~ **atmak (-i)**, *vc.* cause/allow to live; keep alive; (*th., etc.*) bring to life, recreate. ~ **ay**, living: ~ **ağacı**, (*bot.*) arbor vitae: ~

şartları, (*soc.*) living conditions. ~**ayabilirlik,** viability. ~**ayış,** manner of living; life; livelihood. ~**daş/**~**ıt(lık),** (a being) of the same age, coeval. ~**dönümü**ⁿᵘ, birthday. ~**landırmak (-i),** (*ind.*) age. ~**lanmak,** *vi.* grow old, age. ~**lanmaz,** ageless. ~**lı¹,** old, aged; veteran: ~ **başlı,** of mature years: ~**laryurdu,** old people's home. ~**lıca,** getting on in years. ~**lılık,** old age; advanced years: ~ **ayrılması,** (*fin.*) retirement.

yaş·lı² Wet; suffused with tears. ~**lık,** wetness; moisture; dampness; damp weather; (*bot.*) juiciness: ~ **içeriği,** (*phys.*) moisture content. ~**lıkölçer,** (*met.*) hygrometer.

yaşma¹kᵍ¹ (*mod.*) Yashmak, veil. ~**lamak (-i),** veil; put on a yashmak. ~**lanmak,** *vi.* be veiled; put on the yashmak; (*fig.*) become nubile. ~**lı,** veiled.

yat¹ ¹ (*obs.*) Armour; arms.

yat¹ ² (*naut.*) Yacht.

yatağan (*mil.*) Heavy curved knife, yataghan.

yata¹kᵍ¹ Bed, couch; base; (*zoo.*) lair, den; (*naut.*) anchorage, berth; (*rly.*) berth; (*eng.*) (shaft) bearing; (gun) chamber; (*geo.*) river-bed; (*geol.*) stratum, ore-bed, deposit; (*leg.*) receiver (of stolen goods); screen (for illicit activities); den (of thieves); (*agr.*) drill (for plants). ~ **çarşafı,** (*dom.*) bed-sheet: ~ **esiri,** (*med.*) bed-ridden: ~ **lazımlığı,** (*med.*) bedpan: ~ **limanı,** (*naut.*) deep-water harbour: ~ **madeni,** (*min.*) Babbitt metal: ~ **odası,** bedroom; cubicle: ~ **örtüsü,** (*dom.*) quilt, bedspread: ~ **salmak,** spread a bed: ~ **tahtakurusu,** (*ent.*) bedbug: ~ **takımı,** (*dom.*) set of bedding/bedclothes: ~ **yorgan,** bed and bedding: ~**a düşmek,** (*med.*) be confined/take to one's bed: ~**a girmek,** go to bed: ~**a serilmek,** lie down, stretch out: ~**ına kaçırmak,** (child) soil its bed: ~**lar çekmek (-i),** want to go to bed.

yatak·hane Dormitory. ~**lanma,** (*geol.*) deposit formation. ~**lı,** with a bed; having . . . beds; residential; deep-channelled (river): ~ **bıyık,** trained moustache: ~ **vagon,** (*rly.*) wagon-lit, sleeping-car. ~**lık,** bedstead; bed-store; for . . . beds; (*leg.*) receiving and concealing (stolen goods); (*live.*) bedding: ~ **etm.,** act as a receiver: ~ **hasta,** ill enough to be confined to bed: ~ **kadın,** (*pej.*) woman only fit to go to bed with. ~**sız,** non-residential.

yat·alak (*med.*) Confined to bed. ~**ar,** ~ **koltuk (komple),** (*mot.*) (fully) reclining seat. ~**arlık,** (*med.*) clinic. ~**ay,** (*math.*) horizontal: ~ **ağaç,** (*sp.*) beam. ~**ı,** guest's staying the night: ~ **izni,** (*mil., etc.*) sleeping-out pass: ~**ya misafir gelmek/ gitmek,** visit s.o. to stay overnight. ~**ık,** leaning to one side; sloping; recumbent; (*bot.*) decumbent; (*math.*) oblique; (*naut.*) with a list, listing: ~ **yollu top,** (*mil.*) gun with a flat trajectory. ~**ıkkenar,** (*math.*) hypotenuse. ~**ılı,** (*ed.*) boarding; boarder: (*dom.*) living-in (servant). ~**ılmak,** *vp.* = YATMAK. ~**ım,** (*naut.*) rake. ~**ır,** (*rel.*) entombed saint.

yatır·ga (*fin.*) Deposit. ~**ıcı,** depositor. ~**ılmak,** *vp.* ~**ım,** deposit; investment: ~ **bankası,** savings-bank: ~ **yapmak,** make an investment. ~**ımcı,** depositor, investor. ~**mak (-i, -e),** *vc.* = YATMAK; lay down; deposit; cause to lie down; make lean/

slope; throw to the ground; overthrow; (*cul.*) dip/ soak (meat); (*fin.*) invest, deposit. ~**man,** investor.

yatısız (*ed.*) Day-(school/pupil).

yatış (*aer.*) Banking. ~ **dönüş**//**tırmanış,** bank and turn//climb.

yatış·mak *vi.* Calm down; become quiet; subside. ~**tırıcı,** calming; conciliatory; (*med.*) tranquillizer, sedative, anodyne. ~**tırmak (-i),** calm, quieten, tranquillize; sedate; alleviate, assuage; appease.

yat·kı (*mod.*) Crease; fold. ~**kın,** laid down; inclined; deteriorated, stale: **(-e),** accustomed to, fairly skilful at. ~**kınlaşmak,** *vi.* become accustomed, etc. ~**kınlık,** familiarity; skill; (*med.*) predisposition.

yatmak *vi.* Lie down; go to bed; be in bed; pass/ spend the night; (*med.*) be bedridden; (*naut.*) lie at anchor; become flat; be broken in, be used to; be buried; be imprisoned; be unsuccessful; be unemployed: **(-den)**, (*med.*) be down with: **(-e)**, lie on; lean towards; agree to. **yatıp kalkmak (-de),** live in, lodge at; be always doing.

yatsı About two hours after sunset. ~ **ezanı,** (*rel.*) evening call to prayer: ~ **namazı,** evening prayer: ~**dan sonra ezan okumak,** do stg. too late/at an unsuitable moment.

yat·uğan/~**u¹k**ᵍᵘ (*mus.*) Any instrument held in the lap.

yavan (*cul.*) Plain, dry; without oil; tasteless, insipid; (*geol.*) lean. ~**lamak,** *vi.* (*sl.*) be stony-broke. ~**laşmak,** *vi.* be tasteless/insipid. ~**laştırmak (-i),** *vc.* ~**lık,** being dry/without oil; insipidity.

yavaş *a.* Slow; gentle; mild; quiet, soft (sound); docile. ~**!,** *int.* be careful!, gently!: ~ **gel/ol!,** (*sl.*) take it easy!: ~ **konuşmak,** talk in a low voice: ~ **tütün,** mild tobacco: ~ ~**!,** gently!; steady!; don't get excited!: ~ **yürümek,** walk slowly; walk quietly: ~**tan almak,** take things gently/slowly.

yavaş·a (*live.*) Blacksmith's barnacles. ~**ça,** quite gently/slowly. ~**çacık,** very gently/slowly. ~**lama,** *vn.* deceleration. ~**lamak,** *vi.* become slow/mild; be retarded; slow down, decelerate; (rain) slacken. ~**latılmış,** ~ **hareket,** (*cin.*) slow motion. ~**latmak (-i),** slow down, retard, decelerate. ~**lık,** slowness; gentleness; mildness.

yave Foolish talk; nonsense.

yaver Assistant, helper; (*mil.*) adjutant, aide-de-camp. ~ **gitmek,** fit in, be suitable. ~**lik,** rank/ duties of aide-de-camp.

yavru (*zoo.*) Young; cub, foal, chick, etc.; (*fig.*) child, junior. ~ **atmak,** drop (foal, etc.): ~ **çıkarmak,** hatch (chickens): ~**m,** darling!

yavru·ağzıⁿ¹ Light pink. ~**cak,** poor child! ~**cuk,** sweet child! ~**kurt,** (*soc.*) Cub, Brownie. ~**lamak,** *vi.* (*zoo.*) bring forth young; cub, foal, etc.

yav·sı (*zoo.*) Tick. ~**şak,** (*ent.*) young louse. ~**şan,** thorny, spiny. ~**şanotu**ⁿᵘ, (*bot.*) brooklime.

yavuk·lamak (-i, -e) Betroth. ~**lanmak (-e),** be betrothed/engaged to. ~**lu,** betrothed, engaged; fiancé(e).

yavuz Stern, ferocious, grim, cruel; resolute, inflexible. ~ **hırsız ev sahibini bastırır,** s.o. who bluffs his way out of trouble. ~**luk,** sternness, ferocity; resolution.

ay (*mil.*, *mus.*) Bow; arch; (*eng.*) spring; watchspring; (*math.*, *el.*) arc. ~ **(burcu)**, (*ast.*) (constellation of) Sagittarius: ~ **kirişi**, bowstring: ~ **lambası**, arc-lamp.

aya *a.* Walking; afoot. *n.* Pedestrian, walker. ~ **geçidi**, pedestrian crossing: ~ **kaldırımı**, pavement, sidewalk: ~ **kalmak**, be compelled to walk; be in a difficult situation; be left without help: ~ **kaldın, tatar ağası!**, now you're stranded!; you are in a sorry plight!; you're on the wrong track!: ~ **korkuluğu**, pedestrian guard-rail: ~ **yolu**, footpath. ~ **n**[1], on foot; of little account; unskilled: ~ **yapıldak**, walking barefoot. ~ **nlık**, going on foot. **ay·a**[l]**ç**[c1] (*rad.*) Transmitter station. ~ **an**[2], publisher.

ay·çizer (*math.*) Pair of compasses. ~ **dırmak (-i, -e)**, *vc.* = YAYMAK.

yaygara Shout; outcry; clamour. ~ **yı basmak/koparmak**, raise an outcry; make much ado (about nothing). ~ **cı**, *a.* noisy; brawling; loud (in taste): *n.* noisy fellow; brawler; cry-baby. ~ **cılık**, noisiness; brawling.

yay·gı Stg. spread out as a covering. ~ **gın**, wellknown; extensive; widespread; world-wide; (*phil.*) diffused: ~ **kullanışlı**, widely used: ~ **söylenti**, hearsay, common knowledge: ~ **yanlış**, common(ly accepted) error. ~ **gınlaşmak**, *vi.* be(come) well-known/widespread. ~ **gınlık**, being widespread, etc.: ~ **kazanmak**, become popular. ~ **ıcı**, (*rad.*) broadcaster; transmitter; (*pub.*) distributor. ~ **ık**[1], *a.* spread out; broad, wide; (*med.*) astigmatic: ~ **ağızlı**, s.o. who drawls: ~ ~, in a dawdling manner; drawling one's words. ~ **ıkgörü**, (*med.*) astigmatism.

yayı[l]**k**[ğ1 2] *n.* (*cul.*) Butter-churn. ~ **ayranı**, buttermilk: ~ **yaymak**/~ **ta çalkalamak**, churn butter.

yayıl·gan Popular. ~ **gı**, (*phys.*) spectrum. ~ **gıölçer**, spectroscope. ~ **ı**, spread out. ~ **ım**, (*pol.*) expansion. ~ **ımcı(lık)**, imperial·ist/(-ism); expansion·ist/ (-ism). ~ **ış**, spread. ~ **ma**, *vn.* being spread out, etc.; (*mil.*) deployment; (*pub.*) publication; (*phys.*) diffusion; propagation; (*soc.*) diaspora. ~ **macı(lık)**, (*ethn.*) diffusion·ist/(-ism). ~ **mak (-e)**, *vp.* be spread out; be deployed; be broadcast/published; be diffused: *vi.* spread (out).

yayım (*pub.*) Publication, edition; publishing; (*rad.*) broadcasting. ~ **postası**, broadcasting station. ~ **cı(lık)**, publish·er/(-ing); edit·or/(-ing). ~ **lamak (-i)**, publish; broadcast. ~ **lanmak**, *vp.* ~ **lan(ma)mış**, *a.* (un)published.

yayın[1]**(balığı**[n1]**)** *n.* (*ich.*) European catfish, wels.

yayın[2] *n.* (*pub.*) Publication, book, etc.; (*rad.*) broadcast, show, etc.; (*phys.*) diffusion. ~ **etm.**, broadcast; distribute: ~ **müdürü**, editor.

yayın·ca (*pub.*) Bulletin. ~ **dırıcı**, (*phys.*) diffuser. ~ **dırma**, diffusion. ~ **düzen**, (*pub.*) editing. ~ **düzenci**, editor. ~ **evi**, publishing-house, bookpublisher's. ~ **ık**, (*phys.*) diffuse, diffused. ~ **ım**, diffusion. ~ **ıntı**, rumour; news. ~ **lamak (-i)**, publish; (*phys.*) emit. ~ **ma**, (*phys.*) scatter. ~ **man**, publisher.

YAYKO = YAYIMCILAR KOOPERATİFİ.

yayla (*geo.*) High plateau; (nomad's) summer camping-ground. ~ **cı(lık)**, nomad(ism). ~ **çiçeği**[ni], (*bot.*) Mexican tea. ~ **ık**[ğ1], (*live.*) summer pasture. ~ **kıye**, rent for summer pasture. ~ **mak**, *vi.* spend the summer at the YAYLA.

yay·landırmak (-i) *vc.* ~ **lanmak**, *vi.* rock (on a spring); sway (as on a spring); (*sl.*) go away. ~ **lı**, with a bow//spring; sprung; carriage with springs: ~ **çalgı/sazlar**, (*mus.*) instruments played with a bow: ~ **çizgi**, (*pub.*) swung dash, tilde (~): ~ **gözlük**, pince-nez: ~ **perde**, roller blind: ~ **pergel**, (*math.*) bow-compass: ~ **terazi**, spring balance.

yaylım *vn.* Spreading; (*live.*) summer pasture. ~ **ateşi**, (*mil.*) volley, broadside, running fire.

yay·ma *vn.* Act of spreading; (*fin.*) dealer's stall. ~ **maca**, (*pol.*) propaganda. ~ **macı(lık)**, (trade of) small dealer/stallholder. ~ **mak (-i, -e)**, spread; extend; scatter; disperse; disseminate; broadcast; publish; (*phys.*) diffuse, propagate; (*live.*) pasture. ~ **man**, (*pol.*) propagandist. ~ **paca**, propaganda. ~ **van**, broad and shallow; spreading out: ~ ~ **gülmek**, laugh uproariously: ~ ~ **konuşmak**, drawl. ~ **vanlık**, shallowness, being spread out.

yaz Summer. ~ **kış**, all the year round: ~ **saati**, summer time; daylight saving: ~ **türlüsü**, (*cul.*) summer fricassée: ~ **uykusu**, (*zoo.*) aestivation: ~ **a çıkmak**, reach summer: ~ **ı getirmek**, put on light summer clothes. *v.* = YAZMAK.

yaz·a[l]**ç**[c1] (*ling.*) Letter. ~ **ana**[l]**k**[ğ1], (*fin.*, *pub.*) report; certificate. ~ **anakçı**, reporter. ~ **ar**, (*lit.*) writer, editor, author: ~ **çizer**, given to writing: ~ **hattı**, autograph. ~ **arlık**, (*lit.*) writing, authorship. ~ **çizçilik**, (*adm.*) bureaucracy, red tape. ~ **dırım**, dictation. ~ **dırmak (-i, -e)**, *vc.* = YAZMAK; dictate. ~ **gı**, (*rel.*) fate; predestination: ~ **payı**, one's lot in life. ~ **gıcı(lık)**, (*phil.*) fatal·ist/(-ism). ~ **gılı**, fateful, fated. ~ **gısal**, fatalistic.

yazı[1] *n.* (*geo.*) Plain; flat surface.

yazı[2] *n.* Writing; alphabet; calligraphy; manuscript; inscription; correspondence; written article; (*rel.*) fate; (*cin.*) caption, subtitle. ~ **bölümü**, (*pub.*) paragraph. ~ **çoğaltıcı**, duplicator. ~ **dili**, (*ling.*) written language: ~ **hayatı**, (*lit.*) writing/creative period: ~ **ile**, in writing: ~ **işleri**, documents; (*pub.*) editorial work: ~ **işleri müdürü**, (*adm.*) secretary general; (*pub.*) editor: ~ **kâğıdı**, writing-/ note-paper: ~ **makinesi**, typewriter: ~ **masası**, desk: ~ **mı tuğra mı?**, heads or tails?: ~ **tahtası**, (*ed.*) blackboard: ~ **taslağı**, rough copy, draft: ~ **taşı**, (*ed.*) slate: ~ **tuğra atmak**, toss a coin: ~ **ücreti**, (*pub.*) royalty: ~ **vermek**, (*pub.*) contribute: ~ **ya dökmek/geçirmek**, put down in writing: ~ **ya gelmemek**, be unable to explain in writing/put pen to paper: ~ **yı çıkarmak/sökmek**, decipher, read: ~ **yla**, in writing.

yazı·bilim(ci) G\rapholo·gy/(-gist). ~ **boya**, ink. ~ **cı**, writer, secretary; clerk; (*cin.*) scenarist; (*phys.*) recorder, recording-instrument: ~ **barometre**, (*phys.*) barograph: ~ **kadın**, (*mod.*) woman making up brides. ~ **cılık**, clerkship; (*mod.*) making-up. ~ **düzen**, (*pub.*) editing. ~ **düzenci(lik)**, editor(ship). ~ **hane**, (*fin.*) office; bureau; desk; writing-table.

yazı[l]**k**[ğ1] *n.* A pity; a shame; a sin. *int.* Deplorable;

what a pity/shame! ~ **olm. (-e)**, be regrettable: ~ **günah/**~**lar olsun!**, shame!: ~ **ki ...**, I'm afraid that . . .. ~**lanmak (-e)**, regret, be sorry for. ~**sız**, innocent.

yazı·lama (*cin.*) Titling. ~**lı**, *a.* written, inscribed; registered; (*fin.*) nominal; (*rel.*) destined, fated: *n.* (*ed.*) written examination: ~ **antlaşma**, (*leg.*) contract: ~ **hani**, (*ich.*) banded sea-perch; painted comber: ~ **ifade,** (*leg.*) deposition: ~ **olarak**, in writing: ~ **orkinos**, (*ich.*) albacore, tunny: ~ **tartışma**, (*pol.*) polemics. ~**lık**, register; ledger. ~**lım**, entry; report; note: ~ **eki**, postscript. ~**lımlı**, (*fin.*) nominal. ~**lış**, method of writing; spelling. ~**lmak**, *vp.* = YAZMAK: **(-e)**, (*ed.*) be registered/entered/enrolled. ~**m**, (*ling.*) orthography; spelling; (*ed.*) registration.

yazın[1] *adv.* In summer. ~**ki**, *a.* summer.

yaz·ın[2] *n.* Literature: ~ +, *a.* literary. ~**ıncak(çı)**, typ·ing/(-ist). ~**ıncı(lık)**, (work of) man of letters. ~**ınlık**, literature. ~**ınsal(lık)**, litera·ry/(riness). ~**ısıvı**, ink. ~**ısız**, blank; without text. ~**ış**, act/ manner of writing. ~**ışma**, *vn.* correspondence. ~**ışmak (-le)**, correspond, write to each other. ~**ıt**[1], (*archaeol., art.*) inscription. ~**ıtbilim**, epigraphy. ~**ıvermek**, scribble.

yaz·lamak *vi.* Spend the summer. ~**lı**, ~ **kışlı**, for all seasons, summer and winter alike. ~**lık**, *a.* suitable for/used in summer: *n.* summer clothes; accommodation (rented) for the summer: ~ **konut**, summer villa: ~**a çıkmak**, go to one's summer house: ~**ına**, for the summer.

yazma *vn.* Act of writing; (*tex.*) hand-painted/ -printed article; (*med., col.*) mumps. *a.* Handwritten, manuscript; (*tex.*) hand-painted/-printed. ~ **çekmek**, make a copy: ~ **yitimi**, (*psy.*) agraphia. ~**cı(lık)**, (*tex.*) (work of) hand-painter/-printer.

yazmak (-i) *vt.* Write; (*mus.*) compose; inscribe; (*adm.*) register; enrol, take on; make up (bride): **(-de)**, (*pub.*) write in/for: **(-e)**, write to, communicate with: *aux. v.* [191] almost have done stg. [**öleyazdı**, he almost died]. **yaz boz tahtası**, (*ed., obs.*) 'in-out' board: **yaz boz tahtasına çevirmek/ yazıp bozmak**, issue counter-orders, continually change one's mind; be capricious: **yazıp çizmek**, set down/compose in writing.

yazman Secretary. ~**lık**, secretaryship; secretary's duties.

Yb. = (*ch.s.*) İTERBİYUM.

YB. = (*phys.*) YÜK BİRİMİ.

Yd. (Sb.) = YEDEK (SUBAY).

-ydi/-ydı/-ydu/-ydü *v. suf.* [99] = İDİ [OKULDAYDIM].

-ye *n. suf.* (*after vowel*) [28] = -E [GECEYE].

Yecuc ~ **ve Mecuc**, (*myth.*) Gog and Magog.

yed Hand; possession. ~**i kudret**, (*rel.*) Providence: ~**i kudretinde olm.**, be within one's power.

yede[l]**k**[g][i] *n.* Halter; tow-rope; led animal; reserve horse; (*mil.*) reserve; (*sp.*) substitute. *a.* Spare; extra, stand-by, in reserve; auxiliary, emergency. ~ **akça**, (*fin.*) reserves: ~ **(te) çekmek**, (*mot., naut.*) tow: ~ **kuvvetler**, (*mil.*) back-up troops: ~ **oyuncu**, (*cin., th.*) stand-in: ~ **parça**, (*eng.*) spare part: ~ **subay**, (*mil.*) reserve conscript officer: ~ **teker**,

(*mot.*) spare wheel: ~ **üye**, (*adm.*) substitute/part-time member: ~**e almak**, take in tow: ~**e çekmek**, put aside, keep in reserve: ~**e vermek**, have (horse) led//(boat) towed: ~**ten sarfetmek**, break into one's reserves.

yedek·çi Man leading a spare horse//towing a boat: ~ **yolu**, tow-path. ~**lemek (-i)**, keep in reserve/as spare; take in tow; (*cin.*) double. ~**li**, in tow; with a spare part; (*lit.*) part added to make a rhyme.

yedi Seven; (*fig.*) many, all. ~ **ada**, *pr.n.* (*geo.*) Ionian Islands: ~ **başlı (yılan)**, (*myth.*) seven-headed hydra; (*fig.*) dangerous person: ~ **canlı**, having nine lives, invincible: ~ **ceddine tövbe etm.**, forswear for good and all: ~ **düvel**, (*col.*) all nations: ~ **iklim dört bucak**, everywhere: ~ **kat el**, stranger, foreigner: ~ **kralla barışık**, on good terms with everyone; (*pej.*) (woman) with many lovers: ~ **kubbeli hamam kurmak**, build castles in Spain/the air: ~ **mahalle**, everybody: ~ **tuğ çıkmak**, (*his.*) the Sultan go forth to war: ~ VEREN: ~**de bir**, one-seventh part: ~ **sinden yetmişine kadar**, every man alive, everybody. [*Further phrases* = BEŞ.]

yediemin (*leg.*) Depository, trustee.

yedi·gen (*math.*) Heptagon. ~**gir**, (*ast.*) Great Bear constellation. ~**kule**, *pr.n.* (*his.*) Castle of the Seven Towers (Istanbul): ~ **marulu**, (*bot.*) fine type of cos lettuce. ~**li**, having seven (parts); worth seven (units); (*gamb.*) the seven (at cards). ~**lik**, costing/weighing/measuring seven units. ~**nci (7.)**, (*math.*) seventh.

yedir·ilmek *vp.* ~**im**, (*fin.*) corruption, bribery. ~**me**, *vn.* feeding; (*eng.*) hempen bonding (for sealing pipes). ~**mek (-i, -e)**, cause to eat/be eaten; feed; make swallow; cause to be absorbed; make accept (bribe, etc.); expend; depreciate: **yedirip barındırma**, board and lodging: **yedirip içirmek (-i)**, feed/board s.o. ~**melik**, bribe.

yedi·şer Seven each; seven at a time. ~**uyuklayan**, (*zoo.*) dormouse. ~**veren**, (*agr.*) prolific plant; one producing several crops a year: ~ **gülü**, floribunda rose. ~**z**, (*bio.*) septuplet(s).

yedmek (-i) Lead/tow with a rope.

yegâh (*Or. mus.*) A very old melody.

yegân Singly; one by one. ~**e**, single; sole, unique.

yeğ [55] Better; profitable; preferable. ~ **tutmak**, prefer, choose.

yeğen (*soc.*) Nephew; niece.

yeğin Active, intense; violent; victorious. ~ **deprem**, (*geol.*) strong earthquake. ~**ce**, fairly strong. ~**leme**, *vn.*; (*cin.*) intensification. ~**lemek/ ~leşmek**, *vi.* become violent; intensify; be victorious. ~**lik**, (*phys.*) intensity, strength. ~**mek**, make a great effort. ~**sel**, intensive.

yeğ·leme *vn.* Preference, choice: ~ +, *a.* preferential. ~**lemek (-i, -e)**, prefer, choose. ~**lenmek**, *vp.* ~**lik**, preference; choice.

yeğni Light; slight; easy. ~ **ağırlık**, (*sp.*) lightweight. ~**ce**, lightly. ~**k**, (*med.*) mild (attack); abortive. ~**l(ce)**, light(ly). ~**(l)lik**, lightness. ~**lmek**, be(come) lighter. ~**ltmek (-i)**, *vc.* make lighter, lighten. ~**semek (-i)**, consider unimportant, despise.

yeğrek [55] Preferred, chosen; better, best; preferable.

yel'is'si Despair, despondency, desolation. ~ **vermek**, demoralize.

yek One; (*gamb.*) one; ace. ~ TA: ~ TEN. ~ **diğeri**ni, one another; each other. ~ **dil**, of one heart and mind.

yeke (*naut.*) Tiller.

yek·kalem At one stroke; straight away. ~ **nazarda**, at a single glance. ~ **nesak**, in a single row; uniform; even; monotonous, drab. ~ **nesaklık**, uniformity, monotony. ~ **pare**, in a single piece: ~ **döküm**, (*min.*) monobloc casting. ~ **renk**, all in one colour, monochrome; of the same mind. ~ **san**, one with, level; together. ~ **ser**, from end to end; all together; all at once. ~ **ta**, single, sole, unique; matchless. ~ **ten**, all at once; without any reason.

yekûn Total, sum; all told. ~ **tutmak**, add up, total: ~ **u nakletmek**, (*fin.*) bring/carry forward.

yel (*met.*) Wind; (*med.*, *col.*) flatulence; (*med.*) rheumatic pain. ~ +, *a*. Wind-; anemo-: ~ **aşındırması**, (*geol.*) abrasion, erosion: ~ **değirmeni**, windmill: ~ **gibi**, quickly, at speed: ~ **gibi gelmek**, slip in unobserved: ~ **ölçeği**, (*met.*) anemometer: ~ **üfürdü sel/su götürdü**, easily and without effort; 'gone with the wind': ~ **yanı**, (*naut.*) windward side: ~ **yeperek yelken kürek**, hurriedly and in confusion: ~ **e vermek**, scatter to the winds; destroy.

yeldir·me (*mod.*) Light cloak with hood (instead of ÇARŞAF); (*ich.*) very long mackerel net. ~ **mek (-i)**, *vc.* = YELMEK.

yele(li) (*zoo.*) Mane(d); crest(ed). ~ **sırtlan**, aardwolf.

yel·eç/ ~ **eken** High and airy (place).

yele'kği (*mod.*) Waistcoat, vest; (*orn.*) wing-feather, pinion; (*mil.*, *sp.*) (arrow) feathering. ~ **lemek (-i)**, feather (arrow).

yeleme Fanciful, flighty; not serious.

yelengeç = YALINGAÇ.

yelken (*naut.*) Sail. ~ **açmak**, hoist/unfurl sails: ~ **balığı**, (*ich.*) sailfish: ~ **bezi**, canvas, sailcloth: ~ **gemisi**, sailing-boat/-ship: ~ **kürek** = YEL: ~ **leri indirmek/mayna etm.**, lower the sails: ~ **leri suya indirmek**, (*fig.*) climb down, knuckle under; (s.o.'s anger) blow over.

yelken·ci Sail-maker; sailor (on sailing-vessel). ~ **lemek**, *vi.* make sail; sail away. ~ **li**, *a*. with sails: *n*. sailing-boat.

yel·kesen (*sp.*, *etc.*) Wind-break, windscreen. ~ **kovan**, minute-hand (of watch); (*met.*) weathercock; (*arch.*) bargeboard; smoke-cowl. ~ **kovankuşu**, (*orn.*) Manx/Bosphorus shearwater. ~ **lemek (-i)**, blow upon; fan. ~ **lenmek**, (*bio.*) break wind, fart. ~ **li**, (*met.*) windy; (*bio.*) flatulent; (*med.*) rheumatic.

yelloz Whore.

yelmek *vi.* Run; move hurriedly/in confusion. **yellim yelâlım/yeperek**, running swiftly; in great haste.

yel·ölçer (*met.*) Anemometer. ~ **paze**, fan; (*naut.*) rudder-blade: ~ **kuyruklu**, (*orn.*) fantail: ~ **olm.**, fan out. ~ **pazelemek (-i)**, fan. ~ **pazelenmek**, *vi.* fan o.s.

yelpi'kği (*med.*) Severe asthma.

yeltek Frivolous; capricious; unstable.

yeltenmek (-e) Strive/dare to do stg. beyond one's powers.

yel·ve (*orn.*) Snipe; greenfinch. ~ **veler**, buntings. ~ **vuran**, (*ind.*) fan, ventilator. ~ **yutan**, (*orn.*) alpine swift; (*live.*) crib-biting (horse).

yem Food; fodder; (*ich.*) bait; (*mil.*) priming (of muzzle-loader); (*fig.*) deception. ~ **borusu**, (*mil.*) bugle-call for horse-fodder: ~ **borusunu çalmak**, (*fig.*) put s.o. off with idle promises: ~ **dökmek/ koymak**, (*sp.*) spread bait; (*fig.*) deceive: ~ **istemez su istemez**, it's no trouble at all!: ~ **kestirmek**, stop and feed the horses: ~ **i yemek**, rise to/take the bait.

ye·me *vn.* Eating; food; taste: ~ **-içme**, refreshments. ~ **mece**, corruption. ~ **me'k**ği 1 *n*. (*cul.*) eating; food; course, dish; meal; dinner, supper: ~ **borusu**, (*mil.*) bugle-call for food; (*bio.*) oesophagus: ~ **çıkarmak**, serve food: ~ **kitabı**, cookery-book: ~ **meraklısı**, epicure: ~ **odası**, dining-room: ~ **pişirme**, cookery: ~ **seçmek**, be fastidious about food: ~ **sodası**, (*cul.*) baking powder: ~ **takımı**, dinner service: ~ **tezgâhı**, buffet: ~ **üstü**, just at mealtime: ~ **vermek**, invite to a meal: ~ **yemek**, eat food: ~ **yeri**, dining-hall: ~ **e saldırmak**, fall to: ~ **i sokakta yemek**, eat out (at a restaurant, etc.).

yemek2 (**yer**, **yiyecek**, **yiyen**, **yiyor**) **(-i)** Eat; feed; (*live.*) crop; consume; spend; dissipate; (*chem.*) eat, corrode, erode; suffer (stg. unpleasant); take bribes, etc.; not repay a debt. **ye kürküm ye!**, don't judge by appearances!: **yediği naneye bak!**, look at his clumsiness!; what a silly thing to say!: **yediği zehir zıkkım olsun!**, curse him!: **yediğin ekmek gözüne dizine dursun!**, curse his ingratitude!: **yeme de yanında yat!**, delicious food (too good to eat!): **yemeden içmeden**, straight away: **yemeden içmeden kesilmek**, lose one's appetite completely: **yemedik nane bırakmamak**, behave very badly: **yemez**, cunning: **yiyip bitirmek**, devour, consume utterly, exhaust; wear out: **yiyip içmek**, eat and drink.

yemek·hane Dining-hall, refectory. ~ **li**, with food; with a meal; of . . . courses/dishes. ~ **lik**, serving as food; foodstuff; edible; to be eaten; money for food. ~ **siz**, without food/a meal. ~ **üstü**, at dinnertime.

Yemen (*geo.*) The Yemen. ~ **ellerinde Veyselkarani**, utterly lost/at a loss: ~ **kahvesi**, (*bot.*) true Mocha coffee: ~ **safranı**, (*bot.*) dyer's rocket, weld. ~ **li**, (*ethn.*) Yemeni.

yemeni (*mod.*) Light peasant's shoe; coloured cotton kerchief. ~ **ci(lik)**, (trade of) YEMENİ maker/seller. ~ **li**, wearing a YEMENİ.

yemin (*leg.*) Oath; attestation. ~ **billah etm.**, swear in God's name: ~ **bozmak**, violate an oath: ~ **etm.**, swear, take an oath: ~ **ederek vazgeçmek**, abjure: ~ **etsem başım ağrımaz**, I can swear it with a clear conscience (though it's a half-truth): ~ **ettirmek/ verdirmek**, administer an oath: ~ **yükümü**, burden of an oath: ~ **inden hanis olm.**, perjure o.s. ~ **li**, sworn, bound by an oath: ~ **bilirkişi**, sworn expert: ~ **ve yazılı bildiri**, affidavit: ~ **yim oraya ayak basmam!**, I have sworn never to set foot there again!

yemiş (*bot.*) Fruit; fig. ~ **kabuğu**, peel, skin: ~ **vermek**, bear fruit: ~ **yaprağı**, carpel.

yemiş·çi(lik) Fruiterer('s trade). ~ **çil**, (*zoo.*) carpophagous, fruit-eating. ~ **li**, fruit-bearing. ~ **lenmek**, *vi.* fructify. ~ **lik**, fruit-garden, orchard; fruit-store; fruit-dish; fig-orchard.

yemle·me *vn.* Bait; alluring words; (*mil.*) priming. ~ **mek (-i)**, bait (hook/trap); entice, deceive; prime. ~ **nmek**, *vi.* (birds) feed.

yemlik (*live.*) *a.* Suitable for fodder. *n.* Trough; manger; (*fin.*) bribe; (*fig.*) providing a livelihood; (*sl.*) gamblers' victim. ~ **torbası**, nose-bag.

yemyeşil Very green; bright green.

yen[1] (*mod.*) Sleeve; cuff; (*bot.*) spathe.

yen[2] (*fin.*) Japanese currency unit, yen.

yençmek (-i) Pull, tighten; shake down.

yenen (*sp.*) Winner.

yenge (*soc.*) Sister-in-law; brother's wife; aunt-in-law. ~ **lik**, this relationship.

yenge·lç[ci] (*zoo.*) Crab. ~ **(burcu)**, (*ast.*) (constellation of) Cancer: ~ **dönencesi**, (*ast.*) tropic of Cancer: ~ **gibi**, walking sideways; crabwise: ~ **sepeti**, crab-pot: ~ **yağmur kuşu**, (*orn.*) crab plover.

yengi Victory, triumph. ~ **takı**, triumphal arch. ~ **n(lik)**, victor·ious/(-y).

yeni *a.* New; unused, unworn; most recent, latest; original; raw, inexperienced; neo-. *adv.* Recently, newly; just. ~ **başlayan**, novice, beginner: ~ **baştan**, over again, anew, afresh: ~ **çıkma**, latest fashion, new-fangled: ~ **gerçekçilik//izlenimcilik// klasikçilik**, (*art.*) neo-realism//-impressionism// -classicism: ~ **Güney Gal**, *pr.n.* (*geo.*) New South Wales: ~ **kantar**, (*math.*) 100 kilos: ~ **kelime/ sözcük**, (*ling.*) neologism: ~ **kuşak**, (*soc.*) the younger generation: ~ **okka**, (*math.*) one kilogram: ~ **oluşum**, (*bio.*) neoplasm: ~ **unsurlar**, (*soc.*) 'fresh blood', new workers: ~ **yapmak**, do over again, repeat: ~ **Zelanda(lı)**, *pr.n.* (*geo.*) New Zealand(er): ~ **den**, again from the beginning, anew, afresh; re-: ~ **den düzenlenmiş**, (*pub.*) revised: ~ **den** ~ **ye**, very recently; ever anew.

yeni·ay (*ast.*) New moon. ~ **bahar**, (*bot., cul.*) red pepper, pimento, capsicum, paprika. ~ **cami**, *pr.n.* (*arch.*) the New Mosque (Istanbul): ~ **traşı**, (*mod.*) a rough-and-ready hair-cut. ~ **ce**, fairly new/ recent: ~ **eleğim seni nerelere asayım**, fussily over-attentive to stg. new. ~ **çağ**, (*his.*) modern times. ~ **çeri**, (*his.*) Janissary; (*fig.*) swashbuckler, bully: ~ **ağası**, Janissary commander-in-chief: ~ **odası**, Janissary corps: ~ **traşı** = ~ CAMİ: ~ **çerilik**, (*his.*) qualities/duties of Janissaries; Janissary period; (*fig.*) roistering breach of the peace. ~ **den** = YENİ. ~ **dendoğuş**, rebirth, new start; (*his.*) Renaissance. ~ **doğan**, (*med.*) new-born. ~ **dünya**, (*geo.*) the New World; (*bot.*) loquat; (*dom.*) ornamental glass ball: ~ **aslanı**, (*zoo.*) puma. ~ **hisar**, (*geo., his.*) Didyma.

yeni·lk[gi 1] *a.* Nibbled, gnawed; corroded. *n.* (Insect, etc.) bite.

yenik[2] *a.* Defeated. ~ **düşmek**, be defeated: ~ **saymak**, consider defeated.

yeni·le (*sp.*) False start, restart. ~ **leme**, *vn.* replacement; renewal. ~ **lemek (-i)**, renew; renovate; replace; repeat. ~ **len**, (*sp.*) let. ~ **lenme**, *vn.* regeneration. ~ **lenmek**, *vp.* ~ **leşmek**, *vi.* become

new/modern. ~ **leştirmek (-i)**, make new; repair modernize. ~ **letmek (-i, -e)**, *vc.* ~ **leyici**, innovator

yenilgi Defeat.

yenilik Newness; novelty; (*fig.*) rawness, in experience. ~ **korkusu**, (*psy.*) fear of change neophobia: ~ **yapmak**, make/bring about changes, ~ **çi**, s.o. loving change/reform.

yenil·me *vn.* Defeat. ~ **mek**[1], *vp.* = YENMEK[1]; b defeated/overcome; (*sp.*) lose. ~ **mez**, undefeated invincible.

yenilmek[2] *vp.* = YEMEK[2]. Be eaten; be edible. **yenilir** edible: **yenilir yutulur gibi değil**, it's not fit to eat (*fig.*) it's intolerable; unpleasant.

yenim (*min.*) Corrosion. ~ **önler**, (*chem.*) anti corrosive.

yenimaden (*min.*) German silver.

yenir *v.* = YENMEK[2]. *a.* Edible. ~ **salyangoz**, (*zoo.* escargot. ~ **ce**, (*bot.*) canker; (*bio.*) decay.

yenisömürgecilik (*pol.*) The new (economic, ideological) colonialism.

yeniş·ememek (*vi.*) Be unable to defeat each other, (*sp.*) tie, draw. ~ **mek**, struggle/wrestle with each other.

yeni·türeti(m) (*ling.*) Neologism. ~ **yetişenler**, the younger generation. ~ **yetme(lik)**, at the age o puberty; (*iron.*) (being) the budding generation.

yenli (*mod.*) Having sleeves/cuffs.

yen·me[1] *vn.* Conquest, defeat. ~ **mek**[1] **(-i)**, overcome, conquer; be victorious; (*sp.*) win; (chess) checkmate; (*fig.*) get the better of.

yen·me[2] *vn.* Erosion, corrosion; attrition. ~ **mek**[2] *vp.* = YEMEK[2]; be eaten, etc.; be edible; (*tex.*) be worn/frayed; (*min.*) be corroded: **yenenle yanana n dayanır**, food and fuel don't last long: **yenmez**, *a* inedible: **yenmiş**, bitten, gnawed; corroded.

yepelek Slim, slender; graceful; tender.

yepermek *vi.* Run quickly; rush about in confusion.

yepyeni Brand new, mint.

yer[1] *v.* = YEMEK[2].

yer[2] *n.* Earth; ground; floor; place, position; (*th.*) seat; site; space, room; landed property; situation, employment, duty; mark, scar, trace; (*ast.*) World, Earth. ~ **+**, *a.* Earth, ground; geo-; terrestrial; (*zoo.*) ground-: ~ **açmak**, make room for: ~ **almak (-de)**, appear; be involved in: ~ **ayırtma**, reservation: ~ **belirteci**, (*ling.*) adverb of place: ~ **bulmak**, find a place, get employment: ~ **cücesi**, short/small but very cunning: ~ **değiştirmek**, displace; (*sp.*) change ends: ~ **demir gök bakır**, a hopeless outlook: ~ **döşemesi**, (*dom.*) floor-covering: ~ **etm.**, leave a mark; (*fig.*) impress, make an impression: ~ EŞEĞİ: ~ **fiziği**, geophysics: ~ **göçmesi**, (*geol.*) landslide: ~ **gösterici**, (*th.*) usherette: ~ **hızı**, (*aer.*) ground speed: ~ **hostesi**, (*aer.*) ground hostess: ~ KABUĞU: ~ **kabul etmez (-i)**, a great sinner: ~ MEŞE/PALAMUDU: ~ **odası**, ground-level room: ~ **olm. (-e)**, be room for: ~ **ölçme bilgisi**, (*math.*) geodesy: ~ **öpmek**, kiss the ground (in salutation): ~ PIRASASI: ~ SARSINTISI: ~ **seçimi**, choice of site: ~ **sofrası**, (*dom.*) cloth spread on the ground: ~ **solucanı**, (*zoo.*) earthworm: ~ **tezeği**, (*bot.*) peat: ~ **tutmak**, take one's place/seat; reserve/book a place; (*adm.*) fill a position: ~

vermek (-e), bring about; cause to happen: ~ **yarılıp içine girmek**, be swallowed up in the ground, disappear: ~ **yatağı**, bed on the floor: ~ ~, in several places: ~ ~**inden oynamak**, be all over the place/in confusion: ~ **yok!**, no room!: ~ **yurt**, dwelling: ~ YÜZÜ.

yerde, on the ground; on the Earth: ~ **(-ecek)**, [187] instead of (do)ing [**gelecek yerde**, instead of coming]: ~ **kalmak**, not be appreciated/respected: ~ **sürünmek**, crawl: ~ **yenik**, (*sp*.) knock-out.

yerden, from the ground; from the Earth: ~ **bitme**, short, squat; (*fig*.) upstart, parvenu: ~ **çıkarmak**, get rid of; disinfest: ~ **göğe kadar**, completely, utterly: ~ **selam**, very respectful greeting (touching the ground): ~ **yapma**, very short: ~ **yere çalmak**, misuse, illtreat: ~ **yere çarpmak**, discredit, run down: ~ **yere vurmak**, throw to the ground violently.

yere: ~ **bakar yürek yakar**, not so innocent; full of tricks: ~ **bakmak**, cast one's eyes down (in shame/modesty); (elderly) be near to death: ~ **batası âdet**, an accursed custom: ~ **batmak**, perish: ~ **çalmak**, defeat, discredit: ~ **çarpmak**, knock down: ~ **düşmek**, (order) be disregarded/ignored: ~ **geçmek**, feel ready to bury o.s. for shame: ~ **geçsin!**, may he perish!: ~ **göğe koyamamak**, greatly honour: ~ **kapanmak**, prostrate o.s.: ~ **vurmak** = ~ ÇALMAK.

yeri: ~ **göğe birbirine katmak**, move heaven and earth: ~ **olm.**, be appropriate/suitable: ~ **ölçmek**, fall prostrate: ~ **öpmek**, (*jok*.) kiss the ground, fall down: ~ **soğumadan**, he's just left: ~ **yok**, it is uncalled for/out of place: ~ **yurdu belirsiz**, vagabond, tramp:

yerin: ~ **dibi**, (*geo*.) abyss: ~ **dibine batmak/ geçmek/girmek**, be full of shame/confusion: ~ **kulağı var!**, walls have ears!

yerinde, in its place; *in situ*; suitable; to the point, well put; on the mark; correct, right: ~ **bırakmak**, (*adm*.) make (an official) permanent; (*ed*.) keep down (a pupil): ~ **iş görmek**, do just the right thing: ~ **olarak**, rightly, deservedly: ~ **saymak**, make no progress; (*mil*.) mark time: ~ **söz söylemek**, say just the right words: ~ **su çıkmak**, leave one's place without reason: ~ **yeller esmek**, be gone for ever: ~ **lik**, appropriateness; (*leg*.) priority.

yerinden: ~ **ayırmak**, move stg. from its place: ~ **çıkarmak**, displace; depose; (*med*.) dislocate: ~ **oynamak**, leave one's place; be dislocated; get excited: ~ **oynatmak**, (*adm*.) transfer; dislodge: ~ **yönetim**, (*adm*.) decentralized government.

yerine, *post*. [94] instead of, in place of: ~ **bakar**, deputy; agent: ~ **bırakmak**, appoint as deputy: ~ **geçmek**, replace s.o.: ~ **gelmek**, be done; come back into place; act for: ~ **getirmek**, do; complete; fulfil; carry out (an order): ~ **kaim olm.**, act for, take the place of: ~ **konulamaz**, irreplaceable: ~ **koymak/kullanmak**, replace stg.; consider: ~ **masruftur**, it's well spent: ~ **oturmak**, fit well.

yerini: ~ **almak**, take s.o.'s place; displace s.o.: ~

beğenmek/sevmek, (*bot*.) grow well: ~ **bulmak**, (order) be carried out; (man) find the right job: ~ **doldurmak**, be adequate for the job; compensate: ~ **ısıtmak**, hang on to one's job: ~ **sevmez**, (*bot*.) not grow well: ~ **tutmak (-in)**, take stg.'s place, do duty for.

yer-: ~ **le beraber**, level with the ground: ~ **le bir/ yeknesak etm.**, raze to the ground: ~ **le gök bir olsa!**, whatever happens!: ~ **lerde sürünmek**, be in a pitiable state: ~ **lere geçmek** = YERE: ~ **lere kadar eğilmek**, show excessive respect: ~ **leri süpürmek**, (*mod*.) be very long (and sweep the ground): ~ **lerinize!**, (*sp*.) on your marks!

yer(b). = YERBİLİM.

yer·altı[nı] *n*. (*geol*.) Subsurface; (*arch*.) tunnel; underground chamber; foundation: *a*. subterranean, underground; (*fig*.) secret, underground: ~ **su seviyesi**, water table: ~ **suyu**, groundwater. ~ **beri**, (*ast*.) perigee. ~ **betim(sel)**, topograph·y/ (-ical). ~ **bilgini**, geologist. ~ **bilim(ci)**, geolo·gy/ (-gist). ~ **bilimsel**, geological. ~ **bölüm**, plot of land. ~ **çekimi**[ni], (*phys*.) gravitation, gravity: ~ **ivmesi**, gravitational acceleration: ~ **kuvveti**, force of gravity. ~ **çekimsel**, gravitational. ~ **çekirdeği**[ni], (*geol*.) earth's core, nucleus. ~ **değişim**, transposition. ~ **değiştirme**, (*math*.) displacement. ~ **deş**, compatriot; (*chem*.) isotope. ~ **deşsel**, isotopic. ~ **domuzu**[nu], (*zoo*.) aardvark. ~ **edici**, (*eng*.) spacer. ~ **edoğrulum**, (*bot*.) geotropism. ~ **el**, local; regional; ambient; localized, discontinuous: ~ **saat**, (*ast*.) local time: ~ **uyuşturum**, (*med*.) local anaesthetic: ~ **Yönetim Bakan(lığ)ı**, (*adm*.) Minis·ter/(-try) for Local Government. ~ **elleşmek**, become localized. ~ **elleştirmek (-i)**, *vc*. ~ **ellik**, localization. ~ **elması**[nı], (*bot*.) Jerusalem artichoke. ~ **eşeği**[ni], (*ent*.) stag-beetle. ~ **ey**, land; terrain; (*geol*.) rock. ~ **feslеğeni**[ni], (*bot*.) marjoram. ~ **fıstığı**[nı], (*bot*.) groundnut. ~ **ısıl**, geothermal.

yer·gi(ci) (*lit*.) Sati·re/(-rist). ~ **gin**, ugly, unpleasant. ~ **ginlik**, evil; unpleasantness. ~ **gisel**, satirical. ~ **ici**, critical. ~ **ilmek**, *vp*. = YERMEK.

yeri// ~ **n//** ~ **nde//** ~ **nden//** ~ **ne//** ~ **nin** = YER.

yer·ine[l]**ç**[ci] (*geol*.) Trough, geosyncline. ~ **inel**, (*lit*.) allegorical.

yerin·me *vn*. Regret. ~ **mek (-e)**, be sorry for/regret stg.

yer·kabuğu[nu] (*geol*.) Earth's crust. ~ **katı**[nı], (*arch*.) ground floor. ~ **küre**, (*geo*.) earth, world; sphere. ~ **lahanası**[nı], (*bot*.) type of rape.

yerleş·ik Settled; established; resident; permanent; (*med*.) endemic. ~ **ilmek**, *vp*. ~ **im/** ~ **me**, *vn*. settling; inhabiting; housing: *a*. residential: ~ **merkezi**, centre of population. ~ **ke**, (*ed*.) campus. ~ **mek (-e)**, settle down; become established; take root; find work/employment: **(-de)**, settle/live in; establish o.s. at: *imp.v*. become accepted, be used. ~ **tirilmek**, *vp*. ~ **tirme**, *vn*. settling; siting. ~ **tirmek (-i, -e)**, *vc*. settle; populate; put into place, arrange in order; accommodate; find employment; (*eng*.) bed down.

yer·li *a*. Fixed; local; (*soc*.) autochthonous; indigenous, native; (*fin*.) domestic: *n*. native: ~ **çekirge**, (*ent*.) Anatolian locust: ~ **çit**, (*agr*.) fence; hedge: ~ **dolap**, (*dom*.) built-in cupboard: ~ **mal**,

domestic/local produce: ~ **yerinde**, each in his/its own place; ship-shape: ~ **yerine**, each into his/its own place: ~ ~**si**, local inhabitant: ~ **yersiz**, disorderly. ~**lik**, locality. ~**mantarı**[m], (*myc.*) Périgord/French truffle.
yer·me *vn.* Loathing; criticism; blame. ~**meci**, (*lit.*) satirist. ~**mek (-i)**, dislike, loathe; criticize, disparage; satirize. ~**meli**, critical, pejorative.
yer·merkezli (*ast.*) Geocentric. ~**meşesi/ palamudu**[nu], (*bot.*) germander. ~**mumu**[nu], (*geol.*) ozocerite. ~**ölçümcü**, surveyor. ~**örümceği**[ni], (*zoo.*) (?) spider bug. ~**öte**[si], (*ast.*) apogee. ~**özekçil**, (*ast.*) geocentric. ~**pırasası**[m], (*bot.*) motherwort. ~**sakızı**[m](**lı**), (*geol.*) bitu·men/ (-minous). ~**sarmısağı**[m], (*bot.*) ground ivy. ~**sarsıntısı**[m], (*geol.*) earthquake. ~**sel**, terrestrial; earth, ground. ~**seme**, localization. ~**sıçanı**[m], (*zoo.*) mole. ~**siz**, homeless; (*fig.*) unfounded, out of place, inappropriate: ~ **telaş**, false alarm: ~ **yurtsuz**, homeless; stranger. ~**sizlik**, homelessness; unsuitability. ~**sizme**, (*geol.*) displacement. ~**solucanı**[m], (*zoo.*) earthworm. ~ **şekli**, (*geo.*) relief. ~**ucu**[nu], (*geo.*) pole. ~**yağı**[m], (*geol., chem.*) oil, petroleum. ~**yazım**, land registration. ~**yuvar(lağ)ı**[m], (*geo.*) terrestrial globe. ~**yüzü**[nü], earth('s surface): ~**nde öyle bir şey yok**, there's nothing like it in the world, it's unique.
yestehlemek *vi.* (*jok.*) Relieve nature, defecate.
yeşer·mek *vi.* Become/turn green; (*bot.*) produce leaves. ~**ti**, green place. ~**tmek (-i)**, *vc.* make green.
yeşil Green; verdant; fresh (vegetables); unripe (fruit). ~ **çekirge**, (*ent.*) great green grasshopper: ~ **karga**, (*orn.*) roller: ~ **lahana**, (*bot.*) type of small cabbage: ~ **nadas**, (*agr.*) green manuring: ~ **oy**, (*adm.*) abstention, neutral vote: ~ **ötleğen**, (*orn.*) greenish warbler: ~ **şist**, (*geol.*) greenstone.
yeşil·ay *pr.n.* Green Crescent (Tk. temperance society). ~**baca**[l]**k**[ğı], (*orn.*) greenshank. ~**bağa**, (*zoo.*) tree-frog. ~**baş**, (*orn.*) mallard drake: ~**ın geri**, mallard duck. ~**imsi/**~**imtırak**, greenish. ~**lenmek**, become/turn green; be freshened: (-e), (*sl.*) be sexually excited by; be envious of. ~**li**, mixed with green; wearing green. ~**lik**, greenness; verdure; (*agr.*) meadow; silage; (*cul.*) salad; green vegetables, greens. ~**sazan**, (*ich.*) tench.
yeşim (*geol.*) Jade.
yetene[l]**k**[ği] Capacity, capability, aptitude; faculty. ~ **kazanmamış**, novice. ~**li**, capable, apt. ~**siz**, incapable; unskilled.
yeter *a.* Sufficient, enough, ample. *int.* Enough! *v.* = YETMEK. ~ **bulmak**, be satisfied: ~ **çoğunluk**, (*adm.*) simple majority: ~ **de artar**, enough and more than enough: ~ **derecede**, sufficiently: ~**i kadar/**~**ince**, adequately, sufficiently.
yeter·li Sufficient, adequate; capable, competent, qualified. ~**lik**, capacity, competence; efficiency; qualification: ~ **belgesi**, (*adm.*) licence: ~ **eylemi**, (*ling.*) potential verb [151]: ~ **önergesi**, (*adm.*) motion declaring discussion sufficient. ~**lilik**, sufficiency. ~**sayı**, (*adm.*) quorum. ~**siz**, insufficient; incapable; under-. ~**sizlik**, insufficiency; incapacity; disability.

yet·i (*psy.*) Natural faculty. ~**iklik**, capacity, aptitude.
yetim Orphan; fatherless child. ~**ler bakımı**, child care. ~**hane**, orphanage. ~**lik**, being an orphan, orphanhood.
yet·ingen Contented, satisfied. ~ **ingenlik**, contentment, satisfaction. ~**inmek (-le)**, be satisfied/ contented with. ~**irmek (-i, -e)**, (*fin.*) manage on/ with; bring up (children).
yetiş·ici(lik) (*med.*) Intern(ship). ~**ilmek**, *vp.* ~ **kin**, quite mature; adult; skilled; (girl) marriageable, nubile: ~ **ler eğitimi**, adult education. ~**im/** ~ **me**, *vn.* training. ~**mek (-e)**, reach; attain; catch up; suffice; attain maturity, grow up, be brought up; be ready/on hand in time; catch (train, etc.); come to the help of; live to see (an event); be contemporary with; (*bot.*) grow: **yetiş(in)!**, help!: **yetişme(yesi)!**, curse you/(him)!: **yetişmekte olan**, (*ed.*) a budding (scholar, etc.). ~**men(lik)**, apprentice(ship); trainee(ship). ~**miş** or ~ KIN.
yetiştir·ici (*live.*) Breeder; producer; (*ed.*) coach. ~**ilmek (-e)**, *vp.* ~**im**, (*ed., live.*) training. ~**me**, *vn.* bringing up; breeding; cultivation: ~**si (-in)**, brought up by . . .. ~**mek (-i, -e)**, *vc.* = YETIŞMEK: cause to arrive/reach, etc.; (*ed.*) bring up, educate; (*live.*) breed; train; (*agr.*) cultivate, grow, produce; make do, manage; convey (news); be overhasty in giving information.
yetke (*adm.*) Authority, competence; (*psy.*) trust. ~ **taraftarı/**~**li**, authoritarian.
yetki Authority, capacity, power; competence; qualification. ~ **belgesi**, diploma; licence: ~ **vermek**, authorize: ~**si dışına çıkmak**, get out of one's depth: ~**sini kaldırmak**, disqualify.
yetki·deş(lik) (*leg.*) Attorney(ship): ~ **belgesi**, power of attorney. ~**le(ndir)mek (-i)**, consider competent. ~**li**, authorized, competent; qualified: ~ **kişi/kurul/makamlar/merciler**, (*adm., leg.*) competent authori·ty/(-ties): ~ **olm.**, be empowered: ~ **yargılık**, (*leg.*) competence, jurisdiction. ~**lilik**, competence.
yetkin Perfect; (*bot.*) ripe. ~**ci(lik)**, perfection·ist/ (-ism). ~**leşmek**, *vi.* become perfect; ripen. ~**leştir-mek (-i)**, *vc.* perfect; ripen. ~**lik**, perfection.
yetkisiz Without authority; not competent; unqualified. ~**lik**, lack of authority//competence// qualifications.
yet·mek (-e) Suffice, be enough; reach, attain: **yeter ki**, it is enough that . . .: = YETER. ~**mez(lik)**, insufficient/(-ency).
yetmiş Seventy. ~ **yedi göbekten beri**, for (many) generations: ~**te bir**, one seventieth. ~**er**, seventy each; seventy at a time. ~**inci (70.)**, seventieth. ~**lik**, having seventy (parts); worth seventy (units); seventy years old. [*Further phrases* = KIRK.]
yevm Day. ~**i**, daily. ~**iye**, *n.* daily pay/wage: *adv.* every day: ~ **defteri**, (*fin.*) day-book. ~**iyeci**, day-wage worker. ~**iyeli**, *a.* connected with day-wage.
yey- = YEĞ-.
Yezi·di (*rel.*) Yazidi. ~**l**[t][di], impious, cruel; vile fellow. ~**tlik**, treachery, evil.
-yı *n. suf.* (*after vowel*) [28] = -i[1] [HALIYI].
yığ·a (*phys.*) Enthalpy. ~**a**[l]**k**[ğı], (*min.*) bunker.

~dırmak (-i, -e), *vc.* = YIĞMAK. ~ılı, heaped, piled up. ~ılım, *(phys.)* population. ~ılışma, congestion, bottle-neck. ~ılma, *vn.* concentration; piling up. ~ılmak, *vp.* be heaped up: *vi.* accumulate; crowd together; be congested; fall in a faint; collapse.

yığım *(fin.)* Freezing, pegging. ~cı(lık), stock·ist/ (-ing). ~lamak (-i), stock. ~lık, storage fee.

yığın Heap; mass; pile; crowd; batch, collection. ~ buzla, *(geo.)* pack-ice: ~ ~, in heaps: ~la, heaps of . . .: ~lar, *(soc.)* the masses.

yığın·a¹k^{g_1} Heap, pile, mass; *(mil.)* concentration; *(bot.)* colony; *(geo.)* gentle slope. ~bulut, *(met.)* strato-cumulus. ~lık, crowd, mass. ~mak, *vp.* be concentrated. ~tı, accumulation; heap; drift (snow, etc.); crowd.

yığış·ık Piled up. ~ım, *(geol.)* conglomerate. ~ımlı, *(math.)* cumulative. ~ma, *vn.* crowd; congestion. ~mak, *vi.* crowd together; collect, gather; pile up.

yığ·ma Stowage. ~mak (-i, -e), collect in a heap; stow; stack, pile up; accumulate; *(mil.)* mass (troops).

yıka·ma *vn.* Act of washing; bathing; flushing; *(cin.)* developing: ~makinesi, washing machine: ~tozu, washing powder. ~ma¹ç^{c_1}, *(cin., chem.)* developer. ~mak (-i), wash; bath; *(chem.)* leach; *(cin.)* develop. ~nır, *a.* washable. ~nma, *vn.* washing; *(rel.)* ablution: ~odası, washroom: ~teknesi, bath-tub. ~nmak, *vp.* be washed: *vi.* wash o.s.; have a bath. ~tmak (-i, -e), *vc.* ~yıcı, *(cin.)* developer; washer.

yık·ı Ruins. ~ıcı, *a.* destructive; disastrous: *n.* ship-breaker; demolisher; junk-dealer. ~ık, demolished; broken down, ruined; devastated. ~ılım, *(med.)* deterioration. ~ılma, *vn.* demolition. ~ılmak, *vp.* be demolished: *vi.* fall down; collapse; crumble; become decrepit; clear out, take o.s. off: yıkıl git!, clear out! ~ım, disaster, destruction, ruin; *(fin.)* great expense/loss; crash; *(med.)* catabolism: ~döküm, damage: ~olm., be ruined. ~ımcı, demolisher. ~ımlık, destruction. ~ıntı, heap of ruins, debris: ~olm. (-e), be the ruin of. ~ışma, contradiction; *(sp.)* wrestling. ~kın, ruinous; dilapidated, about to collapse. ~ma, *vn.* demolition, destruction. ~mak (-i), pull down; demolish; destroy; ruin; overthrow; *(for.)* fell; *(live.)* unload. ~tırılmak, *vp.* ~tırmak (-i, -e), *vc.* have pulled down, etc.

yıl *(ast.)* Year; any twelve-month period. ~BAŞI: ~DÖNÜMÜ: ~ on iki ay, throughout the year; continuously: ~da, per year, *per annum*: ~lar ~ı, for many a long year: ~larca, for years.

yılan *(zoo.)* Snake; *(fig.)* s.o. cunning and treacherous. ~akbabası, *(orn.)* secretary-bird: ~ gibi, cold and calculating; treacherous, repulsive: ~ dili, *(bot.)* adder's tongue: ~ gömleği, snake's skin; its slough: ~ hikâyesi, long-winded story, stg. that never ends: ~ iğnesi, *(ich.)* pipe-fish: ~ kartalı, *(orn.)* short-toed eagle: ~ kemiği, torturing sense of guilt: ~ kuşu, *(orn.)* African darter: ~ oynatan, snake-charmer: ~ sokması, snake-bite:

~ın kuyruğuna basmak, arouse the spite of s.o. powerful/venomous.

yılan·balığı^{n_1} *(zoo.)* Eel: ~ anası, viviparous· blenny. ~başı^{n_1}, *(zoo.)* panther cowry. ~cı, snake-charmer. ~cı¹k^{g_1}, *(bot.)* sage; *(med.)* erysipelas. ~cıkçı, quack-doctor. ~cıl, *(orn.)* snake-eating bird; sacred ibis. ~kavi, spiral, winding. ~lama, snaking. ~sı, serpentine, snake-like: ~ balık, *(ich.)* ophidium, cusk eel. ~taşı^{n_1}, *(geol.)* serpentine. ~yastığı^{n_1}, *(bot.)* dragon arum; cuckoo-pint. ~yastığıgiller, *(bot.)* Araceae, arum family. ~yıldızı^{n_1}, *(zoo.)* brittle-star.

yıl·başı^{n_1} The New Year; New Year's Day. ~beyıl, year by year.

yıldır·ak *a.* Bright, shining: *n.* lightning: *pr.n.* (*ast.*) Canopus. ~amak, *vi.* shine.

yıldır·gan Terrifying. ~ı, terror(ization). ~ıcı, terrifying; causing fear/anxiety. ~ılmak, *vp.* = YILDIRMAK.

yıldırım *(met.)* Lightning; thunderbolt; *(fig.)* express. ~ cezası, *(leg.)* on the spot/automatic fine: ~ gibi, with great speed/urgency: ~ nikâhı, *(leg.)* special-licence wedding: ~ savaşı, *(mil.)* blitzkrieg: ~ takla, *(sp.)* wrestling hold: ~ telgrafı, express telegram: ~la vurulmuşa dönmek, be thunderstruck (with terror, etc.). ~kıran/~lık/~savar/ ~siperi, lightning conductor.

yıldır·ma *vn.* Act of terrifying, terror. ~macı, terrorist. ~mak (-i), frighten, daunt, terrorize.

yıldız *(ast.)* Star, heavenly body; Pole Star; *(geo.)* north; *(pub.)* asterisk; *(fig.)* destiny; *(cin.)* star. ~ +, *a.* (*cin.*) Star-; *(ast.)* star, stellar; sidereal: ~ akmak/kaymak/uçmak, shooting-star appear: ~ avcısı, *(cin., sp.)* talent scout: ~ bağlantılı, *(el.)* star-connected: ~ barışıklığı (ile), being on good terms: ~ im/işareti, *(pub.)* asterisk: ~ kümesi, *(ast.)* star cluster: ~ şeklinde, asteroidal, stellate: ~ üçgen, *(el.)* star-delta: ~ yılı, *(ast.)* sidereal year: ~ı barışmak (-le), be on good terms with: ~ı dişi, sympathetic, popular: ~ı düşkün/düşük, unfortunate, ill-fated: ~ı kara, unlucky: ~ı parlak, lucky: ~ı parlamak, be lucky/successful: ~ı sönmek, be unlucky/unsuccessful: ~LARARASI: ~ları saymak, *(med.)* count sheep, suffer from insomnia.

yıldız·bilim Astrology. ~bilimci(lik), (work of) astrologer. ~böceği^{n_i}, *(ent.)* firefly; glow-worm. ~cı¹k^{g_1}, *(cin.)* starlet. ~cılık, star system. ~çiçeği^{n_i}, *(bot.)* dahlia. ~karayel, *(geo.)* north-north-west; *(met.)* NNW wind. ~lamak, *(met.)* wind blow from the north; clouds disperse and stars appear. ~lararası, *(ast.)* interstellar. ~lı, starry; covered with stars; astral: ~ vatoz, *(ich.)* starry ray. ~lık, *(ast.)* planetarium. ~poyraz, *(geo.)* north-north-east; *(met.)* NNE wind. ~sal, *(ast.)* sidereal. ~sı, quasi-stellar. ~taşı^{n_i}, *(geol.)* aventurine. ~yağmuru^{n_u}, *(ast.)* star stream. ~yeli^{n_i}, *(met.)* north wind.

yıldönümü^{n_ü} Anniversary.

yılgı Terror, fear. ~cı(lık), *(pol.)* terror·ist/(-ism). ~n, terrified, cowed, daunted. ~nlık, being terrified.

yılhalkası^{n_1} *(bot.)* Annual ring.

yılık Crooked; bent; cross-eyed.
yılış·ık Sticky; importunate; grinning unpleasantly. ~ **ıklık**, stickiness. ~ **kanlık**, stickiness; impudence. ~ **ma**, *vn.* ~ **mak**, *vi.* grin unpleasantly/impudently.
yılkı (*live.*) Herd of horses/donkeys, etc.
yıl·ki ~ (**bu**), this year's . . . . ~ **lamak** *vi.* be a year in one place; become a year old. ~ **lanmak**, *vi.* become . . . years old; remain several years; grow old; (affair) drag on for a long time: **yıllanmış Yahudi aklı**, (*pej.*) great cunning. ~ **latmak** (**-i**), keep for years; delay for a long time. ~ **lık**, *a.* . . . years old; yearly, annual: *n.* (*fin.*) annual cost/rent, etc.; (*pub.*) almanac, directory, annual; (*live.*) yearling: ~ **ödenek/taksit**, (*fin.*) annuity: ~ **ına**, for a year. ~ **lıkçı**, s.o. employed by the year. ~ **lıklı**, paid by the year.
yıl·mak (**-den**) Be afraid; dread. ~ **maz**, undaunted; dreadnought.
yıp·rak Dilapidated, worn out. ~ **ranma**, *vn.* wear and tear: ~ **payı**, (*fin.*) amortization, depreciation. ~ **ranmak**, *vi.* wear out; become worn; grow old/ tired prematurely; (*fig.*) lose face. ~ **ratıcı**, wearing; exhausting; toilsome. ~ **ratma**, *vn.* wearing out, erosion: ~ **savaşı**, (*mil.*) war of attrition. ~ **ratmak** (**-i**), wear out; wear (by friction).
yır (*mus.*) Song, folk-song. ~ **lamak**, *vi.* sing.
yır·ık Torn, split. ~ **ılmak**, *vp.* ~ **mak** (**-i**), tear/split slightly. ~ **tıcı**, tearing, rending; (*fig.*) cruel, bloodthirsty: ~ **hayvan//kuş(lar)**, beast(s)//bird(s) of prey: ~ **kartal**, (*orn.*) tawny eagle. ~ **tıcılık**, preying; bloodthirstiness. ~ **tıcımartıgiller**, (*orn.*) skuas. ~ **tıcısine¹kᵍⁱ**, (*ent.*) robber-fly. ~ **tık**, torn; ragged, tattered; (*live.*) broken-in; (*fig.*) shameless, brazen-faced: ~ **pırtık**, all in pieces/rags. ~ **tılma**, *vn.*: ~ **direnci**, (*phys.*) tearing strength. ~ **tılmak**, *vp.* be torn; (*live.*) be broken in: *vi.* become insolent/ shameless. ~ **tınmak**, *vi.* shriek in desperation/fear; struggle hopelessly. ~ **tlak**, (eye, etc.) gaping as if torn. ~ **tma¹çᶜⁱ**, *n.* (*mod.*) slit. ~ **tmaçlı**, *a.* slit. ~ **tmak** (**-i**), tear; rend; burst; tear to pieces; (*live.*) break in; assault. ~ **ttırmak** (**-i, -e**), *vc.*
yısa *int.* (*naut.*) Heave!, hoist!, pull! ~ **beraber!**, all together now!: ~ **etm.**, heave, hoist: ~ ~, with all one's strength; at the most.
-yış *vn. suf.* (*after vowel*) [172] = -iş [ANLAYIŞ].
-yi *n. suf.* (*after vowel*) [28] = -i¹ [GEZİYİ].
yiği¹tᵈⁱ *a.* Brave; strong-hearted; intrepid, confident. *n.* Young man; manly youngster.
yiğit·başıⁿⁱ (*his.*) Guild inspector. ~ **çe**, bravely; confidently. ~ **lendirmek** (**-i**), *vc.* ~ **lenmek/** ~ **leşmek**, *vi.* grow up; become brave; pluck up courage. ~ **lik**, courage, pluck, heroism: ~ **çıbanı**, (*med.*) acne: ~ **sende kalsın!**, keep up the good work!: ~ **taslamak**, pretend to be brave: ~ **e leke sürmemek**, save one's face.
yin (*bio.*) Body. ~ **bilim**, anatomy.
yine *adv.* [204] Again, still: = GENE. ~ **de**, however: ~ **işini uydurdu!**, he's managed it again!: ~ **olm.**, be repeated: ~ **yolcu olduk**, I must be on my travels again: ~ **yüz yüze bakmak**, meet again.
yine·leme *vn.* Repeating; (*ling.*) repetition. ~ **lemek** (**-i**), repeat; reiterate. ~ **lemeli**, repeated; repetitious;

~ **eylem**, (*ling.*) repetitive verb [148]: ~ **olarak**, repeatedly. ~ **lemeyle**, repeatedly. ~ **lenme**, *vn.* repetition. ~ **lenmek**, *vp.* ~ **li**, *adv.* again, re-.
yirmi Twenty. ~ **beşlik**, twenty-five kurush coin: ~ **yaş dişi**, (*bio.*) wisdom tooth: ~ **de bir**, one twentieth. ~ **lik**, containing twenty (parts); worth twenty (units): ~ **bir genç**, twenty-year old youth. ~ **nci (20.)**, twentieth. ~ **şer**, twenty each; twenty at a time. ~ **şerlik**, containing twenty (units). [*Further phrases* = KIRK.]
-yiş *vn. suf.* (*after vowel*) [172] = -iş [SÖYLEYİŞ].
yit·ik Lost: ~ **ler**, losses. ~ **ikçi**, beachcomber. ~ **iklik**, absence. ~ **im**, loss. ~ **imlik**, disappearance. ~ **irce**, (*naut.*) average. ~ **irim/** ~ **irme**, *vn.*; disadvantage. ~ **iriş**, loss. ~ **irmek** (**-i**), lose; cause to go astray, ruin; (*ling.*) elide. ~ **mek**, *vi.* be lost; be wasted; go astray; go to ruin.
yiv Groove; fluting; line; (*mil.*) rifling; (*eng.*) chamfer; (*mod.*) hem; stripe. ~ **açmak**, groove; rifle: chase. ~ **açar**, diestock; grooving/rifling tool: ~ **lokması**, (*eng.*) die. ~ **li**, grooved, lined; rifled; chamfered; striped.
yiy·ecek *v.* = YEMEK²: *a.* edible; to be eaten: *n.* food; eatables: ~ **güvesi**, (*ent.*) meal moth. ~ **en**, *v.* = YEMEK²: *n.* eater: *suf.* -eater. ~ **esi**, appetite. ~ **esizlik**, (*med.*) anorexia, lack of appetite: ~ **sayrılığı**, anorexia nervosa. ~ **ici**, (*adm.*) corrupt, taking bribes; (*chem.*) corrosive. ~ **icilik**, corruption; corrosion. ~ **im**, food: ~ **yeri kullanmak** (**-i**), use for one's profit. ~ **imli**, pleasant to eat. ~ **inti**, edibles; foodstuff. ~ **ip** = YEMEK². ~ **iş**, way of eating.
YK·B = YAPI VE KREDİ BANKASI. ~ **K** = YÜKSEK KÜLTÜR KURULLARI.
-yken *v. suf.* [190] = İKEN [GELMEKTEYKEN].
-yle/-yla *post.* [86] = İLE [GEMİCİYLE; KARISIYLA].
-ymiş/-ymış/-ymuş/-ymüş *v. suf.* = İMİŞ [İZCİYMİŞ].
Y. M(üh). = YÜKSEK MÜHENDİS.
yo *int.* Hey!, what are you up to?; I won't have it!
YO = (*ed.*) YÜKSEK OKULU.
yobaz (*rel.*) Extreme fanatic; bigot. ~ **laşmak**, become fanatical. ~ **lık**, fanaticism; bigotry.
yo·ga (*phil.*) Yoga. ~ **gi**, yogi.
yoğ- = YOK. ~ **almak**, *vi.* disappear. ~ **altılmak**, *vp.* ~ **altım**, consumption, use. ~ **altmak** (**-i**), consume, use up.
yoğ-ruk(luk) (*min.*) Plastic(ity). ~ **rulmak**, *vp.* = YOĞURMAK; be dented/bent. ~ **rum**, (*psy.*) development, formation. ~ **rumlu/** ~ **rumsal**, (*art.*) plastic: ~ **sanatlar**, plastic arts.
yoğun Thick; stout; coarse; compact; concentrated; (*phys.*) dense. ~ **la¹çᶜⁱ**, (*el.*) condenser. ~ **lam**, (*phys.*) condensation; (*chem.*) concentration. ~ **laşım/** ~ **laşma**, *vn.*; (*phys.*) condensation; (*chem.*) concentration. ~ **laşmak**, *vi.* become dense; concentrate. ~ **laştırıcı** = ~ LAÇ. ~ **laştırmak** (**-i**), condense; concentrate, thicken. ~ **luk**, density: ~ **şişesi**, (*chem.*) pycnometer. ~ **lukölçer**, densimeter, density-meter.
yoğurmak (**-i**) (*cul.*) Knead.
yoğur¹tᵈᵘ (*cul.*) Yog(h)urt, yaourt. ~ **çalmak**, make yoghurt: ~ **u üfliyerek yemek**, be unnecessarily cautious.
yoğurt·çu(luk) (Trade of) yoghurt-maker/-seller.

~**lu**, (*cul.*) served with yoghurt. ~**mak (-i, -e)**, *vc.* = YOĞURMAK. ~**otu**ⁿᵘ, (*bot.*) bedstraw.
yoğuş·turucu (*phys.*) Condenser. ~**uk**, (*min.*) condensed. ~**ma(k)** = YOĞUNLAŞMA(K). ~**um**, condensation.
yo¹kᵍᵘ/ᵏᵘ [142] *a.* Non-existent; absent; negative. *n.* Non-existence; nothing. *adv.* No. *v.* There is/are not; not have [= VAR]. ~ **canım!**, impossible!; I absolutely refuse!; you don't say!: ~ **değildir**, there is/are; it exists: ~ **demek**, deny, reject: ~ **devenin başı!**, incredible!: ~ **edici**, destroying; catastrophic; -cide: ~ **etm.**, annihilate, destroy; remove: ~ **oğlu** ~, nothing at all: ~ **olm.**, cease to exist; die out; not be; be absent: ~ **pahasına**, (*fin.*) for a mere song: ~ **satmak**, have nothing for sale: ~ **yere**, without reason; unnecessarily; in vain: ~ ~, there's everything; *int.* no!, no!: ~**tan var etm.**, make stg. out of nothing: ~**tan yere** = ~ YERE: ~**una**, very cheaply.
yok·edim Eradication; destruction. ~**istan**, *pr.n.* (*iron.*) the land of 'there is not'. ~**ken**, while absent; in the absence of . . .. ~**lam(a)**, *vn.* examination; inspection; (*ed.*, *mil.*) roll-call; (*mil.*) call-up. ~**lamacı**, (*mil.*) inspector; registrar. ~**lamak (-i)**, examine; inspect; grope for; search; try, test; visit (the sick). ~**lanmak**, *vp.* be examined, etc.: *vi.* examine o.s. ~**laştırmak (-i)**, feel; search minutely. ~**latmak (-i, -e)**, *vc.* ~**luk**, absence; non-existence; dearth, lack; poverty: ~**unda**, for want of . . .; in his absence.
yoksa *conj.* [219] If not; otherwise; or; if there is not; but not; I wonder if . . .; it only needs . . .. ~ **gelmiyecek mi?**, perhaps he isn't coming after all.
yok·sama(k) = YADSIMA(K). ~**sayıcı**, *n.* (*phil.*) nihilist. *a.* nihilistic. ~**sayıcılık**, nihilism. ~**sul**, possessing nothing; destitute; in need of; lacking. ~**sullaşmak**, *vi.* become destitute. ~**sullaştırmak (-i)**, *vc.* ~**sulluk**, destitution. ~**sun**, deprived; disappointed: ~ **kalmak**/~**mak (-den)**, be deprived of. ~**sunlu**, (*phil.*) showing lack of. ~**sunluk**, deprivation. ~**sunum**, abstinence. ~**suz(luk)** = ~SUL(LUK). ~**umsama(k)**, = YADSIMA(K).
yokuş *n.* Rise; ascent; slope; ramp. *a.* Rising/sloping (ground). ~ **aşağı**, sloping down; downhill: ~ **yukarı**, sloping up, rising; uphill: ~**a koşmak**/ **sürmek**, create difficulties. ~**çu**, (*sp.*) good climber. ~**lu**, rising, sloping upwards.
yol Way; path, road, street; (*naut.*) channel, canal; (*aer.*) route, line; journey; speed; (*eng.*) conduit; (*fig.*) means; medium; manner, method; aim; behaviour; rule, law; career; (*tex.*) stripe. ~ **açık!**, all clear!: ~ **açmak (-e)**, bring about, make possible; cause; engender; make way for; blaze a trail: ~ **almak**, acquire momentum, get up speed; advance: ~ **aramak**, seek a way: ~ **belgesi**, safe conduct: ~ **bilmek**, know the way; know how to do stg.; know how to behave: ~ **boyu**, along the way: ~ **bulmak**, find a way: ~ **çivisi**, (*mot.*) stud: ~ **dışı**, across country: ~ **düzeni**, (*mot.*) highway code: ~ **erkân**, social conventions: ~ **etm. (-i)**, visit frequently: ~ **evlâdı**, (*rel.*) disciple: ~GEÇEN: ~ **görünmek**, have to travel: ~ **göstermek**, show the

way; assist: ~ **imi**, (*sp.*) route indicator: ~ **iz bilmek**, (*soc.*) know the rules/conventions: ~ **kenarı**, roadside: ~ **kesmek**, waylay s.o.; stage a hold-up: ~ **masraf/parası**, travelling expenses; (*rly.*, *etc.*) fare; (*mot.*) toll: ~ **şaşmak**, take the wrong route: ~ **tepmek**, walk a long way: ~ **tezkeresi**, (*adm.*) pass, travel permit: ~ **tutmak**, (*rel.*) follow one's principles; (*mil.*) blockade the road: ~ **uğrağı/üstü/üzere**, lying on one's road; overlooking the road: ~ **üslup**, mode, manner: ~ **vermek**, give passage, make way; give (a horse) his head; let go his own way; increase one's speed; (*adm.*) dismiss, discharge; open the way to, cause: ~ **vurmak** = ~ KESMEK: ~ **yakınken**, while the going's good; before it's too late: ~ ~, (*tex.*) striped; in lines: ~ **yordam**, (*soc.*) ceremony; custom: ~ **yordam bilmek**, know the proper way to do stg.: ~ **yürümek**, walk along a road; go walking.
yola: ~ **çıkarmak**, provoke, incite: ~ **çıkmak/ düşmek**, set out on a journey, etc.: ~ **dökülmek**, take a certain course: ~ **düzelmek/düzülmek/ koyulmak**, set out for, go straight to: ~ **gelmek**, get into line; think better of stg.; come to see reason, listen to advice: ~ **getirmek**, bring s.o. round to the right way; reform; persuade: ~ **girmek**, come right somehow, be reformed: ~ **gitmek**, travel, make a journey: ~ **koymak**, send s.o. off on a journey: ~ **revan olm.**, (*obs.*) set out: ~ **sokmak (-i)**, put stg. right: ~ **vurmak**, see s.o. off on a journey: ~ **yatmak**, be made to see reason.
yol-: ~**dan çıkma**, aberration: ~**dan çıkmak**, go off the rails; take the wrong road; go astray, go to the bad: ~**dan kalmak**, be kept back; be detained: ~**lara dökülmek**, everyone come out on the streets: ~**lara düşmek**, set out in search of s.o. (urgently): ~**larda kalmak**, be delayed on the road.
yolu: ~ **açılmak**, have the world at one's feet: ~ **almak**, reach the end of the road: ~ **düşmek (-e)**, one's road lead to/pass through; its turn come: ~ **sapıtmak**, take the wrong turning; turn into another road: ~ **tutmak**, (*sl.*) make off, clear out: ~**n açık olsun!**, pleasant journey!, happy landings!; good luck!: ~**n tıkanması**, traffic block/jam: ~**na**, for; for the sake of: ~**na bakmak**, await s.o.'s arrival: ~**na çıkmak**, go out to meet s.o.; meet s.o. on the road: ~**na girmek**, (matter) come right; (problem) sort itself out: ~**na koymak**, set right; arrange: ~**nca**, suitably; legally: ~**nda**, for the sake of; all in order, working properly: ~**nda(ki)**, in the sense that, to the effect that: ~**ndadır**, it's under control: ~**ndan çıkarmak**, derail; pervert; lead astray: ~**ndan koymak**, prevent, detain, delay: ~**nu beklemek**, await s.o.; lie in wait for s.o.: ~**nu bulmak**, find a way to do stg.: ~**nu değiştirmek**, divert: ~**nu kaybetmek**, not know which way to go: ~**nu kesmek**, stop s.o.: ~**nu sapıtmak/şaşırmak**, go astray: ~**nu yapmak**, make possible: ~**nu yordamını şaşırmak**, lose one's bearings; not know where one is: ~**yla**, via, by way of; by means of; properly, duly.
yol·ağzıⁿ¹ Entrance to a road. ~**a¹k**ᵍ¹, footpath; (*phys.*) trajectory. ~**bilir**, well-mannered; adroit,

skilful. ~ **bilmez**, ill-mannered; awkward, clumsy.
~ **cu**, traveller; passenger; child about to be born;
(*med.*) hopeless case, s.o. dying; prostitute: ~
arabası, coach: ~ **eşyası**, baggage: ~ **etm.**, say
goodbye to s.o.: ~ **geçirmek**, accompany s.o. at the
start of a journey: ~ **geçmeliği**, (*adm.*) pass, permit:
~ **gemisi**, (*naut.*) passenger ship, liner: ~ **malı**,
passenger baggage: ~ **salonu**, (*rly., etc.*) waiting-
room: ~ **topluluğu**, caravan; crowd: ~ **uçağı**, (*aer.*)
air-liner: ~ **yolunda gerek**, it's time to be on one's
way. ~ **culuk**, travel; travelling: ~ **etm.**, travel: ~
ne zaman?, when do you leave/set out? ~ **çatağı**[ni],
cross-roads. ~ **daş**, fellow-traveller; colleague;
companion; (*pol.*) comrade. ~ **daşlık**, being a
fellow-traveller; companionship; comradeship: ~
etm., accompany. ~ **demiri**, (*rly.*) rail. ~ **dışı**, off-
street.
yoldurmak (**-i, -e**) *vc.* = YOLMAK.
yoldüzler (*eng.*) Bulldozer.
yole (*naut.*) Yawl.
yol·geçen ~ **hanı**, a much-frequented but undistinguished place. ~ **harcı**[ni], travelling expenses/
allowance. ~ **içi**, on-street. ~ **kesen**/~ **kesici**,
highwayman, brigand. ~ **lama**, *vn.* act of sending;
(*rly.*) goods department; (*mil.*) transport section;
(*arch.*) large beam. ~ **lamak** (**-i**), send; dispatch.
~ **lanmak**, *vp.* be sent: *vi.* set off; advance. ~ **lu**,
having . . . roads; (*tex.*) striped; (*mot.*) fast (vehicle);
(*fig.*) having . . . a way/manner; proper, correct,
regular; of the nature of: ~ **yolsuz işler**, irregular
actions: ~ **yordam bilmek**, behave properly: ~
yordamlı, in the proper way. ~ **luk**, provisions (for
a journey); travelling allowance/expenses; travelling rug.
yolmak (**-i**) Pluck; tear out; strip; eradicate; cheat.
yolsuz Without roads, trackless; contrary to law/
custom/morals; slow-moving (vehicle); (*adm., sp.
etc.*) banned. ~ **etm.**, ban, strike off (member): ~
kadın, prostitute: ~ **kalmak**, (*sl.*) be penniless: ~
yöntemsiz, irregular, improper. ~ **luk**, lack of
roads; irregularity, impropriety; corruption,
malversation.
yol·uk Plucked; hairless. ~ **unmak**, *vp.* = YOLMAK;
be plucked; be robbed: *vi.* (*gamb.*) lose one's
money; (*fig.*) tear one's hair (with grief).
yom Good luck/omen/news. ~ **tutmak**, consider
lucky. ~ **suz**, unlucky.
yoma (*naut.*) Ship's cable.
yon·ca (*bot.*) Clover, trefoil; lucerne: ~ **yaprağı
kavşak**, (*mot.*) cloverleaf junction. ~ **calık**, clover-
field. ~ **da**, (*orn.*) under-feathers. ~ **ga**, (*carp.*) chip,
chipping; kindling. ~ **gar**, (*mus.*) small three-
stringed lute. ~ **(ul)mak** = YONT(UL)MAK.
yont[u] (*live.*) Unbroken mare. ~ **ar**, (*carp.*) plane.
~ **arlamak** (**-i**), plane. ~ **kuşu**[nu], (*orn.*) wagtail.
~ **ma**, *vn.* act of chipping: *a.* chipped; cut out: ~
taş, dressed stone: ~ **taş çağı**, (*archaeol.*)
palaeolithic age. ~ **mak** (**-i**), cut/chip into shape;
dress (stone); pare (nails); sharpen (pencil); (*fig.*)
get money out of s.o. gradually. ~ **u**, (*art.*) carving,
sculpture, statue. ~ **ucu(luk)**, sculp·tor/(-ture).
~ **uk**, *n.* chip; chipped place: *a.* chipped; sharpened;
(*geol.*) eroded, worn: ~ **düz**, (*geol.*) peneplain.

~ **uklaşma**, (*geol.*) erosion, wear; undulation.
~ **ulmak**, *vp.* be cut, etc.; (*fig.*) be polished/
educated: **yontulmamış**, rough, uneducated,
boorish: **yontulmuş yapıtaşı**, (*arch.*) ashlar.
-yor- *v. suf.* [108] *Basis of the present tense*, -ing
[**gidiyorum**, I am going].
yordam Agility, dexterity. ~ **lı**, agile, dextrous.
yorga (*live.*) Jog-trot. ~ **lamak**, *vi.* go at a jog-trot.
yorgan (*dom.*) Quilt, duvet. ~ **döşek yatmak**, (*med.*)
take to one's bed: ~ **gitti kavga bitti**, the dispute
is ended: ~ **iğnesi**, (*tex.*) quilting-needle: ~
kaplamak, sew a sheet to the quilt: ~ **kavgası**,
quarrel faked (to involve s.o. else); fight for one's
immediate interests: ~ **yüzü**, outer covering of a
quilt.
yorgan·cı(lık) (Trade of) quilt-maker/-seller.
~ **lamak** (**-i**), cover with a quilt. ~ **lık**, (material)
suitable for quilts.
yor·gun Tired, weary: ~ **argın**, dead-tired: ~ ~,
wearily. ~ **gunluk**, weariness, fatigue: ~ **kahvesi**,
(*cul.*) reviving cup of coffee: ~ **unu almak**, rest.
~ **mak**[1] (**-i**), tire, fatigue.
yormak[2] (**-i, -e**) Interpret (dream, etc.); presage;
attribute.
yorsu (*psy.*) Interpretation of dreams.
yort·mak *vi.* Wander about. ~ **u**, (*rel.*) Christian
feast; holiday.
yor·ucu Fatiguing, laborious, exhausting;
wearisome. ~ **ulma**, (*eng.*) fatigue: ~ **dayanıklığı**,
fatigue limit. ~ **ulmak**[1], *vp.* = YORMAK[1]; be tired;
tire o.s. in vain.
yor·ulmak[2] *vp.* = YORMAK[2]; be interpreted/
attributed, etc. ~ **um**, interpretation; comment.
~ **umbilim**, (*phil.*) semantics. ~ **umcu(luk)**, (work
of) commentator//(*mus.*) interpreter. ~ **umlama**,
vn. commentary. ~ **umlamak** (**-i**), comment on, explain; (*mus.*) interpret. ~ **umlanmak**, *vp.* ~ **umsal**,
explanatory, interpretative; semantic.
yosma *a.* Pretty; graceful; attractive. *n.* S.o. graceful
and attractive; coquette. ~ **m!**, my pet! ~ **lık**,
gracefulness, charm; coquetry.
yosun (*bot.*) Moss. ~ **bağlamak**, be covered with
moss: ~ **bilgisi**, bryology: ~ **hayvanları**, (*zoo.*)
bryozoa. ~ **lanmak**/~ **laşmak**, *vi.* become mossy.
~ **lu**, mossy.
yoz (*live.*) Untrained, wild; (*agr.*) unworked,
fallow; (*fig.*) degenerate. ~ **laşım**/~ **laşma**, *vn.*;
degeneration. ~ **laşmak**, *vi.* become wild; lose
acquired qualities; degenerate. ~ **laştırmak** (**-i**), *vc.*
~ **luk**, wildness; degeneration.
YÖK = YÜKSEKÖĞRETIM KANUNU// KURULU.
yön Direction; quarter; regard; relation. ~ **bulucu**,
(*rad.*) direction finder: ~ **vermek**, (*naut.*) set a
course: ~ **yöntem**, (*soc.*) customs; etiquette:
~ (**ün)den**, as regards; from the standpoint of.
yön. = YÖNETIM. ~ **kur.** = YÖNETIM KURULU.
yöndeş With the same direction. ~ **açılar**, (*math.*)
corresponding angles. ~ **lik**, correspondence.
yönel·dirim Guidance. ~ **ik** (**-e**), directed/aimed at;
devoted to. ~ **im**, (*bio.*) tropism; (*phil.*) intention;
(*psy.*) tendency, orientation: ~ **bozukluğu**, (*psy.*)
disorientation: ~ **iş**/~ **me**, *vn.* turning towards;
direction, course; orientation: ~ **durumu**, (*ling.*)

dative case. ~ **mek (-e)**, turn towards; direct o.s. towards; intend. ~ **meli**, (*ling.*) in the dative: ~ **tümleç**, indirect object. ~ **te¹ç**ᶜⁱ, cycle handlebar. ~ **ti**, direction. ~ **tici**, *a.* steering. ~ **tik**, turned towards, oriented. ~ **tme**, (*ast.*) orientation. ~ **tmek (-i, -e)**, direct, turn towards, orientate; (*naut.*) con, steer.

yön·erge (*adm.*) Directive. ~ **eşmek (-le)**, *vi.* go in the same direction.

yönet·ici(lik) (Work of) controller/operator/ director/administrator/manager. ~ **ilmek**, *vp.* ~ **im**, control, administration, direction, management: ~ +, *a.* executive, managerial: ~ **biçimi**, (*pol.*) regime: ~ **kurulu**, (*adm.*) board/council of management: ~ **yeri**/ ~ **evi**, (*fin.*) head-office: ~ **e katılmayan ortak**, (*fin.*) sleeping partner. ~ **imsel**, directing, managing, controlling. ~ **ke**, (book of) instructions/regulations. ~ **ken**, ~ **telek**, (*orn.*) tail feather. ~ **me**, *vn.* direction, management: ~ **siyle**, under his direction. ~ **mek (-i)**, direct, control, administer; dominate. ~ **melik**, book of instructions; code, bye-law; regulations. ~ **men(lik)**, (status/office/work of) manager/controller/director/administrator. ~ **sel**, managerial, administrative.

yön·ey (*math.*, *phys.*) Vector. ~ **eylem**, ~ **araştırması**, (*ind.*, *mil.*) operational research. ~ **lem**, tactics. ~ **lemci**, manager. ~ **lendirmek (-i)**, channel; orientate; guide. ~ **lenim**/ ~ **lenme**, orientation. ~ **lü**, directed/turned towards; orientated. ~ **sel**, directional. ~ **seme**, (*psy.*) tendency. ~ **semek (-e)**, *vi.* tend towards.

yöntem Method, way; technique; system; procedure. ~ **bilim(sel)**, (*phil.*) methodolo·gy/ (-gical). ~ **li**, with a method/system; systematic. ~ **lilik**, regularity. ~ **sel**, methodic; systematic. ~ **siz**, without any system, unsystematic, irregular. ~ **sizlik**, irregularity, lack of system.

YÖO = YÜKSEKÖĞRETİM OKULU.

yöre Side; region; environs; neighbourhood; district. ~ **sinde**, in the region of. ~ **kent**, *n.* suburb: ~ +, *a.* suburban. ~ **l**/ ~ **sel**, local. ~ **sellik**, localization.

yörük = YÜRÜK.

yörün·ge (*math.*) Course taken, track, trajectory; (*ast.*, *phys.*) orbit: ~ +, *a.* orbital: ~ **sine oturmak**, (*aer.*) go into orbit; (*ind.*) go into operation. ~ **geç**, orbital.

Yr·b. = YARBAY. ~ **d.** = YARDIMCI.

YSE = YOL SU ELEKTRİK (GENEL MÜDÜRLÜĞÜ).

-yse/-ysa *v.* *suf.* (*after* *vowel*) [99] = -İSE [OKULDAYSAM].

YTP = YENİ TÜRKİYE PARTİSİ.

-yu *n.* *suf.* (*after vowel*) [28] = -i¹ [BORUYU].

yudum *n.* Mouthful; draught (of liquid), sip. ~ **lamak (-i)**, drink in sips; drink slowly. ~ **lanmak**, *vp.* ~ **luk**, *a.* mouthful.

yuf *int.* (*of scorn/disgust*) (*vulg.*) ~ **borusu çalmak (-e)**, boo s.o.: ~ **ervahına!**, curse him!: ~ **sana!**, shame on you!

yufka *n.* (*cul.*) Thin sheet of dough; wafer; unleavened bread in thin sheets. *a.* Thin; weak; poor. ~ **açmak**, roll out the dough: ~ **ekmeği**, very

thin bread: ~ **yürekli**, (*fig.*) compassionate, soft-hearted.

yufka·böreğiⁿⁱ (*cul.*) Ready-made thin sheet of dough; BÖREK made of thin dough sheets. ~ **cı(lık)**, (trade of) YUFKA-maker/-seller. ~ **lı**, in pastry.

Yugoslav·(yalı) *n.* (*ethn.*) Yugoslav. ~ **ya**, *n.* (*geo.*) Yugoslavia: ~ +, *a.* Yugoslav.

yuğ (*rel.*) Memorial service; (*his.*) funeral feast.

yuh *int.* (*of displeasure/anger*).

yuha *int.* (*of contempt/derision*). ~ **çekmek**/ ~ **ya tutmak**/ ~ **lamak (-i)**, hold up to derision; barrack, cat-call, hoot. ~ **lanmak**, *vp.*

yuka¹çᶜⁱ (*geol.*) Anticline.

yukar·da/ ~ **dan** = ~ ı. ~ **ı**, *adv.* [198] above; upstairs; upwards; on high: *a.* high; upper; top: *n.* upper/topmost part: ~ **(-den)**, greater/higher than . . .: ~ **tükürse bıyığı aşağı tükürse sakalı**, between the devil and the deep blue sea; on the horns of a dilemma. ~ **(ı)da**, on high; above; upstairs; overhead: ~ **ıda zikredilen**, afore-mentioned/-said: ~ **(ı)dan**, from above/upstairs: ~ **ıdan almak**, treat harshly; behave condescendingly: ~ **ıdan aşağı**, downwards: ~ **ıdan bakmak (-e)**, look down on: ~ **(ı)sı**, the upper part: ~ **ıya yığmak**, pile up high; (*fig.*) exaggerate.

yu·laf (*bot.*, *cul.*) Oats. ~ **lar**, (*live.*) bridle, halter.

yuma (*naut.*) Mooring-rope.

yumak[1] *v.* = YIKAMAK.

yumak[2] *n.* (*tex.*) Ball (of string, etc.). ~ **bulut**, (*met.*) cirro-cumulus. ~ **çık**, (*bio.*) glomerulus. ~ **lamak (-i)** wind into a ball. ~ **lanmak**, *vp.*

yum·durmak (-i) *vc.* ~ **mak (-i)**, squeeze tight together; shut; close (eye/fist).

yumru *a.* Round, globular; modular. *n.* Stg. round; (*arch.*) boss; (*med.*) boil; (*min.*) nodule; lump; (*fig.*) lump in the throat. ~ **arısı**, (*zoo.*) gall mite: ~ **aşındırıcı(lı püskürtme)**, (*min.*) shot(-blasting): ~ **(kök)**, (*bot.*) tubercle.

yumru·aya¹kᵍ¹ (*med.*) Clubfoot. ~ **cak** = YUMURCAK. ~ **cu¹k**ᵍᵘ, small round object; (*bot.*) tubercle; (*geol.*) nodule.

yumru¹kᵍᵘ (*bio.*) Fist; (*sp.*) blow with the fist. ~ **eklemek (-e)**, catch s.o. a blow: ~ **eldiveni** (*sp.*) boxing-glove: ~ **göstermek**, threaten; frighten: ~ **hakkı**, stg. obtained by force: ~ **kadar**, tiny (stg. that should be big): ~ **a tutuşmak**, come to blows.

yumruk·lamak (-i) Strike with the fist. ~ **lanmak**, *vp.* ~ **laşma**, *vn.* (*sp.*) boxing: ~ **alanı**, boxing-ring. ~ **laşma (-le)**, box. ~ **oyuncusu**ⁿᵘ, boxer. ~ **oyunu**ⁿᵘ, boxing(-match): ~ **topu**ⁿᵘ, (*sp.*) punch-ball.

yumru·lanmak/ ~ **lmak** *vi.* Become round. ~ **luk**, roundness.

yum·uk (Eye) closed by swelling; (eye) half-shut: ~ ~, plump; soft. ~ **uklaşmak**/ ~ **ulmak**, *vi.* become closed, etc.

yumur·ca¹kᵍ¹ (*med.*) Bubo; plague; (*fig.*) pestilential child, brat. ~ **mak**, *vi.* become swollen.

yumurta (*bio.*, *cul.*) Egg; (*ich.*) roe; (*fig.*) testicle; (*dom.*) darning-egg/-mushroom. ~ **akı**, (*bio.*) albumen; (*cul.*) egg-white: ~ **çılbır** = ÇILBIR: ~ **gözesi**, (*bio.*) oocyte; (*bot.*) oosphere: ~ **hazır**

lop = HAZIRLOP: ~ **kabuğu**, egg-shell: ~ **kabuğunu beğenmemiş**, ungrateful (towards one's parents, etc.): ~ **kanalı**, (*bio.*) oviduct: ~ **kapıya dayanmak/gelmek**, situation become urgent/desperate: ~ **oluşması** (*bio.*) oogenesis: ~ **ökçeli**, (*mod.*) with medium-high heels: ~ **patlıcanı**, (*bot.*) whitefruited aubergine: ~ **piçi**, (*orn.*) little grebe: ~ **sarısı**, (*bio.*) egg-yolk; yellow: ~ **zarfı**, (*dom.*) eggcup: ~**dan çıkma**, (*ent.*) eclosion: ~**dan daha dün çıkmış**, pretentious parvenu; s.o. very conceited: ~**ya kulp takar**, good at making excuses: ~**yı çalkamak**, (hen) turn its eggs.

yumurta·cı Egg-seller. ~**cı¹k**ᵍ¹, (*bio.*) ovule. ~**cılık**, egg-selling. ~**lı**, (*cul.*) with egg. ~**lık**, (*dom.*) eggcup; (*bio.*) ovary: ~ **kalkanı**, (*sp.*) box; (*th.*) codpiece: ~**ı altta//üstte**, (*bot.*) inferior//superior ovary. ~**msı**, egg-shaped; ovoid; (*geol.*) oolite. ~**sız**, eggless.

yumurt·lama *vn.*: ~ **borusu**, (*bio.*) ovipositor. ~**lamak (-i)**, (*orn.*, *zoo.*) lay eggs: (*ich.*, *zoo.*) spawn; (*ent.*) blow; (*fig.*) invent (story, etc.); blurt stg. out, be indiscreet. ~**lanmak**, *vp.* ~**latmak (-i, -e)**, *vc.* ~**layanlar**, (*zoo.*) egg-layers. ~**layıcı**, (*zoo.*) oviparous.

yumuş·acık Very soft/mild. ~**ak**, soft; mild; flexible; yielding; amenable; effeminate: ~ **ağızlı**, (*live.*) soft-mouthed: ~ **başlı**, amenable, docile: ~ **damak**, (*bio.*) soft palate: ~ **dolu**, (*met.*) sleet: ~ **ge**, (*ling.*) soft G (ğ): ~ **huylu**, benign: ~ **iniş**, (*aer.*) soft landing: ~ **su**, (*chem.*) soft water: ~ **yüzlü**, too kind to refuse. ~ **akçalar**, (*zoo.*) molluscs: ~ **bilimi**, malacology. ~**aklık**, softness; mildness; flexibility; clemency. ~ **ama**, *vn.*; softening; (*ling.*) voicing. ~ **amak**, *vi.* become soft; become pliant/yielding: (*ling.*) be voiced. ~ **atıcı**, emollient. ~ **atılmak**, *vp.* ~**atma**, *vn.*; (*pol.*) détente; (*min.*) softening; (*sp.*) relaxation. ~**atmak (-i)**, soften; assuage; (*ling.*) voice; (*eng.*) damp. ~**atmalık**, (*eng.*) damper, shock-absorber.

Yun. = YUNAN; YUNANCA(DAN); YUNANİSTAN; YUNANLI.

yuna (*live.*) Small felt saddlecloth.

yuna¹kᵍ¹ Wash-house; public bath; (*dom.*) place for washing clothes on a river bank; (*ind.*) bath. ~ **teknesi**, wash-bowl.

Yunan *n.* (*his.*) Greece; the Greek nation/people. ~ +, *a.* Greek. ~**ca**, (*ling.*) Greek: ~**dan**, taken/ translated from Greek. ~**istan**, (*geo.*) Greece: ~ **kaplumbağası**, (*zoo.*) Grecian tortoise. ~**istanlı**, resident in Greece. ~**lı**, (*ethn.*) Greek.

yunmak (*dial.*) *vi.* Wash.

Yunus (*rel.*) Jonah. ~**balığı**ⁿ¹, (*zoo.*) porpoise; common dolphin. ~**lama**, (*naut.*) pitching.

yurdu (*dom.*) Eye of a needle. ~**lu iğne**, needle.

yur·tᵈᵘ (*pol.*) Native country; fatherland; home; habitation; estate; (*dom.*) large Turkoman tent; (*bio.*) habitat; (*ed.*) hall of residence; teaching institute; (*med.*) sanatorium, convalescent home. ~ **bilgisi**, (*ed.*) civics: ~ **dışında**, abroad: ~ **dışındaki işçilerimiz**, Tk. guest-workers (in Germany, etc.): ~ **özlemi**, nostalgia, homesickness: ~ **satma**, treachery, treason: ~ **tutmak (-de)**, settle/make one's home (in a country): ~ **yönetimi**, politics.

yurt·landırmak (-i) Settle s.o. ~**lanmak**, *vi.* settle; cease to be a nomad, lead a settled existence; acquire an estate. ~**luk**, estate, domain. ~**sal**, *a.* country; home. ~**sama**, *vn.*; nostalgia, homesickness. ~**samak**, *vi.* feel homesick/nostalgic. ~**sever/** (-lik), patriot·ic/(-ism). ~**taş**, fellow-countryman, compatriot. ~**taşlık**, being a compatriot: ~ **yasası**, (*leg.*) civil code. ~**taşsal**, (*leg.*) civil.

yusufçu¹kᵍᵘ (*orn.*) Turtledove; (*ent.*) dragonfly.

yus·yumru/ ~ **yuvarlak** Completely round; very swollen.

-yuş *vn. suf.* (*after vowel*) [172] = -iş [OKUYUŞ].

yut·a¹kᵍ¹ (*bio.*) Pharynx: ~ **yangısı**, (*med.*) pharyngitis. ~**argöze/** ~ **arhücre**, (*bio.*) phagocyte. ~ **kunmak**, *vi.* swallow one's spittle; (*fig.*) gulp. ~**mak (-i)**, swallow, devour, gulp down; (*phys.*) absorb; (*bio.*) ingest; (*fig.*) swallow (insults); endure (injuries) in silence; believe (lies), swallow (tall stories); fail to see (jokes); acquire wrongfully; (*gamb.*) win stg.; (*col.*) learn stg. to the last detail. ~**turmaca**, subtle joke against s.o. ~**turmak (-i, -e)**, cause to swallow (*esp.* lies); swindle. ~**turulmak**, *vp.* be taken in (by lies). ~**ucu**, who swallows/devours; (*phys.*) absorptive; (*gamb.*) who wins. ~**ulmak**, *vp.* be swallowed, etc.; (*gamb.*) lose. ~**um**, (*ling.*) haplology, syncope.

yuva (*orn.*) Nest; (*zoo.*) lair, den; (*ed.*) play-school; (*soc.*) crèche, orphanage; (*fig.*) home; (*bio.*, *eng.*) socket; (*eng.*) slot; (valve-)seating; (*bio.*) cell, alveolus. ~**sını yapmak**, (*sl.*) cook s.o.'s goose.

yuva¹kᵍ¹ Cylinder; roller (esp. for flat mud roofs).

yuva·lamak *vi.* Nest. ~**lanmak**, *vi.* become a householder; (*mil.*) be concealed/camouflaged. ~**lı**, ~ **mafsal**, (*eng.*) ball and socket joint; (*bio.*) enarthrosis.

yuvar (*bio.*) Corpuscle; globule; (*ast.*) globe. ~ +, *a.* Corpuscular. ~ ~, rolling. ~**cı¹k**ᵍ¹, globule; (*chem.*) globulin; (*eng.*) ball(-bearing). ~**cıksıl**, globular.

yuvarla¹kᵍ¹ *a.* Round; spherical; cyclo-. *n.* Ball; globe, sphere; (*child.*) marble; disc; (*mil.*) limber; (*pub.*) cylinder, roller. ~ **hesap//sayı**, (*math.*) round sum//figure: ~ **sıra**, (*ling.*) series of rounded vowels: ~ **solucan**, (*zoo.*) round worm: ~ **testere**, (*carp.*) circular saw: ~ **ünlü**, (*ling.*) rounded vowel: ~ **yüzgeçli**, (*ich.*) lump-sucker.

yuvarlak·laşma *vn.* (*ling.*) Rounding. ~**laşmak**, *vi.* become rounded. ~**laştırmak (-i)**, *vc.* make round. ~**lık**, roundness.

yuvar·lamak (-i) Rotate; roll; roll up; (*sp.*) trip up; (*cul.*) swallow greedily; toss off (drink); (*fin.*) round off/up; (*col.*) utter (incredible lies). ~**lanmak**, *vi.* rotate, revolve; turn round; roll; topple over; (*fig.*) be tormented (by grief, etc.); lose one's job, be sacked; (*sl.*) die suddenly: **yuvarlanan taş yosun tutmaz**, a rolling stone gathers no moss: **yuvarlanıp gitmek**, worry along somehow. ~**laşmak**, *vi.* become round. ~**latmak (-i)**, cause to rotate, etc.; make round. ~**sal**, spherical. ~**sı**, spheroid.

yuvgu = YUVAK. ~**lamak (-i)**, flatten with a roller.

-yü *n. suf.* (*after vowel*) [28] = -i¹ [GÖZCÜYÜ].

yüce *a.* High; exalted; sublime. *n.* High place. ~ **bilmek**, think highly of; recognize as great: ~

Divan, (*leg.*) High Court, special Court dealing with cases arising from Ministers' decisions.
yüce·lik Height; loftiness; exalted rank. ~ **lim**, (*ast.*) culmination: ~ **noktası**, apex. ~ **lmek**, *vi.* become high; rise. ~ **lti**, exaltation. ~ **ltilmek**, *vp.* ~ **ltmek** (**-i**), cause to rise; raise. ~ **yargılık**, (*leg.*) High Court.
yükü Load; (*el.*) charge; (*naut.*) cargo; freight; burden; (*fig.*) heavy task/responsibility; (*bio.*) unborn young; (*dom.*) = ~ LÜK. ~ **altına girmek**, take on a heavy task: ~ **araba(cı)sı**, cart(er): ~ **beygiri**, (*live.*) carthorse: ~ **bildirgesi**, (*naut.*) ship's manifest: ~ **boşalması**, (*geol.*) decompression: ~ **dubası**, (*naut.*) barge: ~ **gemisi**, (*naut.*) cargo-boat/ -ship: ~ **hayvanı**, (*live.*) pack-animal: ~ **katarı** (*rly.*) goods-train: ~ **olm.** (**-e**), give s.o. a heavy task; be a burden to/a charge on s.o.: ~ **taşıma gücü**, (*eng.*) load-bearing capacity: ~ **vurmak (-e)**, load (pack-animal): ~ **te hafif pahada ağır**, light in weight but valuable: ~ **ü çıkarmak**, (*naut.*) break out cargo: ~ **ü üzerinden atmak**, decline/shift responsibility: ~ **ün altından kalkamamak**, find one's duties too heavy a burden: ~ **ünü almak**, take all it can hold; become crowded: ~ **ünü tutmak**, become rich: ~ **ünü yüklenmiş**, wealthy.
Yük. = YÜKSEK. ~ **Müh.** = YÜKSEK MÜHENDİS.
yük·çü(lük) (Work of) porter. ~ **lem**, (*ling.*, *phil.*) predicate. ~ **leme**, *vn.* loading; (*el.*) charging: ~ **boşaltma giderleri//müddeti**, (*naut.*) demurrage// lay-days: ~ **durumu**, (*ling.*) (absolute) accusative case: ~ **kâğıdı**, (*naut.*) bill of lading: ~ **sahası**, (*aer.*) apron: ~ **ve boşaltma**, loading and unloading. ~ **lemek (-i, -e)**, load; place a load on; (*fig.*) throw the blame on; impute; attribute; (*el.*) charge. ~ **lemlik**, (*leg.*) undertaking, contract. ~ **lenci**, (*leg.*, *fin.*) guarantor, surety. ~ **lenici**, contractor. ~ **lenilmek (-e)**, *vp.* be loaded. ~ **lenim**, (*leg.*) engagement, undertaking. ~ **lenme**, *vn.*; commitment; liability: ~ **kabiliyeti**, (*eng.*) bearing capacity. ~ **lenmek (-i)**, load onto o.s.; (*fig.*) take upon o.s., undertake: (**-e**), lean/press against; (*fig.*) throw o.s. upon, attack; keep on at s.o. ~ **lenmelik**, (*fin.*) bond. ~ **lenti**, burden, heavy task. ~ **ler**, (*mot.*) loader. ~ **let**, lorry. ~ **letçe**, small lorry, van. ~ **letçi**, lorry-driver. ~ **letilmek**, *vp.* ~ **letmek (-i, -e)**, place a load on; load (ship, etc.); impose (duty, etc.); impute, attribute. ~ **leyici**, loader; charger. ~ **lü**, loaded (with); (*el.*) charged; overburdened with work; (*bio.*) pregnant; (*fin.*) in debt; rich; (*leg.*) encumbered; (*sl.*) drunk: ~ **ağırlık**, (*mot.*) gross weight: ~ **saat**, peak hour: ~ **uç**, (*el.*) electrode. ~ **lük**, (*dom.*) large cupboard/closet for bedding; luggage rack, baggage-holder.
yüksek *a.* High; alto-; loud (voice); (*fig.*) virtuous; exalted; eminent; (*ed.*) advanced. *n.* (*geo.*) High altitude. ~ **araştırma**, (*ed.*) advanced studies/ research: ~ **atlama**, (*sp.*) high-jump: ~ **basınç**, (*met.*) high pressure: ~ **basınçlı**, (*med.*) hypertonic: ~ **eğitim**, higher education: ~ **fırın**, (*min.*) blast furnace: ~ **fiyat**, (*fin.*) high price, expensiveness: ~ **frekans(lı)**, *n.*/(*a.*) (*el.*) high frequency: ~ **görevli**, (*adm.*) senior official: ~ **güç**, strength, intensity: ~ **hız(lı)**, *n.*/(*a.*) high speed/velocity: ~

irtifa, altitude: ~ **kabartma**, (*art.*) high relief: ~ **katına sunmak**, offer stg. to s.o. important: ~ **kavuşum**, (*ast.*) superior conjunction: ~ **perdeden konuşmak**, talk in a high pitch; (*fig.*) talk big/ challengingly: ~ **nitelikli**, high-quality: ~ **rütbeli**, high-ranking: ~ **seçim kurulu**, (*adm.*) central election commission: ~ **ses**, loud voice; (*mus.*) high-pitched voice: ~ **sesle okumak**, read aloud: ~ **sıcaklık**, high temperature: ~ **tiraj**, (*pub.*) mass circulation: ~ **lerde**, (*naut.*) aloft: ~ **lerde dolaş-mak**, aim high, be ambitious: ~ **ten atmak**, boast; bluster: ~ **ten bakmak (-e)**, look down upon s.o.: ~ **ten kopmak**, set out with great pretensions: ~ **ten uçmak**, be ambitious/presumptuous.
yüksek·ısı ölçer//ölçme, (*phys.*) pyrome·ter// (-try). ~ **lik**, height; altitude; elevation; eminence; (*math.*) vertical. ~ **likölçer**, (*phys.*) altimeter. ~ **okul**, (*ed.*) high school, college. ~ **öğrenim**, higher studies. ~ **öğretim**, higher education: ~ **okulu**, teachers' training college.
yüksel·im (*ast.*) Declination. ~ **iş**, (*fin.*) increase, rise. ~ **me**, *vn.*; (*ast.*) ascension; (*geol.*) uplift, upheaval; (*geo.*) flow (of tide). ~ **mek**, *vi.* mount; rise; ascend; climb; (*adm.*) be promoted; (*naut.*) gain the open sea. ~ **te¹çⁱ**, (*phys.*) amplifier. ~ **tgen**, (*chem.*) oxidizing agent. ~ **tgenme**, oxidation. ~ **ti**, *n.* dimension; altitude: *a.* barometric. ~ **tici**, elevator. ~ **tilmek**, *vp.* ~ **tmek (-i)**, cause to rise; elevate, raise; (*adm.*) promote; (*math.*) raise to a power; (*fin.*) escalate; (*el.*) amplify, boost; (*fig.*) praise excessively, exalt.
yüksü¹kᵍü (*dom.*) Thimble; (*bot.*) acorn-cup; (*bot.*) calyptra, coif. ~ **kadar**, in small quantities. ~ **otu**ⁿu, (*bot.*) foxglove, digitalis.
yük·süz Unburdened; (*naut.*) in ballast, light; (*el.*) no-load. ~ **sünmek (-den)**, regard as burdensome; begrudge.
yüküm (*fin.*) Obligation, liability. ~ **cü**, surety, security. ~ **lenme**, *vn.* being sponsor/surety: ~ **belgesi**, written guarantee/surety. ~ **lenmek**, stand as surety; act as guarantor. ~ **lü(lük)**, (being) obliged/liable/responsible.
yükün (*phys.*) Ion. ~ **leşme**, *vn.* ionization. ~ **sel** ionic.
yükünmek *vi.* Bow/kneel (out of respect).
yül·gü 'Cut-throat' razor. ~ **ük**, (clean-)shaven smooth. ~ **ümek (-i)**, shave off.
yün *n.* (*tex.*) Wool. *a.* Woollen. ~ **lü**, *a.* woollen: *n* woollen cloth.
yüpürmek *vi.* Run about in confusion.
yüre¹kᵍⁱ (*bio.*) Heart; (*col.*) stomach; (*fig.*) boldness; pity; sincerity [*also* = GÖNÜL; iç]. ~ +, (Cardiac; cardio-; heart-: ~ **akımyazımı**, electr cardiography: ~ **akımyazısı**, electro-cardiogram ~ **çarpıntısı**, (*med.*) palpitations; (*fig.*) misgiving ~ **dayanmaz**, unbearable; heartbreaking: ~ ge şemesi, (*bio.*) diastole: ~ **gücü**, morale: ~ **içzar** (*bio.*) endocardium: ~ **karası**, remorse: ~ **kas** (*bio.*) myocardium: ~ **kasıntısı**, (*bio.*) systole: midyesi, (*zoo.*) cockle: ~ **oynaması**, excitemen ~ **oynatıcı**, sensational: ~ **oynatma**, sensation: sayrılığı, (*med.*) cardiopathy: ~ **sayrısı**, cardi patient: ~ **Selanik (-de)**, very fearful, cowardly:

şeklinde, heart-shaped, cordate: ~ **vermek**, hearten, give courage: ~ **yangısı**, great sorrow: ~ **yağı**, happiness, contentment: ~ **zarı**, (*bio.*) pericardium.

yüreği: ~ **ağzına gelmek**, one's heart come into one's mouth, be suddenly frightened: ~ **atmak/ çarpmak**, one's heart beat (with emotion): ~ **bayılmak**, be very hungry: ~ **cız etm./cızlamak**, feel great pity: ~ **dar**, impatient: ~ **dayanmaz**, unbearable: ~ **delik**, full of woes: ~ **dolu**, with a long-nourished grudge: ~ **ezilmek**, suddenly feel hungry: ~ **ferahlamak**, feel relieved: ~ **geniş**, light-hearted, easy-going: ~ **hop etm./hoplamak**, one's heart jump (for joy/fear): ~ **kabarmak**, be nauseated, feel sick: ~ **kalkmak**, be alarmed/very upset: ~ **kararmak**, be dismayed, despair: ~ **katı**, obstinate; obdurate: ~ **katılmak**, be unable to breathe (from cold/emotion, etc.): ~ **oynamak**, one's heart flutter; have misgivings: ~ **parça parça olm.**, greatly pity s.o.: ~ **parçalanmak/sızlamak**, pity (s.o.): ~ **pek**, stout-hearted: ~ **rahatlamak**, make happy: ~ **serinlemek**, lighten one's worries: ~ **sıkılmak**, be depressed/bored: ~ **şişmek**, get very bored/worried: ~ **tükenmek**, wear o.s. out trying to explain stg.: ~ **yağ bağlamak**, feel relieved/happy: ~ **yanmak**, be grieved; feel pity; meet with disaster: ~ **yaralı**, stricken by disaster: ~ **yufka**, easily moved; compassionate.

yüreğine: ~ **dert olm.**, be troubled by s.o./stg.: ~ **inmek**, be struck with great fear, etc.; die suddenly: ~ **işlemek**, affect deeply: ~ **kar yağmak**, suffer pangs of jealousy: ~ **od düşmek** = YÜREĞİ YANMAK: ~ **su serpilmek**, be comforted, rejoice.

yüreğini: ~ **kaldırmak**, thoroughly upset/excite s.o.: ~ **pek tutmak**, hang on to one's courage: ~ **tüketmek**, wear s.o. out (asking for explanations); = YÜREĞİ TÜKENMEK: ~**n yağı erimek**, be terribly anxious/grieved.

yürek-: ~**ler acısı**, heart-breaking event/condition: ~**ler sızlatıcı**, heart-breaking: ~**ten**, sincerely; heartfelt.

yürek·bilim (*med.*) Cardiology. ~**lendirmek (-i)**, encourage; give strength. ~**lenmek**, *vi.* take heart, be emboldened. ~**li**, bold, stout-hearted, plucky; -hearted. ~**lilik**, courage. ~**sel**, cardiac. ~**siz(lik)**, faint-hearted(ness), timid(ity); lukewarm(ness), apath·etic/(-y).

yürü·lkᵍᵘ *a.* Fast-walking, fleet of foot. *pr.n.* (Member of) Turkoman nomadic tribe; (*his.*) Janissary foot-soldier. ~ **at yemini artırır**, striving increases resistance: ~ **semai**, (*Or. mus.*) form of vocal melody.

yürü·me *vn.* ~**mek**, *vi.* walk; go for a walk; (*mil.*) march; hurry along; (*fin.*) be calculated; (*adm.*) come into force, apply, have effect; advance; (*fig.*) develop, make progress; (*sl.*) die: (**-e**), reach; advance on: **yürü!**, (*mil.*) quick march!: **yürür**, *a.* moving, travelling; (*adm.*) effective. ~**nmek**, *imp. v.* be walked (in/on). ~**rlük**, (*leg.*) validity, being in force: ~**e girmek**, come into force, become valid: ~**te kalmak**, be in force: ~**te olmamak**, be in abeyance: ~**ten kaldırmak**, abrogate, annul.

~**tme**, *vn.* enforcement; application: *a.* executive. ~**tmek (-i, -e)**, *vc.* cause to walk, etc.; put forward (ideas, etc.); (*adm.*) apply, execute; (*leg.*) bring/put into force, execute, enforce; (*sl.*) pilfer, walk off with; (*adm., sl.*) sack, dismiss. ~**tmelik/**~**tümce**, regulations; conventions. ~**tücü**, *a.* (*eng.*) driving. ~**tülmek**, *vp.* ~**tüm**, (*leg.*) enforcement; (*adm.*) application, execution. ~**yen**, walking: ~ **merdiven**, escalator, moving staircase. ~**yüş**, gait; (*mil.*) march; (*sp.*) walking: ~ **kapısı**, (*arch.*) wicket-gate: ~ **yapmak**, march; (*pol.*) demonstrate: ~**e çıkmak**, go out for a walk: ~**e geçmek**, begin to walk; **(-e)** (*mil.*) advance on. ~ **yüvermek (-i, -e)**, walk quickly.

yüsrü (*carp.*) Type of black timber.

-yüş *vn. suf.* (*after vowel*) [172] = -iş [YÜRÜYÜŞ].

yüz¹ *a.* [79] Hundred. *n.* One hundred. ~ **adet**, (*live.*) a hundred head (of cattle): ~BAŞI: ~ **kere**, time and time again: ~ **kişilik**, (*stg.*) for a hundred people: ~ **liralık**, (*fin.*) one-hundred lira note: ~ **misli**, one hundredfold: ~NUMARA: ~ **yaşında olan**, centenarian: ~ **yataklı**, hundred-bed (hotel, etc.): ~YIL: ~**de (bir)**, one hundredth; one per cent: ~**de** ~, without a doubt, definitely; all-in, completely, one hundred per cent: ~**lerce**, in (their) hundreds; hundreds of; in great numbers.

yüz² *n.* Face; countenance; aspect; surface; (*tex., etc.*) the right side, face; outer covering of stg.; side; (*arch.*) façade, elevation; (*fig.*) boldness, effrontery; shame; cause, reason, motive. ~ +, *a.* Facial: ~AKI: ~ **bağlamak**, form a crust/skin; (*med.*) heal up: ~ **bulmak**, be emboldened; become presumptuous; be spoilt: ~ **bulunca** = ~ VERİNCE: ~ **çevirmek (-den)**, be estranged from s.o.; turn away from: ~ **etm.**, hand stg. over; (*carp.*) face up (two boards): ~ **geri dönmek/etm.**, face about, turn around; (*mil.*) retreat: ~ **göre**, just to please/ flatter: ~GÖRÜMLÜĞÜ: ~ **görünüşü**, (*med.*) facies: ~ **göstermek**, show one's face, appear: ~ **göz**, the whole face: ~ **göz olm. (-le)**, be too intimate/ familiar with s.o.: ~ **ifadesi**, one's expression: ~ **kalıbı**, (*art.*) face mask: ~KARASI: ~ **kızartıcı**, shameful; disgusting: ~ **kızartmak**, ask a favour unwillingly: ~ **kızdırmak**, feel ashamed: ~ **lekesi**, birthmark: ~ÖLÇÜMÜ: ~ **pudrası**, face-powder: ~ **siperi**, (*eng.*) face-shield: ~ **sivilcesi**, (*med.*) acne: ~ **surat davul derisi/hak getire/mahkeme duvarı**, brazen-faced, shameless: ~SUYU: ~ **sürmek**, prostrate o.s. humbly, show great respect: ~ **tornacısı**, (*eng.*) face: ~ **tutmak (-e)**, turn towards; begin (to do): ~ **tüyü**, down (on face): ~ÜSTÜ: ~ **verince astar istemek**, be given an inch and take a yard: ~ **vermek**, be indulgent to, spoil; give encouragement: ~ **verme cıvır!**, don't encourage him or he'll take advantage of you!: ~ **vermemek**, give a cold reception; be disagreeable: ~ **vurmak (-e)**, have recourse to, apply to: ~ **yastığı**, (*dom.*) pillow: ~ **yazısı**, (*soc.*) decorations stuck on a village bride's face: ~ **den utanır**, it is difficult to say such things to a person's face; it is hard to refuse personally: ~ ~**e**, face to face: ~ ~**e bakmak**, look s.o. in the face; meet: ~ ~**e bakamam**, I can't look him in the face (for shame): ~ ~**e gelmek**, come face to face, meet.

yüze: ~ çekmek/içmek, (*phys.*) adsorb: ~ çıkmak, come to the surface; (*fig.*) be arrogant/insolent: ~ gelen, select, superior: ~ gelmek, come to the surface/top: ~ gülmek, appear loving; show (insincere) friendship: ~ gülücü, hypocritical.

yüzü: ~ açılmak (-in), reveal its beauty/brightness: ~ ak, honest, upright, sincere: ~ ak olsun!, good luck!: ~ asılmak, be sulky/churlish: ~ ekşitmek, frown, look cross: ~ görmek, reach, obtain, find: ~ gözü açılmak, become shameless: ~ gülmek, be happy/delighted; show one's pleasure: ~ güler, with smiling face, happy: ~ kalmamak, lose one's courage: ~ kara, who has done stg. to be ashamed of: ~ kasap süngeriyle silinmiş, brazen-faced: ~ kızarmak, be ashamed: ~ KOYUN: ~ olmamak (-e), not dare, not have the face to; be unable to refuse: ~ pek(iştirmek), (become) brazen-faced/shameless: ~ sıcak, sympathetic, attractive: ~ soğuk, dour, frightening: ~ suyu, honour, self-respect: ~ suyu hürmetine/suyuna (-in), out of respect for; thanks to: ~ teneke kaplı, brazen-faced: ~ tutmamak, shrink from; be afraid to: ~ yazılı kalmak, remain unmoved: ~ yerde, humble, modest: ~ yere gelmek, be ashamed for/of s.o.: ~ yok, he has not the face to; he dare not: ~ yumuşak, too kind to refuse stg./s.o.

yüzünde, on; on the surface of.

yüzünden: = YÜZÜNDEN: ~ akmak, the reason be very clear: ~ çekmek, suffer at the hands of: ~ düşen bin parça olm., be very gloomy/sour-faced about stg.: ~ kan damlıyor, he is in robust health: ~ okumak, understand from s.o.'s face; read (from a book, etc.).

yüzüne: ~ aklatmak, bring honour upon: ~ bağırmak, shout disrespectfully at s.o.: ~ bakılacak gibi/bakılır, good-looking: ~ bakılmaz, ugly, horrible: ~ bakmak, face s.o.: ~ bakmaya kıyılmaz, one can't help looking at s.o. very beautiful: ~ bakmamak, attach no importance to; be angry with: ~ bir daha bakmamak, break off relations with s.o.: ~ çarpmak, cast in s.o.'s teeth: ~ duramamak, be unable to refuse s.o.: ~ gözüne bozmak/bulaştırmak, spoil stg., completely, make a mess of stg.: ~ güldürmek, rejoice the heart of: ~ gülmek, smile at, be friendly towards (insincerely): ~ kan gelmek, (*med.*) recover one's health/strength: ~ kapıyı kapatmak, shut the door on s.o.: ~ karşı (-in), to s.o.'s face: ~ tükürsen yağmur yağıyor sana der, he's completely shameless: ~ vurmak, cast stg. in s.o.'s teeth; reproach s.o. with stg.

yüzünü: ~ ağartmak, please; do honour to: ~ buruşturmak/ekşitmek, pull a sour face: ~ gözünü açmak, explain the facts of life (to a child): ~ gözünü çarpıtmak, pull a wry face: ~ gözünü oynatmak, make/pull faces: ~ güldürmek (-in), please, make happy: ~ kara çıkarmak, put s.o. to shame: ~ kızartmak/kızdırmak, *vi.* be/feel ashamed: ~ kızartmak (-in), make s.o. ashamed/blush: ~ şeytan görsün!, how disgusting he is!: ~ yazmak, decorate a village bride's face: ~ yere getirmek, make s.o. ashamed: ~n akıyla çıkmak

(-den), come through with honour: ~n derisi kalın, thick-skinned: ~n perdesi yırtılmak, become insolent/shameless: ~ze güller!, (*col.*) excuse the expression!

yüzakı Personal honour.

yüz·başı(lık) [49] (Rank/duties of) (*mil.*) captain// (*naut.*) lieutenant//(*aer.*) flight-lieutenant. ~de/ (-lik), (*math.*) percentage; (*phys.*) fraction; (*fin.*) commission. ~de(lik)çi, (*fin.*) commission-agent. ~deyüz = YÜZ[1].

yüz·den *a.* Superficial. ~dürme, *vn.* (*phys.*) buoyancy; flo(a)tation: ~ kuvveti, buoyancy. ~dürmek[1] (-i, -e), *vc.* = YÜZMEK[1], let swim; (*naut.*) float, salvage. ~dürülmek, *vp.* ~ebilir, (*phys.*) buoyant. ~egelen, (*soc.*) prominent, important. ~el, ~ erime, (*geol.*) ablation.

yüzdürmek[2] (-i, e) *vc.* = YÜZMEK[2], have flayed.

yüzer[1] *a.* (*math.*) One hundred each; one hundred at a time. ~ ~, in groups of one hundred. ~lik, *a.* one hundred.

yüzer[2] *v.* = YÜZMEK[1]. *a.* Floating. ~ buz, (*geo.*) ice-floe: ~ havuz, (*naut.*) floating-dock: ~ kınkanatlısı, (*ent.*) water-beetle: ~gezer, (*bio.*) amphibious. ~me, (*nuc.*) absorption. ~top[u], (*eng.*) float, ball-cock (valve); (*naut.*) sea-mark, mooring-buoy.

yüzey (*math.*) Surface, plane; area. ~ gerilimi, (*phys.*) surface tension. ~sel(lik), surface, superficial(ity).

yüzge[l]ç[ci] *a.* Swimming, floating; able to swim. *n.* Swimmer; (*ich.*) fin; (*aer.*) float. ~ ayaklısı, (*orn.*) sungrebe. ~ ayaklılar, (*zoo.*) pinnipeds.

yüz·görümlüğü[nü] (*soc.*) Present from the bridegroom (on first seeing the bride's face). ~karası[nı], shame, dishonour, disgrace.

yüzle·mece To s.o.'s face; face to face; in person. ~mek (-i), accuse/reproach s.o. to his face. ~nmek, *vp.*

yüzleş·mece Coming face to face. ~mek (-le), meet face to face; be confronted with one another. ~tirmek (-i), bring face to face; confront.

yüz·lü[1] *a.* Having/with a . . . face//surface: ~ ~, brazen-faced, unashamed(ly). ~lük[1], (*mod.*) face covering/protection; mask. ~lülük, state of having a . . . face.

yüz·lü[2] *a.* (*math.*) Having/with a hundred . . . .. ~lük[2], worth one hundred (units); containing one hundred (parts).

yüz·me *vn.* ~ havuzu, swimming-bath/-pool: ~ kabiliyeti, (*phys.*) buoyancy: ~ kesesi, (*ich.*) swim/ (-ming) bladder: ~ yeleği, (*naut.*) life-jacket. ~mek[1], *vi.* swim, float; (*fig.*) be swimming in.

yüzmek[2] (-i) (*live.*) Skin; flay; (*fig.*) despoil; (*gamb.*) strip, ruin. yüzüp yüzüp kuyruğuna gelmek, have nearly finished (a long job).

yüznumara (00) (*col.*) Toilet, WC.

yüz·ölçümü[nü] (*math.*) Square measure, surface area; (*agr.*) acreage. ~suyu[nu], honour, self-respect: ~ dökmek, degrade o.s. ~süz, brazen-faced, shameless; cheeky: ~ vurgunculuk, (*fig.*) daylight robbery. ~süzleşmek, *vi.* become shameless, etc. ~süzleştirmek (-i) *vc.* ~süzlük, shamelessness; cheekiness.

yüzücü (*sp.*) Swimmer; (*col.*) exploiter; (*live.*) skinner.

yüzü'kᵍü Ring; (*eng.*) collet. ∼ **çevirmek**, (*child.*) play. ∼ **oyunu**, a game where a ring is hidden under mugs: ∼ **ü geriye çevirmek**, break off an engagement. ∼ **parmağı**ⁿ¹, (*bio.*) ring-finger.

yüzükoyun Face downwards; prone; lying on one's face; upside down.

yüzülmek¹ *imp.v.* Swim.

yüzülmek² *vp.* Be flayed; (*fig.*) be exploited.

yüzüncü (100.) (*math.*) Hundredth. ∼ **yıldönümü**, centenary.

yüz·ünden *post.* [93] Because of; on account of. ∼ **üstü**, unfinished; neglected; face downwards; prone: ∼ **bırakmak**, leave things as they are/unfinished/incomplete: ∼ **kapanmak**, lie prostrate.

yüzyıl *n.* Century. ∼ **lar boyu**, for centuries. ∼ **lık**, *a.* century-long.

YY. = YÜZYIL. ∼ **K** = YENİ YAZIM KILAVUZU.

yz. = YAZIN. ∼ **b.** = (*mil.*) YÜZBAŞI.

Z

Z, z [ze] Twenty-ninth Tk. letter, Z.

-z *n. suf.* [84] = -iz [İKİZ].

zaaf Weakness: infirmity; (*adm.*) lack of control.

za'bıtᵖᵗ¹ A recording; (*adm.*) minutes; report; legal proceedings. ~ **tutmak**, take legal proceedings.

zabıt·a Police. ~ **alık**, a matter for the police. ~ **name**, (*adm.*) minutes; proceedings; protocol.

zabitⁱ (*mil.*) Officer; (*fig.*) commander, disciplinarian. ~ **lik**, rank/status/duties of an officer; commission.

zaç¹ (*chem.*) Iron sulphate; vitriol. ~ **yağı**ⁿ¹, (concentrated) sulphuric acid.

zade *a.* Born; noble. *n.* Son. *suf.* Son of . . . [MEHMETZADE]. ~ **gân**, (*soc.*) aristocracy: ~ **sınıfı**, the nobility. ~ **lik**, noble birth.

zafer Triumph; victory. ~ **bulmak**, be triumphant/ victorious: ~ **takı**, triumphal arch.

zafiyetⁱ Weakness; thinness.

zağ¹ (*orn.*) Carrion crow. ~ **anos**, (*orn.*) hawk-owl; (*zoo.*) = ÇAĞANOZ. ~ **ar(cı)**, (*live.*) (keeper of) hound. ~ **ara**, (*mod.*) fur collar.

zağ² Keenness of edge (sword, etc.). ~ **cı(lık)**, (work of) knife-grinder. ~ **lamak (-i)**, sharpen. ~ **lanmak**. *vp.* ~ **lı**, sharpened, keen-edged.

zahir¹ *n.* Helper, supporter, backer.

zahir² *a.* Outward, external; apparent. *n.* Outside, exterior; (*soc.*) outsider. *adv.* Clearly, evidently; apparently. ~ **olm.**, become apparent: ~ **de**, apparently. ~ **en**, outwardly; apparently. ~ **i**, external, outward; artificial; apparent, virtual.

zahire (*cul.*) Provisions; cereals, corn. ~ **ambarı**, (*agr.*) granary: ~ **tüccarı**, corn-chandler.

zahi'ıtᵈⁱ**(lik)** (*rel.*) Abstemious(ness); ascetic(ism); devout(ness).

zahmetⁱ Trouble; difficulty; distress; fatigue. ~ **buyurdunuz!**, you have put yourself to great trouble!: ~ **çekmek**, suffer trouble/fatigue: ~ **etm.**/ ~ **e girmek**, give o.s. trouble; put o.s. to inconvenience: ~ **etmeyiniz!**, don't disturb/trouble yourself!: ~ **olmazsa!**, please!; if it is no trouble!: ~ **vermek**/ ~ **e sokmak**, cause pain/trouble; put s.o. to great trouble/expense.

zahmet·li Troublesome; painful; arduous, difficult; fatiguing. ~ **siz**, free from trouble; painless; easy. ~ **sizce**, easily; without trouble.

za'ıfᶠ¹ Weakness; poverty, misfortune.

zail Declining, transitory; disappearing; past. ~ **olm.**, disappear; fade; go away.

zaim (*his.*) Feudal chieftain.

zai'ıtᵈⁱ *a.* Unnecessary, superfluous. *n.* (*math.*) Plus (sign).

zakkum (*bot.*) Oleander. ~ **giller**, dogbane family, Apocynaceae.

zalim *a.* Unjust; tyrannical; cruel. *n.* Tyrant. ~ **ce**, cruelly. ~ **lik**, cruelty.

zamᵐ¹ (*fin.*) Addition, supplement. ~ **gelmek**, price be increased: ~ **görmek**, get a rise in salary. **zam.** = ZAMİR.

zaman *n.* Time; period; season; (*ling.*) tense; (*geol.*, *his.*) age, era; (*mus.*) time. *adv.* [185] When (*with participles*; = -DİĞİ; -ECEĞİ). ~ **adamı**, time-server, opportunist: ~ **belirteci**, (*ling.*) adverb of time: ~ **bırakmak**, leave/set aside time for: ~ **bildirimi**, (*rad.*) time signal: ~ **birimi**, unit/interval of time: ~ **eki**, (*ling.*) verbal time suffix [-ECEK, -İYOR, -MİŞ]: ~ **farkı**, (*geo.*) time difference: ~ **hakemi**, (*sp.*) time-keeper: ~ **kazanmak**, gain time: ~ **kollamak**, await its turn: ~ **ölçeği**, time scale: ~ **ölçeri**, chronograph, chronometer: ~ **öldürmek**, kill time, pass the time: ~ **sana uymazsa sen zamana uy**, if the times don't suit you, you must suit yourself to the times: ~ **ulacı**, (*ling.*) gerund of time: ~ **vermek**, devote time to: ~ **a uymak**, conform to contemporary requirements: ~ **ı geçmek**, cease to be useful; its time/season pass: ~ **ın adamı olm.**, keep abreast of the times: ~ **ında**, in due course: ~ **la**, with/in the course of time. [*Also* = VAKİT.]

zaman·aşımıⁿ¹ (*leg.*, *fin.*) Prescription. ~ **daş(lık)**, contemporane·ous/(-ity); simultane·ous/(-ity). ~ **dizin**, chronology. ~ **e**, the age; the present time; fortune: ~ **adamı**, (*iron.*) modern/up-to-date person: ~ **çocukları**, the children of today. ~ **lama**, timing. ~ **lı**, (*eng.*) -stroke.

zamazingo (*sl.*) Mistress.

zamba'ıkᵍ¹ (*bot.*) Lily. ~ **şeklinde**, crinoid. ~ **giller**, lily family, Liliaceae.

zambur = KAMBUR.

zamir Inner consciousness/thought; (*ling.*) personal pronoun. ~ **ine girmek (-in)**, (thought) enter one's mind.

zamk¹ Gum, glue, adhesive.

zamkinos (*sl.*) The what's-its-name; the thing-ummy(bob); running off. ~ **etm.**, (*sl.*) slip away, run off.

zamk·lamak (-i) Gum. ~ **lanmak**, *vp.* ~ **lı**, gummed.

zamm- = ZAM. ~ **letmek**ᵉᵈᵉʳ, add; increase.

zampara Womanizer, debauchee, rake. ~ **lık**, womanizing. ~ **etm.**, chase after women.

zanⁿ¹ Opinion; surmise, conjecture; suspicion. ~ **altında bulunmak**, be suspected/accused: ~ **na kapılmak**, be carried away by an idea: ~ **nıma göre**, in my opinion.

zanaat¹ Craft; handicraft. ~ **çı**/~ **kâr**, craftsman, artisan.

zangır (*ech.*) ~ ~ , trembling(ly); with teeth chattering; clanking, rattling. ~ **dama**, *vn.* ~ **damak**, *vi.* one's teeth chatter with fear; clank; rattle. ~ **datmak (-i)**, *vc.*

zango'ıçᶜᵘ**(luk)** (*rel.*) (Work of) verger, sexton.

zanka Two-horse sleigh.

zan·lı Suspect, accused. ~ n- = ZAN. ~ n'etmek^{eder}/ ~ neylemek (-i), think, suppose.

zaparta = SAPARTA.

zapt[1] Seizure; control, restraint; (*leg*.) recording (in writing). ~ etm., hold firmly; seize, capture; take possession of, confiscate; control, restrain, master; grasp, understand; remember; take down in writing. ~ iye, (*his*.) gendarme(rie). ~ urapt[1], orderliness; discipline.

zar[1] (*bio*.) Membrane, film, diaphragm; (*bot*.) thin skin; (*mod*.) headscarf. ~ gibi, very thin.

zar[2] (*gamb*.) Die, (*pl*.) dice; (*sl*.) pleasure. ~ almak, win: ~ atışı, throw of the dice: ~ atmak, throw dice: ~ gelmek, be lucky: ~ oynamak, dice: ~ tutmak, cheat in throwing dice: ~ ını bozmak, spoil s.o.'s luck; interfere with the dice.

zarafet[i] Elegance; grace; delicacy. ~ ile, easily.

zarar Damage; injury; loss; (*fin*.) deficit; harm, disadvantage. ~ etm./görmek, suffer harm/loss; have a deficit: ~ gelmek, loss/damage occur: ~ gidermek, compensate: ~ vermek/ ~ ı dokunmak, cause harm, etc.; damage, injure; (*fig*.) cripple: ~ ı olmamak, produce no harm: ~ ı yok!, it doesn't matter!; never mind!: ~ ın neresinden dönülse kârdır, any reduction of loss counts as a profit: ~ ına satmak, sell at a loss.

zarar·lı Harmful, destructive; who suffers harm: ~ çıkmak, come out the loser. ~ sız, harmless; innocent; safe, unhurt; (*med*.) benign; (*col*.) not so bad, quite good.

zarb'etmek^{eder} (*math*.) Multiply.

zarf Receptacle; envelope; cover; case; cup-/glass-holder; (*med*.) capsule; (*ling*.) adverb. ~ tümleci, adverbial phrase.

zarf·çı Crook, confidence-trickster. ~ çılık, confidence trick. ~ ında, during, the course of. ~ lamak (-i), put in an envelope. ~ lanmak, *vp*.

zargana (*ich*.) Garfish, garpike.

zari ~ ~ ağlamak, weep bitterly.

zarif Elegant, graceful; delicate; cute; witty, clever (idea, etc.) ~ lik, elegance; delicacy, etc.

zarkanatlılar (*ent*.) Hymenoptera.

zarp = DARP. (*col*.) Strong effect. ~ musluğu, (*eng*.) stop-cock. ~ lı, very effective.

zart ~ zurt etm., give orders/talk in a loud blustering manner. ~ a, (*vulg*.) fart: ~ yı çekmek, (*sl*.) die.

zarur·et[i] Need, want, necessity; distress, poverty: ~ halinde, in case of emergency/necessity: ~ inde kalmak, be obliged to. ~ i, necessary; essential; imperative; unavoidable; involuntary.

zarzor Willy-nilly; barely, only just.

zat[1] Essence; substance; person, individual. ~ işleri, personal matters; (*adm*.) personnel affairs: ~ ı âliniz, [68] Your Honour, you.

zat·en/ ~ i Essentially; in any case; besides, as a matter of fact; of course: *for emphasis* [zaten her zaman geliyor, he *always* comes]. ~ i, essential; original; personal. ~ işerif, Your Honour, (*iron*.) you. ~ ülcenp, (*med*.) pleurisy. ~ ülkürsi, *pr.n.* (*ast*.) Cassiopeia. ~ ürree, (*med*.) pneumonia.

zavallı Unlucky; miserable. ~ (adamcağız), poor fellow. ~ lık, unluckiness; misery.

zaviye Corner; (*math*.) angle; (*rel*.) recluse's cell.

zavurt = AVURT.

zayıf Thin; weak(ly); (*med*.) atonic; (*fig*.) of little weight/authority. ~ akım, (*el*.) low-voltage current: ~ düşmek, become thin/weak: ~ düşürmek, make weak: ~ mizaçlı, (*med*.) of weak constitution: ~ nahif, very weak.

zayıf·lamak *vi*. Become enfeebled/slim/thin. ~ latıcı, (*rad*.) attenuator. ~ latmak (-i), make thin/ weak; debilitate; depress. ~ lık, weakness; (*med*.) debility, adynamia; emaciation, thinness.

zayi[i] Lost; destroyed. ~ etm., lose: ~ olm., be lost, perish. ~ at[1], losses; (*mil*.) casualties: ~ vermek, suffer casualties: ~ verdirmek, inflict casualties.

zayiçe (*ast*.) Astronomical table; horoscope. ~ sine bakmak, cast a horoscope.

ZB = ZİRAAT BANKASI.

zeamet[i] (*his*.) Large fief (held by ZAİM).

zebani Demon of hell; cruel monster.

zebanzet Commonly used in speech.

zebella Huge, thick-set man.

zeberce'l^{di} n. (*geol*.) Chrysolite; beryl. *a*. Pale bluish green.

ze·bir/ ~ bra, (*zoo*.) Zebra: ~ balığı, (*ich*.) zebra firefish.

zebun Weak, helpless. ~ u olm. (-in), be captivated/ duped by s.o. ~ küş, cruel and cowardly/oppressing the weak. ~ küşlük, cruelty; oppression. ~ laşmak, *vi*. become weak/thin.

Zebur (*rel*.) The Psalms of David.

zec·'ir^{ri} Restraint; violence; forcing to labour. ~ ren, forcibly; with violence. ~ ri, violent; compulsory; forcible: ~ tedbir, forceful measure.

-zede n. suf. Stricken by [kazazede, stricken by disaster].

zede·lemek (-i) Damage by striking; maltreat; bruise. ~ lenmek, *vp*.

zefir[1] Deep sigh; expiration.

zefir[2] (*tex*.) Thin striped cotton shirting.

zeha'p^{bı} Belief; imagination.

zeh'ir^{ri} (*chem*.) Poison; stg. very bitter. ~ dişi, (*bio*.) fang: ~ gibi, very bitter; (*met*.) bitterly cold; (*fig*.) very skilful; excessive: ~ yutmak, take poison; (*fig*.) brood over stg.: ~ zemberek, extremely bitter; s.o. very cantankerous.

zeh·irlemek (-i) Poison; (*fig*.) poison s.o.'s mind. ~ irlenmek, *vp*. ~ irli, poisonous, toxic, venomous; (*col*.) poisoned. ~ r- = ZEHİR. ~ retmek (-i), spoil stg. completely. ~ rolmak, *vi*. have one's pleasure spoilt.

ze·kâ(vet[i]) Alertness; intelligence; perspicacity. ~ ki, sharp, quick-witted, intelligent.

zekât[1] (*rel*.) Obligatory alms.

zeker (*bio*.) Penis.

zelil Low, base, contemptible.

zelve (*live*.) Stick holding yoke in position.

zelzele (*geol*.) Earthquake. ~ merkezi, epicentre.

zem^{mi} Blame; censure; disparagement.

zembere'k^{ği} Spring (of watch, etc.); spring mechanism. ~ i boşalmak, (*fig*.) burst with laughter.

zembil Woven basket. ~ otu^{nu}, (*bot*.) quaking-grass.

zemheri (*met.*) Extreme cold; deep midwinter. ~ **zürafası**, (*jok.*) s.o. inadequately dressed for winter.

zemin (*geo.*) The earth, the world; soil, ground; (*art.*) (back)ground; (*ed.*) subject-matter; (*fig.*) basis. ~ **açmak (-e)**, give grounds for: ~ **hazırlamak (-e)**, prepare the ground for: ~ **katı**, (*arch.*) ground floor: ~ **mekaniği**, (*eng.*) soil mechanics: ~ **ve zaman**, conditions of time and space: ~ **ve zamana uygun**, at a propitious moment: ~ **de (bu)**, in this sense; on this subject. ~ **lik**, underground room/shelter; cave; dungeon.

zemm- = ZEM. ~ **¹etmek**ᵉᵈᵉʳ **(-i)**, censure, denigrate, slander.

zemzem (*rel.*) Sacred well in Mecca. ~ **kuyusuna işemek**, do stg. revolting just to acquire notoriety: ~ **le yıkanmış olm.** (**yanında**), be a perfect paragon by comparison.

zencefil (*bot.*, *cul.*) Ginger. ~ **giller**, Zingiberaceae.

zenci (*ethn.*) Negro. ~ **ticareti**, slave trade.

zencir = ZİNCİR.

zendost Womanizer, rake.

Zengibar *pr.n.* (*geo.*) Zanzibar. ~ **lı**, Zanzibari.

zengin *a.* Rich, affluent, wealthy; showy. *n.* Rich person. ~ **adamın harcı**, only within a rich man's means: ~ **arabasını dağdan aşırır, fakir düz ovada yolunu şaşırır**, wealth opens all doors: ~ **kafiye**, (*lit.*) polysyllabic rhyme: ~ **olm.**, be(come) wealthy: ~ **vesaitli**, richly equipped: ~ **yatağı**, (*soc.*) residential quarter: ~ **in malı züğürdün çenesini yorar**, we all know he's wealthy!

zengin·erkiⁿⁱ (*soc.*) Plutocracy. ~ **le(ş)mek**, *vi.* become rich. ~ **leştirmek (-i)**, enrich. ~ **lik**, riches, wealth, affluence.

zenit (*ast.*) Zenith.

zenne *n.* Female sex; a female; (*th.*) female impersonator. *a.* Female; women's. ~ **ci**, seller of women's clothes. ~ **lik**, *n.* womanhoood: *a.* women's.

zeolit (*geol.*) Zeolite.

zephiye (*his.*) Tax on slaughtered animals.

zeplin (*aer.*) Zeppelin, dirigible.

zer (*obs.*) Gold.

zerdali (*bot.*) (Wild) apricot.

zerde (*cul.*) Dish of saffron-flavoured sweet rice (at weddings).

zerdeçal (*bot.*) Turmeric.

zerdeva (*zoo.*) Pine-marten.

Zerdüştü *pr.n.* (*rel.*) Zoroaster. ~ **i**, Zoroastrian; fire-worshipper. ~ **lük**, Zoroastrianism.

zer·¹iʼⁱ (*agr.*) Sowing.

zerkⁱ (*med.*) Injection. ~ **etm.**, inject.

zerre Atom; mote. ~ **kadar**, (not) in the slightest degree: ~ **kadar . . . olsaydı**, if there were just a little . . . : ~ **nin ~ si**, absolutely none.

zerrin *a.* Golden, like gold. *n.* (*bot.*) Jonquil.

zerzevat¹ (*bot.*, *cul.*) Vegetables. ~ **çı**, greengrocer.

zevahir Outside; visible parts; appearance. ~ **e kapılmak**, be deceived by appearances: ~ **i kurtarmak**, save appearances/'face'.

zevalⁱ Decline, decadence; adversity; destruction. ~ **bulmak**/ ~ **e ermek**, (nation, etc.) decline, fall: ~ **vakti**, midday, noon: ~ **vermek**, harm, destroy: ~ **vermemek**, protect: ~ **e yüz tutmak**, begin to decline:

~ **i olm.** **(-e)**, be hurtful. ~ **i**, ~ **saat**, noon; European time. ~ **siz**, eternal.

zev·at¹ *pl.* = ZAT. People. ~ **ce(lik)**, wife(hood). ~ **¹cᶜⁱ**, husband, consort, mate.

zeveban Melting, fusion.

zevkⁱ Sense of taste; (*cul.*) taste, flavour; appreciation, good taste; enjoyment, pleasure. ~ **almak**/ **duymak (-den)**, be appreciative of; enjoy: ~ **bulmak (-de)**, derive pleasure from: ~ **meselesidir**, there's no accounting for tastes: ~ **etm.**, enjoy o.s.: ~ **ine bak!**, enjoy yourself!: ~ **ine gitmek**, find amusing/ pleasant: ~ **ine mecbur**, voluptuary: ~ **ine varmak**, appreciate stg.: ~ **ini bozmak**, spoil s.o.'s pleasure: ~ **ini çıkarmak**, enjoy stg. to the full: ~ **ini okşamak**, please s.o.

zevk·lendirmek (-i) Delight, please. ~ **lenmek**, *vi.* amuse o.s.: **(-le)**, mock at, make fun of. ~ **li**, pleasant, amusing; in good taste. ~ **perest**, pleasure-worshipper. ~ **siz**, tasteless; drab, ugly; in bad taste; lacking taste. ~ **sizlik**, bad taste.

zevzek Silly; talkative. ~ **lenmek**, *vi.* behave · foolishly; talk nonsense. ~ **lik**, foolishness; foolish behaviour. ~ **etm.**, behave foolishly.

zeybe·¹kᵍⁱ (*ethn.*) (Young) Turk from the Aegean coast. ~ **havası**, (*mus.*) folk-tune for: ~ **oyunu**, local folk-dance.

zey·¹il¹ⁱ (*lit.*) Appendix; postscript; supplement.

zeyrek(lik) Intelli·gent/(-gence).

zeytin (*bot.*, *cul.*) Olive. ~ **ağacı**, olive-tree: ~ **iklimi**, (*met.*) hot dry summer, warm moist winter: ~ **kabuklu biti**, (*ent.*) black-scale insect.

zeytin·ci(lik) (Work of) olive-grower/-dealer. ~ **giller**, (*bot.*) olive family, Oleaceae. ~ **lik**, olive grove: ~ **mukalliti**, (*orn.*) olive-tree warbler: ~ **si**, ~ **meyve**, drupe. ~ **yağı**ⁿ¹, (*cul.*) olive oil: ~ **gibi üste çıkmak**, come off best; get the better of an argument. ~ **yağlı**, (*cul.*) prepared/cooked with olive oil.

zeytuni Olive-green.

zf. = (*ling.*) ZARF (YERİNE).

ZF = (*ed.*) ZİRAAT FAKÜLTESİ.

zıbarmak (*live.*) Die; (*col.*) go to sleep.

zıbın (*mod.*) Baby's wadded jacket; sleeveless jacket.

zıdd- = ZIT. ~ **iyet**ⁱ, opposition; apposition; repugnance, antipathy.

zıh (*mod.*) Edging; (*pub.*) border; (*carp.*) fillet, moulding. ~ **lamak (-i)**, put on a border/edge, etc. ~ **lanmak**, *vp.*

zıkkım (*cul.*) Bitter/unpleasant food; poison. ~ **lanmak (-i)**, (*pej.*) stuff o.s. with food.

zılgıt (*sl.*) Threat; scolding. ~ **vermek**, scold: ~ **ı yemek**, get a scolding.

zımba (*carp.*) Drill; bit; (*eng.*) punch, die. ~ **lamak (-i)**, drill; punch; (*sl.*) stab. ~ **lanmak**, *vp.* ~ **lı**, punched: ~ **defter**, notebook with perforated leaves.

zımbır·datmak (*mus.*) Twang, strum. ~ **tı**, twanging, strumming.

zımn·en By implication; between the lines; tacitly: ~ **anlatmak**, imply. ~ **ında**, with a view to; for the purpose of. ~ **i**, implied, indirectly/tacitly understood.

zımpara (*min.*) Emery. ~ **kâğıdı**, (*carp.*, *eng.*) emery paper: ~ **madde**, corundum. ~**lamak (-i)**, rub down with emery. ~**lanmak**, *vp.*
zındık (*rel.*) Misbeliever; atheist. ~**lık**, atheism.
zın·gıl/ ~**gır** = ZANGIR.
zınk¹ ~ **diye durmak**, suddenly stop. ~**adak**, suddenly and with a start.
zıp¹ (*ech.*) Suddenly; pop! ~ **diye çıkmak**, pop up all of a sudden: ~ ~ **sıçramak**, jump about wildly.
zıp·çıktı Upstart, bounder: ~ **bir halde**, (*mod.*) ridiculously dressed. ~**ır(lık)**, (being) hare-brained/ madcap. ~**ka**, (*mod.*) tight-fitting breeches. ~**kın**, fish-spear, harpoon. ~**lamak**, *vi.* jump/skip/ bounce about. ~**latmak (-i)**, *vc.*; bounce. ~**padak**, suddenly, unexpectedly; with one bound. ~**zıp**¹, (*child.*) marble.
zır (*ech.*) ~ ~, any continuous/tiresome noise. ~**deli**, raving mad.
zırh (*mil.*) Armour; (*naut.*) armour-plating. ~ **levhası**, armour plate. ~**lanmak**, *vi.* wear armour; be armour-plated. ~**lı**, *a.* armoured; armour-plated: *n.* (*naut.*) battleship: ~ **kule**, gun-turret.
zırıl (*ech.*) ~ ~, in streams; endless chatter. ~**damak**, *vi.* chatter/clatter incessantly. ~**tı**, *n.* continuous chatter/clatter; squabble; thingummy/ (-bob): *a.* (*sl.*) dirty, silly, useless.
zır·lak Senselessly yelling; bawling. ~**lama**, *vn.* ~**lamak**, *vi.* make an incessant noise; (*live.*) bray; (*pej.*) weep.
zırnı·ıkğı (*chem.*) Orpiment; yellow arsenic. ~ **bile almamak (-den)**, not get a brass farthing out of s.o.: ~ **bile koklatmamak**, avoid giving the smallest mite: ~ **bile vermemek**, give nothing at all.
zırt ~ ~, frequently; at unexpected/awkward times.
zırtapoz Crazy. ~**luk**, craziness.
zırva (*cul.*) Sheep's trotters stewed with garlic; (*fig.*) nonsense, silly chatter. ~ **tevil götürmez**, there's no sense in such foolish talk. ~**lama**, *vn.* ~**lamak**, *vi.* talk nonsense.
zı·ıtddı The opposite; the contrary; anti-; opposition; detestation. ~ **gitmek**, do just the opposite; be contrary: ~ **tedavi usulü**, (*med.*) allopathy: ~**dı olm.**, dislike, be bored with: ~**dına basmak**, do stg. to spite s.o.: ~**dına gitmek**, act contrary to s.o.'s wishes; oppose.
zıt·laşma *vn.* Opposition. ~**laşmak**, *vi.* oppose each other; be opposite. ~**lık**, (*phil.*) antinomy.
zıvana Small pipe; inner tube; (*carp.*) tenon; mouthpiece (for cigarette/narghile). ~ **testeresi**, (*carp.*) tenon saw: ~**dan çıkarmak (-i)**, (*fig.*) enrage s.o.: ~**dan çıkmak**, be befuddled; be in a rage.
zıvana·lı With a tube/tenon: ~ **sigara**, cigarette made with a paper tube. ~**sız**, without a tube, etc.; (*fig.*) raving, crazy.
zıy·a¹ Loss. ~**pak**, slippery.
zibidi Oddly dressed; eccentric, crazy. ~**lik**, eccentricity.
zifaf (*soc.*) Bridegroom's entry into the nuptial chamber. ~ **gecesi**, wedding night: ~ **odası**, bridal chamber.
zifir Nicotine-tar deposit. ~ **gibi**, very dark. ~**i**, pitch-black: ~ **karanlık**, pitch darkness.

zifos Splash of mud. ~ **atmak (-e)**, (*fig.*) annoy besmirch: ~ **yemek**, be spattered with mud.
zift¹ (*chem.*) Pitch, tar, bitumen, asphalt. ~(i** pekini) yesin!**, he may starve for all I care!
zift·lemek (-i) Daub with pitch, etc. ~**lenmek**, *vp* be daubed with pitch: *vi.* (*pej.*) overeat; squander consume; misappropriate, embezzle. ~**li**, bitumin ous; coated with pitch.
zig·otᵘ (*bio.*) Zygote. ~**zag** = ZİKZAK.
zihaf (*lit.*) Shortening a long syllable.
zihayat Alive, living.
zih·inⁿⁱ (*psy.*) Mind; intelligence; memory. ~ **açmak**, develop the mind: ~ **açıklığı**, power o thought: ~ **bulanıklık/karışıklığı**, confusion o thought: ~ **durmak**, one's mind cease to work; b unable to take stg. in: ~ **hesabı**, (*math.*) menta arithmetic: ~ **yormak**, think hard, rack/cudge one's brains: ~**de tutmak**, bear in mind: ~**de geçirmek**, ponder: ~**e nakşetmek**, fix in the mind ~**i açılmak**, one's understanding be increased: ~ **bulanmak/karışmak**, be confused, lose the thread ~**i dolaşmak**, be confused: ~**i saplanmak (-e)**, ge the wrong idea about stg.: ~**i takılmak (-e)**, one' attention be caught by stg.: ~**i toplamak**, concen trate: ~**ini bozmak**, worry one's head about stg ~**ini bulandırmak**, make one suspicious about stg ~**ini çelmek**, mislead; pervert: ~**ini karıştırmak** confuse s.o.: ~**ini kurcalamak**, stg. make on think: ~**ini oynatmak**, go mad.
zihn·en Mentally; in one's head. ~**i**, *n.* = ZİHİN: *a* mental, intellectual. ~**iye**, (*phil.*) intellectualism ~**iyet**ⁱ, mentality.
zikıymetⁱ Precious, valuable.
zik·irʳⁱ Remembrance; mention; (*rel.*) recitin God's name; dervish service: ~**i geçmek**, be men tioned/remembered. ~**retme**, *vn.* ~**ır·etmek**ᵉᵈᵉ (-i), mention; cite; (*rel.*) recite prayers. ~**rolunmak** be mentioned.
zikzak Zigzag. ~ **kelebeği**, (*ent.*) gypsy moth: ~ **yapmak**, change direction/thoughts frequently ~**lı**/~**vari**, zigzagging.
zil Bell; gong; (*mus.*) cymbals, bells on a tam bourine; (*sl.*) hungry. ~ **çalıyor!**, there's the bell' ~ **düğmesi**, call button; bell-push: ~ **takınmak** make merry: ~ **takıp oynamak**, give o.s. up t merriment.
zil·hicce (*ast.*) Twelfth lunar month. ~**kade**, (*ast.* eleventh lunar month.
zilletⁱ Abasement, degradation; contempt.
zil·li (*mus.*) With cymbals/bells; having a bell; (*fig.* quarrelsome, shrewish. ~**limaşa**, (*mus.*) forke tongs with bells/cymbals. ~**siz**, without a bell: ~ **oynamak**, dance for joy. ~**zurna**, ~ (sarhoş), blin drunk.
zilye·ıtᵈⁱ Owner; possessor, holder. ~ **bulunma (-e)**, be in possession of.
zimam (*live.*) Reins. ~**dar**, (*pol.*) leader, statesman
zimmetⁱ (*fin.*) Debt. ~ **bakiyesi**, debit balance: ~ **(hanesi)**, debit side: ~**ine geçirmek**, debit to s.o. embezzle.
zina¹ (*ent.*) Bumble-bee.
zina² Adultery; fornication. ~ **işlemek**, commi adultery; fornicate.

zincifre (*chem.*) Vermilion; cinnabar.
zincir Chain; catena; fetters; (*fig.*) succession, series. ∼ **baklası**, link: ∼ **çizgisi**, (*math.*) catenary: ∼ **dolabı**, (*naut.*) chain-locker: ∼ **işi**, (*tex.*) chain stitch: ∼ **reaksiyonu**, (*phys.*) chain reaction: ∼**e vurmak** (**-i**), put s.o. in chains: ∼**i koparmak**, lose all control of o.s.
zincir·leme *vn.* Chaining: *a.* continuous: ∼ **ad tamlaması**, (*ling.*) serial genitive construction: ∼ **tepkime**, (*phys.*) chain reaction: ∼ **usulüne göre**, continuously. ∼**lemek** (**-i**), chain; connect in series. ∼**lenmek**, *vp.* ∼**li**, with a chain; chained, in chains; in a continuous manner, serially.
zindan Dungeon; dark place. ∼ **etm.**, make uninhabitable/unbearable: ∼ **gibi**, very dark; oppressive: ∼ **kesilmek**, become very dark: ∼ **odası**, cell: ∼ **olm.**, become uninhabitable. ∼**cı**, warder, jailer. ∼**delen**, (*ich.*) medium-sized PALAMUT.
zin·de Alive; active, energetic. ∼**har**, *int.* beware!
zir. = ZİRAAT.
zira *conj.* [215] Because, for.
zira·at¹ Agriculture, farming. ∼ **atçı**, agriculturalist; farmer. ∼**i**, agricultural: ∼ **mücadele ilaçları**, agricultural insecticide chemicals.
zirkon (*geol.*) Zircon. ∼**yum**, (*chem.*) zirconium.
zirve (*geo.*) Summit, peak; (*bot.*) cusp; (*math.*) apex; (*fig.*) acme. ∼ **toplantısı**, (*pol.*) summit meeting.
zirzopᵘ Silly ass. ∼**laşmak**, become crazy. ∼**luk**, craziness.
ziya Light. ∼**dar**, luminous; well lit.
ziyade *a.* More, much, too much; extra; superfluous. *adv.* Very: (**-den**), [197] more than, rather than. *n.* Increase, surplus; (*arch.*) mosque courtyard. ∼ **olsun!**, may it [your food] be plentiful!: ∼**siyle**, very much, excessively. ∼**ce**, somewhat. ∼**leşmek**, *vi.* increase.
ziyafet¹ (*cul.*) Feast, banquet; dinner-party. ∼ **çekmek**, give a feast: ∼ **ödenek/tahsisatı**, entertainment allowance.
ziyan Loss, damage; detriment, disadvantage. ∼ **çekmek/görmek**, suffer loss/damage//prejudice: ∼ **etm.**, waste; suffer loss: ∼ **sebil olm.**, (*col.*) be wasted: ∼ **vermek**, damage, harm: ∼**ı yok!**, it doesn't matter!, it's not important!
ziyan·cı/∼**kâr** Harmful, hurting; injurious. ∼**kârlık**, harmfulness. ∼**lı**, injured; the loser. ∼**sız**, harmless; quite good.
ziyaret¹ Visit; (*rel.*, *etc.*) pilgrimage. ∼ **etm.**, pay a visit; make a pilgrimage: ∼**ine gelmek**, pay s.o. a visit: ∼**lerinin arasını soğutmak**, curtail their visits to each other. ∼**çi**, visitor, caller; pilgrim. ∼**gâh**, much visited place; place of pilgrimage.
ziynet¹ Ornament, decoration. ∼ **iğnesi**, (*mod.*) brooch. ∼**lemek** (**-i**), adorn, decorate. ∼**li**, ornamented.
m. = (*ling.*) ZAMİR.
Zn. = (*chem.*) ÇİNKO.
zodyak¹ (*ast.*) Zodiac.
zoka (*sp.*) Artificial bait, spinner. ∼**yı yutmak**, (*sl.*) swallow the bait, be duped.
zona (*med.*) Shingles.
zonk ∼ ∼, throbbing. ∼**lama**, *vn.*; pulsation. ∼**lamak**, *vi.* (*med.*) throb with pain; pulsate. ∼**latmak** (**-i**), *vc.* ∼**layan**, (*ast.*) pulsating.

zoo. = ZOOLOJİ.
zoo·coğrafya Zoogeography. ∼**log**, zoologist. ∼**loji(k)**, zoolo·gy/(-gical). ∼**spor**, (*bio.*) zoospore. ∼**tekni**, (*live.*) animal-breeding.
zor *n.* Strength; violence; compulsion; difficulty; (*med.*) dys-. *a.* Difficult, hard; fatiguing; compulsory, forced. *adv.* With difficulty; only just. *int.* You won't manage it! ∼ **bela**, with great effort, after great troubles: ∼ **durum**, dilemma: ∼ **kullanmak**, use force: ∼ **nikâh**, forced marriage: ∼ **oyunu bozar**, it's a case of *force majeure*: ∼ **zar** = ZARZOR: ∼**a gelmek**/∼**u altında kalmak**, be forced/constrained: ∼**a koşmak**, raise difficulties: ∼**u ne?**, what's the matter with him?; what does he want?; why should he (do it)?: ∼**u olm.**, have difficulties: ∼**u** ∼**una**, with great difficulty: ∼**unda kalmak**/**olm.**, be obliged to.
zor·aki Forced; involuntary; under compulsion; far-fetched: ∼ **geçim**, a bare living. ∼**akilik**, stg. forced/not natural. ∼**alım**, (*leg.*) confiscation, seizure. ∼**ba**, *a.* violent, brutal; despotic: *n.* bully; rebel. ∼**balık**, use of force; violence; bullying; despotism: ∼ **sökmez!**, force won't work. ∼**gulu**, (*psy.*) enforced. ∼**la**, by force; with difficulty: ∼ **alım**, confiscation; extortion: ∼ **almak**, seize, commandeer; usurp: ∼ **ayırmak**, disrupt: ∼ **girmek**, break into: ∼ **güzellik olmaz**, it can't be achieved by force: ∼ **ilişme**, indecent assault: ∼ **kandırmak**, twist s.o.'s arm. ∼**lama**, *vn.* compulsion; (*med.*) rupture: *a.* forced, compulsory. ∼**lamak** (**-i**, **-e**), (use) force; coerce; exert one's strength; handle roughly; misuse; urge strongly. ∼**lan** = ∼**LA**: ∼ **değil!**, you don't have to!; only if you wish! ∼**lanmak**, *vp.*: *vi.* force o.s.; make vain efforts. ∼**laşma**, *vn.* ∼ **laşmak**, *vi.* grow difficult; become harder. ∼**laştırmak** (**-i**), complicate. ∼**layıcı**, compelling, compulsory: ∼ **nedenler**, (*leg.*) force *majeure*. ∼**lu**, strong; forced; violent; powerful; influential: ∼ **çalıştırma**, (*leg.*) forced labour. ∼**luk**, difficulty; arduousness: ∼ **çıkarmak**, raise difficulties/objections. ∼**unlu**, compulsory; mandatory; essential: ∼ **durum**, *force majeure*: ∼ **kılmak**, make necessary. ∼**un(lu)luk**, compulsion; necessity. ∼**unsuz**, optional.
Zr. = (*chem.*) ZİRKONYUM.
zuhur A becoming manifest; appearance; happening. ∼ **etm.**, appear; happen; come into existence: ∼**a gelmek**, happen: ∼**a getirmek**, bring about; cause to happen.
zuhur·at¹ Chance/unexpected events. ∼**i**, (*Or. th.*) clown: ∼ **kolu**, band of clowns: ∼**ye çıkar gibi**, ludicrously dressed.
zula (*sl.*) (Thieves'/smugglers') secret store. ∼ **etm.**, steal.
zul·men Cruelly. ∼**met¹**, darkness. ∼**m'etmek**ᵉᵈᵉʳ (**-e**), do wrong to; treat unjustly. ∼**'üm**ᵐᵘ, wrong; oppression; cruelty: ∼ **gören**, downtrodden.
zurna (*Or. mus.*) Shrill pipe (accompanied by a drum); (*ich.*) skipper, Atlantic saury; (*sl.*) big nose. ∼ **gibi**, (*mod.*) narrow (trousers): ∼**da peşrev olmaz (ne çıkarsa bahtına)!**, don't expect too much! ∼**cı**, pipe-player: ∼**nın karşısında limon yemek gibi**, distracted from his work. ∼**cılık**, pipe-playing.

zur·napa (*col.*) = ZÜRAFA. ~ **t** = ZART.
zücac(iye) Glass(ware).
züğürt Destitute; bankrupt; stony-broke. ~
tesellisi, cold comfort. ~ **le(ş)me**, *vn.* ~ **le(ş)mek**, *vi.*
become destitute; go bankrupt. ~ **lük**, destitution;
bankruptcy.
Züh·al[i] (*ast.*) Saturn. ~ **re**, (*ast.*) Venus. ~ **revi**,
(*med.*) venereal.
züht (*rel.*) Pious asceticism.
zühul[u] Negligence; forgetfulness. ~ **en**, by
error.
zükâm (*med.*) Cold, catarrh.
zül[lü] Degradation; humiliation.
zülal[i] Cool/pure water; (*chem.*) albumen.
zül·faris/ ~ **farüz** (*bot.*) Flower branches of cara-
calla bean.

zül'üf [fü] Side-lock of hair; love-lock; (*mod.*) tassel
~ **ü yâre dokunmak**, offend s.o. important. ~ **lü**, ~
patka, (*orn.*) tufted duck.
zümre Party; body; group; class.
züm·rüdüanka (*myth.*) Phoenix: ~ **gibi**, existing
only in name. ~ **rü'lt**[dü], (*geol.*) emerald: ~ **gibi**, ver·
green: ~ **yeşili**, deep/emerald green. ~ **rütlenmek**
~ **rütleşmek**, *vi.* turn green.
züppe *n.* Dandy; affected person, dude, snob. *a*
Affected, snobbish. ~ **leşmek**, *vi.* become snobbish
~ **lik**, affectation; snobbery.
zürafa (*zoo.*) Giraffe.
Zürih *pr.n.* (*geo.*) Zurich.
zürra[1] *pl.* Farmers, cultivators.
zürriyet[i] Progeny, descendants.
züyuf *pl.* Base coinage; counterfeit coins.